WELCOME TO THE FOURTH EDITION OF THE CREATURE FEATUR

COMPLETELY REVISED, EXPANDED, UPDATED SINCE THE THIRD EDITION IN 1988:

- **Capsulized reviews of 5,614 genre films of Science Fiction, Horror and Fantasy . . . includes Foreign Films, Animation, Silent Classics, Anomalies**
- **Reviews of Films, TV Movies, Original Videos and Novelty Items ignored by other major movie guides. *Science Fiction & Fantasy Book Review Annual* estimated that 30% of these are not included in major mass-market movie guides**
- **Each review now contains the names of video and laser companies that have released that title for home viewing. Great for searching for titles, and for the historical record in decades to come**
- **230 Photographs of Popular Monsters, Actors and Historic Scenes plus 24 new sketches**
- **Vivid Descriptions of Graphic Murders and Numerical Body Counts of Gore and Slasher Flicks**
- **A total of 1,709 cross references to secondary titles and tricky retitlings so you know when schlocky film makers are trying to fool you**
- **The author, John Stanley, is an acknowledged expert in his field. For six years he was the host of the popular "Creature Features" TV series in the San Francisco-Bay Area, and for 30 years he covered the horror scene for the San Francisco Chronicle. He was dubbed by Fangora Magazine the "Leonard Maltin of horror."**
- ***Reference Books Bulletin* has called this series "a useful guide for public libraries and academic collections supporting film programs." Shades of culture on top of crass commercialism!**

PREPARE FOR A MACABRE JOURNEY INTO THE REALM OF FANTASTIC CINEMA AS YOU HAVE NEVER EXPERIENCED BEFORE

Dedicated To

ERICA STANLEY

The love of my life

ATTENTION: SCHOOLS AND CORPORATIONS

JOHN STANLEY'S CREATURE FEATURES MOVIE GUIDE STRIKES AGAIN is available at quantity discounts with bulk purchase for educational, business or sales promotion ("premium") use. For more information contact Creatures at Large Press, P. O. Box 687, 1082 Grand Teton Drive, Pacifica CA 94044 or call (415) 355-7323.

ATTENTION: INDIVIDUAL READERS

You can purchase additional copies of this book, including a deluxe hardcover edition numbered and signed by the author, by writing to Creatures at Large Press and including check or money order for $22.50 for the trade paperback edition, or $52.50 for the deluxe hardcover. These prices include postage and handling.

A few copies of the now-coveted first edition in this series (published in 1981) are still available from Creatures at Large Press for $22.50 per copy (includes postage and handling).

Enclose check or money order (no cash, please) and send to Creatures at Large Press, 1082 Grand Teton Drive, Pacifica CA 94044. You will also receive a catalogue of our latest releases. Other books now offered are Robert Bloch's **LOST IN TIME AND SPACE WITH LEFTY FEEP** and John Mitchum's 1989 autobiography **THEM ORNERY MITCHUM BOYS.**

JOHN STANLEY'S CREATURE FEATURES MOVIE GUIDE STRIKES AGAIN

(FOURTH REVISED EDITION, TOTALLY REVISED AND UPDATED)

AN A TO Z ENCYCLOPEDIA
TO THE CINEMA OF THE FANTASTIC
OR
IS THERE A MAD DOCTOR/DENTIST
IN THE HOUSE?

BY JOHN STANLEY

COVER AND INTERIOR ILLUSTRATIONS
BY KENN DAVIS

TYPOGRAPHY BY JIM ROSE

CREATURES AT LARGE PRESS
SAN: 281-577X
1082 GRAND TETON DRIVE
PACIFICA CA 94044
(415) 355-7323

COPYRIGHT INFORMATION

**THE CREATURE FEATURES MOVIE GUIDE STRIKES AGAIN. Fourth Revised Edition of THE CREATURE FEATURES MOVIE GUIDE Series.
First printing @1994 by John Stanley**

 Published in the United States of America by Creatures at Large Press, P.O. Box 687, 1082 Grand Teton Drive, Pacifica CA 94044.

The first edition of this book was published by Creatures at Large in 1981. The second edition, with updated material, was reprinted by Warner Books Inc. in 1984. The third revised edition was published by Creatures at Large in 1988. This fourth edition has been completely revised and updated by the author.

Cover painting and 24 brand-new interior illustrations by Kenn Davis, who also illustrated the previous three editions.

Typography by Jim Rose.

Library of Congress Catalogue Card No. 93-074251

Library of Congress Cataloging in Publication Data:

**Stanley, John, 1940-
The Creature Features Movie Guide Strikes Again
(Fourth Revised Edition, Totally Revised and Updated) or
An A to Z encyclopedia to the cinema of the fantastic or
Is there a mad doctor in the house?
1. Fantastic films--Plots, themes, etc. 1.
Creature Features (Television program II.
Title. PN1995.9F36S7 1994 791.43'09'0915**

International Standard Book Numbering Information:

**ISBN: 0-940064-09-X (Trade Paperback)
ISBN: 0-940064-10-3 (Hardcover Deluxe Edition)
ISBN: 0-940064-08-1 (Creature Features Series)**

INTRODUCTION

DAY OF THE TERMINATING DINOSAUR: ARE HUMANS BECOMING EXTINCT?

By John Stanley

IN AN ERA of imaginative and unique film making that now seems long ago and far away, George Lucas had a director of marketing named Sid Ganis. Short in height but tall in reputation and long on affable personality, Ganis enjoyed the early years of Lucas' brilliant film successes. Sid and I had make contact in the early '80s when I covered many of Lucas' triumphs for **CREATURE FEATURES**, a popular Saturday night movie series on KTVU-TV (Channel 2), an independent Bay Area TV station (on the edge of beautiful downtown Oakland). It was a fabulous vehicle that had allowed me to interview genre actors, directors, writers and assorted guests and discuss new film releases, among a variety of pleasurable duties.

My most vivid recollection of Sid was a phone call he made to me one Saturday morning in May 1984 when I was guest-hosting a talk show at radio KGO in San Francisco. I had been discussing the newly released *INDIANA JONES AND THE TEMPLE OF DOOM,* which Ganis' boss had co-produced and which had taken him to the land of Sri Lanka as part of the production crew. Ganis was driving across the bay when he heard my opening critique and invitation for listeners to call in their opinions about the film's violence (a controversial issue in the media that week) and the effect it was having on younger movie goers.

Although he had no need to change into a superhero's costume, Ganis pulled off to the side of the road in search of a phone booth. I immediately put him on the air and he shared some fascinating and insightful information about how nervous Steven Spielberg, the film's director and co-producer, had become over the issue of violence on the eve of the film's release. Spielberg was so upset about the opening reviews, Ganis related, that he had been reduced to walking the streets restlessly on the night of the premiere, unable to sit comfortably in the theater and enjoy the fruits of his cinematic labor. Spielberg was having very grave doubts about his judgment of the Indiana Jones audience, and it would change his attitude about screen violence forever. That Ganis would go to the extra trouble to make the call, and share such a personalized story with my radio audience, was a clear indication of his devotion and loyalty to the film profession, and his loyalty for speaking up on behalf of his employers at a time when they were under media attack.

After Lucas separated from his wife, and fewer projects were on the Lucas film boards, Ganis left the fold in San Rafael, Ca., to take up a more personally satisying position at Paramount in Hollywood as its president of world-wide marketing. He further enhanced his reputation by joining Sony Pictures Entertainment in 1991 as a vice president, then became president of world-wide marketing and distribution at Columbia, a branch of Sony.

It was during this period, in the early months of 1993, that I saw Ganis for the first time in many years. The occasion was a movie junket, which is a kind of ritual gathering of media reporters (press, radio, TV) from all over the country to see a new motion picture and to interview its creators and stars. The hope of the studio or releasing company is that the resulting media blitz will give the film an identity and help it gross big on opening weekend. (This is a concept that doesn't always work. The public knows when a turkey is a turkey, and no amount of hype is going to convince them otherwise. Neverthless, it's a fascinating institution that has allowed me the opportunity to interview many film makers.)

During this event at the Four Seasons Hotel in San Francisco for a new release, *AMOS AND ANDREW*, we met and exchanged pleasantries for a few minutes. Then I shared with him a feeling that had been on my mind for some time. "You know, Sid," I said, "there was something wonderful and special happening back in the early '80s when you were working for Lucas and I was at Channel 2. But it's something I don't feel anymore. Something's gone."

As if he could read my mind, Sid nodded. "Those were great days. And you're right. It doesn't feel the same anymore."

What we had shared, and now seemed lost to us both, was a golden age of science-fiction and fantasy on film. While Sid had been a major force in marketing the *STAR WARS* trilogy and the first two Indiana Jones adventures, and I had hosted one of the most popular and long-running TV shows in Bay Area history, we had seen special effects suddenly escape their barbaric confines to blossom like never before. It had seemed in those halcyon days that fantastic images were reaching the screen as their creators dreamed them, with no technology or expense spared. There was a newfound respect for movie science-fiction and fantasy, which previously had been looked down on as lowbrow fare. Sid and I watched, awed, as the plots of the B movies of yesteryear became the driving force and inspirations behind the effects-laden blocckbusters of the '80s.

SID GANIS

These were the days (roughly 1977-1983) when *STAR WARS* and its sequels breathed new excitement into science fiction, when a plethora of films was exploring new horizons and crashing down old barriers and limitations. When such fare as *THE HOWLING* and *AN AMERICAN WEREWOLF IN LONDON* revealed just how innovative monster special effects were becoming, when Indiana Jones reminded us that the cliffhanger action genre was as durable as ever, when John Carpenter's *THE THING* presented some of the most imaginative (and unsettling) monster images the movies had ever seen, when special effects seemed startlingly mindboggling in *RETURN OF THE JEDI*, *THE LAST STARFIGHTER*, *DRAGONSLAYER*, *TRON* and *MAX HEADROOM.*

"Those days, working for George Lucas, were the most exciting of my life," said Sid, the same nostalgic tone permeating his voice that permeated mine. "It was a time that I don't think will ever quite happen again that way. But that's the nature of life. We move on."

Later, I gave Sid a call at Columbia and he elaborated further: "It's funny, but when I look back on those days with George, it seems almost prehistoric, like we were playing with Tinker Toys. As if we were in a prenatal state. But what we were doing then was absolute state of the art, in terms of story telling and special effects. What George did was take the then-dormant world of effects and turn it into a phenomenon. Another thing about George, even back then he was always talking about things to come. Dreaming about the technology of tomorrow. He was using the word cyber-optics before anyone even knew what it meant. He talked about digitized sound and, in fact, when he built the Skywalker Ranch outside San Rafael, he provided a digital postproduction facility long before such a thing was in vogue."

Perhaps one of the reasons Sid and I felt the way we did is that during the past decade there has been a moving away from this more personalized touch that Lucas and his peers brought to the movie-going public in the '70s and '80s. Genuine entrepreneurs who had the guts and talent to make their sharing of their visions a reality were being replaced by something that seemed wonderful in some ways but disturbing in others.

For during this past decade, we have seen a shifting away from the personal to the mechanical, to the computerized, to the technological. While talented people are still at the helm, something subtle seems to be happening—a dehumanization process that could have a profound effect on the future of movie-making.

While it's true that computer-generated imagery (CGI) has achieved a level of technical excellence, it also poses the threat that the ability to create any image imaginable on a computer screen, without leaving the comforts of an office or editing room, will eventually lead to a programmed system that will eliminate the need for human actors entirely, and create synthetic stars that never really exist. Max Headroom, move over. In short, the day now seems inevitable when movies won't need studios, sets, props or actors. Just a team of computer wizards behind their consoles, letting their imaginations run helter skelter.

Reality? Or just my own personal nightmare?

THE AGE OF MORPHING

One of the first signposts that this new age was coming, and certainly one of the most ground-breaking movies of the 1990s, was James Cameron's *TERMINATOR 2: JUDGMENT DAY*. The 1991 film, its effects overseen by six-time Oscar winner Dennis Muren, one of the masterminds at Lucas' Industrial Light & Magic, contained 40 CGI shots of Robert Patrick's liquid-metal robot assassin (the T-1000) pouring himself into various shapes. This process is called "morphing" (short for metamorphosing), a technique invented by Tom Brigham, an East Coast art student and Harvard graduate. An object or person is smoothly transformed from one image into another, seamlessly and realistically. In the spring of '93, shortly before receiving a technical achievement Academy Award, Brigham described it to me this way: "Pictures are stretched until they match. You treat images as if they were printed on silly putty. By stretching and pulling the silly putty, the objects in both pictures are warped until they match each other."

ROBERT PATRICK AS T-1000

"Morphing" was the first clear indication that after a decade of clumsy pioneering, CGI was state of the art. And, two years later, it went the way of the dinosaur.

Enter *JURASSIC PARK*, Spielberg's adaptation of Michael Crichton's best-selling and wildly popular novel. Released in the summer of '93, it was the first feature movie to depend for its artistic and storyline integrity on CGI. Without computer imagery, *JURASSIC PARK* might have still been a good film, and certainly Spielberg relied on other tricks to pull off his boxoffice hit. But total reliance on the old-fashioned ways, such as Willis O'Brien's/Ray Harryhausen's stop-motion techniques, would have not yielded such satisying results. For as good as stop motion can be, it can't compare to today's computer graphics.

However, *JURASSIC PARK* was also a forewarning, under the guise of blockbuster entertainment, that any imagery was possible—imagery so realistic and convincing that it couldn't have been conveyed more perfectly. But down what path is *JURASSIC PARK* leading us? While the blockbuster trumpets things to come of a technical excellence, with its thundering Tyrannosaurus rex, long-necked brachiosauruses and carnivorous and predatory velociraptors, it also poses dark, perplexing mysteries about where, ultimately, the machine could take man's most important form of 20th Century pop culture.

Sid Ganis envisions the future of the computerized movement in a positive light. "The breadth of motion picture production," he told me from his office at Columbia, "has broadened tenfold since my days with George. That old expression, 'you can do anything now,' is an absolute truism. *JURASSIC PARK* is a perfect example of how intimate a story can be when you use the computer. What appears to be cold technology actually provides warm and alive stories, in which you see and know everything. And by God, you believe it!"

Dennis Muren is similarly inclined. When I interviewed him at ILM in 1991, he said that computers were absolutely vital to the future of movie special effects. However, he added, "it isn't going to be the end-all, but another important tool." I hope he's right.

While impersonal technology may give us our most humanistic movies of tomorrow, the unfortunate dehumanization of our entertainment is reflected, more and more, by the ubiquitous closing of large movie theaters, which once afforded us one of the greatest reactions that movies offer—the group experience, the sharing of exciting images on a giant screen. No film better reminded us of this nearly lost heritage than *THE FUGITIVE*, which opened the same summer as JURASSIC PARK. Audiences were ow-ing and aw-ing a 45-mile-an-hour train crash and several action-chase sequences so visceral that they applauded when they concluded, partly to congratulate the film makers and actors, partly to relieve the unmitigated tension director Andrew Davis brought to the pursuit. (If you don't believe the group-event theory, see THE FUGITIVE in an empty theater. The effect is not the same.)

ELECTRONIC HOME DELIVERY

What we now have, except for a few giant theaters in large cities that have somehow escaped the wrecker's ball, are small shopping-center multiplexes, where it's far more difficult (if not impossible) to find any semblance of the shared experience. But what has brought the greatest degree of dehumanization to the viewing process is the ever-deepening and fanatical trend toward home viewing. It's now quite clear that home video (whether rental or sellthrough) is a dominating force in the entertainment world.

With the closing of drive-in theaters, with the death of the theatrical double feature and the "hardtops" that once unspooled them, the watching of movies for most Americans has become a lonely business. While movie lovers worldwide are seeing more flickers unreel before their very eyes, it's in the privacy of their own homes.

During an interview for the San Francisco Chronicle, where until December 1993 I was employed as an entertainment writer for many years on the Sunday Datebook staff, Irish writer-director Neil Jordan told me on the eve of the opening of his *THE CRYING GAME*, before that movie catapulted him from obscure cult film maker into one of the hottest directors in the world, that he was already earning about 50 per cent of his income from the sale and rental of his old movies to home video. Henry Jaglom, who produces independent movies for well under $1 million each, informed me in the spring of 1993 that he too was receiving half his income from a video distribution deal with Paramount.

And Roger Corman, the man who had helped to re-invent the B movie after TV had destroyed it in the early 1950s, first through American-International and then his own company New World, said in the summer of '93 about his company New Horizon, which releases about 15 low-budget features a year: "Ten years ago, 75 per cent of our income was theatrical; today, our theatrical income is under 25 per cent. Home video—including domestic and foreign—is over 50 per cent of our market."

U. S. tape rental revenues climbed from 3.3 billion in 1991 to 3.5 billion in 1992. In terms of dollars, Americans spent $12 billion to rent/buy videos in 1992, but only forked over $4.9 billion at the movie box office. It's easy to see who's winning this war.

And sales are climbing at a staggering rate. According to Variety, of 19.6 million cassettes sold in 1992, about 11 million were sellthroughs, the other 8.6 million being purchased by rental stores. For sellthrough, this represented an increase of 15 to 20 per cent over the previous year. And as sellthrough retail prices plummet, a plethora of new material is available. First-run features, direct-to-video movies, full-length dual cassette serials, documentaries, exercise tapes, children's programming . . . a rich vein of material.

The market for home video, in fact, has become so lucrative that many producers no longer worry about theatrical release beforehand. They make their films with a clear understanding of audience and genre, and release them directly into the video marketplace.

The best example of this is Charles Band, whose Full Moon production company is reportedly the most successful business making direct-to-video movies. Band, brimming with energy at 42, makes genre movies in Hollywood and in Romania with the help of his father Albert (a king of spaghetti westerns and foreign-produced fare during the 1960s) that are distributed by Paramount. According to Band, he sells anywhere from 32,000 to 50,000 units per title to video stores for rental. He calls Full Moon "a high-profile label," meaning its movies fill a niche in the market place and carry a reputation. "I think of Full Moon," he told me in the spring of '92, "as being synonymous with quality fantasy, just as Disney is synonymous with family entertainment. I make movies that are the comic books of the '90s."

Band is an important figure in the establishment of home video. "I started out on the cutting edge of the video market in 1976 and became one of the first distributors of movies on tape. The very first person, the Godfather of home-movie packaging, was Andre Blay. People thought he was crazy when he started buying the tape rights to *PATTON* and *THE FRENCH CONNECTION*. But I could see something was going to happen, so I acquired 20 independent features myself, including *TUNNELVISION*, *FLESH GORDON* and *THE GROOVE TUBE*. I released them on the Meda label." Band sold the company in 1981 and in new hands it became Media, which grew into one of the most successful video-movie distributors. "It became worth millions," said Band with no regrets. "I could have stayed in the cassette market, but I wanted to produce. I'm much happier this way."

Band admitted that when he was producing from 1983-87, under the banner of Empire-International, he was making such films as *RE-ANIMATOR*, *FROM BEYOND*, *GHOULIES* and *TROLL* for theatrical release. "But then," he recalled, "marketing conditions changed drastically. The dollar weakened, and suddenly almost over night revenue from theatrical plummeted. I had to sell my studio in Rome and regroup as Full Moon. Suddenly there was this incredibly lucrative video market. It was the way to go. Now we have comic books published by Malibu, we have merchandising of Puppet Master and Demonic Toys, a fan club of 30,000 members, audiocassettes and CDs of our soundtracks."

David Winter is another major figure in home video. He is one of Hollywood's leading producers/distributors of low-budget genre movies designed to feed the world's need for explosions, car chases, martial-arts donnybrooks, blazing machine guns and celluloid mayhem in general. A one-time teenage actor on Broadway, who became a dance choreographer, TV director and eventual ministudio mogul, Winter operates West Side Studios (also known as Action International) in Culver City. He produces about six movies a year and picks up another 20 from independent producers and sends them into the world under the Action-International and West Side Video labels. Winter designs his product without pretentions, concerned only with satisfying the vicarious needs of the action-movie fan. Who is looking for sophistication from *ALIEN SPACE AVENGER*, *THOR AND THE AMAZING WOMEN*, *MANIAC WARRIORS* and *FUTURE FORCE* anyway?

"The reason action movies are so popular," Winter told me in the spring of '93, "and the reason they can be moved all over the world, is because the scenes need no translation—no subtitles or explanations. Comedy movies that are funny to one culture are often not funny to another, but physical action . . . ha, that's easily understood in any land."

Winter abandoned his TV career in 1981 when he went to the Cannes Film Festival to shoot *THE LAST HORROR FILM*. "It was while I was shooting the movie, and became exposed to the buying-and-selling market that is Cannes, that I realized I could sell product all over the world myself, without the help of film brokers." By then the video business was just beginning to boom and "I decided to form my own company and with my own money made *DEADLY PREY* and *MAN KILLERS*. They went directly to video. *Boom!* There was this huge, incredible worldwide market for action. On each title we grossed 500 to 600 per cent of the budget. We knew then we were in a good place and we just kept growing."

Also a "growing" concern are animated features from Japan, which finally began to see U.S. theatrical distribution in 1989 through Carl Macek's Streamline Pictures. A Pennsylvanian who re-edited the *ROBOTECH* series for American consumption, and who has written several

CHARLES BAND, BROTHER RICHARD BAND AND FATHER ALBERT BAND

good books on film, Macek has overseen the English dubbing and release of such hits as *AKIRA*, *VAMPIRE HUNTER D*, *LENSMAN* and *TWILIGHT OF THE COCKROACHES*. "We've also set up a videotape company," he told me just before this book went to press, "that has distributed about 60 Japanese animation films. About 75 per cent of our revenue comes from home video, and although we pioneered Japanese animation in this country, other companies are now jumping on the band wagon."

The VCR is here to stay.

FOURTH EDITION—READ ALL ABOUT IT

As you peruse this, the heavily updated and expanded fourth edition in THE CREATURE FEATURES MOVIE GUIDE series, you will realize that a majority of the new entries are B movies made exclusively for the home video market. And many older films have been reevaluated, often with totally new opinions. I've grown and changed since the first edition of this book in 1981, and movies that gave off certain vibes in one decade often age or improve and give off totally different meanings in later years. Unlike other movie guides that hire large staffs of reviewers, this is a one-man operation. As it should be. Otherwise, how can there be any consistent point of view toward the plethora of material produced?

I have made a major change, since the last edition, in how the titles are alphabetized. I now do it the way that seems to have become popularized by Leonard Maltin's excellent and indispensable annual, TV MOVIES AND VIDEO GUIDE. This is a run-all-the-letters-together system. In other words (pardon the pun), eliminate all spaces between words and forms of punctuation and the first article of the title and look up the title by consecutive letters.

I have tried like never before to see as many new and old films as possible since the third edition (REVENGE OF THE CREATURE FEATURES MOVIE GUIDE) was published in the spring of 1988, and a lot of people wonder how this is possible without ultimately suffering from brain damage or a complete physical and spiritual breakdown.

Sometimes I have to wonder myself. In the summer of 1991 I decided to monitor myself to see how many films I see per year. And I arbitrarily set some rules: I would try to see one movie a day, or a maximum of seven per week. At the end of that year, to my personal delight, I discovered I had seen more than the 365 minimum—it came to exactly 400 titles. So the seemingly impossible is possible, if you just make up your mind to do it.

While in the past I've listed as many titles as possible, in this edition I've been forced to retire many inactive titles due to a shortage of space. However, for the sake of handy reference I've kept a reference to the film's title and the edition(s) of previous guides in which it can be found. Most guides simply drop old titles to make way for the new, but this seemed like a good compromise. My wish is one day to see a complete guide with all these titles restored. And, of course, should an inactive title become active again, I shall restore it.

I still believe that this series as a whole reflects the history of fantastic cinema. This includes brand-new theatrical releases, movies made exclusively for home video, movies presented on syndicated TV or cable, seminal silent films, and foreign films that find their way into our theaters and/or video stores. I am still including some titles that have not been put on video, for they remain an important part of the historic record.

Thus, in this widespread compendium, you will find the exploitation films, axe-and-gore murder flicks, the slashers, gashers and bashers. It seems unfair to exclude the superagents with their supergadgets and superchicks, or the old dark houses with their drafty corridors, secret panels and chest-thumping gorillas. We've even included the wrestling superhulks of Mexico and the musclebound warriors of Italy, for what are they but mythology and legend revived. Many new mysteries have found their way into this fourth edition because they overlap into aberrant psychology, and certainly the *PSYCHO*-type movie is a legacy handed to us by Alfred Hitchcock and Robert Bloch that should not go ignored.

One of the nastiest tricks that unscrupulous producers and distributors constantly pull is the retitling ploy. A film bombs as *PSYCHO-A-GO-GO* so it's re-released as *FIEND WITH THE ELECTRONIC BRAIN* and when that fails, it's re-re-released as *BLOOD OF GHASTLY HORROR*. Does it stop there? Nope. Next you've got *MAN WITH THE SYNTHETIC BRAIN*. It's ruthless, it's treacherous, it's devious and it should be outlawed, but you've got this happening by the hundreds, by the thousands.

I've done everything I can to catch these unscrupulous renamings, but for the future you should keep a close eye on Video Watchdog, a bimonthly publication from Tim Lucas that can be ordered at P.O. Box 5283, Cincinnati OH 45205-0283. Tim has people all over the world keeping their eye on retitlings. And you should have his magazine because it discusses

"AWE SHUCKS" FROM JOE BOB BRIGGS

Only days before this book went to press, drive-in theater critic/social commentator/humanitarian Joe Bob Briggs insisted he get his two cents in about this new edition. From his Dallas headquarters, he wrote in his inimitable style: *"I keep two reference works by my bed at all times. One is Eric Weber's* HOW TO PICK UP GIRLS. *The other is John Stanley's* REVENGE OF THE CREATURE FEATURES MOVIE GUIDE. *Never has so much worthless information been gathered together in one place. I'm in awe of the man."*

genre movies with a literacy you will not find elsewhere.

Many films are retitled in foreign countries for cultural or lingual reasons, and that is another matter I have tried to address in this addition by cross-referencing as many variant titles as possible. Included are countless British and European secondary titles that will hopefully make this book more useful, and therefore coveted, by readers far from America.

Coverage of old movie serials has vastly improved. Republic Pictures Home Video has been at the forefront of this vidmovement and has been releasing 8 to 10 cliffhangers each year in high-quality, dual-cassette packaging. Glenn Ross, Republic's director of marketing, told me in 1992 that while the serials were initially released to "a narrow audience of die-hard collectors, the trend has slowly spread to a wider audience through the advent of Indiana Jones adventure movies directed by Steven Spielberg. He's openly admitted that his style was influenced by the cliffhangers he saw as a boy." While Republic remains the Tiffany of the chapter play, its *ADVENTURES OF CAPTAIN MARVEL* outselling all other titles, other companies have proven to be the Woolworth's of the business by releasing many four-hour serials for as little as $9.95, in poor to middling condition. Falling somewhere in between are the releases of Video Communications Inc. of Tulsa. These dual-cassette offerings are in the LP or SP mood and sell for about $19.95, and usually are acceptable.

VIDEO/LASERBLAST

This new edition features extensive information about home video and laser disc releases—coverage that was totally lacking in past editions. The VCR now sits comfortably in about 80 per cent of all TV-viewing homes. But coming up fast is the laser disc machine, and the man responsible for correcting our ignorance about this burgeoning market, and opening our eyes to its mindboggling capabilities, is Bob Stephens, the world's most devoted laser disc viewer, and the author of a damn good review column that runs each Saturday in the San Francisco Examiner.

Bob has repeatedly told us that the laser is the machine of tomorrow, and will eventually replace the vastly inferior VCR unit. The picture is 60 per cent sharper than vidtape, the music tracks are comparable to compact discs, and the use of Surround Sound makes for an unbeatable aural experience. Another thing about lasers—they boast auxiliary soundtracks, trailers, restored scenes . . . in short, a plethora of exclusive material.

At the end of applicable paragraphs, you will find the name or names of those major videotape companies that, at one time or another, have released that particular title into the home-video market. The name of the laser distributor (if any) follows in separate paratheses. This has been compiled so that you can search for your missing video or laser through the company names given; and in the case of videos and lasers that have gone "out of print" or been withdrawn from the market for legal reasons, the information is there for the historical record. No attempt, however, has been made to keep track of things "out of print."

By no means are these video/laser aids a guarantee that you will find what you're looking for. Consider it an informational starting place. While I have not listed all the addresses of video and laser companies, I am providing this short list that I feel will be most helpful to the genre movie fan in his search for lesser-known or esoteric or rare titles:

IMPORTANT VIDEO/LASER COMPANIES

ACADEMY: 9250 Wilshire Blvd., Suite 303, Beverly Hills CA 09212.
ACTION INTERNATIONAL: 10726 McCune Ave., Los Angeles CA 90034.
ARTS & ENTERTAINMENT: 1 - 800 - 423-1212.
BARR ENTERTAINMENT: P.O. Box 7878, Irwindale CA 91706-7878.
BLACKHAWK CATALOG: 5959 Triumph St., Commerce CA 90048-1688.
BUENA VISTA: 500 S. Buena Vista St., Burbank CA 91521.
CAPTAIN BIJOU: P.O. Box 87, Toney AL 35773.
CBS/FOX: 1330 Avenue of the Americas, 5th Floor, NY NY 10019.
CINEMACABRE: P.O. Box 10005-D, Baltimore MD 21285-0005.
CINEMA CLASSICS: P.O. Box 174, Village Station, NY NY 10014. (800 925-6684).
CINEMA SHOP: San Francisco's most unusual place for genre videos and older serials. Ask for Dan Faris or Steve Imura. 606 Geary. (415) 885-6785.
COLUMBIA/TRISTAR: 3400 Riverside Dr., Burbank CA 91505-4627.
CRITERION COLLECTION: 2139 Manning Ave., Los Angeles CA 90025- 6315.
DISCOUNT VIDEO: P.O. Box 7122, Burbank CA 91510.
DISNEY HOME VIDEO: See BUENA VISTA.
EMBASSY: 335 N. Maple Dr., Suite 350, Beverly Hills CA 90210.
FACETS VIDEO: 1517 W. Fullerton, Chicago IL 60614 (catalogue sales-rentals).
FILMFAX: P.O. Box 1900, Evanston IL 60204.
FRIGHT VIDEO: P.O. Box 179, Billerica MA 01821.
FRONT ROW: P.O. Box 5891, Edison NJ 08818-5891.
GOODTIMES: 16 E. 40th St., NY NY 10016.
IMAGE ENTERTAINMENT: 9333 Oso Avenue, Chatsworth CA 91311.
KARTES: See Barr Entertainment.
LASER ISLAND: 1810 Voorhes Ave., Brooklyn NY 11235 (Japanese lasers).
LASER PERCEPTION: San Francisco's best laser shop at 3300 Judah Street. (415) 753-2016. Ask for Eldon.
LASER'S EDGE: 2103 N. Veterans Parkway, Suite 100, Bloomington IL 61704.
LIGHTNING: 60 Long Ridge Rd., PO Box 4000, Stamford CT 06907.
LIVE: 15400 Sherman Way, Suite 500, Van Nuys CA 91401-0124.
LOONIC: 2022 Taraval St., Suite 6427, San Francisco CA 94116.
LUMIVISION: 1490 Lafayette Street, Suite 305, Denver CO 80201.
MCA/UNIVERSAL: 70 Universal City Plaza, Universal City CA 91608-9955.
MGM/UA: 1000 W. Washington Blvd., Culver City CA 90232.
MIDNIGHT VIDEO: 3960 Laurel Canyon Blvd., Suite 275, Studio City CA 91604.
MONARCH: P.O. Box 7006, La Vergne TN 37086-7006.
MOVIES UNLIMITED: 6736 Castor Ave., Philadelphia PA 19149.
MPI: 15825 Rob Roy Dr., Oak Forest IL 60452.
NEW LINE: 116 N. Robertson Blvd., LA CA 90048.
NEW WORLD: See STARMAKER.
NOSTALGIA: P.O. Box 606, Baker City OR 97814.
ORION: 1888 Century Park E., LA CA 90067.
PARAMOUNT: 5555 Melrose Ave., Los Angeles CA 90038-3197.
PHOENIX: 6253 Hollywood Blvd., #818, Hollywood CA 90028.
PIONEER LASER DISC: 2265 E. 220 St., P.O. Box 22782, Long Beach CA 90801-5782.
PRISM: 1888 Century Park E., Suite 1000, Los Angeles CA 90067.
RCA/COLUMBIA: See COLUMBIA TRISTAR.
REPUBLIC: 12636 Beatrice St., Los Angeles CA 90066-0930.
REX MILLER: Route 1, Box 457-D, East Prairie MO 63845.
RHINO: 2225 Colorado Ave., Santa Monica CA 90404-3555.
SCIENCE FICTION CONTINUUM: P.O. Box 154, Colonia NJ 07067.
SIMITAR: 3850 Annapolis Lane, Plymouth MN 55447.
SINISTER CINEMA: P.O. Box 4369, Medford OR 97501-0168 (coded as Sinister/C).
SOMETHING WEIRD: P.O. Box 33664, Seattle WA 98133 (coded as S/Weird).
STARMAKER: 151 Industrial Way E., Eatontown, NJ 07724.
TAMARELLE'S: 11101-A E. 53rd St., Denver CO 80239.
TURNER: #1 CNN Center, Atlanta GA 30348.
VIDEO CITY: 4266 Broadway, Oakland CA 94611. (510) 428-0202. (Ask for Bob Brown, who produces UFO documentaries.)
VIDEO COMICS (STREAMLINE PICTURES): 971 N. La Cienega, Suite 209, LA CA 60069. (Japanese animation)
VIDEO COMMUNICATIONS INC.: 6535 E. Skella Drive, Tulsa OK 74145. (Important for public-domain serials.)
VIDEO DIMENSIONS: 530 W. 23rd St., NY NY 10011.
VIDEO OYSTER: 62 Pearl St., NY NY 10004. (Does rare-video searches.)
VIDEO SEARCH OF MIAMI: P.O. Box 16-1917, Miami FL 33116.
VIDEO TREASURES: 500 Kirts Blvd., Troy MI 48084.
VIDEO VAULT: 1015 Wisconsin Avenue, Washington DC 20007.
VIDEO YESTERYEAR: Box C, Sandy Hook CT 06482.
VIDMARK: 2644 30th St., Santa Monica CA 90405.
VOYAGER CO.: 1351 Pacific Coast Highway, Long Beach CA 90801- 5782.
WARNER BROS.: 4000 Warner Blvd., Burbank CA 91522.
WHOLE TOON CATALOG: 1450 19th Avenue NW, PO Box 369, Issaquah WA 98072 (cartoons only).
WORLDSHIP: 3665 29th St., Grand Rapids MI 49512.
WORLDVISION: 1700 Broadway, 11th Floor, NY NY 10019.

THANKS FOR THE . . .

Besides Bob Stephens, there are a few others I want to thank for helping out in ways large and small during the years that this project has obsessed and absorbed me and driven me to the very brink of madness. For offering sagacious advice about publishing and printing and for being a shoulder to lean and cry on more than a few times, I bow to Malcolm Whyte. For allowing me to see hundreds of genre movies in the darkness of San Francisco's St. Francis Theater, I bow to its manager Harry Ho and his affable doorman, Johnson Shih. For getting me started on the trail of self-publishing (for better or worse), and for making the first two editions of this book possible, I bow to long-time friend Gregory Frazier. And to Gary Meyer, manager of Berkeley's UC Theater. For setting up a number of exciting genre movie festivals at San Francisco's Roxie Theater, which has allowed me to see many films totally unavailable in any other gauge or format, I bow to booker and film enthusiast Elliot Levine. And thanks goes to Brian Waller and the Red Vic Movie House staff for their support, and to San Francisco publicists Jeff Diamond, Walter Von Hauffe and Bill Lanese and his working staff.

Accolades are in order to Dan Faris and Steve Imura of the Cinema Shop, 606 Geary Street, San Francisco's finest browsing place for movie memorabilia and the strangest collection of exploitation movies in the country (call 415 885-6785); to Steve Anker and David Gerstein of the San Francisco Cinematheque, that esoteric film society that still can find a place for schlock horror movies in its excellent Halloween programs, and which has always supported this book series; to long-time collaborator and friend Kenn Davis for putting up with me to do the cover and interior illustrations and his wife Elizabeth for putting up with Kenn; to Kevin Gilligan for financial and tax advice; to Joe Bob Briggs for checking this sucker out when no one else would; to Leonard Maltin for his unflagging support; to Mick Martin, co-author of VIDEO MOVIE GUIDE, for good advice about this book; to Tommy Lee, Enoch Wong and Mary Armstrong for handling all the mail through Pacifica's great post office. I thank my wife Erica, whose abilities to put up with my eccentricities and mood shifts qualifies her as the angel of the century.

LOVING HORROR

I'm glad to be able to write in the year 1994 that genre movies are still favorite with a majority of viewers and doing handsomely for their makers. Let's face it, Creature Features fans. You guys and gals still love scary stuff. Thunder and lightning storms; creepy corridors; screaming women in negligees; teenagers making love as Jason sneaks up on them, spear or javelin or machete in hand; Freddy's steel hand popping through the wall of another dimension; eerie beams of Spielbergian light blasting through windows and holes in the fabric of manmade things; heavy breathing on the other side of the threshold. The submerged sexual/terror lust in all of us eternally wants to be satisfied—vicariously, of course.

We still love to be reminded that lurking just outside the shadows of the darkness surrounding each of our souls are the demons of our worst nightmares. Evil lives and evil makes money and evil pleases us and hurray for evil. Well, movie evil, anyway.

Richard Leskosky, described as "a University of Illinois cinema expert," has remarked that "these movies are a way of seeing our fears dealt with in a manageable way. It has a satisfying effect in the sense we have confronted our worst fears and coped with them. We have seen these horrors and we come out okay."

So, the themes underlying this astral anthology thrive. I hope I will be back for a fifth edition in a few years. Watch the skies. Never let down your vigil.

When the screaming starts, when the bloodletting rolls, and when the bodies flop horridly in their own gore and gooey liquids, I shall be lurking on the periphery, taking notes with my blood-ink pen, scribbling on parchments of dried human skin. And now, before the commercial announcement, here is a horrifying message from our first movie . . .

ABADON. See **VAMPIRES.**

ABBOTT AND COSTELLO GO TO MARS (1953). A misleading title—the comedy duo lands not on the Red Planet but on Venus (inhabited by an Amazonian race of lovely pin-ups) after wandering aboard an experimental rocketship and blasting off by accident. Provocative Mari Blanchard is the Queen of Venus and Anita Ekberg and Martha Hyer are among her shapely servants. One of the duo's most nostalgic comedies. Directed by Charles Lamont. Robert Paige, Jack Kruschen, Jean Willes.

ABBOTT AND COSTELLO MEET DR. JEKYLL AND MR. HYDE (1953). Frolicking satire with Boris Karloff's bitter half running down London's foggy streets. Robert Louis Stevenson must have rolled over in his literary grave as Bud and Lou run wild . . . fans will be less offended by liberties taken with the tale of dual personality. Nice support from identity-confused Craig Stevens and Helen Westcott, decent scripting by that split personality team of John Grant and Leo Loeb, good schizophrenic direction by Charles Lamont. John Dierkes, Reginald Denny, Eddie Parker. (Video/Laser: MCA)

ABBOTT AND COSTELLO MEET FRANKENSTEIN (1948). Beloved spoof designed for Bud Abbott and Lou Costello, their bid to kid the cinema's most-adored monsters. Bela Lugosi re-creates Dracula, Lon Chaney Jr. is tormented Larry Talbot (the Wolfman) and Glenn Strange is the hulking Frankenstein Monster. Even Vincent Price's voice gets into the act as The Invisible Man. Madly uninhibited plot concerns Dracula's attempt to transfer Costello's brain into the head of the Monster. It almost fits. Directed by Charles T. Barton with a flair for the silly and enlivened by damsels Lenore Aulbert and Jane Randolph. (Video/Laser: MCA)

ABBOTT AND COSTELLO MEET THE INVISIBLE MAN (1951). Comedy-duo programmer has amusing moments as Arthur Franz materializes and dematerializes in "Invisible Man"-genre spoofery. A potpourri of prizefighting, gangsters, rigged bouts, and the obligatory scientific formula that renders invisibility. Directed by Charles Lamont with a knockout comedy punch. Sheldon Leonard, Nancy Guild. (Video/Laser: MCA)

ABBOTT AND COSTELLO MEET THE KILLER: BORIS KARLOFF (1949). Satire of the murder-mystery, done by the yuckity-yuckity team with its usual turmoil and louting. Central feature is Boris Karloff as a sinister hypnotist. Directed by Charles T. Barton. Lenore Aubert, Alan Mowbray, Roland Winters. (MCA; Goodtimes) (Laser: MCA)

ABBOTT AND COSTELLO MEET THE MUMMY (1955). You'll get gypped in the crypt and you're a dummy for the mummy if youse gurus waste your taste on this abominable slow-man in gauze, who shambles from his Egyptian tomb to chase two dumb desecrators . . . too bad the creep never caught them and wrung their ridiculous necks. The least of the A & C film spoofs. Marie Windsor, Michael Ansara, Richard Deacon, Dan Seymour, and Eddie Parker (as the mummy) cannot resurrect Howard Christie's production. Director Charles Lamont slams home the sarcophagus lid for good measure. (Video/Laser: MCA)

ABBY (1974). Black exploitation ripoff of THE EXORCIST with Carol Speed falling victim to demonic possession with the spirit Eshju and killing men in the most abominable ways. William Marshall (BLACULA) is a bishop fighting evil. Mediocre effort by genre director William Girdler. Terry Carter, Juanita Moore. (Cinefear)

ABOMINABLE DOCTOR PHIBES, THE (1971). Vincent Price at his grotesque best, hamming it up as Dr. Anton Phibes, who employs the Seven Curses of the Pharaohs to avenge his wife's death. Each murder becomes more horrendous, and the morbidity and necrophilia of the nervy ending will have your nerve endings crawling. You'll also laugh to death at the campy elements emphasized by British director Robert Fuest. Phibes is a hideous parody of a man with a skinless face, a speaking tube in his neck and a bad case of acne that fails to repulse lovely assistant Vulnavia (Virginia North). Joseph Cotten, Terry-Thomas, Hugh Griffith. The rousing sequel: DR. PHIBES RISES AGAIN. (Vestron) (Laser: Image, with **DR. PHIBES RISES AGAIN**)

ABOMINABLE SNOWMAN OF THE HIMALAYAS (1957). Hammer production, written by Nigel Kneale from his BBC play, THE CREATURE, is suspensefully directed by Val Guest. Peter Cushing and Forrest Tucker search for the legendary Yeti in the snowy heights of Tibet. The explorers meet terror at the hairy hands of the ancient creatures. An unusual, thought-provoking ending lifts this out of the potboiler category. This has some very chilling moments, especially when a hairy paw reaches under a tent and gropes for human contact. Maureen Connell, Richard Wattis.

ABOMINATION (1988). Centuries-old monster-beast-creature possesses a youth in sunglasses and makes him tear eyeballs out of human sockets and commit other acts of mayhem. An ugly business, this, as envisioned by writer Bando ("Spread the guts") Glutz, a clutz at the typewriter. Van Connery, Victoria Chaney. Produced-directed by Max Raven. (Hound)

ABRAXUS, GUARDIAN OF THE UNIVERSE (1990). Pro wrestler Jesse Ventura portrays a "Finder," a 10,000-year-old policeman who comes to Earth in search of a renegade cop (Sven-Ole Thorsen, who does an impersonation of Arnold Schwarzenegger). Most of this Canadian film written-directed by Damien Lee has the two grunt guys fighting it out in snow country while each searches for a child that holds the eye to the future of the Universe—or some such tripe. Michael Copeman, Marjorie Bransfield. (MCA)

ABSENT-MINDED PROFESSOR, THE (1961). Disney fantasy-farce with slapstick for the young and satire for the aults, so popular it led to a sequel, SON OF FLUBBER. Fred MacMurray is a bumbling, lovable scientist who discovers Flubber, a compound that gives it users oddball abilities—such as the ability to fly or bound unimpeded across a basketball court. Scenes of a model-T flying across the sky are standouts. Bill Walsh based his screenplay on A SITUATION OF GRAVITY by Samuel Taylor. Wonderful cast includes Nancy Olson as the wife, Keenan Wynn as the villain trying to steal the formula, Ed Wynn, Leon Ames, Edward Andrews. Directed by Robert Stevenson. (Disney)

ABSENT-MINDED PROFESSOR, THE (1988). Disney update of its 1961 Fred MacMurray hit vehicle is typically inferior TV time-killer starring Harry Anderson as a physics professor who re-creates Flubber, a form of rubber that enables lubbers to fly. Directed by Robert Scheerer. Cory Danziger, Mary Page Keller.

ABSURD (1981). This sequel to THE GRIM REAPER (known as ANTHROPOPHAGUS II in Europe) was marketed in America with the name Peter Newton as director. He's really Aristide Massaccesi (aka Joe D'Amato) and this is purely Italian spaghetti dripping with blood. George Eastman is back as the cannibalistic monster. Annie Belle, Ian Danby, Edmond Purdom. (From Wizard as **MONSTER HUNTER**)

ABYSS, THE (1989). Writer-director James Cameron (THE TERMINATOR; ALIENS) stretches beyond the confining genre forms of previous works in this spectacular underwater fantasy adventure. It's a series of cliffhangers as a rescue team (led by Ed Harris, Mary Elizabeth Mastrantonio and Michael Biehn) dives to dangerous depths to find out why a U.S. nuclear sub sank. An alien presence deepens the mystery. Emphasis is on disasters, rescues, and underwater chases and the alien pseudopod effect is revolutionary. But Cameron shifts from ultra-realism to a Spielbergesque fairy-tale ending that gravely dampens the film's climax. The high-tech and fantasy don't mix so well. Leo Burmester, Todd Graff, John Bedford Lloyd, J. C. Quinn, Kimberly Scott. (Video/Laser: CBS/Fox)

ABYSS: SPECIAL EDITION, THE (1989). Re-edited version of James Cameron's underwater epic, this time with the complete ending of the film running 30 minutes longer than the original. (CBS/Fox)

ACCEPTABLE RISKS (1986). TV-movie set in a chemical plant that is leaking toxic waste into the city of Oakbridge. Played as a conspiratorial thriller as the plant manager (Brian Dennehy) tries to keep the leak hush hush and a city manager (Cicely Tyson) closes in on the plot. Directed by Rick Wallace. Kenneth McMillan, Christine Ebersole, Richard Gilliland. (Prism)

ACCIDENTS (1989). Slow-moving paranoia thriller, made in England, in which neurophysical researcher Edward Albert discovers his device for peace (Project Scout, a miniature flying saucer that fires death rays) is being developed for military use by technology chief Jon Cypher. When co-workers begin to die in "accidents," Albert sets out to prove a conspiracy. Director Gideon Amir allows Albert to go bananas in this action film with minimal science fiction. Leigh Taylor-Young, Ian Yule, Candice Hillebrand, Tony Caprari. (Trans World)

ACE DRUMMOND (1936). Above-average adventure serial based on the comic strip inspired by war ace Eddie Rickenbacker. John "Dusty" King is a square-jawed, oft-singing hero ("the G-Man of the Air") and Noah Beery Jr. is wonderful as his sidekick Jerry as they join forces with the Mongolian Secret Service (!) to discover the identity of The Dragon, a villain attempting to stop International Airways with a death ray that blows out pilots' eardrums. Although many elements are dated, directors Ford Beebe and Cliff Smith pack each episode with corny, exciting stuff. Jean Rogers, Guy Bates Post, Arthur Loft. (VCI, Video Treasures, Nostalgia Merchant, Hollywood Home Theater, Video Connection)

ADAM AND EVE (1958). See editions 1-3.

ADDAMS FAMILY, THE (1991). To recreate Charles Addams' macabre cartoon, Paramount assembled a superb cast: Raul Julia as Gomez, Anjelica Huston as Morticia and Christopher Lloyd as Uncle Fester. Sets and costumes provide an additional touch that keeps faith with Addams' graveyard humor. However, first-time director Barry Sonnenfeld has a hard time holding together a lightweight script by Larry Wilson and Caroline Thompson that fails to propel the Addamses into intriguing situations. What minute plot there is concerns a con woman trying to steal the Addams fortune and planting a Fester lookalike in the ghoulish clan. Still to be savored: morbid love dialogues between Gomez and Huston; Christina Ricci's superb rendering of daughter Wednesday Addams; hilarious sight gags, one-liners and mordant touches; and the appearance of Thing, a severed hand that runs all over the landscape; and Carel Steruycken's wordless performance as Lurch the butler. Lloyd plays Fester in every scene with eyeballs bulging and his face on the verge of bursting. Dan Hedaya, Elizabeth Wilson, Judith Malina, Dana Ivey. (Video/Laser: Paramount)

ADDAMS FAMILY VALUES (1993). Charles Addams' cartoon creations, first adapted to fit a TV series during the '60s, then recycled into a box-office smash in 1991, returns as a lavish, big-budgeted sequel with Raul Julia and Anjelica Huston as the heads of the horrorhouse. Carel Struycken is back as Lurch and Christopher Lloyd replays Fester. Other family members include Christina Ricci, Jimmy Workman and Joan Cusack. The Gomez's are blessed with a newborn, which the other kids try to snuff out in a series of macabre, cartoonish sight gags; and Fester falls prey to a femme fatale. (Video/Laser: Paramount)

ADDING MACHINE, THE (1969). See editions 1-3.

ADRENALINE (1990). Anthology of 13 tales of the fantastic and horrific, the main theme being objects that have supernatural powers. Seven Frenchmen directed.

ADVENTURES IN DINOSAUR CITY (1991). Copying elements of TV's DINOSAURS and the Ninja Turtle movies, this fantasy-adventure depicts three teenagers whisked through their father's time-vortex device to the

LON CHANEY JR. AS THE WOLF MAN IN 'ABBOTT AND COSTELLO MEET FRANKENSTEIN'

land of their favorite TV show. In Tar Town and Saur City, walking-talking lizard and dinosaur creatures ("the hippest dudes from the primordial ooze") mingle with anachronistic cave humans. The kids get caught up in intrigue and battle Mr. Big and his cavemen minions. Especially good is a cantina sequence filled with a plethora of creatures. This pleasing albeit dumb concoction was vigorously directed by Brett Thompson. Omri Katz, Shawn Hoffman. (Video/Laser: Republic)

ADVENTURES OF AN AMERICAN RABBIT (1986). Animated feature spinning off from the Superman and Captain Marvel myths. Mild-mannered Rob Rabbit transforms into American Rabbit when danger is at hand. In this adventure he goes after a pack of jackals on motorcycles and helps a band of night-club owners fight off a protection racket. (Kartes) (Laser: Image)

ADVENTURES OF BARON MUNCHAUSEN, THE (1989). British director Terry Gilliam, infected with Monty Python insanity, is in a world of chaotic extremes, where technology malfunctions and the dark side of man reigns. It's an odd framework for an enduring piece of fantasy literature (The Munchausen stories were written in 1785 by R. E. Raspe). The $40 million film, which went through a chaotic production, is a sight to behold as that irascible soldier of fortune, Baron Munchausen, plunders a sultan's treasure trove and starts a war in which Turkish forces assault a European city. He embarks on an odyssey to round up fellow adventurers and encounters a Man on the Moon whose head floats on a platter (played with wild abandon by Robin Williams), has a race with a speeding bullet, rides a cannonball—and pauses occasionally to tell a flashback adventure. The film sports a superb cast: Oliver Reed as Vulcan, king of Mt. Etna; Eric Idle as a member of an acting troupe; Valentina Cortese as the Queen of the Moon; and John Neville in the title role, a tour de force. Whatever its contradictions, see this warped masterpiece. (Video/Laser: RCA/Columbia)

ADVENTURES OF BATMAN AND ROBIN. See **BATMAN AND ROBIN.**

ADVENTURES OF BUCKAROO BANZAI: ACROSS THE EIGHTH DIMENSION (1984). Esoteric sci-fi/fantasy adventure, too clever for its own good as it heaps plot on plot that drown the viewer. Buckaroo (Peter Weller) is a contemporary Doc Savage, an intrepid leader of a team of action specialists, who crashes his nuclear-powered racer through solid matter, causing a disturbance in the Eighth Dimension and unleasing aliens on Earth. The Oscillation Overthruster is necessary to prevent global destruction, so Buckaroo and his Hong Kong Cavaliers pursue mad scientist Dr. Emilio Lizardo (John Lithgow, in a campy performance) and his ugly aliens. Although Earl Mac Rauch's script is unnecessarily complex, first-time director W. D. Richter does well with the action sequences. Ellen Barkin, Jeff Goldblum, Christopher Lloyd, Rosalind Cash, Robert Ito, Matt Clark, Vincent Schiavelli. (Video/Laser: Vestron)

ADVENTURES OF CAPTAIN MARVEL, THE (1941). Excellent 12-chapter Republic serial, one of the best of the '40s, with one-time cowboy star Tom Tyler donning the cape of the comic-book superhero (the word "Shazam" changes newsboy Billy Batson into this veritable man of steel) to pursue the evil Scorpion, a supervillain designing a matter transference machine for world domination. The action is slam-bang nonstop thank you, with veteran serial directors William Witney and John England in peak form as the Scorpion attempts to steal lenses that, when fitted together, will give him incredible power. Frank Coghlan Jr. is corny but adorable as Batson. Harry Worth, Louise Currie, William Benedict, Reed Hadley. (Video/Laser: Republic)

ADVENTURES OF FREDDIE. See **MAGNIFICENT MAGICAL MAGNET OF SANTA MESA.**

ADVENTURES OF HERCULES II. Video version of **HERCULES II** (MGM/UA).

ADVENTURES OF ICHABOD AND MR. TOAD (1949). Two Disney animated adventures in one: "The Wind in the Willows," narrated by Basil Rathbone, and

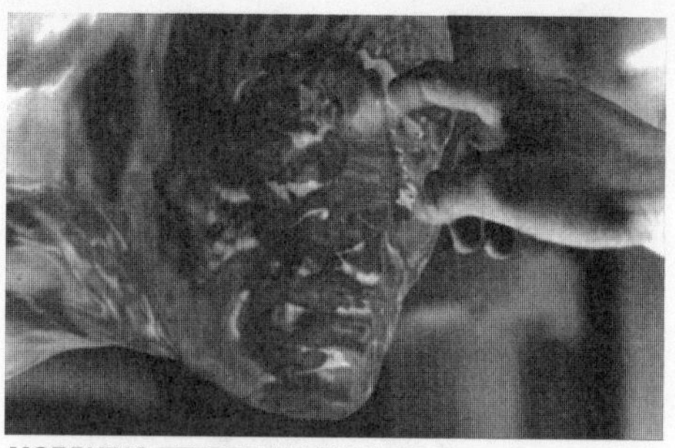

MORPHING EFFECT IN 'THE ABYSS'

"The Legend of Sleepy Hollow," narrated by Bing Crosby. Each is in separate video versions.

ADVENTURES OF MARK TWAIN, THE (1986). Claymation, an animated process used in commercials and short subjects as well as the feature RETURN TO OZ, brings Samuel Longhorn Clemens to life as he, Huck Finn and Tom Sawyer set sail in a balloon that takes them to a rendezvous with Halley's Comet. Twain's voice by James Whitmore. Directed by Will Vinton. (Kartes) (Laser: Paramount)

ADVENTURES OF MILO IN THE PHANTOM TOLLBOOTH. See **PHANTOM TOLLBOOTH, THE.**

ADVENTURES OF SINBAD (1962). This Japanese cartoon, based on Arabian Nights legends, is a curiosity piece for animation completists. In a simplistic style, it spins the familiar story of Sinbad (with friend Ali) embarking on a voyage to find Treasure Island and protect a princess from a caliph and "Hellbat" creature. There's a few unmemorable songs, weak comedy relief from two sailors, and Disneyesque figures: a cat, Pepe, and a mother whale and baby. There's an okay battle between Sinbad and the flying roc, transparent octopus monsters and a good vs evil battle. Directed by Taiji Yabushita.

ADVENTURES OF SUPERMAN, THE. See **SUPERMAN: THE SERIAL.**

ADVENTURES OF TAURA. See **STARSLAMMER.**

ADVENTURES OF ULTRAMAN, THE (1981). Repackaged episodes of the famous Japanese kiddie sci-fi series. See **ULTRAMAN.** (Family Home Entertainment)

AELITA (1924). The avant-garde movement in the Soviet Union during the post-Revolution decade was responsible for this bold, breathtaking adventure set in Russia and on Mars. Its imagery of a futuristic Martian society was a forerunner for the design of American sci-fi (FLASH GORDON and BUCK ROGERS). Its director was Yakov Protazanov, one of Russia's most successful film makers. Designers from the Moscow stage contributed the unique Martian look (heavy on glass and plastics). Based loosely on a story by Alexei Tolstoy, this depicts the love affair between an Earth engineer and the sovereign queen of Mars. Also involved are Gor, "the guardian of planetary energy," the Council of Elders, the dictator Tuskub, and a cast of thousands of Martian laborers. Also known as AELITA: QUEEN OF MARS. (King on Video; Kino; Sinister/C) (Laser: Image)

AERODROME (1983). See editions 2-3.

AFRAID OF THE DARK (1992). Offbeat study in abnormal child psychology with such a remarkably lowkey performance by young Ben Keyworth that it makes your skin crawl. It's full of startling surprises as Keyworth goes blind and his reveries and nightmares are played out as suspense-terror sequences. Many may find it baffling without being enlightening, but it is full of symbolism and allegory for those willing to search. To say more would be giving away too much. This most unusual thriller—giving new shadings of horror to blindness—was directed by Mark Peploe. James Fox, Fanny Ardant, Paul McGann. (New Line) (Laser: Image)

AFTER DARKNESS (1985). Before David Cronenberg's DEAD RINGERS there was this misguided psychological horror yarn about twin brothers who undergo childhood traumas. As adults, seemingly sane John Hurt takes disturbed Julian Sands from an asylum to live with him, but that only makes matters worse as Hurt takes on problems of his sick sibling. Writers-directors Dominique Othenin-Girard and Sergio Guerraz (identified in some U.S. prints as James Foley) create such ambigious characters there's little room for sympathy as they journey from rational to insane. More baffling and irritating than scary or thought provoking, this Swiss-British flick gets lost in its own murkiness. Pamela Salem, Victoria Abril. (Celebrity)

AFTERMATH, THE (1985). Well-directed and -edited post-holocaust adventure in which astronaut Steve Barkett (who also wrote and directed) returns from a mission to discover civilization has been ripped apart by nuclear war. The special effects work (with contributions from Jim Danforth) is remarkably good in creating a convincing nuked-out world. Also, Barkett injects considerable emotion into the relationship between the astronaut and an orphan (Christopher Barkett) he adopts from a radioactive-infected museum curator (Forrest J. Ackerman in a cameo). While evil gang leader Cutter (Sid Haig) ravages the countryside, slaughtering survivors, the astronaut builds up his own following, eventually facing Cutter and his gang in a bloody shootout. John Morgan's evocative music score is reminiscent of Bernard Herrmann. A bravura piece of film-making. Lynne Margulies, Alfie Martin. (Prism; Starmaker)

AFTER MIDNIGHT (1989). Effective horror anthology produced-written-directed by Ken and Jim Wheat. Marc Helgenberger portrays a high school instructor who teaches the "psychology of fear." His students gather to swap three terror yarns, with the framework device providing a fourth climax. #1: Two travelers seek refuge in a lonely mansion after their car breaks down. #2: Four girls are pursued by a madmen and his three killer dogs. #3: An answering service operator is trapped with a slasher. #4: The class is subjected to supernatural walking-dead horrors. Fans should enjoy this Wheat crop. Judie Aronson, Marc McClure, Ed Monaghan, Alan Rosenberg, Tracy Wells. (MGM; CBS/Fox)

AFTER PILKINGTON (1986). Eccentric albeit original British TV-movie, rich with subtleties of characterization and dialogue. University professor Bob Peck meets old flame Miranda Richardson and is trapped by her neurotic needs and his penchant for lying. He realizes she's a murderess who did in an anthropologist—his body is still in the woods behind the house with scissors protruding from his neck. Simon Gray's offbeat mystery has slight slasher overtones. Watch for clues in Christopher Morahan's direction. Giving a bloody fine performance is Barry Foster as Richardson's unsuspecting but far from dumb husband. (CBS/Fox)

AFTERSHOCK (1989). Uneven post-Armageddon adventure, its strongest assets well-staged, prolonged martial arts fights, interesting personalities and actual ruins of old factories. A futuristic society is controlled by a "Central Government" (represented by Richard Lynch and John Saxon) that is slaughtering Christopher Mitchum's rebel forces. A compelling twist is that an alien entity (Elizabeth Kaitain) is involved in the war. Jay Roberts Jr. makes for an uninteresting hero, and one wishes his pal (Chuck Jeffreys, an Eddie Murphy type) had been beefed up. Russ Tamblyn's happy-go-lucky bartender proves a bright light in the drab terrain. Michael Berryman is thrown into the soup too. Chris Derose plays an "apprehender" (read "gunfighter") whose change of heart makes for a few compelling moments. Directed by Frank Harris. (Prism)

AFTER THE FALL OF NEW YORK (1983). Italian-French imitation of MAD MAX is a glimpse at a post-holocaust world where splinter factions wage war. A cynical lone wolf is coerced by rebel forces (The Pan-American Federation) to penetrate the ruins of Manhattan where the evil Euraks hold sway, to rescue the only fertile woman on Earth so she can be rocketed to Alpha Centurai. Parsifal's comrades are a cyborg with a hook hand and a gray-haired warrior who downs foes with steel balls on a wire. The rubble of the Bronx and rat-infested sewers provide effective settings. The acting is unsophisticated and Martin Dolman's direction conventional, but the film gallops along. Michael Sopkin, Valentine Moonier, Roman Geer, George Purdom, George Eastman (as Big Ape, who looks like a Caribbean pirate.) (Vestron; Live)

AFTERWARD (1985). British TV-movie about a haunted house and the family that moves unsuspectingly into its eerie confines. Michael J. Shannon, Kay Harper, John Grillo. (Prism)

AGAINST ALL ODDS. Video version of **KISS AND KILL** (Republic).

AGENCY (1979). Conspiracy thriller involving the use of subliminal hate symbols in TV commercials, created by a secret organization to destroy political candidates. Robert Mitchum runs the agency where advertising man Lee Majors and an iconoclastic writer (Saul Rubinek, who dies a macabre death in a refrigerator) stumble on the secret. Moderately exciting, good tension. Directed in Canada by George Kaczender. Valerie Perrine, Alexandra Stewart, Hayward Morse. (Vestron; MNTEX; from Simitar as **MIND GAMES**)

AGENT FOR H.A.R.M. (1965). Third-rate spy crap starring Mark Richman as Adam Chance, operative of the Human Aetiological Relations Machine assigned to Operation Spore. A scientist has a bacteria that, when fired from a raygun, penetrates flesh and devours the body from within, emerging as a hungry fungus among us. Director Gerd Oswald puts sharper focus on the bikini-clad Barbara Bouchet than the fungus. Robert Quarry appears in a small role and Wendell Corey is the colorless H.A.R.M. assignment chief. Martin Kosleck, Rafael Campos and Carl Esmond contribute little to a film H.A.R.M.-ful to your viewing health.

AIRHAWK (1984). TV clone of BLUE THUNDER depicting the world's deadliest helicopter, piloted by Jan-Michael Vincent as Stringfellow Hawke, reclusive ex-Vietnam pilot for a government agency headed by Alex Cord. An exciting introduction to the TV series, this pilot is enhanced by Ernest Borgnine as Dominic Santini, father figure to Hawke, and Belinda Bauer, an undercover agent posing as a bellydancer in the employ of Dr. Moffett (David Hemmings), a dastard who steals his own helicopter and turns it over to foreign powers. The action scenes are lively and the romance between Vincent and Bauer sensuous. Created by Don Bellisario.

AIR HAWKS (1936). See editions 1-3.

AKIRA (1988). Animated Japanese feature (based on a comic-book series) set in the 21st Century, when Tokyo is ruled by a military government that has brought on urban blight and a disillusioned youth. With imaginative camera angles, director Katsuhiro Otomo brings an unusual sense of cartoon excitement to this convoluted though fascinating morality tale. Two members of a bike gang uncover a secret experiment to develop telekinetic humans to be used in warfare. It's a richly textured tale, demanding full attention. (Streamline) (Laser: Voyager)

ALABAMA'S GHOST (1972). Producer-director Fred Hobbs' descent into ambiguity and esoteric irrelevance as vampires (or facsimiles) chase around California on choppers. Don't expect continuity from this avant garde filmmaker. In fact, you might consider giving up Hobbs' ghost. Christopher Brooks, E. Kerrigan Prescott. (Thrillervideo)

ALADDIN (1986). Italian production, filmed in Miami, Fla., with a monotone, colorless Bud Spencer portraying a genie who befriends kidnapped youth Al Hadden. The gags are uninspired, Bruno Corbucci's direction is lackluster and the dialogue is bland. A waste of time for all. Luca Venantini, Janet Agren, Julian Voloshin. (Media)

ALADDIN (1992). Smash hit animated feature highlighted by the voice work of Robin Williams in the role of a hip genie, an action-prone youth on a magic carpet ride

JAFAR IN 'ALADDIN'

to adventure in the age of the Arabian Nights, fighting the evil sorcerer Jafar and winning the heart of beautuous Princess Jasmine. Music by Alan Menken and lyrics by Howard Ashman, with six songs woven into the tapestry. Produced-directed by John Musker and Ron Clements. Other voices by Scott Weiner, Brad Kane, Linda Larkin, Lea Salonga and Jonathan Freeman. (Video/Laser: Disney)

ALADDIN AND HIS LAMP (1952). Derring-do and Arabian Nights hokum in which a distressed young man finds a magic lamp. John Sands and Patricia Medina should have been called on The Carpet for accepting these shag-gy roles. Directed by Lew Landers, King of the Hollywood lamp scamps. John Dehner, Noreen Nash, Ned Young, Billy House.

ALADDIN AND HIS MAGIC LAMP (1983). Usual stuff about the Arabian Nights adventurer. (Prism)

ALADDIN AND HIS WONDERFUL LAMP (1984). Episode of Showtime's FAERIE TALE THEATRE, directed by Tim Burton. Valerie Bertinelli, Robert Carradine, Leonard Nimoy, James Earl Jones. (CBS/Fox)

ALAKAZAM THE GREAT (1961). Monkey thinks he's smarter than Einstein, but undergoes an object lesson that teaches him even a monkey can be made a monkey of. Japanese animated cartoon dubbed with Occidental voices: Jonathan Winters, Dodie Stevens, Frankie Avalon, Arnold Stang, Sterling Holloway. Score by Les Baxter. Pleasantly diverting. (HBO)

ALBINO (1976). West German-South African co-production, set in Africa, in which a killer with bleached-white skin terrorizes for revenge. Christopher Lee, Trevor Howard, Sybil Danning, Horst Frank, James Faulkner. Directed by Juergen Goslar. (Media)

ALCHEMIST, THE (1983). In 1871, Delgado the Alchemist has the hots for raven-haired Lucinda Dooling and forces her lover (Robert Ginty, a Virginia glass maker) to fight for her honor. When she dies the warlock turns Ginty into a tormented man who eats deer. Flash to 1955, when a woman who looks like Dooling happens to drive by Ginty's cabin and is ESPed into his lair in the company of a benevolent hitchhiker. Everyone fights for soul possession as demons jump through a portal of Hell, a grandmother is impaled on a spike and a man is torn in half by the time-continuum threshold. Whew! Charles Band production directed by James Amante. Viola Kate Stimpson. (Lightning; Vestron; Live)

ALI AND THE TALKING CAMEL (198?). That talking camel, Mehari, is the only fantasy element in this children's adventure as Arab youth Mohamed Rifai tangles with diamond thieves in the Middle East desert. Good locations enhance this ordinary kiddie flick, with Mehari not an endearing character, what with a heavy-handed British accent booming from his slavering jaws. Written-produced-directed by Henry Geddes.

ALIAS JOHN PRESTON (1956). Psychological British thriller with Christopher Lee undergoing nightmares and splitting into good and evil. Directed by David MacDonald. Alexander Knox, Betta St. John, Peter Grant, Sandra Dorne. (Sinister/C; S/Weird)

ALIAS NICK BEAL (1949). Offbeat allegorical fantasy (directed with a satanic wit by John Farrow) has a touch of offbeat casting with Ray Milland as a hornless Beelzebub recruiting souls for Hell. His target is an honest politician (Thomas Mitchell) whom he would corrupt prior to the Grand Descent. Jonathan Latimer's script has Frank Capra-like touches, giving depth to this supernatural drama-comedy. Lovely Audrey Totter employs her own form of seduction. George Macready, Fred Clark, Darryl Hickman, King Donovan. (Filmfax)

ALI BABA GOES TO TOWN (1937). Editions 1-3.

ALICE IN WONDERLAND (1933). A cast indigenous to the 1930s (W.C. Fields, Gary Cooper, Jack Oakie, Richard Arlen, Cary Grant, Charles Ruggles, Baby Leroy, Mae Marsh) populates this expensive Paramount version of Lewis Carroll's classic, directed by Norman Z. McLeod and written by Joseph L. Mankiewicz and William Cameron Menzies. Disappointing effort in which the Carroll characters are reduced to costumed Hollywood personalities. Music by Dimitri Tiomkin. Charlotte Henry, Mae Marsh, Edna May Oliver, Roscoe Ates.

ALICE IN WONDERLAND (1951). Full-length Disney feature, a super-deluxe cartoon blending Lewis Carroll's ALICE'S ADVENTURES IN WONDERLAND with THROUGH THE LOOKING GLASS, reflects the ultimate in Disney's standards. Voices: Kathryn Beaumont, Ed Wynn, Verna Felton, Pat O'Malley, Sterling Holloway, Stan Freberg. (Disney)

ALICE IN WONDERLAND (1951). Rare adaptation of Lewis Carroll's satirical classic, a sparkling blend of live action and stop-motion animation with three-dimensional puppets. Producer-director Lou Bunin found himself in competition with Disney (see above) and unable to secure wide distribution. His film languished and died, not enjoying a revival until 1985. Bunin is faithful to Carroll in this stylized, esoteric whimsy crafted by loving hands, which now suffers from outdated techniques, poor sound and color. Carol Marsh is a beautiful blonde Alice, and the opening features Stephen Murray, Pamela Brown, Felix Aylmer portraying the British royalty that Carroll satirized. (Media; Monterey)

ALICE IN WONDERLAND (1985). Would you believe a $14-million TV-movie adaptation of Lewis Carroll by Irwin Allen, Hollywood's Mad Hatter? A journey into a rabbit hole, indeed, as Allen tackles this four-hour musical with updated language and situations. Directed by Harry Harris (of FAME fame), it has enough guest stars to make a March Hare leap into April. How about Sid Caesar as the Gryphon, Roddy McDowall as the Hare, Lloyd Bridges as the White Knight, Telly Savalas as the Cheshire Cat, Karl Malden as the Lion, Carol Channing as the White Queen, Jonathan Winters as Humpty Dumpty. Alice is portrayed by Natalie Gregory.

ALICE'S ADVENTURES IN WONDERLAND (1972). British musical based on the Lewis Carroll classic, graced by Fiona Fullerton, Sir Ralph Richardson, Peter Sellers, Dudley Moore, Flora Robson. Directed by William Sterling. (Children's Video Library; Vestron; Rentertainment; Impulse)

ALICE, SWEET ALICE (1978). Grueling suspense with well-developed characters and psychiatric background, also known as COMMUNION and HOLY TERROR. A knife-wielding murderer wearing a doll's mask provides the film's engrossing puzzle. The Catholic Church is the dominating motif, with its omnipresent statues of Christ, madonnas and saints, and its themes of pain and suffering, guilt and innocence. Unknowns (Paula Sheppard, Linda Miller, Mildred Clinton) are supported by Lillian Roth and Brooke Shields. Directed by Alfred Sole. (Goodtimes; Spotlite)

ALICE THROUGH THE LOOKING GLASS (1966). Carroll's fantasy enlivened with an all-star cast: Judi Rolin, Ricardo Montalban, Nanette Fabray, Robert Coote, Agnes Moorehead, Jack Palance. Directed by Alan Handley. (Children's Treasures; Kartes)

ALIEN (1979). Just when you thought it was safe to go back into space, along came this ingenious mixture of Gothic horror and sci-fi, a monster movie that lambasts you with shock after shock even after the evil creature is exposed in all its hideous fascination. Credit goes to Swiss designer H. R. Giger for creating the extraterrestrial, ever-changing in its stages of evolution into something larger and deadlier. This revolutionary film unfolds aboard the space freighter Nostromo, ordered to set down on an unexplored planet in response to a distress signal. Soon the organic life form is on board, tracking crew members John Hurt, Tom Skerritt, Ian Holm, Yaphet Kotto, Harry Dean Stanton, Veronica Cartwright and Sigourney Weaver. Director Ridley Scott loves cat-and-mouse games, alternating false scares with genuine jolts. Dan O'Bannon's screenplay not only touches our sense of wonder but reminds us of our fear of the dark and everything unknown or ugly. A splendid paradox giving us those things we dread most, but love to scream at in the dark. It was followed by ALIENS (another classic) and ALIEN 3. (Video/Laser: CBS/Fox)

ALIEN 2. See **ALIENS.**

ALIEN 3 (1992). If ever there was a set designer's movie, devoted totally to moody, nihilistic ambience, it is this third effort in the popular series. Under the direction of David Fincher, who won this assignment through innovative rock videos, ALIEN 3 carries over the pictorial qualities and atmosphere of the first two films. Ridley (Sigourney Weaver) crashlands in a shuttlecraft on a farflung prison planet, Fiorina 161. The only survivor, Ridley learns the ship has brought an alien with it, and one by one the religious fanatics in the dilapidated penal colony are torn asunder. Since the previous films were more interested in hairraising suspense and pyrotechnics than characters, it is not surprising ALIEN 3 lacks any interesting humans other than Ridley, a sympathetic

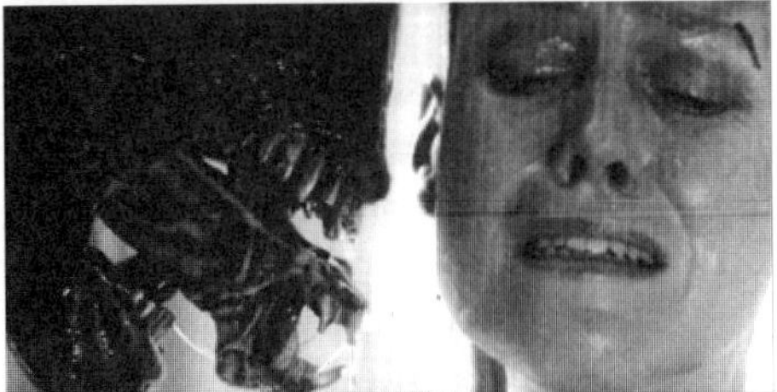

SIGOURNEY WEAVER IN 'ALIEN 3'

doctor (Charles Dance, who disappears too fast from the story) and a convict (Charles S. Dutton). One of the neat twists to the David Giler-Walter Hill-Larry Ferguson script (Vincent Ward is credited with story): the planet is so rundown, it has no weaponry with which to fight the alien. Unfortunately, the film's climax seems lifted from TERMINATOR 2 and some maudlin business involving Ripley doesn't work at all. But these quibblings aside, ALIENS 3 is a gripping horror and sci-fi. Brian Glover, Lance Henriksen. (Video/Laser: CBS/Fox)

ALIENATOR (1989). Another Fred Olen Ray special, derivative of THE TERMINATOR. Rebel leader Ross Hagen escapes prison and comes to Earth to wipe out his own youngsters to affect the future. Watch for Teagan Clive in a sexy role. Robert Clarke, Robert Quarry, Jan-Michael Vincent, John Phillip Law. (Prism) (Laser: Image)

ALIEN ATTACK (1975). TV compilation of episodes from SPACE: 1999, a British series with Barbara Bain and Martin Landau as members of an experimental station on the moon who face hardships when the moon is blasted out of Earth's orbit and hurtles through space. Catherine Schell, Tony Anholt, Nick Tate, Zienia Merton.

ALIEN CONTAMINATION (1980). When a freighter is found with its crew turned into grisly gruel and a cargo of pulsating egg-shapes, you know you're dealing with body-snatched filmmakers contaminated by ALIEN. When the egg sacs burst open, they spread smoky goo and kill. A conspiracy for world conquest is controlled by a one-eyed Martian glob with a big mouth who hypnotizes humans. The effects in this Italian import are as inferior as the dubbing and the monster will have you laughing, not gagging. Writer-director Luigi Cozzi provides an inept charm that makes this fun, especially the inane dialogue. Ian McCulloch, Louise Monroe. (Cannon; Regal; Paragon; in a heavily edited version from European Creative Films as **CONTAMINATION** and from Lettuce Entertain You as **TOXIC SPAWN**)

ALIEN DEAD, THE (1980). ETs ride to Earth on a meteorite, crashlanding and turning a boatful of kids into raving zombies and other nonsocial creatures. Joining forces to fight them are newsman Ray Roberts and game warden Mike Bonavia. An undistinguished work (also known as IT FELL FROM THE SKY) from prolific Fred Olen Ray, who gave us BIOHAZARD (and indigestion). Buster Crabbe, in his final role, plays Sheriff Kowalski. (Academy; Genesis; Paragon)

ALIEN ENCOUNTERS (1979). Writer-director James T. Flocker churned out this empty UFO muddle in semi-documentary fashion, following an investigator in search of a man in black and a floating silver ball allegedly sent to Earth by aliens as part of a probe. Nothing for the mind or the eye. Augie Tribach, Matt Boston.

ALIEN ENCOUNTERS. See **UFO's ARE REAL.**

ALIEN FACTOR, THE (1979). Baltimore filmmaker Don Dohler focuses on a spaceship that crashlands on Earth. Three aliens emerge to terrorize folks around Perry Hill: The Leemoid, a reptilian being that sucks the life force from humans; the Inferbyce, a clawed gooey-looking creature; and the Zagatile, a tall, furry being. Don Leifert, Tom Griffin. (Media; United; VCI)

ALIEN FROM L.A. (1987). The "Alien" is Wanda, a nerdy woman who leaves Malibu to search for her archeologist father, missing in the underground city of Atlantis. This traditional worm-turns fairy tale is a pleasant, oft funny series of misadventures with Kathy Ireland meeting sappy/zappy characters, and endearing her own character with squeaky voice and childlike innocence. In this funky variation on "Alice in Dunderland" that avoids violence, Albert Pyun (SWORD AND THE SORCERER, CYBORG) proves he's a developing director. Thom Mathews, Don Michael Paul, Linda Kerridge, Richard Haines. (Media) (Laser: Image)

ALIEN HIGH (1987). Dumb (or is it stupid?) Canadian teenage comedy, in which two high school nerds in the Bill & Ted mode (only before Bill & Ted) uncover a plot by a humanoid E.T. to turn students into zombies by mind control devices involving rock 'n roll music. This unfolds on the principle that if you can control minds of teeners, you can control any mind. A true-enough axiom. Ron Thinnes is embarrassingly wasted as a screaming principal of another kind. Directed by Eugenie Joseph. Skip Lackey, Lee Tergesen.

ALIEN INTRUDER (1992). Unusual mixture of hardware sci-fi and virtual reality (in the WESTWORLD vein) when a seductress E.T. named Ariel (Tracy Scoggins) seduces spacemen to murder for her. Commander Billy Dee Williams brings a ragtag band of ruffians to a floating space station to investigate, where they become involved with "realities" parodying CASABLANCA, Western and motorcycle movies. The mediocre effects waylay the film's good intentions, spearheaded by writer Nick Stone and director Ricardo Jacques Gale. Maxwell Caulfield, Gary Roberts, Jeff Conaway, Richard Cody.

ALIEN LOVER (1975). TV-movie with Kate Mulgrew and Pernell Roberts involved with a teenage orphan who makes friends with an E.T. beamed down in a TV signal from another galaxy. Directed by Lela Swift.

ALIEN MASSACRE. Video version of **RETURN FROM THE PAST** (Doris Chase).

ALIEN MASSACRE. Video version of **WIZARD OF MARS, THE** (Regal).

ALIEN NATION (1988). Unusual sci-fi thriller, borrowing touches from the buddy-buddy crime flicks to spin its refreshing concept. In the immediate future a shipload of humanoid aliens, labeled "newcomers," crashland on Earth and are assimilated into working-class society, evoking a racist reaction among Earthlings. When a gang of aliens begins a wave of crime, cop James Caan volunteers to team with an alien officer to track the killers. What they uncover, while learning about each other's culture, makes for interesting twists while the drug plot unfolds. Writer Rockne S. O'Bannon gives unusual traits to his aliens (they get drunk on milk, and have peculiar body odors) and makes them believable. Caan walks a fine line between tough-guy hardness and his soft spot for his alien buddy. Mandy Patinkin is memorable as Sykes the alien cop. Produced by Gale Anne Hurd and Richard Kobritz, and directed by Graham Baker, this superior action fantasy became the basis for a syndicated TV series. Terence Stamp, Kevin Major Howard, Leslie Bevins. (Video/Laser: CBS/Fox)

ALIEN ORO, THE (1973). Episodes from THE STAR-LOST, a short-lived TV disaster set aboard the colossal starship Ark, seeking new worlds so its passengers can begin new civilizations. These re-edited episodes deal with Keir Dullea meeting an alien named Oro, who plans to take over the craft. STAR TREK's Walter Koenig portrays Oro. Robin Ward, Gay Rowan.

ALIEN P.I. See **ALIEN PRIVATE EYE.**

ALIEN PREDATOR (1985). Three bumblebutt youths in a rec vehicle (Dennis Christopher, Martin Hewitt, Lynn-Holly Johnson), traveling through Spain, stop in a town where citizens are controlled by living microbes brought from the Moon by a Skylab satellite. Written-directed by Deran Sarafian, from Noah Bloch's script MASSACRE AT R.V. PARK, this inferior sci-fier includes a subplot involving Professor Tracer (Luis Predes) and his attempts to find an antidote at a NASA lab. The heroes play the weak material for laughs, but nothing helps this tedious derivative of ALIEN. Also known as THE FALLING. (Trans World; Video Treasures)

ALIEN PREY (1983). Lousy British cheapie, a feeble excuse for torrid, X-rated lesbian scenes between insufferable bitches living in a country estate. Along comes a humanoid alien that eats chickens, foxes and birds, doesn't know how to swim, and turns into a vampire when he's making love. Shoddy exploitation, with terrible make-up and cliched effects. Directed tastelessly by Norman J. Warren. Barry Stokes, Glory Anann, Sally Faulkner. (Comet; Cinema Group)

ALIEN PRIVATE EYE (1990). Inferior direct-to-video nonsense about a humanoid (Nikki Fastinetti) named Lemro from the Styx (planet Styx, that is) who uses martial arts to battle enemies while she's on Earth searching for a drug sent to our planet on a black disc. Cliff Aduddell, John Alexander, Robert Axelrod. Written-produced-directed by Vik Rubenfeld. (Raedon)

ALIENS (1986). Riveting action-suspense movie, a supreme sequel to Ridley Scott's ALIEN. Writer-director James Cameron, fresh from THE TERMINATOR, concocts a thunderyarn reeking with tension and fear, and structured so tightly it moves at lightning pace, so masterful is Cameron at building cliffhangers within cliffhangers. Sigourney Weaver returns as the resourceful, hard-driven Ripley, who is rescued 57 years after ALIEN ended and faces a bleak future. Haunted by nightmares of the face-hugger and the belly-busting E.T., she returns to Rhea-M to locate colonists who have disappeared. Accompanied back to the windswept planet by commandoes equipped with futuristic weapons, she again faces the most hideous creatures of all time. Cameron's focus is the battle between the cynical, well-trained commando team and devious creatures in the dingy corridors and labs of the compound. The humans are only lightly delineated, but some of them come off good, including Michael Biehn, Bill Paxton, Lance Henriksen, Carrie Henn and Jenette Goldsten. Thrills build on thrills until Ripley takes on Mother Alien and her brood in a sequence that qualifies Weaver as the female Rambo of the '80s. Like ALIEN, this exploits our worst fears and carries them to an extreme. All-time classic, brilliantly conceived. (Video/Laser: CBS/Fox)

ALIENS ARE COMING, THE (1980). Except for a mother ship hovering in Earth's atmosphere, this TV-movie features few effects and little excitement under Harvey Hart's listless direction. It's a compendium of cliches, from the alien energy forces that take over humans to glowing green eyes indicating someone is about to be zapped by strange science. Hoover Dam near Las Vegas is the scenic setting to an otherwise predictable invasion plot. The story ends on a "the nightmare is just beginning" warning. Gosh, what excitement! Tom Mason, Eric Braeden, Caroline McWilliams, John Milford, Max Gail. (Worldvision; Goodtimes)

ALIENS, DRAGONS, MONSTERS & ME (1991). TV documentary about the career of effects artist Ray Harryhausen, featuring clips from his features and rare early works. Narrated by Gary Owens, the report includes Ray Bradbury explaining Harryhausen's importance. (Cerebus) (Laser: Lumivision)

ALIEN SEED (1989). Earth woman becomes pregnant via alien presence on Earth as part of an E.T. scheme to create a new "Messiah" to rule the world. Her sister calls on dedicated newsman Erik Estrada to solve the mystery. Okay direct-to-video fare. Heidi Paine, Steven Blade. Written by director Bob James and Douglas K. Grimm. (Action International)

ALIENS FROM ANOTHER PLANET (1966). Episodes of TV's THE TIME TUNNEL. James Darren and Robert Colbert search for a man in 1547 who has hidden a time bomb in the Time Tunnel Complex; then, the time travelers land in 2268 to face aliens from Alpha One. Produced by TV schlockmeister Irwin Allen. For details, see **TIME TUNNEL, THE.**

ALIENS FROM SPACESHIP EARTH (1977). Mixture of documented facts and Hollywood hokum—but which is which? This film asks the burning question: Are we being visited by aliens? Then the question is illustrated by dramatic reenactments of close encounters. Quick, said the alien to the garbage man, take me to your litter. Lynda Day George, Donovan. (Video Gems)

ALIEN SPACE AVENGER (1988). This parody of alien-invasion movies vacillates between tongue-in-cheek physical comedy/campy dialogue and overdone graphic violence, in which humans are blasted into eternity for no particular reason. In 1939, an alien ship carrying escaped prisoners crashlands and four ugly snake-like monsters take over two men and two women. The story leaps to today as the foursome ventures to New York to tangle with the artist of the "Space Avenger" comic book. The effects consist of showing how the humanoids regenerate new body parts after being blasted to bits. The inability of writer-director-co-producer Richard W. Haines to find a style and stick with it eventually alienates the viewer. A movie in search of fun without finding it. Robert Prichard, Gina Mastrogiacomo, Charity Staley. "Kirk Fairbanks Fogg" is credited as "Space Avenger," but no space avenger appears. (Action International)

ALIEN'S RETURN, THE (1980). UFO hovers over a desert community, bathing a boy and girl in eerie light and fog. Years later he's a deputy marshal, she's a satellite research expert. Man meets woman in town while she's investigating strange emanations from rocks. There's also a crazed prospector responsible for cattle mutilations with his Laser Beam Killer Gun. Low-budgeter from producer-director Greydon Clark's lacks "high tech" clout. Jan-Michael Vincent (deputy), Cybill Shepherd (research expert), Raymond Burr (Cybill's scientist-dad), Vinnie Schiavelli (crazy miner), Neville Brand (sarcastic rancher), Martin Landau (stupid marshal).

ALIEN TERROR. Video version of Boris Karloff's **INCREDIBLE INVASION** (Sony; MPI).

ALIEN II. See **ALIEN CONTAMINATION.**

ALIEN WARNING. See **IT CAME . . . WITHOUT WARNING.**

"My body can't take this any more. The blood of these whores is killing me." —Count Dracula in **ANDY WARHOL'S DRACULA.**

ALIEN WARRIOR (1985). On a beam of light, a man from another dimension (Brett Clark) arrives on Earth to fight "Great Evil." Clark walks around like he's in a trance, rescues Pamela Saunders from rape, fights drug dealers, and converts minority types at Saunders' reading center. A feeble-minded excuse for voyeuristic sex and bloody shoot-outs with Clark behaving like a superhero as he crashes through walls and heals his wounds with an inner power. If there's a moral, it's lost in the mindless violence. Ed Hunt directed. Reggie DeMorton, Nelson D. Anderson. Originally released as KING OF THE STREETS. (Vestron; Live)

ALIEN WITHIN, THE (198?). Rank-amateur film-making, an insufferable mess clearly two movies in one. The filmed portions (originally THE DEADLY STING) depict sexy Bobbie Bresee as aging actress Lynn Roman, who takes a serum that turns her into a monster that sees through a multiple-image prism. She goes after her agent and others who shafted her career. Except for Bresee's performance, this is unconvincing, the monster looking like a reject from a '50s flick. Kenneth J. Hall is said to have directed. The taped portions, directed by Ted Newsom, have Richard Harrison and Gordon Mitchell as movie-world types involved with the serum's creator, Dr. Zeitman, played by an ill-looking John Carradine. Forrest J. Ackerman has an unnecessary cameo as a surveillance expert, and there's a hand-puppet monster no more convincing than the thing Bresee turns into. Producer Fred Olen Ray admitted he had a hand in this. Jay Richardson, Suzanne Ager, Melissa Moore, Crystal Shaw. (MNTEX Entertainment; from Camp as **EVIL SPAWN**, the theatrical title)

ALIEN WOMEN. Video version of **ZETA ONE** (Front Row Entertainment; Prism; Sinister/C).

ALIEN ZONE (1975). Anthology of macabre tales told by ghoulish mortician Ivor Francis to John Ericson, an adulterer fleeing an irate husband. Production values are mediocre but the stories are compelling: A child-hating woman is terrorized by youngsters; a killer photographs women he is about to strangle; two rival detectives try to outwit each other; and a Scrooge-minded man is subjected to mental and physical torture. Ericson's fate provides the fifth tale. Made in Oklahoma, ALIEN ZONE is a diverting novelty directed by Sharon Miller. Judith Novgrod, Burr DeBenning, Charles Aidman, Bernard Fox. (In video as **HOUSE OF THE DEAD** and also known as **ZONE OF THE DEAD**)

ALISON'S BIRTHDAY (1979). Australian supernatural flick written-directed by Ian Coughlan and produced by David Hemmings with a Down Under cast. It's the old possession-of-the-soul serving, with little icing on the cake, as Joanne Samuels (Alison) undergoes a reign of terror so her soul can be transferred to the body of an old hag. Lou Brown, Bunney Brooke, Margie McCrae. (Satori; VidAmerica)

ALLAN QUATERMAIN AND THE LOST CITY OF GOLD (1986). Richard Chamberlain returns as H. R. Haggard's adventurer (sans British accent) trekking through dangerous Africa in search of his missing brother in an inferior sequel to KING SOLOMON'S MINES (1986). Quatermain treks with sexy Sharon Stone, native warrior James Earl Jones and cowardly Indian shaman Robert Donner to a shimmering-white metropolis ruled by evil Henry Silva (in an awful fright wig) and Cassandra Peterson (she of Elvira infamy, in a push-up bra). Only the first half has the charm and humor of its predecessor. Fantasy elements involve snake monsters and Indiana Jones-type ripoffs. Directed by Gary Nelson. (MGM/UA)

ALL DOGS GO TO HEAVEN (1989). Entertaining animated musical-comedy feature from the Don Bluth factory, which portrays the adventures of an unsympathetic con-artist dog named Charlie B. Barkin (voice by Burt Reynolds) who dies and goes to heaven, then returns to Earth to carry out one decent deed. He and his dachshund pal (voice by Dom DeLuise) befriend a young orphan girl, finding redemption for their lawless ways. A few of the musical pieces are wonderful, one involving a giant singing alligator. The ending gets maudlin, but all ages should find this amusing. Bluth directed-produced with Gary Goldman, John Pomeroy and Dan Kuenster. Voices: Loni Anderson, Vic Tayback, Charles Nelson Reilly. (Video/Laser: MGM/UA)

ALLEGRO NON TROPPO (1977). Italian animator Bruno Bozzetto pays homage to Disney's FANTASIA with six vignettes illustrated to classical music. A scroungy cat is the hero of Sibelius' "Valse Triste"; a Coke bottle figures prominently in Ravel's "Bolero," a tour de force depicting the evolution of life; and a honeybee housewife wreaks revenge on picnickers in Vivaldi's "Concerto in C." The story of Adam and Eve is recounted to Stravinsky's "Firebird"; a white-bearded satyr can no longer please the nymphs to Debussy's "Prelude to the Afternoon of a Faun" and a fable is the core of Dvorak's "Slavic Dance No. 7." This world-famous feature sports live-action wraparound about an orchestra recording music for the cartoons and its silly maestro Maurizio Nichetti, who co-wroter the script with Bozzetto. (RCA/Columbia) (Laser: Image)

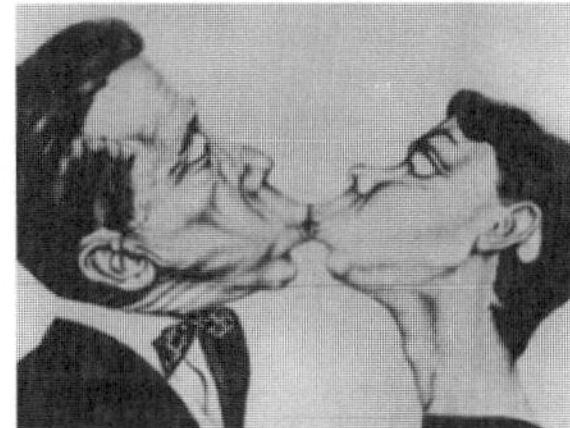

'ALLEGRO NON TROPPO'

ALLIGATOR (1981). Tongue-in-cheek spoof by writer John Sayles (THE HOWLING) sets the skin-tone for this takeoff on giant-monsters-on-a-rampage movies. A 35-foot-long gator is loose in the sewers and cop Robert Forster is in pursuit—when the monster isn't in pursuit of Forster, jaws slobbering for policeman meat. The creature swims to a theme not unlike John Williams' JAWS and carries away entire bodies (look out, gator hunter Henry Silva, you don't stand a chance). Director Lewis Teague (LADY IN RED, CUJO) takes none of it seriously and spices the sewer walls with such graffiti as "Harry Lime lives!" If you hate the sight of amphibious entities, you might take along Gator Aid. Dean Jagger, Sue Lyon, Angel Tompkins. (Lightning; Live)

ALLIGATOR II: THE MUTATION (1990). Unconnected sequel to the 1981 ALLIGATOR, in which an oversized gator monster living in the sewers of L.A. decides to have a coming out party—by munching on fishermen and bums. Cop Joseph Bologna rallies forces with the help of police captain Brock Peters and a colorful gator hunter named "Hawk," played with a southern accent by Richard Lynch. Written by Curt Allen, and directed by Jon Hess, this is a phony-baloney monster movie with crummy effects and unconvincing gore attacks. Steve Railsback plays an equally unconvincing villain running an amusement park next to the lake—gosh, does this mean the patrons will also be eaten? Dee Wallace Stone is wasted as Bologna's wife/scientist, and there's a dumb affair between cop Woody Brown and mayor's daughter Holly Gagnier. (New Line)

ALLIGATOR PEOPLE, THE (1959). Orville Hampton's screenplay is swamped with cliches, but still an entertaining B effort. George Macready is a hypo-happy scientist experimenting with a serum to restore accident victims to normal but which results in scaly skin and glutinous gills. You see, he's been extracting hormones from gators. Richard Crane (TV's Rocky Jones) is one of the doc's guinea pigs who's just wed Beverly Garland. When he runs away, she rushes to his Everglades plantation to become a dame in peril. The film is notable for Lon Chaney Jr. as a modern Captain Hook, and he has a bog-day with his over-the-top role. There's also a great scene of rain-soaked Garland stumbling through a gator-infested swamp. Bruce Bennett lends authority as a psychiatrist. Directed by Roy Del Ruth with a slimy feeling for a swampland horror tale.

ALLIGATORS. See **GREAT ALLIGATOR, THE.**

ALL NEW TALES FROM THE CRYPT. See **TALES FROM THE CRYPT** (the TV series).

ALL OF ME (1984). Disappointing Steve Martin supernatural "comedy"—a waste of the wild and crazy guy, and of Lili Tomlin. He plays a legal attorney (moonlighting as a jazz magician) sent to draw up the will of a dying millionairess. Lili is the insufferable moneybags who croaks only to have her soul transferred to Martin's body. Now half of him is him, half of him is her. The Phil Alden Robinson script (based on an Ed Davis novel) is vacuous, giving director Carl Reiner little to work with. A waste of Madolyn Smith, Richard Libertini, Dana Elcar and Victoria Tennant. (Video/Laser: HBO)

ALL THAT MONEY CAN BUY. See **DEVIL AND DANIEL WEBSTER, THE**.

ALMOST AN ANGEL (1990). Belabored, painful-to-watch fantasy-comedy in which Paul Hogan portrays a bank-robbing rogue who is killed saving a young boy's life and goes to Heaven—there to be confronted by Charlton Heston. Call it CROCODILE DUNDEE MEETS GOD. Described by the robed Heston as "a scumbag," and designated as "a probationary angel," Hogan returns to Earth to do the obligatory good deed. That deed is to befriend wheelchair-bound Vietnam veteran Elias Koteas. It's pure schmaltz with the gags falling as flat as an angel without wings. An empty, misconceived project Hogan co-produced and wrote. He wears many hats, but none fits as well as the one he wore as Dundee. Directed without pizazz by Hogan's pal, John Cornell. The music is by Maurice Jarre. Linda Kozlowski, Parley Baer, Hank Worden. (Paramount)

ALMOST HUMAN. See **SHOCK WAVES.**

ALONE IN THE DARK (1982). Three whacko cases (Jack Palance, Martin Landau, Erland Van Lidth) escape the asylum of doctor Donald Pleasence, as fruitcake as his patients. The homicidal threesome surrounds the house of a psychiatrist and terrorizes his family. The headshrinker finally resorts to violence to save his loved ones. The bloodbath is gratuitous, and there are moments when writer-director Jack Sholder doesn't explain events. The most depraved scene has Palance under a woman's bed, thrusting upward with a knife through the mattress, the point of the blade emerging between her thighs. A real mixed bag of genres from producer Robert Shaye, who went on to greater success with New Line Pictures. Dwight Schultz, Deborah Hedwall, Lee Taylor-Allan. (RCA/Columbia)

ALPHA INCIDENT, THE (1978). A living micro-organism from Mars, brought to Earth on a space probe, terrorizes a motley bunch at a railroad office. The folks bicker and talk and bicker while back at the lab scientists seek an antidote. There's nonsense about not being able to sleep (it's then the microbe destroys the body) so the characters stay awake by playing poker and having sex. Ralph Meeker is wasted as a dim-witted depot manager, and his death scene provides the only effect—his head turning into a puddle of goo. Produced-directed by Bill Rebane, this low-budgeter made in Wisconsin was no incident. Stafford Morgan, John Alderman, John Goff, Carol Irene Newel. (Media)

ALPHAVILLE (1965). Director Jean-Luc Godard also wrote this film set in the near-future in which private eye Lemmy Caution (Eddie Constatine) is assigned to rescue a doctor from a city controlled by a computerized brain, Alpha 60, and its creator, Dr. Von Braun (Howard Vernon). Film noir, science vs. intellect, and romance and mythology, vacillating between art film and detective actioner. Anna Karina, Akim Tamiroff, Christa Lang. (Vintage; S/Weird; Filmfax) (Laser: Japanese)

ALTERED STATES (1980). Sci-fi metamorphosis picture given distinguished treatment by Warner Bros. and ballyhooed for its prestigious director (Ken Russell) and screenwriter (Paddy Chayefsky). But in reality it's the same old mad-scientist story, redressed with special effects razzle dazzle by Dick Smith and others. Genetics investigator William Hurt climbs into a deepwater think tank and regresses to a primeval state, turning into a hairy ape. There's a real freak-out sequence at the end. Blair Brown, Bob Balaban, Charles Haid, Drew Barrymore. (Video/Laser: Warner Bros.)

ALUCARDA. See **SISTERS OF SATAN.**

ALWAYS (1989). Steven Spielberg is a wonderful director but sometimes he overinflates his films with emotion and turns his characters into schmaltzy goofballs, defeating good intentions. ALWAYS is an intimate romance, but Spielberg (working with a Jerry Belson script) gives it such epic proportions that the story's flimsiness is apparent. And yet, it's such a good-natured movie, full of charming characters and enhanced by a rousing John Williams score, you can't help but like it. In this loose update of A GUY NAMED JOE, Richard Dreyfuss is an airman fighting fires in Montana, making dangerous runs over burning forests. Holly Hunter is his lover and John Goodman his best buddy. After Dreyfuss dies in a heroic attempt to save Goodman, he finds himself in a netherland where angel Audrey Hepburn tells him he has to perform one last good deed. Yeah, a lot of ALWAYS is corny, but . . . Brad Johnson, Roberts Blossom, Keith David. (Video/Laser: MCA)

AMAZING CAPTAIN NEMO, THE (1978). Absurd Irwin Allen TV-movie in which two naval officers find the submarine Nautilus abandoned on the ocean floor, with Captain Nemo (Jose Ferrer) preserved in a cryogenic chamber. Nemo leaps out and, forgetting he's just slept for 100 years, pursues a sub commanded by evil Burgess Meredith, who threatens to destroy Washington with a missile. A series of chases featuring force fields, radiation-contaminated waters, laser zap guns, underwater swimming, etc. Robert (PSYCHO) Bloch obviously wrote this to Allen's Neanderthal specifications. Lynda Day George, Mel Ferrer, Horst Buchholz, Warren Stevens. Directed perfunctorily by Alex March.

AMAZING COLOSSAL MAN, THE (1957). Co-writers Bert I. Gordon (producer-director) and Mark Hanna explore the mental anguish undergone by Army colonel Glenn Langan who's growing ten feet a day after exposure to a plutonium explosion. For one thing, his sex life goes all to hell, to the disappointment of Cathy Downs. Instead of staying on this compelling track, Gordon opts for a rampage of destruction and shoddy effects as the colonel stomps across Vegas to face military forces at Hoover Dam. Good score by Albert Glasser. Camp classic of minimal importance. William Hudson, Larry Thor, Russ Bender, Judd Holdren. (Columbia TriStar)

AMAZING DR. G, THE (1965). See editions 1-3.

AMAZING MR. BLUNDEN, THE (1972). Old gentleman (Lionel Jeffries) from the past turns up in the present via the Wheel of Time, and manipulates two children to alter a tragic incident of 100 years ago. Hence, a supernatural tale with paradoxes of time travel and touches of the fairy tale blended with the traditional Victorian ghost story. Based on Antonia Barber's THE GHOSTS, this is an entertaining, clever British film written-directed by Jeffries. Laurence Naismith, Lynne Frederick, Garry Miller, Diana Dors. (Media)

AMAZING MR. X, THE (1948). Undeservedly forgotten miniclassic originally released by Eagle Lion as THE SPIRITUALIST. Memorable for its ghostly ambience and atmospheric photography of John Alton, this has dated qualities that now give it a nostalgic patina. Lynn Bari stars as a wistful, lonely woman living in a luxurious cliffside mansion who hears ghostly whisperings of her dead husband (Donald Curtis). On the beach she meets an exotic spiritualist (Turhan Bey, with a raven perched on his shoulder) who puts her in communication with the dead, over the objections of bland boyfriend Richard Carlson, naive sister Cathy O'Donnell and cop Harry Mendoza. This documents the techniques of the phony-baloney medium: floating ectoplasm, ghostly music, spirit cabinets, etc. (Sinister/C; Rex Miller; Filmfax) (Laser: Lumivision)

AMAZING SPIDERMAN, THE (1977). Fans of the

Marvel comic book should enjoy this pilot episode of the TV series (depicting a dastardly extortionist at work) for which Stan Lee acted as consultant. Production values are strong, the acting is good and the effects well rendered in depicting the wall-climbing crimefighter who has been bitten by a radioactive spider and can change himself into an "amazing" individual. Directed by E. W. Swackhamer. Nicholas Hammond, Thayer David, David White, Michael Pataki. (CBS/Fox; several episodes have been edited and re-released as: **CON CAPER/CURSE OF RAVA, ESCORT TO DANGER/NIGHT OF THE CLONES, MATTER OF STATE/PHOTO FINISH, WOLFPACK/THE KIRKWOOD HAUNTING.** Some are on video.)

AMAZING SPIDERMAN, PARTS II-VI, THE (1977-78). Episodes of the TV series re-edited for TV.

AMAZING SPIDERMAN, THE. Episodes of the TV series: "Doctor Doom, Master of the World" and "Curiosity Killed the Spiderman." (Laser: Image)

AMAZING STORIES (1985-87). Steven Spielberg's NBC anthology, which today plays better than when it premiered, was re-edited into TV-movies and video tapes, each a separate series. The oft-duplicated ingredients are listed here, starting with the commercial videos and going to TV fare. These fantasies range from poignant to comedic to tragic to dark horror, featuring topnotch casts, good scripting and directing, and the ever-present hand of the amazing Spielberg.

AMAZING STORIES: BOOK ONE. In an hour-long episode, "The Mission," Kevin Costner portrays the skipper of a B-17 bomber during World War II who faces a dilemma when his landing gear won't go down and his belly gunner is trapped at his firing position. The ending is pure Spielberg, who directed. "The Wedding Ring" was directed by Danny DeVito and stars DeVito and Rhea Perlman. He's a horror wax-museum employee who steals a ring that turns his wife into an amusing serial killer. (MCA)

AMAZING STORIES: BOOK TWO. "Go to the Head of the Class," a fantasy-comedy revenge tale, stars Christopher Lloyd as the instructor set upon by Scott Coffey and Mary Stuart Masterson and turned into a headless corpse. It was directed by Robert Zemeckis. "Family Dog," an animated piece by Tim Burton, features the voice of Stan Freberg. (Video/Laser: MCA)

AMAZING STORIES: BOOK THREE. In "The Amazing Falsworth," Gregory Hines portrays a night club psychic who uses his powers to identify a serial killer; in ""Life on Death Row," Patrick Swayze plays a criminal electrocuted in the strangest way; and in "One Day at the Beach," a black-and-white episode, Charlie Sheen miraculously saves his combat buddies during an amphibious assault. (Video/Laser: MCA)

AMAZING STORIES: BOOK FOUR. This reprise of episodes from Spielberg's NBC series includes Martin Scorsese's "Mirror, Mirror," "Mr. Magic," and "Blue Man Down." (Video/Laser: MCA)

AMAZING STORIES: BOOK 5. Polly Holliday and June Lockhart star in "The Pumpkin Connection"; Billy Green Bush, Dianne Hull and Gennie James star in "Without Diana." The third episode is "Fine Tuning." (Video/Laser: MCA)

AMAZING STORIES—THE MOVIE (1985). The first of six compilations made for TV syndication. Part I contains "The Mission" (the B-17 wartime fantasy) and "Go to the Head of the Class," a comedy with Christopher Lloyd as a headless corpse.

AMAZING STORIES—THE MOVIE II. Four half-hour episodes make for a superior anthology. "Santa" is a whimsical Christmas Eve tale directed by Philip Joanou. Don't miss Douglas Seale's portrayal of St. Nick and Pat Hingle's cynical sheriff. "The Wedding Ring" is that rollicking black comedy directed by and starring Danny DeVito. "Ghost Train" is pure Spielberg as a grandfather tries to warn his family that a phantom version of the old "Highball Express" is due to run right through their tract home. This was directed by Spielberg. In "The Doll," lonely John Lithgow buys a doll from Leibermacher's Toy Shop that magically leads him to the woman of his dreams. A nostalgic, poignant drama written by Richard Matheson and directed by Phil Joanou.

AMAZING STORIES—THE MOVIE III. Four half-hour episodes. "Mummy Daddy" is William Dear's hysterically funny parody of monster movies, focusing on an actor (Bronson Pinchot) starring in a mummy film. "Family Dog" is an animated piece by Brad Bird, with voices by Stan Freberg, Annie Potts and Mercedes McCambridge. "Remote Control Man," directed by Bob Clark, stars Sydney Lassick as a hen-pecked husband who trades in his selfish family members for characters out of TV shows. In "Guilt Trip," directed by Burt Reynolds from a Gail and Kevin Parent script, Dom DeLuise plays the embodiment of guilt who meets Loni Anderson.

AMAZING STORIES—THE MOVIE IV. Rockne S. O'Bannon's weird prison tale "Life on Death Row," directed by Mick Garris, depicts execution and resurrection; "Mirror Mirror," directed by Martin Scorsese from a Joseph Minion script, stars Sam Waterston as a horror novelist finally haunted by his own creations; in "The Amazing Falsworth," written by Mick Garris and directed by Peter Hyams, night club mentalist Gregory Hines learns the identity of the Keyboard Strangler; and "Vanessa in the Garden," directed by Clint Eastwood from a Spielberg script, stars Harvey Keitel as an artist grieving over the sudden death of beautiful Sondra Locke.

AMAZING STORIES—THE MOVIE V. "The Sitter" is a voodoo comedy, written by Mick Garris and directed by Joan Darling, in which two mean little kids (Seth Green, Joshua Rudoy) find they are not such holy terrors when a Jamaican witch woman comes to sit. "Grandpa's Ghost," scripted by Michael DeGuzman from an idea by director Timothy Hutton, is a melancholy mood piece about aging and death, done with a gentle touch. "Dorothy and Ben," written by Michael DeGuzman and directed by Thomas Carter, deals with a man who's been unconscious for 40 years and his efforts, through telepathy, to help a child in a deep coma. Joe Seneca and Lane Smith star. "Gershwin's Trunk," written by Paul Bartel and John Meyer and directed by Bartel, depicts a declining songwriter (Bob Balaban) and his use of a psychic (Lainie Kazan).

AMAZING STORIES—THE MOVIE VI. The Mick Garris-Brad Bird script for "The Main Attraction," directed by Matthew Robbins, is a one-joke gag for a story about a popular high school guy (John Scott Clough) magnetized by a meteor. "Gather Ye Corns" is a Stu Krieger script, directed by Norman Reynolds, starring Mark Hamlin as a wastrel who proves that collecting can be profitable, if you'll just listen to your friendly leprechaun. "You Gotta Believe Me," starring Charles Durning, tells of a man who has a premonition of a plane crash and does something to prevent the accident. It was written by Stu Krieger and directed by Kevin Reynolds. "Lane Change" is a subtle story of character and time manipulation starring Kathy Baker and Priscilla Pointer; script by Ali Marie Matheson, direction by Ken Kwapis.

AMAZING TRANSPARENT MAN, THE (1960). The plot by Jack Lewis is also transparent, the dialogue is vaporous, the acting is invisible and the direction imperceptible in this pellucid piece of nothingness. Douglas Kennedy as a bank robber, Marguerite Chapman as the obligatory skirt and James Griffith as the insidious inventor (planning to create an invisible army of zombies) have every reason to blush unseen as they play shootemup games before the whole thing vanishes into thin air. You'll see through director Edgar G. Ulmer. (J & J; Sinister/C; S/Weird; Filmfax)

AMAZING TRANSPLANT, THE (1970). Sexual organ transplant gives its donor a hard time because the stiff-minded recepient has memories of the former owner's perversions. At least that's how director Louis Silverman translates Dawn Whitman's bizarre script. Transplant yourself to another channel to avoid this limp medical science-fiction hogwash that goes flaccid and never reaches an exciting climax. Juan Fernandez, Linda Southern. (Electric; S/Weird; American)

AMAZING WORLD OF GHOSTS (1978). Phony documentary as Sidney Paul's voice drones on about "evils hiding in the dark" and "things that go bump in the night" and "ghosts on the threshold of our world," without supporting evidence. Not even the visuals are interesting, consisting of a boy walking through a plaza, and famous statues in museums. What an amazing world of tedium from producer-director Wheeler Dixon.

AMAZING WORLD OF PSYCHIC PHENOMENA, THE (1976). Questionable documentary about everything weird from acupuncture to Kurlian photography to Edgar Cayce the healing prophet. While Raymond Burr as host lends a professional element, there are dubious claims presented as straight facts by writer-director Robert Guenette. One interesting section is on psychic detectives (Peter Hurkos included); another is about a man who *thinks* images onto film. It's strange to see professional actors playing real-life people. Why couldn't the real people have been presented? The whole thing seems contrived and concocted. (VidAmerica)

AMAZONS (1984). Lost race of Amazon women, depicted in the style of a WONDER WOMAN comic book, is brought into the modern world as busty, crusty conspirators out to pull off a political plot. The paranoia scheme has doctor Madeline Stowe accused of malpractice, and, in investigating the mystery with cop Jack Scalia, uncovering a drug that turns men mad with fear, a bow-and-arrow charm bracelet and several crossbows. Director Paul Michael Glaser brings more style and mood to this half-baked, confusing tale than it deserves. Tamara Dobson, Jennifer Warren, Stella Stevens, William Schallert. (Western World)

AMAZONS (1986). Lousy acting pulls this Roger Corman sword-and-sorcery adventure to the depths of viewers' despair. It's amateur night in Shanar, land of the Emerald Queen, where huge-breasted, buttocks-busting babes, their bosoms heaving with battle might, square off against "omnipotent" Lord Kalungo, who intends to acquire the Sword of Azendotti and the magical Spirit Stone. Penelope Reed and Danitza Kingsley are gallant wenches who expose their female charms for cinematic art, warring against Kalungo and his one-eyed associate who resembles a Mohawk Indian. As heavy-handed as fingers holding a cannonball, this is dead weight, charmless and produced on the cheap, no doubt in some foreign land where Corman gets discount rates. Directed by Alex Sessa. Joseph Whipp and Jacques Arndt are among the males who are but dirt bumps in the shadows of mighty women. (MGM/UA)

AMAZON WOMEN. Video version of **GOLD OF THE AMAZON WOMEN** (America's Best).

AMAZON WOMEN ON THE MOON (1987). Compendium of satirical vignettes on TV programs, presented as "switched channels" pieces. Some are funny, some not. The title piece is a clever pastiche of '50s low-budget sci-fi with Steve Forrest as Commander Nelson, who leads a moon expedition to find scantily-clad beauties ruled by Sybil Danning. Even the music parodies the period. Also funny is SON OF THE INVISIBLE MAN, with Ed Begley Jr. as a scientist who thinks he's invisible but isn't. VIDEO PIRATES is an amusing take-off on buccaneer movies. There's a Siskel-Ebert parody that has moments, an amusing roast for average guy Harry Pitkin, presided over by Steve Allen and other comedians. And Henry Silva is a stand-out lampooning Leonard Nimoy and IN SEARCH OF, now called BULLSHIT OR NOT? Directed by Joe Dante, Earl Gottlieb, Peter Horton, John Landis and Robert K. Weiss. And the "Lots of Actors" referred to in the credits? Ralph Bellamy, Carrie Fisher, Russ Meyer, Rosanna Arquette, Griffin Dunne, Paul Bartel, Howard Hesseman, B.B. King. (Video/Laser: MCA)

AMBULANCE, THE (1990). Fascinating study in paranoia from writer-director Larry Cohen, one of the best independent film makers from anywhere. This urban cautionary tale depicts a strange ambulance that picks up diabetic people and whisks them away to the secrert quarters of mad doctor Eric Braeden. Cohen paints eccentric portaits and introduces unexpected plot twists as comic-book artist Eric Roberts searches for Janine Turner with gum-chewing cop James Earl Jones, lady policeman Megan Gallagher and crusty newspaper reporter Red Buttons. Marvel Comics editor Stan Lee appears in a cameo. (RCA/Columbia)

AMBUSHERS, THE (1967). The shapely females in the cast might be "fantastic" to chauvinists, but a flying saucer and its gadgetry are the real fantastic features in this Matt Helm-Dean Martin vehicle (second in the series) played for bad puns, sexual double entendres, leering looks and lecherous repartee by director Henry Levin and scenarist Herbert Baker, spinning off the books by Donald Hamilton. The weapons packed by the lightly-clad sexpots (Senta Berger, Beverly Adams, Janice Rule) are not secret, but do provide diversion. The males are less fetching: James Gregory, Kurt Kasznar, Albert Salmi. (Video/Laser: RCA/Columbia)

AMERICAN CHRISTMAS CAROL, AN (1979). Henry Winkler, "The Fonz" of TV's HAPPY DAYS, becomes Mr. Scrooge in this contemporary version of Dickens' A CHRISTMAS CAROL. David Wayne, Dorian Harewood. Directed by Eric Till. (Vestron)

HENRY WINKLER

AMERICAN CYBORG: STEEL WARRIOR (1993). Well-made futuristic actioner set in a ruined society (a wartorn city in the Holy Land?) where roving soldier of fortune Joe Lara helps Nicole Hansen take the only living fetus on Earth to safety, battling murderous cyborg John Ryan in a series of exciting combat and hand-to-hand encounters. Directed by Boaz Davidson.

AMERICAN GOTHIC (1987). Effective horror thriller generates shudders in probing the thin line between sanity and insanity. Sarah Torgov, recovering from a breakdown after the death of her baby, goes on a vacation with two couples and is stranded on an island off Seattle. They find Rod Steiger and Yvonne De Carlo, demented parents of three murderous adults with the minds of children. The film is less concerned with how the vacationers are disposed of than with Torgov's descent into madness. How she resolves this tale is what the film is ultimately about. Director John Hough spares no punches. Michael J. Pollard, Fiona Hutchison, Mark Lindsay Chapman. (Vidmark; from Virgin as **HIDE AND SHRIEK**) (Laser: Image)

AMERICAN NIGHTMARE (1981). Canadian slasher flick in which a cut-and-ask-questions-later madman is on a rampage in Toronto, destroying prostitutes and other wanderers. Meanwhile, pianist Lawrence S. Day searches for his prostitute sister and cop Michael Ironside seeks the razor murderer. Directed by Don McBrearty. Lawrence S. Day, Lora Stanley. (Interglobal; Media; from Prism as **COMBAT SHOCK**)

AMERICAN NINJA III: BLOOD HUNT (1989). David Bradley is no replacement for Michael Dudikoff in this Cannon martial-arts actioner, a pale comparison to its forerunners when Bradley (as Sean Davidson) and Steve

James (as Curtis Jackson) tangle with The Cobra, a crazed doctor (Marjoe Goertner) with a lab virus that can kill the world's strongest man. Bradley overcomes his injection by calling on inner resources, glowing white under the lights as he kills the germ in his system. Harry Allan Towers' production is routine under Cedric Sundstrom's direction. Michele Chan, Calvin Jung, Yehuda Efroni. (Video/Laser: Cannon)

AMERICAN ORPHEUS (1992). Modernized version of Jean Cocteau's ORPHEUS from Rick Schmidt (he wrote, produced, directed and edited) in which love extends from beyond the grave between a mother and her young daughter. Jody Esther, Karen Rodriguez.

AMERICAN SCREAM, THE (1988). Vacationing family in the Sierra Mountains is terrorized by local freakos and weird dudes, but the Benzingers turn the tables on their tormentors in this horror-comedy written-directed by Mitchell Linden. Kevin Kaye, Jennifer Darling, Kimberlee Kramer. (21st Genesis)

AMERICAN WEREWOLF IN LONDON, AN (1981). This film, with THE HOWLING, established new trends in monster movie effects. Rick Baker demonstrates a brilliance in transforming David Naughton into a hairy creature—not with old-fashioned time lapse techniques but by showing Naughton's body stretching, twisting, expanding and agonizingly popping into its new lycanthropic shape. It's enthralling to watch the transformation—and you know movies can never be the same again. John Landis' scripting and directing are homages to old-fashioned werewolf movies, but he contributes his own tongue-in-cheek comedy through innovative dialogue when a dead friend, Griffin Dunne, keeps returning, in various stages of decomposition, to warn Naughton he will suffer transmutation. Jenny Agutter provides love interest. (Video/Laser: MCA)

AMERICATHON (1978). Neil Israel, that rascally creator of TUNNELVISION, is back as director-writer with more satirical fun and games, this time in a futuristic setting. The First Executive (John Ritter) holds a telethon with Harvey Korman as the Jerry Lewis surrogate. The humor is too sophomoric to register on the Richter Scale and the concept quickly crumbles like a used bar napkin. Production qualities are good and the cast rushes pell mell through the colorful sets, and you'll see Fred Willard, Chief Dan George, Terry McGovern, Meatloaf and Dorothy Stratton. But it's an unsalvagable misfire. (Lorimar; Warner Bros.) (Laser: Image)

AMERICA 3000 (1986). A hundred years after the Great Nuke, a band of Amazon women is led by Vena of Frisco, known as the "Tiara," or Queen. This silly example of post-holocaust movie-making is so absurd that it almost becomes entertaining as the warrior dames (the "fraus") engage in political intrigue with other female tribes and hold sway over the "Machos" (male slaves) in a place called Camp Reagan. Writer-director David Engelbach created his own oddball lingo for this picture—thus "negi" is used for "no," "woggo" means crazy, etc. There are times you can't even tell what people are saying, it gets so "woggo." Two young wanderers join a band of guys (Men's Lib?) to stage an uprising in this satirical, never-take-it-seriously action-comedy flicker. "Negi" way, Jose. Chuck Wagner, Laurene Landon, William Wallace, Sue Glosa, Victoria Barrett, Camille Sparv. (MGM/UA)

AMERIKA (1987). Seven-part TV-movie, controversial when first televised, rousing the heckles of Russians and Americans. The Soviet Union has bloodlessly conquered our land and martial law holds sway, with many entering Siberian-like labor camps, some consorting with the enemy and others fighting for freedom. At 14 1/2 hours it's an ordeal requiring an appreciation of political fantasy. Written-directed by Donald Wrye. Kris Kristofferson, Robert Urich, Sam Neill, Cindy Pickett, Mariel Hemingway.

AMITYVILLE HORROR, THE (1979). Jan Anson's best-selling haunted house chiller was allegedly true, documenting the supernatural experiences of a family on Long Island. This version, with James Brolin and Margot Kidder as husband and wife taking over the haunted residence, deviates frequently from the so-called true events, adding to the confusion as to what is fact and/or fiction. There are harrowing moments as the couple experiences ghostly phenomena and a chilling religious subplot unfolds with Catholic priest Rod Steiger, but neither director Stuart Rosenberg nor screenwriter Sandor Stern come close to capturing the terror of Anson's narrative. Good score by Lalo Schifrin and a supporting cast (Murray Hamilton, Don Stroud, Val Avery, John Larch) keep the film on a professional course. (Warner Bros; Goodtimes) (Laser: Vestron)

AMITYVILLE II: THE POSSESSION (1982). This U.S.-Mexican production begins before THE AMITYVILLE HORROR, depicting allegedly true events about a family that lived in the "spirited" house in 1974 and was subjected to supernatural horrors and demonic possessions. (These events were documented in Hans Holzer's book, MURDER IN AMITYVILLE.) One night the young son is thoroughly possessed by an evil demon and kills his family in cold blood. Shown in all its bloody details, this crime becomes a tasteless exploitation device. Then the film slides into sheer idiocy as priest James Olson tries to exorcise the youth after helping him to escape jail. The finale—set in the Amityville house—has nothing to do with demonology but everything to do with effects and make-up. The performances by Olson, Burt Young, Rutanya Alda, Moses Gunn and Andrew Prine are on a level of hysteria. A sickening movie, directed by Damiano Damiani and written by Tommy Lee Wallace. (Video/Laser: Nelson)

AMITYVILLE III: THE DEMON. Video version of **AMITYVILLE 3-D** (Vestron).

AMITYVILLE 3-D (1983). Third entry in the series about an alleged haunted house on Long Island, first popularized in a "true" book by Jan Anson and kept alive by Hollywood exploitation. Unlike its predecessors, this is based on no facts whatsoever, being loosely connected vignettes. Magazine writer Tony Russell buys the accursed estate, laughing contemptuously at the legends, but finds himself sucked into a supernatural netherland. So much for respectable realtors. The effects are decent (a corpse comes to life; a fire-breathing monster emerges from the well in the cellar; and the house goes berserk in the final reel) but the film's power is limited by the weak William Wales screenplay and limpid direction of veteran Richard Fleischer. Tess Harper, Robert Joy, Candy Clark, John Beal. (In 2-D video from Orion and Vestron.) (Laser: Vestron)

AMITYVILLE 4: THE EVIL ESCAPES (1989). This plays more like an episode of the FRIDAY THE 13TH series than a sequel to the Amityville series, and it's strictly TV caliber. Based on a book by John G. Jones, director Sandor Stern's telescript focuses on a lamp (set on the base of a gnarly tree stump with personified features) that becomes the new home for the supernatural Amityville evil. This "transmigration" finds the lamp being taken to California, where Jane Wyatt's household is terrorized by all the horror cliches from the earlier Amityville entries. Patty Duke looks totally lost as she joins with priest Fredric Lehne to fight the wicked lamp. Lou Hancock, Brandy Gold, Geri Betzler, Aron Eisenberg, Norman Lloyd. (Video/Laser: Vidmark)

AMITYVILLE '92: IT'S ABOUT TIME (1992). By now the phenomena introduced in THE AMITYVILLE HORROR has been overused within the genre—but it's refreshing when film makers can parade out cliches and still make them work. This time the connection to the 1979 adaptation of Jay Anson's book about a case of haunting on Long Island is a 15th Century clock once owned by a French necromancer who ate the flesh of boys. Architect Stephen Macht brings the clock to his tract home in San Gabriel Valley, where "pure evil" goes into action, slowing down or stopping time to make bad things happen. Macht is bitten by a crazed dog, his daughter becomes a sexual seductress, his son is accused of painting swastikas on a neighbor's door, and his ex-wife and boyfriend are

First Cop: "What do you suppose she's talking about? . . . a big black monster with big claws?" Second Cop: "I don't know, but I hope your mother-in-law has an alibi." **—AMSTERDAMNED.**

caught up in inexplicable events. Only the neighborhood supernatural expert, Nita Talbot, knows the truth. You get black, runny goo before the final showdown in Burlwood Estates. Tony Randel effectively directed the script by producers Christopher DeFaria and S. Antonio Toro. Shawn Weaverly, Megan Ward, Damon Martin, Jonathan Penner, Dick Miller. (Video/Laser: Republic)

AMITYVILLE: A NEW GENERATION (1993). This spinoff of AMITYVILLE II: THE POSSESSION, which depicted a teenager killing his family with a rifle, picks up with the son of that teenager, living in a rundown building in L.A., inheriting a haunted mirror from his derelict father. Spirits from behind the glass cause grisly supernatural murders in the building owned by David Naughton as the troubled young man fights internal demons from his family's past. This exploitation thriller places emphasis on psychological aspects and has rewarding moments. It also has a strange twist in the presence of Terry O'Quinn as a special "psychopathology" cop on the case. But much of it is familiar OMEN-style gore effects with not much done with the mirror, a weakness John Murlowski might have rectified in his directing. Oh well, one must patiently accept the bad with the good in the script by producers Christopher Defaria and Antonio Toro. Ross Patridge, Julia Nickson-Soul, Lala Sloatman, Richard Roundtree. (Republic)

AMOK. See **SCHIZO.**

AMONG THE LIVING (1941). Early PSYCHO-style thriller will be of interest to film students for its scrpt (by blacklisted writer Lester Cole and Garrett Ford) and cast: Albert Dekker (in a dual role as sane/insane twin brothers), Susan Hayward, Harry Carey, Gordon Jones, Frances Farmer. Stuart Heisler directed.

AMONG THE LIVING DEAD (1980). Eerie mansion is the setting for this standard foreign-made shocker in which a beautiful woman, on hand for the reading of the will, faces new horrors in the night. Howard Vernon, Christina von Blanc, Britt Nichols, Paul Muller.

AMPHIBIAN MAN, THE (1960). Russian production deals with a young man who discovers he has the lungs of a shark and will soon have to sacrifice his landlubberish romance, which makes for a drowning situation. The dark side of SPLASH. Directed by Gennadi Kazansky and Vladimir Chebotaryov. Anastasia Vertinskaya, Nikolai Simonov and Mikhail Kozakov star. (Sinister/C; S/Weird; Filmfax)

AMSTERDAMNED (1987). Dutch film maker Dick Maas takes elements of the slasher/underwater/chase genres and does wonders with them in this superior horror tale about a mysterious scuba diver who uses the canals of Amsterdam to conceal his presence until he's ready to strike. In addition to the many suspense and graphic-death sequences, writer-director Maas (best known for THE LIFT) also throws in an exciting underwater sequence a la JAWS and stages a fabulous motorboat chase through city streets that is technically flawless and full of dangerous stunts. Amsterdam cop Huub Stapel and girl friend Monique van de Ven are the principals caught up in the "diver of death" plot, which is full of witticisms and twists. (Vestron) (Laser: Image)

AMUCK (1978). Farley Granger and Barbara Bouchet star in this psychoterror malarkey produced-directed by Jurgen Goslar. Granger is a novelist who terrorizes Bouchet, a secretary looking for a lost friend in Venice. AMUCK is amiss and amess.

AMUCK. Video version of **MURDER MANSION** (Continental).

ANATOMIST, THE (1961). British resurrection of Burke and Hare of old Edinburgh, where bodysnatching was a necessary evil in the 18th Century for anatomical schools to procure cadavers for medical purposes. Director Leonard William employs an undercurrent of black wit as Alastair Sim, George Cole and Michael Ripper participate in digging up newly interred corpses. Done better as DOCTOR AND THE DEVILS.

ANATOMY OF A PSYCHO (1961). In the wake of PSYCHO came this horror thriller directed by Brooke L. Peters, of THE UNEARTHLY infamy. It stars Ronnie Burns (son of George and Gracie), Pamela Lincoln, Darrell Howe and Michael Grainger. (S/Weird)

AND MILLIONS WILL DIE (1973). Australian TV-movie in which E Force, disaster-fighting good guys, searches Hong Kong for a time bomb that will release a deadly nerve gas. Predictable suspense actioner moves briskly, but director Leslie H. Martinson lacks the knack for staging realistic action. Richard Basehart and Peter Sumner are loyal operatives racing against time, Leslie Nielsen is a sleazy underworld figure and Susan Strasberg is the demented daughter of a Nazi war criminal.

AND NOW THE SCREAMING STARTS (1973). Gratuitous Gothic grue from Amacus is set in the House of Fengriffin where a severed hand crawls in the drafty corridors. It's a legendary curse the tormented characters must endure. Directed by Roy Ward Baker. Peter Cushing, Herbert Lom, Stephanie Beacham, Patrick Magee, Guy Rolfe. (Media; Prism; Nostalgia Merchant)

ANDROID (1982). Better-than-average sci-fi adventure, exploring man's relationships with robots. Klaus Kinski, bordering on the psychosis of Dr. Frankenstein, lives on a far-flung space station with Max 404, an android assistant (Don Opper, who co-wrote with James Reigle). The doctor creates a beautiful blonde android to keep Max company. Conflict erupts when three escaped convicts hide on the station. Directed by Aaron Lipstadt, onetime assistant to Roger Corman. Brie Howard, Nobert Weisser. (Media) (Laser: Image)

ANDROMEDA STRAIN, THE (1971). Robert Wise's adaptation of Michael Crichton's best-seller is a sci-fi thriller brilliantly designed, well-acted and -plotted in the style of an exciting detective story. A deadly bacterium brought to Earth by a U.S. satellite destroys a desert community (except for an old man and newborn baby). The survivors are isolated in an underground research center where Arthur Hill, Kate Reid, James Olson and Paula Kelly unravel the nacterium mystery. Although the climax is contrived, the film is brilliant in all departments. Scripted by Nelson Gidding. (Video/Laser: MCA)

AND SOON THE DARKNESS (1970). British terror thriller in which two women bicycle across Europe while a slasher waits in the bushes. Directed by Robert Fuest, who gave us THE ABOMINABLE DR. PHIBES. Screenplay by Terry Nation and Brian Clemens. Pamela Franklin, Michele Dotrice, John Nettleton. (HBO)

AND THE WALL CAME TUMBLING DOWN (1985). Workmen uncover the 300-year-old remains of an ancient devil cult in this cheap British TV-movie. Barbi Benton, Gareth Hunt, Brian Deacon.

AND THEN THERE WERE NONE (1945). Outstanding "isolated mansion" murder mystery (remade several times as TEN LITTLE INDIANS but never topped) in which victims die one by one as a diabolical killer stalks them. It's from a novel/play by Agatha Christie but director Rene Clair and adapter Dudley Nichols toned down the comedy to emphasize the claustrophobic, oppressive horror hanging over the doomed characters. The twist ending will come as a jolt. Louis Hayward, June Duprez, Walter Huston, Barry Fitzgerald, Roland Young. (United; Vestron) (Laser: Image)

ANDY COLBY'S INCREDIBLE VIDEO ADVENTURE (1988). Below-average Roger Corman TV-movie in which Randy Josselyn, while watching a video, is sucked into the tube by Lord Chroma (Chuck Kovacic), the ruler of a world within the TV set. The Jed Horovitz-Deborah Brock script is an excuse for Corman to reuse footage from SPACE RAIDERS. Bo Svenson plays . . . Kor the Conqueror? (RCA/Columbia)

AND YOU'LL LIVE IN TERROR! THE BEYOND. See **SEVEN DOORS TO DEATH.**

AND YOU THOUGHT YOUR PARENTS WERE WEIRD (1991). This weak-kneed comedic imitation of SHORT CIRCUIT is a failure, and its attempts to be sentimental are cloying. Joshua Miller and Edan Gross are brother inventors who create an R2-D2-looking robot endowed with the spirit of their deceased father, who helps them outwit dim-witted thief John Quade and his inventor son (Eric Walker) from stealing the robot. Writer-director Tony Goodson makes this an irritating bore. The voice of Alan Thicke serves as the robot-father. Sam Behrens, Susan Gibney. (Vidmark)

ANDY WARHOL'S DRACULA (1974). A most singular vampire movie (also called BLOOD FOR DRACULA and ANDY WARHOL'S YOUNG DRACULA) which has dated badly and now is more laughable than horrific. Its European accents ("virgin" emerges "where-gin") and faggish, foppish performances by the androgynous-looking Udo Kier and Arno Juerging give it an unintentional comedic edge it didn't have in the '70s. The dialogue is uproariously campy ("the blood of this whore is killing me!") and Joe Dallesandro's American accent creates howls when he takes his axe and goes after the vampire. The plot has Kier as a Romanian count looking for a virgin in the family of Vittorio DeSica, but his daughters keep coming up ravished by Dallesandro, leaving Kier to drink tainted blood. You really need patience and a love for Warhol's memory to sit through this. Written-directed by Paul Morrissey. (Video Gems)

ANDY WARHOL'S FRANKENSTEIN (1974). Bloodletting, excessive violence, necrophilia, gore murders. A sickening exercise in black humor... You'll need a strong stomach, and an even stronger sense of curiosity, to endure this low point in cinema, also known as FLESH FOR FRANKENSTEIN. Paul Morrissey directed (and co-wrote the awful screenplay with Tonino Guerra), Carlo Rambaldi handled the gore effects. Joe Dallesandro, Monique Van Vooren, Carla Mancini. (Video Gems)

ANDY WARHOL'S YOUNG DRACULA. See **ANDY WARHOL'S DRACULA.**

ANGEL COMES TO BROOKLYN, THE (1945). See editions 1-3.

ANGEL FOR SATAN, AN (1960). Low-budget Italian chiller, of interest to fans of Barbara Steele, Queen of the Bs during the 1960s. In 1860, a woman's statue—recovered from a lake—is linked to strange events of 200 years ago and a series of murders disrupts the villagers. Beware an evil spirit with hypnotic powers and watch as Steele splits into two personalities. Directed by Camillo Mastrocinque. Anthony Steffen, Ursula Davis.

ANGEL HEART (1987). One strange private eye story in the film noir tradition, seguing into a startling supernatural thriller. Director Alan Parker has a bleak vision of this dark tale, giving it ambience, atmosphere and intriguing symbolism. In 1955, private eye Harry Angel (Mickey Rourke) is hired by Mr. Cyphere (Robert De Niro) to find singer Johnny Fortune, missing since 1943. The trail leads Angel to New Orleans and voodoo rites, and it's littered with corpses as Angel gets closer to the occult solution. Clever viewers will spot the surprise ending in advance, but it's still a staggering viewing experience with its nihilstic views. Lisa Bonet (of the Cosby TV show) engages in a heavy R-rated sex scene. Charlotte Rampling. (IVE) (Laser: Image)

ANGEL LEVINE, THE (1970). Black Jewish angel Harry Belafonte is about to have his wings "clipped" when Heaven gives him one more chance: to create a miracle on Earth by helping an aging tailor and his dying wife. Heavy-winged satire directed by Jan Kadar. Belafonte co-produced. Zero Mostel, Ida Kaminska, Milo O'Shea, Eli Wallach, Anne Jackson, Gloria Foster.

ANGEL OF DEATH (1986). Dr. Mengele, the butcher of Auschwitz who conducted "medical experiments," is found alive in Brazil by Nazi-hunters Fernando Rey and Christopher Mitchum. Mengele is conducting new experiments in genetics with a monkey monster. Directed by Andrea Bianchi and Jesse Franco. Howard Vernon, Jack Taylor, Robert Foster. (New World)

ANGEL OF DEATH (1990). Undistinguished guy-trying-to-kill-the-girl-so-she-won't-talk TV-movie with Gregory Harrison and Jane Seymour. A disappointment from director Bill L. Norton, who should have asked producers-writers Paul and Sharon Boorstin for a rewrite.

ANGEL OF H.E.A.T.—THE PROTECTORS: BOOK #1 (1982). There's a green door and Marilyn Chambers goes behind it but doesn't find an orgy of excitement—it's mad scientist Dan Jesse with a sound-frequency device that shatters metal, and a gang of horny androids. This nutty professor, plotting to steal microchips programmed with high-security data, is too daffy to be an interesting villain and the film fails as soft-core exploitation, having too little sex and nudity. Marilyn may be well-suited (or un-suited?) for X-rated fare, but as sexy spy Angel Harmony (leader of Harmony's Elite Assault Team), her shapely body does little for forward thrust. Even Mary Woronov's lesbian role adds nothing. The best thing in this film, produced-directed by Myrl A. Schreibman (CLONUS HORROR), is Lake Tahoe scenery. If you can't stand H.E.A.T., get out of the kitsch. (Video/Laser: Vestron)

ANGEL OF PASSION (1991). Adultress wakes up in Limbo Heaven with Dr. Guardian, who assigns her to atone for her sexual wrongdoings by returning to Earth and casting a spell that will give pleasures to others. A flimsy excuse for softcore sex scenes and stripteases, performed lustfully if not artistically. Written-directed by Jason Holt as amateurishly as the acting. Lisa Petrund, Douglas McHail, Lynn Chase, Tim Sullivan, Tuscany.

ANGEL OF VENGEANCE. See **MS 45.**

ANGEL ON EARTH (1961). See editions 1-3.

ANGEL ON MY SHOULDER (1946). Deliciously wonderful supernatural comedy with Claude Rains as a devious Devil who arranges for deceased gangster Paul Muni to return to Earth to pose as a well-respected judge. The H. Segall-Roland Kibbee script is witty and Archie Mayo directs with a fine blend of melodrama and tongue-in-cheek. Anne Baxter, Onslow Stevens, Jonathan Hale, Fritz Leiber. (Sinister/C; Nostalgia)

ANGEL ON MY SHOULDER (1980). Superb TV-movie remake of the '46 fantasy-comedy has the advantage of a looser moral code that doesn't straitjacket the writers. With gusto and insight, Peter Strauss portrays a wisecracking crook who's sent to the chair. Next stop: Hell, where he weaves a deal with the Devil to return to Earth and take over the body of a D.A. and sit him up for a political fall. It's delightful to watch Strauss undergo subtle changes and pull a double-cross on old Satan (underplayed by Richard Kiley) and make passes at Barbara Hershey. Directed by John Berry. Janis Paige, Scott Colomby, Murray Matheson. (Sultan)

ANGEL ON THE AMAZON (1948). See editions 1-3.

ANGELS (1992). Influences of Dennis Potter and

"My father is dead. He fell down a bottomless pit."

—Wanda (Kathy Ireland) in **ALIEN IN L.A.**

Charles Dickens hang over this British TV-movie in which guardian angels Tom Bell, Cathy Tyson and Eric Mallett become guides for three tormented souls, one of whom has torn the "cosmic fabric" by not dying at his appointed time. How the spirits, operating out of a heavenly way-station (distinguished by a bleached-out black and white look) come to terms with these confused humans makes for comedy and pathos. Directed by Philip Saville. Warren Clarke is especially good as a sadistic entertainer. Louise Lombard, James Purefoy.

ANGELS IN THE OUTFIELD (1951). A miracle occurs during a ball game when an orphan sees angels hovering above a bottom-of-the-league team. Even more miraculous is the change of heart this creates in the foul-mouthed manager (Paul Douglas imitating Leo Durocher). Producer-director Clarence Brown walks a fine baseline between piousness and comedy and Dorothy Kingsley and George Wells score a hit with their screenplay. And Janet Leigh homers as an omnipresent newspaperwoman. What a powerhouse line-up: Keenan Wynn, Lewis Stone, Spring Byington, Bruce Bennett, King Donovan, Bing Crosby.

ANGEL WHO PAWNED HER HARP, THE (1956). See editions 1-3.

ANGER OF THE GOLEM. See **IT!**

ANGRY RED PLANET, THE (1960). Low-budget space thriller strains to be different but the effects crew only gets H for hernias. Astronauts Gerald Mohr, Les Tremayne, Jack Kruschen and Nora Hayden land on an expressionistic Martin landscape. They encounter a giant spider-bat and globular entities, but none of these goofy E.T.s is convincing. The script by director Ib Melchoir and Sidney Pink evokes unintended chuckles. This was called "Cinemagic"—referring to a tinting that of orange cellophane. Stanley Cortez's cinematography is superior to the material. (HBO) (Laser: Image, with **JOURNEY TO THE SEVENTH PLANET**)

ANGUISH (1987). This might have been a masterpiece of psychoterror had Spanish director Bigas Luna opted for a less disgusting story (he cowrote with Michael Berlin) and gone for classy suspense and shocks. That criticism aside, ANGUISH is still a humdinger. For 20 unsavory minutes we watch crazyman Michael Lerner, a hospital orderly, slice up innocent victims and remove their eyeballs. He also endures hypnotic trances induced by daffy mother Zelda Rubinstein (Tangina in the POLTERGEIST series). Suddenly we realize we're watching a movie called THE MOMMY, playing at a theater in Culver City where a serial killer with a mother fixation is on the verge of a murderous rampage. An odd parallel develops when, in THE MOMMY, Lerner enters a Barcelona theater where Willis O'Brien's THE LOST WORLD is playing. Now we have two movies of almost identical storylines (and don't forget you, watching ANGUISH.) This overcomes poor taste with clever construction. Talia Paul, Angel Jove, Isabel Garcia Lorca. (Video/Laser: Fox)

ANIMAL FARM (1954). Louis de Rochemont's adaptation of George Orwell's cautionary fable about how false governments rise up to enslave their people is still as effective as when it was made. Orwell couched his message as a parable about Manon Farm, run by drunken farmer Jones. When they are badly mistreated, the animals revolt and take over under Napoleon the boar hog. The parallels to communism are obvious as Napoleon turns into a Stalin, fattening his own stomach at the expense of others. Providing an interesting irony is the fact the animals are Disneyesque—but there's nothing cute about their suffering. Under the direction of producers John Halas and Joy Batchelor, this is a powerful film, showing how animation can be a propaganda tool. (Vestron; Media; Video Yesteryear; Amvest)

ANIMAL WORLD (1956). Writer-director Irwin Allen's semidocumentary of the creature kingdom digressing into speculative anthropology with effects by Willis O'Brien and Ray Harryhausen of dinosaurs and other prehistoric monsters. Otherwise, a standard compilation of animal footage taken all over the world.

ANIMATED ADVENTURES OF GENE RODDENBERRY'S "STAR TREK" (1973-74). Eleven volumes of cartoon shows. Voices by William Shatner, Leonard Nimoy, DeForest Kelley. (Paramount)

ANNA TO THE INFINITE POWER (1982). Unusually sensitive film, based on a book by Mildred Ames, depicts telekinetic teenager Martha Bryne and her involvement with spies, who misuse her in a scientific experiment. An intriguing, oblique narrative produced-directed by Robert Wiemer. Dina Merrill, Mark Patton, Jack Gilford, Donna Mitchell. (RCA/Columbia)

ANNIHILATOR, THE (1986). Ripoff of THE TERMINATOR, with the villains in this TV-movie having radar-vision, mechanical heads beneath their faces, and glowing red eyes to indicate they're about to attack. They're "Dynamatars"—strange creatures plotting to take over our world. Newspaperman Mark Lindsay Chapman is the only man who knows the secret and he's trying to save a list of victims, never sure when seemingly ordinary humans will turn into human-machine monsters. Despite cliches, this has driving intensity and style. Geoffrey Lewis, Susan Blakely, Lisa Blount. Directed by Michael Chapman.

ANOTHER FLIP FOR DOMINICK (1982). Intriguing sequel to the intriguing THE FLIPSIDE OF DOMINICK HIDE. In this British TV-movie, Peter Firth portrays a time-traveling agent for a governmental agency in the 21th Century, which tampers with the past to make the future better. Assignment chief Patrick Magee sends Hide into the past after a missing agent, but Hide gets mixed up with a woman whose son he sired. How Hide solves his new mystery and untangles family complications provide a poignant, offbeat fantasy. Directed by Alan Gibson, who co-wrote with Jeremy Paul. Pippa Guard, Caroline Langrishe, Michael Gough.

ANTHROPOPHAGUS. See **GRIM REAPER, THE.**

ANTHROPOPHAGUS II. See **ABSURD.**

ANTICHRIST (1974). See **TEMPTER, THE.**

ANTS. Video version of **IT HAPPENED AT LAKE WOOD MANOR**. Great if you're planning to take your VCR on a picnic. (USA)

APACHE DRUMS (1951). This conventional Western was the last effort of producer Val Lewton, admired for his '40s films stressing unseen horrors. When bloodthirsty Apaches raid the desert town of Spanish Boot, citizens and soldiers seek refuge in a church with high windows through which attacking redmen suddenly leap into the ranks of women and children. Lewton fans will appreciate these suspense sequences. Directed by Hugo Fregonese. Stephen McNally, Coleen Gray, Willard Parker.

APARTMENT ON THE THIRTEENTH FLOOR (1972). Slaughterhouse worker Vincent Parra carries his work home at night, hacking and hewing people instead of animals. Then, taking a tip from Sweeney Todd, he stuffs the parts into a meat grinder. My, isn't this a gristly book. Directed by Eloy de la Iglesia. Emma Cohen.

A*P*E (1976). U.S.-Korean production in which a 36-foot-high relative of K*I*N*G K*O*N*G is discovered on a Pacific island, captured, lost and then stalked by pursuers to Korea, where the hairy one wreaks revenge. Not very O*R*I*G*I*N*A*L, is it? Directed and co-produced by P*a*u*l L*e*d*e*r. Rod Arrants, Joanne De Verona, Alex Nicol. (New World)

APE, THE (1940). Moronic Monogram mess, a waste of Boris Karloff even though the Englishman gallantly attempts to bring the Curt Siodmak-Richard Carroll material up from the primeval muck. Karloff portrays a misunderstood doctor developing a spinal fluid to cure paralysis. His heart is in the right place but his twisted methods (running around in an ape costume to extract fluid from humans) are purely macabre. Directed by William Nigh. Maris Wrixon, Henry Hall, George Cleveland. (Kartes; Sinister/C; Filmfax; Video Yesteryear)

APE CREATURE, THE (1970). Incomprehensible German thriller based on Edgar Wallace's DARK EYES OF LONDON. The Gorilla Gang preys on foreigners, drowning their bodies in a strange contraption. Part of the gang is The

Ape, an ugly man in a monkey costume. As Scotland Yard investigates, there's a Bond-type agent named Sergeant Pepper, death traps, mistaken identities and general mayhem. Alfred Vohrer directed it with a tongue-in-cheek flavor, and apparently never understood the plot any better than you will. First shown in the U.S. as THE GORILLA GANG. Horst Tappert, Uschi Guas, Herbert Fux.

APE MAN, THE (1943). This inexpensive Monogram monstrosity depicts Bela Lugosi mutating into a hairy beast—it shouldn't happen to a gorilla. Wallace Beery, Henry Hall, Louise Currie and Emil Van Horn (as the ape) are wasted under William Beaudine's inept direction. Sam Katzman-produced cheapie. (Cable; Video Yesteryear; Kartes; Filmfax; Nostalgia)

BELA LUGOSI

APE WOMAN, THE (1964). See editions 1-3.

APOLOGY (1986). Taut TV psychothriller in which a killer of homosexuals stalks Manhattan artist Lesley Ann Warren who has an "apology" answering service for those who want to get sins off their chests. Hitchcockian in structure, this unfolds with cop Peter Weller following the clues. George Loros, Ray Weeks, Harvey Fierstein. Directed by Robert Bierman. (HBO)

APPLE, THE (1980). Borrowing from PRIVILEGE, this is a futuristic parable about a rock 'n roll star manipulated by fascistic forces. At its core is an intriguing idea, set in 1994 at the Worldvision Song Contest. Buggallow (all satanic symbolism) seduces a young singer into perversion, while he seeks solace with hippies left over from the '60s. Good intentions are destroyed by the piousness of producer-director-writer Menahem Golan, who spews out an ending in which a man in a white suit comes to Earth in a '60s automobile and takes good souls to Heaven. Grace Kennedy, Catherine Mary Stewart, George Gilmour, Allan Love. THE APPLE shouldn't be picked. (Cannon; Paragon)

APPLEGATES, THE. Video version of **MEET THE APPLEGATES** (Media).

APPOINTMENT, THE (1981). Intriguing though problematic British film about Edward Woodward having a communications problem with daughter Samantha Weyson. Is she creating nightmares for Woodward, or taxing him with adolescent witchcraft power? In his nightmares, Woodward's car is attacked by dogs and it runs off a cliff. Slowly we see the dream (the appointment, or rendezvous with fate) come true. Writer-director Lindsey C. Vickers lets monotonous scenes run too long (filled with Trevor Jones' music of doom) but the film pays off with a hair-raising accident sequence. Shot in England. Jane Merron, John Judd. (Sony)

APPOINTMENT WITH FEAR (1986). Okay video movie distinguished by eccentric characters. Michele Little is appealing as an individualist who spends her time recording private conversations with her long-range microphone; Douglas Rowe is memorable as a bumbling but thorough homicide cop named Kowalski. They're involved with a mental patient possessed by a tree spirit named Attis, King of the Woods, the God of Nature. It unfolds as a slasher flick (teenagers gather for a pre-graduation party) and has dumb, unnecessary stretches of dialogue. It's the offbeat characters and a fluid camera that make it watchable. The Alan Smithee directing credit is a pseudonym. Kerry Remsen, Garrick Dowhen (as Attis), Deborah Voorhes. (Video/Laser: Live)

APPRENTICE TO MURDER (1987). A fire-and-brimstone preacherman (Donald Sutherland) called a "Powwow Doctor," believing Satan walks in various guises, trains young Chad Lowe in detecting evil, and commits a murder with the boy's help in the name of fighting Satan. For this they are sentenced to prison. This offbeat film, based on a true-life murder case, was directed by R. L. Thomas. Mia Sala, Rutanya Alda, Knut Husebo. (New World/Starmaker; Hollywood Home Entertainment) (Laser: Image)

APRIL FOOL'S DAY (1985). See **SLAUGHTER HIGH.**

APRIL FOOL'S DAY (1986). Frank Mancuso Jr., producer of the FRIDAY THE 13TH series, attempts a variation on the slasher flick by placing prank-oriented teenagers in a deserted island mansion where they meet violent demises. Because of a pending surprise twist, the murders cannot be graphically depicted, with director Fred Walton preferring to treat his story as a poor man's TEN LITTLE INDIANS. Genre fans will find this tedious going, with a payoff that may not please everyone/anyone. Jay Baker, Pat Barlow, Deborah Foreman, Lloyd Berry. (Video/Laser: Paramount)

AQUARIAN, THE (1972). See editions 1-3.

AQUARIANS, THE (1970). When nerve gas is discovered leaking from a sunken ship, divers splash down to patch up the holes. Better they should have patched up plot holes in the Leslie Stevens-Winston Miller teleplay. This Ivan Tors TV-movie features a futuristic apparatus called Deep Lab. Ricardo Montalban, Jose Ferrer, Leslie Nielsen, Chris Robinson, Kate Woodville. Underwater footage by Ricou Browning, who played The Black Lagoon creature. Score by Lalo Schifrin.

AQUARIUS. Video version of **STAGE FRIGHT.**

ARABIAN ADVENTURE (1979). Pallid kiddie matinee material in the vein of THE THIEF OF BAGDAD but without the magic. Director Kevin Connor needs a sturdier Flying Carpet than Brian Hayles' screenplay. Christopher Lee as the evil Alquazar, ruler of the jeweled city of Jaddur, chews up the Arabian sets while Milo O'Shea (who is as exciting as counting grains of sand in a wizard's hourglass) battles conjurer's tricks, palace guards and other Allah-be-praised wonders for the bejeweled hand of Emma Samms. From the same team that made those Doug McClure fantasy-adventures in the 1970s. Mickey Rooney (as a comedy-relief inventor), Peter Cushing, Capucine, Oliver Tobias.

ARACHNOPHOBIA (1990). Tongue-in-cheek scare flick about the fear of spiders (see title) and how a lethal prehistoric crawler escapes from a Venezuelan jungle to hide out in the barn of Jeff Daniels and Harley Jane Kozak, urbanites newly moved to a California town. Director Frank Marshall (long-time associate of Steven Spielberg) parades out every "scare thrill" imaginable. The Don Jakoby-Wesley Strick script allows Daniels' phobia to build to a crescendo in a climax that pits him against a nest of killer spiders. The kind of flick that puts "fun" back into movie-going. John Goodman stands out as an obese bug exterminator. Julian Sands, Stuart Pankin, Brian McNamara, Henry Jones, Mark L. Taylor, James Handy. (Video/Laser: Hollywood Pictures)

ARCADE (1993). A Charles Band fantasy in the vein of TRON, depicting how "virtual reality" becomes exactly that when Vertigo Tronics introduces a new video game, Arcade, in Dante's Inferno, a video arcade run by sinister John DeLancie. When the souls of their friends are trapped inside the seven-level game, Megan Ward (a teenager troubled by the recent suicide of her mother) and boyfriend Peter Billingsley work their way to the final level, facing death within an assortment of landscapes loaded with computerized effects ("digital imagery"). David S. Goyer's script emphasizes Ward's problems and so you care about her during the life-and-death ordeal inside Arcade. Directed by Albert Pyun. Sharon Farrell (as Ward's mom), Seth Green, Humberto Ortiz, Jonathan Fuller. (Paramount)

ARCHER: FUGITIVE FROM THE EMPIRE (1981). Sword-and-sorcery TV-movie with little out of the ordinary—just decent fare. A bow-and-arrow warrior, capable of legerdemain, confronts sorceress Estra and some sinuous snake people. Written-produced-directed by

'ARMY OF DARKNESS': BRUCE CAMPBELL GETS ALL STRETCHED OUT OF SHAPE

Nicholas Corea. Lane Caudell, Belinda Bauer, Victor Campos, George Kennedy. (MCA)

ARENA (1990). All the boxing cliches are recycled through this refreshingly different sci-fi fight movie produced by Charles Band and Irwin Yablans. On a "work world" spaceship that resembles a wrench, floating through the Quasar Nebula, Paul Satterfield (who looks like a young Christopher Reeve) is forced to box aliens (including a centipede creature) to pay off his debts and is trained by a four-handed manager and sexy good girl Claudia Christian. (Four-armed is forearmed, I guess.) The Danny Bilson-Paul DeMeo script is a throwback to CHAMPION and ROCKY, with champ pugilist Steve Armstrong manipulated by a corrupt promoter and lured from training by exotic Shari Shattuck. Director Peter Manoogian brings a vitality to this unusual floating world. Hamilton Camp, Armin Shimerman, Jack Carter. Score by Richard Band. (Video/Laser: Columbia TriStar)

ARE WE ALONE IN THE UNIVERSE? (1978). "Factual" reports (hah!) on the possibility of alien life coming to Earth and fooling around with nature and man, but one wonders if producer-director George Gale isn't out to make a fast buck. The narrator of this pseudodocumentary is Hugh Douglas. Superlonely.

ARIES COMPUTER, THE (1972). See editions 1-3.

ARIZONA RIPPER. Alternate TV title for **BRIDGE ACROSS TIME**.

ARK OF THE SUN GOD, TEMPLE OF HELL, THE (1986). Italian-Turkish ripoff of RAIDERS OF THE LOST ARK (as its title subtly suggests) in which safecracker David Warbeck) is assigned to Istanbul (and that's a lot of bull, Istan) to recover a jeweled scepter once belonging to Gilgamesh and now reposing in the Temple of the Sun God. Similar to HUNTERS OF THE GOLDEN COBRA. John Steiner, Susie Sudlow. (Trans World)

ARMY OF DARKNESS (1993). This is actually EVIL DEAD 3, but Universal was afraid the title would debauch society and concealed its true origins. ARMY OF DARKNESS still made money all over the world. This time that warm-hearted, marshmallowy director Sam Raimi (writing with brother Ivan) has concocted a marvelous horror parody in which smart alec Bruce Campbell (also co-producer) travels back in time with his trusty chain saw to encounter terrors of the Dark Age as he (Ash) is assaulted by Deadites, an army of skeletal monsters on horseback; demons; and time-space distortions. Again, it's stylish film making, refusing to take itself seriously but still building to effective shocks. In short, it's "groovy." Danny Elfman's "March of the Dead" theme figures prominently. (Video/Laser: Universal)

ARNOLD (1973). Contemporary Grand Guignol spoof in which curvaceous Stella Stevens marries a corpse, but a necrophilous nut she's not—she wants to inherit a wad of delicious money. The corpse, Arnold, hails from a family of kooks, nuts, perverts, misfits and other everyday people who are murdered in comedic-horrible ways. This whacky horror comedy, directed by George Fenady, has macabre humor and graphic bloodletting. Elsa Lanchester, Roddy McDowall, Farley Granger, Victor Buono, Patric Knowles. (Lightning; Live)

AROUND THE WORLD UNDER THE SEA (1966). Shirley Eaton (the GOLDFINGER girl) looks great in a bathing suit, but there is precious little else to entice your weary eyeballs in this silly underwater adventure. Not even a giant moray eel, a colossal submarine-bathysphere called the hydronaut, ocean earthquakes and other Ivan Tors-style seafaring nonsense. Andrew Marton directs. Lloyd Bridges, Brian Kelly, David McCallum, Keenan Wynn, Marshall Thompson. (MGM/UA)

AROUSERS, THE (1970). The only way Tab Hunter can become sexually aroused in this psychothriller (also known as SWEETKILL and A KISS FROM EDDIE) is by killing women. Directed by Curtis Hanson. Sherry Lattimer, Isabel Jewell, Nadyne Turner, Roberta Collins, Angel Fox, John Aprea. (Nelson/Embassy; Sultan)

ARREST BULLDOG DRUMMOND (1938). Dated but nostalgic entry in Paramount's Drummond series, in which an Incredible Ammunition Detonating Machine is activated. John Howard assumes the British agent's role. George Zucco, H.B. Warner, Heather Angel. James Hogan directed. (Paramount; Rex Miller; Sinister/C)

ARRIVAL, THE (1990). Offbeat mixture of a vague sci-fi plot with a sympathetic portrait of a serial killer and his attempt to find true love. There's an unusual element of sensitivity in director David Schmoeller's handling of the Daniel Ljoka script, which opens in the town of Mayfair on the night a beam of light smashes into a field near grandfather Robert Sampson. An unseen alien presence enters his body and reverses his aging process, so that within months he's a handsome man in his 20s, played by Joseph Culp. However, the alien presence needs estrogren to survive and turns into a killer of women. John Saxon plays the thoughtful agent who tracks the murderer. A shortage of exposition about the alien is puzzling, but the film achieves a level of emotional power. Gore is at a minimum. Robin Frates, Geoff Hansen, Danny Fendley, Joseph Culp, Michael J. Pollard (in a cameo). (Prism) (Laser: Image)

ARTHUR C. CLARKE'S MYSTERIOUS WORLD (1989). Repackaged video versions of the syndicated TV series in which one of the best sci-fi writers discusses the greatest mysteries of our universe. (Six volumes on Pacific Arts video)

ARTHUR THE KING. See **MERLIN AND THE SWORD**.

ASPHYX, THE (1972). An ambience of morbidity hangs over this British supernatural terrorizer, creating a queasiness about death singularly fascinating in the hands of director Peter Newbrook. Scientist Robert Stephens discovers that within each person is a soul (or spirit) called for at the moment of death by a being from another dimension called the Asphyx. Using a special beam-control device, Stephens captures an Asphyx coming to claim his own soul; hence, this develops into a thoughtful, atmospheric tale of immortality. The themes are thoroughly intriguing, and there's a shock ending. Effectively photographed by Freddie Young. Robert Powell, Alex Scott, Fiona Walker, Jane Lapotaire. (Interglobal; VCI; Magnetic; in video as **ASPHYX** and from Media as **SPIRIT OF THE DEAD**)

ASSASSIN (1986). TV-movie clone of THE TERMINATOR, of no particular distinction. Humanoid robot Richard Young is designed to be the perfect killer, but something goes ker-spung and he/it goes on a killing spree. Retired agent Robert Conrad is coercised into tracking him with scientist Karen Austin, who designed him. Young, whose face alternates between deadpan and maniacal glee, plays the role as if he were cast in a slasher movie. Robert Webber is the CIA chief. Written-directed by Sandor Stern. (Academy)

ASSAULT (1970). School for women is under attack from a sex fiend in this pre-slasher-trend British psychoterror flick. Lesley-Anne Down and Suzy Kendall are among the beauties. Frank Finlay, Freddie Jones, James Laurenson, Tony Beckley. Also known as TOWER OF TERROR and IN THE DEVIL'S GARDEN. Directed by Sidney Hayers. (Embassy; Sultan)

ASSAULT ON PRECINCT 13 (1976). John Carpenter pays tribute to NIGHT OF THE LIVING DEAD by depicting a youth gang, a mindless army of kill fanatics, attacking an isolated police station without regard for life or limb. The hoodlums show no more emotion than George Romero's walking corpses. The defenders are led by a black policeman and a hard-boiled office employee, who behave in the macho manner of Howard Hawks' characters. A cult favorite among Carpenter aficionados. Darwin Joston, Austin Stoker, Laurie Zimmer, Martin West, Tony Burton. (Media)

ASSIGNMENT ISTANBUL. See **CASTLE OF FU MANCHU, THE**.

ASSIGNMENT OUTER SPACE (1960). A satellite is out of control and Earth is threatened, but Rik Von Nutter is at the controls, ready to sacrifice everything for our safety. Also known as SPACE MEN, this Italian flotsam merely clutters up our satellite signals. Fine tuners beware. Directed by Anthony Dawson. Archie Savage, Alain Dejon. (Sinister/C; S/Weird; Filmfax; Nostalgia)

ASSIGNMENT TERROR (1970). Humanoid aliens from a freezing, dying planet exploit our superstitions as part of an invasion plot. The ridiculous idea, set forth by writer Jacinto Molina Alvarez (actor Paul Naschy) and further muddled by producer-director Tulio Demichelli, is to revive the Frankenstein Monster, the Mummy and other monsters to terrorize humans. Hey, these freaked-out E.T.'s have seen too many Universal monster movies! Poorly dubbed for the U.S. market—Michael Rennie's real voice wasn't even used. Rennie, assistant Karin Dor and the Werewolf (Naschy) are all that can prevent our destruction. Zounds! Craig Hill, Patty Sheppard. (From UAV as **DRACULA VS. FRANKENSTEIN**)

AS TIME GOES BY (1987). Australian-produced sci-fier depicting a surfer's closest encounter with aliens in a spaceship disguised as a 1940s-style greasy spoon. Turns out that the alien is a nice one who recites lines from old sci-fi movies (shades of EXPLORERS) and does impressions of famous actors. Hmm. Written-directed by Barry Peak. Bruno Lawrence, Nique Needles, Max Gillies (as Joe Bogart, the E.T.), Ray Barrett.

ASTOUNDING SHE MONSTER, THE (1957). This brainless movie will astound no one, not even genuine she-monsters. Frank Hall's non-astonishing script depicts an E.T. femme in a metallic suit (surrounded by a force field) whose body has more curves than the Indy 500, and whose mere touch kills. The critic who called this "pitiful" was merciful. It didn't do astounding things for the career of Shirley Kilpatrick (but what a build) or Robert Clarke. The yet-to-astound-us producer-director: Ronnie Ashcroft. Keene Duncan, Marilyn Harvey. (Sinister/C; S/Weird; Filmfax; Cinemacabre)

ASTRONAUT, THE (1972). See editions 1-3.

ASTRO-ZOMBIES (1969). Grade Z abomination is so incompetently handled, it's a must see. Mad scientist Dr. De Marco (John Carradine) murders for body organs so he can assemble a new being. Wendell Corey is the G-man hot on the trail of the human leftovers. Director Ted V. Mikels (THE CORPSE GRINDERS) co-wrote with Wayne Rogers. Rafael Campos, Wally Moon, Joan Patrick. (VCI; from Wizard as **SPACE ZOMBIES** and Cult as **SPACE VAMPIRES**)

ASYLUM (1972). Ripping good Amicus anthology film (known on TV as HOUSE OF CRAZIES) cleverly scripted by Robert Bloch and adroitly directed by Roy Ward Baker. Four terror tales from the Bloch canon ("Frozen Fear," "The Weird Tailor," "Lucy Comes to Stay" and "Mannikins of Horror") are told through patients in an insane asylum. There's even a fifth story (a payoff for the framework) with a jolt ending. Superior fare. Britt Ekland, Herbert Lom, Peter Cushing, Patrick Magee, Barry Morse, Barbara Parkins, Robert Powell. (Prism; Starmaker; Media) (Laser: Image)

ASYLUM EROTICA. Video version of **SLAUGHTER HOTEL** (Nostalgic Merchant; Meteor; Amvest).

ASYLUM OF SATAN (1971). This first feature from William B. Girdler stars Charles Kissinger as Dr. Jason Spector, a Devil worshipper who maintains Pleasant Hill Hospital for torturous reasons. He kills his charges with (1) a gas chamber filled with killer spiders; (2) snakes set loose in a swimming pool and (3) a burst of fire that turns human flesh into cinders. Carla Borelli is brought to him for sacrifical purposes, but it turns out she's not the virgin everyone thought. You could say the doctor makes a spector-cal of himself. Girdler directed and co-wrote with producer J. Patrick Kelly III. Louis Bandy, Nick Jolley. (United; VCI)

ASYLUM OF THE INSANE. See **FLESH AND BLOOD SHOW, THE**.

ATLANTIS. See **SIREN OF ATLANTIS.**

ATLANTIS, THE LOST CONTINENT (1961). Elaborate George Pal spectacle vacillates between Greek tragedy-melodrama and sword-and-sandal action with special effects by Jim Danforth. Daniel Mainwaring's screenplay (from a play by Sir Gerald Hargreaves) focuses on Greek fisherman Anthony Hall rescuing Atlantis princess Joyce Taylor and finding his way into her underwater kingdom, where intrigue is afoot to take over the world with an Atlantean death ray. Producer-director Pal makes it visually appealing. John Dall, William Smith, Edward Platt, Frank de Kova. (MGM/UA)

ATLAS AGAINST THE CYCLOPS (1961). Italian import showcasing that one-eyed monstrosity of mythical infamy—and the muscles of Mitchell Gordon. A sexy babe, Capys (daughter of Circe), shafts Penelope the Queen and forces Atlas to attack the Cyclops. Not a legendary movie, but it has its share of grunts and groans.

Directed by Antonio Leonviola. Chelo Alonso, Aldo Padinotti, Vira Silenti. (From S/Weird as **ATLAS IN THE LAND OF THE CYCLOPS**)

ATLAS AGAINST THE CZAR. See **SAMSON VS. THE GIANT KING.**

ATLAS IN THE LAND OF THE CYCLOPS. Video version of **ATLAS AGAINST THE CYCLOPS** (Sinister/C; Video Yesteryear).

ATOLL K. Video title for **UTOPIA.**

ATOM AGE VAMPIRE (1960). Italo-French horror film, of interest to fans of cinematographer Mario Bava, who later became a major horror director. Here his work is moody in a film-noir vein. The film is better than average with a good cast headed by Alberto Lupo as an obsessive doctor whose Derma 28 formula restructures human cells and restores the beautiful face of blonde stripper Susanne Loret after she's badly burned. This works not only as a throwback to the 1950s but develops Lupo's flawed doctor, turned into the mad beast Sadak, who makes nocturnal excursions to murder women for hormones. Director Anton Guilio Majano emphasizes the doctor's perverted love and study of A-bomb victims. Sergio Fantoni, Roberto Berta. (Loonic; Sinister/C; S/Weird; Filmfax; V/Yesteryear; Nostalgia)

ATOMIC AGENT (1959). See third edition.

ATOMIC BRAIN, THE (1964). Also known as MONSTROSITY, a fitting description for this mad-scientist melodrama in which the doc transplants brains from cranium to cranium. Low I.Q.s result for everyone. Directed brainlessly by Joseph Mascelli. Erika Peters, Judy Bamber. (Sinister/C; S/Weird; Filmfax; Nostalgia)

ATOMIC KID, THE (1954). Designed by Mickey Rooney as a vehicle for himself, this contains a heap of cheap laughs as Mick is exposed to an atomic blast and becomes radioactive, tangling with foreign spies while glowing in the dark. Yock yock yock. Good cast (Robert Strauss, Whit Bissell, Joey Forman, Bill Goodwin, Hal March, Elaine Davis) can't raise the radium count. Directed by Leslie Martinson. (Republic)

ATOMIC MAN, THE (1956). Adaptation of Charles Eric Maine's THE ISOTOPE MAN, by Maine, emerges a British thriller (also known as TIMESLIP) ticking like a Geiger counter. Exposed to radiation, scientist Gene Nelson is out of synch with time, reacting to events before they happen. That gives him an edge over things to come. Ken Hughes directed. Faith Domergue, Donald Gray, Peter Arne. (Sinister/C; S/Weird; Filmfax)

ATOMIC MONSTER. See **MAN-MADE MONSTER.**

ATOMIC ROCKETSHIP. Re-edited first half of the 1936 **FLASH GORDON** serial.

ATOMIC RULERS OF THE WORLD (1964). Starman, a Japanese superhero from the Emerald planet, flexes his muscles against the evil Meropol Nation to prevent Earth from being blown up. This English version of SUPER GIANTS 3 and SUPER GIANTS 4 is for moppets only. Ken Utsui. (S/Weird)

ATOMIC SUBMARINE, THE (1959). UFO hidden in the ocean depths disrupts routine aboard Arthur Franz's submarine. Before long a one-eyed E.T. invader is creating havoc for the crew. This has so many recognizable B-movie faces, it's worth seeing: Dick Foran, Brett Halsey, Tom Conway, Bob Steele, Sid Melton, Joi Lansing, Jack Mulhall. Directed by serial king Spencer Bennet, written by Orville Hampton, produced by Alex Gordon. (Monterey; Sinister/C)

ATOM MAN VS. SUPERMAN (1950). Sequel to Sam Katzman's 1948 SUPERMAN stars a more affected Kirk Alyn as the Man of Steel, but it holds up as an entertaining depiction of Superman vs. archvillain Lex Luthor, well portrayed by Lyle Talbot. Luthor doubles as Atom Man, a weird dude in a helmet who talks with a metallic voice and intends to take over the world using fantastic gimmicks: a coin that makes a man appear or disappear, a disintegrator ray, and a device that sends enemies into the Empty Doom, a void of lost souls. Directed by King of the Cliffhangers, Spencer Bennet, this is enhanced by Noel Neill as Lois Lane and Tommy Bond as Jimmy Olson. The rich, booming voice of Knox Manning opens and closes each chapter. Call it silly, call it naive, but it's irresistible. (Warner Bros.)

ATOR. See **ATOR THE FIGHTING EAGLE.**

ATOR THE BLADE MASTER (1984). Inconsequential sequel to ATOR with Miles O'Keefe still in a blond wig and wielding a sword with less than astounding agility. Sagacious inventor Akronos has harnessed atomic energy ("Geometric Nucleus") so he sends daughter Lisa Foster to fetch Ator to fight villainous Zovv (Charles Borromin). Meanwhile, Ator, the daughter and karate-swordsman Thong (Chen Wong) protect a tribe against cutthroat warriors who worship a serpent god. The only good scene: cuties being fed to the snake, and Ator battling the colossal asp. Marred by stilted acting and less than artistic directing-writing by David Hills. (From Media as **THE BLADE MASTER**)

ATOR THE FIGHTING EAGLE (1983). Dumbest sword-and-sorcery picture imaginable with Miles O'Keefe as a sword wielder in loincloth and blonde wig. When O'Keefe's virgin bride is abducted on her wedding day by the Spider King, Ator is in hot-blooded pursuit, abetted by an outlaw (Sabrina Siani) in laughable adventures in The Cave of the Ancient Ones, The Cavern of Blind Warriors, The Land of the Walking Dead, The Room of the Shadow Warrior, The Temple of the Spider, etc. Written-directed by David Hills. Sequels: ATOR THE BLADE MASTER, IRON WARRIOR and QUEST FOR THE MIGHTY SWORD. (HBO)

ATOR THE INVINCIBLE. See **ATOR THE FIGHTING EAGLE.**

ATOR III. See **IRON WARRIOR.**

ATOR III: THE HOBGOBLIN. Mistitled series entry. It's actually the fourth, on tape from Columbia, with Aristide Massaccesi credited as writer-director. The U.S. version (Al Bradley credited as director) is **QUEST FOR THE MIGHTY SWORD.** See that entry.

ATRAGON (1964). Japanese sci-fi destruction in the Godzilla tradition, directed by Inoshiro Honda, with effects by Eiji Tsuburaya. A flying nuclear submarine defends mankind against the undersea kingdom of Mu, ruled by the Goddess Wenda. All very noisy, so you should stay awake. Tadao Takashima, Kenji Sahara. Also called ATRAGON, THE FLYING SUPERSUB.

ATTACK FROM SPACE (1958). Sequel to ATOMIC RULERS OF THE WORLD, consisting of portions of Japan's SUPER GIANT 5 and SUPER GIANT 6. Once again Emerald Planet sends the man of steel-plated chrome to Earth to defeat the insidious Sapphire Galaxy. Kids will cheer for more. (S/Weird)

KIRK ALYN AS SUPERMAN

ATTACK OF THE BEAST CREATURES (1985). The "Beast Creatures" aren't the beastliest beasts you've ever seen, but you might get a few laughs out of this amateurish tale, made in Connecticut, in which shipwreck survivors meet zombies as miniature people. The Puppetmaster is at work! Robert Nolfi, Robert Lengyel, Julia Rust. Directed by Michael Stanley. Also known as HELL ISLAND. (Western World)

ATTACK OF THE BLIND DEAD. See **RETURN OF THE BLIND DEAD**.

ATTACK OF THE CRAB MONSTERS (1957). Roger Corman exploitationer (he produced-directed), cheap in depicting stranded travelers on a Pacific island inhabited by giant nuclear-poisoned crustaceans. Strictly in the shrimp league, yet by being shoddy and laughable, Corman creates an entertaining framework with Charles Griffith's script. A charming naivete is at work as monsters gobble up characters (some scenes are gruesome) and then send out victims' thought patterns to lure the living into a trap. Richard Garland, Pamela Duncan, Russell Johnson, Leslie Bradley, Mel Welles.

ATTACK OF THE 50-FOOT WOMAN (1958). Women's Lib should embrace this cheapie as a determined dame rises above the men in her life; men will be intrigued by the largest breasts in the world towering above them. This has earned cult status as an incompetent example of '50s sci-fi but should be viewed from a modern perspective as a metaphor for woman's revenge. Direction (Nathan Juran) and scripting (Mark Hanna) are on a poverty-row level when an alien crashlands in the desert and detours voluptuous Allison Hayes, causing her metabolism to accelerate. The well-endowed Ms Hayes, her bosom heaving with passion, takes it out on the men in her life, including a jerkola husband. Still, she isn't head and shoulders above the rest of the cast: William Hudson, Yvette Vickers, Roy Gordon, Ken Terrell. (Key) (Laser: CBS/Fox, with **THE HOUSE ON HAUNTEDHILL**)

ATTACK OF THE 50 FT. WOMAN (1993). This TV-movie remake of the 1958 sci-fier, produced by Debra Hill, presents Daryl Hannah as quite a hunka woman who's exposed to a ray from a flying saucer and grows to towering proportions. Because she's been so abused by lousy husband Daniel Baldwin and uncaring father William Windom, she goes on a short-lived rampage for revenge. Some of it is fun, but a lot of script possibilities are missed in Joseph Dougherty's rewrite and the effects seem only half-hearted. You wonder why they didn't improve more on an old B movie. Directed by Christopher Guest.

ATTACK OF THE GIANT HORNY GORILLA. See **A*P*E**.

ATTACK OF THE GIANT LEECHES (1959). Leo Gordon's plot is as crudely shaped as the mutated beasts in a swamp, stealing bodies and storing them as food for their leech-erous appetite in an underwater cavern. This unconvincing swamp water is the pathetic producing efforts of Gene and Roger Corman. The aquarian bloodsuckers, caused by falling debris from rockets from nearby Cape Canaveral, are human forms with canvases pulled around their bodies and sucker pods stuck on their faces. The only time the film comes alive is when a sluttish woman (Yvette Vickers) shows off her shapely legs and seduces a good-looking guy while her fat cuckolded husband runs around the marsh firing his shotgun. Such absurdities abound, including inept underwater shots. The direction by Bernard L. Kowalski is limbo-esque. Ken Clark, Bruno Ve Sota, Jan Shepperd. (Sinister /C; S/Weird; Filmfax; Nostalgia)

ATTACK OF THE KILLER CAVE BABES (198?). Slasher psychokiller women are out to kill everyone they can. Arrrgggghhhh! (Standard).

ATTACK OF THE KILLER TOMATOES (1979). Rampaging red-colored monsters of a circular shape attack mankind in San Diego in an intentional spoof of horror movies. It's much talked about by those who haven't seen it, but those who have are less impressed, for its humor tends to wither on the vine. (Even so, three sequels have resulted.) Writer-director John De Bello scores fewer misses than "splats" with his shotgun approach, but some of the giant killer tomatoes, rolling to the attack, are funny—for a while. A curiosity garden piece with its threadbare plot finally getting squished. Love that fruit! David Miller, Sharon Taylor, Eric Christmas. Sequels: RETURN OF THE KILLER TOMATOES, THE KILLER TOMATOES STRIKE BACK and KILLER TOMATOES EAT FRANCE. (Media)

ATTACK OF THE MAYAN MUMMY (1957). Video version of **AZTEC MUMMY, THE** (Sinister/C; Loonic; Nostalgia; S/Weird; Filmfax).

ATTACK OF THE MONSTERS (1969). This has "Made in Japan" stamped all over it. From what other part of the world would you find a film with Gamera the giant turtle battling Guiron to rescue Earthlings from brain-eating space beauties from planet Tera? Also known as GAMERA VS. GUIRON. Directed by Noriaki Yuasa. Nobuhiro Kashima, Chris Murphy. (From Celebrity as **GAMERA VS. GUIRON**)

ATTACK OF THE MUSHROOM PEOPLE (1963). Pull up a toadstool and see tourists on a luxury yacht washed onto a fog-shrouded Pacific isle. They decide a fungus is among us when face-to-face with monstrous walking incredible edibles. Akiro Kubo and Yoshio Tsuchiya head the Japanese cast. That GODZILLA team, director Inoshiro Honda and effects artist Eiji Tsuburaya, pick the mushrooms. (S/Weird)

ATTACK OF THE PHANTOMS. See **KISS MEETS THE PHANTOM OF THE PARK**.

ATTACK OF THE PUPPET PEOPLE (1957). Producer-director-writer Bert I. Gordon pulls the wires but his marionette melodrama dances short of THE INCREDIBLE SHRINKING MAN. John Hoyt gives a sympathetic performance as a lonely, deranged puppetmaster named Franz who runs a toy shop, Dolls Inc. No matter how crazy he seems, you still like the guy, he's so sweet with kids who love the tiny cat he keeps in a matchbox. Franz designs a machine that miniaturizes John Agar and June Kenny so they are "wee the people," but he only belittles himself in the process. Gordon did his own effects, but their cheapness leaves you dangling. Nice "strings," though, by composer Albert Glasser. Scott Peters, Susan Gordon, Michael Mark.

ATTACK OF THE ROBOTS (1967). This French-Spanish production stars Eddie Constantine as an Interpol agent on the trail of an insidious madman (Fernando Rey) and his evil female companion (Francois Brion) who are controlling everyone with Type O blood via an army of zombie monsters. Strictly a computerized programmer with automated acting. Directed by Jesse Franco. (Sinister/C; S/Weird; Video Yesteryear)

ATTACK OF THE SWAMP CREATURES (1975). Produced in Florida, this is a most unwatchable movie. Also known as THE BLOOD WATERS OF DR. Z and ZAAT, it is an incompetent mess written-directed by Arnold Stevens, depicting how a scientist (Frank Cromwell), after being scoffed at for requesting humans for mutation experiments, turns into an amphibious monster. He remarks, while admiring himself in a mirror, "Nothing at all like the catfish, but it's beautiful." While the waterlogged monster kills those who laughed at his theory for a superrace made from radioactive catfish serums, an investigative team clumsily follows in his wake. Meanwhile, the ZAAT-created aquaman picks a bikini girl to be his mate. Thrillervideo's video features Elvira.

AT THE EARTH'S CORE (1976). Second in the Edgar Rice Burroughs adaptations produced in England (thus a sequel to THE LAND THAT TIME FORGOT) with Doug McClure as an adventurer isolated in the kingdom of Pellucidar, an underworld inhabited by loathsome Sagoths. The Wing People are dominated by the Sagoths, giving cause for McClure and explorer Peter Cushing to lead an uprising. Effects consist of mock-up monster models. Kevin Connor directed the John Dark screenplay. Cy Grant, Caroline Munro, Keith Barron. (Warner Bros.)

ATTIC, THE (1980). In-depth psychodrama with Gothic touches (sinister house, electric storms, a corpse in a closet) and a horrific climax in which repressed Wichita librarian Carrie Snodgrass is trapped in her ultimate nightmare. This is a clinical portrait of a sexually deprived spinster forced to care for her sadistic father (Ray Milland). She imagines his death or humiliation, revealing her own psychotic tendencies. Writer-director George Edwards is sensitive to the plight of the lamentable librarian. More intriguing for its insights into the aberrant mind than for visual shocks. Ruth Cox, Rosemary Murphy. (Unicorn; Monterey; CBS/Fox)

AUDREY ROSE (1977). Compelling study of reincarnation, superbly directed by Robert Wise but deteriorating when the issue of life after death is introduced as courtroom melodrama. Anthony Hopkins (as an Englishman who believes his dead daughter has been reincarnated) is most intense and believable. The other characters wallow in self-pity and unreasoning hysteria. The film states an unusually positive case for believing in reincarnation. Scripted by Frank DeFelitta from his own novel. Marsha Mason, John Beck, Susan Swift, John Hillerman, Norman Lloyd. (MGM/UA)

AURA. See **WITCH, THE (1966).**

AURORA ENCOUNTER, THE (1985). Cantankerous Jack Elam playing checkers with a bald-headed midget from space (Mickey Hays) and snorting Dr. Neptune's Elixir is as enthralling as this family-oriented morality tale gets. The time is the 19th Century, in the town of Aurora, which is visited by a "flying craft" and the benevolent little E.T. A female newspaperwoman tries to expose the story, visits governor Spanky McFarland and argues with town sheriff Peter Brown, while three little girls go into a cave where they find a magical crystal. This saccharine, gentle story, with film maker Charles B. Pierce appearing as a preacherman, was produced at the Big D Ranch near Dallas by producer-director Jim McCullough and son Jim Jr., who wrote and co-produced. Carol Bagdarsarian, Dottie West. (New World)

AUTOMAN (1984). See third edition.

AUTOPSY (1974). An Italian morgue is an eerie place with Ennio Morricone's music swelling on the soundtrack—but don't expect much in the way of visual thrills. This is about as scary as walking through your local horror wax museum blindfolded. Mimsy Farmer portrays a young woman working in the morgue, and she's so silly, she deserves every touch of terror thrown at her by writer-director Armando Crispini. Barry Primus, Angela Goodwin. Also known as TAROT. (Mogul; Prism; MPI)

AUTUMN CHILD. See **REFLECTION OF FEAR.**

AVENGER, THE (1960). Heads up! Scotland Yard is receiving packages from "The Executioner," each containing a human intelligence from the neck up. A hunchback, wreaking his revenge, is responsible for these heinous murders. Can the intrepid inspectors catch him? Heads they win, tales they lose. An Edgar Wallace terror-thriller (based on his 1925 novel THE HAIRY ARM) directed by Karl Anton. Klaus Kinski, Heinz Drache, Ingrid van Bergen. (Sinister/C; S/Weird; Filmfax)

AVENGING SPIRIT. Video version of **DOMINIQUE IS DEAD** (Impulse; Simitar).

AWAKENING, THE (1980). Adaptation of Bram Stoker's JEWEL OF SEVEN STARS becomes scrambled mumbo jumbo not even an Egypotologist could decipher. Archeologist Charlton Heston uncovers a long-lost tomb of a wicked princess, whose spirit is transmitted into Heston's newborn daughter. Stephanie Zimbalist becomes the possessed girl, but she never conveys a captured spirit. The Egyptian tomb set is magnificent and Jack Cardiff's desert photography is stunning. But in trying to imitate the gore of THE OMEN, director Mike Newell merely looks like a copycat. Susannah York, Jill Townsend. (Warner Bros.)

AWESOME LOTUS (1986). Comedic martial-arts actioner with Loraine Masterson as a karate killer called out of retirement because silkworms are threatening to put the silk industry out of business. Can she and her associates (a blind karate man and a guy named Tuna who uses his tennis racket as a clobbering device) stop the Federation of Associated Rayon Textiles? Directed by David O'Malley.

AWFUL DR. ORLOFF, THE (1961). Howard Vernon portrays a sadistic doctor who fondles beautiful victims before plunging his scalpel into their wriggling, screaming bodies in his sanguinary experiments to graft their skin onto the face of his horribly disfigured daughter. This Spanish shocker, written-directed by Jesse Franco and also known as CRIES IN THE NIGHT, spawned the sequels DR. ORLOFF'S MONSTER, DIABOLICAL DR. Z and ORGIES OF DR. ORLOFF. Perla Cristal, Diana Lorys. (With subtitles from Video Search; S/Weird)

AXE! (1974). Originally CALIFORNIA AXE MASSACRE and then LISA, LISA, this was re-released in 1983 to cash in on the slasher-movie craze. It's as low budget as they come, about a gang of cheap, sadistic hoods terrorizing a southern belle and her crippled grandfather. The young woman turns on her assailants and gives 'em what fer, yes indeedie. Written-directed by Frederick R. Friedel, who plays a criminal. Jack Canon, Leslie Lee. Dull-edged. (Astrovideo; from Best Film & Video with SCREAM IN THE STREETS)

AXE FOR THE HONEYMOON. See **HATCHET FOR THE HONEYMOON, A**.

AXE MURDERS, THE. See **AXE.**

AZTEC MUMMY, THE (1957). Mexican "classic" that started the "Aztec Mummy" series. If ever a film demanded total imbecility and moronic attention spans, here it is, amigos (also known as ATTACK OF THE MAYAN MUMMY). Rafael Portillo directed this depiction of the mummy Popoca and the vengeance it wreaks. Ramon Gay, Rosita Arenas. Sequels were THE ROBOT VS. THE AZTEC MUMMY, CURSE OF THE AZTEC MUMMY and THE WRESTLING WOMEN VS. THE AZTEC MUMMY. (In 1963, schlock producer Jerry Warren recut the film for the U.S. market, adding scenes with Richard Webb, Nina Knight, John Burton and Bruno Ve Sota. They didn't help.)

AZTEC MUMMY DOUBLE FEATURE. Video packaging of **ROBOT VS. THE AZTEC MUMMY, THE** and **CURSE OF THE AZTEC MUMMY.**

AZTEC MUMMY VS. THE HUMAN ROBOT (1957). Variant title for **ROBOT VS. THE AZTEC MUMMY, THE**.

"This creature fought with more than arms and legs. I'm convinced it has a brain."—Investigator in **ATTACK OF THE SWAMP CREATURES.**

BABA YAGA—THE DEVIL WITCH. See **KISS ME, KILL ME.**

BABES IN TOYLAND (1934). Perennial Laurel and Hardy Christmas favorite; a whimsical version of the Victor Herbert-Glenn McDonough operetta set in a kingdom where toys come to life. Only the soldiers are wooden—everything else in Hal Roach's production is animated: the clowning of the duo, the charming Frank Butler-Nick Grinde script, the playful direction of Gus Meins and Charles Rogers. Marie Wilson toys with her charms. Charlotte Henry, Johnny Downs, Felix Knight, Henry Kleinbach. (Orion; colorized from Goodtimes as **MARCH OF THE WOODEN SOLDIERS**)

BABES IN TOYLAND (1961). Disney version of the Herbert-McDonough operetta, shot on lavish sets by director Jack Donohue, but without the enduring qualities of the Laurel and Hardy version. Still, a colorful if juvenile adaptation with Ray Bolger, Annette Funicello, Tommy Sands, Ed Wynn, Kevin Corcoran, Gene Sheldon and young Ann Jillian sparking the scenery. (Disney)

BABES IN TOYLAND (1986). With music by Leslie Bricusse, this TV remake of the Herbert-McDonough operetta stars Drew Barrymore, Pat Morita, Richad Mulligan, Eileen Brennan and Keanu Reeves. Directed by Clive Donner. (Orion) (Laser: Image)

BABY, THE (1972). A 21-year-old Mongolian idiot—still wearing diapers and called "Baby" by mother Ruth Roman—is befriended by social worker Anjanette Comer. When it appears Roman and her two sisters are homicidal, Anjanette kidnaps the "infant"—but for reasons that will startle you. Ted Post's direction is first-rate. Not pablum . . . grotesque. Marianna Hill, Suzanne Zenor, David Manzy. (Western World; King of Video)

BABY BLOOD (1990). French horror/monster flick in which a snake-like creature crawls up a woman's legs into her womb, then comes out a monster craving blood. It's IT'S ALIVE again with ample gore and ALIEN-like effects. Emmanuelle Escourrou, Jean-Francois Gallotte. Directed by Alain Robak.

BABY DOLL MURDERS, THE (1992). Cliched psychokiller thriller in which a knife-wielding strangler in a black jumpsuit murders big-breasted woman always naked at the time of attack. The masked murderer leaves a doll by the corpses as a calling card. Obsessed cop Jeff Kober thinks he knows who the killer is but boss John Saxon and you the viewer know better as writer-director Paul Leder trods on familiar territory. Other than watching the buxom women, this offers too little too late. Melanie Smith, Bobby Di Cicco, Tom Hodges. (Republic)

BABYLON 5 (1993). TV-pilot in the vein of DEEP SPACE NINE, depicting life aboard a five-mile-long space station that serves as a neutral zone for governments hailing from different solar systems. Someone is trying to destroy Babylon 5 and it's up to Commander Jeffrey Sinclair (Michael O'Hare) to find out who—or what. Imaginative amalgam of space hardware, space-age costumes, exotic alien life forms, model work and computer-generated graphics, so well produced that this led to a syndicated series. Jerry Doyle, Tamlyn Tomita. Created by J. Michael Straczynski. (Warner Bros.)

BABY: SECRET OF THE LOST LEGEND (1985). Entertaining Disney adventure-fantasy set in Africa where paleontologist Sean Young and sports writer-husband William Katt find a mother and father brontosaurus (known to natives as mokele-mobembe) hovering over a newly hatched "baby." Anthropologist Patrick McGoohan and African mercenaries tranquilize the mother, kill the father and pursue the infant, who is befriended by Young and Katt. The creatures are believable, and a warmth is generated for the "brontes," giving this fantasy an unusual versimilitude. Directed on the Ivory Coast by Bill W. L. Norton. (Video/Laser: Touchstone)

BABYSITTER, THE (1980). The theme of the stranger (an embodiment of evil) entering a household to seduce its members has been explored in THE SERVANT and SOMETHING FOR EVERYONE, but in this TV-movie the seductress (Stephanie Zimbalist, in a fine performance) is a murderess, and might be a spawn of a devil force, for she talks to an unseen entity. Zimbalist disrupts the household of William Shatner (a Seattle doctor) and alcoholic wife Patty Duke Austin on a Canadian island. The range of the woman's influence moves from the sublime to the dastardly under Peter Medak's direction. John Houseman is good as the neighbor who suspects foul play and Shatner has good scenes as he falls under Zimbalist's sexual spell. Kenneth Tigar, Virginia Kiser. (Cannon) (Laser: HBO)

BACCHANTES, THE (1961). Euripides' Greek play was the basis for this French-Italian slice-of-myth in which the god Dionysus visits Thebes, a city rivaling Athens in splendour. Ballerina Taina Elg and boisterous Akim Tamiroff co-star. Giorgio Ferroni directed. (Timeless)

BACK FROM THE DEAD (1957). Quickie programmer exploiting the "possessed soul" theme popular during the Bridey Murphy craze, sluggishly directed by Charles Marquis Warren. Catherine Turney's script, based on her novel THE OTHER ONE, never returns from the land of the lifeless. Peggy Castle, Arthur Franz, Marsha Hunt.

BACK TO THE FUTURE (1985). Delicious Steven Spielberg production, a time-travel comedy with Michael J. Fox as a teenager involved with zany scientist-inventor Christopher Lloyd, who has a sports car with a "Flux Capacitor" capable of time jumping. Circumstances whisk Fox back to his hometown in 1955 to make sure his father and mother fall in love to ensure his own birth. Characters are charming, dialogue crisp and witty. Director Robert Zemeckis (who collaborated on the script with producer Bob Gale) builds to an exciting climax as Fox, with the help of a younger Lloyd, races against "time" to get back to the future, which is our present. This deals wonderfully with the paradoxes of time travel. The filmmakers rely on the cleverness of story and character, using effects sparingly. Crispin Glover, Claudia Wells, Marc McClure, Lea Thompson. (Video/Laser: MCA)

BACK TO THE FUTURE II (1989). Bob Gale's clever sequel script picks up where BACK TO THE FUTURE left off, with Michael J. Fox being whisked ahead into time with professor Christopher Lloyd aboard his time-traveling Delorean. They're tampering with time to prevent Fox's future family from going wrong. However, they affect the past and time-hop back to 1955, where scenes from the original picture are repeated, but from a different perspective. And therein is the fun. With director Robert Zemeckis at the wheel, it's energetic, imaginative and sometimes slapstickish—a fascinating, funny blend. The unresolved ending was a teaser for the third BACK TO THE FUTURE. Lea Thompson, Thomas F. Wilson, Harry Waters Jr. (Video/Laser: MCA)

BACK TO THE FUTURE III (1990). This sequel to the sequel is every bit as funny and intriguing as preceding installments in the misadventures of time travelers Michael J. Fox and Christopher Lloyd who, this time, land in 1885 in Hill Valley. The cliches of the Wild West are brought to life by director Robert Zemeckis, and there's the unusual fillip of a romance between Lloyd and school teacher Mary Steenburgen. Especially wonderful is the cliffhanging sequence in which the characters attempt to return to the future aboard a speeding train. You won't be killing time watching—you will improve your disposition and increase your smile. Thomas F. Wilson, Lea Thompson, Elisabeth Shue, Matt Clark, Pat Buttram, Harry Carey. (Video/Laser: MCA)

BACK TO THE PLANET OF THE APES (1974). Pilot episode for TV's short-lived PLANET OF THE APES with Roddy McDowall returning as Galen the Chimpanzee and Ron Harper and James Naughton as astronauts trapped in a society of hairy creatures in our distant future. Highly inferior to the original film series. Directors: Don Weis, Arnold Laven. Royal Dano, Biff Elliot, Cindy Eilbacher, Mark Lenard.

BACKWOODS (1987). Subhuman being (Jack O'Hara) and his neanderthal-like father (Dick Kreusser) terrorize folks in the forest by biting them in the neck. Also known as GEEK, this is about as lowbrow as movies get. Directed by Dean Crow. Christina Noonan, Brad Armacost. (Cinema Group; New Star)

BACKWOODS MASSACRE. Video title for John Russo's **MIDNIGHT** (Midnight).

BAD BLOOD (1989). Psychological horror thriller from director Chuck Vincent is a showcase for pornie actress Georgina Spelvin, who plays a wealthy painter who gets caught up in a murder-poison-confused identity thriller. Troy Donahue, Gregory Patrick, Ruth Raymond, Linda Blair. AKA A WOMAN'S OBSESSION. (Academy)

BAD CHANNELS (1992). One of producer Charles Band's more creative sci-fi comedies, fashioned by director Ted Nicolaou to make fun of rock and roll music, Alien-like monsters, CNN-styled networks and gooey effects. Paul Hipp plays hip, nasty radio disc jockey "Dangerous" Dan O'Dare, 666 on the radio band. His studio is besieged by a tall E.T. with a giant bug-like head and a cutesy-pie robot who cover everything with a green fungus and miniaturize beautiful girls, zapping them into tiny bottles. For listeners they produce a hallucination of a rock and roll band (Blue Oyster Cult, which wrote the musical soundtrack). The satire is thick as cable network news-types gather outside, as the Pahoota townspeople disappear mysteriously and as O'Dare finds a way out of his fungus-covered dilemma. None of it is adequately explained, but then nobody watches Full Moon productions for logic . . . do they? Martha Quinn, Aaron Lustig, Ian Patrick Williams. (Paramount) (Laser: Full Moon)

BAD DREAMS (1988). Gratuitously gory shocker is a rehash of familiar horror material, focusing on a survivor of the Unity Fields cult massacre, in which guru leader Richard Lynch set fire to the members. Thirteen years later Jennifer Rubin awakens to find herself in a "borderline personality" therapy group under Bruce Abbott, and hallucinates that Lynch is back, luring her and friends into OMEN-style murder situations. Chopped up bodies, impalings, a car/body squash and suicide leaps from buildings are among the bloody deaths which baffle Abbott and cop Sy Richardson. The script by Steven E. de Souza and director Andrew Fleming makes interesting comment about modern drugs for mental patients. Produced by Gale Anne Hurd. Dean Cameron, Harris Yulin, Susan Barnes. (Video/Laser: CBS/Fox)

BAD GIRLS FROM MARS (1990). Serial killer is knocking off the leading ladies of the flick BAD GIRLS FROM MARS. Fred Olen Ray directed, co-produced and wrote as Sherman Scott. The good thing here is the undulating body of Edy Williams, who fondles her ample bazooms and has a lesbian bit with Brinke Stevens. Jay Richardson, Gary Graver, Oliver Darrow, Grant Austin Waldman (the latter also produced). (Vidmark)

BADLANDS 2005 (1989). Rejected TV pilot blending the western formula with sci-fi, directed by George (MAD MAX) Miller in Australia. Lewis Smith plays the Matt Dillon-like marshal, Sharon Stone is the gal.

BAD RONALD (1974). Absorbing TV thriller, directed by Buzz Kulik, in which a youth (Scott Jacoby) commits a murder and is hidden in a secret room by his mother. When she dies, a new family takes up residence, unaware of the boy. Jacoby peeps on the newcomers and ultimately terrorizes them. A curious study of claustrophobic psychosis. Kim Hunter, Pippa Scott, John Larch, Dabney Coleman, Cindy & Lisa Eilbacher. (USA; IVE)

BAD SEED, THE (1956). Maxwell Anderson's Broadway play, based on a William March novel, sprouts into a fascinating film under the green thumb of producer-director Mervyn LeRoy. Nancy Kelly believes her mother was a murderess and that she has genetically transferred homicidal traits to her own 8-year-old daughter (Patty McCormack). Sure enough, the sweet thing turns into a horrid, deceiving little killer, at heart a conniving monster. Eileen Heckart, William Hopper, Paul Fix and Jesse White add to the believability of the premise, as does Henry Jones as a dim-witted handyman bright enough to recognize Rhoda Penmark's deceit. Screen adapter

John Lee Mahin was forced to tack on an undesirable deus ex machine ending demanded by Hollywood's morality code, but otherwise it's a fascinating watch. (Video/Laser: Warner Bros.)

BAD SEED, THE (1985). Updated TV-movie version of the Maxwell Anderson play about an amoral youngster, Rhoda Penmark, who diabolically murders a schoolmate. This is more explicit than the 1956 version in depicting how Penmark (Carrie Wells) does in her victims and retains the play's downbeat ending. The most chilling moment is when mother Blair Brown learns of her inherited sociopathological traits. David Carradine, outstanding as the handyman, is supported by Lynn Redgrave and David Ogden Stiers as neighbors and Richard Kiley as grandfather. Directed by Paul Wendkos.

BAD TASTE (1988). A government group, the Alien Investigation and Defense Service, whose job is to keep Earth safe from invasion, discovers a small town is being taken over and moves in for the kill. A bloody battle ensues that should please splatter and action fans, so graphic are the disembowelments and other acts of mayhem in this New Zealand-produced gorefest. Peter Jackson, Terry Potter, Mike Minett, Craig Smith. Written-produced-directed by Peter Jackson. (Magnum)

BAFFLED! (1972). The only baffling thing about this unbaffling TV-movie is why Leonard Nimoy, Vera Miles, Susan Hampshire, Rachel Roberts and Christopher Benjamin bothered. Nimoy is a race driver who suffers from futuristic visions—and an ESP expert fears the people in his visions are in mortal danger. Most of the story unfolds in a stately, stuffy English manor. Produced-directed by Philip Leacock. (CBS/Fox; Avid)

BAIT (1954). The Devil (Sir Cedric Hardwicke) is watching this very movie (he must really be torturing himself), providing narration about how man can be seduced by a curvaceous, fleshy female body. A strange low budgeter produced-directed by actor Hugo Haas, who repeatedly displays a fetish for buxom blondes. The demonstrative peroxide bombshell here is Cleo Moore, involved in infidelity and murder. John Agar, Emmett Lynn.

BALLAD OF HILLBILLY JOHN. See **LEGEND OF HILLBILLY JOHN.**

BALLAD OF VIRGIL CANE. See **SHADOW OF CHAKIRA.**

BAMBOO SAUCER, THE (1967). After test pilot John Ericson claims he was buzzed by a UFO, he is assigned to parachute into China with Dan Duryea's combat team to locate an alien saucer. The squad works with a Russian team and behind-enemy-lines cliches abound as the men bicker over ideologies, Ericson falls for Russian scientist Lois Nettleton, etc. Finally there's a poorly staged shootout with Chinese regulars and Ericson and Nettleton fly the saucer at the speed of light toward Mars. Minor message movie from director-writer Frank Telford. Bernard Fox, Vincent Beck. (Republic)

BANANA MONSTER. Video version of **SCHLOCK** (Western World).

BANDITS OF CORSICA, THE (1953). In this version of Alexandre Dumas' THE CORSICAN BROTHERS, directed by Ray Nazarro, Siamese twins separated at birth retain a metaphysical link—each feels the other's pains and joys. While the 1941 Douglas Fairbanks Jr. version, under the original title, was superior, this is still a decent programmer ably acted by Richard Greene, Paula Richmond, Raymond Burr and Lee Van Cleef.

BANG BANG KID, THE (1968). Italian-Spanish cowboy parody, strained when inventor Tom Bosley shows up in the wild town of Limerick to introduce CXA-107, a remote-controlled gunslinger. Most of the gags fall flat as the stupid-looking mechanical shooter makes an oily fool of himself against cow boss Bear Bulloch (Guy Madison). Produced by Sidney Pink, directed by Stanley Praeger. Clank, went the outlaw, slapping hardware. Sandra Milo, Dianik Zurakowska. (Western World)

BANKER, THE (1989). This slasher flick didn't draw much interest and was deposited directly on video. It's a no-account account of a serial killer (Duncan Regehr) who lays away prostitutes, mutilating and spindelling them as he undergoes a South American ritual, splashing paint on his face like a fanatical native. He also uses a crossbow to stalk victims. Hot on his trail is cop Robert Forster. We suggest an immediate withdrawal. Shanna Reed, Jeff Conaway, Richard Roundtree. Directed by William Webb. (Video/Laser: MCEG)

BARBARELLA: QUEEN OF THE GALAXY (1968). Imaginative adaptation of the French cartoon strip by Jean-Claude Forest with Jane Fonda as the wide-eyed innocent space traveler of 40,000 A.D. with bulging bosom and an incompetency for sex as she encounters close extraterrestrial adventures of the bizarre kind. Roger Vadim directed with an eye for psychedelic detail and treats matters neither seriously nor inanely, allowing the viewer to indulge in the fun. The set design is wonderfully, incredibly weird; Barbarella is attacked by man-eating Barbie dolls, trapped in the Chamber of Dreams and blows the fuse of the Pleasure Machine. Silly, absurd, funny, outrageous, utterly visual . . . the ridiculousness won't stop. John Phillip Law, Milo O'Shea, David Hemmings and Ugo Tognazzi are among the oddly garbed grotesqueries. (Video/Laser: Paramount)

BARBARIANS, THE (1987). Musclemen brothers Peter and David Paul (billed as the Barbarian Brothers) star in this ridiculous Cannon spoof of the sword-and-sorcery canon. The brothers start out as kids with a tribe called Ragniks, whose queen Canary possesses a magical ruby. Richard Lynch (as villainous Kadar) wants the stone for evil purposes and imprisons the group. The boys grow into strongarm louts Kutchet and Gor, who proclaim their prowess with Tarzan-style battle cries and escape to lead a revolt against Lynch and his sorcerers, and partake in battles with warriors, swamp skeleton monsters and a dragon. You might call this BUTCH CASSIDY AND SUNDANCE MEET CONAN. Filmed in Italy under director Ruggerio Deodato, the film's cast plays it for laughs, using anachronisms. Michael Berrymore is especially campy as the Dirtmaster. Eva La Rue, Virginia Bryant. (Media) (Laser: Image)

BARBARIC BEAST OF BOGGY CREEK, THE, PART II. Alternate title for **BOGGY CREEK II.**

BARE-BREASTED COUNTESS, THE. See **EROTIKILL.**

BAREFOOT EXECUTIVE, THE (1971). Chimpanzee develops ability to pick hit TV shows. Too bad networks never followed his formula. Kurt Russell becomes vice-president of a network, thanks to the chimp. Joe Flynn, Wally Cox, Harry Morgan, John Ritter, Alan Hewitt. Directed by Robert Butler. (Disney)

BARN OF THE NAKED DEAD. Video title for **TERROR CIRCUS** (Showcase Productions Inc.).

BARON BLOOD (1972). Mario Bava directed this Gothic tale about the spirit of Baron Otto von Kleist haunting the halls of the family castle and wreaking vengeance with torture devices. Taut chase sequences, grisly gore effects and eerie photography give Bava's cliched script vitality, as do Joseph Cotten (as the Baron) and heavy-breathing Elke Sommer, who does wonders for the low-cut blouse/miniskirt industry. Also called CHAMBER OF TORTURES, THE BLOOD BARON, THE THIRST OF BARON BLOOD. Antonio Cantafora, Massimo Girotti, Alan Collins. (From HBO as **TORTURE CHAMBER OF BARON BLOOD**) (Laser: Image, with **CIRCUS OF HORRORS**)

BARON MUENCHHAUSEN (1943). During World War II, Hitler ordered his UFA film division to produce a non-propaganda entertainment for his Third Reich. This spectacular, richly textured film was the result, but released into a society so devastated by war that few saw it. This subtitled version is a film historian's delight with its period costumes, elegant sets, excellent color, and fine cast. It features many of the fantasy-adventures that Terry Gilliam re-created in THE ADVENTURES OF BARON MUNCHAUSEN. Watch for the funny sequences in

Catherine the Great's court and in the Sultan's harem. The effects were unusually good for their time, but more important is the film's sense of fairy-tale charm. Directed by Josef von Baky. Hans Albers is wonderful as the Baron, Brigitte Horney is exactly that as the sensuous Catherine of Russia, and Wilhelm Bendow is the Man on the Moon. (Video City)

BARON OF TERROR. See **BRAINIAC, THE.**

BARON'S AFRICAN WAR, THE (1943). Whittled-down TV version of the Republic serial **MANHUNT IN THE AFRICAN JUNGLE**, made as **SECRET SERVICE IN DARKEST AFRICA.**

BARRACUDA (THE LUCIFER PROJECT) (1978). Fish poisoned by mankind's pollution take a human to lunch in the waters off Florida. Munch munch with plenty of crunch. This tale of ecological revenge involves Dr. Jason Evers and his experiments in low blood sugar that could affect the entire town. Wayne David Crawford, the blandest hero ever cast in a horror movie, sets out to solve the mystery. Harry Kerwin directed and co-wrote with Crawford. Comedy relief consists of an obese deputy sheriff. Bert Freed, Roberta Leighton, William Kerwin, Cliff Emmich. (VidAmerica)

BARRY McKENZIE HOLDS HIS OWN (1974). Madcap, vulgar Australian comedy; a zippy olio of satire and jokes aimed at, and against, Australians by director Bruce Beresford. Barry McKenzie (Barry Crocker) is traveling with Aunt Edna (Barry Humphries in drag) to Paris, when they are mistaken as the Queen of England and her bodyguard by minions of Count Plasma (Donald Pleasence), a Transylvanian nobleman-vampire who wants her kidnapped to improve tourism in the Carpathanian Mountains. Amidst the crude beer, vampire, vomit, toilet and sex jokes are some clever puns and situations. Wild, woolly and nonstop in its assault on your senses (and sensitivities), especially if you are an Aussie. Roy Kinnear, Dick Bentley. (VidAmerica)

BARTON FINK (1992). A metaphor for the expression "writer's hell"—that region of the mind where wordsmiths suffer when they face creative constipation. New York playwright John Turturro is hired in 1941 by a Hollywood studio to write a wrestling movie. The Earl Hotel, where the motto is "a day or a lifetime," becomes Turturro's hell, his neighbor in the next room (John Goodman) a form of the Devil. There are portions of this Coen brothers film (they co-wrote together; Ethan produced and Joel directed) that explore other aspects of the writer's difficulties in creating, one of the studio's writers (John Mahoney) being based on William Faulkner. Michael Learner's performance as the studio boss is an undisguised satire of Louis B. Mayer, one-time king of MGM, and it's a gem. An exercise in style that blends realistic and surreal elements, and which is fascinating in the enigma it presents. (Video/Laser: CBS/Fox)

BASKET CASE (1981). Cinema of the Grotesque lives! The wicker basket Kevin Van Hentryck carries into Times Square contains something that snarls and chomps on burgers. It's director Frank Henenlotter's homage to monster macabre, full of spattering blood a la Herschell G. Lewis (to whom the film is dedicated) and visually unsettling: "it" is a blob with monstrous head and gnarly arms, a Siamese twin mutant, avenging itself on the flaky doctors who separated him from brother Kevin at birth, and on low-life city trash. Henenlotter uses Times Square's derelicts, whores, drug addicts and quacks for an outrageous acting effect. (Media) (Laser: Japanese import)

BASKET CASE 2 (1991). Because an R rating was desired, writer- director Frank Henenlotter (a "film making subversive") played down this sequel to his 1981 black-comedy shocker. This is the continuing saga of Kevin and Belial—the former a normal-looking guy, the latter a grotesque parody of a man concealed in a basket when he isn't out murdering. In this love story (!), Belial ends up in an attic of monsters and falls in love with a huge operatic mouth called Lorenzo, while his brother Kevin has an affair with a normal woman. The ending is comically dark. Kevin Van Hentenryck, Annie Ross, Ted Sorel. (Shapiro Glickenhaus) (Laser: Image)

BASKET CASE 3: THE PROGENY (1991). Writer-director Frank Henenlotter scores high marks for his imaginative, over-the-top filmmaking bravura, though some may find his grotesque themes more than they can bear. Henenlotter continues to explore the world of freak-monsters (where normal-looking people are the real monsters) for new nuances, so each sequel plunges into new horror territory. Picking up where Part 2 left off, Belial's bride gives birth to "12 baby Belials" when a menagerie of monsters under Annie Ross' care goes to the countryside to escape the "horrors" of the city. The gory effects are more comedic than real, and a sense of twisted satire works on one's sensibilities rather than shock or outrage. These films remain anomalies of the video marketplace—amusing, outrageous, but stylish, with an insightful sense of irony and comedy. Kevin Van Hentenryck, Gil Roper. (Video/Laser: MCA)

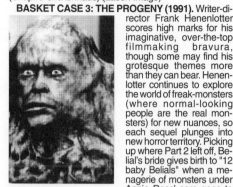

BABY BELIALS

BAT, THE (1959). "Old dark house" horror-drama based on the creaky Mary Roberts Rinehart-Avery Hopwood play, and originally made in 1915, 1926 and 1930 as THE BAT WHISPERS. Vincent Price is a cop investigating a caped figure flitting about a weird mansion, The Oaks, inhabited by "batty" dames. Agnes Moorehead, John Sutton and Gavin Good keep the old-fashioned concepts moving under Crane Wilbur's direction. (Sinister/C; S/Weird; Filmfax)

BATES MOTEL (1987). Disappointing TV pilot spinning off from Robert Bloch's novel PSYCHO and Hitchcock's film adaptation. Bud Cort portrays a lovable nerd locked up in an asylum who befriends Norman Bates and inherits his rundown motel when the psychopathic killer dies. Cort remodels and opens for business with street-smart waif Lori Petty and carpenter Moses Gunn. He is mysteriously bothered by a strange figure (Mrs. Bates?). The motel's first customer, a woman about to commit suicide, has a fling with the supernatural. Cort is too silly and the thrills too weak. Written-produced-directed by Richard Rothstein. Kerrie Keane. (MCA)

BATMAN (1966). Spinning off from the hit TV series with Adam West and Burt Ward, this feature seems better today than when it was released. Batman and Robin fight four archcriminals (The Catwoman, The Joker, The Penguin and The Riddler) who plan to use a Dehydration Machine to convert us to dust. Screenwriter Lorenzo Simple Jr. unfolds this superhero tale in the zany tradition of TV and there's not much more to say about it. Director Leslie H. Martinson treats it like just another quickie TV episode. Lee Meriwether, Cesar Romero, Burgess Meredith and Frank Gorshin are the villains. Stafford Repp, Neil Hamilton. (Video/Laser: Fox)

BATMAN (1989). Director Tim Burton carries the comic-book concept into a dark realm, creating a vision of Gotham City and its crimefighters in a gothic style. Because the Sam Hamm-Warren Skaaren script gives a psychological cause for Batman's Robin-less crusade against crime, Burton spins a tale with all the ironic comedy, tragedy and doom of a Shakespearean saga. The surrealistic imagery by designer Anton Furst provides an unrelenting sense of fear for the lost society in which Bruce Wayne-Batman must tread. As Batman, Michael Keaton brings a brooding angst to the character that is refreshing. Jack Nicholson shines as The Joker, driven by an inner demon that never loosens its maniacal grip. Sinister and brooding, as is Danny Elfman's doom-laden score. Visually it's stunning—to the point it's underdeveloped screenplay suffers. But so much is going on, the portrayals so larger than life, and the hardware so fabulous, it's a gripping experience. Kim Basinger plays Vicki Vale to good effect. Robert Wuhl, Pat Hingle, Billy Dee Williams, Michael Gough, Jack Palance. The sequel: BATMAN RETURNS. (Video/Laser: Warner Bros.)

BATMAN (1943). Columbia's 15-chapter serial is one of the studio's best cliffhangers and holds up well despite its anti-Japanese sentiments and J. Carrol Naish's peformance as Dr. Daka, an enemy agent with a brain-zapping device that turns men into zombies. Naish is out to steal a radium supply, and also steals the show with his campy performance. Lewis Wilson (Batman) and Douglas Croft (Robin) prove worthy crimefighters. Directed by Lambert Hillyer. William Austin, Shirley Patterson, Charles Middleton. (Goodtimes)

BATMAN. Eight videos featuring Batman and Robin in animated adventures. (Video/Laser: Warner Bros.)

BATMAN AND ROBIN (1949). Sam Katzman's 15-chapter Columbia serial stars Robert Lowery as Batman and John Duncan as Robin as they battle the insidious Wizard, a hooded madman who has stolen a valuable invention that could lead to mankind's destruction. Spencer Bennet directed this slugfest of cliffhanging fun. Jane Adams, Lyle Talbot, Ralph Graves, Don Harvey, House Peters Jr. (Goodtimes)

BATMAN: MASK OF THE PHANTASM (1993). Animated feature in the "Dark Knight" vein as a troubled Batman/Bruce Wayne fights the Joker and falls in love with a woman whose father is mixed up with crooks. Moody, loaded with angst and action. Directed by Bruce Timm and Eric Radomski, story by Alan Burnett. Voices by Kevin Conroy, Hart Bochner, Abe Vigoda.

BATMAN RETURNS (1992). Triumphant sequel to the 1989 smash, with Tim Burton displaying a flashy directorial style in one groovy comic-book adaptation. Michael Keaton is back as the angst-riddled crimefighter who faces formidable adversaries: The Penguin, played to the max by Danny DeVito, and Catwoman, one supersexy villainess as scratched out by Michelle Pfeiffer. These psychotic whackos team with city tycoon Max Shreck (wig-covered Christopher Walken) to bring about Batman's downfall in bizarre battles. There are holes in the Daniel Waters script, but this is where powerful, overwhelming visuals are everything. Michael Murphy, Pat Hingle, Vincent Schiavelli, Michael Gough. (Video/Laser: Warner Bros.)

CATWOMAN

BATMEN OF AFRICA (1936). Chopped-up TV-feature version of **DARKEST AFRICA.**

BAT PEOPLE, THE (1973). Low-budget vampire-drama in which John Beck and Marianna MacAndrew suffer from vampire bat bites and undergo transformation. A grisly climax is the only payoff to producer Lou Shaw's screenplay, set in a desert community. Sluggishly directed by Jerry Jameson. Stewart Moss, Michael Pataki, Arthur Space, Paul Carr. (HBO)

BATTERIES NOT INCLUDED (1987). This Steven Spielberg production is a soft-hearted, warm fantasy parable with cutesy-pie hardware. The setting is a building in the Bronx where a cafe is run by Hume Cronyn and Jessica Tandy. Evil forces are at work to remove them, but miniature alien saucers (their crews are never shown; the ships take on human personification) act as fairies for the good folks in the building. The UFO effects are wonderful, and director Robbins gives the film a blend of fantasy and harsh realism without making it depressing. Frank McRae, Elizabeth Pena. "E.T."-type music score by James Horner. (Video/Laser: MCA)

BATTLE BENEATH THE EARTH (1968). British "yellow horde" fantasy about a Chinese scheme to tunnel beneath America with a laser gun and invade with swarms of Asians. Thwarting this insidious plot is Sinbad himself, Kerwin Mathews, whose adversary is a Fu Manchu type (Martin Benson). Montgomery Tully directed L. Z. Hargreaves' script with a straight face, playing none of it for its satire and comedy. Vivian Ventura, Robert Ayres, Peter Arne. (MGM/UA)

BATTLE BEYOND THE STARS (1980). Roger Corman's version of STAR WARS is also a space-opera remake of SEVEN SAMURAI, with Richard Thomas flying through the Universe seeking mercenaries to help his planet Akirian combat warlord John Saxon, who's blowing up everyone with his Stellar Converter. John Sayles' script has a redeeming tongue-in-cheek quality often subservient to the space effects. George Peppard is an amusing cowboy who loves to drink; Robert Vaughn revives his THE MAGNIFICENT SEVEN role as a "gunfighter" haunted by his past; and Sybil Danning is a buxom space jockey whose breasts threaten to pop out of her bra and through the screen. The film's spirit of fun (under Jimmy T. Murakami's direction) should send you into orbit. (Vestron) (Laser: Image)

BATTLE BEYOND THE SUN (1963). Some battle! Two monsters (one an upended pea-pod with a blood-shot eye at the top of its misshapen body, the other a headless toadstool with a jaundiced eye on a tentacle tip) clash for about two minutes. The USSR and USA are in a race to reach Mars, so most of this consists of space stations, rockets, satellites, androids and astronauts, without excitement. Originally a Soviet film, then re-edited by Roger Corman, with new footage by director Thomas Colchart. (Sinister/C; S/Weird; Filmfax)

BATTLE FOR THE PLANET OF THE APES (1974). Fifth and final entry in Arthur Jacobs' PLANET OF THE APES series, and the least effective. This was relegated to the B category, as witness the decreased production values and a less incisive script by John William Corrington and Joyce Hooper Corrington. Upstart apes plot to promote a culture that treats men and apes equally, but insurrectionist gorillas thwart this movement with the help of mutant humans. Roddy McDowall is back as Caesar and Claude Akins is the leader of the growlin' dissidents. Director J. Lee Thompson throws it all away in favor of action, but even shootemup mayhem can't keep everyone from looking like monkeys. Lew Ayres, Paul Williams, John Huston, France Nuyen, Paul Stevens, Pat Cardi, John Landis. (Playhouse)

BATTLE IN OUTER SPACE (1960). Those Godzilla movers, director Inoshiro Honda and effects artist Eiji Tsuburaya, destroy Venice, New York City and the Golden Gate Bridge just to get warmed up for this super-spectacle in which aliens attack Earth, but a counterforce meets the E.T. enemy and blasts E.T. (everything) in sight. Interplanetary conflagration on a grand scale. Ryo Ikebe, Kyoto Anzai, Minoru Takada.

BATTLE OF THE ASTROS. See **MONSTER ZERO.**

BATTLE OF THE STARS (1979). No, not a TV tug-of-war between Bill Cosby and Michael J. Fox. It's a low-grade Italian sci-fi adventure directed by Al Bradly and set in deep space where the Earth cruiser Magellan finds a malevolent race, the Dragonians, zombies with faces of crawling worms. Decaying in body and spirit, these entities need a new home so it's a drag-out battle to save Earth from invasion. The effects are of the electronic zap school and the giant spacecraft resembles a robot toy or a giant slot machine, however you look at it.

BATTLE OF THE WORLDS (1961). Italian director Antonio Margheriti (Anthony Dawson) has the advantage of Claude Rains as a dedicated scientist. Rains keeps the story moving, and lends versimilitude to the otherwise pedantic, unexciting proceedings. Rains warns Earth of an approaching meteor—a sphere for a computerized brain system programmed to launch war on Earth. Out go the rockets and "space wars" technology to prevent our destruction. Bill Carter, Umberto Orsini, Maya Brent. (Sinister/C; S/Weird; Filmfax)

BATTLESTAR GALACTICA (1979). A 125-minute space adventure re-edited from the three-hour pilot which opened the TV series. It's intergalactic war between the Cylons, robots programmed to destroy mankind, and a ragtag fleet of starships returning to Earth after colonies are attacked and nearly destroyed by the Cylons. John Dykstra, contributor to the STAR WARS effects, has ingenious spacecraft, aerial dogfights, massive explosions, alien landscapes. Glen A. Larson's script is derivative of STAR WARS with Richard Hatch and Dirk Benedict emulating Luke Skywalker and Han Solo as warriors racing to their battlecruisers. Richard A. Colla began directing but was replaced by uncredited Alan J. Levi. Lorne Greene, Jane Seymour, Ray Milland, Lew Ayres, Wilfrid Hyde-White. (MCA; Goodtimes) (Laser: MCA)

BATTLESTAR GALACTICA (TV compilations). Re-edited episodes of the popular TV series: "Curse of the Cylons," "Experiment in Terror," "Greetings from Earth," "Gun on Ice Planet Zero," "The Living Legend," "Lost Planet of the Gods," "Murder in Space," "Phantom in Space," "Space Casanova," "Space Prison" and "War of the Gods." MCA offers these on video: "Baltar's Escape," "Fire in Space," "The Long Patrol," "The Lost Warrior," "The Man With Nine Lives," "Murder on the Rising Star," "The Young Lords."

BATTLETRUCK. See **WARLORDS OF THE 21ST CENTURY.**

BAT WHISPERS, THE (1930). Adaptation of THE BAT, the Rinehart-Hopwood play set in a mansion where a caped menace darts about. Roland West's writing-direction are old-fashioned and if you can accept a dusty antique as a decorative piece, this should fit well on your viewing mantel. Remade in 1959 as THE BAT. Chester Morris, Una Merkel. (Captain Bijou) (Laser: Image)

BATWOMAN (1968). Mexican nonsense as a masked heroine (Maura Monti) and pals battle an evil doctor and his cadre of scaly monsters. Wrecked and wretched, with Rene Cadona misdirecting the tamale traffic and writer Alfred Salazar slinging untasty salsa.

BAY COVEN (1987). Despite swipes from ROSEMARY'S BABY and THE OMEN, this TV-movie has intriguing moments when yuppies Pamela Sue Martin and Tim Matheson escape the rat race to live on an island off the East Coast haunted by a witchcraft past. It appears Matheson is part of a cult staging a conspiracy trip on Martin, who keeps seeing things that later aren't there. You've seen it before, but there are scary moments and the climax pays off. Directed by Carl Schenkel. Barbara Billingsley, Jeff Conaway, Inga Swenson. (From Vidmark as **EYE OF THE DEMON**)

BAXTER (1988). A bull terrier narrates this strange French depiction of canine angst as a psyched-out pooch from Paris searches for the perfect master, but brings to humans only unhappiness and death. This is not a "killer dog" movie, but a sincere attempt to get inside a dog's head and find out why man's best friend isn't always so. Based on HELL HOUND, a novel by Jacques Audiard, it was written-directed by Jerome Boivin, who feels this is a "shaggy-dog story in which the dog is more human than the humans." Lise Delamare, Jean Mercure. (New Video Group) (Laser: Lumivision)

BAY OF BLOOD, A. Video version of **CARNAGE** (Gorgon; MPI).

BEACH BABES FROM BEYOND (1993). The aliens are women wearing bikinis and led by Space Babe when they crash a beach party. Saints preserve us. Directed by Ellen Cabot. Joe Estevez, Jacqueline Stallone, Burt Ward, Linnea Quigley, Don Swayze. (Paramount)

BEACH GIRLS AND THE MONSTER. Video version of **MONSTER FROM THE SURF** (Sinister/C; S/Weird; Filmfax).

BEAKS THE MOVIE (1986). Also known as BIRDS OF PREY, this is a steal of Hitchcock's THE BIRDS with nothing new—just inferior thrills when the bird population, rebelling against pollution, hunts and pecks humans to death. Some of the attack sequences are well done but writer-director-producer Rene Cardona Jr. lines his cage at every opportunity, relying on cliches. Rather than rent this strictly-for-the-birds video, pick up THE BIRDS again. BEAKS, which wreaks, was filmed in Madrid. Christopher Atkins, Michelle Johnson, Salvador Pineda. (IVE)

BEAR, THE (1970). Polish folk lore inspired this fantasy involving a man who is part bear. Beautifully photographed. Written-directed by Janusz Majewski. Josef Duriasz, Edmund Fetting. Also called LOKIS.

BEAST, THE. Video version of **EQUINOX** (Wizard).

BEAST AND THE MAGIC SWORD, THE (1983). Jacinto Molina's werewolf series continues with this Spanish-Japanese frighter job with Paul Naschy (writer-producer-director Molina). Shigeru Amachi, Junko Asahina.

BEAST FROM HAUNTED CAVE (1960). Director Monte Hellman dovetails a gangster and monster story (by Charles Griffith) into an unusual melange. Crooks are holed up in a ski resort when a creature in a nearby cave begins a reign of terror. Made in Deadwood, S. Dakota. Sheila Carol, Michael Forest, Wally Campo. Produced by Gene Corman. (Sinister/C; S/Weird; Filmfax)

BEAST FROM 20,000 FATHOMS (1953). Colossal-monster-on-a-rampage thriller, enhanced by the effects of Ray Harryhausen, working solo after an apprenticeship with KING KONG mover Willis O'Brien. Although his stop-motion was to undergo refinement, this remains a trend-setting miniclassic, tense and ferocious. The titular entity is a dinosaur freed from its ten-million-year hibernation by an atomic blast at the North Pole. The creature ravages New York City, swallowing one traffic cop whole and attacking a roller coaster. Directed by Eugene Lourie and co-written by Fred Freiberger (STAR TREK's producer in its final season) and Lou Morheim (of THE OUTER LIMITS). Inspired by Ray Bradbury's "The Foghorn." Paul Christian, Paula Raymond, Cecil Kellaway, Kenneth Tobey, Donald Woods, Lee Van Cleef, King Donovan. (Warner Bros.; Sinister/C) (Laser: Warner)

BEAST IN THE CELLAR (1970). Sleep-inducing, talkative British picture has minimal horror effects and atmosphere. Yak yak yak between Beryl Reid and Flora Robson and little else. James Kelly wrote-directed this forgettable bore. As for the "beast," it's a scrawny non-brawny. (Paragon; Front Row Entertainment)

BEASTMASTER, THE (1982). Sword-and-sorcery adventure from producer-director Don Coscarelli: Bronzed hero Dar (Marc Singer), searching for barbarians who slaughtered his village, telecommunicates with animals and birds and uses an eagle, a panther and two ferrets to carry out his bidding. Some effects are nice, but the plot suffers from bad dialogue. Tanya Roberts is merely decorative as a slave girl who bares her breasts briefly in a pool sequence, and Rip Torn is horribly unrestrained as the villain Maax. John Amos shines as Seth, Dar's fighting companion, even though it is a silly role. There's much to be enjoyed: Bird Men, Zombie Monsters, and a night battle. (Video/Laser: MGM/UA)

BEASTMASTER 2: THROUGH THE PORTAL OF TIME (1990). Suitable sequel to the 1982 adventure, with Marc Singer back as Dar, the benevolent barbarian who travels through the land of Arok in the company of an eagle (Rhu), a tiger (Sharak) and two ferrets (Kodo and Podo) in his new battles against the evil ruler Arklon (Wings Hauser). Sarah Douglas, as a wicked sorceress, learns the secret to a time portal that takes them all to modern-day L.A. where Arklon seeks the Neutron Detonator for world dominance. The comic-book action is plentiful, Douglas makes for a fetching, humorous villainess and Singer is a likable presence, no matter how hokey the R.J. Robinson-Jim Wynorski-Ken Hauser-Doug Miles script gets in adapting a novel by Andre Norton. Director Sylvio Tabet holds the nonsense together. And there's an above-average score by Robert Folk. Kari Wuhrer, Charles Young, James Avery, Robert Z'Dar, Michael Berryman. (Video/Laser: Republic)

BEAST MUST DIE, THE (1973). Assorted types are invited to the mansion of millionaire Calvin Lockhart, who knows one of them is a werewolf. He has electronic lycanthropic-detecting equipment in and around the estate to trap the four-legged attacker. This modern touch is okay but it still boils down to old Wolf Man cliches with a dog dressed to look like a werewolf. Directed by Paul Annett; from a Michael Winder script based on James Blish's novelette, "There Shall Be No Darkness." Peter Cushing, Charles Gray, Anton Diffring. (Starmaker; from Impulse as **BLACK WEREWOLF**) (Laser: Image)

BEAST OF BLOOD (1970). Filipino sequel to MAD DOCTOR OF BLOOD ISLAND, in which insidious Dr. Lorca (Eddie Garcia) keeps a decapitated creature alive. Writer-producer-director Eddie Romero needed to inject more life into this listless horror film, as abominable as the dead forces it depicts. John Ashley, Celeste Yarnall.

BEAST OF BORNEO (1935). See third edition.

BEAST OF HOLLOW MOUNTAIN (1956). Willis O'Brien, the major contributor to stop-motion animation with KING KONG, utilized Regiscope to animate a cattle-hungry Tyrannosaurus Rex in this U.S.-Mexican production made in Mexico by Edward and William Nassour. It's your basic Western but with monster touches, starring Guy Madison as a rancher being forced out by a land baron. Matters pick up with the arrival of Patricia Medina wearing low-cut blouses . . . and finally comes the long-awaited attack by the Rex with the pex from his mountain lair, but the beast isn't on screen long enough. Directorial chores were shared by Edward Nassour and Ismael Rodriguez. From an idea by O'Brien.

BEAST OF MOROCCO (1966). Dreary, pain-in-the-neck flick about a hapless chap (William Sylvester) obsessed with a beautiful woman who turns out to be a vampiress in charge of a bloodsucking cult. Also known as THE HAND OF NIGHT. Terence De Marney, Diane Clare. William Dexter. Directed by Frederic Goode.

BEAST OF PARADISE ISLAND. See **PORT SINISTER.**

BEAST OF THE DEAD. See **BEAST OF BLOOD.**

BEAST OF THE YELLOW NIGHT (1971). Filipino splatter production written-directed by Eddie Romero. John Ashley sells his soul to the Devil so he can turn into different creatures at night, including a werewolf. Eddie Garcia, Mary Wilcox. (United; Sinister/C; Nostalgia)

BEAST OF YUCCA FLATS, THE (1961). Tor Johnson, a brutish actor often seen sneaking up on Bela Lugosi in grade-Z horror jobs, has his sole leading role as a scientist exposed to radiation who goes berserk. Johnson is too typecast, and limited an actor, to bring off the part. Writer-director Coleman Francis resorts to narration to fill in the holes. Douglas Mellor, Barbara Francis. (Sinister/C; S/Weird; Filmfax; Cinemacabre)

BEASTS. Video version of **TWILIGHT PEOPLE, THE** (Direct).

BEASTS. Video version of **CLAWS (1985)** (ANE).

BEAST THAT KILLED WOMEN (1965). Giant gorilla runs wild through a nudist camp. Is nothing sacred in the sunbelt? Blemishes in Barry Mahon's production are as noticeable as those on the extras' behinds; the bad acting is nakedly exposed.

BEAST WITH A MILLION EYES (1958). Cheapo sci-fi without much of a beast (a punctured teakettle) and without a million eyes. Roger Corman produced it, according to Samuel Z. Arkoff. Set near Indio, Calif., Tom Filer's script showcases an obscure E.T. life form that turns beasts against humans. One scene has birds attacking a car (prophesizing THE BIRDS) but otherwise it's a dud. Chances are, millions of eyes never watched Paul Birch, Lorna Thayer and Chester Conklin run around desert country. Directed blindly by David Kramarsky.

BEAST WITH FIVE FINGERS (1947). No need to give Warner Bros. the finger: the studio did an adept job palming off W. F. Harvey's short story to screenwriter Curt Siodmak, who turned it into a superior piece of psychological horror. The severed hand of a maddened pianist scuttles repulsively to and fro . . . or is Peter Lorre imagining an old friend has returned from the grave to strangle him? Lorre goes mad as only Lorre can, nailing the ghastly quintet of digits to a board and flinging it into a fire. Give a big hand to director Robert Florey and a round of applause with sweaty palms to Robert Alda, Andrea King, Victor Francen and J. Carroll Naish. And kudos to Max Steiner for his enriched score. (MGM/UA)

BEAST WITHIN, THE (1982). THE OMEN producer Harvey Bernhard fashioned a horror-monster entertainment with good transformation effects by Thomas Burman. Ronny Cox's wife is raped by an unseen spirit; a son is born possessed by an evil being who takes on new shape before launching a homicidal rampage. One of the film's virtues is the bravura acting by Paul Clemens, who conveys the teenager's demonic pain without makeup in early scenes. There is a dark, moody atmosphere to Philippe Mora's direction. Made in the small town of Raymond, Miss. Edward Levy's novel was loosely adapted by Tom Holland. Bibi Besch, Don Gordon, R. G. Armstrong, L. Q. Jones. (MGM/UA)

BEAUTIES AND THE BEAST, THE (1985). Ushi Dagard and other bountiful babes are attacked by a Yeti who doesn't even have to rip off their clothes. They're all practicing nudists. Some practice. Directed by Ray Naneau and Marius Mazmanian. Also called THE BEAUTIES AND THE VIXENS. (Action Inc.; Applause)

BEAUTIFUL WOMEN AND THE HYDROGEN MAN. See **H-MAN, THE.**

BEAUTY AND THE BEAST (1946). Jean Cocteau's adaptation of the classic fairy tale is a poetic, dreamlike fantasy that still delights new generations. Costuming, sets, music—it is a synthesis of the cinema arts. A surrealistic autumn air hangs over a decaying mansion where Belle (Josette Day) encounters candelabra held by human hands thrust from wall sconces, wooden faces that come to life, walls that whisper to her and the Beast (Jean Marais), a prince trapped in a werewolf's body until he finds a woman to love him. Marais' creature, although fanged and hirsute, is a poet-intellectual who expresses the pain of the human heart. French director Rene Clement acted as technical adviser to Cocteau. Marais portrays three roles: the Beast, Belle's handsome but uninspired village suitor, and the Prince Charming waiting to be restored. Marcel Andre, Mila Parely, Michel Auclair. Music score by Georges Auric. (Embassy; Nelson) (Laser: Nelson; Voyager; Criterion)

BEAUTY AND THE BEAST (1963). Commercialized version of the fairy tale, a standard programmer by director Edward L. Cahn. The George Bruce-Orville Hampton storyline has a cursed duke turning into a creature on nights of the full moon. Make-up by Jack Pierce. Eduard Franz, Mark Damon, Joyce Taylor, Michael Pate.

BEAUTY AND THE BEAST (1976). TV adaptation of the fairy talestarring the husband-wife team of George C. Scott and Trish Van Devere, with supporting roles filled by Bernard Lee (James Bond's M), Virginia McKenna and Patricia Quinn. Scott, who performed his role in a boar's head mask, was nominated for an Emmy. Directed by Fielder Cook.

BEAUTY AND THE BEAST (1979). Czech version of the classic allegory, written-directed by Juraj Herz, with Vlastimil Harapes as the ugly creature and Zdena Studenkova as the beauty.

BEAUTY AND THE BEAST (1984). Episode from Showtime's FAERIE TALE THEATRE starring Susan Sarandon and Klaus Kinski. Directed by Roger Vadim. (Video/Laser: CBS/Fox)

BEAUTY AND THE BEAST (1987). Another entry in the Cannon series of screen adaptations of famous fairy tales, this follows the traditional classic with Rebecca DeMornay as the Beauty and John Savage in the dual roles of Beast and Prince. Directed by Eugene Marner. Yossi Graber, Michael Schneider, Ruth Harlap.

BEAUTY AND THE BEAST (1987). "Once Upon a Time in New York," the two-hour pilot for the cult TV series, introduces Vincent, a warm, sensitive man living in a subterranean society beneath New York City. His only problem is, he's half monster, resembling a hairy werewolf. He rescues a beautiful D.A.'s assistant and takes her into his world where they fall in love. It's a fascinating relationship that was to fuel this unusual TV series for several seasons. Ron Perlman and Linda Hamilton make a great team. (Video/Laser: Republic)

BEAUTY AND THE BEAST: ABOVE, BELOW AND BEYOND (1989-90). Episodes from the classy CBS-TV series: "To Reign in Hell" and "Orphans." Linda Hamilton, Ron Perlman. (Republic)

RON PERLMAN: BEAST

BEAUTY AND THE BEAST: THOUGH LOVERS BE LOST (1989). When Catherine (Linda Hamilton) becomes pregnant with Vincent's baby, she's abducted by an industrialist with grand designs on the child's future. Oddball material, but fascinating. Ron Perlman. (Video/Laser: Republic)

BEAUTY AND THE BEAST (1991). One of the best Walt Disney cartoons and a winner of the Academy Award for best picture. An effervescent adaptation of Madame De Beaumont's eternal fairy tale about an enchanted beast and his love affair with a beautiful young woman during the late 18th century. It is in a musical tradition, with several production numbers—superb renderings thank to lyrics by Alan Menken and music by Howard Ashman. The main characters have charm and depth, and the supporting "cast" is made up of household items (candlestick, clock, tea kettle and tea cup, etc.) that are unforgettably funny. Linda Woolverton's script, the direction by Gary Trousdale and Kirk Wise and the voices of Robby Benson (the beast), Paige O'Hara (Belle the beauty), Angela Lansbury, David Ogden Stiers and many others contribute to the excellence of this tale, Disney's 30th feature cartoon. (Video/Laser: Disney)

BEAUTY AND THE ROBOT (1960). Would you believe Mamie Van Doren has 13 degrees, speaks 18 languages and is head of a college science department? That isn't the only ingredient that makes this Albert Zugsmith programmer fantastic: It also has a gadget that predicts racetrack results and a chimpanzee that types text with its feet. Come to think of it, that isn't so fantastic, since it was probably the chimp that typed the script. Originally released as SEX KITTENS GO TO COLLEGE. Tuesday Weld, Mickey Shaughnessy, Louis Nye, John Carradine, Vampira, Pamela Mason, Harold Lloyd Jr.

BECAUSE OF THE CATS (1975). Murders in a seaside village lead an inspector to a devil cult. Directed by Fons Rademakers. Bryan Marshall, Alexandra Stewart, Sylvia Kristel, Alex Van Rooyen. (Prism)

BEDAZZLED (1968). When a cook is about to hang himself because his first love refuses to acknowledge his existence, the Devil grants him seven wishes in exchange for his soul. But the wishes are thwarted by such ugly beasts as infidelity, bigamy, etc. Director Stanley Donen uses the satirical revue, Beyond the Fringe, to fine advantage: Dudley Moore, Eleanor Bron and Peter Cook (the latter also wrote the screenplay, which takes effective jabs at society, religion and nunneries). Even Raquel Welch comes off looking good as Lust. You will find it uproarious or offensive depending on your liberal threshold. (Video/Laser: CBS/Fox)

BEDEVIL (1993). Trilogy of horror tales from Australian writer-director Tracey Moffatt. In "Mr. Chuck," with Diana Davidson and Jack Charles, the spirit of a U.S. soldier haunts a suburban home; "Choo Choo Choo Choo," with Moffatt and Banula (David) Marika, concerns the spirit of a blind girl; "Lovin' the Spin I'm In," with Lex Marinos and Dina Panozzo, has lovers as ghosts.

BEDFORD INCIDENT, THE (1965). Well-intended attempt to depict events leading up to atomic holocaust when a destroyer commander (Richard Widmark) tracks a Russian sub in North Atlantic waters. It's too heavy-handed to work as propaganda but it does have mounting suspense under director James B. Harris. Sidney Poitier portrays a newspaperman tracking the story. James MacArthur, Wally Cox, Martin Balsam, Eric Portman, Donald Sutherland. Written by James Poe from Mark Rascovitch's novel. (RCA/Columbia) (Laser: Image)

BEDKNOBS AND BROOMSTICKS (1970). Delightful Walt Disney comedy intermingling live action with masterful animation. Based on Mary Norton's THE MAGIC BEDKNOB, this is clever satire in which Angela Lansbury takes a correspondence course in witchcraft just in time to repel invading Germans by bringing to life suits of armor and swords. Imaginatively directed by Robert Stevenson and adapted by Don DaGradi and producer Bill Walsh. David Tomlinson, Roddy McDowall, Sam Jaffe, John Ericson. (Video/Laser: Disney)

BEDLAM (1946). Last of the horror films produced by Val Lewton for RKO. Mark Robson directed his screenplay (inspired by Hogarth's painting, "Bedlam") which depicts horrific conditions in the St. Mary of Bethlehem Asylum of London in 1761. Anna Lee is incarcerated for meddling in the affairs of the cruel asylum-keeper, Master Sims, devilishly played by Boris Karloff. The costuming and mood of the period are expertly evoked and the cast is superb: Ian Wolfe, Jason Robards Sr., Robert Clarke, Ellen Corby, Billy House. (Nostalgia Merchant; Media; Fox Hill) (Laser: Image)

BEDROOM EYES (1984). Strange, offbeat Canadian murder mystery with psychoterror overtones, and an unusual study of voyeurism. Jogger Kenneth Gilman sees two women making love through a bedroom window and confides his Peeping Tom urges to a beautiful psychiatrist. Gilman is swept into murder, becoming an innocent hero on the run. Hypnotism is used to unlock the key to the crime while three policemen follow up the leads. Barbara Law plays an exotic exhibitionist. (Video/Laser: CBS/Fox)

BEDROOM EYES II (1989). Canadian portrait of the dark side of passion and voyeurism is convoluted, but Gerard Ciccoritti's script holds one rapt with its surprises as New York stockbroker Wings Hauser is caught up in shady Wall Street manipulations and a double case of murder. Sexual betrayal, revenge and doublecross figure prominently among Kathy Shower, Linda Blair and Jane Hamilton. A surreal, this-can't-be-happening-to-me quality hangs over the handsome Hauser as he is manipulated by ironic forces in this mixture of knife-gore murders, plots-within-plots and sexual depravity. Joe Giardina, Kevin Thomsen. (Vidmark) (Laser: Image)

BED SITTING ROOM, THE (1969). Offbeat British black comedy directed by Richard Lester, based on Spike Milligan-John Antrobus play—a madman's glimpse at a devastated Britain after nuclear holocaust. But the narrative is so disjointed, and the characters and situations so nonsensical, it is impossible to make any coherency out of the mishmash. It's unfunny to begin with, so what's to laugh at? Rita Tushingham, Ralph Richardson, Peter Cook, Dudley Moore, Spike Milligan.

BEES, THE (1978). If you've seen one swarm, you've seen them all. Yet another "B" thriller movie (written-produced-directed by triple-stinger Alfredo Zacharias) about South American killer bees attacking our hemisphere, with John Saxon, Angel Tompkins and John Carradine out to destroy the little sneaks. Expect to break out in hives. (Warner Bros.)

BEETLEJUICE (1988). A bizarre, outrageous comedy you will love. In a mood of no-holds-barred, exploratory story-telling, writers Michael McDowell and Warren Skaaren concoct an afterlife where recently deceased

Alec Baldwin and Geena Davis are trapped in their home unless they step outside, in which case they find themselves in this crazy waystation where souls wait for reclassification. The thrust of the story has the couple trying to scare a new family in their house—weirdos nuttier than the ghosts. In desperation the ghosts turn to the titular whacko who exorcises humans. As played by Michael Keaton, Betelguese is an absolute trouble-making rascal. Director Tim Burton allows uninhibitedness to rule and the characters' bizarre non sequitur antics are utterly insane. The goofiest supernatural comedy ever made. Jeffrey Jones, Catherine O'Hara, Glenn Shadix, Winona Ryder, Sylvia Sidney, Dick Cavett, Annie McEnroe, Robert Goulet. (Video/Laser: Warner Bros.)

BEFORE DAWN (1933). The limping ghost of crook Joe Valerie, his face a gleaming white mask, stalks an eerie mansion where it's rumored a million dollars in gold is stashed. It's an "old dark house" thriller with Dorothy Wilson as psychic Mlle. Mystera, who comes to the house with Stu Erwin to solve the mystery. Based on Edgar Wallace's short story "Death Watch." Directed by Irving Pichel. Warner Oland, Dudley Digges. (From RKO with **THE BRIGHTON STRANGLER**)

BEFORE I HANG (1940). Effective programmer designed for Boris Karloff. As Dr. John Garth, he seeks a serum to fight off aging, even after being sent to prison for a mercy killing. Some fanciful pseudoscience enhances all the double-talk about medicine for the good of mankind, but it finally boils down to Karloff turning into a human monster a la Dr. Frankenstein. Directed by Nick Grinde. Evelyn Keyes, Bruce Bennett, Edward Van Sloan, Don Beddoe, Robert Fiske. (RCA/Columbia)

BEFORE MIDNIGHT (1933). Isolated mansion is the scene for yet another mystery in which a man has successfully predicted his own death. Was he clairvoyant or just lucky? Lambert Hillyer directed. Ralph Bellamy, June Collyer, Betty Blythe, Arthur Pierson.

BEFORE THE FACT. See **ECOLOGY OF A CRIME.**

BEGINNING, THE (1973). Re-edited footage from the STARLOST TV series created (and then disowned) by Harlan Ellison. Keir Dullea and Robin Ward are passengers aboard a huge ship passing through deepest space in search of new worlds. In this adventure set on the Ark, a certain passageway leads to a tribe made up entirely of males. Barry Morse.

BEGINNING OF THE END (1957). Atomic radiation affects the genes of nature, and hopping out of the grass hoppin' mad are the biggest grasshoppers you'll ever see. But the buggy behemoths move as haltingly as the dialogue, so you know you must be watching a Bert I. Gordon epic. You are! Hence, you're watching one of the weakest of the Giant Bug movies of the 1950s. Peter Graves is unconvincing as a scientist who devises a supersonic sound-wave device to stop the juggernauts. This does not have legs. Peggie Castle, Morris Ankrum, Thomas Henry, Richard Benedict. (Video Treasures)

BEGOTTEN (1991). Written-produced-directed by E. Elias Merhige, this experimental fantasy depicts (without dialogue) a day in the life of God Killing Himself and his wife Mother Earth, who is giving birth to a son. Bloodletting accompanies this inexplicable allegory/metaphor/enigma/call-it-what-you-will. Oh, by the way. The son's name is Son of Earth-Flesh on Bone. Brian Salzberg, Donna Dempsey.

BEHEMOTH, THE SEA MONSTER. See **GIANT BEHEMOTH.**

BEHIND THE CELLAR DOOR. Video version of **REVENGE** with Joan Collins.

BEING, THE (1982). Blatant ripoff of ALIEN: the titular monster has slavering jowels, gnashing teeth and an ornery disposition. The spawning ground for this one-eyed monstrosity is nuclear waste at a plant outside Pottsville, Idaho. Pornie film king William Osco turned legit to produce this schlocker, which under the direction of wife Jackie Kong (she penned the script), is boring cliches. Osco co-stars as Rexx Coltrane, portraying a gallant hero who rescues Marianne Gordon from ludicrous cliffhangers. Martin Landau, Dorothy Malone, Ruth Buzzi and Jose Ferrer are townspeople who become fodder for the beast. Also known as EASTER SUNDAY. (HBO)

BELA LUGOSI MEETS A BROOKLYN GORILLA (1952). So awful it's enjoyable watching Bela Lugosi portray a mad doctor with a serum that turns men into gorillas. Tim Ryan's script focuses on stranded USO entertainers Duke Mitchell and Sammy Petrillo, Dean Martin-Jerry Lewis imitators who parody their counterparts well. Muriel Landers is a native girl pursuing Duke, while Sammy is chased by an overweight gal through jungle sets. Directed by William Beaudine, a specialist at schlock. Associate producer was Herman Cohen. (Sinister/C; S/Weird; Filmfax; Admit One)

BELIEVERS, THE (1987). Gripping tale of black magic and voodoo set in Manhattan, where police psychiatrist Martin Sheen is recovering from his wife's death while investigating gruesome cult murders, the victims children. Sheen is caught up in a conspiracy that also involves hard-boiled cop Robert Loggia. Director John Schlesinger maintains an intense sense of foreboding. A subtexture deals with our powers of belief in the supernormal, so this is a thinking man's horror film with ample gore and violence. Helen Shaver, Lee Richardson, Elizabeth Wilson. (Video/Laser: HBO)

BELL, BOOK AND CANDLE (1959). Witch Kim Novak casts a spell on Jimmy Stewart so he'll give up Janice Rule. The funny moments are too few in this version of John Van Druten's play, adapted by Daniel Taradash and directed by Richard Quine. The cauldron just doesn't bubble enough to make a substantial witch's brew. Oh, hex! Jack Lemmon, Ernie Kovacs, Hermione Gingold, Elsa Lanchester. (Video/Laser: RCA/Columbia)

BELL FROM HELL, A (1973). Spanish-French horror film depicting a dementee who plays jokes on his aunt and sexy cousins. Surreal visuals include a bee attack and a man walled up alive in an old bell tower. Directed by Claudio Guerin Hill, who died the last day of shooting when he fell from the film's church tower. Viveca Lindfors, Renaud Verley. (Unicorn/Viva)

BELLS. TV title for **MURDER BY PHONE.**

BEN (1972). Sequel to WILLARD is cheapjack exploitation, poorly scripted by Gilbert Ralston and routinely directed by Phil Karlsen. Demented Lee Harcourt Montgomery finds the survivors of the first movie (a pack of well-trained rats) and hides them in the city's sewers. Joseph Campanella is in charge of stopping the rats. Arthur O'Connell, Rosemary Murphy, Meredith Baxter, Kenneth Tobey. (Prism) (Laser: Image)

BEN AND ME (1953). Walt Disney animated short subject in which a mouse comes to the aid of Benjamin Franklin. Quaint historic comedy, enhanced by the voice of Sterling Holloway. (Disney)

BENEATH THE PLANET OF THE APES (1970). First sequel to PLANET OF THE APES, less than its predecessor but still an exciting actioner. Astronaut James Franciscus, in search of the first lost expedition, is swept up in a time warp and lands on Earth to find it devastated by atomic war. In an underground city (remnants of New York), he stumbles across humans with ESP powers. On the surface, meanwhile, apes, gorillas and orangutans form an attack party. The direction by Ted Post is taut, the screenplay by Paul Dehn is lean and literate, and John Chambers' make-up is in the tradition of the origin film. Beneath the masks: Kim Hunter, Maurice Evans, Jeff Corey, Thomas Gomez and James Gregory. Among the humans: Linda Harrison (as Nova, speechless native girl), Victor Buono, Tod Andrews, Paul Richards and Charlton Heston, returning as the lost-in-time astronaut Taylor. (Video/Laser: CBS/Fox)

BERKELEY SQUARE (1933). Time-traveling Leslie Howard finds himself half-a-century in the past, socializing with the elite, in this stylish melodrama based on a famous play. Outstanding performances by Howard,

Heather Angel, Beryl Mercer, Samuel S. Hinds, Alan Mowbray and Irene Browne. Credit the direction of Frank Lloyd. Remade in 1951 with Tyrone Power as I'LL NEVER FORGET YOU.

BERMUDA DEPTHS, THE (1978). Above-average TV-movie with a small touch of JAWS and a big touch of MOBY DICK in depicting an expedition searching for a giant sea turtle. Burl Ives is the Ahab obsessed with the capture of the turtle and Connie Sellecca portrays Jennie Haniver, a mysterious brunette believed to be the spirit of a woman who once made a pact with the turtle and is still aqua-maiding 300 years later. Effects are surprisingly good. Written by William Overgard, directed by Tom Kotani. Leigh McCloskey, Carl Weathers.

BERMUDA TRIANGLE, THE (1978). Nonsense based on Charles Berlitz's two books explaining disappearances in the Atlantic Ocean, with a rambling script by Stephen Lord and unfocused direction by Richard Friedenberg. Strictly for squares. (VidAmerica)

BERMUDA TRIANGLE, THE (1978). Italian-Mexican programmer cashing in on sensational material about strange disappearances taking place off the Florida coast. Written-directed by Rene Cardona Jr. John Huston, Claudine Auger, Marina Vlady.

BERNARD AND THE GENIE (1991). This BBC-TV fantasy, written by Richard Curtis and directed by Paul Weiland, is a whimsical entertainment made fun by Lenny Henry's performance as a lively, hip genie who's been corked away for 2,000 years when nerdish art dealer Alan Cummings uncorks him. With each of his wishes granted, Bernard Bottle (Cummings) wreaks revenge on the boss who just fired him and his cheating girlfriend. Light, frothy and frivolous, it's Henry's film all the way as he plays "Joe Sephis." (CBS/Fox)

BERSERK (1968). Joan Crawford is the dearest owner of a big top plagued by mysterious deaths: one performer is impaled on bayonets, another has a spike driven into his head, yet another is sawed in half. Despite its Grand Guignol trappings, it's a glorified whodunit, ably directed by Jim O'Connolly from a script by producer Herman Cohen and Aben Kandel. Ty Hardin, Diana Dors, Michael Gough, Judy Geeson. (RCA/Columbia)

BERSERKER (1987). Students tramping through the woods hear about an old legend in which "berserkers," Viking warriors, were once cursed by the Nordic gods. Who should turn up but one of those resurrected warriors, who tears apart flesh with his bare hands. Written-directed by Jef Richard. Joseph Alan Johnson, Valerie Sheldon, Gregg Dawson. (Starmaker; Prism)

BEST OF RAY BRADBURY THEATER. Three-disc laser set highlighting half-hour episodes from the cable series. Vol. I: "Gotcha," "Skeleton," "The Emissary," "The Fruit at the Bottom of the Bowl." Vol. II: "Punishment Without Crime," "On the Orient, North," "The Coffin" and "The Small Assassin." Vol. III: "And So Died Riabouchinska," "The Man Upstairs," "There Was an Old Woman" and "Tyrannosaurus Rex." (Image)

BEST OF SEX AND VIOLENCE, THE (1981). Horror-fantasy producer Charles Band collected previews from 40 movies released during the 1970s. John Carradine hosts. These include TERMINAL ISLAND, TOURIST TRAP, ZOMBIE, etc. (Wizard)

BETRAYED. See **WHEN STRANGERS MEET.**

BETWEEN TWO WORLDS (1944). Sutton Vane's classic play, about a handful of souls sailing on a phantom ship to destiny, is a fascinating premise in this Mark Hellinger version directed by Edward A. Blatt. It's updated to World War II, which adds to the images and symbols of death important to the theme. John Garfield, Edmund Gwenn, Eleanor Parker, Syndey Greenstreet, Faye Emerson. Music by Erich Wolfgang Korngold.

BEVERLY HILLS BODYSNATCHERS (1989). Unpleasant mortuary humor—embalming jokes and the lot—is the main motivation behind this comedy that is an undertaker's equivalent to the Bill & Ted misadventures. Two nerds (Rodney Eastman and Warren Selko) are forced by their underworld "Uncle Vito" (Art Metrano) to take jobs as mortician's assistants. They end up stealing bodies for boss Vic Tayback and mad doctor Frank Gorshwin, who does an imitation of Boris Karloff as he invents a formula that brings life to the dead. Gorshin is the only funny actor in this misfire of a black comedy. Director Jon Mostow knows nothing about comedy or the timing it requires, and the jokes fall flat when Gorshin is offscreen. Seth Jaffee, Brooke Bundy, Keone Young. (Shapiro Glickenhaus; South Gate) (Laser: Image)

BEVERLY HILLS VAMP (1989). Another effort from prolific genre film maker Fred Olen Ray. This one mixes Hollywood satire (Britt Ekland is a vampire running a brothel in the hills of Beverly) and bloodsucking thrills as Eddie Deezen becomes an enthusiastic vampire hunter with a cross fashioned on his shorts and the words: "Eat crucifix bitch!" Tim Conway Jr., Jay Richardson, Michelle Bauer, Debra Lamb, Robert Quarry. (Vidmark)

BEWARE! THE BLOB (1971). This sequel to THE BLOB, produced by Jack H. Harris and directed by actor Larry Hagman, is a poor horror film tries to be satirical without much success. Robert Walker Jr., Richard Webb, Godfrey Cambridge, Carol Lynley, Shelley Berman and Burgess Meredith appear in cameos, becoming Blob food. Without redeeming social values, and with mediocre effects, beware! THE BLOB is a slob. (From Video Gems as **SON OF BLOB**)

BEWARE THE BRETHREN (1972). Taut British thriller in which beautiful women are murdered by a Londoner practicing soul possession. Produced-directed by Robert Hartford-Davis. Patrick Magee, Ann Todd, Suzanna Leigh. (From Monterey as **FIEND, THE**)

BEWITCHED (1945). Writer-director Arch Oboler borrowed his radio play, "Alter Ego," from LIGHTS OUT and expanded it into a feature that is an intriguing idea routinely executed. Phyllis Thaxter, looking very angelic or very evil, portrays a dual personality who murders her fiance and is sentenced to die. Psychiatrist Edmund Gwenn conducts an experiment in which he separates the personalities and exorcises the bad half. Studio bound and talkative, the film benefits from a good cast: Henry Daniels Jr., Addison Richards, Will Wright.

BEWITCHED (1985). British TV-movie in which a dead woman plagues an aging couple. Directed by Edmund Oboler. Eileen Atkins, Alfred Lynch. (Prism)

BEYOND, THE (1981). See **SEVEN DOORS OF DEATH.**

BEYOND AND BACK (1978). Pseudodocumentary about people who claimed they died but returned from the grave. These "survivors" recount supernormal experiences, describing sensations and the sights one beholds when stepping across the threshold. (VCI)

BEYOND ATLANTIS (1975). Good fantasy-adventure with excellent underwater photography. Add to that shapely Leigh Christian and this comes up a winner. Adventurers John Ashley and Patrick Wayne track Atlantean pearls to a native-inhabited island. Eddie Romero's direction is okay and Charles Johnson's script features a neat twist of fate. George Nader looks a bit silly as a native chief, but what counts is the two-fisted action. Eddie Garcia, Vic Diaz. (United)

BEYOND BELIEF (1976). Trudging pseudodocumentary gives a "glimpse" at faith healers, ESP and reincarnation, with Uri Geller bending spoons. BEYOND BELIEF is beyond relief. (United)

BEYOND DREAM'S DOOR (1988). Effective low-budgeter, made at Ohio State, tells the surrealistic tale of Nick Baldasare, whose nightmares unleash a monster. Clever editing keeps the inferior effects to a minimum and powerful camera angles suggest more than is there. Above-average for a video production. Written-directed by Jay Woelfel (who also wrote the score). Rick Kesler, Susan Pinsky, Norm Singer, Daniel White. (VidAmerica)

BEYOND EVIL (1980). When Lynda Day George takes possession of a house on a Pacific island, she's possessed by the spirit of the previous owner, who needs her for sacrificial ceremonies to the Devil. Director Herb Freed co-wrote with Paul Ross, John Saxon, Michael Dante, David Opatoshu. (Media)

BEYOND TERROR (1980). Spanish horror entry, written-directed by Tomas Aznar, in which spirits rise from their resting places in a monastery and put the whammy on hoodlums who commit crimes against the innocent. Francisco Sanchez, Grajera Raquel Ramirez.

BEYOND THE BERMUDA TRIANGLE (1976). TV-movie exploits the hysteria surrounding the Devil's Triangle theory in a low-key, subtle fashion with a tasteful telescript by Charles McDaniel and the sensitive direction of William A. Graham. Fred MacMurray, after losing his fiancee off the coast of Florida, begins an obsessive search in strange waters. There's a melancholy gentleness about his remorse that MacMurray pulls off without sentimentality. Sam Groom, Donna Mills, Suzanne Reed, Dana Plato. (Magnum)

BEYOND THE BRIDGE. See **TASTE OF SIN, A.**

BEYOND THE CURTAIN OF SPACE (1953). The debutting TV adventures of Rocky Jones and the Space Rangers starring Richard Crane and Sally Mansfield. (Sinister/C; S/Weird; Filmfax)

BEYOND THE DARKNESS (1974). German exploitationer combines ROSEMARY'S BABY with THE EXORCIST to come up with a weak tale about a busty fraulein who has sex with a demon. Strictly for dummkopfs. Directed by Michael Walter (aka Aristide Massaccesi aka Joe d'Amato). AKA BLUE HOLOCAUST.

BEYOND THE DOOR (1975). Italian imitation of THE EXORCIST, set in San Francisco, in which Juliet Mills has a baby in her tummy tum-tum capable of opening/closing doors, knocking crockery off shelves and turning mama into a bitch witch who spits up greenish vomit. How this bratty beastie got into her womb only the Devil would know, if you get our drift. Nice photography of Sausalito and the Golden Gate Bridge, but also long, dull stretches of Richard Johnson walking around (he's supposed to be a go-between for the Devil) and the cliche playroom scenes where the toys come to life. Writer-director Oliver Hellman (aka Sonia Ovidio Assonitis) fails to breathe life into this ripoff. (Media; RCA/Columbia)

BEYOND THE DOOR II (1977). Sequel to BEYOND THE DOOR with Daria Nicolodi in the Juliet Mills role—a mother still suffering the terrors of a son possessed by the spirit of her deceased husband, a son who plays terror games and uses wicked psychokinetic powers. The kid even tries to get sexual. Mom gets hysterical, boy goes bonkers, audience dozes off. Director Mario Bava allows the door to close on his own screenplay without much of a slam. David Colin Jr. is the mean little kid, Ivan Rassimov the dense new husband. Lamberto Bava contributed to the script. Aka SHOCK (TRANSFER SUSPENSE HYPNOS). (Media)

BEYOND THE DOOR III (1991). This has nothing to do with BEYOND THE DOOR—better it should be called RUNAWAY TRAIN OF HORROR. L.A. students ("junior ambassadors") are sent to Belgrade, Serbia, only to fall prey to a Balkan devil cult that wants a virgin (Mary Kohnert) to mate with Lucifer. The group is trapped on a train out of control and the students die horrible deaths one by one. The best parts of Ovidio G. Assonitis' production are the sequences dealing with attempts to stop the train, and not the blood-and-gore scenes. Bo Svenson is wasted in the role of a Yugoslav professor. William Geiger, Renee Rancourt, Jeremy Sanchez, Alex Vitale. Directed by Jeff Kwitny. (Video/Laser: Columbia TriStar)

BEYOND THE FOG. Retitling of **HORROR ON SNAPE ISLAND.** See **TOWER OF EVIL.**

BEYOND THE GATE. See **HUMAN EXPERIMENTS.**

BEYOND THE GRAVE (1973). Spanish thriller from by Jesus Franco about a woman (Emma Cohen) descending into madness by the spirit of her dead dad. Robert Woods, Phillipe Lemaire, Howard Vernon.

BEYOND THE LIVING (1977). Muddled supernatural thriller in which a cult leader dies in a hospital just as his spirit possesses the curvy body of a nurse. She knocks off the characters with cleavers, knives and other sharp/blunt instruments. Meanwhile, there's an absurd subplot in which a black football star-patient turns up with a voodoo amulet to ward off evil. Poorly directed by Al Adamson. Released as NURSE SHERRI. Jill Jacobson, Marilyn Joi, Mary Kay Pass, Geoffrey Land. (From World's Worst Videos as **HOSPITAL OF TERROR**, from Marathon as **TERROR HOSPITAL**, from Lettuce Entertain You as **HANDS OF DEATH** and from Iver as **KILLER'S CURSE**)

BEYOND THE LIVING DEAD (1974). Spanish fright flick stars Paul Naschy as a nasty nut resurrecting corpses and programming them to knock off folks standing in the way of scientific progress. Beyond the comprehension of most living viewers. Directed by John Davidson. (Unicorn; from Western World as **THE HANGING WOMAN** and from Wizard as **RETURN OF THE ZOMBIES**)

BEYOND THE MOON (1954). Spliced together episodes of **ROCKY JONES, SPACE RANGER.**

BEYOND THE RISING MOON (1988). Effects-laden sci-fi adventure set in the next century when an alien spaceship is sought by vying factions on Earth. Among those investigating is bionic woman Tracy Davis who teams with space trader Hans Bachmann to fight the bad guys. Written-produced-edited by Philip Cook.

BEYOND THE STARS (1989). Heartfelt, moving story of an Apollo astronaut (Martin Sheen) who discovers a secret on the moon and is exposed to radiation, and the effect these have upon him when he becomes a recluse in Cedar Bay, Oregon. It's told from the viewpoint of a teenager (Christian Slater) undergoing problems with his divorced parents, who builds a friendship with Sheen and a love affair with Olivia D'Abo. Writer-director David Saperstein sometimes gets too preachy (especially with F. Murray Abraham as a man who studies whale communications) but he spins a compassionate story. Sheen, Slater and Robert Foxworth (as the boy's estranged father) are wonderful, as is Sharon Stone as Foxworth's girlfriend. (Video/Laser: IVE)

BEYOND THE TIME BARRIER (1960). Robert Clarke takes off in an experimental supersonic rocket and, after passing into a time warp, lands in 2024 to find a subterranean world that has survived a cosmic nuclear plague. It's a dreary civilization, making our present-day world, even with its faults, seem Utopian in comparison. Although directed by cult favorite Edgar G. Ulmer, it is marred by terribly amateurish acting, chintzy production values, and an awful script by Arthur G. Pierce. Darlene Tompkins, John van Dreelen, Arianne Arden, Vladimir Sokoloff. (Sinister/C; S/Weird; Nostalgia)

BEYOND THE UNIVERSE (1981). Well-intended, serious-minded science fiction set in the 21st Century after a nuclear war when mankind is undergoing a shortage of oxygen. A dedicated scientist and his loyal band, believing Earth to be in need of healing, try to contact an all-powerful intelligence in space, while dictatorial forces on Earth plan the genocide of old people to preserve precious air. The ambitious script by producer Allan Sandler, director Robert Emenegger, Steven Posner and Seth Marshall III is marred by poor effects and limited sets; but it's the thought that counts. David Ladd, Jacqueline Ray, Henry Darrow.

BEYOND TOMORROW (1940). Sentimental fantasy-comedy focusing on three old men who return from the grave to share Christmas "spirit" with lovers Richard Carlson and Jean Parker. The old fogies are Harry Carey, C. Aubrey Smith and Charles Winninger, with Maria Ouspenskaya and Helen Vinson in supporting roles. Directed by A. Edward Sutherland. (Sinister/C; Hollywood Home Theater; Discount)

BIG (1988). Warm fantasy-comedy in which a 13-year-old is given the body of an adult by a fortune-teller machine at an amusement park. Before you can say G.I. Joe, the boy turns into Tom Hanks and is made vice-president of a toy company under boss Robert Loggia—for who understands toys better than a kid. When Elizabeth Perkins falls in love with him, and Hanks responds as a youth, this becomes a delightful comedy under Penny Marshall's poignant direction. Charm and good humor grace the Gary Ross-Anne Spielberg script. John Heard, Jared Rushton. (Video/Laser: CBS/Fox)

BIG BANG, THE (1987). Sex and sci-fi are satirized by writer-director Jean-Marc Picha (SHAME OF THE JUNGLE) in this French animated feature. Earth is menaced by a new war (hence, the title) so a superhero is dispatched to avert the disaster.

BIG BUS, THE (1976). What is 106 feet long, weighs 75 tons, is bigger than 80 Volkswagens and has a swimming pool? Shucks, it's the world's first nuclear-powered bus, Cyclops, on its maiden voyage from New York to Denver. The gears of this "Grand Hotel" on wheels don't always mesh, but the vehicle still sputters its share of guffaws with James Frawley at the director's wheel. Stockard Channing, Rene Auberjonois, Jose Ferrer, Ruth Gordon, Lynn Redgrave, Larry Hagman. (Paramount)

BIG FOOT (1969). How serious is this movie? When aviatrix Joey Lansing unzips her flying suit, she's wearing a Baby Doll nightie—that's how serious. An exploitation cheapie in which two conmen (John Carradine, John Mitchum) and wimpy roughnecks on Yahamas pursue a tall, disfigured man with oversized feet wearing a mangy ape suit. Tacky, tacky. Big Foot, legendary manthing, is Small Stuff as he carries away Lansing and other women in bikinis for breeding. What this breeds most is contempt. The odd cast includes Chris and Lindsay Crosby, Ken Maynard (an old cowboy star as a general store owner) and Doodles Weaver as a forest ranger. Scenes of sexy Joey being terrorized by the monster are hilarious. Directed by Robert F. Slatzer. (Western World)

BIG FOOT—MAN OR BEAST? (1975). Heavy-footed pseudodocumentary with footage of forests and rugged wilderness and a few so-called authentic scenes of Sasquatch. But it would never hold up in court. Written-directed by Lawrence Crowley. (VCI)

BIGFOOT—THE MYSTERIOUS MONSTER. See **MYSTERIOUS MONSTERS, THE.**

BIG GAME, THE (1972). Radar device, capable of controlling armies of men, is fought over in this spy thriller, which emphasizes action, double-crosses and commando raids more than sci-fi. France Nuyen uses her beauty to win the affections of the son of the weapon's inventor. Most of the action is aboard a freighter as Stephen Boyd and Cameron Mitchell fight to protect Ray Milland and his invention.

BIGGEST BATTLE ON EARTH. See **GHIDRA, THE THREE HEADED MONSTER.**

BIGGLES: ADVENTURES IN TIME (1986). Offbeat time-travel adventure depicting how frozen-food executive Alex Hyde-White travels through time and space whenever his life is in jeopardy to World War I, where he meets Sopwith Camel ace Neil Dickson who is trying to destroy a supersonic device the Germans use to knock down Allied airships. Hyde-White pops in and out of the time-stream at the oddest moments. It's rousing good fun enhanced by Peter Cushing as an officer giving exposition. Directed by John Hough. (New World/Starmaker)

BIG MAN ON CAMPUS (1989). A gallant attempt to satirize THE HUNCHBACK OF NOTRE DAME in modern guise (made as THE HUNCHBACK OF UCLA) but a failure for not coming to terms with the sociological satire inherent in screenwriter Allan Katz's premise—that a "wild man" can be educated and brought into the folds of society despite man's fear to the contrary. Katz also portrays the primitive dude living in the campus belltower who becomes the student body's strangest body when he's assimilated into the educational system by professor Tom Skerritt and tutor Gerrit Graham. Only during the second half does this misguided project seem to move toward its truth, but not even prestigious director Jeremy Paul Kagan can overcome deficiencies of narrative. Melora Hardin, Corey Parker, Cindy Williams, Jessica Harper. (Vestron) (Laser: Image)

BIG MEAT EATER (1982). This comedy-parody of movie genres (directed by Chris Windsor) blends so many together into a "kitchen sink" approach that the drain gets clogged. It's a musical with lampoonish production numbers, it's an alien-invader story with toy robots inside a flying saucer, it's a comedy set in a butchershop where a crazed black named Abdullah destroys meat with his cleaver and cuts up the town Dalmatian into delicacies. There's also a Russian family involved and a mayor who is killed and restored to life by aliens. If any of it makes any sense, write us an explanation. George Dawson, Big Miller, Andrew Gillies. (Media)

BIG NOISE, THE (1944). See editions 1-3.

BIG TROUBLE IN LITTLE CHINA (1986). Ghosts, kung fu, a monster, a subterranean Chinese city and a touch of mysticism . . . ingredients for a lively fantasy-adventure, but director John Carpenter is only partially successful. The main problem is, nothing about this martial arts-ghost story ever ignites the viewer. The best thing is Kurt Russell as a wise-cracking truckdriver who thinks he's John Wayne; he's swept into a mystery in which a 2000-year-old demon must marry the heroine in order to turn back into a man. Action, comedy and light-show effects are part of the brew, but it still emerges lightweight. Dennis Dun, Kim Cattrall. (Video/Laser: CBS/Fox)

BIKINI ISLAND (1991). Girls in skimpy bathing suits are the main reasons to watch this ogler's fantasy in which the chicks turn up on an island for a photo spread, and then are killed one by one. Produced-directed by Anthony (INVISIBLE MANIAC) Markes. Holly Floria, Alicia Anne, Jackson Robinson, Shannon Stiles, Sherry Jackson. (Video/Laser: Prism)

BILL AND TED'S BOGUS JOURNEY (1991). Sequel to BILL AND TED'S EXCELLENT ADVENTURE is inferior horseplay; the material is no longer fresh but retread stuff, stupidly plotted. Writers Chris Matheson and Ed Solomon are back with cyborg versions of Bill and Ted that time-travel from the future to kill our heroes. They do, and the dudes (Keanu Reeves and Alex Winter) go to Hell, where they play Battleship and Clue with the Grim Reaper (William Sadler) in order to return to Earth alive to stop a plot engineered by futuristic dictator De Nomolos (Joss Ackland). This means we also get to visit a bleached-white Heaven and its Pearly Gates. The bodacious vocabulary of the lovable if dumb guys from San Dimas, Ca., is still in evidence, and George Carlin appears briefly as Rufus with his time-traveling phone booth. The best part is the closing titles, in which Bill and Ted appear on magazine covers. Now that's "Excellent." Directed by Peter Hewitt. (Orion) (Laser: Image)

BILL AND TED'S EXCELLENT ADVENTURE (1989). A box office success among teens because of the appeal of Keanu Reeves and Alex Winter as Ted Logan and Bill S. Preston—two "cool dudes" who hope to launch a rock band, the Wyld Stallyns, but first they must pass their history course. To accomplish this, they travel through time with Rufus (George Carlin) in a telephone booth, picking up Napoleon, Billy the Kid, Socrates, Genghis Khan, Abraham Lincoln, Mozart and Sigmund Freud and bringing them to the present for a high school show. The Chris Matheson-Ed Solomon screenplay is very clever or totally dumb, or perhaps both. In spite of its imbecilities, it does have a way of grabbing you. The crazy vocabulary of the boys, and their reactions to the people and customs of assorted time zones, contribute to the appeal, if not the intellectualism. Director Stephen Herek keeps this thing moving, ignoring the huge holes in logic. Terry Camilleri, Dan Shor, Tony Steedman, Rod Loomis. (Video/Laser: Nelson/Orion)

BILLION DOLLAR BRAIN, THE (1967). Imaginative spy thriller based on a Len Deighton novel in the Harry Palmer series, with dazzling gadgetry, colorful European locations and manipulative direction by Ken Russell. Ed Begley is outstanding as a radical Texas multimillionaire with a plan to invade Russia with his own army to defend democracy. Script by John McGrath. Michael Caine (as Palmer), Karl Malden, Francoise Dorleac, Oscar Homolka, Guy Doleman. (Imperial)

BILLION DOLLAR THREAT, THE (1979). Dale Robinette is a superspy 007-style pursuing a typical madman who plans to fiddle with the Earth's ozone layer while mankind burns. A five-and-dime threat at best and a substandard TV-movie that sacrifices everything for action. Directed by Barry Shear, scripted by Jimmy Sangster. Ralph Bellamy, Keenan Wynn, Patrick MacNee.

BILLION FOR BORIS, A (1984). G-rated children's movie, based on a book by Mary Rodgers, in which an incorrigible lad picks up TV transmissions 24 hours in advance and is wise to winning horses and lottery numbers. This Ned Kandel production never ignites and the characters are bland at best. Lee Grant is the only interesting adult, a writer named Sascha, but even the tedium overtakes her too. Kiddie stuff directed by Alex Grasshof. Scott Tiler, Mary Tanner, Seth Green. (Imperial)

BILLY THE KID VS. DRACULA (1965). When he was alive, John Carradine considered this his worst film. Watch and find out why. Directed by William "Crankem-Out-Fast" Beaudine, who abounds in absurdities and vampire lore miscalculations, such as having Carradine/Dracula creeping around in daylight. By all means, don't see it if you can't miss it. Bing Russell, Roy Barcroft, Harry Carey Jr., Olive Carey, Roy Barcroft. (Embassy; S/Weird; Nostalgia; Video Yesteryear)

BIOHAZARD (1984). Awful monster movie, poorly executed by writer-producer-director Fred Olen Ray, who during the closing credits resorts to amusing outtakes, writing off the picture as a joke. An ALIEN ripoff with psychic Angelique Pettyjohn not only making contact with an alien ship and teleporting it to Earth but showing off her enormous breasts. When the alien escapes its container, it's on a rampage of gory death. Christopher Ray plays the cheesy monster. Aldo Ray, William Fair, Frank McDonald. (Cinema Group; Continental)

BIONIC SHOWDOWN (1989). TV-movie based on TV's THE SIX MILLION DOLLAR MAN and THE BIONIC WOMAN, with Lee Majors and Lindsay Wagner re-creating their roles. An enemy bionic man has infiltrated OSI and a new bionic woman helps Steve, Jamie and Oscar fight the enemy at the World Unity Games. Typical TV action stuff moves under director Alan J. Levi. Majors and Richard Anderson served as co-producers. Bill Conti wrote the music. Sandra Bullock, Jeff Yagher, Martin E. Brooks, Lee Majors II, Robert Lansing.

BIONIC WOMAN, THE (1976). TV pilot for the spinoff from THE SIX MILLION DOLLAR MAN, with Lindsay Wagner as Jaime Sommers, a female counterpart to Lee Majors' Steve Austin. When Jaime is almost killed skiing, the science teams puts her back together and she becomes an operative for the Office of Scientific Information. Routine action stuff, a lot of it in slow motion. Directed by Henry Mankiewicz. Monica Randall. (MCA)

BIRD OF PARADISE (1950). See editions 1-3.

BIRDS, THE (1963). Alfred Hitchcock's masterpiece of suspense, scripted by Evan Hunter from the Daphne du Maurier story. For reasons never explained, only pontificated on, winged creatures turn against mankind and attack without warning. Rod Taylor and Tippi Hedren are trapped in a farmhouse and the attacks are spinetingling. (Hedren claims Hitch set hungry birds against her to capture ultimate realism.) The ending is ambiguous, as was the short story, but Hitchcock's masterful direction makes it work. Bernard Herrmann provided the eerie bird "sounds" and Lawrence A. Hampton pulled off the complicated effects, combining real and fake birds in stunning fashion. An all-time favorite worth reseeing. Jessica Tandy, Suzanne Pleshette, Veronica Cartwright, Charles McGraw, Doodles Weaver. (Video/Laser: MCA)

BIRDS II: LAND'S END, THE (1994). Colorless sequel to Hitchcock's '63 classic set on an island off the coast of Florida, where unhappily married Brad Johnson and Chelsea Field bring their two kids and lovable dog for a holiday, only to become pecking targets for seagulls and crows as the winged creatures lead a new revolt against mankind, presumably because of polluted ocean waters. The problems of the couple, which consume most of the film's 90 minutes, seem at odds with the horrific elements, as if writers Ken and Jim Wheat and Robert Eisele needed padding. Padding for a sequel to Hitchcock's great '63 special-effects extravaganza? Daphne Du Maurier's short story was ill-served with this TV-movie that recycles Tippi Hedren from the original—but even she is wasted in a nothing role. BIRDS II just never flies. James Naughton, Jan Rubes.

BIRDS DO IT (1966). See editions 1-3.

BIRDS OF PREY. See **BEAKS THE MOVIE.**

BIRD WITH THE CRYSTAL PLUMAGE, THE (1971). Intense psychological crime-horror thriller (a trend-setter in its day) written-directed by Italy's Dario Argento, in which Tony Musante portrays a writer who tracks down a killer of women. Of seminal importance to the Argento canon, and a must-see for his fans. Eva Renzl, Suzy Kendall. (United) (Laser: Image)

BIRTH OF FRANKENSTEIN. See **CURSE OF FRANKENSTEIN, THE.**

BISHOP'S WIFE, THE (1947). Samuel Goldwyn film revived seasonally for its heart-tugging warmth and sentimentality. Cary Grant is the spirit Dudley, sent to Earth to help a bishop (David Niven) and his wife (Loretta Young) build a new cathedral, and to help the bishop re-establish contact with his "flock." A memorable element is the wine bottle that never empties. Directed by Henry Koster. Monty Woolley, James Gleason, Gladys Cooper, Elsa Lanchester, Regis Toomey. (Embassy; HBO)

B. J. LANG PRESENTS. See **MANIPULATOR.**

BLACK ABBOT, THE (1961). West German adaptation of a 1927 Edgar Wallace mystery featuring a hooded figure terrorizing folks at Lord Chelford's abbey. Directed by Franz Josef Gottlieb. Joachim Fuchsberger, Klaus Kinski, Werner Peters. (Sinister/C)

BLACKBEARD'S GHOST (1968). Peter Ustinov stars in this "cutesy" Disney film as an 18th Century swashbuckler forced to wander in a spiritual limbo until he performs a good deed, in this case helping the track coach of a contemporary college. Directed by Robert Stevenson. Dean Jones, Suzanne Pleshette, Elsa Lanchester. (Video/Laser: Disney)

BLACKBOARD MASSACRE. See **MASSACRE AT CENTRAL HIGH.**

BLACK CASTLE, THE (1952). Call this an "old dark castle" thriller. Swashbuckler Richard Greene visits baron Stephen McNally in his medieval digs to seek a missing friend. Lurking at the arras as castle retainers, and giving this a touch of the sinister, are Boris Karloff and Lon Chaney Jr. Now-classic Gothic suspense programmer with additional villainy from Michael Pate and John Hoyt. Directed by Nathan Juran. (MCA)

BLACK CAT, THE (1934). One of the strangest of Universal's horror films thanks to surreal direction by Edgar G. Ulmer and the abstract script by Peter Ruric, who threw away Poe's tale for more bizarre proceedings. Boris Karloff, leader of a cult of devil worshippers, lives in a strange house constructed over a fort, where he is keeping the corpse of Bela Lugosi's wife. Karloff and Lugosi are antagonists to the death, symbolized by a game of chess. Eerie images (credit photographer John

Mescall), sado-masochism and torture, bizarre gimmicks, unexplained characters. It's enigmatic, but chillingly so. (Media; on MCA cassette and laser with **THE RAVEN**)

BLACK CAT, THE (1941). Nothing to do with Poe; it's about a gathering of heirs in a castle to read the will. What makes it palatable are its cast (Basil Rathbone, Broderick Crawford, Bela Lugosi, Anne Gwynne, Gale Sondergaard, Gladys Cooper, Alan Ladd) and Stanley Cortez's photography. Directed by Albert S. Rogell.

BLACK CAT, THE (1968). See editions 1-3.

BLACK CAT, THE (1980). Just how scary is a black pussy? This Italian supernatural thriller directed by Lucio Fulci answers that question. Not a helluva lot. And how scary are close ups of Patrick Magee's eyeballs? Not a helluva lot. Magee is a village nut recording tapes with voices from the dead whose evil is transported into a black cat . . . or is the evil of the cat overtaking him? Scotland Yard cop David Warbeck investigates murders linked to Magee and his cat and nosy photographer Mimsy Farmer thinks the pussy is pulling off the homicides. Murders include a body falling on a pitchfork, a woman burned alive, claws across hands and other feline felonies. Please, no catty remarks. (Rhino; Media)

BLACK CAT (1990). Luigi Cozzi wrote-directed this movie about a cast making a horror film in a haunted house. Brett Halsey, Caroline Munro. (Columbia)

BLACK CAULDRON, THE (1985). Long-awaited (five years in the making) and expensive ($25 million) animated feature from Disney, based on Lloyd Alexander's THE CHRONICLES OF PRYDAIN. The evil Horned King seeks The Black Cauldron, that Spectral Stewpot with the power to conquer the world. Standing in his way is Taran, a naive hero who proves his nettle with a magic sword, a beautiful scullery maid, a roving minstrel, a fuzzy cute animal creature that mutters, and an oracle-divining pig. An odd blend of styles (some cartoonish, some grittily realistic) and characters (some old-fashioned Disney, others like extras from CONAN) results in a stunningly visual piece that still seems trivial. Directed by Ted Berman and Richard Rich. John Huston narrates the introduction; voices: John Hurt as the Horned King, Grant Bardsley as Taran and Susan Sheridan as Eilonwy. (Disney)

BLACK CHRISTMAS (1974). This predates the slasher cycle and establishes tone and ambience for which the subgenre was to become known, so producer-director Robert Clark deserves credit for establishing precedent in this Canadian film, also known as STRANGER IN THE HOUSE and SILENT NIGHT, EVIL NIGHT. A fiendish killer remains hidden in the attic of a sorority house while police run weary looking for missing persons who are dead in the garret. The killer's identity is never known (writer Roy Moore sets it up so it doesn't matter) but knowledge of the killer's whereabouts contributes to the tension. Olivia Hussey, Margot Kidder, Keir Dullea, John Saxon, Art Hindle. (Warner Bros.)

BLACK COUNTESS, THE. See **EROTIKILL.**

BLACK DEMONS (1991). Brazilian voodoo terror stalks Keith Van Hoven, Joe Balogh and Sonia Curtis during a Rio vacation in this Italian horror thriller directed by Umberto Lenzi.

BLACK DEVIL DOLL FROM HELL (1985). Vidjunk in which a woman is trounced on by a ventriloquist's dummy, a monster programmed by its creator to murder. Directed by Chester T. Turner. Shirley T. Jones, Rickey Roach. (Hollywood Home Theater)

BLACK DRAGONS (1942). Monogram programmer with Bela Lugosi wasted as a plastic surgeon operating on Japanese spies so they can infiltrate America. It's the "yellow horde" menace, a polemic mangled by writer Harvey Gates and squashed to death by director William Nigh. Has the dubious distinction of Lugosi in two roles. Clayton Moore, Joan Barclay. (Sinister/C; Filmfax; Nostalgia)

BLACK DRAGONS OF MANZANAR (1943). Re-edited TV version of the Republic serial **G-MEN VS. THE BLACK DRAGON.**

BLACK ELIMINATOR. Video version of **DEATH DIMENSION** (Unicorn).

BLACKENSTEIN (1973). Unsavory take-off on BLACULA, in which mad doctor John Hart turns a Vietnam basket case into a monster. BLACKENSTEIN only blackens the names of producer-writer Frank Saletri, director William Levey. Andrea King, Liz Renay. (Media)

BLACK EVIL. Video version of **BLOOD COUPLE** (Lettuce Entertain You).

BLACK FRANKENSTEIN. See **BLACKENSTEIN.**

BLACK FRIDAY (1940). Boris Karloff portrays a sympathetic scientist who transplants the brain of a criminal into an injured colleague, with the patient taking on gangster characteristics. Bela Lugosi appears in a small role as a hoodlum. Curt Siodmak's script bears resemblance to his own DONOVAN'S BRAIN. Not a distinguished Universal horror film of the period, but of interest for its cast. Arthur Lubin directed. Stanley Ridges, Anne Nagel, Anne Gwynne, Paul Fix, James Craig.

BLACK HARVEST OF COUNTESS DRACULA, THE. See **WEREWOLF VS. THE VAMPIRE WOMEN, THE.**

BLACKHAWK (FEARLESS CHAMPION OF JUSTICE) (1952). Kirk (Superman) Alyn portrays the noble leader of an international band of flyers fighting foreign agents led by sultry Carol Forman, who is out to steal an Electronic Combustion Ray. This 15-chapter Sam Katzman serial for Columbia has the flyers driving around in black-painted 1950 Fords most of the time, with only an occasional airplane in sight. The action serial is based on the comic drawn by Reed Crandall.

BLACK HOLE, THE (1979). The Black Hole of Space is an astonomical theory that when a star dies it becomes a compressed mass, where laws of physics cease to exist. This Disney effort, an answer to STAR WARS, is a compressed mess. Many effects artists (including Peter Ellenshaw) were brought in to assist, but the Jeb Rosebrook-Gerry Day screenplay belies their efforts with cardboard characters and feeble premises. A survey ship, dangerously close to a Black Hole, is approached by another ship from which robots (cutesy-pie creatures) zap the expensive sets with their blasters. Even the trip through the Black Hole, intended as an abstraction, is a misfire for director Gary Nelson. Anthony Perkins, Robert Forster, Joseph Bottoms, Yvette Mimieux, Ernest Borgnine, Maximilian Schell. Robot voice by Slim Pickens. (Video/Laser: Disney)

BLACK MAGIC (1949). Atmospheric tale about 18th Century hypnotist Cagliostro, who keeps beautiful Nancy Guild under his spell. Producer-director Gregory Ratoff (better remembered as an actor) gives this a gloominess that is all-permeating. Worth seeing for Orson Welles' spellbinding performance as the mesmerizer. Akim Tamiroff, Raymond Burr, Frank Latimore, Barry Kroeger, Valentina Cortesa. (Nostalgia Merchant; Media)

BLACK MAGIC (1991). There's a Preston Sturges zaniness to this whacky comedy set in Istanbul, S.C., where Judge Reinhold shows up to find out how his brother was killed. Seems his sibling has returned from the dead to torment Reinhold to find his killer. The madcap search leads to a would-be witch (Rachel Ward, in a sensuous, ambiguous role), a town crazy (Brion James) and other oddball characters. A most unusual supernatural comedy, so more power to writer-director Daniel Taplitz. Anthony Lapaglia, Richard Whitting, Wendy Markena. (Video/Laser: MCA)

BLACK MAGIC MANSION. TV title of **CTHULHU MANSION.**

BLACK MAGIC RITES—REINCARNATIONS. See **REINCARNATION OF ISABEL, THE.**

BLACK MAGIC TERROR (1979). Suzanne, Queen of Black Magic, raises hell for those who jilt her in this badly dubbed Japanese flicker featuring such appetizing visuals as food turned into maggots, voodoo rituals, etc. Also called QUEEN OF BLACK MAGIC. J. P. Suzanna, W. D. Mochtar. Directed by L. Sujio. (Twilight)

BLACK MAGIC WOMAN (1990). Exotic and sexy Apollonia Kotero provides an eyeful when she falls for gallery curator Mark Hamill, over objections of girlfriend Amanda Wyss. Black magic rituals (dead rooster hanging above his bed, poisonous snake under his pillow, severed human fingers) soon have Hamill voodooized. When a dead servant winds up as "cold cuts" in a refrigerator, you can figure the hexer means business. The twist ending to Gerry Daly's screenplay is neat if predictable. A smooth whodunit directed by Deryn Warren. Victor Rivers, Larry Hankin. (Vidmark)

BLACK MASSES OF EXORCISM, THE. French-Belgian concoction from director Jesus Franco mixing sex and religious fanaticism into an unholy, unsavory stew that has been edited into many versions, some with hardcore sex. Also known as THE RIPPER OF NOTRE DAME. Nadine Pascal, Rosa Amiral, Lina Romay.

BLACK MOON (1975). See editions 1-3.

BLACK NOON (1971). Supernatural TV-movie, written-produced by Andrew J. Fenady, is set in the American West in the 19th Century. A traveling preacher and wife are victims of a witch cult headed by Ray Milland. Fenady throws in a nice twist ending. Yvette Mimieux is gorgeous in billowing, silky nightgowns as she lures men to their doom. Roy Thinnes, Gloria Grahame, Lyn Loring, Henry Silva. Directed by Bernard Kowalski.

BLACK ORPHEUS (1958). Modernization of the Orpheus legend by director Marcel Camus. Death pursues Eurydice at a carnival in Rio De Janeiro. Brazilian production is a favorite outre film because of atmosphere and lyrical score. Oscar and Cannes winner. Breno Mello, Marpessa Dawn, Lea Garcia. (Connoisseur; CBS/Fox) (Laser: Criterion)

BLACKOUT: THE MOMENT OF TERROR. Video version of **BLOOD COUPLE** (Fantasy).

BLACKOUT (1985). Intriguing psychothriller with Richard Widmark as a policeman obsessed by a quadruple family murder—presumably committed by the missing husband. What gives this a wrenching twist is that Keith Carradine, an accident victim, could be the father suffering from amnesia. Does he now have a split personality, reverting to homicidal tendencies at times? Is he terrorizing his bride Kathleen Quinlan? Or is a former lover plotting to drive her bonkers? Intriguing questions to hold your interest. Michael Beck, Gerald Hiken. Directed by Douglas Hickox. (Fox Hills)

BLACKOUT (1988). Has Gail O'Grady's father come back from the death to haunt her attic? And what are those strange dreams she's having about her childhood? Since the screenwriter is by producer Joseph Stefano, you know you're in PSYCHO territory. Directed by Doug Adams. Carol Lynley, Michael Keys Hall. (Magnum)

BLACK PIT OF DR. M, THE (1959). Prepare for the black pit of despair. This Mexican film, simply put, is simply awful. An insane scientist returns from the grave to invade another body and seek revenge. The party most wronged is you, the viewer. Gaston Santos, Rafael Bertrand. Directed by Ferdinand Mendez. Also known as MYSTERIES FROM BEYOND THE GRAVE.

BLACK RAINBOW (1989). Solid work by writer-director Mike Hodges about an evangelist (Rosanna Arquette) with prescient abilities who inadvertently gets involved in a murder plot to cover up a chemical plant scandal. The real story, though, involves Arquette's relationship with alcoholic father Jason Robards and reporter Tom Hulce. Arquette is an actress of unusual calibre and her fans will be delighted when she goes nude in a sizzly love scene with Hulce. The film's theme is summarized when a traveling preacherman remarks, "We steal when we touch tomorrow. It's God's." Mark Joy, Ron Rosenthal, John Bennes, Linda Pierce. (Media; Fox)

BLACK RAVEN, THE (1943). Minor horror overtones of the "old, dark house" school permeate this ordinary whodunit of the '40s in which horror figure of the period George Zucco, as the owner of the Black Raven Inn, plays host to stranded travelers, who die one by one at the hands of a shadowy, hooded figure. It's woefully written (by Fred Myton) and directed (by Sam Newfield). Glenn Strange, strangely enough, is the comedy relief, and Charles Middleton plays a dumb sheriff to no particular avail. (Sinister/C; Rex Miller)

BLACK ROOM, THE (1935). Identical twins (Boris Karloff & Boris Karloff) are caught up in macabre events that lead to the fulfillment of an ancient curse. Assorted bodies are thrown on spikes or skewered in a torture chamber. Karloff, portraying a sympathetic and a hateful character in the same film, shows his mettle under the direction of Roy William Neill. Thurston Hall, Edward Van Sloan, Katherine DeMille, Marian Marsh. (RCA/Columbia; Goodtimes) (Laser: RCA/Columbia; Image)

BLACK ROOM, THE (1981). Ghoulish brother-and-sister team lures unsuspecting victims into the family mansion, photographs them having sex through two-way mirrors in the titular bedroom, and murders them so the brother can have a transfusion to stave off a blood disease. My, what a fun-loving movie. Directed by Elly Kenner and Norman Thaddeus Vane. Stephen Knight, Cassandra Gaviola, Jim Stathis, Linnea Quigley. (Vestron)

BLACK ROSES (1988). Above average video horror flicker that vacillates between thoughtful, almost literate portions of characterization and dialogue, and the cheap thrills of the slasher genre. The town of Mill Basin is in an uproar over satanic rock 'n roll group Black Roses, led by singer Damian. Bluenose Julie Adams predicts disaster—and her forecast comes true when Damian (a demon in human form) hypnotizes the town's youngsters to commit murders. English professor John Martin tries to stop the terror. Ken Swofford, Sal Viviano, Frank Dietz. Directed by John Fasano. (Imperial)

BLACK SABBATH (1963). One of the best Italian horror pictures directed by Mario Bava, and the film that best reflects his attitude toward psychothrillers. He once said that a man alone in a room, confronting his own fears, intrigued him most, and BLACK SABBATH is three studies in abject fear, each introduced by an amusingly morbid Boris Karloff. In "A Drop of Water," based on a Chekhov story, nurse Jacqueline Soussard removes a ring from a dead body and is stalked by the corpse. This is absolutely chilling, for Bava uses color for psychological effect. "The Telephone" concerns strange calls to a beautiful woman from a man believed to be dead. Although the least effective yarn, it has ironic twists and brilliant use of color. This stars Michele Mercier and Lydia Alfonsi. Tolstoy's "The Wurdalak" stars Karloff as a vampire who can only kill those he loves. This is reeking with the kind of gothic atmosphere that Bava was best at achieving. Mark Damon, Suzy Anderson. The music is by Les Baxter. Also known as THE THREE FACES OF FEAR and THE THREE FACES OF TERROR. (HBO; Sinister/C) (Laser: Image, with **BLACK SUNDAY**)

BLACK SAMURAI (1976). Lowbrow actioner with mild fantasy overtones as D.R.A.G.O.N. agent Jim Kelly seeks high priest Bill Roy and priestess Synne (Marilyn Jo) when they kidnap the daughter of an official, Kelly's girlfriend. One long series of martial arts battles with Janicot the priest throwing victims to his rattlesnakes, holding voodoo rights and siccing his beefcake baddies on Kelly. Al Adamson directed. (Continental)

BLACK SCORPION, THE (1957). Willis O'Brien's effects are the only commendable feature in this multi-legged monsterama in which a Mexican volcano spews up king-size mutant spiders. Richard Denning and Mara Corday race through south-of-the-border locations in search of a way of stopping the attack. Edward Ludwig directed this Warner Bros. flick. Unless you like scuttling bugs, you'd better scuttle elsewhere. (Fright)

BLACK SLEEP, THE (1956). Film lacks acting character but has plenty of character actors: Lon Chaney, John Carradine, Akim Tamiroff, Bela Lugosi, Tor

Johnson—what a menagerie. Mad doctor Basil Rathbone performs perverted surgery to create a "gallery of creeps." Lowbrow script by Reginald Le Borg (who also directed) and John Higgins. Barely watchable despite zoo-like cast. (Channel 13)

BLACK SUNDAY (1960). Milestone Italian film marked cinematographer Mario Bava's directing debut and made a horror star of Barbara Steele. Bava pumps so much Gothic atmosphere into this adaptation of Gogol's THE VIJ that it's a masterpiece continually coming back to haunt the viewer. It opens with a horrific sequence in which a spiked mask is placed over Steele's face (she's a witch being burned at the stake) and a curse is placed on her family. Two centuries later Steele's corpse rises to stalk her modern counterpart (also played by Steele). Helping her bring terror to the family is her evil brother, his face a countenace of twisted hate. Arturo Dominici's performance in this role is remarkable. John Richardson, Ivo Garrani, Andrea Cecchi. Music by Les Baxter. Also known as THE DEMON'S MASK, REVENGE OF THE VAMPIRE and HOUSE OF FRIGHT. (Filmfax; Movies Unlimited; S/Weird; Sinister/C carries a British version; in heavily edited form as **MASK OF SATAN, THE**) (Laser: MCA, with **BLACK SABBATH**)

BLACK TORMENT, THE (1964). British thriller in which a lord remarries and goes home to his Gothic mansion to encounter sorcery and murder. John Turner, Ann Lynn and Heather Sears work to make all this unbelievable stuff believable. Directed by Robert Hartford-Davis. (CIC; from VCL as **ESTATE OF INSANITY**)

BLACK VAMPIRE (1973). Heavily altered video version of **GANJA AND HESS,** which is also in video as **BLOOD COUPLE.** This version is of poor quality, featuring some credits as pseudonyms. The box carries another set of fictional names that don't match the credits at all. Puzzling. (Simitar)

BLACK WIDOW, THE (1947). Republic's 12-chapter serial about Sombra the Spider Woman. What excitement, gang, as this daughter of an asinine Asian (portrayed by that femme fatale of '40s femme fatales, Carol Forman) tries to steal a new atomic rocket engine but is thwarted every four or five minutes by criminologist Steve Colt (Bruce Edwards), this in spite of her curvaceous body. As well as gunsels, Sombra employs matter transmitters and other take-over-the-world gadgetry. The abridged TV version is SOMBRA THE SPIDER WOMAN. Directed by Spencer Bennet and Fred C. Brannon, masters of the hang-by-your-thumbs crowd. (Video/Laser: Republic)

BLACK ZOO, THE (1963). Michael Gough is the insane proprietor of a private zoo, in such rapport with his beastly charges that he metaphysically touches them with his lust for vengeance. The animals disappear into the night to do his killing but then the worm, er, we mean lion, turns. Herman Cohen film directed by Robert Gordon, scripted by Cohen. Rod Lauren, Jerome Cowan, Virginia Grey, Elisha Cook Jr., Marianna Hill.

BLACULA (1972). Racist twist on the old vampire cliche: A black African Prince (William Marshall) is resurrected in Transylvania and shipped to L.A. As if the city isn't cursed enough, Prince Mamuwalde inflicts his own pain via punctures in the neck. Blacula falls for a reincarnated princess and pursues low-life types and cops through ghetto streets. It's such bloody good fun, it's a crying shame when the sun comes up. William Crain directed. Vonetta McGee, Denise Nicholas, Thalmus Rasulala, Elisha Cook Jr., Charles Macauly (as Dracula). Sequel: SCREAM, BLACULA, SCREAM. (HBO)

BLADE IN THE BODY. See **MURDER CLINIC.**

BLADE IN THE DARK, A (1983). Italian psychothriller, directed by Lamberto Bava, in which a movie composer isolates himself in a villa to write a horror score while a killer armed with a razor and/or knife stalks victims. Clues the composer uncovers suggest each woman in the cast is a suspect, but clever viewers (like you) will figure out the killer's identity aided by pseudopsychiatric flashbacks. A fair time-killer, cutting slowly into your credulity veins. Andrea Occhipinti, Anny Papa, Fabiola Toledo. (Lightning; Vestron; Live)

BLADE MASTER, THE. Video version of **ATOR THE BLADE MASTER** (Media).

BLADE OF THE RIPPER (1984). Surprise twists heaped atop each other during the climax of this German chiller make up for mediocre production values and lousy U.S. dubbing/scanning. The "Razor Killer" is slashing the throats of Vienna's rich women. An intended victim is the neglected wife (Edwige Fenech) of the first secretary of the American Embassy. She receives flowers from a former lover, strikes up an affair with mysterious George Hilton and is blackmailed by a stranger. Which one—if any—is the murderer? Nothing is what it seems in this Euro-erotic psychothriller loaded with nudity and bloody slashings. Also called NEXT. (Saturn; the Regal video carries no writing/directing credits)

BLADE RUNNER (1982). A visual stunner, directed by Ridley Scott with the same eye for atmosphere that made ALIEN a hit. Graphic designers have created an L.A. of 1999 brilliant in its acid-rain wretchedness. The Hampton Fancher-David Peoples script, based loosely on Philip K. Dick's DO ANDROIDS DREAM OF ELECTRIC SHEEP?, is such a downer the film operates without a soul. Harrison Ford is washed-out private eye Deckard, assigned to destroy rebellious replicants (humanoid robots). Deckard is world-weary, his voice-over monotonic narration, in the Mike Hammer style, contributing a nihilistic touch. Rutger Hauer is the head replicant, suggesting character complexities with the mere twist of a smile. The final confrontation in the Bradbury Building is an atmospheric, action-packed knockout. All style and no humanity; yet, recommended for compelling visuals and Scott's directorial eye, as well as Douglas Trumbull's effects. (Reissued theatrically in 1991 without the narration and with a different ending, it was described as "the director's original cut." However, this was untrue, according to Scott, who claimed it was a test work print. So in 1992 another version was released as the "director's cut," or what Scott wanted. Got that straight?) Sean Young, Joanna Cassidy, Daryl Hannah, Edward James Olmos, Hy Pyke, Joseph Turkel, Brion James. (Embassy; Nelson; RCA/Columbia) (Laser: Nelson; Criterion; Voyager; Warner Bros.)

BLADES (1988). An absurd premise (lawn mower comes back from the junkpile, unmanned, to get even for being replaced by Japanese equipment) is played straight by screenwriter William R. Pace, who sold his bill of goods to director Thomas R. Rondinella. The mind boggles, watching this traumatic Troma production, how Pace's script exactly follows the events of JAWS, the mulcher replacing the killer shark. An unexciting hero and heroine (Robert North, Victoria Scott) slow the Pace-ing down as they join with greens keeper Jeremy Whelan at the Tall Grass Country Club to track the killer machine. Everyone's behavior is as inexplicable as where the machine gets its gas and oil. (Media) (Laser: Image)

BLAKE OF SCOTLAND YARD (1937). The Scorpion, wearing a claw-like hand, is hired by an unscrupulous munitions figure to steal a Death Ray. Blake sets out to recover the invention, tangling with blackguards. This 15-chapter serial has few dull moments. Robert Hill directed Sam Katzman's production. Ralph Byrd, Joan Barclay, Dickie Jones. (in 15 chapters from Captain Bijou; feature version from Video Yesteryear)

BLANCHEVILLE MONSTER, THE (1962). Out of the eons of the misty past it rose, this towering hulk of monstrous flesh and hideous putrescence, to lay its moldly claws on humans who chance to cross its bloody path. Yep, another movie horror, this one from Spanish-Italian producers, who borrowed ideas from Edgar Allan Poe. Directed by Alberto de Martino. Gerard Tichy, Leo Anchoriz, Joan Hills, Richard Davis, Helga Line.

BLAST OFF (1954). Zap! Clap! Trap! Re-edited episodes of TV's **ROCKY JONES, SPACE RANGER** (Nostalgia; Video Yesteryear).

BLAST OFF (1967). Jules Verne-style adventure/fantasy set in Victorian days with Burl Ives, Troy Donahue, Gert Frobe (remember GOLDFINGER?), Hermione Gingold and Lionel Jeffries. It's a zany plot about sending a ship to Venus. Jolly silly fun. Also called THOSE FANTASTIC FLYING FOOLS. Directed by Don Sharp.

BLIND BARGAIN, A (1922). See editions 1-3.

BLIND DATE (1983). Above-average psychothriller unfolds in the style of a Dario Argento jolter. The fascinating premise is that Joseph Bottoms is blinded while fleeing a killer, and agrees to have Dr. Steiger (Keir Dullea) implant a device in his brain that feeds computer-like images to his mind, allowing him to "see." Using the device, he sets out to find the killer in Athens, where this was photographed. The women are sexy (the killer has a penchant for TV models) so it's easy on the eyes. Unfortunately, Kirstie Alley's role is never heavily integrated and one wishes she were around more. James Daughton, Lana Clarkson, Gerald Kelly. Written-produced-directed by Nico Mastoranis, who no doubt digs those Argento thrillers. (Lightning; Vestron)

BLIND DEAD, THE (1972). Spanish horror flick has eerie atmosphere and decent effects in recounting the legend of a 13th Century cult, the Templarios, who murdered thousands of women in blood sacrifices. Known in Spain as TOMB OF THE BLIND DEAD. Written-directed by Amando De Ossorio. Cesar Burner, Lon Fleming, Joseph Thelman, Helen Hays, Rufing Ingels.

BLIND FEAR (1989). Blinded Shelley Hack is trapped in a mountain lodge with killers and must use her wits to save herself. Is this WAIT UNTIL DARK all over again, or what? Canadian feature directed by Tom Berry. Jack Langedijk, Kim Coates. (Academy) (Laser: Image)

BLIND FURY (1989). Rutger Hauer, blinded during the Vietnam War, is trained in martial arts by native rescuers. When he returns stateside to see an old buddy, he gets caught up in a fight with the mob in Reno, using his fighting prowess to help his dead friend's son. Hauer has a psychic sense when he battles, similar to the metaphysical powers of Japan's blind swordsman, Zatoichi. Directed by Philip Noyce. Brandon Call, Terrance O'Quinn, Lisa Blount, Nobel Willingham, Meg Foster, Nick Cassavetes. (Video/Laser: RCA/Columbia)

BLIND MAN'S BUFF. Video version of **CAULDRON OF BLOOD** (Vidcrest).

BLIND MAN'S BLUFF (1991). Foolish, unconvincing TV-movie that is a hodge podge of pseudopsychiatry, split personality behavior, serial murders performed with a hammer, and a little touch of WAIT UNTIL DARK tossed in. Robert Urich portrays a blind novelist stalked by a murderer and gets involved with stolen coins, suspicious cops, his best friend, his psychiatrist and a former flame. Whew! Lisa Eilbacher, Patricia Clarkson, Ron Perlman. Directed by James Quinn.

BLIND WITNESS (1989). TV-movie terror tale of a woman trapped in her home environment with killers (a genre established by WAIT UNTIL DARK). Victoria Principal, whose husband has been murdered, is terrorized in the aftermath of his death. Produced-directed by Richard Colla. Paul LeMat, Stephen Macht, Matt Clark.

BLINK (1993). After an eye operation that restores her sight, Madeleine Stowe experiences "ocular flashback"—images out of their proper sequence in time. Since her visions involve a serial killer, she's quickly embroiled with cop Aidan Quinn. This offbeat thriller with mild supernatural overtones is stylishly directed by Michael Apted. Laurie Metcalf, James Remar. (New Line)

BLISS (1986). Australian comedy of the macabre in which advertising man Barry Otto dies and goes to Heaven and Hell to glimpse both extremes, then returns to Earth to question the meaning of life. Directed by Ray Lawrence from Peter Carey's novel. (Starmaker)

BLITHE SPIRIT (1945). Noel Coward's popular play was turned into a memorable screen adaptation by director David Lean and Coward, who wrote the script. Jolly good the way those British handle a comedy ghost story. Rex Harrison is a chap haunted by his wives. Not the alimony-seeking kind—the dead kind! Constance Cummings, Kay Hammond, Joyce Carey, Margaret Rutherford. (Mike LeBell's)

BLOB, THE (1958). Gelatin-like lumpy-glumpy substance comes to Earth aboard a meteor and grows each time it sucks up a human being, which is often, as Theodore Simonson and Kate Phillips don't want any blobs growing under their script. Steve McQueen and town juveniles set out to warn folks, but nobody listens . . . until the icky-sicky invades a movie theater and then it's too late to stop the ever-growing glunky junky. Tongue-in-cheek fun if you can roll with the World's Biggest Jello Ball. Director Irvin S. Yeaworth Jr. deserves credit for turning this into a cult favorite known for being icky sicky. Aneta Corseaut, Olin Howlin, Earl Rowe. (Video Gems; Video Warehouse) (Laser: Criterion)

BLOB, THE (1988). This remake of the classic 1958 Steve McQueen vehicle is a monster movie with a capital M—a wonderful send-up of the original, ashine with gross but fun special effects. Director Chuck Russell (who co-authored with Frank Darabont) knows what elements of the scare genre make us leap from our seats or pull our feet up from the floor when the film re-creates the famous movie theater scene when the ploppy gloppy pores through the projection portal. Once again the glob Blob is a mindless force but this time was created during a human-genetics experiment in space. We see it ingesting people, changing its shape, and behaving as a scary monster should, at one moment literally sucking a human victim down a tiny drain. Kevin Dillon and Shawnee Smith flee the creature in the sewer system and fight it out (aided by the townspeople) in a battle royal. Hoyt Yeatman spearheaded the effects team and Lyle Conway designed the Blob. Donovan Leitch, Candy Clark, Del Close. (RCA/Columbia) (Laser: Image)

BLOBERMOUTH (1990). Remember when Woody Allen took an old Japanese gangster movie, redubbed the sound track with gags, and called it WHAT'S UP, TIGER LILY? Well, producer Jack H. Harris took his 1958 THE BLOB and redubbed it with voices of the L.A. Connection comedy group. The gag is that McQueen is now a stand-up comedian and the Blob has come to town to steal his thunder with one-liners. It's enough to make you blob-er!

BLOOD (1973). Don't bleed for sexploitation specialist Andy Milligan, even if he bleeds his cast in this sanguinary story of Dr. Lawrence Orlovski (Allan Berendt), a werewolf in 1930's London who keeps company with man-eating plants and an offspring of Dracula. Thinner than water. Eve Crosby, Pamela Adams.

BLOOD AND BLACK LACE (1964). Italian-French horror thriller focused on a fiendish killer and the step-by-step enactment of crimes against beautiful models in a fashion salon run by Eva Bartok. The killer wears a stocking that makes the face an empty blank and there is a merciless choice on director Mario Bava's part to show gore murders in drawn-out, excruciating sequences. One woman has her face shoved against a hot grill, for example. One-time cinematographer Bava uses primary colors to psychological effect, creating the paradox of a beautiful-looking movie about death. Also known as FASHION HOUSE OF DEATH and SIX WOMEN FOR THE MURDERER. Cameron Mitchell, Thomas Reiner, Harriet White. (Media) (Laser: Polygram)

BLOOD AND LACE (1964). Feeble-minded Grand Guignol set in an orphanage where bodies are preserved in a freezer by a hammer-slamming, cleaver-carving killer in a mask. A comedown for Gloria Grahame, Melody Patterson and Vic Tayback. Dennis Christopher is in a small role. Directed by Philip Gilbert.

BLOOD AND ROSES (1961). Director Roger Vadim's version of J. Sheridan Le Fanu's CARMILLA was brutalized by U.S. censors years ago who removed 13 minutes of lesbian activity. What's left of this tale tells of a woman with a family history of vampirism who is obsessed by an ancestor's spirit and an overpowering craving for blood of both sexes. Mel Ferrer, Elsa Martinelli, Annette Vadim. (Paramount/Gateway, with much lesbianism and violence restored.)

BLOOD BARON, THE. See **BARON OF BLOOD.**

BLOOD BATH (1966). Schizophrenic beatnik painter in the L.A. suburb of Venice murders women, lowering their still-warm bodies into a boiling vat. He thinks he's the reincarnation of a vampire. This exploitation flick will be of interest to fans of William Campbell, who co-stars with Marissa Mathes, Lori Saunders, Sandra Knight and Jonathan Haze. Written-directed by Jack Hill and reportedly finished by Stephanie Rothman after Hill was fired by producer Roger Corman. Also contains re-edited footage from a Yugoslavian film. (From Sinister Cinema and 21st Genesis as **TRACK OF THE VAMPIRE**)

BLOOD BATH (1976). A gore film this is not—there's nary a drop of blood and only one bath . . . bubble at that. In this anthology, the cast of a horror film in production dines with the director and exchange stories: (1) a bomb assassin is handed a strange twist of fate; (2) a magic coin transports a man to the Napoleonic wars; (3) a miser is locked into a vault with a ghost; (4) a karate champ knowing the Nine Secrets of Martial Arts learns the tenth. After dinner, the director goes home to (5) a locked room and a monster. Played tongue-in-cheek but amateurishly acted and photographed. Appears to have been shot half on tape, half on film. Directed by Joel (BLOODSUCKING FREAKS) Reed.

BLOODBATH AT THE HOUSE OF DEATH (1984). In one bloody night, 18 died in Headstone Manor: four skewered, two killed by lightning, six frozen in a locker, two axed, one hanged, one blown up and two sliced open. Now investigators and psychics are in the house to check out why it's radiating radioactivity. This parodies specific horror films and was intended by writer-director Ray Cameron as a vehicle for British comedian Kenny Everett, who plays Dr. Lucas Mandeville. Vincent Price stars as The Sinister Man, a cult leader. For the farcically minded. Pamela Stephenson, Gareth Hunt, Don Warrington, Joe Fortune, John Stephen Hill. (Media)

BLOODBATH BAY OF BLOOD. See **CARNAGE.**

BLOOD BEACH (1980). Bathers are sucked into sandy Santa Monica beach by an unseen subterranean creature, baffling cops John Saxon and Burt Young. Writer-director Jerry Bloom builds a modicum of suspense, but the sandsucker is an uninspired blob creature, its origins unexplained. Marianna Hill, David Huffman, Otis Young, Stefan Gierasch. (Media)

BLOOD BEAST FROM HELL. See **BLOOD BEAST TERROR, THE.**

BLOOD BEAST FROM OUTER SPACE. See **NIGHT CALLER FROM OUTER SPACE.**

BLOOD BEAST TERROR, THE (1967). Although Peter Cushing considers this his worst, it doesn't seem that bad on re-review. Backed by Hammer production qualities and a strong cast, Cushing portrays a 19th Century police inspector who goes undercover to discover that mad doctor Robert Flemying has turned beautiful Wanda Ventham into a Death's-Head moth. Cushing's daughter (Vanessa Howard) is threatened as she also goes undercover. Vernon Sewell does a good job of directing. Russell Napier, David Griffin. Also known as THE VAMPIRE BEAST CRAVES BLOOD. (Monterey)

BLOODBEAT (1982). Writer-director Fabrice-Ange Zaphiratos deserves a nod for making a gore film in which he blends psychic and slasher genres. A samurai warrior with a glowing aura terrorizes a rural family gathered for Christmas, in which mother and sister have mental powers. Gore is minimal as Zaphiratos goes for weirdness through music (some classical), enigmatic characters and a sexual link between the sister and the spectral samurai. Helen Benton, Terry Brown, Claudia Peyton, James Fitzgibbons. (Trans World)

BLOOD BRIDE (19??). Catholic girl marries a British antique dealer to discover, to her utter horror, that he murders for pleasure. What a bloody bastard! Philip English, Ellen Barber. (Magnum)

BLOOD BRIDES. See **HATCHET FOR THE HONEYMOON, A.**

BLOOD BUTCHERS. See **TOXIC ZOMBIES.**

BLOOD CASTLE (1970). Alternate video version of **SCREAM OF THE DEMON LOVER** (Lightning).

BLOOD CASTLE (1972). Video version of **LEGEND OF BLOOD CASTLE.**

BLOOD CEREMONY. See **FEMALE BUTCHER.**

BLOOD CIRCUS (1985). See third edition.

BLOOD COUPLE (1973). Released as GANJA AND HESS, and known as DOUBLE POSSESSION, this heavily cut version is the vampiric tale of a black doctor's assistant inflicted with a desire for blood after stabbed with a knife from a long-extinct black Nigerian civilization called Myrthia. This deals with black traditions in a well-intended but mind-dulling fashion, its pacing slow and its moments of action infrequent. Director-writer Bill Gunn appeared in the cast with Duane Jones, Marlene Clarke, composer Sam Waymon and Leonard Jackson. Good black music accompanies the tale, but nothing saves this from its own stuffiness. (Video Gems; from Simitar and Impulse as **BLACK VAMPIRE,** from Lettuce Entertain You as **BLACK EVIL,** from Fantasy as **BLACKOUT: THE MOMENT OF TERROR**)

BLOOD CREATURE. Video version of **TERROR IS A MAN.**

BLOOD CULT (1985). At a Midwest college, co-ed murders lead to the discovery of a witches' coven that dates back to the Salem trials. A sheriff and girlfriend close in on the hags and crones. Made in and around Tulsa, Oklahoma, by Linda Lewis (producer) and Christopher Lewis (director), this was one of the first video movies. Julie Andelman, Charles Ellis. (United)

BLOOD CULT OF SHANGRI-LA. See **THIRSTY DEAD, THE.**

BLOOD DEMON. See **CASTLE OF THE WALKING DEAD, THE.**

BLOOD DINER (1987). Tasteless sleazeball low-budgeter redeemed by its satirical humor directed at the artificialities of horror films. Director Jackie Kong makes fun of the genre as two nerds running a greasy spoon dig up their long-dead uncle, remove his brain and construct a new body from severed virgins' limbs and torsos. Purpose: to summon the great Goddess Sheetar. Mighty Kong allows every crummy joke and sick gag imaginable and spares none of the gore, although it's poorly done (on purpose, one hopes). If ever there was an armpit movie, this is it. Rick Burks, Carl Crew. (Vestron)

BLOOD DRINKERS, THE (1966). Even in the Philippines, according to Cesar Amigo's script, they have a problem with bloodthirsty vampires. The evil incarnate is Satan himself. Drips with gore in a cheap, unpleasant way. Directed by Gerardo De Leon. Amelia Fuentes, Ronald Remy, Eddie Fernandez, Eva Montez. (From Sinister/C as **VAMPIRE PEOPLE**)

BLOODEATERS. See **TOXIC ZOMBIES.**

BLOOD EVIL. Video version of **DEMONS OF THE MIND** (Academy).

BLOOD FEAST (1964). Exploitation gore flick—directed-photographed-scored by Herschell Gordon Lewis, who also did special effects. Lewis is legendary as the Grossest Film-maker of All, and this is exemplary of his "work." We're talking gore gore here. Women are dissected, organ by organ, as a madman restores life into an Egyptian goddess. A sickening spectacle as Lewis preys on vicarious needs of lowbrows. The squeamish are advised not to watch, although intellectuals and other thinkers might get off on the sociopathic implications. Co-produced by another master of exploitation, David F. Friedman. Connie Mason, Thomas Wood. (Comet; Rhino; VCI; S/Weird) (Laser: Hollywood Home Theater)

BLOOD FEAST (1974). Video version of **NIGHT OF A THOUSAND CATS** (Academy).

BLOOD FIEND, THE. See **THEATER OF DEATH.**

BLOOD FOR DRACULA. Japanese laser title for

ANDY WARHOL'S DRACULA.

BLOOD FREAK (1985). A vampire's myths are punctured when he learns the blood of drug addicts taint so good. Steve Hawks, Heather Hughes, Dana Cullivan. (Video Treasures; Simitar offers an edited version; Regal's is said to be unedited)

BLOOD FRENZY. Either a video of **BLOODY FRENZY** or a misspelling in some listings.

BLOOD FROM THE MUMMY'S TOMB (1972). Seth Holt's final directorial assignment—he died during production and was replaced by Michael Carreras. Acting and cinematography in this Hammer production are topnotch but Christopher Wicking's script, about a buxom young woman who resembles a long-dead Egyptian princess, is turgid stuff. Based on Bram Stoker's THE JEWEL OF SEVEN STARS. Andrew Keir, Valerie Leon, George Coulouris. Remade as THE AWAKENING.

BLOOD GAMES (1989). This manipulative, exploitative burst of violence is another revenge metaphor for the war between men and women. Babe and the Ballgirls, an all-women's baseball team, outplay some rednecks, so insulting their macho pride that they go after the sexy gals with intent to do bodily harm, especially since they've killed their boss' sadistic son (in self defense is beside the point). How the women unite into formidable fighters against male aggressors (using baseball bats, rifles and sex) is an intriguing if repulsive procedure in the hands of director Tanya Rosenberg, working from a script by four men. Artistic photography and a cast of fair-complected women raise this blood-and-gore thriller to greater heights than the material deserves. Gregory Cummings, Laura Albert, Shelley Abblett, Ernest Wall. (Video/Laser: RCA/Columbia)

BLOOD HARVEST (1986). Tiny Tim tiptoes through the bloody tulips in this low-budget, lowbrow imitation of the slasher genre in which he portrays Marvelous Mervo, a crazed hayseed in the whiteface and costume of a circus clown. But is he the demented dork who's kidnapping local folks, hanging them up like so many pigs to the slaughter and slitting their throats? This regional horror film was made in Wisconsin by writer-director Bill Rebane. Itonia Salochek sheds her clothes for lightcore sex scenes. Dean West, Frank Benson. (UAV)

BLOOD HOOK (1987). One of the stranger variations on FRIDAY THE 13TH, set at a lake in Muskie, Wisconsin, where fishermen gather for a contest. A killer uses a giant hook to "catch" his prey and then yank them apart. The murderer also shoves a hook through their mouths after they're dead and ties them together like a string of fish, this cheap movie's most ghastly effect. Other effects are amateurish (blame that on director James Mallon). The kind of movie you can fast-forward through because the majority of it is idle chatter among boring characters. Mark Jacobs, Patrick Danz, Sara Hauser, Christopher Whiting. (Prism; Paramount)

BLOOD HUNGER. Video version of **VAMPYRES—DAUGHTERS OF DARKNESS** (Lettuce Entertain You).

BLOOD HUNT. Video version of **THIRSTY DEAD, THE** (Simitar).

BLOOD IS MY HERITAGE. See **BLOOD OF DRACULA.**

BLOOD ISLAND. Video version of **SHUTTERED ROOM, THE** (Ace).

BLOOD LEGACY. Video version of **LEGACY OF BLOOD** (Video Gems).

BLOOD LINK (1983). Clinically detailed portrait of a perverted psychokiller murdering women in Hamburg and Berlin. It's also the study of Siamese twins: Michael Moriarity plays the killer and a doctor experimenting in brain control. Intriguing twists and good production make this Italian thriller above average. However, the sexual violence is a turn-off, creating a fascinating story unpleasant to watch. Penelope Milford, Geraldine Fitzgerald, Cameron Mitchell, Virginia McKenna. Music by Ennio Morricone. Directed by Albert de Martino. (Embassy)

BLOODLUST (1961). Variation on "The Most Dangerous Game": Crazed hunter Dr. Balleau (Wilton Graff) chases humans with a bow-and-arrow rig, displaying the remains as trophies in glass containers. Written-produced-directed with a minimum of lustiness by Ralph Brooke and starring unknowns except for Robert Reed, who became a TV star in THE BRADY BUNCH. Lilyan Chauvin, June Kenny, Joan Lora. (Sinister/C; S/Weird; Filmfax)

BLOODLUST (1981). Video of **DR. JEKYLL AND MISS OSBOURNE** (Citadel; King of Video).

BLOODLUST (1992). Australian-produced vampire shocker in which three femme fatale bloodsuckers rove Melbourne searching for sex-seeking men. Gore, softcore sex and mediocre everything. Written-directed by Richard Wolstencroft and Jon Hewitt. Jane Stuart Wallace, Kelly Chapman, Robert James O'Neill.

BLOODLUST: SUBSPECIES 3 (1993). Third and final bloodspatter in Charles Band's SUBSPECIES series—is this the end for vampire Radu (Anders Hoe) and Mummy dearest (Pamela Gordon)? Picking up right where BLOODSTONE: SUBSPECIES 2 left off, Melanie Shatner is back looking for sister Denice Duff, imprisoned in Radu's Transylvanian castle. Gooey, gory and blood-smeared with some great death scenes enhanced by good effects. Certain to please bloodsucking fans. Written-directed by Ted Nicolaou. (Paramount)

BLOOD MANIA (1970). Wicked, wanton sexpot speeds up her father's demise so she can help her depraved boyfriend pay off a blackmail debt. These unsavory characters finally get chopped into little pieces, but this merciful acts comes too late to benefit the viewer. Directed by Robert O'Neil. Peter Carpenter, co-producer with Chris Marconi, stars. (Academy; VCI)

BLOOD MOON. Video version of **WEREWOLF VS. THE VAMPIRE WOMAN, THE** (AIR).

BLOODMOON (1989). The first half of this Australian psychothriller is deadly dull. Teenagers in Cooper's Bay, which happens to have St. Elizabeth School for Girls and the Winchester School for Boys in close proximity, are being murdered by a killer with a barbed-wire garrot as they have sex, so there's nudity and love-making to keep you awake. The second half builds to a suspenseful climax, aided by Brian May's music. Leon Lissek is memorable as an impotent biology teacher-serial killer protected by wife Christine Amor. In Australia the film featured a "Fright Break" (an idea stolen from William Castle's HOMICIDAL). Directed by Alec Mills. Ian Williams, Helen Thomson, Suzie MacKenzie. (Live) (Laser: Image)

BLOOD OF DR. JEKYLL, THE (1981). Polish film maker Walerian Borowczyk's interpretation of Stevenson's classic is fraught with erotic imagery and bloodletting. Udo Kier, Marina Pierro, Patrick Magee, Howard Vernon.

BLOOD OF DRACULA (1957). Would you believe a vampire movie with songs? Would you believe hypnosis turning Sandra Harrison into a bloodsucker? Would you believe an all-girls' school where the head mistress has evil powers? Would you believe . . . naw, you wouldn't believe. Director Herbert L. Strock and screenwriter Ralph Thornton have justifiably remained obscure but producer Herman Cohen went on to I WAS A TEENAGE FRANKENSTEIN, KONGA, etc. Louise Lewis, Gail Ganley. Also known as BLOOD IS MY HERITAGE and BLOOD OF THE DEMON. (RCA/Columbia)

BLOOD OF DRACULA'S CASTLE (1967). Dreadfully produced flop (also known as DRACULA'S CASTLE) which drains weak laughs from the formula by updating it to modern California, but results are anemic, even with cinematographer Laszlo Kovacs assisting and with John Carradine (as a faithful butler to the Dracula clan) and Lon Chaney Jr. A gross misuse of the Count's non-good name by producer-director Al Adamson, assisted in directing by Jean Hewitt. Alex D'Arcy and Paula Raymond are Mr. and Mrs. Dracula, chaining up beautiful chicks in the cellar. Robert Dix, Ray Young, Vicki Volante. (Interglobal; United; Grand Entertainment; VCI)

BLOOD OF FRANKENSTEIN. See **DRACULA VS. FRANKENSTEIN.**

BLOOD OF FU MANCHU. See **KISS AND KILL.**

BLOOD OF GHASTLY HORROR (1970). Video version of **MAN WITH THE SYNTHETIC BRAIN, THE** (VidAmerica; Movies Unlimited).

BLOOD OF HEROES, THE (1989). Surprisingly good existential glimpse into a futuristic world—a welcome change in the post-Armageddon genre. In a desert landscape, battered bands of warriors rove, training for battlegames ("The League") staged for the upper crust. Rutger Hauer teams with feisty Joan Chen and other scarred "heroes" to take on the best the League offers in bone-crunching gladitorial contests. The games become a metaphor for man's fight to achieve and survive and the script by director David Peoples builds to a satisfying climax despite barren production values. It's Hauer and Chen who make it work intellectually and viscerally. Max Fairchild also shines as Hauer's adversary, giving his brutish character dimension. Made in Australia as SALUTE OF THE JUGGER. Vincent Phillip Donofrio, Anna Katarina, Delroy Lindo. (HBO) (Laser: Image)

BLOOD OF NOSTRADAMUS (1960). His thirst unquenchable, his fangs dripping with gore, notorious Mexican vampire German Robles brags of his ability to murder the police chief at midnight—a vow which gravely upsets law enforcement and forces cops to remain on vigil against this brazen bloodsucker. Consists of footage taken from a Mexican serial and re-edited. Old footage was directed by Frederick Curiel, the new by Stim Segar. Julio Aleman, Domingo Soler. (S/Weird)

BLOOD OF THE DEMON. See **BLOOD OF DRACULA.**

BLOOD OF THE IRON MAIDEN. See **IS THIS TRIP REALLY NECESSARY?**

BLOOD OF THE MAN-BEAST. See **HOUSE OF THE BLACK DEATH.**

BLOOD OF THE MAN-DEVIL. See **HOUSE OF THE BLACK DEATH.**

BLOOD OF THE UNDEAD. See **SCHIZO.**

BLOOD OF THE VAMPIRE, THE (1958). Inspired by the sanguinary efforts of Hammer, screenwriter Jimmy Sangster offers up sinister Callistrastus (Donald Wolfit, of grand theatrics) who conducts blood experiments in an asylum. A superior British chiller, reeking with period atmosphere and doom. Full of the blood and gore Hammer made so fashionable, enhanced by Barbara (CAT WOMAN) Shelley as a heroine undergoing blood transfusions and Victor Maddern as the Igor-style aide-decampy to the mad doc. Directed by Henry Cass. Milton Reid, John Le Mesurier. (Magnet; MPI; Gorgon)

BLOOD ON HIS LIPS. See **HIDEOUS SUN DEMON, THE.**

BLOOD ON SATAN'S CIAW, THE (1971). Gruesome British supernatural chiller (tensely directed by Piers Haggard from Robert Wynne-Simmons' script) concerns the Devil afoot in 17th Century England, turning the kiddies in surrounding farmlands into cauldron-stirring witches and warlocks. Exorcism is employed by a noble Englishman (Patrick Wymark) sworn to destroy the cult. Period atmosphere and costuming are excellent. Also known as SATAN'S SKIN. Linda Hayden, Barry Andrews, Tamara Ustinov. (Paragon; Cannon)

BLOOD ORGY. See **GORE GORE GIRLS, THE.**

BLOOD ORGY OF THE SHE-DEVILS (1973). Quadruple threat Ted V. Mikels (writer/director/producer/editor) offers little blood during sacrificial rites, a few hardly-dressed she-devils (their choreography would roll Busby Berkeley over in his grave) and no orgy at all. It's black magic mumbo jumbo as a queen of the witches, living in a California mansion (in Orange County, maybe?), practices the blackest of arts on the lowest of budgets. Lots of dialogue about psychometry, regression, white magic, etc., but it builds to a big letdown. Lila Zaborin, Tom Pace. (Western World; from Lettuce Entertain You as **FEMALE PLASMA SUCKERS**)

BLOODRAGE (1979). Pointless bloodbath as a mental case stalks the sleazy districts of New York City, attacking anyone he can get his homicidal hands on. Also known as NEVER PICK UP A STRANGER. Directed by Joseph Bigwood. Lawrence Tierney, Ian Scott, James Johnston. (Best of Film & Video; Marquis)

BLOOD RAGE (1983). Video version of **NIGHTMARE AT SHADOW WOODS** (Prism).

BLOOD RELATIONS (1977). Wim Lindner directed this vampire spoof set in a European town where bloodsuckers are tapping into the town's supply of plasma. Maxim Hamel, Gregoire Aslan, Sophie Deschamps, Eddie Constantine.

BLOOD RELATIONS (1988). Fair Canadian-produced chiller set in a mansion where surgeon Jan Rubles is grieving over his wife's death when his son (Kevin Hicks) and girlfriend (Lydie Dernier) visit. What they don't know: Rubles has stored his wife's brain in a fresh cranium. Ray Walston plays an an old man in the house who is dying. Frankenstein horror mixed with who'll-get-the-inheritance plot. Directed by Graeme Campbell. (Video/Laser: Nelson)

BLOOD RELATIVES (1977). Lowkey psychokiller melodrama with mild slasher touches, from French director Claude Chabrol, who focuses on mature teenager Audre Landry having a passionate affair with her first cousin. Donald Sutherland portrays a sensitive cop investigating the girl's stabbing. He suspects David Hemmings, the dead girl's flirtatious boss, but answers to this whodunit are to be found in a red diary. Characterizations are well developed by Chabrol and co-writer Sydney Banks, who adapted a novel by Ed McBain. Lisa Langlois, Stephane Audran, Laurent Malent. (UAV; CIC)

BLOOD RITES. See **GHASTLY ONES, THE.**

BLOOD ROSE, THE. Video version of **RAVAGED.**

BLOOD SABBATH (1972). Wandering guitarist Tony Geary falls for Yala the water nymph (Susan Damante) and is willing to sacrifice his soul to Aloyta, Queen of the Witches (Dyanne Thorne), for Yala's love. Good ideas in William Bairn's script are weakened, however, by gratuitous nudity (granted us by sexy members of Aloyta's coven) and mediocre gore effects. Its shoddy visuals designed by Hugo Grimaldi are in contrast to a languid love mood. (JLT Films)

BLOOD SALVAGE (1989). In the dark-comedy jugular vein of the TEXAS CHAINSAW series, this macabre tale depicts rednecks running a wrecking yard who rig highway accidents and take surviving victims to a barn of horrors, where the family's daffy patriarch (Danny Nelson) slices-dices the bodies. The choicest parts he sells to black marketeer Ray Walston. "Mad Jake" and demented sons close in on traveler John Saxon and family. Crippled daughter Lori Birdsong is subjected to a litany of indignities and horrors. It's a battle of moribund humor as Birdsong outfoxes the brothers, Saxon escapes the barn-dissection center and an alligator slithers around. Done to the tune of "Bringing in the Sheep." Director Tucker Johnston co-wrote the subversive script with producer Ken C. Sanders. Christian Hesler, Ralph Pruit Vaughn. (Magnum; Turner; from Malo as **MAD JAKE**) (Laser: Image)

BLOOD SHACK. See **CHOOPER, THE.**

BLOOD SHED. Video version of **CRAZED** (Regal).

BLOOD SISTERS. See **SISTERS.**

BLOOD SCREAMS (1988). Monastery is haunted by the ghost of a high priest who once ordered a slaughter for the local coven. Trouble begins when traveling magician Russ Tamblyn comes to town. Stacey Shafer, Ron Sands, James Garrett. Written-directed by Glenn Gebhard. (Warner Bros.)

BLOOD SISTERS (1986). New sorority pledges are taken to an old house where they spend the night. Unknown to all, someone connected with murders 13 years before is stalking the premises, murdering the gals in graphic fashion. The women also hallucinate images of ghosts and eerie phenomena wandering the creepy joint. Written-directed by Roberta Findlay. Amy Brentano, Shannon McMahon. (Sony; RCA/Columbia)

BLOOD SONG (1982). Something to sing about: An unusually tense psychothriller with Frankie Avalon forsaking his clean image to portray a mental patient who escapes from an asylum and stalks a young woman (Donna Wilkes) after axing her father (Richard Jaeckel) to death. Good scary thriller. Directed by Alan J. Levi and Robert Angus. Antoinette Bower, Dane Clark. (Abacus; Coast to Coast; from HQV as **DREAM SLAYER**)

BLOOD-SPATTERED BRIDE, THE (1969). Spanish variation on Le Fanu's CARMILLA, as newlyweds Simon Andreau and Maribel Martin, after a slow wedding night, finally get to depravity and perversion. This sets the mood for a shrouded woman (Alexandra Bastedo), a reincarnation of long-dead Carmilla who enjoys blood from a human wrist and making lesbian passes at Maribel. The first hour moves slowly under Vincente Aranda's writing-direction. When murders occur, it's too late. Dean Selmier, Monserrat Julio. (Gorgon; MPI; heavily edited from Vestron as **TILL DEATH DO US PART**)

BLOODSPELL (1988). This video feature has plot twists that make it semi-endurable. Anthony Jenkins is possessed by his father's spirit, a form of monster who intends to live inside his son's body and draw off energy. The invaded youth, staying at St. Boniface, a center for disturbed youngsters, turns telekenetic powers to evil means, creating force fields that cause accidents and death for companions. Effects are okay, acting passable. Aaron Teich, Alexandra Kennedy, John Reno. Directed by Deryn Warren. (Forum; MCEG)

BLOOD SPLASH. Video version of **NIGHTMARE (1981)** (Platinum).

BLOODSTALKERS (1976). A thinking buff's gore flick, structured by writer-director Robert W. Morgan as a metaphor for man's indifference to his fellow man, and man's isolationism from responsibility. Also known as THE NIGHT DANIEL DIED, it starts as a psychological study of two men and two women vacationing in the Florida Everglades. Themes of cowardice and redemption arise when hairy creatures (called "Bloodstalkers" by rural yokels) close in and one of the men (Jerry Albert) seeks help from a community that treats him as an outsider. In a spinoff from STRAW DOGS, Albert turns into the very character that has spawned his predicament. If this sounds profound, rest assured the film has graphic violence: two are dispatched with an axe, a scythe pinions two more to a wall, and one is hung up to bleed to death. Morgan (who also plays a redneck killer) meshes it into an intriguing tale, and even gets artsy at a gospel church where the action is pantomimed and the soundtrack taken over by black singers. Kenny Miller, Celea-Anne Cole, Toni Crabtree. (Vidmark)

BLOODSTONE: SUBSPECIES II (1993). This sequel to SUBSPECIES benefits from Transylvanian/Romanian locations, but Charles Band's vampire thriller is full of disgusting blooddrinking, flesh ripping and other distasteful depictions that rob the tale of potential charm. Anders Hove is back as Radu, that Nosferatu-like vampire with the clawy hands, and Denice Duff is the innocent in a filmy nightgown fleeing his clutches, taking with her the mythical relic (the Bloodstone) said to contain the blood of saints. Pamela Gordon steals the show as Radu's "Mummy," a Crypt Keeper type of ghoulish crone who cackles her way into your heart. Meanwhile, Melanie Shatner shows up as Duff's sister and Kevin Blair is an ineffectual State Department jerkola. If you like 'em gross, by all means. Written-directed by Ted Nicolaou. Next: BLOODLUST: SUBSPECIES III. (Paramount)

BLOODSUCKERS, THE (1970). Vampirism is treated as sexual perversion in this British adaptation of Simon Raven's novel, DOCTORS WEAR SCARLET. Released in England as INCENSE FOR THE DAMNED, it stars Peter Cushing and Patrick Macnee and is enhanced by Cypriot location shooting. A woman searches for her lost fiancee amidst a cult of Satan lovers. Directed by Robert Hartford-Davis. Edward Woodward, Patrick Mower, Imogen Hassal. (Media; Sinister/C; VCL)

BLOODSUCKERS. See **MAN-EATER OF HYDRA.**

BLOOD SUCKERS. Title for **DR. TERROR'S GALLERY OF HORRORS,** which was re-retitled **RETURN FROM THE PAST.**

BLOODSUCKERS FROM OUTER SPACE (1984). Attempt to parody the sci-fi genre, shot around Hamilton, Texas, is an example of a misfire in the hands of amateurs. An invisible life force "from beyond our atmosphere"—its presence signalled by a strong wind—takes over one's bloodstream, bleeds out all the blood through orifices, then reanimates the body. Effects and acting are substandard and attempts by writer-director Glen Coburn to poke fun at warmongering army officers, mad doctors and narrow-minded Southerners are strained. Thom Meyers, Laura Elis. Pat Paulsen cameos as the U.S. President. (Lorimar; Warner Bros.)

BLOODSUCKING FREAKS. Video version of **INCREDIBLE TORTURE SHOW, THE** (Vestron).

BLOODSUCKING NAZI ZOMBIES. Video version of **OASIS OF THE ZOMBIES** (Trans World).

BLOODSUCKING PHARAOHS IN PITTSBURGH (1989). In the vein of the POLICE ACADEMY series, stuffed with vomiting, dildo jokes and other gaggery in poor taste, this regionally produced attempt at comedy-horror is as exciting as visiting Pittsburgh. A mysterious figure, pulling a power unit to which electrical tools are plugged in, kills women and takes their bodies to perfect a formula for eternal life. Two dumb cops follow the trail of Jackie Cairo to the Egyptian part of town (full of camels and snake charmers). One funny slasher gag has the killer jamming a parking meter into a victim's stomach as the "Time Expired" flag pops up. Make-up by Tom Savini; script by director Dean Tschetter. BLOODSUCKING PHARAOHS is the pitts. Jake Dengel, Joe Sharkey, Susann Fletcher, Shawn Elliott. (Paramount)

BLOOD THIRST (1965). Another "Blood-Runner" from the Philippines, depicting bloodthirsty sun cultists. Watch this too long and you'll see spots in front of your eyes. Directed by Newt Arnold. Robert Winston, Yvonne Nielson, Judy Dennis, Vic Diaz Eddie Infante.

BLOOD THIRST. Retitled video version of **SALEM'S LOT** (On Line Cinema).

BLOODTHIRSTY BUTCHERS (1970). Terrible rehash of DEMON BARBER OF FLEET STREET, the Sweeney Todd sanguinary saga. Grotesque oddity that panders to the lowest common denominator, dripping with intestines and blood. A batty barber and a psychotic pastry preparer meld their perversions into one to mutilate

"We're not dealing with some supernatural being from Eastern European folklore popularized by horror cycles in America, Europe and Britain cinema. We're up against a superintelligent life form from another world."

—A dumb doctor in **BLOODSUCKERS FROM OUTER SPACE.**

victims and sell the leftovers as bargain basement pies. It's the work of infamous director Andy Milligan. John Borske, John Miranda. (Midnight/Select-A-Tape)

BLOODTHIRSTY EYES. See **LAKE OF DRACULA.**

BLOODTHIRSTY SEX (1981). Spanish chiller-diller from writer-producer-director Manuel Esteba Gallego about a woman who foresees pending doom for herself and two companions, and can do nothing to stop the horrors that come. Mirta Miller, Diana Conca.

BLOOD TIDE (1981). Also known as THE RED TIDE, this is a ripoff of JAWS in which archaeologist James Earl Jones disturbs a sea monster from its "ancient sleep." Island natives Jose Ferrer and Lila Kedrova know legends about the slimy, gnashing Kraken requiring a virginal sacrifice but aren't telling Jones, Mary Louise Weller, Lydia Cornell and Deborah Shelton. Poor Lydia gets eaten while swimming without a bra. Director Richard Jeffries (who wrote with co-producer Nico Mastorakis) never shows the brimy beast, just slobbering jaws in flash cuts. It's ebb tide for BLOOD TIDE. (Continental; Cinema Group; Planet)

BLOOD TIES (1991). Failed TV-pilot created by Esther and Richard Shapiro—a blend of vampire horror with the DALLAS-type series. BLOOD TIES still offers interesting variations on the theme. Belgian actor Patrick Bauchau is the corrupt patriarch of a vampire family working its way up in the business world in Long Beach, Ca., and is a kind of "globfather" image to bloodlusting relatives. A nephew (Harley Venton) who works as a newsman tries to escape his heritage by romancing D.A. Kim Johnston-Ulrich, but sex brings out the beast in him and this creates conflicts. And there are times when suave Bauchau turns into a snarling beast—a compelling metaphor for the ruthless businessman. Well produced and directed by Jim McBride. New Horizon)

BLOOD TRACKS (1986). Rock group in the Rockies (ha ha) shooting a Rock(ies) Video (ha ha) is attacked by crazies living beneath an old factory. Gore and sex aplenty. Directed by Mike Jackson. Jeff Harding, Michael Fitzpatrick, Naomi Kaneda. (Vista)

BLOOD VIRGIN, THE. See **SYMPTONS.**

BLOOD VOYAGE (1977). Pleasure sailboat bound for Hawaii is the claustrophobic world in which a psychokiller armed with meat cleaver and knives knocks off passengers. These include a troubled Vietnam vet, a buxom, bleached blond scheming to murder her stepfather, a drug addict and a lecherous cook. The horror effects are minimal and director Frank Mitchell brings little style or tension to the thriller, which ends with a twist that seems unnecessary immorale. The only recognizable actor is John Hart, who once played The Lone Ranger. Here he's white haired with matching beard. Jonathan Lippe, Laurie Rose, Mara Modair. (Cinematex; Monterey's version is cut)

BLOOD WATERS OF DR. Z. See **ATTACK OF THE SWAMP CREATURES.**

BLOOD WEDDING. See **HE KNOWS YOU'RE ALONE.**

BLOOD WILL HAVE BLOOD. See **DEMONS OF THE MIND.**

BLOODY BIRD. See **STAGEFRIGHT.**

BLOODY BIRTHDAY, THE (1980). THE BAD SEED played as a slasher film: Two boys and a girl (all born during a solar eclipse) are instilled with homicidal tendencies on their tenth birthday. Emotionlessly, they beat a man over the head with a shovel, strangle his girlfriend with a rope, kill dad (the sheriff of peaceful Meadowvale) with a bat, shoot a schoolteacher (Susan Strasberg) and ogle a naked girl through a peephole. Is this sick or what? Director Ed Hunt proves you can have your cake and slice people too, but it can't hold a candle to other slasher movies. It'll just frost you. Jose Ferrer, Ellen Geer, Melinda Cordell. (Prism; Starmaker)

BLOODY CEREMONY. See **LEGEND OF BLOOD CASTLE, THE.**

BLOODY FIANCEE. See **BLOOD-SPATTERED BRIDE,**

THE.BLOODY FRENZY (1987). Psychiatrist takes his confused clients into the desert for tranquil analyses, but the group is beset by a psychokiller. Directed by Hal Freeman. Wendy MacDonald, Lisa Loring. (Vestron; Hollywood Family Entertainment)

BLOODY GIRL. Video version of **FANGS OF THE LIVING DEAD.**

BLOODY JUDGE, THE. See **NIGHT OF THE BLOOD MONSTER.**

BLOODY MOON (1981). Two killers on a rampage during the Festival of the Moon terrorize Olivia Pascal in this Italian gorefest directed by Jesus Franco. Christopher Brugger, Nadja Gerganoff. (CIC; Trans World)

BLOODY NEW YEAR (1987). A boatload of teenagers occupies an old hotel on a island haunted by attendees of a 1960 New Year Eve's party, who somehow have gotten mixed up in a time-space continuum warp-bend. At least that's what screenwriter Frazer Pearce says. Directed by Norman J. Warren. Also known as WARP TERROR. Suzy Aitchison, Nikki Brooks, Colin Heywood. (Academy)

BLOODY PIT OF HORROR (1965). Italian mishmash of torture scenes should delight sadists, masochists and other flagellators. Mickey Hargitay, one-time hubbie of movie queen Jayne Mansfield, cracks a mean whip as The Crimson Executioner in a castle equipped with the latest torture devices. Visiting the highstone are beautiful models to pose for book covers, but instead they pose their last for Mickey. Massimo Pupillo directed this form of viewing torture. Allegedly based on the memoirs of the Marquis de Sade; his spirit should return and sue for defamation. Walter Brandi, Louise Barrett, Ralph Zucker. Also known as THE RED HANGMAN, THE CRIMSON EXECUTIONER and THE SCARLET HANGMAN. (Sinister/C; S/Weird; Filmfax)

BLOODY POM-POMS. See **CHEERLEADER CAMP.**

BLOODY SCREAM OF DRACULA. See **DRACULA, PRINCE OF DARKNESS.**

BLOODY SECT, THE (1982). The sperm of the Devil is deposited in an artificial insemination bank and used to impregnate three women. Will one of them give birth to a little Devil? Spanish film directed by Steve McCoy. Carlos Martos, Josephine Varney.

BLOODY SPA. See **WARLOCK MOON.**

BLOODY VAMPIRE, THE (1960). Footage from a Mexican serial re-edited by American producer A. K. Gordon Murray. It's Count Cagliostro, good aristocracy, against Count Frankenhausen, evil aristocracy. Directed-written by Michael Morayta. Carlos Agosti, Begona Palacios, Raul Farrell. The sequel was INVASION OF THE VAMPIRES. (Sinister/C; S/Weird; Filmfax)

BLOODY WEDNESDAY (1985). Offbeat study of a man (Raymond Elmendorf) who slowly sinks into madness to become a mass murderer. Based on the 1984 incident at a San Diego hamburger shop where diners were killed by a rampaging gunman, this was written and co-produced by veteran screenwriter Philip Yordan. The incidents are an odd mix of reality and hallucination. Harry is staying in a deserted hotel and he meets an old bellboy who tells him of a past that begins to recur. Another oddity is the presence of hoodlums, who pursue Harry and become involved in sparking his final act of insanity. Directed by co-producer Mark G. Gilhuis. Pamela Baker, Navarre Perry. (Prism)

BLUEBEARD (1944). Edgar G. Ulmer brings good direction to this PRC quickie and John Carradine gives a compelling performance as a Parisian puppeteer who knocks off his models by putting his fingers around their necks and squeeezzziiinnnggg. Nils Asther, Jean Parker, Ludwig Stossel. (Sinister/C; Kartes; Nostalgia; Filmfax)

BLUEBEARD (1962). French-Italian version of the true-life Landru murder case, directed by Claude Chabrol. Charles Denner, Michele Morgan, Danielle Darrieux, Hildegarde Neff. (Charter; Sinister/C)

BLUEBEARD (1972). Ladykiller Richard Burton can't make love to ladies so he kills them as they surrender sexually. And what lovely victims: Raquel Welch (as a nun), Nathalie Delon, Karin Schubert, Marilu Tolo, Virna Lisi, Sybil Danning. Each curdling murder is recounted by Bluebeard to his bride/next-victim-to-be Joey Heatherton, who psychoanalyzes the Count one dark night. Director Edward Dmytryk provides titillation, soft-core nudity, lesbianism, sadism. But scenes are played so flatly, one doesn't know if to laugh or scream. So just cry. (USA; IVE)

BLUEBEARD'S TEN HONEYMOONS (1960). Inexpensive release, shot in England with George Sanders as a strangler of beautiful spouses. Directed by Lee Wilder. Corinne Calvet, Patricia Roc.

BLUE BIRD, THE (1940). Classic fantasy by Maurice Maeterlinck in the tradition of WIZARD OF OZ: Shirley Temple searches for the Bird of Happiness in a land of doom and pessimism, where Gale Sondergaard is the Wicked Witch. Walter Lang directed. Nigel Bruce, Sterling Holloway, Spring Byington, Ann Todd, Helen Ericson, Sterling Holloway. (Trans World; CBS/Fox)

BLUE BIRD, THE (1976). See editions 1-3.

BLUEBLOOD (198?). Demonic powers are unleashed in Swanbrook Mansion. Derek Jacobi, Oliver Reed, Fiona Lewis. Written-directed by Andrew Sinclair. (Video Gems; VCL)

BLUE DEMON VS. THE INFERNAL BRAINS (1967). Mexican horror inanities: a wrestling fool (Alejandro Cruz) and the police against a mad doctor and his female zombies. Directed by Chano Urueta. David Reynoso, Barbara Angely. (Video Latino)

BLUE DESERT (1991). Sexy Courtney Cox lives alone in the desert, drawing her comic strip about a female gladiator, Iron Medusa, when she comes under the scrutiny of a rapist. Written by Arthur Collis and director Brad Battersby. D.B. Sweeney, Craig Sheffer, Sandy Ward. (Academy)

BLUE EYES OF THE BROKEN DOLL, THE. See **HOUSE OF THE PSYCHOTIC WOMEN.**

BLUE HOLOCAUST. See **BURIED ALIVE.** (1979).

BLUE MAN, THE. See **ETERNAL EVIL.**

BLUE MONKEY (1987). Monster thriller set in a county hospital where a man cut by a thorn on a flower plant spits up a caterpillar-like form, which turns into an insect. When the leggy creature is sprayed with NAC-5, a life-force accelerator, it turns into a giant monster spawning new larvae. After the thing go cop Steve Railsback, doctor Gwynyth Walsh and entomologist Don Lake. While this Sandy Howard production is an ALIEN ripoff, it builds suspense and has believable characters, thanks to George Goldsmith's script, which brings in a laser experiment and a quarantine. Director William Fruet rolls his camera through a labyrinth of corridors and photographs the final battle, in a laser lab, breathlessly. Above average for a video movie. John Vernon portrays the head of the hospital. Susan Anspath, Robin Duke, Joe Flaherty, Judith Glass. (RCA/Columbia; from Winson as **INSECT**)

BLUE MURDER (1985). Amateurish acting and an uninspired script by director Charles Wiener and Jim Murray undermine this Canadian film about a madman shooting everyone connected with a pornographic movie racket. So insipid are the protagonists—a sassy black cop and an ill-behaved news investigator—there's no way this becomes compelling as its turgid mystery-horror unfolds. Jamie Spears, Terry Logan. (Video to Video; from AVEC as **PORN MURDERS, THE**)

BLUES BUSTERS (1950). That idiotic Bowery Boy Sach (Huntz Hall) develops an excellent singing voice after a throat operation. You'll only choke on this Monogram programmer that is totally offkey; for diehard Bowery bums only. Directed in D-flat (D for dumb) by William Beaudine. Leo Gorcey, Gabriel Dell, Craig Stevens, Adele Jergens. (Warner Bros.)

BLUE SUNSHINE (1977). LSD derivative causes students to lose their hair and sanity. Writer-director Jeff Lieberman (he who gave us SQUIRM) weaves a detective story (Zalman King searches for the source of "blue sunshine") and a political cover-up plot. But it doesn't cover up what amounts to a bad trip. You'll feel blue and need sunshine. Deborah Winters, Robert Walden, Mark Goddard, Ann Cooper. (Vestron)

BLUE THUNDER (1983). State-of-the-art helicopter (with infrared and eavesdropping devices, not to mention knockout firepower) traverses the skies over L.A., eventually engaging in combat with another superchopper. It's a rousing high-tech actioner with pilots Ray Scheider and Daniel Stern picking up on a military conspiracy and shooting it out in superexciting fashion with bad guy Malcolm McDowell amidst skyscrapers. Great movie action, technically superior. Directed by John Badham, scripted by Dan O'Bannon and Don Jakoby. Warren Oates, Joe Santos, Candy Clark. (Video/Laser: RCA/Columbia)

BOARDING HOUSE (1982). Pretty girls move into a haunted house, oblivious to warnings about its bloody past. Sure enough, a woman's spirit haunts the premises, and blood flows only after it's run cold. Directed by John Wintergate. Alexandra Day, Joel Riordan. (Paragon; from Classical as **HOUSEGEIST**)

BOARDING SCHOOL, THE. Video version of **HOUSE THAT SCREAMED, THE** (Vestron).

BOCCACCIO '70 (1962). Three sexy tales by European directors, one with fantasy appeal. "The Temptation of Dr. Antonio" is Federico Fellini's satire on censorship and bluenoses in which a giant poster of busty Anita Ekberg comes to life and walks through the city, disturbing the prudish and bringing out the red blooded. Other segments (directed by Luchino Visconti and Vittorio De Sica) are sex romps with nothing fantastic except the women, Romy Schneider and Sophia Loren. (Mike LeBell's)

BODIES BEAR TRACES OF CARNAL VIOLENCE, THE. See **TORSO.**

BODY AND THE WHIP, THE. See **WHAT!**

BODY BENEATH, THE (1970). Andy Milligan's flick is a painful, tedious experience in which reverend Gavin Reed and wife Susan Heard take over Carfax Abbey. Aha, they're from a long-descending line of vampires that in-breeding is destroying. Now the Rev needs to rev up with a blood transfusion. Meanwhile, innocent descendant Jackie Skarvellis shows up (the in-house coven wants her child to shore up the family tree) to be terrorized by an Igor-style assistant. One maid gets her eyes punctured with stakes, a man is nailed to the door of Old Soul's Church and other bloodletting abounds, and all one can do is pray it will end quickly—the film, we mean. Also known as VAMPIRE'S THIRST. Berwick Kaler, Richard Ross, Emma Jones. (Western World)

BODY COUNT (1988). Slasher thriller starring Bernie White as a nutty guy who escapes from a mental institution and kills all those he meets. Marilyn Hassett, Dick Sargent, Steven Ford, Greg Mullavey. Also called THE ELEVENTH COMMANDMENT. Produced-written-directed by Paul Leder. (Forum; MCEG)

BODY DISAPPEARS, THE (1941). Warner Bros.' answer to Universal's INVISIBLE MAN series, an out-of-sight farcical comedy that is still bubblingly refreshing as daffy professor Edward Everett Horton discovers a serum that turns Jeffrey Lynn invisible on his marriage day. In this madcap TOPPER-like spoof, Horton kids Dr. Frankenstein by exclaiming "He's alive! He's alive!" and Jane Wyman, as his daughter, was never more beautiful. Horton's "refraction-pigmentation" formula also turns laboratory monkeys invisible—resutling in the doc being incarcerated. Nonstop gags under director D. Ross Lederman. Willie Best was never funnier, no matter how racist his comedy. Herbert Anderson, Craig Stevens.

BODY DOUBLE (1984). Brian De Palma's most outrageous work—he takes narrative liberties and defies credulity to spin this strange story about a horror film actor (Craig Wasson) fascinated by a woman he spies on through a telescope. Soon Wasson is into a mystery that includes a terrifying electric drill murder and a sleazy glimpse into the L.A. underground of pornographic movie-making. De Palma is a master at suspense in the Hitchcock tradition, and uses bits from his own films, even satirizing DRESSED TO KILL in the closing credits. Gregg Henry, Melanie Griffith (as Holly, pornie queen), Deborah Shelton (as erotic, alluring Mrs. Revelle), Guy Boyd (as the cop). (Video/Laser: RCA/Columbia)

BODY IN THE WEB. See **HORRORS OF SPIDER ISLAND.**

BODY MELT (1994). During the testing of a "miracle drug," a mad doc goes berserk and subjects his town to unspeakable horrors. Gerard Kennedy, Andrew Daddo, Ian Smith. (Video/Laser: Prism)

BODY PARTS (1991). It took Hollywood 25 years to make this, but it was worth the wait, for it's a macabre horror tale establishing good characters and suspense before delivering a ghoulish climax. It was inspired by CHOICE CUTS, the award-winning 1965 novel by French writers Pierre Boileau and Thomas Narcejac, whose earlier fictions became the films DIABOLIQUE and VERTIGO. Prison psychiatrist Jeff Fahey loses his arm in an auto accident and sinister Dr. Webb (Lindsay Duncan) grafts on the arm of an executed killer. When the arm starts to control itself with acts of cruelty, Fahey discovers three others also have parts of the killer's body and are suffering similar symptons. What follows makes for one helluva thriller. The adaptation is by Norman Snider and Eric Red, who also directed with a sure hand (his own, of course.) Give an arm and leg to see this one. Brad Dourif, Peter Murnik. (Video/Laser: Paramount)

BODY SNATCHERS (1993). This third adaptation of Jack Finney's popular paranoia sci-fi novel (made twice as THE INVASION OF THE BODY SNATCHERS) keeps the essence but changes characters and settings. The "pod people" are apparently here to stay. Directed by Abel Ferrara from a script by Stuart Gordon, Dennis Paoli and Nicholas St. John. Gabrielle Anwar, Meg Tilly, Forest Whitaker, R. Lee Ermey. (Warner Bros.)

BODY SHOP (1971). Goremeister Herschell Gordon Lewis would have applauded this pastiche of his bloodworks—a direct steal of THE BRIDE OF FRANKENSTEIN in which mad doctor Don Brandon (billed in the credits as ""America's No. 1 Magician") slices up bodies of sexy women with the help of snarling hunchback assistant Gregory, who smokes cigars during the breaks and is told at one point, "You may as well clean up the mess." Without any story, or even an ending (it just suddenly stops), BODY SHOP is distinguished only by the fact that William B. Girdler, who went on to a brief career as a horror director, wrote the music and contributed to the effects. Written-produced-directed by J.G. Patterson. Jenny Driggers. (Paragon; from United as **DR. GORE**)

BODY SNATCHER, THE (1945). Val Lewton, specialist in low budget films suggesting the unseen, produced this literate adaptation of Stevenson's macabre tale in which body snatcher Boris Karloff inherits the trade of Burke and Hare, creating his own corpses when the cemetery runs dry. Directed by Mark Robson from a Philip McDonald-Carlos Keith script (Keith is a Lewton nom de plume). Henry Daniell, Bela Lugosi, Edith Atwater, Robert Clarke, Rita Corday. (RKO) (Laser: Image)

BODY SNATCHER FROM HELL. Video version of **GOKE, BODY SNATCHER FROM HELL** (VCR).

BODY STEALERS, THE (1969). Subtitled THIN AIR . . . describing what Mike St. Clair's plot went into. A sci-fi belly flop in which parachutists keep disappearing in a strange reddish mist. Agents George Sanders and Neil Connery leap into the mystery to find out why. Maurice Evans (believe it or don't) appears as an alien. What will director Gerry Levy and producer Tony Tenser think of next. Robert Flemyng, Patrick Allen.

BOG (1978). There's this Bog Lake, see, where a fisherman is dynamiting fish, only he shakes up the slumbering Incredible Slime Creature. The rubber-suited hulker kills while baffled sheriff Aldo Ray seeks answers from pathologist Gloria De Haven and doc Marshall Thompson. (He should know, he conquered THE FIEND WITHOUT A FACE.) They stare into microscopes and speculate about the creature's blood and breeding habits, since it appears he thrives on type A and loves to smooch with females—human. Finally we see the Bog Monster. Wow! Glug glggglggg . . . Directed by bogged-down Don Keeslar. Leo Gordon turns up as a bayou monster expert from the city. A witch named Adrianna has a psychic link with the monster, and in an odd bit of casting, De Haven plays her too. Thoroughly glgg glgg glgglggg. (Prism)

BOGEY MAN, THE. See **BOOGEYMAN.**

BOGGY CREEK II (1985). When word leaks out old "Boggy" is on the rampage again, terrifying folks in the South, an anthropologist leads an expedition into the bayou with computerized equipment. Meanwhile, a hermit captures Big Foot's offspring, holding him captive. This is producer-director Charles B. Pierce's soggy sequel to THE LEGEND OF BOGGY CREEK. Retitled THE BARBARIC BEAST OF BOGGY CREEK PART II. Cindy Butler, Serene Hedin. (Video/Laser: Media)

BOMBA ON PANTHER ISLAND (1950). See editions 1-3.

BONEYARD, THE (1990). Psychic Deborah Rose, aided by a detective getting long in the tooth, tracks a cult killer and the trail leads to zombie critters. Written-directed by James Cummins. Ed Nelson, Norman Fell, Phyllis Diller, Denise Young. (Prism) (Laser: Image)

BOOBY HATCH (1985). Superscientist with supererotic scientific equipment sets out to test sexual responses in this sci-fi comedy of the flesh written-directed by John Russo and Rudy Ricci. Sharon Joy Miller, Ruby Ricci, Doug Sortino. (Super)

BOOBY TRAP. See **WIRED TO KILL.**

BOOGENS, THE (1982). A mine shaft on the outskirts of Silver City, abandoned since 1912, is reopened with dynamite blasts, setting free tentacled creatures who wrap razor-sharp arms around victims and suck out the blood before engulfing the faces. Four young people caught up in the mystery (Rebecca Balding, Anne-Marie Martin, Fred McCarren, Jeff Harlan) are appealing types, adding to the film's character. Director James L. Conway allows only brief glimpses of the monsters during the climactic chase through the mine shafts, a highlight of this lightweight but enjoyable low-budgeter. (VC)

BOOGEYMAN (1980). Supernatural exploitationer kicks off as a psychostudy of an adolescent knife murderer who grows into a troubled mute. Storyline veers to a haunted mirror, pieces of which cause grisly murders a la THE OMEN. Then it segues into a poor man's EXORCIST as all hell breaks loose with a Catholic priest, flying knives, glowing windows, etc. Finally, disjointed elements refuse to jell and the film babbles to an incoherent closing. Directed by Ulli Lomell, an arty West German filmmaker who went "commercial." Suzanna Love, John Carradine, Nicholas Love. (Wizard; Magnum; Hollywood Home Entertainment) (Laser: Image)

BOOGEYMAN II (1982). This picks up where BOOGEYMAN left off with Suzanne Love (also credited with writing the script with producer Ulli Lommel) recapping the plot, which permits director Bruce Starr to use footage from the original and save a buck. But, this is twice as awful as its predecessor as a spirit with a piece of mirror embedded in his palm terrorizes half of Hollywood's aspiring young performers. Its only statement is about the filmmaking culture of Hollywood as aspirants (Shannah Hall, Ashley Dubay) gather poolside to discuss vagaries of producers. Otherwise, Ulli still seems hung up on impalings and things shoved into victims' mouths. Barely watchable, said the Elgin salesman without his clothes on. Also known as REVENGE OF THE BOOGEYMAN. Shoto von Douglas, Bob Rosenfarb. (VCII)

BOOGIE MAN WILL GET YOU, THE (1942). Did you hear the one about the traveling salesman who stopped off at the old Colonial Inn and ended up in a state of suspended animation? He (Boris Karloff) was only a mad scientist but he sure knew how to make his thunder bolt. Bless Karloff's patriotic heart—he wants to transform ordinary men into superheroes for the war effort. Director Lew Landers and writer Edwin Blum play this for light farce, as do Peter Lorre, Maxie Rosenbloom, Jeff Donnell, Don Beddoe and Larry Parks.

BOOM (1968). See editions 1-3.

BORIS & NATASHA (1992). Incredibly boring live-action version of the cartoon characters from the BULLWINKLE series. Nothing seems to be right—neither Charles Martin Smith's direction nor the performances of Dave Thomas and Sally Kelllerman in the titular roles. The incompetent spies from Pottsylvania are assigned to find a kidnapped professor who has invented a microchip that reverses time. Corey Burton's voice narrates at lightning speed, and that is about the only amusing element. A sad disappointment. Andrea Martin, Alex Rocco, Paxton Whitehead, Anthony Newley. (Academy)

B.O.R.N. (1989). Title is an acronym for Body Organ Replacement Network, a secret organization run by mad sawbones William Smith, who kidnaps women for their organs and sells them for black market transplants. Amanda Blake, in one of her last roles, helps in the search for Ross Hagen's missing daughter. P. J. Soles, Russ Tamblyn, Clint and Rance Howard. Hagen doubled as director and co-writer with Howell. (Prism)

BORN IN FLAMES (1982). Writer-director Lizzie Borden takes an axe and gives our society 40 whacks in this political satire set in the future when the U.S. Government becomes a one-party system and extremist women spearhead a revolution. Music by the Bloods and Red Crayolas. Honey, Jeanne Satterfield. (Icarus)

BORN OF FIRE (1984). Eastern mysticism and religion are the keynotes of this limited-interest tale about a flutist (Peter Firth) and his search for the Master Musician (Oh-Tee), a supernormal being planning to blow up the world. How Firth and girlfriend Suzan Crowley (an ethereal astronomer named Anoukin) will "learn to control forces of the earth" is one of many vaguenesses of this esoteric movie. A djinn runs around (it takes form as snake, scorpion, beast of prey, man or woman) and figures pop in and out to give the film an hallucinatory quality. But watching a deformed man (The Silent One, played by a deformed man, Rabil Shaban) scuttle and seeing Crowley give birth to an insect monster is unpleasant. Far East theologians will dig it the most. Directed by Jamil Dehlavi. (Vidmark) (Laser: Image)

BORROWER, THE (1989). John McNaughton, director of HENRY: PORTRAIT OF A SERIAL KILLER, combines his penchant for chilling horror with a sci-fi theme to spin this bizarre tale about a buglike creature from another planet that is sentenced to exile to Earth, the worst place in the Universe. The alien has been given a human body but keeps losing his head, so he rips off the head of another human and sticks it atop his bloody torso, absorbing that person's pesonality (???) So the alien goes from being Tom Towles to Anthony Fargas to . . . meanwhile, hardboiled cop Rae Dawn Chong and her more sensitive partner Don Gordon are on the thing's trail. THE BORROWER is occasionally fun, frequently perverse and gallops toward a double twist-ending. Neil Giumtoli, Pam Gordon. (Video/Laser: Cannon)

BORROWER: DON'T LOSE YOUR HEAD OVER HIM

BORROWERS, THE (1973). Quaint story of a miniature family living under the floorboards of a Victorian house, leading a cozy life by "borrowing" items from normal-size people. Adapted from a Mary Norton book. Directed by William C. Miller. Eddie Albert, Tammy Grimes.

BORROWERS, THE (1993). British adaptation of Mary Norton's fantasy novels about a family of people only six inches high living under the floorboards of a normal family is tediously executed, capturing little of the story's effects possibilities. Adapted by Richard Carpenter, directed by John Henderson. Ian Holm, Penelope Wilton, Rebecca Callard. (Turner)

BOURBON STREET SHADOWS. See **INVISIBLE AVENGER.**

BOWERY AT MIDNIGHT (1942). Lowbrow Monogram potboiler runs out of steam even with Bela Lugosi as the star. In a dual role (as Professor Brenner and as Karl Wagner), Lugosi deposits the victims of his murderous sprees in his basement. What wretched behavior—and what a creaky old Sam Katzman movie. Directed by Wallace Fox. John Archer, Tom Neal, Wanda McKay, Dave O'Brien. (Sinister/C; Filmfax; Nostalgia; from Admit One with **DICK TRACY VS. CUEBALL**)

BOWERY BOYS MEET THE MONSTERS, THE (1954). Late-in-life attempt by Leo Gorcey, Huntz Hall and the gang to recapture their goofy encounters with supernatural/sci-fi creatures (a la SPOOKS RUN WILD). In this menagerie of mirthy monsters, the guys fall prey to mad doc John Dehner, whose mansion contains a clumsy robot, Gorgog; sweet old lady Ellen Corby who nourishes a man-eating plant; a formula that turns men into hairy beings; a femme fatale in the tradition of Morticia (Laura Mason); a Lurch-like butler, "Gruesome" Grisham; and a gorilla with an IQ higher than Gorcey and Hall combined. Written by Elwood Ullman and Edward Bernds, who also directed.

BOXING HELENA (1993). Jennifer Chambers Lynch, daughter of film maker David Lynch, made an auspicious debut as writer-director with this psychological horror tale—an uncompromising study into aberrant human behavior and sexual obsession. Doctor Julian Sands has a thing for the town slut (Sherilyn Fenn, who plays her beautiful, self-indulgent bitch to perfection) and turns her into a captive after an accident leaves her without arms and legs. This macabre joke becomes grounds for a study of sexual behavior as Lynch examines each character's possessive nature. There's no blood or gore; it's the exploration of things hidden in the darkness of man's subconscious that makes this a memorable study. Kurtwood Smith, Bill Paxton. (Orion)

BOWERY TO BAGDAD (1955). See editions 1-3.

BOX OF DELIGHTS, THE (1984). British TV-movie based on John Masefield's fantasy-adventure about an English youth projected into bizarre adventures via a small box that allows him to fly, makes him into an incredibly shrunken fair-haired lad and sends him into the past. An evil vicar and his henchmen (who occasionally turn into wolves) are the adversaries. Live action is blended with effects and animation. The strong British flavor combined with limited production values may hamper American enjoyment. Directed by Renny Rye. Devon Stanfield, Patrick Troughton. (Video: Facets Video)

BOY AND HIS DOG, A (1975). Harlan Ellison's prize-winning novella about life after nuclear holocaust, faithfully adapted by producer-director L.Q. Jones and assistant producer Alvy Moore. In 2024, young Vic (Don Johnson) roves the devastated surface searching for food and encountering mutant bands. His canine companion, Blood, is capable of ESP and has a radar-like mind. Love among the ruins with beautiful Susanne Benton leads Vic to Down Under, a subterranean society where the males are sterile and Vic is needed to inseminate the gals. Less successful once Up Above is left behind, but still an engrossing sci-fi experiment. Jason Robards, Charles McGraw, Alvy Moore. (Media; Front Row Entertainment; Critics' Choice) (Laser: Image)

BOY AND THE PIRATES, THE (1960). See editions 1-3.

BOY FROM ANDROMEDA, THE (1991). Insufferable Australian TV-movie for kids in which a three-fingered, ten-year-old E.T. child from another star system interreacts with children on Earth. With such poor special effects, this borders on the unwatchable. Directed by Wayne Tourell. Katrina Hobbs, Jane Cresswell, Fiona Kay.

BOY GOD (1986). Lackluster Filipino production for juveniles, but with such poor effects today's young will sneer at it with adults. Nino Muhlach portrays a youngster blessed with Immortality and superhero powers, who goes on a quest to free his parents from a purgatory in which they are doing pentence. He meets bearded guy Vulcan (resembling Old Shazam from Captain Marvel) and fights vampire and lizard men (i.e., actors in ill-fitting animal skins) in poorly choreographed battles. Dreary stuff, dreadfully dubbed. Directed by J. Erastheo Navoa. Jimi Melendrez, Isabel Rivas. (Video City)

BOYS FROM BRAZIL, THE (1978). From the bestseller by Ira Levin, who delivered ROSEMARY'S BABY and married us to THE STEPFORD WIVES. The clever plot deals with a Nazi DNA cloning scheme by master German war criminal Dr. Mengele, played unevenly by Gregory Peck. Hot on Mengeles' trail, trying to solve a mystery surrounding 94 Hitler clones, is Jewish avenger Lieberman, played with dogged weariness by Laurence Olivier. Franklin J. Schaffner directed. Lilli Palmer, James Mason, Uta Hagen, Michael Gough, John Dehner, Denholm Elliott. (Video/Laser: Fox)

BOYS FROM BROOKLYN, THE. Video version of **BELA LUGOSI MEETS A BROOKLYN GORILLA.**

BOY WHO COULD FLY, THE (1986). The resourcefulness of the human spirit, and the power of positive thought, are the themes of this moving drama written-directed by Nick Castle, best known for LAST STARFIGHTER. A mute lad, who has withdrawn into himself and dreams of flying, is befriended by a new family next door undergoing its share of trauma. The small-town ambience, Castle's ability to parody movie form, a collection of benevolent characters, and a lilting musical score enhance this fantasy. Lucy Deakins, Jay Underwood, Bonnie Bedelia, Fred Savage, Colleen Dewhurst, Fred Gwynne. (Warner Bros.) (Laser: HBO)

BOY WHO CRIED WEREWOLF, THE (1973). Director Nathan Juran and actor Kerwin Mathews teamed for this lycanthropic tale, but the winning combination that made THE SEVENTH VOYAGE OF SINBAD a hit is nowhere in evidence. Mathews is bitten by a werewolf and turns into same, threatening the life of his son. Bob Homel's script is a rehash of wolf man cliches. Elaine Devry, Robert J. Wilke, Jack Lucas, Paul Baxley.

BOY WHO TURNED YELLOW, THE (1972). An obscure British film made by the team of director Michael Powell and producer Emeric Pressburger about an English youth who turns yellow and seeks his pet mouse at the Tower of London. Mark Dightam, Robert Eddison.

BOY WITH GREEN HAIR, THE (1948). Joseph Losey, who was later blacklisted, directed this anti-war allegory about orphan Dean Stockwell who wakes up one morning to find he has green hair. He is ostracized by his small community except for a band of war orphans (spirits of the dead) who tell him how to put his uniqueness to good use. Gentle, thoughtful, underrated film. Robert Ryan, Pat O'Brien, Barbara Hale, Dwayne Hickman, Russ Tamblyn, Regis Toomey, Walter Catlett. (Nostalgia Merchant) (Laser: Image)

BRAIN, THE (1962). Variation on Curt Siodmak's DONOVAN'S BRAIN: Well-meaning doctor Peter Van Eyck keeps alive the brain of a sadistic millionaire who gradually compels the doctor to carry out his evil bidding. This German/British co-production effectively makes the old material work. Directed by Freddie Francis. Anne Heywood, Cecil Parker, Bernard Lee, Miles Malleson. Also known as VENGEANCE. (Media; Monterey; Nostalgia; Sinister/C; S/Weird; Filmfax)

BRAIN, THE (1971). Sleazy, amateurish mad doctor clunker with Kent Taylor transplanting the brain of a Middle East ruler into the body of Gor, a brute with a putty face who took lessons at the Tor Johnson Acting School. Poor are the performances and wretched are the camera work and music score. Even the sound stinks. There's a dwarf (the doc's assistant), a blond femme (Vicki Volante) and a doltish hero (Grant Williams). Meanwhile, Reed Hadley's voice keeps coming out of Gor's mouth until the brain is switched to Hadley's body. Difficult stuff to endure. Filipino production, directed by Al Adamson. Also called BRAIN OF BLOOD and THE CREATURE'S REVENGE. (Star Classics; New Horizon)

BRAIN, THE (1988). David Gale, whose "severed" head was an unforgettable element in RE-ANIMATOR, returns as another crazed doctor, a TV show host using airwaves to brainwash viewers. In his lab is a giant head which keeps gnashing its teeth and waving its tail. Somehow this oversized cranium hypnotizes everyone. A paranoia plot is activated when Tom Breznahan and Cyndy Preston are involved with Blake's Psychological Research Institute. While this comments on misuse of TV, and our fear of authority, Barry Pearson's script relies too much on ALIEN cliches. Director Edward Hunt is laden with dreary Canadian locations. Watch for Gale's head in a homage to RE-ANIMATOR. (IVE) (Laser: Image)

BRAIN DAMAGE (1988). Writer-director Frank Henenlotter, mastermind behind BASKET CASE, offers another cult favorite with funky sets and bizarre characters. The monster is Aylmer ("all inspiring famous one"), a thick worm-like thing with teeth and hooks. The hooks he sinks into Rick Herbst's neck, giving his brain a jolt of psychedelic goodies, "color, music and euphoria." Aylmer enjoys boring into your brain and eating it up. For those who think deep, there's a penis fixation to the phallic-looking Aylmer, with sexual references as Aylmer shoots "juice" to the youth. And there's a prostitute who remarks "you've got a monster in there" before undoing Herbst's zipper and coming face to face with Aylmer. The theme comments on our drug culture and dependence on "monsters" such as cocaine and heroin. Gordon MacDonald, Theo Barnes, Lucille Saint-Peters. One subway scene pays homage to BASKET CASE with Kevin Van Hentenryck in a cameo. (Paramount)

BRAIN DAMAGE. See **BRAIN, THE (1971).**

BRAIN DEAD (1989). Director Adam Simon found an unproduced 1963 Richard Beaumont script and updated it. Result: An instant video movie. In a lab of jars filled with brains, neurologist Bill Pullman studies the aberrations of the mind, in particular a mad mathematician played by Bud Cort. There are dreams within dreams within nightmares within fantasies as this convoluted, twisted pretzel

"Take these bodies down to the laboratory at headquarters. I gotta examine 'em to find out who drilled those holes in their skulls. It probably was some maniac who thought he was cracking a safe."

—Benny the dumb cop in **THE BRAINIAC.**

'BRAM STOKER'S DRACULA': FRANCIS FORD COPPOLA'S VERSION STARS GARY OLDMAN (LEFT AND FAR RIGHT) IN VARIOUS GUISES AS THE TRANSYLVANIAN COUNT; WINONA RYDER (CENTER) IS MINA MURRAY

of a movie unfolds in the craziest way. Bill Paxton, Nicholas Pryor, Patricia Charbonneau, George Kennedy. (MGM/UA)

BRAINDEAD. Theatrical title of **DEAD ALIVE.**

BRAIN EATERS, THE (1958). This exemplifies the atomic-era paranoia genre, with director Bruno Vesota creating a bleak world through tilted camera angles and black-and-white photography. Although he stages the action sequences stiltedly, a semi-documentary effect emerges. From inner earth comes small crawling parasites that bore into victims' necks, taking over their brains. The community of Riverdale faces the onslaught with Ed Nelson (who produced the film) heading the scientific investigators. Leonard Nimoy (billed as "Nemoy") plays an old man in a robe but the script by Gordon Urquhart (based on Robert Heinlein's PUPPET MASTERS) muddles up what he's doing there. Alan Frost, Jack Hill. (Columbia TriStar; Nostalgia; Cinemacabre)

BRAIN FROM PLANET AROUS, THE (1956). Delightfully campy sci-fi schlocker with John Agar as a nuclear scientist whose head is invaded by Gor, a floating brain that looks like a huge golf ball with half moons for eyeballs. Gor plans to take over Earth but Val, a good-brain "golf ball" from Arous, hides in a dog's head and waits to strike at Gor's "fissure of Orlando," which when injured will render Gor useless. Does one dare call Ray Buffum's script brainless? This "hot blast of gamma" will send you into convulsions of laughter or bore you to tears with the incompetence of Nathan Hertz's direction. Joyce Meadows plays Agar's long-suffering wife. Make-up by Jack Pierce. (Cinemamacabre; Interglobal; Rhino; S/Weird; Filmfax) (Laser: Image)

BRAINIAC, THE (1961). He munched on brains, this wretched-smelling abomination who, 300 years ago, was a respectable baron, until he was burned at the stake by the Spanish Inquisition. He returns to Earth aboard a meteor (?!) in the shape of a hairy monster with long snout, pincer-like hands and droopy forked tongue (?!), thirsting for vengeance. Watch out as that tongue slurps up your intellect. It came from Mexico but it refused to die and it comes back to haunt us on The Late Show. An Abel Salazar production (he also appears in the cast) directed with complete ineptitude by Chano Urueta. German Robles, Rene Cardona. A U.S. version was prepared by K. Murray Gordon. (Hollywood Home Theater; Filmfax; Sinister/C; Dark Dreams; S/Weird)

BRAIN MACHINE, THE (1956). Taut, well-acted British thriller with minor fantasy overtones. An apparatus that reads psychotic brain waves sets off a night of terror that involves a woman being taken hostage by a drug smuggler. British film noir directed by Ken Hughes. Patrick Barr, Elizabeth Allen.

BRAIN MACHINE, THE (1972). Alternate video version of **GREY MATTER** (Paragon).

BRAIN OF BLOOD. Alternate video version of **BRAIN, THE (1971)** (Magnum; Regal).

BRAINSCAN (1994). Unusually dark and intense horror film about a young computer user (Edward Furlong), recently scarred in a car accident and living alone, who becomes trapped in the nightmarish world of a new computer game (Brainscan), where he commits a murder and is pursued by a strange cop (Frank Langella). Out of the computer pops The Trickster (T. Ryder Smith), a vile character that represents Furlong's uglier side. This has more depth of character than most horror films thanks to director John Flynn. Amy Hargreaves, Jamie Marsh.

BRAIN 17 (1985). A robot, asked by a young boy to save the world, obeys the Asimov Law of Robots: Thou shalt save the world from evil forces. (FHE)

BRAINSNATCHER, THE. See **MAN WHO LIVED AGAIN, THE.**

BRAINSTORM (1983). Offbeat sci-fi thriller distinguished by the visuals of director Douglas Trumbull, whose effects excelled in Kubrick's 2001: A SPACE ODYSSEY. Scientists Christopher Walken and Louise Fletcher develop a sensory gadget that records thoughts and emotions onto tape and plays them back via a headpiece, so the receiver undergoes an identical experience. The research sequences are fascinating, with implications that the device allows one to pass to a higher plane of being through a recording of the death experience. Benevolent research director Cliff Robertson gives in to clandestine military forces (who want the device for war), and Walken fights to keep the system out of the wrong hands. The climax is an abstract neoreligious death sequence, but what Trumbull intended is as nebulous as the heavens in which it is set. BRAINSTORM valiantly tries to reach a metaphysical level, but gets locked out of the Pearly Gates. Joe Dorsey, Alan Fudge, Jordan Christopher. Natalie Wood drowned before finishing her role. (Video/Laser: MGM/UA)

BRAINSUCKER, THE (1988). A murderer posing as a psychiatrist named Dr. Suck uses a corkscrew to knock off his victims in this horror corker from writer-director Herb Robins (THE WORM EATERS). Shot in Santa Fe, New Mexico. Jonathan Middleman. (Raedon)

BRAIN THAT WOULDN'T DIE, THE (1959). Transplanted plot about transplanted brains is lifted from brainless horror flicks that should have died. Jason Evers is your run-of-the-slab scientist keeping his fiance's head alive after her decapitation in a car crash. Now his only problem is to find a female body that turns him on. Once the head is attached, he can proceed with wedding plans. Yucky stuff, as lowbrow as Z movies get, with an awful scene where a monster in a closet yanks a man's arm from its socket. Joseph Green wrote-directed this cheapie which has developed a cult following among weirdos. Virginia Leith, Adele Lamont. (Warner; Rhino; Filmfax; S/Weird; Sinister/C offers an unedited version)

BRAIN TWISTERS (1991). A conspiracy is afoot within a software company to carry out mind-control experiments on its buyers through computer games. Written-directed by Jerry Sangiuliano. Terry Londeree, Farrah Forke, Joe Lombardo.

BRAINWAVES (1982). German writer-producer-director Ulli Lommel helmed this fascinating thriller: Accident victim Suzanne Love, suffering brain damage, is fed (via computer) the thought impulses from a brain donated to a lab run by strange Dr. Clavius (Tony Curtis). While the impulses are designed to return her to normal, she has memories of a murdered woman. How Love and Keir Dullea track down the murderer and deal with the psychological terrors make for an unusual plot. Curtis has an odd role as hoarse-voiced Clavius. Vera Miles, Percy Rodrigues, Paul Willson. (Embassy; Sultan)

BRAM STOKER'S DRACULA (1992). Francis Ford Coppola cleverly concocted an entertainment designed for the art crowd, his own cult followers and aficionados of traditional vampire movies. This opulent, imaginative version of Stoker's classic novel unabashedly plunges into self-indulgence on occasion, yet producer-director Coppola maintains a sure experimental hand. Co-produced by Michael Apted and Robert O'Connor, it was written by James V. Hart and closely follows Stoker's novel, evolving its own visual style and moods. Gary Oldman is superb in the title role, appearing in various guises and special make-ups as he matures from Vlad the Impaler in a surrealistic sequence (a highpoint of many highpoints) to a centuries-old Dracula to a chilling gargoyle-like version. It's a perverse love story as Oldman's Dracula pursues Winona Ryder's Mina; their "romance" soars to new heights of screen erotica in this movie for the senses. Anthony Hopkins is an eccentric Von Helsing, Keanu Reeves is Jonathan Harker, Richard E. Grant is Dr. Jack Seward, Tom Waits is Renfield. (Video: Columbia TriStar) (Laser: Voyager)

BRASS BOTTLE, THE (1964). Unfunny farce with Tony Randall, Burl Ives Barbara Eden and Edward Andrews struggling with an inept plot (by Oscar Brodney) about a down-at-the-heels architect who buys a bottle with a genie. If you had three wishes, one would be never to see this movie. Directed by Harry Keller.

BRAVE NEW WORLD (1980). TV adaptation of Aldous Huxley's classic premonition of things to come, dire visions of man's dehumanization, is unrealized here. The good cast (Keir Dullea, Bud Cort, Ron O'Neal, Kristoffer Tabori, Julie Cobb) cannot cope with Doran William Cannon's adaptation. Directed by Burt Brinkerhoff.

BRAVESTARR (1988). American cowboy and supernatural sidekick Tex Hex are asssigned to rescue the planet of New Texas from a robot-monster invasion in this animated feature directed by Tom Tataranowicz. Voices: Charles Adler, Susan Blu, Pat Fraley. (Celebrity)

BRAZIL (1986). Prepare for two hours of the bizarre in this high-tech, high-energy surrealistic fantasy set in a futuristic quasidictatorship, where everything is askew in a Monty Python way, thanks to writer-director Terry Gilliam. Jonathan Pryce, as a worker in the Ministry of Information, plots against a bumbling "Big Brother" government in hilarious ways and fantasizes himself as a warrior always rescuing a blonde from a giant samurai. Imaginative and free-wheeling, sometimes to the detriment of story and character: It's difficult to relate to people who act so unpredictably. The sets and model work are fabulous, but one wishes Gilliam had restrained his indulgencies to tell a more impactful narrative. Don't miss it, however. Robert De Niro assists as a furnace repairman acting as a terrorist-commando against the regime. Ian Richardson, Kim Greist, Bob Hoskins, Michael Palin. (Video/Laser: MCA)

BREAKDOWN. See **FREEWAY MANIAC.**

BREAKFAST AT MANCHESTER MORGUE. See **DON'T OPEN THE WINDOW.**

BREAKFAST OF ALIENS (1989). Milquetoast Vic Dunlop swallows a miniature alien and is taken over by the E.T. force within him. It's enough to put a lump in your throat. Written by Dunlop (a stand-up comedian) and co-producer/director David Lee Miller. Indy Shriner, John Hazelwood, Steve Franken. (Hemdale)

BREAKFAST WITH THE DEAD. See **DON'T OPEN THE WINDOW.**

BREEDERS (1986). Uneven attempt to blend visual sci-fi with softcore sex, the latter cheapening an idea better played without titillation. Manhattan virgins are impregnated by an other-world beast to the puzzlement of doctor Teresa Farley and cop Lance Lewman. They discover the breeding grounds beneath the hospital, where babes drench themselves in a tub of alien sperm. Effects are good but director-writer Tim Kincaid goes wrong in casting the virgins against type. There isn't a single one that could pass the test—these women have been around! Ed French, a doctor under the alien's spell, designed the effects. (Wizard; Vestron)

BRENDA STARR (1976). Unsold TV-pilot features Dale Messick's comic strip reporter (Jill St. John) flying all over the world for her paper, The Flash. Tabi Cooper is Hank O'Hare, her stalwart companion, and Sorrell Booke is Livwright, her bellowing editor who assigns them to investigate a voodoo cult in Brazil. The body of Jill is wonderful to look at—if only the finished product from director Mel Stuart was as well rounded. Barbara Luna, Torin Thatcher, Victor Buono, Jed Allan.

BRENDA STARR (1992). Campy, flashy and fun, this adaptation of Dale Messick's comic strip stars Brooke Shields as the perky, well-dressed, ultra-coiffured, sparkling reporter for the Flash. At first she's just a drawing by her nerdball creator (Tom Peck) but she turns to flesh and blood when he enters her post-World War II adventures and follows her to South America to find an ex-Nazi (Henry Gibson) and his formula for a new aviation fuel. Shields is always vivacious and a delight to behold, climbing, running and jumping in her chic outfits and showing off her lovely legs. Timothy Dalton is memorable as the mysterious adventurer Basil St. John, the man with the black eyepatch always turning up to rescue her and woo her. Ultimately it is the flashy style of Shields and director Robert Ellis Miller (who is in the cast) that makes this a winner. Diana Scarwid, Jeffrey Tambor, June Cable, Tom Aldredge. In cameos are Charles Durning (as Starr's editor, Livwright), Ed Nelson as President Truman and Eddie Albert as a police chief. Director of photography was Freddie Francis. Messick's strip was first adapted into a 1945 serial, then became a TV-movie for Jill St. John in 1976. (Columbia TriStar)

BREWSTER McCLOUD (1971). M*A*S*H director Robert Altman tackled this difficult-to-grasp fantasy about a youth (Bud Cort) who wants to fly and goes about achieving his lofty task in the Houston Astrodome with the help of sexy bird woman Sally Kellerman. Parodies of TV cops and arrows of outrage fired at contemporary standards never quite satisfyingly jell in this allegorical film that goes off in too many directions. Nice try, Robert, but no wings. Michael Murphy, Stacy Keach, William Windom, Shelley Duvall, Margaret Hamilton. (MGM/UA)

BRICK BRADFORD (1947). Fifteen-chapter Columbia serial based on the adventure comic strip by William Ritt and Clarence Gray, starring Kane Richmond as an adventurer who travels to the moon through a "crystal door" in an effort to stop madman Charles Quigley from using the Interceptor Ray, a new guided missile that could destroy Earth. Directed by Spencer Gordon Bennet, produced by schlockmeister Sam Katzman. Rick Vallin, Linda Johnson, John Merton, Pierre Watkin.

BRIDE, THE (1985). Excellent variation on Shelley's FRANKENSTEIN, beginning where THE BRIDE OF FRANKENSTEIN left off and reminiscent of Hammer's gothic thrillers. After a rousing opening as lightning bolts bring a woman to life in the Baron's lab, this follows the Baron (played sensitively by Sting) teaching worldly ways to the bride-to-be; and the Monster (Clancy Brown, wearing little make-up and emphasizing the emotional rather than physical) joining a dwarf circus performer (David Rappaport) on the road to Budapest to learn he must "follow your heart." A fresh visualization of the parable aspects of Shelley's book, handsomely directed by Franc Roddam. Jennifer Beal, as the Bride, develops into an independent woman. Anthony Higgins, Geraldine Page. (Fox) (Laser: RCA/Columbia)

BRIDE AND THE BEAST (1960). "Nightmare from the jungle! A human bride, enslaved victim of gargantuan HORROR!" But that's the ad; the movie is never as exciting. Hunter Lance Fuller decides an African safari is what wife Charlotte Austin needs—until she's stolen away by an ape. Produced-directed by Adrian Weiss; scripted by Edward D. Wood Jr., who gave us PLAN 9 FROM OUTER SPACE. Johnny Roth, Stevel Calvert. (Weiss Global; Admit One)

BRIDE OF FENGRIFFEN. See **AND NOW THE SCREAMING STARTS.**

BRIDE OF FRANKENSTEIN, THE (1935). James Whale's sequel to FRANKENSTEIN is a masterpiece of macabre humor and Gothic horror. Colin Clive is again at work in the lab as the ambitious, misguided doctor resurrecting the dead and seeking to create a "mate" for The Monster. A delightful subplot involves the miniaturization of beings by the glint-eyed Dr. Pretorious (Ernest Thesiger), and there's the meeting between the Monster and the blind beggar, spoofed so well in YOUNG FRANKENSTEIN. Boris Karloff re-creates his shambling entity of evil and pathos, while Elsa Lanchester doubles as the bride and Mary Wollstonecraft Shelley. Valerie Hobson, Dwight Frye, John Carradine, Una O'Connor, Billy Barty. Music by Franz Waxman. (Video/Laser: MCA)

BRIDE OF RE-ANIMATOR (1989). Although not as impactful as Stuart Gordon's trend-setting RE-ANIMATOR, this sequel is worth seeing for its surreal, nightmarish climax. Dr. Herbert West (Jeffrey Combs), the creation of H. P. Lovecraft, is back with his green serum that gives life to dead tissue. It's eight months later at Miskatonic Medical School and Dr. West joins Dr. Cain (Bruce Abbott) to graft the head of Cain's dead lover onto various body parts: the feet of a ballet dancer, the legs of a prostitute, the womb of a virgin, the hand of a sculptress, another hand of a murderess, and the arms of a lawyer. Meanwhile, the head of Dr. Hill (David Gale) returns to life, zombie creatures break loose and a cop with a severed hand runs rampant. It's one helluva horror scene when these components merge. Brian Yuzna produced-directed the Woody Keith/Rick Fry script. Grand effects work by David Allen, the K.N.B. EFX Group and Screaming Mad George. Claude Earl Jones, Fabiana Udenio (as the thankless, jeopardized love interest), Kathleen Kinmont (as the Bride), Mel Stewart. (Live) (Laser: Image)

BRIDE OF THE GORILLA (1951). Low budgeter set on a jungle plantation where witch Giselle Werbisek uses leaves of the "plant of evil" to turn foreman Raymond Burr into a "sukaras," a mythical animal assuming sundry shapes. Burr turns into a standard Hollywood gorilla—or is the metamorphosis only in his mind? This subtlety by writer-director Curt Siodmak doesn't belong in this cheap monster thriller, reminscient of 1940s' Universal in style and ambience. Barbara Payton is the voluptuous wife, Lon Chaney the superstitious commissioner, Tom Powers the wise doctor and Woody Strode a policeman. (Sinister/C; S/Weird; Filmfax)

BRIDE OF THE MONSTER (1955). Edward D. Wood Jr. "classic," originally BRIDE OF THE ATOM, revealing a Bela Lugosi ravaged by drugs and alcohol. The plot (Alex Gordon helped Wood with the concept) has Lugosi creating a race of atomic supermen, without a lot of luck, and feeding victims to a swamp monster that looks like half of an octopus. Tor Johnson, the obligatory brainless brute, makes a grab for Lugosi in one of the most pathetic fights ever photographed. And dig those amateurs, Tony McCoy and Loretta King. You have to see it to believe it. (Video Yesteryear; Sinister/C; Filmfax)

BRIDES OF BLOOD. See **BRIDES OF THE BEAST.**

BRIDES OF DRACULA (1960). After HORROR OF DRACULA, Christopher Lee refused to play the caped count for a few years, so David Peel assumed the role. Peter Cushing returns as Dr. Van Helsing, the "exorcist" of Transylvania. This excellent Hammer film features silver chains, holy water and a strangely formed "cross" which repels the handsome Peel. Terence Fisher directed using heavy Freudian symbolism. Anthony Hinds produced; Jimmy Sangster cowrote. Martita Hunt, Yvonne Monlaur, Freda Jackson. (Video/Laser: MCA)

BRIDES OF DR. JEKYLL. See **DR. ORLOFF'S MONSTER.**

BRIDES OF FU MANCHU, THE (1966). In this sequel to THE FACE OF FU MANCHU, the insidious, inscrutable Asian mastermind (Christopher Lee) has another incredible scheme—to kidnap sexy daughters of government officials and throw the world into political chaos. Out to thwart the scheme is Nayland Smith (Douglas Wilmer) of The Yard. Lee also has a new Death Ray. Directed by Don Sharp, who co-scripted with Harry Alan Towers, this was followed by THE VENGEANCE OF FU MANCHU. Howard Marion-Crawford, Burt Kwouk, Tsai Chin, Marie Versini, Rupert Davies.

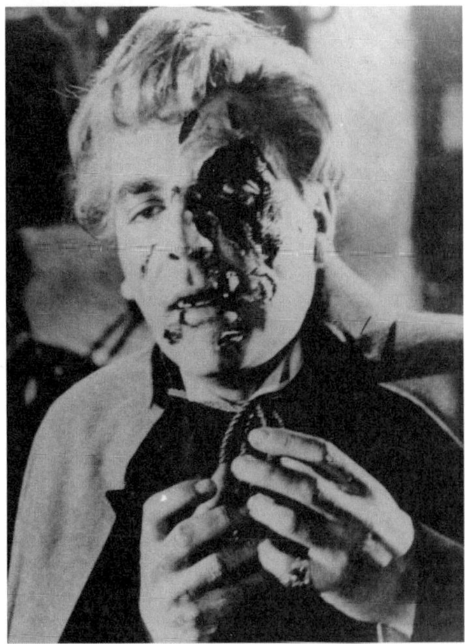

DAVID PEEL IN 'BRIDES OF DRACULA'

BRIDES OF THE BEAST (1968). First in the "Blood Island" Filipino series produced by Eddie Romero, and also known as BRIDES OF BLOOD. Mad doctor Kent Taylor uses radiation to turn the living into monsters that love to munch on normal folk. Romero was so overcome as director, he hired Gerrardo de Leon to help him direct the traffic. John Ashley is the hero, Beverly Hills and Eva Darren the screaming heroines. (Regal)

BRIDES WORE BLOOD, THE (1972). Lackluster vampire flop in which not even the fangs look genuine. Produced in Florida by director Robert R. Favorite, this spins the Legend of the DeLorca Family Curse. In order to make the curse work, old man De Lorca lures four beauties to his mansion. Pedantic and productionless, BRIDES unfolds at a plodding pace, never arousing interest, no matter how much gibberish from Madame Van Kirst, psychic medium, or "conjurations" by De Lorca. Dolores Heiser, Chuck Faulkner, Jan Sherman. (Regal; New Horizon; from Magnum as **BLOOD BRIDE**)

BRIDGE ACROSS TIME (1985). The London Bridge—transported to Lake Havasu, Arizona, and reconstructed there stone by stone—is the showpieçe for this TV-movie in which Jack the Ripper reappears to murder women in his inimitable style. William F. Nolan's teleplay, though an inspired idea, is predictable and follows the standard cat-and-mouse games of stalked victims, baffled police, town politicians wanting to cover up lest tourism decline, etc. E. W. Swackhamer directs with a constant eye on the bridge. It's not bad, just ordinary. David Hasselhoff, Randolph Mantooth, Clu Gulager, Lindsay Bloom, Rose Marie, Adrienne Barbeau. Also known as ARIZONA RIPPER and on video from Fries as **TERROR AT LONDON BRIDGE.**

.**BRIGADOON (1954).** The dance team of Gene Kelly and Cyd Charisse brings to life Lerner and Loewe's Broadway musical as discoverers of a Scottish village which only appears every hundred years. An exciting blend of fantasy and choreography, with a great score. Directed by MGM's master of musicals, Vincent Minnelli, with superb photography by Joseph Ruttenberg. Elaine Stewart, Jimmy Thompson, Barry Jones, Albert Sharpe. (Video/Laser: MGM/UA)

BRIGHTON STRANGLER, THE (1944). Actor John Loder is so obsessed with his role as a strangler in a British stage hit that a concussion during the London Blitz deludes makes him into thinking he's the murderer he's playing. He takes the train to Brighton to carry out a murder, but the girl he meets, June Duprez, tries to help him sort out his confusion . . . right up to the twist ending. Similar to the 1947 Academy-Award winner, A DOUBLE LIFE, but not as classy. Max Nosseck directed. Ian Wolfe, Miles Mander, Rose Hobart, Gilbert Emery. (On a "double bill" from RKO with **BEFORE DAWN**)

BRING ME THE VAMPIRE (1961). Mexican thriller about heirs to a fortune gathering in haunted Black Castle for the night. What they don't know is, the drafty corridors are haunted by a vampire. Made as three separate episodes. Directed by Alfredo E. Crevena. Maria Eugenia San Martin, Hector Godoy, Mantequilla, Carlos Riquelme. (S/Weird; Sinister/C; Movies Unlimited)

BRITANNIA HOSPITAL (1983). Bizarre British film wavering between satire and outrageous black comedy, well directed by Lindsay Anderson. While it makes sport of English institutions, David Sherwin's script has a universality. The setting is a London hospital undergoing turmoil on the day Her Royal Highness visits. A subplot involves a mad doctor who pieces together a Frankenstein Monster from assorted body organs and limbs. When the Creature is brought to life and bites the hand of the doctor that fed it life, this is gruesome and requires strong stomachs. There's also a giant brain called Genesis controlling the administrators. The most irreverent scene has police clubbing rioters while H.R.H. listens to "God Save the Queen." Leonard Rossiter, Malcolm McDowell, Mark Hamill, Alan Bates. (HBO)

BRONX EXECUTIONER (1989). Cyborg killers on a rampage (aren't those mean old cyborg killers always?) in the futuristic Manhattan you loved so much in ESCAPE FROM NEW YORK. Woody Strode, Margie Newton, Chuck Valenti. Directed by Bob Collins. (Cannon)

BRONX WARRIORS. See **1990: BRONX WARRIORS.**

BROOD, THE (1979). Disturbing tale from Canada's "king of horror," David Cronenberg, depicting a therapy called psychoplasmics in which the patient changes cell structure through internal anger. Doctor Oliver Reed experiments with Samantha Eggar, who produces a womb-like sac on her tummy and gives birth to a brood of deformed, monstrous dwarves who enjoy hammering innocent people to death. In one sickening sequence, Samantha breaks open the membrane of her sac, removes a malshaped human form and licks away the blood. An intriguing idea, but blatantly offensive. Art Hindle, Cindy Hinds, Susan Hogan, Henry Beckerman, Nuala Fitxgerald. (Embassy) (Laser: Image)

BROTHER FROM ANOTHER PLANET, THE (1984). A thoughtful, esoteric sci-fier, so satiric in its overview of humans that it becomes precious. Joe Morton portrays a black humanoid alien with three-toed feet and an ability to touch anything broken and make it work. The Brother, stranded on Earth, never speaks during his adventures in Harlem, object lessons in human behavior. Trailing the alien are two interstellar cops. Writer-director John Sayles (one of the aliens) plays them for laughs. A low-budget experimental film, gritty yet charming, with Morton's mimed performance a tour de force. Darryl Edwards, Steve James. (Key)

BROTHER FUTURE (1991). Rapper Phill Lelas of modern Detroit is transported through time to Charleston, 1822, awaking to find himself in the midst of a slave revolt. This dramatized history lesson, with no scientific explanation of how Lelas travels through time, shapes into a serious drama with only mild comedic touches when Lelas introduces modern rap lingo to fellow slaves. Based on a true incident, BROTHER FUTURE is mildly interesting with good performances by Lelas, Carl Lumbly, Moses Gunn and Frank Converse. Written-directed by Roy Campanella II.

BROTHERHOOD OF SATAN, THE (1971). Produced by Alvy Moore and L.Q. Jones, and directed by Bernard McEveety, this low-budget supernatural thriller is well photographed and acted by Struther Martin (as the leader of a Satanic cult), with Moore and Jones also in the cast. A coven in a Southwestern town needs children to feed the Devil during sacrificial offerings. William Welch's script has many chilling moments as well as one eerie dream sequence. Charles Bateman, Anna Capri. (RCA/Columbia; Goodtimes) (Laser: Image)

STROTHER MARTIN

BROTHERHOOD OF THE BELL, THE (1970). See editions 1-3.

BROTHER JOHN (1972). Angelic being descends to Earth to see if we're worth saving, decides we're terribly racist—and since the angel is Sidney Poitier, who's to say he isn't right? TV-movie directed by James Goldstone, written by Ernest Kinoy. Will Geer, Bradford Dillman, Beverly Todd, Paul Winfield. (RCA/Columbia)

BRUCE GENTRY—DAREDEVIL OF THE SKIES (1949). A remote-controlled flying disc of explosive powers is the deadly weapon of The Recorder, an enemy agent who learns it isn't easy to be a dastard when daredevil pilot Bruce Gentry is around. Gentry, created for the comics by Ray Bailey, is played by Tom Neal with gusto in this 15-chapter Columbia serial directed by Spencer Gordon Bennet and Thomas Carr and produced by Sam Katzman. Judy Clark, Ralph Hodges, Forrest

Taylor.

BRUTAL SORCERY (1984). Hong Kong horror thriller starring Lai Hon Chi, Lily Chang. (Ocean)

BRUTE MAN, THE (1946). Rondo Hatton was a limited talent who enjoyed brief fame as a film ugly. He needed no makeup, for he suffered from a pituitary gland disease. Hatton's popularity was due to his portrayal of The Creeper, a character introduced in THE PEARL OF DEATH. That character's origin is recounted in this shoddy thriller. A football hero is disfigured in a lab explosion and, in a beauty-and-beast variation, falls in love with a blind pianist between strangulations. These murders are depicted with Hatton's grotesque shadow on a wall as he moves his gnarly hands toward human throats. Call it pathos/bathos terror. Universal considered it repulsive (though it is only dull today) and sold it to PRC, a grade-Z studio. Hatton died the same year THE BRUTE MAN was released. Directed by Jean Yarbrough. Tom Neal, Jane Adams, Jan Wiley. (Sony; Republic; Admit One) (Laser: Sony)

BUBBLE, THE (1966). Arch Oboler produced-directed this sci-fi mystery about a community surrounded by a force-field where humans are under alien scrutiny. Some 3-D effects are startling (such as a tray of beer floating out to the audience), others fail miserably. What's really unforgivable: Oboler's script is one dimensional. Re-released as FANTASTIC INVASION OF PLANET EARTH. Michael Cole, Deborah Walley, Johnny Desmond, Virginia Gregg, Vic Perrin.

BUCKAROO BANZAI. See **ADVENTURES OF BUCKAROO BANZAI, THE.**

BUCKET OF BLOOD (1959). This classic American-International release (produced-directed by Roger Corman as an exercise in dark humor) depicts the Beat Generation, when pretentious poets wore berets and sat in coffeehouses reciting their works. Dick Miller plays Walter Paisley, a browbeaten busboy at the Yellow Door Coffeehouse who kills a cat and turns it into a sculpture, "Dead Cat." Admired for his "talent," Walter turns to murdering people (a nosy cop, a nude model) and "sculpting" them too for his one-man show. Charles Griffith's hip, flip script is full of amusement, such as when a newsboy croaks, "Read all about the man cut in half! Police can find only part of the body!" Paisley was resurrected in Corman's 1985 CHOPPING MALL. Barboura Morris, Anthony Carbone, Ed Nelson, Bert Convy. (Rhino; Sinister/C; S/Weird; Filmfax)

BUCK ROGERS (1939). In the style of FLASH GORDON serials also starring Buster Crabbe, this 12-episode Universal cliffhanger depicts Buck and Buddy Wade (Jackie Moran) crashlanding their dirigible on a mountaintop and put into suspended animation by a "nirvano" gas. They awaken 500 years later to find the world taken over by Killer Kane (Anthony Warde). Buck battles Kane with Dr. Huer (C. Montague Shaw), Wilma (Constance Moore) and a race of Saturnians. Not as well-produced or -written as the FLASH GORDON shows, but still great fun. Feature versions are PLANET OF OUTLAWS (1953) and BUCK ROGERS: DESTINATION SATURN (1965). (Unedited from UAV and Foothill; in feature form from CBS/Fox as **BUCK ROGERS CONQUERS THE UNIVERSE**)

BUCK ROGERS CLIFFHANGER SERIALS VOLS. I & II. The 1939 full-length serial in a two-box video set. (United)

BUCK ROGERS CONQUERS THE UNIVERSE. Video version of **BUCK ROGERS (1939)** (CBS/Fox).

BUCK ROGERS IN THE 25TH CENTURY (1979). Theatrical version of the TV-pilot produced by Leslie Stevens and Glen A. Larson. A pastiche of STAR WARS with awesome mothership, comedy-relief robots and cardboard heroes and heroines. Sexual double entendres give it a false sense of being "adult," but it's cornball space opera with Gil Gerard as Buck, Erin Gray as space jockey Wilma Deering, Henry Silva as Killer Kane and Pamela Hensley as the sexually arousing Princess Ardala Darco. The voice of Twiki the robot is Mel Blanc's. So is the voice of Dr. Theopolis, a miniaturized computer in the shape of a neon disc worn about Twiki's neck. Daniel Haller directed the Larson-Stevens script. Tim O'Connor, Julie Newmar. (This and many one-hour episodes from MCA) (Laser: MGM)

BUCK ROGERS: FLIGHT OF THE WAR WITCH (1979). Episodes of the Gil Gerard TV series, strung out like derelict spacecraft, mostly space opera cliches. Pamela Hensley, however, is worth ogling in her scanty harem costumes. And this has the "well-roundedness" of Julie Newmar. Larry Stewart directed. Erin Gray, Tim O'Connor, Michael Ansara, Vera Miles. (MCA)

BUCK ROGERS: PLANET OF OUTLAWS (1939). Compilation of highlights from the 1939 Universal serial. (Video Yesteryear)

BUFFY THE VAMPIRE SLAYER (1992). This is not a great vampire comedy but it's fun to watch attractive Kristy Swanson use somersaulting abilities as a cheerleader to battle vampires sucking blood out of the L.A. population. The Valley Girl's chief antagonists are cult leader Rutger Hauer and daffy aide Paul Reubens, but they're too campy to be menacing, so you have to settle for the laughs. Buffy is the descendant of a vampire stalker from the Dark Ages and it's her heritage to carry on the anti-bloodsucker war. Her mentor is Donald Sutherland, a joy to watch as he trains her in fangbusting, and Kristy learns martial arts. Directed by Frank Rubel Kuzui. Luke Perry, Michele Abrams. (Fox)

PAUL REUBENS IN 'BUFFY THE VAMPIRE SLAYER'

BUG (1975). Bradford Dillman reaches for Black Flag when an earthquake releases an insect swarm capable of starting fires. Poor horror film, a low for producer William Castle, best remembered for more gimmicky horror films. Jeannot Szwarc directed the Castle-Thomas Page script based on Page's THE HEPHAESTUS PLAGUE. Joanne Miles, Jesse Vint, Patty McCormack. (Paramount) (Laser: Japanese)

BULLDOG DRUMMOND AT BAY (1937). See third edition.

BULLDOG DRUMMOND IN AFRICA (1938). Unengaging Drummond series film with John Howard as Her Majesty's stalwart hero, this time out to stop a mad doctor armed with a Disintegrator Death Beam. Quaint black-and-white thriller of modest proportions. Directed by Louis King. Heather Angel, J. Carrol Naish, H.B. Warner, Anthony Quinn. (Embassy; from Sultan with ARREST BULLDOG DRUMMOND)

BULLSHOT CRUMMOND (1983). Unharnessed parody of H. C. McNeil's stalwart undercover agent, a gas of a movie played like a Victorian melodrama in Edwardian costumes. Crummond is a complete klutz out to stop his bitter nemesis Otto von Bruno from conquering the world. It starts when inventor Rupert Fenton is kidnapped, and Rupert's naive daughter seeks help from Crummond. Madcap adventures involve a giant tarantula, an "involuntary slippage chair," a force field, a new explosive and a superintelligent octopus. Nonstop gags Monte Python style, frenetically directed by Dick Clement. Stars Diz White, Alan Shearman and Ron House also wrote the script, based on the popular stage play. (Thorn EMI)

BURBS, THE (1989). When weird ADDAMS FAMILY types move into his neighborhood, Tom Hanks and his buddies go dingy, suspecting the newcomers of murder, mayhen and things even worse. Although this is a dumb comedy, aiming for the lowest common denominator, there are sections that look like they were lifted out of horror movies. For that reason, its pseudosupernatural elements might appeal to buffs. Directed by Joe Dante. Carrie Fisher, Rick Ducommun, Corey Feldman, Brother Theodore, Bruce Dern. (Video/Laser: MCA)

BURIAL GROUND (1979). Guests at a country mansion are attacked by the Incredible Walking Dead, George Romero style, after they emerge from an ancient crypt. Director Andrea Bianchi contributes nothing new to the zombie pantheon, but the murders are gory. Karin Well, Peter Bark, Gian Luigi. Also known as ZOMBIE HORROR and ZOMBIE 3. (Vestron; Live)

BURIED ALIVE (1980). Italian gore thriller from director Aristide Massaccesi (Americanized as Joe D'Amato) about a deranged taxidermist who does strange things with corpses following a fouled-up childhood—such as injecting them with a preservation serum. Kieran Canter, Ann Cardini. (Thrillervideo)

BURIED ALIVE (1990). South African horror flicker features John Carradine in reportedly his last role and is bolstered marquee-wise by Robert Vaughn and Donald Pleasence. The setting is Ravenscroft Asylum where horror is enhanced by the themes of Edgar Allan Poe. Harry Alan Towers production directed by Gerard Kikoine (pornie film maker). Karen Witter, Nia Long, Ginger Lynn Allen. RCA/Columbia)

BURIED ALIVE (1990). A black-comedy sense of revenge is at work in this TV-movie,,directed by Frank Darabont, in which secret lovers Jennifer Jason Leigh and William Atherton plot to do away with her husband (Tim Matheson) with a drug that makes it look like he had a heart attack. However, Matheson awakens in his grave and, in a harrowing sequence, claws his way to the surface. How the schemers get their come-uppance is ingeniously presented. Hoyt Axton is the town sheriff. Wayne Grace, Jay Gerber. (MCA)

BURKE AND HARE. See HORRORS OF BURKE AND HARE, THE.

BURNDOWN (1989). Corpses clicking with high radiation counts are found outside a coastal Florida town, where sheriff Peter Firth fights a local-government coverup and reporter Cathy Moriarty uses sexual wiles on the lawman to investigate the gory murders. A nuclear power plant nearby makes it obvious where the killer is coming from. Stuart Collins' novel was adapted for this mediocre whodunit with apocalyptic overtones by Anthony Barwick and producer Colin Stewart. James Allen's direction gives the low-budget film a nihilistic touch. Hal Orlandini, Hugh Rouse. (MCEG/Virgin) (Laser: Image)

BURNING, THE (1982). At Camp Blackfoot, stupid teenagers pull a prank on Cropsy the caretaker, who is horribly burned. When he's released from hospital, Cropsy returns armed with giant shears and eager to wreak vengeance. Another sleazy scuzz-bag slasher-sickness flick with gory murders. Features the massacre of several stupid kids simultaneously, adding to its close-your-eyes-before-the-knife-descends gruesomeness. Producer Harvey Weinsten, a stickler for realism, claims the Cropsy tale is true; or maybe he just saw FRIDAY THE 13TH. Directed by Tony Maylam. Makeup by Tom Savini. Brian Matthews, Leah Ayles. (Thorn EMI)

BURNING COURT, THE (1966). French version of John Dickson Carr's novel in which a family is cursed by ghostly visitations and the ravings of an 18th Century seer turn out to be prophetic. Produced-directed by Julien Duvivier. Also called THE CURSE AND THE COFFIN. Charles Spaak, Nadja Tiller. (Sinister/C)

BURNT OFFERINGS (1976). Modern Gothic with excellent effects, and fine performances by Oliver Reed, Karen Black and Bette Davis (*not* playing a crazy old bat). But alas, it goes awry because of an ambiguous script by producer-director Dan Curtis and William F. Nolan. The theme of the "house possessed by evil" never comes off due to a lack of expository material. Instead, it's a mish-mash. Even a twist ending cannot save it. Nice try turns to ashes. Burgess Meredith, Eileen Heckart, Dub Taylor. (MGM/UA)

BURN, WITCH, BURN (1962). Based on a Fritz Leiber novel, CONJURE WIFE, this better-than-average British supernatural thriller (also known as NIGHT OF THE EAGLE) stars Peter Wyngarde as a professor lecturing against witchcraft and Janet Blair as his wife, armed with charms to ward off evil. Some wild things happen and you'll be unnerved, even if you can see wires propelling a killer bird when it pops off the face of the campus tower. Directed by Sidney Hayers, written by George Baxt, Charles Beaumont and Richard Matheson.

BUTCHER, THE. Video verison of **PSYCHO FROM TEXAS** (Bronx).

BUTCHER, THE (1988). Mute girl Talia Shire discovers a butcher is using his shop for murder. Robert Walden, Vic Tayback. Directed by Paulmichael Miekhe. (Entertainment International Ltd.; from Star Classic as **MURDERERS' KEEP**)

BUTCHER, BAKER, NIGHTMARE MAKER. See **NIGHT WARNING.**

BUTCHER'S WIFE, THE (1991). Warm, wonderful study of the needs and absurdities of romance as filtered through a sweet, naive but clairvoyant farm girl who marries a New York City butcher on impulse and resettles in Manhattan. Her ability to foresee the romantic futures of her husband's customers leads to unforseen complications for her (Demi Moore), the butcher (George Dzundza), the neighborhood psychiatrist (Jeff Daniels) and a mousy woman turned bar-lounge singer (Mary Steenburger in a tour de force role). An unusual commentary on romance, told in a lightly comedic vein by screenwriters Ezra Litwak and Marjorie Schwartz, and tatefully directed by Terry Hughes. Frances McDormand, Margaret Colin, Max Peelich. (Paramount)

BY DAWN'S EARLY LIGHT (1990). Tense, effective doomsday thriller with Powers Booth as a bomber pilot dispatched on a mission that could begin World War III. Ambitionists within the upper level of the Pentagon have dreams of taking over the government and manipulate a psychotic substitute president to carry out their bidding. Meanwhile, Air Force officer James Earl Jones races against time to save civilization. Directed by Jack Sholder. Martin Landau, Rebecca DeMornay. Also known as RED ALERT. (Video/Laser: HBO)

"Oh great! We've got Jason upstairs and Cujo in the yard!"

—William Atherton as the trapped doctor in **BURIED ALIVE** *(1990).*

CABINET OF CALIGARI, THE (1962). Robert Bloch scripted this updated version of the silent German classic THE CABINET OF DR. CALIGARI, but claims producer-director Roger Kay butchered his script. This is loaded with Freudian symbolism and dream sequences, and despite Bloch's reaction is still an interesting experiment, for nothing is what it seems as distraught Glynis Johns, after her car breaks down, stays in a strange house in the country presided over by sinister Dan O'Herlihy. J. Pat O'Malley, Estelle Winwood, Lawrence Dobkin.

CABINET OF DR. CALIGARI (1919). Silent German classic in Expressionism, an attempt to explore psychological horror. It's a nightmare told by an asylum inmate, depicting a carnival hypnotist, his somnambulistic zombie, murders, etc. Contemporary audiences may find this cumbersome with outmoded acting but it remains a hallmark in experimentation. Robert Wiene directed. Werner Krauss, Conrad Veidt, Lil Dagover. (Kino; Sinister/C; Republic; Moore) (Laser: Republic)

CABIN IN THE SKY (1942). Film version of Lynn Rott's epic play depicting the Devil vs. folks in Heaven, featuring an all-black cast: Ethel Waters, Eddie "Rochester" Anderson, Lena Horne, Duke Ellington, Rex Ingram, Mantan Moreland, Willie Best. Directed by Vincente Minnelli. (MGM/UA; Family Home) (Laser: MGM/UA)

CAGE, THE (1965). The original STAR TREK pilot with Jeffrey Hunter as Captain Pike, never shown in its entirely on network but used in a two-parter in the first season, "The Menagerie." Scenes never shown before are in black and white, repeated footage is in color. Creator Gene Roddenberry introduces the pilot, giving background as he walks the set of a STAR TREK movie. If you've seen "The Menagerie" there isn't much point in renting this, but Trekkies will consider it a must-see curio. Nimoy is an excitable Spock, John Hoyt the ship's doctor. Majel Barrett, Susan Oliver. (Paramount)

CAGE. Video version of **MAFU CAGE** (Magnum).

CAGED TERROR (1972). Young couple on a countryside visit is pursued by maniacal killers. Percy Harkness, Elizabeth Suzuki. (Prism; New World)

CAGED VIRGINS (1973). France's Jean Rollin specialized in sex films with vampire themes—or were they vampire films with sex themes? In this blatant helping of eroticism and neck-biting, which Rollin directed-wrote-produced, a European castle is where sexy babes fall into the hands of a vampire. Known as CRAZED VAMPIRE, SEX VAMPIRES, REQUIEM FOR A VAMPIRE and VIRGINS AND VAMPIRES. Virgins? A matter of opinion. Phillipe Gaste, Marie-Pierre Castel.

CAGE OF DOOM. See **TERROR FROM THE YEAR 5000.**

CALIFORNIA AXE MASSACRE. Video version of **AXE!** (Malibu).

CALIFORNIA AXE MURDERS. See **AXE!**

CALLING, THE. See **MURDER BY PHONE.**

CALLING DR. DEATH (1943). Hypnotism solves a murder—the only interesting element in this routine entry in Universal's "Inner Sanctum" series. Directed by Reginald LeBorg, Lon Chaney Jr. portrays a neurologist plagued by his subconscious. J. Carrol Naish is far better as a suspicious cop. Patricia Morison, David Bruce.

CALTIKI, THE IMMORTAL MONSTER (1959). Caltiki, god of Mayan legend, loves humans a la carte and rolls out of his sacred waters in an Aztec temple to infect snoopy scientists. In this U.S.-Italian film photographed by Mario Bava in Spain, and directed by Riccardo Freda, there's nobody to cheer except the monster. Eat those fat-headed scientists, Caltiki, you blithering blob. Daniela Rocca, John Merivale. (J & J)

CAMERON'S CLOSET (1989). Intense thriller about a youngster (Scott Curtis) with telekinetic powers who brings an ancient Mayan demon out of hibernation to live in his closet. Although Gary Brandner (adapting his own novel) is unable to avoid convoluted plot devices, the film intriguingly pulls cop Cotter Smith and psychiatrist Mel Harris into the supernatural shenanigans. Armand Mastroianni's direction is hampered by dull lighting, but otherwise this little movie gallops along, aided by Tab Hunter as Cameron's father. Chuck McCann, Leigh McCloskey, Kim Lankford. (Sony) (Laser: Image)

CAMPSITE MASSACRE. See **FINAL TERROR.**

CAMPUS CORPSE (1977). Repackaging of THE HAZING, a non-horrific, regionally produced college-initiation story with an O. Henry twist ending more disappointing than shocking. Charles Martin Smith, Jeff East, Brad Davis. Directed by Douglas Curtis. (Vestron)

CANADIAN MOUNTIES VS. ATOMIC INVADERS (1947). Rousing 12-chapter Republic serial with the Canadian wasteland (studio backlot?) serving as the setting for a battle royal between Mountie Don Roberts (Bill Henry) and the villain Marlof (Arthur Space), who intends to launch atomic missiles against the U.S. and Canada. Nonstop duel across the icy terrain—even features a reindeer stampede. Directed by Franklin Adreon. Harry Lauter, Tom Steele, Susan Morrow. (Republic)

CANDLE FOR THE DEVIL, A. See **NIGHTMARE HOTEL.**

CANDY (1968). Innocent alien (Ewa Aulin), sexually provocative, lands her saucer on Earth and is sexually assaulted by Marlon Brando, John Huston, Ringo Starr, Richard Burton, Walter Matthau and other stars wasting their time in this grotesque version of Terry Southern's pseudoporno novel. Don't take strangers from CANDY. Directed by Christian Marquand; scripted by Buck Henry.

CANDYMAN (1992). As a supernatural-horror thriller this is a superb adaptation of Clive Barker's story "The Forbidden." Writer-director Bernard Rose skillfully crafts a blood-and-guts tale that has a fascinating subtext about urban legends and how they affect our culture. Virginia Madsen portrays a brave woman studying the legend of "Candyman," a boogeyman-figure within a black ghetto. Her nosing around highrise slums leads to a confrontation with an evil spirit (equipped with a hook hand) and nightmarish events refreshing to the horror genre. Barker acted as executive producer, which may account for the superiority of this to most gore flicks. Tony Todd is electrifying as the slave returned to life as a serial killer. Vanessa Williams is good as Madsen's assistant. Evocative Philip Glass score. (Video/Laser: Columbia TriStar)

CANNIBAL CAMPOUT (1988). Beautiful women are tasty morsels for a gang of flesh-eating freakos. Directed by Jon McBride and Tom Fisher. Carrie Lindell, Richard Marcus. (Donna Michelle)

CANNIBAL FEROX. See **MAKE THEM DIE SLOWLY.**

CANNIBAL GIRLS (1972). In a Canadian town, three dead women with a penchant for human flesh haunt a restaurant where Eugene Levy and Andrea Martin spend the night. Avant-garde supernatural thriller of interest because it was the first work of producer-director Ivan Reitman. Original theatrical prints contained a buzzer sound to warn viewers of pending violence. Ronald Ulrich, Bonnie Neilson. (No buzzer on CIC's version)

CANNIBAL HOLOCAUST (1979). Of the Italian "Human Flesh Eaters" genre in which film makers travel to the Amazon to document cannibalism, only to fall prey to jungle dwellers' appetite. Directed by Ruggero Deodato (JUNGLE HOLOCAUST). Frencesca Ciardi, Luca Barbareschi, Robert Kerman. (Laser: Japanese)

CANNIBAL HOOKERS (1987). Amateurish video movie written-produced-directed by Donald Farmer in which two chicks pose as prostitutes and are turned into zombies with a taste for human flesh. Gary J. Levinson, Eric Caiden, Sheila Best. (Camp)

CANNIBAL MAN. See **APARTMENT ON THE 13TH FLOOR, THE.**

CANNIBAL MASSACRE. See **CANNIBALS ARE IN THE STREETS.**

CANNIBAL ORGY. See **SPIDER BABY.**

CANNIBALS ARE IN THE STREETS (1980). Italian-Spanish "zombies on the loose" flick from director Anthony M. Dawson, with gore by Gianetto De Rossi, who splashed blood in ZOMBIE. The flesh-eaters are Vietnam veterans in downtown Atlanta. Can cop John Saxon stop the plague? Elizabeth Turner, John Morghen. Also known as CANNIBAL MASSACRE, SAVAGE APOCALYPSE and THE SLAUGHTERERS. (From Vestron as **INVASION OF THE FLESH HUNTERS**)

CANNIBAL VIRUS. See **NIGHT OF THE ZOMBIES (1983).**

CANNIBAL WOMEN IN THE AVOCADO JUNGLE OF DEATH (1988). This sendup of APOCALYPSE NOW, safari adventures and sex comedies is talkative and full of tongue-twisting rhetoric on a satirical level. The blend is not the rollicking parody its title suggests. Shannon Tweed portrays Margo Hunt, a feminist on safari with bumbling hunter Brett Stimely and sexy Karen Mistal (that gal from RETURN OF THE KILLER TOMATOES) to find "Kurtz," another feminist (Adrienne Barbeau in loincloth) leading a tribe of Piranha Women in the wilderness of California where they eat men after sex. This hodgepodge is by writer-director J. D. Athens. Barry Primus, Bill Maher. (Video/Laser: Paramount)

CANTERVILLE GHOST, THE (1944). Whimsical, hilarious version of the Oscar Wilde story, directed by Jules Dassin. A cowardly ghost (Charles Laughton, in one fine role) is doomed to walk the family castle until a descendant performs an heroic deed. Updated to incorporate the Nazi threat. Robert Young, Margaret O'Brien, Peter Lawford and Rags Ragland. (MGM/UA)

CANTERVILLE GHOST, THE (1986). TV version of Wilde's comedy, set in modern England when Andrea Marcovicci and Ted Wass inherit a castle in Worcester, where this was filmed. Stalking its halls, with supernatural ball and chain, is Sir John Gielgud as the irascible, blustering spectre; he alone makes this worthwhile. Good effects enhance this old tale in which the ghost must force earthlings to perform an heroic act. Directed by Paul Bogart. (RCA/Columbia)

CAPE CANAVERAL MONSTERS, THE (1960). Phil Tucker, who established new incompetency levels in ROBOT MONSTER, dips to even greater lows. Two bathers are attacked by beams of light (what a great effect!), die in a car crash and return possessed by alien energy fields. Nadja and Hauron (aliens) foul up rocket launchings by pointing a bazooka-shaped zap gun and firing. They address their ET boss on an "interplanetary receiver"—a TV set in which a pancake floats. Katherine Victor and Jason Johnson convey no menace as the turgid invaders, who grow uglier as more putty is heaped on their faces. At control center, a Jewish scientist operates phony-looking equipment while Scott Peters and Linda Connell stumble around the aliens' cave. Mercifully short (69 minutes) but still not short enough!

CAPRICORN ONE (1978). After faking a manned flight to Mars, so Congress will okay expenditures, the U.S. space program arranges for the death of the "astronauts." Wise to their pending demise, James Brolin, Sam Waterston and O. J. Simpson run for their lives. Media reporter Elliott Gould uncovers the conspiracy and tracks the men into the desert. This exciting thriller makes only derogative inferences about our conquest of space and U.S. agencies. Written-directed by Peter Hyams. Hal Holbrook, Karen Black, Telly Savalas, Brenda Vaccaro, Robert Walden. (Video/Laser: Fox)

CAPTAIN AMERICA (1944). This 15-chapter Republic serial, based loosely on the Marvel comic-book character, is an exciting action cliffhanger with Dick Purcell as a D.A. who takes to the Captain America costume to fight the evil Scarab, who uses a poison called "The Purple Death" to kill his enemies and steal such new devises as a "dynamic vibrator" called the Thunder Bolt that knocks down a skyscraper, a Re-Animation Machine that brings a criminal back to life, and other weapons of the "Death Ray" school. The fistfights are great, the action is nonstop, Lorna Gray is fine as the obligatory heroine, Lionel Atwill shines as a perverted sophisticate, and the direction by John English and Elmer Clifton has unusually good camera angles for the period. (The Video Treasures transfer is mediocre; for some strange reason, Republic has not released this on tape.)

CAPTAIN AMERICA (1979). Superlousy superhero TV-movie fails to capture the Simon and Kirby comic-book character popular during World War II and revived in the '60s by Stan Lee. Captain America, or Steve Rogers, is only a distant memory as writer Don Ingalls introduces us to his son (Reb Brown), a wimp who just wants to be left alone and refuses to take FLAG (Full Latent Ability Gain), a serum that would give him "100 per cent human capabilities—strength and agility." But when Steve Forrest and his gang steal the Neutron Bomb and plan to blow up Phoenix, you know Steve Rogers Jr. will don dad's red-white-and-blue costume. The image of Captain America riding across the desert on a motorbike is really the pits. This is superheroism? Directed routinely by Rod Holcomb. Heather Menzies, Robin Mattson, Joseph Ruskin, Lance LeGault. (MCA)

CAPTAIN AMERICA II: DEATH TOO SOON (1980). In this TV-movie sequel to CAPTAIN AMERICA, Reb Brown is back as a superpatriotic superhero fighting Christopher Lee, a bad guy with a substance that, when sprayed into the air, accelerates the aging process in those who breathe it. To find the gang, Steve Rogers poses as a mild-mannered painter who roves the countryside, seeking the help of citizens and taking care of ruffians with a baseball bat. Although based on the comic-book series, this never captures its look or spirit. Directed by Ivan Nagy. Lana Wood, Connie Sellecca, Christopher Cary, Len Birman, Katherine Justice. (MCA)

MATT SALINGER

CAPTAIN AMERICA (1989). Unlike previous versions based on the comic-book hero of World War II, who was revived in the '60s by Marvel, this captures the flavor of the original by pitting Captain America (Matt Salinger) against his grand Nazi nemesis, The Red Skull (Scott Paulin). It's grand, uninhibited comic-book action as the warriors clash in 1943. Through circumstances that could only happen in a four-color magazine, Steve Rogers/Captain America (product of a top-secret experiment) is left in suspended animation in the Arctic while the Red Skull plots the assassinations of the Kennedys and Martin Luther King. Revived from the ice, the red-white-and-blue superhero, armed with a boomerang-like shield, takes on the Skull and his sexy assassins led by his daughter after they've kidnapped the U.S. President (Ronny Cox). Director Albert Pyun ignores logic and goes for pacing to make this a satisfying adaptation. Ned Beatty, Darren McGavin, Michael Nouri, Melinda Dillon, Bill Mumy. (Video/Laser: Columbia/TriStar)

CAPTAIN AMERICA (1991). Laser disc with four animated episodes of a TV series based on the comic book hero: "The Origin of Captain America," "Midnight in Greymoor Castle," "Revenge of Captain America" and "The Sentinel and the Spy." (Image)

CAPTAIN CLEGG. See **NIGHT CREATURES.**

CAPTAIN KRONOS—VAMPIRE HUNTER (1972). Exciting Hammer actioner, also known as VAMPIRE CASTLE and KRONOS. Horst Janson is the dedicated Kronos, who embarks on Quixotic hunts for bloodsuckers with hunchback Professor Grost (John Cater). Writer-director Brian Clemens creates a blend of satire and swashbuckling action with overtones of an old-fashioned serial. Exotic Caroline Munro is Kronos' helper. Shane Briant, Ian Hendry. (Paramount) (Laser: Japanese)

CAPTAIN MEPHISTO AND THE TRANSFORMATION MACHINE (1945). Feature version of Republic's **MANHUNT OF MYSTERY ISLAND.**

CAPTAIN NEMO AND THE UNDERWATER CITY (1970). Stylish variation on Jules Verne's 20,000 LEAGUES UNDER THE SEA, with U.S. Senator Chuck Connors and others falling into the hands of Captain Nemo (Robert Ryan), in command of a city under a glass bubble, Templemere. Emphasis is on intrigue between the Senator and Nemo as their differing politics clash. The underwater action is good but panning and scanning of TV prints is poor. The strong cast and decent effects make this worthwhile. Directed by James Hill. Luciana Paluzzi, Kenneth Connor, Nanette Newman.

CAPTAIN SINBAD (1963). Made in Germany by Frank and Henry King (of GORGO fame), this colorful fantasy stars Guy Williams as the sailor of the Arabian Nights adventures who pursues his fiancee, a damsel trapped in the clutches of wicked Pedro Armendariz (in his final screen role). Sinbad is tortured, battles a giant hand (winning thumbs down) and seeks to cut out the evil caliph's heart. All ages will enjoy the costumes, sets and Byron Haskin's stylish direction. (MGM/UA)

CAPTAIN VIDEO (1951). A 15-chapter Columbia serial spinning off from a once-popular TV show, produced by serial schlockmeister Sam Katzman and directed by Spencer Gordon Bennet and Wallace A. Grissell. Judd Holdren stars as Captain Video, who takes on Vultura (Gene Roth) on the farflung planet of Atoma.

CAPTAIN YANKEE. See **JUNGLE RAIDERS.**

CAPTIVE (1980). Grade B cheapie in which the planet Styrolia engages in war with Earth over possession of Dirathium crystals. Two recon aliens, shot down by our fighters, hold an old farmer and family captive, until one alien has a change of heart. Unexciting and predictable, with an anti-climactic ending. The terrible spaceship-model work finishes off whatever good intentions producers-directors Allan Sandler and Robert Emenegger had. For captive audiences only. Cameron Mitchell, David Ladd, Lori Saunders.

CAPTIVE PLANET: A NIGHTMARE OF LIVING HELL. See **STAR ODYSSEY** (Mogul).

CAPTIVE WILD WOMAN (1943). Acquanetta walks zombie-like as a mysterious native woman transformed into a member of the monkey family by a mad doctor—but everyone associated with this Universal quickie, including John Carradine as Dr. Sigmund Walters and Milburn Stone and Evelyn Ankers as the sympathetic heroes who are members of a circus, is engaged in monkey business. Surprisingly, this tasteless B effort sparked sequels: JUNGLE WOMAN and JUNGLE CAPTIVE, equally as cheap, Jack. Edward Dmytryk directed. Lloyd Corrigan, Paul Fix, Grant Withers.

CAPTIVE WOMEN (1952). New York City ruins in 3000 A.D. are the setting for this yarn by writers-producers Aubrey Wisberg and Jack Pollexfen (fresh from THE MAN FROM PLANET X) in which hideous Mutants raid handsome Norms to snatch away buxom, blond-haired women. There's a third band, the Uprivers, who live—you guessed it, upriver. Robert Clarke, Margaret Field, Gloria Saunders, William Schallert, Ron Randell. Producer was Albert Zugsmith, famed for oddball B flicks. Directed by Stuart Gilmore.

CAPTURE OF BIGFOOT, THE (1979). An insufferable kid, two bad-guy hunters, a forest ranger and his girlfriend, a dumb, disbelieving sheriff, an old trapper named Jake, and a wise Indian are the inept characters running around Cloud Lake in winter, pursuing two extras from Central Casting in furry white suits and monster faces. Hell, them abominations look more like Yetis. Oh well, it's the Legend of Aurak unleashed on us hapless movie-watchers by producer-director Bill Rebane. The cast stumbles through snow drifts without ever getting the drift: Stafford Morgan, Richard Kennedy, Katherine Hopkins, Otis Young, John Goff. (Active)

CAPTURE THAT CAPSULE. See **SPY SQUAD.**

CAR, THE (1977). Disappointing Universal film imitates JAWS with a killer auto supplanting Bruce the Shark. Elliot Silverstein's direction is singularly hindered by a muddled Dennis Shryack-Michael Butler-Lane Slate screenplay, which fuzzily sketches characters and has a murky logic in explaining from whence the vulgar vehicle came. The real stars are stunt driver Everett Creach and "The Car," a squat, evil-looking creation by designer George Barris. The wheeled killer takes on a satanic personality as it zooms, careooms, whirls, spins and roars through a desert community (in and around St. George, Utah), crushing human bodies. James Brolin stars as the sheriff. John Marley, Kathleen Lloyd, R. G. Armstrong.

CAREFREE (1938). Your basic Fred Astaire-Ginger Rogers musical comedy, but this time the wonderful dances and Irving Berlin songs showcase an odd romance between a psychoanalyst (Astaire) and a society dame (Rogers). Compelling psychiatric talk (for its time) and post-hypnotic suggestions make Rogers behave like a little girl—an adolescent behavior she repeated in MONKEY BUSINESS. Outstanding dream-dance sequences and a scene in which Astaire talks to his alter ego in a mirror are highlights of this spoof of psychiatry. Directed by Mark Sandrich. Ralph Bellamy, Luella Gear, Jack Carson. (RKO; Turner; Media) (Laser: Image)

CARNAGE (1967). See **CORRUPTION.**

CARNAGE (1972). Italian scarer (also TWITCH OF THE DEATH NERVE, BLOODBATH BAY OF BLOOD and THE ECOLOGY OF A CRIME) about sadistic murderers fighting over the estate of Countess Federica and featuring 13 gore murders, each carried out in a diabolically bloody way. Graphically revolting, stained with blood from beginning to end. Mario Bava wrote-directed-photographed this bloodbath that features such "cutting-edge" technology as cleavers, spears and other flesh-penetrating weapons. Claudine Auger, Claudio Volonte, Luigi Pistilli. (From Gorgon as **BAY OF BLOOD, A**)

CARNAGE (1984). Rock-bottom clunker from producer-writer-director-cameraman Andy Milligan, depicting newlyweds in a haunted house, where guests are murdered by restless spirits. Poor in all departments, including gore murders. Leslie Den Dooven, Michael Chiodo. (Media; Video Treasures)

CARNATION KILLER, THE (1974). Cheap but effective British TV-movie depicts a serial murderer (Norman Eshley) who has strangled nine women when he is arrested, found insane and sent to an asylum. But he escapes to begin a series of cat-and-mouse games with seemingly innocent Katharine Schofield. Brian (THE AVENGERS) Clemens' script has surprise twists. Half-film, half-tape, this quickie was directed by Robert Tronsom. Derek Smith, Garrick Hagon. (Thrillervideo)

CARNIVAL OF BLOOD (1971). Also known as DEATH RIDES A CARNIVAL, this is set at Coney Island where a slasher with a mother complex knocks off victims. A sick story, in which organs are extracted by the psychokiller, lacks the wallop of an ordinary spin on a Ferris wheel. Written-produced-directed by Leonard Kirtman. Burt Young, Judith Resnick. (Wizard)

CARNIVAL OF SOULS (1962). Obscure cult favorite was revived in 1989, with missing footage restored by producer-director Harvey (Heck) Harvey. It's funky and crude but compelling, for its story avoids cliches—in fact, George Romero credits it with inspiring NIGHT OF THE LIVING DEAD. Candace Hilligloss wanders in limbo between life and death, with death symbols tugging at her. The mood generated by Harvey and co-writer John Clifford and the oddball characters overwhelm the amateurishness to give this a unique touch. The film was created around a deserted pavilion near Salt Lake City, which became a central location for this low-low budgeter made in and around Lawrence, Kansas, and Salt Lake. It lacks graphic shocks but its psychological content is superior. (Goodtimes; S/Weird; Filmfax) (Laser: VidAmerica; Image)

CARNOSAUR (1993). Although an attempt to cash in on the JURASSIC PARK hoopla, this Roger Corman low-budgeter is a good monster-gore movie, well written-directed by Adam Simon. Genetics scientist Diane Ladd, as mad as a hatter, crosses chicken eggs with DNA from dinosaurs (gosh, does this sound familiar or what?) and gets a modest-sized T-Rex creature monster juggernaut that shreds plenty of human flesh. Raphael Sbarge, Jennifer Runyon, Harrison Page. (New Horizons)

CAROL FOR ANOTHER CHRISTMAS (1964). See editions 1-3.

CAROLINA CANNONBALL (1955). Editions 1-3.

CAROUSEL (1956). Ferenc Molnar's LILIOM, readapted by Rodgers and Hammerstein from their Broadway dance musical about loud-mouth carnival baker Billy Bigelow, who returns from the dead to help his daughter grow up. Gordon MacRae portrays Bigelow and the songs include "You'll Never Walk Alone" and "If I Loved You." A great cast (Shirley Jones, Cameron Mitchell, Gene Lockhart, John Dehner, Barbara Ruick) led by director Henry King. (Fox) (Laser: Image)

CARPATHIAN EAGLE (1981). Repackaged episode from British TV's HAMMER HOUSE OF HORROR, depicting serial killer Suzanne Danielle who assumes the modus operandi of killers from the past, and then carries out new waves of horror. In this tale directed by Francis Megahy, the woman poses as a prostitute and murders with a ritualistic knife. There's also a subplot involving an old family curse and a female impersonator. Muddled at times, but the murder sequences are good and there's spicy sex to keep one awake. Suzanne Danielle, Sian Phillips, Barry Stanton. For TV this is packaged with a second one-hour episode. (Thrillervideo, with Elvira)

CARPENTER, THE (1988). Canadian supernatural film, directed by David Wellington, is an offbeat comedy about a woman (Lynn Adams) who falls in love with a ghost of an executed murderer. The troubled spirit (Wings Hauser) has returned as a carpenter. The murders are in tongue-in-cheek fashion. Pierre Lenoir, Barbara Jones. (Video/Laser: Republic)

CARPET OF HORROR (1962). A criminal mastermind a la Dr. Mabuse uses a poison gas to wipe out his enemies. German horror in the vein of Edgar Wallace, directed by Harald Reinl. Joachim Fuchsberger, Karin Dor. (Sinister/C; S/Weird; Filmfax)

CARRIE (1976). Producer-director Brian De Palma's treatment of Stephen King's first novel, a lurid tale of modern Gothic horror, has two sequences that'll make you leap from your seat. It's a psychological study of mousy teenager Sissy Spacek who uses telekinesis power to wreak vengeance after a macabre joke is played on her at the high school prom. Tension between Spacek and mother Piper Laurie, a religious fanatic, is riveting and her "Crucifixion" scene is unforgettable. A powerful horror films of the '70s. John Travolta, Nancy Allen, Amy Irving, William Katt. (MGM/UA; Paramount) (Laser: Voyager; Criterion)

CARRIER, THE (1988). When an isolated community is struck by an epidemic (an allegory to AIDS?) the infected turn into gooey piles of custard. Produced in Michigan on a shoestring budget, this was written-directed by Nathan J. White and stars Gregory Fortescue, Steve Dixon, Paul Urbanski, N. Paul Silverman. (Magnum)

CARRION. See **JAR, THE.**

CARRY ON SCREAMING! (1966). Hilarious spoof in the "Carry On" series pokes spirited fun at Universal's horror movies: a mad doctor who regenerates corpses, his Vampira-like assistant Valaria (exotic Fenella Fielding), a wolfman named Ozbod, and a stuffy butler. Two inept Scotland Yard cops, Bung and Slowbottom, bungle through an investigation to find out why six women disappeared from Hocombe Woods. Turns out our crazed physician has a way of turning them into solid statues with a special dip. Jolly good fun directed by Gerald Thomas. Harry H. Corbett, Kenneth Williams, Charles Hawtrey, Jim Dale, Joan Sims. (Movies Unlimited)

CARRY ON SPYING (1964). England's "Carry On" gang levels its sights on James Bond and comes up with a few laughs, if not avalanches of guffaws. Three dumb agents are after a mysterious concoction stolen by STENCH, an organization under Dr. Crow, half-man, half-woman. Directed by Gerald Thomas. Kenneth Williams, Barbara Windsor, Charles Hawtrey. (Sinister/C)

CARRY ON VAMPIRE. See **CARRY ON SCREAMING.**

CARS THAT EAT PEOPLE, THE (1974). Peter Weir began his directing-writing career in Australia with this bizarre technological horror story set in the Down Under town of Paris, where the young generation drives automobiles covered with decor of other autos they've cannibalized through road traps. Meanwhile, a crazy Frankenstein-style doctor experiments on captured tourists, turning them into monsters. Well, it's a living. Terry Camilleri, John Meillon, Kevin Miles. Also called CARS THAT ATE PARIS. (RCA/Columbia)

CASE OF JONATHAN DREW, THE. See **LODGER, THE (1929).**

CASE OF THE FULL MOON MURDERS (1971). X-rated spoof of horror and sex films, directed by Sean Cunningham. Strictly hardcore at the seams, with "big" actor Harry Reems. Also known as SEX ON THE GROOVE TUBE and THE CASE OF THE SMILING STIFFS. Fred Lincoln, Ron Browne, Cathy Walker.

CASE OF THE MISSING BRIDES. See **CORPSE VANISHES, THE.**

CASE OF THE SMILING STIFFS. See **CASE OF THE FULL MOON MURDERS, THE.**

CASINO ROYALE (1967). Five directors—John Huston, Ken Hughes, Val Guest, Robert Parrish, Joe McGrath—out to make the ultimate James Bond adventure with $14 million still ended up with a fuzzy fiasco. This despite dazzling sets, a plethora of effects and superspy gadgets. Don't confuse this with the Connery series—it was an independent effort satirizing Ian Fleming's character. Despite the fine screenwriters (Wolf Mankowitz, John Law, Michael Sayers, John Huston, Ben Hecht, Joseph Heller, Terry Southern) the cast wanders through the lovely framework hopelessly lost. David Niven portrays Sir James Bond, brought out of retirement to tackle SMERSH, Joanna Pettet is his daughter Mata Bond and Woody Allen plays nephew Jimmy Bond. Peter Sellers, Peter O'Toole, Orson Welles, Ursula Andress, Deborah Kerr. (Video/Laser: RCA/Columbia)

CASSANDRA (1987). A psychokiller writes "Who Killed Cock Robin?" on the mirrors of his victims in this muddled Australian psychological profile of a prescient child and her parents. As Cassandra, Tessa Humphries relives her mother's death-by-shotgun and has psychic flashes of new murders as they happen, including the slasher-death of her father's girlfriend. Deep family secrets are at the root of the script by director Colin Eggleston, Chris Fitchett and John Ruane. Shane Briant, Kit Taylor, Lee James. (Virgin Vision) (Laser: Image)

CAST A DEADLY SPELL (1991). Offbeat, catchy TV-movie combines the private eye genre with cosmic horror of H. P. Lovecraft. Set in a parallel universe in 1948, where everyone can perform magic tricks, L.A. private eye H. Phillip Lovecraft (Fred Ward) is after "The Necronomicon," which holds the key to unleashing evil Elder Gods from their dimensional prisons to earthly environs. Rich recluse David Warner wants the book to control the world; so does night club gangster Raymond O'Connor, while sexy torch singer Julianne More just wants Lovecraft. Director Martin Campbell keeps it moving with gremlins, zombies and beasts as part of the black magic. Producer Gale Anne Hurd includes atmospheric matte paintings that enhance this low-budget effort. You'll enjoy this kooky world in which the cop is named Bradbury. Clancy Brown, Alexandra Powers, Charles Hallahan. (Video/Laser: HBO)

CASTLE, THE (1969). Franz Kafka's allegorical fantasy produced by and starring Maximilian Schell. A stranger, "Mr. K," arrives at an institution called The Castle and is mysteriously caught up in red tape and befuddlement. Metaphysical as hell, and a companion piece to Orson Welles' THE TRIAL. Directed-written by Rudolf Noelte. Cordula Trantow, Trudik Daniel. (Cinema Group)

CASTLE IN THE AIR (1953). Delightfully droll British comedy (a bit screwball at times) in which David Tomlinson, Earl of Locharne and owner of a Scottish castle, uses the ghost of a beautiful woman (Patricia Dainton) as a tourist attraction to beef up income. Based on a witty play by Alan Melville, the film's emphasis is less on ghosts than on Tomlinson's romances with American socialite Barbara Kelly and old friend Helen Cherry. Margaret Rutherford is a batty dame studying Tomlinson's family tree. Directed by Henry Cass with enough satirical jabs to keep the comic bagpipes blowing.

CASTLE OF BLOOD (1962). Above-average Italian horror flick in which George Riviere spends a night in a haunted castle after accepting a bet from Edgar Allan Poe. Naturally, he proceeds to lose his mind as he bears witness to ghostly spirits. Among them is Barbara Steele, who provides a great lift. Directed by Anthony Dawson, who remade the story as WEB OF THE SPIDER. Ah, but that's another night of horror. Also known as CASTLE OF TERROR, THE LONG NIGHT OF TERROR, TOMBS OF HORROR, COFFIN OF TERROR and DIMENSIONS IN DEATH. Margaret Robsahn, Sylvia Sorente, Henry Kruger. (Sinister/C; Filmfax)

CASTLE OF BLOODY LUST. See **CASTLE OF THE CREEPING FLESH.**

CASTLE OF DEATH. Video version of **DEVIL'S NIGHTMARE, THE** (Premiere).

CASTLE OF DOOM. See **VAMPYR.**

CASTLE OF EVIL (1966). Relatives of deceased madman Kovec gather in an eerie mansion for the reading of the will. Suddenly a facsimile of Kovec begins murdering the heirs. Directed by Francis D. Lyon. Scott Brady, Virginia Mayo, Hugh Marlowe, Lisa Gaye, David Brian, Shelley Morrison. (Republic)

CASTLE OF FU MANCHU (1968). Final entry in the British series with Christopher Lee as the insidious Asian with another nefarious scheme to throw the world into chaos. Helping old Fu in this new grue is his dastardly daughter, death rays and torture devices in the Sax Rohmer tradition. Directed by Jesus Franco. Also known as ASSIGNMENT ISTANBUL. Richard Greene, Maria Perschy. (American Videotape; Moore)

CASTLE OF LUST. See **CASTLE OF THE CREEPING FLESH.**

CASTLE OF TERROR. Video version of the Barbara Steele horrifier, **CASTLE OF BLOOD** (S/Weird).

CASTLE OF TERROR. See **HORROR CASTLE.**

CASTLE OF THE CREEPING FLESH (1968). Mad doctor Howard Vernon tries to bring his murdered daughter back to life by killing for body organs. Also called CASTLE OF BLOODY LUST. Directed by Percy G. Parker (Adrian Hoven). Elvira Berndorff, Claudia Butenuth, Janine Reynaud. (Magnum; Videodrome)

CASTLE OF THE DOOMED. See **KISS ME MONSTER.**

CASTLE OF THE LIVING DEAD (1964). Troupe of entertainers stops at Christopher Lee's castle, where bizarre murders commence. Ample lurking through secret passageways before the show biz gang (dwarf and all) discovers Count Drago (Lee) is preserving the dead. You'll get a kick out of Donald Sutherland as a comedy relief policeman (he also appears as an old witch). Directed by Luciano Ricci (Herbert Wise). Gaia Germani, Philippe Leroy. (Sinister/C; S/Weird; Filmfax)

CASTLE OF THE MONSTERS (1957). Mexican spoof of Universal's horror films of the '40s with the comedy team of Clavillazo and Elizondo. The menagerie of cinema monsters is paraded out by director Julian Soler—mummy, werewolf, vampire, Frankenstein.

CASTLE OF THE WALKING DEAD, THE (1969). German-produced excursion into 19th-Century horror with haunted woods (body parts embedded in branches and trunks) and spooky castle of torture chambers, trap doors, snake pit and mad-doctor laboratory. Lex Barker and Karin Dor portray aristocracy invited to Andimi Castle, home of the dreaded Count Regula. They watch helplessly as the Count is brought to life as Christopher Lee, who plays the madman without charm. Seems he has the blood of 12 virgins, but needs Dor's to complete his formula for eternal life. Manfred Kohler's script borrows Poe's THE PIT AND THE PENDULUM for one sequence. The acting, sets and direction by Harald Reindl make this watchable despite its datedness. Also called BLOOD DEMON. (Interglobal; from Magnum as **TOR-**

TURE CHAMBER OF DR. SADISM)

CASTLE OF UNHOLY DESIRES. See **CASTLE OF THE CREEPING FLESH.**

CATACLYSM. See **NIGHTMARE NEVER ENDS, THE** and **NIGHT TRAIN TO TERROR.**

CATACOMBS. See **WOMAN WHO WOULDN'T DIE, THE.**

CATACOMBS (1988). Original video title of a Charles Band film re-released as **CURSE 4** (Transworld).

CAT AND THE CANARY, THE (1927). Silent version of John Willard's play set in a mansion where a killer with a clawed hand sneaks through secret corridors. Directed by Paul Leni. Laura La Plante, Creighton Hale, Flora Finch, Tully Marshall. Remade in 1930 as THE CAT CREEPS. (Budget; Video Yesteryear; Nostalgia)

CAT AND THE CANARY, THE (1939). Paramount's rollicking comedy version of the John Willard "old dark house" play starring Bob Hope and Paulette Goddard, in top form as they make their way through spooky trappings that blend comedy with the supernatural. Superb fun under Elliot Nugent's direction. John Beal, Gale Sondergaard, George Zucco, Elizabeth Patterson.

CAT AND THE CANARY, THE (1978). Tongue-in-cheek version of the famous tongue-in-cheek play by John Willard—which means it's twice as dumb. Heirs gather once again for the reading of the will. Some of the updated novelty devices are cute, but the film wallows in its own antiquity. It's a good cast (Honor Blackman, Edward Fox, Michael Callan, Wendy Hiller, Carol Lynley, Wilfrid Hyde-White), so put the blame on writer-director Radley Metzger. (RCA/Columbia)

CATASTROPHE 1999. See **LAST DAYS OF PLANET EARTH, THE.**

CAT CREATURE, THE (1973). Robert Bloch supernatural teleplay with in-jokes about movie cats, but it's pallid stuff. Gale Sondergaard, one-time Spider Woman, is a cat goddess claiming victims to possess a golden amulet. Kent Smith, of CURSE OF THE CAT PEOPLE, has a cameo. Curtis Harrington needed nine lives to direct David Hedison, Stuart Whitman, Keye Luke, John Carradine; Peter Lorre Jr. turns up in one scene with a knife in his back. Has the bite of a kitten instead of a jungle marauder.

CAT CREEPS, THE (1930). Early talkie, a version of John Willard's THE CAT AND THE CANARY, starring Montague Love, Jean Hersholt and Helen Twelvetrees. It's the "old dark house" with sliding panels, the clawed hand grabbing for the heroine and other "midnight tinglings." Directed by Rupert Julian.

CAT CREEPS, THE (1946). Does the spirit of a dead girl possess a black cat? Vintage Universal material of the '40s. Not a classic but it will be of minor interest to buffs, even if it bears no relation to THE CAT CREEPS of 1930. Directed by Erle C. Kenton. Lois Collier, Noah Beery Jr., Paul Kelly.

CAT FROM OUTER SPACE, THE (1978). Zoolar J-5, a Persian feline, emerges from a disabled UFO in this childish Disney comedy written by Ted (HAZEL) Keys. With a magical collar, Zoolar levitates people and places them into suspended animation in his efforts to rendezvous with the mother ship. Sally Duncan, Ken Berry, McLean Stevenson, Roddy McDowall and Harry Morgan add little to the uninspired plot. Ronnie Schell plays an army sergeant but his voice was dubbed so he could supply the voice of Zoolar. In short, the cat has his tongue. Directed by Norman Tokar. (Disney)

CAT GIRL, THE (1957). Barbara Shelley, in her first British film, inherits a family curse that promises "the craving for warm new flesh and blood." Cuckolded by her devious husband, Barbara unleashes a phantom cheetah on him and girlfriend—a transference that in turn unleashes the curse and sets into motion vengeful murders. Alfred Shaughnessey directed. Robert Ayres, Kay Callard, Paddy Webster. Also known as THE CAT WOMAN.

CATHY'S CURSE (1976). French-Canadian horror flick borrowing from CARRIE in dealing with an eight-year-old girl possessed by the demonic spirit of her aunt, who was killed in a fiery auto crash. Housekeeper plunges from an upper window to her death, family dog is destroyed, other "web of horror" cliches ensue. Special effects are undistinguished, Eddie Matalan's direction is tedious, and Randi Allen as Cathy seems more insufferable than evil. Curses on everyone involved. Alan Scarfe, Beverly Murray, Roy Wiltham. (Planet; Continental)

CATMAN OF PARIS, THE (1946). Claw-ripping murders leads a tormented man to believe he is a werecat (or is it a vampwolf?). Gerald Mohr and John Dehner purr, Lenore Aubert loves to have her ears scratched, Robert J. Wilke just loves a saucer of milk. Director Lesley Selander prowls at night and screenwriter Sherman L. Lowe digs cat litter. Adele Mara, John Dehner.

CAT O'NINE TAILS (1971). Karl Malden, who portrays a blind man specializing in solving crossword puzzles, considers this one of his best low-budget features, a tribute to the talents of writer-director Dario Argento. This blends mystery and psychoterror in telling of a murderer whose blood is tainted with homicidal tendencies. James Franciscus is a reporter on the killer's trail. Catherine Spaak. (Simitar; Bingo) (Laser: Japanese)

CAT PEOPLE, THE (1942). Classic supernatural shocker from RKO producer Val Lewton, who stressed unseen horror in his low-budget assignments. Simone Simon is a fragile European bride fearful she is turning into a panther whenever her sexual desires are aroused. We never witness the transformation, only shadowy figures on windswept streets and the hint of something prowling just out of camera range. A genuinely eerie atmosphere created by director Jacques Tourneur, with Dewitt Bodeen's script remarkably literate. Kent Smith, Tom Conway, Jane Randolph, Jack Holt, (Nostalgia Merchant; Media; King of Video; RKO) (Laser: Image)

CAT PEOPLE (1982). Paul Schrader directed this barely-a-remake of the '42 version, emphasizing the sexual side of humans turning into animals. It's kinky: Malcolm McDowall mutates into a panther whenever sex is on his mind, and so should his relative Nastassia Kinski, only she's a virgin and hasn't developed the impulses. Schrader deals with this depravity in vivid visuals. Yet the exposition is so uncertain, he suggests more than he ultimately shows, an ironic twisting of Lewton's technique. Even the effects by Tom Burman (human arm popping out of leopard's stomach; arm being ripped out of its socket; man-to-animal transmutation) are brief, as if Schrader was afraid to include shocks lest he not be taken seriously. In his vain attempt to remain "honorable" and still be trendily "box office" he creates a film that isn't enough to satisfy harcore horror/gore buffs, and that is too obscure to please a mass audience. The Alan Ormsby script borrows sequences from the '42 version, but is not an improvement. John Heard, Annette O'Toole, Ruby Dee, Ed Begley Jr. (Video/Laser: MCA)

CAT'S EYE (1985). Anthology film combining screenwriter Stephen King and director Lewis Teague, who first dealt with King material in CUJO. A well-made film (superbly photographed by Jack Cardiff) of three tales linked by a superintelligent tail—a tabby who intervenes in affairs of men for non-evil purposes. The opener is black

---

"I got vampires in West Hollywood and big salamanders coming out of the fire hydrants in Santa Monica."

—*The cop in* **CAST A DEADLY SPELL.**

comedy in which habitual smoker James Woods seeks help from Quitters Inc. and finds that Alan King employs a harsh cure. The middle narrative concerns underworld kingpin Kenneth McMillan forcing his wife's lover (Robert Hays) to walk a high building ledge on a bet. Nice O'Henry twist here. Final story is the strongest: Our tabby follows a gnome-like minimonster (created by Carlo Rambaldi) into a rural home to defend Drew Barrymore from ferocious attacks. The menacer is a gremlin dressed as a court jester and the battle in the toy-ridden bedroom is a classic. One of the better King movies. Candy Clark, Jared Naughton. (Video/Laser: Fox)

CAT WITH THE JADED EYES, THE. See **WATCH ME WHEN I KILL.**

CAT WOMEN OF THE MOON (1953). Dreadful 3-D programmer, so unconvincing and stodgy it isn't even so-bad-it's-good. It's just so-bad-it's-unbearable. See it if you must but don't believe that baloney about it rivalling PLAN 9 FROM OUTER SPACE for sheer ineptitude. Some schlock has it, some doesn't. This don't. Sonny Tufts, Victor Jory, Douglas Fowley and Marie Windsor are on a loony lunar expedition but you'll howl at the Sears spacesuits and Woolworth zap guns. The "cat women" are ballet dancers in tights. Cat-o'-nine tails for producer Al Zimbalist (ROBOT MONSTER), director Arthur Hilton and scripter Roy Hamilton. Remade in 1960 as MISSILE TO THE MOON, and also known as ROCKET TO THE MOON. (Nostalgia Merchant; Filmfax; from Rhino in 3-D)

CAUGHT BY TELEVISION. See **TRAPPED BY TELEVISION.**

CAULDRON OF BLOOD (1971). Spanish-American grue (produced in 1967 in Madrid, but not released until after Boris Karloff's death) in which Karloff portrays a blind artist (mis)used by murderous wife Viveca Lindfors to dispose of corpses in a most unusual fashion. Karloff is in a wheelchair most of the time because he was ill. This is one cauldron that fails to boil under the stirring of director-writer Santos Alcocer (Edward Mann). Jean-Pierre Aumont doesn't bubble the pot, either. AKA as BLIND MAN'S BUFF, THE CORPSE COLLECTORS, DEATH COMES FROM THE DARK and THE SHRINKING CORPSE. (Republic; Vidcrest)

CAVEGIRL (1985). Lightweight spoof in the tradition of CAVEMAN, but without effects, monsters or satiric cleverness. It's a dumb sex comedy as Daniel Roebuck portrays a nerd who dresses like Indiana Jones. The military is conducting a "harmonic" time continuum test and accidentally sears Roebuck into prehistoric times where he meets perky blond cave dweller Cindy Ann Thompson in a bikini and chases her through the Cro-Magnon district, populated by the "Homo Erectus" species. There are smutty sex jokes, anal humor and a shaving cream squirting melee. Highlight is when Cindy removes her bra and shows off her wonderful breasts. David Oliver produced-directed Phil Groves' script. (Video/Laser: RCA/Columbia)

CAVEMAN (1981). Carl Gottlieb assumes directorial reins to bring his script (co-written with Rudy De Luca) to the screen—a hilarious send-up of prehistoric monster movies. Unfortunately, the comedy is thin but the stop-motion monsters by David Allen and Roy Arbogast are goofily cute. The cast (Barbara Bach, Ringo Star, Dennis Quaid, Jack Gilford) is lost in time and space. Nice try, Carl, but it's back to the cave to rub two sticks together again. Avery Schreiber, Shelley Long. (CBS/Fox)

CAVE OF THE LIVING DEAD (1963). The cave is the hiding place of vampires clad in black slips and panties who terrorize (seduce?) a German village with their biting attitude, under mad scientist Wolfgang Preiss. To the village comes an Interpol copper and a witch to fight for right. This German-Yugoslav whopper-flopper was produced by Richard Gordon and directed by Akos Von Ratony. Adrian Hoven, Erika Remberg. Also known as THE CURSE OF THE GREEN EYES and NIGHT OF THE VAMPIRES. (Modern Sound)

CELIA—CHILD OF TERROR (1989). Although released in theaters as CELIA, Trylon Video added CHILD OF TERROR to make it look like a horror film a la THE BAD SEED. Exploitation aside, it's a psychological profile of an Australian girl (Rebecca Smart) growing up in a rural area during the 1950s and encountering corruption, indifference, sadism and other "normal" aspects of mankind. Except for brief moments involving imaginary Aussie creatures called Hobyahs, and unexpected acts of violence during its climax, horror fans will feel misled. Directed-written by Australian film maker Ann Turner, who was appalled by the lurid packaging. (Trylon)

CELLAR, THE (1989). A Comanche legend tells of the evil spirit Queg-Why, the "bastard of the raven." The four-legged, ugly creature feasts on human flesh, lives beneath a desert ranchhouse and pops up just for meals. A kid new to the territory (Patrick Kilpatrick) sees it but nobody believes him—including father Chris Miller, whose domestic life is on the verge of collapse. This rendering of a story by Dr. David Henry Keller, adapted by John Woodward, boils down to the familiar confrontation between man and beast. And director Kevin S. Tenney fails to build suspense by showing too much of the creature too soon. Suzanne Savoy, Michael Wren, Lou Perry. Only old-time actor Ford Rainey, as an old desert rat, brings character to the film. (South Gate; Hemdale)

CELLAR DWELLER (1988). This monster thriller, filmed by Charlie Band in Rome, is distinguished by comic-book horror art cleverly intercut with live action to create a nice fantasy effect. John Carl Buechler, a special effects man who turned director with TROLL, again shows he has an appreciation for the genre as director. Artist Debrah Mullowney arrives at lonely Throckmorton Institute for the Arts as a specialist in horror imagery, her inspiration the work of a famous comic-book artist who died there 30 years before. By reading "The Curse of the Ancient Dead," she resurrects a monster, and by drawing comic pages highlighting the killer-beast she kills off her real-life enemies: Unlikable headmistress Yvonne De Carlo, old rival Cheryl-Ann Wilson, and snoopy private eye Vincent Edwards. Comic-book fans will dig the artwork, a homage to mags. Jeffrey Combs, Brian Robbins, Pamela Bellwood. (New World) (Laser: Image)

CEMETERY GIRLS. See **DRACULA'S GREAT LOVE.**

CEMETERY HIGH (1989). Incredibly unwatchable comedy send-up on splatter movies follows four dumb "teenage slasher sluts" running around campus murdering sexually aggressive, rude jocks. The guys get blown away in a variety of ways (except the way they would like to) while the dames make wise cracks. This incomprehensibly bad movie was directed by Gorman Bechard. It features "The Gore Gong" (to warn you things are turning bloody) and "The Hooter Honk" (to warn you sexual material is coming). Two more reasons not to waste your time. Debi Thibeault, Karen Nielsen, Lisa Schmidt. (Unicorn; Hollywood Home Entertainment)

CEMETERY OF TERROR (1984). Mexican import in which mad doc Hugo Stiglitz, resurrecting a corpse in a rite for Satan, meets nosy teenagers armed plan with the

"He who has wisdom wonders not of the beast / For nothing in Hell lives without man's consent. / Woe unto you that gives the beast form / To contemplate evil is to ask evil home."

—From "The Curses of the Ancient Dead" in **CELLAR DWELLER.**

Black Book of the Dead. Written-directed by Ruben Galindo Jr. in Texas. Usi Velasco, Rene Cardona III.

CEMETERY TRAMPS. See **DRACULA'S GREAT LOVE.**

CENTERFOLD GIRLS (1977). Sexually depraved slasher (Andrew Prine) is after "loose" beauties with staples in their navels who posed for a PLAYBOY-style magazine. CENTERFOLD GIRLS is creased and doesn't unfold neatly. Directed by John Peyser. Tiffany Bolling, Aldo Ray, Ray Danton, Francine York. (Media)

CHAIN REACTION (1980). Australian thriller, imaginatively directed by Ian Barry, is full of twists as a worker at WALDO, an atomic waste disposal project, is exposed to radiation and flees hospital to warn of contamination. The escapee is befriended by a race car driver and his nurse-wife, who become prey for "company men" covering up the leak. Exciting car chases in the MAD MAX style. Steve Bisley, Ross Thompson. Known on TV as NUCLEAR RUN. (Video/Laser: Embassy)

CHAIR, THE (1986). Quirky characterizations and a non-genre approach to this story about an old prison haunted by a warden electrocuted two decades earlier should have turned THE CHAIR into a comfortable offering. But it doesn't set easy. The action centers around High Street Correctional Facility when psychologist James Coco and warden Paul Benedict (once a guard at High Street) reopen the old prison to look after "eight fragile psychies." Helping out is naive, neophyte psychologist Trini Alvarado, unaware Benedict is going off the deep end. Electricity becomes an evil force, leading to deaths, amputations, etc. Director Waldemar Korzeniowsky's tone vacillates between horror and comedy. Gary McCleery, Stephen Geoffreys, Ron Taylor. (Video/Laser: Imperial)

CHAIRMAN, THE (1969). A brain transistor is implanted in Gregory Peck, a Nobel scientist, when he journeys to China to learn about a new enzyme which permits food crops to grow in any climate. What Peck doesn't know is: the transistor is a bomb that can be detonated back at Central Control. Peck's escape from behind the Bamboo Curtain turns into a chase/suspense escapade with spy antics and heroics. Directed by J. Lee Thompson. Anne Heywood, Arthur Hill, Keye Luke.

CHALLENGE, THE (1970). TV-movie is food for thought when a satellite crashes into the Pacific; Americans and Russians race to salvage the craft, each placing one soldier on an island to have them shoot it out, winner taking all. Marc Norman's script pulls off the silly idea with director Allen Smithee (an alias) manipulating the cast: Darren McGavin and Mako as the warriors, Broderick Crawford, James Whitmore, Paul Lukas as authority symbols. Skip Homeier co-stars.

CHALLENGER, THE (1991). An evil spirit stalks the woods in this horror film produced-written-directed by Grant Austin Waldman, who also stars. Dan Haggerty, Jay Richardson, Robin Sims. (Magnum)

CHAMBER OF FEAR. Video version of Boris Karloff's **FEAR CHAMBER, THE** (Unicorn).

CHAMBER OF HORRORS (1940). Entertaining Edgar Wallace story (based on SECRET OF THE DOOR WITH SEVEN LOCKS) set in a weird mansion where Dr. Manetta (Leslie Banks, a great of the 1930s) houses torture instruments. Lilli Palmer is a lovely heroine who falls into his trap, and Gina Malo is refreshing comedy relief as a vacationing American. "I love frolicking in a morgue," remarks Ms Palmer when trapped with boyfriend Richard Bird. There's nothing supernatural about it but it's charming in its antiquated fashion. Directed by Norman Lee. (United; Sinister/C; Filmfax; Nostalgia)

CHAMBER OF HORRORS (1966). Diabolical murderer Patrick O'Neal, who lost a hand escaping the hangman, uses detachable paws as murder weapons in this TV-movie (produced-directed by Hy Averback), pilot for an unsold series, HOUSE OF WAX. It was considered too graphic for TV and released to theaters, then put on TV anyway. O'Neal is Jason Cravatte, who changes his murder weapon at the drop of a . . . finger. In theaters it was gimmicked up with a "Horror Horn" and "Fear Flasher" (devices that must have warmed William Castle's heart) but these are excised from TV prints. Suzy Parker makes a fetching heroine in low-cut bodices, but Cesare Danova is a watered-down hero. Written by Stephen Kandell and Ray Russell. Wilfrid Hyde-White, Patrice Wymore, Jeanette Nolan, Marie Windsor, Barry Kroeger, Tony Curtis (in a cameo).

CHAMBER OF TORTURES. See **BARON BLOOD.**

CHANCES ARE (1989). This has such appealing characters it transcends its dumb premise—that of a dead husband returning from Heaven in a new body to fall in love with his former wife and to have (but reject) the opportunity to have sex with his own daughter. It also overcomes our suspension of belief in its casting of characters who never seem to age during a 23-year period. Credit screenwriters Perry and Randy Howze and director Emile Ardolino for taking the chance. Cybill Shepherd, never looking lovelier, plays the widow pursued these 23 intervening years by Ryan O'Neal, but remaining in love with her deceased husband. Mary Stuart Masterson is beautiful as the daughter and adds a strong romantic rival for the attentions of Robert Downey Jr. as the returning spouse. Maurice Jarre's music fleshes out this love tale, as does the camera work of William Fraker. Chances are, you're going to be richly entertained by CHANCES ARE. (Video/Laser: RCA/Columbia)

CHANDU ON THE MAGIC ISLAND (1934). Last eight chapters of the serial RETURN OF CHANDU, with Bela Lugosi as Frank Chandler, also known as Chandu. He's a drab magician (once a popular radio hero) fighting the Black Magic Cult of Ubasti on Lemuria. The first seven reels were also re-edited as RETURN OF CHANDU. Directed by Ray Taylor. (Video Yesteryear has a feature version; Sinister/C has the full-length serial)

CHANDU THE MAGICIAN (1932). Feature version of the radio serial, with Edmund Lowe as a magician who materializes and dematerializes at will. Bela Lugosi, who would later play Frank Chandler in a Chandu serial (CHANDU ON THE MAGIC ISLAND), portrays Roxor, a mad priest who intends to conquer the world. Directed by William Cameron Menzies and Michael Varne. Photographed by James Wong Howe. (Rex Miller)

CHANGELING, THE (1980). Superior haunted house tale heavy with creepy atmosphere, structured by writers William Gray and Diana Maddox. Composer George C. Scott, recovering from the deaths of his wife and child, discovers the mansion is haunted by a murdered child. Director Peter Medak keeps this tense story unfolding on several levels—as a pure ghost story, as a psychological study of Scott's recovery from tragedy, as a morality tale of good vs. evil. The ending is far out but enhances this unusually excellent supernatural tale. Trish Van Devere, Barry Morse, Melvyn Douglas, Jean Marsh, John Colicos. (Video/Laser: Vestron)

CHANGE OF MIND (1969). Brain transplant story, done with sensitivity, and not cackling mad scientists. This treads into racial territory, exploring what happens when the brain of a prominent white D.A. is transplanted into a black man's body. Made in Canada by director Robert Stevens, with music by Duke Ellington. Raymond St. Jacques, Susan Oliver, Leslie Nielsen.

CHARIOTS OF THE GODS? (1974). French "documentary" based on Erich Von Daniken's best-seller purporting that aliens once walked our Earth and influenced the human race. Pyramids, artifacts, cave wall dwellings and possible rocket landing sites on the plains of Peru are "supporting evidence" of Van Daniken's theories. Some have called him hare-brained, others ponder and wonder. It's weak evidence but at least Erich has started us thinking about unexplained mysteries of our planet. Directed by Harold Reinl. (United) (Laser: Image)

CHARLEY AND THE ANGEL (1973). Poor producer's version of IT'S A WONDERFUL LIFE, set in a rural town during the Depression, in which shopkeeper Fred MacMurray, taking his family for granted, is warned by angel Harry Morgan he had better mend his ways. MacMurray, too nice a guy to seem even remotely negligent, sees the light but has troubles with bootleggers. Lightweight Disney comedy with little conviction, although the cast is pleasant and reflects a different age of Disney film-making. Cloris Leachman is the confused but faithful wife and Kurt Russell has a small role. Roswell Rogers based his script on Will Stanton's novel GOLDEN EVENINGS OF SUMMER and Vincent McEveety directed. Vincent Van Patten, Kathleen Cody, Barbara Nichols, George O'Hanlon, Ed Begley Jr. (Disney)

CHARLIE BOY (1980). Two episodes of Britain's HAMMER HOUSE OF HORROR: In the title show, directed by Robert Young, a voodoo doll (a "fetish") causes puncture-wound deaths. There's a good twist ending to this tale of jungle evil. In "The 13th Reunion," directed by Peter Sasdy, a newswoman is assigned to cover the "Think Thin" Fat Farm and lose weight, only she's caught up in a funeral directors' reunion that ends on a sickening note. Leigh Lawson, Marius Goring, Julia Foster. (Thrillervideo packages these separately.)

CHARLOTTE'S WEB (1973). Animated version of E.B. White's story of a pig who foresees himself becoming sausage links and pork roast; a spider befriends him with its magical web. Voices by Debbie Reynolds, Charles Nelson Reilly, Paul Lynde, Henry Gibson. Directed by Charles A. Nichols. (Video/Laser: Paramount)

CHARLY (1968). Based on a short story by Daniel Keyes, "Flowers for Algernon," this brought an Academy Award to Cliff Robertson as Best Actor. He portrays a mentally retarded bakery worker who undergoes surgery and develops an incredibly high I.Q. A bittersweet love story is woven into this fragile tragedy; produced-directed by Ralph Nelson. Written by Stirling Silliphant. Claire Bloom, Lilia Skala, Dick Van Patten. (Video/Laser: Fox)

CHEECH AND CHONG'S 'THE CORSICAN BROTHERS' (1984). Cheech Marin and Thomas Chong drag out that old Alexandre Dumas chestnut about Siamese twins who share a psychic link, experiencing eachn other's pains and joys. Tasteless gags and non sequiturs are set against the French Revolution, with emphasis on homosexual and transvestite behavior. The Brothers Corsican escape beheading at the guillotine of dandy-randy heavy Roy Dotrice and become embroiled in parodies of the swashbuckler. Thomas Chong directed and co-wrote with associate producer (Cheech's wife) Rikki Marin, who doubles as a princess. Robbi Chong, Rae Dawn Chong. (Lightning; Live) (Laser: Vestron)

CHEERLEADER CAMP (1988). This was made so teenagers could watch nubile, bouncing young girls in short skirts and tight sweaters rehearsing at Camp Hurrah. Poor Betsy Russell keeps having strange dreams and darned if a killer doesn't start knocking off the babes one by one. Could it be Leif Garrett, who wants to love Betsy but she won't let him? Or could be it sleazy handyman Buck Flowers? Anyhow, one girl gets clippers through the back of her head and out her mouth. She's left speechless. John Quinn produced-directed this cheerless FRIDAY THE 13TH clone, also called BLOODY POM-POMS. Lucinda Dickey, Lorie Griffin, Terri Weigel. (Prism; Paramount)

CHEERLEADER CAMP II (1990). If you saw CHEERLEADER CAMP I there isn't much point in seeing CHEERLEADER CAMP II unless you enjoy eyeballing retread psychomurder cheapie bombs. (Prism)

CHERRY 2000 (1986). Intriguing action/sci-fi adventure set in 2017 when female robots are love-making machines. When his Cherry 2000 model shorts out while making love in an overflow of soap suds, a dumb male (David Andrews) decides to find a replacement in The Zone—an area of Nevada where outlaw bands and crazy characters rove. His guide is Melanie Griffin (a character named E. Johnson), who leads him into bizarre situations—some of them cliffhangers. Old-timers Ben Johnson and Harry Carey Jr. add professionalism to the raucous proceedings. Director Steve de Jarnatt does all he can to beef up the Michael Almereyda script. Tim Thomerson, Brion James. (Video/Laser: Orion)

CHILD, THE (1977). Rip-off of THE EXORCIST, in which a murderous moppet calls upon ghoulish graveyard demons to carry out her revenge against despicable characters. Directed by Robert Voskanian. Rosalie Cole, Laura Barnett. Also known as ZOMBIE CHILD. (Best; from FHE and Paragon as **KILL AND GO HIDE**)

CHILD OF DARKNESS, CHILD OF LIGHT (1991). The Angel of Death is back in this fascinating OMEN-style TV-movie based on VIRGIN, a novel by James Patterson. Brian Taggert's teleplay compellingly depicts the efforts of priest Anthony John Denison (a "church cop") to investigate the virgin pregnancies of two 15-year-olds (Kristen Dattilo and Sydney Penny). One of the babies will be the Antichrist—but which one? Meanwhile, the world is plagued by disease and pestilence. Denison is aided by nun Sela Ward, who soon falls prey to the Devil's manipulation of her repressed sexual desires. Director Marina Sargenti moves it at a brisk pace and doesn't telegraph a climactic twist that'll hit hard. Brad Davis, Paxton Whitehead. (Paramount)

CHILD OF GLASS (1977). Children's TV-movie is made palatable by a top cast and a good George Duning score. To a southern farm come young Biff McGuire and his family—before long he's having encounters of a singular kind with of a French girl's ghost, who gives him the riddle of the "Child of Glass," the answer to which could lead to a diamond fortune. The gentle Jim Lawrence script is based on Richard Peck's novel, THE GHOST BELONGED TO ME. Directed by John Erdman. Barbara Barrie, Anthony Zerbe (portraying a drunken handyman), Nina Foch (as a could-be witch), Steve Shaw, Katy Kurtzman. (Disney)

CHILD OF SATAN. Video version of **TO THE DEVIL A DAUGHTER** (Olympus).

CHILDREN, THE (1980). Kind-of-fun variation on THE NIGHT OF THE LIVING DEAD in which leakage from a nuclear plant causes a cloud of radiation that turns a busload of children into hollow-eyed zombies. You're in for juvenile jars, kiddie killings and moppet mayhem because the merest touch from a child's atomic-charged fingers causes adults to smoke and turn into rotting flesh. The disgusting idea that adults must go out with machetes and cut off the kids' hands gives this a perverse twist. Producer Max Kalmanowicz directs it like a monster flick of the '50s. Also known as THE CHILDREN OF RAVENSBACK. Martin Shakar, Gil Rogers, Gale Garnett. (Vestron; Rhino)

CHILDREN OF BLOOD. Video version of **CAULDRON OF BLOOD** (Republic).

CHILDREN OF THE CORN (1984). Lousy adaptation of a story from Stephen King's collection NIGHT SHIFT and a prime example of filmmakers (director Fritz Kiersch, screenwriter George Goldsmith) taking a master's work and turning it into schlock. Peter Horton and Linda Hamilton are travelers detoured into a rural community in Nebraska lorded over by a cult of youngsters slaughtering adults as a sacrifice to a corn god. The corncob icon shows up in the climax but is so poorly photographed, one never knows what "it" is. Lend Horton an ear to make this fiasco work. R. G. Armstrong, John Franklin. (Embassy; Starmaker) (Laser: Image)

CHILDREN OF THE CORN: DEADLY HARVEST (1992). Corn stalks Hollywood again when Stephen King's revengeful cornfield god, He Who Walks Behind the Rows, returns to Gatlin, Neb., to manipulate the town's young ones to carry out his/hers/its evil bidding, a form of vengeance for man's toxic poisoning of the corn industry. Ned Romero as Dr. Frank Red Bear, an Indian professor, steals the show. Director David F. Price fails to pick up the pacing and this horror film drags except for a few homicidal set pieces: a man bleeds to death in church during a hellfire sermon; a house falls on an old woman; a doctor is punctured to death by hypos; an invalid in a wheelchair crases through a plateglass window, disturbing a bingo game. Terence Knox, Paul Scherrer, Ryan Bollman, Christie Clark. (Paramount)

CHILDREN OF THE DAMNED (1963). Sequel to VILLAGE OF THE DAMNED is superior thanks to a literate script by John Briley that touches on aggressive behavior. A group of highly intelligent children, created by an alien race which impregnated Earth mothers from deep space, is brought to London where the government intends to destroy them. The kids are wise to the conspiracy and wrest control. Thoughtfully directed by Anton M. Leader; based on ideas from John Wyndham's THE MIDWICH CUCKOOS. Alan Badel, Ian Hendry, Clive Powell, Bessie Love, Frank Summerscales. (MGM/UA) (Laser: MGM, with **VILLAGE OF THE DAMNED**)

CHILDREN OF THE FULL MOON (1980). Repackaged episodes of Britain's HAMMER HOUSE OF HORROR. In the title story, directed by Tom Clegg, Diana Dors portrays a nanny in a strange house in the forest who terrorizes a man and woman. Very bleak, with a downbeat ending. In "Visitor From the Grave," directed by Peter Sasdy, a weak but wealthy woman kills an intruder. Her husband covers up for her, but then she sees the dead man in the darnedest places. There's a twist ending on top of a twist ending. Christopher Cazenove, Celia Gregory, Robert Urquhart, Simon MacCorkindale. (CHILDREN is from Thrillervideo with Elvira.)

CHILDREN OF THE NIGHT. Video version of **DAUGHTERS OF DARKNESS** (Ariel).

CHILDREN OF THE NIGHT (1991). Produced by the Fangoria Magazine empire, this monster-gorefest should satisfy undemanding horrror fans, but it offers nothing fresh or unusual to the vampire genre. The children in Allburg USA ("a quiet town") are imprisoned in suspended animation to provide blood for the number one adult vampire (David Sawyer). A few of the images are memorable—such as teenage girls swimming in a water-filled crypt, and a truck careening with a giant stake thrust ahead of it—but it's all derivative, and its attempts at black humor are out of place. Tony Randel directed in Michigan. Karen Black, Peter DeLuise, Ami Dolenz. (Columbia TriStar)

CHILDREN SHOULDN'T PLAY WITH DEAD THINGS (1972). A hammy traveling troupe journeys to an island to stage a satanic play, pretending to raise the dead. But corpses in the graveyard aren't pretending—they're out for blood! This vacillates between stupidity and cheap thrills in the hands of producer-director Bob Clark, who co-scripted with Alan Ormsby, doubling as the troupe's director. Intelligent viewers shouldn't waste time with dumb movies. Anya Ormsby (Alan's wife), Bruce Solomon. (Gorgon; MPI; from True World as **REVENGE OF THE LIVING DEAD**) (Laser: Japanese)

CHILD'S PLAY (1972). This falls into "metaphorical" or "allegorical horror," a subgenre that includes Shirley Jackson's "The Lottery" and THE SAILOR WHO FELL FROM GRACE WITH THE SEA. adapted by Leon Prochnik from a play by Robert Marasco, it's about the unseen, and hence a provocative work. In a staid Catholic boarding school for boys, a conflict erupts between instructors James Mason and Robert Preston. Into this turbulent milieu comes fledgling gym instructor Beau Bridges, whose innocence is demolished by the secrets he learns about the feud and the twisted students it has bred. A horror story about ideas rather than monsters, and if there are any monsters, they are in human form. Sidney Lumet directed this compellingly.

CHILD'S PLAY (1985). British TV-movie, produced by Hammer for "The Fox Mystery Theater," depicts a family trapped within their home when an invisible wall pops up. Mary Crosby, Nicholas Clay, Debbie Chasen.

CHILD'S PLAY (1988). Considering how preposterous the precise is, this horror tale works thanks to director Tom Holland's suspension of our disbelief. A strangler is tracked down by cop Chris Sarandon and killed, but not before he transfers his soul into a department store doll. The doll finds its way into the hands of a youngster and sets out to kill for revenge. including Sarandon. The boy's mother, Catherine Hicks, has a thankless role, exclaiming such lines as "My God, the doll's alive!" But it is her bravura and acting abilities that also help to save the picture. There are moments when the doll, designed by producer David Kirschner, captures a note of terror despite its small size. Alex Vincent, Brad Dourif, Dinah Manoff. (Video/Laser: MGM)

CHILD'S PLAY 2 (1990). Chucky, the doll's body inhabited by the spirit of the Lakeside Strangler, is back for more cat-and-mouse games in producer David Kirschner's followup to his box office smash. There are few surprises in Don Mancini's script—just more of the same terror tactics. After Chucky is brought back to life by a toy corporation's research department, he turns into a demonic killer, seeking out the youth of the first film to claim his body as a new hiding place. The best sequence comes at the toy manufacturing center's assembly line with a chase involving Chucky. (Video/Laser: MCA)

CHILD'S PLAY 3: LOOK WHO'S STALKING (1991). A despicable horror film, crassly made to cash in on the overworked "Chucky the Killer Doll" concept. Chucky goes on his third (and one hopes final) rampage at a military school for boys after his evil spirit is brought back to life when the Chucky-toy assembly line is reactivated. Don Mancini's screenplay is devoid of originality—once again it's a set-up for chuckling Chucky to trap victims and close in for the kill. The climax, set in a horror-amusement ride in a carnival, is gratuitous. Directed by Jack Bender, who deserved a better feature debut after helming TV's THE DREAMER OF OZ. Justin Whalin, Perrey Reeves. (Video/Laser: MCA)

CHILLER (1985). Producer Richard Kobritz (SALEM'S LOT, CHRISTINE) adds to his good credits with this TV horror movie. Writer-producer J. D. Feigleson's story centers on a malfunction in a Cryonics "mausoleum" that allows doctors to restore life to long-dead Michael Beck—but Beck returns to life without a soul, subjecting everyone to physical and mental tortures. Director Wes Craven sustains suspense and tension. Paul Sorvino is the family minister, Beatrice Straight is the devoted mother. Make-up work by Stan Winston.

CHILLERS (1989). Direct-to-video anthology horror tales told by passengers in a lonely depot waiting for a bus that never seems to come. Five narratives in all, all spun without much luster, on a nothing budget by writer-producer-director Daniel Boyd. Jesse Emer, Marjorie Fitzsimmons. Jim Wolff. (Raedon; Simitar; Prism)

CHILL FACTOR. See **COLD NIGHT'S DEATH, A.**

CHILLING (1974). Offbeat British horror film is a Grand Guignol mixture of slasher murders, violent soap opera and psychoterror as a killer strikes against residents of a small community for a wrong committed at childhood. The film has twists and turns, and unusual characters, as the elaborate death plot unfolds. The gimmick is that victims appear to die of strokes, although death also comes in such forms as exploding auto, harpoon gun, etc. Kevin O'Neill, David Bunt, Guy Doleman.

CHILLING, THE (1989). Lab assistant Linda Blair, mad doctor Troy Donahue and security guard Dan Haggerty are Kansas City residents facing cryogenic corpses returned to life on Halloween by bolts of electricity. Written-produced-directed by Jack A. Sunseri. Ron Vincent co-stars. (Coyote; Hemdale; Satellite)

CHIMERA (1990). In the vein of the Quatermass films, this British TV-movie depicts science out of control and the efforts of society to clean up the mess. Originally made as MONKEY BOY in four one-hour installments, but edited to two hours for U.S. TV, this opens at the Jenner Clinic, where an experiment is underway to create a chimera, a creature with the DNA of man and monkey. A slaughter of the doctors leads to an investigation headed by the powerful and strange Hennessey (Kenneth Cranhaw), essayed in the style of Dr. Quatermass. Stephen Gallagher fashioned the telescript from his novel, and it was directed by Lawrence Gordon Clark. Christine Kavanagh, John Lynch. (Prism) (Laser: Image)

CHINA SYNDROME, THE (1979). Superb "what if?" science thriller set in a nuclear power station that almost causes a catastrophic chain reaction, prevented only by plant foreman Jack Lemmon's expedient actions. The government hushes it up but newswoman Jane Fonda and cameraman Michael Douglas probe for the truth. Excellently directed by James Bridges and written by Bridges, Mike Gray and T. S. Cook. Gripping drama with the Three Mile Island near-tragedy (which occurred the same year this was released) lending credence to the chilling conclusions this makes about our rush to self-destruction. Scott Brady, Peter Donat, Wilford Brimley, James Hampton. (Video/Laser: RCA/Columbia)

CHINCHERO. TV title for **LAST MOVIE, THE.**

CHINESE GHOST STORY, A (1987). Directed by Ching Siu Tung, this is a striking supernatural film blending action, fantasy, martial arts, horror, rock and roll and comedy. A 19th century gothic tale with Taoist philosophy accompanying its genre ingredients, it's a nonstop Hong Kong example of superb, unbridled film making. Leslie Cheung, Wong Tsu Hsien.

CHINESE WEB, THE (1978). Episodes of TV's SPIDERMAN, with the wall-climbing, web-spinning hero helping a Chinese diplomat charged with selling secrets to foreign powers. Directed by Don McDougall. Nicholas Hammond, Robert F. Simon. (Fox)

CHITTY CHITTY BANG BANG (1968). Critics junked this $10 million musical "lemon" about a flying car from the assembly line of producer Albert Broccoli. Hardly anyone liked the songs, John Stears' effects were sneered at and many felt this version of Ian Fleming's book for children had been de-Samonized by adaptors Roald Dahl and Richard Maibaum and director Ken Hughes. Dick Van Dyke portrays the father who tells this Detroit fairy tale to his kids. Sally Ann Howes, Lionel Jeffries, Gert Frobe, Benny Hill, James Robertson Justice. (MGM/UA; Fox; Time-Life) (Laser: MGM/UA)

CHOKE CANYON (1984). Rousing adventure with a minor sci-fi theme: physicist Stephen Collins sets up a computer in a Utah canyon to capture soundwaves (from Halley's Comet) to be turned into "safe energy." But the Pilgrim Corp. is dumping toxic waste and a battle-to-the-death erupts. Although the aerial scenes between a bi-winged plane and helicopter are exciting, an irony is a work: If Collins wants energy for peaceful reasons, why is he willing to destroy property and lives? That aside, director Chuck Bail gets lively performances by Janet Julian as the corp. daughter who turns against her father, Lance Henriksen as a slimy henchman, Bo Svenson as a sympathetic hitman (Capt. Oliver Parkside) and Victoria Racimo as Collins' loyal lab assistant. (Media)

C.H.O.M.P.S. (1980). Juvenile comedy produced by Joe Barbera, king of Saturday cartoons. The title stands for Canine Home Protection System, a shaggy dog robot built with X-ray vision, superstrength, in-house sound effects and the ability to detect crime. Industrialist Jim Backus plots to steal the "dog" from inventor Wesley Eure. The cast plays for cute: Conrad Bain, Valerie Bertinelli, Chuck McCann, Red Buttons, Hermione Baddeley, Robert Q. Lewis. At best, a lightweight diversion, something to catch between buses. Don Chaffey directs with an eye on the nearest fire hydrant. (Orion)

CHOOPER, THE (1971). "The Chooper Man," a legendary Indian spirit haunting a farmhouse, turns out to be a silly-looking man in black who runs around with a long sword, killing snoopers. This crude effort by cult director Ray Dennis Steckler is substandard, with sound as unintelligible as the storyline. Even Steckler's followers will find this excruciatingly painful as the frequent killings are padded out with useless rodeo footage and scenes of pensive Carolyn Brandt walking around as she narrates the threadbare plot. Also known as BLOOD SHACK. Jason Wayne, Laurel Spring, John Bats, Peanuts the Pony. (From Premiere as **CURSE OF THE EVIL SPIRIT**)

CHOPPER CHICKS IN ZOMBIETOWN (1990). Troma drama doesn't live up to its promising title as it plumbs lower depths of the "walking dead" genre. Call it "Dikes on Bikes" when motorcycle mamas ride into the desert town of Zariah (pop: 128) where the dead are resurrected to work in a mine and shambling corpses eat flesh of the living. The klutz sluts with the struts have guts and fight against the flesh-munching undead, knocking off their heads with bats, setting them afire, etc. The chopper-boppers then ride off into the sunset. It's a dreary, uninspired effort to blend parody with gore. Written-directed by Dan Hoskins and Vicki Frederick, Jamie Rose, Catherine Carlen, Lycia Naff, Kristina Loggia. (Video/Laser: RCA/Columbia)

CHOPPING MALL (1986). A combination of WESTWORLD, ALIENS and any movie about malfunctioning robots, this Julie Corman production is loaded with in-jokes and Roger Corman memorabilia. Mary Woronov and Paul Bartel appear as Mr. and Mrs. Bland from EATING RAOUL, there's a store called "Roger's Little Shop of Pets," and Dick Miller is janitor Walter Paisley (a character he created in BUCKET OF BLOOD). Otherwise it's your basic robots-run-amok in the Park Plaza 2000 Shopping Center, where teenagers are spending the night. Director Jim Wynorski cheapens the effect with unnecessary nudity and cliches as the "killbots" (the original title) mindlessly murder, concluding each homicide with "Have a nice day." The kids are well-armed (from "Peckinpah's Sporting Goods") but bullets bounce off the robots as our heroes dodge killer zap rays, and they must resort to more exotic weaponry. Karrie Emerson, Kelli Maroney, Barbara Crampton. (Lightning)

CHOSEN, THE (1977). Italian-British production, originally HOLOCAUST 2000, is a rehash of THE OMEN, with Kirk Douglas as an industrialist who specializes in nuclear power plants and suspects he is fulfilling Biblical prophesies and setting the world on a disaster course. You see, Simon Ward, his son, is the Son of Satan, or the Antichrist. A fine international cast struggles with a muddled screenplay: Anthony Quayle, Virginia McKenna, Alexander Knox. Directed by Alberto De Martino. (Vestron; Fox)

CHOSEN SURVIVORS (1974). See editions 1-3.

CHRISTINE (1983). Stylish, well-lubricated adaptation of Stephen King's novel about a 1958 Plymouth Fury possessed by evil powers. Director John Carpenter shifts into high gear as the car knocks off its "rivals." The car, you see, is "Fury-iously" jealous. For this is a love story about a boy and his car. Call it auto-eroticism. There's a great scene of the auto in flames, speeding through the night. The movie works because of our love affairs with cars, an extension of our sexual energies. Gee, are we getting deep. But don't worry about subtext—focus on that Plymouth as it becomes a frightening "character." Keith Gordon, John Stockwell, Alexandra Paul, Harry Dean Stanton. (Video/Laser: RCA/Columbia)

CHRISTMAS CAROL, A (1938). The best tune to this MGM adaptation of the Dickens classic is another Carroll: Leo G., who co-stars with Reginald Owen, Gene Lockhart and Ann Rutherford. Stodgy but servicable. Directed by Edwin L. Marin. (Video/Laser: MGM/UA)

CHRISTMAS CAROL, A (1951). A heavy atmosphere prevails in this British version of Dickens' tale about Mr. Scrooge, miserly, heartless Londoner, and his fateful encounters with spirits of Christmases past, present and future. Alastair Sim is superb as Scrooge. Mervyn Johns, Ernest Thesiger. Produced-directed by Brian Desmond Hurst. (United; VCI) (Laser: United)

FRANK FINLAY

CHRISTMAS CAROL, A (1984). Superior TV adaptation of Dickens' classic, rich in character acting, insightful characterizations and Victorian ambience—and heartwarming to boot. The Roger O. Hirson teleplay faithfully captures the setting and language of the British master. Under Clive Donner's direction, George C. Scott delivers a tour de force performance as Scrooge undergoes his exposure to the Christmas spirits. Nigel Davenport, David Warner, Frank Finlay (as Marley's ghost), Michael Gough, Angela Pleasence.

CHRISTMAS EVIL. Video version of **TERROR IN TOYLAND** (Saturn).

CHRISTMAS MARTIAN, THE (1971). E.T. saucer slingers land on Earth to help lost children find their way home. They in turn help the Martians get back to their own world. Ho ho ho! Canadian-French yuletide-message film directed by Bernard Gosselin.

CHRISTMAS PRESENT (1985). British reworking of Dickens' A CHRISTMAS CAROL, starring Peter Chelsom as Nigel Playfayre, a Scrooge-like character. Gentle, mild-mannered TV-movie, written-directed by Tony Bicat.

CHRISTMAS THAT ALMOST WASN'T, THE (1966). Folksy Italian children's fare in which Rossano Brazzi (who also directed) plays Phineas T. Prune, multi-billionaire who hates children so much he buys the North Pole and plans to evict Santa, charging him with flagrant violation of child labor laws for using elves and fairies. Santa must work in a department store to raise funds—proving even the best of us go commercial. Script and lyrics by Paul Tripp, who also appears in the cast. (HBO)

C.H.U.D. (1984). Contamination Hazard Urban Disposal is dumping toxic wastes into N. Y. sewers. Also out there are Cannibalistic Humanoid Underground Dwellers, a clan infected by radioactivity. Parnell Hall has shaped an intelligent script focusing on cop Christopher Curry trying to solve his wife's disappearance, and uncovering a conspiracy between government and Manhattan authorities. C.H.U.D. has more class than other films about creatures in slimy sewers. Director Douglas Check photographed underground New York with atmospheric know-how and Tim Boxell's monster designs are effective (creatures have drippy fangs, white glowing bulbs for eyes, stretchable necks). What gives it versimilitude are its Soho locations, grubby street people and T-shirts stained with perspiration. The film sports the tag: "Filmed in and under New York City." John Heard, Laurie Mattos, Justin Hall. (Media) (Laser: Image)

C.H.U.D. II: BUD THE CHUD (1989). A sequel in name only, this failure indulges in tongue-in-cheek comedy, none of which works in the hands of director David Irving. The screenplay by Ed Naha, writing as "M. Kane Jeeves," a one-time pseudonym for W. C. Fields, is a compendium of stolen ideas and completely fizzles in detailing how a cannibal-zombie, the result of a military project, turns the town of Winterhaven into ghoulish killers. Robert Vaughn has fun as the demented officer in charge of the aborted project and is surrounded by Larry Linville, Bianca Jagger, Norman Fell, June Lockhart, Clive Revill—even the director's mother, Priscilla Pointer, joins in the idiotic activities. There's no way to describe adequately how awful this crud C.H.U.D. is. Brian Robbins, Bill Calvert, Tricia Leigh Fisher. (Video/Laser: Vestron)

CHUMP AT OXFORD, A (1940). Milestone Laurel and Hardy comedy in which Stan sustains a concussion and awakens a genius—with aristocratic mannerisms yet. One of the duo's best efforts. Directed by Alfred Goulding. Peter Cushing, Forrester Harvey. (Media; Nostalgia Merchant; Critics' Choice) (Laser: 3M)

CHURCH, THE (1988). Italy's gore master, Dario Argento, concocted this horror tale with director Michele Soavi. Curiously, it fails to engage the viewer despite powerful images of a Budapest church—it's a case of bland characters. Seems Teutonic Knights once buried bodies and an encoded parchment beneath the church. When a librarian-cataloguer deciphers it, and slides open a long-locked hatch leading to a pit below, he unleashes demons that possess his body and that of a woman working in the church. In fact, everyone gets possessed and all hell breaks loose when tourists are locked inside the cathedral. There are unpleasant overtones of child molestation and the usual fright-monsters and spooky imagery, not to mention the oppressive atmosphere of the church. Hugh Quarshie, Tomas Arana, Feodor Chaliapin. (South Gate)

CINDERELLA (1950). Walt Disney's version of the oft-repeated fairy tale (chronicled by Charles Perrault and Brothers Grimm) about the lovely scullery maid mistreated by evil stepsisters who goes to the ball and falls for Prince Charming. Exaggerated storybook prettiness works well here. Voices include Verna Felton, Ilene Woods, Eleanor Audley and Lucille Bliss. (Disney)

CINDERELLA (1977). Sexually explicit R-rated version of the fairy tale, starring Cheryl Smith as the adventuress who gains the upper hand through more than sweetness and light. Directed by Michael Pataki. Kirk Scott, Brett Smiley. (Lightning)

CINDERELLA 2000 (1977). Costumed sci-fi version of the kiddie tale, but it's soft porn for adults, set in 2047, when love-making is not allowed and Big Brother watches with robots. Director Al Adamson is no Prince Charming and scripter Bud Donnelly turned into a pumpkin. No glass slipper, this. (Specialty)

CINDERFELLA (1960). Reversal of the sexes has Jerry Lewis as the brow-beaten lackey with evil brothers (Henry Silva and Robert Hutton). Ed Wynn appears as the fairy "godfather." Get the idea? Director Frank Tashlin's script is a clumsy thing with Lewis (who also produced) mugging maladroitly. Anna Maria Alberghetti, Judith Anderson. (IVE)

CINEMAGIC (1985). Compilation of horror/sci-fi vignettes: "Nightfright"; "Illegal Alien" (see that entry); "Dr. Doberman," "The Thing in the Basement." (MPI)

CIRCLE OF IRON (1979). Martial arts film, produced by Sandy Howard in Israel, is an odd mix of kung fu/Zen philosophy, based on a Bruce Lee-James Coburn idea expanded by Stirling Silliphant and Stanley Mann. Blind sage David Carradine holds the key to all knowledge in a mythical kingdom ("a land that never was and always is") where warrior Jeff Cooper is on The Odyssey of Knowledge, passing ordeals which test strength and cunning. Each adversary is Carradine in make-up—as the Monkey Man, the Rhythm Man and Death. When Cooper reaches Christopher Lee, he learns the meaning of life: Beware Pretentious Movies Bearing Messages. Roddy McDowall plays the White Robe and Eli Wallach is a man in a tub of oil. Dialogue runs to lines like "Tie two birds together; they have four wings yet cannot fly" and "The fool is the twin of the wise." Potential fools have been forewarned. (Embassy)

CIRCUITRY MAN (1990). Stylish, amusing sci-fi hardware actioner set in a near future when society, the environment completely poisoned, has moved underground. This has a rogues' gallery of oddball characters: Plughead (Vernon Wells), a criminal kingpin with sensory inputs in his head; female kingpin Juice (Lu Leonard), adventurer Leech (Dennis Christopher) and lesbian-tough broad Yoyo (Barbara Alyn Woods). The titular character (Jim Metzler) is a humanoid synthetic man who joins bodyguard Lori (Dana Wheeler-Nicholson) to take microchips across country to New York. Two sequences stand out: when Circuitry Man and Plughead meet in Plughead's mind, and when Circuitry Man creates a romantic environment for his affair with Lori. Directed by Steven Lovy, who scripted with Robert Lovy. (Video/Laser: RCA/Columbia)

CIRCUS OF BLOOD. See **BERSERK.**

CIRCUS OF FEAR. Video version of **PSYCHO CIRCUS,** featuring new footage and a new introduction with John Carradine. (Saturn; Sinister/C; Nostalgia)

CIRCUS OF HORRORS (1959). Engrossing British shocker about a plastic surgeon (Anton Diffring) who leaves his patients hideously deformed. Meanwhile, Diffring runs his three-ring circus like a madman, causing grisly gore murders under the Big Top. Wonderfully graphic deaths in all three rings. Sick but engaging. Directed by Sidney Mayers from an engaging script by George Baxt. Yvonne Monlaur, Erika Remberg, Yvonne Romain, Donald Pleasence. (HBO) (Laser: Image, with

BARON BLOOD)

CIRCUS OF TERROR. See **BERSERK.**

CITY BENEATH THE SEA (1971). Irwin Allen, Hollywood's sophomoric producer of TV juvenilia, crash-dived to his usual low for this TV-pilot with an absurd script by John Meredyth Lucas. In 2053, Stuart Whitman, boss of a submerged metropolis, is faced with several crises, some natural, some man-made. Robert Wagner, Rosemary Forsyth, Richard Basehart, Paul Stewart, Joseph Cotten, James Darren, Whit Bissell, Also known as CITY BENEATH THE SEA.

CITY LIMITS (1985). Fifteen years "from now" a plague decimates mankind, and for no reason discernible, society ends up as gangs of survivors, bikers called the DAs and the Clippers, who maintain an uneasy truce and hold jousting contests. One gang is influenced by evil Robby Benson (who never moves from behind his desk) and does the forbidden—uses weapons to gain control. From the team that made ANDROID, this is a pointless excuse for biking stunts, though it avoids being a MAD MAX imitation. Directed by Aaron Lipstadt, scripted by Don Opper. Darrell Larson, Kim Cattrall, Rae Dawn Chong, James Earl Jones. (Vestron; HHE)

CITY OF BLOOD (1987). Prehistoric tribal witch doctor materializes in Johannesburg, killing prostitutes. A medical examiner (Joe Stewardson) pursues the supernatural spectre. Directed-written by Darrell Roodt. Ian Yule, Dudu Meltize, Susan Coetzer. (New World)

CITY OF FEAR (1959). What is Copat 60? A lethal radioactive powder that could blow L.A. off the map. So what's so terrible about that? Some Copat 60 is in a metal box in the hands of an escaped convict (Vincent Edwards). Tense, low-budget thriller, enhanced by location realism. Directed by Irving Lerner. John Archer, Patricia Blair, Lyle Talbot.

CITY OF LOST MEN (1935). Truncated version of Mascot's 12-chapter serial **LOST CITY, THE.**

CITY OF THE DEAD. See **HORROR HOTEL.**

CITY OF THE LIVING DEAD. Video version of **GATES OF HELL** (Pacesetter).

CITY OF THE WALKING DEAD (1980). If you savor zombie monsters slaughtering with guns and knives and if you relish bodies torn asunder and the blood sucked from their throats, you'll rollick in the bloodthirsty joy of this Italian-Spanish goreburst, a loose sequel to Lucio Fulco's ZOMBIE. This is the retitled U.S. version of NIGHTMARE CITY, aka INVASION BY THE ATOMIC ZOMBIES. These vampiric creatures have been subjected to atomic radiation and their cells given "abnormal strength." Director Umberto Lenzi brings nihilism to this doomsday thriller, suggesting through military leaders Mel Ferrer and Francisco Rabal that mankind is doomed. Newsman Hugo Stiglitz and wife Laura Trotter flee across country, barely escaping perilous encounters with bloodsuckers. The violence is ultra-graphic: a woman's breast is cut open and an eye gouged out, etc. Maria Rosaria Omaggio, Sonia Viviani. (Cinema Group; Continental; New Star)

CITY UNDER THE SEA. See **WAR GODS OF THE DEEP.**

CLAIRVOYANT, THE (1935). Antiquated but fascinating story of ashyster seer who discovers he has genuine ESP and must convince citizens a mine cave-in will occur. Claude Rains, as the soothsayer, projects a haunted, tormented soul. Fay Wray, the girl in Kong's paw, provides sympathetic love interest. Directed by Maurice Elvey. (From Kartes as **EVIL MIND, THE**)

CLAIRVOYANT, THE (1982). Refreshingly offbeat slasher flick, with believable characters caught up in a maelstrom of mayhem. "The Handcuff Murders" are sweeping Manhattan when TV talk-show host Perry King begins a vendetta against the killer, helping psychic artist Elizabeth Kemp who draws impressions of the murders. She is caught between the manipulative host and sincere cops as the web tightens. Armand Mastroianni directs with restraint. Norman Parker, Kenneth McMillan. (Magnum; from CBS/Fox as **KILLING HOUR, THE**)

CLAN OF THE CAVE BEAR, THE (1986). Adaptation of Jean Auel's best-selling novel dramatizing man's/woman's earliest days, when he/she still lived in caves and was ruled by tribal customs. Daryl Hannah is Ayla, a Cro-Magnon raised by Neanderthals to become the first woman hunter. John Sayles' script emphasizes the mysticism and destiny of early man. In the vein of ONE MILLION B.C. but without dinosaurs. Pamela Reed, James Remar. (Video/Laser: Fox)

CLARENCE (1990). Substandard TV-movie that is an insult to its inspiration. Clarence is a retread of the Guardian Angel from IT'S A WONDERFUL LIFE but any similiarities are as distant as Heaven itself. Clarence (Robert Carradine) is assigned to help a fellow angel straighten out his family problems back on earth. It's tired, it's cliched and it's un-Heavenly as directed by Eric Till. Kate Trotter, Louis del Grande. (Republic)

CLASH OF THE TITANS (1981). The last work of stop-motion pioneer Ray Harryhausen and producer Charles Schneer (who teamed on many fantasy successes), and hence the end of an era. Harryhausen's techniques seem outmoded (coming in the wake of the effects revolution) and one senses TITANS spelling doom for hand-crafted stop motion. This paean to Greek mythology has all that Grecian royalty atop Mt. Olympus in the personages of Laurence Olivier, Claire Bloom, Maggie Smith and Ursula Andress. The hero (Harry Hamlin) and heroine (Judi Bowker) are—Zeus bedamned!—purely squaresville. When Harryhausen unleashes the horned brute Calibos (Lord of the Marsh), the Medusa, the Kraken (a monster of the deep), the two-headed Dioskilos wolf dog and other beasties, the film finally comes alive. Script by Beverly Cross; direction by Desmond Davis. Burgess Meredith is a standout as chronicler Ammon. (Video/Laser: MGM)

CLASS OF 1999 (1990). There's a vitality and spirit to this action film, the handiwork of director Mark L. Lester, who keeps it moving even when the C. Courtney Joyner script crumbles. It's a freaky blend of THE TERMINATOR, every post-holocaust movie ever made, MAD MAX craziness, ROBOCOP and CLASS OF 1984, to which this could be a loose sequel. By 1999 gangs have taken over our high schools, forcing educators to drastic measures—in this case Stacy Keach brings to Seattle's Kennedy High three androids programmed to teach without sparing the rod. When the robots go out of control, good guy Bradley Gregg unites rival gangs. The pyrotechnics, battle effects and android work are powerful, and Pam Grier, Patrick Kilpatrick and John P. Ryan as the berserk humanoids give the film a tongue-in-cheek tone that matches the campy lines in Joyner's script (based on an idea by Lester). (Vestron)

CLASS OF NUKE 'EM HIGH (1986). Loose sequel to TOXIC AVENGER, set in the same town: Tromaville, the "nuclear waste capital of the world." Again there's a spillage (from the Tromaville Nuclear Facility) into the drinking water at the local high school that causes teens to go berserk, regurgitating ALIEN-like monsters and behaving in a farcical style. It took two directors (Samuel Weil and Richard W. Haines) but it's still out of control—a wild parody of catastrophe movies. Hell, nuke the movie. Janelle Brady, Gilbert Brenton. (Media)

CLASS OF NUKE 'EM HIGH PART II: SUBHUMANOID MELTDOWN (1990). You need the mentality of MTV-watching to endure this out-of-control Troma bombardment of gross images and depraved behavior. We return to Tromaville, where students were exposed to radiation and turned into creatures. Things are no better as campus newspaper reporter Brick Bronsky (looking more like a blond jock than a writer) discovers that crazed Professor Holt (Lisa Gaye) has created monsters (stop-motion style) and is keeping "subhumanoids" in the Tromaville Institute of Technology. "Bizarre" is the only word that describes costumes, characters and behavior as everyone runs amok as if attending an orgy of sex and rock 'n roll. It climaxes (no pun intended) with a tiny squirrel mutating into a giant Godzilla-like monster and stomping hell out of everything. Director Eric Louzil fails the coherency test. Leesa Rowsland, Michael Kurtz, Scott Resnick. (Media) (Laser: Image)

CLASS REUNION MASSACRE (1977). Video version of **REDEEMER, THE** (Continental).

CLAW MONSTERS, THE. Feature version of Republic's serial **PANTHER GIRL OF THE KONGO.**

CLAWS. Video version of **GRIZZLY** (UAV).

CLAWS (1985). A farm lad is attacked by "feline mutants." Jason Roberts, Brian O'Shaughnessy, Sandra Prinsloo. (Western World; from ANE as **BEASTS**)

CLEO/LEO (1989). Male chauvinist pig Scott Baker is turned into a woman (Jane Hamilton/Veronica Hart) and learns the true meaning of understanding between the sexes. Silly comedy produced-written-directed by Chuck Vincent. Alan Naggar, Ginger Lynn Allen (one-time porn actress). (New World; Media)

CLIMAX, THE (1944). Boris Karloff portrays Dr. Hohner, a Svengali impresario casting a hypnotic spell over opera singer Susanna Foster, whom he believes is the reincarnated soul of his dead wife. PHANTOM OF THE OPERA sets (circa 1943) were reused in this Universal thriller which has a tense atmosphere despite a too-chatty script by Curt Siodmak and Lynn Starling. George Waggner directed. Turhan Bey, Gale Sondergaard, June Vincent, Scotty Beckett.

CLOAK AND DAGGER (1985). Unusual espionage adventure blending action and psychological fantasy to point out our penchant for role-playing games and hero worship. Henry Thomas, having relationship problems with father Dabney Coleman, becomes involved with spies and creates imaginary commando-hero Jack Flack (also Coleman) to help him outwit saboteurs. A fun blend of menace and comedy by writer Tom Holland and director Richard Franklin. Michael Murphy, Jeanette Nolan, John McIntire. (Video/Laser: MCA)

CLOCKWORK ORANGE, A (1971). Stanley Kubrick's masterpiece on brainwashing and the price we pay for conformity, based on Anthony Burgess' novel. The setting is the not-too-distant future of England when "droogs" (ruffians and malcontents) rove the countryside, pillaging and raping. When one of these youths (Malcolm McDowell) is arrested for murder, he is processed through a rehab center until he reaches a pacificist state. The Kubrick Touch dominates this unusual tale. Patrick Magee, Michael Bates, Adrienne Corri, David Prowse (Darth Vader). (Video/Laser: Warner Bros.)

CLONE MASTER (1978). Fascinating John D. F. Black script dominates this TV-movie directed by Don Medford. Black deals with the psychological problems a clone might face in a complicated society as scientist Art Hindle makes duplicates of himself. Compelling. Ralph Bellamy, Ed Lauter, Robyn Douglass, John Van Dreelen.

CLONES, THE (1974). Low-budget sci-fier about asexual reproduction is a dull B thriller. The Government duplicates four scientists 52 times and places them in meteorological stations to control the weather. A real scientist discovers the plot and escapes—the rest is standard chase material across rooftops and down boulevards. Lamar Card and Paul Hunt co-directed Steve Fisher's script. Gregory Sierra, Michael Greene, Otis Young, Alex Nichol, Bruce Bennett. (Lightning; Live)

CLONES OF BRUCE LEE, THE (1979). Title gives away the plot of this Hong Kong-produced martial arts actioner. Directed by Chiang Hung. (Media)

CLONING OF CLIFFORD SWIMMER, THE (1974). See editions 1-3.

CLONING OF JOANNA MAY, THE (1991). Excellent writing, deep characterizations and insightful acting raise this three-hour British TV-movie to intriguing heights. It depicts the love-hate relationship between powerful nuclear industrialist Brian Cox (superb as Carl May) and former wife Patricia Hodge (superb in the title role). That relationship is tinged with murder, lust, infidelity and a "DNA implantation" that leads this emotionally involving story into speculative science. The three cloned daughters (Emma Hardy, Helen Adie, Laura Eddy) become a symbolic threesome that leads to Carl May's own downfall—one of many singular twists under Philip Saville's taut direction. Billie Whitelaw, Jean Boht.

CLONUS HORROR, THE (1979). Terse low-budgeter depicting a "breeding farm" where a race is created through cloning. One subject breaks free to warn of this diabolical conspiracy, so you're in for chase excitement as writer-director Robert Fiveson maintains a brisk pace. Dick Sargent, Paulette Breen, Peter Graves, Keenan Wynn, Timothy Donnelly. (Lightning)

CLOSE ENCOUNTERS OF THE THIRD KIND (1977). Steven Spielberg's awesome masterpiece in special effects sci-fi . . . depicting man's first contact with aliens in a spiritually uplifting style. Spielberg draws on documented lore of UFOs and, with the cinematic trickery of Douglas Trumbull, creates staggering effects. The "Mother Ship" is a mind-blower and the smaller saucers flit behind glaring lights, looking solid one moment, multi-dimensional and transparent the next. Less effective is Spielberg's script about power lineman Richard Dreyfuss, who is subjected to the saucer phenomena. But, the meager plot is overshadowed by the beauty of the saucers, the integrity of the effects, and the neoreligious mood. French director Francois Truffaut portrays a UFO investigator heading an international team which travels the world in pursuit of the saucer mystery. What a positive way to prepare us for our next step in space exploration. Another great score by John Williams. Teri Garr, Melinda Dillon, Bob Balaban, Cary Guffey, Carl Weathers, Bill Thurman, Hal Barwood. (Columbia Tristar) (Laser: Voyager; Criterion; Columbia)

CLOSE ENCOUNTERS OF THE THIRD KIND: SPECIAL EDITION. In 1980 Steven Spielberg released this revised version of his theatrical print, featuring new material and deleting old. The film's thrust is, however, basically unchanged. (Video/Laser: Columbia Tristar)

CLOUDS OVER EUROPE. See **Q PLANES.**

CLOWNHOUSE (1987). Teenagers trapped in a mansion with escaped maniacs dressed as circus clowns is such a hackneyed premise you hope these obnoxious kids get killed fast. Alas, screenwriter-director Victor Salva is not so kind. The main kid (Nathan Forrest Winters) behaves so contrary to someone his age that the film defies all plausibility and fails to generate more than a modicum of thrills, and then only cliched ones. Brian McHugh, Sam Rockwell. (Video/Laser: RCA/Columbia)

CLOWN MURDERS, THE (1975). Halloween evening finds those in costumes getting less of a treat than they expected in this cuttem-up-alive thriller. John Candy, Susan Keller, Al Waxman, Lawrence Dane. Directed by Martyn Burke. (Trans World)

CLUB, THE (1994). On prom night, six teenagers are exposed to the Devil during a series of initiation rites. Kim Coates, Rina Romano, Zack Ward, Andrea Roth. (Video/Laser: Imperial)

CLUB DEAD. Video version of **TERROR AT RED WOLF INN** (Electric).

CLUB EXTINCTION (1989). Compelling, complex thriller with sci-fi overtones, inspired by Fritz Lang's silent classics about Dr. Mabuse. (And hence, also known as DR. M.) In this updated version from director Claude Chabrol, Alan Bates portrays the insidious mastermind Dr. Marsfeldt, who designs a method of broadcasting subliminal messages on Berlin TV that makes thousands commit suicide, often taking others with them in spectacular accidents. This German/Italian/French co-production becomes a metaphor for the Berlin Wall and the trapped feelings of Berliners. Outstanding is Jan Niklas as policeman Klaus Hartman, who tracks the mystery of the "suicide virus" through Jennifer Beals, a model whose face appears on citywide "videoboards." This fantasy deals with ideas and is recommended for thinking viewers. Hans Zischler, William Berger, Andrew McCarthy,

Wolfgang Preiss. (Video/Laser: Prism)

CLUTCHING HAND, THE (1936). Creaky, dated serial about a nutty professor with a formula for synthesizing gold (he calls himself the Clutching Hand, hee hee hee hee) and the intrepid detective (Jack Mulhall) and chickadee (Marion Shilling) who pursue him. Stunt man Yakima Canutt, William Farnum and Reed Howes contribute. Directed by Albert Herman. (Captain Bijou; Sinister/C; Nostalgia; Video Dimensions)

COBRA WOMAN (1944). Colorful fantasy of the most entertaining kind, no matter how hokey it gets. A South Seas island is ruled by a hooded cobra, who can be placated only by beautiful princess Maria Montez. She's a great looker but a terrible actress . . . but who cares when we can groove on her voluptuous figure, sacrifices to the volcano, sequined fabrics, and jungle boy Sabu. This Universal hooey bears no resemblance to H. R. Haggard's story. Directed with a flash for trash by Robert Siodmak. Lon Chaney Jr., Lois Collier.

COCOON (1985). Richard Zanuck-David Brown's production, about aging seniors and how they face dying, is only slightly sugar-coated by its fantasy premise. Aliens from another Galaxy wearing human skin (Brian Dennehy, Tahnee Welch, Tyrone Power Jr.) retrieve pods from the ocean floor off Florida. These contain life forms in need of nourishment. Senior citizens (Don Ameche, Wilford Brimley, Hume Cronyn) swim with the pods, emerging with renewed sexual drive and proof hearts can be young and gray. Tom Benedek's script (from a David Saperstein novel) sincerely deals with the problems of the men; with wives Jessica Tandy, Gwen Verdon and Maureen Stapleton; with Jack Gilford's negativism; with greediness destroying a good thing. Ron Howard directs without becoming sentimental, and never succumbs to effects unless needed. Steve Guttenberg, Linda Harrison, Clint Howard, Rance Howard. (Video/Laser: Fox)

COCOON: THE RETURN (1988). This sequel to the 1985 hit was a flop, failing to recapture the magic. The lovable characters are back, but the directorial touch of Daniel Petrie cannot compare to Ron Howard's. Perhaps the story is too sentimental to work, although the feel of the film is similar to the original. Whatever the reason for failure, it is a subtle one. Anyway, the characters that left for the planet of Antarea return to St. Petersburg, Fla., for a holiday, only to be faced with new crises. The Jack Gilford character is harder to take in this new context, one of the film's failings. Don Ameche, Wilford Brimley, Hume Cronyn, Steve Guttenberg, Maureen Stapleton, Jessica Tandy, Gwen Verdon, Elaine Stritch, Courtney Cox. Produced by Richard D. Zanuck/David Brown. (Video/Laser: Fox)

COCKEYED MIRACLE, THE (1946). Editions 1-3.

CODA (1987). Australian slasher retread set at a university where a killer is knocking off women. It's a steal of PSYCHO, so blame writer-director Craig Lahiff. Penny Cook, Arna-Maria Winchester, Liddy Clark, Olivia Hammett. (Palace Home)

CODE NAME: HERACLITUS (1967). Editions 1-3.

CODE NAME: MINUS ONE (1975). Retitled version of the TV pilot for THE GEMINI MAN, a short-lived series. Ben Murphy, after exposure to radiation during an underwater mission, turns invisible for short stretches. He employs his talent to rescue a kidnapped aircraft industrialist. Production values? As invisible as Murphy. Allegedly based on H. G. Well's THE INVISIBLE MAN, but a blind man could see through that. Scripted-produced by Leslie Stevens. Directed by Alan Levi. Katherine Crawford, Dana Elcar, Paul Shenar, H. M. Wynant.

CODE NAME: TRIXIE. See **CRAZIES, THE.**

COFFIN OF TERROR. See **CASTLE OF BLOOD.**

COLD-BLOODED BEAST. See **SLAUGHTER HOTEL.**

COLD EYES OF FEAR (1978). A young man is stalked by his uncle—a killer escaped from prison. Directed by G. Castellari, music by Ennio Moricone. Frank Wolf, Fernando Rey. (Trans World)

COLD HEAVEN (1992). A study of guilt and infidelity told with a walking dead man and religious miracle—hence, a strange movie with a unique ambience. Credit goes to director Nicolas Roeg, working with a script by producer Allan Scott based on a novel by Brian Moore. Theresa Russell is at the heart of this allegory—her infidelity causes dead husband Mark Harmon to return to life and brings about a visitation of the Virgin Mary. Outre as only Roeg can make them. James Russo, Talia Shire, Will Patton. (Video/Laser: Hemdale)

COLD NIGHT'S DEATH, A (1973). Offbeat TV-movie in which scientists Robert Culp and Eli Wallach, isolated in an Arctic research lab, are on the receiving end of a colossal joke on science. Unusual idea from Christopher Knopf; Jerrold Freedman directed. Also known on TV as THE CHILL FACTOR.

COLD ROOM, THE (1984). Amanda Pays portrays a spoiled co-ed who travels to East Berlin to patch up a shaky relationship with father George Segal. She undergoes hallucinations which create two time streams: Her own deterioration set in the present, and her transformation into a girl in Nazi Germany caught up in love and betrayal. The time streams flow together for a nice climax. Intriguing premise, helmed by writer-director James Dearden in Berlin. Renee Soutendijk, Warren Clarke, Anthony Higgins. (Media)

COLD SUN, THE. Re-edited episodes of **ROCKY JONES, SPACE RANGER** (Video Yesteryear).

COLLEGE GIRL MURDERS, THE (1967). Sequel to THE SINISTER MONK, in which acid-gas murders are committed by a killer in a white robe and hood. This Edgar Wallace adaptation (featuring characters from his play THE TERROR) was directed by Alfred Vohrer. Joachim Fuchsberger, Siegfried Schurenberg.

COLOR ME BLOOD RED (1966). Blood-dripping obscenity from writer-director Herschell G. Lewis, gore specialist, and exploitationer David F. Friedman. A deranged artist retains blood of female victims to splash on his impressionistic canvases. Color it Morbid. Don Joseph, Candi Conder. (Comet; Rhino; Video Dimensions; S/Weird; from BFPI as **MODEL MASSACRE**)

COLOR OF LOVE, THE. Video version of **LORD SHANGO** (Aries).

COLOSSUS AND THE AMAZONS (1960). Reverse chauvinism: Gianna Maria Canale and sexpot tribeswomen utilize Rod Taylor and Ed Fury as sex objects. But will the dolls respect the guys in the morning? Where's Men's Lib when you need it? Italian grunt-and-strain actioner directed by Vittorio Sala. (From Video Yesteryear and Sinister/C as **COLOSSUS AND THE AMAZON QUEEN**)

COLOSSUS OF NEW YORK (1958). Excellent low-budget sci-fi thriller, intelligently directed by Eugene Lourie. When genius Ross Martin is struck down by a truck, his father (Otto Kruger) removes his brain and

"COLOSSUS OF NEW YORK'

forces his second son (John Baragrey, who looks and sounds like MacDonald Carey) to create a robot to house the mind. It's a mixture of DONOVAN'S BRAIN, Gort the Robot, Svengali the Hypnotist and DEMON SEED as the brain is stricken by insanity and the robot goes on a murderous spree at the U.N., killing with an X-ray beam through its visor. Ed Wolff plays the ten-foot metal man, Mala Powers is the beautiful wife and Robert Hutton is the colorless love interest.

COLOSSUS: THE FORBIN PROJECT (1968). Tense, exciting sci-fi about a supercomputer designed to maintain peace in the world but which takes control of missile systems, forcing all people to bow to its demagogic whims. Fine effects by Albert Whitlock, sharp direction by Joseph Sargent and a well-honed script by James Bridges (from the D. F. Jones novel). Eric Braeden, Susan Clark, William Schallert. (MCA)

COMA (1978). Robin Cook's best-seller, faithfully adapted by director Michael Crichton. Nurse Genevieve Bujold discovers patients are dying mysteriously under comatose conditions and with Michael Douglas reveals a shocking plot. Good thriller, ample suspense. Richard Widmark, Elizabeth Ashley, Rip Torn, Lois Chiles. (Video/Laser: MGM/UA)

COMBAT SHOCK. Video version of **AMERICAN NIGHTMARE** (Prism).

COMEBACK, THE (1977). Singer Jack Jones is writing new material in an eerie estate when he is haunted by his wife's ghost. Her murderer comes to the mansion, where a confrontation is played out with buckets of blood. Produced-directed by Peter Walker. Richard Johnson, David Doyle. Also known as THE DAY THE SCREAMING STOPPED. (Warner Bros.; Lorimar)

COMEDY OF TERRORS (1963). Sidesplitting parody: Undertakers Vincent Price and Peter Lorre plot to finish off landlord Basil Rathbone but bumble to their own demises. Boris Karloff is in a hysterical role as an old geezer, with Joe E. Brown and buxom Joyce Jameson adding to the macabre merriment. Director Jacques Tourneur (CURSE OF THE DEMON) makes sport of horror cliches with a cast that made the cliches famous. Classic "black comedy" script by Richard Matheson. (HBO; Movies Unlimited) (Laser: Image, with **THE OBLONG BOX**)

COMIC, THE (1985). Not to be confused with the Dick Van Dyke comedy of 1969, this is a British experiment in esoterica too enigmatic, too incomprehensible and too downbeat to make sense. In a future time, in a fascist state, would-be comedian Steve Munroe murders an associate to get his job, and then is haunted by surrealistic nightmares and has an unhappy personal life with a stripper. Some dialogue is completely inaudible. Blame this mess on writer-producer-director Richard Driscoll, who covers up a lack of production values with swirling fog. Joy Lane, Jeff Pirie, Bob Flag. (Magnum)

'COMIC BOOK CONFIDENTIAL'

COMIC BOOK CONFIDENTIAL (1988). Intriguing documentary on the comic books with emphasis on the 1954 congressional hearings that led the industry to impose a censorship code on itself. Film maker Ron Mann focuses on the E.C. comics of the period and interviews Al Feldstein, William M. Gaines and Harvey Kurtzman for memories of those turbulent times. Several horror comics of the period are dealt with—but the film also covers comics up to modern time, with Stan Lee explaining why superheroes became popular in the 1960s and underground artists (Robert Crumb, Gilbert Sheldon, Bill Griffith, Art Spiegelman) commenting on how they brought about changes in the '60s. Highlighted is Will Eisner, whose "Spirit" comic is documented as a major artistic force. Any self-respecting comic book fan will not want to miss this informative, amusing film. (VC)

COMING, THE (1980). Alan Landsburg-produced TV-movie, written-produced-directed by Bert I. Gordon, a witchcraft tale set in Salem, 1692, when a youngster named Ann Puttnam points an accusing finger at a family of innocents. Flash to modern times, when a reincarnation of Ann turns up as shapely Susan Swift, plagued by bad dreams and the spectral image of the father of the family she once accused. There's a good performance by Albert Salmi as the sheriff and Beverly Ross as a witch, but the story is predictable. Tisha Sterling.

COMING OF ALIENS. Video version of **VERY CLOSE ENCOUNTERS OF THE FOURTH KIND.**

COMING OF DRACULA'S BRIDE, THE. See **DRACULA SUCKS.**

COMING SOON (1984). Compilation of footage from Universal's horror and sci-fi movies, as well as trailers and behind-the-scenes footage, such as Steven Spielberg making E.T. Written by Mick Garris and producer John Landis. Narrated by Jamie Lee Curtis. (MCA)

COMIN' ROUND THE MOUNTAIN (1951). All-time low for Bud Abbott and Lou Costello, though Margaret Hamilton is flying high as a witch who concocts a love potion for loony Lou. You'll be comin' round the bend with this lackluster comedy directed by Charles Lamont. Kirby Grant, Glenn Strange, Dorothy Shay.

COMMANDO CODY. Feature-length video version (85 minutes) of the Republic serial **RADAR MEN FRM THE MOON** (Worldwide).

COMMUNION (1989). Whitley Strieber's 1986 best-seller, in which he claimed to have been subjected to medical testing by alien life forms, became an independent feature co-produced and written by Strieber and directed by Philippe Mora. Hence, it is Strieber's point of view—a disturbing fact if you are less than convinced the well-read horror novelist lived through these weird events. However, in all fairness, the film is a compelling study of the abduction phenomenon, and submerges itself into the metaphysical side of the mystery. The creatures—androgynous saucer-eyed humanoids and dark blue, rotund reptilians—are presented as benevolent beings and the film ends on an uplifting note. Christopher Walken as Strieber limns an eccentric, ironic character as he undergoes his sinister encounters. Lindsay Crouse, Joel Carlson, Francis Sternhagen, Andrea Katsulas. (MCEG Virgin) (Laser: Image)

COMMUNION. See **ALICE, SWEET ALICE.**

COMPANION, THE (1976). Weak, talkative psychothriller in which Jack Ging hires nurse Antoinette Bower to kill shrewish sister Edith Atwater. Kent Smith and Robert Emhardt add strength to the cast but Tony Sawyer's lukewarm script and Randall Hood's limp direction do nothing to make this rise above a competent TV movie. (From Gorgon as **DIE, SISTER, DIE!**)

COMPANY OF WOLVES, THE (1985). Beautiful British film mixing man-into-animal effects with ominous symbolism and literary metaphor to retell "Little Red Riding Hood" as a werewolf story. Director Neil Jordan makes this audacious idea work because the fictional never-never land is a foreboding forest, and the theme depicted in graphic horror terms. (One sequence shows a man skinning his own head while wolf parts pop out of his body; another has a wolf's tongue darting out of a human mouth.) Sarah Patterson dreams she and her family are in a village in a past century, threatened by killer wolves or men with "the beast within them." Angela Lansbury is gnarly and wise as the grandmother who tells "once upon a time" werewolf tales. Several wolf-narratives within wolf-narratives build to the confrontation between Patterson (Ms Riding Hood) and Huntsman-turned-fang-monster (Micha Bergese). This works as an exercise in art design, mood and allegory. The photography is exquisite, capturing an autumnal tone that adds to the sinister qualities of the medieval times. David Warner. (Video/Laser: Vestron)

COMPUTERCIDE (1977). See editions 1-3.

COMPUTER GHOSTS (1987). Silly Australian TV-movie depicting the efforts of a bogus security company, Crooksnatchers, to create phony computer-generated hauntings in order to buy up abandoned property cheaply at auction. This innocuous comedy, directed by Marcus Cole, is nearly worthless as an entertainment, especially when the supernatural themes are intermingled with a "Heavenly" subplot in which an old man (who could be the son of God) sends a pair to Earth to circumvent the devious minds behind Crooksnatchers. The comedy is labored beyond belief. Nicholas Ryan, Peter Whitford.

COMPUTER KILLERS. See **HORROR HOSPITAL.**

COMPUTER WORE TENNIS SHOES, THE (1970). Electronic memory bank of a computer is injected into Kurt Russell's brain in this Disney comedy written by Joseph L. McEveety. Cesar Romero is the bumbling bad guy trying to steal the new discovery. Directed by Robert Butler. Joe Flynn, William Schallert. The sequel was NOW YOU SEE HIM, NOW YOU DON'T. (Disney)

CONAN THE BARBARIAN (1982). Robert E. Howard's sword-and-sorcery hero with bulging biceps, who prays to the god Crom, reached the screen as Arnold Schwarzenegger, one-time muscle champ. Despite a "barbaric" Austrian accent, it was good casting. John Milius' direction and script (with cowriter Oliver Stone) give the first half-hour an episodic sense, then indulges the cliches of the quest. The main thrust is Conan's search for his parents' murderer: Thulsa Doom, a snake cultist etched in acid by James Earl Jones. Of interest is Conan's romance with a female warrior, Sandahl Bergman. Mako and Gerry Lopez are of minor interest as Conan's chronicler and sidekick. Ron Cobb's visual designs are imaginative. Sequel: CONAN THE DESTROYER. William Smith, Franco Columbo, Max Von Sydow. (Video/Laser: MCA)

CONAN THE DESTROYER (1984). Strong follow-up to CONAN THE BARBARIAN, directed by Richard Fleischer and scripted by Stanley Mann. Arnold Schwarzenegger is back as the sword-wielding warrior, assigned to escort a teenage princess to a castle where awaits a precious stone with magical powers. His band includes two-faced Wilt Chamberlain, a beanpole of a warrior (Grace Jones) and witty chronicler Mako. The villain is a warlock, Dagoth (created by Carlo Rambaldi), who indulges his fighting whims in a room of mirrors. Tracey Walter, Sarah Douglas, Jeff Corey. (Video/Laser: MCA)

CON CAPER/THE CURSE OF RAVA (1978). Re-edited segments of TV's SPIDERMAN with Nicholas Hammond as the misunderstood superhero. In these stories he meets a bank robber and a telekinetic-minded cult figurehead planning to conquer the world with psychic powers. Directors: Tom Blank, Michael Caffey. Robert F. Simon, Chip Fields, Theodore Bikel, Michael Pataki, Andrew Robinson, Ramon Bieri.

CONDEMNED MEN (1940). See editions 1-3.

CONDEMNED TO LIVE (1935). A monster, thinking it is a bloodsucker, grows up in a remote European village to learn it is really a werewolf. Even creatures need an analyst! Directed by Frank R. Strayer, this is an unusual study in vampirism. Ralph Morgan, Maxine Doyle, Mischa Auer, Maxine Doyle. (Sinister/C; Filmfax)

CONDOR (1986). Routine TV-movie set in a futuristic L.A. where a peace-keeping corps, Condor, fights The Black Widow, a female criminal who steals the code for our national security and threatens to blow up Hollywood unless an old adversary (Ray Wise, the hero) doesn't surrender. Race against time, cars with rocket launchers, other TV mentality sci-fi. Directed by Virgil Vogel. Wendy Kilbourne plays a "mandroid," whom Wise tediously antagonizes. Assignment chief: Craig Stevens.

CONDORMAN (1981). Cartoonist Michael Crawford experiences the adventures he creates for his hero, Condorman, by donning his Condorman costume to fight for the CIA, surrounded by beautiful operatives (Barbara Carrera for one) and gadgets that enable him to fly, drive supercars, etc. Disney spoof of James Bond is watered down kids' stuff. Directed by Charles Jarrott. Oliver Reed, Dana Elcar, James Hampton. (Disney)

CONEHEADS (1993). A spinoff from the SATURDAY NIGHT LIVE sketches depicts a family of pinheaded aliens accepted as normal by people on Earth, from producer Lorne Michaels. Dan Aykroyd and Jane Curtin (from the original cast) are back to have a silly time as they portray "illegal aliens" pursued by INS agents. The sci-fi elements are stylish and the direction by Steve Barron appropriately fast-moving to keep one from noticing any lack of logic. Produced by Lorne Michaels. Michelle Burke, Michael McKean, Jason Alexander. (Paramount)

DAN AYKROYD

CONFESSIONAL, THE (1976). Blasphemy of blasphemies: A Catholic priest tapes confessions of his parishioners, then blackmails them, as though he were a disciple of the Devil. And that's the implication in this film written by David McGillivray and produced-directed by Peter Walker. Anthony Sharp, Susan Penhaligon, Stephanie Beacham, Mervyn Johns. Also known as HOUSE OF MORTAL SIN. (Prism)

CONNECTICUT YANKEE, A (1931). Early sound version of Mark Twain's novel about a blacksmith who travels through time to the days of King Arthur to have an influence on Round Table procedures. Will Rogers stars with Maureen O'Sullivan, William Farnum, Frank Albertson and Mryna Loy. Directed by David Butler. (Fox)

CONNECTICUT YANKEE IN KING ARTHUR'S COURT, A (1949). Musical-comedy based on Mark Twain's fantasy about a man who travels in time to King Arthur's court. It's a handsome showcase for Bing Crosby and his crooning, colorfully directed by Tay Garnett. Neat time-travel paradoxes as Crosby croons and clowns. Victor Young's score is memorable and the cast well chosen: Rhonda Fleming, William Bendix, Sir Cedric Hardwicke, Henry Wilcoxon, Alan Napier, Virginia Field. (Video/Laser: MCA)

CONNECTICUT YANKEE IN KING ARTHUR'S COURT, A (1989). An amusing satirical TV-movie that deviates from Mark Twain's fantasy. Instead of a man traveling through time to the days of yore, a young girl (Keshia Knight Pulliam, star of the Bill Cosby TV show) faces the lance of Sir Lancelot and becomes involved in the king's court, imposing women's lib attitudes and taking advantage of Dark Age superstitions to appear magical. There's a fairy-tale quality and a spirit of fun that director Mel Damski maintains throughout the adventurous tomfoolery. Jean Marsh, Rene Auberjonois, Emma Samms, Whip Hubley, Michael Gross.

CONQUEROR WORM (1968). The final film of director Michael Reeves, a cult filmmaker who died at 25 from a drug overdose, is a stylish horror thriller about witchhunter Vincent Price burning women at the stake when Cromwell was deposing the King of England. Based on a Poe poem, it was written by co-producer Louis M. Heyward and Tom Baker. Ian Ogilvy, Hillary Dwyer, Patrick Wymark, Rupert Davies. Also known as THE WITCHFINDER GENERAL. (HBO) (Laser: Image)

CONQUEST (1984). Italian-Spanish-Mexican job from Italian director Lucio Fulci, a specialist in graphic horror. It's sword and sorcery in a setting where muscular warriors do battle with she-devil Ocron (Sabrina Siani) and hairy beasts. Script and direction are poor, although Claudio Simonetti's rock score is exciting, if inappropriate to Neanderthal locations. Jorge Rivero. (Media)

CONQUEST OF SPACE (1954). Chester Bonestell's paintings of alien landscapes are the highlight of this science-minded adventure about a flight to Mars and the psychological problems of the crew. Directed by Byron Haskin, from James O'Hanlon's script, George Pal's film is an attempt to reflect space travel in a realistic fashion, but that realism is in contrast to the unconvincing characters. Walter Brooke, Eric Fleming, Phil Foster, Ross Martin, William Hopper. (Paramount)

CONQUEST OF THE EARTH. Video version of the pilot for **BATTLESTAR GALACTICA** (MCA).

CONQUEST OF THE PLANET OF THE APES (1972). One of the best in the PLANET OF THE APES series, depicting a futuristic Earth when apes are trained as slaves. Milo the chimpanzee (Roddy McDowall), who has powers of speech and reasoning, forms the slaves into gorilla guerrillas and stages a revolt. Fine direction by J. Lee Thompson, an excellent script by Paul Dehn and intriguing morality lessons make this compelling. Don Murray, Ricardo Montalban, Hari Rhodes, Natalie Trundy, John Randolph. (Video/Laser: CBS/Fox)

CONSPIRACY OF TERROR. See **HOUSE OF SECRETS (1993).**

CONTAGION (1988). Real estate man John Doyle is lured to a dilapidated mansion and forced by ghosts to commit crimes of sex and passion for reasons never made clear by director Karl Zwicky. Nicola Bartlet, Roy Barrett, Nathy Gaffney. (Sony) (Laser: Image)

CONTAMINATION. Heavily edited version of **ALIEN CONTAMINATION** (European Creative).

COOL WORLD (1992). This wasted opportunity to follow in the paw tracks of Roger Rabbit is a mixture of live action and animation that is so far off the mark one wonders what producer Frank Mancuso Jr. and director Ralph Bakshi had in mind when they concocted this schizophrenic glimpse into a cartoonist's mind. There's wonderful animation but the Michael Grais-Mark Victor script is disconnected from cohesive storytelling. Gabriel Bryne plays the whacko cartoonist who travels between Las Vegas and "Cool World," a netherland in his own mind (?) where his cartoons live as "doodles"—drawn characters set against real backgrounds. Sexy Yankee "doodle" dancer-singer Holli Would (patterned after counterpart Kim Basinger) wants to "get real" so she can stay in our world, but why she keeps going from flesh to animation and back again, and why Brad Pitt is a "Cool World" private eye are never made clear. One memorable highlight is a "Superduperman" parody image that deserves more screen time. Michele Abrams, Deidre O"Connell, Carrie Hamilton. (Video/Laser: Paramount)

HOLLI WOULD

COOPERSTOWN (1992). Alan Arkin plays an eccentric in this light-hearted character study. He's an aging baseball coach who never had the pitching career that he dreamed of, and who is haunted by the spirit of his dead catcher friend (Graham Greene). For years Arkin has harbored a grudge against his one-time playing companion, and this details how he revisits people and places from his past to find a new inner peace. It's a pleasant mixture well directed by Charles Haid, who also appears in the cast. Ed Begley Jr., Josh Charles, Paul Dooley, Hope Lang. (Turner)

COPPERHEAD (1984). Video release, made in Missouri, focusing on a crazy swamp family fleeing with a rare necklace. The father is a crazy guy who enjoys blowing away poisonous snakes, but those slimy critters get their revenge. Written-directed by Leland Payton. Jack Renner, Gretta Ratliff. (VCI)

COPS AND ROBIN (1978). Episodes of TV's FUTURE COP, in which policeman Ernest Borgnine is teamed with an android (Michael Shannon). The incompatible pair is assigned to protect a woman from criminals. Later remade as a feature, SUPER FUZZ, also with Borgnine. Directed by Allen Reisner. Carol Lynley, John Amos, Natasha Ryan.

CORPSE, THE. See **CRUCIBLE OF HORROR.**

CORPSE COLLECTORS, THE. See **CAULDRON OF BLOOD.**

CORPSE GRINDERS, THE (1971). Bad, bad exploitationer, as stomach-churning as its title subtly suggests. At a cat-food factory, house tabbies, fed human flesh turned into hamburger patties, become snarling beasts, attacking innocent cat-lovers. The canning was done by producer-director Ted V. Mikels, who (mis)conceived ASTRO ZOMBIES. Arch Hall and Joseph Cranston wrote the tin labels. Tasteless. Sean Kenney, Monika Kelly. (Western World)

CORPSE VANISHES, THE (1942). Vapid potboiler with Bela Lugosi as an unhinged botanist restoring youth to his aging wife by stealing brides' blood. Barrel-bottom production with hammy performances by Lugosi, Luana Walters (wife), Minerva Urecal (crazy old lady), Frank Moran (crazy son) and Angelo Rossitto (cackling dwarf) send this up in a disappearing wisp. Directed by Wallace ("Vanishing") Fox, produced by Sam ("Thin Air") Katzman and written by Harvey ("Evaporation") Gates. (Kartes; Sinister/C; Filmfax; Nostalgia)

CORRIDOR OF MIRRORS (1948). Are Eric Portman and Edana Romney reincarnated lovers? You'll have to endure this turgid British melodrama (with Christopher Lee in an early role, and Alan Wheatley) to find out. Directed by Terence Young. (World)

CORRIDORS OF BLOOD (1957). Interesting pseudo-historical melodrama from Britain with Boris Karloff as a doctor seeking a way to operate without inflicting pain on his patients, and developing the first anesthesia. Unfortunately, he also goes crazy and becomes a hopeless addict. Christopher Lee plays a body snatcher in the Burke & Hare tradition. Robert Day directed. Nigel Green, Adrienne Corri. Finlay Currie. Also known as DOCTOR FROM SEVEN DIALS. (MPI)

CORRUPTION (1967). One of Peter Cushing's best films and a treat with its gore murders, Frankensteinian experimentations (a la THE HORRIBLE DR. HICHCOCK) and surreal sequences shot with wide-angle lenses. Donald and Derek Ford's script focuses on physician Cushing, obsessed with restoring his fiancee's badly burned face. How the doctor and Susan Lloyd become morally corrupt and turn into crazed murderers is an intriguing element director Robert Hartford-Davis handles with finesse if not taste (you see the severed head in the refrigerator and various pituitary and thalamas glands as he steals from the dead). The ending features two surprise twists, one involving an out-of-control laser. David Lodge, Noel Trevarthen, Anthony Booth, Kate O'Meara.

CORRUPTION OF CHRIS MILLER, THE. See **SISTERS OF CORRUPTION.**

CORSICAN BROTHERS, THE (1941). Alexandre Dumas' classic about Siamese twins, who experience each other's pains and joys through a psychic link, is an entertaining premise in this version directed by Gregory Ratoff. Ratoff directed with buckets of swash and plenty of double exposures so Douglas Fairbanks Jr. slaps himself on the back, shakes hands with himself, etc. Akim Tamiroff, J. Carrol Naish, H. B. Warner, Ruth Warrick. (Nostalgia Merchant; Media)

CORSICAN BROTHERS, THE (1960). French adaptation of the Alexandre Dumas novel about Siamese twins stars Geoffrey Horne and Jean Servais. Directed by Anton Giulio Majano.

CORSICAN BROTHERS, THE (1985). TV-movie version of the Dumas classic starring Trevor Eve as the brothers with a psychic link. Directed by Ian Sharp. Geraldine Chaplin, Olivia Hussey, Simon Ward.

CORSICAN BROTHERS, THE. See **CHEECH & CHONG'S CORSICAN BROTHERS.**

COSMIC EYE (1985). Animated sci-fi in which Earth is faced with peace or total destruction when visited by "jazzmen" from another world. Animation by Faith and John Hubley; voices by Maureen Stapleton and Dizzy Gillespie. (Disney)

COSMIC MAN, THE (1959). Direct steal of THE DAY THE EARTH STOOD STILL with alien John Carradine crashlanding on Earth in an attempt to help us feeble-minded Earthlings reconcile our political differences so we can live in peace with the universe. Directed by Herman Green. Lyn Osborne, Bruce Bennett, Paul Langton. (Rhino; S/Weird; Sinister/C)

COSMIC MAN APPEARS IN TOKYO, THE. See **WARNING FROM SPACE.**

COSMIC MONSTERS (1959). Scientist Forrest Tucker blows a hole in the ionosphere with his new invention, allowing rays from space to turn bugs into jumbo Insidious Insects and Behemoth Bugs in Breilly Woods. Adapted from Rene Ray's BBC serial STRANGE WORLD OF PLANET X and directed by Robert Gunn, this is the sort of quickie that gives '50s sci-fi a crummy name. The monster effects are unconvincing, no matter how much scientific gibberish Tucker exchanges with a humanoid visitor from space, who speaks with a British accent yet. Yikes! Gaby Andre, Martin Benson. Also known as THE CRAWLING HORROR. (Media; Rhino; VCI; S/Weird; Filmfax; Sinister/C)

COSMIC PRINCESS (1976). Two episodes of the British series SPACE 1999, in which part of the moon has shot into space with Moonbase Alpha still intact, commanded by Martin Landau and Barbara Bain. In "The Metamorph," directed by Charles Crichton, series regular Maya (Catherine Schell) is introduced—a woman capable of taking on shapes of many life forms. In "Space Warp," directed by Peter Medak, the Alphans discover a flotilla of old spacecraft.

COSMO 2000: PLANET WITHOUT A NAME. See **COSMOS—WAR OF THE PLANETS.**

COSMOS KILLER. See **MIAMI HORROR.**

COSMOS—WAR OF THE PLANETS (1978). Italian attempt to capture the STAR TREK flavor, but coming up flavorless. After maverick space captain John Richardson takes over a new command (punishment for fighting with a fellow officer), his ship encounters unmanned spacecraft from another planet, and eventually he's drawn to the alien world where a robot that resembles a giant slot machine raises hell. This disjointed effort has one interesting idea—a "cosmic love" chamber—but even that is poorly exploited by director Al Bradley. Yanti Somer, West Buchanan, Elly King, Max Karis. (Paragon)

COUNTDOWN (1968). Semidocumentary approach to problems astronauts face in preparing for a moon landing and their race to beat cosmonauts. James Caan, Robert Duvall, Steve Ihnat, Charles Aidman, Ted Knight, Joanna Moore. Director Robert Altman dislikes the film, but it's better than he realizes. (Warner Bros.)

COUNTDOWN TO LOOKING-GLASS (1984). Similar to SPECIAL BULLETIN, this TV-movie is structured as newscasts that show how political circumstances lead to nuclear war. It's chillingly realistic, imitating news shows with a deadpan best exemplified by anchorman Don Tobin (Patrick Watson) and foreign correspondent Scott Glenn. Nancy Dickerson and Eric Sevareid portray themselves, lending versimilitude to Albert Ruben's script. Michael Murphy and Helen Shaver appear in dramatized scenes. Directed by Edward Zwick.

COUNT DRACULA (1970). Spanish-British adaptation of Bram Stoker's DRACULA, produced by co-writer Harry Alan Towers and directed by Jesus Franco. However, a gap remains between honorable intentions and execution and the film still falls short of its goals, with sloppy camera work and bad zooms. Christopher Lee believes this to be among his best work but it's certainly not the best DRACULA. Herbert Lom is Van Helsing and Klaus Kinski is Renfield. Fred Williams, Soledad Miranda. Also known as BRAM STOKER'S COUNT DRACULA, DRACULA '71 and THE NIGHTS OF DRACULA. (Republic)

COUNT DRACULA (1978). Honorable British adaptation of the Stoker novel, presented originally in three 60-minute segments on PBS. Louis Jourdan brings an unusual grace and charm to the title role and makes this a prestigious production with the help of Frank Finlay and Susan Penhaligon. Recommended.

COUNT DRACULA AND HIS VAMPIRE BRIDE (1973). Lacking in Hammer's usual Gothic flavor and detail, Christopher Lee is surrounded by a cheap devil cult and speaks—a blasphemy that destroys the mystique Lee established in earlier films. Lorimar Van Helsing is again essayed by gaunt, indefatigable Peter Cushing, an extra staying power. The final showdown is contrived and half-hearted, as if director Alan Gibson hoped this would be the series' death knell. It was. Lee never again donned the Dracula cape. Joanne Lumley, Michael Coles, William Franklyn. Also known as THE SATANIC RITES OF DRACULA and DRACULA IS DEAD . . . AND WELL AND LIVING IN LONDON. (From Liberty as **SATANIC RITES OF DRACULA, THE**)

COUNT DRACULA'S GREATEST LOVE. Video of **DRACULA'S GREAT LOVE** (S/Weird; Filmfax).

COUNTERATTACK OF THE MONSTERS. See **GIGANTIS, THE FIRE MONSTER.**

COUNTESS DRACULA (1970). Based on Valentine Penrose's historical study THE BLOODY COUNTESS, this Hammer slammer tells the "true" story of Countess Elizabeth Bathory who, in the 16th Century, slaughtered virgins in her dungeons and bathed in their blood. Meanwhile, cop Nigel Green investigates the corpses littering the countryside. Not for the squeamish. Directed by Peter Sasdy. Lesley-Anne Down, Maurice Denham.

COUNT YORGA—VAMPIRE (1970). Producer Michael Macready and writer-director Bob Killjan teamed to make this low-budget horror film, successful enough to be followed by a sequel, RETURN OF COUNT YORGA. In an eerie castle outside L.A., Transylvania count Robert Quarry sets up headquarters invaded by stake-wielding teenagers. Goofy today, trendy when released. Roger Perry, Michael Murphy, Donna Anders, Judith Lang. Narrated by George Macready, Michael's dad. (HBO) (Laser:

Image, with **CRY OF THE BANSHEE**)

COVEN. Video of **DEMON LOVER, THE** (BFPI).

COVENANT (1985). Imagine THE OMEN and DYNASTY blended (with touches of DALLAS) into a supernatural soap opera . . . The influential Noble family, operating the world's most powerful banks, has a pact with Satan to help evil forces (such as Hitler) to power. A band called the Judges has the avowed task to stop the Nobles. This 90-minute TV-movie pilot focuses on the efforts of the Judges (led by Barry Morse) to prevent an initiation ceremony involving the youngest Noble daughter. Director Walter Grauman makes it an entertaining package. Jane Badler, Jose Ferrer, Kevin Conroy, Judy Parfitt, Michelle Phillips, Bradford Dillman.

CRACKED NUTS (1941). Confidence man tries to sell a mechanical man (Shemp Howard of Three Stooges fame) to a small town. Edward Cline directed this dated nonsense. Listen to the creaky joints! Stu Erwin, Mischa Auer, Una Merkel. (Rex Miller)

CRACK IN THE WORLD (1965). Exciting special effects film depicting what happens when scientist Dana Andrews sets off an atomic explosion deep within the earth. Catastrophe is in store as the planet's core splits open. Filmed in Spain by director Andrew Marton, this is loaded down with destruction and suspense sequences. Janette Scott, Alexander Knox, Kieron Moore.

CRACKLE OF DEATH (1974). Episodes of THE NIGHT STALKER with Darren McGavin as Kolchak, a reporter pursuing supernatural beings. "The Doppelganger" is a monster that appears in more than one place at a time and "Matchemonedo" is a bear-creature haunting Chicago's Lakefront Hospital. Directed by Don Weis and Alex Grasshoff. Philip Carey, Simon.

CRADLE WILL FALL, THE (1983). James Farentino's eyeballs roll madly as a doctor seeking the formula for a "Fountain of Youth" serum—the better to inject into his patient, Lauren Hutton, a hardworking D. A. TV-movie based on a novel by Mary Higgins Clark and directed by John Llewelyn Moxey. Ben Murphy co-stars. (Lorimar; Warner Bros.)

CRAFT, THE. See **TO SAVE A CHILD.**

CRASH! (1977). A total wreck that merely rusts in the sun. An antique auto possesses powers to kill, sending Sue Lyon scurrying for a traffic cop. Jose Ferrer, John Carradine and John Erricson pop their clutches. CRASH is a mangled mess with director Charles Band at the wheel. Also known as DEATH RIDE.

CRASH AND BURN (1990). Offbeat Full Moon Production, directed by Charles Band from a J.S. Cardone script, set in July 2030, when the ozone layer is depleted and Earth is bombarded with ultraviolent light and men wear "cool suits" outside. The setting becomes a TV station-power center where several characters are stranded, and a killer "synthoid" (a government humanoid-robot) is on a rampage to protect the UNICOM government. Paul Ganus, a UNICOM agent, learns the truth but turns against the company to protect the innocent people the robot stalks. There's nothing supergreat about this video movie but there are unusual effects and the cast is competent. Ralph Waite, Megan Ward, Bill Moseley, Eva Larue, Jack McGee, Katherine Armstrong, John Davis Chandler. (Video/Laser: Paramount)

CRASHING LAS VEGAS (1956). See editions 1-3.

CRASH OF MOONS. Episodes of **ROCKY JONES, SPACE RANGER** (Sinister/C; S/Weird; Filmfax).

CRATER LAKE MONSTER, THE (1977). Ambitious Harryhausen imitation falls short, mainly because animator David Allen fails to inject personality into his hulking beast, a "plesosaurus" that bellows offkey, waddles awkwardly on flippers and gnashes teeth unevenly while eating human hors d'oeuvres. William R. Stromberg's direction is adequate, but the story wanders, overemphasizing sophomoric comedy relief and a subplot about a sheriff chasing a killer. Glenn Roberts, Mark Siegel, Cardella, Kacey Cobb. (VCI; United)

CRAVING, THE (1980). Ninth entry in Paul Naschy's werewolf series, with the hairy guy meeting up with Hungary's reigning blood queen, Liz Bathory. In the Carpathians, an evil chick digs up Liz and brings her to life by dripping blood over her face. Yech! It's the old silver-dagger-in-the-heart-on-the-night-of-the-full-moon. Spanish gore; ya want more? Directed by Jacinto Molina. Also known as RETURN OF THE WOLF MAN. (Media; Vestron)

CRAWLERS, THE (1990). Nuclear waste from a rural power plant is sucked up by the roots of trees, turning the roots into snake-like monster-tentacles that attack human beings. Mary Sellers and Jason Saucier organize the town to fight off the attackers. Poorly done effects and lousy acting earmark this Canadian sci-fi thriller with ecological overtones. Bubba Reeves, Chelsi Stahr, Vince O'Neil. Directed by Martin Newlin. (Columbia Tristar)

CRAWLING EYE, THE (1958) Old-fashioned alien invader-monster movie with the hoary cliches and bad effects of the '50s. On the plus side is crisp black-and-white photography and a sense of doom when a cloud formation hovers around Mt. Trollenberg in the Alps, something in its interior killing mountain climbers. U. N. investigator Forrest Tucker is drawn into the mystery by sisters (Janet Munro and Jennifer Jayne) who have a mind-reading stage act. The "Eye Monster" is a tentacled blob that's pretty corny when the showdown arrives. Jimmy Sangster based his tense, stereotyped script on a BBC teleplay by Peter Key, "The Trollenberg Terror." Great to curl up and watch, even if you have to laugh occasionally. Directed by Quentin Lawrence. Warren Mitchell, Laurence Payne. Also known as THE CREATURE FROM ANOTHER WORLD. (Fox Hills; Sinister/C; Dark Dreams; Filmfax) (Laser: Image)

CRAWLING HAND, THE (1963). Delightfully sleazy B in which the X-20 lunar rocket returns with a madman aboard, his molecules stricken with Cosmic Rayitis. After his ship is blown up by scientists Kent Taylor and Peter Breck, Rod Lauren finds his severed arm and takes it home. The hand comes alive, clutching human throats and hypnotizing victims. What makes this watchable are Allison Hayes as lab assistant, Tris Coffin as cop, Richard Arlen as lunar project boss and Alan Hale as sheriff. The digited "hand-me-down" beast is finally trapped in a city dump. Tension mounts. Moral: Never fight the hand that bleeds you. Written-directed by Herbert L. Strock. (Video Gems; Rhino; Nostalgia) (Laser: Image)

CRAWLING TERROR, THE. See **COSMIC MONSTERS, THE.**

CRAWLSPACE (1986). Pointless psychokiller movie exploiting human madness without insight into the madman's character. Klaus Kinski, son of a Nazi war criminal, has inherited his father's desire to murder. "Killing is my opiate, my fix," mumbles Kinski, during one of his soul-searching sessions, which are frequent in this Empire film produced in Rome. An ex-doctor from Buenos Aires, who was responsible for 60 deaths, KK rents flats to young women, then spies on them from the ventilator shaft (crawlspace) or kills their sex partners after watching them coupling. In his lab of horrors, KK keeps a woman in a cage and body pieces in bottles. Blood and gore are minimal. Directed by David Schmoeller. Talia Balsam, Barbara Whinnery. (Lightning; Vestron)

CRAZE (1973). Antique collector Jack Palance sacrifices humans to an African idol, going bonkers in eyeball-rolling fashion and bringing his wonderful maniacal menace to this dreadful dreck. A Herman Cohen film made in England, directed by Freddie Francis. Co-written by Cohen and Aben Kandel, who adapted Henry Seymour's THE INFERNAL IDOL. Diana Dors, Julie Ege. (Saturn; from VCR as **DEMON MASTER, THE**)

CRAZED (1982). Quirky psychological portrait of an impotent man (Laszlo Papas) living in a boardinghouse with a cranky, chatty old woman (Belle Mitchell) unfolds in an offhanded way and is loaded with eccentric characters, such as a skid-row hotel owner and a writing instructor. Beverly Ross portrays the lonely woman/diabetic with whom the social misfit falls in love. Circumstances finally force him to commit murders. Writer-director Richard Cassidy, who has a penchant for the bizarre, maintains a sense of sympathy for this demented character. (Trans World; from Regal as **BLOOD SHED** and Genesis as **SLIPPING INTO DARKNESS**)

CRAZED VAMPIRE. See **CAGED VIRGINS.**

CRAZIES, THE (1975). Director George Romero attempts to duplicate his NIGHT OF THE LIVING DEAD by depicting the population of Evans City, Pa., going stark raving bananas after exposure to a deadly virus unleashed by the military into the town's drinking water. Grim civil-war sequences ensue as the debilitating virus brings on madness, then death, while the militia tries to restore order. A frightening commentary on martial law. Fast-paced editing breathes an exciting tempo into this low-budget film, Romero's personal favorite. Originally made as CODE NAME: TRIXIE. Lane Carroll, Harold Wayne Jones. (Vista) (Laser: Japanese)

CRAZY FAT ETHEL II (1987). This sequel to CRIMINALLY INSANE ranks as a rank amateur video-movie showcasing terrible camera work, atrocious sound and pathetic acting. Writer-director Nick PhilLips is the culprit. Priscilla Alden portrays Ethel Jaznowski, who has spent 13 years in Napa State Hospital for murdering her grandmother and five others. Now, because of slashed (ha ha!) funds, she is sent to Bartholomew House, where she meat-cleavers every character in sight. Alden spends her time hatcheting, in an up-and-down motion, her victims. The effects are so poor, the knives don't even stick into the corpses. Michael Flood, Jane Lambert, Robert Copple, Gina Martine. (Video City)

CRAZY HOUSE. See **HOUSE IN NIGHTMARE PARK.**

CRAZY KNIGHTS. See **GHOST CRAZY.**

CRAZY RAY, THE (1923). Silent Rene Clair French film, about an inventor who can make time stand still. Touched by witty scenes and the Clair eye for composition. Henri Rollan. (Video Archives; Sinister/C)

CREATED TO KILL. Video of **EMBRYO** (Ace).

CREATION OF THE HUMANOIDS, THE (1962). Although plagued by cheapness, and static scenes, this is an earnest attempt to tell a postatomic-war cautionary tale, depicting life thousands of years after the Appocalypse when mankind has robots to tend to his needs. Robotic science leads to humanoid robots, but a guerrilla war breaks out when these are programmed to feel emotion and the militant Order of Flesh and Blood stamps out the new models. Reportedly Andy Warhol's favorite movie, CREATION has a strange atmosphere due to the stylized (if inexpensive) sets, a prejudicial theme reflected through humanoid robots ("clickers") treated as inferiors, the color cinematography by Hal Mohr, the make-up by Jack Pierce (of FRANKENSTEIN fame) and occasional brilliant bits of dialogue by Jay Simms. Head android is Dudley Manlove of PLAN 9 FROM OUTER SPACE fame. Don Megowan, Frances McCann. (Raedon; Monterey)

CREATOR (1985). Heartfelt story about a crusty but loveable scientist (Peter O'Toole) who tries to re-create his long-dead wife in his lab by fertilizing an embryo with her cells. So wonderful is O'Toole as Harry Dr. Wolper, and so witty and philosophical is Jeremy Leven's script (adapted from his novel), this is a joy to behold. It's a love story—of O'Toole's undying feelings for his wife, of his platonic relationship with a sexually free nymph named Mellie (Mariel Hemingway). It's also about love between O'Toole's lab assistant (Vincent Spano) and a technician (Virginia Madsen). Accolades to director Ivan Passer for a sensitive film that says so much about the joy and pain of life. David Ogden Stiers, John Dehner, Jeff Corey. (Video/Laser: HBO)

CREATURE (1984). Obvious steal of ALIEN, at best an ambitious failure. What detracts is a spirited attempt to duplicate the ALIEN look but without striving for originality. An archeological expedition travels to Titan, a moon of Jupiter, to discover a derelict ship inhabited by a hideous beast that munches avidly on victims or attaches control devices to victims. Numerous gory touches and resurrected corpses, but director William Malone does not create tension or suspense. The cast is slightly above the teen-age acting level, taking its sense of hysteria from Klaus Kinski, who turns up as a Mad German. Also known as THE TITAN FIND. Stan Ivar, Wendy Schaal, Lyman Ward. (Media; Magnum) (Laser: Media)

CREATURE FROM ANOTHER WORLD. See **CRAWLING EYE, THE.**

CREATURE FROM BLACK LAKE (1976). Two anthropologists search for a long-armed relative of Big Foot, seen loping around a sinister lake. Dub Taylor and Jack Elam as good ole swamp boys give the film character, and the Louisiana bayou photography is okay, but the younger characters and their search is hampered by tomfoolery. The film (aka DEMON OF THE LAKE) ends with a harrowing chase, but it comes too late. Directed by Joy Houck Jr. (Lightning; Vestron)

CREATURE FROM THE BLACK LAGOON (1954). A truly classic monster movie, one of Universal's best ever, originally shot in 3-D. The excellent underwater photography lifts the somewhat mundane Harry Essex-Arthur Ross storyline out of the doldrums as scientists travels to South America in search of a "gillman." Ben Chapman and Riccou Browning share credit for playing the Monster, one of Hollywood's best rubber-suit jobs. Richard Denning and Richard Carlson head the expedition, fighting over lovely Julia Adams. In one sequence she goes swimming alone and the monster swims with her, creating an eerie "beauty and the beast" aquatic ballet. Jack Arnold directed in inspired fashion, contributing ambience and action. Equally fine are Whit Bissell, Nestor Piava (as the superstitious captain) and Antonio Moreno. The H. J. Slater/Henry Mancini musical score is suitably horrendous—and memorable. With the sequels REVENGE OF THE CREATURE and THE CREATURE WALKS AMONG US, this is one series that swam all the way to the bank. (MCA; Goodtimes; Hollywood Movie Greats) (Laser: MCA)

CREATURE FROM THE HAUNTED SEA (1960). Roger Corman directed-film (shot in Puerto Rico) blends horror and satire in a spoof of the Warner Bros. gangster films of the '30s. Charles Griffith's script has gangster Anthony Carbone helping members of Batista's government flee Cuba with a gold cache. Carbone plans to kill them and blame it on a sea monster. Remade as UP FROM THE DEPTHS. Betsy Jones Moreland, Edward Wain, Robert Bean. (Sinister/C; Viking; Video Home Library; S/Weird; Filmfax; Nostalgia)

CREATURE OF DESTRUCTION (1967). Incompetent schlock, plain utterly awful. Les Tremayne portrays a stage hypnotist who puts beautiful Aron Kincaid into a trance, turning her into a sea monster that rises from the surf to murder, kill and slaughter, but not necessarily in that order. Described as a remake of SEA CREATURE, this is the botched work of producer-director Larry Buchanan. Pat Delaney, Neil Fletcher. (S/Weird)

CREATURE OF THE DEVIL. See **DEAD MEN WALK.**

CREATURE OF THE WALKING DEAD (1960). U.S. producer Jerry Warren bought a turgid Spanish film, added new turgid footage and released it as a neoturgid torturer. Dreary stuff, with a voice-over narrator spewing out exposition and interminable scenes of people talking about things unrelated to the plot. A mad doctor experimenting in immortality dies and returns to life to take the place of a lookalike descendant. Frederic Corte directed the original. Rock Madison, Ann Wells, Willard Gross. (Sinister/C; Nostalgia; S/Weird; Filmfax)

CREATURES FROM BEYOND THE GRAVE. See **FROM BEYOND THE GRAVE.**

CREATURES OF EVIL. See **CURSE OF THE VAMPIRES.**

CREATURES OF THE PREHISTORIC PLANET. See **VAMPIRE MEN OF THE LOST PLANET.**

CREATURES OF THE RED PLANET. Alternate title for **VAMPIRE MEN OF THE LOST PLANET.**

CREATURE'S REVENGE. See **BRAIN (1971).**

CREATURES THE WORLD FORGOT (1971). A Hammer prehistoric fantasy-adventure, but producer-writer Michael Carreras dropped stop-motion dinosaurs and focused on a different creature—the kind that arouse men in a special way. The creature he picked was Julie Ege. There's nothing prehistoric, though, about Julie's figure, which bulges out of her animal skins. Carreras' monosyllabic screenplay shows how Julie, daughter of a tribal chief, is given to the chief of a rival clan. Don Chaffey directed this entertainment, which has not a serious bone in its cinematic body. Brian O'Shaughnessy, Tony Bonner, Robert John. (RCA/Columbia)

CREATURE WALKS AMONG US, THE (1956). Third and final release in Universal's BLACK LAGOON series is still better than most B efforts. Scientists Jeff Morrow and Rex Reason capture the Gillman and mutate its lungs so it can live on land. But the murderous passions of man and some hints of sex send the Creature into a primeval rage. Arthur Ross' script builds sympathy for the Creature and deals with unusual philosophical issues. Directed with an ambience of moral decay by John Sherwood. Ricou Browning repeats his underwork role as the Creature, Don Megowan takes over on dry land. Leigh Snowden, Gregg Palmer. (Video/Laser: MCA)

CREATURE WASN'T NICE, THE (1981). See **SPACESHIP.**

CREATURE WITH THE ATOM BRAIN (1955). They were mindless humanoid robots, their brains wired with vengeful circuitry and programmed to kill, kill, kill. These monstrosities multilate, bash, crash and make hash of human targets. Standing tall in this sea of mangled bodies is Richard Denning, who short-circuits the mad doc responsible for the destruction. Delightfully inept Sam Katzman production, totally watchable. Thank writer Curt Siodmak and director Edward L. Cahn for the yocks. Angela Stevens, Harry Lauter, Tris Coffin.

CREATURE WITH THE BLUE HAND (1971). West German version of an Edgar Wallace thriller depicting the Blue Hand, a masked murderer named after his Freddy Kroeger-type killing paw. Klaus Kinski has a dual role (twin brothers). Will Scotland Yard never bring the terror to an end? Directed by Alfred Vohrer. Harald Leipnitz, Siegfried Schurenberg. (Platinum; Front Row)

CREEPER, THE (1948). Not to be confused with the Rondo Hatton "Creeper" series . . . this is about some other creep(er). By way of the cliche fiendish serum, the titular terror is transmutated into a "cat killer" with claw-like hands. Jean Yarbrough directed. Onslow Stevens, Eduardo Ciannelli, Julie Morgan, Philip Ahn. (King Bee)

CREEPER, THE (1980). See **RITUALS.**

CREEPER, THE (1984). Video version of **DARK SIDE OF MIDNIGHT, THE** (AVR).

CREEPERS, THE (1970). Video version of **ASSAULT** (Genesis; Saturn).

CREEPERS (1984). Italian director Dario Argento returns to his SUSPIRIA themes to spin this shivery yarn about Jennifer Connelly at a girls' school in "Swiss Transylvania" who finds crawling maggots and/or worms while detective Donald Pleasence seeks a hooded killer who murders with a knife on a pole. This has that surreal quality that made Argento a cult favorite; his camera follows Jennifer as she chases a fallen telephone down a tunnel and as she plunges into a pit of gooey slime. Despite its murders and "perils of Pauline," though, CREEPERS never sustains the drive of DEEP RED. Daria Nicolodi, Dalila Di Lazzaro. Also called PHENOMENA. (Media)

CREEPING FLESH, THE (1973). British chiller with Peter Cushing as a scientist exploring New Guinea who discovers a skeleton that, when injected with a serum mixed with his blood, comes to life and causes havoc. Cushing injects daughter Lorna Heilbron with serum and she too develops anti-social tendencies. Christopher Lee lends strong presence as an asylum curator. Don't try to make sense of it, just enjoy. Directed by Freddie Francis. Lorna Heilbron, George Benson, Michael Ripper. (Media; RCA/Columbia((Laser: Image)

CREEPING TERROR, THE (1964). Reputedly "the worst film of all time," although PLAN 9 FROM OUTER SPACE deserves equal rank. Made at Lake Tahoe, Nev., it depicts an elongated alien resembling a clumsy shag rug that devours people through a gaping maw, overturns cars and takes forever to shamble ten feet. Surely an example of superior ineptitude, so kudos to director Art Nelson and unwriter Arthur Ross. There's no dialogue, just narration—reportedly, the soundtracks were lost in the lake. Maybe the creature gobbled them up. Vic Savage, Shannon O'Neill. (United; VCI; Rhino)

CREEPING UNKNOWN, THE (1956). Hammer's version of Nigel Kneale's TV play THE QUATERMASS EXPERIMENT, the first in the Quatermass trilogy that includes ENEMY FROM SPACE and FIVE MILLION YEARS TO EARTH. Brian Donlevy portrays a driven scientist who tracks down the only surviving member of a rocket crew infected by an alien spore that turns into a putrescent blob and engulfs the Tower of London. It's up to Quatermass (naturally!) to stop it. Directed by Val Guest. Margia Dean, Jack Warner, Richard Wordsworth, Lionel Jeffries. (Discount; from Sinister/C as **QUATERMASS EXPERIMENT, THE**)

CREEPOZOIDS (1987). Substandard ALIEN ripoff set in 1998 in a post-holocaust world where five deserters from the U.S. Army take refuge from acid rainstorms in an isolated lab. It's a "containment center" for a Government experiment that's created a Hideous Monster (once human, now mutated by "internal genetic synthesis") and a Giant Killer Rat. The effects are really bad, the rat and the monster obviously puppets pushed around by hand. Especially bad is a fight between a deserter and a newborn baby monster that looks identical to the one in IT'S ALIVE. Directed by David Decoteau. Linnea Quigley, Ken Abraham, Michael Aranda, Richard Hawkins. (Urban Classics) (Laser: Full Moon)

CREEPSHOW (1982). George Romero, a lover of horror comics, directs five tales plus a wraparound from Stephen King's script, a homage to the E.C. comics of the '50s, a blending of Gothic horror and black humor. "Father's Day" is a graveyard tale of a walking corpse wreaking revenge; King appears in ""The Lonesome Death of Jordy Verrill," portraying a bumpkin who sees a meteor crash near his farmhouse and spread green fungus ("meteorcrap") over everything; "The Crate" is the grisliest, showing how a creature caged up for a century is freed to feed on humans; the weakest entry, "Something to Tide You Over," is another walking-corpse story and thus redundant; the creepiest entry, "They're Creeping Up on You," is a man-vs.-nature allegory about an eccentric millionaire (E.G. Marshall) vs cockroaches. Tom Savini's effects are outstanding. Hal Holbrook, Adrienne Barbeau, Fritz Weaver, Leslie Nielsen, Viveca Lindfors. (Video/Laser: Warner Bros.)

CREEPSHOW II (1987). Inferior sequel to the 1982 collaboration between writer Stephen King and director George Romero, copying the format of an old E.C. comic book with a character named The Creep (Tom Savini, the make-up artist) introducing three stories by King. (This time Romero produced, with Michael Gornick directing). "Old Chief Wood'nhead" is a revenge yarn in which a general store wooden Indian in the dying town of Dead River comes alive after storeowners George Kennedy and Dorothy Lamour are shot by killers. "The Raft" is a touch better, depicting four teenagers trapped on a lake where an oil-slick monster waits to take each of them to a gooey death. Only with "The Hitchhiker" does the film come to life, with Lois Chiles as an adultress who runs over a pedestian only to be pursued by his spirit. The tales are interspersed with Saturday morning-style animated sequences. (New World) (Laser: Image)

CREEPY CLASSICS (1987). Produced for direct sale through Hallmark card stores, this half-hour compilation

'CREEPSHOW 2': TWISTED OUT OF SHAPE

of clips and trailers from horror and sci-fi movies is hosted by a flippant Vincent Price, who sits in a theater and pun-ishes us. Among the clips: THE BLOB, I WAS A TEENAGE WEREWOLF, THE RAVEN, THE NIGHT OF THE LIVING DEAD, INVASION OF THE BODY SNATCHERS, ATTACK OF THE PUPPET PEOPLE, DAY OF THE TRIFFIDS, DINOSAURUS! and GORGO. (Fox/Lorber)

CREMATORS, THE (1972). Free-rolling adaptation of J.C. May's classic novella, THE DUNE ROLLER, in which an ALIEN sphere is living matter capable of rolling across beaches, absorbing people like so much sand. Written-produced-directed by Harry Essex, of OCTAMAN infamy. Maria Di Aragon, Marvin Howard, Eric Allison. (Action Inc.; Western World)

CRESCENDO (1969). Hammer psychothriller directed by Alan Gibson and written by Jimmy Sangster and Alfred Shaughnessy. Stephanie Powers travels to France and falls into the clutches of James Olson, the demented son of a composer who just died, and other nutty family members. Blood, sex, nudity (including bare bottoms). Margaretta Scott, Joss Ackland, Jane Lapotaire.

CRIES IN THE NIGHT. See **FUNERAL HOME.**

CRIES IN THE NIGHT (1964). See **AWFUL DR. ORLOFF, THE.**

CRIME OF DR. CRESPI, THE (1935). Erich von Stroheim and Dwight Frye star in this Republic low-budgeter, based on Poe's "The Premature Burial." As crazed Dr. Crespi, von Stroheim injects a man with a drug that induces a cataleptic condition, and the man is buried—alive. Scream for your life! Paul Guilfoyle, Harriet Russell, John Bohn. (Filmfax; Nostalgia; Sinister/C)

CRIMES AT THE DARK HOUSE (1940). British actor Tod Slaughter portrayed human fiends who cackled as they committed murder and twisted their mustaches as they leered at beautiful women. In this, a typical example of his Oil-Can Harry style, Slaughter impersonates an Englishman named Percival Glyde after murdering the real thing by driving a spike into his heart. Ensconced in the eerie mansion, Slaughter slaughters most of the cast by strangulation. Overwrought and overdone, CRIMES is a curiosity piece. Based on Colin Wilkins' THE WOMAN IN WHITE, it was directed by George King. (Sinister/C; Nostalgia)

CRIMES OF DR. MABUSE. Video version of **TESTAMENT OF DR. MABUSE, THE** (Sinister/C; Filmfax).

CRIMES OF PASSION (1984). Primarily the study of a prostitute and her sexual games and roles in life, but included here because of Anthony Perkins' role as a defrocked, perverted man of the cloth who hangs around skid row and gets his jollies by wielding a knife. Director Ken Russell opts for an ending that steals from PSYCHO and plays as an obscene joke. Kathleen Turner portrays the whore-by-night, working-woman by day. As freakish as it sounds. (Video/Laser: New World)

CRIMES IN THE WAX MUSUEM. See **NIGHTMARE IN WAX.**

CRIMES OF THE BLACK CAT, THE (1972). See third edition.

CRIMES OF THE FUTURE (1970). David Cronenberg's first feature, set in Dr. Antoine Rouge's House of Skin, where a dermatologist creates Rouge's Malady. A "monster from within"—a foam that flows from the mouth, ears and other orifices—causes subjects to indulge in weird foot fetishes and metaphoric acts of homosexuality. Also involved is the Institute of Neo-Venereal Disease, where a doctor has regenerated defective organs and created new ones. Recommended to hardcore Cronenberg buffs. General audiences will only be baffled.

CRIMES OF VOODOO. See **OUANGA.**

CRIME ZONE (1988). Offbeat post-Armageddon society story that avoids MAD MAX cliches and has the feel of an allegory. In a futuristic society, Soleil, a militant police force (bossed by David Carradine) controls a population of social classes and has "sex" checks to make sure you're not breaking any procreation rules. Peter Nelson and Sherilyn Fenn are "subgrades," lowlife types trying to escape the bleakness of their world. They pull off a heist to earn that escape, but are caught up in double-crosses and betrayals. There are moments of the Orwellian world of 1984, and there's even a touch of Bonnie and Clyde in the Daryl Haney screenplay. There's a funkiness about the characters and settings that is grating, but a sense of tragic character holds one's interest thanks to producer-director Luis Llosa. Roger Corman and Carradine produced. (MGM/UA)

CRIMINAL ACT (1989). Any criminal act involved is on the part of the film makers who cranked out this video movie. Catherine Back and Charlene Dallas portray news investigators tracking down giant humanoid rats in the city's sewer system. Vic Tayback plays the exterminator. Directed by Mark Byers, scripted by producer Daniel Yost. Nicholas Guest, John Saxon. (Prism)

CRIMINALLY INSANE (1974). This, the predecessor to CRAZY FAT ETHEL II, depicts in incompetent fashion the murders committed by a fat dame with a butcher knife. Priscilla Alden, Michael Flood. The utter pits of movie making. Directed by Nick Phillips. Another sequel is DEATH NURSE. (Western World)

CRIMSON CULT, THE (1970). Produced as THE CURSE OF THE CRIMSON ALTAR, and also known as THE REINCARNATION and SPIRIT OF THE DEAD, this is one of Boris Karloff's last films. He portrays a hero, Professor Marshe, an expert in witchcraft. In the English village of Greymarsh, the ancestor of a witch burned at the stake forms a cult and is preparing new sacrifices. Said to be based on Lovecraft's DREAMS IN THE WITCH HOUSE. Directed by Vernon Sewell. Christopher Lee, Michael Gough, Barbara Steele, Mark Eden. (On laser from HBO/Image as **CURSE OF THE CRIMSON ALTAR** with **HAUNTED PALACE, THE**)

CRIMSON EXECUTIONER. See **BLOODY PIT OF HORROR, THE.**

CRIMSON GHOST, THE. (1946). Cliffhanger fans! Here's all 12 chapters of a rousing Republic serial featuring a crude dude who wears a skeleton's mace face, strobe robe and scowl cowl. His henchmen are out to steal the Cyclotrode, a cool tool capable of short-circuiting electrical current. Charles Quigley, as criminologist Duncan Richards, fights the kook spook with the yelp help of Linda Stirling ("Queen of the Serials"). Plenty of action and action and action from matinee kings William Witney and Fred C. ("Cannon") Brannon. Clayton Moore, "The Lone Ranger," is the Crimson Ghost's chief henchman. Stanley Price, Rex Lease. There's a feature-length TV colorized version, and a condensed TV version, CYCLOTRODE X. (Republic; Video Connection)

CRIMSON PIRATE, THE (1952). Delightful farce, with athletic Burt Lancaster swinging from the parapets with his gang of jovial buccaneers; full of non sequiturs and inventions peculiar to the 18th Century: submarines, air balloons, machine guns and tanks. One of the funniest adventure parodies ever made, credit going to producer

Harold Hecht, director Robert Siodmak and writer Roland Kibbee. Nick Cravat, Eva Bartok, Torin Thatcher, Christopher Lee. (Video/Laser: Warner Bros.)

CRIMSON THE COLOR OF BLOOD (19??). When a leading gangster suffers head injuries, a mad doctor grafts a new head on his shoulders and the criminal turns into another criminal, a maniac who roves the landscape slaughtering. Directed by Jean Fortuny. Paul Nash, Sylvia Solar. (Wizard)

CRITICAL LIST. See **TERMINAL CHOICE.**

CRITTERS (1986). Entertaining sci-fi/horror comedy. Criminal aliens (Krites, small fur balls with teeth) escape a space prison and fly to Earth, pursued by two bounty hunters with shape-changing powers. Director Stephen Herek goes for laughs and thrills, and while the latter are least effective, the film maintains a constant charm by not taking itself seriously and by having fun with the Jekyll-Hyde bounter hunters. Above average and popular enough to warrant many sequels. Dee Wallace Stone, M. Emmet Walsh, Billy Green Bush, Scott Grimes, Don Opper. (Video/Laser: Columbia/Tristar)

CRITTERS 2: THE MAIN COURSE (1988). This sequel is equal to the original in maintaining a balance between thrills and comedy as those outer-space porcupine balls, the Kritens, return to Grover's Bend. Again, all hell breaks loose, and this time the Bounty Hunters from space—Ug, No-Face and Charlie—aren't as effective in stopping them. It's left up to adolescent Brad Brown (Scott Grimes), Harv the ex-sheriff and the townspeople to stop the slime-balls. The Chiodo Brothers have again done a commendable job in keeping the creatures rolling along (literally) and in presenting an image of these teethy beasts that vacillates between menace and parody. Good directorial job by Mick Garris, who co-wrote with D. T. Twohy. Don Opper, Tom Hodges, Sam Anderson, Liane Curtis. (Video/Laser: RCA/Columbia)

ORNERY CRITTER

CRITTERS 3: YOU ARE WHAT THEY EAT (1991). "I gotta go where the cosmic winds blow me," remarks Charlie Bounty Hunter (Don Opper) when he turns up to help families trapped in an L.A. apartment building under siege from those furry, rolling fuzzballs with teeth that came from space in CRITTERS and its sequel. Although inferior to the first two entries, this works okay as a video feature and establishes continuity for a long-running series featuring Opper as the alien-blasting good guy/nerd. Written by David J. Schow and directed by Kristine Peterson. Aimee Brooks, John Calvin, Katherine Cortez, Leonardo Dicaprio. (RCA)

CRITTERS 4 (1992). This commences where the fourth film left off, with bounty hunter Charlie McFadden (Don Keith Opper) going into space with the only surviving Krite in an effort to prevent the species from dying out. Cut to the Saturn Quadrant 2045 A.D. aboard a space research station where the crew of the spaceship RSS Tesla is soon engaged in battle with Krites. Opper, awakening from suspended animation, tries to warn the crew of the dangers from the critters. The most amusing aspect of this oddball mixture of comedic horror and sci-fi is Brad Dourif's battle of wits with the central computer, Angela—a metaphor for our ability to create a technology we cannot control. The Joseph Lyle-David J. Schow script is clever in its development of character and director Rupert Harvey (co-producer with Barry Opper) injects satiric elements. Paul Whitthorne, Angela Bassett, Anders Hove, Eric DaRe. (New Line; RCA/Columbia) (Laser: Image)

CROCODILE (1986). JAWS-style plot about an atomic-poisoned crocodile that grows to enormous size (its tail can destroy whole grass villages) and a boatload of adventurers who pursue the creature. Filmed in Thailand, and purely a croc. Directed by Sompote Sands. Nat Puvania, Kirk Warren. (HBO)

CROSSROADS (1986). Americana Negro folk tale, nostalgic in its music and languid in its mood. It's the old one about a man selling his soul to the Devil for fame and fortune, only Old Scratch is short-changing Blind Dog, a harmonica blues artist who's fallen on hard times despite having sacrificed his soul years before. A youth nicknamed Lightnin' Boy helps the geezer by confronting the Devil's minion in a musical playoff, aided only by Blind Dog's Louisiana voodoo charm. The characters are warm and poignant, the music right on, and director Walter Hill and writer John Fusco capture the grass-roots essence of soul and gospel country. Ralph Macchio, Joe Seneca, Jami Gertz, Joe Morton, Harry Carey Jr. Music by Ry Cooder. (Video/Laser: RCA/Columbia)

CROWD, THE/THE WIND. Two half-hour TV adaptations of Ray Bradbury stories. (Laser: MGM/UA).

CROWHAVEN FARM (1970). Supernatural TV thriller produced/directed by Walter Grauman, in which Paul Burke and Hope Lange, as Ben and Maggie Porter, inherit a farmhouse—and a haunting legacy of the 1692 witchcraft trials to go with their marital difficulties. Neat surprise ending surrounding an evil child is provided by John McGreevey's script. Lloyd Bochner, John Carradine, Milton Selzer.

CRUCIBLE OF HORROR (1971). British return-from-the-dead chiller directed by Viktor Ritelis in which Michael Gough is a spirit wreaking revenge on wife Yvonne Mitchell and daughter Sharon Gurney. A viewing crucible. Simon Gough, David Butler. Also known as THE CORPSE and THE VELVET HOUSE. (Paragon)

CRUCIBLE OF TERROR (1971). An insane sculptor coats his victims with wax or bronze when his body is inhabited by the spirit of a dead artist. But don't be upset, it is in the name of art. Oh well, by now you must have the picture . . . oops, we mean bust. And this is, indeed, a bust. British folderol starring Mike Raven as the artist, Mary Maude, James Bolam, Ronald Lacey. Directed by Ted Hooker. (Goodtimes; Video Gems; Prism)

CRUEL ONES, THE (1971). Spanish psychothriller in which Capucine torments the man responsible for the death of her lesbian lover. Directed by Tonino Cervi. Haydee Politoff, Raymond Lovelock. Also known as THE EXQUISITE CADAVER.

CRUISE INTO TERROR (1978). A sarcophagus from Egypt, containing the Son of Satan, brings out the worst in passengers aboard a dilapidated pleasure ship in this TV-movie featuring the latest in sexy clothes for Stella Stevens (as a washed-up divorcee) and Lynda Day George (unhappy wife searching for new romance with tired hubby Christopher George). Bruce Kessler helmed the cameras. Avast, it's scurvy! Ray Milland, Dirk Benedict, Frank Converse, John Forsythe. (Prism)

CRY DEMON. See **EVIL, THE.**

CRY FOR THE STRANGERS (1982). TV-movie from producer David Gerber finds Patrick Duffy as a newcomer to a coastal town where murders are committed by supernatural apparitions called "Clickashaw storm dancers." J.D. Feigelson turned John Saul's novel into a mishmesh of cliches, even though it has been moodily photographed by Frank Stanley (with the help of storm footage) and directed by Peter Medak with competence. Cindy Pickett, Lawrence Pressman, Brian Keith, Jeff Corey.

CRY OF THE BANSHEE (1970). Ugly witch Oona calls up a spirit from the beyond—a servant of Satan to claim a psychotic witchhunter. Villain Vincent Price chews the scenery in this British chiller directed by producer Gordon Hessler. Stylish fun, with surprise ending. Sally Geeson, Quinn O'Hara, Hugh Griffith. (HBO) (Laser: Image, with **COUNT YORGA, VAMPIRE**)

CRY OF THE BEWITCHED. See **YAMBAO.**

"One of these days we're going to look into our microscope and find ourselves looking into God's eyes, and whoever blinks will lose his testicles."

—Peter O'Toole as Dr. Harry Wolper in **CREATOR.**

CRY OF THE WEREWOLF (1944). Nina Foch portrays Celeste La Tour, Queen of the Trioga Gypsies, who inherits the lycanthropic curse from her mother (her transformation takes place offscreen, unfortunately, for you werewolf lovers). This mild Columbia horror thriller, set in New Orleans, was directed by Henry Levin. Fritz Leiber, Barton MacLane, John Abbott.

CRY WILDERNESS (1987). After Eric Foster helps Bigfoot out of a jam (strawberry?), he receives a psychic message from the creature that his father is in trouble. So back into the wilds he goes to save everyone's skin—including Bigfoot's. Scripted by Philip Yordan, directed by producer Jay Schlossberg-Cohen. Maurice Grandmaison, Griffin Casey.

CRYPT OF DARK SECRETS. See **MADRI GRAS MASSACRE.**

CRYPT OF HORROR. See **TERROR IN THE CRYPT.**

CRYPT OF THE BLIND DEAD. See **BLIND DEAD, THE.**

CRYPT OF THE LIVING DEAD (1972). A turkey made in Turkey with new U.S. footage directed by Ray Danton. Archeologists Andrew Prine and Mark Damon warn superstitious natives on an island that a long-dead bloodsucker is about to awaken and drink their life fluid. The first hour is spent with the Wild Man, a one-eyed henchman, murdering all interferrers; the last half-hour details how Prine rescues Patty Sheppard from killer Teresa Gimpera. Originally called HANNAH—QUEEN OF VAMPIRES, by someone who doesn't know the difference between vampires and witches. The gore was edited for TV but the tedium is intact as Julio Salvador wrote-directed it. Also called VAMPIRE WOMAN, YOUNG HANNAH, QUEEN OF THE VAMPIRES and VAMPIRE WOMEN. (Direct; United; VCII)

CRYPT OF THE VAMPIRE, THE. See **TERROR IN THE CRYPT.**

CTHULHU MANSION (1990). "Inspired" by H.P. Lovecraft, this horror film produced in Spain depicts a mansion in which a satanic force is unleashed by hoodlums who hold magician Chandu (Frank Finlay) and daughter (Marcia Layton) hostages. Chandu once tampered with the supernatural (using a book of Cthulhu incantations) and caused his wife Leonor (a homage to Poe?) to burn to death. There are a few good touches amidst the chaos: amphibian-like claw hands that emerge from a frig, demon make-up, and a woman's body being engulfed by tendrils of ivy. Nondiscriminating fans will find it diverting. Brad Fisher, Melanie Shatner, Paul Birchard, Kaethe Cherney. The TV version is BLACK MAGIC MANSION. (Republic)

CUJO (1983). Dogged adaptation of Stephen King's best-seller about a rabid St. Bernard that traps Dee Wallace and son Daniel Hugh-Kelly in a Ford Pinto and holds them at bay, attacking maniacally. Director Lewis Teague displays expertise as a suspense-genre craftsman as the siege becomes a harrowing ordeal. The St. Bernard portraying Cujo (Spanish for "unconquerable force") is deserving of a lifetime supply of Alpo for meeting script demands for a rabies-maddened critter that slobbers, drools and goes for the throat on the theory man is dog's best din-din. Ed Lauter, Christopher Stone, Mills Watson. (Video/Laser: Warner Bros.)

CULT OF THE COBRA (1955). Faith Domergue metamorphizes into a cobra and attacks GIs who infiltrate a snake cult in the Far East in 1945. No attempt is made by director Francis D. Lyons to capture a '40s ambience and Domergue lends nothing to her role (she might have tried to look sinuous instead of sensuous) as Marshall Thompson, Richard Long and David Janssen fall under her spell. No cult movie, this. (MCA)

CULT OF THE DEAD. Video version of **SNAKE PEOPLE, THE** (MPI).

CURIOUS FEMALE, THE (1969). Curious title for a sci-fi picture: The year is 2177, when society is under dictatorial control of a computer. For kicks, citizens watch X-rated tapes. Of minimal curiosity. Written-directed by Paul Rapp. Angelique Pettyjohn, Bunny Allister.

CURSE, THE (1987). Get beyond the stomach-churning graphics of this Ovidio G. Assonitis film, made as THE FARM, and you'll find food for thought. When a meteor crashes in Tellico Plans, Tenn., it contaminates the water of farmer Claude Akins, mutating vegetables and fruits and turning livestock and people into monsters. Fundamentalism gets a swift kick in the seat when Akins becomes a religious fanatic who closes his eyes to the poisoned environment, and there is a cynical attitude toward land developers destroying nature for condos. The tale has a touch of innocence from the view of young Wil Wheaton, an outsider in a family of repressed personalities. Director David Keith maintains an eerie sense of doom and ends on an apocalypic note. Malcolm Danare, Cooper Huckable, John Schneider, Ann Wheaton, Steve Carlisle. (Video Treasures; HBO) (Laser: Image)

CURSE II: THE BITE (1989). The best of the "Venom-Fanged Killer Snake" movies. Although this has no relationship to THE CURSE (1987), it's a superbly slithery tale that will give snake-lovers and -haters mongoose bumps. Jill Schoelen and boyfriend J. Eddie Peck are crossing the Arizona desert, which has been lambasted by radioactive fall-out that gives snakes a venom that replaces the DNA structure in human flesh. Peck's hand turns into a serpent's head, and scaly critters are dropping out of his mouth faster than quarters from a Vegas slot machine. There's a great scene where their car runs over serpents stretched across the desert highway. The whole film has a creepy quality and was directed with style by Fred Goodwin. Jamie Farr is good as a salesman and Bo Svenson is also good as a redneck sheriff. Frankly, we were bitten by this movie. (Trans World)

CURSE III: BLOOD SACRIFICE (1990). It's reassuring to hear Christopher Lee (as a doctor in East Africa circa 1950) remark, "I've seen things that can't be explained by modern science." The reassuring presence of Lee, however, is the only asset of this British-produced voodoo movie, unrelated to THE CURSE or CURSE II. A plantation owner's pregnant wife (Jenilee Harrison) interrupts a witch doctor's sacrifical rite and is singled out to be sacrified to a scaly beast conjured up by voodoo. Chris Walas' monster is another rubber-suited entity (although he carries a machete—an interesting touch). Directed by Sean Barton. Also known as PANGA. (Video/Laser: RCA/Columbia)

CURSE IV: THE ULTIMATE SACRIFICE (1988). Originally made as CATACOMBS by Charles Band, this was initially released on video by Worldvision, then retitled for the CURSE home-video series. As with most films Band produced in Italy, this is well photographed and acted. It is also well directed by David Schmoeller. Set in the church at St. Pietro, Italy, a demon (imprisoned in the church's catacombs) is unleashed when a new Father Superior takes over. The drama is limited to a few encounters with the demon and the death of a few characters; effects are also limited. Timothy Van Patten, Laura Schaefer, Jeremy West, Feodor Chaliaplin. (Video/Laser: Columbia TriStar)

CURSED (1990). When a gargoyle falls off a church during a thunderstorm, pieces are taken to a lab by a scientist and his female assistant; the debris is possessed by evil and acts against the doctor's genetic experiments. Directed by Mychel Arsenault. Ron Lea, Catherine Colvey, Tom Rack.

CURSED MEDALLION, THE. See **NIGHT CHILD.**

CURSED MOUNTAIN MYSTERY, THE (1993). Sher Mountain provides sheer horror in this thriller involving a rare gem with magical powers that falls into the wrong hands. European boxing champ Joe Bugner, making his film debut, portrays the "Protector" of the rock and knocks off bad guys one by one. Directed by Vince Martin. (Columbia TriStar)

CURSE OF BIGFOOT (1972). Everything in this not-sure footed movie is cursed—from the accursed script to the cussed cast. A lousy-looking movie with nary a thrill as square-headed archeologist students find an Indian burial ground. Nerdy professor Wyman and his dorky diggers uncover a stone slab beneath which rests a hairy monster still alive. This Petrified Bigfoot goes on an unimaginative killing spree and sputters to a nonclimax. Director Don Fields' object lesson in how not to make a movie. William Simonsen, Robert Clymire.

CURSE OF DARK SHADOWS. See **NIGHT OF DARK SHADOWS.**

CURSE OF DEMON MOUNTAIN. Video version of **SHADOW OF CHIKARA** (United American).

CURSE OF DRACULA, THE (1958). Francis Lederer sinks his aching fangs into his role as the Transylvanian Count, turning up in California as a refugee artist who infects neighbors with vampirism. Directed by Paul Landres. Norma Eberhardt, Ray Stricklyn, Norbert Schiller. AKA THE RETURN OF DRACULA and THE FANTASTIC DISAPPEARING MAN.

CURSE OF FRANKENSTEIN (1957). Opener in the Hammer FRANKENSTEIN series with Peter Cushing as the inspired albeit demented doctor who yearns to resurrect the dead and Christopher Lee as the Monster, in new make-up. Outstanding horror picture (an international hit) with a Gothic flavor and set design that established standards for scores of Hammer films. Written by Jimmy Sangster, directed by Terence Fisher. Hazel Court, Robert Urquhart, Valerie Gaunt, Noel Hood. (Warner)

CURSE OF FRED ASTAIRE, THE (1982). See third edition.

CURSE OF KING TUT'S TOMB (1980). Legendary incidents behind the curses surrounding the boy king's burial chamber, and the deaths of those who desecrated the treasure trove, are exploited at a hysterical pitch in this TV-movie directed by Philip Leacock, narrated by Paul Scofield and starring Raymond Burr (in a turban), Eva Marie Saint, Harry Andrews, Wendy Hiller and Tom Baker. How much is true? You'll have to reread history to separate fact from the fiction of Herb Meadow's script. Perhaps BEHIND THE MASK OF TUTANKHAMEN, the Barry Wynne book on which this pyramid of sensationalism is based. (RCA/Columbia; Goodtimes)

CURSE OF NOSTRADAMUS, THE (1959). One of four imported films re-edited from a Mexican serial, the U.S. version produced by K. Gordon Murray and directed by Stem Segar. German Robles stars as an aristocratic vampire who vows to kill his father's enemies and warns each one of pending doom. Robles, abetted by a cackling hunchback, turns into a wing-flapping bat each time his adversaries flash a cross at him, and clads himself in the garb of Dracula. Well produced (looking like a Universal horror flicks of the '40s) and tinged with charming naivete. Directed by Frederick Curiel. Julio Aleman, Domingo Soler. Others: THE BLOOD OF NOSTRADAMUS, MONSTER DEMOLISHER, GENII OF DARKNESS. (Sinister/C; S/Weird; Filmfax)

CURSE OF SIMBA. See **CURSE OF THE VOODOO.**

CURSE OF THE ALLENBYS, THE. See **SHE-WOLF OF LONDON.**

CURSE OF THE ALPHA STONE (1985). Obscure horror flick depicts the experiments of a doctor who creates a mad killer who slaughters women. This alleged excitement is interspersed with sex. Directed by Stewart Malleson. Jim Scotlin, Sandy Carey, Lowell Simon. (United)

CURSE OF THE AZTEC MUMMY (1957). Crummy mummy confronts bumbling dummy (a weary dreary superhero dubbed the Angel) when his flipped crypt is desecrated by cinematic defilers. Another unforgivable Mexican production (shambling in the wake of THE AZTEC MUMMY) imported by K. Gordon Murray, from the forgettable "Aztec Mummy" series with Roman Gay. Dr. Krupp squares off against the heroic gauzeman, Popoca. Followed by THE ROBOT VS. THE AZTEC MUMMY and WRESTLING WOMEN VS. THE AZTEC MUMMY. Directed by Rafael Portello. (Sinister/C; S/Weird; Filmfax; as **AZTEC MUMMY DOUBLE BILL**)

CURSE OF THE BLACK WIDOW (1977). Dan Curtis repeats the formula of his NIGHT STALKER with a Giant Killer Spider. There's the investigator hot on the legs of the creature, a research expert who spots the spidery clues, and innocent, sexy victims. The plot scampers along, supported by Anthony Franciosa, Donna Mills, Patty Duke Astin, June Lockhart, June Allyson, Jeff Corey, Sid Caesar and Vic Morrow as the cop. Originally shown as LOVE TRAP. (Continental)

CURSE OF THE BLOOD GHOULS. See **SLAUGHTER OF THE VAMPIRES.**

CURSE OF THE BLUE LIGHTS (1988). Uninspired, derivative video "tale of terror" set in the hick town of Dudley, where stupid teenagers discover a band of ghouls and the statue of a monster that once walked the land. The campy creature make-up and dialogue are strictly from hunger, and the acting pathetic. Don't blame Mame, blame the lame (brained, that is). That would be writer-producer-director John Henry Johnson. Also guilty are Brent Ritter as the leader of the Ghouls, Loath (some actor), Bettina Julius (as The Witch), Patrick Keller and Becky Golladay. (Magnum)

CURSE OF THE CAT PEOPLE, THE (1944). This sequel to THE CAT PEOPLE has Kent Smith and Simone Simon recreating their characters, but has nothing to do with cats. Producer Val Lewton was cashing in on the success of his previous low-budget winner, agreeing to the title but refusing to compromise story. Scripter DeWitt Bodeen came up with a poetically moody tale about a girl's fantasies which produce a fairy godmother (Simone) to protect her from a mysterious stranger in the woods. An eldritch fairy tale, so different it will surprise you. Co-directed by Robert Wise and Gunther V. Fritsch. Ann Carter, Elizabeth Russell, Jane Rudolph. (RKO; Turner has a colorized version) (Laser: Image)

CURSE OF THE CRIMSON ALTAR. Laser title for **CRIMSON CULT, THE** (HBO/Image).

CURSE OF THE CRIMSON CULT. See **CRIMSON CULT, THE.**

CURSE OF THE CRYING WOMAN, THE (1960). Mexican import is a curse on the viewing public. Rosita Arenas inherits a legacy of horror via a mansion haunted by witches, warlocks and other evils. You'll curse, you'll cry. Written-directed by Rafael Baledon. Abel Salazar, Rita Macedo. (Budget; Sinister/C; S/Weird; Filmfax)

CURSE OF THE CYLONS. See **BATTLESTAR GALACTICA.**

CURSE OF THE DEAD. See **KILL, BABY, KILL.**

CURSE OF THE DEMON (1957). Based on "Casting the Runes," a classic short story by M. R. James, a British historian noted for quiet, antiquarian tales of supernatural horror. This British chiller, which has won cult status, was directed by Jacques Tourneur, a disciple of Val Lewton. Psychic investigator Dana Andrews comes to England to probe a devil cult, only to find the supernatural. The Charles Bennett-Hal F. Chester script is full of suspense and highlights a classic climax. Peggy Cummins, Niall

MacGinnis, Maurice Denham, Athene Seyler, Liam Redmond, Percy Herbert. Also known as NIGHT OF THE DEMON. (Goodtimes) (Laser: Image)

CURSE OF THE DEVIL (1973). A hodgepodge of confusing details plagues this Spanish horror thriller, seventh in the series with Paul Nashy (Jacinto Molina) as the nobleman Valadimir Daninsky of Transylvania, who is always turning into a hairy wolfman. First a witch being burned at the stake curses her inquisitors. Then Nashy shoots a running dog, the corpse of which turns into a man. Then a sexy gal drops by the manor and gives him a bite that transforms him into a monster when the moon is full. Only when the tormented Valadimir meets his true love, the seductive Faye Falcon, does the film evoke compassion amidst its bloody murder sequences. The women are knockouts and Nashy/Molina comes off sympathetically. Directed by Charles Aured. AKA THE RETURN OF WALPURGIS and THE BLACK HARVEST OF COUNTESS DRACULA. (United American; Sinister/C; Dark Dreams; S/Weird; Filmfax)

CURSE OF THE DOLL PEOPLE (1961). Better-than-average Mexican horror flick (aka DEVIL DOLL MEN) depicting how four Mexicans witness a taboo voodoo show and are marked for death. "Dolls," living horrors possessed with spirits, go into action with their tools to kill, kill, kill. Directed by Benito Alazraki. Elvira Quintana, Ramon Gay. (Sinister/C; S/Weird; Filmfax)

CURSE OF THE EVIL SPIRIT. Alternate video version of **CHOOPER, THE** (Premiere).

CURSE OF THE FACELESS MAN (1958). Screenwriter Jerome Bixby concocted a variation on the mummy movie, the evil being a stone man, Quintillis Orilius, turned to rock during the destruction of Pompeii in 79 A.D. Painter Elaine Edwards is a reincarnation of a woman the creature loved and now, 2000 years later, he's risen from an archeology "dig" to fulfill his affair. Described as "the son of Etruscan gods," Quintilius is a shambling creature anyone could escape if they just left the room. Archeologists Richard Anderson and Adele Mara try to save the day, but it's a compendium of monster-menacing-woman cliches, with old-fashioned voice-over narration. Charles Gemmorah is the monster. Luis Van Rooten, Gar Moore. Directed by Edward L. Cahn.

CURSE OF THE FLY (1965). Third and least effective entry in THE FLY series. The DeLambres, experimenting with a teleportation machine that still has bugs in it (ha), is suffering from genetic mutations and frequently family members turn into hideous creatures. Director Don Sharp's pacing is slow, the action in Harry Spalding's script too long in coming. Half-hearted attempt features Brian Donlevy as a DeLambres, but not even that old pro, who did so much to bring Professor Quatermass to life, can overcome the inadequacies. George Baker, Carole Gray, Michael Graham, Burt Kwouk.

CURSE OF THE FULL MOON. See **THE RATS ARE COMING! THE WEREWOLVES ARE HERE!**

CURSE OF THE GOLEM. See **IT.**

CURSE OF THE GREEN EYES. See **CAVE OF THE LIVING DEAD.**

CURSE OF THE HEADLESS HORSEMAN, THE (1972). Phantom who rides on a nightly errand of revenge, a human head tucked under an armpit one hopes is deodorized, is a legendary figure in search of hired guns. Amateurish direction by John Kirkland prevents this from ever getting its head on right. Ultra-Violet.

CURSE OF THE KARNSTEINS. See **TERROR IN THE CRYPT.**

CURSE OF THE LIVING CORPSE (1964). Roy Scheider is caught in the jaws of death in this exercise in Grand Guignol in which torso murders appear to be the handiwork of a dearly departed spirit (a millionaire who was buried alive). Writer-producer-director Del Tenney makes this a lively, stylish gore flick. Candace Hilligoss, Helen Waren, Margo Hartman. (Prism)

CURSE OF THE LIVING DEAD (1967). Alternate video version of **KILL, BABY, KILL** (Electric).

CURSE OF THE MAYAN TEMPLE (1977). See third edition.

CURSE OF THE MOON CHILD, THE (1972). See editions 1-3.

CURSE OF THE MUMMY (1971). British TV-movie depicts an Egyptologist resurrecting a long dead queen, unaware his daughter bears a resemblance to the corpse. Naturally, when Ra-Antef awakens, there are murderous events ahead. If only that Egypotologist had read Bram Stoker's JEWEL OF SEVEN STARS, he would have closed down the crypt and sailed home to jolly old England. Isobel Black, Patrick Mower, Donald Churchill.

CURSE OF THE MUMMY'S TOMB (1964). Gauze-enwrapped, bandage-plastered shambler inscribed with hieroglyphics strangles those who desecrate his sarcophagus. The long-dead mummification, Ra-Antef, goes to great lengths to track down the reincarnation of the man who sent him to the crypt. These mummies—such bores. Terence Morgan, Fred Clark, Ronald Howard. Dickie Owen is the mummy. Produced-directed by Michael Carreras and written by Anthony Hinds.

CURSE OF THE SCREAMING DEAD (1982). Sleazy deer hunters arouse Civil War-killed corpses in a churchyard, setting into motion a gorefest of the you-all kind. Produced-directed by Tony Malanowski. Steve Sandkunler, Christopher Gummer. (Mogul)

CURSE OF THE STONE HAND (1959). U.S. producer Jerry Warren purchased two films, added new footage with John Carradine, and released a new monstrosity to an unsuspecting public as a fresh feature. The Mexican footage revolves around a story about an Incredible Creeping Crawling Hand (you've seen it before, only done better), the Chilean footage is about a suicide club. Accursed viewing. (Loonic; Nostalgia)

CURSE OF THE SWAMP CREATURE (1966). In the steaming depths of the deadly Everglades a maniacal doctor is crazily at work creating a half-human reptile monster. You'd think the Alligator People would have knocked him off by now. John Agar looks as though he's still searching for the brain from planet Arous. Produced-directed by bogged-down Larry Buchanan, king of swamp schlock. Francine York, Bill Thurman, Shirley McLine. (S/Weird; Movies Unlimited; Video Dimensions)

CURSE OF THE UNDEAD (1959). Refreshing vampire shocker—a horror Western depicting fanged Michael Pate as a gunfighter (he hires out gun and teeth) brought into a range war to invoke revenge. This strange man in black, Don Drago Robles, gets revenge by sinking those fangs into ornery owlhoots, jeerin' jaspers and cussin' critters. Succeeds where BILLY THE KID VS. DRACULA failed. Eric Fleming, John Hoyt. Directed by Edward Dein. Also known as MARK OF THE WEST.

CURSE OF THE VAMPIRE (1960). One stormy night five showgirls seek refuge in a spooky castle. The gals reveal a penchant for Baby Doll nighties and stiletto heels while Count Gabor Kernassy (Walter Brandi) lurks about, mixing chemicals in his lab and amazed how one babe resembles an old relative. Gosh, it sounds like "Carmilla." Fang marks in a woman's throat are the height of effects in this dreary Italian job, written-directed by Piero Regnoli. Not even the strip-tease sequence is exciting. This picture, dated even when it was produced, just rolls over and dies. Lyla Rocco, Mario Giovbannini. AKA THE PLAYGIRLS AND THE VAMPIRE, DESIRES OF THE VAMPIRE, DAUGHTERS OF THE VAMPIRE and THE VAMPIRE'S LAST VICTIM. Whew!

CURSE OF THE VAMPIRES (1970). Filipino terror (sequel to THE BLOOD DRINKERS) depicts a family of vampires. Directed by Gerardo De Leon. Amalia Fuentes, Eddie Garcia, Romeo Vasquez. Also known as CREATURES OF EVIL.

CURSE OF THE VIKING GRAVE (1991). Canadian TV-movie in which an expedition to Manitoba seeks a crucifix buried in an old Norse grave. Directed by co-producer Michael Scott. Cedric Smith, Nicholas Shields.

CURSE OF THE VOODOO (1964). When great white

hunter Bryant Halliday kills a sacred lion, the jungle tom-toms beat a tattoo of revenge. Halliday thereafter is "haunted" and director Lindsay Shonteff plays up the "unseen" horrors of the bush as the curse closes in for a weak-end Halliday. Shot in England. Dennis Price, Lisa Daniely, Mary Kerridge. Also known as CURSE OF SIMBA, LION MAN and VOODOO BLOOD DEATH.

CURSE OF THE WEREWOLF, THE (1961). Shapely wench Yvonne Romain is raped by a madman and gives birth to a baby which grows into a werewolf in this version of Guy Endore's THE WEREWOLF OF PARIS, transported to Spain in the 1830s. Hammer's production values are high and Oliver Reed is an excellent tormented monster. Sexual frustrations finally bring out the beast in Reed and he attacks. Directed by Terence Fisher. Clifford Evans, Anthony Dawson, Michael Ripper. (Video/Laser: MCA)

CURSE OF THE WRAYDONS (1946). See third edition.

CURSE OF THE YELLOW SNAKE (1963). West German adaptation of a 1926 Edgar Wallace mystery in which an evil Chinese cult stages a "yellow horde" uprising using an objet d'art, the Golden Reptile. Directed by Franz Josef Gottlieb. Joachim Fuchsberger, Eddie Arent, Werner Peters. (Video Images; Video Yesteryear)

CURTAINS (1982). Irritating Canadian slasher film paints characters in muddy fashion. Actress Samantha Eggar commits herself to an asylum to experience madness so her next film will be more believable. Hubby-producer John Vernon leaves her in the nuthouse and gathers six beauties in his isolated mansion, subjecting them to degrading sexual games. That's when the slasher, wearing an old hag's mask, strikes, and that's when it's curtains for CURTAINS. There's nothing clever or suspenseful about the murders, and the climax is neither riveting nor surprising. Jonathan Stryker's direction rambles. Linda Thorson, Annie Ditchburn. (Vestron)

CURUCU, BEAST OF THE AMAZON (1956). Prickly grotesquerie of the Amazon commits hideous murders, throwing John Bromfield and Beverly Garland into confusion (perhaps it's director Curt Siodmak's script that confuses them). Although the ending is a cop-out that nullifies the "fantastic" elements, the film still has gory murders, menacing Brazilian locations (always with the snakes) and bush denizens.

CUTTING CLASS (1989). Here's how the characters get knocked off by a slasher in a high school: A math teacher gets a fireaxe through the brain, an art teacher is baked alive in his kiln, a gym instructor is pinioned with a U.S. flag pole, a vice principal is strangled with her face against a Xerox machine, and a teenager has his throat mundanely cut open with a knife. It's the usual body count amidst the usual inane teenagers who enjoy playing grab ass and smooching while everyone around them is dying. This perversion of teenage sex and blood-spilling is the work of director Rospo Pallenberg, who gets an F. Donovan Leitch, Jill Schoelen, Brad Pitt, Nancy Fish and Mark Barnet are assisted by Roddy McDowall (as a lecherous principal) and Martin Mull in a comedy cameo. (Video/Laser: Republic)

CYBORG (1989). Granted, this has empty-headed characters and gratuitous violence, but director Albert Pyun makes these things with panache and style. CYBORG is memorable for its dynamic editing and stunt coordination. That aside, this is your basic Mad Max retread with Jean-Claude Van Damme as a muscle guy trapped in a post-holocaust world where the Flesh Pirates are after a Cyborg programmed with the new cure to a plague. Damme, playing Gibson (haha!) Rickenbacker, has prolonged battles with troops of the blackest pirate of all, Fender Tremolo (Vincent Klyn), and finally with Tremolo himself. Dayle Haddon plays Pearl Prophet, the pivotal cyborg. (Cannon) (Laser: Warner Bros.)

CYBORG 2 (1993). The insidious Pinwheel Robotics Inc. designs a humanoid cyborg to destroy a rival Japanese corporation in this action-packed, violent glimpse into a chaotic future. Production values are high as writer-director Michael Schroeder has cyborg Angelina Jolle and heroic guy Elias Koteas fighting bounty hunter Billy Drago (playing one of his crazies) and stormtroopers sent out by evil president Allen Garfield. Jack Palance plays an oddball named Mercy. (Vidmark)

CYBORG: THE SIX MILLION DOLLAR MAN. See **SIX MILLION DOLLAR MAN, THE.**

CYBORG COP (1993). Derivative but diverting actioner with sci-fi overtones, depicting the efforts of maverick DEA agent David Bradley to find his brother, taken captive during a drug raid on the Caribbean HQ of nutty scientist John Rhys-Davies and turned into a cyborg killing machine. Rhys-Davies' Kessel is a larger-than-life villain with homosexual suggestions, but the real concern of writer Greg Latter is formula action between cyborgs and mortal men, plus a little rolling in the hay between Bradley and Alonna Shaw, who plays an international reporter without conviction. Bradley is a one-dimensional actor who only shines during fight scenes, when he brings intensity to his combat. But basically it's slam-bam, thank you, viewer. Directed by Sam Firstenberg. Todd Jensen, Rufus Swart.

CYBORG 2087 (1966). Pathetic, rock-bottom sci-fier dealing with time travel in an inept fashion by director Franklin Adreon and writer Arthur C. Pierce. Michael Rennie is a robot policeman from the future who returns to the present to prevent Eduard Franz from carrying out experiments in telepathy that will alter the future. Wendell Corey, Warren Stevens, Karen Steele.

CYCLE PSYCHO (1972). Serial killer Joseph Turkel (what's he doing in this stinker?) kills the wife of businessman Tom Drake for money, then blackmails Drake into getting him young girls he can carve up with his knives. Drake hires the Savage Disciples motorcycle gang to carry off the abduction of two innocents just arrived in wicked L.A. This movie is as depraved as its sleazy characters and not even the motorcycle shots are good. Non-credit goes to writer-producer-director John Lawrence. Aka SAVAGE ABDUCTION. Stephen Oliver, Sean David Kenney, Amy Thomson, Stafford Repp. (Academy)

CYCLONE (1987). This exploitation shootemup stars the shapely torso of Heather Thomas, who comes into possession of a supercycle that the government and other forces are fighting over. It's one blazing firefight and vehicle chase after another with no plot twists to brag about or motivated characters. Another whizbang from captain/director Fred Olen Ray. Jeffrey Combs, Ashley Ferrare, Dar Robinson, Martine Beswick, Martin Landau, Huntz Hall. (Video/Laser: RCA/Columbia)

CYCLOPS, THE (1956). Horror fans prefer to watch this Bert I. Gordon production (he wrote-produced-directed) with one eye shut; general audiences prefer both eyes shut. You have a choice as Gloria Talbot leads an expedition into Mexico in search of her missing lover boy, a crashed aviator grown into a 50-foot monstrosity who moans and groans most of the time. Lon Chaney Jr. hams it up as a berserk uranium hunter always undermining the expedition and James Craig and Tom Drake are along to watch modern lizards in macrophotography scenes and other incompetent special effects. (IVE)

CYCLOTRODE X (1946). Re-edited feature version of the Republic serial **CRIMSON GHOST, THE.**

"Jeez, dad, maybe if you don't eat anybody, nobody'll notice you're a zombie."

—*David Knell in* **CHOPPER CHICKS IN ZOMBIETOWN.**

DADDY'S DEADLY DARLING (1972). This unappetizing psychothriller focuses on disgusting elements: Toni Lawrence, a demented young woman, knive-kills her father when he tries to rape her; she escapes an asylum to meet pig farmer Marc Lawrence, who feeds victims to his hogs and finds in Toni a kindred murderous spirit. Jesse Vent portrays the good ole boy sheriff and Katherine Ross (but not that Katherine Ross) believes pigs are possessed by reincarnated people souls. Lawrence produced-directed this slop, which he wrote as F. A. Foss. Need we add Lawrence makes a boor of himself as he hogs the screen? Also known as THE KILLER. (Paragon; from Simitar and Home Video as **PIGS**; from HVQ as **HORROR FARM**)

DADDY'S GONE A-HUNTING (1969). Good psychomystery in which jilted lover Scott Hylands terrorizes ex-girlfriend Carol White, with many visual touches a la Hitchcock by producer-director Mark Robson. The "McGuffin" is a kidnapped baby carried through San Francisco in a poodle basket. Mild horror touches are combined with the suspense and shocks. Paul Burke, Rachel Ames, Mala Powers. (Warner Bros.)

DAFFY DUCK'S QUACKBUSTERS (1988). Warner Bros. compilation of only mildly pleasing old-cartoon footage with new wraparound storyline as Daffy, Bugs Bunny and Porky Pig parody GHOSTBUSTERS. Sequences have been lifted from "Daffy Dilly," "Prize Pest," "Water Water Ever Hare," "Hyde and Go Tweet," "Claws for Alarm," "The Duxorcist," "The Abominable Snow Rabbit," "Transylvania 6-5000," "Punch Trunk" and "Jumpin' Jupiter." The show kicks off with the new but disappointing "Night of the Living Duck." (Warner Bros.)

DAGORA, THE SPACE MONSTER (1963). Out of the depths of the Pacific it undulates, a quivering mass of octopod mutation jelly jiggling across land to turn cities into seaweed-stained rubble. The monstrosity absorbs diamonds, so why isn't it after Mae West? Japanese monster sci-fier directed by Inoshiro Honda. Hiroshi Koizumi, Yoko Fujiyama. (Video Yesteryear; S/Weird)

DALEKS—INVASION EARTH 2150 A.D. Video of **INVASION EARTH 2150 A.D.** (HBO/Cannon).

DAMIEN—OMEN II (1978). Murderous moppet of THE OMEN, the Antichrist as predicted in the Book of Revelation, is now 13 and using supernatural powers to the max. Grisly death scenes again—including a humdinger in an elevator. Although Harvey Bernhard's production never achieves the horror of its predecessor, cast and direction still make this a must-see. Directed by Don Taylor from a Michael Hodges-Stanley Mann script. William Holden, Lee Grant, Jonathan Scott Taylor, Robert Foxworth, Lew Ayres, Elizabeth Shepherd, Sylvia Sidney. (Video/Laser: CBS/Fox)

DAMN YANKEES (1958). Cinematic pitch of the George Abbott-Douglass Wallop musical (based on Wallop's walloping novel THE YEAR THE YANKEES LOST THE PENNANT) met with mixed reaction—some critics felt Tab Hunter as baseball star Joe Hardy was a homer; others thought he was a casting strike-out. All agreed, however, dancer Gwen Verdon was a hit as Lola the temptress ("whatever Lola wants, Lola gets . . .") who consorts with Satan, who in turn tempts the young ballplayer with promises of eternal youth if he'll throw the World Series. Choreographed by Bob Fosse, scripted by Abbott, directed by Stanley Donen. Ray Walston is fiery as the Devil. (Video/Laser: Warner Bros.)

DAMNATION ALLEY (1977). Roger Zelazny's post-Holocaust novel, turned into a hackneyed version of STAGECOACH by scripters Alan Sharp and Lukas Heller. Civilization has been wiped out by atomic missiles and the terrain is littered with giant scorpions and armor-plated cockroaches. In place of the 'coach is the Land Master, a futuristic tank piloted by Air Force officer George Peppard, underling Jan-Michael Vincent and other dull characters. There's nice effects work when the Earth returns to its proper axis, but other effects are downright awful. Jack Smight directed. Paul Winfield, Murray Hamilton, Dominique Sanda. (Key)

DAMNED, THE. See **THESE ARE THE DAMNED.**

DANCE MACABRE (1991). Robert (Freddy Kreuger) Englund leads a group of dancers training in Russia, but his personality takes a pirouette for the worse and splits into evil and good halves. One of those halves is a serial killer. Directed by Greydon Clark. Michelle Zeitlin, Marianna Moen. (RCA Columbia)

DANCE OF DEATH. Video version of Karloff's **HOUSE OF EVIL** (MPI; Sony).

DANCE OF THE DAMNED (1989). Call this LAST TANGO IN SHADOWLAND. It's a sexual encounter between handsome vampire Cyril O'Reilly and brooding stripper Starr Andreeff, who spend a night discussing the meaning of life, the ennui of an eternal vampire in search of blood, and the importance of sun on the body. There's little here but mood, and there's tons of mood. From the

"Spooks spooked, goblins gobbled, UFOs KO'ed, aliens alienated, vampires vaporized and monsters remonstrated. Daffy Duck, Ace Paranormalist at your service."

—DAFFY DUCK'S QUACKBUSTERS

team that made the STRIPPED TO KILL flicks: Andy and Katt Shea Ruben, he producing, she directing, together writing. Deborah Ann Nassar, Maria Ford, Athena Worthy. Remade by producer Roger Corman as TO SLEEP WITH A VAMPIRE. (Virgin Vision) (Laser: Image)

DANCE OF THE DWARFS (1983). Faltering adventure in the Philippines when anthropologist Deborah Raffin hires drunken helicopter pilot Peter Fonda to locate a scientist investigating a tribe of reptile-men. However, the hideous monsters (designed by Craig Reardon) are too small a part of this adaptation of the Geoffrey Household novel—the story is devoted to bickering and jokes about Fonda's drinking and chauvinism. A drawn-out affair under Gus Trikonis' direction. John Amos is wasted as a snake-loving witch doctor. Carlos Palomino. (From Trans World as **JUNGLE HEAT**)

DANCE OF THE VAMPIRES. See **FEARLESS VAMPIRE KILLERS, THE.**

DANCER AND THE VAMPIRE, THE. See **VAMPIRE AND THE BALLERINA, THE.**

DANGER!! DEATH RAY. See **DEATH RAY.**

DANGER: DIABOLIK (1968). Colorful fantasy based on a French comic strip, with John Philip Law as arch criminal Diabolik, who loots with bemused indifference. He steals a king-size gold ingot, blows up tax offices and makes love to Marisa Mell amidst $10 million. Delightfully iconoclastic. Directed by Mario Bava. Michel Piccoli, Adolfo Celi, Terry-Thomas. (Paramount)

DANGEROUS GAME (1990). A computer expert and pals penetrate the security system of a department store, only to be stalked by a killer. Miles Buchanan, Sandy Lillingston, Kathryn Walker, John Polson. Directed by David Lewis. (Academy)

DANIEL AND THE DEVIL. See **DEVIL AND DANIEL WEBSTER, THE.**

DANSE MACABRE. See **CASTLE OF BLOOD.**

DANTE'S INFERNO (1935). Excellent melodrama featuring a sequence re-creating Gustave Dore's illustration of Dante's classic poem. The engravings are brought to life with startling accuracy: Legions of naked, writhing bodies in eternal banishment to Hell. The non-fantasy plot concerns the rise and fall of a con artist (Spencer Tracy) in a carnival of horrors. Directed by Harry Lachman. Claire Trevor, Rita Cansino (Rita Hayworth).

DARBY O'GILL AND THE LITTLE PEOPLE (1959). Spooky Irish legends are the meat of sport in this lighthearted Disney comedy with Sean Connery in a pre-Bond role. Leprechauns, wailing banshees, a headless coachman—are all blarney for the stoned. A delightful folklore romp in which the King of the Leprechauns, as big as Tom's thumb, is captured by an old Irishman who uses the little one's powers to unite lovers and fight off the Coach of Hades. Aye, it was inspiration that caressed the bones of director Robert Stevenson. Albert Sharpe, Janet Munro, Estelle Winwood, Jack McGowran, Kieron Moore, Jimmy O'Dea. (Video/Laser: Disney)

DAREDEVILS OF THE RED CIRCLE (1939). One of Republic's best serials, primarily because of on-location action pieces directed by cliffhanger kings William Witney and John English. Master criminal #39013 (Charles Middleton) disguises himself as a millionaire and uses deadly Delta Killer Rays against three ex-circus daredevils. Non-stop, rugged action, the kind men (and kids) like. Charles Quigley, Herman Brix (Bruce Bennett), David Sharpe, Carole Landis, Miles Mander, C. Montague Shaw. (Republic; Video Connection)

DARIO ARGENTO'S INFERNO. See **INFERNO.**

DARIO ARGENTO'S WORLD OF HORROR (1986). Vid-documentary on Italian writer-producer-director Dario Argento, best known for DEEP RED and SUSPIRIA. Features segments from CREEPERS, THE BIRD WITH THE CRYSTAL PLUMAGE, DEMONS, etc. Directed by Michele Soavi. (Vidmark) (Laser: Image)

DARK, THE (1979). Hare-brained mixture of sci-fi/horror when an unfrightening 7-foot alien in a fright mask (with glowing red eyeballs) tears off victims' heads and disintegrates them with a laser. Cathy Lee Crosby, Bill Devane, Keenan Wynn, Richard Jaeckel, Casey Kasem and Biff Elliott run around Hollywood looking bewildered, no thanks to director John "Bud" Cardos and scripter Stanford Whitmore. It's the old Frankenstein Monster resurrected in alien form and killing without motive. (Media; from Simitar as **MUTILATOR, THE**)

DARK, THE (1994). Beneath a graveyard, two men battle to save and destroy a creature. Brion James, Jaimz Woolvett, Cynthia Belliveau. (Video/Laser: Imperial)

DARK, THE. See **HORROR HOUSE.**

DARK AGE (1988). Remember JAWS? Remember ALLIGATOR? Remember CROCODILE? Well, now remember (or would you rather forget?) Australia's DARK AGE, the tale of the legendary 25-foot-long Numunwari, a demon salt-water croc/gator/jawsbreaker feared and revered by the Arnhem Land Aborgines. Three men—a ranger and two natives, one of them with an ESP connection to ole Numunwari—set out to find the creature after he's enjoyed human hors d'ouevres. Sound familiar, or what? The difference here is that they want to keep the croc alive, the last of its species. Written by Sonia Borg (from a Grahame Webb novel) and directed by Arch Nicholson. John Jarratt, Nikki Coghill, Max Phipps, Burnam Burnam. (Video/Laser: Charter)

DARK ANGEL. See **I COME IN PEACE.**

DARK AUGUST (1976). Slow-moving, predictable tale of the supernatural in which an old man curses the driver of the jeep that accidentally ran down his daughter. The cursed guy (J. J. Barry) seeks help from a mystic named Adrianna Puttnam (Kim Hunter), but his efforts to follow her advice are thwarted by ironic intervention. This low-budget quickie never builds momentum. Scripted by Martin Goldman (who also directed) and the female lead, Carole Shelyne. (Lightning; Vestron)

DARK BACKWARD, THE (1991). This intriguing attempt to make a morbid comedy within a surreal setting fails because of frequent lapses of taste and an ugly attitude toward people. A little restraint by writer-director Adam Rifkin could have guided this into a more acceptable area. Judd Nelson plays the ultimate nobody—a shy, repressed nerd who grows a third arm out his back when he turns stand-up comedian. His friend (Bill Paxton) is an obnoxious, disgusting character who fornicates with three fat women, licks a woman's corpse in a garbage pit and cackles hysterically. Wait until you see Wayne Newton as talent manager John Chrome, or Rob Lowe as a talent scout, or Lara Flynn Boyle as a sexually repressed hash slinger. Ugh.

DARK CRYSTAL, THE (1982). Muppet mastermind Jim Henson and STAR WARS producer Gary Kurtz collaborated on this fantasy on a faraway planet ruled by Skekses, a race of lizard creatures. It's a kingdom where characters are hand puppets or people in costumes and face masks. David Odell's script, from an idea by Henson, has two Gelflings setting out to find a crystal piece that, when restored to the mystical Dark Crystal, will remove blight from the land. The Skekses and the Mystics, a race of ponderous thinkers, are brilliantly designed, but the Gelflings are lifeless puppets. Brian Froud's fantasy world is well realized, but anyone expecting this to be a cutesy romp will be disappointed. Co-directed by Henson and Frank Oz. (Video/Laser: HBO)

DARK DREAMS (1971). Usual devil cult, usual innocent victims who wander unwittingly into the coven. Usual boredom of sitting through something you've seen before. Usual uninspired direction by Roger Guermontes. Tina Russell, Tim Long, June Dulu, Arlana Blue.

DARK DREAMS. Video title for **EROTIC DREAMS.**

DARK ENEMY (1984). British post-Holocaust sci-fier, made by and with children, for children. The setting is an isolated farm where youngsters ponder the outside world—until one of them (Rory Macfarquhar) investigates. Slow and depressing. Directed by Colin Finbow.

DARKER SIDE OF TERROR, THE (1978). Research professor Robert Forster is passed over for an appointment, so he creates a self-clone which sets out to seduce the wife of the man who got the job. TV-movie directed by Gus Trikonis. Ray Milland, Adrienne Barbeau, David Sheiner, Denise DuBarry, John Lehne.

DARKEST AFRICA (1936). Republic's first serial ever, with wild-animal trainer Clyde Beatty trekking with jungle boy Baru (a chubby lad well-versed in subduing wild animals with a whip) and Bonga the ape in search of the lost city of Joba. They're also looking for Baru's sister—a missing beauty named Dagna, the unwilling Goddess of Joba—but thwarting them are winged warriors (called Bat Men) and two crooks after a fortune in diamonds. Did we forget to mention the volcano and earthquake? Directed breathlessly by B. Reeves Eason (an action specialist) and Joseph Kane, although the acting is pretty corny. Lucien Prival, Manuel King, Edmund Cobb, Elaine Shepard. (Video/Laser: Republic)

DARK EYES (1980). Huge-breasted Lana Wood (sister of Natalie) is some eyeful in this weak-kneed supernatural thriller (originally SATAN'S MISTRESS) in which a "lonely spirit" from beyond (Kabir Bedi) rapes Ms Wood as frequently as writer-director James Polakof can reload his cameras. Tedious, predictable and taking forever to build to its nonarousing climax. John Carradine is wasted in a thankless cameo as a priest. Britt Ekland (as a psychic) and Ms Wood appear in semistages of undress, but this needs more than tantilizing flesh. Tom Hallick. (From HarmonyVision as **DEMON RAGE**)

DARK EYES OF LONDON (1940). See **HUMAN MONSTER, THE.**

DARK EYES OF LONDON, THE (1961). See **DEAD EYES OF LONDON, THE.**

DARK FORCES. Video of **HARLEQUIN (Media).**

DARK HALF, THE (1993). Stephen King's popular novel is given a bang-up job by writer-director George Romero, and Timothy Hutton does a bang-up job as best-selling writer Thad Beaumont, and as his alter ego, a serial killer. Eventually "the dark half" works his way toward Beaumont's New England home. Only during an acopalyptic ending, involving swarms of sparrows, does the tale turn ridiculous and overwrought. But during its suspenseful build-up, with Romero utilizing the conventions of the slasher genre, the film is compelling. Amy Madigan is Beaumont's wife, Michael Rooker is the sheriff, and Julie Harris is Beaumont's colleague. (Orion)

TIMOTHY HUTTON

DARK HERITAGE (1989). Produced-directed by David McCormick, this alleged horror movie depicts innocent campers in contact with killers. (Cornerstone)

DARK INTRUDER (1965). TV pilot (originally BLACK CLOAK) was ignored by networks then released to theaters. It's an above-average thriller, with themes reminiscient of H. P. Lovecraft. The setting is a Victorian-style San Francisco in 1900 where psychic investigator Mark Richman traces ghastly murders to Sumerian devil creatures led by Warner Klemperer. Script by Barre Lyndon, direction by Harvey Hart. (Shocktoons)

DARK INTERVAL (1950). Pre-Hammer British thriller with mild shock overtones which depicts bride Zena Marshall discovering her husband (Andrew Osborn) is off his trolley in his mansion of horrors. Directed by Charles Saunders. John Barry, Mona Washbourne.

DARKMAN (1990). Sam (THE EVIL DEAD) Raimi distinguishes himself again as a director of style, whose visual virtuosity is striking. DARKMAN is reminiscient of the old serials and pulps of the '40s but with a modern black-comedy twist when Dr. Peyton Westlake (Liam Neeson) discovers a formula for synthetic skin, but then is mutilated by gangsters. Barely surviving, and gruesomely disfigured, Dr. Westlake moves from light into darkness to wreak his revenge on enemies by wearing masks that allow him to assume other identities. This watershed movie has the gothic spirit of BATMAN, the split personality of DR. JEKYLL AND MR. HYDE, the deformities of THE PHANTOM OF THE OPERA and the doomed romantic relationship of THE FLY. Frances McDormand, Jenny Agutter, Larry Drake, Nelson Mashita. (Video/Laser: MCA)

DARK MANSIONS (1986). TV-movie, of the slick Aaron Spelling-Douglas S. Cramer variety, in which "volatile passions" and "Gothic supernatural forces" affect a woman when she joins the mysterious Drake family on a "windswept estate" in Oregon to write the family's history. She resembles a deceased member of the family and seems destined to follow in her fatal footsteps. A lot of in-fighting and bedroom love-making, but not a lot of excitement or coherence. Nor is the supernatural element strong until the conclusion. Directed by Jerry London. Joan Fontaine, Michael York, Paul Shenar.

DARK NIGHT OF THE SCARECROW (1981). Unusually gory, violent TV-movie, startlingly refreshing. Bubba, a halfwit accused of murder, is shot by angry farmers, who pump 26 bullets into his quivering body before learning he is innocent. The town acquits the men but Bubba returns as a scarecrow, killing farmers with their own equipment. One gets dropped into a thrashing machine, another is suffocated in a grain silo. The J. D. Feigelson teleplay is filled with surprises, ending on a shocker director Frank De Felitta never tips beforehand. Charles Durning, Larry Drake, Lane Smith, Jocelyn Brando. (Fox/Key; Front Row Entertainment)

DARK OF THE NIGHT (1984). New Zealand imitation of CHRISTINE recycles the theme of the haunted automobile but in a slow-moving, eccentric way that makes this low-budget effort of minimal interest. A Jaguar Mark IV becomes the property of Heather Bolton who soon discovers its former owner was a young woman (Perry Percy) who was murdered. Strange things happen when a stranger (David Letch) turns up. Written by co-producer/director Gaylene Preston from a story by Elizabeth Jane Howard. (Live)

DARK PLACES (1972). Christopher Lee, Herbert Lom and Joan Collins scheme to conceal from gold-hungry Robert Hardy a cache of stolen money hidden in a house reportedly haunted. Violence follows, ending in a bloody mess for all. Directed by Don Sharp. Jan Birkin, Linda Gray, Jean Marsh. (Embassy; Sultan)

DARK POWER (1987). Lash LaRue, one-time western hero who specialized in cracking a whip in a black outfit, made a modest comeback in this tale about evil Indian spirits that haunt a home in North Carolina, only to feel the sharp sting of Lash's whip. For sadists only. Directed by Phil Smoot. (Midwest; Magnum)

DARK REFLECTION (1993). Good suspense thriller with sci-fi genetics overtones as computer expert C. Thomas Howell comes to realize he is the result of a cloning experiment and his lookalike brother (also Howell) plans to replace him. That old ploy, which-one-is-which?, is cleverly used by director Jack Sholder. Lisa Zane, Miko Hughes, Ethan Phillips. (Fox)

DARK RIDE (1977). Fictionalized case history of serial killer Ted Bundy, spun as a mixture of police procedure (with cop James Luisi doggedly on the killer's trail) and gore murder thriller, although the gore is minimal and lacks impact. The only thing this low-budgeter offers is John Karlen as the murderer. Set in San Francisco but filmed mostly in L.A. Directed by Jeremy Hoenack. Susan Sullivan, Martin Speer. (Media)

DARK ROMANCES: Vol. 1 & 2 (1986). Gratuitous gore, vicious violence and sizzling sex are the ingredients of this anthology, shot on tape and released on video. Plots range from bloody film noir to mad doctor sci-fi to gothic chills. Many writers, many directors. Brinke Stevens, Larry Hankin, Julie Carlson. (Film Threat)

DARKROOM (1990). Something never gets developed in the think-tank as director Terrence O'Hara overexposes the plot. The image: a slasher on the loose, motivated by incest. Negative results. Aarin Teich, Jill Pierce. (Quest Entertainment; VCL)

DARK SANITY (1984). Video version of Aldo Ray's **STRAIGHT JACKET** (Marquis; Genesis; Prism).

DARK SECRET OF HARVEST HOME, THE (1978). Tom Tryon's excellent novel was made into a TV-movie by producer Jack Laird, depicting life in a New England village, Cornwall Coombe, where cult-like activities suggest human sacrifice and satanism. Faithful to Tryon's concepts, including the unsettling ending. Bette Davis stars as Widow Fortune, a dowager with powers of witchcraft. Directed by Leo Penn. Joanna Miles, David Ackroyd, Rosanna Arquette, Earl Keyes. (MCA)

DARK SHADOWS (1991). This two-part TV-movie revived Dan Curtis' daytime supernatural serial of the 1960s—and served as the pilot for a shortlived series that brought a new sense of horror and darkness to the sanguinary history of a family of vampires. Barnabas Collins is not here as Jonathan Frid (that part passed to Ben Cross) and that may disappoint fans—but those same fans should be happy about this well-produced, atmospheric and oppressive fang-fantasy. Barbara Blackburn, Jim Fyfe, Joanna Going, Roy Thinnes, Barbara Steele, Jean Simmons. Curtis directed.

BEN CROSS

DARK SHADOWS. Three cassettes from MPI, each containing five episodes from the daytime serial.

DARK SHADOWS. See **HOUSE OF DARK SHADOWS** and **NIGHT OF DARK SHADOWS.**

DARK SIDE OF MIDNIGHT, THE (1984). Trauma-inducing film from the Troma folks about The Creeper, a slasher-smasher-basher knocking off people in Fort Smith, Arkansas. Watching the second hand of your clock ticking toward midnight might be more exciting. James Moore, Wes Olsen. Written-produced-directed by Olsen. (Prism; from AVR as CREEPER, THE)

DARK SIDE OF THE MOON, THE (1989). Taut, well-produced, no-nonsense sci-fi mystery set in 2022 aboard Spacecore 1, a ship on a mission to repair (or "refab") nuclear-armed satellites rotating Earth. When the ship malfunctions it drifts into "Cypress B-40" (code name: dark side of the moon). There, the crew encounters a derelict shuttlecraft that leads to a mystery involving the Bermuda Triangle, walking corpses, and the Devil. The Carey W. Hayes-Chad Hayes script presents the scientific puzzles in an intriguing fashion. Director D. J. Webster keeps it tense. Joseph Turkel, Will Bledsoe, Alan Blumenfeld, Robert Sampson, John Diehl, and Wendy MacDonald. (Vidmark) (Laser: Image)

DARK SIDE, THE. See **REINCARNATE, THE.**

DARK STAR (1975). Sci-fi with the shining: A starship roves the Universe, armed with thermonuclear bombs to explode unstable suns. The John Carpenter-Dan O'Bannon script captures the claustrophobia of space travel and the mental deterioration of ennui-softened crewmen. A malfunctioning computer results in one of the strangest villains in any space movie. The only flaw is a form of alien life, obviously an inflated beachball with clawed feet. Carpenter produced-directed. (Video Dimensions; VCI) (Laser: Image)

DARK TOWER (1987). Sandy Howard production shot in Barcelona, Spain. The first half-hour of this tale of a haunted highrise has a few twists and only minor chills as accidents and murders occur in the building. But then it completely crumbles. Architect Jenny Agutter, who designed the building, is haunted by her dead husband. Michael Moriarty, striving to bring characterization to a woefully written cop role, probes the case with quirky psychics Theodore Bikel and Kevin McCarthy. All these actors—including Carol Lynley in a thankless part as Agutter's secretary—deserve better. This turned out so poor, director Freddie Francis used the pseudonym Ken Barnett. (Forum; MCEG Virgin) (Laser: Image)

DARK WATERS (1944). Merle Oberon hears strange voices calling her from the bayou, and her night light keeps popping off and on. Too bad she never saw GASLIGHT or she might get wise. The waters of the script by Joan Harrison and Marian Cockrell run too still to run deep. Directed by Andre de Toth. Franchot Tone, Thomas Mitchell, Fay Bainter, Rex Ingram, Elisha Cook Jr., Alan Napier. (New World) (Laser: Image)

D.A.R.Y.L. (1985). Boring juvenile fantasy about young robot D.A.R.Y.L. (Data Analyzing Robot Youth Lifeform), labeled a "test tube experiment in artificial intelligence," who escapes from the lab and seeks refuge from Mary Beth Hurt and Michael McKean. He learns the meaning of "human" as he demonstrates his powers and learning abilities. The baddies come looking for him and he becomes an object lesson. Uninspired; dully photographed. Directed by Simon Wincer. Colleen Camp, Kathryn Walker. (Video/Laser: Paramount)

DATE WITH AN ANGEL (1987). There are warm moments in this fantasy morality tale written-directed by Tom McLoughlin—and there's a tenderness too. Emmanuelle Beart is wonderful as an angel found floating in a swimming pool by Michael E. Knight, who's about to marry Phoebe Cates. Beart is so beautiful you believe she's an angel as Knight finds himself caught up in misunderstandings with his fiancee, her parents and his teen-age pals. The story takes on social issues when Cates' father (David Dukes), president of a cosmetics firm, exploits the angel. Fluffy entertainment, but harp-and-halo above most of its ilk. Phil Brock, Albert Macklin. (Video/Laser: HBO)

DAUGHTER OF A WEREWOLF. See **LEGEND OF THE WOLFWOMAN.**

DAUGHTER OF DARKNESS (1990). Location footage of Bucharest, Romania, highlights this TV-movie about Mia Sara's search for her long-lost father. Although the plot is familiar—and the cliches come rattling out of the closet as Sara discovers (1) her father might have been Dracula, (2) she has vampire blood in her veins, and (3) the emblem around her neck symbolizes a cult of bloodsuckers—this will please horror fans with its effects and the performance of Anthony Perkins, who goes absolutely crazy bonkers. Director Stuart Gordon gives it pacing and atmosphere, and allows his heroine to behave in irrational, erratic ways that doesn't always make her an easy character to like. This creates extra tension. Robert Reynolds, Jack Coleman, Dezso Baras.

DAUGHTER OF DR. JEKYLL (1957). Wonderfully ridiculous premise for a cheesy B flick: Gloria Talbot thinks she's tainted by the split personality of her infamous father, and stalks hapless victims at night. The monster myths really go awry in producer-writer Jack Pollexfen's script when a werewolf gets a stake through the heart. Directed by Edgar G. Ulmer. John Agar, Arthur Shields, John Dierkes, Martha Wentworth. (Fox/Key)

DAUGHTER OF DRACULA, THE (1972). French-Spanish-Portuguese film with Howard Vernon as Count Karnstein. Directed by Jesus Franco. Britt Nichols, Dennis Price.

DAUGHTER OF FRANKENSTEIN, THE (1971). Intrepid wrestler Santo (Rodolf Guzman Huerta) is back to do battle with a mad doc's daughter in this Mexican series entry that pits a muscleman in a silver suit against monsters and insane humans. It's Gina Romand's hope to get Santo's blood for her formula to restore youth to aging bones, but the bones of Fernando Oses' script creak louder. Directed by Miguel M. Delgado.

DAUGHTER OF HORROR (1953). A powerful, shocking film noir in black and white, from the imagination of writer-producer-director John Parker, who displays great understanding of psychology and mood film-making. Originally released as DEMENTIA, this is the nightmare of a woman (Adrienne Barrett) whose mental deterioration blurs the line separating reality from fantasy. She drifts through a nocturnal world populated by a fat man, a sadistic policeman and other lowlifes. Parker's strengths lie in his depiction of the woman's illness through her whorish mother and cruel father. Ed McMahon narrates the lurid prose for this avant-garde masterpiece. Great music by George Antheil, enhanced by Marni Nixon's vocals. (S/Weird; Thunderbird; Sinister/C)

DAUGHTER OF THE DRAGON (1931). See third edition.

DAUGHTER OF THE MIND (1969). TV-movie, produced-directed by Walter Grauman, has the makings of a chilling ghost story, involving the spirit of a young girl being investigated by a parapsychologist. But Luther Davis' script cops out to become a counter-espionage intrigue tale. Subject matter and approach, however, will enthrall ESP fans. Ray Milland, Pamelyn Ferdin, Gene Tierney, Don Murray, George Macready, John Carradine, Edward Asner.

DAUGHTERS OF DARKNESS (1971). Belgium's Harry Kumel wrote-directed this contemporary vampire tale which projects Elisabeth Bathory, 16th Century Hungarian countess who bathed in the blood of virgins, into a luxury hotel on the coast of Belgium. As Bathory, Delphine Seyrig gushes with sophistication, glamour and lesbian innuendo which turns blatant when she seduces a newlywed and her husband. While there is blood and gore, Kumel explores the dark side of human sexuality in fascinating fashion, using erotica and symbolism. Achieves an aura of decadence strangely compelling. Aka THE PROMISE OF RED LIPS and THE RED LIPS. Daniele Ouimet, John Karlen. (Cinema Group; from AIR as **CHILDREN OF THE NIGHT**)

DAUGHTERS OF DARKNESS (1974). See **VAMPYRES—DAUGHTERS OF DARKNESS.**

DAUGHTERS OF SATAN (1972). A cliched plot—witch's face in old painting resembles modern woman—is given a boost by Tom Selleck, by a good music score by Richard LaSalle and by picturesque Manila locations. Selleck portrays an art critic who buys a painting that haunts him and his wife. A strange housekeeper arrives, a killer hound lopes across the landscape, and the number 666 pops up. Outside of watching future star Selleck, there's little in John C. Higgins' script, or Hollingsworth Morse's direction, to raise this from humdrum. Barra Grant, Tani Phelps Guthrie. (Wood Knapp)

DAUGHTERS OF THE VAMPIRE. See **PLAYGIRLS AND THE VAMPIRE, THE.**

DAWN OF THE DEAD (1979). George A. Romero's sequel to NIGHT OF THE LIVING DEAD. The unrestricted movie code now allows writer-director Romero to be more graphic, and while overshock lessens the impact, he still has a primitive power that sets him apart from (if not always above) his contemporaries. This succeeds as a stomach-churning glimpse at man's prowess to destroy himself with up-to-date weaponry, and as a spoof on LIVING DEAD itself. For sometimes the walking zombies are treated menacingly, other times as jokes. The plot involves a small band trapped in a shopping mall. DAY OF THE DEAD was the third and final chapter in this sanguinary saga. David Emge, Ken Foree, Scott H. Reininger. (HBO; Republic) (Laser: HBO)

DAWN OF THE MUMMY (1981). Hashish smokers in a Cairo square is as exciting as it gets in this tale of a bandaged-enwrapped hunk of Egyptian royalty circa 3000 B.C. who rises from his desecrated crypt to create an army of flesheating monsters. Heads are ripped off with wild abandon and one unfortunate Egyptian is skewered on a hook. Egyptian pyramid locations are a plus, but the only plus. The script by producer-director Frank Agrama, Darda Price and Ronald Dobrin depicts magazine models posing for cheesecake shots in the crypt of royal king Zevraman. Definitely a lowbrow shambling-dead flick. The sun sets quickly on DAWN OF THE MUMMY. Brenda King, Barry Sattels. (HBO)

DAY AFTER, THE (1983). TV-movie written by Edward Hume and directed by Nicholas Meyer for $8 million depicting nuclear war in and around Lawrence, Kansas. It begins as an average day for several citizens . . . then news of pending attack creates panic. Finally, the Apocalypse comes with twin explosions in which Kansas City is destroyed, women and children vaporized and thousands radiated in the aftermath. The day after is more terrifying as countless bodies are heaped on pyres, people die of radiation poisoning, etc. As grim as anything made for TV. Jason Robards, Georgann Johnson, Kyle Aletter, Bibi Besch, Steve Guttenberg, JoBeth Williams, John Lithgow. (Video/Laser: Embassy)

DAY AFTER TOMORROW, THE. See **STRANGE HOLIDAY.**

DAY BEFORE HALLOWEEN (1983). Australian paranoia thriller depicts a woman chased by a lecherous photographer, a half-crazed boyfriend, a notorious lesbian and a sculptor who puts a severed pig's head in her bed. All of them want to exploit and drive this innocent (Chantal Contouri) bonkers. Simon Wincer directed this strange novelty. Also known as SNAP-SHOT. Music by Brian May. (Catalina)

DAYBREAK (1993). Bleak glimpse into a "near future" when a sexual disease affects society to the point many are being quarantined under mysterous circumstances and an underground resistance movement has risen up. Writer-director Stephen Tolkin brings a social conscience to this TV-movie but it's too downbeat and unapproachable to pass as entertainment. Cuba Gooding Jr., Moira Kelly, Omar Epps, Alice Drummond. (HBO)

DAYDREAMER, THE (1966). Mixture of live action and puppetry to tell Hans Christian Andersen fairy tales: "The Little Mermaid," "The Emperor's New Clothes," "Thumbelina" and "The Garden of Paradise." Ray Bolger, Jack Gilford, Paul O'Keefe, Margaret Hamilton. Voices by Tallulah Bankhead, Burl Ives, Boris Karloff. Directed by Jules Bass. (Children's Treasures)

DAY IT CAME TO EARTH (1977). Radioactive meteorite falls to Earth, unleashing E.T. forces of evil into the corpse of a criminal who comes to life and goes on a rampage. Directed by Harry Z. Thomason. Roger Manning, Wink Roberts, George Gobel. (Paragon)

DAY MARS INVADED EARTH, THE (1962). Boring low-budget feature from producer-director Maury Dexter doesn't have a Martian in it. Communications scientist Kent Taylor and wife Marie Windsor walk through a Hollywood estate, puzzled when they see facsimiles of themselves and children. A probe unit to Mars is being used as a beaming device to bring invisible beings to Earth, where they possess human bodies. Or something. Unusual downbeat ending by writer Harry Spalding.

DAY OF ANGER. See **DAY OF WRATH.**

DAY OF JUDGMENT, A (1981). This could be the

world's only religious slasher flick, a lesson in following the Ten Commandments—or else. It's couched as a parable and the climax has all the excitement of a Sunday sermon. Anyway, a man in black, carrying a scythe and symbolizing Retribution, rides into a Southern town in the '20s and stalks less-than-genteel types: a banker foreclosing on a farmer, a half-crazed widow who poisons a harmless goat, an adulterer and adultress, a son who schemes to send his mom and dad to an asylum. The gore is largely offscreen. From North Carolina producer Earl Owensby. Directed by C.D.H. Reynolds. William T. Hicks, Harris Bloodworth. (HBO)

DAY OF THE ANIMALS (1977). Earth's ozone layer is damaged by aerosol (!?) and turns animals into killers. A little of JAWS, a little of THE BIRDS. Beware of anything on four legs as an expedition is attacked, each member dying a horrible death. Christopher George heads the snivelers and arguers: Leslie Nielsen, Lynda Day George, Richard Jaeckel, Paul Mantee, Ruth Roman, Michael Ansara. Directed by William Girdler. (Media; from Action Inc. as **SOMETHING IS OUT THERE**)

DAY OF THE DEAD (1985). Third and final installment in the NIGHT OF THE LIVING DEAD series from writer-director George A. Romero. The world is now made up of walking zombies with only a few "normals" left. Survivors hide in an underground center where Dr. Logan (Richard Liberty) experiments on the dead. Loco Logan comes into conflict with a military unit which wants to curtail the sickening experiments. (This modern Frankenstein has the dedication of a quack at Dachau.) This conflict seems unnecessary when 9000 zombies are trying to break in. Romero, who once had fun with zombies, here takes himself seriously, relying on effects for horror scenes that revolt rather than entertain. There's the expected chomping on body parts and unstringing of intestines, and thanks to Tom Savini we see a human body ripped apart. A clumsy, unresolved conclusion to the trilogy. Lori Cardille, Terry Alexander, Howard Sherman. (Media; Video Treasures) (Laser: Image)

DAY OF THE DOLPHIN, THE (1973). Mike Nichols misfire in which George C. Scott talks to dolphins. Blame screenwriter Buck Henry. He does Flipper one better by depicting an articulate dolphin who follows commands and saves the U.S. President from assassination. Blackmailing and double-dealing is going on—frequently without story clarity. John Dehner, Trish Van Devere, Paul Sorvino, Fritz Weaver, Edward Herrmann. (Magnetic) (Laser: CBS/Fox)

DAY OF THE MANIAC (1977). Video version of **DEMONS OF THE DEAD** (Super; from Vogue as **THEY'RE COMING TO GET YOU**).

DAY OF THE NIGHTMARE (1965). Dead woman returns from the grave to wreak vengeance. Director of photography Ted Mikels went on to make THE CORPSE GRINDERS. John Ireland, Elena Verdugo, John Hart, Liz Renay, James Cross. Directed by John Bushelman.

DAY OF THE TRIFFIDS (1963). John Wyndham's novel was mangled by screenwriter Philip Yordan in this British version, at one point deteriorating into man-battling-rampaging monsters. Still, some of Wyndham's unusual end-of-mankind story remains intact, showing how most of the world's population is blinded by a meteor shower. Spared their vision, Howard Keel and Nicole Maurey flee to safety, surrounded by armies of Triffids: spores from the meteors which grow into unpruned plant-like beings which yank up their roots and stalk mortals, their pods delivering a lethal sting. Directed by Steve Sekely and Freddie Francis. Janette Scott, Mervyn Johns, Kieron Moore. (Media) (Laser: Fox; Image)

DAY OF THE TRIFFIDS (1980). BBC-TV adaptation of the John Wyndham novel about a different Armageddon: After most of mankind has been blinded by a meteor storm, strange plant-like mutant plant-monsters stalk the Earth. This follows the adventures of a couple struggling for survival. John Duttine, Emma Relph. Directed by Ken Hannam. (Prism)

DAY OF THE WOMAN. See **I SPIT ON YOUR GRAVE.**

DAY OF WRATH (1943). Somber, fascinating study of the witch hunts of the 1620s by Denmark's Carl Theodore Dreyer—a dark story of a woman (Ann Svierkier) fleeing Danish puritans who want to burn her at the stake. Inquisition executions are staged with impact. (Cable; Sinister/C; Filmfax; from Imperial as **DAY OF ANGER**)

DAY THE EARTH CAUGHT FIRE, THE (1961). Doff your fire helmet to the British for giving us an intelligent sci-fi thriller. Two governments set off atomic explosions that result in a shift of the Earth's axis and an eccentric, unstable path for our planet. Mankind heads inexorably toward its doom. Edward Judd is a drunken newspaperman, Leo McKern a crusading science editor, Janet Munro the love interest. Val Guest directed. Michael Goodliffe, Bernard Braden. (HBO; Republic)

DAY THE EARTH FROZE, THE (1959). IT CAME FROM OUTER SWEDEN might be the subtitle for this Finnish-Russian import in which a witch requests the sun not rise. Nature listens, and a new Ice Age is upon us. There's a Nordic fairy-tale quality to this unusual film, which was heavily re-edited by American-International with new narration by Marvin Miller. Directed by Aleksander Ptushko and Julius Strandberg. Nina Anderson, Jon Powers. (Shock Theater; S/Weird; Sinister/C)

DAY THE EARTH GOT STONED, THE (1978). Campside spoofery on our penchant for raucous music as a villain, the Lightning Bug, hopes to destroy civilization by overmodulating rock 'n roll soundtracks. Many scenes from old Republic serials will make this of interest to buffs. Written-directed by Richard Patterson.

DAY THE EARTH MOVED, THE (1974). TV-movie depicts considerable destruction when an earthquake strikes a desert community. Because of an anomaly in a batch of film, a photographer discovers he can predict pending earthquakes. He hurries to the next disaster site to airlift the people out before the quake hits—but it isn't quite that easy. Directed by Robert Michael Lewis. Jackie Cooper, Stella Stevens, Beverly Garland.

DAY THE EARTH STOOD STILL, THE (1951). One of the finest sci-fi movies of the '50s, thanks to director Robert Wise's concern for atmosphere and characterization. Harry Bates' short story, "Farewell to the Master," was altered by writer Edmund North but the essence is kept. Michael Rennie is Klaatu, an alien who lands his flying saucer in Washington D.C., to warn us we must settle our geopolitical differences, or else. Wounded by soldiers, he is hospitalized, but goes undercover to locate a brilliant scientist (Sam Jaffe) in order to gather the intelligentsia to hear his plea. To prove he means business, Klaatu stops all machinery on Earth for one hour. The score by Bernard Herrmann is a classic and even theologians have studied the peculiar Christ symbolism North inserted into the script. Patricia Neal is the love interest who befriends the alien and seeks out a seven-foot robot, Gort, to utter "Klaatu barada nikto," to keep Gort from destroying the world. Gort was Lock Martin, a 7'7" doorman. Hugh Marlowe, Billy Gray, Harry Lauter, Drew Pearson. (Video/Laser: Fox)

DAY THE FISH CAME OUT, THE (1967). Satirical parable misses by a mile, so heavy-handed is writer-director Michael Cacoyannis. A nuclear bomb is accidentally jettisoned onto a Greek island and the idyllic setting is turned into an absurd tourist attraction. Candice Bergman, Tom Courtenay, Sam Wanamaker, Colin Blakely, Ian Ogilvy, William Berger.

DAY THE SCREAMING STOPPED, THE. See

COMEBACK, THE.

DAY THE SKY EXPLODED, THE (1958). Italian-French sci-fi in which a missile from Earth hits the sun, sending meteors on a collision course with our planet. As in WHEN WORLDS COLLIDE, worldwide destruction begins, only this time scientists decide to fire atomic bombs at the hurtling bodies to stop them. Directed by Paolo Heusch. Cinematography by Mario Bava. Also known as DEATH FROM OUTER SPACE. Paul Hubschmid. (Nostalgia; Timeless)

DAY THE WORLD ENDED, THE (1955). Alex Gordon/Roger Corman horror/sci-fi flick, as ludicrous as it is entertaining. Paul Birch has designed a modernistic house free from radioactive contamination in which he and daughter Lori Nelson take refuge on the day of Armageddon. However, a strip teaser, gigolo, gold prospector, gangster and moll turn up for shelter. While they bicker, a hideous mutant (a reminder of atomic horrors in the world beyond) pokes around with the hope of carrying away Lori in her high heels. Richard Denning, Paul Dubov, Adele Jergens, Jonathan Haze. Mike Connors is billed as Touch Connors.

DAY TIME ENDED, THE (1978). Filmed as VORTEX, this Charles Band effort stars Jim Davis as head of a family in a desert solar home as the effects of a supernova reach Earth. A green pyramid appears and tiny creatures dance in stop-motion animation. The house is in a time warp (dig those fighting dinosaurs, gang). Effects by Jim Danforth and David Allen are nice, and the cast is watchable (Christopher Mitchum, Dorothy Malone, Scott Kolden, Marcy Lafferty), but the story is slight and pseudo-Spielbergish. Directed by John "Bud" Cardos from a script by producer Wayne Schmidt, Larry Carroll and David Schmoeller. (Media)

D DAY ON MARS. Edited version of the Republic serial **PURPLE MONSTER STRIKES, THE.**

DEAD AGAIN (1991). This Kenneth Branagh-directed murder-mystery thriller with supernatural/reincarnation overtones is a compelling bit of bravura film making and acting. Amnesia victim Emma Thompson has nightmares about a 1948 Hollywood murder (shown in black-and-white flashbacks) as private eye Branagh helps her to unravel her past aided by hypnotist Derek Jacobi. Unfortunately, Frank goes off the deep end with too many coincidences and the film plunges into self-parody, its excesses overwhelming the cast. Still, many portions are superb, with Andy Garcia contributing as a jaded prize-winning journalist. Robin Williams, in an uncredited cameo, plays a disbarred psychiatrist. Sydney Pollack produced. (Video/Laser: Paramount)

DEAD AIM (1987). This starts as a STRIPPED TO KILL kind of slasher thriller as striptease gals are murdered, with cop Ed Marinaro hot on the trail. Then it becomes a complicated spy mystery involving the FBI and Russian agents. Only a few scenes quality it as horror, and the burlesque segments lack the surrealism that inspired it. Directed by William Vanderkloot. Darrell Larson, Cassandra Gava, Isaac Hayes, Corben Bernsen, William Windom. (Vestron) (Laser: Image)

DEAD ALIVE (1992). Outrageous gore-splatter comedy blending the morbid parody of Frank (BASKET CASE) Henelotter and the macabre styles of Sam Raimi and George Romero. Made in New Zealand, it depicts what happens when simian raticus ("the rat monkey of Sumatra") is brought from Skull Island in 1957 and placed in a zoo. The creature's bite (rendered in stop animation) instantly turns a woman into a monster that ferociously kills. The mom's nerdy son and girlfriend try to contain the corpses in mom's mansion but the living dead keep increasing. The only way to control them? Stick a hypodermic up their nostrils. This features chopped off limbs and heads by the score, a lawnmower that churns bodies into puree gore, hypos into noses and eyes, exploding bodies, a mutant baby running rampant and a karate trained minister. This blatant attempt to offend and still bring a smile to your lips is the work of director Peter Jackson. A must for genre fans, but general audiences will find this too subversive. (Vidmark)

DEAD AND BURIED (1981). Offbeat Dan O'Bannon-Ronald Shusett horror tale, set in coastside Potter's Bluff, where townspeople slaughter strangers by setting them afire or poking them with knives, pitchforks and other handy tools. And snapping photos all the while, for the scrapbooks. It's up to sheriff James Farentino to solve the puzzle. By keeping us in the dark about the why (if not the who), the film under Gary A. Sherman's direction builds to a suspenseful climax. The odd mixture includes witchcraft, voodooism, zombiism. Melody Anderson is Farentino's schoolteacher wife and Jack Albertson is the town coroner. Effects by Stan Winston. (Vestron)

DEAD ARE ALIVE, THE (1972). Alex Cord portrays an alcoholic archeologist photographing Etruscan ruins in Italy, and meeting walking corpses in the process. Directed by Armando Crispino. John Marley, Samantha Eggar, Nadja Tiller, Horst Frank.

DEAD CALM (1989). This Australian adaptation of Charles Williams' novel was reshaped by screenwriter Terry Hayes into a slasher-horror shocker set aboard a yacht manned by Sam Neill and Nicole Kidman, who are on a sailing holiday. The lone survivor (Billy Zane) of a ship massacre comes aboard and the terror begins. It's a fascinating concept to have victims isolated on the ocean with a killer, and director Philip Noyce captures a sense of claustrophobic horror. (Video/Laser: Warner Bros.)

DEAD DON'T DIE, THE (1974). Robert Bloch's teleplay pays homage to the '30s "weird thriller" pulps in this TV-movie directed by Curtis Harrington. During the Depression, George Hamilton discovers there's a plot afoot in Chicago by mad doctor Varek (Ray Milland) to create an army of zombies. It's surreal within its perpetual-night atmosphere, with everyone behaving sinisterly. Ralph Meeker, Joan Blondell, Linda Cristal. (Worldvision)

DEAD END CITY (1989). Evil forces in U.S. Government implement a new "urban renewal" policy by forcing gangs to wipe themselves out, making it safe for law-biding citizens. As the gangs shoot it out, factory owner Greg Cummins refuses to vacate and defends his property. Dennis Cole, Christine Lund, Robert Zdar. Written-produced-directed by Peter Yuval. (Action International)

DEAD-END DRIVE IN (1986). In the 1990s, after civilization collapses and anarchy sets in, teenagers are trapped in a drive-in movie lot in their '56 Chevy. It's a compound for teenagers, and our young hero sets out to escape. What results in this Australian political fantasy are car crashes, blazing submachine-guns and cliffhanging chases. Directed by Brian Trenchard-Smith. (New World)

DEAD EYES OF LONDON, THE (1961). West German remake of the 1940 horror flick THE HUMAN MONSTER, also known as THE DARK EYES OF LONDON, based on Edgar Wallace's THE TESTAMENT OF GOR-

TREAT WILLIAMS/JOE PISCOPO: "DEAD HEAT"

DON STUART. Heavily insured old men are dying too frequently and the clues lead Scotland Yard's Joachim Fuchsberger to a ring of blind murderers led by a reverend. Directed by Alfred Vohrer in Hamburg. Klaus Kinski, Karin Baal. (S/Weird; Sinister/C; Filmfax)

DEAD GIRLS (1990). Women, hearing the song "Life is a Total Bummer—Death Ends All," decide to commit suicide. One survives and goes to a hideway to recover with friends—and the friends are murdered by a masked killer, who uses weapons described in songs she wrote. Directed by Dennis Devine. (Raedon)

DEAD HEAT (1988). Pushing outrageously into the zone of THE REANIMATOR and other wall-busting films, this is many things (the press book calls it a "gleeful mixture of action, adventure, fantasy, horror, mystery, romance and flat-out comedy"). It's best as a comedy of zombie and buddy-cop movies as mad Arthur P. Loudermilk (Vincent Price) rejuvenates dead humans with a machine of electric bolts and sends out zombies to hold up jewelry stores. L.A. cops Treat Williams and Joe Piscopo, a Butch Cassidy-Sundance Kid comedy duo, trail the monsters with coroner Lindsay Frost. The picture, directed by Mark Goldblatt, takes a bizarre turn when Williams becomes a zombie and goes after the bad guys. The best sequence occurs in a restaurant when the carcasses of dead animals (pig, chicken, duck, etc.) attack the cops. Darren McGavin, Keye Luke, Toru Tanaka, Robert Picardo. (New World) (Laser: Image)

DEAD KIDS. See **STRANGE BEHAVIOR.**

DEADLIER THAN THE MALE (1966). Colorful, updated look at British agent Bulldog Drummond in a James Bond mold. Jimmy Sangster stuffs his script with scientific gadgets and assassination devices as shapely murderesses Elke Sommer and Sylva Koscina do the evil bidding of master criminal Nigel Green. The women are dressed in minicostumes, the action is explosive and nonstop—the entertainment value is high. Ralph Thomas directs with a flair for pop art, and Richard Johnson portrays the gentleman spy with aplomb.

DEADLOCK (1991). Rutger Hauer brings a light touch to his role as a jewel thief who is doublecrossed and sent to Camp Holliday, a futuristic prison in which convicts wear collars set to explode. When Hauer and Mimi Rogers escape, the film becomes a poor man's DEFIANT ONES, with the mismatched pair forced to stick close or risk being blown up. Hot on their tails is Hauer's former flame, Asian killer Joan Chen. Although there are not enough futuristic gimmicks to create an intriguing society of tomorrow, Broderick Miller's script has enough action and amusements to make this a pleasing entertainment, and it's well directed by Lewis Teague. James Remar, Stephen Tobolowsky. (HBO)

DEADLY AND THE BEAUTIFUL. Video retitling of **WONDER WOMEN** (Media).

DEADLY BEES, THE (1967). Amicus' adaptation of H. F. Heard's A TASTE FOR HONEY, scripted by Robert Bloch, is more a murder mystery than a horror film as an insane beekeeper develops a strain of mutant bee that attacks a certain scent. Two of the sting-attack sequences are nicely wrought, with terrifying effects. Frank Finlay, Suzanne Leigh, Guy Doleman and Michael Ripper were directed by Freddie Francis. The dialogue drones on, but so bee it.

DEADLY BLESSING (1981). Botched Wes Craven effort, an imitation of many genre films, has little logic as a family of Hittites, a religious sect, terrorizes women living in a farmhouse. One memorable scenes has a rattlesnake crawling into a hot tub with a naked woman. We defy you to keep your eyes open during this sequence. The rest is raunchy sex and violence. Maren Jensen, Susan Buckner, Jeff East, Lisa Hartman, Lois Nettleton (in a going-bonkers role), Ernest Borgnine. (Embassy)

DEADLY DREAM, THE (1971). Unusual TV-movie dealing with the razor-sharp line separating dreams from reality, and reality from dreams. Research scientist Lloyd Bridges repeatedly dreams a group has formed a conspiracy against him. Director Alf Kjellin captures a dreamlike quality matching the surreal story. Janet Leigh, Carl Betz, Leif Erickson, Don Stroud, Richard Jaeckel.

DEADLY DREAMS (1988). Mitchell Anderson is haunted by dreams of when his parents were murdered by a man in an animal mask. Has the killer returned from the dead to kill Anderson? Directed by Kristine Peterson. Juliette Cummins, Xander Berkeley, Thom Babbes. (Virgin Vision) (Laser: Image)

DEADLY DUST (1978). That web-spinning superhero leaps out of Marvel comics to star in this TV-film, edited from episodes of THE AMAZING SPIDERMAN in which Spidey searches for a missing atomic bomb. Nicholas Hammond doubles as Spidey and Peter Parker. Michael Pataki, Robert Alda. (Playhouse; MCA)

DEADLY EYES (1982). Mutant rodents grow to giant size in the London subway, devouring babies and other innocents. The rabid rats finally meet their match when science teacher Sam Groom buys giant mousetraps. Meanwhile, Scatman Crothers goes to an eerie doom while inspecting a sewer. Creatures average the size of dachshunds—in fact, those are dachshunds under the rat skins. An insult to James Herbert's novel, being a typical horror film (directed by Robert Clouse) in which most characters are gnawed on before the final fade. The low budget shows in Ron Wisman's effects and there's a distracting (but sizzling) love affair between Groom and Lisa Langlois. Cec Linder, Lesleh Donaldson. Also known as THE RATS. (Warner Bros.)

DEADLY FRIEND (1986). Writer Bruce Joel Rubin (adapting Diana Henstell's FRIEND) wants to tell a bittersweet love story between a Polytech student (who studies human brains and designs robots) and his next-door girlfriend (a victim of fatherly abuse). Director Wes Craven wants to retell NIGHTMARE ON ELM STREET, loading up on nightmares, tacked-on shock scenes and effects for their own sake (i.e., the basketball bit). Sympathy for the girl, after she's killed and restored to life (via a robot circuitry in her damaged brain), is nil once she begins killing those who wronged her. Matthew Laborteaux, Anne Twomey. (Video/Laser: Warner Bros.)

DEADLY GAME (1991). Several individuals are summoned to an island and set loose as prey for a killer named Osiris. They flee for their lives and avoid death traps a la "The Most Dangerous Game." Each character's guilt is revealed in a flashback (the settings are Vietnam, Cambodia, the Mardi Gras, etc.) and a profile of Osiris builds. Director/co-producer Thomas J. Wright keeps it moving. Among the fleers are Roddy McDowall, Marc Singer, Mitchell Ryan, Jenny Seagrove, Soon-Tech Oh, Frederic Lehne, John Pleshette. (Paramount)

DEADLY GAMES (1982). Esoteric slasher film dealing with the relationship between killer and victim. A black-mask killer is murdering women, but writer-director Scott Mansfield narrows the possibilities to demented policeman Sam Groom or melancholoy theater manager Steve Railsback. The murders are not gory, suggesting Mansfield prefers dealing with drama rather than cliche knife murders. His subtleties cause the film to go in and out of focus, and there are counterpoint idyllic moments when a would-be victim (Denise Galin) enjoys fun and games with the two suspects, unaware one of them is the slasher. Jo Ann Harris, June Lockhart, Colleen Camp, Alexandra Morgan, Dick Butkus. (Monterey)

DEADLY HARVEST (1976). Canadian film set in the near future when food is running low, and citizens tighten belts around empty stomachs to face a bleak tomorrow. Directed by Timothy Bond. Clint Walker, Nehemiah Persoff, Roy Davies. (New World) (Laser: Image)

DEADLY INTRUDER (1985). Unimpressive psychokiller flick: A slasher villain escaped from a nuthouse is loose in a community, where cop Stuart Whitman is always a few clues behind an arrest. Most of the violence is kept off screen by director John McCauley. Writer/co-producer Tony Crupi turns up as Drifter. Molly Cheek, Chris Holder. (HBO)

DEADLY INVENTION, THE. See **FABULOUS WORLD OF JULES VERNE, THE.**

DEADLY LESSONS (1983). Tame TV-movie cashing in on the slasher cycle, but without blood and gross thrills—this plays more like a whodunit. The setting is Starkwater Hall, an exclusive school for pedigree teenage girls. Donna Reed stands out as the cold-blooded school mistress; Ally Sheedy is dull as the newcomer. Directed by William Wiard. Larry Wilcox, David Ackroyd.

DEADLY MANTIS, THE (1957). Sci-fi effects thriller (aka THE INCREDIBLE PREYING MANTIS) in which a giant mantis is released from an iceberg by an earthquake and begins a wave of destruction, knocking over Washington Monument and hiding in Holland Tunnel. This will appeal to those who enjoy '50s' rampaging monsters. Craig Stevens is the officer out to stop the creature, William Hopper the scientist looking for a killing device and Alix Talton the love interest. Directed by Nathan Juran; effects by Clifford Stine. (Video/Laser: MCA)

DEADLY RAY FROM MARS (1938). Video of **FLASH GORDON'S TRIP TO MARS** (Questar).

DEADLY REACTOR (1989). Although this is set in a post-holocaust world, it has the trappings of the old-fashioned Hollywood western as a mean old motorcycle gang terrorizes folks. The "sheriff" is also the film's writer and director, David Heavener. He goes after Hog (Darwyn Swalve) and his sadists. Stuart Whitman, Allyson Davis. (Action International)

DEADLY SANCTUARY (1970). Bad rendering of Marquis De Sade's writings (also called JUSTINE), which captures nothing of the man or his search for sadistic pleasure. It's a half-hearted, R-rated portrait of Justine, who is sexually abused by perverts and freaks. The philosophies of the historic, if not beloved, nobleman who sought the ultimate in self-gratification is reduced to devil cult behavior, bloodletting and sacrifices at the altar of pain. Jack Palance is a cackling idiot as De Sade, and Mercedes MacCambridge plays an awful bitch. Despite its nudity sequences, this never captures an ounce of eroticism under Jesse Franco's direction. Sylva Koscina, Akim Tamiroff, Maria Rohm. (Monterey)

DEADLY SPAWN, THE (1983). An E.T. monster, ripped out of ALIEN, crashlands on Earth in a meteor and proceeds to a dank cellar where it opens its toothsome mouth and swallows up the first person it sees. It's an ugly creation, surrounded by smaller mouths, with tadpole-like babies on the rafters and swimming through greasy puddles. Pretty soon the mother ejects a half-eaten head, which the infants swarm over, devouring with (hamburger?) relish. The only intelligent cast member is a kid who loves horror movies, so he figures out a home-made weapon to combat the gobbling mouth-thing. Very grotesque and poorly shot in 16mm. Obscure is writer-director Douglas McKeown. (On video as **RETURN OF THE ALIEN'S DEADLY SPAWN**)

DEADLY STING, THE. See **ALIEN WITHIN, THE.**

DEADLY VISITOR (1973). Unseen presence in a boarding house is the ghost of a previous inhabitant, back to haunt a writer. Gwen Verdon, Perry King, Stephen Macht, Ann Miles. Cheap British TV production.

DEADLY WEAPON (1988). Unusually sensitive Charles Band production with an underlying, subtle theme about teenage suicide. Rodney Eastman gives a moving performance as a troubled youth in rural King Bee, Arizona, who finds a pistol that fires anti-gravity X-ray beams—zap rays to you. From a dysfunctional family (runaway mother, drunken father, nasty sister), Eastman uses the weapon for self-defense but this only gets him into trouble during a siege. Surrounded by military forces out to retrieve the lethal weapon, the youth tries to find a peaceful way out. Director Michael Miner's script has an element of tragedy. Kim Walker, Gary Frank, Michael Horse, Barney Martin, Ed Nelson. (Trans World)

DEAD MAN WALKING (1987). Unpleasant sci-fi cautionary tale set in a depressing future when a plague has wiped out most of mankind and a corporation called Unitus rules. Those dying of the plague are Zero Men, and clubs have been designed for them to play out games of suicide. Such a Zero Man is Luger (Wings Hauser), hired by corporation man Jeffery Combs to find his boss' daughter, kidnapped by escaped criminal Decker (Brion James). They enter the Plague Zone, and murder, mayhem and car crashes result. Drearily unappealing, set against drab Southern California and styled without pace, sympathetic characters or purpose. It features such revolting images as men playing suicide with a chainsaw and pistols, and a man set on fire in a nightclub act. Produced-directed by Gregory Brown. (Republic)

DEAD MAN'S EYES (1944). Entry in Universal's "Inner Sanctum" series with Lon Chaney Jr. as an artist who has acid thrown into his eyes by jealous Acquanett. After undergoing an eye transplant, Chaney is accused of murder by detective Thomas Gomez. Directed by Reginald Le Borg. Jean Parker, Paul Kelly, Eddie Dunn.

DEAD MATE (1989). David Gregory plays a multiple wife-murderer who uses electricity to bring their corpses back to life. He whisks wiatress Elizabeth Mannino away into his trap of death. Plenty of gore as she tries to escape. Written-directed by Straw (Boss) Weisman. Lawrence Bockins, Adam Wahl, Judith Mayes. (Prism)

DEAD MEN DON'T DIE (1990). When TV newsman Elliott Gould is killed when pursuing a drug story, cleaning woman Mabel King uses voodoo to bring him back to life. Gould goes after his killers posing as a live man and trying not to look like a dead one. Melissa Anderson, Mark Moses, Philip Bruns, Mabel King. Written-directed by Malcolm Marmorstein. (Academy)

DEAD MEN WALK (1943). George Zucco, Practitioner of the Black Arts, dies but doesn't go to Heaven. He sits up in his coffin and tells chortling assistant Dwight Frye he's a vampire. His target is Mary Carlisle, whose life force he sucks out through the neck. Meanwhile, his lookalike brother (another doctor, also played by Zucco) wonders about the two punctures in Mary's neck and reads from a book about witches and warlocks. Dreary PRC quickie, hacked out by director Sam Newfield. (Nostalgia; Sinister/C; VCI; Filmfax)

DEAD OF NIGHT (1945). Superlative British ghost story anthology—possibly the most influential horror film of the '40s. In a drawing room several characters recount frightening incidents. Basil Dearden directed the first story (by E.F. Benson) in which a race driver receives a supernatural warning. The second, directed by Alberto Cavalcanti, is the brooding tale (also adapted from Benson) of the ghost of a little boy murdered by his sister in a tower room. "The Haunted Mirror," directed by Robert Hamer, is a gripper in which an ornate looking-glass reflects a Victorian bedroom and almost compels its owner to commit murder. H.G. Wells' "The Inexperienced Ghost," set on a golf course and directed by Charles Crichton, is of a comedic nature and the weakest tale. "The Ventriloquist" (directed by Cavalcanti) is the most frightening, with entertainer and dummy shifting personalities. The final tale involves the storytellers. Michael Redgrave, Googie Withers, Mervyn Jones, Miles Malleson, Sally Ann Howes. (HBO; Republic) (Laser: Image)

'DEAD OF NIGHT'

DEAD OF NIGHT (1972). Aka THE NIGHT WALK, DEATHDREAM and THE NIGHT ANDY CAME HOME, this is from director-producer Bob Clark (PORKY'S) and screenwriter Alan Ormsby, who borrowed from "The Monkey's Paw." Richard Backus portrays a dead Vietnam soldier whose spirit is brought home by his grief-stricken mother, but now he's a vampire killer. Well-staged chases and a macabre climax. John Marley, Anya Ormsby. (From MPI as **DEATHDREAM**)

DEAD OF NIGHT (1976). During the '70s Universal resurrected the anthology format with two pilots directed by Dan Curtis. The first was TRILOGY OF TERROR; this, the second, features three tales written by Richard Matheson. "Second Chance" is a TWILIGHT ZONE clone with Ed Begley Jr. as a man traveling through time in his 1926 Jordan Playboy. "No Such Thing as a Vampire" stars Patrick MacNee, Anjanette Comer, Elisha Cooke and Horst Bucholtz in a revenge yarn with pseudo-horror overtones. "Bobby" is the best one, about a grieving mother (Joan Hackett) who asks for her drowned son back and gets more than she bargained for when Lee H. Montgomery knocks on her door. (Thrillervideo, hosted by Elvira.)

DEAD OF NIGHT (1987). How can you take a movie seriously when one character says "Who knows how to deal with evil spirits floating out of mirrors?" and another says "Why don't we just look in the yellow pages!" What makes it worse: they do hire an exorcist through the phonebook, who rides to the exorcism on a bike. This minimally developed tale of witchcraft and possession focuses on a battered wife who seeks revenge by creating a doppleganger that leaves her body and, in sexy outfits, kills off the men she picks up. Directed by Deryn Warren. Julie Merrill, Kuri Browne, John Reno, J.K. Dumont.

DEAD ON: RELENTLESS II. See **RELENTLESS II: DEAD ON.**

DEAD ONE, THE (1961). Voodoo tale in which Monica Davis sends a relative corpse out for blood. Voodoo venture vacillates, totally disintegrates when the zombie is zapped by rays of the sun. Written-produced-directed by Barry Mahon. John MacKay.

DEAD PEOPLE. See **MESSIAH OF EVIL.**

DEAD PIT (1989). Take your average SNAKE PIT environment, mix in NIGHT OF THE LIVING DEAD zombies and this is what you get from director Brett Leonard, working with a script he co-wrote with producer Gimel Everett. Cheryl Lawson, playing a mentally disturbed woman haunted by traumatic childhood incidents, ends up in the State Institute for the Mentally Ill, underrgoing psychohypnosis under Dr. Jeremy Slate. She's haunted by the spectre of a mad "surgeon" with eyes that glow red who once performed horrible lobotomies. An earthquake breaks open a pit of corpses and they rove the hospital, murdering fresh victims. It's familiar territory that should sate gore buffs. Danny Gochnauer. (Imperial)

DEAD RINGERS (1988). This study of twin brothers (based on TWINS by Bari Wood and Jack Geasland) is loaded with psychological twists, and pushes this Canadian-produced film into the arena of psychiatric horror. It is so morbidly presented by writer-director David Cronenberg that one is prevented from sympathezing with the characters. It's disturbing to watch two brilliant gynecologists, who have spent their lives together building careers and are now so locked together in spirit they are destroying themselves. Again, Cronenberg turns to the theme of our bodies being invaded by foreigners—the twin doctors are always inserting gynecological tools into their patients, and designing their own instruments judged "radical" by the medical industry. Jeremy Irons is brilliant in the dual roles but even he cannot generate enough sympathy to cancel out the unsettling feelings. The same is true of Genevieve Bujold, who turns on the doctors when they discover she has a freakish vagina. An unnerving experience. Heide Von Palleske, Barbara Gordon, Stephen Lack. (Media) (Laser: Image)

DEAD SLEEP (1991). Nurse Linda Blair, working in the experimental ward of a Brisbane, Australia, hospital, discovers that patients subjected to deep sleep testing are dying. This imitation of COMA was directed by Alec Mills. Tony Bonner, Andrew Booth. (Vestron)

DEAD SPACE (1990). Remember Roger Corman's 1981 ripoff of ALIEN, called FORBIDDEN WORLD? Well, he ripped that off too and cranked out this cheap remake. With footage borrowed from previous Corman sci-fiers, DEAD SPACE has a red face when space jockey Marc Singer and his half-functioning robot Chim-Pan arrive on Phabon, where a genetic experiment with the Delta 5 virus results in a "metamorphic mutant." The creature races around the space station murdering folks, while "freelance contributor" Singer can never hit it with his laser zap gun, he's such a lousy shot. Onions to director Fred Gallo. Laura Tate, Bryan Cranston, Judith Chapman, Lori Lively. (Video/Laser: RCA/Columbia)

DEAD THAT WALK, THE. See **ZOMBIES OF MORA TAU, THE.**

DEAD, THE DEVIL AND THE FLESH, THE (1973). Spanish supernatural thriller in which a writer's dead wife returns to tease him with her spectral sexuality. Written-directed by Jose Maria Oliveira. Carlos Estrade, Patricia Wright, Emiliano Redondo.

DEADTIME STORIES (1986). "Nobody lives happily ever after," promise the producers of this anthology film, made in Greenwich, Conn., as FREAKY TIME TALES. It's a trilogy of tongue-in-cheek horrors told by daddy to a sleepless junior. "Peter and the Witches" is a medieval grim fairy tale in which a fisherman's son helps two cackling crones prepare a human sacrifice. "Little Red Runninghood" is a modern variation on the fairy tale but it's predictable, including the verbal punchline. "Goldilox and the Three Baers" is the weakest of the threesome, played tongue-in-cheek by director Jeffrey Delman. Scott Valentine, Melissa Leo, Cathryn De Prume, Phyllis Craig. (Cinema Group; Continental) (Laser: Image)

DEAD ZONE, THE (1983). Loyal adaptation of Stephen King's best-seller, a riveting portrait of Johnny Smith, who wakes up from a five-year coma to discover he can predict the future. How he copes with this "gift" is enthralling, with director David Cronenberg avoiding cliches. Christopher Walken's performance is tops, Brooke Adams is excellent as Johnny's girl (their affair is bittersweet) and Martin Sheen chillingly plays politician Greg Stillson, whom Johnny intends to assassinate when he foresees Stillson's psychotic condition leading America into war. The film poses difficult, controversial issues but doesn't offer simple solutions. Cronenberg's restraint (except for one death sequence involving the Castle Rock Killer) makes for a thoughtful ESP melodrama, insightfully structured by screenwriter Jeffrey Boam. Tom Skerritt is the sheriff, Herbert Lom is Dr. Weizak, Anthony Zerbe is the influential Roger Stuart, Colleen Dewhurst the mother. (Video/Laser: Paramount)

DEAFULA (1975). Vampire feature produced in sign language, with alimited soundtrack of music and English translation. If you don't understand the language of the hearing impaired, you will have difficulty following this tale about a theology student turned bloodsucker. and his hunchback pal. Written-directed by Peter Wechsberg.

DEAN R. KOONTZ'S THE SERVANTS OF TWILIGHT. See **SERVANTS OF TWILIGHT, THE.**

DEAN R. KOONTZ'S WHISPERS. See **WHISPERS.**

DEAR, DEAD DELILAH (1972). Writer-director John Farris centers on matriarch Agnes Moorehead and her weird Nashville mansion. A murderess is on the premises, axing off heads, in her search for $500,000. Michael Ansara, Dennis Patrick, Will Geer. (Embassy)

DEAR DEPARTED (1987). Whacked-out Australian comedy, so unrestrained in creating a zany universe in which the real world and the afterworld intermingle, it reaches remarkable heights of incomprehensibility. Sexy Pamela Stephenson kills actor-husband Garry McDonald and others to be haunted by their "wronged spirits." There are monster faces, electrical charges of light that encircle bodies and a kind of Halloween nonsense about the hauntings. The characters are so unapproachable that only the most tolerant viewer will endure to the ironic ending. Dear, depart early from DEAR DEPARTED. Su Cruickshank, Marian Dworakowski.

DEATH AND THE GREEN SLIME. See **GREEN SLIME, THE.**

DEATH AND THE MAIDEN. See **FERRYBOAT WOMAN MARIA.**

DEATH AT LOVE HOUSE (1975). Pseudosupernatural TV-movie—poppycock about a writer and wife (Robert Wagner, Kate Jackson) who move into the mansion of a once-famous movie star to write a script of her life. (The location is the old Harold Lloyd estate.) Wagner's father once had an affair with fiery Lorna Love, and Wagner becomes obsessed by the spirit of the depraved actress. Jim Barnett's teleplay is pure baloney, with a mysterious woman in white flitting around the mansion. If only director E. W. Swackhamer hadn't played it so straight. Sylvia Sidney, Marianna Hill, Joan Blondell, Dorothy Lamour, John Carradine, Bill Macy. (Prism)

DEATH BECOMES HER (1992). This dark comedy is a blend of satire, sex, special-effects jokes and commentary on man's greed, with touches that spoof Hitchcock movies. Revenge is the motif when aging Broadway actress Madeline Ashton (Meryl Streep, never looking lovelier) steals plastic surgeon Ernest Menville (Bruce Willis) from fiance Helen Sharp (Goldie Hawn). After Hawn turns into a superfat blob grieving the loss, she vows come-uppance, and plots to steal Willis back and arrange Streep's "accidental" death. Enter Isabella Rossellini in an exotic, erotic role as a half-naked seductress who sells the elixir of eternal youth to Streep. Ken Ralston's effects and Dick Smith's make-up come into play, with characters bodily damaged in hilarious ways. The morality of this is brought into crystal focus in a marvelously zany ending. The script by Martin Donovan-David Koepp is ingenious and producer-director Robert Zemeckis photographs it on magnificent sets, creating a rich Beverly Hills lifestyle contrasted by the unpleasant characters. Ian Ogilvy, Adam Storke, Nancy Fish, Alaina Reed Hall, and movie director Sydney Pollack in a cameo. (Video-Laser: MCA)

MERYL STREEP

DEATH BED. See **TERMINAL CHOICE.**

DEATH BITE. Video of **SPASMS** (Thorn/EMI).

DEATH BY DIALOGUE (1988). Movie script is possessed by evil and monsters leap off the page. If only that much excitement would leap off the screen. Directed-written by Tom DeWier. Jude Gerrard. (City Lights)

DEATH BY INVITATION (1971). Witchcraft thriller written-directed by Ken Friedman in which the descendant of a woman burned as a witch retaliates with an axe. More gore on the floor. Shelby Leverington.

DEATH CAR ON THE FREEWAY (1979). The Fiddler—a maniac driver in a van, who loves to play blue grass music as he attacks—roves L.A. freeways, seeking helpless woman whom he kills in fiery crashes. "Fiery crashes" are the key to this TV-movie, designed by director Hal Needham, onetime Hollywood stunt man, and writer William Wood as an effects vehicle. Some crashes are great, but the story is banal as TV reporter Shelley Hack tracks the killer. There's a weak relationship with TV exec George Hamilton to pad out the script. Peter Graves is an ineffectual cop. Harriet Nelson, Dinah Shore, Abe Vigoda, Frank Gorshin, Barbara Rush.

DEATH COLLECTOR (1988). Dumb, immature blending of sci-fi and westerns when Daniel Chapman, in a future time period, goes ater the guys who killed his brother. Philip Nutman, Ruth Collins. Produced-directed by Tom Gniazowski. (Raedon)

DEATH COMES FROM SPACE. See **DAY THE SKY EXPLODED, THE.**

DEATH COMES FROM THE DARK. See **CAULDRON OF BLOOD.**

DEATH CORPS. See **SHOCK WAVES.**

DEATH CRUISE (1974). Couples think they've won a free cruise but someone has lured them into a trap and wants to murder them on the high seas. Directed by Ralph Senensky. Richard Long, Polly Bergen, Edward Albert, Celeste Holm, Kate Jackson. (Academy)

DEATH CURSE OF TARTU (1966). From the writer-director of STANLEY comes this nonthriller about an Indian witch doctor who stirs in his crypt while natives beat on drums. But William Grefe does little to bolster his supernatural theme by picking teenagers who dance rock 'n roll in the Everglades and swim in shark-infested waters. You want to see them get killed quickly, so insufferable is their behavior. Grefe uses a snake as a killing device but the cottonmouth is made of rubber, so not even the creepy-crawlie aspects are challenging. But the color photography is . . . colorful. Fred Pinero, Babbette Sherrill, Bill Marcus. (Active)

DEATH DIMENSION (1978). Killer bomb could freeze our planet—and ruin TV viewing. Or damage brain cells from underfed story. Dimensionless feature, death to watch, directed by Al Adamson. Jim Kelly, George Lazenby, Harold Sakata. (Budget; from Unicorn as **BLACK ELIMINATOR**, from Movietime as **FREEZE BOMB, THE** and Academy as **KILL FACTOR**)

DEATHDREAM. Video title of **DEAD OF NIGHT (1972)** (MPI).

DEATH DREAMS (1991). Offbeat TV-movie based on the William Katz novel in which a mother accuses her husband of drowning her child. Marg Heldenberger's evidence against stepdaddy Christopher Reeve is based on ESP dreams in which the child returns from the dead to give her clues. Robert Glass does an excellent job of adapting the offbeat narrative into a supernatural thriller (and director Martin Donovan gives it chilling moments) that retains verisimilitude when it turns into a courtroom conflict. Fionnula Flanagan is good as an occultist who befriends Heldenberger. (Laser: Image)

DEATH GAME (1977). Depraved psychodrama depicting perverted, sicko chicks (Sondra Locke, Colleen Camp) who invade Seymour Cassel's home and proceed to (1) seduce him, (2) tie him up and (3) torture him with sleazy sex games. Along comes a delivery boy, whom the busty, sensuous babes drown in a fish tank. Then the fun-happy dolls decide to castrate Seymour. Compellingly degenerate . . . you won't take your eyes off the screen as the bi-sexual chicks swing. Directed by Peter Traynor. Also known as THE SEDUCERS. (VCI)

DEATHHEAD VIRGIN, THE (1973). The last virgin princess of a legendary Moro tribe of the Philippines guards a treasure in a galleon sunk in 1850. Her spirit is aroused when a treasure hunter finds an ancient medallion. The unconvincing monster is a sexy gal wearing a skull-face mask. Philippine locations help this poverty-stricken production, poorly written by Ward Gaynor (an alias for cast members Larry Ward and Jock Gaynor, who portray underwater adventurers) and indifferently directed by Norman Foster. Diane McBain provides plot turns but one wishes she had more scenes in a bikini—she's the only visual excitement. (Academy)

DEATH HOUSE (1988). John Saxon directed and stars in this prison horror thriller as a federal agent with a bad streak who is utilizing a new drug to create unbeatable warriors. Dennis Cole, Tane McClure, Anthony Franciosa, Michael Pataki. (Action International)

DEATH IN SPACE (1974). TV-movie with George Maharis, Cameron Mitchell and Margaret O'Brien. Astronaut chief disappears through the airlock while his ship is 250 miles above Earth. Was his death accidental or murder? Directed by Charles Dubin.

DEATH IN THE HAND (1947). British programmer in which a pianist, riding aboard a train, predicts the deaths of passengers by reading their palms. Sounds like DR. TERROR'S HOUSE OF HORRORS. Based on Max

Beerbohm's SEVEN MEN. Directed by A. Barr-Smith. Esme Percy, Ernest Jay.

DEATH IS CHILD'S PLAY. See **ISLAND OF THE DAMNED.**

DEATH ISLAND. See **MAN-EATER OF HYDRA.**

DEATH KISS (1932). Listed for completist elitists who must see every Bela Lugosi movie. In this Hollywood whodunit, as old-fashioned as Kleig lights and catwalks, our Dracula star portrays the manager of Tiffany Studios, where a murder is committed on the set of a thriller. Turgid and predictable, with Lugosi behaving strangely. Maybe he's scowling at John Wray, Edward van Sloan and David Manner for overacting under Edwin L. Marin's direction. (Prism; Kartes; Thunderbird)

DEATH LINE. See **RAW MEAT.**

DEATH LIST. See **TERMINAL CHOICE.**

DEATH MACHINES (1976). "Mod Squad Goes Bananas" is an apt subtitle for this actioner in which a Caucasian, a Black and an Asian are injected with a Strange Serum and turned into assassins by an insidious Dragon Lady Who Overacts. Kung fu/karate ballets, explosions, fistfights, shoot-outs, bazooka blasts, mass slaughters, crashing autos and body bashings—but no characterizations, plot, intelligent dialogue. Black Belt hero Ron Marchini produced-stars. Made in Stockton, Ca., with Paul Kyriazi directing. (VCI; VidAmerica)

DEATHMASTER (1972). Actor Ray Danton directed this turgid terror tale, cashing in on Robert Quarry's success as a vampire in COUNT YORGA. In this low-grade cheapie, Quarry (associate producer) is a gruesome guru who washes up on a California beach and hypnotizes hapless hippies in a deserted mansion. One by one, the teeners are snuffed vampire style. Should have been entitled TEDIUMMASTER.

DEATHMOON (1978). TV-movie, filmed in Hawaii, dramatizing how businessman Robert Foxworth turns into a werewolf after being jinxed by a native curse. This puts a damper on his affair with France Nuyen. Directed by Bruce Kessler. Joe Penny, Barbara Trentham, Debralee Scott, Charles Haid. (VCL)

DEATH NURSE (1987). Do yourself a favor by not ringing for NURSE, from writer-director Nick Phillips, the entity who brought you CRAZY FAT ETHEL II, sequel to CRIMINALLY INSANE. He's using the same wretched cast in depicting a demented pair running a nursing home and slaughtering patients. Its unstar is Priscilla Alden as Edith Mortley, RN (raunchy nutcake). The less said the better. (Video City; Chop-em Up Video)

DEATH OF A HOOKER. See **WHO KILLED MARY WHATS'ER NAME.**

DEATH OF OCEAN VIEW PARK, THE (1979). Playboy purchased Ocean View Park in Virginia then wrote a script around its destruction. Special effects men used 150 sticks of TNT and 400 gallons of napthalene to destroy the roller coaster. The feeble plot is about a supernatural force that leaves every concession overturned. Diana Canova undergoes premonitions and psychic warnings of the coming disaster. Directed by E.W. Swackhamer. Mike Connors, Martin Landau.

DEATH OF THE INCREDIBLE HULK, THE (1990). In this final installment of the TV-movie series, based on the Marvel Comics character, director Bill Bixby (who plays scientist David Banner) evokes a tragic feeling for the misunderstood scientist who turns into a green entity when angered. The Hulk portions, as usual, feature Lou Ferrigno on a rampage, but thanks to Bixby's sensibilities it's a better-than-average entry. Banner becomes involved with spies leaking secrets from a top-secret security lab, and falls for Elizabeth Gracen before facing his final "demise." Philip Sterling, Barbara Tarbuck, Ann Katerina, John Novak. (Rhino)

DEATH ON THE FOUR POSTER (1963). Atmospheric chiller (aka SEX PARTY) set in a mansion where young people gather for an experiment in the occult, in which deaths are predicted by a psychic. Sure enough . . . what begins as fun and games turns into a nightmare. Italian-French film directed-written by Jean Josipovici. John Drew Barrymore, Gloria Milland.

DEATH PENALTY. See **SATAN KILLER, THE.**

DEATHQUAKE (1983). The first half of this Japanese disaster movie is tedious as a well-meaning scientist warns Tokyo's government that an earthquake will destroy the city. Soap opera sets in when the man's relatives worry about "besmirched" family honor, and he undergoes troubles with wife and girlfriend. Finally, DEATHQUAKE gets down to the catastrophic destruction of Tokyo as a miniature city is destroyed in less-than-convincing shots. So the second half is not worth staying for as the scientist and his women are trapped in the rubble. Directed by Teruyoshi Nakano. Hiroshi Katsuno.

DEATH RACE 2000 (1975). Roger Corman cult favorite, directed by Paul Bartel. It's a real-with-it script by Robert Thom and Charles B. Griffith (from an Ib Melchoir idea) set in the future during a transcontinental race. Since America is a fascist land, anything goes, and that includes running over pedestrians, bombing opponents and taking whatever steps are necessary to win. David Carradine is a maniacal driver (nicknamed "Frankenstein" because he is so brutally scarred). Sylvester Stallone scores big as Machine Gun Joe Viterbo. Other standouts: Simone Griffith, Mary Woronov, Roberta Collins, Joyce Jameson. (Warner Bros.)

DEATH RAY (19??). A James Bond wannabe, Gordon Scott as agent Bart Fargo, is assigned to rescue a kidnapped inventor and prevent terrorists from destroying the world with a disintegrator ray ("more powerful than a laser beam") in this European-produced 007 carbon copy. The effects (phony-looking models of cars, a submarine, a helicopter) are as cheesy as they get. Scripted by Paul Fleming (fat chance!) and directed by Frank G. Carroll. (Star Classics; Best on Film & Video)

DEATH RAY OF DR. MABUSE. See **SECRET OF DR. MABUSE.**

DEATH RAY 2000 (1979). TV-pilot for the superspy series A MAN CALLED SLOANE. See **T. R. SLOANE.** (On video from Worldvision)

DEATH RIDE. See **CRASH!**

DEATH RIDES THE CARNIVAL. See **CARNIVAL OF BLOOD.**

DEATH RING (1993). Mediocre, slow-paced actioner based loosely on "The Most Dangerous Game," with crazed Billy Drago playing a "game master" who kidnaps survivalist Mike Norris to his isolated island where sadists and murderers pay for the pleasure of pursuing him for the kill. A sound idea is given only half-hearted treatment by director R. J. Kizer. Chad McQueen shines as Norris' pal to the rescue, with Drago taking second-place honors for his portrayal as a sociopath. Don Swayze, Elizabeth Fong Sung, Isabel Glasser. (New Line)

DEATHROW GAMESHOW (1987). In an alternate universe, where the U.S. government allows deathrow inmates to gamble their lives on a TV game show, emcee Chuck Toedan (John McCafferty) leads a hard life—pursued by criminals, threatened by kooks and nuts, and the target of feminist Gloria Sternvirgin (Robin Blythe). This parody of how TV sets trends and enforces revised values on our morality is amusing, but forces the issue with vulgarities and tasteless gags. Mark Lasky, Darwyn Carson. (Media) (Laser: Image)

DEATH SCOUTS (1977). Episodes of TV's MAN FROM ATLANTIS series, with gillman Patrick Duffy thwarting a plot by underwater aliens to take over Earth. Directed by Marc Daniels. Belinda Montgomery, Alan Fudge, Tiffany Bolling.

DEATH SCREAMS (1982). "The last scream you hear . . . is your own!" Psychohorror flick depicting the machete murders of college beauties, with plenty of nudity. Directed by David Nelson. Susan Kiger, Jody Kay, Martin Tucker. (Video Gems)

DEATH'S DIRECTORS. See **MANIPULATOR.**

DEATHSHEAD VAMPIRE, THE. See **BLOOD BEAST TERROR, THE.**

DEATH SHIP (1980). A freighter deserted on the high seas, haunted by the misery and sadism of the Nazis who once had a torture chamber aboard, is boarded by Richard Crenna, George Kennedy and other survivors of a sea disaster, who learn of its horrors too late. There's the torture gallery, decomposing bodies, parts that move supernaturally, and Kennedy who thinks he's a murderous captain. Directed by Alvin Rakoff. Sally Ann Howes, Kate Reid, Nick Mancuso. (Embassy)

DEATH SMILES ON A MURDERER (1974). Italian shocker in which Klaus Kinski discovers the secret to an ancient Incan formula for resurrecting the dead, setting into motion a flurry of supernatural revenge killings. This moves fast, is often bewildering, and doesn't bear up under scrutiny. Directed by Aristide Massaccesi. Angelo Bo, Ewa Aulin. (Demonique)

DEATH SPA (WITCH BITCH) (1987). Starbody Health Spa is run by a computer that fouls up, turning a shapely customer into a human lobster. Subsequent foul-ups include flying shower tiles, broken diving board, a hand chopped off in a Quasar, and broken pipes that emit scalding water on nubile bodies. It's not so much the computer as the guy who runs it, whose sister was burned alive. It appears her spirit is invading his body, turning him into a murderous transvesite. This supernatural flick is one strenuous workout with its OMEN-style deaths. What can you say when a dead fish comes alive and bites a man to death except "Cod damn it!" Director Michael Fischa emphasizes other red herrings that won't scare anyone. William Bumiller, Brenda Bakke, Merritt Butrick. (MPI)

DEATHSPORT (1978). A thousand years from now the good guys are Ranger Guides who use swords to make their point. The bad guys are Statesmen (we aren't kidding about this) who ride cycles called "death machines." So they do battle, with crashes and exciting stuff like that. Meanwhile, David Carradine and Claudia Jennings are gladiators in a sporting arena who escape into the desert. Carradine does his kung fu bit against Richard Lynch while Jennings looks fetching in glamorous rags. Unintentional comedy from writer-director Henry Suso and co-director Allan Arkush. (Warner Bros.)

DEATHSTALKER (1983). Sword-and-sorcery fantasy (produced by Roger Corman) with a Conan-style hero who kills mercilessly, grabs pretty girls and never lets scruples stand in his way. "I steal and kill to stay alive—not for the luxury of glory," he remarks, but deep inside Deathstalker is a good guy pursuing the Amulet of Light, Chalice of Magic and Sword of Justice. There are soft-core sex scenes (wow, you see the bare boobs of Barbi Benton, former Playmate) and abundant violence in Howard Cohen's script that director John Watson does not spare. Richard (Rick) Hill is a hero-hunk in a phony blond wig, and Barbi makes for a beauteous damsel. Richard Brooker snarls as the villain Oghris, but what do you expect in a witchcraft/action flick—subtlety? Lana Clarkson, Bernard Erhard. (Video/Laser: Vestron)

DEATHSTALKER II: DUEL OF THE TITANS (1987). Entertaining satire on sword-and-sorcery flicks, capturing a comedic element that makes the hokey production values and acting bearable. Director Jim Wynorski treats Neil Ruttenberg's script with just the right touch. Everyone speaks in a modern idiom, with timely in-jokes sustaining the quest plot. Stealing the show are John Terlesky as the devil-may-care adventurer and Monique Gabrielle, who plays a princess posing as a fortune teller. She also plays a clone femme fatale, showing a sexier, seductive side—say, this gal has talent. John La Zar is the villain-magician Jarek. Tony Naples is attractive and hammy as Sultana, and Maria Scocas leads a gang of Amazons with a twinkle in her eye. Filmed for producer Roger Corman in Argentina. (Vestron) (Laser: Image)

DEATHSTALKER III: THE WARRIORS FROM HELL (1988). This lacks the roguish charm of Rick Hill in the first film and the tongue-in-cheek anachronisms of the second, but it does have a lot of swordplay as John Allen Nelson (third and least Deathstalker) seeks a diamond crystal and find the secret treasure city of Erendor. This tired quest formula limps along (blame it on Howard R. Cohen's script) with bursts of energy from Carla Herd (playing twin sisters—one a sweet thing, the other a princess who falls into evil ways), Claudia Inchaurregui (as a sexy warrior proficient with bow and arrow), Terri Treas (as evil Queen Camisarde) and Thom Christopher (as daffy necromancer Troxartas, who creates zombie soldiers). Another Roger Corman epic, made in Mexico under director/co-producer Alfonso Corona. Aaron Hernan, Roger Cudney. (Vestron) (Laser: Image)

DEATHSTALKER IV: MATCH OF TITANS (1990). That wise-cracking barbarian is back, longer in the tooth but still living by that old axiom, "It's a man's instinct to hunt, to fight and to ravish women." However, the joy has dissipated since his satirical romp through the second film, and writer-director Howard R. Cohen treats this new adventure indifferently, as though he were vacationing in Bulgaria, where this was produced. Deathstalker (Rick Hill), searching for his missing magical sword, attends a tournament of champions in a castle ruled by empress Kana and her army of zombie stone men. Involved is a deposed princess, Kana's henchman and a strongman virgin. Huh? (New Horizons)

DEATH TAKES A HOLIDAY (1934). For three days the personification of Death appears as Prince Sirki (Fredric March), desiring to experience human emotions. For three days death is denied to those who should die. Beautiful Evelyn Venable gives up her earthly lover for the Prince, unaware of his identity. This Hollywood version of Alberto Cassella's popular play was adapted by Maxwell Anderson and Gladys Lehman and directed by Mitchell Leisen. Henry Travers, Edward van Sloan, Gail Patrick, Kent Taylor, Otto Hoffman, Guy Standing.

DEATH TAKES A HOLIDAY (1971). TV remake of the 1934 Fredric March film is inferior, reminding one of that old adage: Never tamper with a good thing. Robert Butler directed. Monte Markham plays Death. Melvyn Douglas, Yvette Mimieux, Myrna Loy, Kerwin Mathews.

DEATH: THE ULTIMATE MYSTERY (1975). Phony baloney pseudodocumentary studying mummies in Mexico and Egypt with depressing narration. Cameron Mitchell and Gloria Prince study reincarnation, regression and other life-after-death subjects. The work of Robert Emenegger, Allan Sandler and Hans Beimler.

DEATH TRAIN, THE (1978). Slow-chugging Australian TV-movie of eccentric characters and supernatural ambiguities. After a man is apparently run over in his backyard by a train, his ankle bone protruding through his neck, an insurance investigator uncovers a land-development plot. Whether a "phantom train" exists or not remains a head-scratching mystery as Hugh Keays Bryne probes for the answer. This film becomes extremely strange when Bryne flees through the night in his underwear, pursued by a killer bulldozer. And just when you think the enigma has been explained, the occult rears its ugly head. Directed by Igor Auzins. (Paragon)

DEATH TRAP. See **EATEN ALIVE.**

DEATH VALLEY (1981). Director Dick Richards is saddled with a sleazy slasher script and his efforts to make it significant are wasted as soon as the graphic violence begins. Then the poor writing and dumb characterizations completely befuddle him. The plot has young Peter Billingsley witness to murder and pursued by mad-dog killers in Death Valley. Paul Le Mat, Catherine Hicks, Edward Herrmann, A.W. Brimley. (MCA)

DEATH WARMED UP (1984). Grotesquely unpleasant New Zealand film, unrestrained in gore as surgeon Gary Day experiments in brain surgeries that turn men into kill-happy zombies. Four people come to Day's island headquarters, Trans Cranial Applications. One of them (Michael Hurst, his hair bleached snowy blond) has a strange link to the doctor as the quartet is subjected to zombie horrors and a chase through red-lit tunnels. An axe in the stomach, exposed intestines, a man impaled on a spike and a gun that fires light beams into the zombies (the only way to kill them) are among the "gorities" by director David Blyth and co-writer Michael Heath. Grim stuff; wishy-washies beware. (Vestron)

DEATHWATCH (1980). Set in a bleak futuristic society (Glasgow, Scotland) in which an evil TV network holds sway over depressed people, this German-French tale is more didactic than visual. Co-producer-director Bertrand Tavernier brings tragedy and pain to its characters, giving heart to their desolation. Based on David Compton's novel THE CONTINUOUS KATHERINE MORTENHOR (or THE UNSEEING EYE), it depicts Harvey Kietel as a man with a video camera device in his head who can transmit pictures and Romy Schneider as a dying woman. The network under Harry Dean Stanton (playing a likable villain) wants to show Romy withering away and Kietel is treacherous in befriending her. But when they fall in love, the film detours into character exploration. Max Von Sydow is as a philosopher who guides the characters toward a final destiny. (Embassy)

DEATH WEEKEND. Video title for **HOUSE BY THE LAKE, THE** (Vestron).

DEATH WHEELERS. See **PSYCHOMANIA.**

DEBORAH (1974). Confused, driven woman (Marina Malfatti) is blessed (or cursed) with psychic powers. Her desire to have a child, even though she cannot, is so strong it creates supernatural forces. Italian film directed by Albert Verrecchia. Gig Young, Bradford Dillman.

DECEIVERS, THE (1988). This fanciful retelling of how the British occupational forces of India discovered a gang of murderers—Thugges worshipping the goddess of destruction, Kali—is structured by Michael Hirst (adapting John Masters' novel) as a thriller with overtones of eastern mysticism. British officer Pierce Brosnan goes undercover as a Thugge to discover that the spirit of Kali is more real than he thought. This Ismail Merchant production, directed by Nicholas Meyer, captures the perverseness of what Brosnan is undergoing, and Brosnan fascinates as the civilized man exposed to barbarism. Shashi Kapoor, Saeed Jaffrey, Helene Michell, Keith Michell. (Video/Laser: Warner Bros.)

DECEPTION (1973). Re-edited episodes of the STAR LOST TV series about a giant starship, The Ark, traveling on an eternal voyage through space. In this episode a computer that can induce hallucinations threatens the crew. Keir Dullea, Ed Ames.

DECOY FOR TERROR. See **PLAYGIRL KILLER.**

DEEP RED: THE HATCHET MURDERS (1976). Mini-masterpiece of psychoshock from Italian director-writer Dario Argento, with David Hemmings as a pianist who witnesses the knife murder of a psychiatrist in Rome. Ingenious killing after ingenious killing follows, with the murderer playing cat-and-mouse games with victims. Among the highlights: a woman being scalded to death in her bathroom, a man being dragged to pieces by a truck. Then Hemmings himself becomes the target for the killer. Also known as DRIPPING DEEP RED and THE SABRE TOOTH TIGER. Daria Nicolodi. (HBO)

DEEP SPACE (1987). Low-budget director Fred Olen Ray rises above his previous programmers, for this sci-fi/horror meringue is well handled and the screenplay (by Ray and T.L. Lankford) has good characters and dialogue. The U.S. Government has created an unstoppable Alien-like monster but the space lab containing the ugly thing crashlands in an L.A. junkyard and begins killing. Cops Charles Napier and Ron Glass are hot on its trail, browbeaten by Bo Svenson. Napier and Ann Turkel (unconvincing as a cop) track the giant bastard to Arkham Alley for a battle to the death with a chainsaw, an axe, assorted firearms and bare hands. Part of the fun is watching character actors Anthony Eisley, Peter Palmer, James Booth and Julie Newmar. (TransWorld)

DEEPSTAR SIX (1989). Above-average blending of the best elements of disaster films with touches of ALIEN. Sean Cunningham's direction captures tension in an underwater lab besieged by a behemoth fish-monster. Rather than rely on tried-and-grue cliches, the Geof Miller-Lewis Abernathy script emphasizes human endurance under duress, relegating the flesh-eating amphibian to second position. One weakness are the so-so underwater effects, but the cast and realism of the lab make up for it. Nancy Everhard, Greg Evigan, Miguel Ferrer. (Video/Laser: Live)

DEF BY TEMPTATION (1990). Troma's answer to Spike Lee is James Bond III (not a gag pseudonym), who wrote-produced-directed this all-black portrait of a female vampire who preys on men in New York bars; it's also the story of a divinity student lured into her seductive traps. An unusual intelligence is at work here, and the low-low budget film is loaded with angst, mood and colorful dialogue. The horror aspects (barful of zombies; the vampire turning into a demon) are the least effective parts of this allegorical study of today's black society. Kadeem Hardison, Samuel L. Jackson, Minnie Gentry, John Canada Terrell. (Shapiro Glickenhaus) (Laser: Image)

DEF-CON 4 (1985). Astronauts orbiting Earth in a satellite watch as the U.S. and Russia are obliterated in nuclear holocaust. When the spacecraft crashes, survivor Maury Chaykin is caught in a war between cannibals, ordinary people and a sadistic militant band. Odd mixture of A BOY AND HIS DOG and MAD MAX as the gangs shoot it out. All the while, unknown to the parties, a missile is counting down to detonation. The space scenes are good high-tech stuff under Paul Donovan's direction but the land warfare footage is commonplace. Kate Lynch, John Walsch. (New World/Starmaker)

DEFENDERS OF THE EARTH: THE STORY BEGINS (1986). Cartoon TV-movie in which Flash Gordon, the Phantom and Mandrake the Magician team against Ming the Merciless. (Avid)

DEFENDING YOUR LIFE (1991). Albert Brooks' films are always oddball mixtures of social comedy and quirky relationships but in this outing he steps into the Twilight Zone to make points about the human condition. After Brooks is killed in a collision with a bus he winds up in a pleasant purgatory, where he must defend his recent existence to determine what new incarnation he will affect. His defense attorney (Rip Torn) locks horns with the prosecution (Lee Grant) as his past life is examined. The gags are amusing as Brooks evaluates his life, falling in love with another defendant (Meryl Streep). Very strange but poignant. (Warner Bros.) (Laser: Pioneer)

DEJA VU (1985). Unconvincing reincarnation story (based on the novel ALWAYS by Trevor Meldal Johnsen) finds novelist Nigel Terry regressing to the 1930s when he was a choreographer in love with ballerina Brook Ashley. Who does Ashley turn out to be but the previous soul of Terry's wife, Jaclyn Smith. The regression scenes evolve around tarot reader Shelley Winters, as unbelievable as the rest of this British film with Clair Bloom as the dancer's domineering mother. Director Anthony Richmond wasn't on his toes—he slouched when he should have pirouetted. (MGM/UA)

DELICATESSAN (1991). A crazy post-holocaust movie and winner of several awards for directors Jean-Pierre Jeunet and Marc Caro. This French film defies description as it depicts events in a rundown building in a ruined city. The inhabitants are bizarre individuals driven to the edge of insanity by whatever has happened to the rest of the world (that part is never explained). The owner of the hotel-deli is a cannibal who keeps meat in the shop by cutting up his tenants; a woman keeps attempting suicide without success; a man lives in a basement of frogs; and there's a commando team that travels through sewers, acting as a police force. The camera plunges into dark holes and travels through pipes and conduits creating a macabre mood. The horrific elements of the script by comic book writer Gilles Adrien, Jeunet and Caro are tinged with a satirical quality, and the action exaggerated. One weird movie, bon ami. Marie-Laure Dougnac, Jean Claude Dreyfus, Karin Viard. (Miramax/Paramount)

DELIRIA. See **STAGEFRIGHT.**

DELIRIUM (1974). Italian psycho-gore murder thriller

from the team (director Ralph Brown, writer Renato Polselli) that did REINCARNATION OF ISABEL. A series of bloody murders appears to have been committed by a prominent doctor, who could be harboring a perverted love for violence. There's a surprise ending—how surprising depends on your ability to second-guess lurid Italian plots. Mickey Haggitay, Rita Calderoni. (Academy)

DELIRIUM (1978). Fair blending of two mystery plots. One is about a psychokiller who slaughters shapely women (one is impaled on a spear, another is pickforked in the neck, another is drowned), the other is about respectable St. Louis businessmen on "The Council," a secret vigilante band that kills murderers and makes their deaths look like suicides. Two homicide cops with the help of a woman close in on the two elements. Directed by Peter Maris. Turk Gekovsky, Debi Chaney, Terry Tenbroek, Barron Winchester. (Paragon; Caravan; from Viz as **PSYCHO PUPPET**)

DELUGE (1933). S. Fowler Wright's tale of Earth's catastrophic destruction, climaxed by a massive tidal wave blanketing New York City. Some holocaust scenes showed up in SOS TIDAL WAVE and other Republic serials. Two surviving males (Sidney Blackmer and Fred Kohler) fight over the only surviving female (Peggy Shannon). Felix E. Feist directed. (Mossman Williams)

DELUSION (1981). Psychological thriller of the PSYCHO school, underplayed by director Alan Beattie who emphasizes the subtleties of Jack Viertel's script. Patricia Pearcy is a nurse who arrives at Joseph Cotten's home to care for him, discovering a crazy son locked up in the house. The characters die one by one . . . but it won't take a genius to figure out the "surprise" ending. David Wayward, John Dukakis. Also known as THE HOUSE WHERE DEATH LIVES. (Sultan)

DEMENTED (1980). Sallee Elyse is no Catherine Deneuve but she tries to pull off a portrayal of a demented woman in the style of Roman Polanski's REPULSION. It's strictly a poor man's version in this thriller directed by Alex Rebar. After being gang-raped in a horse stall, Elyse returns halfway around the bend to her husband-surgeon Bruce Gilchrist, who's two-timing her for a nymphomaniac. When Elyse flips, she corners pranksters in clown masks and eliminates them with cleaver, shotgun, piano wire, etc. The horrific aspects are minimal and, despite pretensions at characterization, it's a dud. Deborah Alter, Kathryn Clayton. (Media)

DEMENTIA. See **DAUGHTER OF HORROR.**

DEMENTIA 13 (1963). Francis Ford Coppola's first directorial-writing job was this Roger Corman cheapie shot in and around an Ireland castle. Luana Anders arrives to claim her family inheritance (after helping her weak-hearted husband take a dive into a lake). She unlocks ghastly secrets in the family closet, unleashing an axe murderer. The death-gore scenes are moderately exciting but it's easy to spot the killer. William Campbell, Patrick Magee, Barbara Dowling, Bart Patton. (World Video Picture; Cable; Hollywood Home Theater; K-Tel; Filmfax; S/Weird; Nostalgia; Sinister/C)

DEMOLITION MAN (1993). Refreshing futuristic action-comedy blockbuster that includes a tongue-in-cheek look at tomorrow. That world (2032 A.D.) is one in which violence has been eliminated and police are benevolent beings incapable of stopping a master criminal (Wesley Snipes, wearing a white wig and playing it for laughs) who has escaped from a cryogenic prison. Thawed out from his deep-freeze container because he's the only man who can stop the evil Simon Phoenix is another criminal, framed ex-cop John Spartan, wonderfully played by Sylvester Stallone. The film's action pieces, when it isn't satirizing social mores, are fabulously directed by Marco Brambilla. Sandra Bullock is a standout as a lady cop who works with Spartan and introduces him to a form of "virtual reality" sex. Nigel Hawthorne, Benjamin Bratt. (Video/Laser: Warner Bros.)

DEMON (1976). See **GOD TOLD ME TO.**

DEMON, THE. See **ONIBABA.**

WESLEY SNIPES: 'DEMOLITION MAN'

DEMON, THE (1981). A slasher, dispatched by the Devil, wears a mask and uses clawed hands and strangulating plastic bags on victims. Psychic cop Cameron Mitchell tracks the monster. The film comes alive when a blonde is trapped with the Demon and runs naked through a house. Directed-written by Percival Rubens. Jennifer Holmes, Craig Gardner. (VidAmerica; HBO)

DEMON AND THE MUMMY (1975). Episodes from THE NIGHT STALKER, the series with Darren McGavin as Kolchak, the newsman tangling with supernatural beings. In "Demon in Lace," directed by Don Weis, Kolchak encounters a succubus inhabiting the bodies of women who cause the death of men who love them; in "Legacy of Terror," directed by Don McDougall, an Aztec mummy rampages. Keenan Wynn, Jackie Vernon.

DEMON BARBER OF FLEET STREET, THE (1936). Throat-slitter Sweeney Todd inspired this dainty British thriller in which a murderous barber turns over his deceased customers to a pieman who uses the cadavers as meat in his delicacies. Starring Tod Slaughter, London's answers to Boris Karloff. Directed by George King. Bruce Seton. (Rhino; Sinister/C; from Video Yesteryear as **SWEENEY TODD: THE DEMON BARBER OF FLEET STREET**)

DEMON FROM DEVIL'S LAKE, THE (1964). Filmmaker Russ Marker wanted to leave his mark but was off the mark with this low-budget sci-fi/horror combo in which a U.S. spaceship crashes into a lake in Texas, causing wildlife to turn into the titular "demon." Remade as NIGHT FRIGHT.

DEMON, DEMON (1975). Modestly produced British TV-movie in which Bradford Dillman falls for his secretary, who demands full possession maritally. When that fails, she demands full possession of his soul. Directed by Richard Dunlop. Juliet Mills, Robert Emhardt.

DEMON HUNTER. Video version of **LEGEND OF BLOOD MOUNTAIN** (Camp).

DEMONIAC (1979). After a religious nut witnesses a satanic rite staged by a scandal magazine publisher, he employs medieval torture to get even. Originally made as THE RIPPER OF NOTRE DAME. Lina Romay, Oliver Mathot. Directed by Jesse Franco. (Wizard)

DEMONIC TOYS (1991). Imaginative night of horror and gory violence in a toy warehouse begins when cop Tracy Scoggins, pursuing illegal-arms dealers, is trapped with an evil spirit ("The Demon Kid") who brings to life playthings that attack and kill. Among them: Baby Oopsy-Daisy ("I can even shit my pants"), a clown jack-in-the-box, a robot that shoots laserfire, and a flesh-eating bear that grows into a giant. Trapped with Scoggins: fat security cop Pete Schrum, "Chunky Chicken" delivery man Bentley Mitchum (Robert's grandson), derelict Ellen Dunning and sadistic killer Michael Russo. This Charles Band production is earmarked by rambunctious, lively direction by Peter Manoogian. Toys by John Buechler. (Paramount) (Laser: Full Moon)

DEMON IN MY VIEW, A (1991). No one portrayed madness better than Anthony Perkins, and in this German production shot in Hamburg and London he is "The Kenbourne Killer," a serial murderer who strangles streetwalkers. Plagued by hallucinations, this guy is so warped and wretched that he makes love to a mannikin and writes poison pen letters. Writer-director Petra Haffter, from a Ruth Rendell novel, structures an unusual portrait of a lonely, sick man, and in one of his last roles Perkins restrains his performance. The romantic subplot involving Uwe Bohm and Sophie Ward seems out in left field until it brings a ironic film-noir touch to the action. Stratford Johns, Brian Bovel, Terence Hardiman, James Aubrey. (Video/Laser: Vidmark)

DEMON KEEPER (1994). Several attendees of a seance must spend a night of horror in a house with an unleashed monster from Hell. Dirk Benedict, Edward Albert, Katrina Laltby. (Video/Laser: New Horizon)

DEMON LOVER (1976). Despite stupid gore killings and a dumb teen mentality, this is grisly stuff that sticks in the memory (and the craw) thanks to writers-directors Donald G. Jackson and Jerry Younkins. Enough idiotic kids to fill a cemetery get involved with a witchmaster who conjures a horned demon from Hell. Especially memorable is the kid who gets an arrow through his groin and grovels on the floor. Luridly compelling if thoroughly tasteless. This stars Guntar (Leatherface) Hanse. (Unicorn; from Regal as **DEVIL MASTER** and from Premiere as **MASTER OF EVIL**)

DEMON MASTER (1973). Video of **CRAZE** (VCR).

DEMON MASTER (1976). A more complete video version of **DEMON LOVER** (Regal).

DEMON MURDER CASE, THE (1983). Because scriptwriter William Kelley leaves no doubt the Devil is at work in Connecticut, and because the story is based on a true trial, this ranks as an exploitative TV-movie lacking objectivity. Believe half of what you see; doubt the rest. A boy is seemingly possessed by a demon; when his brother challenges the invisible entity, it infects his body and uses it to commit murder. A sensational murder case follows. (This story is told in THE DEVIL IN CONNECTICUT.) Directed by William Hale. Eddie Albert, Kevin Bacon, Andy Griffith, Cloris Leachman.

DEMON OF THE LAKE. Video version of **CRATURE FROM BLACK LAKE.**

DEMONOID—MESSENGER OF DEATH (1982). A 300-year-old hand (severed from a desecrator of a Mexican devil cult) is crawling in modern times when Roy Cameron Jenson discovers the tomb with wife Samantha Eggar. It's one severed hand after the other and mumbo jumbo about possession as the "hand" life force passes from person to person. It's a meandering storyline writer-director Alfred Zacharias and co-author David Lee Fein are handing us. Stuart Whitman is a boxing Inglewood priest. Also entitled MACABRA. (Media)

DEMON PLANET, THE (1965). Italian space opera directed by Mario Bava combines elements of the supernatural with sci-fi when rocket jockey Barry Sullivan investigates the planet Aura to discover inhabitants are disembodied spirits. Aura resembles a Transylvanian moor more than a foreign world. Also known as PLANET OF BLOOD, THE HAUNTED PLANET, THE PLANET OF TERROR, TERROR IN SPACE, THE OUTLAWED PLANET and THE PLANET OF THE DAMNED. (On video as **PLANET OF THE VAMPIRES**)

DEMON POND (1980). See third edition.

DEMON POSSESSED (1989). Unusually restrained supernatural tale about six snowmobile explorers trapped on Black Friar Lake. They seek refuge in abandoned Camp St. Dominic, where satanic activities once were held. A hooded shadow is brought out of limbo when the explorers find a ouija board called "The Devil's Eye." Finally, the gore murders: one body chopped up by a freeze locker fan; one punctured through the head with a falling icicle; another hanged; another impaled on barbed wire; yet another crushed under a snow plow. It's told as a memory flashback and the narration captures a quality the rest of the film lacks. Produced-directed by Christopher Webster in Wisconsin. Dawn Laurrie, Aaron Kjenaas, Connie Snyder, David Fields. (Action International)

DEMON QUEEN (1986). Vampire chick on a rampage. Written-directed by Donald Farmer. Mary Fanaro, Dennis Stewart, Cliff Dance. (Mogul)

DEMON RAGE. Video version of **DARK EYES** (Harmonyvision).

DEMONS (1972). See editions 1-3.

DEMONS, THE (1972). Portuguese-French film helmed by writer-director Jesus Franco, a loose sequel to NIGHT OF THE BLOOD MONSTER, about a witch whose kisses turn men into skeletons. Sexually explicit. Anne Libert, Britt Nichols, Howard Vernon. (Unicorn)

DEMONS, THE (198?). Witchcraft thriller in which a woman accused of being a supernatural old crone vows revenge against her attackers. Directed by Lawrence Merrick. Clancy Syrko, Des Roberts.

DEMONS (1985). Dario Argento production, shot in Berlin, and directed by Lamberto Bava, who brings surrealism to this shocker set in the Metropol theater. The audience is watching a film about Nostradamus when a viewer turns into a demon and it's a zombiethon with hideous make-up, foaming green bile, claws, fangs. Really weird things happen (our hero rides through the auditorium on his motorbike, killing zombies with a sword; a helicopter crashes through the roof; two lovers are strangled while they kiss) and it turns out the whole world is infected with demon-mania. (New World) (Laser: Image)

'DEMONS'

DEMONS 2: THE NIGHTMARE RETURNS (1986). Worthy follow-up to DEMONS, strictly for gore lovers as it depicts an army of humans, infected by a strange blood malady, terrorizing sections of Rome. Director Lamberto Bava (son of Mario Bava), with producer Dario Argento, creates a surrealistic world in which a young woman watching a horror movie is attacked by a demon through a TV set. This mingling of reality and media is a fascinating subtext touching on our penchant for violent movies. Anyway, the demon creates an army (contagion is spread through the fingernails) rampaging through the highrise apartment building. There's a memorable battle to the death between a pregnant woman and a newly born demon baby. David Knight, Coralina Cataldi Tassoni, Bobby Rhodes. (Imperial) (Laser: Japanese)

DEMON SEED, THE (1977). Sci-fi thriller combines dazzling computer effects with a literate story (from a Dean R. Koonz novel) dealing with man's rape of Earth and machine's rape of man, in this case lovely Julie Christie. The ultimate computer decides it is greater than its creator and malfunctions to conceive a child that will embody its own genius. Among the effects: a machine having a sexual climax. Donald Cammell directed. Computer voice: Robert Vaughn. Fritz Weaver (as the creator of Proteus IV), Gerrit Graham, Berry Kroeger. (Laser/Video: MGM/UA)

DEMON'S MASK, THE. See **BLACK SUNDAY.**

DEMONS OF LUDLOW, THE (1983). Low-budget supernatural tale with woefully inadequate effects, made in Wisconsin by producer-director Bill Rebane. The New England town of Ludlow faces horror when a long-dead puritan-warlock returns as a haunted piano (?!). Among the out-of-tune weirdo stuff is a phantom noose from another dimension, a demon hand that pops up from the floorboards, haunted toy dolls and sword-wielding duelists. Paul Von Hausen, Stephanie Cushna, Carol Perry, James R. Robinson. (Trans World)

DEMONS OF PARADISE (1987). Filmed in and

around Kihono, on the island of Hawaii, this grade-B monster movie is predictable from stereotyped beginning to hackneyed ending. Nothing can save this movie relying on stolen JAWS subplots and BLACK LAGOON replays. Akua, an ancient fish-demon feared by the natives, is disturbed by fishermen using dynamite and begins kills natives and tourists. The creature, of the unconvincing rubber-suit school, is impervious to bullets and explosions and has the strength to down a helicopter. Directed by Cirio H. Santiago. Kathryn Witt, William Steis, Laura Banks. (Warner Bros.)

DEMONS OF THE DEAD (1975). Effective Italian psychothriller, made in England, is best when the camera is swirling and spinning to capture the fright of a woman recovering from a car accident that caused her to lose her unborn baby. Made in "Chill-O-Rama," DEMONS follows her into a coven of witchcraft practitioners. If you love pseudopsychology, you'll dig this mess. Directed by Sergio Martino. George Hilton, Edwige Fereck, Ivan Rassimor. (From Super as **DAY OF THE MANIAC** and from Vogue as **THEY'RE COMING TO GET YOU**)

DEMONS OF THE MIND (1972). Hammer shocker deals with satanic possession resulting from incestuous sex and is "intense." Shane Briant and Gillian Hills are children kept imprisoned by their father, Patrick Magee is the family physician who learns the dark secrets. The visual horror only comes at the end. Directed by Peter Sykes. Paul Jones, Michael Hordern, Yvonne Mitchell. Also called NIGHTMARE OF TERROR. (HBO; Republic; from Academy as **BLOOD EVIL.**)

DEMONS OF THE SWAMP. See **GIANT LEECHES, THE.**

DEMONSTONE (1989). R. Lee Ermey and Jan-Michael Vincent as fun-loving, shit-kicking Marine Corps buddies out to solve grisly murders in Manila are the best things in this action-horror thriller that uses Filipino political unrest as a subplot. The supernatural amulet of the title involves a 400-year-old curse; Ermey and Vincent have to find out what has unleashed a ferocious supernatural power, but the film's structure is that of an action film with careening automobiles and blazing submachine-guns. The Demonstone gets second billing, with limited effects. Director Andrew Prowse is to be commended for making his shoot-outs believable. Pat Skipper, Peter Brown. (Fries) (Laser: Image)

DEMON TOWER. See **DEMON LOVER.**

DEMONWARP (1987). Dumb movie filled with young people behaving stupidly, and abounding with monsters and masks, gore and goo. In Demonwood, a Bigfoot creature attacks George Kennedy and daughter. Then the teenagers turn up and the hunt is on for the beast. Turns out an alien craft landed in the vicinity and an E.T. beasty is responsible. The story by John Buechler—who designed the monster—was turned into a worthless script by Jim Bertges and Bruce Akiyama and directed with empty-headedly by Emmett Alston. David Michael O'Neill, Billy Jacoby, Pamela Gilbert. (Vidmark)

DEMON WIND (1989). Monster and gore fans will enjoy this variation on THE NIGHT OF THE LIVING DEAD with demonic overtones, a production by Paul Hunt, Michael Bennett and Peter Collins. The setting is a farmhouse (sound familiar?) in which young people amass to fight off legions of walking dead, a cloven-footed, horned demon and gooey-faced freaks. Writer-director Charles Philip Moore fills it with dream sequences and other tricks-within-tricks that undercut the horror, but he still manages a fast pace, horrendous make-up and a few surprises. Eric Larson, Francine Lapensee, Bobby Johnston, Lynn Clark. (Paramount) (Laser: Prism/Image)

DEMON WITCH CHILD (1976). Innocent toddler is taken over by an evil spirit, a worshipper of Satan who adopts a wizened face to do in his victims. Tepid Spanish import written and directed by Amando De Ossorio. (Simitar; from Wizard as **POSSESSED, THE**)

DEMON WITHIN, THE. Video version of **MIND SNATCHERS, THE** (Ace).

DERANGED (1974). Events in the life of Ezra Cobb (Robert Blossom), who murders women, then wears their skin or stuffs their bodies taxidermist-style. It's even more horrible than it sounds, because Cobb is based on the real-life killer Ed Gein, the inspiration for Norman Bates in Robert Bloch's PSYCHO. Scripted by Alan Ormsby, who co-directed with Bob Clark. Tom Savini provided the corpses. Cosette Lee, Robert Warner. (Fright; Moore)

DERANGED (1973). Video version of **IDAHO TRANSFER** (Satellite).

DERANGED (1987). A cheap imitation of Roman Polanski's REPULSION, in which pornie star Jane Hamilton (formerly Veronica Hart) kills a burglar in self-defense and kills anyone who comes near her. Paul Siederman, Jennifer Delora. Directed by Chuck Vincent. (Republic)

DERANGED. See **IDAHO TRANSFER.**

DESERT WARRIOR (1985). Rip-off of MAD MAX with anti-hero Trace (Gary Watkins) battling the villainous Scourge who has kidnaped his sister. Trace's pals are a fast gun (Laura Banks) and a kid with ESP (Linda Grovenor). Made in the Philippines by director-producer Cirio H. Santiago. (Prism)

DESIRES OF THE VAMPIRE. See **PLAYGIRLS AND THE VAMPIRE, THE.**

DESTINATION INNER SPACE (1966). Laughable low-budget "junkie" with an alien that looks like a rejected version of the Black Lagoon creature. An underwater lab commanded by Scott Brady is invaded by a monster from a spaceship that splashed down nearby. Scripter Arthur C. Pierce duplicates the tricks of THE THING but director Francis D. Lyon is no Howard Hawks. Sheree North, Gary Merrill, Roy Barcroft, Mike Road.

DESTINATION MOON (1950). George Pal production depicting man's first flight to the moon—19 years before it happened. The pseudodocumentary style emphasizes difficulties of space walks, weightlessness and other scientific curiosities. Authentic for its day, it now seems tame. Chesley Bonestell's lunar drawings are excellent. Irving Pichel directed. Good score by Leith Stevens. Robert Heinlein co-wrote the script. Warner Anderson, John Archer, Erin O'Brien-Moore, Tom Powers. (Nostalgia Merchant; S/Weird) (Laser: Image)

DESTINATION MOONBASE ALPHA (1975). Two episodes of TV's SPACE: 1999. In one, the crew of Alpha is dying from a mysterious malady; in another, a planet appears to be invading our solar system. Directed by Gerry Anderson. Martin Landau, Barbara Bain, Barry Morse. (CBS/Fox)

DESTINATION NIGHTMARE (1958). Episodes from the unsold TV series THE VEIL, re-edited and introduced by Boris Karloff: "Mme Vernoy," "Girl on the Road" and "Destination Nightmare." Directed by Paul Landres. Whit Bissell, Tod Andrews, Myron Healy. Other episodes were repackaged as THE VEIL and JACK THE RIPPER. (Sinister/C; Filmfax)

DESTINATION SATURN (1939). Re-edited video version from Cable Films of Universal's 12-chapter BUCK ROGERS serial. See **BUCK ROGERS.**

DESTINY TO ORDER (1989). Frustrated writer (Stephen Ouimette), through an electrical jolt to his computor, is suddenly in touch with his characters and takes on different guises to save them from bikers led by Michael Ironside. Canadian film written-directed by Jim Purdy. Alberta Watson, Victoria Snow. (Off Hollywood)

DESTROY ALL MONSTERS (1969). Inoshiro Honda, who brought us Godzilla, unites Japan's hulkers (Godzilla, Godzilla Jr., Ebirah, Wenda, Rodan, Anzilla, Gorasorus, Barugan, Mothra, Varan) in a destruction marathon. When Earth is attacked by spacemen called Kilaaks, they unleash the monsters from Ogaswara Island, sending each to destroy a city. Effects by Eiji Tsuburaya, including a battle atop Mount Fuji. Akira Kubo, Jun Tazaki. Also known as OPERATION MONSTERLAND and THE MARCH OF THE MONSTERS. (Fright) (Laser: Japanese)

DESTROY ALL PLANETS (1968). Japanese monster mauling as "hero monster" Gamera the Flying Turtle (making his fourth appearance, by contractual arrangements with producer Hidemasa Nagata), falls under the evil control of aliens. But two small children set the thick-shelled creature free and he attacks Viras the Incredible Sea Squid. Eastern enthrallment directed by Noriyaki Yuasa. Also known as GAMERA VS. OUTER SPACE MONSTER VIRAS and GAMERA VS. VIRAS. (S/Weird; Sinister/C) (Laser: Japanese)

DESTROYER (1988). The corpse of electrocuted convict Ivan Moser (played by a hulk, Lyle Alzado) stalks an abandoned prison, murdering members of a film crew making "Death House Dolls." Moser is subjected to assorted deaths along with his victims. The screenplay by producers Peter Garrity and Rex Hauck makes little sense, and director Robert Kirk is stuck trying to make something out of nothing. An oddity is the presence of Anthony Perkins as a film director. Deborah Foreman, Clayton Rohner. (Virgin Vision) (Laser: Image)

DESTRUCTORS, THE (1968). A substance called "laser rubies" is sought by foreign powers and undercover agents who use a killer laser beam dubbed "Cyclops." Standard espionage-action flick with fistfights and shootouts, directed by Francis D. Lyon. Michael Ansara, Richard Egan, John Ericson, David Brian.

DEVIL, THE (198X). Gore bore from Hong Kong about an ugly old witch who casts spells on unfortunate Asians who turn all bubbly and gooey inside, with worms and snakes crawling out of their mouths. Visually repulsive, this movie is for people who enjoy torturing themselves by watching horribly dubbed movies from the Orient. Directed by Chang Jen Chieh. (Video City)

DEVIL AND DANIEL WEBSTER, THE (1941). Stephen Vincent Benet's classic story, directed by William Dieterle, is an American folk tale depicting how Senator Webster, an orator-statesman in the rotund shape of Edward Arnold, defends farmer James Craig when Old Scratch, grandiosely etched in brimstone by thunderous Walter Huston, comes to claim his soul. The jury is made up of Benedict Arnold, Captain Kidd and Blackbeard. Robert Wise was editor, Bernard Herrmann wrote the score. Also known as ALL THAT MONEY CAN BUY. H.B. Warner, Jeff Corey, Simone Simon, Anne Shirley, Jane Darwell, William Alland. (Embassy; RCA/Columbia) (Laser: Criterion; Voyager; Nelson)

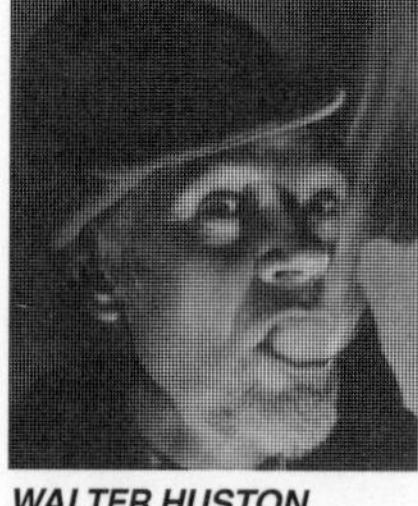

WALTER HUSTON

DEVIL AND DR. FRANKENSTEIN, THE. See **ANDY WARHOL'S FRANKENSTEIN.**

DEVIL AND MAX DEVLIN, THE (1981). A flop Disney comedy in which Elliott Gould, killed in an accident, descends to Hell where he confronts the Devil (Bill Cosby), who will save him from eternal damnation if Gould can find three people to sign over their souls to ol' Nick. The marks are Adam Rich, Julie Budd, David Knell. Directed by Steven Hilliard Stern. (Disney)

DEVIL AND MISS SARA, THE (1971). Is Gene Barry the Devil incarnate? Or an outlaw being escorted to stand trial by a prairie family (James Drury, Janice Rule)? This TV-movie keeps you wondering as Barry schemes to possess Rule. Directed by Michael Caffey. Charles McGraw, Slim Pickens.

DEVIL AND THE DEAD, THE. See **HOUSE OF EXORCISM, THE.**

DEVIL BAT, THE (1941). Depressing reminder of Bela Lugosi's plummeting career in the '40s, this PRC release stars him as a mad scientist who trains a killer bat to carry out his evil bidding. Lugosi guides the night flapper to the target by giving victims a special perfume. Directed by Jean Yarbrough. Suzanne Kaaren, Dave O'Brien, Guy Usher, Hal Price. Also known as KILLER BATS. A loose sequel was DEVIL BAT'S DAUGHTER. (Prism; Sinister/C; Filmfax; Nostalgia)

DEVIL BAT'S DAUGHTER (1946). Rosemary LaPlanche (one-time beauty queen) believes she is possessed by the spirit of her father, who presumably turned into a bat when he died. This sequel to DEVIL BAT is borderline horror with whodunit overtones. It wasn't the butler, but you won't have much trouble figuring out who is guilty, due to no subtleties from producer-director Frank Wisbar. Eddie Kane, John James, (RCA; Sony)

DEVIL BEAR. See **CLAWS.**

DEVIL COMMANDS, THE (1940). Boris Karloff gives another riveting performance as a driven, obsessed man of science determined to unlock nature's secrets: Dr. Julian Blair, who discovers a way of recording human brain waves in his mansion isolated on Barsham Harbor. After the accidental death of his wife, he finds a method of communicating with the dead through an odd head contraption and joins with phony spiritualist Anne Revere (her cold, evil demeanor makes for a chilling performance) in macabre experiments that require corpses from a nearby cemetery. Based on William Sloane's superb novel THE EDGE OF RUNNING WATER, the Robert D. Andrews/Milton Gunzburg script is highlighted by an eerie narration read by Karloff's daughter and laboratory scenes depicting corpses in odd body and head rigs.

DEVIL DOG: THE HOUND OF HELL (1978). Uninspired TV-movie, directed by Curtis Harrington. The Mangy Mutt from Beyond terrorizes suburbanites Richard Crenna and Yvette Mimieux. The yip is a gyp. Kim Richards, Victor Jory, Ike Eisenmann, R. G. Armstrong, Martine Beswick. (Vestron; Lightning)

DEVIL DOLL, THE (1936). This well-produced MGM revenge-fantasy, one of the last films directed by Tod (DRACULA) Browning, is a superior film for its era with enthralling miniaturized effects. It was adapted from Abraham Merritt's BURN WITCH BURN! and Browning's own THE WITCH OF TIMBUCTOO by Garrett Fort, Guy Endore and Erich von Stroheim. Lionel Barrymore goes drag to pose as a sweet old lady who sells life-like dolls in Paris. What his/her purchasers don't realize is that the dolls are real—a doctor has devised a formula for shrinking people and now Barrymore, escaped from Devil's Island after being sent there for a crime he didn't commit, uses these creatures to carry out his revenge. Henry B. Walthall, Maureen O'Sullivan. (MGM/UA)

DEVIL DOLL (1963). Compelling British shocker blending touches of Svengali with the ventriloquist tale from DEAD OF NIGHT. Bryant Halliday is the Great Vorelli, a stage magician-hypnotist with a dummy that walks and talks. Vorelli, a dabbler in the mysteries of India, is no dummy—he knows secrets of soul transference. Lindsay Shonteff directs with a starkness matched by Gerald Gibbs' photography. William Sylvester, Yvonne Romain. (Gorgon; MPI)

DEVIL DOLL MEN. See **CURSE OF THE DOLL PEOPLE, THE.**

DEVILFISH (1984). Video version of **MONSTER SHARK** (Vidmark).

DEVIL GIRL FROM MARS (1954). Patricia Laffan, in a fetching outfit all the rage on the canals this season, and her robot Chani invade Earth with an eye on the men—she has breeding in mind. Directed by David MacDonald, this has no subtleties in depicting how a big-breasted woman would conquer mankind. Hazel Court, Hugh McDermott, Adrienne Corri. (Nostalgia Merchant; Rhino; MPI; Sinister/C; S/Weird)

DEVIL GOT ANGRY, THE. See **MAJIN, MONSTER OF TERROR.**

DEVIL IN THE HOUSE OF EXORCISM. Video version of **HOUSE OF EXORCISM, THE** (Gorgon).

DEVIL KISS (1977). Zombies and other lifeless living inhabit this horror thriller. Oliver Matthews, Evelyn Scott. (Home Vision Cinema)

DEVIL MASTER (1976). Another video version of **DEMON LOVER.** This, from Regal, is said to be more complete than the Unicorn tape.

DEVIL RIDES OUT, THE. See **DEVIL'S BRIDE.**

DEVIL'S BRIDE, THE (1968). Hammer's superb version of Dennis Wheatley's THE DEVIL RIDES OUT. While weaknesses in Richard Matheson's script cannot be denied, Terence Fisher's direction is remarkably fluid, the juxtaposition of scenes excellent and the flavor of Britain in the '20s well preserved. Christopher Lee fights to destroy Charles Gray's devil cult. The "Death on Horseback" sequence is a shocker, and suspense mounts as Lee and force seek protection in a pentagram under assault from supernatural forces.

DEVIL'S COMMANDMENT. Video of **I VAMPIRI** (Sinister/C; Dark Dreams; S/Weird; Filmfax; Weiss).

DEVIL'S DAUGHTER (1973). Insipid TV-movie about a woman (Belinda Montgomery) befriended by batty Shelley Winters who wants to please the Devil. Undistinguished, even with Joseph Cotten, Robert Foxworth and Robert Cornthwaite. Jonathan Frid turns up as a butler—what happened to all those dark shadows? Directed by Jeannot Szwarc.

DEVIL'S DAUGHTER, THE. Video version of **POCOMANIA** (Sinister/C; Video Yesteryear; Discount).

DEVIL'S DAUGHTER, THE (1991). With Herbert Lamb and Kelly Curtis. Directed by Michele Soavi. Produced and co-written by Dario Argento. Also called THE SECT. (Video/Laser: Republic)

DEVIL'S EXPRESS (1975). Martial arts actioner set in New York City, where a practitioner of chop suey kung fu takes on a demon in the subway. Directed by Barry Rosen. Warhawk Tanzania, Sam DeFazio.

DEVIL'S EYE (1960). Ingmar Bergman wrote-directed this Swedish import in which Spanish lover Don Juan's soul is returned to Earth to seduce a virgin whose chastity is an "eyesore" for Satan. Jarl Kulle, Bibi Andersson, Stig Jarrell, Gunnar Bjornstrand. (Nelson; Sultan)

DEVIL'S EYE. See **EYEBALL.**

DEVIL'S GIFT, THE (1984). Monkey doll with sinister eyes (it's inhabited by a demon) carries out evil deeds by hypnotizing a housewife. Filmed in the Santa Rosa-Petaluma area, this low-budgeter is incredibly chintzy, lacking in production except for a weird opening that is partially animated. The drabness of the people and locales, plus the fact the script by Hayden O'Hara, Jose Vergelin and producer-director Kenneth J. Berton was lifted from Stephen King's "The Monkey," make this an excruciating experience. THE DEVIL'S GIFT is no gift to you. Bob Mendlesohn, Vicki Saputo. (Vestron)

DEVIL'S HAND, THE (1959). Linda Christian fertilizes Robert Alda's dreams in hopes the nightmarish seeds will inspire him to "grow" with her voodoo varsity. But it looks like cult chief Neil Hamilton will still have to endanger Alda's life when he proves an enemy of the devil-doll makers. Directed by William J. Hole Jr. Make-up by Jack Pierce. Jeannie Carmen. Also known as THE NAKED GODDESS, WITCHCRAFT and LIVE TO LOVE. (S/Weird; Sinister/C; Loonic; Filmfax)

DEVIL'S LONGEST NIGHT, THE. See **DEVIL'S NIGHTMARE, THE.**

DEVIL'S MASK (1946). Entry in Columbia's I LOVE A MYSTERY series, adapted from Carlton E. Morse's radio series. Based on Morse's "Faith, Hope and Charity Sisters" radioplay, it involves a crashed plane carrying a shrunken head, the only clue to a code and a mystery. Jim Bannon portrays Jack Packard and Barton Yarborough (a radio regular) is Doc Young. Directed by Henry Levin. Anita Louise, Michael Duane. Others in this series: I LOVE A MYSTERY and THE UNKNOWN.

DEVIL'S MEN. See **LAND OF THE MINOTAUR.**

DEVIL'S MESSENGER, THE (1962). Feature version of the Swedish TV series 13 DEMON STREET, created-directed by Curt Siodmak. Lon Chaney Jr. is the Devil and Karen Kadler is Satanya, his messenger. Three narratives: Satanya's image forces weak-willed men to suicide; a woman 50,000 years old is found frozen in the ice; a man's death is foreseen in dreams. New footage was directed by Herbert (THE CRAWLING HAND) Strock. (Sinister/C; S/Weird; Filmfax)

DEVIL'S MISTRESS, THE (1966). In the Wild West, a female vampire drains the life from cowboys not at home on her range. Look out, wranglers, that gal is giving you a bum steer. Joan Stapleton, Arthur Resley, Forrest Westmoreland, Robert Gregory. Written-directed by Orville Wanzer. (Sinister/C; S/Weird)

DEVIL'S NIGHTMARE (1971). Campy dialogue and silly premise provide laughs in this Italian-Belgian flop chiller about a Nazi general whose family has a pact with the Devil. Each generation's eldest daughter is born an evil witch lusting to kill. Flash to present day as seven travelers seek refuge one stormy night in Castle von Rhoneberg. These idiots (bubbleheaded sexy blondes, a glutton, and so on) meet grisly deaths: quicksand, guillotine, Iron Maiden, impalement on spikes, etc. The priest in the group stands to fight a religious battle. Erika Blanc, Jean Servais. Directed by Jean Brismee. Also known as THE DEVIL'S LONGEST NIGHT. (Monterey; New Horizon; from Premiere as **NIGHTMARE OF TERROR,** from Regal as **DEVIL WALKS AT MIDNIGHT, THE** and Applause as **SUCCUBUS**)

DEVILS OF DARKNESS (1965). Stilted British dud which deals with a vampire cult in need of human sacrifices, carried out in a secret hideout beneath the town cemetery. Directed uncomfortably by Lance Comfort. William Sylvester, Hubert Noel, Tracy Reed.

DEVIL'S OWN, THE (1966). Joan Fontaine is the sole interest in this dull Hammer blend of voodoo and satanism. Nigel Kneale's script (based on a Peter Curtis novel) is talk talk talk, and the minimal action comes at the climax during an attempted sacrifice. Setting is a staid English village where witches stir up a cauldron of trouble. Directed by Cyril Frankel. Kay Walsh, Duncan Lamont, Leonard Rossiter. Aka THE WITCHES.

DEVIL'S PARTNER, THE (1958). Negligent nonsense about Ed Nelson bloodizing a pact with Satan and transformed into a wild stallion/serpent. Directed by Charles Rondeau. Edgar Buchanan, Jean Allison, Richard Crane. (Sinister/C; Moore; Cinemacabre; Filmfax)

DEVIL'S PEOPLE. See **LAND OF THE MINOTAR.**

DEVILS POSSESSED (1986). Ruler uses terror to keep the common folk in line, but they revolt—and in this movie the natives are really revolting. Also called THE MARSHAL OF HELL. (All Seasons)

DEVIL'S RAIN (1975). Ernest Borgnine is Jonathan Corbis, a goat demon heading a coven. Innocent passers-by stumble across the secret in Mexico and must be silenced. Trashy film, barely salvaged in the final minutes when the Evil Ones are drenched in a satanic rainstorm, turning into oozing, melting puddles of multi-colored wax. Not even director Robert Fuest (ABOMINABLE DR. PHIBES) comes in out of the rain. William Shatner, Ida Lupino, Eddie Albert, Tom Skerritt, John Travolta, Keenan Wynn. (United; VCI) (Laser: Image)

DEVIL'S TRIANGLE, THE (1974). Cheapjack pseudo-documentary from producer-writer-director Richard Winer which purports unsubstantiated theories about ships, planes and people disappearing in the area of the Atlantic bounded by Miami, Bermuda and Puerto Rico. Inept narration read by Vincent Price. (MGM/UA)

DEVIL'S UNDEAD, THE (1979). Video version of **NOTHING BUT THE NIGHT** (Monterey).

DEVIL'S WEB, THE (1974). Mildly compelling TV-movie starring an aging, grotesque Diana Dors (once a British sexpot) portraying a disciple of Satan who possesses human souls. She turns up at the home of an English gentleman whose daughter is paralyzed and needs care. Dors gives her care all right, teaching her the black arts, until she turns evil. Shaun O'Riordan directed Brian Clemens' script. Andrea Marcovicci, Linda Liles, Cec Linder, Ed Bishop. (Thrillervideo)

DEVIL'S WEDDING NIGHT, THE (1975). Dracula's Nibelungen ring, which lures virgins to a sacrificial party, is the pivotal device in this Italian film, which offers ample nudity. Another variation on the Countess Bathory legend, in which Sara Bay caresses her skin with virgins' blood. Undistinguished mix of blood and sex, directed by Paul Solvay. Mark Damon has a dual role without doubling your pleasure. (Wizard; VCI)

DEVIL'S WIDOW, THE. See **TAM LIN.**

DEVIL TIMES FIVE (1974). During the snowy season around Lake Arrowhead, lodge owner Papa Doc (Gene Evans) is caught up in a supernatural mystery involving five strangers led by a child who could be possessed by the Devil. Low-budget schlock-bottom job is dully paced by writer John Durren (who couples as an actor) and director Sean MacGregor. Sorrell Booke, Taylor Lacher, Joan McCall. Also called PEOPLE TOYS and THE HORRIBLE HOUSE ON THE HILL. (Video Treasures; Media; Sinister/C)

DEVIL WALKS AT MIDNIGHT. Video version of **DEVIL'S NIGHTMARE, THE** (Regal; Saturn).

DEVIL WEARS CLODHOPPERS, THE. See **THIS STUFF'LL KILL YA!**

DEVIL WITHIN HER, THE (1976). British rip-off of THE EXORICST, as messy as Nicholas Carlesi's diapers, who by the tender age of 30 days has pushed his nanny into the Thames and dunked a dead mouse in a teacup. Joan Collins, who birthed this cradled creature after being hexed by a sinister dwarf, wonders why so much mayhem from a toddler. Doctor Donald Pleasence has suspicions. Lack of motivation and obscure demonic background turn this (also known as I DON'T WANT TO BE BORN, THE MONSTER, THE BABY and SHARON'S BABY) into a cinematic nightmare for director Peter Sasdy. Ralph Bates, Caroline Munro. (Axon)

DEVIL WOLF OF SHADOW MOUNTAIN (1964). Western horror tale in which a cowboy drinks from a wolf's print and turns into a beast. Director Gary Kent was last seen gibbering madly as he shambled into the darkness of Shadow Mountain. John Cardoz.

DEVIL WOMAN. See **ONIBABA.**

DEVIL WOMAN (1970). Filipino film focusing on a village Gorgon who sends serpents crawling to attack natives who have wronged her. Directed by J.F. Sibal. Divina Valencia, Roger Calvin. (Sinister/C; S/Weird; Filmfax)

DEVONSVILLE TERROR, THE (1983). German filmmaker Ulli Lommel directed this slow-moving witchcraft/sorcery tale. It begins centuries ago with a Salem witch burning and jumps to modern day, when descendants of the witchstalkers are plagued by a curse. Suzanna Love, one of three women new in town, would appear to be a witch, but it takes forever for townspeople to catch on. Meanwhile, worms infect doctor Donald Pleasence. The script by Lommel, Love (his wife) and George T. Lindsey never comes to life. Robert Walker, Paul Willson, Angelica Rebane. (Embassy; Sultan)

DIABOLICAL DR. MABUSE, THE. See **THOUSAND EYES OF DR. MABUSE, THE.**

DIABOLICAL DR. Z, THE (1966). Murky atmosphere enhances, rather than detracts from, this Spanish-French sequel to THE AWFUL DR. ORLOF with Howard Vernon back as the mad doc. His daughter (Mabel Karr) takes lab center to gain control of a woman dancer nicknamed Miss Death (Estella Blain) for revenge by using a long needle that plunges into victims. Directed by Jesse Franco. Antonio J. Escribano, Guy Mairesse. Also known as MISS MUERTE, MISS DEATH and MISS DEATH AND DR. Z. (Sinister/C; S/Weird; Filmfax)

DIABOLICAL PACT (1968). John Carradine is back in a Mexican horror film directed by Jaime Salvador playing another mad doctor seeking another formula for youth. Regina Torne, Miguel Angel Alvarez. Also known as THE PACT WITH THE DEVIL.

DIABOLIK. See **DANGER: DIABOLIK.**

DIABOLIQUE (1955). French shocker, produced-directed by Henri-Georges Clouzot, is contrived but so cleverly so, it remains a classic. Without giving away too much, we can say it shows how Simone Signoret and Vera Clouzot murder the dreadful principal of their boys' school (he's also the insufferable husband of Ms Clouzot). They hide his corpse in the pool, then discover it missing . . . The headmaster has returned from the dead! And one of the women sees him alive! At this point we will politely shut up. Based on THE WOMAN WHO WAS NO MORE by Pierre Boileau and Thomas Narcejac. A subplot involves the detective working the case. Remade twice as TV-movies: REFLECTIONS OF FEAR and HOUSE OF SECRETS. (Crown; Nostalgia; Foothill; Filmfax; S/Weird) (Laser: Criterion)

DIAL: HELP (1989). Spinning, tonish Italian supernatural thriller epitomizes the frustration of long distance dialing when Charlotte Lewis taps into a psychic energy field containing the spirit of a dead operator. Suddenly her friends are dying and psychic doctor William Berger investigates. Directed by Ruggero Deodato co-wrote the taut script. (Prism)

DIAMOND MOUNTAIN. Video version of **SHADOW OF CHIKARA** (Mintex).

DIAMONDS ARE FOREVER (1971). Seventh entry in the 007 series stars Sean Connery in his last fling in the role prior to quitting in 1972. In this adaptation of Ian Fleming's novel, 007 searches for Blofeld, who is firing his diamond laser at missile bases. The settings range from the lunar landscape to Las Vegas to the Nevada desert. There's a car chase down the mainstreet of Vegas, a race with a moonmobile, lady karate attacks and two gay villains. Jimmy Dean portrays a Howard Hughes-type recluse, Jill St. John is the beautiful Tiffany Case (oh does she love diamonds), Lana Wood appears as sexy Plenty O'Toole, and Charles Gray is the dastardly cat lover, Blofeld. Directed by Guy Hamilton in flashy fashion and written tongue-in-cheek by Richard Maibaum and Tom Mankiewicz. (CBS/Fox) (Laser: MGM/UA)

DIARY OF A MADMAN (1963). Tormented performance by Vincent Price enhances the threadbare script by producer Robert E. Kent, based on Guy de Maupassant's "The Horla." Price is a 19th Century Parisian magistrate, haunted by an invisible entity that forces him to slash beautiful Nancy Kovack to pieces. A quasi-religious ending is in keeping with the morality of the times. The "invisible man" tricks are unimpressive and the weight falls on Price's shoulders. Directed by Reginald LeBorg. Chris Warfield, Ian Wolfe. (Wood Knapp)

DIARY OF THE DEAD (1976). Macabre overtones enhance this oddly structured Hitchcockian thriller starring Hector Elizondo as a pure heel, an out-of-work crossword solver with a shrew of a mother-in-law (Geraldine Fitzgerald). How he sets out to knock her off for her $80,000 inheritance leads to a labyrinth of deadly twists and turns under Arvin Brown's subtle direction. Salome Jens is Elizondo's brow-beaten wife. (Vista)

DICK TRACY (1937). Republic's first serial based on Chester Gould's comic-strip book character has Ralph Byrd portraying the jaw-jutting detective. In this adventure he's up against The Spider (George Morgan), who uses a death ray and operates on Tracy's brother, turning him into a zombie. The 15 chapters were directed by Ray Taylor and Alan James. Kay Hughes, Smiley Burnette. (Burbank; United; Sinister/C; Video Yesteryear; VCI)

DICK TRACY MEETS GRUESOME (1947). Comic-book movie based on Chester Gould's cop (Ralph Byrd) stars Boris Karloff as a heavy who robs banks with a paralyzing nerve gas. He borrowed it from the Green Hornet, maybe? Directed perfunctorily by John Rawlins. Anne Gwynne is Tracy's wife, Tess Trueheart. Howard Ashley, June Clayworth, Robert Clarke, Lex Barker. (Video Yesteryear; Sinister/C; Nostalgia; Rhino; United American; Silver Screen)

DICK TRACY'S G-MEN (1939). In this, the third in Republic's DICK TRACY serials, Ralph Byrd goes against scientist Zarnoff, who uses a drug to bring himself back from the dead after his prison execution. It's nonstop action under directors William Witney and John English. Irving Pichel, Ted Pearson, Walter Miller. And dig that Phylis Isley—she became Jennifer Jones! (United)

DICK TRACY VS CRIME INC. (1941). William Whitney and John English directed this 15-chapter Republic serial (the studio's fourth and last) in which Chester Gould's comic-strip cop tangles with the Ghost, a dastard capable of making himself invisible as he terrorizes the city. Action-packed. Ralph Byrd reprises his role as Tracy, assisted by Frank Morgan. (United; VCI)

DIE, DIE! MY DARLING! (1966). Grand Guignol horror (also known as FANATIC) with Stephanie Powers trapped in a house of crazies governed by religious zealot Tallulah Bankhead, who goes bonkers in eye-rolling, scenery-chomping fashion. The graphic murders are of such an abhorrent nature, the film has a singular gripping fascination. Donald Sutherland is Tallulah's nutty handyman, and he's impressive. Directed by Silvio Narizzano, scripted by Richard Matheson from Anne Blaisdell's NIGHTMARE. Maurice Kaufman. (RCA/Columbia)

DIE LAUGHING (1980). A formula for altering atomic waste into plutonium bomb components is the McGuffin in this spy spoof with Robby Benson as a cabbie who falls into possession of a cute monkey holding the key to the secret. Accused of murder, Benson rushes all over San Francisco with dumb villain Bud Cort in pursuit. A spirit of fun is at work. Directed by Jeff Werner. Charles Durning. Elsa Lanchester. (Warner Bros.)

DIE, MONSTER, DIE (1965). Loose-as-a-goose adaptation of H. P. Lovecraft's COLOUR OUT OF SPACE, produced in England as a vehicle for Boris Karloff and also known as MONSTER OF TERROR. The setting is H.P.'s infamous Arkham County where a desolate tract of land has been stricken by a diseased power from space that turns everyone into monsters. Director Daniel Haller provides isolated moments of fear and mystery, but the majority of Jerry Sohl's script is muddled. Nick Adams is the American who comes to a weird mansion looking for his bride-to-be (Suzan Farmer). Freda Jackson is a woman who keeps her hideous appearance hidden beneath a veil, and Patrick Magee is a doctor. (HBO) (Laser: Image, with **LUST FOR A VAMPIRE**)

DIE, SISTER, DIE. Video version of **COMPANION, THE** (Gorgon; MPI).

DIGBY, THE BIGGEST DOG IN THE WORLD (1974). Rollicking British satire in the "Carry On" tradition . . . a shaggy dog film for young and old in which Project X powder is lapped up by Digby, who becomes an "incredible 50-foot" dog. The effects by Tom Howard aren't great but this Michael Pertweek adaptation of a Ted Key book has a light-hearted lampooning spirit. Directed by Joseph McGrath. Jim Dale, Spike Milligan. (Prism)

DIMENSION FIVE (1966). Fantasy/spy thriller with secret agent Justin Power (Jeffrey Hunter) using a device that whisks him from time zone to time zone to prevent dirty Commies from destroying L. A. with atomic weapons. Directed dimensionlessly by serial producer Franklin Adreon and written without depth by Arthur C. Pierce. Frances Nuyen, Harold Sakata, Donald Woods.

DIMENSIONS IN DEATH. See **CASTLE OF BLOOD.**

DINNER FOR ADELE (1977). A man-eating plant in a Nick Carter detective story? It's Czech director Oldrich Lipsky's frothy, free-wheeling spoof on cops, robbers and monsters. Carter (portrayed by solemn Michal Docolomansky) and sausage-eating Inspector Ledvina are hot on the trail of a mad botanist, The Gardener, whose prize creation is Adele. Adele, you see, is the hungry plant, whose appetite is unleashed by the sound of Mozart's "Lullaby." Crazy props and wild chases.

DINOSAUR: SECRET OF THE LOST LEGEND. See **BABY: SECRET OF THE LOST LEGEND.**

DINOSAURUS (1960). The funniest sci-fi movie ever made— unintentionally, that is. This bizarre variation on the Three Stooges—a prehistoric caveman, a tyrannosaurus and a friendly brontosaurus—will have you in stitches as they run wild on a tropical island after being blasted out of their hibernational digs. One hilarous scene has the caveman (Gregg Martell) fleeing in terror from a woman in pincurlers. Side-splitting from beginning to end . . . kids will love it. Ward Ramsey, Kristina Hanson. Directed by Irvin S. Yeaworth Jr., of BLOB fame. (New World/Starmaker; Sinister/C; S/Weird; Filmfax)

DISAPPEARANCE OF FLIGHT 412, THE (1974). Two jets chase a UFO, forcing an investigation division of the military to quarantine the crews. Officer-in-charge Glenn Ford doesn't appreciate the mistreatment and locks horns with superiors. This never resolves the issue of UFOs but it's fascinating to see their effect on military authority and the common soldier. Directed by Jud Taylor. Bradford Dillman, Guy Stockwell, David Soul, Kent Smith.

DISAPPEARANCES, THE (1977). Re-edited episodes of THE MAN FROM ATLANTIS, with Patrick Duffy as an underwater humanoid. In this adventure an insane lady scientist kidnaps Dr. Merrill. Belinda J. Montgomery, Alan Fudge, Darlene Carr. Directed by Charles Dubin.

DISCIPLE OF DEATH (1972). Insanely inept, ludicrously laughable British mishmash with Mike Raven as a minion of the Devil posing as a priest for easier access to virgins, whom he sacrifices to Satan. Raven is so hammy, and the cast so underdirected by co-producer/co-screenwriter Tom Parkinson, this is hopeless junk. The setting is 18th Century England and there are "Dracula's Brides" and a cackling dwarf. (Unicorn)

DISCIPLE OF DRACULA. See **DRACULA, PRINCE OF DARKNESS.**

DISCONNECTED (1986). Minor slasher film, produced in Connecticut, in which Frances Raines portrays twin sisters implicated in a series of slasher murders. Producer-director Gorman Bechard emphasizes the whodunit aspects of the Virginia Gilroy script. Mark Walker, Carl Koch, Ben Page. (Active; Video Treasures)

DISCREET CHARM OF THE BOURGEOISIE (1972). Luis Bunuel's surrealism switches between reality and fantasy so continuously, most audiences found this befuddling. Bunuel merges ghost stories and narratives-within-narratives in his glimpse at hypocrisy in French society. Fernando Rey, Delphine Seyrig. Oscar-winner for Best Foreign Film. (Corinth; Media; Applause)

DISEMBODIED, THE (1957). Join "The Disinterested" after a few minutes of this jungle gibberish about a voodoo cult which puts the whammy on handsome photographer Paul Burke. The girl who does the native dance in a sarong, Allison Hayes, became "The 50-Foot Woman." Directed by Walter Grauman.

DISTANT EARLY WARNING (1975). TV-movie set at an Arctic research station invaded by aliens capable of clouding men's minds. Directed by Wes Kenny. Michael Parks, Herb Edelman, Tony Geary.

DISTANT LIGHTS (1987). Italian sci-fi/supernatural thriller with above-average storyline. Disembodied spirits from space come to Earth to take over bodies of the newly dead, but in no way are they malevolent—hell, they haven't even seen any George Romero films. Directed by Aurelio Chiesa. Tomas Milian, William Berger.

DISTANT SCREAM, A. See **DYING TRUTH.**

DISTORTIONS (1986). Slow-paced psychothriller in which it appears Olivia Hussey is having hallucinations following the death of her husband at the hands of a homosexual killer. Insanity, you see, runs in her family. A

"I've done lives. Now I'm doing deaths."

—The crazy mad surgeon of lobotomies in **DEAD PIT**

charred face pops up to haunt her, but discerning viewers will see through the red herrings in John Goff's screenplay. It's saved from total tedium by Steve Railsback as the understanding boyfriend, Piper Laurie as the scheming aunt, June Chadwick as a friend of Olivia's, Rita Gam as a grocery store lady, and Edward Albert as the handsome husband. Director Armand Mastroianni never overcomes the limitations. (Academy)

DISTURBANCE, THE (1989). Disturbing portrait of a crazy guy (Timothy Greeson) with a mother complex who has a demon inside his body and kills women. Directed by MTV's Cliff Guest and written by Laura Radford. Lisa Geoffrion, Ken Ceresne. (VidAmerica)

DISTURBED (1990). Goofball study of psychiatrist (Malcolm McDowell) who goes crazy within the walls of Bergen Field Clinic. Seems that Dr. Russell rapes his pretty patients and forces them to commit suicide. It's goofball because McDowell plays as if he were in a screwball comedy while everyone else maintains straight faces. Director Charles Winkler, who co-wrote the whacky script with Emerson Bixby, achieves a dark macabre overtone. The proceedings, including hallucinations and comedy acting by McDowell and Geoffrey Lewis, leads to a twist ending. McDowell's campy performance is joined to Winkler's askew camera angles to suggest madness. Priscilla Pointer is a gas as a devoted nurse and Irwin Keyes and Clint Howard go bonkers as inmates. Pamela Gidley is a victim. (Live) (Laser: Image)

DOC SAVAGE—MAN OF BRONZE (1975). George Pal's campy treatment of a pulp magazine superhero (created by Kenneth Robeson) is one of his last—and least—efforts in a distinguished career as a producer of fantasy movies with trend-setting effects. Ron Ely (TV's TARZAN) has eyes that literally sparkle as he embarks on a mission to South America to find the killers of his father. His Fabulous Five, associates skilled in sciences and martial arts, are far from the characters conceived in the stories, making this seem unfaithful to the source novels. Michael Anderson directed, Pal and Joe Morheim adapted. Paul Gleason, Paul Wexler, Pamela Hensley, Carlos Rivas. (Warner Bros.)

DOCTOR AND THE DEVILS, THE (1985). Dylan Thomas' script, resurrecting the Burke and Hare case of old Edinburgh, was first written in 1945, but considered too Grand Guignol for a movie until producer Mel Brooks and director Freddie Francis turned it into a morality drama. Timothy Dalton is the self-righteous anatomical instructor Dr. Rock (based on Dr. Knox) who buys corpses from body snatchers Jonathan Pryce and Stephen Rea. Pryce's portrait of a totally evil man is chilling and the period detail fascinating; in fact, it's so real, capturing the poverty of Edinburgh, that it becomes uncomfortable viewing. Twiggy, Julian Sands. (Key)

DOCTOR BLOODBATH. Video version of **HORROR HOTEL** (Bingo).

DOCTOR BLOOD'S COFFIN (1961). Sidney J. Furie cut his directorial teeth on this British programmer enhanced by ancient Cornwall settings. Peter Blood, son of a doctor who dabbled in the arcane, discovers a curare poisoning that brings the dead to life. Kieron Moore is a compelling mad doctor, torn between science and evil. Fetching is his nurse, buxom Hazel Court, who screams so beautifully. Ian Hunter, Fred Johnson, Paul Stockman. (Sinister/C; Dark Dreams; S/Weird; Filmfax)

DOCTOR FROM SEVEN DIALS. See **CORRIDORS OF BLOOD.**

DOCTOR MANIAC. See **HOUSE OF THE LIVING DEAD.**

DOCTOR OF DOOM (1960). First in Mexico's "Wrestling Women" series (also called WRESTLING WOMEN VS. THE AZTEC MUMMY and SEX MONSTER) in which brain transplants by a mad doctor leave several empty craniums, one of which was the producer's. Heroic Golden Rubi and Gloria Venus take on gorilla Gomar and her pain-brain companion, Vendetta, in this attempt to liven up the Aztec Mummy by surrounding him/it/whatever with shapely femmes. Written with grunts and groans by Alfred Salazar, directed by Rene Cardona. Armando Silvestre, Lorena Velasquez. (Sinister/C; Hollywood Home; Timeless; Filmfax; from Rhino as **ROCK 'N ROLL WRESLTING WOMEN VS. THE AZTEC MUMMY**)

DOCTOR'S HORRIBLE EXPERIMENT, THE. See **TESTAMENT OF DR. CORDELIER, THE.**

DOCTORS WEAR SCARLET. See **BLOODSUCKERS, THE.**

DOCTOR X (1932). This early Warner Bros. horror Technicolor whodunit is set in the Gothic house of Blackstone Shoals, where "The Full Moon Killer" is one of several eccentric doctors Lionel Atwill has gathered to re-enact the crimes, which consist of a scalpel insertion at the base of the neck and cannibalism. Atwill's performance is intriguing, but other characters are stereotyped, such as Fay Wray as the daughter always screaming at the sight of her mysterious father, and Lee Tracy's wisecracking reporter, disruptive to the somber mood established by director Michael Curtiz. Despite predictabilities, DR. X retains a nostalgic charm and morbid fascination. Preston Foster, Mae Busch. (Video/Laser: MGM/UA)

DOG, A MOUSE AND A SPUTNIK, A (1961). See editions 1-3.

DOGS (1976). Man's Best Friend does an about-tail and doglegs to the left to chase after (or retrieve, in the case of bird dogs) human flesh as though it were upgraded Kal-Kan. This film's bite is worse than its bark as the murderous mutts, cursed curs and psychopurebreds take over management of all pounds and kennels. What a time they have with fire hydrants, with the SPCA out of business. David McCallum leads the human pack, with Linda Gray nipping at his heels. No puppy love in this family. Directed by Burt Brinckerhoff on point, who hounded the cast for better performances, and written by O'Brian Tomalin, who loves to be scratched behind his ears. Therein lies the tail of this tale.

DOGS OF HELL (1982). Regional filmmaker Earl Owensby shot this in Georgia in 3-D as ROTTWEILER. An Army experiment involving surgical implants in animals turns Rottweilers into killers, a "loss of human affection response." The dogs escape and invade the Lake Lure resort, where campers, farmers and passersby die horribly in the jaws of the killer pack. Tom McIntyre's script takes forever to get yipping and director Worth Keter dogs it. Producer Owensby also plays the sheriff but he's without bite. Robert Bloodworth, Bill Gribble, Kathy Hasty, Ed Lilliard, Jerry Rushing. (Media)

DOIN' TIME ON PLANET EARTH (1988). Oddball comedy about misfit Nicholas Strouse in Sunnydale, Ariz., who is told by his computer that he is an alien and it's time to go home. He's visited by other oddballs (Adam West and Candice Azzara) who claim they too are aliens, and they want Ryan to turn his father's revolving restaurant atop a Holiday Inn into a flying saucer for the flight home. Screenwriter Darren Star never makes it explicit if this is real or in Ryan's imagination, but one thing is sure: Andrea Thompson plays a sexy lounge singer who helps Ryan "explode" the DNA knowledge in his system. Directed by Charles Matthau (son of Walter), this has cute moments, but ultimately is forgettable. Hugh Gillin, Gloria Henry, Hugh O'Brian, Martha Scott. Roddy McDowall, Maureen Stapleton. (Warner Bros.)

DOKTOR FAUSTUS (1982). See third edition.

DOLL, THE (1962). See editions 1-3.

DOLL, THE (1963). Swedish fantasy allegory, directed by Arne Mattsson and starring Per Oscarsson as a lonely nightwatchman who finds solace in the companionship of a department store dummy he steals and takes home. Dummy comes to life as Gio Petre and . . . (Facets Multimedia; Discount)

DOLLMAN (1990). One of the lesser efforts of video producer Charles Band, beneath his usual production standards. The effects never believably integrate a 13-inch-high humanoid policeman with the full- scale humans. This wee guy hails from the planet Arturos and crashlands on Earth while in pursuit of a villain in the form of a floating head (and we don't mean a portable toilet). Tim Thomerson essays the psychotic, triggerhappy cop Brick Bardos in a flat fashion and director Albert Pyun fails to trick up shots convincingly. Screenwriter Chris Roghair deals with the characters on a shallow level, especially a young mother and her son trapped in the ghetto of New York. This only snorts to life when Pyun uses documentary techniques to capture street life in the Bronx, where the film was shot. Jackie Earle Haley, Kamala Lopez. The sequel: DOLLMAN VS. THE DEMONIC TOYS. (Paramount) (Laser: Pioneer)

DOLLMAN VS. THE DEMONIC TOYS (1993). Charles Band crossover vidflick teaming space cop Brick Bardo (13 inches in height) from DOLLMAN with the shrunken nurse Ginger ("Doll Chick") from BAD CHANNELS to fight the ugly entities introduced in DEMONIC TOYS. Back as cop Judith Grey (from DEMONIC TOYS) is Tracy Scoggins, who hires Bardo (Tim Thomerson, star of the TRANCERS series) and Ginger (sexy and appealing Melissa Behr) to do battle against the evil playthings, including Baby Upsy Daisy and a new one, Zombie Man. Despite all the tricks, producer-director Band can't make the miniaturization theme believable and Craig Hamann's script, in spite of all the talent at work, falls flat. Phil Brock, Phil Fondacardo, William C. Carpenter. Soundtrack by Quiet Riot. (Paramount)

DOLLS (1986). Ed Naha's predictable script has stranded travelers trapped in the mansion of a couple that specializes in making dolls—more to the point, of turning humans into miniaturized entities they control for evil purposes. Guy Rolfe and Hilary Mason are good in these benevolent-malevolent roles. Carrie Lorraine is a lovable child who discovers the couple's secret and tries to warn the adults. There's enough gore to please the splatter freaks, and one or two nice scenes as the dolls, en masse, close in for the kill. But there's nothing in this film that hasn't been done before, and one wonders what extraordinary director Stuart Gordon saw in it. Ian Patrick Williams, Carolyn Purdy-Gordon. (Vestron)

DOLLY DEAREST (1991). You thought Chucky was yucky. Here's a ripoff that humiliates the screen's goriest killer doll with a female counterpart that can be just as homicidal. The body of a toy is filled with the spirit of Sanzia the Devil Child, a Mexican spawn of Satan. When a tomb is desecrated, the spirit escapes to a toyshop where the Dolly Dearest models are infected with evil—so you got skirt-wearing Chuckies running round trying to kill archeologist Rip Torn, toymaker Sam Bottoms, wife Denise Crosby and their two kids (Chris Demetral, Candy Hutson). Writer-director Maria Lease should pay residuals to the Chucky creators. Lupe Ontirveros, Will Gotay, Alma Martinez. (Video/Laser: Vidmark)

DOLPHIN, THE (1987). A woman gives birth to a dolphin-man who seduces women of fishermen in this Portuguese fantasy written-directed by Walter Lima Jr. (Fox Lorber, with English subtitles)

DOMINIQUE IS DEAD (1978). Millionaire Cliff Robertson is grieving over the death of wife Jean Simmons when he sees her spectral image in the hall. The spirit continues to haunt him, and while he should wise up to the possibility of Hitchcockian tricks, he's a real fall guy to the end. This kind of pseudosupernatural thriller has been done to death, but director Michael Anderson injects it with class. Edward and Valerie Abraham adapted Harold Lawlor's WHAT BECKONING GHOST. Jenny Agutter, Simon Ward. (Prism; from Impulse and Simitar as **AVENGING SPIRIT**)

DONKEY SKIN (1971). French fairy tale, based on a story by Charles Perrault with music by Michel Legrand and direction by Jacques Demy. Catherine Deneuve stars as a princess who must disguise herself so she won't have to marry the wrong man, with Delphine Seyrig as a fairy godmother. Suitable for children and adults. (Tamarelle's; Sultan)

DONOR (1991). Macabre, gory TV-movie is a rehash of COMA and X-RAY in which an aspiring, easily-made-hysterical doctor (Melissa Gilbert-Brinkman) uncovers a hospital conspiracy to exploit indigent patients for their pituitary glands and create a new formula for agelessness. A scalpel killer stalks Melissa, leading to a grisly sequence in a formaldehyde corpse tanks. Effective script by Michael Braverman, directed for shock values by Larry Shaw. Jack Scalia is Melissa's love interest, Pernell Roberts is the chief of staff, Marc Lawrence is an aging patient and Gregory Sierra a baffled cop.

DONOVAN'S BRAIN (1953). Curt Siodmak's classic novel (first produced in 1943 as THE LADY AND THE MONSTER) was remade by producer Tom Gries into a superior version thanks to the literate writing and direction by Felix Feist. Well-meaning scientist Lew Ayres keeps a tyrannical tycoon's brain alive in a solution, but the brain gains mental control, forcing Ayres to commit acts against his will. Chillingly effective. Nancy Davis, Steve Brodie, Gene Evans, Tom Powers. (MGM/UA) (Laser: Image)

DON'T ANSWER THE PHONE (1981). Also known as THE HOLLYWOOD STRANGLER, this was (un)inspired by the L.A. Hillside Strangler case. A disturbed Vietnam vet (Nicholas Worth) rushes around Hollywood, choking women with a stocking. The violence is gratuitous and has no redeeming values, nor does the Michael Castle script shed insight into psychopathic killers. The couch is empty for director-producer Robert Hammer. James Westmoreland, Pamela Bryant. (Media)

DON'T BE AFRAID OF THE DARK (1973). Gnomes and other creatures are frightening Kim Darby, who must convince hubby Jim Hutton she isn't going bonkers. Minor supernatural TV-movie. Directed by John Newland. William Demarest, Barbara Anderson. (IVE)

DON'T GO IN THE HOUSE (1980). Sicko moviemess about a psycho (Dan Gramaldi) whose mother burned him as a kid, so now he sets naked women on fire with his flame-thrower and watches them burn, all because he hates his now-deceased mother—and all women remind him of her. He keeps the charred corpses in his private charnel house. Written-directed by Joseph Ellison; produced by Ellen Hammill, who co-wrote this insultive diatribe against women with Ellison and Joseph Masefield. Don't go in the theater. (Media)

DON'T GO IN THE WOODS (1980). Knife-killer low-budget exploitationer from producer-director Jim Bryan and word-chopper Garth Eliasson. Buck Carradine, Mary Gail Artz and James P. Hayden can't see the forest through the trees. (Media; Vestron)

DON'T GO TO SLEEP (1982). After a young girl dies in a fire, parents Dennis Weaver and Valerie Harper undergo changes as the spirit of their daughter returns for revenge. The family dies off one by one in bloody OMEN style, But since this is a TV-movie the graphics are kept to a minimum. Directed by Richard Lang. This is not a sleeper but a yawner, its prophetic title justified. Ruth Gordon, Robert Webber. (Unicorn)

DON'T LOOK IN THE ATTIC (1981). A film about a haunted house that contains the spirits of cows. Say, are they trying to milk the supernatural theme? One hopes the producers had plenty of pull. Directed by Carl Ausino. Jean-Pierre Aumont. (Mogul)

DON'T LOOK IN THE BASEMENT (1973). An aura of madness clings to this low-budgeter, a credit to producer-director S.F. Brownrigg and writer Tim Pope. In an insane asylum, nurse Rosie Holotik takes over after the previous director was axed to death. Gradually the inmates seize the asylum and the film sinks into a snake pit of insanity. Full of thrills and shocks. Ann McAdams, William McGee, Gene Ross. (VCI; Gorgon; MPI; VidAmerica)

DON'T LOOK NOW (1973). Daphne du Maurier's story becomes an engrossing psychological horror film directed by Nicolas Roeg, featuring erotic love scenes between Donald Sutherland and Julie Christie. Sutherland, a restorer of European churches, foresees his daughter's drowning. His power of prescience increases—and so does the inexplicable mystery. Ambiguous and enigmatic, but its psychic themes are fascinating. Hilary Mason, Clelia Matania. (Video/Laser: Paramount)

DON'T OPEN THE DOOR (1979). The maker of DON'T LOOK IN THE BASEMENT, S.F. Brownrigg, is back with another woman (Susan Bracken) faced with madness when she returns to Texas to ponder who stabbed mother to death. A sense of sexual depravity makes this unpleasantly compelling when Ms Bracken realizes a transvestite killer is in her house. Psycho whackos galore. Gene Ross, Annabelle Weenick. (Video Gems)

DON'T OPEN THE WINDOW (1974). A sound machine designed to kill bugs in the soil has a profound effect on the dead with sonic impulses—it makes them "desoil" and walk like zombies, killing living beings. This spaghetti-shocker is graphically sickening but it will please gore fans. Arthur Kennedy is awful as a disbelieving cop. Ray Lovelock, Christine Galbo. Jorge Grau directed. Also known as THE LIVING DEAD AT THE MANCHESTER MORGUE and BREAKFAST AT THE MANCHESTER MORGUE.

DON'T OPEN TILL CHRISTMAS (1984). He's making a kill list and checking it twice in Britain's answer to SILENT NIGHT, DEADLY NIGHT, with a psychokiller knocking off English Santas. The murders are graphic: a spear through the mouth, a cleaver across the face, two strangulations, a terrifying castration and knife plunges into stomachs. The suspense is well handled by director Edmund Purdom, especially a stalking sequence in the London Dungeon. Purdom also plays a Scotland Yard cop on the case. Caroline Munro appears in a skin-tight dress. Written by Derek Ford. Belinda Mayne. (Vestron)

DON'T WALK IN THE PARK. See **KILL, BABY, KILL.**

DOOM ASYLUM (1988). Long-dead Michael Rogan springs to life like a trampoline acrobat to kill in this comedy slasher flick, shot in New Jersey by Richard (DEATHMASK) Friedman. Gore aplenty plus clips from Tod Slaughter pics. Patty Mullen, Ruth Collins. (Academy)

DOOMSDAY CHRONICLES (1979). William Schallert narrates this pseudodocumentary about the day on which our world will close its doors forever. Would you believe the year of doom will be 1999? We're all doomed if TV keeps throwing us these cheap reports based on thin air. Directed by James Thornton.

DOOMSDAY MACHINE (1967). Sci-fi space film lacking in everything except Stanley Cortez's cinematography. A rocket piloted by Henry Wilcoxon and Grant Williams is halfway to Venus when nuclear war destroys Earth. What to do next? Scriptwriter Stuart James Byre settles on bickering among the passengers (Ruta Lee, Bobby Van, Mala Powers, Denny Miller) and a meeting with a superintelligence deep in space that will provide the answer for mankind's new beginnings. The film doesn't end—it just stops. Directed by Lee Sholem. (from Academy as **ESCAPE FROM PLANET EARTH**)

DOOMWATCH (1972). Chemicals dumped into waters surrounding a British island create human mutations when fish netted from the waters are eaten. Directed by Peter Sasdy. Some hideously good monster make-up. Ian Bannen, Judy Geeson, George Sanders, Percy Herbert, Simon Oates, George Woodbridge. (Monterey; Embassy)

DOORMAN, THE. See **TOO SCARED TO SCREAM.**

DOOR-TO-DOOR MANIAC. See **FIVE MINUTES TO LIVE.**

DOOR WITH THE SEVEN KEYS (1962). West German remake of the 1940 British shocker, CHAMBER OF HORRORS, about a woman who comes to a lonely mansion and meets a madman who keeps a torture chamber well stocked—with victims. Directed by Alfred Vohrer. Klaus Kinski, Heinz Drache. (Sinister/C)

DOPPELGANGER (1969). See **JOURNEY TO THE FAR SIDE OF THE SUN.**

DOPPELGANGER: THE EVIL WITHIN (1992). A better-than-average genre horror film thanks to writer-director Avi Nesher for creating two interesting L.A. culture characters, the sexy performance of Drew Barrymore and a couple of gooey but effective monsters. The characters are movie writer Patrick Highsmith (George Newbern), a likable nerd who klutzes his way to victory over evil, and his co-writer, a sharp-tongued, amusing young woman played by Leslie Hope. The pouty, exotic Barrymore—always in high heels and minidresses when she isn't stripping to make love to Newbern—undergoes a split personality, or a supernatural evil half is walking around outside her body. Nesher's ability to create ambiguity enhances the film's suspense. At the climax, in a bit of monster-shop tour de force, Barrymore splits into two alien-looking entities, fights a battle with evil, then merges back together. George Maharis and Sally Kellerman are wasted in bit roles. Dennis Christopher, Stanley De Santis, Peter Dobson, Dan Shor. (CBS/Fox's videobox bears this title, but the print itself reads only DOPPELGANGER.) (Laser: CBS/Fox)

DREW BARRYMORE

DORIAN GRAY. Video version of **SECRET OF DORIAN GRAY, THE** (NTA).

DORM THAT DRIPPED BLOOD, THE (1981). Formula stuff from producers-directors Jeffrey Obrow and Stephen Carpenter, a killer-on-the-loose, dumb-trapped-teenagers story set in Dayton Hall, which is closed for renovation. That gives the characters lonely rooms to wander in while the slasher-basher stalks them. The kids are given little to do but scream and die. Downbeat ending. Laurie Lapinski, Stephen Sachs. (Media)

DOUBLE DECEPTION (1960). Puzzling mystery about twins; you never are doubly sure which is doubly which. This convoluted enigma is deliciously posed by French masters of suspense Pierre Boileau and Thomas Narcejac, who concocted the original, on which VERTIGO is also based. Alice and Ellen Kessler portray the twins. Directed by Serge Friedman.

DOUBLE, DOUBLE TOIL AND TROUBLE (1993). This light-hearted Halloween TV-movie proves to be a worthy showcase for Cloris Leachman, who portrays twin sisters—one is an evil witch who uses a green moonstone to work her diabolical stuff, the other is a benevolent lady trapped in a mirror by magic. Leachman plots against young twin sisters Mary-Kate and Ashley Olsen when they join forces with a black vagrant, a gnome and a frightened grave digger to steal the moonstone and free the imprisoned sister. A delightful touch prevails throughout this pleasant family diversion. Meshach Taylor, Phil Fondacaro, Eric McCormach.

DOUBLE EXPOSURE (1981). A slasher film (also called THE PHOTOGRAPHER) about an ice-pick murderer stalking L.A. prostitutes . . . focus shifts to a girly mag photographer (Michael Callan) who fears he is the killer. He suffers from dreams in which he slaughters his models (in one case by sticking her head into a bag containing a rattlesnake). Is he dreaming or did he commit these heinous crimes? Not even psychiatrist Seymour Cassel knows for certain. Callan's relationship with his one-armed, one-legged brother (James Stacy) is a mixture of repressed affection, macho backslapping and sibling rivalry. Pamela Hensley and Robert Tessier are cops working with chief Cleavon Little but their contributions are minor as writer-director William Byron Hillman keeps focus on Callan and girlfriend Joanna Pettet. A peculiar non sequitur to the genre. (Vestron)

DOUBLE FACE (1968). German-Italian thriller based on Edgar Wallace's THE FACE IN THE NIGHT, directed by Riccardo Freda. Klaus Kinski is an industrialist whose lesbian wife leads him into murder. (Unicorn)

DOUBLE GARDEN, THE (1970). Mad doctor James Craig uses thunder and lightning to turn carnivorous plants into man-eating bloodsuckers. (From Regal as **REVENGE OF DR. X, THE**)

DOUBLE JEOPARDY. See **TASTE OF SIN, A.**

DOUBLE PLAY (1972). TV-movie composed of two episodes from network series. The pilot for GHOST STORY, a series of one-hour supernatural dramas produced by William Castle, stars Barbara Parkins as an expectant mother who moves into her dreamhome with lawyer husband David Burnie. Unaware they have built on the site of a two-century-old gallows, Parkins undergoes psychic hauntings from a woman who was executed and buried on the hill, and who now wants to take Parkins' baby from her. Directed by John Llewelyn Moxey, this episode is typical TV stuff with a script by Richard Matheson (based on an Elizabeth M. Walter short story). The second half is an episode from MOVIN' ON, a motorbike road series.

DOUBLE POSSESSION. See **GANJA AND HESS.**

DOWN TO EARTH (1947). A star-studded cast in a dull, dreary musical-comedy. Terpsichore, Goddess of Dance, materializes on our mortal plane (i.e., Broadway) to dally with producer Larry Parks. Rita Hayworth was at her loveliest as Terpsichore and co-stars George Macready, Edward Everett Horton, Adele Jergens and James Gleason pant and puff to support her, but there's no magic tricks from director Alexander Hall. (Columbia/TriStar) (Laser: Pioneer)

DRACULA (1931). Bela Lugosi's performance is the saving grace of this Universal milestone movie, establishing the vampire formula for all time. Tod Browning's direction is strangely static, and the Garrett Ford-Dudley Murphy adaptation (from the Hamilton Deane-John Balderston play, in turn from Bram Stoker's novel) is as stuffy as the drawing room in which too much of the action is set. Only the early Transylvania sequences, when Renfield (Dwight Frye) coaches across the eerie moor and arrives at the Gothic Dracula castle, conveys the atmosphere the rest of the film screams for. It is the affected stage-style acting of Lugosi, the malignant evil he suggests, and the hypnotic spell he holds over females that keeps one rapt. The supporting cast becomes mired in the stilted style of the period. Edward Van Sloan portrays the Van Helsing character, Helen Chandler one of Dracula's victims. Make-up by Jack Pierce (who also did Karloff's Frankenstein Monster), cinematography by Karl Freund. (Video/Laser: MCA)

DRACULA (SPANISH) (1931). A Spanish-language version of Tod Browning's DRACULA with a different cast but on the same sets and with the same costumes, lighting and production values. George Melford directed, and some feel he did as good a job, if not better, as Browning. Carlos Villarias plays Dracula. Lupita Tovar, Eduardo Arozamena, Pablo Alvarez Rubio. (MCA)

DRACULA (1958). See **HORROR OF DRACULA.**

DRACULA (1973). Richard Matheson scripted this Dan Curtis TV-film which met mixed reaction: Many critics felt it was slow-paced and dull, others were encouraged to see Jack Palance attempt a sympathetic, tormented portrait of the King of Vampires. This refreshing shift of pace is worth the serious buff's attention. Nigel Davenport appears as Van Helsing. Simon Ward, Fiona Lewis. Directed by Curtis. (MPI; IVE) (Laser: MPI)

DRACULA (1974). See **ANDY WARHOL'S DRACULA.**

DRACULA (1979). Stylish, atmospheric remake of the hoary old Hamilton Deane-John Balderston play (based on Bram Stoker's historic novel). Frank Langella, fresh from the Broadway version, is a sensual, sexy vampire radiating an uncommon amount of lust as he seduces Van Helsing's daughter. That foe of vampires is essayed with passionate histronics by Sir Laurence Olivier. Walter Mirisch's production reeks with period decor and costumes, with enough bloodletting and "undead" chills to satisfy specialty crowds as well as general audiences. Well directed by John Badham, with some great shots of Dracula crawling along the side of a building. Donald Pleasence, Kate Nelligan, Trevor Eve. Score by John Williams. (Video/Laser: MCA)

DRACULA (1984). Japanese animated feature of the Dracula legend, full of graphic violence and gore, and not suitable for young viewers. (Vestron)

DRACULA: A CINEMATIC SCRAPBOOK (1991). History of the infamous vampire traced through film trailers and other oddball tidbits, including most of the Universal and Hammer vampire flicks. Written and directed by Ted Newsom. (Rhino)

DRACULA A.D. 1972 (1972). Hammer broke tradition by placing Dracula in contemporary England, where he is resurrected by a gang of modish rock 'n rollers and avenges himself against a descendant of Professor Van Helsing. Peter Cushing, after an 11-year absence from the series, is back as the updated Van Helsing, tracking the vampire to an old church after his granddaughter (the wonderfully busty Stephanie Beacham) has been lured into Drac's domain. Christopher Lee is still imposing as the bloodsucker with the bloodshot eyes and his battles with Cushing are well staged, although some of the demises are based on now-predictable cliches and some effects have dated. Still, quite well done. Directed by Alan Gibson, written by Don Houghton. Caroline Munro, Marsha Hunt, Philip Miller, Michael Kitchen, Christopher Neame. (Japanese laser: Warner Bros.)

DRACULA AGAINST FRANKENSTEIN. See **DRACULA VS. DR. FRANKENSTEIN.**

DRACULA AND SON (1976). Mixture of horror, comedy and political polemic: The Communists ruling Transylvania feel vampires are bad for the party's image, so Dracula and son are exiled to England, where the film community welcomes them as stars. But talk about typecasting: the boys are hired to play cinema vampires. Directed by Eduardo Molinaro. Christopher Lee, Bernard Menez, Raymond Bussieres, Anna Gael. (Goodtimes)

DRACULA AND THE SEVEN GOLDEN VAMPIRES. See **LEGEND OF THE SEVEN GOLDEN VAMPIRES, THE.**

DRACULA BLOWS HIS COOL (1979). West German softcore sex comedy in which an ancestor of Dracula (Gianni Garko, who doubles as Count Stanislaus) turns up as a photographer, shooting sexy models against the eerie setting. Plenty of undraped beauties and double entendre vampire-sex gags. The castle, for example, is called Van Screw. Directed by Carlo Ombra. Betty Verges, Giacomo Rizzo. (Luna)

DRACULA CHASES THE MINI GIRLS. See **DRACULA A.D. 1972.**

DRACULA CHELSEA '72. See **DRACULA AD 1972.**

DRACULA EXOTICA (1981). X-rated horror porn in which Jamie Gillis, as the vampire, sheds his cloak (and everything else) to put the bite on lesbian "twins" who are ready to kiss more than necks. Also known as LOVE AT FIRST GULP. Samantha Fox.

DRACULA/GARDEN OF EDEN, THE. Double bill of the silent classic **NOSFERATU** and **THE GARDEN OF EDEN.** (Critics' Choice)

DRACULA HAS RISEN FROM THE GRAVE (1968). Heavy (handed) use of religious symbolism earmarks this third film in Hammer's series to star Christopher Lee as the infamous count. In John Elder's script he is reduced to a one-dimensional vampire suggesting tons of evil but unsupported by a strong plot. Two priests climb to Castle Dracula to resurrect the antihero and control his bloodletting for purposes of revenge. A giant crucifix figures ludicrously in the blood-gushing climax. Many scenes were shot through a red filter to cast a sanguinary motif, but this technique, a poor choice by director Freddie Francis, calls attention to itself whenever the camera pans. The beauteous Veronica Carlson is an eyeful in her flimsy nightgowns. Rupert Davies, Barbara Ewing, Michael Ripper. Good music by James Bernard. (Japanese laser: Warner Bros.)

DRACULA IS DEAD AND WELL AND LIVING IN LONDON. See **COUNT DRACULA AND HIS VAMPIRE BRIDE.**

DRACULA—PRINCE OF DARKNESS (1965). After HORROR OF DRACULA, Christopher Lee refused to reappear as the Count for several years. This Anthony Nelson Keys-produced film, however, lured him back into the fold of the cape, so it is often referred to as the sequel to HORROR even though another Hammer feature, THE BRIDES OF DRACULA, was produced in 1960. Two English couples traveling through Transylvania spend the night at tyou-know-who's castle, where the bloodsucker is restored to life in a bizarre ceremony, a perversion on religious resurrection. Then old Drac goes after Barbara Shelley and Suzan Farmer to make them new "brides." One of the best films in the series, directed by Terence Fisher from a script by John Samson and Anthony Hinds writing as John Elder. Also known as DISCIPLE OF DRACULA, REVENGE OF DRACULA and THE BLOODY SCREAM OF DRACULA.

DRACULA, PRISONER OF FRANKENSTEIN. See **DRACULA VS DR. FRANKENSTEIN.**

DRACULA RISING (1992). Unusually ethereal, metaphysical vampire tale from producer Roger Corman, with Stacey Travis as a painter hired to restore old paintings in a European monestary where she is introduced to the ways of bloodsucking by vampire Vlad (handsome Christopher Atkins). With good location work under director Fred Gallo, and a literate script by Rodman Flender and Daniella Purcell, this comes off as one of Corman's better efforts. Doug Wert, Tara McCann. (New Horizon)

DRACULA'S CASTLE. Video version of **BLOOD OF DRACULA'S CASTLE.**

DRACULA'S DAUGHTER (1936). Vintage Universal production picks up where DRACULA left off—with Professor Van Helsing (again played by Edward Van Sloan) under arrest for murdering the Transylvanian Count (after all, he did drive a stake through the chap's cold, cold heart). Female offspring Gloria Holden goes on a new spree of murder. Let the name of Countess Marya Zaleska drip with blood! The film is okay as a time-killer but has none of the legendary proponents of its predecessor. Directed by Lambert Hillyer, scripted by Garrett Fort. Otto Kruger, Marguerite Churchill, Irving Pichel, Hedda Hopper, E.E. Clive. (MCA)

DRACULA'S DESIRE. See **MY SON, THE VAMPIRE.**

DRACULA'S DOG (1978). Nonclassic goes to the dogs with a howling-funny plot in which a Romanian tomb under Soviet guard is disturbed and a vampire slave (Reggie Nalder) escapes his coffin. Since the last descendant of Dracula now lives a normal life in L.A., the gnarly-faced entity, accompanied by the vampiric hound Zoltan, travels to America. The untainted Dracula (Michael Pataki) has taken his family on a vacation, so most of this cheap Albert Band-directed film takes place at a lake with the toady siccing devil dogs (the Baskerville variety, with blazing demonic eyes) on hapless humans. One harrowing sequence has Soviet policeman Mel Ferrer and Pataki trapped in a tiny one-room shack; another has Pataki trapped in his car that anticipates CUJO. Jan Shutan, Libbie Chase. (United; from Thorn EMI and VCI as **ZOLTAN—HOUND OF DRACULA**)

DRACULA'S GREAT LOVE (1973). Re-edited version of a Spanish film imitating the Hammer style. Hence, this has good set designs and costumes, but acting and storyline are as anemic as the victims of the old Count, four lovely senoritas hanging out in an abandoned sanitorium. Dubbing is listless, blood effects are heavily edited and plot sorely in need of a hero. Drac seeks a virgin so he can restore his "evil superiority" and allow his long-dead daughter to rise from her crypt. Paul Naschy is the fanged creature with a more gentle side than most vampires. The swell swelling bosoms belong to Rossana Yanni, Ingrid Garbo and Mista Miller. Also known as CEMETERY GIRLS, CEMETERY TRAMPS and DRACULA'S VIRGIN LOVERS. Written-directed by Javier Aguirre. (MPI; Gorgon; Sinister/C)

BELA LUGOSI IN THE CLASSIC 'DRACULA'

DRACULA'S LAST RITES (1980). Alucard is now in the cover-up business: He's the mortician in a town where folks don't catch on when you murder them by sucking their blood. Spell his name backwards (as they did in SON OF DRACULA) and you discover the nature of the walking dead around him. Also known as LAST RITES, something this film needed from the start. Written-directed by Dominic Paris. Patricia Lee Hammond, Gerald Fielding. (Paragon; Warner Bros.; Cannon)

DRACULA'S SAGA. See **SAGA OF DRACULA.**

DRACULA SUCKS (1978). Hardcore X-rated fare which we include here for "purists." Sex stars John Holmes, Serena, Seka and Annette Haven, while flitting around castle sets, demonstrate unabashedly that Dracula is interested in areas below the neck. Not for kiddies, obviously. Rereleased as LUST AT FIRST BITE. Also known as THE COMING OF DRACULA'S BRIDE. Directed by Philip Marshak. (Media; Unicorn)

DRACULA'S VIRGIN LOVERS. Video version of **DRACULA'S GREAT LOVE.**

DRACULA'S WIDOW (1988). That "Emmanuelle" gal, Sylvia Kristel, as a vampire named Vanessa, "the true wife of Dracula"? Just because Sylvia did a lot of sucking in some of her previous films was no reason to typecast the poor girl in this, a cheapie, creepy, sleepy little nothing movie. Her coffin is delivered to the Hollywood House of Wax where she begins a reign of terror, mesmerizing museum curator Lenny Von Dohlen, wiping out a devil cult and chasing after a descendant of Van Helsing (his grandson is now an L.A. antiques collector). The numerous murders are done without style or imagination, and Sylvia is really a terrible vampire, performing without charm or menace, and not even providing anything sexy to the part. Stephen Traxler, who gave us SLITHIS, was one of the producers. Written by Kathryn Ann Thomas and Christopher Coppola; Coppola also directed this undistinguished, ho hum affair. Josef Summer, Marc Coppola, Rachel Jones. (HBO)

DRACULA: THE BLOODLINE CONTINUES. Video of **SAGA OF DRACULA** (All Seasons).

DRACULA, THE DIRTY OLD MAN (1969). Sexploitation all the way—and they go all the way in depicting a scarlet-cloaked Dracula (Vince Kelly) with a lair of corpses and a newsman-turned-werewolf (Bill Whitton) who supplies female victims. Then Dracula and Wolfman have a falling out over the newsman's girlfriend (Ann Hollis), ending their relationship and all those orgiastic occasions. Written-directed by William Edwards. (S/Weird)

DRACULA, THE GREAT UNDEAD (1985). Recycled TV documentary hosted by Vincent Price, detailing the myths surrounding bloodsucking vampires. Strictly historical stuff with a few clips of Bela Lugosi. (Active; Videotakes; Facets Multimedia)

DRACULA: THE LOVE STORY. See **TO DIE FOR.**

DRACULA TODAY. See **DRACULA A.D. 1972.**

DRACULA VS. DR. FRANKENSTEIN (1972). Spanish-French concoction blending werewolves, vampires and beasties of the night. Written-directed by the indomitable Jesus Franco. Dennis Price plays the bad doctor badly, Howard Vernon plays the vampire vampily. Also called DRACULA, PRISONER OF FRANKENSTEIN. (From VCI as **SCREAMING DEAD, THE**; with subtitles as **EROTIC RITES OF FRANKENSTEIN**)

DRACULA VS. FRANKENSTEIN (1970). Video of **ASSIGNMENT TERROR** (United American).

DRACULA VS. FRANKENSTEIN (1971). Depressingly bad pastiche of Universal horror pictures of the '40s has a campy nostalgia, brought about by a cast that has gone to that great graveyard in the sky. Lon Chaney Jr. and J. Carrol Naish were in their declining, almost decrepit, years. The make-up is dreadful, the lighting amateurish and the music track horrendous, and yet one pines for these gallant scare-stalwarts of the screen. The ludicrous plot is a hodgepodge of creatures and motiveless actions Al Adamson directed in his shamelessly bad way. Forrest J. Ackerman has a bit role as a victim. Also known as TEENAGE DRACULA. Anthony Eisley, Regina Carol, Jim Davis, Zandor Vorkov, Russ Tamblyn. (VidAmerica; Sony; Super; from Duravision as **REVENGE OF DRACULA**)

DRAGONFIGHT (1990). Fascinating metaphor for the immoral behavior of corporations during the '80s, couched in metaphysical images and presented as a morality play within an action frame. In a futuristic society, corporations earn millions by staging gladiatorial contests. But fighter Falchion (Paul Coufos) rebels against the system, refusing to do battle in the Arizona desert with a bellowing warrior (Robert Z'Dar) named Lockaber. So Lockaber goes on a rampage, killing tourists while fleeing Falchion is befriended by ranger Charles Napier and desert rat George "Buck" Flower and his daughter. A mystical quality prevades over the desert footage. A sexy high priestess, who has power to rejuvenate Lockaber, gives the film another unusual push. Budd Lewis' script is never predictable and reveals a sense for sensitive characters. Director Warren Stevens balances these elements. Akexa Hamilton, Michael Pare, Joe Cortese, James Hong. (Warner Bros.)

DRAGON LADY. See **G.I. EXECUTIONER.**

DRAGON'S BLOOD, THE (1963). Magical sword is employed by the brave and loyal Siegried in his fight against a towering, fire-breathing dragon. Unfortunately, the plot is also draggin' and the dub job of this Italian tale of legendary knights is a drag. Directed by Giacomo Gentilomo. Rolf Tasna.

DRAGONSLAYER (1981). Outstanding fantasy-adventure capturing a sense of action, mystery, menace and magic, thanks to the doting care doled out by Matthew Robbins (director) and Hal Barwood (who co-scripted with Robbins). Effects master Dennis Muren pioneered new animation techniques in bringing to life a fire-breather named Vertithrax that flies and breathes fire. The tone is set by Ralph Richardson as the delightful sorcerer Ulrich, while Peter MacNichol as young hero Galen and Caitlin Clark as his maiden are suitably naive and venturesome. Baby dragons provide some of the best moments. Albert Salmi, Peter Eyre, John Hallam. Score by Alex North. (Paramount) (Laser: Columbia)

DRAGON ZOMBIES RETURN (1983). Hong Kong fantasy, directed by Hau Ching, finds a woman discovering the Heartbreak Sword in the Treasure Cavern of Heartbreak Gorge, which allows her to learn the secrets of Dragon Kung-Fu.

DR. ALIEN. Video version of **I WAS A TEENAGE SEX MUTANT** (Video/Laser: Paramount).

DR. BLACK AND MR. HYDE (1975). Black exploitationer with Bernie Casey (as Dr. Henry Pride) experimenting with the regeneration of dying cells in liver patients and finding a formula that turns him into an albino-white killer. He has a childhood phobia about prostitutes and kills the streetwalkers in Watts. This puzzles policeman Ji-Tu Cumbuka, who looks almost as tall and lean as the Watts Towers. A genre film needs an aura of entertaining fantasy, but director William Crain captures the drabness and squalor of Watts, inflicting depression rather than terror. Also known as THE WATTS MONSTER. Rosalind Cash, Stu Gilliam, Marie O'Henry. (VCI)

DR. BREEDLOVE OR HOW I LEARNED TO STOP WORRYING AND LOVE. See **KISS ME QUICK.**

DR. BUTCHER M.D. (MEDICAL DEVIATE) (1979). Originally QUEEN OF THE CANNIBALS, this spaghetti-scarer belongs to the "cannibal school" with its torture and mutilation. It's a mad-doctor-on-a- lonely-Pacific-island tale in which Donald O'Brian creates zombies while Alexandra delli Colli and Ian McCullough investigate. Flesh-munching and organ-ripping keep this lively in the hands of writer-director Frank Martin. AKA ZOMBIE HOLOCAUST and ISLAND OF THE LAST ZOMBIES. (Paragon; Thrillervideo) (Laser: Japanese)

DR. CADMAN'S SECRET. See **BLACK SLEEP.**

DR. CALIGARI (1989). The titular, tit-plated doc is granddaughter of the silent-screen Caligari, and she's so insane, running the Caligari Insane Asylum, that she's using folks for hormone experimentation. A stylish, campy film directed by Stephen (CAFE FLESH) Sayadian. Madeleine Renal, Laura Albert, Fox Harris. (Shapiro Glickenhaus) (Laser: Image)

DR. COOK'S GARDEN (1971). Superb psychochiller with Bing Crosby as a small-town physician who isn't operating with a full set of scalpels. He treats his patients like flowers in his garden—rooting out the sick to make way for the strong. Ted Post directed. Based on a play by Ira Levin. Blythe Danner, Frank Converse.

DR. COPPELIUS (1966). See editions 1-3.

DR. CYCLOPS (1940). Ernest B. Schoedsack, co-creator of KING KONG, returned to the genre with this tale of a mad scientist (Dr. Thorkel, played by Albert Dekker) who miniaturizes people to doll size. Unfortunately, the rear projection and matte shots are unimaginatively executed and the characters are stereotypes, including Dekker's unbalanced doc. Still, this has period charm and is one of the first features to use Technicolor for menacing effect. Janice Logan, Thomas Coley, Victor Killian, Frank Yaconelli. (Video/Laser: MCA)

DR. DEATH: SEEKER OF SOULS (1973). Need a soul for that dead body lying around the house? Just pick up the phone and call Dr. Death ("This is Dr. Death. I'm not in right now, but if you'll leave your name after the beep . . . "). All he has to do is make a house call, pop open the vial around his neck and instruct the wispy vapor that drifts out to enter the cadaver. John Considine is the physician; co-souls belong to Barry Coe, Florence Marley, Cheryl Miller, Jo Morrow and TV horror host Seymour. Directed-produced by Eddie Saeta. (Prism)

DR. DOOLITTLE (1967). Musical comedy based on Hugh Lofting's stories about a British veterinarian-surgeon who talks with animals in the kingdom of Puddlebyon-the-Marsh. Doolittle (Rex Harrison) ventures to the South Seas to find the Great Pink Sea Snail and talks to Polynesia the Parrot, Gub Gub the Pig, Jip the Dog, and Chi-Chi the Chimp. Screenwriter Leslie Bricusse also penned the sometimes-charmless music and lyrics for such numbers as "Talk to the Animals" (an Oscar winner). Herbert Ross did the choreography, which most critics considered limp. Director Richard Fleischer spent $18 million on this "talking dog." Samantha Eggar, Anthony Newley, Richard Attenborough. (CBS/Fox)

DR. DRACULA (1977). Re-edited version of SVENGALI, released in 1974 and later re-released as LUCIFER'S WOMEN. This has new footage by Al Adamson (featuring John Carradine) and was released to TV. See LUCIFER'S WOMEN for a review of the semi-porno as it existed in 1974. This blends devil cult hogwash with a vampire plot. Morgan Upton, Don Barry.

DREAM A LITTLE DREAM (1989). An intelligence and conviction is behind this fantasy-comedy, and an emotional ring in the dialogue sets it apart from other personality-transference movies, but the fantasy premise is so intellectualized this eventually loses its impetus. It's difficult to explain why the minds of aging Jason Robards and teenager Corey Feldman are merged, but how each faces life afterward provides the gist for this morality fable, with emphasis on Feldman's romance with lovely Meredith Salenger. Director Marc Rocco, who produced and co-wrote the script with Daniel Jay Franklin and co-proudcer D.E. Eisenberg, hired his dad, Alex Rocco, to play Feldman's dad. Piper Laurie, Harry Dean Stanton, Corey Haim, Susan Blakely. (Vestron) (Laser: Image)

DREAMANIAC (1986). Sleaz-iac quickie-sickie (made for video) about a heavy metal composer who heavily composes up a succubus to suck a bust or two at a sorority hash-brownies party. Amateurish production marked by buckets of unconvincing blood, tons of sex and nudity and tons of sex and nudity. The bare-skinned monotony and bad acting just won't quit. You will become a blithering screamaniac. Directed by David DeCoteau. Thomas Bern, Kim McKamy. (Wizard)

DREAMCHILD (1985). Alice Hargreaves, who inspired Lewis Carroll to write ALICE IN WONDERLAND, is portrayed by Carol Browne in this wonderful blend of realism and fantasy. In 1932 Hargreaves is invited to Columbia U to receive an honorary degree during a Carroll centenary. She relives her youth in a blend of nostalgic memories and hallucinatory dreams, imagining a tea party with the Mad Hatter and March Hare. Offbeat art picture for the erudite. Directed by Gavin Millar. Ian Holm. (Thorn/EMI)

DREAM DEMON (1988). Virgin Jemma Redgrave, presumably because she's fearful of sexually consummating her pending marriage, has terrifying nightmares, only the demons in them converge with the real world and gruesome, gory murders result. This British flicker has plenty of monsters and hideous make-up for shock lovers. Directed by Harley Cokliss.

DREAMER OF OZ, THE (1990). Warm TV-movie chronicling the life of L. Frank Baum, who wrote THE WONDERFUL WIZARD OF OZ and 13 other books about Dorothy in the magic land of the Emerald City. Richard Matheson's teleplay (from an idea by exec producer David Kirschner) shows the ups and downs of Baum's career and how he became a best-seller in his twilight years, writing fables that fascinated children and adults. This features excellent fantasy sequences with makeup by Craig Reardon and effects by Sam Nicholson. As Baum, John Ritter captures the boy trapped in a man's body, Annette O'Toole is good as his faithful wife and Rue McClanahan is amusing as Baum's mother-in-law. An enchanting, fascinating biodrama. Directed by Jack Bender. Charles Haid, David Schramm.

DREAMING, THE (1988). Slow-moving Australian shocker (make that mild shocker) in which doctor Penny Cook, after treating an aborigine who has defiled a sacred cave, is visited by weird dreams that leads to a 200-year-old mystery. Directed by Mario Andreacchio. Arthur Dignam, Gary Sweet. (Nova)

DREAM LOVER (1986). After Kristy McNichol undergoes a traumatic rape experience, in which she kills her assailant with a knife, she is so plagued by nightmares she seeks the help of dream researcher Ben Masters but only gets in deeper when her dreams become reality. Elements of this psycho-mystery are fascinating, but McNichol portrays the troubled woman with such coldness, one can never feel empathy for her. Directed by Alan J. Pakula. Paul Shenar, Justin Deas. (MGM/UA)

DREAM NO EVIL (1970). Half-baked ripoff of Robert Bloch's PSYCHO, and a hapless career moment for Edmond O'Brien, who portrays a farmer who rises from the autopsy table to kill undertaker Marc Lawrence by ripping open his back with a surgical knife. He also uses a scythe to dispense with an obese sheriff. O'Brien talks hellfire and brimstone with his nymphomaniac daughter (sexy Brooke Mills). Its pseudo-Freudian overtones are explained by hare-brained psychiatrist Arthur Franz. As for writer-director John Hayes, don't dream of seeing his "evil." (Active; Star Classics)

DREAMSCAPE (1984). Tightly honed script by David Loughery, Chuck Russell and director Joseph Ruben makes for an exciting excursion into the subconscious mind (the dreamscape) as telepathic subjects undergo dream testing. Psychic Dennis Quaid is hired by research scientists Max Von Sydow and Kate Capshaw to link with sleeping subjects and experience their nightmares. Christopher Plummer is a sinister government man who wants the dreamlink for assassination purposes, Eddie Albert is a U.S. President troubled by nuclear nightmares. Although Peter Kuran's effects are limited, they capture the spirit of bad dreams, especially in the form of a Snake Creature. Make-up specialist Craig Reardon contributes cadaverous faces. Fine music track by Maurice Jarre. (Video/Laser: HBO)

DREAMS COME TRUE (1985). "Soul traveling" is a psychic projection enjoyed by factory worker Michael Sanville and nurse Stephane Shuford, who leave drab lives to dine in Paris, visit a carnival, etc. From director Max Kalmanowicz (THE CHILDREN). (Media)

DREAM SLAYER. Video of **BLOOD SONG** (HQV).

DREAMS LOST, DREAMS FOUND (1987). Ballyhooed as a "Harlequin Romance," this tear-jerker is saved by Kathleen Quinlan as a widow who sells her San Francisco art gallery and moves to Scotland to buy a castle haunted by the spectre of a crying woman. Quinlan also meets a dashing lover (David Robb). William Corbett's script (based on a novel by Pamela Wallace) relies on the cliche of the romantic genre but does little with the haunted aspect—hence, this is of minimal interest to horror fans. Charles Gray lends support as Quinlan's friend. Colette O'Neil, Betsy Brantley. (Paramount)

DRESSED FOR DEATH. Video version of **STRAIGHT ON TILL MORNING** (Academy).

DRESSED TO KILL (1980). Lulu of a horror film from writer-director Brian De Palma—a macabre black joke as he follows sex-starved housewife Angie Dickinson to her death at the hands of a knife murderess in an unforgettable elevator sequence. More jolting surprises are in score when the murdered woman's son and a prostitute (Nancy Allen) join forces to track the killer. De Palma's direction is brilliant, the film opening and closing with erotic shower sequences. They don't make shockers better than this. Michael Caine, Keith Gordon. (Warner Bros.; Goodtimes) (Laser: Warner Bros.)

DR. FAUSTUS (1967). Richard Burton directed himself (with Nevill Coghill's help) in this British version of the Christopher Marlowe play filmed at Oxford. Guess what bosomy female he sells his soul to the Devil to possess. Elizabeth Taylor as Helen of Troy breathes deeply, almost falling out of her barely-existent costume. But is this art? (RCA/Columbia)

DR. FRANKEN (1980). Robert Vaughn, offspring of the creator of the Frankenstein Monster, is alive and well, thank you, in a Manhattan hospital, specializing in heart transplants. But in private he switches organs body to body. The theme of memory transference within the organs is another fillip to this TV-movie co-directed by Marvin J. Chomsky and Jeff Lieberman. Sometimes the theme is treated seriously, other times it depicts Vaughn's home-made "creature" shambling in a whimsical vein. Vaughn is in top form as the doc. Teri Garr is an innocent young woman. Robert Perault, David Selby.

DR. FRANKENSTEIN. See **FRANKENSTEIN: THE TRUE STORY.**

DR. FRANKENSTEIN ON CAMPUS. See **FRANKENSTEIN ON CAMPUS.**

DR. FRANKENSTEIN'S CASTLE OF FREAKS (1973). Boring Italian menagerie horror film that wastes Rossano Brazzi, Michael Dunn and Edmund Purdom. Same old hoary cliches as the evil doc creates freako anomalies with his Electric Accumulator. And dig the results: Goliath the Giant, Kreegin the Hunchback and Ook the Neanderthal Man. Directed by Robert H. Oliver. Only watchable things: busty lovelies who reveal their enormous breasts. (Magnum; Sinister/C)

DR. GIGGLES (1992). True-grue horror fans will find this a delightfully evil formula of slasher-movie gags brilliantly woven by director Manny Coto, who co-wrote the satirical script with Graeme Whifler. Larry Drake is hysterically macabre as a doctor who uses every instrument in his black bag to slaughter townspeople responsible for hanging his father. So what if dad was stealing the hearts of his patients—literally. Now dear Dr. Evan Rendell, his warped offspring, is stealing them and the body count is climbing! What makes this bloodbath so delightful are the tasteless doctor puns that punctuate (pardon that word) each murder. This is one of the funniest put-ons within the horror-film canon. Drake is over the top as the doctor who makes house calls—without being asked! If you want a second opinion, go ahead, but we urge you to see this. Now, open wide . . . Holly Marie Combs, Cliff De Young, Glenn Quinn. (Video/Laser:MCA)

LARRY DRAKE

DR. GOLDFOOT AND THE BIKINI MACHINE (1966). Comedy-mystery starring Vincent Price as the titular madman who plans world domination with lady robots, capable of seducing the average male. A hodgepodge of ideas and performers, directed by Norman Taurog and written by Elwood Ullman and Robert Kaufman. Followed by DR. GOLDFOOT AND THE GIRL BOMBS. Dwayne Hickman, Frankie Avalon, Fred Clark, Deborah Walley, Susan Hart, Annette Funicello. (AIP)

DR. GOLDFOOT AND THE GIRL BOMBS (1966). Vincent Price, that creator of robotic pulchritude, is back from DR. GOLDFOOT AND THE BIKINI MACHINE with a hot plot to start a war between major powers with his mass-produced androids—literal sexbombs set to explode while making love to military leaders. "Bomb" is the word for this indulgence in idiocy directed by Mario Bava. Fabian, Franco Franchi, Laura Antonelli.

DR. GORE. Video of **BODY SHOP** (United).

DR. HACKENSTEIN (1987). Quaint send-up of FRANKENSTEIN, directed with style by Richard Clark, who wrote the spoofy script. Hackenstein is a misguided scientist with no moral judgment, but he's still an amusing figure as he murders for assorted body parts to put his wife back together. Phyllis Diller appears as a complaining town socialite; Anne and Logan Ramsey are body snatchers in a black-comedy vein. The gore never is offensive as this pleasant comedy unfolds. David Muir, Stacey Travis, Catherine Davis Cox. (Forum; MCEG)

DR. HEKYLL AND MR. HYPE (1980). Incredibly unfunny-unsavory spoof of Stevenson's classic tale of schizophrenic personality, botched by writer-director Charles B. Griffith. Oliver Reed is awful as a podiatrist whose normal countenance is ugly, and who turns normal when his monstrous side surfaces. Switching the faces of good and evil might sound clever but it's presented as non sequiturs with stupid characters: the fragile, sexy young girl who thinks ugly Dr. Hekyll is beautiful; a crazed guy with a feather fetish, Dr. Who; detective Lt. Mac Druck (or "Il Topol"); dumb uniformed cop Sgt. Flea Collar (Jackie Coogan); and Flynn the trash-bin man (Dick Miller). The only decent feature about this flop is Richard Band's music and the only funny line is: "There's a vile, green, garbage-eating monster on the loose." Well, sort of funny. Corinne Calvert. (Paragon)

DRIFTER, THE (1988). Fashion designer Kim Delaney crossing the desert meets handsome Miles O'Keeffe and enjoys a sexual fling—a decision she later regrets when he romances her. Meanwhile, Delaney has troubles with boyfriend Timothy Bottoms who suspects her of infidelity and murder. Reversal of FATAL ATTRACTIONS is done with barren production values and without sharp characterizations. Writer-director Larry Brand fails to bring a ambience to the twisted relationships. Brand doubles as the cop working the case. (MGM/UA)

DRILLER KILLER (1979). Sickening gore-garbage about an artist who goes off the deep end and uses a carpentry drill to do in his foes. You could say this film is full of bit parts. And holes, especially in Nicholas St. John's script. The biggest "bore" of all turns out to be director Abel Ferrara, who doubles as killer. Carolyn Marz, Harry Schultz. (Wizard; Magnum)

DRIPPING DEEP RED. See **DEEP RED.**

DRIVE-IN MADNESS (1989). Anthology of horror trailers intermixed with interviews with genre film makers (George Romero, John Russo, Tom Savini) who describe the making of THE NIGHT OF THE LIVING DEAD. And Sam Sherman talks about SATAN'S SADISTS. Sexy heroines Linnea Quigley and Bobbie Bresee also appear. Written-produced-directed by Tim Ferrante. (Imagine)

DRIVE IN MASSACRE (1976). Producer-director Stuart Segall's tribute to the "passion pit" consists of two overweight cops looking for a killer who terrorizes moviegoers with a long sword, severing their heads from their bodies or piercing two bodies with a single thrust while they make out in a car. The Buck Flower-John Goff script is slow going, failing to achieve style. We can't even recommend that you see this at a drive in. Adam Lawrence, Jake Barnes. (Magnum) (Laser: Image)

DRIVING FORCE (1989). In a post-nuked world, bad guys called the Black Knights terrorize Sam J. Jones and other holocaust survivors. Cheapjack job directed by A.J. Prowse. Katherine Bach, Don Swayze. (Academy)

DRIVING ME CRAZY (1990). The Edsel of "fantasy car" movies—a shiftless mess that will drain your mental battery. German inventor Thomas Gottschalk (who speaks with a British accent) invents a car that runs on "tubular vegetables" and exceeds 200 mph. When this naive jerk arrives in L.A., mogul Dom De Luise steals the car and forces Gottschalk, his pal Billy Dee Williams and his girl Michelle Johnson to chase after him. But first the film runs out of gas and pistons a lot of comedians (Milton Berle, Morton Downey Jr., etc) through its hollow cylinders before breaking down. The jokes are flat—ach, it's a lemon. Steve Kanaly, James Tolkan, George Kennedy, Richard Moll. Directed without gas by Jon Turteltaub.

DR. JEKYLL AND MISS OSBOURNE (1981). Directed by Walerian Borowczyk. Patrick Magee, Udo Kier, Howard Vernon. (From Citadel as **BLOODLUST**)

DR. JEKYLL AND MR. BLOOD. See **MAN WITH TWO HEADS, THE.**

DR. JEKYLL AND MR. HYDE (1920). Silent-screen classic (and the first version of Stevenson's novel) with John Barrymore as the well-intended doctor who tampers with science to create a monster within himself. A tour de force for Barrymore, who underwent the transformations without the aid of trick photography or make-up. Directed by John S. Robertson. Nita Naldi, Brandon Hurst. (Kino; Viking; Republic; Sinister/C; Moore)

DR. JEKYLL AND MR. HYDE (1932). Rouben Mamoulian's direction and the acting of Fredric March and Miriam Hopkins have held up well over the years, making this an endurable film version of Stevenson's oft-abused narrative. The Samuel Hoffenstein-Percy Heath script is unusually adult. As the split personality, March underwent on-camera transfigurations achieved with special lenses and unique make-up by Wally Westmore. Hopkins as the prostitute is extremely seductive and her smouldering sensuality is wonderful to behold. March won an Oscar for his performance, but it is the whole that is greater than any part. Rose Hobart, Holmes Herbert, Edgar Norton. (Video/Laser: MGM/Turner)

DR. JEKYLL AND MR. HYDE (1941). MGM's version of the Stevenson horror classic, with Spencer Tracy in the dual role as the doctor whose evil side surfaces while taking a drug that by today's standards would be "hallucinogenic." While its production standards are high, and its cast includes Ingrid Bergman, Donald Crisp, Lana Turner and Ian Hunter, it lacks the impact of the 1932 version. Still, it's worth seeing. Victor Fleming directed the John Lee Mahin script. Barton MacLane, C. Aubrey Smith, Sara Allgood. (Video/Laser: MGM/UA)

DR. JEKYLL AND MR. HYDE (1968). TV-movie version of Stevenson's classic tale of dual identity, with Jack Palance delivering a tour de force performance. (IVE)

DR. JEKYLL AND MR. HYDE (1973). A musical of the Stevenson classic? With Kirk Douglas as the schizophrenic doctor? From a major TV network? What's the world of horror coming to? But what a cast! Susan George, Stanley Holloway, Michael Redgrave, Donald Pleasence. David Winter directed. (Sony) (Laser: Image)

DR. JEKYLL AND SISTER HYDE (1972). Bizarre variation on the Jekyll-Hyde theme: Instead of a good man metamorphosizing into a bad man, a good man metamorphosizes into a bad woman. This turnabout is considered fair play in Brian Clemens' script. Ralph Bates is the doctor, Martine Beswick his counterpart. Directed by Roy Ward Baker. (HBO; Republic)

DR. JEKYLL AND THE WEREWOLF. Video of **DR. JEKYLL AND THE WOLFMAN** (Sinister/C)

DR. JEKYLL AND THE WOLFMAN (1971). Spanish sequel to MARK OF THE WOLFMAN with Paul Naschy as the hirsute hanger-on (returning for the sixth time in this series). Directed by Leon Klimovsky, scripted by Jacinto Molina. (From Sinister/C as **DR. JEKYLL AND THE WEREWOLF,** from S/Weird as **DR. JEKYLL VS. THE WOLFMAN,** from Filmfax as **DR. JEKYLL VS. THE WEREWOLF**)

DR. JEKYLL'S DUNGEON OF DARKNESS. See **DR. JEKYLL'S DUNGEON OF DEATH.**

DR. JEKYLL'S DUNGEON OF DEATH (1979). Great-grandson of Dr. Jekyll-Mr. Hyde has a serum that transforms criminals into martial-arts battlers. Unwieldy mixture of genres from San Francisco producer-director James Wood. Writer James Mathers stars as Jekyll, and Wood did his own lighting, music and sound. Threadbare, stretched as thin as Wood himself. John Kearnery, Tom Nicholson. Also known as DR. JEKYLL'S DUNGEON OF DARKNESS. (Wizard; Magnum; Genesis)

DR. JEKYLL'S MISTRESS. See **DR. ORLOFF'S MONSTER.**

DR. M (1959). See **BLACK PIT OF DR. M, THE.**

DR. M (1989). See **CLUB EXTINCTION.**

DR. MABUSE, THE GAMBLER (1922). Fritz Lang's earliest depiction of Norbert Jacques' supervillain, a mathematical genius who turns his creativity to evil with murderers, rapists, thieves and counterfeiters engaged in bringing about social upheaval. The architectural madman (Rudolph Klein-Rogge) assumes disguises (banker, psychiatrist, gambler, drunken sailor) to flood the economy with fake money. In 1933 Lang produced a sound version, THE TESTAMENT OF DR. MABUSE, followed in the '60s with a series of German productions, the first of which (THE THOUSAND EYES OF DR. MABUSE) was directed by Lang. Followed by THE RETURN OF DR. MABUSE, DR. MABUSE VS. SCOTLAND YARD and THE SECRET OF DR. MABUSE. (Embassy; Sinister/C; Nostalgia; Moore)

DR. MABUSE VS. SCOTLAND YARD (1964). German madman, out to conquer the world, just might pull it off this time. No matter that Mabuse is dead. He returns to life and takes possession of an invention that turns citizens into killers and conquerers. This German production, directed by Paul May, was part of a series that gave rebirth to Norbert Jacques' archvillain, first popularized by Fritz Lang in the '20s. Peter Van Eyck, Klaus Kinski. (Video Yesteryear; Sinister/C; S/Weird; Filmfax)

DR. MABUSE'S RAYS OF DEATH. See **SECRET OF DR. MABUSE, THE.**

DR. MANIAC. See **MAN WHO LIVED AGAIN.**

DR. MORDRID: MASTER OF THE UNKNOWN (1992). Subdued, sometimes sublime fantasy co-directed by producer Charles Band and his father Albert, depicting a wizard (Jeffrey Combs) who stands guard over the gateway "between our world and darkness" in his Manhattan apartment. His only companion is the raven Edgar Allan. Brian Thompson is Dr. Mordris' nemesis, Kabal, but the battles they fight are tame (a few lightning bolts, a few magical tricks) and the payoff a bit disappointing. Emphasis is more on criminologist Yvette Nipar, who lives in Dr. Mordrid's building and helps him on the earthly plane. The highpoint of C. Courtney Joyner's script is Dave Allen's stop-motion animation of two dinosaur skeletons battling in a museum. Jay Acovone, Ritch Brinkley, Keith Coulouris. Features a moody score by Richard Band. (Paramount)

DR. NO (1963). Granddaddy of the superspy films—first in the James Bond (Agent 007) series. The suave, cold-blooded British spy was created in popular novels by ex-British intelligence agent Ian Fleming, and these early films produced by Harry Saltzman and Albert R. Broccoli have slick, tongue-in-cheek action with glittering gadgets, superweapons and abundant female pulchritude. In his screen debut, 007 battles SPECTRE, a gang of terrorists headed by Dr. No, a mastercriminal operating an underwater city off Jamaica. Sean Connery is slick with the femme fatales, yet ruthless with his Baretta, shooting a man in cold blood, or coolly watching enemies die in fiery traps. Terence Young's stylish direction set the standard. Ursula Andress is provocative as Honey, bikini-clad adventuress; Joseph Wiseman is slimy-great as the evil Dr. No; Jack Lord is contact agent Felix Leiter. Bernard Lee and Lois Maxwell bow as assignment chief M and his secretary, Miss Moneypenny. (CBS/Fox) (Laser: MGM/UA)

SEAN CONNERY

DROP DEAD FRED (1990). Phoebe Cates' imaginary childhood playmate Drop Dead Fred comes back to haunt her during adulthood in the form of Rik Mayall. Red-headed, wild-buoffant Fred (only Phoebe can see him) is a crazy BEETLEJUICE-style character who behaves like a Warner Bros. cartoon character, smoke drifting out of his ears and his eyeballs bulging while helping Phoebe handle her problems, which include a philandering husband and a bossy mom. The zany antics wear thin and it's the cast (Marsha Mason, Tim Matheson, Carrie Fisher) that keeps the premise afloat. Ate de Jong (a pseudonym?) directed. (IVE) (Laser: Pioneer)

DROPS OF BLOOD. See **MILL OF THE STONE WOMEN.**

DR. ORLOFF'S INVISIBLE HORROR (1972). Evil scientist Howard Vernon is at it again, creating an invisible ape-man. (Sinister/C; S/Weird; Filmfax)

DR. ORLOFF'S MONSTER (1964). An evil scientist creates a stalking hulk of abominable mankind, putrescent of flesh, hideous of countenance. Spanish/Austrian sequel to THE AWFUL MR. ORLOF (notice how one "f" got lost in translation, along with coherence) was written-directed by Jesse Franco. AKA THE SECRET OF DR. ORLOFF, THE BRIDES OF DR. JEKYLL and DR. JEKYLL'S MISTRESS. Agnes Spaak, Hugh White, Jose Rubio. (Sinister/C; S/Weird; Filmfax)

DR. OTTO AND THE RIDDLE OF THE GLOOM BEAM (1986). Spy comedy with superagent Jim Varney (in five roles: Dr. Otto, Rudd Hardtact, Laughin' Jack, Guy Dandy, Auntie Nelda) out to stop a doctor from conquering the world. Juvenile jokes, amateurish action. Directed by John Cherry. (KnoWhutimean)

DR. PHIBES RISES AGAIN (1972). Sequel to THE ABOMINABLE DR. PHIBES with Vincent Price (under the direction of Robert Fuest, who co-wrote the imaginative script with Rorbert Blees) again on a rampage, seeking an eternal elixir in Egypt to restore his long-dead wife to life. Robert Quarry (Count Yorga) isn't the best hero material but he works overtime to outwit the devious Phibes. More macabre murders, each attempting to top the last in grisliness. Valli Kemp plays Vulnavia. Hugh Griffith, Terry-Thomas, Beryl Reid, Fiona Lewis, Peter Cushing. (Vestron) (Laser: Image)

VINCENT PRICE

DR. RENAULT'S SECRET (1942). Scientist George Zucco wants to make a man out of a monkey. The idea sounds cliche but, with all due respect, this low-budget Fox release has ample suspense and a fine cast: J. Carrol Naish, Sheppard Strudwick, Mike Mazurki, Jack Norton. It's quick (58 minutes), leaving you scant time to consider the absurdities. Harry Lachman directed.

DR. SATAN (1966). No-calorie Mexican junkfood; voodoo vapidity directed by Miguel Morayta. Also known as DR. SATAN AND THE BLACK MAGIC.**DR. SATAN'S ROBOT (1940).** Feature version of **MYSTERIOUS DR. SATAN, THE** (Video Connection).

DR. SEUSS' 5000 FINGERS OF DR. T. Video version of **5000 FINGERS OF DR. T, THE.**

DR. SEX (1960). Oddball item from director Ted V. Mikels with ample nudity and suggested sex as three sexologists describe their goofiest cases. (S/Weird)

DR. STRANGE (1978). TV-pilot based on the Marvel comic-book character created by Steve Ditko and Stan Lee. Dr. Peter Strange (Peter Hooten), a prominent surgeon, gives up his practice after an accident and joins force with "The Ancient One," a practitioner of white magic (John Mills) who teaches him how to use supernatural forces against evil. Jessica Walter portrays his antagonist, Morgan Le Fay, Queen of the Sorcerers. Philip DeGuere wrote-directed. Clyde Kusatsu, Eddie Benton, Philip Sterling, Sarah Rush. (MCA)

DR. STRANGELOVE, OR HOW I LEARNED TO STOP WORRYING AND LOVE THE BOMB (1964). Director Stanley Kubrick's masterpiece, a tour de force of black comedy. By accident, SAC dispatches planes armed with H-bombs against Russia; one plane in the flotilla is piloted by Major King Kong (Slim Pickens), determined to deliver his payload on Moscow. Back in the states a military uprising is headed by Col. Jack D. Ripper (Sterling Hayden), who believes our water supply has been poisoned by Russians, and General Turgidson (George C. Scott) thinks we can survive despite millions of dead; hell, let the bomb drop. Peter Sellers is in three roles—as President Muffey (who calls the Soviets on the Hot Line, with hilarious results), as Captain Mandrake (a Briton putting down the uprising) and as Dr. Strangelove, an ex-Nazi inventor confined to a wheelchair. An iconoclastic, irreverent statement on our idiotic attitudes toward nuclear weapons; on the muddled thinking of the military; on our race to destruction. The brilliantly original script is by Kubrick, Terry Southern and Peter George. Keenan Wynn (as Colonel Bat Guano), Tracy Reed, James Earl Jones. (Video/Laser: RCA/Columbia)

DR. SYN (1937). This lacks a sense of supernatural horror under director Roy William Neill when skeleton figures on horseback terrorize a British village in the 18th Century. Certainly it has none of the spectral images in the 1962 Hammer remake, NIGHT CREATURES. It's the Russell Thorndyke tale about the evil Captain Clegg (swashbuckled by George Arliss) posing as a minister, but coming to terms for his actions when his daughter is desired by one villager too many. Margaret Lockwood, John Loder. (Video Yesteryear; Moore; Cable)

DR. SYN. See **NIGHT CREATURES.**

DR. SYN, ALIAS THE SCARECROW (1964). Re-edited version of a Walt Disney TV-movie that retells Russell Thorndyke's famous story about evil Captian Clegg and how his skeleton riders terrorize a British village. Patrick McGoohan, George Cole, Michael Hordern. Directed by James Nielsen. (Disney)

DR. TARR'S PIT OF HORRORS. Video version of **DR. TARR'S TORTURE DUNGEON** (Electra).

DR. TARR'S TORTURE DUNGEON (1972). Alleged adaptation of Poe's "The System of Dr. Tarr and Professor Fether," directed in Mexico by Juan Lopez Moctezuma. But don't believe for a moment this is faithful to Poe. Avoid it like the Red Death; tell-tale signs of no heart. Call it Moctezuma's Revenge. (Magnum)

DR. TERROR'S GALLERY OF HORRORS. Video version of **RETURN FROM THE PAST** (Ingram).

DR. TERROR'S HOUSE OF HORRORS (1943). See second/third editions.

DR. TERROR'S HOUSE OF HORRORS (1965). Amicus anthology with Peter Cushing as an uncanny tarot-card reader who confronts five passengers aboard a speeding train and "reads" their futures. Hence, five tales: Art critic Christopher Lee is pursued by a beast with five fingers; Roy Castle is haunted by a voodoo curse; Neil McCallum wishes he hadn't when he wrestles with a werewolf; Alan Freeman is attacked by a peculiar vine plant; and Donald Sutherland sharpens his stake for a vampiric kill. The framework aboard the train provides one final, fatal twist. Directed by Freddie Francis, scripted by Milton Subotsky. Max Adrian, Peter Madden, Katy Wild, Michael Gough, Jennifer Jayne. (Republic)

DRUMS OF JEOPARDY (1931). A strange power in native drums exerts control on others. Warner Oland, June Collyer, Mischa Auer. Directed by George B. Seitz. (Sinister/C; Nostaliga; Discount; Filmfax)

DRUMS OF THE JUNGLE. See **OUANGA.**

DRUMS O'VOODOO (1934). Long-lost voodoo thriller based on a J. Augustus Smith play, LOUISIANA, featuring Smith and the Broadway black cast: Laura Bowman, Gus Smith, Morris McKenny. Hagar, a voodoo priestess, holds sway over a superstitious community in the swamp country. (Sinister/C; Filmfax)

DR. WHO. Fox has several British TV episodes: DR. WHO: DEATH TO THE DALEKS; DR. WHO: PYRAMIDS OF MARS; DR. WHO: SPEARHEAD FROM SPACE, DR. WHO: TERROR OF THE ZYGONS; DR. WHO: THE ARK IN SPACE; DR. WHO: THE SEEDS OF

DEATH; DR. WHO: THE TALONS OF WENG-CHIANG; DR. WHO: THE TIME WARRIOR. Playhouse has DR. WHO: THE DAY OF THE DALEKS; DR. WHO: THE DEADLY ASSASSIN; DR. WHO: PYRAMIDS OF MARS; DR. WHO: THE FIVE DOCTORS.

DR. WHO AND THE DALEKS (1965). DR. WHO remains a popular British sci-fi TV series in America; this feature version is aimed at the same youthful, fantasy-oriented audience. As the kindly inventor, Peter Cushing journeys forward in time to a planet where the good Thals fight off the evil Daleks, strange beings who wear metallic coverings to keep out lethal radiation. Directed by Gordon Flemying, scripted by producers Milton Subotsky and Max J. Rosenberg. Jennie Linden, Roy Castle, Robert Tovey, Geoffrey Toone. (Thorn EMI; Goodtimes)

DUCK SOUP (1932). Beefy broth, bubbling with zaniness and flowing nonstop from the Hollywood kettle of the zesty Marx Brothers. Rufus T. Firefly (Groucho) is the ruler of the kingdom of Freedonia, and there is no end to the political-military satire, slapstick, and double entendres. Directed by Leo McCarey. Margaret Dumont, Louis Calhern, Charles Middleton. (Video/Lasr: MCA)

DUCKTALES: THE MOVIE—TREASURE OF THE LOST LAMP (1990). Fantasy adventure in the style of the Indiana Jones movies. Scrooge McDuck (voice by Alan Young) takes his nephews (voices by Russi Taylor) to Egypt to find a pyramid that houses a seemingly unimportant lamp. Of course, out pops a wish-granting genie (voice by comedian Rip Taylor). Out to get the magical lamp back is evil shape-changer Merlock (voice by Christopher Lloyd). Loads of fun, the animation rich in texture and color. (Video/Laser: Disney)

DUDES (1987). When three New York punkers (Jon Cryer, Daniel Roebuck and Flea) head for a better life in L.A., they are attacked by sadists in Montana. Seeing their pal murdered, two of them mysteriously take on the persona of western heroes to wreak revenge: One becomes a gunslinger, the other a wild Indian. The mythos of the Old West turns DUDES into a neo-Western, with J. Randal Johnson's script never clear why the mystical elements are occurring, and director Penelope Spheeris never making up her mind if this is a comedy about myth, or a violent revenge movie. Catherine Mary Stewart, Lee Ving. (IVE) (Laser: Image)

DUEL (1971). Although this appears to be a non-fantasy suspense TV-movie about a motorist (Dennis Weaver) pursued by an insane trucker, director Steven Spielberg never allows the homicidal driver to be seen and the semi takes on an evil personification, sliding into the realm of THE TWILIGHT ZONE. Weaver's building sense of terror and the cat-and-mouse tactics of the trucker build to a nerve-wracking climax of action and menace. Richard Matheson's script (from his short story) functions on several levels, but viewed just as a shocker, it's a pip. First made for TV, this was released abroad in a longer version, now available to TV. (MCA)

DUEL IN SPACE. Edited episodes of TV's **ROCKY JONES, SPACE RANGER.**

DUEL OF THE GARGANTUAS. See **WAR OF THE GARGANTUAS.**

DUEL OF THE SPACE MONSTERS. See **FRANKENSTEIN MEETS THE SPACE MONSTER.**

DUMBO (1941). Walt Disney's full-length cartoon about the baby elephant who joins a circus and learns to fly by flapping its floppy ears is a visual delight, a high point in animation. Based on the book by Helen Aberson and Harold Pearl. Voices by Sterling Holloway and Verna Felton. (Video/Laser: Disney)

DUNE (1984). Long-awaited version of Frank Herbert's classic novel is a complicated, disappointing Dino de Laurentiis film. David Lynch seems incapable of bringing cohesiveness to his script or direction. The story desperately needs humor and levity to contrast the bleakness of Lynch's unrelenting sobriety. Plot: Everyone needs the planet Dune for a spice from its sands that enables a race of mutants to provide astral space travel to migrating alien cultures. Protecting the spices are worm creatures with mystical links to mankind. DUNE is the story of a Messiah who leads the people of Dune out of bondage. The Messiah is Kyle MacLachlan; Kenneth McMillan is the hated Baron Harkonnen, whose corpulent body floats in astral projection; Jose Ferrer is Emperor Shaddam IV; Linda Hunt is Shadout Mapes (a wasted role); Silvana Mangano is Rev. Mother Ramallo; Sting is Feyd Rautha; Max Von Sydow is Dr. Kynes. And on and on, just like this 140-minute movie. DUNE is all grit, no substance. This was recut in a longer version and rereleased to TV. (Video/Laser: MCA)

DUNE WARRIORS (1992). This imitation of ROAD WARRIOR is also a remake of THE MAGNIFICENT SEVEN without the magnificence. Set in New California in 2040 A.D., Roger Corman's production pits roving Samurai warrior David Carradine against bad guy Luke Askew, who pillages the countryside with bandits. Jillian McWhirter commissions Carradine and good-hearted mercenaries to defend her village. The fighting, while well-staged, is overloaded with mock heroics and doesn't make up for the poor writing by T.C. McKelvey. Produced-directed in the Philippines by an old hand at this MAD MAX nonsense, Cirio H. Santiago. Rick Hill, Blake Boyd, Val Garay. (Video/Laser: RCA/Columbia)

DUNGEONMASTER (1985). Purveyors of sword-and-sorcery computer games will find this tedious going—as much fun as watching an Apple or Atari crashing. Charles Band's production overinvests in effects without a plot to support its gross-outs. Hence, hero and heroine are swept from adventure to adventure with a disregard for logic, undergoing seven encounters to reach . . . what? It's a ripoff of role-playing without the psychological undercurrents of role-playing. The script by Allen Actor provides ill-defined roles for swashbuckling Jeffrey Byron, tied-to-the-stake heroine Leslie Wing and scenery-chewing Richard Moll as Mestema, a minion of the Devil. Seven directors are credited with the stew: Rosemarie Turko handled "Ice Gallery"; John Buechler was responsible for ""Demon of the Dead"; David Allen helmed "Grand Canyon Giant"; Stephen Ford carved a name for himself with "Slasher"; Peter Manoogian caved in to do "The Cave Beast"; Ted Nicolaou megaphoned "Desert Pursuit"; and Band provided the wraparound stuff. Buechler also designed the make-up. Also known as

SPECIAL EFFECTS MAN JOHN BUECHLER

SCROOGE McDUCK and the nephews (Huey, Dewey, Louie) tangle with Merlock the evil wizard in 'Ducktales the Movie —Treasure of the Lost Lamp,' a spinoff from the popular TV series 'Duck Tales'

RAGEWAR. (Lightning) (Laser: Vestron)

DUNGEON OF HARROW. Video version of **DUNGEON OF HORROR** (Sinister/C; S/Weird).

DUNGEON OF HORROR (1962). Low-budget Texas quickie in which a sadistic count lives in a creepy castle with crazy family members. The survivor of a shipwreck falls into his clutches. Directed by Pat Boyette. Russ Harvey, Lee Morgan. (From Sinister/C, S/Weird and Filmfax as **DUNGEON OF HARROW**)

DUNGEONS AND DRAGONS. Video of **RONA JAFFE'S MAZES AND MONSTERS** (Showtime).

DUNWICH HORROR, THE (1969). Producers have major difficulties adapting the cosmic horror tales of H. P. Lovecraft, as evidenced by this fiasco with Dean Stockwell and Sandra Dee (voted the girl least likely to succeed in a horror film role) as students at Miskatonic University. Someone has lifted the infamous Necronomicon volume from the campus library and is using its incantations to summon "The Old Ones" (ancient, banished gods of pure evil) from another dimension during orgiastic, satanic rites. Sounds like pure Lovecraft, but this remains far from the Arkham territory H.P. so vividly explored in his literate, blood-chilling tales. Directed by Daniel Haller. Les Baxter's music is the best thing in this James H. Nicholson-Samuel Z. Arkoff production. Ed Begley, Sam Jaffe, Lloyd Bochner. (Embassy)

DUPLICATES (1992). Well-produced TV-movie depicting how Gregory Harrison and wife Kim Greist, while searching for their missing son and her missing brother, stumble across a government-sponsored brainwashing program conducted by doctors Kevin McCarthy and Cicely Tyson. Honorable intentions (to replace the criminal mind with a clean one) are being subverted to create secret assassins and Harrison and Greist become victims of mind-controlling experiments. Director Sandor Stern, who co-wrote the script with Andrew Neiderman, provides clever twists to familiar material. Lane Smith, William Lucking, Scott Hoxby. (Paramount)

DUST DEVIL (1992). Pretentious and heavyhanded as it is, this is an unusual film told by an unseen narrator as a South African folk tale about a supernatural spirit, a "wind from nowhere," that wanders the earth as a "black magician, a shape shifter, gaining power through the ritual of murder." That evil entity in human form is Robert Burke, who commits his ritualistic murders with a knife and takes a finger from each victim. His newest "intended" is an unhappy wife (Chelsea Field) fleeing a bad marriage with her upset husband in pursuit. Zakes Mokae makes for an unusual black detective on the trail of the Dust Devil. Weird African symbolism, music and sound effects are used by writer-director Richard (HARDWARE) Stanley, who stresses mood and ambience more than plot. Shot in Manibia. John Matshikiza, Rufus Swart, William Hootkins, Marianne Sagebrecht. (Paramount)

DYBBUK, THE (1938). Polish classic of the surreal directed by Michal Waszynski, based on a famous play by S. Ansky. Newly restored in 1989, the story concerns a woman stricken by an evil spirit; she's taken to an exorcist with tragic results. Abraham Morewski, Isaac Samberg. (International Heroic; Facets Multimedia)

DYBBUK, THE (1982). See editions 1-3.

DYING TO REMEMBER (1993). Fashion designer Melissa Gilbert is plagued by nightmares from her previous life—or so her psychiatrist tells her—in this modest reincarnation thriller set in San Francisco. You'll be smarter than Gilbert in solving the 1963 murder case she finds herself tracking with the help of two cops and a real-estate developer. Directed by Arthur Allan Seidelman. Scott Plank, Jay Robinson, Ted Shackelford. (Paramount)

DYING TRUTH (1984). David Carradine enjoys a double role in this TV-movie produced by Hammer for British TV. He plays a photographer vacationing with wife Stephanie Beacham at a coastside hotel, and a man from the future who predicts things to come. Directed by John Hough. Originally entitled A DISTANT SCREAM. Stephen Chase, Fanny Carby. (Cornerstone)

DYNASTY OF FEAR. Video version of **FEAR IN THE NIGHT** (1973) (Magnum; Academy; HBO).

"Every man dreams of being well hung and that fantasy is about to come true for [Prisoner] #1768 with the new Ponderosa model 4000-pound test-strength rope from the Yankem High Rope Shop of Gallows, Montana. And the noose was especially handbound and braided by our friends over at Knotts Landing. It's all yours compliments of 'Live or Die.' Total value . . . Your life!"

—Announcer Don Stewart in **DEATHROW GAMESHOW**

EARTH ANGEL (1991). Insipid, uninspired variation on the saintly story of an angel returned to Earth to fulfill a mission. Intended as a TV pilot, this unheavenly mass is a mess—with Cindy Williams as a pom-pom girl who ends up in heaven where her mentor is former teacher Roddy McDowall. Director Joe Napolitano loves busty girls, and this is full of them, including Ms Williams in form-hugging dresses. Mark Hamill, Cathy Podewell, Rainbow Harvest, Erik Estrada, Alan Young.

EARTHBOUND (1940). See editions 1-3.

EARTHBOUND (1981). Disabled alien spacecraft lands near Gold Rush, where dumb sheriff John Schuck and even dumber deputy Stuart Pankin can't control the crowd when word gets out E.T.s have invaded Earth. It's actually a benevolent humanoid family (led by parents Christopher Connelly and Meredith MacRae) seeking the help of grandfather Burl Ives and his grandson Todd Porter. Hot on their trail is Joseph Campanella as a government guy plotting betrayal of the aliens. Directed witlessly by James L. Conway.

EARTH DEFENSE FORCE. See **MYSTERIANS.**

EARTH DIES SCREAMING (1964). U.S.-British sci-fi thriller with walking zombies for added flavor. Test pilot Willard Parker discovers a handful of Earthlings has survived an apocalyptic attack perpetrated by robots roving the devastated landscape. Parker seeks the power source that will destroy the invaders. Virginia Field, Dennis Price. Directed by Terence Fisher. (Shock)

EARTH GIRLS ARE EASY (1990). A goofy pop-bop sci-fi comedy-parody with the odd look of a Day-glo Buck Rogers comic strip. Three dumb space jockies (Jeff Goldblum, Jim Carrey, Damon Wayans) from another planet crashland into the swimming pool of Valley Girl Geena Davis and go on a spree to experience the L.A. life style, love and sex. This odball comedy features dance numbers well staged by director Julien Temple and satiric slaps at social mores. Although an eccentric burlesque, it's a fetching concoction, refreshing and funny in a dumb way. Charles Rocket and Michael McKean co-star. (Video/Laser: Vestron)

EARTHQUAKE (1974). In the immediate future, L.A. is devastated by a killer quake, which this Universal special-effects disaster epic depicts in microscopic detail. Albert Whitlock's matte work is outstanding, and all the falling glass, bricks and debris are so realistic you'll feel crushed. Where the film falters, under Mark Robson's direction, is in cliched characters and situations conceived by writers Mario Puzo and George Fox. Charlton Heston, Ava Gardner, Lorne Greene, George Kennedy, Richard Roundtree, Walter Matthau. (Video/Laser: MCA)

EARTH STAR VOYAGER (1988). Drawn-out Disney two-part TV pilot featuring teenage cadets on a space adventure in the next century. Ed Spielman's telescript tries to emulate STAR WARS but misses by a lightyear as the juvenile jockeys outmaneuver the evil commander (Peter Donat) tailing them through the void. Richard Edlund provided the less than spectacular effects, Lalo Schifrin's music drones on, and director James Goldstone is weightless, incapable of a single ounce of energy to set Duncan Regehr, Brian McNamara, Julia Montgomery, Jason Michaels and Tom Breznahan and Sean O'Byrne into motion.

EARTH II (1971). Space opera TV-movie (written by William Woodfield and Alan Balter; directed by Tom Gries) has superb effects but only a mediocre story. Gary Lockwood and Tony Franciosa operate a space station between Earth and the moon and must deactivate an unharnessed atomic bomb. Gary Merrill, Mariette Hartley, Lew Ayres, Scott Hylands, Hari Rhodes.

EARTH VS. THE FLYING SAUCERS (1956). Although Ray Harryhausen's stop-motion effects are blatant swipes from George Pal's WAR OF THE WORLDS, and this Columbia release directed by Fred F. Sears is hampered by a low budget, it's of historic importance for helping to keep '50s science fiction in the forefront, and for advancing special effects. The George Worthington Yates-Raymond T. Marcus script has Earth satellites being knocked out of the sky, followed by alien saucers staging a full-scale invasion against tourist attractions in Washington D.C. On the downside is Hugh Marlowe, miscast as a scientist-hero who forever slows down the already-lumbering plot to romance Joan Taylor. And just when the film needs original music, producer Sam Katzman throws themes swiped from other pictures. Still, it's a must-see. Harry Lauter, Morris Ankrum, Donald Curtis. (RCA/Columbia; Goodtimes) (Laser: Image)

EARTH VS. THE SPIDER. Video version of **SPIDER, THE** (RCA/Columbia).

EAST SIDE KIDS MEET BELA LUGOSI, THE. See **GHOSTS ON THE LOOSE.**

EAT AND RUN (1986). Dumb comedy-satire on sci-fi and legal-system movies, with the jokes falling as flat as tasteless food. Heavyset R. L. Ryan, portraying an alien dubbed Murray Creature, starts eating up Manhattan's Italian section when he develops a taste for human salami. Cop Ron Silver (deserving of better material) captures Ryan but is thwarted when a liberal judge (Sharon Schlarth), who happens to be his bedmate, is too lenient. Any attempt at satire is lost. Belch! (Starmaker)

EATEN ALIVE (1976). After THE TEXAS CHAINSAW MASSACRE, Tobe Hooper directed this sickening misfire (the ultimate underbelly of sleaze movies) with an utterly bananas Neville Brand running a dilapidated hotel (The Starlight) in the Louisiana swamp. Next door is a pit containing a hungry alligator who eats animals—and individuals. An unwatchable film (unless you're a hopeless sadist), especially when the beast is going to eat a little puppy. Mel Ferrer, Stuart Whitman, Carolyn Jones, Marilyn Burns. Aka DEATH TRAP, HORROR HOTEL MASSACRE, STARLIGHT SLAUGHTER. (Prism)

EATEN ALIVE (1980). From the warm-hearted sentimentalists who gave you MAKE THEM DIE SLOWLY comes this molar-moving cannibalistic tale of human flesh frying on the barbie. Italian director Umberto Lenzi provides a story involving a jungle cult that parallels the James Jones tragedy of 1978 and a woman seeking her lost sister in the jungles of New Guinea. Rather than satisfy your appetite it will undoubtedly grumble your stomach juices. Also known as EATEN ALIVE BY THE CANNIBALS. Ivan Rassimov, Mel Ferrer. (LD Video; from Continental as **EMERALD JUNGLE**)

EATING RAOUL (1982). Writer-director Paul Bartel concocted (with co-writer Richard Blackburn) this outre black comedy about Paul and Mary Bland (Bartel and Mary Woronov), an average L.A. couple who lure creeps into their home pretending to be swingers, when what they really want to do is kill the deviates for their money. Demurely, Mary seduces them and Paul bangs them—over the head with a skillet, with no visible damage to their moral sensitivities. A hilarious movie, great satire on the L.A. culture. Robert Beltran, Ed Begley Jr., Buck Henry, Garry Goodrow, Charles Griffith. (CBS/Fox)

EAT OR BE EATEN (1986). Video original from the Firesign Theater, a satirical parody of monster movies in which a "koodzoo" vine (whatever the hell that is) takes over a town. Phil Proctor, Peter Bergman. Directed by Phil Austin. (RCA/Columbia)

EBIRAH, TERROR OF THE DEEP. See **GODZILLA VS. THE SEA MONSTER.**

ECHOES (1983). Moody supernatural chiller directed by Arthur Allan Seidelman in New York City, capturing a Manhattan ambience that enhances this weird psychological tale of an artist (Richard Alfieri) haunted by dreams in which he is a once-famous Spanish painter befouled by love, passion and murder. Psychic Gale Sondergaard believes he is plagued by a "twin spirit" from another dimension, while mother Ruth Roman tells him about a miscarriage she had that might be responsible for an "unborn brother." Nathalie Nell, Mercedes MacCambridge, Michael Kellin. (VidAmerica)

ECOLOGY OF A CRIME. See **CARNAGE.**

ED AND HIS DEAD MOTHER (1993). After dear old mom is dead and buried, small-town hardware store owner Steve Buscemi can't adjust, and is ripe for an offer from a cryogenics pitchman (Ned Beatty) to resurrect her. But when she shows up, mom (Miriam Margolyes) has this strange need for human flesh. Wacky dark human directed by Jonathan Wacks. John Glover, Sam Jenkins, Rance Howard.

EDGAR ALLAN POE'S BURIED ALIVE. See **BURIED ALIVE** (1990).

EDGE OF HELL, THE (1989). The incompetence is complete and the ineptitude is exquisite in this amateurish horror flick that throws monsters and special effects at the audience. In an inexplicable turn of events the film segues from a slasher yarn, in which hard-rock musicians gather in a country estate to rehearse their act, into a religious parable in which Triton the Arch Angel squares off against Satan in the form of a beast. At no time do director John Fasano and writer Jon-Mikl Thor (who doubles as Triton) give any indication they are making a rollicking comedy. Jillian Peri, Frank Dietz. (Academy)

EDGE OF SANITY (1989). A must-see film for the overwrought performance of Anthony Perkins, who brings to Dr. Henry Jekyll (aka Jack Hyde) the madness that earmarks his deliveries in PSYCHO and CRIMES OF PASSION. Perkins is indeed on the "edge of sanity" in this foreign-produced R-rated thriller. And if Perkins also teeters on the edge of campiness, it still doesn't detract from this offbeat remake of the Stevenson classic, which throws in Jack the Ripper. Director Gerard Kikoine, known for pornie flicks, crosses into mainstream with a plethora of perversion and Victorian Era sex. Unfortunately, Kikoine's garish excesses (and depiction of sexy clothing styles too modern to belong here) eventually sicken and repel, with only Perkins' performance to bring one back to the fold. The perversity, mixed with many slashed throats, makes this for the strong of heart. Made in Hungary. Glynis Barber, Sarah Maur-Thorp, David Lodge. (Virgin Vision) (Laser: Image)

EDGE OF THE AXE (1989). Crazed madman carrying a long-handled wood-chopping, stump-smashing woodcutter's sharply-honed tool terrorizes hapless citzens of a rural community. Directed by Joseph Braunstein. Barton Faulks, Marie Lane, Page Moseley. (MCEG; Forum)

EDWARD SCISSORHANDS (1990). Masterpiece from director Tim Burton is a contemporary fairy tale with black-comedy overtones, commenting on good and evil within the human spirit. Burton's surrealisitic style matches Caroline Thompson's script (from an idea by Burton) about a young man with pruning shears for hands who lives in a strange castle perched above a tract community. It's a unique world of Burton's own making, seemingly normal but definitely off-kilter. And he captures a warm, magical feeling for his characters that makes the film very approachable. An Avon lady (warm-heartedly portrayed by Dianne Wiest) takes the misfit youth (Johnny Depp) home to care for him, never questioning his oddities—nor does Wiest's husband, Alan Arkin, who essays another eccentric character. Depp is an intriguing image dressed in black, with white face, who pantomimes his part with minimum dialogue, and whose steel-bladed hands (designed by Stan Winston) become a fascinating prop. Winona Ryder, the film's love interest, was never more beautiful. Anthony Michael Hall, Kathy Baker. (Video/Laser: CBS/Fox)

EEGAH! (1962). Arrrrggghhhhh!! What an incredibly astonishing fantasy for brainless teenagers! The dumbest caveman in film history chases a pretty girl through the desert. Arrrrggghhhh!!! Director Nicholas Merriwether's camera work has to be seen to be disbelieved. Unknown cast reaches unsurpassed heights of ineptitude. Did we say unknown? The caveman is Richard Kiel, destined to become Jaws in the James Bond series. Arch Hall Jr., Marilyn Manning, Ray Steckler. Aaarrrgghhh!!! (Rhino; Sinister/C; Cinema) (Laser: Image)

EERIE MIDNIGHT HORROR SHOW, THE (1978). Released as TORMENTED, and also known as THE SEXORCIST, this is an Italian imitation of THE EXORCIST, depicting a young woman's terror when she is possessed by a spirit embodied in a statue. Undistinguished and contrived, featuring R-rated soft porn and sadism. Directed by Mario Gariazzo. Stella Carnacina. (Continental; Planet; from HQV as **ENTER THE DEVIL**)

EFFECTS. See **MANIPULATOR, THE.**

EGGHEAD'S ROBOT (1970). British kiddie comedy in which the son of a robot-inventing scientist picks up the pieces Dad left in the workshop and constructs his own robot-athlete. Calling all moppets! Directed by Milo Lewis. Roy Kinnear, Keith and Jeffrey Chegwin.

EIGHTEEN AGAIN! (1988). Pleasant fantasy-comedy in the switched-bodies tradition, with 81-year-old George Burns trading personalities with 18-year-old grandson Charles Schlatter, who swaggers through the role, cigar in hand, capturing the witty, sagacious manner of the oldtimer. It's moderate, oft-underplayed humor and director Paul Flaherty plays up the characters' charm and appeal. Jennifer Runyon as the girl friend, Red Buttons as an old family friend and Tony Roberts as the misunderstood son of cantankerous Burns provide morality subplots. Only Anita Morris, as a supersexy sexpot, seems a little out of place, as if the film makers felt they had to comment on Burns' legendary "sex prowess." (New World) (Laser: Image)

ELECTRIC DREAMS (1984). This "fairy tale for computers" is a light-hearted look at our computerized fetishes: a love story between Lenny Von Dohlen (nerdish architect) and Virginia Madsen (happy cello player) and a love story between Von Dohlen and Edgar, an entity created within his home computer. Rusty Lemorande's script is gentle and whimsical, often told in computerized images, with Giorgio Moroder's score capturing an electronical "passion." Director Steve Barron (he helmed the first Ninja Turtles movie) tells a pleasant story with pleasant images. Filmed in San Francisco. Maxwell Caulfield, Bud Cort. (Video/Laser: MGM/UA)

ELECTRIC GRANDMOTHER, THE. Video version of **RAY BRADBURY'S THE ELECTRIC GRANDMOTHER** (New World).

ELECTRIC MAN, THE. See **MAN-MADE MONSTER.**

ELECTRONIC MONSTER, THE (1960). Rod Cameron is the head of a mental institution conducting dream experiments in this British adaptation of Charles Eric Maine's ESCAPEMENT. Cameron induces hallucinations electronically to cure mental aberrations, but his plan backfires and results in greater psychoses. Cheap, lackluster film, directed by Montgomery Tully, who threw in some strange dream dance sequences. Mary Murphy, Meredith Edwards. (S/Weird; Sinister/C)

ELEPHANT BOY (1937). Alexander Korda's version of the Rudyard Kipling tale (adapted by John Collier, Akos Tolnay and Marcia de Sylva) introduced Sabu, "the jungle boy," who has a mystical rapport with elephants. The jungle footage, featuring remarkable elephant shots, is by documentarian Robert J. Flaherty. Zoltan Korda, Alexander's brother, directed this British classic. Walter Hudd, Wilfrid Hyde White. (Video/Laser: HBO)

ELEPHANT MAN, THE (1980). John Hurt is John Merrick, a real-life freak of the last century who suffered terrible physical and mental discomforts from his malformities until befriended by a doctor (Anthony Hopkins) who nursed his anguish. Merrick was a learned man, which makes his internal grief all the more touching. A tearjerker in many ways, but memorable for Hurt's make-up as the grotesque-looking Merrick, his pain-racked performance, and Freddie Francis' black-and-white photography, which captures the drabness of industrial England. Anne Bancroft, John Gielgud. Directed by David Lynch, produced by Mel Brooks. (Video/Laser: Paramount)

ELEPHANT MAN, THE (1982). Taped version of the Broadway play starring Philip Anglim. Directed by Jack Hofsiss. (CBS/Fox) (Laser: J2)

ELEVENTH COMMANDMENT, THE. See **BODY COUNT.**

ELIMINATORS (1986). Lively adventure-satire from producer Charles Band depicting a "mandroid" and how he/it seeks the help of a lady scientist, soldier-of-fortune and martial arts champ to do battle with a mad scientist and his army. Filmed in Spain under Peter Manoogian's direction, the film has Patrick Reynolds as a half-man, half-machine character but he's uninteresting compared to the female lead (Denise Crosby), the adventurer (Andrew Prine) and the ninja (Conan Lee). Indiana Jones isn't sweating over this film, but it certainly has its moments of action and humor. John Carl Buechler did his usual good effects job. (Fox/Playhouse)

ELMCHANTED FOREST, THE (198?). Animated feature about artist Peter Palette who has magical powers from an elm tree in Fantasy Forest. (Celebrity)

ELM STREET: THE MAKING OF A NIGHTMARE. Behind-the-scenes documentary about NIGHTMARE ON ELM STREET. (UAV)

EL TOPO (1970). South American director Alexandro Jodorowsky is unarguably outrageous: A gunfighter in black (Jodorowsky) stalks the West, murdering, raping and resurrecting the dead. Rampant with symbolism; sadistic, religious and irreverent in the same breath.

ELVES (1990). Neo-Nazis hiding in Colorado Springs plan to breed an elf with a virgin to create a new Master Race. Along comes Dan Haggerty as a department store Santa Claus to thwart the plot. Directed by Jeff Mandel. Julie Austin, Deanna Lund. (Action International)

CASSANDRA PETERSON (LEFT) AS SHE APPEARS BEFORE DONNING THE SEXUALLY CHARGED COSTUME OF ELVIRA

ELVIRA, MISTRESS OF THE DARK (1988). Cassandra Peterson was always sexually sizzling as L.A.'s horror-movie hostess, her enormous bosom falling out of her slinky black slit-dress as she cracked wise about some awful cinematic wonder. In the starring role of a film, Peterson still looks sexually sizzling and is a total gas. Best moments are at film's end when Elvira performs a fabulous tassle-twirling act in Las Vegas, her gigantic boobs overfilling the screen (or boob tube). The Mystery Hostess leaves her L.A. show for Massachusetts when her great aunt dies and bequeaths her a dark old house. It's a puritan center where old fogies are up tight about Elvira, and all young people love her (or wish they could, in the case of guys.) Fantasy elements: a monster Elvira has to shove down a sink, a shape-changing poodle, and a wicked uncle (W.W. Morgan Sheppard) who turns into a warlock. The workable script is by Peterson (her husband, Mark Pierson, helped but he is uncredited), Sam Egan and John Paragon. Directed by James Signorelli. Edie McClurg, Pat Crawford Brown, William Duell. (New World) (Laser: Image)

EMANUELLE AND THE CANNIBALS. See **TRAP THEM AND KILL THEM.**

EMBALMER, THE (1964). Bloodless Italian movie (also known as THE MONSTER OF VENICE) with an anemic plot about a jocular journalist in Venice looking for an imbecilic embalmer impeccably clad in a robe and wearing a death mask. Directed by Dino Tavella. Maureen Brown, Elmo Caruso, Jean Mart.

EMBRYO (1976). B-movie material about a scientist (Rock Hudson) experimenting with a human fetus, elevated by moody photography (Fred Koenekamp's) and direction (Ralph Nelson's). In only a few days the fetus evolves into a woman (Barbara Carrera), tutored by Hudson in mathematics and sex—emphasis on the latter. But she turns into a homicidal maniac looking for a new formula to prevent her accelerated aging. Diane Ladd, Roddy McDowall, Dr. Joyce Brothers. (USA; IVE; Starmaker; from Ace as **CREATED TO KILL**)

EMERALD JUNGLE, THE. Video version of **EATEN ALIVE (1980)** (Continental).

EMPEROR'S NEW CLOTHES, THE (1987). Entry in Cannon's fairy tale series, sparked by Sid Caesar as the Emperor. Directed by David Irving. Clive Revill, Robert Morse. (HBO)

EMPEROR'S NEW CLOTHES, THE (1984). An episode of FAERIE TALE THEATRE, directed by Peter Medak, narrated by Timothy Dalton and starring Art Carney, Alan Arkin, Dick Shawn. (Knowledge Unlimited; Fox, Facets Multimedia)

EMPIRE OF ASH II (1985). The setting is "New Idaho" in a post- holocaustic time as horseback guys fight motorcycle guys. Horsebacker Thom Schioler teams up with Melanie Kilgour to search for her missing sister. Produced-directed by Lloyd Simandl and Michael Mazo. See EMPIRE OF ASH III for more (less!) (From AIP as **MANIAC WARRIORS**)

EMPIRE OF ASH III (1985). This clone of MAD MAX, set in the post-Armageddon world of 2050, is not simply below average—it's beneath contempt. Has there ever been one of these after-the-nuclear-bombs-fall movies as bad as this? Probably, but we'd rather not search for it. We lasted 60 minutes through this atrocity to set a world record—and we're not bragging. And what's a good actor like William Smith doing as the evil leader who now rules Earth? Digging ditches would have been better, Bill. The blame for this series of incoherent submachine-gun battles, vehicles racing through a jungle and liberal doses of lesbianism and sado-masochism can be placed on producer Lloyd A. Simandl, the indescribable script of Chris Maruna and the direction by Simandl and Michael Mazo. Melanie Kilgour, Ken Farmer.

EMPIRE OF DRACULA (1967). "Empire" refers to a handful of witless women in a blood-guzzling harem who gang up on hapless males. There is no veil of mystery—it's dreadfully predictable horror stuff in turgid Mexican style. Directed by Federico Curiel.

EMPIRE OF PASSION (1978). Japanese ghost story about two lovers who plot the demise of the woman's husband, only to be haunted for their infidelity. Written-directed by Nagisi Oshima.

EMPIRE OF THE ANTS (1977). Subtitled HOW THE PEST WAS WON, this is superschlock from producer-director Bert I. Gordon. Dull characters (Joan Collins, Robert Lansing, Albert Salmi, John David Carson, Robert Pine, Jacqueline Scott) are trapped in a seaside resort with mutant ants, grown to enormous size from radiation. Gordon's special effects are slipshod and the plot (from an H.G. Wells novel) is ludicrous. The giant picnic crashers have taken over a nearby town and hypnotized the residents and . . . see what we mean by superschlock? (Embassy; Sultan)

EMPIRE OF THE DARK (1991). Steve Barkett (THE AFTERMATH) is an all-around film maker: writer, director, editor, actor. This work excels with its pacing, kinetic editing and Bernard Herrmann-like score by John Morgan. This fantasy-adventure has a satanic cult that exists in an alternate dimension; a 50-foot demon from Hell (stop-motion style); serial killings; a private eye-bounty hunter searching for a killer; and ninja-type battles. While Barkett's film suffers from cliches and clumsy acting, this video flick is worth enduring. Barkett stars as the private eye. Christopher Barkett (Steve's son), Richard Harrison, Terry Hendrickson, Dan Speaker. (Nautilus)

EMPIRE STRIKES BACK, THE (1980). Sequel to STAR WARS didn't disappoint fans who returned time and again to cheer Luke Skywalker, Princess Leia, C3PO, R2D2, etc. Darth Vader, still the Scourge of the Universe, sends Imperial forces against rebels on the ice planet Hoth, where battles with Emperial Walkers are the major highlight of the film, but only the beginning of new adventures. Luke searches for Yoda, a mentor who furthers his knowledge of the Force; Han Solo and Chewbacca the Wookie escape the Imperial fleet in an exciting Asteroid Belt sequence; Lando Callrissian, rogue adventurer, is introduced; and Luke faces Vader in a light saber showdown that is a splendid piece of choreographed action. Producer George Lucas turned direction over to Irvin Kershner, and the script (by Leigh Brackett and Lawrence Kasdan) has greater philosophical interest. Lucas' third in this series (RETURN OF THE JEDI) rounded out the unresolved elements of this script but this proved to be the most mature. Hence, it seems to have greater depth, though the emphasis remains on action. Mark Hamill, Carrie Fisher, Peter Mayhew, Harrison Ford, David Prowse (as Vader with voice by James Earl Jones), Anthony Daniels (as the golden robot), Billy Dee Williams (as Lando), Alec Guinness (as a spectral image). (Video/Laser: Fox)

ENCHANTED COTTAGE (1945). It's hokey, this adaptation of the Arthur Pinero play, but it has the appealing magic of a well-told moralistic tale. Robert Young is a wounded vet and Dorothy McGuire is a homely woman but inside their "enchanted cottage" they are healed and beautiful in each other's eyes. Herbert Marshall, Mildred Natwick, Spring Byington, Robert Clarke. Directed by John Cromwell. (RKO) (Laser: Image)

ENCHANTED FOREST, THE (1945). Edmund Lowe is in commune with Nature—he hears music in trees and talks to animals. He teaches these talents to a boy lost in the deep woods. Enchantingly directed by Lew Landers. Brenda Joyce, John Litel, Harry Davenport, Billy Severn. (Video/Laser: New World)

ENCHANTING SHADOW, THE (1959). See third edition.

ENCINO MAN (1992). Dumb teenage comedy becomes so silly that one gives up in abject frustration and rolls with the slap-happy punches. Sean Astin (in a role beneath his talents) finds a Cro-Magnon man in suspended animation and proceeds, with the help of buddy Pauly Shore, to dress him up and pose him at their high school as an exchange student. Brendan Fraser (as Encino Man) is too good to be wasted in such ridiculous fare. Directed by Les Mayfield. Megan Ward, Robin Tunney, Michael DeLuise, Mariette Hartley. (Disney)

ENCORE (198?). In the horror tradition of HALLOWEEN and FRIDAY THE THIRTEENTH. (Axon; Saturn)

ENCOUNTER AT FARPOINT. Video title for the pilot of **STAR TREK—THE NEXT GENERATION** (Paramount).

ENCOUNTERS IN THE DEEP (1985). Underwater fantasy, set in the Bermuda Triangle, in which an oceanographer discovers a subterranean world of wonders—and dangers. Carol Andre, Andy Garcia.

ENCOUNTER WITH THE UNKNOWN (1975). Three slow-paced, allegedly true supernatural stories narrated by Rod Serling. The first "encounter" concerns a prophecy of death that begins with a burial in a graveyard; the second is about a pit inhabited by a monster; and the last is about a man who meets a strange girl. Directed by Harry Thomason. Gene Ross, Rosie Holotick. (VCI; United)

ENDANGERED SPECIES (1982). Enthralling, offbeat suspenser dealing with mutilated cattle. This explores the mystery with research and taste, offering a solution that involves a secret military organization conducting tests as part of a clandestine germ-warfare program. Around this semi-plausible premise director-writer Alan Rudolph and co-writer John Binder fashion a melodramatic mystery in which burned-out New York cop Robert Urich settles in a Wyoming community, only to become caught up in the enigma. JoBeth Williams, Paul Dooley, Hoyt Axton, Harry Carey Jr. (MGM/UA)

ENDGAME (1983). In the post-holocaust world of 2025 A.D., warriors square off in a bloodsport called "Endgame" while stormtroopers in Nazi helmets gun for them. The best Endgame player, Shannon (Al Cliver), talks his roughest opponents (burly brute, martial arts oriental, etc.) into helping him escort mind-reading Mutants to safety, promising them a fortune in gold. Endless

THE FAMILY THAT PREYS TOGETHER

In September 1991 Joe Bob Briggs gathered his four favorite horror-movie TV hosts of all time for a special series on The Movie Channel. Those who took part in the unique retrospective, taped at the Magic Castle in Hollywood, were (clockwise from left) the drive-in movie critic himself; John Stanley (author of the book you are now holding in your sweaty palms and one-time horror host at Channel 2 in Oakland, Calif.); John Zacherly, who portrayed New York's horror host Zacherly; Elvira, Mistress of the Dark, well-known for her warmth, motherly touch, and penetrating intellect; and Ernie 'Ghouldardi' Anderson, better known in modern times as the announcer on 'The Love Boat.'

battles as the band encounters sadists, killers and blind priests. Italian Mad Max imitation directed by Steven Benson. Laura Gemser, George Eastman. (Media)

ENDLESS DESCENT (1989). In the vein of THE ABYSS and LEVIATHAN: Sub inventor Jack Scalia dives in Siren II with by-the-book Captain R. Lee Ermey to find out why Siren I vanished in the depths. Turns out a DNA cloning experiment created monsters with tentacles, and human-shaped monstrosities, in an underwater cavern. This tries for the thrills of ALIENS but misses by leagues. Ray Wise, Deborah Adair, John Toles Bey. Originally produced as THE RIFT. (Live) (Laser: Image)

ENDLESS NIGHT (1971). Agatha Christie adaptation (written-directed by Sidney Gilliat) focusing on a woman hired to scare someone to death. Hayley Mills, Hywel Bennett, Britt Ekland, George Sanders. (HBO; Republic) (Laser: HBO)

END OF AUGUST AT THE OZONE HOTEL, THE (1965). See first edition.

END OF THE WORLD, THE. See **PANIC IN YEAR ZERO.**

END OF THE WORLD (1977). Poverty level sci-fier from producer Charles Band and director John Hayes, whose plodding work (also reflected in his pitiful editing) is tedious. Christopher Lee portrays Zandi, who possesses the body of a priest and plots to blow up Earth because (get this, readers) mankind is contaminating the Universe. Ends on a whimper! Dean Jagger, Lew Ayres, MacDonald Carey, Sue Lyon. (Media)

ENEMY FROM SPACE (1957). Second in Hammer's series about determined scientist Bernard Quatermass, again played by Brian Donlevy, who established the role in THE CREEPING UNKNOWN. A superior effort, from Nigel Kneale's screenplay (based on his TV serial) to Gerald Gibbs' stark photogrpahy to Val Guest's direction. Quatermass discovers a malevolent alien race in control of an isolated industrial station at Wynerton Flats. Vera Day, Bryan Forbes, Michael Ripper. (From Corinth under this title and as **QUATERMASS II: ENEMY FROM SPACE**)

ENEMY MINE (1985). A promising theme kicks off this big-budgeted adventure: An Earthman (Dennis Quaid) and a lizard creature called a Drac (Louis Gossett Jr. in heavy makeup and scaly costume) laser each other out of the heavens during a space war and crashland on a barren planet where they must learn tolerance over mutual hatred. The arms-length relationship shapes into friendship; a twist of fate leads to an exciting rescue situation. The landscapes are realistically harsh and the action sequences superbly designed, with the story making its human points while remaining solid entertainment. Directed by Wolfgang Petersen. (Video/Laser: CBS/Fox)

ENTER THE DEVIL (1975). Reporter Irene Kelly, probing an Indian devil cult, gets more than she bargained for in this quickie from writers-directors F. Q. Dobbs and David Cass. Fine Mojave photography helps to maintain interest but the unknowns (Cass, Josh Bryant, Linda Rascoe) have an impossible time coming to grips with a tumbledown script. Parched throats guaranteed.

ENTER THE DEVIL (1978). Video version of **EERIE MIDNIGHT HORROR SHOW, THE** (HQV).

ENTITY, THE (1983). Above-average supernatural thriller, allegedly based on a true case that occurred in L.A. and adapted by Frank de Felitta. A widowed mother (Barbara Hershey) is attacked by an invisible demon and raped. On a literate level this deals with believers vs. nonbelievers and science vs ESP. Focus is on characters, dialogue and tension as director Sidney J. Furie maintains a fearful atmosphere and refuses to show the "entity" in detail. Excellent make-up by Stan Winston. Ron Silver, David Labiosa, Alex Rocco. (CBS/Fox)

ENTITY FORCE. See **ONE DARK NIGHT.**

EPITAPH (1987). Cop covers up his wife's bloody murder. Seems she's an axe murderess. Written-directed by Joseph Merhi. Natasha Pavlova, Jim Williams, Deolores Nascar. (City Lights)

EQUALIZER 2000 (1987). Ripoff of the Mad Max genre, produced by Roger Corman in the Philippines, where wall-to-wall action unfolds in furious, ludicrous fashion under Cirio H. Santiago's direction. A narrator tells us it's "one hundred years after the Nuclear Winter," and we're in an "arid desert" where the Ownership (i.e. bad guys) has control and a rebel wing is trying to restore order. A loner hero named Slade (Richard Norton, never cracking a smile in a black leather outfit) and a sexy gal (Corinne Wahl, ex-Penthouse pin-up) join forces to fight Mordon, a villain who is after Slade's fantastic weapon, which seems to have more firepower than all the Rambo movies together. It ain't dull as armies of men in black leather scamper over old mining digs, blazing away with machine-guns. William Steis, Robert Patrick, Frederick Bailey, Rex Cutter. (MGM/UA)

EQUINOX (1971). Four teen-age hikers find an ancient witchcraft tome that unleashes supernatural entities, including a horned creature with pterodactyl wings and pitchfork tail. Well-intended effort by writer-director Jack Woods has early David Allen-Jim Danforth effects. Prize-winning sci-fi writer Fritz Leiber turns up as a geologist. The film took four years to complete, so the characters age before your very eyes. Producer Dennis Muren became an award-winning effects artist. Frank Bonner, Edward Connell, Barbara Hewitt. (From Wizard and VCI under this title and from Lightning as **BEAST, THE**)

ERASERHEAD (1978). Surrealistic nightmare from avant-garde filmmaker David Lynch (writer-director-producer-special effects), who suffers from an obsession with prenatal dreams. The camera plunges into black holes, squishy worm-things float like spermatozoa and a hideous mutant baby squawls its anger. "Midnight" cult film has stunning moments, with unsettling visuals and low-live characters. Jack Nance, Charlotte Stewart, Jeanne Bates, Laurel Near. (Video/Laser: RCA/Columbia)

ERIK THE VIKING (1989). Monty Python-styled parody of adventure movies, written-directed by Python alumnus Terry Jones. Tim Robbins stars as a sword-wielding member of a plundering-blundering gang of warriors pillaging during the Age of Ragnarok. Eric decides he's tired of raping and murdering and searches for the Halls of Valhalla. The comedy-adventures are plentiful (see the Dragon of the North Sea, look out for Halfdan the Black, behold the Pit of Hell, keep an eye out for the Edge of the World, and scale the Rainbow Bridge at your own risk). Robbins is supported by John Cleese as the villain, Mickey Rooney as the grandfather, Eartha Kitt as Freya the Witch, Tim McInnerny as Sven the Berserk and Freddie Jones as Harald the Missionary. Never has pillaging been so much fun. (Video/Laser: Orion)

ERNEST SAVES CHRISTMAS (1988). Jim Varney's hammy mugging as inept cabbie Ernest P. Worrell is offset by whimsical touches in this fanciful fable about how a tiring St. Nicholas (Douglas Seale) passes on his North Pole legacy to movie actor Oliver Clark, with an assist given by Varney and vagrant Noelle Parker. Varney shines when he assumes identities (an official resembling Pee-wee Herman, an old lady, and a snake handler) to fool authorities. Bits of yuletide humor include reinder on a ceiling, two elves, and a sleigh on a New York airport runway. This is good family fare. Directed by John Cherry, who created Ernest. Robert Lesser, Gailard Sartain, Billie Bird. (Video/Laser: Touchstone)

ERNEST SCARED STUPID (1991). This fourth feature showcasing the Ernest P. Worrell character essayed by the rubbery-faced Jim Varney is a Halloween horror romp with the dumb-stupid-incredibly inept Ernest driving a garbage truck in Briarville, Mo., where he unleashes the spirit of an evil troll from a tree trunk. The real fun is watching the supernatural creature turn children into wooden dolls and scaring the hell out of everyone. Ernest and his dog-pal Rimshot take on the creature and offspring. The credits, featuring clips from horror non-classics, are a gas. Directed by John Cherry. Eartha Kitt is sassy and campy as an old witch. Austin Nagler, Shay

Astar, Jonas Moscartolo (he's the troll). (Touchstone)

EROTIC ADVENTURES OF SNOW WHITE, THE. See **GRIMM'S FAIRY TALES FOR ADULTS.**

EROTIC ADVENTURES OF THE FOURTH KIND. See **WHAM! BAM! THANK YOU, MR. SPACEMAN!**

EROTIC DREAMS (1988). Softcore sex-fantasy comedy in which Robert Miles, a practitioner of black magic, might lose his soul to the Devil if he doesn't control his sexual desires. Strictly for flesh purveyors. Directed by Robert F. Pope. Nathan Lanes, Stephanie Goldwin. (Celebrity; also in video as DARK DREAMS)

EROTIC RITES OF FRANKENSTEIN. Video version of DRACULA VS. DR. FRANKENSTEIN (Nightmare; from Video Search with English subtitles).

EROTIKILL (1975). Also known as THE BLACK COUNTESS, this is a rock-bottom Spanish vampire atrocity, poorly acted, incompetently photographed, feebly dubbed. Linda Romay bares her considerable assets as Irina, a bloodsucker who terrorizes love-hungry men. Devoid of story, suspense and everything else filmmakers put into movies. Directed by J. P. Johnson. Alice Arno, Monica Swin. (Lightning; from Luna and Media in more erotic form as LOVES OF IRINA, THE)

ESCAPE (1971). Implausible TV-movie with Christopher George as Cameron Steele, one-time escape artist (a la Houdini) now an investigator using his skills to elude torture predicaments. Paul Playdon's story unfolds like a pastiche of an old-fashioned serial: Mad scientist creates a virus that turns men into incredibly mixed-up, walking zombies. Is this "escapism"? Directed by John Llewellyn Moxey. William Windom, Marlyn Mason, Avery Schreiber, John Vernon, Gloria Grahame, Huntz Hall, William Schallert.

ESCAPE FROM GALAXY 3 (1986). "Star Lovers" confront an evil conqueror on a planet in a distant galaxy. Italian space actioner directed by Ben Norman. Cheryl Buchanan, James Milton, Don Powell. (Prism)

ESCAPE FROM NEW YORK (1981). One of John Carpenter's best, moving at a roadrunner's pace as escapist fantasy. The writer-director (with co-writer Nick Castle) populates this imaginative narrative with hard-boiled characters. The plot is an outrageous joke (Manhattan, by 1997, is a maximum-security prison) and gallops headlong with stark atmosphere. Kurt Russell, an eyepatch over one eye, does his Clint Eastwood impression as Snake Plisskin, a rebel assigned by security chief Lee Van Cleef to penetrate NYC to bring out the U.S. President (Donald Pleasence), whose Air Force I jet has crash-landed. Adrienne Barbeau, Harry Dean Stanton, Isaac Hayes, Season Hubley, Ernest Borgnine. (Embassy; Nelson; RCA/Columbia; New Line's version has new footage and interviews) (Laser: Nelson)

ESCAPE FROM PLANET EARTH. Video version of **DOOMSDAY MACHINE** (Academy).

ESCAPE FROM SAFEHAVEN (1989). Nuked-out New York City: in the holocaustic ruins a gang called the Colts is atacked by an evil gang led by Roy MacArthur. It's one hairy battle in this derivative MAD MAX clonehouse. Directed by Brian Thomas Jones and James McCalmont. Rick Gianasi, Mollie O'Mara. (Sony)

ESCAPE FROM THE BRONX (1984). Sequel to 1990: THE BRONX WARRIORS, in which the Bronx is a danger zone of roving gangs and ROAD WARRIOR-type freakos. Trash, the bash-boss, leads his men against Henry Silva, assigned by the Corporation to wipe out everyone in the Bronx. There's plenty of action—but that's all there is in this Italian release directed by Enzo G. Castellari. Mark Gregory, Valeria D'Obici. (Media)

ESCAPE FROM THE PLANET OF THE APES (1971). Third entry in the PLANET OF THE APES series is a talky effort, with screenwriter Paul Dehn overindulging in comedic comparisons between man and monkey. A trio of chimps travels back in time in a space capsule to present-day. But because the talking creatures pose a threat, the government forms a conspiracy. This film's outcome led to CONQUEST OF THE PLANET OF THE APES. Dehn and director Don Taylor score best in generating empathy for the beleaguered chimps, are less successful with satiric jabs. Roddy McDowall, Kim Hunter, Sal Mineo, Eric Braeden (as the villain), Ricardo Montalban, Jason Evers, Albert Salmi, Natalie Trundy. (Video/Laser: Fox)

ESCAPE IN THE FOG (1945). See editions 1-3.

ESCAPEMENT. Video version of **ELECTRONIC MONSTER** (Sinister/C; Filmfax).

ESCAPE OF MEGAGODZILLA, THE. See TERROR OF MECHAGODZILLA.

ESCAPES (1986). Five stories in the tradition of THE TWILIGHT ZONE, but not as satisfying. Host Vincent Price has little to do but look sinister as he spins mini-yarns: "A Little Fishy" is a swipe of a famous EC tale about a fisherman who picks up a sandwich on the beach; "Coffee Break" is the strange-town-visited-by-an-outsider story in which a van driver gets his comeuppance; "Who's There" is a flop of a story about a jogger who meets forest elves; "Jonah's Dream" features an old woman meeting a flying saucer; and "Think Twice" is about the thin line separating fantasy from reality. Directed by David Steensland. (Starmaker; Prism)

ESCAPE TO WITCH MOUNTAIN (1975). Fantasy-adventure produced by Jerome Courtland—strictly moppet material as two children (humanoid aliens who don't know it) flee Donald Pleasence, who wants to harness their telekinesis powers for evil. Eddie Albert is a likable vacationer with a flying Winnebago camper, and there are the friendly faces of Ray Milland, Denver Pyle and Reta Shaw. The only groovy visual is one UFO sequence. Directed by John Hough. Kim Richards, Ike Eisenmann. Followed by THE RETURN FROM WITCH MOUNTAIN. (Video/Laser: Disney)

ESCAPE 2000 (1983). Unusual Australian futuristic adventure, set in a an Orwellean society. A concentration camp for "deviates" is run by sadistic guards under a perverted commandant. Three sexual sickos drop in for sport in the style of "The Most Dangerous Game." Five prisoners are set free and the commadant and his sporting pals follow with high-powered rifles, explosive arrows and other flesh-rending weaponry. The bloody action is almost nonstop. Much gore was cut for the U.S. Produced by David Hemmings, directed by Brian Trenchard-Smith. Music by Brian May. Olivia Hussey, Steve Railsback, Michael Craig, Carmen Duncan. Released to theaters as TURKEY SHOOT. (Embassy; Starmaker)

E.S.P. (1983). Jim Stafford has the power to see into the future. George Deaton. (Best Film & Video)

ESPIONAGE IN TANGIERS (1965). Third edition.

ESTATE OF INSANITY. Video version of **BLACK TORMENT, THE** (VCL).

ETERNAL EVIL (1985). Made in Montreal as THE BLUE MAN, this unusual astral-projection horror tale stars Winston Rekert as a film maker undergoing a series of dreams in which he commits out-of-body murders. He seeks the help of psychiatrist Karen Black. Meanwhile, Montreal cop John Novak carries on his own investigation. Directed by George Mihalka with a fluid camera, but it's quite bewildering. Andrew Bednarsky, Patty Talbot, Lois Maxwell. (Lightning) (Laser: Image)

ETERNAL FIST. See **FIST OF STEEL.**

ETERNITY (1989). At two hours/five minutes, this reincarnation feature runs on eternally—but it's still a sincere movie that marked Jon Voight's return to the screen after a five-year hiatus. Voight portrays a TV news investigator who has dreams about a former life, during a medieval age, when he and Armand Assante were rivals for maiden Eileen Davidson. Now Assante is a ruthless TV station mogul and Davidson an actress whom Assante tries to wrest from Voight. An unlikely TV trial-for-libel on Assante's network gives Voight opportunity to deliver a plea for the brotherhood of man. Voight helped shape the preachy script with director Steven Paul and Paul's wife, Dorothy Koster Paul. Wilford Brimley, Kaye Ballard, Eugene Roche. (Academy)

E.T. THE EXTRATERRESTRIAL (1982). To think: the great box office smash is a simplistic but heartfelt parable in which boy meets alien, boy loves alien, boy loses alien. Steven Spielberg's masterpiece was fashioned from a script by Melissa Mathison, who borrowed such Spielbergian themes as suburban settings; ordinary kids and adults coping with realities; an awesome attitude toward lights in the sky and alien life. Comedy touches keep E.T.

'E.T. THE EXTRATERRESTRIAL'

from becoming too sentimental, and even when the story turns serious, and men are shown as menaces, one feels for E.T.'s plight in wanting to overcome prejudice on Earth to return home. Carlo Rambaldi created E.T., and although the cutie at times seems clumsy and too cute, the cuteness wins you over. Great score by John Williams; fine flying sequences by Dennis Muren. Dee Wallace, Peter Coyote (the man with keys), Robert MacNaughton, Drew Barrymore, Henry Thomas, Milt Kogan. (Video/Laser: MCA)

EUREKA (1983). Surrealistic portrait of the world's richest man, overburdened with the esoterica and eccentricities of cameraman-director Nicolas Roeg to the point of excruciation. Gene Hackman does a good job of etching Jack McCall, a man made unhappy by his good fortune, but the narrative is incoherent, full of symbolic asides (such as a voodoo orgy) and erotic extravagances. Others lost in this muddle: Theresa Russell, Rutger Hauer, Ed Lauter, Joe Pesci. (MGM/UA)

EVE (1968). Celeste Yarnall is an eyeful in costumes as skimpy as the budget for this jungle adventure with overtones of SHE. Celeste portrays an Amazon princess who keeps her natives in line with strange powers—or maybe it's her Max Factor look. Big Game Hunter Christopher Lee and explorer Robert Walker Jr. find her and want to possess her. Can you blame them. Herbert Lom provides the villainy. Directed by Jeremy Summers.

EVE OF DESTRUCTION (1991). Good combination of high-tech sci-fi and action in which humanoid robot Eve VIII goes haywire during a holdup in San Francisco and is locked in "battlefield mode." The robot's creator, who programmed Eve VIII with her own memories, personality and image, joins anti-terrorist specialist Gregory Hines to stop the monster. There's a balance of suspense and action in the script by director Duncan Gibbins and Yale Udoff, with an apocalyptic element that adds a race against time. Hines is effective as the agent and Sweden's Renee Soutendijk shows a wide range in portraying Eve VIII and her creator. Michael Greene, Kurt Fuller, John M. Jackson, Kevin McCarthy. (RCA/Columbia; Orion, Sultan) (Laser: Nelson/New Line)

EVERYTHING YOU ALWAYS WANTED TO KNOW ABOUT SEX BUT WERE AFRAID TO ASK (1972). This has nothing to do with David Reuben's best-selling bedroom guide and everything to do with the uninhibited Woody Allen, who has concocted bizarre sex comedy sketches, such as Gene Wilder loving a sheep, or the giant breast that is sweeping the country, or the army of sperm cells, depicted as shock troops about to be "launched" on a mission. John Carradine, Louise Lasser, Tony Randall, Burt Reynolds, Lynn Redgrave, Robert Walden. (CBS/Fox) (Laser: Pioneer)

EVERYTHING'S DUCKY (1961). Nothing's "ducky" in a movie hinging on talking-duck jokes. Duck out on this quackery when sailors Buddy Hackett and Donald O'Connor (they get star "billing") find a duck that speaks. The daffy duck direction was by Don Taylor. Jackie Cooper, Joanie Summers and Roland Winters are also "billed." This ultimately takes a tern for the worst.

EVE, THE WILD WOMAN (1968). Italian monster mishmash with Brad Harris and Marc Lawrence controlling gorillas. Directed by Robert Morris.

EVICTORS, THE (1979). Writer-producer-director Charles B. Pierce purports this is a true story of a "haunted" farmhouse but his execution lacks conviction or the pseudodocumentary air that earmarked his LEGEND OF BIGFOOT. Surprises are telegraphed and cat-and-mouse suspense is tepid. Michael Parks and Jessica Harper as victims of scheming realtor Vic Morrow. Toss out THE EVICTORS. (Vestron) (Laser: Japanese)

EVIL, THE (1978). Along come Joanna Pettet and Richard Crenna to convert a mansion into a rehab center, unaware of the house's bloody history. First thing they know, people and animals are going crazy at the height of electric storms, the house trembles as though it were '06 again and there's a corpse in the dumbwaiter. There's also the lurking presences of Andrew Prine and Victor Buono, the latter as a demon from Hell. "This house is trying to kill us all," remarks Crenna once he catches on to Donald Thompson's plot gimmick. The rent would kill anyone. Directed by Gus Trikonis. (Embassy)

EVIL ALTAR (1989). The best thing about this video-movie is villain William Smith, who portrays evil on a level few other actors can attain. As a minion of the Devil, Smith's is collecting souls for Hell in the community of Red Rock with the help of cop Robert Zadar. Directed by Jim Winburn. Pepper Martin, Theresa Cooney, Tal Armstrong. (South Gate)

EVIL BELOW (1889). Mixture of underwater action and ersatz supernatural thrills when Wayne Crawford and June Chadwick search for a treasure that went down off the coast of Africa in the 17th Century. Art Payne's script was directed by Jean-Claude Dubbois. (Raedon)

EVIL BRAIN FROM OUTER SPACE (1964). Japanese superhero Starman—or Super Giant—saves Earth from invasion in re-edited episodes 7, 8, and 9 of the juvenile sci-fi serial SUPER GIANT. Others in this series: ATOMIC RULERS OF THE WORLD, ATTACK FROM SPACE, INVADERS FROM SPACE. (S/Weird)

EVIL CLUTCH (1988). Excessively gory Italian film executed without artistic finesse or an understanding of what makes the genre bleed best. In short, this was made to sicken you without artistic merit. A vacationing couple comes to a village haunted by a malignant supernatural force. (No further explanation given.) The couple is set upon by ghouls, demons and the walking dead, depicted as ugly, depraved creatures. For your money you get a man's penis ripped off by a woman's vagina (in the shape of a clawlike hand), arms, hands and heads yanked (or chopped) off, blood spurting through severed arteries, zombie monsters and people screaming, cackling and going crazy without subtlety. A chaotic film with lengthy countryside shots that pad the storyless plot. Written-directed by Andreas Marfori. Coralina C. Tassoni, Diego Ribon. (Rhino offers the uncut version)

EVIL COUNTESS, THE (1973). Variation on "The Most Dangerous Game," with Howard Vernon as the Count Zaroff character who hunts down human prey and turns them over to the titular entity, played by Lina Romay. Jesus Franco directed as Clifford Brown. Kali Hansa, Alice Arno, Robert Woods.

EVIL DEAD, THE (1983). Powerful cult favorite appreciated for excessive gore effects and sledgehammer techniques from a triumvirate of producers (line executive Robert Tapert, writer-director Sam M. Raimi and actor Bruce Campbell). Made in Tennessee and Michigan, the film concerns young adults finding a Book of the Dead from the Sumerian period in a wilderness cabin. Recited incantations open portals to another dimension and hideous demons wreak havoc. And havoc it is, as bodies are hacked to pieces—the only way to stop the evil entities. A crude effort full of visual shocks, reflecting gore talents to come. Duck those flying body parts and look out for the spattering blood. Sarah York, Betsy Baker, Ellen Sandweiss, Hal Delrich. (HBO) (Laser: Image)

EVIL DEAD 2: DEAD BY DAWN (1987). This is so stylishly, hysterically overdone that it stands out as a first-class comedy gore flick. "There's something out there" (a line from the film, believe it or not) exemplifies the tongue-in-cheek approach of director-writer Sam Raimi, who works with co-writer Scott Spiegel in keeping close to the original film's story. Once again the Book of the Dead allows invisible demons to rove the forest, animating inanimate objects and possessing animate ones. Raimi is out to startle you with the most blatant visuals. A man chainsawing off his own hand, a woman gulping an eyeball, tree roots and tendrils strangling humans, and demons cackling their evil are among the perverted delights. There's a wonderful parody of the Rambo trailer in which hero Campbell arms himself, concluding with "Groovy." The overacting finds acceptability within the gushing blood (sometimes green, sometimes red), the flesh-destroying effects and wide-angle-lens shots that are, well, "groovy." Denise Bixler, Kassie Wesley, Dan Hicks, Theodore Raimi. (Video/Laser: Vestron)

EVIL DEAD 3. See **ARMY OF DARKNESS.**

EVIL EYE, THE (1962). Historically this is the first of the Italian "giallo" films, in which more attention is paid to the stalkings and the murders than to the investigations, and the killer is presented as a disguised fiend who shows no bounds in depravity. Directed by Mario Bava in Rome, it depicts a tourist (Leticia Roman) who is witness to a terrible street murder and is caught up in bloody slayings. Years later, Dario Argento took the genre to new heights of horror with THE BIRD WITH THE CRYSTAL PLUMAGE and DEEP RED. John Saxon, Valentina Cortese. (Sinister/C)

EVIL EYE. See **MANHATTAN BABY.**

EVIL EYE. See **POSSESSOR, THE.**

EVIL FINGERS. See **FIFTH CORD, THE.**

EVIL FORCE. See **4D MAN, THE.**

EVIL IN THE SWAMP (1989). Children living in a swamp are stalked by photographer James Keach. John Savage, Robby Benson, Samantha Eggar. Also called ALL THE KIND STRANGERS. (Chiron Industries; MNX)

EVIL JUDGEMENT (1985). Is a psychopathic judge responsible for a series of vicious murders? Pamela Collyer plays an investigator checking out that very question. Directed by Claude Castravelli. Jack Langedyk, Nanette Workman. (Video Treasures; Media)

EVIL LAUGH (1988). A rundown, empty orphanage serves as the setting for this psychokiller screamer in which a killer is knocking off volunteer medical workers. Directed by Dominick Brasscia, who scripted with co-producer Steven Baio. Baio is also in the cast with Kim McKamy, Tony Griffin, Jody Gibson. (Celebrity)

EVIL MIND. TV/video title for the 1935 **CLAIRVOYANT, THE** (Kartes; Sinister/C; Nostalgia).

EVIL OF DRACULA (1975). Japanese pastiche of a Hammer vampire thriller replete with lesbian overtones since there are plenty of Dracula's brides with fang punctures on their breasts. The story parallels Hammer's LUST FOR A VAMPIRE when a new instructor shows up at an all-girls school to discover that the principal has no principles about plunging his teeth into soft necks. Directed by Michio Yamamoto. Toshio Kurosawa.

EVIL OF FRANKENSTEIN, THE (1964). Hammer's third entry in its Frankenstein series, produced by Anthony Hinds, is one of its least efforts, providing only laboratory-worn results. Director Freddie Francis and writer John Elder (Hinds) needed a good solid bolt of electricity in the as . . . pirations. Peter Cushing is back as the Baron with a yen for resurrecting the dead, and Kiwi Kingston, as the Monster, lumbers in caves and laboratories under Francis' own lumbering direction. The Monster, preserved in a glacier, doesn't get moving until late in the proceedings. A new prologue was added for U.S. TV with William Phipps. Peter Woodthorpe, Duncan Lamont, Katy Wild. (Video/Laser: MCA)

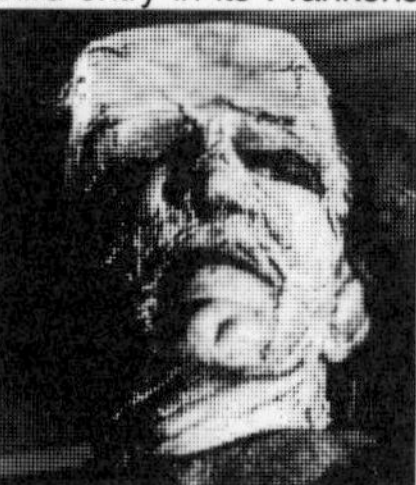

'THE EVIL OF FRANKENSTEIN'

EVILS OF DORIAN GRAY, THE. See **SECRET OF DORIAN GRAY, THE.**

EVILS OF THE NIGHT (1983). Neville Brand and Aldo Ray portray pawns of outer space invaders who terrorize teenagers. John Carradine, Tina Louise, Julie Newmar. Produced-directed by Mardi Rustam. (Lightning; Live)

EVILSPEAK (1982). Dressed-up revamping of the-worm-that-turns tale. Clint Howad (Ron's brother) is a klutzy cadet at a military academy, picked on by juvenile peers. Uncovering a volume on satanic rituals, Clint conjures up Estabar the Demon, who chops off the heads of virgins. Howard uses a computer to call up the devil in a dungeon beneath the school's chapel. This is not a particularly good film and becomes slightly disgusting when a puppy is slaughtered by Howard's tormentors. What makes the film work, though, is Howard's ability to engender sympathy. R. G. Armstrong is wasted as a drunken nightwatchman. Eric Weston's direction is adequate. Some critics speak evil of EVILSPEAK. Don Stark, Claude Earl Jones, Haywood Nelson. (CBS/Fox)

EVIL SPAWN (1987). Originally released by Camp Video, this horror vehicle for sexy Bobbie Bresee was re-edited and new material added by Fred Olen Ray. The result was THE ALIEN WITHIN. See that entry.

EVIL SPIRITS (1990). Take a gloomy mansion, populate it with eccentrics, give it a landlady who murders boarders and you have a "black humor" shocker with an above-average cast. Directed by Gary Graver, whose lighting and gothic imagery give this low-budget effort class, EVIL SPIRITS focuses on Karen Black, a "lovely" landlady as whacky as a gold-plated axe. Among her roomers: Martine Beswick as a spaced-out dancer; Michael Berryman as a Peeping Tom; Bert Remsen and Virginia Mayo as Beverly Hills folk; Mikel Angel (the screenwriter) as a sot; and Debra Lamb as a psychic. Oh, don't forget the wheelchair-bound husband with whom Black communicates psychically, and the guy chained in the cellar who gnaws on human hands. Along comes Social Security inspector Arte Johnson. That still doesn't stop batty Black from burying new bodies in her yard, the smell of which bothers nosy neighbor Yvette Vickers. Robert Quarry is a doctor and Anthony Eisley is a cop. (Prism) (Laser: Image)

EVIL STALKS THIS HOUSE (1981). Multi-chaptered syndicated series re-edited to TV-movie length, with thief Jack Palance taking refuge in an isolated house during a storm and terrorizing the old ladies living there. But these are dames out of ARSENIC AND OLD LACE, who are part of a witch cult. It's cheaply directed by Gordon Hessler on videotape but the Louis M. Heyward story has a perverse charm. There's a quicksand pit, a handiman named Bull, and a tarantula spider. Frances Hyland, Helen Hughes.

EVIL TOONS (1990). The monster in this Fred Olen Ray horror spoof is an animated creature—a demon in a deserted mansion unleashed by shapely cleaning women. David Carradine, Dick Miller, Monique Gabrielle, Suzanne Ager, Arte Johnson, Michelle Bauer. (Prism)

EVIL TOWN (19??). A stranger in town discovers zombies created by a traditional mad scientist. Directed by Edward Collins. Dean Jagger, James Keach, Robert Walker Jr. (Transworld; Starmaker)

EWOK ADVENTURE, THE (1984). Endor's moon, as any RETURN OF THE JEDI viewer knows, harbors intelligent creatures known as Ewoks, who speak an unintelligible language in groans and sighs and are adept with crude weapons. In this TV-movie from George Lucas, a starcruiser carrying a family of four crashlands. The parents are kidnapped by a snorting giant called the Gorax and two kids (Aubree Miller and Eric Walker) are befriended by the little furry ones and trek to find the Gorax. They encounter a vicious Tree Snake, hulking beasts, a lake that entraps those who fall into it and a firefly named Izirna. Bob Carrau's script is juvenile entertainment, but refreshing. Produced by Tom Smith and directed by John Korty in and around Marin County. Special effects by Dennis Muren, Michael Pangrazio, Phil Tippett and Jon Berg. Released in Europe as CARAVAN OF COURAGE: AN EWOK ADVENTURE. Fionnula Flanagan, Guy Boyd. (Video/Laser: MGM/UA)

EWOK: THE BATTLE FOR ENDOR (1985). Sequel to THE EWOK ADVENTURE, less a children's story and more an action adventure in the STAR WARS tradition. Aubree Miller is back as the lost Earthling, Cindel, who

AN EWOK WITH TOM SMITH

sees her parents killed in an attack by the evil alien Kerak and his seven-foot henchmen (lizardmen called Marauders). She escapes with Wicket the Ewok to begin adventures that lead her to a derelict named Noa (Wilford Brimley) and a cute little creature, Teek, who zips around the Endor landscape like a flash. Action is nonstop when Cindel and Wicket are kidnaped by the evil witch Charal and taken to Karek's castle. Climactic battle is a steal from RETURN OF THE JEDI, but still a rousing time. Again, Tom Smith (the genius behind Industrial Light and Magic) is producer and again the story idea is George Lucas'. Jim and Ken Wheat co-wrote and co-directed. The effects are plentiful, featuring a killer dragon in a cave, stop-motion beasts of burden, a flying spaceship, and other delights for which Lucas is famous. Warwick Davis is good as Wicket, but it's Teek who almost steals this show. (Video/Laser: MGM/UA)

EXCALIBUR (1981). John Boorman's interpretation of the King Arthur legend etches a brutal vision of the Middle Ages, intermingling myth and magic with gritty day-to-day hardships. Arthur (Nigel Terry) pulls the mystical Excalibur sword from a rock and with Merlin the Magician (Nicol Williamson) forges a kingdom symbolized by the gallant Knights of the Round Table. But there is also betrayal from his Queen Guinevere (Cherie Lunghi) and the royal knight Sir Lancelot (Nicholas Clay), and the ordeal of the Quest for the Holy Grail. Themes of success, failure and redemption run throughout this strange, lengthy period saga. (Video/Laser: Warner Bros.)

EXO-MAN (1977). David Ackroyd portrays a professor paralyzed by a hitman, so he designs a cumbersome suit in which he can move around, terrorizing gangsters. Ridiculous superhero material by Martin Caidin and Howard Rodman. Directed by Richard Irving. Harry Morgan, Jose Ferrer, Kevin McCarthy.

EXORCISM (1974). Devil cult terrorizes British countryside. Directed by Juan Bosch Palau. Paul Naschy (who wrote as Jacinto Molina), Maria Perschy. (All Seasons; Hollywood Home Entertainment)

EXORCISM AT MIDNIGHT (1979). Two movies in one. First we have color footage of Dr. Lawrence Tierney conducting experiments on a Jamaican in a trance. Tierney explains he's going to bathe the subject in amber light, an experiment designed to control human brain waves, or Chromology. Then we flash back in an amber color called "Spectrum-X"—tinted black-and-white footage from a British thriller about a detective solving a series of murders involving Jamaicans and voodoo. This is colorless in more ways than one—dare we call it boring? Finally we flash ahead to Tierney (in color again) for a less-than-rousing climax. It will take fortitude to sit through this without dozing. John Bates, Bob Allen, Nuba Stuart. Written-directed by Stanley Goulder.

EXORCISM'S DAUGHTER (1974). Spanish attempt to cash in on the EXORCIST craze is a viewing hex also known as WOMEN OF DOOM. The setting is a 19th Century insane asylum where Amelia Gade is incarcerated. Her doctor realizes she is buggy because of an exorcism ceremony she witnessed, but he is attacked for witchcraft as he uses Freudian techniques. Written-directed by Rafael Morena Alba. (From Sinister/C as **HOUSE OF THE INSANE WOMEN**)

EXORCIST, THE (1973). Thinking man's horror picture juxtaposing graphic shock with allegorical levels of religion vs. evil, with William Peter Blatty adapting his best-seller for director William Friedkin. Everyone was shocked by the nauseous horrors suffered by young Linda Blair as she is possessed by an evil spirit: green vomit, ghastly makeup, foul-mouthed blasphemy, glassy sulphurous green eyes, a head that makes a 360-degree turn, etc. In the process, viewers overlooked many of the story's subtleties, which are of greater interest. How, for example, does the mother of priest Jason Miller fit in? How did the amulet come to be found by cop Lee J. Cobb? Concern yourself with these details, and less with bilious visuals, and you will find it richly rewarding. Excellently photographed by Owen Roizman and Billy Williams. Max von Sydow, Ellen Burstyn, Jack MacGowran, Kitty Winn. Mercedes McCambridge provided the ugly voice of the Demon that blurts from Blair's mouth. (Warner Bros.; RCA/Columbia) (Laser: Warner Bros.)

EXORCIST II: THE HERETIC (1977). An absolute fiasco directed by John Boorman—audiences laughed this hunkajunk off the screen, and it deserved debasing, emerging an unintentional parody. Richard Burton, as a priest assigned to investigate the death of Father Karras (from THE EXORCIST) overplays to absurdity. And Louise Fletcher, as a psychiatrist probing the mind of Regan (Linda Blair), is amateurish. The plot involves James Earl Jones as African chief Kokumo and more mumbo jumbo than most witch doctors hear in a lifetime. The only good things about this failure are the cinematography by William Fraker, the set design, and the Ennio Morricone score. Max von Sydow returns in flashbacks. Ned Beatty, Kitty Winn, Paul Henreid. (Warner Bros.)

EXORCIST III: LEGION (1990). William Peter Blatty, who wrote the novel on which THE EXORCIST was based, wrote-directed this third film in the series (based on Blatty's LEGION), which stars George C. Scott as Lt. Kinderman (Lee J. Cobb in the original). New murders lead Kinderman to conclude that the spirit of a serial killer nicknamed Gemini has possessed the body of incarcerated criminal Brad Dourif, who promises to escape to murder again. Blatty goes for unusual scare tactics. Ed Flanders is a priest, Nicol Williamson is the new exorcist, and Patrick Ewing (the Knicks basketball player) is a guardian angel (!?). (Video/Laser: CBS/Fox)

EXORCIST—ITALIAN STYLE, THE (1975). Italian spinoff of THE EXORCIST, with a difference: Director Ciccio Ingrassia plays demons for comedy. After all, isn't possession nine tenths of the laughter? Lean back and enjoy. Starring Ingrassia (isn't self-casting sweet?), with additional devilment by Lino Banfi and Didi Perego.

EXOTIC ONES, THE. See **MONSTER AND THE STRIPPER, THE.**

EXPEDITION MOON. See **ROCKETSHIP X-M.**

EXPERIMENT ALCATRAZ (1950). Minor B-flick, offbeat in telling how doctor John Howard discovers a way of fighting blood diseases with atomic radiation when he uses "guinea pig" volunteers from Alcatraz Prison. The slight sci-fi elements are overshadowed by a typical crime plot by Orville Hampton. Directed by Edward L. Cahn. Harry Lauter, Joan Dixon, Robert Shayne.

EXPERIMENT IN EVIL. See **TESTAMENT OF DR. CORDELIER, THE.**

EXPERIMENT IN TERROR. See **BATTLESTAR GALACTICA.**

EXPERIMENT PERILOUS (1944). Unusually literate psychodrama capturing a Victorian air of mystery when doctor George Brent meets an old lady on a train that is imperiled by a storm. Brent is thrown headfirst into the enigmatic relationship between Paul Lukas and Hedy Lamarr, a couple who seem happily married . . . but beneath she is being slowly terrorized to death by Lukas, who is plagued by hereditary madness. An internalized detective story, cerebral until the climax. Directed by Jacques Tourneur. Albert Dekker. (Media)

EXPLORERS (1985). The gentler side to director Joe Dante, who focuses on three teenagers: One is a dreamer, another is a junior scientist while the third is a youth alienated from his family. They make contact with space creatures, discover how to build a rocket and fly to meet the E.T.s. That meeting is the funny side to CLOSE ENCOUNTERS as the bug-eyed creatures are TV lovers, who recite lines from cartoons and movies. A charming science fantasy, written by Eric Luke, with cute aliens by Rob Bottin. Ethan Hawke, River Phoenix, Jason Presson, Mary Kay Place. (Paramount) (Laser: MCA)

EXPLORING THE UNKNOWN (1977). ESP documentary narrated by Burt Lancaster. TV quality.

EXPOSE. See **HOUSE ON STRAW MOUNTAIN.**

EXQUISITE CADAVER, THE. See **CRUEL ONES.**

EXTERMINATING ANGEL, THE (1967). Allegorical Luis Bunuel film set in a mansion where opera-goers gather for supper. Guests find they cannot leave the mansion; crowds gather outside yet cannot enter. Sheep wander in and are cooked over fires of furniture; a bear climbs a column; and an unattached hand drifts into view. Is this the Hell of the sterile rich? Hmm. Sylvia Pinal, Claudio Brook. (Tamarelle's; Hen's Tooth; Facets)

EXTERMINATORS OF THE YEAR 3000 (1984). Italian-Spanish ripoff of THE ROAD WARRIOR set in a post-holocaust world where men fight for water after the ozone belt is destroyed. Our Mad Max lookalike drives a beat-up wreck equipped with weapons and radar called "The Exterminator," and battles a funky fleet of wheels commanded by Crazy Bull, a grotesque guerrilla who calls his men "Mother Grabbers." Directed by Jules Harrison. Alicia Moro, Alan Collins, Eduardo Fajardo. (HBO)

EXTRATERRESTRIAL NASTY. See **NIGHT FRIGHT.**

EYEBALL (1974). Here's one to turn on gore lovers: murderer kills, then pops out his victim's eyeballs. Nearsighted Italian-Spanish release is about as exciting as watching an eye chart in an optician's office. Director-writer Umberto Lenzi is in need of seeing-eye dogs. John Richardson, Martine Brochard. Also known as THE DEVIL'S EYE. (Prism)

EYE CREATURES, THE (1965). E.T. invaders resembling huge upright marshmallows with black gaping holes for mouths invade a rural community while stupid Army personnel surrounds their flying saucer. Action centers on kids making out on lovers' lane and how they outsmart the hulking entities. This crude TV quickie is an inferior remake of INVASION OF THE SAUCERMEN, produced-directed ineptly by Larry Buchanan. It's only interesting feature is a severed alien hand that does an impression of The Beast With Five Fingers. John Ashley, Cynthia Hull, Chet Davis, Warren Hammack. (Sinister/C; S/Weird; Filmfax; Nostalgia)

EYE OF THE CAT (1969). Michael Sarrazin and Gayle Hunnicutt (gorgeous in miniskirts) plot to get rid of cat-lover Eleanor Parker—only Sarrazin suffers from ailurophobia, a fear of cats. Clever camera angles and exaggerated sound effects hint of a supernatural feline, but how scary can a cat be? Producer Leslie Stevens' film also suffers from bad dialogue by Joseph Stefano and only toward its climax does it take on a macabre air. San Francisco photography (under David Lowe Rich's direction) is okay. Laurence Naismith, Tim Henry.

EYE OF THE DEMON. Video version of **BAY COVEN** (Vidmark).

EYE OF THE DEVIL (1967). French vineyard owner David Niven sacrifices himself to the grape gods to stop a three-year famine. The demands of hooded demon worshippers are fought by wife Deborah Kerr. Donald Pleasence, Sharon Tate, Flora Robson, David Hemmings and Edward Mulhare are wasted in this film butchered for the U.S. Directed by J. Lee Thompson.

EYE OF THE EVIL DEAD. See **MANHATTAN BABY.**

EYE OF THE STORM (1992). Offbeat psychothriller with surprise twists: Two brothers, after surviving the murder of their parents, turn into maladjusted adults running a roadside cafe-hotel, stopping place for drunken millionaire Dennis Hopper and wife Lara Flynn Boyle. Craig Sheffer and Bradley Gregg bring interesing nuances to the whacked-out brothers, one of whom . . . well, we don't want to give it away. Amospheric direction by Yuri Zelser. (New Line)

EYES BEHIND THE STARS (1972). Photographer and model are taking photos when the cameraman senses an alien presence. Eventually he has an encounter too close for comfort. Cheap UFO pseudothriller showing how the government suppresses flying saucer reports. Directed by Roy Garrett. Martin Balsam, Nathalie Delon, Robert Hoffmann. (United; National)

EYES OF A STRANGER (1980). The Miami Strangler is terrorizing women with obscene calls, then strangling and sexually abusing them. Some charmer. Lauren Tewes is a TV newswoman who goes after him when she suspects he's a resident of her apartment building. Jennifer Jason Leigh portrays a vulnerable blind girl. The Mark Jackson-Eric L. Bloom script is sleazy, demeaning to women, unnecessarily brutal and simple-minded. Tom Savini's graphic make-up grotesqueries seem subdued. Director Ken Wiederhorn adds no directorial tricks. John DiSanti, Peter DuPre. (Warner Bros.)

EYES OF ANNIE JONES, THE (1964). ESP combined with a girl who walks in her sleep add up to a corpse. Her strange mumblings become less strange as an ordinary murder plot unfolds. The eyes do not have it. British-U.S. production directed by Reginald LeBorg. Richard Conte, Francesca Annis, Joyce Carey.

EYES OF CHARLES SAND, THE (1972). Peter Haskell portrays the title character who has been given ESP through mother Joan Bennett. He uses his power to help a woman (Sharon Farrell) who appears to be insane, or are members of her family trying to drive her crazy? The best thing in this ESP and psycho madness, besides Reza Badiyi's atmospheric direction is Barbara Rush's homicidal fruitcake act as she who runs around a mansion with a butcher knife, cackling her insanity. Adam West as a psychiatrist, Bradford Dillman as Rush's husband and Gary Clarke as a mysterious young man.

EYES OF DR. CHANEY. See **MANSION OF THE DOOMED.**

EYES OF EVIL. See **THOUSAND EYES OF DR. MABUSE, THE.**

EYES OF FIRE (1984). This artistic, melancholy period supernatural tale is only partly successful. Its photography, capturing a dank, dark forest with strong beams of light and clouds of mist etching its characters, is strong and sensual. But the story by director Avery Crounse is ponderous and a hodgepodge of imagery. The time is 1750 when the townspeople of Dalton's Ferry attempt to hang their adulterous preacher. The man of the cloth is saved by a witch girl and flees to set up a new stockade in a valley inhabited by mud people and a demon. Symbolism and allegory make it literate but nothing about the characters or "monsters" creates suspense. Also called CRY BLUE SKY. Dennis Lipscomb, Guy Boyd. (Video/Laser: Vestron)

EYES OF HELL. See **MASK, THE.**

EYES OF LAURA MARS (1978). Chic photographer Faye Dunaway, a specialist in blending sex and sadism in her morbid lay-outs, is inexplicably linked to a psychokiller, but this link is never explored, and the film becomes a simple-minded one-murder-after-the-other plot until the maniac closes in on Dunaway. John Carpenter's original concept was revised by David Zelag Goodman. Directed by Irvin Kershner. Tommy Lee Jones co-stars as the investigating cop. Intriguing premise ultimately suffers from producer Jon Peters' blindness to story quality. Brad Dourif, Rene Auberjonois, Raul Julia. (RCA/Columbia; Goodtimes) (Laser: Columbia)

EYES OF THE AMARYLLIS, THE (1982). Gentle, restrained ghost story about a young girl (Natalie Babbitt) who comes to Nantucket Island in 1880 to live with her grandmother—a strange woman who keeps an even stranger vigil for the return of a lover who drowned at sea. This is more a coming-of-age tale than a supernatural thriller, as writers Frederick O'Harra and Stratton Rawson emphasize character and atmosphere. Director Frederick King Keller plays the same game. Ruth Ford, Jonathan Bolt, Guy Boyd. (Vestron; Live)

EYES OF THE PANTHER (1990). Repackaged version of an adaptation of Ambrose Bierce's story about how the spirit of a wild animal plagues a young woman. First presented on Shelley Duvall's NIGHTMARE CLASSICS. Directed by Noel Black. Daphne Zuniga, C. Thomas Howell, John Stockwell. (Cannon)

EYES WITHOUT A FACE. Video version of **HORROR CHAMBER OF DR. FAUSTUS, THE** (Interama; Filmfax) (Laser: Image).

FABULOUS BARON MUNCHAUSEN, THE (1961). From the Czechs who made THE FABULOUS WORLD OF JULES VERNE . . . an ingenious blending of live action with animation, based on Gustav Dore engravings. A first-man-on-the-moon story told by writer-director Karel Zeman with panache. On Image laser as **ORIGINAL FABULOUS ADVENTURES OF BARON MUNCHAUSEN (BARON PRASIL), THE.**

FABULOUS JOE (1947). Joe is a dog. So is this Hal Roach film, directed by Harve Foster. You see, Joe talks, and there's nothing duller in Hollywood farces than talking dogs. Walter Abel, Marie Wilson, Sheldon Leonard, Donald Meek. (Nostalgia; Unicorn)

FABULOUS JOURNEY TO THE CENTER OF THE EARTH (1977). See **WHERE TIME BEGAN.**

FABULOUS WORLD OF JULES VERNE, THE (1958). Czech live action/animation technique (dubbed Mystimation) is a visual delight, withb Verne's stories woven together with threads of fantasy. Whether in the clouds in novel airships, under the sea in a submarine or on the ground, this flight-into-fantasy-adventure is charming and exciting. Written-directed by Karel Zeman. (VCI)

FACE, THE. See **MAGICIAN, THE (1958).**

FACE AT THE WINDOW, THE (1939). Tod Slaughter, specialist in evil characters, pulls out all the stops in his portrayal of the Wolf, a serial killer terrorizing Paris in the 19th Century. Directed by George King. Marjorie Taylor, John Warwick. (Nostalgia; Moore; Horizon)

FACE BEHIND THE MASK (1941). Worth seeing for Peter Lorre's performance as a fire-victim who hides his disfigurement behind a mask, then falls in love with a blind woman. Despite the low budget and B-quality direction by Robert Florey, this has a tragic quality instilled by Lorre's performance. Evelyn Keyes, Don Beddoe.

FACE IN THE FOG, A (1936). Hunchbacked killer, The Fiend, uses an unusual bullet for revenge in this low-budget Sam Katzman flick directed by Robert Hill. June Collyer, Lloyd Hughes, (Filmfax; Nostalgia, Sinister/C)

FACELESS (1988). Dr. Flamono (Helmut Berger) attempts to restore a woman's beauty after her face has been disfigured by acid. Also being held in the batty doc's lab is Caroline Munro, whose father (Telly Savalas) sends private dick Christopher Mitchum to find her. Howard Vernon and Anton Diffring also appear in this horror entry from Italian director Jesus Franco. The French version (from Import Horror) is uncut.

FACELESS MONSTERS, THE. See **NIGHTMARE CASTLE.**

FACELESS VAMPIRE KILLERS. See **FEARLESS VAMPIRE KILLERS, THE.**

FACE OF ANOTHER, THE (1966). Hiroshi Teshigahara, director of WOMAN IN THE DUNES, offers another haunting tale with allegorical overtones: A man horribly disfigured in an accident turns into an outcast and is driven to a psychiatrist-plastic surgeon who produces a life-like mask of a stranger's face. Nakadai assumes the stranger's personality. (From Sony with English subtitles)

FACE OF EVE. See **EVE.**

FACE OF FEAR. See **PEEPING TOM.**

FACE OF FEAR. See **FACE OF TERROR.**

FACE OF FEAR, THE (1990). This TV-movie, based on a Dean R. Koontz novel, was adapted by Koontz and Alan J. Glueckman. It's a contrived slasher thriller in which a serial killer, The Butcher, traps magazine editor Lee Horsley and girl friend Pam Dawber in an office building one night and pursues them floor by floor. Although Horsley has a fear of heights, he and Dawber, with a convenient mountain-climber's rig, escape by descending the side of the building. There's some tense moments but the silliness of the situation, and the unbelievable characters established by director Farhad Mann, defeat an all-too obvious contrivance.

FACE OF FIRE (1958). James Whitmore is excellent as a handyman who tries to save a child during a fire and is so badly burned that he is nauseating to look at. Weak of mind and spirit, he becomes an outcast. Based on Stephen Crane's "The Monster." Directed by Albert Band. Cameron Mitchell, Bettye Ackerman, Royal Dano.

FACE OF FU MANCHU, THE (1965). Hammer's resurrection of the Sax Rohmer villain, with Christopher Lee as the insidious Asian planning to destroy the world with a poison invented by a German he holds prisoner. Nigel Green is Sir Nayland Smith of Scotland Yard. Don Sharp directed Harry Alan Towers' production, which Towers wrote. Tsai Chin is Fu's daughter, Karin Dor a hapless captive, Walter Rilla the scientist.

FACE OF MARBLE (1946). While creaky in terms of its antiquated techniques, this Monogram thriller from the Frankenstein school has such an unusual plot that it's entertaining and offbeat. John Carradine, in one of his sympathetic roles, and Robert Shayne portray doctors in a cliffside mansion conducting electrical experiments in restoring life to the dead. Brutus, the family Great Dane, becomes a test experiment, but the dog turns into a phantom that passes through solid walls and drinks the blood of its prey. Not much of this is explained but there's an attraction in watching the female leads, Maris Wrixon and Claudia Drake, run around the castle in nightgowns that emphasis their heaving bosoms. Willie Best is a servant, Thomas E. Jackson is a cop. (Fang)

FACE OF TERROR (1962). Spanish import—about a disfigured girl who undergoes beauty transfiguration—underwent its own surgery at the hands of U.S. film doctors. Hence, a plastic movie. Only a special fluid will keep a young woman alive—you'll need a transfusion to stay awake. Directed by Isidoro Martinez Ferry; U.S. footage by William Hole Jr. Lisa Gaye, Fernando Rey.

FACE OF THE SCREAMING WEREWOLF, THE (1958). A Mexican production (HOUSE OF TERROR) starring Lon Chaney Jr., originally a horror-comedy vehicle for the comedian Tin Tan, but when U.S. repackager Jerry Warren recut it, he left the laughs on the editing room floor. You might still think it's funny, but for the wrong reasons. Directed by Gilberto Martinez Solares, it offers Chaney Jr. in a performance clumsy and inept. SCREAMING WEREWOLF will give you the screaming mimies. (Sinister/C; S/Weird; Filmfax)

FACES OF FEAR. See **TASTE OF SIN, A.**

FADE TO BLACK (1980). Compelling study of lonely Dennis Christopher who fantasizes images from movies and assumes guises of such monsters as the Mummy, Dracula, etc. Finally, reality and fantasy are indistinguishable and Christopher turns on his abusers. These killings are cleverly conceived—in fact, the film feels original (credit writer-director Vernon Zimmerman). Linda Kerridge is a wonderful Marilyn Monroe lookalike, Tim Thomerson is a cop. Clips from THE CREATURE FROM THE BLACK LAGOON. (Media)

FAHRENHEIT 451 (1966). The title refers to the temperature at which paper catches fire—apropos to a plot set in the future when books have been outlawed and special "firemen" seek out and destroy any volumes still in existence. Oskar Werner is such a fireman who discovers the delights of reading and rebels against the regime. Based on the novel by Ray Bradbury, and directed by Francois Truffaut, this has met with mixed emotions—some feel it captures the poetry of Bradbury, others feel the premise is too absurd. I think it's a literate contribution to the film genre. Julie Christie appears in a dual role. Nicolas Roeg photographed it, Bernard Herrmann wrote the wonderful music. Anton Diffring, Cyril Cusack, Anna Palk. (Video/Laser: MCA)

FAIL SAFE (1964). Sidney Lumet's version of the Eugene Burdick-Harvey Wheeler best-seller approaches impending nuclear war as a politico-horror thriller, a portrait of inexorable doom. Stark black-and-white photography by Gerald Herschfeld and electrifying acting by Henry Fonda, Dan O'Herlihy and Walter Matthau make this superior apocalypse science fiction which comments on our militancy and inability to control technology. A U.S. bomber accidentally unleashes a nuclear device on Moscow. To keep peace, the President (Fonda) faces sending one of our own planes to bomb New York City. Dark and gripping. Larry Hagman, Dom DeLuise, Fritz Weaver. (RCA/Columbia; Goodtimes) (Laser: Columbia)

FAIR GAME (1988). This Italian film (made as MAMBA) has a fascinating premise: a woman (Trudie Styler) is trapped in her apartment with a deadly black mamba while her husband uses a TV-monitoring system to interfere with her efforts to avoid the fatal bite. Unfortunately, the direction by Mario Orfini is mediocre and the snake's point-of-view shots ineffectual and cliched. What should have been the ultimate in horror loses its bite (excuse us). Gregg Henry is superb as the crazed husband. The music is by Giorgio Moroder, who also served as associate producer on this threadbare film. Fangs, but no fangs. (Charter/Nelson; Vidmark)

FAIRY TALES (1978). Once upon a time there was an abominable movie filled with smutty jokes, degrading homosexual gags and insults to dwarves and midgets. This parody of Mother Goose features Little Bo Bee, the Old Lady in the Shoe and Snow White in sexual situations filled with foul language and a leering sexual attitude that in the post-AIDs era seems disgusting. A childlike king goes on a quest to find the one woman who turns him on. Plenty of frontage nudity and shapely femmes, and even some musical numbers that spoof Cole Porter. Directed by Harry Tampa. Von Sparks, Irwin Corey, Sy Richardson, Brenda Fogarty. (Cannon; Media)

FALCON'S GOLD (1982). Pulp adventure with mild sci-fi overtones: A chunk of meteorite holds the key to laser power, and various governments are after the secret of its destructiveness. The action is slam-bang and there's little time to consider the story holes and absurdities. Simon MacCorkindale, Louise Vallance and John Marley star. Directed by Bob Schulz. (From Prism as

ROBBERS OF SACRED MOUNTAIN)

FALL BREAK. See **MUTILATOR, THE.**

FALLING, THE. See **ALIEN PREDATOR.**

FALL OF THE HOUSE OF USHER (1948). British geezers at the Gresham Club drink Scotch while one reads Edgar Allan Poe. The famous tale is mangled terribly, parts of its faithful to the original, other parts mere fabrication. Most of the time Lady Madoline flits around the castle in a negligee with a candelabra while Roderick Usher tries to prevent a curse caused by his mother's severed head. Ultimately unwatchable under the misdirection of the blighter Ivan Barnett. Gwendoline Watford, Kay Tendeter, Irving Steen. (Sinister/C; Filmfax)

FALL OF THE HOUSE OF USHER, THE. Video version of Roger Corman's **HOUSE OF USHER, THE** (Warner Bros.; Goodtimes).

FALL OF THE HOUSE OF USHER, THE (1979). Terrible TV version of Poe's classic with wild-eyed, wild-haired Martin Landau overacting as Roderick Usher while his sister (Charlene Tilton) walks hallways in a zombie-like trance. Ray Walston is the faithful retainer who mumbles mumbo jumbo jumpily just as the foundations tremble and tumble. This falls apart faster than Usher's estate. Directed by James L. Conway. (VCI)

FALL OF THE HOUSE OF USHER, THE (1983). Another version of Poe's classic story, this time from director Jesus Franco. Howard Vernon plays the crazed Usher and Lina Romay his wife. Robert Foster is the doctor.

FALSE FACE. See **SCALPEL.**

FAN, THE (1981). Weak slasher film failing to believably portray disturbed Michael Biehn and his reign of terror directed against an aging but attractive Broadway actress (Lauren Bacall). James Garner is wasted as Lauren's husband, although Maureen Stapleton is good as the actress' personal secretary caught up in the knife horrors. Directed by Edward Bianchi. From a novel by Bob Randall. Aka TRANCE. (Video/Laser: Paramount)

FANATIC. See **DIE! DIE, MY DARLING!**

FANGORIA'S WEEKEND OF HORRORS (1986). Footage of a horror convention features interviews with make-up artist Rick Baker, directors Tobe Hooper and Wes Craven and actor Robert Englund. (Media)

FANGS (1978). Killer reptiles and serpents put the bite on the enemies of a snake lover. Proved to be poisonous at the box office. Directed by Vittorio Schiraldi. Les Tremayne, Janet Wood, Bebe Kelly. (United America; Video Gems; Moore)

FANGS OF THE LIVING DEAD (1968). "The coldness of the grave is in my blood," remarks a buxom, frilly-gowned vampire woman in this Italian rehash of DRACULA. The star is Anita Ekberg, who plays (hold your breath) a virgin. Inheriting a castle, she arrives to discover a suspicious baron and a harem of busty, lusty bloodsuckers. The color, production and ladies are nice on the eyes but this is an exercise in tedium. Anyway, fangs for the mammaries, Anita. Written-directed by Armando De Ossorio. Also known as MALENKA THE VAMPIRE, THE NIECE OF THE VAMPIRE, THE VAMPIRE'S NIECE and BLOODY GIRL. Julian Ugarte, Diana Lorys. (Sinister/C; S/Weird; Filmfax)

FANTASIA (1941). Amalgam of cartoon art set to classical music (by Leopold Stokowski and the Philadelphia Symphony Orchestra) was a revolutionary experiment by Disney, animated by artists visually interpreting the music. Each sequence explores an element of the fantastic—from a Bach of abstract designs to a "Nutcracker Suite" of magical sprites and dancing mushrooms; from Mickey Mouse in "The Sorcerer's Apprentice" to Stravinsky's "Rite of Spring," a pageant of life's evolution depicting primeval ooze, dinosaurs and global holocaust. Centaurettes, cupids and winged horses frolic in Beethoven's "Pastoral Symphony," followed by Ponchielli's "Dance of the Hours" featuring pirouetting hippotami. Moussorgsky's "Night on Bald Mountain" is of macabre design. (Disney) (Laser: Disney; Image)

FANTASIES (1982). This average TV-movie, cashing in on the theatrical slasher craze in watered-down style, depicts a standard mad-dog killer out to wipe out the cast and crew of a TV soap opera—and if you've ever seen a soap opera, you know why. Also known as STUDIO MURDERS, it was written-produced by David Levinson. Directed by William Wiard. Suzanne Pleshette, Barry Newman, Patrick O'Neal, Robert Vaughn, Madlyn Rhue.

FANTASIST, THE (1986). A strange literate psychokiller movie thanks to the direction and writing by Robin Hardy, better known for THE WICKER MAN. Adapting Patrick McGinley's novel GOOSEFOOT, Hardy etches the portrait of Dublin teacher Moira Harris, whose sexually repression is caused by her Protestant upbringing in a dysfunctional family. Eccentric American Timothy Bottoms could be "The Phone Call Killer," who calls women with non-obscene erotic poetry that appeals to their repressions, then attacks them with a knife. Policeman Christopher Cazenove is as odd as the rest of the gallery of eccentric personalities in this metaphorical statement about the Irish character. Harris' final confrontation with the killer is psychological and arousing, featuring a bizarre love-making sequence. (Republic)

FANTASTIC ADVENTURES OF UNICO, THE (1982). Japanese animated feature film for children, depicting the life of a heroic unicorn. (RCA/Columbia)

FANTASTIC ANIMATION FESTIVAL (1977). Melange of cartoons from all over the world in a variety of styles—from Max Fleischer's SUPERMAN to the famed BAMBI MEETS GODZILLA. An exciting, eclectic bag of animated goodies. (Media)

FANTASTIC DISAPPEARING MAN, THE. See **CURSE OF DRACULA, THE.**

FANTASTIC INVASION OF PLANET EARTH. See **BUBBLE, THE.**

FANTASTIC JOURNEY (1977). Pilot for a short-lived series, in which scientists are stranded in the Bermuda Triangle, a time continuum limbo area from which characters can enter past or future. Hodgepodge of ideas and cliches (of TV mentality) as the cast encounters pirates, aliens and hooligans from Atlantis. Directed by Andrew V. McLaglen. Carl Franklin, Scott Thomas.

FANTASTIC PLANET (1973). Imagine a world in which humanoids are only inches high and treated like frivolous pets or domestics. Such a world is Ygam, where the masters are the 40-foot-tall Draags, and we earth beings are Oms. Winner of the Grand Prix at Cannes, this French animated film is the work of artist Roland Topor and director Rene Laloux. The parable aspects are fascinating, for they tap into the roots of human existence. Also impressive are the organic drawing styles and oddball flora and fauna of the planet. The plot involves occasional exterminations of the Oms and the outlaw band's attempt to escape to Fantastic Planet, a satellite world where Draags go to meditate. A fascinating sci-fi fable. Voices for the U.S. version: Marvin Miller, Barry Bostwick, Jane Waldo. (Video Yesteryear; United America; Sinister/C; Filmfax; from Vidcrest as **PLANET OF INCREDIBLE CREATURES**)

FANTASTIC VOYAGE (1966). Submarine and crew are miniaturized to microscopic size and injected into the bloodstream of a scientist who has been shot by foreign agents and will die unless the crew can voyage through his body to his brain and destroy a bloodclot with a laser beam. Imaginatively executed, with tremendous effects for their time. In this bizarre inner world of the body, the simplest things become obstacles: an artery is a whirlpool, blood corpuscles are deadly attackers, etc. Richard Fleischer directed. Stephen Boyd, Arthur Kennedy, Raquel Welch, Donald Pleasence, Arthur O'Connell, Edmond O'Brien. (RCA/Columbia) (Laser: CBS/Fox)

FANTASTIC WORLD OF D.C. COLLINS (1984). Imaginative child Gary Coleman is caught up in spy shenanigans with Soviet agents over possession of a videotape that holds the key to the prevention of nuclear war. As he undergoes the chase, Coleman daydreams he's Clint Eastwood, James Bond, Indiana Jones and Luke Skywalker in parody flashbacks. Routine TV-movie, strictly for kids. Bernie Casey, Shelly Smith, Michael Ansara, George Gobel, Marilyn McCoo. Directed by Leslie Martinson. (New World/Starmaker)

FANTASY FILM WORLD OF GEORGE PAL, THE (1986). Fascinating documentary on one of Hollywood's most beloved producers of fantasy and sci-fi, whose DESTINATION MOON, WHEN WORLDS COLLIDE and WAR OF THE WORLDS established new trends. Tony Curtis, Ray Bradbury and Ray Harryhausen discuss Pal's warm character and contributions to cinema. Footage from many of Pal's productions. Written-directed by Arnold Leibovit. (Starmaker) (Laser: Image)

FANTASY ISLAND (1976). Two-hour pilot for the long-running TV series starring Ricardo Montalban as Mr. Rourke, the director of a tropical paradise which caters to satisfying guests' fantasies for a mere $50,000. Ricardo's little pal Tattoo, Herve Villechaize, exclaims "De plane, boss, de plane!" There's only a slight touch of fantasy in this Aaron Spelling-Leonard Goldberg production—mainly in how Montalban pulls off those fantasies. Directed by Richard Lang. Bill Bixby, Sandra Dee, Peter Lawford, Carol Lynley, Hugh O'Brian. (Prism)

FARAWAY, SO CLOSE! (1993). Wim Wenders' sequel to WINGS OF DESIRE, picking up where that film left off with angel Cassiel (Otto Sander) atop the Angel of Victory tower in Berlin. Joining him is Nastassja Kinski as the angel Raphaela. Horst Buchholz, Heinz Ruhmann, Bruno Ganze, Willem Dafoe. (Sony)

FAREWELL TO THE PLANET OF THE APES (1974). Re-edited episodes of the TV series PLANET OF THE APES with Roddy McDowall as Galen the chimp, a fugitive in a kingdom of monkeys and orangs along with two Earthlings who have to keep hiding from search parties. Directed by Don McDougall and J. M. Lucas. Roscoe Lee Browne, Joanna Barnes, Frank Aletter.

FAR FROM HOME (1989). Lightweight killer-on-the-loose terror tale with unusual desert photography. Magazine writer Matt Frewer and teenager daughter Drew Barrymore (of E.T. fame) are stranded in a rundown Nevada burg, where a series of murders dogs them. Predictable and only occasionally exciting, with Susan Tyrrell shining as a shrew of a mother who runs a trailer park. Based on a script by Tommy Lee Wallace and directed by Meiert Avis. Richard Masur, Karen Austin, Jennifer Tilly, Dick Miller. (Video/Laser: Vestron)

FARM, THE (1987). See **CURSE, THE.**

FASHION HOUSE OF DEATH. See **BLOOD AND BLACK LACE.**

FATAL ATTRACTION (1985). Minor psycho-game thriller set in Toronto where Sally Kellerman literally runs into scientist Stephen Lack in a head-on collision. Later, they are sexually attracted and develop a penchant for playing odd games with each other. Mildly mind-bending, but climax is predictable. John Huston appears as Lack's father. Produced-directed by Michael Grant. (Vestron)

FATAL CHARM (1991). Set in Ukiah, Calif., this psychokiller flick went through enough production ills that the director used the pseudonym Alan Smithee. Nicolas Niciphor's script deals with teenager Amanda Peterson falling for a serial killer and writing to him in prison after he's found guilty of heinous crimes. Why? Because he's handsome and has "fatal charm." Ha! The film attempts to set up the viewer for a surprise twist, but that surprise is telegraphed. This cynicism is distasteful and FATAL CHARM is a hollow cliche. The cast is wasted, especially Christopher Atkins as the accused killer. Mary Frann, James Reman, Andrew Robinson, Peggy Lipton, Lar Park Lincoln, Robert Walker Jr. (MCEG)

FATAL GAMES (1983). An awful slasher flick in the hands of total incompetents. The setting is the Falcon Academy of Athletics, where teenagers preparing for the 1984 Olympics don't realize they are guinea pigs for a doctor with a new superstrength formula not unlike steroids. They are also cannon fodder for a mad killer armed with a javelin, who spikes his victims while they work out. The most ridiculous scene has the javelin jerkola lurking underwater while a beautiful swimmer passes above him—an obvious homage to the Black Lagoon Creature. The incoherent script was speared to death by Rafael Bunuel and director Michael Elliot. Sally Kirkland, Lynn Banashek, Sean Masterson, Michael O'Leary, Teal Roberts. Produced as THE KILLING TOUCH. (Media)

FATAL PULSE (1988). Uninspired dash of slash that imitates so many predecessors that it doesn't have an original thought in its doltish script. A killer wearing black gloves closes in on sorority chicks who always happen to be naked or semi-undressed. The dumbest of the murders has the killer using the edge of a record to slit a student's throat. Producer-director Anthony J. Christopher brings nothing special to the material, although Martin Mayo's synthetic score works when it's jazzy. Joe Phelan (Martin Sheen's brother), Michelle McCormick, Ken Roberts, Cindra Hodgson join porn actor Herschel Savage, billed as Harvey Cowen. (Celebrity)

FATAL SKY (1990). Set in central Norway, but shot in Yugoslavia, this thriller blends every "unsolved mystery" imaginable: UFOs, mutilated cattle, meteor showers, humanoid forms in spacesuits, a disease that poxes its victims and kills them, weird black helicopters, a military conspiracy, a top-secret medical installation, etc. Michael Nouri plays a photojournalist tracking an explosion over Norway with sexy pilot Darlene Fluegel. The script by Anthony Able plays off our phobias about government secrets and reinforces them with the cliche army general essayed by Charles Durning. It moves at a brisk clip and its characters are colorful, but genre fans may be disappointed by the clean resolution of the mysteries. Director Frank Shields gets good performances out of Maxwell Caulfield (as a pretty-boy news broadcaster from a super-news station), Dereen Nesbitt and Ray Charleston. (On video/laser from Vidmark as **PROJECT ALIEN**)

FAT SPY (1966). See editions 1-3.

FEAR, THE. See **GATES OF HELL, THE.**

FEAR (1980). Italian psychothriller set in a country home where women are slaughtered by a killer, but not before they've flitted about undressed or tossed off their duds to make love. Some black magic touches give this a sense of weirdness, but it's typical for the genre. Directed by Riccardo Freda. Stefano Patrizi, Martine Brochard. (Wizard; from HGV as **WAILING, THE**)

FEAR (1988). A brutal film about a Vietnam vet who freaks out and goes on a killing spree, this is also an attempt by director Robert A. Ferretti to capture the chaotic, schizophrenic mind of a victim of war. It may repel you, but its nightmarish interpretations of the berserk killer's mind make this unusual. The plotline follows four escapees (including Frank Stallone) who go on a murder spree, terrorizing vacationers Cliff DeYoung and Kay Lenz. (Virgin Vision) (Laser: Image)

FEAR (1990). Psychic Ally Sheedy helps police track serial killers, writing best sellers with her manager Lauren Hutton. The twist to director Rockne S. O'Bannon's script is that a serial killer known as "The Shadow Man" is just as much a psychic as Sheedy, and he uses his power to terrify her because her fear turns him on. "I give great fear," Sheedy cries. This is notches above the usual dame-in-peril fare, enhanced by a Henry Mancini score and John Agar (as the killer), Stan Shaw (cop), Keone Young (another cop) and Dina Merrill (publisher's wife). Produced by Richard Kobritz. (Vestron)

FEAR CHAMBER, THE (1974). One of four Mexican-produced cheapies made by Boris Karloff in 1968 shortly before his death, but not released for years. Karloff fans will not be impressed—the Master has only a few scenes as a benevolent scientist who keeps a living rock in his laboratory, unaware underlings are feeding it women to control its appetite. Written by Jack Hill and directed by Juan Ibanez. Yerye Beirut, Julissa, Carlos East. (Filmfax; from Sinister/C as **CHAMBER OF FEAR** and from MPI as **TORTURE CHAMBER, THE**)

FEAR CITY (1984). Although this has minor horrific overtones in depicting a slasher killer terrorizing topless dancers who work for sleazy New York club owners, fans of MS .45 will want to study the style of director Abel Ferrara, who has a unique way of filming the less-than-desirable elements of Manhattan. Melanie Griffith buffs will also grove on her sexy topless dance sequences. A knife killer who also practices karate is on the loose, and a war has erupted between topless booker Jack Scalia, hard-nosed cop Billy Dee Williams and ex-boxer Tom Berenger. (Video/Laser: HBO)

FEAR IN THE CITY OF THE LIVING DEAD. See **GATES OF HELL, THE.**

FEAR IN THE NIGHT (1947). Cornell Woolrich's "Nightmare" is the basis for this low budgeter with DeForrest Kelley as a musician who wakes up thinking he committed a murder. He turns to a policeman relative (Paul Kelly) for help but evidence mounts that he did it. Written-directed by Maxwell Shane, who remade this in '56 as NIGHTMARE. Ann Doran, Kay Scott, Jeff York, Robert Emmett Keane. (Sinister/C; Filmfax; HBO)

FEAR IN THE NIGHT (1973). Hammer psychothriller with Judy Geeson as a bride being terrorized at a deserted school for boys. Everyone thinks she's recovering from a breakdown and is still nuts, but we know better, right fans? Trick ending by writers Jimmy Sangster and Michael Syson is telegraphed, so this shocker has few surprises. Sangster directed. Joan Collins, Ralph Bates, Peter Cushing. (HBO; Republic; from Magnum as **DYNASTY OF FEAR**)

FEARLESS FRANK (1967). See editions 1-3.

FEARLESS VAMPIRE KILLERS, THE, or PARDON ME, BUT YOUR TEETH ARE IN MY NECK (1967). Roman Polanski's lampoon of the vampire genre is an uneven olio, a mixture of cleverness and inanity that still deserves a look. There's plenty of idiotic clowning as professor Jack MacGowran and his assistant (Polanski) invade the castle of Count Von Krolock (Ferdy Mayne). Because these characters are dunderheads, the foils (and fools) of parody, they are of little interest no matter how much fun is made of wooden stakes and other vampire-hunting accoutrements. Sharon Tate is a girl in a bathtub, and her scene is the funniest. Also known as DANCE OF THE VAMPIRES. Alfie Bass, Fiona Lewis, Ian Quarrier, Ron Lacey. (Video/Laser: MGM/UA)

FEAR NO EVIL (1969). One of two Universal TV-movies (the other is RITUAL OF EVIL) to star Louis Jourdan as psychic ghost chaser David Sorell and Wilfrid Hyde-White as his Watson-like companion, Harry Snowden, an expert in the occult. Bradford Dillman portrays a scientist who buys an old mirror but is killed shortly after in a car crash. His fiance discovers the mirror has strange properties to bring his spirit back. Atmospheric supernatural thriller, tensely directed by Paul Wendkos, adapted by Richard Alan Simmons from a Guy Endore story. Lynda Day, Carroll O'Connor, Marsha Hunt.

FEAR NO EVIL (1981). Director Frank LaLoggia helms this above-average, below-expensive supernatural tale featuring some zippy effects. The plot is implausible (three Archangles descend to Earth to take on human guises to combat Lucifer and his zombies), and there's too much emphasis on a plot involving teenagers, but overall execution and artistry are good. Made as MARK OF THE BEAST. Elizabeth Hoffmann, Dick Burt, R. J. Silverthorn. (Embassy; Columbia)

FEAR STALK (1989). While its physical horror is minimal, this TV-movie reaches a peak in psychological terror thanks to Jill Clayburgh in the leading role as a TV producer who is plagued by a stranger who uses computers to frighten her in every way he can. Her bravura performance gives this otherwise minor offering an edge that makes it worth seeing. Directed by Larry Shaw. Equally good is Sada Thompson as Clayburgh's mother; Stephen Macht is the ineffectual boyfriend. Lynne Thigpen, Sandy McPeak, Loran Luft, Cheryl Anderson.

FEAST FOR THE DEVIL (197?). Woman visits a small coastal European village searching for her missing sister, only to fall under the jurisdiction of a mad doctor. Krista Nell, Thomas Moore, Teresa Gimera. (Mogul)

FEAST OF FLESH. See **BLOOD FEAST.**

FEDERAL AGENTS VS. UNDERWORLD INC. (1949). Republic's 12-chapter serial spotlights an evil network of criminals that has stolen a famous artifact, the Golden Hands, which an ancient legend says is cursed. A nonstop battle erupts between the evil Nila (Carol Forman) and her henchmen against square-jawed federal agent Dave Worth (Kirk Alyn, who that same year played Superman). Alyn battles hired guns and seeks to stop Nila from using an Asian drug that controls men's minds. Fred Brannon directed with all the cliffhangers in place. Rosemary La Planche, Roy Barcroft, James Dale, Bruce Edwards, Tris Coffin. The edited TV-movie version is GOLDEN HANDS OF KURIGAL. (Republic)

FEET FOREMOST (1983). Teenager takes possession of an industrialist and wife when they renovate a 14th Century castle, killing them from "inside out." Based on an L.P. Hartley story, it was directed by Gordon Flemying. Jeremy Kempt, Joanna Van Gyseghen. (Prism)

FEMALE BUTCHER. See **LEGEND OF BLOOD CASTLE, THE.**

FEMALE FIEND. See **THEATER OF DEATH.**

FEMALE PLASMA SUCKERS. Video of **BLOOD ORGY OF SHE-DEVILS** (Lettuce Entertain You).

FEMALE SPACE INVADERS. See **STARCRASH.**

FEMALE TRAP. See **NAME OF THE GAME IS KILL, THE.**

FENGRIFFEN. See **AND NOW THE SCREAMING STARTS.**

FERAT VAMPIRE (1983). Czech horror-fantasy, intended as a comedy-parody of vampire flicks, but with a twist: The bloodsucker is a sports car that runs on blood, not gasoline. Put your foot on the accelerator and a needle pops through the foot pedal, sucking your life's fluid. And we don't mean oil. Directed by Juraz Herz.

FER-DE-LANCE (1974). Promising premise for a TV-movie shocker—a deadly serpent loose aboard an atomic sub—has minimum suspense values. Directed by Russell Mayberry, scripted by producer Leslie Stevens. David Janssen is the captain. Hope Lange, Ivan Dixon, Jason Evers, Ben Piazza. (Worldvision)

FERTILIZING THE BLASPHEMIZING BOMBSHELL (1990). Made as MARK OF THE BEAST (Rhino Video), this TV version has an inappropriate title (it's a serious movie, not a comedy) supposedly describing what happens when a woman looking for her missing sister in the desert region of the Devil's Playground stumbles across a satanic cult. If the title was supposed to set this movie apart, it only sets it apart into the scrap heap of hunkajunk movies one should avoid. The heroine, intended as a human sacrifice, runs around the dunes in panties and blouse until sheriff Bo Hopkins comes to her rescue. It's blasphemy this was even produced. Sheila Caan, Denise King, Rick Hill.

FERRYBOAT WOMAN MARIA (1936). German film directed/co-written by Frank Wisbar that he remade as STRANGLER OF THE SWAMP after fleeing Germany and reestablishing in Hollywood. Like the 1946 remake, this is an atmospheric, eerie intepretation of an old Nordid legend, a metaphor for the crossing from life to death. Sybille Schmitz, Peter Voss, Aribert Mog.

FIELD OF DREAMS (1989). An extraordinary fantasy that is a metaphor, an allegory, a parable. It is an American fairy tale standing for desires and unfulfilled dreams, the search for inner contentment, and the fight against the Establishment to be special. Kevin Costner is a farmer who hears a voice telling him to build a baseball field in his pasture. Costner does—and soon the field is filled with ballplayers long dead, and Costner is sent on an odyssey in search of the truth. Based on SHOELESS JOE, a novel by W. P. Kinsella (whom Costner plays), this involves a drop-out advocate of the 1960s (James Earl Jones) and a long-dead doctor (Burt Lancaster) who lives again before Costner returns to the field for an encounter with his dead father. Writer-director Phil Alden Robinson pulls these elements together in a fascinating way. Amy Madigan, Ray Liotta. (Video/Laser: MCA)

FIEND, THE (1971). Video version of See **BEWARE THE BRETHREN** (Monterey).

FIEND (1980). Regional horror thriller from writer-producer-editor-gofer Don Dohler (THE ALIEN FACTOR) about a supernatural firefly that takes over music teacher Tom Leifert and eats its way into corpses, bringing them to life. Richard Nelson, Elaine White. (Monterey; Prism)

FIENDISH GHOULS, THE. See **FLESH AND THE FIENDS.**

FIENDISH PLOT OF DR. FU MANCHU (1980). Peter Sellers' last film is not his best as he portrays Sax Rohmer's insidious Asian in search of an eternal youth serum, with fantasy contraptions randomly thrown in. Sellers plays Fu Manchu at 168, a younger Fu after drinking the youth elixir, an antiques dealer, and detective Nayland Smith. Smith's stuffiness and British demeanor are the funniest touches in this mess directed by Piers Haggard. David Tomlinson, Helen Mirren, Steve Franken, Burt Kwouk. (Video/Laser: Warner Bros.)

FIENDS, THE. See **DIABOLIQUE.**

FIEND WITHOUT A FACE (1958). A favorite "alien invader" thriller with grotesque brain-spine creatures which attach to heads and suck away human brains . . . positively unsettling monsters. Locale is a Canadian Air Force base where rocket experiments have caused human thoughts to be turned into the attacking brain creatures. This Richard Gordon production is recommended for its macabre overtones. Directed by Arthur Crabtree. Marshall Thompson, Kim Parker, Terence Kilburn. (Video/Laser: Republic)

FIEND WITH THE ATOMIC BRAIN. See **BLOOD OF GHASTLY HORROR.**

FIEND WITH THE ELECTRONIC BRAIN. See **BLOOD OF GHASTLY HORROR.**

FIFTH CORD, THE (1975). Routine Italian psychothriller in which director Luigi Bazzoni attempts to capture the perversity and tension of Dario Argento, with only piddling success. Investigative newspaperman Franco Nero is on the trail of the Aries Killer, a knife-wielding madman who strikes on Tuesdays. There's a couple of exciting sequences (crippled woman crawling to escape killer; boy trapped in narrow tunnel as killer with hands outstretched closes in) but it's too disjointed. Good jazz score by Ennio Morricone. Silvia Monti, Wolfgang Preiss, Edmund Purdom, Pamela Tiffin.

FIFTH MISSILE, THE (1986). TV-movie based on the Frank Robinson- Thomas Scortia novel THE GOLD CREW, in which a Polaris sub, on a mission to simulate war with the Soviets, is stricken by toxic poison and hallucinating Captain David Soul prepares to launch a real missile on Russia. Robert Conrad, Richard Roundtree, Sam Waterston. Directed by Larry Peerce.

FIGHTING DEVIL DOGS (1938). Twelve-chapter Republic serial, directed by that unbeatable triumvirate of action directors: William Witney, John English and Robert Beche. Marine Corps lieutenants Lee Powell and Herman Brix (soon to be Bruce Bennett) square off against The Lightning, a caped hooligan who destroys things with bolts of electricity. The artifical thunderbolt machine (a clap trap?) becomes their target and the action is nonstoppable. The feature version is **TORPEDO OF DOOM.** (Republic; Video Connection)

FILM FACTS REUNION. Writer-director Dominic Paris offers clips from genre films. (Vestron)

FILMGORE (1983). Compilation of blood-and-gore scenes from horror movies: THE TEXAS CHAINSAW MASSACRE, DRILLER KILLER, SNUFF, 2000 MANIACS, BLOOD FEAST, etc. etc. Produced by Charles Band, directed by Ken Dixon, with music by Richard Band. Hosted by Elvira. (Wizard; Force)

FINAL APPROACH (1991). Psychological sci-fi technological thriller in which amnesiac fighter pilot James B. Sikking undergoes interrogation by psychiatrist Hector Elizondo to find out the truth behind a coverup in the military ranks involving a new bomber. Directed by Eric Steven Stahl. Madolyn Smith, Kevin McCarthy, Cameo Kneuer, Wayne Duvall. (Video/Laser: Vidmark)

FINAL CONFLICT, THE (1981). Third and final film in THE OMEN series, as godless as its predecessors. Damien Thorn (Sam Neill), the Antichrist, has become Ambassador to the Court of St. James to be near the birth site (near London) of the Son of God, whose Second Coming is prophesized in the Book of Revelation. The gory murders are numerous (though not as imaginative as in THE OMEN and DAMIEN: OMEN II) as the Son of Satan defends himself against priest-assassins armed with the Seven Sacred Daggers of Meggido. The "final conflict" between the Antichrist and the Son of God is poorly developed by scriptwriter Andrew Birkin, but producer Harvey Bernhard's film still has a compelling "sickness" and a good pseudo-religious score by Jerry Goldsmith. Rossano Brazzi, Don Gordon, Lisa Harrow, Mason Adams. (Video/Laser: Fox)

FINAL COUNTDOWN, THE (1980). Filmed aboard the USS Nimitz, this is an excellent semidocumentary approach to showing the U.S. Navy and Air Force in action. The plot—in which the carrier is caught in a time warp and sent back to Pearl Harbor in 1941 on the eve of the Japanese attack—sounds ingenious, but assorted screenwriters never came to grips with the promising twists. Kirk Douglas, Martin Sheen, Katharine Ross, James Farentino, Ron O'Neal and Charles Durning work with limited material; the pilots and jetfighters come off looking better. Directed by Don Taylor. (Video/Laser: Vestron)

FINAL EXAM (1981). Tame slasher made in South Carolina, a clone of HALLOWEEN. Writer-director Jimmy Huston saves the goriest scenes for last as a fiendish murderer slaughters dumb college students. Most of the time FINAL EXAM deals with campus pranks, hazings and crude jokes, and engages in idle chatter designed as character "development." Huston's writing is so weak, the killer's identity is never given, and his motives are never made clear. Cecile Bagdadi, Joel S. Rice, Ralph Brown. (Embassy; Columbia)

FINAL EXECUTIONER, THE (1983). Lame-brained Mad Max imitation, set in a post-Holocaust world where "Hunters" kill off contaminated people. In search of the woman he loves, William Mang is trained in combat by ex-cop Woody Strode, then invades the stronghold of the hunters, killing them off one by one. The murders on both sides are so violent, one can never feel sympathy for Mang and this becomes nothing but a bloodbath. Directed with neanderthal elan by Romolo Guerrieri. Marina Costa, Harrison Muller. (MGM/UA)

FINAL EYE. See **COMPUTERCIDE.**

FINAL MISSION (1992). Jet fighter pilots testing a new "virtual reality" training system begin to die off so hot-shotter Billy Wirth noses into the truth: an Air Force conspiracy to use men as guinea pigs for a new post-hypnotic zombie-making computer system. Meanwhile, he makes love to beautiful Elizabeth Gracen. Okay thriller co-written and directed by Lee Redmond. Steve Railsback, Corbin Benson, Richard Bradford.

FINAL NOTICE (1989). Lightweight slasher/private-eye thriller that drags out every cliche imaginable. Gil

"I am a Leo with a Scorpio rising and my money is in Scorpio and my Venus is five inches below my bellybutton. Better there than in Uranus."
— Irwin Corey as a Sex Nut in ***FAIRY TALES***

Gerard portrays less-than-thrilling PI Harry Stoner who's in search of the Library Slasher, a knife-plunging maniac who cuts up female forms in art books, and real female forms, too. John Gay's telescript (based on a Jonathan Valin novel) is predictable, with Melody Anderson turning up as a librarian with glasses who takes them off to become . . . wow, a raving beauty. You'll spot the killer in advance of the climax. Directed by Steven H. Stern. Jackie Burroughs, Kevin Hicks, Louise Fletcher, David Ogden Stiers. (Paramount) (Laser: Pioneer)

FINAL PROGRAMME, THE. Video version of **LAST DAYS OF MAN ON EARTH, THE** (HBO).

FINAL ROUND (1993). Another variation on "The Most Dangerous Game," in which champion boxer Lorenzo Lamas, girlfriend Kathleen Kinmont and former baseball star Arne Olsen are stalked by sadistic killers inside an industrial complex. The twist: a computer-based gang is taking million-dollar bets from all over the world as to the outcome. A mediocre action movie, done half-heartedly by all concerned. Olsen wrote the script directed by George Erschbamer. Anthony De Longis, Clark Johnson, Stephen Mendel.

FINAL SANCTION (1989). After war breaks out between the U.S. and Russia, the factions decide to settle the dispute by putting two men into an arena in a fight to the death. Ted Prior is the American, Robert Z'Dar is the Commie. Directed by David A. Prior. (Action International; Hollywood Home Entertainment)

FINAL TERROR, THE (1983). Samuel Arkoff's film (made as CAMPSITE MASSACRE) stars Rachel Ward and Daryl Hannah before they found big-time success. A busload of fire rangers and girlfriends travels into the gloomy woods near Crescent City, Calif., to be stalked by a toothless hag who eats raw dogmeat and keeps severed hands in her Mason jars. A sunless forest and always-dreary sky provides a chilly mood but body count is low, making this of minimum interest to splatter seekers. Director Andrew Davis went on to make topnotch action movies. John Friedrich, Adrian Zmed, Mark Metcalf and Lewis Smith are the louts messing up our beautiful forests. (Video/Laser: Vestron)

FINAL WAR, THE. See **LAST WAR, THE.**

FINGERS AT THE WINDOW (1942). Hypnotist doctor Basil Rathbone mesmerizes mentally deficient patients into carrying out axe murders against his enemies. Director Charles Lederer seems to emphasize the absurdities rather than gloss them over. Contributing to this fatuous foul-up are reporter Lew Ayres and girlfriend Laraine Day, whose behavior defies all credibility. The Rathbone role is one-dimensional and the horror elements are underplayed in favor of "humorous" dialogue. Walter Kingsford, Miles Mander, Charles D. Brown.

FINIAN'S RAINBOW (1968). It took Hollywood two decades to make a film from the popular 1947 play by E. Y. Harburg and Fred Saidy, which featured the songs "How Are Things in Glocca Morra?", "Old Devil's Moon" and "When I'm Not Near the Girl I Love," primarily because the story dealt with race relations. Directed by Francis Ford Coppola and scripted by Harburg and Saidy, the story seems dated although the Burton Lane music is still great. Fred Astaire is Finian, who raises crops near Fort Knox by planting a pot of gold he swiped from leprechauns. Petula Clark, Tommy Steele, Keenan Wynn, Don Francks. (Warner Bros.) (Laser: Pioneer)

FIRE AND ICE (1982). Excellently animated sword-and-sorcery fantasy-adventure set in a world where evil ice king Nekron uses glacial spears to destroy his enemy, namely the kingdom of Firekeep. His mother Juliana orders the kidnapping of Firekeep's princess, a sexy number who is rescued by a young hero during a series of exciting adventures. What makes this outstanding is the superb art by Frank Frazetta, who worked under writer-producer-director Ralph Bakshi. The film was rotoscoped to give it a life-like quality. Comic-book fans will grove on it. Voices by Leo Gordon, Susan Tyrrell, Randy Norton, Sean Hannon, Cynthia Leake. (Video/Laser: RCA/Columbia)

FIREBIRD 2015 A.D. (1981). Political fantasy in the vein of ROAD WARRIOR in which gasoline is no longer available and motorcyclists search for fuel. Mostly action and car maneuvers, very little fantasy. Directed by David M. Robertson. Darren McGavin, Doug McClure, George Touliatos, Mary Beth Rubens. (Embassy)

FIREFIGHT (1987). Gangs of convicts rove a post-holocaust world in an attempt to gain power. James Pfeiffer, Janice Carraher, Jack Turner. Directed by Scott Pfeiffer. (TransWorld; Star Classics)

FIREFOX (1982). One of Clint Eastwood's lesser pictures: dark, melancholy, clumsy, when it should be zappy and fast-paced. FIREFOX depicts has-been pilot Mitchell Gant (Eastwood) being sent to Russia to steal a jet fighter equipped with weapons controlled by human thought. Little is made of this premise—the plot unfolds like a grade-B spy movie. John Dykstra provides nice flying sequences, but they don't make up for deficiencies in the Alex Lasker-Wendell Wellman script, adapted from Craig Thomas' novel. Freddie Jones, David Huffman, Ronald Lacey. (Video/Laser: Warner Bros.)

FIREHEAD (1990). The only interesting feature about this espionage thriller with light fantastic overtones is the pleasant appearance of Chris Lemmon (son of Jack Lemmon), who acts and sounds like his famous father, thus giving this dreary piece a touch of comedy. He portrays a scientist called on by government guy Christopher Plummer to track down Russian defector Ivan (Brett Porter, a Dolph Lundren type) who has the power to shoot lasers from his electrified eyeballs. Helping out is sexy spy Gretchen Becker, a body beautiful with great gams. Plotting to take over the planet, meanwhile, is "The Upper Order" with a "parapolic phase shifter," designed to knock out Ivan's superpowers. Directed by Peter Yuval. (Action International) (Laser: Image)

FIRE IN THE SKY, A (1978). A comet is on a collision course with Earth—destined to hit Phoenix, Ariz. Astronomers Richard Crenna and Joanna Miles warn mankind. But do you think mankind listens? Don't expect much in effects; this consists of characters running around frantically, ignoring Crenna's predicitons or behaving selfishly. Directed by Jerry Jameson. Andrew Duggan, Elizabeth Ashley, Lloyd Bochner, David Dukes.

FIRE IN THE SKY (1993). A controversial UFO abduction case, the singular affair of Travis Walton, is dramatized in this Paramount release written by Tracy Torme (INTRUDERS) and directed by Robert Lieberman. In 1975 Arizona lumberjack Walton allegedly observed a saucer with six other woodsmen. Walton ran toward the UFO, was zapped by a bolt of blue and thrown ten feet, according to eyewitnesses. Thinking Travis dead, the axemen fled. Walton turned up five days later, claiming to have been kidnapped and examined by aliens. How true the Walton incident is has been debated. That aside, FIRE IN THE SKY is a heightened experience of sight and sounds. The saucer interior sequence is gruesome, with Walton awakening in a womb-like, organic environment. These scenes resemble a nightmare with life and death symbols and is a gross exaggeration of what Walton says he experienced, but as film it's chillingly awesome. James Garner is a disbelieving sheriff. D. B. Sweeney, Robert Patrick, Craig Sheffer, Henry Thomas, Bradley Gregg. (Video/Laser: Paramount)

FIRE MAIDENS FROM OUTER SPACE (1956). British sci-fi with a ridiculous plot concocted by director-writer Cy Roth: Space explorers (ineptly led by Anthony Dexter) discover women carrying out sacrifices to the black gods on a moon near Jupiter. By all means, catch it if you want to have a thousand laughs at the expense of Susan Shaw, Paul Carpenter and Harry Fowler. And dig the females dancing to Borodin's music! (Cinemacabre)

FIRE MONSTER. See **GIGANTIS THE FIRE MONSTER.**

FIRE MONSTERS AGAINST THE SON OF HERCULES (1962). Too much brawn and not enough brain in this Italian muscle epic set during the Ice Age, with pecs champion Reg Lewis fighting off a three-headed monster.

Grunt and bear it. Written-directed by Guido Malatesta. Margaret Lee, Myra Kent. (Sinister/C; S/Weird)

FIRESIGN THEATER PRESENTS "HOT SHORTS" (1983). In the style of Woody Allen's WHAT'S UP, TIGER LILY?, the comedy group has written new soundtracks for old Republic serials (SPYSMASHER; MANHUNT OF MYSTERY ISLAND) and grade-Z movies (SHE DEMONS). Many of the bits are funny but it's a one-joke gimmick that wears thin fast. (Video/Laser: RCA/Columbia)

FIRESTARTER (1984). Stephen King ranks this among the worst of his adaptations, and he struck the match right on the head. It's an effects movie, at the expense of a cohesive narrative, adapted by Stanley Mann and directed by Mark L. Lester. Flying fireballs and other inflammatory bolts of energy are hurled by Drew Barrymore, a kid who can turn her anger into flaming revenge. In short, she lights up your life. Government agents and foreign powers are after Barrymore to harness her ESP abilities. George C. Scott fulfills a very odd role. Filmed in North Carolina; the Mike Wood-Jeff Jarvis effects are the best things in this never-catches-fire picture. David Keith, Martin Sheen, Heather Locklear, Art Carney, Louise Fletcher, Moses Gunn. (Video/Laser: MCA)

FIRST MAN INTO SPACE, THE (1958). Cosmic rays turn Earth's first astronaut—an obsessed man who takes his spacecraft higher than ordered—into a hideous, encrusted monster who craves human blood. Writers John Cooper and Lance Z. Hargreaves engender sympathy for the malformed being instead of making him a killer monster. A commendable effort from producer Richard Gordon and director Robert Day. Marshall Thompson is the scientist attempting to communicate with the gnarly man. Carl Jaffe, Marla Landi, Bill Nagy. (Filmfax; Rhino; Media; S/Weird; Discount; Monterey)

FIRST MEN IN THE MOON (1964). Marvelous adaptation of H. G. Wells' novel about a Victorian spaceship blasting off from Earth and flying to the lunar surface; the expedition's adventures are riveting. Ray Harryhausen (also associate producer) provides excellent stop-motion effects, notably the insect moonmen. His lavish alien civilization and its creatures are a satisfying example of what a ton of imagination on a nominal budget can achieve. Edward Judd, Martha Hyer, Lionel Jeffries, Peter Finch. Written by Nigel Kneale and Jan Read; directed by Nathan Juran. Charles H. Schneer produced. (RCA/Columbia) (Laser: Pioneer)

FIRST POWER, THE (1990). Lou Diamond Phillips portrays L.A. cop Russ Logan, who specializes in capturing serial killers. Sadistic killer Patrick Channing (Jeff Kober) is electrocuted and his spirit returns from the hereafter to terrorize Logan—a plot similar to SHOCKED and THE HORROR SHOW and hence not as fresh as writer-director Robert Resnikoff might have thought. Logan teams with psychic Tracy Griffith and has religious help from nun Elizabeth Arlen . . . all these derivative ingredients are blended with ample fights, usually high above the ground. Resnikoff shows promise but needs to get out of the cliche bin. Mykel T. Williamson, Dennis Lipscomb, Carmen Argenziano. (Video/Laser: Nelson)

FIRST SPACESHIP ON VENUS, THE (1960). East German-Polish film is technically superior in presenting a space odyssey adventure, but dubbing and story are weak. A spaceship from Earth, carrying an international crew, lands on Venus to find civilization destroyed by nuculear holocaust. Depiction of the once sophisticated society is imaginative. Ethnic cast includes Yoko Tani, Oldrich Lukes, Ignacy Machowski. Directed by Kurt Maetzig; based on Stanislaw Lem's novel THE ASTRONAUTS. Recut for the U.S. market by Hugo Grimaldi. (VCI; S/Weird; Sinister/C; Moore; Filmfax)

FIRST WOMAN IN TO SPACE. See **SPACE MONSTER.**

FIST OF STEEL (1991). This post-holocaust actioner, set in a desert where roving bands of men fight for ownership of water, is just an excuse for Dale "Apollo" Cook (world kickboxing middleweight champion) and Don Nakaya Nielsen (U.S. kickboxing heavyweight champion) to square off in an endless series of duels. What little plot there is has Cook helping Cynthia Khan find revenge against the roving renegades that destroyed her village, led by Mainframe (Nielsen). Directed by Irvin Johnson. Gregg Douglass, James Gaines. Originally made as ETERNAL FIST. (Video/Laser: Action International)

FIVE (1951). Strange end-of-the-world story, with writer-producer-director Arch Oboler lending it a dark, troubled mood. Mankind has been destroyed by the Bomb, but five survivors try to implement a new society, with unhappy results. The characters are a peculiar bunch but then Oboler is commenting on the absurdity of people who live on a planet where atomic bombs are used to destroy. FIVE ranks as one of the first films to deal with Atomic Armageddon. William Phipps, Susan Douglas, James Anderson, Earl Lee.

FIVE GRAVES FOR A MEDIUM. See **TERROR CREATURES FROM THE GRAVE.**

FIVE MILLION YEARS TO EARTH (1968). Third in the Quatermass series (see THE CREEPING UNKNOWN and ENEMY FROM SPACE) is perhaps Nigel Kneale's best—it is the most outre, replete with religious and mythical overtones. An alien spaceship is uncovered during excavations in London, and corpses of giant grasshoppers are found onboard. Mankind is related to these E.T.s through experiments carried out centuries before. Then it really gets weird as ESP and energy force fields come into play. Andrew Keir assumes the Quatermass role. Directed by Roy Ward Baker, written by Kneale. Also known as QUATERMASS AND THE PIT. Barbara Shelley, James Donald, Duncan Lamont.

FIVE MINUTES TO LIVE (1961). Johnny Cash as a psychokiller? Hey, even a country and western singer has to make a living. Donald Woods, Pamela Mason, Ron Howard. Also called DOOR-TO-DOOR MANIAC. (Video Dimensions; from Discount as **LAST BLOOD**)

FIVE THOUSAND FINGERS OF DR. T, THE (1953). Producer Stanley Kramer's offbeat fantasy reflects the ultimate nightmare for children forced to learn music against their will. One such child (Tommy Rettig) dreams he is imprisoned with 500 others in the prison of Dr. Terwilliker (Hans Conried), a crazed piano instructor owning the world's largest piano. The Dr. Seuss fantasy attempts to recapture a WIZARD OF OZ flavor but the choreography is so odd and listless, the film remains consistently offkey. Retuning was in order, maybe? Directed by Roy Rowland, scripted by Dr. Seuss and Alan Scott. Peter Lind Hayes, Mary Healy. (Xenon; from RCA/Columbia as **DR. SEUSS' 5000 FINGERS OF DR. T.**) (Laser: Columbia TriStar)

FLAME BARRIER, THE (1957). Extraterrestrial substance crashes on Earth aboard a satellite and slurps into a cave for refuge. The entity, which turns flesh into puddles of ooze, is evil and wants to conquer our world (what, again?). A flameout. Directed by Paul Landres. Arthur Franz, Kathleen Crowley, Robert Brown.

FLASH, THE (1990). Well-produced TV-movie depicting the comic-book superhero who moves faster than light and is but a blur in the eyeball of mankind. This pilot for the CBS series has delightful effects of the speeding Flash, and also captures the angst of his alter ego, Barry Allen, a forensic specialist for the LAPD. Written by Danny Bilson and Paul De Meo (also producers) and directed by Rob Iscove. John Wesley Shipp is effective in both roles. Amanda Pays, Alex Desert, Paula Marshall, Tim

'THE FLASH'

Thomerson, Priscilla Pointer. (Video/Laser: Warner Bros)

FLASH GORDON (1936). First of three Universal serials to star Buster Crabbe as the space hero created for the comics by Alex Raymond. (The other two are FLASH GORDON'S TRIP TO MARS and FLASH GORDON CONQUERS THE UNIVERSE.) In one of the best action cliffhangers ever, Flash, girlfriend Dale Arden and scientist Dr. Zarkov try to prevent the planet Mongo (ruled by Ming the Merciless) from conquering Earth. On Mongo, it's all-out action as Flash and followers meet Ming's sexy daughter Aura, the Lion Men, the dragon-lizard monster Gocko, and an underwater race led by King Kala. Jean Rogers is Arden, Charles Middleton the evil emperor, Priscilla Lawson the busty Aura and Frank Shannon the dedicated Zarkov. Stylishly directed by Frederick Stephani. The 12-chapter serial has been released in abbreviated versions as SPACESHIP TO THE UNKNOWN, SPACE SOLDIERS and ATOMIC ROCKETSHIP. (VCI;From Video Yesteryear and Prism as **FLASH GORDON: ROCKETSHIP**)

FLASH GORDON (1980). Dino de Laurentiis' paean to Alex Raymond's comic-strip space hero features a Lorenzo Semple Jr. script that walks a fine balance between action and satire. The costumes and sets are fabulous and the cast finely picked: Sam Jones as Flash is perhaps too naive but his enthusiasm makes him acceptable; Max von Sydow makes movie history as one of the great villains, Ming the Merciless; Melody Anderson is a liberated Dale Arden, and Topol a daffy, dedicated Dr. Zarkov. Brian Blessed thunders his way through the stylish action as Vultan the Hawkman. The great sky battles are faithful to Raymond's designs. Only the rock score by Queen seems out of place. A real fantasy funhouse directed by Mike Hodges. (Video/Laser: MCA)

FLASH GORDON CONQUERS THE UNIVERSE (1940). The third serial in Universal's FLASH GORDON series finds Earth subjected to Ming the Merciless' latest ploy to conquer Earth: The Plague of the Purple Death, a "death dust" that Ming's minions radiate into our atmosphere. Flash, Dale Arden, Dr. Zarkov and Prince Barin, ruler of Arboria, take on Ming with renewed strength, their adventures rocketing them to Frigia, a frozen wasteland. This marked the series' end and is the least of the trilogy, but it's still great fun. Directed by Ford Beebe and Ray Taylor. Carol Hughes, Charles Middleton, Frank Shannon, Beatrice Roberts, Anne Gwynne. Re-edited as PURPLE DEATH FROM OUTER SPACE, SPACE SOLDIERS CONQUER THE UNIVERSE and PERILS FROM THE PLANET MONGO. (From Video Yesteryear, United and Filmfax in 12 chapters)

FLASH GORDON: THE DEADLY RAY FROM MARS. Feature video version of **FLASH GORDON'S TRIP TO MARS** (Questar; Nostalgia; Sinister/C).

FLASH GORDON: MARS ATTACKS THE WORLD. Feature video of **FLASH GORDON'S TRIP TO MARS** (VCI; Cable).

FLASH GORDON: THE PERIL FROM PLANET MONGO. Feature video of **FLASH GORDON CONQUERS THE UNIVERSE** (Questar).

FLASH GORDON: THE PURPLE DEATH FROM OUTER SPACE. Feature video of **FLASH GORDON CONQUERS THE UNIVERSE** (Questar).

FLASH GORDON: ROCKETSHIP. Feature video of **FLASH GORDON** starring Buster Crabbe (Video Yesteryear; Prism, Cable).

FLASH GORDON: SPACESHP TO THE UNKNOWN. Feature version of the original **FLASH GORDON** serial (Questar).

FLASH GORDON'S TRIP TO MARS (1938). Second Buster Crabbe Flash Gordon serial by Universal finds Flash, Dale Arden and Dr. Zarkov flying to Mars to stop Ming the Merciless from stealing the nitrogen from Earth's atmosphere. Adventures involve the Clay People, Azura the Queen of Magic, the White Sapphire, the Tree People, Prince Barin, Tarnak and Happy. Rousing action directed by Ford Beebe and Robert Hill. Jean Rogers, Frank Shannon, Charles Middleton, Beatrice Roberts. Re-edited as DEADLY RAY FROM MARS and MARS ATTACKS THE WORLD. (On video as **FLASH GORDON: MARS ATTACKS THE WORLD**)

FLASH GORDON—THE GREATEST ADVENTURE OF ALL (1982). Animated TV-film starring the popular characters from the comic strip and serials . . The evil emperor Ming drips with sadistic evil as his sexy daughter lures Flash into her den of iniquity. The action is plentiful and there's a lusty bevy of shapely femmes, giving this an unusual touch of decadence. Voices by Robert Ridgely, Diane Pershing and Bob Holt.

FLASHMAN (1966). See editions 1-3.

FLATLINERS (1990). Eschewing genre-film stereotypes, this unusual film probes the frontier of death—specifically the near-death experience. A group of medical college students experiments by "killing" one of its kind and bringing the individual back from complete death at the last possible moment. The suspense is sometimes unbearable. But each student who survives the self-imposed ordeal is haunted by his or her past. Director Joel Schumacher injects a surreal style into Peter Filardi's screenplay in trying to visualize the realm of death (in the same way that Douglas Trumbull explored it in BRAINSTORM). Kiefer Sutherland, Julia Roberts, Kevin Bacon, William Baldwin, Oliver Platt. Recommended. (Video/Laser: RCA/Columbia)

FLAVIA, PRIESTESS OF VIOLENCE (1976). Potential material for a nunnery (Florinda Bolkan) turns monster instead, slaughtering all the men she meets. Italian shocker co-written, produced and directed by Gianfranco Mingozzi. Anthony Corlan, Maria Casares. Also known as THE REBEL NUN.

FLESH AND BLOOD SHOW, THE (1973). British actors audition for a Grand Guignol show as part of a film, but it turns out the auditioner in a sinister hood is setting them up for the kill—literally. A sputtering "splatter" movie, originally shot in 3-D by director Peter Walker. Jenny Hanley, Luan Peters. (Wizard; Monterey)

FLESH AND FANTASY (1943). A dream-like quality pervades over this trilogy dealing with that primitive level of the imagination giving birth to fear and superstition. In the framework for the weird tales, Robert Benchley is disturbed by a bad dream and a friend reads from an old book to allay his dread. Betty Field and Robert Cummings star in a story about a homely seamstress whose love for a man causes a miracle; Charles Boyer is a tightrope walker haunted by images of circus aerialist Barbara Stanwyck. The best tale is Oscar Wilde's "Lord Arthur Seville's Crime," with Edward G. Robinson as an American solicitor in London who meets fortune teller Thomas Mitchell with dire predictions. A fourth story, "Destiny," was cut from the script, expanded and released as DESTINY. Directed by Julien Duvivier.

FLESH AND THE FIENDS, THE (1960). Gruesome twosome, Burke and Hare, are down to their old grave-robbing tricks in this British chiller, brutally chopped for the U.S. market. Also known as THE FIENDISH GHOULS, this deserved better, being well directed by John Gilling. Peter Cushing stars as Dr. Knox, the Edinburgh anatomist forced to purchase classroom cadavers from murderers Donald Pleasence and George Rose. Dark and bleak, similar to THE DOCTOR AND THE DEVILS. (Sinister/C; from United American as **MANIA**)

FLESH CREATURES. See **VAMPIRE MEN OF THE LOST PLANET.**

FLESH CREATURES OF THE RED PLANET. See **VAMPIRE MEN OF THE LOST PLANET.**

FLESH EATER. See **REVENGE OF THE LIVING ZOMBIES.**

FLESH EATERS, THE (1964). Assorted squabblers are stranded on a secluded island where an idiotic scientist has created amoeba monsters which devour people with considerable glee and gnashing. Some effects aren't bad, but overall quality is poor and the visuals are sickening. Directed by Jack Curtis. Martin Koslek is the insane inventor, Rita Morley, Ray Tudor and Byron Sanders the victims. (Monterey; Sinister/C)

FLESH EATING MOTHERS (1988). The gore crowd should get a few laughs out of this send-up depicting lovable mothers being turned into cannibals when they contract a virus after having sex with a promiscuous husband about town. Besides the AIDS metaphor, James Aviles Martin offers a nice directorial style. Its numerous arm-and leg-chewing sequences (Carl Sorenson's effects are grossly amusing), its funny bit in which an alley cat is stretched into two pieces, and its pun lines add up to a good time. Robert Lee Oliver, Valorie Hubbard. (Academy has two tape versions, one unrated)

FLESH FEAST (1970). Veronica Lake, a hair style-setting '40s star, was co-producer of this low-budget flop with a ghastly, repelling premise: Flesh-hungry maggots result in a formula for a rejuvenation serum involving Adolf Hitler. Yech. (Read Ms Lake's autobiography, VERONICA, for details about the film's making in Miami Beach, Fla.) Lake also stars as a scientist. Directed by Brad F. Ginter. Max Baer, Phil Philbin. (WesternWorld)

FLESH FOR FRANKENSTEIN. Japanese laser title for **ANDY WARHOL'S FRANKENSTEIN.**

FLESH GORDON (1974). Rollicking sex parody of FLASH GORDON serials was heavily pornographic when produced by William Osco in 1972, but later was cleaned up for theatrical release. It's a lively romp with Flesh, a half-naked Dale Ardor and Dr. Flexi Jerkoff penetrating the kingdom of Emperor Wang's world of Porno. The props and creatures are visualized sex jokes or phallic imagery. Overshadowing the sophomoric humor, amateurish acting and raunchy sex and gropings are imaginative effects of E.T. monsters in the Ray Harryhausen vein, achieved by Dave Allen and Jim Danforth. Mike Light wrote-directed what remains an anomaly. Jason Williams, Suzanne Fields, William Hunt, John Hoyt, Lance Larsen, Candy Samples. (Media; Video Dimensions; Front Row Entertainment) (Laser: Image)

FLICK. See **FRANKENSTEIN ON CAMPUS.**

FLICKS (1981). A hodgepodge of material, designed as a parody of a night at the movies, with animation ("Cat and Mouse" by Kirk Henderson), coming attractions ("No Way Jose"), newsreel (a spoof on "The March of Time") and scenes from the "main feature," HOUSE OF THE LIVING CORPSE. Joan Hackett stars in "Philip Alien, Space Detective." Pamela Sue Martin, Martin Mull, Betty Kennedy. Directed by Peter Winograd. (Media)

FLIGHT OF BLACK ANGEL (1990). Uncompromising, hard-edged, disturbing TV-movie about a "loose cannon"—a U.S. fighter pilot turned renegade who shoots down his own planes after he's stolen an atomic warhead. He intends to blow up Vegas, and you know this religious nut will do it. It's up to Peter Strauss to stop him. William O'Leary is all too real as the warped pilot. Taut direction by Jonathan Mostow. James O'Sullivan, K. Callan. (Vidmark)

FLIGHT OF THE NAVIGATOR (1986). Charming juvenile sci-fi adventure from Disney, in which David Freeman, 12, returns one day after he's been missing for eight years, having not aged a day. A government investigation reveals that he went into space at the speed of light for four hours. Freeman escapes testing headquarters to find he was befriended by an alien collecting specimens for an intergalactic zoo. The benevolent alien is only a voice controlling an E.T. ship, and an amusing relationship develops. Meanwhile, NASA official Howard Hesseman is trying to find Freeman. Takes a while to get going, then it soars. Directed by Randal Kleiser. Veronica Cartwright, Cliff de Young, Sarah Jessica Parker. (Video/Laser: Disney)

FLIGHT THAT DISAPPEARED, THE (1961). Glorified TWILIGHT ZONE episode with padding: a prop-job flight from L.A. to Washington DC is carrying the inventor of the "beta thermal nuclear warhead" (Daytom Lummis), a rocket designer (Craig Hill) and a mathematician (Paula Raymond) when suddenly it climbs to an unbelievable altitude, to a limbo-land that transcends time and space. There, a "jury of the future" (men and women yet unborn) put the three on trial for designing the ultimate weapon of annihilation. This is more a polemic than an entertainment, and Reginald LeBorg directed it without verve, handicapped by a minuscule budget. Even the surprise ending is pure Rod Serling. Dayton Lummis, Nancy Hale, Gregory Morton.

FLIGHT THAT VANISHED, THE. See **FLIGHT THAT DISAPPEARED, THE.**

FLIGHT TO FAME (1938). Mixture of aviation heroics and a power-mad villain's misuse of a newly invented Ray of Death. Directed by C.C. Coleman Jr. from a script by Michael J. Simmons. Charles Farrell, Jacqueline Wells, Alexander d'Arcy, Jason Robards.

FLIGHT TO MARS (1951). Cheap Monogram space opera in which Martians turn out to be humanoids from the Screen Actors Guild, women's costumes are miniskirts (at least that part of the film came true) and the plot is pure pulp nonsense. A rocket crew from Earth (including Cameron Mitchell and Arthur Franz) finds an underground city of dying Martians ruled by Ikron the Heinous. Because the society needs a gas called Corium to survive, PG&E intrigue is rampant. Morris Ankrum, Marguerite Chapman, John Litel, Robert Barrat and Virginia Huston are among those misdirected by Leslie Selander. (Nostalgia Merchant; Media) (Laser: Image)

FLIPSIDE OF DOMINICK HIDE, THE (1980). Intriguing British TV-movie dealing with time paradoxes and set in a society 150 years from now. Time travel is a government business (watched over by Patrick Macnee) in which time-hoppers return to the past to correct history so things will turn out better in the present. Peter Firth keeps returning to 1980 in a flying saucer contraption and begins a romance that, unbeknownst to him, will have an effect on the future. Written intelligently by Jeremy Paul and director Alan Gibson. Pippa Guard, Caroline Langrishe. The sequel was ANOTHER FLIP FOR DOMINICK.

FLOWERS IN THE ATTIC (1987). Faithful in some ways to V.C. Andrews' best-selling book, and faithless in others, this version is the compelling work of screenwriter-director Jeremy Bloom, an allegory about how we imprison ourselves in pursuit of life's riches, and often turn evil for material needs. The film introduces a happy family but with a sense it's really dysfunctional. When the father dies, mother Victoria Tennant takes her four children to Foxworth Hall, there to be restored into her father's will. But because Victoria has married her own uncle, the kids are deemed the "Devil's spawn" and locked into a room with adjoining attic by their grandmother, played evilly by Louise Fletcher in a role that rivals her Nurse Ratched for hissability. The four prisoners create their own world of love and hate. The four youths (Kristy Swanson, Jeb Stuart Adams, Ben Granger, Lindsay Parker) excellently convey the reactions of teens and adolescents to the plight, and Tennant goes bonkers in believable style. (New World) (Laser: Image)

FLUTEMAN (198?). Australian retelling of "The Piped Piper of Hamelin," set Outback in the town of Minyana (Aborigine for "tomorrow"). Lone stranger John Jarratt, whom the kiddies recognize as a hero, makes it rain for the drought-stricken community, but when the town council refuses to pay him his $5000 fee, he "kidnaps" the young ones with his flute rendition. Innocuous and slow-moving, and except for some silly characters (including Michael Caton's mortician) even youngsters will probably find this boring. Directed by Peter Maxwell. Emil Minty, Peter Gwynne, Patrick Dickson.

FLY, THE (1958). If you can overlook inconsistencies in this version of George Langlaan's story (scripted by James Clavell), you will enjoy this unsettling sci-fi/horror classic about research scientist David (Al) Hedison, who discovers the secret of teleportation. During an experiment, a housefly buzzes into the transfer chamber. The result is two incredibly mixed-up beings: a tiny fly with human head, a human with the fly's head. Think about it and it doesn't bear scrutiny. Even so, it's well directed by Kurt Neumann and enhanced by the histrionics of Vincent Price (as a member of the cursed Delambre family) and Herbert Marshall (as investigating cop). The sequels were RETURN OF THE FLY and CURSE OF THE FLY, with two remakes in the '80s. Patricia Owens portrays the long-suffering wife. (CBS/Fox) (Laser: CBS/Fox, doubled with **RETURN OF THE FLY**)

FLY, THE (1986). Scientific update of the 1958 classic, utilizing gene-splitting and computers to explain how the molecules of a human and a housefly are intermixed. Director David Cronenberg (who co-wrote with Charles Edward Pogue) is again fascinated with deformity and the "beasts from within" theme as scientist Jeff Goldblum devises "telepods" to teleport matter. Chris Walas' Oscar-winning human/fly effects are a knockout, but the story defies credulity when girlfriend Geena Davis still loves this ugly man in metamorphosis. Sympathy is shown the monster once it emerges, but some may find it hard to get past the gore, especially when the fly-creature vomits on a man's hand and foot with an icky goo that dissolves them. John Getz plays a magazine editor involved with the fly-by-night. (Fox) (Laser: CBS/Fox)

FLY II, THE (1989). Chris Walas, an Oscar winner for creating the horrific effects in the 1986 THE FLY, was further rewarded with his first directorial assignment, and he does a good job in re-creating the disgusting but effective Fly creature. However, the script by Mick Garris, Jim and Ken Wheat and Frank Darabont recycles the

DIRECTOR CHRIS WALAS OF 'THE FLY II'

sentimental love story from the original without success, but does succeed with its thrills, effects and gooey gore. This tale of son-like-father begins with the birth of the Fly's son, who grows at an accelerated rate. Soon he's Eric Stoltz, a guinea pig in a rich industrialist's research center, where teleporter pods are again in action. As the Son of the Fly undergoes genetic change, the film races to an exciting, scary conclusion. The last half-hour is every horror fan's delight as the hideous monster goes on a murdering spree, but still retaining human traits. Daphne Zuniga gets lost as the love interest, Lee Richardson is good as the industrialist Bartok. John Getz, Frank Turner, Ann Marie Lee. (Video/Laser: Fox)

FLYING DISC MAN FROM MARS (1950). Twelve-chapter Republic serial is nonstop action in the cliffhanger vein. Walter Reed stars as Kent Fowler, a pilot who does battle with the evil Martian Mota (Gregory Gay). The Thermal Disintegrator and other wild gadgets provide the fantasy elements. By 1951 Republic was giving its serials short shrift/thrift so compared to previous studio efforts this might seem a touch shoddy in the writing and effects. But director Fred C. Brannon gives it that Saturday-matinee feeling that former kids will love re-experiencing. (The whittled-down TV version is called MISSILE MONSTERS.) If you love nostalgia, you couldn't find a better example. Lois Collier, James Craven, Harry Lauter, Tom Steele. (Republic)

FLYING SAUCER, THE (1950). A travelogue/espionage thriller more than a sci-fi adventure with Mikel Conrad as an unlikely Secret Service agent posing as a sportsman/playboy dispatched to Alaska to track the mystery surrounding a UFO. Filmed in and around Juneau under Conrad's direction, this minor independent feature sports long stretches of beautiful aerial photography, but there's little drama, a dollop of romance (with lovely Pat Garrison) and no effects to mention. Hanz von Teuffen, Lester Sharpe, Denver Pyle, Roy Engel. (United; Rhino)

FLYING SAUCER (1965). English-dubbed Italian film (known as a "spaghetti saucer") with Alberto Sordi in four roles as he struggles comedically to prevent a Martian invasion, but keeps getting locked up in asylums. Directed by Tinto Brass. Monica Vitti, Silvano Mangano.

FLYING SAUCER MYSTERY, THE (1950). Old-fashioned documentary about UFOs. Sinister/C, S/Weird and Filmfax offer this in video with other films and trailers of sci-fi flicks related to flying saucers.

FLYING SAUCERS OVER HOLLYWOOD (1992). A documentary report on the making of PLAN 9 FROM OUTER SPACE and its creator, Ed Wood Jr., produced-scripted-directed by his greatest fan, Mark Carducci. Cast members and industry figures comment on how the film influenced them. These include Joe Dante, Sam Raimi and Harry Medved. (Atomic)

FLYING SERPENT, THE (1946). PRC flick of the so-bad-it's-hilarious-school, with George Zucco outstandingly atrocious as a mad doctor who cages Quetzalcoatl (the Killer Bird God) and sends the winged killer out to murder after he has placed a feather from the bird on the intended victim. Acting and music are equally laughable; wires propelling the creature are discernible even to the most non-discerning eyeball. Loose remake of DEVIL BAT; Quetzalcoatl was updated in 1982 for Q. Directed by Sam Newfield. Ralph Lewis, Hope Kramer.

FOES (1977). Uninspired cheapie kicks off with a midair collision between an F-16 and UFO reconnoitering Earth, then spirals downward into copouts: E.T.s are mere multi-colored, floating lights and everything is explained (not shown) by research scientist MacDonald Carey (playing Dr. MacCarey, ha ha). The setting is Perish Island, where a lighthouse keeper and wife are sucked into a radiation whirlpool and spit back out. An ambiguous project, tedious and dull. Director-writer John Coats designed the lousy effects and appears in a minor role. Jerry Hardin, Robert D. E. Alexander.

FOG, THE (1980). Memorable exercise in supernatural horror as a sinister fog engulfs a coastal California town; within the swirling mist are maggot-decaying pirates armed with pikes, hooks and other flesh-ripping weapons, seeking revenge for wrongs committed last century. Director John Carpenter (who co-wrote with producer Debra Hill) plays against our innermost fear of the dark, delivering shock after shock as the fog draws closer. Adrienne Barbeau, Jamie Lee Curtis, Janet Leigh, Hal Holbrook, John Houseman. (Video/Laser: Columbia)

FOG ISLAND (1945). More fog shrouds the logic behind this PRC cheapie than the setting; oh well, enjoy the overacting of Lionel Atwill and George Zucco, gentlemen perched in a lonely island's mansion peopled with weird characters, secret rooms, skeletons, sinister shadows, etc. You couldn't cut through this peasoup with a butcher's knife. Directed by Terry Morse. Jerome Cowan, Veda Ann Borg, Ian Keith. (Thunderbird; Filmfax; Sinister/C; Nostalgia; Video Connection; from Nostalgia Merchant with **RETURN OF THE APE MAN**)

FOLKS AT RED WOLF INN, THE. See **TERROR AT RED WOLF INN.**

FOLLOW ME QUIETLY (1949). More '40s film noir than a horror flick, this offbeat thriller depicts cop William Lundigan pursuing a strangler known as The Judge.

When the cops set up a mannequin in their office, the killer takes the figure's place to keep abreast of what the police are up to. Tight little shocker, well directed by Richard Fleischer. Dorothy Patrick, Jeff Corey, Nestor Paiva. (Turner; Rex Miller)

FOOD OF THE GODS, THE (1976). Bert I. Gordon wrote-produced-directed this horrible horror movie based on an H. G. Wells story. At least a portion of it—the title—is based on Wells. It's lowgrade schlock as Marjoe Gortner goes hunting with pals to encounter giant wasps, extra-large chickens and overgrown rats. If only Marjoe, Ralph Meeker, Ida Lupino and Pamela Franklin had 5000 pounds of American cheese, they might stand a chance. On second thought, Swiss would be better—it would match the thousands of holes in the plot. John Cypher, Belinda Balaski. (Orion; Vestron)

FOOD OF THE GODS II (1989). Only loosely joined to its 1976 inspiration, this Canadian production (also known as GNAWS) is a misfire, trying to follow in the pawtracks of such fare as WILLARD, BEN and other rat-infested flicks but ending up a mouse. The effects (consisting mainly of giant rat heads) are ludicrous rather than frightening, and there is more comedic result than horror. Paul Coufos is a lab scientist experimenting with 192 Mathianol, a growth hormone that results in the king-sized rodents. Directed by Damian Lee. Lisa Schrage, Karen Hines, Colin Fox, Frank Moore. (Video/Laser: IVE)

FORBIDDEN JUNGLE (1950). See editions 1-3.

FORBIDDEN LOVE. See **FREAKS.**

FORBIDDEN MOON (1953). Forbidden viewing; re-edited from TV's **ROCKY JONES, SPACE RANGER.** (Sinister/C; Filmfax; Video Dimensions; Discount)

FORBIDDEN PLANET (1956). Classic film science fiction, set in the year 2200 A.D. on the planet Altair II, where an Earth ship lands to contact Professor Morbius (Walter Pidgeon) and his beautiful daughter Alta (Anne Francis). Suddenly the ship (C-57-D) is attacked by an invisible entity, whose beast-like outline is only visible when it touches the vessel's force-field shield. Nicholas Nayfack's MGM production has overtones of a whodunit thriller (what is this bizarre alien killer and where does it come from?) and has outstanding technology—from Robby the Robot to the subterranean city of the long-dead Krell race to Morbius' futuristic home to the spacecraft and land cruisers. Spacemen Leslie Nielsen, Earl Holliman and Warren Stevens remain second bananas to the witty Robby. Cyril Hume's screenplay is most satisfying. Odd electronics score by Louis and Bebe Barron. Directed by Fred McLeod Wilcox from a Cyril Hume script said to be inspired by Shakespeare's THE TEMPEST. (Video/Laser: MGM/UA; Voyager)

FORBIDDEN ROOM, THE (1977). Italian mystery with a better cast (Vittorio Gassman, Catherine Deneuve) than plot: weird events transpire in an old mansion. Something weird is up there in the attic. At least the atmosphere is eerie. Directed by Dino Risi, who co-wrote with B. Zapponi. Also known as LOST SOUL.

FORBIDDEN SUN (1989). The most distinguishing feature about this British release, originally called BULLDANCE, is the fact that the script is by Robin Hardy, director of THE WICKER MAN. Olympic hopefuls, coached by Lauren Hutton, are on the isle of Crete when one of the women is attacked and violently raped. The others set out for revenge. Cliff DeYoung, Rene Estevez. Directed by Zelda Barron. (Video/Laser: Academy)

FORBIDDEN WORLD (1982). ALIEN ripoff depicting space ranger Mike Colby (Jesse Vint) at a research station on a far-flung world. An experiment in genetic engineering has spawned a mutation that's turning humans into piles of gooey leftovers. However, gore can't take the place of suspense. The attitude of director Allan Holzman is so condescending to his characters that the film lapses into laughableness. The women, for example, quickly strip and leap into bed with Colby, or rush stupidly through the corridors, trying to communicate with "it" or fleeing from its gnashing, slobbering jaws. Dawn Dunlap, Linden Chiles, June Chadwick. (Nelson; Embassy; Sultan) (Laser: Image)

FORBIDDEN ZONE (1982). Sci-fi musical starring the Mystic Knights of the Oingo Boingo as they tour the Sixth Dimension, where Herve Villechaize and Susan Tyrrell reign supreme over devils and demons. Strictly for the midnight cult crowd. Made by Richard and Marie-Pascale Elfman; the latter co-stars with Viva. (Media)

FORBIN PROJECT, THE. See **COLOSSUS: THE FORBIN PROJECT.**

FORCE BEYOND, THE (1978). See **EVIL, THE.**

FORCE BEYOND, THE (1978). Some insufferable kids sight a UFO and try to warn adults of what they've seen. Low-budget time consumer from director William Sachs. Don Elkins, Peter Byrne.

FORCE BEYOND (1982). Millions disappear every year. Are they being abducted by aliens and taken to another planet? This mildly hysterical pseudodocumentary examines psychic phenomena and other mind-boggling puzzles of our universe. It's enough to peel back the layers of your mind. (Media)

FORCED ENTRY (1975). Sicko mean-to-women portrait of a psychokiller (Ron Max) who has an obsession against prostitutes and stalks Tanya Roberts into her home. There are lengthy sequences showing Max raping and beating women. There isn't an ounce of entertainment in this despicable movie. A failure when first released, this was re-edited with new footage in 1980 . . . no amount of doctoring could help this disgusting mess directed by Jim Sotos. Nancy Allen, Robin Leslie. Also called THE LAST ENTRY. (Harmony Vision)

FORCE OF EVIL. Video version of an episode of TV's **TALES OF THE UNEXPECTED** (Goodtimes).

FORCE ON THUNDER MOUNTAIN, THE (1978). Cheapie depicts wilderness folks under attack from an alien crash-landed on Earth. He has a device that turns human thought to evil use. Directed by Peter B. Good, who needs to be better. No thunder, no force. Just the mountain. Todd Dutson, Borge West. (United; VCI)

FOREPLAY (1976). Tepid sex anthology film, with premises barely touching the erogenous zones. In one fantasy, Pat Paulsen buys a life-size Polish sex doll and takes "her" home—only to have mother intervene. It's a limp Dan Greenberg idea. The second, by Bruce Jay Friedman, is about a writer's Muse (in red bikini briefs) who whisks the author into the past so he can consummate unsuccessful sexual conquests. The final episode is equally poor: Zero Mostel as a U.S. President is blackmailed into performing intercourse with his wife on live TV. John G. Avildsen directed this latter embarrassment. (Other directors were Robert J. McCarthy and Bruce Malmuth.) There are frequent cutaways of Professor Irwin Corey, consisting mainly of foul language. FOREPLAY, sorry to say, never builds to an arousing climax. (From Vestron in a heavily edited form)

FOREST, THE (1983). Poorly executed low-budget indie, in which a wife killer turned cannibal (Michael Brody) terrorizes four dull campers. Writer Evan Jones provides plot twists, such as having two children wandering the woods turning out to be ghosts, but it's all predictable (with drawn-out flashbacks and a lack of effects to complement the gore killings). Producer-director Don Jones fails to evoke believable performances from Dean Russell, Elaine Warner, John Batis and Ann Wilkinson. Aha, a critic can see the sleaze through THE FOREST, after all. (Prism; Starmaker)

FOREST OF FEAR. See **BLOODEATERS, THE.**

FOREST PRIMEVAL. See **FINAL TERROR, THE.**

FOREVER (1992). Unusual supernatural comedy-drama blended with softcore sex as rock-music-video director Keith Coogan rents the one-time home of murdered Hollywood director William Desmond Taylor and is haunted by Mabel Normand and other real-life movie stars of the '20s. Sally Kirkland, as a movieland agent, spends most of her time seducing Coogan and disbelieving his story. This is an oddball offering that generates only mild interest despite its probing of a real unsolved murder case. Sean Young, Diane Ladd, Terence Knox, Renee Taylor, Steve Railsback. Directed by Thomas Palmer Jr.; written by Palmer and Jackelyn Giroux. (Crystal Vision)

FOREVER DARLING (1956). One of the few features made by Lucille Ball and Desi Arnaz during their popularity on I LOVE LUCY, and almost forgotten. Lucille and Desi are having marital problems when angel James Mason appears to give them a guiding hand. A curiosity item Lucy fans should take a gander at. Directed by Alexander Hall from a Helen Deutsch script. John Emory, Louis Calhern, John Hoyt. (MGM/UA)

FOREVER EVIL (1987). Video original made in Houston and Coldspring, Texas, involving a demon baby with red-glowing eyes, an Elder God (Yog Cothar, a name stolen from H.P. Lovecraft) imprisoned on a quasar, and a humanoid monster whose identity is kept a secret. Cheaply shot, with amateur talent, this only comes to life with the appearance of a zombie-like creature that cannot be killed, and the efforts of hero and heroine to do the monster in. Oh, there's also some crap about a mythical dagger. If you're a masochist, go ahead and rent it. Roger Evans directed. Charles Trotter, Howard Jacobson, Red Mitchell. (United; VCI)

FOREVER YOUNG (1992). Entertaining family picture that recaptures many of the storytelling values of the '40s, a definite feather in the cap of its producer and star, Mel Gibson. He portrays a test pilot in 1939 whose fiancee is paralyzed in an accident. So stressed out, he puts himself into a deep-freeze experiment under scientist George Wendt, hoping to be reawakened when she comes out of her coma decades later. When he is revived, the disoriented Gibson begins a series of heart-tugging adventures with Jamie Lee Curtis and her two adolescents. Sure, it's corny and manipulative, but it has so many wonderful and sweet moments, you can't help but like Gibson's sympathetic performance. Credit director Steve Miner for also capturing an adolescent romance. Forever successful! Elijah Wood, Isabel Glasser, Joe Morton, Nicholas Surovy. (Warner Bros.)

FORGOTTEN CITY OF THE PLANET OF THE APES (1974). Re-edited from the TV series PLANET OF THE APES, with Roddy McDowall as Galen and Ron Harper and James Naughton as pursued astronauts.

FORGOTTEN ONE, THE (1989). Slow-moving ghost story with few scares, produced in Denver, in which Terry O'Quinn (THE STEPFATHER) takes over an old house haunted by the spirit of a woman who committed suicide there in 1891. Even though O'Quinn would rather be in love with neighbor Kristy McNichol, he's gradually seduced by the beautiful spectral brunette in a series of unexciting incidents with unimaginative effects. Lethargically written-directed by Phillip Badger. Elisabeth Brooks, Blair Parker. (Academy)

FOR HEAVEN'S SAKE (1951). George Seaton tried to duplicate the success of his MIRACLE ON 34TH STREET, but fell on his halo. Dated picture is about angels involving themselves in men's affairs. Clifton Webb is the angelic one in the guise of a rangy Montana rancher, visiting on behalf of an unborn child in Heaven waiting to find a womb to slide into. Webb's entanglement is with the squabbling parents-to-be. Bad Heavens! Joan Bennett, Robert Cummings, Edmund Gwenn, Joan Blondell.

FOR HEAVEN'S SAKE (1986). Sentimental, tug-at-your-heart-strings movie for which Ray Bolger came out of retirement. He portrays Simon, an angel who enjoys hotdogs, beer and meddling in the affairs of basketball player Kent McCord who suffers being a clown on the court even though he thinks he's a champion. Simon is an insufferable Heavenly Body who engages in idiotic conversations with another angel named Malcolm, and looks to offcamera director Jerry Thorpe for much-needed help. This movie is like receiving a telegram that gives the plot in advance. The only interesting character is a dog named Holy Moses. Harvey Jason, Susan Page, Joanna Pettet, Kenneth Mars. (IVE)

FORMULA, THE (1980). Steve Shagan's best-seller was a compelling detective-mystery and this film version emphasizes the cynical theme as cop George C. Scott uncovers a formula that can produce gas from synthetic products, first used by Hitler in World War II. There is a conspiracy by a major oil company to suppress the formula. Marlon Brando exemplifies the conspiratorial side as a cynical, greedy oil magnate. John Avildsen directed Shagan's script. Marthe Keller, John Gielgud, G. D. Spradlin. (CBS/Fox; MGM) (Laser: Japanese)

FORTRESS (1992). Well-produced, intense sci-fi thriller set in a maximum-security prison of the future, run by a private corporation called Mentel. Prisoner behavior is controlled by an explosive ("intestinate") placed in the stomach of each convict; a "mind wipe chamber" where one's memories are erased; and "enhancers," prison officials who have been turned into creatures that live on amino acids. Although the basic form is that of the prison action picture, this has so many intriguing ideas that one is swept along with its effectively brutal torture sequences and the climactic escape attempt. Christopher Lambert and Loryn Locklin play husband and wife who have been imprisoned for breaking the breeding laws—Loryn is pregnant with child. Kurtwood Smith is slimy as the head "enhancer"—his evilness steals the picture. Directed with the gore and violence one expects from Stuart Gordon, who re-animated himself into a first-class director with this superb fantasy-action flick. Jeffrey Combs, Lincoln Kilpatrick, Tom Towles.

FORTY YEARS OF SCIENCE FICTION TELEVISION (1990). The only reason to collect this superficial study of TV sci-fi from 1959-90 is its inclusion of the STAR TREK bloopers. Otherwise, it's clips with cursory commentary from a droning voice. Scenes lifted from early stuff (TOM CORBETT, SPACE CADET) through SCIENCE FICTION THEATER through BATMAN, THE PRISONER, KOLCHAK, etc. Also called A HISTORY OF SCI-FI TELEVISION. (Simitar)

FOR YOUR EYES ONLY (1981). The 12th James Bond adventure, more restrained than many, though it still features exciting chases, futuristic gadgets and vehicles designed to keep Agent 007 one step ahead of the villains. Director John Glen emphasizes character and suspense, allowing 007 (Roger Moore) to appear more human than superman. The British agent is after the tracking system of a sunken nuclear submarine stolen by a ruthless mercenary. The Derek Meddings-John Evans effects are outstanding, Alan Hume's cinematography is topnotch and Bill Conti's music is whistleable. The acting by Topol, Lynn-Holly Johnson and Carole Bouquet is just strong enough to hold attention until the next action sequence. A mountain-scaling feat is one of the film's more suspenseful bits. (Video/Laser: CBS/Fox)

4-D MAN, THE (1959). Jack Harris' production does 3-D one better by having scientist Robert Lansing charged with rays from the fourth dimension and passing through solid objects. But this new power also makes him greedy and homicidal. Has a period-sleaze fascination about it. Also known as MASTER OF TERROR and THE EVIL FORCE. Directed by Irwin S. Yeaworth Jr. and featuring Patty Duke as a kid. Lee Meriwether, James Congdon, Robert Strauss. (New World)

FOUR FLIES ON GREY VELVET (1972). Offbeat Italian psychothriller directed by Dario Argento (DEEP RED, SUSPIRIA) and written by Luigi Cozzi and Mario Foglietti, in which an intrepid hero uses a strange laser device to capture the image of a murderer on a victim's retina. Suspense builds admirably. Music by Ennio Morricone. Michael Brandon, Mimsy Farmer, Bud Spencer.

FOUR-SIDED TRIANGLE (1953). When two scientists fall for Barbara Payton, they stick her in their duplicating machine so each can own her voluptuous body. But the solving of quantity leads to a problem of quality: Will the duplicate be as good as the original? Curious, literate British film (early Hammer, actually) directed by Terence Fisher. James Hayter, John van Eyssen. The American title was THE MONSTER AND THE WOMAN. (Sinister/C; Filmfax; S/Weird; Nostalgia)

FOUR SKULLS OF JONATHAN DRAKE, THE (1959). Familiar beware-the-family-curse is at work in this low-budget special from Robert E. Kent. Eduard Franz, Valerie French and Henry Daniell are employed in Orville H. Hampton's tale about a family whose members are always beheaded at 60. Daniell is Jonathan Drake, who keeps track of all the heads in his private collection. Turns out Drake is a 2000-year-old walking zombie. "Zounds!" four times! Grant Richards, Paul Cavanagh.

FOURTH MAN, THE (1984). Paul Verhoeven, director of TOTAL RECALL, spins a weird allegorical tale about a homosexual writer who suffers hallucinations and undergoes horror when he meets a Black Widow woman whose husbands have all died mysteriously. A multi-layed Dutch film (with subtitles), this may offend some with its sexual and violent content, but art-film lovers should find it of interest. Jeroen Krabbe, Renee Soutenduk, Jon De Vries. (Media; Xenon) (Laser: Image)

FOURTH STORY, THE (1991). Mark Harmon's quirky private eye turns this TV-movie into an intriguing psychothriller in which Mimi Rogers is looking for her missing husband. Although Andrew Guerdat's script is contrived, it is the twists and turns that director Ivan Passer uses to take you on a psychological-mystery ride. Paul Gleason, M. Emmet Walsh, Cliff DeYoung. (Video/Laser: Media)

FRANCIS (1950). A talking mule with Chill Wills' voice? Yep, it's time for that fun-loving Universal-International comedy with Donald O'Connor as a World War II dogface who gets thrown into a psycho ward when he tries to explain about the articulate ass that saved his life in a Japanese ambush. Written by David Stern from his novel and directed by Arthur Lubin, with Zasu Pitts, Eduard Franz, Mikel Conrad, Patricia Medina and Ray Collins providing platoon support. This rollicking comedy was the "pilot" for a long-braying, money-making series: **FRANCIS GOES TO THE RACES (1951), FRANCIS COVERS THE BIG TOWN (1953), FRANCIS JOINS THE WACS (1954), FRANCIS IN THE NAVY (1955)** and the final entry, **FRANCIS IN THE HAUNTED HOUSE (1956),** in which O'Connor was replaced by Mickey Rooney. (Descriptions of these titles are in editions 1-3.) Lubin went on to create TV's talking horse series, MR. ED. FRANCIS IN THE NAVY (Goodtimes) has Clint Eastwood in an early role. (from MCA: FRANCIS, FRANCIS JOINS THE WACS, FRANCIS GOES TO THE RACES, FRANCIS IN THE NAVY.)

FRANKENHOOKER (1989). Black-comedy parody of FRANKENSTEIN in the RE-ANIMATOR vein from writer-director Frank Henenlotter, coming after BASKET CASE and BRAIN DAMAGE. It's madcap lampoonery of the darkest kind as mad doctor James Lorinz salvages body parts of his sister after she's mulched up in a mowing machine. After hilarious adventures in Times Square with hookers, he puts her together again. A cult "midnight" movie, designed for those who enjoy gory horror and aren't easily offended. There's nudity and softcore sex. Patty Mullen, Charlotte Helmkamp, Lia Chang, Louise Lasser. (Shapiro Glickenhaus) (Laser: Image)

'FRANKENHOOKER'

FRANKENSTEIN (1931). Granddaddy of the Walking Monster films, so cleverly directed by James Whale it takes on greater classicality with each viewing. Boris Karloff, as Frankenstein's Monster in the make-up of Jack Pierce, projects a paradoxical mixture of pathos and horror. Whale's vision was years ahead of its time, influencing a superb adaptation of Mary Shelley's novel (by Garrett Ford, Robert Florey, Francis E. Faragoh) and crisp, Gothic-inspired camerawork by Arthur Edeson. Whale went on to make BRIDE OF FRANKENSTEIN, which many feel is superior to the original . . . but unquestionably this established a cinema trend. Whale's superb cast includes Colin Clive as Dr. Frankenstein ("It's alive! Alive!"), Mae Clarke, John Boles, Edward van Sloan, Dwight Frye. A new video version contains the controversial scenes cut from the original of the Monster drowning a little girl in the village pond. (Video/Laser: MCA)

FRANKENSTEIN (1969). See **ASSIGNMENT TERROR.**

FRANKENSTEIN (1973). See **ANDY WARHOL'S FRANKENSTEIN.**

FRANKENSTEIN (1973). Originally shown on ABC-TV in two parts, this is a long, tedious Dan Curtis production (exceeding two hours) in which Robert Foxworth plays an unlikeable, intense Dr. Frankenstein and Bo Svenson is his monstrous creation—an articulate, intellectual shambler who spends too much time talking. The low-budget, lumbering production never escapes the sound-stage look, and director Glenn Jordan zooms his camera too much. Strasberg provides love interest. Heidi Vaughn, Robert Gentry, Philip Bourneuf. (Thrillervideo)

FRANKENSTEIN (1984). U.S./British TV video blending Hammer's Gothic influences with Mary Shelley into an entertaining brew. Robert Powell portrays Dr. Victor Frankenstein with an element of depraved madness, while Carrie Fisher is his innocent sister who is always lifting her period bustle to walk room to room. John Gielgud appears as the blind man in the forest. Terence Alexander is the young assistant and Susan Woolridge his love interest. David Warner brings little pathos to the Monster and his make-up is hideous without being stunning or original. James Ormerod's direction has that anonymous clarity that plagues all taped dramas. Ripley Castle in England is the setting. (Lightning; Live)

FRANKENSTEIN (1984). Japanese animated version of Shelley's classic, full of violence and gore, and not recommended for faint-headed kiddies. (Vestron)

FRANKENSTEIN (1993). Shot in England and Poland for cable TV by British writer-producer-director David Wickes, this adaptation of Shelley's novel stars Randy Quaid as the Monster, Patrick Bergin as Dr. Frankenstein and John Mills as the blind man in the forest. It's a richly ornate version with the obsessed doctor creating his monster with a force-field device that provides the film with its goriest sequence. Quaid is effective as the Monster, and Wickes is faithful to some parts of the book if not to others. Lambert Wilson, Fiona Gillies. (Turner)

FRANKENSTEIN: A CINEMATIC SCRAPBOOK (1990). A "treasury of movie trailers" of all the Frankenstein movies in Universal's and Hammer's horror series, with a sprinkling of oddball and independent movies such as FRANKENSTEIN 1970 and FRANKENSTEIN'S DAUGHTER. The narration by producer-director Ted Newsom isn't much, but occasionally there's a tidbit. Such as Bela Lugosi in a Golem-like make-up for a 1932 FRANKENSTEIN screen test. Such as Boris Karloff appearing in monster makeup at a 1941 baseball game. (Rhino)

FRANKENSTEIN AND THE GIANT LIZARD. See **FRANKENSTEIN CONQUERS THE WORLD.**

FRANKENSTEIN AND THE MONSTER FROM HELL (1973). Final entry in Hammer's Frankenstein series, at its best with laboratory black humor. Shane Briant, a young disciple of Baron Frankenstein, is sent to Carlesbad Asylum for the Insane for his heinous acts, but once there is befriended by Frankenstein (the utterly delightful, and mad, Peter Cushing). Assisted by mute Madeline Smith, the team takes a genius violinist's brain and places it in David Prowse's cranium, resulting in new mayhem. The John Elder script is cliched and half-hearted; Terence Fisher's direction is weary; it's but a ghostly shadow of earlier films in this historic series. Bernard Lee, Charles Lloyd-Pack. (Paramount/Gateway) (Laser: Japanese)

FRANKENSTEIN (BY ANDY WARHOL). See **ANDY WARHOL'S FRANKENSTEIN** (Triboro).

FRANKENSTEIN CONQUERS THE WORLD (1966). Made as FRANKENSTEIN VS. THE GIANT DEVIL FISH . . . but in a cutting room the Devil Fish was spliced out. Destructive mayhem, however, was not cut, so rampage-mayhem-chaos fans can rejoice. The battle royal is between Baragon, a rampaging dinosaur, and a human who is 30 feet high after swallowing a heart created by Dr. Frankenstein for the Nazis. Nick Adams headlines the cast to give the film international appeal. GODZILLA director Inoshiro Honda helms the action, with effects by his pal Eiji Tsuburaya. Tadao Takashima.

FRANKENSTEIN CREATED WOMAN (1967). A Hammer horror film for transsexuals. Peter Cushing, as Baron Frankenstein, has mastered the black science of capturing the spirit of a corpse. A male wraith is transplanted into the body of a beauty with heaving bosom (Susan Denberg), who goes around stabbing folks with a knife, her bosom still heaving. Production values are outstanding and the cast ably manipulated by director Terence Fisher, a specialist at motivating heaving bosoms. Screenplay by John (Heaving) Elder, produced by Anthony Nelson-Keys. Thorley Walters, Robert Morris.

FRANKENSTEIN 80 (1972). Italian rehash of the Frankenstein legend is a blood-splattered flicker with effects by Carlo Rambaldi and direction by Mario Mancini. Gordon Mitchell portrays a mad doctor who creates "Mosaico," a hulking evil that escapes the lab to wreak revenge on sexy women. Marisa Travers, John Richardson. (Gorgon; MPI)

FRANKENSTEIN '88. See **VINDICATOR, THE.**

FRANKENSTEIN EXPERIMENT, THE. See **ANDY WARHOL'S FRANKENSTEIN.**

FRANKENSTEIN GENERAL HOSPITAL (1988). Improv-comic genius Mark Blankfield (JEKYLL AND HYDE . . . TOGETHER AGAIN) stars in this spoof as Dr. Robert Frankenheimer who, with the help of assistant Iggy (Leslie Jordan), puts together a new body from body leftovers. The scenes in his subterranean lab are in black and white because it has been "drained of color"—one of the few gags in this film that works. Another cute bit is set in Tushman's Terminated Teenager Mortuary. Most of the flat humor evolves out of smutty scatology tomfoolery, body parts' jokes, nerdy nurse nutties, sexual depraved puns and pratfalls. Irwin Keyes, as the Monster, is cute and never menacing. Kathy Shower and Katie Caple show off their ample bosoms—it does liven up the tedium. Direction by Deborah Roberts is as flat as the jokes. Jonathan Farwell, Hamilton Mitchell, Ben Stein. (Video/Laser: New Star)

FRANKENSTEIN ISLAND (1981). So bad it has to be seen to be appreciated: Balloonist-cum-scientist Robert Clarke and three pals plus Melvin the dog land on an island where alien women in leopard-skin bikinis dance to tom-toms, pirate Steve Brodie wears an eyepatch and cackles like a madman, schooner captain Cameron Mitchell recites poetry locked in a cage, and the floating head of John Carradine (Dr. Frankenstein) screams "Power! Power! Power!" You also get mad Dr. Van Helsing and his peroxide-blond wife Sheila, and a Frankenstein Monster in a tub of water, surrounded by zombie guards in dark glasses. What does it all mean? Producer-director Jerry Warren never does say. Andrew Duggan, Robert Christopher, Patrick O'Neil, Katherine Victor. (Monterey)

FRANKENSTEIN—ITALIAN STYLE (1977). X-rated spoof with a hulking creature better endowed than his predecessors as he rushes from one female assistant to another to "consummate" the relationship. There hangs the tail. Directed by Armando Crispino.

FRANKENSTEIN MADE WOMAN. See **FRANKENSTEIN CREATED WOMAN.**

FRANKENSTEIN MEETS THE SPACE MONSTER (1965). And you'll meet with boredom from this poverty-stricken heap about an "astro-robot" with half a face (and less a brain) fighting Princess Marcuzan and her alien-invader hordes. This has nothing to do with the Frankenstein Monster, but who cares? Produced in Puerto Rico (as MARS INVADES PUERTO RICO); directed by Robert Gaffney. James Karen, Nancy Marshall. Aka DUEL OF THE SPACE MONSTERS. (Prism)

FRANKENSTEIN MEETS THE WOLF MAN (1943). Fanged, drooling battle between the Frankenstein Monster and Lawrence Talbot, the misunderstood lycanthrope, was declared the "Clash of the Century" by Universal. The rematch of these box-office monsters, written by Curt Siodmak and directed by Roy William Neill, is fun movie-watching. Lon Chaney Jr. is back as Talbot and Bela Lugosi proves he's no Boris Karloff as he shambles ineptly as the Monster. Boy, what a cast of horror favorites: Partric Knowles as Dr. Mannering, who resurrects the Monster; Lionel Atwill as the village mayor; Maria Ouspenskaya as the gypsy woman who intones the classic "wolfbane curse." Dwight Frye, Dennis Hoey, Ilona Massey. (Video/Laser: MCA)

FRANKENSTEIN MUST BE DESTROYED (1970). In this, fifth in Hammer's FRANKENSTEIN series, Peter Cushing cuts apart cadavers to create a hulking entity of evil. The Bert Batt script succeeds in being nauseating, as in a Grand Guignol sequence where a busted water-pipe forces a buried victim up through the mud. Buffs will enjoy this hokum from producer Anthony Nelson-Keys and director Terence Fisher; others may find it unstomachable or tedious as Cushing dons a fright mask to attack victims, cuts open skulls to extract human brains, and forces assistant Simon Ward to claim the body of Veronica Carlson, quite beautous in her diaphonous nightgowns. Freddie Jones plays the Monster.

FRANKENSTEIN 1970 (1958). Instead of harnessing electricity to resurrect man-mad monsters, Baron Victor Von Frankenstein (Boris Karloff) uses atomic energy. Oh well, even horror films have to swing with the modern age. Anyway, the unhinged Baron (victim of Nazi torture) allows a movie crew (feisty Don "Red" Barry is its director) onto his castle grounds, horrified to discover the tinsel-town troupe is making a fright flick. How horrible! But the Baron knows cast and crew will supply the bodies he needs for his nuclear reactor. The surprise ending is quite predictable. Directed by Howard Koch. Tom Duggan, Jana Lund, Mike Lane, Charlotte Austin.

FRANKENSTEIN ON CAMPUS (1970). Canadian flick, also called DR. FRANKENSTEIN ON CAMPUS and FLICK, is a youth-oriented endeavor enlivened by nifty special effects at the climax. Otherwise, it's tedious going when Simon Ward (Viktor Frankenstein IV, descendant of the crazy Bavarian) turns his fellow classmates into monsters. There are subplots involving campus protest rallies and drugs. If you can sit through this, go to the head of the class. Directed by Gil Taylor. Kathleen Sawyer, Austin Willis.

FRANKENSTEIN'S BLOODY TERROR (1971). Spanish import, redesigned for U.S. consumption, has nothing to do with Frankenstein or his Monster—it's about a clan called Wolfstein and depicts a man becoming a werewolf, and then watching helplessly (while chained to a wall) while two vampires seduce his girl. Despite poor dubbing, this has good color photography and nice nocturnal scenes of the vampire playfully leading a young woman into the night. Directed by Enrique L. Equiluz. Paul Naschy portrays the werewolf in this, the first of eight wolfman dim-witted dilemmas. Also known as HELL'S CREATURES, THE MARK OF THE WOLFMAN, THE VAMPIRE OF DR. DRACULA and THE WOLFMAN OF COUNT DRACULA. Whew.

FRANKENSTEIN'S CASTLE OF FREAKS. Video version of **DR. FRANKENSTEIN'S CASTLE OF FREAKS.** (S/Weird; Filmfax; AstroVision; from Best Film & Video with **MAD BUTCHER, THE**)

FRANKENSTEIN'S DAUGHTER (1958). Wretched Z

flick, so compellingly awful it's required viewing for schlock fans. Exemplary of '50s genre, with amateurish actors, condescending script (by H. E. Barrie) and uninspired direction by Richard Cunha. The grandson of Dr. Frankenstein perfects the drug Degeneral, which degenerates Sandra Knight into a hideous, fanged she-creature comparable to what you see on Halloween night at the front door, asking for a treat. Meanwhile, some teenagers try to solve the mystery while a cop dumbly investigates. Wonderfully incompetent. John Ashley, Harold Lloyd Jr., Voltaire Perkins. Also known as SHE MONSTER OF THE NIGHT. (Media; Rhino; Nostalgia; VCI)

FRANKENSTEIN'S GREAT-AUNT TILLIE (1985). Mexican production, shot in English with a U.S.-British cast—figure that one out. Writer-director Myron J. Gold goes for laughs when the Transylvanian town of Mugglefugger lays claim to the Frankenstein Castle because of unpaid taxes. Along come Victor Jr. (Donald Pleasence), buxom June Wilkerson and 109-year-old Great-Aunt Tillie (Yvonne Furneaux) to search for the family fortune hidden in the castle. Nothing aloof about this spoof. Zsa Zsa Gabor, Rod Colbin, Garnett Smith. (Video City)

FRANKENSTEIN: THE COLLEGE YEARS (1991). Good natured, if frequently dumb, TV-movie making slapstick out of the Frankenstein Monster legend. When college scientist Lippzigger dies he leaves his formulae to young student William Ragsdale and pal Christopher Daniel Barnes. Together they resurrect a benevolent creature (Vincent Hammond) who is integrated into campus life as a student and football quarterback. Most of the characters behave stupidly or nerdish, and the humor is of the a-belch-is-funny school. A few of the parody gags will evoke chuckles, but the tee-hes are few. Directed by Tom Shadyac. Larry Miller, Andrea Elson.

FRANKENSTEIN: THE TRUE STORY (1973). The spirit of Shelley's novel is captured in this four-hour TV version. The Christopher Isherwood-Don Bachardy script (also known as DR. FRANKENSTEIN) is literate and the acting is superb. Michael Sarrazin plays the monster, but not as a grotesquerie; rather, the problem is how to keep his flesh from rotting. Dr. Frankenstein (Leonard Whiting) joins ranks with David McCallum to help, then is blackmailed by Dr. Polidori (James Mason) to create a female mate for Sarrazin. One memorable scene shows a woman's head being ripped off her neck. But it is not so much the horror that director Jack Smight stresses; it is the traumas the characters undergo. Agnes Moorehead, John Gielgud, Sir Ralph Richardson, Tom Baker.

FRANKENSTEIN, THE VAMPIRE AND COMPANY (1961). Mexican remake of ABBOTT AND COSTELLO MEET FRANKENSTEIN, with Manuel Loco Valdes and Jose Jasso as the comedy team involved with monsters. Directed by Benito Alazraki.

FRANKENSTEIN 3-D. See **ANDY WARHOL'S FRANKENSTEIN.**

FRANKENSTEIN UNBOUND (1990). Roger Corman's first directorial effort in 20 years is a well-made film if not a great one. But whoever expected greatness from the master of the B horror movie? This adaptation of a popular Brian W. Aldiss novel by screenwriter F.X. Feeney (with rewrite help from Roger baby) follows Dr. Buchanan (John Hurt) in the year 2031 when he's hurled backward through time to 1817 just as Dr. Frankenstein (Raul Julia) is creating a mate for his first monster, which is on a murderous rampage. Filmed in Italy, this has many fascinating elements. Bridget Fonda, Nick Brimble, Catherine Rabett. (Video/Laser: CBS/Fox)

FRANKENSTEIN VS. GIANT DEVIL FISH. See **FRANKENSTEIN CONQUERS THE WORLD.**

FREAKMAKER, THE. Video version of **MUTATIONS** (Vidcrest).

FREAKS (1932). Tod (DRACULA) Browning produced-directed this disturbing portrait of carnival life, also known as FORBIDDEN LOVE, NATURE'S MISTRESS and THE MONSTER SHOW. A stickler for realism, Browning hired real circus freaks to act out a macabre tale about the circus world. Two normal-sized performers try to swindle an inheritance from a well-to-do midget by poisoning him on his wedding night. The sympathetically portrayed freaks turn against the pair, providing a shock ending that disgusted '30s viewers. A Classic of the Grotesque based on Tod Robbins' "Spurs." Among the misshapen: a living torso, pinheads, a "living skeleton" and Siamese twins. Wallace Ford, Roscoe Ates, Olga Baclanova, Edward Brophy. (Video/Laser: MGM/UA)

FREAKY FAIRY TALES. See **DEAD TIME STORIES.**

FREAKY FRIDAY (1977). Disney comedy-fantasy in which teenager Jodie Foster and her suburban mom Barbara Harris exchange personalities (but not bodies). Daughter copes with housekeeping while mom handles classroom. Director Gary Nelson and screenwriter Mary Rodgers deal well with the satiric implications, but the latter half deteriorates into car chases and slapstick antics. John Astin, Patsy Kelly, Dick Van Patten. (Disney)

FREDDIE AS F.R.O.9 (1992). Animated British feature about a superspy frog fighting evil forces named Messina and El Suypremo, who want to put everyone to sleep with a snooze-ray. Directed by Jon Acevski. Voices by Ben Kingsley, Jenny Agutter, Brian Blessed, Michael Hordern and Nigel Hawthorne. (Miramax)

FREDDY'S DEAD: THE FINAL NIGHTMARE (1991). Sixth entry in the NIGHTMARE ON ELM STREET series is as much a fizzle as the previous three, offering nothing new for Freddy Krueger to do but make tepid wisecracks and threaten teenagers with his knife-hand. In this final adventure, Freddy (Robert Englund) terrorizes more troubled teens: Lisa Zane, Ricky Dean Logan, Lezlie Deane, Shon Greenblatt. And there's flashbacks showing how Freddy killed his wife and went after his own child—tasteless material for what is basically an entertainment. The last 10 minutes were filmed in 3-D but it's cheesy stereovision, the images similar to those in a Disneyland horror ride. If Freddy's really dead, good! (Video/Laser: New Line)

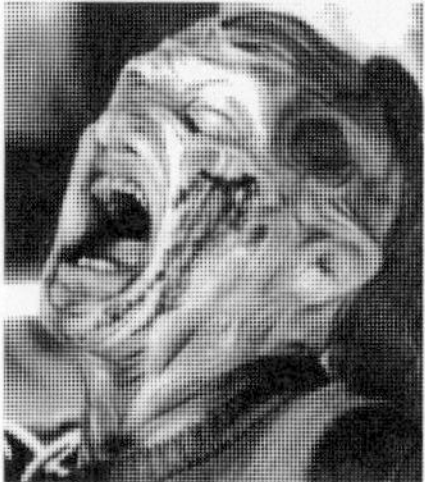

FREDDY KRUEGER

FREDDY'S NIGHTMARE: THE SERIES (1988-90). Five episodes from the syndicated series starring Robert Englund as Freddy Krueger. Directors were Tobe Hooper, Ken Wiederhorn, Tom De Simone, William Mallone. (New Line)

FREE FOR ALL (1949). See editions 1-3.

FREEJACK (1992). Robert Sheckley's IMMORTALITY INC. was the basis for this sci-fi/adventure in which racing car driver Emilio Estevez is yanked forward into time by Mick Jagger, to serve the evil purposes of corporate bigwig Anthony Hopkins. Most of this is action and vehicle chases, never rising above the ordinary as Estevez escapes the cliffhangers. However, when the film enters Hopkins' mind and duplicates his mental landscape, it comes to life in a unique way. Computerized images, however, are still not enough to make up for the clumsily constructed Ron Shusett-Steve Pressfield-Dan Gilroy script. Rene Russo, Jonathan Banks, David Johansen, Grand Bush. (Video/Laser: Warner Bros.)

FREEWAY (1988). A haunting ambience hangs over this study of an excommunicated priest turned religious nutcake who cruises the L.A. freeway system, killing randomly with his .44 revolver. Besides giving it mood, director Francis Delia etches the unhappy, obsessed characters of Darlanne Fluegel, whose husband was a victim of the freeway killer, and nihilistic ex-cop James Russo. Other disturbing albeit fascinating characters: Richard Belzer as a radio talk host whom the murderer calls during his attacks, Michael Callan as a harassed but caring cop, Clint Howard as a sex-crazed mechanic, and Billy Drago as Heller, the killer who uses quotations from the Bible. (Nelson; Starmaker) (Laser: New World)

FREEWAY MANIAC (1989). Paul Winters directed this exercise in murderous behavior that depicts a madman taking refuge on the set of a sci-fi movie and killing again and again. The script was fashioned by Gahan Wilson, the (in)famous macabre cartoonist. Loren Winters, James Courtney, Shepard Sanders. A "thank-you" credit salutes Robert Bloch and Stan Lee, for reasons not explained. Also known as BREAKDOWN (Media).

FREEZE BOMB. Video version of **DEATH DIMENSION (Movietime).**

FRENCHMAN'S FARM (1987). Tracey Tainish witnesses a murder that police tell her was committed in 1944. She and law student David Reyne try to unravel the supernatural mystery. Directed-written by Ron Way. Norman Kaye, John Meillon. (Magnum)

FRENZY (1945). British horror thriller (also called LATIN QUARTER) depicts how a woman is murdered and encased in stone, and how her whereabouts and murderer are discovered through a seance. Written-directed by Vernon Sewell. Derrick de Marney, Frederick Valk, Joan Greenwood. (Sinister/C; Filmfax)

FRENZY (1972). Alfred Hitchcock's good suspense shocker, depicting in unusually graphic style (with some nudity) the strangulations committed by London's infamous Necktie Murderer. There's a classic scene in the back of a potato truck and other clever directorial touches to this unsettling psychological tale of sex and murder, which Hitch jokingly links to food. Jon Finch, Sandra Knight, Barbara Leigh-Hunt, Barry Foster. (Video/Laser: MCA)

FRIDAY THE THIRTEENTH (1980). A lucky day for producer-writer-director Sean Cunningham: This trend-setting slasher movie was a runaway smash, followed by an endless series of sequels, all in a similar vein. A blood-drenched psycho killer named Jason is knocking off his victims (for revengeful purposes) at Camp Crystal Lake. This is a curiosity piece, mainly to see the different ways the victims are done in—there are no two deaths alike. Some of the modus operandi are clever, others ludicrous. Tom Savini made his reputation for gore effects on this film. Adrienne King, Betsy Palmer, Harry Crosby, Mark Nelson. (Video/Laser: Paramount)

FRIDAY THE THIRTEENTH PART 2 (1981). A vast crowd-pleaser under Steve Miner's direction, delivering numerous graphic murders with impalings being the favorite of scripter Ron Kurz. The mutilations are ghastly as that beloved unstoppable killer, Jason Voorhees, returns to Camp Crystal (a.k.a. "Camp Blood") to knock off ill-mannered teenagers just asking for swift dispatching via a poker through the eye, a machete through the jugular, a spear through two bodies at once. Oh, there's also a pitchfork, a chainsaw, and decapitating mechanisms. The cast is negligible (except as cannon fodder) and technical credits adequate if not stunning. Adrienne King, John Furey, Amy Steel, Warrington Gillette, Betsy Palmer. (Video/Laser: Paramount)

FRIDAY THE THIRTEENTH PART 3 (1982). The main titles leap out at you in 3-D and it's a whopper of an effect. And then the movie begins. There isn't a whopper to follow it as the body count builds at Lake Crystal, where more dumb teenagers are on an outing, laughing at that old legend about Jason the Killer. Well, before you can say "Son of the Chainsaw Massacre Meat Cleaver Driller Killer Strikes Again," Jason is back in his funny mask to knock off juvenile jerks one by bloody one. And do those kids deserve what they get! Directed by Steve Miner. Dana Kimmell, Richard Brooker, Catherine Parks. (Video/Laser: Paramount)

FRIDAY THE THIRTEENTH PART 4: THE FINAL CHAPTER (1984). A tepid entry in the series, depicting the slaughterous adventures of Jason Voorhees (an unkillable supernatural wraith) in and around Crystal Lake. Writers Barney Cohen and Frank Mancuso couldn't dream up new ways for bodies to be slashed, skewered or impaled, so Paramount kept the bloodletting and gore effects by Tom Savini to flash cuts. Six teens rent a summer cottage and face death by butcher-knife beheading, hackshaw hacking, corkscrew twisting, stomach knife-punctures, etc. The characters are witless, the dialogue inane and Joseph Zito's direction feeble. Despite the title, the denouement set up an obvious sequel in which Jason returned. Kimberley Beck, Peter Barton, Corey Feldman, Alan Hayes. (Video/Laser: Paramount)

FRIDAY THE THIRTEENTH PART V: A NEW BEGINNING (1985). Fifth in the popular slasher series, a tired formula affair with nothing new about Jason Voorhees, the inhuman killer who delights in wearing a hockey mask. So, this collapses like a balloon with a butcher knife shoved into it. This time the isolated rural setting is a rehab center for the mentally deranged, where ill-defined characters are knocked off by road-flare-shoved-into-mouth, commonplace beheadings and impalings, an axe in the brain, garden shears in the eyeballs, a spike in the brain, ad nauseum. Danny Steinmann directed, but telegraphs every punch. The cast (Melanie Kinnaman, John Shepherd, Shavar Ross, Marco St. John) behaves like refugees from a school for the teen-aged deranged. An unnecessary and mean exercise in gratuitous violence. (Video/Laser: Paramount)

FRIDAY THE THIRTEENTH PART VI: JASON LIVES (1986). Not quite the same old gore murder crap centered around the masked madman, Jason Voorhees. writer-director Tom McLoughlin has seen fit to inject touches of humor into his script, suggesting none of us should take this too seriously. Not that anyone would. By now Jason is a menaceless parody of himself as he stalks his youthful victims in rural settings. One of the gags is that Crystal Lake has been renamed Forest Green County and the cemetery is called Eternal Peace. Here's the body count: machete thrust for two, impaling on a spear, broken bottle into throat, bare fist through a stomach, 360-degree head twist, and assorted stabbings and decapitations. Duck the splatter from the head on a platter. Thom Mathews, Jennifer Cooke, David Kagen. (Video/Laser: Paramount)

FRIDAY THE THIRTEENTH PART VII: THE NEW BLOOD (1988). A weak entry in the Paramount series starring Jason Voorhees, the world's greatest hockey mask salesman, as he is resurrected from the cliffhanger in Part VI. There's nothing new under the electrical storm as Voorhees again stalks the grounds of Camp Crystal, this time faced with the telekinetic powers of a young woman (Lar Park Lincoln) who sets everything on fire everytime she gets pissed off. Director John Carl Buechler hasn't the slightest idea what to do with this retreaded tired tire, as he telegraphs each murder. The thin storyline has Ms Lar undergoing psychiatric testing by cruel headshrinker Terry Kiser and arguing with her mother (Susan Blu) while the usual dumb teenagers provide cannon fodder for Jason's pointed instruments. Jennifer Banko, John Orrin, Kevin Blair, Susan Jennifer Sullivan. (Video/Laser: Paramount)

FRIDAY THE 13TH PART VIII: JASON TAKES MANHATTAN (1989). The title suggests a parody of the Jason Voorhes series, but not so. The hockey-masked killer is back with a vengeance, using spearguns, knives, and other "penetrating" weaponry to kill off young people. But there are twists: Part of the film is set aboard a ship, getting the series away from Crystal Lake and that damn barn. And there are good scenes of Jason in the Big Apple—Times Square, the subway, the rat-infested alleys, the waterfront, etc. Writer-director Rob Hedden should have set the entire picture there. It would have been a real gas. There's also a decent subtext in which the ghost of young Jason comes back to haunt Jensen Daggett. At least they seemed to be trying with this one, even though the endless murders are, by now, all tired retreads. Scott Reeves, Peter Mark Richman, Barbara Bingham. (Video/Laser: Paramount)

FRIDAY THE THIRTEENTH PART 9. See **JASON GOES TO HELL: THE FINAL FRIDAY.**

FRIGHT (1957). Produced during the Bridey Murphy reincarnation craze, this low-budget quickie muddles up reincarnation with multiple personalities. Psychiatrist Eric Fleming hypnotizes Nancy Malone, who reveals that in a former life she was the lover of Prince Rudolf of Austria. Screenwriter Myles Wilder then concocts some incredibly stupid business about Fleming hypnotizing a hardened criminal (Frank Martin) into shooting Malone with blanks so she'll think her alter ego is dead. Huh? Produced-directed by W. Lee Wilder. Dean L. Almquist, Humphrey Davis. (Sinister/C; S/Weird; Filmfax)

FRIGHT (1971). Peter Collinson directed this British shocker with babysitter Susan George trapped in a spooky house with an escapee from an insane asylum. An interesting undercurrent of sexual energy develops as killer Ian Bannen develops fixations. Honor Blackman portrays Bannen's wife. John Gregson, George Cole, Dennis Waterman. (Movies Unlimited; Republic)

FRIGHT HOUSE (1989). Two tales of blood-curdling (you hope!) terror: "Fright House" depicts witches prepping for a meeting with the Devil; "Abandon" is about a teacher who never ages and must explain to her pupils. Directed by Len Anthony. Al Lewis, Duane Jones—the latter in his final role. Produced-directed by Len Anthony. (Studio Entertainment; Shooting Star)

FRIGHTMARE (1974). Disgusting but effective British chiller about a mother (Sheila Keith) who craves (and carves) human flesh and a husband (Rupert Davies) who covers up for her. There's a hot poker murder, a pitchfork homicide and an axe murder or two in David McGillivray's script, and producer-director Peter Walker has the decency to look the other way when the gore splatters. Well, some of the time, anyway. Deborah Fairfax, Paul Greenwood. Also known as ONCE UPON A FRIGHTMARE. (From Prism as **FRIGHTMARE II**)

FRIGHTMARE (1981). "I've never died before, but I want to do it right," proclaims vampire film actor Conrad Radzoff, "The Prince of Ham." And after pushing his director to his death for exhibiting boorish temperamental symptons, Radzoff dies from acute overacting. Where do washed-up horror players go after death? Right back to the living: He's conjured up from the dead by a medium. So Radzoff (Ferdinand Mayne) continues to chew scenery—and bodies—by terrorizing the dumb teenagers who stole his corpse from a mausoleum. It's a campy send-up by writer-director Norman Thaddeus Dane. Luca Bercovici, Nita Talbot, Jennifer Starrett. (Vestron)

FRIGHTMARE II. Video of 1974's **FRIGHTMARE** (Prism).

FRIGHT NIGHT. TV title of **NIGHT FRIGHT.**

FRIGHT NIGHT (1985). Writer-director Tom Holland (author of PSYCHO II) uses the "boy cried werewolf" plot but with ingenious twists. William Ragsdale is convinced a vampire lives next door—but mom, his girlfriend and best friend aren't. Roddy McDowall is marvelous as a late-night "Creature Features" host to whom Ragsdale turns for help. Eventually the girl (Amanda Bearse), a school chum (Stephen Geoffreys) and McDowall enter the vampire's abode, and a "night of terrors" begins, with Richard Edlund providing effects in all their fury. Chris Sarandon has great fun as the vampire, knowing when to be subtle and when to ham it up. He has a handsome assistant (Jonathan Stark) and a homosexual relationship is suggested but never elaborated on. And dig that sequence in a disco when the vampire mesmerizes Bearse. (Video/Laser: RCA/Columbia)

FRIGHT NIGHT PART 2 (1988). This is one sequel that borrows the elements of success from the original. Back from Tom Holland's 1985 hit are Charley Brewster (William Ragsdale) and "Fright Night" TV host Peter Vincent (Roddy McDowall) to stalk new vampires. Director Tommy Lee Wallace and writers Tim Metcalfe and Miguel Tejada-Flores understand what made the first film work—the Brewster-Vincent relationship, the erotic aspects of vampirism, a clever use of effects. Outstanding in the erotic department is Julie Carmen as Regine, a vampire related to the one killed off in the original. With effectively sensual choreographed dances, she proves to be a worthy foe. Traci Lin, Russell Clark, Brian Thompson, Jonathan Grieg. (IVE) (Laser: Image)

FRIGHT SHOW. Video of **CINEMAGIC** (MPI).

FRISSONS. See **THEY CAME FROM WITHIN.**

FROG DREAMING. See **QUEST, THE.**

FROGS (1972). Frightened by the image of frogs, toads and related amphibians leaping to the attack, croaking a melody of death? Then you'll quiver in your wading boots as nature rampages against man (presumably because of our polluting habits). Personifying man's evil side (along with DDT and insecticides) is landowner Ray Milland, who feels the attack just isn't cricket and then orders frogleg soup. The attacking frogs, leaping to the music of Les Baxter and the directorial commands of George McCowan, also have control over snakes and other swamp crawlies as the crowd closes in on Milland's private island, inhabited by quibblers Sam Elliott, Joan Van Ark, Adam Roarke, Judy Pace and William Smith. (Warner Bros.; Vestron) (Laser: Japanese)

FROGTOWN II (1990). This is not quite as amusing or as clever as HELL COMES TO FROGTOWN, but it has campy moments as the Texas Rocket Rangers (inspired by Republic's trilogy of serials that began with KING OF THE ROCKET MEN) fight against the evil Star Frogmeister, who is planning to "turn the world green" by injecting all humans with a frog serum. Rocket Ranger Sam Hell, with the help of his computer F.U.Z.Z.Y., goes up against Commander Toty on the "Frogtown Mutant Reservation." The film works best when its oddball characters (a nerdy scientist played by Brion James; a frog handpuppet; a sexy mutant nurse who only gets turned on by humans) chew up the scenery. Writer-director Donald G. Jackson pays homage at the same time he spoofs movie cliff-hanger conventions. Robert Z'Dar, Denise Duff, Charles Napier, Don Stroud, Lou Ferrigno.

FROM A WHISPER TO A SCREAM. See **OFF-SPRING, THE.**

FROM BEYOND (1986). Director Stuart Gordon (RE-ANIMATOR) has such a distinct style (frenetic pacing, bizarre characters, no-holds-barred horror) that he overcomes the shortcomings of this unrestrained horror thriller from producer Charles Band. Crazy Doc Pretorious (name sound familiar?) has invented the Resonator, which taps into another dimension, allowing a grotesquely awful monster into our world, at the cost of everyone's sanity. Despite all the gooey effects and horrific visuals, the film works because of the overwrought performance of Barbara Crampton as Dr. Roberta Bloch, a psychiatrist who loses all control (sexually and otherwise) to become a kinky anti-heroine (and her bared breasts get pawed by the monster, too). Jeffrey Combs is Crawford Tillinghast. (Characters have genre names provided by scripter Dennis Paoli, who based this loosely on a story by H. P. Lovecraft.) (Video/Laser:Vestron)

'FROM BEYOND'

"More Freeway Attacks: Like Mad Max Out There."

—Newspaper headline in **FREEWAY**

FROM BEYOND THE GRAVE (1973). Amicus anthology film featuring four stories by R. Chetwynd-Hayes, linked by an antique shop setting where owner Peter Cushing foresees the doom of customers trying to cheat him. The stories are "The Gate Crasher," "An Act of Kindness," "The Elemental" and "The Door." Director Kevin Connor presents them with a flourish of atmosphere and production value; recommended. David Warner, Margaret Leighton, Donald Pleasence, Ian Bannen, Diana Dors, Lesley-Anne Down, Nyree Dawn Porter. Also known as THE UNDEAD, TALES FROM BEYOND THE GRAVE, TALES FROM THE BEYOND and THE CREATURES. (Warner Bros.)

FROM HELL IT CAME (1957). A tree trunk named Tabanga branches out when possessed by the radioactive spirit of a dead native. But what a sap! Leaving its shady past behind, the trunk stalks the jungles of a Pacific island, murdering anyone passing through. The performance of the tree (Paul Blaisdell, who was soon after put out to pasture) is equalled only by the wooden acting of Tod Andrews and Tina Carver (but she does have shapely limbs). The ROOTS of horror. The seeds for this were sown by writer Richard Bernstein and planted by producer Jack Milner and director Dan Miller.

FROM RUSSIA WITH LOVE (1964). Second in the James Bond series produced by Harry Saltzman and Albert R. Brocolli, and still a superior spy thriller. The bone of contention is a Soviet decoding machine, the Lektor, which S.P.E.C.T.R.E. is trying to steal from Russia's cryptographic headquarters in Istanbul. Bond is employed by M (Bernard Lee) to steal the device aided by agent Kerim Bey (Pedro Armendariz). And soon our heroic British spy is embroiled with beautiful women (Daniela Bianchi is ravishing) and enemy agents Red Grant (Robert Shaw) and Rosa Klebb (Lotte Lenya). Director Terence Young keeps the pace brisk and the visuals dazzling, capturing every nuance of Richard Maibaum's adaptation of Ian Fleming's novel. The action includes chases in motorboats and helicopters, a fiery belly dance contest climaxed by a gunbattle, and a fight aboard a speeding train. Martine Beswick, Aliza Gur, Lois Maxwell. (CBS/Fox) (Laser: MGM/UA)

FROM THE DEAD OF NIGHT (1989). Despite its use of horror genre cliches and frequent red herrings, and despite its heroine behaving stupidly at times, this four-hour TV-movie sweeps one along. Based on Gary Bradner's novel, WALKERS, it's the mystery of fashion designer Joanna Darby (Lindsay Wagner), who undergoes a harrowing life-after-death experience, only to discover she is pursued by six dead spirits who have one month to get her—so watch for six supernatural attackers. Wagner is bolstered by two boyfriends: Robin Thomas as a jerkola who never believes any of it, and Bruce Boxleitner, a tarot card reader who buys it all. It's director Paul Wendkos who keeps the dubious plot going when William Bleich's script doesn't. Diahann Carroll, Robert Prosky, Merritt Butrick, Joanne Linville.

FROM THE EARTH TO THE MOON (1958). The best features in this adaptation of Jules Verne's scientific adventure are Victorian settings and costumes. Inventor Joseph Cotten uses a new explosive to launch a missile to the moon. He and Debra Paget end up in each other's arms, facing the hazards of space flight. Literate, well-produced but not very exciting. Directed by Byron Haskin. George Sanders, Don Dubbins, Patric Knowles, Morris Ankrum. (United; VCI) (Laser: Image)

FROZEN ALIVE (1964). More experimentation in the art of preserving dead bodies with freezing techniques, tinged with sci-fi overtones. The Evelyn Frazer script deals mostly with the legal ramifications when scientist Mark Stevens is arrested for killing his wife, when her body is really in suspended animation. Directed by Bernard Knowles. Marianna Koch. (Movies Unlimited)

FROZEN DEAD, THE (1966). Don't give it a cold shoulder—it's a chilling (ha ha!) tale depicting a loyal Nazi (Dana Andrews, speaking with an accent that borders on parody) who devises a method to keep German soldiers alive in suspended animation. But something is wrong with their brains and the doctor has a cellarful of mindless Nazis. The doc drills a hole in a brain, severs the head of a strangled woman and keeps it alive, and creates a wall of severed arms that he can tingle back to life with electrity. Mad, you say? Yes, isn't writer-producer-director Herbert J. Leder wonderful. Anna Palk portrays the doctor's niece who enters into telepathic rapport with the detached head, and Philip Gilbert (a specialist in severed heads from America) provides bland love interest. Kathleen Breck, Karel Stepanek, Philip Gilbert. Produced in England.

FROZEN GHOST (1945). Entry in Universal's minor "Inner Sanctum" series, B mysteries introduced by a head floating in a crystal ball—or was it a goldfish bowl? Lon Chaney Jr. plays another misunderstood character: Gregor the Great, a hypnotist who fears he committed murder. Chaney is stiff in the thankless role, and gets no help from director Harold Young. Evelyn Ankers, Milburn Stone, Elena Verdugo, Douglas Dumbrille.

FROZEN SCREAM (1980). Incompetently made time-waster about crazy doctors creating zombie creatures who cackle and look bug-eyed. It's so muddled, there's voiceover narration to explain the plot involving a dumb cop and his terrorized girlfriend, but even that only adds to the confusion. The acting is pathetic, the direction by Frank Roach totally inadequate. The plot is about pre-frontal cranial circuitry lobotomies. It's enough to freeze anyone's mind. Renee Harmon, Lynne Kocol. (VEC; from Continental with EXECUTIONER II)

FROZEN TERROR (1980). First feature from Lamberto Bava is a wild beginning for the son of Mario Bava, famed horror director. Bernice Stegers stars as a whacky broad who keeps the severed head of her husband in her bed—a head endowed with supernatural powers. Originally produced as MACABRO. Veronica Zinny, Robert Posse, Stanko Molnar. (Lightning; Vestron; from CIC as **MACABRE**)

FUGITIVE ALIEN (1986). Japanese sci-fi film in which an alien is wanted by his own race for treason because he won't kill humans. Tatsuya Azuma, Joe Shishido, Miyuri Tanigawa. What a rat! (Celebrity)

FULL CIRCLE. See **HAUNTING OF JULIA, THE.**

FULL ECLIPSE (1993). Fascinating variation on the werewolf theme when heroic urban cop Mario Van Peebles is asked to join a secret group of police who take a serum that gives them superpowers and brings out the animal instincts in them. The kinetic, stylish direction of Anthony Hickox gives the Richard Christian Matheson-Michael Reaves script an added boost, especially when Hickox resorts to violence in the John Woo style. Above average HBO movie. Patsy Kensit, Jason Beghe, Paula Marshall.

FULL MOON. See **MOONCHILD.**

FULL MOON HIGH (1982). Writer-producer-director Larry Cohen's answer to THE HOWLING; a werewolf story about a bitten teen (Adam Arkin, son of Alan Arkin) and his high school adventures. Roz Kellym, Elizabeth Hartman, Ed McMahon, Kenneth Mars, Pat Morita, Alan Arkin, Louis Nye. (HBO) (Laser: Japanese)

FULL MOON OF THE VIRGINS. See **DEVIL'S WEDDING NIGHT, THE.**

FU MANCHU AND THE KEYS OF DEATH. See **KISS AND KILL.**

FU MANCHU'S CASTLE. See **CASTLE OF FU MANCHU, THE.**

FU MANCHU'S KISS OF DEATH. See **KISS AND KILL.**

FUNERAL HOME (1981). Busty Lesleh Donaldson helps grandmother Kay Hawtry run a tourist home, formerly a funeral parlor until her grandfather, Mr. Chalmers (rhymes with "embalmers"), disappeared. In the cellar, late at night, strange voices can be heard. Is Grandma keeping a dark secret? This Canadian film is half-hearted exploitation, not quite a gore movie and not quite a character study. Barry Morse has a minor role as a husband looking for his missing wife. William Fruet's direction is workaday, and Ida Nelson's script is too derivative of PSYCHO to stand on its own. Good track by Jerry Fielding. Also known as CRIES IN THE NIGHT. (Paragon)

FUN HOUSE, THE. See **LAST HOUSE ON DEAD END STREET.**

FUNHOUSE, THE (1981). That TEXAS CHAINSAW MASSACRE lovable, Tobe Hooper, restrains himself for the first half hour of this chiller to establish four teenagers who spend the night in a spooky carnival. But then Tobe pulls out the stops! A sexually repressed midway helper (mime Wayne Doba) wears a fright mask to hide the fact that underneath is an even worse countenance—something to give the Frankenstein Monster nightmares. Sylvia Miles, Kevin Conway, William Finley, Cooper Huckabee, Elizabeth Berridge, Miles Chapin. Effects by Craig Reardon and Rick Baker. (Video/Laser: MCA)

FURTHER ADVENTURES OF TENNESSEE BUCK, THE (1988). Unusual lesbian overtones earmark this satire of the Indiana Jones series made in Sri Lanka, directed by and starring David Keith as the adventurer who leads a jungle expedition with inadequate husband Brant van Hoffman and sexy wife Kathy Shower, who looks great in same with clothing off. A rubdown of Kathy's inspiring body is the highpoint of this sexually activated actioner. (Media) (Laser: Image)

FURTHER TALES FROM THE CRYPT. See **VAULT OF HORROR, THE.**

FURTHER THAN FEAR. See **BEYOND TERROR.**

FURY, THE (1978). Insufficient exposition weakens this Brian De Palma horror-adventure about a young man (Andrew Stevens) with psychic powers who becomes a pawn between spy factions. Superspy Kirk Douglas (Steven's father) tries to rescue him from the villainous John Cassavetes. Emphasis of the John Farris script is on suspense and pursuit, with smashed-up cars, special effects and make-up (Rick Baker). Carrie Snodgress, Amy Irving, Charles Durning. (Video/Laser: CBS/Fox)

FURY OF THE CONGO (1951). Johnny Weissmuller, retired from Tarzan to play Jungle Jim, comes across a jungle where nature has produced a man-eating plant (gulp!) and a spider big enough to challenge the creatures in THEM. It's dreary Sam Katzman-produced stuff for Columbia, unimaginatively directed by William Berke. Even Lyle Talbot and Sherry Moreland look lost in the Congo. Some fury! (Goodtimes)

FURY OF THE SUCCUBUS. See **DARK EYES.**

FURY OF THE WOLFMAN (1971). Paul Naschy tries to get it off his chest—the sign of the Pentagram, we mean. If he doesn't, he'll turn into a hairy killer when the moon is full, just as he did in FRANKENSTEIN'S BLOODY TERROR, to which this is a sequel. Directed by Jose Maria Zabalza, FURY will only make horror fans furious. Naschy (Jacinto Molina) also scripted. Perla Cristal, Veronica Lujan, Mark Stevens. (Unicorn; Charter; Sinister/C; Loonic; Filmfax; S/Weird)

FURY ON THE BOSPHORUS (1965). Editions 1-3.

FUTURE COP (1976). One-joke concept teaming cop Ernest Borgnine with a robot cop (Michael Shannon) who is poorly programmed and always klutzing it up. Poorly programmed is right. This TV-movie directed by Jud Taylor became a series that brought back Borgnine, Shannon and John Amos, then it was the inspiration for another TV-movie, COPS AND ROBIN, with the same cast. And the concept was recycled for the 1980 feature SUPERFUZZ, again with Borgnine. (Paramount)

FUTURE COP (1985). See **TRANCERS.**

FUTURE FORCE (1989). This claptrap actioner features such a laid-back performance by David Carradine that it's almost worth enduring—almost. Carradine is John Tucker, top gun of Civilian Operated Police Systems, an organization of bounty hunters that has replaced the police, so ineffectual has law enforcement become in fighting lawlessness. Carradine, acting like John Wayne, blasts the heavies (led by crooked "cop" William Zipp) and his own men to protect a TV reporter with good-looking legs (Anna Rapagna) who knows too much about Zipp's organization. Carradine even has a metal armpiece that fires laser bolts. Credit writer-director David A. Prior, who went on to make a sequel, FUTURE ZONE. Can nothing stop this man? Robert Tessier, Patrick Culliton. (Action International)

FUTURE HUNTERS (1988). Filipino director Cirio H. Santiago usually turns out MAD MAX imitations, but here he indulges in Indiana Jones-type fantasy adventures energetic and swiftly paced. In a long prologue in 2025, in a post-Holocaust setting, hero Richard Norton finds the head of the magical spear that pierced Jesus Christ's body on the Cross. To prevent the doom of mankind, Norton must find the spear's missing head. He travels to his past, our present (1986), and turns over his mission to an anthropology student (vivacious Linda Carol) and her boyfriend (Robert Patrick). They embark on a series of adventures involving neo-Nazis (Ed Crick and Bob Schott), Amazon warriors, a Mongolian horde and a benevolent race of dwarves in the Philippine jungle. Patently ridiculous, yet entertaining. (Vestron) (Laser: Image)

FUTURE KICK (1991). Lively if frequently cliched Roger Corman production set in a society ruled by corporations with "cyberons" to enforce peace. However, since these android lawmen have morals, they must be destroyed by the men who created them. The soul surviving robot warrior (played woodenly by kickboxing champ Don "The Dragon" Wilson) helps Meg Foster find the psychotic assassin who murdered her husband with a double-bladed device in a smog-ruined world reminiscent of BLADE RUNNER. Writer-director Damian Klaus pads his movie with footage lifted from at least ten other Corman actioners. Christopher Penn, Eb Lottimer, Al Ruscio, Jeff Pomerantz. (New Horizons)

FUTURE KILL (1985). Look at Splatter: He's the leader of a punk gang, an android-man whose hand is a claw device that rips flesh at the wriggling of a finger. Big Splatter and his Little Splatters are cruising the city, following social collapse, looking for members of a fraternity who witnessed Splatter commit a murder. A sickening movie (originally SPLATTER) with nothing to counterbalance its violence and nihilistic viewpoints. As Ronald W. Moore has written-directed it in Austin, Texas, this has zero entertainment values. Edwin Neal, Marilyn Burns. (Video/Laser: Vestron)

FUTURE SCHLOCK (1984). Political satire on Australia's current battle between middle-class suburbanites and non-comformists, set in the 21th Century when the non-comfortists have lost a civil war and are prisoners. Rebels Cisco and Pancho drive their Corvette through the night to harass authorities with prankish tricks. Produced-written-directed by Barry Peak and Chris Kiely. Michael Bishop, Tracey Callander.

FUTURE SHOCK (1993). A failed attempt of recut footage from three movies tied together by having the main character of each visit psychiatrist Martin Kove, who sends them into a trance or listens to their woeful tales. "Jenny Porter" is about a paranoiac woman (Vivian Schilling) trapped in her home by mad dogs. Directed by Eric Parkinson and costarring Brion James. "The Roommate" stars Scott Thompson as a nerdy morgue attendant plagued by a roommate from hell (Bill Paxton). Directed by Francis G. Oley Sassone. "Mr. Petrified Forest" is a surreal, terribly confused tale of Sam Clay going through a death experience, or so it seems. Di-

rected by Matt Reeves. The only horrific sequence opens the film: mad scientists experiment with virtual reality on a dumbbell. What does it all mean? Who knows. (Hemdale)

FUTURE WOMEN (1975). Loosely (and we mean loosely) based on characters created by Sax Rohmer. Shirley Eaton stars as Samanada, a scantily-dressed seductress-ruler of the all-female kingdom of Femina, who plans taking over the world with her machine-gun packing femmes. Director Jesse Franco treats this as a James Bond spoof, but gadgets and effects are shoddy and the action is fake looking. Not even oglers will find much to satisfy them despite all the beautiful women. Richard Wyler, Eliza Montes, Marta Reeves.

FUTUREWORLD (1976). This sequel to WESTWORLD (about a bizarre fantasy paradise that malfunctioned and killed vacationers) picks up when the malfunctions are corrected and Westworld functions alongside Futureworld, where your sci-fi dreams come true. However, crusading reporters Peter Fonda and Blythe Danner suspect a cabal of power-mad villains is using the facilities to take over the world. The Mayo Simon-George Schenk script makes for an exciting thriller with wonderful sets (including the real Houston Space Center) and ample intrigue. Yul Brynner reappears as the Gunfighter in Black. Directed by Richard T. Heffron. Arthur Hill, Allen Ludden, John Ryan, Stuart Margolin, Robert Cornthwaite. (Warner Bros.; Goodtimes; Vestron)

FUTURE ZONE (1990). Sequel to FUTURE FORCE, with David Carradine recreating his role as maverick lawman of the future John Tucker, who draws his weapon according to his own code. In a plot by David A. Prior (who also directed), a cowboy (Ted Prior) rides in from the future to alter the destiny of the gunfighter. Gail Jenson, Patrick Culliton, Ron Taft, Renee Cline. (Action International) (Laser: Image)

FUTZ (1969). Sty in the eye from writers Joseph Stefano and Rochelle Owens: man falls in love with his pig, is persecuted by his fellow man. As directed by Tom O'Horgan, FUTZ takes gutz to sit through; you have to be a little nutz. (Independent United)

GALACTICA III: CONQUEST OF THE EARTH. Video of **CONQUEST OF THE EARTH** (MCA).

GALAXINA (1980). Through the 31st Century soars a starship piloted by Captain Butt (Avery Schreiber) and his misfits, creatures and robots. Their mission: retrieve the Blue Star, a powerful crystal, from robot villain Ordric. This comedy-parody, written-directed by William Sachs, is not a rollicking lampoon but does have isolated laughs. Title character is a sexy robot (Dorothy Stratten, a Playboy centerfold who was murdered shortly after production). Nice try, but no extraterrestrial cigar. Stephen Macht, James D. Hinton. (Video/Laser: MCA)

GALAXY EXPRESS (1979). Japanese animated sci-fi repackaged by Roger Corman. A "space train" of the 35th Century passes through a time continuum, taking passengers to their hopes and dreams. Directed by Taro Rin. (Nelson; Sultan)

GALAXY HIGH SCHOOL (1986). Four episodes from the TV series about an outer-space high schol class, whose president has six hands. (FHE)

GALAXY INVADER (1985). Alien is hunted by Earthlings after it crashlands. Low budgeter directed by Don Dohler. Richard Ruxton, Faye Tilles, Don Liefert, George Stover. (VCI; United; National Entertainment)

GALAXY OF TERROR (1981). Well-produced B job from Roger Corman, a horror/sci-fi tale about a crew on a desolate planet. Each member meets a horrible death—opportunities for blood, gore and multitentacled monsters. The best attack scene is when a sluglike monster "rapes" a beautiful astronaut after stripping away her spacesuit. This moves so fast under Bruce Clark's direction, there's no time to contemplate illogical behavior. Graphic design is satisfying but the ending is needlessly metaphysical. Ray Walston, Erin Moran, Edward Albert. Also known as PLANET OF HORRORS and MINDWARP: AN INFINITY OF HORRORS. A loose sequel was entitled FORBIDDEN WORLD. (Video/Laser: Nelson)

GALLERY OF HORRORS. Video version of **RETURN FROM THE PAST** (Academy).

GAME OF DEATH, A (1945). Richard Connell's horror-adventure classic "The Most Dangerous Game" is the yarn in which man pursues man for bloodsport. The best version was made in 1932; this suffers from budgetary sickness, which hampers the ambitious talents of director Robert Wise. John Loder (as the stranded Rainsford),

Edgar Barrier (as the sadistic Nazi-like hunter Zaroff) and Audrey Long (a love interest not in the original) labor to make Norman Houston's script workable. Jason Robards, Robert Clarke, Noble Johnson.

GAME OF SURVIVAL (1989). Zane, a warrior from another planet, battles six warriors from various parts of the Universe. Directed by Armand Gazarian. Nikki Hill, Cindy Coatman. (Raedon)

GAMERA (1966). First in a series of Japanese-made monster movies starring Gamera as a wannabe Godzilla—actually he/she/it is a flying turtle always sticking its neck out to save mankind from a fate worse than watching Japanese monster marathons. In this origin tale directed by Noriaki Yuasa, Gamera is cantankerous and intends to stomp on Tokyo. The U.S. version contains footage with Brian Donlevy, Albert Dekker and Diane Findlay. Eiji Funakoshi, Harumi Kiritachi. (Filmfax; Just for Kids; Sinister/C; Celebrity's **GAMERA THE INVINCIBLE** is without the U.S. footage.) (Laser: Image, with **GAMERA VS. GUIRON**)

GAMERA VS. BARUGON. Video of **WAR OF THE MONSTERS** (Celebrity) (Laser: Japanese).

GAMERA VS. GAOS. Video/Laser version of **RETURN OF THE GIANT MONSTERS** (Celebrity; Just for Kids) (Laser: Image, with **GAMERA VS. ZIGRA**).

GAMERA VS. GIGER. See **GAMERA VS. MONSTER X** (Celebrity).

GAMERA VS. GUIRON. Video/laser version of **ATTACK OF THE MONSTERS** (Celebrity; Just for Kids) (Laser: Image, with **GAMERA**).

GAMERA VS. MONSTER X (1970). Aka MONSTERS INVADE EXPO '70, this Japanese monster marathon stars that giant flying turtle at Expo '70, where ferocious, noisy battles occur between Gamera and Jiger, a bitchy female who spits spears (!) through her jagged mouth. Crash bam thud. Directed with subtlety by Noriaki Yuasa. (From Celebrity as **GAMERA VS. GIGER)**

GAMERA VS. OUTER SPACE MONSTER VIRUS. See **DESTROY ALL PLANETS.**

GAMERA VS. THE DEEP SEA MONSTER ZIGRA. See **GAMERA VS. ZIGRA.**

GAMERA VS. VIRAS. Video version of **DESTROY ALL PLANETS** (Celebrity).

GAMERA VS. ZIGRA (1971). Aliens called Zigrans plot to conquer Earth, but first have to kill the heroic turtle Gamera. Call it the old shell game. Kids bring Gamera to life and it engages in a rousing battle with a monster-battleship. Incomprehensible for adults; matinee fodder for the toddler. Directed by Noriyaki Yuasa. (Celebrity) (Laser: Image, doubled with **GAMERA VS. GAOS**)

GAMES (1967). Director Curtis Harrington's thriller with Hitchcockian overtones: James Caan and Katharine Ross conceive diabolical mind- playing "games" . . . but Simone Signoret turns sport into nightmare. Resolution of the supernatural elements may disappoint buffs but suspense fans will enjoy Gene Kearney's twist ending, if they haven't seen through the gossamer fabrications. Don Stroud, Kent Smith, Estelle Winwood, Ian Wolfe.

GAMMA PEOPLE, THE (1956). Political sci-fi thriller with Communist madman Walter Rilla turning children into babbling idiots or savant geniuses via radiation treatment. Wobbly, didactic material directed by John Gilling gets trapped behind an ironic curtain. Paul Douglas, Leslie Phillips, Eva Bartok, Martin Miller, Olaf Pooley. (Goodtimes; RCA/Columbia)

GAMMERA THE INVINCIBLE (1966). Wow! Look at that! A hot-breathed, jet-propelled, bi-winged prehistoric monster! And a turtle to boot! Yes fans, another fun-loving, panic-happy, Japanese-inspired creature on the rampage. And look! They've added U.S. footage with Brian Donlevy and Albert Dekker. Now there are two M's in ""Gammera," while his/its other six films had only one. Something got lost in the translation, maybe? Gammera obscura? (Sinister/C; S/Weird)

GANDAHAR. Rene Laloux's original French-language version of what was retitled **LIGHT YEARS.**

GANJA AND HESS (1973). This vampire film directed by Bill Gunn was recut after its release and retitled BLOOD COUPLE, but was so altered it qualifies as a totally different film. See BLOOD COUPLE for details about various video versions and retitlings.

GANJASAURUS REX (1987). Parody/satire/lampoon of Japanese monster movies in which a 400-feet-high dinosaur terrorizes California marijuana growers, looking for a bed of grass to rest his tale in. Paul Bassis, David Fresh. Directed by Ursi Reynolds. (Rhino)

GAPPA—TRIPHIBIAN MONSTER. See **MONSTER FROM A PREHISTORIC PLANET.**

GARBAGE PAIL KIDS MOVIE, THE (1987). Writer-director Rod Amateau has turned out a mean-spirited satire based on the offensive creatures in the Topps Bubble Gum card set. It's a mixed bag of foul frolicking, in which violence and grotesque humor are blended with the ugly characters from space who land on Earth in a garbage can and live in Anthony Newley's magic shop. The songs are forgettable as the characters (Valerie Vomit, Ali Gator, Greaser Greg and Messy Tessie, among others) romp with Mackenzie Astin and Katie Barberi in an absurd plot that involves senseless gang violence and the Home for the Ugly guarded by Leo Gordon. John Buechler did the monster creations. A misfire that belongs in the bucket. It pails beside garbage. (Atlantic; Kartes) (Laser: Paramount)

GARDENER, THE (1974). Offbeat film produced in Puerto Rico with Joe Dallesandro as a shady weed chopper who turns into a tree and has rapport with flowers. Writer-director Jim Kay makes this a tough row to hoe. Rita Gam, Katharine Houghton, James Congdon. (From Unicorn as **SEEDS OF EVIL**)

GARDEN OF THE DEAD (1972). Deceased convicts rise from the grave to scatter-splatter the guards and warden who wronged them. Writer-director John Hayes finds life to be a tough death's row to hoe. My, what a seedy joke. Duncan McLeod, Lee Frost, John Dennis, Susan Charney. (Video Bancorp; from Silver Mine as **TOMB OF THE UNDEAD**)

GARGON TERROR. See **TEENAGERS FROM OUTER SPACE.**

GARGOYLES (1972). Unusually good monster/effects TV-movie with make-up by Ellis Burman and Stan Winston winning an Emmy. Cornel Wilde investigates strange reports about winged creatures in the desert; the Carlsbad Caverns (where this was filmed) are headquarters and nesting place for gargoyle-like aliens planning to take over Earth. Tautly directed by B. W. L. Norton. Jennifer Salt, Bernie Casey, Grayson Hall. (Star Classics)

GAS HOUSE KIDS IN HOLLYWOOD, THE (1947). See editions 1-3.

GAS-S-S-S or IT MAY BECOME NECESSARY TO DESTROY THE WORLD IN ORDER TO SAVE IT (1971). Right on, hey-baby, swing-with-it, daddy-o movie. A nerve gas is loose which kills everyone over 25. Is this instant Utopia for the younger set or is this instant Utopia? An odyssey of fun-loving adventure for 20-year-olds who dress like tourists, fight it out with Hell's Angels and shout obscenities. Is this producer-director Roger Corman's idea of a grand time? Ben Vereen, Bud Cort, Elaine Giftos, Cindy Williams. (Lightning)

GATE, THE (1987). This is purely an effects movie without much logic, a box-office hit without a soul. Stephen Dorff is a kid troubled by a hole in his backyard after a tree is hit by lightning and removed. The hole is a passageway for killer imps to come from another dimension and terrorize Dorff and fellow dorks. It ends up five kids trapped in a house where energy manifests itself in various forms until the Big Monster a la Spielberg arrives. How Dorff defeats the beast is dorfy dumb. Directed by Tibor Takacs. Louis Tripp, Christa Denton, Kelly Rowan, Ingrid Venninger. (Video/Laser: Vestron)

GATE II (1989). Except for good monster effects ranging from a man in a scaly suit to stop-motion animation, this sequel to the 1987 hit offers little with its juvenile storyline and dull characters. Nerdy Louis Tripp makes contact with the Trinity of Demons and has fantasy-horror adventures with girlfriend Pamela Segall and pals Simon Reynolds and James Villemaire. One never senses peril for the oddball foursome, for this is harmless fun from director Tibor Takacs. It sat for three years before a release in '92. Neil Munro, James Kidnie. (RCA/Columbia) (Video/Laser: Vision P.D.G./Sony)

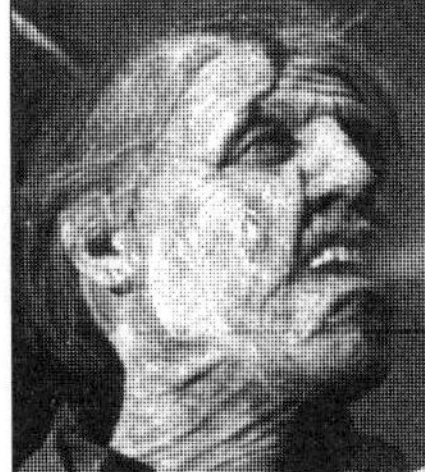
DEMON IN 'THE GATE'

GATES OF HELL, THE (1981). In Dunwich, USA, stomping grounds of H. P. Lovecraft, a priest hangs himself in a graveyard, opening portals to Hades. Christopher George has three days to close that door or every corpse on Earth will never rest again. (Won't George Romero like that!) Director Lucio Fulci (ZOMBIE), who co-wrote this with Dardano Sacchetti as TWILIGHT OF THE DEAD, is more interested in showing a woman vomit her guts out, a drill penetrate a man's head and a brain squashed out of a woman's head. Very pointless (except for the drills) and revolting. Strong stomachs required. Katherine MacColl, Venantino Venantini. Known as THE FEAR, FEAR IN THE CITY OF THE LIVING DEAD and TWILIGHT OF THE DEAD. (Paragon; New Vision; Embassy offers a subtitled version; from Iver as **CITY OF THE LIVING DEAD**)

GEEK. See **BACKWOODS.**

GEEK MAGGOT BINGO (1983). Amateur 16mm monster-horror parody for midnight audiences, written-produced-directed by Nick Zedd. With Dr. Frankenberry (Robert Andrews), vampire queen Scumbalina (Donna Death), sleazy effects and crude camera work and lighting. Narrated by Zacherley, one-time horror host. Enough Zedd? (Monday/Wednesday/Friday; Movies Unlimited)

GEMINI MAN, THE. See **CODE NAME: MINUS ONE.**

GEMINI TWINS, THE. See **TWINS OF EVIL.**

GENERATION (1985). Boring, talkative TV-movie soap opera with mild sci-fi touches about a family in 1999. The main interest here is new gear for a form of "combat hockey" and how it should be tested on the playing field. People bicker, just like in the soaps. Directed by Michael Tuchner. Richard Beymer, Hannah Cutrona, Cristina Raines, Priscilla Pointer. (Embassy)

GENESIS II (1973). Disappointing TV-movie produced-written by Gene Roddenberry, directed by John Llewellyn Moxey. Alex Cord, in suspended animation, awakens in 2133 to find civilization destroyed by atomic war. Surviving factions are broken down into Masters and Slaves and Cord is enmeshed in politics and shoot-outs. Similar characters were utilized in the Roddenberry pilots STRANGE NEW WORLD and PLANET EARTH. Mariette Hartley is sexy in this one . . . Ted Cassidy, Percy Rodriques, Lynne Marta.

GENII OF DARKNESS (1960). One of four films re-edited from a Mexican serial and redubbed for gringos. (The others are CURSE OF NOSTRADAMUS, MONSTER DEMOLISHER and BLOOD OF NOSTRADAMUS.) More nocturnal adventures with German Robles as a bloodsucker whose wardrobe is as shabby as the production. Good guys try to steal the ashes from his coffin to keep him from coming back to life. Ashes to asses . . . Directed by Frederick Curiel. (Sinister/C; Loonic; Nostalgia; Filmfax; S/Weird)

GENIUS AT WORK (1946). Wally Brown and Alan Carney (in the vein of Abbott and Costello) are radio actors with a detective show. Lionel Atwill is their adversary Cobra, a fan of torture chambers. Best for its '40s nostalgia and cast. Directed by Leslie Goodwins. Anne Jeffreys, Robert Clarke, Bela Lugosi, Ralph Dunn.

GENOCIDE (1968). See editions 1-3.

GET SMART, AGAIN! (1989). This retread of the TV spoof of the 1960s returns with Don Adams as Agent 86 and Barbara Feldon as Agent 99. Other agents (Hymie the Robot, Larabee, etc.) are also back, and they lend their humor to Leonard B. Stern's script, which brings the bumbling agents out of retirement to track down a weather-controlling machine in the hands of KAOS. Meanwhile, Agent 99 has written her CONTROL memoirs and that subplot dovetails with Dr. Hottentot's stolen climate formula. The "Would you believe . . . ?" and "And loving it!" gags are repeated and still evoke a chuckle. Directed by Gary Nelson. Bernie Kopell, Dick Grautier, Robert Karvelas, Harold Gould, Kenneth Mars.

GETTING EVEN (1986). A high-tech slam-bam action film with horror/fantasy overtones, first made as HOSTAGE—DALLAS. Industrialist soldier-of-fortune Taggar (Edward Albert) steals a Russian nerve gas from a secret base in Afghanistan (code name Project Viper) so it can be analyzed . . . meanwhile, evil rancher Joe Don Baker plots to steal it. The gas "ravages the flesh" and "devours people" as it "feeds on the atmosphere." (Well, that's what they say!) There are disturbing scenes of victims being turned into jelly and puddies of goo and action bits with helicopters, submachine-guns, hand grenades and other modern devices. Director Dwight H. Tittle sure keeps it lively. Audrey Sanders, Billy Streater. (Vestron)

GETTING LUCKY (1989). No luck for you, the viewer. An unbearable teen comedy appealing to prurient interests as nerdy Steven Cooke finds an Irish "genie" in a bottle (nicknamed "Lepre") who will grant the stupid hero three wishes to win a girlfriend and marry her. As conceived by writer-director Michael Paul Girard, it's unwatchable. Leslie Z. McCraw, Rick McDowell, Jean Stewart. (Raedon, Hollywood Home Entertainment)

GHASTLY ONES, THE (1969). Also known as BLOOD RITES, this period gore thriller was cowritten/produced/directed by Andy Milligan, with a madman running around a mansion chopping folks into little pieces and eating animals alive. The really ghastly one is Milligan who remade this as LEGACY OF HORROR in 1978—it was just as terrible bad ugh. Veronica Radbur, Maggie Rogers. (Video Home Library)

GHASTLY ORGIES OF COUNT DRACULA. See **REINCARNATION OF ISABEL, THE.**

GHIDRAH, THE THREE-HEADED MONSTER (1965). Another of director Inoshiro Honda's exercises in global destruction and monstrous mayhem when Ghidrah, the fire-breathing E.T. dragon, battles Godzilla (in his first role as a good creature), Rodan and Mothra atop Mt. Fuji. Made when Eiji Tsuburaya's effects were still well produced. Eiji Okada, Yosuke Natsuki. Also known as THE BIGGEST BATTLE ON EARTH and MONSTER OF MONSTERS. (Goodtimes; Interglobal; Prism; Hollywood Home Theater; Video Connection; VCII; S/Weird; Video Treasures)

GHOST, THE (1963). Scotland, 1919. Peter Baldwin and Barbara Steele have an affair that drives husband Leonard Elliott to twisted jealousy. Elliott dies but returns from Deathland (using his housekeeper as a medium) to wreak revenge on the ill-tempered lovers. Elliott plays the titular character from THE HORRIBLE MR. HICHCOCK, so this is a loose sequel. Directed by Riccardo Freda. Also known as THE SPECTRE. (United; Sinister/C; Filmfax; Liberty; S/Weird)

GHOST (1990). Take an old cliche (man is terrorized by a ghost) and switch it around (ghost is terrified by man) and you have an original premise and a delightful supernatural comedy-drama that works as a morality lesson. Bruce Joel Rubin's script is a beautiful cinematic device that Jerry Zucker directs with taste. Patrick Swayze portrays a murdered New York banker still existing on the earthly plane, invisible except for his voice, which is heard only by phony spiritualist Whoopi Goldberg. The film deals with how Swayze learns to become a ghost (with the help of eternal subway dweller Vincent Schiavelli), communicate with wife Demi Moore and find his killer.

Nominated for Best Picture. Tony Goldwyn, Rick Aviles, Gail Boggs. (Video/Laser: Paramount)

GHOST AND MR. CHICKEN (1966). Universal programmer is as feeble-minded as the character Don Knotts plays: a bumbling typesetter who proves his worth(lessness) by solving a murder case in a haunted house. Directed by Alan Rafkin. Joan Staley, Dick Sargent, Skip Homeier, Ellen Corby, Hope Summers.

GHOST AND MRS. MUIR, THE (1947). In this atmospheric supernatural comedy with a whimsical, witty touch, widow Gene Tierney lives in a seacoast mansion and collaborates on a best-seller with the salty spirit of sea captain Rex Harrison. Excellent period flavor, superbly directed by Joseph L. Mankiewicz. George Sanders, Natalie Wood, Vanessa Brown. This inspired a '60s sitcom. (Video/Laser: CBS/Fox)

GHOST AND THE GUEST, THE (1944). Comedy-mystery in the OLD DARK HOUSE tradition, with newlyweds James Dunn and Florence Rice honeymooning in a country estate formerly owned by a criminal who strangled his victims with a noose. If he's supposed to be dead, who's dropping those ropes from the secret panels? Morey Amsterdam's script is without inspiration and director William Nigh treats this lightweight material indifferently. Mabel Todd, Robert Dudley, Sam McDaniel. (Sinister/C; Filmfax)

GHOST BREAKERS (1940). Hilarious comedy directed by George Marshall, proving Bob Hope was a master at screen spoofery. A haunted house in Cuba is owned by Paulette Goddard and frequented by ghosts and zombies. Dean Martin and Jerry Lewis did the same story in 1952 as SCARED STIFF, thought with lesser results. Richard Carlson, Anthony Quinn, Paul Lukas, Paul Fix, Willie Best, Pedro de Cordoba. (MCA)

GHOST BUSTERS, THE (1975). After the success of GHOSTBUSTERS, three episodes of a never-aired series were dubbed onto video. Superawful sitcom with Forrest Tucker (Kong), Larry Storch (Spencer) and Tracy (a gorilla) as occult private eyes hunting supernatural prey with a Ghost Dematerializer. Produced on tape on phony studio sets. Directed by Norman Abbott, these superstupid shows parody the Maltese Falcon, the Canterville Ghost and haunted house cliches. (Continental)

GHOSTBUSTERS (1984). Inspired, ingenious supernatural comedy of refreshing images from writers Dan Akyroyd and Harold Ramis and producer-director Ivan Reitman. Bill Murray (Dr. Peter Venkman), Akyroyd (Dr. Raymond Stantz) and Harold Ramis (Dr. Egon Spengler) are Manhattan spirit smashers who transfix spirits with laser guns and imprison evil protoglops in a ghost gaol. An official feels they're polluting the environment, and allows the wraiths and spectral creatures to escape. Now the city is threatened with a "ghost wave." Richard Edlund's effects are brilliant. Murray is the aloof ghostbuster who would rather bed beautiful clients, and his asides are hysterical. Akyroyd is the buffoon and Ramis the straight-faced, text-book expert spouting jargon about multi-dimensional ectoplasmic invasions. Sigourney Weaver discovers an ancient God in her refrigerator. (RCA/Columbia) (Laser: Voyager)

GHOSTBUSTERS II (1989). Once again the premise of men working as demon exterminators with the attitude of firemen is wonderful, with the added twist that evil supernatural slime gains strength through millions of unhappy New Yorkers. But this attempt is strained and often silly without the underpinings of satire. The gang is back (Bill Murray, Dan Aykroyd, Harold Ramis, Ernie Hudson) and so is Sigourney Weaver, whose baby is the target of a sacrifice. The script is by Ramis and Aykroyd, with Ivan Reitman back as director. Despite faults, there's still enjoyment to be derived from this sequel. Rick Moranis, Peter MacNicol, David Margolies. (Video/Laser: RCA/Columbia)

GHOST CATCHERS, THE (1944). Boy, is this old Universal programmer corny as Ole Olsen and Chic Johnson—a cheaper version of Abbott and Costello—yock it up in a parody of OLD DARK HOUSE movies. It just so happens a haunted house is located next to a club where Olsen and Johnson are performing routines. So they drop in to discover a dead body and a gang staging supernormal events. Turns out there's a real ghost in the house too. The club footage—apache dancing, jitterbugging, Morton Downey at the piano—is fun, especially when Andy Devine and Lon Chaney Jr. show up in silly costumes. Gloria Jean, Martha O'Driscoll, Leo Carrillo, Kirby Grant, Tor Johnson, Mel Torme.

GHOST CHASE (1989). Pleasant, innocuous supernatural-comedy set in Hollywood and depicting how a grandfather clock gives off the spirit of an old familiar retainer. The spirit, inhabiting the "body" of a cute alien (in the style of E.T.) being readied for a feature film, sets out with two film makers to track down an old house, which will provide the solution to a family scandal. The Roland Emmerich-Thomas Kubsch screenplay, as slight as it is, is given a nice directorial touch by Roland Emmerich. Jason Lively, Tim McDaniel, Leonard Lansky, Jill Whitlow, Toby Kaye. (MCEG) (Laser: Image)

GHOST CHASERS (1951). Edgar the Friendly Ghost Chaser helps the Bowery Boys capture crooks led by a flipped-out sawbones, Philip Van Zandt. You'll need a chaser too to sit through this William Beaudine-directed programmer. Leo Gorcey, Huntz Hall and the usual gang of adults acting like teenagers. (Warner Bros.)

GHOST CRAZY (1944). Lowbrow horror-comedy vehicle for Shemp Howard and rotund Billy Gilbert, carnival conmen who travel with a caged gorilla. They stop off at a creepy old house to help a damsel in distress and see a sheeted ghost popping out of a secret passageway built into the family graveyard next door. Maxie Rosenbloom is a dumb chauffeur, Minerva Urecal is the sinister housemaid and Jayne Hazard is the harassed heiress. Also known as GHOST KNIGHTS. Directed by William Beaudine. John Hamilton, Bernie Sell, Tim Ryan.

GHOST CREEPS, THE (1940). In this entry in the East Side Kids series (before they were the Bowery Boys), aka BOYS OF THE CITY, Leo Gorcey, Bobby Jordan and others track ghosts of dubious ectoplasmic heritage. It's a night of pseudoterror under director Joseph Lewis and producer Sam Katzman. Call it nocturnal omission. Vince Barnett, Dave Gorcey. (Filmfax)

GHOST DAD (1990). "Can I take you to show-and-tell?" a child asks her father, when he turns up at home as a ghost. And that's about as funny as this vehicle for Bill Cosby gets. Most of the highpoints are special effects as Cosby falls through floors and ceilings, flies through the air, poses as "The Invisible Man," passes through the center of a bus and transports himself through a telephone wire to confront his caller. And the sequence leading up to his "death" is a masterful series of near-disasters and stunts. Sidney Poitier brings a sense of vitality to his direction. Music by Henry Mancini. Kimberley Russell, Denise Nicholas, Barry Corbin. (Video/Laser: MCA)

GHOST DANCE (1982). Indian spirit possesses medicine man and sets him killing. Good Arizona photography but the film is amateurish—from Peter Buffa's direction to the (non)acting of Henry Ball and Julie Amato. Like unkept tomahawk: plenty dull. (Transworld)

GHOST DANCE (1983). See third edition.

GHOST FEVER (1986). Stupefyingly dumb comedy spoofing the "old dark house" genre with stupid cops Sherman Hemsley and Luis Avalos (playing Buford and Benny) assigned to evict tenants from Magnolia House, haunted by a black man (Hemsley in heavy make-up as a black assigned to "keeping spooks in line"), a Southerner (Myron Healey with a Robert E. Lee accent) and an invisible rebel (Pepper Martin) who finally appears as a vampire with a a torture chamber, operating room and walking zombies. "Groins of the Darker Species," a book Hemsley reads in a library sequence, is the only funny joke. Smokin' Joe Frazier plays a goofy boxer and Deborah Benson and Jennifer Rhodes are Southern belles. Directed in Mexico by Lee Madden, who uses the alias Alan Smithee. (Charter) (Laser: Nelson)

GHOST GALLEON, THE. See **HORROR OF THE ZOMBIES.**

GHOST GOES WEST, THE (1935). Classic British comedy directed by Rene Clair with loving care. Robert Donat is romantically delightful as a Scottish spirit doomed to haunt an old drafty castle. When an American millionare moves the structure stone by stone to the American West, the ghost helps his descendants out of a jam. Produced by Alexander Korda. Jean Parker, Elsa Lanchester, Eugene Pallette, Evelyn Gregg. (HBO)

GHOST GOES WILD, THE (1947). Editions 1-3.

GHOSTHOUSE (1988). Undistinguished "possessed house" shock-crock in which the spirit of a juvenile girl and her life-size clown-doll haunt a rundown joint near Boston. Hanging around the environs is a crazy handyman with axe and pitchfork—and along comes human fodder. Lara Wendell screams so much, you wish the killer would get her. Insomniacs will find this a sure cure. Greg Scott, Mary Sellers and Kristen Fougerousse are unknowns whom director Humphrey Humbert directs. Foundationless script by Cinthia McGavin. (Imperial)

GHOST HUNTER (1975). See third edition.

GHOST IN THE INVISIBLE BIKINI, THE (1966). AIP's "Beach" series—bikinied teen girls, motorcycles, robots and monsters—reached an all-time low in this effort with teens rollicking in a haunted house. Boris Karloff, dead and gone to Heaven, is told by Susan Hart he can't get through the Pearly Gates unless he performs a good deed, such as helping Tommy Kirk stay out of the clutches of swindler Basil Rathbone. Don Weis directed this brainless exercise in futility. Deborah Walley, Nancy Sinatra, Patsy Kelly, Jesse White, Harvey Lembeck.

GHOST IN THE MACHINE (1994). The spirit of murderer Karl Hochman (Ted Marcoux) is trapped inside a computer and comes back with demonic powers to haunt Karen Allen, Wil Hornneff and Chris Mulkey. (Fox)

GHOST IN THE NOONDAY SUN (1973). Obscure Peter Sellers/Spike Milligan comedy, never released to theaters until 1984, when it walked the plank into oblivion. Sellers is Dick Scratcher, a buccaneer chef (but hardly gourmet) who kills his captain after learning where the booty is stashed. But his memory grows foggy, and he relies on the captain's ghost to help him. Directed by Peter Medak. Anthony Franciosa, Clive Revill, Peter Boyle, Richard Willis. (Virgin Vision; VCL)

GHOSTKEEPER (1980). Snowbound travelers are trapped in a house on Canada's icy tundra, terrorized by a ghost-cannibal. Riva Spier, Murray Ord, Sheri McFadden. Directed by James Makichuk. (Starmaker)

GHOST MOM (1993). In this Halloween TV-movie, an obnoxious, possessive mother (Jean Stapleton) returns from the dead to help her surgeon son (Geraint Wyn Davies) find the Stone of Ise (a Japanese artifact with magical powers) and avoid an Asian gang. Stapleton is so grating it's hard to care for her or her son, and it's a long time before one's sympathy kicks in. Directed by Dave Thomas. Denis Akiyama, Shae D'Lyn, Jayne Eastwood, Zachary Bennett.

GHOST OF A CHANCE (1987). TV-movie with a sensitive touch, about a piano player (Redd Foxx) coming back from heaven to fulfill a mission under a guardian angel. Foxx forces the detective who accidentally shot him (Dick Van Dyke) to help his son audition for a talent search. Van Dyke also cracks a drug ring and helps the youth go straight. The one amusing sequence has Foxx visiting the Cotton Club in Black Heaven where Satchmo, the Duke and Billie Holliday jive up a storm. Directed by Don Taylor. Brynn Thayer, Richard Romanus, Kimble Joyner, Geoffrey Holder.

GHOST OF DRAGSTRIP HOLLOW, THE (1959). See editions 1-3.

GHOST OF FLETCHER RIDGE (1988). Supernatural elements don't come into play until the conclusion of this tale about city boy Campbell Scott falling for hillbilly girl Virginia Lantry and getting caught in a shotgun feud between two families. Of minimal interest to genre fans; mainly a backwoods morality piece. Directed by Michael Borden. Bernie White, Len Lesser, Bernie White, Sean McGuick, John Durbin. (Simitar)

GHOST OF FLIGHT 401, THE (1978). Alleged true story of a haunting documented in a John Fuller book. After an airliner crash in the Florida Everglades on December 29, 1972, the spectral image of flight engineer Ernest Borgnine is witnessed aboard other planes using salvaged parts from the wreckage. A compelling, offbeat TV-movie retains respectability thanks to director Steven Hilliard Stern and writer Robert Malcolm Young. Gary Lockwood, Kim Basinger, Russell Johnson.

GHOST OF FRANKENSTEIN, THE (1942). Fourth film in Universal's Frankenstein series, directed by Erle C. Kenton, has Bela Lugosi returning as the revengeful Ygor (from SON OF FRANKENSTEIN) and Lon Chaney Jr. lurching uncontrollably as the Monster. W. Scott Darling's script involves Lionel Atwill putting Ygor's brain into the monster. A must see. Sir Cedric Hardwicke, Ralph Bellamy, Evelyn Ankers, Dwight Frye. (MCA)

GHOST OF RASHMON HALL, THE (1947). Dreary adaptation of Edward G. Bulwer-Lytton's classic tale, "The Haunted and the Haunters." It drags like the spirit of a dead sea captain with a bowling ball chained to his peg leg. In the drawing room of an old manor, several British gentry exchange ghost narratives. Psychic investigator Valentine Dyall spins a tale about the very house they're in and what happened when it was recently taken over as a fix-it-up by a young couple. The ghosts of a sailor, his wife and her lover are still on the premises. Complete with a socko ending. If you enjoy dusty period pieces, try it but have "spirits" around. Directed by Denis Kavanagh. Anne Howard, Alec Faversham, Howard Douglas. (Filmfax; Sinister/C)

GHOST OF SLUMBER MOUNTAIN, THE (1919). Willis O'Brien, pioneer in stop-motion animation (KING KONG), provided effects for this short depicting dinosaurs and other prehistoric beasts. The story opens with Uncle Jack telling children about Mad Dick, an old hermit with a telescope to see the creatures. Among the highlights: a battle between a giant bird and snake, a fight to the death between triceratops, and Jack being chased by a dinosaur. Of importance to O'Brien aficionados.

GHOST OF YOTSUYA (1958). Japanese tale of the supernatural. Directed by Nobuo Nakagawa. Shigeru Amachi, Noriko Kitazawa. (Video Action)

GHOST PATROL (1936). Colonel Tim McCoy is the hero of this G-man adventure in which he tracks a gang that hijacks the air mail with a ray gun. Sam Newfield directed. Claudia Dell, Walter Miller. (VCI; Filmfax)

GHOSTRIDERS (1987). Cheap regional supernatural thriller (produced around Dallas) that doesn't have a single spectral effect worth mentioning. An outlaw gang returns from 1886 to terrorize researchers. Not one scene is scary, an attempt to emulate NIGHT OF THE LIVING DEAD is misguided, and a dire lack of pacing, editing and story blasts this worthless crap out of the saddle. It's lynching time for director Alan Stewart. Bill Shaw, Jim Peters, Cari Powell. (Prism; Starmaker)

GHOSTS CAN'T DO IT (1989). John and Bo Derek have made oddball films before (TARZAN, BOLERO) but none quite as oddball as this. Bo, still possessing that spectacular body, is distraught after the suicide death of husband Anthony Quinn. In Heaven, Quinn is confronted by fledgling angel Julie Newmar (whose body is as gorgeous as Bo's) who sends him back to Earth to be with Bo. They can talk but sex is a no-no so Quinn (depicted as a floating head) plots to kill handsome Leo Damian and take over his body. Meanwhile, Bo dances in the rain (the water pressing her dress' thin material against her braless breasts), Bo strips to the buff on a beach, Bo takes a shower and Bo goes for a naked swim. Hubbie John's camera lingers lovingly on her lumpy lovelies. Don Murray portrays Bo's traveling companion, Donald Trump appears at a negotiating table, and attorney Gerry Spence presides over Quinn's mountaintop funeral. Huh? (Video/Laser: RCA/Columbia)

GHOST SHIP, THE (1943). A frightening psychology voyage produced by Val Lewton and directed by Mark Robson set on a sailing ship commanded by homicidal captain Richard Dix, who hides behind a veneer of respectability. Third officer Russell Wade suspects the truth, but can't prove it, even to an inquiry board. One unforgettable sequence has Lawrence Tierney being crushed by an anchor cable in a cargo hold; another has Wade trapped in his quarters and under siege. Edith Barrett, Skelton Knaggs, Ben Bard.

GHOST SHIP (1953). Trim, skimming British supernatural tale, set aboard the Cyclops, a luxury yacht haunted by apparitions ever since it was found adrift with no one aboard. Hazel Court and Dermot Walsh purchase the craft, then learn of its ugly history. Finally, a medium discovers there are corpses of two tormented souls buried below deck, and a murderous captain on the loose. Writer-director Vernon Sewell has tacked on a whodunit ending to give it that is-the-supernatural-real-or-not? A tenseness pervades that will have you clutching your preserver. Hugh Burden, John Robinson. (VCI; Filmfax; Nostalgia; S/Weird; United)

GHOSTS—ITALIAN STYLE (1968). Amusing Italian farce with Vittorio Gassman as a spirit. Satire on foreign customs and mores, as they are affected by the supernatural. Sophia Loren provides this Carlo Ponti film with her own ectoplasmic energy! Directed by Renato Castellani. Mario Adorf, Carlo Giuffre. Marcello Mastroianni cameos as a sprightly spirit. (Sinister/C; Filmfax)

GHOSTS OF HANLEY HOUSE, THE (1968). Owners of the titular mansion can't sell it, so they hold a ghost-story party to make everyone relax. That's when the ghosts come to life and rattle their chains. Party poopers! Elsie Baker, Wilkie De Martel. (Sinister/C; Filmfax)

GHOSTS OF ROME (1961). See editions 1-3.

GHOSTS ON THE LOOSE (1943). Despite its appealing title, this is not one of Monogram's better vehicles for the East Side Kids (Leo Gorcey, Huntz Hall, Bobby Jordan, Stanley Clements) nor does it feature anything supernatural. The Kids find a house being used by Nazi saboteurs led by Bela Lugosi—but not even Lugosi's horror potential is exploited. The only thing of interest is ingenue Ava Gardner. Directed by William Beaudine. (Goodtimes; Hollywood Movie Classics)

GHOSTS THAT STILL WALK (1977). Young boy is possessed by an Indian medicine man spirit in this low-budget pseudodocumentary about ghosts and spirits. It's terribly disjointed and hard to follow but does have one exciting sequence in which an elderly couple traveling in a rec vehicle is attacked by boulders rolling across the desert. Otherwise, tedious going. And boring. Written-directed by James T. Flocker. (VCI; United)

GHOST STORIES: GRAVEYARD THRILLER (1986). Actors stand in a graveyard and relate tales of terror. That's it. No reenactments, no special effects, no production of any kind. (Vestron)

GHOST STORIES. See **KWAIDAN.**

GHOST STORY. See **DOUBLE PLAY.**

GHOST STORY (1974). Video version of **MADHOUSE MANSION** (Comet; Cinema Group)

GHOST STORY (1981). Peter Straub's convoluted best-seller (possessing the chilling qualities of M. R. James) was clumsily transferred to the screen; screenwriter Lawrence D. Cohen oversimplifies Straub's narrative, limiting the variety of ghosts, among other deficits. One horrible face after another (from the "walking dead" school of graphic countenances) is all you get. However, the premise is intriguing: The Chowder Society, a group of old men, gathers to swap ghost stories. Its members—Douglas Fairbanks Jr., John Houseman, Fred Astaire, Melvyn Douglas—share a dark secret from their youth. How a wronged wraith (a drowned woman) avenges herself across the veil of death makes for the supernatural thrills—but oh, Straub's novel was so much more. Directed by John Irvin. Craig Wasson, Alice Krige, Patricia Neal, Ken Olin. (Video/Laser: MCA)

GHOST TOWN (1988). Offbeat Charles Band production is set in a desert ghost town outside Tucson, where modern-day deputy sheriff Franc Luz tracks a missing woman—only to be thrown into the past where he confronts a gunslinging demon (Jimmie F. Skaggs) and the other townspeople of the 19th Century. Director Richard Governor is stuck with a slender storyline to go with cinematographer Mac Ahberg's groovy imagery blending the old West with the supernatural. Catherine Hickland, Bruce Glover. (New World) (Laser: Image)

GHOST TRAIN (1941). Passengers waiting in a British country terminal are subjected to the phenomenon of an express roaring past—one that crashed years before. And this is the anniversary of the accident! Captures the Gothic flavor of the English ghost story. Directed by Walter Forde. (Sinister/C; Nostalgia; Filmfax)

GHOST WALKS, THE (1934). Outdated comedy-horror clunker involving hidden passageways, ghosts who aren't really ghosts and a madman who intends to perform operations that the AMA would never approve. Directed by Frank Strayer. John Miljan, June Collyer, Richard Carle. (Sinister/C; Discount; Filmfax)

GHOST WARRIOR (1985). An Iceman cometh: A 400-year-old samurai warrior, a kind of "Frozen Shogun" in a cavern in Motosuka, Japan, is revived at a cyrogenics hospital in L.A. where Dr. Jane Julian introduces him to modern life. But this warrior out of time and place must wield his sword against evil in this offbeat Charles Band fantasy-actioner produced as SWORDKILL. Hiroshi Fujioka is good as Yoshita as he tangles with modern gangs and is etched in stark relief against skyscrapers, cars, TV sets and pursuing helicopters. Directed by Larry Carroll. John Calvin, Charles Lampkin. (Vestron)

GHOST WRITER (1990). Lightweight, innocuous comedy with Audrey Landers as a writer who settles in a haunted Malibu beachhouse, where 30 years before sexy actress Billie Blaine committed suicide by drowning in the surf. Actually, she was poisoned . . . and now she's rematerialized to ask the writer's help to find the murderer. The most compelling aspect of this TV-movie is Judy Landers, a poor man's Marilyn Monroe. There are the usual invisible (wo)man shticks in director Kenneth J. Hall's script. Jeff Conaway is Audrey's boyfriend, David Doyle a tabloid editor and Anthony Franciosa the heavy. Joey Travolta, John Matuszak, the Barbarian Brothers, Dick Miller, Kenneth Tobey. (Prism)

GHOUL, THE (1933). British chiller of the "walking dead" school . . . Boris Karloff is a Professor of Egyptology in possession of the Eternal Light, a priceless jewel of mysterious properties. Vowing to rise from the dead should anyone tamper with the stone, Karloff dies . . and lives up to his promise when his servant (Ernest Thesiger) steals the Eternal Light. Now it's going to be Eternal Night for that dude. Directed by T. Hayes Hunter. Anthony Bushell, Cedric Hardwicke, Ralph Richardson, Kathleen Harrison. (Sinister/C; Nostalgia; Filmfax)

GHOUL, THE (1974). British Gothic horror thriller (also THE THING IN THE ATTIC) is set in the 1920s and based on THE REPTILE: Wild flappers hold a car race across foggy moors. When one car breaks down, its beautiful driver seeks refuge in Peter Cushing's mansion, unaware he is a defrocked minister whose son is infected with a love for Kali. Now he is a ghoul, feeding on fresh flesh. John Hurt, in an ugly role, plays the crazed ground's-keeper who rapes the beauties before the son munches at lunches. A lumbering, disgusting, pointless movie with nihilistic overtones in John Elder's script. Veronica Carlson, Don Henderson, Alexandra Bastedo. Directed by Freddie Francis. (Media; Electric; VCL; Active)

GHOULIES (1985). Charles Band's turgid imitation of GREMLINS, unimaginatively plotted by producer Jeffery Levy and director Luca Bercovici, and only coming to life in a few effects sequences. The setting is a creepy old house in Hollywood where Peter Liapis and wife Lisa Pelikan come under Black Magic. Mischievous monsters pop in and out to provide the only moments of vitality and humor. Michael Des Barres, Jack Nance, Peter Risch and Tamara de Treaux are among the midgets in make-up. (Vestron) (Laser: Japanese)

GHOULIES II (1988). Innocuous morality tale is a weak sequel to the popular GHOULIES, so it has nowhere to go but down. There's something quaint about its beginnings: Four of the creatures escape to a carnival, where they become part of an attraction, murdering patrons and hiding bodies in the props. A subplot has a money-minded owner threatening to close the show down. This Charles Band production, made in Rome, was directed by Albert Band and sports the hand puppets of John Buechler, Damon Martin, Royal Dano, Phil Fondacaro, Anthony Dawson. (Vestron) (Laser: Image)

GHOULIES III. See **GHOULIES GO TO COLLEGE.**

GHOULIES GO TO COLLEGE (1990). He who possesses a copy of the comic book Ghoulish Tales possesses the key to controlling those mischievous little gremlin imitations from another dimension, who always pop up out of a toilet. The setting for this third entry in the GHOULIES series is Glazier College, appropriate to the sophorific teenage pranks, sex jokes and other lowbrow content. Humanities teacher Kevin McCarthy brings the impish ones back while college factions vie for the "Prank Wee" crown. The stiff, not-always convincing ghoulies were designed by John Carl Buechler, who also directed what amounts to a series of PORKY-like sequences ranging from burping jokes to panty raids in reverse (the women strip the men) to firing squirt guns of "goofy glue." Evan MacKenzie, Eva La Rue. (Vestron)

GHOUL IN SCHOOL. See **WEREWOLF IN A GIRLS' DORMITORY.**

GHOUL SCHOOL (1990). Spoof on teen-age splatter flicks. Joe Franklin, Nancy Siriani, William Friedman. (Hollywood Home Entertainment)

GIANT BEHEMOTH, THE (1959). Stop-motion animator Willis O'Brien provides only mediocre effects for this British creature-on-the-rampage production. The brontosaurus hulker ravages downtown London with its radioactive eyes, burning flesh from bodies. Scientist Gene Evans should have seen THE BEAST FROM 20,000 FATHOMS for monster-destroying pointers. Eugene Lourie, who co-directed with Douglas Hickok, wrote the screenplay. Also known as BEHEMOTH THE SEA MONSTER. Andre Morell, Leigh Madison, Jack MacGowran, John Turner, Henry Vidon.

GIANT CLAW, THE (1957). Inane, incredulous, incompetent—one of the truly laughable sci-fi turkeys of the '50s and a classic low-water mark for schlockmeister producer Sam Katzman. The titular talon is attached to a giant bird from space, which resembles a stuffed Thanksgiving turkey and is obviously pulled by wires. The size of a battleship, the E.T. winged warlord is surrounded by an antimatter force field which makes it impervious to atomic bombs. Jeff Morrow and Mara Corday devise a "mu-meson projector" to down the combed conquerer, cheered on by "bird-watchers" Morris Ankrum, Edgar Barrier and Robert Shayne. The asinine avian avenger, with long neck, bulging eyeballs and a plucked look, will have you rolling in the aisles. Directed by Fred F. Sears, who winged it. (Movies Unlimited)

GIANT FROM THE UNKNOWN (1958). Buddy Baer is a king-size Conquistadore (brought to life by lightning) who haunts a deserted California town. Produced by Arthur Jacobs, who went on to the PLANET OF THE APES series. Jack Pierce's make-up cannot help create a scary monster this time. Tediously directed by Richard E. Cunha. Edward Kemmer, Morris Ankrum, Bob Steele, Sally Fraser. (Media; VCI; Sinister/C)

GIANT GILA MONSTER, THE (1959). Produced by actor Ken Curtis, this low-budget quickie is an uninteresting potpourri of hot rods and teenagers facing a mystery in the New Mexican desert. "What do you suppose is out there?" and "I think I saw something moving" exemplify the dialogue by director Ray Kellogg and Jay Sims. The monster is a harmless lizard enlarged by a macro lens. Kellog went on to direct John Wayne's THE GREEN BERETS, Curtis became Festus on GUNSMOKE. The gila monster's contract was not renewed. Don Sullivan, Lisa Simone, Shug Fisher, Yolanda Salas. (Sinister/C; Rhino; S/Weird; Filmfax) (Laser: Image)

GIANT LEECHES, THE. See **ATTACK OF THE GIANT LEECHES.**

GIANT OF METROPOLIS, THE (1963). Beefcake in the shape of Gordon Mitchell in 10,000 B.D. (Before Dumbbells), when a bulging hero crashes Atlantis, where scientists have perfected immortality and can train their Death Beam on enemies. Grunts and groans—Italian style. Directed by Umberto Scarpelli with a sense of humor. A saving grace, in this case. Bella Cortez, Roldano Lupi. (Sinister/C; S/Weird; Filmfax)

GIANTS OF THESSALY (1961). Re-enactment of the search for the Golden Fleece with decent special effects. Directed by Riccardo Freda. Roland Carey, Ziva Rodann, Moira Orfei. (Sinister/C; S/Weird)

GIANT SPIDER INVASION, THE (1975). The opening to another dimension permits all sizes of spiders to attack Earth. The bigger ones are multi-legged mock-ups propelled by Volkswagens in their pseudobellies. Blame this mess on voice-trainer/actor Robert Easton, for playing the rustic dumbbell who finds radioactive spider eggs and for writing it (with Richard Huff). Steve Brodie, Barbara Hale, Leslie Parrish and Alan Hale Jr. are wasted by director Bill Rebane. (VCL; Movies Unlimited)

G.I. EXECUTIONER (1971). Produced in Singapore as WIT'S END but not released until 1985 as DRAGON LADY. An antimatter device invented by a defecting Chinese scientist is the weak fantasy element in this intrigue flick. Journalist Tom Keena is in the thick of espionage. Star attraction is Angelique Pettyjohn as a stripper who shoots it out with a fat spy while totally naked. Victoria Racimo, Janet Wood, Brian Walden. Directed-written by Joel M. Reed in rambling style. (Vestron)

GIFTED ONE, THE (1989). Average TV-movie about a young man (Pete Kowanko) "5,000 years ahead of his time" with the ability to channel body energy into ESP and healing powers. While undergoing experiments with professor John Rhys Davies, he runs away to learn the secrets of his past. Directed by Stephen Herek. G. W. Bailey, Wendy Phillips, Gregg Henry.

GIGANTIS THE FIRE MONSTER (1955). Sequel to GODZILLA, KING OF THE MONSTERS features the towering infernal as Gigantis. The destructor of Tokyo is trailed to an island where he/she/it battles Angurus, a spiked creature with wings. After some soothing mayhem, Gigantis-Godzilla stomps towar Tokyo to make it a tail of one city. Directed by Motoyoshi Oda, with effects by Eiji Tsuburaya. The 1959 U.S. version was directed by Hugo Grimaldi. Also known as THE VOLCANO MONSTER, THE RETURN OF GODZILLA, GODZILLA'S COUNTERATTACK and COUNTERATTACK OF THE MONSTER. (From Paramount/Video Treasure as **GODZILLA RAIDS AGAIN**)

GILDERSLEEVE'S GHOST (1943). Charming entry in the "Great Gildersleeve" film series based on the popular radio character of the '40s. Ghostly spirits come to Gildie's aid when he's running for city government, and it's a madcap "Topper" kind of situation. Pleasing B-picture directed by Gordon Douglas. Harold Peary, Marian Martin, Richard LeGrand, Amelita Ward, Charles Gemora (as the gorilla).

GILL WOMEN. See **VOYAGE TO THE PLANET OF PREHISTORIC WOMEN.**

GILL WOMEN OF VENUS. See **VOYAGE TO THE PLANET OF PREHISTORIC WOMEN.**

GINGERBREAD HOUSE. See **WHOEVER SLEW AUNTIE ROO?**

GIRLFRIEND FROM HELL (1990). A female Satan turns Liane Curtis into a devilish femme fatale at a birthday party. A clever genre spoof written-directed by Daniel M. Peterson. Dana Ashbrook, Lezlie Deane, James Daughton. (IVE) (Laser: Image)

"In the darkness there is evil. Within the evil there is Death."
—Opening legend of **GIRLS SCHOOL SCREAMERS**

GIRL FROM MARS, THE (1991). Engaging and thought-provoking TV-movie depicts teenager Sarah Sawatsky, who has telekinentic powers and claims to be from Mars. This latter point remains ambiguous to the end, one of the charms of this Canadian-New Zealand production. Sawatsky's father (Edward Albert) is a politician struggling with conservation issues that also touch a scientist (Eddie Albert) who befriends the girl. Something very gentle and touching is at work here under Neill Fearnley's direction. Gary Day, Christianna Hirt.

GIRL FROM SCOTLAND YARD, THE (1937). See editions 1-3.

GIRL FROM S.E.X. (1982). Softcore porn mixing love and war. Plenty of explicit action (you know the kind) as lovely bodies are contoured to fit a James Bondish spy plot. Directed by Paul G. Vatelli. Annette Haven, Lisa Deleeuw, Don Hart, Nicole Noir. (Laser: Image)

GIRL FROM STARSHIP VENUS, THE (1957). See third edition.

GIRL FROM TOMORROW, THE (1990). Entertaining children's TV-movie in which teenager Katherine Cullen, resident of the year 3000 A.D., becomes a pawn in a time-travel experiment gone awry that sends her to 1992 with James Findlay, a fugitive from the year 2500. How Cullen convinces earthlings of her true origins and overcomes the evil intentions of Findlay (with the help of a laser beam called the "transfuser") comprises this Australian production directed by Kathy Mueller. Melissa Marshall, Andrew Clarke, Helen O'Connor, John Howard.

GIRL IN A SWING, THE (1989). Meg Tilly marries a rich Englishman (Rupert Frazier) but they can't find happiness when she is plagued by ghostly visitations from her past . . . or does she have some strange psychic power? Directed by Gordon Hessler, from the novel by Richard Adams. Elspet Gray, Lynsey Baxter, Jean Boht. (HBO) (Laser: Image)

GIRL IN HIS POCKET (1960). French sci-fi comedy with professor Jean Marais shrinking his girlfriend but without minimizing his girl problems. Pleasing farce directed by Pierre Kast. Genevieve Page. (Sinister/C)

GIRL IN ROOM 2A, THE (1975). Poor Italian gore flick about a cult of sadists led by a killer in red mask and gloves, who sticks spears into beautiful women after abducting them. Newly paroled Daniela Giordano appears to be next when she takes residence in a strange house. While she hallucinates, we see a man's hand burned on a fireplace grate, bodies probed with pokers and knifes, a blood spot that appears on the floor, and dull characters searching for missing persons. The dubbing is atrocious, the gore without redeeming social values and the performances, under director-producer William L. Rose, are lousy, including Raf Vallone's. (Prism)

GIRL IN THE KREMLIN, THE (1957). Editions 1-3.

GIRL IN THE MOON (1929). Early German sci-fi film directed by Fritz Lang depicts man's building of a rocket and the trip to the moon. Film historians will find the effects and scientific viewpoints of interest. Gerda Maurus, Willy Fritsch. Klaus Pohl. Also known as BY ROCKET TO THE MOON. (From Video Ten as **WOMEN IN THE MOON**)

GIRL OF THE NILE, THE (1967). See third edition.

GIRLS' NITE OUT (1983). A slasher dressed in a giant bear suit, equipped with razor-sharp talons, runs around Dewitt University on Scavenger Night, knocking off young women. This imitation of FRIDAY THE 13TH is strengthened only by the presence of Hal Holbrook as a campus security chief trying to get a handle on the killer's MO. Directed by Robet Deubel. Richard Barclay. Julie Montgomery, James Carroll, David Holbrook. (HBO)

GIRLS OF SPIDER ISLAND. See **HORRORS OF SPIDER ISLAND.**

GIRLS' SCHOOL SCREAMERS (1984). At the Trinity School for Girls, exemplary students are singled out to spend a few days at the Wildwood Estate (allegedly haunted) to take inventory of valuable antiques. A feeble excuse for giggling teen-agers to become victims of a slasher-killer who uses knife, pitchfork and meat hooks. Written-directed by John P. Finegan Jr. Mollie O'Mara, Sharon Christopher, Mari Butler. (Lightning)

GIRL, THE GOLD WATCH AND DYNAMITE (1981). A sequel to THE GIRL, THE GOLD WATCH AND EVERYTHING, continuing the adventures of a timepiece that freezes the spatial continuum and allows its wearer to walk among frozen figures. This time the watch becomes a pawn in a land swindle. Directed by Hy Averback. Philip MacHale, Lee Purcell, Burton Gilliam, Jack Elam, Zohra Lampert, Gary Lockwood.

GIRL, THE GOLD WATCH AND EVERYTHING, THE (1980). Light-hearted adaptation of John D. MacDonald's fantasy about a nerd (Robert Hays) who inherits a pocketwatch from his late grandfather to discover it stops time. This allows him to carry out ridiculous pranks against criminals trying to steal the watch. The humor is bantamweight and smacks of sitcom. Pam Dawber, Zohra Lampert, Ed Nelson, Peter Brown, Maurice Evans, Larry Hankin, Jill Ireland. Directed by William Wiard.

GIRL WHO DARED, THE (1944). See editions 1-3.

GIRLY (1970). Houseful of psychokillers provides the "no place like home" setting for this British exercise in mayhem and murder, also known as MUMSY NANNY SONNY AND GIRLY. Nobody dies easy under Freddie Francis' direction. Michael Bryant, Vanessa Howard, Ursula Howells, Michael Ripper. (Prism)

GLADIATOR, THE (1938). See editions 1-3.

GLADIATORS, THE (1970). Futuristic anti-war parable masterfully directed by Peter Watkins in pseudo-documentary style on Swedish locations, depicting how East and West, instead of maintaining armies and nuclear stockpiles, hold televised Peace Games—forms of warfare with crack teams of combat specialists. Watkins overplays his symbolic allegory, but it's still imaginative, chilling fantasy. Also known as THE PEACE GAME. Arthur Pentelow, Frederick Danner. (Wizard; VCI)

GLASS SLIPPER, THE (1955). Leslie Caron is an alluring Cinderella and her dreams are lavish—ballets by Roland Petit, set in a Graustrakian castle. Estelle Winwood is the eccentric fairy godmother, Michael Wilding the Prince Charming, Elsa Lanchester the ugly stepmother and Amanda Blake and Lisa Daniels the (hiss hiss) stepsisters. Director Charles Walters wrings charm out of this old Perrault fairy tale. (MGM/UA)

GLEN AND RANDA (1971). Avant-garde Apocalyptic-vision film set 40 years after The Bomb. The title characters are members of a tribe that lives in ignorance of mankind's past. But Glen (Adam?) is curious about Metropolis (the city he read about in old Wonder Woman comics) and he and a pregnant Randa (Eve?) trek through the wilderness of Idaho. Images linger afterward of a tree growing through a rusting car, gas pumps in a weedpatch, Randa eating grass like a horse, the pair eating bugs from old boards, and Glen brutally beating salmon trapped in a stream. Director Jim McBride goes for esoteric effect—this could be viewed as hippies seeking the answers to life's riddles. Steven Curry, Shelley Plimpton. (United; IME) (Laser: VCI)

GLEN OR GLENDA? (1953). A sympathetic study of transvestism from transvestite writer-director Edward D. Wood Jr., who went on to become the diabolical designer of PLAN 9 FROM OUTER SPACE and BRIDE OF THE ATOM. It opens with non sequitur shots of Bela Lugosi reading from a tome, but nothing he says has anything to do with the rest of the film. Cop Lyle Talbot visits doctor Timothy Farrell to discuss two sexually confused men, Glen/Glenda and Alan/Ann. Flashbacks consist of humdrum documentary footage mixed with staged shots absolutely hysterical for their bad acting and writing. Occasionally Wood makes a salient point in building empathy for the transvestites, then he negates it with scenes of two struggling women in bondage-sadism-lesbian footage, or indulges in heavy-handed symbolism. (Video Yesteryear; Sinister/C; Nostalgia)

BELA LUGOSI

GLUMP. See **PLEASE DON'T EAT MY MOTHER!**

G-MEN VS. BLACK DRAGON (1943). Twelve-chapter Republic serial starring Rod Cameron as good old American Secret Service investigator Rex Bennett, a role he played in the sequel SECRET SERVICE IN DARKEST AFRICA. Bennett fights the evil Haruchi and his insidious Black Dragon Society, baddies armed with fantastic devices. (The whittled-down TV version is BLACK DRAGONS OF MANZANAR.) It's all sinisterly administered by director William Witney with some of the finest fightfights ever filmed. In short, the action serial at its best. Constance Worth, C. Montague Shaw. (Republic; Nostalgia Merchant) (Laser: Republic)

GNAW. See **FOOD OF THE GOODS II.**

GNOME-MOBILE (1967). Pleasant Walt Disney musical-comedy fantasy with Walter Brennan, Tom Lowell, Jerome Cowan, Ellen Corby and Ed Wynn. Several children encounter elves and gnomes in California and protect them from carnival exploitation artists. Kids will love it. Directed by Robert Stevenson. (Disney)

GNOMES' GREAT ADVENTURE, THE (1987). Unimaginative TV-movie cartoon lacking in charisma in depicting David the Gnome (voice by Tom Bosley) in adventures with Swift the Fox to find a cache of gold stolen by trolls. Based on THE GNOMES by Rien Poostvleit and Wil Huygen. Directed by Harvey Weinstein. Narrated by Christopher Plummer. Other voices: Bob and Ray, Frank Gorshin, Tony Randall.

GOBOTS: BATTLE OF THE ROCK LORDS (1986). In this animated feature from Hanna-Barbera, the GoBots come to the rescue of the Rock People. Voices: Roddy McDowall, Telly Savalas, Margot Kidder. (VC)

GODDESS OF LOVE (1988). TV-movie with "Wheel of Fortune" hostess Vanna White, in the tradition of I DREAM OF JEANNIE, but more fitting to junior high repertory, so amateurish is the game-show beauty. She portrays Venus, turned to solid marble by Zeus (John Rhys-Davies) but returned to life on contemporary Earth to pester David Naughton. The big effect here is that Vanna zaps everything she doesn't like with electricity from her finger. Better the NBC execs who approved this project should be zapped. David Leisure, Betsy Palmer.

GODSEND, THE (1979). Mysterious woman leaves her newborn baby girl with English farmers. When the child grows up, she is responsible for several deaths through evil emanations. What sounds like an OMEN rip-off is a fair British chiller focus on psychology rather than gore. Produced-directed by Gabrielle Beaumont. Cyd Hayman, Malcolm Stoddard. (Vestron)

GOD TOLD ME TO (1976). Writer-producer-director Larry Cohen's revisionistic look at the Jesus Christ legend will never be sanctioned by the Catholic Church but will fascinate sci-fi fans, iconoclasts, atheists and agnostics. Indiscriminate killings are linked to a Jesus figure (Richard Lynch) conceived when a virgin was artifically inseminated in a flying saucer in 1951. Equally bizarre is the cop (Tony Lo Bianco) investigating the case who was similarly conceived and has psychic powers. Then comes confrontation between the "brothers" as they use their energy beams in a death duel. Irreverent film provides religious food for thought—and controversy. An odd, misunderstood project that was banned, boycotted and theatrically distributed minimally as DEMON. Sandy Dennis, Deborah Raffin, Andy Kaufman, Sylvia Sydney, Harry Bellaver. (Charter) (Laser: Image)

GODZILLA FIGHTS THE GIANT MOTHRA. See **GODZILLA VS. THE THING.**

GODZILLA OF THE MONSTERS (1954). Japanese classic directed by Inoshiro Honda, with effects by Eiji Tsuburaya. It was imported to the U.S. with new footage of Raymond Burr as newspaperman Steve Martin. In this trend-setting monsterthon (the first in a long-running series) Godzilla, a 400-foot-high Tyrannosaurus rex, is aroused from hybernation by an A-bomb and rampages through Tokyo. Serious critics have interpreted Honda's inspiration to present a fire-breathing, radioactive monster as an allegory of the nuclear age. Meanwhile, kids filled the theaters of the world to cheer the dueling titan. Akira Takarada, Momoko Kochi. (Video/Laser: Vestron)

GODZILLA: 1985 (1984). After a ten-year hibernation, Japan's reigning King of Monsters returns mean and snarling as he blows his radioactive breath on downtown Tokyo while giving it his famous two-step stomp. Like the origin movie, this features Raymond Burr as an newspaperman in footage shot for the U.S. Nothing new in this revival—the effects are what you would expect, and there are obligatory scientists and military leaders declaring the dangers of Godzilla's wrath. What's different is a sympathy toward the monster, as if the juggernaut was just looking for a little love. Forget that the large lizard just crushed 3000 Asians. Directed by Koji Hashimoto. Shin Takuma, Ken Tanaka. (New World) (Laser: Image)

GODZILLA ON MONSTER ISLAND (1972). The leapin' lizard (with monster pal Angorus) battles three-headed Ghidrah and Gigan (an obnoxious bird creature with a buzzsaw in its chest cavity) near an amusement park featuring a Godzilla tower. All this is instigated by cockroach aliens invading Earth. Buildup to the battle is repetitive and tedious. Directed by Jun Fukuda. Hiroshi Ichikawa, Yuriko Hishimi. (Sinister/C; Filmfax; from Starmaker as **GODZILLA VS. GIGAN**)

GODZILLA RAIDS AGAIN. Video version of **GIGANTIS THE FIRE MONSTER** (Paramount).

GODZILLA'S COUNTERATTACK. Another title for **GIGANTIS THE FIRE MONSTER.**

GODZILLA'S REVENGE (1969). By now the Godzilla series was shamelessly borrowing footage from earlier films to keep Eiji Tsuburaya's special effects costs down. The setting is Monster Island, where Godzilla and son Minya fight Baragon and other monster stereotypes without compelling personalities. Bad dubbing, although the grunts are more articulate than usual. Directed by Inoshiro Honda. Kenji Sahara. (Simitar) (Laser: Japanese)

GODZILLA VS. BIOLLANTE (1989). A colossal mutated plant is the latest enemy of the Giant Lizard from Tokyo in this sci-fi monster marathon directed by Kazuki Omori. Kunihio Mitamura, Yoshiko Tanaka.

GODZILLA VS. GIGAN. Video of **GODZILLA ON MONSTER ISLAND** (Starmaker; IME) (Laser: Image, with **GODZILLA VS. MECHAGODZILLA**).

GODZILLA VS. HEDORAH. Japanese laser version of **GODZILLA VS. THE SMOG MONSTER.**

GODZILLA VS. MECHAGODZILLA. Video of **GODZILLA VS. THE COSMIC MONSTER** (Starmaker) (Laser: Image, with **GODZILLA VS. GIGAN**).

GODZILLA VS. MEGALON (1973). Clumsy-footed entry in the Godzilla series. The 400-foot-tall green lizard is aided by a jet-packed robot in fighting off Megalon (a giant cockroach with Zap Killer Beam), Baragon the stomper, and a race of underground Earthlings, the Seatopians. Written-directed by Jun Fukuda. Katsuhiko Sasaki, Hiroyuki Kawase. (Goodtimes; Nostalgia; United

American; S/Weird)

GODZILLA VS. MONSTER ZERO. Video version of **MONSTER ZERO** (Paramount; Simitar).

GODZILLA VS. MOTHRA. Video version of **GODZILLA VS. THE THING** (Paramount).

GODZILLA VS. THE BIONIC MONSTER. Video version of **GODZILLA VS. THE COSMIC MONSTER** (Sinister/C; Filmfax).

GODZILLA VS. THE COSMIC MONSTER (1974). This sequel to TERROR OF MECHAGODZILLA is Japanese sci-fi sukiyaki with the King of Monsters battling a cyborg Godzilla controlled by aliens bent on conquest. A huge rodent creature said to embody Asian spirits comes to the real Godzilla's aid when the languid lizard squares off against antagonistic Angorus. Directed by Jun Fukuda. (United American; from Sinister/C as **GODZILLA VS. THE BIONIC MONSTER** and New World as **GODZILLA VS. MECHAGODZILLA**)

GODZILLA

GODZILLA VS. THE GIANT MOTH. See **GODZILLA VS. THE THING.**

GODZILLA VS. THE SEA MONSTER (1966). Also known as EBIRAH—TERROR OF THE DEEP and BIG DUEL IN THE NORTH SEA, this exercise in cardboard mayhem stars the saucy saurian, the King of Monsters, as a crusty critter suffering a case of crabs when he's attacked by colossal crustaceans and does battle with the Red Bamboo bad-guy gang. Jun Fukuda directed, Eiji Tsuburaya did the still-classy effects. Akira Takarada, Toru Watanabe. (Interglobal; Discount; Hollywood Home Theater; Video Treasures)

GODZILLA VS. THE SMOG MONSTER (1972). A Japanese industrial city has an ecology woe: its miasmic bay of waste and rotting animal life breeds Hedorah, which shoots laser beams from its eyepods and flies at will. It intakes nourishment by sitting atop smokestacks and ingesting waste, which is expelled as human-killing smog. To the rescue comes the flat-footed Godzilla to indulge in a duel-of-the-titans. Directed by Yoshimitsu Banno. Akira Yamauchi. (Orion; Simitar) (Laser: Image, with **MONSTER FROM A PREHISTORIC PLANET**)

GODZILLA VS. THE THING (1964). The giant saurian wars with the giant moth Mothra, which lays an egg—literally speaking, of course. From the egg hatch two caterpillar progeny which weave a shroud of silk around hapless Godzilla, leaving him "stranded." A subplot about miniaturized people makes for a good laugh. Directed by Inoshiro Honda; effects by Eiji Tsuburaya. Akira Takarada, Yurito Hoshi. (Under this title from Paramount and as **GODZILLA VS. MOTHRA**)

GOG (1954). Duo-duped during a 3-D craze, Ivan Tors' production is set in an underground research center where infiltrators short out a computer and take over robots Gog and Magog to commit murders. Elements of the whodunit are blended with sci-fi themes. GOG will not leave you agog, but it will keep you entertained. Directed by Herbert L. Strock. Richard Egan, Constance Dowling, Herbert Marshall, William Schallert.

GOKE, BODY SNATCHER FROM HELL (1968). Japanese airliner crashlands on an island after the pilots see a UFO. The survivors (a crooked businessman, a Caucasian woman and an heroic pilot, among others) are attacked by the Gup-madero people, aliens intending to take over Earth. The creature is a lump of goo that enters humans, turning them into vampires. Cheaply and sloppily made, but compelling as it hysterically unfolds in a way purely Japanese. Hideo Ko, Teru Yoshida, Tomomi Sato, Cathy Horan. Directed by Hajime Sato. (On video as **BODYSNATCHER FROM HELL**)

GOLDEN ARROW, THE (1964). See editions 1-3.

GOLDEN CHILD, THE (1986). When Eddie Murphy is on camera, making delightful wise-guy cracks, GOLDEN CHILD is all that glitters. But when co-producer Dennis Feldman's script resorts to action and monster-movie cliches, he's fool's gold, barely rising above a TV-movie. Director Michael Ritchie glitzes up the weaknesses but when fantasy can make anything happen, there's no sense of fun—just hodgepodge. This blends martial arts impossibilities, a demon from hell (Sardo Numspa, played by Charles Dance) and a quest for a magical sword. Murphy portrays The Chosen One, decreed by an ancient Asian scroll to rescue the kidnapped Golden Child in the City of Angels. Charlotte Lewis, Victor Wong. (Video/Laser: Paramount)

GOLDENGIRL (1979). Curt Jurgens subjects daughter Susan Anton to an neo-Nazi experiment to create a superathlete. Interesting character study strengthens a routine plot of political intrigue. Directed by Joseph Sargent. James Coburn, Robert Kulp, Leslie Caron, Harry Guardino. (CBS/Fox)

GOLDEN HANDS OF KURIGAL (1949). TV-feature version of **FEDERAL AGENTS VS. UNDERWORLD INC.**

GOLDEN MISTRESS, THE (1954). Editions 1-3.

GOLDEN RABBIT, THE (1962). See editions 1-3.

GOLDEN VOYAGE OF SINBAD, THE (1974). Ray Harryhausen's effects excitingly capture the Arabian Nights in this excellent fantasy adventure. Marvel at the duel wth the six-armed Kali; a battle between a centaur and a griffin; a ship's masthead painfully coming to life and attacking; and a devious homunculus. For these visual treats alone this Charles Schneer production is worth repeated viewings, as well as for the score by Miklos Rozsa. Brian Clemens' script is weak on character development and John Phillip Law portrays the familiar sword-swinging hero with indifference, but it is Harryhausen who keeps it alive. Another outstanding feature is Tom Baker as the Black Prince, whose villainy is convincing. Also appealing is the semi-draped Caroline Munro, whom fans will want to ogle. A miniclassic. Martin Shaw, Douglas Wilmer. Directed by Gordon Hessler. (RCA/Columbia) (Laser: RCA/Columbia; Pioneer)

GOLDEN YEARS. See **STEPHEN KING'S GOLDEN YEARS.**

GOLDFINGER (1964). Best of the James Bond 007 glossy thrillers for tongue-in-cheek thrills, comedy, gimmicks and gadgets, thanks to scripters Richard Maibaum and Paul Dehn. Director Guy Hamilton provides style and pacing and there has never been a better supervillain than Gert Forbe as gold-hungry Auric Goldfinger. Connery is in top form and so is Shirley Eaton as the bikini girl. The plot concerns the robbery of Fort Knox, a nuclear bomb (to which Bond is handcuffed) and a unique Asian villain, Odd-Job (Harold Sakata). Also a flying team of shapely femmes led by Pussy Galore (Honor Blackman). (MGM/UA) (Laser: MGM/UA; Criterion)

GOLD OF THE AMAZON WOMEN (1979). The fabled Cities of El Dorado are sought by explorer Bo Svenson in this absurd TV-movie. Svenson, after a bow-and-arrow fight in downtown Manhattan, finds a tribe of Amazons in form-fitting Playtex zebra skins. Their leader is buxom

Anita Ekberg, who looks uncomfortable in her Maidenform leopard spots. Donald Pleasence is after the treasure too. Fortunately, director Mark L. Lester emphasizes the camp elements. Richard Romanus, Robert Minor, Bond Gideon. (Embassy; Sultan; from America's Best as **AMAZON WOMEN**)

GOLDSTEIN (1965). See editions 1-3.

GOLEM, THE (1915). Earliest of films about the Jewish avenger, which legend states stormed Prague in the 1580s to save the Jews from a pogrom. German actor Paul Wegener and screenwriter Henrik Galeen directed and wrote with Wegener playing the animated statue crashing through modern-day Prague in his search to find the daughter of an antique dealer whom he loves. (Video Yesteryear)

GOLEM: HOW HE CAME INTO THE WORLD, THE (1920). Director Paul Wegener again worked with writer Henrik Galeen and cinematographer Karl Freund and tried to remain true to the legendary aspects of the Jewish savior. An important contribution for its make-up and scenes of the hulking monster, which inspired many Frankenstein entities to come. Again, Wegener played the monster. (Video Yesteryear; Sinister/C; Nostalgia)

GOLEM'S LAST ADVENTURE, THE (1921). A comedic treatment of the Golem legend, directed in Austria by Julius Szomogyi.

GOLEM: THE LEGEND OF PRAGUE, THE (1936). Czech version of the legend about the Jewish savior, directed by Julien Duvivier. This is set in the 17th Century and depicts the clayman coming to life to protect the Jews against a pogrom. This has several worthwhile moments—including a ballroom sequence in the palace of Emperor Rudolph II when the Golem advances like a juggernaut through the horrified crowd.

GOLIATH AGAINST THE GIANTS (1961). Beefcake bumbling and biceps babbling as Brad Harris grunts and bemoans his way through a mythical fantasy populated by a sea monster, a valley of non-jolly, non-green giants and a bevy of Amazonian femmes quite fatale. Directed by Guido Malatesta. Gloria Milland, Fernando Rey, Barbara Carrol. (Sinister/C; S/Weird)

GOLIATH AND THE DRAGON (1960). Mark Forest can't see through the trees as Hercules (not Goliath) when he battles a three-headed dog, a fire-breathing St. George hater and a king-size killer bat. Everyone else—including Broderick Crawford as the scheming emperor—battles the impossible script. Directed by Vittorio Cottafavi. Gaby Andre, Leonora Ruffo. (Sinister/C; S/Weird)

GOLIATH AND THE GOLDEN CITY. See **SAMSON AND THE SEVEN MIRACLES OF THE WORLD.**

GOLIATH AND THE ISLAND OF VAMPIRES. See **GOLIATH AND THE VAMPIRES.**

GOLIATH AND THE SINS OF BABYLON (1964). More muscle-flexing and superhuman strength when Mark Forest, as a Babylonian bodybuilder, struts his stuff through the palace, impressing kings, subduing villains and seducing beautiful wenches. What a life! Directed by Michele Lupo. Eleanora Bianchi, Scilla Gabel, John Chevron. (S/Weird; Sinister/C)

GOLIATH AND THE VAMPIRES (1964). One-time Tarzan, Gordon Scott, portrays a muddled muscleman who flexes his biceps (but seldom his brain) to destroy zombie slaves and bloodsuckers. Maciste (his name isn't Goliath or Hercules) misses by a mile. Also known as THE VAMPIRES, GOLIATH AND THE ISLAND OF VAMPIRES, and MACISTE VS. THE VAMPIRE. Directed by Giacomo Gentilomo. Gianna Maria Canale.

GOLIATH AWAITS (1981). An ocean liner, hit by a Nazi torpedo in 1939, is on the ocean floor but peculiar air pockets permit survivors to live on. As subsequent generations grow up, a new society is formed. This four-hour TV-film directed by Kevin Connor deals with a fight for power within the ship's compartments while rescue operations take place above. Frank Gorshin is a heavy and Christopher Lee is a leader staving off anarchy. Mark Harmon, Eddie Albert, John Caradine, Alex Cord, Jeanette Nolan, Robert Forster. (Video/Laser: Vidmark)

GOLIATHON (1977). The titular entity is a variation on a Yeti in this Chinese production set in Hong Kong, which serves as a punching bag for Goliathon's misbehavior—as Tokyo serves as a "stomping ground" for Godzilla. Li Hsiu-Hsien, Evelyne Kraft, Hsiao Yao.

GOMAR THE HUMAN GORILLA. See **NIGHT OF THE BLOODY APES.**

GOOD AGAINST EVIL (1977). TV-movie, made in San Francisco, focuses on a young couple terrorized by satan worshippers. Dack Rambo portrays a writer who meets a woman (Elyssa Davalos) selected to bear the Devil's child. Where's Rosemary when you need her? Dan O'Herlihy is the exorcist. Tepid terror. Directed by Paul Wendkos, scripted by Jimmy Sangster. Richard Lynch, Lelia Goldoni.

GOODBYE CHARLIE (1964). George Axelrod's play reached the screen directed by Vincente Minnelli with Debbie Reynolds as the reincarnated spirit of a screenwriter shot dead by an irate husband. A male screenwriter, that is. Yes, it's the old ploy of a man's soul in a woman's body. Scrambled souls and hapless hams. Tony Curtis, Pat Boone, Roger Carmel, Walter Matthau, Joanna Barnes, Martin Gabel, Donna Michelle.

GOOD NIGHT GOD BLESS (1987). A psychokiller priest described as "from Hell" is on a murderous rampage. And God bless you too. Emma Sutton, Frank Rozelaar Green. Directed by John Eyres. (Magnum)

GOONIES (1985). Overdone children's fantasy produced by Steven Spielberg, directed by Richard Donner and written by Chris Columbus. A group of kids is propelled into an exotic adventure in underground Oregon caverns in search of pirates' treasure. It has the madcap tempo of a roller coaster ride, but there is never a real sense of jeopardy even though the caves have death traps and the featherweight story is treated as an epic when modesty was needed. GOONIES is skilled filmmaking, and certainly has youthful vitality provided by Sean Astin, Josh Brolin, Jeff Cohen and Corey Feldman. (Video/Laser: Warner Bros.)

GOR (1987). John Norman's sword-and-sorcery novels make for a wild fantasy adventure with armies of swordsmen, harem women in scanty costumes and larger-than-life characters. Urbano Barberini portrays American college professor Cabot who travels to another dimension ("The Counter Earth") via a magical ring. The nerdy Cabot is quickly turned into a warrior when he helps a subservient band fight evil King Sarm (Oliver Reed). Director Fritz Kiersch fills the tavern and harem scenes with ample naked flesh and there's battle after battle as Cabot infiltrates the barbarian's fortress. Rebecca Ferrati in a sexy costume, Paul L. Smith as an obese ruffian and Jack Palance as a villain for a sequel add to the color. (Warner Bros.)

GOR II. See **OUTLAW OF GOR.**

GORATH (1962). GODZILLA director Inoshiro Honda, with effects pal Eiji Tsuburaya, weaves more sublime outer-space thrills with giant monsters. A planet on a collision course with Earth forces scientists to move our planet from its orbit by firing rockets into the stratosphere, but the noise disturbs a walrus-shaped monstrosity called . . . GORATH! Ryo Ikebe, Akihiko Hirata. (Discount; Video Gems; Prism)

GORE GORE GIRLS, THE (1972). The last of the exploitation films produced-directed by Herschell Gordon Lewis. Also known as BLOOD ORGY, this has amusing moments (some of them intended) as it parodies the movie whodunit, and forecasts slasher flicks to come. Private eye Abraham Gentry is investigating the deaths of strippers Suzy Creampuff and Candy Cane—go go broads sliced up by a masked killer. You see a hot iron dropped on a face, a knife stuck into an eyeball and a bare buttocks flailed in an act of "tenderization." Thrown in are an anti-stripper protest movement, a Vietnam vet who chops up vegetables and fruits, a girl Friday for Mr.

Gentry and comedian Henny Youngman as a club owner. There's an element of fun at work here. Frank Kress, Hedda Lubin. (Midnight)

GORE-MET ZOMBIE CHEF FROM HELL (1987). A spoof of gore flicks, in which a bloodsucker opens a seafood cafe and knocks off customers to sate his evil appetite. Directed by Don Swan. Theo Depuay, Kelley Kuricki, C. W. Casey, Alan Marx. (Camp)

GORGO (1961). Britain's King brothers (Herman, Maury and Frank) produced this sentimental, if still destructive, tale of mother's love. A baby saurian is discovered in the Irish Sea and taken to London to be exhibited. Its 200-foot-high mother comes for baby, wrecking Westminster Abbey and seeing that London Bridge is literally falling down. Unsurpassed for bathos, handkerchief-wringing and a fondness for the marternal instinct. The monsters are men in dinosaurus suits. Directed by Eugene Lourie (THE BEAST FROM 20,000 FATHOMS). Bill Travers, William Sylvester, Vincent Winter. (United; Video Dimensions; VCI) (Laser: Image)

GORGON, THE (1964). Greek legend claims three sisters (Stheno, Euryale and Medusa) can turn bone to stone should you chance to glance the flakes of snakes writhing atop their dead heads. From that theme, Anthony Nelson-Keys has fashioned a Hammer vehicle with Christopher Lee as an investigator who realizes that brain surgeon Peter Cushing is harboring beauty Barbara Shelley for reasons slitheringly sinister. Directed by Terence Fisher. Richard Pasco, Michael Goodliffe, Jack Watson. (RCA/Columbia; Goodtimes) (Laser: Image)

GORILLA, THE (1927). First of several film versions of a play by Ralph Spence in the OLD DARK HOUSE genre, the chief curiosity being a homicidal ape. Produced-directed by Alfred Santell. Charlie Murray, Fred Kelsey, Walter Pidgeon.

GORILLA, THE (1930). First sound version of the Ralph Spence stage smash with Walter Pidgeon. Directed by Bryan Foy. Joe Frisco, Harry Gribbon, Lila Lee.

GORILLA, THE (1939). The Ritz Brothers, a sophisticated Three Stooges, are hired by millionaire Lionel Atwill to protect him from a murderer, The Gorilla. In this, the third film version of Ralph Spence's play, the private eye triumvirate runs wild through Atwill's mansion during a storm as a gorilla slips through secret panels and as butler Bela Lugosi behaves sinisterly. Old-fashioned farce with a sparkling cast. Anita Louise, Patsy Kelly, Edward Norris, Joseph Calleia. Directed by Allan Dwan. (Kartes; Sinister/C; Nostalgia) (Laser: Image)

GORILLA AT LARGE (1954). Produced during the 3-D craze, this emerges a campy entertainment. A gorilla in a sleazy carnival is suspected of committing murders, but anyone can see this is a whodunit. Anne Bancroft is beautiful as an aerialist, Raymond Burr is sinister as the carnival owner, Lee J. Cobb lends a modicum of believability as the cop and Cameron Mitchell and Charlotte Austin are the love interests. Watch for Lee Marvin as a dumb Irish cop—he's hysterical. Harmon Jones directed it straight. Warren Stevens, Billy Curtis.

GORILLA GANG, THE. See **APE CREATURE.**

GORY MURDER, THE (1982). Body parts are displayed throughout this Hong Kong production, which focuses graphically on the murder of a woman at the hands of a sex fiend.

GOTHAM (1988). Call it a Manhattan ghost story. Down-at-the-heels private eye Eddie Martel Mallard (Tommy Lee Jones) has hit the skids when a guy hires him to make his wife stop bothering him. It sounds like a routine 'tec job, until Mallard learns the wife (Virginia Madsen) drowned ten years ago. A moody, offbeat tale of the supernatural as Mallard falls in love with the woman. Writer-director Lloyd Fonvielle blends a ghost story with the P.I. genre. Jones is excellent as the tormented Mallard, and Madsen is sexy as the ghost. Denise Stephenson, Kevin Jarre, Frederic Forrest. (Video/Laser: Cannon; Warner Bros.)

GOTHIC (1987). On the night of June 16, 1816, poet Lord Byron played host at his Villa Diodati to writer Percy Shelley, his future bride Mary Wollstonecraft, her half-sister Claire Clairmont and Percy's physician, Dr. Polidori. Yes, but what is this movie about? Since the director is Ken Russell, it's an exercise in Russellian grotesqueries with incoherent plotline. It was on this famous night Mary Shelley conceived the idea for FRANKENSTEIN. These haunted characters take drugs, have an orgy, rush through drafty corridors and behave as if in a Shakespearean nightmare. Color it depraved, call it freako as Russell explores homosexuality, masochism and decadence. Leeches, maggots, demons, monsters. Gabriel Byrne (Byron), Julian Sands (Percy Shelley), Natasha Richardson (Mary), Myriam Cyr (Claire), Timothy Spall (Dr. Polidori). (Vestron) (Laser: Image)

GRADUATION, THE. See **PROWLER, THE.**

GRADUATION DAY (1981). Above-average slasher film with clever camera work, good point-of-view shots and pacing. Forty years ago a soldier received a Dear John letter and came home to shove a pitchfork into the backs of his faithless wife and lover at the graduation dance. When the graduation-dance tradition is revived, the uniformed killer strikes at the track team. Herbert Freed produced-directed. Christopher George, Michael Pataki, E. J. Peaker. (RCA/Columbia)

GRAMPA'S SCI-FI HITS. Twenty-eight previews of coming distractions, hosted by Al Lewis. (Amvest)

GRANDMA'S HOUSE (1988). Anyone going to Grandma's house, if they know about the Big Bad Wolf, is a fool, but a brother and sister go anyway and find out the hard way. Directed by Peter Rader. Eric Foster, Kim Valentine, Brinke Stevens. (Academy) (Laser: Image)

GRAND TOUR: DISASTER IN TIME (1992). David N. Twohy wrote-directed this excellent adaptation of the sci-fi novel VINTAGE YEAR by Lawrence O'Donnell and C. L. Moore. In this superior time-travel yarn, Jeff Daniels is a hotel owner who encounters travelers from the future who venture to past time zones to watch spectacular disasters—and a disaster is on its way to Daniels' town, and he must tamper with time to avert tragedy. This is the way science fiction should be told on the screen—with taste, interesting characters and respect for the source material. Emilia Crow (as a sexy lady from tomorrow), Ariana Richards (as the "tour guide"), Jim Haymie, David Wells, Nicholas Guest, Robert Colbert. (Academy)

GRASP OF THE LORELEI. See **WHEN THE SCREAMING STOPS.**

GRAVE DESIRES. See **BRIDES OF BLOOD.**

GRAVE OF THE LIVING DEAD (1982). Jesus Franco directed this tale of an army of dead Nazis standing guard over a treasure in the African desert. Also known as THE TREASURE OF THE LIVING DEAD. Manuel Gelin, Eduardo Fajardo, Lina Romay.

GRAVE OF THE VAMPIRE (1972). Michael Pataki portrays a vampire who rapes a pretty co-ed near a mauseoleum. The offspring, brought up on mother's blood, is William Smith, who spends years seeking the rapist—only to confront dear dead dad, and realize heritage is everything in life, after all. Directed by John Hayes. Lyn Peters, Jay Adler. (Unicorn)

GRAVE ROBBERS FROM OUTER SPACE. See **PLAN NINE FROM OUTER SPACE.** Or don't see **PLAN NINE FROM OUTER SPACE.** See if we care.

GRAVE SECRETS (1989). Offbeat ghost story in the POLTERGEIST tradition in which Paul LeMat, a college professor obsessed with contacting the dead, is asked by Renee Soutendijk to investigate her haunted bed-and-breakfast inn. Spectral manifestations, moving objects (i.e., a flying axe), ghostly sounds and eerie winds are the phenomena that plague Le Mat and transmedium David Warner. A headless man and the unlocking of dark family secrets becomes the thrust. Sincere effort by director Donald P. Borchers to weave an original supernatural tale. Olivia Barash, Lee Ving, John Crawford. (Shapiro Glickenhaus) (Laser: Image)

GRAVE SECRETS: THE LEGACY OF HILLTOP

DRIVE (1992). This TV-movie, based on an alleged true incident recounted in the book THE BLACK HOPE HORROR, could be the real-life counterpart to POLTERGEIST. Patty Duke and David Selby move into a rural tract home and undergo hauntings and ghostly manifestations. An intelligently told tale dealing with the legal ramifications of hauntings. Effectively chilling in the hands of director John Patterson. David Soul, Blake Clark, Kelly Rowan, Jonelle Allen. (Worldvision)

GRAVEYARD, THE. Video version of **TERROR OF SHEBA.** (VCL; Interglobal; Electric)

GRAVEYARD OF HORROR (1971). Cemetery, hidden cave, grave robber, hairy corpse that comes to life, innocent victims—all blended by Spanish writer-director Miguel Madrid into substandard horror genre material. They'll dig you . . . you won't dig them. Also known as NECROPHAGUS. William Curran, Catharine Ellison. (Super; from All American as **NECROMANIAC**)

GRAVEYARD SHIFT (1987). Canadian quickie about a taxi driver who also happens to be a vampire, and his adventures with a TV director seeking a sexual experience. Boy, does she get it! The experience we mean. Written-directed by Gerard Ciccoritti. Silvio Oliviero, Helen Papas, Cliff Stoker (any relation to Bram, Cliff?) (Virgin Vision) (Laser: Image)

GRAVEYARD SHIFT II. See **UNDERSTUDY: GRAVEYARD SHIFT II, THE.**

GRAVEYARD SHIFT (1990). Disappointing adaptation of a Stephen King story, which translates here as a series of hoary cliches. The setting is a cotten mill next to a cemetery—and living in the subterranean depths is a

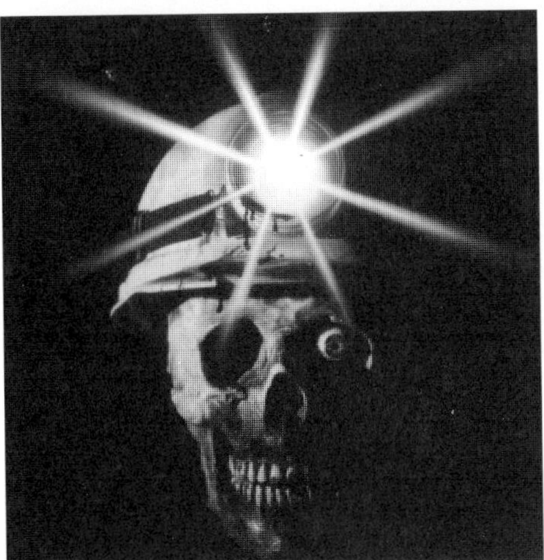

STEPHEN KING'S 'GRAVEYARD SHIFT'

tentacled blob that eats anything it can. The characters are so dark and unappealing that sympathy for their eventual plight, when trapped in the monster's breeding grounds beneath the rat-infested mill, is virtually nil. Adaptor John Esposito's script never escapes the B-movie category, rendering director Ralph S. Singleton as helpless as the cast. David Andrews, Kelly Wolf, Stephen Macht, Brad Dourif. (Video/Laser: Paramount)

GRAVEYARD TRAMPS. See **INVASION OF THE BEE GIRLS.**

GREASER'S PALACE (1972). Writer-director Robert Downey intermingles religious symbolism and irreverent parody in this fantasy allegory. A dude in a zoot suit drops by air into the Old West, where he assumes the stance of a Jesus Christ, resurrecting the dead and healing the sick. Luana Anders, Albert Henderson, Stan Gottlieb, Allan Arbus, Ron Nealy. (RCA/Columbia)

GREAT ALASKAN MYSTERY, THE (1944). Thirteen-chapter Universal serial with Milburn Stone as an adventurer on the trail of a new death ray called the Peragron and German spies. Directed by Ray Taylor and Lewis D. Collins. Marjorie Weaver, Edgar Kennedy, Martin Kosleck, Ralph Morgan.

GREAT ALLIGATOR, THE (1981). Tropical island tourists Barbara Bach and Mel Ferrer could be dinner for an angry tribal god, Kuma, who assumes the form of an overgrown, scaly creature that would one day make about 5000 pairs of walking pumps. This Italian film, directed by Sergio Martino, was made as BIG ALLIGATOR RIVER. Richard Johnson, Claudio Cassinelli, Romano Puppo. (Gorgon; MPI)

GREAT AMERICAN MASSACRE, THE. See **BLOODY WEDNESDAY.**

GREAT GABBO, THE (1929). A curious antique, based on Ben Hecht's "The Rival Dummy," about a ventriloquist (Erich Von Stroheim) with a sophisticated act in a lavish revue. The theme of the dummy taking over the master is presented in an unusual way by director James Cruze. Von Stroheim finally freaks out during one of the film's interminable musical production numbers. The supporting cast (Betty Compton, Don Douglas, Marjorie Kane) is new to sound, so performances tend to be a bit hysterical. (Kartes; Sinister/C; Nostalgia)

GREAT GAMBINI, THE (1937). See editions 1-3.

GREAT IMPERSONATION, THE (1935). See third edition.

GREAT LAND OF SMALL, THE (1986). Evil confronts two children when they enter a fantasy kingdom. (Starmaker; Hollywood Home Entertainment)

GREAT MONSTER YONGARY. See **YONGARY, MONSTER FROM THE DEEP.**

GREAT MOVIE STUNTS AND THE MAKING OF "RAIDERS OF THE LOST ARK." Well-produced behind-the-scenes documentary with footage of George Lucas, Steven Spielberg, Harrison Ford and other key principals. (Video/Laser: Paramount)

GREAT RACE, THE (1965). This riotously falls into the category of THE CRIMSON PIRATE and other spoofs spotlighting weapons and inventions out of their time. Jack Lemmon and Peter Falk are insidious inventors who create devices to thwart Tony Curtis and other drivers in a car race from New York to Paris in the early 1900s. Hilarious Blake Edwards production (he directed and co-wrote with Arthur Ross), filled with vintage automobiles, bizarre gadgets, Roadrunner-style gags and pie-throwing slapstick. Natalie Wood, Keenan Wynn, Arthur O'Connell, Vivian Vance, Larry Storch, Ross Martin, George Macready. (Warner Bros.) (Laser: Pioneer)

GREAT RUPERT, THE (1950). George Pal fantasy-comedy directed by Irving Pichel, in which squirrel Rupert is really an animated puppet—which is more than you can say for Terry Moore, Jimmy Durante and Tom Drake, who are allegedly real. They're all mixed up with Rupert in a mystery surrounding a cache of money hidden in an old mansion. (Discount)

GREAT SPACE CHASE, THE (1979). Feature-length version of the MIGHTY MOUSE TV series featuring the caped superstrong rodent against Harry the Heartless and his heartless-heartless Catomaton.

GREAT WHITE (1982). See third edition.

GREED OF WILLIAM HART, THE (1948). British horror star Tod Slaughter is at his best in this variation on Burke and Hare. Written by John Gilling, directed by Oswald Mitchell. Henry Oscar, Aubrey Woods.

GREEN MAN, THE (1990). Intriguing ghost tale in the British tradition, based on a novel by Kingsley Amis. It's a psychological portrait of alcoholic Albert Finney, proprietor of the Green Man, a country inn haunted by the spirit of a 17th century occult practitioner who comes to symbolize the self-destruction within Finney. This British TV-movie also glimpses into the dark side of Finney's sexuality. Effective hair-raiser directed by Elijah Moshinsky. Linda Marlowe, Sarah Berger, Nicky Henson, Michael Hordern. (A & E; Tamarelle's)

GREEN MANSIONS (1959). Offbeat melodrama-fantasy based on the William Henry Hudson novel, with Audrey Hepburn as the legendary Bird Girl of the Amazon, Rima, who is not permitted to leave her forest even when she meets political refugee Anthony Perkins and falls in love. Mel Ferrer directed from a screenplay by Dorothy Kingsley. Lee J. Cobb, Sessue Hayakawa, Henry Silva, Nehemiah Persoff. (MGM/UA)

GREEN PASTURES (1936). Marc Connelly's stage hit, an unbridled whimsical fantasy presenting a Negro's impression of life after death (i.e. "de lawd" and His Angels holding a fish fry behind the Pearly Gates). All-black cast is headed by Rex Ingram, Eddie "Rochester" Anderson, Oscar Polk and George Reed. Connelly adapted his own play and co-directed with William Keighley. (Key)

GREEN SLIME, THE (1969). U.S.-Japanese sci-fi serving set on Gamma III, a space station where astronauts Robert Horton and Richard Jaeckel confront protoplasmic aliens of a hue between yellow and blue on the color spectrum. Producers Ivan Reiner and Walter Manley were not green with envy about the inadequate effects work, and fans have remained an indifferent hue due to technical deficiencies. The monsters are one-eyed entities with tentacles they want to wrap around curvy Luciana Paluzzi. Directed by Kinji Fukasaku. Also known as DEATH AND THE GREEN SLIME and BATTLE BEYOND THE STARS. (MGM/UA)

GREETINGS FROM EARTH. See **BATTLESTAR GALACTICA.**

GREGORIO AND THE LITTLEST ANGEL (1968). This U.S.-Mexican production is a warm-hearted morality comedy distinguished by Broderick Crawford's amusing performance as a tequilla-besotted rummy who loses his janitorial job in an orphanage and stumbles off to Taxco, where he is befriended by a little girl angel. Crawford's sot is tempted to drink by the Devil in the personification of Tin Tan, who twirls the ends of his mustache in a campy performance. Connie Carol is cute as the Angel, and there's pretty travelogue footage of Mexico. Directed by Gilbert Martinez-Solares. Jacqueline Evans, Evangelina Elizondo, Victor Eberg.

GREMLINS (1984). Steven Spielberg's production is the brainchild of screenwriter Chris Columbus, director Joe Dante and producer Mike Finnell, who have concocted a morality fable blending dark macabre humor with serious horror and the air of a fairy tale. Chris Walas designed and articulated the gremlins. Madcap inventor Hoyt Axton brings home a cuddly, wide-eyed creature he calls "Gizmo." Although Gizmo is benevolent, he passes through an odd reproductive stage leading to the birth of impish, malevolent critters who create havoc. The gremlins are repulsive and amusing. Polly Holliday, Harry Carey Jr., Dick Miller, Edward Andrews, Scott Brady, Kenneth Tobey and Belinda Balaski bring an added touch of fun. (Video/Laser: Warner Bros.)

GREMLINS 2: THE NEW BATCH (1990). A sequel worth seeing—a worthy successor to the 1984 hit—that breaks down the fourth wall to let us laugh at film-making itself. Director Joe Dante and writer Charlie Haas have pulled out the stops to make this zanier and crazier than the original. There are new wrinkles when the Gremlins take over a high-tech office building in Manhattan: one talks, one turns into a giant spider monster, another into a bat flier. Rick Baker's gremlins are incredibly realistic (Gizmo less so) and the gags they pull are nothing but fun. It's Mad Magazine, Hellzapoppin' and William Castle rolled into a satisfying monster comedy. Zach Galligan and Phoebe Cates are back as young lovers challenged by the rampaging gremlins; John Glover is hysterically funny as the rich building designer, Clamp; Christopher Lee is marvelous as a genetics scientist (would you believe "designer genes"?). (Video/Laser: Warner Bros.)

GREY MATTER (1973). Metaphysical ideas are lost to poor production and mediocre acting in this scientific thriller originally made as THE BRAIN MACHINE. A government conspiracy allows for an experiment involving a Brain Machine in the National Environmental Control Center, but questions of immortality and truth lead to human disintegration. Directed and co-written by Joy N. Houck Jr. James Best (as a reverend), Barbara Burgess, Gil Peterson, Gerald McRaney. (Bancorp; Premiere)

GREYSTOKE: THE LEGEND OF TARZAN, LORD OF THE APES (1984). Fresh approach to the cinematic rendering of Edgar Rice Burroughs' jungle hero, with director Hugh Hudson and writers P.H. Vazak (a pseudonyn for Robert Towne) and Michael Austin showing the nitty gritty of growing up as the son of a pack of apes. The film is fascinating as little Tarzan passes through various ages until he emerges a disciplined jungle man. It's when he's domesticated and taken back to Victorian England that the film becomes a strange love story more difficult to relate to. Tarzan fans may resent the heavy realism, while Burroughs purists will have to respect this attempt to recapture the spirit of the Tarzan novels. Christopher Lambert is fine as John Clayton-Tarzan and Sir Ralph Richardson is superb as the Sixth Earl of Greystoke. Ian Holm, James Fox, Andie MacDowell, Cheryl Campbell, Nigel Davenport, Ian Charleson. (Video/Laser: Warner Bros.)

GRIMM'S FAIRY TALES FOR ADULTS (1970). German "bloody horror-sex" exploitationer repackaged for the U.S. Fairy tale characters are depicted doing things Mother Goose would never have allowed. Grimm has become grim in the style of black comedy horror. Grimm and bear it. Directed-written by Rolf Thiele. Marie Liljedah, Eva V. Rueber-Staier.

GRIM PRAIRIE TALES (1990). Offbeat anthology horror flick with two strangers sitting around a desert campfire spinning western terror tales. In this low-budget feature (the first for writer-producer-director Wayne Coe), the storytellers (Brad Dourif as a sensitive intellectual; James Earl Jones as a grubby, snarling bounty hunter) build to such interesting dimensions that their wraparound material overpowers the vignettes, structured like old E.C. comic stories with twist endings: (1) A cowhand dares to cross an Indian burial ground; (2) a man encounters a strange prairie woman who proceeds to seduce him; (3) a young girl learns the truth about her bigoted frontier father; and (4) a rich rancher has hired guns shoot it out to find the fastest. There's a low-key element that makes the stories sublime. Will Hare, Marc McClure, Michelle Joyner, William Atherton, Lisa Eichhorn. (Academy) (Laser: Image)

GRIM REAPER, THE (1981). Italian platter of splatter for nongourmets with Tisa Farrow leading a pack of American tourists to a Greek island where a murderous cannibal is eager to become part of the have-a-tourist-for-lunch bunch. Also known as ANTHROPOPHAGUS, this slowly gnaws away at you as the corpses pile up and as knife after knife is shoved into human flesh. The victims die horribly, by throat-biting, hair-pulling and other unrelenting, sickening means. A flood of blood with bash and splash. The sequel was ABSURD (or ANTHROPOPHAGUS II). Directed by Joe D'Amato. George Eastman, Bob Larson. (Fries Entertainment; Monterey)

GRINDHOUSE HORRORS (1992). Movie trailers of obscure horror and exploitation fare from the 1960s through the '80s. Titles include CULT OF THE DAMNED, DEEP RED, JOURNEY INTO THE BEYOND and THE VIRGIN WITCH. Most is high-class trash. (Ecco; Killgore)

GRIP OF THE STRANGLER. See **HAUNTED STRANGLER, THE.**

GRIZZLY (1976). This imitates JAWS in every detail, but on dry ground. A 15-foot-tall superbear terrorizes Georgia State Park, devouring backpackers and hunters until forest ranger Christopher George and Richard Jaeckel track it down using neomodern weapons. William Girdler directed. Andrew Prine, Lynda Day George, Joan McCall, Joe Dorsey. Also known as KILLER GRIZZLY. (Media) (Laser: Japanese)

GROOVE ROOM (1974). British "old dark house" comedy with Sue Longhurst, Diana Dors and Martin Ljung as Jack the Ripper. Vernon P. Becker wrote-directed. Aka WHAT THE SWEDISH BUTLER SAW.

GROTESQUE (1987). Linda Blair and Donna Wilkes show up at Linda's place for a weekend outing to become targets for Robert Zdar (MANIAC COP) and his gang of bikers. Tab Hunter plays a plastic surgeon. Penty of lousy film-making to please those who like a good bad movie. Directed grotesquely by Joseph Tornatore. Brad Wilson, Guy Stockwell. (Media) (Laser: Image)

GROUNDHOG DAY (1993). Delightful mixture of Bill Murray-style comedy and an unusual fantasy situation in which a cynical TV newscaster is caught in a 24-hour time loop, always waking up at 6 a.m. to face covering the annual Groundhog Day event on Gobbler's Knob in Punxstutawney, Pa., an event he absolutely loathes. At first the lecherous, snobbish Murray uses his knowledge of what's going to happen next to seduce women and carry out other obnoxious acts. But as he keeps repeating the cycle, he undergoes a change of character by shucking his less-admirable qualities, befriending the cameraman (Chris Elliott) he earlier despised and sincerely romancing TV producer Andie MacDowell. Written by Danny Rubin and directed by Harold Ramis. (Video/Laser: Columbia TriStar)

GROUNDSTAR CONSPIRACY, THE (1972). Intriguing if confusing espionage thriller with fantastic overtones, adapted from L.P. Davies' THE ALIEN and directed in Vancouver by Lamont Johnson. George Peppard is a security chief trying to find out who blew up a giant computer. His key to the mystery is Michael Sarrazin, a possible enemy agent—but for whom? The twist: Sarrazin has lost all memory and doesn't know who he's working for. Christine Belford, Tim O'Connor. (MCA)

GROUND ZERO (1973). An atomic device is fastened to a tower of the Golden Gate Bridge by a madman. Up the tower goes special agent Ron Casteel to get his man. This movie is the pits. So is the direction by producer James T. Flocker. And the acting is lousy—even attorney Melvin Belli. Cinematic ineptitude of the highest order. Augie Treibach, Kim Friese, Yvonne D'Anger (onetime topless star). (Genesis)

GROWING PAINS (1982). Video version of an episode from HAMMER HOUSE OF HORROR. See **HOUSE THAT BLED TO DEATH.** (Thrillervideo)

GRUESOME TWOSOME, THE (1967). The inane tone for this gorebore from producer-director-cameraman Herschell Gordon Lewis is set by wigged mannikin heads holding a conversation that leads into the story of an old lady (Elizabeth Davis) who runs "The Little Wig Shop." She turns her beautiful customers over to her slobbering son (Chris Martel), who works on them with an electric carving knife, scalping them and pulling out their intestines. Snoopy teenager Gretchen Wells, a "female James Bond," tracks the missing nubile co-eds. What makes this bearable is its parody. (Midnight; VCI; Rhino)

GUARDIAN, THE (1990). A major disappointment from director William Friedkin—at best a grade-B supernatural thriller. The Steven Volk/Dan Greenburg/Friedkin script (based on the novel THE NANNY by Greenburg) is a bloody fable about a tree in a forest that lives on the blood of newborn babies—babies provided by a sexy wood nymph in the shape of Jenny Seagrave. The characters are so poorly developed, one can never quite get into their emotional states. Dwier Brown, Carey Lowell, Brad Hall, Miguel Ferrer. (Video/Laser: MCA)

GUARDIAN OF THE ABYSS (1982). Episode of the British HAMMER HOUSE OF HORROR series, repackaged for TV with CARPATHIAN EAGLE. The David Fisher teleplay features a haunted mirror, through which images of a devil cult emerge. Director Don Sharp gives this traditional terror tale a nice gloss. Ray Lonney, Rosalyn Landor, John Carson. (Thrillervideo, with Elvira)

GUESS WHAT HAPPENED TO COUNT DRACULA (1970). Des Roberts plays Count Adrian in a Hollywood setting. Claudia Barron, John Landon. Directed by Laurence Merrick.

GUESS WHO'S COMING FOR CHRISTMAS? (1990). Schmaltzy TV-movie with morality lessons about the vagaries of human behavior. Richard Mulligan portrays a happy-go-lucky rural resident of Grover's Mill (the town where Martians landed in WAR OF THE WORLDS) who meets a stranded humanoid alien (Beau Bridges) from the planet Zabar. Bridges carries a briefcase and looks like a businessman. No one in town believes Mulligan that Bridges' saucer needs repairs and his friends turn against him. Mulligan has to examine his own inner feelings. Directed by Paul Schneider. Barbara Barrie, Paul Dooley, James McEachin, John Furey.

GUILTY AS CHARGED (1991). Rod Steiger gets to play one of his nutty characters, a tycoon who turns vigilante and electrocutes criminals in a special electric chair. (What a shocking title!) Steiger is a religious kook (God made him do it!) and this unusual movie is really wired. Sorry about that. Directed by Sam Irvin. Lauren Hutton, Heather Graham, Isaac Hayes, Zelda Rubinstein. (Video/Laser: RCA/Columbia)

GULLIVER'S TRAVELS (1939). In the wake of Disney's SNOW WHITE AND THE SEVEN DWARFS came this animated feature by Max and Dave Fleischer, a loose adaptation of Jonathan Swift's satire classic, with a prince and princess added to the cast. While the Disney influences are obvious, this has superb animation and a satisfying Victor Young score. (Kartes; Crown; Video Warehouse) (Laser: LVA Film Classics; Image; Republic)

GULLIVER'S TRAVELS (1977). Anglo-Belgian blend of animation and live action with Richard Harris as the shipwrecked adventurer who gets mixed up with little people and giants. Not an auspicious credit for Peter Hunt, whose direction is static. The Don Black script makes only token effort to deal with Jonathan Swift's political satire; mainly for children. Catherine Schell, Norman Shelley. (United; Lucerne Media; HHE)

GULLIVER'S TRAVELS BEYOND THE MOON (1966). Japanese sci-fi version of Swift's satiric classic. Directed by Yoshio Kuroda.

GULLIVER'S TRAVELS: JOURNEY TO THE LAND OF THE GIANTS (1983). Animated Spanish version of Swift's classic satire. Directed by Cruz Delgado.

GUN ON ICE PLANET ZERO. See **BATTLESTAR GALACTICA.**

GURU THE MAD MONK (1970). Andy Milligan sexploitation in which a torturer drinks the blood of young girls in his confessional. The setting is allegedly the Middle Ages, but contemporary sets slipped past the graphic designers—they must have been distracted by the nubile bodies. Neil Flanagan, Judy Israel.

GUY NAMED JOE, A (1943). Big-budgeted MGM fantasy scripted by Dalton Trumbo and directed by Victor Fleming, with touches of World War II propaganda. Spencer Tracy, a flying hero who dies in battle, returns to train new recruits and instill new hope in Van Johnson and Irene Dunne, who provide the obligatory love interest. Remade by Steven Spielberg as ALWAYS. Lionel Barrymore, Ward Bond, James Gleason, Esther Williams. (MGM)

GUYVER, THE (1991). A wild and crazy monster-action entertainment mixing martial arts, genetics sci-fi and creatures usually found in Japanese movies. David Gale, portraying an unrestrained crazy scientist, sends his minions (including Michael Berryman) after the Guyver, a device that turns man into the ultimate warrior, ULTRAMAN style. Gale's minions are a motley collection of ugly but funny beasties battling Mark Hamill, the underdog who fights back as the Guyver. Producer Brian Yuzna put together this amusing actioner, which features spectacular fistfights among the monsters. Special effects man Screaming Mad George directed Jon Purdy's energetic script with Steve Wang, and George and Wang also teamed to create the monster effects. Jeffrey Combs and Linnea Quigley in cameos, Vivan Wu, Jack Armstrong, Jimmy Walker, Peter Spellos. (New Line)

GYPSY MOON (1953). See **ROCKY JONES, SPACE RANGER.** (Sinister/C; S/Weird; Filmfax)

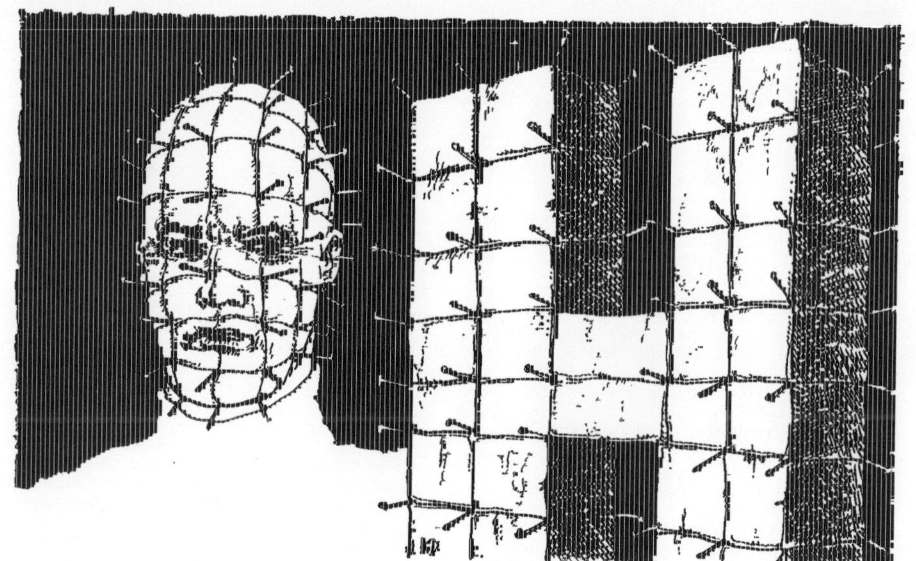

H. G. WELLS' NEW INVISIBLE MAN (1962). Arturo De Cordova and AnaLuisa Peluffo in a Mexican version of the Wells classic. Directed by Alfredo Crevena.

H. G. WELLS' THE SHAPE OF THINGS TO COME (1979). The title is an outright lie! This is not even a remake of the 1936 British mini-masterpiece, THINGS TO COME. Hell, it's not even H. G. Wells. It's a Canadian hunkajunk set "tomorrow after tomorrow," when Earth is ravaged by robotic wars. A moon colony (in need of substance RADIC-Q2) sends scientist Barry Morse, Sparks the robot and a couple of heroic types to Delta 3 to get RADIC-Q2, and they encounter dictator Umas (Jack Palance in a Flash Gordon costume) and robots at war with Carol Lynley and her rebels. The robot comedy relief is pitiful. Directed by George McCowan. John Ireland, Mark Parr, Eddie Benton.

HACK-O-LANTERN (1987). An hysterical, stylized movie villain, Hy Pyke, plays a grandfather in control of a satanic band who kills to protect its secrecy on All Hallows' Eve. Years later, Pyke must pick his successor in the cult. Direct-to-video chiller-diller-thriller of minimum importance directed by Jag Mundhra. Gregory Scott Cummins. (From Legacy as **HALLOWEEN NIGHT**)

HAIL TO THE CHIEF (1972). . . . but nothing hearty about this heavy-handed attempt at political satire in which Richard B. Shull portrays an advisor to a megalomaniacal U.S. President—the parallels to Richard Nixon are prophetic. Shull is appalled to discover the President has an army of vigilantes and concentration camps for hippies. Poorly photographed, HAIL! (its alternate title) suffers from its low budget and high aspirations that cannot be articulated. Directed by Fred Levinson. Dan Resin, Dick O'Neill, Joseph Sirola, Gary Sandy, Lee Meredith. Aka WASHINGTON D.C. (Monterey)

HALF HUMAN (1957). Japanese fantasy-horror directed by Inoshiro Honda, which sheds new light on the Abominable Snowman of the Himalayas. New footage with John Carradine and Morris Ankrum was shot by Kenneth Crane for the U.S. but in any language HALF HUMAN is half-baked. Special effects by Inoshiro's pal, Eiji Tsuburaya. Akira Takarada, Kenji Kasahara, Russ Thorson. (Media; Rhino; S/Weird; Filmfax)

HALL OF THE MOUNTAIN KING. Video version of **NIGHT OF THE HOWLING BEAST** (Majestic).

HALLOWEEN (1978). This low-budget money maker, which launched director John Carpenter's career, is a paean to October 31—a series of jolts designed to shock, rock and knock as it depicts a psychopathic madman who escapes from an asylum and terrorizes babysitters and their boyfriends in a small Midwestern town. The killer is unkillable, allowing for a surprise ending. Director Carpenter, who scripted with producer Debra Hill, knows his scare tactics, never letting the viewer relax. The graphic, stylish murders helped establish the slasher trend. Donald Pleasence portrays the psychiatrist; Jamie Lee Curtis is the screaming target who experiences the ultimate in blood-curdling horror. Nancy Loomis, Nick Castle, Charles Cyphers. (Media) (Laser: Image)

HALLOWEEN II (1981). This picks up on the same night as the original, as Jamie Lee Curtis is hospitalized with psychiatrist Donald Pleasence close at hand. The Bogeyman Slasher, as you suspected, is alive and well—well-angered, that is, shambling zombielike to get poor Jamie in the hospital. Unfortunately, it's a weak premise (co-authored by producers Carpenter and Debra Hill), with the hospital so poorly lit, one wonders how the nurses can find patients. A hypodermic needle thrust into an eyeball, slashed throats and a head dipped into scalding water are among the jolly sights. You almost wish the killer would hurry up and knock off Curtis. Directed by Rick Rosenthal and Carpenter. Charles Cyphers, Jeffrey Kramer, Lance Guest. (Video/Laser: MCA)

HALLOWEEN III: SEASON OF THE WITCH (1982). See a man's eyes squeezed out of their sockets. See a man set himself on fire. See a head twisted off its torso. See a boy's face explode in a shower of beetles, roaches and rattlesnakes. Had enough? If not, catch this John Carpenter/Debra Hill-produced flick, with all the imagery of a Halloween nightmare. But don't be misled by the title. This has nothing to do with the first two HALLOWEEN flicks. Dan O'Herlihy is a designer of children's fright masks (creations of Don Post) with a fiendish plot: In each mask is a device that will explode while children are watching a TV commercial. It's up to Tom Atkins and Stacey Nelkin to thwart the diabolical plan. Director-writer Tommy Lee Wallace creates a few scary sequences, but an element of fun is missing. (Video/Laser: MCA)

HALLOWEEN 4: THE RETURN OF MICHAEL MYERS (1988). Disappointing sequel to HALLOWEEN and HALLOWEEN 2, with the Boogeyman Slasher committing more mayhem. Sorely needed is writer-director John Carpenter, for he understood what made the slasher-killer theme work; stand-in director Dwight H. Little does not. It's more an imitation of the FRIDAY THE 13TH series, so Michael Myers is a substitute Jason Voorhes. Myers is being transferred to a new mental hospital and escapes. He plans to knock off blood relatives in Haddonville, so a handful of characters lock themselves in a dark, eerie house, becoming perfect targets. Not a single murder is believable or shocking, and Donald Pleasence (as the headshrinker) reaches new heights of hysteria. Ellie Cornell, Danielle Harris. (Video/Laser: CBS/Fox)

HALLOWEEN 5: THE REVENGE OF MICHAEL MYERS (1989). Surprisingly good of its kind, capturing an intensity through the overwrought performance of young

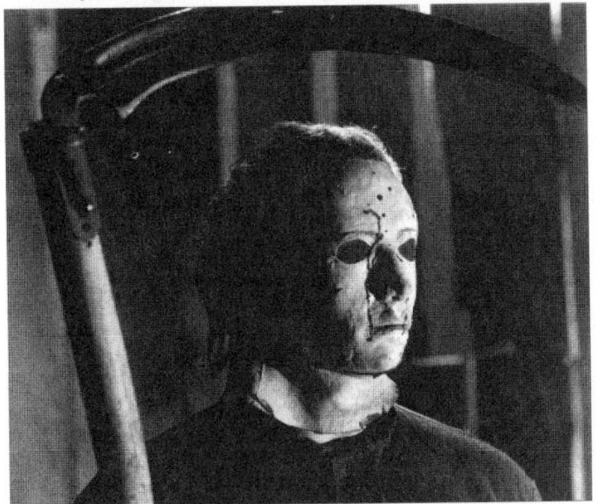

MICHAEL MYERS: A SCYTHE FOR SORE EYES

Danielle Harris as Jamie, niece of the infamous Boogeyman Slasher, who's psychically linked to her uncle and knows when he's going to kill. Another overwrought performance is given by Donald Pleasence as Dr. Loomis, who is now quite mad and a delight to watch as he goes bonkers. These key performances aside, No. 5 is an endless series of cliches, although to his credit director Dominique Othenin-Girard keeps his camera fluid, and the editing makes it more thrilling than it really is. The victims fall prey to Myers in the usual dumb ways, with costumed teenagers retiring into dark places to carry out pranks and sex games. Wendy Kaplan, Ellie Cornell, Donald L. Shanks. (Video/Laser: CBS/Fox)

HALLOWEEN NIGHT. Video version of **HACK-O-LANTERN** (Legacy).

HALLOWEEN NIGHT (1990). Small town is attacked by evil on that grand night for goblins, ghosties and things that go thump in the night. Hy Pyke, Katrina Garner. Directed by Emilio P. Miraglio. (Atlantic)

HALLOWEEN PARTY. See **NIGHT OF THE DEMONS.**

HALLOWEEN WITH THE ADDAMS FAMILY (1979). TV-movie revival of the series of the 1960s with John Astin, Carolyn Jones, Jackie Coogan and Ted Cassidy (Goodtimes)

HAMMER HOUSE OF HORROR DOUBLE FEATURE. Repackaging of the British series HAMMER HOUSE OF HORROR, with two episodes combined in each. TV Guide lists these under the first episode title so see **CHARLIE BOY; CHILDREN OF THE FULL MOON; HOUSE THAT BLED TO DEATH; TWO FACES OF EVIL** and **WITCHING TIME.**

HAMMOND MYSTERY, THE. See **UNDYING MONSTER, THE.**

HAND, THE (1960). Grisly British revenge mystery: Three English POWs refuse to cooperate with Japanese captors and each has a hand cut off. A fourth man talks to save himself and later the three one-handed chaps track him down. Ironic twist-of-fate climax. A hand-me-down movie? Directed by Henry Cass. Derek Bond, Ronald Leigh-Hunt. (Sinister/C; S/Weird; Filmfax)

HAND, THE (1969). See editions 1-3.

HAND, THE (1981). Thinking man's BEAST WITH FIVE FINGERS, in which cartoonist Michael Caine, after losing his right hand in a freakish car accident, sinks into madness, with the severed hand knocking off anyone who has wronged him. Or is Caine committing the murders and hallucinating? Writer-director Oliver Stone has done a thoughtful job of adapting Marc Brandel's THE LIZARD'S TAIL, exploring Caine's insanity with the use of black-and-white film, distorted camera angles, etc. Make-up and effects by Stan Winston, Tom Burman and Carlo Rambaldi. Music by James Horner. Andrea Marcovicci, Viveca Lindfors, Annie McEnroe. (Warner Bros.)

HANDMAID'S TALE, THE (1990). Interesting adaptation of Margaret Atwood's allegorical novel about the kingdom of Gilead, where women undergo a tyrannical training program at the hands of Aunt Lydia (Victoria Tennant) to become nun-like child bearers. Natasha Richardson becomes a symbol of rebellion after she undergoes the horrors of being forced to have sex with a commander (Robert Duvall, who brings many nuances to his basic-villain role) while wife Faye Dunaway assists. However, director Volker Schlondorff demonstrates taste in these kinky sequences. Harold Pinter adapted the book. Aidan Quinn, Elizabeth McGovern, Blanche Baker, Traci Lind, David Dukes. (HBO) (Laser: Image)

HAND OF DEATH, THE (1961). John Agar, after experimenting with a formula that should-not-have-been-conceived-because-it-tampers-with-the-forces-of-natu re, turns into something that looks like a leftover from THE ALLIGATOR PEOPLE. Directed by Gene Nelson. Paula Raymond, Steve Dunne, Roy Gordon.

HAND OF NIGHT. See **BEAST OF MOROCCO.**

HAND OF POWER (1967). West German production of an Edgar Wallace thriller is preposterous yet has a fascination to its campiness. An avenging murderer dressed like a skeleton and calling himself "The Laughing Corpse" commits murders with a Scorpion-shaped ring that contains a poisonous puncture needle. Also known as THE ZOMBIE WALKS. Directed by Alfred Vohrer. Joachim Fuchsberger, Siv Mattson, Pinkas Braun.

HANDS OF A KILLER. See **PLANETS AGAINST US.**

HANDS OF A STRANGER (1962). Interesting variation on Maurice Renard's THE HANDS OF ORLAC in which a doctor must severe the damaged hands of a concert pianist and graft on the hands of "a stranger." While in previous versions the hands belonged to a killer, in this version we never do find out who they belonged to. Writer-director Newton Arnold creates good characters and dialogue but there are times when he goes off the Freudian end. Paul Lukather delivers an intense performance as the pianist driven by his own madness rather than anyone else's and the murders are treated as "accidents." As powerful as this film-noirish effort is, the best version is still MAD LOVE. Joan Harvey, Ted Otis, Irish McCalla, Larry Haddon, Sally Kellerman, Barry Gordon. (Worldvision; Sinister/C; S/Weird; Filmfax)

HANDS OF A STRANGLER (1960). Second film version of Maurice Renard's classic tale of a physician (Donald Wolfit) who grafts the hands of a murderer onto the wrists of a pianist (Mel Ferrer). Christopher Lee co-stars as a stage magician. French-British film was directed by Edmond T. Greville. Donald Pleasence, Danny Carrel, David Peel, Felix Aylmer, Basil Sydney. (From Sinister/C and S/Weird as **HANDS OF ORLAC, THE**)

HANDS OF DEATH. Video version of **BEYOND THE LIVING** (Lettuce Entertain You).

HANDS OF ORLAC, THE (1924). Silent version of Maurice Renard's horror tale, produced-directed in Austria by Robert Wiene (THE CABINET OF DR. CALIGARI) and starring Conrad Veidt and Fritz Kortner.

HANDS OF ORLAC, THE (1935). See **MAD LOVE.**

HANDS OF ORLAC, THE (1960). Video title for **HANDS OF A STRANGLER** (Sinister/C; S/Weird; Filmfax).

HANDS OF STEEL (1986). Cyborg assassin (Daniel Greene) can't carry out his new assignment when his human side prevails, so he goes on the run. Italian copy of THE TERMINATOR directed by Martin Dolman. John Saxon, Janet Agren, George Eastman. (Vestron; Lightning)

HANDS OF THE RIPPER (1971). Offbeat Hammer thriller directed by Peter Sasdy with Angharad Rees as the daughter of jolly Jack the Ripper. The L. W. Davidson script emphasizes psychological effects as Rees is obsessed with memories of gory murders and possessed by the spirit of not-so-dear old dad. Now she must carry out his unholy cravings and carvings. Eric Porter portrays the headshrinker helping her. Ripping good. Jane Merrow, Keith Bell, Derek Godfrey. (VidAmerica)

HANGAR 18 (1980). Intriguing variation of a legendary story in UFO annals (the 1947 Roswell incident) in which a flying saucer and a NASA missile collide in space and the bodies of aliens are retrieved from a desert crash site, then taken to a top-security military base. Where the film falters is in its cheap effects. Directed by James L. Conway. Robert Vaughn, Darren McGavin, Gary Collins, Philip Abbott, William Schallert, H. M. Wynant. (Worldvision) (Laser: Image)

HANGING WOMAN, THE. Video of **BEYOND THE LIVING DEAD.** (Western World; VCI; Unicorn)

HANGOVER SQUARE (1945). Following his performance as Jack the Ripper in THE LODGER, Laird Cregar, an obese, sinister-looking actor who looked years older than his age, again works with director John Brahm to penetrate to the depths of schizophrenic behavior as concert pianist George Harvey Bone, driven to murder in a repressive Victorian society. With this predictable story, success hinges on atmosphere and Cregar's aggravated performance. Brahm and screenwriter Barre Lyndon make it work. The ending is a concerto sequence edited to the Bernard Herrmann score. George Sanders, Linda Darnell, Glenn Langan, Alan Napier.

HANNAH—QUEEN OF THE VAMPIRES. See **CRYPT OF THE LIVING DEAD.**

HANS CHRISTIAN ANDERSEN (1952). Here's one moppets will slurp up as avidly as chocolate sodas: a sweet-flavored, sugar-coated biography of the Danish story-teller in music and song. This Samuel Goldwyn production, directed by Charles Vidor from a script by Moss Hart, spotlights a Frank Loesser score that includes ballet fantasies. Danny Kaye at his best. Jeanmarie, Farley Granger, John Qualen. (Embassy; HBO)

HANSEL AND GRETEL (1954). Costumed puppets enact the famous Grimm fairy tale, with music and songs by the Apollo Boys Choir. Voices by Constance Brigham, Anna Russell, Mildred Dunnock, Frank Rogier. Directed by John Paul. (Media; RCA/Columbia)

HANSEL AND GRETEL (1970). West German version of the old Grimm fairy tale, which is grim indeed, played more as a horror story by writer-director F. J. Gottlieb than as a kiddie yarn. The witch and the gingerbread house are all here, but watch for those Freudian overtones. Barbara Klingered, Francy Fair, Dagobert Walter, Herbert Fux. (Media)

HANSEL AND GRETEL (1982). FAERIE TALE THEATER episode starring Joan Collins as the wicked b . . . er, witch . . . with Ricky Schroder and Bridgette Anderson as the kids. Directed by James Frawley. (Video/Laser: CBS/Fox)

HANSEL AND GRETEL (1987). The Brothers Grimm tale is brought to the screen full-length by Cannon, with Len Talan directing. Hugh Pollard is Hansel, Nicola Stapleton is Gretel. Emily Richard, David Warner, Cloris Leachman. (Cannon)

HAPPINESS CAGE, THE. See **MIND SNATCHERS, THE.**

HAPPY BIRTHDAY TO ME (1981). Above average slasher flick, featuring a top star (Glenn Ford), a name director (J. Lee Thompson) and a major studio (Paramount). While this qualifies as an imitation of HALLOWEEN, it has ingenious twists and turns of its own. The plot revolves around teen-agers who are murdered one by one, and it seems obvious who the killer is . . . or does it? Pseudopsychiatrist motivations and mental-breakdown nonsense give the film a compelling perversity and sense of madness. Don't be put off by the shish-kebab skewering . . . it's only the tip of the . . . fork? Melissa Sue Anderson, Sharon Acker, Lawrence Dane. (Video/Laser: RCA/Columbia)

HAPPY GHOST II (1985). Chinese comedy in which the ghost is a high school teacher who becomes the brunt of student pranks. His use of spectral powers only gets him in trouble with the faculty. Directed by Clifton Ko Chisium. Raymond Wong stars as Hoi Sum-Kwai, the smiling, happy-go-lucky entity.

HAPPY HELL NIGHT (1991). Slasher crasher built around a "Hell Night," derivative of several serial-killer movies you will instantly recognize. Two students, as part of a hazing, are ordered to photograph a madman in an asylum, unaware he is a supernatural entity who, 25 years before, slaughtered fraternity members of Phi Delta Sigma at Winfield College. Those students who aren't massacred by the evil one's ice axe perform a ritual to send the demon back to Hell, under the guidance of Darren McGavin, who unleashed the creature way back when. Despite its potential for mayhem, HAPPY HELL NIGHT is peculiarly unexciting, for director Brian Owens completely fails to generate suspense or menace. In fact, the ugly-faced killer makes an occasional wisecrack in the Freddy Kroeger vein, unbecoming his evil character. Made in Canada and Yugoslavia. Nick Gregory, Laura Carney, Ted Clark, Charles Cragin.

HAPPY LAND, THE (1943). Sentimental mixture of nostalgia and propaganda, at times cloying, at times moving. In Santa Rosa, Calif., druggist Don Ameche and wife Frances Dee lead an ordinary lifestyle until a telegram informs them of their son's death. Devastated, Ameche slides into decline . . . until arrival of his long-dead grandfather (played with a wisp of Americana gentleness by Harry Carey), who recalls, in flashbacks, the wonderful life Ameche's son led before going to war. The film presents the son (Richard Crane) as a young man with many feelings and moods. Irving Pichel directed with quiet sensitivity. Adapted from a MacKinlay Kantor novel. Henry Morgan, Ann Rutherford, Cara Williams.

HAPPY MOTHER'S DAY, LOVE GEORGE. See **RUN, STRANGER, RUN.**

HARD ROCK ZOMBIES (1984). Tombstoned rock 'n rollers rise from their beat-meat peat graves to engage in a little bunk junk funk punk. The metal's heavy, man, heavy, when you're trying to push open the mausoleum door. The great-filled dead include E. J. Curcio, Geno, Sam Mann and Mick McMains. Produced-directed by Krishna Shah. (Vestron; Cannon)

HARD TIMES FOR VAMPIRES. See **UNCLE WAS A VAMPIRE.**

HARDWARE (1990). A messy post-holocaust world is the setting for this punk-funk flick in which an elaborate cyborg killing machine, dubbed Mark 13, goes on a rampage, allowing the effects boys to destroy property and life. Human characters include scavengers who cross the blighted, rubbled landscape and their women. Written-directed by Richard Stanley, who brings an unusually good feel for doom to otherwise familiar material to fans of the MAD MAX genre. Dylan McDermott, Stacey Travis, John Lynch, William Hootkins. Iggy Pop appears as Angry Bob. (HBO) (Laser: Image)

HARDWARE WARS (1977). Laugh-a-second, 13-minute parody of STAR WARS is a cult favorite, coming from the whacky mind of Berkeley filmmaker Ernie Fosselius. This bright, inspired send-up of Lucas' characters and concepts has ordinary home appliances replacing the spaceships and weaponry. On video, coupled with OTHER FILM FARCES that include "Bambi Meets Godzilla," "Porklips Now" and "Closet Cases of the Nerd Kind." (Warner Bros.; Pyramid)

HARLEM GLOBETROTTERS ON GILLIGAN'S ISLAND, THE (1981). Gilligan's Island is reinhabited by the characters from the popular comedy series along with the Globetrotters, stranded when their plane slam- dunks into the ocean. Professor J. J. Pierson (Martin Landau) and femme fatale associate Olga (Barbara Bain) discover a power source called Supremium and bilk the series regulars out of their share of the island. It's resolved with a basketball game between the boys from Harlem and The New Invincibles, a team of ridiculous-looking robots invented by Landau. It's feeble comedy but one can't help but feel nostalgia for the return of Bob Denver, Alan Hale, Jim Backus, Natalie Schafer, Russell Johnson and Dawn Wells. Constance Forslund is now the movie star and David Ruprecht has been added as Thurston Howell IV. Scatman Crothers guest stars as the coach of the Globetrotters. Peter Baldwin directed.

HARLEQUIN (1980). Puzzling Australian film with Robert Powell as a supernatural clown with powers of healing who saves a politician's dying son. The politician (David Hemmings) is a puppet of unscrupulous industrialist Broderick Crawford and must decide between righteousness, as dictated by the Harlequin, or corruption. The moral battle is compelling, Powell's performance is sympathetic and Simon Wincer's direction is tense. Also known as THE MINISTER'S MAGICIAN. (From Media as **DARK FORCES**)

HARRY AND THE HENDERSONS (1987). Excellent comedy in the vein of E.T., in which a middle-class Seattle family takes in a Bigfoot creature and learns to love him despite his clumsy, destructive ways and strong body odor. Rick Baker's hairy Harry is the real star of this Spielberg/Amblin production, which constantly tugs at the heart strings and isn't afraid to wallow in a little sentiment. The result is above-average entertainment with John Lithgow and Melissa Dillon heading the loveable Spielbergite family. David Suchet is an intense but still sympathetic villian (a hunter in pursuit of Bigfoot) and Don Ameche brings charm as an anthropologist. Oscar winner for make-up. (Video/Laser: MCA)

HARRY CREATURE

HARVEY (1950). This superb whimsical fantasy won a Pulitzer Prize for playwright Mary C. Chase and an Oscar for supporting actress Josephine Hull as a wonderfully daffy old aunt. More than just the story of oddball Elwood P. Dowd (James Stewart) who insists his constant companion is a six-foot-high invisible rabbit . . . it is a commentary on our society and the thin line dividing sanity from insanity. This screen version, adapted by Chase and Oscar Brodney, also makes poignant comments about our lack of communication. But enough heavy-handed analysis! This is a wonderful satiric comedy involving classic misunderstandings, character mix-ups and other old devices cleverly revitalized. It will stir your funny veins and touch your sensitive bones. Directed with a deft touch by Henry Koster. Cecil Kellaway, Jesse White, Wallace Ford, Charles Drake, Peggy Dow, Nana Bryant. (Video/Laser: MCA)

HATCHET FOR THE HONEYMOON, A (1971). One of Mario Bava's best directorial jobs is to be savored in this Spanish-Italian co-production. This assumes the point of view of a handsome designer (Stephen Forsyth), but beneath the charm is a psychotic killer who loves to hack up shapely models in wedding gowns. It is disconcerting to see someone mild-mannered turn into a fiend. Forsyth, a character patterned loosely on the Bluebeard legend, is haunted by visions of a childhood trauma that accounts for his antisocial behavior with the hatchet. His wife (Laura Betti) wonders: Whatever happened to nuptial happiness? And just when Forsyth thinks he's a masterful hacker, Betti's recently departed spirit returns in the form of a ghost to give him the abject willies. Bava demonstrates an understanding of how color adds effect to horror themes. A major contribution to European horror cinema. Also known as BLOOD BRIDES, AN AXE FOR THE HONEYMOON and THE RED SIGN OF MADNESS. (Charter; VCII; Media; Timeless)

HATCHET MURDERS, THE. Video title for Dario Argento's **DEEP RED** (HomeVision).

HAUNTED (1976). Enigmatic supernatural thriller written-produced-directed by Michael De Gaetano (UFO TARGET EARTH), focusing on an Englishwoman who fears she is the reincarnation of an Indian woman who practiced black magic. Stalking her is Aldo Ray. Virginia Mayo, Ann Michelle. (Direct Video; VCII; Simitar)

HAUNTED, THE (1957). See **NIGHT OF THE DEMON.**

HAUNTED, THE (1991). Restrained TV-movie in the vein of THE AMITYVILLE HORROR but without the special-effects exploitation. Based on a true story, it details the ten-year-long experiences Janet and Jack Smurl underwent in their Pennsylvania home. The real core of Darrah Cloud's script is the ordeal of Janet Smurl (Sally Kirkland) and how she kept her spiritual faith while demons tried to possess her family. This also deals with the Smurls' rejection by the Church when they sought exorcism help. Demonologists Lorraine and Ed Warren are portrayed by Diane Baker and Stephen Markle. Effective directing by Robert Mandel provides some chilling moments during the ectoplasmic materializations. Jeffrey DeMunn is cast as the long-suffering husband.

HAUNTED AND THE HUNTED, THE. See **DEMENTIA 13.**

HAUNTED BY HER PAST (1987). Cliched, substandard TV-movie relying on the old chestnut of the Haunted Mirror. In this case it's lovely Susan Lucci possessed by the wickedness and wanton abandon of a murderess from the days of witches, a spirit she is linked to by blood. Lucci is nice to look at and a real bitch when she gets mean but the story just limps along. John James plays her loving but dumb husband, Marcia Strassman and Robin Thomas are friends who help the stricken couple. Douglas Seale, Madeleine Sherwood.

HAUNTED CASTLE, THE (1969). See editions 1-3.

HAUNTED HONEYMOON (1986). Gene Wilder wrote-produced-directed and stars in this spoof, bringing only a faint-hearted glow to his protoplasm. It starts off promisingly in the 1940s when Wilder and fiance Gilda Radner—co-stars on radio's "Manhattan Mystery Theater"—perform a program with funny sound-effects gags. Wilder is riddled with phobias, and the only way to get rid of them is to scare him half (or fully) to death. When he and Radner arrive at the family mansion on their honeymoon, he's subjected to terrors (ugly man who walks on walls, hairy werewolf, etc.). But here the script flags and almost every gag sputters and dies. The exception is Dom DeLuise who appears in drag as the family heiress. Now he/she is funny! Jonathan Pryce, Paul L. Smith. (Video/Laser: HBO/Cannon)

HAUNTED HOUSE OF HORROR, THE. See **HORROR HOUSE.** (A house of another holler!)

HAUNTED PALACE, THE (1963). Good horror film produced-directed by Roger Corman, based on a poem by Poe and H.P. Lovecraft's novella, "The Case of Charles Dexter Ward." But any similarities are purely by accident. Charles Beaumont's script describes a warlock (Vincent Price) who possesses a descendant to wreak revenge against those who burned him at the stake. The most interesting device, besides creepy characters with fright faces, is a Thing in a well, a banished "Elder God," the one real Lovecraftian touch. Lon Chaney Jr., Debra Paget, Elisha Cook Jr., Leo Gordon. (HBO) (Laser: Image, with **CURSE OF THE CRIMSON ALTAR**)

HAUNTED PLANET, THE. See **DEMON PLANET.**

HAUNTED STRANGLER, THE (1957). "The Haymarket Strangler" was executed 20 years ago for garroting and slashing five women and now, in 1880 London, obsessed mystery writer/criminologist Boris Karloff is afraid the wrong man was accused. Soul possession sets in when Karloff picks up a scalpel at Scotland Yard's Black Museum and duplicates the heinous murders, his face a twisted, gnarly frightmess. Interesting variation on the Jekyll-Hyde theme; produced in Britain by Richard Gordon, directed by Robert Day with nice can-can scenes. Aka GRIP OF THE STRANGLER. Anthony Dawson, Elizabeth Allan, Jean Kent. (Media; MPI; Gorgon)

HAUNTED SUMMER (1988). This covers the same ground as Ken Russell's GOTHIC, but without the hysterical melodrama or startling images or sexual perversity. Once again it's the summer 1815 and those literary greats-to-be Lord Byron (Philip Anglim), Mary Wollstonecraft Godwin (Alice Krige), Percy Shelley (Eric Stoltz) and Dr. Polidori (Alex Winter) have gathered for games of sex, drugs and philosophical interchanges. The monumental crux is that Mary will become Mary Shelley and write FRANKENSTEIN. But the potential for horror is limited to a couple of drug-crazed sequences—hardly enough to warrant listening to Lewis John Carlino's turgid dialogue or enduring director Ivan Passer's melancholic pacing. Based on the novel by Anne Edwards, the film is well-intended but it plods along, more mysterious than enlightening. Laura Dern. (Media)

HAUNTED: THE FERRYMAN (1986). Horror novelist and his wife, resting in the country, realize one of his books is coming true when they are haunted by a drowned ferryman. British TV-movie directed by John Irvin. Adapted by Julian Bond from a Kingsley Amis story. Jeremy Brett, Natasha Parry, Leslie Dunlop. (Prism)

HAUNTING, THE (1963). Robert Wise's production is one helluva scary supernatural thriller, among the best ever made. Credit Wise's incredibly precise direction and Nelson Gidding's adaptation of Shirley Jackson's HAUNTING OF HILL HOUSE. It's truly scary because the horrors remain unseen and play heavier on the imagination. Richard Johnson, a psychic ghost chaser, picks "sensitives" to help him investigate an old mansion steeped in psychic phenomena. (Much of this is based on true cases.) Psychological problems of spinstress Julie Harris are related to the ghostly events. Guaranteed to chill you, and recognized as a classic. Clair Bloom, Russ Tamblyn, Lois Maxwell. (Video/Laser: MGM/UA)

HAUNTING FEAR (1990). Inspired by Poe's THE PREMATURE BURIAL, this Fred Olen Ray production would have been better titled THE IMMATURE BURIAL, so silly is Ray's attempt at an erotic thriller with PSYCHO underpinnings. Brinke Stevens is suffering from nightmares and hallucinations, unaware her husband (Jay Richardson) is having an affair with sexpot secretary Delia Sheppard. Brinke's only really good nightmare features Michael Berryman as a ghoulish morgue attendant. Most of Sherman Scott's slow-moving script focuses on the lovers as they plot to bury Brinke alive—a phobia caused by her father's death. Ray spices up the cast with Jan-Michael Vincent as a strongarm man posing as a cop, Karen Black as a hypnotist-psychiatrist, Robert Clarke as the family doctor, and Robert Quarry as a hoodlum but the story falls to pieces when Brinke goes on a cackling rampage in her nightgown. (Rhino)

HAUNTING OF HAMILTON HIGH. Theatrical title for **HELLO, MARY LOU: PROM NIGHT II.**

HAUNTING OF HARRINGTON HOUSE (1982). Dominique Dunne portrays a young inhabitant of an alleged haunted house whose camera picks up images of ghosts. Oddball characters (fortune teller, magician, suspicious maid, 95-year-old sisters, etc.) spring to life under Murray Golden's direction. Roscoe Lee Browne, Edie Adams, Phil Leeds, Vitto Scotti. (Video Gems)

HAUNTING OF JULIA, THE (1976). Moody, slow-moving British-Canadian horror film (produced in London), based on a lesser known Peter Straub novel. Mia Farrow, who has just lost her daughter, moves into a strange house haunted by a perverted young girl. Mia becomes obsessed with investigating the child's past. This is lyrical and full of ambience. under the subtle direction of Richard Loncraine. Tom Conti, Keir Dullea, Jill Bennett, Cathleen Nesbitt. (Media; Magnum)

HAUNTING OF M, THE (1979). Stylistic period piece (set in 1906) has the flavor of a Henry James ghost story and is steeped in subtlety. Gregory Nava's photography is exquisite and his wife, Anna Thomas, is a good director with a detail for character nuances. Be forewarned: the pacing is slow and the supernatural thrills almost nonexistent when a family is haunted by the ghost of a previous generation. Produced in Scotland. Sheelagh Gilbey, Nini Pitt, Evie Garratt.

HAUNTING OF MORELLA (1990). Morella is a witch who was burned at the stake and who now needs fresh corpses to restore life to her rotting corpse. This loose-as-a-goose adaptation of an Edgar Allan Poe yarn was directed by Jim Wynorski. David McCallum, Nicole Eggert (who keeps taking her cloths off, for intellectual reasons), Christopher Halsted. (New Horizons)

HAUNTING OF PENTHOUSE D, THE (1974). See editions 1-3.

HAUNTING OF ROSALIND, THE (1973). See third edition.

HAUNTING OF SARAH HARDY, THE (1989). TV-movie recycles the shopworn premise of the woman being driven crazy by a ghost—or is a plot afoot to drive her bonkers so someone can inherit the family fortune? Sela Ward portrays a sweet thing who once watched her mother drown in the surf near their mansion, The Pines. Now she's happily married to Michael Woods, but the spectral image of dear ole mom haunts her. Thomas Baum's adaptation of Jim Flanagan's novel, THE CROSSING, segues midstream from Sarah's point of view to her husband's, allowing for new surprises. Director Jerry London concludes with a snap ending. Polly Bergen, Morgan Fairchild. (Video/Laser: Paramount)

HAUNTING PASSION, THE (1983). Restrained TV-movie which handles its sexual theme tastefully: Jane Seymour is romanced by an invisible ghost in her coastside home. This deals as much with Seymour's problems with her TV newscaster husband (Paul Rossilli); he's undergoing a midlife crisis and cannot perform sexually, leaving an opening for the surrogate ghost. Hiro Narita's camera captures the rugged Pacific Coast and it comes together under John Korty's direction. Millie Perkins, Gerald McRaney, Ruth Nelson. (USA; IVE)

HAUNTS (1976). Only the bad scripting by Anne Marisse and directing by Herb Freed will haunt you . . . A madman wielding scissors attacks pretty girls in a small community, while in a farmhouse outside town May Britt fears that her father, Cameron Mitchell, is responsible for the scissors attacks. Aldo Ray hangs around town as the sheriff. E. J. Andre, William Gray Espy. (Media; Twilight)

HAUNTS OF THE VERY RICH (1973). TV-movie directed by Paul Wendkos borrows from the OUTWARD BOUND premise: Passengers aboard an airliner don't know how they got there or where they're going. Eventually they reach a tropical island (a la FANTASY ISLAND) where weird things happen. It's apparent Lloyd Bridges, Cloris Leachman and Anne Francis are caught up in a Is-it-Heaven-or-Hell? plot. The allegory is contrived by writer William Wood but compelling. Edward Asner, Tony Bill, Moses Gunn, Donna Mills. (Vidmark)

HAUSER'S MEMORY (1970). Based on a novel by Curt (DONOVAN'S BRAIN) Siodmak, this TV-movie explores the premise that scientist David McCallum can inject himself with the memories of another man. This knowledge also gives him the key to a baffling mystery, and he is pursued by spies. Directed by Boris Sagal. Susan Strasberg, Lilli Palmer, Robert Webber.

HAVE ROCKET, WILL TRAVEL (1959). Sci-fi slapstick, directed by David Lowell Rich, with such inanities as the Three Stooges, giant spiders, robots, a botched flight to Venus and cliches spoofing CAT WOMEN OF THE MOON and other howlers. Have TV/will switch . . . unless you're a diehard Stooges fan. Moe, Larry and Joe

De Rita, Jerome Cowan, Anna-Lisa, Bob Colbert.

HAWK OF THE WILDERNESS (1938). A 12-chapter Republic serial directed by William Witney and John English, and starring Mala and Herman Brix (soon to be Bruce Bennett). An uncharted island is inhabited by a jungle boy and superstitious natives living in dread of a volcano. An expedition arrives to rescue the boy and that sets into motion a series of narrow escapes. Monte Blue, Jill Martin, Noble Johnson, Tom Chatterton, William Royle. (Nostalgia Merchant; Video Connection)

HAWK THE SLAYER (1980). British sword-and-sorcery actioner, about rival brothers in search of supernatural powers, is structured like a Western, with fights staged as gunbattles. It reeks of Oedipus overtones as the evil brother Voltan (Jack Palance) seeks to destroy the good (John Terry, armed with Mindsword, a blade that appears out of thin air when needed). Settings are foggy and mystical, characters gritty and determined, and the effects, though not stupendous, are palatable. Director Terry Marcel tends to take it too seriously: acting is of the grandiose, scenery-chewing school. Roy Kinnear, Patrick Magee, Harry Andrews. (USA; IVE)

HAXAN (1921). Subtitled WITCHCRAFT THROUGH THE AGES (its video title from New York Film Annex or Embassy), this Swedish pseudodocumentary may strike an irreverent note with religious viewers lacking senses of humor. There are frolicking witches, warlocks and promiscuous friars, symbolic of the violence of the Catholic Church during the Inquisition. Re-released in 1969 with new music and narration. An antique piece, quaint, irresistibly laughable, written-directed by Ben Christensen. (On video as **WITCHES, THE**)

HEAD, THE (1959). Dr. Ood transfers the beautiful body of a strip-tease queen to the head of a hunchback. Or does he put the hunchback's noogin on the stripper's curvaceous body? Hmm . . . anyway, the result is that two equal one. Dr. Ood (Horst Frank) proves to be an oodle bit farfetched, and by calling the substance that keeps the body organs alive Serum Z, he has provided the film with a suitable grading. A German film also known as HEAD FOR THE DEVIL and THE SCREAMING HEAD. Written-directed by Victor Trivas. Michel Simon, Karin Kernke. (Sinister/C; S/Weird; Filmfax)

HEADHUNTER (1989). A voodoo curse resurrects an evil spirit named Chitatikumo that flies through the air, destroying natives before it moves on to Miami where it runs amok, much to the chagrin of cops Kay Lenz and Wayne Crawford. It always rips off its victims' heads, causing Lenz to remark, "Maybe we can find this guy's head around here somewhere. That would be nice, huh?" Sure would be more sanitary. Since the only way it can be destroyed, according to an old medicine man, is to dismember its body parts, scripter Len Spinelli has a chainsaw-massacre climax. Standard gore-fest stuff directed by Francis Schaeffer. Steve Kanaly, June Chadwick, John Fatooh. (Academy) (Laser: Image)

HEADLESS EYES (1971). Despicable junk that has zero entertainment value and disgusts from beginning to end. Down-on-his-luck New York artist Bo Brudin has his eye poked out while robbing a woman's apartment. This turns him into a serial killer with a patch over one eye. He kills women he sees on the street, then hangs their eyeballs from the ceiling or implants them in his works of "art." An insult to women in particular and mankind in general. Call it blind filmmaking with unsightful writing. Directed by Kent Bateman. (Vestron; Wizard; VCI)

HEADLESS GHOST, THE (1959). Herman Cohen is up to his usual cheap tricks, producing and co-writing (with Kenneth Langtry) a cheap movie not only headless but brainless. Made in England, this alleged supernatural comedy sports a juvenile plot about a spectral entity that has misplaced his head and terrorizes stupid teenagers. Don't worry, you won't lose your head over this movie. Directed by Peter G. Scott. Richard Lyon, Clive Revill.

HEARSE, THE (1980). Nicely crafted vehicle of horror (pun intended). Trish Van Devere, recovering from a mental collapse, settles in a town where she is unwelcome because the house she has inherited is allegedly haunted. At night, an antique corpse wagon turns up to terrorize her. The terror builds well under George Bowers' direction. Joseph Cotten, David Gautreaux. (Media)

HEARTBEEPS (1981). "Mechanical" comedy-love story with Andy Kaufman and Bernadette Peters as shelved robots who meet in a circuitry-adjustment factory and get oiled on each other, with Kaufman hoping he can soon get his piston into Bernadette's camshaft. The robot characters, however, are dumb and without charm, and their face masks are the five-and-dime variety. One funny feature is a comedy robot that tells Henny Youngman jokes. Now that's funny. Stan Winston and Albert Whitlock did the effects. Directed by Allan Arkush. Melanie Mayron, Christopher Guest, Randy Quaid. (MCA)

CATSKIL-55602

HEART CONDITION (1990). Dark comedy from director James O. Parriott in which racist, insubordinate L.A. cop Bob Hoskins dies from a coronary (bad eating habits, angry temper) and is given the heart of a black attorney just killed in a car crash. The ghost of the attorney (Denzel Washington) is visible only to Hoskins as they set out together to find the guys who set up Washington's car "accident." This partnership is tough for the guys to handle because Washington once took away Hoskins' white girl friend (Chloe Webb). Parriott vaccilates between comedy and serious crime and goes for some sentiment, but the drabness of the L.A. milieu and the grim climactic shootout make the film difficult to take to heart. It's also difficult to like Jack Moony (Hoskins' character), the way he barnstorms through this desolate movie. (Video/Laser: RCA/Columbia)

HEART OF MIDNIGHT (1988). Interesting more for its psychological portrait of a confused woman with a psychiatric history than for its supernatural elements, which are errantic and never brought into perspective by writer-director Matthew Chapman. Jennifer Jason Leigh is excellent as Carol Rivers, who inherits a night club called The Midnight from her deceased Uncle Fletcher, a sex pervert who ran a house of "sex games" in the upstairs rooms. Leigh lives in this haunted environment in a state of confusion, receiving help from crisis worker Denise Dummont (a strangely exotic woman), a stranger (Peter Coyote) and policeman (Frank Stallone) who doubts Rivers' sanity. There are a few suspenseful moments as Leigh creeps around the eerie night club, but the menacing factors of Uncle Fletcher remain muddled. Gale Mayron, Sam Schact, Brenda Vaccaro, James Rebhorn. (Virgin Vision) (Laser: Image)

HEAVEN CAN WAIT (1943). Worthwhile comedy produced-directed by Ernst Lubitsch, featuring Laird Cregar as the Devil, who must listen to playboy Don Ameche explain why he shouldn't be dispatched to Hell following his demise. A colorful depiction of American life at the turn of the century, fired up by a musical score by Alfred Newman, Gene Tierney, Charles Coburn, Spring Byington, Signe Hasso, Allyn Joslyn. Not to be confused with the 1978 Warren Beatty fantasy-comedy—that was based on HERE COMES MR. JORDAN. (Video/Laser: CBS/Fox)

HEAVEN CAN WAIT (1978). Amusing escapism comedy starring Warren Beatty who co-wrote with Elaine May and co-directed with Buck Henry. Beatty stars as a football star whose soul is prematurely taken and who demands a replacement body. What he gets is the aging carcass of a millionaire industrialist—and naturally he wants to play quarterback for the L.A. Rams. A remake of the 1941 HERE COMES MR. JORDAN with Julie

Christie, James Mason (as the overseer from above), Jack Warden, Dyan Cannon, Charles Grodin, Vince Gardenia, Buck Henry. (Video/Laser: Paramount)

HEAVENLY BODY, THE (1943). See third edition.

HEAVENLY KID, THE (1985). Unusually sappy teen-age fable in which dragster Lewis Smith is killed when his car plunges off a cliff and is doomed to ride a subway train for eternity . . . unless, he's told by a heavenly emissary named Rafferty (Richard Mulligan), he redeems himself by returning to Earth and helping nerdish Jason Gedrick make it with the chick of his dreams. That's what writers Cary Medoway (who also directed) and Martin Copeland call a premise. There's nothing heavenly about it. It's just plain dull and maudlin. (HBO)

HEAVENLY MUSIC (1943). MGM theatrical short depicting a boogie-woogie musician (Fred Brady) going to a Heaven that resembles an Art Deco night club where he enters a "Hall of Music" and faces a panel of composers (Beethoven, Wagner, Brahms) to see if he is worthy of becoming a new member of the board. Quite schmaltzy, but the music is good and the idealized view of Heaven is a curious one. Directed by Josef Berne.

HEAVENLY PLAY, THE (1943). See first edition.

HEAVEN ONLY KNOWS (1947). Also known as MONTANA MIKE . . . another Hollywood fantasy in which an angel descends from Heaven to become entangled in the affairs of mortals. The setting is the West; Archangel Robert Cummings has been chosen to reform a gun-slinger. Directed by Albert S. Rogell. Brian Donlevy, Marjorie Reynolds, Bill Goodwin, John Litel.

HEAVY METAL (1981). Spinoff from the illustrated fantasy magazine, an imaginative mixture of sci-fi, fantasy, horror and surrealism in different animation styles. The results are uneven but the highs outnumber the lows. The youth market was attracted by the hard-rock music track (Black Sabbath, Cheap Trick, Blue Oyster Cult) and comic fans dug the adaptations of Richard Corben and Berni Wrightson. One tale is about a cabbie in a half-destroyed, futuristic New York City, another is about a haunted B-17 during World War II. A green ball of "universal evil" threads in and out of the narratives, but otherwise the stories have little connection. A dazzling anthology. Directed by Gerald Potterton.

HEAVY TRAFFIC (1973). X-rated cartoon from Ralph Bakshi in the style of the underground comic magazines is certain to be heavy going for squares but grand fun for the drug generation as an artist, suffering from the malaisse of city life, retires to his drawing board to let his imagination run free. (Warner Bros.)

HE KILLS NIGHT AFTER NIGHT. Video version of **NIGHT AFTER NIGHTAFTER NIGHT (HE KILLS)** (Monterey).

HE KNOWS YOU'RE ALONE (1980). Psychokiller flick in which women are terrorized then murdered in a manner most foul. The slaughterer of brides-to-be plays ugly cat-and-mouse games with victims, striking when you least expect the knife to fall. It's terrifying in an excruciating way, and bloodcurdling. Directed by Armand Mastroianni. Don Scardino, Caitlin O'Hearney, Tom Rolfing. Tom Hanks appears in a cameo. (MGM/UA)

HELICOPTER SPIES, THE (1967). Episodes of TV's MAN FROM U.N.C.L.E. series with spies Robert Vaughn and David McCallum in two separate adventures. Leo G. Carroll is the assignment chief. Bradford Dillmann, Carol Lynley, Lola Albright.

HE LIVES. Video version of **SEARCH FOR THE EVIL ONE, THE** (Camp).

HELLBENT (1989). Down-and-out band leader Phil Ward makes a deal with the owner of a bar (the Devil) for success in exchange for his soul. Some deal. Lyn Levand, Cheryl Slean, David Marciano. Written-directed by Richard Casey. (Raedon)

HELLBOUND: HELLRAISER II (1988). Clive Barker's HELLRAISER was a dark, disturbing horror film, which reached new heights in horrifying imagery. This followup is just as unsettling as once again Kirsty (Ashely Laurence) must enter the labyrinth of Hell to confront the Cenobites and solve the Lament Configuration Puzzle Box. The eeriness is unrelenting, somber to its core, and the images are stark and painful. Peter Atkins' script (based on a Barker outline) is concocted from no logic known to man, and the story is chaotic. First-time director Tony Randel still manages to make it an auspicious debut. Clare Higgins, Kenneth Cranham, Imogen Boorman, William Hope. (New World) (Laser: Image)

HELL COMES TO FROGTOWN (1988). One whacked out MAD MAX imitation, which laughs at itself and has a modicum of directorial style from R. J. Kizer and Donald G. Jackson. Sam Hellman (Roddy Piper) is singled out in a post-Armageddon society as a breeding machine needed to "impregnate fertile women" and assigned to accompany Sandahl Bergman and Cec Verrell in a pink van into mutant territory, where fertile babes have been taken by renegades. The community of Frogtown is a campy one, inhabited by a race of toads and ruled over by Commander Toty. (characters destined to croak?) Adding to the whimsical nature of this nonsense is Rory Calhoun as old prospector Looney Tunes; adding to the villainy is William Smith as Count Sodom, a sadist with a vendetta against Hellman. The sequel is FROGTOWN II. (New World) (Laser: Image)

HELL CREATURES. See **INVASION OF THE SAUCERMEN.**

HELLEVISION (1939). See third edition.

HELL FIRE. See **INVASION OF INNER EARTH.**

HELLFIRE ON ICE. Video version of **SWEET SUGAR** (Hurricane).

HELLGATE (1989). Direct-to-video junk designed for visual shocks rather than coherency. A motorcycle gang, The Strangers, rapes the daughter of the man who owns Hellgate, a ghost-town attraction. Years later the father finds a crystal that (1) restores life to the dead and (2) exudes a destructive laser. The dead daughter lures Ron Palillo and pals into a trap for a showdown in Hellgate. None of this hangs together—but director William A. Levey and cast hang together, by the neck until dead. Abigail Wolcott (she of big chest dimensions), Carel Trichardt, Petrea Curran. (Vidmark) (Laser: Image)

HELL HIGH (1989). A little girl playing in a rural dollhouse accidentally kills an obnoxious biker and his girlfriend . . . 18 years later she's a science teacher on the edge of insanity, tormented by four dumb students. Of course, the tormentors soon become the stalked when the gal flips out and goes on a rampage. This is an excruciating viewing experience, probably more painful than the few deaths that it depicts in usual slasher-movie style. Producer-director Douglas Grossman is to blame. Maureen Mooney, Christopher Stryker. (Prism)

HELLHOLE (1985). Women-behind-bars sleazebagger from producer Samuel Z. Arkoff, who breaks tradition with asses-and-jugs-in-the-jug by adding a Frankenstein plot: Doctor Marjoe Gortner tests a brain serum on inmates of Ashland Sanitarium for Women, assisted by psychiatrist Mary Woronov to satisfy her bisexual perversities. (She offers an intense depiction of a lesbian.) But Gortner's "chemical lobotomies" create madwomen. Meanwhile, inmate Judy Landers (a dull actress) is

"Med-Tech's main assignment is to locate and impregnate fertile women in the wasteland. . . . Do you feel up to it?"

—A nurse to Sam Hellman (Roddy Piper) in ***HELL COMES TO FROGTOWN***

stalked by humming killer Ray Sharkey. Edy William fans will delight in watching her fondling women in soft porn segments. Director Pierre De Moro gives this trash style. Terry Moore, Robert Darcy. (Video/Laser: RCA/Columbia)

HELL HUNTERS (1988). Stewart Granger stars in this West German production as a Nazi who invents a spider serum that turns people into fascists. However, war criminal hunters Maud Adams and William Berger thwart the insidious plot. Produced-directed by Ernst R. von Theumer. George Lazenby, Eduardo Conde, Candice Daly. (New Star)

HELL ISLAND. See **ATTACK OF THE BEAST CREATURES.**

HELLMASTER (1990). "If God created the world in six days, and I can make Hell of it in one night, then God must be dead," cackles John Saxon as the evil biochemist conducting the Nietzsche Experiment in this gory, gooey, God-awful ghastfest. Wearing a three-needle hypo hand, which he shoves into victims, the crazed doc has a serum that turns teenagers and a nun into murderous monsters. In turn, the deformed maniacs attack teachers and students on the campus, killing with a scythe. More unpleasant than entertaining, but if you like to see puncture wounds, you'll get the points. Written-produced-directed by Douglas Schulze. David Enge, Amy Raasch, Edward Stevens.

HELL NIGHT (1982). Clever blending of slasher and haunted house cliches, building to many successful suspense sequences—you even grow to like four teen-agers locked in the old Garth Mansion overnight as part of the Alpha Sigma Rho initiation rites. The killers are deformed creatures hiding in tunnels under the house or in secret passageways within. Linda Blair runs screaming through the house, killer in hot pursuit. Well directed by Tom De Simone. Kevin Brophy, Vincent Van Patten. (Media)

HELLO AGAIN (1987). Misfire from director Frank Perry that asks: Can a once-mean dead woman come back from the grave and find acceptance from those she mistreated? A good answer is never provided. Shelley Long is Lucy Chadman, a pathetically clumsy, unliked woman who is the wife of a yuppish plastic surgeon. She chokes on a South Korean chicken ball and dies. Her zany sister (Judith Ivey) brings her back to life with astrological mumbo-jumbo. How she's rejected by hubby (Corbin Bernsen), re-establishes a relationship with her kitchen-loving son and finds romance with Kevin Scanlon form the core of this lethargic movie, which fails to generate any enthusiasm. Just say goodbye and forget it. Sela Ward, Austin Pendleton. (Video/Laser: Touchstone)

HELLO DOWN THERE (1969). See editions 1-3.

HELL OF FRANKENSTEIN, THE. See **ORLAK, THE HELL OF FRANKENSTEIN.**

HELL OF THE LIVING DEAD. See Vincent Dawn's NIGHT OF THE ZOMBIES (1983).

HELLO MARY LOU: PROM NIGHT II (1987). PROM NIGHT was your standard slasher flick—this is more a remake of CARRIE with dabs of THE EXORCIST. In 1957, superslut Mary Lou is accidentally set ablaze as Homecoming Queen. Thirty years later, on the eve of Hamilton High's Homecoming dance, sweet Wendy Lyon is possessed by the spirit of Mary Lou, with demonic winds blowing. Principal Bill Nordham (Michael Ironside, who helped to kill Mary Lou in '57) tries to save his son from death as the evening ends in an explosion of special effects—including a body breaking open and a different person popping out. Ron Oliver's script is predictable, as is Bruce Pittman's direction. Justin Louis, Richard Monette. (Video/Laser: Virgin Vision)

HELLRAISER (1987). Stephen King proclaimed British writer Clive Barker "the future of horror," and to prove it Barker wrote-directed his first feature, believing that "good fantastique should be dangerous, leading us into dreams and night, giving us a map of unexplored territory." HELLRAISER is certainly that: Its "charnel house" subject matter is truly graphic, and Barker is in a bloody rush to show us all the grotesqueries he can. Three demons called Cenobites escape from a small box in which they are trapped to create havoc in a house in England. A corpse is resurrected in the film's best sequence, then lures an old flame into a new love affair. An undercurrent of sexual perversity, coupled with blunt hammer murders, gives Barker's story a disgusting twist. There is a terrific monster guarding the corridor to Hell, and the Cenobites suggest intriguing concepts about pleasure and pain. (New World) (Laser: Image)

HELLRAISER II. See **HELLBOUND: HELLRAISER II.**

HELLRAISER III: HELL ON EARTH (1992). Despite the influence of Clive Barker as executive producer, this is a tired retread of those boys from Hell, the Cenobites, as they battle with Terry Farrell for possession of the Lament Configuration Puzzle Box, the gateway to Hell. Peter Atkins' script (from a story concocted with director Tony Randel) has Farrell crossing an eerie battlefield in a limbo between Heaven and Hell; the removal of a prostitute's skin; the slaughter of a night club's decadent rock 'n rollers; and Farrell's flight down a street as supernatural explosions occur around here. It's loaded with pyrotechnics, electrical zap rays and a plethora of other effects, and the rules of the game keep changing so you never can figure out what's happening. But the fans for whom this was intended could no doubt care less. Anthony Hickox (WAXWORK) directed. Doug Bradley, Paula Marshall. (Video/Laser: Paramount)

HELL'S CREATURES. See **FRANKENSTEIN'S BLOODY TERROR.**

HELLSTROM CHRONICLE, THE (1971). Nils Hellstrom is a scientist (Lawrence Pressman) with a theory the insect world will inherit the Earth, while mankind will die out, because bugs adapt faster than people to change. This theory is espoused with close-up footage of the insect world and its marvelous "beasts": bees, termites, carnivorous plants, spiders, locusts, etc. David Seltzer wrote the script. (RCA/Columbia)

HELP! (1965). Richard Lester's cinema verite/staged masterpiece blends the music and imagery of the Beatles at work and play with a wild, whacky plot in which the mod British musicians search for Ringo Starr's magic ring, stolen by a crazy cult headed by high priest Clang (Leo McKern). A marvelous satire on genre movies (dig that crazy incredible shrinking man parody) as well as a brilliant compendium of their best songs sung in the unlikeliest places. Victor Spinetti, Roy Kinnear, Eleanor Bron, Alfie Bass. (MPI) (Laser: Criterion)

HELP ME, I'M POSSESSED. See **POSSESSED, THE (1974).**

HENDERSON MONSTER, THE (1980). Talkative, actionless TV-movie is a thinking man's FRANKENSTEIN. Jason Miller is a lab investigator studying genetic diseases by improving genetic codes through "gene-splicing," a form of separating DNA to creates new forms of "super-bacteria." Scientists, politicians and journalists clash when Henderson (Miller) refuses to sign a paper that would force him to follow safety procedures. Ernest Kinoy's literate script deals with moral, political implications of man tampering with nature, which since has become a real controversial concern. Directed by Waris Hussein. Stephen Collins, Christine Lahti, David Spielberg, Nehemiah Persoff. (IVE)

HENRY: PORTRAIT OF A SERIAL KILLER (1989). An unsettling film attacked when released for being of questionable "moral content." That's putting it mildly. However, HENRY is not an exploitation movie but a sincere attempt by director John McNaughton (who co-wrote with Richard Fire) to profile a man who murders random victims. The nihilistic point of view, realistic psychological touches and downer ending add up to one shocking film, which never cops out to the bitter end. Michael Rooker is unforgettable as the serial killer. Also excellent are Tracy Arnold (as a young woman who falls in love with Henry) and Tom Towles as a low-life accomplice to some of Henry's crimes. (Video/Laser: MPI)

HENRY THE RAINMAKER (1949). See editions 1-3.

HERBIE GOES BANANAS (1980). Love Bug Volkswagen with a motor all its own is back for its fourth Disney comedy, breaking up counterfeiters in Mexico. On the wild ride: Cloris Leachman as Aunt Louise and Harvey Korman as Captain Blythe. Strictly for the Hot Wheels set. Directed by Vincent McEveety. Charles Martin Smith, John Vernon, Alex Rocco. (Disney)

HERBIE GOES TO MONTE CARLO (1977). Disney was hardly gambling with this comedy about a flying Volkswagen—it was the third entry in a popular series (following THE LOVE BUG and HERBIE RIDES AGAIN), although the engine is starting to break down. It's more car-velous fun and games in France and Monte Carlo. Dean Jones, Don Knotts, Julie Sommars, Roy Kinnear. Directed by Vincent McEveety. (Disney)

HERBIE RIDES AGAIN (1974). Disney's sequel to THE LOVE BUG stars Helen Hayes as Mrs. Steinmetz, the good witch, and Keenan Wynn as Alonzo Hawk, fierce ogre. Hawk wants to erect a skyscraper where Mrs. Steinmetz lives but she enlists the help of a flying Volkswagen (a former racing car) to stop him, leading to merry chases over the hills and streets of San Francisco. Ms Hayes flits through the proceedings oblivious to her perils, giving this tire-squealing fluff an added delight. Directed by Robert Stevenson. Ken Berry, Stephanie Powers, John McIntire. (Video/Laser: Disney)

HERCULES (1959). First in the Italian series about the son of Jupiter (Steve Reeves) using superhuman biceps in his search for the Golden Fleece. Sylva Koscina is lovely to look at, and delightful for Reeves to hold during romantic clenches, but there's little else to recommend in this poorly dubbed sword-and-sandals enterprise. Cinematography by Mario Bava. Directed by Pietro Francisci. Gianna Maria Canale. (Embassy; VidAmerica; S/Weird; VCI; Embassy)

HERCULES (1983). Stupefying Italian interpretation of Greek mythology, imitating CLASH OF THE TITANS by having Zeus and lesser Gods on Mt. Olympus overseeing the affairs of mortals. What makes this so unviewable is Lou Ferrigno (TV's "Incredible Hulk") . . . the muscleman is a helluva hunk, but when he tries to emote, it makes you realize how great Arnie Schwarzenegger is. Writer-director Lewis Coates sinks beneath camp to become insufferably dull. Sybil Danning (her breasts threatening to pop out of her halter like overripe tomatoes), Brad Harris, Rossana Podesta and William Berger are at the mercy of wretched dialogue. The special effects are amateurish . . . One's mind gibbers insanely. (Video/Laser: MGM/UA)

HERCULES II (THE ADVENTURES OF HERCULES) (1984). He's back, that invincible Son of Zeus, and the gods can have him. Lou Ferrigno continues to grunt with macho gusto as he searches for the Seven thunderbolts of Zeus, stolen by "rebel gods." So Herc the Jerc, on yet another odyssey, finds the warrior Goris, a Chewbacca-like beast; the Mire People in the Forbidden Valley; the Lair of Lakunt in the Land of the Little People; the Amazons of Sythia; and the Oracle of Death. Oh, we almost forgot to mention the Wasteland of Hisperia and Normacrill, the only substance in the entire Universe that can face Antus the Fire Monster. Ferrigno delivers his usual Method Acting. Written-directed by Lewis Coates. William Berger, Milly Carlucci, Sonia Viviani, Carlotta Green, Laura Lenzi, Margi Newton. (MGM)

HERCULES AGAINST THE MOON MEN (1964). Straight from wars on the lunar surface comes a race of moon mongrels ruled by a sorceress, Queen of the Lunar Loonies. The only man who can stop their moon-iacal deeds is Hercules, bulging to life as Alan Steel (brace yourself!). Written-directed by Giacomo Gentilomo. Jean Pierre Honore. (Sinister/C; S/Weird; Goodtimes)

HERCULES AND THE CAPTIVE WOMEN (1961). The lost kingdom of Atlantis is the setting for this Italian mess featuring Reg Park as a succulent strongman. He battles, in grunting fashion, an army of automatons and one big dragon. Fay Spain provides glamor as evil Queen Antinea. Directed by Vittorio Cottafavi. Ettore Manni, Gian Maria Volonte. (Rhino; Sinister/C; S/Weird)

HERCULES AND THE HAUNTED WOMEN. See **HERCULES AND THE CAPTIVE WOMEN.**

HERCULES AND THE HYDRA. See **LOVES OF HERCULES, THE.** (Muscles amore?)

HERCULES AND THE PRINCESS OF TROY (1966). Gordon Scott rides a mythical white horse impervious to arrows, muscle his way out of assorted death traps set by treacherous Trojan warriors, and stop a slug-like, sluggish sea creature from devouring Diana Hyland, she in a flowing white robe. Paul Stevens makes with the jokes as Diogenes. Everett Sloane narrates. Directed by Albert Band. (Sinister/C; S/Weird)

HERCULES AND THE TYRANTS OF BABYLON (1964). Stone-faced Rock Stevens is compelled to put his arms around sorceress Helga Line. Yes, she's handing him a Line; she's evil and must be stopped before half the world is destroyed and the other half is wiped out. In Babylon, events just babble on. Directed by Domenico Paolella. Mario Petri, Livio Lorenzon.

HERCULES AT THE CENTER OF THE EARTH. See **HERCULES IN THE HAUNTED WORLD.**

HERCULES GOES BANANAS. Video version of **HERCULES THE MOVIE** (Unicorn).

HERCULES IN NEW YORK. Video version of **HERCULES THE MOVIE** (MPI).

HERCULES IN THE HAUNTED WORLD (1961). "Hercules Descending" might be the subtitle for this adventure in Hell, where old Herc (beefcaker Reg Park) searches for the Magic Apple which will allow him to rescue a beauty held in bondage by evil sorcerer Christopher Lee. While the story is tired, and the action unconvincingly choreographed, there is a visual power to the fantasy sequences from director Mario Bava. Memorable images include Hercules crossing a rope above a pit of boiling lava, and an army of corpses charging while he hurls huge stones into their ranks. Also known as HERCULES AT THE CENTER OF THE EARTH, HERCULES VS. THE VAMPIRES, THE VAMPIRES VS. HERCULES and WITH HERCULES TO THE CENTER OF THE EARTH. Eleonora Ruffo, Giorgio Ardisson, Marisa Belli. (Saturn; Rhino; Sinister/C; S/Weird)

HERCULES IN THE VALE OF WOE (1962). "Woe" describes what you're in for. Not only must you endure beefcake hero (Kirk Morris) boxing with Mongolians but two confidence men from Rome who jump into a time machine and travel back to Hercules' days. Groan ohh ouch yikes . . . Frank Gordon, Bice Valori.

HERCULES OF THE DESERT (1964). Legendary muscleman isn't Hercules, he's Maciste. You'll be further baffled by men who cause avalanches and other disasters through echoing techniques, I think . . . I think . . I think . . . I think . . . The hero is Kirk Morris; the villain is writer-director Amerigo Anton. (Filmfax)

HERCULES, PRISONER OF EVIL (1967). Reg Park, who sucked away your breath in HERCULES AND THE CAPTIVE WOMEN, smashes up papier-mache scenery again as an over-muscled, empty-craniumed grunt hero of the loincloth vs. a sorceress who turns men into werewolves. Directed by Anthony Dawson. Ettore Manni, Maria Teresa Orsini. (Sinister/C; S/Weird)

HERCULES, SAMSON AND ULYSSES (1964). Three times as much grunting in this Italian spectacle, for as the title hints, you're in for a triple treat of muscle-flexing. Kirk Morris, Richard Lloyd and Enzo Cerusico comprise the tiresome threesome hunting a sea monster. For biceps bionics. Directed-written by Pietro Francisci.

HERCULES THE INVINCIBLE (1963). Italian potboiler has muscle maniac Dan Vadis battling a giant dragon. They should have breathed more fire into the script instead of the mouth of the creature. Directed by Alfredo Mancori. Spela Rozin, Ken Clark.

HERCULES THE MOVIE (1970). Zeus is ticked off because Hercules is knocking over pillars and throwing papier-mache boulders, so he banishes the sinew-swelling strongman to contemporary Earth, where his loin-

ARNOLD SCHWARZENEGGER AS HERCULES

cloth is in fashion. Of historical interest because Arnold Schwarzenegger stars (but as Arnold Strong). Directed by Arthur A. Seidelman. (From MPI as **HERCULES IN NEW YORK** and Unicorn as **HERCULES GOES BANANAS**) (Laser: Disc Factory)

HERCULES UNCHAINED (1960). Mythology-happy sequel to HERCULES, directed by Pietro Francisci. Steve Reeves returns as the biceps-bulging beefcaker and lovely Sylva Koscina is his wife with her own well-rounded muscles. Hercules loses his memory to a magical water and is a prisoner in the male harem of the Queen of Lidia. Dreadfully dubbed, but Mario Bava's camera work is excellent, and this Italian film is superior to its countless imitators. Primo Carnera does battle with Reeves. (VidAmerica; S/Weird; Sultan) (Laser: Nelson)

HERCULES VS. THE GIANT WARRIORS (1965). Zeus figures prominently in this Italian-French production, robbing Hercules (Dan Vadis) of his superstrength. What is the poor weakling to do now that the Giant Warriors are on the march? What else but throw sand into their faces. Directed by Alberto De Martino. Moira Orfei,

HERCULES VS. THE HYDRA. TV title for **LOVES OF HERCULES.**

HERCULES VS. THE VAMPIRES. See **HERCULES IN THE HAUNTED WORLD.**

HERE COMES MR. JORDAN (1941). Light-winged fantasy that established the trend for angels-from-Heaven-come-to-Earth plots. A dumb but ambitious prizefighter dies in a plane crash . . . kindly, white-haired heavenly emissary Mr. Jordan (Claude Rains) must find the boxer another body. The body picked is that of a just-murdered millionaire. Edward Everett Horton appears as Messenger #7013. Remade in 1978 as HEAVEN CAN WAIT. Directed by Alexander Hall. Robert Montgomery, Evelyn Keyes, James Gleason, John Emery. (RCA/Columbia) (Laser: RCA/Columbia; Criterion)

HERE IS A MAN. See **DEVIL AND DANIEL WEBSTER, THE.**

HER HUSBAND'S AFFAIRS (1947). Scientist discovers a fluid that removes one's hair and replaces it with thick new sprouts. Were Ben Hecht and Charles Lederer getting bald when they batted out this comedy? Directed by S. Sylvan Simon. Lucille Ball, Franchot Tone, Edward Everett Horton, Gene Lockhart. (Goodtimes)

HERITAGE OF CALIGULA—AN ORGY OF SICK MINDS, THE. Video version of **INCREDIBLE TORTURE SHOW, THE** (Magnum).

HERITAGE OF DRACULA, THE (1970). Jesus Franco-directed vampire flicker repeats DRACULA cliches in graphic fashion. Susan Korda, Dennis Price, Ewa Stromberg. Also known as LESBIAN VAMPIRES and THE SIGN OF THE VAMPIRE.

HERO AND THE TERROR (1988). This Chuck Norris vehicle, an urban thriller with horrific overtones, is based on actor Michael Blodgett's sexually explicit novel about mass murderer Simon Moon. Norris is a dedicated L.A. cop (nicknamed Hero) haunted by nightmares of his one-on-one with Moon, during which he was almost drowned. When Moon escapes an insane asylum, Norris musters up the courage to face the mindless killer again. While there are never any doubts of the battle royal to come, Norris registers more emotional response than usual, and there's a heavy emphasis on his romance with Brynn Thayer. Directed by William Tannen. Jack O'Halloran is menacing as Terror. Steve James, Jeffrey Kramer, Ron O'Neal. (Media) (Laser: Image)

HERO AT LARGE (1980). John Ritter plays Captain Avenger, a facsimile of a superhero promoting a new movie. A hired actor, Ritter takes on characteristics of the superhero and is soon in trouble. A signficiant comedy about the bravery and stalwart qualities we enjoy in our heroes, but which are hard for ordinary people to achieve. Funny and moving. Directed by Martin Davidson. Anne Archer, Bert Convy, Kevin McCarthy, Harry Bellaver. (MGM/UA)

HER PANELED DOOR (1950). See third edition.

HE, SHE OR IT. See **DOLL, THE (1962).**

HEX (1973). Theatrical title for **SHRIEKING, THE.**

HIDAN OF MOUNT BIENJOW, THE. See **INVASION OF THE GIRL SNATCHERS.**

HIDDEN, THE (1987). Exciting sci-fi thriller set (a la THE TERMINATOR) in an urban environment, which adds to the versimilitude of Bob Hunt's far-fetched tale. An alien creature that enters human bodies by way of mouth and controls the mind is loose in L.A. with strange FBI agent Kyle MacLachlan hot on the E.T.'s trail. Humans inhabited by the alien can't be killed easily, so this film is loaded with grim violence and slam-bang action sequences as MacLachlan and homicide cop Michael Nouri pursue the seemingly unstoppable killer. It's told mostly through action, with a minimum of exposition. Director Jack Sholder whisks the cast along, making this a knock-out action picture. Ed O'Ross, Clu Gulager, Claudia Christian. (Video/Laser: Media)

HIDDEN II, THE (1994). That hideous alien-demon from THE HIDDEN is back to wreak more havoc amidst special effects and action. (New Line)

HIDDEN HAND, THE (1942). See third edition.

HIDDEN POWER (1939). See editions 1-3.

HIDDEN RAGE. See **PERFECT VICTIMS.**

HIDE AND GO SHRIEK (1987). What begins as a cliched slasher-film set-up (eight purposely lock themselves into a furniture warehouse for a night of hide-and-seek games and love-making) develops into an interesting affair despite extreme brutality toward women. The fact the warehouse is full of mannequins allows director Skip Schoolnik to have some unusual fun. If you get through the excruciating first half, you'll find the second half, with large-breasted women stripping, rewarding enough. Donna Baltron, Brittain Frye, Annette Sinclair. (New Star) (Laser: Image)

HIDE AND SHRIEK. Video version of **AMERICAN GOTHIC** (Virgin).

HIDEOUS SUN DEMON, THE (1959). Robert Clarke produced, directed and stars in this cheapie, demonstrative of the mutated-monster craze of the '50s. He portrays a physicist exposed to radiation who, under sun rays, transmutates into a scaly, homicidal creature. Clarke conveys the torment this brings to the human soul, but such sympathetic touches are secondary to the murder and mayhem he wreaks. Just plain hideous. Also known as BLOOD ON HIS LIPS, TERROR FROM THE SUN and THE SUN DEMON. Patricia Manning, Del Courtney. (Rhino; Nostalgia Merchant; S/Weird)

HIDER IN THE HOUSE (1989). Chilling and disturbing psychological thriller in which escaped killer Gary Busey hides in the home of a wealthy family (Mimi Rogers and Michael McKean), spying on them and becoming obsessed with intervening in their affairs. Directed by Matthew Patrick. Candy Hutson, Christopher Kinder. (Vestron) (Laser: Image)

HIGH DESERT KILL (1989). Three mountain hunters and an old-timer in the New Mexico highlands are subjected to terror from an unseen alien presence. Old sci-fi hands will quickly see that the humans are being experimented on by Mr. E.T. Bad Creature. Chuck Connors is good as the old man and Marc Singer strikes an interesting chord as a macho hunter, and some of the desert photography is striking, but it's confusing cliches. Directed by Harry Falk. Anthony Geary. (MCA)

HIGHLANDER (1986). Stupendous fantasy-adventure, directed with great imagination by Russell Mulcahy, who employs a fluid camera to tell this cosmic-level story about a race of immortals who duel over the centuries with magical swords to claim "The Prize." This covers four centuries by cross-cutting between past and present to dramatize the growth of a Scotsman (Christopher Lambert) trained by mentor Sean Connery. Their common enemy is Kurgen, a malevolent immortal. The fights are brilliantly staged in this stylish screen fantasy. Watch for the great stairway sword duel. Roxanne Hart, Clancy Brown. (HBO) (Laser: Image)

HIGHLANDER 2: THE QUICKENING (1991). Australian director Russell Mulcahy is a visual stylist and once again he dazzles with camera movement combined with well-choreographed swordfights as the immortal warriors of the planet Zeist battle each other for power on Earth. Back are Christopher Lambert as Macleod and Sean Connery as his teacher Ramirez, resurrected from the dead to help fight Katana (Michael Ironside). The botched plot, which never makes clear the rules by which the immortals function, involves the depleted ozone layer in the 21th century, a barrier around Earth that has created perpetual night, a scheme between an Earth corporation and Katana, and a pretty woman (Virginia Madsen) thrown in for a perfunctory romance. (Video/Laser: Columbia Tristar)

HIGHLANDER: THE GATHERING (1993). This is the pilot for the syndicated series and one other episode. The main character is a relative (Adrian Paul) of Macleod, created by Christopher Lambert in the movie version. In the pilot Lambert guest stars to do battle with immortal villain Richard Moll; in the second adventure Paul seeks an old adversary with Vanity and Tim Reid guest starring. Directed by Thomas J. Wright. (Hemdale)

HIGHLY DANGEROUS (1951). See third edition.

HIGH PLAINS DRIFTER (1973). The oddest spaghetti Western ever—a Clint Eastwood vehicle so he can re-enact his Man With No Name. However, there's more to it when Eastwood, a sadistic gunfighter, rides into a small town and turns its people against each other. Get this: Eastwood is Death, avenging his own murder. Eastwood proves he is a superior director, capturing the fury and violence of this supernatural (?) oater. Verna Bloom, Billy Curtis, Marianna Hill, Jack Ging, Mitchell Ryan. (Video/Laser: MCA)

HIGH RISE. See **SOMEONE IS WATCHING ME.**

HIGH SPIRITS (1988). Madcap comedy set in a drafty Scottish castle which owner Peter O'Toole turns into a "haunted" tourist attraction. Writer-director Neil Jordan (A COMPANY OF WOLVES) keeps the slender idea afloat like so much ghostly ectoplasm by having riotous characters flapping about like the Three Stooges. The players (O'Toole as a balmy Scotsman, Steve Guttenberg as an American with a yen for 200-year-old ghost Daryl Hannah, and Beverly D'Angelo as Guttenberg's sexy wife) bolster the spectral elements. It will certainly lift your—ahem—spirits. Jennifer Tilly, Peter Gallagher, Liam Neeson. (Media) (Laser: Image)

HIGH TOR (1956). See first edition.

HIGH TREASON (1930). See first edition.

HIGHWAYMAN (1987). Supercorny superhero TV-movie, a clone of MAD MAX. Directed by Douglas Heyes in "A Team" style, this has government agent Sam Jones wearing Road Warrior garb and driving the battletruck STEALTH, which carries superweapons, a helicopter and a device that renders it invisible. Claudia Christian, Stanford Egi, Wings Hauser, G. Gordon Liddy. The opening narrative poem read by William Conrad has the line: "They say his father was a fiery rock." Fat chance.

HIGHWAY TO HELL (1991). Imaginative "black comedy" in which Chad Lowe and Kristy Swanson take a desert shortcut to Vegas. But it's a time-space continuum to Hell, where "Hell Cop" C.J. Graham kidnaps Swanson and Lowe pursues in his beat-up coup to Hell City. It's nonstop action-mayhem, puns, jokes about death, and the Devil as Beezle (Patrick Bergin, who brings comedy to the role). Plenty of pizzazz/energetic direction by Ate De Jong. There's such mind-blowing set pieces as a roadside cafe for the dead, a hall where famous evil men sit and bore each other, the river Styx, and severed hands that serve as "handcuffs." Adam Storke, Pamela Gidley, Robert Farnsworth. (HBO)

HI HONEY, I'M DEAD (1990). Angel from Heaven (one of those TV- movies!) helps a dead realtor return to Earth to assist his neglected family. Yech. Directed by Carl Kleinschmitt. Curtis Armstrong, Catherine Hicks.

HILLBILLYS IN A HAUNTED HOUSE (1967). Two music world celebs in a haunted house are subjected to floating apparitions, a gorilla and eyeballs peeping from behind paintings. They also tangle with a gang of spies and crazy doctors. Directed by Jean Yarbrough. The world's first—and last—Country and Western horror comedy! Ferlin Husky, Joi Lansing, Lon Chaney Jr., John Carradine, Basil Rathbone. (United; VCI)

HILLS HAVE EYES, THE (1977). A man's skull is split open with a crowbar; a caveman mutant rips the head off a canary and drinks its blood; a German Shepherd rips open a man's foot and throat; a knife plunges into a twitching torso; a man is tied to a yucca plant, drenched in gasoline and set aflame; a baby is kidnapped and prepared for barbecue. And that's during the prologue . . . yes, it's fun and games from Wes Craven, that modern intellectual who gave us THE LAST HOUSE ON THE LEFT. Craven's screenplay has a Cleveland family searching for a desert mine when it is attacked by degenerate cavemen and women who carry walkie-talkies and cackle withb homicidal glee. This pandering plunge into depravity and death does, however, have a social comment: When innocent people resort to violence, they become no better than their nemeses. John Steadman, Dee Wallace, Susan Lanier, Martin Speer, Robert Houston, James Whitworth, Michael Berryman. (Magnum; Harmony Vision) (Laser: Image)

HILLS HAVE EYES II, THE (1984). Back we go into Wes Craven territory, those hills around Yucca Valley where young folks inevitably meet their deaths at the hands of barbaric cannibals. A bus-load of eight youthful ones is stranded—among them a survivor of the original film plus a reformed cannibal from that same movie, now a vegeterian. What we get is a rock crushing a cyclist's head, a spear into a human chest cavity, a hatchet into a brain and other grisly deaths ending up in a charnal house of corpses. One of two survivors is blind, so writer-director Craven gets to play WAIT UNTIL DARK too. James Whitworth and Michael Berryman fare best as the bone-chompers. (HBO; Republic)

"She's possessed—Linda Blairsville!"

—One of the students in **HELLO MARY LOU: PROM NIGHT II**

HISTORY OF SCI-FI TELEVISION, A. See **40 YEARS OF SCIENCE FICTION TELEVISION.**

HITCHER, THE (1986). Psychokiller movie with such ill-defined motives and surreal plotting that the easiest way to watch is to accept it as a nightmare from which one can't wake up. David Howell, driving across Texas, picks up hitchhiker John Ryder (Rutger Hauer) to become the victim of Hauer's conspiracy to make him look guilty of grisly murders. Howell goes through harrowing experiences, with Hauer involving him with police and then protecting him from capture. There's an undercurrent of homosexual masochism in Eric Red's terse script with images of chains and leather, and a weird psychic link between the two men. There's a human finger on a plate of French fries, a woman tied between trucks and shotgun murders. Many find this despicable, others are intrigued by its enigmas. Directed by Robert Harmon. Jennifer Jason Leigh, Henry Darrow. (Video/Laser: HBO)

HITCHHIKER VOL. 1, THE. Video-packaged episodes of the half-hour horror/mystery series introduced on cable. In "WGOD Talk Radio," with Gary Busey and Geraldine Page, a radio preacher's past catches up to him. In "Hired Help," with Karen Black, a businessman meets an avenger from Hell. In "The Curse," Harry Hamlin portrays an amoral young man who goes to bed with a sexy woman and wakes up to find a snake tattoo on his arm coming to life. (Lorimar) (Laser: Image)

HITCHHIKER VOL. 2, THE. "Dead Man's Curve," "Nightshift" and "The Last Scene." Peter Coyote, Margot Killer, Darren McGavin. (HBO) (Laser: Image)

HITCHHIKER VOL. 3, THE. "Ghost Writer," "And If We Dream" and "True Believer." Ornella Muti, Willem Dafoe, Barry Bostwick. (HBO) (Laser: Image)

HITCHHIKER VOL. 4, THE. "Man's Best Friend," "Face to Face" and "Videodate." Michael O'Keefe, Sybil Danning, Shannon Tweed, Robert Vaughn. (Lorimar) (Laser: Image)

H-MAN, THE (1959). Lime jello lives, fans. A quivering puddle of ooze, radioactively stimulated, creeps, seeps and bleeps through Japanese streets, sucking up hapless humans. The eating scenes, prepared by GODZILLA special effects genius Eiji Tsuburaya, are scrumptuous as human flesh dissolves. You'll then laugh yourself silly at the dubbed soundtrack. That GODZILLA director, Inoshiro Honda, was at the helm. Rated H—for Hokum. Yumi Shirakawa, Kenji Sahara. (RCA/Columbia)

HOBBIT, THE (1977). Animated TV-feature based on J.R.R. Tolkien. Voices by Orson Bean, John Huston, Paul Frees, Hans Conried. Produced-directed by Jules Bass and Arthur Rankin Jr. (Sony; Warner Bros.)

HOCUS POCUS (1993). Witches who keep alive by sucking up the life essence of little children? Doesn't sound like a promising Disney premise, but since it's played as a comedy, with the trio of witches etched by Bette Midler, Sarah Jessica Parker and Kathy Najimy, this comes off as a pleasing grue. Described as "The Three Stooges on Broomsticks," HOCUS POCUS was directed by Kenny Ortega from a script by co-producer Mick Garris and producer David Kirschner and is set in Salem, Mass., where the tricky threesome is conjured up by teenager Omri Katz. (Video/Laser: Disney)

TRIO OF WITCHES IN "HOCUS POCUS'

HOLD THAT GHOST (1941). Frivolous Bud Abbott-Lou Costello comedy of haunted house antics. The screaming and yelling will keep you from dozing, and there are a few funny moments amidst the total nonsense. Richard Carlson and Joan Davis co-star with Evelyn Ankers, Universal's horror heroine. Directed by Arthur Lubin. Mischa Auer, Shemp Howard, Marc Lawrence, the Andrews Sisters. (MCA)

HOLD THAT HYPNOTIST (1957). See editions 1-3.

HOLD THAT LINE (1952). See editions 1-3.

HOLLOW GATE (1988). Four kids on a Halloween spree meet a killer who slices-dices trick or treaters to feed to his fun-loving dog. Katrina Alexy, Richard Dry. Written-directed by Ray Di Zazzo. (City Lights)

HOLLYWOOD CHAINSAW HOOKERS (1987). This campy spoof depicts—hold your breath—a cult of chainsaw-sacrifice worshippers with a demented, pot-bellied guru (Gunnar Hansen, Leatherface in THE TEXAS CHAINSAW MASSACRE) and sexually-charged prostitutes who murder in blood-spattered orgies. Script is credited to Dr. S. Carver and B. J. Nestles who are really director Fred Olen Ray and writer T. L. Lankford. This "Savage Cinema" production, loaded with bare breasts and clumsily simulated sex, is shaped as a private eye thriller as shamus Jack Chandler (Jay Richardson) looks for a missing teenager. Don't miss the Virgin Dance of the Double Chainsaws! The closing credits promise a sequel: STUDENT CHAINSAW NURSES. Michelle Bauer, Linnea Quigley, Dawn Wildsmith. Ray is now deserving of an anthropological study. (Camp)

HOLLYWOOD DINOSAUR CHRONICLES. Doug McClure plays host to a documentary about the prehistoric monsters that have stomped through Hollywood movies, covering "over 75 years of man-eating monsters and special effect!" (Rhino)

HOLLYWOOD GHOST STORIES (1986). Pseudo-documentary about Hollywood stars whose ghosts have reportedly haunted Tinseltown, including spectral sightings of George Reeves and Valentino. Sexy German actress Elke Sommer talks about a haunted house she once lived in. Narrated by John Carradine. Directed by James Forsher. (Warner Bros.)

HOLLYWOOD HAUNTING. Edward Mulhare hosts this excursion into the people who allegedly haunt Hollywood, such as Jean Harlow, Lionel Barrymore, Harry Houdini and other stars. A seance is held to raise the spirit of John Wayne. (MPI)

HOLLYWOOD HORROR HOUSE. See **SAVAGE INTRUDER.**

HOLLYWOOD MEATCLEAVER MASSACRE. See **MEATCLEAVER MASSACRE.**

HOLLYWOOD STRANGLER. Video version of **DON'T ANSWER THE PHONE** (Active; Video Treasures).

HOLLYWOOD STRANGLER MEETS THE SKID ROW SLASHER, THE (1979). One sleazy slasher flick, trying to pass itself off as a psychological study of a serial killer who photographs prostitutes and then strangles them. The strangler (Pierre Agostino) is searching for a "pure" woman. Meanwhile, the Skid Row Slasher kills winos and then runs to cleanse the spirit. It's one murder after the other, each unconvincingly staged, providing elongated glimpses at nude bodies. Although direction is credited to Wolfgang Schmidt, Ray Dennis Steckler has admitted he made this in rundown sections of L.A. It's thoroughly depressing, and you want to take a shower after seeing it. Carolyn Brandt. (Program Releasing Corp.; from Regal as **MODEL KILLER, THE** and Active as **HOLLYWOOD STRANGLER**)

HOLOCAUST 2000. Video version of **CHOSEN, THE** (Vestron).

HOLY TERROR. Video version of **ALICE, SWEET ALICE** (FHS).

HOMEBODIES (1974). Offbeat tidbit in which elderly folks in a highrise knock off those responsible for condemning their tenement. Dark macabre comedy, in the vein of ARSENIC AND OLD LACE but with perverse meanness. Written-directed by Larry Yust. Paula Trueman, Peter Brocco, Frances Fuller, Ian Wolfe, Kenneth Tobey. (Embassy; Sultan)

HOMECOMING NIGHT. See **NIGHT OF THE CREEPS.**

HOMEGEIST. Video of **BOARDING HOUSE** (Air).

HOME SWEET HOME (1980). Thanksgiving dinner is interrupted by a maniac just escaped from the local asylum; he wants the drumsticks for himself. Directed by Netti Pena. Jake Steinfield, Sallee Elyse. (Media; from Front Row as **SLASHER IN THE HOUSE**)

HOMEWRECKER (1992). After his attempt to create a nuclear-weapons-system computer ends in disaster, scientist Robby Benson decides to reprogram Star Shield with a woman's personality named "Lucy" (voice by Kate Jackson). Gradually, "she" falls in love with Benson and gets so jealous when he re-establishes a relationship with his estranged wife that she turns homicidal. This TV-movie, written by Eric Harlacher and director Fred Walton, works neither as a sensitive love story between man and machine nor as a sci-fi horror story about technology gone awry. Sarah Rose Karr. (Paramount)

HOMICIDAL (1961). Producer-director William Castle claimed the idea for this came to him in his sleep; we suspect it came while he watched Hitchcock's PSYCHO. There are similar plotting tricks in Robb White's script. Butcher knife murders are committed by a crazed woman, but nothing is really what it seems, so be prepared for surprises. Castle's gimmicks and sneaky tricks included a special "Fright Break" (not in TV prints). Jean Arliss, Glenn Corbett, Patricia Breslin, James Westerfield.

HONEY, I BLEW UP THE KID (1992). This follow-up to HONEY, I SHRUNK THE KIDS is a rollicking delight bringing back Rick Moranis' daffy inventor Wayne Szalinski, who is working on a secret project that results in the enlargement of his two-year-old son. The kid reaches a height of 50 feet and walks down Glitter Gulch in Las Vegas with his brother and his girlfriend in his pocket. The oversized effects are marvelous and the film unfolds at an amusing clip under the direction of Randal Kleiser. Lloyd Bridges, Ken Tobey, John Shea, twins Daniel and Joshua Shalikar, Marcia Strassman, Robert Oliveri. (Video/Laser: Disney)

HONEY, I SHRUNK THE KIDS (1989). Wacky Walt Disney fantasy-comedy that shows the comedy side to THE INCREDIBLE SHRINKING MAN and his household milieu. Rick Moranis portrays a nerdy but lovable inventor who can't get his electromagnet shrinking machine to work. And when it does, it's pointed at a group of youngsters, who are made so small they can't be seen floating in a bowl of Cheerios. The children have to make their way across the grassy backyard to home so fumbling dad can restore them to human size. Their adventures are highlighted by a ride on a bumblebee, a friendly and heroic ant, a killer scorpion and other things too large and small to mention. It's a joyous, innocuous adventure that scripters Ed Naha and Tom Schulman make palatable for young and old. Directed by Joe Johnston. Matt Frewer, Marcia Strassman, Kristine Sutherland. (Laser/Video: Disney)

RICK MORANIS

HONEYMOON (1985). Nonhorrific, psychological study of a killer who enjoys cat-and-mouse games with his victims. A French film made in New York, HONEYMOON depicts the plight of Nathalie Baye, stranded in America when her husband is sent to prison on a drug charge. She agrees to marry a man to acquire citizenship, realizing too late he's a jerk. Although John Shea as the killer portrays a slimy nice guy, this is so slowly paced, and so lacking in excitement, that it becomes hard to endure. Directed by Patrick Jamain. Greg Ellwand, Peter Donat, Cec Linder. (Lorimar; Warner Bros.)

HONEYMOON HORROR (1982). Clone of FRIDAY THE 13TH, amateurish in its effects—so bad, in fact, when an axe sinks into a human's brain, it falls out before the cut. At Honeymoon Cove, on Lover's Island in Texas, a husband finds his wife with another man and is trapped in a fire. Later, three pairs of newlyweds stop at the rundown resort to frolick, but meet bloody demises at the hands of a badly burned maniac. William F. Pecchi steals the movie (a mean achievement) as a pot-bellied redneck sheriff who chomps on an old cigar. No honeymoon, this. Directed by Harry Preston. (Sony)

HONEYMOON MURDERS (1991). Cheap, amateurish flicker shot in Florida by director Steve Postal, an unwatchable hunkajunk about newlyweds (Angela Shepard and Dave Knapp) terrorized by a phony looking monster at their honeymoon hideaway. Awful. (Postal)

HONEYMOON MURDERS II (1991). As awful as the nonflick that preceded it, this followup to the newlywed murders features more newlyweds (Donna Kozlowski and Tom Eckert) faced with a ghost of a characters killed earlier. The Postals (Steve and Gail) have undone it again. (Postal)

HOOK (1991). Steven Spielberg's paean to J. M. Barrie's PETER PAN finds Robin Williams portraying Pan as an adult who has forgotten his adventures in Neverland and doesn't know how to fly anymore. It's overflowing with warmth, sentiment and comedy-adventure as Williams forsakes his business as a financial "pirate" to return to Neverland to recover his kidnapped son and daughter from Captain Hook. As the blustering pirate, Dustin Hoffman so well submerges himself into the part that one forgets it's Hoffman. Williams is perfect for this child-adult role, because what is he but a grown-up kid. A brightly lit, opulent production that really comes to life when Williams flies, and when young pirates do battle with adult pirates aboard Hook's ship. Julia Roberts is an okay Tinker Bell and Bob Hoskins is a standout as the pirate Smee. Maggie Smith, Caroline Goddall, Amber Scott, Charlie Korsmo. it. (Video/Laser: Columbia TriStar)

HOOKER CULT MURDERS, THE. Video version of **PYX, THE** (Cinema Video Theater).

HOOK OF WOODLAND HEIGHTS, THE/ATTACK OF THE KILLER REFRIGERATOR (1990). Two amateur videos: HOOK OF WOODLAND HEIGHTS is a 40-minute job, made in Massachusetts by Mark Veau and Michael Savino. An escaped convict uses a barbecue fork for a hand and kills teenagers. ATTACK OF THE KILLER REFRIGERATOR is mercifully shorter (15 minutes) and depicts an angry kitchen appliance wreaking revenge against those who misuse its ice compartment. (Donna Michele)

HOPPITY GOES TO TOWN. Video of **MR. BUG GOES TO TOWN** (Spotlite; Republic) (Laser: Image).

HORN BLOWS AT MIDNIGHT, THE (1945). Mark Hellinger's comedy fantasy (directed by Raoul Walsh) stars Jack Benny as an angel sent to Earth to herald the Coming of Doom. For years Benny made derogative comments about this film on his radio and TV shows, and everyone agreed the comedian was justified in his long-running pentence. For nostalgia freaks. Dolores Moran, Alexis Smith, Allyn Joslyn. (MGM/UA)

HORRIBLE DR. HICHCOCK, THE (1962). Robert Flemying, as a lover of corpses who fondles the dead, seeks new blood to inject into his long-dead first wife in 1885 London. He selects Barbara Steele but she resists and screams (as is befitting the Queen of Horror) for her life, flitting through dank corridors and pursued by lightning storms. And then the first wife returns, looking a little grave-worn. Part of this movie's fun is watching for the visual references to Alfred Hitchcock (the doc's name was no accident). This Italian chiller, directed by Riccardo Freda (anglo-ized as Robert Hampton) with a sense of Gothic style and heightened hysteria, was trimmed for the U.S. The sequel was THE GHOST. Also known as THE TERRIBLE SECRET OF DR. HICHCOCK and THE TERROR OF DR. HICHCOCK. Teresa Fitzgerald. (Republic; S/Weird; Sinister/C; Filmfax)

HORRIBLE HORROR (1986). Hosted by the great TV host Zacherley, this contains clips from 50 "vintage" examples of "the best and the worst in horror and sci-fi." Included are SANTA CLAUS CONQUERS THE MARTIANS, GLEN OR GLENDA?, THE SNOW CREATURE, KING OF THE ZOMBIES, etc. (Goodtimes)

HORRIBLE HOUSE ON THE HILL. See **DEVIL TIMES FIVE.**

HORRIBLE ORGIES OF COUNT DRACULA. See **REINCARNATION OF ISABEL.**

HORRIBLE SEXY VAMPIRE, THE (1973). The title of this Spanish import with a mixture of nudity and bloodletting sums up its subtleties as directed by Jose Luis Madrid. Waldemar Wohlfahrt portrays the bloodsucking baron. Aka THE VAMPIRE OF THE HIGHWAY.

HORROR! See **CHILDREN OF THE DAMNED.**

HORROR AND SEX. See **NIGHT OF THE BLOODY APES.**

HORROR AT 37,000 FEET (1973). Airborne TV-movie about a jetliner suspended in midair because it is carrying a sacrificial druid stone. GRAND HOTEL in the sky becomes tedium at 37,000. Directed by David Lowell Rich. William Shatner, Roy Thinnes, Chuck Connors.

HORROR CASTLE (1963). Madman nicknamed "The Executioner," believed to be 300 years old, runs maniacally through an old German structure, killing with ancient torture devices. Christopher Lee portrays the caretaker, who should have taken greater care to protect guests Rossana Podesta and Georges Riviere. Directed by Anthony Dawson. Also known as TERROR CASTLE and CASTLE OF TERROR. (From Panther and Twin Tower as **VIRGIN OF NUREMBERG**)

HORROR CHAMBER OF DR. FAUSTUS (1958). Mad doctor Pierre Brasseur believes he can restore his daughter's marred beauty by grafting on the faces of kidnapped lasses. This French film, directed by Georges Franju, who collaborated with mystery writers Pierre Boileau and Thomas Narcejac, has numerous plot holes, as do the faces of victims when the doc gets through. The grafting sequences have an overabundance of hideous detail but that's what gives this cult favorite its charm. (Sinister/C; S/Weird; Filmfax; from Interama as **EYES WITHOUT A FACE**)

HORROR CONVENTION. Video version of **NIGHTMARE IN BLOOD** (Imperial).

HORROR CREATURES OF THE LOST PLANET. See **VAMPIRE MEN OF THE LOST PLANET.**

HORROR CREATURES OF THE PREHISTORIC PLANET. See **VAMPIRE MEN OF THE LOST PLANET.**

HORROR CREATURES OF THE RED PLANET. See **VAMPIRE MEN OF THE LOST PLANET.**

HORROR EXPRESS (1972). All aboard for terror and destruction! Cataclysmic evil emanates from the remains of a prehistoric monster being railed to Moscow via the trans-Siberian Railroad. The will of the monster invades the minds of the passengers because it needs to build a starship to return to its own galaxy. British-Spanish chiller with superior production values and gory effects. Also known as PANIC IN THE TRANS-SIBERIAN TRAIN. Directed by Eugenio Martia. Christopher Lee is an archeologist, Peter Cushing a scientist and Telly Savalas a Hungarian cop. (Media; Sinister/C; S/Weird; Goodtimes; Prism; Interglobal; Worldvision; Filmfax)

HORROR FARM. Video version of **DADDY'S DEADLY DARLING** (HQV).

HORROR HIGH. See **TWISTED BRAIN.**

HORROR HOSPITAL (1973). Emergency! Acting coach needed in Ward B to restrain Michael Gough from going bonkers in a fright mask as he tampers with patients' brains and cuts off their heads. Gory British import (also known as COMPUTER KILLERS) directed by Anthony Balch. Calling all film doctors . . . (MPI; Gorgon; from Bingo as **DOCTOR BLOODBATH**)

HORROR HOTEL (1960). British thriller reeking with atmosphere in crisp black-and-white photography. The setting is a New England community taken over by a witches' coven. Into the sinister town come a young man and woman seeking one of the coven's victims. Also known as CITY OF THE DEAD. Directed by John Llewellyn Moxey. Patricia Jessel, Christopher Lee, Betta St. John. (United; S/Weird; Amvest; Filmfax; Sinister/C)

HORROR HOTEL MASSACRE. See **EATEN ALIVE.**

HORROR HOUSE (1970). Psychotic killer attacks teen-agers in an old mansion outside London . . . which of the boppers is the attacker? Weak terror whodunit, also known as THE HAUNTED HOUSE OF HORROR, barely kept alive by writer-director Michael Armstrong. Jill Haworth does look good in miniskirts, though. Frankie Avalon, Dennis Price, Mark Wynter, Richard O'Sullivan.

HORROR HOUSE ON HIGHWAY 5 (1975). College students are targets for a killer wearing a Richard Nixon mask. Directed by Richard Casey. (Simitar)

HORROR ISLAND (1941). See editions 1-3.

HORROR MANIACS (1953). Britain's horror film star Tod Slaughter is grubby as hell as a corpse snatcher. Directed by Oswald Mitchell. Henry Oscar, Denis Wyndham. Also known as GREED OF WILLIAM HART.

HORROR OF DEATH. See **ASPHYX, THE.**

HORROR OF DRACULA, THE (1958). Hammer shocker, scripted by Jimmy Sangster and directed by Terence Fisher, was responsible for reviving Bram Stoker's classic vampire villain. This Gothic production brought international acclaim (and box office receipts) to the British studio, which continued in the same vein for 20 years. Christopher Lee captured the more subtle nuances of the Transylvanian count and the film is punctuated by its own miasma of Gothic mistiness. Peter Cushing essayed the Van Helsing role. Sometimes known as DRACULA 1958. Michael Gough, Melisa Stribbling, Carol Marsh. (Video/Laser: Warner Bros.)

HORROR OF FRANKENSTEIN, THE (1970). Writer-director Jimmy Sangster demonstrates less subtlety and more black comedy in this lowbrow entry in the Hammer-Frankenstein series. Ralph Bates, as the industrious Baron, is no replacement for Peter Cushing and David Prowse (Darth Vader's body in STAR WARS) is no surrogate for Christopher Lee as the Monster. The least effective of the Hammer outpourings. Veronica Carlson, Kate O'Mara, Dennis Price. (HBO)

HORROR OF IT ALL, THE (1964). See editions 1-3.

HORROR OF IT ALL, THE (1985). Documentary study of horror and mystery movies with material from classic films and interviews with key writers and film makers. Jose Ferrer narrates. (MPI)

HORROR OF PARTY BEACH, THE (1964). Bikini beach girls are ruthlessly attacked, the flesh ripped from their succulent bodies, by "Black Lagoon"-style amphibians created from radioactive waste dumped in the ocean. Wonderfully inept as the creatures crash a slumber party and carry the girls away—from the Neanderthal production values to the Stoned age cast headed by John Scott and Alice Lyon to the non-direction of Del Tenney. A classic of superior ineptitude. (Prism)

HORROR OF THE BLOOD MONSTERS. Video version of **VAMPIRE MEN OF THE LOST PLANET** (VidAmerica; Republic; Super).

HORROR OF THE STONE WOMEN. See **MILL OF THE STONE WOMEN, THE.**

HORROR OF THE WEREWOLF (1975). Spanish-produced entry in the Paul Naschy-Werewolf series, high on production but mediocre on special effects. It's a spirit of adventure that holds the viewer as an expedition embarks for the mountains of Tibet in search of the Yeti. But at the Pass of the Demons of the Red Moon, Naschy turns wolfman, attacking bloodthirsty bandits and searching for a magic plant that, when mixed with a maiden's blood, will restore him to normal. It's done in the Universal tradition with time-lapse photography and a sympathetic Naschy. Directed in snow country by M. I. Bonns. Grace Mills, Silvia Solar.

HORROR OF THE ZOMBIES (1973). Third entry in the Spanish "Blind Dead" series, also known as THE GHOST GALLEON, with writer-director Amando De Ossorio at the helm, features the long-dead Templar priests returning as rotting, cloaked corpses aboard a Spanish galleon that floats in a mysterious "other dimensional" fog, trapping seafarers. The victims are two buxom babes adrift in a motorboat, soon engulfed by the flesh-munching skeletal knights. Next comes a wealthy sporting goods magnate, a goofball scientist and more dames—fodder for the flesh fondlers. Effects are cheesy, but De Ossorio does inject atmosphere. Maria Perschy, Jack Taylor, Barbara Rey, Carlos Lemos. (Super; World's Worst Video/VidAmerica; Video Tours)

HORROR ON SNAPE ISLAND. Video version of **TOWER OF EVIL.**

HORROR PLANET (1981). Awful British ripoff of ALIEN, with touches of FRIDAY THE 13TH and DRACULA thrown in. On a research lab on a farflung planet in some faraway galaxy, a bug-eyed monster impregnates researcher Judy Geeson. With superhuman strength she vampirizes her research workers, pausing to give birth to mini- monsters. A bloody mess, literally, with plenty of weird electronic noises to keep you on edge. Nick Maley, who co-wrote with Gloria Maley, also did the sickening gore effects and creatures. Directed by Norman J. Warner. Robin Clarke, Jennifer Ashley, Stephanie Beacham, Victoria Tennant. Also called INSEMINOID. (Embassy) (Laser: Image)

HORROR RISES FROM THE TOMB (1972). Spanish rotboiler stars Paul Naschy as a beheaded knight who turns up in modern times as a sorcerer, terrorizing the inhabitants of an old castle. Directed by Carlos Aured and written by Jacinto Molina (Naschy). Emma Cohen, Victor Winner, Helga Line. (Embassy; S/Weird; Western World; Sinister/C; Filmfax)

HORROR SHOW, THE (1989). Made as HOUSE III by producer Sean Cunningham, then strangely retitled, this is a minimally effective tale, weak on all levels and built with poor foundations. L.A. cop Lucas McCarthy (Lance Henriksen) helps to put serial killer Max Jenke (the growling Brion James) into the electric chair, but Jenke's spirit returns to terrorize McCarthy with hallucinations. Jenke's target is the policeman's family—wife Rita Taggart and daughter Deedee Pfeiffer. An unending series of fumbled set-ups, anticlimactic and uninvolving. The film finally hits rock bottom when a turkey on a platter comes to life with Jenke's face on it. Directed by James Isaac. Aron Eisenberg, Matt Clark, Lawrence Tierney, Alvy Moore. (New World; MGM/UA)

HORRORS OF BURKE AND HARE, THE (1971). A few nights in the careers of the Body Snatchers, those grave disturbors of old Edinburgh who sold "goods" to surgical colleges in need of cadavers for anatomy classes. Directed by Vernon Sewell as BURKE AND HARE. Derren Nesbitt, Harry Andrews, Glynn Edwards. (New World) (Laser: Image)

HORRORS OF SPIDER ISLAND (1959). German-Yugoslav effort set on a tropical island where plane-crash survivors (talent scout and good-looking models) meet eight-legged monstrosities with vampire overbite. Producer Gaston Hakim lured writer-director Fritz Bottger into his spider's web. Also known as IT'S HOT IN PARADISE, BODY IN THE WEB, THE SPIDER'S WEB and GIRLS OF SPIDER ISLAND. Helga Frank, Harald Maresch, Barbara Valentin, Alex d'Arcy. (S/Weird)

HORRORS OF THE BLACK MUSEUM (1959). Herman Cohen titillator with sexually suggestive murders committed by a museum curator (Michael Gough). Each homicide is depicted in all its gory glory and Gough stirs up a formaldehyde float in a huge vat so he can "dissolve" his relationships with victims. Features the infamous needles-in-the-binoculars scene. Directed by Arthur Crabtree. Shirley Ann Field, June Cunningham, Graham Gurnow, Beatrice Varley.

HORRORS OF THE RED PLANET. Video version of **WIZARD OF MARS, THE** (Star Classics; Genesis; Republic).

HORROR STAR. See **FRIGHTMARE (1981).**

HORSE'S MOUTH, THE (1954). Waggish Irish oracle forecasts track results to newspaperman Joseph Tomelty. All of England, in the meantime, is in an uproar over how this affects the odds. Directed by Pennington Richards. Robert Beatty, Mervyn Johns.

HOSPITAL MASSACRE. Video version of **X-RAY** (MGM/UA; Embassy).

HOSPITAL OF TERROR. Video version of **BEYOND THE LIVING** (World's Worst; Super Sitters).

HOSTAGE—DALLAS. See **GETTING EVEN.**

HOT TO TROT (1988). A horse is a horse unless of course—he's a talking horse. Yes, that old chestnut, the articulate equine, was revived as a schtick for comedian Bob (Bobcat) Goldthwait, but he doesn't even place or show much. When the talking Don (voice by John Candy) is smarter than humans, it's a depressing comment on society. The script by Stephen Neigher (an alias no doubt, ha ha), Hugh Gilbert and Charlie Peters is so dumb no cannot help but whinny. The film's one funny sequence has "party animals" (dogs, cat, birds, duck, pig) invading Goldthwait's apartment, but otherwise this makes repeated plops. Plot has Bobcat inheriting his family's investment business, and getting hot tips from the horse, while battling with father Dabney Coleman. Directed bareback by Michael Dinner. Virginia Madsen, Jim Metzler, Cindy Pickett. (Video/Laser: Warner Bros.)

HOUND OF THE BASKERVILLES, THE (1939). First film to team Basil Rathbone and Nigel Bruce as Sherlock Holmes and Dr. Watson is not a masterpiece but still a good attempt to recapture the flavor of Doyle's novel. Setting is the foggy moors surrounding Baskerville Hall and the curse that taints its inhabitants. Directed by Sidney Lanfield. Richard Greene, Lionel Atwill, John Carradine, Wendy Barrie. (Video/Laser: CBS/Fox)

HOUND OF THE BASKERVILLES, THE (1959). Hammer's version of the Doyle classic stars Peter Cushing as the Baker Street sleuth, Sherlock Holmes, and Andre Morell as the winsome Watson. This is more effective than the Rathbone-Bruce treatment and will grip your interest with its hellish hound, mist-bound swamps and devious characters, even if the story about a family living under a dreaded curse is familiar. Directed by Terence Fisher. Christopher Lee is Baskerville. Miles Malleson, David Oxley. (CBS/Fox; Magnetic; United Artists)

HOUND OF THE BASKERVILLES, THE (1972). TV-movie strains for the Doyle touch but is an inferior version.

"The full red moon will soon shine in the sky. The demons will come out of their hiding places and their howls will be heard in the night, announcing death."

—Tibetan guide in **HORROR OF THE WEREWOLF**

Stewart Granger as Holmes doesn't project the mandatory qualities for the Baker Street sleuth and there is a lacking in budget and script to pull it off. Bernard Fox is a passable Watson. Directed by Barry Crane. William Shatner, Anthony Zerbe, Sally Ann Howes, John Williams.

HOUND OF THE BASKERVILLES, THE (1977). A genuine dog. British spoof of Doyle's Sherlock Holmes yarn that critics found singularly unfunny. The game is definitely not afoot with Paul Morrissey directing and Peter Cook and Dudley Moore writing. Re-edited for the U.S. and made all the worse for it. Moore, Cook, Denholm Elliott, Joan Greenwood, Spike Milligan. (Atlantic)

HOUND OF THE BASKERVILLES, THE (1983). British remake of the classic Doyle horror novel set on the English moors, with Sherlock Holmes (Ian Richardson) and Dr. Watson (Donald Churchill) hurrying to the aid of Sir Henry Baskerville, plagued by a family curse and a "hound from Hell" that stalks the bogs, tearing out human throats. Martin Shaw portrays Baskerville, Denholm Elliott is Dr. Mortimer and Ronald Lacey is Inspector Lestrade. Directed by Douglas Hickox. Nicholas Clay, Brian Blessed, Glynis Barber. (Laser: Japanese)

HOUNDS OF ZAROFF. See **MOST DANGEROUS GAME, THE** (from the producers of KING KONG).

HOUSE: DING DONG, YOU'RE DEAD (1986). Sean S. Cunningham's production blends supernatural and horror but can't decide whether to play it straight or zoom into camp. Hence, it unwinds with a troubled sense about its own soul. William Katt is mystery writer Roger Cobb, so haunted by his Vietnam experiences that he moves into a sinister Gothic house (where his aunt committed suicide) to write his memoirs. He relives his 'Nam experiences in flashbacks, a bug-eyed monster is coming out of a closet to get him, and he's off into another dimension in search of his long-missing son. The film, directed by Steve Miner, vacillates between stark thrills and comedic laughs played straight-faced by George Wendt (as a neighbor), Kay Lenz (as Katt's ex-wife, who still loves him) and Richard Moll as a soldier returned from the dead. HOUSE is a mood piece of loosely knit vignettes, vague characters and a sense of displacement. Call it weak foundations. (New World) (Laser: Image)

HOUSE II: THE SECOND STORY (1987). Inferior sequel in no way related to the first HOUSE. Director Ethan Wiley's script is neither funny nor scary as it takes on overtones of a stupid teenage comedy when Jesse MacLaughlin, dead 60 years, is dug up by his great great nephew. Royal Dano, in "dead man" make-up, plays it cantankerous and ornery as malevolent forces of the dead pursue a priceless Aztec crystal skull with magical powers. The protagonists are nerds who run around with a friendly worm with the face of a dog and a baby pterodactyl. Arye Gross, Jonathan Stark, Bill Maher, Lar Park Lincoln, Amy Yasbeck (the mermaid in SPLASH TOO). (New World) (Laser: Image)

ROYAL DANO

HOUSE III. See **HORROR SHOW, THE.**

HOUSE IV (1991). William Katt is back from the original HOUSE as Roger Cobb, who refuses to sell his old family manor because it was built over a sacred Indian spring. Cobb's soul is trapped there after his death in a car accident, and it's up to wife Terri Treas and crippled daughter Melissa Clayton to protect the spring from evil brother Scott Burkholder. Sean Cunningham's production, directed by Lewis Abernathy, vacillates between a sensitive portrayal of Cobb's wife and daughter coping with his death and a kitchen-sink horror thriller with an abundance of special effects. Ned Romero stands out as a wise old Indian. Denny Dillon, Dabbs Greer, Ned Bellamy. (New Line) (Laser: Image)

HOUSE AND THE BRAIN, THE (1973). See editions 1-3.

HOUSE AT THE END OF THE WORLD, THE. See **DIE, MONSTER, DIE.**

HOUSEBOAT HORROR (1989). Lake Infinity, where a crew is photographing a music video, is the setting for a series of slasher killings in this Australian imitation of FRIDAY THE THIRTEENTH. Directed by Kendal Flanagan. Alan Dale, Christine Jeston.

HOUSE BY THE CEMETERY, THE (1982). Writer-director Lucio Fulci, that sweet Italian who gave us GATES OF HELL, restrains himself (slightly) to tell this tale, aka THE HOUSE OUTSIDE THE CEMETERY, about a mother, father and son who move into Oaks Mansion, a creepy place (yep, next door to the graveyard), only to find it haunted by a ghoul named Freudstein, who once carried on "illegal experiments" with corpses. There are buckets of gushing blood as the killer's knife slits throats and plunges into torsos, a weird babysitter, a tomb in the hallway, a vampire bat that clings to the wife's head and hero's hand for several minutes, sinister rooms, a dark cellar, etc. Katherine MacColl, Paolo Malco, Ania Pieroni. Exteriors were filmed near Boston. (Vestron)

HOUSE BY THE LAKE, THE (1977). Canadian kill-thrill flick, produced by Ivan Reitman, who would make GHOSTBUSTERS and other major features. The stars, Brenda Vaccaro and Don Stroud, are an asset to writer-director William Freut who has set his story in a pastoral location to contrast the murderous mayhem of sadistic killers. Ample gore effects. Chuck Shamata, Richard Ayres. Also known as DEATH WEEKEND. (VC)

HOUSEGEIST (19??). Young girls check into a Beverly Hills boarding house run by Hank Adly, but some don't check out—alive. Detective Dean Disco investigates the murders. Cindy Williamson, Belma Kora. (Ariel)

HOUSE IN MARSH ROAD. Video version of **INVISIBLE CREATURE, THE** (Sinister/C; S/Weird; Filmfax).

HOUSE IN NIGHTMARE PARK (1973). British horror comedy about a house of deadly serpents, controlled by a family of snakes-in-the-brass. Director Peter Sykes thought of making a sequel but decided the plot had no re-coil. It's okay to laugh, though: this was designed as a vehicle for British comedian Frankie Howerd. Ray Milland, Kenneth Griffith. Also called CRAZY HOUSE and NIGHT OF THE LAUGHING DEAD. (Meteor)

HOUSE IN THE WOODS, THE (1957). Patricia Roc, Michael Gough and Ronald Howard bring to life a lifeless British supernatural nonthriller about a spirit of a murdered woman who returns from beyond for her revenge. Written-directed by Maxwell Munden.

HOUSEKEEPER, THE (1985). This adaptation of Ruth Rendell's novel "Judgment in Stone" is a tour de force for Rita Tushingham: Under Ousama Rawi's direction, she superbly portrays a psychotic woman who suffocates her cruel father, then moves to America to become a maid for a wealthy family. She captures the antisocial traits of a sexually repressed woman who disintegrates into a diabolical murderess. Ross Petty, Tom Kneebone, Shelly Peterson. (Lorimar) (Laser: Image)

HOUSE OF CRAZIES. TV version of **ASYLUM.**

HOUSE OF DARK SHADOWS (1970). Daytime serial DARK SHADOWS prompted producer Dan Curtis to make two features, of which this is the first. (NIGHT OF DARK SHADOWS was a sequel.) Jonathan Frid recreates Barnabas Collins, who rises from the grave and does the Dracula bit, turning residents of the family mansion into "blood brothers." Joan Bennett is Elizabeth, a fellow Collins. Barnabas ages to 150 years in one sequence, an effect achieved by Dick Smith. Produced-directed by Curtis. Grayson Hall, Kathryn Leigh Scott, Roger Davis, John Carlen. (MGM/UA)

HOUSE OF DARKNESS (1948). British film is a series of ghost narratives presented in flashbacks. Laurence Harvey, in an early role, is the stepbrother of a murdered man whose spirit is "restless." Directed by Oswald Mitchell. Leslie Brooks, John Stuart.

HOUSE OF DEATH (1981). This slasher flick, made in and around Shelby, N.C., depicts teen-agers frolicking at a carnival, then telling stories in Sunset Cemetery. That's when the machete-wielding killer attacks. You get a girl with an arrow in her shoulder who is decapitated on a merry-go-round, a double decapitation in a truck, a guy trapped in a grave whose hands are cut off, and other stabbings, slittings and torso penetrations. Also, two dead bodies floating down a river. Not a bad body count. And let's not forget the creamy breasts of the girls. Directed by David Nelson with total indifference. Susan Kiger, William T. Hicks. (Video Gems; Virgin Vision)

HOUSE OF DIES DREAR (1984). Quasisupernatural TV-movie, produced by the Children's TV Workshop, depicts the plight of young Howard E. Rollins Jr. when he and his family move into an old rural Ohio home once owned by a Dutchman who helped slaves escape through the pre-Civil War underground. The house's reputation for being haunted results in a spectral-like image scaring the black family half to death on a stormy night as well as the appearance of an old man, Pluto, who could be a ghost too. Based on a Virginia Hamilton novel, this is distinguished by a climax that spoofs NIGHT OF THE LIVING DEAD. Joe Seneca, Clarence Williams III, Moses Gunn (as contankerous River Lewis Darrow). (Home Vision/Public Media; Pied Piper)

HOUSE OF DOOM. TV title for one version of **HOUSE OF PSYCHOTIC WOMEN.**

HOUSE OF DRACULA (1945). Sequel to HOUSE OF FRANKENSTEIN, in which Universal amalgamated its popular monsters for maximum box office potential. You get Lon Chaney Jr. as the Wolf Man, John Carradine as Dracula and Glenn Strange as the Frankenstein Monster. There's a hunchbacked nurse, Lionel Atwill as a police inspector, and an assortment of creepy characters. This romp was to mark the finale to the studio's pseudoserious monster movies, and paved the way for Abbott and Costello horror comedies. Directed by Erle C. Kenton. Jane Adams, Martha O'Driscoll, Ludwig Stossel, Skelton Knaggs, Dick Dickinson. Make-up by Jack Pierce. (Video/Laser: MCA)

HOUSE OF EVIL (1968). One of four low-budget features made with Boris Karloff two years before his death. The film was caught up in courtroom battles after the death of producer Luis Vergara. The Jack Hill screenplay centers on a castle equipped with a torture chamber, and "torture" is exactly what this Mexican-financed movie is. Karloff plays sinister piano music when relatives gather for the reading of the will. It turns out he's a toy maker whose playthings are endowed with a homicidal spirit. Directed by Juan Ibanez and Hill. (Sinister/C; Filmfax; from MPI as **DANCE OF DEATH** and Unicorn as **MACABRE SERENADE**)

HOUSE OF EVIL. Video version of **HOUSE ON SORORITY ROW, THE** (Dura Vision).

HOUSE OF EVIL (1974). British TV cheapie starring Salome Jens as the sister to Jamie Smith Jackson . . . they're supposed to be in league with the Devil. And the Devil can keep them. Dabney Coleman, Andy Robinson, Sara Cunningham, Lou Frizzle. Directed by Bill Glenn.

HOUSE OF EVIL. TV title for **EVIL, THE.**

HOUSE OF EXORCISM (1976). What's needed here is a priest to exorcise awful imitations of THE EXORCIST, of which this Italian film is one. Excellently curved Elke Sommer brings sensuousness to her role as a possessed woman who spits out frogs! And there's Telly Savalas, doing an imitation of Kojak in search of Kolchak. Re-edited version of LISA AND THE DEVIL, with new footage of Robert Alda as a priest. Also known as THE DEVIL AND THE DEAD. Directed by Mario Bava. Alida Valli, Sylva Koscina. (Maljack; Amvest; from MPI as **DEVIL IN THE HOUSE OF EXORCISM, THE**)

HOUSE OF FEAR (1939). See editions 1-3.

HOUSE OF FRANKENSTEIN (1944). This followed FRANKENSTEIN MEETS THE WOLFMAN and marks Universal's first attempt to unite its money-making monsters. For price of admission you get Lon Chaney Jr. as the Wolf Man, John Carradine as Dracula and Glenn Strange as the Frankenstein Monster. Boris Karloff is Dr. Niemann, who escapes prison with hunchback killer J. Carrol Naish to restore supernatural creatures to life. This was such a hit, it was followed by HOUSE OF DRACULA. Lionel Atwill as the inspector, Elena Verdugo as the gypsy and George Zucco as a showman. Directed by Erle C. Kenton. (Video/Laser: MCA)

HOUSE OF FREAKS. See **DR. FRANKENSTEIN'S CASTLE OF FREAKS.**

HOUSE OF FRIGHT. See **TWO FACES OF DR. JEKYLL, THE.**

HOUSE OF HORRORS (1946). Rondo Hatton, who suffered from a disease of the pituitary gland and needed no makeup for his elongated, fearful face, was featured in a handful of pictures as the Creeper. In this, the first of the short-lived Universal series, Hatton is saved from death by a sculptor (Martin Kosleck) who sends him out to commit revenge murders. Hatton was an inept actor badly exploited in these shockers, which included PEARL OF DEATH and THE BRUTE MAN. He died the year this was released. Directed by Jean Yarbrough. Made as JOAN MEDFORD IS MISSING. Virginia Grey, Robert Lowery, Kent Taylor, Alan Napier, Bill Goodwin.

HOUSE OF INSANE WOMEN. Video of **EXORCISM'S DAUGHTER** (Sinister/C; S/Weird; Filmfax).

HOUSE OF MADNESS. See **DR. TARR'S HORROR DUNGEON.**

HOUSE OF MORTAL SIN. See **CONFESSIONAL.**

HOUSE OF MYSTERY, THE (1934). When a sacred Indian temple is violated, an old curse goes into effect, and the usual suspects gather in a mansion to face death one by bloody one. Gabby Hayes, Brandon Hurst, Ed Lowry and Verna Hillie trample the sets. Directed by William Nigh. (Sinister/C; Filmfax; Discount)

HOUSE OF MYSTERY (1942). See **NIGHT MONSTER.**

HOUSE OF MYSTERY (1960). Weird British film about a young couple (Jane Hylton, Peter Dyneley) out buying a house who listen to a macabre narrative from a mysterious woman. Another couple once lived in the house and a strange power afflicted their TV screen. Director Vernon Sewell's story delves into psychic phenomena, materializations, etc. Snap ending enhances a film pervaded by unseen horror and menace.

HOUSE OF PSYCHOTIC WOMEN (1975). Spanish psychokiller thriller—aka BLUE EYES OF THE BROKEN DOLL and HOUSE OF DOOM—with Paul Naschy, a man haunted by nightmares of strangling women, hired as a handy man by three strange women: One is bound to a wheelchair, another is a nymphomaniac and the third suffers from an injured hand in a restraining device. A killer armed with hatchets, knives, and garden rakes begins slaughtering blond, blue-eyed women, dropping their eyeballs into a bowl of water. None of this makes much sense and the removal of Naschy before the story's end is another oddball bit of plotting by Jacinto Molina and director Carlos Aured. When the killer is finally unmasked, the film goes all to hell. A curiosity piece with fine-looking femmes. Diana Lorys, Eduardo Calvo, Maria Perschy. (World's Worst Video/VidAmerica)

HOUSE OF SECRETS (1936). Hoary hokum with Sidney Blackmer and Holmes Herbert caught up in the mysteries of an old mansion: hidden panels, torture dungeon, mad scientist, outre experiments. Directed by Roland Reed. (Media; Filmfax; Sinister/C)

HOUSE OF SECRETS (1993). A TV-movie remake of Clouzot's DIABOLIQUE, reset in New Orleans with voodoo and the walking dead—touches not found in the novel by Pierre Boileau and Thomas Narcejac, THE WOMAN WHO WAS NO MORE. In that thriller a man and woman plot to kill another woman. But Clouzot switched it around to two women killing one man—a more perverse idea that appealed to the French director, to those who helmed the 1974 TV remake REFLECTIONS

OF MURDER, and to the makers of this lowkey piece of suspense. Bruce Boxleitner, the sadistic owner of a sanitarium, becomes the target of his weak-of-heart wife (Melissa Gilbert) and former mistress (Kate Vernon), who feed him spiked lemonade and drown him in a tub. But it soon appears that his restless, vengeful spirit has returned from the grave to haunt the wife. More cannot be revealed. This version is told as a flashback by voodoo priestess Cicely Tyson to investigating cop Michael Boatman. HOUSE OF SECRETS, except for a couple of by-now classic set pieces borrowed from the Clouzot film, is ordinarily filmed by director Mimi Leder. Originally called CONSPIRACY OF TERROR.

HOUSE OF SEVEN CORPSES (1972). Low budgeter with a decent cast forced into a wasteland of shoddy material. John Ireland, John Carradine and Faith Domergue wander through a feeble plot about the making of a horror film in a mansion (shades of FRANKENSTEIN '80). A resurrected ghoul knocks off a movie producer, a couple of performers and anyone else who wanders through the script. Maybe the ghoul didn't like producer-writer-director Paul Harrison's dialogue. (Video Gems; Hollywood Home Theater)

HOUSE OF SHADOWS (1983). Spanish horror thriller in which a woman, alone on the moor, witnesses a murder, but when authorities can't find the body, she begins to suspect she is hallucinating. Yvonne De Carlo, John Gavin, Directed by Richard Wulicher. (Media)

HOUSE OF TERROR (1972). Slow-moving psychological horror tale with little violence or gore when sexy nurse Jennifer Bishop takes a job tending a neurotic woman played with wonderful bitchiness by Jacquelyn Hyde. After Hyde kills herself in a tub filled with blood, she reappears as a lookalike sister and the plot thickens. Jennifer and boyfriend are out to get the family fortune and a series of doublecrosses and betrayals make this more a game of cat-and-mouse than of horror. Directed by Sergio Goncharoff. John "Bud" Cardos worked second unit. Arell Blanton, Mitchell Gregg. (Transworld)

HOUSE OF THE BLACK DEATH (1965). B-film cast (Lon Chaney Jr, Andrea King, John Carradine, Tom Drake, Jerome Thor) is wasted in this bleak duel between two warlocks. Chaney must resort to wearing the horns of the Devil. Director Harold Daniels lingers his camera on the shapely body of a belly dancer, proving he's an intellectual. Katherine Victor plays Lila the Witch. Dolores Faith, Sabrina, Sherwood Keith. Also known as BLOOD OF THE MAN BEAST, BLOOD OF THE MAN DEVIL and NIGHT OF THE BEAST. (Loonic)

HOUSE OF THE DAMNED (1963). Haunted house thudder exploits circus freaks living in a weird mansion. Harry Spalding's script features walking bodies missing vital pieces—heads, arms, legs, stuff like that. Maury Dexter produced-directed. Merry Anders, Richard Crane, Erika Peters, Richard Kiel. (Continental)

HOUSE OF THE DAMNED (1971). A young woman recently returned home from a mental institution is confronted by horrors in the family mansion. Donald Pleasence, Michael Dunn. Directed by Gonzalo Suarez. (Monterey; New Star)

HOUSE OF THE DARK STAIRWAY. See **BLADE IN THE DARK, A.**

HOUSE OF THE DEAD. Video version of **ALIEN ZONE, THE** (Dig that unreal estate!) (JLT Films).

HOUSE OF THE INSANE WOMEN. Video version of **EXORCISM'S DAUGHTER** (Sinister/C).

HOUSE OF THE LIVING DEAD (1973). Psychotic killer in a cape, who imagines he's out of an Edgar Wallace thriller, rushes around a plantation, Brattling Manor, knocking off family members. A mixture of Black Magic and the Old Family Curse. Aka DOCTOR MANIAC. Mark Burns, Shirley Anne Field. Directed by Ray Austin. (VCI; United; from S/Weird as **KILL, BABY, KILL**)

HOUSE OF THE LONG SHADOWS (1983). Updated version of George M. Cohan's mystery-comedy play, SEVEN KEYS TO BALDPATE, couched in Gothic imagery. Director Peter Walker assembled Vincent Price, Christopher Lee, Peter Cushing and John Carradine to portray weirdos in the eerie mansion Bllyddpaetwr (the setting is now Scotland) on the same night American writer Des Arnaz Jr. settles into the house to write a novel within 24 hours to win a $20,000 wager with publisher Richard Todd. Thrills are played tongue-in-cheek and the violence suggestive rather than overt. Sheila Keith is the blonde in the "long shadows." (MGM/UA)

HOUSE OF THE SEVEN CORPSES. Video version of **HOUSE OF SEVEN CORPSES.**

HOUSE OF THE SEVEN GABLES, THE (1940). A family curse hangs heavy over brothers Vincent Price and George Sanders in this adaptation of Nathaniel Hawthorne's ghost novel in which spirits return to haunt the living. Directed by Joe May. Margaret Lindsay, Dick Foran, Alan Napier, Cecil Kellaway, Nan Grey.

HOUSE OF THE YELLOW CARPET (1984). The aura of a knife killer rises up from the surface of a Persian Rug. Shag on you, murderer. Erland Josephson, Beatrice Romand. Directed by Carlo Lizzari. (Lightning)

HOUSE OF USHER (1960). Roger Corman's adaptation of Poe's short story, "The Fall of the House of Usher," makes excellent use of color to convey a sense of foreboding horror. Vincent Price essays Roderick Usher, a demented aristocrat who unwittingly entombed his sister alive. He spits out the scenery while the rest of the cast creeps along passageways, stares at degenerate Usher paintings and breathes Victorian decay. Scripted by Richard Matheson. (From Warner Bros. as **FALL OF THE HOUSE OF USHER, THE**)

HOUSE OF USHER, THE (1988). Unfaithful adaptation of Poe's "The Fall of the House of Usher," turned into a cheapjack damsel-in-distress thriller with cliches of the "old dark house" genre. Oliver Reed, as the super-sensitive Roderick Usher, holds back none of the histrionics when Romy Windsor falls into his clutches, nor is Donald Pleasence guilty of under-restraint when he appears as a demented degenerate with a killer-drill on his hook-hand. The sickening and unnecessary murder of a child would have offended Mr. Poe—a final insult to the memory of that great writer, whose uncopyrighted material serves producer Harry Alan Towers, director Alan Birkinshaw and irreverent screen adapter Michael J. Murray. Rent Roger Corman's 1960 version—that remains the definitive movie adaptation. Rufus Swart, Norman Coombes, Anne Stradi. (Video/Laser: RCA/Columbia)

HOUSE OF WAX (1953). Superb remake of MYSTERY OF THE WAX MUSEUM, horror in the Grand Guignol tradition, with Vincent Price as a "mad wax" museum curator/sculptor who covers victims with wax and displays them in his Chamber of Horrors. The setting is turn-of-the-century Baltimore, from fogbound streets to gaslit morgues. The 3-D composition lends maximum effect and there is an excellent fire sequence, as well as a memorable chase through dark streets. And, of course, the great paddle-ball scene. Frank Lovejoy is the concerned policeman, Phyllis Kirk and Carolyn Jones are among potential victims. Watch for Charles Buchinsky as the mute assistant—he later became Charles Bronson. Directed by one-eyed Andre de Toth. Paul Picerni, Roy Roberts. (Video/Laser: Warner Bros.)

BURNING WAX DUMMY

HOUSE OF WHIPCORD (1975). British chiller directed by Peter Walker in which Patrick Barr is a former prison warden who keeps a torture chamber to dole out punishment. Barbara Markham, Ray Brooks. (Fries; Monterey;

"I suffer from a morbid acuteness of the senses. Any food more exotic than the most pallid mash is unendurable to my taste buds. . . . The grating of the door bolt is like a sword struck to my ears. I can hear the scratch of rats' claws within the stone wall."

—Vincent Price as Roderick Usher in **THE HOUSE OF USHER**

IVE; American)

HOUSE ON BARE MOUNTAIN (1962). Vampire nudie flick set at Granny Good's School for Good Girls. Count Dracula, werewolves and babes run rampant in a romp of lascivious lechery. Directed by Lee Frost. Co-producer Bob Cresse stars with Jeffrey Smithers.

HOUSE ON HAUNTED HILL (1959). William Castle's best gimmick flick with Vincent Price as a sophisticated madman who invites five guests to Haunted Hill with the offer of $10,000 to anyone who can spend the night and still collect in the morning. Floating sheets, ghostly faces, skeletons, bubbling pits, doors and windows that fly open mysteriously, etc. etc. It's really great fun . . . Robb White's script even has a few genuinely frightening moments. Castle directed with his usual lack of subtlety, but here it worked. Richard Long, Elisha Cook Jr., Carol Ohmart, Carolyn Craig. (Key) (Laser: CBS/Fox, with **ATTACK OF THE 50-FOOT WOMAN**)

HOUSE ON SKULL MOUNTAIN (1973). It's the old "Ten Little Indians" theme with touches of voodoo and black magic when heirs gather in a weird house outside Atlanta. Directed by Ron Honthaner. Mike Evans, Victor French, Ella Woods, Janee Michelle. (CBS/Fox)

HOUSE ON SORORITY ROW, THE (1983). Yet again, another slasher terrorizer in which sorority sisters, on the night of a grad party, are murdered one by one. This marked the writing-directing debut of Mark Rosman, who filmed at an old house in Baltimore. Special effects by Rob E. Holland. Also called HOUSE OF EVIL. Kathryn McNeil, Eileen Davidson. (Vestron; from Dura Vision as **HOUSE OF EVIL**) (Laser: Vestron)

HOUSE ON STRAW HILL, THE (1976). Linda Hayden sees a murder committed in an old mansion, but authorities can't find a body. Eventually she discovers that a similar murder happened in the house 20 years ago. Udo Kier, of Andy Warhol's FRANKENSTEIN, portrays a novelist in the local village, and he starts having hallucinations. Also known as EXPOSE and TRAUMA. Written-directed by James Clarke. Fiona Richmond, Patsy Smart. (New World; Luna)

HOUSE ON THE EDGE OF THE PARK (1984). Despicable Italian film, shot in America, depicts razor-wielding murderer David A. Hess slicing up women's bodies, bashing in a man's head and performing disgusting acts of rape when he and an equally sadistic accomplice terrorize a number of hostages. This is an awful, gratuitous film to endure, even though it tries to pull off a moralistic ending. Annie Belle, Cristian Borromeo, Lorraine DeSelle. Directed by Ruggero Deodato. (Vestron)

HOUSE OUTSIDE THE CEMETERY, THE. See **HOUSE BY THE CEMETERY, THE.**

HOUSE THAT BLED TO DEATH, THE (1980). Episode of Britain's HAMMER HOUSE OF HORROR TV series re-edited for U.S. consumption. The setting is a middle-class home for a family plagued by weird happenings and ghastly sights (such as a severed hand in the refrigerator). A wall pipe breaks during a birthday party, spattering everyone with blood and gore. A twist ending is followed by another shock surprise. Tom Clegg directed. Rachel Davies, Milton Johns, Sarah Keller. Available on video from Thrillervideo with Elvira. On TV, this is featured with **GROWING PAINS**, a tale of possession: An adopted youth is taken to a country manor where a research botanist is working on DL-83, a diet supplement. The boy is taken over by the spirit of the step-father's real son. Francis Megahy directed. Barbara Kellerman, Gary Bond, Norman Beaton.

HOUSE THAT DRIPPED BLOOD, THE (1971). Good Amicus horror film (produced in Britain) written by a prestigious master of horror tales, Robert Bloch. The macabremeister interweaves four stories to recount a strange mansion's history. The main thread is an investigator, searching for a missing film star, who checks out previous tenants. Story one: A horror writer (a chip off the old Bloch?) is haunted by his creations. Story two: Ghostly figure haunts a wax museum managed by a lunatic. Story three: Witchcraft and voodoo dolls with Nyree Dawn Porter and Christopher Lee. Story four: The investigator discovers what happened to that missing star—and wishes he hadn't. Directed by Peter Duffell. Peter Cushing, Ingrid Pitt, Denholm Elliott. (Prism)

HOUSE THAT SCREAMED, THE (1969). Polished Spanish horror film set in a 19th Century boarding school for young women. A touch of class is provided by Lilli Palmer as the head mistress. The film excellently captures the oppressive sexual needs of the girls with erotic artsy intercutting. Heavy lesbian overtones and one intense hazing scene. Suddenly the girls are attacked by a knife killer. It's the style of director Narciso Ibanez Serrador that makes this enjoyable. Cristina Galbo, Mary Maude, John Moulder Brown, Candida Losada. Also called THE BOARDING SCHOOL.

HOUSE THAT VANISHED, THE (1974). A case of The Movie that Vanished once exhibitors got the word about this British-produced misconstruction about a madman with a knife who kills beautiful women. Various titles were tried (SCREAM AND DIE and PSYCHO SEX FIEND) but nothing helped. Directed by Joseph Larraz. Andrea Allan, Maggie Walker, Karl Lanchbury. (VCI; Media; from Lightning as **SCREAM AND DIE**)

HOUSE THAT WOULD NOT DIE, THE (1970). Genuine haunted house with spirits, witchcraft and black magic is spotlighted in this TV-movie. Directed by John Llewellyn Moxey from a telescript by Henry Farrell. Barbara Stanwyck, Richard Egan, Katherine Winn, Doreen Lang, Michael Anderson.

HOUSE WHERE DEATH LIVES, THE. See **DELUSION.**

HOUSE WHERE EVIL DWELLS, THE (1982). Lackluster, predictable "haunted teahouse" tale begins in Japan in 1840 and depicts a cuckolded samurai chopping up his wayward wife and her lecherous lover. Heads roll, arms fly, legs gambol and blood spatters. So much for the prologue. Cut to modern times as Edward Albert and Susan George move into the house, aided by U.S. Ambassador Doug McClure, an old family friend. Susan is haunted by three Japanese spirits superimposed over the footage, leaving nothing to the imagination. Gradually (as certain as death and taxes), the Americans are caught up in a love triangle and restage the samurai violence with karate and swingin' swords. Very unscary, even when Susan's daughter is attacked by crawling spider creatures (where did they come from?). Uninspired except for torrid love scenes in which bare-breasted Susan gives all she has—which is considerable. Directed by Kevin Connor. (MGM/UA)

HOUSE WHERE HELL FROZE OVER, THE. Video version of **KEEP MY GRAVE OPEN** (Clockwork).

HOWARD THE DUCK (1986). Expensive flop that never makes a duck character from another planet, trapped on Earth, believable. For one, the duck costume and make-up are phony—Howard looks like a midget in a Halloween costume. For another, the duck is stupid, when he should have been played seriously, in contrast to the ridiculous premise. Yes, the effects are stupendous . . . but without a story they produce only yawns. Howard, a quacker living on a parallel Earth, is sucked into an astronomical beam and swept across the Universe to Earth, where he falls for musician Lea Thompson and thwarts an alien overlord from conquering our planet. A monumental fowl-up for producers George Lucas and Gloria Katz, and director Willard Hyuck. Duck, you suckers. (MCA)

HOWARD THE DUCK

HOW AWFUL ABOUT ALLAN (1970). Strong Hitchcockian overtones permeate this TV-movie psychothriller about a blind man (Anthony Perkins), living with a daffy sister, who is either bonkers or is being subjected to a bizarre conspiracy. Directed by Curtis Harrington. Julie Harris, Kent Smith, Joan Hackett, Robert H. Harris. (United American; Edde)

HOW DOOO YOU DO (1946). See editions 1-3.

HOW I WON THE WAR (1967). British spoof on World War II in which director Richard Lester depicts a platoon of soldiers killed one by one—but each continues to fight as a ghost. Offbeat approach to an anti-war statement. Michael Crawford, John Lennon, Roy Kinnear, Alexander Knox, Jack MacGowran. (Video/Laser: MGM/UA)

HOWLING, THE (1981). Outrageous werewolf film based on the lousy paperback by Gary Brandner, which director Joe Dante threw away for a tongue-in-cheek narrative by John Sayles and Terence H. Winkless, reinforced by Rob Bottin's great state-of-the-art effects. Transmutation of man into werewolf is one of the most harrowing ever filmed—done with special masks and apparatus that permit us to see jaws growing into shape (complete with dripping teeth). Dante has loaded his yarn with visual in-jokes (Roger Corman and Forrest J. Ackerman have cameos). Dee Wallace, Patrick Macnee, Elizabeth Brooks, John Carradine, Slim Pickens, Kenneth Tobey howl it up. (Video/Laser: Embassy)

HOWLING II: YOUR SISTER IS A WEREWOLF (1986). Not a sequel, just crass exploitation. Psychic investigator/occult practitioner/wolf expert Christopher Lee is hot on the spoor of werewolves and subsidiary monsters, aided by Anne McEnroe (her sister was murdered by beasts) and boyfriend Reb Brower. The bloody trail leads to Transylvania and the Queen of the Werewolves (Sybil Danning). Just to watch her rip off her robe, or grow hair when she makes love to her male werewolf, makes this worth seeing. Grrrrrrrrr. A noisy morsel, loaded with effects, transmutating wolves and a gargoyle-like monster. Philippe Mora directs with emphasis on the action and Ms Danning's spectacular body, no doubt hoping to shore up the weak story co-scripted by Gary Brandner, creator of the HOWLING books. (HBO; Republic) (Laser: Image)

HOWLING III (1987). Somewhere in this third attempt to deal with the werewolves created by novelist Gary Brandner is a kitchen sink—just watch for it. What a mess: There's a town called Flow (wolf backwards), scenes from a movie IT CAME FROM URANUS, footage of Aborigines taken in 1905, three goofy nuns who turn into werewolves, and a movie director who looks like Hitchcock making THE SHAPE SHIFTERS PART 8. What's it really about? A tribe of werewolf people living in Australia and a runaway girl who gives birth to a marsupial human and stuffs it into her stomach pouch. Writer-director Philippe Mora makes this RETURN OF THE WILDERNESS WOLF FAMILY. HOWLING III is not even a howl—it simply defies description. Barry Otto, Max Fairchild, Imogen Annesley, Frank Thring, Michael Pate. (IVE; Vista) (Laser: Image)

HOWLING IV: THE ORIGINAL NIGHTMARE (1988). At least the first three HOWLING films weren't dull! This boring thudder, made in South Africa and L.A. by producer Harry Alan Towers, is set in a town called Drago—where howling can be heard from the woods. Only in the last minutes is there any action, and the special effects—except for a man melting down to his skeletal components—are shoddy. Romy Windsor suffers through as the innocent misunderstood heroine. Directed by John Hough, without his heart in it. Michael T. Weiss, Susanne Severeid. (IVE) (Laser: Image)

HOWLING V: THE REBIRTH (1989). Decent entry in this erratic series based on the novels by Gary Bradner, shaped as a whodunit in a castle outside Budapest. The castle has been closed since the 15th century because of a family curse, but one of several visitors is a hideous werewolf (a descendant of the family) that is killing guests in the secret chambers of the eerie place. Trying to figure out who is the hairy one is the game to be played. Directed with appropriate focus on suspense by Neal Sundstrom. Philip Davis, Citoria Catlin, Elizabeth She, Ben Cole. (IVE) (Laser: Image)

HOWLING VI: THE FREAKS (1990). Sharp improvement over previous sequels in this catch-all series, various elements having been borrowed from three books by Gary Bradner. The centerpiece is Harker's World of Wonders, a carnival of freaks and misfits featuring an alligator boy, a half-man/half-woman combination and assorted vagaries of nature. It unfolds under Hope Perello's direction with surprises and twists. Effects and monster make-up are better than competent and there's one good monster that resembles Nosferatu. Brendan Hughes, Michele Matheson, Carlos Cervantes, Antonio Fargas, Carol Lynley. (Live) (Laser: Image)

HOW TO MAKE A DOLL (1967). Gore specialist Herschell Gordon Lewis' sex comedy with a robot theme, in which a scientist creates beauties solely for sex. Robert Wood, Jim Vance. (S/Weird)

HOW TO MAKE A MONSTER (1958). Herman Cohen horrifier bravely dares to mock its own genre, making its weak script and mediocre make-up effects worth enduring. Hollywood make-up man Robert H. Harris, working at American-International Studios, is told monster movies are passe and his services no longer needed. An ingredient mixed into his cosmetics turns young actors into monsters—enabling Cohen to use all the fright masks from his earlier horror flicks. Targets of these monstrous murderers are studio bosses; they couldn't have picked a more deserving bunch. Gary Conway portrays the monsters. Directed by Herbert L. Strock. Paul Brinegar, John Ashley, Gary Clarke, Morris Ankrum, Walter Reed, Robert Shayne. (RCA/Columbia)

HOW TO STEAL THE WORLD (1968). Episodes of TV's MAN FROM U.N.C.L.E. Napoleon Solo (Robert Vaughn) and partner Illya Kuryakin (David McCallum) chase mad doc Barry Sullivan to prevent him from using poison gas to dominate human will. Eleanor Parker, Tony Bill, Leo G. Carroll. Directed by Sutton Roley.

HOW TO STUFF A WILD BIKINI (1965). . . . with the curvaceous body of Annette Funicello, that's how . . . plus half the starlets wandering Hollywood Boulevard. Buster Keaton (in one of his last roles) is a crazy witch doctor who conjures up a floating bikini. Then he floats Annette into the bikini, and then she floats all the way to America to meet Dwayne Hickman, Frankie Avalon and other beach party boys who dance to Les Baxter music. American-International beach movie drowns in campy waves directed by William Asher. Beverly Adams, Brian Donlevy, Mickey Rooney, Jody McCrea. (Warner Bros.)

HUDSON HAWK (1991). A grand disaster known in some quarters as HUDSON THE DUCK or BRUCE WILLIS MEETS ISHTAR. Star Willis talked producer Joel Silver into overinflating a simple idea into a spectacular action epic empty at its core. Safecrackers Willis and Danny Aiello perform some cute business when they retrieve a gold-making machine invented by Leonardo Di Vinci. The cute business stops when they come up against bizarre, oddball characters also after the machine. The story jumps willy nilly and goofy characters pop in and out. It's depressing to watch Andie MacDowell, James Coburn, Richard E. Grant and Sandra Bernhard wasted on such a chicken Hawk. A major comedown for director Michael Lehmann after HEATHERS. (Video/Laser: Columbia TriStar)

HUDSUCKER PROXY, THE (1994). A masterful satire on American industry and corporate business uniquely shaped as a fairy tale by writers-producers Ethan and Joel Coen, the latter also directing. This stylish, oft-surreal comedy depicts how a rube (Tim Robbins) takes over a major New York firm in 1958 and makes his success by creating the Hula Hoop. It is an allegory for many themes, and the Coens satirize film genres and introduce touches of Frank Capra and Preston Sturges into this weird, intriguing concept. The sets are as sumptious as they are weird, and the characters (such as Jennifer Jason Leigh's fast-talking reporter, Bruce Campbell's wise-guy newsman and Paul Newman's crusty, unfeeling executive) are cliches from an earlier Hollywood. A must-see for anyone who loves movies. (Warner Bros.)

HU-MAN (1976). French art film, described by writer-director Jerome Laperrousaz as "a reworking of the Orpheus myth," that proposes an odd concept: An actor (Terence Stamp) will put himself in dangerous situations and his fear will be televised to the world. Emotional energy from viewers will send him into the future or the past. Jeanne Moreau is Stamp's mistress. Agnes Stevenin, Frederick Van Pallandt. Music by Eric Burdon.

HUMAN DUPLICATORS, THE (1965). Unsubstantiated rumors have it this was financed by Xerox . . . Richard Kiel, E.T. humanoid Kolos, dispatched to conquer Earth, is so ridiculously stilted that his ineptitude is topped only by blonde sexpot Barbara Nichols portraying an undercover woman. Then there's the automaton-like performance of George Nader as the most wooden secret agent since Pinocchio the Spy. George Macready tries to make his mad scientist tolerable. One film you won't want to copy. Directed by Hugo Grimaldi. Richard Arlen, Hugh Beaumont. (IVE; Thrillervideo; from Star Classics as **JAWS OF THE ALIEN**)

HUMAN EXPERIMENTS (1980). Prison doctor believes that shock treatment will make criminals go straight. Crooked thinking, for sure. Sleaze-bag stuff directed by J. Gregory Goodell. Experiment ultimately fails. Linda Haynes, Jackie Coogan, Aldo Ray, Geoffrey Lewis, Lurene Tuttle. (VidAmerica)

HUMAN FEELINGS (1978). Nancy Walker plays God (!) who sends angel Billy Crystal to Earth to find honest folks in Las Vegas. TV pilot, directed by Ernest Pintoff. Pamela Sue Martin, Armand Assante.

HUMAN MONSTER, THE (1940). Bela Lugosi in a dual role could double your pleasure. On one hand, he is Professor Dearborn, proprietor of the Dearborn Institute for the Blind. On the other, he is Dr. Orloff, who tortures the blind and electrocutes them to collect insurance. Directed by Walter Summers in England as DARK EYES OF LONDON. Based on an Edgar Wallace novel. Remade in 1961 as THE DEAD EYES OF LONDON. (Thunderbird; VCI; Kartes; Filmfax; Sinister/C)

HUMANOID, THE (1979). Italian space adventure in which Richard "Jaws" Kiel portrays a rocket jockey who prevents Arthur Kennedy and Barbara Bach from conquering the Universe with the help of an E.T. guru. Routine STAR WARS clone, cheaply produced. Directed by George B. Lewis. Corinne Clery, Leonard Mann.

HUMANOID, THE (1991). Japanese sci-fi set on a farflung planet where a scientist creates a woman robot. Directed by Shin-Ichi Masaki. (Central Park Media)

HUMANOID DEFENDER. Retitled video version of **J.O.E. AND THE COLONEL** (MCA).

HUMANOIDS FROM THE DEEP (1980). Grotesque zombiemen from the depths answer the mating call by sexually attacking young women. Originally this was a less-violent film directed by Barbara Peeters, but producer Roger Corman shot new footage emphasizing amorous amphibians ripping clothes from wriggling sexpots. Starring Doug McClure, Vic Morrow and Ann Turkel, this climaxes (excuse me!) with a battle at a dockside carnival. (Warner Bros.)

HUMANOID WOMAN (1981). Russian film about Earthlings helping an alien (Helen Metelkine) whose planet Dessa is endangered by pollution and an evil ruler. Mady Sementsov. (Celebrity)

HUMAN VAPOR, THE (1960). Japanese film directed by Inoshiro Honda, that GODZILLA gyrator, in which a convict turns into a cloud of smoke to carry out crimes. This is anything but a gas. Performance by airy Yoshio Tsuchiya is vapid; others are full of hot air. Effects by Eiji Tsuburaya. (Video Gems; Prism)

HUMONGOUS (1982). Teenagers accidentally sink their yacht off a strange island where, back in 1946, a pretty woman was raped. The shipwrecked clods find the island deserted, but one by one are knocked off by a hairy wild man. There's nothing surprising or special about the "creature," and the characters are cannon fodder, without personalities. From director Paul Lynch and writer William Gray. Janet Julian, David Wallace, Janet Baldwin. (Embassy)

HUNCHBACK. Video version of **HUNCHBACK OF NOTRE DAME, THE (1981)** (Vidmark).

HUNCHBACK OF NOTRE DAME, THE (1923). Lon Chaney is Quasimodo, the deformed bellringer who falls in love with gypsy girl Esmeralda. This features the sequence in which the misshapen freak is publicly whipped on a turntable. For mastery of make-up and acting, this was Chaney's finest midnight hour. Directed by Wallace Worsley. Chaney closely followed Victor Hugo's description of the humped man and wore a device so he could not stand erect. Ernest Torrence, Patsy Ruth Miler. (Blackhawk; Kino) (Laser: Republic; Image)

HUNCHBACK OF NOTRE DAME, THE (1939). As the hunchback Quasimodo, the misshapen bellringer of Paris, Charles Laughton is more hideous than the stone gargoyles. Directed by William Dieterle, this second film version of Hugo's tumultuous tale of 15th Century France explores the murky medieval mind in a Gothic setting. High production makes this a masterpiece. Maureen O'Hara is the beautiful Esmeralda; Sir Cedric Hardwicke is the villainous Frollo and Walter Hampden is the Archbishop. Thomas Mitchell, George Zucco, Edmond O'Brien, Fritz Leiber, Rondo Hatton. (Nostalgia Merchant; RKO; Media; VidAmerica) (Laser: Image)

HUNCHBACK OF NOTRE DAME, THE (1957). Anthony Quinn is the bellringing gnome in this French adaptation lacking the classical elements of the 1939 version. Quinn portrays Quasimodo as though he were a Mongolian idiot—mumbling and slobbering a la Brando. Provocative Gina Lollobrigida is Esmeralda, the beauty Quasimodo hides in the cathedral. Directed by Jean Delannoy. Alain Cuny, Jean Danet. (Laser: Japanese)

"I feel as if Rod Serling is going to appear at any second."

—A doctor examining a werewolf in **HOWLING III**

HUNCHBACK OF NOTRE DAME, THE (1976). BBC-TV version of Hugo's novel, directed by Alan Cooke, is an early experiment in tape-to-film techniques. Warren Clark is the titular freak, Kenneth Haigh is Archdeacon Frollo and Michelle Newell is Esmeralda.

HUNCHBACK OF NOTRE DAME, THE (1981). Distinguished TV version of Hugo's tale of the bellringer Quasimodo, and his search for love in a world of hate. Writer John Gay etches fine characterizations and period dialogue that isn't stilted. Anthony Hopkins brings warmth to the misshapen human-gargoyle. Derek Jacobi, John Gielgud, Robert Powell, Lesley-Anne Down. Directed by Alan Hume. (From Vidmark as **HUNCHBACK**)

HUNCHBACK OF THE MORGUE, THE (1972). Repulsive Spanish debacle with the titular monstrosity (Paul Naschy, the poor producer's Vincent Price) stockpiling dead girls in his cellar, fighting off hungry rats and keeping company with a mad scientist and his Monster, a head floating in liquid. It's The Movie Theme That Never Dies. Directed by Javier Aquirre. (From All Seasons as **RUE MORGUE MASSACRES, THE**)

HUNCHBACK OF UCLA. See **BIG MAN ON CAMPUS.**

HUNDRA (1984). Thundra-ing U.S.-Spanish sword-and-sorcery actioner, a Conan imitation in the spirit of RED SONJA. Hundra (Laurene Landon) is the sole survivor of a village of massacred females and the femme warrior sets out in sexy costumes to wreak revenge. Turgidly directed by Matt Cimber, who co-wrote with John Goff. John Ghaffari. (Media) (Laser: Japanese)

HUNGER, THE (1983). Bizarre, offbeat vampire tale, directed with razzle dazzle by Tony Scott, brother of Ridley. While the shots are boggling and the ambience effective, this Ivan Davis-Michael Thomas adaptation of Whitley Strieber's novel has enigmatic characters in search of a plot. At times the narrative disintegrates into eye-zapping images and effects. The outre story deals with two vampires (Catherine Deneuve, David Bowie) living off human blood—until Bowie's aging accelerates and Deneuve needs a new partner. She picks Susan Sarandon, a researcher in human longevity, and seduces her in a tasteful lesbian sequence. The "makeup illusions" are by Dick Smith and Carl Fullerton. Dave Allen and Roger Dicken did the monkey effects. Cliff De Young, Beth Ehlers, Dan Hedaya. (Video/Laser: MGM/UA)

HUNGRY PETS. See **PLEASE DON'T EAT MY MOTHER!**

HUNGRY WIVES (1973). Writer-director George Romero's attempt to deal with witches in modern suburbia functions better as a psychology study of sexually frustrated, alcoholic housewives. This has the unorthodox editing of early Romero but it's a tedious ordeal, without sympathetic characters or a plot structure. Virginia Greenwald, Ray Laine. Originally entitled JACK'S WIFE. (From Vista as **SEASON OF THE WITCH**)

HUNK (1987). Charming fantasy-comedy in which nerdy Steve Levitt makes a pact with Satan's emissary (beautiful Deborah Shelton) to be turned into a beach bum with a body women can't resist (John Allen Nelson, some hunk indeed). Director Lawrence Bassoff's script is also nicely developed, emphasizing that beauty is only skin deep, etc. There are beautiful women to ogle and James Coco turns up as the Devil, assuming assorted disguises and, since he can travel back and forth in time, making amusing historical references to tragedies past and present. Robert Morse does a parody of Robin Leach as a TV personality named Garrison Gaylord. (Video/Laser: RCA/Columbia)

HUNTED, THE (1974). Variation on Richard Connell's famous story, "The Most Dangerous Game," in which a madman hunter pursues humans for sport. Lee Remick is one of the quarry the hunter would love to have mounted for his trophy room. Directed by Douglas Fithian. Michael Hinz, Ivan Desny. (Direct; Film Classics)

HUNTER (1971). TV-pilot that sat for two years before being tossed out on the network. Special agent David Hunter (John Vernon) poses as conceited scientist Dr. Praetorius, involved in killer-gas experiments and brain-washed by enemy agents. Elements from THE WIZARD OF OZ are incorporated into the brainwashing and drive Vernon unconvincingly to the edge of madness. Huh? Borders on the undistinguished. Steve Ihnat, Sabina Scharf, Edward Binns, Fritz Weaver. (Lorimar)

HUNTER, THE. See **SCREAM OF THE WOLF.**

HUNTER'S BLOOD (1987). Father-son Clu Gulager and Samuel Bottoms take three pals on a hunting trip on the Arkansas border, encountering murderous rednecks who operate the Razorback Meat Co. A bloodbath ensues. Missing the characters, poetry and deeper themes of DELIVERANCE, this is a senseless retread. Directed by Robert C. Hughes. Ken Swofford, Joey Travolta. (Video/Laser: Embassy/Nelson)

HUNTERS OF THE GOLDEN COBRA (1982). Italian adventure-fantasy in the Indiana Jones style . . . not as classy but still rousing good action as a British Intelligence officer and an American soldier (David Warbeck) pursue the precious Golden Cobra, a relic containing supernatural destructive powers. Warbeck meets a tribe of blow-gun-packin' natives, ruled by a white woman, but is wounded and passes out. Later, he and the English spy undergo adventures in the Philippines with a native cult called the Awoks. Directed by Anthony Dawson. Rena Abadesa, Almanta Suska. (Vestron)

HURRICANE ISLAND (1950). See editions 1-3.

HUSH, HUSH, SWEET CHARLOTTE (1964). Following the success of WHAT EVER HAPPENED TO BABY JANE?, producer-director Robert Aldrich duplicated the formula of daffy old crones played by one-time Hollywood greats. Bette Davis is a demented spinster, haunted by a 30-year-old murder and seeing dead bodies all over the old family mansion. It's treated by Aldrich as a macabre joke and you'll see through the red herrings without much difficulty. What makes this memorable is the decaying Southern plantation and decadent characters to match. Joseph Cotten, Olivia de Havilland, Agnes Moorehead, Victor Buono, Bruce Dern, Mary Astor, William Campbell. (Video/Laser: CBS/Fox)

HYDRA. Variant video version of **ATTACK OF THE SWAMP CREATURES** (Lettuce Entertain You).

HYENA OF LONDON, THE (1963). Italian horror flick directed by Gino Mancini and starring Tony Kendall, Alan Collins, Claude Dantes. (Loonic)

HYPER SAPIEN: PEOPLE FROM ANOTHER STAR (1986). Innocuous, pleasant sci-fi fantasy-comedy for children. Humanoid aliens (Sydney Penny as Robyn and Rosie Marcel as Tavy) teleport to Earth to prove that their Taros is a good planet, taking with them a furry, three-eyed creature called the Tri-Lat Kirbi—which provides this Canadian film with its best comedy when Tri-Lat is befriended by Keenan Wynn as a cantankerous grandfather. (It was Wynn's last role.) British director Peter Hunt took over this heart-warming project from Michael (WOLFEN) Wadleigh. Talia Shire, who appears in the cast, was also a producer. Ricky Paul Goldin, Dennis Holahen, Gail Strickland, Chuck Shamata. (Video/Laser: Warner Bros.)

HYPERSPACE (1987). Earl Owensby sci-fi comedy depicting the misadventures of a ship from space that arrives in North Carolina. Directed by Todd Durham. Alan Marx, Paula Poundworth, Chris Elliott.

HYPNOSIS (1962). What a la+gh! Those dumb It@lian& G&#man Sp^nish p*odu+ers cla@med their fr)ght cla%%ic would p;ut the vieAwer into a d&&p sleep. Wha# a lot of @#$% no5en^5e. AnyonW k{ows tha] a dum{ (mov!e like this c-n't po$$ibly h)rm any*ne. Don't you beXieve a w"rd of ~t.

HYPNOTIC EYE, THE (1959). Low-budget Allied Artists release, designed to cash in on a hypnotism craze, has an unusual twist on sexual obsession and depicts an aberrant relationship between unethical stage hypnotist Jacques Bergerac and busty assistant Allison Hayes. Although the relationship is never explained, its suggested perversions are at the core of a series of self-inflicted mutilations involving 12 beautiful women, brought about with the help of a "human eye" Bergerac uses to seduce them. Hayes, Marcia Henderson and Merry Anders are quite sensuous and lend the film an unusual femme mystique. The script by Gitta and William Read Woodfield is fresh, although one wishes they had made cop Joe Partridge not so witless. Director George Blair and cinematographer Archie Dalzell bring a weird quality to the film's atmosphere. Definitely offbeat and worth a look. Guy Prescott, Fred Demara, James Lydon.

HYPNOTIST (1927). See **LONDON AFTER MIDNIGHT.**

HYPNOTIST, THE (1956). Borderline fantasy deals with use of hypnotism to force a pilot to commit murder. This idea was brought to full flower in THE MANCHURIAN CANDIDATE; here it is a weak premise for a whodunit. Directed-written by Montgomery Tully. Roland Culver, Patricia Roc. Aka SCOTLAND YARD DRAGNET.

HYSTERIA (1964). Hammer psychothriller produced-written by Jimmy Sangster and directed by Freddie Francis. It's a blending of amnesia and hallucinations, asking the question: Is Robert Webber as crazy as he thinks, or is there a logical explanation? Lelia Goldoni, Anthony Newlands, Jennifer Jayne. (MGM/UA)

HYSTERICAL (1983). Pathetic parody of horror movies, with dumb jokes coming fast but never attaining wit. In a lighthouse in Hellview, Oregon, the Hudson Brothers (Bill, Mark, Brett) investigate a long-dead lighthouse keeper (Richard "Jaws" Kiel), whose corpse is restored to life by his also-long-dead wife (Julie Newmar). Half the cast walks with zombie death faces and the other half grimaces at the non sequiturs and weary sight gags. Supporting players helpless to support even themselves are Franklyn Ajaye, Keenan Wynn, Charlie Callas, Richard Donner, Murray Hamilton and Clint Walker. They're as much at sea as the lighthouse keeper. Let's hear it for gross incompetence for director Chris Bearde and the Hudsons, who wrote this mess with Trace Johnston. (Embassy) (Laser: Image)

I BOUGHT A VAMPIRE MOTORCYCLE (1990). British gore-comedy about a motorbike that's cursed by a satanic cult and made to operate sole(less)ly on blood. Revved-up attempt never runs on a full tank. Written by co-producer Mycal Miller and directed by Dirk Campbell. Neil Morissey, Amanda Noar.

I BURY THE LIVING (1958). Weird graveyard chiller with Richard Boone as a cemetery curator who thinks he has power over life and death by shifting stickpins in a cemetery map. Superior tombstone mood established by director Albert Band and "plotter" Louis Garfinkle, although the film is marred by a cop-out ending. Theodore Bikel, Herbert Anderson, Peggy Maurer, Russ Bender. (Goodtimes; S/Weird; Sinister/C; Filmfax)

ICARUS XB-1. See **VOYAGE TO THE END OF THE UNIVERSE.**

ICEBOX MURDERS, THE (1986). Fiendish killer chases beauties through a maze of corridors, then stuffs their freshly-slain corpses into his deep freeze. Give it the cold shoulder. Jack Taylor, Mirta Miller. (Mogul)

ICED (1988). An "Ice Crusher," snow country equivalent to Jason Voorhees, breaks the ice at Snow Peak Resort by (1) killing a guy with a snowplow; (2) thrusting a skipole through a man's chest; (3) driving an icicle through a woman's heart; (4) electrocuting a woman in a hottub; (5) catching a guy's foot in a beartrap and (6) plunging a butcher knife into a pie-eating skiier's chest. While the ski blades are sharp, this is a dull variation on the slasher flick, turgidly scripted by Joseph Alan Johnson, who also plays a skiier. Director Jeff Kwitny slips on the slopes of this slushy saga. Doug Stevenson, Debra DeLiso, Ron Kologie, Alan Johnson. (Prism)

ICE HOUSE, THE. See **LOVE IN COLD BLOOD.**

ICEMAN (1984). This starts as a fascinating, pseudoscientific examination of how Arctic anthropologists uncover a 40,000-year-old Neanderthal Man. The film loses its impetus when the Iceman is placed in an artificial environment for study. Although John Lone is excellent as the primitive man, and Timothy Hutton and Lindsay Crouse compassionate as his befrienders, the story moves into muddled quasi-religious ideas. One wants to feel more for the Iceman, a good guy trapped in a world he can't understand, but he never develops beyond his ice-age soul. A gallant attempt, ably directed by Fred Schepisi. Danny Glover, Josef Sommer, David Strathairn. (Video/Laser: MCA)

ICE PIRATES, THE (1984). Rollicking parody of space adventures in which warp-drive buccaneer Robert Urich and spaced-out laserbucklers Michael D. Roberts, Anjelica Huston and John Matuszak embark to the only planet in the galaxy having water to battle the evil Templar Empire. The funniest elements are (1) a castrating assembly line complete with gay "barber"; (2) the grungiest looking robots in any universe and (3) a time warp sequence in which the action is speeded up as the characters age at accelerated pace. Credit the stylishness to director Stewart Raffill, who co-wrote with Stanford Sherman. For a switch, Urich is a sometimes-cowardly hero. Mary Crosby, as the kidnapped Princess Karina, is so beautiful, she alone is reason to keep your eyes glued to the foolishness. (Video/Laser: MGM/UA)

I CHANGED MY SEX. See **GLEN OR GLENDA?**

I COME IN PEACE (1990). The cliche of buddy cops trying to crack a drug case is given a science-fictional twist in this brutally graphic, unsettling urban tale. An alien drug king lands in L.A. and drains vital fluids from victims—on his planet they make for a great "high." A good alien is tracking the bad one while cop Dolph Lundgren and ill-matched pal Brian Benben crack the crack E.T. A series of violent, bloody encounters with nary an ounce of restraint on the part of director Craig R. Baxley. Betsy Brantley, Matthias Hues, David Ackroyd. Also called DARK ANGEL. (Media) (Laser: Image)

ICON. Video version of **MILL OF THE STONE WOMEN** (American).

ICY DEATH. Video version of **DEATH DIMENSION** (Lettuce Entertain You; Bennu).

IDAHO TRANSFER (1973). Well-intended but emotionally flat message film directed by Peter Fonda. Keith Carradine and other young scientists invent a time machine that carries them ahead into a post-catalysmic world. (MPI; from Satellite as **DERANGED**)

IDENTITY CRISIS (19??). Robin Ward portrays twins. One crucified his girl and is in fruitcake prison. But when he escapes, he takes over his brother's girl (Wendy Crewson) with the evil intentions: to split her into two—just like his personality. Directed by Bruce Pittman. Deborah Grover, Anthony Parr. (Command; from Metropolitan as **THE MARK OF CAIN**)

IDENTITY CRISIS (1990). At the incantational demands of a witch with a perverted sense of humor, the body of a white fashion designer and a black rapper musician are switched, causing "identity crisis" with racial overtones. Directed by Melvin Van Peebles, this oddball comedy was written by and stars Melvin's son, Mario. Ilan Mitchell-Smith, Nicholas Kepros. (Academy)

I, DESIRE (1982). TV-movie with fascinating man vs. supernatural premise, dealing with an L.A. prostitute. David Naughton is lured into the digs of this femme fatale hooker, Desire (Barbara Stock), a vampire subjecting the city to terror. Climactic sequence has Naughton trapped in her web. Directed by John Llewellyn Moxey. Dorian Harewood, Marilyn Jones, Brad Dourif.

I DISMEMBER MAMA (1972). Screenwriter William Norton comments on the sexual perversions of contemporary society when a psycho case flips out and wants to kill his mother. First he goes after another older mother, slaughtering her and befriending her daughter. But this attempt at pathos amidst bloodletting is feeble, misguided sentimentality. This guy is a psychokiller and deserves to be put away! Zoey Hall is the "I" of the title, a freaked-out killer living in Movieland, but it's Greg Mullavey as a hard-nosed cop who's far more interesting. Also known as POOR ALBERT AND LITTLE ANNIE. Directed by Paul Leder. (AstroVideo; Video Gems)

I DON'T WANT TO BE BORN. Video version of **DEVIL WITHIN HER, THE** (Intra; Axon).

I DREAM OF JEANNIE: 15 YEARS LATER (1985). Barbara Eden still looks great in a harem costume in this TV-movie revival, directed by Bill Asher. She's up to her magical mischief against her sister (Jeannie II, also Eden) who is enticing Jeannie's boyfriend Tony Nelson with a sexy astronaut (Wayne Rogers, not Larry Hagman). Series regulars Bill Dailey (as clumsy Capt. Roger Healey) and Hayden Rorke (as psychiatrist Bellows) are on the Magic Carpet ride.

I DRINK YOUR BLOOD (1971). Foreign feature recut and thrown into the U.S. market by exploitation producer Jerry Gross. Writer-director David Durston's premise will turn your stomach: Hippies munch on meat pies infected by a disease and turn into rabies-crazed idiots. To describe more details could bring about regurgitation. Ronda Fultz, Bhaskar, Jadine Wong. (Flamingo; Fright)

I EAT YOUR SKIN (1964). Re-edited version of ZOMBIES, a 1961 feature written-produced-directed by Del Tenney which still turns up on TV in its original form under that title. (It is also known as VOODOO BLOOD BATH.) I EAT YOUR SKIN was a new version that was released in 1971 with I DRINK YOUR BLOOD. See ZOMBIES for a full report. William Joyce, Heather Hewitt. (Wizard; Sinister/C; Rhino; S/Weird; Filmfax)

IGOR AND THE LUNATICS (1985). Devil cult kills women in awful ways (how about putting them through the saw at the nearby mill?) so the police close in. Years later, the leader of the crazies gets out of prison and begins a new assault. Sleazy and cheap. Directed by Billy Parolini. Forget Igor and don't be a lunatic and watch. Joseph Eero, Joe Niola. (Lightning; Live)

I HAVE NO MOUTH BUT I MUST SCREAM. This is an alternate title for **AND NOW THE SCREAMING STARTS** and has nothing to do with a famous short story by Harlan Ellison. Maybe Harlan should sue.

I LED TWO LIVES. See **GLEN OR GLENDA?**

ILLEGAL ALIEN (1982). Lampoon of ALIEN, with unusually excellent sets for an amateur production. However, producer Gregory Keller fails in giving us a funny substitute for the monster. In space, no one can hear you not laughing. (Included on MPI's **CINEMAGIC**)

I'LL NEVER FORGET YOU (1951). But you may forget this movie, in which Tyrone Power travels backward in time for no explainable reason, finding a new romantic life in the 18th Century. This remake of BERKELEY SQUARE, produced in England, finds Power adapting well to the new time and falling in love. Directed soapily by Roy Baker. Ann Blyth, Michael Rennie.

ILLUSION OF BLOOD (1966). Bizarre Japanese mixture of supernatural and samurai when a sword-swinging warrior is haunted by his first wife and driven to self-destruction. Directed by Shiro Toyoda. Tatsuya Nakadai, Mariko Okada.

ILLUSTRATED MAN, THE (1968). A major disappointment, for producer Howard B. Kreitsek's script fails to capture the poetry or imagination of Ray Bradbury's famous anthology. Jack Smight is too conventional a director to give this the technique it screams out for. Three tales are linked by Rod Steiger, a stranger tattooed from head to foot except for a bare place on his back. In this space weird images appear: "The Veldt" is about children living in a playroom with a holograph-projected African setting; "The Long Rains" is about a rocket crew stranded on a rain-pelted Venus and trying to make its way to safety; "The Last Night of the World" depicts a family of the future which beds down in anticipation of Armageddon. Claire Bloom, Jason Evers, Robert Drivas, Don Dubbins, Tim Weldon. (Warner Bros.)

I LOVE A MYSTERY (1945). First film adaptation of Carlton E. Morse's beloved radio series about a trio of private eyes (Jack Packard, Doc Long, Reggie Yorke) from the A-1 Detective Agency who frequently encounter the occult. This Columbia short-lived series was hampered by low budgets and indifferent scripting. The team (minus Reggie) meets a millionaire (George Macready) who fears a devilish cult is after his head for shrinking purposes. Jim Bannon portrays Packard while Barton Yarborough is drawlin' Doc. Directed by Henry Levin. Sequels THE DEVIL'S MASK and THE UNKNOWN.

I LOVE TO KILL. Video of **IMPULSE (1974)** (VCII).

I LOVE YOU, I LOVE YOU. See **JE T'AIME, JE**

T'AIME.

I, MADMAN (1989). Dig Malcolm Brand, a demented '50s writer whose prose makes Stephen King read like fairy tales. He was so crazy he carved off his ears, nose and mouth. Now it's modern L.A. and bookstore employee Jenny Wright picks up a copy of Brand's opus, I, MADMAN. Suddenly Brand is back in all his hideous disfigurement, murdering. This supernatural thriller has moments of weird mood, but the script by David Chaskin is formula and cliched. There's a good stop-motion monster—created by Randall William Cook (he also plays the Brand)—but it's a device that doesn't belong in this film. Directed by Tabor Tikacs. Clayton Rohner, Steven Memel, Stephanie Hodge. (Media) (Laser: Image)

IMAGES (1972). Director Robert Altman indulges in a bit of is-it-real-or-isn't-it? in depicting the schizoid behavior of Susannah York. This British release might please Altman fans but general audiences will find it esoteric. Rene Auberjonois, Cathryn Harrison.

I-MAN (1986). I stands for indestructible, and that describes cabbie Scott Bakula after he's exposed to an alien planet's environment brought to Earth aboard the Galaxy space probe. A good-natured guy, Bakula wants to be left alone but is forced by security chief Herschell Bernardi to track down a stolen laser gun with spy Ellen Bry. As Bakula pursues millionaire villain John Anderson, he keeps rejuvenating himself. Director Corey Allen stages magnificent stunts to round out this TV-movie diversion. Joey Cramer, John Bloom.

I MARRIED A MONSTER FROM OUTER SPACE (1958). Superior bug-eyed monster material from director Gene Fowler Jr. and writer Louis Vittes focuses on newlyweds Gloria Talbott and Tom Tryon when an alien inhabits Tryon's body. Gloria suspects something is wrong—Tom acts emotionless—and by sticking to her viewpoint the film builds as a satisfying mystery. Sexual implications, unfortunately, are barely dealt with. The story is more concerned with conspiracy (a la INVASION OF THE BODY SNATCHERS). Limted effects are good for their time. Ken Lynch, John Eldridge, Valerie Allen, Maxie Rosenbloom. (Video/Laser: Paramount)

I MARRIED AN ANGEL (1942). Rodgers and Hart's stage musical-comedy—fanciful, amusing fantasy in which an angel descends from Heaven to marry a mortal—was drastically altered by screenwriter Anita Loos so that it is no longer light-footed but plodding under W. S. Van Dyke II's direction. And the casting by MGM of Jeanette MacDonald and Nelson Eddy was a mogul's mistake, for she lacks ethereal quality and he emerges a stiff-necked, giddy Hungarian playboy. Reginald Owen, Anne Jeffreys, Janis Carter. (MGM/UA)

I MARRIED A VAMPIRE (1981). Down-on-her-luck Rachel Golden finally encounters the man of her dreams—a century-old vampire (Brendan Hickey)—in this low-budget first feature from writer-director Jay Rankin. Ted Zalewski, Deborah Carroll. (Prism)

I MARRIED A WEREWOLF. See **WEREWOLF IN A GIRLS' DORMITORY.**

I MARRIED A WITCH (1942). Classic Rene Clair comedy full of bitchy battle-of-the-sexes dialogue and "ghostly" effects by Gordon Jennings. Witch spirit (Veronica Lake) is freed from imprisonment and haunts the descendant (Fredric March) of a witchhunter who sent her to the stake 300 years before. Adapted from the Thorne (TOPPER) Smith novel. Robert Benchley, Susan Hayward, Cecil Kellaway, Chester Conklin. (Lightning) (Laser: Warner Bros.; Vestron)

I'M DANGEROUS TONIGHT (1990). Based on a tale by Cornell Woolrich in name only, this TV-movie projects dollops of sex and violence, conveying neither the anguish nor torture that dominates the source material. A cursed red Aztec cloak, after it's removed from a sacrificial altar-sarcophagus, contains powers that turns its wearers evil, and among those who don it (converted into a sexy red dress) are Madchen Amick, Corey Parker and Dee Wallace Stone, the latter as a morgue attendant turned serial murderess. Only Anthony Perkins, as an oddball professor, and R. Lee Ermey as Captain Akman, an even odder cop, bring character to this ineffectual effort. A low-water mark for director Tobe Hooper. Mary Frann, Natalie Schafer, William Berger. (MCA)

IMMEDIATE DISASTER. Video version of **STRANGER FROM VENUS** (Amvest).

IMMORAL MR. TEAS, THE (1958). Night-goer Russ Meyer made light-core history with this low-budget sex fantasy that earned millions and established a new trend among flesh peddlers. Teas (a real-life character playing himself) is a sex tease given a new drug that enables him to see through clothing—which in turn allows viewers to see nubile young women, bounding and jiggling through life. Pretty tame by today's gait, but what a shocker in '58. (Meyer Bosomania)

IMMORAL TALES (1974). Four stories from writer-director Walerian Borowczyk that stride between art and pornography. Only one yarn has fantastic overtones: Paloma Picasso (daughter of artist Pablo) is Elizabeth Bathory, 16th Century Hungarian noblewoman (see DAUGHTERS OF DARKNESS and COUNTESS DRACULA) seeking virgins' blood to summerize her wintry body. Paloma skinny dips in ruby-red liquid before the orgiastic bloodlust begins.

IMMORTAL, THE (1969). Quinn Martin's TV-movie is a frightful mangling of James Gunn's fine novel by scriptwriter Robert Specht. Racing car hero Christopher George has a blood type sought by dying millionaire Barry Sullivan and this turns into escapes, car crashes and other action hogwash. THE IMMORTAL became a short-lived tired-blood series. Directed by Joseph Sargent. Jessica Walter, Ralph Bellamy, Carol Lynley.

IMMORTALIZER, THE (1989). Crazed plastic surgeon, charging a fee that would make your skin crawl from your neck to your thighs, transfers the brains of the old to the bodies of the young. Ron Ray, Chris Croner, Melody Patterson. Script by Mark Nelson; direction by Joel Bender. (Video/Laser: RCA/Columbia)

I, MONSTER (1970). Adaptation of Stevenson's Jekyll-Hyde tale with Christopher Lee, Peter Cushing and Mike Raven superior to co-producer Milton Subotsky's script. Lee portrays the doctor meddling with a schizophrenic formula. Production standards are high and capture Victorian London, but one wishes director Stephen Weeks had plugged up script shortcomings. Richard Hurndall, George Merritt, Kenneth J. Warren.

IMP, THE. See **SORORITY BABES IN THE SLIME BALL BOWL-A-RAMA.**

IMPULSE (1974). Demonic seizure of the brain of Mathew Stone (William Shatner with bulging sideburns) forces him to commit murders and child molestations in a William Grefe production made in Florida. Shatner must have done this one on an . . . impulse? Harold (Oddjob) Sakata, Ruth Roman, Kim Nicholas, James Dobson. Also called WANNA RIDE, LITTLE GIRL? (IVE; from VCI as **I LOVE TO KILL**)

IMPULSE (1984). When Meg Tilly's mother tries to blow out her brains, Meg and husband-doctor Tim Matheson journey to her small rural hometown, where people are acting strangely; something is not allowing them to censor out their own unacceptable, antisocial urges. Soon the whole town is going crazy. Director Graham Baker emphasizes compelling ambience and mystery and a conspiratorial air. The visual and verbal clues are given early on; see if you can figure it out. Hume

"I was perfectly all right before I became indestructible."

— Scott Bakula in **THE I-MAN**

Cronyn, John Karlen, Bill Paxton. (Video/Laser: Vestron)

IMPURE THOUGHTS (1986). Religious film angled for Catholics in which four dead men wait in a nebulous room (purgatory?), describing their lives. Hence, four flashbacks to see if the men can confess their sins and move on (to Heaven?). If you're looking for entertainment, pray for a miracle. Directed by Michael A. Simpson. John Putch, Brad Dourif, Terry Beaver. (Charter)

IN A GLASS CAGE (1982). This Spanish import, written and directed by Agustin Villaronga, is the portrait of a sex pervert, accomplished in a sickening, non-entertaining fashion. A Nazi war criminal, who sexually abused and murdered children in a concentration camp, carries his unnatural desires into civilian life, but a youth he corrupted stalks him for revenge. Had the youth merely used irony for that revenge, this might have been bearable. But because the lad himself is a killer, twisted as the war criminal is twisted, his vengeance is merely disgusting. The murders include a graphic hanging, the slitting of a young boy's throat, and acts of fornication between males. Gunter Meisner, Marisa Paredes. (Cinevista with subtitles)

IN BETWEEN (1991). Turgid morality tale in which Wings Hauser, Robin Mattson and Alexandra Paul wake up in a strange house from which they cannot escape. As they bicker, Heavenly messenger Robert Forster shows up to tell them that one has to return to the land of the living, and asks them to reexamine their lives to decide which one. Writer-producer-director Thomas Constantinides fails to bring any humor or charm to the situation. And with no unusual special effects, it's a monumental yawner. (Monarch)

INCENSE FOR THE DAMNED. See **BLOODSUCKERS, THE.**

INCREDIBLE FACE OF DR. B, THE (1961). Incredible excuse for a Mexican horror film which blends themes of magic with eternal life. The most incredible face of all must have belonged to the producer when he saw rushes. Jaime Fernandez, Erick del Castillo.

INCREDIBLE HULK, THE (1977). Adult approach to a popular green-tinted comic book hero results in a better-than-average TV-movie starring Bill Bixby as scientist David Bruce Banner, conducting experiments that enable test subjects to perform superhuman feats in time of anger and duress. Through gamma rays and ire, Bixby is transformed into a giant brute, primitive and uncontrollable (the creature is Lou Ferrigno). Teleplay by producer-director Kenneth Johnson deals with Bixby's anguish and romance with lab assistant Susan Sullivan. Jack Colvin, Susan Batson. (MCA) (Laser: Image)

THE INCREDIBLE HULK

INCREDIBLE HULK RETURNS, THE (1988). This will go down in history as the TV-movie that introduced Mighty Thor, a Marvel Comics superhero, into the thick of action with the Hulk. While the Hulk (Lou Ferrigno in green paint) is a visceral anti-hero, all brawn and no brain, Thor (Eric Kramer) is a dunderhead with a stylish sense of amusement. The comic-book plot, scripted by director Nick Corea, has David Banner (the Hulk's alter ego) taking a new identity as a scientist at the Joshua Lambert Institute and developing the Gamma Transponder, a laser that could keep him from turning into the Hulk whenever he gets angry. Meanwhile, qausi-nerd Jack Colvin has found the Viking tomb of Thor in a fjord agency, and with his hammer brings him magically back from the land of Odin. Joining forces, Thor and the Hulk fight thugs who've kidnapped Banner's girl (Lee Purcell, in a thankless imperiled-female role). None of the action is inspired (with the slow motion cliche overused once again). Charles Napier, John Gabriel, Tim Thomerson. (Video/Laser: New World)

INCREDIBLE INVASION, THE (1968). Jack Hill assisted Juan Ibanez in directing this U.S.-Mexican film, historically the last Boris Karloff made. Hill also wrote the script. Karloff portrays the inventor of a machine that destroys with radioactive powers. Extraterrestrial entities, in the bodies of unsavory humans, infiltrate Mayer's home, attacking his daughter (Christa Linder). Karloff was ill and his movements are restricted. (From Unicorn and Sinister/C as **SINISTER INVASION**)

INCREDIBLE MELTING MAN, THE (1978). Make-up specialist Rick Baker creates a hideous countenance stripped of human flesh—eyeballs are exposed and atilt, ears are ready to drop off and the face is oozing with bubbly goo. Unfortunately, writer-director William Sachs does nothing exciting with the melter. Alex Rebar, only survivor of a flight to Saturn, is infected with radiation poisoning and becomes a Frankenstein Monster bashing everyone in sight and throwing their body parts around while he decomposes at an alarming rate. A throwback to the sci-fiers of the 1950s. Myron Healy, Jonathan Demme, Burr DeBenning. (Vestron)

INCREDIBLE MR. LIMPET, THE (1963). Melange of live action comedy and animated underwater sequences is strictly for the Don Knotts set. He plays a 4-F reject during World War II who wants to serve his country so badly he turns into a dolphin. Limpet, in short, is limpid. Directed by Arthur Lubin. Carole Cook, Andrew Duggan, Jack Weston. (Video/Laser: Warner Bros.)

INCREDIBLE PETRIFIED WORLD, THE (1957). Incredible petrified script by John Steiner creates wooden acting and a director, Jerry Warren, who is "stumped" by the material. John Carradine, Robert Clarke, Phyllis Coates and other B players are trapped in a diving bell in a submerged world (the bottom of a goldfish bowl, maybe? (Sinister/C; S/Weird; Nostalgia; Filmfax)

INCREDIBLE PREYING MANTIS, THE. See **DEADLY MANTIS, THE.** (And now, let us prey.)

INCREDIBLE SEX-RAY MACHINE, THE (1978). Voyeuristic scientist develops machine that can see through walls and turn people horny. A patch quilt of softcore porn and stupid science. Uschi Digart.

INCREDIBLE SHRINKING MAN, THE (1957). A special-effects classic, brilliantly designed by Universal-International's Clifford Stine and featuring a 15-foot mousetrap, an 18-foot pencil, a four-foot pin and a 40-pound pair of scissors. Thus is Grant Williams dwarfed and made to appear shrinking at the rate of an inch a week. Based on a Richard Matheson novel, and adapted by Matheson, Albert Zugsmith's production transcends the limitations of the fantasy thriller to deal with the metaphysical aspects of a shrinking human. It begins when Williams is inundated in a strange cloud while at sea and follows him "down" until a house cat, a spider and water drops are staggering nemeses in his miniaturized world. Jack Arnold directed it beautifully. Randy Stuart (the wife), William Schallert, Billy Curtis. (Video/Laser: MCA)

INCREDIBLE SHRINKING WOMAN, THE (1981). Delightful parody combining slapstick and satire. Lily Tomlin portrays a housewife (among several roles) exposed to chemical products that shrink her to minuscule size. In one scene she literally stands on a soap box to deliver a tirade to her long-suffering (but talllll) husband, Charles Grodin; in another she is (again, literally) washed down the drain. Finally she's kidnapped by corporation boss Ned Beatty, who wants to learn her secret so he can shrink anyone who stands in the way of company progress. Lily and a gorilla (make-up man Rick Baker) bring the film to an hysterical conclusion. Photographed in pastel shades by Bruce Logan. Effects by Baker and Roy Arbogast. Intelligently directed by Joel Schumacher; Jane Wagner's script works on several levels. A treat for big and little people. Henry Gibson, Maria Smith, Mike Douglas. (Video/Laser: MCA)

GRANT WILLIAMS: 'INCREDIBLE SHRINKING MAN'

INCREDIBLE TORTURE SHOW, THE (1977). A Grand Guignol show presented by Sardu the Great. But offstage he's performing the real thing. Yes, fans, see a woman's brains popped out of her cranium, see eyeballs eaten before your very . . . eyeballs? See . . . yuch! The mastermind behind this blood-and-gore thriller is writer-producer-director Joel Reed. Seamus O'Brien, Louie de Jesus, Niles McMaster. (From Vestron as **BLOOD-SUCKING FREAKS** and **HERITAGE OF CALIGULA**)

INCREDIBLE TWO-HEADED TRANSPLANT, THE (1971). Stomach-churning nonsense about the head of a homicidal maniac being grafted onto the body of a thorough idiot by crazy doctor Bruce Dern. What's incredible about this movie is that it was ever produced. Directed by Anthony Lanza. John Bloom, Pat Priest, Casey Karem, Berry Kroeger. (TransAtlantic; Vintage)

INCREDIBLE VOYAGE OF STINGRAY. Producer Gerry Anderson's "Supermarionation" use of live-action puppets highlights this Image laser disc that depicts the adventures of submarine skipper Troy Tempest.

INCREDIBLY STRANGE CREATURES WHO STOPPED LIVING AND BECAME MIXED-UP ZOMBIES, THE (1964). Madame Estrella, a fortune teller at a sleazy carnival, gets angry at customers if they mock her prophecies, throws acid in their faces and has her Igor assistant toss their bodies into a pit. So much for the zombies. Along comes a shiftless bum (Cash Flagg) who falls prey to her influences, becoming a knife murderer. Meanwhile, back at the midway, hapless audiences are subjected to outrageous production numbers, some featuring talentless stripper Carmelita. It's the work of producer-director Ray Dennis Steckler. Meanwhile, the Theater Marquee Dressers of America complain about this movie—every time it plays, they run out of letters. Atlas King, Carolyn Brandt. (Oh yeah, Cash Flagg is an alias for Steckler. A Steckler for details? (Camp)

INCUBUS (1965). Experimental film written-directed by Leslie Stevens, largely ignored because of its soundtrack in Esperanto, the artificial language which dulled, rather than whetted, appetites of audiences. Filmed at Big Sur, Calif., it is set on a mythical island inhabited by demons, where William Shatner engages in good vs. evil combat. Cinematography by Conrad Hall.

INCUBUS (1982). John Hough (LEGEND OF HELL HOUSE) helms this grisly Canadian horror-charger in which the town of Galen is terrorized by an invisible, sex-starved demon that materializes during the dreams of a man whose mother was once a witch. Or so it seems . . . Trying to solve the mystery is doctor John Cassavetes, cop John Ireland and newspaperwoman Kerrie Keane. Not an outstanding terrorizer, but it has enough oddball characters and screams to sustain attention. Scripted by George Franklin from Ray Russell's novel. Helen Hughes, Dirk McLean. (Video/Laser: Vestron)

INDESTRUCTIBLE MAN, THE (1956). Bottom-of-the-barrel pulper with Lon Chaney Jr. as an electrocuted criminal restored to life (yeah, one of those plots) who goes around town knocking off guys who sent him up the river. Said to be a remake of MAN-MADE MONSTER, but don't believe it. So poorly scripted (by Sue Bradford and Vy Russell) and directed (by Jack Pollexfen) it's bad enough to be entertaining. Robert Shayne, Marian Carr, Ross Elliott. (Sinister/C; S/Weird; Filmfax)

INDIANA JONES AND THE LAST CRUSADE (1989). This third (and final?) installment in the series from Steven Spielberg and George Lucas is a wonderful lark—as good as the first film for its ingenuity of plot and action. The opening is a classic example of visual storytelling, without the need of exposition, as we meet a young Boy Scout named Jones (River Phoenix) pursuing a Spanish artifact. The adventure in this prolonged sequence cleverly blends a bag of action-tricks with a visual explanation of all the gadgets and phobias of the Indiana Jones character (leather jacket, hat, whip, fear of snakes, etc.). Especially memorable is a chase aboard a circus train. Cut to the 1930s and we're now with Jones as he leaps into a new adventure—the search for the Holy Grail. A major twist in THE LAST CRUSADE is the introduction of Sean Connery as Dr. Henry Jones, Indy's father, who has been kidnaped by Nazis. The interplay between Harrison Ford (as Indy) and Connery is delightful. Highlights include a Nazi rally complete with Adolf Hitler, motorcycle and speedboat chases, a ride on a dirigible, a search through a tunnel beneath Venice, and the finding of the Grail. It is then that the film takes on mythical proportions that zooms Indiana into pure fantasy. Screenwriter Jeffrey Boam makes it all work, and director Spielberg never allows the pace to let up. Denholm Elliott returns as the bumbling museum curator Marcus Brody and Alison Doody provides the minimal love interest. (Video/Laser: Paramount)

INDIANA JONES AND THE TEMPLE OF DOOM (1984). A rousing cliffhanger that sweeps one headlong into the second screen adventure of soldier-of-fortune/archeologist Indiana Jones. And because the "thrill ride" is nonstop, one has no time to consider the absurdities and excesses screenwriters Willard Hyuck and Gloria Katz pump into George Lucas' original idea. Like RAIDERS OF THE LOST ARK, it's a fast-paced, exciting saga produced by Lucas and Steven Spielberg, with Spielberg directing. The action is tongue-in-cheek, but there are also moments of severe intensity. The madcap plot begins in Shanghai 1935 with Jones and dancer Kate Capshaw and the kid Shortround (homage to the orphan in Samuel Fuller's STEEL HELMET) fleeing from insidious Asians. After a great night club dance sequence, the three escape via a wild airplane ride that leads them to a hair-raising parachute jump (but without a parachute), a ski ride and a "white rapids" excursion. Then the trio winds up in India where they help recover a magical glowing rock from a Kali cult. There's a fiery pit, secret caverns, torture chambers, creepies and crawlies, a variation on a roller coaster ride, a tidal wave and a suspension bridge with Indie trapped and crocodiles snapping below. Harrison Ford leaps and jumps and runs through it all, always managing to recover his hat and whip. Ke Huy Quan is cute as the Chinese youth and Amrish Puri and Roshan Seth make for good cardboard villains. Don't miss the eating scene—it's the funniest gross-out ever. (Video/Laser: Paramount)

INFERNAL IDOL, THE. See **CRAZE.**

INFERNAL TRIO, THE (1974). French-Italian-German mixture of terrors: gore murders, a Count Dracula character and black humor. Francis Girod directed and wrote. Romy Schneider, Michel Piccoli. (Connoisseur)

INFERNO (1980). Italy's Dario Argento, famed for DEEP RED, is up to his usual writing-directing scare tactics in this tale of witchcraft, suspended animation and other supernatural delights set in a New York apartment where a gloved killer stalks. Mario Bava was credited with some effects. Irene Miracle, Leigh McCloskey. (Key)

INFERNO IN SPACE (1954). See **ROCKY JONES,**

SPACE RANGER. (Inferno: Pure hell!)

INFINITY OF HORRORS, AN. See **GALAXY OF TERROR.**

INFRA-MAN (1975). Kids will cheer the wonderful menagerie of extraterrestrial creatures, the kung fu fighting and other comic book elements of this Asian mishmash. Adults may become fascinated watching this awfulness carried to ultra-ludicrous extremes as a superpowerful hero in funny clothing (he's a bionic man!) fights a dragon lady (Dragon Mom) who sends these boggling creatures—Octopus Man, Beetle Man, etc.—out from her headquarters in the bowels of the Earth to do battle. It Came From Hong Kong. Directed by Hua-Shan. Hsiu-Hsien portrays Infra-Man. (Prism; S/Weird)

INFRA SUPERMAN. See **INFRA-MAN.**

INHERITOR (1990). When her twin sister dies in Windsor Lake, Lisa McGuire turns up to investigate with local cop John Rice. Seems an old Indian curse might have done in the girl—as a bloodlusting minotaur. Directed by Brian Kendal-Savegar. Barnaby Spring, Dan Haggerty, John Russo. (Vidamerica)

INITIATION, THE (1982). Unusual slasher film with more meat than usual: In addition to members of a sorority pulling pranks during Hell Week, there is a member (Marilyn Kagan) undergoing nightmares of a childhood trauma when she saw her mother in bed with another man, and a man burst into flames. There's an odd relationship with her mother (Vera Miles) and father (Clu Galager). Meanwhile, seven inmates escape from an insane asylum. The climactic bloodbath comes during a night in a shopping mall when the killer strikes with bow and arrow, hatchet, crossbow, speargun, etc. Directed by Larry Stewart. (HBO; Starmaker)

INITIATION OF SARAH, THE (1978). Undistinguished TV-movie ripoff of CARRIE, complete with girl-being-hazed scenes. Shy, reticent Kay Lenz attends college only to come into conflict with a rival sorority to which her more outgoing sister belongs. Kay has strange psychic powers, you see, so on the night of the initiation who should urge her to utilize them but batty sorority mistress Shelley Winters. Directed by Robert Day. Tony Bill, Kathryn Crosby, Morgan Fairchild (as a great bitch), Tisa Farrow. (Worldvision)

INITATION: SILENT NIGHT, DEADLY NIGHT 4. See **SILENT NIGHT, DEADLY NIGHT 4: INITATION.**

IN LIKE FLINT (1967). Sequel to OUR MAN FLINT is another pleasantly satiric Bond spoof. James Coburn is cool superagent Derek Flint, a gadget-equipped sex symbol with a computerized brain and a mastery of martial arts. A band of women, intent on conquering Earth, is replacing political leaders with doubles by using a numbing face cream. Delightful weapons and gimmicks, beautiful women and creative set designs; Directed by Gordon Douglas. Lee J. Cobb is the befuddled assignment chief. Among the sexy gals: Jean Hale, Anna Lee, Yvonne Craig (Batgirl herself) and Erin O'Brien. Andrew Duggan, Hanna Landry. (Trans World; Fox) (Laser: CBS/Fox)

INNER SANCTUM (1947). This has nothing to do with the radio horror series of the 1940s that featured a host with ghoulish puns; the titled was purchased for exploitative reasons. Strange Dr. Velonious (Fritz Leiber) meets a woman on a train and tells her a weird story about a man who commits murder and seeks refuge in a boarding house in a small town. Uninspired poverty plot ploddingly directed by Lew Landers. Mary Beth Hughes, Charles Russell, Billy House. (Sinister/C)

INNERSPACE (1987). Shades of FANTASTIC VOYAGE with touches of THE INCREDIBLE SHRINKING MAN: Space astronaut Dennis Quaid is miniaturized and injected into the buttocks of a nerdish supermarket cashier (Martin Short), who is then chased by the hired killer of mad scientists Kevin McCarthy and Fiona Lewis, in pursuit of the microchip that permits the shrinkage. This Steven Spielberg production is played for comedy and while director Joe Dante injects his usual in-jokes, it's too long to sustain its light themes. Dennis Muren and Rob Bottin contributed the effects. Vernon Wells, Robert Picardo, Orson Bean, Henry Gibson, Dick Miller, Kenneth Tobey. (Video/Laser: Warner Bros.)

INNOCENT BLOOD (1992). Offbeat vampire comedy-thriller starring Anne Parillaud as a sexy bloodsucker who feasts on gangsters and makes it appear that the underworld did it. She chews their necks ravenously, her eyes glowing red and green, but the vicious tearing turns victims into vampires. Gang boss Robert Loggia decides to take over the rackets by turning his gang into vampires. Realizing her mistake, Parillaud joins cop Anthony LaPaglia to wipe out the fanged hoods. Director John Landis emphasizes the comedy of Michael Wolk's script with homages to vampire and monster movies. Made in Pittsburgh, INNOCENT BLOOD is refreshing, with Frank Oz, Sam Raimi and other Landis cronies popping up. And Don Rickles gives a lively performance as Loggia's mouthpiece. David Proval. (Columbia TriStar)

ANNE PARILLAUD

INNOCENTS, THE (1961). Superior cinematic version of Henry James' TURN OF THE SCREW, directed with unbearable tension by Jack Clayton, scripted by Truman Capote and William Archibald with insight, and capturing the decay, depravity and haunted possession which reek in the novel. Deborah Kerr is the prim governess dispatched to a country mansion to tend the children of ice-cold baron Michael Redgrave. Beneath the serene exterior are undercurrents of menace. Are the children possessed by a former governess and valet who were sadistic lovers before their deaths? Or is it all in Kerr's imagination? Much of the horror is only suggested. One of the best ghost movies ever made. Martin Stevens, Pamela Franklin.

INNOCENTS FROM HELL. Video version of **NUNS OF SAINT ARCHANGELO, THE** (Showcase).

INN OF THE DAMNED (1974). This Australian horror western (set in Gippsland, 1896) is worth seeing for Dame Judith Anderson as a crazed, homicidal Austrian innkeeper who murders her guests with her demented husband. The first half, however, moves with the agility of a wombat with two Achille's tendons cut as no one has the wits to figure out why all the travelers are checking in but not checking out. Finally, lawman Alex Cord uses his wits against the pair in a hairraising cat-and-mouse sequence. Produced-written-directed by Terry Bourke. Michael Craig, Joseph Furst, Robert Guilte. (Paragon)

INN OF THE FLYING DRAGON, THE. See **SLEEP OF DEATH, THE.**

INN OF THE FRIGHTENED PEOPLE. See **REVENGE** (with Joan Collins, 1971).

IN POSSESSION (1985). Carol Lynley and Christopher Cazenove play a couple that sees apparitions on a Brighton holiday. These apparitions return two years later to haunt the couple.

INQUISITION (1974). Spanish torture-chamber melodrama written-directed by Jacinto Molina, who also stars under the name of Paul Naschy as a fanatic who falls in love with the daughter of a warlock, whom he has sentenced to death. She makes a pact with the Devil to get even. Juan Luis Galiardo, Ricardo Merino. (Video City)

IN SEARCH OF . . . See **LEONARD NIMOY IN SEARCH OF . . .**

IN SEARCH OF ANCIENT ASTRONAUTS (1975). Re-edited footage from CHARIOTS OF THE GODS?, the German feature based on Erich Von Daniken's book about alleged visitors from space and the so-called proof of their visitations. Repackaged for TV by Alan Landsburg, narrated by Rod Serling. Don't take it too seriously . . . (Thunderbird)

IN SEARCH OF ANCIENT MYSTERIES (1975). More footage from CHARIOTS OF THE GODS? repackaged for U.S. TV by Alan Landsburg with Rod Serling narrating. Pure speculation, inconclusive evidence.

IN SEARCH OF BIGFOOT (1976). Standard poor man's documentary about the legendary creature, with alleged footage of the Incredible Mind-Boggling Hulking Hairy Beast-man Thing running upright on two legs. Produced-directed by Lawrence Crowley and William F. Miller. Narrated by Phil Tonkin.

IN SEARCH OF DRACULA (1976). U.S.-Swedish horror documentary narrated by Christopher Lee, produced-directed by Calvin Floyd. This discusses the history of vampires via paintings, drawings and film footage of early Murnau, Dreyer and Lugosi. Scholarly, not scary. From a book by Raymond T. McNally/Radu Florescu.

IN SEARCH OF HISTORIC JESUS (1980). Dull pseudodocumentary about the Shroud of Turin, alleged to be the robe Jesus Christ wore when he was Crucified. Some good actors lend their support: Royal Dano, Nehemiah Persoff, John Anderson, John Rubinstein. Thoroughly unconvincing as fact or fiction. Directed by Gary Conway. (VCI; Vestron) (Laser: Image)

IN SEARCH OF NOAH'S ARK (1976). Noah account pseudodocumentary which investigates wreckage on Mt. Ararat as remnants of the Biblical vessel. Directed by James L. Conway. (VCI; Vestron)

INSECT. Video version of **BLUE MONKEY** (Winson Entertainment).

INSEMINOID. See **HORROR PLANET.**

INSIDE A DARK MIRROR. See **BEYOND THE GRAVE.**

INSIDE THE LABYRINTH (1986). One-hour video goes behind the scenes of the making of Jim Henson's LABYRINTH to reveal how the creatures were designed and articulated. (Embassy; Sultan)

INTERFACE (1984). Silly, poorly conceived computer-theme fantasy, made in Dallas by regional filmmakers (dare we call them hackers?). Its saving grace is a couple who play it strictly for laughs as they search for the secret to a group of masked, costumed computerites ("We are the interpreters of the Master Process") who sit around their consols speaking with metallic voices and killing by remote control devices. The ending falls apart. Maybe director Andy Anderson forgot his modum operandi. John Davies, Laura Lane. (Vestron)

INTERNATIONAL HOUSE (1933). Hearty Paramount comedy with an all-star cast (W.C. Fields, Rudy Vallee, Burns and Allen, Sterling Holloway, Stu Erwin, Bela Lugosi) focuses on eccentrics lodging in a Chinese hotel where skullduggery is afoot to wrest the Radioscope (a device that can pick up sight and sound anywhere in the world) from the inventor Wang Wu-Hu. Directed by Edward Sutherland. (Video/Laser: MCA)

IN THE AFTERMATH: ANGELS NEVER SLEEP (1987). Offbeat blending of live action and animation to spin an intriguing post-holocaust tale depicting an angel on earth, helping us to straighten out problems. Directed by Carl Colpaert. Tony Markes, Rainbow Dolan. (New World)

IN THE CASTLE OF BLOODY LUST. See **CASTLE OF THE CREEPING FLESH.**

IN THE DEVIL'S GARDEN. See **ASSAULT.**

IN THE GRIP OF THE SPIDER. See **WEB OF THE SPIDER.** (A well-spun yarn?).

IN THE MIDNIGHT HOUR (1985). Violent TV-movie vacillating between graveyard humor and shock thrills in telling its satirical tale of the town of Pitchford Cove, where teenagers on Halloween night violate the graveyard to enact a ritual that unleashes scores of corpses. These walking dead are ghouls who crash a teen party and go for yocks; the vampires go for the jugular; others are werewolves. A lively affair, full of laughs and thrills. Dick Van Patten has fun as a silly dentist and Kevin McCarthy is the drunken judge who gets his comeuppance. Lee Montgomery, Shari Belafonte-Harper, LeVar Burton. Directed by Jack Bender. (On TV as THE MIDNIGHT HOUR and from Vidmark under that title)

IN THE NICK OF TIME (1991). Lloyd Bridges dons the garb of old St. Nick and rushes to New York to find a replacement for himself—or else there will be no Christmas. You see, he's up for mandatory retirement after 300 years. Walt Disney production directed by George Miller. Michael Tucker, Cleavon Little.

IN THE SHADOW OF KILIMANJARO (1986). Dramatization of a true incident that took place in Kenya during the drought of 1984, when 90,000 starving baboons went on a killing spree, terrorizing natives and settlers alike. Director Raju Patel treats this topic as though it were a remake of JAWS, emphasizing gore and building suspense each time the critters amass in the darkness. Well done, with interesting characters, good photography. Timothy Bottoms, Michele Carey, Don Blakely, John Rhys-Davies, Irene Miracle. (IVE)

IN THE SPIRIT (1990). Oddball supernatural comedy in which Marlo Thomas and Elaine May portray the guests of a nutty psychic who lives next door to a murderer. Peter Falk, Olympia Dukakis, Melanie Griffith. Directed by Sandra Seacat. (Academy)

IN THE YEAR 2889 (1965). Uncredited remake of Roger Corman's THE DAY THE WORLD ENDED, depicting holocaust survivors who gather in a sheltered valley to bicker with each other and fight off a mutant monster. Corman's version was watchable—this work from director-producer Larry Buchanan isn't. Les Tremayne, Paul Petersen, Quinn O'Hara, Charla Doarty. (S/Weird)

INTO THE BADLANDS (1991). Macabre TV-movie (possibly inspired by GRIM PRAIRIE TALES) is a failed anthology, all mood and little substance. The trilogy features unsatisfactory twist endings as bountyman-narrator-storyteller T. L. Barston (Bruce Dern) roves the West in search of outlaw Red Roundtree. In the first yarn, an outlaw flees a lawman and takes up with a prostitute; in the second, two women rivals for the same man are snowbound in an isolated cabin and attacked by wolves; and in the third Barston closes in on Roundtree. Director Sam Pillsbury pumps sardonic touches into the creaky old wagon, but ultimately it groans. Helen Hunt, Dylan McDermott, Lisa Pelikan, Andrew Robinson. (MCA)

INTO THE DARKNESS (1986). Beautiful models are knocked off in this blood-splasher, enhanced by the menacing presence of Donald Pleasence. Ronald Lacey, Polly Pleasence. Double your Pleasances? Directed by

Back in the days of the Old West, there were these stretches of territory that God and nature just plain forgot. Dark and parched and empty as all the moons of Mars. Places where sensible men never ventured. Where only dreams and phantoms walked . . . smack between civilization and the ninth Circle of Hell."

—Bruce Dern as the narrator/bounty hunter in **INTO THE BADLANDS**

Michael Parkinson. (Video Pictures; Westernworld)

INTRUDER, THE (1977)."Psychopath-loose" movie, starring Jean-Louis Trintignant driving with his stepson across Europe and facing danger from a stranger in a panel truck. Directed by Serge Leroy. Mireille Darc, Adolfo Celi. (VidAmerica)

INTRUDER, THE (1983). The Stranger (Tony Fletcher) comes to Holoway (actually Brantford, Ontario) driving a trailer emblazoned with the sign: "Coming Soon." What is coming soon is entertainer Howard Turt, who gives everyone a glowing aura that forces them to tell the truth. This parable is touched with pretentious symbolism and heavy-handed religious overtones, and instead of coming to a resolution, the movie fizzles. Somewhere in THE INTRUDER is an idea, but writer Norman Fox and director David F. Eustace never tap into it. Pita Oliver, Gerald Jordan, Jimmy Douglas.

INTRUDER (1989). Better-than-average "trapped with a slasher" genre flick thanks to writer-director Scott Spiegel's clever use of camera angles and point-of-view shots. His ironic juxaposing of images holds one's interest while story and characters do not. This time the human fodder is trapped in a supermarket at night with a crazed killer who uses tools of the produce-butcher trade to commit his murders. Bodies on meat hooks, sliced on meat cutters, cracked open with butcher knives, hatchets, axes—if your butcher has it, Spiegel uses it. Spiegel taints his story meat with a forced ending that speaks poorly of our police—a disturbing element unnecessary in a gory, spoofy entertainment. Elizabeth Cox, David Byrnes, Sam Raimi. (Video/Laser: Paramount)

INTRUDERS (1992). True-life UFO abduction cases documented in Budd Hopkins' book have been blended into a dramatization in this four-hour TV-movie directed by Dan Curtis. Richard Crenna is a disbelieving psychiatrist who comes to realize these bizarre cases cannot be explained in traditional psychiatric terms; he takes up the cause of helping abductees find inner peace. What emerges from the Barry Oringer-Tracy Torme teleplay is a convincing, chilling study of a phase of UFO-ology that is little understood. Mare Winningham and Susan Blakely portray sisters who have been terrorized by strange aliens since they were children. What is shockingly revealed through G. D. Spradlin's cynical Air Force general is the government's contemptuous attitude of keeping the truth hidden from the public while their own researchers carry out a clandestine study of abductions. Daphne Ashbrook, Alan Autry, Ben Vereen, Steven Berkoff. (Fox)

ALIEN VISITORS IN 'INTRUDERS'

INTRUDER WITHIN, THE (1981). Okay TV-movie, but too imitative of ALIEN to generate its own unique suspense. Chad Everett is a "tool-pusher" on an oil rig for the Zorton Oil Company, who drills to 19,000 feet to uncover a hideous creature from our ecological past, a spawn that implants reproductive sperm within a human being. When that man goes crazy and attacks a woman crew member, she is destined to give birth to . . . you know what, don't you? The monster passes through evolutionary stages before becoming a man in a glistening fright suit. Directed by Peter Carter. Joseph Bottoms, Jennifer Warren. (Transworld)

INVADER (1992). Exciting, high-tech sci-fi thriller jam-packed with ambitious computerized effects and model work ranging from mediocre to excellent. Although an adventure, the film manages to comment on wasted government spending, if subtext is your thing. An alien entity (in the form of a miniaturized flying saucer) takes over the military and plans nuclear war, with only three standing in its way: a wise-cracking reporter for a scandal sheet, a Defense Department investigator and an Air Force general. The pacing is swift under writer-director Philip J. Cook as the trio faces giant robot HAR-V (Heavily Armed Rampaging Vaporizer) and jet fighters equipped with ASMODS (Automated System Managing Offense & Defense Strategies). Hans Bachmann, A. Thomas Smith. (Video/Laser: Vidmark)

INVADERS FROM MARS (1953). A cult following has built over the years because this touches a sensitive cord in people, who remember those things which first frightened them, and the gap between youth and adults. Jimmy Hunt wakes up one night to spy an E.T. craft submerging itself in a hill outside his house, but no one will believe him, not even when aliens take over humans in a widespread conspiracy. It's the ultimate in paranoia-for-kids. Director William Cameron Menzies, who directed THE MAZE, brings abstract styles to the strange sets, giving this a surreal touch. While Richard Blake's script cops out at the end, the story does have wonderful moments. Arthur Franz, Helena Carter, Leif Erickson, Morris Ankrum, Milburn Stone. Remade in 1986. (Nostalgia Merchant; Media) (Laser: Image)

INVADERS FROM MARS (1986). Sincere remake of Menzies' 1953 cult favorite, with writers Dan O'Bannon and Don Jakoby sticking to the original story and director Tobe Hooper trying to recapture what made the original so memorable to the young. In ways they do a better job in capturing the paranoia of a lad who sees everyone being turned into zombies but whom nobody will believe. This excels with its effects by John Dykstra and its Stan Winston-designed monsters. Wonderful cave and spaceship interiors too as Hunter Carson and Karen Black lead the Marines in an exciting old-fashioned rescue. The film is simple and fast-moving with cliff-hangers and visual delights: soldiers being sucked into the sand, Louise Fletcher swallowing a frog whole, and a machine that bores needles into humans being zomboided. Jimmy Hunt, who played the boy in the original, is back as the town's police chief; as he walks up to the hill toward the sandpit, he remarks, "I haven't been up here since I was a kid." Timothy Bottoms, Laraine Newman, James Karen, Bud Cort. (Cannon) (Laser: Image)

INVADERS FROM SPACE. Video version of **ATTACK FROM SPACE** (S/Weird).

INVADERS FROM THE DEEP: STINGRAY. "Supermarionation" puppet adventures of sub captain Troy Tempest and his underwater gadgets. (Laser: Image)

INVADERS FROM THE PLANETS. See **ATOMIC RULERS OF THE WORLD** (They don't measure up.)

INVADERS FROM THE SPACESHIP. See **PRINCE OF SPACE.**

INVASION (1966). Atmospheric British chiller in which an alien "Lystrian" craft crashes near a country hospital, with the ETs aboard being a policewoman and prisoner. When they're taken to the hospital, a force field pops up around the building. A peculiar ambience is generated by director Alan Bridges. Edward Judd, Yoko Tani, Tsai Chin. (S/Weird; Movies Unlimited)

INVASION, THE (1973). Re-edited episodes of TV's STAR LOST, about a ship on a thousand-year journey through space. A deranged commander plans to increase the intellectual capacity of the Ark through brain implants. Keir Dullea, Stephen Young.

INVASION BY THE ATOMIC ZOMBIES. See **CITY OF THE WALKING DEAD.**

INVASION EARTH: THE ALIENS ARE HERE (1988). When insect-like aliens invade a small town, the creatures have a close encounter with an audience watching clips from monster movies, ranging from THE BLOB to WAR OF THE WORLDS to THEM to THE GIANT CLAW to FIEND WITHOUT A FACE. These scenes give the kids in the audience what they need to fight the monsters. Directed by George Maitland. Janice Fabian, Christian Lee. (New World) (Laser: Image)

INVASION EARTH 2150 A.D. (1966). Sequel to DR. WHO AND THE DALEKS, featuring that lovable curmudgeon doctor (Peter Cushing) who moves through the dimensions in his time machine. In this adventure written by producer Milton Subotsky, Dr. Who (a character created on the BBC) squares off against the Daleks (mutated beings in R2D2-like movable units) who have conquered our planet. Directed by Gordon Flemying. Bernard Cribbins, Ray Brooks, Andrew Keir. Also known as DALEKS—INVASION EARTH 2150 A.D. (HBO)

INVASION FORCE. See **HANGAR 18.**

INVASION FROM INNER EARTH (1977). Filmed in the snow wastes of Wisconsin, this low-budget cheapie depicts stranded travelers being knocked off by red-glowing death rays generated by off-camera aliens. The plot plods as often as the snowbound characters, and director Ito Rebane's idea of an ET is to have a heavy-handed voice boom over a radio receiver. The effects are awful and the film lumbers to an incomprehensible ending. (VCI; from Platinum as **HELL FIRE**)

INVASION FROM THE MOON. See **MUTINY IN OUTER SPACE.**

INVASION OF CAROL ENDERS, THE (1974). Meredith Baxter transfers her personality into the body of a woman killed in an "accident" in this Dan Curtis TV-movie. Chris Connelly, Charles Aidman. (Thrillervideo)

INVASION OF MARS. See **ANGRY RED PLANET.**

INVASION OF PLANET X. See **MONSTER ZERO.**

INVASION OF THE ANIMAL PEOPLE (1960). Swedish smorgasbord recut for the U.S. with new footage by Virgil Vogel and Jerry Warren. An alien creature on the loose is recaptured by its other-world masters, who closely encounter some mountain folks. Aliens should better observe the leash laws. Minor sci-fier by Arthur C. Pierce. John Carradine, Robert Burton, Barbara Wilson, Stan Gester. Also known as TERROR IN THE MIDNIGHT SUN and SPACE INVASION FROM LAPLAND. (Vidmark; Loonic; Sinister/C; Nostalgia)

INVASION OF THE ASTRO MONSTERS. See **MONSTER ZERO.**

INVASION OF THE BEE GIRLS (1973). Quickie horror thriller with fantasy overtones scripted by Nicholas Meyer, who claims he got stung when his script was tampered with. What should have been a stinger about women turning into men-destroying insects is instead a stinker—Meyer is hereby vindicated. William Smith is a G-man buzzing around the hive of sexy Victoria Vetri and other "Bee Girls." Strictly for the Birds—and B fans. Directed with a buzz-on by Denis Sanders. Anitra Ford, Rene Bond. (Embassy; Sultan)

INVASION OF THE BLOOD FARMERS (1972). Druid cult seeks a special blood type to rejuvenate its dying queen, kept secreted in a coffin. Lifeless film produced-directed by Ed Adlum could use a transfusion too. Cynthia Fleming, Tanna Hunter. (Thunderbird; Regal)

INVASION OF THE BODY SNATCHERS (1956). The political ramifications of director Don Siegel's classic have been well expounded on (it was produced during the McCarthy hysteria of the 1950s and its subtext is rooted in fear of conspiracy) but it can be enjoyed strictly for its thrills. It's a tale of mounting suspicion and horror as Kevin McCarthy, resident of Santa Mira, discovers an alien race (creatures encased in strange pods which froth and crack open) is creating duplicates of the townspeople and turning them into zombies. The literate Daniel Mainwaring-Sam Peckinpah script (from Jack Finney's novel) and the supporting cast (Dana Wynter, Carolyn Jones, King Donovan) contribute good work, but it is Siegel's direction that makes it a classic. Remade in '78 and '93. (RCA/Columbia; Republic has a colorized version) (Laser: Republic; Criterion; Voyager)

INVASION OF THE BODY SNATCHERS (1978). Inspired by Jack Finney's novel and first produced in 1956, this has undergone so many changes in W.D. Richter's adaptation that it stands apart from Don Siegel's version. This time we are introduced to alien spores as they leave their home planet and drift through space; it's a striking sequence. The spores settle in San Francisco near victims-to-be: Donald Sutherland, Brooke Adams, Leonard Nimoy, Veronica Cartwright. Slowly the humans are replaced by pod creatures, but we're still not sure how much is conspiracy and how much is paranoia and hysteria. The pod effects are revoltingly good and there are several startling scenes, including a mutation dog, that make this Philip Kaufman-directed film memorable. Don Siegel turns up in a cameo as a cab driver, and Kevin McCarthy plays his character from the original. (Video/Laser: MGM/UA)

INVASION OF THE BODY STEALERS. Video version of **BODY STEALERS, THE** (USA; IVE; Vestron).

INVASION OF THE FLESH HUNTERS. Video version of **CANNIBALS IN THE STREETS** (Vestron).

INVASION OF THE FLYING SAUCERS. See **EARTH VS. THE FLYING SAUCERS.**

INVASION OF THE GIRL SNATCHERS (1973). A detective hires hippies to rescue Earth women from insidious aliens. Directed by Lee Jones. David Roster, Ele Grigsby. Also known as THE HIDAN OF MOUNT BIENJOW. (Majestic International; United; VCI)

INVASION OF THE HELL CREATURES. See **INVASION OF THE SAUCERMEN.**

INVASION OF THE LOVE DRONES (1977). Porn corn about crazy inventor Dr. Femme (Viveca Ash) who arrives on Earth in a craft powered by a "sex drive." Her foreplay: to create a race of sexy love creatures possessing energy to create a worldwide orgy of pleasure. This film has some climax! Jerome Hamlin is the crew of one (an astronaut of position?) who puts many porn figures through their stances.

INVASION OF THE NEPTUNE MEN (1961). Humanoids in spacesuits with cone-shaped headpieces, hailing from the eighth planet, attack a band of Earth children who are rescued by a silver-suited hero they call Space Chief. Later, the children watch as scientists and military leaders band together to put an electronic bubble over Tokyo to stave off another Neptunian attack. Again, Space Chief comes to the rescue, blowing the Neptune villains out of the skies. Infantile antics, horrendously dubbed, with effects of the GODZILLA genre. Directed by Koji Ota and starring Shinichi Chiba (otherwise known as Sonny Chiba) as the steely dull Space Chief, whose name in the Japanese version was Ironsharp. (S/Weird)

INVASION OF THE ROBOT DINOSAURS. A boring scientific study of Tyrannosaurus Rex, Triceratops and other prehistoric creatures, including a look at the environment in which they stalked the Earth and the assorted theories about why they died out so quickly. In "Dinamation," but so what? (Rhino)

INVASION OF THE SAUCER MEN (1957). American-International double-biller slanted for teenagers and featuring wonderful bug-eyed, head-bulging Martians. The film has a reputation for being so-bad-it's-good. The Robert Gurney Jr.-Al Martin mishmash of a plot (from a Paul Fairman story) has teeners being injected with alcohol by the aliens in an attempt to have them arrested for drunk driving. The hero is Lyn Osborne, Cadet Happy on TV's SPACE PATROL. Frank Gorshin, Steve Terrell, Gloria Castillo, Russ Bender, Ed Nelson. Directed by Edward L. Cahn. Would you call this a Cahn Job? Remade as THE EYE CREATURES. (Columbia TriStar)

INVASION OF THE SPACE PREACHERS (1990). An asinine accountant and a dumb dentist—pale imitations of Bill & Ted—head for West Virginia for a vacation and nerd their way through pallid misadventures when they encounter a lizardlike alien from a farflung planet, on Earth to capture a fugitive from her own world posing as a preacherman. Lash of God, who wields a whip in barrooms to convert the sinners, has an insidious plan to hypnotize his radio-show listeners into obeying his orders but our insipid heroes save the day with the help of a militant gun nut. Writer-director Daniel Boyd stages one flop sequence after another, and not a single gag for 100 minutes is funny. Pray this movie goes away. Jim Wolfe, Gary Nelson, Elisha Hahn, Gary Brown. Musician Jimmy Walker plays himself. (Rhino)

INVASION OF THE STAR CREATURES, THE (1962). Lowbrow premise played for laughs—a spoof directed by Bruno Ve Sota. However, you won't be guffawing or chortling. Some va-va-voom babes from space with size E bras invade Earth with Vege-Men, but two Army deadbeats thwart the dumb plot—not difficult for two idiots. Frankie Ram, Bob Ball, Gloria Victor.

INVASION OF THE VAMPIRES (1961). Mexican spinoff of DRACULA, a sequel to THE BLOODY VAMPIRE, with the old fanged killer (Count Frankenhausen, played by Carlos Agosti) in 16th Century costume. Stalking the Count is a doctor who asks "Do you suppose there are forces of darkness?" You better believe it, Doc. Written-directed by Miguel Morayta; the American version was tampered with by K. Gordon Murray. Rafael del Rio, Tito Junco. (Sinister/C; S/Weird; Filmfax)

INVASION OF THE ZOMBIES (1961). Second in a Mexican series detailing the ridiculous behavior of a masked wrestler called Samson (or Santo) who fights evil scientists and other forces of evil—when he isn't wrestling a bad script. In this epic, he throws down a scientist who has created an army of zombies and pins him with a brain lock. Written-directed by Benito Alzraki. (Sinister/C; Filmfax)

INVASION: UFO (1972). Re-edited episodes of a British series which took the kind of model work in the THUNDERBIRDS series and combined it with live action. SHADO is an Earth organization designed to fight off attacking aliens, who are human in shape and often trick us Earthlings by infiltration methods. Standard TV fare directed-written by Gerry Anderson and David Tomblin. Ed Bishop, Wanda Ventham Sewell. (VC)

INVASION U.S.A. (1953). Albert Zugsmith low-budget feature directed by Alfred E. Green that reflects the "Red Menace" hysteria of the Cold War. Patrons in a bar meet a soothsayer who predicts what might happen if the U.S. was invaded by the enemy following nuclear holocaust. Bingo: The invasion happens, with the Commies blasting us to pieces. Hampered by a lack of effects if not a lack of paranoiac ideas. However, the trick ending just doesn't work. Gerald Mohr, Dan O'Herlihy, Peggie Castle, Phyllis Coates, Noel Neill.

INVASION U.S.A. (1985). Bloodthirsty Communist commando Richard Lynch leads Soviet terrorists to the Florida coast in barges, then has squads attack homes in the suburbs, shopping centers, etc. The only man to stop this invasion is Chuck Norris, portraying secret agent Mark Hunter, who proceeds to act as a one-man army, killing the invaders ruthlessly, often in cold blood. This is an awful movie, full of stupid story holes, plagued by sadistic, gratuitous violence, with motives and behavior defying all logic. Directed by Joseph Zito. (Video/Laser: MGM/UA)

INVISIBLE ADVERSARIES (1978). Austrian import from Export—producer-director Valie Export, that is. It's hard to see what he saw in this tale about unseen entities called Hyksos who are up to the usual Alien Invasion Plot and the efforts of a photographer and boyfriend to save mankind. Invisible production values. Susanne Widi, Peter Weibel. (Facets, with English subtitles)

CHUCK NORRIS

INVISIBLE AGENT (1942). Cigarettes floating in air and Gestapo agents being kicked in the seat of their pants by an unseen presence are highpoints of this propagandistic comedy-adventure in which Jon Hall is rendered "unsightly" by taking a drug intravenously. Traveling to Nazi Germany, he gives the Fuhrer what for. Curt Siodmak's script is preachy and preposterous and director Edward L. Marin glorifies mock heroics as Hall indulges in espionage situations, but it's great fun. Peter Lorre overplays a Japanese baron and Ilona Massey slinks through Berlin as a femme fatale. Cedric Hardwick, Keye Luke, John Litel, Holmes Herbert. (MCA)

INVISIBLE AVENGER (1958). "The Shadow," the invisible crimefighter (real name: Lamont Cranston) of pulps and radio, is the hero in this Republic film made in New Orleans and directed by cameraman James Wong Howe and John Sledge. Cranston ("who clouds men's minds so they cannot see him") uses his hypnotic cloak of invisibility to thwart a political assassin while also investigating the murder of a jazz figure. Richard Derr is the playboy investigator. Marc Daniels, Helen Westcott. (Sinister/C; S/Weird; Filmfax)

INVISIBLE BATMAN, THE (1985). Italian mishmash in which a costumed superhero fights disorganized crime. Etore Gunadi, Ercole Tassi.

INVISIBLE BOY, THE (1957). A vehicle designed for Robby the Robot following FORBIDDEN PLANET, with Richard Eyer as a likable youth who puts Robby back together. As a reward, Robby (voice by Marvin Miller) turns the boy invisible. Unfortunately, the robot comes under the spell of a central computer, Univac, which plans world conquest. Nice special effects and refreshing comedy sparkle throughout Cyril Hume's screenplay. Philip Abbott, Diane Brewster, Harold J. Stone. Directed by Herman Hoffman.

INVISIBLE CREATURE (1960). Made in Britain, this supernatural thriller is about a husband who plans to murder his wife but finds she is protected by a spirit. Directed by Montgomery Tully. Tony Wright, Patricia Dainton. (From Sinister/C and S/Weird as **HOUSE IN MARSH ROAD, THE**)

INVISIBLE DEAD, THE. Video version of **ORLOFF AGAINST THE INVISIBLE MAN** (Wizard; VCI).

INVISIBLE DR. MABUSE, THE (1961). Mediocre German revival of the super archvillain created by Norbert Jacques and made famous by Fritz Lang in the 1920s. Dr. Mabuse (Wolfgang Priess) schemes to steal a formula for invisibility and take over the world. His nemesis is government man Les Barker. Karin Dor, Werner Peters. Directed by Harold Reinl. (S/Weird)

INVISIBLE GHOST, THE (1941). Monogram mess produced by Sam Katzman with Bela Lugosi as confused, mixed-up Charles Kessler who hypnotizes his wife into committing murders. Directed by Joseph H. Lewis. Betty Compson, John McGuire. (Video Yesteryear; Nostalgia; Sinister/C; United American; Filmfax)

INVISIBLE HORROR, THE. See **INVISIBLE DR. MABUSE, THE.**

INVISIBLE INVADERS, THE (1959). Riotously inept low budgeter, each scene a treat for buffs who take perverse delight in watching celluloid disasters. Invisible aliens, hiding on the moon, fly to Earth and, changing molecular structure, take possession of corpses to become an army of walking dead. They start with Dr. Noymann (John Carradine). Bad special effects and terrible acting by John Agar, Jean Byron and Robert Hutton provide a laugh-a-minute, as do the solemn narrator and documentary footage. Director Edward L. Cahn has a style as stiff as a zombie. By all means, see it and revel in its absolute ineptitude.

INVISIBLE KID, THE (1987). Nerdish teenage scientist Jay Underwood, searching for the formula of invisibilty once sought by his late father, creates a greenish, gloopy goo that, when combined with pigeon shit, renders him unseeable. Getting revenge on the jerks at Valleyville High, spying on naked, large-breasted girls in the shower and evoking gasps from dumbbell mom Karen Black are Underwood's applications of his formula in this vapid excuse for a fantasy-comedy, in which pigeon shit is the most compelling commodity. The invisibility effects are impoverished, the acting is pitiful and a curse of invisibility should be wished on writer-director Avery Crounse. Wally Ward, Chynna Phillips, Brother Theodore. (Media) (Laser: Image)

INVISIBLE KILLER, THE (1940). PRC mystery thriller in which sound is diabolically used as an instrument of murder. Sounds unsound, looks unsound. Directed by Sam Newfield. Roland Drew. (Sinister/C)

INVISIBLE MAN, THE (1933). The irony of Universal's adaptation of H. G. Wells' novel about scientist Jack Griffin (who discovers monocaine, a drug that renders him invisible) is that it made a star of Claude Rains, even though he is seldom seen, only heard, while swathed in bandages and wearing black goggles. Because of the formula, he is turned into a power-mad killer. "Suddenly I realized the power I had, the power to rule, to make the world grovel at my feet," he proclaims. James Whale's direction and the effects are marvelous. So are character bits by Una O'Connor, John Carradine, Dwight Frye, E. E. Clive and Gloria Stuart. Adapted by R. C. Sherriff. (Video/Laser: MCA)

INVISIBLE MAN, THE (1958). Mexican adaptation of the H.G. Wells novel, directed by Alfredo B. Crevenna. Arturo de Cordova, Ana Luisa Peluffo.

INVISIBLE MAN, THE (1975). This Universal TV-pilot is an updated, science-fictional version of the H. G. Wells novel. David McCallum is Dr. Daniel Weston, a scientist involved in the development of a laser beam who stumbles across the secret of invisibility. He decides to keep it a secret from mankind and flees. Of course, others who want the secret chase after him. Directed by Robert Michael Lewis, written-produced by Steven Bochco. Melinda Fee, Jackie Cooper, Henry Darrow.

INVISIBLE MANIAC (1990). A pubescent attitude hangs over this semi-comedic stab at the INVISIBLE MAN formula, making it a tasteless variation on the dumb-teenager slasher flicks. Numerous nubile, naked female bodies dominate the shower and locker rooms of a high school where a brilliant but insane physics professor (Noel Peters) is hiding from the law, posing as a physics teacher. The cackling madman (and he cackles a lot) turns himself invisible with a "molecule reorganization" serum and pinches bare fannies and titties before a rampage of destruction, first by killing the nymphomaniacal principal and then the students. Gore effects are substandard and writer-director Rif Coogan doesn't know how to bring out the humor in his script, and it fails as a gorefest. Shannon Wilsey, Melissa Moore. (Republic)

INVISIBLE MAN RETURN, THE (1940). Sequel to THE INVISIBLE MAN stars Vincent Price as the brother of scientist Jack Griffin. Price is seldom seen but often heard once he takes a duocaine inoculation and is rendered unseeable. Escaping prison (where he has been unjustly sent), he searches for Jack's real killer. The effects are startling as Price wraps and unwraps himself and as objects float. Quite enjoyable. Joe May directed the Lester Cole-Curt Siodmak script. Nan Grey, Sir Cedric Hardwicke, John Sutton. (MCA)

INVISIBLE MAN'S REVENGE, THE (1944). Sequel to a sequel has little to do with Wells' fantasy, or to the two films preceding it. Scientist John Carradine discovers a formula for invisibility via injection, which he gives to wrongly-accused Jon Hall so he can escape pursuers and track down the culprits who cheated him out of a diamond mine. More floating objects and invisible man trickery, but producer Ford Beebe's direction is lackluster. Evelyn Ankers, Alan Curtis, Gale Sondergaard, Ian Wolfe.

INVISIBLE MONSTER, THE (1950). A 12-chapter Republic serial depicting an incredibly inept madman (Stanley Price) who calls himself the Phantom Ruler and intends to conquer the world with an army of invisible warriors. Wearing a cloak chemically treated with a magical formula, he makes himself disappear while standing in the beam of a light ray, but the Phantom Idiot rarely uses this device effectively in his capers to steal money or equipment. Seems that insurance investigator Lane Carson (square-jawed Richard Webb) always outsmarts him. And then there's his assistant Carol Richards (Aline Towne), who runs around the hills of Hollwyood in her high heels, occasionally pulling a pistol from her oversized purse and taking potshots at bad guys she can never hit. But no matter how naive it gets, this is nonstop fun. Directed by Fred C. Brannon. Lane Bradford, John Crawford, Marshall Reed. The TV edited version is SLAVES OF THE INVISIBLE MONSTER. (Republic)

INVISIBLE RAY, THE (1936). Boris Karloff is scientist Janos Rukh, who captures light rays from the past and finds an ancient meteor in the Carpathians imbued with "Radium X," a substance that infects Karloff with a luminous radioactivity that kills anything he touches. On the expedition is Bela Lugosi as Dr. Felix Benet, a sympathetic scientist. The effects are innovative in this unusually lively Universal horror thriller directed by Lambert Hillyer. Frances Drake, Frank Lawton, Beulah Bondi. (Video/Laser: MCA)

INVISIBLE STRANGLER (1984). Produced in 1976 as THE ASTRAL FACTOR, this remained unreleased for years—for obvious reasons. It's a muddled mess as an imprisoned murderer learns the art of making himself invisible and escapes to knock off those who sent him up. Robert Foxworth plays the stupefied cop and nice looking ladies pop in and out (Elke Sommer, Mariana Hill, Leslie Parrish, Sue Lyon, Stephanie Powers). The awful script is by Arthur C. Pierce; the bland direction is by John Florea. Insignificant cameos by Alex Dreier, Percy Rodrigues and John Hart. (Trans World)

INVISIBLE TERROR, THE (1963). This West German swipe of THE INVISIBLE MAN—despite amateurish acting and poor action—takes on a life of its own, its absurdities encouraging one to ask: How could this have been produced? Director Raphael Nussbeaum knows nothing about pacing, writer Wladimir Semitjof knows nothing about plots. It's about a doctor who discovers a serum for invisibility. In short, total human ineptitude that's a kick to watch. So be a masochist and enjoy. Ellen Schwiers, Hans Borsody. (Filmfax)

INVISIBLE: THE CHRONICLES OF BENJAMIN KNIGHT (1993). This sequel to MANDROID requires that you see the original first to get the drift. This picks up the adventures of how Benjamin Knight (Michael Dellafemina) turns invisible when he takes "Super-Com Crystal" tablets designed by scientist Jennifer Nash, and how wheelchair-bound inventor Brian Cousins controls a robot warrior through a headpiece now reduced to a pair of dark glasses. Nash (as Zanna) becomes a kind of female Rambo when she battles Eastern European police and a gang of misfits and cutthroats led by the ugly Drago (Curt Lownes). Written-directed by C. Courtney Joyner, INVISIBLE was produced in Romania by Charles Band and is notable for its "Invisible Man" special effects if not coherence. (Paramount)

INVISIBLE WOMAN, THE (1940). No connection to THE INVISIBLE MAN outside of the title. John Barrymore, in one of his last roles, invents a machine that renders fashion model Virginia Bruce invisible. Foreign spies pursue the machine and Miss Bruce. The usual invisibile sight gags, but worth watching for its cast: Shemp Howard, John Howard, Charles Ruggles, Oscar Homolka, Maria Montez, Margaret Hamilton. Directed by Edward Sutherland. (MCA)

INVISIBLE WOMAN, THE (1983). Empty TV-movie, the most invisible production of our time. Director Alan J. Levi, who gave us an INVISIBLE MAN series in 1975 with David McCallum, might have faded into nothingness after this nonsubstance about a research scientist (Bob Denver) whose test chimpanzee accidentally mixes a formula and vanishes. Along comes Alexa Hamilton to become the Invisible Woman. Watch a cast waste away to nothing: Jonathan Banks, David Doyle, George Gobel.

INVITATION TO HELL (1982). Amateurish British horror film, ineffectual in shock and make-up effects. When the film's virginal heroine shows up at a college reunion, she's used as a sacrifice to the spring equinox. A walking, burned-up corpse evokes laughter rather than thrills. This waste of time is to be avoided at all costs. Directed by Michael J. Murphy. Becky Simpson, Joseph Sheahan. (Mogul; Western World; Videoline)

INVITATION TO HELL (1984). Wes Craven-directed TV-movie inspired by POLTERGEIST in which inventor Robert Urich arrives at a strange corporation, Micro Digitech, to begin experiments on a new spacesuit (designed for a Venus expedition) that has laser weaponry built into its sleeves and a helmet that detects non-human lifeforms. Meanwhile, a seductive demon from Hell (Susan Lucci) is luring everyone through the portals of her country club into the depths of hell to seize control of their souls. When Urich's wife (Joanna Cassidy) and children are mind-zapped, he dons the spacesuit for his descent into Hell. Silly premise never convinces. (Sony)

IRON MAN. See **TETSUO: THE IRON MAN.**

IRONMASTER (1983). Conan imitation in which muscle-bound swordsman with a way of communicating with the gods of war discovers a talisman to help fight off evil forces. Sam Pasco, Elvire Audray, George Eastman. Directed by Umberto Lenzi. (Prism; ANE)

IRON WARRIOR (1986). This sequel to ATOR THE FIGHTING EAGLE and BLADE MASTER in the easily forgettable ATOR series stars that Poor Man's Conan, Michael O'Keefe, on the island of Malta as he does battle with monsters and assorted villains to protect Princess Janna (Savina Gersak). Directed by Italian potboiler king Al Bradly. Tim Lane, Elizabeth Kaza. (Media)

ISABEL (1968). Genevieve Bujold is going mad, seeing illusions, apparitions and visions in this confusing Canadian psychological study written-produced-directed by Paul Almond. What does it all mean? You tell us.

I SAW WHAT YOU DID (1965). Gimmicky William Castle-directed potboiler in which two teenage baby sitters phone at random, exclaim "I saw what you did!" and hang up. One man they call (John Ireland) has just finished slaughtering his wife (Joan Crawford) in a shower scene inspired by PSYCHO. William McGivern's script (from an Ursula Curtiss novel) has mysteriously opening and closing doors and windows as the mad killer stalks the teeners. A minor film that satisfies more for its campiness than its outdated thrills. Leif Erickson, Pat Breslin.

I SAW WHAT YOU DID (1988). This TV-movie remake of the 1965 William Castle feature is the medium at its worst—plodding direction by Fred Walton, a mediocre script by Cynthia Cidre (from the Ursula Curtiss novel) and a sincere cast in need of all the help it can get. Castle's work had a tongue-in-cheek endearment, but this lacks it all. The plotline has been shifted around so the killer is now film-music composer Adrian Lancer (Robert Carradine) who goes berserk. He loves to tie you up and set you on fire. Out of tune, isn't he? The teenagers who becry "I saw what you did and I know who you are!" are a wearisome lot, and the whole thing unfolds predictably. Shawnee Smith, Tammy Lauren, Candace Cameron, David Carradine.

ISLAND, THE (1980). This Zanuck-Brown production of Peter Benchley's novel proposes a solution to the Bermuda Triangle mystery: All those boats and people are vanishing because modern descendants of 17th Century pirates are still flying the skull and crossbones. An exciting premise, but Benchley's script is insipid and the characterizations are atrocious. Magazine researcher Michael Caine and son seek an answer to the mystery by acting as decoys. David Warner and his pirates are supposed to have a code all their own, but it's a ridiculous life they lead, plunging the film into laughability. Director Michael Ritchie's worst. Angela McGregor, Frank Middlemass. (Video/Laser: MCA)

ISLAND AT THE TOP OF THE WORLD (1974). Inferior Disney adventure-fantasy with poor effects and a horribly mangled story—a cinematic massacre of Ian Cameron's THE LOST ONES. David Hartman, hardly the stuff movie heroes are made of, leads an expedition to the polar regions in the airship Hyperion in 1908. The team discovers a long-forgotten kingdom ruled by bloodthirsty Vikings. This "adventure epic" misses by miles, turning its potential fun into turgidity. Directed by Robert Stevenson. Donald Sinden, Mako. (Disney)

ISLAND CLAWS (1982). Old-fashioned giant-monster-on-the-rampage flick, enhanced by Florida photography and the personas of Robert Lansing and Barry Nelson. A research team is experimenting with crustaceans when an atomic energy malfunction creates one huge monster crab killer and forces the little crabbers to turn against mankind, with a taste for People Thermidor. Thrills are minimal until the monster crab attacks. The story (by Jack Cowden and underwater stuntman Ricou Browning) is predictable. Herman Caredenas directs. Jo McDonnell, Nita Talbot. (Vestron)

ISLAND OF BLOOD (1986). Actors working on a rock 'n roll film on a deserted island begin dying according to a song's lyrics. Crime of a rhyme. Jimmy Williams, Dean Richards. (Action International)

ISLAND OF DEATH. See **ISLAND OF THE DAMNED.**

ISLAND OF DR. MOREAU, THE (1977). Effective adaptation of H. G. Wells' novel with Burt Lancaster as the demented albeit earnest doctor who converts animals into half-men through vivisection. The "creative make-up" is excellent, resulting in a menagerie of "manbeasts" led by Richard Basehart as the Sayer of the Law. The tropical rain forests near St. Croix in the Virgin Islands are a superb location for director Don Taylor. Michael York and Barbara Carrera as the lovers confronted with Moreau's horrors make for a sympathetic couple. ISLAND OF LOST SOULS was the 1933 version starring Charles Laughton, and that was a good one too. Watch for Nick Cravat as M'Ling. (Warner Bros.)

ISLAND OF LIVING HORROR, THE. See **BRIDES OF BLOOD.**

ISLAND OF LOST SOULS (1933). One of the most chilling horror films of the 1930s, a repellant though intriguing adaptation of H. G. Wells' novel about the mad Dr. Moreau, who grafts animals into men in his "House of Pain" to change the process of evolution. Charles Laughton, as the vivisectionist who presides God-like over his creatures, is on the hammy side, but his overplaying is what makes Moreau seem above the affairs of ordinary men, destined to change science. Bela Lugosi as the wolfman has a grotesquely satisfying role. Not for the squeamish as the beasts-men scamper about in mental and physical anguish. Written by Philip Wylie and Waldemar Young, directed by Erle C. Kenton and starring Richard Arlen as the shipwrecked hero. Remade in 1977 as THE ISLAND OF DR. MOREAU. (MCA)

ISLAND OF LOST WOMEN (1959). Stranded fliers find a lost scientist (Alan Napier) and his daughters . . . there's a death ray and other overused fantasy elements to round out this pulp-inspired adventure tale. Directed by Frank Tuttle. Jeff Richards, Diane Jergens, John Smith.

ISLAND OF TERROR (1967). An isolated community

is under attack from man-produced silicate monsters that suck human bone marrow. Director Terence Fisher and writers Alan Ramsen and Edward Andrew Mann infuse tongue-in-cheek with the macabre to avoid the humdrum in this sickening nightmare. Silicates are snake-like tentacles that slither around corners when you least expect them. They'll have you jumping as they wriggle up stairways and latch onto human flesh. There's a great sequence where Peter Cushing has to cut off his own hand to save himself. Niall MacGinnis, Edward Judd, Eddie Byrne. Also known as NIGHT OF THE SILICATES. (Sinister/C; S/Weird; MCA)

ISLAND OF THE ALIVE. See **IT'S ALIVE III: ISLAND OF THE ALIVE.**

ISLAND OF THE BURNING DOOMED (1967). Produced in Britain as NIGHT OF THE BIG HEAT, and also known as ISLAND OF THE BURNING DAMNED, this is a simmering adaptation of a John Lymington novel in which Christopher Lee, Peter Cushing, Patrick Allen, Sarah Lawson and Jane Merrow are attacked by aliens capable of burning measly humans to death with a heat wave. But the film, unlike the characters, never catches fire. Directed by Terence Fisher. (New Star)

ISLAND OF THE DAMNED (1976). Spanish horror thriller is an exciting exploitation film in which a pregnant wife and her husband visit a pleasure island to find all the adults dead and homicidal children eager to slaughter more. On a less obvious level, it points out how children become victims of adult madness through civil war and strife. Hence, their revenge! Luis Perafiel's script is food for thought and explicitly violent as the children close in on the couple, forcing them to commit acts of mayhem. Directed by Narciso Ibanez Serrador. Also known as WHO CAN KILL A CHILD?, WOULD YOU KILL A CHILD?, DEATH IS CHILD'S PLAY and ISLAND OF DEATH. Lewis Fiander, Prunella Ransome.

ISLAND OF THE DEAD/ISLAND OF THE DOOMED. See **MAN-EATER OF HYDRA.**

ISLAND OF THE FISHMEN. See **SCREAMERS.**

ISLAND OF THE LAST ZOMBIES, THE. See **DR. BUTCHER M.D.**

ISLAND OF THE LIVING DEAD. See **ZOMBIE (1979).**

ISLAND OF THE LOST (1968). Insignificant Ivan Tors TV-movie in which explorer-anthropologist Richard Greene and five young travelers discover a Pacific island inhabited by prehistoric sabertooth wolves, nine-gill sharks, ferocious ostriches, etc. A blending of FLIPPER and SWISS FAMILY ROBINSON as the stranded band meets a native living on the island as part of a survival course imposed by his tribe. Written by Tors and Richard Carlson, with Ricou Browning handling the underwater photography. (Republic; Genesis)

ISLAND OF THE SNAKE PEOPLE. See **SNAKE PEOPLE, THE.**

ISLAND OF THE TWILIGHT PEOPLE. See **TWILIGHT PEOPLE, THE.**

ISLE OF THE DEAD (1945). Arnold Boecklin's painting, "Die Todinsel," inspired this low-key Val Lewton horror chiller, strongly atmospheric but slow under Mark Robson's direction. One of Boris Karloff's strangest roles—he portrays a tyrannical Greek general in the year 1912 (the Balkan War is raging) who believes in "vrykolakas," Greek vampires. When a sinister plague infects the island, Karloff quarantines everyone and, one by one, the assorted characters meet their doom. Ellen Drew, Jason Robards Sr., Alan Napier, Marc Cramer. (Fox Hills; Nostalgia Merchant; Turner) (Laser: Image)

ISLE OF THE FISH MEN. See **SCREAMERS.**

ISLE OF THE SNAKE PEOPLE. See **SNAKE PEOPLE, THE.**

ISN'T IT SHOCKING? (1973). Psychomurder TV-movie with Edmond O'Brien as gentle, peace-loving Justin Oates, who is killing old folks in an Oregon community with an electronic device, and watching as fledgling sheriff Alan Alda bumbles his way to a solution. Directed by John Badham. Louise Lasser, Ruth Gordon, Will Geer, Lloyd Nolan.

I SPIT ON YOUR GRAVE (1979). The epitome of rape-woman's revenge pictures, a cult favorite written-directed-edited by Meir Zarchi. A bloody tale (also known as DAY OF THE WOMAN) about four men who gang-bang vacationing Camille Keaton. After a second go-around of debasement, the chauvinistic pigs are wasted by the avenging angel who uses every weapon at hand from butcher knife to hangman's rope to woodman's axe to . . . not for the squeamish. Eron Tabor, Richard Pace. (Wizard; VidAmerica) (Laser: VidAmerica; Image)

IT! (1966). The Golem is the Jewish Avenger, a creature of clay wreaking havoc on desecrators. Roddy McDowall is a batty museum curator keeping the mummified body of the Golem as an exhibit who finally misuses the creature for evil revenge. The thing goes berserk, destroying Hammersmith Bridge and kidnapping Jill Haworth. Written-produced-directed by Herbert J. Leder. Paul Maxwell, Aubrey Richards, Ernest Clark.

IT! See **STEPHEN KING'S IT!**

ITALIAN MOUSE, THE. See **THE MAGIC WORLD OF TOPO GIGIO.**

IT CAME FROM BENEATH THE SEA (1955). Collaboration between producers Charles Schneer and Sam Katzman and stop motion animator Ray Harryhausen resulted in an historic monster flick about a giant octopus awakened by an atomic blast and attracted to San Francisco Bay. The creature (with only six tentacles, due to Katzman's insufficient budget) attacks the Golden Gate Bridge and Embarcadero. This has its fun moments as directed by Robert Gordon from a George Worthington Yates-Hal Smith script. Donald Curtis and Kenneth Tobey still have time to woo scientist Faith Domergue during the mayhem. Ian Keith, Harry Lauter, Del Courtney. (RCA/Columbia; Goodtimes) (Laser: Columbia TriStar)

IT CAME FROM HOLLYWOOD (1982). Compilation of the best "worst" scenes from genre movies, emphasis on monsters, horror and drugs. Comedians appear in camped-up cameos covering specialized themes. Gilda Radner does Gorillas and Musical Memories; Cheech and Chong cover (naturally) Getting High, Giants, and Animal Kingdom Goes Berserk; Dan Aykroyd deals with Brains, Aliens and Troubled Teenagers. There's a salute to Edward Wood Jr. (PLAN 9 FROM OUTER SPACE) and Prevues of Coming Attractions and Technical Triumphs. The guest hosts are superfluous—the clips can stand alone. Anyway, fans, you'll see scenes from WHITE GORILLA, BRAIN THAT WOULDN'T DIE, etc. Hollywood at its funniest—and dumbiest. (Video/Laser: Paramount)

IT CAME FROM OUTER SPACE (1953). One of the finest science-fiction thrillers of the 1950s, inspired by a Ray Bradbury outline that was modified for Universal-International by Harry Essex, and originally released in 3-D. Essex's screenplay, while being among the first to portray benevolent aliens, is alo a plea for better understanding between races. This is Jack Arnold's best directorial work, for he captures a desert eeriness as bug-eyed aliens crashland their ship near astronomer Richard Carlson's isolated home. The E.T.s, dubbed Xenomorphs, are giant eyeball creatures capable of assuming human forms. A "fish-eye" lens is used to simulate the point of view of the creatures. Barbara Rush provides love interest, Charles Drake is the disbelieving sheriff, and Russell Johnson and Joe Sawyer are possessed telephone linemen. (Video/Laser: MCA)

IT CAME UPON THE MIDNIGHT CLEAR (1984). Sappy TV-movie starring Mickey Rooney as a New York cop who suffers a fatal heart attack and goes to Heaven, requesting of St. Peter (George Gaynes) that he be allowed to spend one final Christmas with grandson Scott Grimes. Sentimental cornpone in Central Park, directed by Peter H. Hunt. Barrie Youngfellow, Hamilton Camp, Annie Potts. (RCA/Columbia; Goodtimes)

IT CAME . . . WITHOUT WARNING (1980). Here's a warning: Beware this sci-fi terror tale (a predecessor to PREDATOR) in which an alien stalks Earthlings for trophies to adorn his spaceship walls. Martin Landau (playing Fred Dobbs, get it?) and Jack Palance deserve the Overacting Awards of 1980; they are genuinely terrible as would-be victims of the creature, who uses ugly disc-shaped suckers for "bullets." Slurp sqwk glump: those are sounds made by the Incredibly Hungry Disc Beasties. They are effective, even if Greydon Clark's direction isn't. Cameron Mitchell, Neville Brand, Sue Ane Langdon, Larry Storch, Ralph Meeker. (From HBO as **WITHOUT WARNING**)

IT CONQUERED THE WORLD (1956). "It" does nothing of the sort—"it" is one sad-looking Venusivian hiding in a cave that blows its invasion because "it" is dumb enough to rely on Lee Van Cleef to carry out "its" evil bidding. And dumb enough to send a squad of bat creatures to kill Beverly Garland, thereby tipping off Peter Graves to what is happening. This Roger Corman produced-directed quickie (remade as ZONTAR, THE THING FROM MARS) ranks as one of his all-time worst, yet fans continue to enjoy its campiness. Dick Miller, Russ Bender, Sally Fraser, Jonathan Haze, Charles B. Griffith, Paul Blaisdell. (RCA/Columbia)

IT FELL FROM THE SKY. See **ALIEN DEAD.**

IT GROWS ON TREES (1952). Charming, heartwarming fantasy-comedy in which a wholesome American family discovers that two unusual trees planted in the backyard are capable of greenery—greenbacks, that is. The Leonard Praskins-Barney Slater script satirically deals with the legal implications of spending money the government didn't make and draws a pleasant portrait of Irene Dunne, hubby Dean Jagger and typical teenage son and daughter Joan Evans and Richard Crenna. This Universal-International release directed by Arthur Lubin nostalgically captures the innocence of another time.

IT HAPPENED AT LAKEWOOD MANOR (1977). Lake Wood is minor as far as horror is concerned. This TV-movie is preposterous: Swarms of irate ants attack a resort, imprisoning dull and unimaginative individuals inside. Ants' antisocial behavior is blamed on pesticides and man's carelessness toward nature, but hasn't that already been overworked by frogs? The suspense is ersatz, the menace of these Hymenopteras uninvolving . . . you wouldn't hesitate to go on a picnic. In fact, do—it beats this dreary stuff. Directed by Robert Scheerer. The best screamer in the cast is Suzanne Somers. Robert Foxworth, Lynda Day George, Myrna Loy, Bernie Casey, Steve Franken. (From USA as **ANTS**)

IT HAPPENED AT NIGHTMARE INN. Video version of **NIGHTMARE HOTEL** (Sinister/C; S/Weird).

IT HAPPENED HERE (1966). Two Englishmen (Kevin Brownlow and Andrew Mollo) spent eight years and $20,000 to produce this pseudodocumentary depicting what might have happened had Hitler invaded England in 1943 and conquered the Empire. Britain is depicted under Fascist rule (Gestapo troops march past Big Ben; SS troopers flirt with girls on the Thames) but an underground group fights the invaders. Rough camera work and an unintelligible soundtrack are deficits that give this flight-of-fiction a hard-edged reality.

IT HAPPENED ONE CHRISTMAS (1977). Inferior remake of IT'S A WONDERFUL LIFE, with the Jimmy Stewart role rewritten for Marlo Thomas, who now fights despair after a life of self-sacrifice. Cloris Leachman, Wayne Rogers, Orson Welles, Doris Roberts, Barney Martin. Directed by Donald Wrye.

IT HAPPENED TOMORROW (1944). Dick Powell can read tomorrow's news today, provided by an old ghost. What happens when he reads his own obituary? Directed by Rene Clair. Linda Darnell, Jack Oakie.

IT HAPPENS EVERY SPRING (1949). For fantasy fans, baseball lovers, romanticists and scientists. Professor Ray Milland invents an anti-wood substance. Think what that could mean if applied to a baseball. So, as his spitball curves around every swinging bat in the majors, he becomes a big league pitcher and carries a losing team to the World Series. It's the whimsical side to THE NATURAL, a marvelous comedy starring Jean Peters as the love interest and Paul Douglas as a blustering manager. A film like this should happen every spring. A hit directed by Lloyd Bacon. Alan Hale Jr., Ray Collins, Ed Begley, Ray Teal, Gene Evans.

IT LIVES AGAIN. Video version of **IT'S ALIVE II** (Warner Bros.).

IT NEARLY WASN'T CHRISTMAS (1989). Alternate title for **NEARLY WASN'T CHRISTMAS, THE.**

IT'S A DOG'S LIFE (1955). See editions 1-3.

IT'S ALIVE (1968). Credit writer-producer-director Larry Buchanan for botching this one thoroughly. A crazy rancher who collects snakes and crawlies has also found a "lizard amphibian" in a cave, so he feeds it passers-by. Along comes paleontologist Tommy Kirk plus another couple, and they're all thrown to the Masasaurus. The most exciting thing is not the creature—it's a rubber-suited fake—but watching blonde Shirley Bonne walk around in a yellow miniskirt. (S/Weird; Nostalgia; Loonic)

IT'S ALIVE (1975). Larry Cohen wrote-directed this gruesome shocker about an infamous infant who slides from the womb with claws, fangs and sharp teeth and kills doctors and nurses before they even have time to spank his spiked behind. While it sounds like the ultimate nightmare, rolling birth and death into one act, Cohen creates the ambience of an abnormal world tainted by birth control pills, poisonous chemicals, smoggy air and atomic fallout. Your skin will crawl as the bloodthirsty bambino (created from the nightmares of Rick Baker) lurks around every corner. Cohen keeps his monster out of camera range most of the time, thereby building suspense and shocks. John Ryan, Sharon Farrell, Guy Stockwell, Andrew Duggan, Michael Ansara. (Warner Bros.)

IT'S ALIVE II (1978). Larry Cohen's IT'S ALIVE was a powerful indictment against our misuse of atomic power and drugs, but this sequel fails in the delivery room. Call it stillborn. Cohen's writing and directing are utterly off the mark in depicting another baby-faced killer sliding from a womb with claws and teeth to kill. Parents Frederic Forrest and Kathleen Lloyd flee with the mutant to an incubation hideout where other baby-monsters are under study by scientist Andrew Duggan and the father from the first film, John Ryan. (Duggan believes the babies are "the next step in evolution so we can survive the pollution of our planet.") Credit Rick Baker for the hideously fanged creatures infrequently shown during Cohen's hide-and-seek direction. John Marley, Eddie Constantine. (From Warner Bros. as **IT LIVES AGAIN**)

IT'S ALIVE III: ISLAND OF THE ALIVE (1986). An unusual performance by Michael Moriarty earmarks this second sequel to writer-director Larry Cohen's 1975 hit. A wave of baby monsters is hitting society and Moriarty decides that love and not death is the way to deal with the teethy tykes when their fate must be decided in a court of law. Judge MacDonald Carey decrees they be sent to a desert island. Moriarty goes a little paranoid, turned cynical by how society exploits the mutant monsters through the media, and he returns to the island with an expedition to help the freaks. Moriarty's nuttiness and the social issues touched on by Cohen's script make this above-average. The monsters are depicted with live action and stop-motion animation. Karen Black, Laurene Landos, Gerrit Graham, James Dixon. (Warner Bros.)

IT'S A WONDERFUL LIFE (1946). Capra-corn as Hollywood's producer-director Frank Capra indulges in whimsical nostalgia to present a slice of unforgettable Americana. Guardian Angel Clarence (Henry Travers) is dispatched to a small Wisconsin town to show Jimmy Stewart, a disillusioned young man, what might have happened had he never been born. A touch of A CHRISTMAS CAROL makes this an exceptionally penetrating slice of life, which Capra scripted with Frances Goodrich and Albert Hackett. Donna Reed, Lionel Barrymore, Thomas Mitchell, Gloria Grahame, Ward Bond. Wonderful music by Dimitri Tiomkin. (Hal Roach; Republic; Nostalgia Merchant; a colorized version also exists) (Laser: Republic; Criterion)

IT'S GROWING INSIDE HER. TV title for **DEVIL WITHIN HER, THE.**

IT'S HOT IN PARADISE. See **HORRORS OF SPIDER ISLAND.**

IT'S NOT THE SIZE THAT COUNTS (1974). Sequel to PERCY, known in England as PERCY'S PROGRESS . . . a continuation of the adventures of the man with the first penis transplant . . . but here the concept shrinks to nothing. On top of the misplaced organ theme, this deals with a chemical in the water making men impotent. Ooops, there goes sex. Denholm Elliott, Elke Sommer, Vincent Price, Judy Geeson, George Coulouris. Directed by Ralph Thomas. (Sultan)

IT STALKED THE OCEAN FLOOR. See **MONSTER FROM THE OCEAN FLOOR.**

IT! THE TERROR FROM BEYOND SPACE (1958). Epitome of the sci-fi monster movies of the 1950s, more bearable than its title would suggest thanks to a decent script by Jerome Bixby. Ray "Crash" Corrigan dons the rubber suit to play a vampire-style Martian which stows away on a rocketship and then, when deep in space, develops a thirst that can't be quenched at the snack bar. That's when astronauts Marshall Thompson, Shawn Smith, Ann Doran and Kim Spalding get it in the neck. Frequently compared to ALIEN. Directed by "quickie master" Edward L. Cahn. (MGM/UA)

I VAMPIRI (1957). Gianna-Maria Canale, one-time queen of Italian B movies, pulls a Countess Bathory routine by bathing her body in the blood of striptease beauties while carrying on before the public as a stately actress. Routine psychomurders are enhanced by Mario Bava's cinematography and nifty aging effects. For voyeurs and gore fans. Directed by Riccardo Freda. (On video as THE DEVIL'S COMMANDMENT)

IVANNA. See **SCREAM OF THE DEMON LOVER.**

I'VE LIVED BEFORE (1956). Low-budget, mildly interesting tale of reincarnation from Universal-International. Jock Mahoney, a sympathetic airline pilot, believes he is the reincarnation of a flyer shot down over France on April 29, 1918. John McIntire is the doctor who talks about psychoses and neuroses and helps Mahoney to sort out his life. Ann Harding is the girl who provides a link between Mahoney and the Spad flyer. Directed by Richard Bartlett. Leigh Snowden, April Kent, Jerry Paris.

IVORY APE, THE (1980). You thought King Kong had problems . . . Rangi is an ape that wants to be alone, but no such luck. Captured and placed aboard a freighter, she breaks her bonds and escapes to Bermuda, where the local constabulary wants to shoot her down after she attacks and kills her trackers. Anthropologist Cindy Pickett and Steven Keats want to take Rangi alive, while big game hunter Jack Palance has more fatal ideas in mind. Never very exciting—the William Overgard script unfolds in a predictable fashion, and there's more dialogue than action. The best moment comes when Palance recounts how a crocodile once carried away his son in its jaws. Directed by Tom Kotani on location.

I WALKED WITH A ZOMBIE (1943). RKO low budgeter is producer Val Lewton's classic, a loose adaptation of JANE EYRE (scripted by Curt Siodmak and Ardel Wray) in which nurse Frances Dee is brought to a Caribbean island to care for a woman in a zombie-like state, victim of mental paralysis. Hauntingly directed by Jacques Tourneur, with a Calypso-inspired score by Roy Webb. J. Roy Hunt's cinematography is punctuated by striking visuals, such as a voodoo native (Darby Jones) with a cadaverous face stalking two women through a canefield. James Ellison, Tom Conway, Edith Barrett. (Nostalgia Merchant; Media; RKO; Turner)

I WAS A TEENAGE BOY. See **SOMETHING SPECIAL.**

I WAS A TEENAGE FRANKENSTEIN (1957). Herman Cohen's sequel to I WAS A TEENAGE WEREWOLF, with Whit Bissell reappearing as a mad doctor, relative of the infamous Baron. Ludicrous as its title, with severed limbs graphically offered up for their shock value (and severed limbs in 1957 were an onscreen rarity). Despite its trend-setting virtues, and the fact it was an early proponent of black-macabre humor, Kenneth Langtry's script is hopelessly laughable, often in the wrong places. You too will be a teenage zombie if you sit through this. Phyllis Coates, Gary Conway. (RCA/Columbia)

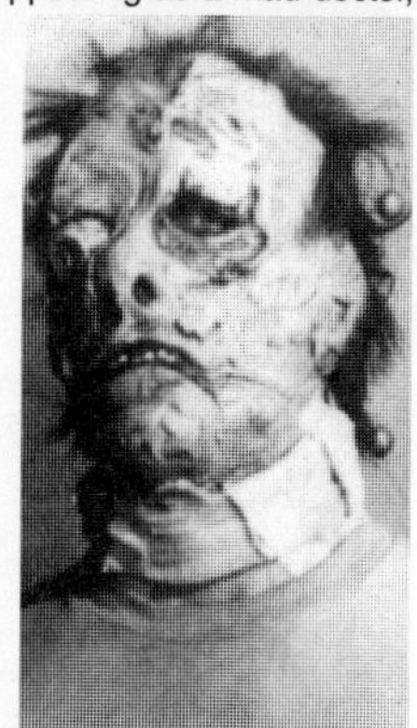

TEENAGER GARY

I WAS A TEENAGE SEX MUTANT (1989). Poor Billy Jacoby. Every time a tubular, humming creature pops out of his head all the women rip their clothes off and claw his body. It's worse than acne. That creature got there because of alien Judy Landers, a biology teacher in miniskirt and high heels who's on earth to conduct experiments in human (and inhuman) behavior. Kenneth J. Hall's kitchen-sink script (with emphasis on sex rather than mutant) is pretty dumb with nerdy Jacoby turning into a rock star, an excuse for a musical number. Directed by Dave Decoteau. Olivia Barash, Stuart Fratkin, Bobby Jacoby, Arlene Golonka, Edy Williams. (From Paramount as **DR. ALIEN**)

I WAS A TEENAGE WEREWOLF (1957). An American-International classic with Michael Landon as a troubled youth etched in the style of James Dean. When he falls under the control of wicked doctor Whit Bissell, Landon regresses to a primitive, animalistic state (make that werewolfian) on a rampage of killing. The suspense is minimum under Gene Fowler Jr's direction, but the point of view of the story's young people, the depiction of adults, and the time-lapse transformation special effects, although dated, now seem nostalgic and quaint. For decades Landon disavowed this film, then came to Arkoff in the 1980s and asked permission to use some footage for an episode of HIGHWAY TO HEAVEN he called "I Was a Middle-Aged Werewolf." Yvonne Lime, Guy Williams, Robert Griffin. (RCA/Columbia)

I WAS A TEENAGE ZOMBIE (1987). An amateurish, almost unwatchable piece of crapola. Better it should have been called I WAS A TEENAGE NERD. Some jerks hanging around Woodbridge High discover that a drug dealer named Mussolini (Moose for short), whom they killed and threw in the bay, has been brought back to life by high-energy radioactive contamination from the Mohawk Nuclear Power Plant. Mix the contamination with "kinetic energy" and presto—a dreaded zombie killer. Director John Elias Michalakis tries to shock by having a tongue pulled out of a man's mouth and a young woman bent in half while she's being raped by "Moose," but these effects leave everything to be desired. Michael Ruben, George Seminara. (Video/Laser: Charter)

I WAS A ZOMBIE FOR THE FBI (1984). An alien monster presented in stop-motion animation, a silver ball that turns humans into zombies, the secret formula for a soft drink, Unicola—these are the bizarre ingredients that make this an offbeat sci-fi spoof played straight by writer-director Marius Penczner. The time is the 1950s when the criminally-inclined Brazzo brothers survive a plane crash, stumble across an alien plot and involve the FBI in a kidnapping—and that's only the beginning. Refreshing oddity; unusual in that it was produced at Memphis State University. John Gillick, James Rasberry, Larry Rasberry. (Cinema Group; Continental)

JABBERWOCKY (1977). British satire, inspired work by Monty Python alumnus Terry Gilliam, who directed and co-wrote (with Charles Alverson). King Bruno the Questionable (Max Wall) must defeat a dragon monster that is so awful, peasants would rather catch the plague. In the vein of MONTY PYTHON AND THE HOLY GRAIL, with blood, dismemberment, wallowing in dirt. For those who like humor as dark as the ages in which this medieval parody is set. Michael Palin plays a dragon-stalking peasant. (Video/Laser: RCA/Columbia)

JACK AND THE BEANSTALK (1952). Fantasy-comedy with Lou Costello as a babysitter reading the famed fable to an obnoxious brat. Presto: Costello becomes Jack and Bud Abbott plays the village butcher "boy." Buddy Baer is the ogre—ferocious but appealing enough not to scare the kids for whom this fluff was intended. Directed by Jean Yarbrough. (MGM/UA; Amvest; VCI; from Goodtimes with AFRICA SCREAMS)

JACK AND THE BEANSTALK (1976). Animated feature version of the classic fairy tale, directed by Peter J. Solmo. (RCA/Columbia)

JACK AND THE BEANSTALK (1983). An episode from TV's FAERIE TALE THEATER. Dennis Christopher, Katherine Helmond, Elliott Gould, Jean Stapleton. (Video/Laser: CBS/Fox)

JACK ARMSTRONG (1947). Fifteen-chapter cliff-hanger from schlockmeister Sam Katzman, starring John Hart as the all-American boy who goes after mad Dr. Grood (Charles Middleton) and his Death Ray, placed on a spaceship orbiting Earth. Directed by Wallace Fox. Rosemary La Planche, Joe Brown Jr, Claire James.

JACK'S BACK (1987). Intriguing update to Jack the Ripper is set in L.A. where a slasher-killer is duplicating the infamous 1888 crimes and the city is in a grip of terror. There's a psychic link between twin brothers John and Rick Wesford (James Spader) and when John is found hanged, and assumed to be the Ripper, Rick comes forth to clear his name. Nice plot twists involve a police hypnotist, a short-tempered doctor and a brute named, naturally, Jack. The script by director Rowdy Herrington is above average. Cynthia Gibb, Rod Loomis, Rex Ryon. (Video/Laser: Paramount)

JACK'S WIFE. See **HUNGRY WIVES.**

JACK THE GIANT KILLER (1962). Director Nathan Juran and actors Kerwin Mathews and Torin Thatcher re-teamed again after THE SEVENTH VOYAGE OF SINBAD, but this fantasy-adventure (written by Orville Hampton) sorely needs the Harryhausen touch. While Don Beddoe is effective as a leprechaun, the giants, sea serpents, griffins and flying witches leave something to be desired. Mathews is brave of heart, Thatcher is treacherous as Pendragon the Sorcerer and Judi Meredith is enchantingly beautiful. Youngsters will enjoy. Jim Danforth effects. (Video/Laser: MGM/UA)

JACK THE MANGLER OF LONDON. See **JACK THE RIPPER OF LONDON (1971).**

JACK THE RIPPER (1958). Boris Karloff anthology of four mild tales, each introduced by Karloff, who also has roles in three. These studio-bound yarns rely on dialogue and acting, and hence are of minimal impact. "Jack the Ripper" (made in London) is the best, with a clairvoyent aiding Scotland Yard's Inspector McWilliams in solving the Whitechapel murders. "Summer Heat" has Harry Bartell as a man with precognition powers who witnesses the murder of a blonde—before it happens. Karloff is the police psychiatrist. "Vision of Crime" involves rival brothers whose father returns from the grave. Karloff is the family attorney. "Food on the Table" features Karloff as a scheming sea captain who poisons his wife, only to have her return as a mischievous spirit. Michael Plant wrote the Ripper segment; no other writing credits given. The only director's credit is David MacDonald. These episodes were produced by Hal Roach Jr. for the series THE VEIL, but it was a flop and sold into syndication as three anthologies. The others are THE VEIL and DESTINATION NIGHTMARE. Paul Bryar, Gretchen Thomas,

Robert Griffin, Niall MacGinnis. (S/Weird)

JACK THE RIPPER (1958). This version of the Whitechapel murders of the 1880s has little bearing on facts but is still an effective thriller. While not as graphic as subsequent versions, it was considered controversial in its time and banned in some states when released in America by Joseph E. Levine. Written by Jimmy Sangster, and produced, directed and photographed by Robert S. Baker and Monty Berman, the film presents the traditional figure (Ewen Solon) in cape and slouch hat, carrying a black satchel. An American cop joins Scotland Yard to solve the case. Lee Patterson, Eddie Byrne. (Paramount; Sinister/C; S/Weird; Filmfax)

JACK THE RIPPER (1971). See **JACK THE RIPPER OF LONDON.**

JACK THE RIPPER (1976). This Jack tears it! A totally inaccurate German-Swiss depiction of the infamous London murders, with facts discarded by screenwriter-director Jesse Franco for exploitation. Klaus Kinski portrays the sexual brute as a despicable freako who stops at nothing to murder-fornicate. Clinically sickening in details. Josephine Chaplin, Herbert Fux. (Vestron)

JACK THE RIPPER (1988). Engrossing and intense TV-movie that offers a solution to the unsolved Jack the Ripper case. This dramatization of the five horrendous slasher-crimes covers the investigation, political intrigue and near-rioting of citizens. At the heart of the film's power is Michael Caine as Inspector Frederick George Abberline, who heads the investigation with Sergeant George Godley (Lewis Collins). Producer-director David Wickes' script takes on a whodunit aspect as suspects are established, among them the Queen's grandson (Marc Culwick), a psychic (Ken Bones), a vigilante leader (Michael Gothard), American actor Richard Mansfield (Armand Assante), even members of the police. The last half-hour is especially fascinating as Caine's behavior rises to a fever pitch as he closes in on the Ripper. Ray McAnally, Jane Seymout, Susan George. Harry Morgan, Edward Judd. (MPI; Vestron)

JACK THE RIPPER OF LONDON (1971). Modernized treatment of the infamous Whitechapel murders, showing the killer to have cannibalistic instincts. An unsavory Spanish-Italian version that is beneath contempt. Co-written by the film's star Paul Naschy (as Jacinto Molina) and director Jose Luis Madrid. Patricia Loran.

JACOB'S LADDER (1990). Intriguing cinematic puzzle that offers numerous clues to its surprise conclusion but only if you're watching carefully, and can see where screenwriter Bruce Joel Rubin is headed. In Vietnam in 1971, a platoon is attacked under odd circumstances. Flash ahead to the present as Tim Robbins, a GI wounded in the assault, undergoes visions, in which it appears demons are determined to kill him. We also flashback to his life before Vietnam, and elements from all three realities intermingle, and we are adrift in Robbins' mind. Directed by Adrian Lyne in brilliant style. Elizabeth Pena, Danny Aiello, Matt Craven. (IVE) (Laser: Image)

JALOPY (1953). Broken-down Bowery Boys vehicle with stripped gears never gets out of first and stalls after the credits. Huntz Hall creates a formula that is a love potion and a high-powered auto fuel. Directed by William Beaudine without overdrive.

JANE AND THE LOST CITY (1986). "Jane" was first a comic strip in the London Daily Mirror about a blonde whose clothes were always falling away to reveal her shapely form in panties and bra—she alone kept up the morale of British troops during World War II. This film version, with Kirsten Hughes playing Jane, is a take-off on the adventures of Indiana Jones with Jane venturing into Africa in 1940 to find a lost city's diamond fortune. With Jack Buck or "Jungle Jack" (a square hero dumbly played by Sam Jones) she fights a Nazi beauty (Maud Adams) and her inept henchmen. There's a leopard queen with a British accent, a British colonel and his butler, and tribes of lizard and water warriors. A bland spoof at best. Jasper Carrott, Robin Bailey. Directed by Terry Marcel. (New World)

JAR, THE (1984). For 90 minutes little happens while Gary Wallace sits and looks either blank or frightened. Following an auto accident (filmed so darkly one can barely see it), Wallace finds a bottle containing a demon that proceeds to drive him out of his mind. This attempt at surrealism and horror (also called CARRION) with very few visuals (corpse rising out of tub of blood; slaughter of American troops in Vietnam) isn't worth one's time. Directed by Bruce Toscano. (Magnum)

JASON AND THE ARGONAUTS (1963). Superb mythological fantasy, directed by Don Chaffey, with stop motion animation by the incomparable Ray Harryhausen. A recounting of the adventures of Jason and his warriors who dare the dangers of a bronze giant named Talos, the winged harpies, the seven-headed Hydra and sword-wielding skeletons to claim the Golden Fleece. Todd Armstrong is a superb Jason, watched from on high by the Gods of Mt. Olympus. The link between mortal and immortal becomes a compelling element to the Jan Read-Beverly Cross script. As a picturesque, picaresque fantasy, this is hard to top. Nancy Kovack is Medea, Honor Blackman and Niall MacGinnis are Goddess and God, Nigel Green is the brave Hercules. A great score by Bernard Herrmann enhances this British-U.S. effort. (RCA/Columbia) (Laser: RCA/Columbia; Criterion)

JASON GOES TO HELL: THE FINAL FRIDAY (1993). Is this really the last of the FRIDAY THE 13TH flickers? Yes . . . until Hollywood decides to make a few million more from the Jason-Voorhees-in-a-hockey-mask-formula. In this, the ninth series entry, Jason is back as a supernatural entity transferring his evil soul from body to body by injecting a piece of his heart into a new recipient's mouth. Hot on his trail: bounty hunter Creighton Duke (Steven Williams), the only man on Earth who knows that only a descendant of Jason can kill him, if equipped with a magical sword that Duke just happens to carry. This remains a relative unimaginative blood-and-violence fest, with the usual variety of death devices to dispatch the cannon-fodder characters. Nobody in the cast is memorable—only Kane Hodder as the hockey-masked Jason. According to the script, Jason murdered a total of 83 people in the preceding films. Not bad. Not great, but not bad. Jon D. LeMay, Karl Keegan, Steven Culp, Erin Gray. (New Line)

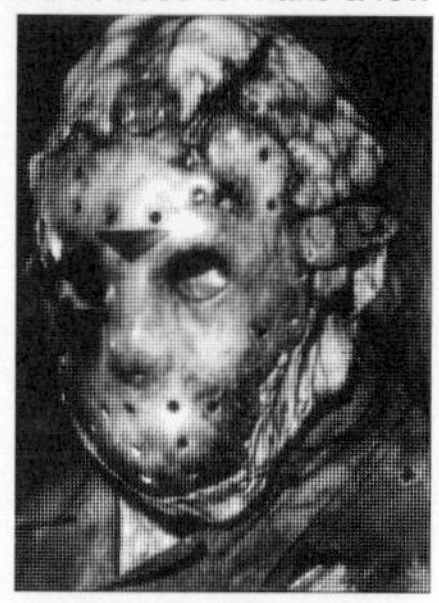

JASON VOORHEES

JASSY (1948). By using her wits and a psychic ability to foresee disasters, a beautiful gypsy girl (Margaret Lockwood) rises from poverty to become the bitter, cynical head of a British estate in this high-quality Technicolor adaptation of a novel by Norah Lofts. It's basically an overwrought costume drama, with the minor ESP subplots to qualify it for this book, and should be seen in color for maximum enjoyment. The direction by Bernard Knowles is of such a high quality that the rougher edges of the story can be overlooked. Sassy, classy, not too trashy. Patricia Roc, Dennis Price, Basil Sydney, Cathleen Nesbit, Ernest Thesiger, Torin Thatcher.

JAWS (1975). Box-office smash based on the so-so albeit best-seller by Peter Benchley. Under Steven Spielberg's direction, this becomes a classic adventure saga, ingeniously mounted to evoke our primeval fears as a Great White Shark (25 feet long) attacks the New England community of Amity. After episodes in which humans are bait or narrowly escape the superfish, sharkfighters Robert Shaw, Richard Dreyfuss and Roy Scheider set out aboard the Orca to kill the monster. In addition to taut action sequences and great shark effects, there are subtle horrors too, such as when Shaw, a survivor of the sinking of the U.S. Indianapolis in 1945, describes how men were eaten alive. Carl Gottlieb and Spielberg hashed out the final story. This all-time fish whopper did for public beaches what ALIEN did for space travel. The great "shark machine" music is by John Williams. Lorraine Gray, Murray Hamilton, Jeffrey Kramer. (Video/Laser: MCA)

JAWS 2 (1978). This sequel to the smasheroo inspired by Peter Benchley's novel is afloat in too-familiar waters and lacks the bite of the original. Director Jeannot Szwarc imitates Spielberg in shameless style, but captures none of the visceral terror. Bruce the Mechanical Shark looks exactly that as he "attacks" youngsters trapped on the high seas. Surely a colossal case of overbite. Carl Gottlieb co-scripted with Howard Sackler. Returning are Roy Scheider as the sheriff, Lorraine Gary as his wife and Murray Hamilton as the obnoxious mayor. Jeffrey Kramer, Collin Wilcox. (Video/Laser: MCA)

JAWS 3 (1983). What could have been gnashing thrills, Bruce the Shark in 3-D, is a disappointment when a baby Great White and 35-foot-long mother enter the lagoon of a Florida seaworld park and attack swimmers and the underwater observation rooms and corridors. Except for scenes where the behemoth swallows a man, or bumps its snout against plucky heroine Bess Armstrong, JAWS 3-D strangely lacks excitement. It's hard to understand why some scenes are underlit, the stupid characters (did Richard Matheson and Carl Gottlieb really write this dribble?), and the juvenile, almost Porky's approach. A few 3-D effects are fine (such as a floating severed arm), but stereovision adds little to the dimensions of this mediocre attempt. Lou Gossett Jr., Dennis Quaid, Lisa Mauer. Production designer Joe Alves directed. Simon MacCorkindale, Barbara Eden. (Video/Laser: MCA)

JAWS 3-D. See **JAWS 3.**

JAWS 4. See **JAWS THE REVENGE.**

JAWS OF DEATH. Video version of **MAKO: THE JAWS OF DEATH.** (King of Video; Paragon)

JAWS OF SATAN (1983). Terrible killer-snake movie: a King Cobra on a rampage is a demon serpent sent from Hell to terrorize priest Fritz Weaver. If that sounds absurd, consider the awful Neanderthal special effects, the absurd screenplay by Gerry Holland and the unskilled direction of Bob Claver. The cobra commands other poisonous creatures (asps, rattlers, cottonmouths, water mocassins) to carry out its biting, so the coiled critters are everywhere, harassing Gretchen Corbett and Jon Korkes, both of the Wimp School of Acting. A wretched wreck filmed in Alabama. (Wood Knapp)

JAWS OF THE ALIEN. Video version of **HUMAN DUPLICATORS, THE** (Star Classics).

JAWS THE REVENGE (1987). Anyone who has been to Universal Studio's tour knows that Bruce the Great White Shark rises out of the water to scare everyone on the tourist tram. Well, that's exactly how Bruce looks when he/she/it goes on the attack in this third sequel in the JAWS series. With that all-important illusion shattered, JAWS THE REVENGE is a waste of viewing time. Bruce is now endowed with a supernatural ability to single out members of the Brody family: Lorraine Gary's two sons, and Gary herself during the climactic encounter. Producer-director Joe Sargent gives away the shark's presence prior to each attack, so no tension builds. Michael de Guzman's script defies all credibility, and not even Michael Caine as a pilot helps much. Mario Van Peebles, Karen Young. (Video/Laser: MCA)

J.D.'S REVENGE (1976). Well-acted supernatural tale in which law student/cabbie Glynn Turman (in an excellent performance) is possessed by the spirit of a razor-wielding black lowlife murdered in 1942. Turman undergoes transformation, becoming the deceased J. D. Walker. Motivation for the possession is a night club hypnosis act—a weakness in Jaison Starkes' otherwise compelling story. Produced-directed by Arthur Marks. Lou Gossett, Joan Pringle, David McKnight. (Orion)

JEKYLL AND HYDE (1990). Elaborate sets and period costumes enhance this British TV-movie version of Robert Louis Stevenson's classic tale of dual personality, written-directed by David Wickes. Michael Caine is Dr. Henry Jekyll, whose experiments have turned him into a monstrous murderer terrorizing London. The effects of the metabiological transmutation are familiar though well done. Caine's performance captures the doctor's psychic pain. His Jekyll is a doomed man, and really tears apart the scenery. A new element is the doctor's romance with Cheryl Ladd, which leads to a startling conclusion. Wickes and Caine previously collaborated on a JACK THE RIPPER TV-movie. Joss Ackland, Lionel Jeffries.

JEKYLL AND HYDE PORTFOLIO, THE (1972). Mad killer with a split personality has nothing to do with Robert Louis Stevenson, but isn't it fun for producer-director Eric J. Haims to exploit famous titles. Portfolio permanently closed. Gray Daniels, Mady Maguire.

JEKYLL AND HYDE . . . TOGETHER AGAIN (1982). Comedian Mark Blankfield creates a white powder that, when sniffed, brings out an alter ego. It's a "beast of the '80s" that sprouts kinky hair and jewelry (yes, jewelry). And then this hybrid Hyde grows platform heels (yes, platform heels) and a gold tooth with Love inscribed on it (yes . . .) This is a self-respecting monster? Blankfield's talent could not salvage this mess from writer-director Jerry Belson, who demonstrates no taste or respect for "an audience of the '80s." Bess Armstrong, Tim Thomerson, George Chakiris. (Paramount)

JEKYLL'S INFERNO. See **TWO FACES OF DR. JEKYLL, THE.**

JENNIFER (1978). Thinly disguised copy of CARRIE, about withdrawn Lisa Pelikan, who possesses supernatural powers in time of jeopardy. Jennifer is harassed by the campus bitch at Green View School for Girls but, because she once reached into a box of poisonous serpents without being bitten, she can call upon the Winds of Fury. That's when the snake gods attack. "Give me the vengeance of the viper," she demands. You should say, "Give me the Power to resist imitation B-movies." Nina Foch, John Gavin. Directed by Brice Mack. AKA JENNIFER: THE SNAKE GOD. (Vestron)

JENNIFER 8 (1992). A tour de force for Andy Garcia, who offers vulnerability and menace in the same breath. On the surface this is a criminologist's (Garcia's) search for a serial killer of blind women, and underneath it's a dark, psychological study of (Garcia's) schizophrenic personality. The film's real powers lie in the direction by writer Bruce Robinson and the lighting by Conrad Hall, who photographs this as a pure horror picture. The suspense pieces are starkly unforgettable, even if the negligible whodunit fails to wash. Uma Thurman is the blind-girl victim-to-be, as fragile as a butterfly, Lance Henriksen is Garcia's loyal friend, and John Malkovich is St. Anne, an interrogator who brings an element of sleazy menace to the stark proceedings. (Video/Laser: Paramount)

JESSE JAMES MEETS FRANKENSTEIN'S DAUGHTER (1966). Outre oater with monster motifs, a blend of cowboys and mad doctor. Result: A laughable disaster that bites the dust. This abomination depicts a pardner of fast-drawing Jesse transmutated into a cactus-chewing Monster dubbed "Igor" when the daughter of the title implants Dr. Frankenstein's brain in his cranium. Directed by William Beaudine. John Lupton, Nestor Paiva, Narda Onyx, Jim Davis. (Embassy; Nostalgia; Sultan)

JETSONS, THE (1962). Four of the early episodes from the half-hour series about a commonplace family in the 21st Century, with voices by Mel Blanc, George O'Hanlon, Penny Singleton and Janet Waldo. (Hanna-Barbera; many episodes also available) (Laser: Image)

JETSONS MEET THE FLINTSTONES, THE (1987). Made-for-TV animated feature finds Elroy Jetson developing a time machine that sends his space-age family back to the Stone Age. Their new home is Bedrock, their new friends are the Flintstones. George O'Hanlon and Henry Corden provide voices. Directed by Ray Patterson. (Hanna-Barbera) (Laser: Image)

JETSONS: THE MOVIE (1990). Feature-length cartoon version of the TV series about a family of tomorrow is a bland effort, never transcending the TV medium to soar to new heights. George Jetson is promoted by boss Mr. Spacely to work on an asteroid mining operation. Voices by George O'Hanlon, Mel Blanc, Penny Singleton, Tiffany. (Video/Laser: MCA)

JIGSAW MURDERS, THE (1989). Mild horrific overtones (mad killer is leaving body parts of a beautiful model all over L.A.) is all that will appeal to horror lovers in this low-budget police procedural. Emphasis is on cops Chad Everett (a drunk unable to control his petulant daughter) and Paul Kent (a likable partner on the verge of marriage) who build a vendetta against the killer (Eli Rich). Since the murderer's identity is no secret, there's no suspense, nor does director Jag Mundhra give it a hard edge. Yaphet Kotto stands out as a medical examiner. Michelle Johnson, Dena Drotan. (MGM/UA)

JITTERS, THE (1989). Kyonshee, the Chinese walking dead, become trapped on Earth and are sought by Marilyn Yokuida and boyfriend Sal Viviano, plus some magicians who know a few incantations of the undead. It's pretty silly, played for laughs, and has miminal impact. A brick falling on your head from 12 stories—that has impact. Produced-directed by John M. Fasano. James Hong, Frank Dietz, Handy Atmadja. (Prism)

JOAN MEDFORD IS MISSING. See **HOUSE OF HORRORS.**

J.O.E. AND THE COLONEL (1985). "Project Omega" creates a superperfect human by a recombining of molecules in a controlled environment. The result is "J-type Omega Elemental," a perfect soldier. This comic-book idea is improved by producer-writer Nicholas Corea by allowing J.O.E. to have compassion for the scientists who created him. The rest is formula action as J.O.E. carries out dangerous missions to satisfy a need for excitement. Directed by Ron Satlof. Terence Knox, Gary Kasper, Aimee Eccles, William Lucking, Marie Windsor. (From MCA as **HUMANOID DEFENDER**)

JOE VS. THE VOLCANO (1990). John Patrick Shanley wrote-directed this parable (with overtones of fantasy and comedy) in which Tom Hanks, diagnosed as having a terminal illness, agrees to jump into a South Pacific volcano to appease the angry island gods. Why he wants to sacrifice himself and why Lloyd Bridges hires him are just two cloudy issues surrounding this eccentric movie. Shanley errs by not letting us know this is a fantasy until the climax. Meg Ryan portrays half-sisters, each diametrically opposed to the other, Ossie Davis shines as a philosophical chauffeur, and Robert Stack is authoritative and sinister as Hanks' doctor, who diagnoses that Hanks has a "brain cloud." But it still doesn't jell. (Video/Laser: Warner Bros.)

JOHN CARPENTER PRESENTS 'BODY BAGS' (1993). Acting if he were an out-of-control Crypt Keeper, with "blab on the slab," John Carpenter portrays a ghoulish morgue keeper who introduces three tales. In "Gas Station," directed by Carpenter, Alex Datcher is an attendant at an all-night service booth who is terrorized by a serial killer. Standard slasher, woman-in-peril stuff, with only a clever tag line to set it apart from the zillion other slashers. In "Hair," also directed by Carpenter, Stacy Keach learns the hard way that his phobia about growing bald, and his deal with hair-restoring Dr. Locks (David Warner), are terrible prices to pay. And in "Eye," directed by Tobe Hooper, Mark Hamil plays a guy who loses his right eye in a car accident and has it replaced with the eye of a serial killer. Roger Corman has a cameo in this one. Carpenter's tongue-in-cheek gore gags are the best thing this has to offer. In short, he puts hip zip in the flip trip to the body shop. (Republic)

JOHN CARPENTER

JOHNNY GOT HIS GUN (1971). Dalton Trumbo's classic antiwar novel of World War I, about an American doughboy who has his arms and legs blown away and his face destroyed (along with speech and hearing), was brought to the screen by Trumbo as writer-director. Timothy Bottoms as the hopeless quadriplegic fantasizes into his past to retain his sanity. He also devises a way of thumping his torso on the sheet to communicate with nurse Diane Varsi. In one sequence, Donald Sutherland appears as Jesus Christ. An uncompromising portrait of war's ruinous aftermath. Marsha Hunt, Charles McGraw, Eduard Franz, Donald Barry. (Media) (Laser: Image)

JOHN TRAVIS—SOLAR SURVIVOR. See **OMEGA COP.**

JONATHAN (1969). The West Germans tackle the Dracula theme, throwing in political overtones for Greater Social Significance. But it's still a vampire blitz, Fritz, and wins Han's down. Written-directed by Hans W. Geissendorfer. Jurgen Jung, Ilse Kunkele.

JOURNEY BACK TO OZ (1971). Animated version of the L. Frank Baum classic, with Liza Minnelli's voice for Dorothy, who is transported via cyclone into a magical land with all the familiar characters. Lyrics by Sammy Cahn and Jimmy Van Heusen. Directed by Hal Sutherland. Milton Berle (Cowardly Lion), Herschel Bernardi (Woodenhead the Horse), Ethel Merman (Wicked Witch) and Margaret Hamilton (Aunt Em). Mel Blanc, Jack E. Leonard, Paul Lynde, Mickey Rooney. (MGM/UA; Family Home Entertainment; Kartes)

JOURNEY BENEATH THE DESERT (1961). French-Italian actioner finds director Edgar G. Ulmer struggling with an arid script and coming up lost in the middle of story desolation. An atomic explosion reveals an entrance to the Lost City of Atlantis, ruled by the wicked queen Antinea (Haya Harareet), who gives nosy explorer Jean-Louis Tritignant a bad time. Georges Riviere, Rad Fulton. (Sinister/C; S/Weird; Filmfax)

JOURNEY INTO DARKNESS (1969). See editions 1-3.

JOURNEY INTO MIDNIGHT (1969). See editions 1-3.

JOURNEY INTO THE BEYOND (1973). West German ESP documentary with John Carradine as narrator. Cameras rove the world to record bizarre rituals, sacrificial offerings and other forms of human behavior. Directed by Rolf Olsen. (Family Home Entertainment)

JOURNEY THROUGH THE BLACK SUN. Repackaged episodes of TV's SPACE 1999 (IVE).

JOURNEY TO THE BEGINNING OF TIME (1955). Czech melange of live action, animation and puppet work in depicting youths drifting down the river of time and encountering dinosaurs and other beasts of the prehistoric past. Although good work from director Karel Zeman, this was drastically altered and released in America in 1966 by producer William Cayton.

JOURNEY TO THE CENTER OF THE EARTH (1959). Bernard Herrmann's music sets the mood for this spirited version of Jules Verne's novel about an expedition into the bowels of our planet, directed by Henry Levin with style. Light-hearted touches contribute to the entertainment. The underground sets are stunningly imaginative, the adventures replete with giant lizards and an erupting volcano and the cast colorful: James Mason and Pat Boone lead the expedition while Arlene Dahl keeps her lips well painted to lessen our fears she might be too far from civilization. Diane Baker, Alan Napier. (Video/Laser: CBS/Fox)

JOURNEY TO THE CENTER OF THE EARTH (1987). youngsters fooling around in a Hawaiian cave drop through a hole into a subterranean world containing the lost continent of Atlantis. A mess of a movie, worked over by two directors (Rusty Lemorande and Albert Pyun) and pasted together into something that only vaguely resembled a feature film. Nicola Cowper, Ilan Mitchell-Smith, Kathy Ireland. (Video/Laser: Cannon)

JOURNEY TO THE CENTER OF THE EARTH. See **WHERE TIME BEGAN.**

JOURNEY TO THE CENTER OF THE EARTH (1993). Jules Verne might want to strangle those responsible for this TV-movie, so far is it removed from his 1864 fantasy novel about explorers descending into a beautiful but deadly subterranean world. That criticism aside, this is an over-the-top sci-fi extravaganza depicting a bullet-shaped vessel, the Adventure, which is fired into volcanic molten lava and "swims" to the center of the Earth, a world of alien creatures, a race of wise Yetis (as represented by 7-foot Carel Struycken, who plays Lurch in the ADDAMS FAMILY movies), a humanoid shape in a life-support unit, and prehistoric cavemen. It gets ridiculous at times, yet it has a thrusting vitality. Aboard the ship is a woman's head floating in a bubble (a computer nicknamed "Devin," short for Digital Electro-Plastic Virtual Intelligence Navigation) and several stereotypes. Directed by William (HARRY AND THE HENDERSONS) Dear. David Dundada, Farrah Forke, Kim Miyori, Jeffrey Nordling, Tim Russ, Fabiana Undenio. Standouts are John Neville as an eccentric expert on inner world myths and F. Murray Abraham as a professor who goes nuts.

CAREL STRUYCKEN

JOURNEY TO THE CENTER OF TIME (1968). Back and forth in time—centuries into the future when mutants battle a dictatorship, centuries into the past when dinosaurs are savage—keeps this fantasy clipping along, even if it fails to come to grips with logic. Directed by David L. Hewitt. Scott Brady, Gigi Perreau, Anthony Eisley, Lyle Waggoner. (Academy; Genesis; also from American as **TIME WARP**)

JOURNEY TO THE FAR SIDE OF THE SUN (1969). The Doppelganger theory, that there is a parallel world matching our own detail for detail, is put to the test in this commendable space thriller, directed by Robert Parrish and written by Gerry and Sylvia Anderson and Donald James. European Space Exploration Centre uncovers a planet on the other side of the sun and sends a manned vehicle with Roy Thinnes. The film is also a study in conspiratory paranoia. Made as DOPPELGANGER. Herbert Lom, Ian Hendry, Lynn Loring. (MCA)

JOURNEY TO THE PAST. See **I'LL NEVER FORGET YOU.**

JOURNEY TO THE SEVENTH PLANET (1961). Sluggish Swedish space saga depicts a rocketship landing on Neptune in 2001 and the crew meeting aliens who read minds and put up defenses that play on human fears. The script (by director Sidney Pink and Ib Melchior) borrows Ray Bradbury themes. The expedition includes John Agar and Carl Ottosen, with Greta Thyssen and Ann Smyrner as beautiful alien humanoids. It's tedious going, showing little visual imagination to pull off the effects. (Laser: Image, with ANGRY RED PLANET)

JOURNEY TO THE UNKNOWN (1969). See editions 1-3.

JUDGEMENT DAY (1989). Video flick is an uneven supernatural thriller set in the village of Santana, where once a year the Devil and disciples drop in from Hell to claim souls. There's good dialogue by writer-director Ferde Grofe Jr. and a professional air lent by Monte Markham, Peter Mark Richman and Cesar Romero; and yet, elements are muddled, and Kenneth McLeod and David Anthony Smith, portraying wanderers trapped in the village, range from good to poor. Grofe captures an eerieness in some ruins in the Philippines, and there's chilling scenes of marching demons, but one wishes it could be better than it is. (Magnum)

JULES VERNE'S ROCKET TO THE MOON. See **BLAST OFF.**

JUNGLE, THE (1952). Terrific adventure made in the jungles of India; authenticity carries this Robert L. Lippert low budgeter. Rod Cameron, Marie Windsor and Cesar Romero search for prehistoric mastodons—and find them in a hair-raising climax. Far Eastern musical score, depiction of native customs and real battles among wild animals make this very viewable. Directed by William Berke, scripted by Carroll Young. (Weiss Global)

JUNGLE BOOK, THE (1942). Alexander Korda's imaginative adaptation of Rudyard Kipling's famous story, treated here as a fairy tale and set in an impressionistic jungle of cobalt blues and magentas. Sabu portrays Mowgli, raised by wolves from infancy to become a jungle boy who talks to monkeys, snakes, elephants and other denizens of the verdane. Mowgli's world is interloped upon by three turbaned villains searching for a Legendary Lost City's jewel treasure. The Miklos Rozsa score is a classic. Directed by Alexander's brother, Zoltan Korda. Rosemary De Camp, Ralph Byrd, Joseph Calleia, Patricia O'Rourke, John Qualen. (Embassy; Goodtimes) (Laser: Nelson)

JUNGLE BOOK, THE (1967). Animated version of the Mowgli stories by Kipling is passable, but not up to Disney's usual standards. Although enchanting at times, the film is old-fashioned in its music and stereotyped voices. The story has a panther escorting the jungle boy to his village after the animals agree he cannot survive in the wilds. Voices: Phil Harris, Louis Prima, Sebastian Cabot, George Sanders, Sterling Holloway. Directed by Wolfgang Reitherman. (Video/Laser: Disney)

JUNGLE CAPTIVE (1945). Universal's third and final entry in its hairy apewoman series (see CAPTIVE WILD WOMAN and JUNGLE WOMAN) is campish fun in which Otto Kruger (mad doctor) and Rondo Hatton (mad doctor's mad assistant) revive an ape woman from the twilight of death and monkey around with her ancestral genes. Vicky Lane endures the ape make-up. Also known as WILD JUNGLE CAPTIVE. Directed by Harold Young. Amelita Ward, Jerome Cowan, Eddie Acuff.

JUNGLE HEAT. Video version of **DANCE OF THE DWARFS** (Transworld).

JUNGLE HELL (1956). Sabu, of JUNGLE BOOK fame, is sadly miscast in this bad film written-produced-directed by Norman A. Cerf involving a flying saucer, a death ray and nonsense about a radioactive rock. And that, viewer, is the real hell of JUNGLE HELL. K. T. Stevens, David Bruce. (Sinister/C)

JUNGLE HOLOCAUST. Video version of **LAST SURVIVOR, THE** (Video City).

JUNGLE JIM (1948). First in a series of cheap African adventures from producer Sam Katzman and starring Johnny Weissmuller as a pith-helmeted he-man (created as a comic strip by Alex Raymond) who walks past potted plants, mumbles monosyllabic sentences and pats Tamba the chimp on the noggin. It kept the one-time Tarzan star active for years in low-budget junglejunk featuring footage from countless other movies. Jungle Jim is seeking a rare drug that combats polio. The villain is George Reeves, TV's SUPERMAN. Virginia Grey, Lita Baron. Directed by William Berke.

JUNGLE JIM IN THE FORBIDDEN LAND (1952). Khaki-clad scout of the potted jungle fights a greedy ivory hunter who is upsetting the natives with the help of a "giant apeman" believed to be the missing link. A midget idea from the brain of Samuel Newman, directed by Lew Landers. Johnny Weissmuller mutters tired dialogue. Angela Greene, Jean Willes.

JUNGLE MANHUNT (1951). Johnny Weissmuller, as a man of the bush, helps a reporter find a missing football player. This Sam Katzman programmer is padded with dinosaur footage from other pictures which only points out major deficiencies in this potted jungle fiasco. Directed by Lew Landers. Bob Waterfield, Lyle Talbot.

JUNGLE MOON MEN (1955). The Jungle Jim character was dropped so Johnny Weissmuller could portray himself, although what significance that would have on this movie is questionable. For nothing seems changed as Weissmuller walks by the same potted plants he passed as Jungle Jim. In this junglemess he's searching for the secret to eternal youth from a jungle tribe that prays to the moon god. Directed by Charles S. Gould. Myron Healey, Jean Byron, Bill Henry.

JUNGLE RAIDERS (1985). Expedition searches for a cursed jewel (the Ruby of Gloom) in the verdant thick. Aka CAPTAIN YANKEE. Lee Van Cleef, Christopher Connelly. Directed by Anthony Dawson. (MGM/UA)

JUNGLE TREASURE (1951). Entry in the British "Old Mother Riley" comedy series in which a supernatural manifestation turns out to be an antiquated pirate who knows the whereabouts of a buried fortune. Directed by Maclean Rogers. Arthur Lucan, Sebastian Cabot.

JUNGLE WOMAN (1944). Sequel to CAPTIVE WILD WOMAN continues the adventures of Acquanetta, an unfortunate who keeps transmutating into a gorilla woman when doctor J. Carrol Naish fools around with her genes. (And we don't mean Levis, gang.) Occasionally the she-creature reverts to type and kills. Either you will view this as a stilted, turgid mess or you will find it nostalgically pleasing, reflecting the values of Universal horror movies of the '40s. Reginald Le Borg directed. Third and final film in this series was JUNGLE CAPTIVE. Evelyn Ankers, Lois Collier and Milburn Stone are all competent, but Acquanetta walks through her role in a trance.

JUNGLE WOMAN (1944). See **NABONGA.**

JUNIOR (1985). Two busty hookers just released from prison start a new life on an abandoned riverboat but are terrorized by a low I.Q. pervert and his equally crazed mother. The best moment is when Junior (Jeremy Ratchford) cuts apart their house with his chainsaw; another socially redeeming scene has Junior fondling one of the girl's privates. A movie with a contradiction: It depicts the women as gutsy and liberated, yet exploits their sexuality. Strictly for intellectuals and (lame)brains. Directed by Jim Hawley. Suzanne Delaurentiis, Linda Singer. (Starmaker; Prism)

JURASSIC ENCOUNTER

JUPITER MENACE, THE (1982). Offbeat pseudo-documentary, hosted by George Kennedy, who proposes a "mythical theory" that the world is doomed and there's nothing mankind can do about it. Too bad for all you human beings reading this book. You see, the Earth will go "tilt" in the year 2000, and that will be the end of that. So keep your eye on the pinball machine. Directed by Lee Auerbach and Peter Matulavich. (HBO)

JURASSIC PARK (1993). One of the most important movies in the technological use of computers, proving that nothing is impossible in the world of film as long as artists have the imagination to pull it off. This adaptation of Michael Crichton's best-seller is a fascinating example of how electronic technology can be blended with live-action footage to produce an ultimate thrill-adventure movie. In this case, we are taken to an amusement park on a small island off the coast of Costa Rica where Richard Attenborough has established a zoo-park for prehistoric creatures. (He's extracted DNA from ancient fossils and bred several species.) Unfortunately, he didn't reckon on everything going wrong when paleontologists Sam Neill and Laura Dern visit the island with scientist Jeff Goldblum. The script by David Koepp, from an adaptation by Crichton and Malia Scotch Marmo, spends little time on characterizations, as this was designed to thrill us with dinosaur footage unlike any dinosaur footage you've seen before. Under Steven Spielberg's direction, this marvelous shocker features a thundering Tyrannosaurus Rex attacking two amusement park vans; angry Velociraptor's chasing two children through a kitchen; a herd of galloping Triceratops bounding across a meadow past three human figures; and a poison-spitting Bilophosaur trapping a human during a rainstorm. Dennis Muren headed the staff of special effects workers that included Phil Tippet, Stan Winston and Michael Lantieri. Every trick was paraded out and blended into a seamless whole. JURASSIC PARK made box-office, and technological, history. (Video/Laser: MCA)

JUST BEFORE DAWN (1982). Youthful campers, with a deed to a section of wilderness, ignore warnings of forest ranger George Kennedy not to go into the woods. They go anyway, only to be terrorized by evil mountain-men. Director Jeff Lieberman (SQUIRM, BLUE SUNSHINE) creates suspenseful moments but has nothing new to offer. Kennedy gives a good limited performance, and Deborah Benson is the best of the teen-agers, proving in the climactic struggle that a woman can be effective in the most terrifying of situations. Chris Lemmon, Gregg Henry, Mike Kellin. (Paragon)

JUST IMAGINE (1930). Musical comedy-fantasy of historical interest: El Brendel, a citizen of 1930, awakens to find himself in 1980 surrounded by bewildering gadgetry. Then he blasts off for Mars! Songs by Henderson, DeSylva and Brown. Directed-written by David Butler. Maureen O'Sullivan, Frank Albertson.

JUSTIN CASE (1988). This Walt Disney TV-movie from writer-director Blake Edwards is a dreary mystery-comedy in which Molly Hagan (as an out-of-work dancer) teams up with the ghost of a newly deceased private eye (George Carlin, in a wasted role) to find his murderer, a beautiful "Lady in Black." He materializes in and out, permitting Edwards to vent tired Invisible Man gags. And since only Hagan sees/hears Carlin, everyone wonders why she's talking to herself, why she's kissing empty air, ad nauseam. Timothy Stack, Kevin McClarnon. Music by Henry Mancini. Watch this Justin A. Pinch.

JUSTINE. See **DEADLY SANCTUARY.**

KADOYNG (1972). Spaceship piloted by a benevolent being (Leo Maguire) lands on Earth to help a family in need. Minor British effort for children, directed by Ian Shane. Teres Codling, Adrian Hall.

KAMIKAZE (1986). Offbeat French sci-fi/horror thriller in which an electronics expert creates a Death Ray that kills when projected into TV sets. A detective investigates, donning Japanese kimono and hachimaki (suicide pilot's headband) for battle. Directed by Didier Grousset. Richard Bohringer, Dominique Lavanant.

KAMIKAZE '89 (1983). A futuristic society, run by a totalitarian government controlling all media, is the setting for this German film with Rainer Werner Fassbinder as a cop investigating a series of bombings. Similar to the French CLUB EXTINCTION, but with a flavor all its own provided by director Wolf Gremm. (MGM/UA)

KARATE KILLERS, THE (1967). Re-edited episodes of TV's MAN FROM U.N.C.L.E., starring Robert Vaughn and David McCallum as superagents for a clandestine American security agency, with Leo G. Carroll their assignment chief, Mr. Waverly. In two glued-together stories the agents are after a formula that could turn water into gold, and then they go after a special aircraft. Curt Jurgens, Joan Crawford, Telly Savalas, Herbert Lom, Diane McBain. Directed by Barry Shear.

KARNSTEIN. See **TERROR IN THE CRYPT.**

KARNSTEIN CURSE, THE. See **TERROR IN THE CRYPT.**

KEEP, THE (1983). When writer-director Michael Mann adapted F. Scott Wilson's vampire novel, he dropped all references to vampires—and took himself so seriously he fell flat on his egg-covered face. So there is Mr. Mann, face down in the mire over this solemnly pretentious affair. The only saving grace are the special effects, light show extravaganzas with thick white beams of light. An immortal guardian, Glaeken Trismegestus (Scott Glenn), arrives in a Rumanian village in 1941 after Nazi troops have unleashed a demonic power (Molasar) from a castle. Jewish language expert Ian McKellen and daughter Alberta Watson are brought to the Keep to translate runes for Wehrmacht officer Jurgen Prochnow and SS major Gabriel Byrne. McKellen believes Molasar to be a savior of the Jews (a Golem?) but the Nazis believe it to be only evil. The vampire that's never called a vampire rips asunder the crummy Nazis and is ready for a showdown with that Glaeken guy, eyes glowing like emeralds, and squares off in a battle of Killer Zap Rays, music by the Tangerine Dream swirling around them with the fog. Figure it out and give us a call. (Video/Laser: Paramount)

KEEPER, THE (1976). Canadian film written-directed by Tom Drake, with Christopher Lee as an insane asylum director who has a plan to insure his patients and murder their heirs, giving him the dough he needs to conquer the world a la Dr. Mabuse. Lee accomplishes this with a hypnosis machine. A private detective, Dick Driver, acting melodramatic to the max, is hired by a man whose brother is an inmate and to whom he is psychically linked. There are strange twists and turns, plus a police chief who falls under Lee's spell and acts as if he's in a comedy and not a horror film. Tell Schrieber, Sally Gray. (Interglobal; Trans World)

KEEP MY GRAVE OPEN (1980). Strange Camilla Carr, living in a strange house, kills strangers. A strange movie, with strange motivations until the trick ending. Produced-directed by S.F. Brownrigg, responsible for DON'T LOOK IN THE BASEMENT. Strange enough, strangely enough, to hold your interest. Gene Ross, Stephen Tobolowsky, (Unicorn; from Clockwork as **HOUSE WHERE HELL FROZE OVER, THE**)

KEMEK (1970). Minor cautionary tale about the misuse of modern drugs. Kemek is a pharmaceutical company using people as guinea pigs to test a new concoction that affects one's memory and brings on bursts of violence. David Hedison portrays a man misused by an unscrupulous gang of opportunists and killers. The writing-direction by Theodore Gershuny and Don Ray Patterson is so convoluted and the editing so choppy, it's impossible to tell what's going on. This movie was a drug on the market. Diagnosis: Don't take it. Mary Woronov, Cal Haynes, Alexandra Stewart. (Genesis; from Neon as **FOR LOVE OR MURDER**)

KGOD (1980). KRUD, a rundown TV station in San Poquito, is taken over by Dabney Coleman and turned into a rousin' religious rete—but at the expense of decency and fair play, the message writers Dick Chudnow and Nick Castle throw out as the final amen. But first come on-air program parodies with religious motifs, such as the game show "Healed for a Day," an exorcism reported on the morning news, and "One Life to Lose," a soap opera starring Joseph and Mary of Nazarus. This comedy in the vein of Mad Magazine may grow on you despite its ineptitudes; its witlessness is charming. Jamie Lyn Bauer, Sidney Miller, Joyce Jameson, Ruth Silveira. (From Vestron and on Image laser as **PRAY TV**)

KID WITH THE BROKEN HALO, THE (1982). Saccharine TV-movie designed to tug at heart strings, bring tears to eyes and make one feel good about humanity. And who's to say those aren't good values in a saccharine TV-movie? One just wishes telewriter George Kirgo had tried for something less hackneyed than this vehicle for the cutesy-pie talents of Gary Coleman. Little ol' Gary is an angel earning his halo who goes to Earth with fellow angel Robert Guillaume to help three families straighten out worldly problems. June Allyson is an ex-actress who hates the world and her snotty behavior is the only realistic counterpoint to the helpings of granulated sugar. Two other families are troubled by more domestic problems, but it's hohum city. Ray Walston is cute as the angel bookkeeper, but hohum to him too. Directed by Leslie Martinson. (USA)

KILL AND GO HIDE. Video version of **CHILD, THE** (Monterey; Paragon).

KILL AND KILL AGAIN (1981). Amusing, tongue-in-cheek martial arts romp with James Ryan (South African action star) leading a team of fighters (with mystical and levitational powers) into a tyrant's stronghold, where a mind-controlling drug is being tested for world conquest. This never takes itself seriously and spoofs superspy-kung fu flicks with a passion. Directed by Ivan Hall. Anneline Kriel, Ken Gampu, Norman Robinson. (Media)

KILL, BABY, KILL (1966). One of director Mario Bava's great gothic supernatural thrillers, revealing his power in the use of color for psychological effect. Coroner Giacomo Rossi-Stuart arrives in a 19th Century village to conduct an autopsy, and soon realizes that the ghost of a child, murdered by the citizens, is haunting the town. Erica Blanc, one of Bava's beautiful heroines, is Rossi-Stuart's assistant who discovers that witch Fabienne Dali is also spinning diabolical magic. But the real dread remains unseen, punctuated by the dead girl's laughter. And there are fine scenes of Rossi-Stuart and Blanc trapped in eerie rooms. Aka CURSE OF THE DEAD, CURSE OF THE LIVING DEAD, DON'T WALK IN THE PARK and OPERATION FEAR. (Sinister/C; S/Weird; Filmfax) (Laser: Polygram)

KILLBOTS. See **CHOPPING MALL.**

KILLDOZER (1974). TV-movie, directed by Jerry London, will make you doze when it should kill you with its unusual theme. Sci-fi writer Theodore Sturgeon adapted his short novel with the help of Ed MacKillop, but what emerged is hackneyed TV. A construction crew on a Pacific island is building a landing strip when an inexplicable invisible force from another world invades a bulldozer, giving it life . . . the animated inanimate object attacks the crew. Deteriorates into stock situations with stock characters played by Clint Walker, Carl Betz, James Wainwright, Robert Urich and Neville Brand.

KILLER, THE. Video title for **DADDY'S DEADLY DARLING,** also in video under that title. Original title was **PIGS.** It's a porker under any snout.

KILLER, THE (1990). Made in super-8 for around $9,000, this has found a cult following through Joe Bob Briggs' encouraging critiques, which have ranked it up there with HENRY: PORTRAIT OF A SERIAL KILLER. Duke Ernsberger plays a guy made crazy by medical experiments who's murdering and threatening to chomp on human flesh. Directed by producer Tony Elwood.

KILLER APE (1953). Ridiculous Jungle Jim movie with the natives restless because of a giant gorilla with homicide in mind. The creature is controlled by villains concocting a serum that will destroy all of mankind's will to resist. Use your own will to resist this junky Sam Katzman-produced movie starring Johnny Weissmuller. Directed by Spencer Gordon Bennett. Nestor Paiva, Carol Thurston, Max Palmer, Ray "Crash" Corrigan.

KILLER BAT. Video version of **DEVIL BAT** (Kartes).

KILLER BEES, THE (1974). This has very little sting despite director Curtis Harrington and a bravura performance by Gloria Swanson, making a "rare appearance." Gloria portrays the matriarch of a family in Napa Valley (where exteriors were filmed) raising hives of a rare African bee. Eventually the winged creatures attack and kill under her guidance. After this, did Gloria become known as "the queen of the bees"? Kate Jackson, Edward Albert, Craig Stevens.

KILLER BEHIND THE MASK, THE. See **SAVAGE WEEKEND.**

KILLER GRIZZLY. See **GRIZZLY.** (Grrrrrrrrr!)

KILLER IN EVERY CORNER, A (1974). Mediocre British TV-movie, only watchable for the sinister performance of Patrick Magee as Professor Carnaby, a psychologist experimenting in conditioned behavior designed to create murderers—a homicidal variation on Pavlov's dog. The mad doc invites Joanna Pettet and Petra Markham to study with him, but he's really using them as fodder for his experiments. Brian Clemens' script is without much subtlety and Malcolm Taylor's direction is restricted to a few cheap studio sets. Max Wall, Eric Flynn. (Thrillervision without Elvira)

KILLER INSTINCT, THE (1981). This hillbilly horror saga set in Tennessee is distinguished by a ferocious performance by Henry Silva as a murderous, sadistic redneck who goes completely out of control, torturing and murdering to protect the good name of rednecks everywhere. Interesting death devices are used (watch for the TV antenna sequence) as well as the usual explosions, hot tar, feathers and other homicidal methods common in the Deep South. This Canadian effort, of minimal consequence, was directed by William Fruet. Nicholas Campbell, Barbara Gordon. (Cineplex Odeon)

KILLER KLOWNS FROM OUTER SPACE (1988). Hilarious spoof of sci-fi alien invader movies finds the town of Santa Cruz invaded by E.T. humanoids who dress up as clowns and use "funny" props to zap humans into cocoon-like containers. The funnymen are never explained but it doesn't matter as the movie clips along with a blend of thrills and laughs. The only way to kill a killer "klown" is to shoot it in the nose, which sends it off into another dimension. The effects are zany and the characters memorable, especially John Vernon as a paranoid cop. About those clowns: While they seem funny at first glance, they're really quite ugly and their laughter is the stuff of dark comedy. Grant Cramer, Suzanne Snyder, John Allen Nelson, Royal Dano. Directed by Stephen Chiodo. (Video/Laser: Media)

KILLER LACKS A NAME, THE (1966). Variation on THE INDESTRUCTIBLE MAN and MAN-MADE MONSTER, in which the villain finds that his steel hand contains enough voltage to knock off enemies. This Italian effort, directed by Tullio Domichelli and starring Lang Jeffries and Olga Omar, will not give you much of a charge. Lacks a jolt. The amps went oomph.

KILLER NERD (1991). Toby Radloff, a face in MTV spots, portrays a maniac with a mother complex who gets over it by burying the hatchet—in mom's head. He also turns his ire on fire by sticking it to his adversaries with TNT sticks. Written-produced-directed by Mark Steven Bosko Ohio. (Hollywood Home)

KILLER NUN (1978). One-time sexpot Anita Ekberg portrays a man-murdering nun who kills patients in a women's prison. Directed by Giulio Berruti. Alida Valli, Massimo Serator, Joe Dallesandro.

KILLER PARTY (1986). April Fool's Day saga only for fools: When three pledges in the Sigma Alpha Phi sorority undergo initiation on "Ghost Night," real horrors begin at a costume party when a killer in a diving suit (isn't this synopsis incredible?) kills with electricity, hammer, guillotine, pitchfork and standard kitchen knife, then stuffs body parts into a frig. Then this slasher flick turns into supernatural hogwash when a spirit takes over a live body. Paul Bartel (as a nerdy professor), Martin Hewitt, Ralph Seymour. Directed by William Fruet. (Key)

KILLERS ARE CHALLENGED (1966). Transparent 007 imitation from Italy, originally SECRET AGENT FIREBALL, with Richard Harrison as a spy-hero who poses as a scientist to protect a petroleum project. His gadgets include a ring that forewarns him of pending death. You too have been forewarned. Directed by Anthony Dawson. Susy Andersen, Wandisa Guida.

KILLER'S CURSE. Video version of **BEYOND THE LIVING** (Iver).

KILLERS FROM SPACE (1954). Humanoids with bulging eyeballs and jumpsuits resurrect Peter Graves from the dead as part of their plot to take over Earth. Don't they know hundreds of other E.T.s have tried without success? Some aliens just never get the message. Dull sci-fi directed by W. Lee Wilder (brother of Billy Wilder). Barbara Bestar, James Seay, Frank Gerstle. (VCI; Sinister/C; S/Weird; Rhino; Filmfax)

KILLER SHREWS, THE (1959). This is not about ugly wives going on a murderous rampage. According to Jay Simms' script, shrews are the tiniest of rodents, but some crazy scientist has enlarged them to 100 pounds each. Strange how these giant killer shrews resemble Irish setters in blackface. Maybe they'll bark the hero (James Best) or his Norwegian girlfriend (Ingrid Goude) to death. There's such a wonderful sense of ineptitude to Ray Kellogg's direction that this is fun to watch. Producer Ken Curtis doubles as a victim, proving he's a "shrewed" guy. Baruch Lumet, Gordon McLendon. (Sinister/C; S/Weird; Filmfax)

KILLER'S MOON (1978). Drug-crazed fanatics flee an asylum and attack a busload of beautiful babes. British psychothriller written-directed by Alan Birkinshaw. Anthony Forrest, Tom Marshall. (VCL)

KILLERS OF THE CASTLE OF BLOOD. See **SCREAM OF THE DEMON LOVER.**

KILLER SPORES (1977). Space capsule returns to Earth contaminated by an alien substance which takes over control of humans. Patrick Duffy, who has gills that enable him to live underwater, is assigned by NASA to investigate. Re-edited episodes of TV's MAN FROM ATLANTIS series. Directed by Reza Badiyi. Belinda Montgomery, Alan Fudge.

KILLER TOMATOES. It started with **ATTACK OF THE KILLER TOMATOES,** continued with **RETURN OF THE KILLER TOMATOES,** went to **KILLER TOMATOES STRIKE BACK** and then splattered again with **KILLER TOMATOES EAT FRANCE.**

KILLER TOMATOES EAT FRANCE (1991). Another squishy sauce of mirth and gory madness when those rolling homicidal love fruits take to the French landscape to squash humans anew. Wow, those are some tomatoes! Marc Price, Angela Visser, I.M. Seedless, Steve Lundquist. Directed by John DeBello. (Video/Laser: CBS/Fox)

KILLER TOMATOES STRIKE BACK (1990). The murderous love fruits are on another roll, squashing mankind into oblivion and making a lot of people stew. Directed by John DeBello. John Astin, Rick Rockwell, Crystal Carson, John Weatherspoon. (Video/Laser: Fox)

KILLER WHALE. See **ORCA.**

KILLER WITH TWO FACES (1974). British TV cheapie starring Donna Mills as a screaming heroine frightened by a mad strangler who could be one of two brothers. Undistinguished production on to the level of a thriller soap opera. Ian Hendry, David Lodge, Roddy McMillan. Directed by John Scholz-Conway. (IVE)

KILLER WORKOUT (1986). A serial killer is on the loose again (NOT AGAIN!!!) in this typically bloody but boring intellectual treatise on man's inhumanity to his fellow man in the form of murdering them in a gym. As strained as the face of Arnold Schwarzenegger when he lifts a weight too heavy for him. (Academy)

KILL FACTOR, THE. Video version of **DEATH DIMENSION** (Academy).

KILLING CARS (1986). West German science thriller, made in England, stars Jurgen Prochnow as Ralph Korda, an automotive engineer who designs a new power source for cars—but before he can introduce it, agents from a sinister oil cartel intervene. Directed-written by Michael Verhoeven. (Vidmark)

KILLING EDGE, THE (1986). With no production values, this imitation-MAD MAX isn't even an imitation, it's just an amateurish time-waster filmed in the countryside. Produced in Britain, it's set "in the middle of the Nuclear Winter" following atomic war, when Terminators enslave the innocent to harvest crops. Along comes lone survivor Bill French in search of Guard #7, the joyous being who murdered his wife and son. Robert Bauer's script is no script at all, and director Lindsay Craig Shonteff can give it no dressing. Al Lambert, Marv Spencer. (Video City; Hollywood Home Entertainment)

KILLING HOUR, THE (1982). Video version of **CLAIRVOYANT, THE** (Clair who?) (CBS/Fox).

KILLING KIND, THE (1973). John Savage, suffering from a mama's complex, stalks his victims while ever-loving mom Ann Sothern bakes apple pies and coos her affection to calm down her killer boy. Slow, lethargic pacing by director Curtis Harrington. Cindy Williams, Luana Anders. (Unicorn; Paragon; American)

KILLING OF SATAN, THE (1983). Filipino supernatural fantasy in which "The Prince of Magic" (a wizard in a red jump suit) calls forth Satan (with a tail and a pitchfork) to do battle with "Coronado," a parolee who has inherited superpowers from the dead village shaman and runs around in Levis and tennis shoes. Bolts of magic zap juice are fired, seductive women turn into killer snakes, snakes turn into serpent-tongued succubi and on it goes, with the supernatural magic accomplishing little excitement, especially when "Coronado" blows one of his adversaries over a cliff using just his breath. Directed without wit or style by Efron C. Pinon. Ramon Revilla, Elizabeth Oropesa. (Paragon)

KILLINGS AT OUTPOST ZETA (1980). Low-budget adventure in the tradition of STAR TREK which attempts an intriguing story, even if production is hampered by lousy effects. After three expeditions to a farflung planet have disappeared, a fourth team of space rangers is sent and finds 11 corpses, their insides eaten away. It seems that in exploring the planet, the previous scientists discovered a form of rock life. Nice try by producer-directors Allan Sandler and Robert Ememegger (he also wrote the electronic music score). Gordon Devol, Jacquelyn Ray, Jackson Bostwick. (United)

KILLING SPREE (1990). Man reads diary by wife, unaware that it's fiction, and thinks she's dallying with other men and flips out, killing in the worst ways: Gutting human torsos, decapitating them and removing scalps. Then the corpses come to life and return for revenge. Overdone by producer-writer-director Tim Ritter. Asbestos Felt, Courtney Lercara. (Twisted Illusions)

KILLING TOUCH, THE. See **FATAL GAMES.**

KILL OR BE KILLED (1966-67). Episodes of TV's TIME TUNNEL series including one in which the two scientists trapped in time (see TIME TUNNEL) turn up at Pearl Harbor on the eve of the Japanese sneak attack. One of them must seek out his own father to warn him. James Darren, Robert Colbert, Sam Groom.

KILL TO LOVE (1981). Hong Kong production about a mad-dog killer knocking off his victims in horrible ways. Chop suey holiday. Directed by Tam Kav Ming. Ching Hsia, Chung Cheung Lin.

KINDRED, THE (1986). Ripoff of ALIEN, without an original thought, and an embarrassment for Rod Steiger. He's a nutty scientist on the fringes of an experiment in gene-splicing that results in "Anthony," a tentacled monster hiding in subterranean chambers underneath a doctor's country home. What are catacombs and deep pits doing under the floorboards? Just one of the many dumb aspects of this goo movie. From Jeffrey Obrow and Stephen Carpenter, the schlockmeisters who gave us THE DORM THAT DRIPPED BLOOD. One critic thought the title referred to a benevolent Communist. No, it stands for trash of the sleaziest kind. David Allen Brooks, Talia Balsam, Kim Hunter. (Video/Laser: Vestron)

KINDRED SPIRITS. See **LOVE CAN BE MURDER.**

KING ARTHUR, THE YOUNG WARLORD (1975). Legendary tale of the most gallant knight of all, told in traditional form in this British TV-movie. Directed by Peter Sasdy, Sidney Hayers and Pat Jackson. Oliver Tobias, Jack Watson. (Video Gems)

KING DICK (1982). French-Italian animated feature, released as LITTLE DICK, THE MIGHTY MIDGET. A midget forces an ugly witch to return him to full size, along with a prince and princess. Sex themes, poor dubbing and substandard animation make this unsuitable for children . . and adults.

KING DINOSAUR (1955). First effort by producer-director Bert I. Gordon focuses on four astronauts who land on an alien planet, Nova, and walk past Benedict Canyon boulders, reacting to offscreen prehistoric monsters. On screen, the monsters turn out to be stock footage beasties from ONE MILLION B.C. The turgid screenplay was by Tom Gries, who became a film-TV director. The narrator is Marvin Miller. Gordon's co-producer was Al Zimbalist. Bill Bryant, Wanda Curtis, Douglas Henderson. (Video/Laser: Weiss Global)

KINGDOM OF THE SPIDERS (1977). Several thousand tarantulas, bola, crab, wolf and funnel-web spiders attack an Arizona community to get even for man's misuse of insectides. Director John "Bud" Cardos makes this absurdity work with the help of William Shatner in one of his better movie roles as a veterinarian who joins up with bug expert Tiffany Bolling, who's really bug-eyed over Captain Kirk. The effect of 5000 spiders swarming over everything (and everybody) is chilling and will have you watching where you step for days afterward. Woody Strode, Nancy Lafferty, Natasha Ryan. (United; VCI)

KING KONG (1933). The granddaddy of giant-ape movies, so skillfully conceived by producers-directors Merian Cooper and Ernest B. Schoedsack that it has lost little of its charm and suspense. Willis O'Brien's stop-motion effects are still startling for their time, ingeniously depicting the 50-foot-tall gorilla presiding over prehistoric Skull Island. A filmmaking expedition headed by Carl Denham (Robert Armstrong) and an adventurer (Bruce Cabot) pursues the creature after it abducts Fay Wray. The chase includes battles with dinosaurs, a marauding pterodactyl, a giant snake and other monstrous spectacles. Captured and returned to civilization as a stage display, mighty Kong breaks free to provide this unbridled fantasy with a grand climax atop the Empire State Building. It features a great Max Steiner score and its cast includes Wray as Ann Darrow, the woman Kong rips the clothes from, Frank Reicher as Captain Englehorn, Noble Johnson as the native chieftain, and Sam Hardy as Charles Weston. The script was begun by British mystery writer Edgar Wallace and finished after his sudden death by Ruth Rose (Schoedsack's wife) and James A. Creelman. David O. Selznick was executive producer. Dino de Laurentiis remade it in 1976 but this remains the definitive giant ape movie. (RKO; Turner; Media) (Laser: Criterion; Image, with **SON OF KONG**)

KING KONG (1976). Producer Dino De Laurentiis proclaimed this $24 million remake a "cinema event"—and while it may be undeniably an event, it is far from recommendable cinema. The Lorenzo Semple Jr. screenplay calls on the TV BATMAN traditions of high camp and emerges a mishmash of satire, thrills, fantasy and spectacle under John Guillermin's direction. This leaves only the special effects to marvel at, and while some of them are good, there is no sense of tradition, balance or proportion. The hairy paw picking up screaming Jessica Lange, so deftly handled in the 1933 original, is so overdone here it becomes ludicrous. No stop motion animation—it was all done with men in monkey suits or with unconvincing giant mock-ups. It finally topples from its own weight. Jeff Bridges, Charles Brodin, John Randolph, John Agar, Rene Auberjonois, Ed Lauter. Rick Baker wears the monkey suit. (Video/Laser: Paramount)

KING KONG ESCAPES (1968). More Toho Studio mass destruction (special effects by Eiji Tsuburaya) as the hairy desecrator of Tokyo battles Gorosaurus, a relative of Godzilla, plus an exact replica of himself, Mechanikong, the work of a nutty scientist (dubbed Dr. Who). American footage featuring Rhodes Reason was appended. You really have to like these Japanese things to enjoy. Also known as THE REVENGE OF KING KONG and KING KONG'S COUNTERATTACK. Directed by Inoshiro Honda. Mie Hama, Linda Miller.

KING KONG LIVES (1986). How the mighty have dropped with a leaden thud since Kong plummeted from the Empire State Building in Dino De Laurentiis' 1976 remake. Here Dino offers a sequel wherein dedicated doctor Linda Hamilton keeps Kong in the world's biggest animal hospital to give him a heart transplant. Who should adventurer Brian Kerwin find on Kong Island—just when Linda needs a transfusion for Kong—but a Young Chick Kong with the hots for the hairy guy. The most hilarious scene comes when Kong is operated on, the surgical tools like props from THE INCREDIBLE SHRINKING MAN. Kong and his Chick thunder across the plains, stomping everything in sight, in some of the funniest scenes imaginable. The idea of trying to take a romance, complete with mother's love, and turn it into a thundering-plundering-blundering Kong movie is the most ludicrous thing imaginable—yet director John Guillermin (who helmed the 1976 adaptation) does it with a straight face. So bad it's not even good. (Lorimar) (Laser: Image)

KING KONG'S COUNTERATTACK. See **KING KONG ESCAPES.**

KING KONG VS. GODZILLA (1963). Clash of the century between "two world-shaking monsters" is in reality a Japanese thud as loud as Kong's footfall. The hairy ape of Skull Island battles a king-sized octopus and Godzilla in a seemingly endless series of fisticuffs and body bashings. Additional footage with Michael Keith was shot for the U.S. Directed by Inoshiro Honda. Based on an idea by animator Willis O'Brien. James Yogi, Tadao Takashima. (Goodtimes) (Laser: Japanese)

KING OF KONG ISLAND (1968). Also known as EVE THE WILD WOMAN. With remote-control devices, giant gorillas become robot killers. A descendant of the King himself happens along and decides enough is enough already and starts crunching skulls—and remote-control devices. Left to its own devices, this Spanish-produced job (made as EVE THE WILD WOMAN) would fall flat on its ugly kisser. Directed by Robert Morris. Brad Harris, Marc Lawrence. (VCI)

KING OF THE JUNGLE (1933). Buster Crabbe considered this take-off on Tarzan one of his few "A" movies and was proud of his "lion man" performance. Philip Wylie and Fred Niblo Jr. co-authored the screenplay about a jungle youth raised on the vine by lions who is brought to the U.S. as a carnival attraction. Good jungle and wildlife footage; holds up better than most '30s jungle flicks. Frances Dee, Irving Pichel. Directed by Bruce Humberstone and Max Marcin.

KING OF THE MOUNTIES (1942). Action-packed 12-chapter Republic serial in which Allan Lane as "King of the Royal Mounted" fights Axis agents who intend to bomb America with a new kind of aircraft. Gilbert Emery, Russell Hicks, Peggy Drake, Duncan Renaldo.

KING OF THE ROCKET MEN (1951). Republic serial, all 12 chapters, in which Tris Coffin, a member of Science Associates, dons a jet-propelled flying suit to become "Rocket Man," a high-flying hero who soars against Mr. Vulcan, an evil nerd trying to steal the Sonutron (a rock disintegrator) and wreak havoc on the world. Instead, he should have concentrated on disintegrating the rocks in his head—he and his henchmen bungle the job so badly. Straight out of the comic books, and lively directed by Fred C. Brannon. Don Haggerty, Mae Clarke, House Peters Jr. Released to TV in a shortened version as LOST PLANET AIRMEN. (Video/Laser: Republic)

KING OF THE STREETS. See **ALIEN WARRIOR.**

KING OF THE ZOMBIES (1941). Not king of the zombie movies, for sure. Horridly hoary and ingratiatingly insipid "walking dead" melodrama in which mad doctor

Henry Victor creates zombies for the Axis. Mantan Moreland rolls his eyes and runs at the slightest sign of a "spook." As dated as whalebone corsets and Easter bonnets. Dick Purcell, Joan Woodbury. Directed by Jean Yarbrough. (Video Archive; Sinister/C)

KING ROBOT. See **MY SON, THE VAMPIRE.**

KING SOLOMON'S MINES (1937). This British version of H. Rider Haggard's epic adventure about an African expedition in search of a priceless diamond treasure, featuring Quartermain the Great White Hunter, is crude by today's standards, with far too much emphasis on the gospel singing of Paul Robeson (playing a native bearer). Sir Cedric Hardwicke and Roland Young are the explorers who dare the dangers of the Dark Continent, coming up against a witch who brings about a volcanic explosion and puts a curse on the trekkers. The 1950 MGM version was better, although that featured none of the fantasy. Directed by Robert Stevenson. John Loder, Anna Lee. (Embassy; Sinister/C; Nostalgia; Home Vision)

KING SOLOMON'S MINES (1985). This has such a spirited sense of light-hearted adventure, and moves at such a lightning clip, that one is almost willing to overlook the fact it has nothing to do with H. R. Haggard's novel and everything to do with Indiana Jones. The exciting action sequences are almost direct steals, right down to the line "Trust me." Richard Chamberlain proves a virile, rugged Quartermain helping feisty heroine Sharon Stone find her lost father and a diamond mine in Africa prior to World War I. Full of derring-do and mock heroics in a tongue-in-cheek vein, with the villains (Herbert Lom as a German officer, John Rhys-Davies as a Turkish adventurer) more caricature than menace. There's an hysterical cannibal pot sequence, a madcap flying chase, a strange tribe of tree-hanging Africans, a couple of village massacres and one lengthy cave sequence that features a wicked witch, a giant spider and death devices a la TEMPLE OF DOOM. Production values are grand, with half the tribes of Africa working as extras. Directed by J. Lee Thompson. (MGM/UA)

CHAMBERLAIN

KING SOLOMON'S TREASURE (1978). Light-hearted, minor fantasy-adventure based loosely on H. R. Haggard's novel about Allan Quartermain, a Great White Hunter searching for a lost fortune in the wilds of Africa. John Colicos makes for a different Quartermain, but equal emphasis is put on comedy relief: naval officer Patrick Macnee and David McCallum, who help in rescuing a young woman from a prehistoric monster and in finding a lost Roman-style city ruled by a Cleopatra-like Britt Ekland. Harry Alan Towers' production, directed by Alvin Rakoff. Wilfrid Hyde-White, Ken Gampu. (VCI)

KIRLIAN WITNESS, THE (1978). Minor but interesting effort from writer-producer-director Jonathan Sarno, depicting a murder that is "witnessed" by a plant and the efforts of the victim's sister to track the murderer. Kirlian photography, a method of photographing an object's aura, is used to solve the case. This offbeat film is marred by a muddled script. Nancy Snyder, Lawrence Tierney, Joe Colodner. Photographed in Soho. (From Magnum as **PLANTS ARE WATCHING, THE**)

KISS, THE (1988). Felice (Joanna Pacula) is a witch after the daughter of her sister. When the sister dies in an auto accident right out of THE OMEN series, the beguiling witch moves in on the daughter (Meredith Salenger) and father (Nicholas Kilbertus), and begins murders that involve a cat-like familiar, solidified from Felice's mumbo-jumbo incantations and curses. The climax is such an unbelievable series of actions that it becomes laughable. The hero is Mimi Kuzyk, a friendly neighbor who comes to the daughter's rescue. Unclarified story points and unexplained reasons for a monster emerging from Felice's mouth are just two unexplained things this film poses. Directed by Pen Densham. (Video/Laser: RCA/Columbia)

KISS AND KILL (1968). Christopher Lee essays the insidious Fu Manchu role for the fourth time with sadistic glee. This time Fu's plot to rule the world involves hypnotized women who transfer a deadly poison to anyone who touches their passionate lips. Call it the Hacks Factor application. Richard Greene portrays the Scotland Yard pursuer Nayland Smith and Shirley Eaton is chief among the "black widows." Producer Harry Alan Towers wrote as Peter Welbeck. Aka BLOOD OF FU MANCHU, FU MANCHU AND THE KISS OF DEATH, AGAINST ALL ODDS and FU MANCHU AND THE KEYS OF DEATH. Directed by Jess Franco. (Trans Atlantic; Moore; American; from Republic as **AGAINST ALL ODDS** and from Bingo as **KISS OF DEATH**)

KISS DADDY GOODBYE (1981). Brother and sister with ESP powers resurrect their father after he's been killed by a motorcycle gang, and the dead parent goes after people whom his children consider "bad guys." Strangle strangle mangle mangle. Meanwhile, social worker Marilyn Burns and county deputy Fabian Forts try to solve the mystery and have a little G-rated sex but both are slow on the uptake and remain mentally behind while a predictable plot flows like molasses, and with about as much excitement as watching molasses flow. Director Patrick Regan's kids, Nell and Patrick III, portray the adorable let's-get-revenge-kids. Jon Cedar, Marvin Miller. (Monterey; Twilight; from Premiere as **THE VENGEFUL DEAD** and from IVE and Genesis as **REVENGE OF THE ZOMBIES**—a misnomer since there is only one zombie in the movie)

KISS FROM EDDIE, A. See **AROUSERS, THE.**

KISS KISS, KILL KILL (1966). German-Italian-Yugoslav hodgepodge spy thriller featuring a drug that induces a zombie-like state; apparently the drug affected the entire cast, which walks vacant-eyed through their mindless roles. A dismal adaptation of Bert F. Island's "Kommissar X" books. Directed by Gianfranco Parolini. Tony Kendall, Brad Harris, Maria Perschy.

KISS KISS, KILL KILL (1974). Bluebeard wife killer Michael Jayston uses strangulation techniques, sometimes in the bathroom. He's looking for a third victim when he meets a blonde (Helen Mirren) he's really falls for. But he cannot resist the temptation of a rich widow's pocketbook and two-times both women. Brian Clemens' script has a twist ending on top of a twist ending—it should catch you by surprise. Produced-directed by John Sichel. Michael Gwynn, Richard Coleman.

KISS ME DEADLY (1955). What's a Mike Hammer thriller by Mickey Spillane doing in this book? Because Ralph Meeker, as the blood-and-guts private eye, is in pursuit of a suitcase that could have a holocaustic effect on anyone who opens it. Director Robert Aldrich, with A.I. Bezzerides' script, has fashioned one of the strangest of film noir thrillers. Albert Dekker, Paul Stewart, Cloris Leachman, Leigh Snowden, Strother Martin, Jack Elam, Robert Cornthwaite. (Video/Laser: MGM/UA)

KISS MEETS THE PHANTOM OF THE PARK (1978). Outrageous TV vehicle for the rock group Kiss, its title giving away the storyline about mad doctor Anthony Zerbe trying to turn the musicians into sideshow freaks who're so far out, it's hard to distinguish them from rockers. They end up a menagerie of monsters (Frankenstein Monster, werewolf, Dracula) under Gordon Hessler's direction. Our advice: Kiss it off. Peter Criss, Ace Frehley, Gene Simmons. Aka ATTACK OF THE PHANTOMS. (Worldvision) (Laser: Image)

KISS ME GOODBYE (1982). If you set your brain on zero, this could be a mildly charming comedy with supernatural overtones. This is a fluffy throwback to the light-hearted comedies of the 1960s. Broadway choreographer Jolly Villano (James Caan), dead these past five years, turns up to pester ex-wife Sally Field, who is about to marry an Egyptologist (Jeff Bridges). The Charlie Peters script has Jolly invisible to all but Sally, who keeps saying something dumb and then something even dumber to cover up for the first dumb statement. This leads to pointless conversations, confusions and other devices that barely move the story. Too, Bridges is stuck with a nerdish character no one would want to marry, and you wonder why Sally is bothering. You also wonder why producer-director Robert Mulligan picked this project. Mildred Natwick, Claire Trevor, William Prince, Maryedith Burrell. (CBS/Fox)

KISS ME, KILL ME (1969). Photographer Carroll Baker thinks she's befriended a witch—but is it fact or fantasy? Italian-made thriller, based on a cartoon strip by Guido Crepar, co-stars George Eastman and Isabelle DeFunes. Evil spells, ample nudity. Also called BABA YAGA—THE DEVIL WITCH. (Paragon; Unicorn)

KISS ME, KILL ME. See **T.A.G.—THE ASSASSINATION GAME.** (You're It!)

KISS ME, MONSTER (1968). Caribbean island is the haven for a mad doc carrying out experiments on animals and naked women as though he had just seen THE ISLAND OF DR. MOREAU. Writer-director Jesus Franco is responsible for another Spanish flicker with grotesque imagery. Janine Reynard, Rossana Yanni, Adrian Hoven. Aka CASTLE OF THE DOOMED. (Value)

KISS ME QUICK! (1963). The sex life of the Frankenstein Monster is the key issue when an alien from Sterilox joins forces with Dr. Breedlove. There's a menagerie of monsters (including a mummy and vampire) but the public kissed it off quick. Also known as DR. BREEDLOVE. Co-directed by producer Pete Perry and Max Gardens. Jackie DeWit, Althea Currier. (S/Weird)

KISS OF DEATH. Video of **KISS AND KILL** (Bingo).

KISS OF EVIL (1962). Made in Britain as KISS OF THE VAMPIRE and re-edited heavily for the U.S. It was produced during that long period when Christopher Lee refused to don the cape of Dracula, and Hammer was forced to cast a surrogate count, in this case Noel Willman, who portrays Dr. Ravna. The good doc invites an English couple honeymooning in Bavaria to his chateau, where he and his disciples practice the black arts and drink plenty of blood to keep their strength up. A professor resembling Van Helsing turns the tables on the vampire gang with the help of a squadron of bats. One of the better Hammer offerings. Directed by Don Sharp and scripted by producer Anthony Hinds (as John Elder). Clifford Evans, Edward De Souza, Isobel Black.

KISS OF THE BEAST (1990). This variation on THE BEAUTY AND THE BEAST is a rich-looking production, having been filmed on Italian locations. But the Dennis Paoli script is a mess of stuff about the owner of a castle (Sherilyn Fenn) who encounters a traveling "World of Wonders" sideshow that brings distress into her life. She discovers there's a beast living in the walls who materializes in and out of her reality-fantasy reveries. Meanwhile, the statues on the castle grounds are actually the frozen spirits of those who have sinned and other family secrets are contained in a painting. There's a lot of R-rated sex between beautiful woman and ugly beast but producer-director Charles Band never brings the elements together. Malcolm Jamieson, Hilary Mason, Alex Daniels, Phil Fondacaro. (On video and laser from Paramount as **MEREDIAN: KISS OF THE BEAST**)

KISS OF THE TARANTULA (1972). A lonely, misunderstood child, befriended by her undertaker father but hated by her unfaithful mother, realizes mom is committing adultery with dad's brother and unleashes a tarantula spider into her bedroom. It's the beginnings of a spider murderess. This independent low budgeter, directed by Chris Munger, does for spiders what WILLARD did for rats. You'll shudder as scores of tarantulas scurry up the arms and legs of a pair of kissers in Lover's Lane when the demented Suzanne Love unleashes her pretty pets as eight-legged avengers. She cackles such commands as "Spin faster" and "Scuttle you creepers" as they scurry into the night to spread their web of horror. A strange subplot involves a rural policeman who falls in love with Suzanne (as though she were a hypnotic spiderwoman) and covers up her crimes, but his faith/fate is a chilling one. Eric Mason, Patricia Landon. Also known as SHUDDER. (Monterey; Gorgon; United)

KISS THE GIRLS AND MAKE THEM DIE (1967). Lightweight spoof of the James Bond genre, made by Dino De Laurentiis in Rio de Janeiro. Although a pale copy of 007's exploits, it has a sparkle to its comedy, gorgeous women in figure-flattering wardrobes, and scenic action set against picturesque Rio. The villain is industrialist Ardonian (Raf Vallone), who intends to bombard the U.S. with emissions of "cordize" to "kill the sex drive in men" and allow Chinese hordes to invade America. For his own sexual amusement, Ardonian has a bevy of beauties in suspended animation. Michael Connors walks somnambulistic through his role as super agent Kelly who has minipistols hidden in his clothing and is always eating bananas. A standout is Terry-Thomas as a chauffeur secret agent. Directed by Henry Levin and Dino Maiuri. Dorothy Provine portrays Connors' charming, sexy contact. Beverly Adams, Marilu Tolo, Margaret Lee, Sandro Dori.

KNIFE FOR THE LADIES, A. See **SILENT SENTENCE.**

KNIFE IN THE BODY. See **MURDER CLINIC.**

KNIGHT MOVES (1993). Excellent blending of Hitchcockian whodunit trickery and a serial-killer plot: Christopher Lambert is a chess grandmaster in a seaside resort tournament when several beautiful women are murdered. Clues indicate the killer is playing cat-and-mouse games with Lambert, who is also suspected by cops Tom Skerritt and Daniel Baldwin. Director Carl Schenkel treats Brad Mirman's script as a horror thriller, a Sherlock Holmes mystery and brings literary and cinematic twists to this riveting, taut suspense shocker. Diane Lane, Charles Bailey-Gates, Ferdinand Mayne. (Republic)

LAMBERT

KNIGHT RIDER 2000 (1991). TV-movie revival of the popular '82-86 series with David Hasselhoff as the crime-fighting driver of a computerized car. Typical TV action stuff when he takes on crooked cops in the year 2000 and befriends crusading policewoman Carmen Argenziano. Directed by Alan J. Levi. Megan Butler, Edward Mulhare returns as assignment chief Devon Miles. William Daniels returns as the voice of KITT.

KNIGHTS (1992). Does the world need another cyborg movie? Hardly, but writer-director Albert Pyun brings such kinetic energy to the feeble plot that one cannot help but enjoy the flying bodies and mindless action. Once you get past the absurd idea of Kris Kristofferson playing a cyborg warrior named Gabriel, you've got clear sailing into Armageddon land ("another age, another place") where evil cyborg Lance Henriksen (chewing scenery, growling under his breath and waving a mechanical arm) searches for fresh humans so that he might feast on their blood, a "fuel" for him and his machinemen. Kick boxing champ Kathy Long makes for a believable warrior as she takes on Henriksen's fighters in the butte country around Moab, Utah. The film's conclusion suggests a sequel. Scott Paulin, Gary Daniels, Nicholas Guest. (Paramount)

KNIGHTS OF THE DRAGON, THE. Theatrical title for **STAR KNIGHT.**

K-9000 (1991). Compendium of cops-and-robbers cliches: high-speed car chases; shootouts; bodies crashing through windows; punches that would destroy an average human. Providing a fantasy twist to this TV-movie is "Niner," a German shepard (experimental model K-9000) cybernetically able to communicate mentally with cop Chris Mulkey. Scientist Catherine Owenberg's Piper Institute has developed the dog as a peaceful weapon, but bad guy Judson Scott and gang want it for a wartime weapon. You've seen it B4-1000 times. Directed by Kim Manners. Dennis Haysbert, Danna Gladstone. (Fries)

KNUCKLE MEN. See **TERMINAL ISLAND.**

KONGA (1961). Herman Cohen production, unconscionably made as I WAS A TEENAGE GORILLA. Biologist Michael Gough is raising man-eating plants when he branches out into bigger things. Twenty-five feet bigger: that's the size of a chimp-turned-killer-gorilla injected with a New Scientific Serum That Will Advance Mankind Into a New Epoch. Gough also has an ogling eye for Claire Gordon, a bouncy young thing who wears tight sweaters, much to the jealousy of lab assistant Margo Johns. The gorilla comes off looking all right, but you can't say the same for Gough when Konga picks up the hapless doctor and carries him into the London street to do an imitation of King Kong. Quite terrible, but its high incompetency level makes it fun. John Lemont directed and Cohen co-scripted with Aben Kandel. Jess Conrad, Austin Trevor, Jack Watson.

KONGO (1932). Hard-hitting, two-fisted sound version of the 1928 Lon Chaney silent classic WEST OF ZANZIBAR, a horror-melodrama based on a play by Chester DeVonde and Kilbourn Gordon. This tale of revenge, as tough as they come, stars Walter Huston (in the Chaney role) as a hate-driven ivory trader in the African jungle who is motivated by a perverse desire to humiliate and control others. Huston brings a bitter intensity to his bravado performance, and equally effective are Conrad Nagel as a drunken doctor, Lupe Velez as a nymphomaniacal native girl and Virginia Bruce as a woman wallowing in alcoholism and self-pity. Directed by William Cowen.

KONRAD (1985). Lightweight TV-movie which, despite its threadbare production and obvious scripting, takes on a charm. Huckleberry Fox portrays an "Instant Child," a creation by goofy doctor Max Wright who accidentally delivers the youth to the wrong address. Spiritually down-and-out Polly Holliday falls in love with Konrad, teaching him that the state of perfection sought by "the factory" only dehumanizes him. Yes, the object lessons are too obvious and there's hokum with Ned Beatty wanting to marry Polly and raise Konrad, yet it seems bearable with director Nell Cox's touch. (Public Media)

KRONOS (1957). A different kind of alien invasion thriller, even if it is hampered by a low budget, and average direction by producer Kurt Neumann. A UFO deposits a towering hunk of computerized machinery on Earth, which then pistons its way across the landscape, sucking up energy and squashing everyone who gets beneath its size 45 sneakers. Jeff Morrow, John Emery and Morris Ankrum are experienced hands with this kind of material, but it's that gigantic mechanical block that steals the show. Barbara Lawrence, Robert Shayne. (Nostalgia Merchant) (Laser: Image)

KRUG AND COMPANY. See **LAST HOUSE ON THE LEFT, THE.**

KRULL (1983). A fairy-tale quality instills this sword-and-sorcery adventure with a sense of childlike wonder, making it more palatable for the young than the grittier Conan sagas. Emphasis is on dazzling effects and innovative designs on the planet Krull, where a rock-fortress spaceship commanded by the Beast unloads an army of Slayers. Warrior Ken Marshall is separated from his lovely princess (Lysette Anthony) and joins forces with Ergo the Magician and a band of thieves to challenge the Beast in his Black Fortress. The odyssey unfolds with a deadly bog, two murderous changelings, a cavern of

WITCH AND CYCLOPS IN "KRULL'

webs housing the Widow of the Spider, a herd of sky-riding Firemares and assorted quest perils. Final assault on the Beast is a rousing one—plenty of thunder, fire and clashing steel—and there's an opulent score by James Horner. KRULL is fine matinee material, blazing with color and action. Peter Yates' direction is first-rate, giving Stanford Sherman's script a sense of the majestic. Freddie Jones is the wise man, Ynyr; Francesca Annis is the Widow of the Web; Bernard Bresslaw is the one-eyed Cyclops; David Barttley is Ergo the Magician and Alun Armstrong is Torquil, bandit leader. (Video/Laser: RCA/Columbia)

KUNG FU EXORCIST (1976). Hong Kong blending of horror and martial arts. Kathy Leen, billed as the "lady Bruce Lee," fights her way to victory against the Shaolin Holy Man, who has aligned himself with the Devil so his flying dropkicks will have greater impact.

KUNG FU FROM BEYOND THE GRAVE (1982). As in HAMLET, a murdered spirit from beyond the grave requests his son to seek revenge and our hero, Sonny Sing, does just that, aided by a vampiric count at one point in the non-stop martial arts action. Call it BLOOD AND CHOP SUEY. Directed by Li Zhao. (Ocean)

KUNG FU VAMPIRE BUSTER (198?). Hong Kong blending of martial and bloodsucking arts with the likes of Lu Fang, Wang Hsiao Feng, Chien Hsiao Hou. (Ocean)

KUNG FU ZOMBIE (1981). Love that title! Martial arts master almost gets the chop suey kicked out of his noodles when he confronts a vampire proficient in kung fu. Just a lot of fighting with little motive behind the supernatural elements. Should please action buffs, though. Directed by Hwa I Hung. Billy Chong. (Ocean)

KWAIDAN (1965). Japanese anthology film by Masaki Kobayashi plunges into the shadowy valley of Lafcadio Hearn's ghost stories, once described as "permanent archetypes of human experience." Yoko Mizuki's script masters the paradox of being horrifying and beautiful with its four-part, two-and-a-half-hour format. The first tale is the surrealistic vignette of a defeated Samurai warrior who leaves his wife for a wealthy highborn who turns out to be an unbearable bitch. "In the Cup of Tea" deals with a man who peers into his teacup one morning and finds the reflection of a stranger gazing back. "Koichi, the Earless" is the most ghostly of the yarns, depicting a man summoned by ancient spirits to serve as their storyteller. "The Woman of the Snow" is about a secret whispered by one friend to another which must never be repeated. A color film of lush composition featuring superb dreamlike special effects. Excellent cast headed by Renato Mikuni, Michiyo Aratama and Tatsuya Nakadai. (S/Weird; Video Yesteryear; Filmfax; Sinister/C; Nostalgia) (Laser: Criterion)

LABORATORY (1980). Prepare for total tedium when humanoid aliens in metallic suits abduct Earthlings (alcoholic rich bitch, Chinese woman, fanatical priest, woman musician, black athlete, etc.) and place them under observation in a deserted clinic. Nothing happens for the next hour while the aliens talk in echoing, hard-to-understand voices and the humans bicker. Produced-directed by Allan Sandler and Robert Emenegger. Martin Kove, Ken Washington, Camille Mitchell. (United; VCI)

LABYRINTH. See **REFLECTION OF FEAR.**

LABYRINTH (1986). Curious mixture of Muppet humor, THE WIZARD OF OZ and ALICE IN WONDERLAND: Obnoxious teenager Jennifer Connelly is plunged into the kingdom of the King of Goblins (David Bowie) as she pursues gremlins who whisked away her baby brother. The premise is weak (the infant is never in any real danger) and not even a 13-hour time limit imposed on Connelly adds suspense as she has adventures with fairies, goblins and dwarves. While Brian Froud's designs and Jim Henson's creatures are amusing (especially a shaggy dog with eyepatch, a clumsy dwarf named Hoggle and a dimwit fuzzball called Bluto), there is an air of ersatz to the thrills in Terry Jones' script, and Bowie is much too charming. Produced by George Lucas and directed by Jim Henson. (Video/Laser: Embassy/Nelson)

LADY AND THE MONSTER, THE (1943). First screen adaptation of Curt Siodmak's novel DONOVAN'S BRAIN in which a financial genius' brain is preserved after his death and takes over others by telepathic communication, is inferior to the 1953 version. The classic idea was misshaped by Republic into an ordinary horror flick. Directed by George Sherman, the film is a dated atmosphere piece, chiefly memorable for John Alton's noir lighting. Vera Ralston is miscast as the heroine. Erich von Stroheim, Richard Arlen, Sidney Blackmer.

LADY DRACULA. See **LEMORA—LADY DRACULA.**

LADY DRACULA (1977). German vampire comedy with Brad Harris as a cop involved with a bloodsucker seeking a blood supply. Directed by Franz-Joseph Gottlieb. Evelynb Kraft, Christine Buchegger.

LADY FRANKENSTEIN (1971). Women's Lib comes to the laboratory! Smock-wearing "femme fatale" Sara Bey (as evil as her father) is a cut-up as she switches brains in two bodies to create a new Frankenstein Monster, copying daddy's techniques. Daddy is Joseph Cotten, who wanders through this European Hammer-clone a bit lost. The monster is a frightful make-up job but Bey is well built, exposing her beautiful breasts in sizzling love scenes. Mel Welles forgot to direct Mickey Hargitay, who stands around looking very brawny—and also lost. Also known as MADAME FRANKENSTEIN. Herbert Fux, Paul Muller. (Sinister/C; Embassy; S/Weird; Filmfax; Sultan)

LADYHAWKE (1985). Topnotch fantasy adventure filled with derring-do and swashbuckling; it's also a pleasing fairy tale romance in which gallant knight Rutger Hauer turns into a wolf at night, and beautiful princess Isabeau (Michelle Pfeiffer) transmutates into a hawk by day. This means they can never fulfill their love—until there happens along a flippant squire (Matthew Broderick), who conspires with old Imperius (Leo McKern) to undo the evil spell imposed by evil bishop John Wood. The Italian castles and ruins lend authenticity to this gritty costume drama with high energy performances. Directed by Richard Donner for producer Harvey (THE OMEN) Bernhard. (Video/Laser: Warner Bros.)

LADY IN WHITE (1988). A movie for your Top Ten list. Writer-producer-director Frank La Loggia, who showed promise with the 1981 FEAR NO EVIL, has fashioned a supernatural tale that captures the "sense of wonder" Ray Bradbury often speaks of. La Loggia blends life in a small Eastern Seaboard town in 1962 (in the nostalgic style of Spielberg) with ghost and gothic elements. Lukas Haas is superb as Frankie Scarlotti, 10, who encounters the spectral spirits of a girl who was violently murdered and her mother, a legendary "Lady in White" who haunts the environs of Willowpoint Falls. The story is told as a voice-over memory—that and its racial subplot are reminiscent of TO KILL A MOCKING BIRD. While adults might think its menacing qualities will be frightening to children, it is this very quality that will attract youngsters. Len Cariou, Alex Rocco, Katherine Helmond. (Virgin Vision) (Laser: Image)

LADY POSSESSED (1951). Vague personality transference melodrama about an American (June Havoc) in London who begins to behave like the late wife of pianist James Mason. Compared to today's "possession" films, this is tamed and underplayed. LADY POSSESSED is so dated it has assumed a watchability it may not have had in 1951. Mason also produced and co-wrote with wife Pamela. Directed by William Spier and Roy Kellino.

Stephen Dunne made his film debut.

LADY, STAY DEAD (1982). Australian shocker from producer-writer-director Terry (INN OF THE DAMNED) Bourke about a gardener (Chard Hayward) who kills a woman, then covers his tracks by attacking someone else who saw the crime being committed. Sleaze fans will be disappointed to learn this is only slightly tacky. Movie, stay lost. Roger Ward, Louise Howitt. (Video City)

LADY TERMINATOR (1989). An evil queen's reincarnation—a student on an anthropological quest—goes on a rampage, killing half the population of Indonesia. Barbara Anne Constable, Christopher J. Hart. Directed by Jalil Jackson. (Studio Entertainment)

LAIR OF THE WHITE WORM, THE (1988). Writer-director Ken Russell takes a standard horror-movie plot and gives it his usual bizarre twists and sense of perversity. The result: a decadent, perplexing mixture of campy one-liners, absurd visuals and unapproachable characters. The setting is the mansion of Lady Sylvia Marsh (Amanda Donohoe), the head of a snake cult preparing virginal sacrifices to the Worm God, who lives in a deep pit and only emerges for fresh munchies. Lady Marsh claims her victims, sways to music like a cobra, and sharpens her fangs for the next attack. With hysteria and garish style, Russell again proves he's one of the wildest film makers in the world. Hugh Grant, Catherine Oxenberg, Peter Capaldi. (Vestron) (Laser: Image)

LAKE OF DRACULA (1971). Japanese horror film made with compassion. A woman is saved from a vampire by an old man and the experience lingers with her for years, even though others treat it as a bad dream. Events come to a climax when Dracula's grandfather turns up. Also known as DRACULA'S LUST FOR BLOOD, BLOODTHIRSTY EYES and JAPULA. Directed by M. Yamamoto. Midori Fujita, Mori Kishida.

LAKE OF THE LIVING DEAD. See **ZOMBIE LAKE.**

LAND BEFORE TIME, THE (1988). Outstanding cartoon feature from the team of Don Bluth, Gary Goldman and John Pomeroy, produced by Steven Spielberg and George Lucas. It's a warm, thrilling account about a young dinosaur named Littlefoot who survives a prehistoric cataclysm and leads young survivors on a trek to a promised land. The terse 66 minutes have some wonderful set pieces and are reminiscent of the best Disney cartoons of yore. Youngsters might be frightened when the band is imperiled by the carnivorous Sharptooth, but that is counterbalanced by wonderful characters and a warm humor. Voices by Pat Hingle (narrator and Rooter), Helen Shaver (Littlefoot's mom), Candice Houston (Cera), Judith Barsi (Ducky), Will Ryan (Petrie), Burke Barnes (Daddy Topps). (MCA; Applause) (Laser: MCA)

YOUNG ANATOSAURUS

LAND OF DOOM (1984). Another after-the-Bomb Mad Max-style adventure, the focus on a warrior named Harmony (Deborah Rennard), a man-hater forced to join forces with nomad Garrick Dowhen as they trek to a legendary paradise. Wall-to-wall action with crazy vehicles and zap guns, with bands of sadists pillaging and raping and finally being outgunned by midgets in robes. That's about all director Peter Maris can offer, and if that's all you need, by all means . . . (Lightning)

LAND OF FARAWAY, THE (1987). Limited special effects by Derek Meddings and tedious stretches make for a fair children's fantasy spun as a sword-and-sorcery fairy tale. Stockholm orphan boy Nicholas Pickard is carried away on the white beard of an old man to a kingdom ruled by benevolent king Timothy Bottoms. But to earn happiness the boy (renamed Mio) decides to venture with Jum-Jum (Christopher Bale) to the Land Outside, to kill evil knight Kato (Christopher Lee). Aided by a magical sword and a cloak of invisibility spun by Susannah York, the youths close in on Kato for a showdown, the film's one exciting moment. Directed by Vladimir Grammatikov. (Prism; Starmaker)

LAND OF THE LOST (1974). Sid and Marty Krofft produced this children's TV series about the Porter family, which is sent back in time through a "dimensional gate" to prehistoric days, where the clan meets such creatures as Tasha the pet dinosaur, Sarface the Tyrannosaurus rex, Shung the Terrible and other stoned Stone Age characters. (Worldvision has six tapes, each containing two episodes)

LAND OF THE LOST (1974). More episodes of the Porter family in a kingdom of friendly creatures. In "Chaka," they meets the chimp people, the Pakuni, and in "Dopey" the teeners find an unhatched brontosaurus egg and baby it along. (Embassy)

LAND OF THE LOST (1974). Another two episodes from the TV series set in a weird prehistoric world. This time a displaced forest ranger and two kids meet up with a confederate soldier from the Civil War. (Embassy)

LAND OF THE MINOTAUR, THE (1977). Dreadful British-Greek production, made in Greece and also known as THE DEVIL'S PEOPLE and THE DEVIL'S MEN, in which minister Donald Pleasence utilizes religious symbols (cross, holy water, etc.) to fight off a devil cult commanded by Peter Cushing. Bereft of logic, characterizations, suspense and anything else that makes watchable cinema. Directed by Costas Carayiannis. Luan Peters, Vanna Revilli, Nikos Verlakis. (VCI)

LAND THAT TIME FORGOT (1975). First entry in a series of Edgar Rice Burroughs adventure-fantasy yarns produced by John Dark and directed by Kevin Connor. When a British merchant is sunk by a U-Boat during World War I, the survivors (Doug McClure, Susan Penhaligon) seek refuge on an uncharted island forgotten by time. All the monsters (dragon, pterodactyl, etc.) are full-scale mock-ups moved mechnically, and sometimes it shows. Yet, there is a spirit of rousing adventure that makes this enjoyable. The sequel was AT THE EARTH'S CORE, followed by THE PEOPLE THAT TIME FORGOT. John McEnery, Anthony Ainley. (Vestron)

LAND UNKNOWN, THE (1956). Potentially exciting lost-world theme (helicopter carrying explorers bumps into a pterodactyl and crashlands in a primeval jungle) becomes the hackneyed plot for a cheap-jack (and we mean cheap, Jack) Universal-International potboiler, marred by what appears to be stock footage of attacking dinosaurs from previous prehistoric sagas. Clifford Stine's effects are ultimately too limited. Directed by Virgil Vogel. Jock Mahoney, Douglas Kennedy, William Reynolds. (MCA)

LASERBLAST (1978). Teenager Kim Milford discovers a laser cannon in the desert (dropped during a war between alien armies) and uses it for revengeful purposes. This low-budget quickie from producer Charles Band is one zap after the other, with Milford turning green whenever he blows up cars and buildings. There's some nice stop motion work of the aliens by Dave Allen—it's the story that's nonanimated. Keenan Wynn and Roddy McDowall are wasted in stupid cameos. Directed with a one-track mind to blow everything up by Michael Rae. (Media) (Laser: Shadow Entertainment)

'THE LAND UNKNOWN'

LASERBLAST II (1985). "The ultimate alien weapon is back" with special effects by Mechanical and Makeup Imageries Inc. Charles Band-Paul Levinson production written by Robert Amante. This has never shown up on TV or in video. Anyone out there seen it?

LASER MAN, THE (1988). Japanese-American film maker Peter Wang wrote-directed this offbeat tale that makes a statement about our misguided development of technology, in this case a laser weapon that an industrial firm intends to use in an assassination. Wang stars as New York cop Lt. Lu (a blend of Judge Dee and Charlie Chan) who investigates a laser technician (Arthur Weiss) being manipulated into the plot. It's a curious mix of cultural interchange, Zen philosphy, action and artistic direction. The results are interesting and well-intended. Marc Hayashi, Maryann Urbano, Tony Ka-Fei Leung.

LASER MOON (1992). A crazed doctor, in possession of a laser Death Ray to do in his victims, plays a cat-and-mouse game with a radio disc jockey, proclaiming his next kill on the air and forcing authorities to send in a ringer (Traci Lords) to capture him. One zapped movie. Crystal Shaw, Harrison, Leduke. Directed by Bruce Carter. (Hemdale)

LAST ACTION HERO (1993). An $80-million misfire for Arnold Schwarzenegger, who parodies his screen

SCHWARZENEGGER DOES SHAKESPEARE (!?)

persona in a mishmash of ingredients. There is promise in the Shane Black-David Arnott script, but it's buried within worthless debris and a sense of chaos evoked by producer-director John McTiernan, whose dark style doesn't match this comic-book material. Austin O'Brien portrays a youth who loves Schwarzenegger's Jack Slater movies, and is watching the latest ("Jack Slater IV") when a magical ticket (given to him by old projectionist Robert Prosky) transports him into the film. Now he lives Slater's adventures against gang boss Anthony Quinn, hit man Charles Dance and crooked cop F. Murray Abraham. Look at this mess: in-parody with references to Hollywood movies, violent action and sudden death, spectacular fireworks and choreography and a host of secondary characters, including police captain Frank McRae, obligatory girl Mercedes Ruehl and cameos by Jim Belushi, Chevy Chase, Little Richard, Art Carney, Sharon Stone, Jean-Claude Van Damme. Only Dance seems to be having any fun. How do you sum up this movie? As Slater would say, "Big mistake!" (Video/Laser: Columbia TriStar)

LAST BLOOD. Video version of **FIVE MINUTES TO LIVE** (Discount).

LAST BRIDE OF SALEM, THE (1974). Cheapo TV-movie, in which painter Bradford Dillman and goody-two-shoes wife Lois Nettleton move to Salem Village, a community haunted by witches. Everyone pooh-poohs the old legends except the minister who knows evil is afoot when he discovers Dillman is a descendant of a cursed family. Now Dillman and daughter are marked for sacrifice. Also sacrificed: good acting and production. Don't sacrifice your time. Directed by Tom Donovan.

LAST CANNIBAL WORLD, THE. See **LAST SURVIVOR, THE.**

LAST CHASE, THE (1981). Racer Lee Majors' career is cut short when oil reserves are depleted and an epidemic kills millions. Speeding around in his red Porsche, Majors survives by swiping gas from deserted stations. Ecological warning in the guise of sci-fi is a minor diatribe. Directed by Martyn Burke. Burgess Meredith, Chris Makepeace. (Vestron)

LAST CHILD, THE (1971). TV-movie set in 1994 when the government, to cut overpopulation, limits families to one child. Parents Michael Cole and Janet Margolin flee authorities, aided by sympathetic senator Van Heflin (excellent in his last role). Directed by John Moxey. Kent Smith, Ed Asner, Harry Guardino.

LAST DAYS OF MAN ON EARTH (1973). Robert Fuest, director of the Dr. Phibes films, certainly has a penchant for the bizarre. He "designed," wrote and directed this tale of the future (based on Michael Moorcock's THE FINAL PROGRAMME) in which the son of a renowned scientist, Jerry Cornelius, seeks a microfilm that has the formula for creating a synthetic human, a "New Messiah." His adversary is beautiful Miss Brunner (Jenny Runacre), a Death-Black Widow figure luring men to sudden demises. The action is well staged with unusual comedic touches. Jon Finch (as Jerry Cornelius), Sterling Hayden, Hugh Griffith, Patrick Magee, Julie Ege, Harry Andrews, George Coulouris, Sarah Douglas. (Embassy) (Laser: Image)

LAST DAYS OF PLANET EARTH, THE (1978). Vignettes of doom as Earth heads for the last round-up, Japanese style. Armageddon begins when the ocean turns blood-red and sealife expires, vegetation blooms and becomes man-eating stalkers, and radioactive monsters rove the planet. A visionary nightmare from director Toshio Masuda.

LAST DINOSAUR, THE (1977). U.S.-Japanese TV-movie in which an expedition discovers a lost world inhabited by wild natives and a dinosaur. Characters and dialogue are hopelessly banal (Richard Boone is the insufferable leader of the expedition) and the effects are from the Godzilla school of destruction. Directed by Alex Grasshof and Tom Kotani. Joan Van Ark, Steven Keats.

LAST ENTRY, THE. See **FORCED ENTRY.**

LAST HORROR FILM, THE (1982). Amusing satire on horror movies with Joe Spinell as a neurotic New York cabbie, Vinny Durand, who has the hots for actress Jana Bates (Caroline Munro) and imagines himself a movie director making THE LOVES OF DRACULA. He follows her to Frances' Cannes Film Festival, where this was filmed, so there's a rich amount of moviedom detail to intrigue buffs. A series of gore murders begins with Durand hanging around the edges, taking films of Jana and making love to her projected image. And dig those hilarious scenes between Spinell and his little old Jewish mother (played by his real mom, Mary). A way-out derivative of slasher flicks directed and co-produced by David Winter. (Media; Video Treasures)

LAST HOUSE ON DEAD END STREET (1981). Filmmakers murder their stars to make snuff movies, then when they get cheated by their distributor, they kill the executives and use their death scenes in new snuffers. That'll teach the bastards who keep screwing over film makers. Steven Morrison, Dennis Crawford. Directed by Victor Janos. (Sun)

LAST HOUSE ON THE LEFT, THE (1972). Pandering effort of producer Sean S. Cunningham and writer-director Wes Craven, made to shock in the grossest manner with its tale of retribution. Aka SEX CRIME OF THE CENTURY, NIGHT OF VENGEANCE and KRUG AND COMPANY, this depicts a family under attack from sadists: rape, castration, buzzsaw killings, crucifixions, torture. Craven leaves out nothing. And yet this has an unrelenting power that makes it compelling despite crudities. You'll still need a strong stomach. David Alex Hess, Lucy Grantham. (Vestron; CIC offers the complete version) (Laser: CIC; Vestron)

LAST HOUSE ON THE LEFT II. See **CARNAGE.**

LAST HUNTER, THE. See **CANNIBALS IN THE STREETS.**

LAST JAWS, THE. See **GREAT WHITE, THE.**

LAST KIDS ON EARTH, THE (1983). Two one-hour British TV films for children: "Nutcase" is a farce in which bungling policemen search for a nuclear bomb planted by a gang of singing villains. Meanwhile, our young heroes find a Time-Space Warp Control Machine that could save the city. "Zero Hour" is a serious look at two runaway children who find themselves in a deserted town, where a research station is about to blow up. Andrew Ashley, Jayne Collins.

LAST MAN ON EARTH, THE (1964). First adaptation of Richard Matheson's classic novel, I AM LEGEND, is far more faithful than the second, THE OMEGA MAN. Filmed in Italy by director Ubaldo Ragona (with U.S. insert shots by Sidney Salkow), it stars Vincent Price as the only non-tainted survivor of a worldwide plague; all others are walking corpses, a mutated form of vampirism. Price burns their bodies during the day and, with the coming of dusk, rushes to his fortress to fight off the nocturnal marauders. Co-written by Matheson (who uses the penman Logan Swanson). Emma Danieli, Giacomo Rossi Stuart. (Sinister/C; S/Weird)

LAST MOVIE, THE (1971). Following EASY RIDER, Dennis Hopper chose to direct this outre story—so bewildering that Universal gave it the toss. Produced in Peru, it depicts the making of a Western movie (with real-life director Samuel Fuller portraying the crazed director) but quickly turns into a Moebius Strip, twisting and winding upon itself with its illusions-within-reality, reality-within-illusions, and time-space psychological distortions. Bizarre and baffling. Peter Fonda, Julie Adams, John Phillip Law, Sylvia Miles, Rod Cameron, Kris Kristofferson. Released to TV as CHINCHERO. (United American)

LAST OF THE SECRET AGENTS, THE (1966). Marty Allen and Steve Rossi portray spies in this James Bond spoof with such gimmicks as a spy agency, GGI (Good Guys Inc.), which is fighting T.H.E.M.—art thieves after the Venus De Milo. Art this ain't. Produced-directed by Norman Abbott. Nancy Sinatra, John Williams, Edy Williams, Lou Jacobi, Sig Ruman.

LAST PREY OF THE VAMPIRE, THE. See **PLAYGIRLS AND THE VAMPIRE, THE.**

LAST REUNION (1955). British chiller about a reuning World War II bomber squadron and a series of supernatural events. Michael Gough, Eric Portman. (Sinister/C; S/Weird; Filmfax)

LAST RITES. See **DRACULA'S LAST RITES.**

LAST STARFIGHTER, THE (1984). Superior space adventure with excellent effects and an interesting love story fleshed out by writer Jonathan Betuel. Lance Guest is living a bleak existence in a trailer park and excelling only at video games when he is picked by humanoid alien Robert Preston (portraying loveable conman Centauri) to help the Star League of Planets fight off a flotilla of invaders. Guest is trained by Dan O'Herlihy as Grig, the only remaining E.T. who knows intergalactic warfare. Designers Ron Cobb and James D. Bissell give this fairy tale a glossy look, but it is the sensitive love between Guest and Catherine Mary Stewart that makes this work. Directed by Nick Castle. (Video/Laser: MCA)

LAST SURVIVOR, THE (1976). Another cannibalistic indulgence in blood and gore from the meateating-conscious Italians. This time it's director Ruggero Deodato up to no-good exploitation as his cameras track a legendary maneating tribe on Mindanao. Massimo Foschi, Me Me Lay. Also known as THE LAST CANNIBAL WORLD. (From AIR as **CANNIBAL** and Video City as **JUNGLE HOLOCAUST**)

LAST UNICORN, THE (1982). Pleasing animated version of Peter S. Beagle's novel about a beautiful unicorn searching for the rest of her breed and battling the Terrible Red Bull. Wizardry and magic are at work, making this suitable for all. Voices: Alan Arkin, Jeff Bridges, Mia Farrow, Robert Klein, Angela Lansbury, Christopher Lee, Paul Frees. (CBS/Fox; Kartes) (Laser: J2)

LAST VICTIM, THE. See **FORCED ENTRY.**

LAST VICTIM OF THE VAMPIRE. See **PLAYGIRLS AND THE VAMPIRE, THE.**

LAST WAR, THE (1961). Japanese production, with special effects by Eiji Tsuburaya, depicts massive destruction: earthquakes, tidal waves, atomic explosions, the shattering of London Bridge, the pulverization of the Arch of Triumph, the crumpling of the Statue of Liberty and the nuclearization of the Kremlin domes. Now let's see, did they leave any landmark out? It's all caused by faulty wiring in a missile base Fail-Safe System. The only thing missing from this Japanese-created mayhem is Godzilla battling Rodan. Directed with a spectacular sense for destruction by Shue Matsubayashi. Also known as THE FINAL WAR. Frankie Sakai. (Video Gems)

LAST WARRIOR, THE. See **FINAL EXECUTIONER, THE.**

LAST WAVE, THE (1978). Australia's Peter Weir directs an intriguing if mystifying tale of prophecy and doom. The symbolism is fascinating, though, and the atmosphere of pending death heavy as Sydney-based attorney Richard Chamberlain defends Aborigines accused of murder, but he is plagued by visions of horrors to come. A film that works on several levels, and which challenges the intellect as well as pleases the eye. Olivia Hamnett. (Warner Bros.; Rhino) (Laser: Japanese)

LAST WILL OF DR. MABUSE, THE. See **TESTAMENT OF DR. MABUSE, THE.**

LAST WOMAN ON EARTH, THE (1960). Director Roger Corman trivializes post-Armageddon survival into a cheap triangular love story. Two men and one female, instead of worrying about how to build a better world after nuclear holocaust, engage in fatiguing dialogue and clumsy clenches. The screenplay is by Robert Towne. Towne also plays one of the argumentative males opposite Anthony Carbone and Betsy Jones-Moreland. (Sinister/C; S/Weird; Filmfax; Nostalgia)

LATE FOR DINNER (1991). Surprising mixture of genres from director W. D. Richter, who helmed THE ADVENTURES OF BUCKAROO BANZAI. Scripted by Mark Andrus, this opens in 1962 as two innocents—Brian Wimmer and Peter Berg—are caught up in a land swindle. They fall into the hands of a doctor doing a cryonics experiment—and wake up 29 years later without aging a day. The film then abandons sci-fi gimmicks and deals with what happens when the boys return to their New Mexico home and resume old relationships. This odd movie maintains a sense of freshness. Marcia Gay Harden, Colleen Flynn. (New Line) (Laser: Image)

LATE GREAT PLANET EARTH, THE (1978). Compendium of prophesies of evil events yet to come, including the emergence of the Antichrist, based on the best-seller by soothsayer Hal Lindsey. This intriguing pseudo-documentary (written-directed by Robert Amram) makes a strong case for mankind's demise in the near future, when Apocalypse will be Now! Narrated with conviction by Orson Welles. (Video Treasures)

LATHE OF HEAVEN, THE (1980). TV adaptation of Ursula K. LeGuin's novel about a man (Bruce Davison) whose dreams change the course of the world. A psychologist (Kevin Conway) investigating the phenomenon tries to use the dreamer to make the world a better place, but his plan backfires. Recommended. Produced-directed by David Loxton and Fred Barzyk. (WNET/13)

LATIN QUARTER. See **FRENZY.**

LATITUDE ZERO (1969). Japanese adventure with Americans (Joseph Cotten, Cesar Romero, Patricia Medina, Richard Jaeckel) borrows Jules Verne devices when war rages between two submarine captains equipped with zap guns, nuclear torpedos and assorted destructive weapons. Hulking monsters are thrown in should you get bored with underwater action. That GODZILLA team, director Inoshiro Honda and effects artist Eiji Tsuburaya, collaborated. Final coordinate: Zero.

LAUGHING DEAD, THE (1989). Travelers in Mexico participate in a "festival of the dead" celebration, only to become some of the dead when Mayans decide it's sacrifice time. Zombies run amok, pulling off body parts (credit special effects man John Buechler for that). Produced-written-directed by J.T. Somtow. Tim Sullivan, Forrest J. Ackerman (as a dead body).

LAWLESS LAND (1988). Another post-holocaust world a la MAD MAX, depicting the arid adventures of two young people who try to escape from a totalitarian ruler of the devastated landscape, and their predictable adventures staying ahead of a bad guy called Road Kill. Directed by Jon Hess. Leon Berkeley, Xander Berkeley, Nick Corri. (MGM/UA)

LAWNMOWER MAN, THE (1992). That tired plot about the mental retard who's turned into a genius gets "virtual reality" technology in this overblown adaptation of a story from Stephen King's NIGHTSHIFT. Jeff Fahey is a simple-minded gardener-grasscutter who falls into the clutches of scientist Pierce Brosnan, whose experiments with computers turns Fahey into a psychic superman. "The Shop," a secret organization behind Brosnan's research, wants Fahey to carry out evil deeds. Only the computerized nightmare sequences stand out from the myriad of cliches in the script by the husband-and-wife team of Brett Leonard (who also directed) and Gimel Everett (who also co-produced). Jenny Wright, Mark Bringleson, Geoffrey Lewis, Jeremy Slate. (New Line)

JEFF FAHEY

LEATHERFACE: THE TEXAS CHAINSAW MASSACRE III (1989). This second sequel to the 1974 trend-setter in U.S. Grand Guignol comes close to being a remake. The script by "splatter punk" writer David J. Schow (heavily tampered with by producer Robert Engelman and director Jeff Burr) has desert travelers Kate Hodge, William Butler, Toni Hudson and Ken Foree falling prey to Leatherface Sawyer and his new surrogate family of all-American perverts, murderers and sadists. Finally it's Hodge who is subjected to one horror after the other as she is captured, tortured and escapes—only to find herself in a bog of bubbling yuck. The black humor is suitably gruesome but the sum total is less than expected. The film was extensively cut for an R rating, and Schow says many of his set pieces (such as a man being cut down the middle) were as brutally mutilated as his characters. R. A. Mihailoff (Leatherface), Viggo Mortensen. (Video/Laser: RCA/Columbia)

LEECH WOMAN, THE (1960). Coleen Gray, seeking eternal life, learns from Africans that a brain secretion can restore the aging body. One murder, however, leads to more before she and the plot turn to powder. Edward Dein directed the David Duncan screenmplay. Gloria Talbott, Grant Williams, John Van Dreelan. (MCA)

LEFT HAND OF GEMINI, THE (1972). See first edition.

LEGACY, THE (1980). Botched horror thriller never focused sharply by director Richard Marquand. Travelers Katharine Ross, Sam Elliott, Roger Daltrey, Charles Gray. etc. gather in a European chateau where "a legacy of evil" is passed from generation to generation—or something like that. Supernatural gore murders go on interminably. Aka THE LEGACY OF MAGGIE WALSH. (MCA)

LEGACY OF BLOOD (1978). Incompetent psychothriller in which four heirs to a country estate spend the night in the homestead to qualify for the family fortune. Each is murdered in horrible fashion; even the head of sheriff Rodolfo Acosta ends up on a turkey platter in the frig. Jeff Morrow, John Carradine, John Russell and Faith Domergue are all squandered by producer-director Carl Monson. A pox on the horror house of writer Eric Norden. (From Video Gems as **BLOOD LEGACY**)

LEGACY OF HORROR (1978). Primary primer in how not to make a movie—a masterpiece of choppy editing, poor lighting, camera noise, uneven acting and rank cinematography. Credit tacky Andy Milligan the exploitationer—he wrote-directed this mess about three silly sisters who spend a night on Haney Island with their inane husbands to collect an inheritance. A slouch-hatted slouch leaves a head on a platter, shoves a pitchford into a fat stomach and saws a man in half. Elaine Boies, Chris Broderick. A remake of Milligan's THE GHASTLY ONES. Ghastly is right! (Vidcrest; Gorgon; MPI)

LEGACY OF MAGGIE WALSH. See **LEGACY, THE.**

LEGACY OF SATAN (1973). Gerard Damiano, of porno fame, directed this flicker in which an evil cult selects Lisa Christian as its new queen. (Abacus)

LEGEND (1985). Ridley Scott's fairy tale fantasy is in a never-neverland rendered in autumnal detail, all falling leaves, mysticism and magic. So beautiful is the scenery that exquisite detail overshadows the weak story. Peasant Tom Cruise and Princess Lili (Mia Sara) seek the last unicorn in the kingdom, unaware that Darkness (Tim Curry, excellent as a world-weary demon) is using them to set a trap for the horned creature (designed by Rob Bottin. A disappointment because the script by William Hjortsberg lacks humor or clever development, and the romantic leads are real wimps, hardly the stuff of quest-fantasy. Billy Barty, Alice Playten, David Bennett. (Video/Laser: MCA)

LEGENDARY CURSE OF LEMORA. See **LEMORA, LADY DRACULA.**

LEGEND IN LEOTARDS. See **RETURN OF CAPTAIN INVINCIBLE.**

LEGEND OF BIGFOOT, THE (1976). See editions 1-3.

LEGEND OF BIG FOOT (1982). Misguided attempt to portray that misunderstood beast of the forest, who only seeks companionship. Poor little thing. No wonder it stomps on folks. Stafford Morgan, Katherine Hopkins. (Active)

LEGEND OF BLOOD CASTLE (1972). Another sanguinary variation on the Countess Bathory myth, with Lucia Bose bathing in the blood of victims and husband Esparatco Santoni becoming a vampire. Jorge Grau directed this Spanish-Italian fiasco also known as COUNTESS DRACULA, LADY DRACULA, BLOODY CEREMONY and THE FEMALE BUTCHER. Ewa (CANDY) Aulin, Ana Farra, Franca Grey. (Simitar; CVC; also in video as **BLOOD CASTLE**)

LEGEND OF BLOOD MOUNTAIN, THE (1965). Obscure fright flick about a small-town newspaperman in Georgia on the trail of a killer monster. Poor regional film-making by director Massey Cramer. Gregory Ellis, Erin Fleming. (From Camp as **DEMON HUNTER**)

LEGEND OF BOGGY CREEK, THE (1973). Producer-director Charles B. Pierce uses pseudodocumentary techniques to tell this allegedly true story of a Bigfoot haunting the Arkansas swamp. Pierce uses local residents who claim to have seen the monster and re-enacts close encounters with such veracity, you almost believe them. Earl E. Smith's script is told in voiceover, as though it were a misty memory. Willie E. Smith, John Hixon. (Lightning; Vestron)

LEGEND OF DOOM HOUSE (1972). Orson Welles, portraying an old man of the sea, is trapped in a house haunted by Greek gods, and proceeds with taxidermist Charles Janssens to encase their ancient souls within human skins. Weird French-Belgian-German adaptation of a novel by Jean Ray directed by Harry (DAUGHTERS OF DARKNESS) Kumel. Susan Hampshire, Jean-Pierre Cassel, Sylvia Vartan, Walter Rilla.

LEGEND OF HELL HOUSE (1973). In adapting his

own novel HELL HOUSE, Richard Matheson eschewed garishness and gory imagery for unseen grotesqueries. Hell House, accursed estate of the perverse Emeric Belasco, has been haunted by psychic phenomena since his death years before. A dying millionaire hires psychist Clive Revill to prove the existence of life after death and Hell House becomes the proving ground. Members of Revill's team are wife Gayle Hunnicutt, mental medium Pamelan Franklin and medium Roddy McDowall, sole survivor of an earlier attempt to exorcise Hell House. This atmospheric film (in the league of THE HAUNTING) is tense under John Hough's direction. Watch for Michael Gough. (Video/Laser: CBS/Fox)

LEGEND OF HILLBILLY JOHN (1972). ONE STEP BEYOND host John Newland directed this version of Manly Wade Wellman's book WHO FEARS THE DEVIL?, a collection of supernatural stories about a guitarist, Silver John, who roves the Appalachians, warding off evil with his guitar's silver strings. Hedge Capers, Denver Pyle, Susan Strasberg, Percy Rodriguez, R. G. Armstrong. (New World) (Laser: Image)

LEGEND OF HORROR (1972). See editions 1-3.

LEGEND OF LIZZIE BORDEN, THE (1975). A spinstress living in Fall River, Mass., allegedly picked up an axe one morning in 1892 and gave her mother 40 whacks. When she saw what she had done, she gave her father 41. But that's the old legend—this TV-movie offers new theories about the infamous case. As the accused murderess, Elizabeth Montgomery is coldly indifferent, bringing a macabre touch to the docudrama approach of this intriguing study in abnormal behavior. Directed by Paul Wendkos. Fritz Weaver, Ed Flanders, Katherine Helmond, Don Porter.

LEGEND OF LOCH NESS (1976). Pseudodocumentary about the Scottish loch where it is believed a prehistoric sea beast dwells, occasionally rearing its snake-like head above water. Explorers use modern equipment to seek the creature, but come away with inconclusive evidence. Produced-directed by Richard Martin. Narrated by Arthur Franz. (VCI)

LEGEND OF LYLAH CLARE, THE (1968). Bizarre, surreal story of film producer Peter Finch who finds a lookalike for a dead actress and trains her to imitate the glamour queen. Is Kim Novak, who begins behaving oddly, possessed by the woman's spirit? Is she a reincarnation? Is she a walking corpse? These questions are left dangling as producer-director Robert Aldrich makes devastating statements about TV advertising and failings of the media. Ernest Borgnine, Coral Browne, George Kennedy.

LEGEND OF PRAGUE, THE. See **GOLEM, THE (1936).**

LEGEND OF SLEEPY HOLLOW (1949). Walt Disney's animated version of Washington Irving's childhood classic about Ichabod Crane's terrifying Halloween-night ride through a forest frequented by The Headless Horseman. Narrated by Bing Crosby. (Video/Laser: Disney)

LEGEND OF SLEEPY HOLLOW (1980). TV-movie adaptation of Washington Irving's Headless Horseman parable. Directed by Henning Schellerup. Jeff Goldblum, Paul Sand, Meg Foster, Laura Campbell, Dick Butkus. (VCI; Starmaker; Lucerne Media)

LEGEND OF SPIDER FOREST, THE (1971). British shocker about a spider-venom nerve gas being developed by a Nazi scientist and a woman described as a "spider goddess." Peter Sykes directed the script by Donald and Derek Ford. Simon Brent, Sheila Allen, Neda Arneric. Also known as VENOM. (Wizard; Media; from Lettuce Entertain You as **SPIDER'S VENOM**)

LEGEND OF THE BAYOU. See **EATEN ALIVE.**

LEGEND OF THE CHAMPIONS (1983). Offbeat British TV-movie appears to be the origin for a series (THE CHAMPIONS?) that combines elements of THE PRISONER with comic-book superhero antics. Secret agent Craig Sterling (Stuart Damon) is undergoing brainwashing by his own boss Tremayne (Anthony Nichols) and The Interrogator (Colin Blakely), who suspect him of being a double agent. In flashback sequences it's revealed that Sterling and two fellow agents (Alexandra Bastedo and William Gaunt), on a mission in Red China to steal locust being used in a mutation program, crash-landed in the Tibetan mountains and were endowed with superhuman powers by a guru (Felix Aylmer). An intriguing idea that is handicapped by unconvincing special effects and Cyril Frankel's routine direction.

LEGEND OF THE DINOSAURS (1983). Japan's answer to JAWS—a monster extravaganza in which a sleeping plesisaurus, after hibernating for millions of years, is awakened by a trembling Mt. Fuji and attacks attendees of a lakeside Dragon Celebration. This gaping toothsome creature with long scrawny neck and teeth gnashes its way to destruction. Before it's over, several prehistoric monsters have joined in the mayhem. Tsunehiko Watase, Nobiko Sawa. (Celebrity)

LEGEND OF THE MOUNTAIN (1979). Chinese-Mandarin ghost tale, based on an 11th-century legend called "A Caveful of Ghosts in the West Mountains," which gives away the plot. Directed by King Hu.

LEGEND OF THE SEVEN GOLDEN VAMPIRES (1973). Co-production between Hammer and the Shaw Brothers of Hong Kong results in satisfying sukiyaki—an east-west blending of martial arts, kung fu and vampire bloodletting. In 1804, Count Dracula inhabits the body of a Chinese priest in order to resurrect seven vampire corpses in Samurai armor who terrorize villagers. Flash-ahead to 1904: Peter Cushing, as Van Helsing, joins his heroic son, Swedish beauty Julie Ege (in low-cut gowns, blouses and high-heeled boots) and a troupe of Chinese warriors to destroy the demons. The action is nonstop, the fights are tremendous jobs of choreography and the monster make-up effective. A rousing entertainment. Directed by Roy Ward Baker. Aka DRACULA AND THE SEVEN GOLDEN VAMPIRES. Robin Stewart, David Chiang, John Forbes Robertson. (Sinister/C; 21st Genesis; from Media and Electric as **SEVEN BROTHERS MEET DRACULA, THE**)

LEGEND OF THE WEREWOLF (1975). British horrorizer in the Hammer mood, with Gothic atmosphere, superior direction by Freddie Francis and a fine cast headed by Peter Cushing as an investigating medical examiner and Ron Moody as a man plagued by lycanthropy, who goes on multi-murder sprees when the moon is full. (He was raised by a wolfpack as a child.) Anthony Hines scripted as John Elder, his plot reminiscent of CURSE OF THE WEREWOLF. (Interglobal; VCL; Moore)

LEGEND OF THE WOLFWOMAN (1977). A degenerate, lowbrow Spanish horror film with helpings of sadism, violence and sex as Ann Borel, reincarnation of a wolf creature from a previous century, rips, tears and slashes her way to oblivion. Directed-written by Rino di Silvestro. Frederick Stafford, Dagmar Lassander. (United; VCI; VIP; from VBG as **SHE WOLF** and from Mogul as **TERROR OF THE SHE WOLF**)

LEMORA—THE LADY DRACULA (1973). Surrealis-

MIA SARA AS PRINCESS LILI IN 'LEGEND'

tic vampire flick with arty overtones—some scenes pretentious as hell, others traditionally imitative of DRACULA. A young girl's odyssey through a nightmarish landscape is filled with grotesque people and maintains curiosity if you don't take it literally. Cheryl Smith carries the picture as the 13-year-old girl. Directed by Richard Blackburn, who wrote EATING RAOUL. Aka THE LEGENDARY CURSE OF LEMORA and LEMORA—A CHILD'S TALE OF THE SUPERNATURAL. Lesley Gilb, William Whitton, Hy Pyke. (Demonique; Fright)

LEMRO, PRIVATE EYE. See **ALIEN PRIVATE EYE.**

LENSMAN (1989). Computer animation enhances this Japanese cartoon about the cosmic adventures of Edward E. (Doc) Smith, in which war breaks out between the Galactic Alliance (good guys) and the Bosconian War Lords (bad guys). Painstakingly drawn, with ample battles to hold one's attention. Directed by Uoshiaki Kawajiri and Kazuyuki Hirokawa. (Laser: Lumivision)

LEO CHRONICLES, THE (1972). See first edition.

LEONARD NIMOY IN SEARCH OF: VOL. 1 (1978-81). Three half-hour episodes of the once-popular TV series IN SEARCH OF, hosted by Leonard Nimoy. These three cover the theme of London: Sherlock Holmes, Jack the Ripper and the Tower of London murders.

LEONARD PART 6 (1987). If Bill Cosby can pick any property he wants, this is a travesty on his own fame. The title refers to secret agent Leonard Parker, brought out of retirement to track down a crazy woman (Gloria Foster) trying to take over the world with animals, birds and insects trained to kill. It's told in narration by Parker's aide-de-camp Tom Courtenay, who looks embarrassed to be present. Spectacle destruction scenes were created by Richard Edlund but it's otherwise a bad idea which director Paul Weiland puts the final destructive touches to. The funniest lines: "Amardillos awaiting activation, caterpillars on the march in Sausalito, possums in Piedmond awaiting orders." Composer Leonard Bernstein attempts to parody movie forms, but his score is lost under the chaos. Moses Gunn, Pat Colbert, Joe Don Baker. (Video/Laser: RCA/Columbia)

LEONOR (1975). Offbeat Spanish-French-Italian period horror film directed by Juan Bunuel, Luis' son, and based on a vampire story by Luidwig Tieck. Liv Ullmann rises from her crypt to suck the life from children. Slow going, with strange Bunuel-type imagery to keep you wondering. Ornella Mutti, Antonio Ferrandis. (CBS/Fox)

LEOPARD MAN, THE (1943). Cornell Woolrich's novel BLACK ALIBI was adapted by screenwriter Ardel Wray for producer Val Lewton. It emerges a superb low-budget, high-thrills masterpiece of "quiet horror." Director Jacques Tourneur provides memorable sequences greater than the sum total—including one in which a gypsy girl's blood flows under a door after she is locked outside and attacked by an unseen force. That force is believed to be an escaped leopard, but all is not what it seems. Minimal focus is placed on hero and heroine (Dennis O'Keefe, Jean Brooks) as they track down the source of evil. (Fox Hill; Media) (Laser: Image)

LEPRECHAUN (1992). This low-budget quickie turns the fun-loving elf of Irish lore into a serial murderer who makes nasty quips in the style of Freddy Krueger. Short on cinematic stature, just like the titular entity, who is played on a one-dimensional mean and ugly note by Warwick Davis. The minuscule plot revolves around a family that settles in a rural shack where the leprechaun's sack of gold is hidden. Written and directed by Mark Jones, whom the Irish should sue. Jennifer Aniston, Ken Olandt, Mark Holton, Robert Gorman. (Vidmark)

LEPRECHAUN 2 (1994). In the same vile vein of its predecessor, this slap against Irish folk legend stars Warwick Davis (again) as a shortish but effectual imp seeking a new bride. Directed by Rodman Flender. Charlie Heath, Shevonne Durkin, Sandy Baron, Clint Howard. (Vidmark)

LESBIAN TWINS. See **VIRGIN WITCH, THE.**

LESBIAN VAMPIRES. See **HERITAGE OF DRACULA, THE.**

LETHAL GAMES. See **ONCE UPON A SPY.**

LET'S KILL UNCLE (1966). Unusual William Castle film in which a young boy and girl are trapped in a mansion on an island with Nigel Green, who tries to knock off the kiddies. Pat Cardi, Mary Badham, Linda Lawson.

LET SLEEPING CORPSES LIE. Video version of **DON'T OPEN THE WINDOW.**

LET'S LIVE AGAIN (1948). See editions 1-3.

LET'S SCARE JESSICA TO DEATH (1971). Director John Hancock is to be congratulated for a multi-layered horror film with frightening visuals. There isn't much logic to the story yet the overall effect is unsettling. Zohra Lampert, newly released from an asylum, never knows if she's hallucinating or something weird is happening on her Connecticut farm. Are those spaced-out inhabitants in town vampires or zombies? The film has a dream-like quality in depicting her nightmares. Gretchen Corbett, Barton Heyman, Kevin O'Connor. (Paramount)

LEVIATHAN (1989). Whatever possessed director George P. Cosmates to make a demeaning imitation of ALIEN is more mysterious than anything in the David Peoples-Jeb Stuart script. Emerging in the wake of DEEPSTAR SIX, this is inferior underwater horror-action set on a mining station two miles deep. The crew discovers a sunken Russian ship and the genetic-experiment infection that killed the Soviets begins to kill the Americans, one of them turning into an amphibian-fishman, a Stan Winston accomplishment. Peter Weller and Richard Crenna (as the boss and doctor of the crew) fare best with the underwritten roles, while Amanda Pays, Daniel Stern, Ernie Hudson, Michael Carmine, Hector Elizondo and Lisa Eilbacher are mere monster fodder. It never gels, even with composer Jerry Goldsmith and designer Rob Cobb contributing. (Video/Laser: MGM/UA)

LICENSED TO KILL. See **SECOND BEST SECRET AGENT IN THE WHOLE WIDE WORLD, THE.**

LICENSED TO LOVE AND KILL. See **MAN FROM S.E.X., THE**

LICENSE TO KILL (1964). See editions 1-3.

LICENSE TO KILL (1989). Superior entry in the James Bond series (marking Timothy Dalton's second portrayal and the fifth time that John Glen directed) has 007 going after the killers of agent Felix Leiter (David Hedison). The stunts are spectacular, the fantastic gadgets kept to a minimum and Dalton brings a no-nonsense versimilitude to Bond, who races through Florida and South America in search of a drug operation commanded by Robert David and Frank McRae. Carey Lowell, Talisa Soto, Anthony Zerbe, Wayne Newton. (Video/Laser: CBS/Fox)

LIFE AND ADVENTURES OF SANTA CLAUS (1986). Animated TV-movie based on a L. Frank Baum novel in which Santa is accepted into The Immortals (a race that rules over the elements) so he can battle the bad Awgwas and bring pleasure to kids. Voices: Earl Hammond, Earle Hyman, Larry Kennedy. Produced-directed by Arthur Rankin Jr./Saul Bass. (Warner Bros.)

LIFEFORCE (1985). Colin Wilson's intellectual novel SPACE VAMPIRES becomes an uneven but still recommended space-horror film by director Tobe Hooper and adaptors Dan O'Bannon and Don Jakoby. Hooper helms macabre scenes of corpses popping to life—these horrific visuals will have you shivering. A spaceship discovers an alien vessel which harbors bat-like creatures and three incubated humanoids. One of them, a big-busted female, sucks energy from Earthlings, turning them to cadavers. The gripping and eerie fascination builds as inspector Peter Firth and astronaut Steve Railsback attempt to solve the soul-transference, lifeforce-energy mystery. It is when London is ablaze, and half the population turns into zombies, that the film falls apart, its effects too metaphysical and its ending too ridiculous to live up to earlier thrills. Frank Finlay, Mathilda May, Patrick Stewart. Music by Henry Mancini; effects by John Dykstra and John Gant. (Vestron) (Laser: Image; Vestron)

LIFE IS A CIRCUS (1958). British comedy (written-directed by Val Guest) depicts how members of the Big Top utilize Aladdin's Lamp to save their tent. Bud Flanagan, Shirley Eaton, Lionel Jeffries (as the genie), Jimmy Nervo. Known as part of the "Crazy Gang" series.

LIFE, LIBERTY AND PURSUIT ON THE PLANET OF THE APES (1974). Earth astronauts Ron Harper and James Naughton are subjected to perilous brainwashing techniques by chimps and orangutans in this TV-movie of episodes re-edited from the short-lived PLANET OF THE APES. Roddy McDowall, Beverly Garland, Mark Lenard.

LIFEPOD (1980). A spaceship is plagued by a computer that goes crazy. Joe Penny, Jordan Michaels, Kristine DeBell. (VCI; United)

LIFEPOD (1993). This "stranded in space" adventure, with a script by M. Jay Roach and Pen Densham that was inspired by Alfred Hitchcock's film LIFEBOAT, is an exciting, fast-moving TV-movie directed by Ron Silver, who is also in the cast. On Christmas Eve, 2169, a civilian space cruiser (the Lutrania) is returning from Venus ("across an ocean of 10 billion light years") when it's sabotaged. A handful of survivors escapes aboard an emergency "lifepod." But from the start, things go wrong and it's obvious there is a traitor in the ranks, as well as social issues to be discussed. This is a pure genre film done with style by Silver, who uses claustrophobic tricks to good advantage. The outer-space effects and hardware are excellent, twists come frequently, and the characters (including a dwarf called Q-3) are interesting enough to warrant caring about the "whodunit" aspect. Robert Loggia, Jessica Tuck, Stan Shaw, Adam Storke, Ted Gale, CCH Pounder. (Cabin Fever)

LIFE PROPHECIES AND MYSTIQUE OF NOSTRADAMUS, THE (198?). Another video cash-in on the Nostradamus craze, with a likeness of Orson Welles on the box. (American)

LIFESPAN (1975). A short life span, that's what this U.S.-British-Belgian production experienced. The aged story: a doctor experiments with a serum to lengthen life, his subjects members of an old folks' home. Alexander Whitelaw wrote-produced-directed in Amsterdam. Hiram Keller, Tina Aumont, Klaus Kinski. (Vestron)

LIFETIME, A (1974). See first edition.

LIFT, THE (1983). Fascinating Dutch import, a cross between an exploitation shocker and an art film. A new elevator system in a high-rise reprograms its organic microchips to kill passengers in grisly ways—at least that's what writer-director Dick Maas intimates as his tale tersely unfolds. Maas conveys a sense of classy horror and then lapses into graphic slayings—including one hair-lift-ing sequence in which a security guard is decapitated. The mystery involves a conspiracy between the elevator designer and the electronics programmer as a lift repairman (Huub Stapel) searches for the truth. Gripping stuff, "up-lifting." Willeke Van Ammelrooy, Josine Van Dalsum. (Media) (Laser: Image)

LIGHT BLAST (1985). Mad physicist with a ray machine (it resembles a prop from a Buck Rogers serial) burns the flesh right off your bones when he terrorizes San Francisco by demanding $10 million in ransom money. It's up to homicide cop Erik Estrada and his partner (comedian Michael Pritchard) to stop the madman. This kicks in with a gritty, pseudodocumentary feeling with its scenic locations, fast editing and dynamic camera angles. But writer-director Enzo G. Castellari and co-writer Titus Carpenter have too feeble a story and too vapid a set of characters to sustain what is finally an empty-headed action film with interminable chases with cars, trucks, motorboats and anything that moves. Thomas Moore, Peggy Rowe, Bob Taylor, Nancy Fish. (Lightning)

LIGHTNING BOLT (1967). Anthony Eisley is a lackluster superspy trying to prevent an insidious madman from exploding U.S. spacecraft with a laser beam death ray vortex blaster atom-smashing burp buster. Italian-Spanish thriller directed by Antonio Margheriti (Anthony Dawson). Also known as OPERATION GOLDMAN. Wandisa Leigh, Diana Lorys, Fulco Lulli. (Sinister/C)

LIGHTNING FIELD, THE. See **LIGHTNING INCIDENT, THE.**

LIGHTNING INCIDENT, THE (1991). Intriguing story about a mother-to-be (Nancy McKeon) who undergoes strange incidents before the baby's birth, which suggest her aging mother (Polly Bergen) is haunted by a Central American devil-worship cult that will place the baby in jeopardy. Daughter and mother are led into a labyrinth of horror involving a killer snake, a tattoo of a lizard, and a field of pillars that attracts lightning bolts. Directed by Michael Switzer. Elpidia Carrillo, Miriam Colon, Tim Ryan. (Paramount)

LIGHT YEARS (1987). Superb French animated feature from Rene Laloux (FANTASTIC PLANET) showcasing his impression of the human experience through science-fiction. In this parable of good vs. evil, Laloux deals with the kingdom of Gandahar, a playground where man and organic life live in peace. But something begins turning men into stone, so Queen Ambisextra sends her handsome son, Sylvain, to investigate. Accompanied by a beautiful, bare-breasted woman, Airelle, Sylvain is led into a world of chaos, meeting killer robots called Men of Metal, a race of mutants called the Deformed (who speak only in past or future tense), a godlike brain, the Metamorphis, and a mystery involving the time-space continuum. A thinking man's action cartoon about the paradoxes of time, the misuse of power and science, the impersonalization of machines, the poisoning of our atmosphere, and the danger of peace without vigilance. "Adapted" into English by Isaac Asimov. (Vidmark) (Laser: Image)

AIRELLE

LIGHT YEARS AWAY (1981). Allegorical French-Swiss film by writer- director Alain Tanner about a strange old man (Trevor Howard) who claims birds have taught him how to fly, and who imparts philosophies to drifter Mick Ford. Odd offering, more thoughtful than action-oriented, enhanced by Scottish backgrounds.

LIKE FATHER LIKE SON (1987). A stuffy heart specialist (Dudley Moore) and his wild teenage son (Kirk Cameron) undergo personality transferrance with an Indian brew mistakenly put in a Tabasco bottle. The youth attends school with all the knowledge of the doctor and the father attends to his hospital rounds with zero knowledge. The situations and gags fall pretty flat, with director Ron Daniel unable to bring much oomph or merriment to the lackluster premise. Sean Astin as the boy Trigger, inadvertently responsible for the change of souls, Catherine Hicks as a sympathetic nurse, and Patrick O'Neal as the snobbish head of the hospital all do their best, but it fizzles. Margaret Colin as a sexpot adds a sizzle, then dissipates and dies. (RCA/Columbia) (Laser: Image)

LI'L ABNER (1940). Infrequently shown version of Al Capp's comic strip fails to capture the flair of the printed page, but is still an interesting period piece. The main problems were the low budget and the uninspired direction of Albert S. Rogell. Buster Keaton appears as Lonesome Polecat. Chester Conklin, Doodles Weaver, Edgar Kennedy. (Video Yesteryear; Nostalgia; Discount)

L'IL ABNER (1959). The Norman Panama-Melvin Frank Broadway play came to the screen with all the crazy ingredients and flavor of Al Capp's cartoon strip. Dogpatch has been selected as an atomic bomb site, which brings out the worst in Evil-Eye Fleagle—he puts the "whammy" on folks. Yokumberry is a drink that gives Abner Yokum his abnormal strength, but in the process he loses his sex drive—upsetting to Daisy Mae's own dogpatch. Peter Palmer is wholesomely naive as Abner and Leslie Parrish is absolutely stunning in the original HotPants. Frank directed, Panama produced. Stubby Kaye is Marryin' Sam, Al Nesor is Fleagle. Julie Newmar, Stella Stevens, Bern Hoffman, Billie Hayes, Robert Strauss. (Paramount)

LILA. See **MANTIS IN LACE.**

LIMIT UP (1989). Nancy Allen shines in this amusing fantasy-comedy as a soybeans commodity trader at Chicago's Midwest Grain Exchange, working her way up from runner to the cover of Time as saleswoman. However, she has to make a deal with Danitra Vance, a rep for Lost Souls Inc. ("You sin, we win") who will claim Allen's soul some day. (Her license plate: CU-N-HELL). However, the thrust of the script by director Richard Martini and Lu Anders is on Allen's positive qualities and her warm relationship with Brad Hall. There's a neat surprise ending with Ray Charles as a street musician. Dean Stockwell is good as Allen's hard-driven boss. (Video/Laser: MCEG/Virgin)

LINK (1986). Offbeat suspense thriller with horror overtones—an oddity from Australian producer-director Richard Franklin and writer Everett DeRoche. Terence Stamp, specialist in the behavior of chimpanzees, brings student Elizabeth Shue to his isolated mansion where she meets a superintelligent chimp named Link, who dresses like the family retainer, smokes cigars and watches her take a bath with a lecherous look. Franklin mounts the suspense during the siege portion, but a weak character for the woman, and a small role for Stamp create an unsatisfying, unfocused film. (HBO; Republic)

LINK, THE (1982). See **BLOOD LINK.**

LINNEA QUIGLEY'S HORROR WORKOUT (1991). The queen of the B horror flicks, star of such sophisticated fare as CREEPOZOIDS, headlines this parody of exercise videos in which she leads assorted monsters and fright characters through aerobics. Directed by Kenneth J. Hall. (Cinema Home)

LION MAN, THE (1937). See editions 1-3.

LION MAN (1980). Get beyond the turgid beginnings of this swashbuckling Greek production and you'll discover a campy action flick with ridiculously choreographed battles as the Son of Solomon does combat with evil. Having been raised by lions, this son of a witch has clawlike hands that penetrate into enemies' bodies like knives and kills them. Later on, when his hands are destroyed by acid, he dons appendages to wipe out a hundred soldiers (no kidding) in one encounter. Get into a mood for a great awful movie and you'll groove. Directed by Natuch Baitan. Steve Arkin, Barbara Lake. (Best Film & Video)

LION MAN. See **CURSE OF THE VOODOO.**

LION, THE WITCH AND THE WARDROBE (1979). Animated fantasy based on C.S. Lewis' "Chronicles on Narnia," depicting how some kids use their closet as a means of traveling to another kingdom. (Republic; Vestron; Public Media)

LIQUID DREAMS (1991). Stylish first effort by director Mark Manos is set in a futuristic "Big Brother Is Watching" society where homes are bombarded with Neuro-Vid, designed to keep them desensitized to the rest of the world's problems. Through this oddball world of fashion and music moves Candice Daly, in search of the murderer of her sister. Richard Steinmetz, Barry Dennen, Juan Fernandez. (Academy) (Laser: Image)

LIQUID SKY (1983). New wave/punk rock/heavy metal/western decadence flick depicting freaked out adrogyne Margaret whose penthouse rooftop is visited by a flying saucer. Once she's been infected by an alien organism, her orgasms result in the deaths of her partners. What a way to go in the land of debauchery. Sardonic and funk punk bunk, with video graphics and reverse polarity taking the place of sexual encounters of the closest kind. More MTV than movie as Anne Carlisle (as the borderline man-woman) writhes through her torrid affairs with Manhattan low life. Smartly produced by Russian emigre Slava Tsukerman, who co-wrote with wife Nina Kerova. (Video/Laser: Media)

LISA (1989). Cat-and-mouse psychokiller thriller that tries to emulate the Hitchcockian touch with little success. D. W. Moffett portrays "The Candlelight Killer," who uses answering machines in the homes of victims as part of his terror ploy. troublesome teen-ager Staci Keanan unwittingly makes sexy calls to the killer, trying to set up a date for mom. Unaware that mom Cheryl Ladd is in danger, Lisa carries out her duplicity as only a teen-ager can. The script by director Gary Sherman and Karen Clark tries to deal with the problems of teenagers growing up in a fatherless household as it unfolds its tale of suspense and murder, and the mixture is only mildly effective. Tanya Fenmore, Jeffrey Tambor, Edan Gross. (CBS/Fox)

LISA AND THE DEVIL. See **DEVIL IN THE HOUSE OF EXORCISM. LISA, LISA.** See **AXE.**

LITTLE ARK, THE (1971). See editions 1-3.

LITTLE GIRL WHO LIVES DOWN THE LANE, THE (1976). Psychological chiller with 13-year-old Jodie Foster knocking off folks to keep a dark secret: Mother is buried in the cellar. Tautly directed by Nicolas Gessner. Alexis Smith, Martin Sheen, Scott Jacoby. (Vestron) (Laser: Image)

LITTLE MATCH GIRL, THE (1987). Comedienne-actress Maryedith Burrell wrote this TV-movie based on Hans Christian Andersen's tale about a beam of light that falls to Earth and turns into an 8-year-old girl (Kesiah Knight Pulliam) who sells matches to bring magical happiness to others. Burrell, who also has a featured role, sets it during the Depression around the forced eviction of poor people at Christmas and a rich man's conflict with his two sons. Pulliam pulls off her role with just the right touch. Directed with a nice touch by Michael Lindsay-Hogg. Jim Metzler, John Rhys-Davies, William Youmans, Rue McClanahan. (Academy)

LITTLE MERMAID, THE (1989). Hans Christian Andersen's classic fairy tale is excellently rendered in this animated Disney musical feature directed by John Musker and Ron Clements. A mermaid named Ariel (voice by Jodi Benson) lives with her father, Triton, in an underwater kingdom. After she saves a handsome prince from drowning, she trades her singing voice to an evil octopus to live on land and marry him. Her companion is a crab named Sebastian, and his plight in the kitchen of a French chef is one of the most charming sequences in the film. Great songs and music by Howard Ashman and Alan Menken. (Video/Laser: Disney)

ARIEL THE MERMAID

LITTLE MONSTERS (1989). Fred Savage stars in this vicious fantasy-comedy about a kid's encounter with Maurice, a wart-hog creature (Howie Mandel). They venture into a realm of monsters—inspired by BEETLEJUICE, perhaps? This film has a mean edge and is offensive without being funny. Directed as if it were a Halloween special for kids by Alan Greenberg. Ben Savage (Fred's brother), Daniel Stern, Margaret Whitton. (MCA)

LITTLE NEMO: ADVENTURES IN SLUMBERLAND (1992). Winsor McCay's comic strip character, conceived for the screen by Ray Bradbury, is a superior example of Japanese animation, with the youthful Nemo being carried off to Slumberland to be the playmate of Princess Camille, daughter of King Morpheus. The Chris Columbus-Richard Outten script was directed by Misami Hata and William T. Hurtz. Voices by Gabriel Damon, Mickey

Rooney, Rene Auberjonois. (Hemdale)

LITTLE PRINCE, THE (1973). Charming philosophical music-fable based on the book by Antoine de Saint-Exupery, produced-directed by Stanley Donen, with script/lyrics by Alan Jay Lerner and music by Frederic Loewe. Singing pilot Richard Kiley crashes in the Sahara and meets an emissary from Asteroid B-612, a child in search of life's meaning. In surreal flashbacks the youth tells of odd characters he's met in the galaxies. A child with a British accent, Steven Warner seems a strange choice for the prince, but he looks endearing. In one musical sequence, Gene Wilder plays a fox and Bob Fosse is a choreographed snake. (Video/Laser: Paramount)

LITTLE RED RIDING HOOD (1959). Editions 1-3.

LITTLE SHOP OF HORRORS, THE (1960). Producer-director Roger Corman's macabre comedy parodies horror-monster flicks with a vengeance. Jonathan Haze is in a daze as Seymour Krelboing, a flower shop clerk who raises a giant plant that repeatedly burps "Feed me, I'm hungry!" Seymour does—human food. Belch! Mel Welles is shopowner Gravis Mushnik, Jackie Joseph is the love interest and Dick Miller is a customer. Jack Nicholson as a crazy cameo in a dentist's chair. Scripted by Charles Griffith, who wrote the story around a set Corman had seen in a studio. The film developed a cult following and became a stage musical and then was remade as a film in 1986. (Hollywood Home Theatre; Vestron; Filmfax) (Laser: Japanese)

LITTLE SHOP OF HORRORS (1986). Corman's B-film and intimate musical were turned into an overinflated horror musical, following the music and storyline of the play but much darker and crueler in depicting how a nerd falls in love with a bimbo and feeds human body parts to a man-eating, talking plant. What was once a charming comedy becomes an uncomfortable experience, for the screen overemphasizes the slum area of Mushkin's Floral Shop and the monstrousness of the plant, Audrey II, as it sways humans with its Svengali-like hold. Especially unfunny are Steve Martin as a sadistic dentist and Bill Murray as his masochistic patient, carrying to extremes what in the original film was a funny moment. Director Frank Oz was escaping his G-rated Muppet image—even Warner Bros. had to lighten up the unpleasantries before the film was released. (Video/Laser: Warner Bros.)

LIVE AGAIN, DIE AGAIN (1974). TV-movie explores Cryonics, a form of suspended animation in which a diseased person is frozen with the hope the body can be thawed out later when the disease is curable. Director Richard A. Colla leans on psychological aspects as a family faces the reality of a Cryonics-treated mother (Donna Mills) returning after 34 years. The startled husband is Walter Pidgeon and the children, now grown up, are Vera Miles and Mike Farrell. Written by Joseph Stefano.

LIVE AND LET DIE (1973). Roger Moore's first time out as British spy 007, James Bond . . . He attempts the droll indifference and sophisticated snobbery of the licensed-to-kill superagent, but he's a connoisseur strictly for philistines. The series had begun to deteriorate to the point screenwriter Tom Mankiewicz was resorting to a stereotyped Southern sheriff, J. W. Pepper. Director Guy Hamilton maintains the visual standards he established in GOLDFINGER with a plot about Negro drug king Kananga (Yaphet Kotto) and how Bond tracks him to his lair in the Louisiana swamps. This features a wild motorboat chase, an alligator pit and other jeopardy devices. Jane Seymour, David Hedison. (CBS/Fox) (Laser: MGM)

LIVER EATERS, THE. See **SPIDER BABY.**

LIVE TO LOVE. See **DEVIL'S HAND, THE.**

LIVING COFFIN, THE (1965). Mexican horror film blends supernatural and Western-action elements when a buckskin hero and his comedic sidekick meet a ranching family haunted by "The Curse of the Crying Ghost." A mysterious veiled witch, a bog of quicksand and a coffin with a built-in alarm are featured in this goofy melding of genres. It's fun, in an incompetent way. American producer K. Gordon Murray brought it across the border with new footage directed by Manuel San-Fernando. The original spooks-and-sombrero stuff was shot by Ferdinand Mendez. Gaston Santos is the cowboy hero. Mary Duval, Peter D'Aguillon. (Sinister/C; S/Weird; Saturn; Filmfax)

LIVING DAYLIGHTS, THE (1987). Timothy Dalton's first outing as James Bond proved that he could carry off the role with a more serious demeanor than his predecessor, Roger Moore, and a greater sense of depth. The fantasy-weapon elements are minimal as everyone tries harder for suspenseful realism, without sacrificing the visual qualities of previous 007 adventures. The Richard Maibaum-Michael G. Wilson script has Bond involved with Soviet defectors, KGB agents, gunrunners and a beautiful Czech concert cellist (Maryam d'Abo). The climactic fight aboard a cargo plane is a stunning action piece that puts this with the best of the Bonds. Directed with an adventurous flair by John Glen. Jeroen Krabbe, Joe Don Baker, John Rhys-Davies, Art Malik, Caroline Bliss (Miss Moneypenny). (CBS/Fox) (Laser: MGM/UA; CBS/Fox)

TIMOTHY DALTON

LIVING DEAD, THE (1934). Antiquated British mystery mellow-drama in which a Scotland Yard dick invents a serum that induces death—part of a scheme to collect insurance money. Only he has the antitoxin when he kidnaps his partner's daughter and puts her into a coma. You too will slide into catatonia. Directed by Thomas Bentley. Gerald Du Maurier, George Curzon. (Thunderbird; Filmfax; Sinister/C; Discount)

LIVING DEAD AT MANCHESTER MORGUE. See **DON'T OPEN THE WINDOW.**

LIVING DOLL (1990). Medical student Mark Jax, working parttime in a morgue, collects the corpse of flower girl Katie Orgill and takes her home to study her beauty, his romantic fantasies blinding him to her rotting condition. Even though his landlady is Eartha Kitt, this low-budget, New York-based horror flicker is nothing to sing about as Jax fantasizes that the corpse is talking to him. For necrophiliacs only. Directed by George Dugdale and Peter Litten. (MGM)

LIVING GHOST, THE (1942). Moldy Monogram monstrosity, raggedy around the edges but of mild interest for its old-fashioned "haunted house" techniques and comedy. James Dunn portrays Nick Brother, the Sympathetic Ear, a "good listener" who turns private eye to investigate the disappearance of a rich man. Seems a machine called a "cyclo-propane" had something to do with it. William Beaudine was gravely (ha ha ha!) handicapped by a weak budget. It's a parody of the Charlie Chan school of detection, but at least it's mercifully short. Joan Woodbury, Minerva Urecal.

LIVING HEAD, THE (1959). Mexican horror importer K. Gordon Murray jazzed up this Abel Salazar flicker for U.S. consumption. This abomination is head but not shoulders above others of its (stereo)type. When a tomb is opened by an archeological expedition, its members find the head of an Aztec warrior, who's been waiting centuries to fulfill a curse. Directed by Chanto Urueta. German Robles, Ana Luisa Peluffo. (Sinister/C; Video Yesteryear; S/Weird; Filmfax)

LIVING IDOL, THE (1957). Steve Forrest and James Robertson Justice enliven this U.S.-Mexican film (made in Mexico) in which an idol of stone is responsible for several deaths and a young woman turns out to be reincarnated. Only for those with idol time on their hands. Directed by Albert Lewin and Rene Cardona.

LIVING LEGEND, THE. See **BATTLESTAR GALACTICA.**

LIZARD IN A WOMAN'S SKIN, A. See **SCHIZOID (1971).**

LIZZIE (1957). Hugo Haas-directed version of Shirley Jackson's novel THE BIRD'S NEST. Eleanor Parker has three personalities: Elizabeth, a mousy worker in a museum; Beth, who seems well adjusted; and Lizzie, a wild party girl. Which will dominate her soul? Psychiatrist Richard Boone probes her psyche to find out. Joan Blondell co-stars with director Haas who plays a friend of Elizabeth's—or is it Beth's—or Lizzie's—or—

LOBSTER MAN FROM MARS (1989). Sci-fi buffs of '50s movies will find this parody a treat—a movie-within-a-movie that starts when sleazy producer Tony Curtis (as J. P. Sheildrake) sits down in his screening room to see LOBSTER MAN FROM MARS, a schlocker in which a flying saucer crashlands and regurgitates an alien invader accompanied by flying bat-creatures. In pursuit of the monsters go private eye Tommy Sledge (the stand-up comic), the young couple (Deborah Foreman and Anthony Hickox), and scientist-professor Patrick Macnee. Directed with the right touch by Stanley Sheff. Billy Barty, Dean Jacobsen, Fred Holiday, Dr. Demento. (Video/Laser: IVE)

LOCH NESS HORROR, THE (1982). One sorry monster movie, filmed at Lake Tahoe, Calif., by writer-director Larry Buchanan. A papier mache neck and head, with rows of serrated teeth, is more a lovable toy than a ferocious sea beast. Buchanan throws in subplots (Nazi plane that crashed in 1940 has cargo of dangerous bombs aboard; nut tries to kidnap beautiful girl; dynamite expert is blackmailed by military to perform a dangerous dive) but the harder he tries the sillier it gets. And some of the Scottish accents are not to be believed! What an embarrassment to the real-life Nessie. Sandy Kenton, Miki McKenzie, Barry Buchanan. (Monterey)

LOCKET, THE (1946). The oddball psychodrama touches of this film herald trends to come in psychological-horror dramas of later decades. Laraine Day is a "Black Widow" with a power to drive men to madness and/or suicide. She appears the essence of purity but beneath the facade is a female bitch-monster, often blind to, or confused by, her own neuroses. Despite dated techniques, this has a sinister drive swathed in melodramatic and intriguing psychiatric nonsense. Directed moodily by John Brahm, famous for THE LODGER. Robert Mitchum, Brian Aherne, Gene Raymond.

LOCK UP YOUR DAUGHTERS (1956). A collection of scenes from cheap Bela Lugosi movies, thrown together by producer Sam Katzman, who hired Lugosi to narrate shortly before the actor died. Footage includes scenes from THE APE MAN and THE VOODOO MAN.

LOCK YOUR DOORS. See **APE MAN, THE.**

LODGER, THE (A STORY OF THE LONDON FOG) (1926). Alfred Hitchcock's first major thriller and the film that many critics feel is seminal to the horror and suspense sound films on which he would sharpen his teeth in later years. This was the first of several versions of the 1913 Marie Belloc-Lowndes novel about Jack the Ripper, thinly disguised here as "The Avenger," a knife-wielding madman who specializes in murdering women with blond tresses. Tilted angles and an influence of German expressionism earmark this effective chiller. Ivor Novello, Marie Ault, Malcolm Keen. (Video Yesteryear; Video Image; Nostalgia; Grapevine)

LODGER, THE (1932). First sound adaptation of the Belloc-Lowndes novel with Ivor Novello repeating the role of the Jack the Ripper-style killer he first etched in Alfred Hitchcock's 1926 silent version. Directed by Maurice Elvey. Elizabeth Allan, A.W. Baskomb, Jack Hawkins. Released in U.S. as THE PHANTOM FIEND.

LODGER, THE (1944). Atmosphere and performance are everything in this fogbound, eerie version of Marie Belloc-Lowndes' novel depicting fear-stricken London during the horrendous Jack the Ripper rippings in Soho. Laird Cregar, a superb heavy of the early 1940s, provides an undercurrent of menace and smouldering psychosis in a fine portrayal of a heinous villain. Barre Lyndon's adaptation is brooding with Victorian ambience. Merle Oberon is the music hall dancer who becomes Cregar's target; George Sanders is her compassionate lover. Congratulations to director John Brahm, cinematographer Lucien Ballard and composer Hugo Friedhofer for haunting contributions to this horror classic. This remake of a 1926 Alfred Hitchcock thriller was in turn remade by Fox in 1953 as THE MAN IN THE ATTIC. Sir Cedric Hardwicke, Sara Allgood, Doris Lloyd.

LOGAN'S RUN (1976). MGM's version of the William Nolan-George Clayton Johnson novel (adapted by David Zelag Goodman) was thoroughly botched into a bastardization of glaring inconsistencies, peopled by uninteresting characters and often ineptly directed by Michael Anderson. The setting is a subterranean future society where everyone is brainwashed into going to their deaths at age 30; if they try to "run" they are cut down by "Sandmen." Sandman Michael York rebels and escapes to the outside world. Peter Ustinov lives in the ruins of the nation's capital, Roscoe Lee Brown plays a robot named Box, Jenny Agutter is the love interest, and Farrah Fawcett-Majors delivers an appalling performance. (Video/Laser: MGM/UA)

LOKIS. See **BEAR, THE.**

LONDON AFTER MIDNIGHT (1927). Tod Browning wrote-produced-directed this MGM silent thriller with vampire overtones. Remade by the studio in 1935 as MARK OF THE VAMPIRE. Lon Chaney, Percy Williams, Conrad Nagel, Henry B. Walthall.

LONE WOLF (1988). Two computer whizzes track a series of murders committed by a werewolf in this regional horror thriller produced in Denver. Directed by John Callas. Dyann Brown, Kevin Hart. (Prism)

LONG DARK NIGHT, THE. Condensed TV version of **PACK, THE.** (A dogged film!)

LONG HAIR OF DEATH (1964). Italian shocker, in the vein of BLACK SUNDAY, in which Barbara Steele, the daughter of a witch burned at the stake, dies and returns from the dead after her tomb is opened by a burst of lightning. Directed by Anthony Dawson (Antonio Margheriti). Based on J. Sheridan Le Fanu's CARMILLA. Giorgio Ardisson. (Sinister/C; S/Weird; Filmfax)

LONG NIGHT OF TERROR, THE. See **CASTLE OF BLOOD.**

LONG, SWIFT SWORD OF SIEGFRIED (1971). U.S.-West German fantasy adventure with plenty of sex depicting the heroic knight in pursuit of the fire-eating dragon. Long all right, but not too swift. Originally directed by Adrian Hoven in German, with English scenes written-directed by sex exploitationer David F. Friedman. One of Sybil Danning's first films . . . now she's swift—if you get our drift. Raymond Harmstorf, Heidi Bohlen. (From Private Screenings as **MAIDENQUEST**)

LONG WEEKEND (1986). Australian nature-is-awry thriller in which John Hargreaves and Briony Behets go to the country and find themselves surrounded by animals on the prod. Produced-directed by Colin Eggleston. (Trans World)

LOOKER (1981). Michael Crichton wrote-directed this strange mixture of sci-fi, suspense and horror, never quite finding the right blend. It's gimmicky and tricky, about a TV-commercial production company that has an artificial way of creating laser projections of beautiful models. But first the company must eliminate the real women on whom these clone lovelies are patterned with a strange time-continuum blaster. Sinks into utter confusion at times but the set designs are outstanding and the cast (Albert Finney as the hero, James Coburn as the heavy, Susan Dey and Leigh Taylor-Young as love interests) is accomplished. (Video/Laser: Warner Bros.)

LOOK WHAT'S HAPPENED TO ROSEMARY'S BABY (1976). Look what's happened to a hit movie when they made a breeched TV sequel. They gave birth to a

LAST-MINUTE UPDATES

ALIENATOR (1989). This Fred Olen Ray sci-fi special is derivative of THE TERMINATOR, but with a female warrior (Teagan Clive) armed with a laser gun who comes to Earth to capture an escapee (Ross Hagen) from a top-security prison in space operated by warden Jan-Michael Vincent. On Earth, game warden John Phillip Law joins with some young travelers and Korean War vet Leo G. Gordon to protect the rebel and fight off the zap gun-packing lady. She's quite an unusual image in sexy costume, packing that death-ray rod, but she's the only pleasant surprise in this otherwise predictable, cliched actioner with little brain power to propel the script by Paul Garson. Robert Clarke, Robert Quarry, Richard Wiley, Dyana Ortelli, Jesse Dabson, Dawn Wildsmith. (Prism) (Laser: Image)

ANGELS IN THE OUTFIELD (1994). This starts out as a soapy, sappy film about a foster child trying to get back together with his wayward, hapless father, but then segues into a delightful comedy that builds speed by the second until it finally wins you over completely and makes you feel great. Based only loosely on the 1951 film that inspired it, this zooms off into its own fly-ball territory once young Joseph Gordon-Levitt gets into the good graces of gruff baseball coach Danny Glover, whose team, the California Angels, is in last place—until a band of angels led by Al (Christopher Lloyd) makes miraculous things happen on the diamond and the baseball Angels soar toward winning the Pennant. The special effects of the angels are warm and wonderful and director William Dear, a master at fantasy comedy, makes all the sentiment and cornball stuff work together into a homerun. Tony Danza strikes just the right note as a pitcher who doesn't know he's dying, Ben Johnson is an old pro as the forgiving team owner, and Brenda Fricker is memorable as the foster mother. Written by Dorothy Kingsley, George Wells and Holly Goldberg Sloan. (Video/Laser: Disney)

BEHIND THE MASK (1946). Although based on The Shadow character from the pulp magazines, this features none of the supernatural or metaphysical attributes of Lamont Cranston to cloud men's minds so they cannot see him. All Kane Richmond does as the playboy about town is cast a sinister shadow while wearing a cape, mask and fedora and threaten his adversaries. Most of George Callahan's script wastes its time making fun of Margo Lane (Barbara Reed) as she's always getting in the way of the investigation of a murdered newspaper columnist. Directed by Phil Karlsen, the film is fun to watch for its good-natured comedy but has little action and no fantasy whatsoever. Robert Shayne, George Chandler, Dorothea Kent.

BLIND JUSTICE (1994). Inspired by, but not attributed to, the Jonah Hex comic-book character, this HBO TV-movie is a dark, macabre western with strange religious symbolism that draws a parallel to the Jesus Christ legend. Armand Assante is effective as a near-blind Civil War survivor named Canaan who travels the West with a newborn baby (shades of the Babycart series from Japan!), has keen senses, and is haunted by nightmares of his wartime experiences. Director Richard Spence captures a surreal feeling for the Arizona landscape and the Daniel Knauf telescript, while drawing on many derivative elements. is nevertheless full of excellent dialogue and unexpected characters and situations. Elisabeth Shue, Robert Davi, Adam Baldwin. (HBO)

BODY MELT (1993). Gruesome gore stuff, from Australia, in which mad doc Ian Smith discovers a vitamin pill that causes its takers to hallucinate and undergo self-destruction, such as exploding when it's least appropriate. Plenty of graphic carnage earmarks this film from writer-diretor Philip Brophy. Gerard Kennedy, Andrew Daddo, Vince Gil.

BODY SNATCHERS (1993). "They get you when you sleep," says one who knows of the conspiracy. If that sounds familiar, then be prepared for the fact that there's nothing new in this third adaptation of Jack Finney's classic sci-fi novel, except that this time we get to see how the seed pods from space steal one's soul and shape a lookalike humanoid form inside the organic pod itself. This is more a sequel than an adaptation, being set in and around a military installation where toxic waste is stored. The pods, as one might expect, are taking over the surrounding communities one by one, and it's up to Gabrielle Anwar and Terry Kinney to escape the clutches of the human monsters and destroy them and warn the rest of mankind—if anyone is left to listen, that is. The paranoia that earmarked the first two versions called **INVASION OF THE BODY SNATCHERS** (Don Siegel's in 1956; Philip Kaufman's in 1978) is here with all the subtext about alienation, indifference and what happens when we lose the power and humanity of our emotions. It's just disappointing that the excellent film makers involved (Abel Ferrara directed; Stuart Gordon, Dennis Paoli and Nicholas St. John wrote the new script) didn't come up with some fresh twists. R. Lee Ermey, Billy Wirth, Christine Elise, Meg Tilly, Forest Whitaker. (Video/Laser: Warner Bros.)

BOUNTY HUNTER 2002 (1992). Another cheaply produced MAD MAX wannabe, although it does have the advantage of a sense of humor as reflected through Phil Nordell (as the bounty hunter), who roves the desert in search of a virgin, which in 2002 A.D. brings big bucks. Nordell portrays a traditional antihero, in this case an alcoholic working for a Japanese consortium that wants the virgin. She's played by Francine Lapensee, and she's one tough fighter (and an unconvincing virgin). Jeff Conaway, who plays a crazed religious fanatic, and Vernon Wells, who is Nordell's rival, were associate producers on this crudely made actioner. (Action International)

BRAIN SMASHER . . . A LOVE STORY (1992). A failed vehicle for comedian Andrew Dice Clay, in which he portrays a hapless night club bouncer (whose reputation is so ferocious he's called "The Brain Smasher," ha ha ha) who befriends photo model Teri Hatcher when she's pursued by a gang of Asians (in Green Hornet-type masks and black overcoats) for the rare "Red Lotus," a flower said to possess "the key to ultimate power." Written and directed by Albert Pyun, who is better suited to sci-fi actioners, most of this film (shot in Portland almost entirely at night) depicts the pair fleeing Yuji Okumoto and his gang of athletic kung fu fighters. Brion James and Tim Thormerson, members of Pyun's club, are wasted in colorless roles as a team of unlikable cops. Other guest players include Deborah Van Valkenburgh, Charles Rocket and Nicholas Guest.

CLASS OF 1999 II (1993). This sequel to Mark Lester's 1990 box-office hit is a lesser piece of film-making that is uncomfortably violent. That discomfort comes from a mixed sense of morality as high school students of a vicious kind are murdered by their teacher because they are rebellious. That teacher appears to be a "battle droid, A-77 series," a leftover from the cyborgs that were all allegedly destroyed in the previous film. The bloodletting is extreme as the "droid" engages in numerous unpleasant murders, including some with a combat knife. A blood bath is featured as the film's climax, and there's a "surprise" ending that makes little sense. A poorly structured project (blame it on the neanderthalic script by Mark Sevi) that director Spiro Razatos photographs with a penchant for bloody violence. Sasha Mitchell, Nick Cassavetes, Caitlin Dulany, Jack Knight, Gregory West, Rick Hill. (Vidmark)

CLUB, THE (1993). Following a high school prom dance, several graduates are trapped in an ancient mansion which once housed a Suicide Club, and an evil force is unleashed on them. This is a rather infuriating Canadian horror thriller that is more noisy than scary, and which offers a few morphing special effects but precious little else to thrill one. The castle-like setting and atmosphere are good but dull characters make you want to quit THE CLUB. Witten by Robert C. Cooper, directed by Brenton Spencer. Joel Wyner, Andrea Roth, Rino Romano, Zack Ward, Kelli Taylor. (Imperial)

COLD SWEAT (1993). Routine erotic thriller that qualifies for this book only because hit man Ben Cross is haunted by the ghost of one of his victims (Maria Del Mar). This fascinating premise could have been a movie in itself but it's only a subplot of little consequence, and all that's left is a series of double crosses within double crosses as sizzly Shannon Tweed and lover boy Adam Baldwin plot to do in her hubby (Dave Thomas) etc etc. Written by Richard Beattie, directed by Gail Harvey. (Paramount)

CROW, THE (1994). This is the film that claimed the life of its star, Brandon Lee (son of Bruce Lee), who was accidentally shot on the set in early '93. It's a dark, surreal version of James O'Barr's comic-book series about Eric Draven, a rock musician who is murdered and returns from the dead to wreak revenge against the sleazy criminals who did in him and his fiancee. The title refers to a supernatural bird that leads Draven through his bloody, vengeful experiences. The plot is nothing special but the film is notable for its atmosphere (a decaying city with wet, glistening streets), kinetic editing, dynamic action pieces and the unique directorial style of Alex Proyas. Not a work of art but certainly an example of bravado film-making. Script by David Schow and John Shirley. Ernie Hudson, Michael Wincott.

CURSE OF THE CANNIBAL CONFEDERATES (199?). Does anyone out there in the world of sane people know anything about this Troma Team Release about how the South rises again through reb troops who get up from their graves to give the Yankees what fer? I haven't seen it but I have been informed that it stars Steve Sandkuhler, Christopher Gummer and Rebecca Bach, and was produced-directed by one Tony Malanowski. (Troma)

DARK, THE (1993). Eerie photography in a tunnel beneath a cemetery enhances this Canadian horror thriller in which a maverick ex-FBI agent (Brion James) pursues a genetic monster that feeds on dead bodies. One twist in Robert C. Cooper's script is that the toothy, hairy creature is semi-benevolent when a drifter (Stephen McHattie) and greasy-spoon waitress (Cynthia Belliveau) join in the search. However, Cooper's narrative is muddled—a deficient that Craig Pryce's direction cannot overcome. Jaimz Woolvett, Dennis O'Connor, Neve Campbell. (Imperial)

DARK WIND, THE (1991). Mild Indian mysticism and witchcraft overtones are woven throughout this excellent mystery thriller starring Lou Diamond Phillips as Novajo reservation cop Jim Chee, who is caught up in a mystery involving a cache of drugs, crooked Federal agents and an assortment of colorful Novajo and Hopi characters. The New Mexico landscapes are beautifully and eerily captured through the unusual direction of documentary film maker Errol Morris. Co-produced by Robert Redford. Gary Farmer, Fred Ward (as Joe Leaphorn), John Karlen. The Neal Jimenez-Eric Bergin script was adapted from a Tony Hillerman novel. (New Line)

DEMON KEEPER (1993). After a bare-breasted beauty is burned at the stake, unleashing flashes of lethal energy-light that kill her inquisitors, we flash to modern day as psychic investigator Edward Albert conducts a druid "Prohibition Sabbath" to raise the sleeping spirit of Amadeus the Horned Demon (played by Mike Lane in a devil suit). Once Amadeus is unleashed in a mansion cut off from the rest of the world by an intense thunderstorm, the seance attendees are murdered one by one, the demon preying on their weaknesses. This is an uninspired Roger Corman thriller, made in South Africa to save a buck, that dredges up every Demon cliche imaginable (with plenty of bare breasts to spice the tasteless broth). Not a single spark of originality is to be found in Mikel Angel's script. Produced-directed by Joe Tornatore. Dirk Benedict, Andre Jacobs, Adrienne Pearce, David Sherwood. (New Horizons)

FOUR SKULLS OF JONATHAN DRAKE, THE (1959). Familiar beware-the-family-curse plot is at work in this cheapie from producer Robert E. Kent. Despite its abundance of shrunken heads, the appearance of a Jivaro native with his mouth sewed shut and threads dangling from his chin is as horrific as it gets as Orville Hampton's threadbare story, about a family whose male members are always beheaded at 60, unfolds. Henry Daniell is appropriately menacing as Jonathan Drake, who keeps all the skulls in his private collection. Turns out Drake is a 2000-year-old walking zombie. Zounds four times. Inexpensive sets, lethargic direction by Edward L. Cahn and a long sharp stiletto that bends like a piece of rubber are in store for you, the cursed viewer. Valerie French and Eduardo Franz bring a grain of versimilitude to the otherwise cheapjack proceedings.

A GNOME NAMED GNORM (1993). An amusing and sometimes charming fantasy blending a cops-and-robbers whodunit plot with the bonding of a furry creature from Inner Earth with a blundering cop (Anthony Michael Hall) working on a murder case. What elevates this out of the ho-hum humdrum of videomovies is the presence of a delightful and sympathetic being who digs his way to the surface to recharge a crystal that gives life to his subterranean world. Gnorm, who bears witness to a homicide, is just realistic enough to tug at your heart a little and provide some nice comedy touches to the script by co-producer Pen Densham and John Watson. It was directed by special-effects wizard Stan Winston. Jerry Orbach lends strength as Hall's cop boss and Claudia Christian is good as Hall's girl pal. Eli Danker, Robert Z'Dar, Mark Harelik. (PolyGram)

GEORGE LUCAS: HEROES, MYTHS AND MAGIC (1993). This is based on 20 hours of interviews with Mr. Lucas at his Skywalker Ranch outside San Rafael, CA, conducted by documentary film makers Jane Paley and her husband Larry Price. Lucas expresses his theories about mythology and how he applied them to the STAR WARS trilogy (and how he hoped to tap into our fears of the dark with shocking images in the Indiana Jones movies), how he created new film making technology, and how all his work is based on "trying to figure out what we are and what life is and some of the truths that lie beyond the surface." Interviews with his collaborators include comments by Ron Howard, Lawrence Kasdan, Carrie Fisher, Kate Capshaw, Francis Ford Coppola, Harrison Ford and Steven Spielberg. Atheme throughout this enlightening portrait is Lucas' emotional and intellectual connection to special effects and the new technologies he has spearheaded. Fans won't want to miss this special, originally aired on PBS.

HIDDEN II, THE (1993). This sequel is inferior to the 1987 sci-fi actioner that inspired it, with Raphael Sbarge taking the place of Kyle McLachlan as the good-guy alien inside a human body who is on Earth to destroy an evil alien (a bug-like monster) that, as a parasite, passes from body to body. The one interesting twist here is that Sbarge is slowly being consumed by a kind of cancer that will inexorably turn him into an evil alien, and this endangers his relationship with Kate Hodge, the daughter of cop Michael Nouri from the first film. Other than that, this is predictable, cliched action pieces with bodies being blasted full of lead, and the slug-like creature choosing new bodies. Written-diected by Seth Pinsker, THE HIDDEN II never reveals itself to be much more than another lousy sequel. Jovin Montanaro, Christopher Murphy, Michael Weldon, Michael A. Nickles. (New Line)

LIQUID DREAMS (1991). Offbeat mystery thriller with sci-fi overtones, set in a futuristic society, where Candice

LAST-MINUTE UPDATES

Daly searches for her sister's killer in a surreal night-club world where a mad doctor conducts experiments on beautiful strippers. He is searching for an extract that recaptures the ultimate sexual climax—just one of several bizarre elements in the Zack Davis-Mark Manos script that captures an intriguing perverse atmosphere. Its only downfall is a threadbare production look. Also directed by Manos. Richard Steinmetz, Barry Dennen, Tracey Walter, Juan Fernandez, Paul Bartel. (Academy offers rated and unrated versions)

MAN'S BEST FRIEND (1993). Better this should have been called MAN'S BEAST FRIEND or MAN'S BEST FIEND. Yes, Alpo salespeople, it's another "killer dog" movie, this time with a big lovable pooch called Max 3000, who's being groomed as a powerful weapon in lab experiments conducted by Lance Henriksen. Along comes snoopy TV newswoman Ally Sheedy, who ends up taking Max 3000 home with her, unaware in her own inept way that on occasion Max becomes a drooling killing machine, with a penchant for cookie snacks. There isn't much more to the dogeared script by director John Lafia. Robert Costanzo, Fredric Lehne, John Cassini, J.D. Daniels, William Sanderson. (New Line)

M.A.N.T.I.S (1994). Rousing special-effects superhero TV-movie in which M.A.N.T.I.S. (Mechanically Augmented Neuro-Transmitter System), a crippled black man in a metallic suit who flies around Ocean City in a futuristic air machine, wages war against a crooked political who is pitting black gangs against each other as an excuse to use excessive, dictatorial force on the streets. Produced by Sam Raimi, Robert Tapert and Sam Hamm (the latter also wrote the telescript), this is pure genre stuff that action fans will dig—from the technological hardware to the groovy supersuit to the pyrotechnics. Directed by Eric Laneuville. Carl Lumbly, Bobby Hosea, Gina Torres, Steve James, Obba Basatunde.

MASK, THE (1994). A live-action comedy that pays tribute to the zany style of Tex Avery and other Warner Bros. animators from the Golden Age of cartoons. There's a touch of Roger Rabbit at work here, although THE MASK never quite becomes an animated film. The effects appear to have been computer generated. It's an ideal vehicle for the daffy Jim Carrey, who portrays the worm that turns. He's an ineffectual banker and lady's man, searching for his own identity, when he finds a magical mask (allegedly the property of the Viking God Loki) and can fulfill his wildly fantasy by turning into a "superhero" with the capabilities of behaving just like an Avery character: moving with the speed of a whirlwind; popping his eyeballs and changing other parts of his anatomy in cartoonish style; producing wild and crazy props at the blink of an eyelid; changing costumes and characterizations at will; and practicing a form of wild abandon found only in the world of Bugs Bunny. Set in the metropolis of Edge City, THE MASK has a nominal plot (by Mike Webb) about a gangster trying to get the facepiece for his own evil designs, but it's all just an excuse that's a mile high and three miles wide for Carrey to go bonkers as only he can go bonkers. Director/co-producer Chuck Russell gives this unusual novelty piece just the right comic book touches. Peter Riegert, Peter Greene, Amy Yasbeck, Richard Jeni, Nancy Fish. (Video/Laser: New Line)

MASTER KEY, THE (1945). A 15-chapter Universal serial that is typical for the studio's output during World War II: Its emphasis is on a strong cast of B-picture players, a lot of plot that doesn't require more than an occasional outburst of action, and fistfights that can't compare to those in the Republic cliffhangers. In short, expect plenty of story and dialogue as government agent Tom Brant (Milburn Stone, who went on to become Doc on GUNSMOKE) fights a gang of Nazis in 1938 America that is out to use the Orotron Machine to turn seawater into gold. Helping Stone in his multi-chapter quest are Dennis Moore as a fellow agent and girlfriend Jan Wiley. Directed by Ray Taylor and Lewis D. Collins. (VCI)

MERLIN (1992). Originally produced as OCTOBER THE 32ND, this fantasy-adventure has a reincarnation theme in which counterparts to characters from the King Arthur legend are still warring against each other in modern times. Standouts in the cast are Richard Lynch as Pendragon, a sorcerer who uses black magic; James Hong as Leong Tao, "Guardian of the Sword" of Excaliber; and Rodney Wood as the titular magician ("older than time, older than stars"). Shot in England, MERLIN is an ambitious if sometimes poverty stricken production that was directed vigorously by Peter Hunt (John Stewart directed the action sequences). Nick McCarthy's script vacillates between poetic passages, "mumbo jumbo" as Pendragon calls up his demons and magic, and standard action stuff. Peter Phelps, Nadia Cameron, Robert Padilla, Ted Markland, Desmond Llewelyn. (Hemdale)

NEO-TOKYO (1986-91). This trilogy of excellent Japanese animation, commissioned for a futuristic exposition in Japan many years ago, opens with Rin Taro's "Labyrinth," the story of a little girl who lives in a surreal city with her big house cat. Suddenly she's pulled through a mirror into another dimension. Things pick up considerably with Yoshiaki Kawajiri's "Running Man," the depiction of the world's greater race-car driver and his disintegration as he races toward oblivion. (An edited version of this once ran on MTV.) Katsuhiro Otomo's "The Order to Stop Construction" depicts an executive sent to the jungles of South America where he finds that the robot workers have taken over. (Streamline)

NIGHT LIFE (1989). Teenage mortician's assistant Scott Grimes is in for one gory zombie attack on the night when a bolt of lightning turns dead teenagers into flesh-munching shamblers. The blood, severed limbs and torn throats are abundant in this NIGHT OF THE LIVING DEAD mixture of macabre comedy and shocks. As the mean old mortician who browbeats Grimes, John Astin has the film's best scenes, especially the one in which his stomach is pumped full of embalming fluid. You'll laugh, cry and scream at this revolting gore flick written by Keith Critchlow and directed by David Acomba. Cheryl Pollak, Anthony Geary, Lisa Fuller, Alan Blumenfeld. (Video/Laser: RCA/Columbia)

NIGHTMARE CLASSICS (1989). Two excellent period classics from Shelley Duvall's Showtime series, singularly well produced for the medium. "The Strange Case of Dr. Jekyll and Mr. Hyde" is the traditional story but sports an unusual performance of evil by Andrew Stevens and fine direction by Michael Lindsay-Hogg. Laura Dern and Nicholas Guest co-star. "The Turn of the Screw" is based on Henry James' famous ghost novel and offers a fine performance by Amy Irving, who co-stars with David Hemmings. It was directed by Graeme Clifford.

NIGHT OF THE DEMONS 2 (1994). That demonic bride Angela is back to Hull House to terrorize a few students from St. Rita's Academy, who are dumb enough to pay her a visit on Halloween night. This time for your money you get a lot of dark sex humor and visual horror with (1) a spiked bat through a human brain; (2) breasts that turn into hands that kill; (3) a snake that crawls into a woman's vagina; (4) a nun's head chopped off with a

"I can hear an angel fart."

—Robert Loggia as the gangster boss in **INNOCENT BLOOD.**

sword; (5) a priest who turns into a pile of goo and gore; (6) a head that's used as a basketball; and (7) a snake-lady monster with a swishing tail. Well, that's a few of the more enlightening moments in this special-effects extravaganza that might upset the Catholic Church but which is certain to please diehard fans of monster-zombie flicks that spare no expense to splash blood on all walls and ceilings. Directed by Brian Trenchard-Smith, NIGHT OF THE DEMONS 2 is a real chomp, klomp, ker-plonk romp. Christi Harris, Darin Hearnes, Bobby Jacoby, Merle Kennedy, Amelia Kinkade, Zoe Trilling. (Video/Laser: Republic)

ONE NIGHT STAND (1984). In Sydney, Australia, on the evening when nuclear war breaks out in eastern Europe, four teens in a Sydney theater listen to news of the coming Armageddon while playing strip poker, arguing, loving and finding fellowship to fight off pending doom. This unusual Australian film was produced by Simon Wincer and written-directed by John Duigan with the best of anti-war intentions, but there isn't an ounce of excitement or action to go with characters who try to be appealing but are ultimately bloody bores. Tyler Coppin, Cassandra Delaney, Jay Hackett, Saskia Post. (Trans World; Sultan)

PAST MIDNIGHT (1991). This psychological horror tale, made on location in the Seattle area, is classically structured by screenwriter Frank Norwood in the Hitchcock tradition, but it's still slight stuff. Social worker Natasha Richardson falls for ex-con Rutger Hauer, refusing to believe he murdered his wife with a butcher knife and took 8 mm movies while committing the crime. However, the finger of suspicion points toward him and Richardson is on the horns of a dilemma, especially when she realizes she's pregnant. The film only comes to life during the climactic revelations, but it's a long wait, and the direction by Jan Eliasberg is only occasionally flashy as she moves the crazy around like crazy; there are still too many lengthy, lethargic stretches. Clancy Brown portrays Richardson's old boyfriend who provides her with an essential plot device: a pump-action shotgun. Guy Boyd, (Columbia TriStar)

PHILADELPHIA EXPERIMENT II (1993). This picks up nine years after the end of THE PHILADELPHIA EXPERIMENT with time traveler Brad Johnson from 1943 being sent into an alternative universe where Hitler won World War II because he got his grubby hands on a Stealth fighter equipped with atomic weaponry that went through a time anomaly. It's up to Johnson to go back and change history and prevent a totalitarian world from happening, after Hitler won the war using the fighter plane. This is a taut, well-produced action fantasy written by Kevin Roch and Nick Paine and directed by Stephen Cornwell. Marjean Holden, Gerrit Graham, John Christian Graas, Cyril O'Reilly. (Vidmark)

PRINCE OF THE SUN (199?). Hong Kong fantasy-martial arts actioner starring Cynthia Rothrock as a warrioress in a red robe who is assigned to protect a child said to be a "living Buddha," a reincarnation from "a neverending reality." Chuck fully of nutty special effects, kung fu fighting and bizarre, silly characters. Directed by Welson Chin. Conan Lee, Sheila Chan.

RECKLESS KELLY (1993). This is Yahoo Serious' follow-up to YOUNG EINSTEIN, in which the Australian comedy actor/film maker, who has a penchant for the weird and the bizarre stretched to extremes, portrays the spirit of outlaw Ned Kelly, passed down to one of his descendants. Serious, whose island is populated by characters out of THE WIZARD OF OZ, sets out on an odyssey of adventure to raise $1 million If you like 'em whacky, by all means. Serious wrote-directed, seriously. Melora Hardin, Alexei Sayle, Hugo Weaving, John Pinette.

RETURN OF THE LIVING DEAD III (1993). Not since RE-ANIMATOR has a gore-horror film had the impact and the style of this masterpiece of grisly effects. A large part of the credit must go to producer-director Brian Yuzna as he keeps up an unrelenting pace and builds step by step, taking the graphic horror to new heights as this bloody, mayhem-filled film unfolds. J. Trevor Edmond portrays a young man whose military father (Kent McCord) is involved in the latest experiments with Trioxin, the gas that brings the dead to life. In a secret lab, the new horrors unfolding are witnessed by Edmond and girlfriend Mindy Clarke. Soon, both are caught up in the ghastliness of events, trapped in an old sewer as the walking dead (who must dull the terrible pains they feel by eating human brains) close in. The last 20 minutes features a gallery of human corpses on the move, and the effect is riveting. This is one gore flick that really pays off, thanks also to a well thought-out script by John Penney. Sarah Douglas assists as an uptight militarist who wants to use the living corpses as combat troops. James T. Callahan, Sal Lopez, Mike Moroff, Basil Wallace. (Vidmark)

REVENGE OF THE RED BARON (1993). Roger Corman's answer to those lightweight Full Moon vidmovies blending comedy and fantasy, but without some of the intrinsic charm that Charles Band can bring to the genre. This walks a fine line between tragedy and farce when young Tobey Maguire, coming from a split home, goes to live with his father (Cliff De Young), a jerk of the first order, and a wheelchair-bound grandfather (Mickey Rooney), the World War I aviation hero who shot down the Red Baron. A bolt of electricity strikes Rooney's remote-controlled model-version of Richtoffen's warship, giving life to the miniplane and doll pilot in the form of a reincarnated Richtoffen. The doll delivers quips in the style of Chucky the Killer Doll while Maguire has to prove he's innocent of murder and isn't insane. The contrast between comedy and real-life tragedy gives this film a difficult balance, and makes it impossible for director Robert Gordon to make the film work on all the levels it strives to reach. Ronnie Schell, Don Stark, Joe Balogh, Laraine Newman. (New Horizons)

ROSWELL (1994). A fascinating TV-movie account of what has come to be known as one of the best documented cases of a crashed UFO, based on a well-researched nonfiction book by Kevin D. Randle and Donald R. Schmitt, "UFO Crash at Roswell." Roswell is Roswell, New Mexico, where in July 1947 Roswell Army Air Force Base reported that a flying saucer had crashed nearby in the desert. However, the military immediately changed its story and began a massive cover-up that involved hundreds of civilian and military personnel. What was suppressed was the discovery of four or five alien corpses, and one extraterrestrial that was still alive. This adaptation by Arthur Kopit follows the intelligence officer (played by Kyle MacLachlan) who was one of the first to the crash site, and who had to bear the burden of silence, and of not knowing the full truth for many years. Told through the device of a 30-year reunion at the Air Force Base, ROSWELL unfolds as a mystery jigsaw, many of the pieces fitting into place, but others remaining lost. Finally, through a strange character played by Martin Sheen, MacLachlan learns of an alleged cover-up that extended all the way to the White House, and of subsequent events and encounters between the U.S. Government and UFOs. It gets wild and woolly, but you can't deny it's engrossing. And director Jeremy Kagan photographs many portions of this eerie "true tale" with odd camera angels, slightly out-of-focus lenses, and a real sense for the shivery quality such a story produces in all of us. Charles Martin Smith, John M. Jackson, Dwight Yoakum, Bob Gunton, Xander Berkeley, Kim Greist, Peter MacNicol. (Showtime)

SAND FAIRY, THE (19??). BBC-TV two-part children's production running well over two hours, designed solely for moppets by writer Helen Cresswell and director Marilyn Fox. Based on E. Nesbit's "Five Children and It," this series of kiddie adventures presents a fuzzy gnome called a Psammead who grants a family of Edwardian children a series of wishes that allows them to (1) grow wings and fly like angels; (2) travel back in time to a castle where two armies are fighting it out in armor; and (3) rescue a kidnapped baby. Adults will want to put their kids in front of this while they rush off to more important things. Simon Godwin, Nicole Mowat, Charlies Richards, Tamzen Audas. (Fox)

SHADOW, THE (1940). Columbia's 15-chapter cliffhanger, based on a dark-avenger character who was popular in pulp magazines and on radio during the '30s and '40s, offers little of the eerie-horror mystery for which the series was best known. Directed by James W. Horne, this is more in keeping with the traditional serial plot of the day, as "eminent scientist and good citizen" Lamont Cranston goes against a supervillain known only as The Black Tiger. This guy is an invisible being who is unseen because he walks in a beam of light, a gimmick later used by Republic in its serial INVISIBLE MONSTER. The Black Tiger is after "supreme financial power" so he can take over the world with his Death Ray and other sophisticated weaponry. Victor Jory assumes the disguise of Chinese gentleman Lin Chang to fool the underworld when he isn't assuming the guise of The Shadow, a caped figure who laughs menacingly each time he pops up suddenly to thwart the criminals. (There are many plot parallels between this and THE SPIDER'S WEB, another vigorous, action-packed cliffhanger.) Veda Ann Borg is Margot Lane, Frank La Rue is Commissioner Weston, Philip Ahn is Cranston's faithful servant, and Jack Ingram heads up the baddies working for the ungrateful Black Tiger. (Available on video from specialty houses.)

SHADOW, THE (1994). The famous pulp-magazine anti-hero of the 1930s, and a radio staple throughout the '40s, comes to the screen full-blown in the style of BATMAN, with great emphasis on "the look" and "the feel" of a world in which Lamont Cranston, a wealthy playboy, assumes the guise of a masked avenger who has the power "to cloud men's minds so they cannot see him," and goes after a descendant of Genghis Khan (John Lone), who intends to conquer the world with a pre-World War II nuclear device. Alec Baldwin is enormously powerful as Cranston/The Shadow, and Penelope Ann Miller makes for a very sexy and adorable Margo Lane ("the only person who knows to whom the voice of the invisible Shadow belongs"). Although there are campy elements that give THE SHADOW a sense of fun, and David Koepp's screenplay is stuffed with the cliches of the "dark avenger" genre, the spectacle of the production design remains overpowering and is the key to this movie's success. So is the fluid direction of Russell Mulcahy, a master at action and intriguing visuals. Atotally satisfying adventure. Ian McKellen, Tim Curry, Jonathan Winters, Andre Gregory. (Video/Laser: MCA)

SILENT MOBIUS (1990). A fascinating account, told through Japanese animation, about the Abnormal Mystery Police, women of the future with psychic powers who fight monsters that break thorugh another dimension to invade Earth. Their chief adversary is Lucifer Hawke, one of the key characters from the famous comic strip on which this cartoon feature is based. Directed by Michitaka Kikuchi. (Streamline)

SNAPDRAGON (1993). Offbeat psychological serial killer thriller in which police psychologist Steven Bauer falls in love with a beautfiul, mysterious young woman whom he begins to suspect is slitting the throats of men with "the dragon's tongue," a Chinese razor concealed in her mouth, under her tongue. This lowkey cop/killer drama is strangely compelling and underplayed all the way by director Worth Keeter, who treats Gene Church's psychological-leaning script with respect. Chelsea Field, Pamela Anderson, Matt McCoy, Rance Howard. (Prism)

SPIDER'S WEB, THE (1938). One of the best, and most exciting, of the serials produced by Columbia. There's a breathless sense to the pacing uncommon to most Columbia chapter plays, and directors Ray Taylor and James W. Horne keep it bouncing along with energetic stunts, explosive special effects and a strong cast headed by Warren Hull (as The Spider, his alter-ego, "famed criminologist" Richard Wentworth, and a disguised underworld figure named Blinky McQuade) and Kenneth Duncan as faithful companion Ram Singh. The Spider (based on a "dark avenger" character from a popular pulp magazine series) is after "The Octopus," a villain in a white sheet who plans to disrupt American society through sabotage and take over with his own government. It's neat how The Spider swings on ropes and drops numerous villains with a volley of pistol fire, and follows a vigilante doctrine in stopping the bad guys. Iris Meredith, Richard Fiske, Marc Lawrence.

TAINTED BLOOD (1993). Spinning off from the thesis of THE BAD SEED, this derivative TV-movie is a whichisit, in which one of two teenagers is the offspring of a family that always passes along homicidal tendencies to offspring. Investigative writer Raquel Welch is trying to determine which one, while telescripter Kathleen Rowell plants dozens of red herrings to throw you off the track. Average for its kind, except for Joan Van Ark's over-the-top performance as a neurotic, hard-drinking mother of one of the teens. Directed by Matthew Patrick. Alley Mills, Kerri Green. (Paramount)

TEENAGE CATGIRLS IN HEAT (1991). You'll feel cold for the duration of this low-budget, regionally produced horror nonthriller depicting how the statue of an Egyptian cat goddess transmutates cats into naked women and causes mortals to commit sacrificial suicide while a nerd with cat-hunting equipment runs around the countryside. One scene has it literally raining cats without dogs. Words are inadequate to describe just how awful this piece of trash is. Directed by Scott Perry, who cowrote with Grace Smith. Gary Graves, Carrie Vanston, Dave Cox.

TIGER CLAWS (1991). A serial killer known as "The Death Dealer" damages the interior organs of his victims without leaving exterior markings except for claw marks across their cheeks. Swinging into action are martial arts cops Jalal Merhi (who also produced) and Cynthia Rothrock, who demonstrate karate and kickboxing skills in what is basically an action picture with minor horror overtones. The well-endowed Rothrock and Merhi are personable players who bring likeability to their characters, and director Kelly Makin makes it a workable albeit formula picture. Script by co-producer J. Stephen Maunder. Bolo Yeung, Ho Chow. (Video/Laser: MCA)

WEEKEND AT BERNIE'S 2 (1993). This ridiculous sequel to the comedy about two jerkolas trying to conceal a dead body while being pursued by racketeers qualifies for this movie guide because the dead body (Terry Kiser) is brought back to life by voodoo magic and dances whenever music plays. Andrew McCarthy and Jonathan Silverman are back as the nerds who, this time, end up on St. Thomas in the Caribbean to look for a buried treasure, the whereabouts of which is known only to the Calypso-happy Bernie. As absurd as it is, you can't help but laugh at some of the slapstick antics through which Kiser's "corpse" must fly. Barry Bostwick appears for writer-director Robert Klane. (Columbia TriStar)

"You don't know L.A. It's like New Jersey with earthquakes."
—Harvey Korman in **MUNCHIES.**

Mongolian. Stillborn. The story (by producer Anthony Wilson) picks up years later when the Devil's son Adrian is a young boy and is taken away from Rosemary (now Patty Duke). The narrative then skips to when Adrian is a young man (Stephen McHattie) involved with a demon cult. Only Ruth Gordon as the witch next door repeats her role from the original—everything else is second-rate substitution. And director Sam O'Steen is no Roman Polanski. Broderick Crawford, George Maharis, Tina Louise, Donna Mills, Ray Milland.

LOONIES ON BROADWAY. See **ZOMBIES ON BROADWAY.**

LOOSE IN LONDON (1953). Leo Gorcey, Huntz Hall and the Bowery Boys find their hair standing on end in a British manor complete with torture devices, a belltower that tolls the hour of murder and the "ghost" of a hangman. If you love dumb delinquents, you'll love LOOSE IN LONDON. Directed by Edward Bernds.

LORCA AND THE OUTLAWS. See **STARSHIP.**

LORD OF THE FLIES (1963). On the eve of atomic holocaust, English schoolboys crashland on a tropical island. The youths splinter into bands and deteriorate into practitioners of cruel barbarism. This strange allegory on social and political behavior, based on the novel by William Golding, has uneven acting and suspense, but still yields a high rate of cinematic allegory. A good effort from screenwriter-director Peter Brook. James Aubrey, Tom Chapin. Diamond; King of Video) (Laser)

LORD OF THE FLIES (1990). This version of William Golding's novel is superior to the 1963 film in that it has a better cast and a slicker production, but generally it tells the same allegorical tale about British school boys stranded on a tropical island and how they break into groups, one representing the thoughtful side the man, the other man's primitivism. The obvious symbolism doesn't detract from this compelling object lesson about human behavior. Directed by Harry Hook. Balthazar Getty, Badgett Dale. (Video/Laser: Nelson)

LORD OF THE RINGS (1978). Director Ralph Bakshi injects a flavor of reality into this animated version of J. R. R. Tolkien's epic narrative set in Middle Earth, specifically the novels THE TWO TOWERS and THE FELLOWSHIP OF THE RING. All the likeable and evil characters have been re-created: the Hobbits, wizards, the Gollum, Ring Wraiths, etc. But none recaptures the poetic, sensitive qualities of Tolkien's tomes. Bakshi abandoned sequels but there were TV movies by other animators: THE HOBBIT and RETURN OF THE KING. Voices by John Hurt, Christopher Guard, William Squire, Andre Morell. (HBO; Top; Diamond; Connoisseur)

LORD SHANGO (1975). All-black cast dominates this programmer in which Lord Shango, a tribal priest, returns from the dead to keep superstitious folks in line. Marlene Clark, Lawrence Cook. Directed by Raymond Marsh. (From Aries as **COLOR OF LOVE, THE)**

LORDS OF MAGICK (1989). Two young magicians from the 10th Century (Jarrett Parker and Mark Gauthier) travel through time to the future (our present day) to battle an evil power named Saladin and save a princess (Ruth Zackarian) from harm. David Marsh produced and directed and co-wrote the script with Sherman Hirsch. Brendan Dillon Jr., David Snow, John Clark. (Prism)

LORDS OF THE DEEP (1989). You can hear producer Roger Corman's mind turning over: "Hey, guys, underwater lab movies are in; let's churn out a quickie to cash in." So, Howard Cohen and Daryl Haney cranked out a potboiler script set in 2020 about an underwater lab crew trapped with a creature that looks like a swimming bat. This isn't even as good as the science-fiction pastiches Corman used to produce in the early '80s—it's a throwback to the '50s with its antiquated set design, costumes and stilted dialogue, all with a Buck Rogers look. Not even the monster is interesting—DEEP is a shallow way to spend your time. Directed without an ounce of flair by Mary Ann Fisher. Corman appears in a cameo role as a corporate official. Bradford Dillman, Priscilla Barnes, Daryl Haney, Ed Lottimer. (MGM/UA)

LORELEI'S GRASP, THE. See **WHEN THE SCREAMING STOPS.**

LORNA THE EXORCIST (1974). A European-produced supernatural tale made in the wake of THE EXORCIST, depicting a man's seduction by a witch who wants to claim the child from their union when the daughter turns 18. The film's blatant sexuality is commingled with themes of possession and retribution. Directed by Jesse Franco as Clifford Brown. Guy Delorme, Lina Romay, Howard Vernon. (Video Search of Miami)

LOST ATLANTIS (1932). See editions 1-3.

LOST BOYS, THE (1987). Premise with promise is never exploited to its max: In a coastal town (Santa Cruz, Calif.) a punk gang is made up of vampires who terrorize newcomer kids. This launched the career of Kiefer Sutherland and is full of effects and rock music that should appeal to a young audience, but it fails to render a strong payoff. Directed by Joel Schumacher, written by Janice Fischer, James Jeremias and Jeffrey Boam. Jason Patric, Corey Haim, Dianne Wiest, Barnard Hughes, Ed Herrmann. (Video/Laser: Warner Bros.)

LOST CITY, THE (1935). Mascot's 12-chapter serial is nonstop jungle action as electrical engineer Kane Richmond discovers Magnetic Mountain, hideaway of Zolok (stage actor William Boyd), who plans to take over the world with his earthquake-making machine. Watch for George "Gabby" Hayes as the slave trader. Fun if you overlook outmoded acting and filming techniques. Directed by Harry Revier. (Foothill; Sinister/C; Nostalgia; Filmfax offers the serial and a feature version)

LOST CITY, THE (1982). Robert Dukes directed this imitation of SHE which features a long-undiscovered metropolis, a queen with a headdress, crumbling ruins and a quest for romance and riches. Bernadette Clark, David Cain Haughton, Margot Samson.

LOST CITY OF ATLANTIS, THE (1978). Phony and groany documentary speculates on Atlantis and other enigmas. Plenty of conjecture but few answers and little conviction. Unimaginatively slapped together by "lost" director Richard Martin.

LOST CONTINENT, THE (1951). Robert L. Lippert fantasy-adventure has atmospheric production values, a memorable score by the excellent but underrated Paul Dunlap, and a strong performance by Cesar Romero as a flight commander looking for a rocket that crashed on a high plateau of a lost island. His flight crew (John Hoyt, Hugh Beaumont, Sid Melton) is surrounded by man-eating dinosaurs. Surprisingly good for a low-budget quickie. Hillary Brooke, Acquanetta, Whit Bissell, Chick Chandler. Directed by Sam Newfield. (Weiss Global; Moore)

LOST CONTINENT, THE (1968). Hammer adaptation of a Dennis Wheatley novel with touches of William Hope Hodgson splashed in for added monster moisture by producer-director Michael Carreras. A freighter is jeopardized by a cargo of high explosives; survivors of this ordeal face another: A Sargasso Sea of Lost Ships, menaced by seaweed serpents, colossal crabs and shipwrecked Spanish nuts who worship a wriggling octopus god. This pulp adventure with middling effects goes dead in the water. Eric Porter, Hildegard Knef, Suzanna Leigh.

LOST EMPIRE, THE (1985). As dumb as this is, it has moments to please oglers, for producer-writer-director Jim Wynorski has made a male sexual fantasy first, an adventure second. Unlikely L.A. cop Angel Wolfe (buxom Melanie Vincz) is out to avenge a fellow cop's death and

"We totally annihilated his night-stalking ass."

—One fair-haired youth to another in **THE LOST BOYS**

find the Eye of Avatar, an energy-packed gem belonging to a lost race of Lemurians. Her adversary is Dr. Sin Do (hammily rendered by Angus Scrimm, the Tall Man from PHANTASM) who runs an island called Golgotha, where Angel goes with Raven de la Croix, an endowed woman on a white charger, and karate-kicking Angela Aames. It's the bouncing breasts that will make you say: So who wants subtlety? Bob Tessier is superawful as Scrimm's toady. Linda Shayne, Angelique Pettyjohn, Kenneth Tobey, Garry Goodrow. (Lightning)

LOST HORIZON (1937). James Hilton's romantic fantasy set in Shangri-la, a luxuriant valley hidden in the Tibetan Mountains, is given poetic, sensitive interpretation by producer-director Frank Capra. Shangra-li, where aging, greed and brutality are nonexistent, is an idyllic symbol for everything man searches for. Ronald Colman was never more appealing as Robert Conway, brought to the valley with other stranded airline passengers aboard a pilotless plane. Jane Wyatt is Conway's sweetheart; H.B. Warner is wise old Chang, Sam Jaffee is the High Lama, and Edward Everett Horton is a fussy paleontologist. Thomas Mitchell, Noble Johnson, Margo. (Video/Laser: RCA/Columbia)

LOST HORIZON (1973). Although Ross Hunter's musical version of the James Hilton book was severely panned (Rex Reed called it "Brigadoon with chopsticks"), it is not nearly as static or plastic as you might fear. True, its musical sequences are absurd within the framework of such a time and place, yet this version (directed by Charles Jarrott) follows the spirit of Capra's 1937 film. Charles Boyer as the High Lama, John Gielgud as wise old Chang, Peter Finch and Michael York as the stranded travelers. Olivia Hussey, Sally Kellerman, George Kennedy, Liv Ullmann. (Laser: Pioneer)

LOST IN TIME (1977). Re-edited pilot for TV's **FANTASTIC JOURNEY, THE.**

LOST ISLAND OF KONGA (1938). Feature version of Republic's **HAWK OF THE WILDERNESS**.

LOST JUNGLE, THE (1934). Feature version of Mascot's serial with animal trainer Clyde Beatty as an African explorer looking for his fiance's missing father. He crashes his dirigible on an island and stumbles across a subterranean metropolis that has everything but Rapid Transit. It's poorly directed by Armand Schaefer and David Howard and the acting is atrocious but if you like serials, it's a must. Warner Richmond, Cecelia Parker, Syd Saylor, Mickey Rooney. (Nostalgia; Video Connection; Video Dimensions)

LOST MISSILE, THE (1958). Footloose rocket from Russia streaks into our stratosphere and could destroy Peoria. But don't sweat, democracy lovers. Robert Loggia is on hand to produce a countermissile that will save us. Directed by Lester William Berke. Ellen Parker, Larry Kerr, Philip Pine, Joe Hyams. (Fright)

LOST PLANET, THE (1953). A craft called a "cosmojet" from the planet Ergro crashes on Earth, giving newspeople Judd Holdren and Vivian Mason something to cover in this 12-chapter Columbia serial produced by Sam Katzman. Bent on conquering Earth is Dr. Grood (Michael Fox), who engages in battles with the Earthlings back on his native planet. Directed by Spencer Bennet. Ted Thorpe, Forrest Taylor, Gene Roth.

LOST PLANET AIRMEN (1949). Feature version of Republic's **KING OF THE ROCKET MEN**.

LOST PLANET OF THE GODS. See **BATTLESTAR GALACTICA.**

LOST PLATOON, THE (1989). Four dead soldiers-vampires wander the battlefields from the Civil War to Vietnam, their presence spotted by a combat cameraman who's wise to their eternal wanderings. Directed by David A. Prior. William Knight, David Parry, Stephen Quadros, Lew Pipes. (Action International)

LOST SOUL. See **FORBIDDEN ROOM, THE.**

LOST TRIBE, THE (1949). Jungle Jim . . . pith helmets . . . Tamba the chimp . . . jungle Shangri-La . . . potted plants . . . a lost race of natives . . . Columbia sound stage sets . . . rubber crocodiles . . . Elena Verdugo in a sarong . . . tired-and-blue Johnny Weissmuller vehicle from venerable Z-producer Sam Katzman and director William Berke. Munga bunga crumba.

GEORGE HAMILTON IN 'LOVE AT FIRST BITE'

LOST TRIBE, THE (1983). Writer-director John Laing attempts to tell a metaphysical tale about an anthropologist in the jungle of New Zealand searching for a missing race of Indians and becoming missing himself. His twin brother (both roles by John Bach) is suddenly possessed with weird tendencies, including a yen for his brother's wife. The characters' behaviors are irritating rather than compelling and this evolves into an inexplicable mystery never satisfactorily resolved. Darien Takle, Emma Takle, Terry Connolly. (Thrillervideo; Fox Hills; Media)

LOST WOMEN (1952). Turgidly written-directed-acted sci-fi thriller about a mad scientist (Jackie Coogan) who creates a race of superwomen (hah!) injected with the emotions of spiders. So incompetent you won't believe your eyes. A lost cause for Richard Travis, Lyle Talbot, Allan Nixon, Tandra Quinn. Directed by writer Herbert Tevos and Ron Damond. Also known as LOST WOMEN OF ZARPA. (In video as **MESA OF LOST WOMEN**)

LOST WORLD, THE (1925). Silent milestone, first major feature to spotlight the stop motion work of special effects pioneer Willis O'Brien, the man who moved King Kong. It's the Sir Arthur Conan Doyle story about explorers, led by Professor Challenger, who find a prehistoric world of brontosauruses and tyranosaurus rexes. Wallace Beery, Bessie Love, Lewis Stone. Directed by Harry Hoyt. (Video Yesteryear; Nostalgia) (Laser: Lumivision)

LOST WORLD, THE (1960). Producer-director Irwin Allen fails to do justice to Conan Doyle's Professor Challenger adventure, in which Claude Rains leads an expedition in search of a high plateau forgotten by time. The gloss is there but Allen caters to simplistic thrills. The "monsters" are real lizards shot with macro lenses—and the thrills involving a tribe of cannibals are just as phony. David Hedison, Jill St. John, Michael Rennie, Fernando Lamas, Richard Haydn.

LOST WORLD, THE (1992). Very good adaptation of

the famous Professor Challenger fantasy-adventure by Sir Arthur Conan Doyle, with John Rhys-Davies giving a vigorous performance as Challenger and David Warner equally effective as his rival. They join ranks in this Canadian film (made in Zimbabwe by producer Harry Alan Towers) with reporter Eric McCormic, photographer Tamara Goeski, young stowaway Darren Peter Mercer and native girl Nathania Stanford to discover prehistoric life on a plateau in Africa. Peter Welbeck's telescript is slanted for family viewing and has modern save-the-species overtones. Directed by Timothy Bond. (Worldvision)

LOST WORLD OF LIBRA, THE (1968). See first edition.

LOST WORLD OF SINBAD, THE (1965). Toshiro Mifune portrays a Japanese swordsman-adventurer who challenges a Medusa-like enchantress and assorted demons to save an island's people from an evil takeover. Effects by Eiji Tsuburaya, of GODZILLA fame. Directed by Senkichi Tangiguchi.

LOUISIANA. See **DRUMS O' VOODOO.**

LOVE AND CURSES . . . AND ALL THAT JAZZ (1991). TV-movie designed for Gerald McRaney and Delta Burke, who portray a mild version of Nick and Nora Charles. He's a doctor, she's a snoop and together they investigate a dead woman returned to life, a voodoo "death powder" and other mumbo jumbo common to New Orleans, but emphasis remains on cute dialogue between the stars. McRaney also directed, though his handling of the mildly horrific script is ordinary. Elizabeth Ashley shines as a relative of Burke who runs a New Orleans hotel. Tony Todd, Harold Sylvester.

LOVE AT FIRST BITE (1979). New wrinkles are painted onto the 800- year-old face of Dracula in this funny satire on movie monsters. George Hamilton is marvelous as the Transylvanian shut-in who yearns for the 20th Century so much that he jets to New York to claim a fashion model. Dracula is an anachronism adapting to 20th Century Manhattan, and the gags are fast and furious. Classic scenes: the disruption of a funeral in a Harlem chapel, a midnight raid on a New York blood bank, Dracula disco dancing. Susan St. James is the lovely fashion model hypnotically falling for Hamilton's charms, and Richard Benjamin is the whacky psychiatrist who gets his monster lore scrambled. Robert Kaufman's script is a delight and director Stan Dragoti pulls it wonderfully together. Dick Shawn is a zany cop and Arte Johnson is Drac's Igor. (Warner Bros.) (Laser: Vestron)

LOVE AT FIRST GULP. See **DRACULA EXOTICA.**

LOVE AT STAKE (1986). Mad Magazine-styled slapstick comedy about the Salem Witch trials, consisting of sexual innuendos and anachronisms of a dumb nature. The Terry Sweeney-Lanier Laney script never rises above such "yocks" as a baker named Sara Lee and the appearance of Dr. Joyce Brothers as an expert trial witness. The witch is Barbara Carrera, who uses her sexual aura and black magic to trick and mislead our forefathers in puritanical New England. John Moffitt was cursed to be director. Patrick Cassidy, Kelly Preston, Bud Cort, David Graf. (Video/Laser: Nelson)

LOVE BUG, THE (1969). First of four Walt Disney comedies about an intelligent Volkswagen (Herbie the Love Bug). Designed for moppets, but even older folks should enjoy the cute antics as Herbie runs wild. Directed by Robert Stevenson. David Tomlinson, Dean Jones, Michele Lee, Buddy Hackett, Joe Flynn, Joe E. Ross. (Video/Laser: Disney)

LOVE BUTCHER, THE (1975). Sleazo stuff from directors Mikel Angel and Don Jones, who play this psychothriller for laughs. A wimpy gardener (Erik Stern) is abused by the women who hire him, so he turns into a killer who beds the broads before he butchers them. What makes this unique is the use of garden tools by the killer. Gee, what a tough row to hoe . . . shear terror . . . should we call the killer a rake? But enough, we must be shoveling off. Kay Neer, Jeremiah Beecher. (Monterey)

LOVE CAN BE MURDER (1992). Lightweight TV-movie in which fed-up lawyer Jaclyn Smith becomes a fledgling private eye, only to meet the ghost of a shamus (Corbin Bernsen) murdered back in 1948. The unsuited pair goes to work to solve the crime, and gradually fall in love. Smith and Bernsen play well together. Directed by Jack Bender. Anne Francis, Tom Bower, Susan Brown, Nicholas Pryor. Also known as KINDRED SPIRITS.

LOVE CAPTIVE, THE (1934). See editions 1-3. **LOVE EXORCIST.** See **DADDY'S DEADLY DARLING.**

LOVE FACTOR, THE. Video version of **ZETA ONE.** (Sinister/C; S/Weird; Filmfax)

LOVE FROM A STRANGER (1936). British variation on Bluebeard with Basil Rathbone setting out to knock off another beautiful wife. Based on an Agatha Christie story. Directed by Rowland V. Lee. Ann Harding, Bruce Seton. (Sinister/C; Nostalgia; New World; Filmfax)

LOVE IN COLD BLOOD (1969). Sleazy production, shot in blight-riddled L.A. David Story is an ice house worker, a whacko who murders buxom, platinum-haired Sabrina and other sexpots, hiding their bodies in cold storage. We're talking cold shoulder here. David has a real-life lookalike brother Robert, who portrays a cop, and David also murders him and takes his place. The Storys must have taken their training at the Neanderthal school of acting. A mess, even with Jim Davis and Scott Brady helping. Directed by Stuart E. McGowan.

LOVE MANIAC. See **MAN WITH THE SYNTHETIC BRAIN.**

LOVE ME DEADLY (1972). Necrophilia involves a coven of devil worshippers operating out of an L.A. funeral home. Mary Wilcox plays the lover of corpses. Never widely released—one of the movie world's small favors to you. Directed-written by Jacques LaCerte. Lyle Waggoner, Christopher Stone. (Video Gems)

LOVE PILL, THE (1971). Recommended to horny viewers only: A candy doubles as a contraceptive when chewed just right. Women are turned into flaming nymphomaniacs, their bodies quivering with passion—and then the fun begins in this raunchy British comedy. Directed by Kenneth Turner. Toni Sinclair, Melinda Churcher. (Academy)

LOVE POTION NO. 9 (1992). The Jerry Leiber-Mike Stoller song inspired this amusing fantasy-comedy in which nerdy biochemists Tate Donovan and Sandra Bullock discover an aphrodisiac and become the worms that turn. Writer-producer-director Dale Launer brings cute twists to the battle of the sexes. Mary Mara, Dale Midkiff, Anne Bancroft (as fortune teller Madame Ruth).

LOVERS BEYOND THE TOMB. See **NIGHTMARE CASTLE.**

LOVERS OF THE LORD OF THE NIGHT, THE (1983). Mexican witchcraft thriller directed by actress Isela Vega, who also portrays the film's governess. Elena de Haro, Emilio Fernandez.

LOVESICK (1983). Psychiatrist Dudley Moore falls for playwright patient Elizabeth McGovern—which so irritates the ghost of Sigmund Freud that he appears as Alec Guinness. Only Moore can hear Guinness' pearls of couched wisdom, so characters keep wondering why Moore talks into thin air (into which this Marshall Brickman movie evaporates). John Huston is a shrink warning Moore about his infidelity. Alan King, Renee Taylor, Ron Silver, Gene Saks. You won't love LOVESICK but you may get sick, luv. (Video/Laser: Warner Bros.)

LOVE SLAVES OF THE AMAZON (1957). Tall, beautiful women, their bodies pulsating with lust, capture wilderness explorers and imprison them to serve as "love slaves." Lowbrow action adventure, rather intense for its time, written-produced-directed by Curt Siodmak. Don Taylor, Eduardo Ciannelli, Gianna Segale, John Herbert.

LOVES OF HERCULES, THE (1960). Muscleman Mickey Hargitay should be a gallant he-man fighting the Cyclops, the Hydra and the Incredible Forest of Tree Men. But he spends more time in this French-Italian "spectacle" breathing passionate breath over his thinly clad real-life lover-wife Jayne Mansfield. Can't say we blame him; who needs myths when you have the rounded substance of Mansfield? Directed by Carlo Bragaglia. A TV version exists as HERCULES VS. THE HYDRA. (Sinister/C; S/Weird; Vidmark)

LOVES OF IRINA, THE. Re-edited version of **EROTIKILL** that eliminates the supernatural element (Media; Private Screenings/Luna).

LOVE TRAP (1978). Sexy British spoof, in the fashion of old music hall revues, with plenty of naked female flesh and comedy antics as serviceman Robin Askwith, returning from World War II, becomes involved in a series of murders and mistaken identities over a miniaturized cigarette lighter that has an effect on electronic power. Despite its silliness, it's entertaining. Directed by James Clarke. Anthony Steel, Fiona Richmond.

LOVE TRAP. See **CURSE OF THE BLACK WIDOW.**

LOVE: VAMPIRE STYLE (1971). West German comedy-satire of the Dracula genre in which a descendant of the old Count knocks off fellow villagers one by one. Herbert Fux, B. Valentin.

LOVE WAR, THE (1970). Unconvincing TV-movie: Earth is fought over by two alien races; Lloyd Bridges and Angie Dickinson get caught up in the E.T. showdown. The fate of our wonderful planet hangs in the balance when opposing parties come face to face in a deserted town to shoot it out. Resembles an episode of THE INVADERS. Directed by George McGowan.

LOVING TOUCH, THE. See **PSYCHO LOVER.**

LUCAN (1977). Wolf Boy (Kevin Brophy) with orange-glow eyes returns to civilization to be studied by John Randolph. TV-movie (directed by David Greene) led to a series that loped on ABC for two years, then was lopped, never to lope again. Stockard Channing, Ned Beatty, William Jordan.

LUCIFER COMPLEX, THE (1978). Mountain hiker enters a cave where a computer is stored with tapes of man's history. For 20 minutes he watches footage of warfare and moralizes in stream-of-consciousness dribble. Jump to 1986 as spy Robert Vaughn uncovers a Nazi plot to clone Hitler. The Vaughn footage (directed-written by David L. Hewitt) appears to be an unsold pilot added to James Flocker's cave junk. An editor's nightmare. Keenan Wynn, Aldo Ray. (VCI; United)

LUCIFER'S WOMEN (1974). Director Paul Aratow's twist on TRILBY, the story of Svengali hypnotically luring a woman, is a poorly shot, feebly written sex exploitationer blending lesbianism, satanism and other distasteful themes. Made in San Francisco, and wrenching the talents of Larry Hankin and Morgan Upton, it's a lowbrow travesty. See DOCTOR DRACULA for how this was re-edited into a TV-movie with new footage.

LUCK OF THE IRISH, THE (1948). All you O'Flahertys, McGillicutties and O'Hoolihans take note: Here's a fittin' Irish fantasy that'll pop your Cork County. Cecil Kellaway is an overimbibing leprechaun affecting the conscience of reporter Tyrone Power who is manipulated by publisher Lee J. Cobb. Can the good fairy of folklore lead Power and girlfriend Anne Baxter to the pot o' gold? A viewing rainbow from director Henry Koster.

L Is For Lorre

From the time he played the child serial killer in "M," Hungarian actor Peter Lorre was doomed to play psychotics, misfits and sociopaths in a career that spanned three and a half decades.

LUCKY STIFF (1988). Anthony Perkins directed this comedy about a rejected fat man (Joe Alaskey) picked out by cannibals to be the main course at Christmas dinner. Donna Dixon seduces him at Lake Tahoe and takes him to the family spread, where sex gags and visual tomfoolery unfold. Alaskey makes wise-guy jokes as he tries to avoid becoming an entree. Jeff Kober, Elizabeth Arlen, Charles Frank, Barbara Howard, Leigh McCloskey, Bill Quinn. (Video/Laser: RCA/Columbia)

LUGGAGE OF THE GODS! (1983). Labored takeoff on CAVEMAN in which primitive cave people meet the 20th Century and deal with modern people and inventions. Played by writer-director David Kendall solely for comedy as Yuk, Hubba, Zoot, Kono and Tull fight off modern crooks. Mark Stolzenberg, Gabriel Barre, Gwen Ellison. (Academy)

LUNATICS—A LOVE STORY (1991). Cute comedy with light fantasy overtones in which Theodore Raimi portrays a nerdish agoraphobiac who, locked in his apartment, imagines spiders crawling in his brain and a mad doctor with a hypo chasing him. Yeah, he's a lunatic. Deborah Foreman runs around Pontiac, Mich., also fantasizing her worst fears. She's a lunatic too. They finally meet and face their fears together. Director Josh Becker's script includes a stop-motion giant spider. Produced by Bruce Campbell, who is also in the cast. A production from Sam Raimi/Robert Tapert. (Video/Laser: SVS/Triumph)

LUNCH MEAT (1987). Sickening ripoff of THE TEXAS CHAINSAW MASSACRE, written-directed on a shoestring by Kirk Alex. It's full of cut-up bodies as it depicts a demented family that slaughters humans for meat and sells these unkindest cuts of all to a hamburger stand. Garden tool are used to hack the cast to pieces. Kim McKamy, Chuck Ellis, Elroy Wiese. (Tapeworm)

LURKERS (1988). Study in abnormal psychology (what other kind is there in a horror movie?) from director Robert Findlay, focusing on a young girl tormented during her childhood who grows up to be a tormented cello player. The woman's dead mother keeps coming back to torment her more in visions. Totally abnormal. Christine Moore, Gary Warner. (Media)

LURKING FEAR (1994). The only element of H. P. Lovecraft's short story retained by writer-director C. Courtney Joyner is family inbreeding and how it creates a family of ghouls living beneath a cemetery in Arkham County, Mass. For this Full Moon-Charles Band production, Joyner has enjoined gangsters looking for buried money, a plot to blow up the cemetery, a normal member of the ghoul family searching for identity, and two women who fight it out in a muddy graveyard in pouring rain. LURKING FEAR is loaded with graphic violence, monsters and gore, so fans of this fare will not be disappointed. And the cast is good: Jon Finch as the head of the gangsters who loses his head over money (ahem), Ashley Lauren as a Rambo-style participant, Jeffrey Combs as a crazed doctor (again?), Alison Mackie, Paul Mantee, Blake Bailey. And Vincent Schiavelli plays undertaker Skelton Knaggs. It's a gas. (Paramount)

LUST AT FIRST BITE. See **DRACULA SUCKS.**

LUST FOR A VAMPIRE. Video version of **TO LOVE A VAMPIRE.** (HBO) (Laser: Image, with **DIE, MONSTER, DIE**)

LUST OF THE VAMPIRE. See **I VAMPIRA.**

LUTHOR THE GEEK (1989). Director Carlton J. Albright (THE CHILDREN) spins a tale of a guy who likes to bite off the heads of chickens (an old carnival "geek" act he saw as a kid) and slaughter people. Gore fans should derive satisfaction from watching the body-maiming mayhem. Edward Terry, Joan Roth, Tom Mills. (Quest)

LYCANTHROPUS. See **WEREWOLF IN A GIRLS' DORMITORY.** (A sorority row?)

M (1930). Fascinating portrait of abnormal sexuality, years ahead of its time in technique and psychological insight. This trend-setting German film was directed by Fritz Lang, who used real Berlin underworld characters in small roles. Peter Lorre made his screen debut as a perverted child murderer who wants to stop but can't resist his homicidal impulses. The role made Lorre famous but typecast him for life. Lang was an imaginative filmmaker, a fact reflected in every frame of this innovative work. (Budget; Kartes; Crown; Embassy; Sinister/C; Nostalgia)

M (1951). Joseph Losey's remake of Lang's portrait of a child murderer is inferior but still a compelling study. David Wayne essays the Lorre role, fondling the shoes of his victims and playing melancholy tunes on a flute. Howard Da Silva is the detective, Martin Gabel the underworld kingpin who organizes a search for the killer. Raymond Burr, Steve Brodie, Karen Morley.

M3: THE GEMINI STRAIN. See **PLAGUE, THE.**

MACABRA. TV title for **DEMONOID.**

MACABRE (1958). The first of producer-director William Castle's "gimmicky" shriekers: Audiences were insured by Lloyds of London against death by fright. Based on THE MARBLE FOREST, a novel by 15 mystery writers, and adapted by Robb White, it tells of a doctor (William Prince) with just five hours to find his daughter, who has been buried alive. Delightful closing credits. Castle was off and running for the next 15 years as a purveyor of horrifying and pleasing hokum. Jim Backus, Ellen Corby, Christine White, Susan Morrow.

MACABRE SERENADE. Video version of Karloff's **HOUSE OF EVIL** (Unicorn).

MACABRO (1980). Video version of Lamberto Bava's **FROZEN TERROR** (CIC).

MAC AND ME (1988). A ripoff of E.T. depicting a space probe landing on a moon of Saturn and accidentally sucking a family of four aliens aboard. On Earth, alien tyke Mac is separated from his parents and moves in with a suburban family. This retread finally comes to life when the aliens are reunited with the help of the earth youngsters but even then the outcome is predictable, since writers Steve Feke and Stewart Raffill (also the director) swipe again from E.T. The Alan Silvestri music is a plus, as is the cast: Christine Ebersole (as the struggling widowed mom), Jonathan Ward, Katrine Caspary. (Orion) (Laser: Image)

MACISTE AGAINST HERCULES IN THE VALE OF WOE. Video version of **HERCULES IN THE VALE OF WOE** (S/Weird).

MACISTE IN HELL (1962). Strongarm fool Kirk Morris can lift lead weights but has trouble lifting a curse off a Scottish village, so he travels to Hell to confront bitch-witch Helene Chanel. This Italian action spectacle (also called THE WITCH'S CURSE) was directed by Riccardo Freda. Vira Silenti, Andrea Bosic, Angelo Zanolli. (Movies Unlimited; Unicorn; Sinister/C)

MACISTE VS. THE VAMPIRES. See **GOLIATH AND THE VAMPIRES.**

MACUMBA LOVE (1960). Voodoo thriller (made in Brazil by producer-director-actor Douglas Fowley) is as topheavy as its two main attractions, June Wilkinson, a buxom blonde with a 44-inch chest. Walter Reed plays a writer exposing withcraft as fakery. Wilkinson went on to pose for Playboy au naturel and Reed retired to Santa Cruz. Also hanging around the edges is Ziva Rodann, who like the well-endowed Wilkinson wears sexy outfits. A lot of snakes, voodoo music and the song "Danse Kalinda." Macumba Dumba Dumba. (S/Weird)

MAD ABOUT MEN (1954). Husky-voiced, musky-mannered Glynis Johns in a dual role—as a young woman and as Miranda the Mermaid. The latter decides to switch places with her human counterpart for a different kind of splash. This British sequel to MIRANDA is aswim with fun and awash in light-heartedness. Directed by Ralph Thomas. Donald Sinden, Margaret Rutherford.

MADAM WHITE SNAKE (1962). See editions 1-3.

MADAME DEATH (1968). John Carradine essays a Dr. Frankenstein-like madman who joins forces with disfigured beauty Regina Torne to perform ungodly operations to make her look good again. Nothing looks good in this Mexican abomination. Directed by Jaime Salvador. Elsa Cardenas, Miguel Angel Alvarez.

MADAME FRANKENSTEIN. See **LADY FRANKENSTEIN.**

MADAME SIN (1971). Robert Wagner was exec producer and star of this TV-movie, with Bette Davis as a female Fu Manchu who plans to conquer the world with financial genius Denholm Elliott. She makes it appear undercover agent Wagner is a defector, and then tricks him into helping her kidnap a naval officer so she can hijack an atomic sub. Unusual downbeat ending. Directed by David Greene in England and Scotland. (CBS/Fox)

MAD AT THE MOON (1991). Ssslllooowww-moving, pretentious werewolf western that doesn't even deliver a werewolf—just a guy with a little hair on his hands and face. In fact, this "supernatural tale of the Old West" directed by Martin Donovan doesn't even have much of the supernatural. What we do have is a frontierswoman with hot pants (Mary Stuart Masterson) getting married to a man for name and prestige when she really loves gunfighter Hart Bochner. A ponderous, pretentious and enigmatic movie. Fionnula Flanagan, Cec Verrell, Stephen Blake. (Video/Laser: Republic)

MAD BUTCHER, THE (1972). Italian black-comedy variation on Sweeney Todd with Victor Buono as Otto Lehman, a crazed Viennese meat-cutter who is released from an asylum to resume his practice . . . of strangling people and grinding them into delicious sausages he sells to the police. Director John (Guido) Zurli goes for laughs with a lilting Viennese waltz in the background. Buono brings a charm to his madman who calmly does his thing while newspaperman Brad Harris and frustrated cop John Ireland try to solve the mystery. There's no blood or gore—the horror underlying this whimsically macabre tale is implied. "Buono appetito!" Karin Field, Carl Stearns. (Magnum; Star Classics; Genesis)

MAD BUTCHER OF VIENNA. See **MAD BUTCHER, THE.**

MADDEST STORY EVER TOLD, THE. See **SPIDER BABY.**

MAD DOCTOR, THE (1941). Psychopathic physician Basil Rathbone knocks off wealthy wives with the help of creepy pal Martin Koslek. We prescribe you watch it. Directed by Tim Whelan. Ellen Drew, John Howard, Ralph Morgan.

MAD DOCTOR OF BLOOD ISLAND (1969). Sanguinary companion to BEAST OF BLOOD (same monster appears in both), shot in the Philippines with John Ashley and Angelique Pettyjohn. A monster of chlorophyll turns green everytime it sees a fresh victim. Directed by Eddie Romero and Gerry DeLeon. Also called TOMB OF THE LIVING DEAD. (Magnum; Regal issued a tape under this title but it's actually **DOUBLE GARDEN, THE**)

MAD DOCTOR OF MARKET STREET, THE (1941). San Franciscans can relax—the main artery of downtown bleeds only slightly in this Universal horror thriller showcasing Lionel Atwill as a scientist who flees the city by the Bay to a tropical island where he holds sway over superstitious natives. A shipwreck survivor arrives to upset his tyranny. Joseph Lewis directed this un-Marketable ugly. Al Martin, Una Merkel, Nat Pendleton.

MADE IN HEAVEN (1987). Poetic, lyrical fantasy that is a hallmark in the career of director Alan Rudolph. This remarkable film touches on human destiny, love at first sight and our purpose for being—without infringing on personal religious concepts. Timothy Hutton is charming as a heroic young man who dies in his prime and finds that Heaven is an idyllic region where there is room for romance and the better emotions of man. He and angel Kelly McGillis fall in love, but she's reincarnated in a new life and Hutton is given 30 years to find her by heavenly boss man Emmett (He is really a she—Debra Winger in disguise.) How McGillis and Hutton live new lives on Earth, and unwittingly search for each other, touches the heartstrings. Maureen Stapleton, Don Murray, Marj Dusay, Ray Gideon, Mare Winningham. Music figures Neil Young, Tom Petty, Tom Robbins do cameos. (Lorimar) (Laser: Image)

MAD EXECUTIONERS, THE (1965). Edgar Wallace mystery set in London (but produced in Germany) depicting axe murders—but at the same time a sex fiend is loose, raping, so Scotland Yard has double trouble: Rape and scrape. Directed by Edward Zbonek. Wolfgang Preiss, Chris Howland. (Sinister/C)

MAD GENIUS, THE (1931). Variation on the Svengali theme: a crippled puppeteer (John Barrymore) maintains strange sway over a young man he turns into a groovy dancer. When the dancer falls in love with Barrymore's secret love, the mesmerist exercises his power to its fullest—ending in an axe murder. Directed by Michael Curtiz. Donald Cook, Marian Marsh, Boris Karloff.

MAD GHOUL, THE (1943). David Bruce is a laughable walking monster when George Zucco (a mad scientist, cackling with sadistic glee) discovers a poisonous vapor that forces Bruce to kill at Zucco's bidding. Robert Armstrong, Evelyn Ankers, Turhan Bey, Milburn Stone and Charles McGraw work hard with the feeble idea. James P. Hogan directed this helping of tasteless ghoulish ghoulash.

MADHOUSE (1972). Sleazy spooker filmed in London (also known as THE REVENGE OF DR. DEATH) about a hammy actor (Vincent Price) suspected of committing gore murders during the filming of a TV series. The climax is so unbelievable and forced even horror fans will wonder what's happening. Made by the kind of mentality that thinks the sight of a spider is the height of horror. Eeeekkkkk! Directed by Jim Clark. Adrienne Corri, Linda Hayden, Robert Quarry, Peter Cushing. (HBO)

MADHOUSE (1983). U.S.-Italian production written-produced-directed by Ovidio G. Assonitis. Psychological thriller about twin sisters who meet after one escapes from an insane asylum. Involved in the gory proceedings: a killer dog, a power drill, rotting corpses and other ingredients designed to soothe your shattered nerves. Trish Everly, Michael Macrae. (VCL; Virgin Vision)

MADHOUSE MANSION (1974). Ghost story in the M. R. James tradition, so damn bloody British that Americans might find it too fey and slow-moving when a sexually repressed young man shows up at a baronial house in the 1920s. He's haunted by a doll that inflicts him with psychic images of a hundred years ago when the mansion was next door to Borden's Insane Asylum and plots were afoot to incarcerate an innocent woman. The minimum gore scenes are forever in coming and one must look for subtleties within the excellent period milieu. Produced-directed by Stephen Weeks at Penhow Castle. Marianne Faithfull, Leigh Lawson, Barbara Shelley. Also called GHOST STORY. (Comet; Cinema Group)

MAD JAKE. Video of **BLOOD SALVAGE** (Malo).

MAD LOVE (1935). Peter Lorre brilliantly conveys madness and compassion as Dr. Gogol in this excellent adaptation of Maurice Renard's THE HANDS OF ORLAC, the story of how the hands of a murderer, recently guillotined, are grafted onto the wrists of a musical pianist whose own hands have been crushed in an accident. Lorre, the surgeon who has a fatal obsession for the lovely star of a Grand Guignol show in Paris, descends ever deeper into madness, yet retains a sense of the pathetic. Karl Freund's direction is ahead of its time for atmosphere and camera angles. Ted Healy is intrusive as a comic-relief reporter but he does not interfere with the scenes between Lorre and the actress (Frances Drake) or the pianist (Colin Clive). Gregg Toland photographed it beautifully and Dimitri Tiomkin wrote the score. Definitely a must see. (MGM/UA)

MAD, MAD MONSTERS (1972). When Baron

Frankenstein holds his wedding at the castle, all monsters are invited in this animated feature for kids. Similar to MAD MONSTER PARTY. (Prism)

MAD MAGICIAN, THE (1954). Inspired by HOUSE OF WAX, this has remained an appreciated thriller in which Vincent Price hams it up as an stage illusionist's assistant who kills his employer and takes his place. John Brahm directed Crane Wilbur's script which features among its death devices a crematorium designed for stage work and a buzz-saw trick that isn't a trick. Patrick O'Neal portrays the hero. Not as good as HOUSE OF WAX but still compelling. Jay Novello, Corey Allen, Eva Gabor, Mary Murphy.

MADMAN (1981). Old "Madman Marz," a farmer who dangled from a rope after murdering his family, is said to prowl the woods at night. Children around the campfire are warned not to speak his name or he may come back to murder again. Sure enough, Marz goes on a marvelous murder march, knocking off the characters of writer-director Joe Giannone as fast as possible. Tony Fish, Alexis Dubin. (HBO)

MAD MAX (1979). Australian landmark film that instigated a new trend in futuristic fantasies set in an anarchistic world of roving warrior bands. Mel Gibson portrays a policeman after industrial collapse who foresakes his badge to pursue cutthroats who wiped out his family. The car chases and crashes are spectacularly staged, establishing a new state-of-the-art for breathless pursuits and grinding collisions. And the brutality is extreme. After MAD MAX, action movies were never the same. The mastermind was George Miller, who co-directed with Gibson. Two wildly successful sequels followed: ROAD WARRIOR and MAD MAX BEYOND THUNDERDOME. (Vestron; Goodtimes) (Laser: Vestron)

MAD MAX II. See **ROAD WARRIOR, THE.**

MAD MAX BEYOND THUNDERDOME (1985). Third action-packed saga in the career of Mad Max, from the rip-roaring imaginations of directors George Miller and George Ogilvie, who give full vent to the fantasy of a post-holocaust world in which a roving warrior (Mel Gibson) fights daily to survive. Max (played with greater sensitivity by Gibson this time) faces Aunty Entity (Tina Turner), dictatorial champion of Bartertown, where he squares off against a brute named Blaster in a gladiatorial arena of bone-cracking action. Ever-changing scenery and creative plot twists keep one enthralled as Max faces not only Thunderdome but a wheel of fortune, a blistering desert crossing, a society of youngsters that keeps old traditions alive, and a climactic train-and-car chase that includes the chief villain (Ironbar, played by Angry Anderson) and the zany pilot Jedediah (Bruce Spence) from the second film. Totally satisfying action-fantasy. (Video/Laser: Warner Bros.)

MADMEN OF MANDORAS. See **THEY SAVED HITLER'S BRAIN.**

MAD MISSION 3 (1984). Rotund Harold Sakata (Oddjob of GOLDFINGER) and Richard Kiel (Jaws of the Bond films) harass a bumbling Japanese agent who is tricked by James Bond and Queen Elizabeth lookalikes to steal the Star of Fortune from a well-guarded security system. Madcap parody, vigorous but dumb, with Peter Graves doing a gag on his own MISSION: IMPOSSIBLE TV series. Directed by Tsui Hark. (HBO)

MAD MONSTER, THE (1942). PRC quickie, directed by Sam Newfield, with scientist George Zucco (what, again?) as a madman mainlining a transfusion of wolf's blood into a farmer's bloodstream. And guess what that turns him into . . . Fangs McDonald. Zucco whips the hairy creation into submission and sends him on errands of revenge. And don't forget a quart of milk on the way home. Rock bottom material, so bad it fascinates. Glenn Strange, who was to play the Frankenstein Monster at Universal, is the wolf creature. Anne Nagel, Johnny Downs, Mae Busch, Sarah Padden. (Video Archive; Loonic; Sinister/C; Nostalgia; Filmfax)

MAD MONSTER PARTY (1967). "Animagic" puppet film blending horror and comedy, the scenario by Ken Korobkin and Harvey Kurtzman, the latter the creator of Mad Magazine. The puppet characters are a melange of cinema monstrosities: Frankenstein Monster, Dracula, Wolfman, the Creature, Dr. Jekyll and Mr. Hyde, the Mummy and the Hunchback of Notre Dame. Boris Karloff provides the Baron's voice. Enchanting. Directed with style by Jules Bass. (Embassy; RCA/Columbia)

MADONNA OF THE SEVEN MOONS. See editions 1-3.

MAD PLUMBER, THE. Video version of **PLUMBLER, THE.**

MAFU CAGE, THE. Video version of **MY SISTER, MY LOVE.**

MAGIC (1978). Low-key version of William Goldman's novel depicting a demented ventriloquist whose dummy Fats overpowers his personality. The slasher aspects are minimized as director Richard Attenborough focuses on the warped character of Anthony Hopkins. Ann-Margret delivers a laid-back performance as a childhood sweetheart whom Hopkins returns to during his descent into madness. Goldman adapted from his own novel. Ed Lauter, Burgess Meredith. (Video/Laser: Nelson)

MAGIC CARPET, THE (1951). See editions 1-3.

MAGIC CHRISTIAN, THE (1969). Hodgepodge of non sequiturs, with Peter Sellers as a millionaire traveling the world to prove everyone has a price (even Vincent). Some sequences are surrealistic; some designed for sight gags; some relate to nothing in the universe. Despite madcap images (Raquel Welch whipping slaves, Christopher Lee spoofing Dracula, Laurence Harvey stripping, Yul Brynner going drag), the cast cannot make this adaptation of Terry Southern's novel magically. Directed by Joseph McGrath. Ringo Starr, Wilfrid Hyde-White, Richard Attenborough, Roman Polanski, John Cleese. (Video/Laser: Republic)

MAGIC CHRISTMAS TREE, THE (1985). Seasonal fairy tale featuring Santa and other holiday fare in a fantasy framework. Directed by Richard C. Parish. Chris Kroegen, Charles Nix, Terry Bradshaw. (VCI; United)

MAGIC FACE, THE (1952). See editions 1-3.

MAGIC FOUNTAIN, THE (1961). See editions 1-3.

MAGICIAN, THE (1926). Silent mini-classic directed-written by Rex Ingram is based on a Somerset Maugham novel and was inspired by the career of Aleister Crowley. Mad magician Paul Wegener prepares Alice Terry for a transfusion to create a new life force. Comes complete with hump-backed assistant.

MAGICIAN, THE (1958). Genuinely chilling moments dominate this Swedish mystery from Ingmar Bergman about a mesmerizing legerdemain expert who travels the countryside, claiming ESP powers. It's a dark mood that Bergman projects, and he does it brilliantly. Ingrid Thulin, Bibi Andersson, Max von Sydow. (Video/Laser: Nelson)

MAGICIAN OF LUBLIN, THE (1978). Fascinating portrait of a Jewish entertainer who rises to the top of Warsaw society as a magician/escape artist, then throws it all away to greed, ego and lust. Alan Arkin's portrayal is unusually anachronistic for a turn-of-the-century drama, but the German locations, period costumes and co-performances (Louise Fletcher, Valerie Perrine, Lou Jacobi, Shelley Winters) make it work. Yasha (the magician) believes he can fly and this fantasy element provides this adaptation of Isaac Bashevis Singer's "The Magician" with some startling moments and a supernatural climax. Directed by Menahen Golan. (HBO/Cannon)

MAGIC MOMENTS (1989). Harlequin Romance TV-movie has a compelling premise: stage illusionist/escape artist John Shea uses trickery to lure TV producer Jenn Seagrave into his romance trap. Or is he using the supernatural? Shea is a compelling screen presence, whose mere glance is erotic, and Seagrave too vulnerable to resist, so there are no surprises. In fact, a shortage of conflict hampers what could have been a neat twist. Directed by Lawrence Gordon Clark.

MAGIC SERPENT (1966). Japanese fairy tale: Heroic

young man searches for the murderer of his father, a wicked wizard. When he finds the sorcerer, the dude turns into a dragon, so the young man turns into a king-size frog. Directed by Tetsuya Yamauchi. Also called GRAND DUEL IN MAGIC. (S/Weird)

MAGIC SNOWMAN, THE (1987). Yugoslav children's fantasy focusing on a fisherman's young son who talks to Lumi-Oku, a spirit that takes the form of a snowman (voice by Roger Moore). The plot is episodic, dealing with the boy's problems with an evil fishing captain, a pair of skates needed for an upcoming race, and an accident and rescue on thin ice. Adults will find the whole affair thin ice. Directed by C. Stanner. Joshi Fried, Jack Aronson.

MAGIC SWORD, THE (1962). Bert I. Gordon fantasy-adventure yarn for the young set, based on the St. George-Dragon legend. Basil Rathbone is a chilly sorcerer, Estelle Winwood a maladroit witch, Gary Lockwood the heroic St. George, Anne Helm the fair Helene. Also on hand: an ogre, a bubbling pond that dissolves flesh, a French shepherdess who turns hag, and assorted magic. Above average, capturing the quality of a rousing fairy tale. Richard Kiel is a giant. (Sinister/C; S/Weird; Video Yesteryear; MGM/UA; Filmfax)

MAGIC TOYSHOP, THE (1986). This British adaptation of Angela Carter's maturation novel is for a specialized audience appreciative of the Englishness of its idiocyrancies; its ethereal attitude and nonsensational approach may leave some fans cold. Hence, this film requires you to bring much of your own childhood to its theme so you can relate to Melanie, 15, who is sent to London to live with an uncle after her parents are killed. The uncle (who has a supernatural power to make toys move) maintains a dictatorial spell over his family and begins a metaphorical rape of Melanie. The characters are warm except for the uncle, essayed with brooding psychosis by Tom Bell. Carter adapted her own novel without making it mawkish. There's always a hard edge to this urban fairy tale. Caroline Milmoe, Kilian McKenna. Directed by David Wheatley.

MAGIC VOYAGE OF SINBAD (1953). This is a Soviet version of an ancient legend, which leads one to suspect the Sinbad title was capitalistic exploitation for the U.S. version. Whatever . . . an adventurous wanderer seeks the Bird of Happiness with an underwater maiden. Directed by Alexander Ptushko . . . for the U.S. edition, new scenes were shot by James Landis and written by Francis Ford Coppola. (Sinister/C; S/Weird)

MAGIC WORLD OF TOPO GIGIO, THE (1961). See editions 1-3.

MAGNETIC MONSTER, THE (1953). Producer Ivan Tors and director Curt Siodmak teamed to write this low budgeter dealing with sci-fi theories difficult to depict—which makes this more oriented to ideas than visuals. The "monster" is a new isotope sucking up energy and giving off radiation as it grows in size. The good cast makes up for the intangible "monster": Richard Carlson, King Donovan, Strother Martin. (Monterey)

MAGNETIC MOON (1954). Unattracting viewing. See **ROCKY JONES, SPACE RANGER.**

MAGNIFICENT MAGICAL MAGNET OF SANTA MESA (1977). Lighthearted, innocuous David Gerber TV-movie starring Michael Burns as a wimpy inventor who discovers a magnetic force-field that could revolutionize the face of modern industry. Only Burns' boss, Mr. Undershaft, and devious millionaire Harry Morgan plan to steal the formula and reap a greedy harvest. On the level of a sitcom, with little attraction or pull. Watch for Loni Anderson in a minor secretarial role. Directed by Hy Averback. Susan Blanchard, Tom Poston.

MAGNIFICENT MS (1979). See third edition.

MAGUS, THE (1969). Bewildering adaptation of a John Fowles novel, its ending as ambiguous as its story. Anthony Quinn is the magus (magician) on a Greek island where Michael Caine teaches. Caine is enmeshed in a maze of role-playing games involving Quinn and the mysterious Candice Bergen. There are plots within plots and a World War II flashback involving betrayal and heroism. Under Guy Green's direction, a psychic journey into the peculiar patterns of the mind. Certain to be too abstract and complex for viewers seeking pat solutions. Anna Karina, Julian Glover, Corin Redgrave.

MAIDENQUEST. Video version of **LONG, SWIFT SWORD OF SIEGFRIED, THE.**

MAID TO ORDER (1987). Get past an awkward beginning, and a clumsy Cinderella premise, and this evolves into a funny, warm comedy that takes satirical jabs at Hollywood. Beverly Hills philanthropist Tom Skerritt, angry at spoiled daughter Ally Sheedy, wishes her out of his life—a wish Good Fairy Beverly D'Angelo grants him. Homeless, Sheedy takes a job as a housecleaner with a wealthy Malibu Beach family. Director Amy Jones balances the hokiness with amusing characters: Dick Shawn's music entrepreneur, Valerie Perrine's whacky Lotusland wife, Michael Ontkean's chauffeur and Merry Clayton's maid. (Video/Laser: IVE)

MAIN STREET KID, THE (1948). See editions 1-3.

MAJIN, MONSTER OF TERROR (1966). Well produced Japanese supernatural actioner with fine destruction effects when a legendary "golem" of Asia (a stone statue imbued with a warrior's spirit) comes to life for revenge against an evil chamberlain. Before the rampage, when villains are crushed underfoot or swallowed up by gaping holes in the earth, the film is a Samurai warrior saga with ample sword action. Directed by Kimiyoshi Yasuda. Follow-ups were THE RETURN OF GIANT MAJIN and MAJIN STRIKES AGAIN. (S/Weird)

MAJIN II. See **THE RETURN OF GIANT MAJIN.**

MAJIN STRIKES AGAIN (1966). You've heard of rock 'n roll idols—here's a rock idol who rolls with the punches when fighting evil. Yes, it's Rock Head himself, that legendary warrior statue imbued with a soul who does for the Japanese what the Golem did for the Hebrews in this third entry in Japan's Majin series. Directed by Issei Mori and Yoshiyuki Kuroda. See MAJIN, MONSTER OF TERROR and the sequel, RETURN OF GIANT MAJIN, to find out you can't keep a stoned guy down.

MAJIN, THE HIDEOUS IDOL. See **MAJIN, MONSTER OF TERROR.** (Majin Japan!)

MAJORETTES, THE (1987). John Russo, co-writer of NIGHT OF THE LIVING DEAD with George Romero, scripted this variation on the slasher theme (also known as ONE BY ONE) with a "broad" mixture of uncovered breasts and sliced up body organs in depicting the slaughter of cheerleaders by a maniac killer. Directed by Bill Hinzman. Kevin Kindlin, Terrie Godfrey. (Vestron)

MAKE THEM DIE SLOWLY (1983). Italian cannibal shocker stars Lorainne de Selle as an anthropologist who wants to prove that cannibalism doesn't exist and goes to South America. She's wrong—or there wouldn't be a movie. One stomach-churning atrocity after another as members of her expedition are put to death. The most appalling device is a head-holder which allows a machette-wielding native to slice off a scalp and pluck out the brains for a feast. Allegedly banned in 31 countries, but don't believe it. Written-directed by Umberto Lenzi. John Morghen, Robert Kerman. Aka CANNIBAL FEROX. (Thrillervideo without Elvira)

MAKING CONTACT (1986). Well-produced, well-directed fantasy from German filmmaker Roland Emmerich is filled with Spielbergisms: the weird lights and moving toys of CLOSE ENCOUNTERS, the telepathy and scientific teams of E. T., the supernatural voice from beyond on the phone of POLTERGEIST, etc. Joshua Morrell, after his father's death, makes contact with a voice that turns out to be that of a turn-of-the-century magician, represented by a devil doll. MAKING CONTACT never connects. Tammy Shields, Eva Kryll. (New World)

MAKING MR. RIGHT (1987). Well-intended but tedious fantasy-comedy in which nerdy professor John Malkovitch creates android Ulysses in his own image for Chemtec Corporation. When PR expert Ann Magnuson is called in to hype him, she teaches the naive robot the art of romance—causing him to short circuit. This tries to make comments about love, loneliness and the human condition, but it's full of dumb humor (mistaken identities, people falling into swimming pools) that leaves director Susan Seidelman with Mr. Wrong. Polly Bergen, Ben Masters. (Video/Laser: HBO)

MAKO: THE JAWS OF DEATH (1976). Sonny Stein (Richard Jaeckel) makes friends with killer Mako sharks and learns to communicate. When the sharks are borrowed by marine biologists for experiments, they turn into killers. Produced-directed by William Grefe. Jennifer Bishop, Harold Sakata, John Davis Chandler. (Video Media; from United American as **JAWS OF DEATH**)

MALATESTA'S CARNIVAL OF BLOOD (1973). Horror thriller with Herve Villechaize (destined for FANTASY ISLAND) involved in an unsavory plot of murder, gore and cannibalism. Written-directed by Christopher Speeth. Janine Carazo, Jerome Dempsey, William Preston.

MALENKA THE VAMPIRE. See **FANGS OF THE LIVING DEAD.**

MALPAS MYSTERY, THE (1960). British adaptation of Edgar Wallace's FACE IN THE NIGHT, in which a murderer without a face terrorizes Maureen Swanson, Allan Cuthbertson and Geoffrey Keene in the traditions of "the old dark house." Directed by Sidney Hayers.

MALTESE BIPPY, THE (1969). Made at the height of the popularity of TV's LAUGH IN, this is an awful vehicle for Dan Rowan and Dick Martin. Norman Panama is responsible for writing-directing this outrageous turkey, which depicts the boys as witless wonders exchanging dumb banter as they enter a Yonkers house haunted by werewolves from next door. Julie Newman, Fritz Weaver, Dana Elcar, Carol Lynley, Robert Reed. This was a bomb so SON OF THE MALTESE BIPPY was abandoned. Thank your lucky bippy.

MAMBA. See **FAIR GAME.**

MAMMA DRACULA (1980). French-Belgian effort with Louise Fletcher as a vampire (unaffected by daylight or religious symbols) who must periodically bathe in the blood of virgins. But did you know there's a short supply? Society is so perverted, you see. Maria Schneider portrays a policewoman and the whole thing, as the title indicates, is played for broad farce by farcical broads. Directed by Boris Szulzinger. Jimmy Shuman, Alexander Wajnberg. (Trans World; RCA/Columbia)

MAN ALIVE (1945). See editions 1-3.

MAN AND THE MONSTER, THE (1958). Second-rate pianist with a nagging mother ("Your mind is gone, son!") sells his soul to the Devil in exchange for brilliance, but finds that everytime he plays, he turns into a cheap version of the Wolfman. Call it long-hair music. This Mexican thriller is a non-chiller with its turgid dialogue by producer-leading man Abel Salazar. As the evil pianist, Salazar gives a grind-tuned performance. Directed by Raphael Baledon. Repackaged across the border by infamous schlock packager K. Gordon Murray. (Sinister/C; S/Weird; Filmfax)

MAN BEAST (1956). The worst is Yeti to come. A search for the Abominable Snowmen leads an expedition into the mountains of Tibet, unaware that the high-altitude creatures are luring good-looking women into the snow country to improve the breeding stock. Sex in a snowdrift? And who the devil is Rock Madison, the man in the monster suit? More cheap thrills from producer-director Jerry Warren. Virginia Maynor, George Skaff. (Rhino; Nostalgia; S/Weird; Filmfax)

MANBEAST! MYTH OR MONSTER (1978). Hammy TV pseudodocumentary purports the existence of the Yeti and Bigfoot with footage shot in exotic locations, including restaged shots. Hardly the final word in scientific investigation, but interesting speculation when the hokum doesn't overpower heavy-footed writer-director Nicholas Webster. Rob Bottin effects.

MAN CALLED DAGGER, A (1967). Laszlo Kovacs' cinematography is the highlight of this Bond imitation superspy thriller directed by Richard Rush in which secret agent Dick Dagger (Paul Mantee) prevents a wheelchair-bound former Nazi (Jan Murray) from taking over the world with a mind-conquering gadget. Dagger's girl is Terry Moore and Sue Ane Langdon is Murray's sexy mistress. Richard Kiel has a "giant" role.

MAN CALLED FLINTSTONE, THE (1966). Theatrical version of Hanna-Barbera's animated TV series is for young adults. It has the voices of Alan Reed, Mel Blanc, Gerry Johnson and Jean Vanderpyl, and a storyline that satirizes James Bond movies. Fred Flintstone, the cave dweller, looks just like Secret Agent Rock Slag, so old Fred is up against the Green Goose, insidious leader of S.M.I.R.K. (Hanna/Barbera) (Laser: Image)

MAN CALLED SLOANE, A. See **T. R. SLOANE.**

MANCHURIAN CANDIDATE, THE (1962). One might interpret that the intriguing premise to this Howard Koch production—Communists brainwash a loyal American and turn him into an assassin—came true when Lee Harvey Oswald assassinated John F. Kennedy. George Axelrod's adaptation of Richard Condon's novel will have you outraged and entertained as it depicts Laurence Harvey as a brainwashed GI conditioned to murder—and the murder is to be a U.S. candidate for the presidency. Audacious theme is handled brilliantly by director John Frankenheimer, even if it defies credulity. Frank Sinatra, Janet Leigh, Angela Lansbury, James Gregory, Henry Silva, Leslie Parrish, John McGiver, Whit Bissell, James Edwards. (Video/Laser: MGM/UA)

FRANK SINATRA

MANDINGO MANHUNTER. Video version of **MAN HUNTER** (Wizard).

MANDRAKE (1978). TV-movie version of the comic strip magician created by writer Lee Falk and artist Phil Davis. This routine TV-pilot has Mandrake (Anthony Herrera in black costumes), who works for the government, called in to pull something out of his sleeve to solve why explosions are being set off by people programmed to act on post-hypnotic suggestions. Mandrake's comrade-in-arms is jungle prince Lothar (Ji-Tu Cumbuka), but he's given too little to do by writer-producer Rick Husky. Mandrake also has a talisman which gives him his magical powers of thought projection. Directed by Harry Falk. Harry Blackstone Jr. plays a scientist.

MANDROID (1993). On-location filming in Romania enhances this above-average Charles Band/Full Moon production, in which a Supercon plant-spore process leads to the creation of a metal warrior piloted by a human soul. The Earl Kenton-Jackson Barr screenplay focuses on the intrigue surrounding the selling of Mandroid to the West and the attempts by the Russians to wrest it away. There's plenty of action and special effects as the parties outfox each other and as Mandroid gets into the fray. Well directed by Jack Ersgard, whose brother Patrick Ersgard portrays an Interpol agent in need of a shave. Brian Cousins, Jane Caldwell, Michael Dellafemina, Curt Lowens. (Paramount)

MAN EATER. See **GRIM REAPER, THE.**

MAN-EATER OF HYDRA (1966). "My beauties," chortles insane baron Cameron Mitchell to mutant plants—carnivorous cactii, fiendish fronds and terror tendrils. And the crazy count loves earthworms! A collection of upper-crust Europeans, gathered at his estate, are murdered one by one by an unseen presence while the baron blithely shows off his cross between a Venus Flytrap and a Century Plant. Beg pardon, sire, but something in the garden is eating the guests. Spanish-German production is crudely photographed and acted, and plays almost like a stereotyped whodunit, yet has a compulsion in the way the decadent characters behave, setting themselves up for the slurping green creepers and wriggling branches. Also known as BLOODSUCKERS, ISLAND OF THE DEAD, DEATH ISLAND and ISLAND OF THE DOOMED. Directed by Mel Welles.

MAN FACING SOUTHEAST (1986). Allegorical film from Buenos Aires depicts what happens at a mental institution when a man shows up, claiming to be an alien. Directed by Eliseo Subiela. Lorenzo Quinteros, Hugo Soto. (New World)

MANFISH (1956). Colorful tale in which adventurers John Bromfield, Victor Jory and Lon Chaney Jr. sail the South Seas in search of treasure and other action-packed quests. Said to be based on Edgar Allan Poe's TELL-TALE HEART and THE GOLD BUG, although the adaptation is loose. Produced-directed by W. Lee Wilder. Barbara Nichols. (S/Weird; Sinister/C; Nostalgia)

MAN FROM ATLANTIS, THE (1977). Two-hour pilot for a short-term series with Patrick Duffy (DALLAS) as a young man equipped with gills, webbed hands and feet. In this origin yarn, directed by Lee H. Katzin, Duffy (as an extraterrestrial known as "Mark Harris") washes up on a beach and is rushed to a Navy hospital. Once the military knows his capabilities, he is assigned to find a sunken submarine. Belinda Montgomery portrays Duffy's assistant; Victor Buono is the villain always trying to destroy Duffy. Lawrence Pressman, Dean Santoro. (Goodtimes; Worldvision)

MAN FROM PLANET X, THE (1951). Scientist Raymond Bond informs newspaperman Robert Clarke a new planet is headed toward Earth . . . sure enough, on a foggy moor in Scotland, a spaceship lands to spearhead an invasion. The twist here is that a human, for his own evil ends, captures the bubble-headed alien and tortures it for information. This sci-fier was directed in only a week by Edgar G. Ulmer. The script by producers Aubrey Wisberg and Jack Pollexfen is unusual. Margaret Field, William Schallert, Roy Engel, Charles Davis.

MAN FROM S.E.X., THE (1983). British-produced James Bond spoof from producer Lindsay Shonteff, starring Gareth Hunt as Charles Bind, a supersecret agent dispatched by boss Geoffrey Keen to America to fetch a missing lord. Hunt comes up against supervillain Senator Lucifer Orchid (Gary Hope) who is manufacturing human clones and substituting them in high positions. Comic-book action farce. Nick Tate, Fiona Curzon. (Catalina)

MAN FROM THE FIRST CENTURY. See **MAN IN OUTER SPACE.**

MAN FROM THE PAST, THE. See **MAN IN OUTER SPACE.**

MAN FROM YESTERDAY (1949). Editions 1-3.

MANHATTAN BABY (1984). Ancient Egyptian curse turns archeologist Christopher Connelly blind and gives his daughter ESP. Italian film made in New York/Egypt by Lucio Fulci. Also known as EYE OF THE EVIL DEAD. Martha Taylor, Brigitta Boccolli. (Lightning)

MAN HUNTER, THE (1980). Italian-Spanish-West German co-production belongs to the school of cannibal thrillers and was directed by Jesus Franco (as Clifford Brown) without many redeeming social values. The plot has movie starlet Ursula Fellner kidnapped by a gang of freaks and involved with a cannibal tribe. Al Cliver, Ursula Fellner. (Trans World; from Wizard as **MANDINGO MANHUNTER**)

MANHUNTER (1986). Offbeat crime thriller with baffling twists, based on Thomas Harris' RED DRAGON, the book that introduces Hannibal (Cannibal) Lecter, who figured more prominently in THE SILENCE OF THE LAMBS. Retired FBI operative William Petersen has the psychic ability to enter the minds (or dreams) of the serial killers he pursues. He's brought back by his former chief Dennis Farina to pursue a madman (known as "The Tooth Fairy") who is slaughtering entire families. Director Michael Mann gives this the glitz and pop appeal of a MIAMI VICE episode, and further enhances it with startling violence and death. Kim Greist, Brian Cox. (Karl/Lorimar) (Laser: Karl/Lorimar; Warner Bros.)

MANHUNT IN SPACE (1954). See **ROCKY JONES, SPACE RANGER** (Sinister/C; S/Weird; Filmfax).

MANHUNT IN THE AFRICAN JUNGLE (1943). Originally made as SECRET SERVICE IN DARKEST AFRICA, this superb Republic serial is nonstop action featuring great choreographed fights. Cliffhanging situations, skullduggery among spies, death ray beams, wonder drugs, a forged legendary scroll and the Dagger of Solomon are among its rousing ingredients. Rod Cameron is heroic Rex Bennett, undercover man who infiltrates the Gestapo. This is said to be the serial that inspired Steven Spielberg to create Indiana Jones. Directed by Spencer Bennet. Joan Marsh, Duncan Renaldo, Kurt Kreuger. The sequel was **G-MEN VS. THE BLACK DRAGON** with Cameron returning. The feature TV version is THE BARON'S AFRICAN WAR. (Video/Laser: Republic)

MANHUNT OF MYSTERY ISLAND (1945). Outstanding 15-chapter Republic serial with Roy Barcroft as a bloodthirsty buccaneer who uses a zingy electric chair (the Atomic Power Transmitter) to change into one of four owners of Mystery Island—but which one? Guessing Captain Mephisto's true identity is but one fun element of this wonderful serial. Linda Stirling, queen of the cliffhangers, and Richard Bailey, a square-jawed hero, search for her kidnapped father (a scientist with a Death Ray Machine) and fight Mephisto's pirate gang led by Kenne Duncan. Plenty of chuckles and thrills, and some of the finest speedboat chases and fistfights ever staged by the studio. Barcroft, Republic's ubiquitous villain, is superb in the role of Captain Mephisto. Directed with flair by stunt specialist Yakima Canutt, Spencer Bennet and Wallace Brissell. The shortened TV version is CAPTAIN MEPHISTO AND THE TRANSFORMATION MACHINE. (Republic; Nostalgia Merchant) (Laser: Republic)

ROY BARCROFT

MANIA (1960). Video of **FLESH AND THE FIENDS** (United American; Sinister/C; S/Weird; Filmfax).

MANIAC (1934). Crude exploitationer of the 1930s, fascinating for its insight into how schlock producers of the period pandered to unsophisticated audiences. This defied the movieland moralists to become an X-rated product in defiance of existing levels of taste and decency. Producer Dwain Esper, heralded as the first of grade-Z movie-makers, passed off this trash under the guise of mental health education in drawing pseudoparallels between criminal behavior and manias. Dreary story has a mad doctor discovering a life-restoring serum and with his crazed assistant stealing a woman's corpse. Women bare their breasts and thighs, a cat's plucked-out eyeball is devoured by the doc and a body is entombed with a black cat a la Poe. The forerunner of bargain-basement sleaze, unforgettable in its ineptitude. Any self-respecting schlock watcher must see this. (Video Yesteryear; Video Dimensions; Sinister/C)

MANIAC (1963). Hammer psychothriller has several plot twists as Kerwin Mathews, an artist living in France, is pursued by his girlfriend's husband and faces death by blowtorch. Startlingly good shocker in the Hitchcock tradition, directed by Michael Carreras and written by producer Jimmy Sangster. Nadia Gray, Donald Houston, Justine Lord. (RCA/Columbia)

MANIAC (1980). Penultimate "sicko" movie about a depraved murderer with a mother fixation who scalps his victims and nails their hair onto mannikins. Makeup specialist Tom Savini lets the blood flow from severed throats, decapitated heads and body cavities as psychokiller Frank Zito (Joe Spinell) kills with knives, shotgun, garroting wire and other delicate instruments. This movie sinks pretty low in its exploitation of schizophrenic, psychopathic bloodletting: it is so obsessed with scenes of death that director William Lustig doesn't even bother to titillate us with nudity when he has ample opportunity. Caroline Munro appears as a curvaceous fashion photographer. The killer rattles on with a stream-of-consciousness dialogue, but there is no insight into a fiendish sex murderer. This is ultimately more sickening for what it implies than what it graphically depicts. Gail Lawrence, Kelly Piper. (Media)

MANIAC COP (1988). Lively psychokiller flick, inspired a little by THE PHANTOM OF THE OPERA in depicting the murder spree of a crazy cop terrorizing a city. He was once a good cop who was wronged by the department, sent to Sing Sing and murdered by inmates. However, he returns from the dead with a vengeance, murdering with a long knife built into his night stick. Despite plot holes and deck stacking, producer Larry Cohen's script is full of twists, and director William Lustig keeps the action moving. Bruce Campbell is a cop accused of the crimes, Laurene Landon is a cop in love with Campbell; Richard Roundtree is a dense-headed commissioner, William Smith is bald cop Captain Ripley, Sheree North is a cripple with an odd relationship with Maniac Cop, and Robert Z'Dar is the uniformed fruitcake. (RCA/Columbia; Star Classics)

MANIAC COP 2 (1990). Effective sequel brings back dead policeman Matt Cordell (Robert Z'Dar) as a supernatural entity who perversely keeps turning up at crime scenes to aid the criminal, not the victim. Producer-writer Larry Cohen demonstrates a knack for blending cops-and-robbers action with slasher-horror elements and director William Lustig brings a noir style to the revengeful mayhem. The car chase material and action sequences are spectacular, culminating in an exciting incident in Sing Sing. An amusing "skat" song has Maniac Cop proclaiming: "You have the right to remain silent . . . forever!" Robert Davi, Claudia Christian, Michael Lerner, Bruce Campbell, Laurene Landon, Clarence Williams III, Charles Napier. (Live) (Laser: Image)

MANIAC COP 3: BADGE OF SILENCE (1992). Another energetic, violence-prone study in mayhem from beyond the grave when that dead cop Matt Cordell is resurrected by voodoo magic on the day of his funeral and returns with a new vengeance to get even again. Robert Z'Dar is back as Cordell with a messed-up, rotting face, and Robert Davi is good cop Sean McKinney, trying to protect a female cop who's been shot and is bordering on death. Co-producer Larry Cohen's script is an imaginative array of action set pieces, concluding with a great ambulance-car chase with Cordell's body engulfed in flames behind the wheel. Directed by William Lustig and Joel Soisson. Caitlin Dulany, Gretchen Becker.

MANIAC MANSION. See **AMUCK.**

MANIACS ARE LOOSE, THE. See **THRILL KILLERS, THE.**

MANIAC WARRIORS. Video version of **EMPIRE OF ASH II** (AIP).

MANIKA: THE GIRL WHO LIVED TWICE (1989). Young Ayesha Dharker, growing up in an Indian fishing village, believes she has lived before and teacher Julian Sands helps her resolve her dilemma. France-Swiss flick, made in Sri Lanka and Nepal, was directed by Francois Villliers. Suresh Uberoi, Stephane Audran.

MAN IN BLACK, THE (1950). See editions 1-3.

MAN IN HALF MOON STREET, THE (1944). Miklos Rozsa's music graces this "mad scientist" thriller in which 120-year-old scientist Nils Asther needs new glands to stay young and in love. Based on a play by Barre Lyndon, later remade as THE MAN WHO COULD CHEAT DEATH. Directed by Ralph M. Murphy. Helen Walker, Brandon Hurst, Paul Cavanaugh.

MAN IN OUTER SPACE (1961). Czech sci-fi satire about a workman accidentally sent into the galaxies where he meets an alien capable of invisibility. They return to Earth in 2447 to engage in comedic situations. Directed-written by Oldrich Lipsky. Milos Kopecky, Radovan Lukavsky. Aka THE MAN FROM THE FIRST CENTURY and THE MAN FROM THE PAST.

MAN IN THE ATTIC (1953). Twentieth Century-Fox's low-budget remake of its excellent 1944 production THE LODGER is still a good film thanks to Jack Palance, whose face is a mask of evil as he captures the sympathetic, horrific aspects of Mr. Slade, a pathologist whose psychosis is explained by a mother fixation. Made before graphic screen gore and violence, the film's power is in performance, costuming, Victorian sets and Hugo Fregonese's direction. Constance Smith, Byron Palmer, Frances Bavier, Rhys Williams, Lillian Bond.

MAN IN THE BACK SEAT, THE (1961). See editions 1-3.

MAN IN THE DARK (1953). Routine crime melodrama hyped by fantastic overtones (criminal Edmond O'Brien undergoes a brain operation that erases his underworld tendencies) was an early 3-D film experimenting with roller coaster rides, doctors' scalpels and objects designed "to leap into your lap" in stereovision. O'Brien can't remember where he stashed $130,000 while the audience ducks flying glass and hurtling automobiles. Audrey Totter, Ted De Corsia, Horace McMahon. Directed by Lew Landers. A remake of 1936's THE MAN WHO LIVED TWICE.

MAN IN THE MIRROR (1937). See editions 1-3.

MAN IN THE MOON (1961). Modest British comedy, directed by Basil Dearden, is quaint in its foolishness and unpretentious in its satire. Kenneth More is William Blood, guinea pig for tests on the common cold. He's trained for a mission into space—mainly to pave the way for more valuable astronauts. Droll and delightful, with Shirley Anne Field (a tasty distraction in low-cut evening dress and feathery boa) in the role of a stripteaser who lures More into her own cosmos. Michael Hordern, Noel Purcell, Charles Gray.

MAN IN THE SANTA CLAUS SUIT, THE (1979). Seasonal TV-movie with a yuletide warmth. Fred Astaire is an elfin character in a dozen roles (chauffeur, cabbie, hot dog salesman, on and on) but mainly runs a costume shop. Each customer who dons his Santa suit undergoes a crisis. Zany pacing keeps this moving as if Donner and Blitzen were yanking the team. Among the likeable people: a destitute restaurateur (John Byner) pursued by gangsters, an unhappily married senator's aide (Bert Convy) and Gary Burghoff as a nerd trying to land a beautiful model. Nanette Fabray and Harold Gould are memorable as a couple re-enacting their old vaudeville routines. Directed by Corey Allen. (Media)

MAN IN THE TRUNK, THE (1942). Editions 1-3.

MAN IN THE WHITE SUIT, THE (1952). Rollicking, irreverent satire on British big business and labor. Research chemist Alec Guinness discovers, in his bubbling laboratory, a formula for indestructible suit fabric. He's hailed, then hated when it dawns on England's textile industry that this discovery could put it out of business. Directed by Alexander Mackendrick. Joan Greenwood, Michael Gough, Ernest Thesiger, Cecil Parker. (HBO)

MANIPULATOR, THE (1971). Mickey Rooney has a powerful range, but not even he can carry this avant garde study in psychological disintegration. Using distorted camera angles to capture bewilderment, this experiment in madness (also known as B. J. LANG PRESENTS) is set in a loft of props and mannikins, where Rooney imagines he is directing movies in 1947. His captive audience is actress Luana Anders tied to a chair. Lang imagines all kinds of oddball scenes, allowing director-writer Yabo Yablonsky to escape total claustrophobia with crowds of weirdo people at orgies and hippie parties. (The only other character is a janitor played by Keenan Wynn.) It's like a dream, enhanced by slow motion and other tricks, but what could have been a tour de force becomes overindulgence. Co-produced by Burt Sugarman. (Vestron)

MANIPULATOR, THE (1980). A production crew is making a horror movie when suddenly the killers in it are real murderers for a "snuff" film. Written-directed by Dusty Nelson. Gore effects by Tom Savini. Aka DEATH'S DIRECTORS and EFFECTS. John Harrison, Susan Chapek.

MANITOU, THE (1978). A 400-year-old Indian medicine man spirit, Misquamacus, is reborn in the body of Susan Strasberg and bursts from her back in a harrowing birth sequence. Sound absurd? It is, and yet this adaptation of Graham Masterson's novel (directed by William Girdler, who co-wrote with Jon Cedar) transcends its own ridiculousness by virtue of its cinematic power. Mechanical effects by Gene Grigg and Tim Smythe and horrific make-up by Tom Burman are superb and will have your own skin crawling. Also a far-out special effects ending by Dalt Tate and Frank Van Der Veer. Tony Curtis as a charlatan mystic heads the cast: Ann Sothern, Stella Stevens, Paul Mantee, Michael Ansara (as exorcist Indian Singing Rock) and Burgess Meredith. (CBS/Fox; Charter) (Laser: Nelson)

MAN MADE MONSTER (1942). Excellent effects and Jack Pierce's make-up lend class to this B production from Universal which was Lon Chaney Jr's first monster role. Sole survivor of a bus crash, he emerges an anomaly of glowing electricity. He joins a carnival as Dynamo Dan the Electrical Man and is experimented on by evil Dr. Rigas (Lionel Atwill) who foresees a race of walking electric men, their mere touch lethal. Deemed a killer, Chaney is sent to the electric chair, but all that does is add to the glow in his cheeks. The sympathetic, misunderstood monster finally goes berserk and decides to light up everyone's life. A "shocking" ending. Directed by George Waggner. Originally released to theaters as THE ATOMIC MONSTER. Anne Nagel, Frank Albertson.

MANNEQUIN (1987). Okay comedy about mannequin maker Andrew McCarthy who brings to life one of his creations (imbued with the spirit of a long-dead Egyptian princess). Romantic comedy is strained at times, but there's a light-hearted spirit that prevails. Kim Cattrall, Estelle Getty, G. W. Bailey, James Spader. Written-directed by Michael Gottlieb. (Media) (Laser: Image)

MANNEQUIN TWO: ON THE MOVE (1991). This sequel to MANNEQUIN has its moments of humor, mostly provided by Meshach Taylor's faggish department store decorator. This time the mannequin that comes to life is the Enchanted Peasant Girl, a 1000-year-old citizen cursed into a state of rigidity by an evil necklace until she finds a lover. That occurs when she meets William Ragsdale in a department store, and the buffoonery is on as she learns the ways of the U.S. while eluding an evil Prime Minister. Kristy Swanson as the mannequin/live girl is gorgeous and showing off her wondeful figure and sparkling personality makes up for many story deficiencies. Directing pro Stewart Raffill makes it look better than it is as Terry Kiser, Stuart Pankin and Cynthia Harris go for the strained yocks. (Video/Laser: Live)

MAN OF A THOUSAND FACES (1957). Universal's biography of Lon Chaney Sr., the pliable actor who specialized in grotesque monster roles during the Silent Era. As a melodrama about Chaney's marital strife it's on the hokey side, but the studio atmosphere and re-created scenes from Chaney's classics are ably captured by director Joseph Pevney. James Cagney is a feisty, memorable Chaney, Dorothy Malone and Jane Greer provide teary love interest, Roger Smith appears as Chaney Jr. and Robert Evans is studio honcho. (MCA)

MAN OF STONE, THE. See **GOLEM, THE** (1936).

MAN ON A SWING (1974). Confusing, unresolved mystery-thriller with ESP themes: Cliff Robertson is the

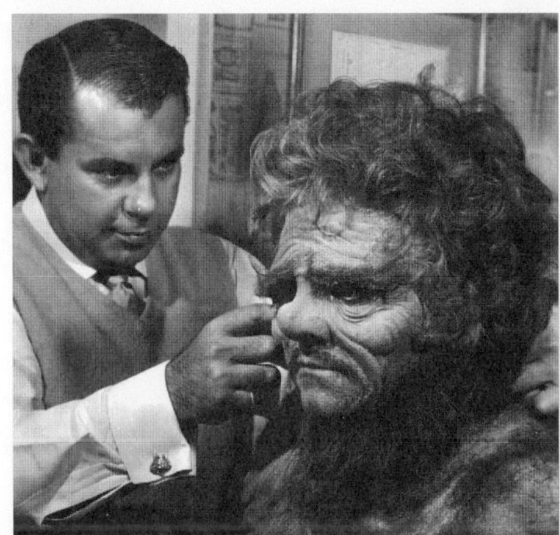

BUD WESTMORE MAKING UP JAMES CAGNEY IN '57

police chief in a small community where a young girl has been murdered. Joel Grey informs Robertson he has facts about the case—but these turn out to be facts known only by police. Does Grey have clairvoyant powers? Or is he playing a sick game with the law? Directed by Frank Perry. Elizabeth Wilson.

MANOS, HANDS OF FATE (1966). Wretched supernatural non-chiller about a cult of demon-worshippers, "The Night People," who terrorize a family crossing the desert. The main torture is the burning off of hands as a sacrifice to the ungodly ones. "Tuning out" with your hands is the answer to any telecasts beamed your way. Hal P. Warren, described as a fertilizer salesman (move over, Bandini), made this in El Paso, Texas. Hands off! (Sinister/C; S/Weird; Filmfax)

MAN'S BEST FRIEND (1993). MAX is a DNA-engineered guard dog, created by Dr. Paul Jarret (Lance Henriksen), in this sci-fi thriller co-starring Ally Sheedy. (Video/Laser: New Line)

MANSION OF MADNESS, THE. See **DR. TARR'S HORROR DUNGEON.**

MANSION OF THE DOOMED (1975). Unqualified revulsion is generated by this crude horror film . . . certainly it demeaned the careers of Richard Basehart and Gloria Grahame. Basehart portrays Dr. Chaney, an eyeball transplant experimenter. When his daughter is blinded, he stops at nothing to restore her sight, including the taking of eyeballs from others. Not only does this Charles Band production show the operations graphically, but victims are depicted by director Michael Pataki in all their sightless misery. The bloody, shocking ending of eyeless victims avenging themselves remains one of the sickest in memory. Vic Tayback, Arthur Space. Also called EYES OF DR. CHANEY. (Bingo)

MANSTER, THE (1959). This U.S.-Japanese co-production epitomizes the thrills in the monster-horror movies of the '50s: pseudoscientific explanations, cheesy effects and hammy acting. And that's exactly why it's so fun. American accountant Peter Dyneley is turned into a two-headed creature by a Japanese doctor experimenting with new body-altering drugs, who also keeps his deformed wife locked in a cell. Made in Japan with a mixed cast. Directed by G. P. Breakston and Kenneth G. Crane. (J & J; Sinister/C; S/Weird; Filmfax)

MAN THEY COULD NOT ARREST, THE (1933). See editions 1-3.

MAN THEY COULD NOT HANG, THE (1939). Prophetic horror thriller has a fascinating sequence in which Boris Karloff, on trial for murder, pronounces that body transplants will one day become a vital field of science. In this Columbia scientific thriller, Karloff is Dr. Savaard, whose experiments to arrest the body's metabolism, so transplants can be carried out, causes a patient's death. Sentenced to hang, Savaard is resurrected by a loyal lab assistant. Then all those responsible for sending Savaard to prison are gathered in a mansion and murdered one by one. Directed by Nick Grinde. Roger Pryor, Lorna Gray, Ann Doran, Don Beddoe, James Craig. (RCA/Columbia; Goodtimes)

MANTIS (1993). Special effects superhero TV-movie in which MANTIS (Mechanically Augmented Neuro Transmitter System) fights crime in the style of DARKMAN—that being no coincidence since this was produced by Sam Raimi and Robert Tapert. The script by Sam Hamm (BATMAN) was directed by Eric Laneuville. Carl Lumbly, Bobby Hosea, Gina Torres.

MANTIS IN LACE (1968). Cleaver murders galore from producer-writer Sanford White, who spins a bloody tale of a topless dancer (Susan Stewart) who drops acid and murders the men she entraps with garden tools. William Rotsler directs all the whacks and whangs with dollops of sex. Only saving grace is Laszlo Kovacs' cinematography. Steve Vincent, Pat Barrington. (S/Weird)

MAN WHO CAME FROM UMMO, THE. See **ASSIGNMENT TERROR.**

MAN WHO CHANGED HIS MIND, THE. See **MAN WHO LIVED AGAIN, THE.**

MAN WHO COULD CHEAT DEATH, THE (1959). Classy Hammer remake of THE MAN IN HALF MOON STREET, starring Anton Diffring as the 100-year-old madman who needs new glands to maintain a youthful appearance. Diffring is entranced by a former lover, Hazel Court, now in love with doctor Christopher Lee, whom Diffring forces to perform unspeakable deeds. High-class production combined with Terence Fisher's sleek direction make for a handsome horror flick. Scripted by Jimmy Sangster, produced by Michael Carreras.

MAN WHO COULD WORK MIRACLES, THE (1937). Alexander Korda's version of H. G. Wells' story about George McWhirter Fotheringay, an Essex draper's clerk endowed with miraculous powers, is a playful blending of the cosmic and the comic. Roland Young as Fotheringay performs minor miracles at first, then graduates to bigger stuff. Directed by Lothar Mendes, scripted by Wells. Beautifully arresting film with pleasing effects for their time. Ralph Richardson, Ernest Thesiger, George Zucco, Torin Thatcher. (Embassy) (Laser: Image)

MAN WHO FELL TO EARTH, THE (1976). Enigmatic Nicolas Roeg sci-fi film is complex and will be indecipherable to some—but a rich mosaic of study to others. Davie Bowie, in his screen debut, conveys the asexual manner and features of an E.T. humanoid from a dying planet, who crashlands on Earth. Using a scientific formula, he establishes a corporate empire and raises money to build a rocketship so he can return to his family. But he becomes a victim of a corrupt society, dwindling away to a hopeless alcoholic. An unusually sensitive film, beautifully photographed (Roeg began as a cinematographer) with offbeat effects. Claudia Jennings, Buck Henry, Bernie Casey, Candy Clark, Rip Torn. (Video/Laser: RCA/Columbia)

MAN WHO FELL TO EARTH, THE (1987). TV-movie version of the Nicolas Ray feature with Lewis Smith and Beverly D'Angelo. A mere imitation. Directed by Robert J. Roth.

MAN WHO HAUNTED HIMSELF, THE (1970). Roger Moore undergoes surgery after an auto accident and suddenly doctors can hear two heartbeats. After recovery, Moore realizes he has an exact double—a doppleganger conspiring to take his place. The ending is extremely weird; in fact, the Michael Relph-Basil Dearden script is very original. Dearden also directed. Hildegard Neil, Olga Georges-Picot, Anton Rodgers. (HBO)

MAN WHO LIVED AGAIN, THE (1936). Boris Karloff is the creator of a brain transference machine. Unfortunately, Dr. Laurience goes bonkers when his financial backer stops funding the project, and he sets out to exchange his mind with that of John Loder, with whom his lab assistant Anna Lee is in love. A British film directed by Robert Stevenson. Cecil Parker, Lynn Harding, Donald Calthrop. (Sinister/C; Nostalgia; Filmfax)

MAN WHO LIVED TWICE, THE (1936). Ralph Bellamy is a criminal who undergoes an operation to change identity. Surgery results in the loss of his memory and a change of heart from evil to good, and the once-ugly man becomes a doctor. Loosely remade in 3-D in 1953 as MAN IN THE DARK. Marian Marsh, Ward Bond. Directed by Harry Lachman.

MAN WHO MADE DIAMONDS, THE (1937). See editions 1-3.

MAN WHO SAW TOMORROW, THE (1981). Orson Welles narrates (on and off camera) this fascinating pseudodocumentary that reexamines the predictions of Michel de Nostradamus, the 16th Century French physician who jotted down thousands of quatrains, all of which are believed to be forecasts of history, right down to one that predicts a tyrant named "Hister" will terrorize the world. The latter part of the film deals with predictions of a nuclear war in 1999—following which there will be a thousand-year peace. Welles' voice (if nothing else) will hold you riveted. Much of the footage was staged by director Robert Guenette. (Warner Bros.)

MAN WHO TURNED TO STONE, THE (1957). Incredibly dull, poorly produced Sam Katzman quickie for Columbia—with nothing to bring its boring horror/sci-fi mishmash to life. The setting is the LaSalle Detention School for Girls, where crazed doctor Victor Jory drains the life from women to keep himself and his sycophants alive. When too many girls turn up dead, administrator Charlotte Austin (with colorless William Hudson) investigates the odd Dr. Murdock. Jory walks through it with a stone face with a zombie-like assistant. The project is petrified and that includes Leslie Kardos' direction. Paul Cavanagh, Frederick Ledebur, Ann Doran.

MAN WHO WAGGED HIS TAIL, THE (1961). Whimsical Italian fantasy-comedy with Peter Ustinov as a hard-hearted Brooklyn landlord-lawyer hexed by a magician and turned into a canine. He will remain so until he can find someone who loves him. The mongrel, Caligula, starts nosing around for a master. Produced-directed by Ladislao Vajda. Pablito Calva, Aroldo Tieri. (Sinister/C)

MAN WHO WALKED THROUGH WALLS, THE. See **MAN GOES THROUGH THE WALL, A.**

MAN WHO WANTED TO LIVE FOREVER, THE (1970). Suspenseful TV-movie with a few beautiful Canadian skiing sequences, directed tautly by John Trent. Stuart Whitman and Sandy Dennis are trapped in a mountain sanctuary ruled by millionaire Burl Ives, who brings would-be victims to his stronghold so body organs are available for transplanting the moment he needs them. Intriguing premise. Jack Creley, Ron Hartman.

"You better watch out when you hear that sound / It means that the Maniac Cop's around. / Once upon a time he was a supercop, / But the bad guys framed him to make him stop. / They put him in prison where they tried to kill him / But he broke out and now he's a villain."

*—The "Skat" song from **MANIAC COP***

MAN WHO WASN'T THERE, THE (1983). Abysmal attempt to create a mystery-comedy a la FOUL PLAY with THE INVISIBLE MAN blindly thrown in. Director Bruce Malmuth and writer Stanford Sherman give this a teenage mentality that will make you evaporate. The sexual jokes are a leering slap against women; the 3-D is pointless; and the plot so incomprehensible that the twists only irritate. State department official Sam Cooper finds an egg-shaped device loaded with vials of green serum that render their drinkers invisible. An invisible criminal has three dumb henchmen a la The Three Stooges running around Washington D.C. after Cooper and girl friend (Lisa Langlois, who has some silly scenes making love to empty air). The only member of the woe-begone cast who makes anything funny of this is Jeffrey Tambor as a Soviet official. (Paramount)

MAN WHO WOULDN'T DIE, THE (1942). See editions 1-3.

MAN WITH NINE LIVES, THE (1940). Premonitory glimpses at Cryonetics, the science of freezing bodies into suspended animation, long before it was called that. Boris Karloff stars as Dr. Kravaal, whose intentions are far from mad when he entombs a dying patient. A drug accidentally knocks out everyone in the cave and when Karloff awakens ten years later, he has a cancer cure but the good doc goes bonkers, forcing scientists Roger Pryor and JoAnn Sayers to become guinea pigs. Directed by Nick Grinde. Hal Taliaferro, Charles Trowbridge.

MAN WITHOUT A BODY, THE (1958). British horror never released in the U.S. for reasons apparent when you endure this mess in which Robert Hutton, dying of a brain tumor, arranges to have the brain of prophet Nostradamus (Michael Golden) transplanted in place of his own. Directed brainlessly by W. Lee Wilder and scripted on a Mongolian level by William Grote. George Coulouris, Sheldon Lawrence, Kim Parker.

MAN WITH THE GOLDEN GUN, THE (1974). Ninth in the James Bond series, with Christopher Lee as the $1-million assassin Scaramanga. Bond and Scaramanga fight over a Solar Energy Laser Beam on a Pacific island but it's not very exciting stuff. with Roger Moore (as 007) seeming fatigued and indifferent. Re-introduction of a Southern sheriff during a car chase indicates writers Richard Maibaum and Tom Mankiewicz were running low on ideas. Britt Ekland and Maud Adams are lovely to behold but this still needs more attractions. One of the villain's aides, Nick Nack, is Herve Villechaize, who went on to FANTASY ISLAND. Directed by Guy Hamilton. Clifton James, Richard Loo, Marc Lawrence, Bernard Lee. (CBS/Fox) (Laser: MGM/UA)

MAN WITH THE POWER, THE (1977). Good-natured TV-movie starring Bob Neill as a likeable young man who discovers from scientist Tim O'Connor that his father was an alien who crossbred with an Earthling. Now, Neill has a psychokinetic power to concentrate explosive energy to stop objects or manipulate them. A spy plot involves the kidnapping of foreign princess Persis Khambatta with whom Neill is in love. No great shakes, just pleasantly diverting. Vic Morrow turns up as an abductor. Written-produced by Allan Balter. Directed by Nicholas Sgarro. Roger Perry, Austin Stoker. (MGM)

MAN WITH THE SYNTHETIC BRAIN. In the beginning, producer-director Al Adamson hacked out PSYCHO A GO GO in 1965. When that was a no-go-go he shot new footage and called it FIEND WITH THE ELECTRONIC BRAIN. When that short-circuited, he went back and filmed Kent Taylor, John Carradine and buxom blonde Regina Carroll in revised footage, calling it BLOOD OF GHASTLY HORROR. And when that emerged a ghastly horror, he retitled it MAN WITH THE SYNTHETIC BRAIN. So what's it all about? You tell us. A murder in an alley leads to a flashback about a diamond robbery which leads to a flashback about mad doctor Carradine with a high-pitch voltage machine who creates a man with an electronic brain. The man's father (Taylor) kidnaps Carradine's daughter and holds her hostage while cop Tommy Kirk chases the robbers in the hills near Lake Tahoe. Filmed in "Chill-O-Rama."

MAN WITH THE X-RAY EYES, THE Video version of **X—THE MAN WITH THE X-RAY EYES.**

MAN WITH THE YELLOW EYES. See **PLANETS AGAINST US.** (Jaundiced science-fiction?)

MAN WITH TWO BRAINS, THE (1983). That wild and crazy guy, Steve Martin, in a wild and crazy picture—make that wild and uncontrolled. It's a hodgepodge of mad-doctor cliches and tongue-in-cheek Frankenstein jokes, a roller-coaster ride with laugh peaks and nonguffaw valleys too. And yet, it's enchantingly watchable, with a barrage of sex jokes downright hilarious. Carl Reiner directed with an eye for colorful visual parody. Martin falls in love with a brain floating in a solution created by doctor David Warner and can't get sexy wife Kathleen Turner to make love to him. Paul Benedict, Peter Hobbs, James Cromwell, Merv Griffin. (Video/Laser: Warner Bros.)

MAN WITH TWO FACES, THE (1934). See editions 1-3.

MAN WITH TWO HEADS, THE (1972). In this case, two are not better than one, for writer-director Andy Milligan deals ineffectually with the Jekyll and Hyde theory. In the 1830s in England, a scientific gent (Denis De Marne) mixes up a formula that brings out the worst in him—a dastard named Mr. Blood. Instantly forgettable. Julia Stratton, Jacqueline Lawrence. Made as DR. JEKYLL AND MR. BLOOD. (Midnight)

MAN WITH TWO LIVES, THE (1942). Grounded plot about a man brought back from death at the same moment a criminal is electrocuted at the state pen, only now the decent guy has been taken over by the evil soul of the gangster, who begins a wave of crime to get even. Directed without charge by Phil Rosen and acted without kick by Edward Norris and Addison Richards.

MARCH OF THE MONSTERS, THE. See **DESTROY ALL MONSTERS.**

MARCH OF THE WOODEN SOLIDERS. Video version of **BABES IN TOYLAND.** (Video Dimensions; Independent United; Goodtimes offers a colorized version) (Laser: Image)

MARDI GRAS FOR THE DEVIL (1993). Effective supernatural thriller set in New Orleans at Mardi Gras time when cop Robert Davi tangles with the Devil (Michael Ironside). Satan killed Davi's father 20 years before and now wants to destroy everything that Davi loves—ex-wife Lesley Anne Down, girlfriend Lydia Denier and partner Mike Starr. There's ample pyrotechnics and stunt work and cross-cutting between the Devil making love to a sadistic prostitute and Davi and Denier coupling. The script by director David A. Prior captures the emotional involvement of the characters and offers well-defined roles for police chief John Amos and voodoo expert Margaret Avery (as Sadie), who provides background that the Mardi Gras holiday began in Europe 800 years ago to celebrate the rites of spring and involved bloody sacrifices by the church. Made as NIGHT TRAP. (Prism)

MARDI GRAS MASSACRE (1978). Low-budget exploitationer, shot in New Orleans. Writer-producer-director Jack Weis offers hogwash about an Aztec priest who slices up women on his altar. Plenty of gore, little else. Curt Dawson, Gwen Arment. (Midnight Video; VCII)

MARIANNE. See **MIRRORS.** (For reflective moods?)

MARK OF THE BEAST. See **FEAR NO EVIL.**

MARK OF THE BEAST. Video version of **FERTILIZING THE BLASPHEMIZING BOMBSHELL** (Rhino).

MARK OF THE DEVIL (1970). Sickening German-British gore bore about 17th Century witchhunter Herbert Lom and his ghastly torture methods. Features the jolly sight of a woman's tongue being cut out of her head, and other nubile desirables with their blouses ripped open, undergoing heinous forms of sadism. This revolting material went over with the public, for a sequel was also embraced by viewers. Directed by Michael Armstrong. Udo Kier, Reginalf Nalder. (Vestron; Lightning)

MARK OF THE DEVIL PART II (1972). Blood flows in gushing streams from broken, twisted bodies and ripped-asunder flesh as alleged witches and heretics are tortured by fun-loving purveyors of the Inquisition (what a sedate period in history!) Producer Adrian Hoven leaves his devilish mark again by writing and directing. Anton Diffring, Erica Blanc. (Video Dimensions; Vidmark)

MARK OF THE DEVIL PART III. Video version of **SISTERS OF SATAN** (Fame Entertainment).

MARK OF THE DEVIL (1985). British TV-movie of the supernatural in which murderer Dirk Benedict is plagued by a tattoo that spreads to the rest of his body. Jenny Seagrove, George Sewell, John Paul.

MARK OF THE GORILLA (1950). Johnny Weissmuller as Jungle Jim tangles with meat-headed Nazis looking for a gold treasure guarded by a giant ape. Tired Sam Katzman picture for Columbia, directed wearily by William Berke. MARK OF THE GORILLA is the mark of the fool. Onslow Stevens, Trudy Marshall.

MARK OF THE VAMPIRE (1936). Tod Browning's horror thriller sets itself up as a graveyard-vampire chiller, closely following the silent film LONDON AFTER MIDNIGHT. However, it too soon turns into a whodunit with preposterous premises, certain to disappoint fans expecting supernatural thrills. Bela Lugosi duplicates his Dracula image as Count Mora, Carol Borland is his "bride" who flaps him across the dungeons, Lionel Barrymore appears as the vampire chaser and Lionel Atwill, for the umpteenth time, is the probing policeman. Elizabeth Allen, Jean Hersholt, Donald Meek. (MGM/UA)

MARK OF THE VAMPIRE (1957). See **VAMPIRE, THE.**

MARK OF THE WEST. See **CURSE OF THE UNDEAD.**

MARK OF THE WITCH (1970). Old-timer hag (shall we say around 300 years old?) terrorizes nonbelievers in a college town. Marie Santell is the witch. Robert Elston, Anitra Walsh, Darryl Wells, Marie Santell. Directed by Tom Moore in Dallas. (AIP)

MARK OF THE WOLFMAN, THE See **FRANKENSTEIN'S BLOODY TERROR.**

MAROONED (1970). Astronauts Richard Crenna, James Franciscus and Gene Hackman are orbiting Earth when the retroactive rockets refuse to fire. And they have only 42 hours of oxygen left. On the ground, NASA executive Gregory Peck and slide-rule expert David Janssen launch a rescue through the eye of a hurricane passing over Launch Pad Seven. The effects won an Oscar and there's exciting business among the astronauts when they realize one must be sacrificed. Lee Grant, Nancy Kovack and Mariette Hartley are wives back at Control Center. Directed by John Sturges, with Mayo Simon's script based on Martin Caidin's novel. Scott Brady, Walter Brooke. (Video/Laser: RCA/Columbia)

MARS ATTACKS THE WORLD (1938). Feature-length version of **FLASH GORDON'S TRIP TO MARS**; available in all 12 chapters on video, too.

MARS INVADES PUERTO RICO. See **FRANKENSTEIN MEETS THE SPACE MONSTER.**

MARS NEEDS WOMEN (1966). . . . but you don't need this TV-movie, a dreadful outing in which the dying Martian race sends us messages proclaiming they need our best-looking women to procreate a new species. Please send Jayne Mansfield, Sophia Loren and Elke Sommer! Hopelessly silly time-waster produced-written-directed by Larry Buchanan, said to be a remake of PAJAMA PARTY. By whatever title, it's a slumber bummer. Tommy Kirk, Yvonne Craig. (Sinister/C; S/Weird; Filmfax)

MARSHAL OF HELL, THE. See **DEVILS POSSESSED, THE.**

MARSUPIALS: THE HOWLING III. See **HOWLING 3.**

MARTA (1971). Italian-Spanish Grand Guignol horror thriller starring Stephen Boyd as a madman with a torture chamber. Jesus Puente, Marisa Mell, Isa Miranda.

MARTIAN CHRONICLES, THE (1979). Ray Bradbury's classic novel of Mars colonization (a loose-knit collection reprinted from pulps) arrived as a six-hour miniseries with Rock Hudson as John Wilder, the one character who links the disjointed narratives. Bradbury's book is poetic style and atmosphere, difficult qualities for film. Occasionally director Michael Anderson works well within the limited sets and skimpy effects, but he cannot prevent the meager budget (for so huge an undertaking) from showing. Richard Matheson has written a thoughtful teleplay recounting man's colonization of the Red Planet, the chameleon qualities of the Martians, and other fantasy premises that make Bradbury's work one of the finest of the 20th Century. Darren McGavin, Gayle Hunnicutt, Bernadette Peters, Fritz Weaver, Roddy McDowall, Maria Schell, Barry Morse, Jon Finch, Chris Connelly. Available in a three-set video series: Vol. I: "The Expeditions" (IVE); Vol. II: "The Settlers" (USA); Vol. III: "The Martians" (USA) (Laser: Image)

MARTIANS GO HOME (1990). Composer Randy Quaid is writing a score for a sci-fi movie when the music is piped into space. As a result, Martians invade Earth, showing up as green-skinned beings in green clothing who behave like obnoxious stand-up comedians. This adaptation of Fredric Brown's popular novel, written by Charlie (GREMLINS II) Haas, is a misfire that is excruciatingly unfunny. Haas' every attempt at something original is either destroyed by director David Odell or just doesn't work in the hands of Quaid, Margaret Collin (as his love interest), the sexy Anita Morris (as an insufferable talk show psychologist) and Barry Sobel (doing his fast patter stand-up shtick). (IVE) (Laser: Image)

MARTIN (1976). Portrait of an 18-year-old vampire, directed-written by George A. Romero (NIGHT OF THE LIVING DEAD), who demythologizes the living-dead legend. Martin (John Amplas) imagines he is a descendant of Nosferatu but in reality he uses a razor blade to slash victims' wrists, and he is bothered by neither garlic cloves nor Christian crosses. There are two outstanding sequences—the assault of a woman in her train compartment, and the snaring of two lovers in a large home—and as a black comedy of exploitation, MARTIN comes off nicely. Romero's most thoughtful work. Make-up man Tom Savini co-stars with Lincoln Maazel and Christine Forrest. (HBO) (Laser: Image)

MARVELOUS LAND OF OZ, THE (1982). Sequel to THE WIZARD OF OZ, with Baum's characters traveling with Dorothy back to Kansas. A musical production by the Children's Theater Co. of Minneapolis. (MCA)

MARY, MARY, BLOODY MARY (1973). Viewer, viewer, unfortunate viewer. You are in for a bloody Mexican vampire tale about a female blooddrinker (Christina Ferrare, onetime wife of John DeLorean) down Mexico way, with John Carradine showing up briefly as her vampire father. Directed by Juan Lopez Moctezuma (who certainly got his revenge). David Young, Helene Rojo. (Summit International; Continental)

MARY POPPINS (1964). Disney delight with Julie Andrews in her all-time best role—a nanny in London with the ability to fly and perform magic. It's an ingenious mixture of live action and animation, the epitome of family entertainment. Dick Van Dyke, Glynis Johns, Hermione Baddeley, Arthur Treacher, David Tomlinson. Directed by Robert Stevenson. (Video/Laser: Disney)

MASK, THE (1961). A hokey but mildly fun Canadian horror film with segments shot in 3-D; viewers are forewarned to put on their glasses each time psychiatrist Paul Stevens starts to have one of his hallucinations. These stereovision bits are full of arbitrary horror images (witches, misty swamps, killer snakes, corpses coming to life, evil spirits reaching out for you, etc.). The storyline is like a TWILIGHT ZONE episode with OUTER LIMITS lighting as Stevens comes into possession of a South American art treasure—a mask that brings out homicidal tendencies in its wearer. Produced-directed by Julian Roffman. Claudette Nevins, Bill Walker. In 1982 a version was released to TV with the 3-D segments in red-and-green tinting, introduced by magician Harry Blackstone. (From Rhino in 3-D) (Laser: Image)

MASKED MARVEL, THE (1943). A 12-chapter Republic serial with a switch: Instead of the mastermind villain's identity withheld, the identity of the heroic Masked Marvel is kept secret—you only know it has to be one of four insurance cops. Super-explosives and super-powerful weaponry are used as the Marvel prevents Japanese saboteurs from blowing up America. Yet another excursion into wonderfully staged nonstop action. Just marvel-ous, darling. Directed by Spencer G. Bennet. Tom Steele, William Forrest. (Republic; Video Treasures)

MASK OF DIJON (1946). The only reason (we mean the only!) to endure this PRC cheapie is for Erich von Stroheim as a retired stage illusionist whose attempt to make a comeback results in his humiliation. He resorts to hypnotism ("stare into my eyes . . . you are getting sleepy") to force others to carry out revenge murders. It's a gas to watch this artist at work. Directed by Lew Landers. Jeanne Bates, Edward Van Sloan.

MASK OF FU MANCHU, THE (1932). This marks the only time Boris Karloff played the ruthless Asian madman created by Sax Rohmer, and it is a classic in artful campiness. This serves as a reminder of the excellent sets, costumes and production values MGM once indulged in, no matter how inconsequential the material. Fu Manchu is out to grab the sword of Genghis Khan so he may lead his Yellow Hordes against the world. Racism and slurs ("You hideous yellow monster!"), Death Ray gadgets, the Room of the Golden Peacock, and traps and torture devices employed by Fu Manchu against his nemesis, Nayland Smith (Lewis Stone). Myrna Loy is superbly salacious as Fu's decadent daughter, suggesting the most licentious sexuality. Charles Starrett, Karen Morley, Jean Hersholt. Directed by Charles Brabin. (MGM/UA)

MASK OF SATAN, THE. Heavily edited version of **BLACK SUNDAY.**

MASKS OF DEATH (1984). Stylish British TV-movie, bringing Peter Cushing back as the Baker Street sleuth, with a rather sedate John Mills portraying Dr. Watson. Parallel plots unfold: the finding of several corpses with twisted, hideous expressions, and a mystery involving the Home Secretary. The setting is London 1913, on the eve of World War I—a clue to a diabolical scheme involving English and German associations. Directed by Roy Ward Baker. The cast is enhanced by Anton Diffring as German royalty, Ray Milland as the secretary under fire and Anne Baxter as Irene Adler. Aka SHERLOCK HOLMES AND THE MASKS OF DEATH. (Warner Bros.; Lorimar) (Laser: Image)

MASQUE OF THE RED DEATH, THE (1964). Edgar Allan Poe's allegory about aristocrats who hold a costume ball at the height of a virulent plague to keep away Death has been strongly adapted to a full-length horror thriller directed by Roger Corman, written by Charles Beaumont and R. Wright Campbell and starring Vincent Price as Prince Prospero, a sadistic Italian nobleman of the 12th Century, surrounded by decadence and deceit in the form of Hazel Court (she makes a deal with the Devil) and Patrick Magee in an ape's outfit. One of the best in Corman's Poe series. Nigel Green, Jane Asher, David Weston. (Lightning; Live) (Laser: Image, with **THE PREMATURE BURIAL**)

MASQUE OF THE RED DEATH (1989). It's hard to understand why producer Roger Corman would take one of his best movies, American-International's superb 1964 version, and turn it into this inferior remake. Adrian Paul as the sadistic Prince Prospero is no match for Vincent Price, nor is Larry Brand (who co-wrote the script with Daryl Haney) half the director that Corman is. The production values are woeful, as is most of the acting. Only Patrick Macnee as the Red Death brings any professionalism to this wrong movie. Clare Hoak, Jeff Osterhage, Tracy Reiner. (Video/Laser: MGM/UA)

MASSACRE AT CENTRAL HIGH (1976). Pre-slasher teen flick, so it doesn't follow the more established genre cliches. This assumes a sympathetic attitude toward student Derrel Maury, who doesn't like the way snarling nasties are behaving at the local high, and decides it's time for a high of his own—retribution. Minor cult film. Directed by Renee Daalder. Andrew Stevens, Kimberly Beck, Robert Carradine. (MPI; Gorgon)

MASSACRE HOSPITAL. See **X-RAY.**

MASSACRE IN DINOSAUR VALLEY (1985). Despite its title this foreign-produced adventure film has no fantasy elements, but rather falls into the category of the "jungle holocaust" genre, being filled with gruesome torture effects, killer piranha fish, spears, blow guns and machete body chops. Michael Sopkiw is an adventurer in the Indiana Jones vein, a dinosaur-bone hunter forced down in the South American jungle with other travelers. An odd mixture of adventure, explicit violence and sex (including a torrid lesbian number) without being much fun, with the morbid elements taking hold. The dubbing is pretty terrible, and the acting without subtlety. Susane Carvall, Milton Morris, Martha Anderson. Written-edited-directed by Michael E. Lemick. (Lightning; Live)

MASSARATI AND THE BRAIN (1982). Minor TV-movie with lightweight James Bond-style gadgets and weapons which secret agent Christopher Hewett uses to fight neo-Nazi Christopher Lee (wearing a black Gestapo trenchcoat) in his search for a sunken treasure of rare coins. The cast (sexy Ann Turkel, also sexy Carmilla Sparv, also also sexy Kathy Witt) has to compete with the precocious 10-year-old Peter Billingsley, the genius kid who helps Hewett with the electronic equipment. The kid almost wins. Directed by Harvey Hart.

MASSIVE RETALIATION (1984). In the tradition of PANIC IN YEAR ZERO, but without the excessive violence, this anti-war film is a fascinating, well-written study in human behavior under duress. On a Fourth of July, several families gather at a ranch in Marin County when nuclear war breaks out between the U.S. and Russia. Led by militant Peter Donat, the families shut out the rest of the world—or try to, with disastrous results. Producer-director Thomas A. Cohen spins this cautionary parable in realistic style and explores character, though at the expense of action. Comedians Michael Pritchard and Bob Goldthwait have relatively straight roles, although Goldthwait's deputy sheriff does have his bizarre streak. Marilyn Hassett, Susan O'Connell, Jason Gedrick, Mimi Farina, Johnny Weissmuller Jr. (Video/Laser: Vestron)

MASS MURDER. See **MURDER LUST.**

MASTER MINDS (1949). When Sachs (Huntz Hall) eats too much sugar he slips off into a trance that allows him to predict the future. Leo Gorcey exploits him as a carnival fortune teller until mad scientist Alan Napier kidnaps him—mainly to exchange intelligences with a humanoid ape creature named Atlas (Glenn Strange). It's the usual Bowery Boys nonsense from Monogram, directed in the usual vaporous fashion by Jean Yarbrough. Jack Pierce did the monster makeup but it's all laughs and no thrills. Leo Gorcey, Gabriel Dell, Bernard Gorcey, Gabriel Dell, Minerva Urecal, Jane Adams.

MASTER OF EVIL. Video version of **DEMON LOVER** (Premiere).

MASTER OF HORROR (1960). Produced in Argentina and consisting of three Edgar Allan Poe short stories—"Case of Mr. Valdemar," "The Cask of Amontillado" and "The Tell-Tale Heart." Enrique Carreras directed with Narcisco Ibanez Menta heading the cast. Jack Harris issued this in 1966 in an Americanized version without "The Tell-Tale Heart" episode.

MASTER OF TERROR. See **4-D MAN, THE.**

MASTER OF THE WORLD (1961). A mingling of Jules Verne's MASTER OF THE WORLD and ROBUR THE CONQUEROR results in an uneven fantasy adventure. What is good is The Albatross, a marvelous Victorian craft kept aloft by whirling blades and electrical current. Also good: The decorative staterooms and 19th Century costumes. What isn't so good is Richard Matheson's adaptation: Robur is portrayed as just another mad genius who hates war but inflicts it on others. Also not so good is the hammy acting of Vincent Price. Also not so good is the presence of Charles Bronson as the hero. A hero in this kind of movie he is not. A mixed bag of air directed by

William Witney. Henry Hull, Mary Webster, Wally Campo. (Warner Bros.; MGM/UA)

MASTERS OF THE UNIVERSE (1987). A live-action version of TV's animated "He-Man and the Masters of the Universe." What we have are wind-up characters fighting a cosmic battle to save the Universe. (You expected less?) An obvious clone of STAR WARS and other fantasy-quest films yet it has a life of its own, unfolding at a feverish pitch, with imaginative costume and set designs. Dolph Lundgren as He-Man is some hunk as he pursues the "Cosmic Key," a device that holds the power of good over evil. His adversary is Frank Langella as Skeletor, who sends his ugly minions after He-Man and pals: Man-at War (Jon Cypher) and his daughter Teela (Chelsea Field), and a dwarf-alien named Gwildor (Billy Barty in a lot of costume and make-up). Ultimately, MASTERS suffers from David Odell's campy dialogue, the superficially glittering direction of Gary Goddard, and mock heroics of monumental proportion as He-Man takes on armies of laser-armed robots. Bill Conti's music is a ripoff of STAR WARS and SUPERMAN. Meg Foster is Evil-Lyn, James Tolkan is the cop Lubic, and Courteney Cox and Robert Duncan McNeil portray Earthlings caught up in the war when it shifts to Earth through a time-space continuum. (Video/Laser: Warner Bros.)

DOLPH LUNDGREN

MASTERS OF VENUS (1962). Re-edited version of a British serial about a spaceship from Earth that finds a race on Venus descended from Atlantis. Norman Wolland, Robin Stewart. (Sinister/C; Vidmark; Filmfax)

MATANGO, THE FUNGUS OF TERROR. See **ATTACK OF THE MUSHROOM PEOPLE.**

MATCHLESS (1966). Matchless only in its witlessness in spoofing the Bond thrillers: Agent Patrick O'Neal has a ring that renders him invisible for ten hours at a stretch. Isn't that ingenious? O'Neal is seeking the whereabouts of a criminal mastermind (Donald Pleasence) but must constantly fight off adversary Henry Silva, who desperately wants the ring. Doesn't bell a ring? Directed in Italy by Alberto Lattuada.

MATILDA (1978). The sight of a man in a kangaroo suit, bouncing around a boxing ring, is so outlandish, this feeble flick becomes a rollicking "fantasy." Despite a name director (Daniel Mann) and top-flight cast (Elliott Gould, Robert Mitchum, Harry Guardino), this adaptation of Paul Gallico's comedy novel is not a knockout. But it is a dragout. It goes down for the count early, even if the kangaroo stays on its bounding paws. Joke: Did you know kangaroos had a navy? Yeah, pocket battleships. (Orion; Vestron; Live)

MATINEE (1993). Director Joe Dante and producer Michael Finnell (the GREMLINS team) are back for this homage to moviegoing that is set in a Florida town in 1962 at the height of the Cuban Missile Crisis. Producer Lawrence Woolsey (John Goodman), molded after the gimmick king William Castle, arrives with his latest exploitation horror flick "Mant!" to be shown in Atomo-Vision and Rumble-Rama. Much of the black-and-white "Mant!" is shown during the matinee, and it's a wonderful send-up of sci-fi/monster movies of the '50s ("Half Man, Half Ant, All Terror!"), starring Kevin McCarthy, William Schallert and Robert Cornthwaite, who actually appeared in these things. The rest of Charles Haas' plot focuses on a family and its reaction to the crisis. All the teenagers attend the matinee and become caught up in the gimmicks of the afternoon. Haas also deals with the bomb scare of the day, the craze for bomb shelters and other nostalgia of the 1960s. It's a satisfying comedy, enhanced by Cathy Moriarty's performance as a jaded actress and mistress of Goodman's who attends the screening dressed as a nurse. Simon Fenton, Omri Katz, Lisa Jakub, Jesse Lee, Lucinda Jenney, James Villemaire. Jesse White, Dick Miller and John Sayles make brief appearances. (Video/Laser: MCA)

MATTER OF LIFE AND DEATH, A. Video title for **STAIRWAY TO HEAVEN.**

MATTER OF STATE/PHOTO FINISH (1978). Rare coins figure in an insurance fraud . . . a case stolen from a government official holds top-secret reports . . . Spider-man TV adventure episodes from the series that starred Nicholas Hammond and Michael Pataki. Jennifer Billingsley, John Crawford, Charles Haid, Geoffrey Lewis.

MAUSOLEUM (1982). Minor supernatural tale with hokey effects. Would you believe dry-ice mist in the family crypt with rats in the shadows and thunder and lightning outside? Totally devoid of thrills since we know from the outset that sexy Bobbie Bresee, member of the cursed Nomed Family, is possessed by a demon that forces her to act like a nymphomaniac and slaughter her lovers. None of these bloody deaths is particularly exciting, nor are the gore effects believable. John Buechler's makeup and fright masks are only fair. Bresee is the highlight, frequently baring her wonderful breasts with wild abandon. Too bad her acting isn't as magnificent. Marjoe Gortner is wasted as Bresee's dumb husband and La Wanda Page has an embarrassing cameo as a maid whose feet don't fail her when it's time to run. Directed by Michael Dugan. Norman Burton, Maurice Sherbanee. (Video/Laser: Nelson/Image)

MAX HEADROOM (1985). High-tech British black comedy fantasy with imaginative computer graphics and TV transmissions. In a near-future world, a crusading investigative TV reporter for the 23rd Network discovers a conspiracy to telecast a subliminal "blip" commercial that will cause viewers to overload and literally explode. A check of network officials and the adolescent genius who created the "blips" leads to weird confrontations and chases through a depressed industrialized England as an entity named Max Headroom is sent over the airwaves. Success of this TV-movie led to TV specials and a network series starring Max, who also became featured in U.S. commercials. Life imitates art. Directed by Rocky Morton and Annabel Jankel. Matt Frewer, Nickolas Grace. (Karl/Lorimar) (Laser: Warner Bros.)

MAXIE (1987). This adaptation of MARION'S WALL by Jack Finney is a gallant, but failed, attempt at screwball humor with a twist of TOPPER. A long-dead nymphomaniac of the Flapper Era returns to possess meekish Glenn Close, secretary to a Catholic priest. For Close it might have been a tour de force performance—switching from a sex-starved hussy to a straitlaced married woman—but Paul Aaron's direction and the script by Patricia Resnick are weak. Mandy Patinkin, Ruth Gordon, Valerie Curtin,

MANT AND CATHY MORIARTY IN 'MATINEE'

Barnard Hughes. (HBO) (Laser: Image)

MAXIMUM OVERDRIVE (1986). Stephen King's debut as a director tells us he should stick to writing. He's taken a story from NIGHT SHIFT, the one about killer semi-trucks trapping travelers in a roadside diner, and added sci-fi overtones. Seems a comet passing Earth has affected electrical and gas machines and instilled in them a homicidal urge to wipe out mankind. So trucks run people down, lawn mowers mow and Walkmans strangle. King falls back on the old cliche siege story, but his characters are unbelievable and unsympathetic, and one ends up laughing at, and not gasping with, this hapless bunch. Lacking suspense, a human villain and any sense of form, MAXIMUM OVERDRIVE delivers minimum underthrust. Emilio Estevez, Pat Hingle, Laura Harrington. (Video/Laser: Lorimar)

MAXIMUM THRUST. See **OCCULTIST, THE** (Urban Classics).

MAXIM XUL (1991). Professor of ancient lore (Adam West) discovers nine demons that he believes are responsible for all evil on Earth, but policeman Jefferson Leinberger isn't convinced as he tries to solve a series of murders. Filmed in Baltimore by director-producer Arthur Egeli. Mary Shaeffer, Billie Shaeffer. (Magnum)

MAZE, THE (1953). Three-dimensional thriller directed-designed by William Cameron Menzies (of GONE WITH THE WIND fame) who poured considerable talent into this low-budget chiller, which today seems decrepit and laughable. The setting is an isolated Scottish castle where a family curse hangs over Richard Carlson, who is suddenly called home from fiance Veronica Hurst to fulfill a family destiny. While there are suggestions of Lovecraftian horror in Dan Ullman's screenplay, and nifty scenes in the hedge labryinth from which the film takes its title, the ending deteriorates into ludicrous non-shock. On the other hand, for a look at outmoded techniques, and a special corniness you can't find anywhere else, THE MAZE is worth a look. Michael Pate, Hillary Brooke, Katherine Emery.

MAZE, THE (1985). British TV-movie in wich a ghost haunts a country estate. Francesca Annis, James Bolam, Sky McCatskill. (Prism)

MAZES AND MONSTERS (1982). Rona Jaffe's popular novel about the mental effect of game-playing roles on four college students, and how one student loses his mind, is an above-average TV-movie directed by Steven H. Stern. There are moments of hallucinatory madness, of medieval magic and mythical monsters. But the real emphasis is on the quintet of Dungeons & Dragons players and their psychological imbalances. Tom Hanks, Wendy Crewson, David Wallace, Anne Francis, Lloyd Bouchner, Murray Hamilton, Peter Donat, Louise Sorel, Vera Miles, Susan Strasberg. Aka RONA JAFFE'S MAZES AND MONSTERS. (Lorimar; Warner)

MEATBALLS PART II (1984). Raunchy teenage comedy of snide sex jokes and dumb behavior with an E.T. parody in which a saucer lands near Camp Sasquatch and drops off a nerdy kiddie alien. Nicknamed Meathead, the jerkola E.T. uses levitation to help campmates win a boxing match. Feeble stuff. Directed by Ken Wiederhorn. Richard Mulligan, Hamilton Camp, Misty Rowe. (Video/Laser: RCA/Columbia)

MEATBALLS III (1987). Sally Kellerman is wasted in this despicable teenage sex comedy as Roxy Du Jour, a porno queen who dies while filming a heated sequence and isn't allowed inton Heaven until she's done a good deed—such as helping nerdy Patrick Dempsey get laid. Dempsey is either a wimp or a macho-man as he vacillates under Roxy's magical powers. One of the worst of sequels, insipidly directed by George Mendeluk. Al Waxman, Isabelle Mejias, Shannon Tweed. (IVE)

MEATCLEAVER MASSACRE (1977). Rated R—for Raunchy. Four killers are targets for forces from beyond, called up by an occult professor. Christopher Lee appears as the storyteller. Directed by Evan Lee. Aka HOLLYWOOD MEATCLEAVER MASSACRE.

MEATEATER (1979). Mentally unbalanced pervert with a thing for Jean Harlow movies goes on a murderous rampage. Arch Jaboulian, Diane Davis, Emily Spendler. Directed by Derek Savage. (Active)

MEAT IS MEAT. See **MAD BUTCHER, THE.**

MEDICAL DEVIATE. See **DR. BUTCHER M.D.**

MEDIUM, THE (1934). British ESP thriller, directed by Vernon Sewell with a chilly atmosphere. Remade as THE LATIN QUARTER and HOUSE OF MYSTERY.

MEDIUM, THE (1951). Written-directed by Gian Carlo Menotti and based on his opera about a phony-baloney spiritualist. Watch for a young Anna Maria Alberghetti. Marie Powers, Leo Coleman. (Video Artists)

MEDIUM, THE (1985). See third edition.

MEDIUM, THE (1992). In Singapore an Australian journalist interviews a medium on trial for murder, realizing his powers may be greater than she suspected. Directed by Arthur Smith from a script by Margaret Chan and Rani Moorthy that is based on a true incident. Dore Kraus, Margaret Chan.

MEDUSA TOUCH, THE (1978). Richard Burton, looking as though he can't understand what went wrong with EXORCIST II: THE HERETIC, wanders haplessly about as a man with the power of telekinesis, which he unconsciously uses to crash giant airliners and murder people. He seeks the help of psychiatrist Lee Remick, but even with Freudian techniques she's powerless to stop his destruction of a cathedral containing Queen Elizabeth. The subtle touch is lacking in Jack Gold's direction and John Briley's screenplay. Lino Ventura, Harry Andrews, Alan Badel, Derek Jacobi. (CBS/Fox)

MEDUSA VS. THE SON OF HERCULES (1962). Italian-Spanish production is a standard muscle-happy flick with bicepted beefcaker Perseus going against a one-eyed monster. Richard Harrison walks through the proceedings as though he's afraid the producers won't have his next paycheck. Directed by Alberto de Martino. Anna Ranalli, Leo Anchoriz. (Sinister/C; S/Weird)

MEET ME IN LAS VEGAS (1956). Whenever rancher Dan Dailey holds the hand of ballerina Cyd Charisse, he can't lose at the gambling tables. Exactly why is never explained (unlucky at love?) in this otherwise fantasy-less MGM musical-comedy with Agnes Moorehead, Lena Horne, Jerry Colonna. Directed by Roy Rowland. (MGM/UA; Turner)

MEET MR. LUCIFER (1953). See editions 1-3.

MEET THE APPLEGATES (1991). An absurd cautionary tale (written by director Michael Lehman and Redbeard Simmons) about a family of jumbo-jet beetles living in a South American rain forest who mutant into human beings and move to Median, Ohio. Still with us? The "Applegates" assimilate into society, making enough dumb mistakes to pad out this excuse for a comedy. Has to be seen to be believed, but do you want to waste the time? Ed Begley Jr., Stockard Channing, Bobby Jacoby, Cami Cooper, Dabney Coleman (in drag yet). (From Media as **THE APPLEGATES**)

MEET THE HOLLOWHEADS (1989). Makeup specialist Tom Burman made his directing debut with this comedy set in a futuristic society that resembles a parody of a TV sitcom as it focuses on the Hollowhead family (John Glover, Nancy Mette, Matt Shakman, Juliette Lewis and Lightfield Lewis) coping with tomorrow's world. (Video/Laser: Media)

MEGAFORCE (1982). One of the worst of movies—totally botched by director Hal Needham. Barry Bostwick is miscast as the leader of an international strike force of good guys, supposedly armed with the latest weapons. Bostwick leads his force against old school chum Henry Silva and they behave as schoolboys, not as leaders of men. In one scene Bostwick's motorcycle sprouts wings; in another, a detachment of men aboard motorcylces parachute to the ground. As if that wasn't absurd enough, characters spout stupid dialogue. Persis Khambatta is nothing more than feminine decoration, and Edward

Mulhare is a wishy-washy general who knows he's in a turkey. (CBS/Fox) (Laser: Japanese)

MEGAVILLE (1990). Overdone, unconvincing futuristic tale in the "Big Brother" mold with J.C. Quinn as a brain-washed cop for a corporate-ruled society who is assigned by boss Daniel J. Travanti to infiltrate a gang offering uncensored TV shows to the public, including one that shows the President being strangled to death. Quinn's programming is unstable and he keeps short-circuiting and undergoing weird hallucinations and illnesses. Why anyone would pick him for a spy is a major weakness in the script by director Peter Lehner and Gordon Chavis. Billy Zane, Grace Zabriskie, Hamilton Camp. (IVE)

MELODY IN THE DARK (1948). See editions 1-3.

MEMOIRS OF AN INVISIBLE MAN (1992). Disappointing adaptation of H.F. Saint's novel about an average working man rendered invisible when a scientific experiment goes awry at a research plant. Its failure is all the more distressing because John Carpenter directed and Chevy Chase starred and neither rise to the occasion. Chase underplays Nick Halloway, failing to engage us on a comedic or dramatic level. The script by William Goldman, Dana Olsen and Robert Collector stresses a routine chase as Halloway is pursued by maverick agents of the CIA led by Sam Neill. And where's the romantic spark between Chase and Daryl Hannah as the girlfriend who agrees to help him escape his pursuers? (The fact they meet and have a quick fuck in the ladies' room doesn't help the relationship.) Some of the invisible-man effects are interesting but it's not enough to recommend this tired failure. Michael McKean, Jim Norton, Patricia Heaton. (Video/Laser: Warner Bros.)

HANNAH AND CHASE

MEMORIAL VALLEY MASSACRE (1988). Axe-wielding madman plagues campers who thought they were getting a holiday, and instead get a hollow slay. Directed by Robert C. Hughes. William Smith, Cameron Mitchell, John Kerry. (Video/Laser: Nelson)

MENACE FROM OUTER SPACE (1954). Menace is right! See **ROCKY JONES, SPACE RANGER** (S/Weird; Filmfax).

MEN MUST FIGHT (1933). MGM curiosity piece, based on an anti-war play brought to the screen as a forerunner of special-effects disaster films. During World War I pilot Robert Young loses his life, but not before leaving Diana Wynyard pregnant. In 1940, war with Eurasia erupts and now that offspring chooses not to bear arms. This speaks out sharply against misguided patriotism and the senselessness of war. Of special interest is an air raid on New York resulting in massive destruction. Old-fashioned, but the themes are intriguing and director Edgar Selwyn brings tension to this cautionary tale. Lewis Stone, Phillips Holmes, May Robson, Hedda Hopper.

MEN OF ACTION MEET WOMEN OF DRAKULA (1969). See editions 1-3.

MEPHISTO WALTZ, THE (1971). This Quinn Martin production did not dance circles at the box office—it turned out to be lame-footed under Paul Wendkos' direction. It's a supernatural thriller that still has moments with Alan Alda, Curt Jurgens, Jacqueline Bisset, Barbara Parkins and William Windom struggling to overcome script deficiencies. Jurgens portrays a dying pianist who transfers his soul to a journalist (Alda). (CBS/Fox)

MERIDIAN: KISS OF THE BEAST. Video/laser version of **KISS OF THE BEAST** (Paramount).

MERLIN AND THE SWORD (1983). Just seeing Candice Bergen in a fright wig in her pre-Murphy Brown days, playing a mean witch-bitch, makes this TV-movie worthwhile. This retelling of the Arthurian legend (originally ARTHUR THE KING) has an outstanding cast (Malcolm McDowall as King Arthur, Edward Woodward as Merlin) action, intrigue and an occasional magic trick and monster. Dyan Cannon is visting Stonehenge when she's transported to an ice cave where Merlin has been imprisoned, and he relates in flashback the legend. Directed by Clive Donner, this is not a superepic, but its good acting carries it over its low-budget rough spots. Joseph Blatchley, Rupert Everett, Liam Neeson, Michael Gough. Narrated by John Smith. (Vestron)

MERMAIDS OF TIBURON, THE (1962). Writer-producer-director John Lamb goes on the rocks with his "tail tale" about a half-human, half-fish gal (Diane Webber, and we kid you not about her last name) who swims along the California-Mexican coast. A Marineland operator is looking for a legendary pearl fortune and pursues the sexy fishwoman through underwater channels to where she abides with her pet shark. Timothy Carey portrays the heavy. Later re-released as AQUASEX in an adult version that featured nude footage of Gaby Martone. George Rowe, Jose Gonzales-Gonzales. (Fright)

MESA OF LOST WOMEN. Video version of **LOST WOMEN** (S/Weird; Filmfax).

MESMERIZED (1984). Gothic thriller in which Jodie Foster is terorized by John Lithgow, who uses hypnosis to keep her under his spell. Written-directed by Michael Laughlin. (Vestron; from Edde as **SHOCKED**)

MESSAGE FROM SPACE (1978). SEVEN SAMURAI reset in a faraway galaxy, with a dash of STAR WARS. Inhabitants of Jillucia seek eight soldiers-of-fortune to stave off an attack by the Gavanas Empire, a battle which culminates with an attack on a space station. Decent effects (including an interstellar ship that has sails, of all things) cannot salvage a mediocre script—nor can director Kinji Fukasaku save the day. Vic Morrow and Sonny Chiba beef up U.S. box office, but their help is minimal in any language. (Laser: Japanese)

MESSIAH OF EVIL (1973). Writers-producers-directors Willard Huyck and Gloria Katz created this muddled mess about a town of zombies. It failed under its own title and was reissued as DEAD PEOPLE, RETURN OF THE LIVING DEAD and REVENGE OF THE SCREAMING DEAD. Nothing helped. Michael Greer, Marianna Hill, Joy Bang, Royal Dano, Elisha Cook Jr. (Video Gems; Media)

METALSTORM: THE DESTRUCTION OF JARED-SYN (1983). Blatant rip-off of ROAD WARRIOR from producer-director Charles Band and writer Alan J. Adler, jampacked with grim-jawed, steely-eyed characters and overacting. Some effects are unusual for a 3-D movie, and production is occasionally ambitious, but this has no heart. "Peacekeeping Ranger" Jeffrey Byron is sent to quell an uprising on Lemuria and arrest head insurrectionist Jared-Syn. It plays like a cowboys-and-Indians nonsaga, with Western cliches creeping into the imbecilic dialogue. The dusty auto chases are routine, the zap gun shootouts are dumbly staged and the climax never happens—Jared-Syn simply vanishes into another dimension with promise of a sequel. METALSTORM II never happened. Richard Moll, Mike Preston, Tim Thomerson. (Video/Laser: MCA)

METAMORPHOSIS (1975). Arty Swedish adaptation of Franz Kafka's 1912 allegory-fantasy about a drab warehouse salesman who metamorphoses into a giant cockroach and must live under his domineering father, mousy mother and repressed sister as a rejected "thing." Czech director Ivo Dvorak makes fascinating use of point-of-view as his camera climbs the walls and walks the ceilings, peers from beneath tables and beds and turns 360 degrees to capture the anguish and claustrophobic feeling of the unfortunate youth. The human-size cockroach is revolting yet Dvorak builds sympathy by showing the cruel side to human nature. Shunned as so much vermin for more than a decade, this was finally shown in San Francisco in 1987. Crisply shot in sepiatone and color, METAMORPHOSIS will please the art-house set but commerical movie-goers may feel all the bugs are not out of the story. Ernst Gunther, Peter Schildt, Gunn Wallgren.

METAMORPHOSIS: THE ALIEN FACTOR (1991). All hell breaks loose when doctors experiment once too often with tissue samples of an E.T. in their top-security laboratory. One of the docs turns into a monster big enough to require stop-motion animation. Well produced but you've seen it all before. Derivative script by writer-director Glenn Takakjian. Tara Leigh, Tony Gigante, Dianna Flaherty. (Imperial)

METEOR (1979). About to collide with Earth is a five-mile-wide hunk of space debris . . . which leaves the military feuding with the politicians, the politicians feuding with the civilians, the Communists arguing with the President, etc. A lot of time is spent building up to the disaster, but when it comes its impact is not what it should have been. The theme is trivialized by personal problems of Sean Connery (U.S. scientist), Natalie Wood (Russian physicist), Henry Fonda (the President), Karl Malden, Martin Landau, Trevor Howard, Sybil Danning. Directed by Ronald Neame. (Warner Bros.; Goodtimes)

METEOR MAN, THE (1993). Excellent black cast is wasted in this lightweight albeit well-intended parody of Superman, recast here as a black man who uses his superpowers in a benevolent way. Writer-director-star Robert Townsend is a pleasant personality but the funniest moments are too infrequent, and come too late, to save the premise. This "Tinsel Townsend Production" stars Townsend as an ineffectual schoolteacher who is hit by a meteor and absorbs a gooey green ball into his body. Before you can spell kryptonite, he's transformed into . . . METEOR MAN, and going up against the vicious Golden Lords street gang. That excellent cast has James Earl Jones as Mr. Moses (a silly guy wearing funny wigs), Bill Cosby as a street bum, Nancy Wilson, Sinbad, Lawanda Page, Eddie Griffin, Don Cheadle and rap artists Biz Markie, Big Daddy Kane and Bobbie McGee. (MGM)

ROBERT TOWNSEND

METEOR MONSTER (1957). Also known as TEENAGE MONSTER, this is set within the cliches of the Western as a mysterious ray shoots out of an asteroid and infects the body of a young boy. Slowly he turns into a monster who commits outrages against a desert community. Produced-directed by James Marquette. Gilbert Perkins, Anne Gwynne. (Monterey; Sinister/C)

METROPOLIS (1927). Silent German classic, directed by Fritz Lang, is an expressionistic view of a city in 2026, a complex skyscraper system built for slavery. The enslaved population's only hope is a woman Messiah, so the totalitarian rulers plot to substitute her with a robot. Revolt and destruction follow. This landmark classic is viewed in modern times with mixed reactions: some feel it is naive and outdated; others feel it is a masterpiece of political sci-fi and a forerunner of the special-effects picture. In '84 a reconstructed version was released (scenes missing since the film was cut for the U.S. market in the '20s were restored) with new sound effects, color and a score by Giorgio Moroder. A controversy developed over whether or not a new score was suitable for an old picture. Within the score were eight new songs, with many lyrics by Pete Bellotte. Karl Freund was one of the cinematographers. Brigitte Helm, Alfred Abel, Gustav Froehlich, Fritz Rasp, Rudolf Klein-Rogge (Vestron; Kino; Cable; Video Yesteryear; with THINGS TO COME from Goodtimes). (Laser: Vestron)

MIAMI GOLEM. See **MIAMI HORROR.**

MIAMI HORROR (1987). E.T. force controls Earthlings with psychic energies but TV reporter David Warbeck fights the alien invaders as well as John Ireland's gang of thugs. Also called MIAMI GOLEM, this was directed by Martin Herbert. Lawrence Loddi, Laura Trotter, George Favretto. (Action International; Panther)

MICROWAVE MASSACRE (1979). Comedian Jackie Vernon, playing a construction worker, chops up his wife (Claire Ginsberg) and stuffs the tidbits into the freezer. He develops a taste for those morsels and stockpiles human flesh—the coldest cuts of all. Director Wayne Berwick plays this rancidly macabre meatloaf for laughs; if you find cannibalism funny, you'll guffaw up an appetite. Loren Schein, Al Troupe, Lou Ann Webber. (Rhino; Select-A-Tape; Midnight)

MIDNIGHT (1980). John Russo, who co-authored THE NIGHT OF THE LIVING DEAD with George Romero, wrote-directed this horror effort (based on his novel) in the vein of THE TEXAS CHAINSAW MASSACRE. A teenager runs away from home and falls into the hands of a family of demented killers who worship the Devil. It's familiar territory enlivened by the make-up of Tom Savini. Lawrence Tierney is a drunken cop who attempts sexually to molest the teenager in the opening scenes and later comes to her rescue—an odd morality. Melanie Verlin, John Amplas, Greg Besnak. (Vidmark)

MIDNIGHT (1989). Lynn Redgrave goes over the top as a shrilly, bitchy TV horror-movie hostess named Midnight, and Tony Curtis goes with her as a TV producer conniving to get the copyright to her character. This is more an indictment of Hollywood than a horror film, with the scary stuff coming toward the end when a mysterious killer knocks off Midnight's associates. Producer-writer-director Norman Chaddeus Vane allows the cast to overindulge and you end up with unpleasant profiles, hardly the stuff of a riveting movie. Frank Gorshin stands out as an actor turned agent. Steve Parrish, Karen Witter, Rita Gam, Wolfman Jack, Gloria Morrison. (Sony) (Laser: Image)

MIDNIGHT AT MADAME TUSSAUD'S (1936). George Pearson directed this British film set in London's infamous wax museum of horrors. Charles Oliver, James Carew, Bernard Miles, William Hartnell. (Filmfax)

MIDNIGHT CABARET (1990). Devil-worship cult plots for a young actress to become impregnanted with the child of Satan, using a New York night club as the base of operation. (Warner Bros.)

MIDNIGHT HOUR, THE. Video version of the TV-movie **IN THE MIDNIGHT HOUR** (Vidmark).

MIDNIGHT MANHUNT (1945). See third edition.

MIDNIGHT MENACE (1937). See editions 1-3.

MIDNIGHT MOVIE MASSACRE (1986). Producer Wade Williams made this spoof of 1950s sci-fi movies at the Granada Theater in Kansas City, Mo. Set in 1956, it depicts an audience of freaks, nerds, nuts, misfits and rejects watching SWEATER GIRL FROM MARS and SPACE PATROL: GUARDIANS OF THE UNIVERSE. Williams uses the Kitchen Sink principle as he insults you, shocks you, tickles your funnybone and reminds you why you enjoy bad movies. SPACE PATROL (directed by Larry Jacobs) features Robert Clarke and Ann Robinson as heroic types. Meanwhile, an alien monster lands near the theater and closes in, killing the ticket-office gal and moving toward the snack bar. Will the beast get the obese popcorn eater, the back-row smoochers, the trio of stupid tough guys, the girl who keeps dropping snotty rags into a sex-crazed cowboy's beer cup? Stand by for more dripping gore. Mark Stock directed the script by David Houston, John Chadwell, Roger Branit (also the editor) and Williams. David Staffer, Mary Stevens, Tom Hutsler,

Margie Robbins. (VCI; United)

MIDNIGHT OFFERINGS (1981). Stephen J. Cannell TV-movie with themes of witchcraft and exorcism. It's good witch Mary McDonough against bad witch Melissa Sue Anderson in a plot as predictable as the color of a black cat. Rod Holcolm gives indifferent direction to Juanita Bartlett's teleplay, which is about as scary as a black cat running in front of your car. Gordon Jump, Patrick Cassidy, Cathry Damon, Marion Ross.

MIDNIGHT'S CHILD (1992). Subtitle this derivative mixture of ROSEMARY'S BABY and THE HAND THAT ROCKS THE CRADLE as "The Nanny From Hell." Olivia D'Abo, possessing a red crystal pendant with powers to sway men's minds, portrays a Swedish disciple of Satan ("the Prince") who picks the daughter (Elissabeth Moss) of a young L. A. couple (Marcy Walker and Cotter Smith) to be the Devil's next bride. David Chaskin's TV script is obvious and Colin Bucksey's direction of this Victoria Principal production lacks surprises. You'll be calling the shots long before Ms Walker wises up. Jim Norton, Judy Parfitt, Roxann Biggs.

MIDNIGHT WARNING (1933). Man vanishes from an allegedly haunted hotel room and everyone denies his existence. An old Alexander Woolcott story was adapted with a surprise ending that was reused many times afterward in radio, TV and movies. Directed by Spencer G. Bennet (later a serial specialist). Remade without horror overtones as SO LONG AT THE FAIR and DANGEROUS CROSSING. Claudia Dell, William Boyd, John Harron. (Sinister/C; Filmfax; Discount)

MIGHTY GORGA, THE (1970). Variation on KING KONG in which adventurers Anthony Eisley, Kent Taylor and Scott Brady discover a plateau inhabited by prehistoric monsters and one king-size ape (see title). Unimaginative work from director David L. Hewitt, who doubled as Gorga in a gorilla suit. Nothing mighty about it. Just mighty bad. Megan Timothy, Lee Parrish, cinematographer Gary Graver, William Bonner. (Cinema Concepts)

MIGHTY JOE YOUNG (1949). KING KONG mentors Merian C. Cooper and Ernest B. Schoedsack teamed to spoof their giant ape with this mighty adventure showcasing the stop motion of Willis O'Brien, Hollywood's screen-magic pioneer. (O'Brien received a much-deserved Oscar.) Mighty Joe Young, a friendly giant gorilla raised in Africa by Terry Moore, is brought to the states by promoter Robert Armstrong (repeating his role from KONG) where the creature is an attraction in a Hollywood night club, the Golden Safari. While Moore plays "Beautiful Dreamer" on her piano, Joe goes bananas and demolishes the nitery, escaping. It's up to sympathetic cowhand Ben Johnson and Moore to rescue the hapless Joe. A fire in an orphanage climaxes the script by Ruth Rose (Mrs. Schoedsack). John Ford, although he received no credit, directed some second unit. Ray Harryhausen assisted O'Brien. Remarkably well-made if old-fashioned picture produced by Cooper and directed by Schoedsack. Frank McHugh, Regis Toomey, Nester Paiva, Primo Camera, Douglas Fowley. (Nostalgia Merchant; Turner) (Laser: Image, also in a tinted version)

MIGHTY JUNGLE, THE (1964). Explorers Marshall Thompson and David Dalie split up to pursue different adventures. Dalie goes to the Amazon where he finds a lost city; Thompson ventures to Africa to undergo perils of the Congo River and Pygmies. Their adventures are padded with real footage of battling iguanas, snakes, rampaging elephant herds, etc. Written-directed by Arnold Belgard and Dave DaLie. Music by Lex Baxter. (Paragon; King of Video)

MIGHTY PEKING MAN, THE (1977). Hong Kong flick copying KING KONG but with the addition of a blonde (Evelyn Krafty) who is a giant ape's companion. An expedition takes both of them back to Hong Kong. Directed by Homer Gaugh.

MIKE AND THE MERMAID (1964). Editions 1-3.

MILLENNIUM (1989). John Varley adapted his short story, "Air Raid," into this feature that seems to be two separate movies welded together. It opens with a grim depiction of two airliners colliding and investigator Kris Kristofferson examining the wreckage. This portion is uncannily realistic. Suddenly, Varley introduces time travelers from 1000 years in the future, led by Cheryl Ladd. It is then the plot gets bogged down in an unconvincing love story, many scenes of which are repeated when Ladd messes with time, jumping from time zone to time zone. Seems that in the distant future mankind will be faced with the danger of becoming sterile, and people from the present day are needed to procreate the race. And that's Ladd's job. Ultimately, the time-travel/Armageddon plot is too full of holes to take seriously and the picture crashes as grimly as those jetliners. Directed by Michael (LOGAN'S RUN) Anderson. Daniel J. Travanti, Robert Joy, Lloyd Bochner. (IVE) (Laser: Image)

MILLION DOLLAR DUCK (1971). Disney fantasy about a radioactive duck laying the proverbial Golden Egg. Our advice to the kids: Take a gander. To the adults: Duck it. Directed by Vincent McEveety. Dean Jones, Sandy Duncan, Joe Flynn, James Gregory, Tony Roberts, Arthur Hunnicutt. (Disney)

MILLION DOLLAR LEGS (1932). See editions 1-3.

MILLION EYES OF SU-MURU, THE (1967). Shirley Eaton is a female Fu Manchu masterminding a plot to take over the world. Her most deadly weapon, not counting the ones God gave her at birth, is a Medusa phaser-gun that turns folks into rocks. Yeah, it stones them. It's up to Frankie Avalone and George Nader to put a stop to her nefarious man-chewing. Klaus Kinski and Wilfrid Hyde-White are among the colorful characters. Followed by a sequel, RIO '80, released to TV as FUTURE WOMEN.

MILL OF THE STONE WOMEN, THE (1962). Based on THE FLEMING TALES by Peter van Weigan, this Italian-French effort was made in Holland and relates the affairs of a mad doctor who drains blood from female corpses to keep his daughter alive. The setting is a windmill where a museum of notorious female murderers is open for business. Run-of-the-windmill. Directed by Giorgio Ferroni. Wolfgang Preiss, Pierre Brice, Scilla Gabel. (Paragon; Sinister/C; from American Video as **ICON**)

MILPITAS MONSTER, THE (1975). After being the brunt of jokes by Steve Allen and Jack Benny, the Bay Area community of Milpitas, Calif., pulled a joke on the public by producing a horror film. The town of 32,500 helped in the production, which took two years and cost $11,000 in 16mm. The titular titan is a creature with bat-like wings and a gasmask face, spawned in the embryo of pollution. "Milpy" rises from the ooze to wipe out a town drunk and ends up atop a TV transformer tower. Quite amateurish, from Robert L. Burrill's direction to Davie E. Boston's script to the acting of half of Milpitas. Ben Burtt, who went on to win an Oscar for his sound effects in STAR WARS, contributed to the effects. Paul Frees narrates. And Milpitas lives! (United; VCI)

MIND BENDERS, THE (1963). Philosophical British study of men who undergo isolation tests in deep submergence tanks and experience changes in personality. Dirk Bogarde is subjected and his brain becomes putty—posthypnotic suggestions bring about a total alteration in his behavior. James Kennaway's script deals seriously with personal complications that result with wife Mary Ure and comments on tampering with the human psyche. Directed by Basil Dearden. John Clements.

MINDFIELD (1989). In this Canadian production, an experiment with LSD to turn men into mindless murderers has left Michael Ironside living a nightmarish existence. Doctor Christopher Plummer is in on the plot. Directed by Jean-Claude (VISITING HOURS) Lord. Lisa Langlois, Stefas Wodoslowsky, Sean McCann. (Magnum) (Laser: Image)

MIND GAMES (1979). Video of **AGENCY** (Simitar).

MIND GAMES (1988). Mildly compelling psychological thriller told subtly, in the vein of THE SERVANT. Lone traveler Maxwell Caulfield is befriended by vacationers Edward Albert, wife Shawn Weatherly and son Matt Norero, but manipulates each for devious purposes—corrupting the innocent youth, seducing the unhappy wife and making life miserable for angst-ridden Albert. The film has its most ironic moment when Albert reads the deranged hitchhiker's diary, which lucidly describes his family's psychological needs and hang-ups. But Kenneth Dorward's script is without enough depth or horror to make this worthy of a fan's attention. (CBS/Fox)

MIND KILLER (1988). Threadbare, sloppily produced video feature, with unpleasant graphics that are not backed up by a strong story or good acting. Joe McDonald is a nerdy librarian whom the girls ignore—until he finds an old manuscript that gives him the secret to controlling the will of others. But the one librarian (Shirley Ross) whom he would like to get his hands on is too smart for him. The script by Dave Sipos, Curtis Hannum and director Michael Krueger has the final twist of McDonald producing a creature within his exploding brain. A real mind-numbing experience. Christopher Wade, Kevin Hart, Tom Henry. (Prism)

MIND OF MR. SOAMES, THE (1970). Amicus version of Charles Eric Maine's novel is a thoughtful psychological study of a young man in a coma since birth who, awakened by electrical stimulation, must be taught like a newborn child. Terence Stamp is excellent as the bewildered young man, Robert Vaughn has one of his finest roles as a sympathetic scientist, and Nigel Davenport is coldly clinical as the project boss who has no compassion. This maintains a high level of intelligence and avoids a contrived climax, leaving some problems unresolved. Sensitively directed by Alan Cooke.

MIND OVER MURDER (1979). Offbeat TV-movie, rather explicit for its time, stars Deborah Raffin as a commercial model who begins having what doctor Christopher Cary calls "precognitive audio-visual hallucinations"—periods when time stands still and she sees and hears flashes of events to come. The recurring image in these brief but disorienting nightmares is an evil-looking bald man, played with menace by Andrew Prine. Raffin is finally helped by a government man (David Ackroyd) investigating a plane crash that would also seem to involve the bald man. Robert Carrington's script is often contrived and has Raffin doing inexplicable things (such as walking into a deserted alleyway) yet also deals intriguingly with her confused state of mind and disinitegrating marriage to Bruce Davison. Ivan Nagy's direction captures Prine's sleazy environment and depravity. Robert Englund has a supporting role.

MIND SNATCHERS, THE (1972). Should science tamper with those parts of the human mind that control our emotional levels and personality traits in an effort to create happy people—or do we need to be individuals, even if we are plagued by neuroses and other unstable traits? This literate film explores that issue by establishing a clandestine military laboratory in Germany, where doctor Joss Ackland inserts steel fibers into men's brains to improve their health and eliminate disobedient traits. Excellent performances by two of the guinea pigs, Ronny Cox and Christopher Walken, keep Rony Whyte's screenplay (based on a play, THE HAPPINESS CAGE, by Dennis Reardon) on a heightened edge, as does the presence of sinister Army officer Ralph Meeker. Filmed in Denmark. Tom Aldredge, Marco St. John. (Congress; Prism; from Ace as **DEMON WITHIN, THE**)

MIND WARP. Alternate video verison of **GREY MATTER** (Academy).

MINDWARP (1991). The first of several horror movies produced by the Fangora publishing empire, this post-holocaust retread stars Bruce Campbell as a Mad Max-like hero who's involved with mutants who live in dark tunnels and most folks are tied to a dream-invoking network called Infinisynth. Angus Scrimm stands out as the sadistic villain. Directed by Steve Barnett. Marta Alicia, Elizabeth Kent, Mary Becker. (RCA/Columbia)

MINDWARP: AN INFINITY OF TERROR. See **GALAXY OF TERROR.**

MINISTER'S MAGICIAN, THE. See **HARLEQUIN.**

MINOTAUR, THE WILD BEAST OF CRETE (1961). According to mythology, the Minotaur was a half-bull, half-man monster who fed on human flesh and was kept in a Cretan labyrinth. In this Italian production, half-bull says it all. Theseus (Bob Mathias) struts bravely forward, flexing his biceps, to destroy the maneater with a magical sword. Rosanna Schiaffino, Alberto Lupo, Rik Battaglia. Directed by Silvio Amadio. (S/Weird)

MIRANDA (1948). Pleasant British comedy starring Glynis Johns as a lovely mermaid who takes a liking to a handsome landlubber and forsakes the sea for life inland. And therein hangs a tail. Followed by the 1954 sequel, MAD ABOUT MEN. Directed by Ken Annakin. Googie Withers, Margaret Rutherford.

MIRROR MIRROR (1990). CARRIE meets THE GATE swept open by DEMON WIND. So goes this compendium of cliches enhanced only by Rainbow Harvest as a shy teenager turned into a force of vengeful evil when she falls under the spell of a cursed mirror through which monsters pass to the earthly plane. Such pros as Karen Black (as a self-centered mother), William Sanderson (as a science teacher) and Yvonne De Carlo (as a furniture dealer) cannot salvage a movie as dreary as this. MTV director Marina Sargenti makes her feature debut, and while she does a creditable job, there's no freshness to this endless series of scenes you've seen before, and before, and before. Kristin Dattilo, Ricky Paul Goldin. (Academy) (Laser: Image)

MIRRORS (1974). Video version of MARIANNE, a psychological thriller made in New Orleans. Newlyweds Kitty Winn and William Swetland check into a sinister hotel where Kitty has hallucinations as she wanders through a hall of mirrors. Voodoo lady (Vanessa Hutchinson) has cursed her and is hoping to claim her soul. Peter Donat plays a doctor, but whose side is he on? Directed by Noel Black. Ray Bradbury is listed as "creative consultant." Mary-Robin Redd, William Burns. (Family Home Entertainment; Monterey)

MISADVENTURES OF MERLIN JONES, THE (1964). An Electro-Encephalograph is the do-it-yourself creation of college student Tommy Kirk, which infuses him with power to read men's (and kids') minds. The device also enables him and Annette Funicello to capture crooks. Standard juvenile comedy from Disney. Leon Ames, Stu Erwin, Alan Hewitt, Connie Gilchrist, and a chimp. Directed by Robert Stevenson. The sequel: THE MONKEY'S UNCLE. (Disney)

MISERY (1990). Rob Reiner's triumphant adaptation of Stephen King's best-seller with Kathy Bates coping an Oscar for her crazed Annie Wilks, any writer's ultimate nightmare of a fan gone mad. James Caan, in one of his best roles in years, brings numerous nuances to novelist Paul Sheldon, injured in a car accident during a snow storm and cared for secretly by the infatuated Ms Wilks—infatuated, that is, until her insanity takes over and he becomes her prisoner. The scene with the sledgehammer is guaranteed to evoke a scream, and to Reiner's credit is a most effective shock-violence sequence. One wishes there was more of Richard Farnsworth's homespun sheriff, Buster, but that is a minor flaw. Frances Sternhagen, Laureen Bacall, Graham Jarvis, J. T. Walsh. (Video/Laser: MCA)

MISFITS OF SCIENCE (1985). Pilot for a short-lived series in which a handful of teenagers are each given a special power to help the world out of its constant jams. A not-so-special effects effort that has a few amusing moments, but which ends up as labored as the series. Directed by James Parriott. Kevin Peter Hall. (MCA)

MISS DEATH. See **DIABOLICAL DR. Z, THE.**

MISSILE BASE AT TANIAK (1953). Re-edited TV version of the Republic serial **CANADIAN MOUNTIES VS. ATOMIC INVADERS**. See that entry.

MISSILE MONSTERS (1951). Feature version of Republic's **FLYING DISC MAN FROM MARS.**

MISSILE TO THE MOON (1959). Richard Travis, leader of a lunar expedition, is so dumb he doesn't know some reform school jerks have sneaked aboard his cardboard rocketship. On the moon, he and his crew of nitwits find a Lost Race of women and a cave filled with beasts controlled by wires from the catwalks overhead. Truly an all-time low, based on the lowest of the low to begin with, CAT WOMEN OF THE MOON. Directed by Richard Cunha. Gary Clarke, Laurie Mitchell, Cathy Downs. (Media; Rhino; Thrillervideo; S/Weird; Filmfax)

MISSING ARE DEADLY, THE (1975). Editions 1-3.

MISSING GUEST, THE (1938). Sinister house lures a handful of guests, one of whom disappears from a room; a search is conducted but no explanation is found. Remake of SECRET OF THE BLUE ROOM. Directed by John Rawlins. William Lundigan, Paul Kelly.

MISSING LINK (1989). Set "one million years ago," this oddity from producers Peter Guber and Jon Peters depicts an ape-man (species Australopithecus Robustus) wandering the African veldt, observing wild animals, finding his family slaughtered by lions, and wondering how he can put a stone axe to good use. There's very little in it that will appeal to fantasy fans. Peter Elliott plays the hairy guy, with make-up by Rick Baker. Written-directed-photographed by David and Carol Hughes. (MCA)

MISSION GALACTICA: THE CYLON ATTACK. TV version of the 1978 TV pilot for **BATTLESTAR GALACTICA** (Video/Laser: MCA).

MISSION MARS (1968). Laughable kiddie stuff with Darren McGavin and Nick Adams as hysterically incompetent astronauts on Mars I, the first manned probe to the Red Planet. Their ship looks like an inverted Campbell Soup can, the alien life form (called a Polarite) resembles Gumby and an E.T. sphere is a golf ball magnified. Directed by Nicholas Webster. (Unicorn)

MISSION STARDUST (1968). Spacecraft from Earth is forced down on the moon, where robots lead astronauts to an alien craft. Medical help is needed to overcome a disease. Spanish-Italian-West German co-oper is based on the Perry Rhodan book series. Directed by Primo Zeglio. Lang Jeffries, Essy Persson. (Rhino)

MISS LESLIE'S DOLLS (1972). Filipino flick for lowbrows as an ugly homosexual-transvestite with a mother fixation murders women and slices up their bodies. As for those childish playthings of the title, they aren't Cabbage Patch variety. Directed-written by Joseph G. Prieto. Salvador Ugarte, Terry Juston, Kitty Lewis, C. W. Pitts.

MISS MORRISON'S GHOSTS (1981). British TV-movie is a fascinating true-life case of a ghostly experience undergone by two women from Oxford walking the gardens at Versailles who claim they were thrown into a time-space continuum where they saw the spirit of Mary Antoinette. The women's jobs are jeopardized after they tell their story to the British Psychic Society. Wendy Hiller, Hannah Gordon. Directed by John Bruce.

MISS PINKERTON (1932). See third edition.

MISTRESSES OF DR. JEKYLL. See **DR. ORLOFF'S MONSTER.**

MISTRESS OF THE APES (1979). Larry Buchanan wrote-directed this low-budget film, which tackles none too successfully the ape-man-as-a-missing-link-in-evolution theme. Jenny Neumann, Paula Sils. (Monterey)

MISTRESS OF THE WORLD (1959). The secret of controlling Earth's magnetic fields is discovered by a scientist who is murdered. His daughter wages a fight against evil. This Italian-French-West German production stars Martha Hyer, Sabu, Lino Ventura, Wolfgang Preiss and Carlos Thompson; severely edited for the U.S. Directed by William Dieterle. Wolfgang Preiss. (Vidmark)

MIRACLE, THE (1959). Carroll Baker, a covent postulant about to take holy vows, she runs away with handsome dragoon Roger Moore. The statue of a Madonna pops to life, steps down in the form of Ms Baker and assumes her place. Meanwhile, Carroll is having one helluva time, taking up with gypsy, matador, nobleman. But each lover meets a bloody demise. Is there a religious message in all this? One of the great howlers of the '50s, a film so pious and hypocritical, the human intellect boggles. Irving Rapper directed it with straight face. Walter Slezak, Vittorio Gassman, Katrina Paxinou.

MIRACLE BEACH (1991). Not a single effects shot graces this time-killer about a beautiful green-eyed genie (Ami Dolenz) sent by a heavenly assignment chief (Allen Garfield) to an L.A. beach to help a nerdy guy (Dean Cameron) find true love with Felicity Waterman at the same time he's throwing a beauty contest attended by big-busted babes. Pat Morita and Vincent Schiavelli are wasted in this grant-my-wish comedy directed by Skott Snider. Ample nudity (the T & A kind) is all there is to keep one awake. Alexis Arquette, Brian Perry, Martin Mull.

MIRACLE IN MILAN (1952). Controversy sprang up when this Vittorio de Sica fantasy was released, for everyone had a different political interpretation and de Sica was accused of being a communist. But he denied any political overtones and said he was bypassing the intellect to reach the heart. The screenplay (by de Sica and Cesare Zavattini) concerns an orphan named Toto, visited by his deceased foster mother and given a miracle-working dove. (Home Vision) (Laser: Voyager)

MIRACLE IN THE RAIN (1956). Touching and sentimental to some, pious and corny to others . . . Plain Jane Wyman is leading a dreary life in 1942 until she meets fun-loving Army private Van Johnson. She gives him a token of their romance before he ships out overseas. Now here comes the heavy part: Jane is suffering from pneumonia when she staggers outside into a rainstorm, has a vision and faints—only to wake up and . . . well, we won't spoil the rest. Directed by Rudolph Mate, scripted by Ben Hecht from his own novel.

MIRACLE MILE (1988). Offbeat cautionary tale (call it pre-Armageddon) that scores for mood and unpredictable plot. What would you do if you had 70 minutes to react to pending nuclear attack? That's the situation for musician Anthony Edwards who answers a phone outside Johnnie's restaurant in L.A. and learns the horrible truth. This second feature from writer-director Steve (CHERRY 2000) de Jarnatt is an intriguing study in mass hysteria that builds unrelentingly as Edwards plans an escape route. Be forewarned this is a downer, with no cop-out ending. Denise Crosby is exceptionally good as a stockbroker who represents the intellectual side of man in dealing with a life-and-death crisis. Compelling viewing. John Agar, Lou Hancock, Mykel T. Williams, Kelly Minter. (HBO) (Laser: Image)

MIRACLE OF FATHER MALACHIOS, THE (1967). See editions 1-3.

MIRACLE OF MARCELINO, THE (1954). See editions 1-3.

MIRACLE OF OUR LADY OF FATIMA, THE (1952). Dramatization of an incident that occurred in Fatima, Portugal, in 1917 and which was accepted by the Catholic Church as a miracle. The miracle consisted of the sun seeming to swoop down out of the sky and swing across the Heavens, a phenomenon witnessed by thousands who had gathered at the urging of three children who claimed they had seen the Virgin Mary. When this delves into the political climate of that desperate World War I period, it is an oversimplification of good vs. evil. When director John Brahm focuses on the youngsters, the film becomes credible and touches the heartstrings. Agnostics and atheists will find this difficult viewing. Believers

"I have conquered science. Why can't I conquer love?"

—Peter Lorre in **MAD LOVE**

will rejoice. Those with open minds will find that this only taps the events superficially and additional reading is suggested. Max Steiner's score was nominated for an Oscar. Gilbert Roland, Frank Silvera, Angela Clarke, Jay Novello. (Video/Laser: Warner Bros.)

MIRACLE OF THE BELLS, THE (1948). Pious or provocative, depending on how much you are disturbed by Overstatement and Preaching. Fred MacMurray, a movie publicist, escorts the body of a dead actress (Valli) back to her hometown, where for three days the church bells ring without human aid—or so it would appear. Ben Hecht and Quentin Reynolds wrote the screenplay from Russell Janney's best-seller, but even they had to admit it was a "hunkajunk." Directed by Irving Pichel as though it were the Second Coming. So campily presented, it reaches a point of must-see fascination. Frank Sinatra, Lee J. Cobb, Philip Ahn. (Republic; Spotlite)

MIRACLE ON 34TH STREET, THE (1947). Is there really a Santa Claus? You bet your reindeer, Christmas lovers and Virginia. This delightful slice of Americana was written-directed by George Seaton, who has a Kringly knack for fantasy-comedy in a heart-warming vein. Edmund Gwenn is a department store Santa who insists on the authenticity of his role and forces the issue to trial. The subplot focuses on a romance between Maureen O'Hara and John Payne and orphan Natalie Wood and while it's hokey, it blends beautifully with the Santa fairy tale. (Video/Laser: CBS/Fox)

MIRACLE ON 34TH STREET, THE (1973). Sebastian Cabot, David Hartman, Roddy McDowall and Jim Backus are starred in this TV musical version of George Seaton's 1947 comedy classic. Directed by Fielder Cook.

M.M.M. 83 (1965). See editions 1-3.

MODEL KILLER, THE. Video version of **HOLLYWOOD STRAMGLER MEETS THE SKID ROW SLASHER, THE** (Regal).

MODEL MASSACRE. Video version of **COLOR ME BLOOD RED** (BFPI).

MODERN PROBLEMS (1981). Disappointing Chevy Chase vehicle in which he portrays an air-traffic controller who is bathed in a strange atomic cloud and takes on a green glow and ESP talents. Ken Shapiro, amusing director of THE GROOVE TUBE, blew it here, trying to make his satire socially relevant when in fact it is plain dumb. Shapiro is so uncertain of his material that Chase finally becomes unsympathetic. Mary Kay Place, Nell Carter, Dabney Coleman. (CBS/Fox)

MODESTY BLAISE (1966). The Peter O'Donnell-Jim Holdaway comic strip was adapted with verve by director Joseph Losey and scriptwriter Evan Jones. Monica Vitti portrays the sexy superheroine with all the right equipment—and the most current gadgets and weaponry. Terence Stamp is Willie Garvin, her comrade-in-arms. Modesty is hired to protect a fortune in gems, but villainous Dirk Bogarde (as Gabriel, an amusing heavy with homosexual overtones) begins a series of double crosses aided by Mrs. Fothergill (Rosella Falk). Harry Andrews, Clive Revill, Michael Craig.

MOLE MEN VS. THE SON OF HERCULES (1962). Mark Forest grunts and groans as Maciste, a muscle-bound he-man fighting through an underground city. All brawn and no brain in this Italian sword-and- sandal scandal directed by Antonio Leonviola. Moira Orfei, Paul Wynter, Gianna Garko. (Sinister/C; S/Weird)

MOLE PEOPLE, THE (1956). John Agar leads a Tibetan expedition underground where it encounters mutant human-moles. But the mole moes aren't the bad guys—they're dirt slaves to the Sumerians, a white race dwelling in a typical Hollywood Underground Lost City. This pulp adventure tale is made acceptable by good mole make-up and rubber suits. In a laughable prologue, Dr. Frank Baxter discusses the possibilities of life in the core of the Earth which is as bogus as the plot by Laszlo Gorog. Dig it! Directed by Virgil Vogel. Cynthia Patrick, Hugh Beaumont, Alan Napier. (Video/Laser: MCA)

MOM (1989). Dreary direct-to-video flop predicated on the idea that a sweet old mother turned into a flesh-eating monster makes an intriguing concept. Maybe so, but the guys who made FLESH-EATING MOTHERS did it better. This limps along in depicting serial-killer Brion James taking refuge in the home of sweet Jeanne Bates and turning her into a demon who looks for bums to murder and eat. Mom's son (Mark Thomas Miller) is a TV newscaster who figures out what's going on. Stella Stevens appears as an aging whore, dressed in an outrageous costume, and is the only relief from tedium. Directed-written without flair by Patrick Rand. Mary McDonough, Art Evans. (Video/Laser: RCA/Columbia)

MOM AND DAD SAVE THE WORLD (1991). Imagine a blatant spoof of sci-fi serials of the '30s and you've got the idea for this parody in which a planet of "idiots" plots to blow up Earth with a "Death Ray Laser." Led by Lord Tod (Jon Lovitz) of the planet Spengo, the aliens transport an Earth couple (Jeffrey Jones and Teri Garr) to their world. How the witless Earthlings (Jones is a couch potato, Garr is the ultimate loving mother) outsmart the more-witless aliens, with the help of a tribe of cave-dwelling natives who are the most witless of all, is the basis for the Chris Matheson-Ed Solomon script (they also created Bill & Ted). Directed by Greg Beeson. Thalmus Rasulala, Tod's wise old sage, died after the film was finished. Kathy Ireland, Dwier Brown, Wallace Shawn, Eric Idle. (Warner Bros.)

HANDMAIDEN

MOM FOR CHRISTMAS (1990). Olivia Newton-John portrays a department-store mannikin that comes to life to help a motherless child (Juliet Sorcey). Newton-John also sings a few yuletide numbers to keep it warm and sentimental. Doug Sheehan, Doris Roberts, Carmen Argenziano, James Piddock.

MOMMA'S BOY. See **NIGHT WARNING.**

MOMO (1987). John Huston makes one of his last screen appearances in this obscure Italian-West German fantasy directed and co-written by Johannes Schaaf and based on Michael Ende's THE NEVERENDING STORY. Radost Bokel portrays a ten-year-old orphan who turns to Father Time (Huston) to help her rid a local village of The Grey Men, a gang that stays alive by puffing on cigars. MOMO has been pretty much a no-no.

MONDO LUGOSI: A VAMPIRE'S SCRAPBOOK. Compilation of interviews with horror film star Bela Lugosi and clips from his movies. (Rhino)

MONGREL (1983). Its bite is worse than its bark—so conclude the men and women living in Aldo Ray's rural boarding house when they are killed off one by one by "a killer animal" heard roving the hallways at night. Filmed in Austin, Texas, this cheap horror flick is of little consequence. Writer-director Robert A. Burns found himself in the doghouse when it was finished. Terry Evans, Catherine Malloy, Mitch Pileggi. (Paragon)

MONIQUE (1983). Mentally disturbed wife (Florence Giorgetti) learns her husband has been cheating on her and decides to cheat him—out of his life. Directed by Jacques Scandelari. (VCL)

MONITORS, THE (1969). Misguided satirical misfire, involving Chicago's Second City comedy troupe, in which benevolent humanoids called The Monitors take over an American city, but an underground movement called SCRAG threatens peaceful order. This adaptation of a Keith Laumer novel is played in a dumb, farcical manner that never engages the viewer and meanders all over the landscape. Myron J. Gold's script was directed by Jack Shea with mimimal production values and the good cast is swamped by the material, including Guy Stockwell, Susan Oliver, Larry Storch, Avery Schreiber, Keenan

Wynn, Shepperd Strudwick and Sherry Jackson. Appearing in cameos are Alan Arkin, Stubby Kaye, Xavier Cugat and Jackie Vernon. Don't bother to monitor.

MONKEY BOY. Condensed video version from Prism of the four-hour British TV-movie re-edited to **CHIMERA.** See that entry. (Laser: Image)

MONKEY BUSINESS (1952). Hilarious comedy classic written by Ben Hecht and I.A.L. Diamond and directed by Howard Hawks. It's a screwball affair with Cary Grant as the epitome of the Absent-Minded Professor who is searching for a youth formula for industrialist Charles Coburn. Inadvertently, a chimpanzee mixes chemicals into the lab's drinking water that regresses one's mental state to a puberty level. Grant is aptly aided by Ginger Rogers as his jealous wife (she also portrays a mischievous juvenile to hilarious effect) and Marilyn Monroe as a leggy secretary who amply and unabashedly displays a pair of Grant's latest creation, nonrun stockings. A delight of comedy and satire, one of the greats of the '50s. Hugh Marlowe, Robert Cornthwaite, Larry Keating, Douglas Spencer, George Winslow. (Video/Laser: CBS/Fox)

MONKEY SHINES (1988). With George Romero directing one might assume this would be filled with horrible graphics—but such is not the case. And yet the film (scripted by Romero, from a novel by Michael Stewart) is an unpleasant experience, for its depicts a capuchin monkey as a blood-thirsty killer. Jason Beghe portrays a paraplegic trying to adjust to his miserable milieu when Melanie Parker brings him a well-trained monkey to serve as aide. But mad scientist John Pankow injects the monkey with a serum that turns him rabid. There's an unexplained psychic link between the creature and Beghe during the murders. Not for the psychologically squeamish. Joyce Van Patten, Christine Forrest, Stephen Root. (Orion) (Laser: Image)

MONKEY'S PAW, THE (1932). First sound version of the famous W.W. Jacobs short story, in which a mother wishes for her dead son's return—a wish granted by a severed monkey's paw. Directed by Wesley Ruggles. C. Aubrey Smith, Louise Carter, Ivan Simpson.

MONKEY'S PAW, THE (1948). British treatment of the W. W. Jacobs ghost tale starring Milton Rosmer and Michael Bass. Written-directed by Norman Lee.

MONKEY'S UNCLE (1964). Sequel to THE MISADVENTURES OF MERLIN JONES, depicting new scientific discoveries by a college whiz kid. Tommy Kirk boosts campus spirits by educating football players in their sleep so they won't flunk and be dropped from the team. It worked on a chimpanzee—why shouldn't it work on dumb football heroes? Annette Funicello, Leon Ames and Stanley (the chimp) reappear. Directed by Robert Stevenson. (Disney)

MONOLITH MONSTERS, THE (1957). A meteor, after crashing near a town in Death Valley, expands and grows when touched by water. Different pieces form into rock-like monsters which turn humans into solid stone. Grant (INCREDIBLE SHRINKING MAN) Williams and Lola Albright struggle to evacuate a town in danger of the titular entities. John Sherman directed. Les Tremayne, William Schallert. Effects by Clifford Stine. (Fright; MCA)

MONSTER, THE (1925). Silent miniclassic with Lon Chaney Sr. as the mad Dr. Ziska who restores life to the dead. An important film that established many genre cliches. Directed by Roland West. Gertrude Olmstead, Hallam Cooley. (Classic Video Cinema Collector's Club)

MONSTER (1975). See **DEVIL WITHIN HER.**

MONSTER (1979). K-Tel's, Genesis' and Premiere's video versions of **TOXIC HORROR, THE.**

MONSTER A GO-GO (1965). Any film about an astronaut who lands on Earth in a space capsule and emerges a ten-foot monster has got to go-go. Obscure low budgeter was started by Bill Rebane and finished by Herschell Gordon Lewis as "Sheldon Seymour." Phil Morton, Harry Hite. (United; VCI; S/Weird)

MONSTER AMONG THE GIRLS. See **WEREWOLF IN A GIRL'S DORMITORY.**

MONSTER AND THE GIRL, THE (1941). Vengeful criminal swears to knock off the scoundrels who framed him, is knocked off himself in the electric chair. His brain is transferred into an ape's skull and the ape begins the Simian Shamble, killing scroundrels. Nostalgic material of the '40s, directed by Stuart Heisler. George Zucco essays a mad scientist while Ellen Drew is hapless heroine and Rod Cameron the square-jawed hero. Gerald Mohr, Paul Lukas, Onslow Stevens, Philip Terry.

MONSTER AND THE STRIPPER, THE (1973). Get this plot: A werewolf is the attraction in a New Orleans nitery, working for the mob. This stand-up comedian has them howling! Also known as THE EXOTIC ONES. (Simitar)

MONSTER AND THE WOMAN, THE. See **FOUR-SIDED TRIANGLE.**

MONSTER BARAN, THE. See **VARAN THE UNBELIEVABLE.**

MONSTER CLUB, THE (1981). Fun-filled British horror flick has three bizarre elements: a conversation between Vincent Price (portraying a vampire) and John Carradine (portraying horror writer R. Chetwynd-Hayes); The Monster Club, a disco hang-out for freaks and ghoulies dancing hard-rock musical numbers; and a trilogy of tales told by Price, based on Chetwynd-Hayes stories. One concerns a monster called a "shadmock,"

VINCENT PRICE/FRIENDS IN 'THE MONSTER CLUB'

whose silent whistle is fatal to mortals; the second features Donald Pleasence leading a band of vampire chasers who keep their stakes in violin cases; and the third is about a village of "humgoos," who put the whammy on movie director Stuart Whitman. Roy Ward Baker directed with tongue in his cheek. A must for buffs for its in-jokes. Richard Johnson, Britt Ekland, Simon Ward, Patrick Magee, Anthony Steel. (Thrillervideo) (Laser: Image)

MONSTER DEMOLISHER (1960). One of four horror films sold into the U.S. by schlock producer K. Gordon Murray, who bought a Mexican serial starring German Robles as Nostradamus the Vampire. Cheap and unexciting with poor production values. Directed by Frederick Curiel. German Robles, Julio Aleman, Aurora Alvarado. Sequels: CURSE OF NOSTRADAMUS, GENII OF DARKNESS, BLOOD OF NOSTRADAMUS. (Nostalgia; Loonic; Sinister/C; S/Weird; Filmfax)

MONSTER DOG (1985). Rock star Vince Raven (played by rock star Alice Cooper) returns to his old family mansion to make an MTV video. Wild dogs surrounds the place, killing the sheriff and his deputy, while inside Raven raves about an old legend that his father was a werewolf who commanded the killer canine corps. There's nice atmosphere to this thriller that makes up for mediocre acting. Even Cooper comes off looking good, and Victoria Vera is a beautiful heroine. Written-directed by Clyde Anderson. (TransWorld)

MONSTER FROM A PREHISTORIC PLANET (1967). Gappa (the "Triphibian Monster") is just a baby freshly hatched from his egg, but scientists who have never seen Japanese monster movies take the infant to Tokyo for study. Gargantuan mom and pop rush out to rescue him, trampling over 42 cities, 456 villages and 9362 innocent people. Then they really get mad. Director

Haruyasu Noguchi captures a playful childish touch that makes this more bearable than most Japanese monster movies. (Orion) (Laser: Image, with **GODZILLA VS. THE SMOG MONSTER**)

MONSTER FROM GREEN HELL (1957). Formula "giant creature" flick set in Africa, where gigantic wasps are on the loose, trying to sting Jim Davis and Eduardo Ciannelli after being exposed to extreme radiation inside an experimental beehive. This Al Zimbalist production, directed by Kenneth Crane, epitomizes all the bad "bee" movies. Vladimir Sokoloff, Barbara Turner. (Media; Rhino; Nostalgia; S/Weird; Filmfax)

MONSTER FROM MARS. See **ROBOT MONSTER.**

MONSTER FROM THE OCEAN FLOOR (1954). One of the very first films from Roger Corman in which the titular monstrosity is only intimated or discussed until the climax. Had it been shown any sooner (octopus with a giant eye in the center of its head) it would have destroyed the minimal mood and suspense. The setting is the coast of Mexico where a village is being terrorized by the—dare we say it?—Devil Fish! The worst aspect of this E.C. (Early Corman) film is the dubbing—the voices are clearly in an echo chamber. The cast of unknowns (Stuart Wade, Dick Pinner and Anne Kimball) remained unknowns. And what ever happened to that oddly named director, Wyott Ordung? And who was William Danch, who according to Hollywood legend cranked out the script in one night? (Vidmark)

MONSTER FROM THE SURF (1965). Jon Hall directed and stars in this primitive piece of putrescence (aka THE BEACH GIRLS AND THE MONSTER) about a nutty oceanographer who spends half his time watching bikini girls and the other half creating a creature that preys on the cuties. So what else is new, professor? Sue Casey, Walker Edmiston, Dale Davis, Read Morgan.

MONSTER HIGH (1988). A certain Mr. Armageddon from another world lands on Earth in pursuit of two goofballs who stole an explosive device and are threatening to blow up the Green Planet. Sophomoric mentality mars this feeble attempt at parody. Directed by Rudiger Poe. Dean Iandoli, Diana Frank, David Marriott, Robert M. Lind, Sean Haines. (Video/Laser: RCA/Columbia)

MONSTER HUNTER (1982). Bloodthirsty Italian gore thriller (aka ABSURD and ANTHROPOPHAGUS II) in which priest Edmond Purdom chases a psychokiller with superhuman strength. Directed by Peter Newton. George Eastman, Annie Belle. (Lightning; Wizard)

MONSTER IN THE CLOSET (1986). Outright parody of the monster movies of the '50s. In this case it's an E.T. beast with gaping mouth that shambles through Chestnut Hills, Calif., murdering people in their closets, places from which the creature draws unexplained energy. ("Destroy your closets," one of the characters pleads.) Donald Grant as a nerdy newspaperman is aided by Claude Akins as the sheriff who thinks the monster is a giant snake, Howard Duff as a priest who feels all beings are God's children, Henry Gibson as a scientist who wants to study the thing rather than kill it, Donald Moffat as a crazy Army general, Jesse White as a cranky news editor, Stella Stevens as a woman named Crane taking a shower, Paul Walker as a boy genius nicknamed The Professor, and Denise DuBarry as the heroine. Writer-director Bob Dahlin allows you to participate in the satire without being slammed over the head. (Lorimar) (Laser: Japanese)

MONSTER ISLAND (1980). See **MYSTERY OF MONSTER ISLAND.**

MONSTER MAKER, THE (1944). PRC programmer with J. Carrol Naish as something called Igor who ogles lovely concert pianist Wanda McKay from the balcony. When she rejects his advances, he gets even by injecting a serum into her father, Ralph Morgan, with the help of strange assistant Glenn Strange. Unpleasant movie that must have almost destroyed Naish's career. Sam Newfield directed. Sam Flint, Tola Birell, Terry Frost. (Cable; Sinister/C; Filmfax; Nostalgia)

MONSTER MAKER. See **MONSTER FROM THE OCEAN FLOOR.**

MONSTER OF HIGHGATE PONDS, THE (1960). See editions 1-3.

MONSTER OF LONDON CITY, THE (1964). Well-produced West German psychothriller/whodunit based on an Edgar Wallace novel and set in modern London, where the "New Jack the Ripper" stalks prostitutes in the foggy streets. A Ripper play is being performed at an Edgar Allan Poe theater and it appears its producer could the killer. Belongs to the "clutching-hand" school of horror with touches of mild nudity. Directed by Edwin Zbonek. Hansjorg Felmy, Marianne Koch, Hans Nielsen. (Sinister/C; S/Weird; Filmfax)

MONSTER OF PIEDRAS BLANCAS, THE (1959). A thing from the sea resembling a "Black Lagoon" reject hangs out near a lighthouse. The lighthouse keeper puts food out for the visiting thing. That's when a series of murders occurs. Fans are still laughing their heads off at this mess directed by Irvin Berwick. Les Tremayne, John Harmon, Jeanne Carmem, Don Sullivan. (Video Dimensions; Republic; Vidmark)

MONSTER OF TERROR. See **DIE, MONSTER, DIE!**

MONSTER OF THE WAX MUSEUM. See **NIGHTMARE IN WAX.** (Beware waxy build-up!)

MONSTER OF VENICE, THE. See **EMBALMER.**

MONSTEROID. See **TOXIC MONSTER, THE.**

MONSTER ON THE CAMPUS (1958). Director Jack Arnold flunked out on this Neanderthal Man thriller for Universal-International, falling below standards he established in CREATURE FROM THE BLACK LAGOON and IT CAME FROM OUTER SPACE. The blood from a prehistoric fish is used by college professor Arthur Franz to concoct a coelecanth serum that creates a mutant dragonfly and dog. When Franz cuts himself on the fish, he reverts to primeval barbarism and goes on a rampage. Script by David Duncan. Eddie Parker, Whit Bissell, Joanna Moore, Troy Donahue. (MCA)

MONSTERS ARE LOOSE, THE. See **THRILL KILLERS, THE.**

MONSTERS CRASH THE PAJAMA PARTY (1965). A satire on American-International beach-horror flicks, set in a haunted house and featuring a menagerie of creatures and monsters. Directed by Don Brandon. Peter James Noto stars. (Sinister/C)

MONSTERS FROM AN UNKNOWN PLANET. See **TERROR OF MECHAGODZILLA.**

MONSTERS FROM THE MOON. See **ROBOT MONSTER.**

MONSTER SHARK (1984). Umpteenth ripoff of JAWS, depicting scientist William Berger chasing after a 40-foot, prehistoric-age shark/octopus that's eating the local swimming population. Phony effects destroy what little impact this Italian "monstrosity" possesses after director Lamberto Bava and screenwriters Luigi Cozzi and Sergio Martino get through splashing around. Tiny little cinematic bubbles, indeed. Aka RED OCEAN. Michael Sopkin, Valentine Monnier. (From Vidmark as **DEVILFISH)**

MONSTER SHOW, THE. See **FREAKS.**

MONSTERS INVADE EXPO '70. See **GAMERA VS. MONSTER X.**

MONSTERS, MADMEN, MACHINES (1984). TV documentary in which Gil Gerard examines famous sci-fi figures in Hollywood films. (RKO)

MONSTERS OF DR. FRANKENSTEIN. See **FRANKENSTEIN'S CASTLE OF FREAKS.**

MONSTER SQUAD, THE (1987). A cute idea nicely executed: Count Dracula rises from his tomb to gather the Mummy, the Frankenstein Monster, the Gillman and the Mummy to go after a magical amulet that will give them power to control the world. The only thing blocking their way is a group of kids: The Monster Squad! Director Fred Dekker (NIGHT OF THE CREEPS) has fashioned a Gothic horror comedy with co-writer Shane Black that is amusing and quaint, lambasting viewers with special effects. While it's derivative, Dekker pulls it off with charm and style. Duncan Regehr portrays Dracula in a hammy style, while Tom Noonan is a benevolent Frankenstein creature who grows on you. And the kids are great: Andre Gower, Robby Kiger, Brent Chalem, Ryan Lambert, Ashley Bank. Stephen Macht does what he can with the thankless role of a disbelieving cop. Effects by Stan Winston and Richard Edlund. (Vestron) (Laser: Image)

THE GILL MAN

MONSTER THAT CHALLENGED THE WORLD, THE (1957). Uninspired formula "giant-monster-created-by-radiation" non-thriller. This time the monstrosity is a giant caterpillar (would you believe a mutant mollusk?) rising from the depths to terrorize Tim Holt, Audrey Dalton and Hans Conried. Or is Hans Conried terrorizing us? Poorly done, from the effects to Arnold Laven's direction to Pat Fielder's script. Milton Parsons, Barbara Darrow, Jody McCrea, Casey Adams. (Fright)

MONSTER WALKS, THE (1932). A chattering chimpanzee named Yogi is the suspect when people are murdered in an isolated mansion during a thunderstorm. Mischa Auer, as a servant named Hanns Krug, wields a wicked whip, has hairy arms and tries to do in lovely Vera Reynolds. This antiquated thriller, written by Robert Ellis and directed by Frank Strayer, is exemplary of "old dark house" thrillers with stilted acting, lethargic pacing and no sense of the macabre. See it only if you're curious about relics. Rex Lease, Sheldon Lewis. (Video Yesteryear; Nostalgia; Sinister/C; Filmfax)

MONSTER X. See **GODZILLA VS. MONSTER ZERO.**

MONSTER ZERO (1966). And Zero is what this monster flick scores on the Entertainment Scale. GODZILLA director Inoshiro Honda and effects buddy Eiji Tsuburaya are up to usual tricks with Monster Zero, a hulking entity of evil resembling three-headed Ghidrah. Also involved are Godzilla and Rodan, lured from Earth by Planet X fiends so they won't interfere with a force invading Earth. It's incomprehensible but lean back and enjoy the explosive effects, atrocious dubbing and Nick Adams re-creating his role of the astronaut he played in FRANKENSTEIN CONQUERS THE WORLD. Known in some quarters as INVASION OF THE ASTRO MONSTERS. Akira Kubo, Akira Takarada. (From Paramount as **GODZILLA VS. MONSTER ZERO**)

MONSTROID. See **TOXIC HORROR, THE.**

MONSTROSITY. Video version of **ATOMIC BRAIN.**

MONTEZUMA'S LOST GOLD (1978). Travelogue-adventure (of the pseudodocumentary school) re-enacting an old legend about an escaped convict who found a fortune in gold ingots in a mountain cave. There are lurid suggestions the westerner was cursed by Incan spirits, or some such hogwash. John Burrud (son of Bill Burrud) and Brian Burton follow Bodine's trail, interviewing an old Indian and a Kansas historian. The curse and ghosts never do materialize, and any intriguing ideas completely peter out. Milas Hinshaw and John Burrud produced-directed. Michael Carr, Tom Hinshaw, Tumbleweed Harris.

MONTY PYTHON'S MEANING OF LIFE (1983). Be forewarned: If you find the Python group tastelessly irreverent, expect to be insulted, for this is a vile albeit witty offering. It begins brilliantly with a ten-minute parody of pirate movies and big business, then switches to a pseudoexamination of life—dealing with birth control, sex education, religion, a boys' school, the military aristrocracy and so on. Among the highlights (or lowlights?) is dancing in the streets of Devonshire by the lower classes, a sickening liver removal scene, a spoof of ZULU, a fat man throwing up in a posh French restaurant, and Christmas in Heaven. Terry Jones directed and Terry Gilliam handled the animation. John Cleese, Eric Idle, Michael Palin and Graham Chapman appear in most of the scenes, often in drag. Hilarious one moment, sickening the next. (Video/Laser: MCA)

MOONCHILD (1972). Pretension allegory in which Mark Travis undergoes a reincarnation cycle at an old Spanish-style church where John Carradine is "The Keeper of Words" and Victor Buono symbolizes gluttony. Images are of gargoyles, musty corridors, eyeballs, hooded monks and a girl running free in an aqua negligee. What does it mean? Ask writer-director Alan Gadney. There are flashbacks to the Spanish Inquisition and a one-eyed hunchback named Humunculus among the freaky background players. A lot of artsy-craftsy crosscutting only obscures already clouded issues. MOONCHILD, also known under the title FULL MOON, is too quickly eclipsed by its own enigmatic shadows. Janet Landgard, Pat Renella, Mark Travis, William Challee.

MOON 44 (1990). Expensive adventure in the vein of STAR WARS is set in 2038, when galactic mining colonies are controlled by corporations. Internal affairs agent Michael Pare is sent by company president Roscoe Lee Browne to Moon 44 in the Outer Zone to find out why shuttlecraft are disappearing. Action centers around uncovering company turncoats and fighting off a robot-controlled spaceship. Script by producer Dean Heyde and director Roland Emmerich for this German production is weak but the set designs are realistic. Lisa Eichhorn plays the love interest and Malcolm McDowell is commander of the mining station. Brian Thompson, Dean Devlin, Stephen Geoffreys. (Live) (Laser: Image)

MOON IN SCORPIO (1987). Psychokiller whodunit in which three couples embark on a Pacific voyage aboard a yacht—one of them a murderer who first sticks a butcher knife in the stomach of the victim, and then cuts his/her throat with a multi-bladed speargun. Robert S. Aiken's script attempts to limn the characters—three of whom are Vietnam War buddies—but fails to provide motivation for the killings. Best sequence has John Phillip Law struggling in the water with a half-rotted corpse. That's a macabre image. Otherwise cinematographer/director Gary Graver treats it without much style, and Britt Ekland seems uncomfortable in this genre. Fred Olen Ray was co-producer of this direct-to-video release. William Smith, Louis Dan Bergen, April Wayne, Robert Quarry, Jillian Resner. (Trans World)

MOON MADNESS (1983). French animated sci-fi feature, based on an H. G. Wells story, simplistically drawn and written. An 18th century astronomer and a band of pals (a strongman named Hercules, a man who blows wind, etc.) travel to the moon aboard a sailing ship and encounter a race of beings, Suninites, who possess a talisman that is the source for Eternal Life. Another E.T. race of tiny creatures called "Green Leaves" arrives in flying saucers and war erupts. (Vestron)

MOON OF THE WOLF (1972). TV-movie explores the werewolf legend in the Louisiana bayou, where David Janssen is a sheriff investigating throat-ripping murders. Bradford Dillman, Royal Dano, Geoffrey Lewis and Barbara Rush are caught up in the lycanthropic events. Howling good. Directed by Daniel Petrie. (Worldvision; Goodtimes) (Laser: Worldvision)

MOON PILOT (1962). Disney comedy pokes fun at our predilection for national security, at pompous military officers and at our drive to conquer space. Astronaut Tom Tryon is chosen to circumnavigate the moon and this leads to a meeting with an alien from Beta Lyrae. Directed by James Neilson. Brian Keith, Edmond O'Brien, Kent Smith, Tommy Kirk, Nancy Kulp. (Disney)

MOON RAINBOW (1989). Four cosmonauts return from an exploration of Jupiter's moon with the "black mark"—a psychic power this Russian sci-fi movie never explains beyond being "an ability to influence sensitive control." In fact, few things are explained as director Ermach strives for a metaphysical quality, holding on the faces of his characters for an eternity in a failed attempt to make the space explorers into heroic Soviet figures. The psychedelic effects are old-fashioned, the scenes are plodding and the whole thing can be summed up as the essence of turgidity. Vladimir Yostukhin, Igor Stariguin, Vassill Livanov.

MOONRAKER (1979). Eleventh James Bond adventure, depicting 007's attempt to stop master villain Drax (Michael Lonsdale) from starting a totalitarian colony in space. There's an excellent space station battle, a gondola chase through Venice, motorboat action, ample fistfights and sexual encounters of the closest kind. Richard Kiel repeats his Jaws role. Roger Moore walks indifferently through it all. One of the more fun-to-watch Bonds. Lois Chiles co-stars as Mary Goodhead. Directed by Lewis Gilbert, scripted by Christopher Wood. Brian Keith, Bernard Lee. (Video/Laser: CBS/Fox; MGM/UA)

MOONSHINE MOUNTAIN (1967). Undistilled Herschell Gordon Lewis in which an ape killer stands vigilence over an infamous Kentucky still, knocking off dirty revenooers who chance along. Chuck Scott, Adam Sorg, Jeffrey Allen, Bonnie Hinson.

MOONTRAP (1988). Hardware sci-fi actioner involving a moon-landing expedition that finds a civilization of mechanical robots with murderous intent. The astronauts also find a lone woman alien and this provides for a romance that can only be described as feeble. The Tex Ragsdale script isn't much, and the cast (headed by Walter Koenig of STAR TREK fame) isn't exceptional, but the special effects provide a few thrilling moments in what amounts to a mild diversion. Unfortunately, exposition is never provided for the 14,000-year-old race of machines or how its technology was developed. Bruce Campbell, Leigh Lombardi, Robert Kurcz, Reavis Graham. (Shapiro Glickenhaus) (Laser: Image)

MOON ZERO TWO (1969). Transmutation of cowboy adventure into space opera. James Olson, rocketship pilot in the year 2021, is down on his luck and agrees to help the Beautiful Girl Looking for Her Missing Brother. This Hammer production was written by Michael Carreras and directed by Roy Ward Baker, but MOON ZERO TWO still adds up to zilch. Catherine Von Schell, Adrienne Corri, Bernard Bresslaw, Michael Ripper.

MORE THAN A MIRACLE (1967). CINDERELLA—ITALIAN STYLE was the British title for this Italian/French film. Sophia Loren is the peasant girl in the low-cut blouse and Omar Sharif is the Prince Charming caught up in a plot of witches and magic. Dolores Del Rio, Leslie French. Directed by Franceso Rosi.

MORE WILD WILD WEST (1980). Enchanting sequel to the TV series THE WILD WILD WEST, which featured out-of-time-and-place weaponry and inventions, and frequent sci-fi plots. Secret agents James West (Robert Conrad) and Artemus Gordon (Ross Martin) are back to prevent Jonathan Winters from taking over the world via a mad scheme that involves invisible fighters. Burt Kennedy directed. Harry Morgan, Victor Buono, Avery Schreiber, Joyce Brothers. (CBS/Fox)

MORIANNA (1965). Swedish horror thriller that overlaps into the supernatural. Written-directed by Arne Mattsson. Anders Henriksson, Lotte Tarp, Heinz Hopf.

MORONS FROM OUTER SPACE (1985). Witty British spoof of sci-fi movies and the British classes in which a crew of hapless humanoid aliens bumbles to Earth, crashlanding on a freeway in a hysterically funny sequence. Pompous leaders and the media assume these maladroit fools are superintelligent and efforts are made to display them to the world as superiors. Directed by Michael Hodges, scripted by Mel Smith and Griff Rhys Jones, a comedy team portraying the aliens Bernard and Graham Sweetley. (Cannon; HBO)

MORTAL SINS (1990). Psychokiller thriller with religious overtones when a TV evangelist of the Divine Church of the People is caught up in a series of murders that implicate him in sinful doings. Brian Benben, Debrah Farentino, Anthony LaPaglia. Directed by Yuri Sivo. (Academy) (Laser: Image)

MORTAL SINS (1992). A serial killer who gives his female victims the last rites as they are dying confesses to Christopher Reeve in the St. Mary's confessional one day, and Reeve must hold to the Catholic Church's edict that this information is privileged. The moral issues are about all this TV-movie have going for it. Director Bradford May tries to keep it moving by allowing Reeve to be determined, likeable, confused all in one satisfying whole. Roxann Biggs, Francis Guinan, Weston McMillan, Philip R. Allen, Lisa Vultaggio. (CBS/Fox)

MORTUARY (1981). All of us will have our day with the mortician (or cremator) sooner than we hope, so why watch a madman mortician thrust blunt instruments into bodies and tube out their blood? A wretched excuse for a movie from writer-director Howard Avedis, with Christopher George as an uptight mortician. But is he or his morbid son (Bill Paxton) the caped, pasty-faced killer who stalks Lynda Day George with a skewering device? It's a moot point—you'll only want to divert your eyes when the embalming techniques are dragged out in their bloody horrification. And you'll cringe as a still-living body (Mary McDonough's) is about to be skewered alive and the killer cackles, "This way, heh heh, we'll be together forever." Morbid City. (Vestron)

MORTUARY ACADEMY (1988). Grimm Mortuary and Academy is inherited by Paul Bartel and Mary Woronov and they set out to reanimate a dead heavy metal band in order for the group to perform one last gig to save the funeral home. Directed by Michael Schroeder. Perry Lang, Tracey Walter, Christopher Atkins, Lynn Danielson, Cesar Romero. (RCA/Columbia) (Laser: Criterion)

MOST DANGEROUS GAME, THE (1932). Richard Connell's story was perfect for producers Ernest Schoedsack and Merian C. Cooper, who were themselves adventurers and must have felt rapport with Great White Hunter Rainsford (Joel McCrea) and Evil Hunter Count Zaroff (Leslie Banks). In its day this was hard-hitting and explicit but time has blunted its undercurrents of perverted sex and made apparent its cinematic crudities. Still, one can sense the genius of Schoedsack (who co-directed with Irving Pichel) and Cooper in depicting a madman and how he hunts people for the greatest thrill of all, the human trophy. Remade as A GAME OF DEATH, RUN FOR THE SUN and BLOODLUST. Robert Armstrong, Fay Wray. (Cable; Sinister/C; Media; Kartes)

MOST DANGEROUS MAN ALIVE (1961). Cobalt bomb blast turns escaped convict Ron Randell into a literal "man of steel." Because he was framed, Randell sets out to kill the men who set him up. While this is familiar stuff, director Allan Dwan has a surprise: He explores the man's sex life mistress Debra Paget—or at least as far as they dared to go in those days. Morris Ankrum, Elaine Stewart, Anthony Caruso.

MOTEL HELL (1980). Outrageous black horror-comedy that will make you laugh in spite of your good taste. Rory Calhoun is a good ol' country boy operating the roadside Motel Hello (only the O burned out on the neon sign) and a sausage-packing plant next door. Seems Farmer Smith and his sister have decided smoked people'r better'n smoked pig, so they bury their still-living, let's-fatten-'em-up human guinea pigs up to their necks in a field. (Occasionally Rory, bein' a humane sorta guy, goes out there and snaps their necks.) Calhoun's nonchalance and Kevin Connor's witty direction make this in-bad-taste film palatable, right up to the bloody climax featuring a duel with chainsaws and a tied-down heroine headed toward a buzzsaw. Wolfman Jack, Dick Curtis, Paul Linke, Nancy Parsons. (Video/Laser: MGM/UA)

MOTHER RILEY MEETS THE VAMPIRE. See **OLD MOTHER RILEY MEETS THE VAMPIRE.**

MOTHER RILEY RUNS RIOT. See **OLD MOTHER RILEY MEETS THE VAMPIRE.**

MOTHER'S DAY (1980). Offshoot of THE TEXAS CHAINSAW MASSACRE—macabre humor mixed with bloody, excruciatingly painful attacks on women. Mother (Rose Ross, the epitome of matriarchal love) is training her perverted backwoods sons in the art of attack and rape. Holden McGuire and Billy Ray McQuade are the slobbering oafs who eat their breakfast from swill buckets. The demented lads have their fun with three campers. How two turn against the boys makes for a hair-raising climax that involves a can of Draino and a TV set as murder weapons. Oh, we almost forgot the electric carving knife. You'll cheer the girls in spite of yourself. Nancy Hendrickson, Deborah Luce and Tiana Pierce turn in good performances. Produced-written-directed by Charles Kaufman. (Media; Video Treasures)

MOTHRA (1962). Two Oriental girls called the Peanut Sisters, each six inches high, help a giant caterpillar hatch from its egg. When the girls are kidnapped by a contemporary P. T. Barnum, Mothra goes wild, destroying Tokyo Tower and spinning a cocoon. The usual massive destruction results as it rescues the helpless girlettes. Mothra is not a man in a rubber suit but a mock-up controlled by wires. Directed by Inoshiro Honda, with effects by his pal Eiji Tsuburaya. (RCA/Columbia; Goodtimes) (Laser: Japanese)

MOUNTAIN OF THE CANNIBAL GOD. See **SLAVE OF THE CANNIBAL GOD.**

MOUNTAINTOP MOTEL MASSACRE (1983). Taking her cue from Norman Bates about motel management, proprietor Anna Chappell kills her daughter in a fit of range, then attacks unsuspecting roomers (black carpenter, drunken preacherman, newlyweds, two bimbos and an ad man) with a sickle or throws bugs and snakes on their sleeping bodies. Utterly bad gore effects. Guests check in but don't check out in this sleazy slasher flick poorly shot in Louisiana. Directed by Jim McCullough Jr. Bill Thurman, Will Mitchel. (New World)

MOUSE ON THE MOON (1963). Sequel to THE MOUSE THAT ROARED under Richard Lester's direction is another droll exercise in satire. That poor principality, Grand Fenwick, discovers its only economy, wine, can fuel a moon rocket. Margaret Rutherford, Terry-Thomas and Ron Moody give it wit and charm.

MOUSE THAT ROARED, THE (1959). It's the audience that roared—that's how this British satire-comedy was received around the world. In the fictional principality of Grand Fenwick the grand Duchess declares war on the U.S. (soley for rehabilitation funds). An attack expedition sets out for America and becomes embroiled in slapstick with the deadly Q-Bomb. Peter Sellers plays three roles (the Prime Minister, a soldier in arms and the Grand Duchess) and is ably assisted by Jean Seberg, daughter of the bomb's creator. Directed by Jack (THE CREATURE FROM THE BLACK LAGOON) Arnold. The screamingly funny screenplay was by Stanley Mann and Roger MacDougall. The sequel was MOUSE ON THE MOON. Leo McKern, William Hartnell. (RCA/Columbia)

MOVIE HOUSE MASSACRE (1984). Allegedly haunted film palace becomes the site for new murders in the slasher vein in this weak-kneed horror spoof. Directed by Alice Raley. Mary Woronov, Jonathan Blakely, Lynne Darcy. (Active; Moore)

MR. CORBETT'S GHOST (1990). John Huston made his last on-camera appearance in this TV-movie directed by his son Danny Huston. It's your traditional deal-with-the-Devil plot and it co-stars Burgess Meredith, Paul Scofield and Mark Farmer. (Monterey; Kartes)

MR. DESTINY (1990). Entertaining variation on IT'S A WONDERFUL LIFE, sublimely directed by James Orr, who collaborated on the heartfelt script with Jim Cruikshank. James Belushi portrays an unhappy executive with a baseball bat manufacturing company who wishes things could have gone better—and presto, up pops Michael Caine as the embodiment of destiny. Belushi is projected into a parallel universe where he now has the best of everything, but quickly learns that the best can be superficial and that he has lost more than he has gained. This parable is delightfully developed with a subtle sense of humor and with Caine in peak form in an effective if limited role. This is one fantasy the whole family can enjoy. Linda Hamilton, Jon Lovitz, Hart Bochner, Bill McCutcheon, Rene Russo, Maury Chaykin. (Touchstone)

MR. DODD TAKES THE AIR (1937). Third edition.

MR. DRAKE'S DUCK (1951). Douglas Fairbanks Jr's swan song as a producer is an effervescent, witty comedy about a duck that lays a radioactive egg with explosive properties. Fairbanks plays a newlywed looking for solitude on his rundown Sussex farm but finding only notoriety when the military, press and everyone else turns up to investigate the golden duck. Written-directed by Val Guest. Wilfrid Hyde-White, Reginald Beckwith.

MR. FREEDOM (1968). See third edition.

MR. FROST (1990). Intellectually fascinating study of good vs. evil and the ironic corruption of good in order to fight evil. This French-British production stars Jeff Goldblum as an incarnation of the Devil—or so he claims when he's arrested for 24 heinous murders he confesses to. Psychiatrist Kathy Baker thinks she's dealing with a serial killer until others around her are cursed by Mr. Frost and arresting-cop Alan Bates convinces her of the man's true identity. The war of nerves and wits between Goldblum and Baker, reminiscent of that between Jodie Foster and Anthony Hopkins in SILENCE OF THE LAMBS, becomes the core of this unusually thoughtful study of man and his ambiguously evil ways. Directed by Phillipe Setbon. Roland Giraud, Jean-Pierre Cassel, Daniel Gelin. (Sony) (Laser: Image)

MR. HEX (1946). Huntz Hall, that Bowery man posing as a Boy, is turned into a champion boxer by a post-hypnotic suggestion that has the impact of a left jab and a right cross combined. Only Bowery Boy fans will find this a knock-out; others will be punch drunk. Directed by William Beaudine. Ian Keith, Gabriel Dell. (Kartes)

MR. INVISIBLE. See **MR. SUPERINVISIBLE.**

MR. KRANE (1958). This one-hour TV show from the golden age of live drama is an intriguing sci-fi period piece. In 1970 an emissary in black (Sir Cedric Hardwicke) approaches the Secretary of State (John Hoyt) to inform him he is an alien from a farflung world, here to warn mankind that if we attempt to start an atomic war, the race will be destroyed. With its antecedents in THE DAY THE EARTH STOOD STILL, and with a touch of IT CAME FROM OUTER SPACE, this captures a ring of poetry gone from today's movie and TV writing. The acting by Mary LaRoche and Peter Hansen may seem on the hysterical side, but the message comes through loud and clear. Directed by Boris Sagal.

MR. PEABODY AND THE MERMAID (1948). An amusing idea (50-year-old Bostonian finds a lovely mermaid and takes her home to his bathtub) is heavy-handed comedy in the hands of producer-writer Nunnally Johnson and director Irving Pichel. William Powell looks uncomfortable in his unromantic role, for he already has a wife who frowns on this whole fish story. Only Ann Blyth as the gorgeous seawoman makes a big splash and has fun as she swims, rests in the tub and looks at Powell with wonderful gooey-eyed expressions. Irene Hervey, Fred Clark, Andrea King. (Republic)

MR. PEEK-A-BOO (1951). Marcel Aymes' classic short story, "The Man Who Walked Through Walls," was the basis for this French comedy in which Bourvil is a bureaucrat with the power to pass through inanimate objects. Remade as THE MAN WHO WALKED THROUGH WALLS. Directed by Jean Boyer. (Sinister/C; S/Weird; Filmfax)

MRS. AMWORTH (1977). British adaptation of the famous story by E.F. Benson in which a village is attacked by what appears to be a vampire. Glynis Johns stars, Alvin Rakoff directed. (Learning Corp.)

MR. SARDONICUS (1961). Enjoyable gimmick film from William Castle, in which the audience is given the opportunity to decree the villain's fate during the closing minutes. While critics could argue that this impeded the film's pacing, it's a historic moment in the Castle cannon that, unfortunately, has been dropped from TV prints. This ironic, perverse horror story (by Ray Russell, from his own short story) is about a Transylvanian count with a problem: His face has frozen into a hideous smile and he must wear a mask. He calls on doctor Ronald Lewis for help. Oscar Homolka is the one-eyed, sadistic Igor. Several cuties pass through, for Sardonicus is obsessed by beauty, the thing he cannot have. Offbeat.

MR. SCIENCE FICTION'S FANTASTIC UNIVERSE (1988). A guided tour through the home/museum of Forrest J. Ackerman. Artwork, magazines, books, masks, props and everything else this prominent figurehead in the world of science-fiction has amassed during this career as a gadfly for fantasy. (VC)

MR. SUPERINVISIBLE (1970). Spanish-Italian-West German co-production about a superhero who can't be seen by the naked eye—or the covered eye—after he swallows an Indian potion. Directed by Anthony Dawson. Dean Jones, Philippe Leroy, Gastone Moschin. (Simitar)

MR. SYCAMORE (1975). A movie that's up a tree: The title character, plagued by a dull existence and a wife who picks on him, turns into a wooden plant. A-corny touch of whimsey, which never took root in American theaters, yet it features an oak-kay cast which doesn't go to seed: Jason Robards, Sandy Dennis, Jean Simmons, Robert Easton. This one is a stumper heavily uprooted for TV. (Worldvision)

MR. VAMPIRE (1986). Hong Kong production casts a new slant on the vampire genre, playing it up for laughs from an Asian point of view. Directed and co-written by Lau Kun Wai. Ricky Hu, Moon Lee, Chin Suit Ho.

MS .45 (1980). Disturbing avant garde exploitation film made in Manhattan is fascinating in its surrealistic depiction of an "angel of vengeance." Zoe Tamerlis is a mute Garmet District worker brutally raped twice in the same day. She kills her second attacker, cuts up his body and stores the pieces in her frig. With the dead rapist's .45, she is turned into a cold-blooded murderess, her targets any men she meets on the street. It's not so much a revenge movie as the portrait of a woman driven insane by life's pressures. Zoe is coolly beautiful and frightening, conveying the madness of Nicholas St. John's script. Abel Ferrara has a real sense of stylized direction, ending on a ritualistic touch of symbolism as Zoe, dressed as a nun at a masquerade party, becomes a black image of Death. Also known as ANGEL OF VENGEANCE, this is a knockout, gritty movie, unpleasant but enthralling. (Fries; IVE) (Laser)

MUMMY, THE (1932). This Universal horror feature inspired four sequels and numerous imitations, but this has best withstood the Egyptian sands of time. It holds up thanks to cinematographer Karl Freund, making his directorial debut. Freund often relied on the unseen to convey horror, and this approach has assured Stanley Bergerman's production an immortality of its own. Boris Karloff, in Jack Pierce's superb makeup, portrays Im-Ho-Tep, a 3700-year-old high priest of Egypt resurrected by an archeological expedition. Disguising himself in yet another kind of Pierce makeup, wizened Karloff walks through modern Egypt carrying the Scroll of Thoth in an effort to find his long dead love, reincarnated in the modern body of Zita Johann. Edward Van Sloan, David Manners, Noble Johnson, Bramwell Fletcher. The sequels were THE MUMMY'S HAND, THE MUMMY'S TOMB, THE MUMMY'S GHOST and THE MUMMY'S CURSE. (Video/Laser: MCA)

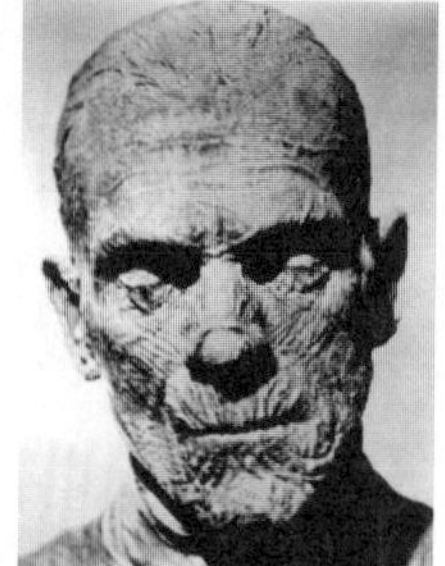

BORIS KARLOFF

MUMMY, THE (1959). Unlike many Universal "Mummy" sequels of the 1940s, in which Kharis shambled around pathetically, this Hammer version captures the murderous ferocity of the gauze-enwrapped high priest as he stomps across foggy 19th Century England, seeking the reincarnation of a princess now married to archeologist Peter Cushing, the man who desecrated Kharis' tomb. It's Christoper Lee in the makeup of Roy Ashton, and he's wonderfully unstoppable. The scene of Lee rising from a bog is especially striking. Directed by Terence Fisher, written by Jimmy Sangster. Yvonne Furneaux, Eddie Byrne, Felix Aylmer, George Pastell, Michael Ripper. (Video/Laser: Warner Bros.)

MUMMY AND THE CURSE OF THE JACKALS, THE (1969). Archeologist Anthony Eisley showing a 4000-year-old Egyptian princess how to hook up a modern bra is about as good as it gets in this amateurish attempt to recapture the spirit of Universal's MUMMY series. The injection of John Carradine as an Egyptologist to explain how the curse works only underscores how pathetic this monsterthon is. And the scenes of a werewolf (described also as a "jackal man") fighting with a mummy in a casino in downtown Las Vegas is hilariously incompetent, causing any incredulous viewer to wonder just what director Oliver Drake had in mind. It couldn't have been an exciting movie. Robert Allen Browne, Marlita Pons, Maurine Dawson, Saul Goldsmith. (Academy)

MUMMY'S BOYS (1936). A dumb comedy vehicle for the team of Bert Wheeler and Robert Woolsey. The Curse of King Pharmatime has killed off nine out of 13 archeologists when the boys apply for a new expedition to Egypt. The horror elements are only slight as the gags run to wisecracks and the routines seem to last forever. Sample joke: "Four little daughters of the Nile? No wonder the Sphinx won't talk." Directed by Fred Guiol. Barbara Pepper, Moroni Olsen, Willie Best, Frank Lackteen. (Rex Miller) (Laser: Image)

MUMMY'S CURSE, THE (1945). The last of Universal's "Kharis the Mummy" films, which had so deteriorated that the hulking high-priest-in-bandages was a laughing, not a screaming, matter. It picks up where THE MUMMY'S GHOST left off—as the swamp is drained and the bodies of Princess Ananka and Kharis are recovered. Soon Kharis (shabbily played by Lon Chaney Jr.) is footloose on a diet of tana leaves, chasing a beautiful woman who can't quite flee the slow-moving shambler. Virginia Christine, Peter Coe, Martin Kosleck. Directed by Leslie Goodwins. (Video/Laser: MCA)

MUMMY'S CURSE OF THE JACKAL. See **MUMMY AND THE CURSE OF THE JACKAL**.

MUMMY'S GHOST, THE (1944). Third in Universal's "Kharis the Mummy" series coming on the heels of THE MUMMY'S TOMB, with Lon Chaney Jr. stumbling around New England to discover that Ananka, his beloved princess, is reincarnated in the shapely form of Ramsay Ames. John Carradine takes over as high priest to force-feed the tana leaves. Makeup by Jack Pierce. George Zucco appears briefly to send Carradine on his mission. Barton MacLane, Robert Lowery. Directed by Reginald Le Borg. (Video/Laser: MCA)

MUMMY'S HAND, THE (1940). This entertaining sequence to Universal's THE MUMMY started a series of low-budget programmers featuring a bandaged high priest named Kharis, who forsakes the Scroll of Thoth for tana leaves. They are all quite similar, with a mummy slowly shambling along, while no one else can ever quite get away from its clutches. The role of the long-dead Egyptian went to former cowboy actor Tom Tyler—his only appearance as a monster. Dick Foran and Wallace Ford provide romantic and comedy relief as a pair of down-and-out archeologists trying to finance an expedition to the Hill of the Seven Jackals through magician Cecil Kelloway and daughter Peggy Moran, who is mistaken by the Mummy for his long-lost love, Princess Ananka. An historic film moment occurs when the High Priest of Karnak (Eduardo Ciannelli) instructs George Zucco in the art of tana leaf cooking, and footage from THE MUMMY is repeated. This is solid B- picture material and better than the three films that followed. Directed by

Christy Cabanne. (Video/Laser: MCA)

MUMMY'S REVENGE, THE (1973). Spanish stew of supernatural curses and Egyptian walking dead is strictly meat and potatoes—basic to the horror viewer's diet, without any rich calories. Ultimately inedible. Directed by Carlos Aured, scripted by Jacinto Molina. Paul Naschy portrays the Nile Valley drifter in bandages. Aka THE VENGEANCE OF THE MUMMY. (Unicorn)

MUMMY'S SHROUD, THE (1967). Despite the cliches that riddle its plot like holes in ancient bandages, this Hammer horror thriller is well done in the acting department. After a cumbersome beginning in Egyptian times, as we're inundated with exposition about a gauze-enwrapped entity, we flash to present day as an expedition desecrates the tomb and removes mummy Eddie Powell to a museum to be resurrected by He Who Possesses an Accursed Blanket. Intense murders follow. Andre Morell is exceptional as the head of the expedition, a spoiled millionaire. Stylishly done with individual details often outshining the sum total. Maggie Kimberley portrays an unlikely archeologist, what with all those flimsy nightgowns and low-cut blouses. Best of the cast is Catherine Lacey as a decaying soothsayer who reads crystal balls. John Gilling directed. Produced by Anthony Nelson-Keys (writing as John Elder).

MUMMY'S TOMB, THE (1942). Second Universal feature in the "Kharis" series, with Lon Chaney Jr. inheriting the gauze from Tom Tyler in THE MUMMY'S HAND. Again it's George Zucco as the High Priest, who turns the evil-doing over to Turhan Bey, who then dispatches Kharis to kill archeologist/tomb defiler Dick Foran, but not until we've seen footage from THE MUMMY'S HAND and the angry villagers from FRANKENSTEIN. In this one Elyse Knox is the reincarnated beauty who is carried away by Kharis. Directed by Harold Young. Make-up by Jack Pierce. (Video/Laser: MCA)

MUMMY STRIKES, THE. See **ATTACK OF THE MAYAN MUMMY.**

MUMMY VS. THE HUMAN ROBOT (1963). Mexican variation on an old theme has the standard bandage-covered personage from a previous Egyptian era fighting it out with a clanking robot while a mad doctor stands in the wings, cackling. The whole production should have been mummified and buried in a crypt.

MUMSY, NANNY, SONNY AND GIRLY. See **GIRLY**.

MUNCHIE (1992). A sequel in name if not spirit to MUNCHIES, this depicts a mischievous but not murderous alien (with the jolly face of a pig, and the voice of Dom DeLuise) wisecracking his way through a comedy misadventure with youth Jaime McEnnan, his beautiful mother Loni Anderson and her simpering boyfriend, a total nerd as played by Andrew Stevens. There are cute moments in the script by R. J. Robertson and director Jim Wynorski, especially when nutty inventor Arte Johnson gets into the fun. Strictly family viewing. (New Horizon)

MUNCHIES (1987). This rank imitation of GREMLINS has nothing to recommend it—not even deep philosophical values. Archeologist Harvey Korman and son Charles Stratton find an alien in a South American cave and bring it back to civilization, where it multiples into several mischievous, murderous Munchies. The creatures are unconvincing, and so the film doesn't even work as high camp. Director Bettina Hirsch fails to bring crunch to this bunch . . . but why go on. Nadine Van Der Velde, Alix Elias, Charles Phillips. (MGM/UA)

MUNSTER, GO HOME (1966). Feature based on TV's THE MUNSTERS with Fred Gwynne, Yvonne De Carlo, Al Lewis and Butch Patrick recreating video roles. The Munsters inherit a haunted house and all its problems, which include a counterfeiting ring led by Hermione Gingold, Terry-Thomas and John Carradine. Directed by Earl Bellamy. (MCA)

MUNSTERS' REVENGE, THE (1981). Reviewed in the context of the '90s, this Universal TV-movie revival of the popular THE MUNSTERS series of the '60s has a charm it seemed to lack in its own time. Is it just nostalgia, or is there something quaint this captures? At the core of its charm are Fred Gwynne as Herman Munster and Al Lewis as Grandpa Munster, with Yvonne De Carlo (as Lily Munster) taking a back seat to the action. The silly Dr. Diabolic (Sid Caesar, in a funny role) instills robotic life in the monsters of a Hollywood wax museum and arranges for them to steal the jewels from a mummy's sarcophagus. One memorable scene has Gwynne and Lewis in drag as coffee shop waitresses fighting off male customers, Lily decorating a Christmas tree with horror symbols, and Caesar doing characters that include his crazed German scientist. It was directed by Don Weiss without much enthusiasm, but time has been good to this minor effort, as if a Beverly Hills plastic surgeon had given it a facelift. K. C. Martel, Jo McDonnel, Bob Hastings, Gary Vinson, Charles Macaulay, Howard Morris, Ezra Stone. (MCA)

MUPPET CHRISTMAS CAROL, THE (1992). Delightful adaptation of the Dickens classic, full of great Muppet gags and visuals and even capturing the darker side of Scrooge's nocturnal journey with the spirits of Christmas. As Scrooge, Michael Caine is a standout—the only human in the cast, otherwise made up of the puppetry magic of Frank Oz and the rest of the Muppet gang. Directed by Brian Henson. (Disney)

MURDER AND THE COMPUTER (1975). An inventor about to unveil the world's most sophisticated computer is murdered . . . it had to be someone on hand during the ceremonies. TV whodunit directed by Paul Stanley. Gary Merrill, Babara Anderson, Kaz Garas.

MURDER AT DAWN (1932). Poverty row production creaks with age but features the interesting DXL Accumulator, a device harnessing solar energy, but the plot focuses more on whodunit in an old dark house. Directed routinely by Richard Thorpe. Mischa Auer, Jack Mulhall.

MURDER BY DECREE (1979). Splendid Sherlock Holmes/Dr. Watson thriller in which the detective heroes stalk Jack the Ripper. It would appear the Whitechapel killings are being covered up by a government conspiracy. Classy material (similar to A STUDY IN TERROR), with murders photographed with taste and Christopher Plummer as a likeable Holmes and James Mason as an articulate Watson. What a singular supporting cast! Anthony Quayle, Donald Sutherland, John Gielgud, Susan Clark, Genevieve Bujold. Directed by Bob Clark. (CBS/Fox; Embassy; Sultan) (Laser: CBS/Fox)

MURDER BY INVITATION (1941). Editions 1-3.

MURDER BY MAIL. See **SCHIZOID.**

MURDER BY MOONLIGHT (1989). Watching Brigitte Nielsen climb out of a spacesuit to reveal she's in a push-up bra makes one realize it's a crying shame there isn't any gravity on the moon to give her a helping hand. This scene is the highpoint of this otherwise static, talkative TV-movie set on a moonstation where U.S. and Soviet personnel argue over how to carry out a murder investigation, and Brigitte and a blond Russian strip off their moon gear to make love. The story, set in 2015, ten years after a near-nuclear war on Earth, was directed by Michael Lindsay-Hogg with a sagging feeling. Gee, did we say sagging? Sorry about that, Brigitte. Julian Sands, Jan Lapotrire, Brian Cox, Gerald McRaney. (Vidmark)

MURDER BY NIGHT (1989). Average TV-movie, produced in Canada, centers on "The Claw Hammer Killer," a serial murderer terrorizing people who once ate at the Puzzles Restaurant. During one murder, Robert Urich is exposed to a car explosion and wakes up with amnesia. Is he the killer or only a passer-by? Detective Michael Ironside and police psychologist Kay Lenz manipulate Urich to remember. Tepid whodunit, in which the killer's identity is easily spotted in advance. Directed by Paul Lynch. Richard Monette, Jim Metzler. (MCA)

MURDER BY PHONE (1980). A literately written Canadian horror film, best for its clever dialogue between ecology fighter Richard Chamberlain and telephone company advisor John Houseman, who meet in Toronto during a save-the-environment convention. Meanwhile,

'THE MUPPET CHRISTMAS CAROL'

certain citizens are answering their phones, only to have blood shoot from their ears, nose, eyes and mouth because of a terrible vibrating force. Then a killer bolt of electricity pours through the receiver and throws them against the wall as if Zeus had struck. Chamberlain, when he isn't dating mural painter Sara Botsford, is hot on the trail of the killer. Slickly directed by Michael Anderson. Hell's Bells, this is pretty good stuff. Barry Morse, Robin Gammell, Gary Reineke. Aka BELLS. (Warner Bros.)

MURDER BY TELEVISION (1935). Fuzzy, unadjusted Bela Lugosi whodunit in which two brothers—one an inventor, the other a murderer—are involved with the development of TV. There's also a Death Ray, a standard ploy of the 1930s. Static direction by Clifford Sanforth. June Collyer, George Meeker, Huntley Gordon. (Video Yesteryear; Video Resources; Sinister/C)

MURDER BY THE CLOCK (1931). Third edition.

MURDER CLINIC, THE (1966). Black-robed fiend (with a cowl yet) stalks the halls of an isolated hospital for weirdos, slashing victims with a razor blade. A young nurse arrives on the Gothic scene to serve as the heroine of this Italian-French horror tale that is overacted but compellingly presented with its period ambience, costumes and baroque settings. William Berger stars as a misunderstood doctor who keeps an ugly secret in one of the upstairs rooms, from which weird sounds emanate. Plenty of gore (some was cut for TV) and creeping around to create tension and suspense. Produced-directed by Michael Hamilton (Elio Scardamaglia). Francoise Prevost, Mary Young, Barbara Wilson. (VCI)

MURDERERS' KEEP. Video version of **BUTCHER, THE** (Genesis; Star Classics).

MURDERERS' ROW (1966). A sequel to THE SILENCERS, this is the second in the Matt Helm series with Dean Martin as the superspy who walks indifferently through bizarre adventures. Brimming with succulent women, gleaming gadgets, ingenious weapons and flippant dialogue, it never for a moment takes itself seriously. You'll enjoy Karl Malden as a villain with a killer ray who hopes to destroy the White House. Stylishly directed by Henry Levin, he allows you to set your brain on "idle" and enjoy. Follow-ups: THE AMBUSHERS and THE WRECKING CREW. Ann-Margret, Camilla Sparv, Beverly Adams, James Gregory. (RCA/Columbia)

MURDER IN LAW (1989). This slap against mother's love might have given new depths of horror to the phrase "mother-in-law" were it not for the fact that its unfolding is far more ludicrous than it is scary. Still, Marilyn Adams is rather deviously delightful as a daffy old bat who spears an orderly to death and escapes from Silver Oak Asylum, in Louisiana, to take up residence later with her son Joe Estevez in his stately San Francisco home. Joe refuses to believe mom might be crazy even though she (1) slaughters the family cat, (2) trashes the bedrooms and (3) pushes an iron into the face of the family's Mexican maid. Talk about denial! Anyway, he finally puts murderous mother away, but she escapes and chases Joe's wife and daughter with a butcher knife. Adams really goes over the top as a total nut. Sandy Snyder, Darrel Guilbeau, Debra Lee Giometti, Rebecca Russell. Directed by Tony Jiti Gill. (Monarch)

MURDER IN SPACE (1985). Gimmick-riddled whodunit originally shown on Showtime with prizes offered to those who could spot clues revealing the murderer of astronauts (male and female) aboard Comestoga, a lab rocketing through space. First a Soviet cosmonaut is strangled to death (it is discovered she was pregnant), then crew members are poisoned, throttled and blasted to pieces. Back on Earth, U.S. and Russian scientists and diplomats hush up the scandalous elements, while figuring out which crew member is the maniac. Directed by Steven Hilliard Stern. Wilford Brimley, Arthur Hill, Michael Ironside, Martin Balsam. (Vidmark)

MURDER IN SPACE. See **BATTLESTAR GALACTICA.**

MURDER IN THE AIR (1940). Ronald Reagan as brash "Brass" Bancroft, intrepid Secret Service agent, and Eddie Foy Jr., as Gabby Watters his falling-down comic sidekick, are the campy highlights of this Warner Bros. propaganda piece in which the less-than-dynamic duo goes after saboteurs out to steal the "Inertia Projector"—a device that paralyzes power at its source, from jetplane engines to electric toasters. Fast-paced under Lewis Seiler's direction. John Litel, Robert Warwick.

MURDER IN THE BLUE ROOM (1944). See editions 1-3.

MURDER IN THE ETRUSCAN CEMETERY. See **SCORPION WITH TWO TAILS, THE.**

MURDER LUST (1986). Low-budget clone of THE STEPFATHER, directed by Donald Jones, who earlier did THE LOVE BUTCHER. Eli Rich portrays a security guard who picks up whores and murders them. The twist: Rich portrays him sympathetically. Rochelle Taylor, Dennis Gannon, Bonnie Schneider, Lisa Nichols. (Prism)

MURDER MANSION (1970). Oddball characters (hitchhiker, motorist, heiress, lawyer, motorcyclist) are caught in a foggy mist and take refuge in the sinister mansion of Martha Clinton. Evelin Stewart, Analia Gade. Directed by Francisco Lara Polop. (Unicorn; Charter; from Continental as **AMUCK)**

MURDER MOTEL (1974). What's that old saying? Human guests check in but don't check out. TV-movie thriller, directed by Malcolm Taylor, stars Robyn Millan and Derek Francis. A young woman investigates the disappearance of her fiance. (Thrillervideo)

MURDER OBSESSION. See **FEAR (1981).**

MURDER ON LINE ONE (1990). British horror flick opens with an eyeball being left on the doorstep of Emma Jacobs by a murderer who slaughtered an entire family. A whodunit unfolds. Written- directed by Anders Palm. Peter Blake, Simon Shepherd, Allan Surtees. (Academy)

MURDEROUS VISION (1991). Unimpressive TV-movie with Bruce Boxleitner as a demoted cop trying to restore his honor by tracking down a mad doctor-killer who skins the faces of his victims. He achieves this with the help of a psychic. Directed by Gary Sherman. Laura Johnson, Joseph D'Angerio, Robert Culp.

MURDERS IN THE RUE MORGUE (1932). The title is the only Poe you'll find in this Universal thriller starring Bela Lugosi as a carnival spielman with a gorilla act. The early promising atmosphere and odd sexual overtones are not sustained as master detective Dupin (Leon Ames billed as Leon Waycroft) tracks Dr. Mirakle to put a stop to his crazy theory that mating ape with virgin will result in a perfect union between man and animal. Directed by Robert Florey, who lingers sadistically on the scenes in which the Darwin-crazed Lugosi tortures prostitutes. Camera work by Karl Freund. (MCA)

MURDERS IN THE RUE MORGUE (1971). Strangely compelling thriller of the Grand Guignol school, though it has nothing to do with Poe's story. The offbeat Henry Slesar-Christopher Wicking script features bizarre relationships, flashbacks within flashbacks and dreams within dreams. Maniac Herbert Lom commits ghastly acid murders while Jason Robards Jr. and Christine Kaufman stage a horror play in Paris' finest theater. Gordon Hessler directed. Adolfo Celi, Lilli Palmer, Maria Perschy, Michael Dunn. (Orion) (Laser: Japanese)

MURDERS IN THE RUE MORGUE, THE (1986). Well-produced TV-movie with George C. Scott as French detective Auguste Dupin, who comes out of retirement to solve two bloody murders and prove his daughter's fiancee is not guilty of the crimes. Paris locations are cleverly used, and Scott is fine, but the pacing is slow. Directed by Jeannot Szwarc. Val Kilmer, Rebecca De Mornay, Ian McShane. (Video/Laser: Vidmark)

MURDERS IN THE ZOO (1933). Lionel Atwill so overacts as a philanthropist/big game hunter that what should be horrifying is ludicrous. Because he's insanely jealous of his unfaithful wife, he sews up the mouth of her paramour and leaves him to die in the jungle. The next lover is killed by a mamba snake. And on it goes, involving lions, tigers and a house of pythons. While today it might seem mild, it was hard-hitting in its day and frequently censored because of Atwill's suggested depravity. Directed by Edward Sutherland with a relish for the distasteful. Randolph Scott, Gail Patrick, John Lodge.

MURDER SOCIETY, THE. See **MURDER CLINIC.**

MUSIC FOR THE MOVIES: BERNARD HERRMANN (1992). Documentary-biography of one of Hollywood's finest composers, who contributed so much to sci-fi and fantasy on the screen. Includes many excellent clips from Hitchcock thrillers and interviews with those who knew the composer well, including Lucille Fletcher, James Stewart, Louis Kaufman, David Raksin, Elmer Bernstein and Norman Corwin. Directed and edited by Joshua Waletzky.

MUSIC OF THE SPHERES (1983). Frightfully dull Canadian idea movie that never overcomes viewer indifference. With a soundtrack half-English, half-French, it unfolds in the next century when supercomputers (called "Beasts") inform Anne Dansereau that a plan to use asteroids as sources of solar energy is throwing the balance of the Universe out of kilter. This movie goes absolutely nowhere. Directed by G. Philip Jackson.

MUTAGEN, THE (1988). Cheesy low-budget thriller with pseudoscientific overtones, produced on a shoestring and a half, if photography and acting are any judge. Another mad doctor is at work, injecting innocent folks with his formula (which would revolutionize the world, of course) and turning them into killers. Cops investigate, always miles behind the forces of evil. Writer-director Eli Necakov does little creatively with Terence Gadsden's story. Jackie Samuda, Les Williams.

MUTANT (1982). See **FORBIDDEN WORLD.**

MUTANT (1983). This time the zombies are on the march because of exposure to toxic refuge, but a zombie is still a zombie with only an appetite for human flesh. Same old "walking dead" cliches with Wings Hauser, Bo Hopkins and Jennifer Warren fighting off monsters. Directed by John "Bud" Cardos. Aka DARK SHADOWS and NIGHT SHADOWS. (Video/Laser: Vestron)

MUTANT II. See **ALIEN PREDATOR.**

MUTANT HUNT (1986). Made-for-video sci-fi/horror combination, with emphasis on hand-to-hand fighting and depressed New York City locations. Writer-director Tim Kincaid does a creditable job with this tale of Delta VII cyborgs out of control after they've been given a drug, Euphoran, that turns them into "psychosexual killers." Rick Gianasi is Matt Ryker, mercenary for hire who sets out with a stripper and a black martial arts dude to track the mindless killers. There are nifty scenes of a cyborg pulling his face apart and a lot of drippy, gooey effects, all done in a less-than-serious style. One character says it all with "Total carnage, uncontrolled fury, what else could you ask for?" Mary Fahey, Ron Reynaldi, Tawnie Vernon. (Wizard; VCI)

MUTANT ON THE BOUNTY (1989). Kyle T. Heffner, a mutated saxophone player, gets beamed into the year 2048 aboard the spacecraft USS Bounty. Ha ha ha. Then he tries to make it with Deborah Benson. Ha ha ha. And other crew people, such as a humanoid robot, female doctor and fat captain. Directed by Robert Torrance. Ha ha ha. And ha ha ha to John Roarke, John Furey and Victoria Catlin. (South Gate; Hemdale)

MUTANTS IN PARADISE (1987). Lame-brained comedy that parodies TV's THE SIX MILLION DOLLAR MAN without an ounce of wit. Nitwit scientist "Oscar Tinman" (Robert Ingham) creates a genetically superior superman named "Steve Awesome" out of a nerd (Brad Greenquist). Mad doctor Edith Massey also creates a female counterpart, "Alice Durchfall," played by attractive Anna Nicholas. The only plot has a gang of Russian agents out to kidnap the pair. The dumb jokes are nonstop and there isn't a laugh in the carload. Stylelessly written-directed by Scott Apostolou, who filmed in Charlottesville, Va. Skip Suddeth, Ray Mancini. (Transworld)

MUTATIONS, THE (1974). This British nightmare thriller, like Tod Browning's FREAKS, features real-life sideshow freaks. Donald Pleasence portrays a biologist who sees the world dying and decides crossbreeding man and plants is the answer to survival. His experiments create hideous mutants and a man-eating plant to dispose of any cadavers left lying around. Directed by Jack Cardiff, this was Michael Dunn's last film before his untimely death. Tom Baker is Pleasence's assistant and Jill Haworth and Julie Ege provide shapely bodies and screaming mouths. Brad Harris, Scott Anthony. (From Vidcrest as **FEARMAKER, THE**)

MUTATOR (1990). This "A Cut Above Production" is barely that, being a familiar genetics-gone-amok, man-shouldn't-tamper-with-nature horror tale with mediocre hairy-monster effects. Directed by John R. Bowey, the cast works hard with the meager characterizations. Tigen Inc. is a chemical engineering corporation that must seal itself off one night when "genetically engineered beings" (caused by an experiment gone awry) cut loose with homicidal intent. Trapped in the huge plant-laboratory are Brion James (in an unusual role as hero), the lovely miniskirted Carolyn Ann Clark, Milton Raphael Murrill and Brian O'Shaughnessy. (Prism) (Laser: Image)

MUTILATED. See **SHRIEK OF THE MUTILATED.**

MUTILATOR, THE (1983). Below-average slasher flick (aka FALL BREAK) bespeckled with weak characterizations and only moderately sickening gore. After a clumsy prologue in which a youngster accidentally shoots his father, the story jumps to the present day to follow six teenagers to a seaside condominium, where they are stalked and slaughtered by the father, a big game hunter. Death by drowning, chainsaw slicing, machete chopping, pitchfork plunging, hook impalement, and battleaxe bleeding. Also for your viewing pleasure: a body severed in half, another body beheaded, still another delegged. My, my, ain't we got fun. Filmed near Atlantic Beach in a dismal coastal location. Buddy Cooper wrote and directed. Matt Mitler, Frances Raines, Morey Lampley. (Video/Laser: Vestron)

MUTILATOR, THE. Video version of **DARK, THE (1979)** (Impulse; Simitar).

MUTINY IN OUTER SPACE (1965). The mutiny is not committed by humans but by a fungus brought aboard Space Station X-7. With the help of stop-motion animation, it turns astronauts into beasts. Poor sci-fier directed by Hugo Grimaldi. William Leslie, Glenn Langan, Dolores Faith, Richard Garland.

MY BEST FRIEND IS A VAMPIRE (1987). Mildly amusing, but never hysterically hilarious or fabulously funny, comedy in which Robert Sean Leonard is infected with lycanthropy and slowly turns into a vampire. But this is a world of benevolent families, similar to the world of benevolent werewolves in TEEN WOLF, so our sympathy is always with Leonard as he faces two misguided vampire hunters, Professor Leopold McCarthy (David Warner, in a parody of the bat-hater he played in NIGHTWING) and Grimsdyke (an Igor-type played by an amusing character actor, Paul Willson). The funniest bit is the title of a vampire book: "A Practical Guide to an Alternative Lifestyle." Directed by Jimmy Huston. Cheryl Pollak, Rene Auberjonois, Evan Mirand, Fannie Flagg. (HBO)

MY BLOOD RUNS COLD (1965). Your blood won't run cold watching this anemic pseudohorror thriller. Allegedly, a mad killer is the reincarnation of an old lover boy once in love with an ancestor of Joey Heatherton. As the killer, Troy Donahue talks Joey into thinking she's been reincarnated too. Phony chills and ersatz thrills bloodlessly directed by William Conrad from John Mantley's pale script. Barry Sullivan, Nicolas Coster.

MY BLOODY VALENTINE (1981). "Roses are red/Violets are blue/MY BLOODY VALENTINE/Is abso-

THE SHAFT KILLER IN 'MY BLOODY VALENTINE'

lute grue" . . . Heart-to-heart Canadian horror film of the slasher school is strangely compelling despite lack of characters and logic. It hinges on grabby visuals as a deranged killer—wearing a miner's uniform and face-mask—attacks citizens of Valentine Village with a pick-axe. Photography and stunt work are excellent as the murderer stalks partygoers in a coal mine. Without getting pickie, we enjoyed it. Sorry, no miners allowed. Directed by George Mihalka. Effects by Tom Burman. Paul Kelman, Cynthia Dale. (Video/Laser: Paramount)

MY BROTHER TALKS TO HORSES (1946). See editions 1-3.

MY DEMON LOVER (1987). This mindless supernatural comedy could have been a total disaster, but screenwriter Leslie Ray wisely injected a sense of the old Saturday matinee into his tale about a young man (Scott Valentine) "po-zassed" by the "Rumanian Blue Balls Curse"—which turns him into a different kind of monster, or "Pazosky," each time he tries to make love. Valentine must perform a "noble deed" to exorcise himself, and he does it with the help of nerdy blond Michelle Little. Meanwhile, there's a killer called The Mangler and it appears Valentine is the killer. Good performances by Arnold Johnson (as The Fixer), Robert Trebor (as a dunderhead suitor of Little's), Gina Gallego (as a sexy newswoman) and Alan Fudge (as the cop), plus that sense of cliffhanger derring-do, make this enjoyable. Directed by Charles Loventhal. (Video/Laser: RCA/Columbia)

MY FRIEND, DR. JEKYLL (1961). The Italians played this for laughs—a shrewd move since audiences would have laughed anyway: A mad scientist invents a personality transference machine and switches bodies with the instructor in a girls' school, where he instigates love-making sessions. Abbe Lane can't resist Ugo Tognazzi. Directed by Marino Girolami. Also known as MY PAL DR. JEKYLL. Carlo Croccolo, Raimondo Vianello.

MY FRIENDS NEED KILLING (1977). Vietnam veteran Greg Mullavey goes on a spree to murder the men he served with (apparently they were involved in a massacre). Mullavey doesn't just murder—he first tortures his victims and their wives. Writer-director Paul Leder (I DISMEMBER MAMA) goes for an unusual ending. Meredith MacRae, Clayton Wilcox, Carolyn Ames.

MY GRANDFATHER IS A VAMPIRE (1991). Al Lewis has a ball as a jovial, fun-loving 280-year-old vampire who never harms a single neck in this New Zealand production for children. It's spun as a fairy tale when the old man dies and returns from the dead to enter into adventures with his grandson, most of them centered around the efforts of an aging suitor to Lewis' sister coming after Lewis as a vampire killer. A light-hearted quality runs throughout Michael Heath's script and David Blyth's direction. Justin Gocke, Milan Borich. (Republic)

MY MOM'S A WEREWOLF (1988). Silly Crown-International comedy along the lines of TEEN WOLF, but with sexually frustrated mother Susan Blakely the member of the family who turns into a hairy beast after she meets Harry Thropen (John Saxon) in his pet shop. The visual gags don't extend much beyond long fangs and hirsute legs. Little fire is added by director Michael Fischa to this weak kettle of guffaw grue, although Saxon gives a menacing performance given the inanities loping around him. Katrina Caspary, John Schuck, Diana Barrows, Ruth Buzzi, Marilyn McCoo. (Prism) (Laser: Image)

MY PAL, DR. JEKYLL. See **MY FRIEND, DR. JEKYLL.**

MYRA BRECKINRIDGE (1970). While critics in general hated this adaptation of Gore Vidal's best-seller, and some cast members (Mae West among them) disowned it as unforgivable trash ruined by director Michael Sarne, this expensive flop has intriguing possibilities. The plot evolves around a man (film critic Rex Reed) being transformed into a beautiful woman (Raquel Welch) during a sex-change operation, and his/her subsequent misadventures in Hollywood. It's daring, it's resourceful, it's irreverent and it's offensive as hell. Outrageous is a better word. Personal taste will dictate personal reaction. Farrah Fawcett, Roger C. Carmel, Calvin Lockhart, Jim Backus, John Carradine, Andy Devine. (CBS/Fox)

MY SCIENCE PROJECT (1985). Boring teenage fantasy-comedy in which an inept science student, poking around an abandoned Air Force installation, discovers a force-field gadget left over from a flying saucer discovered by the military in 1959. The device sucks up all the energy in sight and becomes a time tunnel, out of which emerge monsters and warriors of the past. John Stockwell, Danielle Von Zerneck and Fisher Stevens are the hapless teens, but the picture goes to a freaked-out performance by Dennis Hopper as a science teacher who regresses to his hippie habits when he's sucked into the space-warp continuum. Jonathan Betuel, who wrote THE LAST STARFIGHTER, wrote-directed but no amount of effects can save his sci-fi project. (Video/Laser: Touchstone)

MY SISTER, MY LOVE (1979). Intriguing psychological study of two sisters living in a cluttered mansion, where they keep an ape in a "mafu cage" belonging to their late father, a noted jungle explorer. Lee Grant tries to stay afloat while her sister, Carol Kane, sinks into barbarism, torturing apes and humans alike. Produced largely by women, this low budget effort is strangely compelling and offbeat, with lesbian overtones. Directed by Karen Arthur. Will Geer, James Olson and Badur the Orang. Aka THE MAFU CAGE. (Wizard; VCI; Magnum)

MY SON, THE HERO (1961). Italian-French farce making sport of mythological characters and their accoutrements. So we have Pedro Armendariz with Pluto's helmet of invisibility, the snaky Gorgon, the Cyclops, statues that come to life and other oddities. Legend has it this was made as a serious film, then turned into a comedy by English dubbers in the style of Woody Allen's WHAT'S UP, TIGER LILY? Directed by Duccio Tessari.

MY SON, THE VAMPIRE (1952). Made in England as OLD MOTHER RILEY MEETS THE VAMPIRE, this was released in the U.S. as VAMPIRE OVER LONDON. This present version was re-re-issued in 1964 and is part of the "Mother Riley" series popular for many years in Great Britain. Arthur Lucan appears in drag, capturing a music hall lowbrow humor for which he was famous. Bela Lugosi is Baron Van Housen, who thinks he's Dracula and wears all the regalia, sleeping in a coffin. Produced-directed by John Gilling. Kitty McShane, Dora Bryan. (From Sinister/C as **VAMPIRE OVER LONDON**)

MY STEPMOTHER IS AN ALIEN (1988). The sexually arousing presence of Kim Basinger is the saving grace of this labored sci-fi comedy in which the blond beaut portrays an E.T. life form (some form!) who hooks up with scientist Dan Aykroyd to save her planet from destruction. She has a great time learning about sex—so good, in fact, that Aykroyd becomes her straight man (in more ways than one). If you take this for the parody that it was intended, you might have a good time despite a less-than-great alien that looks like a cross between a sick cobra and a malfunctioning flute, and rather pedestrian direction by Richard Benjamin. Jon Lovitz, Alyson Hanigan, Joseph Maher. (Video/Laser: RCA/Columbia)

MYSTERIANS, THE (1959). Cockroach-headed aliens from Mysteroid, their eyes shooting blue flames, wear uniforms that strangely resemble Asian styles and have a bearing that smacks of Confucian etiquette. Despite this dead giveaway you're watching a Japanese movie, THE MYSTERIANS is a visual delight with ample special-effects destruction. Sympathy is engendered for the Mysterians who claim their planet has been destroyed by Strontium-90 and they have come to Earth to procreate with our beautiful women. From that indomitable GODZILLA pair, director Inoshiro Honda and effects pioneer Eiji Tsuburaya. Kenji Sahara, Yumi Shirakawa. (VCI; United; Star Classics) (Laser: Japanese import)

MYSTERIES FROM BEYOND EARTH (1975). Documentary purports to examine UFOs, Atlantis, pyramids, Mayan temples, the Bermuda Triangle, Black Holes in space and other phenomena "kept secret from our world" or "from beyond the stars." Despite all the hype, this emerges a tedious, pretentious "expose" that resorts to stock footage of flying saucers from old movies. Hosted by Lawrence Dobkin, who delivers the sleep-inducing narration on camera. Produced-directed by George Gale. (United; VCI)

MYSTERIES FROM BEYOND THE GRAVE. See **BLACK PIT OF DR. M, THE.**

MYSTERIES FROM BEYOND THE TRIANGLE (1977). This is supposed to be the documented voyage of a band of scientists and psychics who traveled through the Bermuda Triangle. But it looks like 16mm photography of a yachtsman's holiday blended with travelogue footage. Poor excuse of a movie that never swims but treads in place with wild speculations and unsubstantiated, harebrained conclusions. (VCI)

MYSTERIES OF BLACK MAGIC. See **RETURN FROM THE BEYOND.**

MYSTERIES OF THE GODS (1976). More West German interpretations about man being descended from aliens, taken from the books of Erich von Daniken. Wild theory, with little substantiation or scientific proof to back it up. Directed by Harald Reinl. (United)

MYSTERIOUS CASTLE IN THE CARPATHIANS, THE (1982). Czech comedy in the Gothic tradition, set in the last century in Devil's Castle, where an opera fan keeps the body of his prima donna preserved in a special crypt. Meanwhile, to keep visitors away, the Baron's crazy-mad inventor assistant creates unnatural phenomena to give the place a spooky reputation. Directed-written by Oldrich Lipsky. Michael Docolomanky, Jan Hartl.

MYSTERIOUS DOCTOR, THE (1943). A tall, headless figure (the alleged ghost of Black Morgan) walks through assorted fogbound Warner Bros. studio sets with a butcher knife in an attempt to frighten the God-fearing townspeople of Morgan's Head and keep the work force out of the local Cornwall tin mine. Along comes the titular physician to check out the superstition, and weird events occur. A predictable plot and minimal horror effects are offset by a speedy pace from director Ben Stoloff and some decent performances, but it's mainly a hoary vehicle designed as anti-Nazi propaganda. John Loder, Eleanor Parker, Lester Matthews, Creighton Hale.

MYSTERIOUS DR. FU MANCHU, THE (1929). First sound film to feature the diabolical Fu Manchu. The Asian mastermind with designs to take over the world was Warner Oland, destined to play Charlie Chan in later years. Neil Hamilton (of TV's BATMAN) is on hand as Nayland Smith of Scotland Yard, Fu's nemesis, while Jean Arthur provides skirts and screams. Directed by the mysterious Rowland V. Lee.

MYSTERIOUS DR. SATAN, THE (1940). Republic serial directed by cliffhanging masters William Witney and John English. Dr. Satan (Eduardo Cinnelli) is an archfiend who has invented a robot to terrorize the world. But he needs C. Montague Shaw's remote control device to make it work. That's when a man in a copper mask steps in to thwart the evil gang. Non-stop action and non-stop nonsense will have you alternately gasping and chuckling —it never stops moving along its ludicrous, fun-filled pathways. Robert Wilcox is the hero, Ella Neal the heroine. The feature version is DR. SATAN'S ROBOT. (Republic; Nostalgia Merchant)

MYSTERIOUS INVADER. See **ASTOUNDING SHE MONSTER, THE.**

MYSTERIOUS ISLAND (1929). MGM adaptation of Jules Verne's adventure was begun silent, then sound was added prior to its release. It is not totally faithful to Verne (you will, for example, not find Captain Nemo), but it does deal with stranded Civil War escapees meeting a submarine crew on a lost island. This took three years to complete and three directors contributed: Maurice Tourneur, Lucien Hubbard and Benjamin Christiansen. Lionel Barrymore, Pauline Starke, Warner Oland.

MYSTERIOUS ISLAND (1951). Sam Katzman 15-chapter serial with Karen Randle as a woman from Mercury who visits the isle first created by Jules Verne to dig up a precious metal that will help her conquer our planet. Captain Nemo is on hand to contribute to the cliffhangers and Richard Crane is the young hero. Directed by Spencer G. Bennet.

MYSTERIOUS ISLAND (1961). Visually exciting adaptation of Jules Verne's book with effects by Ray Harryhausen and outstanding music by Bernard Herrmann. The John Prebble-Daniel Ullman-Wilbur Crane script is the weakest element of this Charles H. Schneer production filmed in Spain and England, for the characters are treated as stereotypes and the situations often deteriorate into shopworn thrills. Three Yankee prisoners of war escape Richmond Prison during a storm and make their getaway in an observation balloon to an unexplored Pacific island where a "Swiss Family Robinson" lifestyle is established. The Yanks are joined by shipwreck survivors and all are under attack from giant monsters: an overgrown chicken, a prehistoric Phororhacos, a nautiloid cephalopod and other Harryhausen marvels. Michael Craig, Michael Callan, Gary Merrill and Joan Greenwood are among the stranded, while Herbert Lom emerges from the foamy brine as Captain Nemo. Stylishly directed by Cy Endfield. (RCA/Columbia) (Laser: Voyager)

MYSTERIOUS ISLAND OF CAPTAIN NEMO (1973). French-Spanish production, an adaptation of Jules Verne themes, is sorely lacking in imagination and exciting effects. Omar Sharif portrays the Nautilus-sailing captain, but it is a portrayal inferior to James Mason's in Disney's 1954 TWENTY THOUSAND LEAGUES UNDER THE SEA. Directed by Henri Colpi and Juan Antonio Bardem. Philippe Nicaud, Gerald Tichy, Jess Hann.

MYSTERIOUS MAGICIAN, THE (1964). West German version of an Edgar Wallace novel, focusing on a murderer known as "The Squeaker" who is piling up the corpses in jolly old England. Directed by Alfred Vohrer. Joachim Fuchsberger, Heinz Drache. Sometimes known as THE WIZARD and THE SQUEAKER. (Sinister/C)

MYSTERIOUS MONSTERS, THE (1975). TV documentary, narrated by Peter Graves, which focuses on the Abominable Snowman, the Loch Ness Monster and Bigfoot. Same old rehash. Directed-written by Robert Guenette. Psychic Peter Hurkos appears.

MYSTERIOUS MR. WONG, THE (1935). Bela Lugosi at his worst, portraying a Chinese shopkeeper in search of the 12 coins of Confucius, which will give him mystical powers. Turgid Monogram hambone with Wallace Ford clowning around as the guy who's going to get the insidious Wong. As drab as they come. Directed by William Nigh. (Sinister/C; Nostalgia; Filmfax; Thunderbird)

MYSTERIOUS PLANET (1982). Ambitious but incompetent attempt to blend matte paintings, stop-motion animation creatures and space hardware effects into a grand adventure, allegedly based on a novel by Jules Verne. A spaceship carrying some unconvincing galaxy jockeys crashlands on a life-sustaining planet inhabited by a bikini-clad girl with healing powers and a lost race of superintelligent beings. The actors are too amateurish to create interesting characters, the photography is slapdash and the monsters all look like cute pieces of clay (which is what they are). Technically this is a nightmare, with some of the sound unintelligible and other portions containing an unwanted echo effect. Produced and directed (if you can call it that) by Brett Piper and "starring" Paula Tauper, Boyd Piper, Michael Quigley and Bruce Nadeau. (Video City)

MYSTERIOUS SATELLITE. See **WARNING FROM SPACE.**

MYSTERIOUS STRANGER, THE (1982). Delightful adaptation of a Mark Twain fantasy, a companion piece to his CONNECTICUT YANKEE IN KING ARTHUR'S COURT, in which a printer's apprentice (Chris Makepeace) imagines he is back in Guggenheim's day, helping print Bibles. He conjures up a free-wheeling youthful spirit from the future named No. 44 (Lance Kerwin) who works magical spells over striking printers and confounds an alchemist (a wonderful character essayed by Fred Gwynne). An amusing period fantasy, rich in character and detail, superbly directed by Peter H. Hunt. (From MCA as **MARK TWAIN CLASSICS: THE MYSTERIOUS STRANGER**)

MYSTERIOUS TWO (1979). Alan Landsburg TV-movie stars John Forsythe and Priscilla Pointer as white-robed emissaries from another planet or dimension who hypnotically gather followers and then lead them away to . . . where? Not even you, the viewer, will find out in this allegorical tale inspired by the Jonestown massacre of 1978. Here the lambs to the slaughter believe that "He and She" (as the aliens are called) will provide and make a blissful world. Originally made as FOLLOW ME IF YOU DARE, then shelved before coming to the network in 1982. Director-writer Gary Sherman captures a weird quality with his glaring white lighting. Great build-up to a non-payoff. James Stephens, Robert Pine, Noah Beery Jr., Vic Tayback. (USA; IVE)

MYSTERY IN DRACULA'S CASTLE (1977). Eerie lighthouse is the setting for this mystery-comedy from Disney. Brothers who are horror movie fans tangle with jewel thieves. Nothing supernatural about it, just fanciful window dressing and cheap thrills. Johnny Whitaker, Clu Gulager, Mariette Hartley. Directed by Robert Totten.

MYSTERY LINER (1934). The spectral image of a dead sea captain is observed aboard a passenger ship in this Monogram adaptation of Edgar Wallace's THE GHOST OF JOHN HOLLING. Directed by William Nigh. Noah Beery, Astrid Allwyn, Gustav von Seyffertitz, Edwin Maxwell. (Filmfax; Sinister/C; Nostalgia)

MYSTERY MANSION (1983). Lackluster juvenile adventure made in Oregon, and designed as a family picture, but adults will find it tedious going. Three children and their father seek a treasure map after one kid has prescient dreams about an incident that occurred in an old house in 1889 when an outlaw gang caused the death of a young girl. Two escaped convicts and a benevolent old prospector figure into the scheme, but this never builds up much steam due to the pedantic direction of David E. Jackson. Dallas McKennon, Jane Ferguson, Greg Wynne. (Media)

MYSTERY OF MARIE ROGET, THE (1942). Blatant misuse of the Poe title, since this Universal programmer has little to do with the classic detective story featuring C. August Dupin, the deductive sleuth who set the style for Sherlock Holmes. It's basically a detective tale with Patrick Knowles excellently conveying the personality of the eccentric French investigator. It has nice Gothic touches, and is enhanced by Maria Ouspenskaya, John Litel, Charles (Ming the Merciless) Middleton and sexy Maria Montez. Directed by Phil Rosen.

MYSTERY OF MONSTER ISLAND (1980). Ineptly juvenile U.S.-Spanish production, based on an adventure story by Jules Verne but don't believe it. It's quite a stupid tale in which a young scholar and his elocution teacher are stranded on an island overrun by prehistoric beasts (which walk upright on two legs), seaweed monsters, steam-blowing worms and other rubber-suited entities. Peter Cushing, as a benevolent island owner, and Terence Stamp as a gold-hungry villain are wasted. Directed by J. Piquer Simon. Paul Naschy, Ian Sera.

MYSTERY OF THE GOLDEN EYE (1978). Re-enactment of an allegedly true story about three adventurers searching for the lost son of a U.S. Senator on the island of Komodo, famed for its prehistoric dragons. Footage of the lizard creatures is good, and shows a family of them munching on a deer. The human footage is less stimulating, since the camera team was incapable of getting the synch sound correct. The narration (read by actor Arthur Franz) unconvincingly tries to inject intrigue into the dull travelogue footage. Produced-directed by Richard Martin. The phony-baloney adventurers are Robert White, K. K. Mohajan and Basil Bradbury.

MYSTERY OF THE MARIE CELESTE, THE. Video version of **PHANTOM SHIP**

(Blackhawk; Critics' Choice; Video Yesteryear).

MYSTERY OF THE 13TH GUEST, THE (1943). See third edition.

MYSTERY OF THE WAX MUSEUM, THE (1932). One of the first films made in the two-strip Technicolor process; it also served as the model for the 1953 3-D remake, HOUSE OF WAX. Lionel Atwill has one of his finest roles as museum curator Ivan Igor, a genius wax sculptor disfigured in a fire. Now he is a madman, killing his enemies and encasing their corpses in wax to serve as his "horror displays." Has the famous scene in which Fay Wray pounds away at Atwill's face until it cracks to reveal a terribly scarred countenance beneath. Michael Curtiz directed. Glenda Farrell, Frank McHugh, Holmes Herbert, Gavin Gordon. (Video/Laser: MGM/UA)

MYSTIC, THE (1925). Silent terror flick from director Tod Browning in which the title Hungarian, a charlatan, suddenly finds his blood running cold when he raises a spirit from beyond. Aileen Pringle, Conway Tearle.

MY UNCLE THE VAMPIRE. See **UNCLE WAS A VAMPIRE.**

MY WORLD DIES SCREAMING. See **TERROR IN THE HAUNTED HOUSE.**

"I want my molecules back!"

—Chevy Chase in **MEMOIRS OF AN INVISIBLE MAN**

NABONGA (1943). Classic example of How to Set Up Camp in the Jungle: Hire Julie London to play a "great white goddess" raised by gorillas and revered by natives; sign Buster Crabbe to wear jodhpurs as he rushes past potted plants; engage Barton MacLane to scowl villainously. Directed by Sam Newfield. "Nabonga nowanna." (Sinister/C; Nostalgia; Movies Unlimited)

NAIL GUN MASSACRE (1987). Helmeted avenger takes to Texas streets to slaughter construction workers who gang-banged his girl. The only novelty here is the murder weapon, subtly referred to in the title, which is used in a variety of ways so you'll bite your nails. Written-directed by Terry Loftin and Bill Leslie. Rocky Patterson, Michelle Meyer, Ron Queen. (Magnum)

NAKED EVIL. See **EXORCISM AT MIDNIGHT.**

NAKED EXORCISM (1975). Italian chiller, made in the wake of THE EXORICST, with Richard Conte as a priest caught up in demonology. The story (by director Angelo Pannaccio) asks the burning question: Does the Devil possess the brother of a nun? Jean-Claude Verne, Francoise Prevost, Mima Monticelli.

NAKED GODDESS, THE. See **DEVIL'S HAND.**

NAKED JUNGLE, THE (1954). Cancel your picnic plans to see this grand version of Carl Stephenson's classic story, "Leiningen vs. the Ants." It's slow going at first—what with all those smoochy embraces between mail-order bride Eleanor Parker and plantation owner Charlton Heston—until the killer ants mobilize and march on the plantation's crops. Those little ravenous carnivores will scare the hell out of you as men are eaten alive. Directed by an antsy Byron Haskin, written by Philip Yordan and Ronald MacDougall with ants in their pants. Great thrills in this George Pal production co-starring William Conrad. (Video/Laser: Paramount)

NAKED LOVERS (1977). Corpses walk again when aliens from planet Eros bring the dead to live. Isn't it loverly . . . Ursula White, Alban Ceray. French production, produced-directed by Claude Pierson.

NAKED LUNCH (1991). Written and directed by David Cronenberg, this adaptation of William S. Burrough's cult novel is a nightmarish descent into the drugged-out world of a novelist (Peter Weller) who hallucinates reality into a twisted spy adventure where giant centipedes and other monstrous creatures (created by Chris Walis) control him. It's a metaphor of homosexuality that will baffle some, sicken others and intrigue those who appreciate Cronenberg's intepretation of what was generally considered an unfilmable book. Judy Davis, Julian Sands, Roy Scheider. (Fox)

NAKED MASSACRE (198?). Killer nurse is on the loose, spilling blood instead of giving it. Mathieu Carriere, Carol Laurie. Directed by Denis Heroux. (Vidcrest)

NAKED TEMPTRESS, THE. See **NAKED WITCH.**

NAKED VENGEANCE (1986). In the style of I SPIT ON YOUR GRAVE, with a raped woman seeking revenge against her attackers. Strong stomachs required. Directed by Cirio H. Santiago. Deborah Tranelli, Kaz Garas, Bill McLaughlin. (Lightning; Live)

NAKED WITCH, THE (1961). Film maker Larry Buchanan is the one to blame for this tale about an old hag who returns from the dead to terrorize a Texas village. Beth Porter, Lee Forbes, Libby Hall. Also called THE NAKED TEMPTRESS. (Sinister/C)

NAME FOR EVIL, A (1973). Pretentious. esoteric allegory, in which Robert Culp resigns his architectural firm by throwing his TV out the window and moving to Canada to restore his great-great-grandfather's mansion, haunted by a ghost on a white charger. The ghost sleeps with wife Samantha Eggar while Culp seeks solace with a mountain girl. Ambiguous as hell. Written-directed by Bernard Girard. (Premiere; Paragon)

NAME OF THE GAME IS KILL, THE (1968). Jack Lord stars in this psychochiller set in the Arizona desert where an evil family of temptresses (Tisha Sterling, Collin Wilcox, Susan Strasberg) threatens an unsuspecting traveler. Directed by Gunnar Hellstrom.

NANNY, THE (1965). Lowkey, underplayed Hammer production with stress on the psychological implications of a murderous woman (Bette Davis) who, on the surface, is all sweetness. Davis does a fine job working with producer-writer Jimmy Sangster and director Seth Holt. Pamela Franklin, Wendy Craig, Jill Bennett.

NASTY RABBIT, THE (1965). Juvenile spy spoof in which rabid Russian roustabouts rigged as wranglers hop to the task of destroying our nation with a bacteria-laden rabbit. Director James Landis and writers Arch Hall Sr. and Jim Crutchfield forgot to carry a rabbit's foot for good luck—the film died during testing. Hare today, gong tomorrow. Melissa Morgan, Arch Hall Jr. (Rhino)

NATAS: THE REFLECTION (1983). Nosy reporter seeks the truth about an Indian legend that states there is a sentry standing guard over the passageway between

Heaven and Hell. Call it blights-of-passage. Directed by Jack Dunlap. Randy Mulkey, Pat Bolt. Elvira introduces with usual asides. (Thrillervideo)

NATIONAL LAMPOON'S CLASS REUNION (1982). Mildly amusing spoof on slasher movies, in which The Unknown Killer (with a paper sack over his head) terrorizes Lizzie Borden High School when graduates of '72 reune. There's a nerd (Fred McCarren) who's the hero, a Dracula vampire (Jim Staahl), a fire-breathing witch (Zane Buzby) and a sexy beauty (Shelley Smith), a blind girl who can't hear so good (Mary Small), etc. John Hughes' script never fails to stay sophomoric, but Michael Miller's direction is effective for such a ridiculous premise. Misty Rowe, Michael Lerner. (Vestron)

NATURAL, THE (1984). This tale of a baseball player who makes a striking comeback is also an allegory of battle between good and evil, and a metaphor for the indomitable spirit of man. Call it an American fable. Robert Redford stars as Roy Hobbs, a once-promising rookie mysteriously shot by a woman in black. He turns up years later armed with "Wonderboy," a bat made from a tree struck by lightning. When he leads the team to victory, Hobbs is tempted by seductress Kim Basinger, corrupt team owner Robert Prosky and perverted gambler Darren McGavin. Can he overcome his weaknesses and achieve the American Dream? In two great batting sequences, Hobbs performs miraculous (in a literal sense) feats, beautifully punctuated by Randy Newman's music. A great Americana film using baseball as a symbol of our drive for success. Based on the 1952 novel by Bernard Malamud, adapted by Roger Towne and Phil Dusenberry. Barry Levinson directed. Glenn Close, Robert Duvall, Wilford Brimley, Barbara Hershey, Richard Farnsworth, Joe Don Baker. (RCA/Columbia) (Laser: Pioneer)

NAVIGATOR: AN ODYSSEY ACROSS TIME, THE (1988). New Zealand film maker Vincent Ward has created a mini-masterpiece of fantasy with this offbeat, beautifully photographed tale of 14th Century England, when the Black Plague swept the land. In an isolated village, miners are impressed with visionary dreams of young Griffin, who leads select followers on a journey through time and space. Ward's viewpoint is of a stranger in a strange land, so that modern technology to a man from the past looks life-threatening. This unlikely time travel movie is filled with symbolism and layers of meaning as it weaves in and out of dreams and reality in a wondrous way. The film won 19 awards. Bruce Lyons, Chris Haywood, Hamish McFarlane. (Trylon)

NAVY VS. THE NIGHT MONSTERS (1966). Director Michael Hoey's script, based on Murray Leinster's MONSTER FROM THE EARTH'S END, depicts plant creatures with acid in their veins who stalk forth and "stump" Anthony Eisley before launching their invasion against Earth. Mamie Van Doren breaths heavily to push the biggest night monsters of all against the thin material of her blouse, thereby revealing the roundness of the Gargantuas concealed beneath. Bobby Van, Billy Gray, Pamela Mason, Russ Bender. (Paragon)

NEANDERTHAL MAN, THE (1953). Cliched human-into-primeval-creature theme when scientist Robert Shayne discovers how to send a man back through evolutionary stages. In short, another hairy movie monster. Directed by E. A. Dupont from a script by co-producers Aubrey Wisberg and Jack Pollexfen. Richard Crane, Doris Merric, Joyce Terry, Dick Rich.

NEAR DARK (1987). The Bonnie and Clyde of horror films, which shirks cliched Gothic trappings to take on the look of a rural gangster movie, photographed against a stark Americana landscape and peopled by grubby killers who resemble Depression migrant workers. They're really vampires and there's nothing fastidious about these Texas clod kickers. Director Kathryn Bigelow and co-writer Eric (HITCHER) Red create a disturbing, violent, bloody story that many may find too gory to watch. Genre buffs, however, will dig this modern Western in which Jenny Wright hooks Adrian Pasdar with a neck bite and he reluctantly joins the gang. A parable of innocence exposed to evil, with Lance Henriksen and Bill Paxton as fascinatingly grotesque gang members. Offbeat and worth catching—the film, not vampirism. Tim Thomerson. (HBO) (Laser: Image)

NEARLY WASN'T CHRISTMAS, THE (1989). Family-styled TV-movie starring Charles Durning as a disillusioned Santa Claus, so distraught over human selfishness he ventures into the real world to find redeeming individuals. He meets a youngster trying to get mother and father back together and makes an odyssey across America, encountering greedy people who quickly see their nasty ways, and helping others overcome bad circumstances. Durning underplays his role in this warm morality lesson directed by Burt Brinckerhoff. Ted Lange, Wayne Osmond, Annette Marin. Re-released to TV as IT NEARLY WASN'T CHRISTMAS.

NECROMANCER: SATAN'S SERVANT (1988). Slow-moving, predictable horror flick underplays its violence and bloodletting. A demon called from beyond carries out revenge murders by taking possession of a witch, or necromancer. This happens after drama student Elizabeth Cayton is raped by three fellow students but is afraid to tell authorities, and calls on Lisa the Avenger (Lois Masten) to wreak havoc. Softcore sex scenes reveal that Cayton has a fine body, but that's the only appeal this offers. Russ Tamblyn is wasted as a lecherous drama coach. Directed by Dusty Nelson. John Tyler, Rhonda Durton. (Forum) (Laser: Image)

NECROMANCY (1971). Terror tale written-produced-directed by Bert I. Gordon with Orson Welles as toy manufacturer Cato, boss man of a witchcraft cult restoring life to Cato's dead son. Into the community of Lilith comes Pamela Franklin, unwitting (or is it witless?) heroine subjected to tortures from Mr. Cato's so-called toys. For lovers of dead movies only. Lee Purcell, Michael Ontkean. (From Paragon as **WITCHING, THE** and Magnum as **ROSEMARY'S DISCIPLES**)

NECROMANIAC. Video version of **GRAVEYARD OF HORROR** (All American).

NECROPHAGUS. See **GRAVEYARD OF HORROR.**

NECROPOLIS (1986). Sleazy, kinky R-rated supernatural flick, so nihilistic there's nary an entertaining moment in its 77 minutes. After an opening set in 1686 New Amsterdam, where it's revealed Leeanne Baker runs a devil cult, she turns up reincarnated as a blond sex kitten in black miniskirt and nylons in modern Manhattan. Wearing the Devil's Ring, she uses mind control over the street trash and fights a psychological battle with a black priest, a former adversary who has also been reincarnated. She has three sets of breasts which leak this white gooey stuff, a substance her zombies suckle on. Yes, it's pretty weird stuff coming from writer-director Bruce Hickey. Jacquie Fitz, Michael Conte. (Vestron) (Laser: Japanese)

NEEDFUL THINGS (1993). This adaptation of Stephen King's sprawling, dark novel (one of his most complex) combines black comedy and bloody thrills, a mixture that prevents the film from being ultimately satisfying. However, to the credit of writer W. D. Richter and director Fraser Heston (son of Charlton), it's loaded with film-making artistry and sports a fine cast. To Castle Rock, Maine, pure Stephen King territory, comes the devil in the form of Leland Gaunt (Max von Sydow, in a fine performance), who opens a shop (Needful Things) and offers items for sale to lure buyers into pacts. Now in the clutches of evil, these townspeople carry out acts against each other until the town explodes—figuratively and literally. Ed Harris plays Sheriff Alan Pangborn, the film's only heroic figure, and Bonnie Bedelia is outstanding as a cafe proprietress suffering from arthritic pain. Amanda Plummer's Nettie Cobb is an ultimate portrayal of sexual oppression, and J.T. Walsh as the crazed "Buster" carries madness to cartoonish proportions. This film is so stark, and so deeply disturbing in commenting on man's inhumanity, that it is missing one needful thing: more rays of hope to counteract its too-effective darkness. (Columbia TriStar)

NEITHER THE SEA NOR THE SAND (1972). See editions 1-3.

NEMESIS (1992). Slam-bam action thriller set in 2027 A.D., when a movement is afoot to replace human beings with mechanical clones. Oliver Gruner, doing an impression of Jean-Claude Van Damme, portrays Alex Rain, L.A. cyborg cop who undergoes harrowing adventures in his quest to reach the Red Army Hammerheads, a terrorist group that could help prevent evil clone-cop Tim Thomerson from fulfilling the conspiracy. Director Albert Pyum brings such kinetic energy to the rousing battle sequences—filled with acrobatic bodies, explosions and incredibly intense firepower—that the film grabs on and won't let go. Cary-Hirdyuki Tagawa, Merle Kennedy, Deborah Shelton, Brion James, Marjorie Monaghan, Thom Mathews. (Imperial)

NEON CITY (1991). Sci-fi version of STAGECOACH set in MAD MAX country—an enjoyable action derivation masterminded by Monte Markham, who co-wrote (with Buck Finch and Jeff Begun), directed and stars as a corrupt sheriff ranger in a post-holocaustic world of 2053 A.D. While there's plenty of action, there's also good ensemble acting led by Michael Ironside (as ex-ranger Harry M. Stark) and Vanity (as a fugitive who becomes Stark's bounty). They're with motley passengers traveling in a futuristic funky bus across a dangerous desert zone ruled by "Skins." Lyle Alzado, Valerie Wildman, Mick Klar. Shot on the salt flats of Utah. (Vidmark)

MICHAEL IRONSIDE

NEON MANIACS (1985). "When the world is ruled by violence, and the soul of mankind fades, the children's path shall be darkened by the shadows of the . . . Neon Maniacs." That prologue doesn't make much sense, but neither does this exercise in excessive gore effects. The premise—that a gang of grotesque killer-monsters live within a tower of the Golden Gate Bridge in San Francisco—is never developed; instead we're subjected to teenagers who are disbelieved by police when they tell of the slimy creatures they've seen slithering around the bridge, killing their buddies. Director Joseph Mangine manages some harrowing suspense (especially a runaway streetcar sequence) and the monsters are ugly enough, but the story sucks. Just a lot of gooey mayhem as the Samurai, Bowman and Hangman monsters stalk their prey. Donna Locke, Allan Hayes. (Lightning; Vestron)

NEPTUNE DISASTER, THE (1973). Hard to believe a full-grown movie producer (Sandy Howard) would ask his cameraman to photograph fish in an aquarium tank with macro lenses and pass them off as "monsters from the deep." Yet that's what happened in this underwater fantasy. Ben Gazzara, Yvette Mimieux and Ernest Borgnine look through the windows of their "Neptune" craft and react to "monsters" but their expressions are those of the dumbfounded. Directed by Daniel Petrie. (From CBS/Fox as **THE NEPTUNE FACTOR**)

NEPTUNE FACTOR, THE. Video version of **NEPTUNE DISASTER, THE** (CBS/Fox).

NEPTUNE'S CHILDREN (1985). Boring British TV-movie of two episodes: "The Kids Who Found Atlantis" and "Selkie the Seal." In the first, youngsters meets a 300-year-old "boy" who lives in an underwater kingdom. In the second, the insufferable kiddies meet Neptune, king of the sea, in the form of a stuffy old Englishman who hurries about the Empire causing trouble for people indifferent to the poisoning of the seas. Directed by Anthony Squire. Simon Turner, Perry Balfour.

NEST, THE (1987). There's the flavor of a '50s creatures-on-a-rampage flick to this adaptation of Eli Cantor's novel about an island community being attacked by a swarm of genetic-jazzed cockroaches. Scripter Robert King and director Terence H. Winkless bring to this Julie Corman production a mixture of straight thrills and comedy. The roaches are the result of unauthorized testing by the company INTEC. The best moments come when the roaches take on the shape of life forms they've ingested, including humans, giving the special effects team the opportunity to create man and cat monsters. Robert Lansing, Lisa Langlois, Franc Luz and Terri Treas bring a sense of fun to the picture. (MGM/UA)

NESTING, THE (1981). Robin Groves, a neurotic writer suffering from agoraphobia, seeks refuge in a haunted house and is driven to madness by ghostly spectres in this blending of supernatural shocks and psychological terrors. It's a valiant try by writers Daria Price and Armand Weston (the latter, a one-time pornie maker, produced-directed) on a limited budget, but it's a strong supporting cast (John Carradine and Gloria Grahame in pivotal roles) that finally gives convincing clout to an otherwise predictable horror story. Christopher Loomis, Michael David Lally, David Tabor. (Warner Bros.)

NET, THE. See **PROJECT M-7.**

NETHERWORLD (1991). A quieter-than-usual Full Moon Production from producer Charles Band, enhanced by New Orleans locations. Michael Bendetti arrives at his father's Louisiana mansion where a cult of bird lovers uses winged creatures as a means of restoring the dead to life. The best effect by Steve Patino is the Hand of Satan, a severed human paw that floats through the mansion's corridors (shades of PHANTASM!) and thrusts its claws into your eyeballs. A hint of sexual decadence hangs over the script by Billy Chicago (pseudonym for director David Schmoeller, who appears as bartender Billy Chicago). Excellent performances by Denise Gentile, Anjanette Comer, Holly Floria and Alex Datcher add up to one interesting video movie. (Paramount) (Laser: Full Moon)

NEUROSIS. See **REVENGE IN THE HOUSE OF USHER.**

NEUTRON BATTLES THE KARATE ASSASSINS (1964). Muscular wrestler Wolf Ruvinskis takes the full count against automaton killers who deliver death-dealing blows with hands and feet.

NEUTRON TRAPS THE INVISIBLE KILLERS (1964). Not only can you not see villains, but you cannot find plot in this Mexican film in the Masked Wrestler vs. Evil Genius Doctor series. Wolf Ruvinskis again, trying to hitch up his droopy drawers.

NEUTRON VS. THE AMAZING DR. CARONTE (1964). That thick-skulled masked wrestler is still trying to pin an evil genius to the mat but there's never a referee to count to three. So Neutron, against his code of ethics, fights dirty by kicking Dr. Caronte right in his lobotomy. Now that hurts! Wolf Ruvinskis yet again. (Sinister/C; S/Weird; Filmfax)

NEUTRON VS THE BLACK MASK (1962). More hilarious bone-crunching which pits a witless wrestler against an insidious doctor who specializes in new weapons and monsters. Wolf Ruvinskis again, under Frederico Curiel's direction. (Sinister/C; Dark Dreams; S/Weird; Filmfax)

NEUTRON VS THE DEATH ROBOTS (1962). Is Neutron a gallant superhero in a gleaming uniform, an aura of patriotism emanating from his body, a halo of truth ringing his incorruptible head? Naw, he's a wrestler (Wolf Ruvinskis) clad in a Woolworth's black mask (a dyed barley sack) and droopy boxing trunks in his fight against the incredible Dr. Caronte. Directed-written by Frederico Curiel. (Sinister/C; Filmfax)

NEUTRON VS. THE MANIAC (1961). Masked wrestler of Mexico, a superhero among body-hold fans, is back for another round as he floors Dr. Caronte over possession of a deadly explosive, but it's hardly a main event for the viewer. Wolf Ruvinskis. (Sinister/C; S/Weird; Filmfax)

NEVERENDING STORY, THE (1984). Offbeat fairy tale told in striking details by German filmmaker Wolfgang Petersen. A youth, reading a book given to him by a strange shopowner, is projected into the land of Fantasia, which is about to be destroyed by The Nothing. He must find a cure for the dying Empress in her Ivory Tower, and he sets out on his episodic quest. The lad meets a racing snail, a rock-eating stone man, a wise old colossal turtle, statues with laser-beam eyes and other charming creatures. But when the film tries to be philosophical with a form of double think, it is a letdown. Tami Stronach, Moses Gunn, Patrick Hayes. (Video/Laser: Warner Bros.)

NEVERENDING STORY II: THE NEXT CHAPTER, THE (1990). Weak follow-up to Wolfgang Petersen's popular film of 1984, its fantasy elements appealing mainly to the young because of a sanitized script by Karin Howard, who adapted new parts of Michael Ende's novel. However, its visuals are again a delight to behold as youngster Jonathan Brandis, reading a magical book given to him by Mr. Koreander (Thomas Hill), is propelled into the kingdom of Fantasia. Evil empress Xayide (Clarissa Burt) tries to trick Brandis into using up all the wishes granted by Orin the magic medallion, for then he will become her slave. The creatures Falkor and Rock Biter are back, as well as Atreyu, a bird-like entity. John Wesley Shipp, THE FLASH of TV, figures into the story minimally as he reads the narrative from the book. Director George Miller is not the same George Miller who made MAD MAX. Kenny Morrison, Alexandra Johnes, Martin Umbach. (Video/Laser: Warner Bros.)

NEVER PICK UP A STRANGER. See **BLOODRAGE.**

NEVER SAY NEVER AGAIN (1983). Sean Connery's return as James Bond after he forsook the part for 12 years is a loose remake of THUNDERBALL (producer Kevin McClory ended up with story rights after a legal battle; this is not part of the official series). It's a return to adventurous derring-do as British secret agent 007 tries to thwart Largo from detonating two atomic warheads he's stolen from U.S. missiles as part of a SPECTRE plot. The gadgetry, action and sexy ladies are abundant—everything you expect in a Bond thriller. Barbara Carrera is a sadistic SPECTRE assassin, as exotic as she is deadly; Kim Basinger is the innocent (though well-rounded) young thing saved by Bond; Max von Sydow is the insidious SPECTRE chief with the white cat; Klaus Maria Brandauer is one of the best Bond villains yet, giving Largo such human traits as a sense of humor, joviality and jealousy. There are jokes about Bond growing old, but Connery still has the looks to pull it off. Irvin Kershner's direction is slick and unobtrusive. (Video/Laser: Warner Bros.)

NEVER TOO YOUNG TO DIE (1986). Directed by Gil Bettman, this parody of James Bond action thrillers throws in touches of ROAD WARRIOR for bad measure. It's about a dastardly plot to poison the L.A. water supply with superspy Lance Stargrove coming to the rescue. John Stamos, George Lazenby, Vanity, Robert Englund. (Charter)

NEW ADVENTURES OF TARZAN, THE (1935). A 12-chapter serial starring Herman Brix (later to become Bruce Bennett) independently produced by Edgar Rice Burroughs in Guatemala, which provides colorful jungle and old-ruins footage. The jungle hero has left Africa for South America to find a friend kindapped by villainous Mayans. Tarzan locates a valuable artifact that also contains the formula for a revolutionary explosive. The acting is dreadfully passe. Directed by Edward Kull and W. F. McGaugh. Ula Holt, Frank Baker, Dale Walsh, Harry Ernest. In 1938, it was re-released in feature form as TARZAN AND THE GREEN GODDESS. (The complete serial is available from Rhino.)

NEW ADVENTURES OF WONDER WOMAN, THE (1977). WONDER WOMAN TV episodes re-edited to feature length, with shapely Lynda Carter portraying the superhero with bullet-bouncing bracelets. She is forced to leave Paradise Island to protect its secret location from evil forces. Girl watchers, don't miss the bevy of jiggling beauties (scantily clad at that). Lyle Waggoner, Beatrice Straight, Jessica Walter, Fritz Weaver.

NEW BARBARIANS, THE. Video version of **WARRIORS OF THE WASTELAND** (Impulse).

NEW GLADIATORS, THE (ROME 2072 A.D.) (1987) "Kill Bike" is the highest rated show on the World Broadcasting System, in which men fight on "machines of death." It's the greatest in "pain, brutality and human cruelty." But along comes a new show, "Battle of the Damned," in which the best bikers are given old-fashioned gladiatorial weaponry and told to rip each other apart. It's "live until the death." Meanwhile, there's a scheme afoot involving corporate crooks, computers and a distant satellite to gain control of the world, and only the gladiators can stop the nefarious plot. Yes, gang, it's one of those Italian futuristic action films, directed by Lucio Fulci, loaded down with zap guns, stormtroopers, exploding bikes and beheadings. Jared Martin, Fred Williamson, Howard Ross. (Media)

NEW HOUSE ON THE LEFT. See **CARNAGE.**

NEW INVISIBLE MAN, THE (1957). Video version of **H.G. WELLS' NEW INVISIBLE MAN** (S/Weird; Sinister/C; Filmfax).

NEW KIDS, THE (1985). Orphaned teenagers are sent to Florida to work with relatives in a sleazy amusement park, incurring the wrath of a town bully nicknamed Joe Bob, in obvious tribute to the great redneck movie reviewer, Joe Bob Briggs. The bully and his buddy bullies commit heinous acts of torture and murder, concluding in a bloody shootout-battle at the carnival. Sean Cunningham directed this worthless, unmotivated can of trash. But we did like the homage to Joe Bob. Shannon Presby, James Spader, Lori Laughlin, John Philbin, Eric Stoltz. (Video/Laser: RCA/Columbia)

NEW ORIGINAL WONDER WOMAN, THE (1975). World War II adventure off the pages of Charles Moulton's superheroine action strip. Amazonian Lynda Carter is curvaceously perfect as the superheroine with bullet-bouncing bracelets and magical lariat. She leaves Paradise Island to fight Axis powers as military aide-de-camp Diana Prince. This pilot TV-film led to a series which promoted Ms Carter into the awareness of red-blooded Americans who believe in freedom, justice and the American way of showing off sexy women in TV pilots. Directed by Leonard Horn. Red Buttons, Cloris Leachman, Lyle Waggoner, Stella Stevens.

NEW PLANET OF THE APES. See **BACK TO THE PLANET OF THE APES.**

NEW YEAR'S EVIL (1982). Roz Kelly, a sexy chick-emcee for a punk-rock radio special, is the target for a knife killer calling himself Evil (Kip Niven). She tries to act as a psychiatrist for the police, but the killer continues to knock off beautiful women, moving ever closer to the station. Footage is devoted to punk-rock numbers while the plot waits in the wings, so don't anticipate breathtaking pace. There are surprise twists from writer-director Emmett Alston. Chris Wallace, Grant Cramer, Louisa Moritz. (Paragon; Cannon)

NEW YORK RIPPER (1981). Italy's horror director Lucio Fulci is up to his usual graphic close-ups of human flesh being ripped apart in this Manhattan melodrama of murder, in which a knife-wielding killer, who cackles like a duck, slaughters prostitutes. Fulci has added a who-dunit element in the Dario Argento vein, so there are many suspects to suspect. But when it comes to scenes of a woman's stomach and breast being opened by a razor blade, Fulci returns to his primitive level. Jack Hedley, Almanta Keller, Howard Ross, Andrew Painter. (Vidmark)

NEW YORK STORIES (1989). Trilogy of charming, lightweight fables, one with fantasy elements: Woody Allen's "Oedipus Wrecks," a silly yarn (call it the ultimate Jewish nightmare) in which a nebbish business executive (Allen) is troubled by a doddering old mother always criticizing him. One night at a magician's show she disappears, only to reappear as a giant image in the sky, revealing to all New Yorkers what's wrong with her son. The other stories, directed by Martin Scorsese and Francis Ford Coppola, are delightful in their own right. (Video/Laser: Touchstone)

NEXT. U.S. theatrical title for **BLADE OF THE RIPPER.**

NEXT OF KIN (1982). Australian/New Zealand supernatural thriller set in a lonely rest home, where events described in an old woman's diary start to recur to daughter Jackie Kerrin. Directed-written by Tony Williams. John Jarratt, Gerda Nicolson. (Media; VCL) (Laser: Virgin Vision)

NEXT ONE, THE (1982). Weak, tedious Greek-produced fantasy with supernatural-religious overtones, about as exciting as Zorba the Greek on crutches. Adrienne Barbeau and her young son are living in a villa on the isle of Myconos when a stranger (Keir Dullea) washes ashore. He's someone from the time-space continuum, the brother of Jesus Christ, although what significance this has remains a mystery in the hands of writer-director Nico Mastorakis. Dull and slow-moving. Peter Hobbs, Jeremy Licht. (Vestron)

NEXT VICTIM. Alternate video version of **BLADE OF THE RIPPER** (Video Gems; Dominique).

NEXT VICTIM, THE (1974). Carroll Baker stars in this British TV production about a wheelchair-bound woman terrorized by a psychotic murderer. T. P. McKenna, Ronald Lacey, Maurice Kaufman. Directed by James Ormerod. (Thrillervideo)

NEXT VOICE YOU HEAR, THE (1950). Pious idea by Charles Schnee (God's voice is heard over every radio in the world, in the language of the listener) is an impossible assignment for director William Wellman. Sure we should examine our hearts, sure we should glory over the Universe set before us, sure we should have faith, but producer Dore Schary should leave message-sending to Western Union. James Whitmore stars as Joe Smith, factory worker (or Everyman) in this turgid allegory. Nancy Davis, Gary Gray, Jeff Corey. (MGM/UA)

NICE GIRLS DON'T EXPLODE (1987). An amusing and unusual premise (teenager Michelle Meyrink causes objects to burst into flames whenever she makes love) is reduced to screwball cases of mistaken identity and daffy misunderstandings in this fantasy-comedy shot in Lawrence, Kansas. Meyrink's mother (Barbara Harris) tries to prevent the fires from breaking out—literal flames as well as passionate ones. Paul Harris' script deals with sexual themes, although this element is kept on a cutesy level. William O'Leary portrays the bewildered boyfriend and Wallace Shawn is a would-be paramour of Harris' named "Ellen." Directed with a light touch by Chuck Martinez. Irwin Keyes, Belinda Wills, James Mardini. (New World) (Laser: Image)

NICK KNIGHT (1989). A clever idea—L.A. cop is a good-guy vampire who can only work at night—is witlessly carried out in this TV-movie starring Rick Springfield as the detective investigating a series of killings in which the blood of the victims is drained. Knight's old rival, another eternal vampire, is out to get a sacrifical Mayan goble, the key to becoming mortal again. Meanwhile, Knight has a romance with museum curator Laura Johnson that lacks conviction. The level of violence is unusually grim for a TV-movie. There's never a sense that Springfield is a cop, and the premise becomes anemic. John Kapelos, Robert Harper, Michael Nader. (Starmaker) (Laser: Image)

NIECE OF THE VAMPIRE. See **FANGS OF THE LIVING DEAD.**

NIGHT AFTER HALLOWEEN (1983). Chantal Contouri is stalked by a boyfriend who is also a psychokiller. Robert Bruning, Sigrid Thornton. (Magnum)

NIGHT AFTER NIGHT AFTER NIGHT (HE KILLS) (1970). Also known as NIGHT AFTER NIGHT, this depicts a modern Jack the Ripper stalking the streets of London for prostitutes. Jack May, Linda Marlowe. Directed by Lewis J. Force. (Monterey; Media)

NIGHT ANDY CAME HOME, THE. See **DEAD OF NIGHT** (1974).

NIGHT ANGEL (1990). An evil spirit, assuming the shapeliness of a modern sexual female, seduces men to kill them for power. It's the Lilith legend retold in modern gory-story terms by director Dominique Othernin-Girard. Isa Anderson, Karen Black, Linden Ashby. Narrated by Roscoe Lee Browne. (Fries) (Laser: Image)

NIGHTBEAST (1982). Substandard effects and an unconvincing monster mask are compensated for by enthusiastic directing and writing by Don Dohler, who takes every cliche of the alien-invader genre and crams them into this video offering. A spaceship drops from the sky onto the town of Perry Hill and an ugly E.T. leaps out, slaughtering hunters with a laser pistol. So much for intellect. The town sheriff and his female deputy try to save the town while the mean alien kills kills kills. Should satisfy genre lovers with its sheer elan. And girl watchers will appreciate Dohler showing much naked female flesh. Tom Griffith, Jamie Zemarel, Anne Frith, George Stover (editor of Cinemacabre magazine), Richard Dyszel, Don Leifert. (Paragon)

NIGHTBREED (1990). In the wake of the success of HELLRAISER, Clive Barker returns as writer-director with a rip-roaring monster flick, all the stops out and pumping with imagination. Based on Barker's novel CABAL, this is the story of Midian, where monsters dwell after they die. And there are scores of beasts, creatures and "things" so don't miss this if you love effects and monster make-up. Craig Sheffer is a human monster who joins their ranks after his death is set up by a psychiatrist hoping to learn secrets of eternal life. That psychiatrist, in a brilliant bit of twist-casting, is David Cronenberg, the Canadian director. Anne Bobby, Charles Haid, Malcolm Smith, Catherine Chevalier. (Media) (Laser: Image)

NIGHT BRINGS CHARLIE, THE (1990). Low-budget effort, from Orlando, Fla., in which a psychokiller with power tools goes after women at a slumber party. Be careful you don't fall asleep yourself. Directed by Tom Logan. Wally Parks, Paul Stubenrach. (Quest)

NIGHT CALLER FROM OUTER SPACE, THE (1965). Low-budget British effort, in which an egg-shaped object sent to Ganymede (a moon of Jupiter) and back is discovered by scientist John Saxon, working at an astronomy station. The egg is a matter transferrer for a monster sent here to (1) frighten Patricia Haines half to death and (2) kidnap pretty women by posing as a girly magazine editor. Ronald Liles' direction achieves a dreary look distinctively British with a stiff-lipped cast: Maurice Denham, Alfred Burke, Aubrey Morris, Warren Mitchell. (Sony) (Laser: Image)

NIGHT CHILD, THE (1975). EXORCIST ripoff from Italy, lifeless and dull, with Richard Johnson as the man who could save the day if only he'd stop messing with Joanna Cassidy's body and pay attention to the girl (Nicole Elmi) with people-destroying powers. You'll fall asleep waiting for the ESP action. A nadir for director Max Dallamano. Lila Kedrova, Edmund Purdom. (Cocktail)

NIGHTCOMERS, THE (1972). Prequel to Henry James' TURN OF THE SCREW, revealing how evil valet-gardener Quint (Marlon Brando) and governess Miss Jessel (Stephanie Beacham) engage in brutal, voyeuristic bedroom techniques that turn two innocent children into little monsters. Directed by Michael Winner. Harry Andrews, Anna Palk, Thora Hird. (RCA/Columbia;

"I don't think [the] Betty Ford [clinic] takes vampires."

—Rick Springfield as Nick Knight in **NICK KNIGHT**

Nelson; Charter) (Laser: Image)

NIGHT COMES TOO SOON, THE (1947). See **GHOST OF RASHMON HALL, THE.**

NIGHT CRAWLERS. See **NAVY VS. THE NIGHT MONSTERS, THE.**

NIGHT CREATURE (1977). Metaphysical link between big game hunter Axel McGregory (Donald Pleasence) and a killer leopard provides an odd ambience to this strangely compelling tale of cowardice and bravery, photographed in exotic Thailand locations. Pleasence brings the black cat to his private island for a showdown, but unexpected visitors foul up his plans. Good dialogue and mood make up for an ambiguous, unresolved story. Ross Hagen, Nancy Kwan, Jennifer Rhodes. Also called OUT OF THE DARKNESS. (VCI)

NIGHT CREATURES (1962). Skeletons on horseback ride through Romney Marsh, pillaging farmers. Village vicar Peter Cushing warns the populace the Devil is afoot, but cooler heads recognize the presence of pirate captain Clegg and his "Marsh Phantoms." Minor Hammer production is a remake of a 1937 film, DR. SYN (remade again by Disney as THE SCARECROW OF ROMNEY MARSH). Directed stylishly by Peter Graham Scott. Also known as CAPTAIN CLEGG. Oliver Reed, Yvonne Romain, Milton Reid, Michael Ripper.

NIGHT CRIES (1978). Psychiatry and psychic phenomena are skillfully blended by writer Brian Taggart in this TV-movie supernatural mystery story. Well directed by Richard Lang and nicely acted by Susan St. James as the distraught mother who refuses to believe her baby died at childbirth and dreams she is in jeopardy. William Conrad is a scientist conducting experiments in dreams who helps Susan unravel the sex trauma haunting her. Michael Parks, Cathleen Nesbitt, Ellen Geer, Jamie Smith Jackson, Lee Kessler. (WorldVision)

NIGHT DANIEL DIED, THE. See **BLOODSTALKERS.**

NIGHT DIGGER, THE (1971). This British psychothriller (also known as THE ROAD BUILDER) is subtle—no graphic violence or bloodletting in spite of its depiction of a serial murderer (Nicholas Clay) who buries his female victims on the site of new road construction. The thrust of Roald Dahl's script (based on Joy Cowley's NEST IN A FALLEN TREE) is the man's manipulation of an aging blind invalid (Pamela Brown) and her daughter (Patricia Neal), and the subsequent affair between the intruder and Neal, a sexually repressed maid who takes care of her conniving mother. Director Alastair Reid emphasizes the grotesque nature of the seemingly normal people in the neighborhood, and sympathizes with those plagued by neuroses and madness. Sublime score by Bernard Herrmann. Graham Crowden, Jean Anderson, Peter Sallis, Yootha Joyce.

NIGHT EVELYN CAME OUT OF THE GRAVE, THE (1972). Good Italian thriller with quasisupernatural overtones and a strong sense of sexual perversion. Maniac Anthony Steffen enjoys bringing beautiful women to his estate and then . . . but that would be giving away too much. Watch as a number of ghastly sights unfold under Emilio P. Miraglia's direction. Erika Blanc, Giocomo Rossi-Stuart, Marina Malfatti.

NIGHTDREAMS (1981). Lightly pornographic fantasy in which a pair of scientists observes a woman, jolting her with stimulating electrons so she will undergo erotic dreams. Dorothy LeMay, Loni Sanders, Jennifer West.

NIGHTFALL (1988). Night doesn't fall fast enough in this Julie Corman production of Isaac Asimov's famous short story about a race of biblical-like people faced with losing all sunlight every thousand years and coping with the psychological terror of darkness. All the robed characters act like tragic figures out of Sheakespearean dramas, but without poetry or pentameter it plays more like a soap opera made for Julius Caesar. Paul Mayersberg wrote the misguided script, which is a travesty against sci-fi literature, and also directed the dullish events on Arizona desert locations. David Birney is awful in a fright wig as a leader of a cult. Sarah Douglas, Alexis Kanner, Andra Millian, Starr Andreeff. (MGM/UA)

NIGHT FIEND. TV title for **VIOLENT BLOOD BATH.**

NIGHTFLYERS (1987). In adapting George R. R. Martin's novella, screenwriter Robert Jaffe and producers Robert and Herb Jaffe had good intentions to produce a space adventure combining literary and cinematic techniques. Unfortunately, the effects are uneven, the plot is unnecessarily convoluted, and the characters so abrasive that NIGHTFLYERS annoys more than it intrigues. In the 21st Century, Catherine Mary Stewart and a group of scientists set out on an old space freighter, Nightflyer, only to discover that the ship's computer is controlled by the essence of an evil woman, who created a clone male (Michael Praed) before her death. Now she wants the clone, Captain Royd, for herself, and kills the intruders one by one. Director Robert Collector had his name replaced with the alias T. C. Blake, so unhappy was he with the results. John Standing, Lisa Blount, Glenn Withrow, James Avery, Michael Des Barres. (IVE) (Laser: Pioneer)

NIGHT FRIGHT (1968). Low-budget schlock, filmed in the South and strictly from hunger. A rocket sent into space (Operation Noah's Ark) with hundreds of animals is subjected to radiation, turning them into mutations. The ship (now a UFO) lands near Satan's Hollow, and a creature attacks stupid teenagers making out in a convertible. This monster (with the body of Robot Monster and the face of It! The Terror From Beyond Space) runs through the woods after sheriff John Agar and deputy Bill Thurman, pipe-smoking scientist Roger Ready and more dumb stupid teenagers led by Carol Gilley. Deadly dull, without a whit of imagination from director James A. Sullivan. Also known as THE EXTRATERRESTRIAL NASTY. (Sinister/C)

NIGHT GALLERY (1969). Rod Serling's collection of horror stories, THE SEASON TO BE WARY, was adapted by Universal into a trilogy which became the pilot for a popular series. Stories are hung together by the theme of surrealistic paintings in a creepy art gallery, presided over by host Rod Serling. In the first tale, directed by Boris Sagal, Roddy McDowall speeds along the death of a relative, then realizes he is being haunted by a painting. In the second, directed by Steven Spielberg (making his directorial debut), Joan Crawford is a blind woman who buys the eyes of a beggar so she might see again; and in the third, directed by Barry Shear, Richard Kiley is a one-time Nazi butcher seeking refuge from Israeli avengers (and his conscience) by hiding in a painting hanging in an art gallery. (MCA)

ROD SERLING

NIGHT GAME (1989). Contrived, lightweight slasher flick that barely qualifies to be called a thriller. A killer who uses a strange kind of hook is murdering beautiful women in the Galveston area, and local cop Roy Scheider is hot on his trail, realizing that baseball, and the way the Astros have been playing lately, has something to do with the homicides. It would have been far more interesting for director Peter Masterson to deal with Scheider's romance with Karen Young, his conflict with authorities and his friendship with likable boss Richard Bradford. One limp serial-killer movie. (HBO)

NIGHT GAMES (1980). French director Roger Vadim deals with the phobias and traumas of Cindy Pickett and Joanna Cassidy in this tale of a frightened housewife and a phantom killer on the loose. Barry Primus, Mark Hanks. (Embassy; Sultan)

NIGHT GOD SCREAMED, THE (1971). Priest Alex Nichol and wife Jeanne Crain pick a poor neighborhood to move into: It's frequented by devil worshipers who just drowned a women as a sacrifice to Satan, and now they're being terrorized by the religious fanatics. Low budget job, inadequately directed by Lee Madden and leadenly scripted by Gil Lasky. Daniel Spelling, Michael Sugich, Barbara Hancock. Aka SCREAM. (Trans World)

NIGHT HAIR CHILD. See **WHAT THE PEEPER SAW.**

NIGHT HAS A THOUSAND EYES, THE (1948). Cornell Woolrich was a pulp writer of the '40s, excellent at suspense noir, and this adaptation of his '45 novel is a classic in foreboding gloom and inexorable doom. Edward G. Robinson portrays a haunted man who can predict disasters but only wants the "unseen forces" to leave him alone. Finally he predicts that a matron (Gail Russell) will die one night at 11 p.m. sharp—but before that someone will crush a flower under foot, a vase will break and a wind will blow. Yeah, it all starts to happen. Directed by John Farrow with a stronge sense of film noir. John Lund, William Demarest, Virginia Bruce, Jerome Cowan, Richard Webb, Onslow Stevens.

NIGHT HAS EYES, THE. Video version of **TERROR HOUSE** (Sinister/C; Filmfax; Nostalgia).

NIGHT IN PARADISE (1946). Walter Wanger fantasy depicting the court of King Croesus of Lydia in 560 B.C., to which Aesop the writer comes to pen a new fable. But Aesop pays scant attention to blank paper, ogling the scant costumes and Merle Oberon as a Persian princess. Gale Sondergaard is a Phrygian sorceress who makes herself invisible, plaguing others with her mocking laughter, while Thomas Gomez and Turhan Bey contribute to this fancy-dress fol-de-rol. Escapist hokum directed by Arthur Lubin. Ray Collins, Paul Cavanaugh, Marvin Miller, John Litel, Douglass Dumbrille, Julie London, Barbara Bates.

NIGHT IS THE PHANTOM. See **WHAT!** (Huh?)

NIGHT KEY (1937). Kindly Boris Karloff, inventor of a burglar alarm system, is kidnapped by underworld dastards, and pretends to co-operate until he can juryrig the device to fire death rays at the heavies. The British actor is a gentle puppy in this minor Universal programmer directed by Lloyd Corrigan. Ward Bond, Jean Rogers.

NIGHT LIFE (1989). Mortician Scott Grimes, who delights in dissected bodies, has the tables turned on him by four dead high school pals who are resurrected by lightning bolts and chase after him. Directed by David Acomba. Cheryl Pollak, John Astin, Anthony Geary. (Video/Laser: RCA/Columbia)

NIGHTLIFE (1990). Quirky vampire love tale with satirical overtones: A century-old vampire beauty (Maryam D'Abo) is resurrected and wants nothing to do with former vampire flame Ben Cross, falling instead for a doctor (Keith Szarabajka) willing to treat her disorder as a "disease." Szarabajka and D'Abo making love in a coffin, Camille Saviola as a superstitious Mexican woman who looks after D'Abo and Cross as a star-crossed lover all contribute to the atmosphere of this straight-faced, but funny-underneath TV-movie directed by Daniel Taplitz. Jesse Cori, Oliver Clark, Glenn Shadix. (Video/Laser: MCA)

NIGHT LIFE OF THE GODS (1935). Editions 1-3.

NIGHTMARE (1956). Adaptation of Cornell Woolrich's story about a musician who wakes up after a nightmare to find clues that indicate he carried out a murder. Kevin McCarthy, as the New Orleans jazz player, seeks the help of Edward G. Robinson, his brother-in-law policeman. First made in 1947 as FEAR IN THE NIGHT. Maxwell Shane directed-wrote both versions. Virginia Christine, Connie Russell, Barry Atwater, Rhys Williams.

NIGHTMARE (1961). See editions 1-3.

NIGHTMARE (1964). Teen-ager Jennie Linden has terrifying dreams in which she hears the voice of her crazed mother. Seems the old bat went berserk and stabbed a man to death; and now Jennie fears she has mom's madness. A phantom figure in a nightmare haunts her until her birthday, when Jennie flips out and stabs the woman to death. This Hammer suspense thriller has an intriguing Jimmy Sangster script, but if you're sharp, you'll spot the red herrings and figure out what's happening. Directed by Freddie Francis. David Knight, Moira Richmond, Brenda Bruce.

NIGHTMARE (1973). Video of **VOICES** (Mirisch).

NIGHTMARE (1981). Cinematic sleaze scuzz recommended to splatter fans only. A homicidal maniac keeps reliving an incident from childhood during which he axed to death his mother and father while they were engaging in sadistic sexual pleasure. Despite its morbidity and grisly effects, NIGHTMARE has a fascination that holds and repels you. Written-directed by Romano Scavolini. Sharon Smith, Baird Stafford. (New Star; Planet; from Platinum as **BLOOD SPLASH** and Continental as **NIGHTMARES IN A DAMAGED BRAIN**)

NIGHTMARE ALLEY (1947). William Lindsay Gresham's novel was a shocker in depicting a maladjusted young man who joins a carnival and rises to become a successful night club mind reader and then a bilker of millionairesses via a spiritualism racket. The movie code allowed only portions of the book, but Fox still made an earnest attempt to capture Gresham's psychological portrait. Tyrone Power is powerful as Stan Carlisle, repelled when he first sees the "geek"—half-man, half-beast of the midway who tears off heads of chickens. This deterioration of an ambitious man into a dipsomaniac is more shivery than any alleged "monster" movie. Directed by Edmund Goulding. Coleen Gray, Joan Blondell, Helen Walker, Ian Keith.

NIGHTMARE AT NOON (1988). Outstanding photography of Utah desert locations and well-staged action highlight this adventure. Travelers Wings Hauser, Kimberly Beck and Bo Hopkins stop in Canyon Land only to find that everyone has gone crazy from the water and is on a homicidal rampage, their bodies full of green blood. It seems that APE (the Agency for Protection of the Environment), under the guidance of albino Brion James, is conducting an unauthorized experiment, the details of which are never explained. Director Nico Mastorakis includes a well-staged helicopter chase. George Kennedy is Sheriff Hanks and Kimberley Ross is his sexy daughter. (Republic)

NIGHTMARE AT SHADOW WOODS (1983). This HALLOWEEN imitation has but a single twist: A slasher killer recently escaped from an asylum has a lookalike twin, and no one can tell them apart. So, pals, which one is the real killer? And that's all this independent film (made in Jacksonville, Fla.) has to offer. Ed French's make-up and gore effects are nothing special and the murders are all telegraphed. Directed flatly by John M. Grissmer. Louise Lasser, Mark Soper, Marianne Kanter, Julie Gordon. (From Prism as **BLOOD RAGE**)

NIGHTMARE BEACH. See **WELCOME TO SPRING BREAK.**

NIGHTMARE BEFORE CHRISTMAS (1993). A unique and wonderfully imaginative feature that employs three-dimensional models in telling the story of Halloweentown, a kingdom of freakish characters ruled by Jack Skellington, a lean unmean figure who discovers there's also a Christmastown and decides to bring the macabre spirit of his land to the Real World of children by posing as Santa Claus—with disastrous results. This is the dark side to Disneyesque cartoons and while its frequently grotesque images contradict the usual spirit of cartoons, it still captures a sense of warmth and humanity. The idea was Tim Burton's, the adaptation is by Michael McDowell and Caroline Thompson, and San Francisco-based animator Henry Selick directed with an inspired touch. This is a one-of-a-kind experiment in stop motion, which took three years to produce, and features several songs. Danny Elfman wrote the music. (Video/Laser: Touchstone)

NIGHTMARE CASTLE (1966). Standard Italian Gothic chiller distinguished by Barbara Steele in two roles, as a wife cheating on her scientist husband and as a cousin. You've seen it before: mad doctor utilizes electrical impulses in experiments with human blood; murder victims rise from grave to wreak vengeance. Directed-written by Mario Caiano. Paul Miller, Helga Line, Laurence Clift, Rik Battaglia. Also known as NIGHT OF THE DOOMED, ORGASMO, THE FACELESS MONSTER and LOVERS BEYOND THE TOMB. (Hollywood Home Theater; Sinister/C; Filmfax; S/Weird; Budget)

NIGHTMARE CIRCUS. Video version of **TERROR CIRCUS** (Regal).

NIGHTMARE CITY. See **CITY OF THE WALKING DEAD.**

NIGHTMARE CLASSICS I (1989). Two first-rate episodes of a series produced for Showtime by Shelley Duvall. The first is "Carmilla," a version of the Sheridan Le Fanu tale of lesbian vampires, updated to the antebellum South where land owner Roy Dotrice must protect his daughter Ione Skye from the advances of lovely stranger Meg Tilly. Directed by Gabrielle Beaumont. The second is "Eye of the Panther" starring C. Thomas Howell, Daphne Zuniga and John Stockwell. Linda Hunt opens both shows with narration from Edgar Allan Poe.

NIGHTMARE CLASSICS II (1989). Two episodes from a Showtime series: "The Strange Case of Dr. Jekyll & Mr. Hyde," starring Andrew Stevens and Laura Dern, and "The Turn of the Screw," based on the Henry James classic.

NIGHTMARE FESTIVAL. Cheap compilation tape of previews of coming attractions from assorted horror and sci-fi features. (Discount)

NIGHTMARE HOTEL (1970). Spanish horror flick, written-directed by Eugenio Martin, is set in a hostelry of hostility on the Mediterranean coast, where two batty sisters murder tourists when they fail to live up to moral standards. The bodies, with gaping knive wounds in vital organs, are dumped into wine vats before the wine is served to the guests. Meanwhile, innocent Judy Geeson arrives looking for her missing sister and notices how strange it is guests disappear without checking out. Accommodations must be poor. Don't make a reservation. Also known as CANDLE FOR THE DEVIL.

NIGHTMARE HOUSE. Video version of **SCREAM, BABY, SCREAM** (Camp).

NIGHTMARE IN BLOOD (1976). Low-budget horror film depicts the world of fantasy-comic book fandom. While its humor is hip and droll, it's still a genre suspense shocker featuring macabre murders. Jerry Walter brings new facets to the screen vampire as Malakai, an actor specializing in vampire films, and guest of honor at a San Francisco convention. Elements of fandom (horror writer, Sherlock Holmes fan, comic book store owner) band to track Malakai when he turns out to be a real vampire. Malakai's henchmen are publicity men who turn out to be Burke and Hare, infamous body snatchers. The John Stanley-Kenn Davis screenplay incorporates a censor of comic books named Unworth and an Israeli avenger searching for Malakai since the Nazi atrocities. Stanley, host of TV's CREATURE FEATURES in San Francisco for six years, directed and co-produced with Davis. Kerwin Mathews has a cameo in a swashbuckling sequence. Barrie Youngfellow, Hy Pyke, Ray K. Goman, Drew Eshelman, Morgan Upton, Justin Bishop. (Video City; from Imperial as **HORROR CONVENTION**)

NIGHTMARE IN WAX (1969). Variation on the HOUSE OF WAX theme but as limp as a piece of melting candle. Cameron Mitchell is good as Rinaud, disfigured curator of a wax museum who showcases his victims as exhibits. Rex Carlton's story is so ludicrous and sleazy, it's fascinating to watch. The ending, unfortunately, is a cop-out. Directed by Bud Townsend in the Movieland Wax Museum in Los Angeles. Anne Helm, Berry Kroeger, Scott Brady. (United; VCI)

NIGHTMARE MAKER. See **NIGHT WARNING.**

NIGHTMARE NEVER ENDS, THE (1980). In the vein of THE OMEN, this blends biblical prophecy with horror, and with its sense of hysteria emerges a strange film defying description. The script can be accredited to Philip Yordan, but the production is hampered by uneven cinematography, atrocious sound and unrestrained performances. Jewish avenger Abraham Weiss, in search of the SS officer who murdered his family during Hitler's reign, discovers that musician Robert Bristol is the son of Satan, on Earth to create havoc. Cops Cameron Mitchell and Marc Lawrence, after much soul searching, believe Weiss. Meanwhile, surgeon Faith Clift is married to Nobel prize-winning author Charles Moll, whose book GOD IS DEAD becomes a center for controversy. Whew! This can also be seen in truncated form in NIGHT TRAIN TO TERROR. The erratic nature of THE NIGHTMARE NEVER ENDS might be explained by three directors: Tom McGowan, Greg Tallas and Philip Marsak. Also known as SATAN'S SUPPER. Maurice Grandmaison, Klint Stevenson. T.J. Savage. (Nite Flite; Simitar; Premiere; Video BanCorp; from Genesis under its original title, **CATACLYSM**)

NIGHTMARE OF TERROR. Video version of **DEMONS OF THE MIND** (Odds and Ids?).

NIGHTMARE ON ELM STREET, A (1984). A box-office hit with Robert Englund as maniacal killer Fred Krueger who uses a glove-hand of long knifes in place of fingernails. Krueger is a supernatural entity in a slouch hat who turns up in the dreams of teenagers and proceeds to murder them. Director Wes Craven's script is weak on exposition and logic, but it didn't bother audiences, as he focuses in on suspenseful murders and bloody special effects, with atmosphere and spooky shadows abounding. This led to a series of sequels and a TV series. John Saxon, Heather Langenkamp, Ronee Blakley, Johnny Depp. (Media) (Laser: Image)

NIGHTMARE ON ELM STREET, PART 2: FREDDY'S REVENGE, A (1985). In some ways this is better than the original, being capably directed by Jack Sholder and having more character development. On the other hand, it doesn't have as many scares and it barely walks the twilight nightmare world of dreams as the first film did. Anyway, what we have is the return of Freddy Krueger in the dreams of Mark Patton, who moves into the sinister house on Elm Street. Father Clu Gulager and mother Hope Lange, having not seen the original movie, have no idea their son is being taken over by Freddy. It becomes not a symbolic battle but a literal one as the external Mark Patton cracks open and Robert Englund (as Krueger, wearing the knives-for-fingernails device) pops out. This battle of wills is the film's primary strength, with a climactic confrontation in a boiler factory. However, the film's best sequence comes at the beginning as a runaway bus is perched on a precipice—that is straight out of a terrifying nightmare. (Media) (Laser: Image)

FREDDY

NIGHTMARE ON ELM STREET 3: DREAM WARRIORS, A (1987). Another solid follow-up to the Wes Craven box-office hit, exploring new "nuances" of the Freddy Krueger character for shock exploitation. This time youngsters terrorized by Krueger in their dreams take part in a controlled experiment using a new drug. The last 30 minutes are exciting as they link together in the same dream and fight Krueger with various combative techniques. imaginative surprises and creative effects are in store, though as usual the story remains slender and the characters of minimal interest. Directed by Chuck Russell. Heather Langenkamp, Patricia Arquette, Priscilla Pointer, John Saxon, Craig Wasson, Robert Englund. (Media) (Laser: Image)

NIGHTMARE ON ELM STREET 4: THE DREAM MASTER, A (198). The lousiest entry in the Freddy Krueger series—a hodgepodge of horror effects, Krueger's witty one-liners and teenage tomfoolery never makes any sense, and is lacking in a premise. There is no set of rules as Freddy pops in and out of nightmares and reality, wreaking the same old havoc. by now boring. Director Renny Harlin does a good job of capturing the ambience of the series, and accolades to the set designers for creating the Elm Street house. Robert Englund is wonderful as the character, but he sorely needs new business. Rodney Eastman, Andras Jones, Tuesday Knight, Danny Hassel. (Media) (Laser: Image)

NIGHTMARE ON ELM STREET 5: THE DREAM CHILD, A (1989). Audiences seem to love these disjointed plots with little (if any) logic as child murderer Freddy Krueger invades the dreams of intended victims. Under the direction of Stephen Hopkins, this s-s-s-s-sequel becomes graphic shock heaped on graphic shock when Freddy decides to be reborn through the pregnancy of arch-enemy Alice Johnson (Lisa Wilcox). Robert Englund has his usual throwaway lines, and repeats all the cliches as prescribed by writers Sara Risher and Jon Turtle. It's really time to do something new with Freddy—like have him as the antagonist in NEMO IN SLUMBERLAND. Danny Hassel, Whitby Hertford, Kelly Jo Minter, Erika Anderson, Nick Mele. (Media) (Laser: Image)

NIGHTMARE ON ELM STREET 6, A. See **FREDDY'S DEAD: THE NIGHTMARE ENDS.**

NIGHTMARE ON THE 13TH FLOOR, THE (1990). Below-average TV-movie in which something weird is happening on the 13th floor of the Wessex Hotel, where travel writer Michelle Greene is doing an article about the hotel's history. She's soon the-hapless-girl-in-peril, having witnessed a murder on the supposedly non-existent 13th floor that involves a devil cult, a fire-axe murderer, and staff of conspirators. The teleplay by Dan Distefano and Frank De Felitta is a premise that doesn't stand scrutiny. Greene is merely irritating as the heroine, and James Brolin's role is all too obvious. But there are stand-out performances by John Karlen as an ulcer-suffering cop and by Lucille Fletcher as a sassy hotel employee. Director Walter Grauman does not seem suited to this genre, as all surprises are telegraphed, and the horror images repetitive, not frightening. (Paramount)

NIGHTMARE PARK. See **HOUSE IN NIGHTMARE PARK, THE.**

NIGHTMARES (1983). Anthology of eerie tales, directed by Joseph Sargent, without any bonding theme. "Terror in Topanga" is derivative of the slasher genre with a murderer threatening housewife Cristina Raines, who has to go out for cigarettes one night. This is the weakest of the lot, so the film builds with "The Bishop of Battle," detailing how Emilio Estevez, obsessed with video games, challenges a 13-level, 3-dimensional war game. "The Benediction" is a chilling narrative about a man of the cloth (Lance Henriksen) and his lack of faith prior to his encounter with a sinister truck. "Night of the Rat" is the biggest crowd-pleaser, in which a giant demon rodent from German mythology terrorizes a suburbanite family. Suspense mounts as the unhappily married husband and wife (Richard Masur and Veronica Cartwright) face a horrific onslaught. The first three yarns were written by Christopher Crowe, the fourth by Jeffrey Bloom. (MCA)

NIGHTMARES IN A DAMAGED BRAIN. Video version of **NIGHTMARE (1981)** (Continental).

NIGHTMARE SISTERS (1987). Made under the guise of a sex fantasy-comedy, this sequel to SORORITY BABES IN THE SLIMEBALL BOWL-A-RAMA ranks as one dumb dumb-teenagers-on-the-loose flick. It's the mindless concoction of producer-director Dave DeCoteau and writer Kenneth J. Hall as they retread those nerdy Tri Eta Phi gals from SORORITY BABES who turn into sexually charged sexpots during a seance with a crystal ball in which fortune-teller Omar is trapped. The curvaceous threesome proceeds to turn into vampy vampires while sucking on the bodies of three macho guys from the campus. Much of this is softcore raunch as Linnea Quigly, Brinke Stevens and Michelle McClellan pop in and out of their lingerie. A monster doesn't appear until the non-climax when an exorcist shows up. Hitless and witless. Richard Gabai, Marcus Vaughter, William Dristas. Omar is billed as Dukey Flyswatter. (Trans World)

BRINKE STEVENS

NIGHTMARE VACATION. See **SLEEPAWAY CAMP.**

NIGHTMARE WEEKEND (1986). Evil computer scientist Debbie Laster uses software (and soft wear?) to warp human minds and turn college girls into "mutantoids." How? By firing a silver ball into the brain, which turns its owner into a drooling, slavering walking dead shambling rambling zombie freako monster ghoul killer. Directed by Henry Sala. Dale Midkiff, Debra Hunter, Lori Lewis. (Lightning; Live)

NIGHT MONSTER (1942). Metaphysical theme rescues this Universal potboiler from cinematic mediocrity. Ralph Morgan portrays a legless madman who creates new limbs through sheer will power. He behaves in standard crazy-man style by stalking into the night to murder the doctors responsible for his double amputation. Bela Lugosi and Lionel Atwill are present but contribute little. Ford Beebe directed in the style of an "old, dark house" thriller-comedy. Nils Asther, Irene Harvey.

NIGHT MUST FALL (1937). Frightening psychological study of a madman—based on the famous Emlyn Williams supsense play, but so literate it is not the stuff of visceral viewing. It's about a psychotic axe murderer, a Cockney lad charming . . . and deadly. Robert Montgomery conveys this twisted sickness with such smooth deftness we almost forget his evil as he convinces an old woman in a wheelchair (Dame May Whitty) that he's a good boy. And let's not forget what the hatbox contains . . . Directed by Richard Thorpe. Rosalind Russell, Alan Marshall.

NIGHT MUST FALL (1964). What was underplayed horror in the 1937 MGM version of Emlyn Williams' play is commercialized here for visual horror. Albert Finney is Danny, who is no longer a deceptive genius of evil but a brutal butcher, wallowing in sexual debauchery and ceremonial perversion as he dominates the household of a wheelchair-bound woman. Here we see him chopping off a woman's head and throwing her body into a pond, as well as the sexual games. Put the blame on contemporary graphic cinema, director Karel Reisz and screenwriter Clive Exton. Mona Washbourne is the widow, Susan Hampshire is her daughter.

NIGHT MY NUMBER CAME UP, THE (1955). See editions 1-3.

NIGHT NURSE (1977). Davina Whitehouse answers an ad inquiring for a nurse and is soon taking care of a wheelchair-bound opera singer—and trapped in a haunted house. Directed by Igor Auzins. Kay Taylor, Gary Day, Kate Fitzpatrick. (Paragon)

NIGHT OF ANUBIS. See **NIGHT OF THE LIVING DEAD.**

NIGHT OF A THOUSAND CATS (1974). Meow-ish Spanish exploitationer with comely pussycat Anjanette Comer for catnip, but you won't buy the canned goods director Rene Cardona is selling: A crazed nobleman lives in an old Mexican castle with his Igor-type aide and a kennel of hungry cats, to whom nutty Hugo feeds human flesh. Meanwhile, Hugo flies around in a helicopter looking for women in bikinis and has a trophy room where he keeps the heads of beauties with whom he has had sex. The climax hardly lives up to its title, with only a few dozen tomcats rushing through the castle. The film finally tucks its tail and ducks into an alley. (Paragon; from Academy as **BLOOD FEAST**)

NIGHT OF BLOODY HORROR (1969). Terrible title matches bad lighting, lousy acting and sleazy set design in this low-budget incompetence made in New Orleans by writer-producer-director Joy N. Houck Jr. Same old descending meat cleaver and running blood. Night of the Cinematic Bungle. Gerald McRaney, Gaye Yellen, Evelyn Hendricks. (Paragon; King of Video)

NIGHT OF DARK SHADOWS (1971). DARK SHADOWS, TV's daytime serial with supernatural creatures, led to HOUSE OF DARK SHADOWS which in turn led to this sequel which doesn't have Jonathan Frid as Barnabas the Vampire, even though it still deals with the infamous Collins family. David Selby plays Quentin Collins, a painter haunted by the spirit of an ancestor once involved with witches. Evil spirits pop up in his studio in the Collinwood mansion, making wife Kate Jackson think he's cheating. The setting—the Jay Gould estate in Tarrytown, New York—should have been an imposingly menacing location but it isn't, the humor is unintentional and the plot unfolds in haphazard fashion, as though producer-director Dan Curtis was still grinding out mindless TV fodder. Lara Parker, Nancy Barrett, Grayson Hall, John Karlen. (Video/Laser: MGM/UA)

NIGHT OF HORROR (1980). Visitors to an old battlefield are haunted by voices and spirit images of the dead. Produced-directed in Baltimore by Tony Malanowski. Steve Sandkuhler, Gae Schmitt. (Genesis)

NIGHT OF TERROR (1933). See editions 1-3.

NIGHT OF TERROR (1987). Renee Harmon and Henry Lewis co-star in this gore-flow in which a family of psychos conducts brain operations. (Image)

NIGHT OF TERRORS. See **MURDER CLINIC, THE.**

NIGHT OF THE BEAST. See **HOUSE OF THE BLACK DEATH.**

NIGHT OF THE BIG HEAT. See **ISLAND OF THE BURNING DOOMED.**

NIGHT OF THE BLIND DEAD. See **BLIND DEAD.**

NIGHT OF THE BLOOD BEAST (1958). Astronaut passing through Earth's radiation belt is infected by an alien spore and returns a "blood beast." Scientists are trapped in a space center with the creature, allowing director Bernard Kowalski (working for producers Gene and Roger Corman) to imitate scenes from THE THING. Ed Nelson, Jean Hagen, Angela Greene, Michael Emmet. (Sinister/C; S/Weird; Filmfax)

NIGHT OF THE BLOOD MONSTER (1972). Spanish-German-Italian effort in the degenerate tradition of MARK OF THE DEVIL . . . a sickening exercise in sadism and brutality, even after being edited for the U.S. Witchhunter Christopher Lee (patterned after a real personage) scours the England of King Henry V for assorted heretics. More subtly known in Britain as THE BLOODY JUDGE. Directed by Jesus Franco. Maria Schell, Leo Genn, Maria Rohm, Margaret Lee. (GEE)

NIGHT OF THE BLOODY APES (1971). Brunette in shocking red tights and a cat-like face mask wrestles other women while her boyfriend, a police inspector, watches. Meanwhile, a goofy scientist transfers a gorilla's heart into his dying son but the young man turns into an apeman who crashes through Mexican streets on a rampage. Mostly, the simian-man tears clothing off women and mauls them, revealing large bare breasts and creamy thighs. The gore effects are crude and sickening, the wrestling scenes dull and the acting and dubbing pathetically bad. And the title is wrong—there's only one ape. Directed by Rene Cardona, who co-wrote with son Rene Cardona Jr. Armand Silvestre, Norma Lazareno, Jose Elias Moreno. (MPI; Gorgon)

NIGHT OF THE CLAW. See **ISLAND CLAWS.**

NIGHT OF THE CLONES/ESCORT TO DANGER (1978). Two episodes of the SPIDERMAN TV series.

NIGHT OF THE COBRA WOMAN (1972). In a Filipino setting, beautiful Marlene Clark transmutes into a deadly snake whenever she doesn't get her formula—a mixture of sex and serum. Some fix. This U.S.-Philippines venture, written-directed by Andrew Meyer, was defanged for U.S. consumption and is less "striking." Features the subtle acting of Joy Bang and Slash Marks. Audiences hissed back. The pits. (Embassy)

NIGHT OF THE COMET (1984). A juvenile mentality permeates this low-budget horror/fantasy, written-directed by Thom Eberhart, in which the end of the world is trivialized as a visit by teenager survivors to a clothing store, where they run wild. It begins when a passing comet sends out deadly rays that either kill people or turn them into zombies. There are bits and pieces from so many other movies, it's impossible to keep tabs on the pasted-together plot. There's also some indecipherable business with scientists in an underground lab who hope to find a serum to combat lethal cosmic rays. Geoffrey Lewis, Mary Woronov, Sharon Farrell Catherine Mary Stewart, Kelli Maroney. (CBS/Fox)

NIGHT OF THE CREEPS (1986). Low-budget sci-fi/horror thriller derivative of everything: THE THING, NIGHT OF THE LIVING DEAD, FRIDAY THE 13TH, ALIEN and any other innovative special effects movie. It was a promising debut for director-writer Fred Dekker. Made as HOMECOMING NIGHT, it begins in 1959 when an alien probe is launched to Earth, just when an axe maniac is about to murder a couple of college students. Cut to 1986 as Tom Atkins (detective Cameron) tries to solve a series of murders involving walking corpses, worm-like creatures that leap into your mouth and take over your body, and that old axe killer. Atkins is very good as the unorthodox cop. Jason Lively, Lene Starger, Steve Marshall, Jill Whitlow. Above average for its type. (HBO) (Laser: Image)

NIGHT OF THE DAMNED (1971). Italian supernatural thriller in which a Sherlock Holmes-like detective is hired to help destroy a resurrected witch. Directed by Peter Rush. Pierre Brice, Patrizia Viotti, Angelo de Leo.

NIGHT OF THE DARK FULL MOON. See **SILENT NIGHT, BLOODY NIGHT.**

NIGHT OF THE DEATH CULT (1975). Video version of **NIGHT OF THE SEAGULLS** (Sony).

NIGHT OF THE DEMON. Video title of **CURSE OF THE DEMON.**

NIGHT OF THE DEMON (1979). Cheesy "Bigfoot" gore flick, overloaded with bloody, violent deaths, amateurish under Jim Wasson's direction. Five colorless explorers go in search of "Crazy Wanda," a legendary woman of the backwoods who was raped by a beast and gave birth to a malformed hairy infant. When they dig up the baby's grave to prove the story, the hirsute one with bad body odor goes on a rampage. Climactic siege features death by routine saw cut, ordinary broken glass, standard strangulation, typical throttling, mundane disembowelment, and predictable pitchfork. And that doesn't include other deaths revealed in flashbacks-within-the flashback. For blood-and-guts fans only. Mike Cutt, Joy Allen. (VCII; Gemstone)

NIGHT OF THE DEMON. See **TOUCH OF SATAN.**

NIGHT OF THE DEMONS (1988). On Halloween night, insufferable teenagers party in an abandoned mortuary. Sexy chicks Linnea Quigley and Mimi Kinkade unleash demons from Hell and, before you can pull the arms and legs off a human torso, are turned into monsters. The teeners are knocked off in hideous ways, until a miniarmy of zombies hulks around the digs. Director

Kevn S. Tenney (WITCHBOARD) creates a spirit of fun in a carnival house of horror, but never is any of this juvenilia designed seriously. Alvin Alexis, Allison Barron, Lance Fenton. (Video/Laser: Republic)

NIGHT OF THE DEVILS (1971). Italian-Spanish quickie in which a young man fears his girl is part of a witch cult. Loaded with corpses and gore. Directed by Giorgio Ferroni. Based on a short story by Tolstoy. Gianni Garko, Agostina Belli, Maria Monti.

NIGHT OF THE DOOMED. See **NIGHTMARE CASTLE.**

NIGHT OF THE EAGLE. See **BURN, WITCH, BURN.**

NIGHT OF THE FLESH EATERS. See **NIGHT OF THE LIVING DEAD.**

NIGHT OF THE GHOULS (1958). While PLAN 9 FROM OUTER SPACE and other Edward D. Wood Jr. films have a warped perspective and garishness that make them high camp, this supernatural horror tale has only brief flashes of Woodmania, and is mainly dreary. Criswell's narration helps, but Wood's story plods. Undercover cop Duke Moore (described as a "ghostchaser") enters the house on Willows Lake to find old cowboy actor Kenne Duncan (as Dr. Acula) holding phony seances. Nothing quite makes sense as Duke wanders the house, a comic-relief cop does a Stepin Fetchit parody and a couple of women shamble like Vampira. Tor Johnson stomps around as Lobo, and there are suggestions this could be a sequel to BRIDE OF THE ATOM. Maybe. John Carpenter, Paul Marco, Valda Hansen, Bud Osborne. Also known as REVENGE OF THE DEAD. (Rhino; Nostalgia Merchant; Sinister/C; S/Weird; Filmfax)

NIGHT OF THE HOWLING BEAST (1975). Spanish sequel to FRANKENSTEIN'S BLOODY TERROR (aka THE WEREWOLF AND THE YETI), with Paul Naschy as a member of a Tibetan expedition who is attacked by a werewolf and changed into a creature. Then it becomes a battle between the wolfman and a yeti. Miguel Iglesias Bonns directed Jacinto Molina's script. The visuals surpass the weak acting by Gil Vidal, Grave Mills and Silvia Solar. (Republic; Super; from Majestic as **HALL OF THE MOUNTAIN KING**)

NIGHT OF THE HUNTER (1955). Visually artistic film directed by Charles Laughton, surrealistic and macabre in recounting Davis Grubb's hair-raiser about a psychotic, Scriptures-quoting preacher (Robert Mitchum) who has "love" tattooed on one hand, "hate" on the other. He's in pursuit of two children who know where a stash of stolen money is kept, and there's no doubt of his homicidal intentions. Literate screenplay by James Agee; Stanley Cortez's cinematography is outstanding. Shelley Winters, Peter Graves, James Gleason, Lillian Gish, Don Beddoe. (MGM/UA) (Laser: Voyager; Criterion)

MITCHUM

NIGHT OF THE HUNTER (1991). The 1955 version was a masterpiece of cinematic technique, cinematography and acting. In this remake, scripted by Edmond Stevens in a terser storyline that misses many of the gems in Davis Grubb's novel, the only thing commendable is Richard Chamberlain's performance as Preacher Powell —he looks downright evil at times. But the rest of the cast is ordinary and David Greene's direction is unexceptional, given the tough act of having to follow Charles Laughton's inspired vision.

CHAMBERLAIN

Diana Scarwid, Amy Bebout, Reid Binion, Ray McKinnon, Burgess Meredith.

NIGHT OF THE LAUGHING DEAD. See **HOUSE IN NIGHTMARE PARK, THE.**

NIGHT OF THE LEPUS (1972). Jumpin' jackrabbits! The Southwest desert is littered with critters—only they're not so little after being injected with a hormone (designed to decrease breeding habits) which increases growth genes. In short, thousands of rabbits have been photographed in macro close-up by director William Claxton and matted with Rory Calhoun and Janet Leigh looking scared to death. Not as hare-y as you think, it just breeds contempt. This hasenpfeffer speciality costars Stuart Whitman, DeForest Kelley and Paul Fix.

NIGHT OF THE LIVING BABES (1987). Jon Valentine directed this sex-horror comedy in which two guys looking for a brothel find more than they bagained for in the form of female zombies. Michelle McClellan, Connie Woods, Andrew Nichols, Louie Bonanno. (Magnum)

NIGHT OF THE LIVING DEAD (1968). Pittsburgh's George Romero shot this low-budget horror film on weekends, with a cast of unknowns, for $150,000. The result was a classic that built one of the strongest reputations in the horror genre, and it set a trend. It's a miniclassic of eerie proportions due to its black-and-white photography, its clever use of documentary techniques to lend versimilitude, its imaginative editing and its horribly ironic ending. A space probe returning to Earth introduces into our atmosphere a form of radiation which affects dead bodies, bringing them to life. Soon the countryside is crowded with armies of walking dead. Untainted humans seek refuge in a farmhouse—and the horror is unrelenting as the zombies attack, often munching on human flesh. John A. Russo wrote the script for Romero, who got great mileage out of Duane Jones, Judith O'Dea, Karl Hardman, Marilyn Eastman. Re-released to TV in 1986 in a colorized form. There were two sequels: DAWN OF THE DEAD and DAY OF THE DEAD. (Republic; Media; United; Nostalgia Merchant; S/Weird; Filmfax; Vestron; Spotlite) (Laser: Republic; 3M; Collectible Classics; Image; Landmark)

NIGHT OF THE LIVING DEAD—THE REMAKE (1990). Yes, this is a remake of George Romero's 1968 classic, but there are new elements, as if Romero decided that since you already know how the old movie came out, you should be thrown a few surprises. The first half-hour is identical to the original, with Barbara (Patricia Tallman) taking refuge in a deserted farmhouse after she's been attacked by the living dead. The same band of characters are introduced . . . then scripter Romero plays revisionist, changing Barbara from a comatose broad into a female Rambo, tampering with how characters are killed off, and eliminating exposition about why the dead are back to life (elements that made the original work so well). This isn't as effective as the original (the gore effects, for one, don't have the impact after years of imitative exploitation) but it does stand on its own merits, thanks in part to Tom Savini's direction. It just ain't the classic you made the first time, George. John Russo, who wrote the original 1968 script with Romero, co-produced with Russ Streiner. (Video/Laser: RCA/Columbia)

NIGHT OF THE SEAGULLS (1975). Dead knights thirsting for virgins' blood ride through a small village, terrorizing superstitious folks. It takes a doctor and his wife to find a way to stop them in this sequel to THE BLIND DEAD from writer-director Amando De Ossorio. Victor Petit, Maria Kosti, Sandra Mozarosky. (From Sony as **NIGHT OF THE DEATH CULT**)

NIGHT OF THE SILICATES. See **ISLAND OF TERROR.**

NIGHT OF THE SORCERERS (1970). Great Leopard Devil claim sacrifice of blonde white girl. Soldiers come, kill plenty bad natives. Many moons later, expedition comes from sky in great silver bird. God men go to taboo burial grounds. Take long time die, one by one. Leopard

Devil take lives. Angry. Plenty mad. Turn man into creature who belong in black lagoon. Powerful witch doctor say: "My mother the sorceress told me there'd be nights like this." Directed by Amando De Ossorio. Jack Taylor, Simon Andreu, Kali Hansa. (Unicorn; Viva)

NIGHT OF THE STRANGLER (1973). Director Joy N. Houck Jr. (the intellectual who made NIGHT OF BLOODY HORROR) is back with gore-erotica in New Orleans. Beautiful women have dreams they are being strangled—and awaken to find they are being choked to death. Mickey Dolenz, James Ralston. (Paragon)

NIGHT OF THE VAMPIRES. See **CAVE OF THE LIVING DEAD.**

NIGHT OF THE WEREWOLF. See **CRAVING, THE.**

NIGHT OF THE WITCHES (1970). Rapist disguised as a preacher Keith Erik Burt) gets his comeuppance when he falls in with a witch cult, unaware of the satanic rape they have planned. This Canadian production has moments of light-heartedness, but tedium finally prevails. Burt (who wrote and directed) is Keith Larsen.

NIGHT OF THE ZOMBIES (1983). Wretched Italian steal of DAWN OF THE DEAD: New Guinea is exposed to a gas (unleashed during secret experiments) and turned into a landscape of Walking Dead. The whole thing is ludicrous as SWAT-team types set out on a mission (the purpose is never clear) by blasting through the undead. Even though the yokels know to shoot the creatures in the head, they repeatedly waste ammo by firing into bodies, and behave like the Three Stooges. Director Vincent Dawn goes to extremes to make this bloody with exploding heads, maggot-infested bodies, ghouls munching on human organs and intestines. Not a single frightening moment, it's simply repulsive and unwatchable. Also known as ZOMBIE CREEPING FLESH, ZOMBIE INFERNO, CANNIBAL VIRUS and HELL OF THE LIVING DEATH. Frank Garfield, Margit Evelyn Newton, Selan Karay. (Vestron)

NIGHT OF THE ZOMBIES II (1983). This is not a sequel to NIGHT OF THE ZOMBIES (above). Writer-director Joel M. Reed, the intellectualizing sentimentalist of BLOODTHIRSTY FREAKS, is up to his blood-gushing tricks in this walking-dead tale of World War II soldiers who have been kept in suspended animation with nerve gas Gamma 693 and are now terrorizing civilians on a former battlefield in Germany. Sleazy stuff with cheap makeup and effects. Jamie Gillis is an investigating CIA agent, Ryan Hilliard is the doctor and Samantha Grey is the obligatory love interest. And Reed, ever so shy, turns up as a modern-day Nazi. (Prism)

NIGHT OF VENGEANCE. See **LAST HOUSE ON THE LEFT, THE.**

NIGHT OWL (1993). A literate quality hangs over this TV-movie about an evil "feminine power of the universe"—a siren-like "witch voice" that arrives with the full moon of the autumn equinox and lures lonely, unhappy men to their doom. This "collective rage of all women who have been ridiculed by men" picks on jazz musician James Wilder, whose wife Jennifer Beals ends up trying to solve the mystery with the help of Dr. Matthews (Jackie Burroughs), an expert in understanding "female vengeance" and the invisible seductress entity. The fine writing by producers Rose Schacht and Ann Powell, and the atmospheric direction of Matthew Patrick, shape this into something different. Allis Hossack, Justin Louis.

NIGHT RIPPER (1986). Fiendish killer stalks and slashes fashion models. Directed by Jeff Hatchcock. James Hansen, April Anne. (Magnum; International)

NIGHT SCHOOL (1980). Although atmospherically directed by Kenneth Hughes, this slasher-gasher has a silly premise: the headhunter rituals of New Guinea and how they're applied to ghastly killings at a Boston college. After each beheading, the motorcyclist-murderer throws the head into liquid. The killings are repetitive (woman victim screams, slasher closes fast with a knife) and moments of depraved sexuality are gratuitously thrown in. Rachel Ward looks great in a shower strip scene, but is hopelessly lost with her dialogue. You'll spot the killer's identity early on. (Key)

NIGHT SCREAMS (1987). Football hero holds a party for friends just when two psychokillers escape from an asylum. Guess who comes to the party uninvited. Joe Manno, Ron Thomas, Randy Lundsford. Directed by Allen Plone. (Prism)

NIGHT SHADOWS. See **MUTANT (1983).**

NIGHT SLASHER. Video version of **NIGHT AFTER NIGHT (HE KILLS)** (Unicorn).

NIGHT SLAVES (1970). Director Ted Post is to be congratulated for an effective TV-movie, based on a Jerry Sohl novel. The setting is a small town under the hypnotic spell of aliens repairing their rocketship—only James Franciscus is immune because of a metal plate in his skull, and he falls for one of the lovely E.T.s (Tisha Sterling). Lee Grant, Andrew Prine, Scott Marlowe, Leslie Nielsen, John Kellogg, Victor Izay.

NIGHT STALKER, THE (1972). Dan Curtis' production made history as the highest-rated TV-movie of its day as it took a fresh, novel approach to the vampire theme. Kolchak, an impetuous, fast-talking newspaperman (Darren McGavin), believes Las Vegas murders are being committed by an ageless bloodsucker (no, not a slot machine). After frustrating politics with police and city officials, Kolchak faces the creature (Barry Atwater) in a hair-raising showdown. Superbly directed by John L. Moxey and wonderfully scripted by Richard Matheson, from Jeff Rice's story. Carol Lynley, Ralph Meeker, Kent Smith, Claude Akins, Simon Oakland (as Kolchak's city editor). The concept resulted in a sequel, THE NIGHT STRANGLER, and a short-lived series. The series ran down, but not Kolchak. He's forever incorrigible. (Magnetic; CBS/Fox)

NIGHT STALKER: TWO TALES OF TERROR, THE (1974-75). Two episodes of the series based on Dan Curtis' TV pilot. The titles are "The Ripper" and "The Vampire." (MGM/UA)

NIGHT STALKER, THE (1986). The only outstanding aspect of this "killer-on-a-spree" shootemup is Charles Napier as unsympathetic alcoholic cop J. J. Stryker. That aside, this movie defies credulity as a Vietnam vet, believing in Eastern philosphies that involve worshipping of cattle, makes himself impervious to police bullets. The "boogeyman"-style killer is murdering prostitutes in L.A. and painting gibberish on their foreheads. How the criminal is tracked is without imagination and the climactic shoot-out is unnecessarily bloody, with scores of good guys getting slaughtered. Director Max Kleven gives the film a tough, gritty feel by shooting in city slums. Michelle Reese, Katherine Kelly Lang, Robert Zdar, Gary Crosby. (Lightning; Vestron)

NIGHTSTALKER (1979). Two 20,000-year-old flesh eaters (i.e. cannibals) move to L.A., hearing that the meat there is fresh daily. Molar-moving melodrama. Directed by Lawrence D. Foldes. And what the hell is Aldo Ray doing in this mess? (Live)

NIGHT STAR—GODDESS OF ELECTRA (1963). See editions 1-3.

NIGHT STRANGLER, THE (1973). Fascinating sequel to THE NIGHT STALKER stars Darren McGavin as aggressive newsman Kolchak, stalking mysteries that lead him into the supernatural. Richard Matheson's teleplay has Kolchak in Seattle, trailing a "walking corpse" killer who slaughters women. With research help from librarian Wally Cox, Kolchak realizes he is dealing with a 100-year-old madman who needs a serum to stay alive. Jo Ann Pflug is the heroine and Simon Oakland re-creates the harassed assignment editor. Directed by Dan Curtis. Richard Anderson, Scott Brady, Margaret Hamilton, John Carradine.

NIGHT TERROR (1977). Fast-moving suspense tale relying on visual impact. Valerie Harper witnesses the slaying of a patrolman and flees in her car for her life, the killer in hot pursuit. Edge-of-chair material never lets go in this taut TV-movie directed by E. W. Swackhamer. Richard Romanus, Nicholas Pryor, John Quade.

NIGHT TERROR (1989). Dreams plague a man who keeps waking up to discover his worst nightmares are real. Directed by Michael Weaver. Jeff Keel, Guy Ecker, Jon Hoffman. (Magnum)

NIGHT THAT PANICKED AMERICA, THE (1975). Behind-the-scenes dramatization of how Orson Welles' Mercury Theater dramatized H. G. Wells' WAR OF THE WORLDS on radio on Oct. 30, 1938. What was intended to be a Halloween prank was taken to be a real event by the U.S. public, which fled the "invaders from Mars." This documents the production, the real-life cast and crew and the listeners who overreacted. Joseph Sargent directed Nicholas Meyers' script. Vic Morrow, Cliff De Young, Wallace McGinn, Meredith Baxter.

NIGHT THE WORLD EXPLODED, THE (1957). A mineral deep in the Earth is threatening to explode and destroy our world, and only scientists William Leslie and Kathyrn Crosby can prevent it. Give producer Sam Katzman and director Fred F. Sears credit for bringing in another Columbia quickie on schedule with little regard for cinematic values. Tris Coffin, Terry Frost.

NIGHT THEY KILLED RASPUTIN, THE (1962). See third edition.

NIGHT THEY SAVED CHRISTMAS, THE (1984). Light-hearted, entertaining TV-movie highlighted by Art Carney's warm performance as St. Nick and Paul Williams' as an elf. The setting is a storybook North Pole, where an oil drilling company threatens the toy factory with dynamiting. How St. Nick and wife June Lockhart avert tragedy for the children of the world makes for a pleasant yuletide parable, built around Paul LeMat as an engineer whose wife (Jaclyn Smith) and children are on hand to help. Directed by Jackie Cooper. (Prism; Cabin Fever; Starmaker)

NIGHT TIDE (1963). Writer-director Curtis Harrington's first film is set at a seaside carnival where sailor Dennis Hopper is mesmerized by Mora the Mermaid (Linda Lawson), who believes she is part of a race of sea creatures. A fortune teller warns him to stay away, but Hopper is inexorably drawn to this strange woman. A persuasive film. Luana Anders, Gavin Muir. (Film Forum; Sinister/C; S/Weird; Filmfax)

NIGHT TRAIN TO KATHMANDU (1988). Cable TV-movie slanted for family viewing but lacking drama and devoid of special effects, even though it deals with an "invisible city" in the Himalayas which appears twice every royal generation, allowing a young prince to mingle with modern man in an attempt to test his strength against temptations. A magical jade medallion holds the key to the mystery as archeologist teacher Pernell Roberts matches wits with a Nepalese historian and two children who are in Nepal with their parents on an exchange program. Very bland. Eddie Castrodad, Milla Jovovitch. Robert Stoeckle. Written by director Robert Wiemer and Ian Robert. (Video/Laser: Paramount)

NIGHT TRAIN TO TERROR (1985). White-haired God (billed as Himself) and Satan (billed as Lu Sifer) are on a celestial/hellbound train debating good vs. evil and ownership of three souls: hence, three stories made up of parts of unreleased features. "The Case of Harry Billings" is a surreal nightmare in a hospital where the bodies of patients are cut up and sold. John Philip Law wanders through this dream-of-horrors, surrounded by crazy doctors and naked, sexy women. "The Case of Gretta Connors" is about a Death Club, where members subject themselves to dangers for thrills—there's an electrocution sequence, a winged beetle of death (stop motion) and a wrecking-ball torture device. "The Case of Claire Hanson" is footage from CATACALYSM, with Cameron Mitchell and Marc Lawrence as cops in pursuit of the Son of Satan. This features amateurish stop-motion monsters. Several directors are credited: John Carr, producer Jay Schlossberg-Cohen, Philip Marshak, Tom McGowan, Gregg Tallas. (Prism)

NIGHT TRAP. See **MARDIS GRAS FOR THE DEVIL.**

NIGHT UNTO NIGHT (1947). See third edition.

NIGHT VISION (1987). Stolen VCR machine provides visions of demon worship and allows watchers to predict the future. Stacy Carson, Shirley Ross, Tony Carpenter. Directed by Michael Krueger. (Prism)

NIGHT VISION (1990). Maniacally paced TV-movie directed and co-written (with Thomas Baum) by Wes Craven. A burned-out, vicious cop (James Remar in a high energy role) and a sweet psychologist (Loryn Locklin) join forces to find "The Spread-Eagle Killer." Despite the cliches, Remar and Locklin bring so much energy to this oddball serial-killer-vs-cops yarn that the film rushes like a firetruck to the scene of the arson. Dr. Sally Powers (Locklin) is capable of absorbing psychic impressions and thoughts, turning into a dual personality: half normal cop, half innocent-woman-about-to-be-vicitmized-and-enjoying-it. It's weird. Remar grows to like her so much he destroys half of L.A. to save her. Penny Johnson, Bruce MacVittie, Francis X. McCarthy.

NIGHT VISITOR, THE (1971). Many Ingmar Bergman regulars star in this Mel Ferrer production—a horror thriller set in an insane asylum from which Max von Sydow escapes each night to carry out a gruesome murder, returning before morning. Directed by Laslo Benedek in Sweden. Trevor Howard, Liv Ullmann, Per Oscarsson, Andrew Keir, Rupert Davies. (United; VCI)

NIGHT VISITOR (1989). Below (wayyyyyy belowwwwww) average urban horror thriller too technically inferior to be taken seriously by today's demanding audiences. An attempt by director Rupert Hitzig to turn elements of the weak plot into sardonic comedy doesn't work either. Derek Rydall portrays a failing student who becomes infatuated with a sexy neighbor (Shannon Tweed as a sexpot/whore/tease). One night he sees his teacher killing her in a devil-cult ritual, but then nobody believes him because he's always crying wolf. Allen Garfield and Michael J. Pollard as a pair of demented brothers are never convincing, even as campy cut-ups, and Elliott Gould is wasted as a former cop who comes out of retirement to help track the killers. Just as wasted is Richard Roundtree as a plaincloths cop who just stands around. Not even garbled portions of the soundtrack were redubbed. An absolute loser. (MGM/UA)

NIGHT WALK. See **DEAD OF NIGHT (1972).**

NIGHT WALKER, THE (1965). William Castle "gimmick" horror film, written by Robert Bloch and prefaced with gobblydegook about dreams, making producer-director Castle seem as though he is seriously dealing with the subconscious. Of course, Castle was a master showman and movie-world huckster just making another buck. After her husband dies in a mysterious explosion, Barbara Stanwyck has bizarre dreams about a walking man (Lloyd Bochner). Numerous thrills follow, with at least a dozen red herrings and a climax in a room of death more hilarious than frightening. Robert Taylor, Judith Meredith, Rochelle Hudson, Hayden Rourke. (MCA)

BARBARA STANWYCK

NIGHT WARNING (1981). Susan Tyrrell's performance as a demented, getting-battier-by-the-minute broad is the saving grace of this exploitation shocker—and we mean exploitation. This low-budget film (also known as BUTCHER, BAKER, NIGHTMARE MAKER and THRILLED TO KILL and MOMMA'S BOY) rakes homosexual haters over the coals in the form of prejudiced cop Bo Svenson, who wants to nail Susan's nephew (Jimmy McNichol) for murder and for hanging around a "faggot" basketball coach. The situation is contrived and denigrates the film's more honorable intentions, leaving only Ms Tyrrell to go bonkers in her wonderfully unsubtle way. She knives nearly all the cast to death with unrestrained glee. Directed by William Asher. Marcia Lewis, William Paxton. (HBO)

NIGHT WARS (1988). Vietnam War memories plague the dreams of buddies Brian O'Connor and Cameron Smith. Dan Haggerty is a headshrinker who tries to figure it all out. Written-directed by David A. Prior. Steve Horton, Chet Hood, Jill Foor. (Sony)

NIGHT WATCH (1973). Cat-and-mouse suspense thriller based on a play by Lucille Fletcher. Elizabeth Taylor thinks she sees seen the moving figure of a dead man in the house next door. Did she? Or is she crazy? Or is some diabolical plot afoot? Husband Laurence Harvey isn't telling. Brian G. Hutton's direction keeps you guessing. Billie Whitelaw. (Fox Hills; Media)

NIGHTWING (1979). Columbia adaptation of Martin Cruz Smith's novel starts as a study of the plight of American Indians—then shifts to bat exterminator David Warner showing up with a "bat mobile" loaded with scientific tracking equipment. Next, bats attack out of the night, claiming victims. Then the search for the bat cave. A muddled mess because of the meandering screenplay by Steve Shagan, the uninspired direction of Arthur Hiller, and the mediocre bat effects. Nick Mancuso, Strother Martin, George Clutesi, Steven Macht, Kathryn Harrold. (RCA/Columbia) (Laser: Image)

NIGHTWISH (1989). Director-cum-actor Jack Starrett is a doctor conducting experiments in deep-sleep nightmares with four sexy gals who include Elizabeth Kaitan and Alisha Das. His Igor-type assistant is Robert Tessier. Written-directed by Bruce R. Cook. Artur Cybulski, Tom Dugan, Brian Thompson. (Vidmark; Vestron)

NINE EIGHT FOUR—PRISONER OF THE FUTURE (1979). Inspired by THE PRISONER and THX 1138, this never finds its own voice or spirit, and wallows in a netherland of imitation. Did we mention it's also Kafkaesque? Stephen Markle is a corporate executive who finds himself a prisoner when The Movement takes over, and undergoes interrogation at the hands of a ruthless overseer. The characters are thoroughly uninteresting, and the writing and direction so cold and impersonal, the viewer never has a chance to sympathize with Markle. Directed in Toronto by Tibor (THE GATE) Takacs as THE TOMORROW MAN. (VCL)

976-EVIL (1989). Robert Englund, who portrays Freddy Krueger in the NIGHTMARE ON ELM STREET films, made his directorial debut with this slow-moving supernatural tale. A high school tough (Patrick O'Bryan) lives with his nerdy cousin (Stephen Geoffreys) and religious, kooky aunt (Sandy Dennis, who turns out to be the best thing in the picture). But all too soon the story deteriorates into a standard "the-worm-turns" plot in which Geoffreys, in calling a "horrorscope" hot line, meets a hell-ish guy named Mark Dark (Robert Picardo) who gives the nerd the powers of evil to destroy his tormentors. The ending is a steal from the POLTERGEIST movies, and the make-up effects by Kevin Yagher and the supernormal action are never overwhelmingly exciting—just routine. The video contains footage cut from the theatrical release. Jim Metzler, Maria Rubell. (Video/Laser: RCA/Columbia)

976 EVIL II: THE ASTRAL FACTOR (1992). It's the usual Kitchen-Sink blend of horror and comedy from director Jim Wynorski as he spins this sequel in which "The Slate River Serial Killer" (Rene Assa, playing a high school principal) terrorizes citizens, with help from Satan, by turning up as an astral projection of himself. The effects are pretty good (body splattered by truck, a talking mouse's head, an icicle through the chest, fiery crashes, etc.) and there's a bizarre sequence in which a victim is trapped inside a black-and-white movie combining elements of NIGHT OF THE LIVING DEAD and IT'S A WONDERFUL LIFE. It's pure Wynorski although the script was written by one Eric Anjou. Debbie James makes for an attractive heroine and Patrick O'Bryan (from the original) serves as a kind of anti-hero. Brigitte Nielsen guest stars as a sexy occult-shop owner. Paul Coufos, Leslie Ryan, Karen Mayo Chandler, Buck Flower, Phil McKeon. (Vestron)

1984 (1956). If George Orwell intended his novel to be a frightful warning, this British film version isn't even an old- fashioned "boo." The main fault lies in its limited budget: It is imperative the atmosphere of the future totalitarian state of "Big Brother" be realistically conveyed, that there be the paranoia of everybody under surveillance in a grim world. That grimness is lost here. The workload falls on Edmond O'Brien and Jan Sterling as the defiant lovers and on Michael Redgrave as the ruthless leader who subjects Winston Smith (O'Brien) to the ultimate terrors in physical and psychological torture. A well- intended film that just didn't come off. Directed by Michael Anderson. Donald Pleasence, Michael Ripper.

1984 (1983). George Orwell's world of Big Brother—a dictatorship in which men are enslaved by tricks of government—today seems more a parable than a possible future. If ever a movie grimly portrayed an unbearable society, this is it in all its depression. The cast resembles concentration camp victims—gaunt, closely shaven, empty-eyed, traumatized—and there isn't a single humorous moment. The superb acting plays second to the blemishes, bleak settings and somber tone of director Michael Radford. Hence, John Hurt as the trammeled Winston Smith (who has love for his fellow man despite dehumanization) and Richard Burton (as the Interrogator who has neither love nor hate, just obedience) are not pleasant to watch. Orwell's message comes through strong: that once man has lost his freedom, he is totally subservient to propaganda, and will believe what isn't true, and disbelieve what is. In conveying a frightening image, this British film succeeds, but in terms of entertainment, it is depressing. (IVE) (Laser: Image)

1990: THE BRONX WARRIORS (1983). Vic Morrow, in one of his last roles, portrays Hammer the Exterminator, a policeman of the future who infiltrates the Bronx, a battleground for gang wars between Trash (caucasian) and Ogre (black). Inspired by THE ROAD WARRIOR, this Italian production will be of interest to archeologists, for it was filmed in the ruins of the Bronx and affords a depressing look at a major U.S. city. Directed by Enzo G. Castellari. Christopher Connelly, Fred Williamson, Mark Gregory. (Media)

1994 BAKER STREET: SHERLOCK HOLMES RETURNS (1993). Extraordinarily entertaining TV-movie that recycles old Holmesian material in a satirical albeit nonbelittling fashion. The success of this exercise in deduction and old-fashioned sleuthing is due to a bravua performance by Anthony Higgins as the London detective in deerstalker's cap, and to a breathless pace established by writer-director Kenneth Johnson. Holmes, the London cop of the 1880s, awakens in 1993 in a suspended animation machine and sets out with doctor Debrah Farentino through San Francisco to solve a trilogy of murders, all of them involving "tigers," and to track down a heinous descendant of Dr. Moriarty, a ruthless underworld figure played by Ken Pogue. Must-viewing for any Holmes aficionado. Mark Adair Rios, Julian Christian, Joy Coghill.

NINJA TERMINATOR (1985). The Golden Ninja Warrior, a statuette of magical powers, is sought by three martial arts students in this action-oriented karate-klout movie. Sho Kosugi, Wong Cheng Il, Jonathan Wattis.

NINJA, THE VIOLENT SORCERESS (1986). Vampire, ghost and a few live beings do battle. Directed by Bruce Lambert.

NINJA III: THE DOMINATION (1984). An appalling bloodbath of Phoenix policemen sets into dubious motion this sequel in the NINJA series (sword fighting, bodyslamming, car crashing). A samurai warrior, impervious to bullets, kills scores of bluecoats before transferring his evil soul into telephone repairwoman Lucinda Dickey, who slaughters more policemen. The action is adequately directed by Sam Firstenberg but the story is bereft of suspense or characterizations. Sho Kosugi, dedicated hero ninja, is on hand (one eye covered by a black patch) to duel with the supernatural force in fights that kung fu you to death. All formula and no interplay can make even raw action dull. Jordan Bennett, David Chunt, T. J. Castronova. (MGM/UA) (Laser: Japanese)

NINTH CONFIGURATION, THE (1979). Oddball study in schizophrenia by writer-producer-director William Peter Blatty, who adapted his novel TWINKLE TWINKLE, KILLER KANE. In this portrait of madness without heroes or easy answers, several U.S. soldiers (including an astronaut) suffering from breakdowns gather in a castle to act out their fantasies for psychiatrist Stacy Keach. But there is a secret behind Keach's behavior that wrenches the narrative. Not an easy film to endure, but sincere and literate, and well acted. Jason Miller, Scott Wilson, Robert Loggia, Moses Gunn, Tom Atkins, Neville Brand. (New World) (Laser: Image)

NINTH GUEST, THE (1934). See third edition.

NITWITS, THE (1935). See editions 1-3.

NO BLADE OF GRASS (1970). Cornel Wilde distinguished himself as a director with THE NAKED PREY. In this version of John Christopher's novel, scripted by John Forestal, we have a Wilde look at ecological neglect that leads to worldwide famine and anarchy, and a small band that makes its way to a wilderness fortress. But, Wilde degrades the worthy message by focusing on gang rape and unsavory motorcycle gang killings in B-movie fashion. What might have been an important post-holocaust film disintegrates into a shootemup thriller. Nigel Davenport, Jean Wallace (Wilde's wife), Anthony May, Lynn Frederick, George Coulouris.

NOCTURNA (1978). Low-budget quickie, subtitled GRANDDAUGHTER OF DRACULA, opens at Dracula's castle in Transylvania, which has been converted into a hotel where Drac's granddaughter falls for a musician. When she runs away to New York with the rocker, granddad (John Carradine) follows in this poor man's LOVE AT FIRST BITE. Writer-director Harry Tampa plays it for laughs, with Yvonne De Carlo re-creating her role from THE MUNSTERS. Bizarre mixture of rock, sex and vampires. Adam Keefe. (Media)

NO ESCAPE (1994). A rousing first-rate action movie with futuristic overtones, enhanced by rugged, scenic Australian locations, the frenetic, stylish work of director Michael Campbell (working with producer Gale Anne Herd) and Ray Liotta as an anti-hero trapped in the penal world of 2022 A.D. A Rambo of tomorrow, Liotta is sentenced to maximum security prison, only to be transferred by sadistic warden Michael Learned to an island where two convict factions are at war—a band of primitive warriors led by Kevin Dillon and a more peaceable bunch guided by The Father (Lance Henriksen). Campbell stages the numerous action scenes with impact, and Liotta emerges a durable action star thanks to a Michael Gaylin-Joel Gross script that allows him to develop a dimensional character. Stuart Wilson, Ernie Hudson, Kevin J. O'Connor.

NO HAUNT FOR A GENTLEMAN (1952). British supernatural comedy about a long-dead ghost haunting the mother-in-law of the owner of a rural estate. Directed by Leonard Reeve. Sally Newton, Jack McNaughton, Anthony Pendrell.

NO HOLDS BARRED (1952). See editions 1-3.

NOMADS (1985). Avant-garde supernatural tale in which nurse Lesley Anne Down is bitten by a raving patient (Pierce Brosnan) and is possessed by images of the man's past. Through psychic flashes she learns he is an anthropologist who just moved into a home once frequented by "nomads," evil spirits in human form who wander the deserts of the world. Cross-cutting between Pierce's persecution at the hands of the nomads (who take on the persona of a punk motorcycle gang) and the images haunting Down, the film unfolds enigmatically. Written-directed by John McTiernan. Anna-Maria Montecelli, Adam Ant, Hector Mercado, Mary Woronov. (Paramount) (Laser: Japanese)

NON-STOP NEW YORK (1937). Robert Stevenson directed this glimpse into future aviation set aboard an airliner with futuristic gadgets. It's really an excuse for a murder mystery involving a female passenger. Among the script's writers is Curt Siodmak. (Filmfax)

NO. ONE OF THE SECRET SERVICE (1977). Low-brow parody of James Bond from British producer-director Lindsay Shonteff finds Nicky Henson portraying the suave, stupid Charles Bind, a not so super agent dispatched by assignment chief Charles Bind to investigate a secret military organization called KRASH (Killing, Raping, Arson, Slaughter & Hit), a front for a roving sniper-assassin (Richard Todd). This sequel to THE MAN FROM S.E.X. is thoroughly dumb and worthless. Aimi MacDonald, Dudley Sutton, Sue Lloyd.

NO PLACE LIKE HOMICIDE (1962). Editions 1-3.

NO PLACE TO HIDE (1955). Pellets containing a lethal virus are carried by two boys on the run through the Philippines. David Brian is the sympathetic doctor seeking the youths. Feeble travelogue adventure, with no place to go but down. Josef Shaftel directed Norman Corwin's script. Marsha Hunt is the long-suffering mother. Hugh Corcoran, Celia Flor. (Prism)

NORLISS TAPES, THE (1973). Producer-director Dan Curtis teamed with writer William F. Nolan for this rejected TV pilot. Roy Thinnes is psychic investigator David Norliss, faced with a walking corpse and a demon from Hell. Don Porter, Angie Dickinson, Claude Akins, Michele Carey (in a sexy role), Hurd Hatfield.

NORMAN'S AWESOME EXPERIENCE (1989). Science lab assistance Tom McCamus is transported through time to the Roman Empire with cutie Laurie Paton and photographer Jacques Lussier. The threesome engages in witticisms as they fight off a barbarian horde. Written-directed by co-producer Paul Donovan. Lee Broker, David Hemblen. (South Gate; Hemdale)

NORMING OF JACK 243, THE (1975). David Selby, a conformist living in a futuristic society, falls in love with a fugitive who forces him to reconsider his pacificism. Politically minded TV-movie directed by Robert Precht.

NORTHSTAR (1985). Failed TV pilot in which astronaut Greg Evigan is subjected to a force field in space and returns to Earth with superhuman powers and an IQ surpassing Einstein's. Given that, it's nothing more than the usual spy shenanigans. Deborah Wakeham, Mitchell Ryan, Mason Adams.

NOSFERATU (1922). German filmmaker F. W. Murnau changed the names and incidents in Bram Stoker's DRACULA and foisted it on the public as an original story about a bloodsucker living in Bremen in 1838. Stoker's widow recognized the similarities and sued Murnau. All prints were ordered destroyed but a few survived the purge and NOSFERATU has taken its just place among silent vampire classics. There's no doubting the Stoker influence in these chronicles of the nocturnal affairs of Count Orlock (Max Schreck), but the film warrants attention as an historical conversation piece. (Kino; Goodtimes; Foothill; Discount; Republic; Sinister/C; Video Yesteryear) (Laser: Image; Republic)

NOSFERATU—THE VAMPIRE (1979). Decidedly offbeat remake of F. W. Murnau's 1922 pirated version of DRACULA, written-produced-directed by Germany's Werner Herzog. But the pacing is so leisurely, the film plods along when it should leap out at you. Yet, the heavy atmosphere and unnerving make-up of Klaus Kinski in the title role gives this lengthy West Germany production (124 minutes) a compelling attraction-repulsion. Isabelle Adjani. (Crown) (Laser: Japanese)

NOSTRADAMUS (1979). This title adorns the Bargain Video cassette box, but the film inside is actually PROPHECIES OF NOSTRADAMUS, an Australian TV documentary. (See that entry for details.)

NO SUCH THING AS GRAVITY (1989). This 45-minute sci-fi art film with a narrative structure is Alyce Wittenstein's depiction of a futuristic world in which mankind is ruled by LaFont Corp., which tends to man's needs with machinery. Outcasts are sent to the artificial planet Terra Nova (off-Earth scenes are in color; Earth scenes are in black and white), which shifts from orbit and threatens to destroy Earth, and it's up to a computer expert and his girl to save the day. The cast is made up of Nick Zedd as a defense attorney, Taylor Mead as a crazed judge, Michael J. Anderson, Emmanuelle Chaulet and video rock star Holly Adams.

NO SURVIVORS, PLEASE (1963). West German import depicts alien invaders (Orions) taking over Earthlings at their moment of death, as part of an invasion scheme. Producer Hans Albin co-directed with Peter Berneis. Maria Perschy, Robert Cunningham. (S/Weird)

NOTHING BUT THE NIGHT (1972). Christopher Lee produced (and stars in) this adaptation of John Blackburn's CHILDREN OF THE NIGHT, in which kids are injected with serum that contains memory genes of the dead; these memories turn the young ones into terrifying murderers. Directed by Peter Sasdy. Peter Cushing, Diana Dors, Lee, Georgia Brown. Also known as THE RESURRECTION SYNDICATE. (Trend Video Concepts; from Monterey as **DEVIL'S UNDEAD, THE**)

NOTHING BUT TROUBLE (1991). Madcap, Monty Python-styled comedy with horrific overtones in which financial advisor Chevy Chase and sexy Demi Moore are picked up for speeding in a small town and subjected to death traps and other cliffhanging situations at the hands of a crazed justice of the peace (Dan Aykroyd), his assistant John Candy and other whacky characters, including two human piglet twins. This exercise in disguises (Aykroyd and Candy play other characters in dense makeup) quickly turns to slapstick. The funky set design and crazy gadgets are terrific. (Warner Bros.)

NOTHING LASTS FOREVER (1984). Comedy-love story set sometime in the near future when artist Zach Galligan flunks a test and ends up directing traffic in the Holland Tunnel under boss Dan Aykroyd. Somehow Galligan, after a love affair with Apollonia van Ravenstein, goes to the moon on a Lunarcruiser bossed by travel guide Bill Murray. First feature of producer Lorne Michaels and writer-director Tom Schiller.

NOTHING VENTURE (1947). See editions 1-3.

NOT OF THIS EARTH (1956). Paul Birch, alien from the planet Davana, generates Death Rays whenever he removes his dark glasses and concentrates his gleaming, blank orbs. He's on Earth to send specimens of mankind back to his home planet, and he's aided in his vampiric mission (they need blood, you see) by a bat monster. Produced-directed by Roger Corman. Beverly Garland, Jonathan Haze, Dick Miller.

NOT OF THIS EARTH (1988). Entertaining remake of Roger Corman's 1956 cult favorite, opening with a main title with scenes from Corman's horror/sci-fi favorites. This self-homage is appropriate to the pleasing campiness that follows. The story again focuses on a strange man in dark glasses (Arthur Roberts) whose eyeballs zap you to death. The Alien is from planet Darvana to check out human blood. If it works in the Alien's veins, then Darvana (where inhabitants are dying, and need blood) will invade Earth. Ex-pornie movie star Traci Lords (in her first "straight" role) is a nurse assigned to take care of The Alien. Other odd characters include a blond chauffeur (Lenny Juliano), a uniformed policeman (Roger Lodge), a doctor (Ace Mask), a silly vacuum salesman (Michael Delano) and assorted big-busted bimbos. Lords is good, especially in a blue bikini. Directed by Jim Wynorski. (MGM/UA)

NOT OF THIS WORLD (1991). A fun-filled throwback to the sci-fi films of the '50s, reminiscent of ELECTRONIC MONSTER. This other-world life form comes to Earth on a meteor and feeds off electricity, growing in size from a small lizard-like thing into a slobberer the size of the Ritz. It's up to power-plant executive Lisa Hartman (!), her father Pat Hingle, sheriff A Martinez and young kid Luke Edwards to stop the glooky-goop monster as it slithers around the countryside, opening its toothy maw and all but saying "Feed Me!" Writer Robert Glass even throws in a brotherhood theme by having a Japanese exec cooperate with Hartman as she casts aside miniskirt and high heels to battle the enemy from space. Diected by Jon Daniel Hess. Tracey Walter, Michael Greene, Cary-Hiroyuki Tagawa.

NOT QUITE HUMAN (1987). Two-part Disney TV-movie is undistinguished fodder for the video mill, with dense-brained scientist Alan Thicke creating an android (Jay Underwood, from THE BOY WHO COULD FLY) named "Chip" that is programmed to take everything he's told literally—the main source of humor in Alan Ormsby's script, based on books by Seth McEvoy. Steven H. Stern produced-directed. Joseph Bologna, Robyn Lively, Robert Harper. (Disney)

NOT QUITE HUMAN II (1989). A charming improvement over Part I in this series based on the novels by Seth McEvoy and produced by Disney. Alan Thicke returns as the scientist who created the android "Chip Carson." In this misadventure Chip goes to college where he overcomes his built-in naivete, meets a female android and falls in love for the first time, and outsmarts robotic scientists. Good fun, with yocks provided by writer-director Eric Luke. Greg Mullavey, Robyn Lively, Katie Barberi, Dey Young.

NOT QUITE HUMAN III. See **STILL NOT QUITE HUMAN.**

NOW YOU SEE HIM, NOW YOU DON'T (1972). Comedy-farce in the Disney series starring Kurt Russell as the brainiest boy in Chemistry 1A who is always creating a new formula. This time it's a spray that brings about invisibility—a discovery crook Cesar Romero plans to steal. The premise is belabored but the effects during the crazy car chases are amusing. Directed by Robert Butler. Joe Flynn, Joyce Menges, Jim Backus, William Windom, Edward Andrews. (Disney)

NUCLEAR CONSPIRACY, THE (1986). Boring but boring British movie in which a young woman tracks her kidnapped husband and daughter with a free-wheeling photojournalist. It's all talk and dull detective work as they uncover a cover-up. Written-produced-directed by Rainer Erler. Birgit Doll, Albert Fortell. (Vidmark)

NUCLEAR RUN. TV title for **CHAIN REACTION.**

NUDE BOMB, THE (1980). Feature version of TV's GET SMART about CONTROL Agent 86, Maxwell Smart, who fights CHAOS in his delightfully inept style. Don Adams is no different from his TV days as he fights for the freedom, liberty and clothing of all by preventing a plot that would strip us bare-ass nude. Clive Donner directs this compendium of spy gags (by Arne Sutton, Bill Dana and Leonard B. Stern) with monumental indifference. Bomb indeed. Sylvia Kristel, Rhonda Fleming, Dana Elcar, Pamela Hensley. (Video/Laser: MCA)

NUKIE . . . IN SEARCH OF AMERICA (1989). Cutesy pie alien creature is on the move across America. Glynis Johns, Ronald France, Steve Railsback. Directed by Sias Odendal.

NUNS OF SAINT ARCHANGELO, THE (1971). Horror film, also known as INNOCENTS FROM HELL, directed by Domenico Paolella. Anne Heywood, Ornella Muti. (From MPI as **SISTERS OF SATAN**)

NURSE SHERRI. See **BEYOND THE LIVING.**

NURSE'S SECRET (1941). See third edition.

NURSE WILL MAKE IT BETTER. See **DEVIL'S WEB, THE** (Open wide and say "Arrgghh!").

NUTRIAMAN: THE COPASAW CREATURE. See **TERROR IN THE SWAMP.**

NUTTY PROFESSOR, THE (1963). Even those who normally eschew Jerry Lewis comedies have found this fulfilling in exploring the Jekyll/Hyde theme. Lewis portrays clumsy Professor Julius F. Kelp, a myopic, marmot-toothed scientist who discovers a concoction that turns him into an aggressive alter ego, Buddy Love. Lewis also directed and co-wrote the clever script with Bill Richmond. Stella Stevens, Del Moore, Kathleen Freeman, Howard Morris. (Video/Laser: Paramount)

NYLON NOOSE, THE (1963). German nonsense about a daffy doctor trying to mummify bodies and some stockholders gathered in the obligatory weird mansion. The stockholders are strangled, one by one, with a nylon noose. You'll get all choked up too. Directed by Rudolf Zehetgruber. Richard Goodman.

NYMPHOID BARBARIAN IN DINOSAUR HELL, A (1990). If this were only half as good as its title . . . a superlow-budget novelty set in a post-Armageddon world where Linda Corwin (in the briefest of animal skins) fights mutation cave men, stop-motion giant dinosaurs and other prehistoric evils. Most of the unconvincing action is inarticulate, no doubt a match-up to the mentality of writer-director Brett Piper and producer Alex Pirnie, who doubles as actor. Paul Guzzi, Marc deShales, K. Alan Hodder.

NYOKA AND THE TIGERMEN (1942). Rousing, fun-packed 15-chapter Republic serial (made as PERILS OF NYOKA) stars Kay Aldridge as the comic-book jungle girl searching for her missing father and the Tablets of Hippocrates, said to record long-lost secrets of the ancient Greeks, and the cure for cancer. Evil, sexy high priestess Vultura (Lorna Gray, later Adrian Booth), is also after the Tablets and it's one cliffhanger after another, including an encounter with a giant gorilla, Satan. One of the most action-packed, energetic serials ever produced. Gray's slit skirts, which reveal her beautiful legs when she sits on her throne, indicate this was made for an audience other than mere juveniles. Directed with nonstop excitement by serial whiz William Witney. Clayton Moore, Tris Coffin, William Benedict, Charles Middleton. A TV feature version is **NYOKA AND THE LOST SECRETS OF HIPPOCRATES.** (All 15 chapters from Republic) (Laser: Republic)

OASIS OF THE ZOMBIES (1981). Adventurers searching for Rommel's treasure in North Africa face a legion of walking Nazi corpses. Manuel Gelin, Frances Jordon, Jeff Montgomery, Myriam Landson. Directed by A. M. Frank (aka Marius Lasoeur), who borrowed footage from Jesse Franco's unfinished TOMB OF THE LIVING DEAD. (United American; Lightning; Wizard; Filmline; Gemstone; from Trans World as **BLOODSUCKING NAZI ZOMBIES**)

OBEAH (1935). See third edition.

OBLONG BOX, THE (1969). "Far worse things are known to mankind," says Vincent Price, possibly referring to other American-International pics exploiting Edgar Allan Poe titles. Pretty gory stuff, with depravity and bawdiness thrown in by producer-director Gordon Hessler. Price's brother was disfigured by an African witch doctor and buried alive, only someone dug him up and now he's alive, on a rampage of lustful murder. Alastair Williamson, Christopher Lee, Sally Geeson, Rupert Davies. (Key; HBO) (Laser: Japanese)

OBSESSION (1976). Brian De Palma's film pays homage to VERTIGO. Cliff Robertson, grieving over the loss of his wife, is drawn into an affair with a woman who bears a startling resemblance to his dead spouse. Paul Schrader's script becomes artsy-craftsy while Vilmos Zsigmond's cinematography heightens suspense and ambience. In Hitchcock tradition, De Palma chose Bernard Herrmann to write the score. Genevieve Bujold, John Lithgow, Sylvia Williams. (RCA/Columbia; Goodtimes) (Laser: RCA/Columbia)

OBSESSION: A TASTE FOR FEAR (1987). Italian psychosex thriller with more sex than thrills when an unshaven cop searches for a serial killer slaughtering his/her/its way through the depraved of Rome. There's heavy-handed lesbian overtones as director Piccio Raffanini penetrates the sleazy velvet underworld. Contains a minimum of horror; aka PATHOS. Virginia Hey, Gerard Darmon, Gioia Scola, Carlo Mucari. (Imperial)

OCCULT EXPERIENCE, THE (1987). Documentary glimpses at Satanism around the world, including excursions to San Francisco's Satanic Temple of Set and the Church of Satan in Australia. Also examined is ALIEN designer H. R. Giger at his Swiss retreat. Produced-directed by Frank Heimms. (Video/Laser: Sony)

OCCULTIST, THE (1988). Private eye Rick Gianasi goes to the voodoo island of San Caribe to fight zombies. Written-directed by Tim Kincaid. Joe Derrig, Jennifer Kanter, Mizan Nunes, Richard Mooney. (Unicorn; from Urban Classics as **MAXIMUM THRUST**)

OCCURRENCE AT OWL CREEK BRIDGE (1962). French short subject, based on Ambrose Bierce's classic story, was a Cannes Film Festival prize winner that also won an Oscar for best short subject. However, before Academy Award time William Froug, producer of THE TWILIGHT ZONE, offered it as part of the series, with Rod Serling introducing this unusual tale of the Civil War.

Written-directed by Robert Enrico. Roger Jacquet, Anne Cornaly. (Festival Films; Kids Klassics; Video Yesteryear's version also contains THE RED BALLOON)

OCTAMAN (1971). Embarrassing man-in-a-rubber-suit monster movie. Blame writer-director Harry Essex, who stole from his script for CREATURE FROM THE BLACK LAGOON. Essex knows nothing about building suspense or how to photograph a menacing creature effectively. Kerwin Mathews and Pier Angeli endured the humiliation of appearing with the phony-looking monster. Octaman is supposed to be an octopus mutation created by contaminated waters. U.S.-Mexican production drowns in babbling bubbles. Jeff Morrow, Harry Guardini. (Prism; Video Gems; Western World)

OCTOBER 32ND (1992). Original theatrical title for a future film released by Hemdale on Home Video as **MERLIN**. See tjat emtru imder "Last-Minute Updates."

OCTOPUSSY (1983). The 13th James Bond adventure and sixth with Roger Moore as the indefatigable 007. There are the usual super-weapons and the action sequences are among the liveliest for the series. His adversary is Afghan prince Kamal Khan (Louis Jourdan), who operates a palace in India with henchman Gobinda (Kabir Bedi). Kamal plots with power-hungry Russian general Steven Berkoff to explode an atomic bomb in Germany and bring chaos to N.A.T.O. Titular character is an octopus-loving dragon lady (Maud Adams) heading an all-women's smuggling ring. The derring-do is frequently exciting, thanks to high production standards. Especially fun is a fight aboard a speeding train and Bond clinging to the fuselage of a plane in flight. Directed by John Glen, who helmed FOR YOUR EYES ONLY. Script by George MacDonald Fraser, Richard Maubaum and Michael G. Wilson. Music by John Barry. Lois Maxwell, Kristina Wayborn. (CBS/Fox) (Laser: CBS/Fox; MGM/UA)

ROGER MOORE

OFFERINGS (1989). Writer-producer-director Christopher Reynolds borrows heavily from HALLOWEEN in spinning this Oklahoma-based production about a cannibalistic youth who grows up to escape the insane asylum in which he has been incarcerated, terrorizing teenagers and murdering with chainsaw and other body-penetrating weaponry. OFFERINGS offers nothing new—even the music is swiped from Carpenter. Loretta Leigh Bowman, Elizabeth Greene. (South Gate)

OFFICIAL DENIAL (1993). An alien is captured when its spacecraft is shot down by the U.S. Air Force's top-secret E.T. unit. A fight erupts in the military over whether to dissect the creature or spare its life. Chad Everett, Dirk Benedict, Parker Stevenson. Produced by the Sci-Fi Channel.

'OFFICIAL DENIAL'

OFFSPRING, THE (1986). Oldfield, Tenn., is the setting for horror stories reflecting the evil people and activities of the community. Aka FROM A WHISPER TO A SCREAM, it stars Susan Tyrrell as a reporter who witnesses the execution of a mad woman (Martine Beswick) by lethal injection and visits Vincent Price in his musty library to learn the town's history. The first yarn stars Clu Gulagher as a sexually suppressed clod who kills women, only to have one of them return from the grave to haunt him. This is the weakest segment, memorable only for Gulagher's odd albino-like makeup. Story #2 is about a swamp witch doctor who has the secret to eternal life, and the efforts of a criminal to find the elixir. A nice twist ending here. Yarn #3 is set at Lovecraft's Traveling Carnival, where a snake woman uses her voodoo powers to control The Amazing Arden, who eats razor blades and glass. The Civil War tale that follows is the film's most chilling, reminiscent of LORD OF THE FLIES when Union stragglers fall into the hands of youngsters who have formed their own religion based on the horrors of the war. Finally, the Tyrrell-Price footage has its own surprise ending. THE OFFSPRING, shot in Georgia, has good direction by Jeff Burr, who co-scripted with C. Courtney Joyner and Darin Scott. Terry Kiser, Harry Caesar, Rosalind Cash, Cameron Mitchell, Lawrence Tierney. (Video/Laser: Live)

OF GODS AND THE UNDEAD (1969). Editions 1-3.

OF UNKNOWN ORIGIN (1983). Strangely compelling war of cunning erupts in a Manhattan apartment when advertising exec Peter Weller duels with an intelligent mutant rat. Hence, the film becomes a metaphor for man's never-ending war against vermin, and the history of how rats have plagued mankind is graphically described and depicted in this adaptation of "The Visitor" by Chauncey G. Parker III. Director George P. Cosmatos captures a surreal element as Weller is obsessed and sinks into insanity. This psychological exploration in Brian Taggert's script also insightfully deals with Weller's professional life, giving the film a rich subtext. Supporting cast is good (Jennifer Dale, Shannon Tweed, Lawrence Dale) but ultimately the rat and Weller's obsession dominate. (Warner Bros.)

OGRE, THE (1988). Italy's Lamberto Bava helmed this psychological horror tale about a sexually mixed-up author of horror novels (Virginia Bryant) haunted by childhood memories when she moves into a mansion. Out of her disturbed mind emerges the titular entity of evil. (Video Mania)

O'HARA'S WIFE (1982). Standard TOPPER-style supernatural comedy in which Ed Asner, grieving over his wife's death, discovers her spirit has returned to his household. But only he can see her spectral form. So you have jokes with Asner talking to air, misunderstandings, etc. Predictable TV-movie, directed by William Bartman, with Mariette Hartley in the thankless wife role. Tom Bosley, Perry Lang, Ray Walston, Jodie Foster, Nehemiah Persoff, Richard Schaal. (Vestron)

OH, BOY! (1938). "Oh, brother!" is a more apt way to describe this archaic British comedy about a weak-willed scientist (Albert Burdon) who concocts a magical formula that turns him into a strongman. Oh, well! Directed by Albert De Courville. Mary Lawson, Bernard Nedell.

OH, GOD! (1977). Thought-provoking allegorical in which a supermarket manager (John Denver) is asked by the Almighty (George Burns) to tell the human race to straighten up. Denver is judged part of the Lunatic Fringe but finds notoriety on Dinah Shore's TV show. This leads to a courtroom hearing, where Burns appears to prove God's existence. The laughs are gentle, the message obvious, the acting restrained. Director Carl Reiner makes it work without piousness. Ralph Bellamy, Donald Pleasence, Teri Garr, William Daniels, Barnard Hughes, Paul Sorvino, Barry Sullivan. (Video/Laser: Warner Bros.)

OH, GOD! BOOK TWO (1980). In the beginning there was OH, GOD! and lo, it came to pass there was a sequel directed by Gilbert Cates, and audiences looked at it and said it was fair to middling. And God, who does resembleth George Burns with a cigar, said, "I shall choose a child to carry My Word to the people," and the child was Louanne. And she was good. Worldly wickedness was challenged by universal good will, and Box Office Keepers did say, "Receipts, thou art beautiful." And Suzanne Pleshette, David Birney, Howard Duff, Wilfrid Hyde-White, Conrad Janis and Hans Conried were hence employed. (Warner Bros.)

OH, GOD! YOU DEVIL (1984). Third film in the series with George Burns (cigar and all) as The Lord is a whimsical, entertaining allegory about good vs evil, decency vs greed, etc. Podunk musician Ted Wass unwittingly signs a pact with The Devil (also Burns) to be metamorphosized into rock star Billy Wayne (Robert Desiderio), only Billy realizes success isn't so great and just wants his wife back. He calls on God for help, and at a poker table in Las Vegas, God and Satan determine the fate of all. Lowkey and amusing with Paul Bogart directing unobtrusively. Eugene Roche is especially good as Wayne's record agent. Roxanne Hart, Eugene Roche, Ron Silver. (Video/Laser: Warner Bros.)

OH HEAVENLY DOG (1980). Joe Camp, creator of BENJI, puts the pooch to a new use in directing this fantasy-comedy in which private eye Chevy Chase, while investigating a murder, is stabbed to death and winds up in Heaven. He's ordered to return to Earth to solve his own homicide but the only body available is a dog's. So he goes down on all fours, wags his tail and tracks Omar Sharif and other suspects through rainy London streets. Inoffensive fun, with several plot surprises and a good performance by Benji. Jane Seymour, Robert Morley, Donnelly Rhodes, Alan Sues. (CBS/Fox) (Laser: Japanese)

OH, THOSE MOST SECRET AGENTS (1966). See editions 1-3.

OH! WHAT A LOVELY WAR (1969). British comedy patterned after a music hall entertainment, which struggles to keep its balance as director Richard Attenborough walks precariously between fantasy and reality in this overstated satire of World War I and the stupidity of its generals. A seaside resort advertises "World War One . . . Songs, Battles and a Few Jokes." The Len Deighton script shifts between the resort and battlefield, but there are no trenches—only fields of poppies and scoreboards of casualty figures. Laurence Olivier, Ralph Richardson, Jack Hawkins, Dirk Bogarde.

O.K. CONNERY. See **OPERATION KID BROTHER.**

O.K., NERO (1954). See editions 1-3.

OLD DARK HOUSE, THE (1932). Following FRANKENSTEIN, director James Whale made this version of J. B. Priestley's BENIGHTED, creating a subgenre terror-satire genre that persisted for years. A violent thunderstorm (what other kind are there in horror films?) forces travelers to spend the night in a weird mansion inhabited by butler Boris Karloff, a 102-year-old lunatic, a fire-loving brother and a God-fearing sister, all suffering from assorted psychoses, neuroses and halitoses. Tons of fun in an atmosphere of musky decay. Ernest Thesiger, Charles Laughton, Raymond Massey.

OLD DARK HOUSE, THE (1963). Producer-director William Castle's remake of Whale's 1932 mystery-comedy is a failure, capturing none of the decaying atmosphere and droll comedy. The house is too new and airy and the plot has been updated to feature Tom Poston as a car salesman who goes to the old place to sell a car and takes refuge with oddball travelers during a storm. Robert Morley, Janette Scott, Mervyn Jones.

OLD DRAC. See **OLD DRACULA.**

OLD DRACULA (1975). Producer John H. Wiener would have us believe this is a comedy-horror classic destined to take its place beside YOUNG FRANKENSTEIN. Wiener would have us believe David Niven brings exciting interpretations to the vampire count, placing him in the Lugosi-Lee category. Wiener would have us believe a faulty blood transfusion turning a long-sleeping princess into a black vampire (Teresa Graves) is the premise for a funny, invigorating film (directed by Clive Donner). Above all else, Wiener would have us believe he is a film producer. Ha!

OLDEN DAYS COAT, THE (1981). An old coat in Granny's closet sends a ten-year-old girl back in time. (New World)

OLD LEGENDS NEVER DIE (1966). Episodes of Irwin Allen's TIME TUNNEL series. James Darren and Robert Colbert travel back to King Arthur's day to tangle with Merlin the Magician, then find themselves in Sherwood Forest helping Robin Hood and his Merry Men. See **TIME TUNNEL, THE.**

OLD MOTHER RILEY MEETS THE VAMPIRE. See **MY SON, THE VAMPIRE.**

OLD MOTHER RILEY'S GHOSTS (1941). Arthur Lucan in drag really is a drag as a charwoman who breaks up a plot to steal a secret invention from a designer living in an alleged haunted house. Part of the Mother Riley series that includes OLD MOTHER RILEY'S JUNGLE TREASURE and OLD MOTHER RILEY MEETS THE VAMPIRE. Produced-directed by John Baxter. Kitty McShane (Lucan's wife) co-stars with John Stuart, A. Bromley Davenport and Dennis Wyndham. (Nostalgia; Sinister/C; Filmfax)

OLIVIA. Video version of **TASTE OF SIN, A** (VCII).

O LUCKY MAN (1973). Britain is now a fascist state of corrupt corporations, forcing coffee salesman Malcolm McDowell to endure unscrupulous government officials and murdering execs. As usual, the English satirize themselves with devastation. Directed by Lindsay Johnson. Arthur Lowe, Ralph Richardson, Rachel Roberts. (Warner Bros.)

OMEGA COP (1990). Stuart Whitman, Adam West and Troy Donahue enliven this derivative future-cop action yarn starring martial arts fighter Ron Marchini, who's after a gang of slave traders. Pretty ho-hum stuff otherwise. Directed by Paul Kyriazi. (South Gate; Hemdale)

OMEGA MAN, THE (1971). Richard Matheson's I AM LEGEND was first adapted as THE LAST MAN ON EARTH, an Italian cheapie that was faithful to the book, blending mythical vampirism with science-fiction. This Charlton Heston vehicle is less faithful. The year is 1975 and Heston would appear to be the sole survivor of a plague. Gone are the vampires of I AM LEGEND, gone is the one-man battle to survive against blood-drinking zombies. A new plotline has Anthony Zerbe heading religious mutants wishing to kill Heston because he represents the knowledge that poisoned mankind. Then comes a real clunker: Heston finds other untainted survivors and has a miscegenational romance with Rosalind Cash. Director Boris Sagal has made a sow's ear out of a silk purse. (Warner Bros.)

OMEGANS, THE (1967). Lethargic, insufferable non-shocker starring Keith Larsen and Ingrid Pitt as secret lovers plotting to kill her husband (an artist played by Lucien Pan) on an expedition in the jungles of Malaysia. The spirits of an ancient race called the Omegans pollutes a mountain stream, leaving a fluroscent glow on anyone who touches or drinks the poisonous waters. The most exciting aspect of this uninspired quickie is the shapely body and sexual dynamite of Ms Pitt. Otherwise, producer-director W. Lee Wilder could find nothing else to elevate the viewer's blood pressure.

OMEN, THE (1976). Screenwriter David Seltzer borrowed a prophecy from the Book of Revelation, which foredooms the coming of Armageddon, and fashioned the premise for a horror trilogy, of which this is the first. It's a supernatural terror tale of sensational proportions: The Antichrist child, the son of Satan, is reborn and walks among us, destined to rise up through politics and turn "man against his brother . . . till man exists no more." A whopper of a tale—from Jerry Goldsmith's suspenseful score to Gil Taylor's low-key lighting to John Richardson's bloody effects to Richard Donner's taut direction. This features grisly, imaginative murders as Gregory Peck sets out with photographer David Warner to prove the Antichrist exists. There's a ghastly beheading, a hanging, an attack by the Hounds of Hell and other demonic horrors. While sequels (DAMIEN: OMEN II and THE

FINAL CONFLICT) never fully lived up to the premise, this carries it too well. Produced by Harvey Bernhard. Leo McKern, Lee Remick, Billie Whitelaw, Harvey Stephens, Martin Benson, Sheila Raynor. (Video/Laser: CBS/Fox)

OMEN II. See **DAMIEN—OMEN II.**

OMEN III. See **FINAL CONFLICT—OMEN III, THE.**

OMEN IV: THE AWAKENING (1991). Loose remake of THE OMEN, with producer Harvey Bernhard recycling ingredients of his 1976 hit. This TV-movie has a few exciting moments when a female counterpart to Damien is adopted by a U.S. politician, unaware that "Delia" ("Always Visible" in Greek) is the spawn of Satan. A sequence at a psychic fair is especially effective. But the teleplay by Brian Taggert (from a story by Taggert and Bernhard) has the beheading sequence, the evil devil dog that causes a death, and other familiar "horrible deaths" without exploring new territory. Composer Jonathan Sheffer uses Jerry Goldsmith's themes. Faye Grant, Michael Woods, Michael Lerner, Madison Mason. Directed by Jorge Montesi and Dominique Othenin-Girard. (Video/Laser: CBS/Fox)

OMICRON (1963). E.T. who has never seen Italian sci-fi movies thinks he has a brilliant idea: He'll invade the body of an Earthling and take over our planet. These poor dumb beings from beyond our galaxy . . . will they never learn? Written-directed by Ugo Gregoretti. Renato Salvatori, Rosemary Dexter.

OMOO OMOO THE SHARK GOD (1949). Oboy, oboy, Herman Melville would perform aquatic somersaults if he knew what U.S. producers did to his novel about the South Seas and the curse that hangs over valuable pearls. Directed by Leon Leonard. Ron Randell, Devera Burton. (Filmfax; Sinister/C)

ON A CLEAR DAY YOU CAN SEE FOREVER (1970). Despite director Vincent Minnelli, cinematographer Harry Stradling, lyricist Alan Jay Lerner, actress Barbra Streisand, actor Yves Montand, this was a box-office disaster. Streisand plays a Bridey Murphy type who, through regression brought on by her psychiatrist, discovers she lived a previous existence in the 1840s. Large-scale production numbers never involve the viewer. Adapted by Alan Jay Lerner from his play. Bob Newhart, Jack Nicholson. (Video/Laser: Paramount)

ON BORROWED TIME (1939). Based on the Paul Osborne-Lawrence Watkin Broadway play in which Mr. Brink (Sir Cedric Hardwicke) is in reality Mr. Death, fresh from Hell to claim wheelchair-bound Lionel Barrymore. Sentimental fable, well acted. Directed by Hal Bucquet. Beulah Bondi, Una Merkel, Henry Travers, Ian Wolfe.

ONCE BEFORE I DIE (1968). Inexplicable film produced-directed by John Derek in the Philippines as a vehicle for then-wife Ursula Andress. U.S. soldiers escort Andress through the jungles after Pearl Harbor, with Andress appearing to be an "Angel of Death"—her image is freeze-framed over scenes of war and destruction. And the men she kisses all die in battle. A baffling experience, with the only memorable acting by Richard Jaeckel as a war-crazed dogface with a bald head. Derek appears in a brief role, assisted by Ron Ely and Rod Lauren. (Movies Unlimited)

ONCE BITTEN (1985). Teenage sex comedy with supernatural overtones, not as dumb as some but still kind of dumb. Lauren Hutton is "The Countess," a 400-year-old vampiress living in an L.A. mansion. She needs three fixes from a male virgin or she'll show her years, so she picks Jim Carrey, who is also frustrated because his girl (Karen Kopins) won't dish out. The women fight for Hutton's attention while Hutton is dumbfounded. There's funny chase stuff through the Countess' mansion with her manservant, a gay vampire (Cleavon Little), leading the monster followers. Finally fizzles under Howard Storm's direction. They deserve a transfusion for trying, anyway. (Video/Laser: Vestron)

ONCE UPON A FRIGHTMARE. Video version and TV title for the British-made **FRIGHTMARE II** (Monterey).

ONCE UPON A MIDNIGHT DREARY. See **ONCE UPON A MIDNIGHT SCARY.**

ONCE UPON A MIDNIGHT SCARY (1979). Anthology TV-film in which Vincent Price introduces children's ghost stories. "The Ghost Belonged to Me" is about a boy who sees a spectre in the family barn, warning him of a disaster. Washington Irving's "Legend of Sleepy Hollow" is played for laughs, emphasizing silliness rather than the tale's supernatural elements. Longest of the pieces is "The House With a Clock in Its Walls," in which a youth discovers his uncle is a wizard. Designed to get children to rush to the library and get books to read. Good idea. Rene Auberjonis, Guy Boyd, Lance Kerwin. (Video Gems)

ONCE UPON A SPY (1980). Jimmy Sangster, a Hammer faithful, penned this TV-movie clone of James Bond with Christopher Lee as Marcus Valorium, who has perfected a "molecular condensor beam" capable of shrinking objects. First he steals the fabulous X-2 computer by shrinking it, then he shrinks an aircraft carrier, then he plans to bounce his beam off a satellite mirror and destroy everything. Agent K-12 (Mary Louise Weller, a real looker) gets hooked up with nerdish computer guy Ted Danson. Director Ivan Nagy plays this for what it is, comic book fodder. John Cacavas' music (almost wall to wall) emulates Bond themes. Glitzy and glittery with ample derring-do. Eleanor Parker is good as a feisty assignment chief. Aka LETHAL GAMES.

ONCE UPON A TIME (1944). Funny Hollywood fantasy about Broadway impresario Cary Grant down on his luck—until he discovers a caterpillar that dances to the tune of "Yes Sir, That's My Baby." Without getting preachy or heavy-handed, this adaptation of Norman Corwin's radio play "My Client Curly" makes comments on human nature and the flightiness of success—a pun you will better understand when you see this comedy directed by Alexander Hall. Janet Blair, James Gleason, William Demarest, Art Baker, John Abbott.

ONCE UPON A VIRGIN (1975). French sex-horror entertainment directed by Jean Rollin, in which women fall prey to an evil count in his torture chamber. Mylene d'Antes, Jean-Louis Vattier.

ONE BODY TOO MANY (1944). Comedy takeoff on THE OLD DARK HOUSE, full of fright cliches: sinister figure lurking in a mansion, thunder and lightning, hidden passageways and secret panels. Bela Lugosi portrays a butler who keeps trying to serve poisoned coffee to guests, just one of many zany delights. Directed by Frank McDonald. Jack Haley, Lyle Talbot. (Sinister/C; Nostalgia; Hollywood Home Theater)

ONE BY ONE. See **MAJORETTES, THE.**

ONE DARK NIGHT (1982). Writer-director Thomas McLoughlin borrows the bobbing corpses of POLTERGEIST as 154 zombies (designed by Tom Burman) shamble through a shadowy mausoleum, smothering the panicked characters to death. But instead of being macabre, the sequence has the effect of a funhouse of horrors, and shock value is minimized. On the plus side is an underlying premise of telekinesis. Karl Raymar has developed the power to rob young girls of their bioenergy and becomes a psychic vampire. His corpse is placed in the mausoleum, and then a teen-age sorority forces a plebe to spend the night there. Rest in pieces. Aka REST IN PEACE and ENTITY FORCE. Adam West, Robin Evans, Melissa Newman, Meg Tilly, Leslie Spreights. (Thorn EMI/HBO)

ONE DEADLY OWNER (1974). Mildly compelling tale about a Rolls Royce purchased by Donna Mills, a beautiful model who doesn't understand her compulsion for the car. Gradually she realizes its previous owner, wife of a business tycoon, is (re)possessing the car. No special effects or action sequences; Brian Clemens' teleplay depends on characterization. In this respect he is aided by Mills, by her boyfriend Jeremy Brett and by Laurence Payne and Robert Morris. Ian Fordyce directed. (Thrillervideo)

ONE FRIGHTENED NIGHT (1935). Comedy-mystery

in the style of THE CAT AND THE CANARY in which heirs gather to hear the reading of the will. Directed by Christy Cabanne. Charles Grapewin, Regis Toomey, Wallace Ford. (Kartes; Sinister/C; Nostalgia; Filmfax)

ONE HOUR TO DOOMSDAY. See **CITY BENEATH THE SEA.**

ONE HUNDRED CRIES OF TERROR (1965). . . . but only two tales of gothic horror—the first involving a husband and a secret lover who plot to murder the wife; the second about a woman buried alive in a mausoleum. The stories are inspired by Poe. Directed by Ramon Obon. Adriana Welter, George Martinez, Joaquin Cordero. (Sinister/C; S/Weird; Filmfax)

ONE MAGIC CHRISTMAS (1985). Harry Dean Stanton as an angel named Gideon? That's one of many oddities in this dark parable (from Walt Disney yet!) in which he is assigned (by God?) to convince a certain mother the values of the yuletide season. That mother, Mary Steenburgen, has lost her seasonal spirit because (1) hubby was just shot by a bank robber, (2) her kidnapped children have drowned and (3) she's been fired from her supermarket job. Stanton (who looks more like a sinister character than an angel) sends Mary's daughter to the North Pole to meet Santa. A sentimental tearjerker that doesn't have the strength of its schmaltz to pull it off. Gary Basaraba, Elizabeth Harnois, Arthur Hill (playing a white-haired grandfather), Wayne Robson. Directed by Phillip Borsos. (Video/Laser: Disney)

ONE MILLION B.C. (1940). Hal Roach's production depicting men vs. dinosaurs makes for whopping good adventure. This tribute to the Stone Age is filled with visual thrills, not the least of which is Carole Landis in antelope pelt. The Rock People are a crude, meat-eating tribe lorded over by grunting Tomack (Lon Chaney Jr.), who kicks Victor Mature out into the cold. Jutting-jawed Mature goes to the Shell People, a less boorish tribe that savors vegetables and practices manners. Eventually the tribes become gregarious, but not before battles with brontosauri, trachodons and other beasts. There's a climactic volcanic eruption. A classic, directed by Roach, Roach Jr. and D. W. Griffith. Remade with Rachel Welch in 1967 as ONE MILLION YEARS B.C. (Media; Nostalgic Merchant; Fox Hills) (Laser: 3M)

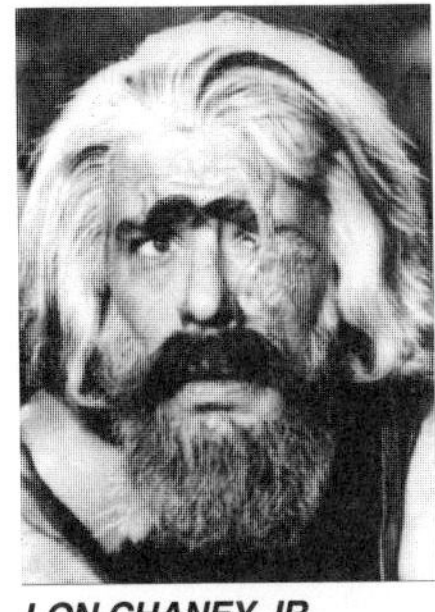

LON CHANEY JR.

ONE MILLION YEARS B.C. (1967). Hammer's remake of Hal Roach's 1940 miniclassic, with Raquel Welch (in fetching animal skins) as the Shell People gal who meets a Rock Tribe guy (John Richardson). Michael Carreras wrote-produced for Hammer, with Don Chaffey directing. A must-see for Ray Harryhausen's stop-motion animation. Like its predecessor, this is grand entertainment. Martine Beswick.

ONE NIGHT STAND (1984). On the evening nuclear war breaks out, four teens in a Sydney apartment listen to news on their transistor while playing poker and coming to a realization that dawn will bring a new world. This unusual Australian film was written-directed by John Duigan. Tyler Coppin, Cassandra Delaney. (Trans World; Sultan)

ONE OF OUR DINOSAURS IS MISSING (1975). Amusing Disney fantasy-comedy spoofs British behavior (nannies, stiff upper lip, that sort of thing, old chap) and monster films. Lotus X is a Chinese secret hidden in the tibia of a museum dinosaur, which restores life into the ancient creature. Fighting over possession of Lotus X are Peter Ustinov (Hnup Wan, of Chinese Intelligence) and Helen Hayes (nanny and backbone of the Empire). Made in England with Robert Stevenson directing. (Disney)

ONE OF OUR SPIES IS MISSING (1966). Episodes of THE MAN FROM U.N.C.L.E. series, re-edited into a feature with Robert Vaughn and David McCallum as supercool superspies with superwry superwits. Maurice Evans, Vera Miles, Yvonne Craig and James (STAR TREK) Doohan are involved with a serum that restores life. Leo G. Carroll appears as Mr. Waverly, assignment chief. Darrell Hallenbeck directed.

ONE SPY TOO MANY (1966). More re-edited MAN FROM U.N.C.L.E. footage with Rip Torn as would-be conquerer of the world, Alexander the Greater, out to steal a new Biological Warfare Gas that makes unwilling people say "I will." Napoleon Solo (Robert Vaughn) and Illya Kuryakin (David McCallum) are surrounded by beautiful women who keep taking their clothes off. It's enough to make you cry "Uncle." Directed by Joseph Sargent. Dorothy Provine, Yvonne Craig, Leo G. Carroll.

1001 ARABIAN NIGHTS (1959). Full-length Near-Sighted Magoo cartoon will disappoint fans eager for the satire of the short subjects, but children will be diverted by a story in which Magoo, uncle of Aladdin, is in love with a princess. Gags are unnecessarily repeated and the film looks padded. The producers might have been as near-sighted as Magoo. Voices by Jim Backus, Kathryn Grant, Hans Conried, Dwayne Hickman, Herschel Bernardi. (RCA/Columbia)

ONE THOUSAND YEARS FROM NOW. See **CAPTIVE WOMEN.**

ONE TOUCH OF VENUS (1948). Light comedy touch keeps this from becoming coy when department store floorwalker Robert Walker kisses a marble statue of the Venus de Milo, granting it life as gorgeous Ava Gardner. Adapted by Harry Kurnitz and Frank Tashlin from the play that originally starred Mary Martin with book by S. J. Perelman and Ogden Nash; music by Kurt Weill. Directed by William A. Seiter. Dick Haymes, Eve Arden, Tom Conway. (Video/Laser: Republic)

ONE WISH TOO MANY (1956). British comedy for the juvenile crowd: Youth discovers glass marble that grants his every wish. Directed by John Durst. Anthony Richmond, John Pike. (Sinister/C; S/Weird)

ON HER MAJESTY'S SECRET SERVICE (1969). George Lazenby replaces Sean Connery in this, the sixth in the James Bond series. Lazenby has neither the diction nor the finesse of Connery, nor does he appear comfortable in the arms of Diana Rigg and other beauties. To take up the slack, director Peter Hunt works extra-hard with action. Villain Ernst Stavros Blofeld (Telly Savalas) is masterminding a takeover of the world using allergies hidden in women's cosmetics that will result in sterility. Richard Maibaum adapted the Fleming novel, providing a love affair between Bond and Rigg (daughter of an international bad guy) that is the best aspect of this spy adventure. Julie Ege, Bessie Love, Catherina Von Schell. (Video/Laser: MGM/UA: CBS/Fox)

ONIBABA (1965). Macabre Japanese allegory horror tale (based on an ancient legend) in which two women survive in a marshland in the 16th Century by preying on soldiers. Artistically grisly stuff as the murderesses, surrounded by reeds bending in the wind, lure males into their love-deathtraps. When the younger woman falls for a samurai, the older preys on the girl's fears of the supernatural. Directed by Kaneto Shindo. Nobuko Otowa, Jitsuko Yoshimura. (Tamarelle's; Connoisseur; S/Weird)

ONLY A COFFIN. See **ORGIES OF DR. ORLOFF.**

ONLY WAY OUT IS DEAD, THE. See **MAN WHO WANTED TO LIVE FOREVER, THE.**

ON THE BEACH (1959). Stanley Kramer's plea for peace is a classy version of Nevil Shute's novel in which mankind has dropped the Bomb and Australia is the only continent yet untouched by radiation. The story pivots on a submarine commander (Gregory Peck), his affair with Ava Gardner and their subsequent acceptance, and rejection, of doom. Kramer's direction emphasizes the gloom of inexorable death. "Waltzing Matilda" is used to haunting effect. Anthony Perkins, Fred Astaire, Donna Anderson. (CBS/Fox) (Laser: Image)

ON THE COMET (1970). Czechoslovakian adventure is enchanting material from writer-director Karel Zeman, who borrowed from a Jules Verne book, HECTOR SERVADAC. When a comet collides with Earth in 1888, it rips away a hunk of Africa containing a French outpost; this piece roars off through space. The survivors, besides arguing about national differences, face prehistoric monsters, sea serpents and a colossal fly through stop-motion animation. Emil Horvath, Magda Vasarykova. (Blackhawk; Facets Multimedia)

ON THE TRAIL OF ED WOOD (1990). Documentary on the career of Ed Wood Jr., responsible for PLAN NINE FROM OUTER SPACE and other schlocky flicks. Actor Conrad Brooks is the host of this excursion into the dark side of an unhappy creative artist and his botched attempts at cinema. Directed by Michael Copner. (Videosonic Arts)

087 MISSION APOCALYPSE (1966). Editions 1-3.

OPEN HOUSE (1987). Routine slasher flick with routine gore murders when the Open House Killer—angered by rising costs of homes in Beverly Hills—slaughters sexy realtors and their clients. Joseph Bottoms portrays radio psychologist Dr. David Kelly, who hosts "The Survival Line," and the killer calls him up during a broadcast, drawing him and his girl, Adrienne Barbeau, into the mystery. Director Jag Mundhra handles the bloody murders well, spicing them up with kinky sex and nudity. Rudy Ramos, Mary Stavin. (Prism)

OPERA. See **TERROR AT THE OPERA.**

OPERATION ABDUCTION (1957). See editions 1-3.

OPERATION ATLANTIS (1962). See editions 1-3.

OPERATION COUNTERSPY (1965). James Bond pastiche (of Italian-Spanish-French origin) featuring death rays and a madman in command of a secret base bristling with superweapons. Directed by Nick Nostro. George A. Ardisson, Helen Chanel.

OPERATION FEAR. See **KILL, BABY, KILL.**

OPERATION KID BROTHER (1967). Sean Connery's kid brother, Neil Connery, pursues supercriminal Adolfo (THUNDERBALL) Celli, who controls an underground city, hypnotizes innocent people with an evil machine and plans to take over the world. Daniela (FROM RUSSIA WITH LOVE) Bianchi is the femme fatale, Bernard Lee is around as M, Lois Maxwell is Moneypenny and Anthony (MR. NO) Dawson is a hit man. Alberto De Martino directed. Also called OK CONNERY. (From Abacus and American Video as **SECRET AGENT 00**)

OPERATION MONSTERLAND. See **DESTROY ALL MONSTERS.**

OPERATION TOP SECRET (1964). See editions 1-3.

ORACLE, THE (1985). The spirit of a murdered businessman (Willliam Graham) is contained in an ancient form of Ouija board that seduces beautiful Caroline Capers Powers and causes her to see visions of his murder. Directed by Roberta Findlay. Roger Neil, Pam LaTesta, Victoria Dryden. (USA; IVE)

ORCA: THE KILLER WHALE (1977). To whales what JAWS was to sharks—but hardly a whale of a movie. Seafaring Richard Harris, after harpooning Orca's mate, is attacked by the superwhale, which also rams its snout into a seacoast town, almost sinking it. Touches of MOBY DICK don't do much to improve the silly story, nor do gratuitous touches of gore false to the nature of killer whales. Among potential whale bait are Bo Derek, Keenan Wynn, Charlotte Rampling and Will Sampson. Munchy munchy. Michael Anderson directed this in the wake of JAWS. (Video/Laser: Paramount)

ORGASMO. See **NIGHTMARE CASTLE.**

ORGASMO. See **PARANOIA.**

ORGIES OF DR. ORLOFF, THE (1966). Madman/aristocrat Howard Vernon invites his livng relatives to his crumbing estate because he hopes they will soon be his dead relatives. When the old guy is found knived to death, the invitees realize there is a serial killer within their midst. Written-produced-directed by Santos Alcocer. Maria Saavedra, Adolfo Arles, Tota Alba. Also known as ONLY A COFFIN.

ORGY OF THE BLOOD PARASITES. See **THEY CAME FROM WITHIN.**

ORGY OF THE DEAD (1965). Campy send-up of horror movies, but whether director A. C. Stephens knew that is debatable. Based on a novel by Edward Wood Jr., and said to be a loose sequel to PLAN 9 FROM OUTER SPACE, this hysterically funny anomaly is set in a cemetery where the Devil (Criswell) and Ghoulita (Fawn Silver) watch exotic dancers perform their stuff in the buff. Criswell and Silver are hilarious as they stumble through their lines and as a pair of innocent bystanders watch while tied to stakes. Also hanging around the graveyard are a mummy and a werewolf who crack jokes about Cleopatra. The dancers are lovely, making this nudie a girl watcher's delight. The color is good and the dry ice swirls dramatically. A must for Wood aficionados and flesh peddlers. (Rhino)

ORGY OF THE VAMPIRES (1972). Video version of **VAMPIRE'S NIGHT ORGY, THE** (Sinister/C; S/Weird).

ORGY OF THE VAMPIRES. See **ORGY OF THE DEAD.**

ORIGINAL FABULOUS ADVENTURES OF BARON MUNCHAUSEN, THE. Variant video/laser versions of **FABULOUS BARON MUNCHAUSEN, THE** (American Video) (Laser: Image).

ORIGINAL FLASH GORDON COLLECTION. Boxed set of four condensations of the FLASH GORDON serials under the titles SPACESHIP TO THE UNKNOWN, DEADLY RAY FROM MARS, PERIL FROM PLANET MONGO and PURPLE DEATH FROM OUTER SPACE. (Questar)

ORIGINAL GHOST BUSTERS. These Continental repackaged TV episodes of a 1975 failed series are described under **GHOST BUSTERS.**

ORLAK, THE HELL OF FRANKENSTEIN (1961). Mexican monster mayhem (and mirth?) from producer/director Rafael Baledon as a remote-controlled entity with a metal head and metal skeleton, created by the typical mad scientist (would you believe Dr. Carlos Frankenstein?), stomps through turn-of-the-century streets, committing revenge murders. Joaquin Cordero, Armando Calvo. (Sinister/C; Filmfax)

ORLOFF AGAINST THE INVISIBLE MAN (1970). Spanish horror thriller in which a nutty scientist creates an unseeable human who kidnaps his partner's daughter. Howard Vernon, Britt Carva. Directed by Pierre Chevalier. (From Wizard as **INVISIBLE DEAD, THE**)

ORPHAN, THE (1979). Mixed-up youth undergoes traumas as a prelude to graphic murders. Children shouldn't play with dead adults. John Ballard wrote-directed; allegedly inspired by Saki's short story "Sredni Vashtar." Mark Owens, Joanna Miles. (Rhino; Prism)

ORPHEUS (1949). Intriguing, baffling, perplexing, irritating, pleasing—all these describe French director Jean Cocteau's retelling of the ancient Greek legend of Orpheus, a dead poet who descended into Hell after being returned to life by a personification of Death. In this modernized version, Jean Marais portrays the poet and Maria Casares is the entrancing, mysterious woman in black. Rather than try to follow a coherent storyline, Cocteau chose a surreal approach with stark black-and-white photography and a range of special effects that are startling. This is a dizzying treat for the eye and the intellect, and a cinematic challenge for anyone who enjoys unusual film making. Music by Georges Auric. Francois Perier, Juliette Greco, Maria Dea. (Embassy; Video Yesteryear; Sinister/C; Sultan)

OSA (1985). Pointless MAD MAX ripoff, poorly written and stylelessly directed by Oleg Egorov. In a vague future society where water is a precious commodity, and anarchy rules in the desert, a gang of cutthroats led by Mr. Big murders a young girl's family. She grows up under the tutelage of "Trooper," who teaches her how to use a crossbow. The climax is a game to the death called Bird

Hunt. Kelly Lynch, Peter Walker, Etienne Chicot, Daniel Grimm. (HBO Cannon)

OSS 117—DOUBLE AGENT (1968). French-Italian spy antics with John Gavin as an agent wiping out assassins in the Mideast. Directed by Andre Hunebelle. Margaret Lee, Curt Jurgens, Luciana Paluzzi. Followed by two sequels: **OSS 117—MISSION FOR A KILLER** (1966), with superspy Frederick Stafford searching for a rare drug, and **OSS 117 TAKES A VACATION** (1969).

OTHER, THE (1972). Tom Tryon's best-selling novel with heavy religious symbolism is such an ingenious storytelling trick it is difficult to describe without giving away its jolting surprises. Under Robert Mulligan's direction, it unfolds on a Connecticut farm in 1935 and shows the strangest abnormal psychology in children since THE BAD SEED. In spite of visual gimmicks (Tryon adapted his novel), Mulligan never cheapens the story, only enhances it with his clever manipulations. We refuse to say anything else—except see it! Chris and Martin Udvaronky, Uta Hagen, Diana Muldaur, John Ritter, Victor French, Christopher Connelly. (CBS/Fox)

OTHER HELL, THE (1980). A blasphemous Italian slap at Catholicism, set in a nunnery where women are slaughtered by supernatural forces, the "work of the devil." But an ecclesiastical detective thinks it's a human murderer and investigates. Jesus, is he in for a surprise. Included are scenes of a dead body having its vagina ripped out, a child stabbed several times, a baby scalded in a cauldron of boiling water, and a priest knived in the groin at least twice. Sit all the way through this and you deserve a few Hail Marys and Amens. Directed by Stefan Oblowsky, who must never go to church on Sunday. Franca Stoppi, Carlo Demejo. (Vestron; Prism; Lettuce Entertain You)

OTHERS, THE (1957). TV version of Henry James' novella, THE TURN OF THE SCREW, with Sarah Churchill as the governess battling to save the lives of two children—or is the supernatural horror all in her imagination? Tommy Kirk, Geoffrey Toone.

OUANGA (1935). The title refers to a Haiti voodoo curse placed by a native priestess on the wife-to-be of a plantation owner. The sacrificial rites lead to a hexed climax. Aka CRIME OF VOODOO and DRUMS OF THE JUNGLE; remade as POCOMANIA. Produced-written-directed by George Terwilliger. Made in the Caribbean. Fredi Washington, Sheldon Leonard.

OUR MAN FLINT (1966). Wonderful spoof of the Bond spy genre with lanky, dapper James Coburn as Z.O.W.I.E. operative Derek Flint. He can control his body organs (oops, did we write that?), has a cigarette lighter with 83 functions (blow torch included) and possesses an astonishing knowledge of bouillabaisse. He pursues G.A.L.A.X.Y., an insidious gang controlling the weather via weird science. Lee J. Cobb is the bureau chief; Gila Golan is among the harem women who surround Flint. The sequel, IN LIKE FLINT, was an equally raucous success. Directed by Daniel Mann. Edward Mulhare, Benson Fong, Russ Conway, Rhys Williams. (Video/Laser: CBS/Fox)

OUR MOTHER'S HOUSE (1967). Mildly macabre British film, directed by cameraman Jack Clayton and written by Haya Harareet and Jeremy Brooks, in which five children growing up with an invalid mother are suddenly faced with caring for themselves. Keeping mom's death a secret is what gives this "children's" tale its bizarre twist—that and the way old dad (Dirk Bogarde) shows up at an inopportune moment. It is the suggested horrors that stand out, rather than the visuals. Pamela Franklin, Margaret Brooks, Mark Lester, Louis Sheldon Williams.

OUTER LIMITS, THE (1963-65). Superb sci-fi series of '60s TV remains famous for its excellent scripts (often structured as morality plays), eerie moods, alien and human monsters and compelling, oft-relevant themes—and only gets better with age, as does the "noir" cinematography of Conrad Hall. Individual one-hour episodes are on video by MGM/UA. (MGM/UA has two superb laser discs, each containing eight episodes.)

OUTER SPACE CONNECTION, THE (1975). Intriguing science speculation from IN SEARCH OF producer Alan Landsburg, in the vein of Erich Van Daniken but done with greater honesty. Written-directed by Fred Warshofsky, this suggests we have been visited in the distant past by aliens who left behind a stone laboratory-museum to which they will return in the next century. Fascinating theory, well thought out, with Rod Serling's voice to back it up. Persuasive. (United; VCI)

OUTER TOUCH (1979). Lowbrow British comedy about shapely women from outer space hunting down humans for their zoo of aliens back home. Directed by Norman J. Warren. Barry Stokes, Tony Maiden.

OUTING, THE (1985). See **SCREAM**.

OUTING, THE (1986). Nothing amusing about the Aladdin's Lamp in this low-budget quickie—it's inhabited by an ugly demon who exerts supernatural powers in OMEN-like revenge murders (spear impales man, rattlesnake crawls up man's trouser leg, cobra attacks woman in bathtub, man is broken in half). The Lamp is first taken from an Old Hag by crooks disposed of by green rays of death, then it goes into an anthropology museum. The murders occur when stupid teenagers have an all-night party (an "outing") in the museum. Fans will dig the gory murders but not groove so much on the demon-monster. Deborah Winters (also associate producer) plays the Old Hag as well as modern woman Eve Farrell. Written-produced by Warren Chaney, directed by Tom Daley. James Huston, Andra St. Ivanyi, Danny D. Daniels. (IVE)

OUTLAND (1981). Superbly crafted mystery-actioner from writer-director Peter Hyams which depicts a farflung world (lo, a moon of Jupiter) where Earthmen mine trinium. The full-scale interior sets are complex, the exterior models mind-boggling and the pace unrelenting as marshal Sean Connery tracks down a company conspiracy to feed its workmen a dangerous drug to improve their output. When Connery won't knuckle under, company boss Peter Boyle imports two hired gunmen. There's even swinging doors for those who want to compare this to HIGH NOON. Frances Sternhagen, James Sikking. (Video/Laser: Warner Bros.)

OUTLAWED PLANET, THE. See **DEMON PLANET.**

OUTLAW OF GOR (1987). Entertaining if corny sequel to GOR, continuing the adventures of Tarl Cabot (a square-jawed square played by Urbano Barberini) who, with a ruby-red magical ring, returns to the harsh, sandy world where Xenos the high priest (Jack Palance) rules with bitchy Lara (Donna Denton). Before you can plunge a sword into the nearest guard, she's usurped the throne, Cabot is her avowed enemy and she's thrown Cabot's beautiful love Talena (Rebecca Ferrati) into the dungeon. Cabot, his stupid friend Watney (Russel Savadier) and the dwarf Hup (Nigel Chipps) fight back. Denton steals the show with her hysterical portrayal of a totally evil bitch-queen, while Palance brings little conviction to his role (being stuck with dialogue by Rick Marx and Peter Welbeck, who adapted the novels by John Norman). Director John "Bud" Cardos holds it all together rather well. (Warner Bros.)

OUTLAWS (1986). Above-average TV-movie blending time travel and the traditional Western. Outside Houston, Texas, in 1899, an outlaw gang is trapped by lawman John Grail (Rod Taylor), and just as the shoot-out begins, a bolt of electricity propels them into the 1980s, where they learn the ways of modern man without giving up their own code of the West. The parable element of Nicholas Corea's script is well done, and the characters (William Lucking, Charles Napier, Patrick Houser, Richard Roundtree) appealing. Director Peter Werner permits the action to get wild and woolly.

OUT OF SIGHT, OUT OF MIND (1989). Horror director Greydon Clark is back with a tale of the Kabuki Killer and how this antisocial guy terrorizes Susan Blakely after he burns her daughter alive. Wings Hauser plays Blakely's husband and Edward Albert is the cop. Lynn-Holly Johnson, Richard Masur. (Prism) (Laser: Image)

OUT OF THE BODY (1988). In Sydney, Australia, a killer is knocking off beautiful women and removing their eyeballs. Musician Mark Hembrow foresees the crimes but police won't believe him. Turns out there's more than meets the eyes—a supernatural monster is afoot. Directed by Brian Trenchard-Smith. Tessa Humphries, Carrie Zivetz, Shane Briant. (Sony) (Laser: Image)

OUT OF THE DARK (1989). An office of young women (call girls?) who specialize in faked orgasms on the phone for a "sex talk" business, Suite Nothings (the boss is Karen Black), becomes target for a pervert who dresses as Bobo the Clown and bludgeons or strangles the cuties. The issue this movie raises—do sex-by-phone businesses contribute to the sickness of America?—is never touched on, only exploited with smutty talk. Director Michael Schroeder treats OUT OF THE DARK, red herrings and all, as a cheapo slasher flick. Paul Bartel makes a cameo appearance along with Tab Hunter, Divine and Geoffrey Lewis. Black has little to do but look worried and scream—a waste of her talents. Also wasted is Bud Cort as a suspect. Sorry, but we kept hearing a wrong number on this one. A lot of Suite Nothings in our ear? Cameron Dye, Lynn Danielson, Starr Andreeff. (Video/Laser: RCA/Columbia)

OUT OF THE DARKNESS. See **TEENAGE CAVEMAN.**

OUT OF THE DARKNESS (1985). British supernatural tale set in an English village where three youths see the ghost of a child who died in the 17th Century Plague. They set out to learn the town's history and free it of the unhappy spirit. Written-directed by John Krish. Garry Halliday, Michael Flowers.

OUT OF THIS WORLD (1954). See **ROCKY JONES, SPACE RANGER.**

OUT OF TIME (1988). Light-spirited, sometimes satirical TV-movie in the vein of BACK TO THE FUTURE, in which future cop Bruce Abbott, tracking a criminal in the year 2088, is transported to modern times in the time-chopper of baddie Adam Ant. He meets his silly great-grandfather (Bill Maher) and begins to shape his ancestor's future as a great cop-hero and inventor. Robert Butler directed in typical TV stlye, with the time-travel effects being a shaky, out-of-focus picture. Did they run out of time on the set? Leo Rossi, Kristan Alfonso.

OUT ON A LIMB (1987). What's a true story doing in this book? It's Shirley MacLaine's search for identity via reincarnation, UFOs, astral travel and E.T. communication, as she described them in her best-selling book, adapted to TV as a five-hour movie. Only during the last two hours, when Shirley reaches Peru and undergoes mysticism and ESP phenomena, does this become fascinating. Well-intended by producer co-writer Colin Higgins and director Robert Butler. Charles Dance, John Heard, Anne Jackson. (Laser: Japanese)

ON 'LIMITS'

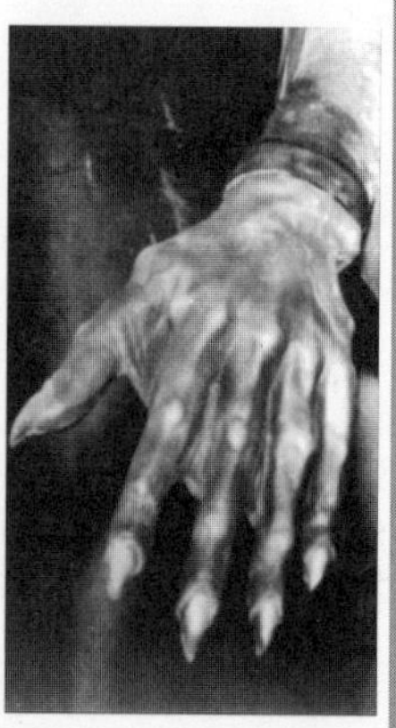

For two seasons (1963-64) 'The Outer Limits' presented some of the best science-fiction stories ever written for television, with almost every show featuring an alien or humanoid monster. Conceived by Leslie Stevens, the series is now considered a classic, with most of the episodes available on videocassette.

OUTRAGE, THE (1964). Remake of the Japanese classic RASHOMON, reshaped into a Western by director Martin Ritt, but a pretentious misfire, overacted by Paul Newman as a greasy Mexican bandit who may have raped a woman and murdered her husband. The same story is told from different points of view with an Indian witch doctor spinning the dead man's side from beyond the grave. Heavy-handed outrage against Japan's Akira Kurosawa. Others who overact are Clair Bloom as the wife, Laurence Harvey as the husband and William Shatner as the disillusioned priest. Faring better are Howard Da Silva as the narrator and Edward G. Robinson as the philosophical peddler who best understands the dark side of human nature.

OUTWARD BOUND (1930). Despite its creaking timbers, this early Warner Bros. talkie (based on a Sutton Vane play) is a compelling message movie about a strange ship that carries passengers to the Afterlife, where "Heaven and Hell are the same place." An Examiner comes aboard to critique the virtues of each passenger, and summerize his or her usefulness (or uselessness). This was directed by Robert Milton in a style of murkiness that was partially intended and partially provided by inferior filming techniques and film stocks. The story was later reused as anti-Nazi propaganda in the 1944 remake BETWEEN TWO WORLDS. Leslie Howard, Douglas Fairbanks Jr., Helen Chandler, Beryl Mercer, Alec B. Francis, Montagu Love.

OVAL PORTRAIT, THE (1972). Wanda Hendrix, Gisele MacKenzie and Barry Coe star in this TV-movie about a woman possessed by a woman's soul trapped in a painting. Based on an Edgar Allan Poe story, it's set during the Civil War. Directed by Rogelio Gonzales Jr. (Platinum Productions; Front Row; Tenth Avenue)

OVERDRAWN AT THE MEMORY BANK (1983). Good sci-fi tale based on a John Varley story set in a Big Brother society ruled by a giant corporation, Novicorp. Raul Julia stars as Aram Fingal, a "processor third class" who discovers the existence of movies and projects himself into a new reality based on CASABLANCA. Julia does a fair impression of Bogart as Rick Blaine but the key to this story is the clever use of dual universes and alternate realities as programmer Linda Griffiths (as Appolonia James) helps Fingal (1) restore his true identity and (2) overcome the dictatorial Mr. Big, who takes on the persona of Sydney Greenstreet from CASABLANCA. Director Douglas Williams does a remarkable job, given his limited budget. Wanda Cannon, Donald C. Moore, Louis Negin, Jackie Burroughs, Maury Chaykin. (Starmaker/New World) (Laser: Image)

OVERLORDS OF THE UFO (1976). Subtitled a "Scientific News Documentary," this purports farfetched, unconvincing theories as if they were irrefutable fact. Did you know that all those UFOs, or flying saucers, we've been observing all these years are from another dimension? Yeah, they're called Estranians. Quick, call the National Inquirer. And while you're at it, have writer-producer-advisor W. Gordon Allen investigated by a bunco squad. The details of several real-life UFO cases are given, and there is footage of Uri Geller bending keys, but what this has to do with the "Overlords" is vague.

OVERSEXED (1974). Dr. Shirley Jekyll mixes a formula that turns her into Ms Sherry Hyde, thereby doubling her need for sexual encounters of the closest kind and breaking the snaps on her now-undersized bra. Veronica Parrish stars for director-writer Joe Sarno, a filmmaker with a cult following. Undernourished.

PACK, THE (1977). Schweinhund of dog-slasher movies as psychopoodles, demonic dachshunds, terror terriers and horror hounds seek human hydrants. A "We're surrounded and got to find a way out" plot with Joe Don Baker as chief canine-kicker. Robert Clouse wrote-directed. Dogs' "worst enemies" are R. G. Armstrong, Richard B. Shull, Richard O'Brien, Hope Alexander-Willis. Also known in some pounds as KILLERS WHO WORE COLLARS—heh heh, just kidding. Aka THE LONG DARK NIGHT. (Warner Bros.; Vestron)

PAJAMA PARTY (1964). Beach-and-bikini exploitationer seemed a shambers when it was first made, but a sense of nutty nostalgia now hangs over it— and a sense of innocence about its tomfoolery. Tommy Kirk plays a Martian who lands on Earth to discover the teen cult of parties and rock 'n roll music and fall for Annette Funicello, while former stars frolic in the strangest roles of their careers: Elsa Lanchester, Buster Keaton, Dorothy Lamour, Harvey Lembeck, Jesse White, Susan Hart. Don Weis directed. (Warner Bros.; Trylon)

PALE BLOOD (1990). Offbeat, stylized vampire thriller with clever twists and a bravura performance by Wings Hauser. The Hong Kong team of writer Takashi Matsuoka and director V.V. Dachin Hsu have concocted a vampire named Michael Fury (George Chakiris), hired to solve the "Vampire Killer" murders. Chakiris, his face pale and drawn, is sinister in his antiheroic role as a supernatural entity. Ultimately, though, it is Hauser's vampire hunter and his maniacal acting that sets this apart. Pamela Ludwig, Diana Frank, Darcy DeMoss. (Video/Laser: RCA/Columbia)

PALE RIDER (1985). Clint Eastwood first played a weird western gunfighter who turned out to be a ghost in HIGH PLAINS DRIFTER. Here he repeats the idea as The Preacher, a spectral-like, mythical stranger who rides out of nowhere to help gold miners fight the encroachment of a mining baron. Writers Dennis Shryack and Michael Butler turn the idea of Death Personified into a heavy-handed affair, unnecessarily symbolic and metaphysical, but Eastwood's powers as a charismatic actor make this a viewing pleasure. John Russell, Michael Moriarty, Carrie Snodgress, Christopher Penn, Richard Drysart, Richard Kiel. Eastwood produced and directed. (Video/Laser: Warner Bros.)

PANDA AND THE MAGIC SERPENT (1958). Ancient Chinese fairy tale, made by the Japanese, depicts the animated adventures of a cute furry animal, a Dragon God and an immortal serpent, The White Snake Enchantress. Narrated by Marvin Miller. Directed by Taiji Yabushita and Kazuhiko Okabe. (Family Home Entertainment; Video Yesteryear)

PANDEMONIUM (1982). This now seems one of the funniest of the FRIDAY THE 13TH parodies that came in that film's wake. A Jason-styled killer, who skewered five girls on a long-long spear in 1963, is back in black stalking the ridiculous men and women undergoing cheerleader training at It Had to Be U. An AIRPLANE-like compendium of parodies and sketches, in which Debralee Scott, Carol Kane and Candy Azzara are subjected to nonsense. The film sparkles with surprise cameos by Tom Smothers, Pee-wee Herman, Tab Hunter, Kaye Ballard, Donald O'Connor and Eve Arden. Enough of the hodgepodge works thanks to the polished direction of Alfred Sole. Originally produced as THURSDAY THE 12TH. (MGM/UA)

PANDORA AND THE FLYING DUTCHMAN (1952). Modern look at the ancient legend: James Mason is skipper of the Flying Dutchman, doomed to sail the seas until he finds a woman willing to die for him. He pursues Ava Gardner, certainly a woman any man would die for. Jack Cardiff's Mediterranean footage is beautiful in color. Written-directed by Albert Lewin. Nigel Patrick, Sheila Sim, Marius Goring.

PANDORA'S BOX (1928). Silent-screen classic from German director G. W. Pabst is worth mentioning because Jack the Ripper becomes a key figure in the life of a beautiful young woman (Louise Brooks) who drifts into prostitution as she craves the decadent life. (Embassy; Sultan; Video Dimensions)

PANGA. See **CURSE III: BLOOD SACRIFICE, THE.**

PANIC (1960. See **TELL-TALE HEART, THE.**

PANIC (1976). Italian flicker, set in Great Britain, is an old-fashioned "Frankenstein on the Loose" plot in which a professor, experimenting in bacteriological warfare, discovers a vaccine, has an accident and emerges a monster with a body that bleeds and a bloated face stripped of flesh. "The Plurima Plan" has backfired and it's up to hero and heroine to prevent a panic in the town under quarantine, and to discover an antidote. Directed by Giovanni Bergamini. David Warbeck, Janet Agren, Frank Ressel. (Gorgon/MPI)

PANIC AT LAKEWOOD MANOR. See **IT HAPPENED AT LAKEWOOD MANOR**.

PANIC IN THE CITY (1967). No-nonsense low-budget feature, shot on L.A. streets, moves fast under Eddie Davis' direction as federal agent Howard Duff tracks down an A-bomb being built by a demented Soviet agent. Semidocumentary approach helps gloss over story holes and Paul Dunlap's music heightens tension. Stephen McNally is a straightfaced assignment chief, Linda Cristal is a radiation expert and Nehemiah Persoff goes bonkers as the crazed Ruskie. Anne Jeffries and Dennis Hopper have limited spy roles.

PANIC IN THE TRANS-SIBERIAN TRAIN. See **HORROR EXPRESS.**

PANIC IN THE WILDERNESS (1975). Bigfoot-type monstrosity decides it's feeding time and goes on a rampage in the Canadian Northwest while human beings wonder what that strange thing is over there behind that clump of trees. The only panic this film caused was audiences scampering for exit doors.

PANIC IN YEAR ZERO (1962). Hydrogen holocaust is upon us and so is anarchy—rape, murder and other human reactions to Armageddon. A family fights off pillagers and rapists to survive. Cheap production values, a vague screenplay and the indifferent direction by Ray Milland (who also portrays Harry Baldwin, average father) make this a weak end-of-civilization yarn. When a doctor comments: "If we scrape the scabs off, and apply disinfectant, civilization might recover," one wishes American-International had applied disinfectant to the script's botched complexion. Milland's family: Jean Hagen, Mary Mitchell, Frankie Avalon. (Fright)

PANIC ON THE AIR (1936). See third edition.

PANIC STATION (1986). Two scientists at a satellite research installation begin to hallucinate. Also known as THE PLAINS OF HEAVEN. Richard Moir, Reg Evans, Gerard Kennedy. Directed by Ian Pringle. (Academy)

PANTHER GIRL OF THE KONGO (1955). One of the last of the cliffhangers from Republic, and only a shadow of the great '40s serials. After realizing how good Phyllis Coates looked in khaki shorts and tight blouse in JUNGLE DRUMS OF AFRICA, she was cast in the Nyoka mold as an African adventurer. But Coates performed without emotion and it's a poorly produced serial. Her adversary is Dr. Morgan (Arthur Space) who turns crawfish into monsters, and uses these mutations to chase away African natives from a diamond mine. The serial, inspired by THEM, is salvaged by Myron Healey as great white hunter Larry Sanders. When seen as 12 chapters there's a certain inept charm that makes you want to forgive director Franklin Adreon and writer Ronald Davidson. Not a lot, just a little. Archie Savage, Mike Ragan. Feature version: THE CLAW MONSTERS. (Video/Laser: Republic)

PANTHER SQUAD (1986). Substandard action flick starring Sybil Danning as a female Rambo who leads scantily clad warrioresses against Clean Space, an ecological group preventing space exploration. All the demure Sybil shows off is her disintegrator zapgun; she doesn't give us a modicum of titillation as her HotPants gang knocks the heck out of the baddies. Her fans will weep as they dream of her lavish figure hidden beneath the fatigues, and will cry additional tears about how poorly this was directed by Peter Knight. (Lightning)

PAPERHOUSE (1987). Poignant psychological fantasy about a 11-year-old (Charlotte Burke) who escapes her unhappy world by dreaming herself into her drawings. Burke finds herself on a windy coastline in front of a strange house and meets a young boy—she also encounters her worst fears in a frightening horror sequence. But basically this is about her internal struggles to find herself, to reconcile her differences with her parents (Glenne Headly and Ben Cross) and to discover first-time love with the boy (Elliott Spiers). The excellent script by Mathew Jacobs was adapted from a Catherine Starr novel. (Vestron) (Laser: Image)

PAPER MAN (1971). The deaths of three college students appear to be caused by a computer intelligence. Solution to the mystery is more mundane but early portions of this TV-movie have eerie qualities. Directed by Walter Grauman. Dean Stockwell, Stephanie Powers, James Stacy, James Olson, Ross Elliott. (Xenon)

PARADISIO (1962). Arthur Howard (brother of British actor Leslie Howard) possesses eyeglasses that see through clothing in this British "nudie," for which audiences wore 3-D glasses. Even though Pop Howard raises his eyebrows, this remains lowbrow stuff. Sample: He visits the Louvre, looks at Goya's painting and sees the Maja stripped. A serpent is in PARADISIO. (New World; S/Weird; Video Dimensions)

PARALLEL CORPSE (1983). Mortuary workman sucks up blood from bodies but also tries to suck money out of a serial murderer after the attendant finds a victim in one of his coffins. Now the killer better coffin up the cash. Buster Larsen, Agenta Eikmanner. (Media)

PARANOIA (1969). Italian-French shocker with Carroll Baker as a woman undergoing psychological terror. Director Umberto Lenzi throws in plenty of sizzling sex. Lou Castel, Tino Carraro. Also called ORGASMO and A QUIET PLACE TO KILL. (Spotlite; Republic; Unicorn)

PARANOIAC (1963). Despite Jimmy Sangster's clever plot, this Hammer mystery is dull, lacking the wallops of a good psychological terror film. Oliver Reed, who killed his brother, is stunned when the brother returns alive. Things get tricky after that, so pay attention. Janette Scott, Alexander Davion, Maurice Denham.

PARASITE (1982). Released to theaters in 3-D, this low-budget sci-fi/horror cheapie takes place in a post-Armageddon world where men are equipped with laser guns. A monster runs around burrowing into people and leaping at the camera. Stan Winston's creature effects are average, the gore is gratuitous. The stuff wrapped around the violence is lethargic as Robert Glaudini discovers there's a worm in his abdomen that could spread to mankind. Produced-directed by Charles Band. Of passing interest, perhaps, as one of Demi Moore's first films. Luca Bercovici, Cherie Currie. (Wizard; Paramount; Embassy) (Laser: Shadow)

PARASITE MURDERS, THE. See **THEY CAME FROM WITHIN** (Intestional subterfuge required).

PARDON ME, BUT YOUR TEETH ARE IN MY NECK. See **FEARLESS VAMPIRE KILLERS, THE.**

PARENTS (1989). This stark, disturbing suburbia psychological horror tale set in the atomic-age of the 1950s can be viewed in three ways: (1) as a grim study of a youth who discovers his parents are cannibals; (2) as a hallucination of a manic depressive child who only imagines the meat on the table is human flesh; (3) as a metaphor for the childhood trauma many go through when well-meaning parents force some awful food down their throats. Director Bob Balaban has done a good job of delivering the goods in Christopher Hawthorne's script. Superb as the Laemle family are Randy Quaid, Mary Beth Hurt and Bryan Madorsky; the latter goes through the film without a single change of expression, and yet reflects the script's needs. Sandy Dennis is good as a flighty psychologist. Graham Jarvis, Juno Mills-Cockett, Kathryn Grody. (Vestron) (Laser: Image)

PARIS PLAYBOYS (1954). Idiot's delight! The Bowery Boys, in the French capital, fight over ownership of a sour cream that doubles as an explosive. TNT for your complexion? The cast got creamed on this one: Leo Gorcey, Huntz Hall and dem udder East Side dopes. How about a sour cream pie for director William Beaudine? He's simply Eiffel.

PARTS—THE CLONUS HORROR. Video version of **CLONUS HORROR, THE** (Catalina).

PASSING CLOUDS. See **SPELLBOUND (1940).**

PASSING OF THE THIRD FLOOR BACK, THE (1936). Strange British allegory, directed by Berthold Viertel, in which a Jesus Christ figure appears on Christmas Eve to help boarding house roomers. Conrad Veidt, Anna Lee, Cathleen Nesbitt. (Sinister/C)

PASSION FLOWER HOTEL. See **BOARDING HOUSE.**

PASSPORT TO DESTINY (1944). Charwoman Elsa Lanchester in a World War II fantasy: She stalks Adolf Hitler, aided by a magical ring which protects her from the Gestapo and SS. A curiosity piece you might enjoy for its outbursts of blatant propaganda. Directed by Ray McCarey. Gordon Oliver, Lenore Aubert, Lionel Royce.

PASSPORT TO HELL (1964). See third edition.

PATHOS. See **OBSESSION: A TASTE FOR FEAR.**

PATRICK (1978). Australian import directed by Richard Franklin, a Hitchcock aficionado who went on to direct ROADGAMES and PSYCHO II. Patrick (Robert Thompson) is a psychotic nerd who murders his mother and lover, then slides into a comatose state to become a "living dead man" used as a guinea pig in a neurologist's research. Patrick develops powers of psychokinesis and terrorizes, in cat-and-mouse style, nurse Susan Penhaligon and hospital staff. Familiar material is given an attractive edge by Franklin's direction and the hip script by Everett De Roche. Music by Brian May. Robert Helpmann, Julia Blake, Rod Mullinar. (Unicorn; Vestron; Harmonyvision; Magnum)

PATRICK IS STILL ALIVE (1980). This Italian sequel to Richard Franklin's PATRICK depicts that bedridden psychotic nerd still in bed and making trouble by picking up evil vibrations from criminals and turning them into psychokinesis projections. Directed by Mario Landi with emphasis on gore. Sascha Pitoeff, Gianni Dei, Carmen Russo.

PATRICK STILL LIVES. See **PATRICK IS STILL ALIVE.**

PEACE GAME, THE. See **GLADIATORS, THE.**

PEACEMAKER (1990). Sci-fi action in which two humanoid aliens end up on Earth fighting it out—each claiming to be the good "lawman." Figuring out which is which is no fun the way writer-director Kevin S. Tenney has it laid out. The aliens crash through windows, leap over walls, fall through trees, crash cars, trucks and bikes, shoot at each other with pistols, rifles, shotguns and submachine guns, and sock each other on the jaw repeatedly. But since they can rejuvenate themselves, so what? You'd think one of them would figure out a way to kill the other. Robert Forster and Lance Edwards (the latter talking like a Russian) run all over L.A. with medical examiner Hilary Shepard. Seems the aliens got to Earth through a Black Hole. They should send this movie back through it. (Charles Fries) (Laser: Image)

PEANUT BUTTER SOLUTION, THE (1985). Canadian children's movie will be of limited interest to anyone since it is bereft of excitement or humor. A youngster visiting the ruins of a burnt-out house sees something so horrific that his hair falls out. Later, he's visited by a dead wino and told to rub an ointment into his hair made of flies, kitty litter and peanut butter. His hair grows all right—down to his waist. Writer-director Michael Rubbo tries to make it a cute package but this movie sticks to the roof of your mouth. Mathew Mackay, Alison Podbrey, Michael Hogan. (New World)

PEARL OF DEATH (1944). Sherlock Holmes feature in the Basil Rathbone-Nigel Bruce Universal series, featuring Rondo Hatton as "The Creeper," a character whose origins are detailed in THE BRUTE MAN. Updated Holmesian adventure, above average for the series, based on Arthur Conan Doyle's "The Adventure of the Six Napoleons." Evelyn Ankers, Dennis Hooey, Ian Wolfe. Directed by Roy William Neill. (CBS/Fox)

PEEPING TOM (1960). Director Michael Powell's unrelenting portrait of a psychopathic young man (who photographs the women he murders with a 16mm camera) was ahead of its time and resulted in Powell's ostracism from Britain's film industry. "Shovel it up and flush it down the sewer," wrote one critic. Yet this has no blood or gore, maintaining an implicit viewpoint toward sex and violence. What disturbed Powell's contemporaries was Leo Marks' screenplay focusing on sexual perversion through metaphor and symbolism. Thus, the film asks viewers to become voyeurs and this evoked negative response. Carl Boehm is superb as the filmmaker. Moira Shearer, Anna Massey, Shirley Anne Field. (Admit One) (Laser: Image)

PEGGY SUE GOT MARRIED (1986). Unusually sensitive love story that uses time travel as a device for Kathleen Turner, portraying an unhappily married housewife, to return to her teen years, ready to rectify the mistakes of her future. But the men she thinks she would prefer all turn out to be less than perfect, and her boyfriend (husband to be) drives her onto the horns of a dilemma. Beautifully directed by Francis Ford Coppola, with fine supporting roles by Nicolas Cage, Leon Ames and Don Murray. Turner portrays her character in the past bereft of make-up. (Video/Laser: CBS/Fox)

PENALTY OF DEATH. See **VIOLENT BLOOD BATH.**

PENETRATION (1976). Re-edited x-rated version of the Italian feature THE SLASHER . . . IS THE SEX MANIAC with new pornographic footage of Tina Russell and Harry Reems. Farley Granger, who plays a policeman, must have been mortified.

PENTAGRAM. See **FIRST POWER, THE.**

PENTHOUSE, THE (1989). Minor horrific overtones tinge this suspense TV-movie in which Robin Givens, daughter of wealthy record producer Robert Guillaume, is trapped in her apartment with a childhood friend who just escaped from an asylum. What makes this interesting is that Givens doesn't want the boy hurt, handicapping the police. Thus, the script by Frank Defelitta and William Wood (based on an Ellston Trevor novel) creates sympathy for the villain, etched in pain and madness by David Hewlett. David Greene directed in a slick, clean style. Donnelly Rhodes, Cedric Smith. (Turner)

PEOPLE, THE (1972). Sensitive adaptation of Zenna Henderson's morality parables about humanoids stranded on Earth, living in an isolated rural community. Their dormant telepathic and levitation abilities are reactivated with the help of new schoolteacher Kim Darby, who gains their trust along with doctor William Shatner. John Korty directs this offbeat Francis Ford Coppola TV production with a gentle, poetic touch. Dan O'Herlihy, Laurie Walters, Diane Varsi. (Prism)

PEOPLE ACROSS THE LAKE, THE (1988). Contrived TV-movie benefits from photography in the wilderness around Vancouver, but takes a beating in the story department because of a suspenseless, telegraphed plot. Fed up with the big city, stockbroker Gerald McRaney and wife Valerie Harper take the kids to an isolated house on a lonely lake, where dead bodies are turning up and an unknown presence stalks the woods with homicidal intent. This suffers from obvious characters and cliche situations, out of which not even Barry Corbin (as a deranged country boy) can salvage anything. Tammy Lauren, Jeff Kizer.

PEOPLE THAT TIME FORGOT, THE (1977). Third in a series of Edgar Rice Burroughs adventures—the others are LAND THAT TIME FORGOT and AT THE EARTH'S CORE. Patrick Wayne and explorers find Doug McClure (star of the previous adaptations) in a kingdom of dinosaurs, pterodactyls and Neanderthal brutes. The effects (mechanized mock-ups) aren't al-

"Somebody look under his jacket. See if he's got a blue suit with a red S on his chest. I think we just killed Clark Kent."

—A policeman in **PEACEMAKER**

ways convincing, but a spirit of adventure makes up for shortcomings. Directed by Kevin Connor. Dana Gillespie, Thorley Walters, Sarah Douglas, David Prowse. Fourth in the series: WARLORDS OF ATLANTIS. (Embassy)

PEOPLETOYS. See **DEVIL TIMES FIVE.**

PEOPLE UNDER THE STAIRS, THE (1991). Satisfying romp through a house of horrors—one of writer-director Wes Craven's best efforts. It's an unusual horror fairy-tale about a black youth (Brandon Adams) who, because his mother needs an operation, breaks into his landlord's home to steal gold coins. But the mansion is inhabited by a homicidal husband-wife team, zombies kept in a dungeon, a killer rottweiler, trapdoors, secret corridors with death traps, a kitchen of cannibal terror and a pit of corpses. The violence and ghastliness is counterbalanced by humorous portrayals of the adult killers by Everet McGill (he runs around in a black leather outfit, blasting everything with a shotgun) and Wendy Robie, who insists they say their prayers before retiring. This avoids the moral ambiguities of Craven's earlier works and has a whimsical conclusion to its subplot about poor ghetto conditions. Ving Rhames, A. J. Langer, Sean Whalen. (Video/Laser: MCA)

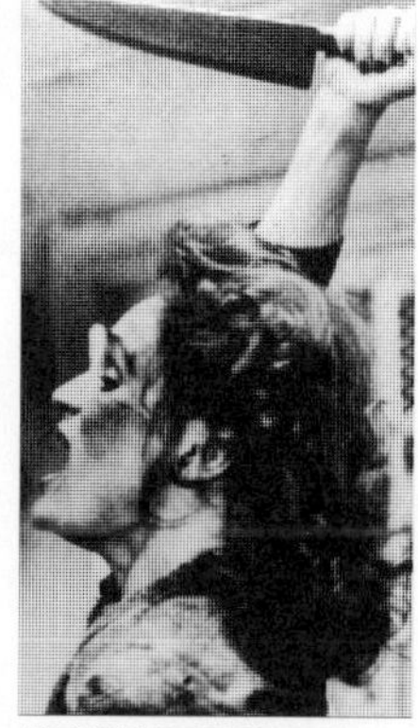

WENDY ROBIE

PEOPLE WHO OWN THE DARK, THE (1975). Spanish end-of-the-world thriller directed by Leon Klimovsky and starring Maria Perschy, Tony Kendall and Paul Naschy as members of a Marquis De Sade coven who are saved from an atomic blast but then fight senselessly among themselves. These folks are welcome to all the dark they can get. Don't sit in it with them. (Sun; Star Classics)

PERCY (1971). Would you believe the first male sex organ transplant? Performed by that stiff-mannered, upright surgeon Sir Emmanuel Whitbread? Smutty British joke, erected from a novel by Raymond Hitchcock and inserted into a screenplay by Hugh Leonard. Director Hywel Bennett tries to pump energy into this flaccid project, but it's limp. There isn't even a climax, offhand. Oh, the film has spurts but suffers from self-abuse and withdrawal symptons as Denholm Elliott, Elke Sommer and Britt Ekland end up rubbing you the wrong way. In the final analysis, sterile and impotent. Call it emasculated. But don't call it irresistible.

PERCY'S PROGRESS. See **IT'S NOT THE SIZE THAT COUNTS.**)

PERFECT BRIDE (1990). Female counterpart to Terry O'Quinn's "stepfather" is essayed by Sammi Davis as she goes from family to family, killing those who suspect she's a murderess with a hypo. John Agar, Kelly Preston. Directed by Terrence O'Hara. (Media)

PERFECT VICTIMS (1988). Originally made as HIDDEN RAGE, this presents a serial killer who has AIDS and is out to humiliate and kill women. His first targets are two models whom he drugs and rapes. Then this demented guy goes after the models' boss, a beautiful woman with a boyfriend who owns a Malibu mansion, and in his spare time sets fire to a guy and knives a woman in the belly. The cop on the case is Clarence Williams III. While the Academy video retains the AIDS angle, the TV version drops it completely so it appears the guy is just another slasher killer. Whichever way you see it, PERFECT VICTIMS is undistinguished. Leading lady Deborah Sheldon was also exec producer and director Shuki Levy also wrote the music. Lyman Ward, Tom Dugan, Nikolete Scorsese. John Agar appears briefly as a neighbor walking his dog. (Academy)

PERFECT WOMAN, THE (1950). British comedy (based on a play by Wallace Geoffrey and Basil Mitchell, scripted by producer George Black and director Bernard Knowles) is heavy-handed and its robotic concept hopelessly clanking. An inventor creates a flawless female amidst belabored situations. Stanley Holloway, Patricia Roc, Nigel Patrick.

PERIL FROM THE PLANET MONGO. Re-edited footage of **FLASH GORDON CONQUERS THE UNIVERSE** (Questar).

PERILS OF GWENDOLINE: IN THE LAND OF THE YIK YAK (1985). Tongue-in-cheek erotic-bondage adventure based on the lesbian-oriented French comic strip by John Willie, with director Just Jaeckin adding Indiana Jones touches. This light-hearted male fantasy has happy-go-lucky Brent Huff reluctantly leading Tawny Kitaen into jungle dangers to find her father and a priceless butterfly. The Kiop kingdom of cannibals and a Forbidden City of breast-plated (ha ha!) beauties pulling chariots are among the points of interest, not to mention the two naked points on most of the women in the cast. Filmed in the Philippines. (Video/Laser: Vestron)

PERILS OF NYOKA. See **NYOKA AND THE TIGERMEN.**

PERILS OF PAULINE, THE (1967). Tedious, unfunny Universal TV-movie comedy makes satiric sport of Pauline White, serial queen of the 1910s, by depicting Pamela Austin in states of undress, suspended animation and assorted disarray. Belabored effort is unbecoming to Pat Boone and Terry-Thomas. Directed by Leonard and Joshua Shelley. Edward Everett Horton, Hamilton Camp, Kurt Kazner.

PERSECUTION. Video version of **TERROR OF SHEBA** (Electric).

PERSEUS THE INVINCIBLE. See **MEDUSA VS. THE SON OF HERCULES.**

PERSONALS (1990). This TV-movie is notable for the performance of Jennifer O'Neill as a homicidal knife killer (her blade is enscribed with "Aloha") who performs her misdeeds in a blonde wig with a cool detachment made all the more terrifying by her sexuality and beauty. Unfortunately for O'Neill, who is suffering from a mother problem, one of her victims is a writer doing a story on lonely women and the man's wife (Stephanie Zimbalist) decides to avenge his death. Has twists that make it above average. Directed by Steven H. Stern. Robin Thomas, Gina Gallego, Rosemary Dunsmore. (Video/Laser: Paramount)

PESTICIDE (1978). Heavy-handed horror flick from France's Jean Rollins with plenty of graphic bloodletting visuals (gore to you) when a young woman (Marie-Georges Pascal) discovers that the spray on vineyards is turning folks into shambling zombie monsters. Serge Marquand, Patricia Cartier, Felix Marten.

PETER CUSHING: A ONE-WAY TICKET TO HOLLYWOOD (1988). British TV documentary about the famed British horror-film actor, with Cushing discussing his career. Directed by Alan Bell. (Blood Times)

PETER IBBETSON (1935). Old-fashioned romanticized fantasy in which imprisoned 19th Century convict Gary Cooper dreams himself into a virtual reality where he is joined by his lover Ann Harding to escape the squalor and unhappiness of their existences. A special-effects avalanche was unique for its time. Good production values and direction by Henry Hathaway make bearable a theme that today seems totally corny. Ida Lupino, Dickie Moore.

PETER PAN (1953). J. M. Barrie's fantasy about a fairy who leads two children into a Never Never Land inhabited by Captain Hook is a Pan-of-gold, a Disney animation masterpiece. Voices by Bobby Driscoll, Hans Conried, Heather Angel, Tom Conway, Stan Freberg, Kathryn Beaumont. Highlights are Tinker Bell, an imp surrounded by a twinkle of light, reckless redskins who wage war on lost human boys and a crocodile hungry for Hook. (Video/Laser: Disney)

PETER PAN (1960). Video rerelease of an NBC-TV production starring Mary Martin in the role she made famous on Broadway; a highly recommended version of J.M. Barrie's fantasy. (Goodtimes) (Laser: Image)

PETE'S DRAGON (1977). Superb Disney musical-comedy blending live action and animation to tell the hilarious saga of Elliott the Dragon, a fire-breather from Fantasy World, on Earth to help children in trouble. He flies, turns invisible and has a sense of humor, snarling at disbelievers and throwing frightening shadows on walls. His lovability ultimately wins you over. Elliott meets 9-year-old Pete (Sean Marshall), a runaway pursued by the nasty Gogans. Setting is Passamaquoddy, where lighthouse keeper Mickey Rooney and daughter Helen Reddy befriend the boy and dragon. Jim Dale pops up as a medicine show man, Dr. Terminus, with Red Buttons as his assistant, Hoagy. Shelley Winters is grotesquely hilarious as Ma Gogan. Don Chaffey directed with a masterful touch. Jim Backus, Jane Kean, Jeff Conaway. (Video/Laser: Disney)

PET SEMATARY (1989). Based on one of Stephen King's most intriguing novels, this is a film rooted in pessimism, and so dark in its statement about life that one comes away with a deep sense of dread. It is set in a landscape of evil where an old Indian burial ground restores life to anything buried in it, and at no time does director Mary Lambert allow a ray of hope to penetrate the doom-laden atmosphere. Its plot roots are borrowed from W. F. Jacob's "The Monkey's Paw," but King (who wrote the screenplay too) imbues it with his own unique vision. The story revolves around a doctor and his family who have just moved into an old house in the country, and what happens to these four decent people will depress you to the core of your soul. Adding a strong presence is Fred Gwynne as an old farmer, who knows all the secrets of the graveyard and becomes the catalyst for the dire events. (Video/Laser: Paramount)

PET SEMATARY II (1992). A mean-spiritedness hangs so triumphantly over this sequel to the popular 1989 Stephen King movie that, rather than being classically morbid, this horror tale is grossly sickening and nihilistic in its statement about man's inhumanity to animals—not to mention man himself. Once again the setting is the rural community of Ludlow, Maine, where new veterinarian Anthony Edwards and son Edward Furlong settle to start over following the death of Edwards' wife (a "scream queen" movie actress electrocuted while making "Castle of Terror"). Before long Furlong and his friend Jason McGuire are burying McGuire's dead dog in the cursed Pet Sematary. This sets into motion horrific events, exploited to their maximum bloodletting by director Mary Lambert, who shows us such sights as a cageful of torn-apart kittens, rabbits being ripped apart, and a bully (Jared Rushton) having his face chopped up in a spinning motorbike wheel. It's a thoroughly unpleasant viewing experience with its touches of physical abuse to children and a scene of deputy sheriff Clancy Brown shooting his stepson's dog in cold blood. Sarah Trigger, Lisa Watty, Darlene Fluegel. (Video/Laser: Paramount)

PHANTASM (1979). Little logic dominates this macabre tale set at Morningside Cemetery, USA, as the sinister Tall Man (Angus Scrimm, shouting "BOOOYYYYY!") sends human victims into another dimension where they are reduced to dwarves and exploited as slaves. This hogwash is a crowd pleaser thanks to the stylish direction-photography by Don Coscarelli, who has included a severed hand and finger, .45 slugs plowing into flesh and a floating silver sphere which thuds into heads and drills out brains and blood. Coscarelli's only concern is to shock us into our early tombstones. A pleasing supernatural thriller. Just lean back into your casket and enjoy. Bill Thornbury, Michael Baldwin, Reggie Bannister. (Embassy; CBS/Fox) (Laser: Nelson; Vestron)

PHANTASM II (1988). The original 1979 hit horror flick remains writer-director Don Coscarelli's crowning achievement, as he attempts nothing new in this sequel. Instead, he relies on The Tall Man (sneeringly revived by menacing Angus Scrimm), the steel ball with knives and drills, the dwarves from another dimension and the portals into that other dimension. Mike (played this time by James Le Gros) and Reggie (repeated by Reggie Bannister) are after Scrimm, who is sucking the souls out of the graveyards of America. They meet up with a couple of chicks (Paula Irvine, Samantha Phillips) who really add nothing to the plot. It's the steel ball that reigns and rains (blood, that is) as it burrows into a man's back, chews up his insides and comes out his mouth. At times this has the feel of the graveyard and mausoleum to it. (Video/Laser: MCA)

ANGUS SCRIMM

PHANTOM BROTHER (1988). Orpahned teenager is haunted by the spirit of his brother, who was killed in a car crash. Directed by William Szarka. Jon Hammer, Patrick Molloy, John Gigante. (South Gate)

PHANTOM CHARIOT (1920). Death drives a hard bargain and a strange Coach of Death in this Swedish adaptation of a classic Selma Legerlof story. Each December 31 he picks up the soul of the last man to have died in the year to replace him as driver. Early horror classic directed-written by Victor Sjostrom. Also known as THE PHANTOM CARRIAGE and THE STROKE OF MIDNIGHT. (Sinister/C)

PHANTOM CREEPS, THE (1939). Campy Universal serial starring Bela Lugosi as Dr. Alex Zorka, an insane inventor who in the first chapter creates an eight-foot robot with an evil face, invents a belt that turns him invisible, sends mechanical killer spiders after his enemies, and plots the overthrow of the world through the powers of a meteor fragment. Captain Bob West (Robert Kent) is Zorka's adversary, accompanied by a pretty newspaperwoman (Dorothy Arnold) in frilly skirts. A bit dated but still an enjoyable serial when viewed with an eye toward Lugosi's over-the-top performance as the mad doctor, and the incompetence of his number-one henchman Monk (Jack C. Smith). Directed by Saul Goodkind and Ford Beebe without a trace of subtlety. Edward Van Sloan, Regis Toomey, Eddie Acuff. (Kartes; Captain Bijou; VCI; Nostalgia; Video Connection)

PHANTOM EMPIRE (1935). Gene Autry serial blending an underground lost city with cowboy action. Autry sings on the air from "Radio Ranch" then rushes off to prevent subterranean tyrants from destroying civilization with death rays, disintegrator units, sonar devices and atom-smashing smasheroos. For loyal Autry fans only—it's very crude toil. Frankie Darro, Smiley Burnette. Directed by action specialists B. Reeves Eason and Otto Brower. (MCA; Rhino; Nostalgia Merchant; Sinister/C; Video Yesteryear; Filmfax; the feature version, RADIO RANCH, is also in video)

PHANTOM EMPIRE, THE (1989). Schlockmeister producer-director Fred Olen Ray, who believes in throwing in the kitchen sink just in case, has concocted a yarn (with collaborator T. L. Lankford) that features cannibalistic mutant cavemen, a secret underground world, a race of women in animal skins, Robby the Robot, stop-motion dinosaurs, and an expedition of idiots. Wow, gang, that's exciting. Actually, gang, it's campy, as only Ray can make them campy. And we're talking master of the camp grounds. Sybil Danning hits an all-time silly high as the Queen of the Underground Chicks, Russ Tamblyn is laughable as an aging prospector, Robert Quarry bumbles his way around caves, Susan Stokey and Michelle Bauer look sexy and Ross Hagen and Jeffrey Combs look tough. (Prism)

PHANTOM FIEND, THE (1932). American title of a 1932 British version of the Marie Belloc-Lowndes novel

THE LODGER about a Jack the Ripper-style murderer. See **LODGER, THE.**

PHANTOM FIEND. See **RETURN OF DR. MABUSE, THE.**

PHANTOM FROM SPACE (1953). Cheapie suffers from lack of production, especially when an invisible E.T. is finally revealed to be human in form. Setting is L.A.'s Griffith Observatory where the alien is pursued. Weak as a new-born kitten. Ted Cooper, Jim Bannon, Noreen Nash, Harry Landers. W. Lee Wilder produced-directed. (Goodtimes; S/Weird; Sinister/C; Filmfax)

PHANTOM FROM 10,000 LEAGUES (1955). Menace from the deep turns out to be shallow. Kent Taylor discovers an amphibious creature but keeps it a secret from overdeveloped spy Helene Stanton, who wears skimpy bathing suits to take our minds off the underdeveloped plot. Dan Milner directed this terrible movie that will give you the bends. Cathy Downs, Michael Whalen, Rodney Bell. (Sinister/C; S/Weird; Filmfax)

PHANTOM IN SPACE. See **BATTLESTAR GALACTICA.**

PHANTOM LOVERS. See **GHOSTS IN ROME.**

PHANTOM OF CRESTWOOD (1932). Ahead-of-its time whodunit thriller in which a high-class mistress (Karen Morley) gathers her lovers at Crestwood to extort them, unaware a killer wearing a death mask and using gaming darts as murder weapons is running through secret passageways. Great flashback device, good effects, a fun whodunit. Directed by David Ruben. Ricardo Cortez, Anita Louise, H. B. Warner, Pauline Frederick. (Rex Miller) (Laser: Image)

PHANTOM OF DEATH (1987). Psychological portrait of a brilliant concert pianist (Michael York) who has a rare disease called Protaria, or Premature Senility, that turns him into a psychokiller. Cop Donald Pleasence takes on the case and develops a vendetta when the pianist harasses him with phone calls, taunting him to solve the murders. Despite its intriguing premise, this Italian production directed by Ruggero Deodato never builds excitement or suspense. The disease prematurely ages York, so by the end he's turned into a wrinkled monster. Edwige Fenech, Mapi Galan. (Vidmark)

PHANTOM OF HOLLYWOOD (1974). Take-off on PHANTOM OF THE OPERA, set in a deteriorating film studio where bigwigs are selling off the backlot to pay off debts. From the depths of movies' past comes a Masked Avenger to preserve low-budget picture values, even at the cost of human life. Standard TV-movie produced-directed by Gene Levitt. Peter Lawford, Jack Cassidy, Skye Aubrey, Jackie Coogan, Broderick Crawford, Kent Taylor, Regis Toomey, John Ireland.

PHANTOM OF PARIS, THE (1931). While its horror overtones are lightweight, this is a seminal film in the development of the weird-horror hero, based on a novel by Gaston Leroux, creator of THE PHANTOM OF THE OPERA. Cheri-Bibi, an illusionist/escape artist a la Houdini, is accused of murdering his fiancee's father (C. Aubrey Smith) and sentenced to the guillotine. Innocent but filled with bitter anguish (a characteristic of the Phantom, The Shadow and Darkman), Cheri-Bibi (John Gilbert in excellent form and voice) escapes prison and goes into hiding from the cop (Lewis Stone) obsessed with his capture. Compelling if dated film captures demented anguish within its abused hero. Well directed by John S. Robertson. Ian Keith, Lelia Hyams, Jean Hersholt.

PHANTOM OF PARIS. See **MYSTERY OF MARIE ROGET, THE** (Hairy in Paree!).

PHANTOM OF SOHO (1963). German-British thriller, based on an Edgar Wallace mystery, MURDER BY PROXY, in which a masked fiend darts through seedy London streets, knocking off British gentry belonging to the Zanzibar Club. Directed by Franz Joseph Gottlieb. Dieter Borsche, Hans Sohnhker, Barbara Rutting. (Sinister/C; S/Weird)

PHANTOM OF THE MALL: ERIC'S REVENGE (1989). Modernized variation on THE PHANTOM OF THE OPERA, in which a wronged young man, burned in a fire started by an unscrupulous land developer, wears a metallic face mask as he wreaks revenge on the occupants of Midwood Mall and protects his one-time girlfriend from harm. All that's missing is the falling-chandelier scene. With its shopper's spree of genre cliches and motley collection of mediocre murders under the direction of Richard Friedman, the film fails to generate suspense. Kari Whitman, Derek Rydall, Jonathan Goldsmith, Morgan Fairchild (as a mayor yet—some politics). (Fries; United America issued MAKING OF PHANTOM OF THE MALL) (Laser: Image)

PHANTOM OF THE OPERA, THE (1925). Appreciation for the silent screen helps but isn't mandatory for enjoying this oldie with make-up genius Lon Chaney as an acid-scarred madman living beneath the Paris Opera House who frightens the sopranos out of their tenors. Based on a Gaston Leroux novel, this Universal classic has marvelous make-up and imagery that would inspire film makers for decades. Despite outdated acting techniques and staginess, this is a must see. Directed by Rupert Julian. Mary Philbin, Norman Kerry. (Kino; Video Yesteryear; Kartes) (Laser: Lumivision; Image)

PHANTOM OF THE OPERA, THE (1943). Second screen version of Leroux's novel is one of the few horror films in Technicolor from the 1940s. Stylized, beautifully

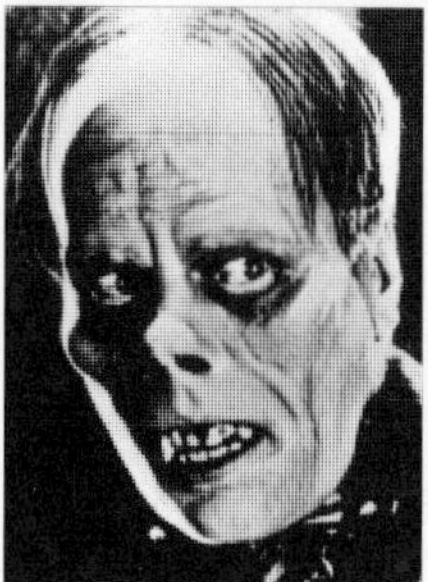

LON CHANEY JR.

ROBERT ENGLUND

photographed by Hal Mohr and very entertaining despite some hokum. Claude Rains portrays a misused-abused composer whose face is scarred by acid and who, in pain-riddled madness, seeks refuge in sewers beneath the Opera House. In revenge, he commits outrages against the establishment he once so loved. Enduring favorite with great sets and costumes and a flamboyant cast: Nelson Eddy, Susanna Foster, Leo Carrillo, Fritz Leiber, Edgar Barrier. Directed by Arthur Lubin. (Video/Laser: MCA)

PHANTOM OF THE OPERA (1962). Hammer's filmization of Gaston Leroux's novel is comparable to the 1943 version in story and opulence. Herbert Lom is the Phantom in a one-eyed mask, Michael Gough is the music pirate and Heather Sears is the beautiful soprano. Polished under Terence Fisher's direction, romantically mysterious and set in London instead of Paris, with the underground chambers of the Phantom now connected with the slimy blimey sewers. Adaptation by producer Anthony Hinds. Thorley Walters, Edward De Souza, Miles Milleson, Michael Ripper.

PHANTOM OF THE OPERA (1983). TV-movie version of Leroux's novel is set in turn-of-the-century Budapest. Maximilian Schell's singing wife is beautiful but incompetent, and commits suicide, driving Schell to the brink of insanity. He is disfigured and, with an accomplice, flees underground into the labyrinth of the city, there to heal his body and scheme revenge. Five years later he reemerges as the Phantom to terrorize American singer Jane Seymour, British opera director Michael York and other hapless figures in the musical landscape. Though this has the ambience of Budapest, it remains inferior to earlier sound versions and unfolds in a most peculiar way. Directed by Robert Markowitz. Jeremy Kemp, Diana

Quick, Philip Stone.

PHANTOM OF THE OPERA, THE (1989). Despite opulent Budapest settings (standing in for London), costumes and sets, producer Menahem Golan still manages to turn Gaston Leroux's gothic horror classic into an exploitation shocker that cashes in on the use of Robert (Freddy Krueger) Englund in the title role. Unlike the actors who have faced this part before, Englund brings little sympathy to Erik, who is no longer an unfortunate victim of circumstances, but a man who exchanges his soul for supernatural powers. Director Dwight H. Little brings ambience and pace to this, the bloodiest version of all the film and TV adaptations. Jill Schoelen, Alex Hyde-White, Bill Nighy, Stephanie Lawrence. (Video/Laser: RCA/Columbia)

PHANTOM OF THE OPERA, THE (1990). Opulent, splendidly rendered variation on Gaston Leroux's novel, originally a four-hour TV-movie made at the Paris Opera and Paris Caves of Mello. Arthur Kopit adapted his own play which depicts Erik the Phantom not as a menacing mystery but as a tragic figure who falls in love with a costume girl "who sings like an angel." The sets, costumes and cast are exquisite, and despite its theatrical origins, director Tony Richardson does a masterful job. Burt Lancaster stars as the benefactor of Erik; Charles Dance is a poetic, reachable Phantom; and Teri Polo is the delicate waif turned into Paris' newest diva. The first half is a comedy sendup, but when Erik is wronged the storyline turns serious. The opera sequences are splendid. One of the best adaptations in the series, even if it does stray quite far from the original material. Andrea Ferreol, Adam Storke, Jean-Pierre Cassel. The above-average score is by John Addison.

PHANTOM OF THE PARADISE (1975). Bizarre Brian De Palma film satirizes PHANTOM OF THE OPERA and comments on our music-oriented rock 'n roll youth and the debased values of the business world. De Palma's script is a retelling of the Faust legend, with crazed songwriter William Finley entering into a blood pact with rock impresario Paul Williams (who wrote music and lyrics). Climactic rock concert is a masterpiece of hysteria, but clarity of plot is often sacrificed for wild visuals. Williams is brilliant as the satanic force of depraved sexuality. For the "turned on" generation(s); squares may find it hard going. (Key) (Laser: CBS/Fox)

PHANTOM OF THE RED HOUSE, THE (1954). Mexican haunted house quickie has heirs to a fortune killing each other while a dead millionaire's spirit watches. Directed by Miguel M. Delgado. Alma Rosa Aguirre, Raul Martinez. Gordon Murray imported the Americanized version. (S/Weird; Filmfax)

PHANTOM OF THE RITZ (1988). Several rock and roll musical groups are highlighted in this excuse for a series of musical numbers that focuses on a haunted theater and the efforts of producers to keep calm as their performers are subjected to hauntings. Directed by Allen Plone. Peter Bergman, Deborah Van Valkenburgh. (Prism) (Laser: Image)

PHANTOM OF THE RUE MORGUE (1954). Warner remake of MURDERS IN THE RUE MORGUE, shot in 3-D, depicts the Surete unsurely pursuing a killer of beautiful women over the rooftops of Paris. Good color and direction by Roy Del Ruth, but 2-D TV prints lose something of the original stereovision. Karl Malden gives his only performance as a mad doctor and tinges his professor with dignity and humanity, but he still seems a bit out of place. Claude Dauphin, Patricia Medina, Steve Forrest, Merv Griffin (!), Anthony Caruso and a gorilla named Sultan (Charles Gemora).

PHANTOM PLANET, THE (1961). Variation on GULLIVER'S TRAVELS has Earthman Dean Fredericks (of Hollywood) landing on an alien planet, Rheton, inhabited by tiny people who need help to fight off an attack by another E.T. race. Fredericks is shrunken to six inches and squares off against the invaders, led by Richard Kiel. Lousy special effects, and as slow moving as an alien rocket without fuel. Directed by William Marshall. Dolores Faith, Francis X. Bushman, Coleen Gray, Anthony Dexter, Dick Haynes. (Sinister/C; S/Weird)

PHANTOM RAIDERS (1940). See editions 1-3.

PHANTOM SHIP (1937). Hammer's second film, first released as MYSTERY OF THE MARIE CELESTE. It deals with the famous brigantine found abandoned in the Atlantic in December 1872, offering a wild interpretation of what happened to the vanished crew. A kind of whodunit, with crew members being murdered one by one during a raging storm at sea. Bela Lugosi portrays a suspicious captain. Denison Clift directed. Shirley Grey, Arthur Margetson, Dennis Hoey. (Cable Films; Kartes; Sinister/C; Bosko)

PHANTOM SPEAKS, THE (1945). Republic quickie follows the story of BLACK FRIDAY very closely in telling of a murderer on Death Row who is electrocuted. His spirit then enters the body of a doctor and commands him to kill, kill, kill. Directed by John English. Richard Arlen, Lynne Roberts, Stanley Ridges, Tom Powers.

PHANTOM TOLLBOOTH, THE (1970). Imaginative cartoon by Chuck Jones, mixing live action with animation. The titular tollbooth is a passageway to a magical world structured on the laws of mathematics and patterned on the written word. Voices by Mel Blanc, Hans Conried, Les Tremayne, Larry Thor, Daws Butler, June Foray. (MGM/UA; also on video as **ADVENTURES OF MILO IN THE PHANTOM TOOLBOOTH, THE**)

PHANTOM TREEHOUSE, THE (1984). Animated cartoon in which two boys and their dog become lost in a world of strange characters. (Vidamerica)

PHARAOH'S CURSE, THE (1956). Slow-moving, poor man's version of THE MUMMY, with pedestrian direction by Lee Sholem and inferior monster make-up for the wizened face of the creature in this bit of desert turgidity. In 1902 a British patrol led by Mark Dana encounters a strange priestess (Ziva Shapir) of a cat cult linked to an Egyptian tomb desecrated by explorer Ben Wright and his archeologists. Members of the expedition die one by one from a curse. If you like old 1950s horror movies in black and white you might enjoy some of its old-fashioned touches, but by modern standards this, like the mummy Ra-Hatib, should be kept under wraps. Diane Brewster, Alvado Guillot. (J & J)

PHASE IV (1974). Saul Bass, famed film-title designer, directed this bizarre sci-fi/horror thriller (a prize winner at Trieste) depicting a war between scientists in a desert outpost and an army of intelligent killer ants that drench their enemies in a sticky yellow substance. The ants, a result of pollution, are diabolical adversaries as they chew their way into the installation and demonstrate hypnotic powers. The excellent cinematography, the special ant documentary footage and John Barry's art direction enhance this offbeat tale with a way-out metaphysical ending. Michael Murphy, Nigel Davenport, Lynne Frederick, Alan Gifford. (Video/Laser: Paramount)

PHENOMENA (1985). Japanese laser title for **CREEPERS.**

PHENOMENAL AND THE TREASURE OF TUTANKAMEN (1984). The curse of King Tut strikes again in this inept French-Italian superhero adventure as a masked hero pursues a golden relic with mystical powers and stops the blundering of a tomb. Slam bam, crash boom. Directed by Ruggero Deodato. Maura Nicola Parenti, Gordon Mitchell. (Wizard; VCI)

PHILADELPHIA EXPERIMENT, THE (1984). Since 1943 unsubstantiated legends have swum through the annals of "unsolved mysteries" about the U.S. Navy conducting experiments with an invisible force field that caused ships to turn invisible. This builds an exciting time-travel story around that legend: Two sailors in the radar experiment (Michael Pare, Bobby Di Cicco) are catapulted to the present to face fish-out-of-water adventures. This sensitively deals with the problems of a young man finding that the woman he loved in 1943 is now beyond his reach. But director Stewart Raffill also emphasizes action and weird effects, balancing plot and adventure. Eric Christmas, Nancy Allen, Miles McNamara. (Thorn EMI/HBO) (Laser: Image)

PHILADELPHIA EXPERIMENT 2, THE (1993). A "monolithic vortex machine" threatens to send invading armies to Earth unless Brad Johnson can stop the Nazi-like scientist behind the invasion. Directed by Stephen Cormwell. (Vidmark)

PHOBIA (1981). Even John Huston had to leap into the horror genre, but his contribution as director is ordinary, displaying no special skill for the field. Dr. Paul Michael Glaser is conducting "implosion therapy" on human guinea pigs, each of whom suffers from a phobia: fear of heights, of falling, of snakes, of crowds. One by one these patients are murdered in graphic ways: by dynamite explosion, by falling, by drowning, by snake bite, by elevator crush. A lack of suspects tips off who the killer is early on but there's still a compelling quality thanks to the intense performance of ruthless, driven investigating cop John Colicos. Susan Hogan, Alexandra Stewart. Robert O'Ree, Lisa Langlois. (Paramount)

PHOBIA. See **NESTING, THE.**

PHOENIX, THE (1978). Taiwanese import in which an alien woman, Flower Fox, travels to Earth and puts under her evil spell a fisherman who has found her magical book, "Magic Vessel of Plenty and Bamboo Book." Since the tome creates wealth, several villains come after it, including Flower Fox's henchman, Steel Hand, standing seven feet tall as Richard Kiel. Directed by Richard Caan and Sadamasa Arikawa. (Video Action; from Planet as **WAR OF THE WIZARDS**)

PHOENIX, THE (1981). TV-movie (pilot for a short-lived series) about an extraterrestrial (formerly a Mayan known as "Bennu of the Golden Light") who walks out of his South American tomb to shake up mankind with Charlie Chan homilies and mystical mutterings. Super-hero action written-produced by Anthony and Nancy Lawrence. Judson Scott, Shelley Smith, E. G. Marshall. Directed by Douglas Hickox.

PHOENIX THE WARRIOR (1988). Welcome to a post-Armageddon world, following bacteriological war and plague, in which only men have survived to rove the wastelands. Kathleen Kinmont is a warrior of the future who befriends a woman who gives birth to a new male—and then the evil Reverent Mother (an ugly mutant) and her henchwoman (Persis Khambatta) are after the child, a symbol of power. It's a series of male-fantasy cliches: dune buggies racing in the desert, a bevy of beauties in bikini outfits, and the attractive Kinmont repeatedly stirring one's libido. Despite the hackneyed script by Robert Hayes and Dan Rotblatt, the film unfolds (under Hayes' direction) in a competent, fast-moving way, and lacks that element of incompetence that makes bad movies better. Peggy Sands, James H. Emery, Sheila Howard. (Sony) (Laser: Image)

PHOENIX 2772. See **SPACE FIREBIRD 2772.**

PHOTOGRAPHER, THE. See **DOUBLE EXPOSURE.**

PHYNX, THE (1970). See editions 1-3.

PICKING UP THE PIECES. See **BLOODSUCKING PHARAOHS IN PITTSBURGH.**

PICKLE, THE (1993). A satire on Hollywood in which failing movie producer Danny Aiello compromises his art to make a sci-fi flick about a flying pickle. Thus, one gets to see a silly fantasy movie-within-a-movie as well as Aiello recovering his self-esteem with mother Shelley Winters, ex-wife Dyan Cannon and French girlfriend Clotilde Courau. Written-produced-directed by Paul Mazursky. Ally Sheedy, Griffin Dunne, Isabella Rossellini, Little Richard. (Video/Laser: Columbia TriStar)

PICNIC AT HANGING ROCK (1975). Australian director Peter Weir has taken a true incident from 1900 and made a mystical, puzzling film that never solves its mysteries, although that very fact is one of its strongest elements. Four school girls picnicking on a precipitous rock formation vanish; later, one of them turns up dazed. But where are the others? For some this may pass as artistic cinema with ample pregnant pauses, but those seeking an answer will call this pretentious. Like it or not, it's beautifully photographed by Russell Boyd and finely directed by the weird Weir. Rachel Roberts, Dominic Guard. (Vestron) (Laser: Japanese)

PICTURE MOMMY DEAD (1966). Stylish psychothriller from producer-director Bert I. Gordon, who shows more film-making savvy than usual. Susan Gordon (Bert's daughter) is effective as a troubled teen on the verge of going bonkers with memories of mommy Zsa Zsa Gabor burning to death. She lives with her morally ambiguous father (Don Ameche) and greedy, nymphomaniacal stepmom (Martha Hyer) in a mansion with a painting of Mom that holds a key to the mystery. It's such an intriguing school of barracuda that it's fun to watch the performances of Ameche, Hyer, Wendell Corey (as a crotchedy old attorney) and Maxwell Reed (family retainer). Anna Lee, Signe Hasso. (Charter)

PICTURE OF DORIAN GRAY, THE (1945). Oscar Wilde's morality horror story, about an evil man (Hurd Hatfield) whose decadence is embodied in a painting that reflects his degradation while he remains young, becomes literate, fascinating cinema in the hands of writer-director Albert Lewin, with George Sanders memorable as the Englishman who introduces Dorian Gray to debauchery. Angela Lansbury (she was nominated for an Oscar), Donna Reed, Peter Lawford, Bernard Gorcey. Narration read by Sir Cedric Hardwicke. (Video/Laser: MGM/UA)

PICTURE OF DORIAN GRAY (1973). Oscar Wilde's classic about a man's search for eternal youth, and his descent into sin, was produced for TV by Dan Curtis. Shane Briant is the artist who stays young while his portrait grows old. Nigel Davenport, Charles Aidman, John Karlen, Fionnula Flanagan. Directed by Glenn Jordan. (Thrillervideo/IVE)

PIECES (1983). Repulsive chainsaw-killer flick, in which a madman dismembers beautiful women, taking "pieces" back to his freeze locker to complete a human "jigsaw puzzle." As degrading as it is absurd, and humiliating to women. Filmed in Boston by writer-director Juan Piquer Simon, who apparently went all to pieces behind the camera, this is awful awful sleazy trash. Christopher George plays an unlikable cop, Lynda Day is an unlikely undercover woman, Edmund Purdom is the campus dean and Paul L. Smith provides red herrings. (Vestron) (Laser: Japanese)

PIED PIPER, THE (1972). Literate, well-acted version of Robert Browning's poem about a mysterious piper in medieval 14th Century England whose magical pipe music mesmerizes plague-bearing rats away from a village. Sets and costumes are realistic in this David Puttman film that walks between adult themes and children's touches. Well-directed by Jacques Demy. Donovan is the piper. Donald Pleasence, Michael Hordern, Roy Kinnear, John Hurt, Jack Wild, Diana Dors.

PIED PIPER OF HAMELIN (1957). TV production recounting in music and dance the legendary tale of the medieval piper who lures children from a German village. Van Johnson, Claude Rains, Jim Backus, Lori Nelson, Kay Starr, Doodles Weaver. Directed by Bretaigne Windust. (Media; Kartes)

PIED PIPER OF HAMELIN (1984). Episode of FAERIE TALE THEATRE, starring Eric Idle and directed by Nicholas Meyer. (CBS/Fox) (Laser: Japanese)

PIGS. Video of **DADDY'S DEADLY DARLING** (Simitar; Home Cinema; Paragon; Studio One).

PILL CAPER, THE (1967). Re-edited episodes from the ghastly sitcom, MR. TERRIFIC. For details, see THE POWER PILL. Directed by Jack Arnold.

PILLOW OF DEATH (1945). Last of Universal's "Inner Sanctum" programmers introduced by a floating head in a crystal ball. Lon Chaney Jr. is going bonkers as a lawyer who murdered his wife (or did he?). Indifferently directed by Wallace Fox. Brenda Joyce, J. Edward Bromberg, Wilton Griff.

PIN (1988). Subtitled "An Unexpected Visit to a Most

Terrifying Place," this adaptation of a popular novel by Andrew Neiderman is a fascinating study of abnormal sexual psychology in depicting a paranoid schizophrenic played by David Hewlett. Country doctor Terry O'Quinn uses a mannikin nicknamed Pin (short for Pinocchio) to teach his son and daughter sex education, and uses ventroloquist talents to project the voice. Hewlett believes Pin is real and sinks ever deeper into his own soulful terror, making life miserable for his sister (Cyndy Preston) and her boyfriend (John Ferguson). Writer-director Sandor Stern not only makes it seem plausible by eliciting good performances, but captures an understanding of mental illness too often lost in "mind thrillers." (New World) (Laser: Image)

PINK CHIQUITAS, THE (1986). This has all the elements of a campy take-off on sci-fi flicks, but falls flatter than a discarded banana peel. After a pink meteor falls near Beansville, sexy gals are turned into nymphomaniacs. Meanwhile, dumb private eye Tony Mareda Jr. (Frank Stallone, brother of Sylvester) tries to outwit the alien force (symbolized by the voice of Eartha Kitt). It's played for farce (especially by John Hemphill as a mayor, Bruce Pirrie as a nerdy TV weatherman and Don Lake as a deputy sheriff) but it's so erratically zany that it never fulfills its promises. Written-directed by Anthony Currie. Elizabeth Edwards, Claudia Udy, McKinlay Robinson. (Starmaker; Prism)

PINK PANTHER STRIKES AGAIN, THE (1976). Pink Panther movies are pretty far out but this goes sci-fi crazy. Herbert Lom returns as the French policeman driven so daffy by Inspector Clouseau that he plays the organ (remember PHANTOM OF THE OPERA?) and prepares his Destruction Device to knock down the U.N. building. Things vanish and reappear in a time continuum as director Blake Edwards flies in a spirit of utter disjointed nonsense and Peter Sellers' bumbling and mumbling reaches perfection. Lesley-Anne Down, Marne Maitland, Burt Kwouk, Burt Kwouk. (CBS/Fox) (Laser: MGM/UA; Fox)

PINOCCHIO (1940). Disney masterpiece about a wooden puppet transformed into a bona fide youth with Jiminy Cricket looking on is a free-handed adaptation of Collodi's classic, replete with Geppetto the gentle woodcarver, Figaro the kitten, Cleo the goldfish and Monstro the Whale. Brilliant animation. Voices by Dickie Jones, Cliff Edwards, Walter Catlett, Evelyn Venable. (Disney) (Laser: Disney; Image)

PINOCCHIO AND THE EMPEROR OF THE NIGHT (1987). Animated feature adapting the 1882 story by Carlo Collodi about a wooden puppet who comes to life and embarks on an odyssey to become a human being. This is slanted for children and uses animation of only moderate interest. Pinocchio, a glow worm named Gee Willikers, a singing marionette named Twinkle and Grumblebee (of the Royal Air Bugs) search for a music box and encounter the villainy of Scalaway and the Emperor of the Night. Despite years of production under Lou Scheimer, and the voice talents of James Earl Jones, Tom Bosley, Don Knotts, Lana Beeson, Ed Asner and Jonathan Harris, this never rises above mediocrity. (New World) (Laser: Image)

PINOCCHIO IN OUTER SPACE (1965). Carlo Collodi's puppet story becomes animated space opera with the voice of Arnold Stang in this U.S.-Belgian cartoon directed by Ray Goosens. Our long-nosed hero journeys to the far reaches of the Universe to do battle with a whale and make friends with an E.T. snapping turtle. Voices: Conrad Jameson, Minerva Pious. (RCA/Columbia)

PIRANHA (1978). On the surface an exploitation "eat 'em alive" picture, but more a fantasy-satire thanks to John Sayles' script and Joe Dante's whimsical direction. A mutant strain of piranha is fed into U.S. waterways and the teeny waterdemons feast on the feet of Keenan Wynn and the facial tissues of Bradford Dillman. Barbara Steele fans will enjoy her as a conspiratorial military officer. There's also unusual stop-motion footage of strange creatures in a laboratory. And some dialogue is wonderfuly witty. (Warner Bros.)

PIRANHA II: THE SPAWNING (1981). Loose sequel to PIRANHA is set at a Caribbean resort where underwater diving coach Tricia O'Neil is in conflict with chief of police Lance Hendriksen (her estranged husband) and tourist Steve Marachuk, a member of a research program that has created a mutant—a cross between a piranha and a flying fish. These winged monsters are munching on hotel guests. It's hard to get suspense out of tiny creatures and the effects are standard blood and gore, with one ALIEN-style attack when a minimonster pops from a victim's stomach. Director James Cameron is strongest in allowing his cast to create believable characters. Cameron went on to make TERMINATOR and ALIENS, two superior thrillers. Aka **PIRANHA II: FLYING KILLERS.** (Video/Laser: Embassy/Nelson)

PIRATES OF PRAH (1953). Re-edited shows of **ROCKY JONES, SPACE RANGER** (Video Yesteryear).

PIT, THE (1981). Horror movie twice as bad as its title—hence, the pits. A perverted look at a perverted kid (Sammy Snyders) who peeps on his sexy babysitter and talks to his friend Teddy, a toy bear who talks back, planting salacious ideas in his "innocent" head. Sammy is also the friend of Trogs, gnarly beasts with blazing yellow eyes in a pit outside town. To keep them fat, Sammy feeds them his friends. The perversity and gore never really gell, with Sammy's abnormal sexuality shallowly explored. The story picks up steam once the beasties escape the pit and reign munching terror on delicious humans. Filmed around Beaver Dam, Wisc. Directed by Lew Lehman. Laura Hollingsworth, Jeannie Elias. (Embassy; Starmaker)

PIT AND THE PENDULUM, THE (1961). Excellent adaptation of Edgar Allan Poe's tale starring Vincent Price, but Poe's narrow storyline about a prisoner tortured by a razor-edged pendulum swinging closer and closer to his restrained body has been expanded by Richard Matheson into a Gothic masterpiece of horror. Nobleman John Kerr arrives at a creepy, seacoast castle to face Price playing a Spanish count haunted by the fact his father was an executioner for the Inquisition. "Am I not the spawn of his depraved blood?" cries out Price. Producer-director Roger Corman was at his inspired height making this AIP masterwork. Barbara Steele, Luana Anders, Anthony Carbone. (Vestron; Warner Bros.) (Laser: Japanese)

PIT AND THE PENDULUM, THE (1990). This Charles Band production, filmed in Giove, Italy, depicts the sadism of the Spanish Inquisition. One is subjected to torture scenes and dungeon bloodletting when breadmaker Rona De Ricci is accused of being a witch and taken captive by the cruel monk Torquemada. (Lance Henriksen, in another of his villain roles, holds back nothing.) While the Dennis Paoli script has its antecedents in Poe (touches are borrowed from "The Cask of Amontillado," "The Premature Burial," and the titular tale), it is director Stuart Gordon having his excesses, such as cutting out a woman's tongue, exploding an old hag being burned at the stake, cutting a swordsman in half with the swaying pendulum, grinding a skeleton to powder, and pouring water down a woman's throat. Oliver Reed appears as a cardinal who remarks, "The good Lord wants us to love our neighbor—not roast him." A roasting is certainly in order. Jonathan Fuller, Frances Bay, Mark Margolis, Jeffrey Combs, Tom Towles. (Paramount) (Laser: Full Moon)

PLACE OF ONE'S OWN (1944). See first edition.

PLACE TO DIE, A (1973). See editions 1-3.

PLAGUE, THE (1979). Scientist working on a mutant bacteria (M3) to nourish plants and provide food for millions causes a leakage to the outside world, where bacteria infects children. The epidemic snowballs as a researcher seeks a virus to counteract the acetylecoline created by the bacteria. Kate Reid, who fought the Andromeda Strain, is a loyal scientist battling the killer disease. Canadian production, directed by Ed Hunt. Aka **PLAGUE M3: THE GEMINI STRAIN.** (VidAmerica)

PLAGUE DOGS, THE (1982). Richard Adams' novel

was a didactic diatribe against vivesection which producer-writer Martin Rosen (WATERSHIP DOWN) distilled into an animated feature. Two dogs escape an experimental station in England's Lake District and begin a trek to a mythical island for animals. They are befriended by the Tod, a fox who teaches them how to live in the wilderness. Meanwhile, the army and populace are in pursuit to destroy the dogs. Animation is state-of-the-art, but the story is depressing and this was a box-office failure despite all its good intentions. Voices by John Hurt, James Bolam, Christopher Benjamin, Judy Geeson, Nigel Hawthorne. (Charter)

PLAGUE OF THE ZOMBIES (1966). Director John Gilling has fashioned a stylish Gothic Hammer horror thriller set in the last century that builds tension with superior production values. Peter Bryan's storyline touches on British hierarchy and its indifference to the working class when a doctor and his daughter come to visit an old friend in an eerie Cornish village and uncover a sadistic squire who turns men into voodoo zombies to work an old tin mine beneath his plantation. Especially memorable are scenes where corpses slither and wriggle out of their graves. One of Hammer's best. Jacqueline Pearce, Andre Morell, Diane Clare, Michael Ripper.

PLAINS OF HEAVEN, THE. See **PANIC STATION.**

PLANETA BURG (1962). This is the Soviet sci-fi film that Roger Corman recut into VOYAGE TO A PREHISTORIC PLANET. Later, footage was used in VOYAGE TO THE PLANET OF PREHISTORIC WOMEN. In its USSR version it is also known as STORM PLANET, COSMONAUTS ON VENUS and PLANET OF STORMS. The original was directed and co-written by Pavel Klushantsev. Gennadi Vernov, Ladimir Temelianov, Yuri Sarantsev. (Sinister/C)

PLANET EARTH (1974). Failed Gene Roddenberry TV pilot is a remake of another unsold pilot, GENESIS II. John Saxon awakens from suspended animation in the 22nd Century, discovering mankind has splintered into strange societies. The rulers are women led by sexy Diana Muldaur and the men are slaves called Dinks. How Saxon and Ted Cassidy save man from a fate worse than death is the substance of the teleplay by Roddenberry and Juanita Bartlett. Janet Margolin, Christopher Carey, Majel Barrett. (Unicorn)

PLANET OF BLOOD. Video version of **QUEEN OF BLOOD** (Star Classics; Sinister/C; S/Weird).

PLANET OF DINOSAURS (1978). Despite its crude shortcomings there is an earnestness behind this low-budget attempt at a science-fictional ONE MILLION YEARS BC. When the spaceship Odyssey explodes in space, survivors aboard a shuttlecraft land on a prehistoric planet ruled by dinosaurs. The various attitudes toward survival become a microscopic look at mankind. It has stop-motion animation work by Douglas Beswick (in the Harryhausen vein) and interesting matte paintings by Jim Danforth. Of the cast members, James Whitworth is most effective as he persuades others that to survive they must become the hunters and not the hunted. Produced-directed by James K. Shea, who shows occasional flair. Ramela Bottaro, Louie Lawless, Harvey Shain. (Active; Star Classics)

PLANET OF HORRORS. Made as MINDWARP: AN INFINITY OF TERROR, but released as PLANET OF HORRORS, then retitled **GALAXY OF TERROR** (see that entry) for cable TV. Call it what you will.

PLANET OF INCREDIBLE CREATURES. Video version of **FANTASTIC PLANET** (Vidcrest).

PLANET OF STORMS (1962). See **PLANETA BURG.**

PLANET OF TERROR, THE. See **DEMON PLANET.**

PLANET OF THE APES (1968). Based loosely on the Pierre Boulle novel, this is a mixture of action, suspense and satire, although the latter element tends toward parody and cheapens the effect. Charlton Heston is a U.S. astronaut caught in a time warp and thrown into the future. He crashlands on a desolate planet ruled by chimpanzees, orangutans and gorillas, where man is a mute slave. There is much ape talk about man's warlike nature and his downfall. John Chambers' makeup is imaginative, Franklin J. Schaffner's direction is brilliant and there is a visually rewarding punchline to the Rod Serling-Michael Wilson script. Jerry Goldsmith's music is excellent. Kim Hunter, Roddy McDowall, James Whitmore, James Daly and Maurice Evans are among many stars who appear in make-up and costumes. Four sequels followed. (Video/Laser: CBS/Fox)

PLANET OF THE DAMNED, THE. See **DEMON PLANET.**

PLANET OF THE DINOSAURS. See **PLANET OF DINOSAURS.**

PLANET OF THE LIFELESS MEN. See **BATTLE OF THE WORLDS.**

PLANET OF THE VAMPIRES. Video version of **DEMON PLANET, THE** (HB0; Orion) (Laser: Image, with **QUEEN OF BLOOD**; Polygram).

PLANET ON THE PROWL. Video version of **WAR BETWEEN THE PLANETS** (Monterey; S/Weird).

PLANET OUTLAWS (1939). Re-edited version of the 1939 serial **BUCK ROGERS.** (Thunderbird)

PLANETS AGAINST US (1961). What happens when the Italians/French/Germans ally to make a sci-fi film? They come up with a humanoid robot (Michel Lemoine) that walks softly on flesh-covered feet and carries a big schtick: eyeballs that hypnotize and zap, and hands that turn humans to household dust. Brutally re-edited for the U.S. market. Directed by Romano Ferrara. Aka **PLANETS AROUND US.** (Sinister/C; S/Weird; Filmfax)

PLAN NINE FROM OUTER SPACE (1956). Ranks with FIRE MAIDENS FROM OUTER SPACE and CAT WOMEN OF THE MOON in sinking to new, inspired depths of cinematic ineptitude. Words such as amateurish, crude, tedious and aaarrrggghhhh can't begin to describe this Edward D. Wood film with Bela Lugosi in graveyard scenes made shortly before his death. Other footage has Lugosi coming out of a drab house. Lugosi died before the film was finished and an obvious "double" was used. The unplotted plot by Wood has San Fernando Valley residents troubled by UFOs of the worst encounter. Humanoid aliens Dudley Manlove (a famous radio voice) and Joanna Lee land their cardboard ship with a ninth plan to conquer the world (the first eight failed, you see). They resurrect corpses, including Vampira, Tor Johnson and Lugosi's double. The results are unviewable except for masochists who enjoy a good laugh derived from watching folks making fools of themselves. Psychic Criswell introduces the film with typical Wood nonsense. Lyle Talbot, Tom Keene, Mona McKinnon. (Nostalgia Merchant; Sinister/C; S/Weird) (Laser: Image)

PLANTS ARE WATCHING, THE. Video version of **KIRLIAN WITNESS, THE** (Magnum).

PLAY DEAD (1985). Yvonne de Carlo has a satanic pact with a Devil Dog, who murders members of her family for revenge. One is strangled, another electrocuted; even an investigating cop dies after the canine pours him a lye-laced cocktail. Pretty well acted and produced, but lacking sufficient exposition and characterizations to give it substance. In short, it finally rolls over and . . . Directed by Peter Wittman. Stephanie Dunnam, David Cullinand. (Academy; from Video Vision as **SATAN'S DOGS**)

PLAYGIRL KILLER (1970). Canadian release in which William Kerwin kills his models and stores their corpses in a freezer. Also known as DECOY FOR TERROR. Directed by Enrick Santamaran. Neil Sedaka, Jean Christopher. (New World)

PLAYGIRLS AND THE VAMPIRE (1960). See **CURSE OF THE VAMPIRE.**

PLAY IT AGAIN, SAM (1972). Woody Allen's comic masterpiece finds him playing his usual inept, impotent self but imagining that the spirit of Humphrey Bogart (Jerry Lacy) is always at his shoulder with tough-guy, amorous advice. The Bogart impression is hilarious and

Allen is excellent as the nerd in search of a proper balance between the way he is and the way he'd like to be. Based on the Broadway play by Allen. Diane Keaton, Tony Roberts, Jennifer Salt, Susan Anspach. Directed by Herbert Ross. (Video/Laser: Paramount)

PLAY MISTY FOR ME (1971). Clint Eastwood made his directorial debut with this odd psychological thriller with a minimum of suspense and "slasher" behavior. Clint is a soft-voiced Monterey disc jockey who is the love object of Jessica Walter—but he rejects her in favor of Donna Mills. This turns love into hate as Jessica sharpens her butcher knife and goes after Clint with a vengeance. There are only a few scary segments; on TV, unfortunately, the closing scenes are too dark. Watch for director Don Siegel as a bartender—Eastwood's private little joke. (Video/Laser: MCA)

PLAYROOM (1990). Variation on the mummy tales, in which an archeologist (Christopher McDonald) opens a tomb and releases the spirit of a long-buried demon prince. Directed by Manny Coto. Lisa Aliff, Aron Eisenberg, James Purcell, Jamie Rose, Vincent Schiavelli. (Video/Laser: Republic)

PLEASE DON'T EAT MY MOTHER! (1973). Revoltingly titled exploitationer—an alleged comedy about a plant that devours human flesh a la LITTLE SHOP OF HORRORS, only with a lot of bare female flesh on the premises. Produced-directed by Carl Monson. Rene Bond, Flora Wisel, Buck Kartalian. (S/Weird; Movies Unlimited; Video Dimensions)

PLUCKED (1967). See editions 1-3.

PLUMBER, THE (1979). Australia's Peter Weir directed this offbeat psychological study of a repairman who terrorizes housewives. Judy Morris, Ivar Karts, Robert Coleby, Candy Raymond. Aka THE MAD PLUMBER. (Media)

PLUTONIUM BABY (1987). A child polluted with nuclear poisoning, after watching his mother die from contamination, sets out to avenge this wrong. Produced-directed by Ray Hirschman. Danny Guerra, Patrick Molloy. (Trans World)

PLYMOUTH (1991). TV-movie might have been titled DAYS OF OUR LIVES ON LUNA. Plymouth (named after Plymouth Rock) is the first city on the moon where Dr. Audie Matheson (Cindy Pickett) raises four kids and tries to keep her pregnancy a secret from space jockey Dale Midkiff. The film's single most intriguing development—that a baby born on the moon can't survive on Earth—is dumped in favor of a disaster theme when a "solar flare" threatens the city. Your basic rescue-mission adventure. Richard Hamilton, Pery Reeves, Matthew Brown, Jerry Hardin.

POCOMANIA (1939). Voodoo thriller set in Jamaica with an all-black cast, a remake of a 1935 feature known as DRUMS OF THE JUNGLE, OUANGA and CRIME OF VOODOO. Nina Mae McKinney is a hexish priestess who curses a rival to acquire a plantation. Produced-directed by Arthur Leonard. Jack Carter, Ida James. (Reel Images)

POINT, THE (1971). Animated TV special, a thoughtful cartoon that will touch sensitivites of adults and children. A round-headed youth in a society of people with pointed heads must learn to adjust to being an "ugly duckling." He finally gets "the point." Directed by Fred Wolff. (Vestron) (Laser: Image)

POINT OF TERROR (1972). One-time actor Alex Nichol directed this Crown-International production, but frankly we missed the Terrorless Point. Peter Carpenter stars as a man who experiences a series of murders, including his own. And then he wakes up! Ah, but then you're in store for a (non)surprise. Dyanna Thorne, Lory Hansen, Paula Mitchell. (VCI; Neon)

POINT OF TERROR. Video version of **BIRD WITH THE CRYSTAL PLUMAGE, THE** (United).

POISON (1990). A prize winner at the 1991 Sundance Film Festival, this surreal story of a boy who kills his father is broken into three parts intercut into a confusing, bizarre mosaic. "Hero" is in the style of a "60 Minutes" documentary, consisting of pseudointerviews with people who know the incarcerated youth, trying to explain the killing. "Horror" is a black-and-white account of a doctor (Larry Maxwell) who has isolated the hormone of the sex drive ("the molecular coagulation theory") but turns into a leper-monster when he drinks his own serum. This is spun in a nightmarish Frankenstein fashion with satirical overtones. "Homo" depicts the disturbing, graphic adventures of a man trapped in the homosexual environment of prison, and features notorious sex sequences. Writer-director Todd Haynes was inspired by the novels of Jean Genet and uses quotations from MIRACLE OF THE ROSE, OUR LADY OF THE FLOWERS and THIEF'S JOURNAL. This enigmatic, moody art film will not be for everyone. Edith Meeks, Susan Norman, Scott Renderer. (Fox Lorber)

POISON AFFAIR, THE (1955). Also known as CASE OF POISONS, this French horror thriller is an atmospheric experiment in black mass, with undercurrents of sadism and masochism. Directed by Henri Decoin. Anne Verdon, Danielle Darrieux.

POLISH VAMPIRE IN BURBANK, A (1988). Failed foreign-produced parody of THE ADDAMS FAMILY with barely a laugh in a coffinload. A family of Dracula clones suffers from a son (writer-producer-director Mark Pirro) who doesn't want to drink blood, so a sexy member of the family introduces him to throat-biting and blood-sucking with lovely Lori Sutton. And then the creepo's brother, also a family outcast, turns up as a walking skeleton. Ugh. The cute title never pays off because we're never given any sense of the L.A. milieu, and the juvenile level to which Pirro resorts ultimately buries him alive. Bobbi Dorsch, Hugh O. Fields. (Simitar)

POLTERGEIST (1982). Smash winner from Steven Spielberg, who gave the directorial reins to Tobe Hooper. Spielberg's goal, with fellow writers Mark Grais and Michael Victor, is one of contrasts: to tell a suburbia haunted-house story and throw in all the ESP and parapsychology tricks in the books on haunting. It's a child's nightmare as unseen entities enter a tract home through the TV and inspire grosser phenomena. Along the supernatural path the daughter is trapped in another dimension, the son is attacked by a tree, and coffins and corpses pop up from the ground to terrorize the housewife. Edge-of-the-seat movie comes complete with a monstrous demon from beyond and glaring white lights. Outstanding effects by Industrial Light and Magic. Heather O'Rourke as the daughter, Craig T. Nelson as the average father, JoBeth Williams as the typical housewife and Zelda Rubenstein as the petite but powerfully weird clairvoyant. (Video/Laser: MGM/UA)

POLTERGEIST II: THE OTHER SIDE (1986). Inferior sequel to POLTERGEIST never captures the intensity of the original, no matter how many monsters or supernatural effects director Brian Gibson throws at the camera. The Freeling family (victims of that first Cuesta Verde haunting) are now staying with JoBeth Williams' mother. This time the evil spirits are members of a religious sect that sought refuge in a cave (the one under the tract home) with their maniacal leader back in the 1800s. But ole man Kane (Julian Beck) is trapped in Purgatory, and must out-magic Indian medicine man Will Sampson who chants and smokes demons up his nose. There's no logic within-the-logic-of-the-supernatural, just disconnected events with ill-defined characters. (Only Beck comes off well, looking genuinely satanic as the brimstone preacher.) Richard Edlund's effects are up to standard, but without a strong story, they float in limbo. Craig T. Nelson is back as the father, Zelda Rubinstein reprises her role as the diminutive, squeaky-voiced psychic investigator and Geraldine Fitzgerald is the dead mother who dons angel's wings in an unintentionally comic scene. (Video/Laser: MGM/UA)

POLTERGEIST III (1988). With each sequel this series becomes more disappointing, considering how good the original was. This time Carol Anne (Heather O'Rourke) is living in a New York skyscraper that her uncle designed. Nathan, that bad old dead man in a black hat, needs Carol Anne for reasons never made clear, but instead of taking her away to the dead zone, he plays horror games by breaking mirrors, shafting elevators, turning the swimming pool into an iceberg and trapping people in other dimensions. There's hardly any plot to the screenplay by Brian Taggert and producer-director Gary Sherman, so it's a tedious series of supernormal incidents. Tom Skerritt and Nancy Allen have thankless roles as the surrogate parents, Zelda Rubinstein seems a parody of the former Tangina character, and O'Rourke almost has to carry the picture herself. Unfortunately, she died not long after the film was finished, adding to the legendary stories about a curse stalking the series. Lara Flynn Boyle, Richard Fine, Kip Wentz. (Video/Laser: MGM/UA)

POOR ALBERT AND LITTLE ANNIE. See **I DISMEMBER MAMA.**

POOR DEVIL (1973). Poor TV pilot has Sammy Davis Jr. as a Devil's apostle bungling his assignments. He's given one last chance by Satan to lay claim to a human being or he'll send Davis to . . . Heaven? Christopher Lee has the Devil to play. Directed by Robert Scheerer. Jack Klugman, Adam West, Madlyn Rhue.

POOR GIRL, A GHOST STORY (1986). Michael Apted directed this one-hour episode from the British series, HAUNTED. Shades of THE INNOCENTS as governess Lynne Miller tutors for a rich family stricken with supernatural events. Angela Thorne. (Prism)

POPCORN (1991). A must-see for movie genre buffs. A film class at UC at Oceanview, taught by Tony Roberts, decides to hold a horrorthon at the Dreamland Theater showing films with William Castle-type gimmicks: "Mosquito!" is a 3-D epic satirizing monster flicks of the '50s; "Attack of the Amazing Electrified Man" (in Shock-a-Rama) is a spoof on electric killing machines; and "The Stench" (in Aroma-Rama) is a pastiche of a Japanese horror flick a la "H Man." Portions are shown as the horrorthon unfolds and takes on elements of THE PHANTOM OF THE OPERA when a masked killer stalks the committee. The film (scripted by Alan Ormsby as "Tod Hackett") goes merrily whacky with death devices, a woman (Jill Schoelen) having dreams about her past, and mysterious film maker Lanyard Gates, who once made the film "The Possessor." This mixture of send-up and thrills is delightful under Mark Herrier's direction despite a skewered sense of story. Ray Walston is a movie-memorabilia shop owner (Dr. Mnesyne) who helps the committee set up the theater. Tom Villard, Dee Wallace Stone, Derek Rydall, Elliott Hurst, Freddie Marie Simpson. (Video/Laser: RCA/Columbia)

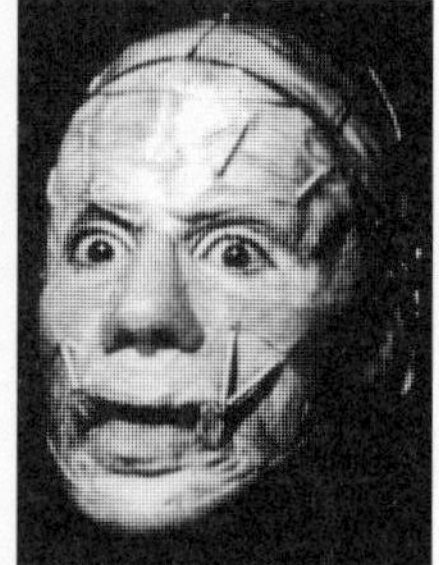

TIM VILLARD

POPDOWN (1968). British pop-up plot takes a potshot at our potent potential for Pop Art by portraying the Alien Op, a snoop cop who opportunely opts to crop up, plunk down and pore over our planet people to perceive our penchant for pop. Peculiar, plodding production for potheads poops particularly. Fred Marshall produced, directed and penned. To put it plentifully: Plop! Plooey! Piff! Pow! Plunk! Per-Klop! Diane Keen, Jane Bates, Zoot Money, Carol Rachell.

POPEYE (1980). A rarity of cinema: an adaptation of a popular comic strip that translates well to screen. Robin Williams makes his pic debut as Elzie Crisler Segar's sailor who loves spinach and Olive Oyl. Director Robert Altman, filming on Malta, captures the look and spirit of the four-color strip with a cast that steps out of the pages of "Thimble Theater." Williams' muscles had to be built up with falsy forearms, but you'd swear Shelley Duvall was born to play the beanpole Olive Oyl. The blustering sailor with the corncob pipe sings "I Yam What I Yam and That's All That I Yam," and there are 11 other songs by Harry Nilsson. Paul Dooley portrays Wimpy the hamburger lover, Paul L. Smith is the villainous Bluto (his song: "I'm Mean"), Ray Walston is Luther Billis. Script by Jules Feiffer, who must have taken his spinach as a boy. (Video/Laser: Paramount)

POPULATION: ONE (1986). See third edition.

PORN MURDERS, THE. Video version of **BLUE MURDERS, THE** (AVEC).

PORTRAIT IN TERROR. Yugoslav horror film re-edited into **TRACK OF THE VAMPIRE.**

PORTRAIT OF JENNIE (1949). Is love so powerful it transcends time, space, mortality? Struggling artist Joseph Cotten thinks so after meeting mysterious Jennifer Jones, who commissions him to paint her portrait. After an affair with Cotten, she perishes in a Cape Cod hurricane, just like another woman many years before. Jones had earlier remarked, "Where I come from, nobody knows; where I'm going, everyone goes." Profound, what? Metaphysical melodrama on the pretentious side—it's an overblown David O. Selznick production, directed by William Dieterle. Ethel Barrymore, Lillian Gish, Cecil Kellaway, David Wayne. (CBS/Fox)

PORT SINISTER (1953). Inexpensive adventure in which Port Royal, a sunken pirates' city, rises during an undersea earthquake, attracting treasure seekers who encounter giant monsters from the deep. Aka THE BEAST OF PARADISE ISLAND. Directed by Harold Daniels. James Warren, William Schallert, Lynne Roberts, House Peters Jr.

POSED FOR MURDER (1989). Playboy pinup Charlotte Helmkamp imitates life by playing a model for Thrill Magazine in an effort to get a major part in the film "Meat Cleavers From Mars." Meanwhile, a killer stalks her with tools of dismemberment. Directed by Brian Thomas Jones. Carl Fury, Rick Gianasi. (Academy)

POSSESSED, THE (1965). When Peter Baldwin turns up in an Italian village, he finds the citizens behaving like zombies—an affliction caused by Valentine Cortese. An offbeat Italian horror entry co-written and co-directed by Luigi Bazzoni and Franco Rossellini. Virna Lisi, Salvo Randone, Pia Lindstrom.

POSSESSED, THE. Video version of **DEMON WITCH CHILD** (Wizard).

POSSESSED (1974). An evil doctor operates a laboratory and death chamber in his desert castle with the help of a hunchback who beats women and dissects corpses. This joyous little horror film (also called HELP ME, I'M POSSESSED) stars Dee Peters and Lynn Marta. Written by William Greer and produced and directed by Charles Nizet. (Video Gems)

POSSESSED, THE (1977). EXORCIST-style special (liquid matter spewing from a human mouth, stuff like that) provides the highpoint for yet another TV-movie about evil spirits taking over people. The setting is a school for girls which must be cleansed by defrocked father James Farentino. Whatever possessed producer-director Jerry Thorpe? Joan Hackett, Eugene Roche, Harrison Ford, Ann Dusenberry. (Unicorn)

POSSESSED, THE (1982). See **MANHATTAN BABY.**

POSSESSION (1973). When marrieds John Carson, Joanne Dunham move into a country home, she hears screams and a whistling of "Green Sleeves." Seance medium Hilary Hardiman reveals a corpse in the cellar is reaching from beyond the grave. Brian Clemens throws in a twist to climax this inexpensive TV-movie produced in England and directed routinely by John Cooper. Poorly staged action, and not a drop of gore. If POSSESSION is nine-tenths of the law, consider this an arresting experience. Richard Aylen, James Cossins.

POSSESSION (1981). German-French production directed by Poland's Andrzej Zulawski, in which a demonic creature (created by Carlo Rambaldi and resembling the newborn babe in ERASERHEAD) takes over Isabele Adjani, forcing her to have violent spells and misbehave in a Berlin subway station. Meanwhile, her husband, Berlin businessman Sam Neill, tracks down her lovers to dispose of them. This film has won foreign awards and is full of bloody excesses, making it simultaneously compelling and repulsive. (Vestron)

POSSESSION OF JOEL DELANEY (1972). Tense, unsettling supernatural thriller in which socialite Shirley MacLaine realizes her brother's soul is possessed by voodoo in downtown Manhattan. Black magic in squalid tenements? This contrast of imagery is nicely visualized by director Waris Hussein. The climax in a lonely beach cottage offers (a) a severed head and (b) a twist ending that might surprise you. Perry King, Michael Hordern, Lovelady Powell. (Paramount)

POSSESSION UNTIL DEATH DO YOU PART (1987). Another despicable example of how movies demean womanhood as nothing more than an object for male desire—and murder. John R. Johnston is a wide-eyed babbling idiot with a mother fixation who kills indiscriminately, using blunt screwdrivers, stakes, shovels, axes and other implements, apparently to make up for the one major tool he's lacking. An excuse for scenes of beautiful women taking baths and showers, dressing and undressing, and behaving like sex objects as they attend drunken orgies and male strip clubs. There isn't an ounce of entertainment as Johnston, his face painted like a wild Indian, goes on his bloody spree. Directed by Lloyd A. Simandl and Michael Mazo. Melissa Martin, Cat Williams. (Marathon; Cinema Group)

POSSESSOR, THE (1972). Italian hokum about a medallion that curses an archeology student to commit murder. A female succubus is responsible. Cheap stuff originally entitled SEX OF THE WITCH, and also known as THE EVIL EYE. Directed by Elo Panaccio. Susan Levi, Jessica Dublin. (Lightning)

POTTSVILLE HORROR, THE. See **BEING, THE.**

POUND PUPPIES AND THE LEGEND OF BIG PAW (1988). "Puppy Power," a magical means of people and dogs talking to each other, is the basis for this animated cartoon based on the Saturday morning TV series. Voices by George Rose, B. J. Ward, Ruth Buzzi and Nancy Cartwright. Directed by Pierre DeCelles. (Family Home Entertainment)

POWER, THE (1968). Producer George Pal took the gourmet novel by Frank Robinson and turned it into a plate of scrambled eggs. John Gay's screenplay is undernourished, and Byron Haskin's direction unfulfilling, as George Hamilton realizes that one of several men in a research project has a terrible "power" to move objects, to blot out entire memories and to kill by telekinesis. In short, one of the finest novels of the 1950s emerged as one of the most disappointing films of the 1960s. Offbeat music by Miklos Rozsa. Suzanne Pleshette, Michael Rennie, Nehemiah Persoff, Earl Holliman, Richard Carlson, Aldo Ray, Ken Murray, Barbara Nichols, Yvonne De Carlo. (Paramount)

POWER, THE (1984). Not an original idea in this low-budget hunkajunk from Jeffrey Obrow and Steve Carpenter, who concocted THE DORM THAT DRIPPED BLOOD. A clay Aztec figurine (housing evil powers of the god Destacatyl) levitates a man and pinions him on a spike, drops a ton of steel on a nightwatchman and harasses a reporter for a tabloid as sleazy at this movie. The exploding arms and throbbing armpits have been done before and the climax is a monster terrorizing Susan Stokey and teen-agers in an ordinary house. They even had the audacity to steal the title of Frank Robinson's sci-fi classic. Shameful. (Vestron)

POWER MAN. See **POWER WITHIN, THE.**

POWER OF THE WHISTLER (1945). "The Whistler" was originally a radio suspense series about a wandering story-teller who "knows many things for I walk by night . . . " The film adaptations were inexpensive but well-produced noir thrillers. In this one, directed by Lew Landers and written by Aubrey Weisberg, a fortune teller predicts the death of Richard Dix, who just happens to be homicidal. Janis Carter, Jeff Donnell.

POWER PILL, THE (1968). MR. TERRIFIC was a short-lived sitcom depicting the nebbish misadventures of gas station nerd Stanley Beemish, who possesses superhuman powers a la Superman when he swallows a pill concocted by the Bureau of Special Projects in Washington, an agency run by John McGiver. Beemish (Stephen Strimpell) is enmeshed in espionage plots as he fumbles his way to victory in this compilation of half-hour episodes; a subplot involves everyone looking for a device that nullifies all sources of power. Companion compilation is THE PILL CAPER, which is just as terrible tasting. Directed by Jack Arnold.

POWER WITHIN, THE (1979). Standard TV-movie/pilot-for-a-proposed series (THE POWER MAN) with Art Hindle as a barnstorming pilot who is struck by lightning and suddenly can point his finger and zap things with an electric ray. Seems his mother was exposed to a blast of radiation on the day of his birth and now he can store up energy like a battery. Spies Eric Braeden and David Hedison mistakenly think that Hindle is part of a suspended-animation project and kidnap his girlfriend scientist. Directed by John Llewellyn Moxey. Edward Binns, Joe Rassulo, Richard Sargent. (MCA; Prism)

PRANCER (1989). Mawkish, unappealing children's fantasy, about a little girl's love for a reindeer she believes to be Santa's. As the centerpiece for a sentimental movie, the reindeer is without charm or warmth and one can only wonder what possessed producer Raffaella de Laurentiis. An unbelievable mess with the girl's mean old wicked father (Sam Elliott) undergoing an unconvincing character change. Even Cloris Leachman's crotchedy old woman, who's supposed to be sympathetic, isn't. The ad proclaims "Something magical is about to happen," but it never does. Also forgettable: John Hancock's direction and Maurice Jarre's score. Abe Vigoda, Michael Constantine, Rutanya Alda. (Orion) (Laser: Nelson)

PRANKS. See **DORM THAT DRIPPED BLOOD.**

PRAYER OF THE ROLLERBOYS (1991). Despite the pseudofuturistic setting and scads of extras on roller skates, this is not part of the ROLLERBALL series. Set in a society that is breaking down, this depicts undercover agent Corey Haim penetrating a gang of extortionists called "Rollerboys" to uncover a plot to sterilize the population. Fantasy elements are minimal—this plays more like a crime thriller. Directed perfunctorily by Rick King, who only wrings a few moments of excitement during roller-skate chase sequences employing a mobile camera. Patricia Arquette, Christopher Collet, Julius Harris, Devin Clark. (Academy) (Laser: Image)

PRAYING MANTIS (1982). The dark side of woman's deceit and deception is dramatized in this British TV-movie adaptation of Hubert Monteilhet's novel, LES MANTES RELIGIEUSES, a complicated but enthralling tale of adultery, lesbianism, murder and revenge involving an aristocratic couple and commoners who blur the class distinctions with their nefarious schemes. The acting is impeccable, with the cast headed by Jonathan Pryce as a weak-willed anthropologist. The "praying mantis" women are etched in subtleties and extremes by Cherie Lunghi and Carmen Du Sautoy. The direction by Jack Gold is cold and calculated, contrasting the lovers' passion. (Karl Lorimar)

PRAY TV. Video of **KGOD** (Vestron) (Laser: Image).

PREDATOR (1987). Tense, action-packed, high-tech sci-fi/horror adventure, forever moving under John McTiernan's direction as Arnold Schwarzenegger and his commando team move into a South American jungle to retrieve a cabinet member held hostage by rebel forces. What Arnie and his men don't know, once they've completed their mission in a blaze of pyrotechnics, is that they are being stalked by an alien creature, on Earth to claim human trophies. Finally it's just Arnie against the alien as he uses his wits Rambo style. Early scenes of the alien using camouflage techniques (by Stan Winston) are effective, the tension sustains and the film ends on a satisfying, uplifting note after an intense bashing match. Carl Weathers, Elpida Carrillo, Bill Duke, Jesse Ventura, R. G. Armstrong. (Video/Laser: CBS/Fox)

PREDATOR 2 (1990). A relentless, driving pace, gory action and a futuristic setting (L.A. 1997) in which drug gangs are making life miserable for police provide an unusual background for this sequel movie about the semi-invisible hunter from another planet who stalks human beings for his trophy room. The script by Jim and John Thomas has lapses but director Stephen Hopkins keeps it moving. Danny Glover stars as the cop Harrigan who is forced to work with creepy FBI agent Gary Busey when drug dealers start turning up dead—victims of the alien offspring of the creature from the first film. Alan Silvestri's score is an enhancement. Seven-foot-tall Kevin Peter Hall is back as the monster. Ruben Blades, Maria Conchita Alonso, Bill Paxton, Kent McCord, Calvin Lockhart, Mortton Downey Jr. (Video/Laser: CBS/Fox)

'PREDATOR'

PREHISTORIC WOMEN (1950). Treated as a pseudodocumentary, with a narrator blabbering about primeval man while primitives in loincloths and animal pelts stand around speaking prehistoric gibberish. In one sequence the hero caveman discovers fire and cooks a side of beef. The first hash slinger! Don't let lipstick on the girls 20,000 B.C. bother you—it didn't bother director Gregg Tallas. Allan Nixon, Laurette Luez. (Rhino; S/Weird; Filmfax)

PREHISTORIC WOMEN (1966). Voluptuous brunettes and fair-skinned blondes in animal-skin bikinis are the primary (and primordial?) reason to watch this Hammer delight primevally produced-directed by Michael Carreras in the wake of his other semi-nude girly-revue triumphs: SHE and ONE MILLION YEARS B.C. Big game hunter Michael Latimore is magically transported through time to prehistoric days when evil ruler Martine Beswick (captivating, shall we say?) holds sway over her fair-haired slaves, among them pouty-lipped, ravenous Edina Ronay and buxom Carol White. This girl-watcher's delight, made in England as SLAVE GIRLS, is utter nonsense, but nonsense men enjoy as the acres of undulating flesh parade past the camera and bevies of babes perform ritual dances that might have been choreographed by Busby Berkeley. And dig that phallic-symbol nose on the rhino, a deep intellectual comment on the primitive urges that motivate mankind. Stephanie Randall, Alexandra Stevenson. (Increase)

PREHISTORIC WORLD. See **TEENAGE CAVEMAN.**

PREHYSTERIA (1993). To cash in on the JURASSIC PARK-dinosaur hysteria of '93, Charles Band and his father Albert co-produced and -directed this light-hearted video comedy in which four dinosaur eggs hatch four cutesy-pie creatures that proceed to mischievously plague a household that includes a couple of nice, affectionate kids. David Allen's special effects and Richard Band's sublime musical score are the highlights of this adolescent romp. Brett Cullen, Colleen Morris, Samantha Mills, Austin O'Brien, Tony Longo. (Paramount)

PRELUDE TO A KISS (1992). It's the old soul transference theme again, this time an aging man taking over the body of a young woman after he kisses her during her wedding ceremomy. Craig Lucas' 1988 Broadway play was adapted by Lucas for director Norman Rene with a sensitive, sophisticated touch that keeps events on a spiritual, moving level. Alec Baldwin, who starred in the play, is back as the husband who realizes bride Meg Ryan is not a woman but a man, and Sydney Walker is the old man whose kiss starts it all. Kathy Bates, Ned Beatty, Patty Duke, Richard Riehle, Stanley Tucci. (Fox)

PRELUDE TO TAURUS (1972). See editions 1-3.

PREMATURE BURIAL, THE (1962). One of the best in Roger Corman's Edgar Allan Poe series, reeking with decay and desolation as nobleman Ray Milland, who lives in a weird house isolated on a foggy moor, is obsessed with the fear of being buried alive. Ray Russell and Charles Beaumont concocted an intriguing if frequently corny storyline that, combined with Daniel Haller's set design and Corman's direction, is a winner. Hazel Court, Richard Ney, Heather Angel, Alan Napier, John Dierkes. (Vestron)

PREMONITION, THE (1975). Despite a ponderous beginning, this emerges an offbeat tale of ESP, with supernatural overtones, in the hands of director Robert Allen Schnitzer. It unfolds like a mystery story as crazed mother Ellen Barber seeks to reclaim the baby she gave away for adoption, aided by a crazy carnival clown (Richard Lynch). Sharon Farrell, the new mother, experiences flashes of things to come and other phenomena as the kidnaping plot unfolds, thickened by the appearance of a female doctor experimenting in telepathetic dreams. Some elements don't blend smoothly, but the film gallops to a rapid conclusion, with policeman Jeff Corey helping out. Filmed in Mississippi. (Embassy)

PRESENCE, THE. See **WITCHTRAP.**

PRESIDENT'S ANALYST, THE (1967). Writer-director Theodore J. Flicker's outre satire on presidential administrations, the FBI and our obsession with violence, conspiracies and counterespionage. James Coburn, headshrinker for the President, learns more than he should and flees for his life, pursued by humanoid robot killers. Outrageous, iconoclastic, thoroughly enjoyable if you like off-the-wall humor. Godfrey Cambridge, Pat Harrington, Will Geer, Arte Johnson. (Paramount)

PRESIDENT VANISHES, THE (1934). Third edition.

PRETTYKILL (1987). Detective David Birney has his hands full as he stalks a serial killer who murders prostitutes, and tries to deal with the split personality of his girl Season Hubley. Directed by George Kaczender. Susannah York, Yaphet Kotto. (Warner Bros.) (Laser: Image)

PREVIEW MURDER MYSTERY, THE (1936). See editions 1-3.

PREY. See **ALIEN PREY.**

PREY, THE (1980). A man in the woods is beheaded by his own axe. Along come three guys and three gals, and guess who are "the prey." A lot of footage of bugs, insects, snakes, spiders, raccoons and other creatures preying on each other, as well as gushing blood, severed throats and detached heads. Someone tells "The Monkey's Paw" at a campfire. Minor slasher movie, very minor. Directed by Edwin Scott Brown. Debbie Thureson, Steve Bond. (Thorn EMI/HBO; Starmaker)

PRICELESS BEAUTY (1989). Better this should be called HIGHLANDER DREAMS OF JEANNIE. Christopher Lambert plays a rock star who feels responsible for his brother's motorcycle death and retires to Italy's coast to become angst-riddled. When he finds China, a "small genie" in an ancient urn who materializes as shapely Diane Ladd, life improves but he still refuses to return to the music world. Lambert's search for love amidst personal pain gets in the way of any enjoyment this minor Italian production might have had. With its ponderous pacing, lengthy shots in which nothing happens, and Lambert's overwrought performance, writer-director Charles Finch should be put in a bottle. Francesco Quinn, J.C. Quinn. (Video/Laser: Republic)

PRIMAL IMPULSE (1974). Bizarre combination of sci-fi (an astronaut is stranded on the moon) and horror (astronaut sends thought waves back to Earth to control a woman's mind). Klaus Kinski stars. (Lightning)

PRIMAL RAGE (1990). The bite of a monkey undergoing lab experiments causes a student to feel basic urges manifesting in strange ways. A reporter uncovers the cause as a mad scientist on a college campus. Special effects by Carlo Rimbaldi. Directed by Vittorie Rambaldi. Patrick Lowe, Bo Svenson. (Warner Bros.)

PRIMAL SCREAM (1987). Imitation of BLADE RUNNER with elements of the private-eye thriller. A new power source, Hellfire, is being developed by a corporation of questionable values. When a space colony near Saturn is destroyed, earthbound PI Corby McHale (Kenneth J. McGregor) gets involved with a beautiful dame (Sharon Mason as Samantha Keller) and others (including Nicky Fingers, played by Joseph White) in an incomprehensible plot ill-conceived by director William Murray. This low-budget effort has moments of sheer energy, but then so do pantyhose. (Magnum; Nova)

PRIME EVIL (1988). Lackluster and tedious bit about a devil cult formed in the 14th Century, at the time of the Black Death, so the Parkman family will have eternal life and carry out acts of "prime evil" for Lucifer. The supernatural elements are boring rather than stimulating, the monster that oversees the sacrifical rites is not convincing, and there's predictable business about beauties in white robes about to be sacrificed. The whole business, directed by Roberta Findlay, is without inspiration. William Beckwith. (New World) (Laser: Image)

PRIME RISK (1984). Diverting spy-superscience flick, derivative of WARGAMES. Computer expert Toni Hudson and pilot Lee Montgomery team up to rip off a bank's automated teller machine, only to stumble across a plot by foreign spies (led by Keenan Wynn) to destroy the U.S. currency system via computers. They rush to Washington D.C. to warn the CIA, but agents Samuel Bottoms and Clu Gulager are hard-headed. Written-directed by Michael Farkas. (Lightning; Live)

PRINCE OF DARKNESS, THE (1987). Writer-director John Carpenter creates an above-average supernatural thriller reminiscent of his ASSAULT ON PRECINCT 13 in that the story is in a single setting where main characters are trapped. It's an abandoned L.A. church watched over by a sect called the Brotherhood of Sleep. A weird container of swirling fluids is a doorway for the Devil to return to Earth. Scientists led by Victor Wong and priest Donald Pleasence study the phenomenon only to fall pray to zombies. Old superstitions vs. computers is an exciting element, and one wishes Carpenter had focused more on that than the gory murders he overuses to keep the plot moving. Carpenter directs with a sense of doom (enhanced by his synthesized score). Jameson Parker, Lisa Blount, Dennis Dun, Susan Blanchard. Alice Cooper has a small role as a street bum. (Video/Laser: MCA)

PRINCE OF SPACE (1959). Japanese superhero stuff, designed for kids, in which the undefeatable Planet Prince comes to Earth in a flying saucer to defend us hapless humans from alien invaders. In the first of two episodes, the priceless Prince tangles with Phantom Mission, a magician trying to swipe a new rocket fuel. In the second, the Phantom teams with giants to kidnap a physicist. Directed by Eijiro Wakabayashi. (S/Weird)

PRINCESS BRIDE, THE (1987). This gallant attempt by director Robert Reiner to recapture the qualities of an old-fashioned fairy tale is a refreshing treat with only occasional moments of fizzle. Adapted by William Goldman from his popular book, Chris Sarandon must rescue his princess lover (Cary Elwes) from kidnappers. On his odyssey, he meets villain Christopher Guest, talkative kidnaper Vizzini (Wallace Shawn in the film's funniest role), lovable brute Fezzik (Andre the Giant), Miracle Max (Billy Crystal, unrecognizable in makeup), old witch Valerie (Carol Kane, also unrecognizable), and a Spanish swordsman (Mandy Patinkin) seeking the six-fingered murderer of his father. For monster lovers there are giant killer eels, a huge muskrat in the Fire Swamp and "The Machine," a contraption that sucks your life away. Peter Falk portrays the grandfather who reads bedridden Fred Savage the tale from an old book. (Nelson) (Laser: Nelson; Criterion)

PRINCESS CINDERELLA (1955). Italian version of the Cinderella fantasy, doctored up to feature fairy tale ingredients. Directed by Sergio Tofano. Silvano Jachino, Robert Villa. (JEF Films)

PRINCESS WARRIOR (1990). One sorry excuse for a low (make that "nonexistent") budget fantasy, and one miserably acted and directed flicker. It opens on Vulkara, a planet of sexy bubbleheaded blondes in negligees. Among them are sisters vying with Queenmother (Cheryl Janecky) for power. A teleporter carries several of them to Earth where the queen partakes in a wet t-shirt contest, meets a motorbike guy (Mark Pacific) and two L.A. cops (Tony Riccardi and Augie Blunt) who are as dumb as the blondes. These antics go on forever. Only funny thing is the name of a Vulkarian: Bulemia. Ha ha ha! Lindsay Norgard directed without revealing talent. Dana Fredsti, Sharon Lee Jones.

PRISON (1987). There's a tough, brutal edge to this supernatural tale set within Wyoming State Penitentiary, in which the spirit of an electrocuted prisoner, William Forsythe, returns from the dead as an energy field. Inanimate objects become very animated as they kill off the prisoners and guards, with a barbed-wire death being quite effective. Charles Band's production, has a strong sense of doom and grittiness provided by director Renny Harlin. Lane Smith, Viggo Mortensen, Chelsea Field, Lincoln Kilpatrick. (New World) (Laser: Image)

PRISONER, THE (1967). Classic fantasy-mystery British TV series, first shown on U.S. TV in 1968 as a summer replacement. Created by Patrick McGoohan, it also stars McGoohan as an intelligence officer who resigns his position and is suddenly kidnapped and taken to a remote village to be brainwashed by agents of an unknown power. There are no pat answers to who, what and why, for this is an experiment in surrealism, a metaphor for man's undying will to escape his captors and enjoy freedom. All 17 episodes of this enthralling series are on video. (MPI; Maljack) (Laser: Image)

PRISONER OF THE CANNIBAL GOD. See **SLAVE OF THE CANNIBAL GOD.**

PRISONERS OF THE LOST UNIVERSE (1983). Fantasy-adventure on the level of a Saturday matinee. TV personality Kay Lenz and workaday electrician Richard Hatch are propelled into another dimension, a medieval world where evil tribesman Kleel (John Saxon) rules with an iron gauntlet. Hatch, who just happens to be an expert kendo swordsman, and Lenz, who has a spicy tongue and liberated attitude, do in the heavies with the help of a comedy-relief thief (Peter O'Farrell) and a Green Man (Ray Charleson). There are moments when director Terry Marcle captures a spirit of fun and action, but otherwise it's colossally stupid. Effects are mediocre. Kenneth Hendel, Myles Robertson. (VCL)

PRISON SHIP STAR SLAMMER. See **STAR SLAMMER.**

PRIVATE EYES (1953). See editions 1-3.

PRIVATE EYES (1981). Tim Conway claims he wrote the script for this mystery-comedy parody over a weekend, and it shows. Conway and Don Knotts are bumbling detectives investigating a millionaire's murder at a castle estate. They encounter all the "old dark house" cliches. Lang Elliott directs so indifferently that the most thrilling thing in this comedy of terrors and errors is the shapely body of Trisha Noble. Now there's something to scream (joyfully) about! Bernard Fox, Grace Zabriskie, John Fujioka. (Video/Laser: Vestron)

PRIVATE LIFE OF SHERLOCK HOLMES, THE (1970). Must-see for Baker Street Irregulars and Holmesphiles . . . a minor masterpiece written by Billy Wilder and I.A.L. Diamond and directed by Wilder, with excellent music by Miklos Rozsa. Robert Stephens makes the

London sleuth a much likable man with a sense of humor and a self-effacing manner. Almost at once the game is afoot when Holmes helps an attempted suicide . . . a plot involving marvelous Jules Verne-style gadgets, Queen Victoria and Holmes' supercilious brother Mycroft (Christopher Lee). Lush, expensive production handsomely mounted, which unfortunately died at the box office and has been brutally edited. Colin Blakely essays an intelligent Dr. Watson. Genevieve Page, Clive Revill. (Key)

PRIVATE LIVES OF ADAM AND EVE, THE (1961). See editions 1-3.

PRIVATE PARTS (1972). Dilapidated hotel in L.A. slums is the setting for this morbid tale of murderous misfits. This weird excursion by director Paul Bartel relies on grotesque visuals without character expansion. A 14-year-old runaway (Ann Ruymen) seeks refuge among residents who behave like asylum inmates: swishy ex-minister, photographer who makes love to plastic mannequins, etc. Pretty kinky; you kids send the adults to bed early if this shows up on the late show. Produced by Gene Corman, Roger's brother. Stanley Livingston, John Ventantonio. (MGM/UA)

PRIVILEGE (1967). Visually fascinating British fantasy, directed by Peter Watkins in pseudodocumentary style (not unlike his WAR GAME), is ruthlessly savage in its use of political satire, unrelenting in depicting greed. In a Britain of the near future popular singer Paul Jones is misused by a coalition government as a propaganda device to persuade young people to conform. Jones, a neurotic, uptight, laconic pawn, finally revolts after he is shrouded in religious neo-Nazi mysticism during a lavish night rally. Required viewing for fantasy buffs and for those with strong political consciences.

PRIZE OF PERIL, THE (1983). Futuristic "death game" movie (based on a short story by Robert Sheckley) in which men must match their skills against each other for cash money on a life-and-death competition that is televised to the public (shades of THE RUNNING MAN). French film directed by Yves Boisset. Gerard Lanvin, Michel Piccoli, Marie-France Pisier. (Astral)

PROBE (1972). Leslie Stevens wrote-produced this pilot for the short-lived series SEARCH, which depicts colorless secret agents using sophisticated electronic gadgets against spies. Commonplace as TV movies go. Directed by Russ Mayberry. Burgess Meredith, Angel Tompkins, Elke Sommer, John Gielgud. (Unicorn)

PROFESSOR, THE (1958). Theatrical short subject relates existence of a werewolf to a communist plot, reflecting Red-Scare hysteria of the '50s. (From S/Weird and Filmfax with wolfman-movie trailers)

PROFESSOR CREEPS, THE (1942). Editions 1-3.

PROFESSOR POTTER'S MAGIC POTIONS (1983). Juvenilistic British comedy by the Children's Film Foundation Ltd. will interest kids only. Potter's an absent-minded fool concocting new discoveries which elementary schoolers use to foul up the system. There's an elixir of truth, a superstrength drink, a spray that turns adolescent warbling into beautiful singing, and a Fountain of Youth formula which reverts the Head Master back to his childhood. Silly and inconsequential. Directed by Peter K. Smith.

PROFILE OF TERROR. See **SADIST, THE.**

PROGRAMMED TO KILL (1987). Instead of a male cyborg a la THE TERMINATOR, this time the killer is a female model, created by the CIA to recover children kidnapped by terrorists. Sandahl Bergman portrays the lady liquidator. Written by Robert Short, who co- directed with Allan Holzman. Robert Ginty, James Booth, Alex Courtney. Also called THE RETALIATOR. (Media)

PROJECT ALIEN. Video/laser version of **FATAL SKY, THE** (Video/Laser: Vidmark).

PROJECTED MAN, THE (1967). British horror thriller with scientific ovetones would have been more watchable with faster pacing and less superfluous material. Bryant Halliday is made hideous during an experiment with matter transference gadgets. Now his mere touch can kill, and he's on a rampage of murder and destruction. Mary Peach, Tracy Crisp, Norman Wooland, Derek Farr. Ian Curteis directed.

PROJECTIONIST, THE (1971). Experimental, offbeat collage of social comment, in-jokes, satire, etc. Written-produced-directed-edited by Harry Hurwitz. Projectionist Chuck McMann is so caught up in his private film fantasy world he superimposes dreams over reality, becoming Captain Flash and constantly saving the world from some disaster. Rodney Dangerfield, Ina Balin, Harry Hurwitz. (Vestron; Live)

PROJECT M-7 (1953). See editions 1-3.

PROJECT MOONBASE (1953). Robert Heinlein helped producer Jack Seaman write this Robert L. Lippert film, about man going to the moon. Directed by Richard Talmadge. Donna Martell, Ross Ford. (Vidmark)

PROJECT NIGHTMARE (198?). Two men flee their worst nightmares, meeting a lone beauty in the desert. Directed by Donald Jones. Charles Miller, Seth Foster, Elly Koslo. (Academy)

PROJECT SHADOWCHASER (1992). Subtitle this "Hospital Die Hard Meets Cyborg Man Under Siege." All flippancy aside, it's a rousing "high tech" sci-fi action thriller starring Martin Kove as a criminal brought out of suspended animation to infiltrate a highrise hospital that's been taken over by terrorists led by Romulus (Frank Zagarino), a billion-dollar android ("a perfect synthetic warrior") turned renegade against his ruthless government-backed creator (Joss Ackland). Kove's aided by the President's daughter (Meg Foster in a miniskirt) while FBI guy Paul Koslo assists from control center. Stephen Lister's script has so many twists and surprises that this plays better than some of the big-budgets actioners it imitates. And it's well directed by John Eyres. (Prism) (Laser: Image)

PROJECT VAMPIRE (1992). "Resurrection by injection" is the tag line for this zero-budget horror thriller with sci-fi overtones, in which crazed German Dr. Klaus and his blond nurse, who decidedly has the hots for his perverted Teutonic profile, carries out "Project Alpha" with cackling, hand rubbing and predictions of world conquest. This daffy duo wants to turn the world into blood-drinking vampires by injecting everyone with a secret-formula serum. Most of the action is of the chase variety, with little linking logic—a technique of writer-director Peter Flynn. Myron Natwick, Brian Knudson, Mary-Louise Gemmill. (Video/Laser: Action International)

PROJECT X (1968). Gimmick specialist William Castle purchased two novels by L. P. Davies—ARTIFICIAL MAN and PSYHCOGEIST—and dovetaild them into a far-out story about scientists circa 2118 who trick secret agent Christopher George into believing he's passed back through time to the 1960s. Motive: to probe his mind and uncover some Deep Dark Secret about how to stop a Soviet-Chinese invasion. Hallucinatory sequences with animation were provided by Hanna-Barbera. Henry Jones, Monte Markham, Harold Gould, Keye Luke. (CBS/Fox)

PROJECT X (1987). An excellent and moving melodrama with comedy overtones starring Matthew Broderick as an Air Force pilot who gets assigned to a secret project involving the study of intelligence in chimpanzees. When Fox learns that the creatures (with whom he can communicate) are to be destroyed, he takes drastic steps. Totally entertaining and satisfying. Directed by Jonathan Kaplan. Helen Hunt, Bill Sadler, Robin Gammell, Stephen Lang. (Video/Laser: CBS/Fox)

PROM NIGHT (1980). In a moment of moppets' malice, four youngsters cause the death of a fifth . . . years later, an axe-packing, black-masked killer turns up at the school prom to wreak revenge. This gore thriller features one harrowing chase through the campus, but is otherwise predictable slasher fare. You'll feel stood up. Directed by Paul Lynch. Jamie Lee Curtis, Leslie Nielsen, Robert Silverman, Antoinette Bower. (Pioneer Artists; MCA) (Laser: MCA)

PROM NIGHT II. See **HELLO MARY LOU: PROM NIGHT II.**

PROM NIGHT III: THE LAST KISS (1990). Following through on the supernatural elements inherent in the second PROM NIGHT film, this is an undistinguished rehash of clumsy cliches and stupefying stereotypes that are moldy hat. Beauty queen Mary Lou Mahoney (Courtney Taylor) is back from the dead to hypnotize student Tim Conlon into helping her carry out murders, with death devices seemingly stolen from PHANTASM. Since it's all been done before, there's not much pizzazz in Ron Oliver's directing or writing. Cyndy Preston, David Stratton. (IVE) (Laser: Image)

PROM NIGHT IV: DELIVER US FROM EVIL (1991). Better-than-average slasher flick, despite cliches and predictable twists, primarily because the Richard Beattie script spends time setting up four characters for the climactic kill. The murderer is a Catholic priest kept locked up since 1957, when he viciously murdered prom nighters for performing sex. In 1991 he escapes his captors and closes in on the four celebrating students gathered in a country manor for fun and sex. The customary association between sex and death in these slasher things is utilized to the utmost as the bloody events unfold. Directed by Clay Borris with the usual POV shots of the killer spying on his victims and an array of religious symbolism. If anyone shines in this bloodbath it is Nikki de Boer, who undergoes harrowing near-death experiences—barefoot yet. Alden Kane, Joy Tanner. (Video/Laser: Live)

PROMISE OF RED LIPS. See **DAUGHTERS OF DARKNESS.**

PROPHECIES OF NOSTRADAMUS (1979). Packaged in video under the title NOSTRADAMUS, this Australian TV documentary is a study of the 16th century prophet Michael Nostradamus, who wrote hundreds of quatrains which might have predicted the future. Of special interest are his quatrains referring to the three Antichrists, two of whom were Hitler and Napoleon, and a description of what would appear to be an atomic war that will occur no later than 1999. The third Antichrist, if you believe the soothsayer, has yet to rise to power. Speculative but intriguing.

PROPHECY (1979). Director John Frankenheimer fails to come to grips with making an effective horror thriller. Scriptwriter David Seltzer disguises this tale with ecological themes and social "significance," but none of it helps to make the monster plot cohesive. Tom Burman's grotesque creatures, created by pollution, are frightening at first, but then become grotesque as the film turns into a chase-action film. Armand Assante, Talia Shire, Robert Foxworth, Richard Dysart. (Paramount)

PROTECTORS, BOOK I. See **ANGEL OF H.E.A.T.**

PROTOTYPE (1983). Thinking man's sci-fi TV-movie, written with dignity by Richard Levinson and William Link in dealing with the dilemma a scientist faces when his creation is used for ill purposes. The new design is a humanoid (David Morse) perfected by scientist Christopher Plummer. When the Pentagon intervenes, Plummer steals his creation and hides him away. Levinson and Link concentrate on the cerebral, intellectual aspects. Arthur Hill, as a Pentagon general, is restrained and sympathetic, indicating the writers feel there are two sides to every weapon. David Greene directs with a sure, restrained hand. Frances Sternhagen, James Sutorius, Stephen Elliott. (King Bee; Live) (Laser: Live)

PROTOTYPE X29A (1992). Good computer graphics and a strong story about the merging of man's soul into the metal body of a programmed robot make this special-effects sci-fi actioner above average. In 2057 A.D., cybernetic humans (Omegans) are hunted down by killer cyborgs (Prototypes) and intrigue surrounds one scientist's attempt to alter the program. Writer-director Phillip Roth captures a nihilistic landscape and the sadness of humans/machines caught up in the bleakness of a shattered society. Lane Lenhart, Robert Tossberg, Brenda Swanson. (Video/Laser: Vidmark)

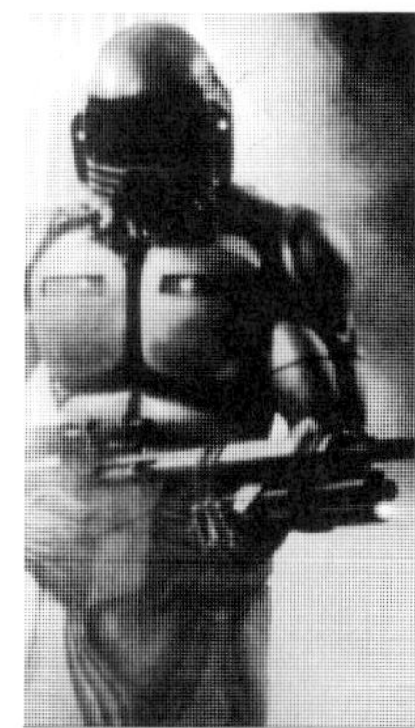
X29A MODEL

PROWLER, THE (1981). One of the better slasher bloodbaths that flowed in the wake of FRIDAY THE THIRTEENTH, with just enough tantilizing mystery to go with Tom Savini's bloodily graphic make-up. The bloodletting begins in 1945 when two prom attendees are impaled on a pitchfork, presumably by a crazed GI just returned from combat. Jump to 1980, when a menacing figure in fatigues and helmet, his face hideously scarred, stalks the campus on prom night, shoving his bayonet through the head of a male victim and impaling a naked woman in a shower with his thematic pitchfork. This is an intense murder sequence and ranks as one of the best in the slasher canon. Director Joseph Zito maintains a gloomy, suspenseful atmosphere in the stalking sequences. Vicky Dawson is credible as the heroine who accompanies sheriff Christopher Goutman. Lawrence Tierney and Farley Granger add touches of professionalism to this cut above the average, if you"ll excuse the pun. Also called THE GRADUATION. (VCII; Direct; from VCI as **ROSEMARY'S KILLER**)

PSI-FACTOR, THE (1980). Low-budget sci-fi thriller: Peter Mark Richman is a scientist working on the secretive Deep Probe Project when he picks up musical sounds from Cyrus III. After a yellow ball of light visits Richman's home, the Air Force personnel attached to the project don't believe him and he and girlfriend Gretchen Corbett flee a conspiratorial cover-up. Director Bryan Trizers tries to bring the characters to life during the pursuit, but the cheesy effects and an unconvincing resolution defeat this effort of good intentions. Tom Martin, Tom Troupe, Don Eitner, Britt Leach. (Monarch)

PSYCHIC, THE (1968). Little-known effort from goremeister Herschell Gordon Lewis, in which a business executive, given psychic powers after an accident, goes totally mad. Dick Genola, Robyn Guest, Bobbi Spencer. (Camp; S/Weird)

PSYCHIC, THE (1977). Jennifer O'Neill's performance as a woman who suffers visions of violent deaths that have happened or will happen elevates this Italian psychothriller from director-writer Lucio Fulci (ZOMBIE), who unfortunately lingers too long on O'Neill's face and zooms the landscape like a maniacal cinematographer, distracting from the suspense of O'Neill's discovery of a body entombed in a country estate. The most effective sequence has O'Neill as a child visualizing her mother's suicidal plunge from a cliff as her face scrapes against the shale and rips to shreds. Gabriele Ferzetti, Marc Porel, Gianni Garko. (Catalina; Lightning)

PSYCHIC (1991). Taut, cat-and-mouse Hitchcockian TV-movie thriller with ESP overtones. College student Zach Galligan has prophetic visions of a serial killer in dark glasses but becomes a suspect when he tries to help disbelieving police. Thin characterizations (including a villain that needed to be fleshed out) and a few slasher-movie cliches are deficiencies director George Mihalka tries valiantly to overcome. Catherine Mary Stewart, Michael Nouri, Albert Schultz. (Vidmark)

PSYCHIC KILLER (1975). Convicted murderer Jim Hutton learns astral projection through a strange medallion and, when released, uses his power against those who wronged him. The revenge killings foreshadow techniques in slasher films to come. Despite inspired moments, this is hampered by an inadequate budget and ordinary direction by Ray Danton, who cast then-wife Julie Adams as a psychiatrist heroine, Paul Burke and Aldo Ray as bewildered cops, Nehemiah Persoff as a believer in ESP and Neville Brand as a butcher. Rod Cameron, Della Reese, Whit Bissell. (Embassy)

PSYCHO (1960). The ultimate in horror thrills, a genuine genre classic. It's a series of cinematic tricks allowing director Alfred Hitchcock to indulge his unique, impactful techniques. The shower sequence, the most famous movie murder of all time, demonstrates the fine art of editing, and there are at least three other sequences which will have you leaping once Hitch focuses on Norman Bates, a reclusive young man who runs a motel and lives in a weird house with his domineering mother. But first there's Janet Leigh embezzling money from her boss and taking it on the lam. Later, her lover John Gavin and her sister Vera Miles search for her, as does investigator Martin Balsam. Then comes the sequence when Miles dares to enter the Bates' cellar and . . . but we can't reveal more without spoiling the many thrills this adaptation of Robert Bloch's famous novel delivers. (It was scripted faithfully by Joseph Stefano.) This ultimate horror in schizophrenia isn't as farfetched as it might seem—Bloch claims his descent into a killer's warped mind is based on a true-life case. The great score is by Bernard Herrmann. Simon Oakland, John McIntire, Frank Albertson. (Video/Laser: MCA)

PSYCHO II (1983). Is it possible to follow in Hitchcock's footprints and successfully make a sequel to the great macabre classic? Sort of . . at least this is not a failure, even if it can't reach the heights of that which inspired it. Richard Franklin, an Australian who had barely distinguished himself with PATRICK and ROADGAMES before being picked to direct Norman Bates' return 23 years later, seems an unlikely choice. But he was a Hitchcock disciple and advised by Hitch in the art of German expressionistic cinema. With writer Tom Holland, Franklin fashions an homage to the themes and characters of Robert Bloch's novel (although, alas, Bloch was not involved) and strives for a film that spins off from, but doesn't copy, the original. Now it is Bates (declared sane and released from Atascadero Hospital) being terrorized by someone dressing up like Mother and murdering with a butcher knife. Behavior of the characters is often confusing, but the shocks keep one's mind off script deficiencies. The macabre ending, comedic one moment and horrifying the next, comes as a jolt. Anthony Perkins is oddly vulnerable as Bates; Vera Miles returns as Lila, fighting to keep Bates institutionalized; Robert Loggia is the sympathetic psychiatrist; and Meg Tilly is Norman's confused love interest. (Video/Laser: MCA)

PSYCHO III (1986). Call it "Daze of His Lives: The Continuing Love Story of Norman Bates." That infamous mother-lover is back in the phantom house on the hill next door to the motel, welcoming travelers in his inimitable style. This time the callers include a defrocked nun on the run from her haunted past and a low-life vagabond with kinky sex habits (not the nun's). Anthony Perkins doubles as director of this offshoot of Robert Bloch's famous novel, bringing unusual touches to Charles Pogue's script. Gore murders liven up the pace, but this lacks the intensity of its predecessors. Just run-of-the- kill. Jeff Fahey, Diane Scarinid, Roberta Maxwell. (Video/Laser: MCA)

PSYCHO IV: THE BEGINNING (1990). Unexpectedly good follow-up to the original themes established in Hitchcock's 1960 classic based on the equally classic Robert Bloch novel, with screenwriter Joseph Stefano again dealing with Norman Bates, this time as a youngster growing up in that sinister house on the hill. It opens with a radio show discussion of matricide (cases where children murder their mothers) with one of the callers turning out to be Bates (Anthony Perkins). In flashbacks, we see the aberrant sexual psychology of Mrs. Bates (wonderfully limned by Olivia Hussey) that led to Norman's character makeup. The murder sequences, in which young Norman (played by "E.T." star Henry Thomas) murders the girls he meets, are so realistic as to be unsettling, and the double homicide-by-poison of Norman's mother and lover is painful to watch. Director Mick Garris does a remarkably good job on this one. (Video/Laser: MCA)

PSYCHO A GO-GO! See **BLOOD OF GHASTLY HORROR.**

PSYCHO BOY AND HIS KILLER DOG. See **BOY AND HIS DOG, A.**

PSYCHO CIRCUS (1966). Christopher Lee's lean figure graces this Harry Alan Towers production designed to follow in the bloody footprints of CIRCUS OF HORRORS, but it's a weak whodunit with only mildly horrific overtones, based on the Edgar Wallace novel of 1928, AGAIN THE THREE JUST MEN. Stolen money is the motive behind a series of murders surrounding the traveling Barberini Circus, and John Moxey's direction plays up the cops-and-robbers elements far more than the horror fans might be expecting. Leo Genn gives a good performance as a Scotland Yard cop, Heinz Drache portrays the ringmaster, Anthony Newlands is the Big Top owner, Cecil Parker is amusing as the blubbering Yard supervisor, Suzy Kendall and Margaret Lee provide beauty, and Victor Maddern is a robber. (From Sinister Cinema and Saturn as **CIRCUS OF FEAR**)

PSYCHO COP (1988). Pseudopoliceman Bobby Ray Shafer kills for his satanic cult, the blood needed for rituals. Semi-illiterate teenagers figure prominently among his many victims. Written-directed by Wallace Potts. Jeff Qualle, Palmer Lee Todd. (South Gate)

PSYCHO FROM TEXAS (1981). Although copyrighted in 1981, this was shot in Texas in 1974. It finally reached the screen with the impact of a redneck's double-barreled shotgun missing both firing pins. It's not Southern Comfort as John King III portrays a wild man who kidnaps an oilman for ransom, murdering an innocent girl to keep her quiet and committing general mayhem. Watch this to ogle Linnea Quigley stripped naked by King III in the middle of an empty barroom and jiggle her breasts while he pours a pitcher of beer over her head. Watch for Jack Collins as the stereotyped sheriff, Joann Bruno as a screaming maid, and Tommy Lamey as a demented southerner named Slick who spends half the film chasing the overweight oilman through the swamp. Written-directed by Jim Feazell. Also known as EVIL + HATE = KILLER. (Paragon; from Bronx as **BUTCHER, THE**)

PSYCHO GIRLS (1987). Poisoner Darlene Mignacco escapes from the insane asylum to kill her sister Agi Gallus, aided by two demented henchmen. Canadian flick directed by Gerard Ciccoritti. John Haslett Cuff, Rose Graham. (MGM/UA)

PSYCHO KILLER. See **PSYCHO LOVER.**

PSYCHO KILLERS. See **FLESH AND THE FIENDS, THE.**

PSYCHO LOVER, THE (1971). Psychiatrist plots to murder his wife, using headshrinker techniques and brainwashing to program the killer. Offbeat but minor, reminiscent of THE MANCHURIAN CANDIDATE. Written-produced-directed by Robert Vincent O'Neil. Lawrence Montaigne, Joanne Meredith, Frank Cuva.

PSYCHOMANIA (1963). Girls' school is always a suitable setting for a bloody horror movie—so many lovely young bodies for a sadistic killer to choose from, and the camera can linger on the gory details as the madman hacks and hews. This will turn your stomach as well as it turned a profit when first released. A Del Tenney production directed by Richard Hilliard, it stars Dick Van Patten as a cop, Lee Philips as the killer, James Farentino, Sylvia Miles and Sheppard Strudwick. Aka VIOLENT MIDNIGHT. (Sinister/C; Filmfax)

PSYCHOMANIA (1973). Upper-crust Britishers George Sanders and Beryl Reid make a pact with a Frog Demon so when their son (Patrick Holt), the leader of motorcyclists called The Living Dead, kills himself in a crash, they resurrect him and he roars out of his grave aboard his hog. He urges his gang members to kill themselves too. So the riders set out to commit suicide in spectacular ways (running their bikes into stone walls and off cliffs, like that). What a bizarre British horror film, especially when the grand dame, Reid, turns into a frog. Defies description. Directed by Don Sharp. (King of Video; Media; Goodtimes; United; Western World)

PSYCHOPATH, THE (1966). A bloody killer leaves tiny dolls beside his corpses. It turns out that all four victims once examined the records of a German tycoon after World War II and his fortune was lost as a result. Now revenge is being wreaked—but by whom? Robert Bloch keeps his often-illogical screenplay moving quickly, providing a framework for red herrings, gore murders and PSYCHO-type thrills. Directed by Freddie Francis. Patrick Wymark, Alexander Knox, Margaret Johnston, Judy Huxtable.

PSYCHOPATH, THE (1968). Klaus Kinski lends his special screen madness to this European-produced tale about a psychiatrist who discovers that his girlfriend's ex-husband is a murderer. Directed by Guido Zurli. George Martin, Ingrid Schoeller. (Lightning)

PSYCHOPATH, THE (1973). Obscure thriller in which Tom Basham, the host of a kiddie TV show, runs across the county murdering the adults who are mean to kids who watch his show. There's a version with many murders and a version with none of the murders. Also features John Ashton. Written-produced-directed by Larry Brown. (Fox Hill; Media)

PSYCHOPHOBIA (198?). Italian poor man's POLTERGEIST, with a touch of THE EXORCIST thrown in. A real estate saleswoman, recovering from the death of her husband, puts out enough psychic emotion to activate supernatural forces within her home. A parapsychologist attempts to help her rid the mansion of evil via ultrasonic waves, but the demonic winds only blow that much harder. The usual exploding head, falling objects and electrical arcs.

PSYCHO PUPPET. Video of **DELIRIUM** (Viz).

PSYCHO RIPPER. See **NEW YORK RIPPER.**

PSYCHO SEX FIEND. See **HOUSE THAT VANISHED, THE.**

PSYCHOS IN LOVE (1987). Black humor predominates in this gory thriller in which a bartender and manicurist kill people just for laughs. Finally they turn their attention on a topless dancer. This film has been compared to EATING RAOUL, but it isn't as good. Produced-edited-directed by Gorman Bechard. Debi Thibeault, Frank Stewart. (Wizard; VCI)

PSYCHO SISTERS (1972). Susan Strasberg screams in the shower and behaves neurotically after her husband dies in this exploitation cheapie. She's consoled by her sweet young sister—or so it appears. Faith Domergue, Charles Knox Robinson, Sydney Chaplin. Directed by Reginald LeBorg. (Prism)

PSYCHOTRONIC MAN, THE (1980). Slow-moving, ponderous independent feature shot in Chicago by director Jack M. Sell, with long stretches where very little happens. A barber (Rocky Foscoe) is possessed with what a scientist calls "psychotronic energy" (submerged power in the subconscious mind) and he wills people to die. One man splatters on the sidewalk in slow motion, others are engulfed by wind and go bonkers. (Unicorn)

PUFNSTUFF (1970). Feature version of a TV kiddie series from Sid and Marty Krofft is a disappointment, tending to talk down to its audience. It depicts a magical kingdom of witches, warlocks, talking animals, etc. Directed by Hollingsworth Morse. Jack Wild, Billie Hayes, Martha Raye, Mama Cass Elliott, Billy Barty.

PULSE (1988). Surprisingly good science-gone-amok thriller with effective close-up work on household appliances, wiring systems and other modern technology. The premise of director Paul Golding's script is that our electrical system is being invaded by bursts (or "pulses") caused by an alien force, although that force is never fully explained. Cliff DeYoung and son Joey Lawrence are trapped in their home and under attack from anything being fed electrical power. The film never overexploits its theme and accomplishes chilling moments when wires and plugs turn quite menacing. Myron Healey, Charles Tyner, Matthew Lawrence, Dennis Redfield. (Video/Laser: RCA/Columbia)

PUMA MAN, THE (1980). Superpoor superhero Italian fantasy-adventure: An ancient Aztec legend claims that aliens descended to Earth at the dawn of time, giving superpowers to a race of men. Now conquest-hungry Donald Pleasence wants those powers and steals a Golden Mask that enables him to put people under hypnotic spells and perhaps knock off Pumaman. Who is Pumaman? Glad you asked. He's a wimpy guy working as a paleontologist in a museum, who is befriended by a South American Indian named Vadinho. Suddenly Pumaman is wearing this cheap cape and can fly. The special effects shots are terrible, the acting even worse. Misconceived by director Alberto De Martino, this stuff gives comic books a rotten reputation. Walter George Alton is Pumaman, Miguelangel Fuentes the Indian and Sydne Rome the heroine. (Prism; Parade)

PUMPKINHEAD (1988). This first directorial effort by special effects genius Stan Winston has the flavor of an old morality horror tale from an E.C. comic. Young Ed Harley witnesses a demon finishing off his prey. Flash ahead to Harley as an adult (Lance Henriksen), living a lonely life in the backwoods with his son. Odd circumstances lead Harley to seek the help of an old crone to resurrect Pumpkinhead (the vengeful monster) so he can kill off a band of irresponsible dirt bikers. Pumpkinhead is a powerful, and awesome, creature and the plot has several twists as the murders are carried out one by one. Genre fans will appreciate the ambience that Winston pumps into every scene. Above average and highly recommended. Jeff East, John DiAquino, Kimberly Ross, Joel Hoffman. (Video/Laser: MGM/UA)

LANCE HENRIKSEN

PUNISHMENT PARK (1970). See editions 1-3.

PUPPET MASTER (1989). One of producer Charles Band's better horror offerings, enhanced by the fine puppet trickery of David Allen, who uses every effects device in the book. Director David Schmoeller also demonstrates style, especially in an opening sequence where a little creature scurries around the lobby of the Bodega Bay Inn in 1939 as Gestapo agents come to murder William Hickey, a puppetmaster considered an enemy of the Third Reich. Jump to the hotel during modern times, when psychics (each with a different power) investigate the suicide of Hickey's son. But the son is still alive, using the minimonsters to commit murders, and the horror is on as Drillhead (a drill for a pate) and other homicidal creatures, each with a murder-shtick, attack and the gore gets thick. Schmoeller's camera is effective in making the puppets plausible, often by having his Steadicam sweeping at floor level. Paul Le Mat, Irene Miracle, Matt Roe, Kathryn O'Reilly, Jimmie F. Scaggs, Barbara Crampton. A topnotch choice. (Paramount) (Laser: Full Moon)

PUPPET MASTER II (1990). The Attack of the Doll People is on again when investigators from the Office of Paranormal Claims turns up at the Scarab Hill Hotel at Bodega Bay, Ca., dying one by one at the bloodied hands of the murderous marionettes of Andre Toulon, the phantom-like puppet master with a formula for giving life to his wired folk. Stop-motion specialist Dave Allen directed this Charles Band production and his workshop provided the effects. While this sequel never reaches the heights of the original, it is not without interesting points, the large breasts of pinup gal Charlie Spradling among them. The puppets are a varied lot, including Drillhead, Death Face, and a Darth Vader-like character with a fire extinguisher arm. And Steve Welles has a ball portraying the evil Toulon, whose face is covered by bandages and weird goggles. Toulon's origin-story is revealed in a 1912 Cairo flashback, a plot element expanded on in the third film. Toulon imagines that psychic investigator Elizabeth MacClellan is his long-dead wife and saves her for an amusing transformation sequence. Gregory Webb, Nita Talbot, Jeff Weston. (Paramount) (Laser: Full Moon)

PUPPET MASTER III: TOULON'S REVENGE (1990). Set in 1941 Germany, this traces the origins of how Andre Toulon (Guy Rolfe in an effective role) came to discover the secrets of animating inanimate objects with the souls of victims of the Hitler regime. Major Krauss (Richard Lynch, in one of his sneering roles) is heading the Death Corps Project—a perverted attempt to restore life to dead German soldiers so they can be used to kill again—and murders Toulon's wife. This forces him to seek his revenge and he accomplishes it in a most hideous way, his Nazi adversaries dying most unpleasantly. Charles Band's PUPPET MASTER series continues to show a sense of intelligence and sardonic wit with this amusing entry written by C. Courtney Joyner (from an idea by Band) and directed by co-producer David DeCoteau. David Allen pulled the strings for the puppets, which this time include a five-gun cowboy. Sarah Douglas, Walter Gotell, Ian Abercrombie, Kristopher Logan. (Paramount) (Laser: Full Moon)

PUPPET MASTER 4 (1993). Another lively entry in Charles Band's popular series depicting the puppet creations of German scientist Andre Toulon (Guy Rolfe), who now directs his creatures to help scientist Gordon Currie fight the Totem monsters. These alien-like minicreepies, commanded by the ancient Egyptian warrior monster Sutek, trap Currie, Chandra West and Teresa Hill in deserted Bodega Bay Inn to prevent them from discovering the secret of life. Pinhead, Drillhead and others, in a resurrection scene out of FRANKENSTEIN, animate Toulon's latest puppet, Decapitron, which has interchangeabe heads, one of them a bank of weapons. And the war between little monsters rages with Richard Band's music accentuating the combat. This lively piece (puppets by David Allen) was directed by Jeff Burr. Jason Adams, Felton Perry. (Video/Laser: Paramount)

PUPPETOON MOVIE, THE (1987). Delightful compilation of cartoon short subjects produced by George Pal from 1942-47 for Paramount. Pal, a Hungarian who had fled the Nazis, was a well-loved artist who used wooden figures with stop-motion techniques to produce some of the most striking animation work of the period, which was honored with Oscar nominations. After an introduction featuring Art Clokey's Gumby, Pokey and Arnie the Dinosaur, you'll see the best of Pal's work in "John Henry and the Inky Poo," a classic based on an old Negro legend, "Tulips Shall Grow," Pal's indictment of Nazi atrocities committed in Holland, "Tubby the Tuba," a wistful, melancholy story of a woe-begone musical instrument (narrated by Victor Jory) and "Jasper in a Jam," about a boy locked in a clock shop for the night. Highly recommended. (IVE) (Laser: Image)

PURPLE DEATH FROM OUTER SPACE (1940). Video version of the serial **FLASH GORDON CONQUERS THE UNIVERSE** (Questar).

PURPLE MONSTER STRIKES, THE (1945). Fifteen-chapter Republic serial, distinguished by Roy Barcroft's campy performance as an alien in tights who intends to steal a rocket engine so he can then invade our planet. "The Purple Monster" (so-called because he came to Earth on a meteor that trailed a purple stream) can make himself invisible and take possession of another body and appear to be that person. Dennis Moore plays the intrepid hero who stands alone against the invasion, with tall, leggy Linda Stirling helping out. Serial king Barcroft utters plenty of purple prose, but it's hardly his best villain. The fights are well staged and there are such sci-fi devices as an "Electro Annihilator." Co-directed by Spencer Bennet and Fred C. Brannon. James Craven, Mary Moore. (Republic; Nostalgia Merchant)

PURPLE PEOPLE EATER (1988). "We've thrown in everything about the 1950s that might trigger nostalgic memories," writer-director Linda Shayne says of this family movie in which an alien entity (inspired by Sheb Wooley's 1958 hit song) joins a young rock 'n roll band led by Neil Patrick Harris. The creature, a cutesy-pie E.T. type with a yellow horn on its head that plays musical notes, proceeds to thwart evil landlord John Brumfield from evicting lovable oldsters Ned Beatty and Shelley Winters, while Chubby Checkers and Little Richard show up for a benefit concert. Wooley appears briefly as a circus manager. Shayne (with an assist from Jim Wynorski) has concocted an innocuous entertainment for the young. Peggy Lipton, James Houghton, Molly Cheek. (Media) (Laser: Image)

PURPLE ROSE OF CAIRO (1986). Brilliant Woody Allen comment on our love for movies, and the thin line that separates their fantasy from our reality. Movie-starved Mia Farrow, a struggling, abused housewife-waitress during the Depression, seeks escape into melodramas, and is astonished one matinee when the main character of the film speaks to her, steps down from the screen and becomes part of her life. The complications this creates are hilarious and poignant. Danny Aiello, Jeff Daniels. (Video/Laser: Vestron)

PURSUIT (1972). Michael Crichton directed this TV-movie based on his novel BINARY. A political fanatic intends to disrupt the 1972 Republican National Convention with a deadly nerve gas as part of his scheme to destroy the President. Tense, fast-moving thriller scripted by Robert Dozier with ample suspense. Ben Gazzara, E. G. Marshall, William Windom, Martin Sheen, Joseph Wiseman. (Republic)

PYGMY ISLAND (1950). Unsurprising entry in Sam Katzman's Jungle Jim series with Johnny Weissmuller as the king of the potted forests. In this one the swimming champ, pal of assorted chimps and chumps, takes on a guy in a gorilla suit, some men impersonating witch doctors and a rubber crocodile. Not to mention a strange plant. Directed by William Berke. Ann Savage, David Bruce, Billy Barty, Tris Coffin.

PYRO (1964). Look what happens when you play with fire: You come up with a smokeless Spanish-U.S. psychothriller—a flame-out. Barry Sullivan's jilted mistress, Martha Hyer, starts a conflagration that destroys Sullivan's family and leaves him horribly scarred. A plastic surgery restores him to normal and he sets out to wreak revenge. Sullivan's makeup is as uninspired as the story, which will burn you. Directed by Julio Coll. Sherry Moreland, Hugo Pimental, Soledad Miranda.

PYX, THE (1973). Strange Canadian film, shot in Montreal, was directed by Harvey Hart and stars Christopher Plummer as a cop investigating the death of prostitute-drug addict Karen Black) and uncovering a Devil cult. Soundtrack songs were written and sung by Ms Black. Jean-Louis Roux, Donald Pilon, Jacques Godin. (Prism; from Cinema Video Theater as **HOOKER CULT MURDERS, THE**)

Am I not the spawn of [my father's] depraved blood? The blood of a thousand men and women was spilled within these walls. Limbs twisted and broken, eyes gouged from bloody sockets, flesh burned black . . ." —*Vincent Price in* **THE PIT AND THE PENDULUM**

Q PLANES (1939). Classy British production (also called CLOUDS OVER EUROPE) depicting a test pilot and Scotland Yard sleuth tracking a new secret Death Ray. High on suspense and good acting: Laurence Olivier, Valerie Hobson and Ralph Richardson contribute finely etched roles. Compelling propaganda. Tim Whelan and Arthur Woods co-directed.

Q: THE WINGED SERPENT (1982). Satisfying monster movie written-produced-directed by Larry Cohen, with stop-motion effects by Dave Allen. Decapitation of a window washer on the Empire State Building is the first in many claw crimes committed by a feathered flying serpent, known in Aztec mythology as Quetzlcoatl. Q, for affectionate brevity, lives atop the Chrysler Building and brings daily terror to residents by skinning them alive. Bizarre sacrificial killings by a believer in Aztec legends has led to the "rebirth" of the bird—that's the theory of cop David Carradine, who has a hard time convincing fellow cops Richard Roundtree and James Dixon. Outstanding is Michael Moriarty as a hood who knows where the bird is hiding. Good score by Richard O. Ragland. Also known as THE WINGED SERPENT. Candy Clark, Lee Louis. (MCA)

QUARANTINE (1989). Eccentric, offbeat Canadian TV-feature set in a futuristic society which is wracked by plague. A dictatorial state has seized power and its Gestapo-styled police subject anyone related to a victim of disease to an area of quarantine. Rebels (represented by Beatrice Boepple) try to assassinate a senator, in the process meeting a computer expert programming a way of tracking the disease. One finds a parallel to AIDS in Charles Wilkinson's script (he also produced-directed) but the message is muddled and the film fails to reach a resolution. Garwin Sanford, Jerry Wasserman, Tom McBeath, Michelle Goodger. (Republic)

QUATERMASS AND THE PIT (1958). Remade in the '60s as **FIVE MILLION YEARS TO EARTH,** but here's the original British three-hour, six-chapter TV series starring Andre Morell as Professor Quatermass. (Sinister/C; S/Weird)

QUATERMASS CONCLUSION, THE (1979). This final chapter in Nigel Kneale's scientific adventures about Professor Bernard Quatermass is not as compelling as the three previous (THE CREEPING UNKNOWN, ENEMY FROM SPACE, FIVE MILLION MILES TO EARTH) but is still arcane enough that it should satisfy series followers. John Mills is a less believable scientist than his earlier incantations but still effective, with a crazed look in his eye, as he roves an England on the verge of anarchy, looking for a missing niece. A strange power is attracting thousands of people to Stonehenge from where they are "beamed up" to an unknown planet. The dialogue and characters all have the Kneale twist so nothing is ordinary about this TV-movie made for the BBC, with Piers Haggard directing. Simon MacCorkindale, Barbara Kellerman, Margaret Tyzack, Brewster Manson. (Thorn EMI/HBO)

QUATERMASS II. Original British theatrical version of **ENEMY FROM SPACE** (Laser: Image).

QUATERMASS II: ENEMY FROM SPACE. Video of the British version of **ENEMY FROM SPACE** (Corinth; Sinister/C).

QUATERMASS EXPERIMENT. Original British theatrical version of **CREEPING UNKNOWN, THE.** (Dark Dreams; Sinister/C; S/Weird) (Lasr:Japanese)

QUEEN KONG (1976). British film (budgeted at $632,000) is a light-hearted, affectionate parody—but Dino de Laurentiis felt it encroached on his $20 million remake of KING KONG and charged copyright infringement. Oh well. The plot by Ron Dobrin and Frank Agrama (the latter also directed) has Queen Kong climbing the London Post Office Tower in emulation of the real King. All you queens take note.

QUEEN OF ATLANTIS. See **SIREN OF ATLANTIS.**

QUEEN OF BLACK MAGIC. Video version of **BLACK MAGIC TERROR** (Lettuce Entertain You).

QUEEN OF BLOOD (1966). Writer-director Curtis Harrington, to make up for a small budget, utilizes color to good advantage and emphasizes character rather than effects in telling of an expedition sent into space in 1990 to a dying planet. Astronauts John Saxon, Judi Meredith and Dennis Hopper find a green-colored woman (Florence Marly), sole survivor of her race, and one by one fall victim to her vampirism. Harrington throws a surprise into the climax. Basil Rathbone in one of his final roles. Forrest J. Ackerman guest stars. Rocket footage was lifted from a Soviet sci-fi movie. (Star Classics; from Sinister/C as **PLANET OF BLOOD)** (Laser: HBO)

QUEEN OF OUTER SPACE (1958). Spaceship crew discovers life on Venus—and what life! Beautifully stacked babes in silk stockings, miniskirts and boots. And wearing Earth-type lipstick yet! Their queen (Zsa Zsa Gabor) cuts down on the divorce ratio by issuing no-men-allowed decrees. She then turns her Beta Disintegrator Ray on Earth. Space heroes Eric Fleming, Paul Birch, Dave Willock and Patrick Waltz keep their jaws jutting and crack chauvinistic jokes about the well-rounded dolls while Zsa Zsa—who can't resist men—gads about helping them. Edward Bernds, who directed Three Stooges vehicles, was at the helm. Script by Charles Beaumont from a one-joke outline by Ben Hecht. The Dolls: Laurie Mitchell, Lynn Cartwright. (Fox)

QUEEN OF SPADES (1948). Stylish British adaptation of Pushkin's fantasy about an aging countess who sells her soul to the Devil to win at cards. Along comes an Army officer who murders her for the secret, then is haunted by her tormented soul. Sensitively rendered with a haunting score by Georges Auric. Thorold Dickinson directed. Anton Walbrook, Edith Evans, Ronald Howard, Anthony Dawson, Miles Malleson. (HBO)

QUEEN OF SPADES (1960). Pushkin's horror story retold through the music of Tchaikovsky in a Russian production written-directed by Roman Tikhomirov that will possibly strike the fancy of opera lovers more than horror fans. But watch and get cultured, lowbrows. (HBO) (Laser: Image, with **EUGENE ONEGIN**)

QUEEN OF SPADES (1966). See editions 1-3.

QUEEN OF THE AMAZON (1947). Great White Goddess rule over jungle people, take care her villagers. Come from giant silver bird that fall from sky. White man come jungle, look for Great White Goddess. Natives no let Great White Goddess go back white man's world. Tom-toms beat message. White man evil. White man take long time die. Robert Lowery, Patricia Morison, J. Edward Bromberg. (Sinister/C; Nostalgia; Weiss Global)

QUEEN OF THE AMAZONS. See **COLOSSUS AND THE AMAZONS.**

QUEEN OF THE CANNIBALS. See **DOCTOR BUTCHER M.D. (Medical Deviate)**.

QUEEN OF THE GORILLAS. See **BRIDE OF THE GORILLA.** (Bride-and-seek in the bush?)

QUEEN OF THE JUNGLE (1935). Feature version of a 12-chapter serial, which in turn featured stock footage from a 1922 cliffhanger, JUNGLE GODDESS. It's set in the lost land of Mu, where a Killer Ray emanates from the eye of an idol. The usual collection of motley natives (posing as leopard men) comes up against the great white hunter, etc. etc. Directed by Robert Hill. Reed Howes, Mary Kornman, Dickie Jones, Marilyn Spinner.

QUEEN OF THE VAMPIRES (1967). Sex, vampirism, blood and other traditional horror elements are blended rather haphazardly by French producer-director-writer Jean Rollin into a mishmash. Also known as VAMPIRE WOMEN and THE RAPE OF THE VAMPIRE. Bernard Letrou, Solange Pradel.

QUEEN'S SWORDSMEN, THE (1962). Editions 1-3.

QUEST, THE (1984). Offbeat Australian quasifantasy (also known as FROG DREAMING) blending metaphysical overtones with coming-of-age object lessons when inquisitive youth Henry Thomas probes the mystery behind a legendary creature living in a lake of Devil's Knob, an area shrouded in frog mysteries. Thomas' meeting with an Aborigine, steeped in the region's legends, leads him deeper into the meaning of life (and lake) until the climax, where the explanation behind the monster offers insight into Thomas' learning process. Beautifully photographed and acted. Tony Barry, Rachel Friend, John Ewart. Written by Everett de Roche, directed by Brian Trenchard-Reed. (Charter)

QUEST FOR FIRE (1982). Gritty, realistic look at Neanderthals, showing how man discovered not only fire but a sexual position other than the standard Missionary grope. Nothing glamorous about these people, who dress in rags and paint their faces with mud. Mammoths and saber-toothed tigers harass them, and their guttural language was created by Anthony Burgess. Directed by Jean-Jacques Annaud. Everett McGill, Rae Dawn Chong, Ron Perlman. (Video/Laser: CBS/Fox)

QUEST FOR LOVE (1971). Unusually sensitive, literate British fantasy-romance, dealing with an outre form of time travel. Scientist Tom Bell awakens in a different time stream, where he is now a novelist unhappily married to Joan Collins. Time "split" back in 1938 on two different parallel courses, and he's trapped in his alter ego, a man who has many traits he despises. He falls in love with Collins, but their newfound relationship is—but that would be spoiling it. Handsomely directed by Ralph Thomas, intelligently scripted by Bert Batt, from John Wyndham's "Random Quest." Simon Ward, Denholm Elliott, Laurence Naismith. (Independent United)

QUEST FOR THE LOST CITY (1990). Independent, low-budget Canadian adventure film none too convincing in depicting how a young man (Christian Malcom) tracks his missing father to a place called Xeon where a devil cult is headed by a demonic guy named Satoris. Made as THE FINAL SACRIFICE, this cheapie has little to recommend . . . and someone forgot to put in a lost city. Brice Mitchell, Shane Marceau. Produced-directed in Alberta by T. Jardus Greidanus. (Action International)

QUEST FOR THE MIGHTY SWORD (1989). Another pathetic entry in the Italian-produced Ator series, this time with the son of Ator (Eric Allen Kramer) on the march to free his mother Dejanira from a magical spell that has entrapped her within the Flame of Thorn, the devious work of an evil wizard who is assisted by dwarf creatures. But first, Ator must find the Treasure of the Kingdom of the West and destroy skeleton warriors as well as an unconvincing fire-breathing dragon that oozes different colors of blood when sliced by Ator's Mighty Sword of Sacred Thrall. Feeble direction by David Hills. Also known as ATOR III: THE HOBGOBLIN, although that title is incorrect since this is actually the fourth ATOR movie. Margaret Lenzey, Donald O'Brien, Dina Morrone, Chris Murphy, Laura Gemser, Melissa Mell. (Video/Laser: RCA/Columbia)

QUESTOR TAPES, THE (1974). Android Robert Foxworth seeks data about his creator (his memory banks have been erased) in this Gene Roddenberry TV pilot—one of his best efforts, even if it never sold as a series—which he co-wrote with Gene L. Coon. An intriguing variation on the theme of man looking for his origins while under the control of aliens for thousands of years. Don't miss this suspenseful, literate offering. Directed by Richard Colla. Lew Ayres, John Vernon, Dana Wynter, Mike Farrell, James Shigeta.

QUIET EARTH, THE (1985). Provocative, compelling morality tale that explores the end of civilization in a vein reminiscent of THE WORLD, THE FLESH AND THE DEVIL. At 6:12 one Sunday morning everyone vanishes from the planet except Zac Hobson (Bruno Lawrence), a scientist working on Operation Flashlight, which apparently has altered and made unstable the fabric of the Universe. The implication is that Zac refused to will himself to go to the Great Beyond with everyone else, and is now faced with the final destruction of Earth. But he's not alone—he finds a woman (Alison Routledge) and a black man (Peter Smith) and a volatile relationship begins. This New Zealand film, based on the novel by Craig Harrison, was directed by Geoff Murphy. (Video/Laser: CBS/Fox)

QUIET PLACE TO KILL, A. Video version of **PARANOIA** (Unicorn).

QUINTET (1979). Frigid tale set in the distant future when a new Ice Age has left mankind in a city buried up to the mezzanine with icicles. Survivors Paul Newman, Vittorio Gassman, Fernando Rey, Bibi Andersson and Tom Hill play an odd game, Quintet, but it's a Big Chill you'll give this Robert Altman film because of its lacxk of warmth. Suffered from bad circulation among exhibitors. Altman directed and co-wrote with Frank Barhydt and Patricia Resnick. (Key)

RABBIT TEST (1978). Tasteless comedy, directed by Joan Rivers, depicting the world's first pregnant man. Rivers fires off a thousand gags in helter-skelter fashion, usually missing the target. Joan, can we talk? Alex Rocco, Billy Crystal, George Gobel, Doris Roberts. (Charter; RCA/Columbia; Magnetic) (Laser: Nelson)

RABID (1977). Porn queen Marilyn Chambers has a wardrobe in this shocker (also called RAGE) written-directed by Canadian horror king David Cronenberg. She's carrier of a blood disease that compels her to inject poison into victims through a phallic-like syringe in her armpit. Deodorant companies, take note. The mad-dog disease sends victims screaming, biting into the world. It's an epidemic of monumental proportions in downtown Montreal! Graphic effects are enough to make you foam at the mouth. Morbidly compelling, with unpleasant ending. Frank Moore, Joe Silver, Patricia Gage. (Warner Bros.)

RABID GRANNIES (1988). Although released as a Troma film, this is a French-Belgian-Dutch production dubbed by a British cast. It's wild black comedy poking fun at the hyprocisy of the Catholic church and human greed when a family gathers to celebrate the birthday of two "grannies" and ponders who will receive the family fortune. Retribution against the greedy ones comes when "grannies" become "whammies," bloodthirsty demons with claws. Family members, trapped in rooms of the estate, are murdered in horrendous ways while survivors bicker and seek escape. Writer-director Emmanuel Kervyn treats the demons with a humorous aside. One gets the feeling he's making a statement about gory American films. Whatever he's up to, it works. Catherine Aymerie, Caroline Braekman, Danielle Daven, Raymond Lescot. (Media) (Laser)

RACE WITH THE DEVIL (1975). Only Jack Starrett's direction injects life into this chase chiller. Starrett keeps the film keen with excitement when two married couples—vacationing in a trailer—accidentally witness a sacrificial murder during a satanic cult meeting. It's a hair-raising, tire-squealing pursuit with a large-scale conspiracy going down. But not even Starrett salvages the lousy ending. Warren Oates, Loretta Swit, Peter Fonda, Lara Parker, R. G. Armstrong. (CBS/Fox/Key)

RADAR MEN FROM THE MOON (1952). Hero in a flying suit—Commando Cody, Sky Marshal of the Universe—jetpacks to the moon to discover a dictator (hammily played by Roy Barcroft, the great serial villain) using atomic weapons against Earth in this rollicking 12-chapter Republic serial. George Wallace runs around in the rocket suit (first worn in KING OF THE ROCKETMEN) against adversary Retlk and his incompetent henchmen. If Commando Cody is your idol, see another serial in which he appears, ZOMBIES OF THE STRATOSPHERE. Directed by Fred C. Brannon, this is corny but wonderful campy fun. Aline Towne, Clayton Moore, Tom Steele. (Republic; Burbank; Filmfax; in feature form as **COMMANDO CODY**) (Laser: Republic)

RADAR PATROL VS SPY KING (1949). Slam-bam action serial, 12 chapters of it, from Republic cliffhanger director Fred C. Brannon. The evil Baroda and his sexy accomplice, Nitra, sabotage radar defenses along the U.S. border, bringing into play the Electro Annihilator and death-producing Gamma Ray. Kirk (SUPERMAN) Alyn stars as government guy Chris Calvert. Chapter-play regulars Jean Dean, Anthony Warde, John Merton, Tristram Coffin, John Crawford. (Republic)

RADAR SECRET SERVICE (1950). Robert L. Lippert quickie depicts G-men with newfangled radar equipment tracking hijackers of atomic materials. Standard chase-action low budgeter with John Howard, Tom Neal, Adele Jergens, Sid Melton, Ralph Byrd, Tris Coffin, Marshall Reed. Directed by Sam Newfield. (Weiss Global)

RADIOACTIVE DREAMS (1986). Somewhere in this mess is an idea for a movie that hasn't been made yet. It's the attempted funny side to MAD MAX when missile-site watchmen Michael Dudikoff and John Stockwell dig to the surface on April 1, 2010 (a joke on us all?) to play private eyes Philip and Marlowe (detective stories being all they've read for years) in a post-holocaust world. What follows is a mishmash in which mutants, little boys in white suits (who keep saying "fuck"), and other grotesque survivors chase after two keys that will launch the only remaining atomic missile. Dudikoff and Stockwell run around Edge City in their BVDs while sexy Miles Archer (Lisa Blouton, a Sybil Danning rival) attempts to seduce the keys from them, and a dude named Dash Hammer pursues with a zap gun. Directed by Albert Pyun. George Kennedy and Don Murray have ridiculous roles. (Vestron) (Laser: Image)

RADIO FLYER (1992). This grimly depicts children exposed to physical abuse from their stepfather, but concludes on a mystical twist that allows one battered youth to escape his pain. It's a wonderful movie about golden moments of adolescence and discovery of new marvels during a summertime of wide-eyed enchantment. Granted, these are difficult elements to reconcile, abuse and fantasy, and yet director Richard Donnor and cinematographer Laszlo Kovacs capture the importance of a belief in the impossible, and David Mickey Evans' script (based on experiences as an abused child) is a delicate masterpiece. Lorraine Braco portrays a single mother who takes her sons Joseph Mazzello and Elijah Wood to the California town of Novato in 1969. RADIO FLYER has moments when the narration (read by Tom Hanks), the color photography and Hans Zimmer's music combine into movie-making at its most powerful. The excellent cast includes Adam Baldwin as the drunken stepfather and John Heard as a sympathetic lawman. (Video/Laser: Columbia TriStar)

RADIO RANCH (1935). Feature-length video version of the serial **PHANTOM EMPIRE** (Video Yesteryear).

RAGE (1973). The first half of this George C. Scott-directed anti-government polemic is exciting in depicting the accidental unleashing of a nerve gas that kills a rancher's son and livestock. The government conspires to cover up, forcing the rancher (Scott) to carry out acts of revenge against military installations. Richard Basehart, Martin Sheen, Barnard Hughes, Stephen Young, Kenneth Tobey. (Warner Bros.)

RAGE. See **RABID.**

RAGE (1984). Italian MAD MAX imitation offering brainless action and stupid plotting. Captain Rage is a survivor of nuclear apocalypse who goes into "The Forbidden Land" (nuked New Mexico?) to Alpha Base to find uranium to save mankind. His adversary, Sergeant Flash, pursues him into "The Land of the Trembling Rocks" where they fight it out in a climactic train chase. Styleless and witless, with inane dialogue that runs to such lines as "It won't be easy building up a new world, but there's no harm in trying." Wanna bet? (Un)directed by Anthony Richmond. Conrad Nichols, Steve Eliot.

RAGEWAR. See **DUNGEONMASTER, THE.**

RAGGEDY ANN AND ANDY, A MUSICAL ADVENTURE (1977). Animated version of Johnny Gruelle's doll characters endowed with life-breathing qualities. Loaded with songs but not too much stuffing. Voices by Didi Conn, Arnold Stang, Joe Silver, Paul Dooley. Directed by Richard Williams. (CBS/Fox)

RAIDERS FROM OUTER SPACE (1966). Three episodes of Irwin Allen's TIME TUNNEL TV series with Robert Colbert and James Darren as scientists trapped in time zones. In the pilot episode, "Rendezvous with Yesterday," we see how our heroes are stuck in a continuous time-warp anomaly. "The Kidnappers" deals with plant people in some future time; "One Way to the Moon" depicts a flight to Mars threatened with sabotage. Gary Merrill, Whit Bissell, Warren Stevens, Michael Ansara, Ross Elliott, J. T. Callahan. For more details see **TIME TUNNEL, THE.**

RAIDERS OF ATLANTIS (1983). Satisfying U.S.-Italian actioner, full of blazing machine-guns, exploding grenades, Molotov cocktails, and bodies falling from parapets. The salvaging of a Russian sub causes lost Atlantis to rise from the ocean just when Chris Connolly and other soldiers of fortune are passing by. Out of nowhere appear mercenaries to restore Atlantis to its full glory. From then on the action is nonstop under Roger Franklin's direction. Mike Miller, Ivan Rassimov, John Blade, Bruce Baron. (Prism; Video Treasures)

RAIDERS OF THE LIVING DEAD (1985). Other than a great title, what does this Canadian film offer? Not much. What might have been amusing satire remains a dreary, unrealized concept involving a crazy doc at a correctional institute who experiments on executed criminals and finds a way to bring them back to life. Meanwhile, a bright kid designs a laser gun and a reporter runs around Ontario to solve the mystery. Watching cement harden is more exciting. Directed by Samuel M. Sherman. Scott Schwartz, Robert Deveau.

RAIDERS OF THE LOST ARK (1981). Dynamite team George Lucas (producer) and Steven Spielberg (director) created this homage to the cliffhangers of yesteryear, accomplished with the flashy, dazzling production and effects expertise of the '80s. Lawrence Kasdan's script has all the cliches, and yet, since they have been unused for so long, they are like newfound gems. The excitement begins with archeologist-adventurer Indiana Jones (Harrison Ford) stealing a sacred stone from temple ruins in South America (actually Hawaii) and escaping death traps and angry natives before flying off in an airplane with a boa constrictor in the cockpit. Then the pacing really picks up when he and the heroine—tough chick Karen Allen—search for the Lost Ark of the Covenant, which has a sinister power the Nazis covet. (This takes place in the 1930s.) There's a great snake-chamber sequence, a wild-and-woolly chase with Ford single-handedly battling a German truck convoy, and climactic special-effects hoopla when the Covenant is opened and Pandora's demons are unleashed. The raw spirit of adventure is beautifully punctuated by John Williams' music. Ronald Lacey, John Rhys-Davies, Denholm Elliott, Paul Freeman. Sequels are INDIANA JONES AND THE TEMPLE OF TOMB and INDIANA JONES AND THE LAST CRUSADE. (Video/Laser: Paramount)

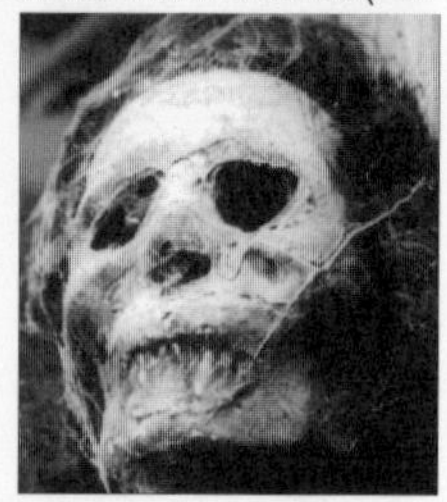

'RAIDERS' MUMMY

RAINBOW BRITE AND THE STAR STEALER (1985). Rainbow Bright is a kid in Rainbow Land who brings "joy and color" to the world . . . she must prevent an evil Princess and her Glitterbots from taking the planet Spectra in this animated feature. (Warner Bros.)

RAINBOW BRITE: MIGHTY MONSTROMURK MENACE (1983). Rainbow and her friends (the Sprites and Color Kids) must prevent the dastardly Murky Dismal from erasing all the colors in the spectrum. Animation for kids. (Video/Laser: Vestron)

RAINBOW ISLAND (1944). See editions 1-3.

RAIN KILLER, THE (1990). A serial murderer strikes when it's raining, viciously slashing women who are ex-drug addicts. ("Round up the usual perverts," remarks a cop.) The twists and turns involve alcoholic cop Ray Sharkey and federal agent David Beecroft as they form an uneasy alliance to track the knife-wielding killer. Directed by Ken Stein. Michael Chiklis, Tania Coleridge, Woody Brown. (Video/Laser: RCA/Columbia)

RAIN WITHOUT THUNDER (1992). A polemic protesting the pro-life abortion movement, couched in documentary style as public figures, in 2042 A.D., discuss "fetal murder." It's cautionary science fiction with the view that if conservatives continue to dictate abortion-rights policy, society could end up treating women found guilty of abortion as common criminals. This sheds sinister light on the Catholic Church and draws a one-sided view of abortion—that women should have the right of choice. Writer-director Gary Bennett forsakes real drama in favor of the talking heads technique, draining the film of full impact. Betty Buckley portrays a mother imprisoned for helping her daughter have an abortion; Fredric Forrest is a sleazy prison warden; Jeff Daniels is a D.A. who has lost his fight in defending women; Linda Hunt is outstanding as an advocate of women's rights; Iona Morris is a ruthless prosecutor; and Sheila Pinkham is a symbolic figure of womanhood who describes the horrors of illegal abortions. Well intended, but filmic potentials are wasted.

RAISE THE TITANIC (1980). Clive Cussler writes rousing adventures with mild sci-fi overtones. This adaptation of his best-selling novel focuses on the finding of the Titanic and getting it resurfaced and returned to port. While the scientific techniques and apparatus are interesting, the characters remain singularly dull. Richard

Jordon doesn't do justice to Cussler's he-man adventurer, Dirk Pitt. Box office disaster for Sir Lew Grade. Directed by Jerry Jameson. Anne Archer, Jason Robards, Alec Guinness. (Video/Laser: CBS/Fox)

RAISING CAIN (1992). One of Brian De Palma's best films—an unpredictable work that will have you hooked from the moment you meet Dr. Carter Nix, a schizophrenic madman (John Lithgow). There's no denying that De Palma is manipulative, but he pulls off this experiment in terror with such outrageous pastiche, you can only admire him for his creative gall. Lithgow gets to play Nix, Nix's evil alter ego, Nix's father and a female nurse. Produced by Gale Anne Hurd, RAISING CAIN uses all the gimmicks in the cinematic book and overcomes disturbing themes of serial murder, child kidnapping and a plethora of abnormal behavior to remain an entertainment designed to scare the daylights out of you. It will. Lolita Davidovich, Steven Bauer, Frances Sternhagen. (Video/Laser: MCA)

RAMAR OF THE JUNGLE (1952). See third edition.

RANA: THE LEGEND OF SHADOW LAKE (1981). Another guy in a phony-looking rubber suit hanging around a polluted-looking lake . . . yep, the umpteenth imitation of THE CREATURE FROM THE BLACK LAGOON. This is a movie you can fast forward through without missing a thing, not even during dialogue sequences. Uninteresting characters walk around the lake or swim while the entity remains offcamera most of the time. The only good scene has a giant bullfrog popping out of the monster's mouth. The rest lacks the frog but has plenty of bull. Producer-director Bill Rebane really blew it with this regional flick (made in Gleason, Wisconsin). Karen McDiarmid, Alan Ross. (Active)

RAPE OF THE VAMPIRE, THE. See **QUEEN OF THE VAMPIRES.**

RAPTURE, THE (1992). Fascinating if baffling parable about man's neverending search for God, his belief in the hereafter and his salvation. This cosmic tale by writer-director Michael Tolkin, who wrote GHOST, uses an unhappy telephone operator (Mimi Rogers, in a tour de force performance) as a metaphor for that search. She's a woman who's wasted her life, indulged in group sex in her quest for love, and now, on the verge of becoming manic depressive, "sees the light" and embraces Jesus. But her confusion reaches new heights when her husband is killed by a crazed gunman and she takes her daughter to Vasquez Rocks, there to wait for Christ's Second Coming. The Horsemen of the Apocalypse are soon on the horizon. This oddball movie, since it questions fundamental beliefs and depicts group sex as well as a murder, is a shocker, and certainly will not be to everyone's liking. Gutsy stuff. David Duchovny, Patrick Bauchau, Kimberly Cullum. (Video/Laser: Columbia/TriStar)

RASHOMON (1951). Japanese director Akira Kurosawa's masterpiece. Set in 8th Century Japan, it tells of three men (priest, woodchopper, servant) who take refuge from a storm under the gate of Rashomon, in the ruined city of Kyoto, where they discuss the recent murder of a Samurai warrior and the seduction of his wife by a bandit. In flashbacks, we see five versions of the same tragedy, including one told by the dead warrior through a medium. A compelling study of objective/subjective truth, of man's lust, greed and prejudice. Toshiro Mifune is the grunting, animalistic bandit and his performance is unforgettable. Hollywood remade this as THE OUTRAGE. (Embassy) (Laser: Voyager)

RASPUTIN (1939). French "biography" of the mad monk who infiltrated the palace of Russia's Nicholas II, to hold royalty under the spell of his hypnotic powers, is essayed by Harry Baur with unkempt beard, peasant's smock and a manner that makes him both repugnant and attractive. More realistic than the 1933 stylized version. Directed by Marcel L'Herbier. Marcelle Chantal.

RASPUTIN AND THE EMPRESS (1933). See editions 1-3.

RASPUTIN—THE MAD MONK (1966). Fictional biography of the monk who held Svengali-like control over the Czar's court is a tour de force for Christopher Lee, who overcomes the limitations of John Elder's script to breath fire into this strange personage from Russian history. Directed by Don Sharp with a flair for atmosphere and costumes, this Hammer film utilizes sets from DRACULA—PRINCE OF DARKNESS, and interjects horror movie-inspired devices. Barbara Shelley, Richard Pasco, Suzan Farmer.

RATBOY (1986). This honorable attempt by actress-turned-director Sondra Locke, produced by Clint Eastwood's Malpaso company, is an American fairy tale about a human freak living in a garbage dump befriended by a journalist (Ms Locke) who wants to exploit him. It's about our media-hungry culture, our penchant for exploitation and our lack of compassion for what is different. Whatever the good intentions, however, it remains an anomaly, trapped in a twilight zone of its own making. It's tough to sympathize with a half-rat person, no matter how cute Rick Baker has designed him. The story is finally self-defeating. Robert Townsend, Larry Hankin, Christopher Hewett. (Warner Bros.)

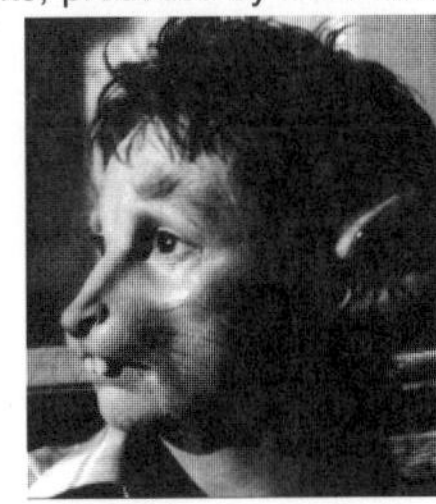

'RATBOY'

RAT PFINK AND BOO BOO (1966). BATMAN spoof is a juvenile mis-mixture of maladroit superheroes (rocker singer and gardener) chasing a motorcycle gang which kidnapS a woman with Kogar the Gorilla. Yes, rat pfink producer-director Ray Dennis Steckler made a boo boo. Carolyn Brandt. (Camp)

RATS, THE. See **DEADLY EYES.**

RATS. See **RATS: NIGHT OF TERROR.**

RATS ARE COMING! THE WEREWOLVES ARE HERE! (1972). Andy Milligan is writing-producing-photographing! The results are here! And are they awful! Man-eating rats WILLARD-style, family werewolves WOLFMAN-style. This low budgeter is style-less. Aka THE CURSE OF THE FULL MOON. Hope Stansbury, Jacqueline Skarvellis. (Select-A-Tape; Midnight)

RATS: NIGHT OF TERROR (1983). Above-average Italian-French post-holocaust shocker starts in a MAD MAX vein, then shifts to horror. In 225 A.B. (After the Bomb) the world is divided into an underground society and "primitives" roving the surface. A motorcycle gang led by Kurt (a Jesus Christ lookalike—this whole movie has a strange Biblical connection) finds a food cache in a desert town taken over by rats. How the rodents devour the characters (often from within, chewing their way to the surface) is the focus while the bikers go hysterical. A surprise ending works nicely. Director Vincent Dawn was going for something different in the genre. Richard Raymond, Richard Cross. (Lightning)

RATTLERS (1976). Not as terrible as its title makes it sound, this exploitative movie from snake-in-the-grass producer Harry Novak depicts vicious attacks by rattlesnakes infected by a secret nerve gas dumped by the military. Herpotologist Sam Chew is hired by the local sheriff to find out why the snakes are attacking, and the script is shaped as an investigational procedural as he tracks the deadly sidewinders with comely photographer Elizabeth Chauvet. Anyone with a fear of snakes will get the creeps, but otherwise there's little to recoil from in writer-director John McCauley's work. Celia Kaye, Dan Priest. (USA; Lorimar)

RAVAGED (1969). Plastic surgeon Howard Vernon steals the faces of beautiful women and grafts them onto the ugly countenances of his patients in this sexually-alive French horror film directed by Claude Mulot. Frederic Lansac, Elizabeth Teissier, Philippe Lemaire, A. Duperey. (In video as **BLOOD ROSE**)

RAVAGERS, THE (1979). Murky, clumsy science fiction, as empty and soulless as the radioactive landscape in which it is set. Mankind has dropped the Big Bomb and now there are two bands of survivors: The Flockers (The Good Guys) and the Ravagers (The Bad Guys). Richard Harris is neither, being a loner-individual seeking the Land of Genesis with pleasure girl Ann Turkel. Ernest Borgnine, Art Carney and Woody Strode are wasted. Adapted from Robert Edmond Alter's novel, PATH TO SAVAGERY, by screenwriter Donald Sanford. Totally ravaged by director Richard Compton.

RAVEN, THE (1935). This has nothing to do with Poe's poem, but it does owe inspiration to Edgar Allan for torture devices used by mad doctor Bela Lugosi, a Poe-phile who turns to the master's literature to wreak vengeance. Boris Karloff has a sympathetic role playing a criminal disfigured by Lugosi as a form of blackmail. Unusually sadistic; a Universal period piece you want to see. Directed by Louis Friedlander, who later became Lew Landers. Irene Ware, Samuel Hinds, Ian Wolfe. (Video/Laser: MCA, with **BLACK CAT, THE**)

RAVEN, THE (1963). The chemistry of Peter Lorre, Vincent Price and Boris Karloff results in a delightful horror parody. Price portrays a queasy magician who hears someone tapping, tapping, tapping at his 15th Century chamber door . . . yes, it's Poe's famous black bird with the refrain "Nevermore," but this bird has a quirk: It keeps transmutating into Lorre (or is it the other way around?). Producer-director Roger Corman winds up with a Duel of the Wizards—a classic piece of comedy and effects. Kudos to screenwriter Richard Matheson. Hazel Court, Jack Nicholson, Olive Sturgess. (Warner Bros.) (Laser: Image)

RAW FORCE (1982). Martial arts action thriller, in which adventurers set sail for Warriors' Island, where kung fu zombies await. Once Cameron Mitchell, Geoff Binney and Jillian Kessner are in action, it's shootouts and skull crashings. Directed-written by Edward Murphy. Jennifer Holmes, Robert Dennis. (Media)

RAWHEAD REX (1987). On the surface, a monster-on-a-rampage movie, depicting a creature that rises from the ruins of a fertility cult site and kills. However, the fact this is set in Ireland and involves the church leads one to believe that screenwriter Clive Barker was saying something about the current religious war there. for example, a scene in which the demon urinates on his disciple in a church graveyard. Barker has disavowed this film, probably because the monster design is less than exciting, and pulls down the imaginative writing. David Dukes portrays the American yanked into the adventure with wife Kelly Piper and children while investigating "sacred sites" near Dublin. Many of the bloody murders are effective, and there are good cat-and-mouse sequences help build tension. Niall Toibin, Ronin Wilmot, Hugh O'Connor, Cora Luinny. (Vestron) (Laser: Image)

RAW MEAT (1972). See editions 1-3.

RAW NERVE (1991). Serial killings performed in a room of mirrors cause Ted Prior to have nightmare visions, but policemen Glenn Ford and Jan-Michael Vincent pooh-pooh the information. The only sympathetic ear is reporter Sandhal Bergman's. Filmed in Mobile, Ala., this features one-time porn queen Traci Lords, Randall (Tex) Cobb and Red West. Directed by Ted's brother, David A. Prior. (Action International)

RAY BRADBURY THEATER, VOL. I and II (1986). Video repackaging of half-hour adaptations of Bradbury stories made for cable TV: "Marionettes Inc." stars James Coco; "The Playground" features William Shatner; and "The Crowd" highlights Nick Mancuso. Modest, low-budget work, written by Bradbury and directed by Paul Lynch, William Fruet and Ralph Thomas. (Disney)

RAY BRADBURY'S THE ELECTRIC GRANDMOTHER (1981). Video version of a TV special written by Bradbury and Jeffrey Kindley—a bittersweet look at the pain of losing loved ones. Edward Hermann and his children go to Fantoccini Ltd. for the answers to their problems: They order a new grandmother who shows up as Maureen Stapleton, who proceeds to teach them love and respect. Poignantly moving. Paul Benedict, Tara Kennedy. Directed by Noel Black. (From New World as **ELECTRIC GRANDMOTHER, THE**)

RAY BRADBURY

RAY BRADBURY THEATER. Please see **STRANGE TALES/RAY BRADBURY THEATER** and **BEST OF RAY BRADBURY THEATER, THE** for laser versions.

RAZORBACK (1983). Australian import is one of the better imitations of JAWS, capturing a shivery element of fear. Here the ruthless predator is a killer boar stalking the Outback, so huge it crashes through walls and drags away victims into the desert. Gregory Harrison plays the husband of a TV reporter researching kangaroo poachers who is attacked by the razorback. Harrison and a big game hunter, whose baby was dragged off by the beast, join ranks to track the killer. Director Russell Mulcahy uses desert locations to great advantage, employing lights and shadows to capture an eeriness similar to the mood in IT CAME FROM OUTER SPACE. There's also disturbing symbolism that enhances the psychology of the horrors Harrison encounters, and a statement about man's inhumanity as reflected through the uncouth kangaroo hunters. Scripted by Everett De Roche. Bill Kerr, Chris Haywood, John Howard, David Argue. (Warner Bros.) (Laser: Japanese)

R.C.M.P. AND THE TREASURE OF GENGHIS KHAN (1948). Canadian Mountie Christopher Royal, his jaw grimly determined, wars with outlaw Mort Fowler over a 13th Century treasure containing the secret to liquefying diamonds. It's a seesaw battle to see who will walk "The Cave of a Thousand Tunnels." Jim Bannon is the red-coated hero in this truncated version of the Republic serial DANGERS OF THE CANADIAN MOUNTED. Directed by Fred Brannon and Yakima Canutt. Virginia Belmont, Anthony Warde, Tom Steele.

REACTOR. Video version of **WAR OF THE ROBOTS** (Mogul).

REAL GENIUS (1985). Talk about a movie that goes brainless: teenagers with high I.Q.s join in a campus project to perfect a laser beam. They bicker, pull pranks, meet girls and wander aimlessly. Director Martha Coolidge seems confused about what to do with the guys and gals—they finally poop out from ennui. Strictly lamebrain. Val Kilmer, Gabe Jarret, William Atherton, Ed Lauter. (Video/Laser: RCA/Columbia)

REALLY WEIRD TALES (1988). Parodies of horror films: "All's Well That Ends Well," directed by Paul Lynch; "Cursed with Charisma," directed by Dan McBrearty; "I'll Die Loving," directed by John Blandard; With John Candy, Joe Flaherty, Catherine O'Hara, Martin Short. (HBO; Video Treasures)

REAL MEN (1987). Goofball fantasy-comedy in which secret agent Jim Belushi leads mild-mannered John Ritter into crazy adventures that include meeting a UFO in order to stop a major threat to the world—in exchange an alien spaceman gets what he considers is the most important Earth commodity. It's nonstop action never making a point, but the soundtrack will keep you awake. Dennis Feldman directed. Barbara Barrie, Gail Bari, Bill Morey. (Video/Laser: CBS/Fox)

RE-ANIMATOR (1985). Topnotch gore flick—disgustingly sickening as it panders terribly on one hand and amuses cleverly on the other. Smart filmmakers give us a sendup while satisfying vicarious, visceral needs. Although based on H. P. Lovecraft's stories about Herbert West, a resurrector of the dead, this is really George Romero-Herschell Lewis-Lucio Fulci in one. The Dennis Paoli-William J. Norris-Stuart Gordon script is outrageous: an intense, nerdish medical student (Jeffrey Combs) discovers a green serum that brings corpses to life. His main adversary is a sadistic, perverted doctor (David Gale) who has eyes only for Barbara Crampton, even after his head is severed. There are graphic encounters with the dead come-to-life, a scene where the doctor's head makes love to the heroine while she's strapped to a table, and a final crescendo of morgue black humor when cadavers attack, their intestines popping out and enwrapping the hero like a vengeful serpent. If it sounds grotesque, blame make-up men Anthony Doublin, John Naulin and John Buechler, and credit director Gordon. You'll "ugh" and "ahh" but you'll love it, perverted viewer that you are. (Vestron) (Laser: Image; Vestron)

REASON TO DIE (1989). Another slasher thriller in which cop Wings Hauser sets up his own girlfriend to trap the razor-wielding killer. Isn't that what girlfriends are for? Directed by Tim Spring. Liam Cundill, Anneline Kriel. (Vidmark) (Laser: Image)

REBELLION OF THE DEAD WOMEN, THE. See **VENGEANCE OF THE ZOMBIES.**

REBEL NUN, THE. See **FLAVIA, PRIESTESS OF VIOLENCE.**

REBORN (1984). In one of his hysterical, fever-pitched roles, Dennis Hopper plays a white-suited, bow-tied TV preacher (Rev. Tom Harley) who heals the sick, has his own church/school/studio, offers a BankonChrist card and has goons run his electronic pulpit. A woman can make her hands and feet bleed (stigmatized stigmata?) and Michael Moriarty tries to keep her from falling into Hopper's clutches. A memorable sequence has Moriarty getting "stuck" in his girlfriend when she passes out during intercourse. It's thoroughly intriguing to watch Hopper's overwrought performance and to see Moriarty rendered "helpless." Directed in Italy by Bigas Luna. Antonella Murgia, Francisco Rabal. (Manson; Vestron)

RED ALERT (1977). Taut, engaging TV version of Harold King's novel PARADIGM RED, about a leak in a nuclear plant that threatens mankind. Director William Hale emphasizes suspense in a race-against-time climax. David Hayward, M. Emmet Walsh, William Devane, Ralph Waite, Adrienne Barbeau. (Paramount)

RED BLOODED AMERICAN GIRL (1990). Heather Thomas' uninhibited role as a guinea pig (in an experiment to find a cure for AIDS) who is turned into an insatiable vampire is the only offbeat thing in this Canadian film with Christopher Plummer as an obsessed doctor in charge of Life Reach Foundation. Andrew Stevens is Dr. Owen Augustus Urban II, an expert in the unscrambling of the genetic code. Screenwriter Alan Moyle ends this scientific adventure on an upbeat note and director David Blyth sustains interest by focusing on the attractive body of Ms Thomas in a torrid love scene with Stevens. Kim Coates, Lydie Denier (she in an all-too-brief sex scene). (Prism) (Laser: Image)

RED DAWN (1984). On a visceral level, this John Milius film is a patriotic depiction of U.S. guerrilla youths killing Soviet and Cuban troops who have invaded America. You'll be caught up in the mock heroics as the teenage Wolverines fire machine-guns and rocket launchers, blowing away the Ruskie army. However, the politics of this movie are so scrambled, and the explanation of how the U.S. is invaded in a war of conventional weapons so unconvincing, the story falls apart when it attempts to justify its own militarism. Patrick Swayze heads the freedom fighters guided by blind hate, while enemy forces are commanded by William Smith, whose guile suggests an updated Fu Manchu. Powers Boothe is a downed jet pilot and Harry Dean Stanton and Ben Johnson are among captured Americans tortured or mowed down by firing squads. This will kick you in the guts or leave you cold with incredulity. (Video/Laser: MGM/UA)

RED DRAGON. See **MANHUNTER.**

REDEEMER, THE (1976). Homosexual actor, lesbian bitch, unscrupulous attorney, athlete, rich woman, louse of a lover—these '67 graduates of Stuart Morse Academy turn up at the creepy school to be imprisoned by a fiend who uses flame thrower, shotgun, swords and washroom basin to kill. It's never clear why this is happening and it's covered over with pseudoreligious overtones. Director Constantine S. Gochis offers nothing redeeming in THE REDEEMER. Nick Carter, T.G. Finkbinder, Jeanette Arnette, Michael Hollingsworth. Subtitled SON OF SATAN! (VCI; Genesis; from Continental as **CLASS REUNION MASSACRE**)

RED HANGMAN, THE. See **BLOODY PIT OF HORROR.**

RED HOUSE, THE (1947). Thanks to screenwriter-director Delmer Daves, and the theremin of composer Miklos Rozsa, this ranks as a super-entertaining horror mystery. True, there are no ghosts or goblins, but the film reeks with a cursed atmosphere and Rozsa's music evokes dreaded things that not even the script suggestsd. (It is a score that should be listened to, and studied, by aficionados of film music.) Never has Edward G. Robinson been so tormented by the horrors of the past, and never have "the haunted woods" been filled with such foreboding. Lon McCallister, Judith Anderson, Rory Calhoun, Julie London. (Crown; Kartes; Congress; Filmfax; Sinister/C)

RED LIPS. See **DAUGHTERS OF DARKNESS.**

REDNECK COUNTY RAPE. See **REDNECK ZOMBIES.**

REDNECK ZOMBIES (1988). Beer infected with radioactivity turns ale-swilling patrons into walking dead. What? Again? In "Entrailvision" yet. Directed by Perceles Lewnes. Lisa De Haven, W.E. Benson, William Decker. (Trans World)

RED PLANET MARS (1952). Radio contact is made with Mars by scientist Peter Graves with a "hydrogen valve" designed by a Nazi war criminal. But it's a ruse . . . the messages (which upset the economy of the world, throwing governments into chaos) are phonies sent by the Nazi, who is controlled by Soviet agents. And then a message from Mars pleads for universal peace and Christianity. The Russian people are so shaken that in one of the most pious moments in movie history, they stage a revolt, knocking Stalin to pieces in 12 days. (See THE 27TH DAY for a similar plot.) The John L. Balderston-Anthony Veiller script (based on a play, and hence preachy and talky) is an exercise in spiritualism and wishful thinking, one of the oddest sci-fi movies of the '50s, a result of McCarthyism and Red Hysteria. Don't miss it. Directed by Harry Horner with a straight face. Andrea King, Marvin Miller, Morris Ankrum.

RED SHOES, THE (1948). Beautiful use of Technicolor by cinematographer Jack Cardiff highlights this classic British film produced-directed by Michael Powell and Emeric Pressburger, a distinguished pair of (shoe-film)makers. This glimpse at ballerinas and music, which was nominated for, and won, several Oscars, focuses on Moira Shearer, an ingenue rising through the ranks under the tutelage of opera-company manager Anton Walbrook, who portrays a fascinating and complex character. The film's centerpiece is an abstract ballet sequence in which Shearer cannot stop dancing when she wears the red shoes (an idea borrowed from Hans Christian Andersen). So distinguished is this production, and so insightful is the acting, writing and directing, I hesitate to include it in this kind of book. Marius Goring, Robert Helpmann, Leonide Massine, Albert Basserman. (Paramount; Videotakes) (Laser: Live)

RED SIGN OF MADNESS, THE. See **HATCHET FOR A HONEYMOON.**

RED SONJA (1986). Sword-wielding heroine of Conan creator Robert E. Howard is brought to life by Danish model Brigitte Nielsen, who had never acted before. She does a credible job under Richard Fleischer's direction. The plot is odyssey stuff (by Clive Exton and George MacDonald Fraser) as Red Sonja and a male counterpart (not Conan, but played by Arnold Schwarzenegger as if he were) seek a green crystal with destructive powers.

Fantasy elements include a pet spider that purrs like a kitten and a viewing screen manipulated by a wizard as wicked as the way Nielsen handles her sword. Could have used more romance between Brigitte and Arnold, but they went for a PG rating. Sandahl Bergman, Paul Smith, Ronald Lacey. Music by Ennio Morricone. (Video/Laser: CBS/Fox)

RED TENT, THE (1971). Italian explorer Umberto Nobile (Sean Connery) is in his 80s, watching a TV show about his ill-fated flight in the airship Italia over the North Pole in 1928. The ghosts of those who died in the crash (Nobile was sole survivor) and the aborted rescue attempts that followed gather to relive the struggle in the snowy wasteland and consider Nobile's guilt. Italian-Soviet film, fascinatingly acted and capturing the chill of ice floes. Directed by Mikhail K. Kalatozov. Claudia Cardinale, Hardy Kruger, Peter Finch. Music by Ennio Morricone. (Video/Laser: Paramount)

RED TIDE, THE. See **BLOOD TIDE.**

REEL HORROR (1985). Egads! Hecate's a queen of creatures confronted with entities that burst forth from old cans of movie film. Un-canny. "Terrifying and hilarious." Oh, reel-y? Catherine Bach, Leslie Caron, John Carradine, Donald Pleasence, Katherine Ross, Talia Shire. Produced-directed by Ross/Claire Hagen.

REFLECTING SKIN, THE (1991). Philip Ridley, award-winning British painter and playwright of the macabre, wrote-directed this disturbing study of an eight-year-old (Jeremy Cooper) whose world is a compendium of horrors: a serial killer stalks his playmates, his mother and father are manic depressives with suicidal tendencies, and a neighbor could be a vampire. This cold, indifferent universe is beautiful on the surface, but dark as a trip down a rabbit hole into hell. It is a contrast of lovely cinematography and graphic horrors, and a film that taps into one's primal fears as it depicts a loss of innocence. Viggo Mortensen, Lindsay Duncan. (Video/Laser: Live)

REFLECTION OF FEAR, A (1971). Weak imitation of PSYCHO, with surprise twists more baffling than enthralling. Sondra Locke is held prisoner in her bedroom by her mother. The cast is good (Robert Shaw, Sally Kellerman, Mary Ure, Mitchell Ryan, Signe Hasso) but the ending muddled. Directed by William Fraker, photographed by Laszlo Kovacs. (RCA/Columbia)

REFLECTIONS OF MURDER (1974). TV-movie reworking of DIABOLIQUE, the French horror thriller directed by Henri-Georges Clouzot and based on the Pierre Boileau-Thomas Narcejac novel. In this version, which follows the major changes from the book Clouzot introduced, Joan Hackett and Tuesday Weld plot to kill cruel Sam Waterston, then face the wrath of his vengeful spirit—or so it seems. Also called AUTUMN CHILD and LABYRINTH. Directed by John Badham and written by Edward Hume and Lewis John Carlino. Remade as HOUSE OF SECRETS in 1993. (Republic)

REFRIGERATOR, THE (1991). Newlyweds David Simonds and Julia Mueller move into a New York apartment, unaware their refrigerator is the doorway to Hell. Tongue-in-cheek horror written-directed by Nicholas Tony Jacobs. Angel Caban, Phyllis Sanz. (Monarch)

REFUGE OF FEAR (198?). Two couples seek refuge in a bomb shelter when nuclear war breaks out, and face post-holocaust conditions. (All Seasons; Home)

REGENERATION (1988). Canadian low-budget effort depicts scientist John Anderson bringing the dead to life through a photography technique that is less than convincing. Directed-written by Russel Stephens. Marek Cieszewski, Suzanne Ristic.

REINCARNATE, THE (1971). Canadian supernatural-black magic thriller in which a dying attorney undergoes sacrificial rituals to transfer his life force into the body of a young artist. But the body-and-soul transference has one black cat too many. Directed by Don Haldane. Jack Creley, Jay Reynolds, Trudy Young. Also known as THE DARK SIDE. (Magnum)

REINCARNATION, THE. See **CRIMSON CULT, THE.**

REINCARNATION OF GOLDEN LOTUS (1989). Hong Kong love-fantasy based on a Chinese legend about a prostitute brought back to life and her search for happiness in modern Hong Kong. Direted by Clara Law. Joi Wong, Eric Tsang, Lam Chun Yen. (Connoisseur)

REINCARNATION OF ISABEL, THE (1973). Mickey Hargitay, one-time muscleman-husband of sex symbol Jayne Mansfield, stars in this Italian chiller about a castle where satanic monks resurrect a witch burned at the stake 400 years before. She has a strange appetite, this beautiful woman: she thrives on virgins' blood. From director Ralph Brown and writer Renato Polselli, the team that collaborated on DELIRIUM. Also known as THE GHASTLY ORGIES OF COUNT DRACULA, THE HORRIBLE ORGIES OF COUNT DRACULA and BLACK MAGIC RITES—REINCARNATIONS. Whew! Rita Calderoni, Max Dorian, Consolata Moschera.

REINCARNATION OF PETER PROUD, THE (1975). Faithful adaptation of Max Ehrlich's best-seller (Max did the script himself), but what works on paper doesn't always translate to screen. The climax is predictable and the pacing is slow under J. Lee Thompson's direction. Michael Sarrazin stars as a man suffering from nightmares who discovers he lived a former life in New England. He tracks down his heritage only to fall in love with his daughter from the previous lifetime. It gets a mite kinky at that point, with a masturbation scene that is erotic but tasteful. Margot Kidder, Jennifer O'Neill, Cornelia Sharpe, Debralee Scott, Steve Franken. (Vestron) (Laser: Image)

REJUVENATOR, THE (1988). A perverse quality hangs over this twisted tale (also called REJUVENATRIX) of the search for eternal youth, in which screenwriters Simon Nuchtern and Brian Thomas Jones (the latter also directed) remind us we are better off to accept ourselves for what we are. Another asset to this grotesque but hypnotic film is John MacKay's performance as a misguided doctor searching for a youth serum. Jessica Dublin portrays an aging actress who finances MacKay's lab tests in hopes she can start a new movie career. But the serum creates a brain-eating monster and Jones indulges in disgusting effects of the gooey kind. An odd film that fascinates as it repels. James Hogue, Katell Pleven, Marcus Powell. (Sony) (Laser: Image)

REJUVENATRIX. See **REJUVENATOR, THE.**

RELENTLESS (1989). Intriguing psychokiller thriller in which Judd Nelson is "The Sunset Killer," who selects victims with his own last name who live on Sunset Boulevard and kills them at sunset. The murders are graphically unappealing (kitchen knife into stomach, piano wire around neck, gunshots to the chest, etc.) but the search by cops Robert Loggia and Leo Rossi is fascinating. Rossi is a New Yorker transplanted to the L.A. milieu and Loggia is the toughened old-timer. Nelson is portrayed as "the mundanity of death"—a wimpy-looking but well-trained killer. Director William Lustig does justice to the script by Jack T. D. Robinson. Meg Foster, Patrick O'Bryan, Mindy Seeger, Angel Tompkins. (Video/Laser: RCA/Columbia)

RELENTLESS II: DEAD ON (1991). This sequel is up to the quality of the original, with Michael Schroeder taking the directorial reins. It's a hard-hitting tale of horror, murder and conspiracy. Driven, out-of-control cop Sam Dietz (again played by Leo Rossi), who solved the case of "The Sunset Killer" in RELENTLESS, is on the trail of another serial killer—or so it appears. His manic behavior leads him into trouble: conflicts occur with ex-wife Meg Foster, FBI agent Ray Sharkey and hired assassin Miles O'Keefe. The murders are in slasher-movie style and supporting cast is strong. Dale Dye, Marc Poppel. (Video/Laser: Columbia TriStar)

RELENTLESS III (1992). This has all the makings for a bang-up third entry in the unrelenting RELENTLESS series, again with maverick cop Sam Dietz (Leo Rossi, back for his third outing) in search of a diabolical serial killer. There's never any mystery about whodunit—these films are about cat-and-mouse games the killers play with

Dietz, who instigates personal vendettas against his adversaries. This time the "repeater" is a charming snake played by William Forsythe. While there are twists during the unfolding, and writer-director James Lemmo brings tension to the characters, examines the emptiness of Dietz's pesonal life, and creates a sense of nihilistic inevitability, the film fails because of a miserably unsatisfactory ending. Robert Costanzo, Edward Wiley, Tom Bower, Savanah Smith Boucher. (New Line)

RELUCTANT ASTRONAUT, THE (1967). Play the reluctant viewer to avoid this Don Knotts programmer, in which a lily-livered janitor (guess who) is picked to be an "astronaut" to undergo dangerous training to make it safer for real spacemen. Produced-directed by Edward J. Montagne. Joan Freeman, Leslie Nielsen, Jesse White, Jeanette Nolan, Arthur O'Connell.

RELUCTANT SAINT, THE (1962). See editions 1-3.

REMARKABLE ANDREW, THE (1942). World War II propaganda entertainment: William Holden, beleaguered bookkeeper, is helped by Andrew Jackson's ghost to maintain integrity and fight corruption. Ironically, this was adapted by Dalton Trumbo (from his own novel), who in later years was blacklisted. Brian Donlevy stars as the spirit. Ellen Drew, Rod Cameron, Richard Webb. Stuart Heisler directed.

REMEMBER LAST NIGHT? (1935). Included here for director James (FRANKENSTEIN) Whale completists, this is a slick, fun-filled murder mystery in the style of THE THIN MAN with light ESP overtones. Constance Cummings and Robert Young are an idle-rich couple who, following a wild party, wake up in a friend's home to find their host murdered in his bed. Cop Edward Arnold pays a call to interrogate suspects. Bright, sophisticated, full of witty dialogue, art deco in design. Based on Adam Hobhouse's HANGOVER MURDERS.

REMOTE (1993). Call this Charles Band video production HOME ALONE MEETS THE REMOTE-CONTROL KID IN E.T. SUBURBIA. Chris Carrara portrays a remote-control expert (he's great controlling toy helicopters, planes and other airborne craft) trapped in a model tract home with three bumbling hold-up men (John Diehl, Tony Longo, Stuart Fratkin). The kid uses his skills to outwit the foolish outlaws and win the heart of girlfriend Jessica Bowman. A yodeling puppet named Gunther, whom Carrara uses to good comic effect, is reminiscent of a creature from PUPPET MASTER. A pleasant family picture written by Mike Farrow and directed with style by Ted Nicolaou. Richard Band provides a light-hearted score. (Paramount)

REMOTE CONTROL (1987). There's this new "sci-fi" video movie out on the market, REMOTE CONTROL, supposedly made in the '50s, that depicts a wife slaughtering her husband with a futuristic sewing machine. However, anyone playing this hot flick on a VCR is instantly turned into a maniacal killer. Vidstore employee Kevin Dillon gets wise and with girl friend Deborah Goodrich tracks the film makers to a studio where employees are under the control of alien invaders. This comment on video and what it's doing to minds and libidos is from writer-director Jeff (SQUIRM) Lieberman. Christopher Wynne, Jennifer Tilly. (IVE)

REMO WILLIAMS: THE ADVENTURE BEGINS (1985). Loose adaptation of the Warren Murphy-Richard Sapir "Destroyer" novels, scripted by Christopher Wood and directed by Guy Hamilton. Despite an incredulous premise (one-time New York cop undergoes plastic surgery to assume new identity to work for clandestine government operation that fights evil forces), this is an engaging fantasy-adventure. As Remo Williams (a name selected off a bedpan), Fred Ward portrays a dour, slighty-likeable hunk who trains with 80-year-old Chiun, a Korean played by Joel Grey. Chiun teaches Remo to dodge bullets, scale walls, climb the Statue of Liberty and other feats of derring-do (would you believe walking on water?). Plot: Industrialist Charles Cioffi misappropriates U.S. funds for a "Star Wars" spaceware program. The action is rousing (especially the Statue of Liberty sequence) and there are mock heroics aplenty. Wilford Brimley and J. A. Preston are secretive government men and Kate Mulgrew the minimal love interest. (Video/Laser: HBO)

RENEGADE SATELLITE (1954). Re-edited episodes of the TV series **ROCKY JONES, SPACE RANGER** (Video Dimensions).

RENO AND THE DOC (1983). Canadian film proposes an interesting psychic link between a con man, Dr. Hugo Billing, and a quiet, hermit-like skiier named Reginold Colt—but writer-director Charles Dennis does little with it except make sex and drinking jokes. It's the story of how Doc forces Reno to make a comeback to win the Whistler's Cup, a skiing championship, with tasteless racist gags about a tribe of drunken Indians (the Cuchamungas) who like to shoot up the countryside. Of absolutely zero interest to fantasy fans. Ken Welsh, Henry Ramer, Linda Griffiths. (New World)

RENTADICK (1972). The title of this lowbrow British comedy sums up the lower level to which it aspires. The limp plot by John Cleese and Graham Chapman concerns a nerve gas that paralyzes all organs from the waist down. Directed by Jim Clark. James Booth, Julie Ege, Ronald Fraser, Spike Milligan. (Virgin Vision)

REPEAT PERFORMANCE (1947). After she commits a murder, Joan Leslie is projected back in time exactly one year—fate has given her another chance at life. Interesting premise goes hammy in the hands of director Alfred Werker. More of a romantic melodrama than a time-travel fantasy. Remade in the 1980s as the TV-movie TURN BACK THE CLOCK. Louis Hayward, Richard Basehart, Virginia Field, Tom Conway.

REPO MAN (1984). Outre blending of punk rock imagery and surrealistic sci-fi by British writer-director Alex Cox. Emilio Estevez is a punker wandering through industrial sections of L.A., searching for meaning to his nihilistic existence, when he teams with Harry Dean Stanton, a cynic who repossesses cars. Meanwhile, there's a 1964 Chevy Malibu driven by a crazed nuclear scientist who has stolen alien corpses from a government lab and hidden them in the trunk. Cox blends the seamy slice of life with metaphysical fantasy into this offbeat meringue of genres. Produced by "Monkee" Michael Nesmith. Tracey Walter, Sy Richardson, Jennifer Balgobin. (Video/Laser: MCA)

REPOSSESSED (1990). Free-wheeling, uninhibited parody of THE EXORCIST with Linda Blair playing a comedy counterpart to her vomit-spewing Regan. Either you'll enjoy this olio of non sequiturs, visual puns, regurgitation gags and other juvenile comedy or you'll find it hopelessly lame-brained. Probably the latter as the genuinely funny bits are far between in director Bob Logan's anything-goes script. However, Blair and Leslie Nielsen (he as the exorcising priest) enjoy themselves, especially Nielsen as he hams it up singing and dancing. Ned Beatty seems less certain as a TV evangelist. Jennifer Daniel, Noel Willman, Ray Barrett. In cameos are Jack LaLanne, Wally George, Army Archerd. (Live) (Laser: Image)

REPTILE, THE (1966). Demonstrative of the excellent Gothic atmosphere, costuming, acting and scripting in Hammer films, this tale of 19th Century Cornwall is a moody, chilling piece from producer Anthony Nelson Keys (writing as John Elder) and director John Gilling. In the not-so-friendly village, a newcomer and wife are involved in murders in which victims turn black with fang marks in their necks. It won't take you long to figure out that a Malayan curse and king cobra venom are at the core of the mystery, but this is a shocker with good monster make-up. Seeing these Hammer films today makes you wish modern producers could be as classy. Noel Willman, Ray Barrett, Jennifer Daniel, Jacqueline Pearce, Michael Ripper.

REPTILICUS (1962). Tale about the tail of a dinosaur which rejuvenates itself into an entirely new beast—a "sweetish" version of GODZILLA scripted by that team of Danish pastry makers, Sidney Pink (who also directed) and Ib Melchoir. Carl Ottosen and Ann Smyrner are the monster stalkers as the creature (a flimsey puppet on wires) stalks through Copenhagen. There's nice pseudo-documentary scenes with military forces, but the effects and crummy-looking monster by Kay Koed are Ineptilicus. Mimi Heinrich, Dirk Passer.

REPULSION (1965). Roman Polanski's masterpiece of psychological horror will unmercifully grip you. For the entire movie you are in the mind of Catherine Deneuve, a demented woman on a killing spree in her apartment. The reasons are not explained, only visually hinted at. Catherine is possessed by a frightening form of madness—you sympathize with her, even after she commits heinous crimes. The detail is realistic, the setting is stark, the music by Chico Hamilton and Gabor Szabo captures a mood of mental aberration. This is about the horrors of the mind. (Studio Entertainment; Video Dimensions; Film Classics; Global Media)

REQUIEM FOR A VAMPIRE. See **CAGED VIRGINS.**

REST IN PEACE. See **ONE DARK NIGHT.**

REST IN PIECES (1987). After daffy aunt Dorothy Malone commits suicide by taking cyanide while performing her will on a tape, young marrieds Loren Jean Vail and Scott Thompson Baker inherit her mansion and $8 million in missing money. At the estate, they discover everyone—from the maid to a minister—is homicidal, having joined Malone's zombie cult by committing suicide in exchange for eternal life. This tale takes too long to get going, but once the murderous creepos go into action, and Ms Vail runs through corridors going bonkers, it's not bad. Directed by Joseph Braunstein with a penchant for showing off the shapely form of Ms Vail as she sinks ever deeper into paranoia. Jack Taylor, Patty Shepard, David Rose. (Video/Laser: IVE)

REST IS SILENCE, THE (1960). See editions 1-3.

RESURRECTED, THE (1992). A dandy horror film and one of the better adaptations of H. P. Lovecraft. Screenwriter Brent V. Friedman borrows from "The Case of Charles Dexter Ward" and in the hands of director Dan O'Bannon it's a winner. Providence, R.I., private eye John March (John Terry) is hired by beautiful Jane Sibbett to find out why hubby Chris Sarandon is behaving so strangely. What March finds is that an ancestor of Sarandon, a wicked wizard, has taken over his body and is conducting experiences in giving life to dead beings. Todd Masters' effects depict half-decayed cadavers that are very much alive; one scene features the flesh being stripped off one body and reapplied to another; and the subterranean pit sequence is memorable. Good music score by Richard Band. Robert Romanus, Laurie Briscoe. Aka SHATTERBRAIN. (Live)

RESURRECTION (1980). Ellen Burstyn is a Kansan who almost dies in an auto crash, undergoing an "out of body" experience in which dead figures beckon for her. Back among the living she is endowed with healing powers. Lewis John Carlino's script deals with faith healing without copping out, and Daniel Petrie directed with conviction. Sam Shepard, Eva Le Gallienne. (MCA)

RESURRECTION OF ZACHARY WHEELER, THE (1971). TV-movie depicts a presidential candidate badly injured in a car crash and taken to a weird clinic in Alamagordo, N.M. where synthetic bodies, "somas," are created, then used in a bizarre blackmail plot. Most of this is chase action, focusing on newsman Leslie Nielsen trying to avoid capture as he tracks the mystery. Directed by Robert Wynn. Angie Dickinson, Jack Carter, Bradford Dillman, James Daly. (United)

RESURRECTION SYNDICATE. Alternate title for **NOTHING BUT THE NIGHT.** In video as **DEVIL'S UNDEAD, THE.**

RETALIATOR, THE. See **PROGRAMMED TO KILL.**

RETIK THE MOON MENACE. Feature version of the serial **RADAR MEN FROM THE MOON.**

RETRIBUTION (1987). The spirit of a man brutally shot and set on fire inhabits the body of a quiet, depressed hotel resident just as he leaps to suicidal death. Dennis Lipscomb returns to life, unaware his body is possessed, and that the spirit goes on nocturnal jaunts to avenge the fiery-bloody murder. This supernatural thriller almost reaches a point of total revulsion when a victim is cut down the middle by a meat saw. RETRIBUTION never recovers after that, and distances itself from empathy, producer-writer-director Guy Magar allowing his story to remain nihilistic. Leslie Wing is okay as a psychologist, but Hoyt Axton is wasted as a cop. Suzanne Snyder, Jeff Pomerantz, George Murdock. (Virgin Vision) (Laser: Image)

RETURN (1985). Lethargic as a corpse . . . tedious as a calculus exam . . as slow as free-flowing molasses . . . You won't go back to resee this Boston product about a man possessed by the spirit of a dead peron. Phony baloney "age regression" melodrama with no action or effects. Yakity yakity yakity. Written-directed by Andrew Silver. Frederic Forrest, Anne Lloyd Francis, Karlene Crockett. (Academy) (Laser: Image)

RETURN, THE. Video version of **ALIEN'S RETURN, THE** (Thorn EMI).

RETURN, THE (1973). After 400 years the Ark, an exploration spacecraft, returns to Earth. This consists of re-edited episodes from STARLOST, the doomed TV series Harlan Ellison created and then severed himself from forever. Incredibly boring stuff, incompetently photographed and acted. Keir Dullea, Lloyd Bochner.

RETURN FROM THE BEYOND (1961). Poverty stricken Mexican tale about a crazed witch who uses her magic to wage war against a doctor and his daughter. Also called MYSTERIES OF BLACK MAGIC. Nadio Haro Oliva, Elsa Cardenas. Directed by Miguel M. Delgado.

RETURN FROM THE PAST (1966). Dreadful anthology of stories about vampires, werewolves, walking dead, etc.—in short, scrapings of the horror barrel. This cheapie, directed by David L. Hewitt, looks like it was performed by a fourth-rate acting troupe with props and wardrobe left over from a school play. Released as DR. TERROR'S GALLERY OF HORRORS . . . or was it THE BLOOD SUCKERS? Should be returned to the past. John Carradine, Lon Chaney Jr., Rochelle Hudson, Roger Gentry. (S/Weird)

RETURN FROM WITCH MOUNTAIN (1978). Inferior sequel to the Disney smash ESCAPE TO WITCH MOUNTAIN, again with Kim Richards and Ike Eisenmann as humanoid kids stranded on Earth who take trips from their sanctuary on Witch Mountain. The alien moppets, who possess "molecular flow," the ability to control objects and people, are on vacation in L.A. when they encounter evil scientist Christopher Lee and associate Bette Davis. John Hough directed. Jack Soo, Anthony James, Denver Pyle. (Disney)

RETURNING, THE (1983). Ancient Indian spirits heap plenty mad! Gallop from great teepee in thunder sky to haunt white eyes living in land of great sand dunes, big Mojave. Angry warrior spirits no want land back—only wantum try out techniques they saw in THE EXORCIST many moon ago. Big Chief Joel Bender and scratching paper man Patrick Nash like Custer—lead'em cast (Susan Strasberg, Gabriel Walsh, Ruth Warrick) and crew to great massacre at Little Big Picture. (Imperial; from Dura Vision and MPV as **WITCH DOCTOR**)

RETURN OF BATMAN. See **BATMAN AND ROBIN.**

RETURN OF CAPTAIN INVINCIBLE (1982). Comedic portrait of a down-and-out superhero (Alan Arkin), complete with musical numbers by Richard O'Brien (of THE ROCKY HORROR PICTURE SHOW) and Christopher Lee as a crazed doctor. Directed by Philippe Mora. Kate Fitzpatrick, Bill Hunter, Graham Kennedy, Michael Pate. (Magnum) (Laser)

RETURN OF CAPTAIN MARVEL. Feature-length version of the Republic serial **ADVENTURES OF CAPTAIN MARVEL, THE.**

RETURN OF CAPTAIN NEMO, THE. See **AMAZING CAPTAIN NEMO, THE.** (Boggling! Not amazing)

RETURN OF CHANDU, THE (1934). Serial with Bela

Lugosi as Chandu the Magician (popular radio hero of the '30s) who goes up against the Black Magic Cult of Ubasti on the isle of Lemuria. Dreary, outdated material in need of action, pacing and decent acting. Directed by Ray Taylor. Maria Alba, Clara Kimball Young. Feature versions are THE RETURN OF CHANDU and CHANDU ON THE MAGIC ISLAND. (On video in serial form from Captain Bijou and Sinister/C; from Rhino as RETURN OF CHANDU THE MAGICIAN, THE)

RETURN OF COUNT YORGA, THE (1971). The success of COUNT YORGA—VAMPIRE dictated this sequel, Robert Quarry again essaying the bloodsucker who runs amuck in California. Now there's better acting thanks to Mariette Hartley, Roger Perry, Walter Brooke, Yvonne Wilder (as a deaf mute) and George Macready. And director Bob Kelljan has greater control, providing frightening moments when corpses attack an orphanage near San Francisco. Bill Butler's cinematography is high class. Once again Michael Macready (George's son) produced. Screenplay by Kelljan and Wilder.

RETURN OF DRACULA, THE. See **CURSE OF DRACULA, THE.** (Curses! Boiled again!)

RETURN OF DR. FU MANCHU, THE (1930). Sax Rohmer's diabolical Oriental goes bonkers in this sequel to THE MYSTERIOUS DR. FU MANCHU. Warner Oland is the madman plotting to take over the world with a secret drug that induces catalepsy; the insidious Asian fiend also contends with Scotland Yard's Nayland Smith (Neil Hamilton). Directed by Rowland V. Lee. Jean Arthur, William Austin, O. P. Heggie.

RETURN OF DR. MABUSE, THE (1961). Well-produced Italian-French-German sequel to Fritz Lang's films of the '30s and the 1960 THE THOUSAND EYES OF DR. MABUSE, depicting an ingenious madman bent on conquering the world. Inspector Lohmann (Gert Frobe) and FBI man Lex Barker join reporter Daliah Lavi to prevent the archvillain (Wolfgang Preiss) from infiltrating a nuclear plant and controlling employees' minds. Interesting, but not up to Lang's originals or the books by Norbert Jacques. Directed by Harald Reinl. Fausto Tozzi, Werner Peters. Next came THE TESTAMENT OF DR. MABUSE, DR. MABUSE VS. SCOTLAND YARD and THE SECRET OF DR. MABUSE. (Sinister/C; S/Weird; Filmfax)

RETURN OF DR. X, THE (1940). Humphrey Bogart in a horror film? There he is with pallid face, sunken cheeks and horn-rimmed glasses, requiring a blood "fix" every few hours, which accounts for the 493 corpses littering his neighborhood. Bogart was being punished by Jack Warner for his iconoclastic attitudes, but never again was he so dumbly wasted in such undistinguished fare. Meanwhile, Wayne Morris endures as a fast-talking (also dumb) newspaperman, Dennis Morgan suffers as the Nice Young Man, John Litel looks embarrassed as the Doctor Who Went Too Far and Rosemary Lane oozes charm as the Friendly Nurse. Directed programmer-style by Vincent Sherman.

RETURN OF GIANT MAJIN, THE (1966). Clomping time again for that ancient God of War who inhabits a stone statue and goes around crushing the worst offenders in a medieval feud. In this sequel to MAJIN, MONSTER OF TERROR, production values are good and the action is well staged. Directed by Kenji Misumi and Yoshiyuki Kuruda. Third film in the series was MAJIN STRIKES AGAIN. Kojiro Hongo, Shiho Fujimura.

RETURN OF GODZILLA. See **GIGANTIS THE FIRE MONSTER.**

RETURN OF JACK THE RIPPER, THE. See **JACK THE RIPPER (1958).**

RETURN OF MAJIN, THE. See **RETURN OF GIANT MAJIN, THE.**

RETURN OF MAXWELL SMART. See **NUDE BOMB, THE.**

RETURN OF PETER GRIMM, THE (1935). More creaky than charming is this sentimental ghost story based on a play by David Belasco, first made as a silent in 1926. Crotchety Lionel Barrymore returns from the grave enwrapped in a gooey substance that suggests cinematographer Glenn Williams smeared Vasoline on the lens. Thin plot has relatives fighting over an inheritance and discussing the recently deceased—who stands to one side, listening. It's gentle and bloodless as Barrymore tries to prevent a wrongful marriage, and it's saccharine sweet when a youngster goes to his maker and walks into the sunset with the cranky Barrymore. Directed by Victor Schertzinger. Helen Mack, Edward Ellis, Donald Meek. (Turner; RKO)

RETURN OF SHERLOCK HOLMES, THE (1986). The first hour of this TV-movie from writer-producer Bob Shayne is a Sherlockian delight: Private eye Jane Watson (Margaret Colin, a wonderfully spunky actress with lovely eyes one could swim in) learns she is the great granddaughter of Dr. John Watson and resurrects Holmes from a deep-freeze sleep, where he has been awaiting a cure for bubonic plague (with which he was injected by James Moriarty's brother). Holmes (a lean, erudite Michael Pennington) is soon caught up in a mystery that unfortunately is far too routine. But oh, does Pennington have fun with the sexy Colin. Recommended to detective fans, although Holmesian buffs may consider this sacrilegious, and becry such spoofery. Lila Kaye, Connie Booth, Nicholas Guest, Barry Morse (in a cameo bigger than it seems).

RETURN OF SUPERBUG (1979). West German Wunderauto, about which you oughta wunder, has become a jeep half-track operated by a robot called "El Guancho" with a voice like Bugs Bunny's. On an island off the coast of Spain, several parties search for an airplane containing the "Treasure of Corleone," lost during World War II. Oddly enough, unlike the two films before it, this has serious themes, such as the Superbug's pilot having a drinking problem. Director Rudolf Zehetgruber proves to be a backseat driver. Brad Harris.

RETURN OF THE ALIEN'S DEADLY SPAWN. Video version of **DEADLY SPAWN, THE** (Continental).

RETURN OF THE APE MAN (1944). Not that it matters, but this is not a sequel to THE APE MAN. Bela Lugosi and John Carradine bring a prehistoric Neanderthal out of its deep freeze—a hairy caveman who loves to run amuck, a nonsocial trait they "exorcise" by giving him the brain of George Zucco. The result is a cultured, refined gentleman who plays "Moonlight Sonata" . . . and then goes on a rampage. All-time low for the cast. Sam Katzman and Jack Dietz produced for Monogram; Phil Rosen directed. (Media; on a "Double Bill" Nostalgia Merchant video with **FOG ISLAND**)

RETURN OF THE BLIND DEAD (1973). Spanish sequel to THE BLIND DEAD (also TOMB OF THE BLIND DEAD and ATTACK OF THE BLIND DEAD) directed by Amando de Ossorio, with Tony Kendall. This "walking dead" series includes HORROR OF THE ZOMBIES and NIGHT OF THE SEAGULLS (also NIGHT OF THE DEATH CULT). (Genesis)

RETURN OF THE EVIL DEAD. Video version of **RETURN OF THE BLIND DEAD** (Bingo; JEF Films).

RETURN OF THE FAMILY MAN (1990). Another interpretation of THE STEPFATHER theme, with Ron Smerczak as a man who wipes out families whenever the mood strikes him. Made in South Africa, this was directed by John Murlowki. Liam Cundill, Terence Reis, Debra Kaye. (Raedon)

RETURN OF THE FLY (1959). Underrated sequel to THE FLY, with a scientist's son (Brett Halsey) picking up the experiment in teleportation where dead old dad left off. With stark black-and-white photography by Brydon Baker, director Edward L. Bernds evokes some horrifying moments in a mortuary and keeps things buzzing. George Langelaan's story gimmick—transposition of body parts on human and fly, so tiny fly has human head and huge human has huge fly's head—is repeated by Bernds (he also scripted), indicating there was nothing new to be achieved in this sequel. But it's still a nice low-budget film. Vincent Price, Dan Seymour, John Sutton. (Video/Laser: CBS/Fox)

RETURN OF THE GIANT MONSTERS, THE (1967). Japanese monster movie with plenty of snap—its main protagonist being that giant turtle Gamera, who comes out of his shell when Gyaos, a winged monstrosity that fires laser bolts through its mouth, attacks Earth without pity. Kazufumi Fujii's effects include earthquakes and spewing lava, in case the titans bore you with routine destruction. Actually the effects are good . . . but you must appreciate these Asian slam-bang affairs to reach the bitter end. Directed by Noriyaki Yuasa. (From Celebrity as **GAMERA VS. GYAOS**)

RETURN OF THE INCREDIBLE HULK, THE (1977). Sequel to THE INCREDIBLE HULK has Bill Bixby back as Dr. Banner, trying to learn why he transmutates into a green monster (strongman Lou Ferrigno with spinach-coloring rubbed all over his body) whenever he gets mad or stressed out. Based on the Marvel comic book character; decently done. Directed by Alan J. Levi. Dorothy Tristan, William Daniels, Laurie Prange.

RETURN OF THE JEDI (1983). Third in the STAR WARS series, culminating the middle trilogy of George Lucas' proposed nine-part saga. JEDI resolves the cliff-hangers in THE EMPIRE STRIKES BACK and moves faster than Imperial fighters as Luke Skywalker, Princess Leia, Chewbacca, Lando Calrissian and that Laurel-and-Hardy team in space, R2D2 and C3PO, penetrate the fortress of vile bandit Jabba the Hutt (a giant toad creature) to rescue Han Solo's carbonized body. After a marvelous opening featuring a menagerie of E.T.s and a hair-raising battle aboard Jabba's land barge, our heroes are off to fight the Empire, personified by Darth Vader and the Emperor (looking like a wicked wizard) and several thousand stormtroopers. Ken Ralston's team at Industrial Light and Magic perfected its equipment so that the effects are great. There's mind-boggling space hardware whizzing past the camera, and a fabulous chase on air bikes through a forest. Phil Tippett's otherworldly beings are a delight to terrestrial eyes. In addition to nonstop action, diehard fans will be intrigued by Luke's quest for his heritage. It's a mythological duel of good vs. evil in its purest form and elevates Lawrence Kasdan's script, often guilty of banal dialogue and indifference to the characters. Director Richard Marquand goes for the glossy and bright; hence, this doesn't have the pessimism Irvin Kershner brought to EMPIRE, and it ends on a positive upbeat note in the camp of the Ewoks, a race of cuddly creatures who help fight the Empire. A super-exciting superpicture. Mark Hamill, Carrie Fisher, Harrison Ford, Peter Mayhew, Billy Dee Williams, David Prowse, Anthony Daniels. (Video/Laser: CBS/Fox)

HARRISON FORD

CHEWBACCA

RETURN OF THE KILLER TOMATOES (1988). This sequel to the 1979 sci-fi farce, remembered more for its title than its content, is quite dumb—and a lot of fun. It's played for broad comedy and spends more time satirizing TV commercials and advertising than malevolent love fruits. This silly romp, directed by director John DeBello, has a thin story built around mad Professor Gangreen (John Astin) who turns a tomato into a sexy woman (busty Karen Mistal) by exposing it to music. Mistal gets mixed up with the hero of the first movie (Anthony Starke), now a pizza parlor owner, and with the help of a black investigator in a cowboy suit, a scuba diver, a guy parodying John Belushi from Spielberg's 1941 and a benevolent little tomato nicknamed "F.T.," they race around San Diego like stooges. Somehow a charming little film emerges from the hodgepodge. George Clooney, Steve Lundquist, Charlie Jones. (New World) (Laser: Image)

RETURN OF THE KING, THE (1979). Subtitled A STORY OF THE HOBBITS, this animated sequel to LORD OF THE RINGS details the search for the Ring of Doom, the only object that can prevent evil from engulfing the world. Adapted by Romeo Muller from the classic fantasy series by J. R. R. Tolkien, this is a complicated sword-and-sorcery tale that doesn't always translate well to film. How the small but mighty Hobbit creatures are involved in the affairs of several races of good and evil beings in a never-never land of magic is at the core of this fable, distinguished by the voices of Orson Bean, William Conrad, Theodore Bikel, John Huston, Roddy McDowall, Paul Frees and the ballads of Glenn Yarbrough as the roving minstrel. A Japanese-U.S. production, guided by producer-directors Arthur Rankin Jr. and Jules Bass. (Xenon)

RETURN OF THE LIVING DEAD (1973). See **MESSIAH OF EVIL.**

RETURN OF THE LIVING DEAD, THE (1985). Dan O'Bannon, author of ALIEN and DEAD AND BURIED, makes his directorial debut with this spinoff from NIGHT OF THE LIVING DEAD and spoofs the genre without sacrificing shocks, making this superior black-comedy horror (O'Bannon scripted too). In a warehouse for the world's oddities are U.S. military cannisters rumored to contain corpses inflicted with a plague from space (there are references to George Romero's 1967 movie). A malfunction frees a corpse and causes a toxic rain to fall on Resurrection Cemetery. Next, the walking dead are everywhere. Absolutely hysterical (if you have a morbid sense of humor) with thrills in the Romero tradition. O'Bannon is to be commended. And thanks also goes to Clu Gulager, James Karen, Beverly Randolph, Thom Mathews and Don Calfa for giving versimilitude to the wild, woolly fun. (HBO; Hemdale) (Laser: Image)

RETURN OF THE LIVING DEAD PART II (1987). This isn't half as much fun as Part I. It duplicates the effects of the first film without exploring the themes in any novel ways, and it never builds up steam. No suspense, no surprises. This time one of those deadly cannisters falls out of an Army truck (Toxic and Hazardous Waste Unit), spreading its gas to a graveyard. Out of the ground pops an army of shambling dead people, eager for "Brains! More brains!" It's finally a small band of survivors escaping in a cherry red Chevy. The cast standout is Philip Bruns as a goofy doctor who has the funniest lines in the picture and mugs for all he's worth, knowing there is no better way to play this material. Written-directed by Ken Wiederhorn. James Karen, Thom Mathews, Michael Kenworthy, Marsha Dietlein, Dana Ashbrook. (Lorimar) (Laser: Image)

RETURN OF THE LIVING DEAD 3 (1993). Reliable old Trioxin, that chemical that restores life to the dead, is back in action in this straight-faced followup in the series, which has ample bloody effects and a plot surrounding J. Trevor Edmond's efforts to bring dead girlfriend Mindy Clarke back to life. Directed by Brian Yuzna. Kent McCord, Basil Wallace. (Vidmark)

RETURN OF THE MAN FROM U.N.C.L.E.: THE 15 YEARS LATER AFFAIR (1983). Resurfacing of T.H.R.U.S.H., the terrorist birdbrains, forces Napoleon Solo and Illya Kuryakin back into action in this TV-movie based on the hit '64-67 series. T.H.R.U.S.H. demands $350 million in ransom or it will explode the H957 nuclear device—the most terrifying weapon in the universe. This is so imitative of the Bond films that some sequences play like direct steals. The devices are strained; the only freshness is provided by Robert Vaughn and David McCallum as the retreads who crack jokes about their ages. George Lazenby also saves the day by breezing through as James Bond (referred to as J.B.) and rescuing Napoleon during a high-speed chase through Las Vegas. With Leo G. Carroll dead, Patrick Macnee is the new chief, Sir John Raleigh. Villains are Anthony Zerbe and Keenan Wynn. Directed by Ray Austin. (Trans World)

RETURN OF THE SHAGGY DOG, THE (1988). Substandard two-part TV-movie update of the popular Disney comedies of the '50s in which a man turned into a dog with the help of a magical ring. This watered-down pap was directed by Gtuard Gillard. The cast is bubbly but it's still no great shakes of a dog's tail. Gary Kroeger, Todd Waring, Michelle Little, Cindy Morgan.

RETURN OF THE SIX MILLION DOLLAR MAN AND THE BIONIC WOMAN (1987). Two old TV series are retreaded into a mediocre TV-movie. Steve Austin (Lee Majors) and Jamie Somers (Lindsay Wagner) are brought out of retirement to stop Fortress, a gang led by Martin Landau trying to get the secret of bionic power. The first hour is bionic soap opera as Austin rekindles a romance with Jamie and seeks the respect of the son he never raised. Phony sentiment and mushy stuffq97until Austin and Jamie team up to toss around the bad guys in slow motion. Richard Anderson is back as the assignment chief, with Lee Majors II playing Austin's son, a bionic warrior with X-ray zap vision. Directed by Ray Austin.

RETURN OF THE SWAMP THING, THE (1989). Another comic-book movie from Jim Wynorski, one-time PR man for Roger Corman. The tragic qualities of the original Berni Wrightson-Len Wein comic book character are foresaken as the creature is used as a springboard device for a tongue-in-cheek comedy. Managing a straight face, Louis Jourdan reprises his role as Dr. Arcane from the 1981 Wes Craven vehicle, conducting new genetic experiments a la H. G. Wells' Dr. Moreau in his antebellum mansion. There's talent here—lovely, sexy Heather Locklear, attractive, exotic Sarah Douglas, Ace Mask as a silly doctor, and Joey Sagal as a security guard. What passes for a story has Swamp Thing (stoically played by Dick Durock in a rubber suit) always at the site of trouble, ready to rescue someone. The attempt at a romance between Swampy and Heather is ludicrous . . . if only this tried to equal the melancholic, tragic feel of the comics. (Video/Laser: RCA/Columbia)

RETURN OF THE TERROR (1934). Editions 1-3.

RETURN OF THE VAMPIRE, THE (1943). Columbia pastiche of horror films of the '40s is crude but fun—if you like cornball premises and corny fog swirling around the vampire as he attacks. Bela Lugosi is a long-dead bloodsucker in cahoots with a werewolf (Matt Willis) he holds under his power in London 1918. A Van Helsing-imitating professor destroys him with a stake, but an air raid in blitz-terrorized London years later resurrects him and he begins a new wave of horror, attacking members of the family that "staked" him. Directed by Lew Landers. Nina Foch, Miles Mander. (RCA/Columbia; Goodtimes) (Laser: RCA/Columbia; Image)

RETURN OF THE WOLFMAN, THE. See **CRAVING, THE.**

RETURN OF THE ZOMBIES. Video version of **BEYOND THE LIVING DEAD** (Wizard).

RETURN OF WALPURGIS. See **CURSE OF THE DEVIL.**

RETURN TO BOGGY CREEK (1978). Not a sequel to LEGEND OF BOGGY CREEK, but a good children's movie under Tom Moore's direction, with many beautiful shots of the swamps, ample banjo music and a "Boggy Creek Ballad" as two brothers and their sister encounter a benevolent, hairy beast of legend. Languidly told, with colorful bayou characters. Worth going back for. Directed by Tom Moore. Dawn Wells and Dana Plato head the regional cast. (CBS/Fox)

RETURN TO FANTASY ISLAND (1977). Second TV pilot for the series that became the long-running hit, FANTASY ISLAND, with assorted wish-fulfillers making

DIRECTOR KEN WIEDERHORN AND FRIENDS

fools of themselves while hanging around Mr. Roarke (Ricardo Montalban). Directed by George McGowan. Adrienne Barbeau, Horst Buchholz, Joseph Cotten, Pat Crowley, Joseph Campanella, George Chakiris, Karen Valentine. Herve Villechaize as Tattoo. (Prism)

RETURN TO HORROR HIGH (1987). Because unsolved murders occurred at Crippen High in 1982, a film crew uses the abandoned institution to make a horror pic. This is not a sequel to HORROR HIGH but rather another belabored spoof of FRIDAY THE 13TH, with a penchant for thinking that buckets of spattering blood is something to laugh about. The story is told within a flashback framework and the plot mixes reality with movie fantasy, which might have been amusing had it all fit together, which it doesn't. Vincent Edwards portrays a biology professor dissected like one of his frogs. Alex Rocco has a few funny moments as a sleazy producer but this is a series of juvenile, unscary gore gags with mediocre characters. Bill Froehlich wrote-directed. George Clooney, Scott Jacoby, Pepper Martin, Panchito Gomez. (New World) (Laser: Image)

RETURN TO OZ (1964). Full-length animated sequel to L. Frank Baum's THE WIZARD OF OZ (Prism).

RETURN TO OZ (1985). Admirable attempt by Disney to recapture the flavor of the adventures of Dorothy in Oz (as originally conceived by L. Frank Baum) was a box-office failure, which critics decried for its somber tone and its failure to be as charming and appealing as the 1939 MGM musical. All that aside, it's an imaginative if slow-paced sequel, following Dorothy as she is subjected to the electrical machine of a doctor (Nicol Williamson) and nurse (Jean Marsh) trying to cure her of insomnia caused by her first adventure in Oz. She awakens in the fanciful kingdom with a talking chicken named Billina and is joined with Tik Tok, a mechanical robot, Jack Pumpkinhead and a moose head named Gump. They must free the Emerald City inhabitants, frozen into marble statues by the evil Gnome King, and his queen, Princess Mombi (also played by Marsh). Memorable sequences include the Wheelers, cackling jokers who move about on wheels, and a chamber where the princess keeps heads encased behind glass. The effects are good, especially Will Vinton's Claymation, a process of animating the rock faces. There's more production quality than zip to Walter Murch's direction, but don't be put off by the bad word of mouth. Fairuza Balk is a good Dorothy, Piper Laurie appears as Aunt Em, and Matt Clark is Uncle Henry. The dark side to THE WIZARD OF OZ. (Video/Laser: Disney)

RETURN TO SALEM'S LOT, A (1987). Enjoyable vampire-horror sequel (unofficial) to Stephen King's SALEM'S LOT, directed by Larry Cohen, who collaborated on the script with James Dixon. Anthropoligist Michael Moriarty resettles in the New England vampire community with estranged son Ricky Addison Reed and their relationship is at the core of this film—each is a loser in life, lured too easily into the world of the vampires, and each recognizes the other's fragilities. Another unusual treat is the presence of film maker Samuel Fuller, who plays Van Meer, a Nazi hunter turned Vampire Killer who has some wonderfully esoteric dialogue as he rushes through the town, staking monsters to death. Leading the vampire coven is Andrew Duggan aided by June Havoc, Evelyn Keyes and Ronee Blakely. (Warner Bros.)

RETURN TO TREASURE ISLAND (1954). See editions 1-3.

REVENGE (1971). Haggy old dame goes bats in a decaying San Francisco Victorian, imprisoning Stuart Whitman. Prisoner's girl, through ESP powers, sets out to rescue him from a fate worse than death—being locked up with Shelley Winters! Joseph Stefano dreamed it up; Jud Taylor directed. Bradford Dillman.

REVENGE (1971). Intense, disturbing tale of retribution filled with quirky, ironic twists. Not a horror film in the traditional sense, but horrific for its comment on man's animalistic side. James Booth portrays a pub owner who kidnaps the man he suspects of murdering-raping his daughter and holds him hostage. It's terrifying in that Booth is an honest citizen caught up in emotional forces that are soon out of control. The people are unusually real for this tale of revenge, and Joan Collins' performance as Booth's wife is a standout. Sidney Hayers directed. Ray Barrett, Sinead Cusack, Kenneth Griffith. Aka BEHIND THE CELLAR DOOR, TERROR FROM UNDER THE HOUSE and INN OF THE FRIGHTENED PEOPLE. (Sultan; Axon; Moore)

REVENGE (1986). Here's a blood cult flick that goes to the dogs: In Tulsa, Okla., some of the best citizens are members of the Kaninas Cult, which worships a demon hound. Patrick Wayne and a farmer lady track down the culprits in a video cheapie described as a sequel to BLOOD CULT. Among the delights: an axe in a farmer's forehead, a co-ed's severed foot, deskinned heads and charred bodies. Written-directed by Christopher Lewis. John Carradine. (United/VCI)

REVENGE IN THE HOUSE OF USHER (1982). European retread of Edgar Allan Poe's tale, directed by Jesso Franco, includes flashbacks lifted from THE AWFUL DR. ORLOFF. Howard Vernon, Olivier Matlhot, Dan Villers. Also known as NEUROSIS. (Trans World; Wizard; Movies Unlimited)

REVENGE OF BILLY THE KID (1991). A woman gives birth to a half-human, half-goat creature that soon kills local citizens. British horror comedy was directed by Jim Groom. Michael Balfour, Samantha Perkins.

REVENGE OF DRACULA (1971). Video version of **DRACULA VS. FRANKENSTEIN** (Duravision).

REVENGE OF DR. DEATH. See **MADHOUSE.**

REVENGE OF DR. X. Video version of **DOUBLE GARDEN, THE** (Regal).

REVENGE OF FRANKENSTEIN, THE (1958). Sequel to THE CURSE OF FRANKENSTEIN and one of the best in Hammer's Frankenstein series, permeated with a satanical sense of humor (thanks to scripter Jimmy Sangster) that does not distract from horrific elements. Peter Cushing returns as the Baron, working in a hospital in Carlsbruck for access to organs and limbs so he might give his hunchback assistant a new body. It's warped (the story, not the body) but that's what makes these British fright flicks so bloody good, old man. Directed by Terence Fisher with a lust for macabre humor. Michael Gwynn replaces Christopher Lee as the Monster, with Lionel Jeffries as a body snatcher.

REVENGE OF GODZILLA. Japanese laser title for **GODZILLA'S REVENGE.**

REVENGE OF KING KONG, THE. See **KING KONG ESCAPES.**

REVENGE OF THE BLOOD BEAST. See **SHE BEAST, THE.**

REVENGE OF THE BOOGEYMAN. See **BOGEYMAN II.**

REVENGE OF THE CREATURE (1955). THE CREATURE FROM THE BLACK LAGOON was too big a hit just to float away, so director Jack Arnold and producer William Alland reteamed for this exciting sequel recapturing the superb underwater photography and brain-bashing thrills of the original. Martin Berkeley's story is nonstop action when the Gill-Man is rediscovered in his Black Lagoon, captured and brought to a sea world park in Florida. Eventually the primeval Creature goes on a rampage—mainly to carry Lori Nelson away to his marshy hideaway in the Everglades. John Agar and John Bromfield fight over the girl, but it's just a half-hearted subplot. Originally produced in 3-D, but few patrons saw it that way in the 1950s. In '82 the film resurfaced on TV in a special 3-D presentation. Nestor Paiva, Clint Eastwood (in his debut as a lab technician), Robert B. Williams, Dave Willock. (Video/Laser: MCA)

THE GILL MAN, LORI NELSON, RICHARD CARLSON

REVENGE OF THE DEAD (1959). See **NIGHT OF THE GHOULS.**

REVENGE OF THE DEAD (1984). By Italian horror standards, one of the tamest spaghetti-shockers ever produced. This TV-movie (also called ZEDER—VOICES FROM BEYOND) is about an unsold novelist who discovers letters written on his typewriter ribbon which refer to "K Zones," areas where the dead return to life. Writer and wife set out for Necropolis and an oracle of the dead. Unfortunately, the emphasis of director-producer Pupi Avati is on dialogue and literacy with a modicum of visual shocks. The film's 100 minutes cannot sustain interest. Gabriele Lavia, Anna Canovas, Bob Tonelli, John Stacy. (Lightning; Wizard; Live)

REVENGE OF THE DEAD (1975). See **MEAT-CLEAVER MASSACRE.**

REVENGE OF THE GODS (1966). Re-edited episodes from Irwin Allen's TIME TUNNEL (see that entry). In their time-hopping adventures, Robert Colbert and James Darren witness the Fall of Jericho and the Siege of Troy. Whit Bissell, Lee Mereiwether, John Doucette, Rhodes Reason, Michael Pate, Lisa Gaye.

REVENGE OF THE HUMANOIDS, THE (1981). French feature cartoon with limited animation and terrible faces on most of the characters—which cuts the appeal considerably. It's a STAR WARS clone, with the Omega Intergalactic Police (and a cutesy-pie robot named Metro) getting trapped on a planet in the convolutions of an intergalactic war. The complicated maneuvering is too hard for kids to understand, and adults will be disappointed by the child-like characters, so this will please neither side. Creator-director Albert Barille needed to bring more appeal to his tale of war and revolution. Music by Michel Legrand.

REVENGE OF THE JEDI. George Lucas announced the third film in his STAR WARS series under this title, but changed his mind before the release date, retitling the project RETURN OF THE JEDI. Some posters and pre-release material carry the REVENGE title.

REVENGE OF THE LIVING DEAD. See **MURDER CLINIC, THE.** (Feeling lifeless? See a doctor!)

REVENGE OF THE LIVING DEAD (1972). Video version of **CHILDREN SHOULDN'T PLAY WITH DEAD THINGS** (True World).

REVENGE OF THE LIVING ZOMBIES (1989). Bill Hinzman, who appeared in George Romero's NIGHT OF THE LIVING DEAD as a zombie, produced- directed this homage to Romero, and it's strictly for cultists, with bloodletting, gore effects and nihilistic attitude. In one respect, you wish Hinzman (who appears as Flesh Eater) was more original in depicting walking zombies—on the other hand, you have to respect his respect for Romero. But there are libel laws and there's little (if any) originality—even the ending is a ripoff. Made near Pittsburgh, in the same area where Romero made the original. Recommended to those who appreciate this sort of bloody thing. John Mowod, Leslie Ann Wick, Kevin Kindlin. Also known as FLESH EATER. (Magnum)

REVENGE OF THE MYSTERONS FROM MARS (1981). TV version of THUNDERBIRD 6, a sequel to THUNDERBIRDS ARE GO, is a full-length puppet space adventure produced in England by Gerry and Sylvia Anderson. Great fun as Captain Scarlett and Spectrum save Earth from destruction, with the model work good. Directed by Brian Burgess, Robert Lynn and Ken Turner. (Family Home Entertainment)

REVENGE OF THE RADIOACTIVE REPORTER (1990). In the satiric (and yes, dumb) vein of TOXIC AVENGER, this Canadian spoof set in Toronto depicts reporter David Scammell's attempts to investigate a nuclear power plant leak, only to be pushed into a contaminated vat by his nemeses and emerge . . . a freak who goes on a rampage. Produced-directed by Craig Pryce. Derrick Strange, Randy Pearlson. (Magnum)

REVENGE OF THE SCREAMING DEAD. See **MESSIAH OF EVIL.**

REVENGE OF THE STEPFORD WIVES (1980). TV-movie sequel to THE STEPFORD WIVES (a popular novel by Ira Levin and a quality feature) is unfaithful to the original, and just stupid exploitation. Surprising, too, since it was directed by DR. PHIBES mastermind Robert Fuest, and it has a good cast: Arthur Hill, Don Johnson, Sharon Gless, Julie Kavner, Mason Adams, Audra Lindley. (Embassy; Sultan)

REVENGE OF THE TEENAGE VIXENS FROM OUTER SPACE (1986). Lightweight spoof has sexy spacegals visiting Earth, one of them to see a human son she sired 16 years earlier. Cheap and easy to forget, its titillation being minimal. Directed by Jeff Farrell. Howard Scott, Lisa Schwedop, Amy Crumpacker, Sterling Ramberg. (Continental)

REVENGE OF THE VAMPIRE. See **BLACK SUNDAY.**

REVENGE OF THE ZOMBIES, THE (1943). The only saving graces of this Monogram flopper is the hammy, bug-eyed performance of John Carradine as a crazed Nazi doctor living in the swampland of Louisiana where he creates shambling zombies for Der Fuhrer, and the somnambulant performance of beautiful Veda Ann Borg, who drifts through this poverty-row low-budgeter in a trance, her shapely body sheathed in a sexy white night-gown. Mantan Moreland, Robert Lowery, Bob Steele and Gale Storm are among the nostalgic faces that help to overcome the threadbare drabness of the Lindsley Parsons production, directed flatly and unimaginatively by Steve Sekely. (Loonic)

REVENGE OF THE ZOMBIES (1981). Video version of **KISS DADDY GOODBYE** (Genesis; IVE).

REVENGE OF THE ZOMBIES (1981). Hong Kong production is gory and bloodthirsty in the extreme. Black magic runs rampant as a hundred-year-old sorcerer retains youthfulness by drinking blood—by the buckets. Torture and martial arts action, too. Directed without subtlety by Horace Menga.

REVOLT OF THE DEAD ONES. See **VENGEANCE OF THE ZOMBIES.**

REVOLT OF THE ZOMBIES (1936). The zombies are revolting! Edward and Victor Halperin (WHITE ZOMBIE), clumsy filmmakers at best, return to the walking dead theme with predictably uneven results. A low point in the career of Dean Jagger as an explorer in Cambodia who finds the secret to creating zombies. Of minor interest to film historians and completists. Edward produced, Victor directed. Dorothy Stone, Roy D'Arcy, Robert Noland. (Hal Roach; Sinister/C; Filmfax; Quintex)

REX HARRISON PRESENTS STORIES OF LOVE (1974). Trilogy of romances by well-known authors. Two of them have elements of fantasy and mystery: "Epicac" is the story of a computer programmer who falls in love with a machine; it's from a Kurt Vonnegut Jr. story. "Kiss Me Again, Stranger" is a Daphne Du Maurier tale about the love between a war veteran and a murderess. Julie Sommars, Bill Bixby, Roscoe Lee Browne, Leonard Nimoy, Lorne Greene.

RHINOCEROS (1974). See editions 1-3.

RICHARD III (1955). British version of Shakespeare's play about the crippled English king who ruthlessly murdered those blocking his way to power. Sir Laurence Olivier directed-produced-starred in the title role, assisted by John Gielgud, Ralph Richardson, Claire Bloom, Sir Cedric Hardwicke, Alec Guinness, Stanley Baker. Highly recommended. (this same story is told as Gothic horror in THE TOWER OF LONDON.) (Embassy; RCA/Columbia; Sultan)

RIDERS OF THE STORM (1986). Politically radical, cinematically bizarre satire set in the near future when Willa Westinghouse is leaning way to the right in her effort to become the first woman president, assisted by an advisor named McCarthy. Meanwhile, Dennis Hopper, Michael J. Pollard and other Vietnam aviation vets are flying around in the democratic skies in an old beat-up bomber, broadcasting S & M-TV, a pirate station projecting a non-Establishment view and a "psy-ops" technique of mind control. The military, in cahoots with Westinghouse, plans to blow Hopper's superstation out of the sky while he manipulates to destroy Westinghouse's career. This is a pillhead's nightmare and contains a few swift kicks at the electronic pulpit. Directed by Maurice Phillips. Eugene Lipinski, James Aubrey, Nigel Pegram. (Nelson; New Line) (Laser: Nelson)

RIDERS OF THE WHISTLING SKULL (1937). The Valley of the Skulls is location of the lost city of Lukachuke, inhabited by Lukachukians. Along comes an archeological expedition with the Three Mesquiteers (Bob Livingston, Ray Corrigan, Max Terhune) riding shotgun. Supernatural themes make this an offbeat entry in the Republic Western series. Remade in 1949 as a Charlie Chan feature, THE FEATHERED SERPENT. Directed by Mack V. Wright. (Filmfax; Sinister/C; Nostalgia; Video Connection)

RIDERS TO THE STARS (1954). Passing meteor swarm attracts three rocketeers, who blast off from Earth to catch hunks of the spacerock. According to scientist Herbert Marshall, the meteors could answer our space problems. The astronauts (William Lundigan, Robert Karnes and Richard Carlson) fly high while lovely Martha Hyer waits on the ground. Realistic details and emphasis on people make this like an old-fashioned service drama. Carlson directed the Curt Siodmak script for this Ivan Tors production. Dawn Addams.

RIDING ON AIR (1937). Joe E. Brown is Elmer Lane—mismanaging editor of the Caremont (Wisconsin) Chronicle—who is involved with swindlers promoting a new airplane radio beam. Rollicking, delightful RKO comedy. Directed by Edward Sedgwick. Guy Kibbee, Florence Rice, Clem Bevans. (Kartes; Nostalgia)

RIDING WITH DEATH (1976). Two episodes of the short-lived GEMINI MAN TV series, a variation on THE INVISIBLE MAN in which Ben Murphy, as a secret agent for INTERSECT, turns invisible with a molecule scrambler. In the first adventure he drives a truck carrying a new volatile rocket fuel; in the other he poses as a race car driver out to get an evil promoter stealing secrets of the new XK-240 jet fighter. In both of these below-average stories he's assisted by bureau chief William Sylvester and femme agent Katherine Crawford. Directed by Alan J. Levi and Don McDougall. (MCA)

RIFT, THE. See **ENDLESS DESCENT.**

RING OF TERROR (1962). Wardrobe and hair styles suggest this was filmed during the mid-1950s but unreleased until the '60s. It's an amateurish story about fraternity students and hazing rituals. A medical student must remove a ring from a corpse in a graveyard, but he dies of fright. You'll die of boredon as this nothing production unfolds. Directed by Clark Paylow. George Mather, Esther Furst, Austin Green, Joe Conway. (Vidmark; Sinister/C; S/Weird; Filmfax)

RIO '80. See **FUTURE WOMEN.**

RIPPER, THE (1982). See **NEW YORK RIPPER.**

RIPPER, THE (1985). Amateurish, low-budget regional thudder shot on tape in Tulsa, Okla. A college instructor teaching "Famous Crimes on Film" finds a ring worn by Mary Kelly, a Jack the Ripper victim. At night he has nightmares in which he sees old Jack slaughtering women and ripping out their intestines. Lumbering, cumbersome hunkajunk with tediously repetitious murders and downright bad acting—not to mention crummy dialogue (by Bill Groves) and slow direction (by Christopher Lewis). An excruciating viewing experience. Robert Brewer and David Powell did the make-up effects. Famed make-up man Tom Savini plays Jack the Ripper by twirling the ends of his mustache and chuckling with fiendish glee. (VCI; United)

RIPPER OF NOTRE DAME, THE. See **DEMONIAC.**

RISING STORM (1989). Set in 2099 A.D., this satirical adventure depicts a tyrannical society run by Reverend Jimmy Joe II, who controls the Oval Office with a hypocritical, dictatorial hand. This film's best moments are its comments about religion and government not mixing, and the humorous personalities of its four main characters. Zach Galligan, a totally naive young man, and his hard-boiled brother Wayne Crawford join freedom fighters June Chadwick and Elizabeth Keifer to find a lost radio station in the desert, and their fresh characterizations give this tired genre retread a shot in the arm. The rest is mock heroics as the rebels close in on Jimmy Joe II for a blazing climax. Director Francis Schaeffer filmed in South Africa. John Rhys Davies, William Katt, Graham Clark, Gordon Mullholland.

RISK, THE (1960). What might have been a boring spy thriller (bubonic-curing serum is discovered but concealed from the medical world) is enhanced by producers-directors Ray and John Boulting, specialists in British thrillers. Tony Britton, Ian Bannen, Peter Cushing, Donald Pleasence, Spike Milligan.

RITES OF DRACULA, THE. Video version of **SATANIC RITES OF DRACULA, THE** (Gemstone).

RITUAL OF EVIL (1970). Too bad Universal didn't continue its series about a ghost investigator (Louis Jourdan) and his wise old assistant (Wilfrid Hyde-White), introduced in FEAR NO EVIL the year before. Both are TV movies of considerable quality. In this sequel, superbly directed by Robert Day, Jourdan investigates the death of an heiress, encountering black magic rituals. Anne Baxter, Diana Hyland.

RITUALS (1978). Engrossing performance by Hal Holbrook, struggling against the wilderness and his fellow man, holds together this Canadian picture which vacillates between DELIVERANCE and a slasher theme. Five physicians take a fishing trip into the "Cauldron of the Moon," a beautiful but isolated region of Ontario, to be terrorized by an unseen madman. The explanation to the mystery is weak, and never worked into the dialogue by writer Ian Sutherland, and Peter Carter is perhaps too introspective to be directing an action picture, but there is a raw energy that works through the mundanities. Not for the squeamish, however. Lawrence Dane, Robin Gammell, Ken James. Also known as THE CREEPER. (Embassy)

ROAD BUILDER, THE. See **NIGHT DIGGER, THE.**

ROADGAMES (1982). Well-crafted though eccentric thriller in the Hitchcock vein, cleverly conceived by writer Everett De Roch and intelligently directed by Richard Franklin. Patrick Anthony Quid (Stacy Keach) is a trucker on his way to Perth with pig carcasses when he suspects the driver of a green van is a Jack the Ripper-style murderer whose game is chopping up women's bodies—and Quid suspects carcasses in his rig might be human. Quid is an independent, good-humored driver who talks to his dingo companion, Boswell. Jamie Lee Curtis turns up as a runaway heiress and joins Quid in his "game" to track the killer. Franklin never compromises the story for shocks and shows insight into screen suspense. (Embassy; Charter)

ROAD TO BALI (1953). Zany Hope-Crosby "Road" picture, with the duo in the South Seas as jobless vaudevillians who hire out as divers for sunken treasure. There's a hilarious squid, a slap-happy gorilla, an erupting volcano, even Dorothy Lamour in sarong. One sequence features Bogart pulling the African Queen through a swamp—another has Jane Russell appearing out of thin air. The non sequiturs go on and on. A ball and a half directed by Hal Walker. (Unicorn; Discount)

ROAD TO HONG KONG (1962). Last of the Hope-Crosby "Road" pictures resembles an elongated vaudeville sketch and is not up to earlier series efforts. The tomfoolery dreamed up by director Norman Panama and producer Melvin Frank involves a space launching and an international gang (led by Joan Collins) out to steal the formula for a new rocket fuel. Dorothy Lamour is also on hand—but it isn't the same old magic. Frank Sinatra, David Niven, Dean Martin, Jerry Colonna and Peter Sellers appear in cameos. (MGM/UA)

ROAD TO MOROCCO (1942). Hope-Crosby "Road" inanities are a pure delight with satire of Arabian Nights cliches—flying carpets, talking camels, magic rings, genii, etc. Directed by David Butler. Dorothy Lamour, Anthony Quinn, Monte Blue, Vladimir Sokoloff. (MCA)

ROAD TO ZANZIBAR (1941). Second of the Hope-Crosby "Road" pictures finds them in the midst of savage natives and performing routines with a crazy gorilla. Zesty, marvelous comedy. Forget your troubles and enjoy. Directed by Victor Schertzinger. Dorothy Lamour, Una Merkel, Eric Blore, Douglass Dumbrille. (MCA)

ROAD WARRIOR, THE (1981). Sequel to MAD MAX is George Miller's masterpiece of the Cinema of the Bizarre, ten times better than its predecessor, with Mel Gibson repeating his role as a lone warrior in a post-Armageddon society where gas and oil are the richest commodities and survivors of industrial collapse fight to claim them. Max, in the tradition of the roving gunslinger aiding the underdog, befriends a benevolent band to keep precious fuels from falling into the hands of a vicious gang led by Humungus. The chase sequences are among the most exciting ever filmed. Characters are often grotesque and unlikeable, but you'll be rooting for the good guys and booing the bad. Miller co-scripted with Terry Hayes and Brian Hannant. Bruce Spence, Vernon Wells, Kjell Nilsson, Mike Preston. Aka MAD MAX 2. (Video/Laser: Warner Bros.)

ROBBERS OF THE SACRED MOUNTAIN. Video version of **FALCON'S GOLD** (Prism).

ROBIN HOOD AND THE SORCERER (1983). The dark side of the Sherwood Forest legend, produced in England by Paul Knight and directed by Ian Sharp from a melancholy script by Richard Carpenter. While this lacks the romance of the Errol Flynn version, it chooses its own sad, shadowy path through shrouded Sherwood. This has a subtext of sword and sorcery as a god of the woods, Hearne, guides Robin to his destiny and as a sorcerer tries to stop him from acquiring an arrow of good fortune. Sharp directs the action with gritty, grunting realism . . . Michael Praed is Robin of Loxley, Nicholas Grace is the ambivalent Sheriff of Nottingham and Clive Mantel is driven Little John. Other CBS/Fox (or Playhouse) releases in this series: **ROBIN HOOD . . . THE LEGEND SERIES: HEARNE'S SON, ROBIN HOOD . . . THE LEGEND SERIES: ROBIN HOOD AND THE SORCERER; ROBIN HOOD . . . THE LEGEND: THE SWORDS OF WAYLAND; ROBIN HOOD . . . THE LEGEND SERIES: THE TIME OF THE WOLF.**

ROBINSON CRUSOE OF CLIPPER ISLAND (1936). Polynesia is the setting for this action-packed tropical 14-chapter Republic cliffhanger. Mala, an imitation of Sabu the Jungle Boy, is an undercover agent for U.S. Intelligence, sent to an island where the villain Porotu is trying to erupt a volcano with the help of a Volcano Eruption Machine. A big canine named Buck the Wonder Dog and a gallant steed named Rex helps Mala to save the island. Mamo Clark, William Newell. (Republic; Nostalgia; Sinister/C)

ROBINSON CRUSOE OF MYSTERY ISLAND. TV-feature version of the serial **ROBINSON CRUSOE OF CLIPPER ISLAND.** (Video Connection)

ROBINSON CRUSOE ON MARS (1964). Fascinating sci-fi version of Daniel Defoe's novel of survival, written by Ib Melchoir and John C. Higgins. Astronaut Paul Mantee is ejected from Gravity Probe One when his

PAUL MANTEE IN 'ROBINSON CARUSO ON MARS'

missile almost collides with a meteor. Landing on the Red Planet, he undergoes incredible hardships, finding a means of breathing and overcoming nightmares in which dead partner Adam West returns alive. Mantee meets an escapee humanoid slave whom he dubs Friday. Aliens with heat rays seek Friday, allowing for exciting space opera with zappy (for their time) effects. Elements of this were borrowed for 1985's ENEMY MINE. Directed by Byron Haskin. (Laser: Criterion)

ROBO-C.H.I.C (19??). Blonde Kathy Showers, one-time intellectual Playboy pinup, portrays a cybernetic creature involved with the drug market who meets up with Burt Ward, Jack Carter and Phil Proctor. Written-directed by Jeff Mandel. (Action International)

ROBOCOP (1987). Glossy, high-tech comic-book action, superior in photography and design and featuring excellent stop-motion work by Phil Tippett, who contributed so much fine material to the STAR WARS trilogy. In a futuristic society controlled by an evil corporation, dedicated cop Peter Weller is blasted by a gang of sadists in a gory death scene. Weller is resurrected as a cyborg, but this is a Six Million Dollar Man with only half a heart; the other half is ruled by computerized directives and a penchant for violence against lawbreakers. It's wall-to-wall action with Tippett's activation of an Enforcement Droid the highpoint. What's contradictive about Paul Verhoeven's direction is the stark violence, which is unsuitable for the young people this Judge Dredd-imitation was intended. In this slam-bam superhero superflick, Weller's partner is Nancy Allen, with Ronny Cox as a corporate villain of the slimiest order. Two sequels followed. (Orion) (Laser: Image)

ROBOCOP II (1990). Colossal action film that ends in colossal frustration for the viewer, with horrible lapses of taste on the part of writers Walon Green and Frank Miller (he of the BATMAN comic books). A youth gang led by adolescent Gabriel Damon is one of the most dubious choices for violent material, and mars whatever good intentions director Irvin Kershner had. This is mindless action from beginning to end, with Peter Weller back to portray the titular half-man/half-android without the humanity of the first box-office success. Phil Tippet is back with his superb stop-motion model effects, but nothing can save this excessive case of screen mayhem. Nancy Allen, Daniel O'Herlihy, Belinda Bauer, Tom Noonan, Felton Perry. (Orion) (Laser: Image)

ROBOCOP 3 (1993). This is a vast improvement over the second film, and returns to the central themes that made the first ROBOCOP such a hit. Robert Burke replaces Peter Weller in the title role as we return to a futuristic Detroit where the evil corporation, Omni Consumer Products, hires thugs to keep disorder so it can carry out nefarious plans. Robocop fights a Japanese cyborg assassin, undergoes trauma when his human/mechanical psyches clash, and even flies to defeat lawbreakers. Nancy Allen returns as Robocop's partner. Well directed and written by Fred Dekker. (Orion)

ROBO MAN. Video version of **WHO?** (Ace; MNTEX).

R.O.B.O.T. See **CHOPPING MALL.**

ROBOTECH: THE MOVIE (1986). Re-edited version of a Japanese TV series, designed for American consumption. Limited animation and concepts. Strictly for moppets. Directed by Carl Macek and Ishiguro Noburo.

ROBOT HOLOCAUST (1985). Video sci-fi that is so bad, camp followers might get a chuckle out of this megamess. The plot is indecipherable. On New Terra, following the Robot Rebellion of '33, a band of Earthlings (stupid heroes, whinny broads in halter tops and a Conan lookalike) faces forces of the Dark One and a chick in spike heels (Angelika Jager, a wonderfully incompetent hamactress) by defying The Cave of Sewage Worms, the Room of Questions, the Pleasure Machine and the Vault of Beasts. Everyone like a refugee from an Edward D. Wood Jr. movie. Unbelievably poor effects, to boot. Speaking of boots, give one to director-writer Tim Kincaid and the cast: Nadine Hart, Norris Culf, Joel von Ornstein. (Vestron; VCI)

ROBOT JOX (1990). Popular sci-fi novelist Joe Haldeman scripts a rousing tale of futuristic gladiators who take to controlling giant robots which fight it out in special arenas. The idea of monstrous upright walking machines controlled by their pilots, or jox, is a novel one but never reaches maximum effectiveness, perhaps because director Stuart Gordon (of RE-ANIMATOR fame) was hampered by a limited budget. Gary Graham is the robot jox who goes through personal trauma before he accepts the ultimate challenge from his arch-rival. Originally released as ROBOJOX. Anne-Marie Johnson, David Koslo. (Video/Laser: RCA/Columbia)

ROBOT MONSTER (1953). Reportedly produced-directed by Phil Tucker in less than a week and written in 30 minutes by Wyott Ordung. Exec producer Al Zimbalist even decided to Contribute to the Arts by filming in 3-D. As the hero, George Nader looks as mechanical as the extra in an ape suit (with a fishbowl over his head) called Ro-Man, who lands on Earth with his Bubble Communications Machine to kill the only six human beings left after a zap ray has wiped out mankind. Once those six are dead, it will be safe for 268,000 Martians to carry out a landing. Meanwhile, in Bronson Canyon, Ro-Man chases Nader, Claudia Barrett and Selena Royle in the funniest footage ever. Must be seen to be (dis)believed. Marvelously incompetent. Yes, see it! (Sony; Rhino offers a 3-D version) (Laser: Image)

ROBOT NINJA (1990). An actor playing a costumed superhero turns into a real superhero to fight the forces of evil. Michael Todd, Burt Ward, Michael Shea, Bogdan Pecic, Maria Markovic. Written-produced-directed by J.R. Bookwalter. (Cinema Home; Phoenix)

ROBOT OF REGALIO (1954). See **ROCKY JONES, SPACE RANGER.** (Get oiled first!)

ROBOT VS. THE AZTEC MUMMY, THE (1959). Third and final entry in the Mexican "Aztec Mummy" series, preceded by THE AZTEC MUMMY (also known as ATTACK OF THE MAYAN MUMMY) and THE CURSE OF THE AZTEC MUMMY. Directed by Raphael Portillo, this depicts Dr. Krupp wandering into a crypt with a clanking robot, which he has given a brain so it won't bump into any sarcophaguses. Krupp wants to loot Aztec treasure, but standing guard is that hulking package of bandages, that walking commercial for plastic strips, that swathed slob . . . the Aztec Mummy. Crash! Bang! Thunk! Boom! Bash! Mangle! Thud! Crunch! Wallop! Re-packaged for U.S. tastes by K. Gordon Murray. Ramon Gay, Rosita Arenas. (Admit One; Goodtimes; Sinister/C; S/Weird; also in video as **AZTEC MUMMY DOUBLE FEATURE**)

ROBOT WARS (1993). Dave Allen has created a wonderful stop-motion battle between the upright walking robot warrior (reprised from ROBOT JOX) and a spider-like walking robot (inspired by the Imperial Walkers from THE EMPIRE STRIKES BACK?) in this Charles Band adventure. It's set in 2041 A.D. when Earth is divided into zones and America is selling "robotic security systems" to foreign powers. An Asian general (Danny Kamekoni) representing the "Centros" schemes to steal a Mega Robot, disrupting rebel robot jock Marion Drake (Don Michael Paul) and his girl Barbara Crampton. Peter Haskell is the boss at control central always in conflict with Drake and James Staley is comic-relief hero Stumpy. Albert Band, father of Charles Band, directed this loose sequel to ROBOT JOX. Lisa Rinna, Kuji Okumoto. (Paramount) (Laser: Full Moon)

ROCKET ATTACK U.S.A. (1960). Spy thriller starring nobody you ever saw before, packaged by producers you never heard of, about characters you wish they hadn't bothered to create. Superspies rush around Moscow trying to convince Commie leaders that atomic war is futile, but the Soviets, who have never heard of the Nuclear Freeze, devastate New York City anyway and World War III begins. That's entertainment! Directed by Barry Mahon. (Sony)

ROCKETEER, THE (1991). This $40 million-plus spinoff from Dave Stevens' popular comic book is a gem of a Disney adventure movie as a young pilot of 1938 (Bill Campbell playing Cliff Secord) battles machinegun-toting gangsters, stoic FBI men and devious Nazis. They're all after Secord for possession of a rocket-propelled jetpack that enables the pilot to streak through the sky at fantastic speeds, in the style of Commander Cody of RADAR MEN FROM THE MOON. The flying sequences (created by George Lucas' Industrial Light & Magic) are superexciting, director Joe Johnston (creator of Yoda and other STAR WARS ingredients) captures the art-deco ambience of L.A. of the '30s, and the script by Danny Bilson and Paul De Meo always maintains a clear-cut distinction between good and evil. The cast is great: Campbell as the naive, unstoppable hero; Jennifer Connelly as his sexy girlfriend Jenny; Alan Arkin is the absent-minded mechanic Peevy; Timothy Dalton as a suave Hollywood movie star; Paul Sorvino as the chief hoodlum, and Ed Lauter as the glib FBI agent. There's a character named Lothar (seven-foot Tiny Ron) who's made up to look like Rondo (The Creeper) Hatton. (Disney) (Laser: Image)

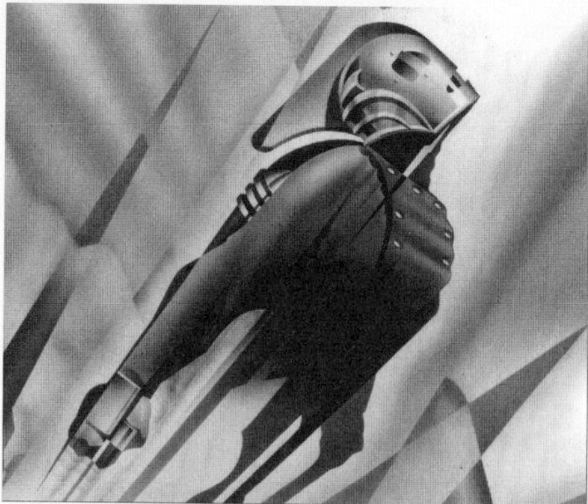

ARTIST'S RENDERING OF 'THE ROCKETEER'

ROCKET MAN, THE (1954). A figure dressed in a spacesuit (it looks like the one Michael Rennie wore in THE DAY THE EARTH STOOD STILL) appears out of nowhere (and is never explained) to give orphan George "Foghorn" Winslow a zap gun that becomes a tool of the youth's wishful thinking whenever he aims it. It makes a car stop from hitting a fellow lad sprawled in the road and it makes politicians and braggarts blurt out the truth at the most damaging moments. This lightweight fable by Lenny Bruce and Jack Henley was directed by Oscar Rudolph without the special-effects magic the picture cries out for. Instead, we're saddled with a dopy romance between John Agar and Anne Francis and Spring Byington's efforts to save an orphanage. Winslow, he with the heavy voice for one so young, is almost lost amidst this schmaltz.

ROCKET SHIP. See **FLASH GORDON (1936).**

ROCKETSHIP X-M (1950). Producer Robert L. Lippert rushed this low-budgeter into production to beat DESTINATION MOON into theaters, and some consider this B effort superior to the more expensive George Pal production. The first rocketship blasting off for the moon malfunctions and lands instead on Mars, where astronauts Lloyd Bridges, Ona Massen, Noah Beery Jr., John Emery and Hugh O'Brian find the atomized remains of a once-great civilization. The remnants are primitive cavemen, blinded by radiation. An unhappy ending is an unexpected twist to this film directed-written by Kurt Neumann. Good production values and a fine score by Ferde Grofe, with effective use of the theremin. (Media; Nostalgia Merchant; a different video version, ROCKETSHIP X-M: SPECIAL EDITION, features new special- effects footage and tinted sequences) (Laser: Image)

ROCKET TO THE MOON. See **CAT WOMEN OF THE MOON.**

ROCKING HORSE WINNER, THE (1950). Slow pacing and underplayed emotions are shortcomings in this John Mills-produced version of D. H. Lawrence's story about a child who can predict race winners if he is riding his toy rocking horse with great frenzy. Mills appears as the handyman, Valerie Hobson is the mother, John Howard Davies is the driven youth. Written-directed by Anthony Pelissier. (Learning Corp.; Films Inc.)

ROCK 'N ROLL NIGHTMARE. Video version of **EDGE OF HELL** (Academy).

ROCK 'N ROLL WRESTLING WOMEN VS. THE AZTEC APE. Video of **WRESTLING WOMEN VS. THE AZTEC APE,** with rock and roll track. (Rhino)

ROCK 'N RULE (1983). Offbeat animated feature set in a future society where only rats, cats and dogs have survived a nuclear disaster. These mutants, who live in Ohmtown—a half-destroyed, half-neomodernistic city—are in awe of Mok, a super-rock star ugly as sin and in search of a code that will release a beast from another dimension and enable him to enslave animalkind. The soundtrack carries work by Cheap Trick, Debbie Harry, Lou Reed, Iggy Pop and Earth, Wind and Fire but the film has an unpleasant look. Directed by Clive A. Smith. (Video/Laser: MGM/UA)

ROCKTOBER BLOOD (1986). "Heavy metal" horror flick in which a psycho singer comes back from the dead to kill members of his former band. Directed by Beverly and Ben Sebastian. (Vestron)

ROCKULA (1990). Every 22 years centuries-old vampire Dean Cameron meets a reincarnated version of a former lover and rescues her from a gang of pirates who always show up to murder her. If that isn't hard enough to swallow, Cameron also has a running dialogue with his mirror reflection, which has a life (and dress) of its own, and he forms a vampire rock 'n roll band. This mess from director Luca Bercovici (who ground out the script with producer Jeffrey Levy and Christopher Vernel) has occasional charming moments (Susan Tyrell as a sassy bartender, Bo Diddley as a band member, a cute animated main title) but it overstretches itself with too many whacky premises. Tawny Fere, Nancy Ferguson, Kevin Hunter. (Video/Laser: Warner Bros.)

ROCKY HORROR PICTURE SHOW, THE (1975). As a London stage musical, this appealed to the transvestite-gay crowds, but soon became the straight "in thing." This film version, like the play, is slanted for the freak-rock

'THE ROCKY HORROR PICTURE SHOW'

crowd. It satirizes Frankenstein, haunted-house mysteries, sci-fi movies and our penchant for sexual-identity confusion. Naive newlyweds Barry Bostwick and Susan Sarandon stumble onto a foreboding castle where aliens from Transsexual are creating the perfect he-man stud under the scientific (and loving) care of Dr. Frank N. Furter (Tim Curry). Full of bizarre props, musical numbers and strange cutting techniques, it has become a successful midnight movie and continues to play in major cities with attendees dressed as the characters. Those who relate to a mixture of depravity and satire will find this diverting. Directed by Jim Sharman, who co-wrote with Richard O'Brien, who also appears in the cast. Jonathan Adams, Charles Gray, Meatloaf, Little Nell, Patricia Quinn, Peter Hinwood. (Video/Laser: CBS/Fox)

ROCKY JONES, SPACE RANGER. Low-budget TV kiddie series produced in 1953-55 with Richard Crane as jockey Rocky jocularly rocketing into space for the United Solar System, fighting evil where he, Winky and Vena Ray find it. These dumb live-broadcast shows were repackaged for TV. These deceptively appear under the titles BEYOND THE MOON, BLAST OFF, CRASH OF MOONS, DUEL IN SPACE, FORBIDDEN MOON, GYPSY MOON, INFERNO IN SPACE, MAGNETIC MOON, MENACE FROM OUTER SPACE, OUT OF THIS WORLD, ROBOT OF REGALIO, SILVER NEEDLE IN THE SKY.

RODAN (1956). Made in the wake of GODZILLA—KING OF THE MONSTERS by Japan's leading director Inoshiro Honda, this Japanese sci-fi epic reflects the Asian predilection for super-ludicrous effects in depicting a giant pterodactyl with a 250-foot wing span and a destructive nature that allows it to destroy several metropolises. Emphasis is on rousing catastrophe, while the dwarfed humans stand in awe or run screaming in terror. Eiji Tsuburaya is responsible for the destruction. Better than later Japanese monster movies, with more care lavished on the spectacle. But the dubbing is atrocious and acting styles hard to take. Kenji Sahara, Yumi Shirakawa, Akihiko Hirata. (Vestron; Video Treasures; Gateway/Paramount) (Laser: Vestron)

ROGER CORMAN: HOLLYWOOD'S WILD ANGEL (1978). Crude but interesting one-hour documentary directed by Christian Blackwood in which Hollywood schlockmeister Roger Corman is examined. Includes interviews with Peter Fonda, Joe Dante, Paul Bartel and other cult directors. Recommended for those into genres. (International Historic; MPI)

ROGER CORMAN'S FRANKENSTEIN UNBOUND. See **FRANKENSTEIN UNBOUND.**

ROLLERBABIES (1976). In the wake of ROLLERBALL came this imitative sci-fi population satire in which a future society passes an anti-lovemaking law. Instead, folks fornicate live on TV to satisfy the needs of the masses. This sex exploitation piece was produced-directed by Carter Stevens. Robert Random, Suzanne McBain, Yolanda Savalas.

ROLLERBALL (1975). Title refers to a futuristic bloodied version of Roller Derby which takes the place of warfare—controlled by six cartels merged to form a world government. Director Norman Jewison creates a sterile picture when depicting the robot-like people of tomorrow—but an exciting, bloody one when depicting the awesome-awful sport. Chief player is Jonathan E. (James Caan), who rebels in one final orgy of Rollerball bloodlust. William Harrison's story was a terse metaphor—millions were expended to give the sport specific rules and bring it to life, as conceived by Harrison in his script adaptation. John Houseman, Maud Adams, Pamela Hensley, Ralph Richardson, John Beck. (MGM/UA) (Laser: Image)

ROLLER BLADE (1986). Unbelievably bad MAD MAX imitation, so incompetent one wonders to what new low Donald G. Jackson (co-writer, producer, photographer, director) will sink next (see below). Set in the post-holocaust "Second Dark Age," this portrays a cult of "Holy Rollers"—religious women of "The Cosmic Order of Roller Blade" who wear skates, fight with knives and take orders from Mother Speed, who talks with a lisp. They're looking for a magic crystal but so is the masked villain Saticon, who commands a hand puppet cackling with lustful glee as it strips cellophane off a nude woman. It's hard to imagine a society that runs on skates and skateboards, but here it is in all its vast stupidity, including a marshal who talks with "thee" and "thou." The action is phony, the attempts at religion blasphemous, the effects laughable and the acting hitting rank amateurism. Has to be seen to be believed. Suzanne Solari, Jeff Hutchinson. (New World)

ROLLER BLADE WARRIORS: TAKEN BY FORCE (1988). Holy rollers! You can't say photographer-director Donald G. Jackson isn't consistent: The bad acting he allowed in ROLLER BLADE is permitted in this new adventure on skates set in a post-holocaust world where Mother Speed (Abby Dalton) reigns over women warriors ("Go forth," she proclaims, "and skate the paths of righteousness.") This time the wheeled wenches are protecting a psychic virgin from falling into the hands of evil-doers who feed beautiful women to a monster in an energy plant. Little sense is to be made from Lloyd Strathen's script (from a Jackson idea), what with tongue-in-cheek characters, exaggerated swordplay and sappy dialogue. Example: One woman says "What's a man like?" and another replies "Like soup on a cold night." And yet the direction has a strange kinetic energy and sincerity of purpose, suggesting Jackson is a dedicated schlock filmmaker. You should see at least one of these things—they defy description. Kathleen Kinmont, Jack Damon, Elizabeth Kaitan, Rory Calhoun (in a cameo), Norman Alder, Suzanne Solari. (Raedon)

ROLLING THUNDER (1991). Obscure but excellently produced cautionary tale written-produced-directed by Scott Dittrich, a surfing film maker who has a statement to make about the way we're destroying the natural things he enjoys so much as a sportsman. Set in 2040 A.D., in a world where all oceans have been poisoned by man's industry, a cave-dwelling storyteller (Ian Abercrombie) relates to children his youth as a surfer "before the poisoned skies." There's fine footage of surfing in the Hawaiian Islands, Baja California, Western Australia and other places where the great waves form, and footage of polluted oceans and beaches. Although the message is obvious, Dittrich's footage is so wonderful, one is willing to forgive him for turning maudlin.

ROLLOVER (1981). Alan J. Pakula directed this futuristic financial thriller in which the Arabs rig a diabolical system to collapse the world money market and bring about financial chaos and anarchy. Its abstractions are not easy to follow but it is an honorable attempt to suggest where today's economic manipulations are taking us. Fine cast is headed by Jane Fonda, Kris Kristofferson and Hume Cronyn. Pakula and screenwriter David Shaber avoid crass commercialism tricks and stick to the intrigue among those who have the power to make our world collapse. (Warner Bros.)

ROMAN SCANDALS (1933). Eddie Cantor's funniest comedy: He travels through time and wakes up in ancient Rome. The gags, non sequiturs and anachronisms are bounced off the Colosseum wall nonstop. Eddie is selected by Nero to be his wine taster; he is surrounded by beautiful Samuel Goldwyn girls in togas and there is a chariot race making sport of BEN-HUR. Directed with panache by Frank Tuttle. Ruth Etting, Alan Mowbray. (Nelson; HBO)

ROME, 2072 A.D.—THE NEW GLADIATORS. See **NEW GLADIATORS, THE.**

RONA JAFFE'S MAZES AND MONSTERS. Video of **MAZES AND MONSTERS** (Lorimar; Warner Bros.).

ROOGIE'S BUMP (1954). Only a bump on a log as far as the movie world was concerned—minor league material about a boy who becomes a major league pitcher due to a protuberance on his throwing arm. Directed by Harold Young. Robert Marriot, Ruth Warrick.

ROOM TO LET (1950). Early Hammer film based on a BBC play by Margery Allingham, recounting the story of Jack the Ripper with Valentine Dyall as the strange lodger, Dr. Fell. The story is set in London 1904 and told in flashback form. Interesting variation on a familiar theme. Directed by Godfrey Grayson, who co-adapted with John Gilling. Merle Tottenham, Jimmy Hanley. (Blood Times; Sinister/C; Nostalgia)

ROSELAND (1971). See editions 1-3.

ROSEMARY'S BABY (1968). Congratulate William Castle for buying Ira Levin's book in galley form (before it became a best seller) and for realizing he needed Roman Polanski (and not himself) to direct and write the adaptation. The results became the high point of Castle's career. This is a quiet exercise in the supernatural that builds gradually, often providing only a suspicion of evil, and sometimes a doubt, that newlywed Mia Farrow is the victim of a conspiracy plot in modern Manhattan. She suspects neighbors Sidney Blackmer and Ruth Gordon are witches, joined in a bloodpact with her husband-actor John Cassavetes. Is it possible he has formed a union with the Devil? Is the baby in her stomach spawned by Satan during one of her nightmares? She becomes the perfect Hitchcockian foil: a misunderstood, sympathetic, vulnerable young woman whose bizarre story is disbelieved by everyone, including doctor Ralph Bellamy. Maurice Evans, Patsy Kelly, Charles Grodin, Hope Summers, Castle (as the man in the phone booth). (Paramount; RCA/Columbia) (Laser: Paramount)

ROSEMARY'S BABY II. See **LOOK WHAT'S HAPPENED TO ROSEMARY'S BABY.**

ROSEMARY'S DISCIPLES. Variant video version of **NECROMANCY** (Magnum).

ROSEMARY'S KILLER. Variant video version of **PROWLER, THE** (VCI).

R.O.T.O.R. (1987). Amateurish ripoff of ROBOCOP, made by regional film makers in Dallas in dire need of a good director and stunt co-ordinator. The film appears to have been dubbed, as if the producers lost the sound tracks or decided the voices weren't right. Dallas cop Barrett Coldyron, with the help of Dr. Steel from Houston, pursues #222, a runaway cop named R.O.T.O.R. (Robotic Officer Tactical Operation Research) programmed "To Judge and Execute." There's behind-the-scenes political shenanigans going on (a senator is backing the project so he can get into the White House, that kind of stuff) but it's all deadened by the acting. Coldyron has discovered "an unknown alloy" that contains molecular memory and enables a metal man to learn by moving its joints. An unbelievably bad flick directed by Cullen Blaine. Richard Gesswein, Margaret Trigg, Jayne Smith, James Cole. (Imperial)

ROTTWEILER. See **DOGS OF HELL** (Some bark!).

RUBY (1977). Weakly directed Curtis Harrington horror film, with Piper Laurie as the former moll of a deceased gangster; the hood returns from the dead and leaves the bodies of victims all over a drive-in theater specializing in old horror movies. Harrington was reportedly fired during production and replaced by Stephanie Rothman. Janet Baldwin, Stuart Whitman, Roger Davis, Fred Kohler. (VCI; United)

RUDE AWAKENING (1981). Thrillervision edition (hosted by Elvira) of a one-hour episode from a British TV horror series, HAMMER HOUSE OF HORROR. See **TWO FACES OF EVIL / RUDE AWAKENING.** (Laser: Image)

RUE MORGUE MASSACRES, THE (1973). Mad doc Gotto brings his dead girlfriend back to life because he needs her body for new experimentation. Aka THE HUNCHBACK OF THE MORGUE. Directed by Javier Aguirre. Paul Naschy, Rossana Yanni, Maria Perschy, Vic Winner. (All Seasons Entertainment)

RULING CLASS, THE (1972). Scathing satire aimed at the British class system and a devastating indictment of the "stupidity" of the power structure, told through the distorted viewpoint of a debauched, schizophrenic madman. Peter O'Toole believes he is God, and spends his resting moments perched on a giant cross. "When I pray to Him," says O'Toole, "I am talking to myself." This paranoid black sheep of an upper-crust family is "exorcised" back to sanity—or so it seems as he takes his seat in the House of Commons. However, the old mugger is still quite bats, imagining everyone to be corpses and himself as Jack the Ripper on a slashing spree. This black comedy scripted by Peter Barnes was not a blooming success in the eyes of the ruling critics, but O'Toole fans will not want to miss his tour de force performance. Equally effective, even when the picture is uneven, are Arthur Lowe, Alastair Sim, Coral Browne, Harry Andrews, Nigel Green, William Mervyn. Directed by Peter Medak. (Nelson) (Laser: Image)

RUNAWAY (1984). Exciting, imaginative sci-fi action-mystery from writer-director Michael Crichton, set in a

"They throw guts around like slapstick cream pies."
—A pending victim of cannibalistic grandmothers in **RABID GRANNIES**

ARNOLD SCHWARZENEGGER: 'THE RUNNING MAN'

near-future when mankind is served by robots which occasionally go haywire. Tom Selleck and Cynthia Rhodes are members of the "Runaway Squad," designed to put amuck metal out of commission. Villain Gene Simmons, armed with a zap gun that fires guided-missile bullets around corners, is after microcomputer chips that will give him control of the robots and he sics an army of mechanical spiders on Selleck in a rousing, outrageous climax. Kirstie Alley, Stan Shaw. (Video/Laser: RCA/Columbia)

RUNESTONE, THE (1990). Rip-roaring old-fashioned monster movie in which a 6th Century Norse runestone is uncovered during a dig in West Pennysylvania and brought to Manhattan. A tall, hairy creature with long scary fingers escapes the stone and kills half the New York City police force, since bullets cannot stop it—only a legendary Viking battle axe can do that. Despite plenty of graphic murders and an eerie atmosphere, the film is loaded by writer-director Willard Carroll (working from a novella by Mark B. Rogers) with pretentious, cryptic crap that keeps slowing down the excitement, especially scenes of Alexander Godunov sitting in a cuckoo clock shop. Stand outs in the solid cast are Peter Riegert and Lawrence Tierney as hardened Manhattan cops. William Hickey, Mitchell Laurance, Tim Ryan, Dawan Scott. (Video/Laser: Live)

RUN FOR THE SUN (1956). See editions 1-3.

RUNNING AGAINST TIME (1990). A straight-faced variation on BACK TO THE FUTURE, in which university professor Robert Hays discovers that campus scientist Sam Wanamaker has designed a "transdimensional physics machine" capable of moving objects through time and space. Hays "transdimensionalizes" himself to Dallas in 1963 to prevent the assassination of President John F. Kennedy—only the beginning of the time continuum screwups in this daffy, gassy TV-movie written by Robert Glass and Stanley Shapiro (based on a novel by Shapiro) and directed by Bruce Seth Green. Hays sometimes seems to be in a comedy rather than a serious time-travel drama but since the absurdities are too many to list, it doesn't make much difference. Fun in a zany way, though meant to be a thriller. Catherine Hicks, Wayne Tippit, Juanita Jennings. (MCA)

RUNNING MAN, THE (1987). While this is a vehicle for the biceps and physique of Arnold Schwarzenegger, it is really Richard Dawson who steals the picture as Damon Killian, the host of a futuristic TV series. The twist is that in 2017, Schwarzenegger is a political undesirable thrown into prison. Following his exciting escape, he grabs the attention of Killian, who wants Schwartzy for his game show in which participants are pursued by assorted killers, and awarded grand prizes if they survive the "contest." All too soon Schwartzy is the guest of honor, and must fight Sub-Zero (Prof. Taru Tanaka), Buzzsaw (Gus Rethwisch), Dynamo (Erland Van Lidth), Captain Freedom (Jess Ventura) and Fireball (Jim Brown). It's rough, tumble action, well staged by director Paul Michael Glaser, but contrived for its shocking deaths and the quippish lines Arnold tosses after his victims. ("He had to split," he says in reference to Buzzsaw, who's just had a whirring blade shoved up his gonads). Schwartz promises Killian "I'll be back" (a line from THE TERMINATOR) but their final showdown is anticlimactic after so many violent confrontations. Stephen E. de Souza's script is based on the novel by Richard Bachman (Stephen King) and it never comes to grips with the pseudopolitical backgrounds to make the action plausible or the characters sympathetic. Supporting cast is good (Maria Conchita Alonso, Yaphet Kotto, Mick Fleetwood) but ultimately it's Dawson you want to run with. (Vestron) (Laser: Image)

RUN, PSYCHO, RUN (1969). Tedious, unwatchable Edwardian horror-melodrama without much horror, directed by Italy's Brunello Rondi. The setting is the Cornwall coast in 1910, where a young wife is suddenly murdered and husband Gary Merrill finds a lookalike to keep her memory alive. It's mostly talk among characters in period costumes with puffy hairstyles. The ultimate in boredom. Elga Anderson, Rosella Falk.

RUN, STRANGER, RUN (1973). Actor Darren McGavin directed this offbeat psychothriller in Nova Scotia . . . Robert Clouse's script involves Ron Howard in a series of graphic murders. Also known as HAPPY MOTHER'S DAY . . . LOVE, GEORGE. Cloris Leachman, Patricia Neal, Bobby Darin, Simon Oakland, Tessa Dahl, Kathie Brown. (RCA/Columbia)

RUSH (1984). Super-chintzy Italian MAD MAX rip-off, relying on action as a Rambo-style survivor (Conrad Nichols) of nuclear war roves the desert's "forbidden zone." In this world you're either a prisoner in tattered rags or a well-armed soldier working for villain Gordon Mitchell . . . Rush rushes to support the former by blasting the latter to pieces in poorly staged, unbelievable action sequences directed by Anthony Richmond. The video version is enhanced by an introduction and closing with Sybil Danning, clad in a camouflaged bra and little else, and carrying a wicked machine-gun as she makes cracks about her .38s and the guys' "big barrels." Now that's worth seeing. (USA)

RUSH WEEK (1989). Generic slasher film is lacking in gory special effects or a plot clever enough to avoid giving away who the killer is. A robed figure carrying an executioner's axe roves the hallways of Tambers College, slicing up sexy coeds posing for girly photos. This vacillates between slasher scenes and unfunny prankster gags being pulled on the campus folks by the Beta Delta Beta—in short, a stupid kill-the-teenagers movie with Pamela Ludwig as a reporter with an inquiring mind, Gregg Allman as her journalism instructor (?) and Roy Thinnes as Dean Grail. Bob Bralver's direction is pretty lousy. Courtney Gebhart, Don Grant, David Denney. (Video/Laser: RCA/Columbia)

"The objective was to build the perfect cop of the future . . . a machine programmed to overcome any obstacle to combat the crimes and corruption which threaten the very existence of our society . . . but, something went terribly wrong."

—R.O.T.O.R.

SAADIA (1953). See editions 1-3.

SABRE TOOTH TIGER. See **DEEP RED.**

SABU AND THE MAGIC RING (1957). Thudding TV pilot was recut into this feature with Sabu as an overaged jungle boy and William Marshall (Blacula) as a genie. Sorry, Sahib, but it's a forgettable night in Arabia; nothing magical about it. Directed by George Blair. Daria Massey, Robert Shafto, John Doucette.

SACRIFICE! (1972). Unsavory entry in Italy's cannibal "eat-em-up-alive" genre. In this culinary outing in Thailand, a tribe of gourmets has a recipe for Human a la Chomp. Directed by Umberto Lenzi.

SADIST, THE (1963). Surprisingly good shocker never resorts to exploitation in telling the taut tale of a serial killer and girlfriend holding waylaid travelers as hostages in a wrecking yard. Blond, blue-eyed Arch Hall Jr. is excellent as the cackling killer who talks like Richard Widmark and taunts victims with cat-and-mouse threats. Writer-director James Landis throws in nifty twists of plot and brings prestige to a story that in lesser hands would be schlock. Excellent photography by William Zsigmond. Richard Alden, Don Russell, Marilyn Manning, Helen Hovey. (Rhino; Sinister/C)

SAFE PLACE, A (1971). See editions 1-3.

SAGA OF DRACULA, THE (1972). Saga is sagging and sanguinary in this sappy Spanish sputterer from director Leon Kilmovski: Count Dracula's granddaughter, heavy with child and bad dialogue, arrives at the old castle homestead with her nonvampiric husband. While she and the audience endure labor pains, hubby dallies with the count's lovely brides. Tina Sainz, Tony Isbert, Narcisco Ibanez Menta (Dracula), Cristina Suriani. Aka DRACULA'S SAGA and DRACULA: THE BLOODLINE CONTINUES. (Sinister/C; Filmfax; from S/Weird and All Seasons as **SAGA OF THE DRACULAS**)

SAGA OF THE VIKING WOMEN AND THEIR VOYAGE TO THE WATERS OF THE GREAT SEA SERPENT. Roger Corman's grab at the longest title of all time! See **VIKING WOMEN AND THE SEA SERPENT.**

SAILOR WHO FELL FROM GRACE WITH THE SEA, THE (1976). Unusual psychological horror tale with a shock ending reminiscent of E.C. Comics. Demented youngster Jonathan Kahn watches mother Sarah Miles making love to sailor Kris Kristofferson. Slowly he and his chums devise a horrifying scheme. Directed-written by Lewis John Carlino. Margo Cunningham, Earl Rhodes. (Magnetic; CBS/Fox) (Laser)

SAKIMA AND THE MASKED MARVEL (1943). Feature version of **MASKED MARVEL, THE.**

SALEM'S LOT (1979). TV adaptation of Stephen King's best-selling vampire novel—the shuddery tale of how a European bloodsucker turns an East Coast community into a graveyard. Reggie Nalder is the vampire Barlow in the Lugosi tradition, with James Mason portraying Barlow's aide-de-vamp. David Soul tries to stop the pair with the help of Lance Kerwin. Written by Paul Monash, directed by Tobe Hooper, the mild-mannered sentimentalist who gave us TEXAS CHAINSAW MASSACRE, and produced by Richard Kobritz (CHRISTINE). Originally four hours but cut to a shorter version for cable TV. Some scenes are stronger than those shown on the network. (The European version, also stronger, is in video/laser from Warner Bros. as **SALEM'S LOT—THE MOVIE**; from On Line Cinema as **BLOOD THIRST**)

SALUTE OF THE JUGGER. See **BLOOD OF HEROES.**

SALVAGE (1979). Amiable TV-movie with junk dealer Andy Griffith building a spaceship to fly to the moon and salvage science equipment littering the lunar surface. Lighthearted fare with interesting characters, this two-hour pilot became a short-lived series that never lived up to its promising debut. Directed by Lee Phillips. Joel Higgins, Trish Stewart, Richard Jaeckel, Peter Brown.

SAMSON AND DELILAH (1949). Cecil B. DeMille's "Biblical True Confessions" about the passionate lovers who ultimately betray themselves, realizing real love too late. The superstrength of Samson (Victor Mature) emanates from his uncut hair but when Delilah (Hedy Lamarr) shears his bangs, his sinewness is also clipped. DeMille is all gaudiness and phony baloney dialogue. Angela Lansbury, Henry Wilcoxon, George Reeves, George Sanders. (Video/Laser: Paramount)

SAMSON AND DELILAH (1984). The late producer Franklin Levy once described this TV-movie as the "Biblical Body Heat," about the Israelite hunk with the muscles and seven long locks of hair who falls for a looker from the valley of Sorek. The hunk is Australian unknown Anthony Hamilton, the femme is Belinda Bauer and they have sizzling love scenes. Levy's production for Gregory Harrison's Catalina Productions has the spirit of an old-fashioned Biblical epic, with Victor Mature in a small role as Samson's father. Directed by Lee Phillips. Max Von Sydow, Stephen Macht, Maria Schell, Jose Ferrer. And Bauer . . . what a femme fatale from Sorek! (Starmaker; Prism)

SAMSON AND THE MIGHTY CHALLENGE (1964). The mighty challenge for the viewer is to endure this monument to muscles as four brawn-happy grunters (Samson, Hercules, Maciste, Ursus) wreak havoc on dumb villains by using incredible superpower. No mental workout, this. Directed by Giorgio Capitani. Alan Steele, Nadir Baltimor. (Sinister/C; S/Weird)

SAMSON AND THE SEVEN MIRACLES OF THE WORLD (1963). The eighth wonder is that this Italian spaghetti strainer about a muscleman with superstrength got produced at all. Even Gordon Scott admirers will concur that his trophy tissue is a dead atrophy issue as he fights saucy Tartars and saves Yoko Tani from a death worse than fate. Not Great Scott! Directed by Riccardo Freda. Dante Di Paolo.

SAMSON IN KING SOLOMON'S MINES (1964). Reg Park replaces Gordon Scott but the grunts are the same and the biceps bulge just as beefily as Maciste (where the hell's Samson?) is forced to slave in an African mine, a magical ring strapped to his leg by a lovely villainess. Now all Maciste has to do is form a union to improve labor conditions. Directed-written by Piero Regnoli. Wandisa Guida, Dan Harrison.

SAMSON IN THE WAX MUSEUM (1964). You thought the "Neutron" series from Mexico (featuring a black-masked wrestler in droopy drawers) was bad? Usted haven't seen nada yet, amigo. A wrestler named Samson (or Santo, depending on translation) tries to get a brain-lock on a mad scientist running a wax museum who has the power to turn people into monsters. No Mexicali rose garden, this. Directed by Alfonso Corona Blake. Claudio Brook. (Sinister/C; S/Weird; Filmfax)

SAMSON VS. THE GIANT KING (1965). The character is actually Maciste, interred in a tomb in Russia. Special salve spread over his powerful beefcake restores his brawn and he's off to fight an evil Czar steppe by steppe. Kirk Morris crumples cardboard pillars, throws papier-mache boulders and knocks down a balsa wood coliseum. Directed by Amerigo Anton.

SAMSON VS. THE VAMPIRE WOMEN (1961). This entry in the Mexican-produced series about a wrestling hero who fights the supernatural on the sidelines (known as Santo, the Silver Maskman) is a potboiler re-edited for the U.S. by producer J. Gordon Murray and director Manuel San Fernando. These flicks from the Churubusco-Azteca studio resemble old Universal horror movies in production and music, and this has good sets, beautiful women and an intriguing visual design, though the wrestling sequences are mundane in comparison. A "Mistress of the Night" resurrects an army of women vampires and uses hypnosis to disguise how ugly they really are. Santo, Maria Duval, Lorena Velazquez, Jaime Fernandez, Augusto Benedico. Original Mexican director was the dis-grunted Alfonso Corona Blake. (Sinister/C; S/Weird; Filmfax)

SAMURAI (1979). Routine TV-movie with Joe Penny as Lee Cantrell, eager-beaver San Francisco assistant D.A. who takes samurai lessons from James Shigeta. When he sees the law abused, and reruns of THE GREEN HORNET, Penny dons Japanese warrior garb and wields a wicked sword to stop tycoon Charles Cioffi who has a supersonic device that causes earthquakes. The Jerry Ludwig script is predictable, the characters cliched. Directed by Lee H. Katzin. Geoffrey Lewis, Morgan Brittany, Beulah Quo, Dana Elcar.

SANDCASTLES (1972). See editions 1-3.

SANTA CLAUS (1960). Check it once, don't check it twice: Beloved St. Nick (Jose Elias Moreno) joins Merlin the Magician to fight the Red Devil and his impish minions when he should be handing out presents to kiddies. Is nothing sacred to Mexican director Rene Cardona? Or to K. Gordon Murray, the U.S. impresario who imported this from down south? Jangled bells. (Sinister/C; S/Weird; United; Silver Screen)

SANTA CLAUS CONQUERS THE MARTIANS (1964). Given this was designed as a children's sci-fi fairy tale, and given it's played like a Dr. Seuss fractured fable, MARTIANS fulfills its limited expectations and is not as awful as some critics say. Because the green-faced children on Mars are distracted by the TV shows beaming in from Earth, the grand ruler Kemar orders his men to kidnap Santa Claus from the North Pole and use him as a propaganda weapon to cheer up the canal kids. Accompanying the invaders on their mission is a Tobor-type robot, Tog. Two Earth children are also kidnapped, and of course they and Santa teach the Martians a few lessons. As a curiosity piece, this production isn't half bad. Directed by Nicholas Webster. John Call plays a jovial Santa and somewhere among the green-faced kids is Pia Zadora. Leonard Hicks, Vincent Beck. (Nelson; S/Weird; Filmfax; from Valley Star as **SANTA CLAUS DEFEATS THE ALIENS**)

SANTA CLAUS DEFEATS THE ALIENS. See **SANTA CLAUS CONQUERS THE MARTIANS.**

SANTA CLAUS—THE MOVIE (1985). Enchanting family movie depicts how a big-hearted Earthling and wife are picked by Father Time to be Mr. and Mrs. Santa Claus, destined to live at the North Pole where elves led by Dudley Moore make the toys. This portion is charming, with elaborate sets to give Santa Claus versimilitude. Then the film switches to modern times and trivializes the spirit of Christmas by focusing on two kids and one evil toy manufacturer (John Lithgow). It's still successful enough that you should put this on your Christmas list. Huddleston is an excellent Santa. Burgess Meredith, Judy Cornwell. (Media) (Laser: Image)

SANTO AGAINST THE ZOMBIES. See **INVASION OF THE ZOMBIES.** (Santo wrestles a bad script!)

SANTO AND DRACULA'S TREASURE (1968). That low IQ-ed masked wrestler Santo is back, struggling with a hapless Alfredo Salazar script involving Dracula's ring (the kind on a finger) and a time machine. Directed by Rene Cardona. Rodolfo Guzman Huerta (he's Santo), Noelia Noel, Aldo Monti.

SANTO AND THE BLUE DEMON VS. DRACULA AND THE WOLF MAN (1967). Nothing like cramming all the ingredients into its title . . . In this Masked Wrestler mindboggler, two dumb wrestlers meet two dumber monsters. Two plus two equal one dumb movie. Directed by Miguel M. Delgado. Aldo Monti.

SANTO ATTACKS THE WITCHES (1964). Masked wrestler of Mexico returns for battles with old witch Lorena Velazquez and serpents she conjures up from Hell. The Hell you say? Directed by Jose Diaz Morales. Ramon Bugarini, Maria Eugenia San Martin.

SANTO VS FRANKENSTEIN'S DAUGHTER (1971). Masked wrestler of Mexico again, doing in a Frankenstein-like monster, a wicked scientist's daughter and other beings of the supernatural. Directed by Miguel M. Delgado. Rodolfo Guzman Huerta, Gina Romand.

SANTO VS THE MARTIAN INVASION (1966). Mexico's savoir of the wrestling ring faces invaders from space. Ugh! Directed by Alfredo B. Crevenna. Maura Monti, Eva Norvind, Wolf Ruvinskis.

SARGOSSA MANUSCRIPT, THE (1965). See editions 1-3.

SASQUATCH (1977). Sole-flattened treatment of Big Foot, directed by Ed Ragozzini, stumbles over its own fallen arches at every bend in the Canadian Northwest scenery. Scientists search for the missing link but prove to be dumber than the hairy apeman who outsmarts them from behind every bush. SASQUATCH is a no watch. (VCI)

SATAN. See **MARK OF THE DEVIL.**

SATAN BUG, THE (1965). Crisp suspense chiller adapted by James Clavell and Edward Anhalt from an Alistair MacLean novel, swiftly paced by director John

Sturges. A virus serum is stolen by a demented doctor (Richard Basehart) who has delusions of power. If allowed to escape its bottle, the "bug" could wipe out mankind. George Maharis portrays a heroic agent, Dana Andrews is a general, Anne Francis is his daughter and Frank Sutton and Ed Asner are oleaginous heavies. John Larkin, John Anderson, Hari Rhodes.

SATANIC RITES OF DRACULA. This Hammer horror thriller was retitled in the U.S. as **COUNT DRACULA AND HIS VAMPIRE BRIDE.** Liberty Entertainment offers a complete tape version under its original title; UAV also offers a version, **RITES OF DRACULA, THE.** For a critique see **COUNT DRACULA AND HIS VAMPIRE BRIDE.**

SATANIK (1968). Director Piero Vivarelli, red-blooded Italian male, has this thing for Magda Konopka, lingering his camera on her shapely thighs and voluptuous breasts. Magda starts the picture as an old hag but turns into a ravishing, miniskirted babe after drinking a youth formula. Despite obvious flaws in Eduardo M. Brochero's script, this has an undercurrent of sexual perversity. Julio Pena, Armando Calvo, Umberto Raho. (Allied Artists Video; Sinister/C; S/Weird)

SATANIS—THE DEVIL'S MASS (1969). Editions 1-3.

SATANISM AND WITCHCRAFT. See **SCREAM GREATS II: SATANISM AND WITCHCRAFT.**

SATAN KILLER, THE (1993). Poorly lit and photographed in Norfolk, Va., incoherently edited and inanely acted, and cruel in its violence toward women, this is a waste-of-time serial killer chase in which cop Steve Sayre goes on a bloody vendetta after his lovely fiance is murdered. Director Stephen Calamari should be chopped up and served in a ketchup sauce. Billy Franklin, James Westbrook, Belinda Creason, Cindy Healy. Aka DEATH PENALTY. (Action International)

SATAN MURDERS, THE (1974). Unscrupulous woman plots with demon lovers to kill her equally unscrupulous husband in this British TV production which stumbles about on cloven feet. Directed slowly by Lela Swift. Larry Blyden, Salome Jens, Susan Sarandon.

SATAN'S BLACK WEDDING (1976). Terrible production standards and awful color—not to mention atrocious acting and horrendous direction by Phillip Miller—negates this tale about devil worshippers and a dead woman who returns to life as a vampire in Monterey. Greg Braddock, Ray Miles. (Western World)

SATAN'S BLADE (1982). The naked female form is the main motif of director L. Scott Castillo Jr. as he fills this film with bountiful titties and ass, but little else. Unless you consider women being ruthlessly knifed to death by a madman a socially redeeming theme. Yes, gore gang, another slasher flick, set at a lake resort being terrorized by a legendary mountain man whose spirit allegedly roves with a knife given to him by evil gods. Two married couples and a bevy of bosomy beauties gather for a weekend—targets for the killer's knife. Tom Bongiorno, Stephanie Leigh Steel, Elisa R. Malinovitz. (Prism; Trend Video Concepts; Starmaker)

SATAN'S BLOOD (1977). Spanish supernatural thriller in which a couple is tricked into entering an old, dark house where satanists await. Directed by Carlos Puerto. Angel Aranda, Sandra Alberti, Marian Karr. (From Mogul as **DON'T PANIC**)

SATAN'S CHEERLEADERS (1976). Writer-director Greydon Clark intermingles THE OMEN with I WAS A RAH RAH BOOM GIRL in this "cheer-y" tale of a witch cult headed by John Ireland and Yvonne DeCarlo which terrorizes big-busted, miniskirted cheerleaders from Benedict High. Remarks a cult member, "Some townspeople feel the Prince of Darkness might desire that the blood of a maiden flow tonight." Incompetently handled, in a bemusing way, with Jack Kruschen and John Carradine on the sidelines. Let's hear it for Satan: Give me E . . . X . . . P . . . L . . . O . . . I . . . T . . . A . . . T . . . I . . . O . . . N . . . Give me F . . . I . . . L . . . M . . . Give me . . . aw hell, give me a raincheck. (United; Interglobal; VCI)

SATAN'S CLAW. See **BLOOD ON SATAN'S CLAW.**

SATAN'S DAUGHTERS. Video version of **VAMPYRES—DAUGHTERS OF DARKNESS** (Majestic).

SATAN'S DOGS. Video version of **PLAY DEAD** (Video Vision).

SATAN'S MISTRESS. See **DARK EYES.**

SATAN'S PRINCESS (1989). This witchcraft movie presents a little of everything to titillate you (lesbian love scenes, man-woman love scenes, cops-and-robbers shootouts, a strangling, an icepick-in-the-back scene, a blow-torch job, etc.) but only adds up to exploitation material from producer-director Bert I. Gordon. Robert Forster portrays a burned-out ex-cop searching for the missing daughter of a friend. The girl is making lesbo love with beautiful French actress Lydie Denier while Forster runs around having bad dreams, kicking and hitting people to learn the truth, being nasty to his girl and trying to take care of his handicapped son. Caren Kaye, Philip Glasser, M.K. Harris, Ellen Geer, Jack Carter. (Video/Laser: Paramount)

SATAN'S SADISTS (1969). Sickening exercise in violence and bloodletting—unredeemed and unrelieved in its trashiness as a motorcycle gang kills for pleasure. Familiar faces are welcome in this wasteland, but are only death fodder for the bikers: Russ Tamblyn, Scott Brady, Kent Taylor. Greydon Clark, a producer of schlock, is a gang member. Directed by Al Adamson. Regina Carrol, Robert Dix, Gary Kent. (Super)

SATAN'S SATELLITES (1952). Feature version of **ZOMBIES OF THE STRATOSPHERE** (Admit One).

SATAN'S SCHOOL FOR GIRLS (1973). Roy Thinnes, of TV's THE INVADERS, as Satan? Yep, they cast against type in this TV-movie set in a girls' school. Directed by David Lowell Rich. Kate Jackson, Pamela Franklin, Lloyd Bochner, Cheryl Ladd. (Prism)

SATAN'S SISTER. See **SHE BEAST, THE.**

SATAN'S SKIN. See **BLOOD ON SATAN'S CLAW.**

SATAN'S SLAVE (1976). British import with Michael Gough as a dabbler in black magic who intends to bring to life a long-dead witch. Directed by Norman J. Warren from a David McGillivray script. Candace Glendenning, Martin Potter, Barbara Kellerman.

SATAN'S STORYBOOK (198?). Two short tales of horror, one about a serial killer who goes to the electric chair for his deeds, the other about an actor who hangs himself and meets a clown in the world of the dead. Pornography actress Ginger Lynn has a straight role. (Even Steven Entertainment)

SATAN'S SUPPER. Variant video version of **NIGHTMARE NEVER ENDS, THE** (Academy).

SATAN'S TOUCH (1984). Blond-haired personification of the Devil (Paul Davies) gives grocery store owner James Lawless the ability to gamble in Las Vegas and Atlantic City without losing, a blessing that is a curse when casino boss Warren Frost investigates him with computers, voice-stress machines and other equipment. Uneven photography and acting detract from this curiosity piece that will be of zero interest to horror fans. Amateurishly written-directed by John Goodell. Shirley Venard, Lou Bellamy. (Regal; VCI)

SATAN'S TRIANGLE (1975). Supernatural TV-movie advances the theory that ships and planes are missing in the Bermuda Triangle because a demon needs the crews and passengers to keep his home fires burning. What begins in promising fashion when Kim Novak is shipwrecked is quickly awash in muddy waters when helicopter rescuers Doug McClure and Alejandro Rey show up. Directed by Sutton Roley. Jim Davis, Ed Lauter, Michael Conrad.

SATELLITE IN THE SKY (1956). Above Earth, a Tritonium bomb accidentally adheres to the hull of a spaceship. Now, unless astronauts risk their lives, our planet could be in terrible danger. British sci-fi is land-locked soap opera focusing on frightened men finding faith in themselves, loving their women fast and hard, etc. Directed by Paul Dickson. Kieron Moore, Donald Wolfit, Lois Maxwell, Bryan Forbes, Thea Gregory.

SATISFIERS OF ALPHA BLUE (1981). Alpha Blue is a vacation planet in the 21st Century where sexual needs are satisfied by computer. A rebel decides it's time again for real kissy poo poo and for everyone to have a name instead of a number. Pornie written-produced-directed by Gerard Damiano. Lysa Thatcher, Hillary Summers, Maria Tortuga.

SATURDAY NIGHT SHOCKERS VOL. I. Video combo of **THE CREEPING TERROR** and **CHAINED FOR LIFE** (Rhino).

SATURDAY NIGHT SHOCKERS VOL. II. Video combo of **MANBEAST** and **HUMAN GORILLA** (Rhino).

SATURDAY NIGHT SHOCKERS VOL. III. Video combo of **THE MONSTER OF PIEDRAS BLANCAS** and **THE MESA OF LOST WOMEN** (Rhino).

SATURDAY THE 14TH (1981). Blame producer Julie Corman, wife of Roger, for this flubbed comedy-spoof directed childishly by Howard R. Cohen. A couple (Richard Benjamin, Paula Prentiss) moving into a haunted house are confronted by aliens, vampires and other monsters and things. Many folks worked on the effects, but men in rubber monster suits still look like men in rubber monster suits and most of the jokes fall as flat as corpses. The only funny sequence is when a shark fin appears in a bathtub. Rosemary DeCamp, Jeffrey Tambor, Severen Darden. (Embassy; Sultan)

SATURDAY THE 14TH STRIKES BACK (1988). This sequel to Julie Corman's 1981 horror spoof is not an improvement on the original but another series of weak gags written-directed by Howard R. Cohen and produced by Corman with the poorest of effects. A weird family living in a strange L.A. house is again the target of a bevy of monsters, unleashed when a crack opens under the mansion. Neither a quintet of sexy young women nor footage lifted from Corman action films can save this fluff, and a good cast (Ray Walston, Avery Schreiber, Patty McCormack, Julianna McNamara, Jason Presson, Leo Gordon) is wasted. (MGM/UA)

SATURN THREE (1980). Astonishing sets and futuristic hardware mean very little when the plot is one big Story Hole in blackest space. The star here is Hector the Demi-God Robot, a masterpiece of technology, blending human features with robotic traits. The less successful human stars are Kirk Douglas and Farrah Fawcett as space dwellers on Titan, a moon of Saturn, living an idyllic Adam-and-Eve existence until Harvey Keitel drops by to malprogram the robot to lust after Farrah's body. This mess of contrivance and confusion never reaches a suitable conclusion. Based on an idea by production designer John Barry, who died before the film was completed, it was finished by Stanley Donen. Douglas Lambert, Ed Bishop. (Video/Laser: CBS/Fox)

SAVAGE ABDUCTION. Variant video version of **CYCLE PSYCHOS** (King of Video; Paragon).

SAVAGE APOCALYPSE. See **CANNIBALS ARE IN THE STREETS, THE.**

SAVAGE BEES, THE (1976). Bruce Geller, creator of MISSION: IMPOSSIBLE, produced-directed this TV-film, swarming with excitement when South American killer bees migrate to Louisiana aboard a banana boat and sting folks to death. Ben Johnson is the efficient sheriff, Michael Parks is the medical aide, Horst Buchholz is the expert on killer bees. Written by Guerdon Trueblood. In the same vein as THE SWARM and THE BEES. (And THE STING?) (USA; Alan Landsburg; IVE)

SAVAGE CURSE, THE (1974). British-produced TV cheapie depicts walled-alive themes borrowed from Poe's "Cask of Amontillado." Scripted by Brian Clemens, directed by John Sichel. Quite tacky. George Chakiris, Jenny Agutter, Anton Diffring, Russell Hunter.

SAVAGE DAWN. Video of **STRYKER** (Media; Bingo).

SAVAGE INTRUDER (1975). Miriam Hopkins, an aging movie star portraying an aging movie star, hires a male nurse (John David Garfield) only to realize too late that he's a psychokiller. Directed by Donald Wolfe. Also called HOLLYWOOD HORROR HOUSE. (Unicorn)

SAVAGE LUST (1989). Weakly plotted "old dark house" mystery in which six teenagers and a runaway fugitive take refuge in a deserted mansion, where in the front yard a demolished automobile has been enshrined. Suddenly, a knife-wielding maniac in a white mime mask starts knocking them off. The explanation behind the almost-nonexistent mystery provided by writer-director Jose Ramon Larraz is barely enough to hold this cliched picture together, and there is only one torrid love-making sequence to justify a title that makes this film appear to be an "erotic thriller" when it is not. Jennifer Delora, William Russell. (Action International)

SAVAGES (1973). Weird idea, enigmatically executed by director James Ivory in Tarrytown, N.Y. Primitive Mud People rise from primeval ooze, exposing their naked behinds with indifference. They're about to make a human sacrifice when a croquet ball drops out of nowhere. Awed at something more perfectly rounded than derrieres, they discover an elegant manor and crash a party. Comparison of modern decadence and ancient barbarism is at work here—thoughtful stuff, but extremely puzzling. Sam Waterston, Salome Jens. (Lightning)

SAVAGE WEEKEND (1978). Also known as THE UPSTATE MURDERS and KILLER BEHIND THE MASK, but by any title it's a slasher movie displaying a fetish for sadism and bordering on abnormal sexuality in depicting what happens to vacationers who become fodder for a killer in a fright mask. Unusual amount of soft porn and nudity, enough to make you head downstate. And the sequence in which a nymphomaniac fondles a cow in vivid close-up leaves no doubt what udder gutter the mind of co-proudcer/writer/director David Paulsen is sprawled in. Murders by strangulation (followed by hangings), by hatpin (through the brain of a raving homosexual), by chainsaw (now, there's an old saw!), by buzzsaw (now, there's a new saw!). Excruciating to watch. Christopher Allport, James Doerr, Kathleen Heaney, David Gale, Marilyn Hamlin. (Paragon)

SCALPEL (1978). First feature effort of Joseph Weintraub and John Grissmer could have used a finer edge in depicting a psychopathic plastic surgeon (Robert Lansing) who creates a "dead ringer" lookalike for his missing daughter (Judith Chapman) so he can collect a $5 million inheritance. Ample twists and turns in director Grissmer's screenplay; a minor suspense melodrama with a surprise ending. Go ahead, take a stab at SCALPEL. (Charter; Embassy)

SCALPS (1983). Juvenile gore thriller poorly written and sloppily directed by Fred Olen Ray, with a terrible soundtrack and an amateurish cast, which at least makes for a few unintended laughs. Archeology students on an expedition to the Black Trees Indian Burial Ground disturb the spirit of the renegade Black Claw (also known as Tom A. Hawk), who scalps the kids, shoots arrows into them and otherwise behaves abominably. Cancel his reservation. Kirk Alyn (one-time serial SUPERMAN) appears briefly as an absent-minded digs specialist, Forrest J. Ackerman has a pointless cameo as "Professor Trentwood" and Carroll Borland pops up as Dr. Reynolds, with nothing to do. Jo Ann Robinson, Roger Maycock, Richard Hench, Frank McDonald. (Imperial; Marquis; on Planet video with **SLAYER**)

SCANNERCOP (1993). This fourth entry in the SCANNERS series is a riveting, well-produced cop thriller in which scanner Daniel Quinn, a member of the LAPD, uses his powers to track down a mad scientist (Richard Lynch) who is using a brainwashing technique to turn innocent people into cop killers. Good effects, suspense and a honed script by George Sanders and John Bryant make this one a winner. Directed by Pierre David. Darlanne Fluegel. (Republic)

SCANNERS (1981). Contrived but fascinating film written-directed by David Cronenberg. Psychics (scanners) have disrupted a government investigation of their powers and gone underground to wage a war of conquest. Scientist Patrick McGoohan sends a scanner into their secret ranks to spy . . . intrigue and violent death follow. Cronenberg achieves a weird atmosphere and the special effects (including an exploding human head) shook up audiences and gave the film word of mouth. If Cronenberg had avoided his muddled plot, he might have scanned better. Three interesting sequels followed. Stephen Lack, Jennifer O'Neill, Michael Ironside, Lawrence Dane. (Embassy; CBS/Fox) (Laser: Nelson)

SCANNERS II: THE NEW ORDER (1990). Although David Cronenberg didn't return to make this sequel to his '81 hit, it's a fair follow-up depicting new adventures of "Scanners," those with power to control others via mental forces, and even explode heads on occasion. The Canadian film, scripted by B. J. Nelson and directed by Christian Duguay, depicts scanner David Kellum (David Hewlett) preventing crooked elements in Toronto's government from taking over with evil scanners. The gory scanner duels are handled well and three sequences stand out: the destruction of a video arcade; the demolition of a mannikin warehouse; and a mental battle between Hewlett and bad-guy scanner Raoul Trujillo. Yvan Ponton, Deborah Raffin, Isabelle Mejias, Tom Butler. (Media/Fox) (Image)

SCANNER STEPHEN LACK

SCANNERS III: THE TAKEOVER (1991). Liliana Komorowska's campy performance as a sweet scanner who takes an experimental drug from her father and turns into a purely evil woman is the highpoint of this Canadian film directed by Christian Duguay. She all but chews the sets as she sways the masses through TV, kills dear old dad in a hottub and seduces a young executive during her ruthless climb to the top. The only person in her way is wayward brother Steve Parrish, who returns from a Thailand monastery to give Liliana's henchmen a piece of his scanner mind, resulting in mayhem and pyrotechnics. Call this one KUNG FU MEETS VIDEODROME. Valerie Valois, Daniel Pilon, Collin Fox, Claire Cellucci. (Video/Laser: Republic)

SCANNERS IV. See **SCANNERCOP**.

SCARAB (1983). Devil-worship exploitation flick with Rip Torn, Robert Ginty and Cristina Hachuel. Directed by Steven-Charles Jaffe. The plot revolves around a resurrected Egyptian god and a former Nazi seeking new sources of power.

SCARECROW, THE (1981). John Carradine turns up in this obscure Canadian film as a slasher-rapist. Directed by Sam Pillsbury. (Pan-Canadian)

SCARECROWS (1988). Above-average video horror flick which, despite derivative plotting devices and typical grisliness, has a fascination conceived by Richard Jefferies and co-writer/editor/producer/director William Wesley. In the Florida jungle paramilitary robbers, after pulling off an army payroll heist, find themselves the hunted when they get mixed up with scarecrows endowed with homicidal tendencies (exactly how is alluded to in some shallow exposition). It's your basic walking-dead story with mildly interesting characters and an avoidance of too many genre cliches. Gang member Ted Vernon was also executive producer. Victoria Christian, Richard Vidan. (Forum) (Laser: Image)

SCARED STIFF (1953). Dean Martin-Jerry Lewis remake of the 1940 Bob Hope-Paulette Goddard horror comedy, THE GHOST BREAKERS, with new musical numbers. The comedians are hamming it up in Jamaica, where they have fled to avoid gangsters. Lizabeth Scott has inherited a haunted castle infested with zombies, secret passageways, flying bats, clanking suits of armor and other "old dark house" cliches rigged by effects master Gordon Jennings. George Marshall directs the Herbert Baker-Walter de Leon script with an appropriate light touch. Carmen Miranda, Dorothy Malone, Jack Lambert. (Paramount)

SCARED STIFF (1987). Slave master of the 1850s comes back to a Southern mansion to terrorize a psychiatrist and his wife and child who apparently have been cursed. Director Richard Friedman co-wrote the script with Mark Frost and producer Daniel F. Bacaner. David Ramsey, Nicole Fortier, Andrew Stevens, Mary Page Keller. (Video/Laser: Republic)

SCARED TO DEATH (1946). The only color film Bela Lugosi ever worked in—a skid-row programmer narrated by a dead girl, her report coming in flashback from the morgue. A stiff, boring plot has several characters coming together under one roof and behaving ridiculously. Slow moving and talkative, with minimal horror elements. Directed by Christy Cabanne. George Zucco, Nat Pendleton, Joyce Compton, Douglas Fowley. (Nostalgia Merchant; Sinister/C; Filmfax)

SCARED TO DEATH (1980). ALIEN lookalike called a Syngenor (Synthesized Genetic Organism), created in a lab DNA experiment, hides in L.A.'s sewers, sucking marrow from victims by inserting its tongue into the mouth. Ugh. Under the direction of Bill Malone, who also wrote the script, the first half is slow going, alternating trapped humans undergoing attack and the domestic life of ex-cop John Stinston and secretary Diana Davidson. The last half picks up in the sewers, where Stinston and scientist Toni Jannotta are pursued by the thing. Climax takes place in an iron metal factory and finally the film becomes harrowing. The characters, unfortunately, are all contrived and boring. (Media)

SCAREMAKER, THE. See **GIRLS NITE OUT.**

SCARLET CLAW, THE (1944). Phosphorescent ghost haunts the moors, ripping out throats of victims with a bloody claw and fleeing—a white, glittering spectre etched against foggy swampland. Who should pick up a glow of his own as he cries "The game is afoot!" but Sherlock Holmes, visiting Canada with the good Dr. Watson. Jolly good item, with thrilling and scary moments, in the Universal series with Basil Rathbone and Nigel Bruce. A fine chap, that producer-director Roy William Neill. And that writer Edmund L. Hartman, now there's a good fellow, hey what? (Key)

SCARLET CLUE, THE (1945). This Charlie Chan programmer features a killer in the garb of a fantastic creature using bizarre poison capsules and radio beams to carry out homicides. Even Sidney Toler as Charlie Chan seems livelier, as though he detected a glimmer of hope in the script. Directed by Phil Rosen. Mantan Moreland, Ben Carter, Benson Fong, Ian Wolfe.

SCARLET EXECUTIONER, THE. See **BLOODY PIT OF HORROR.**

SCARS OF DRACULA (1970). Popular Hammer production in the Christopher Lee/Dracula series—written by John Elder, directed by Roy Ward Baker, scored by James Bernard. Lee, resurrected when his ashes are covered with bat's blood, begins his reign of terror and fights off a revenge seeker. Blood and sadism (lots) have been added to the formula. Dennis Waterman, Christopher Matthews, Jenny Hanley, Michael Gwynn, Michael Ripper. (HBO; Republic)

SCHIZO (1976). Graphic British psychothriller with a topnotch cast, good direction by Peter Walker and a mildly intriguing script by David McGillivray. It's a bloody thing, though, highlighting a darning needle through an eyeball socket, a sledgehammer into a human brain, a body run over by a truck, and a few standard knife slashings. Lynne Frederick portrays a pretty ice-skating star pursued by a strange man (John Leyton) and a memory of maternal homicide. Nice twist ending. Stephanie Beacham adds her charms to the tense tale.

John Fraser, Jack Watson. (Media; VCI)

SCHIZO (1990). Lisa Aliff's 30-minute ordeal to escape the horrors of a Yugoslavian monastery, where a slavic spirit-demon takes over archeologist Aron Eisenberg, is the best thing about this offbeat tale of Eisenberg's search for a lost tomb. Keaton Jones' script gets skewered at times before the focus falls on Eisenberg's possession and the horrors he performs in a chamber of torture. Director Manny Coto succeeds in capturing a claustrophobic and oppressive feeling amidst the Yugoslav locations and emphasizes the obsessed behavior of Eisenberg as he gradually goes bonkers. Vincent Schiavelli has an unusual role as a mental patient. Coto went on to make the superior DR. GIGGLES. Christopher McDonald, Maja, James Purcell, Jamie Rose.

SCHIZOID (1965). See **PSYCHOPATH, THE.**

SCHIZOID (1971). Made in London, this French/Italian/Spanish psychothriller stars Leo Genn, Stanley Baker, Florinda Bolkan and Jean Sorel. Lucio Fulci directed/co-wrote with a mind that has to be schizoid. Also known as A LIZARD IN A WOMAN'S SKIN.

SCHIZOID (1980). Psychiatrist Klaus Kinski's group-therapy patients are knocked off one by one by a scissors-wielding maniac while gossip columnist Marianna Hill investigates. Cheap and tasteless, althought some scenes of Kinski capture an eerie quality whenever director-writer David Paulsen tries to upgrade this sleazy material, aka MURDER BY MAIL. Craig Wasson, Richard Herd, Christopher Lloyd, Flo Gerrish. (MCA)

SCHLOCK (1973). John Landis' first feature (he wrote-directed) is a refreshing change of pain for horror fans, depicting a Neanderthal man (Landis) thawed from his prehistoric haven and on a rampage in an average U.S. city. It's played as a satire on movie monsters. Forrest J. Ackerman and Don Glut guest with Saul Kahn and Joseph Piantodosi. (Lighting; Wizard; from Westernworld as **BANANA MONSTER**)

SCHOOL OF DEATH (1977). An orphanage is the setting for a tale with Dean Selmier and Sandra Mozarauski. Directed by Pedro L. Ramirez. (All American)

SCHOOL SPIRIT (1985). Football player Tom Nolan, on his way to get laid, is killed in an accident. An already dead uncle (John Finnegan) shows up to take him to Heaven, but the star is still eager to get laid and wants another day for unfinished "business." This low-budget Roger Corman comedy was directed by Alan Holleb. Roberta Collins, Larry Linville. (Media)

SCHOOL THAT ATE MY BRAIN, THE. See **ZOMBIE HIGH.**

SCIENCE CRAZED (1990). Instantly forgettable claptrap set in Shelley Institute where "The Fiend" attacks women. Produced in Canada in 1987, this amateurish effort was written/co-produced/ directed/edited by Ron Switzer. Cameron Klein, Tony Dellaventura, Robin Hartsell. (Interamerica Entertainment)

SCORPIO SCARAB (1972). See editions 1-3.

SCORPION WITH TWO TAILS, THE. A woman dreams of horrible deaths. Van Johnson, John Saxon. AKA MURDER IN THE ETRUSCAN CEMETERY. (Cinema Group; Palisades)

SCOTLAND YARD HUNTS DR. MABUSE. See **DR. MABUSE VS. SCOTLAND YARD.**

SCOTLAND YARD DRAGNET. See **HYPNOTIST, THE.**

SCOUNDREL, THE (1935). See editions 1-3.

SCOUNDRELS, THE (1969). Masked hero of Mexico puts a stranglehold on motorcyclists working for a batty babe who worships Aztec gods. Hero acts so much like a blind fool it appears he forgot to cut eyeholes in his face mask. Directed by Federico Curiel. Mil Mascaras.

SCREAM (1973). See **NIGHT GOD SCREAMED.**

SCREAM (1985). Originally shot in 1981 as THE OUTING, this was released four years later and hailed as the worst horror movie of all time. Hopelessly written-directed by Larry Quisenberry with the pacing of a snail, this hunkanothin' follows uninteresting, never-developed hikers to a deserted Western town where a Killer strikes with hatchet and axe. Minimal gore scenes and hardly any explanation about the killer is given. Woody Strode turns up mysteriously on horseback. One long series of dull panning shots with people who act contrary to human nature. Pepper Martin, Hank Worden, Alvy Moore, Gregg Palmer. (Vestron)

SCREAM . . . AND DIE. video version of **HOUSE THAT VANISHED, THE** (Lightning).

SCREAM AND SCREAM AGAIN (1970). Stomach-churning thrill piece from director Gordon Hessler and writer Christopher Wicking, who bring to this British luridness a touch of allegory. Vincent Price is a scientist creating superhumans through fiendish surgical anomalies, mutilating bodies in sickening ways to acquire transplants. That's when Hessler and Wicking get a little carried away . . . again and again. Peter Cushing is an ex-Nazi and Christopher Lee is a British secret agent. Judy Huxtable is a screaming victim. Based on a Peter Saxon novel. Alfred Marx, Uta Levka. (Vestron)

SCREAM, BABY, SCREAM (1969). Hippie artist at work in Miami—he turns nice folks into monsters so he can then paint them. Weasel at the easel. Beware, viewer, beware. Directed by Joseph Adler, scripted by Laurence Robert Cohen. Ross Harris, Eugenie Wingate, Chris Martell, Suzanne Stuart. (Regal; from Camp as **NIGHTMARE HOUSE**)

SCREAM, BLACULA, SCREAM (1972). Sequel to the box office smash BLACULA, a sometimes-amusing, often-chilling portrait of vampirism with William Marshall again "bringing to life" the aristocratic black vampire. This time his bones are used in voodoo rituals, and he reappears in human form to do battle with priestess Pam Grier. Marshall, with his authoritative presence and booming, rich voice, creates a sympathetic vampire. Directed by Bob Kelljan of COUNT YORGA—VAMPIRE fame. Don Mitchell, Richard Lawson, Bernie Hamilton. (Filmways; Orion) (Laser: Japanese)

SCREAM BLOODY MURDER (1972). A psychopath with a hook hand, the result of an accident while he was squashing his dear ol' daddy with a tractor, is freed from a house for the insane and goes on a rampage of mass murder. Written-produced-directed by Robert J. Emery. Paul Vincent, Marlena Lustik, Paul Ecenia. (VCI; United)

SCREAM DREAM (1990). Carol Carr portrays a rock singer whose body is possessed by a witch/demon. Cheap effort in the gore tradition, shot by writer-director Donald Farmer in Tennessee. Melissa More, Nikki Riggins, Jesse Raye. (American; Interamerican Entertainment/New Image)

SCREAMER (1970). See **SCREAM AND SCREAM AGAIN.**

SCREAMER (1974). Surprisingly effective British TV-movie with Pamela Franklin fearful she is being stalked by a homicidal rapist. Recovering from an attack, she superimposes the attacker's face over every man she meets and goes hysterical. Brian Clemens' telescript introduces a few unexpected twists before a satisfying climax. Shaun O'Riordan's direction is better than usual for these cheap productions. (IVE)

SCREAMERS (1978). Roger Corman purchased an Italian flick, THE FISH MEN, added 12 minutes of new footage and re-released it on an unsuspecting world. Mad doc Richard Johnson creates gill guys and daughter Barbara Bach reluctantly cooperates until the shipwreck survivor Claudio Cassinelli helps her escape the volcanic island as it sinks. Special monster make-up by Chris Walas. Italian footage was shot by Sergio Martino, U.S. inserts by Dan T. Miller. Also known as ISLE OF THE FISHMEN. Joseph Cotten, Mel Ferrer, Cameron Mitchell, Beryl Cunningham. (Embassy)

SCREAM FOR HELP (1984). Swift pacing and thrill piled on thrill make this a lively suspense-mystery, scripted by Tom Holland and directed by Michael Winner. Teen-ager Rachael Kelly suspects her stepfather of trying to kill her mother for the family fortune but no one in town (including the police commissioner) will believe her, even though it's apparent from the outset there is a conspiracy afoot. The climax is ludicrous and grossly violent yet you will be compelled to watch. David Brooks, Marie Masters. (Lorimar) (Laser: Warner Bros.)

SCREAM GREATS (1986). Documentary on make-up/special effects man Tom Savini, featuring quotes by Savini and interviews with George Romero and various actors on the set of DAY OF THE DEAD. Fascinating look into low-budget movies. Footage features many films Savini has labored on, with emphasis on his working relationship with Romero. First in a series from Fangoria Magazine. (Video/Laser: Paramount)

SCREAM GREATS II: SATANISM AND WITCHCRAFT (1986). Second video in a series produced by Fangoria magazine, this volume tracks real-life devil cults, witches and other satanic elements in the world of black arts. Directed by Damon Santo Stefano from a Richard Lawton script. (Video/Laser: Paramount)

SCREAMING DEAD, THE (1971). Video version of **DRACULA VS. DR. FRANKENSTEIN** (Wizard).

SCREAMING HEAD, THE. See **HEAD, THE.**

SCREAMING MIMI (1958). Emphasis is on the psychology of the psycho in this literate adaptation of Fredric Brown's horror-crime novel about a burlesque dancer mentally unhinged after being attacked by a lunatic wielding a blood-covered knife. Newspaper columnist Phil Carey wants to befriend the stripper—and who can blame him, she's played by statuesque, stacked Swedish beauty Anita Ekberg, an unbelievingly stunning woman. Director Gerd Oswald's ambience of the night club world is enhanced by Gypsy Rose Lee (as the owner of the strip joint, El Madhouse) and zylophone player Red Yost Norvo. Outstanding is Harry Townes' over-the-edge portrayal of a jealous psychiatrist. Pure '50s noir with light horror overtones. (Sinister/C)

SCREAMING SKULL, THE (1958). American-International thud-crud as dim-witted as the family servant played by Alex Nicol, who directed in a manner as dim as the lighting. To the haunted mansion come John Hudson and Peggy Webber, not overly bright themselves. In fact, everyone seems to have a bulb unscrewed as a diabolical murder plot unfolds that involves a human head stripped of all flesh, gleaming white, which keeps popping up. Gee, the supernatural must be at work. Did we say diabolical? Make that dim-witted. Producer John Kneubuhl scripted from F. Marion Crawford's classic horror story. Tom Johnson, Russ Conway. (Sinister/C; S/Weird; Filmfax)

SCREAMING SKULL, THE (1973). TV-movie version of the story by Francis Marion Crawford, with David McCallum and Carrie Nye. Directed by Gloria Monty from a script by Norman Borisoff.

SCREAMING STARTS, THE. See **AND NOW THE SCREAMING STARTS.**

SCREAMING WOMAN, THE (1972). TV adaptation of Ray Bradbury's story about a child who hears a woman's voice coming from beneath the ground and tries to tell disbelieving adults. However, telewriter Merwin Gerard threw away the concept in favor of cliches: Olivia de Havilland, recovering from a breakdown, finds a woman buried alive, but nobody will believe her—except Ed Nelson, the neighbor who did the burying. So now he has to shut her up . . . and the terror begins. Ray Bradbury this is not. On its own it holds up as a formula suspense chiller, but director Jack Smight is no Hitchcock. Joseph Cotten, Walter Pidgeon, Jan Arvan.

SCREAM OF DEATH. See **LIVING COFFIN, THE.**

SCREAM OF FEAR (1961). Favorite Hammer production in the let's-scare-the-lovely-woman-to-death genre, written by producer Jimmy Sangster and directed by Seth Holt. Susan Strasberg is haunted by the corpse of her father, who turns up in the swimming pool. Decorum dictates we reveal nothing further, lest your enjoyment of this labyrinthine thriller be marred. Take nothing for granted, and be prepared to be jolted by the "haunting" scenes. AKA TASTE OF FEAR. Christopher Lee, Ronald Lewis, Ann Todd. (CBS/Fox; RCA/Columbia)

SCREAM OF THE DEMON LOVER (1971). Spanish-Italian programmer with an all-too-familiar plot (beautiful woman comes to eerie Gothic castle, where sinister nobleman holds sway) is well photographed and acted, suggesting exciting things that never arrive. He's a part-time doctor experimenting with rejuvenating dead flesh, she's a biochemist falling for the baron even though he's suspected by the villagers of heinous crimes against women. There's a decayed hand that crawls over her supple body and a fiend in the cellar—and would you believe a servant named Igor? Director J. L. Merino is worthy of better assignments than E. Colombo's screamplay. Jennifer Hartley and Jeffrey Chase do what they can as the odd couple, but are ultimately defeated by an unsatisfying, illogical ending. (Charter; from Lightning as **BLOOD CASTLE**)

SCREAM OF THE WOLF (1974). Werewolf TV-movie produced-directed by Dan Curtis and adapted by Richard Matheson from a David Chase story. Or are those torn-up corpses some kind of trick? Peter Graves, Clint Walker, Philip Carey, JoAnn Pflug, Don Megowan.

SCREAMPLAY (1986). Spoof on horror flicks starring Rufus Butler Seder as a would-be writer named Edgar Allen (ha ha!) whose characters come to life as he creates them at the typewriter. Unusual, with some nice twists by the real "screamwriters," Ed Greenberg and Seder, who also directed his own scream-pt.

SCREAM, PRETTY PEGGY (1973). Blatantly plagiaristic TV-movie rip-off of Robert Bloch's PSYCHO. Bette Davis stars as a bedridden mother, Ted Bessell is her artistic, misunderstood son. Gee, did we give it away? Scripter Jimmy Sangster and director Gordon Hessler should be ashamed. Charles Drake, Sian Barbara Allen.

SCREAMS OF A WINTER NIGHT (1977). Effective attempt to deal with the fear that mounts to a crescendo if we listen to one horror story too many, told with a minimum of gory effects or monstrous visuals—emphasis is on suggestion. The setting is Lake Durant (called Coyote Lake by the Indians) where young vacationers settle in a cabin for the weekend. Half the script by co-producer Richard H. Wadsack deals with Chataba, a legendary evil spirit of the wind that wreaks havoc. The other half is made up of stories the kids tell each other on a dark night. "Moss Point Man" deals with a Yeti creature stalking two kids; "Green Light" depicts fraternity students spending the night in a hotel haunted by a green light; and "Crazy Annie" is the psychological study of a young woman who kills with a knife. The framework story is most effective as director James L. Wilson builds to the horrifying climax. Filmed in Natchitocines Parish, La., this features William Ragsdale (FRIGHT NIGHT) in a bit part. Matt Borel, Gil Glasgow, Patrick Byers, Mary Anne Cox. (VCI; United)

SCREAMTIME (1983). Anthology of three British TV episodes with wraparound footage shot in New York City of two smalltime hoodlums watching the episodes on cassettes they've stolen. The first is about a maladjusted puppeteer who brings his dummies to homicidal life. The second depicts a woman in a mansion who keeps seeing a child playing in the yard and a man rushing about the house with a butcher knife. In "Garden of Blood" (the only title given to any of the chapters) dirt bikers invade the home of two old ladies to rob them but a spirit in a painting comes to life to wreak revenge. Below par for TV production. The hoods get their comeuppance in the dumbest ways. Produced and directed by Al Beresford. No writing credits. Vincent Russo, Robin Bailey, Dora Bryan. (Lightning; Live)

SCROOGE (1935). British adaptation of Dickens' A CHRISTMAS CAROL, with Seymour Hicks as the miserly one. Hicks also co-wrote the script with H. Fowler Mear. Directed by Henry Edwards. Donald Calthrop, Robert Cochran. (Video Yesteryear; Discount)

SCROOGE (1970). Ebenezer Scrooge, villain of Dickens' A CHRISTMAS CAROL, has never been more avaricious, churlish or penurious as in this dark British musical-comedy directed by Ronald Neame. Give Albert Finney credit but also credit the production design of Terry Marsh for capturing the supernatural. While the songs are mediocre to good, the cast injects charm into the material: Alec Guinness as Marley's Ghost, Edith Evans as the Ghost of Christmas Past and Kenneth More as the Ghost of Christmas Present. A perennial favorite with lavish music productions and faithfulness to the spirit of Dickens. (Video/Laser: CBS/Fox)

BOBCAT GOLDTHWAIT

SCROOGED (1988). This updating of Charles Dickens' A CHRISTMAS CAROL in a TV network setting, with Bill Murray assuming the Scrooge-like role of heartless humbugging president Francis Xavier Cross, is an odd mixture with mixed results. If a character is to undergo a personality transformation—the point of Dickens' classic—he must be presented seriously, and not sillily. Unfortunately, writers Mitch Glazer and Michael O'Donoghue do not establish a character we care enough about to make the visitations of the ghosts (past, present, future) pay off. And yet within this giant failing are funny bits, unconnected to the whole. Especially good are Robert Mitchum as a network vice-president, Carol Kane as the daffy Ghost of Christmas Present, and Michael J. Pollard as a down-and-outer abused by the Murray character. On the other hand, a nutcake character (Bobcat Goldthwait) is out of place in this movie. This needed a great deal of finesse which director Richard Donner failed to bring to it, relying instead on effects and a monstrous Ghost of Christmas Future. Karen Allen, John Forsythe, John Glover, David Johansen, Buddy Hackett. Several personalities (Robert Goulet, Lee Majors, John Houseman) appear in cute cameos. (Video/Laser: Paramount)

SEA BAT, THE (1930). This precursor to JAWS and other killer-fish films is crude in depicting a leviathan of the deep that resembles a giant manta ray, and the effects are never better than primitive. This is far more interesting for Raquel Torres' fiery slut on an island in the Caribbean, whose scanty native costumes fire up the blood of Charles Bickford, an escapee from Devil's Island posing as a preacher. The old corny story about a bible in one hand and a gun in the other (and which will the man choose?) sprang from Bess Meredyth and John Howard Lawson, with director Wesley Ruggles filming in Mexico. Boris Karloff has a very small role as a sponge fisherman named Corsican. Nils Aster.

SEA DEVILS (1985). Slightly exciting Spanish version of a story by Jules Verne, filmed in Africa, Portugal and Spain. A band a la Swiss Family Robinson undergoes adventures with mild fantasy and horror overtones. Part of the odyssey is at sea aboard a whaling ship, the rest is on an island where Arabs, pirates and our heroic band fight over a hidden treasure. Written-directed by J. Piquer Simon. Ian Sera, Frank Brana. (Academy)

SEANCE ON A WET AFTERNOON (1964). Engrossing British film written-directed by Bryan Forbes, chilling and stark in its depiction of an unbalanced woman (Kim Stanley) who forces her milquetoast husband (Richard Attenborough) to kidnap a rich industrialist's daughter. It's the woman's hope to establish herself as a spiritualist by "locating" the youngster. Realization that she is willing to murder the child comes as a jolt to Attenborough. He is thrown into a dilemma, the uncertainty of which holds one in the grip of its ghastly implications. Patrick Magee, Maria Kazan. (Vidamerica)

SEA OF LOVE (1989). Although this depicts how unorthodox New York cop Al Pacino and partner John Goodman track a serial killer suspected of being a woman (male victims are shot in the back of the head during sex), the emphasis of Richard Price's script is on characterizations and relationships when Pacino falls in love with suspect Ellen Barkin. Harold Becker directs this superb thriller with a taut touch and Pacino delivers a great performance. Just remember that terror and suspense are minimal, but effective when used. William Hickey, Lorraine Bracco. (Video/Laser: MCA)

SEARCH. See **PROBE.** (Dig it!)

SEARCH FOR BRIDEY MURPHY, THE (1956). Based on the bestseller by Morey Bernstein, reportedly the true story of a woman who, when hypnotized by Bernstein, regressed to a previous existence in Ireland. A study in reincarnation, never sensational or exploitative, and not too exciting, either. But it is persuasive, leading one to believe Bridey was indeed a woman who lived 150 years ago, and whose memories are retained in the body of a modern woman. Louis Hayward portrays Bernstein; Teresa Wright is Bridey. Written-directed by Noel Langley. Kenneth Tobey, Richard Anderson, Nancy Gates, Walter Kingsford. (Paramount)

SEARCH FOR THE EVIL ONE (1967). Joseph Kane, who once directed Roy Rogers Westerns, turned up in his twilight years to helm this bit of nonsense about Adolf Hitler turning up alive in Argentina (where else?) and plotting a new assault on the world. Sieg Heil! drama designed for Nuremberg burn-outs. Lisa Pera, H. M. Wynant, Henry Brandon (Martin Bormann), Pitt Herbert (Hitler). (From Camp as **HE LIVES**)

SEARCH FOR THE GODS (1975). TV-movie, produced by Douglas S. Cramer, with a Herman Miller-Ken Pettus script playing off the Erich von Daniken theory that aliens walked Earth centuries ago. But this comes off as routine good guys vs. bad guys pap, directed routinely by Jud Taylor. Wandering Kurt Russell, looking for pieces of an ancient medallion with alien-like markings, stumbles around Taos, New Mexico. The search is just as futile for the viewer. Ralph Bellamy, Stephen McHattie, Raymond St. Jacques. (Unicorn)

SEA SERPENT (1985). Atomic explosion arouses an underwater undulater sleeping in the briny deep. Drunken ship's captain Timothy Bottoms espies the slippery serpent, but nobody will believe him—until Taryn Power spots the aquatic assaulter. Off they go to destroy the marine marauder with advise from professor Ray Milland (in his last role). Poorly made Spanish seafarer, of minimum impact; a dozing denizen. Directed by Gregory Greens, who is really Italian horror director Amando de Ossorio, who also wrote the script. Jared Martin and Spanish horror director Leon Klimovsky are also in the cast. (Lightning)

SEASON OF THE WITCH. Video version of George Romero's **HUNGRY WIVES** (Vidamerica; Vista).

SECOND BEST SECRET AGENT IN THE WHOLE WIDE WORLD, THE (1966). British imitation of James Bond from director Lindsay Shonteff, starring Tom Adams as agent Tom Vine, who joins sexy Veronica Hurst to protect a Swedish scientist who has developed an anti-gravity machine. The sequel: WHERE THE BULLETS FLY. Peter Bull, Judy Huxtable. (Charter)

SECOND COMING, THE. See **MESSIAH OF EVIL.**

SECOND COMING OF SUZANNE, THE (1974). Incomprehensible mess that never comes close to making sense. Writer-director Michael Barry (son of Gene Barry) opts for clever editing and artsy-craftsy nonsense as he tries (but fails) to tell of pretentious film makers (art imitating life?) Jared Martin and Richard Dreyfuss making a flick about Jesus Christ, only in this one JC is a woman, played by an angelic, mute Sondra Locke. Barry tries to pack this low-budget effort, shot in San Francisco, with social significance, but Ms Locke has a heavy cross to bear. (From Video Gems as **SUZANNE**)

SECONDS (1966). Multi-tiered John Frankenheimer film, adapted from David Ely's novel by Lewis John

Carlino, is an allegory about our search for identity and a "fresh start," and a whopper of a horror tale, photographed surrealistically by James Wong Howe. A secret organization supplies clients with new identities and faces so they can escape to a new milieu. John Randolph, disillusioned New York banker, emerges from his operation as Rock Hudson. But the "new man" cannot adjust to the artificial world the organization provides and he demands yet another identity. The climax is absolutely shocking; Rock Hudson was never better. Salome Jens, Will Geer, Jeff Corey, Murray Hamilton. A neglected film deserving to be rediscovered.

SECOND SIGHT (1989). Unfunny comedy ripoff of GHOSTBUSTERS, about a detective agency that uses ESP to solve cases. John Larroquette and Stuart Pankin are ordinary PIs who use psi-whacky Bobby McGee (Bronson Pinchot) to find a kidnapped Cardinal. For this goofball premise to work, McGee should be a delightful fruit cake, but as played by Pinchot, he's just plain dumb, performing erratic, wild things. There isn't a single laugh no matter how director Joel Zwick tries to film it. You can only plumb the depths of emptiness when you are bottomed out to start. Bess Armstrong, John Schuck, James Tolkan, William Prince—good actors all—cannot help. (Video/Laser: Warner Bros.)

BRONSON PINCHOT

SECRET AGENT FIREBALL. See **KILLERS ARE CHALLENGED.** (But you won't be challenged!)

SECRET AGENT SUPER DRAGON (1966). Sequel to CODE NAME: JAGUAR is an unimpressive Italian/French/German spy adventure with undercover agent Ray Danton assigned to prevent a mastermind from taking control of Earth with the drug Syncron II. Marisa Mell and Margaret Lee are sexy ladies populating Danton's scrumptious surroundings. Directed by Calvin Jackson Padget. Jess Hahn. (Sinister/C)

SECRET BEYOND THE DOOR (1948). Fritz Lang psychological thriller filled with psychiatric double-talk to cover up incongruities and lapses in Silvia Richards' script about a woman who marries publisher Michael Redgrave and suspects he's a Bluebeard. Joan Bennett is asking for it when she reaches for the knob to the door of the Forbidden Bedroom. The music by Miklos Rozsa provides a lot of what isn't there. And incidentally, there are enough red herrings to open a fish shop. Anne Revere, Paul Cavanagh. (Republic)

SECRET CEREMONY (1969). In a London cemetery, Mia Farrow meets Elizabeth Taylor, a whore putting flowers on the gravestone of her daughter who died ten years earlier. Mia strangely resembles the dead daughter, and damned if the whore doesn't strangely resemble Mia's late mother. Director Joseph Losey blends fantasy and reality along a path that leads to suicide and murder—but can you endure the grimness? Robert Mitchum, Pamela Brown. (Kartes)

SECRET CINEMA, THE (1969). Offbeat short subject directed by Paul Bartel that was later made into a half-hour episode for Spielberg's AMAZING STORIES. A woman (Amy Vane) can't decide if her life is real or she's part of a movie being produced by a crazed producer. Gordon Felio, Connie Ellison. (Rhino)

SECRET GARDEN, THE (1949). Atmospheric, evocative adaptation of Frances Hodgson Burnett's story in which Margaret O'Brien, in her last screen role, portrays a girl who fantasizes a garden outside a country estate as a haven for the abused and sick. The fantasy sequences were shot in Technicolor. Scripted by Robert Ardrey, directed by Fred Wilcox, produced by Clarence Brown. Dean Stockwell, Herbert Marshall, Gladys Cooper, Elsa Lanchester. (MGM/UA)

SECRET LIFE OF WALTER MITTY, THE (1948). Wonderful adaptation of James Thurber's story about a meekish gent who escapes into fantasies, ideally slanted for the comedic talents of Danny Kaye. Mitty, a milquetoast working for a pulp-magazine publisher, fantasizes numerous whimsical adventures, then he's pulled into a real one when he comes in possession of a secret formula which spy Boris Karloff is seeking. Frothily directed by Norman Z. McLeod. Virginia Mayo, Ann Rutherford, Fay Bainter. (Video/Laser: Nelson)

SECRET OF DORIAN GRAY, THE (1971). Absolute cropper . . . Harry Alan Towers' updating of the Oscar Wilde novel, THE PICTURE OF DORIAN GRAY, to satisfy the youth market . . . an Italian-German bomb with writer-director Massimo Dallamano emphasizing the decadence and homosexuality of a young man (Helmut Berger) whose soul is captured in a painting reflecting his aging and sexual debaucheries while he remains vigorously youthful and nocturnally active. Richard Todd, Herbert Lom, Beryl Cunningham. Very, very perverted. (From Republic as **DORIAN GRAY**)

SECRET OF DR. ALUCARD. See **TASTE OF BLOOD, A.**

SECRET OF DR. MABUSE, THE (1964). One of several West German sequels to Fritz Lang's films of the '20s about a mastermind criminal with plans to conquer the world. The mad doctor (Wolfgang Preiss) is a math genius who turns his brilliance to evil with the use of a Death Ray. Peter Van Eyck, Werner Peters, Leo Genn and Yoko Tani drudge drearily through Western Europe, looking like refugees. Directed by Hugo Fregonese. Other entries in this series: THE THOUSAND EYES OF DR. MABUSE, THE RETURN OF DR. MABUSE and DR. MABUSE VS. SCOTLAND YARD.

SECRET OF DR. ORLOFF, THE. See **DR. ORLOFF'S MONSTER.**

SECRET OF MY SUCCESS (1965). Editions 2-3.

SECRET OF NIMH, THE (1982). Splendid adaptation of Robert C. O'Brien's novel about a family of mice seeking a new home and mother mouse searching for mythical characters because a son is sick with pneumonia and needs medicine. A fanciful odyssey with wonderful animal characters, this is stylish, old-fashioned animation by producer-artist Don Bluth. The film was not a big success, perhaps because audiences were asked to accept rats as heroic figures. Too bad . . . the film deserved better with its bursts of vivid imagination. Voices by Elizabeth Hartman, Dom De Luise, Hermione Baddeley, Peter Strauss, Paul Shenar, Derek Jacobi, John Carradine, Aldo Ray. (Video/Laser: MGM/UA)

'NIMH' MOUSE

SECRET OF THE BLACK TRUNK (1962). This West German adaptation of Edgar Wallace's novel DEATH PACKS A SUITCASE depicts a knife killer working over the guests at a Soho hotel. Investigator Joachim Hansen intervenes. (Sinister/C)

SECRET OF THE BLACK WIDOW (1964). Diabolical killer utilizes slugs shaped to resemble black widow spiders as he cuts down his targets one by one, baffling Scotland Yard flatfeet. West German thriller directed by F. J. Gottlieb. O.W. Fischer, Karin Dor, Werner Peters.

SECRET OF THE BLUE ROOM (1933). Kurt Neumann directed this first film version of the tale by Erich

Philippi about a man who dies in a haunted room. (Remakes: MURDER IN THE BLUE ROOM and THE MISSING GUEST.) Standard "old dark house" stuff. Paul Lukas, Onslow Stevens, Lionel Atwill.

SECRET OF THE CHINESE CARNATION, THE (1965). See editions 1-3.

SECRET OF THE LOCH, THE (1934). Diver Seymour Hicks takes a swim in the Scottish loch and discovers an underwater beast—sort of a British Loch Jaws. Directed by Milton Rosmer. Nancy O'Neil, Gibson Gowland. (Nostalgia; Sinister/C; Filmfax)

SECRET OF THE SWORD (1985). Feature spinoff from the animated TV series starring He-Man and She-Ra. He-Man and She-Ra (long-lost brother and sister) join forces to fight off the evil Hordak and his hordes. Voices by John Erwin, Melendy Britt, George DiCenzo. (Magic Window; RCA/Columbia)

SECRET OF THE TELEGIAN (1960). Remove the blood from the body, replace it with electricity and you've got yourself a rechargable monster (sorry, batteries not included). That's one way for Japanese producer Tomoyuki Tanaka to stay "current." The monster is really a man who uses a teleporter device to avenge himself against wartime comrades who betrayed him. Special effects are by Eiji Tsuburaya, who had so much fun moving Godzilla. Socket to them, director Jun Fukuda. Shock them, writer Schinichi Sekizawa. Koji Tsuruta, Akihiko Hirata. (Sinister/C)

SECRET SERVICE IN DARKEST AFRICA. See **MANHUNT IN THE AFRICAN JUNGLE.**

SECRETS OF THE DEATH ROOM. See **LOVE ME DEADLY.** (Step right in, my dear)

SECRETS OF THE FRENCH POLICE (1932). Surely, Shirley, The Surete was surly over this surreal serving. Its real secrets had to be more titillating than those "exposed" here. It's no secret composer Max Steiner's score was the highpoint of this thriller in which a hypnotist uses mirrors to mesmerize a beautiful woman and hides his corpses in plaster . . . of Paris, of course. Odd mixture of routine police work and mad doctor cliches, allegedly based on newspaper articles. Frank Morgan, Julia Gordon, Gregory Ratoff. David O. Selznick produced this creaking curiosity piece.

SECRETS OF THE UNKNOWN. Five-volume video set of the ABC documentary series about unnatural phenomena, including reports on UFOs, the Titanic, the pyramids, Jack the Ripper, dreams, etc. (MPI)

SECRET WITNESS (1931). Killer gorilla is trained to kill for its demented master. Directed by Thornton Freeland. Una Merkel, William Collier Jr., ZaSu Pitts.

SECRET WORLD OF POLLY FLYNT (1987). The Magical World of Another Time, which can only be reached via one's imagination, is visited by Katie Reynolds to escape her loneliness. British TV-movie co-starring Brenda Bruce.

SECT, THE. See **DEVIL'S DAUGHTER (1977).**

SEDUCERS, THE. Video version of **DEATH GAME** (VCI).

SEED OF TERROR. See **GRAVE OF THE VAMPIRE.**

SEEDPEOPLE (1992). Producer Charles Band's video movie borrows heavily from THE INVASION OF THE BODY SNATCHERS for its premise: In Comet Valley, where a meteorite struck centuries before, alien spores scatter to turn folks into hideous killer-monsters with long fangs and terrible-looking mouths covered with drippy slime. The beings change back and forth from monster to human, and when they're humans they are without emotion. Gee, that is familiar. Sam Hennings and Bernard Kates lead the fight to stop the alien takeover in this paranoia thriller flick. Directed by Peter Manoogian. Andrea Roth, Dane Witherspoon, David Dunard, Holly Fields. (Paramount) (Laser: Full Moon)

SEEDS OF EVIL. Video version of **GARDENER, THE** (Unicorn).

SEE NO EVIL (1971). Richard Fleischer's attempt to make a PSYCHO tale: Blind girl Mia Farrow is trapped in a house of corpses and pursued by a killer identified only by his cowboy boots. The macabre touches of Brian Clemens' script have their moments, but shock value is minimal and one wearies of Farrow's pathetic screams and ever-depressing plight. If only these helpless people would learn to lock their doors. Dorothy Allison, Robin Bailey. (RCA/Columbia) (Laser: Image)

SEIZURE (1974). Gore murders galore when a demented writer (Jonathan Frid of DARK SHADOWS) creates characters who spring to life: Martine Beswick is the Queen of Death, Henry Baker plays an executioner and Herve Villechaize is Shorty the Slicer. Director Oliver Stone co-scripted with Edward Mann. Troy Donahue, Mary Woronov. Being that it's Stone's first effort, this is worth seeking out. (Prism; Starmaker)

SENDER, THE (1982). Thought-provoking sophisticated horror film dealing with the psychological traumas of a young man (Zeljko Ivanek) suffering from amnesia. He's placed under the care of psychiatrist Kathryn Harrold, who experiences the mental images of his nightmares. Low-key handling by director Roger Christian and the taut screenplay by Thomas Baum make for a decent shocker. Shirley Knight appears as an apparition (or ghost?) of the boy's domineering mother, who fights Harrold for her son's love. Paul Freeman, Sean Hewitt. (Video/Laser: Paramount)

SENSUOUS VAMPIRES. See **VAMPIRE HOOKERS.**

SENTINEL, THE (1977). Attempt at a classy demonic film in the league of THE OMEN or THE EXORCIST falls short in the hands of director Michael Winner, who allows the climax to deteriorate into a freak sideshow. Too many important events in Jeffrey Konvitz's story are unexplained and characterizations are muddy as a river bottom when fashion model Cristina Raines settles in a New York City brownstone, where priest John Carradine maintains a singular vigil at an upstairs window. One scary sequence has the model confronted with the terrors of her childhood but the film as a whole never jells, this despite a plethora of interesting characters: Eli Wallach as the cop on the case, Ava Gardner as a strange realtor; Sylvia Miles and Beverly D'Angelo as lesbian lovers; Burgess Meredith as a sinister man with a cat; Christopher Walken as Cristina's lover; and Jose Ferrer and Arthur Kennedy as men of the cloth. (MCA)

SERENADE FOR TWO SPIES (1965). See third edition.

SERGEANT DEADHEAD THE ASTRONAUT (1965). Lamebrain American-International excuse for comedy—produced during the "Beach" craze—is strictly for deadheads. Astronaut Frankie Avalon goes into orbit with a chimpanzee. Each returns to Earth with the traits of the other, the chimp plotting rocket trajectories and the astronaut peeling bananas. This throws the military into an uproar. You'll be thrown into a tizzy. Directed by Norman Taurog. Deborah Walley, Cesar Romero, Fred Clark, Buster Keaton.

SERPENT AND THE RAINBOW, THE (1988). Wade Davis is an anthropologist-adventurer who in 1982 went to Haiti in search of a legendary "zombie poison"—a toxic substance that could explain the existence of zombies in the voodoo netherworld. He came back with a sample of a drug (tetrodotoxin) that might explain "voodoo death." This film borrows the concept liberally and turns Davis' quest into a horror tale. Craven, who made the film in Haiti under dangerous conditions, mixes dreams and reality effectively. As long as you understand this is a Hollywood interpretation, and not a literal rendering of Davis' book, watch and enjoy. It has

THE SPIRIT OF DEATH

great visual thrills, a creepy Haitian atmosphere and a superb drum-music soundtrack (by Brad Fiedel) authentic to the island's culture. Bill Pullman, Cathy Tyson, Zakes Mokae, Paul Winfield. (Video/Laser: MCA)

SERPENT ISLAND (1954). Bert I. Gordon's first feature, so impotently produced it was never released to theaters but shown "first-run" on TV. Sonny Tufts and Mary Munday are lovers caught up in a voodoo curse after they are stranded on a Pacific island. Poor acting will evoke a curse from you, too. (Fox Hills; Media)

SERPENT OF DEATH (1990). A cursed statue brings instability into the life of an archeologist. (Prism; Paramount) (Laser: Image)

SERPENT WARRIORS (1986). Eartha Kitt as a snake goddess? Clint Walker as a zoologist? You bet your fangs. An ancient curse by a snake-loving tribe is plaguing a construction site, so Walker, Anne Lockhart and Chris Mitchum fight off wriggling warriors and sinuous slammers. Hundreds of snake extras were needed by director Niels Rasmussen to satisfy Martin Wise's hissing script demands. Coil up and go to sleep.

SERUM. See **DR. BLACK AND MR. HYDE.**

SERVANTS OF TWILIGHT, THE (1991). Chillingly effective variation on THE OMEN theme, in which private eye Bruce Greenwood is hired to protect young Jarrett Lennon and his mother Belinda Bauer from zealots from the Church of Twilight. Led by kooky fanatic Grace Zabriskie, the group believes the boy to be the Antichrist and will stop at nothing to kill him. Although it's a lengthy chase, with ambushes, fistfights and murders, it maintains a strong supernatural flavor thanks to the fine direction of co-producer Jeffrey Obrow and the sharp-edged script by Obrow and Stephen Carpenter, who based it on Dean R. Koontz' novel TWILIGHT. Carel Struycken is effective as one of the religous nuts with homicidal tendencies, and Richard Bradford stands out as one of Greenwood's associates. (Vidmark)

SEVEN BROTHERS MEET DRACULA, THE. Video version of **LEGEND OF THE SEVEN GOLDEN VAMPIRES, THE** (Electric; Media; American).

SEVEN CITIES OF ATLANTIS. See **WARLORDS OF ATLANTIS.**

SEVEN DAYS TO NOON (1950). Gripping doomsday thriller from the British team of John and Roy Boulting in which an atomic researcher (Barry Jones) steals the UR-12 bomb and threatens to blow up London if the Prime Minister doesn't cease bomb production. The City's evacuation is detailed with stark scenes of deserted London landmarks. Meanwhile, Scotland Yard under inspector Andre Morell seeks the professor. Supertense suspense cautionary tale. (J & J)

SEVEN DEADLY SINS, THE (1953). Seven Italian and French directors spin seven vignettes, each dramatizing a provocative sin. Only one episode is touched by fantasy: "Sloth," in which a lazy angel floats to Earth to influence our pedantic pace. Directed by Jean Dreville. Gerard Philipe, Jacqueline Plessis. (Ivy Classics)

SEVEN DEATHS IN THE CAT'S EYE (1972). Italian/French/German production . . . a masterpiece of horror—in a pig's eye! Beastly murders in a European village culminate in new victims in the local castle, allegedly haunted by an old curse involving a killer cat. Meow Owww! Written-directed by Antonio Margheriti (Anthony Dawson). Also known as SEVEN DEAD IN THE CAT'S EYES. Jane Birkin, Anton Diffring. (Prism)

SEVEN DOORS OF DEATH (1983). New Orleans hotel has a subterranean chamber with a door leading to "The Beyond." When opened, the passageway allows walking dead to enter society in this Italian companion piece to GATES OF HELL. Also known as THE BEYOND. Directed by Lucio Fulci. Katherine MacColl, David Warbeck, Sarah Keller. (Thrillervideo)

SEVEN FACES OF DR. LAO (1964). George Pal eggroll captures the Confucius charm of Charles Finney's novel, thanks to most honorable Charles Beaumont script. Tony Randall, playing a Chinese circus owner who turns up in Abalone, Arizona, also essays Merlin the Magician; seer Appolonius of Tyana; Pan; Medusa; the Abominable Snowman; and a mustachioed serpent. Frank Tuttle won an Oscar for his make-up. Unscrupulous businessman Arthur O'Connell is buying up property because a railroad is coming through and things must be set right by the philosophical (but never insidious) Dr. Lao. Barbara Eden, Noah Beery. Jim Danforth provided animation. (Video/Laser: MGM/UA)

SEVEN FOOTPRINTS TO SATAN (1929). See editions 1-3.

SEVEN KEYS TO BALDPATE (1929). First sound version (following two silent ones) of the George M. Cohan play based on an Earl Derr Biggers novel, directed by Reginald Barker. A writer tries to hack out a novel in empty Baldpate Inn but he's harassed by strange visitors and comedic interruptions. This comedy-mystery with overtones of the "old dark house" was made twice more in sound, then converted into a British horror picture, HOUSE OF THE LONG SHADOWS. Richard Dix, Margaret Livingston.

SEVEN KEYS TO BALDPATE (1935). Second talkie version of the Cohan comedy-mystery play, starring Gene Raymond, Eric Blore, Margaret Callahan and Walter Brennan. Directed by William Hamilton and Edward Kelly.

SEVEN KEYS TO BALDPATE (1947). George M. Cohan's stage play was adapted into this, a funny spoof on the "old dark house" genre, with Phillip Terry holing up in a weird house to write a book on a bet. Directed by Lew Landers. Arthur Shields, Jacqueline White.

SEVEN MAGNIFICENT GLADIATORS, THE (1983). Sword-and-sandal remake of SEVEN SAMURAI, but playing more like THE MAGNIFICENT SEVEN, a remake in itself. Bandit leader Dan Vadis, endowed with supernatural powers by his sorceress mother, yearly attacks a village, but the town's women have had enough and, armed with a magical sword, seek a gladiator who can wield it without burning his hands. That warrior is Han (Lou Ferrigno) who joins with Sybil Danning (as a good-natured swordstress) and five other heroes to fight to the death with Vadis. Brad Harris, Carla Ferrigno, Mandy Rice-Davies (one-time prostitute involved in the British Parliament scandals of the 1960s.) Entertaining for its rousing battles and the performance of Danning. Directed by Bruno Mattei. (MCA)

SEVENTH CONTINENT, THE (1968). Editions 1-3.

SEVENTH SEAL, THE (1956). Ingmar Bergman's work is perpetually dark, rampant with heavy symbolism and troubled people. This remains one of his best films, set in the 14th Century when a knight (Max von Sydow), after ten bloody years in the Crusades, pauses for a game of chess with Death on a bleak beach. The burning of a young woman at the stake, the travels of a couple named Mary and Joseph, the disillusionment of people in a time of corrupted Christianity—all are made bawdy, brutal, funny and touching in this Bergman masterpiece. Seal of Approval. (Embassy) (Laser: Criterion)

SEVENTH SIGN, THE (1988). The Bible predicts God will give seven signs to tell us the end is here, that it's time to go out with a bang. In this apocalyptic thriller—a kind of OMEN without the Antichrist—a stranger (Jurgen Prochnov) appears with a parchment in hand, breaks its seal, and drops it to the earth. Dreadful things happen. Such as all the fish in the ocean turn up dead, and an Arab village where Sodom once stood turns to ice. The End of the World is trivialized when average housewife Demi Moore becomes the Seventh Seal, the only thing that can prevent Armageddon. Heaped on that absurdity is the idea that the Roman soldier who refused

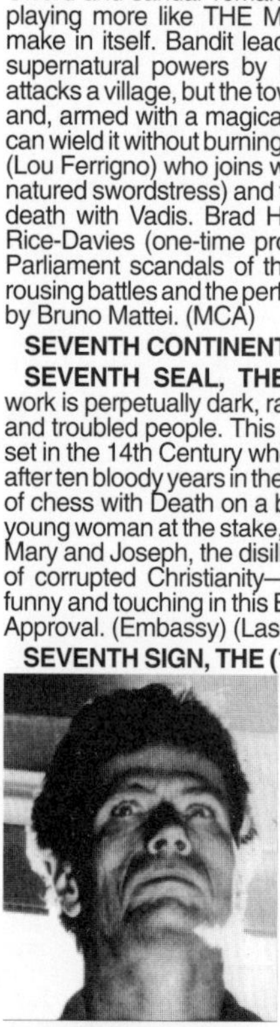

JURGEN PROCHNOV

Christ water on the way to crucifixion has been damned to walk the earth, and is here to make certain the End of the World happens on cue, garbed as a Catholic priest. What the religious symbolism and heavy-handed music from Heaven means could only be explained by Hungarian director Carl Schultz. What makes it all the more appalling is that nobody wanted to make a pseudoreligious turkey. But they did. And got gobbled up. Michael Biehn, Peter Friedman, Manny Jacobs, John Heard. (RCA/Columbia) (Laser: Image)

SEVENTH VEIL, THE (1946). Heavy-handed British melodrama has James Mason maintaining a Svengali control over brilliant pianist Ann Todd, who cannot escape the mesmerizing spell. Strictly for ladies with dry handkerchiefs. Directed tearfully by Compton Bennett. Hugh McDermott, Herbert Lom. (Vidamerica)

SEVENTH VICTIM, THE (1943). Esoteric Val Lewton production for RKO, when he was turning out memorable low-budget horror films. Kim Hunter (in her screen debut) plays a meek student at a strict girls' academy, who ventures to New York City to find her missing sister. Hunter is befriended by a strange private eye who turns up dead on a subway. Then she meets Hugh Beaumont, once married to her sister, who introduces her to an Italian cafe called Dante's, inhabited by disillusioned poets. The sister, acting as one in a trance, is part of a cult worshipping the Devil, and she must die for betraying the cult's code of silence. An allegorical conclusion to the DeWitt Bodeen-Charles O'Neal script has the sister entering a flat with a hangman's rope dangling from the ceiling. Director Mark Robson, in his debut, never compromises the dark pessimism. Tom Conway, Jean Brooks, Isabel Jewell, Evelyn Brent. (RKO)

SEVENTH VOYAGE OF SINBAD, THE (1958). Fruitful collaboration between producer Charles Schneer, director Nathan Juran, writer Kenneth Kolb and stop-motion animator Ray Harryhausen—an enchanting adventure tale, its acting and dialogue appropriately stylized, its creatures often sympathetic and its story capturing the magic of the Arabian Nights. Kerwin Mathews is a robust, romantic Sinbad forced by evil magician Torin Thatcher (he has shrunken princess Kathryn Grant to minuscule size) to seek the egg of a roc on an island dominated by a cyclops. Harryhausen's effects (including an ingenious sword duel with a skeleton) were to improve in subsequent films but the sheer art of his talent is all here: the dancing snake woman, a two-headed roc, a fire-breathing dragon, etc. etc. All beautifully enhanced by Bernard Herrmann's score. An absolute must for fantasophiles. Richard Eyer appears as the genie from "the land beyond beyond." (RCA/Columbia) (Laser: RCA/Columbia; Pioneer)

SEVERED ARM, THE (1973). Sickening revenge yarn in which survivors of a mine cave-in slice off a man's arm for food. In moments they are rescued. Years later the survivors die one by one, each horribly mutilated. In some instances, arms are torn out of their sockets. You'll be revolted. Written-directed by Thomas S. Alderman. Deborah Walley, Marvin Kaplan, John Crawford. (Video Gems)

SEVERED TIES (1991). Produced by the film-making arm of the Fangoria magazine empire, this is about a severed arm. It turns into a lizard-like creature (as part of a regeneration/gene engineering experiment conducted by Billy Morrissette) that scuttles on a pathway to gore and mayhem. Standing out in the cast are Elke Sommer, Oliver Reed and Garrett Morris. Directed by Damon Santostefano, from a script by John Nystrom and Henry Dominic. (Columbia TriStar)

SEX AND THE VAMPIRE (1970). France's Jean Rollin wrote-produced-directed this sexy bloodsucking saga about a couple on a honeymoon dumb enough to stop off in an ancient castle for the night and set upon by vampires. Sandra Julien, Dominique. Aka THE TERROR OF THE VAMPIRES and VAMPIRE THRILLS.

SEX CRIME OF THE CENTURY. See **LAST HOUSE ON THE LEFT, THE.**

SEX DEMONS, THE. See **DEMONS, THE (1972).**

SEX KITTENS GO TO COLLEGE. See **BEAUTY AND THE ROBOT** (but only if you have nine lives).

SEX MACHINE, THE (1975). Italian soft-core porn-comedy set in the next century and purporting the preposterous precept that intercourse and other sexual acts can create an electrical flow, direly needed by mankind because electrical power is no more. Feeble excuse for dumb slapstick and smutty gags without "socially redeeming" values. The film's only amusing sequence comes when a massive orgy is held in a hotel, while in the kitchen a team of scientists note how much voltage is stimulated by copulation, homosexuality, etc. Luigi Proietti, Agostina Belli. Written-directed by Pasquale Festa Campanile. (Media)

SEX MONSTER. See **WRESTLING WOMEN VS. THE AZTEC MUMMY.**

SEX ON THE GROOVE TUBE. See **CASE OF THE FULL MOON MURDERS.SEXORCIST, THE.** See **EERIE MIDNIGHT HORROR SHOW, THE.**

SEX PARTY. See **DEATH ON THE FOUR POSTER.**

SEX VAMPIRES. See **CAGED VIRGINS.**

SEXY CAT (1972). Mysterious killer using horrendously diabolical murder weapons (and in one instance a lethal snake) stalks the cast and crew of a motion picture starring a comic-strip character called Sexy Cat. This Spanish gore thriller was written-produced-directed by Julio Perez Tabernero. Dianik Zurakowska, German Cobos, Lone Fleming. (Telecine Spanish)

SHADEY (1985). Fascinating study in human eccentricities and madness, a parable of good vs. evil told with biting satire. Anthony Sher portrays a garage mechanic who can transfer thoughts onto film. For giving this "talent" to the government, Shadey wants a sex-change operation, but he's betrayed by doctor Billie Whitelaw when his ESP is used by the military. A secondary plot has Shadey involved with financier Patrick Macnee, his daughter (Leslie Ash) and crazy mother (Katherine Helmond). Several acts of violence are effective under Philip Saville's direction, and Sher's performance is a tour de force. The over-the-edge script is by Snoo Wilson. Bernard Hepton, Larry Lamb. (Key)

SHADOW. Variant video version of **TENEBRAE.**

SHADOW, THE (1933). British chiller depicts a hooded figure who behaves like a shadowy substance by flitting through secret passageways of an old mansion, killing inhabitants. Nothing is hiding in the shadows you haven't already seen in this creaky creeper. Directed by George A. Cooper. Elizabeth Allen, Henry Kendall. (Sinister/C; Filmfax)

SHADOW CHASERS (1985). Two-hour TV pilot for a shortlived comedy-supernatural series, created by producer Brian Grazer and director Kenneth Johnson, is an amusing idea blending the humor of GHOSTBUSTERS with the paranormal of TV's SIXTH SENSE. Trevor Eve is a pragmatic professor at Georgetown University teamed with Dennis Dugan, a frivolous tabloid writer who believes in the supernatural. In their first misadventure, they investigate a haunted house where a mysterious fire consumed a man alive. Characters and situations are amusingly developed. Nina Foch is a university scientist giving the team its assignments.

SHADOW DANCING (1988). Ballet dancer Nadine Van der Velde, while rehearsing for MEDUSA, takes on the personality of another dancer. Plenty of dancing, too few shocks. Directed by Lewis Furey. Christopher Plummer portrays the leader of the troupe. James Kee, Gregory Osborne, John Colicos. (SGE) (Laser: Image)

SHADOWHUNTER (1991). Taut chase-action that blends with the supernatural as angst-ridden cop Scott Glenn is assigned to an Arizona Indian reservation to bring back cold-blooded killer Twobear (Benjamin Bratt). Twobear is a "coyote man," a shaman capable of creating "ghost sickness" in enemies, and Glenn undergoes ordeals on a physical and spiritual level as he pursues his quarry across the rugged landscape with Indian guide Angela Alvarado in tow. Writer-director J.S. Cardone (SHADOWZONE) brings an intelligent balance between action and the metaphysical in this above-average thriller. Robert Beltran, Tim Sampson, George Aguilar, Beth Broderick. (Republic)

SHADOWMAN (1973). French TV serial is complete with cliffhangers as supercriminal Jacques Champreux (shaped after Dr. Mabuse) and villainess Gayle Hunnicutt search for a treasure, resurrecting corpses to form a zombie army. Heavily cut for the U.S. Directed by Georges Franju from a Champreux script. Gert Frobe, Josephine Chaplin, Raymond Bussieres. (Cult)

SHADOW OF CHIKARA (1977). What begins as an adventure Western, as Confederate survivors of the last battle of the Civil War set out to find a treasure, shifts into a moody, strange tale of the quasisupernatural. Is a hidden cache of diamonds in a cave watched over by demon hawks or hawk spirits in human form? Writer-producer-director Earl E. Smith fashions his macabre yarn with dandy surprise twists and creepy ambience. Joe Don Baker, Sondra Locke, Ted Neeley, Slim Pickens, John Davis Chandler, Joy Houck Jr. Also known as THE BALLAD OF VIRGIL CANE. (New World; from Mintex as **WISHBONE CUTTER**; from High Desert Films as **THUNDER MOUNTAIN**) (Laser: New World)

SHADOW OF CHINATOWN (1936). Archaic cliffhanger serial with Bela Lugosi as Victor Poten, an insane Eurasian scientist whose racial hatred for Caucasians leads him to slink around Chinatown in a cape, committing murders and hypnotizing innocents with a remote-controlled "You-are-in-my-power" device. Actually, this is clumsily handled by director Robert F. Hill and must have looked old-fashioned even when first released. Released in theatrical form as YELLOW PHANTOM. Dreadful thesping. Herman (Bruce Bennett) Brix, Joan Barclay, Luana Walters, Charles King. (Sinister/C; Nostalgia; Video Connection)

SHADOW OF DEATH. TV title for **BRAINWAVES.**

SHADOW OF EVIL (1966). Made in Bangkok, with Kerwin Mathews as secret agent OSS 117 trying to stop mad doc Robert Hossein and his virulent rats from spreading an epidemic across civilization. Pier Angeli provides love interest. An entry in the French 0SS spy series. Directed-written by Andre Hunnebelle.

SHADOW OF TERROR (1945). See editions 1-3.

SHADOW OF THE CAT, THE (1961). Dead woman's feline wreaks revenge by attacking her killers in this British chiller-diller directed by John Gilling, who cleverly uses his camera to turn an ordinary house cat into a sinister creature. Script by mystery novelist George Baxt. Barbara Shelley, Freda Jackson, Andre Morell.

SHADOW OF THE HAWK (1976). Beautifully photographed supernatural fantasy depicts Canadian Indian Jan-Michael Vincent exorcising a 200-year-old evil spirit. Chief Dan George is the ancient shaman whose sad dignity is touched by "bad medicine," Marilyn Hassett is a reporter. Directed by George McGowan.

SHADOW OF THE WEREWOLF. See **WEREWOLF VS. THE VAMPIRE WOMEN, THE.**

SHADOW ON THE LAND (1968). See editions 1-3.

SHADOW PLAY (1986). Super-boring probe of the supernatural, too ethereal and literate to play well as a horror film—it's all talk and too little action when playwright Dee Wallace-Stone suffers writer's block and hibernates on Ocra's Island, where she sees the spectre of a man who died by falling from a lighthouse. She becomes obsessed with him, writing poetry in his style and going hysterical between play rehearsals. Wallace-Stone and Cloris Leachman strive to make something of this well-intended portrait of obsession, but writer-director Susan Shabourne doesn't have enough intriguing material to jolt the story from its comatose state. When one of the characters remarks, "There's more life in the dead than the living around here," you want to shout back "You said it, sis." Ron Kuhlman, Delia Salvi, Barry Laws. (New World)

SHADOWS IN THE NIGHT (1944). See editions 1-3.

SHADOWS RUN BLACK (1984). Bouncing naked titties, bare asses and other female anatomy men generally find provocative are the most intriguing features in this drearily directed slasher-whodunit in which a serial killer, "The Black Angel," murders sexy co-eds. Chief suspect is Kevin Costner in an uncredited role. It's nothing his fans would want to bother seeing. Meanwhile there's plenty of pubic hair from a frontal view as the killer in a black jumpsuit and mask murders cuties, always when they just happen to be undressed. The dialogue is cliched and vacuous, the killer's motive is pure baloney and director Howard Heard is stuck with a cast as dreary as the locations. William J. Kulzer, Shea Porter, George J. Engelson. (Lightning)

SHADOW WORLD (1983). Animated juvenile space action in which a fair-haired lad of the galaxy saves our star system from invaders. Routine. (Media; Hi-Tops)

SHADOWZONE (1989). "Scientific horror" best describes this Charles Band production which blends bits of ALIEN, THE THING and DREAMSCAPE to spin its claustrophobia nightmare. Investigating officer David Beecroft arrives at an underground lab where Operation Shadowzone is under way: experiments in extended deep sleep, as part of a space program. But the subconscious mind of a subject (big-breasted Maureen Flaherty) opens a portal to another dimension and a monster (code name: John Doe) slips in—one that assumes shapes and identities. The lab personnel (Cutter the obese cook, Shivers the jittery maintenance man, Kidwell the beautiful technician, Von Fleet the Asian scientist) are soon stalked by the shape-changing creature. Louise Fletcher, always rubbing chapstick on her lips, becomes the key to reopening the dimension-portal. Good script by director J. S. Cardone has surprise twists. James Hong, Shawn Weatherly, Miguel Nunez, Lu Leonard. (Paramount) (Laser: Full Moon)

SHAGGY D.A., THE (1976). Sequel to Disney's THE SHAGGY DOG is missing its original cast, but it does have the original scarab ring, once owned by the Borgia family, inscribed with the Latin phrase "Intra Kapori Transmuto." This is the device that turns lawyer Dean Jones into a Bratislavian sheep dog capable of speech and thought, and it happens at a bad time since Jones is running for D.A. against crooked Keenan Wynn. Directed by Robert Stevenson. Tim Conway, Suzanne Pleshette, Vic Tayback, Jo Anne Worley. (Disney)

SHAGGY DOG, THE (1959). Scarab ring of the Borgias, combined with the proper incantation, turns the son of mailman Fred MacMurray into a Bratislavian sheep dog—at the most embarrasing moments. Endearing Disney comedy, capturing the nostalgia of a Saturday matinee. A frustrated policeman ("Follow that dog!") and spies add to this fluffy innocuousness directed by Charles Barton. Tommy Kirk, Jean Hagen, Annette Funicello. (Video/Laser: Disney)

SHAKER RUN (1985). Although there's a science-horror theme that sets this New Zealand film into motion (deadly virus is sought by the military), this is mainly car chases and action sequences that go on too long. Director Bruce Morrison doesn't know when to slow down. Peter Weller, Sam Elliott, Antonio Fargas, Blanche Baker. (Video/Laser: Embassy/Nelson)

SHAKMA (1990). In Roddy McDowall's research lab, experiments with a baboon result in a berserk creature named Shakma, who escapes during a "Dungeons and Dragons" game called Nemesis, played by immature scientists in a closed-off highrise. It becomes a different game when Shakma attacks and kills the participants in gory cat-and-mouse situations. The only unusual thing about Robert Engle's script, besides substituting a baboon for a slasher-killer, is that the heroines don't come out of the horror situation as well as you might suspect. Christopher Atkins finally faces the hairy onslaught one-on-one. Co-directed by producer Hugh Parks and Tom Logan. Amanda Wyss, Ari Meyers, Robb Morris, Greg Flowers. (Quest)

SHALLOW GRAVE (1987). Frustrating, unresolved suspense thriller that owes its allegiance to Alfred Hitchcock. In addition to parodying the PSYCHO shower sequence (which has no business in this movie), it borrows its premise from the innocent-person-caught-up-in-mysterious-circumstances genre. Four teenage students driving to Florida are caught up in the murder of a waitress. Innocent, trying to convince others of the truth, the girls die one by one. It's disturbing when evil wins and a movie ends before it should. This has decent acting and camera work but screenwriter-producer George E. Fernandez digs a deep grave for himself. Directed by Richard Styles. Tony March, Tom Law, Lisa Stahl. (Prism)

SHAMAN, THE (1987). Family is haunted by the spirit of an evil medicine man. Directed by Michael Yakub. Michael Conforti, Elvind Harum. (Imperial)

SHAME OF THE JUNGLE (1975). French-Belgian animated feature which spoofs Edgar Rice Burrough's Tarzan with sci-fi elements thrown in. Voices by Bill Murray, John Belushi, Johnny Weissmuller Jr. Directed by French animator Picha and Boris Szulzinger. (JEF Films)

SHANKS (1974). Singularly offbeat William Castle production (he also directed the Ranald Graham script) starring French mime Marcel Marceau as an insane puppeteer who controls the dead. Given only limited distribution; most critics deemed this a failure. Marceau fans may want to see his first effort of straight dramatic acting; otherwise, of marginal interest. Tsilla Chelton, Philippe Clay, Cindy Eilbacher.

SHARAD OF ATLANTIS (1936). Re-edited feature version of the Republic serial **UNDERSEA KINGDOM.**

SHARK. See **GREAT WHITE, THE.**

SHARON'S BABY. See **DEVIL WITHIN HER, THE.**

SHATTERBRAIN. See **RESURRECTED, THE.**

SHATTERED SILENCE. See **WHEN MICHAEL CALLS.**

SHE (1925). Silent version of H. Rider Haggard's classic novel. Directed by Leander D. Cordova. Betty Blythe, Carlysle Clackwell. (Video Yesteryear; Nostalgia)

SHE (1935). Merian C. Cooper, co-director of KING KONG, produced this version of H. Rider Haggard's novel, with stage actress Helen Gahagan in her only screen role. Unlike the original, set in Egypt, this takes place in the icy Himalayas, where within a Siberian mountain explorers discover a lost kingdom, Kor, ruled by a 500-year-old queen who believes one of the adventurers to be the reincarnation of her former lover. Directed by Irving Pichel and Lansing C. Holden. Max Steiner's eerie score is a major contribution to the fantasy genre. Nigel Bruce, Noble Johnson.

SHE (1965). Hammer's version of the Haggard fantasy novel set in the kingdom of Kuma is the second sound attempt. The problem here seems to be not the set design or costuming—they are exquisite. It is the mundane script by David T. Chantler which relies on "lost city" cliches. For those bored by reincarnation, or by the stereotyped performances of Peter Cushing, John Richardson and Christopher Lee, there are the garments of Ursula Andress (as Ayesha) and Rosenda Monteros, so flimsy as to require excessive scrutiny. Thus the all-important question becomes: Are those shapely wenches wearing anything underneath their Frederick's of Hollywood attire? Directed by Robert Day, produced by Michael Carreras. Bernard Cribbins, Andre Morell. (The loose sequel was VENGEANCE OF SHE.)

S*H*E (1979). Cornelia Sharp is caught up in Bond Age adventure as she sets out, as an agent for Securities Hazards Expert, to prevent a dastardly villain from taking over the world's oil supply. Action-packed 007-like exploits of daring-do. Directed by Robert Lewis from a TV script by Richard Maibaum. Robert Lansing, William Taylor, Isabella Rye, Anita Ekberg, Omar Sharif. (Prism)

SHE (1982). Sandahl Bergman portrays the ruler of a lost kingdom, but this Italian film strays markedly from Haggard's novel, incorporating parody and sci-fi to create a hybrid. In this city of the Urech people, the ruler can levitate his enemies, and mutants can clone themselves each time an arm falls off. Writer-director Avi Nesher (an Israeli) has written a black-comedy adventure of anachronisms. David Goss, Quin Kessler, Harrison Muller, Gordon Mitchell. (Vestron; Lightning)

SHE BEAST (1965). One of the few works of director Mike Reeves, who attracted a cult following after his premature death in 1968 of a drug overdose. Originally made as THE REVENGE OF THE BLOOD BEAST, and later known as SATAN'S SISTER, this stars Barbara Steele as a woman possessed by an ancient witch. She goes on a murderous rampage, while husband Ian Ogilvy searches Transylvania for her. The rampage allows Reeves some interesting juxtaposing of images. He was working with a limited budget (and not the greatest script by Michael Byron) yet he brings it off well. (Gorgon; Rhino; S/Weird; Filmfax; MPI)

SHE CREATURE, THE (1956). Chester Morris prowls California beaches in a black homberg as a hypnotist, the Great Lombardi, who puts the whammy on sexy Marla English. Forcing her soul back to prehistoric times, she emerges from the waves covered with unattractive appendages, carrying out Morris' evil bidding with slashing deaths. American-International release was produced by Alex Gordon, directed by Edward L. Cahn. Tom Conway, Cathy Downs, Ron Randell. Remade as CREATURE OF DESTRUCTION.

SHE DEMONS (1958). Ludicrous, grade-Z Arthur Jacobs abomination suffering from diarrhea of the jungle. Whip-cracking sadistic Nazis dominate a Pacific island where a fiendish doctor strips the beauty off assorted lasses and tries to transfer their good looks to his ugly frau. You'll need a sense of humor to sit through this. Richard E. Cunha directed, if you can call it directing, and co-wrote the script with H.E. Barrie, if you can call it writing. One historical highlight is Irish McCalla as a shipwrecked traveler—that same year she appeared on TV as Sheena the jungle girl. Tod Griffin, Victor Sen Young, Gene Roth. (Media; Rhino; VCI; Sinister/C)

SHE DEVIL (1957). Immaterial fantasy thriller, produced-directed by Kurt Neumann, and written by Neumann and Carroll Young, doesn't even adequately exploit the shapely body of Mari Blanchard, and any resemblance to Stanley Weinbaum's famous story, "The Adaptive Ultimate," is coincidential. The wonderful Ms Blanchard, one of the sexiest actresses of the 1950s, is able through serum injections to adapt herself as she rushes around inexpensive Fox soundstage sets murdering. Jack Kelly, Albert Dekker, John Archer.

SHE-DEVILS ON WHEELS (1968). Motorcycle gore movie, full of dismemberings and bloodlettings. The "mean mothers" are exactly that—women who perform sadistic acts against males. Produced-directed by Herschell Gordon Lewis. Betty Connell, Pat Poston, Nancy Lee Noble. (VCI; Western World)

SHEENA—QUEEN OF THE JUNGLE (1984). The major mistake in bringing the comic-book "Queen of the Jungle" to the screen was to present her as a naive innocent rather than as a hip modern woman. Thus, as sexy as she may be in her leopard skins, Tanya Roberts doesn't convince. Instead, writers David Newman, Leslie Stevens and Lorenzo Semple Jr., spinning off from the character created by Will Eisner and S. M. Eiger in the '30s, concoct a campy adventure which John Guillermin directs with a straight face. Ted Wass and Donovan Scott are newsreel cameramen in Tigorda (an African kingdom) involved in political intrigue and picturesque adventures with Sheena, who bounces along (in more places than one) on a horse painted like a zebra. It becomes a chase with soldiers, trucks, helicopters and other gimmicks. Sheena can talk to the animals and has mystical powers as the silly story unfolds. If you can get into the spirit, you might have fun watching this turkey. Elizabeth of Toro co-stars. (RCA/Columbia; Goodtimes) (Laser: RCA/Columbia)

SHE-FREAK (1967). Exploitation of circus freaks in the style of Tod Browning's FREAKS but without a sense of taste or sympathy for those short-changed by nature. A terrible misuse of the malshaped and malformed by producer-writer David F. Friedman and director Byron

Mabe. SHE-FREAK is she-weak. (Magnum)

SHE MONSTER OF THE NIGHT. See **FRANKENSTEIN'S DAUGHTER.**

SHERIFF AND THE SATELLITE KID, THE (1979). Cary Guffey is an alien humanoid fallen to Earth who meets up with a Spaghetti Western-style lawman (Bud Spencer) in this Italian comedy-drama. Joe Bugner.

SHERLOCK HOLMES AND SAUCY JACK. See **MURDER BY DECREE.**

SHERLOCK HOLMES AND THE MASKS OF DEATH. See **MASKS OF DEATH.**

SHERLOCK HOLMES AND THE SPIDER WOMAN (1944). Fictional spiders from the upper reaches of an African river are employed on an eight-legged basis to bite victims for that wonderful "spider woman," Gale Sondergaard. This murderess-seductress almost outwits the Baker Street sleuth and his loveable companion, Dr. Watson. One of the best films in the Universal series to star Basil Rathbone and Nigel Bruce, with wonderful interplay between Rathbone and Sondergaard and good scenes involving Angelo Rossitto as a midget who helps the spiders along the walkways. (Sondergaard returned in an inferior psuedosequel without Holmes, THE SPIDER WOMAN STRIKES BACK.) Produced-directed by Roy William Neill.

SHERLOCK HOLMES IN CARACAS (1992). The sleuth of Baker Street (Jean Manuel Montesinos) and Dr. Watson (Gilbert Dacournan) find a vampire and pagan cult afoot in this satirical, rather than serious homage to Arthur Conan Doyle. Venezuelan production (in English) directed-written by co-producer Juan Fresan. Carolina Luzardo, Maria Eugenia Cruz.

SHERLOCK HOLMES IN THE BASKERVILLE CURSE (1985). Undistinguished British cartoon feature, its only interesting element being the voice of Peter O'Toole as Holmes. It's Sir Arthur Conan Doyle's HOUND OF THE BASKERVILLES in simplified form—and a waste of time.

SHERLOCK HOLMES: MURDER BY DECREE. See **MURDER BY DECREE.**

SHER MOUNTAIN KILLINGS MYSTERY (1990). See **CURSED MOUNTAIN MYSTERY, THE.**

SHE'S BACK (1989). Carrie Fisher plays a Queens housewife murdered by robbers who returns from the dead. But only husband Robert Joy sees her as she encourages him to get revenge. (Sound a little like GHOST?) Directed by Tim Kincaid. Matthew Cowles, Sam Coppola. (Vestron) (Laser: Image)

SHE WAITS (1972). Unimpressive supernatural TV-movie with Patty Duke possessed by the ghost of David McCallum's first wife (Dorothy McGuire). Lots of talk, few thrills. Produced-directed by Delbert Mann. Beulah Bondi, Lew Ayres, Nelson Olmstead. (Prism)

SHE WAS A HIPPIE VAMPIRE. See **WILD WORLD OF BATWOMAN, THE** (She shoots from the hip!).

SHE WOLF. Video version of **LEGEND OF THE WOLF WOMAN** (VBG).

SHE-WOLF OF LONDON (1946). June Lockhart dreams about hideous murders in Hyde Park and imagines the Allenby Curse has turned her into a hairy monster. There's psychiatric double talk and ample dark photography but the script by George Bricker will neither frighten nor fool any really intelligent she-wolves. Directed by Jean Yarbrough. Don Porter, Lloyd Corrigan.

SHINBONE ALLEY (1971). Delightful cartoon version of Don Marquis' "archy and mehitabel" stories, in which a poet who writes in a free-verse style is reincarnated as a cockroach and jumps from typewriter key to typewriter key to write his material (hence no capital letters). Quaint and entertaining. Voices by Carol Channing, Eddie Bracken, John Carradine, Alan Reed. (Simitar; Kartes; Video Gems)

SHINING, THE (1980). Stanley Kubrick's uneven adaptation of Stephen King's best-seller set in The Overview, a haunted hotel in the Rockies, and a boy with powers of telepathy and prophecy. Kubrick's camera is fluid and there are brilliant sequences: Jack Torrance (Jack Nicholson) and family haunted by a moldy corpse; wife Shelley Duvall discovering a weird manuscript by her husband; a chase through a hedgerow maze; Torrance meeting ghostly bartender Joseph Turkel; and the deterioration of Torrance as he chases his wife with an axe. But director Kubrick and co-writer Diane Johnson have erringly and frequently deviated from King's masterful plot and neglected important exposition; scenes are enigmatic and frustrating when they should be thrilling and enlightening. Scatman Crothers plays the Negro who, like Torrance's son, has "the shining," but it's another misinterpreted role. (Warner Bros.; RCA/Columbia) (Laser: Warner Bros.)

SHIP OF ZOMBIES. See **HORROR OF THE ZOMBIES.**

SHIRLEY THOMPSON VS. THE ALIENS (1972). Australian sci-fi about invading aliens has as much bounce as a kangaroo with two broken legs. A statue of the Duke of Edinburgh comes to life as a way of aliens communicating with earthlings but the film never comes to life. Should be put outback and down under and kept there. And good day to you too, Shirley Thompson. The producer-directorco-writer was Jim Sharman, who made THE ROCKY HORROR PICTURE SHOW. Jane Harders (as Shirley), John Likoxitch, Helmut Bakaitis.

SHIVERS. See **THEY CAME FROM WITHIN.**

SHOCK (1946). Nifty suspense thriller is frugal on budget but frenetic on technique when psychiatrist Vincent Price murders his wife, unaware a young woman has seen the ghastly crime and gone into shock. When he finds out she knows too much, he and his nurse set out to keep her quiet by using drugs and hypnosis. Lynn Bari, Reed Hadley, Anabel Shaw, Frank Latimore, Charles Trowbridge. (Kartes; Cable; Sinister/C; Filmfax)

SHOCK. See **BEYOND THE DOOR II.**

SHOCK CHAMBER (1985). Canadian TV-movie, a trilogy of tales with ironic endings. A mother tells a magazine writer about her three sons: In "Symbol of Victory," a teener tries out a love potion; in "Country Hospitality" a waitress in a greasy spoon poisons a kidnapper, then plans to doublecross her accomplices; in "The Injection" two brothers plan an insurance ripoff by feigning death. The latter has the best twist, but the whole thing is cheaply shot on videotape and the "surprises" have been done before. Doug Stone appears in all episodes. Karen Cannata, Bill Boyle, Bill Zagot. (Vector)

SHOCK 'EM DEAD (1990). Repugnant, horribly acted horror film depicting a nerd (Stephen Quadros) losing his job in a pizza parlor and striking up a deal with voodoo woman Tyger Soope—his soul for a chance to be a great rock 'n roll musician. Only problem is, he has to kill with magical daggers as a source of energy to stay alive. This stupid premise, concocted by director Mark Freed with writers David Tedder and Andrew Cross, makes for one insufferable movie that will shock no one, so incompetent are its effects and bloodletting. Its emptiness only makes the appearances of Traci Lords (as the group manager), Troy Donahue (as the rock promoter) and Aldo Ray (as the pizza parlor owner) all the more pathetic. Tim Moffet, Gina Parks. (Academy) (Laser: Image)

SHOCKER (1989). Writer-director Wes Craven creates a new variation on Freddy Krueger through The Family Killer—a wisecracking ugly guy named Horace Pinker who terrorizes a city as a serial murderer. Pinker is too unappealing and doesn't have the campiness of Freddy as he is propelled through horrific adventures that turn into outright parody, in sharp contrast to sincere attempts to terrify. Craven also borrows the device of the dream (as in NIGHTMARE ON ELM STREET, pick any number) to provide impetus—in this case Peter Berg dreams of Pinker and where he's committing crimes, so Berg and his policeman father (Michael Murphy) can track him. Pinker is electrocuted, but he's made a deal with the evil Gods of TV and passes in and out of TV screens at will. Mitch Pileggi, Cami Cooper, Richard Brooks, Theodore Raimi, John Tesh, Dr. Timothy Leary. (Video/Laser: MCA)

SHOCK! SHOCK! SHOCK! (1988). Outright spoof of horror and sci-fi schlock from directors Todd Rutt and Arn McConnell, involving aliens from space and a knife murderer. Brad Isaac, Cyndy McCrossen. (Rhino)

SHOCK (TRANSFER SUSPENSE HYPNOS). See **BEYOND THE DOOR II.**

SHOCK TREATMENT (1973). Also known as DOCTOR IN THE NUDE, this French-Italian film focuses on physicians at a rejuvenation center who discover a formula to prevent aging, but several youths are murdered for their blood and organs before the diabolical plot is squelched. Written-directed by Alain Jessua. Alain Delon, Annie Girardot, Michel Duchaussoy, Robert Hirsch.

SHOCK WAVES (1970). Low-budget horror favorite with SS officer Peter Cushing creating an underwater corps of Aryan zombies, who rise from the depths as blond figures wearing goggles. Brooke Adams ends up on Cushing's Nazi-happy island after surviving the sinking of a yacht captained by John Carradine. Directed by Ken Wiederhorn, who co-wrote with John Harrison and Ken Pare. Jay Maeder, Luke Halpin. Also known as DEATH CORPS and ALMOST HUMAN. (Prism; Starmaker; American)

SHOES OF THE FISHERMAN (1968). Didactic political-religious fantasy set in the near future when a Russian archbishop, after many years in a Siberian labor camp, is appointed Pope. A famine crisis arises in Red China, and when it appears the Chinese are about to use the atomic bomb, the Pope makes an announcement that shocks the Catholic Church. Oversimplification of complex issues make this pretty hard to swallow. Directed by Michael Anderson. Anthony Quinn, Oskar Werner, Vittorio De Sica, John Gielgud, Rosemary Dexter, Burt Kwouk, Clive Revill, Laurence Olivier, David Janssen. (Video/Laser: MGM/UA)

SHOGUN ASSASSIN (1980). Americanized version of Japan's "Baby Cart" samurai series, depicting Lone Wolf, a freelance killer who travels to and from his bloody assignments with his five-year-old son Kuroso riding in a wooden cart equipped with knives. Two films in the series were re-edited down to one by U.S. producers David Weisman and Robert Houston, and a new soundtrack added. The result is a bizarre, mystical action film, with gallons of spurting gore as Lone Wolf's magical sword kills ninja by the hundreds. There are moments when Lone Wolf seems to be possessed by prophetic visions and a sense of superhearing. Anyway, it's weird (what with that little kid narrating the story) and worth a look. (Pioneer Artists; MCA) (Laser: MCA)

SHOGUN WARRIORS: GRANDIZER (1982). Japanese animated cartoon in the STAR WARS vein. Other films in this series: SHOGUN WARRIORS: GAIKING; SHOGUN WARRIORS: SPACEKETEERS; SHOGUN WARRIORS: STARVENGERS.

SHORT CIRCUIT (1986). Sparkling comedy with cute touches, a spoof on hardware movies starring Robot #5, designed by Syd Mead and activated by Eric Allard. #5, the cutest damn robot in any movie, is part of a line of laser-equipped metal warriors called Saints, created by scientist Steve Guttenberg, who works for Nova Laboratories. During a lightning storm, #5 takes on human characteristics and is befriended by Ally Sheedy. Afraid of being dismantled, #5 flees into madcap, hilarous misadventures during which he is inspired by John Wayne, the Three Stooges and John Travolta, among others. Wonderfully directed by John Badham from the script by S.S. Wilson and Brent Maddock. Don't miss it. (Video/Laser: CBS/Fox)

SHORT CIRCUIT 2 (1988). This sequel to the wonderful SHORT CIRCUIT again presents the amusing Johnny-Five robot, but cannot sustain the charm of the original. This time #5 (with the darling voice of Tim Blaney) turns up in the big city where he helps Fisher Stevens (as the malapropism-speaking Ben Jahrvi) and con man Michael McLean mass produce a slew of tiny Johnny-Fives for toy marketer Cynthia Gibb. Along the way the gullible J-5 is misused by crook Jack Weston for a bank heist, flies through the sky on a hang-glider and helps street crooks rip off car stereos. Kids will love its action scenes and morality lessons, but the film ultimately becomes an endurance test. Directed by Kenneth Johnson, written by J-5's originators, S.S. Wilson and Brent Maddock. (RCA/Columbia) (Laser: Image)

SHORT STORIES OF TERROR. See **MASTER OF HORROR.**

SHOT IN THE DARK, A (1935). Old-fashioned murder mystery thriller in the "old dark house" tradition. A shrouded figure flits through the mansion, using an unusual weapon to carry out his murders. Directed by Charles Lamont. Charles Starret, Robert Warwick, Edward Van Sloan. (Sinister/C; Filmfax)

SHOUT, THE (1978). Thinking man's horror film, based on a story by Robert Graves and directed by Jerzy Skolimowski, who explores in fascinating style the concept that a man can kill by the tone of his voice. Thoughtful and literate. Alan Bates, Susannah York, John Hurt, Tim Curry, Robert Stephens. (Vidamerica; RCA/Columbia; Embassy)

SHREDDER ORPHEUS (1989). A TV signal beamed from Hell is destroying people on Earth who have survived the Apocalypse and are living in The Grey Zone. As if the world wasn't already in bad enough shape, society is now controlled by TV stations that specialize in punk rock. Written-directed by Robert McGinley, who also stars as band leader Orpheus. Stephen J. Bernstein, Megan Murphy. (Action International)

SHRIEKING, THE (1974). Filmed in the hills of South Dakota as HEX, this oddball movie offers many promises but fails to pay off. Keith Carradine, Gary Busey and Scott Glenn portray well-decorated World War I aviation heroes traveling on motorcycles (the first bikers' gang?), searching for whatever the Lost Generation searched for in those days. They meet sexy sisters who appear to be witches—at least one of them sews shut the mouth of a frog. Nothing is made explicit by screenwriters Leo Garen (also the director) and Steve Katz. There's absolutely zero excitement as this fizzles out. Hilarie Thompson, Dan Haggerty, Robert Walker. (Prism) (Laser: Image)

SHRIEK OF THE MUTILATED (1974). Amateurish low budgeter in which a peculiar Dr. Prell (Alan Brock), alleged to be the survivor of an expedition in search of the legendary Yeti, returns to Boot Island with researchers. They are murdered one by one by a creature in a white suit. Also involved is a crazy mute Indian named Laughing Crow and a cannibal-devil cult and the worst acting you've ever seen. The real shrieks came from mentally mutilated theater patrons who wanted their money back after exposure to this bad cheapie. Jennifer Stock, Tawn Ellis, Michael Harris. Directed by Mike Findlay. (Lightning; Live)

SHRINKING CORPSE. See **CAULDRON OF BLOOD.**

SH! THE OCTOPUS (1938). See editions 1-3.

" . . . A sadist, one of the most disruptive elements in human society. To have complete mastery over another, to make him a helpless object, to humiliate him, to enslave, to inflict moral insanity on the innocent."

—The Narrator in **THE SADIST**

SHUDDER. See **KISS OF THE TARANTULA.**

SHUTTERED ROOM, THE (1966). Unfaithful version of a novelette by H. P. Lovecraft and August Derleth. That was a good horror story—this is just a horror. After so many horrendous murders, performed by something locked up in a weird house, it is utterly impossible to swallow the explanation offered about what is hiding in the shuttered room. This "monster" would have a difficult time kicking sand into the face of a 90-pound weakling, let alone throttling half the cast. A waste of Gig Young, Carol Lynley, Oliver Reed, Flora Robson and Bernard Kay. Directed by David Greene. (From Ace as **BLOOD ISLAND**)

SIGN OF THE FOUR (1982). British TV version of the Sherlock Holmes novel by Conan Doyle has Ian Richardson as a breathless Holmes and David Healy as a keen-eyed Watson. Where the Charles Edward Pogue teleplay falters is in showing the mystery rather than telling it from Holmes' viewpoint. Hence, little suspense and few surprises. Holmes and Watson are tracking the Great Mogul, the world's second largest diamond. Directed stylishly by Desmond Davis.

SIGN OF THE VAMPIRE, THE. See **HERITAGE OF DRACULA, THE.**

SILENCE OF THE LAMBS, THE (1991). Dynamite adaptation of Thomas Harris' novel (by Ted Tally) about an FBI woman's efforts to track down the serial killer Buffalo Bill—the nickname he's earned by skinning his victims. Helping her is imprisoned serial murderer Dr. Hannibal Lecter, who eats his victims. Lecter becomes one of the screen's most electrifying fiends thanks to Anthony Hopkins. Under Jonathan Demme's direction, this is a masterful blend of psychological horror and physical violence. "Hannibal the Cannibal," incidentally, appeared in Thomas' novel RED DRAGON, which was produced by Michael Mann in 1986. Jodie Foster is great as FBI agent Clarice Starling; the drama between her and Hannibal is unforgettable. Scott Glenn, Ted Levine, Anthony Heald, Brooke Smith, Diane Baker. Roger Corman and George Romero appear in cameos. (Orion) (Laser: Orion/Image)

SILENCERS, THE (1966). First in the Matt Helm series (the others: MURDERERS' ROW, THE AMBUSHERS, THE WRECKING CREW) stars Dean Martin as Donald Hamilton's superspy, intended as a high-class Bond imitation, but bargain basement with cheap gadgets and a madman-plans-to-conquer-world plot. Villain Victor Buono behaves like an angry grandfather; Martin behaves as though he lost interest in acting after THE YOUNG LIONS. Under Phil Karlson's direction it's clumsy and leering, but the women are great: Stella Stevens, Daliah Lavi, Nancy Kovack, Cyd Charisse, Beverly Adams. (RCA/Columbia)

SILENT DEATH. See **VOODOO ISLAND.**

SILENT MADNESS (1983). Unsavory slasher thriller with COMA-like subplot as Belinda Montgomery, deserving of better material, portrays a nurse in Cresthaven Mental Hospital who discovers that through a computer error a homicidal maniac (who committed the "Sorority Slaughter") was released by mistake. Montgomery tracks the killer (Solly Marx), who is murdering with sledgehammer, drill press, vice, crowbar and whatever device is handy. Meanwhile, sinister doctors at the hospital dispatch their own killers to clean up mistakes. Director Simon Nuchtern handles action sequences clumsily, and gore effects are minimal (or edited from the TV prints, which are poorly scanned off the 'scope original). Sharp instruments are always being thrust at the camera because this was shot in grainy 3-D. Viveca Lindfors, Sydney Lassick. (Media)

SILENT NIGHT, BLOODY NIGHT (1973). Gory thriller as chopped up as the victims of an axe murderer taking revenge on those responsible for an insane asylum revolt that resulted in the death of doctors and personnel. The story gets further chopped up by censors during flashbacks. First released as NIGHT OF THE DARK FULL MOON, this was directed by Theodore Gershuny. Patrick O'Neal, John Carradine, James Patterson and Walter Abel look cut to the quick by the quick cuts. (Paragon)

SILENT NIGHT, DEADLY NIGHT (1984). Controversial (when released) bloodthirsty slasher flick about a killer in a Santa Claus suit. Controversy also flowed from its less-than-lovely portrait of a Catholic school for orphans, operated by a starkly stern Mother Superior who delights in sadistic spankings. All that aside, it's a slasher-genre entry, undeserving of attention. A shallow psychological history of the murderer is presented when, as a youngster, he watches his mother and father being murdered on Christmas Eve by a Santa Claus lookalike. He grows into a tall, muscular teen-ager (Robert Brian Wilson) who thinks Santa punishes those who aren't good during the year. When he's forced to don a St. Nicholas outfit by his boss, he's primed for a rampage of yuletime destruction: a beheading, an impaling and assorted axe penetrations. Directed by Charles E. Sellier. Lilyan Chauvan, Toni Nero, Danny Wagner. (Paragon; USA) (Laser: Image)

SILENT NIGHT, DEADLY NIGHT PART II (1986). Anyone who saw the first entry in this slasher series about a killer in a Santa Claus suit will feel ripped off watching the first half of this sequel: Most of it is footage from the original as the killer's brother, locked up in an asylum, tells his family history in flashback to a headshrinker. Viewers will feel ripped off watching the second half as the brother begins killing. There's a reprehensible sequence in which he walks down a suburban street, killing residents with a pistol, and other sickening crimes while clad as St. Nick, including an attack on a deformed nun. Director/editor Lee Harvey succeeds in making this one of the most mean-spirited slasher films ever made. Eric Freeman, James L. Newman, Elizabeth Cayton. (IVE) (Laser: Image)

SILENT NIGHT, DEADLY NIGHT III: BETTER WATCH OUT! (1989). Third entry in the once-controversial Santa Claus killer series is an improvement over the wretched second entry, but . . . it's okay to pout because this is still a tedious affair that parades out every cliche, without panache or energy. What's equally depressing: it was directed by Monte Hellman (TWO-LANE BLACKTOP). The plot (by Carlos Laszlo, Helmann and producer Richard Gladstein) concerns a blind woman (Samantha Scully) psychically linked to the Santa Claus killer (played without menace by Bill Moseley), who has been restored to life by mad scientist Richard Beymer. Not even the refreshing Robert Culp can bring much vitality to his cop role. Eric Da Re, Laura Herring, Elizabeth Hoffman. (IVE) (Laser: Image)

SILENT NIGHT, DEADLY NIGHT 4: INITIATION (1990). Since there's no killer Santa Claus to terrorize Christmas lovers, here's another crass example of using a title solely for exploitation purposes. All that aside, it's more unpleasant and disgusting than scary in the hands of director Brian Yuzna. Neith Hunter portrays a writer for the L.A. Eye, whose investigations of a woman's fiery deathleap off a building lead her to a Daughter of Isis witch cult led by Maud Adams. Cockroaches, slugs and giant leeches (created by Screamin' Mad George) figure prominently in how the cult terrorizes Hunter, who is needed as a witch replacement. Clint Howard appears in one of his grotesque-evil roles, and commits a sickening murder in Hunter's flat. (He's the only memorable thing.) One hopes that lovely Adams and Allyce Beasley (of TV's MOONLIGHTING) can get their careers back on track, as this nowhere movie is a bottoming out. Tommy Hinkley, Reggie Banister, Jeanne Bates, Laurel Lockhart. (Live) (Laser: Image)

SILENT NIGHT, DEADLY NIGHT 5: THE TOY MAKER (1991). At least a killer Santa Claus, missing from the fourth film in this mediocre series, is on the prowl again in this horror whodunit in which a killer produces toys that come to life through an electrical charge and kill their recepients. Among the toy tinglers are a ball with snake-like arms, a snail monster, rollerskates with jet propulsion, a severed hand, and a flying superhero. Among the suspects is Mickey Rooney as toystore owner Joe Petto (and that name is a joke, son), his weirdo son and a department store Santa who's behaving strangely around a certain mother and mute child. Out of this olio scripting by producer Brian Yuzna and director Martin

Kitrosser comes an adequate twist climax and opportunities for make-up guy Screamin' Mad George to show off his special effects. Jane Higginson, Brian Breyer, Tracy Fraim, William Thorne, Neith Hunter, Clint Howard. (Live)

SILENT NIGHT, EVIL NIGHT. Originally **BLACK CHRISTMAS,** then **STRANGER IN THE HOUSE**.

SILENT RAGE (1982). Chuck Norris' kung fu/karate expertise is worked in with a Frankenstein plot tinged with horror touches. Hence: "Chuck Norris Meets the Bionic Man on Halloween." Feeble in all departments, with the karate action never blending with the horror elements, despite screenwriter Joseph Fraley's double talk about a superserum (Monogen 35) and other gibberish. Just an excuse for director Michael Miller to stage action (including a barroom brawl) showing off Norris' physical dexterity. Ron Silver, Toni Kalem, Steven Keats, William Finley. (Video/Laser: RCA/Columbia)

SILENT RUNNING (1972). "A" for effort to writer-director Douglas Trumbull, who first found favor through his effects in 2001: A SPACE ODYSSEY. Trumbull repeats his spectacular space images: awesome ships floating between planets, exploding suns and a solar storm. A floating space station (the last garden of a defoliaged-Earth) is manned by Bruce Dern and three "drone" robots, Huey, Dewey and Louie. Dern goes psychotic when ordered to destroy his forest, and he mutinies. The effects are wonderful and Dern's demented attitude is justified by the Deric Washburn-Michael Cimino-Steve Bochco script. Adult sci-fi worthy of repeated viewings. (Video/Laser: MCA)

SILENT SCREAM (1980). Writer-director Denny Harris pays homage to Hitchcock's PSYCHO with this tale of a demented household where innocent roomers are murdered by a knife-happy kook daughter (played without restraint by Barbara Steele). Gore murders provide shocks, but the plotting (or is it plodding?) of the Ken/Jim Wheat script is predictable, and characterizations without depth. A moment of silence, please, while we scream for Harris. Yvonne De Carlo, Cameron Mitchell, Avery Schreiber, Rebecca Balding. (Media)

BARBARA STEELE

SILENT SCREAM, THE (1980). Two repackaged episodes from the British TV series, HAMMER HOUSE OF HORROR. In "The Silent Scream," former Nazi camp commandant Peter Cushing runs a pet shop where he carries out experiments in animal behavior. He extends that to human behavior when ex-convict Brian Cox and wife Elane Connelly fall into his clutches. This chilling tale was written by Francis Essex and directed by Alan Gibson. In "Witching Time," 17th Century witch Patricia Quinn comes back to haunt Jon Finch in his country Woodstock House, where she was burned at the stake. Prunella Gee, the long-suffering wife, tries to prevent Finch's downfall to Lucinda's sexual charms, but ends up fighting her own battle against a voodoo doll. Written by Anthony Read and directed by Don Leaver, this is an effective supernatural tale. Ian McCulloch plays the all-knowing doctor. (Thrillervideo)

SILENT SENTENCE (1973). Heavily edited TV version of the feature A KNIFE FOR THE LADIES. Not quite a Western, not quite a horror flick. Call it an oater-bloater. A Jack the Ripper-style killer is stalking saloon girls while sheriff Jack Elam and investigator Jeff Cooper stalk the murderer. Made in Old Tucson, this has Gene Evans, Joe Santos, John Kellog and Ruth Roman in interesting character roles, but it's a minor stab at best. Directed by Larry G. Spangler.

SILENT STAR. See **FIRST SPACESHIP ON VENUS, THE.**

SILHOUETTE (1990). Unconvincing, preposterous woman-in-peril TV-movie starring Faye Dunaway in a role way beneath her dignity. She plays an architect stranded in a small Texas town who witnesses a knife murder, only she can't prove it and the local sheriff is powerless to help her. Thinking she can identify him, the killer tries to kill her time and again, succeeding in only frightening her half to death and boring the audience. The holes in the Jay Wolf-Victor Buelle script are bigger than the shotgun wounds and director Carl Schenkel telegraphs every ersatz surprise. David Rasche, John Terry, Carlos Gomez. (MCA)

SILVER BULLET (1985). Well-produced adaptation of Stephen King's novelette, "Cycle of the Werewolf," which proves to be a slight story. King adapted his own book, emphasizing life in a small North Carolina town, Tarker's Mills, and how it is plagued by brutal werewolf killings. The focus is on crippled Corey Haim (his motorized wheelchair is dubbed Silver Bullet) and his relationship with sister Megan Follows and alcoholic uncle Gary Busey. How they learn the werewolf's identity and set a trap builds to an unexceptional climax. Carlo Rambaldi's werewolf is effective; the moonstalker just needs a stronger story. Daniel Attias directs well, especially a sequence in the swamp when the wolfman stalks his stalkers through nocturnal mist. Everett McGill, Corey Haim, Terry O'Quinn. (Video/Laser: Paramount)

SILVER NEEDLE IN THE SKY (1954). See **ROCKY JONES, SPACE RANGER** (Sinister/C; Filmfax).

SIMON (1980). Under Marshall Brickman's direction this dabbles satirically where ALTERED STATES seriously wallowed, and emerges too intellectualized to be entertaining. Alan Arkin is a genius immersed in a think tank. When he emerges he performs the film's only funny bit: Without makeup or props, he pantomimes man's evolution, from amoeba to monkey to present day. Now, that's funny. The rest of Brickman's gags (he wrote the script too) and concepts aren't. Unrealized premise wastes Austin Pendleton, Judy Graubart, William Finley and Fred Gwynne. (Warner Bros.)

SIMON, KING OF THE WITCHES (1971). Andrew Prine's portrayal of a world-weary magician/warlock is the only unusual aspect of this low budgeter which remains strangely lowkey when Prine befriends a young boy and helps a D.A. find out who's been supplying drugs to his daughter (Brenda Scott). There's just no pacing or excitement. A ride down the Hollywood Freeway around 4:30 p.m. any weekday is scarier. Directed by Bruce Kessler. (Electric; Unicorn; Warner Bros.)

SIMPLY IRRESISTIBLE (1982). Drab, lifeless R-rated comedy-satire that could have been wild and zany had producer Summer Brown and director Edwin Brown let themselves go writing the script. It's about nerdy Richard Pacheco who's so bored with his sex life that he goes to see Miracle Meyer (Lou Ganapoler) who has designed a time machine built from an amusement park "Wild Mouse." Meyer, who talks to what is presumably the Voice of God, sends Pacheco back in time to Cleopatra, where he becomes known as Walter of Marin; to the Shakespearean terrain of Romeo and Juliet; and finally throws him together with spy favorite Mata Hari. What's wrong is a sense of lifelessness and a condescending portrayal of women as cheap, dumb nymphs. (Juliet, for example, is played as a hot lesbian). As it is, it is totally resistible. Samantha Fox, Dorothy LeMay, Starr Wood, Gayle Sterling.

SINBAD AND THE EYE OF THE TIGER (1977). Packed with the visual stop-motion thrills only animator Ray Harryhausen can bring to romantic fantasies, this adventure in the land of Arabian Nights lore is abroil with mythical monsters, exciting duels between man and beast, wizardry and witchcraft. Patrick Wayne is a mediocre Sinbad, as wooden as the dialogue, so it's a showcase for Harryhausen's memorable creations: a chess-playing baboon, three axe-swinging jinns; a Troglodyte; a giant tiger; a king-size walrus and a metal giant called Minaton. What, no Caroline Munro? Directed by actor Sam Wanamaker, scripted by Beverly Cross. Taryn

Power, Jane Seymour, Margaret Whiting, Patrick Troughton. Harryhausen also co-produced with Charles Schneer. (Video/Laser: RCA/Columbia)

SINBAD OF THE SEVEN SEAS (1989). Alleged to be based on Edgar Allan Poe's "The Thousand and Second Tale of Scheherazade," this emerges as a children's fantasy-adventure with Lou Ferrigno as the muscular hero he established in the HERCULES films, although he has a sense of humor this time. There's thrill after thrill (hah!) as the evil vizier is busier than usual flinging the Sacred Gems of Basra to the four corners of the world, forcing Sinbad and his adventurers (the son of a king, a Viking warrior, a dwarf, a bald cook and a Chinese soldier of fortune) to fight the Legions of Death; the Warrior Women (or Amazons) of the Enchanted Island; the Army of Ghost Warriors and the Stone Man with a Shining Face. All manner of magic and wizardry is employed. Produced-directed by Enzo G. Castellari, who co-wrote with Tito Carpi, from an idea by Lewis Coates. John Steiner, Leo Gullotta, Teagan, Haruhiko Yamanouchi. (Video/Laser: Cannon)

SINGLE WHITE FEMALE (1992). Provocative study of two women living in a New York flat and how one takes control, until this unusually classy psychothriller explodes into the violence you find in slasher bashers. Bridget Fonda is superb as a computer businesswoman whose shaky existence is shaken further when she chooses Jennifer Jason Leigh as her room mate. Leigh turns into an unforgettable murderess, endowing this study of depression and madness with rich character not quickly forgotten. Don Roos based his script on John Lutz's novel "SWF Seeks Same," and director Barbet Schroeder proves he's topnotch. Steven Weber, Peter Friedman. (Video/Laser: Columbia Tristar)

SINISTER DR. ORLOFF, THE (1982). That awful physician isn't back—it's a fiendish son following in dear father's slash tracks. Again, hapless females are subjects for perverted surgery as he tries to replace damaged parts on mother's mangled body. Jesus Franco wrote-directed. Howard Vernon, Robert Foster.

SINISTER INVASION (1968). Video of **INCREDIBLE INVASION, THE** (UIV; Sinister/C; S/Weird; Filmfax).

SINISTER MONK, THE (1965). German thriller in the style of Edgar Wallace, depicting a hooded figure with a whip who lashes victims to death. Blackmail, murder, mayhem—all the things that make life worth living. Harold Leiphitz, Karin Dor. Directed by Harald Reinl.

SINS OF DORIAN GRAY, THE (1983). TV-movie switches sexes in Oscar Wilde's morality tale of debauchery/soul disintegration by having "Dorian" a sexpot (Belinda Bauer) who gives up decency by transferring her soul to a piece of film, her screen test. "Dorian" wants to be a successful actress and sleeps with producers and behaves like a superbitch. Unusually trashy material for the tube—audiences will love its luridness. Directed by Tony Maylam. Anthony Perkins, Joseph Bottoms, Michael Ironside. (Playhouse/Fox)

SINS OF THE FLESHAPOIDS (1965). San Francisco underground film maker Mike Kuchar (with brother George) created this parody of sci-fi movies, in which survivors of nuclear war are serviced by robot "fleshapoids." The society is decadent and lolls around the palace all day. A buxom miss in low-cut red gown has fruit dumped on her while a handsome man sprawls on a couch eating a Clark candy bar. When a servant goes amok, it kills the woman and flees to another home, where it joins in sexual union with a humanoid by joining hands and producing electrical sparks. This was made for $1,000 and is remakable for arty lighting techniques and gaudy Arabian Nights sets. A total anomaly. Bob Cowan, Donna Kerness.

SINS OF THE PAST (1984). TV-movie starring Barbara Carrera as the madame of high-class prostitutes who break up when one is murdered. Individually, the beauties (Kim Cattrall, Debby Boone, Tracy Reed and Kirstie Alley) are tracked by a slasher-killer. Standard TV fare (with erotic touches) directed by Peter H. Hunt.

SINTHIA THE DEVIL'S DOLL (1970). Child commits murder. Is she possessed? Wouldn't seem likely, since THE EXORCIST hasn't even been produced yet. Ah, to the Devil with it! . . . The hell you say! Directed by Ray Dennis Steckler. Shula Roan, Diane Webber, Maria Lease. (S/Weird; Sinister/C)

SIREN OF ATLANTIS (1948). "Lost Continent" fantasy with one-time Universal star, campy/exotic Maria Montez. Explorers Jean-Pierre Aumont and Dennis O'Keefe stumble across a missing city ruled by Montez, who had seen better civilizations with Jon Hall. Burning braziers and bulging brassieres as she lolls on divans in skimpy costumes and watches dancers. Slave, peel that grape! Montez's last picture . . . she committed suicide soon after. Three men were needed to direct: Arthur Ripley, Douglas Sirk, John Brahm. Henry Daniell co-stars. Producer Seymour Nebenzal was remaking his 1932 version of this same story, from a novel by Pierre Benoit.

SIREN OF BAGDAD (1953). Hans Conried's comedic talents keep this Arabian Nights parody wriggling like a camel undergoing a flea attack. Although the setting is ancient Egypt, Robert E. Kent's script is loaded with non sequiturs and contemporary gags. Paul Henreid is a daffy magician who uses his magic box to save slave girls. Very campy albeit dumb, with Patricia Medina and assorted harem girls (Laurette Luez, Anne Dore) providing a fetching decor to this Sam Katzman nonsense. Directed so fine by Richard Quine.

SISTERHOOD, THE (1988). Women of a voluptuous nature fight to stay alive in a MAD MAX kind of post-holocaust world. Directed in the Philippines by Cirio H. Santiago. Rebecca Holden, Chuck Wagner, Lynn-Holly Johnson, Barbara Hooper. (Media) (Laser: Image)

SISTERS (1973). Brian De Palma's homage to Hitchcock is black comedy and biting satire, but confused by erratic editing, strange juxtaposing of scenes and lack of logic. Because De Palma's intentions are fuzzy, SISTERS is an intriguing mess. The director (who co-wrote with Louisa Rose) examines one of two Siamese sisters (both played by Margot Kidder) who keeps splitting her personality—not to mention a few heads. Jennifer Salt, an irascible reporter, sets out to prove the sister committed murder. True, the suspense is considerable and there is excellent use of split screen but it's ultimately a bumble of a jumble. Bernard Herrmann wrote the music. Charles Durning, Barnard Hughes. (Warner Bros.)

SISTER SISTER (1987). Moody, heavily Gothic horror melodrama, strong for its ambience and miasma of the decaying swamp and decadent spirit of the South. In the bayou country, in an antebellum mansion dubbed The Willows, the Bonnard sisters (Jennifer Leigh Jason and Judith Ivey) go bonkers because of past and present stimuli. Director Bill Condon (who co-wrote with Joel Cohen and Ginny Cerrella) has the advantage of a real location (the Greenwood Plantation in Napoleonville, La.) as his tale unfolds with all the hysterics and histronics of a fire-and-brimstone damnation preacher sermon. It doesn't make a lot of sense but the atmosphere makes it compelling. Dennis Lipscomb, Eric Stoltz, Anne Pitoniak. (New World) (Laser: Image)

SISTERS OF CORRUPTION (1973). Spanish slash trash about a killer so fickle who strikes with a sickel, swathing then bathing his victims in blood and crud. Directed by Juan A. Bardem. Jean Seberg, Perla Cristal.

SISTERS OF DEATH (1978). Sleazily made albeit entertaining low-budget thriller stars young Claudia Jennings as one of five women lured to the Hacienda del Sol outside Paso Robles. They're former members of a cult group called The Sisters, and one of them harbors a dark secret. They're soon trapped by madman Arthur Franz, who loads bullets for his Gatling gun and plays the flute. Even thought it's shoddily directed by Joseph A. Mazzuca, this has a fascination that most movies of this kind miss by miles. The explanations and surprise ending make no sense—it's in the unfolding. Cheri Howell, Sherry Boucher, Paul Carr. (United; VCI)

SISTERS OF SATAN (1975). Mexican horror film

cashing in on the EXORCIST craze of the '70s in depicting two bloodthirsty nuns and a vampire named Alucarda. Directed by Juan Monteczuma. Also known as ALUCARD. (Academy; Cinema Greats; from Fame Entertainment as **MARK OF THE DEVIL PART III**)

SISTERS OF SATAN (1971). Video version of **NUNS OF SAINT ARCHANGELO, THE** (MPI).

SIX HOURS TO LIVE (1932). See editions 1-3.

SIX MILLION DOLLAR MAN, THE (1973). While the Lee Majors TV series denigrated into a kiddie-oriented SUPERMAN, this pilot is an exciting thriller that does justice to Martin Caudin's novel, CYBORG. Majors is a test pilot horribly mutilated in a plane crash; the U.S. Government spends $6 million to restore him with greater speed, strength, X-ray vision and other superhuman talents. Richard Irving directed. Barbara Anderson, Martin Balsam, Darren McGavin, Robert Cornthwaite, Olan Soule. (In video as **CYBORG: THE SIX MILLION DOLLAR MAN**)

SIX WOMEN FOR THE MURDERER. Variant video version of **BLOOD AND BLACK LACE.**

SKEETER (1993). That old sci-fi standby, the mutated creature of nature (first made popular in such '50s fare as THEM), is recycled in this desert-based action thriller that blends too many characters and subplots for its own good, and fails to generate a sense of building suspense. A "skeeter" is a flesh-munching mosquito monster, a few times bigger than it should be. Young sheriff's deputy Jim Youngs, corrupt sheriff Charles Napier, a crazed man in a limousine (Jay Robinson), another crazed character played by Michael J. Pollard and screaming Tracey Griffith all figure in this olio of special effects, mystery and mosquito attacks. Director Clark Brandon co-wrote the derivative script with Lanny Horn. (New World)

SKELETON ON HORSEBACK (1940). Editions 1-3.

SKETCHES OF A STRANGLER (1978). Psychotic artist Allen Goorwitz murders his female subjects, cackling with glee. Meredith MacRae, Frank Whiteman. (Fox Hill; Media)

SKULL, THE (1965). Based on Robert Bloch's "The Skull of the Marquis De Sade," this has an unusual viewpoint: through the eyes of a skull as it bites victims to death. Director Freddie Francis and screenwriter Milton Subotsky have created an effective thriller showcasing a skull possessed by a sadistic Frenchman. But that doesn't curtail Peter Cushing—a collector of demonology, witchcraft and black magic artifacts—from buying the skull from collector Patrick Wymark. Nice cranium capacity. Same story was retold as part of TORTURE GARDEN. Nigel Green, Christopher Lee, Michael Gough, George Coulouris, Patrick Magee. (Academy; Paramount/Gateway)

PETER CUSHING IN 'THE SKULL'

SKULLDUGGERY (1970). Thoughtful adventure-message film (directed by Gordon Douglas) about man's relationship to his prehistoric past, and the crass exploitation of his soul. Nelson Gidding's script is finally a plea for better understanding among races. Burt Reynolds and Susan Clark lead an expedition into Rhodesia to find benevolent man-ape creatures. The tiny beings are considered for slave labor, and a trial places creatures and mankind on examination. Roger C. Carmel, Chips Rafferty, Wilfrid Hyde-White, Pat Suzuki, Alexander Knox, Rhys Williams. (MCA)

SKULLDUGGERY (1983). Stylish, imaginative glimpse at role-playing games and how they cross from fantasy into reality. This fascinating tale begins in Canterbury in 1382 when The Warlock claims the soul of an unborn child and curses a royal family. Flash ahead to Trottelville USA in 1982 as a group meets to play life-and-death games, unaware Diabolus has dealt himself into the contest. A phantom archer is involved in the deadly play and the murders are cleverly fashioned by director Ota Richter. Thom Haverstock, Wendy Crewson, Clark Johnson, Kate Lynch. (Media; from Paragon as **WARLOCK**)

SKY ABOVE HEAVEN (1964). Dull French film about an aircraft carrier pursued by a UFO, a radioactive probe from space. Warring powers of Earth put aside differences to face a common enemy. Director/co-writer Yves Ciampi makes social commentary on war but it ends up resembling a recruiting film. C'est magnifique, la guerre. Aka SKY BEYOND HEAVEN and SKIES ABOVE. Andre Smagghe, Yvonne Monlaur.

SKY BANDITS (1940). Royal Mounted hero setshis sights on capturing a mad scientist equipped with a Death Ray. Directed by Ralph Staub. Louise Stanley, Dwight Frye. (Sinister/C; Filmfax; Video Connection)

SKY BIKE, THE (1968). British version of Disney's MONKEY'S UNCLE, in which adorable youths rig a bicycle to a flying machine and pedal into the heavens. Directed by Charles Frend. Liam Redmond.

SKY CALLS, THE (1959). This is included so we can make reference to the fact that footage from this Russian production was used in BATTLE BEYOND THE SUN. Its USSR title is NIEBO ZOWIET.

SKY PARADE, THE (1936). See editions 1-3.

SKY PIRATES (1986). In 1945, John Hargreaves flies into a time warp near Easter Island and crashlands in the ocean . . . flash-ahead to his court martial where we learn he and other explorers are involved with a stone of magical powers brought to Earth by aliens. Indiana Jones-style adventure, directed by Colin Eggleston. Meredith Phillips, Max Phipps, Bill Hunter. (CBS/Fox) (Laser: Japanese)

SLAPSTICK (OF ANOTHER KIND) (1982). Disastrous version of the Kurt Vonnegut novel by writer-producer-director Steven Paul, failing to translate Vonnegut's far-out concepts. An alien race, watching over the Galaxies (Orson Welles' voice), sends "twin advisors" to Earth to prevent the Chinese from learning the secret of gravity and upsetting the Universe's balance. The parents chosen for impregnation are Jerry Lewis and Madeleine Kahn. Played straight it might have worked—but not with the mugging of Lewis, Kahn, Marty Feldman (the family retainer), John Abbott (the doctor) and Pat Morita (Chinese spy). Jim Backus, as the President, looks pained as he explains why Air Force I is powered by chickenshit. Film director Samuel Fuller, as a colonel running a military academy for foul-ups, is a treat when he struts out dressed as a frontier scout. Otherwise, SLAPSTICK is the unfunniest comedy ever to hit your kisser with tasteless merengue. (Video/Laser: Vestron)

SLASH. See **BLOOD SISTERS.**

SLASH DANCE (1989). When young dancers turn out to audition for a musical show, a killer goes into action, knocking them off one by one—perhaps because of their questionable acting abilities? Lots of dancing, few thrills. Written-directed by James Shyman. Cindy Maranne, James Carrol Jordan, Jay Richardson. (Glencoe; Simitar)

SLASHER . . . IS THE SEX MANIAC, THE (1976). Well-structured Italian psychokiller thriller enhanced by

Farley Granger as a cop after The Avenger, a knife murderer who targets unfaithful wives of prominent men. The script by director Robert Montero, I. Fasant and Lou Angeli builds tensely to the bloody climax and throws in surprise twists. Also called SO SWEET, SO DEAD; an X-rated version was called PENETRATION. Sylva Koscina, Susan Scott, Jessica Dublin. (Monterey)

SLASHER IN THE HOUSE. Video version of **HOME SWEET HOME.** (Front Row Entertainment)

SLAUGHTER. TV title of **DOGS.**

SLAUGHTER, THE. See **SNUFF.**

SLAUGHTERERS, THE. See **CANNIBALS ARE IN THE STREETS, THE.**

SLAUGHTER HIGH (1985). Derivative slasher flick, close to THE REDEEMER in plot. It begins at Doddsville County High, where nerdy Simon Scuddamore is the brunt of a practical joke when he's photographed nude by callous peers and dumped headfirst down the toilet. Further victimized in a fire-acid scarring accident, Simon is carried away on a stretcher. Flash-ahead to modern times as model Caroline Munro and others who participated in the sick joke are lured to a fake reunion where, in the hallowed halls, they are hollowed out or slaughtered one by bloody one: Crucifixion to door, stomach blown up to spill out intestines, knife through seat of car pinioning driver, acid bath in tub, submersion in sumphole, crushing under weight of car. Finally it's just Caroline in a virginal white pants suit, discovering all the bodies as she flees the killer who wears a Court Jester's mask. George Dugdale, Mark Ezra and Peter Litten double as writers-directors. Munro fans get to see their sweetie in sexy poses. Carmine Iannoccone, Donna Yaeger. Originally released as APRIL FOOL'S DAY. (Vestron)

SLAUGHTER HOTEL (1973). An expose of a popular hotel chain, as some business critics have claimed? Or just another beastly Italian horror film? Viewers will have to ponder subtleties and allegorical overtones for the answer . . . if they can stand the bloodletting and beheadings. The setting is an asylum run by Klaus Kinski. Directed by Fernando Di Leo. Margaret Lee. (MPI; Gorgon; from Amvest as **ASYLUM EROTICA**)

SLAUGHTERHOUSE (1987). Slasher-sleaze bottoms out with this reprehensible, repugnant, repulsive movie. A companion piece to DADDY'S DEADLY DARLINGS, and just as unfit for swine, SLAUGHTERHOUSE depicts a degenerate butcher-knife killer and his evil father (Bacon & Son) murdering people as if they were so many pigs and hanging them on hooks in a dilapidated factory. Writer-director Rick Roessler treats teenagers as dumb fodder and treats hogs with more affection than people. No matter how you slice it, this comes up a porker. Sherry Bendorf (as Lizzie Borden, the sheriff's daughter), William Houck, Don Barrett, Joe Barton, Eric Schwartz. (Embassy; Charter)

SLAUGHTERHOUSE FIVE (1972). Contemporary PILGRIM'S PROGRESS, based on Kurt Vonnegut's novel and directed by George Roy Hill, depicting the fire bombing of Dresden in 1945. But that is only one episode in the life of Billy Pilgrim, who is "unstuck" in time and leaps from time period to time period—or is he "traveling" in his mind? He and Hollywood starlet Montana Wildhack (Valerie Perrine) are captured by invisible beings and placed in a zoo on the planet Tralfamador. Wry commentary on the absurdity of human existence is presented in disjointed fashion by screenwriter Stephen Geller, but cleverly edited to produce a philosophical shrug of the shoulders. Michael Sacks, Ron Leibman, Perry King, Holly Near, John Dehner, Eugene Roche, Sorrell Booke. (MCA) (Laser: Image)

SLAUGHTERHOUSE ROCK (1987). Alcatraz Island in San Francisco Bay once again serves as the site for murderous, monstrous mayhem in another hard-to-sit-through horror flick. Nicholas Celozzi is suffering from horrible dreams caused by the one-time commandant of Alcatraz who turned into a cannibal and formed a pact with the Devil. When Celozzi and friends visit The Rock they meet the spirit of a rock musician (Toni Basil) who solicits Celozzi's help to destroy the forces of evil. It's a muddled mess as people die, souls transfer bodies, etc. All the horror-genre cliches are dragged out by writer Ted Landon and director Dimitri Logothetis. Tom Reilly, Donna Denton, Hope Marie Carlton. (Sony)

SLAUGHTER OF THE VAMPIRES (1962). Italian abomination about a Viennese bloodsucker who gives newlyweds a wedding-night surprise. Edited in 1969 and resold to TV as CURSE OF THE BLOOD GHOULS. Directed by Roberto Mauri. Dieter Eppler, Walter Brandi. (Monterey; Sinister/C; Filmfax; S/Weird)

SLAVE GIRL (1947). See editions 1-3.

SLAVE GIRLS. See **PREHISTORIC WOMEN.**

SLAVE GIRLS FROM BEYOND INFINITY (1987). From the garbage pits of the universe comes this unbelievably bad sci-fi remake of "The Most Dangerous Game," the classic Richard Connell story filmed many times. This is pandering at its worst by producer-director Ken Dixon when shapely femmes land on a jungle planet where hunter Zed and his robots torture them and use them for sport. The three gals run around in bikini bottoms and bras, dodging killer rayguns, zombies and "Phantazoid Warriors." "It's a cold cosmos," remarks Zed. It was an even colder time when this hit the vidshops. One of the worst. Cindy Berl, Elizabeth Cayton, Don Scribner, Brinke Stevens. (Urban Classics) (Laser: Full Moon; Shadow Entertainment)

SLAVE OF THE CANNIBAL GOD (1978). A cross between Italian cannibal movies and jungle adventure a la KING SOLOMON'S MINES, with the former genre overpowering the latter and the film becoming distasteful (pardon the pun, folks). Ursula Andress and her weak-willed brother want to find her missing husband, and she solicits big-game hunter Stacy Keach. The Cesare Frugoni-Sergio Martino script degenerates into cannibals munching on snakes, lizards and human flesh, a mummified corpse with a Geiger counter in its open stomach, a lizard being sliced open and its blood being poured on natives' hands, a native spiked to death in a tree trap, a man eaten by a crocodile, etc. The highpoint comes when the Pukahs strip Andress and rub red paint over legs and thighs—a scene her one-time husband, John Derek, borrowed for his Tarzan movie with Bo Derek. But the scene is a long time arriving. Martino also directed. Antonio Marsina, Claudio Cassinelli. Also known as PRISONER OF THE CANNIBAL GOD. (Wizard; Video City; Vestron)

SLAVES OF THE INVISIBLE MONSTER (1950). Feature version of **THE INVISIBLE MONSTER.**

SLAYER, THE (1982). On Georgia's Tybee Island, an actress who has nightmares and her friends stay in an old house, soon to be stalked by a diabolical killer. Director J. S. Cardone brings an unusual intensity to this slash-bash and creates an eerie electrical storm atmosphere. He also builds up the gore murders—a man decapitated by a trapdoor, a derelict battered with a ship's oar and a woman pitchforked through the breasts. The skimpy plot deals with the actress' childhood phobias. Sarah Kendall, Frederick Flynn, Carol Kottenbrook, Alan McRae, Carl Kraines. (Planet; Marquis; on a Continental video with **SCALPS**)

SLAYRIDE. See **SILENT NIGHT, DEADLY NIGHT.**

SLEAZEMANIA: THE SPECIAL EDITION (1986). Captivating compilation of previews of coming attractions for assorted sex films, nudies and softcorn pornies stretching from the '30s through the '80s, with no redeeming social values. See all the good scenes without having to sit through the bad films. Listen to bombastic announcers recite lurid come-ons ("an orgy overweight with immorality!") and see that wonderful "Explosive Thrills"-type lettering lurch across the screen. While the emphasis is on sex (would you believe "Pin Down Girls" and "Curfew Breakers"?), there are horror trailers, starting with LAST OF THE PENTINENT, an obscure exploitationer of the '30s, proceeding to ORGY OF THE DEAD, incorporating THE PSYCHIC and winding up with Fred Olsen Ray's PRISON SHIP, a women-in-space sci-fi schlocker. Take yourself to the lower depths of depravity with this siren-screaming, bullet-blazing thriller diller "trailers for sailors." (Rhino)

SLEAZEMANIA STRIKES BACK (1987). More previews of coming attractions of some of the worst sex and horror films ever made. Rollick to the rhythm of BEACH BLANKET BLOOD BATH, TWO THOUSAND MANIACS, BLOOD FEAST, GORILLA WOMAN and THE GIRL FROM S.I.N. Subtitled "The Good, the Bad and the Sleazy!" And "coming soon to a theater or cesspool near you." Don't miss it if you can. (Rhino)

SLEAZEMANIA III: THE GOOD, THE BAD AND THE SLEAZY (1988). Here Rhino goes again, this time with previews of coming attractions that highlight DANCE HALL RLACKET, TEENAGE ZOMBIES and other cruddy goodies. (Rhino)

SLEDGE HAMMER (1984). Below par slasher thriller made on videotape about a hammer slammer who kills mom and lover at an early age and grows up to be an adult basher smasher when teenagers come to the family home one weekend. Writer-director David A. Prior hammers home his point, nailing down the characters. Consider this critic a hammer damner. Ted Prior, Linda McGill, John Eastman. (Western World)

SLEEPAWAY CAMP (1983). Weak-kneed slasher flick, without flair for gore. Oh, there are murders galore at Camp Arawak (sex pervert is scalded in vat of boiling water, boy drowns in overturned rowboat, youth is death-stung by angry bees, another kid is knived in the shower) but they're clumsily staged homicides. Mike Kellin runs the dilapidated camp, covering up the killings so his reputation won't suffer. Written-directed by Robert Hiltzik with no understanding of what makes a horror film work. He should be sent to camp to sleep away his career. Felissa Rose, Karen Fields. (Media)

SLEEPAWAY CAMP 2: UNHAPPY CAMPERS (1988). Thoroughly despicable slasher film carried to tasteless extremes with rock and roll yammering on the soundtrack. Pamela Springsteen, sister of Bruce, portrays a counselor at Camp Rolling Hills who meticulously murders each and every vacationer—including her senior male counselor. When she stuffs one poor victim into a latrine, flies buzzing around a face covered with human excretement, you know movie making has reached an all-time low. Murders occur by every device imaginable—not a single one original to Fritz Gordon's pathetic excuse for a script. Directed by co-producer Michael A. Simpson. Brian Patrick Clarke, Renee Estevez, Walter Gotell. (Nelson)

SLEEPAWAY CAMP 3: TEENAGE WASTELAND (1989). Another gratuitous exercise in gross bloodletting and terrible taste, all directed at teenagers. Michael J. Pollard gets to act crazy again as a supervisor when the killer of Part 2 returns to kill again and again and again. Twice was bad enough—three times is unforgivable. Written by Fritz Gordon and directed by co-producer Michael A. Simpson. (Video/Laser: Nelson)

'SNOW WHITE AND THE SEVEN DWARFS'

SLEEPER (1973). Life in America in 2173 as Woody Allen conceives it—he wrote, directed and starred as a man frozen alive in 1973 who awakens 200 years later in a Big Brother society. "I'm 2000 months behind in my rent," he cries. He and Diane Keaton search for the Dictator's Nose in order to destroy the totalitarian society and help a revolutionary movement. Allen displays his talents in visual comedy (such as the giant vegetable scene), in mime as a jerking, jerky robot and in verbal gags that spare none of our institutions. One of Allen's best efforts. Marshall Brickman helped Allen write the script. John Beck, Mary Gregory. (CBS/Fox) (Laser: MGM/UA; CBS/Fox)

SLEEPING BEAUTY (1959). Sentimental Disney cartoon, too cute in its depiction of good fairies and down-home folks and a bit grotesque in presenting Maleficient, her raven and the goblins. There is little story—just sweetness and honey. Voices by Mary Costa, Verna Felton, Barbara Luddy, Bill Shirley, Barbara Jo Allen, Taylor Holmes. (Video/Laser: Disney)

SLEEPING BEAUTY (1966). Full-length version of the Tchaikowsky ballet, danced by members of the Leningrad Kirov Ballet, with Alla Sizova in the role of Princess Aurora. Pure form and beauty in a rewarding series of dances. Directed by Appolinari Dupko and Konstantin Sergeyev. (Thorn EMI)

SLEEPING BEAUTY (1983). FAERIE TALE THEATER version of Tchaikovsky's ballet, directed by Jeremy Paul Kagan. Christopher Reeve, Bernadette Peters, Beverly D'Angelo. (Video/Laser: CBS/Fox)

SLEEPING BEAUTY (1987). Entry in the Cannon series of features based on fairy tales, with Morgan Fairchild in low-cut bodices which increase the tempo of the story. It's well acted in generous costuming and features David Holliday as the King, Tahnee Welch as Rosebud, Nicholas Clay as the Prince, Sylvia Miles as Red Fairy and Kenny Baker as an elf. Directed by David Irving. (Cannon)

SLEEPING CAR, THE (1989). Retread college student David Naughton has hallucinations of ghastly-ghostly manifestations in a sleeping car converted into a rural rental unit after it was recovered from a railroad collision. Naughton resembles the man responsible for causing the accident so the spirit of the train's engineer (turned into a serial killer as a result) comes back as a decaying corpse to murder Naughton's fellow students and journalism instructor. These ghastly gore murders highlight Greg O'Neill's script, which attempts to deal with Naughton's difficulties of adjusting to a new life, a practitioner of "white magic" played by Kevin McCarty, the eccentric wife of the dead engineer, and the engineer played by monster creator John Carl Beuchler. Should satisy genre fans. Produced-directed by Douglas Curtis. Judie Aronson, Jeff Conaway, Dani Minnick, Steve Lundquist. (Vidmark) (Laser: Image)

SLEEPLESS NIGHTS. See **SLUMBER PARTY MASSACRE, THE.**

SLEEP OF DEATH (1978). Slow-paced costume horror melodrama produced in Britain/Ireland and set in France, 1793, when nobleman Per Oscarson sets out for Paris, after his father dies, to learn about the world. Unfortunately, he meets a sinister gentleman (Patrick Magee) and other unsavory characters before it's apparent he's mixed up with vampires who will stop at nothing to put him into a death-like trance. Magee steals the movie with his slimy performance but producer-director Calvin Floyd (who cranked out the script with his wife Yvonne, basing it on a Joseph Sheridan Le Fanu story) never builds the momentum to make this compelling. Marilu Tolo, Brenda Price, Curt Jurgens. Aka INN OF THE FLYING DRAGON. (Prism)

SLEEPWALKERS (1991). The script, a Stephen King original, was hailed as "the first King story written expressly for the screen," but it is minor King, depicting two shape-changing monsters who have assimilated themselves into society as humans but who face discovery when the "boy" falls in love with a mortal, much to the chagrin of his distraught "mother." They also have the power to make themselves and objects (such as cars) invisible, so this dark tale is all over the map, and director Mick Garris is stuck with the wavering narrative. Some of King's pals have cameos (Clive Barke, Joe Dante, John Landis, King himself) but it's an in-joke that falls flatter than the film's attack victims. What with cats coming to the rescue, SLEEPWALKERS is a disappointment. Brian Krause, Alice Krige, Madchen Amick, Ron Perlman. (Video/Laser: RCA/Columbia)

STEPHEN KING

SLIGHTLY PREGNANT MAN, A (1973). "You got knocked up?" a friend asks Marcello Mastroianni. He nods. Because of a hormone imbalance from chemicals in his food, Marcello is the world's first pregnant man. That should provide laughs and satire for French director Jacques Demy. This exercise in unplanned parenthood co-stars Catherine Deneuve as the surprised—what else would you call her?—father. (VidAmerica)**SLIME CITY (1988).** The "slime" refers to what people turn into when they live in a New York apartment—but what's so strange about that? Written-directed by co-producer Gregory Lamberson. Robert C. Sabin, Mary Hunter, T.J. Merrick, Dick Biel. (Camp)

SLIME PEOPLE, THE (1963). Robert Hutton runs through L.A. warning mankind that prehistoric monsters covered with viscous liquid matter, and climbing out of the sewers, are planning to erect a dome above the city to lower the temperature and create a climate suitable for fungi. Strictly for ecocrud-and-erosion crowd. Hutton directed the Vance Skarstedt script. Susan Hart, Les Tremayne, Tom Laughlin. (Video Gems; Rhino)

SLIPPER AND THE ROSE, THE: THE STORY OF CINDERELLA (1977). Bryan Forbes' lavish musical-comedy version of CINDERELLA, moderately successful in lyrics, choreography and touching romance. Richard Chamberlain as Prince Charming and 24-year-old Gemma Craven as the brow-beaten scullery maid are the focus, yet it is often the character players (Annette Crosbie as the Fairy Godmother, Michael Hordern as the blustering King, and Dame May Whitty as the crotchety Queen) who keep the story frothy. This free-wheeling interpretation deals with many facets of the famous storybook romance seldom plumbed before, giving the narrative freshness. Featuring Austrian castles, London's Southwark Cathedral and a dreamy Golden Coach. Christopher Gable, Kenneth More.

SLIPPING INTO DARKNESS. Video version of **CRAZED** (Genesis).

SLIPSTREAM (1989). This starts out as a seemingly cliched imitation of the MAD MAX post-Armageddon genre, depicting an outlaw of the future (Bill Paxton) kidnapping a fugitive with a price on his head from lawman Mark Hamill and his partner Kitty Aldridge. However, the film—produced by Gary Kurtz, who also produced the first two STAR WARS films—turns into something quite different (and special) as it depicts Paxton's flight into the "slipstream," a current of air flowing above Earth that "washes the planet clean." The characters take on dimension as Hamil realizes his charge is an android, capable of healing the sick. The dialogue by Tony Kayden becomes unusually poetic and intriguing, and the performances are sensitive as the excitingly photographed adventures unfold. Director Steven M. Lisberger captures an affinity for soaring in aerial footage, enhanced by the score of Leonard Bernstein. Eleanor David, Ben Kingsley, F. Murray Abraham. (Virgin Vision)

SLITHIS (1978). There's no way for us feeble humans to stop this hulking, anti-social monster—a mixture of radioactivity and organic mud from the Imperial Energy Plant off the L.A. coast. Now the slimy humanoid is stalking folks around Venice and Marina Del Rey, tearing them limb from limb, chomping hungrily on their tasty flesh and slashing their faces to pulp. The monster (ex-Olympic swimmer Win Condict in a rubber suit) is a nice try by fledgling writer-producer-director Stephen Traxler. On TV as **SPAWN OF THE SLITHIS.** (Media)

SLUGS THE MOVIE (1988). It's a familiar plot: toxic waste infects a rural community's slugs and snails until they turn into monster-sized killers in the local sewers. Health inspector Michael Garfield investigates and has to deal not only with marauding mollusks but pesty bureaucrats. Despite the cliches, director J. P. Simon does a credible job with a cast that plays it straight, enhancing the routine script by Ron Gantman, based on a novel by Sharon Houston. Kim Terry, Philip Machale, Alicia Moro, Santiago Alvarez, John Battaglia. (New World) (Laser: Image)

SLUMBER PARTY MASSACRE (1982). Call it SON OF DRILLER KILLER. A murderer escapes from an asylum and terrorizes L.A. teen-agers (well-stacked ones) with his portable battery-operated drill. The unusual aspect about an otherwise not-unusual slasher film: it was written by female activist Rita Mae Brown and produced-directed by Amy Jose. Yes, those who cried loudest about wanton exploitation of womanhood exploit it to the max! When it comes down to the wire, women as well as men exploit bare asses and titties and gobs of violence to make a buck. This features the ubiquitous drill churning through eyeballs, brains, shoulder blades and chest cavities, and slashing open an occasional throat or stomach. What is really sickeningly depressing is that once an innocent character is forced to pick up a weapon for defense, he or she seems to enjoy using it as much as the frenzied, drooling killer. Michele Michaels, Robin Stille. (Embassy)

SLUMBER PARTY MASSACRE II (1987). Not that SLUMBER PARTY MASSACRE was any great shakes, but at least it was made by women who wanted to take pokes at the Establishment, using the slasher theme as its foundation. This sequel is just stupid, and in its own inept way condescendingly puts down rock and roll music and its entertainers, probably without realizing it. The main killer (Atanas Ilitch) is a singer-guitarist in black with an electrical guitar that is also a giant drill, and that drill penetrates several nubile, teenage bodies when a female rock group gets together for a party. Disintegrating flesh, farflung gore and a pillow fight with flying feathers are the highpoints of the script by director Deborah Brock. A genuinely terrible movie in every respect. Crystal Bernard, Kimberly McArthur, Juliette Cummings, Patrick Lowe, Heidi Kozak. (Video/Laser: Nelson)

SLUMBER PARTY MASSACRE 3 (1990). A repeat of the drill-killer attacks of the first two entries in this pitiful series. Strictly boring from top (head) to bottom (ass). Directed by Sally Mattison. Keely Christian, Brittain Frye, M.K. Harris, David Greenlee. (MGM/UA)

SMALL TOWN MASSACRE. Video version of **STRANGE BEHAVIOR** (Scorpio).

SMILING GHOST, THE (1941). Weak comedy makes fun of haunted houses and features a Negro servant (Willie Best) seeking new ounces of bravery to face secret panels, hidden rooms and phony spooks. Wayne Morris is the "aw, gee" reporter hired by heiress Alexis Smith to find out why all her prospective husbands are dying like flies. Brenda Marshall has brunette hair to contrast Alexis' blonde coiffure. Silly but fun. Directed by Lewis Seiler. Alan Hale, Lee Patrick, David Bruce.

SMOKY MOUNTAIN CHRISTMAS, A (1986). Tuneful TV-movie starring Dolly Parton as a country singing star (art imitates life?) who meets a witch (Anita Morris) and a backwoodsman (Lee Majors) in outback Tennessee. Ay-hoo. Bo Hopkins, Dan Hedaya. Directed by Henry Winkler. (CBS/Fox)

SMUGGLER'S COVE (1948). Ersatz haunted-house mystery-comedy starring Leo Gorcey, Huntz Hall and the usual Bowery Boys, who fumble for a few laughs under William Beaudine's direction. Martin Kosleck, Gabriel Dell. (VidAmerica)

SMURFS AND THE MAGIC FLUTE, THE (1984). French-Belgian animated feature set in the Middle Ages in the land of the Smurfs, small bluish creatures. Into their kingdom comes an outlaw, Oilycreep, with the Magic Flute, an instrument capable of making people dance wildly. Pursuing the bandit is Pee Wee from the king's castle. Enhanced by a Michel Legrand musical score. Produced-directed by Jose Dutillieu. Based on a popular series of books. (Video/Laser: Vestron)

SNAKE PEOPLE, THE (1971). One of four Boris Karloff movies made in 1968, but unreleased for several years due to legal complications. In this undistinguished fare, also known as ISLE OF THE SNAKE PEOPLE, Karloff portrays Karl Van Molder, a landowner whose daughter (Julissa) is kidnapped by a snake cult on Coaibai Island. Co-directed and co-written by Jack Hill and Juan Ibanez. (Gemstone; Unicorn; Sinister/C; S/Weird; Filmfax; from MPI as **CULT OF THE DEAD**)

SNAKE PIT, THE. Video version of **TORTURE CHAMBER OF DR. SADISM** (Magnum).

SNAKE PIT AND THE PENDULUM, THE. Another title for **TORTURE CHAMBER OF DR. SADISM.**

SNAKE WOMAN, THE (1960). As torpid as a serpent trapped in an arctic blizzard, this low-budget British film was directed with the bite of a fangless black mamba. In a corny style, thanks to an outdated script by Orville H. Hampton, George Fowler's production depicts a "legendary" event in 1890 in North Cumberland, England. A crazed herpatologist injects his wife with snake poison to cure her mental illness. She gives birth to a baby with characteristics of a reptile, who grows up as sexy Susan Travers, the only appealing element of this unwatchable mess. It was directed by Sidney J. Furie with assistant director being Douglas Hickox, who would go on to make many horror pictures. John McCarthy, Geoffrey Denton, Elsie Wagstan. (Cinemacabre)

SNAP-SHOT. See **DAY BEFORE HALLOWEEN**.

SNOWBEAST (1977). Snowbound, derivative TV-movie, inspired by JAWS, is set at a ski lodge where a Bigfoot creature is on the prowl, killing vacationing skiiers. Owner Sylvia Sidney tries to keep it hushed up, but panic prevails. There are excellent skiing sequences, but Joseph Stefano's script deals with cliches and never affords a look at the monster, going for the point of view technique. One hairy face at a window is about all you see. Not exactly an avalanche of chills; snowbound. Directed by Herb Wallerstein. Bo Svenson, Yvette Mimieux, Clint Walker, Robert Logan. (Worldvision)

SNOW CREATURE, THE (1954). Abominable look at the Abominable Snowman of the Himalayas: The creature is dumb enough to nab the wife of a botanist, which leads to its capture and a journey that takes it to L.A., where it escapes its captors. Strictly a snow job by writer-director W. Lee Wilder, the brother of Billy Wilder. Some like it cold. Paul Langton, Rudolph Anders, Leslie Denison. (VCI; Amvest; Sinister/C; S/Weird)

SNOW DEVILS (1965). See editions 1-3.

SNOW QUEEN, THE (1959). Hans Christian Andersen fairy tale animated by the Russians and intended for moppets, although adults might be touched by its sense of purity. Universal-International supplied a new soundtrack (voices by Sandra Dee, Tommy Kirk, Patty McCormack) and tacked on an unnecessary prologue with Art Linkletter. Icy sliver in the eye of a young boy transforms him into an impish youth swept away to the chilly land of the Snow Queen. Nothing sophisticated or satiric, but visually attractive.

SNOW QUEEN (1984). Showtime's FAERIE TALE THEATRE version of Hans Christian Andersen's story about a boy cursed by a goblin. Lance Derwin, Melissa Gilbert, Lee Remick (as the Queen). Directed by Peter Medak. (CBS/Fox)

SNOW WHITE (1987). Yet another Cannon film based on a classic fairy tale. Diana Rigg shines through as the Mean Queen in this lively costume morality play. Written-directed by Michael Berz. Billy Barty, Sarah Patterson, Nicola Stapleton, Mike Edmunds.

SNOW WHITE AND THE SEVEN DWARFS (1938). Unfettered version of the Brothers Grimm fairy tale, the first feature cartoon from Disney. A triumphant classic, its animation as fresh as the day it established new trends in cartooning. By now it's a familiar story—the stepdaughter of the wicked witch is marked for death but escapes to be befriended by seven little fellows mining jewels. Along comes the Poisoned Apple, Prince Charming, etc. An enchanting viewing experience child and adults never forget. (Disney)

SNOW WHITE AND THE SEVEN DWARFS (1983). Showtime's FAERIE TALE THEATRE adaptation of the Brothers Grimm tale with Vanessa Redgrave, Rex Smith, Elizabeth McGovern. (Video/Laser: CBS/Fox)

SNOW WHITE AND THE THREE STOOGES (1961). Brace yourself for the eye-gouging, scrambled-brains antics of Moe Howard, Joe De Rita and Larry Fine as the Three Stooges return in one of their best features. What makes this fractured fairy tale memorable is beautiful color production and skating numbers featuring Carol Heiss as the lovely princess. Walter Lang directed the Noel Langley-Elwood Ullman script. Guy Rolfe, Buddy Baer, Patricia Medina. (Playhouse)

SNUFF (1974). Set in South America, this variation on the Manson Family massacre was advertised as a real "Snuff" film—i.e. people were really killed on camera—but it was a sick hoax. Written-directed by Michael and Roberta Findlay. Also known as THE SLAUGHTER.

SOCIETY (1989). There are two ways to view SOCIETY. Literally, it's a horror movie about a secret band in Beverly Hills that feasts on "outsiders" at orgies. The bodies of these creatures, when sexually aroused, turn into a putty-like substance, absorbing victims "body and soul." Figuratively, it's an allegory about what society does to us if we are vulnerable—it monstrously feeds on us. Whichever way you view SOCIETY, it is one of the oddest films of its day, the Woody Keith-Rick Fry script functioning on several tiers. Billy Warlock portrays a symbolic 17-year-old teen haunted by hallucinations and caught up in the hysteria of paranoia as he realizes his mother, father and sister are part of the incestuous sex cult. The film's reputation rests largely on its orgy sequence in which the "surrealistic make-up" of Screamin' Mad George depicts grotesque, twisted

'SOCIETY'

bodies oozing in and out of each other, faces where vaginas and buttocks should me, and a woman who walks on her hands. Themes of racism, corruption of law and order and ostracization are part of the rich mosiac that Brian Yuzna directed with a sure hand. Devin Devasquez, Evan Richards, Ben Meyerson, Charles Lucia. (Video/Laser: Republic)

SO DARK THE NIGHT (1946). See third edition.

SOLARBABIES (1986). In the post-Armageddon year 41, the world has been nuked into a desert where children are indoctrinated by a dictatorship, The Protectorate, which allows young ones to act out aggression with skateball teams. In Orphanage 43, ruled by benevolent Charles Durning and showcasing violent arena action similar to that in ROLLERBALL, a group of youths finds Bohdi, a glowing white ball that possesses an alien life force. As Bohdi changes hands we meet Nazi-like policeman Richard Jordan, a gang called the Scorpions, "eco-warriors," and tribes of survivors. Action on roller skates, with futuristic equipment (such as a robot named Terminec), dominates the plot. MAD MAX cliches make you wish SOLARBABIES had more solar energy. Effects by Richard Edlund. Directed by Alan Johnson. Jami Gertz, Jason Patric, Lukas Haas, Claude Brooks, Sarah Douglas. (Video/Laser: MGM/UA)

SOLAR CRISIS (1992). High-tech sci-fi adventure with ample space hardware in which astronauts are sent into the sun to set off an anti-matter bomb and prevent a megaflare that will destroy Earth. But back on Earth, corporate magnate Peter Boyle schemes to sabotage the project by reprogramming the ship's half-android crew member. And there's another plot involving military commander Charlton Heston and his missing grandson Tim Matheson. In fact, too many plots causes confusion and spoils this expensive Japanese-financed project, which underwent enough reshooting for the original director to assume the pseudoym of Alan Smithee. Based on a novel by Takeshi Kawata, and adapted by Joe Gannon and Crispan Bolt, this ambitious project sports Jack Palance as an old desert rat, Annabel Schofield as the android, Michael Berryman, and Paul Koslo. Musical score by Maurice Jarre, effects by co-producer Richard Edlund. Its production problems aside, there's enough good stuff here to satisfy fans.

SOLARIS (1972). Beautifully photographed Russian film, but ponderous and philosophically obscure. On the planet Solaris, Earth has established an observation station. The planet's ocean is capable of sending "visitors" to the space station—who take on substance from the deepest guilt and memories of humans. Written-directed by Andrei Tarkovsky. Dontas Banionis, Natalia Bondarchuk. (Fox Lorber) (Laser: Image)

SOLE SURVIVOR, THE (1970). When the wreckage of a World War II bomber is found in the Libyan desert, an investigating team discovers the only survivor of the crash might have lied about what happened in '43. What the team cannot see are the ghosts of the crew, spirit-bound to the crash site until the truth is known. Guerdon Trueblood's script is literate (if occasionally verbose) and the production values of this Steve Shagan TV-movie are above average. Special praise to Vince Edwards, William Shatner and Richard Basehart, as well as director Paul Stanley.

SOLE SURVIVOR (1982). Offbeat supernatural horror thriller, thinking fan's fare that is too mystifying to bring total satisfaction. Aging actress Anita Skinner has a premonition that her TV producer (Caren Larkey) will survive a catastrophic plane crash—and she does. Why is never made clear by writer-director Thom Eberhardt, but it it intimated she was "overlooked" and weird forces of the undead are coming to claim her. Walking corpses turn up. Eberhardt, in not providing exposition, creates a murky tale as he goes for ambience over visual shocks. Watch for death symbolism. (Vestron)

SOMBRA THE SPIDER WOMAN (1947). Feature version of **THE BLACK WIDOW.**

SOME CALL IT LOVING (1973). John Collier's fable, "Sleeping Beauty," about a girl asleep for eight years who is purchased from a carnival by a lonely man, was expanded by writer-producer-director James B. Harris, with Zalman King as the jazz player and Tisa Farrow as the sleeper. Richard Pryor plays a character on drugs. The full-length form, unfortunately, is more than the short story can bear. Carol White, Logan Ramsey. (Monterey; IVE)

SOME GIRLS DO (1967). Splendid James Bond imitation with Richard Johnson as Hugh "Bulldog" Drummond, a British detective graduated to superspy in this sequel to DEADLIER THAN THE MALE. The old Bulldog is after supervillain James Villiers, who creates an army of robotized sexy women to sabotage the SST-1, an experimental aircraft, and hold up Britain for eight million pounds. A voyeur's romp blending undercovered undercover females with such gadgets as a make-up kit that projects a soul-shattering "infrasonic" killer beam and powerboats operating on infrasupersonic speed devices. Director Ralph Thomas plays all the absurdities for the satire intended. The cast is either very British (Maurice Denham, Robert Morley) or very sensuous (Daliah Lavi, Beba Loncar, Sydney Rome, Virginia North). Never a dull moment, what?

SOMEONE AT THE TOP OF THE STAIRS (1973). Supercheap TV-movie produced in Britain. Talk talk talk and few thrills as Donna Mills, Judy Carne, David Bekeyser, Brian McGrath and Francis Willis work with a creaky Brian Clemens plot about a man in the attic of an old mansion who absorbs the life force of ghosts and projects them as apparitions. Directed by John Sichel.

SOMEONE BEHIND THE DOOR (1971). French psychothriller has a good cast (Anthony Perkins, Jill Ireland, Charles Bronson, Henri Garcin) but a mediocre plot about a brain surgeon trying to force an amnesia victim to commit murder. Directed by Nicolas Gessner. (Saturn; Unicorn) (Laser: Image)

SOMEONE'S WATCHING ME! (1978). This TV-movie, which owes much to Alfred Hitchcock's REAR WINDOW for its voyeurism and persecution paranoia, was written-directed by John Carpenter, who again distills the finest essences of the suspense-horror story. Lauren Hutton portrays a likeable TV director who takes an apartment in an L.A. high rise, only to become the target for a long-range Peeping Tom who harasses her with calls, letters and eventually the promise of death. Hutton makes for a resourceful heroine-in-peril who is willing to go after the killer instead of vice versa. David Birney plays her ineffectual boyfriend (a USC philosophy instructor) and Adrienne Barbeau (a lesbian for reasons never explored) is a fellow office worker who also becomes prey for the killer, whose identity is less important than his tactics. This also works as a parable about modern-day hazards of city living, but just taken for what it is, it's a better-than-average effort for TV with fine music by Harry Sukman. Also known as HIGH RISE.

SOMETHING EVIL (1972). Substantial TV-movie, an early work of director Steven Spielberg, who displays imaginative use of the camera to trick up some supernatural hokum taking place on a farm in Bucks County, Pa. The family consists of Sandy Dennis, Darren McGavin and Johnny Whittaker. The neighbors include Jeff Corey, Ralph Bellamy and Bruno Ve Sota.

SOMETHING IS CRAWLING IN THE DARK (1970). Stranded travelers seek refuge in a haunted house, discovering evil all too quickly. Directed by Mario Colucci. Farley Granger, Stan Cooper. (Value)

SOMETHING IS OUT THERE (1977). Video version of **DAY OF THE ANIMALS** (Action Inc.).

SOMETHING IS OUT THERE (1988). Disappointing four-hour TV pilot for a short-lived series—derivative of ALIEN and other sci-fi plots to distraction. "Something" is ripping people apart on Earth and detective Joe Cortese is hot on the trail, suspecting a woman (Maryam D'Abo) who's always hanging around the murder sites. She turns out to be Ta'ra, a humanoid alien from a prison ship, chasing an escaped convict called a Xenomorph, who just happens to be a shape-changer, although in its natural state it resembles a giant cockroach. The thing gets inside you then pops out. Sound familiar? The only intriguing sequence for four hours is when the "something" escapes from the ship. Pretty weird stuff, the way Richard Colla directs it. But all that dialogue between the cop and girl, and the subplot about the cop's love life—it's insufferable TV mentality stuff. Written by Frank Lupo, co-executive producer with one-time actor John Ashley. Rick Baker created the Xenomorph and John Dykstra concocted the space effects. Robert Webber, George Dzundza, Kim Delaney.

SOMETHING SPECIAL (1987). The "something" of the title is a male sex organ, grown on the body of young teenager Pamela Segall by magical means. While that might sound raunchy, screenwriters Carla Reuben and Walter Carbone (working with the Alan Friedman short story "Willy Milly") make this a thoughtful teen comedy, dealing with teenage behavior on a satirical level. The Milly who becomes an overnight Willy takes on the guise of a male, encouraged by her father to box and curse to be "one of the boys." How she/he learns about the sexes is clever story-telling, enhanced by the sensitive direction of Paul Schneider. Eric Curry, Mary Tanner, Seth Green, Taryn Grimes, John Glover, Patty Duke. Alternate titles: WILLY MILLY and I WAS A TEENAGE BOY. (Continental)

SOMETHING WEIRD (1968). Not as awful as most Herschell Gordon Lewis exploitationers, but improvements can be measured on the head of a darning needle. An accident victim enters into a pact with a hideous witch and emerges with ESP powers, helping the police solve crimes. SOMETHING WEIRD is something wasted. Script by producer James F. Hurley. Tony McCabe, Elizabeth Lee. (Video Dimensions; Vidmark)

SOMETHING WICKED THIS WAY COMES (1983). Ray Bradbury's 1962 best seller reached the screen a Disney production, with Bradbury writing his own screenplay and picking his own director, Jack Clayton, and star, Jason Robards. The result, alas, is not a classic (even Bradbury, apparently, has a hard time adapting Bradbury) but still recaptures the melancholy "dandelion wine" mood of Bradbury's youth in Illinois in 1932 and his poetic imagery. Two boys (one representing the daring side of Bradbury's schizophrenic soul, the other the conservative intellectual) encounter a sinister carnival operated by Mr. Dark, a delicious personification of evil. Dark and his midway freaks steal the youth of victims to replenish themselves (a theme explored in Bradbury's "The Dark Ferris") and it's up to the boys (aided by Robards as a librarian father) to resist the temptations of the insidious Dark, well etched by Jonathan Pryce. While the effects are dazzling and offbeat, the relationship between the intellectual youth and the father doesn't build the fire it needs to consume the viewer. Great character bits by Royal Dano as the Electric Man and Pam Grier as a witch. (Video/Laser: Disney)

SOMETIMES THEY COME BACK. See **STEPHEN KING'S SOMETIMES THEY COME BACK.**

SOMEWHERE IN TIME (1980). Sensitive adaptation of Richard Matheson's time travel novel, BID TIME RETURN. Christopher (Superman) Reeve is a romantic playwright fascinated with a turn-of-the-century stage actress (Jane Seymour). So intense is this fascination he overcomes time flow and travels back through the years to Michigan's Mackinac Island where he finds the actress and conducts a bittersweet love affair. Matheson adapted his book, Jeannot Szwarc directed. Teresa Wright, Christopher Plummer. (Video/Laser: MCA)

SOMEWHERE TOMORROW (1983). Sensitive, gentle love story, employing the lesser sensational elements of the ghost story. A teenager (Sarah Jessica Parker) is the first on the crash site of a small plane carrying two young men. One of the youths (Tom Shea) dies, but he returns from the spirit world to help the girl overcome personal problems, namely her refusal to accept the recent death of her father, and her mother's intentions to remarry. Tenderly told and intelligently written, but writer-producer-director Robert Wiemer fails to inject much excitement, nor is there any clever use of the ghost. The ending will disappoint fans of the supernatural. Nancy Addison, Rick Weber. (Media)

SONG OF BERNADETTE, THE (1943). Film biography of a French woman who claimed to see visions of the Virgin Mary in 1858, and the ostracism, ordeal by trial and self-doubt she suffered until the Catholic Church accepted her experiences as a miracle and the healing waters of Lourdes were established. First-class Fox production directed by Henry King and written by George Seaton, with inspiring score by Alfred Newman. Jennifer Jones, Linda Darnell, Vincent Price, Lee J. Cobb, Gladys Cooper, Sig Ruman, Jerome Cowan, Alan Napier, Fritz Leiber Sr. (Video/Laser: CBS/Fox)

SONG OF THE SUCCUBUS (1975). Editions 2-3.

SONNET FOR THE HUNTER, A. See **WITCHFIRE.**

SONNY BOY (1987). Grotesque movie about a kidnapped child, brought up by a demented family and caged like an animal. Produced by Italy's Olividio G. Assonitis and directed by Robert Martin Carol, this was made in the U.S. desert and stars Michael Griffin as the boy-turned-killer, David Carradine in drag as the woman of the house (!) and Brad Dourif as Weasel. Ugh. Sydney Lassick, Conrad Janis. (Media) (Laser: Image)

SON OF ALI BABA (1952). Just say the secret word—"Sesame"—and the door to the hidden cave will spring open and 40 thieves will pop out. What is more fantastic than that? How about Tony Curtis in the title role of this Universal-International Arabian fantasy actioner? If you can swallow his Brooklyn accent, there's a bridge we'd like to sell you. This Ross Hunter production was directed by Kurt Neumann with his scimitars crossed. Piper Laurie and Susan Cabot provide love interest, Victor Jory and Gerald Mohr provide villainy.

SON OF BLOB. Video version of **BEWARE! THE BLOB** (Video Gems).

SON OF DARKNESS: TO DIE FOR 2. See **TO DIE FOR 2: SON OF DARKNESS.**

SON OF DRACULA (1943). Universal's second sequel to DRACULA (after DRACULA'S DAUGHTER) focuses on Count Alucard (check that spelling, fans), a cloaked entity in Louisiana country who hypnotically draws Louise Albritton into vampirism. Loads of atmosphere, good make-up by Jack Pierce, nifty man-to-bat transitions (done with animation) and a sense of fun, with Chaney enjoying his role. Directed by Robert Siodmak. J. Edgar Bromberg, Evelyn Ankers, Robert Paige. (Video/Laser: MCA)

SON OF DRACULA (1974). With Ringo Starr producing, and filling in as Merlin the Magician, this goes down as the only (we hope) rock 'n roll vampire flick. It vacillates between comedy and what Starr considers "outre." All the standard cliches are here, plus figures from the rock world, and while there is an obvious love for horror movies underlying the project, results are wishy washy. Directed by Freddie Francis. Dennis Price, Keith Moon, John Bonham, Suzanna Leigh.

SON OF DR. JEKYLL, THE (1951). Lightweight variation on the Jekyll-Hyde theme, with Louis Hayward as a scientist trying to prove dear old (dead) dad wasn't as evil as everyone claimed, especially that Robert Louis Stevenson chap. But then his own experiments go awry and he turns bad. Some nights it just doesn't pay to mix secret chemicals. Directed by Seymour Friedman. Alexander Knox, Jody Lawrence, Gavin Muir.

SON OF FLUBBER (1963). Disney's sequel to THE ABSENT-MINDED PROFESSOR revives Fred MacMurray as the forgetful scientist who invents a "flubber gas" that allows him to control the weather (imagine an impromptu rainstorm inside a station wagon). Keenan Wynn is again the bad guy trying to steal the gas, Nancy Olson is suffering Mom and Tommy Kirk is the son. Visually witty fantasy prevails. Directed by Robert Stevenson and written by producer Bill Walsh. Ed Wynn,

Charles Ruggles, William Demarest, Paul Lynde, Stuart Erwin. (Disney)

SON OF FRANKENSTEIN (1939). The third and final time Boris Karloff played the Monster—and the last time the Monster evoked viewer sympathy. Director Rowland V. Lee, imitating James Whale, captures a surrealistic aura—Germanic in its expressionism—and there's a literate ring to the script by Willis Cooper, a famous radio writer (LIGHTS OUT, QUIET PLEASE). Bela Lugosi's Ygor the Shepherd is one of his more menacing roles—he escapes his own hamminess and type-casting. Basil Rathbone as the good doctor chews the scenery, but his histrionics are appropriate to the story. Lionel Atwill is unforgettable as the police chief with an artificial hand which clicks and jerks like a mechanical monster. Superior effort in the series, one which no true-blooded horror fan should miss. (MCA; RCA/Columbia) (Laser: MCA)

SON OF GODZILLA (1968). Bringing up junior can be trying, as this Japanese study in parenthood shows. Out of a giant egg pops a baby Godzilla, Minya. The monster tyke has a slight disadvantage: He has harmless breath and blows only smoke rings. Minya is slapped around by father a bit until he learns good manners—such as how to hulk with style, shamble with grace and crush and maim with finesse. And then a giant praying mantis flies by, challenging the moppet monster to a duel. Children will find this delightful; adults will wonder if the Japanese are putting them on with inept charm. Directed by Jun Fukuda. Tadao Takashima, Akira Kubo, Beverly Maeda. (Hollywood Home; Prism; Budget; Video Treasures) (Laser: Japanese)

SON OF HERCULES IN THE LAND OF DARKNESS (1963). Italian grunt spectacle as Dan Vadis, in the muscle-bound role of Hercules, does battle with a wicked queen in an underground city. Spela Rozin. (Video Yesteryear; S/Weird)

SON OF HERCULES IN THE LAND OF FIRE, THE (1963). Ugh! Strain! Groan! Hercules (Ed Fury) is up to his usual flexing, aiming his superstrength at unnatural forces. Directed by Giorgio Simonelli. Claudia Mori, Luciana Gilli, Adriano Micantoni, Nando Tamberlani.

SON OF HERCULES VS. VENUS (1980). Muscle heroes tackle Olympian Gods in the greatest Olympic Games of all. Directed by Marcello Baldi. (Best Film & Video)

SON OF INGAGA (1940). Romantically-inclined giant ape runs through the jungle in search of his Caucasian heart throb, taking her back to the lab. Played for laughs . . . wasn't it? Let's give director Richard Kahn the benefit of the doubt, shall we? Zack Williams, Laura Bowman. (J & J; Sinister/C; Madhouse; Filmfax)

SON OF KONG, THE (1934). King Kong creators Merian C. Cooper and Ernest B. Schoedsack concocted this sequel, panned by critics and disowned by its stop-motion animator, Willis O'Brien, who resented Ruth Rose's tongue-in-cheek script. That didn't stop it from making money, but it has never attained classic status, remaining in Kong's shadow. Still, it now plays like a film of historic importance with ample comedy and adventure as Carl Denham (Robert Armstrong) returns to Skull Island to pay off debts incurred from Kong's destructive rampage through New York City. (Can you imagine the bill the Empire State Building owners handed him?) The offspring of Kong is a lovable albino creature. Helen Mack replaces Fay Wray as the heroine, but returning are Frank Reicher, Noble Johnson and Victor Wong. (Nostalgia Merchant; Media; Fox Hills) (Laser: Image, with **KING KONG**)

SON OF SAMSON (1962). Mark Forest is not playing Samson but Maciste. By any name he's a muscular dolt who falls prey to a wicked queen wearing a magical locket that puts thoughts of love into his feeble brain. Directed by Carlo Campogalliani. Chelo Alonso, Angelo Zanolli, Vira Silenti. (Sinister/C; S/Weird)

SON OF SATAN. See **WHAT!**

SON OF SINBAD (1955). Made in 3-D but released flat—you might use that same word to describe the impact this Howard Hughes-RKO release had on viewers. Dale Robertson as Sinbad, with a Texas accent? Yech. More at home in this Hollywoodesque fantasy nonsense are Vincent Price (as poet Omar Khayyam) and the stimulating Mari Blanchard, who fills her scanty harem costumes with considerable pulchritude. Other women doing the same are Sally Forrest and Lili St. Cyr. The plot has to do with the secret of Green Fire, a forerunner to TNT, but the only fire this picture needed was under director Ted Tetzlaff. Arabian music by Victor Young. (United; VCI; Republic)

SONS OF STEEL (1988). Australian adventure with heavy metal music, set in the near future in the kingdom of Oceana where a plot is afoot to blow up Sydney Harbor and traveling through time is the means by which to stop it. Written-directed by Gary L. Keady. Rob Hartley, Roz Wason, Jeff Duff.

SORCERERS, THE (1967). One of the few films of wunderkind director Michael Reeves before his untimely death . . . this adaptation of John Burke's novel (by Reeves and Tom Baker) depicts elderly couple Boris Karloff and Catherine Lacey devising a machine that enables them to experience sensations of those under their control. Lacey goes whacky, feeling too many oats, and urges a mod-minded teenager to commit sadistic murders. It's an exciting idea, but Reeves was hampered by an almost non-existence budget and the film looks cheaper than it deserves. Ian Ogilvy, Susan George.

SORCERESS, THE (1956). See editions 1-3.

SORCERESS (1982). High-camp sword-and-sorcery actioner produced by Jack Hill with the subtlety of a cauldron-stirring, cackling witch and directed by Brian Stuart with the finesse of an axeman hacking through bramblebrush. Dialogue by Jim Wynorski will have you howling as two sisters, endowed with supernatural strength as well as healthy chests (which they reveal often), search for the wicked wizard who murdered their mother. There's a satyr-like character who bellows like a goat, a Viking swordsman and a beefcake who introduces the twins to nightly pleasures. Plus an army of zombie swordsmen and effects by John Carl Buechler, added by producer Roger Corman to save the picture. Leigh Harris, Lynette Harris, Bob Nelson. (HBO)

SORORITY BABES AT THE SLIMEBALL BOWL-O-RAMA (1988). The title is the only thing distinctive about this purely pathetic attempt at campy comedy. First you have lowlife Peeping Tom nerds who crash a campus house for dames to watch their sororiety rites, such as having bare fannies spanked and chests squirted with whipped cream. Then you have the broads playing a joke on the guys by having them break into a bowling alley. Gee, really exciting so far, right? Then you have a stupid hand-puppet imp from another dimension that turns the asinine teens into homicidal killers. The monster is as unbelievable as the cast, and the lowest common denominator is always sought by director David DeCoteau. Linnea Quigley, Andras Jones, Robin Rochelle, Hal Havins, Brinke Stevens. (Urban Classics) (Laser: Full Moon)

SORORITY GIRLS AND THE CREATURE FROM HELL (1990). This bears no relationship to David DeCoteau's "Sorority Girls" series, which at least had sophomoric hum. This is unfunny dumb as unappealing gals and guys rendezvous at a mountain cabin and are torn apart by a man with a Neanderthal face turned killer by a giant-skull statue in a secret cave. The stone-age script by producer-director John McBrearty makes no more sense than that. A rank amateur production, stricken by poverty. Len Lesser, Stacy Lynn, Eric Clark, Dori Courtney. (Complete Entertainment)

SORORITY HOUSE MASSACRE (1985). Eternal fraternal is internal and infernal when a cackling knife killer, foaming at the mouth and wide of eyeballs within their sockets, slaughters daughters of the rich and seeks to make dead co-ed Angela O'Neill, who's been dreaming about an escaped psycho case. Written-directed by Carol Frank. (Warner Bros.)

SORORITY HOUSE MASSACRE 2 (1990). Five

sexually arousing babes, their bodies barely covered by Frederick's of Hollywood lingerie, rush about a house of horror pursued by a killer who apparently is the ghost of a demented madman who slaughtered his family in the residence years before. As dumb as it sounds, it's fun to watch how director Jim Wynorski poses the babes for ultimate sexploitation. Melissa Moore, Robyn Harris, Stacia Zhivago, Dana Bentley. (New Horizons)

SORORITY SISTERS. See **NIGHTMARE SISTERS.**

SO SAD ABOUT GLORIA (1973). So sad about SO SAD ABOUT GLORIA, a sad statement of a sadistic shadowplay showing slaughter and the same sanguinary sad plot about seducing a sad skirt into a state of sad insanity. Sad for director-producer Harry Thomason and sad for Dean Jagger, Lori Saunders, Lou Hoffman, Bob Ginnaven, and sad for you, the viewer. For sad-ists.

S.O.S. COAST GUARD (1937). A 12-chapter Republic serial in which Bela Lugosi portrays a scientist (Boroff) who creates a deadly gas capable of disintegrating objects (in case you're wondering, the gas is composed of Arnaltite and Zanzoid, got it?). His opponent is Ralph Byrd (later to play Dick Tracy) as a Coast Guard undercover man. Directed breathlessly by William Witney and Alan James. Maxine Doyle, Carlton Young, Thomas Carr. There's a feature version under the same title. (Video/Laser: Republic)

S.O.S. INVASION (1969). See editions 1-3.

S.O.S. TIDAL WAVE (1939). See editions 1-3.

SO SWEET, SO DEAD. See **SLASHER . . . IS THE SEX MANIAC, THE.**

SOUL OF A MONSTER (1944). Director Will Jason makes this potboiler special with tricked up camera angles, but results are mediocre. George Macready portrays a millionaire on the verge of death, saved when his wife prays for help and salvation comes from female demon Rose Hobart. Jim Bannon, Jeanne Bates.

SOULTAKER (1990). Evil entity comes to Earth to take souls. Written by Vivian Schilling, who also stars, and directed by Michael Rissi. Joe Estevez, Gregg Thomsen, David Shark and Robert Z'Dar as "The Angel of Death." (Action International) (Laser: Image)

SOUND OF HORROR (1967). Spanish producer Gregory Siechristian keeps expenses down by making his monster (a prehistoric dinosaur) invisible. It only becomes "noticeable" by a bellowing cry on the soundtrack each time director Jose Anthonio Nieves Conde moves the camera. The roar sends the Greek expedition that stirred up the monster scurrying for new digs. Arturo Fernandez, Soledad Miranda. (Nostalgia; Loonic)

SOUND STAGE MASSACRE. See **STAGEFRIGHT.**

SOYLENT GREEN (1973). Big-budgeted version of Harry Harrison's MAKE ROOM, MAKE ROOM that graphically, and depressingly, depicts life in 2022. A curious blending of the private eye genre with glimpses of a world to come, scripted by Stanley Greenberg without much faith to Harrison's story. Earth has become a smog-shrouded planet, hopelessly populated, and near-anarchy is at hand as Manhattan cop Charlton Heston investigates a series of murders—perpetrated to protect a secret. This was Edward G. Robinson's last film, and ironically he portrays a dying man who seeks a pleasant form of suicide in this downbeat world of tomorrow. Leigh Taylor-Young, Chuck Connors, Joseph Cotten, Brock Peters. Tautly directed by Richard Fleischer. (Video/Laser: MGM/UA)

SPACE AMOEBA, THE. See **YOG—MONSTER FROM SPACE.**

SPACEBALLS (1987). Another "babbling Brooks" production. In spite of himself, writer-producer-director Brooks manages to sprinkle funny one-liners and puns throughout this spoof of STAR WARS. It begins with "Once upon a time warp . . ." with rolling credits, then introduces Dark Helmet (villain), Lone Starr (young hero), Barf (dog-man, his own best friend), Princess Vespa (heroine), Yogurt (wise old sage with knowledge of that ethereal power, the Schwartz) and Pizza the Hut (monster). Helmet and his Spaceballs try to steal the oxygen from planet Druidia's atmosphere, the lampoonery being of the broadest kind. Not all the characters work and the spoofery comes too late after the success of STAR WARS to seem relevant. (Didn't HARDWARE WARS do it better?) Still, the cast is bright: John Candy, Rick Moranis, Daphne Zuniga, Bill Pullman, Dick Van Patten, George Wyner. Brooks doubles as Yogurt and a human villain, President Skoorb. Joan Rivers provides the voice of a female golden robot who "wants to talk." (Video/Laser: MGM/UA)

SPACECAMP (1986). Spacecamp is where young would-be astronauts undergo simulated flights and learn the meaning of responsibility. A dingbat robot a la R2D2 causes a rocket to be launched with a young crew aboard under adult trainer Kate Capshaw. How the kids face the rigors and perils of space flight make for an intriguing premise enhanced by special effects. Pleasant viewing, directed by Harry Winer. Lea Thompson, Tom Skerritt, Kelly Preston. (Video/Laser: Vestron)

SPACE CASANOVA. See **BATTLESTAR GALACTICA.**

SPACE CHILDREN, THE (1958). Bernard C. Schoenfeld's script is an allegory (about the gap between adolescence and adulthood) set in a seacoast desert community, which allows director Jack Arnold to duplicate the environmental mood effects from his earlier sci-fi films. A new family arrives at a rocket-launching center, where the children see a UFO and meet an intelligent rock-brain that forces them to sabotage an atomic missile project. The telepathic alien, strangely enough, never communicates—it's all shown without exposition. This being a message picture first and an entertainment second, William Alland's production builds to flat-footed honorable intentions. Parents are depicted as dolts—children as wise pacifists. Johnny Crawford, Russell Johnson, Sandy Descher.

SPACE CRUISER (1977). Animated Japanese space adventure (set in 2199) features interplanetary war between Earth and a planet of evil, Gorgon. Not great animation; strictly for space-happy moppets. Directed-written by Yoshinobu Nishizaki, originally for an Asian TV series. Voices by Marvin Miller, Rex Knolls, Mercy Goldman. (Laser: Japanese, with **MY YOUTH IN ARCADIA**)

SPACE CRUISER YAMATO PART II (1979). Further depiction of warfare between our planet and Gorgon, designed by a team of Japanese animators under the writing and direction of Toshio Masuda.

SPACE DEVILS. See **SNOW DEVILS.**

SPACED INVADERS (1990). A kiddie science-fiction parody of "alien invaders attack earth" movies—midget E.T.s who speak in English idioms idiotically are fighting an interstellar war when their radio picks up a broadcast of Orson Welles' "War of the Worlds." Thinking Earth is a rendezvous point for their space fleet, the aliens land in a rural town on Halloween night and are taken by townspeople to be simple treat-or-treaters. It's lowbrow action and comedy juvenilely directed by Patrick Read Johnson. Douglas Barr, Royal Dano, Ariana Richards, J. J. Anderson, Gregg Berger. (Video/Laser: Touchstone)

SPACED OUT (1979). British comedy about sexpots from the Betelgeuse star system who learn about the birds and the bees from Earthling male prisoners. Pretty cheap and pretty silly—and the women are pretty, too—pretty dumb, so don't expect much to challenge the intellect. Barry Stokes, Tony Maiden. Directed by Norman J. Warren. (Vidamerica; Thorn EMI)

SPACE FIREBIRD 2772 (1980). Japanese animated feature is a creative exercise in space adventure as adventurer Godoh and sexy robot Olga rocket into the void to circumvent the destructive activities of a monster. Written-directed by Taku Sugiyama. (Celebrity)

SPACEFLIGHT 1C-1 (1965). See editions 1-3.

SPACEHUNTER: ADVENTURES IN THE FORBIDDEN ZONE (1983). A $12 million space saga released in 3-D but with few "comin' at ya!" thrills. In the 22nd Century, interstellar mercenary Peter Strauss diverts his scow to the plague-riddled planet Terra 11 to rescue tourists in the clutches of villainous Overdog (Michael Ironside), a half-machine entity who soaks up psychic power of beautiful women (without bothering with physical contact). Production design is messy and funky with an eclectic assortment of costumes, weapons and vehicles. The script never develops Strauss' Wolff character or his "Odd Couple" relationship with waif Molly Ringwald. Ernie Hudson is wasted as the sidekick, Washington. Lamont Johnson directs with an eye to continuous action, and there's a conflagration with Overdog. Andrea Marcovicci. (Video/Laser: RCA/Columbia)

SPACE INVASION OF LAPLAND. See **INVASION OF THE ANIMAL PEOPLE.** (And lap it up!)

SPACE KID. See **MEATBALLS PART II.** (For meatheads)

SPACEMAN AND KING ARTHUR, THE. See **UNIDENTIFIED FLYING ODDBALL.**

SPACEMAN IN KING ARTHUR'S COURT, THE (1980). Juvenile-minded time-travel fantasy starring Dennis Dugan as a nerdy inventor who creates a lookalike humanoid robot of himself (named Hermes) and travels aboard the spaceship Stardust back to the days of King Arthur, where he uses modern wizardry to defeat a coup to overthrow the king. This pleasant, innocuous bit of whimsey is enhanced by a British cast headed by Kenneth More (as Arthur), Jim Dale and Ron Moody. Don Tait wrote the telescript directed by Russ Mayberry. (Disney)

SPACEMAN SATURDAY NIGHT. See **INVASION OF THE SAUCER MEN.**

SPACE MASTER X-7 (1958). Lower-berth material of the "blob" school: Fungus off the hull of a space probe mixes with blood and becomes a "Blood Rust"—resembling out-of-control Jello—which goes on a killing spree. Quick, someone, decontaminate it before it spreads. The presence of Moe Howard as a cabbie suggests director Edward Bernds might have intended this as comedy. Screenwriters George Worthington Yates and Daniel Mainwaring might feel otherwise. But Bill Williams, Paul Frees and Joan Barry play it for serious.

SPACE MEN. See **ASSIGNMENT OUTER SPACE.**

SPACE MEN APPEAR IN TOKYO. See **WARNING FROM SPACE.**

SPACE MISSION OF THE LOST PLANET. See **VAMPIRE MEN OF THE LOST PLANET.**

SPACE MONSTER (1965). Of the "Rocky Jones, Space Ranger" school, in which pilots argue among themselves while jockeying to another planet. The titular Space Monster is a rubbery-faced character (never explained) which the crew encounters halfway to its interstellar destination. Finally, after more bickering, the crew crashlands in the ocean of an alien world. Special effects consist of a model rocket floating in a tankful of crabs and lobsters, probably in an L.A. restaurant. Aka FIRST WOMAN INTO SPACE. James B. Brown, Russ Bender, Francine York. Producer-director Leonard Katzman went on to DALLAS. (S/Weird)

SPACE MONSTER DAGORA. See **DAGORA, THE SPACE MONSTER.**

SPACE MUTINY (1989). A spaceship of the Southern Sun is taken over by mutineers. But, you guessed it, one man comes forward to stop the dastardly act. Reb Brown, John Phillip Law, James Ryan, Cameron Mitchell, Cissy Cameron, Graham Clark. Produced-directed by David Winter from a script by Maria Dante. (Action International)

SPACE 1999. Episodes of the 1974-75 British TV series, with Martin Landau and Barbara Bain as inhabitants of a lunar station that is catapulted into space when the moon explodes. In addition to this three-hour pilot from USA, there are **COSMIC PRINCESS, DESTINATION MOONBASE ALPHA** and **JOURNEY THROUGH THE BLACK SUN.** (DESTINATION is from CBS/Fox and JOURNEY is from IVE.) Four episodes are available from ITC/J2 Communications: **VOYAGERS RETURN, A MATTER OF LIFE AND DEATH, EARTHBOUND** and **THE GUARDIAN OF PIRI.** (Laser: Image has 23 discs, each with two episodes.)

SPACE 1999: ALIEN ATTACK. Video of TV episodes introduced by Sybil Danning. (USA/Adventure)

SPACE NINJA. Video version of **SWORDS OF THE SPACE ARK** (King Bee).

SPACE PATROL VOL. I (1955). Early-day TV turkey about Buzz Corey and Cadet Happy fighting to clean up space for the United Planets. You really have to be a fan of these old shows to endure its naivete and rock-bottom budget. Viewed as nostalgic camp, it passes . . . slightly. This video contains four episodes with cast regulars Ed Kemmer, Lyn Osborne, Ken Mayer and Virginia Hewitt. (Nostalgia Merchant)

SPACE PATROL VOL. 2 (1955). Four more episodes of the low-budget TV series. (Video Yesteryear)

SPACE PATROL (1955). Three-volume set of episodes from the early-day TV series. Vol 1: "The Underwater Spaceship Graveyard," "The Theft of the Rocket Cockpit" and "Danger . . . Radiation." Vol. 2: "Revenge of the Black Falcon," "The Androids of Algol" and "The Android Invasion." Vol. 3: "The Exploding Stars" and "The Atomic Vault." (Rhino)

SPACE PRISON. See **BATTLESTAR GALACTICA.**

SPACERAGE: BREAKOUT ON PRISON PLANET (1985). Bank robber Michael Pare is sentenced to imprisonment on Proxima Centauri 3, in New Botany Bay's Penal Colony #5, in the 22nd century. While that may sound like sci-fi, this turns into a basic action film with Pare leading a major breakout. The factions race through the desert in ROAD WARRIOR-style dune buggies, blasting away with ordinary pistols and machine-guns. Screenwriter Jim Lenahan attempts to inject human elements into the mock heroics by focusing on "escaper hunter" John Laughlin, his gorgeous red-headed wife Lee Purcell, ex-LAPD cop Robert Farnsworth, and redneck planet governor William Windom. Farnsworth, a one-time stunt man turned actor, portrays the sagacious, laconic Western hero who straps on his six-guns at the finale, so it's easy to compare this to Hollywood's action Westerns. Despite its mindlessness, this film moves at a fast clip. Directed by Conrad E. Palmisano. (Lightning)

SPACE RAIDERS (1983). What might have been a classic kind of TREASURE ISLAND IN SPACE, with a castaway youth joining star-roving renegades and mercenaries, is a leaden nonadventure in tedium, as characterless as the space pirates it depicts. Roger Corman's film is lacking in style and pace, unfolding mechanically, without heart, under writer-director Howard R. Cohen. Not one of the alien creatures looks like anything more than an actor wearing a rubber face mask, and the space battles are staged without excitement, often consisting of outtakes from earlier Corman space movies. When gang leader Vince Edwards (rough on the outside, all marshmallowy inside when it comes to the kid) goes against the Robot Death Ship, you root for the bad guys. Thom Christopher, Patsy Pease, David Menderhall, Dick Miller. (Warner Bros.)

SPACESHIP (1983). Abominal attempt to satirize ALIEN in the vein of AIRPLANE (hence the title) as the Vertigo, a phony-looking rocket, streaks through space carrying a ridiculous crew commanded by Leslie Nielsen. An alien, as phony as the rocket, sings and dances a little ditty called "I Want to Eat Your Face." Whatever charm this might have had is obliterated by overacting (including Ron Kurowski as the Monster), flat direction and utterly dumb writing. The major blame can be put on Bruce Kimmel, who wrote, directed and plays one of the crew. Eject it through the airlock, quick! Gerrit Graham, Cindy Williams, Patrick Macnee (as wild-eyed Dr. Stark). Aka THE CREATURE WASN'T NICE. (Vestron)

SPACESHIP TO THE UNKNOWN (1936). Newly re-edited version of the first half of the FLASH GORDON serial from Universal. See **FLASH GORDON**.

SPACE SOLDIERS. See **FLASH GORDON (1936).**

SPACE SOLDIERS CONQUER THE UNIVERSE. See **FLASH GORDON CONQUERS THE UNIVERSE.**

SPACE THING (1968). A mild pornie from skin flick specialist David Friedman in which an alien ship lands in L.A. and its inhabitants become involved with goofy humans who spend their time indulging in sex. Produced-directed by B. Ron Elliott. (S/Weird)

SPACE VAMPIRES (1981). Video version of **ASTRO ZOMBIES.**

SPACE WARRIORS 2000 (1980). Children's special effects sci-fi with a doll coming to life to join the Galaxy Council and fight alien invaders.

SPACE-WATCH MURDERS. (1978). Editions 1-3.

SPACEWAYS (1953). Early Hammer foray into the fantastic, and an interesting twist it is. Howard Duff, space scientist, is suspected of placing the corpses of his wife and lover inside a satellite circling Earth. To clear himself, he blasts off to recover the satellite. Early collaborative effort between Michael Carreras (producer), Terence Fisher (director) and Jimmy Sangster (assistant director). Eva Bartok, Alan Wheatley. (Sinister/C; Weiss Global)

SPANIARD'S CURSE, THE (1958). British jury sends an innocent man to the gallows—he vows to get vengeance. Suddenly, the jurors die one . . . heh heh . . . by one. Diabolical, isn't it? Directed by Ralph Kemplen and written by Kenneth Hyde from a novel by Edith Pargiter, THE ASSIZE OF THE DYING. Tony Wright, Susan Beaumont, Lee Patterson, Basil Dignam, John Watson. (Sinister/C; S/Weird; Filmfax)

SPARE PARTS (1984). West German thriller, FLEISCH, is an offbeat, oft-intriguing medical mystery in which honeymooners become victims of a body organ transplant operation. The action drifts from Texas (where trucker Wolf Roth helps Nordic beauty Judith Speidel find her missing husband) to New York City for an unusual climax. Writer-director Rainer Erler avoids many genre cliches. (Vidmark)

SPARKS: THE PRICE OF PASSION (1989). Unconvincing TV-movie in which Victoria Principal stars as the mayor of Albuquerque, New Mexico, and is the target of a serial killer. Principal is totally preposterous in a role obviously tailored for her glamorous TV-star image; there are neither sparks nor passion. And the slasher elements are feeble. Directed without conviction by Richard Colla. Ted Wass, Hector Elizondo, William Lucking, Elaine Stritch, Ralph Waite.

SPASMS (1983). DEATH BITE, a chilling novel by Michael Maryk and Brent Monahan, depicted the horrible attacks of a 19-foot taipan snake, a serpent from the island of Narka-Pintu whose bite kills in three minutes. This Canadian adaptation alters the taipan to a demon serpent from the Gates of Hell. Oliver Reed, a hunter once bitten by the supernatural reptile, has ESP link to the demon and undergoes visions (in black and white) of its vicious, gory, "cold-blooded" attacks. Peter Fonda is the snake expert who talks about "viral telepathy" and Kerrie Keane is the obligatory female. Al Waxman is the uncouth villain who goes out with three "strikes" against him. Screenwriter Don Enright also introduces a pointless snake cult; his adaptation should have been exciting (the book certainly was) but it generates little suspense and uncoils lethargically to an anticlimax. Tangerine Dream provides a "serpent's love theme." Minimum effects footage of the supernatural serpent—director William Fruet doesn't have the bite. (Thorn EMI/HBO)

SPAWNING, THE. Video version of **PIRANHA II: THE SPAWNING** (Embassy).

SPAWN OF THE SLITHIS. See **SLITHIS.**

SPEAK OF THE DEVIL (1989). Belabored comedy in which a lecherous, phony evangalist (Robert Elarton) and his equally phony but quite nymphomaniac wife (Jean Miller) buy a haunted house in L.A. and convert it into "Church of Latter Day Sin"—motto being "Sin today without guilt." The greedy wife, meanwhile, makes a pact with the Devil. The script by producer-director Raphael Nussbaum and Bob Craft is all over the place with subplots: innocent girl threatened with "learning about sin"; rabbi subjected to castigation by a foul-mouthed Christian. The satanic rituals are attended by unconvincing demons and there are weak-willed attempts to have the Reverend get religious. But to what avail? Bernice Tamara Goor, Walter Kay, Louise Sherill. (Action International)

SPEAR OF DESTINY, THE. See **FUTURE HUNTERS.**

SPECIAL BULLETIN (1983). Controversial TV-movie (by producer Don Ohlmeyer and writer-director Marshall Herskovitz) is a pastiche of a network news special. Scenes of an anchor team at a network studio are interspersed with footage shot by "live" cameras on the scene. Suspense is ever-building and the effect of realism ever-numbing as antinuclear protestors hold hostages in Charleston, S.C. These well-intended but warped radicals have an atomic device and threaten to set it off. The ending is a stunner. Ed Flanders, Kathryn Walker. (Karl Lorimar; Kartes; RCA/Columbia)

SPECIAL EDITION OF CLOSE ENCOUNTERS OF THE THIRD KIND. After the theatrical release of CLOSE ENCOUNTERS OF THE THIRD KIND, Steven Spielberg restored excised footage and took out some of the original, hoping to reach a new state of perfection. The end result seems no better or worse than the original, with storyline unchanged. Either gives you satisfying results. (Video/Laser: RCA/Columbia)

SPECIAL EFFECTS (1984). Unusual psychopathic murder-mystery written-directed by Larry Cohen. Eric Bogosian is a legendary pornographic film maker who puts angst into his work—and secretly murders the women in his life, photographing their deaths with a camera hidden in his decorative bedroom. After killing a talentless model, he wins the confidence of cop Kevin O'Connor and plans to make a film about her murder, using her husband as an actor. How Bogosian plays cat-and-mouse games with the cops and the husband makes for a compelling film with surprising twists. Zoe Tamerlis, Brad Rijn. (Embassy)

SPECTERS (1987). Tedious Italian horror job that makes a specter-acle of itself when archeologist Donald Pleasence, digging in the catacombs beneath Rome, uncovers a crypt that contains the spirit of a demon that looks like Nosferatu in silhouette. The film is stretched beyond human endurance, offering nothing frightening. It took three Italians to think up the story and four to write the script for director Marcello Avallone. They do not add up to the Magnificent Seven. John Pepper, Katrine Michelsen, Massimo de Rossi. (Imperial)

SPECTRE, THE. See **GHOST, THE.**

SPECTRE (1977). Intriguing Gene Roddenberry TV-pilot with Robert Culp and Gig Young as fighters of the supernatural who take on Asmodeus, a Prince of Evil controlling a Druid cult. Fans will find this delightful viewing, the Roddenberry-Samuel B. Peeples script full of surprises and Clive Donner's direction angled to capture the sexual side to the cult. John Hurt, Ann Bell.

SPECTREMAN VS. ZERON AND MEDRON (1985). Two episodes of a TV series in which a costumed crimefighter battles Dr. Gori and his monster Zeron, not to mention the villain Karas. (Wonderland)

SPECTRE OF EDGAR ALLAN POE, THE (1973). Grieving over the loss of his loved one, a beauty who died before her time, Robert Walker Jr. (as Poe) seeks rest in the mansion of Cesar Romero, who just happens to be a sadist with a torture chamber of snakes. Director-producer-writer Mohy Quandour allegedly delves into phobias apparent in Poe's stories, but it's exploitation hokum shedding no insight into the real Poe. Tom Drake and Carol Ohmart run around the drafty house to no avail. Nevermore, quoth viewers. (Unicorn)

SPELL, THE (1977). Blatant steal from CARRIE . . .

this TV-film is the story of a teenage girl who uses kinetic powers against her tormentors. Despite obvious parallels, this has a feel of its own and includes a coven of witches nurturing ESP powers in the young. The diabolical theme is overshadowed by a duel between daughter (Susan Myers) and mother (Lee Grant). The Brian Taggart script makes salient comments on the Generation Gap and lack of communication between children and parent. On that level, it is keenly interesting. Directed by Lee Philips. (Goodtimes; Worldvision)

SPELLBINDER (1988). L.A. lawyer Timothy Daly is so many steps behind the viewer in figuring out what this supernatural mystery that he grows into a tedious hero long before the climax to Tracy Torme's script. Without Daly's Jeff Mills to care about, there's little director Janet Greek can bring to this tale of a satanic cult that sets up sacrifices for the full moon. There is Kelly Preston to watch when she seduces Daly in a sizzling bedroom scene, there's the menacing presence of Anthony Crivello and there's Cary-Hiroyuki Tagawa's portrayal of a cop—but this wizened witchcraft tale is bereft of effects, gore or anything else to hold one's interest. Rick Rossovich, Audra Lindley. (CBS/Fox)

SPELLBOUND (1940). British shocker featuring demonic possession and spiritualism, based on THE NECROMANCERS by Hugh Benson. Written by Miles Malleson and directed by John Harlow, this depicts a spiritualist bringing back a dead lover. Derek Farr, Hay Petrie, Vera Lindsay, Felix Aylmer. Also known as PASSING CLOUDS and THE SPELL OF AMY NUGENT. (Sinister/C; Filmfax)

SPELLBOUND (1945). Alfred Hitchcock walks "the dark corridors of the human mind," probing into guilt, fantasy, schizophrenia, paranoia and persecution complexes, but never forgetting this is a psychothriller. What a screenplay Ben Hecht has adapted from Francis Beeding's novel, THE HOUSE OF DR. EDWARDES. You're in for a couchful of tricks as headshrinker Ingrid Bergman attempts to unlock the brain of amnesia victim Gregory Peck. Watch how the "master of suspense" gradually reveals the Freudian clues, and see how he toys with the audience, leaving doubt if Peck is a murderer or not. The dream sequences were designed by Salvador Dali and include blank, staring eyes, mouthless- noseless faces, bizarre landscapes. Miklos Rozsa's music, employing the eerie-sounding theremin, is the best "psychoanalytic" score ever written. Donald Curtis, Leo G. Carroll, Wallace Ford, Rhonda Fleming. (Video/Laser: CBS/Fox)

SPELLCASTER (1988). Unreleased until 1992, this Charles Band production made under his Empire logo is half-horror, half-comedy that unfolds in Bracciano's Castle outside Rome, where a motley collection of contest winners gathers to find a million-dollar check hidden on the premises. A drunken rich-bitch rock star, a fat guy, an Italian crook, a blonde floozy and a TV video-jock are the greedy characters offset by a nice couple from Cleveland. Adam Ant is the host-owner of the castle, named Diablocyril St. Michaels, but obviously the Devil incarnate. The Dennis Paoli-Charles Bogel script (from a story by Ed Naha) has such a cop-out ending that the film falls on its pie-studded face in spite of rich production values, good monsters by John Buechler and satisfying gory murders staged by director Rafal Zielinski. It's a case of the film never taking itself seriously enough. Richard Blade, Gail O'Grady, Harold "P" Pruett. (Video/Laser: RCA/Columbia)

SPELL OF EVIL (1973). Diane Cilento, reincarnation of a 16th Century witch, wields strange powers and inflicts terror on her husband and his secretary. Brian Clemens scripted this low-budget TV-movie directed by John Sichel. Jennifer Daniel, Edward De Souza.

SPELL OF THE HYPNOTIST. See **FRIGHT (1957).**

SPIDER, THE (1958). Producer-director Bert I. Gordon, who works harder than any other producer-director to save a buck, gets entangled in a web of ineptitude in presenting a giant mutant spider living in a cave outside of a town crawling with unbearable two-legged teenagers. Eight-legged monstrosity turns out to be eight times duller than most giant movie spiders. Ed Kemmer, of SPACE PATROL, stars as the adult to the rescue. June Kenney, Gene Roth. Aka EARTH VS. THE SPIDER.

SPIDER BABY or THE MADDEST STORY EVER TOLD (1964). Peculiar and fascinating blend of black humor and macabre horror, designed with a tongue-in-cheek attitude that still does not lessen the impact of chilling moments. The bizarre plot revolves around the Merrye family, which is stricken by Merrye's Syndrome, a "progressive age regression" disease that takes victims "beyond pre-natal to a level of savagery and cannibalism." Two sisters, demented beyond description, live in an "old dark house" with their crazy brother and family chauffeur Bruno, played by Lon Chaney with conviction. Relatives come to the house to win the family inheritance with a lawyer named Schlocker (a nice touch, that) and face the death games, designed by the children in an air of naivete. There's a great dinner-table scene and crazy dialogue that keeps the film working as shock and satire. One of Chaney's best low-budget roles, with director Jack Hill keeping everything in balance despite the wild nature of his script. Carol Ohmart, Quinn Rebeker, Mantand Moreland. (Loonic; Dark Dreams; S/Weird; Filmfax; Admit One)

SPIDERMAN. Video version of **AMAZING SPIDERMAN, THE.** (MCA) (The laser disc from Image features four episodes: "Night of the Clones," "Escort to Danger," "Con Caper" and "Curse of Rava.")

SPIDERMAN (1981). Two TV episodes: "Night of the Clones" and "Escort to Danger." (Prism)

SPIDERMAN: PHOTO FINISH. Video version of TV episodes (Star Classics).

SPIDERMAN STRIKES BACK (1978). Episodes of a two-part TV adventure from THE AMAZING SPIDERMAN, recut for syndicated TV. See **DEADLY DUST.**

SPIDERMAN: THE DRAGON'S CHALLENGE. See **CHINESE WEB, THE.**

SPIDER RETURNS, THE (1941). Feature version of the 15-chapter Columbia serial of the same title, based on a once-popular pulp magazine character who wore a mask and fought supercriminals. The Spider is out to stop The Gargoyle, a foreign saboteur seeking to subjugate mankind with a TV spying gadget called "The X-Ray Eye." Directed by James W. Horne. Warren Hull, Mary Ainslee, Dave O'Brien.

SPIDER'S VENOM. Video version of **LEGEND OF SPIDER FOREST, THE** (Lettuce Entertain You).

SPIDER'S WEB, THE. See **HORRORS OF SPIDER ISLAND**.

SPIDER WOMAN STRIKES BACK, THE (1946). Dreary Universal thriller in which Gale Sondergaard recreates her portrayal from SHERLOCK HOLMES AND THE SPIDER WOMAN. Once again The Creeper (Rondo Hatton), introduced in THE PEARL OF DEATH, is scaring people to death with his malformed acromegalic face while Ms Spidey grows odd plants which feed on blood of young women. Who should happen along but young woman Brenda Joyce, who settles into the house of horror, unaware of the fate-worse-than-death awaiting her. Milburn Stone and Kirby Grant are in the neighborhood, and maybe they can save her. Directed by Arthur Lubin and written by Eric Taylor. (From CBS/Fox as **SPIDERWOMAN**)

SPIES A-GO-GO. See **NASTY RABBIT, THE.**

SPIRAL STAIRCASE, THE (1946). Psychosuspense thriller (produced by Dore Schary) in which speechless housemaid Dorothy McGuire is pursued through a New England mansion in 1906 by a killer who murders women with physical deformities. There are tense sequences directed by Robert Siodmak, and Mel Dinelli's script emphasizes subtle psychological motivations. The whodunit aspects are well treated. Based on Ethel Lina White's SOME MUST WATCH. George Brent, Ethel Barrymore, Kent Smith, Elsa Lanchester, Rhonda Fleming, Rhys Williams. (Video/Laser: CBS/Fox)

SPIRAL STAIRCASE, THE (1975). Thoroughly botched version of Ethel Lina White's SOME MUST WATCH, capturing none of the suspense or mystery of this old-fashioned plot about a speechless nurse trapped in a house with a psycho-killer. There's no feeling of isolation (the house is in the suburbs, not the country) and Peter Collinson's direction is as limp as the corpses. Jacqueline Bisset tries to make her part believable, but the identity of the murderer is easily discerned. Christopher Plummer and Sam Wanamaker deserve better. Mildred Dunnock, Gayle Hunnicutt, Elaine Stritch, John Philip Law. (Warner Bros.)

SPIRITISM (1961). Mexican version of the famous story, "The Monkey's Paw," would have author W. W. Jacobs rising from his grave to throttle director Benito Alazarakl. This Is the old tale of a mother granted three wishes when she comes in possession of the mummified paw. Jose Luis Jimenez, Alicia Caro, Nora Veryan. (Sinister/C; S/Weird)

SPIRIT IS WILLING, THE (1967). Lightweight, bubbly ghost comedy from producer-director William Castle, featuring none of his gimmicks or tricks, now seems terribly dated and inappropriate to the rest of his canon. With a silly music score by Vic Mizzy, the film is a broad farce set on the New England coast, in a house haunted by three 19th Century spirits constantly battling with each other and leaving the house a shambles. Newcomer parents Sid Caesar and Vera Miles (wasted in these roles) think son Barry Gordon caused the mess, and Ben Star's screenplay hinges on this misunderstanding. John McGiver, Cass Daley, John Astin and Jay C. Flippen contribute nice comedy bits to this innocuous fluff, which was based loosely (and we mean loosely) on Nathaniel Benchley's novel THE VISITORS.

SPIRIT OF '76 (1990). Roman Coppola, son of Francis Ford Coppola, produced. Lucas Reiner, son of Carl Reiner, wrote-directed. Susan Landau, daughter of Martin Landau, also produced. Call it ALL IN THE FAMILY. This is a ripoff of BACK TO THE FUTURE and TED AND BILL'S EXCELLENT ADVENTURE in which nitwits from the future (where recorded history is lost because the records were "degoused") lands in 1976 to learn the ways of modern men (rock 'n roll dancing, fast cars, self-identity groups) while trying to repair their busted time machine. The gags are lame and the cast can do little with the threadbare script. In short, a waste of time unless you like to watch celebrity offspring. David Cassidy, Olivia d'Abo, Carl Reiner, Leif Garrett, Rob Reiner, Julie Brown, Moon Zappa, Don Novello, Iron Eyes Cody, Barbara Bain, Geoff Hoyle. (Video/Laser: Columbia TriStar; Sony)

SPIRIT OF THE BEEHIVE (1974). In the year 1940, two Spanish children see the movie FRANKENSTEIN and become obsessed with the Monster Myth. Because the moppets are isolated from their parents, their obsession to understand why the Monster killed the girl in the pond draws them into a fantasy world where the Frankenstein Monster exists and treats them with kindness. Beautifully photographed film that, unfortunately, lacked broad appeal. Written-directed by Victor Erice. Fernando Fernan Gomez. (Connoisseur) (Laser)

SPIRIT OF THE DEAD (1968). See **CURSE OF THE CRIMSON ALTAR, THE.**

SPIRIT OF THE DEAD (1972). Video version of **ASPHYX, THE** (VCL).

SPIRITS (1990). A priest and a team of ESP experts investigate a haunted house. Directed by Fred Olen Ray. Erik Estrada, Carol Lynley. (Vidmark)

SPIRITS OF THE DEAD (1969). Three directors adapted Edgar Allan Poe tales in this French-Italian effort also known as TALES OF MYSTERY. "Metzengerstein" is Roger Vadim's contribution, with Jane and Peter Fonda as a wanton countess and her cousin who attend orgies and fight among themselves. When she kills him, he returns as a black stallion. It's the weakest of the trio. "William Wilson" (Louis Malle directed) stars Alain Delon as a man with a dual personality who tries to win Brigitte Bardot in a card game. The third is the best: Federico Fellini's "Never Bet the Devil Your Head, or Toby Dammit," with Terence Stamp as a drunken British actor called to Rome to receive an award. Narrated by Vincent Price. James Robertson Justice. (Fright)

SPIRITUALIST, THE. See **AMAZING MR. X, THE.**

SPLASH (1984). This comedy hits the water just right—a Disney release that is a gainer and a half. Released under the Touchstone banner, it was that studio's first film with a glimpse of female nudity. Mermaid Daryl Hannah leaves Bermuda waters for Manhattan,

DARYL HANNAH AS THE MERMAID IN 'SPLASH'

where on dry land she falls for Tom Hanks and creates hysterical scenes gnawing on lobsters in a restaurant and screeching fish notes that shatter a dozen TV screens. Ron Howard's direction never jackknives and the Lowell Ganz-Babaloo Mandel-Bruce Jay Friedman script is a series of charming vignettes. John Candy as Hanks' produce district brother, Eugene Levy as the nerd trying to expose Hannah's secret and Richard Shull as Dr. Ross contribute wonderful characterizations. And love those scenes of Hannah, tail and all, floating in a bathtub. Dody Goodman and Shecky Greene also contribute bits. (Video/Laser: Touchstone)

SPLASH, TOO (1988). Disappointing sequel to the 1984 smash SPLASH, made for TV. Amy Yasbeck was an inspired piece of casting and she brings Madison the Mermaid to life again, but the Bruce Franklin Singer script is bland, failing to build momentum and lacking clever comedy. And so director Greg Antonacci is left holding the flipper. This begins where the original left off, with Madison and her lover (Todd Waring) on a paradise island, swimming in the lagoon. The goons back in the States cause problems for Waring's brother (Donovan Scott); there's a scientist mistreating dolphins, and Madison and hubby settle down to marital bless—all failed subplots. No SPLASH, just a ripple. Rita Taggart, Noble Willingham, Dody Goodman.

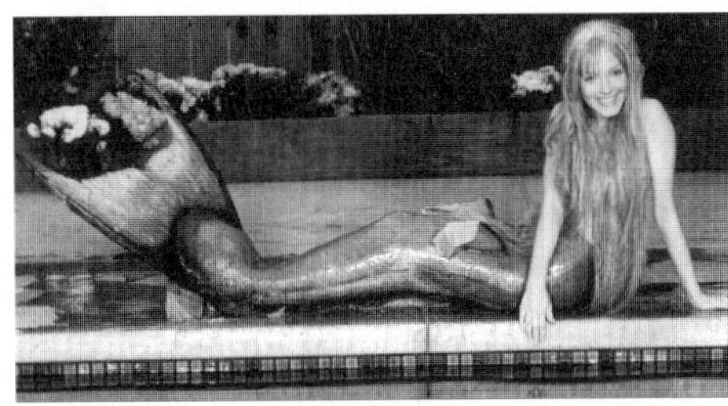

AMY YASBECK AS THE MERMAID IN 'SPLASH TOO'

SPLATTER. See **FUTURE KILL.**

SPLATTER . . . ARCHITECTS OF FEAR (1986). Special-effects artists run wild on a movie location, creating mutants, zombies and Amazon women for the sake of cinema art. Interesting, informative; better than the movies the effects guys are working on, that's for sure. Directed by Peter Rowe. (Synchron)

SPLATTER UNIVERSITY (1984). Described as "where the school colors are blood red"... another Troma slasher flick with the usual line-up of victims. Written-directed by Richard W. Haines. Francine Forbes, Cathy Lacommare, Dick Biel. (Available in two versions, one gorier than the other, from Vestron.)

SPLIT (1988). Avant garde, underground-style feature set in a futuristic time when an "Agency" keeps everyone under surveillance and computerized control. Individualistic Starker (Timothy Dwight) refuses to conform and lives off the land, leading the director of the Agency (played by writer-director Chris Shaw) to instigate an intensive search. Meanwhile, the director undergoes transformation from human to android, and gradually the two plots meld. This is filled with computer graphics and an MTV-style editing that leaves one confused. John Bechtel, John Flynn. (Action International)

SPLIT SECOND (1992). Outstanding aspects of this monster-and-effects extravaganza are the manic performances of Rutger Hauer as the maverick cop Stone and Neil Duncan as a serial-killer specialist who takes on aspects of Hauer's crazed personality when they are assigned to track down a ten-foot-tall Alien-like monster in a futuristic London plagued by rats and flood waters caused by a thermal thaw. Hauer, an anxiety-stricken paranoiac who lives on coffee and chocolate, plays the psychic Stone to maximum effectiveness as the monster turns out to be unkillable and flits about the sewers, ripping the hearts out of victims. The ambience of a deteriorating city is excellently captured in Tony Maylam's direction, and the characters are vividly grotesque. Kim Cattrall plays the heroine and Michael J. Pollard is The Rat Catcher. (Video/Laser: HBO)

SPONTANEOUS COMBUSTION (1989). What appears to be a steal of Stephen King's FIRESTARTER turns into an intense sci-fi paranoia thriller involving a 1955 A-Bomb test and how an experiment leads to a man capable of human combustion—the art of setting his fellow man on fire. Brad Dourif brings a strong intensity to the role, and one gets the feeling that writer-director Tobe Hooper (who crafted the script with Howard Goldberg) was expressing his personal anger against Hollywood. The cast (Cynthia Bain as the girl friend, William Prince as the sinister mastermind and Jon Cypher as the strange doctor) brings to this work a sense of conspiratorial fear. The fire effects by Stephen Brooks (with John Dystraka as consultant) are good. Dey Young, Melinda Dillon. (Media) (Laser: Image)

SPOOK BUSTERS (1946). Huntz Hall's I.Q. approximates the intelligence of a chimpanzee, so surgeon Douglas Dumbrille (The Mad Scientist) decides to implant Huntz's brain into the head of a gorilla. This Monogram lowbrower, directed by William Beaudine, is set in a haunted house. No doubt the title inspired GHOSTBUSTERS. Leo Gorcey, Gabriel Dell. (Warner Bros.)

SPOOK CHASERS (1957). Late-in-the-series Bowery Boys haunted house cheapie, with Stanley Clements (replacing Leo Gorcey, who had dropped out) and Huntz Hall meeting gorillas, ghosts and "apparitions" in a drafty mansion. Directed by George Blair.

SPOOKIES (1985). Two horror movies (one of them TWISTED SOULS) are joined with Elmer's Glue to (1) tell the tale of travelers trapped in a mansion zombies and inhuman monsters and (2) spin the tale of a ghoul who resembles a "Creature Features" TV host and his minions as they terrorize innocent folks. The "kitchen sink" approach should please undemanding fans. It took three directors (Eugenie Joseph, Thomas Doran, Brenda Faulkner) to make nothing out of something. Felix Ward, Dan Scott. (Sony) (Laser: Image)

SPOOKS RUN WILD (1941). The East Side Kids meet Bela Lugosi in a Monogram comedy. The Carl Foreman-Charles Marion script features Lugosi as a killer called The Monster, who travels in a coffin and is pursued by Von Gorsch. Directed by Phil Rosen, produced by Sam Katzman. Huntz Hall, Leo Gorcey, Bobby Jordan. (Sony; Kartes; Budget; Sinister/C; Video Yesteryear; Reel World)

SPOOKY MOVIE SHOW, THE. See **MASK, THE.**

SPRING, THE (1990). Archeologists Dack Rambo and Gedde Watanabe search for Ponce De Leon's Fountain of Youth in Florida jungles. Also searching for "Eternal Youth" is industrialist Steven Keats and guarding the secret are voodoo siren Virginia Watson and Shari Shattuck. Directed by John D. Patterson. (Quest)

SPY IN THE GREEN HAT, THE (1966). More MAN FROM U.N.C.L.E. TV episodes re-edited into a feature with Napoleon Solo (Robert Vaughn) stopping madman Jack Palance from diverting the Gulf Stream with a sound device. David McCallum is Vaughn's fellow agent and Leo G. Carroll is the assignment chief. Directed by Joseph Sargent. Janet Leigh, Maxie Rosenbloom.

SPY IN YOUR EYE (1966). See editions 1-3.

SPY SMASHER (1942). Spy Smasher was a character in Fawcett comic books during the 1940s . . . in thids 12-chapter serial from Republic, which stands out for its glossy production values and is one of Republic's best, the superhero is portrayed by Kane Richmond. He battles valiantly against The Mask, a German dastard heading a sabotage ring in America. Ongoing cliffhangers feature zap guns, supersonic skyplanes, and advanced forms of TV electronics. Directed by serial specialist William Witney. Marguerite Chapman, Tris Coffin, Sam Flint, Hans Schumm, Frank Corsaro. Feature version is SPY SMASHER RETURNS. (Republic)

SPY SQUAD (1962). See editions 1-3.

SPY WHO LOVED ME, THE (1977). One of the best James Bond adventure-fantasies following Sean Connery's retirement from 007 activities. Bond (Roger Moore) is assigned to prevent the builder of an underwater city (Curt Jurgens) from stealing atomic subs and turning their missiles on the free world—an impossible mission made possible with the help of Soviet spy Barbara Bach. The action sequences are terrific, the full-scale freighter sets are impressive and overall the film brims with stylish action. The sex jokes are leeringly sophomoric and the Christopher Wood-Richard Maibaum typically farfetched, but you won't be bored. Richard Kiel almost steals the film as the indefatigable villain Jaws, who survives catastrophes without disrupting a hair on his head. The character, in fact, returned in MOONRAKER. Lewis Gilbert directed the action and mayhem. Caroline Munro is featured in a bikini, chasing Bond in her helicopter. (RCA/Columbia) (Laser: MGM/UA)

SPY WITH MY FACE, THE (1966). When U.N.C.L.E. agent Robert Vaughn thrusts a pistol between Senta Berger's breasts, she remarks, "The one in the middle seems to be a gun." Yes, gang, another feature from one-hour TV shows ("The Double Affair"). Senta is plotting to take over Project Earth Save (a weapon powerful enough to destroy Griffith Park in one afternoon) and substitute a lookalike Napoleon Solo. Then, for laughs, she plans to ransom the USA for 80 zillion bucks. Spy fun with microphones in the lipstick case and cyanide in the Kool cigarette pack. Directed by John Newland. David McCallum, Michael Evans, Leo G. Carroll.

SQUEAKER, THE. See **MYSTERIOUS MAGICIAN.**

SQUIRM (1976). Just try to worm out of watching this one: electrically-charged earthworms, sandworms and bookworms (not to mention such bilateral invertebrates as acanthocephalans, nemertines, gordiaceans and annelids) wriggle, wiggle and squiggle into huge lumps prior to dawn, attacking dumb clucks (Don Scardino, Patricia Pearcy and Jean Sullivan) who drop by the swamp. Yep, it's the early worm that gets the bird. Made in Georgia by writer-director Jeff Lieberman with tongue in cheek. Ludicrous but fun cinema, allegedly populated by 250,000 real-life worms. Glow, worms, glow . . . (Video/Laser: Vestron)

SSSSS (1973). Does the title refer to the sound made by slumped-over viewers 15 minutes into the picture? Or to the cobras mad doc Strother Martin keeps in his lab outside town? It doesn't matter since producers Richard Zanuck and Dick Brown wanted to prove they could make a picture with passable effects and ridiculous premise before making THE STING and JAWS. Turning a full-grown man into a household cobra is a farce in the hands of writer Hal Dresden and director Bernard Kowalski. Would you believe a climax where a man-snake battles a mongoose? Oh well, life is one big snake pit. Dirk Benedict, Richard B. Shull.

STAGE FRIGHT (1983). Demented actress (Jenny Neumann) gets cold feet before the curtain rises, the first of several things that turn frigid during this British horror movie-within-a-movie, aka NIGHTMARES. Drop your drapes! (VidAmerica)

STAGEFRIGHT (1987). Also known as DELIRIA, BLOODY BIRD and AQUARIUS, this is out of the FRIDAY THE 13TH mold, with escaped killer Irving Wallace (a demented actor who went berserk and killed 16 people) amuck in a theater in an owl's costume, murdering a musical-play troupe: egotistical director, lecherous producer, bitchy actress, gay extra, rejected actress, etc. There are gore murders with chainsaw, axe, power drill—one body is literally pulled in half. The film takes a turn for the better once it's the killer pitted against one actress, a resourceful type who has Wallace hanging by his thumbs. Slasher-gore fans will be satisfied, but the nihilistic mood may unsettle sentimentalists and cry-babies. David Brandon, Barbara Cupisti, Don Fiore, Robert Gligorov, Directed by Michael Soavi. (Imperial)

STAIRWAY TO HEAVEN (1946). Philosophical fantasy from British producers-directors-writers Michael Powell and Emeric Pressburger that is literate, imaginative and profound in dealing with a man defying his own fate. Aka A MATTER OF LIFE AND DEATH, this British film (in black and white, with color sequences) follows RAF pilot David Niven who leaps from his flaming bomber without a bloody parachute. But someone slips up in Heaven and he is allowed to survive. Niven demands a trial by the higher celestial court and tells the powers-that-be why he should continue to live. Kim Hunter, Marius Goring, Raymond Massey, Robert Coote, Richard Attenborough.

STALKER (1979). Russia's Andrei Tarkovsky, who gave us SOLARIS, once again demonstrates daring style in this weird tale of a writer and scientist who enter a "mysterious zone" from which no one has ever returned. Their tour guide for this momentous event is called Stalker. Plenty of food for thought with enough messages to open a telegram service. Weighty but not unwieldy. Anatoly Solonitsyn, Alisa Freindlich.

STALK THE WILD CHILD (1976). JUNGLE BOOK update in which Benjamin Bottoms portrays a toddler raised by wolves, who turns into older Joseph Bottoms by the time he's removed from the jungle. It's the job of psychiatrist David Janssen to get him ready for freeways, fast-food restaurants and late-night TV movies. Eventually this pilot became a short-lived TV series, LUCAN, with Kevin Brophy in the title role. Directed by William Hale. (Worldvision)

STAND, THE (1994). Stephen King's colossal novel of an Apocalyptic showdown between good and evil in a world ravished by disease (a man-made virus that has killed millions) is a difficult one to translate to film. After years as a possible movie property, it finally came to the TV screen as a six-hour epic directed by Mick Garris, and it sports many good performances: Ruby Dee as the sweet old woman who gathers the forces of good around herself; Jamey Sheridan as Randall Flag, who symbolizes the Devil. Other distinguished performers: Rob Lowe, Ray Walston, Miguel Ferrer, Ed Harris, Kathy Bates. This is a long one, though, and requires a lot of patience to get through as it skips around to different parts of the country as the opposing forces join ranks to face the Armageddon to come. For King fans, though, it's a must.

STANLEY (1972). Awful exploitationer produced-directed by William Grefe asks the poignant question: Can a rattlesnake named Stanley find happiness with a Seminole Indian who bears a grudge against mankind? As the Indian, Chris Robinson is passable, destined for greater things as a TV soap star on GENERAL HOSPITAL, but Stanley, from Snake Central Casting, really sinks his teeth into Gary Crutcher's plot—and characters including crook Alex Rocco. Sufferers of ophidiophobia should beware. (VCI; Neon; VidAmerica)

STARBIRDS (1982). Space war explodes between Earth and winged creatures from a space station circling Jupiter in this animated U.S.-Japanese cartoon adventure. Focus is on a supership called Dynamo, launched to counter the attack. Directed by Tadao Nagahama and Michael Part. (Media)

STARCHASER: THE LEGEND OF ORIN (1982). Full-length 3-D cartoon feature has breathtaking space battles and weapons of tomorrow, and many stereovision effects are outstanding. But characters and storyline smack of STAR WARS. It's certainly no Disneyesque film Steven Hahn produced-directed from a script by Jeffrey Scott: Orin is a slave digging for power crystals in Mineworld, ruled by robots with electric whips and the tyrant Zygon. Orin breaks out to the land above, undergoing adventures with an obligatory female, a blind youth, a roguish adventurer a la Han Solo and a spaceship operated by Arthur the Computer. Parts of the film, however, move at warp factor five, making up for technical and story defects. One of the best scenes has Orin manhandled by scraggly "mandroids," half-machine creatures. A must-see for 3-D addicts. Voices by Joe Colligan, Carmen Argenziano, Noelle North, Les Tremayne. (Video/Laser: Paramount)

STARCRASH (1979). A return to the delightfully campy dialogue and plotlines of old-fashioned serials. The universe is in the grip of the evil Count Zarth Arn (Joe Spinell) and only Stella Starr, a space pilot who wears high-heeled boots in warp drive, can stop him with the help of alien navigator Akton and Elle the Robot, who speaks like a mentally deficient Texan. As played by Caroline Munro, wearing black leather underwear, Stella stops the star-show. Marjoe Gortner is her partner and Christopher Plummer is The Emperor of Space. A galactic wreck for adults, but kids 6 to 18 will shriek with delight. Flash Gordon never had a girl like Caroline . . . Directed by Lewis Coates, an Italian better known as Luigi Cozzi. (Charter; Embassy)

STARCROSSED (1985). TV-movie ripoff of STARMAN, featuring a female E.T. in humanoid form Earthling male. A secret government organization is after the stranded alien (Belinda Bauer) and her own kind stalk her with super-deadly zap laser guns, which means plenty of explosions, chases and other action from writer-director Jeffrey Bloom. There's an attempt at a poignant love story between Bauer and James Spader but the cheapness of the effects and the lack of production doom this to the graveyard of uninspired time killers. Jacqueline Brookes, Peter Kowanko, Clark Johnson.

STAR CRYSTAL (1985). "High-tech" sci-fi with good effects and spaceship interiors. It begins as a horror-mystery film in the vein of ALIEN when astronauts discover a crystal in Mars' Olympus Mons crater. Later, when a crew is trapped aboard a shuttlecraft with a lifeform from the rock, director Lance Lindsay brings out the cliches: tentacles that wrap around victims, drained corpses, etc. But after the creature taps into the computer and gets Bible religion, it/him/she (?) emerges a cute E.T. copy. This never makes up its mind what it is, and turns into an anomaly. John W. Smith, Faye Bolt, C. Jutson Campbell. (New World)

STARFLEET: THE THALIAN SPACE WARS (198?). Animated adventures of interplanetary warfare.

STARFLIGHT ONE: THE PLANE THAT COULDN'T LAND (1983). Mild sci-fi theme (a hypersonic transport aircraft) is overpowered by standard TV-movie gimmicks about passengers trapped in flight with time and oxygen running out and other suspense ploys that won't have anyone on the edge of their seats. Directed by Jerry Jameson. Lee Majors, Hal Linden, Lauren Hutton, Robert Webber, Ray Milland, Jocelyn Brando. (Vestron)

STAR KNIGHT (1986). Any film with Klaus Kinski, Fernando Rey and Harvey Kietel has to arouse curiosity, but in this case one can ignore the triple billing. This turns out to be an oddball Spanish film (released as KNIGHTS OF THE DRAGON) set in the days of knights rescuing damsels from fire-breathing dragons. Kinski is a benevolent magician for a foolish ruler who surrounds himself with a plotting priest (Rey) and bodyguard knight (Kietel). An alien in a spacesuit lands in a Spielbergesque UFO and communicates to the king's daughter (Marie Lamor) telepathically, while comedy relief with a bumbling "Green Knight" sets a light-hearted mood that predominates the direction by producer Fernando Colombo. (Video/Laser: Vidmark)

STAR MAIDENS (1976). The planet Medusa is dominated by female chauvinist pigs who force men to grovel at their feet, pleading for equal rights. Needed: Men's Lib. Directed by Wolfgang Storch and James Gatward. Judy Geeson, Christiane Kruger, Pierre Brice.

STARK MAD (1929). Lloyd Bacon-directed film, released in silent and sound versions; pretty hoary by today's standards, but interesting nevertheless. A Mayan temple houses a giant ape, whose cries startle a jungle expedition looking for a missing explorer. Also involved: a Hairy Taloned Monster, H. B. Warner, Irene Rich, Claude Gillingwater and Louise Fazenda.

STARLIGHT SLAUGHTER. See **EATEN ALIVE**.

STARLOST: THE INVASION, THE (1973). Re-edited episodes of STARLOST, the disastrous Canadian TV series created by Harlan Ellison, who had his name changed to Cordwainer Bird in the credits. Set aboard the Space Arc, a floating city in 2790, this is the kind of stilted stuff that gives blemish to the good name of science fiction. Two stories—one about contact with an alien ship and the second about "implant" people—are boring, lacking a single moment of excitement. In STAR TREK the characters are smart. In THE STARLOST the characters are dumb. Captain Kirk says "Engage." This says "Disengage." Keir Dullea, Gay Rowan, Robin Ward, Stephen Young, Donnelly Rhodes. The static direction is to be blamed on George McGowan and Joseph L. Scanlan.

STARMAN (1984). One of the few sci-fi movies of the '80s with as much "heart" and emotion as effects—not quite as triumphant as E.T. but trying hard. When a ship crashlands on Earth, its pilot transforms into deceased Jeff Bridges, whose wife (Karen Allen) must accompany him on his odyssey to safety. Starman has the powers of resurrection, and there's a Christ parable in the Bruce A. Evans-Raynold Gideon screenplay. What builds is a love between Earthling and alien, which culminates in her impregnation—the first joining of two races. On their trail is sympathetic scientist Charles Martin Smith and a ruthless government agent, Richard Jaeckel. John Carpenter directed with a feeling for his characters, injecting as much comedy as the serious theme allowed. A commendable effort, with Dick Smith, Stan Winston and Rick Baker contributing topnotch effects. (Video/Laser: RCA/Columbia; Pioneer)

STAR ODYSSEY (1978). In this Italian potboiler, aliens auction off "insignificant" planets, with Earth going for the highest price. The inheritors show up over the green planet in a death ship, blasting away. The only man who can save us is a psychic professor surrounded by adventurers, misfits and comedic robots, who seek to destroy the alien ship's metal, Indirium. The humanoids wear metallic suits and blond wigs, props left over from WAR OF THE ROBOTS, a spaghetti import also directed by Al Bradly. Screen sci-fi at its worst, with inane dialogue and a music track that is a joke. The funniest scenes involve a fight between a human and an android boxer and stupid antics between man-and-wife robots. You have to see one of these to believe they exist. Yanti Somer, Gianni Garko, Sharon Baker. (From Mogul as **CAPTIVE PLANET**)

STAR PILOTS (1966). As soon as STAR WARS became a roaring success, an Italian flop, 2+5 MISSION HYDRA, was dusted off, retitled and distributed to unwitting audiences. Three aliens land on Earth to kidnap homo sapiens for a zoo that will open soon in a solar system near you. Directed by Pietro Francisci. Kirk Morris, Gordon Mitchell, Roland Lesafree, Leontine Snell.

STAR PRINCE, THE. See **INVADERS FROM SPACE.**

STAR QUEST: BEYOND THE RISING MOON (1989). Outer-space adventure starring Tracy Adams as Pentan, an artificially created woman who fights evil. Directed by Phillip Cook. (VidAmerica) (Laser: Image)

STARSHIP (1986). Convoluted Australian sci-fier in the STAR WARS vein, set on a mining station on Ordessa in the 21st Century. It's the Empire vs. the Rebels again as renegades uncover a plot to kill 600 miners and try to take over the starship before the massacre happens. Director Roger Christian has a hard-edged style but the script he and Matthew Jacobs wrote is lacking in humor, in clarity and in sharply defined characters. You know a film is in trouble when robots are more interesting than humans, and that's the case here with a droid named Grid, whose face resembles a Noh-play mask. The most exciting moments occur during a hand-to-hand battle aboard a mining truck. John Tarrlant, Donough Rees, Deep Roy, Ralph Cotterill. Aka LORCA AND THE OUTLAWS. (Cinema Group; Magnum)

STARSHIP INVASIONS (1977). Christopher Lee, playing humanoid alien Captain Ramses in a silly costume, battles another race of E.T.s in order to invade Earth. Robert Vaughn is equally wasted as a UFO expert investigating sightings followed by mass suicides. No one seems to be trying very hard to raise above the level of a juvenile Z movie. A tax shelter deal for writer-director Ed Hunt? Daniel Pilon, Victoria Johnson.

STARSLAMMER (1986). Hilariously bad Jack H. Harris misfire produced-directed by Fred Olen Ray, blending the "women behind bars" theme with a Roger Cormanish space adventure. Sandy Brooke, a miner on Arous, is captured by Ross Hagen, a psycho bad guy with spiked hands, and sent to Vehement, a women's prison in space where female guards dress like sado-masochists and behave like raving lesbians. Sandy and pal Susan Stokey endure adventures with the Sovereign, a space tyrant; the Inquisitor (Aldo Ray in fright make-up); the Deadly Spawn (an awkward Alien-like mess); the Jagger Rat (a rodent with sharp teeth) and assorted depraved freakos. Ray plays it for laughs at times but Michael D. Sonye's script is torturous torture. The film is broken into chapters ("Death on Planet Arous," "Jail Break 3000") and promises Taura will be back in CHAIN GANG PLANET. So far it hasn't happened. Mary Gant, Dawn Wildsmith, John Carradine, Bobby Bresee. Aka STARSLAMMER: THE ESCAPE and PRISON SHIP STAR SLAMMER. (Vidmark)

STAR TREK. All the original TV episodes have been issued in cassette by Paramount, including five two-in-one specials, and are available in stores. So is the famous untelevised pilot; see **CAGE, THE.**

STAR TREK—THE MOTION PICTURE (1979). First movie version of the popular TV series was a $40 million epic. But did director Robert Wise pull off an epic? "Trekkies" came away disappointed, feeling it was talkative and handicapped by weak concepts. Harold Livingston's screenplay—combining the TV episodes "The Changeling" and "The Doomsday Machine"—depicts a cloud-like object on a collision course with Earth and the USS Enterprise speeding from drydock to intercept. Attempts are made to rise above the mock heroics of STAR WARS but it still falls short of being a 2001: A SPACE ODYSSEY with its lack of a living villain and its cloudy characters. The effects are uneven—ranging from excellent (when depicting the cloud's interior) to less-than-adequate (when depicting a San Francisco shuttleport.) The original cast is here: William Shatner, Leonard Nimoy, DeForest Kelley, James Doohan, George Takei, Walter Koenig, Nichelle Nichols and Grace Lee Whitney. Stephen Collins and Persis Khambatta are non-regulars. Despite its flaws, this was a worldwide box-office success and began a series of sequels and spawned two new TV series. (Paramount; RCA/Columbia) (Laser: Paramount)

STAR TREK II: THE WRATH OF KHAN (1982). Rejoice! This is truer to the TV series than the first film. A 1967 episode, "Space Seed," serves as the springboard, with villainous Khan (Ricardo Montalban, playing a su-

THE MANY FACES OF 'STAR TREK'

WILLIAM SHATNER

LEONARD NIMOY

JIMMY DOOHAN

GEORGE TAKEI

DeFOREST KELLEY

NICHELLE NICHOLS

WALTER KOENIG

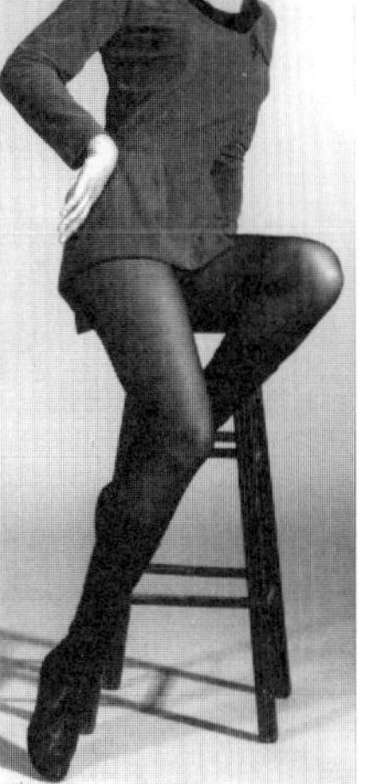

BRENT SPINER

PATRICK STEWART

MARINA SIRTIS

GRACE LEE WHITNEY

perintelligent Earthman) wreaking revenge on Captain Kirk for stranding him on a God-forsaken planet. The crew is back (Shatner, Kelley, Doohan, Koenig, Takei, Nichols), but it's Leonard Nimoy who commands center stage with his death scene and burial in space. It was a brilliant gimmick by writer Jack B. Sowards that beamed up a sequel, STAR TREK III: THE SEARCH FOR SPOCK. An enormous success for Paramount, producer Harv Bennett and director Nicholas Meyer. Non-regulars included Kirstie Alley, Bibi Besch, Paul Winfield and Ike Eisenmann. The one individual shoved into the background was creator Gene Roddenberry, who reportedly did not get along with Paramount during the making of the first film. WRATH OF KHAN is not a classic but its clean-lined effects (by Ken Ralston and the Industrial Light & Magic team) and its unpretentious space-opera yarn make it an A effort worth going to the end of the Universe to see. (Video/Laser: Paramount)

STAR TREK III: THE SEARCH FOR SPOCK (1984). This begins where STAR TREK II left off—with the Enterprise returning to Earth, its crew members grieving over the death of science officer Spock. But while WRATH OF KHAN was classic in its depiction of the STAR TREK regulars, this smacks of TV writing. So it finally resembles an over-inflated one-hour show, brimming with effects you wish they could have done on TV in the '60s. Before he died, Spock transferred his soul's essence to Dr. McCoy, so they must return to Genesis (a planet undergoing a speeded-up evolutionary cycle), recover Spock's corpse while fighting off Klingons, and get back to Vulcan. Leonard Nimoy does a fine job directing—one wishes the script by producer Harve Bennett had contained more emotion and sharper dialogue. Ken Ralston again heads the Industrial Light & Magic team, creating effects that reflect the state-of-the-art level to which this series had ascended. Guest appearances by Mark Lenard as Spock's father, Dame Judith Anderson as the High Priestess of Vulcan, Christopher Lloyd as the Klingon commander. At hand are regulars William Shatner, Nimoy, DeForest Kelley, Jimmy Doohan, George Takei, Nichelle Nichols, Walter Koenig. (Video/Laser: Paramount)

STAR TREK IV: THE VOYAGE HOME (1986). Unquestionably the best of the STAR TREK features, a satisfying blend of story and characters. Picking up where THE SEARCH FOR SPOCK ended, this depicts the regulars returning to Earth aboard the Klingon Bird of Prey, while Earth is under siege from an alien space probe. To save Earth, Kirk and crew travel back to the 20th Century to kidnap two humpback whales. This action takes place in San Francisco and the scenes of Kirk, Spock and others adjusting to modern times are hilarious. A charming idea, beautifully directed by Leonard Nimoy, and a family film in the truest sense, with an ecology message to boot. Catherine Hicks appears as a whale conservationist. William Shatner, Nimoy, DeForest Kelley, George Takei, James Doohan, Nichelle Nichols, Walter Koenig. (Video/Laser: Paramount)

STAR TREK V: THE FINAL FRONTIER (1989). The Enterprise goes in search of God in this fifth series contender, and under the direction of William Shatner, Captain Kirk himself, it emerges an average but enjoyable adventure containing comedy, action, metaphysical dialogue, even the deeper meanings of life, no matter how superficial. Laurence Luckinbill is at the core of the film's strength as a Christ-like figure named Sybok (hailing from Vulcan) who converts disciples for a trek to find the meaning of the Universe. After a burst of action on a planet in the Neutral Zone, Sybok commandeers the Enterprise and heads for the Great Barrier, beyond which lies the legendary Sha Ka Ri, the home of . . . ? The Kirk-Spock-McCoy interplay is here, there's a romance between Uhuru and Sulu, and Scotty gets to camp it up as comedy relief. The ending is ambiguous and you might say that Shatner, producer Harve Bennett and screenwriter David Loughery copped out about the final meaning of life, but you can't expect to learn everything from a STAR TREK adventure. Leonard Nimoy, DeForest Kelley, James Doohan, George Takei, Nichelle Nichols, Walter Koenig, David Warner. (Video/Laser: Paramount)

STAR TREK VI: THE UNDISCOVERED COUNTRY (1991). Outstanding entry in the series, tightly written-directed by Nicholas Meyer, produced efficiently by Leonard Nimoy and starring the world-famous cast in its swan song. It is a darker STAR TREK with less bantering between cast regulars and none of the buffoonery that tinged the fifth film. There are Shakespearean touches in the dialogue and a sense of tragic doom about its characters that even reaches out and touches Captain Kirk, forced to face his prejudice against Klingons. With a plot paralleling world events at the time, THE UNDISCOVERED COUNTRY depicts the Enterprise assigned to establish contact with Klingon leader David Warner, who wants to make peace with the Federation. (The Klingon Empire faces collapse after the explosion of a mining moon that bears a close parallel to the Chernobyl disaster in the Soviet Union.) The story unfolds with Kirk and Dr. McCoy on trial for murder and sentenced to an ice planet while Spock, in command of the Enterprise, encounters treachery and duplicity as loyalties are divided by peace proceedings. Sulu turns up as captain of his own starship, the Excelsior. The film was released only weeks after the death of series creator Gene Roddenberry. A stand-out in the cast is Christopher Plummer as a Klingon warrior, Chang. DeForest Kelley, James Doohan, Walter Koenig, Nichelle Nichols, George Takei, Kim Cattrall, Mark Lenard, Grace Lee Whitney, Brock Peters, John Schuck, Christian Slater. (Video/Laser: Paramount)

STAR TREK: THE NEXT GENERATION (1987). The excellent two-hour pilot to the sequel series to the original STAR TREK—set a century later with different characters aboard a galaxy-class USS Enterprise. The teleplay by D. C. Fontana and series creator/producer Gene Roddenberry is a compelling piece that set the tone and introduced Patrick Stewart as Captain Jean-Luc Picard; Jonathan Frakes as Commander William Riker; LeVar Burton as engineering officer Geordi LaForge; Denise Crosby as security chief Tasha Yar; Michael Dorn as the Klingon, Lt. Worf; Gates McFadden as Dr. Beverly Crusher; Marina Sirtis as the provocative, sensitive Counselor Deanna Troi; Wil Wheaton as youthful Wesley Crusher; and Brent Spiner as the wonderful humanoid robot, Data. This two-hour adventure, "Encounter at Farpoint," directed by Corey Allen, has the Enterprise crew proving mankind's better side to the humanoid alien Q (John de Lancie), who later became a recurring character causing Jean-Luc Picard endless troubles. This oddball "court martial" takes the crew to a farflung planet where another alien, Zorn (Michael Bell), is misusing a life form for his own benefit. It was a great introduction to a great series. Many individual episodes are packaged in video. (Paramount)

STAR TREK BLOOPERS (1969). This now historic reel of outtakes from the making of the TV episodes are always hilariously funny and a must revisit for all fans. (Movies Unlimited)

STAR VIRGIN (1979). Adult flick set on a faraway planet where the only human left is a robot created by a race of machines. They show her assorted sex scenes, some of which involve a Dracula character. Directed by Linus Gator. Kari Klark, Johnny Harden, Tracy Walton.

STAR WARS (1977). Director-writer George Lucas' masterpiece of space-opera adventure. Plotwise, it's nothing more than a rehash of FLASH GORDON narratives, but Lucas treats the material with $10 million of respect. Every penny shows in dazzling effects, futuristic gadgets and costumes. There are laser gun battles; a planet called Tatoonie; hairy space freighter pilot Chewbacca the Wookie; a spaceship squadron attack on the Death Star satellite; Darth Vader, villainous Dark Lord of the Sith; ships moving at the speed of light; robots and more robots; and a spaceport bar sequence featuring a menagerie of grotesque alien life. Laurel-and-Hardy robots (R2D2 and C3PO) provide comedy relief, in some ways becoming more human than the humans. A close look reveals Lucas has a penchant for objects (call them "toys") and this is like an adolescent fantasy, wrought by adult technology. Lucas wisely chose refreshing unknowns (Mark Hamill as Luke Skywalker, Harrison Ford as Han Solo, Carrie Fisher as Princess Leia Organa) and added pros Alec Guinness as an aging space warrior and Peter Cushing as Darth Vader's right-hand henchman. John Dykstra supervised vast teams of effects artists; the popular music is by John Williams. Followed by THE EMPIRE STRIKES BACK and RETURN OF THE JEDI. (CBS/Fox)

STATE OF INSANITY. See **BLACK TORMENT**.

STATIC (1987). Director Mark Romanek's odd independent fantasy (which he wrote with leading man Keith Gordon) is the tale of a youth who builds a machine through which one can see into Heaven. Amanda Plummer, Bob Gunton. (Forum; MCEG)

STAY AWAKE, THE (1987). This South African monster flick is inferior work more aptly titled THE GO TO SLEEP. It's a steal of THE SLUMBER PARTY MASSACRE only instead of a human killer it sports an unconvincing red-eyed, green-hued demon, the Angel of Darkness, that descends on nubile pretties at the St. Mary's School for Girls as they hold an all-night party. As created by screenwriter-director John Bernard, the Angel is the reincarnated spirit of a serial killer who knocked off 11 women before he was executed and vowed to return and kill again. Now he's back, gang, and ready to slaughter with windy demonic powers. Uninspired and cliched, a depressing way to kill 88 minutes. Shirley Jane Harris, Tanya Gordon, Jayne Hutton, Heath Potter. (Video/Laser: Nelson)

STAY TUNED (1992). Entertaining, whacked out supernatural comedy that parodies TV by sending couch potato John Ritter and wife Pam Dawber into TV Hell where they have just 24 hours to escape various cliffhanging situations or their souls will be claimed by the Devil (Jeffrey Jones). The ambitious Tom S. Pakrer/Jim Jennewein script offers pastiches of MTV, STAR TREK, WAYNE'S WORLD, film noir and cat-and-mouse cartoons as Ritter and Dawber leap from program to program. Director Peter Hyams obviously had a good time directing the frisky cast made up also of Bob Dishy, David tom, Eugene Levy and Don Calfa.

STEEL AND LACE (1990). Fair mixture of gory horror and cybernetics sci-fi in which mad doc Bruce Davison, to avenge the suicide of his sister (she was raped but the five guilty men went free), creates a humanoid robot that knocks off the men (now unscrupulous businessmen) by tearing off their heads, drilling holes in their stomachs or doing naughty things to their ding dongs. On the trail is a cop and his girlfriend artist. The Joseph Dougherty-Dave Edison script is predictable after the first half-hour, although Ernest Farino directs in a fast-moving style. Clare Wren, David Naughton, Stacy Haiduk. (Fries) (Laser: Image)

STEEL DAWN (1987). Patrick Swayze is at the center of this film's modest success, for he brings intensity and a sense of mystery to Nomad, a swordsman in the MAD MAX tradition who roves the deserts of a nuked-out world. Doug Lefler's screenplay has a parallel to SHANE and countless Samurai warrior flicks when Nomad stops wandering to help a mother (Lisa Niemi, Swayze's real-life wife) and son (Brett Hool) protect their water purification station from land baron Anthony Zerbe. Contributing minor but interesting characters to the action are Brion James, John Fujioka and the Namib Desert of southwest Africa. It's been done before in the post-holocaust genre, so director Lance Hool, given inferior material, fights a gallant if losing battle. (Vestron) (Laser: Image)

STEEL JUSTICE (1992). Two-hour pilot for a proposed but dropped TV series is set in the 21st Century, when a future society suffers from overcrowding and roving lawlessness within the city structure. Future cop Robert Taylor is plagued by dreams of his son's death at the hands of a gunrunning syndicate and the images of a beckoning black man (J.A. Preston) and a toy in the shape of a dragon. How producer-director Christopher Crowe (writing with John Hill) resolves this with a wish-granting time traveler from the future and the toy turning into a giant fire-breathing monster (a "robosaurus") is absurd and unfitting to the film's seriously intended themes. Roy Brocksmith, John Finn, Neil Giuntoli, Geoffrey Rivas, Joan Chen.

STEEL KEY, THE (1953). See editions 1-3.

STEPFATHER, THE (1986). Above-average portrait of a serial killer, played well by Terry O'Quinn and compellingly written by Donald E. Westlake, who concocted this tale with fellow mystery writer Brian Garfield and Carolyn Lefcourt. O'Quinn's madman is a schizophrenic who needs the family structure in his life, until the urge to massacre overtakes him. Then he moves on, setting up a new identity in a new town, seeking out a new fatherless family. The implications are chilling and director Joseph Ruben never allows the unexpected twists to become too nihilistic—there's always hope that fate will intervene. Shelley Hack, Jill Schoelen, Charles Lanyer. (Video/Laser: Nelson/Embassy)

STEPFATHER II: MAKE ROOM FOR DADDY (1989). This sequel to the video hit is another example of a premise that should not be resurrected. In the original Terry O'Quinn was an average-looking guy who would suddenly go crazy and kill his family, then move on to establish another identity and kill again. This picks up with O'Quinn in a mental institution in Puget Sound—but it doesn't take him long to escape and establish a new identity as a headshrinker living near realtor Meg Foster, with whom he soon sets up housekeeping. Director Jeff Burr is handicapped by John Auerbach's script and directs indifferently, injecting too little suspense into the sluggish events. STEPFATHER II ends up being another slasher flick. Caroline Williams, Jonathan Brandis, Henry Brown, Mitchell Laurance. (HBO) (Laser: Image)

STEPFATHER III (1992). Another inferior sequel that attempts to retread the irony of a psychotic serial killer posing as the perfect family man, and then exploding into homicidal action when his cover is blown. Here the paradox is reduced to Robert Wightman (taking over the Terry O'Quinn role by undergoing plastic surgery in the opening sequence) acting like an automated suburbanite when he resettles in Deer View, Calif., to marry Priscilla Barnes, and making wisecracks ("father knows best . . . come to daddy!") whenever he's just killed—usually with a sharp instrument that allows for blood squirting and dollops of gore splattering on walls. The script by director Guy Magar and Marc B. Ray fails to explore a subplot in which Wightman's new stepson suspects him and uses his home computor to investigate. The use of a leaf mulcher does provide this excursion into bloody violence with a memorably sickening climax. Sickening? Make that disgusting. David Tom, John Ingle, Season Hubley. (Video/Laser: Vidmark)

STEPFORD CHILDREN, THE (1988). This TV-movie is the third go-around to work with material from Ira Levin's novel, THE STEPFORD WIVES. (The second

. . . AND THE FACES OF 'STAR WARS'

Left to right: Robots See-Threepio and Artoo-Detoo; the evil dictator Darth Vader (as played by David Prowse); Mark Hamil as heroic freedom fighter Luke Skywalker, and one of the Jawas on the planet Tatooine

effort was a worthless 1980 TV-film, RETURN OF THE STEPFORD WIVES.) This Paul Pompian production fares better as Don Murray and Barbara Eden settle in the New England community that seems conservative and peaceful, but which harbors a lab where human substitutes are created by crazy doctor Richard Anderson. Murray lived in the village 20 years ago and had a robot wife, so he knows what idyllic bliss this can be. Where the film falls short is in credulity: Murray's behavior is never really dealt with, and all the husbands in town (members of the Men's Association) are so obviously evil, it's hard to believe they could have gotten away with malprogrammed robots for so long. James Coco appears in his final role as the school's cooking teacher. Bill Bleich adapted and Alan J. Levi directed. Randall Batinok, Tammy Lauren, Debbie Barker, Dick Butkus.

STEPFORD WIVES, THE (1975). Superior horror film with an intelligent William Goldman script (from Ira Levin's fine novel) and thoughtful direction by Bryan Forbes. This says more about our obsession with mechanical things than dozens of so-called relevant movies, and it says it in a frightening way: In a complacent upper-crust community in New England a conspiracy is afoot among men to replace their wives with robot-controlled humanoid imitations. And the mastermind is a former employee of Disney (think about that one). Katharine Ross discovers her friends (Paula Prentiss and Tina Louise, among others) are automated replacements and the suspense builds to a finish right out of FRANKENSTEIN. Owen Roizman's cinematography adds to the atmosphere of this scary piece. Patrick O'Neal, Nanette Newman, Peter Masterson. (Embassy)

STEPHEN KING'S CAT'S EYES. See **CAT'S EYE.**

STEPHEN KING'S GOLDEN YEARS (1991). Originally a seven-part TV miniseries, this is one of Stephen King's more eccentric creations, though ultimately a failed one. A top-secret experiment at Falco Plains Agriculture Testing Center results in an explosion set off by a crazed doctor. Exposed to the blast is an aging janitor who comes under the scrutiny of government guys when he starts to grow younger, and glows a bright green. Intrigue, suspicion and double-dealing abound. An assassin from "the shop" is out to kill anyone who knows the secret, and another agent is out to save the janitor. These various factions provide for a lively chase and intriguing characters, but where the script goes wrong is in not developing the fantasy elements. While the payoff is a disappointing one, especially after a four-hour duration, the individual moments make up for some of the letdown. Keith Szarabajka, Felicity Huffman, Frances Sternhagen, Ed Lauter, R.D. Call, Bill Raymond. Directed by Kenneth Fink. (Worldvision)

STEPHEN KING'S GRAVEYARD SHIFT. See **GRAVEYARD SHIFT (1990).**

STEPHEN KING'S IT (1990). Four-hour TV-movie adaptation of the imaginative, nerve-wracking best seller about an entity in the sewer of the town of Derry that wreaks havoc every 30 years. This unseen entity appears in human form as Pennywise the Clown (Tim Curry, in a bravado performance), feeding off the fear of locals and manifesting illusions and fantasies. Seven of the town's adolescents band to destroy it, then return 30 years later to redo the job. It takes nearly two hours just to establish characters and premise, and repeats the same illusions over and over. The characters are interesting and the cast labors valiantly but director Tommy Lee Wallace (writing with Lawrence D. Cohen) provides an unsatisfying ending. John Ritter, Harry Anderson, Annette O'Toole, Richard Thomas, Dennis Christopher, Richard Masur, Tim Reid. (Video/Laser: Warner Bros.)

STEPHEN KING'S NIGHT SHIFT COLLECTION. Video exclusive containing two half-hour adaptations from King's 1978 collection, NIGHT SHIFT. "Woman in the Room," written-directed by Frank Darabont in 1983, is the simple story of an attorney whose mother is dying, and who contemplates euthanasia. This is a strong mood piece. "Boogeyman," written-directed by Jeffrey C. Schiro, is about a father (Michael Reid) who suspects a "boogeyman" murdered his children and put his wife into a nuthouse. He goes to a psychiatrist (Bert Linder) for help. Nice twist ending. Again heavy on ambience. Latter produced in 1982 at the N.Y. University School of Undergraduate Film. (Granite)

STEPHEN KING'S NIGHT SHIFT COLLECTION. This 1989 video consists of two more short films made by students based on stories from King's anthology. "Disciples of the Corn" (1983) was made before CHILDREN OF THE CORN and, because it is succinct and faithful to the original material, is better than the feature. Jonah, "the nicest little town in Oklahoma," is taken over by homicidal children who worship a crow god and attack travelers—including a man and woman passing through. Writer-director-editor John Woodward displays a talent for atmosphere and action. "The Night Waiter" (1987) was made as a student project at San Diego State by writer-director-producer-editor Jack Garrett and is reminiscent of ideas expanded in THE SHINING. To the Bay View Hotel comes new room service waiter Brian Caldwell, who's in immediate conflict with night clerk Ray Adamski. Again, good atmosphere prevails, although the ending is abrupt. (Karl James Associates)

STEPHEN KING'S SILVER BULLET. Video version of **SILVER BULLET.** (Hi yo, King, away!)

STEPHEN KING'S SLEEPWALKERS. See **SLEEPWALKERS.**

STEPHEN KING'S SOMETIMES THEY COME BACK (1991). Supernatural TV-movie, based on a story by the King of horror, is a macabre tale of revenge from beyond the grave. Tim Matheson portrays a school teacher who returns to his home town, where 27 years before his brother was knived to death by teenage hoodlums. A train killed all but one of the attackers . . . and now those dead youths have returned in a phantom car that spits fire to kill Matheson's students and make his life a living nightmare. Matheson stumbles through his hallucinations and dreams conveying a deep sense of dread. Why the dead boys can be seen by everyone else, but their car cannot, makes for a disconcerting ghost story that doesn't stay consistent within its own rules. But it's still engrossing work, nicely directed by Tom McLoughlin and ably adapted by Mark Rosenthal and Lawrence Konner. Brooke Adams, Robert Rusler, Robert Hy Gorman, William Sanderson. (Video/Laser: Vidmark)

STEPHEN KING'S TOMMYKNOCKERS, THE. See **TOMMYKNOCKERS, THE.**

STEPMONSTER (1992). A Roger Corman production, from a story by Fred Olen Ray, in which a hideous creature known as a Tropopkin assumes the human form of a sexy young woman (Robin Riker) to trick Alan Thicke into marrying her. But Thicke's son George Gaynes is wise to the monster and its gargoyle bat-like companion and sets out to stop the nefarious plan. Because the special effects are not convincing, there's little reason to see this exercise in comedy-thrills half-heartedly achieved by director Jeremy Stanford. Ann Dolenz, Edie McClurg, John Astin (as a coughing preacher). (New Horizon)

STEREO (1969). A 65-minute, 16mm black and whiter shot for $3500 in Canada by David Cronenberg. This first effort is set in a bleak institution where Dr. Stringfellow conducts experiments in ESP. While the photography is crisp, the narrative is presented in voiceover, without synch dialogue or music. The pedantic passages are pieces of pseudoscientific information as if taken from a medical journal. Yet one can see the seminal beginnings for Cronenberg's later films. Stringfellow is operating on human guinea pigs to release their psychic powers and discovers that sexual activity results in better communications. Strictly for completists.

STILL NOT QUITE HUMAN (1992). The continuing comedy misadventures of Chip Anderson, the humanoid invented by scientist Alan Thicke, finds the likeable robot-youth attending the Robotics Convention of America. When dad is kidnapped and imprisoned in a white dome by an evil scientist, Chip (played with delightful innocence by Jay Underwood) and his pals (a pickpocket and female cop) go after the dastards. A charming element makes this Disney-produced series appealing. Written-directed by Eric Luke. Christopher Neame, Betsy Palmer, Adam Philipson, Rosa Niven.

STILL OF THE NIGHT (1982). Sophisticated, intelligent whodunit in the psychological vein, detailing how psychiatrist Roy Scheider tracks a slasher killer who murdered a patient. It's writer-director Robert Benton's homage to Hitchcock with slasher-flick touches added—a quiet, underplayed approach as Scheider suspects the killer is a beautiful blonde (Meryl Streep) having an affair with the murdered patient. The symbolic dream sequence is out of Hitchcock's SPELLBOUND; even the Streep character reminds one of Kim Novak in VERTIGO. Little gore or violence—this could be the only cerebral slasher movie ever made. Idea by Benton and David Newman. Jessica Tandy, Joe Grifasi, Sara Botsford. (CBS/Fox; MGM/UA) (Laser: CBS/Fox)

STING OF DEATH (1966). Mad biologist John Vella turns into an underwater monster—described as a "jelly-fish-man," with tentacles that strangle. The kind of horror drama it's impossible to get all wrapped up in. Directed by William Grefe. Valerie Hawkins, Joe Morrison. Neil Sedaka provides soundtrack songs.

STINGRAY. British TV series using live-action puppets (Supermarionation) is on two Image lasers. See **INCREDIBLE VOYAGE OF STINGRAY** and **INVADERS FROM THE DEEP: STINGRAY**.

STOLEN AIRSHIP (1969). Czech fantasy directed by Karel Zeman is a loose adaptation of Jules Verne themes, depicting children at the turn of the century who steal an airship and encounter Captain Nemo. Michael Pospisil, Hanus Bor. Also known as THE STOLEN DIRIGIBLE and TWO YEARS HOLIDAY.

STOLEN FACE, THE (1951). Early Hammer effort, directed by Terence Fisher, produced by Anthony Hinds and written intelligently by Richard Landau and Martin Berkeley. It depicts doctor Paul Henreid fixing the scarred face of Mary MacKenzie to resemble his true love (Lizabeth Scott). Unusual drama of twisted personalities and confused identities. John Wood, Suzan Stephen, Russell Napier. (Weiss Global)

STONE COLD DEAD (1980). Cheaply made Canadian psycho-flicker about a slasher-basher-smasher-crasher who takes photos of the prostitutes he murders with a knife. Richard Crenna is the cop on the case. Paul Williams, Linda Sorenson, Belinda J. Montgomery. Directed by George Mendeluk. (Media)

STONES OF DEATH (1988). Shades of POLTERGEIST: An ancient Australian curse goes into effect when a housing development is built on an old graveyard where the Kadaicha tribe once existed. Directed by James Bagle. Tom Jennings, Natalie McCurray, Zoe Carides, Eric Oldfield. (Sony)

STOOGEMANIA (1985). A comedy-fantasy exploring the nutty behavior of Howard F. Howard (Josh Mostel), a complete idiot whose entire life so centers around The Three Stooges that he admits himself into Stooge Hill, a rehabilitation center for those suffering from hallucinations and zany behavior brought on by too much exposure to Moe, Larry and Curly. It's a wonderful concept but one which is never very funny as presented by director Chuck Workman. By far the best footage is from the old Stooges shorts, some of which have been colorized for this feature. But every time we see the masterful comedy trio, we are reminded of just how pathetically inadequate Mostel, Melanie Chartoff (as his goofy girlfriend), Sid Caesar (doing his neurotic Freudian doctor bit), and Josh Minor are. So knock Workman over the head with a hammer (BONK!!!), strike him on the cheek (KER-SLAPPP!!!) and proceed with the eye-gouging bit (SQUISH!!!) (Paramount)

STOP PRESS GIRL (1949). See editions 1-3.

STORM PLANET. See **PLANETA BURG.**

STORMQUEST (1988). Women rule men in the world of Ishtan, where the male is strictly used for breeding. However, Kai Baker and Christina Whitaker like male muscles too much and lead Brent Huff (with sorceress Dudizile Mkhize) in a revolt against the female chauvinist pigs. Made in Argentina by director Alex Sessa. Rocky Giordani, Anne Marie Ricci. (Media)

STORY OF CINDERELLA, THE. See **SLIPPER AND THE ROSE, THE.**

STORY OF MANKIND, THE (1957). See editions 1-3.

STORY OF THREE LOVES, THE (1953). Trilogy of romanticized tales, bittersweet and lyrical, captures a mystical quality that permeates the moonstruck characters. Although only one story is fantasy, the whole film has an undercurrent of magic, as if the characters are floating in a fantasy realm of true love. "Mademoiselle" is a whimsical vignette in which governess Leslie Caron recites love poetry while trying to teach young Ricky Nelson, who rebels against her smothering care. With the help of witch Ethel Barrymore, he turns into a full-grown man and, controlled by impulses he doesn't understand, proceeds to fall for Ms Caron. This is a wonderful segment directed by Vincent Minnelli, with Farley Granger as the starry-eyed "man-boy." The other stories, "The Jealous Lover" (James Mason, Moira Shearer) and "Equilibrium" (Kirk Douglas, Pier Angeli), still have a magical quality (enhanced by the lush music of Miklos Rozsa) that will find favor with fantasy lovers.

STRAIGHT JACKET (1982). Unconvincing psychokiller drama mixing in two characters who have the ability to foresee the future: a young wife (Kory Clark) who just moved into a house previously the scene of a decapitation murder, and a cop (Aldo Ray) recently kicked off the force. The acting borders on the amateurish and the Phillip Pine/Larry Hilbran script unfolds in a poor manner, so there is no suspenseful climax. Directed by co-producer Martin Green. Chuck Jamison, Bobby Holt, Andy Gwyn. (Genesis; Neon; Ariel International; from Marquis as **DARK SANITY**)

STRAIGHT ON TILL MORNING (1972). Obscure Hammer psychothriller designed for ambience and characterization as it unfolds leisurely. It is fascinating because of imaginative cross-cutting and its sympathy for a man who records the voices of his murder victims. Director Peter Collinson and screenwriter Michael Peacock try to be arty and it works—thanks to the editing tempo and the moods of Rita Tushingham (as a mousy, shy thing) and the killer, Shane Briant, a confused psychotic who befriends Rita, then draws her into his spider's lair. Produced by Michael Carreras. Tom Bell, Annie Ross. (On video as **DRESSED FOR DEATH.**)

STRAIT-JACKET (1964). While this William Castle horror thriller has none of his gimmicks, and its techniques now seem dated, it features a wonderfully campy performance by Joan Crawford as a murderess who chops off the heads of her adulterous husband and lover and is sent to an institution for 20 years. She gets to revive her "cheap tramp" characterization of the '40s, and she does it up without director Castle restraining her, when she shows up to live with daughter Diane Baker. Right away she behaves oddly when handyman George Kennedy, in a great sleaze role, chops off the head of a chicken. And what do you know. Pretty soon heads are rolling again as Crawford turns into one batty broad suffering from hallucinations. Robert Bloch's script is one of his favorites—producer-director Castle left most of it intact. Beware red herrings—the script is full of them. Rochelle Hudson, Howard St. John, Leif Erickson. (RCA/Columbia)

STRANDED (1987). Entertaining sci-fi actioner, in which a family of aliens accompanied by a robot guard escape their war-ravaged world for asylum in a farmhouse on Earth. What follows is a siege situation with black sheriff Joe Morton facing not only the aliens but prejudice from deputies and townspeople. An assassin-alien in human form is also involved as the tense situation unfolds. This Robert Shaye-Sara Risher production is a respectable piece of work. Directed by Tex Fuller. Susan Barnes, Ione Skye, Cameron Dye, Michael Greene, Gary Swanson, Barbara Hughes. Maureen O'Sullivan appears as the beseiged grandmother. (Video/Laser: RCA/Columbia)

STRANGE ADVENTURE (1933). Monogram quickie set in the typically strange house where a hooded killer strikes. Too old to be either strange or an adventure. Directed by Phil Whitman. William V. Mong, Regis Toomey, Dwight Frye. Also called THE WAYNE MURDER CASE. (Sinister/C; Filmfax)

STRANGE ADVENTURE OF DAVID GRAY, THE. See **VAMPYR (1931).**

STRANGE AND DEADLY OCCURRENCE, THE (1974). Is the mansion of Robert Stack and Vera Miles haunted? Or is someone playing tricks on their hyper-imaginations? TV-movie from producer Sandor Stern creeps around the issue too long. John Llewellyn Moxie directed. L.Q. Jones, Herb Edelman, Margaret Willock, Dena Dietrich. (Worldvision)

STRANGE BEHAVIOR (1981). Aussie-New Zealand production (also known as DEAD KIDS) in which a crazed doctor murders high school students after conducting weird experiments on their bodies. The acting is overblown and the plotting by producer Michael Condon and director Michael Laughlin out of a horror pulp, but the film has a sense of freshness and features a strong cast: Michael Murphy, Louise Fletcher, Fiona Lewis, Scott Brady. (RCA/Columbia; from Scorpio as **SMALL TOWN MASSACRE**)

STRANGE BREW (1983). Dave Thomas and Rick Moranis portray Bob and Doug McKenzie, characters they created on TV, in this whacky roller-coaster-ride-of-a-movie in which mad doctor Max Von Sydow plans to conquer the world by addicting everyone to beer. Uncontrolled chaos, directed by Thomas and Moranis, who also co-wrote. (Video/Laser: MGM/UA)

STRANGE CARGO (1940). Many puzzled over this Joseph L. Mankiewicz production based on Richard Sale's allegorical novel, NOT TOO NARROW, TOO DEEP. While on the surface it's a Devil's Island prison picture, it is also a story in which each character is symbolic. Ian Hunter, for example, projects Christ characteristics. Now that we've given you a clue, you figure out the rest. Joan Crawford, Clark Gable, Peter Lorre, Paul Lucas. Directed by Frank Borzage. (MGM/UA)

STRANGE CASE OF DR. JEKYLL AND MR. HYDE, THE (1968). U.S.-Canadian TV production produced by Dan Curtis and starring Jack Palance as one of the most effective Jekyll-Hydes in the cinematic history of Robert Louis Stevenson's horror classic. Directed by Charles Jarrott. Makeup by Dick Smith. Denholm Elliott, Torin Thatcher, Oscar Homolka, Leo Genn, Billie Whitelaw. (On Thrillervideo with Elvira)

STRANGE CASE OF DR. JEKYLL AND MR. HYDE, THE (1989). One-hour TV version of the famous Robert Louis Stevenson novelette. Directed by Michael Lindsay-Hogg. Anthony Andrews, Laura Dern, George Murdock, Nicholas Guest, Rue McClanahan. (Cannon)

STRANGE CASE OF DR. RX, THE (1942). Insidious-type killing agents (poisoned needles, undetectable venom, etc.) are employed by a doctor who kills those who escape imprisonment through legal loopholes. Predictable red herring-packaged Universal potboiler has the avenger desiring to transfer the brain of Patric Knowles into the cranium of a gorilla. Lionel Atwill figures prominently as Dr. Fish. Directed by William Nigh. Anne Gwynne, Mantan Moreland, Shemp Howard, Paul Cavanagh, Mantan Moreland.

STRANGE CONFESSION (1945). "Inner Sanctum" Universal programmer with Lon Chaney Jr. as a tormented man victimized by a drug manufacturer. Based on the play THE MAN WHO RECLAIMED HIS HEAD, first adapted to the movies in 1934 with Claude Rains. Directed by John Hoffman. Brenda Joyce, Milburn Stone, Lloyd Bridges, Addison Richards.

STRANGE DOOR, THE (1951). Robert Louis Stevenson's "The Sire de Maletroit's Door" serves as writer Jerry Sackheim's plot for this torture-chamber Universal-International programmer, with Charles Laughton as an elegantly insane 18th Century nobleman who chews up the Iron Maidens and rushes through his dialogue as though he wanted to get on to more prestigious projects. Quite histrionic, as subtle as a case of Bubonic Plague, but fascinating for its cast and ambience. Laughton so oozes evil that his henchman (Boris Karloff) turns out to be the good guy in comparison. Joseph Pevney directs with florid flourish. Sally Forrest, Michael Pate, Alan Napier.

STRANGE EXORCISM OF LYNN HART, THE. See **DADDY'S DEADLY DARLING** or **PIGS.**

STRANGE HOLIDAY, THE (1942). This Arch Oboler film (he wrote/ directed) is based on his LIGHTS OUT radio play, "This Precious Freedom," in which a businessman returns to his hometown to find a dictatorship in power. The surprise ending will come as a disappointment to those who haven't already suspected a trick is being played. Although made in '42, it was not released until '45, presumably because its theme might have been depressing to wartime audiences in need of a lift, not a morality lesson. Aka THE DAY AFTER TOMORROW. Claude Rains, Barbara Bates, Gloria Holden, Martin Kosleck.

STRANGE ILLUSION, THE (1945). Edgar G. Ulmer appreciators will be delighted to discover this minor PRC quickie in which teen-ager James Lydon dreams his father's death wasn't an accident. He suspects a man he sees in his dreams is also the man wooing his unsuspecting mother. He sets out to prove his dream is true. Crude but effective thriller if you are forgiving of a B approach. Warren William, Regis Toomey, Sally Eiler, George Reed. (Sinister/C; Filmfax)

STRANGE IMPERSONATION (1946). Editions 2-3.

STRANGE INVADERS (1983). In the style of monster invader movies of the '50s, this is a blend of comedy and thrills, effects and chases in telling its genre tale of space creatures plotting our overthrow in a midwestern town in 1958. Paul LeMat gets involved when he discovers his ex-wife is one of *them* and now her pals are coming to look for her daughter, who's an alien too. Well, half an alien. LeMat and Nancy Allen end up on the run. Good direction by Michael Laughlin, who co-wrote with William Condon. Michael Lerner, Louise Fletcher, Fiona Lewis, Kenneth Tobey, June Lockhart. (Vestron) (Laser: Image)

STRANGE MR. GREGORY. (1946). Editions 1-3.

STRANGENESS, THE (1985). Inspired by THE BOOGENS, this is "lost mine" stuff as geologists enter the legendary Golden Spike Mine, closed years before when workmen mysteriously vanished. There's a cruel boss, a writer who talks in deathless prose, an experienced old mine hand and other cliched types. Long stretches of nothing, extended periods of ennui, with an occasional glimpse of a tentacled creature animated by stop motion. No feeling of menace as the film plods to a routine climax. Directed by David Michael Hillman, without any "strangeness." Dan Lunham, Terri Berland. (Transworld; Premiere)

STRANGE NEW WORLD (1975). Episodic adventures in which astronauts—in suspended animation for 180 years in deep space—return to discover Earth has divided into odd cults following nuclear holocaust. Hence, three separate stories, pared from an original two-hour format to 90 minutes. Part of Gene Roddenberry's trilogy of pilot failures that includes GENESIS II and PLANET EARTH. John Saxon, Kathleen Miller, James Olson. Directed by Robert Butler. (Unicorn)

STRANGE OBSESSION. See **WITCH, THE (1966).**

STRANGE PEOPLE (1933). See editions 1-3.

STRANGE POSSESSION OF MRS. OLIVER, THE (1978). Richard Matheson's intriguing tale of dual personality stars Karen Black as a bored housewife married to a boring husband-lawyer (George Hamilton). She gets the yen to wear a low-cut red blouse, blonde wig and slinky skirt. She is also compelled to buy a house in a beach community, where it would appear a woman who looks just like her once resided—before her tragic demise. Director Gordon Hessler builds the mystery with a deft camera, creating ambiguities to intrigue us: Is Black undergoing possession, reincarnation or what? Supernatural mood blends with psychological thrills.

STRANGER, THE (1973). Pilot for a proposed (but unsold) series as U.S. astronaut Glenn Corbett, sole survivor of his flight team, wakes up on a planet identical to Earth (but it's really an alien world on the far side of the sun). He tries to return home with the help of turncoat scientist Lew Ayres and sympathetic Sharon Acker while corrupt power figures Cameron Mitchell and Steve Franken track him. Despite standard TV values, Gerald Sanford's script zips along and director Lee H. Katzin keeps his characters moving so you won't have time to wonder why cars have California plates. George Coulouris, Dean Jagger. (King of Video)

STRANGER, THE (1987). More Hitchcockian than horrific, this U.S.-Argentine suspense-shocker deals with amnesia when Bonnie Bedelia wakes up in a hospital following an escape from a murder scene without remembering who she is. Director Adolfo Aristarain treats some sequences as if there were part of a horror film, with the rest being average cops-and-robbers stuff. Bonnie is beautiful to watch despite her shallow character, but once the surprise twist is revealed in a movie theater, the film unfolds predictably. Peter Riegert, Barry Primus, David Spielberg. (RCA/Columbia)

STRANGER FROM VENUS (1955). Ripoff of THE DAY THE EARTH STOOD STILL, but not as exciting, and pedantic to the extreme. This time the "stranger" with telepathic and healing powers is Helmut Dantine, a benevolent but stern Venusian here to warn us that unless we stop tampering with atoms, we could destroy the order of the solar system. Why he would pick a lonely British inn and ask that the world leaders be brought to him is incomprehensible, and one of the gaping holes in Hans Jacoby's script. And why Patricia Neal, so excellent in THE DAY THE EARTH STOOD STILL, would be involved in this pale carbon copy is just as indecipherable. It might have been well-intended on the part of director Burt Balaban to make this anti-war statement, but it's a bloody bore, chaps. Derek Bond, Arthur Young, Cyril Luckham, Marigold Russell, Willoughby Gray, Nigel Green. (Media; Nostalgia Merchant; Wade Williams)

STRANGER IN OUR HOUSE (1978). Wes Craven directs one of those watered-down TV-movies that offers limp shocks, mediocre effects and a predictable story, in this case based on a Lois Duncan novel. Lee Purcell portrays a witch from the Ozarks who comes to Linda Blair's ranch to hex Linda's horse Sundance, steal her boyfriend and perform other acts of tiresome mayhem. Blair's a capable actress deserving better, as are co-stars Jeremy Slate, Jeff McCracken, Jeff East, Carol Lawrence and MacDonald Carey, the latter as Professor Jarvis. (Thorn EMI/HBO; also on video as **SUMMER OF FEAR**)

STRANGER IN THE HOUSE. See **BLACK CHRISTMAS.**

STRANGER IS WATCHING, A (1982). Unsettling mixture of suspense and violence, directed by Sean Cunningham, the mastermind behind FRIDAY THE 13TH. Even though this is a better-crafted movie and has a superior plot (from a book by Mary Higgins Clark), it was a flop. What Cunningham fails to realize is that audiences prefer slasher movies in which the killer is a faceless killing machine. That rule is broken as we follow killer Rip Torn when he kidnaps a TV reporter and a young girl and hides them in the New York subway system. Also, the reporter (Kate Mulgrew) is so well drawn that it becomes unbearable to watch when a screwdriver is thrust into her stomach. Cunningham might have done better to stress the kidnaping plot and the capital punishment aspects, going for inherent suspense in the Hitchcock tradition. James Naughton, Barbara Baxley, Roy Poole. (MGM/UA)

STRANGER ON THE THIRD FLOOR (1940). Director Boris Ingster has a true sense of style and indulges in surrealistic camera angles for dream sequences in this horror thriller starring Peter Lorre as a homicidal maniac. Call it German Expressionistic. Lorre is excellent in the role and makes up for weaknesses in Frank Partos' screenplay. There's a very strange trial sequence, too, with more cock-eyed camera angles. Elisah Cook Jr., John McGuire. (Fox Hills) (Laser)

STRANGERS (1980). Explorers in a Colorado cave come across strange blue stones linked to a recent space capsule mission—only to find something monstrous lurking in the dark. Hee hee hee hee hee. Belinda Mayne, Marc Bodin.

STRANGER'S GUNDOWN. (1975). Editions 1-3.

STRANGERS IN PARADISE (1986). In 1939, a Nazi undergoes suspended animation, awakening in the '80s to renew his terror. Written-produced-directed by Ulli Lommel. Ken Letner, Thom Jones. (Vestron)

STRANGER WITHIN, THE (1974). Richard Matheson's teleplay concerns a woman (Barbara Eden) whose actions are controlled by her unborn baby. Is the child an alien? A supernatural force? Not one of Matheson's best . . . Standard TV-movie production values at a plodding pace. Directed by Lee Philips. George Grizzard is the puzzled husband. (USA; Lorimar)

STRANGER WITHIN, THE (1990). Ricky Schroeder portrays a psycho case who turns up claiming to be Kate Jackson's long-lost son—but all he has in mind is a campaign of terror. Tom Holland (FRIGHT NIGHT) directs. Chris Sarandon, Clark Sandford.

STRANGEST DREAMS. See **INVASION OF THE SPACE PREACHERS.**

STRANGE TALES/RAY BRADBURY THEATER (1986). Video reissue of episodes shown on Showtime's RAY BRADBURY THEATER. Three literary classics have been handsomely adapted by Bradbury: "The Town Where No One Got Off" (with Jeffrey Goldblum), "The Screaming Woman" (Drew Barrymore) and "Banshee" (Peter O'Toole). (HBO)

STRANGE WORLD OF PLANET X. See **COSMIC MONSTERS.** (X marks the splotch)**STRANGLER, THE (1963).** Misunderstood, insecure fat man Leo Kroll, who suffers from a mother's complex, chokes nurses to death because they symbolize keeping his bedridden mother alive. Victor Buono and Ellen Corby are well cast in the roles and director Burt Topper works diligently with Bill Ballinger's script, but the low budget strangles everyone in the end. (Key; Sinister/C)

STRANGLER OF BLACKMOOR CASTLE, THE (1960). Bryan Edgar Wallace wrote the script for this German thriller featuring British types rushing through a drafty English castle trying to avoid a costumed neck-squeezer who cackles as he murders them, burns the letter "M" into their foreheads, and sends severed heads through the mail. Directed by Harald Reinl. Karin Dor, Hans Nielsen. (Sinister Cinema; Filmfax)

STRANGLER OF THE SWAMP (1946). German director Frank Wisbar adapted his fantasy, FERRYMAN MARIA, into this PRC thriller, low on budget but high on style and decaying ambience. A ferryboat operator has been murdered and now the swamp country is terrorized by the "walking dead" shape of Charles Middleton (Ming of the FLASH GORDON serials) who hangs those responsible for his death. Rosemary LaPlanche is a beautiful actress who overcomes the limited swamp sets and a perfunctory romance with Blake Edwards (later to become a producer-director) to help raise this to a mini-classic in atmosphere. Frank Conlon, Effie Parnell. (Sony; RCA/Columbia)

STRANGLER OF VIENNA, THE. See **MAD BUTCHER, THE.**

STRANGLERS OF BENGAL, THE. See **STRANGLERS OF BOMBAY.**

STRANGLERS OF BOMBAY, THE (1959). Dramatization of the true story of the Kali devil cult and how the

British in the 1820s stamped out cult followers, who murdered for the sheer joy of spilling blood. A crisp, lean Hammer production, directed by Terence Fisher with a touch of the macabre. Allan Cuthbertson, Guy Rolfe, Marne Maitland, Jan Holden. Not for the squeamish. Aka THE STRANGLERS OF BENGAL.

STRAYS (1991). Would you believe a TV-movie with the "horrifying monster" a feral housecat? That's what producer-writer Shaun Cassidy sells you in this absurd catnip. Lawyer Timothy Busfield and novelist Kathleen Quinlan live in a forest, unaware the mean tabbie has invaded their attic with a band of feline accomplices. The film's tone, dialogue and satire are similar to those in ARCHNOPHOBIA as the humans engage in inane chatter and petty jealousies when it appears Busfield's client (beautiful, sexy Claudia Christian) is trying to win him away from Quinlan. Director John McPherson has fun when the cats jump out of the woodwork, what with a lightning storm outside, but the cliches are so drearily familiar that this never has more than half a life. William Boyett provides the film's only relief from tedium as a wise-cracking veterinarian. (MCA/Universal)

STREETS (1988). The only aspect about this Roger Corman cheapie to interest horror fans is Ed Lottimer's highly charged performance as a blond sadistic-masochist L.A. patrolman who takes out his hatreds on homeless kids. Christina Applegate and David Mendelhall are on the run from his brutality when they aren't shooting up or talking interminably about their plight as teenagers. Director Katt Shea Ruben (STRIPPED TO KILL) co-wrote the coincidence-laden script with producer-hubbie Andy Ruben. Had more emphasis been put on crazed Lottimer, this might have been an interesting parable on violence perpetrated on minority groups by the law. Alan Stock, Mel Costello. (MGM/UA)

STREETS OF FIRE (1984). Odd rock-action movie, set in a U.S. city in an unspecified time that amalgamates many styles. A rock 'n roll star (Diane Lane) in this strange landscape is kidnapped by thugs called The Bombers. Boyfriend Michael Pare pursues with tough broad Amy Madigan tagging along, her dialogue some great hard-boiled chick stuff. The action is well staged by director Arthur Hill, who co-wrote with Larry Gross, and the urban streets are a mixture of modish motifs, giving the film a unique ambience. Ten original songs with a throbbing beat provided by Ry Cooder. Rick Moranis, Richard Lawson. (Video/Laser: MCA)

STREET TRASH (1987). Strange booze making the rounds of New York's Skid Row turns derelicts and other alkies into bubbling puddles of goo in this low-budgeter shot in New York by director Jim Muro. The effects team has a field day, but anyone with a modicum of good taste will avoid this like the Bubonic Plague. Mike Lackey, Vic Noto, Bill Chepil. (Lightning)

STRIPPED TO KILL (1987). One can almost hear director Katt Shea Ruben insisting her movie be filled with realistic, gritty glimpses of striptease artists—their angst, sleazy bosses, tough working hours and compromised personal lives—and producer Roger Corman insisting on a slasher-killer plot for box office. Neither seems to win although all those ingredients, and then some, are here. What goes awry is the premise that cop Kay Lenz, going undercover as a stripper, falls in love with the profession, while a strangler-killer knocks off shapely femmes one by one. Another problem with the Andy Ruben-Katt Shea Ruben script is its incoherent ending, which defies description with a chase, a fire, an identity revelation and a mess of other stuff. Greg Evigan as Lenz's macho partner and Norman Fell as the club owner add versimilitude to the anguish and there are some arousing strip dances, but the film is too stripped of humanity. Pia Kamakahi, Tracey Crowder, Debby Nassar. (MGM/UA)

STRIPPED TO KILL 2: LIVE GIRLS (1989). If ogling bountiful titties and asses is what you seek in movie-watching, jump to it, because that's all this Roger Corman production has: sexually desirable women, wearing kinky, provocative outfits and dancing very exotic, erotic numbers. Writer-director Katt Shea Ruben knows the psychology of the stripper, and imbues her topless dancers with male sex-fantasy traits, ranging from lesbian overtones to sadistic undertones. This is as big a mess as STRIPPED TO KILL with its plot contrivances and alleged surprise ending, and vacillating characters. In this mish mash stolen from Cornell Woolrich, dancer Maria Ford keeps dreaming she has a razor between her teeth and is slashing throats of dancers, waking up to find blood on her mouth. Actually she is having psychic dreams (further details would give away the woeful whodunit plot) and becomes suspect in the murder case when L.A. cop Ed Lottimer investigates. You do have to admit, though, that Karen Mayo Chandler, Birke Tam, Marjean Holden and Debra Lamb are something to watch as they perform red-hot strips. (MGM/UA)

STRONGEST MAN IN THE WORLD, THE (1975). Disney teen comedy, sequel to THE COMPUTER WORE TENNIS SHOES. Kurt Russell discovers a formula for superhuman powers. There's funny weightlifting scenes, but it's predictable fun and games. Eve Arden, Cesar Romero (repeating his role as a crook who steals formulas), Phil Silvers, William Schallert. Directed by Vincent McEveety. (Disney)

STRYKER (1983). Low-budget quickie from Howard R. Cohen (of SATURDAY THE 14TH and SPACE RAIDERS infamy) that is a swipe of ROAD WARRIOR set in a post-Armageddon world where tribes of strangely dressed survivors fight over water. Stryker (Steve Sandor) is a unadorable hero who engenders zero sympathy. This mess was directed without care by Cirio H. Santiago in the Philippines, and it's one corny action scene after the other. Andria Savio, William Ostrander. (Starmaker; Embassy; from Bingo as **SAVAGE DAWN**)

STUDENT BODIES (1981). Spoof on the slasher trend has the courage of its convictions, but humor is on such a sophomoric level that this becomes unstomachable, as bad as the films it ribs. Interesting as a parody, but of little substance. Mickey Rose wrote-directed. Kristen Riter, Matt Goldsby, Richard Brando (as an off-screen menace called The Breather), Mimi Weddell. (Video/Laser: Paramount)

STUDIO MURDERS. See **FANTASIES.**

STUDY IN TERROR, A (1966). Who would be better qualified to deduce the identity of that chap who knives his way through the London streets, Jack the Ripper, than the indomitable Sherlock Holmes and his sycophant, Dr. Watson. Ripping good show (written by Donald and Derek Ford) with busty prostitutes shrouded by the Whitechapel fog and a conceited Holmes played by John Neville. Donald Houston assists as Dr. Watson. Quick, Watson, the Morning Express! Directed stylishly by James Hill. (RCA/Columbia) (Laser: Image)

STUFF, THE (1985). Another strange, strange satirical horror tale from the bizarre, bizarre mind of writer-producer-director Larry Cohen. A bubbly, gooey substance pops up from the earth and becomes a delicious yogurt-like dessert called The Stuff. When industrial spy Michael Moriarty tries to learn the formula, he uncovers the real truth: The dreams that the Stuff are made of are nightmares. It's a living substance that takes over mind and body, oozing out of gaping mouths and attacking in a flowing wave of glup. It's kind of THE BLOB, sort of. Cohen treats this horror premise as a joke. One minute he's reminding us of fluoride in water and poisonous preservatives in food, in the next he's spoofing the military and advertising world. Andrea Marcovicci portrays the marketing expert-love interest and Paul Sorvino is an Army officer. Patrick O'Neal, Garrett Morris, Scott Bloom, Alexander Scourby (in his last role). Jim Danforth/David Allen worked on the effects. (New World)

STUFF STEPHANIE IN THE INCINERATOR (1989). A traumadrama from Troma about a gang that delights in torturing shapely femmes and then throwing their carcasses into a roaring fire. This is played for laughs? Directed by Don Nardo. Catherine Dee, William Dame, Dennis Cunningham. (IVE) (Laser: Media)

SUBMERSION OF JAPAN, THE. See **TIDAL WAVE.**

SUBSPECIES (1990). Classical vampire tale, reminiscent of the gothic Hammer species, from the Charles Band-Full Moon production house. European locations enhance this morbid yet fascinating account of three women visiting a Transylvanian castle where Radu—an evil count with bony fingers, and resembling Nosferatu—holds sway over miniature gargoyles and the "bloodstone," a device that gives him powers of evil. David Allen's effects are effectively used by director Ted Nicolaou, who emphasizes the gory as well as more sublime elements in the Jackson Barr-David Pabian script. It moves slowly at times but the film is stamped with good production values. Michael Watson, Angus Scrimm (in a cameo), Laura Care, Anders Hove, Michelle McBride, (Video/Laser: Paramount)

SUBSPECIES II. See **BLOODSTONE: SUBSPECIES II.**

SUBSPECIES III. See **BLOODLUST: SUBSPECIES III.**

SUBURBAN COMMANDO (1991). A real bellyflop for professional wrestler-turned-thespian (a redundancy of terms?) Hulk Hogan, who portrays space ranger Shep Ramsey, a savior of the Universe who defeats galaxy tyrant William Ball in a blaze of sci-fi pyrotechnics and then vacations on Earth, living in the home of nerdy engineer Christopher Lloyd and wife Shelley Duvall. If that doesn't make sense, wait . . . Two bounty hunters from the cosmos (who, strangely enough, resemble wrestlers) drop in on Hulk for a showdown, allowing for Lloyd to be the worm that turns. There's plenty of zappy action when Ball returns from the dead as a lizard monster, but one wonders what drew so much talent to this stranglehold on human brain cells. It was directed by Burt Kennedy (?) and it has Jack Elam as a retired old soldier and Roy Dotrice as Hulk's assignment chief—who deserve to be body slammed for taking such parts. It also has a mean spirit even though it appears to be made for family viewing. Larry Miller, Jo Ann Dearing, Michael Faustino. (New Line) (Laser: Image)

SUCCUBARE (1984). Described as a "blockbuster of bone-chilling horror!" Sure it is!

SUCCUBUS (1969). Beware heavy cuts by TV censors, for this German film directed by Jesus Franco (also called NECRONOMICON) is X-rated. Nothing hardcore, you understand, just bare bosoms and suggestions, rather than depictions, of sordid sexual acts surrounding a night club entertainer who simulates torture and intercourse during her "number." The Devil arrives (shown in double exposure) and taunts her, forcing her to perform murder during her nitery routine. Howard Vernon, Jack Taylor, Adrian Hoven, Janine Reynaud.

SUCCUBUS. Video version of **DEVIL'S NIGHTMARE** (Applause).

SUDDENLY, LAST SUMMER (1960). We include this because of one of the most bizarre acts of cannibalism imaginable—a homosexual youth who mistreats his sexual partners and is "eaten" alive. All symbolic, of course, since it is based on a Tennessee Williams play. Williams and Gore Vidal collaborated on the script for director Joseph L. Mankiewicz. Elizabeth Taylor, beautiful sister of the homosexual, is used to lure boys to the beach in Mexico. Now she is in an insane asylum, threatened with a lobotomy because mother Katharine Hepburn doesn't want the truth known about her son. Only headshrinker Montgomery Clift can get at the truth. Unforgettably strange movie as only Williams can write them. Albert Dekker, Mercedes McCambridge, Gary Raymond. (Video/Laser: RCA/Columbia)

SUGAR COOKIES (1977). After a pornie filmmaker tricks a sexy model to commit suicide in front of the camera, a friend of the dead girl wreaks her revenge. Directed by Michael Herz. Lynn Lowry, Mary Waronov, Monique Van Vooren. (VidAmerica)

SUGAR HILL (1974). Black exploitation pic (sometimes called VOODOO GIRL) depicts black zombies getting revenge on Honkie White Bastards. Marki Bey seeks vengeance after her boyfriend is knocked off by a Mafia group. Don Pedro Colley is the Baron called back from death as her instrument of revenge. Robert (YORGA) Quarry is involved. Directed by Paul Maslansky. Betty Anne Rees, Richard Lawson, Zara Culley. Aka ZOMBIES OF SUGAR HILL.

SUICIDE CULT (1977). The CIA, using astrology as a science, discovers a way to forecast everyone's future. One mad scientist delves into the issue of Jesus Christ's Second Coming and finds himself doing battle with a devil cult. Directed by Jim Glickenhouse. Bob Byrd, Monica Tokell. (Continental; New Star)

SUICIDE MISSION (1971). A Mexican wrestler in droopy trunks and a silver mask, Santo, grunts and groans through another hapless assignment—viewers will surely hope he won't come back alive. But no such luck. Directed by Federico Curiel. Lorena Velazquez.

SUMMER CAMP NIGHTMARE (1987). We're including this simply to tip you off that despite its title, this is not a slasher or horror flick. It's a dumb teenager romp set at separate camps for boys and girls who fall under the tyrannical rule of bluenose camp counsellor Chuck Connors. For the record it co-stars Charles Stratton, Adam Cart and Harold Pruett. Fans: forget it. (Video/Laser: Embassy/Nelson)

SUMMER OF FEAR. Alternate video version of **STRANGER IN OUR HOUSE** (Thorn EMI/HBO).

SUMMER OF SECRETS (1976). Australian film is difficult to categorize or describe—it begins as a psychological thriller about a boy and girl being terrorized by an eccentric, then shifts gears to probe a bizarre variance on the Frankenstein Monster theme. Too ponderous and talkative to be commercial, too unfocused and pseudo-intellectual to appeal to the thinking man. Directed by Jim Sharman, who helmed THE ROCKY HORROR PICTURE SHOW. Arthur Dignam, Rufus Colllins, Nell Campbell. (VidAmerica)

SUNDOWN: THE VAMPIRE IN RETREAT (1989). Offbeat vampire western, loaded with unusual concepts and bubbling with an infectuous cinematic vitality. Purgatory is a town in the Utah desert (where this was filmed) where Count Mardulak (David Carradine) takes his vampire citizens to start a new life without killing, living off artificial blood made in a factory. But preacherman John Ireland wants vampires to kill humans and leads a revolt against benevolent Mardulak. An undercurrent of satire runs throughout this vigorous action-comedy film with Carradine a stand-out. Richard Stone's main theme is an amusing pastiche of grandiose western scores. Accolades to director Anthony Hickox, who co-wrote the amusing script with John Burgess. Jim Metzler, Morgan Brittany, Maxwell Caulfield, M. Emmet Walsh, Bruce Campbell. (Vestron)

JOHN IRELAND

SUPERARGO AND THE FACELESS GIANTS (1967). Better to call this Italian-Spanish potboiler SUPERARGO AND THE BRAINLESS PRODUCERS. It's nonsense about a special agent mastering mind control with the help of a one-time lama. Athletes turned into mummy robots are inflicting damage on the world—as much as this will damage your brain. A sequel to SUPERARGO VS. DIABOLICUS. Directed by Paolo Bianchini. Ken Wood (Giovanni Cianfriglia), Guy Madison. (Sinister/C; S/Weird; Filmfax)

SUPERARGO VS. DIABOLICUS (1966). First in the Italo-Spanish SUPERARGO series, a heap of brainrot about a mind-controlling spy who also has the power of levitation in his fight against a uranium thief (Gerhard Tichey) plotting to take over the world. Ken (Giovanni Cianfriglia) Wood, as limber as a petrified forest, portrays

Superargo. Empty cranium vs. dull uranium. Directed by Nick Nostro. Gerard Tichy. (S/Weird)

SUPERBEAST (1972). Shapely scientist Antoinette Bower ventures to the Philippines to meet a crazy doctor (Craig Littler) experimenting on criminals with a drug that turns them into beasts, which then serve as targets for demented big-game hunter Harry Lauter. It may sound like an interesting variation on "The Most Dangerous Game," but it's superdull, with writer-producer-director George Schenck taking forever and a jungle to get the plot rolling. The good cast has too little to work with, and none of the "superbeast" make-up is that imaginative. Vic Diaz, Jose Romulo.

SUPERBOYS. See **SUPERKIDS.**

SUPERBUG, SUPER AGENT (1976). Witless attempt by the West Germans to rip off Disney's THE LOVE BUG. Dudu the Beetle is a computerized Volkswagen that talks, swims and camouflages itself as a rock. Consider director Rudolf Zehetgruber running low on creative fuel. The dubbing is atrocious, the editing is sloppy beyond belief, the acting disengaging. As dead as a disconnected battery. Dudu is a dud, dude. (JEF)

SUPERBUG—THE WILD ONE (1977). Another unendurable entry in West Germany's series about the Yellow Dudu, an insufferable Volkswagen with a mind of its own and its driver is Ben, a happy-go-lucky but charmless adventurer who wheels Superbug on an African auto endurance race. Other participants are a silly Scotsman on a hovercraft, jungle doctor Daktari Jo, diamond smugglers and their henchmen. Quite unexciting, with no sense of a chase whatsoever, padded with footage of elephants, giraffes, lions and monkeys. Directed by David Mark, which could be an Angloized alias for exec producer Rudolph Zebetgruber, who directed SUPERBUG, SUPER AGENT, first in this witless series. Richard Lynn, Katharina Orginski.

SUPER FUZZ (1980). This U.S.-Italian production (also SUPERSNOOPER) is so dumb and innocuously good-natured it becomes enjoyable as Florida cop Terence Hill (Italian spaghetti-Western star) is exposed to a rocket explosion and develops superhuman powers—telepathy, high-speed movement, etc. Partner Ernest Borgnine flips trying to deal with these talents, and his comedy timing enhances an otherwise vapid showcase. The film's climax degenerates into the broadest of chase slapstick; yet, somehow, that sense of playfulness prevents SUPER FUZZ from becoming totally negligible. Directed by Sergio Corbucci. Joanne Dru, Marc Lawrence, Julie Gordon. Borginine starred in two similar TV pilots, FUTURE COP and COPS AND ROBIN. (Embassy)

SUPERGIRL (1971). Stacked chick from space tries to warn us of an invasion—Frenchmen get so carried away by her voluptuousness they try to get the E.T. babe in the sack for some ooh-la-la. Just goes to prove you *can* keep a good Frenchman down. Directed by Rudolf Thome. Iris Berben, Marquand Bohm.

SUPERGIRL (1984). Wild and woolly Alexander Salkind production featuring wonderful flying scenes and expensive effects. Kara (daughter of Zoltar, brother of Superman's father) loses the Omega Hedran, a life-giving object that spells doom for Argo City (on Krypton) unless she can recover it. Jumping aboard the Binar Shoot, a vehicle for passing through the Sixth Dimension, Kara (Helen Slater) comes to Earth, assumes the guise of college girl Linda Lee and engages in adventures with Selena, a wicked witch (beautifully essayed by Faye Dunaway) who uses the Hedran to conjure up evil. What's lacking in David Odell's episodic script are strong relationships and logic. What saves this is its visual style (thanks to cinematographer Alan Hume) and Dunaway's flamboyant sorceress. She proclaims herself "The ultimate siren of Endor," and becomes Hollywood's greatest villainess. The production is aided by Peter O'Toole (as Kara's father) who reaches Shakespearean heights when he's lost in the Phantom Zone and turns to alcoholism. Slater performs well in her debut role. Effects by Derek Meddings and Roy Fields. Music by Jerry Goldsmith. Directed by Jeannot Szwarc. Mia Farrow appears as Supergirl's mother and Brenda Vaccaro is whimsical as Selena's right-hand gal. Peter Cook, Simon Ward. (USA) (Laser: Image)

SUPER INFRAMAN, THE. See **INFRAMAN**.

SUPERKIDS (1978/79). Two British TV-movies for children, edited back-to-back, are strictly formula comedies about magical powers possessed by youngsters. In "Sammy's Super T-Shirt," a 12-year-old with the power to bound across the ground like a basketball is pursued by bumbling scientists; in "Electric Eskimo," an Alaskan youth is endowed with electrical energy. Strictly for the young set. Kris Emmerson, Lawrie Mark, David Young, Keith Jaynes. Also known as SUPERBOYS.

SUPERMAN—THE MOVIE (1978). Super-spectacular $40 million Ilya Salkind production pays homage to the most famous superhero of the comic books, radio, and serials . . . but never in a single style. This beautifully crafted film begins as a space adventure, depicting the origin of Superman, his father Jor-El (Marlon Brando) and the demise of Krypton, all done seriously. It then shifts to our baby hero landing on Earth and tended to by the Kent family, and a sentimental, lyrical quality in the cornfields of Kansas prevails. The more traditional comic book ambience is generated when Kent shows up in Metropolis, writing for the Daily Planet, and falling in love with reporter Lois Lane. It's a great affair, with Superman carrying Lois through the skies of the city. And finally, we have Superman's adventures with Lex Luthor, evil mastermind who plans to create an earthquake that will send California into the Pacific. Mixture of styles may have been caused by so many writers: Mario Puzo, David Newman, Leslie Newman, Robert Benton. John Williams' musical score gives the film a true sense of heroic grandeur. Richard Donner directed, and did a wonderful job. Christopher Reeve doubles as Superman and Clark Kent and he's perfect casting. Gene Hackman hams it up as Luthor, Ned Beatty likewise as his bumbling sidekick, and Margot Kidder is perfect as Lois. (RCA/Columbia; Warner Bros.) (Laser: Warner Bros.)

CHRISTOPHER REEVE

SUPERMAN II (1981). Entertaining special-effects masterpiece translates the famous comic book to the screen with a joyous sense of wonder. This followup to the 1978 box-office smash is a rich mosaic of action, light-hearted romance ("mushy stuff") and a sense of stylistic spoofery, even if director Richard Lester is somewhat dwarfed by the story's enormity. The cast is wonderful, with Christopher Reeve again doubling as the Man of Steel and as Clark Kent, mild-mannered reporter, Margot Kidder again falling in love with Superman, and Gene Hackman returning as master villain Lex Luthor. Sarah Douglas, Jack O'Halloran and Terence. Stamp appear as Kryptonite heavies who turn the world topsy-turvy with their superpowers. Their destruction of downtown Metropolis is brilliant. The Mario Puzo-David Newman-Leslie Newman script moves moves moves, and you'll love E. G. Marshall as our First Executive with a toupee. Ned Beatty (back as Otis), Jackie Cooper (back as Perry White) and Susannah York (back as Superman's mother) appear briefly. (Video/Laser: Warner Bros.)

SUPERMAN III (1983). Alexander and Ilya Salkind, the Brothers Whim of producers, commit an unpardonable cinematic sin: After establishing high standards for effects and scripting in their first two Superman epics, they allowed mediocrity to set in. The David/Leslie Newman script is a half-witted affair in which the Man of Steel (Christopher Reeve again) pursues archcriminal Ross Webster (unctuously played by Robert Vaughn). But Superman doesn't seem to have his heart in it—and the same can be said for director Richard Lester, whose SUPERMAN II was so much more stylized. There's a dull love affair between Clark Kent (also Reeve) and old high school flame Lana Lang (Annette O'Toole) that never builds, and Richard Pryor is plain stupid as computer whiz Gus Gorman, victimized by Vaughn to reprogram the world so there is a monopolistic hold on the world's oil. The film comes to life when Superman is weakened by ersatz Kryptonite and turns evil—you'll see Superman drinking whiskey and having an affair with sexy Annie Ross. Finally there's a great duel of alter egos when Kent and Superman square off in a junkyard. But the humanity that enhanced the previous films is missing, and no amount of effects magic can make up for it. Jackie Cooper appears as Perry White, and Margot Kidder is in just two scenes as Lois Lane. (Video/Laser: Warner Bros.)

SUPERMAN IV: THE QUEST FOR PEACE (1987). Superman is no longer so super—Menahem Golan and Yoram Globus took over the series from the Salkinds and proved they were made of putty, not steel. The Harrison Ellenshaw effects are so inferior as to be (1) laughable and (2) disappointing, and the Lawrence Konner-Mark Rosenthal script (based on a Christopher Reeve idea) is a spectacular mess, never leaping a single bound. Christopher Reeve as Clark Kent/Superman is so appealing you want to like this movie, but director Sidney J. Furie gets in the way of a good time. Superman is on a kick to dump all nuclear weapons into a space junkpile, but returning to stop him is Lex Luther (Gene Hackman), who creates a mighty solar man to combat our stalwart hero. This battle is an insult to the three films that preceded it. Mariel Hemingway as the new owner of the Daily Planet provides the film's only charm by exposing her beautiful gams. And that, fans, is the highlight of this distressingly disappointing movie. Sam Wanamaker portrays Mariel's greedy father. Margo Kidder returns as Lois Lane, and except for one flying sequence with Superman is left out of the picture. Jon Cryer, Marc McClure. (Video/Laser: Warner Bros.)

SUPERMAN. Compilation of excellent Fleischer Brothers cartoons from the '40s depicting the Man of Steel. Includes "Superman 1," "Magnetic Telescope," "Japoteurs," "Bulleteers," "Jungle Drums," "Mechanical Monsters," "The Mummy Strikes." (Media)

SUPERMAN AND THE JUNGLE DEVIL (1954). Episodes of the George Reeves TV series spliced into a feature, then resold to TV. Noell Neill as Lois Lane.

SUPERMAN AND THE MOLE MEN (1951). George Reeves first played the Man of Steel in this Robert L. Lippert feature, later divided into two chapters and shown on the long-running TV series SUPERMAN. Dwarves emerge from the subterranean depths to throw a town into panic, but Superman appears to act as a go-between. Phyllis Coates is Lois Lane, a role she duplicated on TV during the 1951 season. Jeff Corey, Walter Reed, Stanley Andrews. Directed by Lee Sholem. Also known as SUPERMAN AND THE STRANGE PEOPLE. (Warner Bros.)

SUPERMAN CARTOONS OF MAX AND DAVE FLEISCHER, THE. Laser edition of the superior SUPERMAN cartoons of the '40s. (Image)

SUPERMAN COLOR CARTOON FESTIVAL. Another video packaging of the superb Fleishcer Brother cartoons from the '40s.

SUPERMAN FLIES AGAIN (1954). Three episodes of the TV SUPERMAN series pasted into a feature. The Man of Steel breaks up a band of jewel thieves; he helps a private eye solve a caper; he is exposed to Kryptonite. George Reeves leaps over tall buildings and speeding locomotives with ease. Directed by Thomas Carr and George Blair. Noel Neill, Jack Larson, Robert Shayne. Elisha Cook Jr.

SUPERMAN: THE COMPLETE CARTOON COLLECTION, THE. Two-cassette collection of the 17 cartoons by the Fleischer Brothers, felt to be the best on tape in terms of quality. (Video Dimensions)

SUPERMAN: THE SERIAL (1948). One of the better serials to come out of the Columbia factory from producer Sam Katzman. It's a series of rip-roaring adventures (in 15 chapters) beginning with Superman's origins on Krypton, his coming to Earth in a rocket, his adoption by the Kent family, and his journey to Metropolis to fight crime disguised as Clark Kent. The flying sequences are animated in a cartoonish style—a jarring contrast to the fine live-action footage. Superman's adversary is the sexy Spider Lady, played with a perverse twist by Carol Forman in an appealing black outfit, her main murder device a large electrified web. She's out to possess the "Reducer Ray" and has Kryptonite to keep Superman at bay. Noel Neill is a perky Lois Lane, although her actions are annoyingly dumb. It was directed with style by Spencer G. Bennet and Thomas Carr and stars Kirk Alyn as a square but likable Man of Steel. Pierre Watkin is Perry White and Tommy Bond is Jimmy Olson. In this wonderful cliffhanger can be seen the antecedents for the TV series with George Reeves. The chapter's begin and end with narration read by Knox Manning, who had one of the best voices in radio. (Warner Bros.)

SUPER MARIO BROS. (1993). They took the popular Nintendo video game and turned it into a lavish effects extravaganza, jam-packed with action, comedy and computerized graphics. Even so, the result is a mediocre mixture out of control, and never having the internal logic a good fantasy needs. Bob Hoskins and John Leguizamo are delightful as Brooklyn plumbers who enter another dimension where a kingdom of people descended from dinosaurs is ruled by comical tyrant King Koopa (Dennis Hopper with a crazy hairdo). The plumbers are after a magical pendant and a bevy of kidnapped Brooklyn beauties and the pace is unrelenting as they meet an evil priestess, a pet T-Rex named Yoshi, henchmen called Goombas (tall dudes with tiny lizardheads) and a zillion funky props, sets and costumes. Nobody can fault the energetic direction by Rocky Morton and Annabel Jankel, the creators of Max Headroom. Fiona Shaw, Samantha Mathis, Fisher Stevens, Richard Edson. (Hollywood Pictures)

SUPERNATURAL (1933). See editions 1-3.

SUPERNATURAL (1980). Spanish production in which a deceased husband returns from the grave to avenge his wife's infidelity. An expert in ESP is called in and there's a lot of dialogue about paranormal activities. Directed by Eugenio Martin. Cristina Galbo.

SUPERNATURALS, THE (1986). Well-produced Sandy Howard production that opens in 1865, when Confederate prisoners are forced to walk across a mine field by a Union sadist. A youth surviving that ordeal possesses magical powers that, a hundred years later, plague a detachment of Army recruits training in the area where the Civil War massacre took place. Dead rebels are on the march, killing the soldiers one by one, while the boy's mother, in beautiful form, falls for one of the troopers. Macabre, eerie imagery by director Armand Mastroianni richly enhances this offbeat, above-average horror thriller. Nichelle Nichols, Maxwell Caulfield, Talia Balsam, Scott Jacoby, Levar Burton. Excellent music by Robert O. Ragland. (Embassy)

SUPERSONIC MAN (1979). A humanoid alien cruising through space in a capsule is awakened and told he has a mission to carry out on the endangered planet of Earth, where the mad would-be-dictator Dr. Goolick (Cameron Mitchell) plans to conquer mankind with a fire-breathing robot. So Supersonic Man, cape billowing in airless space, swoops toward the Green Planet to music that was inspired by SUPERMAN—THE MOVIE. Once on

Earth he confronts Goolick's green-garbed minions, the robot and a comic-relief drunk with basset hound in a series of asinine, uninspired adventures. Mitchell, despite mad-doctor dialogue, is drab and non-threatening. The effects are mediocre, and the storyline too stupid for children or adults. Directed and co-written by J. Piquer Simon. Michael Coby, Diana Polakow, Richard Yesteran. (United)

SUPERSONIC SAUCER (1956). Quaint British film for children in which moppets help a UFO from Venus out of a tight spot on Earth. Includes animated sequences. Directed by S. G. Ferguson. Marcia Monolescue, Fella Edmonds, Donald Gray. (Sinister/C)

SUPERSPEED (1935). See third edition.

SUPERSTITION (1982). Haunted house-exorcism package with ample gore effects. Black Lake is haunted by a witch drowned there in 1692, and she also haunts a nearby mansion, allowing for bloody acts of violence that make it appear the house is responsible. What we have here is an exploding head in a microwave oven, a body ripped open by a whirring skillsaw ("My, what teeth you have!"), a body gutted and chopped in half by a descending windowframe, the toes of a swimmer eaten off, a man hanged in an elevator shaft, a man crushed by a wine press, and a woman nailed to the floor with spikes (including one through her brain). The characters are fodder for the deathmill in Donald G. Thompson's script, including Albert Salmi's inquisitive policeman, Larry Pennell's drunken husband, James Houghton's investigating hero and Lynn Carlin's heroine. James W. Robinson's direction is hampered by flat lighting. Also known as THE WITCH. (Lightning)

SUPERTRAIN (1979). A GRAND HOTEL on rails and one of the worst TV premises ever. This pilot for a flop, derailed series (which embarrassed NBC) loses steam immediately as it depicts an atomic-powered choo choo complete with swimming pool, discotheque and other futuristic gadgets. But instead of being sleek and streamlined, this chug chug chugs down the tracks—it's barely the little engine that could. Dan Curtis production with Keenan Wynn as the train's owner. Vicki Lawrence, George Hamilton, Fred Williamson.

SUPERVAN (1977). This low-budgeter made at the "Freak-Out" show for vans in St. Joseph, Mo., would have served better as a documentary. It is lamebrain as a comedy or action-chase film with its solar-powered Vandora the Supervan, equipped with a built-in female voice and laser zap ray. Its young players are uncharismatic and director Lamar Card fails to build excitement into the chases. But when he turns the film into a visual study of vans and drivers, and the beautiful art that adorns their vehicles, the film snaps to life. Only Morgan Woodward as the pompous owner of Mid American Motor Corp., who's out to prevent the solar car from cutting into his business, has fun as he swaggers with his cigar, ogling girls and brushing away sycophants. Mark Schneider, Katie Saylor, Len Lesser.

SUPERWHEELS (1978). Sequel to West Germany's SUPERBUG SUPERAGENT features more inept misadventures of the yellow Volkswagen Dudu, computerized to talk and think like a human. Its programmer, Jim Bondi, is a cowboy-style roustabout who befriends two nuns taking part in a mountainous car race, helping them overcome an evil Count and his henchmen. The snow-covered Alps are littered with junked cars—and this movie. Robert Marck, Sal Brogi.

SURF NAZIS MUST DIE (1986). Despite its campy title, this Troma production takes itself seriously in depicting war between the Samurai Surfers and the Surf Nazis for control of Power Beach. In "the near future," following an earthquake that's left the L.A. basin devastated, these gangs fight it out and spend enough time riding big waves to slow the plot to a backcrawl. The neo-Nazi band, led by "Adolf" and "Mengele," becomes the target of an irate black mother (Gail Neely) after her son is murdered, and she's a sight as she buys firearms (to "blow away honkies"), rides a motorcycle and pursues Nazi rats in a speedboat. Directed by Peter George. Barry Brenner, Dawn Wildsmith, Bobbie Bresee, Dawne Ellison. (Media)

SURF TERROR. See **MONSTER FROM THE SURF.**

SURF II (1982). The big gag: There never was a SURF I. Ha ha ha ha! Glub glub. New Wavers in black outfits are aliens who abduct teen-agers into an underwater UFO . . . Buzz Cola, a new soft drink, turns teens into zombies or women . . . this foolish sexploitation trash consists of unfunny jokes, such as eating seaweed, crunching on glass, jiggling bare breasts into the mouths of overweight boys and kidding a stupid sheriff, Chief Boyardit. The script by director Randall Badat is impossible to describe as infantile jokes are blended like flotsam on the tide. Joshua Cadman, Linda Kerridge, Cleavon Little, Ruth Buzzi, Lyle Waggoner. (Media; King of Video)

SURROGATE, THE (1984). Unhappily married couple (Art Hindle and Shannon Tweed) seek help from sex therapist Carole Laure who tries to free their repressed fantasies . . . second storyline focuses on a serial murderer specializing in stabbings . . . elements are linked by director Don Carmody. Michael Ironside, Marilyn Lightstone, Jim Bailey. (Media)

SURVIVALIST, THE (1987). When war with Russia appears imminent, biker gangs in Texas take over the territory, terrorizing Steve Railsback and son. Mindless action in the MAD MAX vein, without style or interesting characters. This film can't possibly survive. Jason Healey, Marjoe Gortner, Cliff De Young, David Wayne, Susan Blakely. (Vestron) (Laser: Image)

SURVIVAL 1990 (198?). Survivors of a nuclear holocaust scavage the devastated landscape in packs of mutants and still-ordinary men. (VC)

SURVIVAL RUN. See **DAMNATION ALLEY.**

SURVIVAL ZONE (1984). "Welcome to World War IV," proclaims a survivor of nuclear holocaust that has left a handful to rove the nukked landscape. Among them: Bigman and his vicious motorcycle gang, heroic Adam Strong (Morgan Stevens) and Gary Lockwood, who lives with wife Camilla Sparv and children on an isolated farm. The screenplay by producer-director Percival Rubens and Eric Brown has these elements coming together to do battle in what is a predictable (though surprisingly philosophical) portrait of post-Armageddon survival. It finally boils down to routine action and sadistic torture and looks as though it was made in Australia. Zoli Marki, Ian Steadman. (Prism; Starmaker)

SURVIVING THE GAME (1994). Well-written, entertaining variation on "The Most Dangerous Game" in which derelict Ice-T becomes the prey for a small band of hunters led by Rutger Hauer, Gary Busey and Charles S. Dutton. Rugged Canadian terrain enhances the action as Ice-T proves more durable than his stalkers ever imagined. In an odd twist, Eric Bernt's script turns the tables by having Ice-T becoming the stalker, and creates suspense for the baddies. Director Ernest Dickerson spends just enough time on the twisted attitudes of the hunters to elevate this above other "Dangerous Game" remakes. John C. McGinley, William McNamara, Jeff Corey. (New Line)

SURVIVOR, THE (1981). Doom-laden ambience and an eerie Brian May score make this Australian adaptation of James Herbert's novel a satsifying experience. After jumbo-jetliner captain Robert Powell emerges from the wreckage of his crashed 747 he joins psychic Jenny Agutter and priest Joseph Cotten to find out who is responsible. Ultimately the supernatural intervenes in a fiery climax. Powell is good as the mentally confused survivor. Directed by actor David Hemmings from a David Ambrose script. (Lorimar; Warner Bros.)

SURVIVOR (1986). Worthless post-holocaust movie in a quasi-ROAD WARRIOR vein. Richard Moll is astronaut Kragg, who takes off aboard Challenger II to circle Earth 228 times while a nuclear war wipes out mankind. He awakens to find himself shackled to a pipe, and proceeds to enter an adventure with Sue Kiel that makes no sense involving a subterranean city where a madman has Wolf Larsonish dreams of starting mankind over again. There's one good action sequence where men dangling on chains fight it out, but otherwise this is incoherent, from Bima Stagg's script to Michael Shackleton's direction. Chip Mayer, John Carson. (Vestron) (Laser: Image)

SUSPENSE. See **BEYOND THE DOOR II.**

SUSPIRIA (1976). Short on logic but long on thrills, this is a fan's picture—an Italian import written by director Dario Argento and Daria Nicolodi. Jessica Harper is an American enrolled in a German dance academy, when suddenly a thunderstorm sets the mood for a bat attack, falling maggots, a throat-ripping dog and cackling witches. Commendable "cheap thrills" with Joan Bennett, Udo Keir and Alida Valli. (Magnum) (Laser: Image)

SUZANNE. Alternate video title for **SECOND COMING OF SUZANNE, THE** (Video Gems).

SVENGALI (1931). George du Maurier's TRILBY was adapted with John Barrymore as the hypnotic, eye-rolling impresario who seduces Marian Marsh and turns her into a singing star. Directed by Archie Mayo. Marian Marsh, Donald Crisp, Lumsden Hare. (Classic Video; Sinister/C; Filmfax; Cinema Collector's Club)

SVENGALI (1955). Baroque British version of George du Maurier's TRILBY, starring Donald Wolfit as the hypnotist who sways the will of a beautiful singer and turns her into a brilliant performer—but he cannot force honey-haired Hildegarde Neff to love him. Director-writer Noel Langley emphasizes the love affair between Miss Neff and an artist (Terence Morgan). Weird, somber adaptation. (S/Weird; VCI)

SVENGALI (1983). TV version of the George du Maurier classic, directed by Anthony Harvey and written by Frank Cucci. The cast is the thing: Peter O'Toole as the vocal coach, Jodie Foster as singer Zoe Alexander, with Elizabeth Ashley and Pamela Blair in supporting roles. Stripped of diabolical elements, this is an ordinary love story, without good vs. evil conflicts. (IVE)

SWAMP OF LOST SOULS, THE. See **SWAMP OF THE LOST MONSTERS.**

SWAMP OF THE BLOOD LEECHES. See **ALIEN DEAD, THE** (USA).

SWAMP OF THE LOST MONSTERS (1964). Mexico's cowboy star Gaston Santos on his Wonder Horse rides to save a screaming heroine when she is attacked by an amphibian creature in this Mexican Saturday-matinee fodder. U.S. producer K. Gordon Murray re-released the film with new footage by director Stem Segar. The rest of this mess, featuring inept comic relief (a fat Pancho-like character), stupid fistfights, lowbrow slapstick and a superphony gillman suit, was directed by Raphael Baledon. Manola Savedra, Manuel Dondi. (Saturn; Filmfax; Nostalgia; Sinister/C; Genesis)

SWAMP THING (1982). Popular comic-book creature, half-man, half- slime, is the laughing stock of the Okefenokee in the hands of director-writer Wes Craven. The juvenile approach is an ironic shift from his LAST HOUSE ON THE LEFT and THE HILLS HAVE EYES and will disappoint fans expecting hardcore horror. The monster looks exactly like what it is—a strongarm actor in a rubber

SWAMP THING

suit. And Craven lingers lovingly on the phony outfit, allowing us to wince for minutes at a stretch. Louis Jourdan has the thankless role of Arcane, Swamp Thing's nemesis, and Adrienne Barbeau streaks through the wilderness, screaming as she is pursued by the creature (for a moment she pauses to bare her lovely breasts). Though trying to play a "ballsy broad" and make Alice Cable a heroine, Barbeau is merely decorative and rescuable. Nicholas Worth, David Hess. (Video/Laser: Embassy/Nelson)

SWAMP THING II. See **RETURN OF THE SWAMP THING.**

SWARM, THE (1978). Lousiest of the "killer bees" movies, although based on a good book by Arthur Herzog. Sterling Silliphant's adaptation and Irwin Allen's direction dealt too much with cliches and not with Herzog's concepts. The South American killer bees are moving northward, and threaten to destroy civilization. All that's stopping them are Michael Caine, as a bee specialist, Katharine Ross, Olivia de Havilland, Ben Johnson, Fred MacMurray, Richard Chamberlain, Richard Widmark and a beehive of Hollywood actors. You're in for a "sting." The "swarmy" music is by Jerry Goldsmith, a hornet among composers. (Video/Laser: Warner Bros.)

SWEENEY TODD: THE DEMON BARBER OF FLEET STREET. Video version of **DEMON BARBER OF FLEET STREET, THE** (Video Yesteryear).

SWEENEY TODD (1971). British TV version of THE DEMON BARBER OF FLEET STREET, reviving the old legendary plot about the strange alliance between a barber and the owner of a bakery shop located conveniently next door. Seems the hair-cutter also cuts throats, then turns over the bodies to the baker who puts them into his pastries. Here's pie in your eye. Produced by Sidney Pink. Freddie Jones stars.

SWEENEY TODD (1984). Angela Lansbury and George Hearn star in this TV version of the smash Broadway hit (based on the old British tale of a throat-cutter's union with a pie maker), which was nominated for several awards. It's a musical version, dark and atmospheric, not pleasant at all, for the bloodletting is extremely realistic for the stage as Lansbury and Hearn explore the sick side to the human appetite. (RKO)

SWEET KILL. See **AROUSERS, THE.**

SWEET SIXTEEN (1983). Muddled mess of a horror movie, featuring too few murders to satisfy the slasher crowd and too much confusion in the final reel for anyone to make sense of it. Erwin Goldman's script is at fault, for Jim Sotos has done a decent job of directing on a low budget and the cast is composed of good players valiantly bringing quality to an ill-conceived story. In a Texas town a rash of murders centers around newcomer Melissa (Aleisa Shirley), just 16. Her sexual awakening is the cause of the violence, but far more interesting is sheriff Bo Hopkins and his daughter Dana Kimmell. A red herring subplot involves an Indian burial ground—which Patrick Macnee, as Melissa's father, is excavating—but it never dovetails. Susan Strasberg, Henry Wilcoxon (as an old Indian), Sharon Farrell, Larry Storch, Michael Pataki. (Vestron)**SWEET SOUND OF DEATH (1965).** Editions 1-3.

SWEET SUGAR (1972). Voodoo melodrama with a mad doctor up to illegal experimentation with women prisoners, who break out in a blaze of glorious action. A bitter pill to take. Directed by Michel Levesque. Phyllis E. Davis, Ella Edwards, Timothy Brown. (Continental; also in video as **CAPTIVE WOMEN III**)

SWEET, SWEET RACHEL (1971). Unseen presence tries to drive three lovely lasses out of their beautiful skulls. ESP expert Alex Dreier experiments, disturbing the unseen world around him. TV-movie has nice ambience and a feeling for the supernatural via director Sutton Rolley and writer Anthony Lawrence. Stefanie Powers, Pat Hingle, Brenda Scott, Chris Robinson.

SWITCH (1991). Once again writer-director Blake Edwards (VICTOR/VICTORIA) tackles the fascinating theme of confused sexual roles, but this time it's a fantasy clunker. When womanizer Perry King is murdered by three abused lovers, he winds up in Purgatory, where it's decided (by the male and female voices of God) that he should be given a second chance to find a woman who respects him. But then the Devil (Bruce Martyn Payne) gives him the body of a sexy woman (Ellen Barkin) in his/her quest. What results are unfunny situations in which Barkin (remember this is a male trapped in a female's body) embarks on lesbian and hetereosexual relationships. Only toward the climax, when the woman gets pregnant, does the film take on poignancy. Jimmy Smits, JoBeth Williams, Lorraine Bracco, Tony Roberts, Lysette Anthony. (Video/Laser: HBO)

SWITCH IN TIME. See **NORMAN'S AWESOME EXPERIENCE.**

SWORD AND THE DRAGON, THE (1956). The Russians celebrate a legendary swordsman, Ilya Mourometz, the slayer of creatures. In this adaptation of his career as a monster carver, he wields a magic sword against an ogre; a "wind" monster; and a three-headed hydra. Boris Andreyev is the gallant knight, erratic but errant. Directed by V. Kotochnev. Boris Andreyev, Andrei Abrikosov. (United; Sinister/C; S/Weird)

SWORD AND THE SORCERER, THE (1982). Producers Brandon Chase and Marianne Chase offer a fantasy reminiscent of Saturday matinee serials as Lee Horsley battles evil in a mythical kingdom (Eh-Dan) ruled by Cromwell (Richard Lynch) and his demon (George Maharis). Prince Talon (Horsley) must also rescue Kathleen Beller. It was well directed by Albert Pyun (from a script by Tom Karnowsky) and has bloody effects as well as good transformations of men into monsters (by Richard Washington). (Video/Laser: MCA)

SWORD IN THE STONE, THE (1963). T. H. White's account of the early days of King Arthur was turned into a full-length Disney cartoon capturing the fantasy excitement of how Arthur (called Wart) meets Merlin the Magician and undergoes several adventures before pulling the sword Excalibur from the stone and proving he is the rightful ruler of Britain. Young Arthur is changed into a fish so he might witness the wonders of the sea, and he joins in battle with sorcerers in a memorable sequence. Voices by Sebastian Cabot, Karl Swenson and Alan Napier. (Video/Laser: Disney)

SWORDKILL. See **GHOST WARRIOR.**

SWORD OF ALI BABA, THE (1965). Editions 1-3.

SWORD OF HEAVEN (1985). Magical blade, forged hundreds of years ago by Zen priests from a meteor becomes the object of contention between the evil gang that possesses it and a Japanese policeman, naturally skilled in martial arts, visiting California. Directed by Byron Meyers. Tadashi Yamashita, Mel Novak, Bill (Superfoot) Wallace, Venus Jones. (LD Video)

SWORD OF THE BARBARIANS, THE (1983). Sangrai the adventurer, the son of Ator (hero of a series of Italian films), vows when his wife is murdered to destroy the followers of the Goddess Rani, and rides to the Ark of the Templars for a magical crossbow that will help him finish the job. Barbarically cheap Italian sword-and-sandal yarn, directed without flair by Michael E. Lemick. You've seen all the flailing swords before. Peter MacCoy, Sabrina Siani, Margarethe Christian.

SWORD OF THE VALIANT (1984). Entertaining, swashbuckling interpretation of the Legend of Sir Gawain and the Green Knight, awash in colorful dialogue and characters. The Green Knight, a supernatural entity, rides into King Arthur's court and challenges any brave knight to chop off his head. The only catch is, if the swinger misses, the Green Knight (Sean Connery) gets a return swing. A squire (Miles O'Keeffe) accepts the challenge, thus beginning an outre odyssey into adventure, myth and magic as he sets out on a one-year quest for the answer to a riddle of wisdom. His wanderings take him to the land of Leonette, where he finds love, imprisonment and new enemy Ronald Lacey. Sets and costumes in this Golan-Globus production are splendid. Trevor Howard is the disillusioned king, Lila Kedrova is the wife of the protector of Leonette, Peter Cushing is a roving fop, Cyrielle Claire is Sir Gawain's love. Photographed by Freddie Young and Peter Hurst. Leigh Lawson, John Rhys-Davies. (MGM/UA)

SWORDSMAN, THE (1992). Lorenzo Lamas is adept with epees, sabers and swords in this fantasy adventure-mystery cast in the mold of HIGHLANDER. Lamas portrays an L.A. cop undergoing psychic visions connected with the Sword of Alexander the Great, which has fallen into evil hands. Lamas comes under the control of diabolical sorcerer Michael Champion and must break free to duel for possession of the priceless weapon. Writer-director Michael Kennedy has a good sense of ambience and his stunt coordinators stage good swashbuckling sequences, but Lamas is lifeless, whose thrust with a blade is far better than his thrusts with Claire Stansfield in the pallid love-making sequences. Still, this is a notch above most fantasy-action fare. Nicholas Pasco, Raoul Trujillo. (Republic)

SWORDS OF THE SPACE ARK (1981). Video version of a Japanese ripoff of STAR WARS entitled MESSAGE FROM OUTER SPACE, a Saturday matinee-style TV special for the kiddies. The year is 2090, the setting is the 15th solar system where, on the planet Kendall, we are introduced to a Chewbacca-like gorilla spacecraft pilot, a villain in a helmet with plenty of "stormtroopers," a rock god in the shape of a giant ship, another ship in the shape of a 19th Century sailing vessel, etc. Strictly for the undiscriminating. The original was directed by Minoru Yamada, with special effects by Nobuo Ajima; the English version was written/produced/directed by Bunker Jenkins. (From King Bee as **SPACE NINJA: SWORDS OF THE SPACE ARK**)

SWORDS OF WAYLAND, THE (1983). Episode of cable TV's ROBIN HOOD THE LEGEND, starring Michael Praed as the hero of Sherwood who clashes with a devil-worship cult. (Playhouse)

SYBIL (1976). Landmark four-hour TV production is a tour de force for Sally Field as a mentally disturbed woman who harbors within her inner confusions 16 personalities. Although based on a true story, director Daniel Petrie and writer Stewart Stern treat this as a psychological horror story, revealing how Sybil was physically and sexually abused. Field won an Emmy for her performance. (Ironically, her co-star is Joanne Woodward as the psychiatrist who helps Sybil refind herself. Woodward played a character similar to Sybil in 1957's THREE FACES OF EVE, and won an Oscar for it. She was nominated for her role here, but did not win.) There is poetry, horror and insight into the human condition in this moving and often disturbing production. Also winning Emmies were Stern and Leonard Rosenman, Alan and Marilyn Bergman for the music. Brad Davis, Martine Bartlett, Jane Hoffman. (MGM/UA)

SYLVIA AND THE PHANTOM (1945). Alfred Adam's play was adapted by the French into a period comedy in which a young woman meets the spirit of a long-dead gentleman. Directed by Claude Autant-Lara. Odette Joyeux, Jacques Tati. (Embassy; Nelson)

SYMPTONS (1974). Admired Spanish shocker directed-written by Joseph Larraz (with Stanley Miller) depicting bloody events in a country manor. Angela Pleasance, Lorna Heilbron, Peter Vaughan, Ronald O'Neil. Also known as THE BLOOD VIRGIN.

SYNGENOR (1990). Synthetic genetic organism (hence SYNGENOR) is a new cyborg designed to fight our wars in the Middle East. Starr Andreeff fights for her life when the cyborg turns rogue. Directed by George Elanjian Jr. Mitchell Laurance, Charles Lucia, David Gale, Riva Spier. (South Gate; Hemdale)

SYSTEM OF DR. TARR AND PROFESSOR FEATHER, THE. See **DR. TARR'S TORTURE DUNGEON.**

T.A.G.—THE ASSASSINATION GAME (1983). Curious offshoot of the slasher genre, written-directed by Nick Castle. A game's afoot of make-believe assassination on college campuses, with students stalking each other armed with rubber dart guns. But one spoil sport goes psycho and kills opponents with a .45 (try to duck that dart), then stalks Linda Hamilton while Robert Carradine tracks clues for the campus paper. There's a nice jazz score by Craig Safan, but little suspense or payoff to this slight offering. Ready or not, here it comes. Perry Lang, Frazer Smith, Kristine DeBell. (Embassy)

TAKING TIGER MOUNTAIN (1983). Independent production, in black and white, shot in Wales. In the near future, the Soviet Union and U.S. are recovering from three mega-wars. While American boat people flee to Britain, draft dodger Bill Paxton is brainwashed to be an assassin by a feminist terror group. His target: a major selling white slaves. Moody, stark, low-budget grainy. Produced-written by Tom Huckabee.

TALE OF A VAMPIRE (1992). Julian Sands portrays a most unusual vampire in this Gothic tale of romance and neck-obsession set in a rainy London. His lover is Suzanna Hamilton. Directed by Shimako Sato, who cowrote with Jane Corbett. Kenneth Cranham, Marian Diamond, Michael Kenton. (Vidmark)

TALE OF THE FROG PRINCE (1982). Shelley Duvall's FAERIE TALE THEATER originally presented this popular story of how a prince is turned into a frog by a fairy godmother. Directed by Eric Idle. Robin Williams, Teri Garr, Candy Clark. (Video/Laser: CBS/Fox)

TALES FROM BEYOND THE GRAVE. See **FROM BEYOND THE GRAVE** (Graves of Wrath?).

TALES FROM THE CRYPT (1972). Adaptation of five E.C. comic stories published in the '50s by Al Feldstein and William Gaines (the latter became long-time editor of Mad). The famous panels (drawn by such artists as Johnny Craig, Graham Ingels and Jack Davis) have been recreated faithfully; and thanks to Milton Subotsky's script and Freddie Francis' direction, this comes off as a fun-filled horror film. Four individuals trapped with the Crypt Keeper (Sir Ralph Richardson) are told a narrative foreshadowing his/her destiny. "And All Through the House" deals with Joan Collins fighting off a Santa Claus madman on Christmas Eve; "Reflection of Death" is about a dead man who can't get used to the idea; "Poetic Justice" deals with a St. Valentine's Day gift delivered by Peter Cushing, fresh from his grave; "Wish You Were Here" is a variation on "The Monkey's Paw"; and "Blind Alleys" has Nigel Patrick blundering through a mazework of razor blades. VAULT OF HORROR, the sequel, adapted four more shuddery E.C. yarns. And in 1989 a cable TV series brought the Crypt Keeper back as storyteller. (Prism)

TALES FROM THE CRYPT (1989). Three episodes from the HBO cable series: "The Man Who Was Death," directed by Walter Hill and scripted by Hill and Robert Reneau; "And All Through the House," directed by Robert Zemeckis and written by Fred Dekker; and "Dig That Cat . . . He's Real Gone," directed by Richard Donner and written by Terry Black. (Video/Laser: HBO)

TALES FROM THE CRYPT: VOL. 2 (1989). Three more half-hour adaptations from the pages of the E.C. comics: "Only Sin Deep," with Lea Thompson; "Lover Come Hack to Me," with Stephen Shellar; and "Collection Complete" with E. Emmet Walsh and Audra Lindley. (Video/Laser: HBO)

TALES FROM THE DARKSIDE: VOLUME I (1984). Repackaged episodes of George Romero's half-hour TV series. "Word Processor of the Gods?" is a Stephen King story in which a writer changes history on a computer. "Djinn, No Chaser," based on a Harlan Ellison story, is a whimsical farce about a married couple (Colleen Camp, Charles Levin) and a genie in the form of Kareem Abdul Jabbar. "Slippage" depicts how David Patrick Kelly slips through the cracks of time and vanishes. (Thrillervideo) (Laser: Image)

TALES FROM THE DARKSIDE: VOL. 2 (1984). Three shorts from the syndicated series: Danny Aiello stars as a gambler in "The Odds," making a bet with a ghost; Harry Anderson stars in "All a Clone by the Telephone," in which an answering machine drives him crazy; and "Anniversary Dinner" features a hitchhiker and cannibals. (Thrillervideo) (Laser: Image)

TALES FROM THE DARKSIDE: VOL. 3 (1984-85). More half-hour TV jobs from George Romero: "Mookie and Pookie" is a good idea about a whiz at computers who is dying and reprograms himself to live; "It All Comes Out in the Wash" has Vince Edwards seeking an idyllic lifestyle; and "Levitation" is a superb magic story with Joseph Turkel as a magician who carries his sleight-of-brand too far. (Thrillervideo) (Laser: Image)

TALES FROM THE DARKSIDE: VOL. 4 (1984-85). Three more quickies from the Romero series: "The New Man," the pilot episode, stars Vic Tayback as a heavy drinker who finds his past catching up to him; "Snip, Snip" is cute comedy with Bud Cort and Carol Kane as practitioners of magic who use their powers to win a lottery; and "Painkiller" is about a guy being nagged to death. (Thrillervideo) (Laser: Image)

TALES FROM THE DARKSIDE: VOL. 5 (1984). Three more episodes of the syndicated TV series: "Inside the Closet," in which a co-ed's dreamy world becomes a nightmare; "The False Prophet," about a horoscope addict with a Pisces complex; and "Grandma's Last Wish," showing how a neglected old lady gets her revenge. (Thrillervideo) (Laser: Image)

TALES FROM THE DARKSIDE: VOL. 6 (1985-86). More episodes in TV's half-hour series from George Romero: "Bigalow's Last Smoke," about the gasping problems of a chain-smoker; "The Tear Collector," about a lonely woman who falls under a spell; and "The Madness Room," about a millionaire and precocious wife. (Thrillervideo) (Laser: Image)

TALES FROM THE DARKSIDE: VOL. 7 (1985-86). Three half-hour episodes from the TV series: "In the Cards," in which a fortune teller falls prey to an old gypsy curse; "A Case of the Stubborns," in which a dead man refuses to believe he has passed into the beyond; and "Trick or Treat," in which a nasty storekeeper gets his at Halloween. (Thrillervideo) (Laser: Image)

TALES FROM THE DARKSIDE: THE MOVIE (1990). A slight variation on the CREEPSHOW series—a trilogy of horror stories with a "framework" linking device. Based on the syndicated TV series from George Romero, this begins in the kitchen of a woman preparing to cook a boy imprisoned in an adjacent cell. To stall for time, the youth reads her stories from a volume entitled TALES FROM THE DARKSIDE. The first yarn, "Lot 249," is a mummy narrative inspired by Sir Arthur Conan Doyle and written by Michael McDowell—about how a scheming scholar brings a 3000-year-old mummy monster to life. This is only moderately frightening, with a twist ending. "Cat From Hell" is a Stephen King idea scripted by Romero in which a hitman is hired to kill a supernatural feline. Grisly ending to this one. "Lover's Vow," the final yarn, has the strongest potential: a starving artist makes a pact with a murderous gargoyle and finds fame, riches and happiness as a result—but the surprise ending falls flat. The make-up (by Dick Smith) and effects are good. Potential is here but director John Harrison never creates a sense of over-the-edge excitement. Christian Slater, Deborah Harry, David Johanson, Rae Dawn Chong, William Hickey, James Remar. (Video/Laser: Paramount)

GARGOYLE MONSTER

TALES OF HOFFMANN (1951). Producers-directors-writers Michael Powell and Emeric Pressburger collaborated on this first sound version (there were three silent ones) of Jacques Offenbach's opera, beautifully executed in Technicolor. Love and fantasy blend when Hoffman relates his past romances to travelers resting in an inn. In "Olympia," he falls in love with a dancing doll; in "Giulietta," Hoffman loves a girl under the spell of a witch; and in "Antonia," Hoffman struggles to save a girl who will die if he sings. The superb cast is headed by Moira Shearer, the exquisite dancer from another Powell-Pressburger classic, THE RED SHOES. Robert Helpman, Pamela Brown, Robert Rounseville, Ludmilla Tscherina. (Pioneer Artists Inc.) (Laser: Criterion)

TALES OF MYSTERY AND IMAGINATION. See **SPIRITS OF THE DEAD.**

TALES OF TERROR (1962). Roger Corman at his producing-directing best, with Richard Matheson superbly adapting a trilogy of Poe stories in "rococo Gothic." In "Morella," maddened Vincent Price faces his wife's ghost in the shapeliness of Leona Gage... slow but eerie, with Price believably sinking into alcoholic insanity. A combination of "The Black Cat" and "The Cask of Amontillado" teams Price and Peter Lorre in a rollicking wine-tasting contest. This tale is played for laughs, and Lorre comes off in excellent form. (Also in excellent form is Lorre's wife, Joyce Jameson.) In "The Case of M. Valdemar," Price is on his deathbed, kept alive by hypnotist Basil Rathbone. Handsomely mounted and entertaining in a preposterous way. Debra Paget, Wally Campo, Maggie Pierce. (Warner Bros.)

TALES OF THE HAUNTED. Short-lived TV series, re-edited as **EVIL STALKS THIS HOUSE.**

TALES OF THE UNEXPECTED. Four episodes gathered from the syndicated TV series ROALD DAHL'S TALES OF THE UNEXPECTED. These include "People Don't Do Such Things" (with Arthur Hiller and Samantha Eggar; directed by Gordon Hessler); "A Youth From Vienna" (with Dick Smothers; written by John Collier; directed by Norman Lloyd); "Skeleton in the Closet" (with Charles Dance; directed by Paul Annett); "Bird of Prey" (with Sondra Locke; directed by Ray Danton). (Prism) (Laser: Image)

TALES OF THE UNEXPECTED (1977). Is convicted murderer-rapist Teddy Jakes alive or dead? Because Jakes has harassed them and the law can't help, Lloyd Bridges and Pat Crowley have murdered Jakes and dumped his body in a well. But Jakes is very much alive, chewing on his gum, and terrorizing their children again. This re-edited version of a two-part episode ("The Force of Evil") from Quinn Martin's short-lived TV series is strangely lacking in a supernatural approach to a walking-dead-man plot. Blame director Richard Lang and/or scriptwriter Robert Malcolm Young. The film has a few "shock" moments, but mainly its drivel from the TV assembly line, enhanced only by desert-lake locations. John Anderson, Eve Plumb, William Watson, William Kirby Cullent. William Conrad is the ominous announcer. (Prism; from Goodtimes as **FORCE OF EVIL**)

TALES OF THE UNKNOWN (1990). Compilation of four short tales of horror, produced independently from 1983-1989. "Jack Falls Down," directed by John Kim and written by Michael Matlock, deals with a deal with the Devil; "The Big Garage" is director/writer Greg Beeman's parable about a repair garage that traps stranded motorists; "Warped" is writer-director Roger Nygard's tale of revenge and incest; and "Living on Video" is producer-director Todd Marks' comment on how TV invades our privacy. (Action International)

TALES OF TOMORROW I (1953). One of TV's earliest adult sci-fi series, which ran live for three seasons on ABC, plays today as a milestone with its excellent casts. This contains four episodes: "Frankenstein," "Dune Roller," "Appointment on Mars" and "The Crystal Egg." Worth searching out. Lon Chaney Jr., Bruce Cabot. (Nostalgia Merchant)

TALES OF TOMORROW II (1953). Four more episodes of TV's first important sci-fi series: "Past Tense," "A Child Is Crying," "Ice From Space" and "The Window." Boris Karloff, Paul Newman, Rod Steiger, Walter Abel. (Nostalgia Merchant)

TALES OF TOMORROW (1951-53). Two episodes of the classic anthology series of early TV: James Dean and Rod Steiger in "The Evil Within" (a superb Jekyll-Hyde variation) and Henry Jones in "The Spider's Web," a superb sci-fi/horror yarn. (Rhino)

TALES OF TRUMPY. See **UNEARTHLING, THE.**

TALES THAT WITNESS MADNESS (1972). British horror anthology in the style of TALES FROM THE CRYPT, directed by Freddie Francis and written by Jennifer Jayne. Donald Pleasence and Jack Hawkins are strolling through an asylum and meet four crazies who spill their yarns: "Mr. Tiger" is about a boy who creates imaginary beasts; "Mel" stars Joan Collins as a bitchy wife who resents her husband bringing a tree into the living room—a tree that is living in a terrifying sense; "Penny Farthing" is a time-travel tale involving a haunted bicycle; and "Luau" is a voodoo/cannibal story with Kim Novak as a rich doll whose daughter is a sacrificial lamb. The final shocker concerns what happens to Pleasence and Hawkins in the asylum. Involving and unusual. Georgia Brown, Donald Houston. (Paramount)

TAM LIN (1971). Roddy McDowall directed this feature which was never theatrically released. William Spier's script (based on a Robert Burns' poem) is about a witch involved with jet setters. Ava Gardner, Ian McShane, Cyril Cusack, Richard Wattis, Joanna Lumley, Sinead Cusack, Stephanie Beacham. Also known as THE DEVIL'S WIDOW and THE DEVIL'S WOMAN.

TANYA'S ISLAND (1980). Exotic Canadian model D. D. Williams fantasizes she's on an island with a hairy beast—a man in a gorilla suit designed by Rick Baker and Rob Bottin. Obviously, producer-writer Pierre Brousseau had good intentions and hired a good director, Alfred Sole, to carry them out, but nothing quite meshes. Made in Puerto Rico. (Simitar)

TARANTULA (1955). Director Jack Arnold tries to recapture the moods of IT CAME FROM OUTER SPACE and CREATURE FROM THE BLACK LAGOON but this Universal-International "giant creature" thriller (written by R.M. Fresco and Martin Berkeley) comes off as a lesser effort. Leo G. Carroll, seeking a nutrient to feed the increasing world population, turns a spider into a monster which, naturally, escapes. John Agar and Mara Corday have a perfunctory, dull romance soon forgotten when Clifford Stine's effects take over. But the effects are only mildly exciting and the film builds unspectacularly to a fiery climax as the ill-tempered arachnid attacks mankind. Clint Eastwood has a bit part as a jet pilot. Nestor Paiva, Ross Elliott, Eddie Parker. (Video/Laser: MCA)

TARANTULAS: THE DEADLY CARGO (1977). When an aircraft crashes in a California orange-growing region, banana spiders in a shipment of coffee beans from South America escape to begin a campaign of murder against everyone connected with oranges (except Anita Bryant). Claude Akins organizes the townspeople (overcoming the objections of dumb officials) and tracks the deadly critters to the local orange-packing plant. TV spiders act far more intelligent than the TV humans. Directed by Stuart Hagmann. Charles Frank, Howard Hesseman, Pat Hingle. (Alan Landsburg; Star Classics; USA; IVE)

TARGET EARTH (1954). Cheapie Herman Cohen release makes a clunking thud that matches the clunking of metal robots wandering through an American city after Earth has been zapped by a Death Ray and there are only a handful of survivors. At least it keeps the budget down. Richard Denning, Virginia Grey, Whit Bissell, Kathleen Crowley, House Peters Jr. and Arthur Space are among the boring types who behave foolishly while fighting off those clunker robot machines. Not even Paul Dunlap's music helps this exercise in tedium. Directed by Sherman A. Rose. (United)

TARGET . . . EARTH? (1980). Victor Buono is an alien (Homer the Archivist) watching Earth with a computer's help and wondering about our reaction to the Siberian explosion of 1908. Lowbrown sci-fi that tries to mix in pseudofact and quasiknowledge with scenes of Isaac Asimov and Carl Sagan. Billions . . . and billions of people tuned out. Written-produced-directed by Joost van Rees. (VCI)

TARGET FOR KILLING (1966). See third edition.

TARGETS (1968). Roger Corman came to Peter Bogdanovich with out-takes from THE TERROR (1963) and asked the writer-producer-director to construct a movie. Bogdanovich needed only a few scenes to concoct a tale about Byron Orlok, an aging horror star who feels he's passe (the real world's horrors are far worse, he believes) and wants to retire. Orlok is played by Boris Karloff in one of his best roles. Meanwhile, Tim O'Kelly, average American, murders his family with a high-powered rifle and snipes at motorists. Later, these divergent elements merge at a drive-in, where Orlok delivers his farewell address. Bogdanovich co-stars as a Sammy Fuller-type director. In recent years this unusual feature has taken on cult status. It's damn powerful. Sandy Baron, Mike Farrell, Jack Nicholson, Dick Miller, Randy Quaid, James Brown. (Paramount)

JOHNNY WEISSMULLER AS TARZAN THE APE MAN

TAROT. See **AUTOPSY.**

TARZAN AND THE AMAZONS (1945). Entertaining Johnny Weissmuller entry in the Tarzan series in which the vine-swinger and family (Brenda Joyce as Jane, Johnny Sheffield as Boy) find a lost city of sexy amazon women led by an old lady, Maria Ouspenskaya, best known as the gypsy woman in the "Wolf Man" films at Universal. Kurt Neumann directed the action-packed script. Barton MacLane.

TARZAN AND THE GREEN GODDESS. Feature/video version of the 1935 serial **NEW ADVENTURES OF TARZAN, THE** (Hollywood Home Theater).

TARZAN AND THE LEOPARD WOMEN (1946). Using long steel claws built into their leopard pelts, a cult of natives cuts out the hearts of victims and turns them over to their High Priestess (Acquanetta) to appease the angered Leopard God. Fun-filled potted-plant potboiler (28th in the Tarzan series) starring Johnny Weissmuller, Brenda Joyce, Johnny Sheffield, Edgar Barrier, Dennis Hoey, Anthony Caruso, Tommy Cook. Produced-directed by Kurt Neumann.

TARZAN IN MANHATTAN (1989). Lightweight, played-for-laughs TV-movie that doesn't do justice to Edgar Rice Burroughs' jungle man. After his mother gorilla Kona is murdered and Cheetah is kidnapped from the African wilds, a youthful Tarzan (Joe Lara) flies to New York where he joins with a cabbie (Kim Crosby) and her private eye father Archimedes (Tony Curtis) to track down the chimp. What they uncover is a philanthropist (Jan-Michael Vincent) conducting brain operations on monkeys to increase their intelligence. There isn't an ounce of believability in the cliched Anna Sandor-William Gough teleplay, and all the Tarzan gags fall flat. And director Michael Schultz photographs it as just another urban action-comedy. Oh, it's a jungle out there in Manhattan. Joe Seneca, Jerry Meline Taggert.

TARZAN'S DESERT MYSTERY (1943). Burroughs' jungle hero battles prehistoric monsters, but don't think producer Sol Lesser was spending money. He was swiping footage from ONE MILLION B.C. Tarzan (Johnny Weissmuller) wanders across sand dunes instead of jungle, looking for a plant that could cure malaria and fighting off Nazis. Helpings of fun and propaganda are packed into Edward T. Lowe's screenplay directed by William Thiele. Nancy Kelly, Otto Kruger, Joe Sawyer, Robert Lowery, Johnny Sheffield.

TARZAN'S MAGIC FOUNTAIN (1949). Lex Barker became the first Tarzan listed in the New York Social Register, and the tenth actor to essay the Edgar Rice Burroughs role. When a long-lost aviatrix (Evelyn Ankers) is found wandering in the jungle, looking no older than 25, explorers penetrate Tarzan's domain in search of a Fountain of Youth, guarded by the ferocious Leopard People. Also note that Tarzan now wears moccasins. Brenda Joyce is a fetching Jane—dig those crazy jungle skins. Albert Dekker, Alan Napier, Elmo Lincoln, Charles Drake. Directed by Lee Sholem.

TASTE FOR BLOOD, A (1967). Producer-director Herschell Gordon Lewis' updating of the Dracula legend (also known as THE SECRET OF DR. ALUCARD) finds a descendant of the count drinking from a flagon of vampire wine. Whom should he seek out and mark for death? Why, the destroyers of his maligned ancestor. Gore specialist Lewis appears in the cast. Bill Rogers, Elizabeth Wilkinson, Otto Schlesinger. One draggin' flagon, this chalice from no palace. (S/Weird)

TASTE FOR FLESH AND BLOOD, A (1990). Outer space creature has a thing for human flesh and arterial fluids—in short, a ravenous appetite for mortals. Rubin Santiago, Lori Karz, Tim Ferrante. (Legacy)

TASTE OF EVIL, A (1973). Barbara Parkins, recovering from a rape attack, is either going crazy or is the victim of a diabolical plot. This Aaron Spelling TV-movie was written by Jimmy Sangster, directed by John Llewellyn Moxey. Barbara Stanwyck, Roddy McDowall, Arthur O'Connell, William Windom, Bing Russell.

TASTE OF FEAR. See **SCREAM OF FEAR**.

TASTE OF SIN, A (1983). German film maker Ulli Lommel (BOOGEYMAN) cast his wife Suzanne Love as a British woman who previously witnessed her mother murdered by a GI, and who now murders her lovers. She meets an engineer (Robert Walker Jr.) in the process of dismantling the London Bridge and moving it to Arizona. Four years later Walker turns up at the newly located bridge, seeing a realtor who resembles Love but who now speaks without a British accent and doesn't recognize him. This VERTIGO-like twist is about the only interesting thing going in an otherwise slow-moving, would-be suspense thriller. Producer-director Lommel also co-wrote the shadowy script. Bibbe Hansen, Jeff Winchester, Nicholas Love, Amy Robinson. (From VCII as **OLIVIA**)

TASTE THE BLOOD OF DRACULA (1970). A tooth-bite above most of Hammer's Dracula films of the period, with Christopher Lee again conveying an aura of menace when three gentlemen in search of lust and thrills engage in a bit of satanism, inadvertently resurrecting the long-dead Count. These men and their families meet death in horrible albeit traditional vampiric fashion. Dracula, in a genuinely imaginative climax, faces a new form of death in a recently reconstructed church. Above average direction by Peter Sasdy, with screenwriter John Elder atoning for the horrible botch he made of EVIL OF FRANKENSTEIN. Linda Hayden, Isla Blair, Geoffrey Keen, Michael Ripper, Ralph Bates.

TC 2000 (1993). Although set in a futuristic society where criminals are called "breakers" and cops are "trackers," this is your basic martial-arts actioner. But it's a lively one, with a funky set design and well-choreographed battles as two cops are subjected to brutality and a double-cross in their "underworld security force" city. Bobbie Phillips is especially effective in a dual role: as an honest cop and later as a rebuilt sexy android. She's such an attractive woman, she distracts your mind from a lot of this film's ugliness and violence. Written with a lot of plot and directed by T. J. Scott, this Canadian film co-stars Bolo Yeung, Jalal Merhi and Billy Blanks.

TEENAGE CAVEMAN (1958). Despite rock-age production values, an inept performance by Robert Vaughn and horrendous music by Albert Glasser, this is salvaged by the direction of Roger Corman and a strangely shaped script by R. Wright Campbell. Vaughn, from a primitive tribe forbidden to trespass where dwells The Monster That Kills With a Touch, enters the taboo zone anyway, where a surprise ending awaits him (but not you—you can see it coming). There is no truth to the rumor this was originally called I WAS A TEENAGE CAVEBOY, although a correct alternate title is OUT OF THE DARKNESS. Jonathan Haze, Robert Shayne, Frank De Kova, Leslie Bradley. (RCA/Columbia)

TEENAGE DRACULA. See **DRACULA VS. FRANKENSTEIN.**

TEENAGE EXORCIST (1991). Scream queen Brinke Stevens wrote and starred in this spoof of THE EXORCIST which has a few chuckles but most of it lacks spirit. The sexy Stevens portrays a mousy creature who takes possession of a haunted mansion and is turned into a wanton seductress by a horned demon, but there's no way she'll ever pass for a teenager. Although Michael Berryman, Robert Quarry (as a bumbling "Father Karas") and Jay Richardson strive for laughs the material just isn't there. There's an occasional special effect but the whole thing is halfhearted. Directed by Grant Austin Waldman. Eddie Deezen, Tom Shell, Elena Sahagun. (Video/Laser: Action International)

TEENAGE FRANKENSTEIN. See **I WAS A TEENAGE FRANKENSTEIN.**

TEENAGE MONSTER. See **METEOR MONSTER.**

TEENAGE MUTANT NINJA TURTLES: THE MOVIE (1990). The comic book series by Kevin Eastman and Peter Laird tapped into mythology with its four turtles turned into crime-fighters named Raphael, Michelangelo, Donatello and Leonardo, and a Yoda-like philosopher in

RAPHAEL AND SPLINTER

the form of an intelligent rat named Splinter. Brought to the screen in a live-action movie, these characters become a collection of costumes designed by Jim Henson's Creature Shop, without the distinctive personalities of the comic books. The direction by Steve Barron is dark when it should be light and airy, the script by Todd W. Langen and Bobby Herbeck lacks the mythological proportions that might have turned this into a STAR WARS-like classic, and the villain imitates Darth Vader without possessing his memorable qualities. Although a box-office hit when released, this remains a shabby effort, crude when it needed to be smooth, wise-crackish when it needed to have a touch of class. Read the comic books or play the computer games—this is a disappointing addition to the Ninja Turtle phenomenon. Judith Hoag, Elias Koteas, Joch Pais, Michelan Sisti, Leif Tilden, David Forman, Michael Turney. (Family Home Entertainment) (Laser: Image)

TEENAGE MUTANT NINJA TURTLES II: THE SECRET OF THE OOZE (1991). Even worse than its predecessor, this half-hearted commercially shaped entertainment is for small fry—adults will find it difficult going as the mutant turtles get involved with the music world so that Vanilla Ice, Ya Kid K and Cathy Dennis can perform. Once again the nemesis Shredder is on hand, and the origin of the shell-backed heroes reveals that a mad doctor (David Warner) was responsible for the ooze from which they sprang. Script by Todd W. Langen, directed by Michael Pressman. (RCA/Columbia; New Line) (Laser: Image)

TEENAGE MUTANT NINJA TURTLES III: THE TURTLES ARE BACK . . . IN TIME (1993). Those pizza-loving, sewer-dwelling, fun-loving turtlenecks are off on a new adventure, traveling back to 17th Century Japan where they get into a bloody battle with a nobleman waging war against rebels. Most of the script by director Stuart Gillard focuses on slapstick hand-to-hand combat sequences as Raphael, Leonardo, Donatello and Michaelangelo slug it out with Caucasian bad guy Stuart Wilson and warlord Sab Shimono, while that lovely newspaperwoman April O'Neil (Paige Turco) watches from the sidelines. Meanwhile, back in Manhattan, Splinter the intellectual rat puts up with the 17th Century behavior of samurai warriors who travel through time in exchange for the turtle guys. Don't ask—it's too complicated to explain. You either dig the silly humor and slam bang action or you should go to the opera. Elias Koteas, Vivian Wu, Mark Caso, Matt Hill, Jim Raposa, David Fraser, James Murray. (New Line)

TEENAGE PSYCHO MEETS BLOODY MAMA. See **INCREDIBLY STRANGE CREATURES WHO STOPPED LIVING AND BECAME CRAZY MIXED-UP ZOMBIES, THE.**

TEENAGERS FROM OUTER SPACE (1958). Evil teenage aliens land on Earth in the company of Gargon, a lobster creature that walks on its hind legs and turns to jelly when the good-kid alien aims his Blaster Zap Gun. Strictly for the teenage set, if teenagers can sit through it. It's doubtful adults will want to. Produced-written-directed by Tom Graeff. Also known as THE GARGON TERROR. David Love, Dawn Anderson, Bryan Grant. (Sinister/C; S/Weird; Filmfax)

TEENAGE STRANGLER (1964). Co-eds are found dead with lipstick marks on their foreheads and scarves tightly around their necks, and it looks like a member of the Fast Backs gang did it. Low-budgeter produced in West Virginia is well photographed in color but poorly acted and indifferently directed by Ben Parker. The film has an alleged cult following, probably because of its dated rock 'n roll dance sequences and the square parents. But the slasher aspect is underplayed without adequate effects. Bill Bloom, John Ensign, Rick Harris. (Sinister/C; S/Weird; Filmfax)

TEENAGE ZOMBIES (1960). Hulking entities of evil, never exceeding 19, are created by a nerve gas—the brainstorm of a mad doctor (Katherine Victor) living on an island. Unfortunately, these vacationing teenage hulks look as vacuous and hollow-eyed as any teenager walking down a street, mesmerized by rock 'n roll music on a transistor. So this is less a horror film than a social document of unusual realism. Produced-directed by Jerry Warren. Don Sullivan, Steve Conte. (Sinister/C; S/Weird; Video Yesteryear; Filmfax)

TEEN VAMP (1989). Bitten in the neck by a prostitute, Beau Bishop turns into a traditional bloodsucker taken for granted by all his friends—what's so special about a vampire? Regional low-budget effort, shot in Shreveport, La., flops miserably. Written-directed by Samuel Bradford. Karen Carlson, Angie Brown, Clu Gulager. (New World)

TEEN WITCH (1989). Pallid comedy with musical-dance numbers in the MTV tradition, complete with an object lesson for Robyn Lively, a witch who discovers her powers at age 16 and uses them to become the best liked girl in school. Steppin' Lively learns the hard way, however, that you shouldn't always get what you want. Some object lesson. Without special effects, this is so lightweight it blows away on a cloud of nothingness. Director Dorian Walker doesn't even bring the dance numbers to life. Zelda Rubinstein is cute as the fortune teller who guides Lively through her magical stages and Shelley Berman is funny as an English teacher, but they can't salvage this broomstick bomb. Dan Gauthier, Joshua Miller, Caren Kaye, Dick Sargent. (Media)

TEEN WOLF (1985). Werewolf tale avoids genre cliches and goes for a shaggy twist: underdog teenager Michael J. Fox learns from dad about his wolfish genealogy and copes with being hairy on the gym floor during a basketball game. In that respect the Joseph Loeb III-Matthew Weisman screenplay is unique, but nothing is done with the premise, beyond Fox fighting within himself for the human half to succeed without resorting to the wolf, which is capable of break dancing and other physical feats. James Hampton, Scott Paulin, Jerry Levine, Susan Ursitti. Directed by Rod Daniel. (Paramount; Goodtimes) (Laser: Paramount)

TEEN WOLF TOO (1987). Without the charming presence of Michael J. Fox, this sequel to the '86 hit is a bore,

JASON BATEMAN IN 'TEEN WOLF TOO'

duplicating the themes of the original without exploring new territory, and presenting a lethargic cast with little to work with. Jason Bateman, portraying Todd Howard, the cousin of the Fox character, turns up at Hamilton U on a sports scholarship but really wants to study. He's sidetracked into exploiting his werewolf abilities to become the most popular, hairiest guy on campus. Eventually he loses the respect of the good people, and has to regain it in a climactic boxing match that tries to recapture the furor of ROCKY. Director Christopher Leitch is left high and dry with inadequate material by R. Timothy Kring, from a story by TEEN WOLF creators Joseph Loeb III and Matthew Weisman. Stuck with hopeless roles are Kim Darby (sympathetic science instructor), John Astin (insidious Dean Dunn), Paul Sand (absurd boxing coach) and James Hampton (hairy Uncle Howard). Wenches Beth Ann Miller and Rachel Sharp provide the shapeliness the rest of the production direly needs. (Paramount)

TEKWAR (1993). William Shatner produced-directed this adaptation of his popular sci-fi novel set in a "virtual reality" future where mind stimulants have replayed drugs. There are four episodes in all. Greg Evigan, Eugene Clark, Torri Higginson. (MCA)

TELEFON (1977). Much talent is wasted on a feeble premise: A phone call to programmed spies in the U.S. activates them with a post- hypnotic phrase to carry out sabotage. It's dirty Commie rats up to world-conquering tricks . . . but special agent Charles Bronson is calling the long-distance operator for information, to track the baddies from Moscow. Why Don Siegel wanted to direct this, or why Sterling Silliphant and Peter Hyams got involved in the script . . . gee, was it money? Lee Remick, Donald Pleasence, Tyne Daly, Alan Badel, Patrick Magee, Sheree North, John Mitchum. (MGM/UA)

TELEGIAN, THE. See **SECRET OF THE TELEGIAN, THE.**

TELEPHONE BOOK, THE (1971). See editions 1-3.

TELEVISION SPY (1939). See editions 1-3.

TELL-TALE HEART, THE (1960). Intensely acted, well-photographed British horror film (also known as PANIC) based loosely on Edgar Allan Poe's story. Laurence Payne portrays Poe, who dreams he's Edgar Marsh, a librarian in a French town where he falls in love with flowershop worker Adrienne Corri, a femme fatale who would rather dally with Edgar's best friend (Dermot Walsh). The librarian, crazed with jealousy, murders his friend and places his body under the floorboards in the library. Soon, the exaggerated beating of a heart drives him to madness. There's a very macabre sequence in which Payne cuts out the heart of his victim, holding the still-pumping organ in his bloody hands. A memorable sleeper directed by Ernest Morris and written by Brian Clemens and Elden Howard. Watch for subtle literary clues hinting at the surprise ending. (Loonic; Sinister/C; S/Weird; Filmfax)

TEMPTER, THE (1974). Watch Italian director Alberto de Martino's rip-off of THE EXORCIST (made as THE ANTICHRIST) and you won't eat for a week after seeing: possessed woman gulping down severed head of toad; possessed woman licking up spilt blood; possessed woman regurgitating wine; possesed woman vomiting scrambled eggs; possessed woman spitting up green slime; possessed woman spewing into the face of a relative. All this gooiness has to do with reincarnation of a witch burnt at the stake hundreds of years ago. Demonic winds, flying furniture, far-flung objects. What the Devil are Mel Ferrer, Arthur Kennedy and George Coulouris doing in this Anti-Christ pasta? (Embassy)

TENANT, THE (1976). This adaptation of Roland Topol's novel is either a study in paranoia or an old-fashioned ghost story, and it is to the credit of director Roman Polanski that his script (co-written with Gerard Brach) works either way. Polanski is effective as a repressed Pole who rents a Paris flat and is haunted by the spirit of a woman who committed suicide by leaping from a window into the courtyard below. He also believes that the building's owner (Melvyn Douglas as a curmudgeon) and other tenants are conspiring to drive him crazy. The takeover of his personality includes Polanski going drag—a grotesque image that enhances the film's ambiguities. The build-up is slow albeit fascinating and Polanski captures nuances of character brilliantly. A mosaic of oddball characters is played by Isabelle Adjani, Jo Van Fleet, Lila Kedrova, Claude Dauphin and Shelley Winters. (Paramount)

TENDER DRACULA OR CONFESSIONS OF A BLOOD DRINKER (1974). Peter Cushing portrays a movie actor playing a vampire who plays a count who plays . . . French production directed by Pierre Grunstein. Alida Valli, Bernard Menez. (Blood Times)

TENDER FLESH. See **WELCOME TO ARROW BEACH.**

TENDERNESS OF THE WOLVES (1973). Award-winning German film produced by Rainer Werner Fassbinder and directed by Ulli Lommel, who tells Kurt Raab's story of a mass murderer in avant garde, symbolic fashion. The public never took to Ulli's intellectual filmmaking, so he gave up in disgust and made BOOGEY MAN and BRAINWAVES. Jeff Roden, Margit Carstensen, Kurt Raab, Brigitte Mira.

TENEBRAE. See **UNSANE.**

TEN LITTLE INDIANS (1965). Inferior remake of AND THEN THERE WERE NONE, the classic Agatha Christie suspense mystery set on a lonely island where a handful of stranded guests are stalked by a killer. Writers Harry Alan Towners and Peter Yeldham have changed the setting to a snowbound chateau and updated the characters. It doesn't work, making one thirst for the 1945 Rene Clair original (made as AND THEN THERE WERE NONE). Hugh O'Brian, Shirley Eaton, Wilfrid Hyde-White, Fabian, Leo Genn, Daliah Lavi. Directed by George Pollock. Please, no Pollock jokes.

TEN LITTLE INDIANS (1976). Third film version of Agatha Christie's mystery play, and the least satisfying. Producer-screenwriter Harry Alan Towers shifts the setting to Iran, of all places, into a posh hotel. Orson Welles' voice supports a big cast (Elke Sommer, Oliver Reed, Gert Frobe, Herbert Lom, Charles Aznavour, Richard Attenborough). Directedby Peter Collinson. (Charter)

TEN LITTLE INDIANS (1989). The fourth film version of Agatha Christie's stage mystery in which a band of strangers is brought to a mansion isolated on an island and murdered one by one by the mysterious Mr. Owens. This is a perversion of that idea in which the setting is now the wilds of Africa, where the strangers have been invited on a safari by Mr. Owens. Isolated at their encampment, the travelers are knocked off in the usual way, but without the Christie's panache. Donald Pleasence is the judge, Frank Stallone is an ineffectual guide, Sarah MaurThorp is the hapless heroine, Herber Lom is the daffy general, Brenda Vaccaro is a lesbian actress, Warren Berlinger is Blore, Yehuda Efronti is the shady doctor, Paul L. Smith is the suspicious Mr. Rodgers, Moira Lister is Mrs. Rodgers and Neil McCarthy is Anthony Marsden. The abominable script was massacred by Jackson Hunsicker and Gerry O'Hara, which in turn massacred director Alan Birkinshaw. (Cannon)

TENNIS COURT (1984). British Hammer TV production, made for "The Fox Mystery Theater," with supernatural twists: Hannah Gordon's ex-lover from World War II, a victim of burns and unrequited love and now confined to a recuperation center, projects his anger onto the family's old tennis court, where unpleasant events occur to Hannah's son and herself. She hires a parapsychologist to investigate. Peter Graves is on hand as a priest/former lover. The twist ending is nicely done. Directed by Cyril Frankel.

TENTACLES (1977). Italian film is a steal of JAWS, jazzed up with Henry Fonda, John Huston, Shelley Winters and Claude Akins. A killer octopus, an unfrightening creature, terrorizes a seaside town. Slow moving, dim-witted and exasperating! Directed by Oliver Hellman, better known as Olvido Assonitis. Cesare Danova, Bo Hopkins. (Vestron; Orion)

TENTH VICTIM, THE (1965). In the 21st century, war has been outlawed and replaced by "The Big Hunt," a means of venting aggression wherein citizens are "licensed to kill," alternating as hunters and victims. Anyone surviving ten hunts is guaranteed financial rewards for life. The game idea sprang from the fertile imagination of Robert Sheckley, and under Elio Petri's direction is savagely satirical and suspenseful, with Ursula Andress as a "hunter" with a loaded bra (we kid you not) and Marcello Mastroianni as her prey. The adaptation is frequently erratic but the chase and ingenious weapons are engrossing. Not to mention Ursula's bod. Elsa Martinelli is also a shapely huntress. (Embassy)

TEN TO MIDNIGHT (1983). Slasher film with hardened cop Charles Bronson, a Dirty Harry of the '80s, distressed when the legal system thwarts him from taking a sex-crazed killer off the streets. He plants incriminating evidence to put the killer away, but his conscience won't allow him to go through with it. The most interesting characters are Andrew Stevens as Bronson's inexperienced partner and Lisa Eilbacher as Bronson's daughter, chief target of the slasher. The killer is chillingly played by Gene Dare (though his motives are obscure); he murders while totally nude. Polished direction by J. Lee Thompson and a honed script by William Roberts make this a standout. Geoffrey Lewis, Wilford Brimley. (Video/Laser: MGM/UA)

TERMINAL CHOICE (1982). Riveting medical psychothriller, holding you spellbound as its diabolical murder plot unfolds. Joe Spano's patients are dying at Dodson Medical Clinic in Toronto because someone is programming life-and-death hospital equipment to kill patients. Investigators Diane Venora and Don Francks move in; suspicious-looking doctors and medical red herrings crop up in Neal Bell's script. Climactic scenes of Spano trapped in a hospital bed are exciting. Strange blending of mystery, computerized sci-fi and whodunit. David McCallum portrays the clinic's owner. Directed by Sheldon Larry. Aka DEATH BED, DEATH LIST, CRITICAL LIST and TRAUMA. (Vestron)

TERMINAL ENTRY (1986). Inspired by WARGAMES, this forgettable Paul Smith production has minimal fantasy overtones as hackers accidentally tap into a computer used by Arab terrorists led by Kabir Bedi and infiltrating America in death squads. Government fighters Edward Albert, Yaphet Kotto and Smith blaze away in uninspired action sequences. John Kincade directed. Heidi Helmer, Patrick Labyorteaux. (Celebrity)

TERMINAL ISLAND (1973). Socio-political sci-fi set in the not-too-distant future, when man has created San Bruno Maximum Security Detention Center, 40 miles off the California coast where the worst criminals fend for themselves. This lacks the production values of better films with a similar theme (such as ESCAPE FROM NEW YORK) as the Jim Barnett-Charles S. Swartz-Stephane Rothmann script focuses on criminals who fight among themselves until major warfare breaks out. Director Rothmann may have intended this as a metaphor for the world at large, but its vapid qualities negate its social criticisms and reduce it to low-budget action, without inspiration. Tom Selleck appears as a doctor roving the island. Phyllis Davis, Don Marshall, Ena Hartman, Randy Boone, Marta Kristein, Barbara Leigh, Geoffrey Deuel. (Continental; VCI)

TERMINAL MAN, THE (1974). The first half of this version of Michael Crichton's best-seller is a compelling study in modern technology and surgical techniques. Neurosurgeons implant a miniaturized computer in the brain of George Segal, who's suffering from fits of rage (described as temporal lobe epilepsy) following an accident. But the film's second half, following Segal after he escapes the hospital staff, becomes a pointless series of homicides, ending in a graveyard sequence with a crucifixion. The pace is too lethargic for material that should be fast-moving, and the ambiguities of producer-director Mike Hodges' script become transparent as the terminal man terminates. Joan Hackett is fine as a doctor on the operating staff—the flaws are foggy characterizations and inappropriate directorial techniques. Jill Clayburgh, Ian Wolfe, Matt Clark. (Warner Bros.)

TERMINATOR, THE (1984). One of the best action movies of the '80s, blending fantasy with horror and suspense to create an incredibly satisfying viewing experience. Arnold Schwarzenegger portrays a humanoid robot from 2029 A.D., a time when man has been conquered by robot machines. Schwarzie travels back to present day to assassinate a young woman; one day she will give birth to a child who will overthrow the robot society. The machine-killer begins a cold-blooded reign of terror to find the woman, killing anyone in his way. The pacing is relentless as the intended victim (Linda Hamilton) flees with Michael Biehn's help. James Cameron directs with a real sense for pace, and the script by Cameron and producer Gale Anne Hurd not only has an abundance of action but even works in a relevant love story. Stan Winston's effects are wonderfully graphic; the whole thing is one big success. Schwarzenegger's simple line, "I'll be back," is a classic. Paul Winfield, Lance Henriksen, Rick Rossovich, Dick Miller, Earl Boen. (HBO; Hemdale) (Laser: HBO; Hemdale; Image)

TERMINATOR 2: JUDGMENT DAY (1991). A blockbuster classic of high-tech bravura, a worthy follow-up to the 1984 classic and a trendsetting epic in terms of its special-effects razzle dazzle. Arnold Schwarzenegger is back as the cyborg-man from the future, only this time programmed not to kill, and to rescue important individuals from being terminated by his adversary, an advanced form of cyborg-man (Robert Patrick) whose liquid-metal components enable him to change shape and to form

HE'S BACK! SCHWARZENEGGER IN 'TERMINATOR 2'

parts of his body into lethal weapons. The computerized metamorphosis effects are stunning as T-1000 enters the present timestream to assassinate Linda Hamilton (back as Sarah Connor, the role she created in TERMINATOR) and her son John Connor (Edward Furlong). This is one terrific action film, its formula already established by producer-director James Cameron, who co-wrote with William Wisher. Medals for the creators of the metal man, Stan Winston and Dennis Muren. Earl Boen, Joe Morton, S. Epatha Merkerson, Castulo Guerra. (Video/Laser: Live)

TERMINATOR 2: SPECIAL EDITION (1991). Pioneer laserdisc with 15 minutes of new material.

TERMINUS (1987). Obscure futuristic thriller in which Karen Allen pilots the Ferro-glider (a kind of superbus) across a hostile desert with Jurgen Prochnow and Johnny Hallyday. (Hemdale)

TERRIBLE PEOPLE, THE (1960). See editions 1-3.

TERRIBLE SECRET OF DR. HICHCOCK, THE. See **HORRIBLE DR. HICHCOCK, THE.**

TERRIFIED (1963). Dreary, unbelievably bad Crown-International programmer depicting a crazed killer in a black mask who runs around a deserted mining town murdering teenagers. Passe even when it was produced. Directed by Lew Landers. Rod Lauren, Steve Drexel, Tracy Olsen, Denver Pyle, Barbara Luddy, Harry Lauter.

TERRIFYING TALES. Anthology of horror yarns (Front Row Entertainment).

TERROR, THE (1938). See editions 1-3.

TERROR, THE (1963). History of this Roger Corman tricky quickie is more fascinating than the film: After finishing THE RAVEN, Corman realized Boris Karloff owed him two days work, so he fashioned a script and filmed Karloff's scenes back to back. Later, Francis Ford Coppola, Monte Hellman, Jack Hill and Dennis Jacob added new scenes. No wonder the Jack Hill-Leo Gordon script seems disjointed. Napoleonic officer Jack Nicholson (who directed some scenes) pursues ghostly Sandra Knight into a seacliff mansion owned by Karloff. Supporting players: Jonathan Haze, Dick Miller. Some footage of Karloff was also used in TARGETS. (World Video; Goodtimes; Genesis; Prism; S/Weird; Filmfax)

TERROR. Video version of **SHOCK CHAMBER** (North American).

TERROR (1973). See **DR. FRANKENSTEIN'S CASTLE OF FREAKS.**

TERROR (1978). Offtrail British supernatural thriller ingeniously starts off with a film within a film, a fictional rendering of film maker John Nolan's family, once cursed by a witch spirit armed with a mighty sword. Before long that evil spirit is causing objects to leap about, snakes to appear, demonic winds to blow, and gore murders of the grisliest kind to occur at Buttercup Lodge. David McGillivray's script is messed up but director Norman J. Warren brings style to the bloody events. Carolyn Courage, James Aubrey, Sarah Keller, Tricia Walsh, Michael Craze. (VCI)

TERROR ABOARD (1933). See editions 1-3.

TERROR AT LONDON BRIDGE. Video version of **BRIDGE ACROSS TIME** (Charles Fries).

TERROR AT RED WOLF INN (1972). Young woman is lured to a seaside inn for an all-expenses-paid holiday, only to discover the elderly couple running the place is into cannibalism, as is their retarded son. Allen J. Actor's script has tongue-in-cheek subtleties and keeps horror visuals limited to PG. Only the nihilistic ending will leave one feeling let down. Otherwise, a good scare job, a tame TEXAS CHAINSAW MASSACRE. Director Bud Townsend does an okay job, but don't make reservations at the Red Wolf. The food tastes strange there. Also called THE FOLKS AT THE RED WOLF INN and TERROR HOUSE. Linda Gillin, Arthur Space, Mary Jackson. (Academy; from Cougar as **TERROR ON THE MENU**)

TERROR AT TENKILLER (1986). Girls vacationing at a mountain cabin on Lake Tenkiller encounter death at the hands of a psychokiller. Produced-directed by Ken Meyer, script by Claudia Meyer. Mike Wiles, Stacy Logan, Dean Lewis, Michelle Merchant (United)

TERROR AT THE OPERA (1987). Writer-producer-director Dario Argento is back in action as Europe's premiere horror film maker, this time setting his macabre machinations in an opera house where a singer becomes the target for a diabolical serial killer. It's a bloody good show Argento offers. Cristina Marsillach, Ian Charleson, Daria Nicolodi. Aka OPERA. (From South Gate in rated and unrated versions) (Laser: Japanese)

TERROR BENEATH THE SEA (1966). What's a Japanese monster movie without Godzilla or Ghidrah? Not much, if this is any indication. A mad doctor, the ruler of an underwater city, turns humans into water- breathing "cyborgs." A plot is afoot to Take Over the World but two reporters and a physicist turn the tide in the underwater lab. U.S. version (also known as WATER CYBORGS) was shot simultaneously with the Japanese version and stars many English-speaking cast members. Its director is Hajime Sato, who goes by the name of Terence Ford. Star Shinichi Chiba is now known as Sonny Chiba, martial arts specialist. Hideo Murota, Peggy Neal. (Monterey; Sinister/C; Discount)

TERROR CASTLE. See **HORROR CASTLE.**

TERROR CIRCUS (1973). The humiliation of women reaches an alltime exploitation low in this first-feature effort from director Alan Rudolph, who went on to direct major Hollywood features. including the cattle-mutilation thriller ENDANGERED SPECIES. This has no redeeming values in depicting depraved Andrew Prine, a desert hermit with a mother fixation who kidnaps stranded women and ties them up in his barn. He treats Manuella Thiess, Sherry Alberoni and Sheila Bradley like animals in a circus zoo, making them perform despicable acts. Out in the toolshed, meanwhile, there's a mutated monster (caused by Nevada nuclear tests) that likes to break out and kill. (Regal; from Showcase Productions Inc. as **BARN OF THE NAKED DEAD**)

TERROR CREATURES FROM THE GRAVE (1965). Lackluster Italian chiller has the presence of Barbara Steele but not the presence of mind to tell a compelling story, or provide genuine scares. Instead, you're handed nonsense about a terrible plague and how victims are summoned from the dead to avenge an occultist. The photography is okay but gee, what lousy direction by co-producer Ralph Zucker (aka Massimo Pupillo). Sure cure for insomnia. Walter Brandi, Marilyn Mitchell, Alfredo Rizzi. Also called THE TOMBS OF HORROR, FIVE GRAVES FOR A MEDIUM and COFFIN OF TERROR. (Sinister/C; S/Weird; Filmfax)

TERROR EYES. See **NIGHT SCHOOL.**

TERROR EYES (1987). Supernatural comedy in which the Devil sends a sycophant to help an advertising agent write a horror screenplay. Vivian Schilling stars and wrote the screenplay (with the Devil's help?). Lance August, Daniel Roebuck, Vivian Schilling, Dan Bell. Directed by Eric Parkinson. (Action International)

TERROR FACTOR. See **SCARED TO DEATH (1946).**

TERROR FROM THE SUN. See **HIDEOUS SUN DEMON, THE.**

TERROR FROM THE YEAR 5000 (1958). Experimentation with a time machine brings objects from the future—including a malformed woman who needs males to procreate the human race in 5000 A.D. The line forms to the right, gents. She gets the guys she needs through hypnosis and other subterfuges. Real claptrack, a definite failure for writer-producer-director Robert Gurney Jr. Aka CAGE OF DOOM. Joyce Holden, Ward Costello, Beatrice Furdeaux, John Stratton.

TERROR FROM UNDER THE HOUSE. See **REVENGE (1971).**

TERROR FROM WITHIN (1974). Pamela Franklin undergoes psychic dreams, realizing a copse of elm trees, a photo hidden in a painting and a mysterious Rolls-Royce are clues to a mystery. A cheaply produced British TV-movie, a plodding thing without punch. Brian Clemens (creator of THE AVENGERS) gave his idea to telewriter Dennis Spooner. Franklin has little to do but look frightened and toss in her sleep; the real star is Ian Bannen as a strange man always carving on wood. Very ho-hum bum. Directed by James Ormerod.

TERRORGRAM (1990). Horror trilogy about revenge, with tales ranging from the absurd to the serious, and getting better each time. The mastermind here is producer-director Stephen M. Kienzle. The morality yarns are bridged with narration by "The Voice of Retribution" (James Earl Jones), written as a poor man's Rod Serling imitation, and by the appearance in each story of a messenger from hell wearing a lightning bolt on his cap. "Heroine Overdose," cranked out by Kienzle and Donna M. Matson, is the farcical tale of a movie director (played as a bastard by Jerry Anderson) named Alan Smithee (the alias used by real unhappy directors). Smithee, maker of "Cycle Maniacs" and "Driller," mistreats the women in his life (especially the actresses) and finds himself detoured onto Elm Street. It's played for laughs and the effect is less than the next two yarns. "Pandora" (written by Kienzle) depicts TV anchorwoman Angela Pandoras (Linda Carol Toner) when she strikes down a boy with her car and flees. She gets hers through a Pandora's Box substitute, and it's rather effective. The best of the tales is "Veteran's Day," focusing on dirty rat Eric Keller (J. T. Wallace) and how a Vietnam casualty he once offended places Keller on the battlefield to learn the true meaning of war. (Monarch)

TERROR HOSPITAL. Video version of **BEYOND THE LIVING** (Marathon).

TERROR HOUSE (1943). Also known as THE NIGHT HAS EYES, this is a superior British gothic thriller of the damsel-in-distress school, in which lovely schoolteacher Mary Clare and a companion journey to the Yorkshire moors (fraught with perilous quicksand) where a friend disappeared a year earlier. During a storm they meet sinister hermit James Mason, who believes he turns into a frenzied killer under the full moon. There's an odd psychological edge (taken from an Alan Kennington novel) and heavy moor ambience thanks to director Leslie Arliss. After red herrings, there are solid graphic shocks and a satisfying and stark ending. Wilfrid Lawson, Joyce Howard, Tucker McGuire.

TERROR HOUSE. See **TERROR AT RED WOLF INN.**

TERROR IN SPACE. See **DEMON PLANET.**

TERROR IN THE AISLES (1984). Compilation of shock scenes from horror, sci-fi and crime movies. Some are from classy or classic movies while others were lifted from schlock. In short, a hodgepodge that has moments of intensity as we relive Hitchcock's PSYCHO and STRANGERS ON A TRAIN. Other films: Carpenter's THE THING, SUSPIRIA, WHEN A STRANGER CALLS, NIGHTHAWKS, THE EXORCIST, ROSEMARY'S BABY and DRESSED TO KILL. The cassette version has more gore than the TV version. Compiled by Andrew Kuehn and Stephen Netburn. (MCA)

TERROR IN THE CRYPT (1963). Christopher Lee heads the cast of this Spanish-Italian supernatural yarn that approaches its subject leisurely, in a sincere effort to build suspense and atmosphere, and to pay homage to J. Sheridan Le Fanu's CARMILLA. Lee, a nobleman who fears his daughter is possessed by a witch, invites occult experts to his castle to observe her behavior. Several murders occur before the demon is exorcised. Directed by Thomas Miller. Jose Campos, Vera Valmont. Aka CRYPT OF HORROR, THE KARNSTEIN CURSE, THE CRYPT OF THE VAMPIRE, THE VAMPIRE'S CRYPT, KARNSTEIN, THE CRYPT AND THE NIGHTMARE, CARMILLA and THE CURSE OF THE KARNSTEINS. Stop it, already. (Baker; S/Weird)

TERROR IN THE FOREST. See **FOREST, THE.**

TERROR IN THE HAUNTED HOUSE (1958). Newlyweds Cathy O'Donnell and Gerald Mohr reside in a lonely mansion in a mood of happiness, but soon the bride is haunted by dreams and memories of a murder she witnessed as a child—or is she hallucinating? Or is hubby Mohr up to something diabolical? The answers await your curiosity—should you have any after reading this description. Directed by Harold Daniels. John Qualen, Barry Bernard, William Ching. Also known as MY WORLD DIES SCREAMING. (Rhino)

TERROR IN THE JUNGLE (1968). Search party seeks a youth lost in the Amazon after a plane crash; the boy escapes cannibals and other unpleasantries of the steaming jungle with his toy tiger, which turns into the real thing to protect him. Mexican-U.S. co-production directed by that masterly trio: Tom De'Simone, Andy Janzack and Alex Graton. Henry Clayton Jr., Robert Burns, Fawn Silver. (Academy)

TERROR IN THE MIDNIGHT SUN. See **INVASION OF THE ANIMAL PEOPLE** (Reigning cats and dogs?).

TERROR IN THE SWAMP (1985). Poachers' Cave, now there's a place to steer clear of, I'm warnin' ya. Seems folks 'round Houma, Louisiana, are turnin' up plumb dead. Course, the reason's mighty clear, them local scientists tamperin' with the nutria water rodent 'n all, and danged if they didn't done created a giant mootation rat. Reckon it twern't gonna scare ya too much cause it's just oneathem extras in a hairy suit. Dad rat it. Soon's that picture wrapped, folks ran that Joe Catalanotto and his'n crew 'n scribblers Terry Hebb 'n Martin Folse smack outta town and told 'em and them high-falutin' actors, Billy Holliday, Chuck Long and Michael Tedesco, quit givin' us swamp folks a bad name or next time we'll sic them gators 'n cot'n moccasins on you city slickers, hot damn gotohell. Did ya'all know it was to be called NUTRIAMAN: THE COPASAW CREATURE? Gertrude, hand me my shotgun! (New World) (Laser: New World; Image)

TERROR IN THE WAX MUSEUM (1973). Parade of character actors turns this shallow tallow HOUSE OF WAX pastiche into a passable film. If nothing else holds your interest, try identifying familiar faces. A murderer with waxy build-up is adding new trophies to his displays. George Fenady directed. Broderick Crawford, Ray Milland, Elsa Lanchester, John Carradine, Louis Hayward, Maurice Evans, Patric Knowles, Lisa Lu. (Lightning; Vestron)

TERROR IN THE WOODS. See **FOREST, THE.**

TERROR IN TOYLAND (1980). Is nothing sacred? This, the first of the killer Santa Claus movies that set the stage for the SILENT NIGHT, DEADLY NIGHT series, is the ultimate in crass commercialism and execrable exploitation. The world's first killing Kris Kringle is "an emotional cripple"—a sexually repressed worker at the Jolly Dream Toy Co. He's haunted by 1947 memories of his mother being fondled by Santa at the Christmas tree. Keeping records on which children are naughty or nice, he flips out and takes his bag of goodies into the world. To kiddies he delivers gifts—to adults, death. The only memorable sequence has Santa pursued down an alley by angry citizens carrying torches—homage to FRANKENSTEIN. But there's no depth to the killer's characterization and writer-director Lewis Jackson never pulls it all together. And the final scene is outrageously out of place in a pseudostudy of a murderer. Brandon Maggart, Jeffrey DeMunn, Dianne Hull, Andy Fenwick. Aka YOU BETTER WATCH OUT. (Academy; from Saturn as **CHRISTMAS EVIL)**

TERROR IS A MAN (1959). The first in the Filipino-produced "Blood Island" series, in which impassioned mad doctor Francis Lederer conducts experiments in his lab that turn a man into a leopard (tiger?) creature. To Lederer's island comes shipwreck survivor Richard Derr, an engineer who falls for the doc's attractive wife, curvaceous Greta Thyssen, whose sexuality creates a tension. Reminiscent of THE CREATURE WALKS AMONG US in its sympathetic portrayal of the misunderstood beast and the way the shoreline scenes are photographed. Despite a poor monster design, this film is not without interest when human conflict is aroused. Co-directed by Gerry de Leon and Eddie Romero. Oscar Keesee, Lilia Duban. (Filmfax; Sinister/C; S/Weird; on video as **BLOOD CREATURE**)

TERRORNAUTS, THE (1967). British sci-fi is terror-not when an astronomer and his lab are teleported to another planet where events, none of them making sense, occur with monotonous repetition. Indifferently directed by Montgomery Tully. Simon Oates, Zena Marshall, Patricia Hayes. Amicus production adapted by John Brunner from a Murray Leinster novel, THE WAILING ASTROIDS. (Charter; New Line)

TERROR OF DR. CHANEY, THE. See **MANSION OF THE DOOMED.**

TERROR OF DR. FRANKENSTEIN. See **VICTOR FRANKENSTEIN.** (To Victor belongs the spoiled)

TERROR OF DR. HICHCOCK. More complete video version of **HORRIBLE DR. HICHCOCK, THE** (Sinister/C; Duravision; Filmfax).

TERROR OF DR. MABUSE, THE. See **TESTAMENT OF DR. MABUSE, THE.**

TERROR OF FRANKENSTEIN (1976). Unusually faithful adaptation of Mary Shelley's FRANKENSTEIN novel, similar in tone to THE TRUE STORY OF FRANKENSTEIN, and not exploitation claptrap. This does not portray the Monster in a hideous fashion, and even permits him to speak in a heavy voice similar to Richard Burton's. The Irish-Swedish production is boosted by good location photography and a cast that brings depth to the characters. Per Oscarsson portrays the Monster and Leon Vitali is the doctor. The strong supporting players: Nicholas Clay, Stacey Dorning, Jan Ohlsson. Produced-directed by Calvin Floyd, who collaborated on the script with wife Yvonne. Aka VICTOR FRANKENSTEIN. (VC)

TERROR OF GODZILLA, THE. See **TERROR OF MECHAGODZILLA.** (a mecha-nation, Japan!)

TERROR OF MECHAGODZILLA (1975). Giant robot monster attacks Earth, realizing the green planet isn't going to be a pushover when fire-snorting Godzilla shows up, slamming his tail in anger. Also involved in this Japanese mish mash (along with the kitchen sink) are mechanized cyborgs, Ghidrah, Ebirah, Rodan and a bird monster, Chitanoceras. Godzilla's creator, Inoshiro Honda, directed. This sequel to GODZILLA VS. THE COSMIC MONSTER was 15th in the series. Aka THE ESCAPE OF MEGAGODZILLA and MONSTERS FROM THE UNKNOWN PLANET. Katsuhiko Sasaki, Tomoke Ai. (Paramount) (Laser: Japanese)

TERROR OF SHEBA (1974). Superior psychological British thriller: Lana Turner is a vindictive mother subjecting her bastard son to persecution to get even for the way men in her life mistreated her. The boy turns crazy and drowns the family cats in bowls of milk, burying their bodies in a minigraveyard concealed in a labyrinth. As an adult (Ralph Bates), he still bears the brunt of mother's evil when she kills his child and arranges for his wife to find him in the arms of another woman. But, Bates has his revenge. Stark, taut film with first-rate performances by Turner (looking well-preserved), Bates, Trevor Howard as the secret father, Olga Georges-Picot as the seductress and Suzan Farmer as the wronged wife. Directed by Don Chaffey. Aka PERSECUTION. (From Interglobal as **GRAVEYARD, THE**)

TERROR OF THE DOLL. Video of the Karen Black episode from **TALES OF TERROR** (MPI).

TERROR OF THE HATCHET MEN. See **TERROR OF THE TONGS, THE.**

TERROR OF THE LIVING DEAD (1972). Spanish fright flick directed by Jose Luis Merino.

TERROR OF THE MAD DOCTOR. Video version of **TESTAMENT OF DR. MABUSE, THE** (S/Weird).

TERROR OF THE MUMMY. See **MUMMY, THE (1959).**

TERROR OF THE SHE WOLF. Video version of **LEGEND OF THE WOLF WOMAN** (Mogul).

TERROR OF THE SNAKE WOMAN, THE. See **SNAKE WOMAN, THE.**

TERROR OF THE TONGS (1961). Christopher Lee portrays the insidious Chun King, a ruthless tong leader surrounded by torture devices, diabolical weapons, insidious poisons, treacherous doctors, slave girls, opium dens and other pleasures of life. Directed by Anthony Bushell; written by Jimmy Sangster. Also called TERROR OF THE HATCHET MEN. Geoffrey Toone, Yvonne Monlaur, Burt Kwouk, Milton Reid.

TERROR OF THE VAMPIRES, THE. See **SEX AND THE VAMPIRE.**

TERROR ON ALCATRAZ (1987). Aldo Ray is terrible as an ex-convict who burns a cigarette into his girl's chest before he turns killer and razors a retired guard's throat. Then he heads for Alcatraz, where the key to a fortune in stolen money is waiting in Cell #146—but to get it he must cut through a crowd of young people having a party on the island. Ray (playing Frank Morris, a real-life convict who escaped from the island in '62) meat-cleavers a man in the forehead, drowns a female guard in a vat and generally behaves in an anti-social fashion. This instant video non-classic has crummy lighting, bad acting and unbelievable behavior. And you see "The Island of Pelicans" in San Francisco Bay in all its touristic decay. Blame the dumb writing on Donald Lewis and the cruddy direction on Marvin G. Lipschultz. Veronicia Porchall, Scott Ryder. (Trans World)

TERROR ON TAPE (1983). Compilation of grisly scenes from horror/sci-fi exploitation films—we're talking Gross City, men. Clips are frameworked around videostore owner Cameron Mitchell (resembling a ghoul) as he greets customers (a nerd, a macho construction worker, a sexpot in a revealing outfit) and pushes the sickening merchandise. Scenes are from VAMPIRE HOOKERS, RETURN OF THE ALIEN'S DEADLY SPAWN, BLOODTIDE, CATHY'S CURSE, FROZEN SCREAM, ALIEN PREY, COLOR ME BLOOD RED and 2000 MANIACS. You'll see baby alien monsters eat a human head, a hatchet sink into a brain, hairy hands strangle a father in a confessional booth, a needle plunge into an eye, a human arm severed, a boulder dropped on a woman's chest, impaling by pitchfork, a scalping, ad nauseum. For strong stomachs only, and we mean strong! The wraparound was directed by Robert A. Worms III and features Michelle Bauer as the hot tamale let's-romp chick. (Continental)

TERROR ON THE MENU. Video version of **TERROR AT RED WOLF INN, THE** (Cougar).

TERROR ON TOUR (1980). Don Edmonds, noted for his sadistic films about Nazi commandant Ilsa, helmed this minor-league psychoslasher flick in which the stabber runs around murdering prostitutes while dressed as a member of a hard-rock group, The Clowns. It's up to the real Clowns to make fools of themselves while tracking the killer. Mainly an excuse for an abundance of feebly produced rock footage as the amateurish cast misses every beat of Del Lekus' script. Rick Styles, Chip Greeman, Rich Pemberton, Lisa Rodriguez. (Media)

TERROR OUT OF THE SKY (1979). Sequel to THE SAVAGE BEES, in which bumbling bumble bee experts Efrem Zimbalist Jr. and Dan Haggerty of the National Bee Center are attacked by stingers that go buzz in the night. Bees-ily directed by Lee H. Katzin. Ike Eisenmann, Steve Franken. (USA; Alan Landsburg)

TERROR STRIKES. See **WAR OF THE COLOSSAL BEAST.**

TERROR TRAIN (1980). Unsavory college kids, holding a masquerade party on a speeding train, are knocked off one by one by a knife-wielding maniac. Muddled characters created by scriptman Y. T. Drake make it difficult to swallow the preposterous action. The only exciting moments come when Jamie Lee Curtis, scream queen from HALLOWEEN, is pursued by the killer through the train. Ben Johnson as the sympathetic conductor and magician David Copperfield are derailed by one lousy script, as is director Roger Spottiswoode. (Key) (Laser: CBS/Fox)

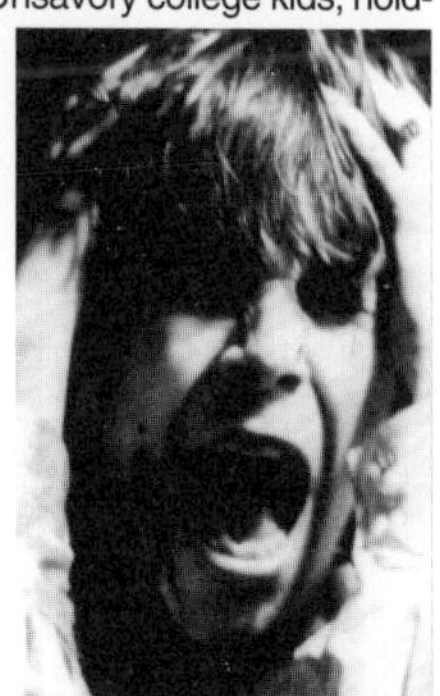

JAMIE LEE CURTIS

TERRORVISION (1986). Failed comedy-satire from producer Charles Band and writer-director Ted Nicolaou. It's a lowbrow insult when a garbage-collecting alien on Pluton accidentally jettisons a monster into space, which comes to Earth on a lightning bolt and enters a home through its TV screens. The monster, designed by John Buechler, is a gross thing with big teeth and a long tongue and it hogs the camera too long. Folks in the invaded home are a swinging couple (Mary Woronov, Gerrit Graham), a militant grandfather (Bert Remsen) and an obnoxious kid (Chad Allen). An Elvira clone, Medusa, is wasted. Made in Italy. (Lightning)

TERRORVISION (1985). TV-anthology of horror short stories, lifted from a syndicated series that never got off the ground. Producers lacked TerrorVision.

TERROR WITHIN, THE (1989). Another crank-out job from Roger Corman's copycat factory—this time the Chestburster from ALIEN and the suspenseful corridor sequences from ALIENS are imitated but never surpassed. The setting is a subterranean research station in the Mojave Desert after most of mankind has been wiped out by a virus. Ugly mutations rove the desert, one of them penetrating the security of the laboratory run by George Kennedy, Andrew Stevens (armed with a crossbow, and accompanied by his real-life dog Butch), Terri Treas and Starr Andreeff. The "Gargoyle" monster (designed by Dean Jones) is a disappointing example of a man in a rubber suit. Granted, there are harrowing chase sequences at the climax, but the script by Thomas M. Cleaver remains derivative and Thierry Notz's direction is journeyman but hardly inspired. John Lafayette, Tommy Hinchley. (MGM/UA)

TERROR WITHIN II, THE (1990). Andrew Stevens, star of the first TERROR WITHIN, reprises his crossbow-packing hero and steps in as writer-director, performing as well as, if not better than, his predecessors. It's pretty much the same old stuff when those "grotesque genetic mutations" penetrate the underground research lab of R. Lee Ermery to carry out the usual killings. This also has the mutations raping women, an ugly birth sequence and the suspenseful battles in the corridors. There isn't anything you haven't seen before in this post-Armageddon world, but undemanding fans will find it an adequate time killer. Stella Stevens (Andrew's mom) portrays a lab asistant. Burton "Bubba" Gilliam, Clare Hoak, Chick Vennera. (Vestron)

TESTAMENT (1983). Powerful anti-war film, depicting in low-key fashion the after-effects of nuclear holocaust. Hamelin is a small California community beyond the major blast area. However, gamma rays, radiation and fallout take their toll. Focus is on a mother and four children (father William Devane is away at the time) as she clutches for hope while despair grows around her. No devastation, no blood and only a few corpses wrapped in sheets—yet this is a gut-wrenching picture. Based on a short-short story by Carol Amen (who says the idea came to her in a vision), scripted by John Sacre Young, and produced by Jonathan Bernstein and Lynne Littman (she also directed) for PBS. Jane Alexander is outstanding as the mother fighting to hold family together. William Devane is strong in the brief father role. Mako, Leon Ames and Lurene Tuttle appear in cameos. Lukas Haas, Clete Roberts. (Video/Laser: Paramount)

TESTAMENT OF DR. CORDELIER, THE (1959). Writer-producer-director Jean Renoir's version of Stevenson's "The Strange Case of Dr. Jekyll and Mr. Hyde," with Jean-Louis Barrault in the dual role of Dr. Cordelier and the evil Opale. Micheline Gary, Teddy Bilis. Aka EXPERIMENT IN EVIL and THE DOCTOR'S HORRIBLE EXPERIMENT. (Facets Multimedia)

TESTAMENT OF DR. MABUSE, THE (1933). In this sequel to Fritz Lang's 1922 DR. MABUSE, THE GAMBLER, the evil genius (Rudolf Klein-Rogge) dies broken and alone in an asylum. But the head of the sanitorium becomes infected with Mabuse's megalomania. Shrewd inspector Lohmann (from Lang's M, also played by Otto Wernicke) tracks the surrogate criminal. Atmosphere, suspense, social melodrama in the best Lang tradition. Oscar Beregi, Karl Meixner, Theodor Loos. Aka THE LAST WILL OF DR. MABUSE. (International Collection)

TESTAMENT OF DR. MABUSE, THE (1962). Second in a series of West German remakes based on Fritz Lang's early films about a math genius who turns his intellect to crimes against humanity. Confined to an asylum, Dr. Mabuse works his devilish schemes through hypnosis and other acts of terror carried out by henchmen—even after his demise. Hardly up to the quality of Lang's version, yet a sincere attempt by director Werner Klinger. Wolfgang Preiss is the doctor, Walter Rilla is in charge of the asylum and Gert Frobe is the cop after Mabuse. Senta Berger, Helmut Schmid.

TESTAMENT OF ORPHEUS (1960). French film written-directed by Jean Cocteau, who plays the central figure: a poet of the 18th Century seeking the meaning of existence in strange landscapes, where reality cannot be distinguished from fantasy. He encounters Minerva, goddess of wisdom; a blind Oedipus and a bald receptionist (Yul Brynner). Imaginative mixture. Pablo Picasso, Charles Aznavour. (Nostalgia; Facets Multimedia)

TEST PILOT PIRX (1979). See third edition.

TETSUO: THE IRON MAN (1988). The spirit of the cinema of the grotesque, established by David Lynch and David Cronenberg, lives anew in this Japanese novelty that epitomizes the cyber-punk movement in film and music. Film maker Shinya Tsukamoto is either a genius or a madman, and his bizarre movie will either turn you on or sicken you. This is a disturbing yet fascinating treatise on man's phobia of the metals he forges and the out-of-control machines he creates. A taxi driver turns into a misshapen hunk of metal (or is he imagining the transmutation?) made up of tubes, wires, gears, cables, steel tentacles and a whirring drill for a penis. The imagery of the transformation is horrendous, making this unsuitable for the squeamish, especially sequences dealing with Iron Man's sexual interludes. One is reminded of GODZILLA movies, the torn face of Schwarzenegger in THE TERMINATOR, and the Japanese obsession with atomic-bomb wounds—which some footage seems to duplicate. Way, way out, so brace yourself or you might bolt. (Fox Lorber)

TETSUO II: BODY HAMMER (1992). Another gory body-mutilation marathon from Japan's Shinya Tsukamoto, who wrote/co-produced/directed/photogrpahed this sequel to TETSUO: THE IRON MAN. Tokyo resident Tomoroh Taguchi is kidnapped by psychopath skinheads and transforms into a cyberman. Gross.

TEXAS CHAINSAW MASSACRE, THE (1974). Strictly an exercise in exploitation, but done with such grotesque style that it now stands as a cult classic in American Grand Guignol. Nowadays it might seem tame but in its day it was controversial, so cruel and sick seemed its macabre touches. Marilyn Burns establishes new screaming records as she is pursued through an orchard by a madman eager to sink his teeth into her neck—the teeth of his chainsaw, that is. Poor Marilyn. She's bound and gagged, beaten, cut with a razor blade, shoved into a canvas sack and forced to sit in an armchair made of real arms. The family of sick characters is played for grotesque comedy. Directed by that mild-mannered sentimentalist Tobe Hooper. Kim Henkel co-wrote with Hooper. Gunnar Hanse plays the crazy guy with the buzzing saw. Two sequels followed. Allen Danziger, Paul Partain. (Video Treasures; Wizard; Media) (Laser: Vestron)

LEATHERFACE

TEXAS CHAINSAW MASSACRE 2, THE (1986). Lawman Lefty Enright (Dennis Hopper), father of one of the victims of the first film, tracks the chainsaw killers using a radio disc jockey named Stretch (Caroline Williams) as bait. Tobe Hooper's new cut-and-tear adventures of the Sawyer family comprise one odd movie—a hip, flip comment on various American mania, personified by the return of Leatherface (chainsaw-whacking specialist), Chop-Top (the idiot with a metal plate in his head) and Grandpa, still trying to hit victims over the head with a sledgehammer, but usually missing. Hooper captures a macabre humor from L. M. Kit Carson's groovy albeit simplistic script which turns to surreal horror once Stretch is trapped in the underground caverns of an abandoned tourist attraction. Hooper turns Grand Guignol into farce and sociological subtext, and Hopper is a standout with chainsaws strapped to his side like six-shooters. Gory, not for the squeamish, but the satire makes it a must-see. (Media) (Laser: Image)

TEXAS CHAINSAW MASSACRE 3. See **LEATHERFACE—THE TEXAS CHAINSAW MASSACRE III.**

THANK YOU, SATAN (1989). French-Candanian effort in which a 14-year-old makes a deal with the Devil so her parents won't break up and lose their apartment. Directed by Andre Farwagi. Marie Fugain, Eric Blanc.

THAT LADY IN ERMINE (1948). Director Ernst Lubitsch died during filming of this Fox costume period comedy, so Otto Preminger helmed the last ten days of shooting without credit. The setting is southeast Europe in 1861 when Douglas Fairbanks Jr. steps from a painting in bodily form to pursue another solid body, Betty Grable. Swirling gowns, dashing colonels and gorgeous countesses in a never-never land of Bavarian customs. This light-hearted Technicolor affair is visually appealing, its characters gallant and beautous. Cesar Romero, Walter Abel, Reginald Gardiner, Whit Bissell. (Media)

THAT MAN IS PREGNANT (1972). Satirical comedy in a reversal of the sexes—the title says it all when a cop is given startling news by his doctor. Directed by Simon

Nuchtern and starring sexy Anita Morris. (Independent United)

THAT RIVIERA TOUCH (1966). See third edition.

THAT'S THE SPIRIT (1945). See editions 1-3.

THEATER OF BLOOD (1972). Macabre black comedy (similar to the Dr. Phibes series with its sick jokes and bloodletting) with Vincent Price as ham Shakespearean actor Edward Lionheart, who so murders scenes from the classics that London's critics murder him in the press. The "murdering" becomes literal when Lionheart has his revenge against the critics and murders them with the help of a band of bums (the true identity of which will surprise you). Death devices are borrowed from Shakespeare, a clever touch to Anthony Greville-Bell's script. Death's labor found, you might say. Diana Rigg, Jack Hawkins, Harry Andrews, Coral Browne, Diana Dors, Robert Morley, Michael Hordern, Dennis Price. Jolly good horror from director Douglas Hickox. (MGM/UA) (Laser: Image)

THEATER OF DEATH (1967). Whodunit-horror story with slasher overtones. Parisian theater presenting Grand Guignol is site of several murders committed by a ghoul or vampire. Could it be that Christoper Lee, head of the troupe, is responsible? Don't count on it, as there are a few surprises. Samuel Gallu directed. Lelia Goldoni, Julian Glover, Jenny Till, Ivor Dean. Aka THE BLOOD FIEND and THE FEMALE FIEND. (VCI; Republic; Sinister/C)

THEIR BIG MOMENT (1934). A diverting supernatural comedy in which a klutchy magician's assistant (Zasu Pitts) is roped into posing as a spiritualist to defraud a widow of her fortune. It's based on a creaky old Walter Hackett play so most of the action takes place in a drawing room, where Pitts and Slim Summerfield go for the laughs and stuffed shirts Ralph Morgan and Bruce Cabot look sinister. There's some odd business with poison in the final reel, and darned if Pitts doesn't begin to have clairvoyant powers. Director James Cruze photographs it for the play it is. Max Steiner was musical director. Kay Johnson, Huntly Gordon.

THEM! (1954). "Giant bug" movies of the '50s tended to be cheapjack affairs, but not this Warner Bros. classic, which holds up as a sci-fi thriller and as a chase suspense-mystery story, wonderfully concocted by screenwriter Ted Sherdemann. Director Gordon Douglas captures a maximum of atmosphere in this taut tale of mutant ants (12 feet high) terrorizing the New Mexico desert near the Alamogordo atomic-test sites. Superior effects by Ralph Ayers will convince you those giant ants are real and attacking! Intriguing chase to track down the queen bee and destroy her nest leads to the L.A. sewers—more opportunity for Douglas to build suspense as armies of men move into the slimy tubes. Edmund Gwenn is the aging expert in myrmecology, the science of ants; heroes are James Arness and James Whitmore, with Joan Weldon as Gwenn's daughter, who's also a scientist. William Schallert, Onslow Stevens, Dub Taylor, Leonard Nimoy, Fess Parker. (Video/Laser: Warner Bros.)

THERE'S NOTHING OUT THERE (1991). Teenagers head for a mountain cabin, only to find themselves stalked by a slasher. But one of the teens has seen all the horror-slasher flicks made and tries to warn everyone by following the guidelines of the movies. Written-directed by Rolfe Kanefsky. Craig Peck, Wendy Bednarz, Bonnie Bowers. (Laser: Image)

THERE'S SOMETHING OUT THERE. Video version of **DAY OF THE ANIMALS** (Vidmark).

THESE ARE THE DAMNED (1961). Joseph Losey directed Hammer's low-key, uncompromising indictment of the misuse of atomic power (also known as THE DAMNED). A government program headed by Alexander Knox uses children for experiments—a cold, ruthless act reflecting the world's battle for political power through nuclear threat. All the themes have been cleverly blended by Evan Jones from H. L. Lawrence's novel, CHILDREN OF LIGHT. MacDonald Carey is the American who discovers the secret project, Oliver Reed is the leader of the youths, Shirley Anne Field is Reed's brother and Viveca Lindfors is a shattered woman.

THEY ALL DIED LAUGHING (1964). See editions 1-3.

THEY CAME FROM BEYOND SPACE (1967). Nine pieces of a meteorite crash into a field in Cornwall—each containing an alien presence that jumps into a human brain and takes over the body. Only Robert Hutton (who has a protective metal plate in his head) escapes control and fights to stop the invasion. This Amicus production, similar to the TV-movie NIGHT SLAVES, is based on Joseph Millard's "The Gods Hate Kansas," has the values of a TV-movie and is hokey in its presentation of ray guns and other E.T. paraphenalia. Its pulpish story (adapted by co-producer Milton Subotsky) never rises to a level of sophistication, nor does director Freddie Francis look for anything more than obvious cliches. When Hutton meets the Master of the Moon (Michael Gough in a cameo) the film especially becomes laughable. A fizzle in all departments. Jennifer Jayne, Zia Mohyeddin, Bernard Kay. (Sultan; New Line)

THEY CAME FROM WITHIN (1975). One of the best of the disgusting zombie-gore movies in the wake of NIGHT OF THE LIVING DEAD, and one of the best samplings of grue from Canadian writer-director David Cronenberg. Produced by Ivan Reitman, it has the atmosphere of George Romero and a touch of ALIEN before ALIEN was made, and qualifies as a trend-setting film. Residents of the Starliner Towers housing unit in Montreal are subjected to worm-like parasites that turn them into sexually lusting monsters. Its sick humor, ghastly murders and oddball sexual encounters as the highrise dwellers are taken over and turn on their neighbors with hearty sexual appetites. There are great scenes of the worm creatures popping out of bodies or jumping into mouths, a chilling bathtub sequence, and an unrelenting sense of chaotic horror. Strong stomachs and a sense of humor are prerequisites for this bloody classic. Aka SHIVERS, FRISSONS and THE PARASITE MURDERS. Paul Hampton, Barbara Steele, Joe Silver, Lynn Lowry, Allan Migicovsky. (Vestron)

THEY LIVE (1988). Ray Faraday Nelson's famous short story "Eight O'Clock in the Morning" served as the inspiration for this John Carpenter-masterminded sci-fi action film, which takes the idea that aliens have infiltrated our society and hypnotized us not to see them. But writer Frank Armitage (working with Carpenter's concepts) broadens the idea into a statement about how we were conditioned to be automatons by the Reagan Administration in a declining society where the middle-class is becoming poorer. Hence, the first half-hour of this is compelling, with director Carpenter framing a tent city on the outskirts of L.A. against the highrises of downtown. (He conveyed a similarly stark view of L.A. in PRINCE OF DARKNESS.) And professional wrestler Rowdy Roddy Piper, in his first legit acting role, seems an interesting character, a laconic construction worker caught up in social deprivation. And then the shooting starts when George Nada (Piper), by wearing special glasses, discovers half the population is made up of aliens who wear their skeletal make-up outside their bodies. From then on it's downhill as Piper goes through adventures to destroy the aliens. Meg Foster provides a very weak romantic angle in this ultimate statement on our paranoia. (Video/Laser: MCA)

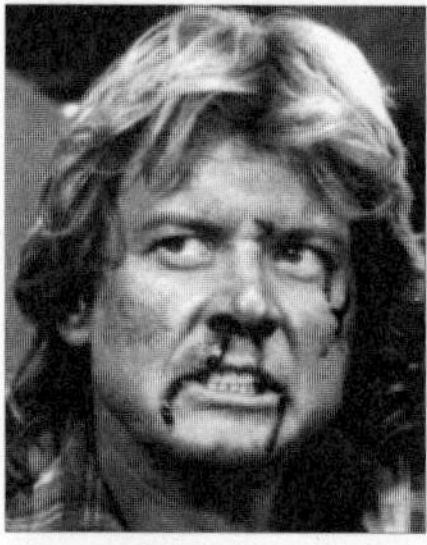

RODDY PIPER

THEY MIGHT BE GIANTS (1971). Escaping an intolerable world in which his wife has just died, lawyer George C. Scott retreats into a fantasy realm in which he thinks he's Sherlock Holmes. This thoughtful premise unfortunately goes awry and becomes a disjointed allegory, so surrealistic in its unfolding that its initial hold dwindles and is lost in an enigmatic climax, where illusion and reality mingle to form a new madhouse. Joanne Woodward co-stars as Scott's psychiatrist, whose name is Dr. Watson. Based on a play by James Goldman, who wrote the script. Directed by Anthony Harvey. Jack Gilford, Lester Rawlins. (MCA)

THEY'RE COMING TO GET YOU (1972). Video version of **DEMONS OF THE DEAD** (Vogue).

THEY'RE PLAYING WITH FIRE (1984). Minor whodunit seriously attempts to be a suspense shocker, then deteriorates into a slasher film featuring a fiend in a ski mask, wielding a wicked axe. The real asset of this low-budget effort written-directed by Howard Avedis is Sybil Danning, who wears bikinis and strips to make love to Eric Brown. She is one incredible woman. Supporting cast: Andrew Prine, Paul Clemens, K. T. Stevens. Marlene Schmidt co-produced with Avedis. And now back to Sybil . . . (Thorn EMI/HBO)

THEY SAVED HITLER'S BRAIN (1964). This has been ranked as one of the worst movies ever made, and while there are moments when it comes close, it never has the ultimate campiness one prefers. The Richard Miles-Steve Bennett story (originally MADMEN OF MANDORAS) is a muddled affair about a deadly G Gas and its antidote (PAM - Formula D). First a scientist is kidnapped, then a U.S. couple is kidnapped to a South America country (Mandoras) where neo-Nazis (led by Marshall Reed) keep Hitler's head in a special solution (pardon that pun, please). Since a secret agent is wearing a minidress circa 1969, one suspects the film may have set on a shelf for years before new footage was added to salvage the mess. The poor cinematography in these scenes is another clue to the padding, as most of the film has a professional look thanks to Stanley Cortez. The music track was lifted from Universal- International horror movies. The direction by David Bradley is pedestrian. Walter Stocker, Audrey Caire, Carlos Rivas, Nestor Paiva, Scott Peters. (VCI; United; Video Yesteryear)

THIEF OF BAGDAD, THE (1940). British producer Sir Alexander Korda's fantasy in the Arabian Nights tradition is still the best of its kind—an allegory of good vs. evil, a love story, an adventure of quest, retribution and restitution, a tale of black magic in which a wizard, tormented by love for a woman, is driven to his doom. Above all, this blends metaphor of language with poetic visuals and lush, exotic music. Sabu possesses an ageless quality as the thief who joins deposed king John Justin to fight the wicked Vizier, played to perfection by Conrad Veidt, and to romance beautiful June Duprez. Screenwriter Miles Malleson doubles as the dopey but loveable sultan who collects the world's strangest toys. Rex Ingram is the towering, thunderous Djinni, who springs from a tiny bottle uncorked by Sabu. Visual effects and cinematography by William Cameron Menzies, music by Miklos Rozsa. Three directors were needed: Michael Powell, Ludwig Berger and Tim Whelan. Splendid Technicolor adventure; cannot be recommended too highly. (Video/Laser: Nelson/Embassy)

THIEF OF BAGDAD, THE (1960). Entertaining Arabian Nights adventure, but a thousand and one adventures away from the 1940 version. This Italian production, imported to America by Joseph Levine, stars Steve Reeves as a muscular hero who must pass seven tests to possess the Blue Rose, the only cure for an ailing princess. But why would anyone face so many dangers for such a flaccid character (played by Georgia Moll)? Made in Tunis and Italy. Directed by Arthur Lubin, Edy Vessel, Arturo Dominici. (Embassy)

THIEF OF BAGDAD, THE (1978). TV version of the Thousand and One Nights tales (directed by Clive Donner) in which a roguish beggar-thief battles the evil wizard, replete with magic carpet, bottled genie, veiled beauties, paradise gardens and magical lamp. Special effects by John (STAR WARS) Stears. Prince: Kabir Bedi; thief: Roddy McDowall; wizard: Terence Stamp. Others in the cast: Peter and Paula Ustinov, Frank Finlay, Ian Holm, Marina Vlady. (Video Gems)

THIEF OF DAMASCUS, THE (1952). Sword-and-sandal scandal, from flickie-quickie producer Sam Katzman, stars Paul Henreid as an Arabian Nights hero consorting with Scheherazade, Sinbad and Ali Baba to put down an evil caliph. Same old "Open Sesame" seeds. John Sutton, Jeff Donnell, Lon Chaney Jr., Elena Verdugo. Directed by Will Jason.

THIN AIR. Video version of **BODY STEALERS, THE.** (Just doing what comes snatch-erally?)

THING . . . FROM ANOTHER WORLD, THE (1951). One-time editor Christian Nyby is credited with directing this RKO version of John W. Campbell's "Who Goes There?" but it is generally known that producer Howard Hawks was on the set as guiding benefactor. Certainly the technique of overlapping, fast-delivered dialogue is a tell-tale giveaway. No matter . . . because of its concern for a strong camaraderie among military men (a standard Hawks trait), for sprightly dialogue (by Charles Lederer), for tingling suspense, and because it captures the frigid atmosphere of an Arctic research station, THE THING remains one of the best sci-fi thrillers of the '50s. Another achievement is composer Dimitri Tiomkin's use of the theremin to create an unholy chilling theme. A small band (U.S. Air Force personnel and scientists, including one woman, Margaret Sheridan) at an isolated outpost near the North Pole retrieves the frozen body of an alien which has come to Earth aboard a flying saucer. Once the creature (described as an emotionless vegetable monster) thaws out, it's on a destructive rampage, needing human blood to survive. The makeup for the creature (James Arness in a jumpsuit with putty nose) is a letdown, but glimpses of the monster are minimized, allowing tension to build unrelentingly. Kenneth Tobey heads the Air Force personnel, Douglas Spencer is great as the wise-cracking newsman Scotty, Robert Cornithwaite is memorable as the misguided scientist. Dewey Martin, Eduard Franz, Paul Frees, John Dierkes, George Fenneman, Tom Steele. (RKO; Nostalgia Merchant; RCA/Columbia; VidAmerica; Goodtimes) (Laser: Turner/Image/VidAmerica)

THING, THE (1982). Outstanding John Carpenter-directed version of John W. Campbell's "Who Goes There?", the classic novella first brought to the screen by Howard Hawks in 1951. While that film is remembered for suspense and characterizations, and not for monster or effects, Carpenter has striven for exactly the opposite values, stressing the shape-changing extraterrestrial beast at the expense of all else. Yet, it is this single facet that makes the film so compelling. Rob Bottin and a team of tricksters create remarkably grisly, gruesome effects—perhaps the most gruesome ever captured on film. According to Bottin, there are 45 different glimpses of the creature as it undergoes change. The stuff of our worst nightmares, this will give children bad dreams and may even upset adults. The cast is topped by Kurt Russell, with strong support from Wilford Brimley, T. K. Carter, Richard Dysart and Richard Masur. The setting is an Antarctic research station where scientists are isolated by a raging storm. Meanwhile The Thing, freed from imprisonment in the ice, where it has been for 100,000 years (next to its crashed saucer), begins taking "shape."

ROB BOTTIN & CREATIONS FOR 'THE THING' (1982)

The screenplay by William Lancaster (son of Burt) is muddled but as a special effects classic, this is the greatest. (Video/Laser: MCA)

THING IN THE ATTIC, THE. See **GHOUL, THE (1975).**

THINGS HAPPEN AT NIGHT (1948). . . . but not much happens in this British version of a Frank Harvey play, THE POLTERGEIST, which depicts a young girl possessed by a mischievous demon. Directed by Francis Searle. Gordon Hacker, Garry Marsh, Olga Linda, Beatrice Campbell. (Sinister/C; Filmfax; Nostalgia)

THINGS TO COME (1936). British production from Alexander Korda—directed by William Cameron Menzies from a screenplay by H. G. Wells, who adapted his own novel—is a minor classic in sci-fi set design and effects, although its philosophies now seem muddled and naively outdated. The epic is broken into three prophetic sections. The first depicts war in 1940 which leads to the Dark Age, when pestilence (the Wandering Sickness) sweeps the world. The second section deals with a feudal system in which neighboring districts wage war. The third part, set in 2036, depicts man on a higher plane devoting himself to art and science. A rocket expedition to the moon is planned, but reactionaries fear man has advanced far enough and stage an uprising. Which leads to war. Thus, history is a cyclical process. Stunning achievement for its time, with a cast that does wonders with the oft-pedantic dialogue: Sir Cedric Hardwicke, Raymond Massey, Ralph Richardson, Margaretta Scott, Edward Chapman. (Kartes; Media; Filmfax; Sinister/C)

THING THAT COULDN'T DIE, THE (1958). Universal-International, once the king of horror, was foundering when it produced this programmer, for David Duncan's script is wretched and Will Cowan's direction double-wretched, with studio composer Joseph Gershenson stealing themes from other films to keep the budget low. The back-lot studio ranch is the setting for a feeble story about a girl with divining powers who finds the head of a 16th Century devil worshipper which maintains a hypnotic hoodoo over the cast as the long-dead dastard, once an enemy of Sir Francis Drake, tries to rejoin his severed head to its body. But believe us, this lacks body. William Reynolds, Andra Martin.

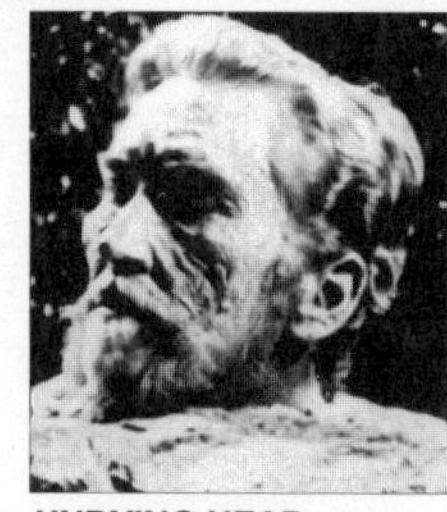

UNDYING HEAD

THING WITH TWO HEADS, THE (1972). Imagine the social satire that might have gone into this horror-fantasy about a hulking black convict (Rosey Grier) who wakes up from an operation to find the head of a bigoted white surgeon (Ray Milland) attached to his neck. But no . . instead we are subjected to gross stupidities as Grier rushes around L.A. to clear himself of a murder charge and Milland acts like a redneck dolt. Every opportunity for something amusing or clever is missed by director Lee Frost. William Smith, Roger Perry, Chelsea Brown, Don Marshall.

THIRD FROM THE SUN (1972). See third edition.

THIRST (1979). Above-average Australian vampire tale has a compelling, perverse nature in its bite when Chantal Contouri is taken to a country farm to be "fattened" for the kill by a vampire gang. Henry Silva has a great death scene and David Hemmings is outstanding in a surprise-twist role. Well directed by Rod Hardy. THIRST, aka THE BLOOD CULT OF SHANGRI-LA, will quench your need for a good horror movie. (Media; Cult)

THIRST OF BARON BLOOD, THE. See **BARON BLOOD.**

THIRSTY DEAD, THE (1974). Filipino production of minor importance; its feeble story barely brings it above the level of episodic TV. Jennifer Billingsley and other beauties are kidnapped from night spots in Manila and taken to a jungle hideaway where a devil cult hangs out, dressed in Baby Doll nighties, sarongs and bikinis. Seems that John Considine and followers believe in the god Rahu, whose head is kept in a red-tinted box. The chicks are needed for blood transfusions, which are gulped down by the cult (they give the chicks eternal beauty). A sensitive love affair develops between Jennifer and John, but it isn't enough to bring Charles Dennis' script out of the pulp jungle. Director Terry Becker offers no style and little adventure when the women break for freedom and a chase ensues. Gore effects are clumsily handled, and the ending unsatisfying. Judith McConnell, Tani Guthrie. (Western World; Applause; King of Video; from Simitar as **BLOOD HUNT**)

THIRTEEN GHOSTS (1960). Campy but pleasing horror film produced and directed by William Castle, prophet of the great god Gimmick. Filmed in "Illusiono," for which viewers were provided "Ghost Finders": glasses with panels of red (enabling them to see the ghosts) and blue (blocking out the ghosts). Robb White's story: A family inherits a haunted house, unaware a fortune is hidden among the bric-a-brac. Ghosts come and go with the blink of an eye. Thirteen was Castle's lucky number on this ghostly outing. Rosemary De Camp, Donald Woods, Martin Milner, Margaret Hamilton. (RCA/Columbia; Goodtimes)

THIRTEENTH CHAIR, THE (1937). Outstanding MGM cast (Dame May Whitty, Lewis Stone, Henry Daniell) enhances a rickety story about a seance faked to elicit a murderer's confession. The film reveals how spiritualists pull off their shoddiest tricks. Based on Bayard Veillier's play; first produced in 1929 by Tod Browning with Bela Lugosi and Conrad Nagel.

THIRTEENTH FLOOR, THE (1988). After she witnesses her father accidentally kill a man with electricity, an estranged girl grows up to become Lisa Hensley and meets the ghost of the deceased youth. They join forces to expose the father. Written and directed by Chris Roache. Tim McKenzie, Miranda Otto, Jeff Truman, Vic Rooney. (Prism; Paramount)

THIRTEENTH GUEST, THE (1932). As creaky as the unoiled doors in the drafty corridor . . . as dusty as the unswept corners of the secret rooms . . . yes, another "old dark house" imitation starring Ginger Rogers and Lyle Talbot among those trapped in the mansion with a black-caped killer equipped with strange weaponry and gadgets. Directed by Albert Ray. J. Farrell MacDonald, James Eagles. (Sinister/C; Video Yesteryear; Filmfax)

THIRTEENTH REUNION. Video version from Thrillervision of an episode of HAMMER HOUSE OF HORROR. See **CHARLIE BOY/THIRTEENTH REUNION.**

THIRTEEN WOMEN (1932). Myrna Loy, still looking like the sadistic, sexually perverted daughter of Fu Manchu, portrays a half-caste who once tried to cross the color barrier but was cruelly rejected by her class mates and thrown out of an all-girls' school. Now she's back with a vengeance, using dire astrology predictions and hypnotic spells to get even with the gals who betrayed her. Half this adaptation of the Tiffany Thayer novel (by Bartlett Cormack and Samuel Ornitz) shows her as a diabolical mystic, the other half treats her as a common criminal as she tries to poison a child and commit other vengeful crimes with a male accomplice. This unevenness throws the film off kilter just when it gets going, and director George Archainbaud never regains footing. Ricardo Cortez is the cop, Irene Dunne is an intended victim in Beverly Hills, Jill Esmond, Florence Eldridge, Kay Jonson and Mary Duncan.

THIRTY-FOOT BRIDE OF CANDY ROCK, THE (1959). Lou Costello's last feature (sans Bud Abbott) stars Lou as a goofy assistant to a crazy inventor who transforms Dorothy Provine into a gigantic representative of the feminist movement and sends her and Lou through a time-travel device. A sad finale to the career of a once-popular film prankster. Directed by Sidney Miller. Robert Burton, Doodles Weaver, Gale Gordon, Jimmy

Conlin, Charles Lane. (RCA/Columbia)

THIS HOUSE POSSESSED (1981). Another house-possessed-by-evil TV-movie, a ripoff of BURNT ASHES and THE EVIL. An architect constructs an estate equipped with surveillance equipment that turns into a death trap for a rock singer (Parker Stevenson) and his girl (Lisa Eilbacher). The perverted forms of housekeeping include death by malfunctioning electrical gate, a demonic mirror, an overheated swimming pool and cords that lash themselves about the victim. A sense of deja vu—that you have been in this house before—will overwhelm you. Directed by William Wiard. Joan Bennett, Slim Pickens, Shelley Smith, K. Callan.

THIS ISLAND EARTH (1955). Sincere adaptation of Raymond F. Jones' novel resulted in a classy Universal-International sci-fi epic with abundant effects by Clifford Stine and Stanley Horsley. The Franklin Coen-Edward G. O'Callighan script is uneven but it's still a pleasure to ogle the space battles and interplanetary travel as Rex Reason and Faith Domergue are transported to the planet Metaluna by E.T. humanoid Jeff Morrow to save the dying world from attack by its rival enemy, Zahgon. It was excitingly directed by Joseph Newman (aided by Jack Arnold and producer William Alland) and crisply edited by Virgil Vogel. The climax is heightened by a six-foot offspring of a giant bug with exposed brain, eyes as big as saucers and blood vessels outside the skin. Lance Fuller, Russell Johnson, Douglas Spencer, Robert Nichols. (Video/Laser: MCA)

THIS IS NOT A TEST (1962). Atomic attack is pending, so highway cop Seamon Glass warns motorists. Marginal sci-fi directed by Frederic Gadete. Mary Morlas, Thayer Roberts. (Sinister/C; S/Weird; Filmfax)

THIS STUFF'LL KILL YA! (1971). Gore specialist Herschell Gordon Lewis wrote-produced-directed this blood-drenched tale of revenooers in an Oklahoma town where a minister is behind the gore murders of college girls. Blood and brimstone, maybe? The last movie of cowboy actor Tim Holt. Aka THE DEVIL WEARS CLODHOPPERS. Jeffrey Allen, Gloria King, Ray Sager. (Trans-World; Fright)

THOR AND THE AMAZON WOMEN (198?). Race of shapely wenches, armed with lethal bows and arrows and other equipment considered standard issue for a lost tribe of sexy babes, calls on an ancient God when word leaks out their Queen is between a rock and a hard place. Directed by Leon Viola. Joe Robinson, Susy Andersen, Harry Baird. (Action International)

THOSE FANTASTIC FLYING FOOLS. Video version of **BLAST OFF.**

THOUSAND AND ONE NIGHTS, A (1945). Cornel Wilde as Aladdin rubs the Magic Lamp and out pops Evelyn Keyes, as well-curved as his scimitar. After lurking through caves, peering at the brocade costumes of harem cuties and fighting off Phil Silvers' bad jokes, Wilde still falls short of 1001 delights. Watch for Shelley Winters—she's sexily positioned among the plotting viziers. And Rex Ingram, still rollicking with delight over THIEF OF BAGDAD, returns as a mighty genie. Hang on, little ones, we're about to fly across the world again on a Magic Carpet. Directed by Alfred E. Green.

THOUSAND CRIES HAS THE NIGHT. See **PIECES.**

THOUSAND EYES OF DR. MABUSE, THE (1960). Fritz Lang returned to West Germany to co-write (with Heinz Oskar Wuttig) and direct this resurrection of his 1932 classic, THE TESTAMENT OF DR. MABUSE, reactivating the evil genius who turns his intellect to nefarious pursuits. Aka THE SECRET OF DR. MABUSE and THE DIABOLICAL DR. MABUSE, this is not up to the original, but still damn good Lang as Commissioner Kraugs (Gert Frobe) tracks the criminal to the Hotel Luxor. This set off a wave of Mabuse remakes: THE RETURN OF DR. MABUSE, DR. MABUSE VS. SCOTLAND YARD and THE SECRET OF DR. MABUSE. Dawn Addams, Wolfgang Preiss, Peter Van Eyck, Howard Vernon. (Sinister/C; S/Weird; Filmfax)

THOU SHALT NOT KILL . . . EXCEPT (1985). Set in 1969, the year Charles Manson committed several murders, this establishes the premise that a Manson-like crazyman is on a killing spree near Detroit, where Sergeant Stryker (homage to John Wayne in SANDS OF IWO JIMA) is recovering from wounds received in Vietnam. Stryker and three Army buddies are all that can stop Manson and his killers from slaughtering hostages. You want to cheer the military guys even though they're as bloody as the Manson-takeoffs and spatter gore all over the place. Make-up man Gary Jones needed buckets of the stuff as the gang is wiped out, each dying a sanguinary death. Brian Schulz, John Manfredi, Robert Rickman and Tim Quill are heroes while film maker Sam Raimi portrays the demented cult leader. It's better than a lot of of revenge-horror films, with a good score by Joseph Lo Duca. director Josh Becker wrote the script. (Prism)

THREADS (1984). Great Britain's answer to THE DAY AFTER, a semidocumentary docudrama (first shown on the BBC) depicting what happens to the city of Sheffield when the USA and the USSR spark a nuclear war. Horribly grim and terrifying, sparing none of the hopelessness and sense of despair that accompanies such a futile act. You won't forget it. Written-directed by Mick Jackson. Karen Meagher, Reece Dinsdale. (New World; Western World)

THREE CASES OF MURDER (1955). Superior British trilogy: While the second narrative is a standard police procedural, the first and third are of a macabre nature. "Lord Mountdrago," by Somerset Maugham, stars Orson Welles as a member of the House of Lords who dreams about a man he once humiliated, and that man's apparent revenge. Directed by George More O'Ferrall, with Alan Badel and Andre Morell. "In the Picture" stars Badel as an insane painter trapped in his own painting in a museum. Directed by Wendy Toye; with Leueen MacGrath.

THREE FACES OF EVE, THE (1957). Although this Oscar-winning film is based on a true story, we include it here because it's the best of the multiple personality films that cross over into the aberrations of the human mind and deal with the theme as psychohorror material. This is effective in dealing with the pain that individuals endure when they can't control a variety of personalities within them. Nunnally Johnson directed. Joanne Woodward, David Wayne, Lee J. Cobb, Nancy Kulp, Vince Edwards. (Video/Laser: CBS/Fox)

THREE FACES OF FEAR/THREE FACES OF TERROR. See **BLACK SABBATH.**

THREE NUTS IN SEARCH OF A BOLT (1964). Licentious comedy spiced up by busty Mamie Van Doren (as sexpot Saxie Symboll) who teams with Paul Gilbert and John Cronin to have a hambone actor (Tommy Noonan) pretend he's a famous psychiatrist (!) so he can analyze their sexual problems and bring them to new peaks of happiness. Whether she can act or not is immaterial as Mamie of the monumental mammaries proceeds to shed Noonan's clothing for reasons that would give Freud a complex. Ziva Rodann, Alvy Moore, L.Q. Jones. Noonan directed. (Simitar)

THREE ON A MEATHOOK (1973). William Girdler wrote-directed this adaptation of the true-life murder case of Ed Gein, the madman who wore the skin of his victims and had a mother complex. Yes, the same real-life homicidal maniac who inspired Robert Bloch to write PSYCHO. Charles Kissinger, James Pickett. (Regal; Video Treasures; Front Row Entertainment)

THREE STOOGES IN ORBIT, THE (1962). Your senses will be spinning too during this wacky feature starring Moe Howard, Larry Fine and Joe De Rita as nitwits who meet crazy inventor Emil Sitka, designer of a submarine-tank battle weapon. Complicating the plot are Martians out to steal the device. This cinematic idiocy is super-lowbrow yet now radiates a special nostalgic flavor, brought on by the fact the Stooges have become entertainment icons, enduring beyond their own time. Even the phony monster masks seem quaint and amusing. My, how time gives the darnedest things a patina of historical significance. Directed by Edward Bernds; scripted by Elwood Ullman; produced by Norman Maurer, one-time editor of Three Stooges comic books. Carol Christensen, Nestor Paiva, Edson Stroll.

THREE STOOGES MEET HERCULES, THE (1962). Spoof on musclemen epics, with Moe Howard, Larry Fine and Joe De Rita working in Ithaca, N.Y., in a soda shop, befriending the guy next door who just happens to be inventing a time machine. They travel back in time to Greece before Christ to that Ithaca to meet Ulysses, Hercules (portrayed as a dumb grunt master) and Achilles the Heel. The funniest scenes feature the Stooges in drag in a harem, mistaken as hand maidens, and partakers in a Ben-Hur parody as they row a king's vessel on a "holiday cruise." Effacious and outrageous, with the Stooges trapped in a low-budget continuum. Directed by Edward Bernds. Gene Roth, Samson Burke. (RCA/Columbia; Goodtimes)

THREE SUPERMEN IN S. DOMINGO (198?). Costumed "supermen" take on a gang of counterfeiters in foreign-produced action-comedy flick. Directed by Italo Martinenghi.

3,000 A.D. See **CAPTIVE WOMEN.**

THREE WORLDS OF GULLIVER, THE (1960). Following THE SEVENTH VOYAGE OF SINBAD, producer Charles H. Schneer and special effects artist Ray Harryhausen collaborated to bring Jonathan Swift's satire to the screen, and the results are impressive. Again, Kerwin Mathews portrays the young hero—a traveler who falls overboard and finds himself captive in the land of the Lilliputians, tiny people under the thumb of the Brobdingnags, unfriendly giants from a neighborhing island. Mathews befriends the Tiny Tims and battles the towering titans. The wonderful effects capture more of a fairy tale quality than other Harryhausen efforts. Romance, action and comedy with the younger set better served. Directed by Jack Sher. Jo Morrow, Peter Bull, June Thorburn, Lee Patterson. Wonderful music by Bernard Herrmann. (RCA/Columbia)

THRILLED TO DEATH. See **NIGHT WARNING.**

THRILLER (1983). Granddaddy of rock music videos with horror and monster motifs inspired by the movies. This vehicle—written-directed by John Landis—shot Michael Jackson into the big time, and features a memorable song voiced by Vincent Price. A special video called THE MAKING OF THRILLER shows the behind-the-scenes view. (MCA)

THRILL KILLERS, THE (1967). Ray Dennis Steckler, an eccentric but likable low-budget filmmaker, directs and stars in this high-energy though often laughable psychokiller smasher-basher in which an escaped maniac, Mad Dog Glick, terrorizes assorted passers-by when he runs into three other escaped nuts, one of whom carries a large axe. A lot of what Steckler does is crude satire and there's an underlying element of naivete that makes it palatable. The film works best as a chase during its last half hour as Liz Renay runs (and repeatedly screams) for her life. Steckler has built up an odd cult following. (Camp)

THRONE OF FIRE, THE (1983). Costume fantasy in which a sword-wielding muscleman must save the world from the son of the Devil and a witch named Azira. Directed in Italy by Franco Prosperi. Sabrina Siani plays the daughter of King Egon. (MGM/UA)

THRONE OF THE BLOOD MONSTER. See **NIGHT OF THE BLOOD MONSTER.**

THROUGH NAKED EYES (1983). Hitchcockian TV-movie has a few surprise twists and offbeat characters when highrise dweller David Soul realizes Pam Dawber—a chick in a nearby building as tall as his—is also spying on him. They strike up a relationship just when a slasher-smasher starts striking folks with his butcher knife. But suspicion is diverted onto Soul, a flutist who behaves oddly and doesn't have easy relationships with people, including his father William Schallert. Contrived suspense situations by writer Jeffrey Bloom will still have you on the edge of your couch. Directed by John Llewellyn Moxey. (Prism; Media)

THROUGH THE MAGIC PYRAMID (1981). Ron Howard-directed TV-movie slanted for the juvenile set, in which Chris Barnes portrays Billy Tuttle, a youth who, with help of a magical ring and a pyramid shape, travels through time to the 18th Dynasty, just prior to King Tut taking the throne as the ruler of Egypt. It's simplistic action-adventure when Tut is kidnapped by an evil general and Barnes and his bloodhound Scout follow the scent. In the vein of THE WIZARD OF OZ, characters from Barnes' world turn up in counterparts: Vic Tayback (as the villain) and Hans Conried (as the high priest). Scripted by Rance Howard (Ron's dad) and Herbert J. Wright. Olivia Barash, Betty Beaird, Gino Conforti, Elaine Giftos, Eric Greene, James Hampton.

THUNDERBALL (1965). Stylish James Bond espionage adventure, set largely underwater and featuring exotic, sophisticated scuba equipment and weapons. Sean Connery, as 007, tracks one-eyed Largo (Adolf Celi) who has hijacked a NATO aircraft armed with atomic bombs and demands a ransom of one million pounds. Several punnish quips by 007 flip through Bond's lips—they are part of the charm that continued to cling to these marvelous adventures. Richard Maibaum and John Hopkins adapted the Ian Fleming novel. The undersea photography and full-scale battles make this an outstanding contribution to the series (this story was remade into NEVER SAY NEVER AGAIN.) Claudine Auger plays Domino, and Luciana Paluzzi is a palaluzzi of a woman in her bathing suits. Directed with pizzazz by Terence Young. (CBS/Fox)

THUNDERBIRD SIX (1968). Sequel to THUNDERBIRDS ARE GO offers more puppet adventures as our heroes face the Black Phantom in their new spacecraft. Gerry and Sylvia Anderson wrote and produced, David Lane directed. (Video/Laser: MGM/UA)

THUNDERBIRDS ARE GO (1966). Gerry and Sylvia Anderson, who produced some top British TV science-fiction, first became known for THUNDERBIRDS, which featured realistic effects and mature storylines around marionette characters. This full-length treatment is demonstrative of the excellent puppet-model work. The International Space Rescue Service blasts off for Mars but the project is threatened by saboteurs. See also REVENGE OF THE MYSTERONS FROM MARS. Directed by David Lane. (Video/Laser: MGM/UA)

THUNDERBIRDS: COUNTDOWN TO DISASTER (1981). Marionette sci-fi with the space adventurers saving the Empire State Building and putting out an oil fire in the Atlantic. Directed by David Elliott, David Lane and Desmond Saunders. (Family Home)

THUNDERBIRDS TO THE RESCUE (1980). Adventures from the British THUNDERBIRDS marionette series featuring imaginative model and puppet work. Novelty film worth watching. (Family Home Entertainment)

THUNDERHEART (1992). While on the surface this is a whodunit, in which FBI agents Val Kilmer and Sam Shepard investigate a murder on the Pine Ridge Reservation in S. Dakota, it's also the spiritual study of Kilmer (whose character is part Sioux Indian) and how he rediscovers his roots through strange visions, dreams and other metaphysical experiences brought on by an old medicine man. THUNDERHEART is a taut thriller with an intriguing conspiracy twist to its unusual story. Graham Greene, Fred Ward, John Trudell.

THUNDER MOUNTAIN. See **SHADOW OF CHAKIRA.**

THUNDER RUN (1985). Minor sci-fi actioner set in the deserts of Nevada and Arizona when an aging trucker (Forrest Tucker in his final screen role) helms a Kenmore Supertruck (with indestructible tires, bulletproof windows and trick weapons) through a gauntlet of foreign agents who drive camouflaged Volkswagens (equipped with heat-seeking rockets) and other ROAD WARRIOR-style vehicles. There's nonsense about a computer code, a tunnel of lasers and a mysterious helicopter. Tuck is carrying a cargo of plutonium for CIA boss John Ireland and wheels the rig with the daring of Mad Max. Crashes are plentiful and well-photographed. Directed by Gary Hudson. John Sheperd, Jill Whitlow. (Media)

THURSDAY THE 12TH. See **PANDEMONIUM.**

THX 1138 (1971). In an underground society, in the distant future, man lives in a drugged stupor, ruled by a computerized police system that denies citizens the right to feel emotions or sexual desires. George Lucas, in his impressive directorial debut, creates an automated, trance-state world that is a visual experience exploring man's darkest side to controlling his own behavior. While the future technology and the emotionless behavior of the robots are fascinating, the Walter Murch-Lucas script also probes into man's need to remain individualistic as captive Robert Duvall breaks loose from the system to escape to the unknown surface world above. Produced by Francis Ford Coppola, who first admired Lucas' short 16mm film which he made at USC entitled THX 1138 4EB, this is a major stepping stone in the path to the STAR WARS series. Donald Pleasence, Maggie McOmie, Don Pedro Colley, Johnny Weissmuller Jr. (Video/Laser: Warner Bros.)

TICKS (1993). Vacationing teenagers Peter Scolari, Ami Dolenz, Rosalind Allen and Alfonso Ribeiro encounter mutant-monster insects in a special-effects sci-fi thriller directed by Tony Randel. (Republic)

TIDAL WAVE (1975). Roger Corman's Americanized version of SUBMERSION OF JAPAN, an Asian epic depicting the sinking of the subcontinent of Japan by tidal waves, land catastrophies and assorted disasters and tragedies. Footage with Lorne Greene was added to give "local" appeal. Unfortunately, excessive U.S. editing destroyed the film's continuity. Still, director Shiro Moritani captures a feeling of doom unusual in Japanese films of this kind. American scenes directed by Andrew Meyer. (New World)

TIGER CLAWS (1992). Serial killer knocks off his victims and leaves trails of "tiger claws" behind as his trademark. Martial arts cops Jalal Merhi and Cynthia Rothrock demonstrate karate and kickboxing skills in what is basically an action picture with minor horror overtones. Directed by Kelly Makin. Bolo Yeung, mo Chow, Ho Chow. (Video/Laser: MCA)

TIGER FANGS (1943). Obscure PRS quickie set in the Far East (on potted jungle sets) in which June Duprez is terrorized by what would appear to be killer humans who assume the form of tigers. Pretty stuffy and predictable; horror elements are minimal. Directed by Sam Newfield. Frank Buck, Duncan Renaldo, Howard Banks. (Sinister/C; Nostalgia; Discount)

TIGER MAN. See **LADY AND THE MONSTER.**

TIGHTROPE (1984). Fascinating, perplexing study of a New Orleans cop (Clint Eastwood) investigating brutal sex murders of women in the kinky velvet underworld of perversion. Eastwood is lured into this sordid world and finds he enjoys it—then discovers the killer has a vendetta against him. The subtext finds Eastwood examining his own values, atlhough the main thrust remains the pursuit, craftily built to an exciting climax by writer-director Richard Tuggle, who treats this more like a slasher-horror thriller than a whodunit. Clint's romance with Genevieve Bujold contributes to the theme. One of Eastwood's best. (Video/Laser: Warner Bros.)

TILL DAWN DO US PART. See **STRAIGHT ON TILL MORNING.**

TILL DEATH (1978). Tepid, lethargically paced supernatural-ghost tale. Keith Atkinson is locked in a mausoleum with the corpse of his wife (Belinda Balaski), who died in a car crash which he caused. He's snared in a state of limbo, where the spouse rises from her crypt and tries to seduce him into joining her in the Great Beyond. None of this makes sense, and the ending, in which transparent entities menace the helpless couple, sheds no light on Gregory Dana's muddled script. Walter Stocker pointed the camera and co-produced with actor Marshall Reed. Not to have and to hold . . .

TILL DEATH DO US PART (1987). Newlyweds arrive at a new estate where a portrait of a blonde woman holds the key to a mystery involving vampires. (Ariel)

TILL DEATH DO US PART. Video version of **BLOOD-SPATTERED BRIDE, THE.** (Vestron)

TIM BURTON'S NIGHTMARE BEFORE CHRISTMAS. See **NIGHTMARE BEFORE CHRISTMAS.**

TIME AFTER TIME (1979). Ingenious time travel yarn written-directed by Nicholas Meyer in which Jack the Ripper flees Victorian London in a machine built by H. G. Wells, landing in San Francisco, November 1979. Wells, pursuing the slasher, becomes an amusing anachronism as he adjusts to 20th Century customs. David Warner is an intriguing Ripper, remarking to Wells, "We haven't gone ahead, we've gone back; man hasn't advanced beyond barbarism," flipping on the six o'clock news to prove it. Malcolm McDowell is the British idealist-writer and Mary Steenburgen the kooky but lovable bank executive who befriends him. This imaginative fantasy is enhanced by a rich Miklos Rozsa score. Charles Cioffi, Shelley Hack, Clete Roberts. (Video/Laser: Warner Bros.)

TIME BANDITS (1981). Thoroughly wacky time-travel comedy zanily directed by Terry Gilliam of Monty Python infamy. Destructive fun as a gang of dwarfs aids a youth (Craig Warnock) lost in a time hole. Gags fly fast and furious, and many stars show up in cameos: Sean Connery is Agamemnon, John Cleese is a hilarious Robin Hood, David Warner is wonderful as the Evil Genius of the Universe. Others in the Gilliam-Michael Palin script: Sir Ralph Richardson, Ian Holm, Kenny Baker, Shelley Duvall. Absolutely bananas at times, but you'll be too busy laughing to tell yourself none of this mayhem makes sense. Producer George Harrison provided songs. (RCA/Columbia; Paramount) (Laser: Paramount)

TIME BARBARIANS (1991). A direct ripoff of BEASTMASTER 2, stealing that film's curious blend of sword-and-sorcery fantasy and timehopping. Set in the magical kingdom of Armana, it depicts a warrior king (Deron Michael McBee) losing his crystal amulet to Mondrok the cutthroat and being sent through time to modernday L.A. by wizard queen Ingrid Vold, she in a long stringy blond wig. Muscle guy McBee, also wearing a blond wig and reciting turgid dialogue by writer-director Joseph J. Barmettler, does battle with modern gangs with his sometimes-invisible sword and tracks the bad-guy warrior with the help of a TV reporter in a miniskirt. The effects are minimal, the fighting less than convincing and the plot and dialogue rancid. Jo Ann Ayres, Daniel Martine, Louis Roth, Michael Ferrare.

TIMEBOMB (1990). Rousing action thriller with overtones of THE MANCHURIAN CANDIDATE in which watchmaker Michael Biehn is the target for superassassins created by a secret government gang run by Richard Jordan and Robert Culp. Writer-director Avi Nesher crams this offbeat adventure with violent action and the pace is unrelenting as Biehn and psychoanalysist Patsy Kensit follow the clues with cop Raymond St. Jacques tagging along. The sequence in which Biehn undergoes "behavior modification experiments" presents unusual holographs. Tracy Scroggins portrays the sexy assassin Ms Blue. (Video/Laser: MGM/UA)

TIMEBURST—THE FINAL ALLIANCE (1988). Offbeat, satisfying fantasy thriller with shootemup action, martial-arts mayhem, convoluted plot twists and pseudo-philosophy (Zen-style). Scott David King portrays a 350-year-old man, Urbane, who discovered the Japanese secret of immortality in feudal times under the guidance of "The Master" (Gerald Okamura) and now is a CIA agent who suffers amnesia and has brief flashes of his past life. Bad guy Jay Richardson and gang are after the secret with a Japanese band led by Craig Ng. Caught in the middle is "The Master" (also immortal) and another CIA operative (Michiko) who provides romantic interest and a partner for Urbane during the chases. The script by producer/director Peter Yugal and co-producer Michael Bogert offers an unusual ending. Chet Hood, Jack

Vogel. (Action International)

TIME FLIES (1944). See editions 1-3.

TIME FLYER (1985). TV-movie starring Huckleberry Fox as a youth who travels through time to 1927 to help his grandfather (Peter Coyote) prevent a rift in the time flow. Art Carney.

TIME GUARDIAN, THE (1987). Fanciful and exciting sci-fi special-effects extravaganza in the STAR WARS mold (with TERMINATOR overtones) set in 4039, when Earth has been destroyed by cyborg killer robots called Jen-Diki. A domed city commanded by Dean Stockwell travels through time and space to escape the Jen-Diki, and warriors Tom Burlinson and Carrie Fisher are sent back to 1988 to set up a final apocalyptic confrontation with the half-human metal monsters. They are aided in their desert adventures by wandering Nikki Coghill as they also square off against corrupt Australian policemen. The effects are well done, the pacing by director Brian Hannant (who concocted the script with John Baxter) is intense, and the action is plentiful enough to make this Australian production a welcome treat. Tim Robertson. (RCA/Columbia; Orion) (Laser: Nelson)

TIME MACHINE, THE (1960). Stylish George Pal version of the famous H. G. Wells novel, charming in its depiction of 19th Century milieu and moving at a fast clip as Rod Taylor hops into his ingenious apparatus and travels through several centuries. He arrives at a bleak world in the year 802,701 to find mankind's remnants: The rulers are the cannibalistic Morlocks and the Eloi serve as slave labor and food, working in underground caverns. It's continuously exciting and has a poignant message that avoids being preachy. Taylor is excellent and Yvette Mimieux is cuddly as the soft, warm heroine, Weena. The effects by Gene Warren and Wah Chang deservedly won an Academy Award. Pal directed the David Duncan script. Alan Young, Sebastian Cabot, Whit Bissell. (Video/Laser: MGM/UA)

TIME MACHINE, THE (1978). Nothing to do with H. G. Wells' classic, just a cheapjack TV-movie, a pilot for an unsold series. Scientist John Beck saves the world from a runaway missile even before he jumps into his gleaming time bus and races from zone to zone. Dreadful scripting by Wallace Bennett has Beck shooting it out with outlaws in a Western town, facing witchhunters in Salem and sailing into the far future to meet the Eloi. Insulting to the memory of Wells and all self-respecting sci-fi enthusiasts. Director Henning Schallerup should get lost in another time zone. Priscilla Barnes, Rosemary De Camp, Whit Bissell, Jack Kruschen, John Hansen, Andrew Duggan. (VCI)

TIME OF THE APES (1987). Overly juvenile (and overly dumb) Japanese TV-movie in which obnoxious children and a pampering adult are trapped in a PLANET OF THE APES world, where the Commander of the simians (a top banana?) has his monkey minions chasing the interlopers. They manage to survive cliffhanger after cliffhanger, the dubbed voices seldom matching. Strictly for kiddies. Reiko Tokunaga, Hirito Saito. (Creature Features; Celebrity)

TIME OF THE BEAST. See **MUTATOR.**

TIME OF THEIR LIVES, THE (1946). Abbott and Costello comedy is a classic example of the team at its best. Lou is murdered and dumped in a well; the time is 1780 and Lou was on his way to warn George Washington of Benedict Arnold's treachery. Now he and fellow ghost Marjorie Reynolds haunt a tavern in modern times to find a letter disclaiming their guilt. Special effects "Invisible Man"-style. Binne Barnes, Kirk Alyn and Gale Sondergaard enliven this wacky spoof directed by Charles Barton. (MCA)

LOU COSTELLO

TIME OF THE WOLF (1986). Video version of one of the TV episodes starring Jason Connery as Robin Hood. (Playhouse)

TIMERIDER: THE ADVENTURES OF LYLE SWANN (1983). Time-travel hogwash depicting how a Baja 500 race motorcyclist gets lost in the desert and passes through time portals, which scientists are experimenting with at control center. Just a poor rehash of TIME TUNNEL as Fred Ward lands in the 1880s to be surrounded by outlaw leader Peter Coyote and his ornery gang of mavericks, who'd love to trade their hooves for wheels. Ample stunt riding and horse chases, but production values are those of a TV-movie and the script by producer Michael Nesmith and William Dear (the latter also directed) is predictable, including the time paradox "surprise" ending. Belinda Bauer provides interesting love interest—in fact, she's the only intriguing character. Ed Lauter, Richard Masur, L.Q. Jones. (Video/Laser: Pacific Arts)

TIME RUNNER (1992). Traditional literary time paradoxes are at play in this action thriller shot in Vancouver and British Columbia, but ultimately its script (uncredited) is too erratic to be satisfying. The time is 2022 when a civil war on Earth has rebels trying to depose the tyrannical leader Neila (check that spelling backwards, pal). Space jockey Mark Hamill (as Captain Michael Rainier) is caught in a wormhole and sent back to Earth in the year 1992, where he fights the forces of the president-to-be and is present at his own birth. So many elements are undefined and so many sequences devoted to mindless action that this stumbles to an unconvincing conclusion. They try to make Hamill "a new kind of terminator," but it doesn't work, in spite of fluid direction by Michael Mazo and fast-paced editing. Brion James portrays the evil president and Rae Dawn Chong is a scientist of dubious loyalties who helps Hamill. Allen Forget, Gordon Tipple, Marc Bauer, Barry W. Levy. (New Line/Columbia TriStar) (Laser: Image)

TIMESLIP. See **ATOMIC MAN, THE.**

TIMESTALKERS, THE (1986). Rather complicated time-travel fantasy explained in bits and pieces, as if it were a jigsaw puzzle in the mind of writer Brian Clemens. This helps to build mystery and curiosity as modern physicist William Devane, following the death of his wife and son in an auto accident, confronts a woman from 2586 A.D. (Lauren Hutton) and begins tracking a strange gunfighter (Klaus Kinski) who keeps bouncing from the past century to the present one via a crystal device. Elements finally come together under Michael Schultz's direction in this diverting entertainment, even if Kinski's performance seems unnecessarily manic. John Ratzenberger, Forrest Tucker, Tracey Walter. (Fries)

TIME TRACKERS (1989). Time-travel fantasy-comedy produced by Roger Corman, who no doubt used props and costumes left over from his remake of THE MASQUE OF THE RED DEATH. In 2033, an evil scientist working on a "time tunnel" project goes back in time to change history so he can have credit for inventing the device. Eventually the characters end up in 1133 when the Red Duke, a Robin Hood-like hero, is fighting forces of evil in a fairy-tale England. The best feature about this Howard R. Cohen screenplay (he also directed) is the comedy relief provided by Ned Beatty as a modern cop whisked back to days of yore. The cast (Wil Shriner, Kathleen Beller, Bridget Hoffman, Alex Hyde-White, Lee Bergere) romps through this nonsense, but it's time worn. (MGM/UA)

TIME TRAVELERS, THE (1964). German scientist Preston Foster and companions Merry Anders and Phil Carey are projected into the future to find Earth burned to a cinder by atomic war. Man-eating creatures ravage the surface (the lava beds near Barstow, Calif.) but underground is a colony of survivors using robots to build a spaceship for escape to another planet. Watch for Forrest J. Ackerman in a cameo. Directed by Ib Melchoir, who co-wrote with David Hewitt. Later, Hewitt adapted this plot for JOURNEY TO THE CENTER OF TIME. John Hoyt, Carol White, Dennis Patrick. (HBO)

TIME TRAVELERS (1976). Undistinguished TV-movie produced by Irwin Allen in the vein of his old TV series, TIME TUNNEL. An epidemic labeled XB, whose cure remains a mystery, forces doctors Sam Groom and Tom Hallick to travel back to Chicago 1871 to seek out cantankerous doctor Richard Basehart, who might unknowingly hold the cure. But they are also unknowing, having plummeted into the Windy City on the day of the fire started by Mrs. O'Leary's cow. Bad timing, mediocre scripting by Jackson Gillis (borrowing from an idea co-created by Irwin Allen and Rod Serling) and a cast that is never convincing (except for the fiery performance by Basehart) make this a dubious time-killer. Directed by Alex Singer. Trish Stewart, Francine York, Booth Colman, Walter Burke. (Thorn EMI)

TIME TROOPERS (1989). Following nuclear war, society creates a special police force to keep everyone in check. Directed by L. E. Neiman. Albert Fortell, Hannelore Eisner. (Prism)

TIME TUNNEL, THE. In 1983, 20th Century-Fox released to TV five compilations of re-edited episodes of Irwin Allen's 1966-67 series. Each consists of two stories: ALIENS FROM ANOTHER PLANET, KILL OR BE KILLED, OLD LEGENDS NEVER DIE, RAIDERS FROM OUTER SPACE and REVENGE OF THE GODS. The series was set at an underground laboratory (Tic Toc Base) where the U.S. Government is conducting experiments in time travel under General Heyward Kirk (Whit Bissell) and engineer Lee Meriwether. Scientists James Darren and Robert Colbert are trapped in the apparatus and emerge in time zones past, present and future. It wasn't a great series, but then hardly anything Allen produced ranks as classic. Notable for its stock footage from epic Fox films and for stealing music from said epics. It's more fun to identify the scenes and music than to follow the storylines.

TIME WALKER (1982). Sci-fi mummy yarn that gets so wrapped up in unbelievable plot developments, it unravels early in the action—or nonaction, since this is a lethargic, lumbering two-bit movie. When archeologist Ben Murphy breaks into King Tut's tomb, he finds a sarcophagus containing an E.T. under wraps. Back at the California Institute of the Sciences, dumb technician Kevin Brophy exposes the long-dead creature to so much gamma force the alien pops up alive, shambling around in search of five glowing "jewels," which will enable him to communicate with his home planet. "E.T., Phone Home"—get it? The cast shambles around like so many dummy mummies in need of a director. So where was director Tom Kennedy all this time? Nina Axelrod, Austin Stoker, James Karen. (Charter)

TIME WARP (1981). Low-budget adventure in which an astronaut on a voyage to Jupiter is zapped by a time paradox malfunction. Mainly played for comedy. Adam West, Gretchen Corbett, Chip Johnson, Kirk Alyn. Directed by Allan Sandler and Robert Emenegger.

TIME WARP. Video version of **JOURNEY TO THE CENTER OF TIME** (American).

TIME WARP TERROR. See **BLOODY NEW YEAR.**

TINGLER, THE (1959). Gimmicked-up fright flick from producer-director William Castle, with theaters originally wired to give audiences a "tingle" at "shocking" moments. Disregarding that hokum, though, this is fine Castle Macabre enhanced by a tongue-in-cheek flavor. Scientist Vincent Price discovers each of us has a mysterious element brought to life by fear that takes possession of our backbones. Removed from the body, the spine becomes a lobster-like monster attaching itself to the nearest human and sucking away bone marrow. The best sequence in this camp-ish miniclassic is when The Tingler is loose in a movie theater and everyone runs like hell as the thing crawls through the projector aperture. There is a hand coming out of a tub of blood shot in color, which some TV prints show. Robb White dreamed up the nifty idea. Daryl Hickman, Philip Coolidge, Judith Evelyn, Patricia Cutts.

TIN MAN (1983). This attempt at a "feel-good" movie has honorable intentions and is shaped in a manner similar to CHARLEY. Stone-deaf auto mechanic Timothy Bottoms creates a speaking computer named Osgood (nickname: The Wizard of Osgood), falls in love with Deana Jurgens and has his hearing restored by doctor John Phillip Law. When a major corporation markets his computer, he realizes some things are more important than the material. How Bottoms finds happiness remains the bulwark of Bishop Holiday's script, with the sci-fi taking second position and undermined by a low budget. Produced-directed by John G. Thomas. Law, who normally plays misfits, here plays a sympathetic doctor and he's quite good. Troy Donahue also shines as an ambivalent executive. (Prism; Media)

TINTIN AND THE BLUE ORANGES (1965). See editions 1-3.

TINTORERA . . . BLOODY WATERS (1977). Open wide . . . it's a British-Mexican ripoff of JAWS, full of chopped nuts created by director Rene Cardona Jr. Involved in the hunt for the Great White: Susan George, Hugo Stiglitz, Priscilla Barnes, Fiona Lewis, Jennifer Ashley. Wider please . . . we want to get the entire body in the fish's mouth . . . ah good, thank you . . . Chomp! Chew chew! Gulp! AAAAAhhhhhh . . . (Media)

TINTORERA . . . TIGER SHARK. See **TINTORERA . . . BLOODY WATERS.**

TITAN FIND, THE. See **CREATURE.**

TO ALL A GOODNIGHT (1980). Another slap at Santa Claus, depicting graphic murders at the Calvin (Klein?) Finishing School for Girls, performed by a homicidal yuletider in a St. Nick costume. Even the blood is slow-moving as the killer fires crossbow arrows into torsos, plants an axe blade in a forehead, hangs a severed head in a shower stall, shoves a knife into a back, and loops a garroting wire around a soft human throat. Directed by David Hess. Jennifer Runyon, Forrest Swanson, William Lauer, Buck West. (Media)

TOBOR THE GREAT (1954). Clanking sounds do not emanate from the mechanical man of the title, but from the rusty mind of director Lee Sholem and the unoiled typewriters of screenwriters Phillip MacDonald and Dick Goldstone, who must have intended this "clunker" for six-year-olds. But even the young will be bored by the spy antics and performances of Charles Drake, Karin Booth, Lyle Talbot, Robert Shayne, Taylor Holmes and William Schallert, who look as though they wanted to get oiled. Ask yourself: Tobor or not Tobor? Remember, TOBOR is a bore. (Video/Laser: Republic)

TO DIE FOR (1989). Two vampires prey on women in L.A. in this trendy video horror film directed by Dean Sarafian and written by Leslie King. One of those bloodsuckers is Vlad Tepish, the original "Dracula" on whom Bram Stoker based his novel. Brendan Hughes, Scott Jacoby, Duane Jones, Steve Bond, Sydney Walsh. Followed by a sequel. (Academy) (Laser: Image)

TO DIE FOR 2: SON OF DARKNESS (1991). Dr. Max Schreck (the name of the actor who starred in the German classic NOSFERATU) turns up at a hospital at Lake Serenity. In actuality he is Vlad Tepish (the madman whom Bram Stoker patterned DRACULA after) turned immortal and trying to live a cleaner vampire's existence by tapping into the hospital's blood bank instead of puncturing humans. However, his communal vampire friends prefer to kill their supper, causing a rift in the local bloodsucking community. Taught between these forces are a mother and her adopted baby (the child is secretly Vlad's) and a vampire hunter a la Von Helsing. Rather well done by director David F. Price, who brings zing to the Leslie King script. Good cast, too, with Vince Edwards as the disbelieving cop. Rosalind Allen, Steve Bond, Scott Jacoby, Michael Praed, Jay Underwood, Remy O'Neill. (Vidmark)

TO KILL A CLOWN (1972). Blythe Danner and Heath Lamberts portray a young couple renting a beach cottage who fall prey to a crazed Vietnam veteran who unleashes his Dobermans on them. Alan Alda as the demented cripple who has undergone horrors in a POW camp delivers a chilling performance. While the ending is not satisfying, there are moments that ring true. Based on a story by Algis Budrys, "Master of the Hounds." Directed by George Bloomfield. (Media)

TO KILL A STRANGER (1985). When singer Angelica Maria is forced to murder sex maniac Donald Pleasence, does she report it to the cops? Hell no, the guy was a war hero. So she conceals the body. Meanwhile, there's long-suffering husband Dean Stockwell and a cop (Aldo Ray) and a military officer (Mad Magazine cartoonist Sergio Aragones). What the hell is a nice guy like Aragones doing in this flick? Directed by Juan Lopez-Moctezuma. (Virgin Vision; VCL)

TO LOVE A VAMPIRE (1970). In the wake of the success of THE VAMPIRE LOVERS, a blatant amalgam of lesbian love and vampirism, Hammer produced this sequel in the Karnstein series, utilizing characters created by J.S. Le Fanu, although any relationship to the original book was abandoned for commercial shock. A girls' finishing school next door to Karnstein Castle provides the perfect setting for dozens of nubile women exercising in flowing white robes and some exercising lesbian contact with a girl named Mircalla (Yvette Stensgaard). Jimmy Sangster directed Tudor Gates' script without subtlety, which forced U.S. distributors to cut heavily. Ralph Bates, Mike Raven, Pippa Steel, Suzanna Leigh. (From HBO as **LUST FOR A VAMPIRE**)

TOMB, THE (1985). Egyptian snake goddess Nefratis, nothing more than a vampire with fangs, is resurrected from her sarcophagus by young dumb adventurers and materializes in L.A. to recover a magical amulet in the possessesion of archeologist Cameron Mitchell. The acting is really bad, full of modern idiom when it should possess feeling for an ancient culture—blame poor direction on Fred Olen Ray. And the bad dialogue ("I've come to kill you, you mummufied bitch!") on Ken Hall. Sybil Danning and John Carradine have pointless cameos. Michelle Bauer is sexy as the vamp but she needs to take acting lessons. Susan Stokey, David Pearson, Richard Alan Hench. (Trans World)

TOMB OF HORROR. See **TERROR CREATURES FROM THE GRAVE.**

TOMB OF LIGEIA (1965). Edgar Allan Poe's poem, in which the spirit of a dead woman returns through the corpse of her husband's second wife, becomes a Roger Corman film made in England. Many consider this one of Corman's best—Poe lovers, on the other hand, objected to its overuse of the walking corpse and the fact Vincent Price must kill it over and over again. The literacy of the production is attributable in part to screenwriter Robert Towne and Corman's direction. The 1820s of England is well captured in the set design. Elizabeth Shepherd, John Westbrook, Derek Francis. (HBO) (Laser: Image, with **CONQUEROR WORM**)

VINCENT PRICE

TOMB OF THE LIVING DEAD. See **MAD DOCTOR OF BLOOD ISLAND.**

TOMB OF THE UNDEAD (1972). Video version of **GARDEN OF THE DEAD**. (Silver Mine; Increase).

TOMB OF TORTURE (1966). Corny Italian-German chiller about a dumb girl who thinks she is the reincarnation of a dead countess and undergoes traumatic nightmares. Torture only in the sense you have to sit and watch this Italian film badly repackaged for the U.S. market by Richard Gordon. Directed by Antonio Boccaci. Annie Albert plays the beleaguered girl. Thony Maky, William Gray. (Dark Dreams; Modern Sound)

TOMBS OF HORROR. See **CASTLE OF BLOOD.**

TOMBS OF THE BLIND DEAD. First in a series of Spanish-Portuguese films from writer-director Amando De Ossorio. See **BLIND DEAD, THE.** Others: RETURN OF THE EVIL DEAD, HORROR OF THE ZOMBIES, NIGHT OF THE SEAGULLS (aka NIGHT OF THE DEATH CULT). (Paragon)

TOMCAT: DANGEROUS DESIRES (1993). Eccentric mixture of genetic sci-fi and cat-and-mouse horror (excuse the term) with erotic overtones and bedroom nudity that give this video movie an unusual mood. Scientist Maryam D'Abo has found a way to transfer a genetic solution taken from a cat into the brain of Richard Grieco, who is suffering from a genetic deficiency (whatever that is). Grieco emerges with the characteristics of a cat, and a primitive instinct to kill the sexy women he mates with. This is basically a four-character scenario (by director Paul Donovan) that moves as languidly as a black cat through a dark alley and has its best erotic scene when blonde sexbomb Natalie Radford masturbates while having a breathless phone conversation with Grieco. There's a good chase sequence through a lumber mill but this is like a cat at the foot of a deadend alley—it has nowhere to go, and simply ends with a mild meow. Too much mood and erotica and not enough story, but if you dig mood and erotica this is catnip. (Video/Laser: Republic)

TOM CORBETT, SPACE CADET: VOL. I. Six 15-minute episodes of a TV sci-fi adventure series, produced around 1950-51 for live telecast. Crude space opera of interest only to historians and TV nostalgia freaks. The great alien landscape painter Willie Ley is said to have been the show's technical advisor, and it was based on a Robert A. Heinlein novel, SPACE CADET. Frankie Thomas was Tom Corbett, Michael Harvey and Edward Bryce played Captain Strong during different seasons, Jan Merlin was cadet Roger Mannings and Margaret Garland was Dr. Joan Dale. (Nostalgia Merchant; Media)

TOM CORBETT, SPACE CADET: VOL. II. Four 30-minute episodes of the continuing space adventures of Corbett, Roger Manning and Astro, produced in the '50s for live TV. Cast off this blast off unless you're into old-fashioned video nostalgia. (Nostalgia Merchant; Media)

TOMMYKNOCKERS, THE (1993). Excellent four-hour adaptation by Lawrence D. Cohen of Stephen King's sprawling, complex novel about an alien force that crash-landed outside Haven Falls (typical of King's New England territory) centuries earlier and now drains the humanity from the people so the aliens can get back into action. It evolves around drunken poet Jimmy Swits and estranged wife Marg Helgenberger and how they come to grips in first unleashing the extraterrestrial menace and then trying to curtail it. Secondary characters include a lovely sheriff (Joanna Cassidy), a town slut (Traci Lords) and the one man who knows about the legend of the "tommyknockers" (E. G. Marshall). A number of weird plot twists are tossed in (the townspeople are inventing crazy new devices, including a novel-writing machine) before the satisfying climax in the haunted woods involving a buried spaceship and some great looking aliens. Directed by John Power. John Ashton, Allyce Beasley, Robert Carradine, Cliff De Young, Annie Corley, Leon Woods. Also known as STEPHEN KING'S THE TOMMYKNOCKERS.

A TOMMYKNOCKER

TOMMY TRICKER AND THE STAMP TRAVELER (1983). It isn't until the second half of this Canadian children's film that its fantasy elements are introduced. But once young Lucas Evans learns the secret of reducing himself onto a postage stamp, and sets out on a series of adventures, writer-director Michael Rubbo finally comes to life. Evans' episodic trek takes him to China and Australia. This modest effort features a pleasant cast: Anthony Rogers, Jill Stanley, Andrew Whitehead, Chen Yuan Tao, Catherine Wright and Paul Popowich. (Family Home Entertainment)

TOMORROW MAN, THE. See **NINE EIGHT SIX—PRISONER OF THE FUTURE.**

TOM THUMB (1958). Delightful George Pal fantasy-musical, based on the fairy tale by the Brothers Grimm, about a woodsman, Honest John, who wishes for a child the size of his thumb—and literally gets it in the form of happy-go-lucky Russ Tamblyn, a trampoline star who bounces bubbly in the role. Enchanting, nonsensical mixture of live-action choreography, animation in the old Puppetoon style Pal introduced in the '40s; and music and songs with a touch of sparkling magic. Terry-Thomas and Peter Sellers are wonderfully corny as the villains in the Black Swamp who misuse the minuscule Thumb to rob the King's Treasury. The plot (by director Ladislas Foder) is slight—it's Pal's ability to capture a cinematic lightheartedness that works. Alan Young, Jessie Mathews, June Thorburn. (MGM/UA) (Laser: MGM/UA; Turner)

TOM THUMB (1958). Spanish version of the Grimm fairy tale, directed by Rene Cardona. Maria Elena Marques, Cesare Quezadas. Narrated by Paul Tripp.

TOM THUMB AND LITTLE RED RIDING HOOD VS. THE MONSTERS. See **LITTLE RED RIDING HOOD AND THE MONSTERS.**

TONIGHT'S THE NIGHT (1954). See editions 1-3.

TOOLBOX MURDERS, THE (1977). Disgusting but imaginative use of power drill, nail gun, hammer and other electrically powered hand tools provides modus operandi for a fiendish killer, played with cackling relish by Cameron Mitchell. He's the manager of an apartment and by night he dons a mask to lay waste to the women he hates because of a mother complex. Strong stomachs required. Directed by Dennis Pamelyn Ferdin, Anita Corsaut, Wesley Eure. (United; Video Treasures)

TOOMORROW (1970). See editions 1-3.

TOO MUCH (1987). Cutesy-pie children's fantasy (and it's strictly for children) about a Caucasian girl (Bridgette Andersen) living in Japan who is teamed with an experimental robot named R-1 or "Ke-Em"—a Japanese-made prototype that resembles R2-D2 from STAR WARS and does cuddly stuff. Meanwhile, evil scientist Dr. Finkle and his fat Asian henchmen are out to steal the creation, but not before the girl and robot run away. It's a short-circuited SHORT CIRCUIT; in short, TOO MUCH is not enough. This is the kind of film that spelled doom for producers Golan & Globus, and surely impaired the career of writer-director Eric Rochat. Masato Fukazama, Hiroyuki Watanabe, Char Fontana.

TOO SCARED TO SCREAM (1983). PSYCHO lives when a knife-wielding murderer attacks victims in a Manhattan apartment building. Obvious suspect is the doorman (Ian MacShane), a repressed ex-actor who spouts Shakespeare and lives with his invalid mother (played catatonically by Maureen O'Sullivan). Mother? Did we say Mother? Hmmmm . . . Cops Mike Connors and Anne Archer meet suspects and sex perverts as director Tony Lo Bianco builds suspense with smelly red herrings. Aka THE DOORMAN. Leon Isaac Kennedy, Ruth Ford, John Heard, Murray Hamilton. (Vestron)

TOPPER (1937). Classically funny Hal Roach adaptation of the Thorne Smith comedy novel. Constance Bennett and Cary Grant portray a rich couple killed in an accident, but fate decrees they remain on Earth until achieving a good deed. So they straighten out the affairs of henpecked Cosmo Topper (Roland Young) and nagging wife Billie Burke. Delightfully madcap, jammed with visual tricks, utterly refreshing. This led to two sequels (TOPPER TAKES A TRIP and TOPPER RETURNS) and in the '50s became a long-running TV series with Leo G. Carroll, Anne Jeffreys and Robert Sterling. (Media; Nostalgia Merchant; Video Yesteryear; Video Treasures offers a colorized version)

TOPPER (1980). Updated TV version of the classic Thorne Smith supernatural comedy, designed as a vehicle for hubby-wife team Kate Jackson and Andrew Stevens. But it's a slow, laborious affair compared to its inspiration, having none of the madcap charm of the '30s. Totally tepid . . . a bottomer. Directed by Charles Dubin. Jack Warden, Rue McClanahan, James Karen.

TOPPER RETURNS (1941). Second Hal Roach sequel to TOPPER is more rollicking high jinks in the Thorne Smith tradition with Roland Young as the sophisticate who solves an "old dark house" murder with the aid of ghost Joan Blondell. The great supporting cast includes Carole Landis, Billie Burke (as Topper's goofy spouse), Dennis O'Keefe, Patsy Kelly and Eddie "Rochester" Anderson. Directed by Roy Del Ruth. (Video Yesteryear; Kartes; United; Video Classics)

TOPPER TAKES A TRIP (1939). The first TOPPER sequel, again with Constance Bennet as the svelte Marion Kerby, a ghost who pops in and out of sight while trying to keep Cosmo (Roland Young) from divorcing pea-brained Mrs. Topper (Billie Burke) during their holiday in Europe. Stuffy characters (such as Alan Mowbray's butler) are an added treat, and Hal Roach's special effects department has objects moving mysteriously as the female ghost performs mischievous deeds. Directed by Norman Z. McLeod. Irving Pichel, Alex D'Arcy, Franklin Pangborn. (Video Treasures; Media)

TORMENT (1986). Made in San Francisco by writers-directors Samson Aslanian and John Hopkins, this psychothriller puts aside the whodunit aspects of the genre to emphasize suspense and surprises without concern for subtlety. A young woman engaged to a hard-working cop working on the case goes to stay with his neurotic mother, only to have the killer show up on the doorstep. The contrived story holds one's interest because of its twists and turns, the aberrant nature of the killer and the questionable behavior of the overwrought mother. Tension and hysteria make the story work. Taylor Gilbert, William Witt, Eve Brenner. (New World)

TORMENTED (1960). Bert I. Gordon-Joe Steinberg production—which means it's schlock time on the old tube tonight. Nice Richard Carlson turns out to be not so nice after pushing his wife (Juli Reding) off a lighthouse platform. The woman's corpse materializes to haunt him. Instead of acting rational, he goes off the deep end to provide this film with a surprise ending. Bert I. Gordon directed the George Worthing Yates script. Susan Gordon, Gene Roth, Joe Turkel, Lillian Adams, Eugene Sanders. (Sinister/C; S/Weird; Filmfax)

TORMENTED. See **EERIE MIDNIGHT HORROR SHOW, THE.**

TORPEDO OF DOOM (1938). Feature version of the Republic serial **FIGHTING DEVIL DOGS.**

TORSO (1973). Italian gore galore murders with touches of sleazy lightcore pornography dominate this crude, rude sick flick. Suzy Kendall and a bevy of glamour models are on the fringes of a series of hacksaw murders committed by a madman in a hood who strangles his female victims and then fondles their nude bodies with bloody hands. This unsettling "entertainment" climaxes when Kendall (one leg in a cast) is trapped in a villa with the killer as he saws up Suzy's beautiful friends. Moreso TORSO? Less-so messo. Directed by Sergio Martino. John Richardson, Tina Aumont, Luc Meranda. (Prism; MPI)

TORTURE CHAMBER, THE. Video version of **FEAR CHAMBER, THE** (MPI).

TORTURE CHAMBER OF BARON BLOOD. Video version of **BARON BLOOD** (Thorn EMI).

TORTURE CHAMBER OF DR. SADISM (1969). Alternate video version of **CASTLE OF THE WALKING DEAD** (Magnum; Regal).

TORTURE DUNGEON (1969). Andy Milligan, purveyor of blood and guts in living color, wishes to entertain you (with the help of co-writer John Borske) with mutilations, dissections, savage beatings and all-around bloodletting as seen from the eyes of the Duke of Norwich. Wallow in the sanguinary joy of it all (along with Jeremy Brooks and Susan Cassidy) as that medieval nobleman knocks off anyone in line for the throne he covets down in the old dank dungeon. (Midnight)

TORTURE GARDEN (1967). Above-average horror anthology, skillfully written by Robert Bloch (he adapted four of his short stories), and imaginatively directed by Freddie Francis. At a British carnival sideshow, barker Dr. Diablo (Burgess Meredith) offers "special terrors" to his visitors—glimpses into their unpleasant futures. Hence, the Bloch Busters: "Enoch" is the Weird Tales classic about a demon cat who eats the heads of its victims; "Terror Over Hollywood" shows why all our favorite movie stars are so beautiful; "Mr. Steinway" is the bizarre look at a haunted piano; and "The Man Who Collected Poe" (the best of the lot) stars Jack Palance as a sorcerer who brings Poe back from the dead much to the shock of Poe collector Peter Cushing. And then, of course, there's the surprise ending with Dr. Diablo. Beverly Adams, Michael Bryant, Maurice Denham, Robert Hutton. (Video/Laser: RCA/Columbia)

TORTURE ROOM, THE. See **TORTURE CHAMBER OF DR. SADISM, THE**.

TORTURE SHIP (1939). Avoid passage aboard this floating carrier of tedium, bound for the port of boredom with ennui just off starboard. Although based on a Jack London story, "A Thousand Deaths," this Victor Halperin-directed film (he of WHITE ZOMBIE) is pure flotsam depicting crazy doc Irving Pichel experimenting with the glands of criminals aboard his floating lab of horror. Lyle Talbot, Sheila Bromley. (Loonic; Nostalgia)

TO SAVE A CHILD (1991). Failed TV-movie pilot for a series, derivative of the ROSEMARY'S BABY genre in which Marita Geraghty, pregnant with child, winds up in a New Mexico community with her doctor-husband. But from the beginning it's apparent the town is evil, and her prenatal paranoia suspicions build quickly. This kind of withcraft-Devil cult tale has been told so many times before, it's totally obvious what's going down, and instead of throwing us surprise zingers, scripter Joyce Eliason simply fulfills our non-expectations. Director Robert Lieberman is stuck with a bad concept, but he pulls good performances from Geraghty, hubby Peter Kowanko, Joseph Runningfox (as the strange Indian Toby Coldcreek), Shirley Knight and Spalding Gray. Especially excellent is Anthony Zerbe, who oozes evil. Also shown on TV as THE CRAFT.

TO SLEEP WITH A VAMPIRE (1992). That old saw about the cheapest way to make a movie—put two actors into a single room and let them talk to each other for 90 minutes—is put to practical use by producer Roger Corman in this remake of DANCE OF THE DAMNED, right down to the dialogue. The two characters are a night club stripper with suicidal tendencies (Charlie Spradling) and a lonely nocturnal wanderer-vampire (Scott Valentine) with the soul of a poet. He locks her up for a night to learn what the daytime is like and they exchange morbid dialogues about the meaning of life and other vital issues for strippers and vampires. The title of this one-note sleep inducer is all too prophetic, its only lively moments depicting big-breasted women stripping. After that, you need No-Doze tablets. Directed by Adam Friedman from a rewrite by Patricia Harrington. Richard Zobel, Ingrid Vold. (New Horizons)

SHARON STONE

TOTAL RECALL (1990). An exciting, breathless sci-fi/action movie, capturing the pure essence of what movies are about, with director Paul Verhoeven knocking down the walls of film violence to incorporate his own dark vision of how terrible the human species can be to itself. It's Arnold Schwarzenegger's best acting job as a worker in the year 2084 who discovers his quiet, boring life is cover for a previous identity as a spy—none of which he remembers. His search for an understanding of himself and the treacherous events that suddenly endanger his life lead to a mining colony on Mars and a string of fascinating characters and situations. The pacing of the script (by Ronald Shusett, Dan O'Bannon and Jon Povill, based on a Philip K. Dick short story, "We Can Remember It for You Wholesale") never lets up and there are exciting twists that move the story to a new level of action, and give it an epic quality, as life on Mars is in jeopardy. The story has the bizarre flavor of the STAR WARS series, though without sympathetic characters. It's a satisfying experience with good-to-excellent effects and make-up (by Rob Bottin). The cast serves the material well: Rachel Ticotin as the mysterious romantic lead; Sharon Stone as the "loving" wife; Michael Ironside as the insidious heavy; Ronny Cox as the conspiracy master. (Live) (Laser: Image)

ROBERT BLOCH CALMS HIS SHATTERED NERVES

TO THE DEVIL . . . A DAUGHTER (1976). Satanist Christopher Lee is out to transform a young child into a devil goddess in this Hammer film based on a Dennis Wheatley novel (Chris Wicking did the adaptation) and directed with a strong sense of evil by Peter Sykes. Richard Widmark (acting with unusual intensity) portrays an occult writer who tries to stop Lee with the help of a book, THE GRIMOIRE OF ASTAROTH. The 16-year-old is Nastassia Kinski, daughter of Klaus Kinski. Sykes zooms all over the gloomy landscapes and the final results are pretty good if somewhat muddled. Honor Blackman, Denholm Elliott. (New Star; Continental; CinemaGroup; Republic; from Olympus as **CHILD OF SATAN**)

TO TRAP A SPY (1966). The very first MAN FROM U.N.C.L.E. TV pilot, re-edited to feature length. Robert Vaughn and David McCallum are undercover agents fighting a crime syndicate cashing in on the misery of an African nation. Don Medford directed producer Sam Rolfe's script. William Marshall, Fritz Weaver, Patricia Crowley, Luciana Paluzzi, Leo G. Carroll.

TOUCH OF MELISSA, THE. See **TOUCH OF SATAN, THE.**

TOUCH OF SATAN, THE (1973). Dull, tedious romance between a friendly wanderer and a witch living on a farm on the road to San Francisco, spiced up only by a pitchfork poking and a hayhook homicide. Oh, there's an ugly witch hanging around the house, but mostly director Don Henderson focuses on the boring couple. The pace is so slow you can fast-forward your VCR through this and miss nothing. Robert Easton, a tall, gangling actor who plays hayseeders and teaches voice elocution/dialects in real life, appears as a mob leader. He must have been brought in to help with the New England accents. Emby Mellay, Lee Amber. Aka THE TOUCH OF MELISSA. (King of Video)

TOURIST TRAP (1979). Low-budget exploitation chiller borrows from PSYCHO, CARRIE and HALLOWEEN, and comes off powerfully with its cat-and-mouse terror, thanks to the imaginative direction of David Schmoeller. Four likable young travelers are lured to a deserted roadside wax museum owned by reclusive Chuck Connors. Stealing the show are numerous mannikins (with gaping, screaming mouths) and masks that litter a madman's torture chamber. The film sinks deeper and deeper into nightmare allegory until reality is nonexistent, and one needn't bother to sort out any logic. Jocelyn Jones, Keith McDermott, Dawn Jeffory, Robin Sherwood, Tanya Roberts. (Media; Paramount)

TOWER, THE (1983). Above-average Canadian TV-movie, inspired by Hal 2000, the rampaging computer in 2001: A SPACE ODYSSEY. This is set in the Sandawn Building, a monument in Ontario to computerized technology. Lola, the system that runs the building, becomes obsessed with "heat units" which "she" feels she needs to keep power, unaware these "heat units" are people. One night she dematerializes office workers one by one. Among the characters are two intelligent office employees, an immature security guard, a guy with a gun, a girl in a bikini, and the boss' wife, who knows her husband is messing around with a secretary. A subplot outside the building involves the computer designer meeting a prostitute in a bar, but he's barely integrated into the story. Written-directed by James Makichuk. George West, Jackie Wray, Ray Paisley. (AVEC)

TOWER, THE (1992). A highrise office building owned by Intercorp. and controlled by a computerized system called Cybernetics Access Structure (CAS), becomes a nightmare for Paul Reiser and Susan Morman, employees trapped overnight when the system has a breakdown and flips into a "terminate intruders" mode. The cliffhangers are good, and the suspense builds steadily under the direction of Richard Kletter (who cowrote this Gregory Harrison-produced TV-movie with John Riley) but where things go awry is in the dumb love affair that dominates when the couple should be fighting for their lives. Still, it has its scary moments and is a decent time-killer. Richard Gant, Annabelle Gurwith, Roger Rees.

TOWER OF EVIL (1974). Snape Island houses a lighthouse and a cache of ancient Phoenician treasures; it is also the romping ground for a murderer who severs hands and heads from corpses and leaves the remains for visitors (including Jill Haworth and Bryant Halliday) to stumble across. Graphic shocker has plenty of bare flesh and sexual activity in addition to its horrors to hold interest—and that's during the film's quieter moments. From British producer Richard Gordon; written-directed by Jim O'Connolly. Dennis Price, George Coulouris, Anna Palk, Jack Watson. Aka HORROR ON SNAPE ISLAND and BEYOND THE FOG. (Gorgon; VCI; Orion; MPI)

TOWER OF LONDON (1939). Boris Karloff's performance as Mord, executioner of the Duke of Gloucester (Richard III), alone warrants a viewing of this study in homicidal royalty. Bodies are strewn in the dungeons and dining halls of 15th Century London as the Duke and Mord knock off those standing in their way—including Vincent Price, who is drowned in a vat of wine, and two young children who are strangled. This is Merrie Olde England? Basil Rathbone is chilling as the power-hungry duke, and Karloff unforgettable when he pleads to fight in the battle of Tewksbury because "I've never killed in hot blood before." Literate script by Robert N. Lee; directed by Rowland V. Lee. (MCA)

TOWER OF LONDON (1962). You thought the '39 Basil Rathbone version was grotesque and bloody? It seems a children's fable compared to this Roger Corman adaptation with Vincent Price as Richard III, a hunchback cripple whose withered arm and twisted leg match his mind—a mind haunted by guilt as he schemes and murders for power to the British throne. Torture and death nonstop . . . the squeamish should beware. Mord is played by Michael Pate. Corman directed, his brother Gene produced, and the script was fashioned by Leo V. Gordon, F. Amos Powell and James B. Gordon. Joan Freeman, Sandra Knight, Bruce Gordon. (Wood Knapp)

TOWER OF SCREAMING VIRGINS (1971). European-made period thriller is more of a swashbuckler in the tradition of Alexandre Dumas than a horror film, although it fulfills the latter category by depicting bloody murders in the Tower of Sin, where the Queen of France and other sexpots hold orgies, concluding them by having brigands slaughter young noblemen the wanton women have lured into their chambers. The action and period production qualities are good and the film satisfies best on an action level. Plenty of nudity and erotic love-making sequences. And this deserves one laugh when a lady in waiting is named Blanche DuBois. Directed by Francois Legrand. Terry Torday, Jean Piet, Veronique Vendell, Armando Francioli. (Video Yesteryear; Video Dimensions; Filmfax)

TOWER OF TERROR (1941). Insane lighthouse keeper creates horror for those around him; eerie setting; slow British pace. Wilfred Lawson, Michael Rennie, Movita, Morland Graham. Directed by Lawrence Huntington. (Sinister/C; Filmfax)

TOWER OF TERROR. See **ASSAULT.**

TOWN THAT DREADED SUNDOWN, THE (1977). In March, 1946, in Texarkana, a schizoid killer wearing a hood began a reign of terror that to this day remains unsolved. Writer-director Charles B. Pierce brings pseudorealism to this true crime drama, but then spoils it with dumb comedy relief involving a maladroit deputy. Ben Johnson and Andrew Prine stand out as toughened lawmen in hot pursuit. The murders are unnerving as the Phantom strikes without mercy. Features elements that foreshadow the slasher films. Ben Johnson, Andrew Prine, Dawn Wells. (Warner Bros.)

TOXIC AVENGER, THE (1984). Flaky farce on monster movies, a scattergun of visual gags with some pellets on target and others missing by miles. It's funky and ugly and gory and cruddy and yet takes on a crude charm. Played for parody, TOXIC AVENGER is set in Tromaville, a center for toxic waste, where nerdish 90-pound janitor Melvin falls into a barrel of atomic poison and emerges a mutated crusader who fights crime, his symbol a wet mop shoved into the face of an unconscious foe. Satirical vignettes ensue, depicting brutish fights and a romance between the dippy crime-fighter and a well-developed (her body, that is) blind girl. Amidst this hodgepodge are raunchy sex jokes and bouncing bare breasts. Produced-directed by Samuel Weis and Michael Hertz. Mitchell Cohen, Andree Maranda, Jennifer Babtist. (Vestron; Live; Lightning) (Laser: Vestron)

TOXIC AVENGER PART II, THE (1989). If you can set your brain control on Zero, and get into the spirit of slapdash fun, you might have an amusing time watching this sequel to Troma's '84 hit. That original was fresh and funny, while this is just madcap mayhem. The bad guys from Apocalypse Inc. are out to take over Tromaville with only the Avenger to stop them—and that's all the plot you'll find. Directors Michael Herz and Lloyd Kaufman (that traumatized Troma team) exercise no control over the barrage of lowbrow sight gags, but at least there's Tokyo location footage (where the Avenger heads to find his missing father). Ron Fazio and John Altamura double as the Avenger, Phoebe Legere reprises her role as Claire, the sexy blind girl, Rick Collins plays the heavy. (Video/Laser: Warner Bros.)

TOXIC AVENGER

TOXIC AVENGER PART III: THE LAST TEMPTATION OF TOXIE, THE (1989). Toxie turns into a Wall Street tycoon in this third entry in the wild and woolly Troma series that goes for the lowest common denominator in screen excitement—in short, it's totally stupid. But there are moments of fun if you can accept the inanities of producer-director Lloyd Kaufman and writers Kaufman and Gay Partington Terry. Ron Fazio, John Altamura, Phoebe Legere, Rick Collins, Lisa Gaye and Jessica Dublin head the whacky cast. (Vestron)

TOXIC HORROR. See **TOXIC MONSTER, THE.**

TOXIC MONSTER, THE (1979). The producers would have us believe this is based on a true story that occurred in Colombia in 1971. Better they should try to sell us a certain bridge in Brooklyn. Subtitled THE LEGEND THAT BECAME A MONSTER, it's another variation on JAWS and the Loch Ness Monster when a small village in Colombia (where this was filmed) is plagued by a series of killings, the victims being chewed up on jagged teeth. A cement plant in the village has been polluting the waters of a nearby lake, and swimming in the toxic waters is a giant amphibious beast. Company troubleshooter Jim Mitchum is dispatched by cynical American boss Phil Carey to investigate. Also on hand is scientist Anthony Eisley and priest John Carradine, who delivers fire-and-brimstone messages about "the dark angel from the depths." This wouldn't be so bad if the monster was half believable. They didn't even try. Produced-directed by Kenneth Hartford. Aka MONSTEROID. (In video from Premiere/Academy as **TOXIC HORROR, THE.**

TOXIC SPAWN. Video version of **ALIEN CONTAMINATION** (Lettuce Entertain You).

TOXIC ZOMBIES (1984). Poor man's imitation of NIGHT OF THE LIVING DEAD, aka BLOODEATERS, in which hippie marijuana growers are sprayed by a herbicide, Dromax, which gives them hollow eyes and bloodlust. Type-0 flows and the gore spurts as the shamblers mindlessly attack picnickers and fishermen. A federal agent enters the area to investigate, discovering a government conspiracy that ordered the spraying. Writer-producer-director Charles McCrann offers little subtext or substance beyond the bloodletting, so this is your basic exercise in exploitation futility. Charles Austin, Beverly Shapiro. (Raedon; Monterey)

TOY BOX, THE (1971). Plaything from schlock exploitation producer Harry Novak has monsters from space turning up on Earth and stimulating humans sexually so they can eat their brains. Written-directed by Ron Garcia. Evan Steele, Ann Myers, Lisa Goodman, Deborah Osborne, T. E. Brown. (S/Weird)

TOY FACTORY. TV title for **NECROMANCY.**

TRACK OF THE MOONBEAST (1976). An Indian talks about the legend of an Incredible Lizard God, then an asteroid shower falls on New Mexico, a fragment lodging in a man's brain as he watches with his HotPants-wearing girlfriend. Yeah, you guessed it—the guy turns into a rubber-suited monster with a bad case of acne. Murder, mayhem and shots of the pretty girl's bare legs follow. Poor in every way; low-budget director Dick Ashe was not helped by Joe Blasco's make-up or phony suit. Chase Cordell, Donna Leigh Drake. (Prism)

TRACK OF THE VAMPIRE. Video version of **BLOOD BATH (1966)** (Sinister/C; S/Weird; Genesis).

TRACKS (1976) Avant garde writer-director Henry Jaglom (A SAFE PLACE) comments on the loss of the American Dream by depicting Vietnam veteran Dennis Hopper accompanying the corpse of a combat buddy to his burial place. The entire film is set aboard a train and zeroes in on the hallucinations and fantasies of Hopper, for the war has destroyed his beliefs. This had little dramatic impact on audiences, but Jaglom's good intentions are boundless. Taryn Power, Dean Stockwell, Topo Swope, Zack Norman. (Monterey; Paramount)

TRANCERS (1984). Muddled cross between BLADE RUNNER and THE TERMINATOR, set in the 23rd Century when half of L.A. is underwater, and a war rages between police and zombie-like "Trancers." These human killers are trained by Whistler (Michael Stefani), whose adversary is hard-boiled "Angel City Trooper" Jack Deth (Tim Thomerson). Whistler has gone into the past to eliminate the relatives of a special peace council so the council will no longer exist. Deth follows him to modern-day L.A. where he uses a time-stopping wrist-watch to save the heroine. A mess of a storyline by director-producer Charles Band, who nevertheless made several sequels. Also known as FUTURE COP. Helen Hunt, Anne Seymour, Richard Herd, Richard Erdman. (Video/Laser: Vestron)

TRANCERS II: THE RETURN OF JACK DETH (1990). An unnecessarily convoluted and hard-to-follow plot showcases the return of future cop Jack Deth (Tim Thomerson), living in present-day "Old California" with new wife Lena (Helen Hunt) after traveling through time. His old wife Alice (Megan Ward) turns up in his time zone on a mission to nail the evil E.D. Wardo (Richard Lynch), an ancestor of the original film's chief villian, the Whistler. (So where's Whistler's Mother through all this?) Wardo runs Green World Mission, turning out "trancer" zombies with Scurb, a drug from 2078 that gives him power over his subjects. Screenwriter Jackson Barr (working from an idea by producer-director Charles Band) tries to make this hodgepodge of time-travel cliches meaningful by giving Deth two romances but there's little that's fresh or interesting if you've already seen BACK TO THE FUTURE. Biff Manard, Martine Beswicke, Jeffrey Combs, Alyson Croft, Barbara Crampton. (Paramount) (Laser: Full Moon)

TRANCERS III: DETH LIVES (1992). "This is the best thing that's happened to me in two centuries!" exclaims Trancer hunter/private eye Jack Deth in this, the third in this series, in which he is taken from 1992 (where he was trapped in Part II) to 2352 and back to 2005 to prevent the origins of the Trancer research. This is by far the least interesting of the TRANCER movies, showing none of the imagination and wildness that earmarked Part II, for example. Produced by Charles and Albert Band, it was written and directed by C. Courtney Joyner and stars Tim Thomerson (his Deth wisecracks are wearisome), Melanie Smith, Andrew Robinson, Tony Pierce, Dawn Ann Billings, Helen Hunt, Megan Ward, Stephen Macht. (Paramount) (Laser: Full Moon)

TRANCERS 4: JACK OF SWORDS (1993). In his time-hopping adventures, Jack Deth (Tim Thomerson) is in a parallel universe in the medieval kingdom of Orpheus, where a gang of Trancers called Nobles preys on humans by sucking out their energy. Call it JACK DETH MEETS ROBIN HOOD when the wise-cracking, trenchcoated Deth joins rebels (nicknamed "tunnel rats") to fight the evil ruler (Clabe Hartley) of the Nobles, and the arrows start to fly. Producer Charles Band brings production value to this Full Moon fantasy-adventure made in Romania. For the first time in the series, Deth doesn't deal with any of his wives. Lucky break for him. Written by Peter David, directed by David Nutter. Lochlyn Munro, Jeff Moldovan, Ty Miller, Stacie Randall, Terri Ivens, Mark Arnold, Steven Macht. (Paramount) (Laser: Full Moon)

TRANS-ATLANTIC TUNNEL (1935). In the vein of THINGS TO COME, a pseudorealistic prophecy film with Curt Siodmak helping in the adaptation. The time is the '40s as a crew, under engineer-designer Richard Dix, gives their blood, sweat and tears to dig a tunnel under the Atlantic with a 50-foot radium drill. Interesting for its predominance of advanced technology. Walter Huston appears as the President, George Arliss is the Prime Minister officiating over tunnel-opening ceremonies, and Madge Evans is Dix's long-suffering wife. Directed by Maurice Elvery. Leslie Banks, Helen Vinson, C. Aubrey Smith. Aka THE TUNNEL. (Budget; Moore Video; Filmfax; Grapevine; Sinister/C)

TRANSFORMATIONS (1989). Oddball mixture of supernatural horror and hardware sci-fi when space-cargo pilot Wolf Shadduck (Rex Smith) is taken over by an evil, sexy incubus demon in a dream fantasy. Landing on a mining planet-penal colony complex, Wolf learns from doctor Lisa Langlois that he's carrying a plague—an opinion reinforced by sympathetic priest Patrick Macnee. This bizarre sci-fier takes a twist when its hero begins killing prostitutes—the demom within him taking over. Scriptwriter Mitch Brian's hodgepodge of ideas isn't reinforced by the sparse production and minimal effects in this New World production made at Empire Studio in Rome under the direction of Jay Kamen. Ultimately it doesn't have the budget or the ambience to make its intermixed themes effective. Christopher Neame, Michael Hennessey. (Starmaker) (Laser: Image)

TRANSFORMERS: THE MOVIE (1986). Feature version of the TV cartoon series in which the fighting robots save the Universe from a planet called Unicron and an army of baddies led by Megatron. The only distinguishing value is the film's voices: Orson Welles, Robert Stack, Leonard Nimoy, Eric Idle, Judd Nelson, Lionel Stander. Otherwise, it's Saturday morning all over again. (Avid; Family Home Entertainment)

TRANSFORMERS, THE: VOL. 1-7 (1984-85). Animated series available in video, depicting the autobots in their never-ending fight against forces of evil. Moppets only. (Family Home Entertainment)

TRANSIT. See **FIRST POWER, THE.**

TRANSMUTATIONS (1985). Clive Barker, who co-wrote this British low budgeter with James Caplin, has disavowed the result, but it's a rather offbeat horror film about unsavory Dr. Savary and his drug Thakanicene, a liquid that gives users hallucogenic euphoria. But the side effects are disfigurement of face and body; the mad doctor (played with wonderful abandonment by Denholm Elliott) is creating an army of zombie-like addicts. This physically marred band kidnaps beautiful prostitute Miranda Richardson, bringing in an underworld gang led by Motherskille (Steven Berkoff) and an old boyfriend hired to track down the femme, who has a fatal attraction for all. They are as addicted to her as the poor saps are to the doc's drug—a fascinating parallel to this odd tale, which ends on a metaphysical twist. Director George Pavlou keeps the unpredictable plot moving briskly. Ingrid Pitt appears as Pepperdine, the whorehouse madam. Larry Lamb, Art Malik. Aka UNDERWORLD. (Vestron) (Laser: Image)

TRANSYLVANIA 6-5100 (1985). Nutty newsmen Ed Begley Jr. and Jeff Goldblum are assigned to find Frankenstein in Transylvania by the editor of a sleazoid tabloid. What they dig up in a backlot Rumanian village are would-be monsters created by the quite insane Dr. Malavaqua (Joseph Bologna) and assistants Lupi (Carol Kane) and Radu (John Byner), who pose as domestic help. There's a hunchback, vampire, Frankenstein hulker, mummy . . . but you'll be depressed to find out what they really are. Script by director Rudy DeLuca. Jeffrey Jones, Geena Davis, Michael Richards, Norman Fell. (New World) (Laser: Image)

TRANSYLVANIA TWIST (1989). A witless series of verbal/visual puns, non sequiturs and movie-fan in-jokes as director Jim Wynorski (onetime Roger Corman neophyte) and writer R. J. Robertson spoof vampire and Frankenstein movies. Nerdish Dexter Ward (Steve Altman) and sexy Teri Copley of Arkham, Mass., are searching for the "Book of Ulthar," a Lovecraft-inspired volume that could release an "elder god" from captivity. Robert Vaughn guest stars as Byron Orlock, vampire, and he's down for the count. Others in gag roles: Angus Scrimm, parodying his PHANTASM character; Steve Franken as a Bavarian constable; Ace Mask; Howard Morris, Jay Robinson, etc. The best sequence in this mess produced by Corman is a musical number, "Give Me Some Action," in which Wynorski reruns every explosion ever used in a Corman film. (MGM/UA)

TRAPPED (1989). Cliched TV-movie, lacking in originality, depicts the plight of Kathleen Quinlan trapped in a new office building with a slasher killer armed with a knife and a baseball bat who's seeking revenge against TNX Industries, a company responsible for dumping toxic waste. Every cat-and-mouse trick is pulled out by writers Fred Walton (he also directed) and Steve Feke as the lovely Quinlan, in a short tight skirt and high heels, dangles from ledges, leaps in and out of elevators, and uses her female wits to stay one leap ahead of the murderer. A surprise ending is thrown in for good measure. Bruce Abbott, Katy Boyer. (MCA)

TRAPPED BY TELEVISION (1936). See editions 1-3.

TRAP THEM AND KILL THEM (1977). Disgusting Italian gore flick of the cannibal school, a travesty on good taste directed by Joe D'Amato (aka Aristide Massacessi), who cooked up this mess with writer Romano Scandariato. D'Amato mixes the lip-smacking sequences with soft-core pornie stuff as an expedition ventures to the Amazon only to be, in most cases, eaten alive. Yummy yummy. Laura Gemser, Gabriele Tinti, Susan Scott, Donald O'Brien, Percy Hogan. (Trans World)

TRAS EL CRISTAL. See **IN A GLASS CAGE.**

TRAUMA (1962). Sweet young Lorrie Richards witnesses the brutal murder of her socialite aunt and lapses into amnesia to escape reality. Supposedly cured, she returns to the lonely mansion to uncover the mystery of her lost years, aided by architect John Conte. Directed-written by Robert Malcolm Young. Lynn Bari portrays the murdered aunt. (Wizard; Vestron)

TRAUMA (1975). See **HOUSE ON STRAW HILL.**

TRAUMA. See **TERMINAL CHOICE.** (Melo-trauma?)

TRAUMA (19??). A private girls' school is located close to a village where murders are occurring and where rich men's fantasies are catered to by the populace. Written-directed by Albert Negrin. Fabio Testi. (From Lettuce Entertain You as **VIRGIN TERROR**)

TREACHERY AND GREED ON THE PLANET OF THE APES (1974). Recycled TV episodes of the short-lived series that tried to recapture the glory of THE PLANET OF THE APES movies but failed. Shoddy sets and effects spell doom for Roddy McDowall, William Smith, John Hoyt, Zina Bethune, Victor Killian. Directed by Don McDougall and Bernard McEveety.

TREASURE OF THE FOUR CROWNS (1983). Writers-producers Tony Anthony and Gene Quintano, who gave the world COMIN' AT YA! in 3-D, blend elements of MISSION: IMPOSSIBLE and RAIDERS OF THE LOST ARK to depict adventurers stealing valuable crystals from a cult of religious nuts. These crystals have magical and atomic powers of "good or evil," depending on who owns them. The main concern is the 3-D; some effects are good, but logic is discarded for cheap thrills. The caper provides suspense, but otherwise it's condescending. Directed by Ferdinando Baldi in Spain. Anthony and Quintano portray adventurers. Ana Obregon, Francisco Rabal, Kate Levan. (MGM/UA)

TREASURE OF THE MOON GODDESS (1987). Mildly entertaining adventure-fantasy in the Indiana Jones tradition, but without the pizzazz. Rich guy Don Calfa and bikini-clad "secretary" are at poolside while he recites the adventure, which is shown in flashback: Calfa is the talent agent of small-time sexy blonde singer Lu De Belle (Linnea Quigley) who is gigging in joints on the fringes of the South American jungle. Turns out her face resembles that of a native idol, so she's worth plenty to the bad guys if they can kidnap her. But Calfa, a sleazy guy, hires adventurer Asher Brauner and his girl (Jo Ann Ayres, a beautiful number) to escort them out. The band winds up in Indian territory with a crooked native chieftain and a cave of magical powers. A light-hearted touch in the Eric Weston-Asher Brauner script makes it bearable, even Joseph Louis Agraz's indifferent direction is forgivable. (Vidmark)

TREASURE OF THE PETRIFIED FOREST, THE (19??). Audra the Witch and the Sword of Valhalla (not to mention a secret valley) figure in this Italian-produced action flick. In the words of Audra, "It's not going to be easy to find a way to the Valley of Petrification." Gordon Mitchell, Ivo Payer, Eleanor Bianchi.

TREASURE OF THE WHITE GODDESS, THE (1983). Blend in a little cannibalism, mix a touch of Tarzan to the proceedings and you have this Spanish potboiler, written-produced-directed by Jesus Franco in which Robert Foster portrays a jungle adventurer seeking a white woman legended to be living with natives. Katia Wiener, Albino Grazianni, Javier Maiza.

TREMORS (1989). Rarely does a horror-monster movie satisfy all the needs of the genre . . . but here's one that's funny, scary, suspenseful, packed with action, gruesome, satirical and well-scripted and -acted. It has the flavor of a "mutant monster" film of the '50s as two desert-community handymen, Kevin Bacon and Fred Ward, discover there's "something out there" under the ground, tunneling at top speed and popping up to feast on sheep and people. These are giant worms, each with a gaping maw that contains smaller snake-like heads. It's a wild romp for our heroes to keep their feet off the ground when trapped in an isolated town with scientist Finn Carter, gun nuts Michael Gross and Reba McEntire (who blast away at an attacking worm in a hilarious send-up on modern firepower) and assorted survivors. The monsters are the frightening-fun kind and director Ron Underwood keeps it moving as fast as the locomotive-like worms. Script by producers S. S. Wilson and Brent Maddock. Produced by Gale Anne Hurd. (Video/Laser: MCA)

TRIAL, THE (1963). An Orson Welles movie—he wrote, directed, portrayed a lawyer, sketched the sets, selected the music, served as cameraman, supervised dubbing and handled the editing. Whew! His artistry is everywhere in this outre version of Franz Kafka's allegorical story of nondescript bank clerk Joseph K. (Anthony Perkins), arrested without reason and placed on trial. There are several interpretations to this Kafka tale, made all the more rich by the Wellesian treatment. Intriguing cameos by Akim Tamiroff, Romy Schneider, Jeanne Moreau and Elsa Martinelli. Expect an enigmatic movie. (Connoisseur; Budget) (Laser: Japanese)

TRIAL OF ROCKY JONES. Recut episodes of ROCKY JONES, SPACE RANGER. (Video Yesteryear)

TRIAL OF THE INCREDIBLE HULK, THE (1989). Dr. David Banner (Bill Bixby) is still suffering a tormented soul, and fighting off new bouts of angst, as he join forces with Daredevil (Rex Smith) to fight a dastard named Fiske (John Rhys Davies) who maintains his headquarters at the top of a building. Daredevil doubles as a blind attorney who wants to defend Banner on a criminal charge, but the Hulk (Lou Ferrigno) breaks out of his body to provide his own escape from prison. An average entry in the Incredible Hulk series and an okay adaptation of the Marvel heroes by writer/co-producer Gerard Dipego, with Bixby contributing as producer-director. Marta Du Bois, Joseph Mascolo, Nancy Everhard, Richard Cummings Jr. (New World)

TRIAL OF THE WITCHES. See **NIGHT OF THE BLOOD MONSTER**.

TRIBE, THE (1974). Boring TV-movie depicting Neanderthals (led by Victor French) and Cro-Magnons fighting it out 100,000 years ago. There's not a dinosaur in sight; just people in pelts sitting around or sneaking over hilltops, waiting for history to overtake them so mankind can begin making movies about prehistoric man. Dullest caveman movie ever made, directed by Richard A. Colla. Warren Vanders, Henry Wilcoxon.

TRIBULATION 99: ALIEN ANOMALIES UNDER AMERICA (1992). By pasting together documentary and feature footage, Craig Baldwin creates a sci-fi "documentary" that blends every known conspiratorial and/or crackpot theory into a narrative about aliens known as Quetzals (from the planet Quetzalcoatl) that has infiltrated our society and is responsible for interplanetary-international events since 1949. Strictly a novelty item, but since it lasts only 48 minutes, its madcap editing and crazy sound track hold one rapt.

TRICK FOR TRICK (1933). See third edition.

TRICK OR TREAT (1986). Ripoff of PHANTOM OF THE PARADISE, focusing on a heavy metal rocker (Sammi Curr, played by Tony Fields) who zaps dancers with electric bolts from his guitar. Curr, who uses sadism and death images in his act, has died and gone to rock heaven only to be brought back when a young fan (Marc Price) plays his last record backwards and is ordered to get out there and kick ass. Price finally realizes he's being manipulated by an evil force, and tries to stop Sammi's returned corpse with the help of girlfriend Lisa Orgolini. In a gag appearance, Ozzy Osbourne appears as a TV crusader against rock music. Good effects at the climax can't save this from its adolescent mentality. Directed by actor Charles Martin Smith, written by producers Joel Soisson and Michael S. Murphey. (Lorimar; American; Warner Bros.)

TRICK OR TREATS (1982). With all the experience Gary Graver has had as cinematographer, producer, director and actor, one would expect he would at least know that a horror film requires a quickened tempo, and not the movements of a lumbago-riddled grandmother. No treat, this HALLOWEEN-inspired slasher yarn, depicting how babysitter Jackelyn Giroux puts up with the Halloween night antics of jokester Christopher Graver while a maniac killer is approaching the house, intent on murdering the woman inside. It takes forever to happen and there's only a minimum of splatter matter. The killer is an escapee from an asylum for the criminally insane dressed as a woman, but all of Graver's attempts at drag humor fall as flat as a man who's just had his throat cut by the Boogeyman. David Carradine, Carrie Snodgress, Steve Railsback and Paul Bartel are wasted in miniroles. Let's all rush over to Graver's L.A. digs and soap up his windows. (Vestron)

TRILOGY (1970). See editions 1-3.

TRILOGY OF TERROR (1975). Anthology TV-movie produced-directed by Dan Curtis for which William F. Nolan adapted stories by himself and Richard Matheson. The unusual feature is that Karen Black appears in all three in four roles. "Julie" is a witchcraft tale involving a sexually unhappy teacher being blackmailed by a student; "Millicent and Therese" permits Black to engage in schizophrenia as she portrays diametrically opposing sisters; and "Amelia" (from Matheson's "Prey") is a horrifying tale of a doll that terrorizes Black in her apartment. Gregory Harrison, Robert Burton, John Karlen, George Gaynes. (MPI; the "Amelia" episode is on tape from MPI as **TERROR OF THE DOLL**)

TRIPODS: THE WHITE MOUNTAINS, THE (1985). British adaptation of three John Christopher novels in which aliens called "Tripods" take over Earth in 2193 A.D. Directed by Graham Theakston and Christopher Barry. John Shackley, Jim Baker. (Sony) (Laser: Image)

TRIP TO MARS. See **FLASH GORDON: MARS ATTACKS THE WORLD.**

TRIUMPH OF THE SON OF HERCULES (1963). "Yuri Men" are beastly creatures, ripping apart human bodies as men pull wings off flies, but they're still no match for the might of Maciste in yet another Italian adventure bulging with beefcake in the form of Kirk Morris. Directed by Tanio Boccia. (Sinister/C; S/Weird)

TROG (1970). Super-ridiculous Herman Cohen production is a thorough time waster—it also wasted the talents of Joan Crawford as an anthropologist helping a caveman (a troglodyte, played by Joe Cornelius) find a place in contemporary society, and occasionally taking him to lunch. (This same idea was presented far more maturely in ICEMAN.) Michael Gough overacts as the villain thwarting her research. Director Freddie Francis does what he can with Aben Kandel's stone-age script. TROG is a dog. Robert Hutton, Bernard Kay.

TROIKA (1969). See editions 1-3.

TROLL (1986). Unusually tame, G-rated Charles Band production directed with taste by John Carl Buechler, a special effects man making his directorial debut. The setting is a San Francisco apartment building where little Jenny Beck is possessed by a troll from another dimension. This ugly undroll troll has a magical ring that turns everyone into mythical creatures or rainforests. The creatures and effects are adequate but the characters are cardboard and the promising themes in Ed Naha's script never developed beyond embryos. Michael Moriarty and Shelley Hack as the parents are wasted, as is Sonny Bono in a cameo (he becomes the rainforest). The standouts are June Lockhart

THE CREATURES IN 'TROLL'

as the guardian over the Tolkien-like creatures, and her lovely daughter, Anne Lockhart. Nice try, but no GREMLINS. (Video/Laser: Vestron)

TROLL 2 (1990). This has the grotesque dwarf-like monsters of the original, and gory make-up and bloodletting to satisfy fans, but its juvenile approach and substandard acting (some of the worst in modern memory) make it inaccessible for shocks or suspense. Writer-director Drake Floyd has no idea how to work with actors and his script, set in the rural burg of Nilbog (check that out backward), jumps all over the place, introducing characters as fodder to kill off. The monsters prey on a family of vacationers, chief of which is young Michael Stephenson. With the help of his dead grandfather's spirit, the youth not only proves he's the best actor in the cast but thwarts those damn dwarfs. George Hardy, Margo Prey, Connie McFarland. (Columbia TriStar)

TROLLENBERG TERROR, THE. See **CRAWLING EYE, THE.** (Trolling for monsters?)

TROMBA, THE TIGER MAN (1949). German film is a pitiful affair about a lion trainer who utilizes a strange drug to maintain control over his creatures—and a beautiful woman. Directed by Helmut Weiss. Rene Deltgen, Gustav Knuth. (Sinister/C)

TRON (1982). Walt Disney's adventure set in an electronic game world broke cinematic territory with splendid computer-generated images, but story and acting are so ineptly ridiculous that what emerges is a novelty piece with nowhere to go. A major problem is writer-director Steven Lisberger's plot. Instead of setting up the characters, he immediately plunges into the computerized Tron world, making one feel lost from the start. A corporate bigwig (David Warner) is stealing the game ideas of designer Jeff Bridges. To find the evidence to prove Warner's conspiracy, Bridges, Cindy Morgan and Bruce Boxleitner are zapped into the other-dimensional world of the computer. Wonderful blending of live action with computerized graphics, but at no time is there a sense of menace—just a playfulness. Nice try, Steven, but no Pac-Man. Barnard Hughes, Dan Shor. (Disney)

TROUBLE IN MIND (1986). Although set in the near-future, in a society plagued by a mood of doom and pending war, this film written-directed by Alan Rudolph has few fantasy elements. It is more a surreal-like situation in which John Hawks (an ex-cop known as "The Hawk" played by Kris Kristoffersen) returns to Rain City (actually Seattle) where he makes a play for old girlfriend Genevieve Bujold (as a crusty cafe owner) but falls for Lori Singer, who is married to cheap gangster Keith Carradine. Hawks also is caught up in a war between two criminal factions (one of them bossed by Divine playing an ugly vermin named Hilly Blue) and there's one very odd shootout. It's a strange film, as only Rudolph can make them, and its character portrayals are superb and real. Joe Morton, George Kirby. (Nelson/Charter) (Laser: Nelson; MCA)

TROUBLESOME DOUBLE (1971). British comedy, sequel to EGGHEAD'S ROBOT, features whiz kids creating new robots in the lab. Moppets only. Keith Chegwin, Julie Collins, Tracy Collins. Directed by Milo Lewis, scripted by Leif Saxon.

T.R. SLOANE (1979). Average Quinn-Martin TV-movie with Cliff Gould's script imitating the James Bond superspy films. It was first telecast as DEATH RAY 2000, then syndicated to TV under this new title. Robert Logan portrays a smooth-talking government man out to recover the hijacked Dehydrator, a device that sucks the moisture out of your body, leaving you a shriveled up raisin (or prune). Villain Clive Revill pets spiders and snakes and sics strong-man Ji-Tu Cumbuka on his enemies. Ji-Tu has a stainless steel hand embedded with claws and knives, so there's nice fights staged by director Lee H. Katzin. And Ann Turkel as Logan's love is a pleasing presence. But this is so cliched and predictable only the most die-hard Bond-imitation fans will be compelled to watch. Dan O'Herlihy (as Logan's assignment chief), Maggie Cooper, Paul Mantee.

TRULY, MADLY, DEEPLY (1990). Totally offbeat ghost story that deals deeply, passionately with the grief that comes after the death of a loved one. Overcoming that grief and finding a new life is the theme of the script by director Anthony Minghella, who brings a sense of uniqueness to his tale of spirits from the beyond who impinge on the material world. Juliet Stevenson is the devastated wife recovering from the death of Alan Rickman, who suddenly pops up with other dead souls. There's nothing frightening about them, they just hang around her house watching TV and moving the furniture. It's all in the emotional depth of Minghella's writing and the way that Stevenson captures the despair, and her attempt to find new relationships. Bill Paterson, Michael Maloney. (Touchstone)

TRUTH ABOUT UFO'S & ET'S, THE (1982). Pseudo-documentary approach to flying saucers and their potential occupants is hosted by Brad Steiger, an author who covers all subjects strange and werid. (VCI)

TUCK EVERLASTING (1980). Gentle, pastoral turn-of-the-century fantasy (based on Natalie Babbitt's novel) in which a girl growing up in the South is befriended by a benevolent family that never ages. Its members, 104 years ago in the pioneer days, drank holy water from a spring and are destined to live forever, but their secret is threatened by a stranger. Director Frederick King Keller approaches this with an autumnal quality, treating the characters with sensitivity. Genuine family movie. Fred A. Keller, Paul Flessa, James McGuire. (Vestron)

TUNNEL, THE. See **TRANSATLANTIC TUNNEL.**

TUNNELVISION (1976). In 1985, the Senate accuses Tunnelvision, the People's TV Network, of altering the fabric of society through programming. An investigation serves as an excuse for dozens of parodies and satires on game shows, news telecasts, commercials, comedy series, etc. At least 50 actors and satirists appear in this spoof of contemporary video-watching. Irreverent and witty. Credit Neil Israel, director-co-writer-executive producer, for this channel hop into the future. Chevy Chase, Phil Proctor, Howard Hesseman, Edwina Anderson, James Bacon. (MPI; HarmonyVision)

TURKEY SHOOT. See **ESCAPE 2000**.

TURNABOUT (1940). TOPPER creator Thorne Smith wrote the whacky novel on which this Hal Roach production is based. The gimmick here is that a married couple (Carole Landis and John Hubbard) exchange bodies. The single joke is stretched a little thin, although director Roach pads it with amusing visuals. Adolph Menjou, William Gargan, Mary Astor, Donald Meek.

TURN BACK THE CLOCK (1989). TV-movie remake of the 1947 fantasy-thriller REPEAT PERFORMANCE in which a woman who has just committed a murder on New Year's Eve is given the chance to relive the last year to circumvent fate and prevent the murder from happening. However, Sheilah Powers, a fading TV actress played by blooming TV actress Connie Selleca, mucks up the waters even worse when her disloyal husband (David Dukes) has an affair with an aspiring, conniving screenwriter (Wendy Kilbourne), and her best friend (Jere Burns) has an affair with rich bitch Dina Merrill. The restructured convoluted plot was concocted by Lee Hutson and Lindsay Harrison from the original 1947 script by Walter Bullock, in turn based on a novel by William O'Farrell. Directed by Larry Elikann with the usual gloss of a glitzy look at Hollywood glamour. Joan Leslie, who starred in REPEAT PERFORMANCE, appears in a cameo.

TURN OF THE SCREW, THE (1974). TV-movie, originally shown in two parts, is an adaptation of Henry James' classic horror novella, written by William F. Nolan and directed by Dan Curtis. The ambiguities of the story are faithfully retained and Lynn Redgrave, as the governess tutoring two children seemingly troubled (or possessed) by a dead spirit (or spirits), is superior. Megs Jenkins, Jasper Jacob, Eva Griffith. (Thrillervideo)

TURN OF THE SCREW, THE (1989). Video version of **NIGHTMARE CLASSICS II** (Video/Laser: Cannon).

TURN OF THE SCREW, THE (1992). This modernized adaptation of Henry James' classic novel of the supernatural by British producer Michael White is told in the form of a flashback by Marianne Faithfull during a gathering at her manor. Patsy Kensit portrays the tutor sent by a depraved Englishman (Julian Sands) to Bly House, his isolated estate, to educate his two children, only to discover they are possessed by the dead spirits of the evil Quint and his lover, Miss Jessels, a fact housekeeper Stephane Audran would rather ignore. Writer-director Rusty Lemorande strains a bit hard, and turns unnecessarily pretentious in the fright sequences, employing obvious religious and sexual symbols to capture themes of faith and depravity. This is an eccentric, stylish film, zinging to life when the hauntings are in force. To Lemorande's credit, he captures an erotic undertone without resorting to blatant sex, and shows off a commendable experimental spirit. THE INNOCENTS (1962) is still the best version, with a grand performance by Deborah Kerr, but it remains unavailable on video. (Live)

TUT AND TUTTLE (1981). Time-travel TV-movie, designed as a comedy for the young 'uns, stars Chris Barnes as a fair-haired youth who, after running the wrong way during a school football game and scoring for the other team, stares into the force field of a pyramid and is propelled back through the centuries to ancient Egypt, where he meets Tutankhamen (Eric Green) and saves the Nile from total defile. Vic Tayback and Jo Anne Worley are among the schemers and Hans Conried, in one of his last roles, appears as an advisor who helps the young king escape the treachery. (Time-Life)

TV CLASSICS: FLASH GORDON AND THE PLANET OF DEATH (1953). Episodes of a '50s TV series with Steve Holland, Irene Champlin and Joe Nash. Directed by Gunther V. Fritsch.

TV'S BEST ADVENTURES OF SUPERMAN. Four volumes of half-hour episodes of the TV series that starred George Reeves. (Warner Bros.)

12:01 (1993). In 1973 Richard Lupoff wrote the short story "12:01 P.M." for the Magazine of Fantasy and Science Fiction, using the idea of "a time loop" in which a man is trapped in a park during his lunch hour and doomed to live it over and over again. In 1990 Jonathan Heap wrote-directed a 25-minute adaptation (starring Kirkwood Smith) nominated for an Academy Award. This two-hour TV-movie was produced by Heap, with his old school chum Philip Morton throwing away the minimal plot and using the "time bounce" as a gimmick. Now we have Jonathan Silverman portraying a clerk in an electronics corporation, UTREL, which is running tests of "particle physics," an attempt to accelerate molecules and harness energy. After a bad day at the office, during which lab assistant Helen Slater is murdered, Silverman wakes up the next morning destined to relive the day over again. He stops being an ineffectual nerd and sets out to prevent Slater's murder and the test-firing of a disintegrator ray, which could put all of mankind into a 24-hour time loop. While this may sound like GROUNDHOG DAY, Lupoff's premise did come first. It's a pretty good thriller and once the time-loop idea is under way, the pacing picks up noticeably under Jack Sholder's direction. Martin Landau plays Dr. Thadius Moxley, the dedicated scientist in charge of the project; Nicolas Surovy is a sinister lab technician, Robin Bartlett is Silverman's bitchy boss and Jeremy Piven is Silverman's prankster pal. (Fox)

TWELVE TO THE MOON (1960). There are a dozen reasons why this poverty-stricken sci-fi thriller doesn't thrill, and Ken Clark, Anthony Dexter, Francis X. Bushman, Tom Conway and Robert Montomgery Jr. are five. Tedium galore as Lunar Eagle One lands in the crater Menelaus to encounter lunatic creatures ruled by the Great Coordinator, who threatens to turn Earth into a giant popsicle. This movie sucks, all right. Directed by David Bradley from DeWitt Bodeen's script. John Wengraf, Cory Devlin, Tema Bey and Michi Kobi are four more reasons why 12 TO THE MOON is less than classic. Photographed by the great John Alton.

TWENTY MILLION MILES TO EARTH (1957). Space probe returning from Venus, damaged by a meteor, crashes into the ocean off Sicily. A tiny dinosaur-like creature (a Venusian specimen) survives the impact but our atmosphere causes it to grow at an accelerated rate—all too quickly it assumes monstrous proportions, crashing through the Roman Forum and the Temple of Saturn while Army combat units pursue with flame-throwers. This Columbia low-budgeter (directed by Nathan Juran; written by Bob Williams and Christopher Knopf) has outstanding stop-motion work by Ray Harryhausen, whose Ymir creature is one of his finest; Harryhausen injects personality into the Ymir and evokes sympathety for its plight. Harryhausen's partner, Charles H. Schneer, produced this minor classic. Joan Taylor, William Hopper, Arthur Space. (Laser: Pioneer)

27TH DAY, THE (1957). Aliens wish to colonize Earth but cannot conduct warfare—it's against their religion—so they send emissary Arnold Moss to abduct five Earthlings from different countries. In his UFO, Moss gives each captive capsules which could, on telepathic command, destroy all human life within 27 days. It's the aliens' way of giving us a chance to commit suicide. Or, if we don't use the capsules, we win and they'll go away. Realizing the power they hold, and how that power could be misused by less scrupulous individuals, the principals disperse to hide and contemplate. Main focus is on Gene Barry and Valerie French as they wrestle with their consciences and fall in love. Message science-fiction with strong anti-Communist overtones in the vein of RED PLANET MARS, adapted by John Mantley from his own novel. This film's blatant political stance definitely reflects its time and place. William Asher directed. George Voskovec, Stefan Schnabel, Paul Birch, Ralph Clanton. (Movies Unlimited)

TWENTY THOUSAND LEAGUES UNDER THE SEA (1916). Silent screen version directed and written by Stuart Paton. Based loosely on the Jules Verne novel. Allen Holubar, Matt Moore, Jane Gail. (Kino; Grapevine) (Laser: Image)

TWENTY THOUSAND LEAGUES UNDER THE SEA (1954). Classic Disney adventure (based on the Jules Verne novel) spares no expense to re-create Captain Nemo's atomic sub, the underwater kingdoms, the giant squid and other Vernesque wonders. Kirk Douglas, Peter Lorre and Paul Lukas are survivors of a whaling ship ramming who find themselves on the Nautilus, under the command of the brilliant but demented Nemo (James Mason), who wages war against those who wage war. The effects are remarkably grand for their day, especially the squid attack as men armed with harpoons try to dislodge the multi-tentacled giant off the sub's hull. This remains the film that best captures the flavor of Verne and his inventions. Directed by Richard Fleischer, written by Earl Fenton. (Video/Laser: Disney)

TWICE BITTEN. Video version of **VAMPIRE HOOKERS** (HQV; Ariel).

TWICE DEAD (1988). The old haunted house tale retold as a juvenile slasher splasher, occasionally diverting but ultimately disappointing with its plethora of cliches. An actor who hung himself in the old Tyler estate in the

'30s is back in the '80s to haunt a newly arrived family. The main problem with director Bert Dragin's script (which he cranked out with producer Robert McDonnell) is that the spirit's intentions are never clear—one minute it's trying to strangle young Tom Breznahan, the next it's warning him his sister Jill Whitlow is being raped. The film deteriorates into disappointing practical jokes when the two teenagers in the family are forced to ward off threatening punks. The concluding supernatural gore murders are humdrum stuff. Sam Melville, Brooke Bundy, Joleen Lutz, Jonathan Chapin. (Video/Laser: Nelson)

TWICE-TOLD TALES (1963). Lushly photographed anthology highlighting three fantasy-horror tales by Nathaniel Hawthorne, Vincent Price in each. Writer-producer Robert E. Kent has selected: "Dr. Heidegger's Experiment," in which Price and Sebastian Cabot experiment with a rejuvenation serum that returns their youth and brings long-dead Mari Blanchard back from the grave; "Rappaccini's Daughter," a strange yarn in which a woman's touch brings instant death, and a plant that destroys any who touch it; and "The House of the Seven Gables," a traditional haunted house/family curse story (and weakest of the three). Director Sidney Salkow's pacing is slow, but rich detail and ensemble acting make the film a stylish one. Brett Halsey, Beverly Garland, Richard Denning. (MGM/UA)

TWICE UPON A TIME (1983). Unique albeit arcane animation piece by John Korty, utilizing the Lumage process, an improvement on the Eastern European technique of miniature cutouts photographed through clear sheets of glass (as opposed to the cel method of animation). This fanciful fairy tale is about the Rushers of Din, who each night dream sweet dreams from Sunny Frivoli—until the Murkworks intervene with their nightmares. It then becomes a race for control of the Cosmic Clock as two whimsical heroes, Ralph the All-Purpose Animal and his sidekick Mum (who speaks in sound effects), fight the raunchy Synonamess Botch, maniacal ruler of the Murkworks Nightmare Factory. Script concocted by Korty, Swenson, Suella Kennedy and Bill Couturie. Voices by Paul Frees, Hamilton Camp, Julie Payne, James Cranna, Marshall Efron. (Warner Bros.)

TWILIGHT OF THE COCKROACHES (1988). The Asian roach (a species known as Blattas orientalis) is given sympathetic treatment by Japanese producer-director Hiroaki Yoshida in this curious blend of live action with animation. The people are real—it's the roaches that have been cartooned into the world as misunderstood, maligned creatures, so dwarved by the lumbering humans that they seem vulnerable to danger. This unusual treatment makes this full-length allegorical cartoon an offbeat entertainment, with Yoshida drawing parallels to the Holocaust and to the behavior of today's Japanese people and their willingness to shut their eyes to the rest of the world. Definitely worth it, even if you hate cockroaches. (Streamline) (Laser: Japanese)

TWILIGHT OF THE DEAD. See **GATES OF HELL**.

TWILIGHT PEOPLE, THE (1972). A spirit of jungle adventure and good location photography are the best things this Roger Corman-David Cohen film (made in the Philippines) have to offer. The Jerome Small-Eddie Romero script is a rehash of THE ISLAND OF DR. MOREAU and ISLAND OF LOST SOULS, featuring a cave prison of half-human, half-animal experimentations gone awry, including a Goat Guy, a Panther Woman, a winged Bat Creature (on wires yet), a Dog Daughter, etc. John Ashley plays adventurer Matt Farrell, kidnapped and taken to a jungle stronghold. He's the perfect specimen for the mad doctor's next experiment, but first there's time to fall in love with the scientist's assistant. Director Romero moves it at a fast clip, with enough action to make it bearable. Also known as ISLAND OF THE TWILIGHT PEOPLE. Good cast all around: Pat Woodell, Jan Merlin, Charles Macaulay, Pam Greer (as that panther gal), Mona Morena and Ken Metcalfe. Ashley doubled as one of the producers. (United; from Direct as **BEASTS**)

TWILIGHT'S LAST GLEAMING (1977). In 1981, former Air Force officer Burt Lancaster and other prison escapees take over a SAC missile room and threaten mankind with nuclear destruction unless secret documents (a la "The Pentagon Papers") are revealed. Director Robert Aldrich focuses on the U.S. President (Charles Durning) and the dilemma he faces to satisfy Lancaster's demands; also afoot is a conspiracy that allows for a shocking conclusion. Aldrich doesn't quite bring off this difficult theme, but there is ample food for political thought. Richard Widmark, Melvyn Douglas, Paul Winfield. (Key; CBS/Fox) (Laser: CBS/Fox)

VIC MORROW IN 'TWILIGHT ZONE -- THE MOVIE'

TWILIGHT ZONE CHRISTMAS (1960). Video version of "Night of the Meek," an episode from THE TWILIGHT ZONE TV series starring Art Carney as a drunken department store Santa Claus who stumbles across a magic bag that allows him to give away any gift asked for. A wonderful seasonal fantasy written by host Rod Serling, directed by Jack Smight and co-starring John Fiedler, Burt Mustin and Meg White. (Fox)

TWILIGHT ZONE—THE MOVIE (1983). Entertaining if not classic homage to the great Rod Serling TV series. Produced by Steven Spielberg and John Landis, this is made up of four tales (three based on TV episodes) and a clever prologue. Landis directed and wrote the prologue and first episode, which stars Vic Morrow as a bigot puzzlingly projected into situations where he is vilified (by Nazis, Ku Klux Klansmen, black American soldiers in Vietnam, etc.). While it has the moralistic turnaround Serling loved, Landis' script is weak and makes this the least of the quartet. Providing a warm glow is Spielberg's segment about how old folks in a rest home rediscover youth with the help of a traveling goodwill magician, Scatman Crothers. It's a spiritually uplifting fantasy. Third and best of the yarns is an adaptation of a Jerome Bixby story (scripted by Richard Matheson, directed by Joe Dante) about a youth with the ability to affect physical things by "willing" them. A good cast (Kathleen Quinlan, Jeremy Licht, Kevin McCarthy, Patricia Barry, William Schallert, Dick Miller) adds to the nostalgia. And there's '30s-style animation by Sally Cruikshank and a novel interpretation of life-size cartoon monsters by Rob Bottin. Final episode, directed by Australia's George Miller, is based on the famous TV episode "Nightmare at 20,000 Feet," in which a neurotic (John Lithgow, in the role originated by William Shatner) sees a gnomelike monster on the wing of a jetliner and goes bananas to prevent it from making the plane crash. (Video/Laser: Warner Bros.)

TWILIGHT ZONE, THE (1959-61). Four episodes from Rod Serling's classic series that set new standards for fantasy story-telling on network TV for well over a decade. The quartet: "The Invaders," the famous Agnes Moorehead episode in which she portrays a lonely lady fighting off miniaturized aliens who have crashlanded in her hovel; "The Lonely," in which Jack Warden meets and falls for a mechanical woman; "One for the Angels," with Ed Wynn holding off the arrival of Death; and "Eye of the Beholder," a classic about a society in which it's hard to tell the mutants from the normal folks. (CBS/Fox has packaged many episodes in eight cassettes, and has issued two lasers, each with four episodes.)

TWINKLE, TWINKLE, KILLER KANE. See **NINTH CONFIGURATION, THE.**

TWINS OF DRACULA. See **TWINS OF EVIL.**

TWINS OF EVIL (1971). Predictably plotted sequel to Hammer's VAMPIRE LOVERS and LUST FOR A VAMPIRE, dealing with the Karnstein family and its vampiric curse. Peter Cushing as a witchhunter of the 19th Century seeking to help two "infected" 19-year-old beauties: Mary and Madeleine Collinson, altogether beauties who are seen in the altogether in several shots. Tudor Gates' script is heavy with heaving bosoms and unsubtle hints of lesbian love-biting. Directed by John Hough. Dennis Price, Isobel Black, Kathleen Byron, Damien Thomas, David Warbeck. Also known as THE GEMINI TWINS, VIRGIN VAMPIRES and TWINS OF DRACULA. (VidAmerica)

TWISTED BRAIN (1973). Harassed student Pat Cardi, too mousy to stand up for his own rights, transforms into a hairy beast who stalks his tormentors on campus in a tired worm-turns plot. An entire segment dealing with the boy's parents has nothing to do with the rest of the film; it was added as padding. Originally released as HORROR HIGH, but it's no high at all; in fact, it was an all-time low for director Larry Stouffer. John Niland, Austin Stoker. (United; VCI)

TWISTED JUSTICE (1990). In a futuristic L.A., where new anti-gun laws require policemen to carry stun guns (or "stingers") instead of lethal firearms, maverick cop James Tucker (played by writer-producer-director David Heavener) uses unorthodox procedure (i.e., a long-barreled revolver) to go after the "Bullseye Murderer," a rapist who uses the drug "Umbra" that turns him into a super-intelligent psychotic, with superhuman strength. Helping Tuck is Shannon Tweed and getting in his way are fellow cops Erik Estrada and Jim Brown. Since this is watered down action trash, wasting Karen Black in an empty cameo, we refer you to a similar film that is much better trash and more stylistic, David Pirie's FUTURE FORCE, which also spotlights an iconoclastic law enforcer named Tucker. (Arena; K-Beech)

TWISTED NERVE (1969). Ray Boulting directed this British chiller about a psychopathic killer (Hywel Bennett) who plans to trap innocent, vulnerable Hayley Mills. The young man has a Mongoloid brother and may be suffering from chromosome defects. Unfortunately, Bennett is never that menacing and the film moves at an ungodly lumbersome pace. Music by Bernard Herrmann. Boulting co-scripted with Leo Marks and Roger Marshall. Billie Whitelaw, Phyllis Calvert, Frank Finlay.

TWISTED NIGHTMARE (1987). After a mentally handicapped youth is killed, a figure lunges out of the darkness for revenge. Written-directed by Paul Hunt. Rhonda Gray, Cleve Hall, Brad Bartrum. (Transworld)

TWISTED SOULS. See **SPOOKIES, THE.**

TWITCH OF THE DEATH NERVE. Video version of **CARNAGE** (MPI).

TWO DEATHS OF SEAN DOOLITTLE (1975). George Grizzard portrays a man who has no fear of dying for he thinks there is a doctor who can restore him to life. British TV-movie. Directed by Lela Swift. Barnard Hughes, Jeremiah Sullivan, Grayson Hall.

TWO EVIL EYES (1990). Inspired by the macabre genius of Edgar Allan Poe, George Romero and Dario Argento teamed up to make this anthology. Romero's contribution, a loose version of Poe's "The Facts in the Case of M. Valdermar," plays more like an episode of THE TWILIGHT ZONE and is the kind of material you see when someone is imitating Romero. Adrienne Barbeau is fleecing her dying husband and supernatural forces from beyond the grave are unleashed when her accomplice-doctor uses hypnotism. It's just okay, with Tom Atkins reprising his cop from NIGHT OF THE CREEPS and Ramy Zada, Bingo O'Malley and Jeff Howell assisting. The better half of this duo is Argento's "The Black Cat," an amalgamation of elements from Poe yarns. Harvey Keitel plays Rod Usher, a crazed crime photographer who murders his wife and hides her blood-spattered corpse behind a bedroom wall. The outcome is predictable but Argento brings stylish touches to "The Black Cat" (which he wrote with Franco Ferrini). John Amos, Sally Kirkland, Kim Hunter, Martin Balsam. (Media/Fox) (Laser: Image)

TWO FACES OF DR. JEKYLL, THE (1961). Hammer pulls a switch on the overworked Robert Louis Stevenson split personality plot: Instead of a good-looking doc turning into an ugly brute, a not-so-handsome chap transmutates into a handsome playboy who falls for London's can-can girls. Directed by Terence Fisher from a Wolf Mankowitz script. Paul Massie, Dawn Addams, Christopher Lee, Oliver Reed. Strictly a game of Hyde-and-seek, produced by Michael Carreras and Anthony Nelson Keys. Aka HOUSE OF FRIGHT and JEKYLL'S INFERNO.

TWO FACES OF EVIL (1981). Two one-hour episodes of the British telly's HAMMER HOUSE OF HORROR, re-edited for the U.S. In "Two Faces of Evil," a husband driving his family through a village is attacked by a hitchhiking Dracula, apparently a doppelganger of the husband. Director Alan Gibson wrings good performances from Anna Calder-Marshall and Gary Raymond. In "Rude Awakening," Denholm Elliott portrays a woman-chasing realtor who keeps returning to Lower Moat Manor in his nightmares. Gerald Savory has structured a savory script directed by another Hammer veteran, Peter Sasdy. Pat Heywood, James Laurenson, Lucy Gutteridge. (Each from Thrillervideo with Elvira.)

TWO LITTLE BEARS, THE (1962). Mild, child-pleasing fantasy fluff in which the two children of parents Eddie Albert and Jane Wyatt turn themselves into bear cubs at night. Now dad wishes they could hibernate for the winter. Directed by Randall F. Hood. Brenda Lee, Soupy Sales, Nancy Kulp, Butch Patrick, Jimmy Boyd.

TWO LOST WORLDS (1950). Hackneyed desert island non-thriller about 19th Century shipwrecked pirates who've kidnapped a girl and must face the wrath of prehistoric monsters and heroic James Arness, who's out to save the chick. The monsters are stock footage from ONE MILLION B.C. Directed by Norman Dawn. Bill Kennedy, Laura Elliott, Gloria Petroff, Tom Hubbard. (Sony)

TWONKY, THE (1953). Man's ultimate fate, that the TV set will one day conquer him and command his existence, is allegorically expressed in this cautionary Arch Oboler production (he wrote-produced-directed) based on an amusing story by Henry Kuttner. The premise has the set being invaded by the energy of an experimental robot (from where is never made too clear) and capable of sending out energy rays to accomplish anything it wants, including putting some of the cast to sleep. The same fate might await some viewers as this low-budget effort is silly to the point of distraction, its slim humor overmilked and its music score overplaying every bit of whimsy. At the heart of the film is Hans Conried's performance as the flustered owner of the out-of-control TV set, but other than his befuddled attitude, Oboler gives him little to work with. "Twonky" is the word given to something that we don't understand. Billy Lynn, Gloria Blondell, Janet Warren, Ed Max.

TWO OF A KIND (1983). Simply awful, revolting vehicle for Olivia Newton-John and John Travolta. It is unforgivable they chose this wimpy fantasy to continue their screen romance begun in GREASE. This is just plain turkey fat. Travolta's a down-at-the-heels nobody who robs a bank to pay off loan sharks, she's the bank teller he holds up. Meanwhile, Gene Hackman is the Voice of God in Heaven, where angels Charles Durning, Beatrice Straight and Scatman Crothers use the earthly couple to prove to God the world doesn't have to start all over again—there is still some good in the worst of mankind. In the hands of writer-director Vincent Bufino it's a botched mess, without warmth, humor or social redeeming value. Oh, we almost forgot: Oliver Reed turns up as the Devil, to tempt our heroes from the path of righteousness. One time when a joker could beat TWO OF A KIND. (USA) (Laser: Fox)

TWO ON A GUILLOTINE (1965). If you think the title is bad, wait until you see producer-director William Conrad try to imitate William Castle, but without knowing how. It was a low point for Warner Bros. the day Henry Slesar and John Kneubuhl banged out this headless script about an illusionist (Cesar Romero) who devises a new guillotine for his magic act, much against the wishes of beautiful wife Connie Stevens, PR man Parley Baer and babysitter Virginia Gregg. Cut to 20 years later and now "The Great Duquesne" is dead in a glass coffin, and his daughter (Connie Stevens again, looking no different) is coming to his funeral. She must live in his spooky house midnight to dawn for seven nights in order to inherit $300,000. Ghostly events happen (weird noises, a skeleton on a wire, a dematerializing bunny rabbit) but nothing that will frighten horror fans. Slanted for a younger audience, with unnecessary rock 'n roll music and Dean Jones as an undercover newsman. This features one of the last music scores by Max Steiner. John Hoyt, Connie Gilchrist.

TWO PLUS FIVE: MISSION HYDRA. See **STAR PILOTS.**

2001: A SPACE ODYSSEY (1968). Producer-director Stanley Kubrick's monumental venture into the realm of science fiction is a landmark film combining visual fascinations with a plethora of ideas often left to individual interpretation. Special effects by Douglas Trumbull are an achievement for their time, the music by Johann and Richard Strauss and other classical composers lends the film distinction, and the screenplay (by Kubrick and Arthur C. Clarke) is stunning in its implications. The boggling story begins with a "Dawn of Man" sequence in which ape-like creatures (the beginnings of man) are given intelligence after touching a monolithic black slab. By 2001, man is on the moon and preparing to journey to other planets when a similar slab is uncovered which transmits a signal to Jupiter. Astronauts Gary Lockwood and Keir Dullea are assigned to investigate, but their odyssey is endangered by a ruthless, malfunctioning computer nicknamed HAL. How the machine is overcome makes for a suspenseful allegory of man vs. machine. Final journey through the Star Gate is a sensory experience of psychedelic colors and psychotic patterns, heightened to a fevery pitch with music to commit suicide to. The "Star Child" ending is enigmatic and complex. Stunning, intelligent film not equalled by the '84 sequel. Best seen on a big screen or letter-boxed for TV. William Sylvester, Daniel Richter, Leonard Rossiter, Robert Beatty. (Video/Laser: MGM/UA)

2010: THE YEAR WE MAKE CONTACT (1984). If Stanley Kubrick's 2001: A SPACE ODYSSEY is the Bible of movie science fiction then this sequel (written-produced-directed-photographed by Peter Hyams) is blasphemy. Although this picks up nine years later as continuing adventures of HAL the malfunctioning computer, David Bowman (the astronaut who vanished into the Star Gate) and the abandoned Intrepid space vehicle, it has none of the epic sense of Kubrick's masterpiece—in fact, it mundanely starts on Earth and wastes a half-hour depicting needless scenes of Roy Scheider's home life, conversations about a Russian-U.S. rescue mission to Jupiter and other trivial junk. When the film finally gets into space to recount the important parts of Arthur C. Clarke's story, it must be rescued by Richard Edlund's effects. Credit him for one of the most exciting sequences set in space: the walk of two men transferring from the Russian spacecraft Leonov to the deserted Intrepid. That enigmatic "black monolith" is back, but the Kubrick ambiguities are gone—replaced by a simplified theme that tells, never suggests, that the floating slab belongs to God. Those who remember RED PLANET MARS will blanch at Clarke's pseudoreligious miracle which finishes the film—and hopefully the thought of any further irrelevant, irreverent sequels. Scheider, John Lithgow and Bob Balaban as the American spacers work with limited roles, but remain second best to Edlund's effects. Keir Dullea appears briefly as Bowman; among the Russian astronauts are Helen Mirren and Dana Elcar. (Video/Laser: MGM/UA)

2019: THE FALL OF NEW YORK. See **AFTER THE FALL OF NEW YORK.**

2020 TEXAS GLADIATORS (1985). A nuked-out Dallas, Texas, is the wild and woolly setting for this rambunctious post-holocaust adventure pitting a band of good-guy warriors called "The Rangers" against the "New Order" that intends to use them as slave labor in a mine. With the trappings of a western (saloon brawls, shootouts and a tribe of noble Indians), this foreign-produced flick gallops along, its endless action sequences holding one in the grip of its momentum as "The Rangers" go up against the outcast Catchdog and an army of soldiers equipped with thermal shields, off which bullets bounce. It's absurd comic-book stuff, directed without pretensions by Kevin Mancuso. Harrison Muller, Al Cliver, Daniel Stephen, Sabrina Siana. (Media)

2069 A.D.—A SENSATION ODYSSEY (1969). Men of the future travel into the past in a time machine to alter history. People of the present, beware. Directed by Cam Sopetsky. Harvey Foster.

2069: A SEX ODYSSEY (1974). West German-Austrian sex comedy in which women from Venus land on Earth to collect samples of male semen so they can impregnate folks on their dying planet. Directed by H. G. Keil. Nina Frederic, Catherina Conti. (Academy)

TWO THOUSAND MANIACS (1964). Revolting exploitation material panders with scenes devoted to dismembered arms and legs, chopped-up bodies and heaped intestines. Setting is the modern South where rednecks are still fighting the Civil War by hacking to death any Northerners who wander through. Rednecks making red necks, get it? It turns out the town of Pleasant Valley, once wiped out by General Grant, periodically appears out of a time warp so the citizens can wreak revenge. Considered the "masterpiece" of gore purveyor Herschell Gordon Lewis, who wrote, produced and directed. One watches at one's own risk. (Wizard; Comet; Rhino; S/Weird) (Laser: Japanese)

TWO THOUSAND YEARS LATER (1969). Good intentions on the part of producer-director-writer Bert Tenzer make this worthwhile, even if the execution is occasionally faulty, and the satiric punches poorly delivered. The god Mercury, who has kept a Roman gladiator in suspensed animation, thaws him out and sends him into the future, to our time and place. The warrior warns us we're headed for the Big Fall, but he himself falls prey to the vultures of society. Terry-Thomas, Edward Everett Horton, Pat Harrington Jr.

TWO WEEKS TO LIVE (1942). Lum 'n Abner were a couple of rustic store managers popular on radio in the 1940s. In this feature version, Lum thinks Abner's dying, so he helps him find jobs to pay the hospital bill. Work includes flying a Martian rocket, clomping through a haunted house and drinking a Jekyll-Hyde formula. Innocuous, old-fashioned fun, as old as the hills of Tennessee. Directed by Malcolm St. Clair. Chester Lauk, Norris Goff, Franklin Pangborn, Charles Middleton.

TWO WORLDS OF JENNIE LOGAN, THE (1979). Plagued by her husband coming off an affair, unhappy housewife Lindsay Wagner finds an old dress in a Victorian home and slides into a time continuum, traveling back to the turn of the century to fall in love with Marc Singer. She passes back and forth between her two worlds, involved with murder, confused identities and the paradox of changing the past to ensure her future happiness. Nicely written by director Frank DeFelitta (he adapted David Williams' novel SECOND SIGHT) with well-etched performances by Wagner, Singer, Linda Gray, Joan Darling and Henry Wilcoxon. (USA; Fries)

UFO (1956). Investigative reporter wanders Washington D.C. interviewing Air Force personnel of Project Bluebook (a study of flying saucers). End result of this Ivan Tors-Clarence Greene pseudodocumentary is not a very close encounter, Francis Martin's script proving inconclusive. "Real life" footage of UFOs is out of focus, shaky and just as inconclusive. Tom Powers narrates.

UFO—EXCLUSIVE (1979). Sheer speculation about unidentified flying objects, alien life forms walking our Earth and other exciting stuff like that, all presented in this phony documentary narrated by Robert Morgan.

UFO INCIDENT, THE (1975). Fact or fiction? You must judge this intriguing TV-movie based on an alleged incident that occurred to Betty and Barney Hill while they drove through lonely countryside (an incident detailed in the book INTERRUPTED JOURNEY). They were hypnotized by aliens and led into a saucer to undergo biological testing. Only later, with a sympathetic psychiatrist's help, did the frightening details emerge. This thoughtful treatment deals with the trauma of UFO abductions but also leaves doubt as to exactly what happened. Provocatively directed by Richard A. Colla, with James Earl Jones and Estelle Parsons convincing as the racially-mixed couple. The doctor is excellently essayed by Barnard Hughes.

UFO JOURNALS (1976). 4-F way to OD on the ABCs of UFOs carrying DNA E.T.s with ESP. On the QT, this 2-D job didn't have IQ or B.O. TNT. It was DOA. OK?

UFORIA (1980). Eccentric but entertaining portrait of three free-spirited souls, with light fantasy touches. Texas drifter-grifter Fred Ward meets a supermarket check-out clerk (Cindy Williams) neurotic as hell and they begin an uneasy romance. Meanwhile, phony evangalist Harry Dean Stanton can genuinely heal although he doesn't know why. Williams' belief in UFOs is twisted by Stanton (against Ward's better wishes) into a new pseudoreligious cult. A compelling character study with surprise ending, although you can probably see it coming. Richard Baskin, Dennis M. Hill. Written and directed by John Binder. (MCA)

UFOS . . . A NEED TO KNOW (1991). Thoughtfully produced, lowkey documentary detailing fascinating aspects of the UFO mystery, produced by Bob Brown of Oakland's Video City. Although he and co-producer Ted Oliphant are believers, they approach cautiously, documenting reports with a sense of balance. This covers the unusual number of UFO reports in and around Fyffe, Ala.; the mutilated cattle mystery, the Roswell crash of 1947 (now well documented). One of the best UFO documentaries of the period. (Vido City)

UFOS ARE REAL (1979). UFOs are real . . . boring, if this pseudocumentary is any indication. It offers nothing to prove its title except "evidence" of grainy, inconclusive film and still photographs, and harps on how reliable eyewitnesses are, how sinister the Air Force is, etc. Some experts and witnesses are convincing, but other films have done it better. Written-directed by Ed Hunt. Aka ALIEN ENCOUNTERS.

UFOS: ARE WE ALONE? Video doc (United).

UFOS: IT HAS BEGUN (1976). Rod Serling narrates this semidocumentary approach to the mystery of flying circular disc craft. Guest appearances by Burgess Meredith, Jose Ferrer and Dr. Jacques Vallee. Directed by Ray Rivas. (United)

UFOS/STRANGE SKIES. Documentary on unmarked airborne circular objects. (Pacific Arts)

UFO SYNDROME (1981). Is the U.S. Government conspiring to cover up the true reason why there are so many strange lights in the sky? Or are we seeing leftover footage from UFO JOURNALS? The possibilities are as endless as the Universe. Produced-directed by Richard Martin, narrated by Anthony Eisley.

UFO: TARGET EARTH (1974). Producer-director Michael A. deGaetano made this cheap ($70,000) off-target bore that misses Earth by miles. An electronics expert picks up signals of an alien craft submerged in a lake near town and tries to uncover its secrets, but this is an exercise in monumental tedium. Too much talk and not enough action. And no visible monster! Nick Plakias, Cynthia Cline. (Simitar; Movies Unlimited)

UFO: THE SERIES (1970). Two volumes of episodes from the British TV series in which the secretive S.H.A.D.O. protects Earth from alien invaders. Directed by David Lane. Ed Bishop, George Sewell, Peter Gordeno, Gabrielle Drake. (Today Home Entertainment)

UFO: TOP SECRET (1978). Boring, redundant pseudodocumentary (emphasis on the pseudo) that drones on interminably with absurd speculations about E.T.s coming from other worlds to invade Earth. Blurry photos described as "startling," "fascinating" and "genuine" are paraded out as evidence while narrator Sidney Raul rambles on about the mysteries of the Universe. Difficult to sit through without wanting to scratch your ass several times. Produced-directed by Wheeler Dixon. (Interglobal; United)

UGETSU (1954). Academy Award-winning Japanese film, based on stories by 18th Century writer Akinari Ueda, is a weird, evanescent blend of violence and fantasy set against 16th Century Japan. Two parallel stories evolve around a potter and a farmer who abandon their wives to fulfill dreams of glory. The farmer turns Samurai warrior and the potter falls for a woman who turns out to be a spirit. Acted in classic Japanese style, often as delicate as brush strokes on a vase, sometimes brutal in its sweaty action, but always beautifully photographed by Kazuo Miyagawa. Translated, the title means "Pale, mysterious moon after the rain." Directed by Kenji Mizoguchi. Machiko Kyo, Masayuki Mori. (Embassy; Western) (Laser: Voyager)

UGLY DUCKING, THE (1959). Comedic Hammer treatment of the Jekyll-Hyde theme in which Bernard Bresslaw portrays a mentally defective descendant of Robert Louis Stevenson's scientist who concocts the old formula and turns into Teddy Hyde, colorful addition to the dance hall crowd and jewel robbery set. Undistinguished comedy, too corny to turn into a swan. Directed by Lance Comfort. Reginald Beckwith, Jon Pertwee, Michael Ripper, Richard Wattis.

ULTIMATE IMPOSTOR, THE (1978). Unsold TV pilot, based on William Zacha's THE CAPRICORN MAN, stars Joseph Hacker as a U.S. agent whose memories are wiped out by the Chinese Reds. Back at HQ, he is considered the perfect guinea pig for receiving alpha-10 wave lengths packed with computerized information, which in turn is transmitted into his brain cells. He can retain this information for only 36 hours, which adds suspense to his first assignment: find a defecting Russian submarine officer kidnapped by Ruskie agents. Average TV actioner, scripted by producer Lionel E. Siegel. Directed by Paul Stanley. Keith Andes (with a bald scalp), Erin Gray, Tracy Brooks Swope. (MCA)

ULTIMATE WARRIOR, THE (1975). A non sequitur among Hollywood's post-Armageddon yarns, predating MAD MAX and thus a curious anomaly from writer-director Richard Clouse, who mixes intellectual content with standard action. The allegory of intellect vs. brute force is told via two groups trapped in a destroyed New York: pacificists led by The Baron (Max von Sydow, in an underplayed role) and sadists and marauders led by Carrot (William Smith). While this has none of the style or combative ingenuity of MAD MAX and countless clones, it has the strengths of von Sydow and Yul Brynner as a "street fighter" named Carson (after frontier scout Kit, who blazed new trails in a wilderness?) to bolster its sagging story. Rivalry is over a tomato patch—symbol of the old world lost and the beginning of a better one. A chase through an abandoned subway is a highlight. Despite good moments, it ultimately falls flatter than the corpses Brynner so easily chalks up. Joanna Miles, Richard Kelton, Stephen McHattie. (Warner Bros.)

ULTRAMAN (1967). Feature version of a Japanese TV comic strip, in which a befuddled Asian turns into a man of steel to fight the monsters of the Universe that have managed to survive Godzilla movies. Strictly for the kiddie-sans. Co-directed by special effects wizard Eiji Tsuburaya. Satoshi Furuya, Shoji Kobayashi. (Family Home Entertainment)

ULTRAMAN—MONSTER BIG BATTLE (1979). More re-edited footage from the Japanese kiddie sci-fi TV series, ULTRAMAN.

ULTRA WARRIOR (1992). Hodge podge of footage from assorted Roger Corman post-Armageddon movies has been inserted into this derivative MAD MAX clone lacking distinction. Dack Rambo portrays a warrior of 2058 assigned to track down Zerconium, a substance needed to make bombs to stop invading aliens from turning Earth into a blazing sun. The Atlantic Seaboard is "Oblivion," a radioactive zone where he confronts a villain (the Bishop) in boring battles. Characters are cliched and made unappealing by an indifferent cast: Meshach Taylor, Clare Beresford, Mark Bringelson, Charles Dougherty. It was, like a hundred other MAD MAX ripoffs, directed without an ounce of ingenuity by Augusto Tamayo and Kevin Tent. (New Horizons)

ULYSSES (1955). The Homeric touch is lost in this Carlo Ponti-Dino de Laurentiis film, better described as a tribute to costume-sword adventures. Kirk Douglas brings a sense of quest and tragedy as the heroic Ithacan who sacks Troy and spends ten years making his way home. The Gods frown on Kirk as he battles from adventure to adventure, meeting the Cyclops, Circe the Enchantress (who turns Ulysses' crew into swine), and the Sirens of the Rocks. It ends in a bloodbath on Ithaca, where Ulysses slaughters suitors of wife Penelope (Silvana Mangano doubles as Circe and the long-suffering wife.) Irwin Shaw and Ben Hecht assisted several Italian writers; Mario Camerini directed. Anthony Quinn, Rossana Podesta. (Warner Bros.)

ULYSSES AGAINST THE SON OF HERCULES (1963). Mythological baloney in which the gods turn their anger against Ulysses and order Hercules to stop his earthly pursuits. The two musclemen join ranks to fight off the Bird People and the Troglodytes ruled by a wicked, insane king. And so it goes for 100 minutes of film, produced by one-eyed Italian and French producers, and directed by Mario Caiano. Georges Marchal, Michael Lane, Raffaella Carra.

UNBORN, THE (1991). Disturbing, cautionary parable about mankind's poisoning of fetuses, told as a paranoid thriller in the vein of ROSEMARY'S BABY but with the horrific elements springing from the scientific and not the supernatural. Brooke Adams is artificially inseminated by seemingly benevolent Dr. Meyerling (James Karen), but he's a geneticist conducting experiments to create a superhuman being. Adams' nightmares are compounded by her manic depression and inability to deal with the "monster" growing inside her. Although the final "baby" is not that convincing, and in the evil vein of Larry Cohen's IT'S ALIVE, the message in Henry Dominic's script comes shrieking through. Producer-director Rodman Flender does a credible job lending this premise ambience and paranoia. Jeff Hayenga, K. Callan, Jane Cameron, Kathy Griffin. (Video/Laser: RCA/Columbia)

UNBORN II, THE (1993). Loose sequel to THE UNBORN has another patient of Dr. Meyerling giving birth to a deformed baby with an urge to chew up people after biting them in the neck. Mother Michele Greene faces the challenge of holding off baby killer Robin Curtis. This Roger Corman production, directed by Rick Jacobson, works best as an action thrilller, with car chases and intense shootouts ovepowering the horror sequences, which are unconvincing because the hideous baby-monster is unconvincing. Scott Valentine portrays a neighbor who befriends Greene. Leonard O. Turner, Brittany Powell. (New Horizon)

UNCANNY, THE (1977). Writer Peter Cushing must convince skeptical publisher Ray Milland that the behavior of felines is deadly by telling him three tales. The first episode, set in London, depicts how cats avenge the death of their owner Joan Greenwood. In the second, a cat with magical powers gets rid of a scummy human, and in the third, Donald Pleasence and Samantha Eggar scheme to commit murder in Hollywood. Directed by Denis Heroux and scripted by the catty Michael Parry. Susan Penhaligon, Roland Culver, Alexandra Steward, John Vernon. British-Canadian production originally produced as BRRRR! (Media)

"You know, people are beginning to eat people out there."
—Yul Brynner as Carson in **THE ULTIMATE WARRIOR**

UNCLE WAS A VAMPIRE (1959). Christopher Lee is in peak form doing a parody of his Hammer version of Dracula in this silly albeit pleasant Italian horror-comedy in which he turns up at a hotel for young romantics, where his nephew-owner (rascally Renato Rascel) has been reduced to working as a bellhop. Once Rascel is bitten by his 400-year-old uncle and grows fangs, he begins biting the necks of all the beautiful women at the resort. Only the kiss of the hotel's sweet gardener (Sylvia Koscina, a fragrant flower herself) can save him from eternal bloodsucking. Rascel's nerdy and hammy performance has its amusing moments, and there are bikini and negligee-covered cuties and scenic coastal photography to hold one's attention in this mild terror-error laughfest directed with the touch of a feather by Pio Angeletti (also known as Stefano Vanzina). Kay Fisher, Lia Zoppelli, Susanna Loret. Also known as HARD TIMES FOR VAMPIRES, HARD TIMES FOR DRACULA and MY UNCLE THE VAMPIRE.

UNDEAD, THE (1957). Roger Corman film inspired by the Bridey Murphy craze of the '50s: Psychiatrist Richard Garland, through hypnosis, sends prostitute Pamela Duncan into the past, where she is destined to be burned as a witch. Knowing events to come, she tries to alter history . . . with unsettling results. Corman directed the Mark Hanna-Charles Griffith script. Allison Hayes, Val Dufour, Billy Barty, Dick Miller, Mel Welles, Richard Devon. (Nostalgia; AIP)

UNDEAD, THE. See **FROM BEYOND THE GRAVE.**

UNDERCOVER LOVER. See **MAN FROM S.E.X.**

UNDERSEA KINGDOM (1936). Rousing 12-chapter Republic serial (the studio's second after DARKEST AFRICA) stars Ray "Crash" Corrigan as a naval officer with superstrength who finds himself on the Lost Continent of Atlantis battling Monte Blue, who has a disintegrator weapon. Robots, submarines and other fantastic weaponry keep the story moving, as does the lively direction of Joseph Kane and action specialist B. Reeves Eason. It's a gas even if the acting is creaky. Lois Wilde, C. Montague Shaw, Lon Chaney Jr. Smiley Burnette. (Nostalgia Merchant; Republic; Filmfax; Sinister/C)

UNDERSEA ODYSSEY. See **NEPTUNE FACTOR, THE.**

UNDERSTUDY, THE: GRAVEYARD SHIFT II (1988). The "blood is the life" theme of DRACULA and CAMILLA and its sense of perversity are the strongest elements of this portrait of a vampire who takes a job as the leading "bloodsucker" in a low-budget flick being shot on an L.A. soundstage. There are times when writer-director Gerard Ciccoritti gets pretentious with dialogue, and the storyline is a jagged mess as the film skips around from reality-reality to the reality of the movie. Although Mark Soper etches an unusual monster, it is Wendy Gazelle as an actress who is central focus as she is seduced away from her editor-boyfriend and turned into a vampire herself. Ciccoritti is aspiring to something different but stumbles in the process, and the film feels staged and claustrophibic, as stifling as the interior of a vampire's dirt-lined coffin. A very loose sequel to the equally strange GRAVEYARD SHIFT. (Virgin Vision) (Laser: Image)

UNDERTAKER AND HIS PALS, THE (1967). Sickening black comedy (minus laughs) in which a mortician increases his profit margin by getting cadavers from motorcycle-riding murderers. Once he has dough for the funeral services, he picks up side money by turning the corpses over to a restaurant, where they are dished up a la carte for gourmets and served au Gratuitous. Robert Lowery, the Batman of 1949, must have been hard up when he accepted his role from producer-director David C. Graham, whose ineptitude reaches classic proportions midway through the first reel. W. Ott, Rad Fulton, Ray Dennis. (Flaming)

UNDER THE SIGN OF CAPRICORN (1971). See third edition.

UNDERWATER CITY, THE (1962). Well-intended pseudodocumentary about the building of Amphibia, a community on the ocean floor where Carl Benton Reid hopes to prove that man can survive for long periods in a communal society. The color is nice and the cast an able one (William Lundigan as a designer, Julia Adams as his love interest, Roy Roberts as an official) but the Owen Harris script is talkative and Frank McDonald directs in a flat fashion. And the effects are unexciting—a feature that matches the plot and consigns this Alex Gordon production to Davy Jones' Locker.

UNDERWORLD (1985). Variant video title for **TRANSMUTATIONS** (Vestron).

UNDYING BRAIN, THE. Video version of **BRAIN OF BLOOD** (Premiere).

UNDYING MONSTER, THE (1942). Odd offshoot of the werewolf genre, based on the novel by Jessie Douglas Kerruish and starring James Ellison, Heather Angel and John Howard. Director John Brahm captures the Cornwall setting in this tale of a family haunted by a centuries-old lycanthropic curse. Mature and thoughtful, with emphasis on ambience rather than a great monster or special effects. Also called THE HAMMOND MYSTERY. Scripted by Lillie Hayward and Michel Jacoby. Bramwell Fletcher, Heather Thatcher. (Sinister/C; Movies Unlimited)

UNEARTHLING, THE (1984). Really bad E.T. imitation, of the it-came-from-outer-space school. A meteor crashlands on Earth in a forest that just happens to be full of (1) dumb teenagers, (2) some nightingale egg poachers and (3) a young boy who has seen the crash. Out of the crash hulks a plastic-suited creature with the nose of an anteater. This is the father alien, who goes around killing everyone. Meanwhile, the insufferable kid finds an alien egg and hatches it. Out pops a cute version of the father, who goes "Coo" to tug at your heartstrings. The script by J. Piquer Simon (who also directed) and Jack Gray goes nowhere. THE UNEARTHLING is the unmovie of the decade. Ian Sera, Nina Ferrer, Oscar Martin, Susan Blake.

UNEARTHLY, THE (1957). Enjoyable sleaze, grade-Z fashion, with John Carradine as a mad doc who discovers a 17th gland containing the secret of youth, "prolonging life for thousands of years." So naturally he kidnaps innocent people and exposes them to electricity bolts and deformities. His assistant, Lobo, is lumbering Tor Johnson. Myron Healey is a sympathetic criminal seeking refuge in the doc's recup center and sexy femme Allison Hayes is an intended victim. Carradine, always on the verge of hysteria, asks "Did you sterilize my #23 scalpel?" and plays morbid organ music during dinner. Producer-director Brooke L. Peters manages a silly "buried alive" sequence. Roy Gordon, Arthur Batanides. (Rhino; Filmfax; Sinister/C)

UNEARTHLY STRANGER (1963). John Neville wakes up to discover his lovely wife (Gabriella Lecudi) sleeps with her eyes open. Her peculiar traits increase—until Neville realizes he has married an alien, sent to Earth to kill scientists in the space project Neville is working on. However, when the E.T. femme falls for Neville, the plan goes awry. Thoughtful British sci-fi thriller from producer

'UNHOLY' :TREVOR HOWARD, NICOLE FRONTIER

'THE UNINVITED': A HAUNTED-HOUSE CLASSIC

Albert Fennell suggests and implies, rather than shows, the horrors at work. John Krish directed the Rex Carlton script. Jean Marsh, Philip Stone, Warren Mitchell, Patrick Newell. (Movies Unlimited; Wade Williams)

UNHINGED (1983). Old mansion in Oregon is the setting for this low-budget regional film in which murders are committed with a variety of horrendous weapons. Those squeaking sounds in the background are the unoiled hinges of the killer's mind. Written-produced-directed by Don Gronquist. Laurel Munsion.

UNHOLY, THE (1988). Well-produced, well-acted but slow-moving and sometimes ponderous religious parable of good vs. evil. A demon from Hell named Daziadarius, which manifests itself on Easter weekend, sucking up priests and/or virgins, is haunting a church to which Ben Cross is assigned after Cross survives a 17-floor fall without injuries. Guiding Cross in his fight are an Archbishop (Hal Holbrook) and a blind priest (Trevor Howard, in one of his last roles) and working to lead him astray is a night club owner (William Russ) who presents a devil-cult show and a young beauty (Jill Carroll). The Philip Yordan-Fernando Fonseca script is high-class though the monster looks like something out of a grade-B effort, and its actions are unsavory, in a sexual manner of speaking. Camilo Vila directs with an emphasis on religious symbols, and Ned Beatty brings unrest to his role as a sympathetic cop. Claudia Robinson, Nicole Frontier. (Vestron) (Laser: Image)

UNHOLY NIGHT (1929). See third edition.

UNHOLY QUEST, THE (1934). See editions 1-3.

UNHOLY THREE (1925). One of director Tod Browning's weird silent films starring Lon Chaney Sr. as a ventriloquist who teams up with a midget, an ape and a muscleman to pull off an unusual caper. Victor McLaglen, Mae Busch, Matt Moore. Rare; pops up sometimes at revival houses. (Classic Video Cinema Collectors' Club)

UNHOLY THREE (1930). Sound remake of Tod Browning's 1925 film, again with Lon Chaney Sr. as the leader of a colorful gang pulling off an ingenious caper. Jack Conway directed. Lila Lee, Elliott Nugent.

UNICO IN THE ISLAND OF MAGIC (1984). Animated Japanese feature depicting the adventures of a unicorn left to fend for itself in a forest. (RCA/Columbia)

UNIDENTIFIED FLYING ODDBALL (1979). Walt Disney comedy update of Mark Twain's A CONNECTICUT YANKEE IN KING ARTHUR'S COURT in which a space engineer and his robot are sent back in time to the Round Table milieu of King Arthur. Don Tait adapted this lighthearted fantasy (a U.S.-British production) and Russ Mayberry directed with the same spoofy touch he gave PETE'S DRAGON. Dennis Dugan, Jim Dale, Ron Moody (as Merlin the Magician), Kenneth More. Also known as UFO and THE SPACEMAN AND KING ARTHUR. (Disney)

UNINVITED, THE (1944). Those who saw this in the '40s, or discovered it on TV in the '50s, always remember it fondly as one of the few good haunted house movies. However, now that we have been carried to the heights of atmospheric and shock film making, one might accuse Paramount's adaptation of Dorothy Macardle's novel UNEASY THRESHOLD of being slow moving and talky. But anyone searching for old-fashioned story-telling values—fascinating characters, strong motives, scintillating dialogue, a setting that serves as a metaphor for character, etc.—will find this demonstrative of '40s Hollywood at its best. Ray Milland and sister Ruth Hussey buy a mansion, Windward House, on the Cornish coast to be confronted with subtle hints of a haunting: wilted flowers, a weeping voice, a gust of wind on the stairs, a room turning cold, the smell of mamosa. Recommended for the fine script by Frank Partos and Dodie Smith, the gentlemanly direction of Lewis Allen, and the performances of Milland, Hussey, Gail Russell, Donald Crisp, Cornelia Otis Skinner and Alan Napier, the latter as the village doctor. (Video/Laser: MCA)

UNINVITED (1987). For a monster movie to work, the terrorizing entity must have a modicum of scariness and/or believability. If not, the horror turns into uninvited comedy. The monster in UNINVITED, resembling a Muppet reject that's always popping out of a cat's mouth, is so obviously faked as to invite uninvited laughter. Writer-producer-director Greydon Clark has assembled a fine cast: Alex Cord as a sleazy underworld character, George Kennedy as his gunsel, Clu Gulagher as a drunken sychopant and Toni Hudson as a woman hired to sail Cord's yacht. And there's possibilities for character relationships as we see Cord—a man of power and wealth—fall pray to evil desires and bubble-headed sexpots. But rather than trust in his own abilities, Clark resorts to ALIEN cliches. Clare Carey, Eric Larson, Beau Dremann. (New Star) (Laser: Image)

UNIVERSAL SOLDIER (1992). What's that old saying? All brawn and no brain? Apply that adage to the script by Richard Rothstein, Christopher Leitch and Dean Devlin and you've got UNIVERSAL SOLDIER. As a sci-fi action picture it's nonstop violence when Vietnam War adversaries Jean-Claude Van Damme and Dolph Lundgren kill each other in combat and reappear years later as cyborgs controlled by "mad doctor" Jerry Orbach. The hardware, technology, combat and martial-art sequences are explosive and exciting but the plot (Van Damme regains part of his humanity and goes on the run with TV news reporter Ally Walker, wih Lundgren on their heels) is comic-book fodder. So, settle in for exploding and overturning vehicles and anticipate the mano-to-mano battle royal between the stars during the last 15 minutes. Directed by Roland Emmerich. Ed O'Ross, Leon Rippy, Ralph Moeller. (Columbia TriStar) (Laser: Live)

UNKNOWN, THE (1927). Although not a horror story

DOLPH LUNDGREN AND JEAN-CLAUDE VAN DAMME IN 'UNIVERSAL SOLDIER'

in the traditional or gothic sense, this silent-screen collaborative effort between director Tod Browning and "Man of a Thousand Faces" Lon Chaney Sr. is a morbid, creepy tale of revenge that will have your skin crawling. Chaney is at his most anguished as a killer fleeing the police who takes the unlikely disguise of Alonzo the Armless, a circus performer who seemingly has no arms and throws knives with his feet. Alonzo falls prey to his own emotions—mainly his love for Nanon, played by Joan Crawford at her most alluring. To win that love Alonzo has his arms surgically removed, only to discover too late that Nanon loves another. How Chaney seeks revenge against his rival (a happy-go-lucky gypsy) is one of the strangest, and most lurid, plot devices ever. It's a hallmark of dark cinema, suggesting the grim overview of life shared by Browning and Chaney and scriptwriter Waldemar Young. S. Norman Kerry, Nick De Ruiz, John George, Frank Lanning. (Enrique J. Bouchard)

UNKNOWN, THE (1946). Third and final entry in Columbia's cheap, short-lived series based on Carlton E. Morse's popular radio thriller, I LOVE A MYSTERY. Jim Bannon stars as ace adventurer Jack Packard and Barton Yarborough is Doc Young in this adaptation of the famous episode, "Faith, Hope and Charity Sisters," although the sisters have been simplified to one to save bucks. The investigators search for a cloaked entity in a haunted mansion to which wayward daughter Jeff Donnell has just returned. The phantom cries of a baby heighten the mystery. Henry Levin directed.

UNKNOWN ISLAND (1948). Paleological potboiler, straight out of a pulp magazine, throws together several prehistoric beasts on an uncharted island in the Pacific discovered by Barton MacLane (tough sea captain), Richard Denning (alcoholic beachcomber), Virginia Grey (obligatory skirt with pouting lips) and Philip Reed (returning war hero). The rubber-suited monsters shuffle around without attacking anyone. Threat factor is zero. There's also a ridiculous gorilla that battles a dinosaur—one of the most ludicrous moments in the history of lost-island movies. Directed turgidly by Jack Bernhard. (Nostalgia; Movies Unlimited)

UNKNOWN POWERS (1980). Three half-hour episodes of a pseudodocumentary TV series witlessly spliced together to create a turgid study of extrasensory (non)perception. Samantha Eggar, Jack Palance, Will Geer and Roscoe Lee Browne are Hollywood personalities who host-narrate these weak studies of occult science. Its power remains unknown. (Video Gems)

UNKNOWN SATELLITE OVER TOKYO. See **WARNING FROM SPACE.**

UNKNOWN TERROR, THE (1957). The known terror is Charles Marquis Warren's sluggish, turgid direction of this unimaginative trash depicting an expedition to the Caribbean to find the Cave of Death, a place of purgatory for local natives. Dr. Ramsey (Gerald Milton) has a fungus-mold formula that, when injected into patients, turns them into gooey-faced beasts whom the doctor exiles to the eerie cave. Meanwhile, that expedition includes Mala Powers (she runs through foliage in a flimsy negligee, pursued by a beast-thing), John Howard (he climbs into the Cave of Death without even a flashlight) and Paul Richards (a gimpy-legged adventurer who gets the hots for the heaving, and outwardly thrust, bosom of Indian girl May Wynn). Eventually the cave becomes the setting as a gooey formula turns into a flood of washday bubbles. Now, dear viewer, you know the real terror of which mankind dares not speak.

UNKNOWN WORLD (1951). Effective Robert L. Lippert sleeper, filmed in the Carlsbad Caverns, depicts an expedition corkscrewing into the core of the earth with a giant duralunin-powered drill mounted on the front of their "mole ship." These human burrowers, searching for a new place for mankind to live so decent people can escape the threat of atomic attack, discover conditions at Earth's center to be harmful to reproduction. The Millard Kaufman script is neat and unpretentious. Directed stylishly by Terrell O. Morse. Bruce Kellogg, Victor Killian, Jim Bannon. (Prism; Sinister/C; Filmfax)

UNMASKED: PART 25 (1990). British spoof of American slasher flicks finds Gregory Cox wearing a mask like Jason's as he knocks off folks. Producer-writer Mark Cutforth and director Anders Palm have fun with black comedy, but it's rather feeble, old chaps. Fiona Evans, Edward Brayshaw. (Academy)

UNNAMABLE, THE (1988). Another adaptation of an H. P. Lovecraft tale, falsely advertised as being in the league of REANIMATOR. Except for an offbeat female monster named Alyda (well played by Katrin Alexandra and imaginatively designed by effects man R. Christopher Biggs) this has nothing to offer but tedious haunted-house cliches as four students from Miskatonic University are pursued from floor to floor by the demonic form, which enjoys (a) ripping out your heart, (b) bashing your head against the floor until it cracks open like an eggshell and (3) slashing your throat so blood gushes out. Another plot has to do with Randolph Carter (named after a Lovecraft character) and his nerdish companion seeking the answer to the mansion's mystery through old musty books and incantations, which may have something to do with tree monsters—writer/director Jean-Paul Ouellette never makes it that clear. UNNAMABLE, unless you're looking for a gore flick with a good monster, is unnecessary. Charles King, Mark Kinsey Stephenson. (Vidmark) (Laser: Image)

UNNAMABLE II, THE (1992). Writer-director Jean-Paul Ouellette returns with an adaptation of H.P. Lovecraft's short stories "The Unnamable" and "The Statement of Randolph Carter," picking up on the same night that THE UNNAMABLE ended, with all the dead bodies being carted away by sheriff Peter Breck. Antiquarian John Rhys-Davies of Miskatonic University (located in Arkham County) joins with Randolph Carter (Mark Kinsey Stephenson) in tracking down the mystery surrounding that winged, big-breasted she-demon named Alyda, who is discovered to be two beings trapped in a cave: within the hideous monster is imprisoned the innocent soul of a young woman (Maria Ford). Girl watchers will appreciate the fact that Ms Ford spends most of the film stark naked, covered only by a mane of wild flowing hair, once she's been separated from the evil spirit through an incantation. The rest of THE UNNAMABLE II is exploitation gore thrills as the creature destroys, with her superhuman strength, most of the characters and as Carter and Ms Ford run around Arkham County. It's an okay horror picture in that regard, but it's far from the literate cosmic-horror level that made Lovecraft so great to read. Charles Klausmeyer, Julie Strain, David Werner, Siobhan McCafferty. (Prism)

UNNATURAL (1952). Erich von Stroheim in a role that fit him to an M—for madman. He's a scientist creating a beautiful woman in his laboratory. Like Barbara Carrera's woman in EMBRYO, she has no morals and destroys those around her. Hildegarde Neff, Karl Boehm. (Sinister/C; Filmfax)

UNSANE (1984). Nobody makes a psychothriller as well as Italy's Dario Argento, and in this retitled version of TENEBRAE, writer-director Argento is at his best. Mystery novelist Anthony Franciosa turns up in Rome to find himself involved with a mad killer enflamed by Franciosa's writings. There's bloody axe murder after axe murder, an excellent sequence in which a Doberman pursues a hapless female victim, and constant twists of plot. It's fun trying to guess what Argento will throw at you next. John Saxon has a small role as Franciosa's agent and the victims include Eva Rubins, Carola Stagnaro and John Steiner (the latter as a policeman hooked on mystery fiction). UNSANE is inspired. (Media; Fox Hills has a heavily edited version; also in video as **SHADOW**)

UNSEEN, THE (1945). Nifty, low budget Paramount mystery with haunted house overtones which don't quite pan out, but the Raymond Chandler-Hagar Wilde storyline has fascinating characters and ghostly ambience, which director Lewis Allen brings full-bodied to the screen with a good cast: Joel McCrea, Gail Russell, Herbert Marshall, Phyllis Brooks.

UNSEEN, THE (1980). Despite a trite-sounding plot (three beautiful TV newscasters are secluded in a house with a madman and, one by one, are brutalized and murdered), this is a strange, sometimes enthralling low-budget flick, made in and around Solvang, Calif., a Danish-style village of windmills and smorgasbord restaurants. Written by Michael L. Grace, it takes one of the hoariest cliches of horror movies—the animalistic, "unseen" entity living in the cellar—and gives it a new sense of mystery, even compassion. Not that the film aspires to anything more than it is—it just does what it sets out to do well under Peter Foleg's direction. Barbara Bach, Sydney Lassick, Stephen Furst, Karen Lamm, Lelia Goldoni. (VidAmerica)

UNTAMED WOMEN (1952). An uncharted island is home for many gorgeous hunks of pulchritude called Druids (Doris Merrick, Midge Ware, Judy Brubaker, Carol Brewster) who specialize in modeling animal skins. The shapely femmes introduce a new line of low-cut wear when shipwreck survivors are beached nearby. Roving the island are prehistoric beasts (outtakes from ONE MILLION B.C.), who dig the new fashions too. The landscape includes man-eating plants and male slaves. Lyle Talbot, Mikel Conrad, Morgan Jones, Autumn Rice. Directed by W. Merle Connell. (J & J)

UNTIL DEATH DO YOU PART. See **POSSESSION UNTIL DEATH DO YOU PART.**

UNTIL THE END OF THE WORLD (1991). Difficult, diffused Wim Wenders oddity that mixes elements of film noir and high-tech sci-fi without it all coming together in a cohesive fashion. The year is 1999 and a nuclear rocket has gone awry over Earth. Exotic, mysterious Solveig Dommartin gets involved with a private eye, a novelist played by Sam Neill, a satchel of stolen money, hold-up men and other types before the meandering story shifts to Australia where her boyfriend William Hurt meets his scientist-father (Max Von Sydow), who has designed a camera that transfers images into brain waves that a blind person can "see." Photographing in 15 countries, the cultish German director intended this as a metaphor for our unending search for ourselves and the meaning of life. It's so dense and pretentious that you might laugh at it, not with it. For diehard Winders fans only, or those who don't mind being baffled (as well as tortured) by inaccessible characters and unfathomable plot. (Video/Laser: Warner Bros.)

WIM WENDERS

UP FRANKENSTEIN. See **ANDY WARHOL'S FRANKENSTEIN.**

UP FROM THE DEPTHS (1979). "Down to the Depths of Despair" better describes this amateurish imitation of JAWS, which features ridiculous characters, phony effects and a holiday feeling that betrays any cinematic drama. Charles Griffith, an old Roger Corman alumnus, directed in the Hawaiian Islands, hamstrung with a terrible script by Alfred Sweeny, who is said to have used THE CREATURE FROM THE HAUNTED SEA as his guide. Sam Bottoms wins worst acting award bottoms up. In this picture, you root for the killer fish and hope the dumb white-eyes get eaten. (Vestron)

UP IN SMOKE (1957). Huntz Hall sells his soul to the Devil in exchange for the names of winning horses. Our racetrack tout tip of the day: Go to the races and avoid this lowbrow, low-budget entry in Allied Artists' cheapie Bowery Boys series — one of the last ever produced at a time when the ideas had long since run their course. Devil-doesn't-care direction by William Beaudine, I-don't-give-a-damnation script by Jack Townley. Stanley Clemens, Byron Foulger (as the Devil), David Gorcey.

UPSTATE MURDERS, THE. See **SAVAGE WEEKEND.**

URBAN WARRIORS (1975). Nuked landscape of devastated America is the setting for this tale of factions that battle it out for survival. Directed by Joseph Warren. Karl Landgren, Alex Vitale, Deborah Keith. (Cannon)

UTOPIA (1951). The last film of the great comedy team of Stan Laurel and Oliver Hardy, this French-Italian production depicts life on an island that has mysteriously popped up from the sea. There, a new society is designed to be the ultimate in living. Far from the comedy team's best work but still of compelling interest to die-hard fans. Also called ATOLL K. Conceived-directed by Leo Joannon. Suzy Delair, Max Elloy, Adriano Rimoldi. (Congress; Vestron; Loonic; Amvest)

V (1983). Four-hour miniseries written-produced-directed by Kenneth Johnson. Fifty giant saucer-shaped motherships from another galaxy appear, crewed by humanoids here to exchange precious commodities to save their dying planet. But these E.T.s are two-faced conquerors, wresting control of TV networks to take over the world. Guerrilla units led by Marc Singer fight back by zapping the humanoids with their own ray guns and stealing their shuttlecrafts. It is then that V (from the World War II phrase, V for Victory) deteriorates into mock heroics and a plot about bigotry and betrayal patterned on Nazi Germany. The special effects are good, the art design derivative. The best touch is when a high school band greets the first aliens to Earth with the theme from STAR WARS. (Laser: Japanese, as **V1**)

V: THE FINAL BATTLE (1984). Six-hour continuation of V, but without creator Kenneth Johnson. Producers Daniel H. Blatt-Robert Singer took the helm, hiring Richard Heffron to direct and a mess of hacks to carry on the story. Primarily action and intrigue in the TV vein, designed to introduce a weekly TV series that was short-lived. Jane Badler stands out as an alien bitch in charge of the invasion. Marc Singer is back at the hero, with Faye Grant. (Laser: Japanese, as **V2**)

VAGRANT, THE (1992). This Mel Brooks production is an interesting but failed experiment in surreal paranoia, with Bill Paxton as a yuppie accountant who buys a fixer-upper to become terrorized by a brute of a man, monstrous in behavior. This unpleasant character is played with relish by Marshall Bell, but motives for the harassment are never clear in Richard Jeffries' script. It's played as a comedy and Paxton is a nerdy klutz, which makes it difficult to root for him since he's his own worst enemy, and not the vagrant. Occasionally the surreal elements serve the premise, and director Chris (THE FLY II) Walas struggles to bring style and pacing to the material, but the ambiguities underlying the vagrant's motives defeat good intentions. And Michael Ironside's cop adds to the lack of focus. Mitzi Kapture, Colleen Camp (as a goofy, horny real estate lady), Stuart Pankin, Marc McClure. (MGM/UA)

VALERIE AND THE WEEK OF WONDERS (1970). See editions 1-3.

VALHALLA (1986). Danish cartoon version of a popular comic strip in which two youngsters are involved with Thor, god of Thunder, Loke, an evil counterpart, and a vicious baby giant named Quark in the land of Udgaard. Directed in the vein of a Saturday morning cartoon by Peter Madsen.

VALLEY OF GWANGI, THE (1969). Excellent Charles H. Schneer production, made in Spain, with brilliant stop-motion effects by Ray Harryhausen and a romantically pleasing story by Willis O'Brien. It's an exciting turn-of-the-century Western (directed by James O'Connolly) in which cowboy James Franciscus discovers a forbidden valley of prehistoric creatures. A Tyrannosaurus rex is lassoed and hogtied in one helluva exciting sequence, then displayed in a traveling circus. Up there with the best of Harryhausen's work. Gila Golan, Richard Carlson, Freda Jackson, Laurence Naismith. (Video/Laser: Warner Bros.)

VALLEY OF THE DRAGONS (1961). Jules Verne story (adapted by director Edward Bernds) served as the premise for this adventure in which a comet swooping past Earth during the 19th Century sucks up two Earthmen in the process of fighting a duel. On their floating rock, Cesare Danova and Sean McClory find prehistoric monsters (or are we seeing outtakes from ONE MILLION B.C.?) and tribes of warring cave people. Joan Staley, Gregg Martel.

VALLEY OF THE EAGLES (1952). Good location photography and a suspenseful script by director Terence Young enhance this British production set in Lapland. An invention that converts sound into energy is stolen by a scientist's assistant, who also has an eye on the inventor's wife. A police inspector comes to the rescue. Jack Warner, Nadia Gray, Christopher Lee, John McCallum,

Anthony Dawson. (Modern Sound)

VALLEY OF THE STONE MEN. See **MEDUSA VS. THE SON OF HERCULES** (Stoned again?).

VALLEY OF THE ZOMBIES (1946). Republic Studio stinker with such a poor budget there aren't any zombies—only mad doctor Ian Keith, resurrected from beyond the pale and keeping himself alive with blood transfusions. Robert Livingston and Adrian Booth (first known as Lorna Gray in Republic serials) creep around eerie graveyards and creepy mansions, while cops are portrayed as dumb characters. A campy element gives this cheapie a charm all its own. Directed by Philip Ford.

VAMP (1986). Above-average teenage comedy blending horror and laughs when members of a frat party step into the After Dark Club—and a comedy Twilight Zone—to meet Grace Jones (as Katrina, an Egyptian mummy goddess). She and her strippers are literal femme fatales who put the bite on the boys. New World comedy has a few scary-fun moments as well as humor. Directed stylishly by Richard Wenk. Chris Makepeace, Sandy Baron, Robert Rusler, Billy Drago, Brad Logan. (New World) (Laser: Image)

VAMPIRA. See **OLD DRACULA**.

VAMPIRE, THE (1956). In modern Mexico, Count Lavud (German Robles) is forced to suck the blood of victims twice before they become truly undead. A bloodsucker sure has to work harder these nights. Directed by Fernando Mendez. Imported to the U.S. by K. Gordon Murray. Abel Salazar is the co-star and producer. Ariadna Welter, Carmen Montego, Mercedes Soler. (Sinister/C; S/Weird; Filmfax)

VAMPIRE, THE (1957). Also known as MARK OF THE VAMPIRE, this minor biter, strictly lower berth (six feet lower?) depicts doctor John Beal pulling a Jekyll-Hyde routine after he swallows the inevitable pill. Coleen Gray, Kenneth Tobey, Lydia Reed, Paul Brinegar. Directed by Paul Landres.

VAMPIRE (1979). Effective vampire tale—one of the better TV productions—features the trappings of the Gothic thriller but crypt-oligizes them intelligently and chillingly. Jason Miller and E. G. Marshall are superb as vampire hunters stalking Richard Lynch, an 800-year-old bloodsucker in San Francisco. Made on location, this is unresolved so the story would segue into a weekly series, but it was never picked up. Well directed by E. W. Swackhammer; written by Steve Bochco and Michael Kozell. Jessica Walter, Barrie Youngfellow.

VAMPIRE AND THE BALLERINA, THE (1960). A shot of Brandi (Walter Brandi, that is) is the only horrific element in this Italian imitation of Hammer and Universal gothic thrillers. Brandi, who vacillates between a wizened, ugly bloodsucker and a handsome count, depending on his blood count, lives in "The Castle of the Damned" with buxom Maria Luisa Rolando, who floats in filmy nightgowns through drafty corridors. The turgidness of writer-director Renato Polselli's staging is enlivened by good black-and-white photography and touches of cheesecake surrounding a troupe of ballerinas practicing in a nearby chateau. This relic belongs to a bygone era of cinematic innocence and is quaint, not scary. Helene Remy, Tina Gloriani, Sarco Ravailoi. Also called THE DANCER AND THE VAMPIRE and THE VAMPIRE'S LOVER.

VAMPIRE AT MIDNIGHT (1988). Bodies drained of blood are dumped out of a limousine as it dashes about the lonely streets of L.A.—the pasttime of a nocturnal bloodsucker who's pretending to be a psychologist. The focus of this low-budget horror feature—with more erotic ambience than most—is a beautiful blond pianist (she looks great in white and red outfits) and her relationship with a cop working on the case, who's trying to keep her from falling under the doc's hypnotic spell. These characters (especially the sexy blonde) put meat on the bones of this lean, mean tale. Directed by Greggor McClatchy. Jason Williams, Gustav Vintas. (Key)

VAMPIRE BAT, THE (1933). Mad scientist Lionel Atwill (as that wonderfully dedicated but demented Dr. Otto von Niemann) sneaks around leaving puncture marks in the necks of victims—but is he a vampire? Edward T. Lowe's script and Frank Strayer's direction are outdated, but this is worth seeing for the cast: Melvyn Douglas as leading man, Fay Wray as screaming heroine, Dwight Frye as crazy henchman. (Sinister/C; Western; Filmfax; Goodtimes)

VAMPIRE BEAST CRAVES BLOOD, THE. See **BLOOD BEAST TERROR. THE**.

VAMPIRE CASTLE. See **CAPTAIN KRONOS—VAMPIRE HUNTER**.

VAMPIRE CIRCUS (1972). Three-ring Hammer midway of horror, set in 1810 Serbia in a village wracked by plague. Paying a visit to the community is a big top with low entertainers: vampires and other types capable of transmutation into animals and grotesque night creatures. The owner of the circus, a vampire himself, is seeking revenge against those who murdered his cousin. Graphically gory in the Hammer tradition. Directed by Robert Young. Adrienne Cori, Laurence Payne, Thorley Walters, David Prowse (Darth Vader), Lynne Frederick, Skip Martin. (Fright)

VAMPIRE COP (1990). The title character (William Lucas) dons blue to evoke red from victims in this regionally produced (Florida) minor horror item. Written-directed by Donald Farmer, who's also in the cast. Melissa Moore, Mal Arnold. (Panorama; Atlas)

VAMPIRE DOLL, THE (1970). Japanese horrorifier avoids cliches of the Dracula genre and deals with a girl with a damned soul. Too artistic for the schlock crowd. Kayo Matsuo. Directed by Michio Yamamoto.

VAMPIRE HAPPENING (1971). Not much about vampires is happening in this German comedy fiasco with uninspired performers who waste their time (and yours) stalking corridors of a dreary castle. The star is Ferdy Mayne, who plays the Dracula spinoff. Directed by Freddie Francis. Yvor Murillo, Ingrid Van Bergen, Pia Degermark, Thomas Hunter. (United; VCI)

VAMPIRE HOOKERS (1979). John Carradine dons the cape of a bloodsucking vampire who uses shapely wenches to bring victims to the local cemetery, where he finishes them off. You won't get hooked watching this Filipino production. Directed by Cirio H. Santiago, scripted by Howard Cohen. Bruce Fairbairn, Trey Wilson, Karen Stride. (Continental; Cinema Group; New Star; from HQV and Ariel as **TWICE BITTEN**)

VAMPIRE HUNTER D (1985). "This story takes place in the distant future, when mutants and demons slither through a young world of darkness." So begins this

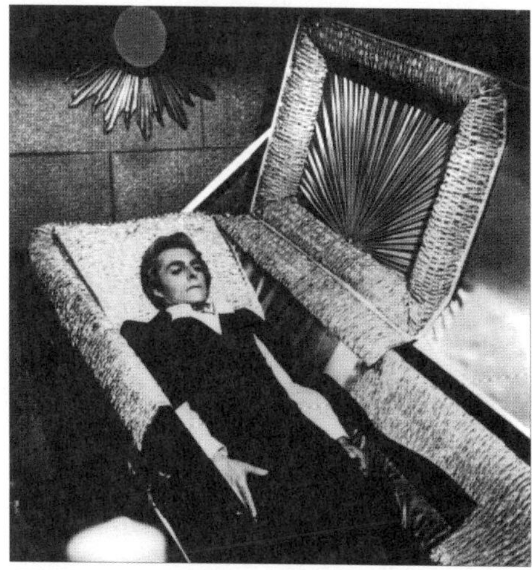

RICHARD LYNCH IN SAN FRANCISCO IN 'VAMPIRE'

superbly animated Japanese adventure in a vein of dark fantasy in 12,090 A.D., when a race of vampires rule like feudal land barons and a sub-class of half-vampire, half-human warriors take on the role of vampire hunters. "D," who resembles a samurai swordsman with a touch of Dr. Strange, is a sinister traveler hired by a young woman to protect her from Count Magnus Lee. She's kidnapped and "D" fights three sisters who turn into deadly serpents and other characters endowed with magical powers. It's a rip-roaring adventure directed by Toyoo Ashida. (Streamline)

THEY CALL HIM 'D'

VAMPIRE KILLERS. See **FEARLESS VAMPIRE KILLERS, THE**.

VAMPIRE LOVERS, THE (1970). Initial entry in Hammer's Karnstein series with Ingrid Pitt as the beautiful, busty Lesbian-inclined Mircalla (sequels were LUST FOR A VAMPIRE and TWINS OF EVIL). It features a sensuous sex romp between two gorgeous babes (heavily edited by U.S. censors) who engage in streaking and breast-biting. Peter Cushing is General Spielsdorf, the exorcist who must behead Mircalla (an anagram of Carmilla). Directed by Roy Ward Baker from a Tudor Gates script. Pippa Steele, Madeline Smith, Kate O'Meara, Douglas Wilmer, Dawn Addams, Ferdy Mayne. (Orion; Embassy) (Laser: Japanese)

VAMPIRE MEN OF THE LOST PLANET (1971). Muddled horror/sci-fi fiasco (written by Sue McNair) in which vampires from another planet attack Earthlings with such frequency that Dr. Rynning (John Carradine) sends rocket XB-13 to the faraway planet, where astronauts discover dinosaurs, squabbling cave people and Spectrum X, a freaky frequency that makes the color red dangerous to have around, and which accounts for scenes tinted a reddish hue. This Al Adamson-directed olio has everything but the sinking kitsch. It's only distinction is that the cameraman was William Zsigmond. Features footage from UNKNOWN ISLAND and ONE MILLION B.C. and there are persisting rumors footage was lifted from a Filipino horror flick. Robert Dix, Vicki Volante, Joey Benson, Bruce Powers. Also called CREATURES OF THE PREHISTORIC PLANET, CREATURES OF THE RED PLANET, FLESH CREATURES OF THE RED PLANET, THE FLESH CREATURES, HORROR CREATURES OF THE LOST PLANET, HORROR CREATURES OF THE PREHISTORIC PLANET, HORROR CREATURES OF THE RED PLANET and SPACE MISSION OF THE LOST PLANET. (From Republic and VidAmerica as **HORROR OF THE BLOOD MONSTERS**)

VAMPIRE OF DR. DRACULA. See **FRANKENSTEIN'S BLOODY TERROR**.

VAMPIRE OF THE HIGHWAY, THE. See **HORRIBLE SEXY VAMPIRE, THE**.

VAMPIRE OVER LONDON. Video title for **MY SON, THE VAMPIRE** (Sinister/C; S/Weird; Filmfax).

VAMPIRE PEOPLE. Video version of **BLOOD DRINKERS, THE** (Sinister/C).

VAMPIRE PLAYGIRLS. See **CEMETERY GIRLS**.

VAMPIRE PRINCESS MIYU (1988). Japanese animated thriller depicting the Oriental occult as an ESP specialist investigates the supernatural. Directed by Toshihiro Hirano. (Central Park Media)

VAMPIRES, THE (1957). See **I VAMPIRI**.

VAMPIRES, THE (1961). Video version of **GOLIATH AND THE VAMPIRES** (Sinister/C).

VAMPIRES (1988). At a private Connecticut school, mad doctoress Jackie James uses a machine to extract the energy from her girl students; Duane Jones plays an occultist. Also known as ABADON. Produced-directed by Len Anthony; written by James Harrigan and Anthony. Orly Benair, Robin Michaels, John Bly.

VAMPIRE'S COFFIN, THE (1957). Campy Mexican pastiche of Universal horror movies of the '40s—stylish in a ridiculous way. Enhanced by good black-and-white photography, the film depicts tomb defilers who unleash a vampire drenched in salsa sauce. Bordering on a Bela Lugosi parody, the sanguinary count turns one of the defilers into an Igor-like minion and stalks beautiful women, who always faint so he can carry them away to his hideout. The climactic battle in a wax museum (reminiscent of HOUSE OF WAX) is a gas, with the vampire needlessly turning into a bat to fool his human foe. There's a laugh a minute, enhanced by a score copying the work of Hans Salter. German Robles portrays the evil Count Lavud, producer Abel Salazar doubles as a cast member to keep the budget down. Directed by Fernando Mendez. The U.S. version was produced by K. Gordon Murray, with new material directed by Paul Nagle. (Sinister/C; S/Weird; Filmfax)

VAMPIRE'S CRYPT. See **TERROR IN THE CRYPT**.

VAMPIRE'S GHOST, THE (1945). The closest thing to a Val Lewton-type movie ever made by Republic Studios. Director Lesley Selander treats this as if it were another jungle flick with bug-eyed superstitious natives. Its strengths lie in its script by Leigh Brackett and John K. Butler, which features literate dialogue and narration and an interestingly developed vampire: Webb Fallon, played by the strange John Abbott. Fallon (Gallic for "the stranger, one who walks in darkness beyond the campfires," according to the script) is an ages-old vampire whose heart is full of poetry and pain living in the town of Bakunda, West Africa, and running Fallon's Place, a saloon/casino of questionable reputation. Abbott's Fallon has a soft spot for Peggy Stewart and tries to take her away from big game hunter Charles Gordon. Grant Withers' priest and Adele Mara's jungle girl talk and behave like Lewton characters, giving the film added fillips when Selander's direction falters. Roy Barcroft. (Sinister/C; Discount)

VAMPIRES IN HAVANA (1986). Full-length horror-comedy cartoon from Cuba's Juan Padron, creator of that popular hero of the people, Elpidio Valdes, the freedom fighter. This shirks Cuban politics to deal with Dr. Werner Amadeus von Dracula, who has a secret formula so vampires can walk in sunlight. His nephew, Pepito, grows up to become a jazz trumpeter in Havana, while various factions (the European Vampire Group and La Capa Nostra) fight for the formula. This is rollicking, madcap-paced animation with characters who resemble escapees from a Gahan Wilson nightmare. Its bizarre imagery, eccentric ideas and broad buffoonery make it compelling.

VAMPIRE'S KISS (1988). And now for something completely different in the vein (heh heh!) of vampire movies . . . here's a strange tidbit about a New York literary

"Africa—the Dark Land where voodoo drums beat in the night, where the jungles are deep and full of secrets and the moon that lights them is still a mystic moon. Africa—where men have not forgotten the evil they do since the dawn of time."

—The narrator (John Abbott) in **THE VAMPIRE'S GHOST**

agent (Nicolas Cage) who gets it in the neck from a Manhattan vampire and goes insane, turning into a bloodsucker—or so he thinks. We can see his reflection in a mirror—but he can't! It is the ambiguities of the Joseph Minion script that no doubt appealed to director Robert Bierman. But in avoiding genre conventions, VAMPIRE'S KISS moves off on such an oddball tangent, into a region of hallucinatory dreams, it's tough to peg. It's more a study in madness as Cage makes life hell for his secretary, stands up his girl friend, fantasizes himself in the office of his shrink (Elizabeth Ashley in a non-responsive role) and carries a stake, requesting he be put to death before he attacks innocents. It works neither as a comedy nor as a satire, and floats in a void of its own. Catch it for something completely different if you're a vampire completist. Maria Conchita Alonso, Jennifer Beals. (HBO) (Laser: Image)

VAMPIRE'S LAST VICTIM, THE. See **PLAYGIRLS AND THE VAMPIRE, THE.**

VAMPIRE'S LOVER, THE. See **VAMPIRE AND THE BALLERINA, THE**.

VAMPIRE'S NIECE. See **FANGS OF THE LIVING DEAD**.

VAMPIRE'S NIGHT ORGY, THE (1973). Softcore Spanish flick in which a European town is taken over by vampires, eager to mix blood-drinking with sexual proclivity. Not exactly an orgy of excitement; call it "touching." Directed by Leon Klimovsky. Helga Line, Jack Taylor. (Filmfax; from Sinister/C as **ORGY OF THE VAMPIRES**)

VAMPIRES OF BIKINI BEACH (1987). Insufferable teen-age monster flick, a rank amateur effort shot in L.A. on a shoestring, and having the appeal of same strung through the eyelets of a raunchy tennis shoe. Two dumb teeners find "The Book of the Dead," and then find themselves in the thick of a vampire cult led by a caped cornball named Demos, who intends to raise an army of vampire zombies to take over the world. The vampires are ham personified, and every cliche is paraded before your weary eyes as this wretched waste of man-hours unfolds. The title is cute, but everything else isn't. Todd Kauffman, Jennifer Badham.

VAMPIRE'S THIRST. Video version of **BODY BENEATH, THE**.

VAMPIRES VS. HERCULES. See **HERCULES IN THE HAUNTED WORLD**.

VAMPIRE THRILLS. See **SEX AND THE VAMPIRE**.

VAMPIRE WOMAN. See **CRYPT OF THE LIVING DEAD**.

VAMPIRE WOMEN. See **QUEEN OF THE VAMPIRES**.

VAMPYR (1932). German masterpiece photographed by Rudolf Mate (he later became a Hollywood director) and produced-directed by Carl Theodore Dreyer, whose script (written with Christen Jul) is based on J. Sheridan Le Fanu's CARMILLA. It remains one of the few horror films to so well capture the nightmarish qualities of a dream. A visitor (Julian West) to a peculiar inn in a strange village is given a book on vampirism and plunged into a cryptic world of shadows, coffins and vampires. VAMPYR has, in recent years, taken on a cult following and been recognized as a minor art classic. Also known as THE STRANGE ADVENTURE OF DAVID GRAY and CASTLE OF DOOM. Henriette Gerard, Sibylle Schmitz, Rena Mandel. (Kino; Video Yesteryear; S/Weird; Filmfax) (Laser: Image)

VAMPYRES. Video version of **VAMPYRES—DAUGHTERS OF DARKNESS**. (Magnum)

VAMPYRES—DAUGHTERS OF DARKNESS (1975). R-rated version of the X-rated VAMPYRES. Lesbian bloodsuckers Fram and Miriam (Marianne Moore and Anulka) prey on campers vacationing on the lawn of their castle—until one of them makes the mistake of falling in love with handsome Murray Brown. The theme is: every lesbian vampire should own a castle. They certainly have a gay time in the crypt with Joseph Larraz directing. (Magnum; from Majestic as **SATAN'S DAUGHTERS** and Lettuce Entertain You as **BLOOD HUNGER**)

VAMPYRES . . . WHEN LIFE IS NOT ENOUGH (19??). Super-cheap quickie flick shot in New Jersey by writer-director Bruce G. Hallenbach. Randy Scott Rozler, Cathy Seyler, John Brent. (Raedon)

VANISHING POINT (1971). Exciting car chase film (with excellent stunt driving by Carey Loftin) has an intriguing metaphysical side underneath Richard Sarafian's direction. Barry Newman is Kowalski, a laconic, enigmatic race driver leading the police on a breathtaking race from Denver to Nevada. A psychic link is established between Kowalski and blind radio disc jockey Cleavon Little, who makes him a hero to listeners, seeing in Kowalski a symbol of rebellion. Symbolism surrounding old desert rat Dean Jagger who collects rattlesnakes is a bit heavy but contributes to existential philosophies about vanishing breeds. And a topless woman on a motorcycle remains one of this film's unforgettable images. Written by Guillermo Cain. Paul Koslo, Robert Donner. (Video/Laser: CBS/Fox)

VANISHING SHADOW, THE (1934). Twelve-chapter Universal serial with Onslow Stevens as an invisible avenger who goes after the murderers of his father with a robot, a death ray and other futuristic inventions. Directed by Lew Landers. Ada Ince, Walter Miller.

VARAN THE UNBELIEVABLE (1958). Varan was described by one critic as a flying squirrel with jet-propelled nuts, by another as a prehistoric bat . . . what the hell is this thing called Varan? Beats the hell out of us, but kiddies will squeal with delight at this U.S. version of a Japanese monster movie directed by Inoshiro Honda. Pure action as the Godzilla carbon copy beelines toward Tokyo, encountering resistance from a naval officer. Scenes with Myron Healey were added for U.S. appeal by director Sid Harris. Effects by Honda's partner, Eiji Tsuburaya. Kozo Nomura. Aka THE MONSTER VARAN. (VCI; United)

VARROW MISSION, THE (19??). A small Utah town undergoes a strange UFO invasion in this film allegedly based on a true incident. (Trend)

VAULT OF HORROR, THE (1973). Sequel to TALES FROM THE CRYPT consists of stories adapted from the E.C. comics of the '50s edited by William Gaines and Al Feldstein. Milton Subotsky's black-macabre script recaptures only some of the E.C. flavor, but horror fans will still enjoy. Five people trapped in an underground tomb with the Vault Keeper listen as he spins five yarns that run the gamut: vampirism, limb dismemberment, body snatching, voodoo, satanism, etc. "Midnight Mess," stars Daniel and Anna Massey; "The Neat Job," Glynis Johns and Terry-Thomas; "This Trick'll Kill You," Curt Jurgens; "Bargain in Death," Edward Judd and Michael Craig; and "Drawn and Quartered," Tom Baker. Roy Ward Baker directed. Aka TALES FROM THE CRYPT PART II. (Nostalgia Merchant; Media)

VEGAS IN SPACE (1991). This homegrown film from San Francisco's drag-queen community is an outrageous, campy spoof of sci-fi space adventures, emphasis on uninhibitedly wild hairdos, glitzy costumes and a self-mocking of the gay scene. As an underground oddity and an anomaly of movie making, it's a popular film-festival item and was released theatrically by Troma Inc. in 1993. It's the work of impresario Phillip R. Ford, who produced, directed, edited and conceived the no-state-of-the-art effects. It was conceived as a showpiece for drag-queen Doris Fish, who helped Ford shape the script with Miss X (another drag queen). Fish plays the captain of a spaceship assigned to investigate the disappearance of jewels on the planet Clitorius. But since no males are allowed on the planet, Fish and other crew members take sex-change pills, turning into women. There's no attempt at serious film making so what gives the film's its unusual edge is it's blatant badness and lack of cinematic art. It works better as an audience-participation experience. Except for a few sexual inuendoes or double entedres, there is nothing sexy about the film—it is never lascivious. Only the clothing and hair are in bad taste. Doris Fish died of AIDS in 1991, the month the film opened in San

Francisco. Two months later another cast member, Tippi, who plays "Princess Angel," died of AIDS. Among the drag queens: Miss X as "Veneer, Queen of Clitorean Police"; Ginger Quest as "Empress Nueva Gabor"; Timmy Spence as "Lt. Dick Hunter"; Ramona Fischer as "Lt. Sheila Shadows"; Jennifer Blowdryer as "Futura Volare"; and Sandelle Kincaid as "Babs Velour." (MCA)

VEIL, THE (1958). Four vignettes from an unsold TV series, with Boris Karloff as introducer: "Crystal Ball," "The Doctor," "Genesis," and "What Happened to Peggy?" Directed by Herbert L. Strock. Patrick Macnee, Robert Griffin, Ray Montgomery. Also built from leftover episodes: JACK THE RIPPER and DESTINATION NIGHTMARE. (Sinister/C; S/Weird; Filmfax)

VEIL, THE. See **HAUNTS**.

VEIL OF BLOOD (1973). Swiss vampire yarn written-directed by Joe Sarno, about a baroness of blood whose soul is kept alive in the bodies of descendants. Nadia Senkowa, Untel Syring, Ulrike Butz.

VELVET HOUSE. See **CRUCIBLE OF HORROR**.

VELVET VAMPIRE, THE (1971). Commendable attempt by director Stephanie Rothman and co-writers Charles S. Swartz and Marice Jules to create an unusual vampire picture. Also known as THE WAKING HOUR, this has strong sexual overtones that heighten the suspense when travelers Michael Blodgett and Sherry Miles stop at the ranchero of Celeste Yarnall, unaware she is a sensual vampire and a descendant of horror writer Sheridan Le Fanu. There's time wasted with desert dunebuggy footage, but once Yarnall focuses on her targets, male and female, the going gets sensuous. How the vampire is laid to rest belongs to the Flower Child Generation. Sherry Miles, Gene Shane. (Embassy; Impulse; Simitar) (Laser: Image)

VENETIAN AFFAIR, THE (1966). Predictable, cliched spy thriller about a nerve-destroying drug that turns men into controllable zombies, but done with a topnotch cast headed by Robert Vaughn as an undercover agent, Karl Boehm as the dastardly villain, Elke Sommer and Felicia Farr as sexy go-betweens and Boris Karloff as a mysterious inventor. The Venice location photography is pleasant and distracts from the muddled story by E. Jack Neuman, who adapted a novel by Helen MacInnes. Directed by Jerry Thorpe. Ed Asner, Luciana Paluzzi, Roger C. Carmel, Joe De Santos.

VENGEANCE. See **BRAIN, THE (1962).**

VENGEANCE LAND (1986). In the year 2030, the Hunters hunt the Hunted. Zap guns in desolation. Directed by Roderick Taylor.

VENGEANCE OF FU MANCHU, THE (1968). Lackluster Harry Alan Towers production (third in the British series) with Christopher Lee as the diabolical Asian mastermind who forces a surgeon to create an exact duplicate of Scotland Yard's Nayland Smith in an insidious plot to substitute the chief law enforcers with killer clones. Strangely lacking in action. Directed by Jeremy Summers from a Towers script. Howard Marion Crawford, Tsai Chin, Horst Frank, Maria Rohm, Tony Ferrer.

VENGEANCE OF HERCULES. See **GOLIATH AND THE DRAGON**.

VENGEANCE OF SHE (1967). The best thing going in this loose Hammer sequel to the Ursula Andress version of H. Rider Haggard's SHE is the sexy Olinka Berova, who turns up on a millionaire's yacht in a daze, uncertain of who she is or why she's being mysteriously drawn to a lost city in the nearby desert mountains. Berova, an exotically attractive blonde with a marvelous figure, parades around in various stages of disarray in the company of heroic Edward Judd while high priest John Richardson tries to lure the beauty into the Eternal Flame and thereby find eternal life in the kingdom of Kuma. Peter O'Donnell's script is compelling enough to hold one's interest, the Hammer production values are strong and director Cliff Owen focuses on the shapely form of Ms Berova frequently enough to take one's mind off any inadequacies of story. Andre Morell, George Sewell, Colin Blakely, Noel Willman, Jill Melford.

VENGEANCE OF THE MONSTER. See **MAJIN, MONSTER OF TERROR**.

VENGEANCE OF THE MUMMY. See **MUMMY'S REVENGE, THE**. (Mummy Deadest!)

VENGEANCE OF THE ZOMBIES (1972). Spanish fright job directed by Leon Klimovsky (the hombre who gave us SAGA OF DRACULA and VAMPYRES) and starring that Holy Toledo monster star Paul Naschy. Indian sage named Krisna (is his first name Harry?) arranges, through a magical chant, to raise a woman from the grave, who is turned into a killing machine for purposes of revenge. Montezuma's revenge could be next. Script by Jacinto Molina. Mirta Miller, Vic Winner, Luis Ciges. Also known as REVOLT OF THE DEAD ONES and THE REBELLION OF THE DEAD WOMEN. (Home; Sinister/C; All Seasons; S/Weird; Filmfax; from Vogue as **WALK OF THE DEAD**)

VENGEANCE: THE DEMON. Once proposed theatrical title for **PUMPKINHEAD**.

VENGEFUL DEAD, THE. Video version of **KISS DADDY GOODBYE** (Premiere).

VENOM (1982). Kidnapping-hostage-siege plot mixed with snake-menace subplot results in a taut suspenser despite melodramatic contrivances and one-dimensional characters. Martin Bregman's production maintains a compelling hold as a black mamba, the most lethal reptile around the house, is loose in a London mansion where kidnappers Oliver Reed, Susan George and Klaus Kinski hold a rich kid for ransom. Tension mounts as the killer snake slithers through the house, ready to strike. Meanwhile, policeman Nicol Williamson barricades the street to engage in standard hostage cliches. Director Piers Haggard keeps Robert Carrington's script uncoiling. Sterling Hayden is the boy's grandfather, a retired big-game hunter (hence knowledgeable about deadly serpents), and Sarah Miles portrays an expert in herpetology trapped in the house. (Vestron)

VENOM. See **LEGEND OF SPIDER FOREST.**

VENUS AGAINST THE SON OF HERCULES (1962). An entire planet against one lousy muscleman? Naw, just a sinew-happy warrior against mangy Italian meeklings as he fights to overcome magical incantations, monsters, man-eating plants and other stuff by writer-director Marcello Baldi. Massimo Serato, Roger Browne, Jackie Lane. (Sinister/C; S/Weird)

VENUSIAN, THE. See **STRANGER FROM VENUS.**

VENUS IN FURS (1969). Harry Alan Towers production features James Darren and Barbara McNair as ghosts unaware they are spirits as they become involved with the underworld of sex and sadism. Director Jesus Franco (who co-scripted with Malvin Wald) spins a weird story about weirdos and perverts. The title was lifted from Sacher-Masoch, but everything else was taken from Hunger. Just goes to prove you can't wrap a sow's ear in a mink stole. Klaus Kinski, Dennis Price, Maria Rohm. Aka BLACK ANGEL. (Republic)

VERTIGO (1958). Alfred Hitchcock classic reeking with a supernatural atmosphere enhanced by Bernard Herrmann's eerie music. Even though suggestions of afterlife and reincarnation are explained logically, it's still a compelling story in which James Stewart, a detective who has survived a bad fall and suffers from a fear of heights, prevents mysterious Kim Novak from committing suicide in San Francisco Bay and falls in love with her as he tries to help her remember her past. The Alec Coppel-Samuel Taylor script is based on an excellent French thriller by Pierre Boileau and Thomas Narcejac. Barbara Bel Geddes, Henry Jones, Tom Helmore. (Video/Laser: MCA)

VERY CLOSE ENCOUNTERS OF THE FOURTH KIND (1979). Three creatures from another world (or so they would appear) have continuous sexual experiences with a physics teacher in the woods. Italian sexploitation of the worst kind. Directed by Mario Garriazzo. Maria Baxa, Monica Zanchi, Mariko Maranza. (In video as **COMING OF ALIENS, THE**)

VETERAN, THE. See **DEAD OF NIGHT** (1974).

VIBES (1988). What might have been a rousing fantasy-adventure in the fashion of ROMANCING THE STONE turns up a lame duck for producer Ron Howard. Psychics Jeff Goldblum and Cyndi Lauper (he has the power of psychometry, she makes predicitons via an Indian Spirit Guide) are lured to Ecuador by a strange character named Harry Buscafusco (Peter Falk) to find a room of gold in a lost city high in the mountains. Little of the adventure and comedy promise of this premise—concocted by screenwriters Lowell Ganz and Babaloo Mandel, who gave us SPLASH—pays off as the romantic team finds that almost everyone else they've encountered in the film is in on one scheme or another. Richard Edlund provides mildly interesting special effects surrounding a pyramid-shaped stone that gives off powerful psychic energy, but director Ken Kwapis has little with which to work. The Goldblum-Lauper duo is quite appealing, though. Julian Sands, Googy Gress, Michael Lerner, Ramon Bieri. (RCA/Columbia) (Laser: Japanese)

VICE VERSA (1948). See editions 1-3.

VICE VERSA (1988). An amusing, oft-clever use of the plot device of switched personalities in two bodies—in this case a somewhat neurotic, humorless department store executive (Judge Reinhold) swaps souls with his adolescent son (Fred Savage) through the magical powers of a Thailand art object that resembles a devil's mask. Reinhold steals this show with his portrayal of a youngster in a man's body, capturing the nuances of a wide-eyed kid having the advantages of an adult's body. To the credit of screenwriters/producers Dick Clement and Ian La-Frenais, they keep the ridiculous Thailand elements to a minimum, and play down the danger element as art collectors-thieves Swoosie Kurtz and David Proval pursue father and son for the relic. Director Brian Gilbert is far more interested in social satire. Corinne Bohrer, Jane Kaczmerek, Gloria Gifford. (Video/Laser: RCA/Columbia)

VICTIMS (19??). Four attractive gals go camping in the desert—an open invitation for a serial killer to stalk them. Produced-directed by Jeff Hathcock. (Simitar)

VICTOR FRANKENSTEIN. TV title for **TERROR OF FRANKENSTEIN.**

GOLDEN GATE BRIDGE RESCUE IN 'VERTIGO'

VIDEO DEAD, THE (1987). Uninspired video original, another variation on NIGHT OF THE LIVING DEAD, only this time the zombie monsters come out of a TV set. Written-produced-directed by Robert Scott in and around San Francisco, this features gore effects, zombie make-up and a dumb plot. Rocky Duvall, Roxana Augesen, Sam David McClelland. (Embassy)

'VIDEO DEAD'

VIDEODROME (1983). Bungled David Cronenberg picture, grotesque and repulsive under his writing and direction. James Wood is a sleazy cable TV station owner, looking for porn programming, who stumbles across a sadistic series called "Videodrome." Watch enough sex and violence and a new organ grows in your brain that creates hallucinations. Eventually your mind and body evolve into something more wholesome. It's a plot by the Moral Majority to cleanse the nation. If you're having trouble following this critique, wait until you see this botched mess. Rick Baker's effects are ugly, and the sex and violence were heavily cut by Universal for an R rating. (Note, however, that Cronenberg restored the footage from his X-rated version for video and laser.) Deborah Harry of Blondie is the beautiful female lead, but her character is so unsavory, she and Wood as sadists are a turn off. Sonja Smits, Peter Dvorsky, Les Carlson. (MCA; A & E) (Laser: MCA)

VIDEO MURDERS (1987). Murderer tapes all his crimes; meanwhile, he's tracked by a police detective. Eric Brown, Virginia Loridans, John Ferita. (Trans World)

VIDEO WARS (1984). Inept Italian spy spoof, in which dumb superspy Scattergood (billed as George Diamond, but don't believe it), the head of SOB (Subversive Operations Bureau), is assigned by a video-happy President to stop a villain named Reichmonger, dictator of the kingdom of Vacabia, which has programmed the video games of the world to brainwash everyone for conquest. Absolutely nothing happens in this Mario Giampaolo produced-directed fiasco except a bevy of beauties show off their breasts and legs, and a dumb Norwegian beauty (Joan Stenn, as Miss Hemisphere) tries to lay the hero. (Best Film & Video)

VIENNA STRANGLER, THE. See **MAD BUTCHER.**

VIEW TO A KILL, A (1985). Something misfired in Roger Moore's seventh (and last) 007 outing. Despite the massive destruction and opportunities for excitement, director John Glen's pacing is strangely lethargic. Part of the trouble is a minimum of offbeat gadgets and machines; a less-than-rugged Moore, whose quips are as weary as his physique; and a Richard Maibaum-Michael G. Wilson script lacking humor or freshness. Master villain Max Zorin plots to destroy Silicone Valley and the world micro-chip market by creating earthquakes to shake up the Andreas Fault. The film's only saving Grace is the lithe Ms Jones as May Day, a tigress who makes Christopher Walken's Zorin a wimp in comparison. Tanya Roberts as heroine Stacey Sutton is an attractive eyeful but her acting abilities are minimal. Patrick Macnee is pleasant as Bond's undercover companion but he never gets a chance to display the ability of Steed the Avenger. There's a shootout on the Eiffel Tower, a high-speed fire engine chase down Market Street in San Francisco, a cliffhanging climax on the Golden Gate Bridge, and the blowing up of an underground cavern . . . but it just sits there and dies. (Video/Laser: CBS/Fox; MGM/UA)

VIKING WOMEN AND THE SEA SERPENT (1958). Rock-bottom Roger Corman programmer (he produced-directed) depicts a water beast that functions as a *deus ex machina* by intervening at the last minute between bands of warring Vikings. Scenes are so dark, the ocean

GRACE JONES AS MAY DAY IN 'A VIEW TO A KILL'

waves so phony and the position of man to beast so ambiguous, the only horror to be pondered is: Who designed the crummy monster? Too bad the creature didn't swallow the good guys along with the bad—that would really give him indigestion. The people are that tasteless. Originally made as THE VOYAGE OF THE VIKING WOMEN TO THE WATERS OF THE GREAT SEA SERPENT. Abby Dalton, Gary Conway, Susan Cabot, Brad Jackson, Jonathan Haze.

VILLAGE OF EIGHT GRAVESTONES (1982). What appears to be a murder mystery soon develops touches of the supernatural when the young heir to a fortune discovers there's a curse on his family, placed there four centuries ago by a band of eight samurai soldiers. Directed by Yoshitaro Nomura. Kenichi Hagiwara.

VILLAGE OF THE DAMNED (1960). Faithful version of John Wyndham's MIDWICH CUCKOOS, thanks to director Wolf Rilla, who co-wrote the adaptation with Stirling Silliphant and George Barclay. A small community in England is isolated by a strange invisible shield and its inhabitants afflicted by prolonged sleep. Later, the village's pregnant women give birth to hollow-eyed children who possess irresistible hypnotic powers, and grow up to dominate adults, especially their fathers. Ultimately, these singular alien children will have a devastating effect on mankind. This British film generated a sequel, CHILDREN OF THE DAMNED, equally well done. George Sanders, Barbara Shelley, Michael Gwynn, Laurence Naismith. (MGM/UA) (Laser: MGM/UA, with **CHILDREN OF THE DAMNED**)

VILLAGE OF THE GIANTS (1965). Bert I. Gordon on an unstoppable, unquenchable rampage—editing, writing, producing, directing, even contributing special effects. Is there no way this man can be chained? Is the world helpless against him? Must we be subjected to the blasphemous suggestion that this fantasy film is based on H. G. Wells' FOOD OF THE GODS? And must we be exposed to stupid teenagers who discover a food that makes them grow to amazing proportions? And must we listen to such dialogue as "It's our world, not theirs" and "It's us against the adults"? Do we not all have the right to close our eyes rather than endure the varied acting styles of Tommy Kirk, Johnny Crawford, Beau Bridges, Ron Howard and Joy Harmon in Perceptovision? This is a mini among giants. (Embassy)

VINCENT PRICE'S ONCE UPON A MIDNIGHT SCARY. See **ONCE UPON A MIDNIGHT SCARY.**

VINDICATOR, THE (1984). Above-average, well-produced Canadian blend of horror and sci-fi (originally FRANKENSTEIN '88) reminiscent of MAN-MADE MONSTER and THE INDESTRUCTIBLE MAN. Obsessed (and certainly mad) scientist Richard Cox takes the victim of an accident (David McIlwraith) and turns him into a cyborg, who escapes and commences a rampage of death and destruction because of his evil programming, even though he's a good guy who would rather go after the crooks. Bounty huntress Pam Grier (her name is Hunter) is hired to track the robot killer with a gun that fires "vaporized acid," and she's one ruthless bitch. There's some nice sewer sequences, good battles and destruction scenes, a violent rape and a sense of cinematic style emerging from director Jean-Claude Lord. Stan Winston created the cyborg look, which is more messy than dressy. Teri Austin, Maury Chaykin, Denis Simpson. (Key)

VINEYARD, THE (1989). Japanese madman with a penchant for blood traps victims on his island. His blooddrinking gives him immortality, but will the theme immortalize this movie? James Hong, Karen Witter, Michael Wong, Cheryl Lawson. Directed by Bill Rice. Script by Hong, Douglas Condo and James Marlowe. (New World) (Laser: Image)

VIOLENT BLOOD BATH (1985). The presence of Fernando Rey as a magistrate haunted by memories of sending a serial killer to the guillotine enhances and upgrades this foreign-produced psychothriller, which co-stars Marissa Mell as his long-suffering wife. It appears that the serial murderer has returned from the grave when a new wave of identical crimes begins, forcing Rey back onto the case to work with police. The script by John Tebar and director Jeorge Grau (said to be based on a "theme" by Guy Maupassant) has enough character content to set this above most of its kind. Aka PENALTY OF DEATH and NIGHT FIEND. Esparaco Santoni, Elisa Laguna. Shown on TV as NIGHT FIEND. (World's Worst; VidAmerica)

VIOLENT MIDNIGHT. See **PSYCHOMANIA** (1963).

VIPER (1993). Crummy TV-movie about an wheelchair-bound inventor (Dorian Harewood) who creates a new law-enforcement vehicle for a futuristic society and a criminal suffering from amnesia (James McCaffrey) who drives the prototype auto to prove its worthiness. Director Danny Bilson co-scripted with Paul De Meo. Joe Nipote, Sydney Walsh, Jon Polito.

VIRGIN AMONG THE LIVING DEAD, A (1971). Young heiress is haunted by her family's secrets after arriving in the family's stomping grounds in British Honduras—where the stomping is literal. Directed by Jess Frank. Footage was used from ZOMBIE LAKE to make this more commercial in the U.S. Paul Muller, Christina Von Blanc, Britt Nichols. (Lightning; Wizard; from Edde as **ZOMBIE 4**)

VIRGIN HUNTERS (1993). Sorry, no sex in the year 2000, but that doesn't stop teens from doing it anyway—causing a team of sex cops to go into action. Morgan Fairchild, Ian Abercrombie, Brian Bremer, Michelle Matheson. Directed by Ellen Cabot. (Torchlight/Paramount)

VIRGIN OF NUREMBERG. Video version of **HORROR CASTLE** (AIP; Twin Tower; Panther).

VIRGINS AND VAMPIRES. See **CAGED VIRGINS.**

VIRGIN SPRING, THE (1960). Superlative Ingmar Bergman classic based on an old Swedish song, "The Daughter of Tore of Vange," which tells of the rape-murder of an innocent girl, the revenge of the father and the gushing forth of a spring at the site of the heinous act. Bergman evokes 14th Century Sweden in memorable detail, his cast in turn capturing the simplicity, and desperation, of the grass-roots characters. Birgitta Petterson is the essence of purity and innocence as the murdered girl and Max von Sydow, as the outraged father, undergoes a strange ritual before pursuing the three rapists with his hunting knife. Powerful material, uncompromising in its depiction of rape, yet gentle in its reverence for the Swedish people. (Nelson)

VIRGIN TERROR. Video version of **TRAUMA** (Lettuce Entertain You).

VIRGIN VAMPIRES. See **TWINS OF EVIL.**

VIRGIN WITCH, THE (1970). British production focusing on black mass and witchcraft as two women arrive in London to work as models, but find themselves in the velvet underground of lesbian sex and seduction. Directed by Roy Austin, scripted by Klaus Vogen from his novel. Ann Michelle, Vicky Michelle, Keith Buckley, Patricia Haines. (Prism)

VIRUS (1980). Well-produced, nihilistic U.S.-Japanese sci-fi thriller with pessimistic overtones, in which mankind is wiped out by a plague, except for a handful of survivors at the South Pole. A sub sails for Washington DC to avert the automatic launching of U.S. nuclear missiles, with Bo Svenson and Sonny Chiba all that stand between another holocaust and salvation. The huge cast includes Glenn Ford, Henry Silva, Chuck Connors (as the sub captain), Robert Vaughn and Cec Linder. Directed-written by Kinji Fukasaku, from a novel by Sakyo Komatsu. (Media; Starmaker)

VIRUS (1980). See **CANNIBALS ARE IN THE STREETS, THE.**

VISIONS (1990). Joe Balogh suffers from visions that could hold the answer to who is killing the hoboes in and around Portland, Oregon. Psychic/slasher film that is all too familiar by now. Produced-directed by Steven Miller from a screenplay he wrote with Tom Taylor. Alice Villarreal, A.R. Newman, J.R. Pella. (Monarch)

VISIONS OF DEATH (1972). Outstanding TV-movie, suspenseful as hell as physics professor Monte Markham is suddenly plagued by psychic visions in which he sees flashes of a mad bomber planning to blow up half of Denver. The tension mounts as policeman Telly Savalas first suspects Markham, then realizes his ESP is genuine. How they work together to capture the madman heaps on more suspense. Tautly written by Paul Playdon and directed with style by Lee H. Katzin. Barbara Anderson provides solid love interest. Tim O'Connor, Joe Sirola, Lonny Chapman, Jim Antonio, Richard Erdman. Also known as **VISIONS.**

VISIONS OF EVIL (1973). Young woman just released from the fruitcake house is in fear of going back when she moves in with her husband and experiences nightmares of her doom that include dreams about an axe murder. Lori Saunders, Dean Jagger, Ben Ginnaven. Aka VISIONS OF DOOM. (Prism)

VISITANTS, THE (1987). E.T. creatures from beyond space land on Earth in the 1950s and, just for laughs, settle down to suburbia living. Directed by Rick Sloane. Marcus Vaughter, Johanna Grika, Nicole Rio. (Star Classics; Trans World)

VISIT FROM A DEAD MAN (1974). Low-budget videotape quickie shot in England. A triangular situation between a wealthy collector of statues, his gorgeous wife and a lawyer results first in murder, then in a supernatural visitation. Directed by Lela Swift. Alfred Drake, Stephen Collins, Heather MacRae.

VISIT TO A SMALL PLANET (1960). Producer Hal Wallis took Gore Vidal's Broadway play (a light-hearted affair that sparkled with ironic wit) and had writers Edmund Beloin and Henry Garson reshape it into a shapeless, hapless vehicle for the slapstick of Jerry Lewis. As Kreton, an E.T. who lands on Earth to observe the Civil War, Lewis discovers he has timed his arrival 100 years too late. He rectifies his mistake by becoming a Peeping Tom to observe American customs. The sight gags and inanities, of unimaginative proportions under Norman Taurog's direction, are set into feckless motion. Example: Lewis has the power to make people recite "Mary Had a Little Lamb" in baby talk. Vidal must have had a little kitten. Joan Blackman, Fred Clark, Earl Holliman, Lee Patrick, Gale Gordon, Jerome Cowan, John Williams, Barbara Lawson. (Musicvision)

VISITING HOURS (1982). Better-than-average slasher film that often follows killer Michael Ironside, so that we are as much with him as the victims. A Canadian production, this also focuses on Lee Grant as a TV reporter fighting for women's rights who is stalked by Colt Hawker (Ironside) in a hospital. Tautly directed by Jean Claude Lord and scripted with an understanding of movie terror by Brian Taggert. Linda Purl, William Shatner, Lenore Zann, Harvey Atkin. (Video/Laser: CBS/Fox)

VISITOR, THE (1980). Offbeat imitation of THE OMEN, dealing with an Archangel who comes to Earth to ward off a force of evil from Hell. This allegorical mumbo jumbo is told with odd camera angles, unexplainable effects and pseudoreligious symbolism that baffles rather than enlightens. Directed by Giulio Paradisi. An Italian-U.S. production with a top cast: Glenn Ford, Mel Ferrer, Shelley Winters, John Huston, Sam Peckinpah, Lance Henriksen. (Embassy; Sam Goldwyn) (Laser: Sam Goldwyn)

VISITOR FROM THE GRAVE (1982). One-hour episode of the British series, HAMMER HOUSE OF HORROR, packaged as a video. This can also be seen as half of a TV-movie coupled with **CHILDREN OF THE FULL MOON**. See that entry. (Thrillervideo)

VISITORS, THE (1988). Swedish variation of THE AMITYVILLE HORROR is an effective supernatural chiller with several scary sequences, undermined only by mediocre English dubbing. Before the haunting begins, however, writers-producers Joakim and Patrik Ersgard take the time to establish the psychological tension between a young insurance executive and his wife and their two children when they move into a country home. Their conflicts set into motion the forces of demons imprisoned in an attic room—wallpaper falls off the walls, a strange sliding noise can be heard behind the walls and finally a demon's image appears. Director Joakim Ersgard brings a peculiar edge to some of the characters that borders on satire, but the atmospheric sequences work well. Keith Berkeley, John Force, Joanna Berg, John Olson. (Vidmark) (Laser: Image)

VOICE OF THE WHISTLER (1945). Richard Dix is forced to commit murder by a post-hypnotic suggestion in this low-budget film noir inspired by THE WHISTLER radio series. William Castle co-wrote the script with Wilfrid H. Pettit, and directed with a sense of doom. Lynn Merrick, Tom Kennedy, Rhys Williams, Donald Woods.

VOICES (1973). Little-known British film with David Hemmings and Gayle Hunnicutt as a couple who arrive at an old mansion and imagine they see ghosts. Neat twist ending may catch viewers offguard. Directed by Kevin Billington. Adapted from a Richard Lortz play by George Kiro and Robert Enders. Lynn Farleigh, Peggy Ann Clifford. (From Mirsch as **NIGHTMARE**)

VOICES FROM BEYOND (1990). Italian horror director Lucio Fulci tells the tale of a man who dies but comes back to confront his daughter and have her investigate his death. Fulci directed and co-wrote the script with Piero Regnoli. Duilio Del Prete, Karina Huff.

VOLCANO MONSTER, THE. See **GIGANTIS THE FIRE MONSTER.**

VOLERE VOLARE (1993). Rollicking, absurd Italian comedy in which a daffy but lovable sound effects man (Maurizio Nichetti) turns into a cartoon version of himself after falling in love with an equally daffy gal (Angela Finocchiaro) who specializes in partaking in kinky (but innocuous) sex games with her goofy clientel. Loaded with zany sound effects, sight gags and a gallery of wonderfully bizarre personalities. Written-directed by Maurizio Nichetti and Guido Manuli. (New Line)

VOLTRON, DEFENDER OF THE UNIVERSE: CASTLE OF LIONS (1984). Animated feature of the STAR WARS school pitting the Galaxy Alliance vs. the evil robots of King Zarkon. The heroic team must find the whereabouts of some vital keys in a castle where Robeast roves relentlessly. (Sony) (Laser: Image)

VOLTRON, DEFENDER OF THE UNIVERSE: PLANET DOOM. Laser disc compilation of four episodes of the cartoon series starring the heroes of the Galaxy Alliance. (Image)

VOODOO BABY (1979). Joe D'Amato directed this exploitationer involving black magic, demons and bizarre sexual practices of the supernatural. Susan Scott, Richard Harrison, Lucia Ramirez.

VOODOO BLACK EXORCIST (1989). Black prince, dead for 3000 years, rises from the grave to wreak revenge. Aldo Sambrel, Tenyeka Stadle, Fernando Sancho. (Vidtape/Duravision)

VOODOO BLOOD BATH. See **I EAT YOUR SKIN** and **ZOMBIES.**

VOODOO BLOOD DEATH. See **CURSE OF THE VOODOO.**

VOODOO DAWN (1989). Weak production values, a lack of tension and a loosely structured storyline by John Russo/Jeffrey Delman/Thomas Rendon/Evan Dunsky make for one cold VOODOO DAWN. Two students go looking for a friend who is researching migrant workers in the south, unaware that their friend has been turned into a flesh-craving zombie by a tall black crude dude with a machete. There's an attempt to repeat plot elements of NIGHT OF THE LIVING DEAD but director Steven Fierberg's pacing is far too lethargic to melt the dew off the grass of this DAWN. Only interesting moment is when a demon head rises up from a man's stomach a la ALIEN. Raymond St. Jacques, Theresa Merritt, Gina Gershon. (Academy) (Laser: Image)

VOODOO DOLLS (1990). School maidens fall victim to the ghoulish ghosts residing in an old institution of learning that teaches them the true meaning of ABC: Apparitions, blood and corpses. Directed by Andre Pelletier. Maria Stanton. (Atlas Entertainment)

VOODOO GIRL. See **SUGAR HILL.**

VOODOO HEARTBEAT (1972). See editions 1-3.

VOODOO ISLAND (1957). Boris Karloff's performance as hoax buster Phillip Knight is the saving grace of this Howard W. Koch-Aubrey Schenck low-budget, low-energy production filmed on Kauai Island, Hawaii. Eager to debunk reports of voodooism, Karloff, associate Beverly Tyler and assorted adventurers end up on an island where man-eating plants (and not very convincing ones at that) are on the attack. Richard Landau's script has Karloff realizing the supernatural does exist, and an affair between angst-ridden explorer Rhodes Reason and the naive, sexually awakening Tyler. Sluggishly directed by Reginald LeBorg. Murvyn Vye, Elisha Cook and Jean Engstrom provide secondary characters.

VOODOO MAN, THE (1944). Fun in a perverse way, this is so appallingly bad. George Zucco is a voodoo cult leader with a TV "spy" device who works in cahoots with hypnotist Bela Lugosi and John Carradine, a drum-beating Igor-type whose light bulbs are rather weak. Lugosi is kidnapping women with a phony roadblock detour, encasing them in sexy nightgowns and putting them into trances in the hopes he can transfer one of their souls into the corpse of his wife, who has been dead 22 years. This is attempted while Zucco utters nutty mumbo jumbo. Under William Beaudine's direction, Lugosi is the world's biggest hambone, with the Carradine character taking close second. The Monogram production values (with producer Sam Katzman at the helm) are distressingly poor, and the acting is so bad it could put you into a catatonic state. Wanda McKay, Louise Currie, Henry Hall, Michael Ames.

VOODOO WOMAN (1957). Slow-moving, shopworn jungle thriller from producer Alex Gordon in which Marla English (whose body English is superb, even if she doesn't shape up much as an actress) falls under mad doctor Tom Conway and resembles a "Living Dead" refugee with fright wig and scare mask. Directed by Edward L. Cahn. Touch (Michael) Connors, Lance Fuller, Paul Dubov, Paul Blaisdell. Remade as CURSE OF THE SWAMP CREATURE. (RCA/Columbia; Paramount)

VORTEX. Video of **DAY TIME ENDED, THE** (Value).

VORTEX (1982). Two hardware government corporations shoot it out for possession of a "Star Wars" laser weapon, with a lady private eye involved. Avant garde, artsy craftsy stuff. James Russo, Lydia Lunch, Dick Miller, Bill Rice. Directed by Scott and Beth B. (Icarus)

VOYAGE INTO EVIL. See **CRUISE INTO TERROR.**

VOYAGE INTO SPACE (1968). Japanese TV series re-edited to feature length and dubbed in English. Result: An outer space mess in which a youth and giant robot fight off imperialistic aliens. Mitsunobu Kaneko.

VOYAGE OF THE ROCK ALIENS (1984). Sci-fi musical comedy with Chainsaw, Dee Dee, Frankie and Diane fighting invading E.T.s Directed by James Fargo. Pia Zadora, Tom Nolan, Craig Sheffer, Ruth Gordon, Jimmy and the Mustangs. (Prism)

VOYAGE TO ARCTURUS (1971). Cheapie space adventure from writer-director B. J. Holloway, with outer space cliches. David Eldred, Tom Hastings, Susan Junge.

VOYAGE TO THE BOTTOM OF THE SEA (1961). Visually exciting, good-humored Irwin Allen production designed for the young set with big names to appeal to parents: Walter Pidgeon, Joan Fontaine, Peter Lorre, Robert Sterling. The biggest star remains the atomic sub Seaview, with panels of flashing lights and fluctuating gauges. (This set was used in the TV series of the same title.) The Van Allen Radiation Belt surrounding Earth has caught fire; the mission of Seaview is to fire a missile to put out the blaze. But complications erupt aboardship when a saboteur goes to work. Barbara Eden, Frankie Avalon, Michael Ansara, Henry Daniell, Regis Toomey. (CBS/Fox/Playhouse) (Laser: Japanese)

VOYAGE TO THE END OF THE UNIVERSE (1964). Czech sci-fi has meritorious values, but is hampered by poor English dubbing and cropped Cinemascope format. Setting is a colossal spaceship carrying a colony to a new habitable world. Emphasis is on problems aboard the craft, encounters with an alien ship and its dead crew, and an adventure in a space nebula. The surprise ending will fool no one, but director Jindrich Polak and cast work hard to pull it off. Zdenek Stepanek.

VOYAGE TO THE PLANET OF PREHISTORIC WOMEN (1968). Not a sequel to VOYAGE TO THE PREHISTORIC PLANET, just more footage lifted from a 1962 Soviet film, PLANET OF STORMS, which Roger Corman repackaged for U.S. consumption. New footage directed by Peter Bogdanovich features Mamie Van Doren and other statuesque cuties in furry bikinis. These buxom dolls portray psychic humanoids who enjoy close encounters with stranded Earthnauts. And nauts to you, too, earthy ones. It was written (?) by Henry Ney. Also called GILL WOMAN and GILL WOMEN OF VENUS. (Sinister/C; S/Weird; Filmfax)

VOYAGE TO THE PREHISTORIC PLANET (1965). Highlights from the Soviet sci-fi movie, PLANET OF STORMS, the story of cosmonauts exploring Venus, plus new footage shot by writer-director Curtis Harrington that features Basil Rathbone, Faith Domergue and Marc Shannon. Roger Corman spliced it together with Elmer's Glue. Same old plot: Earthmen crashland on an alien world to face new dangers from E.T.s, robot men, centuries-old lizards, etc. Voyage to prehistoric tedium. Nostalgia; Sinister/C; Filmfax)

VOYAGER FROM THE UNKNOWN (1982-83). Episodes of TV's VOYAGERS about travelers trapped in different time zones as they try to return to the present. Directed by James D. Parriott and Rick Colby. Jon-Erik Hexum, Meeno Peluce, Ed Begley. (MCA)

VULCAN, SON OF JUPITER (1962). Rod Flash flashes his biceps as he fights off lizard men and other monsters found in beefcake Italian fiascos. Directed by Emmimo Salvi. Gordon Mitchell, Bella Cortez.

VULTURE, THE (1967). Akim Tamiroff as a creature with a bird's body, legs and wings, but retaining human head and arms? That's only the beginning, bird lovers. Dig the inept performances of Robert Hutton and Broderick Crawford, groove on the ersatz, belly-flopping suspense. The vultures must be picking the bones of writer-producer-director Lawrence Huntington. (IVE)

VULTURES (1985). Jim Bailey in five roles (you figure out which characters) is the highpoint of this gore-murder thriller told in whodunit fashion. Yachtsman Stuart Whitman is accused of the crimes, but we know better as he pursues the clues. Average for its type. Written-produced-directed by Paul Leder. Yvonne De Carlo, Aldo Ray, Greg Mullavey, Maria Perschy. (Prism)

WACKO (1981). Producer-director Greydon Clark's parody of FRIDAY THE 13TH features The Halloween Lawn Mower Killer, a weirdo who wears a pumpkin for a face as he terrorizes Alfred Hitchcock High (where the Hitchcock Birds face the De Palma Knives). Most gags in this spoof fall flatter than pancakes—and flattery will get you nowhere. References (visual and verbal) to horror/sci-fi cinema might help buffs to enjoy this in a small way. Everyone else will wince as the town faces an unlucky Friday, 13 years after the original Lawn Mower Killing. Joe Don Baker plays crazy cop Dick Harbinger, George Kennedy and Stella Stevens play nutty parents (he a Peeping Tom, she a demented sexpot), Scott McGinnis plays the young hero and Julia Duffy is a virgin. (Vestron) (Laser: Image)

WACKY WORLD OF DR. MORGUS (1962). Regional film with Dr. Morgus, one-time New Orleans horror-movie host, as a doctor who invents a machine that turns people into sand and back again. Directed by Raoul Haig. Sid Noel, Thomas George, Dan Barton.

WACKY WORLD OF MOTHER GOOSE, THE (1967). Mother Goose characters reshaped into a story of spies, secret agents and undercover men. Featuring the voice of Margaret Rutherford. (Sultan)

WAILING, THE. Video of **FEAR (1980)** (HGV).

WAIT UNTIL DARK (1967). Borderline psychothriller about a blind woman (Audrey Hepburn, who received an Oscar nomination) terrorized by killers who invade her New York apartment for a doll containing heroin. Director Terence Young treats the climax—killer Alan Arkin stalking the helpless woman—as though he wanted to outthrill Hitchcock, and for this sequence we recommend this shocker based on Frederick Knotts' play. Richard Crenna, Efrem Zimbalist Jr., Jack Weston, Samantha Jones. (Video/Laser: Warner Bros.)

WAKING HOUR, THE. See **VELVET VAMPIRE.**

WALKING AFTER MIDNIGHT (1988). Offbeat Canadian documentary in which famous entertainers recount their experiences with reincarnation. Among the celebs are Helen Shaver, Rae Dawn Chong, Martin Sheen, James Coburn, Willie Nelson, Dennis Weaver, Donovan, Ringo Starr and the Dalai Lama.

WALKING DEAD, THE (1936). Recommended Warner Bros. chiller directed by Michael Curtiz with Boris Karloff as an ex-con framed for murder and electrocuted. Doctor Edmund Gwenn, experimenting on dead animals, restores Karloff to the living. As a hollow-eyed, hallow-faced cadaver, he pursues his framers, forcing them into situations where they meet violent deaths because of their own fear-filled stupidity. Gruesome but fun. Ricardo Cortez, Marguerite Churchill.

WALK LIKE A MAN (1987). What old-pro director Melvin Frank (who made films with Norman Panama) is doing as producer-director of this ridiculous comedy is a question to ponder. Howie Mandel portrays a young man raised by wolves brought back to civilization to live with his original family. It's played for farce as Howie chases fire engines, walks like a canine and bays at the moon. Christopher Lloyd and Colleen Camp yock it up as crazed family members out to get the youth's fortune, and they can be funny at times. And despite absurdities and sometimes tasteless slapstick antics, there is a crude charm Mandel brings to Bobo that may evoke a few chuckles. As the sympathetic woman who trains Bobo in the ways of civilization, Amy Steel is a nice counter balance, but this still plays like an inane sitcom. Scripted by Robert Klane. (MGM/UA)

WALK OF THE DEAD. Video version of **VENGEANCE OF THE ZOMBIES** (Vogue).

WAR BETWEEN THE PLANETS (1965). Wayward planet on a collision course with Earth creates tidal waves, land upheavals and panicky dialogue among Earthlings, giving Italian effects "artists" opportunity to play with cheap models. A giant brain controlling the asteroid must be entered by rescuers. Excessively unimpressive. Directed by Anthony Dawson (Antonio Margheriti). Giacomo Rossi-Stuart, Peter Martell. (In video as **PLANET ON THE PROWL**)

WARD 13. See **X-RAY.**

WAR GAME, THE (1966). Shattering shocker by writer-producer-director Peter Watkins depicts nuclear holocaust in a English village. Watkins doesn't spare graphic details: human panic, fire storms, food shortages, atomic wounds, the maimed and the stunned and the dead. Objective, non-hysterical approach gives this TV-film impact. Strikes close to home in the vein of THE DAY AFTER and THREADS. So realistic it was banned from British TV. (Festival; Hollywood Home Theater; Sinister/C; S/Weird; Filmfax)

WARGAMES (1983). Enthralling, suspense-packed fantasy (written by Lawrence Lasker and Walter F. Parkes) in which teeners Matthew Broderick and Ally

Sheedy accidentally gain access to the NORAD computer system and play a "game" of nuclear war between the U.S. and the Soviet Union that becomes the real thing back at control central. This is great edge-of-your-seat viewing with computer controller Dabney Coleman and Air Force General Barry Corbin working against the clock to avert nuclear holocaust. Directed by John Badham. (Video/Laser: MGM/UA; CBS/Fox)

WAR GODS OF THE DEEP (1965). Vernesque underwater fantasy quite fanciful, and watchable, as a band of intrepid heroes discovers the lost city of Lyonesse (off the Cornish coast) in 1903. Its smuggler inhabitants have survived as gillmen and their leader is Vincent Price, who thinks Susan Hart is the reincarnation of an old lover. Satisfying blend of action and humor, directed by Jacques Tourneur. Tab Hunter, David Tomlinson. Aka CITY UNDER THE SEA.

WAR IN SPACE (1977). Japanese action with mediocre effects, overexcited cast members and a plot that reads like it was lifted out of Amazing Stories magazine circa 1942. A meteor swarm approaching Earth turns out to be a flotilla of space hardware from Venus, blasting us with lasers. The aliens are green-skinned humanoids, their leader a jerkola wearing a Roman-style helmet and commanding a giant mother ship. Asian volunteers of the U.N. Space Bureau pursue the invaders back to Venus where they engage in guerrilla tactics and a shootout that involves a man in a hairy suit armed with a laser. Plays like a service melodrama, with Jun Fukuda directing in the tradition of Inoshiro Honda. Also called WAR OF THE PLANETS. Kensaku Morita, Yuko Asano. (Video Action)

WARLOCK (1983). Video version of **SKULLDUGGERY** (Paragon).

WARLOCK (1989). Intriguing idea is executed in a mildly interesting way. Warlock Julian Sands of the 17th Century is transported to modern times and a witch hunter named Giles Redferne (Richard E. Grant) follows after him. The warlock intends to carry out the Devil's plan of destruction but Lori Singer (as L.A. lady Kassandra) joins Redferne in thwarting the evil. Producer-director Steve Miner injects atmosphere and brooding qualities, but the story line by David Twohy is too weak to sustain for long. (Video/Laser: Vidmark)

JULIAN SANDS

WARLOCK 2: THE ARMAGEDDON (1993). Only the recurring presence of Julian Sands qualifies this as a sequel when the titular force of evil (the son of Satan) turns up in modern times in search of powerful runestones in the possession of assorted humans. Only two Earthlings (drab characters played by Chris Young and Paula Marshall) have the supernatural power to fight him in a small California town, and it's a rather ordinary dual of wizards, wherein any special effect is permissible, whether it makes sense or not. The film is dark and humorless and has little appeal beyond Sands' personification of evil, so you could end up rooting for him instead of the boring kids, both of whom have to be killed and brought back to life to have the superpowers to battle Sands. Where's the imagination and humor director Anthony Hitchox brought to the WAXWORK series? It's sorely and blatantly missing. (Vidmark)

WARLOCK MOON (1973). Weak witchcraft flick (shown on TV as BLOODY SPA) was shot in the San Francisco-Bay Area by producer-director-editor Bill Herbert, who had the best intentions but a static directorial style that defeated him. The same can be said for the writing of John Sykes. The plot, which takes forever and a night to move, concerns Laurie Walters and Joe Spano fooling around a strange house on the outskirts of Livermore (actually a deserted Army tuberculosis clinic), where oddballs have a witch cult. Only during the last minutes does real horror build, and there is a perverse twist ending. Walters and Spano went on to star in TV series. Edna Macafee, Ray K. Goman. (Unicorn)

BORIS KARLOFF IN 'THE WALKING DEAD'

WARLORD 3000 (1992). While this has the external trappings of a MAD MAX imitation, set in a futuristic desert when radiation storms ravish the landscape and drug-crazed psychotics drive dune buggies, it has some similance of plot and interesting characters who clash on an emotional level instead of participating in the same-old physical violence. Jay Roberts portrays Nova, a soldier seeking the drug dealer responsible for having his family slaughtered who falls in love with his nemesis' daughter (Denice Marie Duff). The story is told in the memory voice-over, giving the script by Ron Herbst and producer-director Faruque Ahmed a literary element. By no means is this a great picture, but it's engaging (after a clumsy start) and has well-staged action. Steve Blanchard, Wayne Duvall, Dawn Martel, Jeff Sable. (Columbia TriStar)

WARLORDS (1988). If anyone brings to life this umpteenth copy of MAD MAX, it is Dawn Wildsmith as a wild-woolly adventuress who has survived a nuclear war and is in the country (near Vasquez Rocks) escaping bands of mutants. It's another Fred Olen Ray low-budget potboiler, the producer-director working with a skimpy, almost nonexistent script by Scott Ressler. David Carradine, in the Mad Max role, seeks his missing wife, abducted by warlord Sid Haig. There's comedy, but the premise is so weak, the performers (Robert Quarry, Brinke Stevens, Fox Harris and Ross Hagen) have nothing to work with. Especially bad, in this compendium of supertired cliches, is a talking head named Ammo that Carradine carries in an old box. WARLORDS is a dud with a thud. (Vidmark) (Laser: Image)

WARLORDS OF ATLANTIS (1978). Fourth and last film in a series of picturesque fantasy adventures from producer John Dark and director Kevin Connor, starring Doug McClure. He portrays an intrepid hero transported via diving bell into an undersea kingdom of seven cities inhabited by treacherous Martians. Characters and situations in Brian Hayles' script are preposterous but Roger Dickens' monsters are visual delights: a giant octopus; a multi-armed mollusk with rolling eyeballs; a snake-fish; a thing with flippers called a Zarg; a flying fish with bad overbite; a scaly millipede. Cyd Charisse, as Atsil the High Priestess, fares well because she gets to display her shapely legs. Still, it's the octopus with the real class. Shane Rimmer, Peter Gilmore.

WARLORDS OF THE 21ST CENTURY (1981). Gas costs $59 a liter after the great Oil Wars and what's left of mankind on New Zealand (farmers and isolated groups) is subjected to roving bloodthirsty pirates, whose only nemesis is The Hunter (Michael Beck), an avenging warrior a la Mad Max. Made as BATTLETRUCK, for chief villain James Wainwright pillages with an armored oil carrier bristling with firepower, the story (co-written by director Harley Cokliss) centers on how The Hunter and Straker face off, with Straker's daughter (Annie McEnroe) caught in the middle. (Embassy)

WARNING, THE. See **IT CAME . . . WITHOUT WARNING.**

WARNING FROM SPACE (1956). Japanese sci-fi message film, in which friendly E.T.s (shaped like starfish) land on Earth in human guise to warn us of dangers we face if we use atomic weapons, and to offer help in stopping a planet that will collide with Earth. More mature than most Japanese films of this kind. Directed by Koji Shima. Keizo Kawasaki, Shozo Nanbu. Aka THE MYSTERIOUS SATELLITE, THE COSMIC MAN APPEARS IN TOKYO, SPACE MEN APPEAR IN TOKYO and UNKNOWN SATELLITE OVER TOKYO. (Sinister/C; S/Weird; Dark Dreams; Filmfax)

WARNING SIGN (1985). Engrossing action thriller in the style of THE ANDROMEDA STRAIN, tautly directed by Hal Barwood, who co-wrote and co-produced with Matthew Robbins. At the isolated Utah plant of Biotek, a secret government germ warfare plant, a bacteria is unleashed that infects the "rage" area of the brain and turns victims into homicidal maniacs. Trapped in the plant is security guard Kathleen Quinleen, while outside her sheriff-husband Sam Waterston tries to solve the mystery being kept hush-hush by government toady Yaphet Kotto. The performances are excellent, the script exciting, the action full of twists as they seek an antitoxin to stop the monsters. (CBS/Fox)

WAR OF THE COLOSSAL BEAST (1958). Producer-director Bert I. Gordon's sequel to THE AMAZING COLOSSAL MAN finds the ever-growing 60-feet-tall Army Colonel Manning (played this time by Dean Parkin) not destroyed at Boulder Dam but down in Mexico, snatching taco trucks off the highway in hopes of finding something that will stick to his king-size ribs. As in most Gordon films, the effects are pedantic, and the same could be said for George Worthing Yates' script. One of the soldier boys remarks, "There's no place in this civilization for a 60-foot man." He said it. Roger Pace, Sally Fraser, Russ Bender. Aka THE TERROR STRIKES. Music by Albert Glasser. (Columbia TriStar)

WAR OF THE GARGANTUAS (1967). Sequel to FRANKENSTEIN CONQUERS THE WORLD was re-edited for the U.S., with a sequence explaining connection to the first film dropped; hence, connections are tenuous at best. With Inoshiro Honda directing and Eiji Tsuburaya at the effects helm, you're in for a monster extravaganza: A giant octopus battles another entity of green-hued evil and the greeny takes on a brown-hued beast. The only thing that happens by occident is Russ Tamblyn as a scientist. Aka DUEL OF THE GARGANTUAS. Kumi Mizuno. (Paramount/Gateway)

WAR OF THE GODS. See **BATTLESTAR GALACTICA.**

WAR OF THE MONSTERS (1966). Toho's sequel to GAMMERA THE INVINCIBLE, with that friendly snapping turtle, Gammera, doing battle with Barugon the Dinosaur, a creature surrounded by a forecefield. Kids will cheer the chest-pounding, noisy encounters; adults will snooze. Directed by Shigeo Tanaka. Kojiro Hongo. Aka GAMERA VS. BARUGON. (S/Weird)

WAR OF THE PLANETS (1965). Turgid is the best word to describe this uninspired Italian adventure set on space wheel Gamma I, which is invaded (on New Year's Eve yet) by invisible bodiless beings from Mars called Diaphanois. Coming to Gamma I to investigate is Tony Russell and spacesters armed with rifles that spit flame a few feet, and ray guns called .38s. The aliens, described by screenwriter Ivan Reiner as "bodiless patterns of energy," speak through humans, while the human response is "Good God" or "Incredible." The only exciting moments provided by director Anthony Dawson are when astronauts form the words "Happy New Year" while floating through space a la Busby Berkeley, and when they dance to "Auld Lang Syne" while cavorting in the void. This film's sequel was WILD, WILD PLANET. Lisa Gastoni, Franco Nero, Carlo Giustini.

WAR OF THE PLANETS (1977). See **WAR IN SPACE.**

WAR OF THE ROBOTS (1978). Ambitious Italian space opera, but condescending and insulting to audiences. A race of robots (in metallic suits, wearing blond wigs) kidnap a beautiful woman; a squad of rocket jocks (including a Texan, yet) slip into warp drive and pursue across the galaxies, meeting weird aliens in papier-mache caverns and firing laser beams hither and thither. Armies of extras, massive sets and tons of action can't compensate for Alfonso Brescia's inept direction (he's credited as Al Bradly). Special onions to Marcus Griffin for his awful electronics "shuffling" score, the dumbest ever, and to Alan Forsyth for inferior effects. Except for leading man Antonio Sabato, the credits would appear to be Angloized pseudonyms: Melissa Long, Patricia Gore, James Stuart, Robert Barnes and "a special performance" by Mickey Pilgrim. Pilgrim's Progress? (United; from Mogul as **REACTOR**)

WAR OF THE SATELLITES (1958). Aliens you never see (producer-director Roger Corman's economic ingenuity at work) don't want us fooling around in space, so one takes over the body of scientist Richard Devon aboard a satellite. But he (it) falls for Susan Cabot, a foolish act that makes him vulnerable to Earthlings who suspect something is awry. Something is awry—the tepid script by Lawrence Louis Goldman, who banged it out for Corman after the Russians launched Sputnik. According to legend, Corman directed it in eight days—one day longer than it took God to create the Universe. Dick Miller, Michael Fox, Robert Shayne.

WAR OF THE WIZARDS. Video version of **PHOENIX, THE** (Planet).

WAR OF THE WORLDS (1953). George Pal's commendable version of H. G. Wells' novel of a Martian invasion—imaginatively depicted in the Oscar-winning effects of Gordon Jennings. Alien saucers land in isolated areas of California and zap everything in sight with greenish death rays. Barre Lyndon's script, focusing on research physicist Gene Barry and scientist Ann Robinson, sometimes sinks into cliches yet it unfolds with such compelling swiftness and breathless action that the invasion takes on epic proportions. One suspenseful sequence depicts a bug-eyed Martian, another shows Barry searching for Robinson through war-ravaged L.A. The opening prologue is beautifully rendered, with the planets described by the splendid voice of Sir Cedric Hardwicke. One of the few sci-fi classics of the cinema. Directed by Byron Haskin. Carolyn Jones, Robert Cornthwaite, Paul Frees, Jack Kruschen, Les Tremayne, Alvy Moore, Charles Gemora (as the Martian). (Video/Laser: Paramount)

WAR OF THE ZOMBIES. See **NIGHT STAR—GODDESS OF ELECTRA.**

WARP SPEED (1981). Independent cheapie about a man endowed with ESP powers who realizes something strange is happening aboard a spacecraft. Camille Mitchell, Adam West, David Chandler.

WARRIOR AND THE SORCERESS (1984). Interesting, and entertaining, Barbarian-and-sorcery Conan copy, with director John Broderick showing an influence of Japanese samurai movies. Here he copies YOJIMBO when The Dark One, a laconic warrior (and the only survivor of his race), hires out to two warring factions in the village of Yabatar, shifting sides as fortunes of war shift. David Carradine is good in this variation on the wandering gunslinger. Oddities include The Protector (a giant octopus-monster), a green lizard that whispers into the ear of its master, a four-breasted dancing assassin and the sorceress, who forges the mighty sword of Ura for The Dark One and rushes about for the entire picture, her glistening, beautiful breasts bared. Above average for Roger Corman. Luke Askew, Maria Socas. (Video/Laser: Vestron)

WARRIOR OF THE LOST WORLD (1985). Silly MAD MAX ripoff, with the absurd premise that Earth has been devastated by radiation wars and evil Omegans, led by Prosser (Donald Pleasence), are fighting the good guys, the Outsiders. Robert Ginty comes riding by on a rocket-launching "supersonic speedcycle" equipped with Einstein the Computer, which espouses such comments as

"Bad Mothers" (cops) and "Very Bad Mothers" (more cops). Ginty agrees to help Persis Khambatta rescue her father (Harrison Muller) from Prosser's stronghold, so there's plenty of explosive action that allows Fred Williamson (as Henchman) to crash the scene, guns blazing to synthesized music. Director David Worth's script makes little sense, but the action is nonstop. (HBO)

WARRIORS FROM THE MAGIC MOUNTAIN See **ZU: WARRIORS FROM THE MAGIC MOUNTAIN.**

WARRIORS OF THE APOCALYPSE (1987). Another post-Holocaust action-adventure that starts off in the Mad Max mode (civilization wiped out by war; 150 years in the future surviving bands rove a desert-like landscape wiping each other out) and then shifts to a Lost City saga with overtones of SHE. Trapper leads his motley lot into a forest with the promise that somewhere ahead lies The Mountain of Life, a Shangri-la where existence is eternal. On the way they wipe out a tribe of natives led by Giant Bill, discover a pygmy band that can heal wounds and resurrect the dead, and Amazon warriors armed with bows and arrows and huge bosoms. The Lost City is ruled by an exotic wench and a treacherous High Priest and they shoot it out with laser bolts from their eyeball sockets. The lost race, behaving like Aztecs, conducts fertility rites and sacrifices yet has machinery to turn ruined terrain into lush jungle. The monosyllabic script by Ken Metcalfe is a mishmash of cliches and the action is wall-to-wall, stopping only long enough for the Amazon wenches to put on white see-through gowns. Michael James, Debrah Moore, Franco Guerrero, Mike Cohen. (Lightning)

WARRIORS OF THE WASTELAND (1983). Inferior, imbecilic MAD MAX ripoff by Italians finds two unlikable antiheroes (Timothy Brent, Fred Williamson) roving the nuked countryside 2019 A. H. (After Holocaust) in ridiculous automobiles, seeking an evil band (The Templers, Administrators of Revenge) that is slaughtering innocent folks. Absurdly-dressed men ride redesigned motorbikes, fire silly zap guns (which give off inane electronic sounds) and no doubt wonder why director Enzo G. Castellari doesn't demand the Method style of acting. Suitable only for insomniacs in the wasteland of TV. George Eastman, Anna Kanakis, Thomas Moore. (Simitar; HBO; from Impulse as **NEW BARBARIANS, THE**)

WARRIORS OF THE WIND (1985). While portions of this Japanese animated feature resemble a typical Saturday morning sci-fi cartoon, it has an overriding style and air of excitement that set it apart from cheaper competitors. The setting is a post-holocaust world, where a race led by Queen Salina stand watch over The Valley of the Wind, inhabited by giant dragonflies and threatened by toxic poisoning. Giant centipede-like creatures with healing powers were no doubt inspired by the sand worms in DUNE. Directed by Kazuo Komatsubara. (New World)

WASHINGTON D.C. See **HAIL TO THE CHIEF.**

WASP WOMAN, THE (1960). Producer-director Roger Corman gives us a "stinker" in need of more production sting. Strictly a bottom-of-the-hive programmer (scripted by Leo Gordon) with Susan Cabot as a Wacky Anglo-Saxon Protestant . . . a cosmetics manufacturer seeking an eternal youth formula from wasp enzymes. Once she's an oversized member of the Hymentopera clan, she turns predacious and goes on a murderous spree, sticking it to all the guys but good. It's the wasp-ish budget that does in THE WASP WOMAN. Anthony Eisley, Michael Mark, Frank Wolff. (Sinister/C; S/Weird; Rhino; Filmfax)

WATCHED! (1972). This crime film about the downfall of a D.A. specializing in drug cases, who falls prey to cocaine and becomes a defense attorney, highlights surreal, hallucinatory scenes of Stacy Keach undergoing deterioration. Keach, who in later years would serve time in a British prison for possession of cocaine, is shown engulfed in the powdery drug, saying, "Cocaine! My mucus membrane is but a memory." Keach's adversary is drugbuster Harry Yulin, and the two have a compelling duel to the death. Writer-director John Parsons made this unusual film in San Francisco, capturing the Haight-Ashbury in the depressing aftermath of the drug culture that thrived in the '60s. A strange anamoly, this requires patience but is worth seeing for its unwitting prophesies. Brigid Polk, Denver John Collins, Valerie Carter. (Vestron; Simitar)

WATCHER IN THE WOODS, THE (1980). Disney attempted to escape formula kiddie movies with this adaptation of a Florence E. Randall novel, but the results are too silly to make it an adult movie and not silly enough to make it a kiddie treat. Music writer David McCallum, wife Carroll Baker and daughters Lynn-Holly Johnson and Kyle Richards move into a secluded mansion owned by sinister old bat Bette Davis. A strange psychic force emanates from a nearby forest, but is never explained as the teens, overwhelmed by ESP powers, help Davis' long-lost daughter. Apparently an alien probe has taken her, and trapped her in another dimension, and there's a shower of fireworks by Harrison Ellenshaw that passes as effects. The film, directed by John Hough and adapted by Brian Clemens, Harry Spalding and Rosemary Anne Sisson, was never released theatrically, even after new footage was added by doctoring director Vincent McEveety. Ian Bannen, Georgina Hale, Richard Pasco. (Disney)

WATCHERS (1988). Had this modest sci-fi/horror thriller been given decent effects, and had the script by Bill Freed and producer Damian Lee (from Dean Koontz's novel) been developed as a juvenile fantasy, instead of a bloody adult affair, THE WATCHERS might have been watchable. A government experiment produces two creatures: A Golden Retriever with superintelligence and a monster called an OXCOM (Outside Experimental Combat Mammal). There's a third experiment gone awry but you'll have to figure that one out yourself. The monster is never shown and this never delivers as a bloodletting vehicle. Nor does the supersmart dog integrated strongly into the plot to become a dominating element to please younger audiences. Directed by Jon Hess. Corey Haim, Michael Ironside, Duncan Fraser, Blu Mankuma. (IVE) (Laser: Image)

COREY HAIM

WATCHERS II (1990). The Golden Retriever, Einstein, is back in this moderately effective horror/science-gone-awry action film, communicating telepathically with Marc Singer, who must destroy a monster called the Outsider (or AE-73), an escapee from a top-secret military project. Based on Dean Koontz's novel, with adaptation by Henry Dominic. Directed by Thierry Notz. Tracy Scoggins, Jonathan Farwell, Irene Miracle, Mary Woronov. (IVE) (Laser: Image)

WATCH ME WHEN I KILL (1981). Italian psychothriller concocted in the vein of Mario Bava, but lacking the stylistic nuances and cinematic verve of that master of the macabre. Director Anthony Bido turns it into a plodding, almost incomprehensible killer-on-the-loose concoction featuring three mildly interesting deaths: a pharmacist is knived in the back, a woman's head is shoved into a bubbling stewpot, and a man is strangled in his bath with a thick cord. The explanations are ludicrous; no writing credits are provided. Co-produced by Herman Cohen. Aka THE CAT WITH THE JADE EYES. Richard Stewart, Sylvia Kramer. (HBO)

WATER BABIES, THE (1978). Charles Kingsley's novel was brought to the screen in a partly animated British film with James Mason, Billie Whitelaw and Joan Greenwood. Children escape into a watery kingdom—and once beneath the surface the film turns to animation. Actor Lionel Jeffries directed. Bernard Cribbins, David

Tomlinson. Aka SLIP SLIDE ADVENTURES. (Nelson)

WATER CYBORGS. See **TERROR BENEATH THE SEA.**

WATERMELON MAN (1970). Unsophisticated comment on the undeclared war between blacks and whites, directed with a heavy hand by Melvin Van Peebles to entertain blacks and warn whites. Godfrey Cambridge, wearing "white-face," is a Caucasian bigot with a caustic tongue who suddenly turns Negro and is faced with unpleasant racial experiences. Seed-y morality play. Estelle Parsons, Howard Caine, Mantan Moreland, Kay Kimberley. (Video/Laser: RCA/Columbia)

WATERSHIP DOWN (1978). Brilliantly animated version of Richard Adams' best-seller dramatizing the odyssey of rabbits fleeing their doomed warren and seeking a new home in the English countryside. Obeying but not understanding the psychic visions of a young rabbit, the creatures are threatened by a dictatorship under General Woundwort and flee for their lives. The tale is an analogy to the struggle of the British during World War II, ingeniously crafted by producer-director Martin Rosen. Even though there are violence and bloodletting when the fur flies, this offbeat cartoon is recommended to young and old for its object lessons skillfully blended with story. Voices by John Hurt, Ralph Richardson and Zero Mostel. (Video/Laser: Warner Bros.)

WATTS MONSTER, THE. See **DR. BLACK AND MR. HYDE.**

WAVELENGTH (1983). Thoughtful morality tale thanks to writer-director Mike Gray, who fashions a philosophical story that indicts militaristic attitudes toward aliens. Robert Carradine, a burned-out guitarist in Hollywood, meets psychic Cherie Currie who mentally "hears" wails of help from E.T. humanoids (dubbed Beta, Delta and Gamma), captured from a downed UFO and caged in a secret installation near Carradine's home. The couple penetrates the system to help the trio escape. Its one weakness is that youngsters with shaved heads play the aliens, when credibility calls for a more realistic rendering. Keenan Wynn is along to help the escape plan work. Effective soundtrack by Tangerine Dream. (Embassy; Starmaker)

WAXWORK (1988). Intriguing premise—spectators who innocently step inside waxwork horror exhibits are teleported into another world—is enhanced by the imaginative, stylish work of writer-director Anthony Hickox (great-grandson of British film distributor J. Arthur Rank and son of late director Douglas Hickox), who loads this weird tale with effects and bloodletting. Setting is a residental "house of waxy horrors" (presided over by sinister David Warner), where teenagers and investigating police become part of the tableaus after undergoing horrible deaths. A plethora of characters and monsters fight it out in a messy melee during the fiery conclusion. In cameos are Patrick Macnee (an anti-monster nut in a wheelchair), Miles O'Keefe (as Dracula) and John Rhys Davies. Zach Galligan (of GREMLINS) is the male lead, followed by Deborah Foreman and Michelle Johnson. (Vestron) (Laser: Image)

WAXWORK II: LOST IN TIME (1991). Off-the-wall but entertaining sequel to WAXWORK, starting where the first film ended as Zach Galligan and Monika Schnarre flee the burning wax museum, pursued by a severed hand. Accused of killing her stepfather, Schnarre and Galligan travel through time to gather evidence of her innocence, undergoing an odyssey that is essentially parodies of horror movies. The time zones include Dr. Frankenstein's lab, a haunted house (this sequence is in black and white, imitating Robert Wise's THE HAUNTING); a spaceship terrorized by an ALIEN-like creature; and King Arthur's court, where an evil sorcerer tries to take over the throne. These adventures are tongue in cheek and colorfully presented by writer-director Anthony Hickox, who goes a bit berserk by having the climactic battle in a series of time zones, all movie genres: Dr. Jekyll, Jack the Ripper, Godzilla, Romero's walking dead in a shopping mall, and the German NOSFERATU. A definite cassette crowd pleaser. John Ireland (as the king), Martin Kemp (Frankenstein), Bruce Campbell, Juliet Mills, Patrick Macnee, David Carradine, Jim Metzler, Michael Des Barres, Joe Baker, Marina Sirtis, Sophie Ward. (Live)

WAY AND THE BODY, THE. See **WHAT!**

WAYNE MURDER CASE, THE. See **STRANGE ADVENTURE.**

WAY . . . WAY OUT (1966). So-so Jerry Lewis vehicle: In 1999 a replacement is needed to man a U.S. weather station on the moon. Lewis is selected, along with Connie Stevens, but domestic complications, even on the lunar surface, can be trying (and tiresome). Things perk up when Soviet astronaut Anita Ekberg appears, but veteran director Gordon Douglas can't prevent this from becoming weightless. Script by William Bowers and Laslo Vadnay. Robert Morley, Dennis Weaver, Brian Keith, Dick Shawn, Sig Ruman.

WEAPONS OF DESTRUCTION. See **FABULOUS WORLD OF JULES VERNE, THE.**

WEAPONS OF VENGEANCE (1963). See editions 1-3.

WEB OF THE SPIDER (1972). Stylish Italian supernatural thriller holds one's attention as it opens in a country tavern where Edgar Allan Poe (Klaus Kinski at his wildest) is telling a terror tale. Journalist Anthony Franciosa is challenged by Poe to spend one night in Blackwood Villa, a haunted castle. Once ensconced, Franciosa meets two beautiful women who fight over him. The redhead is a real knockout. What Franciosa is really seeing are spectral images of long-dead occupants of the castle, and he must relive the horror of their deeds. This remake of CASTLE OF BLOOD was directed by Anthony M. Dawson (Antonio Margheriti); based on Poe's "Danse Macabre." Also called IN THE GRIP OF THE SPIDER. Michele Mercier, Peter Carsten, Karin Field. (Filmfax; Sinister/C)

WEDNESDAY CHILDREN, THE (1973). Editions 1-3.

WEEKEND (1968). Surrealistic French-Italian fantasy written-directed by Jean-Luc Godard, depicting Parisians out to have a good time on Saturday and Sunday, but encountering dead bodies and strange folks who claim to be historical personages. Hard to explain . . . some audiences were turned off by the unanswered enigmas of this art film. Strictly for the avant-garde crowd. (New Yorker; Facets Multimedia)

WEIRDO (1989). Freaked-out lowlife (Steve Burington) is on a murderous rampage in this Andy Milligan horror thriller that he wrote and directed. It's dripping with ineffectual gore murders. Jessica Straus, Naomi Sherwood, Lynne Angus. (Raedon)

WEIRD ONES, THE (1962). See third edition.

WEIRD SCIENCE (1985). Absolutely awful teenage sex-fantasy comedy, more excruciating than titillating—a complete misfire from writer-director John Hughes. Two idiotic juvenile nerds (Anthony Michael Hall, Ilan Mitchell-Smith) feed ridiculous material into a computer to create a perfect woman. What comes out amidst a lot of pyrotechnic nonsense is Kelly LeBrock, a real beauty. The plot rambles on A.C. (After Creation) with no coherence and LeBrock possesses unexplained witch powers that make things come and go at will, including some appalling biker characters. The cast—Bill Paxton, Suzanne Snyder, Robert Downey—must still be trying to live down this fiasco. Final insult is the title, stolen from the E.C. comic that featured some of the best illustrated sci-fi stories of all time. Editors William Gaines and Al Feldstein would have used Hughes' plot to line garbage cans. (Video/Laser: MCA)

WEIRD TALES. See **KWAIDAN.**

WEIRD WOMAN (1944). Entry in Universal's "Inner Sanctum" series stars Lon Chaney Jr. In this, the second in a series of six programmers, he's a professor in danger of being killed by witchcraft, but who refuses to believe his beautiful bride can protect him with her amulets and

FUN-LOVING PREHISTORICS IN 'WE'RE BACK'

incantations. This version of Fritz Leiber's excellent novel, CONJURE WIFE, is inferior to the 1961 British remake, BURN, WITCH, BURN. Blame it on an oversimplified script by Brenda Weisberg and indifferent direction by Reginald Le Borg. Evelyn Ankers, Anne Gwynne, Ralph Morgan, Lois Collier, Kay Harding.

WELCOME HOME, JOHNNY BRISTOL (1972). Offbeat psychoanalytic TV-movie is reminiscent of CITIZEN KANE in style because its psychological clues are presented as a baffling mystery to a man's true identity. Recently returned from captivity in Vietnam, Johnny (Martin Landau) searches for the clues to his heritage, discovering his hometown has disappeared and the people from his past aren't who they should be. These perplexing puzzles are explained by Freudian symbolism. Compelling atmosphere and intriguing premise pay off. Scripted by Stanley R. Greenberg, directed by George McGowan. Jane Alexander, Brock Peters, Martin Sheen, Pat O'Brien, Forrest Tucker, Mona Freeman.

WELCOME TO ARROW BEACH (1974). An awful title song, "Who Can Tell Us Why?," poses a question that might have been put to producer Laurence Harvey. Alas, Harvey died when it was released, so no answers are forthcoming. This is an incomprehensible mess in its TV version, for any visual reference to its reported cannibalism theme was edited out. (The original title: TENDER FLESH). What remains is a B horror film, poorly photographed, of a beach wanderer (Meg Foster) befriended by a stranger (Harvey in his last role) and taken to his mansion. Korean War flyer/hero Jason Henry (Harvey) lives there with Joanna Pettet, and apparently likes to kill women and eat their flesh—but this is only a guess. Sheriff John Ireland is running for office while deputy Stuart Whitman noses into the mystery. Oddly enough, or maybe not so oddly, writer Wallace C. Bennett drops these elements for a climax where the boy and girl sneak into the house of horrors to confront Harvey. Harvey's direction is undistinguished, perhaps reflecting the cancerous illness that was taking his life. Glory LeRoy, Jesse Vint.

WELCOME TO BLOOD CITY (1977). Peculiar Canadian sci-fi mystery leaves many details clouded in uncertainty and lacks a stylish separation between reality and fantasy sequences. The results are chaotic—and intriguing. Samantha Eggar and Barry Morse are on a research team where potential "kill masters" for an ongoing war are placed into hallucinatory states to determine which are strongest. The fantasy realm becomes a WESTWORLD where test subject Keir Dullea is exposed to the sadism of sheriff Jack Palance and bloody gunfights. The Stephen Schneck-Michael Winder script really gets weird when scientist Eggar projects herself into Dullea's alternate reality, and watches tapes of them making love. The main problem is drab camera work, a lack of effects (these would have enhanced the lab sequences), and indifferent direction by Peter Sasdy. The film ends on a metaphysical note and leaves moral ambiguities as cloudy as ever. (Interglobe; Lightning; Pan-Canadian)

WELCOME TO OBLIVION (1990). Another MAD MAX ripoff, starring Dack Rambo as the silent hero who, in the wake of nuclear war, goes on a mission in a mining zone called Oblivion. He's assisted by mutant Clare Beresford. Directed by Augusto Tamayo, who filmed in Peru. Meshach Taylor, Mark Bringelson.

WELCOME TO SPRING BREAK (1988). Electrocuted biker returns from the dead to terrorize students vacationing in Florida. The police chief is John Saxon, Michael Parks is the doctor, Lance LeGault is the minister. Written-directed by Harry Kirk Patrick. Also called NIGHTMARE BEACH. (IVE; Critics' Choice)

WE'RE BACK! A DINOSAUR'S STORY (1993). Excellent feature cartoon for children, a Steven Spielberg production, in which a scientist (voice by Walter Cronkite) brings a group of dinosaurs to modern day via his time-travel device and the creatures interrelate with the kids. Based on Hudson Talbott's book, this fine animated special was written by John Patrick Shanley and directed by Dick and Ralph Zondag. Other voices by John Goodman, Jay Leno and Martin Short. (MCA)

WEREWOLF, THE (1956). Nifty low-budget monster flick from producer Sam Katzman in which Steven Ritch, suffering from radiation poisoning, is accidentally turned into a wolf man by scientists. Rampage of death and destruction follows, in the vein typified by THE WOLF MAN. Location filming in and around Las Vegas by director Fred F. Sears gives this extra umph. If not a howling classic, certainly better than most werewolf movies of the '50s, with the Robert E. Kent-James B. Gordon script creating sympathy for the wolf human. Don Megowan is the lawman who regretfully pursues Ritch. Joyce Holden, George M. Lynn.

WEREWOLF (1987). Totally dependent on the Rob Bottin-Rick Baker effects that earmarked THE HOWLING and AN AMERICAN WEREWOLF IN LONDON, which means it has no new visual tricks to offer, this is the two-hour pilot for a syndicated TV series. John York is bitten by a wolfman, bleeds when his palm is (dis)graced by the sign of the pentagram and does battle with a werewolf named Skorzeny, played grotesquely, in sickening make-up, by Chuck Connors. Stalking the stalkers is a philosophical, grim-jawed bounty hunter imitating Clint Eastwood. Highlight of this below-standard fare is a battle between two furry monsters with jutting fangs. Lance LeGault, Raphael Sbarge, Michelle Johnson, John Quade.

WEREWOLF AND THE YETI, THE. See **NIGHT OF THE HOWLING BEAST.** (The beast is Yeti to come!)

WEREWOLF IN A GIRLS' DORMITORY (THE GHOUL IN SCHOOL) (1963). Good black-and-white photography, a competent cast and weird characters (crippled caretaker, haughty wife, teen-age blackmailer,

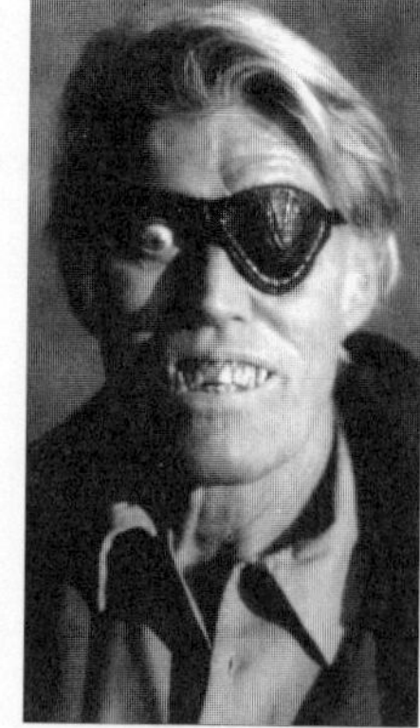

TV'S 1987 'WEREWOLF' WITH CHUCK CONNERS

cold secretary, sinister chauffeur) put this European horror film at the head of the class. Suggested menace (faces at windows, shadows on walls, etc.) as well as a heavy werewolf theme will keep you poised as murders occur in a girls' school that is finishing in more ways than one. Carl Schell, younger brother of Maximilian and Maria, heads the cast for director Richard Benson. Give this one the old college try. Also called LYCANTHROPUS, I MARRIED A WEREWOLF, MONSTER AMONG THE GIRLS, THE GHOUL IN SCHOOL and GHOUL IN A GIRLS' DORMITORY. Barbara Lass, Curt Lowens, Maurice Marsac. (Sinister/C; S/Weird; Filmfax)

WEREWOLF OF LONDON (1935). One of the earliest of Hollywood's werewolf films, not as exciting as Universal's THE WOLF MAN, which established movie-lycanthropy traditions this failed to generate. Robert Harris' script seems very dated as botanist Henry Hull seeks a plant that blooms only in the Tibetan moonlight. During his expedition he is bitten by a savage beast. Returning to London, Hull turns into a four-legged monstrosity. Although Jack Pierce created the memorable make-up, Hull does little to bring the role to life. Directed by Stuart Walker. Warner Oland, Valerie Hobson, Spring Byington. (Video/Laser: MCA)

WEREWOLF OF WASHINGTON, THE (1973). Clever mixture of horror and political satire by writer-director-editor Milton Moses Ginsberg begins in the tradition of THE WOLF MAN with reporter-turned-press-aide Dean Stockwell bitten by a werewolf and warned by a gypsy woman about a curse. Back at the White House, Stockwell suspects a Communist conspiracy and confuses the "pentagram" (which appears in the palms of victims-to-be) with "Pentagon," fearing a military plot. At night, on Capitol Hill, he looks for savory Senators and chewable Congressmen. The make-up is good, reminiscent of Universal's hairy man, and there's a good scene where Stockwell overturns a phone booth with a screaming woman inside. Meanwhile, the President (Biff McGuire)—a parody of Nixon—has a wolfish appetite. When the President sees Stockwell as the wolf man, he says, "Down boy, heel." Clifton James, Beeson Carroll, Jane House, Michael Dunn (as a scientist who appears to be designing a Frankenstein Monster), Thayer David. (Monterey)

WEREWOLF OF WOODSTOCK (1974). Videotape TV-movie, one of the dumbest lycanthropy movies ever. Tige Andrews, of MOD SQUAD fame, portrays a farmer turned into a hippie-hating, beer-swilling monster who terrorizes music lovers by stalking the woods during the '69 Woodstock Music Fair. Directed by John Moffitt. Meredith MacRae, Michael Parks, Ann Doran.

WEREWOLF'S SHADOW, THE. See **WEREWOLF VS. THE VAMPIRE WOMEN, THE.**

WEREWOLF VS. THE VAMPIRE WOMAN, THE (1972). West German-Spanish fly-by-night werewolf film, with Paul Naschy as the monster with a silver bullet in his heart, resurrected by pathologists who should have seen THE WOLF MAN. Waldemar Daninsky pairs with cuddly cuties to create a vampire baby. Writers Jacinto Molina and Hans Munkell mix up the legends a bit, but variety is the spice of death, and the images by director Leon Klimovsky are quite striking if the story is not. Gaby Fuchs, Patty Shepard, Andres Resino. Jacinto Molina, by the way, is Naschy. Also called SHADOW OF THE WEREWOLF, THE WEREWOLF'S SHADOW and THE BLACK HARVEST OF COUNTESS DRACULA. (Hollywood Select; Horizon; Filmfax; S/Weird; Sinister/C; from AIR as **BLOOD MOON**)

WEREWOLF WOMAN. See **LEGEND OF THE WOLF WOMAN.**

WEREWOLVES ON WHEELS (1971). With surfing music blaring on the soundtrack, a motorcycle gang roars through the countryside, hurls curses, attends impromptu orgies, drinks barrels of beer and roughs up monks. In retaliation, the cyclists are cursed with lycanthropy. What follows is unintentional comedy and sleazy bloodletting and nudity. We're all for exploitation but please—do it with class. This dumb release was directed by Michel Levesque. Stephen Oliver, D. J. Johnson, Billy Gray, Barry McGuire. (Unicorn)

WEST OF ZANZIBAR (1929). Tod Browning-MGM silent film starring Lon Chaney Sr. as a crippled, sadistic magician living in the Congo with plans to steal ivory with the help of a "monster." Lionel Barrymore, Warner Baxter, Mary Nolan. For more details see **KONGA**, the sound remake with Walter Huston. (Dark Dreams) (Laser: MGM/UA, with **UNHOLY THREE**)

LON CHANEY SR.

WESTWORLD (1973). In premise and visuals, this is superior sci-fi, written-directed by Michael (THE ANDROMEDA STRAIN) Crichton. What's missing are meaty characterizations for Richard Benjamin and James Brolin and a reason for the malfunctioning of Westworld, an amusement center of the future, where vacationers enact fantasies. This is a rich man's Disneyland, consisting of Western, medieval and Roman themes. The idea is to live the dangers of the periods without undergoing physical harm. But harm is in everyone's way when the center malfunctions and the robots kill tourists. Yul Brynner portrays an android gunslinger who uses real bullets and sets off a chase through the sets. But since we care little for Benjamin, it's hard to take the horrors seriously. FUTUREWORLD is a sequel which fared better as a story. Dick Van Patten, Steve Franken. (Video/Laser: MGM/UA)

WHAT! (1965). Italian-French-British gothic, heavy with atmosphere and period costumes and set in an a mansion on a cliff, where everyone acts sinister or hysterical. Daliah Lavi is haunted by the visions of a murdered count (Christopher Lee as a sadistic chauvinist) and she flits about the castle in negligees, gasping at muddy footprints and a gnarly hand that's interminably reaching for her. For the U.S. market the sexual depravity scenes were heavily cut (What??), so what's left is a lot of skulking around under Mario Bava's direction. If you enjoy corny melodramas, by all means. Tony Kendall, Harriet White, Isli Oberon. Also known as NIGHT IS THE PHANTOM, THE WHIP AND THE BODY, THE BODY AND THE WHIP and SON OF SATAN.

WHAT A CARVE UP. Video version of **NO PLACE LIKE HOMICIDE** (Sinister/C; S/Weird; Filmfax).

WHAT A WHOPPER! (1961). See editions 1-3.

WHAT EVER HAPPENED TO AUNT ALICE? (1969). Another movie about batty old women, starring Geraldine Page as a murderess who keeps knocking off her housekeepers for their dough and burying them in her garden. It's of the WHAT EVER HAPPENED TO BABY JANE? school with Ruth Gordon and Mildred Dunnock contributing to the cast of grand old dames. Directed by Lee H. Katzin. Rosemary Forsyth, Robert Fuller, Joan Huntington. (Magnetic)

WHAT EVER HAPPENED TO BABY JANE? (1962). Contemporary Grand Guignol yarn directed by Robert Aldrich, who established a subgenre of thrillers in the '60s about batty old dames. It helped to rejuvenate sagging careers. Bette Davis and Joan Crawford are sisters who have left acting to live in a gloomy old house. Bette gradually goes off her nut, torturing her crippled sister and driving herself to the brink of insanity. Nothing more horrible than a dead bird on a food tray is shown—the horrors are psychotic ones implied by screenwriter Lukas Heller, taking off from a novel by Henry Farrell. Victor Buono, Anna Lee, Bert Freed. (Video/Laser: Warner Bros.)

POSTER FOR THE '62 ORIGINAL; LYNN REDGRAVE IN THE '91 TV REMAKE

WHAT EVER HAPPENED TO BABY JANE? (1991). TV-movie remake of the Henry Farrell novel that was first adapted by Robert Aldrich in '62 with Bette Davis. This time the actress-sisters are played by Vanessa and Lynn Redgrave. Vanessa is the sympathetic, bedridden former movie star hated by her demented sister and kept a prisoner in her own mansion. The update by Brian Taggert focuses on intriguing if lurid material about the freaky folks in Hollywood these days. The grotesqueries of Lynn's performance are what make this notable; there's little else except graphic murders, but even these do not build suspense; instead, they only add to the unsavoriness of it all. Directed by David Greene. John Glover, Bruce A. Young, Amy Steel, Samantha Jordan, John Scott Clough.

WHAT HAVE YOU DONE TO SOLANGE? (1971). Italian adaptation of Edgar Wallace's 1923 novel THE CLUE OF THE NEW PIN, in which Christina Galbo has psychic visions of murders to come while making love with boyfriend Fabio Testi. Directed by Massimo Dallamano. Joachim Fuchsberger, Karin Baal, Gunther Stoll. Score by Ennio Morricone. (Video Search)

WHAT'S SO BAD ABOUT FEELING GOOD? (1968). Gentle fable from director George Seaton, in the spirit of MIRACLE ON 34th STREET. A toucan in New York harbor infects the city with a virus that brings about euphoria. Cigarette and alcohol sales drop and politicians fear this will restructure American politics. Seaton's approach is too inoffensive for effective Establishment satire. George Peppard, Mary Tyler Moore, Dom De Luise, Susan Saint James, Cleavon Little.

WHAT'S THE MATTER WITH HELEN? (1971). In the vein of WHAT EVER HAPPENED TO BABY JANE?, directed by Curtis Harrington with a tongue-in-cheek quality that alternates with the sharp suspense of Henry Farrell's script. Debbie Reynolds and Shelley Winters are mothers of murderers serving time who move to Hollywood during the '30s to open a dancing school. Shelley, as Helen, gets religion from Agnes Moorehead and goes bonkers in her wonderfully unique way. Dennis Weaver, Pamelyn Ferdin. (MGM/UA)

WHAT'S UP, HIDEOUS SUN DEMON? (1989). A comedy reissue of Robert Clarke's cult classic of 1959, THE HIDEOUS SUN DEMON, with a revised soundtrack that spoofs the film in the style of Woody Allen's WHAT'S UP, TIGER LILY? The new material, by Craig Mitchell, features the voices of Jay Leno, Susan Tyrrell, Barbara Goodson and Bernard Behrens.

WHAT THE PEEPER SAW (1973). Offbeat British psychodrama, interesting for its ambiguities and hints of conspiracy. Mark Lester is a perverted little bastard who might have drowned his mother—or so suspects stepmother Britt Ekland, the only one to penetrate to the roots of the boy's "bad seed" tendencies. Father Hardy Kruger refuses to believe so psychiatrist Lilli Palmer makes it appear Britt is off her rocker and commits her. Screenwriter Trevor Preston is interested in the psychological interplay among his intriguing characters, and how they step in and out of shadows cast by the aberrant mind. Directed with a minimum of flash and dash by James Kelly. (VCI; Interglobal)

WHAT WAITS BELOW (1983). Intriguing fantasy-adventure from producer Sandy Howard, with Robert Powell as a soldier of fortune called upon by a U.S. military unit in South America to help in the installation of a sonar device in an underground cavern. Director Don Sharp captures tension and suspense as the expedition (Timothy Bottoms, Anne Heywood, Richard Johnson, Lisa Blount) works its way into the cavern's depths to discover (1) an ALIEN-like rock monster and (2) a race of albino-skinned Lemurians. When the action erupts there's plenty of it. (Lightning)

WHEELS OF FIRE (1984). There's never a dull moment in this nonstop display of car chases and gunbattles, which amounts to another MAD MAX retread, directed-written by action master Cirio H. Santiago. The hero is Trace, the heroine is Stinger and the villain is Scourge in a post-Armageddon world of dune buggies, souped-up autos and tons of desert dust. There's a tribe of white-haired cannibal Sandmen in a cave, a dwarf fighter, samurai swords, a flame thrower, batteries of artillery and mortars, a clairvoyant woman warrior and peace lovers called The True Believers. What else could you want? Totally mindless, yet fascinating as it unfolds at a dashing pace without logic. Gary Watkins, Laura Banks, Lynda Wiesmeier, Linda Grovenor. (Video/Laser: Vestron)

WHEELS OF TERROR (1990). The first half of this TV-movie, designed in the manner of a slasher flick by screenwriter Alan B. McElroy, resembles THE CAR in its setting (small desert community) and the fact that we never see the killer driver. The second half takes on its own flavor as school-bus driver Joanna Cassidy, after seeing her daughter abducted by the killer car, chases after the black sedan in a prolonged car chase. It is during this exciting sequence that director Christopher Cain struts his artsy fartsy stuff, and WHEELS OF TERROR is at its best. Marcie Leeds, Arlene Dean Snyder. (Video/Laser: Paramount)

WHEN A STRANGER CALLS (1979). Chilling premise: babysitter Carol Kane receives weird calls before realizing a killer is in the house with her, calling from an extension. After this shocking start, the story deteriorates into standard chase fare as cop Charles Durning, years later, pursues the killer after he escapes from an asylum. Finally, the story returns to the babysitter and again becomes a genre scare flick with moments that will make you leap with fright. Recommended to all babysitters. Directed by Fred Walton, who co-scripted with Steve Feke. Rachel Roberts, Colleen Dewhurst, Ron O'Neal, Tony Beckley. (Video/Laser: RCA/Columbia)

WHEN A STRANGER CALLS BACK (1993). Emphasis in this TV-movie sequel to the '79 shocker WHEN A STRANGER CALLS is on the psychological terrors endured by babysitter Jill Schoelen who, five years after an ordeal at the hands of a kidnapper, is terrorized anew by her assailant. Carol Kane, the victimized babysitter in the original, and Charles Durning, the cop on the case, are back as investigators helping Schoelen solve the mystery of someone breaking into her apartment and leaving behind clues to frighten her. The cat-and-mouse aspects of the script by director Fred Walton (who co-created the characters with Steve Feke) dominate, and there are eerie and scary sequences, although explanation of who and how and why is lacking. Gene Lythgow, Karen Austin.

WHEN DINOSAURS RULED THE EARTH (1970). Spectacularly built blonde Victoria Verti is some eyeful in this Hammer sequel to ONE MILLION B.C., which depicts early man squaring off against prehistoric creatures and the elements (including the formation of the moon). Jim Danforth headed a team of effects artists, while Val Guest wrote-directed. Ms Verti is a member of the Rock

Tribe rescued by Robin Hawdon of the Sea Tribe. Cast out from their respective bands, they rove the barren surface, make love in caves and encounter snakes, crabs and dinosaurs. Effects are not up to the Harryhausen standard, but it's solid entertainment. Robin Hawdon, Patrick Allen. (Video/Laser: Warner Bros.)

WHEN DREAMS COME TRUE (1985). Messily plotted TV-movie delves into the nightmares of Cindy Williams, a museum tour guide caught up in the affairs of Dallas' "Perfect Murderer." As she realizes her dreams are prophetic, she seeks the help of boyfriend cop Lee Horsley, but behaves in such a dumb manner, you root for the killer to get her. William Bleich's script never deals with why she's having the dreams, an element that would have been far more interesting, and which would have shored up holes in the script. Director John Llewellyn Moxey is stuck with bad material, and can dream up nothing to improve it. David Morse, Stan Shaw, Jessica Harper.

WHEN KNIGHTS WERE BOLD (1936). British musical fantasy (of the A CONNECTICUT YANKEE IN KING ARTHUR'S COURT school) in which commoner Jack Buchanan is transported in time to medieval days. Fay Wray is the damsel in need of rescuing. Directed by Jack Raymond. Martita Hunt, Robert Horton, Garry Marsh. (Video Yesteryear)

WHEN MICHAEL CALLS (1969). Compelling, sometimes intriguing TV-movie even if its outcome is predictable. Based on a John Farris novel, this walks that gossamer plotline between supernatural chiller and diabolical let's-drive-Sister-Jessica-to-Death as divorcee Elizabeth Ashley receives calls from her long-dead son, while ex-hubby Ben Gazzara investigates. The characters are interestingly etched by telewriter James Bridges and director Philip Leacock does his best on a limited budget. There are effective "dead boy" spectre scenes and a few chilling calls which drive Ashley hysterical. Michael Douglas, Marian Waldman, Albert S. Waxman. (From Platinum as **SHATTERED SILENCE**)

WHEN STRANGERS MARRY (1944). A gem of a low-budget suspense shocker, far ahead of its time, and a precursor to the horror thrillers that William Castle would produce-direct years later. Castle shows imagination and verve in helming this shocker about a woman (Kim Hunter) who marries a mysterious salesman (Dean Jagger) to become caught up in the "Silk Scarf Strangler" murders. Castle completists won't want to miss this yarn, which was scripted by Castle and Philip Yordan. It has Robert Mitchum in an early role.

WHEN THE SCREAMING STOPS (1973). A school of nubile young women . . . a scaly monster brought to life by moonlight . . . an underwater cavern where tigerskin-clad cuties dwell . . . the Sword of Siegfried . . . it's the kitchen-sink theory as applied by writer-director Amando De Ossorio in this naive, silly tale based on an old legend that Lorelei stands guard over the Gold of the Rhine River, killing when the moon is full. The amphibious green slime monster with big teeth is more comedical than frightening and there is an eyefilling parade of curvaceous cuties in bikinis and other skimpy costumes that will please males. But beautiful faces and shapely bodies don't necessarily make for a good movie. Tony Kendall stars as a thick-skulled hunter brought to the school to kill the monster. Mild lesbian overtones rear up. Helga Line, Silvia Tortosa, Josefina Jartin. Also called GRASP OF THE LORELEI or THE LORELEI'S GRASP. (Lightning)

WHEN THE WIND BLOWS (1986). Raymond Briggs' British cartoon book inspired this animated feature showcasing Hilda and Jim (average Britons represented by the voices of Peggy Ashcroft and John Mills) as they face nuclear holocaust. Decidedly offbeat. Directed by Jimmy Murakami. (IVE) (Laser: Image)

WHEN WOMEN HAD TAILS (1970). Senta Berger stars in this Italian send-up of prehistoric monster movies featuring scantily clad cave people by portraying one of the latter, discovered by seven rock dwellers—seven being significant as this is a take-off on SNOW WHITE AND THE SEVEN DWARFS. It seems Ms Bergen wags her tail when she gets horny. Directed by Pasquale Festa Campanile, co-scripted by Lina Wertmuller. (WesternWorld; Sinister/C)

WHEN WOMEN LOST THEIR TAILS (1971). Sequel to WHEN WOMEN HAD TAILS. Get it? Sizzling Senta Berger returns in her scanty animal skins in the continuing adventures of passionate women in days of volcanic, explosive sexuality. They love with a primitive passion! Again directed by Pasquale Festa Campanile, with Lina Wertmuller again rounding out the curvy storyline. (WesternWorld)

WHEN WORLDS COLLIDE (1951). Producer George Pal's above-average version of the Edwin Balmer-Philip Wylie novel, with an intelligent script by Sydney Boehm that deals convincingly with man's social disintegration when a star dubbed Bellus passes so close to Earth it causes destructive earthquakes, tidal waves and other mayhem. Mankind's only hope is to build a rocketship to take a handful of humans to a satellite planet, Zyra—and thus begins the race to survive. Among those in the project are millionaire John Hoyt and lovers Richard Derr and Barbara Rush. Chesley Bonestell was technical advisor; Gordon Jennings won an Oscar for his effects. Directed by Rudolf Mate, who turned this into one of the best sci-fi films of the '50s. Mary Murphy, Larry Keating. (Video/Laser: Paramount)

WHERE ARE THE CHILDREN? (1985). Mildly horrific adaptation of Mary Higgins Clark's novel, but missing the hard edge such a suspense tale needed. For a story about a madman who kidnaps two children and holds them hostage, with the intent to murder them, this has too few graphic shocks—fans are going to call this Zev Braun production "wimpy." Jill Clayburgh portrays the hysterical mother of the children whose history suggests she could be responsible for the kidnapping. The supporting cast is good, especially Frederic Forrest as the kidnapper (wearing a pillow to give him added weight), and Max Gail and Barnard Hughes. Scripted by Jack Sholder and directed by Bruce Malmuth. (RCA/Columbia)

WHERE DO WE GO FROM HERE? (1945). Effervescent 20th Century-Fox musical-comedy with costumed production numbers (lyrics by Ira Gershwin and Kurt Weill) and nonsensical fun as 4-F patriotic Fred MacMurray finds Aladdin's Lamp, frees genie "Alley" (Gene Sheldon) and wishes himself in the army. But the genie fouls up and sends Fred back in time to George Washington's army at Valley Forge. The non sequitur gags remind one of Mad Magazine, MacMurray does a ridiculous parody of Hitler in a barroom of German stereotypes, and there's a delightful musical number aboard the Santa Maria when Mac winds up part of Columbus' expedition. The silly casting includes Alan Mowbray as General Washington, Anthony Quinn as Chief Badger (who sells Manhattan to MacMurray for $24 dollars—the Badger Game, get it?) and June Haver and Joan Leslie as All-American beauties who fall for the bumbling, lovable Mac. Very American, very nostalgic. Directed by Gregory Ratoff.

WHERE HAVE ALL THE PEOPLE GONE? (1974). TV-film combines two bizarre elements: a solar fire that destroys all mechanical devices and a plague that decimates mankind, turning corpses into ashes. A typical video plod-plot as a few survivors struggle to reach Malibu . . . only sci-fi buffs will find the earthbound trek worth making. John Moxey directed the Lewis John Carlino-Sandor Stern script. Peter Graves, Verna Bloom, Kathleen Quinlan. (Lorimar)

WHERE THE BULLETS FLY (1967). One dull cliffhanger after another as super-incredible superagent Tom Adams pursues the formula for a method of draining nuclear energy from the alloy called spurium. This sequel to THE SECOND BEST SECRET AGENT IN THE WHOLE WIDE WORLD fluctuates from mediocrity to ineptitude and back. Directed by John Gilling. Dawn Addams, Sidney James, Michael Ripper. (CBS/Fox)

WHERE THE DEVIL CANNOT GO (1960). See editions 1-3.

WHERE THE TRUTH LIES (1962). See editions 1-3.

WHERE TIME BEGAN (1977). Spanish version of Jules Verne's novel by writer-director Juan Piquer is inferior to the 1959 adaptation, JOURNEY TO THE CENTER OF THE EARTH. The pace is sluggish, the characterizations dull. The film gains life when the monsters appear. Even though they are laughable dinosaur and King Kong imitations, they beat the monotony of the expedition into the bowels of Earth. Kenneth More stars as the professor in charge. Ivonne Sentis, Frank Brana, Pep Munne, Jack Taylor. (Embassy)

WHILE I LIVE (1948). British psychological supernatural thriller about a girl suffering from amnesia who sings a song that could only have been known by a dead girl. This leads the dead girl's relatives to believe she's returned from the dead. Written-directed by John Harlow, from Robert Bell's play, THIS GAME GARDEN. Sonia Dresdel, Clifford Evans. (Sinister/C; Filmfax)

WHIP AND THE BODY, THE. See **WHAT!**

WHIP HAND, THE (1951). William Cameron Menzies, remembered for INVADERS FROM MARS and THE MAZE, designed-directed this "red menace thriller," a RKO release with blatant touches of anti- Communist propaganda. Elliott Reid, Edgar Barrier and Raymond Burr labor against overwhelming odds with a crazy plot in which ex-Nazis hiding in a northwestern town are in search of a germ that could wipe out mankind. If the film seems schizophrenic that's because it was first made by Menzies as THE MAN HE FOUND, from a script by Stanley Rubin. The footage was recut according to a revised script by George Bricker and Frank L. Moss. Chalk it up to the hysteria rampant in Hollywood in those days, what with the House Un-American Activities Committee at work.

WHIRLPOOL (1949). Slick 20th Century-Fox murder mystery with slight fantasy overtones: Charlatan psychiatrist Jose Ferrer uses hypnotism to force kleptomaniac Gene Tierney to carry out his bidding. This sets her up as a suspect in a homicide he committed, although he has a perfect alibi: He was in a hospital recovering from an operation. The scenes where Ferrer hypnotizes himself are of mild interest, but the story (based on a Guy Endore novel) is dated and Otto Preminger's direction is routine, capturing little of the noir elements of the story. Worth seeing, though, for the cast: Richard Conte (as the never-doubting husband), Charles Bickford (as the cynical cop), and Eduard Franza (as the D.A.)

WHIRLPOOL (1970). See editions 1-3.

WHISKEY AND GHOSTS (1967). Obscure Italian western-comedy from producer Carlo Ponti captures a Three-Stooges flavor with its sagebrush silliness, and it's just dumb enough to evoke mild chuckles. Napoleon B. Higgins, a nerdish snake-oil salesman, is pursued across the desert by Mexican outlaws (stereotypes at their worst) while Davy Crockett's ghost (depicted as a chubby, whiskey-guzzling drunk in a derby with ho-ho-ho humor) helps Higgins out of life-threatening situations. Eventually, the spirits of Johnny Appleseed (!) and Pecos Bill (!!) are added to the craziness. An anomaly made when spaghetti westerns were big, so there are overtones of that genre within this melee of western wackiness. The dubbing, though, is bad. Directed by Anthony Dawson. Tom Scott, Fred Harris, Mariel Martin.

WHISKEY MOUNTAIN (1977). Cyclists and their wives seek a legendary treasure but instead find "death and terror." Christopher George, Preston Pierce, Robert Collins, Robert Leslie. Directed by William Grefe. (Best Film & Video)

WHISPERING GHOSTS (1942). Old-fashioned, fun-filled mystery-comedy stuffed with ectoplasmic figures, spectral voices, a cursed ship—all logically explained in the Philip MacDonald story scripted by Lou Breslow. Milton Berle is a radio-program detective who seeks a killer with sidekick Willie Best, a comedy relief figure typically racist for the period. John Carradine, Brenda Joyce, Grady Sutton, Arthur Hohl. Directed by Alfred Werker.

WHISPERING SHADOWS (1933). Mascot serial of 12 chapters in which the evil Professor Strang (Bela Lugosi) brings wax figures to life and has powers to project his shadow at will. He can also kill people with radio death rays. It's excitingly paced but crudely made and dated. Directed by Albert Herman and Colbert Clark. Henry B. Walthall, Karl Dane, Viva Tattersall. (Captain Bijou; Sinister/C; Nostalgia; Video Connection)

WHISPERS (1990). Unusually good Canadian adaptation of Dean R. Koontz's novel about a woman (Victoria Tennant) terrorized by a knife-wielding attacker—but nothing is what it seems when assailant Jean LeClerc returns from the dead to terrorize her anew. She and cop Chris Sarandon set out to find out if he's dead or not. The trail leads to devil worship, vampires and an army of deadly cockroaches, all cleverly arranged by writer Anita Doohan and carefully shot by director Douglas Jackson. The film also has an unusual homosexual touch, which we cannot elaborate on without giving away the ending. Peter MacNeill, Linda Sorenson, Eric Christmas, Jackie Burroughs. (Live) (Laser: Image)

WHISPER TO A SCREAM, A (1989). Stripper Nadia Capone takes a job as a telephone-sex lady, creating sensuous personas that turn on a killer and make him kill the dancers at Nadia's club. Canadian psychokiller flick unfolds in predictable fashion. Director Robert Bergman cranked out the script with producer Gerard Ciccoritti. (Virgin Vision) (Laser: Image)

WHISTLING IN DIXIE (1942). The Old Dark House again, this time with Red Skelton (in his recurring role as that radio detective, The Fox) scampering along eerie corridors, bumping into "ghosts" and hearing strange voices. The so-called "Whistling" series (this is a sequel to WHISTLING IN THE DARK) holds up well thanks to the comedic timing of the irascible Skelton, who was in his prime. Directed by S. Sylvan Simon. Ann Rutherford, George Bancroft, Guy Kibbee.

WHISTLING IN THE DARK (1941). Red Skelton's lovable albeit bumbling radio-detective The Fox was to inspire a sequel, WHISTLING IN DIXIE. In this wild and woolly comedy mystery, Skelton bumps into moon worshippers. Fun from beginning to end with Skelton's undated slapstick a delight. And we're not just whistling, Dixie. Conrad Veidt, Ann Rutherford, Virginia Grey. Directed by S. Sylvan Simon.

WHITE CANNIBAL QUEEN (1974). Flesheating Italian epic in which a father (Al Cliver) spends years tracking down his daughter (Candy Coster, better known as Lina Romay) who was kidnapped by lip-smacking jungle natives. Directed by Jesse Franco. Umm umm good. (Video City)

WHITE GORILLA, THE (1945). Bad film patching, in which footage from a silent 1927 African adventure, PERILS OF THE JUNGLE, was inserted with new footage directed by Harry L. Fraser. A gorilla (Ray "Crash" Corrigan in a hairy white suit) clashes with a black gorilla in "the battle of the century"—but which century? So bad you might enjoy it, if you enjoy punishing yourself. Lorraine Miller. (Weiss Global)

WHITE LIGHT (1990). Offbeat Canadian-produced mixture of cops vs. the underworld action and a mild supernatural plot in which deep-cover cop Sean Craig (Martin Kove) is shot by an assassin and has a six-hour near-death experience, meeting beautiful Rachel (Allison Hossack). Returned to the living, Kove tracks down his old nemesis, searches for the mysterious Rachel and meets a lady scientist conducting experiments with tetradetoxin, a drug that simulates the death experience. Ron Base's script is unusual enough to sustain interest despite familiar ingredients and director Al Waxman brings moments of sensitivity to the romantic interludes. Filmed in Toronto. Martha Henry, Heide von Palleske, James Purcell. (Academy) (Laser: Image)

WHITE MARE'S SON, THE (1982). Inexpensively produced, effective Hungarian animated feature, di-

MADGE BELLAMY, BELA LUGOSI IN 'WHITE ZOMBIE'

rected by Marcell Jankovics, based on an ancient Scythian legend about a dragon princess who disguises herself as a white horse to escape into exile where she can raise her son. Abstract and metaphoric.

WHITE OF THE EYE (1986). Off-the-wall, unusually original portrait of a psychokiller and what happens when he goes off the deep end. This is not a slasher film—it's a study of people in an Arizona town and how they react to a series of wealthy-housewife murders. Sometimes the characters behave in such a bizarre way that credulity is stretched to the breaking point, but director Donald Cammell keeps it balance with his fine cast by always emphasizing the perversensss of the unpredictable script by China and Donna Cammell. This will not be everyone's cup of tea, but those who appreciate the metaphor (complete with apocalyptic climax) will groove on its cinematic delights. David Keith, Cathy Moriarty, Art Evans, Alan Rosenberg. (Paramount)

WHITE PONGO (1945). Laughable, nostalgic reminder of the killer-gorilla genre prolific in the '40s. Pongo, a white ape believed to be the missing link between anthropod and man, carries off screaming Maris Wrixon, threatening to mate with her in his lair. Cheer, don't wince, and have fun with this hoary old horror. Kick him where it hurts, Ms Wrixon. Directed by Sam Newfield, scripted by Raymond L. (Schlock) Schrock. Richard Fraser, Lionel Royce. (Sinister/C; Nostalgia)

WHITE REINDEER, THE (1953). See editions 1-3.

WHITE SLAVE (1985). Englishwoman Elvive Audray is kidnapped and tortured by cannibals. Will Gonzales co-stars. Directed by Roy Garrett. (Lightning)

WHITE ZOMBIE (1932). Long hailed as a lost classic, this was rediscovered in the '60s, then condemned by some fans who wished it had remained lost. Want the truth? It's creaky and awful, only occasionally enhanced by the symbolic imagery injected by producer Edward Halperin and director Victor Halperin. Yet it's historically important because of Bela Lugosi, whose performance makes this worth viewing. Yes, he's in dire need of restraint as he overplays Legendre, a sweetless sugar plantation owner in the West Indies who holds sway over an army of zombies. Heavy-handed, turgid viewing, yes, but it's a wonderful glimpse into Hollywood's schlocky past. Voodoo lore was borrowed by writer Garnett Weston from William Seabrook's nonfictional MAGIC ISLAND. Madge Bellamy, John Harron. (Prism; United; Kartes; Quintex; Sinister/C's and Filmfax's version includes a "lost" interview with Lugosi.)

WHO? (1974). Espionage-fantasy mixture in which U.S. scientist Joseph Bova undergoes Communist cybernetic surgery to become a counter-agent, only to endure an auto accident. The FBI sends Elliott Gould to investigate. Director Jack Gold's script is based on a novel by Algis Budrys. Trevor Howard, Ed Grover, Ivan Desny. (From Ace as **ROBO MAN**)

WHO CAN KILL A CHILD? See **ISLAND OF THE DAMNED.**

WHO DONE IT? (1956). Above-average British comedy thriller (directed by Basil Deardon) in which an inept private eye saves the Empire from spies assigned to steal a weather-controlling device. Belinda Lee, Benny Hill, Ernest Thesiger, Garry Marsh, George Margo.

WHO FEARS THE DEVIL? See **LEGEND OF HILLBILLY JOHN, THE.**

WHO FELL ASLEEP? See **DEADLY GAMES.**

WHO FRAMED ROGER RABBIT (1988). An instant classic, an instant masterpiece, an instant Hollywood innovation—a feature that blends live action with animation in a seamless style, creating a unique universe set in 1947. This is the kingdom of Hollywood where cartoon characters (toons) live and breath with humans, working in cartoons but taking "human" jobs during lean times. You really have to credit animation director Richard Williams and Industrial Light and Magic for major contributions to the effect. Almost every cartoon character conceived through 1947 has a featured role or cameo in this entertaining production from Steven Spielberg and Disney. The Jeffrey Price-Peter S. Seaman script (based on Gary K. Wolf's novel WHO CENSORED ROGER RABBIT?) stars Bob Hoskins as private eye Eddie Valiant trying to help cartoon star Roger Rabbit duck a murder charge. Directed with incredible vitality by Robert Zemeckie, the film really gets weird when Hoskins goes to Toonville, a community where all animated characters live. A subplot involves a scheme to get rid of cable cars to make room for freeways—giving this an odd twist of social relevance. The one human-animated character is sexy songstress Jessica (voice by Kathleen Turner). Christopher Lloyd excels as the villain, Judge Doom, Joanna Cassidy portrays Valiant's girl friend, and Stubby Kaye leads his own cartoonish presence as a comedy writer. Highlights include Daffy Duck and Donald Duck performing a piano duo, cameos by Tweety Bird and Sylvester (voices by Mel Blanc), and a guest spot by Lena Hyena. You'll need to see this more than once to catch all the characters and visual gags. (Video/Laser: Touchstone)

WHO IS JULIA? (1988). Intriguing TV-movie adaptation of the Barbara S. Harris novel about the world's first brain transplant. James S. Sadwith's teleplay deals with the emotional and psychological issues of a new brain in a foreign body, with not a single Dr. Frankenstein cliche.

ROGER RABBIT CONFRONTED BY BOB HOSKINS

Mare Winningham portrays a housewife who receives the brain of a sexy model. How she and hubby Jameson Parker adjust, how the model's husband tries to reclaim what he's lost, and how the medical staff copes with its own confused feelings, make for compelling soap-opera material. Directed by Walter Grauman. Jeffrey DeMunn, Jonathan Banks, Mason Adams.

WHO KILLED AUNT MAGGIE?. See third edition.

WHO KILLED DOC ROBBIN? (1948). Dated comedy of the Old Dark House school, complete with a man (actually a gorilla in a human suit), a gorilla (a man in a suit), secret panels, drafty corridors, ectoplasmic manifestations and one mad doctor. Only George Zucco, the crazy physician with an atomic apparatus, looks comfortable in the haunted surroundings. Virginia Grey and Don Castle look lost. Directed by Bernard Carr. (Hollywood Home Theater; Sinister/C)

WHO KILLED MARY WHATS'ER NAME (1972). It isn't the plot, it's the strange, fascinating characters that bring to life this offbeat whodunit. Ex-boxer, diabetic Red Buttons—appalled at everyone's indifference to the ghastly murder of Mary Di Napoli, a New York streetwalker—investigates. Aided by his feisty daughter (Alice Playten), Buttons meets the oddballs. There's whore Sylvia Miles, cop David Doyle, old partner Conrad Bain, sharp-tongued black cop Gilbert Lewis, suspicious landlord Dick Williams and weird filmmaker Sam Waterston. Director Ernie Pintoff gives the story ambience by filming in sleazy city settings. An obscure movie worth digging up. (Video Gems; Prism)

WHO SLEW AUNTIE ROO? (1971). Minor horror themes barely qualify this as a fright flick, yet it always evokes a rowdy response from viewers who recognize the Hansel-and-Gretel parallels to this modern tale of two children living with auntie Shelley Winters. She wants to toss them into the oven in what passes for a gingerbread house. The script (Gavin Lambert, Jimmy Sangster, Robert Blees) meanders but the cast works hard to make the feeble ideas work: Mark Lester, Ralph Richardson, Hugh Griffith, Lionel Jeffries. Despite its slightness, and only average treatment by director Curtis Harrington, this comes out a winner. (Vestron)

WICKED, THE (1989). Australian horror import depicting a rural family of vampires visited by stranded individuals. Brett Cumo, Angela Kennedy, Richard Morgan. Directed by Colin Eggleston. (Select; Hemdale)

WICKED CITY (1992). A fascinating action-packed animated Japanese fantasy-adventure feature set in a land where mankind is at war with "the black world," from which monsters come through the time-space continuum to attack humans. An uneasy treaty exists between the worlds, but renegades break it and a "black guard" agent is assigned to protect a diplomat for the treaty signing. Monsters (including a spider-lady) and effects are exciting and frequently sexual, the film has a heightened sense of eroticism, and the mood captures the bizarre flavor of the comic-book novel by Hideyuki Kikuchi. Directed by Yoshiaki Kawajiri. (Streamline)

WICKED STEPMOTHER (1989). Writer-director Larry Cohen makes pretty strange films, touched by Cohen peculiarities—but this time he didn't mend his wicked, wicked ways and came up with what ranks as the rankest of his work. Bette Davis plays a witch who presumably shrinks people (why or how is never explained) and tries to move in on Lionel Stander, who shares living space with daughter Colleen Camp and son-in-law David Rasche. Along comes Barbara Carrera (looking exotic as usual) as a witch who casts meaningless spells—an excuse for some meaningless effects poorly done. The only funny scene is a police line-up of old-lady types, but after that it's a misfire. Another good actor unfortunate enough to get involved is Tom Bosley, who portrays the cop on the case. (MGM/UA)

WICKED, WICKED (1973). Curiosity piece by writer-producer-director Richard L. Bare, projected in a split-screen process hyped as "Duo-Vision." It's two bad movies in one as half the screen shows mad killer Randolph Roberts wearing a fright mask, stalking beautiful women with his knife, and embalming them in cold-blooded fashion, the other half showing cop Scott Brady tracking him down. The split-screen concept allows for suspense but that's about all. How is WICKED, WICKED? Lousy, lousy. David Bailey, Tiffany Bolling, Edd Byrnes, Diane McBain.

WICKER MAN, THE (1972). This oft-admired film sports a top British cast (Britt Ekland, Diane Cilento, Ingrid Pitt, Christopher Lee) but received poor distribution on two occasions: when initially released in a butchered form, and again in 1978-79 in re-edited form, with director Robin Hardy touring the U.S. to flack for the film. In its complete form, this retains an unusual power in depicting the inhabitants of a Cornish village who act strangely when a constable turns up to investigate a disappearance. One of the highlights of this unusual story is an erotic nude sequence involving the comely Ms Ekland. And Lee considers it one of his best. The literate script is by Anthony Shaffer. Ian Campbell, Aubrey Morris, Edward Woodward. (Media; Republic)

WILD BEASTS (1985). A strange chemical in the local water turns animals and men against each other in a battle to the death. Italian parable couched in the visuals of the horror genre. Directed by Franco Prosperi. John Aldrich, Lorraine de Selle. (Lightning)

WILD BLUE MOON (1992). Mexican supernatural thriller in which Maira Serbulo (playing the daughter of a witch) uses witchcraft for revenge against the painter (Thom Vernon) who jilted her. Directed-written by producers Taggart Siegel and Francesca Fisher.

WILDEST DREAMS (1987). Brainless sex comedy with a little bare-breasted nudity and simulated rolling in the hay when nerdish James Davies, hungry for love and sex, uncorks Heidi Paine (as the genie Dancee) from an Egyptian vase and is granted the wish of having beautiful women fall in love with him instantly. However, each woman is so overbearing that Davies keeps asking for another. It's a series of tasteless sight gags, dumb verbal jokes, big hooters and other prurient interests from writer Craig Harrall and producer-director Chuck Vincent. Cork it and forget it. Deborah Blaisdell, Ruth Collins, Jill Johnson. (Vestron) (Laser: Image)

WILD IN THE SKY (1972). See editions 1-3.

WILD IN THE STREETS (1968). Far-out premise, like man, dig this: Rock singer Max Frost (Christopher Jones), manipulated for political reasons, turns the tables on congressman Hal Holbrook and manipulates Capitol Hill for his own devious goals. The result is a lower voting age (would you believe 14?) and an election in which the singer is elected President. His first act in Congress: to put everyone over 35 into concentration camps, where they are force-fed hallucinogens. Wild wild wild. Directed with youthful passion by Barry Shear and scripted with unbridled imagination by Robert Thom. Shelley Winters, Ed Begley, Millie Perkins, Diane Varsi, Richard Pryor, Dick Clark. (Video/Laser: HBO)

WILD JUNGLE CAPTIVE. See **JUNGLE CAPTIVE.**

WILD MAN (1989). Magical ring on the finger of secret agent Eric Wilde (Don Scribner) enables him to return to life whenever he gets killed by bad guy James L. Newman. The ring comes from Indian medicine man Fred J. Lincoln, who also directed this video actioner. Michelle Bauer, Kathleen Middleton, Travis Silver, Ginger Lynn Allen. (Celebrity)

WILD PALMS (1993). In 2007 A.D., L.A. attorney James Belushi wakes up from a dream about a rhino in his pool, setting into motion events that lead him to realize he is at the core of a conspiracy that involves a quasireligious communications organization secretly planning to control the world through a form of TV virtual reality. This intriguing theme by Bruce Wagner is told in such an offhanded, convoluted and slow-moving fashion in this six-hour "TV event" that interest drifts unless one is dedicated to keeping track of the many characters, their dual loyalties and a past that is constantly mingled with

A TV EVENT OF '93: 'WILD PALMS'

the present. You will need to appreciate the eccentric and bizarre as this futuristic cautionary tale unfolds. Robert Loggia is strong as the messiah of the cult (The Fathers), David Warner is intense as the leader of the underground fighting the cult, and Angie Dickinson is superb as a torture expert for Loggia. Others who do well with difficult roles are Dana Delany, Kim Cattrall, Ernie Hudson, Bebe Neuwirth, Nick Mancuso, Robert Morse and Brad Dourif. Various episodes were directed by Peter Hewitt, Keith Gordon, Kathryn Bigelow and Phil Joanou. Music by Ryuichi Sakamoto. (ABC)

WILD THING (1986). Unusual urban fantasy patterned after the TARZAN myth, springing from the imagination of screenwriter John Sayles. In 1969 a child witnesses the murder of his mother and father at the hands of drug dealers. The youth escapes and grows up wild in the city slums to emerge in modern day as a Robin Hood on a rope, who swings from the parapets to rescue the innocent from the evil elements of The Zone, a depressed area of an American city, the "home of the down and out, outlaws and outcasts." Rob Knepper plays Wild Thing as a naive innocent (he calls sex, for example, "body bump") and has his first romance with Kathleen Quinlan, who has just arrived to work in a relief mission. Wild Thing's battle is with drug kingpin Chopper and he stalks baddies with a crossbow. A fascinating, though not-always-successful tale of messed-up Americana, with director Max Reid capturing the coarseness of city life and its decadence and decency. Robert Davi, Maury Chaykin, Betty Buckley. (Paramount; Goodtimes)

WILD WILD PLANET (1967). Dull, dull Italian sci-fi set in 2015 A.D. spends too much time setting up a premise that never jells—a miniaturized scientist (Massimo Serato) who plots to kidnap representatives of the United Democracies with the help of intergalactic robot female pirates. This unofficial sequel to WAR OF THE PLANETS was directed by Anthony Dawson (Antonio Margheriti). Tony Russell, Lisa Gastoni, Franco Nero, Massimo Serato, Charles Justin. (S/Weird)

WILD, WILD WEST REVISITED, THE (1979). Another follow-up to the once-popular TV series, with Robert Conrad as secret agent James T. West and Ross Martin as his sidekick, Artemus Gordon. It's all cowboy fun and games with 19th Century clones, nuclear bombs and other out-of-time-and-place inventions springing from the wild, wild mind of scriptwriter William Bowers. Burt Kennedy directed purely for laughs. Jo Ann Harris, Paul Williams, Harry Morgan, Joyce Jameson, Rene Auberjonois. (CBS/Fox)

WILD WOMEN OF WONGO (1958). Ten thousand years before Christ? That's what producer George R. Black, director James Wolcott and writer Cedric Rutherford would like you to believe as they present a film that truly belongs to the Stoned Age of Cinema. Wongo is indeed a world of "wild women" where prehistoric dames, in need of better hairdos, worship the Temple of the Dragon God. Meanwhile, Goona men wish they could get their beady hands on these luscious broads. An actress named Adrienne Bourbeau appears as one of the cave chicks, with the hots for Ed Fury. Wongo wongo bongo bongo slongo. (Rhino; Amvest; Media)

WILD WORLD OF BATWOMAN, THE (1966). Cheapie writer-producer-director Jerry Warren is responsible for this attempt to cash on the BATMAN phenomenon of '66 with this regrettably floppish superheroine nonflick starring Katherine Victor (in her native Greece she's known as Katena Ktenavea) as a queen of costumed women assigned to fight Dr. Neon and his sidekick, Ratfink. George Andre, Steve Brodie, Lloyd Nelson, Richard Banks. Aka SHE WAS A HIPPIE VAMPIRE. (Rhino; Sinister/C; S/Weird; Discount; Filmfax)

WILLARD (1971). Stephen Gilbert's novel, RATMAN'S NOTEBOOKS, is material that proved a difficult mousetrap for director Daniel Mann and scripter Gilbert Ralston to set. You'll never be suckered in by its cheesiness; it's too unbelievable in depicting how a 27-year-old failure (Bruce Davison) trains an army of 500 rats to do his evil bidding, which includes murdering a sadistic boss (Ernest Borgnine). WILLARD had box office snap, especially with black ghetto audiences who sided with the rats as they attacked honkies and Establishment figureheads. Sondra Locke plays Bruce's girlfriend in a miniskirt, Elsa Lanchester is the demanding, dying mother and Michael Dante is a fellow office worker. The sequel, BEN, was also a money-maker but just as mousy. (Prism) (Laser: Image)

WILLIES, THE (1990). Anthology of horror stories suffers from slow pacing and padded material. Three teens (Sean Astin, Jason Horst, Joshua Jon Miller) spend the night trying to gross each other out with bloodcurdlers. Some are sickening vignettes ("Tennessee Frickasee," "Haunted Estate," "Poodle Souffle") but most of the film is devoted to two lengthy tales: "Bad Apples," in which a picked-on kid gets his revenge with a monster in the boys' room at Greeley Elementary High, and "Flyboy," a perverse, pathological study of a fat boy (Michael Bower) with a fetish for collecting dead flies. Naturally, the flies get their revenge for having their wings pulled off with the help of Spivey's Own Miracle Manure. There's something unappetizing about this film (you actually want to see Bower knocked off, he's so despicable) when it should have had a sense of fun. Blame writer-producer-director Brian Peck. Ralph Drischell, Kathleen Freeman, Ian Fried, James Karen, Jeremy Miller, Clu Gulager. (Prism) (Laser: Image)

WILLIS O'BRIEN: A COMPILATION. Highlights from films featuring the stop-motion animation of the man who invented it, Willis O'Brien. Included: KING KONG, LOST WORLD and MIGHTY JOE YOUNG. (VC)

WILLOW (1988). A George Lucas production that tries to regain the magic and excitement of the STAR WARS series, but which misses by a considerable distance. However, Lucas fans will consider it the best game in town until something better happens along. It is full of lavish (if not wondrous) special effects and the action is plentiful, even though the characters don't have the charm and mythical qualities to make them memorable. For what it is, WILLOW is the episodic adventures of a dwarf (called a Nelwyn) returning a lost baby to civilization, unaware the cooing infant, a princess destined to ascend to the throne in Daikini territory, has been ordered killed by the wicked sorceress Queen Bavmorda. As Willow, Warwick Davis leads his miniband into a plot involving a Han Solo-like renegade named Madmartigan (Val Kilmer), the evil general Kael (Pat Roach) and two pocket-sized adventurers. The film conveys three points of view during the action sequences, creating amusing effects. Bob Dolman's screenplay borrows from many sources to spin the far-ranging tale. Since there's never

'WILLOW': BILLY BARTY AS HIGH ALDWIN; VAL KILMER; GENERAL KAEL

any doubt as to a happy ending, one's attention is held by the parade of little people, warriors, magicians, killer animals and monsters. Directed by Ron Howard with a rough edge. Joanne Whalley, Jean Marsh, Billy Barty, Patricia Hayes, Gavan O'Herlihy, Kevin Pollak, Phil Fondacaro. (Video/Laser: RCA/Columbia)

WILLY McBEAN AND HIS MAGIC MACHINE (1965). Japanese puppet feature in AniMagic, which approximates a 3-D look. McBean, a bright child who joins forces with Mexican monkey Pablo, travels through time to prevent Professor Rasputin von Rotten from tinkering with the fabric of history. Quaint and charming. Written-produced-directed by Arthur Rankin Jr. Voices by Larry Mann, Billie Richards, Alfie Scopp. (Prism)

WILLY/MILLY (1986). See **SOMETHING SPECIAL.**

WILLY WONKA AND THE CHOCOLATE FACTORY (1971). Visually attractive adaptation of Roald Dahl's children's book, with enough whimsical humor and satire for adults too. It's a fantasy odyssey through a candy factory conducted by Gene Wilder, a fluffy concoction complete with morality lessons and a superb cast: Jack Albertson, Leonard Stone, Peter Ostrum, Denise Nickerson, Roy Kinnear. Impressionistic sets of the chocolate factory almost steal away the Hershey bar. It'll melt in your mouth . . . (Video/Laser: Warner Bros.)

WIND, THE (1986). Deserted village on the windswept Greek island Monemvassia is the setting for this psychoterror flick with overtones that the ubiquitous breeze sweeping the desolate place is supernatural. Producer-director Nico Mastorakis (who co-wrote with Fred C. Perry) fashions cat-and-mouse slasher games when adventure writer Meg Foster is attacked by next-door neighbor Wings Hauser. Boyfriend David McCallum, back in L.A., is too far away to do anything so his is a thankless role. Every twist is predictable, there's little suspense in Mastorakis' lethargic style, and the setting, with its catacombs and ruinous atmosphere, ultimately has too little story to service. Robert Morley, Steve Railsback, John Michaels, Tracy Young. (MGM/UA)

WINGED SERPENT, THE. See **Q: THE WINGED SERPENT.** (Queue up to see it!)

WINGS OF DESIRE (1987). West German director Wim Wender creates a mesmerizing, poetic effect in this fable about two angels (without wings, halos and harps) hovering above Berlin and listening to the thoughts of inhabitants. (They are beautifully underplayed by Bruno Ganz and Solveig Dommartin.) As they reflect on the human condition, Ganz is overtaken by the desire to be human and transformed into flesh and blood so he can indulge his love for a circus aerialist. The film is told in stark black-and-white images except when Ganz feels human or turns human. Peter Falk, portraying an actor making a movie, becomes a key figure in this philosophical, brooding and moving tale. Sequel: FARAWAY, SO CLOSE. (Orion) (Laser: Image)

WIRED (1989). Very strange biographical movie based on Bob Woodward's study of comedian-actor John Belushi's drug overdose death in 1982. That book was a serious attempt to learn the truth of Belushi's death and to explore the devastation drugs has on our culture, but this movie is a supernatural comedy in which Belushi's spirit (Michael Chiklis) comes alive on the coroner's slab and is led through a life recap by taxi driver Ray Sharkey (playing a chicano variation on the Guardian Angel). J.T. Walsh plays Woodward, shown investigating the death. All of this, plus assorted flashbacks into Belushi's career, is never blended in Earl Mac Rauch's script. Just when you get caught up in the serious drug issues, and the impact of Belushi's self-destruction, the comedic fantasy elements intrude and deaden the effect. Larry Peerce's offbeat direction, in which present and past are often shown in the same scene, is finally defeated by trivialization. Bad taste prevails. Lucinda Jenny, Alex Rocco, Gary Groomes, Patti D'Arbanville. (IVE) (Laser: Image)

WIRED TO KILL (1986). The futuristic post-holocaust world in this low-low-budget actioner is different from Mad Max's, so at least it strives for originality. The time is 1998, and while there is a similance of law and order, the world is pretty screwed up when Emily Longstreth, freshly kicked out of her home, teams with electronics inventor Devin Hoelscher who's just had his legs broken by a sadist (Merritt Butrick) and his band of perverts. The gimmick is that the incapacitated Hoelscher must use the girl to carry out his dirty work with a robot named Winston. Directed-written by Franky Schaeffer. Frank Collison, Tommy Lister Jr., Kim Milford. A little better than usual for this genre. (Lightning)

WISHBONE CUTTER. Video version of **SHADOW OF CHIKARA** (MNTEX).

WISHMAKER, THE (1979). Slow-paced, gentle-mannered German TV-movie based on "The Goosegirl" by the Brothers Grimm, in which the legendary three wishes are granted a poor blacksmith's son as he searches for a beautiful princess who is ostracized by her wicked father-king. The lad learns wisdom through his youthful mistakes and the teachings of a sagacious "witch." Decent production values and a sincere cast turn what might have been a dreary experience into okay family fare. Directed by Ursula Schmenger. Ingrid John, Gunter Nauman, David Schneider. (Video Gems)

WISHMAN (1991). Modern fairy tale set in L.A.: garbage collector Paul LeMat loves from afar beautiful Quin Kessler, who is kept a virtual prisoner by her guardian and a mean-old housekeeper named Crabb. Enter Geoffrey Lewis as Liggett Hitchcock, a genie who has lost his magic bottle and some of his powers, and Staten Jack Rose, a charming con man played by Brion James. The hapless guys team to help Kessler escape her plight and reclaim the bottle, which has ended up in a museum. The humor is only mildly funny and the make-a-wish potential is never fully utilized, but writer-director Michael Marvin makes this a pleasing concoction with his personable characters. Paul Gleason, Nancy Parsons, Gailard Sartan, Liz Sheridan. (Monarch)

WITCH, THE (1966). Redundantly named Damiano Damiani directed and co-wrote (with Ugo Liberatore) this Italian tale based on a novel by Carlos Fuentes that depicts Richard Johnson, a historian translating erotic literature in a castle library, caught up in psychological mystery with horrific overtones and touches of black magic. Also called THE WITCH IN LOVE, THE STRANGE OBSESSION and AURA. Rosanna Schiaffino, Gian Maria Volonte. (S/Weird; Sinister/C)

WITCH, THE (1982). See **SUPERSTITION.**

WITCH AND WARLOCK. See **WITCHCRAFT.**

WITCH BENEATH THE SEA, THE (1962). Who is the alluring, legendary Amazon, her loins throbbing with passion, who attracts men and puts them into a frenzy of lustful desire? Who is the novelist who falls under the spell of her licentious urges? Is the legend of Marizinia true or is there a simpler explanation? Low-budget stuff(ing) for lowbrow viewers. John Sutton, Gina Albert.

WITCHBOARD (1986). Sincere effort to tell a terror tale with good characterizations underlies this low-budget supernatural thriller utilizing the ouija board as a horror device. Unfortunately, the first half could be called WITCHBORED, with writer-director Kevin S. Tenney in need of more panache for his planchette. Finally, the murders begin after Tawny Kitaen dabbles with a ten-year-old spirit, unaware she is communicating with a mass murderer back from the grave and stalking prey with his axe. The gore is light but the impact is there at the chaotic climax, a blending of slasher- and EXORCIST-type thrills. Todd Allen, Stephen Nichols. (Continental; Magnum) (Laser: Image)

WITCHBOARD 2: THE DEVIL'S DOORWAY (1993). A few spectacular effects—that's about all writer-director Kevin S. Tenney brings to this sequel to his '86 hit, which again uses the ouija board as a device linking our world to the spirits. Ami Dolenz moves into a loft apartment, finds the "witchboard" and communicates with the spirit of a dead woman who claims to have been murdered. A series of OMEN-inspired gore-murders occurs, but Tenney doesn't set up interesting characters or circumstances to build on the mystery of who the dead woman is, or who killed her. Timothy Gibbs, John Gatins, Laraine Newman, Julie Michaels. (Republic)

WITCHCRAFT (1959). See **DEVIL'S HAND, THE.**

WITCHCRAFT (1964). British quickie, reportedly made in 20 days under director Don (KISS OF THE VAMPIRE) Sharp, transcends its speedy Robert L. Lippert production values to become a sustaining (albeit minor) chiller starring Lon Chaney Jr. as a man who seeks vengeance after his family plot is bulldozed. Yvette Rees, Jack Hedley, Jill Dixon, Viola Keats.

WITCHCRAFT (1989). Brand-new mother Anat Topol-

BRUNO GANZ AS DAMIEL IN WIM WENDERS' 'WINGS OF DESIRE'

THE OUIJA BOARD IN 'WITCHBOARD'

Barzilai moves into the gothic house of her mother-in-law and has visions that suggest demons are close at hand. This was such a successful video release that it inspired sequels. Directed by Robert Spera. Gary Sloan, Mary Shelley, Deborah Scott. (Academy)

WITCHCRAFT II: THE TEMPTRESS (1989). Ridiculous sequel is supposed to be deadly serious but it turns out hysterically funny. The offspring from the original, now a teenager living with adoptive parents, is the spawn of the devil, and a buxom, blonde witch in black lingerie and high heels (played by supersexy Delia Sheppard) hams it up trying to seduce him into her coven. She acts more like a dancer in a cheap burlesque club than an evil spirit, and eventually the best thing going in this movie are her large breasts, which threaten to rip apart her Frederick's of Hollywood costumes. Charles Solomon, as the young man, is inadequate to the occasion, but his facial expressions are joyful to behold. They aren't what director Mark Woods wanted, but the editor left them in anyway. Mia Ruiz, David L. Homb, Kirsten Wagner. (Academy)

WITCHCRAFT III: THE KISS OF DEATH (1991). A marked improvement over WITCHCRAFT II, with Charles Solomon back as an L.A. D.A. who has the power of a warlock but refuses to use it for evil. He meets a warlock who does use his powers for evil, kissing women and turning them into sex slaves. The warlock falls for Solomon's girl and sets Solomon up for the kill. Solomon turns to an African witch doctor for help. Screenwriter Gerry Daly injects interesting characterizations and director R. L. Tillmans handles his assignment adequately, considering the low budget and limited effects. Lisa Toothman, Domonic Luciano, Leana Hall. (Academy)

WITCHCRAFT IV: VIRGIN HEART (1992). Charles Solomon is back as lawyer Will Spanner, who is again called on to use his warlock abilities when he defends a man accused of a ritualistic murder. Involved are a British talent agent and his sexy charge, a stripper named Belladonna (played by Penthouse pin-up Julie Strain). Call it a Strain on the eyes. Directed by James Merendino. Clive Pearson, Jason O'Gulihur, Lisa Jay Harrington. (Academy) (Laser: Image)

WITCHCRAFT '70 (1970). Italian documentary written-directed-edited by Luigi Scattini, with English narration by Edmund Purdom, which explores contemporary witchcraft. Heavily edited for TV, since it was released theatrically with an X.

WITCHCRAFT THROUGH THE AGES. Video version of **HAXAN** (Embassy; New York Film Annex; Grapevine; Western; MPI).

WITCH DOCTOR, THE. Video version of **RETURNING, THE** (Dura Vision; MPV).

WITCHERY (1988). An island off the coast of New England is haunted by witch Hildegard Knef, the spirit of a one-time sexy movie actress who committed suicide by jumping out an upper-level window. With the help of cackling hags, who make the Crypt Keeper and the Vault Keeper seem beautiful by comparison, she performs assorted OMEN-style murders. Among the unfortunate souls (a boatload of people stranded on the island) are a photographer, a magazine writer, two realtors, Linda Blair and a kid, and an ugly man and his wife. The graphic, unpleasant-to-watch murders include a voodoo-doll puncture job, a human mouth sewn shut by thread (this one will keep you in stitches), a body hung upside down and burned alive in a fireplace, a crucifixion, nails and all, and another body through a window. This Italian gory story was written by Anonymous and directed by Martin Newlin, better known in Rome as Fabrizio Laurenti. Catherine Hickland, David Hasselhoff, Annie Ross. (Vidmark)

WITCHES, THE. See **DEVIL'S OWN, THE.**

WITCHES, THE. Video version of **WITCHCRAFT THROUGH THE AGES.**

WITCHES, THE (1989). Director Nicolas Roeg spins a satisfying witchcraft tale that walks a fine tightrope between being a child's fable and an adult's delight. Outstanding in her first screen role in almost 15 years is Mai Zetterling as the grandmother of bespectacled youth Jasen Fisher. The lad listens with wide-eyed wonder to her tales of witches and their devious ways. Good thing, because when the boy and granny spend a holiday in a seacoast hotel in England they encounter a coven holding a convention, presided over by the grand High Witch—Anjelica Huston in an excellent performance. Her plot is to poison the children of England with sweets and it's up to Jasen, after he's been turned into a mouse, to outsmart the cackling coven. The characters are delightfully funny and the witches convey the witty treachery that Margaret Hamilton conveyed in THE WIZARD OF OZ. Executive producer Jim Henson provided the effects and Allan Scott adapted Roald Dahl's book. Rowan Atkinson, Bill Paterson, Brenda Blethyn. (Video/Laser: Warner Bros.)

WITCHES AND THE GRINNYGOG, THE (1983). British children's TV series re-edited for U.S. telly. It's the supernatural misadventures of a coven and a magic statue. Zoe Loftin, Giles Harper, Heidi Mayo.

WITCHES' BREW (1985). Originally shot in 1978 as WHICH WITCH IS WHICH?, this failed to stir the cauldron and underwent reshooting before being sold to cable TV. It's a comedy rendering of Fritz Leiber's BURN WITCH BURN (though uncredited), showing the humorous side to suburban witchcraft. Richard Benjamin is a university professor whose wife (Teri Garr) uses her witch's powers to help him get ahead, but he forces her to throw away her good-luck charms . . . leaving him wide open to the wives/witches of two rivals and their mentor, witch Lana Turner. The old biddy conspires to enter Teri's body, allowing for cheap effects. The jokes are thin, the production qualities cheap. Directed by Richard Shorr with new footage by Herbert L. Strock. A Strock of bad luck? (Embassy)

WITCHES' MOUNTAIN, THE (1972). Coven of cackling crones and hideous hags terrorizes a young couple in a castle in the Pyrenees Mountains. Directed by Raoul Artigot. Patty Shepard, John Caffari, Monica Randal. (Unicorn)

WITCHES OF EASTWICK, THE (1987). Three divorced women living in a New England village steeped in American tradition discover they have witch-like powers and, one by one, are willingly seduced by a newcomer to town, Daryl Van Horne, who is none other than the Devil incarnate, here to engage in a battle of the sexes that is intellectual and visually exciting thanks to the special effects of Rob Bottin. Jack Nicholson is brilliant as the seductive chauvinist male who employs supernatural tricks (such as levitation) to tease his conquests. The women are equally talented for the occasion: Susan Sarandon is a suppressed music teacher turned into a passionate redhead; Cher is a sculptress, showing her dramatic and comedic acting abilities; and Michele Pfeiffer is a local newspaper reporter, beautiful and vulnerable. Veronica Cartwright should also be singled out for her performance as the woman who realizes what Van Horne is up to and tries to stop him. There's wonderfully witty dialogue by Michael Cristofer, who adapted John Updike's novel, and director George Miller treats the material on an epic scale, suggesting we are seeing the supreme battle of good over evil, man against woman, and other cosmic themes. It is, however, Nicholson's performance that will endure. One could be critical of the ending, which goes berserk with nauseating effects (the Road Warrior coming out in Miller, perhaps?) but this is still a superior entertainment. Richard Jenkins, Keith Jochim, Carel Struycken. (Video/Laser: Warner Bros.)

WITCHES TRIAL, THE. See **NIGHT OF THE BLOOD MONSTER.**

WITCHFINDER GENERAL, THE. See **CONQUEROR WORM, THE.** (Death wormed over?)

WITCHFIRE (1985). Since she's also the associate producer, leading lady Shelley Winters can go bonkers in grand style, cackling with a madness that will delight your perverse soul. When her psychiatrist is killed in a car crash, the madcap Shelley plots to escape the Institute for Living (better known as the Asylum for the Utterly Crazed). She and two other batty dames (Frances De Sapio and Corrine Chateau) take refuge in the rural house where Shelley once set fire to her parents. The babbling old broad thinks she's a witch, but not once does anything supernatural happen, no matter how many incantations she recites from her battered book. One lousy video movie—substandard in every respect. Pay homage to director Vincent J. Privitera. Gary Swanson plays a hunter estranged from his son, but that's a subplot that has nothing to do with anything. Also known as A SONNET FOR THE HUNTER. Peter Masterson, David and James Mendenhall. (Lightning)

'THE WITCHES OF EASTWICK': CHER, SUSAN SARANDON, JACK NICHOLSON, MICHELLE PFEIFFER

WITCHING, THE. Video version of **NECROMANCY** (Paragon).

WITCHING TIME (1980). Elvira-hosted Thrillervideo version of a British-produced HAMMER HOUSE OF HORROR episode. See **SILENT SCREAM, THE.**

WITCH IN LOVE. See **WITCH, THE.**

WITCH KILLER OF BROADMOOR. See **NIGHT OF THE BLOOD MONSTER.**

WITCHMAKER, THE (1969). William O. Brown wrote-produced-directed this poor man's glimpse at witches and warlocks sneaking through the misty Louisiana bayou for producers L.Q. Jones and Alvy Moore. Much of this is ludicrous exploitation, especially the scenes in which Luther the Berserk (John Lodge) hangs up women by their heels, slices their throats and lets the blood drip to the ground. There's chilling, atmospheric sequences in the swamp country. Brown's plot has psychic researchers Moore, Anthony Eisley and the beautiful dolls investigating the bogland. Before long the gals are drifting through the foggy landscape in sexy negligees, which stirs the blood of the creeps back in the cave—and those creeps include horror movie host Seymour. (Cinema Concepts; Interglobal)

WITCH'S CURSE, THE. Video version of **MACISTE IN HELL** (Sinister/C; S/Weird).

WITCH'S MIRROR, THE (1961). The old Haunted Mirror Plot: The ghost of a murdered woman emerges from the accursed glass to wreak revenge on her husband, who acts dumber than most husbands in Mexican horror films produced by Abel Salazar. This splitting image will give you a splitting headache. Seven year's bad luck guaranteed if you watch to the bitter end. Directed with a sense of self-reflection by Chano Urueta. Rosita Arenas, Armando Calvo, Isabela Vorona. (Sinister/C; Filmfax; S/Weird)

WITCHTRAP (1989). Due to flat, nonatmospheric lighting, mediocre actresses and inadequate effects, WITCHTRAP limps along without much conviction. It's also been mistitled as it has a warlock as its chief villain. Writer-director Kevin S. Tenney did a better job with WITCHBOARD than with this haunted house tale involving a warlock (J. P. Luebsen) who returns from the dead to reclaim his missing heart when a team of psychic investigators invade his Gothic domain. Only James W. Quinn as private eye Tony Vicente and Linnea Quigley as a psychic video technician seem at home with this material, the rest of the cast being strangely amateurish. Kathleen Bailey, Rob Zapple and Judy Tatum head the paranormal experts. Tenney appears briefly as the owner of the house who hires the private cops and psychics. (Magnum) (Laser: Image)

WITCH WHO CAME FROM THE SEA (1976). Insightful if gory portrait of a demented, sexually perverted woman who calls herself Molly the Mermaid. Millie Perkins is no witch; she's a homicidal killer of two muscular football stars, slashing them with a razor. She's haunted by memories of her sea-captain father, who raped her as a child, and now she attacks her lovers, often slicing up their sexual organs. This low-budget film directed by Matt Cimber on L.A. beaches is not for children. Richard Thom, Perkins' husband, has written a symbolic screenplay as disturbing as it is enlightening. Some murders are graphic, with Millie rubbing blood over the mermaid tattooed on her stomach, and other scenes are quite erotic as Perkins has sex with a TV star. Vanessa Brown is her friend, Lonny Chapman is bar owner Long John; Peggy Feury is Perkins' equally crazy sister. (Unicorn)

WITCH WITHOUT A BROOM, A (1967). Jeffrey Hunter, in one of his last roles before his untimely death, keeps seeing witch Maria Perschy pop up in his classroom. Fantasy turns to comedy as she ineptly casts spells which never work properly. Amusing Spanish-U.S. co-oper produced by Sidney Pink, directed by Jose El Lorietta (Joe Lacy). Perla Cristal, Gustavo Rojo. (IMA)

WITH HERCULES TO THE CENTER OF THE EARTH. See **HERCULES IN THE HAUNTED WORLD.**

WITHOUT WARNING. Video version of **IT CAME . . . WITHOUT WARNING** (HBO).

WIT'S END. Original title of **G.I. EXECUTIONER.**

WIZ, THE (1978). The idea was to take THE WIZARD OF OZ, cast it with blacks and inject it into a modern setting. The springboard for this expensive Universal musical was a Broadway smash by William Brown and Charles Smalls, but drastic changes were made by screenwriter Joel Schumacher and director Sidney Lumet, and critics were not enamored. The songs and music (by Smalls and Quincy Jones) vary in effectiveness, but all the picture seems to achieve is to cast a dark (no pun intended) pall over one's memories of the vivacious MGM hit of 1939. Here the plot is enmeshed in urban impressionism with the Wicked Witch's monkeys, for example, equipped with motorcycles. Diana Ross, Michael Jackson, Nipsey Russell, Lena Horne, Richard Pryor. (Video/Laser: MCA)

WIZARD, THE (1927). Silent screen predecessor to those mad-scientist-tampering-with-an-ape pictures. Gaston Leroux's story, "Balaoo," directed by Richard Rosson, has insane physician Edmund Lowe sewing the head of a human onto a gorilla's body. A study in needlepoint? Leila Hyams, E. H. Calvert, Barry Norton. Remade in 1942 as DR. RENAULT'S SECRET.

WIZARD, THE (1964). See **MYSTERIOUS MAGICIAN, THE.**

WIZARD OF BAGHDAD, THE (1961). Sam Katzman production, which means it's cheap, with script by Jesse L. Lasky Jr., which means he must have needed the money, with direction by George Sherman, which means it at least has good action sequences. It's your basic Arabian Nights Plot: Prince overthrows vizar with a drunken genie who finally gets his powers back after a long magicless hiatus. Dick Shawn, Diane Baker.

WIZARD OF GORE (1970). One of the great camp-gore classics from the king of blood and guts, producer-director Herschell Gordon Lewis. The Allan Kahn script has a mad magician named Montag the Magnificent (Ray Sager) who performs horrifying mutilations on the stage (all faked), but then does them for real with members of the audience after the show is over. See a woman cut in half and watch another spiked to death. Strong stomaches required. Ray Sager, Judy Cler, Wayne Ratay. (Rhino; Select; New Star; Continental)

WIZARD OF MARS, THE (1964). Low-budget slop of the "gee whiz" school, its schlocky story borrowed from THE WIZARD OF OZ. Three astronauts and one femmenaut rocket to the Red Planet, crash-landing in a wilderness. By following a "golden road" they find a civilization ruled by wizard John Carradine. Time on the planet is frozen, and only by unfreezing it can the Earthlings return home. The effects are inadequate to the ambitions of screenwriter David Hewitt, whose chores extended to producing-directing. Forrest J. Ackerman served as technical adviser, but to what avail is unclear. Turgidly acted by Roger Gentry, Vic McGee, Eve Bernhardt, Jerry Rannow. (Republic; Genesis; from Star Classics/Genesis as **HORRORS OF THE RED PLANET** and from Regal as **ALIEN MASSACRE**)

WIZARD OF OZ, THE (1939). Perennial MGM classic (produced by Mervyn LeRoy, directed by Victor Fleming) continues to be enjoyed by new generations enthralled with the magical story-telling of L. Frank Baum, whose fairy tale was adapted by Noel Langley. Judy Garland is the young Kansan Judy who is knocked out during a tornado (in black and white) and wakes up (in color) in a fantasy kingdom. Taking the Yellow Brick Road to adventure, she meets the scarecrow (Ray Bolger), the Tin Man (Jack Haley) and the Cowardly Lion (Bert Lahr). The fantastic kingdom of Oz is ruled by Frank Morgan and threatened by the wicked witch (Margaret Hamilton) and a swarm of deadly flying monkeys. Then, of course, there are the Munchkins. Cedric Gibbons' art design always looks fresh and vibrant, the songs and music are unfor-

GREGORY HINES, MORGUE TECHNICIAN: 'WOLFEN'

gettable and the exaggerated acting perfectly captures the proper note. Enjoy the Munchkin merriment, because you will never discover a film as wonderful as this one. Billie Burke, Charles Grapewin. (Video/Laser: MGM/UA)

WIZARD OF OZ, THE (1982). Animated version of the L. Frank Baum classic, featuring the voices of Lorne Greene and Aileen Quinn. (Paramount)

WIZARD OF SPEED AND TIME (1986). Stop-motion animator Mike Jittlov took his popular short subject and reworked it into a feature, frameworking his effects sequences into a story about his ongoing difficulties trying to break into Hollywood and produce a TV special. Written-directed-edited by Jittlov, who also stars. Paige Moore, Richard Kaye, Philip Michael Thomas. (Shapiro Glickenhaus) (Laser: Image)

WIZARDS (1976). Tolkienesque masterpiece of animation by Ralph Bakshi, depicting a future when mankind, following atomic holocaust mutation, is divided into two camps: the mechanized armies of Blackwolf the Tyrant, whose followers are a motley collection of frog creatures and demons, and the peace-loving elves who practice wizardry. The art work is stunning, especially the brutal clash of armies in which Bakshi combines animation with live-action stock footage. The influences of comic book artists Wally Wood, Frank Frazetta, Berni Wrightson and Al Williamson are pronounced. The narrative by Bakshi is sometimes garbled and the characterizations uneven, but these minor problems do not distract from the film's visual power. Bakshi's best! (Video/Laser: CBS/Fox)

WIZARDS OF THE DEMON SWORD (1991). Producer-director Fred Olen Ray, a champion of the B movie, tackles sword-and-sorcery themes with tacky, campy, so-bad-it's-good results. The Knife of Aktar, key to unlimited power, is fought over by hammy conjurer Lyle Waggoner and roving swordsman Blake Bahner, who's trying to help maiden Heidi Paine and her imprisoned father Russ Tamblyn, with advise fron the Seer of Roebuck (Hoke Howell). With all of its nonsequiturs and silliness, this has to be seen to be believed. Camera work by Gary Graver. Jay Richardson, Dawn Wildsmith.

WIZARDS OF THE LOST KINGDOM (1984). Cliche-riddled, amateurish sword-and-sorcery nonsense, distinguished only by the blase, tongue-in-cheek performance of Bo Svenson as Kor the Conqueror, a wandering swordsman who befriends a youth who is "Simon, song of the good wizard Wilford, magician of the Kingdom of Axum." Simon and his "fuzzface" companion, a furry thing called Goldpack, are searching for a magical ring, and so is Chirka the evil sorcerer. They throw rays of light at each other but the conflict is minimal and forced, and even Svenson can't sustain his performance under Hector Olivera's feeble direction. There's a hobgoblin, an insect woman who turns into a monster, five dead walking corpses and assorted STAR WARS-style aliens. As the kid says, "Pretty neat stuff, huh?" Vidal Peterson, Thom Christopher, Barbara Stock. (Media)

WIZARDS OF THE LOST KINGDOM II (1990). David Carrdine's presence as legendary swordsman The Dark One helps this Roger Corman production a little, but director Charles B. Griffith's script is slow-paced and generic as Carradine, Bobby Jacoby and wizard Mel Welles unite to fight forces of evil in the sword-and-sorcery tradition. Susan Lee Hoffman, Lana Clarkson, Blake Bahner, Sid Haig, Henry Brandon. (Media)

WIZ KID, THE (1989). Inconsequential German TV-movie has a nerdy kid creating a more-agressive clone of himself and outsmarting some baddies who want to kidnap him. For moppets only. Directed by Gloria Behrens. Martin Forbes, Gary Frobes, Narcisa Kukavica, Jake Wood. (Vidmark)

WOLF (1994). Amazing, isn't it, when skilled film makers can take an old B-movie plot, update it, give it modern sensibilities, and presto—a tired old idea lives again in exciting, new form. This is nothing more than a remake of THE WOLF MAN, with Jack Nicholson as a fiction editor who is bitten by a wolf one snowy, stormy night and slowly transmutates into a hairy creature with all the symptons and anguish of Lawrence Talbot. However, it's full of excellent dialogue (by Jim Harrison and Wesley Strick) and stylish make-up effects by Rick Baker. And director Mike Nichols proves he knows his genres by giving WOLF an odd atmosphere. And Michelle Pfeiffer is superb as Nicholson's lover. A howl of a good film! James Spader, Kate Nelligan, Richard Jenkins, Christopher Plummer, Eileen Atkins. Music by Ennio Morricone. (Columbia Tri/Star)

WOLFEN (1981). This adaptation of Whitley Streiber's novel might have been a winner, but . . . if you excite an audience's expectations for a monster, you'd better pay off. But when the titular entities (mutant wolves with superintelligence) reveal themselves, the film falls faster than a diarrhetic wolf hound's doo-doo. Instead of creatures seemingly capable of ghastly gore murders, we are shown ordinary wolves with slight makeup. The disappointment is ultra-devastating. Up to then, WOLFEN is a graphically suspenseful thriller about a killer pack running in the ruins of the Bronx. Director Michael Wadleigh, who co-wrote with David Frye, also made bad changes in Streiber's plot. There's business about Indians (they were once pushed off their land, just like earlier generations of wolves) but that remains secondary to Albert Finney as the cop in pursuit of the four-legged killers. The Steadicam point-of-view shots in the Bronx ruins are marvelous; if only the payoff had paid off. Gregory Hines, Diane Venora, Edward James Olmos, Tom Noonan. (Video/Laser: Warner Bros.)

WOLF MAN, THE (1941). Classic Universal thriller establishes the mood and lore for the werewolf genre, and presents sympathetic Lon Chaney Jr. as Lawrence Talbot, a student attacked by a werewolf (Bela Lugosi) who, under the full moon, turns into a marauding, slavering monster. Jack Pierce's time-lapse make-up is outstanding and Curt Siodmak's script explores the trauma and torment of lycanthropy in sympathetic fashion. Maria Ouspenskaya recites the famous "werewolf curse" poem and Claude Rains portrays the father who gropes to understand his son's malady. Produced-directed by George Waggoner. Ralph Bellamy, Evelyn Ankers, Warren William. (Video/Laser: MCA)

WOLF MAN, THE (1977). See **LEGEND OF THE WOLF WOMAN.**

WOLFMAN, THE. See **CURSE OF THE WEREWOLF, THE.**

WOLFMAN: A CINEMATIC SCRAPBOOK. See **WOLFMAN CHRONICLES, THE**.

WOLFMAN—A LYCANTHROPE (1978). Although his

films rarely play outside the South, Earl Owensby is a producer of money-making genre flicks. In this one, set in Georgia near the turn of the century, Owensby inherits the Curse of the Glasgow Family and turns into a hairy killer under the full moon. Written by Darrell Cathcart and directed by Worth Keeter. But Owensby was howlin' all the way to the bank. Kristina Reynolds, Maggie Lauterer. (Thorn EMI)

WOLFMAN CHRONICLES (1991). Excellent compilation of movie trailers and clips that traces the cinematic history of the werewolf on screen, described by writer-director Ted Newsom as a tribute to the "wildest beast men and wolf women." It starts with the first attempts by Universal (WEREWOLF OF LONDON, THE WOLF MAN, THE HOUSE OF FRANKENSTEIN, etc.). Lon Chaney Jr., who played the hairy beast frequently, is profiled, and there is rare footage from an episode of TV's ROUTE 66 in which he played a wolf man opposite Boris Karloff and Peter Lorre. Lugosi is shown as a hirsute being in THE APE MAN and RETURN OF THE VAMPIRE. Although the track is occasionally poorly mixed, the previews are wonderful, including CRY OF THE WEREWOLF, SHE-WOLF OF LONDON, THE UNDYING MONSTER, and THE MAD MONSTER. The film also traces the screen history of Jekyll and Hyde monsters. A collector's item. (Rhino)

WOLFMAN OF COUNT DRACULA, THE. See **FRANKENSTEIN'S BLOODY TERROR.**

WOLF PACK/THE KIRKWOOD HAUNTING (1978). Two episodes of the SPIDERMAN TV show recut into a video feature. In the first episode, directed by Joe Manduke, a mind-expanding drug falls into the hands of a criminal who uses it to turn men into zombies. In the second, directed by Don McDougall, a seance crowd stages a phony haunting to bilk a millionairess. Nicholas Hammond, Robert F. Simon, Paul Carr, Marlyn Mason.

WOLFWOMAN. Video version of **LEGEND OF THE WOLFWOMAN** (Lobo Lady Lopes Loosely!) (VCI).

WOMAN EATER, THE (1957). Unchewy, cheap British import from producer Richard Gordon with George Coulouris as a mad doc who feeds females to a tree. Is its bark worse than its bite? In turn, the tree provides insane Coulouris with a serum for bringing the dead to life. Below usual British nourishment standards . . . it will eat up your valuable time and give you severe indigestion. Burp! . . . See? Directed by Charles Saunders on an empty stomach, maybe? Written by Brandon Fleming without an appetite, maybe? Vera Day, Joy Webster, Jimmy Vaughan.

WOMAN FROM DEEP RIVER. See **MAKE THEM DIE SLOWLY.**

WOMANHUNT, THE (1972). John Ashley-Eddie Romero schlockaroo, made in the Philippines, copies "The Most Dangerous Game," but with a mad hunter who prefers blondes, brunettes and redheads in his pith-helmeted pursuits on his private island. No males need apply. Lisa Todd, of HEE HAW, is one of the curvaceous creatures the madman pursues. Oglers, pay attention. Ashley also co-stars and Romero directed. Sid Haig, Pat Woodell.

WOMAN IN BLACK, THE (1989). Chilly British ghost story in the best literary traditions of H. R. Wakefield and M. R. James. Adapted from a Susan Hill novel by Nigel Kneale, creator of the "Professor Quatermass" series, this TV-movie under the direction of Herbert Wise has moments that will freeze your bone marrow as it captures the eeriness and supernatural ambience in and around Eel Marsh House, a manor on a fog-shrouded moor where solicitor Adrian Rawlins is cleaning up the estate of a deceased recluse. A psychological study of Rawlin's mounting fear as he hears ghostly sounds and sees the spectral image of the dead woman, who serves as an omen for dire events. Bernard Hepton, David Daker, Pauline Moran, David Ryall. (BFS)

WOMAN IN THE MOON (1929). Silent Fritz Lang film, also known as BY ROCKET TO THE MOON and GIRL IN THE MOON, depicts man's first trip to the moon and a lunar landscape of sand dunes. Lang was one of the best directors of the '20s in handling sci-fi material, as METROPOLOS so richly proves, but this is definitely a lesser work. Gerda Maurus, Willy Fritsch, Fritz Rasp. (Festival; Video Yesteryear)

CLAUDE RAINS AND LON CHANEY JR. IN 'THE WOLF MAN'

WOMAN'S OBSESSION, A. See **BAD BLOOD.**

WOMAN WHO CAME BACK, THE (1945). Arthritic Republic witchcraft thriller in which a woman suspected of being the reincarnation of a 300-year-old witch returns to New England. Suggestive, rather than blatant material, from director Walter Colmes and writers Dennis Cooper and Lee Willis. Otto Kruger, John Loder, Nancy Kelly and Ruth Ford deserved better. (Sony; RCA/Columbia)

WOMAN WHO WOULDN'T DIE, THE (1964). Murderer is tricked into thinking he is pursued by the ghost of a victim. Or is it a trick by the living to make him talk? For Gary Merrill, it was the British movie that wouldn't live. Directed by Gordon Hessler, adapted by Daniel Mainwaring from Jay Bennett's CATACOMBS. Jane Merrow, Neil McCallum.

WOMBLING FREE (1977). Children's concoction (in the style of The Muppets, but without half the fun) depicting how cutie creatures, Wombles, set out to clean up dirty old London. BBC special based on a popular book by Bernard Spear. David Tomlinson, Ken Baker, Frances De La Tour, Marcus Powell. (RCA/Columbia)

WOMEN OF DOOM. See **EXORCISM'S DAUGHTER.**

WOMEN OF THE PREHISTORIC PLANET (1966). Old-fashioned low-budget sci-fi movie, extinct as soon as STAR TREK showed everyone how it should be done. Cheapies from the '60s era such as this were loaded with inexpensive "interior rocket" sets, studio-bound "exteriors" that always looked it, phony props and awful effects—call it the "dark ages" of space movies. Wendell Corey is a wise starship commander; John Agar is his adventurous second in command; Stuart Margolin appears in an early role; Merry Anders is a sexpot in space; Keith Anders is an officer; Irene Tsu is a crew woman who goes native; and night club comedian Paul Gilbert performs terrible variations on his act. The plot follows a starship to a distant planet on a rescue mission to save the crew of a hijacked ship. The scenes with the lizard monsters are laughable, and the "surprise ending" to director Arthur C. Pierce's script features one of the hoariest cliches in "speculative fiction" history. They sure don't make'em like this anymore—thank God! (Paragon; King of Video)

WONDERFUL WORLD OF THE BROTHERS GRIMM, THE (1962). The first wide-screen Cinerama film with a plotline, this George Pal production uses the process to wonderful advantage in recounting the story of the brothers Grimm (Laurence Harvey and Karl

"That's what makes all of this worthwhile, the adventure. Day after day, week after week, month after month, year after year, ah, the sheer thrill of it all, persuing the planets, unifying the universe, galloping through the galactics."

—Paul Gilbert as an astronaut in **WOMEN OF THE PREHISTORIC PLANET**

Boehm) and their personal hardships, and three fairy tales they concocted: "The Cobbler and the Elves," featuring animated puppets; "The Dancing Princess" with Yvette Mimieux, Jim Backus and Russ Tamblyn; and "The Singing Bone," with Terry-Thomas, Buddy Hackett and Otto Kruger. There is also a memorably sentimental sequence in which one of the brothers imagines the characters he has created visiting him in his sick room. Claire Bloom, Walter Slezak, Ian Wolfe, Barbara Eden, Arnold Stang. Directed by Pal and Henry Levin, scripted by Charles Beaumont, David Harmon, William Roberts. (Video/Laser: MGM/UA)

WONDER MAN (1944). Delightful Samuel Goldwyn comedy, showcasing the multi-talents of Danny Kaye under Bruce Humberstone's fluid direction. Danny plays twins—one of whom is murdered by gangsters. His ghost returns to help his brother overcome complications with the underworld. Kaye has a romp, flashing his many talents. Virginia Mayo, Vera-Ellen, Steve Cochran, Otto Kruger, Huntz Hall, S.Z. Sakall. (Classic Collection; HBO; Sultan)

WONDERS OF ALADDIN, THE (1961). Wonderless U.S.-Italian attempt by producer Joseph E. Levine to cash in on the Arabian Nights genre, with Donald O'Connor miscast as the possessor of the magic lamp. Vittorio De Sica makes an appearance as the genie, but there's nothing wondrous about this comedic swashbuckling bomb directed by Henry Levin and Mario Bava. Aldo Fabrizi, Milton Reid. Michelle Mercier, Noelle Adam. (Charter)

WONDER WOMAN (1974). First TV pilot depicting Charles Moulton's comic book heroine was a failure. John D. F. Black's script updated Wonder Woman and placed her in a liberated society instead of stressing the period of the original strip (the '40s, when a woman had to fight chauvinistic attitudes as well as forces of evil). Cathy Lee Crosby just didn't have enough "wonder" to be the busty supergal with bullet-bouncing bracelets as she battles villain Abner Smith (Ricardo Montalban) with friend Steve Trevor (Kaz Garas). A superior series concept with Lynda Carter (now talk about a busty supergal!) was introduced in '75 and became a hit. Directed by Vincent McEveety. Andrew Prine, Richard X. Slattery.

WONDER WOMEN (1973). Filipino hunkahorror with the insane scientist being a beautiful woman, Dr. Su (Nancy Kwan), and her victims being athletes whom she kidnaps so she can use them as spare parts to sell to aging or dying millionaires. The producer, Ross Hagen, doubles as a hero who arrives on Dr. Su's island to investigate. Suzy Wong was on the skids. Directed by Robert O'Neill. Maria De Aragon. (From Media as THE DEADLY AND THE BEAUTIFUL)

WON'T WRITE HOME, MOM—I'M DEAD. See **TERROR FROM WITHIN.** (Horror you? I'm slime!)

WOOF! (1989). Boring children's TV-movie from Britain in which insufferably boring Edward Fidoe keeps turning into a shaggy Norfolk terrier. And that's exciting as it gets. WOOF! is a poof. Adapted from an Allan Ahlberg story by Richard Fegen and Andrew Norris; produced and directed by David Cobham. Liza Goddard, John Ringham, Thomas Aldwinckle.

WOOF TOO! A GIRL AND HER DOG (1990). As boring as its predecessor, this British whimsey has that Norfolk terrier (whose really a red-headed youth played by Edward Fidoe) starring in TV dog-food commercials and helping girlfriend Sarah Smart win a bicycling championship. The dog Tich does the best acting. Produced-directed by David Cobham.

WORK IS A FOUR-LETTER WORD (1968). See third edition.

WORLD APARTMENT HORROR (1991). From director Katsuhiro Otomo, who gave us AKIRA, comes this live-action horror-action flick depicting a gangster (Hiroki Tanaka) and his efforts to evict Asian immigrants from an apartment building haunted by a supernatural monster. Also written by Otomo with Keiko Nobumoto. Yuji Nakamura. (Video Search of Miami)

WORLD BEYOND, THE (1978). See editions 1-3.

WORLD BEYOND THE MOON, THE (1953). SPACE PATROL was one of TV's early sci-fi shows, designed for juvenile watchers and done live in the studio, which didn't permit many rocketship take-offs or astonishing effects. The series is nostalgically remembered by those growing up at the time, although a re-reviewing reveals terrible plots, cardboard sets and low-caliber acting. Regulars were Ed Kemmer as Commander Buzz Corey and Lyn Osborn as Cadet Happy. See **SPACE PATROL.**

WORLD GONE WILD (1988). Undistinguished MAD MAX-style postholocaust actioner made palatable by the presence of Bruce Dern as Ethan, a guru who throws off funny one-liners and acts out of synch with the rest of the cast and story. The time is 2087 A.D. after the Big War, and mankind suffers from a lack of water except for Lost Wells, a hippie-like community which is besieged by Adam Ant and his army of pseudoreligious followers—men in white robes who keep machine-guns tucked underneath. The Jorge Zamacona screenplay relies on standard action cliches and borrows from THE MAGNIFICENT SEVEN by having Dern and girlfriend Catherine Mary Stewart look for mercenaries to help them stave off a pending attack. These characters are colorful if familiar: Michael Pare as a silent hero-type; Anthony James as a cannibal, Rick Podell as a gunsliner, Julius Carry III as a nitro man and Alan Autry as strongman Hank. Directed by Lee H. Katzin, an old hand who deserves better material than this rehash. (Media)

'WORLD GONE MAD'

WORLD OF DRACULA (1979). Re-edited episodes of a TV series about a modern-day 512-year-old vampire in San Francisco who is pursued by a descendant of Von Helsing. Corny but colorful stuff, with memorable lines of dialogue as the vampire-hunter and girlfriend (whose mother was a victim of Dracula) close in on the articulate, oft-poetic bloodsucker. Directed by Kenneth Johnson (producer/co-writer), Sutton Roley and Jeffrey Hayden. Bever-leigh Banfield, Louise Sorel.

BELOVED CHARACTERS IN 'THE WIZARD OF OZ'

WORLD OF HORROR (1968). Polished Polish TV-film comprised of three famous horror stories: Oscar Wilde's "Lord Arthur Saville's Crime," Wilde's "The Canterville Ghost" and Wilkie Collins' "A Terribly Strange Bed."

WORLD OF HORROR. Video version of **DARIO ARGENTO'S WORLD OF HORROR** (Vidmark).

WORLD OF SPACE, THE. See **BATTLE IN OUTER SPACE.**

WORLD OF THE VAMPIRES, THE (1960). Abel Salazar production, imported from Mexico by American-International for TV, is unique in that music played on a piano built with bones and skulls is used to destroy the bloodsucking monsters. Not the same old tune, amigo. Directed by Alfonso Corona Blake. Mauricio Garces, Jose Baviera. (Sinister/C; S/Weird; Budget; Filmfax)

WORLD'S GREATEST ATHLETE, THE (1973). Innocuous Disney comedy, in which Roscoe Lee Browne resorts to playing a witch doctor and Tim Conway is his usual dumb-cluck self. Jan-Michael Vincent portrays the superathlete. Of course, he gets caught up in voodoo and body shrinking. Silly but enjoyable; for the family. Directed by Robert Scheerer. John Amos, Billy De Wolfe, Nancy Walker, Howard Cosell. (Disney)

WORLD, THE FLESH AND THE DEVIL, THE (1959). Allegory dealing with the morality and racial prejudice of man, set within the framework of an "end-of-the-world" story. Miner Harry Belafonte survives atomic attack and, moving on to New York City, finds other survivors: Inger Stevens and Mel Ferrer, the latter a candidate for the Ku Klux Klan with his racial hatreds. The most striking scenes are those of Belafonte wandering through the deserted streets of New York. Writer-director Ranald MacDougall based his provocative script loosely on M. P. Shiel's THE PURPLE CLOUD. The fine musical score is by Miklos Rozsa.

WORLD WAR III (1982). Political-military sci-fi dominates this TV-movie in which Russia invades Alaska with an eye on seizing the oil pipeline. Should the U.S. go to war or not? President Rock Hudson must decide. This provocative venture was written by Robert L. Joseph (based on a best-selling novel) and directed by David Greene and Boris Sagal. The latter was killed during filming when he backed into the rotor blade of a helicopter. David Soul, Brian Keith, Cathy Lee Crosby, Katherine Helmond, James Hampton (Fox; MCA)

WORLD WAR III BREAKS OUT. See **LAST WAR, THE.**

WORLD WITHOUT END (1956). Entertaining grade-B actioner in which a rocket crew passes through a time warp into 2508 A.D. to discover Earth has been wiped out by atomic war, and the inhabitants are mutant cave types. But underground lives a race of humanoid survivors led by Rod Taylor. Nothing new, but fast moving with its many fights, monsters, etc. Written-directed by Edward Bernds. Hugh Marlowe, Lisa Montell, Paul Brinegar, Nancy Gates, Nelson Leigh. (VC)

WORM EATERS, THE (1981). Crazy Guy (Herb Robins, who also wrote-directed this sleazy exploitationer) talks to worms and forces people to eat them (remarkably disgusting, wouldn't you say?) and turns them into worm monsters. Could have been intended as a horror comedy, although with the eccentric Robins at the helm, and T. V. Mikels producing, anything was possible. Worm your way out of watching unless you have a taste for wriggling, crawly things. (WesternWorld)

WORST SECRET AGENTS, THE. See **OH, THOSE MOST SECRET AGENTS.** (Oh, the worst!)

WORST WITCH, THE (1986). Children's TV-movie, never elevating itself out of the silly league, set at a training school for witches, where recruit Fairuza Balk is an ugly duckling razzed by fellow pupils. Director Robert Young treats the whole thing like a juvenile joke, never allowing head witchmistress Diana Rigg or Grand Wizard Tim Curry the opportunity to soar in their roles (pun intended). The flying broom effects are lousy, the acting belongs to the Arched Eyebrow school. Kids might cheer, but adults will surely wince (and please don't call me Shirley). (Prism)

WOULD YOU KILL A CHILD? See **ISLAND OF THE DAMNED.**

WRAITH, THE (1986). The titular entity is a supernatural spirit in an Arizona town where tough guy Packard Walsh (Nick Cassavetes) holds sway over an odd collection of gang members: Skank, Gutterboy, Oggie, Rughead, etc. The Wraith (Charlie Sheen) is equipped with an Incredible Killer Rifle and a customized sports car to knock off baddies when he isn't making love to Sherilyn Fenn. Pointless revenge fantasy clumsily written by Mike Marvin but at least interestingly directed by him when it comes to car chases and stunts designed by Buddy Joe Hooker. Giving the film its only touch of comedy is Randy Quaid's Sheriff Loomis. He's cynical and funny and provides ironic counterpoint to the mayhem and death. Too bad the story wasn't about him instead of those ridiculous teenagers. Matthew Barry, Griffin O'Neal, Jamie Bozian, Clint Howard, Chris Nash, David Sherrill. (Lightning) (Laser: Image)

WRESTLING WOMEN VS. THE AZTEC MUMMY (1965). Video of **DOCTOR OF DOOM.** (Budget; Filmfax; S/Weird; from Rhino as **ROCK 'N ROLL WRESTLING WOMEN VS. THE AZTEC MUMMY**)

WRITER'S BLOCK (1992). This TV-movie, perhaps inspired by Stephen King's THE DARK HALF, depicts mystery writer Morgan Fairchild undergoing trauma when a serial killer, The Red Ribbon Killer, begins to duplicate the murders in her book. What's intriguing about this psychological study of the writer is whether or not the killer is real or an entity created by her imagination and now stalking her. Better than usual for its genre. Michael Praed, Mary Ann Pascal, Cheryl Anderson, Joe Regalbuto. Written by Elisa Bell and directed by Charles Correll.

"This is the year 2087, 75 years after the two great forces of the world engaged in a war . . . Most of the people of the Earth were destroyed. A cruel trick was played on the survivors. Although there are times when the clouds fill the skies, it has not rained for 50 years. Things are fucked up!" —*Bruce Dern in* **WORLD GONE WILD**

XANADU (1980). Musical fantasy, directed by Robert Greenwald, in which Olivia Newton-John is one of the nine Muses, roller skating in the park and into the life of artist Michael Beck in an effort to make his dreams come true. With such a weak premise for a feature, one would hope the singing-dancing to be of an unforgettable quality. Alas, poor dork, that's not the case. Definitely nothing to muse over. Gene Kelly, James Sloyan, Katie Hanley, Sandahl Bergman. A remake of DOWN TO EARTH. (Video/Laser: MCA)

XAVER (1988). Alien humanoid Carlos Pavlidis lands on the outskirts of Munich and everyone thinks he's just another tourist. Along comes Rupert Seidl (as Xaver, a German hayseeder) who dubs the E.T. "Alois," and off they go to the city with big-breasted Gabi Fischer in tow. Directed-written by Werner Possardt.

XENIA (1990). Unusually literate vampire film opens at the Crest Theater in Sacramento, Ca., where film producer Dennis Edwards (producer-director of XENIA) meets movie critic Dana M. Reeves (also producer-director of XENIA) to see XENIA, PRIESTESS OF NIGHT, a horror film made by mysterious director Andre W. Wiers, who has the credits HOUSE OF VARICOSE VEINS, CRY OF THE SHANKER SORE and THE CRAWLING GALLBLADDER. This becomes a film-within-a-film as they watch the black-and-white movie unfold, opening this up to a parody of movie criticism and genres. And the "Xenia" within XENIA is a turgid piece—purposely designed to spoof techniques of '50s film making. Hmm, some esoteric piece of work. Watch for Bob Wilkins, one-time "Creature Features" host of the San Francisco-Bay Area, in a cameo. Herb Lightman, Matias Bombal, Sharie-Marie Jonsin, Timothy Gray, Dale Meader, Roberta Shepps.

X FILES, THE (1993). This two-hour pilot for the popular Fox network series depicts the exploits of two special FBI agents (played by David Duchovny and Gillian Anderson) who investigate strange phenomena cases. After this episode involving UFOs and abductions, THE X FILES went on to become a TV hit, covering a variety of fascinating subjects. Producer-creator Chris Carter says he was inspired by THE NIGHT STALKER series but wanted to deal with so-called supernormal mysteries instead of supernatural ones.

X FROM OUTER SPACE (1967). X for xcruciating . . . yet again another Japanese creature bonanza for moppets produced by adults with children's minds. Guilala, a giant stegosaurus that spits steel spears, grows from a single cell into a monster after being brought from space attached to a spacecraft's hull. The monster goes on the same old rampage, destroying the nearest city—destruction-prone Tokyo. Co-written and directed by Kazui Nihonmatsu. Starring the impulsive Eiji Okada and the erratic Shinichi Yanagisawa. (Orion) (Laser: Image, with **YONGARY, MONSTER FROM THE DEEP**)

X17 TOP SECRET (1965). See editions 1-3.

X-RAY (1982). Like HALLOWEEN II, this is set entirely in a city hospital in which a mad slasher is on the loose, murdering without discrimination. Director Boaz Davidson's stylishness is weakened by a chamberpot of cliches plotted by Marc Behm. Still, there's a greater sense of fun than in most slasher flicks, thanks to a cast overemphasizing hysteria and paranoia. A flashback shows a 1961 Valentine's Day murder witnessed by an adolescent girl. Flash forward to Barbi Benton entering "massacre hospital" for a check-up—and the body count climbs. There are effective images of horror and death, and Davidson captures an eerie ambience that takes one's attention off the story holes. Barbi does well with her characterless role and is the only non-suspicious character. Chip Lucia, Jon Van Ness, Guy Austin, Lanny Duncay and John Warner Williams always look and sound as one of them is the killer. Nice music by Arlon Ober, even if it is all cliches. Also called HOSPITAL MASSACRE. (In video as **MASSACRE HOSPITAL**)

X—THE MAN WITH THE X-RAY EYES (1963). One of Roger Corman's strangest films, hampered by inadequate effects and other budget woes yet singularly compelling as it unfolds an allegorical plot about Dr. Xavier (Ray Milland), who discovers a way of seeing through objects—to the heart of the Universe! The climax to the Robert Dillon-Ray Russell script was inspired by the Bible and is utterly gross, yet producer-director Corman succeeds in jolting you. John Hoyt, Don Rickles, Dick Miller, Diana Van Der Vlis, John Dierkes. Aka THE MAN WITH X-RAY EYES. (Video/Laser: Warner Bros.)

X—THE UNKNOWN (1957). This Hammer rammer is sometimes confused with the Quatermass series, and although Dean Jean portrays a sympathetic scientist similar to Quatermass, it is a vehicle unto itself, being Jimmy Sangster's first script. It is sci-fi reeking with eerie atmosphere as a sludge monster rises from a Scottish bogland to seek out radioactive materials on which to feed. Good effects and great gloominess achieved by director Leslie Norman. Leo McKern, Anthony Newley, Edward Judd, Edward Chapman.

XTRO (1982). A touch of ALIEN, a little blending of POLTERGEIST and a modicum of VENOM—in short, your average ripoff movie with nothing original thrown into the bargain. This British sci-fier starts with Philip Sayer being abducted by E.T.s, then returning to Earth three years later, reprogrammed to suck on other people's flesh and give his young son psychic powers. There's silly baloney about toy soldiers coming to life that seems at odds with the ALIEN imitations. One doesn't know whether to laugh, scream at the gooey, horrendous effects or just go blind. Is masturbation the answer? A few hideous moments might have your skin crawling, but in general a waste of time. Directed with little imagination by Harry Bromley-Davenport. Bernice Stegers, Simon Nash, Danny Brainin, Maryam D'Abo. (Thorn EMI/HBO) (Laser: Image)

XTRO II: THE SECOND ENCOUNTER (1991). Once in a great while a film derivative of a classic is inspired enough to transcend its own imitative weaknesses to take on a life of its own. This Canadian film is such a "sleeper." Although a spinoff of ALIENS, XTRO II eventually builds a momentum of suspense, action and characterization that sends it spiralling above other imitations. This achieves what ALIEN 3 did not. The setting is a computer-controlled research center for Project Nexus, an attempt to send explorers, after altering their body structure, into a "parallel universe." What's waiting for them returns in the transferrence machine and . . . you guessed it, an Alien-like monster that sets out to kill those sequestered in the project lab. The monster is an effective one, the cast is sharp and the pyrotechnics and effects well produced. But it's the tension captured by director Harry Bromley-Davenport that elevates this to classy status. For once, a ripoff script (this one by producer John A. Curtis, Steven Lister, Robert Smith and Edward Kovach) spurts fresh blood. Jan-Michael Vincent, Paul Koslo, Tara Buckman, Jano Frandsen, Nicholas Lea, W. F. Wadden. (New Line) (Laser: Image)

YAMBAO (1956). Ramon Gay acts queerly as a sugar plantation boss bewitched into romancing an old crone's granddaughter in this Mexican flambe directed by Alfredo Crevena. Also called YOUNG AND EVIL. Ninon Sevilla, Ricardo Roman.

DAVID DUCHOVNY AS MULDAR IN 'THE X FILES'

YANKEE IN KING ARTHUR'S COURT, A. See **CONNECTICUT YANKEE IN KING ARTHUR'S COURT, A.**

YEAR OF THE CANNIBALS (1971). Patterned loosely on Sophocles' ANTIGONE, with Britt Ekland caught up in bizarre social changes following World War III. It is now against the law to bury the bodies of insurgents who are slaughtered by the hundreds but Britt and Pierre Clementi do so under the threat of death. This Italian film gets littered with as many platitudes as there are bodies strewn on the post-Armageddon avenues. Written-directed by Liliana Cavani.

YEAR 2889. See **IN THE YEAR 2889.**

YELLOW CAB MAN, THE (1949). Pleasantly diverting Red Skelton vehicle (pun intended) has the comedian playing a cabbie who invents a glass that can't be shattered and then speeding for his life with spies in pursuit. This MGM comedy immediately shifts into high and stays there, the meter running all the way. Directed by Jack Donohue. Gloria De Haven, Walter Slezak, Edward Arnold, James Gleason, Paul Harvey.

YELLOWHAIR AND THE FORTRESS OF GOLD (1984). Mixture of spaghetti Western violence and Indiana Jones humor when a white woman raised by Indians (Laurene Landon) and Pecos Bill (Ken Roberson) search for the "Treasure of Kings" while pursued by an outlaw gang and Mexican federales, both led by sadistic brutes. The fantasy element surrounds a legendary tribe of Comanches (Tulpan Warriors) who turn to plastic when they're shot. There's the imitative snake attack scenes and temple sequences, and a magic horn. Its light-heartedness makes it palatable. (Lightning)

YELLOW PHANTOM (1936). Feature version of the serial **SHADOW OF CHINATOWN.**

YELLOW SUBMARINE (1968). Full-length cartoon featuring the music of the Beatles and the Beatles as their animated selves, who board Young Fred's submarine to help defeat the Blue Meanies and the Ferocious Flying Glove in Pepperland. Imaginative pop and op art set new trends at the time of the film's release, and the satiric and verbal humor is rollicking. Live-action-with-animation, etchings and footage of the Beatles as well as a soundtrack lovingly loaded with the Beatles sound make for a masterpiece. Directed by George Dunning. (Video/Laser: MGM/UA)

YELLOW WALLPAPER, THE (1989). "Masterpiece Theater" adaptation of Charlotte Perkins Gilman's classic story of a woman who, while recovering from a breakdown, sinks deeper into melancholia and depression with her obsession with the wallpaper in her bedroom. Psychological horror at its most chilling. Directed by John Clive. Julie Watson, Stephen Dillon, Carolyn Pickles.

YESTERDAY MACHINE, THE (1962). Cheaply produced regional sci-fi time-travel adventure, entertaining because of its campy qualities in depicting how small-town, pipe-smoking cop Tim Holt (in his final screen role) and newsman James Britton track down a Nazi fanatic who has figured out a way of accelerating the velocity of time to send test subjects in and out of the past, all for the Third Reich. Professor Ernst Von Hauser (hilariously played by Jack Herman, as if he were doing an impression of Sid Caesar's Professor Von Knowitall) explains his pseudophysics or "superspectronic relativity" to Britton in a hilarious scientific double-talk sequence. Meanwhile, there's fun in watching torch singer, bleach-blonde Ann Pellegrino sing, scream and fall into Britton's arms every time she's in danger. Be forewarned: You have to get a kick out of semiamatuerish efforts to enjoy. Linda Jenkins, Jay Ramsey. (Video City; Sinister/C; S/Weird; Filmfax)

YETI: THE GIANT OF THE 20TH CENTURY (1971). Italian giant-monster nonepic tells the tale of a 50-foot Yeti, discovered in an icefield in the wilds of Northern Canada by a scientific expedition. The Yeti, a tall dude covered with plenty of hair and photographed to look very big against blue-screen backgrounds, shows benevolence toward those who treat him decently. But the bad guys show up to exploit the monster, and the police have no understanding of this poor monster when he decides to take a stroll, so rampaging and mayhem result. The effects are obvious, the acting is of the "gee whiz" school and the attempts to humanize the beast fall flat. Then there's a Lassie-type collie that runs around, creating yocks for the Yeti. Directed by Frank Kramer with no polish; the photography is rough too. Phoenix Grant, Jim Sullivan, Tony Kendall, Eddy Fay.

YOG—MONSTER FROM SPACE (1971). Also known as SPACE AMOEBA, this Japanese sci-fi sukiyaki depicts an alien amoeba that comes from outer space on the hull of a space probe, infecting various life forms on Earth and turning them into Godzilla-like destructors who bear such names as Ganime, Kamoeba and Gezora. Scientists work day and night to devise a method of stopping the infection, finally settling on bat cries from old DRACULA soundtracks. (Sorry, we were only kidding . . . we're just getting punchy as we near the end of this massive book.) What really gets them in the end is an erupting volcano. Oops, did we give something away? Directed by Inoshiro Honda. Akira Kubo, Atsuko Takahashi, Noritake Saito. (Sinister/C)

YOGI AND THE INVASION OF THE SPACE BEARS (1988). Animated TV-movie in which Yogi and his pal Boo Boo encounter E.T. units out to conquer Earth. Voices by Daws Butler, Don Messick. (HBO)

YONGARY, MONSTER FROM THE DEEP (1967). South Koreans joined with the Japanese to produce this "horror" about a hulking monster (who looks not unlike Godzilla) freed from its centuries-old cave by an atomic blast and on his way to destroy Seoul, capital of South Korea. Yongary is different from Godzilla in that he drinks gasoline for breakfast, lunch and dinner . . . but Yongary still runs out of petrol before the first reel is over. You really have to like men-in-monster-suits to tune in. Directed by Kiduck Kim. Starring the unflappable Yugil Oh and the undiscouraged Chungim Nam. (Orion) (Laser: Image, with **X FROM OUTER SPACE**)

YOR: THE HUNTER FROM THE FUTURE (1983). Lowbrow fantasy escapism, but energetically on the level of a Saturday serial and hence palatable entertainment. Italian director Anthony Dawson, a master at cheap imitatons of whatever trend is popular, never aspires to more than he delivers. At least the noisy soundtrack will keep you alert, even if the acting will deaden your brain cells. YOR starts as a caveman pastiche with muscular hunk Reb Brown rescuing beautiful Corinne Clery from a prickly dinosaur and fighting off hairy Neanderthals. Just when you think you're in for another ONE BILLION B.C., the medallion around Yor's neck leads him to a post-holocaust control center ruled by the winner of a Darth Vader lookalike contest, The Overlord, who has an army of robots and a nuclear bomb. The ray guns zap, metal explodes, the rockets burst in air and there's more pyrotechnics than the Fourth of July and World War II combined. The Cro-Magnon plot is from a popular book by Juan Zanotto and Ray Collins. John Steiner, Carole Andre, Alan Collins. (Video/Laser: RCA/Columbia)

YOU BETTER WATCH OUT (1980). Original theatrical title for what is now on tape from Saturn as **CHRISTMAS EVIL** and from Academy as **TERROR IN TOYLAND.** See **TERROR IN TOYLAND.**

YOU'LL FIND OUT (1940). Three reasons to see this RKO sendup of the "Old Dark House" genre are Boris Karloff, Peter Lorre and Bela Lugosi, who spoof themselves as a terrifying trio involved in a phony seance in a mansion where bandleader Kay Kyser and his group (comedian Ish Kabibble, Harry Babbit, singer Ginny Sims) are stranded. A new recording device called the "sonovox" creates weird voices and Kyser indulges in his radio "College of Musical Knowledge" nonsense, with nostalgic musical numbers thrown in. It's an entertaining mix reflecting the essence of the '40s through James V. Kern's nonsensical script. Dennis O'Keefe and Helen Parrish provide obligatory love interest. Lorre is amusing with his bulging eyes and long cigarettes, Karloff is

AAARRGGHH! IT'S YOG -- MONSTER FROM SPACE

charmingly menacing as the mansion host and Lugosi hams it up with a turban as a mystic. Produced-directed by David Butler. (Budget; Hollywood Home Theater) (Laser: Image)

YOU'LL LIKE MY MOTHER (1972). Taut psychological thriller with a sinister ambience in which Patty Duke visits her mother-in-law in a house that becomes snowbound. Once she's trapped she learns horrible secrets about the family she's married into. Rosemary Murphy and Richard Thomas have chilling roles. Directed by Lamont Johnson, scripted by Jo Heims. Sian Barbara Allen.

YOU NEVER CAN TELL (1951). It would be a cheap shot to call this film a dog. Despite its unpromising storyline, it is quite funny. A German Shepard, King, becomes heir to a fortune, then is poisoned by a one-time trainer (Charles Drake) from the K-9 Corps so he can marry Peggy Dow and settle down very rich. King arrives in beastitory, where he is turned into a "humanimal" and allowed to return to Earth to uncover the dastardly trainer. Back on Earth as private eye Rex Shepard (Dick Powell), King is the brunt of jokes about fire hydrants, dogfood and handy tree trunks, and indulges in verbal puns of his own. Sounds like a dog, yeah, but it's done with such a goodheartedness that the "dogeared" script by director Lou Breslow and David Chandler wins you over. Also very funny is Joyce Holden, a one-time race horse reincarnated as a human to help King solve the caper. Albert Sharpe, Sara Taft, Will Vedder.

YOUNG AGAIN (1986). The opposite of BIG—instead of a youth wishing to be in an adult's body, and being granted that wish, 40-year-old business executive Robert Urich wishes he were in the body of a teenager again, and along comes guardian angel Jack Gilford to grant the wish. Now in the body of K.C. Reeves, Urich returns to his home town and to the high school where he strikes up a new relationship with Lindsay Wagner, the girl that got away when he was a teen. This Disney TV-movie deals poignantly with the problems of a teenager trying to date a woman old enough to be his mother, and is a charming morality tale. Directed by Steven Hilliard Stern.

YOUNG AND EVIL. See **YAMBAO.**

YOUNG DRACULA. See **ANDY WARHOL'S DRACULA.**

YOUNG EINSTEIN (1989). An "alternate universe" fantasy-comedy written-produced-directed by Australia's Yahoo Serious, who also plays the title role. The premise is that Alfred Einstein was born on the isle of Tasmania and went to Sydney in 1905 to invent his theory of relativity and make history by also discovering the surf board, rock 'n roll music, the electric guitar and atomic fission. This is a wild, whacky comedy (you're trapped in a different time stream, Luv) that was a sensation in

Australia, but it did a swift nosedive in the U.S., presumably because the parody and satire tapped into something exclusively Down Under. Yahoo has been compared to Monty Python and Pee-Wee Herman, but he's a noncomformist in search of his own daffy twilight zone. Full of visual puns, slapstick inspired by Warner Bros. cartoons, and the humorous use of classical music by Mozart, Rossini, Prokofiev and Beethoven. (Video/Laser: Warner Bros.)

YOUNG FRANKENSTEIN (1974). Hysterically funny Mel Brooks take-off on the Universal horror films of the '30s, in particular THE BRIDE and SON OF FRANKENSTEIN, since sequences those films are parodied. Brooks, who directed/co-wrote the script with Gene Wilder, is wild and ingeniously creative, though some of the satire works and some falls flat. Peter Boyle is the singularly inane creature created by Dr. Frankenstein (Wilder), while Marty Feldman is the hunchbacked Iggor, Cloris Leachman the daffy woman hanging around the Frankenstein castle and Madeleine Kahn the eventual "bride." Watch for Gene Hackman as the blind hermit in the forest. You'll scream—with delight. (Video/Laser: CBS/Fox)

YOUNG HANNAH, QUEEN OF THE VAMPIRES. See **CRYPT OF THE LIVING DEAD.**

YOUNG HARRY HOUDINI (1987). Excellent two-hour Disney movie for TV presenting Harry Houdini as an adult, telling a story of his childhood to an admirer. Flashback to 1886 as young Erich Weiss runs away from home to pursue his dream to become a magician. After a nifty train sequence, in which the lad demonstrates a practical use of escaping from handcuffs, he meets a traveling magic show and becomes a disciple of sleight-of-hander Jose Ferrer, who inspires the boy to keep after his dream. A mute Indian named John Parker teaches young Weiss how supernormal powers (such as the ability to fly astrally) can be brought into play if only you believe in yourself. This is nostalgic and warm, full of colorful period characters and a sense of a boy learning to be a man. Wil Wheaton, Jeffrey Demunn, Kerri Green, Barry Corbin, Roy Dotrice, Ross Harris, J. Reuben Silverbird. Director James Orr co-wrote with Jim Cruickshank.

YOUNG MAGICIAN, THE (1987). Pleasant Polish-Canadian TV production, fourth in the "Tales for All" series, in which a youth named Peter (Rusty Jedwab) learns the power to move objects, often at a rapid velocity, only to discover he's looked upon as a freak—until police need his help to avert a major disaster. Writer-director Walder-mar Dziki never allows the material to ignite as much as one might like, but it's passable entertainment. Edward Garson, Natasza Maraszek. (Family Home Entertainment)

YOUNG MAN, I THINK YOU'RE DYING. See **BEAST IN THE CELLAR, THE.**

YOUNG SHERLOCK HOLMES (1985). Rousing Steven Spielberg-produced action-adventure, perfect in technical aspects, and handsomely cast. It's a tribute to the Victorian detective by portraying him and Watson as students at a boys' school, solving a mystery in the Sir Arthur Conan Doyle tradition. At least the first third, which captures the antecedents of the Holmes canon and the restraint of Doyle's story-telling and has Chris Columbus' best writing. The Holmes stories were, after all, studies in ratiocination and deduction and only occasionally lapsed into wild and woolly adventure. But when the gaslit "Rover Boys" stumble across an Egyptian death cult in the heart of London, it slides into an Indiana Jones adventure with mock derring-do and heroics. And because there's nightmarish hallucinations, Spielberg and gang have an excuse to drag out special effects: a dead squab that comes to life on the dinner plate like a killer buzzard; gargoyles that attack an old inventor in a curio shop; French pastries that become animated cutesy-pie imps; graveyard horrors with rotting corpses; etc. Spielberg twice apologizes in the credits for taking liberties but apparently had permission to use the characters (or was it just a blessing?). Many Holmesian props (pipe, Inverness cape, violin, deerstalker's cap) are cleverly introduced. (Video/Laser: Paramount)

YOUNG, THE EVIL AND THE SAVAGE, THE (1968). Michael Rennie makes one of his last screem appearances in this Italian exploitation thriller, and it's an unremarkable closing to his otherwise fine career. A girls' dormitory is the setting for gore murders. Rennie and Mark Damon lurk on the premises. Directed by Anthony Dawson (Antonio Margherti). Eleanor Brown, Sally Smith.

YOUNG TIME TRAVELERS, THE (1984). Compilation of British TV children's programs depicting youngsters on journeys through time and space. Mark Dightam.

YOU ONLY LIVE TWICE (1967). Lavishly produced James Bond thriller from Albert Broccoli and Harry Saltzman (their fifth), with Sean Connery carrying the load as the urbane, sophisticated, implausable Agent 007. Blofeld (Donald Pleasence), mastermind of SPECTRE, returns with a plan to hijack U.S. and Soviet space capsules and blackmail the world. Gadgets, superweapons, seductive women, unstoppable action—all enhanced by John Barry's music as Bond finds himself in Japan. Durably directed by Lewis Gilbert and swiftly paced by scenarist Roald Dahl. Akiko Wakabayashi, Karin Dor, Bernard Lee, Charles Gray, Robert Hutton, Tsai Chin. After this, Connery left the series not to return until DIAMONDS ARE FOREVER. (Video/Laser: MGM/UA; CBS/Fox)

YOU'RE TELLING ME (1934). See editions 1-3.

YOUR TEETH ARE IN MY NECK. See **FEARLESS VAMPIRE KILLERS, THE.**

ZAAT (1973). See **ATTACK OF THE SWAMP CREATURES.**

ZACARIAH (1971). Say, viewin' pardners, it's "the first electric Western" with high-falutin' rock personalities Country Joe MacDonald, Elvin Jones 'n Doug Kershaw. Them jaspers're packin' six-shooters 'n rovin' through 1880 quippin' in hip lingo and spoutin' modern homilies, with some grits throwed in. But rein up there, amigo. Them shootin' irons're loaded with blanks 'n the script by that there Firesign Theater, it's a misfire, you betchum. Reckon it's time to put this-a-here gang out to pasture. Empty saddles in the ole corral tonight, pardners. 'N now, amigos 'n compadres, like tah strum 'n hum a little song for yah-all. (CBS/Fox)

ZAMBA THE GORILLA (1949). Beau Bridges, in an early juvenile role, portrays a pre-teener lost in the jungle and living with a gorilla. When his mother comes looking

YAHOO SERIOUS IN 'YOUNG EINSTEIN'

for him, Zamba demands more than cookies and milk to relinquish his ape-hold on the 6-year-old. Eagle Lion sepiatone flick, directed by action specialist William Berke and starring Jon Hall as a jungle hero and June Vincent as a woman who feels the passions of the veldt.

ZAPPED! (1982). Pathetic comedy that falls on its face as Scott Baio (onetime TV boy star) discovers he has telekinetic powers after a high school lab explosion. The intellectual height of this undernourishment is to have Baio cause a girl's blouse to pop open or have her dress fly off. Willy Aames (also a onetime TV boy star) is around as a cardboard character to say "Gee Whiz." So belabored that not even teen-agers, for whom producer Jeffrey D. Apple intended it, will sit still for long. Director Robert J. Rosenthal was defeated before he started. Scatman Crothers, Roger Bowen and Sue Ane Langdon have dumb cameos. (Video/Laser: Nelson/Embassy)

ZAPPED AGAIN (1989). Lamebrain sequel to a fantasy-comedy that was lousy to begin with. Rebellious Todd Eric Andrews, a student at Ralph Waldo Emerson High, discovers a prune juice that gives him telekinetic powers, which he uses to elevate Linda Blair's dress over her head or to get even with sadistic co-workers. In fact, too little use of visual humor prevails—director Doug Campbell is stuck with boring dialogue and inane characters. ZAPPED AGAIN zapped him good, as it did Sue Ane Langdon, Karen Black, Lyle Alzado and Kelli Williams in empty-headed roles. (Video/Laser: Embassy/Nelson)

ZARDOZ (1973). Visually exciting sci-fi/fantasy tale set in 2293, but writer-producer-director John Boorman is heavy-handed and unnecessarily symbolic when Sean Connery (as an Exterminator, a man entitled to impregnate women) infiltrates The Vortex, an intellectual society segregated from the rest of the world's savagery. It evolves into a political-social allegory (with esoteric literary overtones) and is composed of incongruous, unfathomable elements. For hardcore fans who appreciate experiments in the outre—general audiences may find this enigmatic. Charlotte Rampling, Sally Anne Newton, Sara Kestelman, John Alderton. (Key; CBS/Fox) (Laser: CBS/Fox)

ZEBRA FORCE (1977). Well-produced cops-and-robbers actioner set in L.A. spotlights Vietnam vets who take on the Mob to rid society of drug-dealers. The twist: the Caucasian soldiers turn into Negroes when they strike against Richard X. Slattery and his guys, then revert back to Caucasians in the blink of an eye. Without explanation! Their leader is a one-armed Lieutenant who needs a sound tube against his throat to speak. An implausible twist ending rounds out the action of this unusual film. Odd, and disconcerting, to say the least. Written-directed by Joe Tornaturi. Mike Lane, Rockne Tarkington, Glenn Wilder, Anthony Caruso. The sequel, CODE NAME: ZEBRA, has no fantasy. (Media)

ZEDER—VOICES FROM THE BEYOND. See **REVENGE OF THE DEAD.**

ZELIG (1983). Brilliant Woody Allen pastiche of biographical-documentary films comprised of staged scenes and historical black-and-white footage into which Allen has been matted. Leonard Zelig is a schmuck of the first order, whose shyness and alienation from society have given him a unique talent: the chameleon ability to take on the characteristics of others. This wonderful parody spotlights Allen with Eugene O'Neill, Herbert Hoover, the crowd at Hearst's Castle, and Hitler during a Munich rally. It's a classic Allen gag carried off ingeniously. Mia Farrow is the mousy psychiatrist who tries to break Zelig of his malady, and you'll see real-life people (such as Susan Sontag) making fun of themselves by participating in this colossal lampoon. Three cheers for the klutzy Mr. Zelig, and four cheers for the unprecedented Allen. (Video/Laser: Warner Bros.)

ZERAM (1991). Japanese sci-fi actioner in which a lovely alien humanoid batles the monster Zeram (a fugutive E.T. from another galaxy), which has a strange mushroom-like flattop from which a snake with a human head emerges. As the fights go on and on, the creature mutates into other forms so the heroine (and two comedy-relief buffoons) keeps bringing out new weapons to blow it asunder. Good visuals, inept plot and acting. Directed by Keita Amemiya. Yuko Moriyama stars. (Fox Lorber)

ZERO BOYS, THE (1986). Gang of youths well-known for wilderness survival takes shelter in a deserted house in the forest only to become targets for drooling killers equipped with Bowie knife and crossbow. It's never explained who the killers are, so it's hard to generate interest in the cat-and-mouse games writer- producer-director Nico Mastorakis plays in this FRIDAY THE 13TH clone. Not even the three big-breasted women in the gang have much to show. Daniel Hirsch, Kelli Maroney, Tom Shell, Crystal Carson. (Lightning)

ZERO POPULATION GROWTH. See **Z.P.G.**

ZETA ONE (1969). Outer-space cuties, Angvians, battle drab undercover ops in this British production from Tony Tenser, which is best described as soft-core pornography. Writer-director Michael Cort adapted his story from a comic strip with help from Christopher Neame. Robin Hawdon, James Robertson Justice, Dawn Addams, Charles Hawtrey, Anna Gael. (From Sinister/C as **THE LOVE FACTOR** and Front Row Entertainment as **ALIEN WOMEN**)

ZIPPERFACE (1992). A serial killer in a black leather suit and mask with a zipper across his lips resembles Jason of the FRIDAY THE 13TH series, what with the machete-like knife he keeps plunging into the beautiful bodies of actresses-prostitutes. Or he uses to chop off their heads. Poor Palm City will never be the same as the female mayor cries for an arrest and female cop Donna Adams searches for the fiend and reads her lines badly. The script by Barbara Bishop and Mark Troy (from an idea by producer-director Mansour Pourmand) is more of a whodunit with an occasional gore murder as red herrings are set up—smelly fish that won't fool you in the slightest if you're wise to slasher flicks fashioned as murder mysteries. A substandard, poorly acted production strikes an extra-bad note of incredulity on several occasions. This sleazy movie with mild nudity and unimaginative R-rated love scenes is easy to miss. Jonathan Mandell, David Clover, Trisha Melynkov. (Action International) (Laser: Image)

ZODIAC KILLER, THE (1971). Chintzy, amateurish rendering of a true murder case that rocked San Francisco in the late '60s, and which remains unsolved to this day. Several citizens were indiscriminately murdered by a man who played a dangerous cat-and-mouse game by taunting police with cyphers and other clues. This version, concocted with the help of one-time S.F. Chronicle reporter Paul Avery, is wretchedly conceived, with little directorial style from producer Tom Hanson or scenarists Ray Cantrell and Manny Mendoza. A couple of the murders are graphically effective—especially sunbathers being stabbed to death by the hooded killer—but otherwise the staging and editing are poor. Oddly enough, the closing voice-over of the killer is chilling as he describes how the law works to protect him. Hal Reed, Bob Jones, Ray Lynch and Tom Pittman comprise the nonprofessional cast, which is aided briefly by the appearance of Doodles Weaver. Note: Another Chronicle employee, former political cartoonist Robert Graysmith, later wrote a best-selling account of his investigation of the case. (Academy)

ZOLTAN, HOUND OF DRACULA. Video version of **DRACULA'S DOG** (Thorn EMI/HBO; Republic).

ZOMBIE (1979). Unauthorized sequel to Romero's DAWN OF THE DEAD, set on St. Thomas Island where Tisa Farrow and Ian McCulloch battle zombies, resurrected via voodoo rituals by fiendish doctor Richard Johnson. Heads are blown off in abundance (that's the only way to stop a zombie, remember?) and director Lucio Fulci and scenarist Elisa Briganti allow this Italian exploitationer to reach ridiculous extremes—such as having a zombie attack and bite a killer shark and having

'Look out! Ahhhhhh!'

— From any movie featuring zombie monsters on a rampage of destruction to rip apart human flesh and munch on mortal meat and chew mankind to bits.

a human eyeball punctured. But that's what this "walking dead" genre is all about, right? Ian McCullough, Auretta Gay. Also known as ZOMBIE 2 and ZOMBIE FLESH EATERS. (Magnum; Wizard; Lightning) (Laser: Image)

ZOMBIE 2. See **ZOMBIE.**

ZOMBIE 3. See **BURIAL GROUND.**

ZOMBIE 4. Video version of **VIRGIN AMONG THE LIVING DEAD, A** (Edde).

ZOMBIE BRIGADE (1988). When the Japanese build an amusement park in the Australian desert, dedicated to the Robotman cartoon hero, a graveyard of Vietnam dead is disturbed and shambling corpses arise from their resting places to bounce around like kangaroos and lust for the blood of Japanese tourists. Written-produced-directed by Carmelo Musca and Barrie Pattison. John Moore, Khym Lam, Geoff Gibbs, Adam A. Wong.

ZOMBIE CHILD. Canadian video version of **CHILD, THE** (CIC).

ZOMBIE CREEPING FLESH. See **NIGHT OF THE ZOMBIES (1983).**

ZOMBIE FLESH EATERS. See **ZOMBIE** (Yummy!).

ZOMBIE HIGH (1987). Honorable intentions to make a meaningful horror film, with social overtones, are handicapped by mediocre filmmaking and sound, so at best this is a poor man's STEPFORD WIVES with conspiratorial overtones thrown in. And the title is misleading, as this is not a "walking dead" melodrama in the George Romero tradition. So don't look for brain-hungry corpses brought back to life. At Ettinger Academy, student Virginia Madsen discovers a plot to turn the alumni into automatons, and she is threatened with a lobotomy to give her eternal life via a crystal implanted in her brain. All she and the others need is a daily fix of blood and brain tissue, a concoction created by the campus' Dr. Frankenstein, Dean Eisner (Kay Kuter). Horror fans will find Ron Link's direction too mild and the social relevancy too weak for this to work either way. Richard Cox, James Wilder, Sherilyn Fenn, Paul Feig. Also called THE SCHOOL THAT ATE MY BRAIN. (Cinema Group; Simitar; Continental)

ZOMBIE HOLOCAUST. See **DR. BUTCHER M.D.**

ZOMBIE HORROR. See **BURIAL GROUND.**

ZOMBIE INFERNO. See **NIGHT OF THE ZOMBIES (1983).**

ZOMBIE ISLAND MASSACRE (1984). A Caribbean island is the setting for this tale of vactioners being slaughtered by what appears to be a killer zombie tree. Huh? But all is not what it seems. Screenplay by Logan O'Neill and William Stoddard. Directed by John N. Carter. David Broadnax, Rita Jenrette. (Fox Hills; Media)

ZOMBIE LAKE (1985). Corpses of Nazi soldiers slaughtered in a World War II battle rise from the depths of a very nonpicturesque lake to attack nude women swimmers, who spread wide their legs while the camera photographs them from below. The rotting troopers fondle bare breasts and asses. Gee, an art horror movie with redeeming values. Directed by Jean Rollin (billed on some prints as J.A. Lazer) and co-written by Jesse Franco. Howard Vernon, Britt Carva, Robert Foster, Fred Sanders. Also called LAKE OF THE LIVING DEAD. (Lightning; Wizard; VCI)

ZOMBIE NIGHTMARE (1987). Mediocre Canadian horror film, shot in Ste Anne de Vellevue, and released to video once distributors saw no hope for theatrical. It goes to the trouble of setting up the character of a young boy who, after seeing his father knived to death by toughs while rescuing a young girl being raped, grows up to be a macho good guy who prevents two hoods from robbing a market. He is promptly run over by a carload of delinquents. Mother comes along and turns the corpse over to a local witch, Molly Mokembe, who proceeds to resurrect him from the dead. Now our hero (Jon-Mikl Thor) becomes a zombie killer with a baseball bat who goes after the gang. The murders (as conceived by scriptwriter David Wellington) aren't exciting and the fights poorly staged by director Jack Bravman. Adam West has a small but pivotal role as a cynical policeman—why he took this part is a bigger mystery than any of the voodoo and mysticism underlying the witch's mumbo jumbo. Music lovers may grove on the rock track that features "Zombie Night" by Knighthawk and other renditions by Motorhead, Girlschool, Thor, Deathmask, Fist, Virgin Steel and Battalion. Tia Carrere, Manuska Rigaud, Frank Dietz. (New World)

ZOMBIES (1961). Crude, dumbly conceived junk piece (originally VOODOO BLOOD BATH) about a Miami Beach writer lured to a Caribbean island to solve the mystery of some fright-faced natives and a doctor (Robert Stanton) searching for a cure to cancer. This exemplifies sleazy thrills as William Joyce runs around with floozy Heather Hewitt to solve the unmysterious mystery. Credit (or discredit) Del Tenney for writing-producing-directing this mess. Assistant director was William Grefe, who went on to direct STANLEY and other schlock. ZOMBIES was repackaged in 1971 as I EAT YOUR SKIN and double billed with I DRINK YOUR BLOOD.

ZOMBIES. See **DAWN OF THE DEAD.**

ZOMBIES OF MORA TAU (1957). Columbia producer Sam Katzman must have been in a trance-like state when he read Raymond T. Marcus' script. Edward L. Cahn must have also been in a deep sleep when he accepted the assignment to direct. Otherwise, why bother? Gregg Palmer and Allison Hayes (the 50-Foot Woman) sleepwalk through roles as adventurers in search of diamonds in an underwater hiding place guarded by hollow-eyed insomniacs. Ray Corrigan, Morris Ankrum, Gregg Palmer . . . zzzzzzz. (RCA/Columbia)

ZOMBIES OF SUGAR HILL. TV title for **SUGAR HILL.**

ZOMBIES OF THE STRATOSPHERE (1952). This 12-chapter entry in Republic's sci-fi serial cycle of the early '50s is the third and final adventure in a trilogy of "flying man" sagas, the others being KING OF THE ROCKET MEN and RADAR MEN FROM THE MOON. In this one the guy with the jet-rocket back pack is Larry Martin (Judd Holdren) of the Inter-Planetary Patrol, a watchdog of the solar system. The "zombies" are actually Martians Marex (Lane Bradford) and Narab (Leonard Nimoy), who land on Earth and persuade an evil scientist (Stanley Waxman) to help construct a hydrogen bomb and explode it, forcing Earth out of its orbit. Fred C. Brannon directed this campy cliffhanger, the charm of which comes from its now-antiquated but-delightful-to-watch space vehicle effects, frequent fisticuffs, and underwater photography in which the Martians appear to walk along the bottom of the ocean. An obvious inspiration for the '91 feature THE ROCKETEER. Aline Towne, Tom Steele, Wilson Wood, Jack Shea. (Republic; Nostalgia Merchant; Video Connection; the TV feature version **SATAN'S SATELLITES** is on video from Admit One) (Laser: Republic)

ZOMBIES ON BROADWAY (1945). When the owners of the Zombie Hut, a night club on the Big Street, an- nounce they'll have real-life dead zombies performing o stage, they're forced to send schmucks Wally Brown a Allen Carney to the West Indies island of San Sebasti to bring back the real dead McCoy. Darby Jones, wonderful bug-eyed zombie corpse in I WALKED W A ZOMBIE, is back for more shenanigans, this

'ZOMBIES OF THE STRATOSPHERE'

strictly for laughs, as he stalks Anne Jeffreys and the two idiots through potted jungles, occasionally carrying off a body. Bela Lugosi portrays Dr. Renault, the madman perfecting his walking dead, in his usual wide-eyed style. Taken as a period piece, it's quite funny with Sheldon Leonard in a good role as the night club owner. Director Gordon Douglas guides the cast through the inanities quite well. Ian Wolfe, Frank Jenks. (Turner; IME) (Laser: Image)

ZOMBIETHON (1986). Compilation video of the goriest scenes from zombie movies, with new wraparound footage produced-directed by Ken Dixon. Various women pursued by walking dead enter the El Rey Theater to sit in a crowd of zombiers and see clips from ZOMBIE (1979), which include the infamous eye-gouging and shark-biting sequences; ZOMBIE LAKE, with emphasis on bare flesh and wide-open legs; OASIS OF THE ZOMBIES, a foreign film with Afrika Corps soldiers stalking the living; and ASTRO-ZOMBIES. Only with this final camp classic does this video take on a fun quality; otherwise, you really have to love zombies to find enjoyment. Other clips from THE INVISIBLE DEAD, A VIRGIN AMONG THE LIVING DEAD, WHITE ZOMBIE and FEAR. (Wizard; Lightning; Force)

ZOMBIE WALKS, THE. See **HAND OF POWER, THE.**

ZONE OF THE DEAD. Video version of **ALIEN ZONE** (Monarch).

ZONE TROOPERS (1986). Simple-minded, mildly enjoyable World War II fantasy from Empire International, which resembles a segment of TV's COMBAT when GI dogfaces in Italy shoot it out with German troops. Four survivors flee into the forest to meet "Bug," an E.T. creature with an insect's head who evaporates Nazi war machines with his disintegrator ray. "Bug" is part of a band of alien troopers stranded on Earth and since they understand war, and the good guys from the bad guys, they side up with the dogfaces to blast dirty Nazi rats into another dimension. Unusually gentle for a Charles Band production, with nostalgic '40s tunes on the soundtrack. Directed by Danny Bilson; okay effects by John Buechler. Tim Thomerson, Timothy Van Patten, Biff Manard, Art LaFleur. (Lightning)

ZONTAR: THE THING FROM VENUS (1968). Described as a new version of Roger Corman's IT CONQUERED THE WORLD . . . but why resurrect that old turkey? Well, don't laugh because this film is so inept, it's a minor cult favorite among those who love good-bad movies. The story reaches new lows in screen sci-fi as John Agar opposes a space monster capable of dominating the human mind. Too bad a spark of creativity didn't dominate the mind of writer-director Larry Buchanan. See it. You won't believe it. Susan Bjorman, Anthony Houston, Warren Hammack. (Video Dimensions; Sinister/C; S/Weird; Dark Dreams; Filmfax)

ZOO SHIP (1985). Huge spaceship, carrying specimens from all over the Universe, crashlands on Earth, and you know what that means. Special effects by Jim Danforth and Sydney Dutton. Directed by Richard Shorr. James Whitmore, Craig Wasson, Keenan Wynn, Audra Lindley, Roddy McDowall.

ZOTZ! (1962). Walter Karig's popular 1940's novel was produced by William Castle, with screenplay by Ray Russell, but the results, despite those years of waiting, were negligible. An old coin possesses strange powers once its holder utters the word "Zotz!" Karig's neat twist on the Aladdin's Lamp theme is reduced to cliches, with enemy spies coming after the owner of the coin, Tom Poston. ZOTZ to you, William Castle. Jim Backus, Fred Clark, Cecil Kellaway, Louis Nye. (RCA/Columbia)

Z.P.G. (1972). Which stands for Zero Population Growth, in case you haven't been following Earth's current population problems. And which stands for Zero Picture Grabber, if you've already seen it. Geraldine Chaplin plays a wife of the 21st Century who defies anti-birth laws and has her baby anyway (hubby Oliver Reed helped, of course). The city is surrounded by a deadly smog, forcing the cast to wear gas masks, but masks might be more in order for the audience to prevent them from gagging on this turgid sociological sci-fier. Directed by Michael Campus, scripted by Max Ehrlich and Frank DeFelitta. (Paramount)

Z-7 OPERATION REMBRANDT (1967). See editions 1-3.

ZU: WARRIORS FROM THE MAGIC MOUNTAIN (1983). Hong-Kong produced fantasy of a wild-and-woolly nature, with adventurers of the 10th Century entering a mountain in China and facing such rivals as Evil Disciples, Blood Crows, Flying Swords, Evil Force, Heaven's Blade and wizards, warlocks, priestesses and other entities endowed with magic. It gets out of hand under Tsui Hark's direction, often becoming ridiculous when the cast is richocheting off the walls, yet there is a free-spirited feeling to this rambuctious production, and sense of breathlessness, that enables a Western audience to embrace this pastiche of the West's sword-and-sorcery quest fantasies. And that's it, pal, there ain't no more.

"...ll films are vampiric in nature. They draw your life's blood and ...ou to the brink of existence. You live for months in darkened ... never seeing the light of the sun. Then while you grow old, ...mains unaltered by time."

—Movie director Andre W. Wiers (Dana M. Reeves) in **XENIA**

453